# 1968
# READER'S DIGEST
# ALMANAC
# AND
# YEARBOOK

PUBLISHED ANNUALLY BY
THE READER'S DIGEST ASSOCIATION, INC., PLEASANTVILLE, NEW YORK

# 1968 READER'S DIGEST ALMANAC AND YEARBOOK

Published annually by The Reader's Digest
Association, Inc.

Compiled by the editors of the
Reader's Digest Almanac.

Special contributions from the thirty
international offices of the
Reader's Digest around the world.

LIBRARY OF CONGRESS CATALOG CARD NUMBER: 66-14383

PRINTED IN THE UNITED STATES OF AMERICA

# CONTENTS

(Special articles are listed under the subject headings. Consult the Index on pages 1000-1024 for page references to tabular data.)

**CONTENTS** (continued)

**CONTENTS** (continued)

Pages

# CONTRIBUTORS

The distinguished authorities listed below were among those who collaborated with the editors in preparing information for the 1968 edition of the *Reader's Digest Almanac and Yearbook.* Their professional affiliations are given, along with the subjects of their contributions.

**Asimov, Isaac,** Associate Professor of Biochemistry, Boston University: SCIENCE

**Barkham, John,** Literary Critic, *Saturday Review:* BOOKS AND AUTHORS

**Boyd, William,** Senior Associate, National Municipal League: STATE REAPPORTIONMENT

**Brace, Richard M.,** Chairman of History Department, Oakland University: ALGERIA

**Bradley, C. Paul,** Chairman, Department of Political Science, Flint College, University of Michigan: MALAYSIA

**Bustin, Edouard,** Professor of African Studies, Boston University: CONGO, DEMOCRATIC REPUBLIC OF

**Butwell, Richard,** Director, Patterson School of Diplomacy and International Commerce, University of Kentucky: LAOS

**Cairns, John C.,** Professor of History, University of Toronto: FRANCE

**Cass, James,** Education Editor, *Saturday Review:* EDUCATION

**Claassen, Harold,** Sportswriter, The Associated Press: OLYMPIC GAMES

**Collins, Robert O.,** Professor of History, University of California: SUDAN

**Durso, Joseph,** Sportswriter, *The New York Times:* BASEBALL

**Fitzgibbon, William,** Editorial Staff, *The New York Times Magazine:* UNITED NATIONS; U.S. FOREIGN AFFAIRS

**Friis, Erik J.,** Editor, *American Scandinavian Review:* DENMARK, ICELAND, NORWAY, SWEDEN

**Gailey, Harry,** Professor of History, San Jose State College: AFRICA

**Hagan, Charles B.,** Professor of Political Science, University of Illinois at Urbana: AUSTRALIA

**Halperin, Ernst,** Professor of Politics, Institute of Inter-American Studies, University of Miami: CUBA

**Hanna, Paul L.,** Professor of Social Sciences, University of Florida: MIDDLE EAST

**Harrison, James P.,** Professor of History, Hunter College: COMMUNIST CHINA—History

**Hartman, Louis F.,** C.SS.R., Executive Secretary, Catholic Biblical Association: PROMINENT BIBLICAL PERSONS

**Hewes, Henry,** Drama Critic, *Saturday Review:* THEATER

**Hoffman, Oswald C.,** Speaker, *The Lutheran Hour:* THE ECUMENICAL MOVEMENT

**Honey, P. J.,** Professor of South East Asian Studies, University of London: VIETNAM

**Hughes, Allen,** Music Department, *The New York Times:* MUSIC AND DANCE

**Kanner, Lee,** Assistant to the Financial Editor, *The New York Times:* U.S. BUDGET; PRESIDENTIAL ELECTIONS 1968

**Karpat, Kemal H.,** Professor of Government, New York University: CYPRUS

**Kauffmann, Stanley,** Associate Editor, *New Republic:* FILMS

**Legum, Colin,** *The Observer* (London): NIGERIA

**McKay, Vernon,** Professor of Asian Studies, The Johns Hopkins University: GABON; SOUTH AFRICA; SOUTH WEST AFRICA

**Morgan, Patrick,** Assistant Professor of Political Science, Washington State University: UNION OF SOVIET SOCIALIST REPUBLICS

**Needler, Martin C.,** Professor of Inter-American Affairs, University of New Mexico: DOMINICAN REPUBLIC

**Palmer, Norman D.,** Professor of Political Science, University of Pennsylvania: CEYLON; INDIA

**Parker, Franklin,** Professor of Education, University of Oklahoma: RHODESIA

**Partner, Peter,** Professor of History, Winchester College (England): EGYPT

**Ranis, Peter,** Assistant Professor of Political Science, State University of New York at Stony Brook: ARGENTINA

**Schneider, Ronald M.,** Associate Professor of Government, Columbia University: BRAZIL

**Schwartz, Harry,** Editorial Board, *The New York Times:* THE COMMUNIST WORLD

**Shafer, Robert J.,** Professor of History, Syracuse University: MEXICO

**Staar, Richard F.,** Professor of Political Science, The National War College: POLAND

**Stern, Fritz,** Seth Low Professor of History, Columbia University: GERMANY, FEDERAL REPUBLIC OF

**Storry, Richard,** Lecturer in Far Eastern Studies, Oxford University: JAPAN

**Sutton, Horace,** Associate Publisher, *Saturday Review:* TRAVEL AND TRANSPORTATION

**Szulc, Tad,** Foreign Correspondent, *The New York Times:* SPAIN

**Taxay, Donald,** Former Curator, Chase Manhattan Bank Money Museum: U.S. CURRENCY

**Turner, Arthur C.,** Professor of Political Science, University of California: EUROPE

**Vandenbosch, Amry,** Professor of Political Science, University of Tennessee: BELGIUM

**von Vorys, Karl,** Associate Professor of Political Science, University of Pennsylvania: PAKISTAN

**Walsh, Agatha,** Head of Reference Section, British Information Services (New York): UNITED KINGDOM

**Williams, Robert J.,** Washington Reporter, *Forbes Magazine:* U.S. ECONOMY

**Wright, Marcia,** Professor of History, Columbia University: KENYA

**Wu, Yuan-li,** Professor of Business Administration, University of San Francisco: CHINA—Economy

# WORLD IN REVIEW: 1967

## Chronology: The Year in Brief • Major Events of 1967 • Obituaries of Prominent Persons

United Press Int'l.

THE WAR IN VIETNAM is but one of many significant topics reviewed in the *1968 Reader's Digest Almanac and Yearbook.* Here are the other events that made the year 1967 one to remember: the six-day Arab-Israeli war, the escape to freedom of Stalin's daughter, the Glassboro summit meeting, space probes to Venus—to name only a few.

THIS 1968 EDITION combines the best features of both a yearbook —a record of the year's events—and an almanac—a book of facts. The articles, statistics, photographs, charts, and maps are carefully organized for instant reference and readability. For convenience, the book is divided into sections, each dealing with a particular subject.

THE FIRST SECTION, World in Review, has three parts: a month-by-month chronology of national and international events; a series of reports reviewing the year's most important developments by areas—Far East, Middle East, Europe, Africa, and the Americas; and a record of the deaths of prominent persons during 1967.

# CHRONOLOGY: THE YEAR 1967 IN BRIEF

## JANUARY

### NATIONAL

**Three Republican Governors,** each regarded as a contender for the 1968 GOP Presidential nomination, were inaugurated *January 2.* Governors Nelson A. Rockefeller of New York and George W. Romney of Michigan were sworn in for their third terms; Governor Ronald W. Reagan of California began his first term.

**Jack Ruby,** 55, died *January 3* at Parkland Memorial Hospital, Dallas. Doctors said the former nightclub owner, who shot and killed Presidential assassin Lee Harvey Oswald in 1963, had been suffering from cancer. However, death was attributed to a blood clot in the lungs.

**The Georgia Supreme Court** ruled *January 6* that the State Legislature had the power to elect a state governor, thus breaking the deadlock that arose when neither major gubernatorial candidate received a clear majority of the popular vote in the November, 1966, election.

**General Motors** announced *January 6* the recall of about 250,000 1967-model cars following the discovery of flaws in the steering mechanism of some automobiles.

**Representative Adam Clayton Powell,** Democrat of New York, was ousted as chairman of the House Education and Labor Committee by a vote of House Democrats *January 9.*

**Julian Bond,** the Atlanta Negro Democrat who had been barred twice from taking his elected seat, was seated in the Georgia Legislature *January 9.* The U.S. Supreme Court ruled that his statements opposing the Vietnam war and defending draft-card burning had not disqualified him as a member of the legislature.

**The 90th Congress** convened *January 10.*

**President Johnson** delivered the annual State of the Union Message to a joint session of Congress *January 10.* The President requested Congressional approval for a 6 per cent surcharge on personal and corporate income taxes in order to help finance domestic Great Society programs and American participation in the Vietnam war. He also said it was the solemn duty of both the U.S. and the Soviet Union to cut back in the arms race.

**Edward W. Brooke,** the Massachusetts Republican, was sworn in as a United States Senator *January 10,* thus becoming the first Negro to hold a Senate seat in nearly a century.

**The House of Representatives** voted *January 10* to deny administration of the oath of office to Representative Adam Clayton Powell, pending the outcome of a special investigation into his qualifications for office.

**The Supreme Court** ruled *January 10* that United States citizens holding valid passports may not be prosecuted if they visit Communist nations where travel by Americans has been prohibited by State Department regulation.

**Lester G. Maddox,** the 51-year old Democratic segregationist and former restaurant owner, was elected Governor of Georgia *January 10* by the State Legislature.

**Harvard archeologists** disclosed *January 13* the discovery in Kenya of an elbow bone that the scientists assert proves the history of man dates back 2,500,000 years.

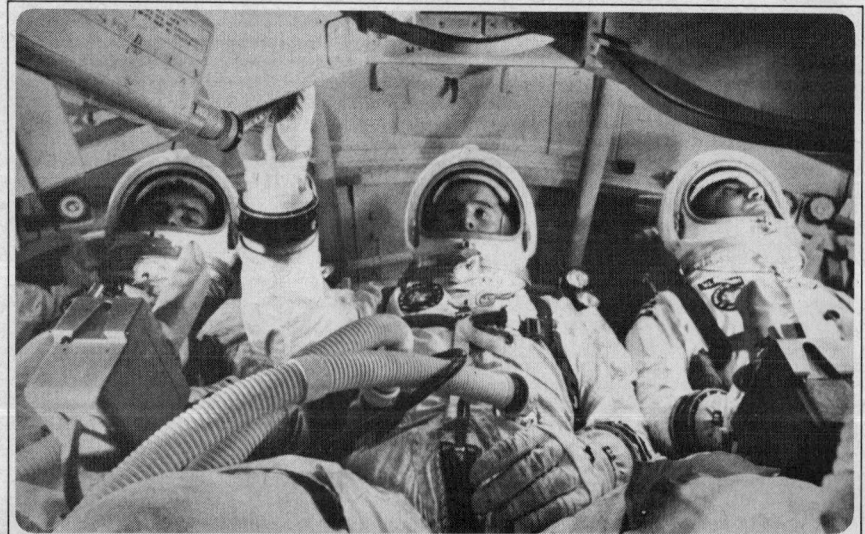

Victims of Apollo spacecraft tragedy: Astronauts (from left) Roger Chaffee, Edward White II, Virgil Grissom

Wide World

Wide World

Bobby Baker prior to his conviction by a Federal court

Wide World

Vietcong suspect takes leave of his wife after arrest.

**The American gross national product**—the total value of the nation's goods and services—rose by 5.4 per cent during 1966, the Department of Commerce announced *January 15*.

**Mrs. John F. Kennedy** withdrew her suit against William Manchester, author of *The Death of a President,* and Harper & Row, the publishers. Settlement of the dispute, announced *January 16,* cleared the way for publication of the book in April.

**Mrs. George C. Wallace** was inaugurated as Governor of Alabama *January 16.* She succeeded her husband, who had been ineligible under state law to seek another term.

**Lucius Amerson,** a 33-year-old former paratrooper, was sworn in as sheriff in Tuskagee, Alabama, *January 16,* thus becoming the first Negro sheriff to take office in the South in this century.

**McCormick Place,** Chicago's vast, lakefront exhibition hall, was virtually destroyed by fire *January 16.* Damage was estimated at $120,-000,000.

**Albert H. DeSalvo,** the 35-year-old mental patient who claimed to be the "Boston Strangler," was convicted *January 18* on ten counts of assault, armed robbery, and sex crimes. He was sentenced to life imprisonment.

**Dr. Clark Kerr** was removed as president of the University of California *January 20.* With California Governor Ronald W. Reagan in attendance, the University Board of Regents voted 14–8 in favor of Dr. Kerr's dismissal.

In a special **"Message on Older Americans"** sent to Congress *January 23,* President Johnson requested approval for major increases in Social Security benefits to become effective July 1, 1967.

**The Supreme Court** ruled *January 23* that New York laws designed to prevent Communists from serving in the state's educational and civil service systems were unconstitutional.

President Johnson submitted the **Federal Budget** for the 1968 fiscal year to Congress *January 24.* The Administration called for expenditures of $169.2 billion and receipts of $167.1 billion, for a deficit of $2.1 billion.

**Astronauts Virgil I. Grissom, Edward H. White II, and Roger B. Chaffee** were killed *January 27* in a fire aboard a spacecraft undergoing tests at Cape Kennedy, Florida.

**Robert G. (Bobby) Baker,** the 38-year-old former secretary to the Senate Democratic majority, was convicted *January 29* by a Federal court in Washington, D.C., on seven counts of theft, fraud, and income-tax evasion. Baker's attorneys announced they would appeal the case.

**Local draft boards** may not punish registrants for publicly protesting the war in Vietnam by re-classifying them IA, a Federal Court of Appeals ruled *January 30.*

### INTERNATIONAL

**The North Vietnamese government** rejected *January 3* the proposals advanced by Britain for a peace conference to be attended by Washington, Saigon, and Hanoi officials. Both the United States and South Vietnam had accepted the proposal earlier.

**Spain and Romania** signed an accord *January 5* establishing diplomatic and commercial relations.

Virtually all **trade between the United States and Rhodesia** was cut off by executive order signed by President Johnson on *January 5.*

Clashes between **Chinese Red Guards** and forces opposed to Chairman Mao Tse-tung were reported *January 8.* Peking Radio broadcast reports of violence erupting in Shanghai and Nanking.

**Roman Catholic and Anglican churchmen** announced *January 12* the formation of a joint commission to study issues that have divided the two faiths for four centuries.

**Britain and France** announced agreement *January 16* on plans for joint development of a supersonic swing-wing jet aircraft.

**The United States and South Vietnam** agreed *January 17* to observe a four-day cease-fire during the lunar New Year. The Vietcong had asked for a seven-day truce period. Both South Vietnam and the United States said they were willing to meet with representatives of North Vietnam to discuss a longer cease-fire.

**The Senate of Chile** voted *January 17* to refuse permission to President Eduardo Frei Montalva to make a state visit to the United States. Unstable domestic politics, rather than anti-Americanism, reportedly prompted the unprecedented action.

**President Charles de Gaulle of France and Prime Minister Harold Wilson of Britain** met in Paris *January 24* to discuss the possibility of British membership in the Common Market.

**Israel and Syria** reaffirmed their armistice *January 25,* pledging to refrain from committing hostile acts along the 45-mile border between the two countries. The move came in the wake of a series of shooting incidents near the border.

**A treaty prohibiting the use of nuclear weapons in outer space** was signed *January 27* in London, Moscow, and Washington. Earlier, 60 other nations had signed the accord.

**Chinese soldiers** waving fixed bayonets shouted anti-Soviet slogans in a mass demonstration outside the Russian Embassy in Peking *January 28.* The protest followed a clash between Russian and Chinese students in Moscow's Red Square.

**Pope Paul VI and Soviet President Nikolai Podgorny** met *January 30* at Vatican City. It was the first meeting between a Roman Catholic Pontiff and a chief of state of the Soviet Union.

## FEBRUARY

### NATIONAL

**Lunar Orbiter 3** was launched from Cape Kennedy *February 4* on a 92-hour photographic mission to the Moon. The spacecraft was scheduled to transmit to Earth pictures of possible landing sites on the Moon for manned space vehicles.

Labor leader James R. Hoffa begins prison sentence.

**The 25th Amendment** to the U.S. Constitution, providing for succession to the Presidency, went into effect *February 10.*

**The National Student Association** admitted *February 13* that it had used funds provided by the Central Intelligence Agency to help finance its international activities between the early 1950s and 1966.

**Secretary of Defense Robert S. McNamara** announced *February 15* plans to call up some 30,000 reservists who had not served two-year terms of active duty.

**First pictures of the surface of the Moon** transmitted by Lunar Orbiter 3 were received at a Madrid tracking station *February 15.* The pictures showed small craters and pitted, broad, level areas thought to be safe for manned spacecraft landings.

**New Orleans' District Attorney Jim Garrison** announced *February 18* that he was conducting an investigation into the possibility of a plot to assassinate President John F. Kennedy.

The Select Committee of the House investigating the conduct of Representative **Adam Clayton Powell** recommended *February 23* that the Harlem Congressman be seated in the House, but be punished with a fine of $40,000, loss of seniority, and public censure and condemnation by the Speaker. The Committee found Powell guilty of "gross misconduct." Powell remained at his Bimini vacation home throughout the course of the proceedings.

**Air Force Academy officials** announced *February 24* that 24 cadets had resigned because of violations of the academy's honor code.

**Ramsey Clark** was named Attorney General *February 28.* His father, Supreme Court Justice Tom Clark, immediately announced that he would retire from the high court in order to avoid the possibility of conflict of interest with the Justice Department.

### INTERNATIONAL

**President Johnson** said *February 2* that he was "not aware of any serious effort" by the North Vietnamese government to end the war in Vietnam.

**The United States** consigned two million tons of grain to India *February 2* in an effort to help avert a major famine.

**The Soviet Union** issued a stern warning to the Communist Chinese government *February 4* declaring that if violence directed against Russians in Peking were not curbed, Moscow would take retaliatory action.

**The U.S. Navy aircraft carrier** *Franklin D. Roosevelt* pulled into Cape Town, South Africa, to refuel *February 4.* However, because of South African apartheid laws, the crew was restricted to the ship.

**Soviet Premier Alexsei Kosygin** arrived in Britain *February 5* for talks with British Prime Minister Harold Wilson. Officials indicated that settlement of the Vietnamese conflict was to be the prime topic of discussion between the two leaders.

**The Soviet Union** signed an accord with Iran *February 7,* under which the U.S.S.R. was committed to supply Iran with almost $100,000,000 worth of military equipment.

Secretary of State Dean Rusk declared *February 9* that the United States would not halt its bombing raids on North Vietnam unless the Hanoi government indicated a willingness to make a reciprocal gesture.

Emperor Haile Selassie of Ethiopia arrived at the White House *February 13* to begin an official visit to the United States.

The 17-nation Disarmament Conference reconvened in Geneva *February 21*.

President Sukarno of Indonesia was reported *February 22* to have surrendered all of his executive power to General Suharto, the Indonesian Army commander in control of the national government.

The Indian Congress Party suffered a major defeat in national elections that ended *February 22*. Food shortages were cited in some reports as a major reason for voter dissatisfaction with the ruling party.

United States officials disclosed *February 26* that American planes had begun dropping mines into North Vietnamese rivers in an attempt to halt the flow of supplies southward aboard junks and sampans.

## MARCH

### NATIONAL

The House of Representatives voted *March 1* to bar Representative Adam Clayton Powell from his seat in the House.

Senator Robert F. Kennedy, the New York Democrat, proposed in a Senate speech *March 2* that U.S. bombing of North Vietnam be suspended.

Betty Furness was named *March 4* by President Johnson to succeed Mrs. Esther Peterson as special assistant for consumer affairs.

President Johnson sent to Congress *March 6* a special message recommending extensive revision of the Selective Service system during the next two years. The President's recommendations called for establishment of a lottery system for drafting men eligible for military service and a re-examination of college student deferments.

James R. Hoffa surrendered to United States marshals in Washington, D.C., *March 7* to begin serving an eight-year prison sentence for jury-tampering.

Representative Adam Clayton Powell filed suit in Federal district court in Washington *March 8* in an attempt to regain his seat in the House of Representatives.

President Johnson requested *March 9* Congressional restoration of tax incentives for business investment. The incentives had been temporarily repealed in 1966.

The new grave of President John F. Kennedy in Arlington National Cemetery was blessed by Richard Cardinal Cushing of Boston in a simple ceremony at 7 A.M. on *March 15*. President Johnson and members of the Kennedy family attended the ceremony.

The Supreme Court ruled *March 20* that law enforcement officials are not required by the Constitution to reveal informants' identities.

A Federal Court ordered all Alabama schools to desegregate in a ruling handed down in Montgomery *March 22*.

Senator Robert F. Kennedy of New York declared *March 27* that he would not enter Presidential primaries in 1968 and that he would move to keep his name off primary ballots.

President Johnson ordered the Central Intelligence Agency to end its financial assistance to private organizations in a directive made public *March 29*.

### INTERNATIONAL

Czechoslovakia and Poland signed a treaty of military assistance and friendship *March 1*. Observers indicated that the treaty was the first of a series of agreements in which East Germany, Poland, and Czechoslovakia were expected to unite in an effort to perpetuate the division of Germany.

U.N. Secretary General Thant predicted *March 5* that the fighting in Vietnam would be "prolonged and bloody." Thant said he believed that cessation of U.S. bombing of North Vietnam would be an important step toward peace.

Svetlana Alliluyeva, the middle-aged daughter of the late Russian dictator Joseph Stalin, was reported *March 10* to have defected to the West from the Soviet Union.

American planes bombed a major North Vietnamese iron and steel manufacturing complex about 40 miles north of Hanoi *March 10*. It was the first time since the start of the war in Vietnam that American pilots had received permission to bomb that type of target.

Svetlana Alliluyeva arrived in Geneva, Switzerland, *March 11* aboard a jet from Rome.

Mrs. Indira Gandhi was re-elected Prime Minister of India *March 12*.

General Suharto of Indonesia took the oath of office as acting President *March 12*.

U.S. military headquarters in France were closed permanently *March 14*, 18 days prior to the deadline set by French President Charles de Gaulle for the evacuation of all American forces from France.

President Johnson announced on *March 15* the resignation of Henry Cabot Lodge as United States Ambassador to South Vietnam. Ellsworth Bunker, U.S. Ambassador-at-Large, was named to replace Lodge in the Saigon post.

Ceremony at closing of SHAPE Headquarters in Paris

Wide World

President Johnson and other leaders at Adenauer funeral

**The West German government** agreed *March 15* to invest some $5,000,000 in U.S. Treasury bonds in order to help ease American balance of payment deficits generated by the maintenance of American forces in Germany.

**The South Vietnamese Constitutional Assembly** unanimously approved the text of a new national Constitution *March 18.* The Constitution, providing for the election of a president and a two-house legislature, was promulgated on March 31.

**President Johnson,** together with key diplomatic and military advisors, arrived at Guam, in the Pacific, *March 19* for talks with South Vietnamese and American military and diplomatic officials. At the conclusion of the two-day conference, the President declared that he was cautiously optimistic about the course of the war.

Washington officials disclosed *March 21* that in early February President Johnson had sent a letter to **President Ho Chi Minh** of North Vietnam in which the American Chief Executive urged direct talks between American and

Demonstrators protested Vietnam war at U.N. Plaza.

North Vietnamese officials in an effort to end the war. Ho Chi Minh rejected the President's proposals in a reply dated February 15.

**The civilian government of Sierra Leone** was overthrown *March 24* in a bloodless coup. It was the tenth coup in an African nation in the last two years.

**The tanker** *Torrey Canyon,* aground off southwest England, broke up on a reef *March 26,* pouring tons of oil toward English resort beaches.

**Vice President Hubert H. Humphrey** left Washington *March 27* on a seven-nation European tour.

**Pope Paul VI** issued his fifth encyclical *March 28.* The Pontiff declared that wealthy nations were obligated to assist in the development of poor nations.

**The first French nuclear submarine,** the 7,900-ton *Redoutable,* was launched *March 29* in Cherbourg.

President Johnson ratified a **consular treaty** with the Soviet Union *March 31.* It provided for the opening of additional consulate offices in several cities of both countries.

The new **NATO Headquarters** at Casteau, Belgium, was opened formally *March 31.*

## APRIL

### NATIONAL

**Postmaster General Lawrence F. O'Brien** announced *April 3* that he had recommended to President Johnson the conversion of the Post Office Department into a nonprofit government agency.

In a statement delivered *April 4,* **Dr. Martin Luther King, Jr.,** called on Negroes and whites to register their opposition to the war in Vietnam by becoming conscientious objectors to military service.

**President Johnson** sent to Congress *April 5* a request for a 4.5 per cent pay increase for civilian Federal employees and members of the armed forces. The President also requested Congressional approval of an increase in the rates for first, second, and third class mail.

**Robert G. (Bobby) Baker,** former secretary to the Senate Democratic majority, was sentenced *April 7* to one to three years in Federal prison after being convicted on charges of income-tax evasion, conspiracy, theft, and fraud.

**William Manchester,** author of *The Death of a President,* said *April 7* that he would earn between $300,000 and $400,000 from sale of the book, while the John F. Kennedy memorial library would realize between $5 million and $10 million.

**A 13-day strike** against major radio and television networks ended *April 10.*

**The Board of Directors** of the NAACP approved *April 10* a resolution stating opposition to the merger of the civil rights and peace movements, as had been proposed by Dr. Martin Luther King, Jr.

**Adam Clayton Powell** was re-elected *April 10* to the Congressional seat from which he had been ousted by a vote of the House of Representatives.

The **Surveyor 3** spacecraft made a soft landing on the Moon and began transmitting pictures of the lunar surface to earth *April 19,* after a 65-hour flight from Cape Kennedy. Surveyor 3 was the second American spacecraft to achieve a soft landing on the Moon.
**Tornadoes** struck northern Illinois *April 21,* leaving more than 50 dead and hundreds injured.
**Cassius Clay,** the world heavyweight boxing champion, refused *April 28* to be inducted into the Army. He was subsequently tried and convicted of violating Federal draft laws, sentenced to five years in prison, fined $10,000, and stripped of his boxing title. The conviction and sentence were appealed.

### INTERNATIONAL
In a statement issued *April 1,* **U.N. Secretary General Thant** publicly requested the United States to declare a truce in the Vietnam war with a view to the possibility that the move might provoke reciprocal action by the Vietcong and Hanoi.
**Roland Michener** was named Governor General of Canada *April 4.*
**North Vietnam and the Vietcong** rejected *April 6* the peace proposals made by United Nations Secretary General Thant.
**U.S. military aid to India and Pakistan** was terminated *April 12.*
**Hemisphere chiefs of state** attending a summit conference in Punta del Este, Uruguay, approved *April 13* an eight-point development program that included plans for creation of a Latin American Common Market.
On *April 15* thousands of **anti-war demonstrators** staged what was described as the most massive peace rally ever held in New York City.
**North Vietnam** rejected *April 16* a four-point peace proposal offered by Canada. Hanoi termed the Canadian plan "at variance with the sovereignty of the Vietnamese people."
Responding to a West German appeal for a détente, **Walter Ulbricht,** the East German Communist leader, proposed *April 17* a meeting between leaders of the two states.
**An attempted coup d'etat** by army officers in Ghana was crushed by government forces *April 17.*
**Former West German Chancellor Konrad Adenauer** died *April 19* at the age of 91. President Johnson flew to Bonn April 23 to attend the state funeral.
**Mihajlo Mihajlov,** the Yugoslav author whose articles had often been critical of the quality of life under Communist regimes, was sentenced to four-and-one-half years in prison by a court in Belgrade on *April 19.*
**Secretary of State Dean Rusk** declared *April 19* that the United States and South Vietnam were willing to withdraw their forces ten miles south of the demilitarized zone if the North Vietnamese would take similar action. Hanoi rejected the proposal.
**A military junta** seized control of the Greek government *April 21.* Constantine V. Kollias, chief prosecutor of the Greek Supreme Court,

King Constantine (r.) with army chief after Greek coup

was named Premier. Asserting that the coup had been staged in order to prevent a leftist revolt, the junta suspended some provisions of the Constitution.
**Svetlana Alliluyeva,** daughter of Joseph Stalin, flew to the United States *April 21* from Switzerland, where she had remained in seclusion since defecting from the Soviet Union in India on March 6.
**Col. Vladimir M. Komarov,** lone pilot of the first manned spacecraft sent aloft by the Soviet Union since 1965, was killed *April 24* when the re-entry parachute of the Soyuz I capsule malfunctioned and sent the craft plummeting to earth.
**Crown Princess Beatrix** of the Netherlands gave birth to a son *April 27.* The child was the first male heir born in the Dutch royal family since 1851.
**Expo 67,** the Canadian world's fair, formally opened *April 27.*

## MAY

### NATIONAL
**The Senate Internal Security Subcommittee** opened an investigation *May 2* into the extent of subversive influences on racial disturbances in the United States.
**The World Journal Tribune,** a New York City afternoon daily, **ceased publication** *May 5,* less than eight months after its first edition appeared.

President Johnson visits U.S. pavilion at Expo 67.

Israeli soldiers celebrate at Jerusalem's Wailing Wall.

"By the Beard of the Prophet—Is It Only a Paper Moon?"

The Defense Department announced *May 10* plans to recommission a **World War II battleship** from the reserve fleet for Vietnam duty. **In a landmark decision** handed down *May 15,* the Supreme Court held that constitutionally guaranteed safeguards applicable to adults in trials must be extended to youths appearing in juvenile courts.

**The United Presbyterian Church in the U.S.A.,** adopting the first major doctrinal change in the church in more than 250 years, approved *May 22* the Confession of 1967, which deals with the relationship between Christian virtues and contemporary issues such as poverty, peace, and race relations.

**Some 85,000 Ford Cougars** were recalled by the Ford Motor Company *May 22* for repair of a headlight defect.

President Johnson named **Alexander B. Trowbridge** Secretary of Commerce *May 22.*

**A trio of masked bandits** brandishing submachine guns ambushed two Brink's Inc. guards in Brockton, Massachusetts, *May 23* and escaped in a stolen armored car with more than $600,000 in cash. It was the sixth armored car robbery in Massachusetts in 14 months.

**The Supreme Court,** in a 5-4 decision handed down *May 29,* ruled that a California statute providing property owners with "absolute discretion" over the rental and sale of housing was unconstitutional because it was discriminatory and thus violated the 14th Amendment. The Court also ruled that the 14th Amendment guarantees an American the right to his citizenship until he relinquishes it; thus, the Court held, Congress was not empowered to revoke an American's citizenship without his consent.

**INTERNATIONAL**

**Hijackers** ambushed a bullion truck in a northeast section of London *May 1,* overpowered three guards with ammonia, and escaped with $2 million in gold bars belonging to N. M. Rothschild & Sons.

**British Prime Minister Harold Wilson** announced *May 2* that Britain would again seek membership in the European Common Market. President Charles de Gaulle of France had blocked Britain's bid for membership in the economic community four years earlier.

**President Chung Hee Park** of South Korea was re-elected *May 3* to a second four-year term by a large majority vote.

**Three captured American pilots** were led through crowds of jeering North Vietnamese in the main streets of Hanoi *May 6.* The State Department registered a stiff protest with the Hanoi government through the International Red Cross, calling the abuse of the Americans a "flagrant violation" of the Geneva convention governing treatment of prisoners of war. **American officials** disclosed *May 8* that air raids against targets near Hanoi had been suspended between mid-December and the end of April in a futile bid for peace. During the same period, the officials said, North Vietnam had been invited, through Polish diplomatic channels, to make a similar gesture of de-escalation, but had refused.

**Cunard Lines** announced *May 8* that two venerable transatlantic liners, the *Queen Elizabeth* and her sister ship, the *Queen Mary,* would be withdrawn from service and sold.

**Dr. Zakir Husain** was elected President of India *May 9.* He was the first Muslim to become chief of state of the predominately Hindu nation.

**Pope Paul VI** flew to Portugal *May 13* to celebrate Mass and to pray for peace at the Shrine of Fátima.

**U.S. planes** bombed a power plant about one mile from the center of Hanoi *May 19.* It was the first time a target in downtown Hanoi had been designated for an Allied air strike.

At the request of the United Arab Republic, the 3,400-man **United Nations Emergency Force** that had served for ten years as a buffer between Egyptian and Israeli forces in the Sinai Peninsula and the Gaza Strip was withdrawn on *May 19.* The U.N. military posts were subsequently occupied by Arab troops.

**The Soviet Union** ratified *May 19* the international treaty banning the use of nuclear weapons in outer space.

**King Constantine of Greece** announced *May 21* the birth of a son, Prince Paul, who is heir to the Greek throne.

**Massive riots** led by supporters of the Peking regime erupted *May 22* in the British Crown Colony of Hong Kong.

A total of 322 persons were reported to have been killed in a fire that destroyed the largest department store in Brussels *May 22* at the height of the afternoon shopping crush. Arson was suspected. The store reportedly had been the target of anti-American demonstrations.

**Pope Paul VI** called *May 24* for a halt in the American bombing of North Vietnam and an end to the infiltration of men and war materiel into South Vietnam by Hanoi.

**Sir Francis Chichester** sailed into the harbor at Plymouth, England, at dusk on *May 28* aboard his 53-foot ketch *Gipsy Moth IV,* thus ending his solo, nine-month voyage around the world. Queen Elizabeth II subsequently knighted the 64-year-old mariner.

Johnson meets Kosygin at Glassboro summit conference.

## JUNE

### NATIONAL

**U.S. Army Captain Howard B. Levy,** the 30-year-old doctor who had refused to obey orders to train Green Beret forces for service in Vietnam, was found guilty *June 2* by a ten-member general court-martial of disobedience, culpable negligence, and seeking to promote disloyalty. Levy was sentenced to three years at hard labor, ordered to forfeit all pay and allowances, and dismissed from the Army.

**Rioting** broke out in the Roxbury district of Boston *June 3*. More than 1,000 Negroes threw bottles, looted stores, and battled with 1,700 policemen.

**The Supreme Court** ruled *June 5* that tenants, businessmen, and property owners may legally refuse to admit to their premises any inspector who does not have a search warrant.

**Cyrus R. Vance** resigned as Assistant Secretary of Defense *June 10*. **Paul H. Nitze,** Secretary of the Navy, was named to replace him.

**Vice President Humphrey** underwent minor surgery *June 10* for removal of a nonmalignant tumor.

**The Supreme Court** handed down 14 decisions on *June 12*, the last day of its current term. In major rulings, the Court held that:

● States do not have the power to outlaw interracial marriages.

● Labor unions have the legal right to fine members who work during a strike.

● A $500,000 libel judgment awarded by a Texas Court to former Major General Edwin A. Walker against the Associated Press was invalid.

● A $460,000 libel judgment awarded to Wallace Butts, former director of athletics at the University of Georgia, against the Curtis Publishing Company was valid.

● The lower court conviction of Dr. Martin Luther King, Jr., and seven others on contempt of court charges growing out of an Alabama civil rights demonstration was valid.

● A New York State law permitting court-approved eavesdropping in investigations was unconstitutional.

● Suspects in criminal cases must be provided with lawyers when they appear in police line-ups.

**Solicitor General Thurgood Marshall** was nominated by President Johnson *June 13* to succeed Justice Tom Clark on the Supreme Court. When Congress confirmed the appointment, Justice Marshall became the first Negro ever to sit on the nation's highest court.

**Robert Kintner,** former president of both NBC and ABC, resigned *June 14* as Special Assistant to the President to undergo eye surgery.

**A merchant marine deck officers' strike** began *June 14* and tied up shipping in Atlantic and Gulf Coast ports for eight days.

**Warren M. Christopher,** a 41-year-old San Francisco lawyer, was nominated Deputy Attorney General by President Johnson *June 15*.

**Luci Johnson Nugent,** younger daughter of the President, gave birth to an 8-pound, 10-ounce boy, Patrick Lyndon, in Austin, Texas, on *June 21*.

**Sixteen members of a Negro revolutionary group** were arrested *June 21* in New York and Philadelphia on charges of anarchist conspiracy. Police said members of the group had planned to assassinate Whitney M. Young, Jr., and Roy Wilkins, both moderate Negro civil rights leaders.

**Senator Thomas J. Dodd,** the Connecticut Democrat, was censured by the Senate *June 23* for using political funds "for his personal benefit." The vote in favor of censure was 92 to 5.

### INTERNATIONAL

**Full-scale war** broke out between Israel and the Middle Eastern Arab States *June 5*. Within six days the Arab military force collapsed, and Israel seized the Sinai peninsula, the Gaza strip, the Old City of Jerusalem, and Jordanian territory on the west bank of the Jordan River. Both sides agreed *June 10* to accept a cease-fire and the presence of a U.N. observer team.

Moving one step closer to the development of a hydrogen bomb, France began a new series of **nuclear tests** in the Pacific *June 5*.

Three decades of formal ostracism of the **Duchess of Windsor** by the British royal family ended officially *June 7* with the appearance of the Duchess at her husband's side, together with Queen Elizabeth II, who had invited her, at a public memorial ceremony in London. The Duke of Windsor, who was King Edward VII, had abdicated his throne in 1936 to marry the American-born divorcée.

The Soviet Union launched an **unmanned space laboratory** on a four-month flight to Venus *June 12*. Two days later the United States launched a Venus probe by **Mariner 5,** a rocket one-fourth the size of the Russian spacecraft.

**Premier Aleksei N. Kosygin** of the Soviet Union flew to New York *June 15* to attend a special session of the U.N. General Assembly, called to consider the Middle East question. En route to the United States, the Russian Premier stopped briefly in Paris to confer with President de Gaulle of France.

**Communist China** announced *June 17* the successful detonation of its first hydrogen bomb.

**President Johnson and Premier Kosygin** of the Soviet Union held talks at Glassboro, New Jersey, on *June 23* and *June 25*. Officials said that discussions at the summit conference had ranged over Vietnam, the Middle East, and a treaty to halt the spread of nuclear weapons. Both men agreed the meetings had been "useful"; President Johnson said they had been "very good." Communist Chinese radio broadcasts condemned the summit meeting, charging that the Russians were close to concluding a "vicious deal with Johnson" directed against Peking. Premier Kosygin remained in the United States for ten days, then flew to Cuba for talks with Premier Fidel Castro.

**Peking** increased pressure on Hong Kong *June 29*, charging that British military planes from the crown colony had violated mainland territory. China also suspended food shipments into Hong Kong, creating severe shortages.

**Premier Nguyen Cao Ky** of South Vietnam withdrew from his nation's presidential race *June 30* and announced that he would run for vice-president on the ticket headed by General Nguyen Van Thieu, South Vietnamese chief of state.

**The Kennedy Round** of trade agreements was signed in Geneva *June 30* by 46 nations.

## JULY

### NATIONAL

**Attorney General Ramsey Clark,** completing the Justice Department's two-year study on electronic bugging devices, issued regulations *July 6* forbidding all wiretapping and virtually all electronic eavesdropping except in cases of national emergency.

**Newark** became the scene of intensive race rioting as Negroes in the city's ghetto began looting stores and firing at police and firemen from rooftops. By *July 14*, the third day of disorders, the violence had spread into Newark's business district, and State Police and National Guardsmen were summoned to attempt to halt the rioting, which persisted for several more days.

**Minneapolis race riot** was quickly halted *July 21* by National Guardsmen.

**Militant black leaders** concluded a Newark conference *July 23* after adopting resolutions against moderate Negro stands on racial issues and fixing the blame for the Newark riot on the white race. On the same day a new riot erupted in Detroit; violence spread throughout large sections of the city and huge fires burned out of control.

**H. Rap Brown,** Negro "Black Power" leader, gave an inflammatory speech *July 24* in Cambridge, Maryland, after which crowds rioted, setting fire to sections of the town. Brown disappeared when authorities began a nationwide hunt for him, but was arrested by the FBI at Alexandria, Virginia, two days later.

**New race riots** erupted *July 24* in the Puerto Rican section of New York City, as well as in Rochester, New York, and Englewood, New Jersey. Rioting in Detroit increased in intensity as Michigan's Governor Romney called in the National Guard and President Johnson rushed 4,700 Army paratroopers into the city. The President called the riots acts of lawlessness that did not represent the vast majority of Negroes in the U.S.

**Detroit's race riot,** worst in the nation's history, was virtually ended by *July 27*, although periodic sniping persisted from some rooftops and fires still burned in many neighborhoods. A curfew and a ban on liquor sales were kept in effect until the end of the week.

© 1967 Register & Tribune Syndicate

"Yes, but what do you think caused the riots?"

Wide World

Detroit police search suspects for weapons during riot.

Biafra rebel troops surrender to a Nigerian soldier.

Earth fissure caused by quake near Adapazari, Turkey.

## INTERNATIONAL

**Moise Tshombe,** former Congolese premier subject to the death penalty upon his return to the Congo, was arrested *July 2* by authorities in Algeria.

**Arab-Israeli** cease-fire violations continued *July 3,* the third day of the truce, as mortar and machine-gun fire was exchanged across the Suez Canal. Meanwhile, at the U.N., a Soviet-backed Yugoslav resolution demanding withdrawal of Israeli forces from Arab territory was defeated, although a resolution condemning Israeli unification of Jerusalem was passed.

**New Congolese war** erupted as Katangese soldiers and foreign mercenaries attacked President Mobutu's troops *July 5* in Bukavu. The attack was generally interpreted as a reaction to former Premier Tshombe's arrest in Algeria.

**Nigerian federal troops** encountered heavy fighting *July 8* as they advanced into Biafra.

Prolonged tensions in **Hong Kong** between the British and Communist elements erupted *July 9* into demonstrations and violence.

**Cairo meeting** of Egyptian President Nasser, Jordanian King Hussein, and Algerian President Boumedienne on *July 11* resulted in plans for Hussein to attempt arrangement of a permanent solution to the dispute between Israel and the Arab states.

**Congolese fighting** was virtually ended when white mercenaries fled *July 13* from Kisangani.

**Britain** announced plans *July 18* for complete withdrawal from all of its territories east of Suez by the mid-1970s.

**The Johnson Administration** announced plans *July 22* for increased troop combat efficiency in Vietnam. General William C. Westmoreland, commander of U.S. forces in Vietnam, was promised an increase of troop strength to 525,000 by late 1968.

**Earthquakes** took 213 lives in Turkey. The most severe tremors struck the community of Adapazari *July 22.*

**Pope Paul VI** met in Istanbul *July 25* with Eastern Orthodox Patriarch Athenagoras. Ceremonies highlighted a historic step in the direction of ultimate unity between Roman Catholicism and Eastern Orthodoxy.

**French President de Gaulle** departed abruptly from Canada on *July 26* after touring Expo 67 in Montreal and making a speech that appeared to encourage Quebec's freedom from the Dominion of Canada. The speech was followed by a rebuke from Canadian Prime Minister Lester Pearson, after which de Gaulle cancelled plans to visit the prime minister in Ottawa.

**Explosions** *July 29* wracked the U.S. aircraft carrier *Forrestal,* on duty off the coast of Vietnam. A total of 129 men were dead or missing in the wake of the worst U.S. naval disaster since World War II.

## AUGUST

### NATIONAL

**Milwaukee** lived through the second day of strict curfew on *August 1.* Wisconsin Governor Warren P. Knowles' strong security measures effectively halted a race riot in its early stages. In Washington, F.B.I. Director J. Edgar Hoover said that there was no evidence of a conspiracy behind the July race riots.

**A ten per cent income tax surcharge** was the subject of President Johnson's special request to Congress *August 3.* The high cost of the Vietnam war was cited as a major reason necessitating additional funds.

**The Senate Judiciary Committee's** hearings on racial rioting was the scene of an attack *August 4* on the Administration's antipoverty program. Evidence from a Nashville, Tennessee, police chief indicated that Federal funds had backed a Negro "liberation" school teaching hatred of whites.

**New York City Negroes** in Washington demonstrated at the House of Representatives *August 7* to protest defeat of the Administration's rat control bill. In a separate racial development in Detroit, two city policemen were charged with the murder of two innocent Negroes during the Detroit rioting in July.

Arab refugees return to Israeli-held sector of Jordan.

**Fairbanks, Alaska,** was hit *August 15* by a severe flood, forcing the evacuation of thousands of residents.

**New Haven racial violence** erupted for the third straight night on *August 21*. Fires and scattered incidents of looting were reported in various parts of the city.

**Forest fires** raged uncontrolled in sections of Washington, Oregon, Idaho, and British Columbia. On *August 22* Portland, Oregon, recorded 61st consecutive day without rain.

**The House of Representatives** cut back the Administration's foreign aid authorization bill by $247,000,000 on *August 24,* as Southern Democrats joined Republicans in effective protest against Administration policies.

**George Lincoln Rockwell,** American Nazi leader, was shot and killed by a sniper in Arlington, Virginia, on *August 25*. The murderer, who was quickly captured, was a disgruntled former member of Rockwell's party.

**Nineteen skydivers** drowned *August 27* in Lake Erie when their aircraft's pilot accidentally dropped them over water. Heavy clouds and faulty radar information had caused the pilot to lose his bearings.

**INTERNATIONAL**

**Communist China** celebrated its army's 40th anniversary on *August 1*. The absence of many important leaders at the ceremonies in Peking led to speculation concerning previously unknown military purges.

**Mercenaries and Katangan rebels** were described as having fled the Bukavu area after their defeat by the Congolese army. Reports reaching Washington on *August 2* tended to confirm Congolese President Mobutu's claims of total victory over the rebels.

**South Vietnam's presidential campaign** opened officially on *August 3*, with all of the major candidates appearing on a Saigon TV program.

**Jerusalem's Arabs** held a general citywide strike *August 7* to protest Israeli occupation. The strike halted all business activity in the city's Old Sector.

**West German Chancellor Kurt Georg Kiesinger** met with President Johnson in Washington on *August 15-16*. They decided that a reduction of military forces in West Germany must be preceded by full consultation between German and U.S. leaders, and that NATO forces should remain intact.

**Chinese demonstrators** broke into the Soviet embassy in Peking, according to a Yugoslavian press report of *August 17*. The mob was said to have smashed windows and started fires.

**Israeli repatriation** of Jordanian war refugees went into effect *August 18*. On the first day 355 Arabs displaced by the war crossed the Jordan River and returned to their homes.

**Nuclear treaty drafts** presented by the U.S. and the U.S.S.R. in Geneva on *August 24* were identical, indicating an unusual degree of accord between the two world powers. Thus hopes were raised for a final agreement on the treaty by early 1968.

**Secretary of Defense McNamara,** testifying before a Senate subcommittee on *August 25,* voiced serious doubts regarding the effectiveness of U.S. bombing in Vietnam. He further stated that there was no evidence that North Vietnam could be "bombed to the negotiating table."

**British Prime Minister Harold Wilson** shuffled his cabinet on *August 28* in the wake of major criticism, from both inside and outside his Labour Party, regarding the government's apparent inability to cope with the nation's economic problems.

**Chinese Communist officials** in London clashed with city police on *August 29* in an alley behind the Chinese diplomatic mission. The incident was related to British difficulties in Hong Kong and Peking.

**The Arab summit meeting** in Khartoum was dominated by Egyptian President Nasser and Jordanian King Hussein. It was reported on *August 30* that they had told other conference delegates of the possible need for a negotiated settlement with Israel.

## SEPTEMBER

**NATIONAL**

**President Johnson** stated *September 1* that there were no serious differences of opinion between Secretary of Defense McNamara and the Joint Chiefs of Staff regarding the conduct of the war in Vietnam.

**Michigan's Governor George Romney** claimed in a *September 4* speech that he had been "brainwashed" by U.S. military personnel during his 1965 visit to Vietnam. He also claimed that the Administration had misled the American people regarding Vietnam.

**The United Automobile Workers** struck the Ford Motor Company *September 7*. Chrysler and General Motors continued to operate.

**The President and Mrs. Johnson** announced *September 10* the engagement of their daughter, Lynda Bird, to Marine Captain Charles Robb of Milwaukee.

**Public school teachers** in various parts of the country protested low salaries and poor working conditions in a series of strikes. The mass resignation of New York City teachers on *September 11* occurred six days after a statewide teachers' strike in Michigan.

Open housing demonstrations in Milwaukee were led by a Roman Catholic priest, the Reverend James E. Gropi. On *September 13* Milwaukee's Archbishop, the Most Reverend William E. Cousins, declared qualified support for Father Gropi's action.

**Hurricane Beulah** struck the Texas coast *September 21,* causing widespread flooding and heavy property damage.

**The teachers strike** was settled in New York City on *September 26.* This was eight days after public school teachers in Michigan had returned to their classes.

**Walter Washington** was sworn in *September 28* as commissioner of the District of Columbia, a post equivalent to mayor of the city of Washington. He thus became the first Negro to head a major municipal governing body in the nation's history.

### INTERNATIONAL

**South Vietnamese voters** elected Nguyen Van Thieu as president and Nguyen Cao Ky as vicepresident on *September 3.* About 83 per cent of the 6,000,000 voters turned out for the nation's first national election. Observers from 24 countries, including a 22-man U.S. delegation, concluded that the balloting was conducted in a reasonably honest manner.

**Secretary of Defense McNamara** announced *September 7* that the U.S. plans to build a complex barrier near South Vietnam's northern border. Consisting of land mines, barbed wire, and electronic devices, the barrier would be designed to halt enemy infiltration.

**Chinese and Indian troops** clashed *September 11* in the Himalaya Mountains. The day-long battle was the area's most serious incident since the Chinese-Indian border war of 1962.

**Cambodian Prince Norodom Sihanouk** removed pro-Peking officials from his cabinet on *September 11* in an effort to reduce Communist Chinese influence over the nation.

**French President Charles de Gaulle** returned to Paris on *September 12,* concluding a week's visit to Poland. De Gaulle's suggestion that Poland pursue policies independent of the Soviet Union was given a cool reception by Polish officials.

**Truong Dinh Dzu,** the peace candidate who finished second with a surprisingly strong showing in the September South Vietnam presidential elections, was convicted *September 15* on charges of illegal currency manipulations.

**Egyptian Field Marshall Abdel Hakim Amer** was reported to have committed suicide on *September 15* in the wake of the Arab military defeat at the hands of Israel.

**The America's Cup** was retained by the U.S. in a major international yachting event on *September 18.* The U.S. yacht *Intrepid* defeated Australia's *Dame Pattie* in four straight races.

**U.N. Secretary General Thant** opened the 22d General Assembly session on *September 19* with a speech requesting associate membership for weak member-states. Thant stated that full membership for such nations could lead to a general weakening of the U.N.

Vietnamese voter studies the list of candidates.

**The Queen Elizabeth II,** Britain's newest ocean liner, was launched in Scotland on *September 20.*

**The Soviet Union** announced *September 23* an agreement by which it would provide massive economic and military aid to North Vietnam in 1968.

**South Arabia's** two rival nationalist groups announced agreement for a cease-fire after concluding a conference in Cairo on *September 25.* They thus took the first major step to end the chaotic political situation plaguing the country.

**An offer to end the bombing** of North Vietnam was made by President Johnson on condition that such action would bring about prompt, productive peace discussions. Johnson's proposal, made *September 29,* came one day after France's assertion at the U.N. that U.S. actions in Vietnam are endangering world peace.

## OCTOBER

### NATIONAL

**Thurgood Marshall** took office as the first Negro associate justice of the Supreme Court on *October 2.*

**The 10 per cent income tax surcharge** proposed by President Johnson was shelved *October 3* by the House of Representatives Ways and Means Committee.

**President Johnson** refused *October 5* to yield to Congressional demands that he propose cuts in Federal spending as a condition for Congressional consideration of his tax surcharge proposal. The President's statement came one day after the Senate made drastic cuts in the Administration's antipoverty bill.

**The St. Louis Cardinals** defeated the Boston Red Sox *October 12* in the seventh and final game of the World Series.

**Secretary of State Dean Rusk** vehemently assailed critics of the Vietnam policy while defending the Administration's stand, *October 12.* On the same day 30 members of the House of Representatives urged the President to halt the bombing of North Vietnam because of its failure to achieve the announced objectives.

**The nation's governors** began an eight-day Caribbean cruise after concluding the National

Patriarch Athenagoras visits Pope Paul VI in Rome.

Governors' Conference in New York on *October 16*. Attending the functions were three potential Presidential candidates: Nelson Rockefeller of New York, George Romney of Michigan, and Ronald Reagan of California.

**A jury in Meridian, Mississippi,** found seven men guilty of participating in the 1964 murders of three civil rights workers. The verdict, reached on *October 20*, was the first pro-civil rights criminal conviction in the state's history.

**Antiwar demonstrators** concluded a weekend of protests at the Pentagon on *October 22*. Among the 400 persons arrested for trying to disrupt operations of the Department of Defense was writer Norman Mailer.

**General Motors** recalled 1,143,000 Chevrolets for replacement of a steering part on *October 24*.

Castro announces death of 'Ché' Guevara on Cuban radio.

**Dr. Martin Luther King** began a five-day jail sentence in Birmingham, Alabama, on *October 30*. His sentence stemmed from a 1963 civil rights demonstration.

### INTERNATIONAL

**North Vietnam** rejected *October 3* the Johnson Administration's peace offers on the grounds that the U.S. has no right to impose conditions on the Democratic Republic of Vietnam.

**Britain's Labour Party** called on the administration of Prime Minister Harold Wilson to dissociate itself from American policy in Vietnam, *October 4*.

**Nigerian federal troops** captured Enugu, the capital city of secessionist Biafra, on *October 4*, in a major step toward ending the civil war.

**Foreign Minister Thanat Khoman** of Thailand supported U.S. bombing of North Vietnam in a speech *October 5* before the U.N.

**Greece's King Constantine** compromised with the ruling military junta by agreeing to the retirement of 144 officers fallen from the regime's favor, *October 9*. The move followed by two days the junta's release of a prime political prisoner, former Premier George Papandreou.

**Indonesia** suspended diplomatic relations *October 9* with Communist China, in a move just short of a total break.

**Bolivian authorities** announced that Cuban Communist leader Ernesto ("Che") Guevara had been killed in a clash between guerrillas and government troops. Guevera's identity was officially confirmed *October 10*, two days after his reported death.

**Soviet space capsule** Venus IV made the first successful landing on the planet Venus on *October 18*, one day before U.S. spacecraft Mariner 5 swept within 2,480 miles of Venus's surface. Both space probes indicated that the planet is unfit for human habitation.

**An Egyptian gunboat** sank the Israeli destroyer *Elath* in a surprise attack *October 21*. While Israel charged the U.A.R. with a cease-fire violation, Egyptian authorities countercharged that the destroyer, sunk in the Mediterranean Sea near Port Said, had violated Egyptian waters.

**Andorra** was visited *October 23* by French President Charles de Gaulle, who is also coprince of the principality. De Gaulle is the first French head of state to visit Andorra in 1,150 years.

**Israeli artillery** in Sinai fired across the Suez Canal *October 24*, destroying Egyptian oil refineries and wiping out about 80 per cent of Egypt's oil resources.

**The Shah of Iran** officially crowned himself Emperor on *October 26*, after which he crowned his wife Empress. It was mainly a symbolical ceremony, since the Shah, Mohammed Riza Pahlevi, has been king since 1941. However, he had opposed an official coronation until a time when he could see indications of success in his efforts to build a progressive nation.

**Patriarch Athenagoras,** leader of Eastern Orthodox Christianity, met with Pope Paul VI in Rome on *October 26* in a return visit after the Pope's trip to Istanbul in July. Goals of Christian unity were restated by both.

The Shah of Iran crowns his wife Empress in Tehran.

Cleveland's new mayor, Carl B. Stokes, with family.

**Britain's House of Lords** had its powers reduced, according to an *October 31* declaration read at Parliament's opening by Queen Elizabeth II. The number of hereditary peers was limited, as was the body's power to delay passage of House of Commons legislation.

**U.S. Vice President Humphrey,** acting as the official U.S. representative, attended the inauguration of South Vietnamese President Thieu in Saigon on *October 31.* Humphrey's arrival was greeted by Vietcong shelling of Saigon's Independence Palace lawns.

## NOVEMBER

### NATIONAL

**President Johnson** chided antiwar demonstrators in the U.S. on *November 1,* saying that they were not making any contribution toward ultimate peace in Vietnam. He was referring primarily to the large Pentagon demonstrations held the previous week.

**Supreme Court Justice Potter Stewart** joined Justice William O. Douglas in stating that the Supreme Court should consider the legality of U.S. military action in Vietnam. The judicial dissent came on *November 6* when the Court declined to hear the appeal of soldiers who refused to go to Vietnam.

**Off-year elections** on *November 7* resulted in dramatic Republican gains in New Jersey and Kentucky. Negro Democrats won two major mayoral contests—Carl B. Stokes in Cleveland and Richard G. Hatcher in Gary, Indiana. In Boston, Mrs. Louise Day Hicks, a proponent of school segregation, was defeated for mayor by Kevin H. White.

**Two major U.S. space missions** achieved success *November 9.* Saturn 5, world's largest launch vehicle designed for eventual manned flights to the Moon, underwent its first flight test from Cape Kennedy, Florida. On the same day Surveyor 6 landed on the Moon and began televising pictures of a possible future landing site for U.S. astronauts.

**President Johnson** appealed for united support of his Vietnam policies while on a 5,100-mile, two-day tour of U.S. military installations on *November 10–11.*

**Bitter antiwar rioting** erupted in New York City on *November 14* outside a hotel where Secretary of State Dean Rusk was giving a major speech on U.S. policy in Vietnam.

**Sixty-three U.S. cities** were chosen *November 16* by the Johnson Administration as participants in a $300,000,000 slum clearance program.

**Michigan's Governor Romney** officially announced his candidacy *November 18* in the 1968 Presidential election.

**The U.S. population** reached 200,000,000 on *November 20,* according to a clock in the national census bureau.

**A jet airliner** crashed in Kentucky near the Cincinnati airport *November 20,* killing 66 of the 82 persons aboard.

**Secretary of Defense McNamara** was nominated as president of the World Bank by President Johnson, according to a *November 27* report. This indicated the imminent appointment of a new Secretary of Defense.

### INTERNATIONAL

**British plans for withdrawal from South Arabia** by late November were announced in London *November 2.* Meanwhile, rival Arab nationalist groups battled for control in Aden.

**Arthur J. Goldberg,** U.S. Ambassador to the U.N., indicated *November 2* a degree of relaxation in U.S. terms for a Vietnam peace settlement. He said that the U.S. was prepared to vote for participation of the National Liberation Front (political arm of the Vietcong) in a peace conference.

**A Soviet satellite system** capable of carrying a nuclear bomb to any point on Earth was being developed, according to a *November 3* statement by U.S. Secretary of Defense McNamara.

**Yemen's President Abdullah al-Salal** was ousted in a bloodless coup *November 5* while he was out of the country. Since Salal had opposed a peace pact between Egypt and Saudi Arabia that would settle the rival interests of those two nations in Yemen, Salal's removal prompted hopes for an end to the long civil war plaguing Yemen.

**Jordan's King Hussein,** appearing on U.S. television *November 6,* stated that he was prepared to recognize Israel's right to exist in peace. He later claimed that his statements also represented the views of Egypt's President Nasser.

**The Soviet Union's 50th Anniversary celebration** reached a climax *November 7* with a mammoth parade in Moscow. Among the many giant rockets displayed was one believed capable of launching a nuclear bomb via a satellite.

**South Vietnamese President Thieu** named his cabinet on *November 9.* Most of the members were military officers.

**Turkish Cypriotes** battled with Greek troops *November 14–15* in skirmishes that took at least 25 lives.

**Portugal** was condemned *November 15* by the U.N. Security Council for its failure to prevent mercenaries from using Angola as a base for attacks against the Congo.

**Japan's Premier Eisaku Sato,** visiting President Johnson in Washington, obtained a U.S. agreement on *November 15* providing for talks leading to the eventual return of Pacific islands captured from Japan during World War II.

**Britain devalued the pound** from $2.80 to $2.40 *November 18* in a measure aimed at reviving international faith in British currency and correcting the nation's chronically unfavorable balance of trade. Reactions were felt throughout the world as Spain, Israel, Hong Kong, Denmark, Ireland, Fiji, Bermuda, Malta, and Malawi also devalued their currency. In the U.S. the Federal Reserve Board acted to maintain the dollar's value by increasing the international interest rate from 4 to 4.5 per cent.

**Flash floods in Portugal** claimed 457 lives on *November 26.* Hardest hit were the towns of Quintas and Odivelas, both near Lisbon.

**Aden** assumed independence *November 30* as the last British troops withdrew from the area.

## DECEMBER

### NATIONAL

**Minnesota Senator Eugene McCarthy** won endorsement *December 3* as the 1968 Presidential candidate by a Democratic Party minority opposed to the renomination of President Johnson.

**Lt. General Leonard F. Chapman, Jr.** was named Marine Corps Commandant *December 4* by President Johnson.

**A two-year extension of poverty funds** totaling $4.16 billion was approved *December 5* by a House-Senate conference committee.

**President Johnson** appealed to business leaders for restraints on price increases *December 6* in wake of cost rises for some steel products.

**Lynda Bird Johnson** became Mrs. Charles Robb *December 9* at a White House wedding ceremony.

### INTERNATIONAL

**Albert B. Bongo** became president of Gabon *December 3,* filling the office left vacant by the death of Léon Mba.

**Resolution of the Cyprus crisis** appeared imminent *December 3* when Greece, Turkey, and Cyprus promptly replied to U.N. Secretary-General Thant's peace proposal. A major point of the proposal was the stationing of U.N. peacekeeping troops on Cyprus.

**A heart transplant operation** was performed *December 3* by South African surgeons. The patient regained consciousness the next day and learned of the operation's success.

**A new French jet-powered train** attained a track speed record of 215 m.p.h. *December 4.*

**Jorge Pacheco Areco** became president of Uruguay *December 6,* a few hours after the death of President Oscar D. Gestido.

United Press Int'l.

U.S.S.R. displayed latest rockets in Moscow parade celebrating 50th anniversary of the Bolshevik Revolution.

# MAJOR WORLD EVENTS OF 1967

## REPORT ON THE FAR EAST

Wide World

U.S. troops secured Vietnamese territory near Cambodian border in Operation Junction City, Feb., 1967.

### THE WAR IN VIETNAM

There was an overall escalation of the Vietnam war in 1967, with increased U.S. bombing in the north, buildup of U.S. military manpower in the south, and use by the Vietcong (Communist) guerrillas and North Vietnamese army of a greater number of highly sophisticated weapons imported from Communist China and the Soviet Union.

During the year some measurable Allied gains were made on the ground, as an increasing number of South Vietnamese hamlets were taken from the Vietcong. U.S. air power maintained its superiority over all of Vietnam, although U.S. Secretary of Defense Robert McNamara confessed serious doubts regarding an air war that appeared to have no demonstrable effect on the North Vietnamese economy and also seemed unable to stop the flow of North Vietnamese troops and supplies into the south. Heavy military action in late 1967 in the Demilitarized Zone dividing North and South Vietnam was taking the unmistakable form of a grim and bloody stalemate.

### THE WAR IN 1967

**Major Ground Operations.** In an effort to secure the South Vietnamese capital of Saigon from Vietcong terrorist attacks and to neutralize the many villages in the adjacent province of Gia Dinh, U.S. forces launched Operation Cedar Falls in January, 1967. A jungle area called the Iron Triangle was surrounded and all of its villages occupied and then razed, necessitating the resettlement of some 8,000 inhabitants. Vast sections of jungle were cleared by bulldozers, thus depriving the Vietcong of vital hiding places.

Beginning in February, U.S. troops launched Operation Junction City to wrest from Vietcong control a 1,000-square-mile section of swamp and jungle near the Cambodian border. The area, known as War Zone C, had long been the main Communist

**THE WAR IN VIETNAM** *(continued)*

stronghold in South Vietnam. However, when 30,000 U.S. troops swept into the territory they found little to attack. Forewarned, the Vietcong had disappeared to the north and into Cambodia.

One of the year's most devastating Vietcong attacks was directed at the U.S. air base at Danang on July 15. Shortly after midnight a Vietcong contingent fired about fifty 120-mm rockets into the base, inflicting heavy damage on barracks and ammunition storage areas and destroying 11 planes and 12 helicopters. Twelve Americans were killed and 145 wounded in the attack.

By midsummer the war's focus had shifted to the Demilitarized Zone (DMZ), a narrow strip of land extending from the Laotian border to the South China Sea. As early as April the U.S. forces had begun clearing a strip of land parallel to the border in an effort to create an obstacle line just below the DMZ. The U.S. Marine outpost at Conthien was repeatedly attacked by North Vietnamese regulars, with heavy casualties on both sides. Conthien, located on high ground within sight of the DMZ, looks out over a vast stretch of North Vietnam and also serves as the western terminus of the incompleted obstacle line.

On September 1 long-range North Vietnamese artillery, placed several miles above the DMZ, began heavy bombardment of U.S. border strongholds. Again, the prime target was Conthien. Marines held the territory, but at the cost of heavy casualties. The possibility of retreating—in order to draw enemy artillery placements forward into South Vietnam where they could be attacked by ground forces—was considered and re-

This Navy medic tried to save a wounded Marine.

jected because of Conthien's strategic importance. Attacks by Thailand-based U.S. B-52 bombers on enemy artillery placements were only moderately successful.

**Air Operations.** What had begun in February, 1965, as limited bombing of a few specified North Vietnamese targets had gradually expanded by 1967 into large-scale bombing of most military and industrial areas of North Vietnam. Prime targets for the early bombing raids were rail and highway supply routes, but this operation proved frustrating. The North Vietnamese succeeded in replacing bridges, highways, and stretches of railroad track almost as quickly as U.S. planes could destroy them.

One by one, target areas previously forbidden to U.S. bombers were removed from the off-limits category, and by late 1967 the air campaign had increased to some 150 bombing missions per day.

In March a squadron of U.S. F-105 Thunderchiefs, based in Thailand, struck Thainguyen (35 miles north of Hanoi), heavily damaging the only steel-producing complex in North Vietnam. In April rail yards only 2¼ miles from the center of Hanoi were bombed, while in the port city of Haiphong two power stations were knocked out of commission. Bombing targets in August included a North Vietnamese military camp at Kepha and a railroad bridge at Langson, only a few miles south of the Chinese border.

In October the air war was further intensified as U.S. planes struck Phucyen Air Base, 18 miles from Hanoi. By that time only a very few potential target areas remained untouched by bombing raids—notably, Gialam airfield on Hanoi's outskirts and the harbor of Haiphong.

U.S. aircraft downed by enemy fire totaled more than 700 by October, 1967.

**Manpower.** By mid-October there were some 480,000 U.S. troops in Vietnam. Approximate figures for the other Allied forces in South Vietnam at that date were: Vietnamese, 700,000; Koreans, 45,000; Australians, 6,500; Thais, 2,500; Filipinos, 2,200, and New Zealanders, 200. Midsummer estimates placed the combined strength of North Vietnamese regulars and Vietcong guerrillas in South Vietnam at about 296,000.

In September the U.S. military command in Saigon announced that the number of Americans killed in action during 1967 had reached 6,721. The U.S. death toll since 1961 was placed at 13,519; the total number of U.S. wounded was 83,433.

**Peace Proposals.** With the four-day February truce during the Vietnamese *Tet* holi-

## THE WAR IN VIETNAM (continued)

day, hopes for peace talks reached a new high, but were doomed by basic disagreement between President Lyndon B. Johnson and North Vietnamese President Ho Chi Minh. Ho's insistence that peace talks could not begin before an unconditional cessation of U.S. bombing in the north was met by Johnson's insistence that bombing could not end until North Vietnam ceased infiltrations of troops and supplies to the south. Neither side was willing to take the first step.

United Nations Secretary-General Thant proposed in April that a general truce be called as a first step toward negotiations. He stated his belief that the U.S. could afford to take the calculated risk of initiating a halt to hostilities, thus opening the way for peace talks. Thant's suggestion was unacceptable to the U.S. Government.

### BACKGROUND OF THE WAR

The history of modern Vietnam has been a chronicle of unrelieved turmoil. In the mid-19th century France conquered the area, which then became part of French Indochina. After World War II (when the area was occupied by Japan) France attempted to regain influence. But in 1946 nationalist and Communist groups (the Vietminh) led by Ho Chi Minh began a civil war that ended with the defeat of French troops at Dienbienphu in 1954.

**Division and Subversion.** In July, 1954, a 14-nation conference at Geneva divided the new nation at the 17th parallel into South Vietnam and Communist North Vietnam. The U.S. was not a party to the accord but agreed to abide by its provisions. The U.S. did ratify the Southeast Asia Mutual Defense Treaty, which specified that South Vietnam, Laos, and Cambodia could enlist the aid of SEATO members against aggression. After the Geneva partition Vietminh veterans began preparations to subvert the South Vietnamese government. The years 1954 through 1959 marked the first phase of the Vietnamese conflict. Communist action consisted of sporadic acts of terror, assassination, and subversion.

**Full-Scale War.** In 1960 North Vietnam overtly proclaimed its intention to seize the south through full-scale guerrilla action. By 1961 all-out war had supplanted subversion. At the request of the South Vietnamese government, President John F. Kennedy increased the number of U.S. troops acting as military advisers in the country from 685 to approximately 2,000 by the end of 1961.

In 1962 large areas of the south fell under Communist Vietcong (the offshoot of the old Vietminh) control, and by 1963 the U.S. had increased its troop strength to 16,500. In November of that year the South Vietnamese government, led by President Ngo Dinh Diem, was overthrown. This began a period of political instability that lasted until the assumption of power by Air Force Vice Marshal Nguyen Cao Ky in early 1965. That period of weakness prompted a quick and effective surge in Vietcong activity.

By 1964 the U.S. had increased its troop strength to 23,000 and had begun a course of planned military actions directed at bringing North Vietnam to the conference table. As more American troops were sent in, their role was officially changed from advisers to active combatants. In February, 1965, President Johnson ordered the bombing of North Vietnam, and a month later 5,000 Marine combat troops landed in South Vietnam.

Although greatly intensified, U.S. military efforts failed to halt the steady stream of troops and equipment flowing from North Vietnam into the south. Thus, in July, 1965, when U.S. troop strength was 72,000 men, President Johnson announced a massive buildup and doubled the monthly draft quota. Within four months the U.S. had 165,700 fighting men in Vietnam.

In 1966 the South Vietnamese political situation brightened when Premier Ky pledged a new constitution and general elections for 1967—promises he fulfilled (see page 245). But battlefield conditions remained grim, and the U.S. Government continued to increase its commitment despite anti-war demonstrations and rising political opposition in the U.S. to the Johnson Administration's Vietnam policy. By October, 1966, American troop strength had increased to 331,000. This trend continued in 1967 and shows every sign of persisting in 1968.

Vietnamese peasants: war's innocent victims

United Press Int'l.

# QUOTABLE QUOTES OF 1967

During 1967 many prominent figures voiced their opinions about a great variety of subjects, ranging from war and riots to the arts and the miniskirt. A representative selection of these memorable quotations about world, domestic, and general affairs appears below.

## WORLD AFFAIRS

United Press Int'l.

• **President Lyndon B. Johnson** (*commenting to reporters on the Vietnam war, Feb. 2*): "I go to bed every night feeling that I've failed that day because I couldn't end the conflict in Vietnam."

• **U.N. General Assembly President Abdul Rahman Pazhwak of Afghanistan** (*addressing the Assembly upon retiring as president, Sept. 20*): "If fools and folly rule the world, the end of man in our time may come as a rude shock, but it will no longer come as a complete surprise."

• **Secretary of State Dean Rusk** (*discussing Red China, Jan. 26*): "These events in mainland China are obviously of greatest importance. We ourselves don't know what they mean, but that doesn't embarrass us because Mao Tse-tung obviously doesn't know what they mean . . . either."

• **Israeli Foreign Minister Abba Eban** (*commenting on the Arab-Israeli war, reported July 9*): "I think that this is the first war in history that on the morrow the victors sued for peace and the vanquished called for unconditional surrender."

• **Pablo Casals,** Spanish cellist and conductor (*commenting to reporters on his 90th birthday, reported Jan. 1*): "I have seen so many wars and revolutions in the world. . . . Men do not know what they are, what they do. They do not know that we are human beings, brothers."

• **Robert Lowell,** American poet (*at recital by Soviet poet Andrei Voznesensky, May 17*): "Both countries . . . have really terrible governments. But we do the best we can with them, and they'd better do the best they can with each other or the world will cease to be here."

United Press Int'l.

• **Indian Prime Minister Indira Gandhi** (*Jan. 3*): "Man today is more obsessed with mysteries of outer space than about . . . the earth . . . the ocean . . . the mountain(s). . . . Man is still a surface scratcher."

## DOMESTIC AFFAIRS

• **Stokely Carmichael,** former head of SNCC (*commenting on the Democrats in Congress, reported Jan. 15*): "Their civil rights bills were not worth the time and energy . . . spent in typing them. They were obviously designed to pacify Afro-Americans . . . but we will not be pacified. . . ."

• **President Johnson** (*denouncing instigators of riots, Sept. 15*): "These wretched, vulgar men, these poisonous propagandists, posed as spokesmen for the underprivileged and capitalized on the real grievances of the . . . people."

Wide World

• **Martin Luther King** (*June 19*): "Everyone is worrying about the long hot summer with its threat of riots. We had a long cold winter when little was done about the conditions that create riots."

## GENERAL

• **Archibald MacLeish,** American poet (*June 13*): "Without those last quartets of Beethoven, without Oedipus the King, without a Hamlet or a Lear, or Michelangelo's ceiling . . . the electronic age could be a nightmare—a brighter, louder nightmare than any that has gone before."

United Press Int'l.

• **Mayor John Lindsay** of New York (*commenting on the miniskirt at a press conference Jan. 6*): "It's a functional thing. It enables young ladies to run faster and because of it they may have to."

• **Yosuf Karsh,** photographer (*April 13*): "Pope John XXIII said to me: 'Almighty God knew 77 years ago that He was going to make me Pope. Wouldn't it have been easier if He had made me more photogenic to simplify Karsh's work?' "

• **Jack Valenti,** president of Motion Pictures Association of America (*on whether he saw signs in Russia of hostility toward American films, July 20*): "No, I didn't see any pickets, so I knew I must be in a foreign country."

# FOCUS ON THE NEWS

## GLASSBORO SUMMIT MEETING

President Johnson listens as Soviet Premier Kosygin makes statement at end of Glassboro meeting.

The New York Times

With the arrival of Soviet Premier Aleksei Kosygin in New York City on June 17 for the United Nations special session on the Middle East crisis, there was immediate speculation regarding the possibility of his meeting with President Lyndon Johnson. The President soon made it clear that although he was unwilling to go to New York to meet Kosygin, he would be happy to see the Soviet leader in or near Washington. Kosygin's reply indicated unwillingness to go to Washington, and hopes for a summit meeting began to fade. Finally, a happy middle ground was found at the quiet college town of Glassboro, New Jersey, halfway between New York and Washington.

The first meeting took place on June 23, and virtually the entire town of Glassboro (population: 11,689) turned out to see the world leaders. The conference, held at the home of the President of Glassboro State College, lasted for over five hours, during which time a wide range of world topics was discussed. A second and final session was held two days later.

After the final meeting, President Johnson said that he and the Soviet Premier had made progress in efforts to improve mutual understanding and also agreed to keep in close touch in the future. Premier Kosygin expressed hope for increased cooperation but restated his government's positions that the U.S. should withdraw from Vietnam and that Israel should give up the territory it had conquered during the Arab-Israeli war.

The Glassboro meeting had not been expected to produce any major breakthrough in diplomatic relations between the United States and the Soviet Union, and in fact it did not. However, it was an encouraging indication of the growing "thaw" in the Cold War. Predictably, the Peking government denounced the meeting as a "vicious deal directed against China."

## THE SIX-DAY WAR

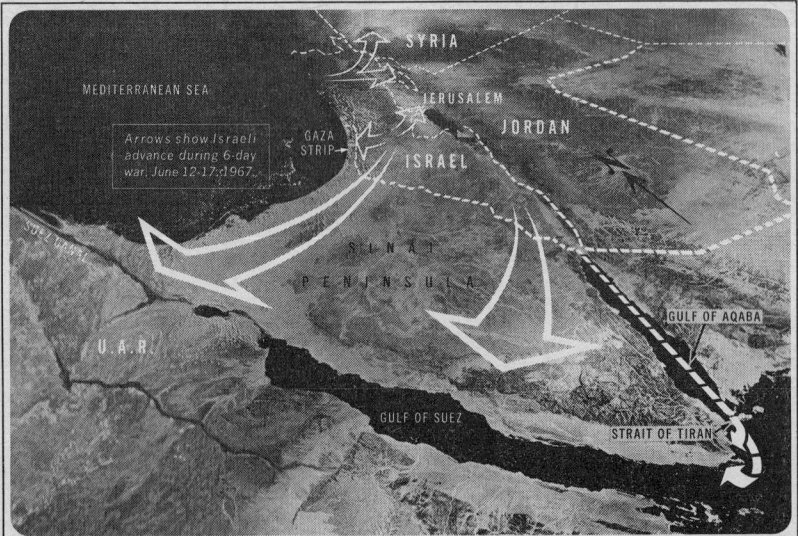

Map superimposed on a photo taken from a U.S. earth satellite shows the area of the Arab-Israeli war.

Based on NASA Photo

On June 5, 1967, war erupted between Israel and its Arab neighbors. Within six days Israel had defeated the combined forces of the United Arab Republic (Egypt), Jordan, and Syria, and controlled an area roughly four times its prewar size.

### BACKGROUND

**Causes of War.** Conflicting nationalism was the major factor leading to the Arab-Israeli War. Zionist Jews had established the modern state of Israel in 1948 in the historic Jewish homeland of Palestine, but Arabs have traditionally claimed the same area as part of their homeland. By early 1967, Arab-Israeli friction (which had resulted in wars in 1948-49 and in 1956) again threatened the peace. Syria was providing support for frequent terrorist raids into the Jewish state, and Israeli reprisals were mounting in severity. Meanwhile, President Gamal Abdel Nasser of the United Arab Republic, sensing that his leadership of the Arab world was being challenged, decided to take dramatic action against Israel.

**Preparations.** On May 14 the United Arab Republic (which had entered into a defense pact with Syria in November, 1966) accused Israel of massing troops on its northern frontier for an assault against Syria. Nasser followed this accusation with action, putting his armed forces on a war footing and moving large numbers of troops into the Sinai Peninsula. On May 20 he forced the withdrawal of the United Nations Emergency Force, which had kept the Gulf of Aqaba open to Israeli shipping, and announced that the Gulf would be closed to Israel. On May 30 King Hussein of Jordan agreed to a military pact with the U.A.R. that placed his army under Egyptian command. Interpreting these maneuvers as equivalent to acts of war, Israel prepared for war.

### THE WAR

**Attack on Egypt.** Early on Monday morning, June 5, the Israeli air force began a massive, non-stop attack on all of the U.A.R.'s air fields, surprising the Egyptians and virtually destroying their air power. Air action against Jordan and Syria was delayed for several hours in the unfulfilled hope that those states would make no military moves. By the end of Tuesday, June 6, Israel commanded the skies over the Middle East, and the Egyptian government was charging that U.S. and British aircraft were participating in the Israeli attack — a charge denied by Washington and London.

Initial Israeli ground thrusts were also

concentrated against the United Arab Republic. Armored columns moved westward along three routes across the Sinai Peninsula, penetrating and outflanking the Egyptian forces. By the time the U.A.R. acceded to a U.N. Security Council demand for a cease-fire on Thursday evening, June 8, Israeli forces were established along the Suez Canal. Two days earlier the Egyptians had rendered the canal temporarily useless by blocking it with sunken vessels. At the time of the cease-fire, the Gaza Strip, all of Sinai, and the Gulf of Aqaba were under Israeli control. On June 8 Israeli aircraft and torpedo boats attacked the U.S. naval vessel *Liberty* in the Mediterranean Sea.

**War with Jordan.** When Jordan entered the war on the morning of June 5, Israeli forces moved to isolate and occupy the Jordanian sector of Jerusalem. On June 7, with the Old City of Jerusalem in Israeli possession, Jordan became the first of the Arab states to accept the U.N. demand for a cease-fire. But Israeli forces did not halt until they were established along the Jordan River and held all of western Jordan.

**War with Syria.** On June 8 the Israeli air force began a massive attack on the Syrian fortifications in the Golan highlands, overlooking the upper Jordan Valley. Early on the following day, the Syrian government announced its acceptance of the cease-fire demand. But fighting continued as Israel launched a major ground attack that penetrated the forward Syrian artillery emplacements. On Saturday, June 10, when the Israelis held the Golan Heights, the cease-fire became effective.

### WAR'S AFTERMATH

In the U.N. Security Council, where the Middle East crisis had been under consideration since May 24, the Soviet Union took the lead in condemning Israel as the aggressor and demanding Israel withdraw behind the 1949 armistice lines.

Israel insisted that it would not retire from the occupied areas until final peace settlements were reached in direct negotiations with the Arab states. The latter, refusing to recognize the state of Israel, maintained that Israel must evacuate all the occupied territories, and steadfastly rejected suggestions for direct negotiations.

Repeated violations of the cease-fire agreements continued to occur long after the six-day war had ended. The most serious Arab violation was the sinking of the Israeli destroyer *Elath* off the Mediterranean coast of Sinai by Egyptian sea-to-sea missiles on October 21. Three days later Israel violated the cease-fire agreement with an artillery barrage across the Suez Canal that destroyed two major Egyptian oil refineries at Port Suez.

Arab-Israeli antagonisms, fears, and intransigence served to delay a negotiated peace, while Soviet-American rivalries rendered unlikely the enforcement of a great-power compromise in the Middle East.

An Israeli soldier watches his countrymen gather at the Wailing Wall in Old Jerusalem, June 14, 1967.

## NATO SANS FRANCE

NATO troops take part in opening of new military headquarters at Casteau, Belgium, on April 5, 1967.

The most significant events in Europe during 1967 included the enforced transfer of the North Atlantic Treaty Organization headquarters from France to Belgium and prolonged discussion and negotiations regarding possible enlargement of the European Economic Community (Common Market) from its present six-nation membership. Also noteworthy were the economic malaise that continued to affect West Europe, and the military coup in Greece that resulted in suspension of democratic government. The most notable European personality of the year—as has been the case during the past several years—was France's President Charles de Gaulle, whose eminence was achieved primarily by his success in pursuing negative policies.

### GAULLIST POLICIES

**NATO.** As the result of a 1966 decision by de Gaulle, the North Atlantic Treaty Organization (NATO) was forced to move its military headquarters out of France. On March 30, 1967, the flags were lowered at Rocquencourt, SHAPE Headquarters for 16 years, and on March 31 they were raised at the new headquarters at Casteau, Belgium. Although de Gaulle was willing to allow NATO's civil headquarters to remain in France, that section was also moved as a matter of convenience. On October 16 the new civil headquarters buildings were opened near Brussels. Now that France has withdrawn military cooperation from

NATO and may totally withdraw from the organization in the near future, the member-nations have begun active studies to determine NATO's future role, which may become less military and more political.

**European Economic Community (Common Market).** On May 11 Britain made its second formal application for membership in the European Economic Community (E.E.C.). Similar bids followed from two of Britain's European Free Trade Association partners, Denmark and Norway, as well as from Ireland. However, expansion of the E.E.C. from its present six-member status is not likely to happen soon.

Britain's request for admission was blocked in October when an E.E.C. special report stipulated that British balance-of-payments problems be solved as a prerequisite for E.E.C. membership. Other major changes in British economic policy were called for, including elimination of sterling as an international currency backed by gold reserves. The report, essentially a French effort to keep Britain out of the E.E.C. despite support for Britain by the other five Common Market members, amounted to an efficient Gaullist stalling device, as opposed to the outright French veto in 1963 of Britain's earlier request for entry.

**De Gaulle in Poland.** As a step in his campaign to enhance France's international prestige, de Gaulle paid an official visit to Poland in early September. Despite a warm welcome, the visit was not an unqualified success. De Gaulle's veiled invitation to Poland to play a more independent role in international politics was firmly rebuffed by the Polish government, which reaffirmed its dependence on the Soviet Union. De Gaulle's emphatic statement of approval of Poland's acquisition in 1945 of the lands east of the Oder-Neisse line served only to anger many West Germans.

## EUROPEAN DISCONTENT

**Faltering Economies.** Although enjoying peace and a measure of prosperity, Europe continued to suffer a decline in its economic growth, with West Germany being particularly hard-hit. Britain introduced austerity measures in July, 1966, that proved to have some beneficial effect, but the nation's chronic balance-of-payments problems and economic sluggishness were still present in late 1967.

**Political Problems.** Largely because of faltering economies, few European governments remained popular with their electors in 1967. In Britain, for example, the deflationary economic policies of Prime Minister Harold Wilson were highly unpopular even with members of his own Labour Party. General British dissatisfaction was indicated in the by-elections of late October, when the governing Labour Party suffered some unexpected losses.

In France the Gaullists won only a small majority in the National Assembly elections held in March, although they did better in the September local elections. In West Germany the long-term future of Chancellor Kurt Georg Kiesinger's "Great Coalition" appeared somewhat problematical in the wake of the country's most serious postwar business recession.

## MILITARY COUP IN GREECE

**Parliamentary Chaos.** Greece's democratic government, long subject to violent internal disorder, completely broke down in early 1967. Political feuding between young and inexperienced King Constantine and veteran former Premier George Papandreou appeared to be working in the latter's favor. On March 30 a non-political caretaker government had collapsed at Papandreou's instigation, and it was generally believed that he would regain the premiership in elections scheduled for May 28.

**Military Junta.** On April 21 high-ranking members of the Greek army, claiming that they were acting in the king's name, initiated a coup and established a military regime. Stating that their intervention had been necessary to save Greece from Communism,

"It's Not THAT Common!"

the junta enforced a curfew and strict censorship throughout the country. Although it became quite obvious that King Constantine was not the leading force behind the junta, he publicly accepted its rule on the understanding that it was to be a temporary step toward a more workable parliamentary system in the future. But the new government showed signs that it intended to stay in power on a long-term basis.

Foreign comment, at first hostile to the new regime, moderated as the year progressed, mainly because Greece had become unexpectedly quiet and orderly, in contrast to its era of hectic and highly imperfect democratic government.

De Gaulle visited Poland in September, 1967.

# FOCUS ON THE NEWS

## STALIN'S DAUGHTER ESCAPES TO FREEDOM

Svetlana Alliluyeva, arriving at Kennedy International Airport, New York City, April 21, 1967

"I have come here in order to seek the self-expression that has been denied to me for so long in Russia." Svetlana Alliluyeva, Joseph Stalin's daughter, was speaking to reporters at Kennedy Airport, New York City. It was April 21, 1967—six weeks after her decision to seek asylum in the U.S.

The sole survivor in the immediate family of a powerful dictator, schooled all her life in the atheistic doctrines of Communism, Mrs. Alliluyeva (who uses her mother's maiden name) quietly denounced the system: "I was brought up in a family where there was never any talk about God. But when I became a grown-up person I found that it was impossible to exist without God in one's heart....Since that moment the main dogmas of Communism have lost their significance for me."

Mrs. Alliluyeva's journey to freedom began in December, 1966, when reluctant Soviet authorities gave her permission to travel to India, her late husband's homeland, to scatter his ashes in the sacred waters of the Ganges. The Soviet government had denied her permission to marry Brijesh Singh, an Indian citizen.

Mrs. Alliluyeva was deeply moved by India, and it was there that she made her decision not to return to the Soviet Union. On March 6 she taxied to the U.S. Embassy in New Delhi where she sought asylum.

Her defection—a propaganda setback for the Soviet Union—came as a shock to her two children, Iosif, a 22-year-old medical student, and his half-sister, Yekaterina, 17.

Mrs. Alliluyeva's personal memoirs, Twenty Letters to A Friend, were published in October, 1967. The book was acclaimed as a deeply personal footnote to modern history. Mrs. Alliluyeva has earmarked profits from the book for philanthropic projects. She already has given $250,000 for a hospital to be built in India.

## AFRICAN DISUNITY

Africa fell victim in 1967 to a continuing breakdown of order, stability, and parliamentary democracy. The greatest chaos occurred in Nigeria, which had survived two bloody military takeovers in 1966, only to slip into a state of civil war.

The main reason for the Nigerian conflict was tribal suspicion and hatred between the Northern Region's Hausa tribe and the Eastern Region's Ibo tribe. After the massacre of thousands of Ibos, the Eastern Regional government decided that it could exist within Nigeria only if the regions were to become strong at the expense of the central government. When denied this privilege the Easterners declared their independence as the Republic of Biafra on May 28. The inevitable civil war began on July 6. Late in the year the central government appeared assured of military victory over Biafra, but solutions to the country's social and political problems were nowhere in sight.

The Congo, which has enjoyed few peaceful days since 1960, was again plagued by conflicts between the army and white mercenaries, who operated almost at will in the east. Somalia, still claiming territory from Ethiopia and Kenya, fostered guerrilla activity in those neighboring states, although in October Kenya and Somalia agreed to end hostilities. The ten-year-old civil war in southern Sudan showed no sign of abating. In Angola, Mozambique, and particularly in Portuguese Guinea, nationalist guerrilla bands pursued their wars of liberation against the Portuguese. The military regime in Ghana, which had ousted Kwame Nkrumah in 1966, found itself the target of another military revolt. Sierra Leone, the last major African state with a functioning two-party system, was wracked by a series of near-comic-opera coups which left the military in control.

In white-controlled Africa, Ian Smith's regime in Rhodesia continued to function despite persisting economic sanctions imposed after the country's secession from the Commonwealth of Nations in November, 1965. And South Africa continued to retain control of South West Africa despite increased protests by representatives of black African states at the United Nations.

Many African states have achieved relative stability by abandoning all pretense of parliamentary rule. For example, Togo, Dahomey, Upper Volta, and the Central African Republic have military rule, while many other African states have one-party regimes. But the potential dangers accompanying the abandonment of parliamentary rule are illustrated by the recent events in Nigeria, Ghana, and Sierra Leone.

One effect of the violent changes in Africa has been to show how ethereal were previous Pan African schemes. The Organization of African Unity has been unable to limit actions of member states where there was a conflict of national interests. It has been even less successful in attempting to prevent civil war in the Congo and Nigeria.

Nigerian federal troops advance against secessionist Biafra forces near town of Ore, in August, 1967.

Wide World

## THE PUNTA DEL ESTE CONFERENCE

Keystone Press

The presidents of the American nations, meeting at Punta del Este, Uruguay, approved long-range plans designed to further the economic development of the Western Hemisphere, in April, 1967.

Nineteen presidents of the American nations met at Punta del Este, Uruguay, from April 12 to 14, 1967, to assess the economic development of the Western Hemisphere and to map plans for increased inter-American progress in coming years. The most significant step taken by the American leaders was agreement on the creation of a Latin American economic community extending throughout Central and South America. The new community was to begin operations in 1970 and to be fully functioning by 1985. This vast new free-trade zone would replace two current organizations—the Latin American Free Trade Association and the Central American Common Market.

U.S. President Lyndon B. Johnson expressed long-range optimism for the success of the conference's program, which was summarized in a joint declaration of the presidents. The declaration set forth the following main goals: (1) expansion of Latin American trade, (2) modernization of Latin American agriculture to meet the needs of an expanding population and to eliminate the need for costly food imports, (3) improvement of educational systems and an end to illiteracy, (4) expansion of health facilities and elimination of epidemic and endemic diseases, and (5) technological development within backward nations.

A strong note of dissent was voiced by President Otto Arosemena Gomez of Ecuador, who completely rejected the declaration. He said that the true solution to Latin America's problems lies in increased aid from the United States. Gomez has often protested that the U.S. spends too much money on Southest Asia and that much of this could be put to better use in inter-American development programs.

However, Gomez's position was rejected by most of the other leaders as an indication of ineffectuality and excessive dependence on the United States. Addressing the Latin American leaders, President Johnson summed up the majority opinion by saying that U.S. assistance "will only be useful as it reinforces your determination and builds on your achievements."

# OBITUARIES OF PROMINENT PERSONS: 1967

**Adenauer, Konrad,** 91, Chancellor of West Germany (1949–63), who led the remarkable reconstruction of that country after World War II; d. Rhöndorf, Germany, April 19.

**Allen, Henry (Red),** 60, for many years one of America's finest Dixieland jazz trumpeters; d. New York City, April 17.

**Andrews, Laverne,** 51, oldest member of the popular Andrews Sisters singing trio ("Chattanooga Choo Choo," "Bei Mir Bist Du Schön"); d. Hollywood, May 8.

**Angell, Sir Norman,** 94, British newsman and author who won the Nobel Peace Prize in 1933. His many books (*The Great Illusion, The Unseen Assassins*), articles, and lectures dealt with the problems of peace and war; d. Croydon, England, October 7.

**Attlee, Earl Clement R.,** 84, Prime Minister of Great Britain (1945–51); a leader of the Labour Party, he was called the architect of the modern welfare state in Britain; d. London, October 8.

**Auer, Mischa,** 62, actor; a comedian and character actor, he starred in films during the 1930s and 1940s (*My Man Godfrey, Three Smart Girls*); d. Rome, March 5.

**Aymé, Marcel,** 65, French novelist and playwright who was best known for *The Green Mare,* a satire of French peasant life; d. Paris, October 14.

**Barden, Graham A.,** 70, U.S. Democratic Congressman from North Carolina (1934–61); d. New Bern, North Carolina, January 29.

**Barnett, Claude A.,** 77, Negro journalist who founded the Chicago-based Associated Negro Press; d. Chicago, August 2.

**Barth, Theodore H.,** 75, co-inventor (with the late Carl L. Norden) of the Norden bombsight, used on U.S. bombers during World War II; d. Wareham, Massachusetts, June 19.

**Bastianini, Ettore,** 43, Italian baritone who sang with the La Scala Opera in Milan and with the New York Metropolitan Opera; d. Sirmione, Italy, January 25.

**Bickford, Charles,** 78, actor; his career on stage, in films (*Song of Bernadette, Johnny Belinda*), and on television (*The Virginian*) spanned nearly 40 years; d. Hollywood, November 9.

**Block, Martin,** 64, disk jockey whose popular "Make Believe Ballroom" was heard on New York radio for 20 years (1934–54); d. Englewood, New Jersey, September 19.

**Bracci, Francesco Cardinal,** 87, Vatican expert on canon law and member of a commission to implement the Lateran Pacts; d. Rome, March 24.

**Buckley, Charles A.,** 76, politician; one of the last big-city political bosses, he was a leader of the Democratic Party in New York City and a U.S. Congressman (1934–64); d. New York, January 22.

**Buckmaster, Leland S.,** 72, labor leader who was international president of the United Rubber Workers Union (1945–60); d. Henderson, Kentucky, January 3.

**Bullitt, William C.,** 76, diplomat; the first U.S. Ambassador to the Soviet Union (1933–36), he was also Ambassador to France (1936–41); d. Neuilly, France, February 15.

**Burlingame, Roger,** 67, editor and author of biographies, novels, magazine articles, and poetry (*The American Conscience, Three Bags Full, Susan Shane*); d. West Redding, Connecticut, March 19.

**Burnette, Lester A. (Smiley),** 55, actor probably best known as the sidekick of Gene Autry and Roy Rogers in early Western movies; d. Encino, California, February 16.

**Cardijn, Joseph Cardinal,** 85, Belgian churchman who founded the Young Christian Workers, an international social and economic welfare organization, in 1925; d. Louvain, Belgium, July 25.

**Carnera, Primo,** 60, Italian prizefighter; the world heavyweight boxing champion (1933–34), he was ruthlessly manipulated by underworld racketeers; d. Sequals, Italy, June 29.

Konrad Adenauer

Sir Norman Angell

Clement R. Attlee

Pictorial Parade

Wide World

Pictorial Parade

Primo Carnera

Nelson Eddy

Ilya Ehrenburg

**Castelo Branco, General Humberto,** 66, President of Brazil (1964–67); he led the military coup in 1964 that ended the oppressive rule of President João Goulart; d. in plane crash near Fortaleza, Brazil, July 18.

**Chaffee, Lt. Commander Roger B.,** 31, U.S. astronaut, who was killed, along with two other astronauts, in a flash fire that broke out during a simulated launching of the Apollo spacecraft; d. Cape Kennedy, Florida, January 27.

**Chamberlain, Edward,** 68, Professor Emeritus of Political Economy at Harvard University; he wrote *The Theory of Monopolistic Competition* (1933), a classic in economic theory; d. Cambridge, Massachusetts, July 16.

**Christophoros II,** 91, Greek Orthodox Patriarch of Alexandria and All Africa (1939–67); d. Athens, July 23.

**Clark, Grenville,** 84, lawyer, influential government adviser, and advocate of world federalism; d. Dublin, New Hampshire, January 13.

**Clyde, Andy,** 75, actor; he perhaps was best known as Hopalong Cassidy's sidekick; d. Los Angeles, May 18.

**Cockcroft, Sir John,** 70, British physicist who was awarded the Nobel Prize in 1951 for splitting the atom for the first time by mechanical means; d. Cambridge, England, September 18.

**Connell, The Very Reverend Francis J.,** 79, dean of Catholic University in Washington, D.C.; he was best known for his interpretations of moral theology; d. Washington, May 12.

**Connor, Sir William,** 57, British journalist; under the pseudonym of Cassandra he wrote a column that appeared in London's *Daily Mirror* for over 30 years; d. London, April 6.

**Darrow, Charles,** 78, inventor of the popular game "Monopoly"; d. Ottsville, Pennsylvania, August 28.

**Darwell, Jane,** 87, actress whose 61-year career stretched from silent movies to *Mary Poppins.* In 1940 she received an Academy Award for her portrayal of Ma Joad in *Grapes of Wrath;* d. Hollywood, August 13.

**De Kallay, Nicholas,** 79, Premier of Hungary (1942–44); he had been living in exile since 1944; d. New York, January 14.

**Denny, Reginald,** 75, British actor who played Colonel Pickering in the Broadway production of *My Fair Lady;* d. Surrey, England, June 16.

**Dick, George,** 86, medical researcher and co-developer of the Dick test for scarlet fever; d. Palo Alto, California, October 10.

**Dreyer, Dave,** 72, pianist and song writer whose hits included "Cecilia," "Me and My Shadow," and "Back in Your Own Back Yard"; d. New York, March 2.

**Dunn, James,** 61, actor who won an Academy Award in 1946 for his performance in *A Tree Grows in Brooklyn;* d. Santa Monica, California, September 3.

**Eagan, Eddie,** 69, athlete who captured two Olympic gold medals, one in boxing (1920) and the other as a member of the U.S. bobsled team (1932); d. New York, June 14.

**Eddy, Nelson,** 65, singer and actor; he starred with Jeanette MacDonald in Hollywood musicals (*The Girl of the Golden West, Bitter Sweet, Naughty Marietta*); d. Miami Beach, March 6.

**Ehrenburg, Ilya,** 76, Soviet novelist and polemicist who twice was awarded the Stalin Prize for Literature. Ehrenburg's novel *The Thaw* (1954) attracted worldwide attention for its candor; d. Moscow, September 1.

**Elman, Mischa,** 76, Russian concert violinist whose long and successful career began at the age of 12 and carried him to Europe and the United States; d. New York, April 5.

**Fall, Bernard B.,** 40, historian who received wide acclaim for his studies of the strife in Vietnam (*Hell in a Very Small Place, Street Without Joy*); d. near Hué, South Vietnam, February 21.

**Farrar, Geraldine,** 85, soprano who starred with the New York Metropolitan Opera (1906–22); d. Ridgefield, Connecticut, March 11.

**Fay, Sidney J.,** 91, historian; his *Origins of World War I* challenged the belief that Germany was solely responsible for that war; d. Lexington, Massachusetts, August 29.

**Fechteler, Admiral William M.,** 71, Chief of Naval Operations (1951–56) and veteran of both World Wars and the Korean War; d. Washington, D.C., July 4.

**Fogarty, John E.,** 53, Democratic Congressman from Rhode Island (1940–67); he was Chairman of the House Appropriations Committee for 17 years; d. Washington, D.C., January 10.

**Foxx, Jimmy (Double X),** 59, baseball player with the Philadelphia Athletics from 1925 to 1945. His record of 534 home runs during his career is surpassed only by Babe Ruth and Willie Mays; d. Miami, July 21.

**Funk, Casimir,** 83, biochemist who discovered vitamins in 1912 and proved that certain diseases resulted from vitamin deficiency; d. Albany, New York, November 19.

**Garden, Mary,** 92, Scottish soprano; one of the great opera prima donnas from 1900 to 1931; her popularity was due more to her excellent dramatic interpretations than to her singing voice; d. Aberdeen, Scotland, January 3.

**Garner, John Nance,** 98, Vice President (1933–41) under Franklin D. Roosevelt; an extremely influential figure on Capitol Hill, he was instrumental in getting Roosevelt's New Deal legislation passed by Congress; d. Uvalde, Texas, November 7.

**Gassner, John W.,** 64, Professor of Playwriting and Dramatic Literature at Yale University; he was a highly respected theater critic, teacher, and anthologist; d. New Haven, Connecticut, April 2.

**Gibbs, William Francis,** 81, naval architect; although he designed thousands of navy vessels, his fondest creation was the luxury liner *United States;* d. New York, September 6.

**Gold, Michael,** 74, writer who was perhaps best known for his novel *Jews Without Money,* which like his other writings was aimed at social protest; d. Terra Inda, California, May 14.

**Grissom, Lt. Colonel Virgil I. (Gus),** 40, U.S. astronaut; one of the seven original Mercury astronauts, he was killed in a flash fire that broke out during a simulated launching of the Apollo spacecraft; d. Cape Kennedy, Florida, January 27.

**Guevara, Ernesto (Ché),** 39, Latin American revolutionary; once the right-hand man of Fidel Castro, he attempted to export the Cuban revolution to other Latin American nations; d. while commanding guerrilla troops in southeast Bolivia, October 8.

**Guthrie, Woody,** 55, folk singer and composer whose many songs ("This Land Is Your Land," "So Long It's Been Good to Know You") told of the beauty as well as the injustice in America; d. New York, October 3.

**Harriman, Florence Jaffray,** 97, U.S. Minister to Norway (1937–40) and an early crusader for social reform; in 1963 President Kennedy awarded her the first Citation of Merit for Distinguished Service; d. Washington, D.C., August 31.

**Heyrovsky, Jaroslav,** 76, Czechoslovak chemist who was awarded a Nobel Prize in 1959 for his discovery of polarography, a method for determining the chemical composition of certain substances; d. Prague, March 27.

**Hinshelwood, Sir Cyril,** 70, British chemist who shared the 1956 Nobel Prize in Chemistry with Soviet chemist Nikolai Somanov for research into the velocity and mechanics of chemical reactions; d. London, October 9.

**Hobart, Alice Tisdale,** 85, writer whose best-selling novels (*Oil for the Lamps of China, The Cup and the Sword*) were set in many parts of the world; d. Oakland, California, March 14.

**Hoffman, Clare,** 92, U.S. Republican Congressman from Michigan (1934–62) who advocated isolationism and opposed federal social legislation; d. Allegan, Michigan, November 3.

**Hopper, Edward,** 84, painter whose starkly realistic canvases (*Night Hawks, Early Sunday Morning*) depicted everyday scenes of contemporary America; d. New York, May 15.

**Howe, Mark DeWolfe,** 60, Professor of American Law at Harvard University; an authority on constitutional law, he completed the first two volumes of a biography of Oliver Wendell Holmes; d. Cambridge, Massachusetts, February 28.

**Hughes, Langston,** 65, writer whose novels, stories, poems, and plays (*The Weary Blues, Not Without Laughter*) described Negro life in America; d. New York, May 22.

**Juin, Marshal Alphonse-Pierre,** 78, the last remaining Marshal in the French army and one of the most controversial military figures in France after 1940 because of his right-wing political views; d. Paris, January 27.

**Kaiser, Henry J.,** 85, industrialist who achieved his first success as a shipbuilder during World War I and went on to build a $2 billion-a-year industrial empire, the Kaiser Industries Corporation; d. Honolulu, August 24.

Geraldine Farrar

Jimmy Foxx

John Nance Garner

Edward Hopper

**Keane, Johnny,** 55, baseball player who later managed the St. Louis Cardinals (1961–64) and the New York Yankees (1964–66); d. Houston, January 6.

**Kesserling, Joseph,** 65, playwright who was perhaps most famous for *Arsenic and Old Lace,* one of Broadway's longest-running plays; d. Kingston, New York, November 5.

**Kilgore, Bernard,** 59, managing editor of *The Wall Street Journal* (1941–66); he built it from a small financial newspaper into a nationwide daily for businessmen; d. Princeton, New Jersey, November 14.

**Kodály, Zoltán,** 84, Hungarian composer and violinist; was considered the greatest living Hungarian composer; d. Budapest, March 6.

**Kohler, Wolfgang,** 80, German research psychologist who was a founder and exponent of Gestalt psychology (perception of an organized whole rather than separate parts added together); d. Enfield, New Hampshire, June 11.

**Komarov, Colonel Vladimir,** 40, Soviet cosmonaut, who was killed on his second space venture aboard the capsule Soyuz I; d. U.S.S.R., April 24.

**Krueger, General Walter,** 86, U.S. Army General who distinguished himself as commander of the Sixth Army in the Pacific in World War II; d. Valley Forge, Pennsylvania, August 24.

**Krupp, Alfried,** 59, German industrialist who was the fifth and last family head of the immense Krupp industrial empire begun in 1911; d. Essen, Germany, July 30.

**al-Kuwatly, Shukri,** 76, President of Syria (1943–49; 1955–59), who agreed to union with Egypt in 1958 but went into exile the next year after a disagreement with Egypt's President Nasser; d. Beirut, Lebanon, June 30.

**Lahr, Bert,** 72, comedian who starred in vaudeville and burlesque, on Broadway, radio and television, and in films. He won acclaim as the Cowardly Lion in *The Wizard of Oz* (1939) and as a hobo in Beckett's play *Waiting for Godot* (1956); d. New York, December 5.

**Lamont, Thomas S.,** 68, Wall Street banker who was once a partner of J. Pierpont Morgan; d. New York, April 10.

**Lane, William P., Jr.,** 74, Democratic Governor of Maryland (1946–50) who introduced that state's first sales tax; d. Hagerstown, Maryland, February 7.

**Leigh, Vivien,** 53, British actress; among her many memorable portrayals were Scarlett O'Hara in *Gone with the Wind,* Blanche du Bois in *A Streetcar Named Desire* (for both portrayals she received Academy Awards); d. London, July 8.

**Luce, Henry,** 68, publisher who founded the Time, Inc., magazine empire. His publications (*Time, Life, Fortune, Sports Illustrated*) have widely influenced the reading habits, political views, and cultural tastes of the American public; d. Phoenix, Arizona, February 28.

**Luthuli, Albert,** 69, South African Negro leader who, in 1960, became the first African to receive the Nobel Peace Prize. Throughout his life he waged a non-violent campaign against racial discrimination in South Africa; d. Sanger, South Africa, July 21.

**McAdoo, Eleanor Wilson,** 77, daughter of President Woodrow Wilson; she married Wilson's Secretary of the Treasury at the White House in 1914; d. Montecito, California, April 5.

**McCullers, Carson,** 50, writer whose short stories, plays, and novels (*The Member of the Wedding, Reflections in a Golden Eye, The Heart Is a Lonely Hunter*) dealt with the relationship between loneliness and love; d. Nyack, New York, September 29.

**Magritte, René,** 68, Belgian surrealist painter whose paintings juxtaposed extreme realism with elements of wildest fantasy; d. Brussels, August 15.

**Malinovsky, Marshal Rodion Y.,** 68, Soviet Minister of Defense (1957–67); a hero of World War II, he was awarded the Order of Lenin seven times and the title of Hero of the Soviet Union twice; d. Moscow, March 31.

**Mansfield, Jayne,** 34, voluptuous film star who generally played the role of a dumb blonde. Among her most popular movies were *The Wayward Bus* and *Will Success Spoil Rock Hunter?*; d. in an automobile accident, New Orleans, June 29.

**Martin, Edward,** 87, Governor of Pennsylvania (1943–47) and U.S. Senator (1947–59); d. Washington, Pennsylvania, March 19.

**Masefield, John Edward,** 88, British poet; the author of "Sea Fever," "Cargoes," "The Everlasting Mercy," and other poems became England's Poet Laureate in 1930; d. Abingdon, England, May 12.

Langston Hughes

Vivien Leigh (with Clark Gable)

**Maurois, André,** 82, French biographer and novelist whose biographies of historical figures (Shelley, Victor Hugo, Balzac) won worldwide acclaim; d. Neuilly, France, October 9.

**Maximos IV Cardinal Saigh,** 89, Melchite Patriarch of Antioch and All the Orient, who earned a reputation for progressive leadership; d. Beirut, Lebanon, November 5.

**Mba, Leon,** 65, President of Gabon (1961–67); d. Paris, November 28.

**Miller, Arthur Lewis,** 74, U.S. Republican Congressman from Nebraska (1953–59); d. Chevy Chase, Maryland, March 16.

**Morgenthau, Henry, Jr.,** 75, Secretary of the Treasury (1934–45) under President Franklin Roosevelt. He formulated the Lend-Lease Program for supplying Britain with arms; d. Poughkeepsie, New York, February 6.

**Mossadegh, Mohammed,** 86, Premier of Iran (1951–53); a controversial leader whose regime was marked by extreme nationalism, he was overthrown in 1953; d. Tehran, March 5.

**Muller, Hermann J.,** 76, geneticist who received a Nobel Prize in 1946 for his discovery that X-ray radiation can cause hereditary defects; d. Indianapolis, Indiana, April 5.

**Muni, Paul,** 71, actor who has been called the man of a thousand faces. Perhaps his finest performances were in *The Story of Louis Pasteur* (for which he received an Academy Award in 1936) and *Inherit the Wind* (which won him a Tony Award in 1956); d. Santa Barbara, California, August 25.

**Muste, Reverend Abraham J.,** 82, pacifist who led anti-war and anti-armament delegations to Moscow and Vietnam during his lifelong crusade for peace; d. New York, February 11.

**O'Neal, Emmet,** 80, U.S. Democratic Congressman from Kentucky (1935–46) and U.S. Ambassador to the Philippines (1947–49); d. Washington, D.C., July 18.

**Oppenheimer, J. Robert,** 63, physicist who directed the development of the atomic bomb (1943). He became a controversial figure when his security clearance as a scientific consultant was withdrawn by the Federal Government in 1953. Ten years later, however, he was awarded the Atomic Energy Commission's $50,000 Fermi Award; d. Princeton, N.J., February 18.

**Orr, Carey,** 77, political cartoonist for the Chicago *Tribune* (1917–63); he won a Pulitzer Prize in 1961; d. Wilmette, Illinois, May 16.

**Paddleford, Clementine,** 67, food editor of the New York *Herald Tribune* (1940–66) and one of the country's best-known writers about food; d. New York, November 14.

**Parker, Dan,** 73, sportswriter for the New York *Daily Mirror* (1926–63) and the New York *Journal-American* (1963–64); d. Waterbury, Connecticut, May 20.

**Parker, Dorothy Rothschild,** 73, humorist whose conversation, poetry, essays, and short stories ("Big Blond," "Telephone Call") were characterized by a spontaneous, biting wit; d. New York, June 7.

**Pinkerton, Robert A.,** 62, head of Pinkerton, Inc., the private detective agency founded by his great-grandfather in 1850; d. Bay Shore, New York, October 11.

**Rains, Claude,** 77, British actor whose films (*The Invisible Man, Caesar and Cleopatra*) and stage performances (*Darkness at Noon, The Confidential Clerk*) won great acclaim; d. Sandwich, New Hampshire, May 30.

**Rathbone, Basil,** 75, British actor; although he starred in a variety of films and in Shakespearean plays, he was best known for his portrayal of the detective Sherlock Holmes; d. New York, July 21.

**Reinhardt, Ad,** 53, painter; called the "black monk" of abstract impressionism, he developed a painting style that reduced form and color to a minimum; d. New York, August 30.

**Rice, Elmer,** 74, playwright; a pioneer in theatrical realism and other modern dramatic techniques, Rice received a Pulitzer Prize in 1929 for his play *Street Scene*; d. Southampton, England, May 8.

**Ritter, Joseph Cardinal,** 74, Roman Catholic Archbishop of St. Louis who was noted for his active support of civil rights, religious liberty, and progressive change; d. St. Louis, Missouri, June 10.

**Roberts, Roy Allison,** 79, journalist; a powerful figure in American journalism, he was president of the Kansas City *Star* (1947–65) and a director of the Associated Press; d. Kansas City, Missouri, February 23.

J. Robert Oppenheimer        Dorothy Parker

Carl Sandburg

Francis Cardinal Spellman

Spencer Tracy

**Rockwell, George Lincoln,** 49, founder and leader of the American Nazi Party; he was slain by a former member of his own party; d. Arlington, Virginia, August 25.

**Ross, Barney,** 57, prizefighter; the former lightweight (1933) and welterweight (1934–38) champion of the world, he was also a Marine hero in World War II; d. Chicago, January 18.

**Sandburg, Carl,** 89, poet and biographer; hailed as the "American bard," his poetry ("Chicago," "Prayers of Steel," "Fog,") and his monumental biography of Lincoln captured the spirit of 20th-century America. He received a Pulitzer Prize in 1940 for *The War Years*, and another in 1950 for his *Complete Poems*; d. Flat Rock, North Carolina, July 22.

**Sargent, Sir Malcolm,** 72, British conductor; the most popular conductor in England, he performed in major cities all over the world; d. London, October 3.

**Sassoon, Siegfried,** 80, British poet; a hero of World War I, he recounted the horrors and brutality of war in his verses ("Aftermath," "The Rear-Guard"); d. Wiltshire, England, September 1.

**Sheridan, Ann,** 51, actress; during her 30-year career she starred in many successful films (*The Man Who Came to Dinner, King's Row*) and on television; d. Hollywood, January 21.

**Smith, Holland M. (Howlin' Mad),** 84, Marine Corps General who commanded the Marine forces in the Pacific (1945–46) and led the U.S. assault on Iwo Jima (1945); d. San Diego, California, January 12.

**Somoza de Bayle, Luis Anastasio,** 45, President of Nicaragua (1956–63), who attempted to liberalize the strong-man regime his father, Anastasio Somoza, had imposed on Nicaragua; d. Managua, Nicaragua, April 13.

**Spellman, Francis Cardinal,** 78, Roman Catholic Archbishop of New York since 1939 and a member of the College of Cardinals since 1946. As Vicar General of the Armed Forces, he visited (since 1951) American soldiers overseas at Christmas; d. New York, December 2.

**Tatum, Reese (Goose),** 45, basketball player; as a member of the Harlem Globetrotters (1942–55) he earned the title of "Clown Prince of Basketball"; d. El Paso, Texas, January 18.

**Tedder, Air Marshal Lord,** 76, British air com-

mander who served as Deputy Supreme Commander during the Allied invasion of Europe (June, 1945); d. Surrey, England, June 3.

**Thaw, Evelyn Nesbit,** 82, Floridora Girl in the early 1900s whose husband, Harry Thaw, murdered the architect Stanford White to "vindicate" her honor; d. Santa Monica, California, January 17.

**Tishman, Norman,** 65, a leading real estate developer who was chairman of the board of the Tishman Realty and Construction Company; d. New York, February 27.

**Toklas, Alice,** 89, devoted friend of Gertrude Stein who helped to preside over their renowned literary salon in Paris from 1907 to 1946; d. Paris, March 7.

**Toto, (Antonio de Curtis),** 69, Italy's leading theater and film comic; d. Rome, April 18.

**Tracy, Spencer,** 67, actor; during his 37-year career he won two Academy Awards (for *Captains Courageous* in 1937 and for *Boys Town* in 1938); d. Beverly Hills, June 10.

**Van de Graaff, Robert J.,** 65, physicist who in 1933 perfected the Van de Graaff particle accelerator, popularly known as the "atom smasher"; d. Boston, January 16.

**Vanier, Major General Georges P.,** 78, Governor General of Canada (1959–67), the first French-Canadian to hold that post; d. Ottawa, Canada, March 5.

**White, Lt. Colonel Edward H.,** 36, U.S. astronaut; the first American to "walk" in space, he was killed in a flash fire that broke out during a simulated launching of the Apollo spacecraft; d. Cape Kennedy, Florida, January 27.

**Wiley, Alexander,** 83, U.S. Republican Senator from Wisconsin (1938–62); d. Philadelphia, October 26.

**Woodring, Harry H.,** 77, Secretary of War under President Franklin D. Roosevelt (1936–40) and Democratic Governor of Kansas (1930–32); d. Topeka, Kansas, September 9.

**Yoshida, Shigeru,** 89, Premier of Japan (1946–54), who led postwar Japan's economic recovery; d. Oisi, Japan, October 20.

**Youssoupoff, Prince Felix,** 81, Russian nobleman who in 1916 murdered the monk Rasputin, who had a mystic control over Czar Nicholas II and the Czarina; d. Paris, September 27.

# INTERNATIONAL AFFAIRS

## United Nations · U.S. Foreign Affairs · The Communist World · International Organizations

United Nations

Soviet Premier Aleksei Kosygin addressed an emergency session of the U.N. General Assembly on June 19, 1967. Kosygin demanded that Israel withdraw from territory she occupied after the Arab-Israeli six-day war.

## THE UNITED NATIONS: 1967

In its 22-year existence the United Nations was seldom put to the test as strenuously as in 1967. Two major military conflicts, several brushfire wars, and political strains that threatened to erupt into steely confrontations were added to the ongoing problems of famine, disease, illiteracy, and overpopulation with which the world organization tries to cope.

In his 1967 annual report U Thant, Secretary-General of the United Nations, said the world body was facing a "crisis of confidence" over its ability to make clear-cut decisions and to take forceful actions on important problems. Some of the U.N.'s strongest members openly defied the organization's edicts. Other nations quietly ignored them. But there were pluses as well as minuses in the U.N.'s 1967 record.

The year began with an auspicious event. On January 27, 1967, 62 nations, including the United States and the Soviet Union, signed a treaty to limit military activities in outer space. This landmark treaty—since ratified by the U. S. Senate—prohibits the placement of nuclear weapons or other weapons of mass destruction into orbit, on the Moon, or on any other heavenly body. Proposed by President Lyndon Johnson, the treaty was negotiated by the U.N. Outer Space Committee.

This treaty, as well as the progress made at the 17-nation Geneva conference on a pact to prevent the spread of nuclear weapons, was basically the result of an improvement of relations between the United States and the Soviet Union. As many students of the U.N. have observed, the effectiveness of the world organization depends largely on the state of the relations between the two great powers.

But U.N. weakness was demonstrated anew on May 19 when the General Assembly adopted a resolution ordering that South *(continued)*

**THE UNITED NATIONS: 1967** (continued)

West Africa be made independent of South Africa by June, 1968. South Africa defied the Assembly and announced that it would not respect the resolution.

Also in May, U Thant acceded to an Egyptian request to withdraw the U.N. peacekeeping forces that for ten years had been patrolling the border between Egypt and Israel. Within three weeks after the removal of the U.N. force, war erupted between Israel and the Arab states (June 5).

A cease-fire resolution by the Security Council, adopted by both sides, was perhaps the U.N.'s greatest accomplishment in 1967. U.N. observer patrols were re-established on both sides of the cease-fire line although sporadic outbreaks of hostilities have continued. Israel, demanding official recognition of her statehood through direct negotiation with the Arab states, declined to work with U.N. intermediaries. The Arab nations, on the other hand, demanded a return to the "truce" conditions and boundaries that existed before the war.

In addition to the Security Council meeting, the war provoked an emergency session of the General Assembly. This inspired one of the most spectacular displays of political oratory in modern times—but without results. The U.S.S.R. came off the loser in its attempts to have the Assembly condemn Israel for aggression, but the U.S. fared little better in its efforts to mediate the conflict. Deadlock was the result in both the Middle East and the General Assembly. The Assembly, mired in dispute, was set back further when Israel rejected the demand that it modify its plans to unify both the New and Old cities of Jerusalem.

Secretary-General Thant appointed a personal representative to Israel to report on conditions in Jerusalem. Israel consented to the envoy's visit but imposed restrictions confining his report to fact-finding and barring its use for political purposes.

Throughout 1967 the U.N.—particularly through the efforts of U Thant—attempted to mediate the Vietnam war. Thant's proposals were keyed to a halt in the U.S. bombing of North Vietnam. His position against the "domino theory" (that is, that other Asian nations will come under Communist domination if South Vietnam falls) brought him into conflict with U.S. Secretary of State Dean Rusk, who called Thant's proposals "fuzzy." Still, the U.S., through Ambassador Arthur Goldberg, offered to accept the offices of the U.N. for mediation of the war, although it demanded a signal of reciprocity from North Vietnam as a condition for a bombing halt.

The U.S. pressed the Soviet Union (which had been publicly declaring that a bombing halt would bring Hanoi to the bargaining table) to accept a Security Council debate on the war. With Russia's refusal the U.N.'s potential usefulness on the Vietnam issue faded, at least for the time being. The situation was unchanged by Soviet Premier Aleksei Kosygin's appearance at the U.N. in mid-June, during which he attempted to recoup some of Russia's diplomatic losses during the Arab-Israeli debate, and by his subsequent meeting with President Johnson at Glassboro, New Jersey.

On September 19, 1967, the 22d annual session of the General Assembly opened, and for the first time a member of the Communist bloc was selected as its head: Foreign Minister Corneliu Manescu of Romania.

In his opening report to the 22d session, Secretary-General Thant warned that "the international situation has not only not improved since the previous regular session of the Assembly, it has in fact deteriorated considerably." He put into effect a previously unused provision of the charter to hold Security Council meetings at the foreign-minister level in an attempt to solve major world problems.

After the sinking of the Israeli destroyer *Elath* in late October by Egyptian patrol boats and the retaliatory shelling of Port Suez by Israeli artillery, the tenuous Middle East truce was seriously undermined. The Security Council unanimously passed a resolution demanding that Israel and the United Arab Republic "cease immediately" all military activity. Ambassador Goldberg continued to meet with the Soviet Ambassador to the U.N. and other delegates in an attempt to hammer out a peace formula acceptable to both sides.

During 1967 the special agencies of the United Nations carried forward their programs steadily if unspectacularly. Among the major efforts were the smallpox eradication and birth-control campaigns of the World Health Organization. The United Nations Educational, Scientific and Cultural Organization (UNESCO) issued a report on the effects of apartheid on education, science, culture, and information in South Africa. The Refugee Organization and the Food and Agriculture Organization (FAO) moved in to help the peoples of the Middle East who had been uprooted by the war. And the FAO joined with the United States to provide grain for famine-threatened India.

What are the prospects for the U.N. during 1968? The politically divided General Assembly is unlikely to be more forceful than it has been in the immediate past. The Security Council's effectiveness will depend largely on the nature of any crisis it faces. If the problem is one that does not collide with U.S. and Soviet interests, the Council's achievement may be high.

Not definitely in sight but always likely is a U.N. crisis on the seating of Red China. Although the U.S. and many of its allies still oppose seating Peking, the bulk of the U.N. membership now appears to be leaning the other way. Another membership problem is that of the "ministates." U Thant has called for a special (less than full) membership for tiny newly independent nations, in order to prevent overpopulating the organization.

Through defeat and deadlock the U.N. retains its value as a world forum. Asked about the U.N.'s tendency to talk rather than act on the problems posed during the early days of the Cold War, Warren Austin, then U.S. Ambassador to the U.N., said: "When we stop talking, watch out."

Wide World

Soviet Foreign Minister Andrei A. Gromyko and U.S. Ambassador Llewellyn E. Thompson chat while British Ambassador Sir Geoffrey Harrison signs the U.N. Space Treaty on January 27, 1967, in Moscow.

## UNITED NATIONS HEADQUARTERS

The present site of the United Nations headquarters is an 18-acre tract along the East River in midtown Manhattan. Purchased with an $8.5 million gift from John D. Rockefeller, Jr., the site is now international territory, owned by the United Nations.

In November, 1947, the world body unanimously approved a design submitted by an international consulting board under the direction of Wallace K. Harrison, an American architect. The United States loaned the organization $65 million, and construction began in September, 1948. The General Assembly met at "United Nations, New York" for the first time in October, 1952. (Interim business had been conducted from temporary quarters at Hunter College in New York City, and at Lake Success, New York.) An expansion program completed in 1964 provided space for the delegations of up to 126 member nations.

The present headquarters comprises three interconnected buildings and a library, surrounded by plazas, gardens, and lawns. The Secretariat Building is a 39-story rectangular column, sheathed in glass and marble, and containing offices and working space for the headquarters staff. The General Assembly Building, facing a landscaped plaza to the north, is a sloping, double-concave structure, topped by a shallow dome. The two are linked by a four-story Conference Building, which is cantilevered over Franklin D. Roosevelt Drive and contains council chambers and conference rooms.

The General Assembly Hall, in which representatives of all the member nations convene in formal session at least once a year, is 165 feet long, 115 feet wide, and three stories high. Seats for 756 delegates and alternates are arranged in curved rows on the floor, facing the officials' podium, and are flanked by seats for advisers and observers. In the rear are places for 472 alternate delegates, representatives' guests, and the press. Public galleries overlook the hall. Translation and press booths line the walls. All 2,070 seats are equipped with earphones, enabling participants and spectators to listen to proceedings in any of the U.N.'s five official languages: Chinese, English, French, Spanish, and Russian. Translation is simultaneous. The Dag Hammarskjöld Library is located on the southwest corner of the headquarters site.

Buildings are open to the public from 9 A.M. to 5:45 P.M. daily, except Christmas and New Year's Day. An international staff of guides conducts tours of the headquarters between 9:00 A.M. and 4:45 P.M. daily, at a cost of $1.25 for adults and 50 cents for servicemen, students, and children over five years of age.

## UNITED STATES MISSION TO THE UNITED NATIONS

Arthur J. Goldberg, *Ambassador Extraordinary and Plenipotentiary,* Permanent Representative to the United Nations

Will B. Buffum, *Ambassador,* Deputy Permanent Representative to the United Nations

Arthur J. Goldberg, *Ambassador,* Representative on the Security Council

Arthur E. Goldschmidt, *Ambassador,* Representative on the Economic and Social Council

Eugenie Anderson, *Ambassador,* Representative on the Trusteeship Council

## CURRENT MEMBERS OF THE UNITED NATIONS

Original members of the United Nations are all those nations that participated in the U.N. Conference on International Organization at San Francisco in 1945, or that signed the Declaration by United Nations of June 1, 1942, and signed and ratified the Charter of the United Nations. Any other nation that applies for membership must be recommended by the Security Council to the General Assembly for a vote. Membership is open to all countries that are willing to accept the obligations of the Charter.

Listed below are the 122 members of the United Nations, with the dates on which they became members and the name of each nation's chief United Nations representative at the beginning of the 22nd session in September, 1967.

| MEMBER NATION | DATE OF MEMBERSHIP | REPRESENTATIVE TO UNITED NATIONS |
|---|---|---|
| Afghanistan | November 19, 1946 | Abdul Rahman PAZHWAK |
| Albania | December 14, 1955 | Halim BUDO |
| Algeria | October 8, 1962 | Tewfik BOUATTOURA |
| Argentina | October 24, 1945 | Dr. José Maria RUDA |
| Australia | November 1, 1945 | Patrick SHAW |
| Austria | December 14, 1955 | Dr. Kurt WALDHEIM |
| Barbados | December 9, 1966 | Frank L. WALCOTT |
| Belgium | December 27, 1945 | Constant SCHUURMANS |
| Bolivia | November 14, 1945 | Fernando ORTIZ SANZ |
| Botswana | October 17, 1966 | Dr. Z. K. MATTHEWS |
| Brazil | October 24, 1945 | José SETTE CAMARA |
| Bulgaria | December 14, 1955 | Milko TARABANOV |
| Burma | April 19, 1948 | U SOE TIN |
| Burundi | September 18, 1962 | Terence NSANZE |
| Byelorussian S.S.R. | October 24, 1945 | Guerodot Gavrilovich TCHERNOUCHTCHENKO |
| Cambodia | December 14, 1955 | HUOT SAMBATH |
| Cameroon | September 20, 1960 | Joseph N. OWONO |
| Canada | November 9, 1945 | George IGNATIEFF |
| Central African Republic | September 20, 1960 | Michel GALLIN-DOUATHE |
| Ceylon | December 14, 1955 | Hamilton Shirley AMERASINGHE |
| Chad | September 20, 1960 | Boukar ABDOUL |
| Chile | October 24, 1945 | José PIÑERA |
| China (Taiwan) | October 24, 1945 | LIU Chieh |
| Colombia | November 5, 1945 | Dr. Julio Cesar TURBAY AYALA |
| Congo (Brazzaville) | September 20, 1960 | Jonas MOUANZA |
| Congo (Democratic Republic of) | September 20, 1960 | Théodore IDZUMBUIR |
| Costa Rica | November 2, 1945 | Luis Demetrio TINOCO |
| Cuba | October 24, 1945 | Ricardo ALARCON QUESADA |
| Cyprus | September 20, 1960 | Zenon ROSSIDES |
| Czechoslovakia | October 24, 1945 | Milan KLUSÁK |
| Dahomey | September 20, 1960 | Maxime-Léopold ZOLLNER |
| Denmark | October 24, 1945 | Hans R. TABOR |
| Dominican Republic | October 24, 1945 | José Rafael MOLINA-UREÑA |
| Ecuador | December 21, 1945 | Dr. Leopoldo BENITES |
| El Salvador | October 24, 1945 | Dr. Hector ESCOBAR SERRANO |
| Ethiopia | November 13, 1945 | Lij Endalkachew MAKONNEN |
| Finland | December 14, 1955 | Max JAKOBSON |
| France | October 24, 1945 | Armand BERARD |
| Gabon | September 20, 1960 | Marcel SANDOUNGOUT |
| Gambia | September 21, 1965 | (Vacant) |
| Ghana | March 8, 1957 | Richard Maximilian AKWEI |
| Greece | October 25, 1945 | Demitris BITSIOS |
| Guatemala | November 21, 1945 | Dr. Ramón CADENA HERNANDEZ |
| Guinea | December 12, 1958 | ACHKAR Marof |
| Guyana | September 20, 1966 | Eustace R. BRAITHWAITE |
| Haiti | October 24, 1945 | Marcel ANTOINE |
| Honduras | December 17, 1945 | Humberto LOPEZ VILLAMIL |
| Hungary | December 14, 1955 | Károly CSATORDAY |
| Iceland | November 19, 1946 | Hannes KJARTANSSON |
| India | October 30, 1945 | Gopalaswami PARTHASARATHI |
| Indonesia | September 28, 1950* | Abdullah KAMIL (Acting) |
| Iran | October 24, 1945 | Dr. Mehdi VAKIL |
| Iraq | December 21, 1945 | Dr. Adnan PACHACHI |

* First admitted September, 1950; withdrew March, 1965; readmitted September, 1966.

| | | |
|---|---|---|
| Ireland | December 14, 1955 | Cornelius C. CREMIN |
| Israel | May 11, 1949 | Gideon RAFAEL |
| Italy | December 14, 1955 | Piero VINCI |
| Ivory Coast | September 20, 1960 | Siméon AKE |
| Jamaica | September 18, 1962 | Keith JOHNSON |
| Japan | December 18, 1956 | Senjin TSURUOKA |
| Jordan | December 14, 1955 | Muhammad H. EL-FARRA |
| Kenya | December 16, 1963 | Burudi NABWERA |
| Kuwait | May 14, 1963 | Muhalhel Mohamad AL-MUDHAF |
| Laos | December 14, 1955 | Khamking SOUVANLASY |
| Lebanon | October 24, 1945 | Philippe TAKLA |
| Lesotho | October 17, 1966 | A. S. MOHALE |
| Liberia | November 2, 1945 | Nathan BARNES |
| Libya | December 14, 1955 | Dr. Wahbi EL-BOURI |
| Luxembourg | October 24, 1945 | Pierre WURTH |
| Madagascar | September 20, 1960 | Louis RAKOTOMALALA |
| Malawi | December 1, 1964 | Nyemba Wales MBEKEANI |
| Malaysia | September 17, 1957 | Radhakrishna RAMANI |
| Maldive Islands | September 21, 1965 | Ahamed HILMY DIDI (Absent) |
| Mali | September 28, 1960 | Moussa Léo KEITA |
| Malta | December 1, 1964 | Dr. Arvid PARDO |
| Mauritania | October 27, 1961 | Abdallahi OULD DADDAH |
| Mexico | November 7, 1945 | Dr. Francisco CUEVAS CANCINO |
| Mongolia | October 27, 1961 | Jhambalyn BANZAR |
| Morocco | November 12, 1956 | Ahmed Taibi BENHIMA |
| Nepal | December 14, 1955 | Major General Padma Bahadur KHATRI |
| Netherlands | December 10, 1945 | Dr. J. G. de BEUS |
| New Zealand | October 24, 1945 | Charles CRAW |
| Nicaragua | October 24, 1945 | Dr. Guillermo SEVILLA-SACASA |
| Niger | September 20, 1960 | (Vacant) |
| Nigeria | October 7, 1960 | Chief S. O. ADEBO |
| Norway | November 27, 1945 | Edvard HAMBRO |
| Pakistan | September 30, 1947 | Agha SHAHI |
| Panama | November 13, 1945 | Aquilino BOYD |
| Paraguay | October 24, 1945 | Miguel SOLANO LOPEZ |
| Peru | October 31, 1945 | Carlos MACKEHENIE |
| Philippines | October 24, 1945 | Salvador P. LOPEZ |
| Poland | October 24, 1945 | Bohdan TOMOROWICZ |
| Portugal | December 14, 1955 | (Vacant) |
| Romania | December 14, 1955 | Gheorghe DIACONESCU |
| Rwanda | September 18, 1962 | Célestin KABANDA |
| Saudi Arabia | October 24, 1945 | (Vacant) |
| Senegal | September 28, 1960 | Ousmane Socé DIOP |
| Sierra Leone | September 27, 1961 | Christopher O. E. COLE |
| Singapore | September 21, 1965 | Dr. WONG Lin Ken |
| Somalia | September 20, 1960 | Abdulrahim Abby FARAH |
| South Africa | November 7, 1945 | Matthys L. BOTHA |
| Spain | December 14, 1955 | Don Manuel AZNAR |
| Sudan | November 12, 1956 | FAKHREDDINE Mohamed |
| Sweden | November 19, 1946 | Sverker C. ASTROM |
| Syria | October 24, 1945 | George J. TOMEH |
| Tanzania | December 14, 1961 | John W. S. MALECELA |
| Thailand | December 16, 1946 | (Vacant) |
| Togo | September 20, 1960 | Dr. Alexandre J. OHIN |
| Trinidad and Tobago | September 18, 1962 | Dr. P. V. J. SOLOMON |
| Tunisia | November 12, 1956 | Mahmoud HESTIRI |
| Turkey | October 24, 1945 | Orhan ERALP |
| Uganda | October 25, 1962 | E. Otema ALLIMADI |
| Ukrainian S.S.R. | October 24, 1945 | Sergei Timofeevich SHEVCHENKO |
| U.S.S.R. | October 24, 1945 | Dr. Nikolai Trofimovich FEDORENKO |
| U.A.R. (Egypt) | October 24, 1945 | Mohamed Awad EL-KONY |
| United Kingdom | October 24, 1945 | Lord CARADON |
| United States | October 24, 1945 | Arthur J. GOLDBERG |
| Upper Volta | September 20, 1960 | Tensoré Paul ROUAMBA |
| Uruguay | December 18, 1945 | Dr. Pedro P. BERRO |
| Venezuela | November 14, 1945 | Dr. Manuel PEREZ GUERRERO |
| Yemen | September 30, 1947 | Abdulaziz A. AL-FUTAIH |
| Yugoslavia | October 24, 1945 | Dr. Anton VRATUŠA |
| Zambia | December 1, 1964 | Joseph Ben MWEMBA |

## PRINCIPAL ORGANS OF THE UNITED NATIONS

■ **THE GENERAL ASSEMBLY** is the main deliberative organ of the United Nations. Including representatives from all the U.N. member nations, it is empowered to discuss and make recommendations on matters within the scope of the organization's Charter. It also approves the U.N. budget and apportions expenses among the members. A president, elected at the beginning of each session, presides. The General Assembly convenes annually in regular session on the third Tuesday in September. It may be called into special session under certain conditions. Each member nation has one vote, and is permitted to send up to five representatives to each session. On ordinary matters, decisions are carried by a simple majority of members present and voting; on more important matters, by a two-thirds majority.

The General Assembly works through seven Main Committees: First Committee (Political and Security, including regulation of armaments), Special Political Committee (shares work of the First Committee), Second Committee (Economic and Financial), Third Committee (Social, Humanitarian, and Cultural), Fourth Committee (Trusteeship, including non-self-governing territories), Fifth Committee (Administrative and Budgetary), Sixth Committee (Legal).

Other committees assisting the General Assembly are: General Committee (supervises Assembly work), Advisory Committee on Administrative and Budgetary Questions, Committee on Contributions, and Credentials Committee.

■ **THE SECURITY COUNCIL** has primary responsibility for maintaining peace and security. It comprises five permanent members—China (Taiwan), France, the United Kingdom, the U.S.S.R., and the United States—and ten nonpermanent members elected to two-year terms by the General Assembly. The Security Council is organized to function continuously. Each member has one vote. Decisions on procedural matters are carried by a majority of nine members. However, on important matters, the nine affirmative votes must include concurrence of the five permanent members. This is known as the "veto" privilege. Abstention does not constitute a veto. The Security Council is empowered to investigate any situation that might lead to friction between two or more countries. It acts on behalf of U.N. member nations, all of whom are pledged to carry out its decisions, as well as to make available to the Council assistance and facilities—including armed forces—which it declares necessary for maintenance of international peace. A country that is a member of the United Nations, but not of the Security Council, may participate in its discussions when the Council considers that nation's interests to be specially affected. Members and non-members are invited to participate in Security Council discussions of disputes to which they are parties. However, a Council member that is party to a dispute may not vote on the decision.

**The Disarmament Commission** includes all U.N. member nations. It prepares proposals for regulation, limitation, and reduction of armed forces and armaments; for elimination of all weapons adaptable to mass destruction; and for international control of atomic energy in order to ensure its use for peaceful purposes.

**The Military Staff Committee** is composed of the Chiefs of Staff of the five permanent members—China (Taiwan), France, the United Kingdom, the U.S.S.R., and the United States —or their representatives. It advises and assists the Security Council on such questions as the Council's military requirements for the maintenance of peace, the strategic direction of armed forces placed at its disposal, the regulation of armaments, and possible disarmament.

■ **THE ECONOMIC AND SOCIAL COUNCIL** examines and makes recommendations on international economic, social, cultural, educational, and health issues, and related matters. The Council comprises 27 members, nine of whom are elected each year to three-year terms by the General Assembly. It is aided by functional and regional commissions.

The seven functional commissions are: Statistical, Population, Social, Human Rights, Status of Women, Narcotic Drugs, and International Commodity Trade. There is also a special Sub-Commission on Prevention of Discrimination and Protection of Minorities.

There is a separate regional commission for each of the following four areas: Europe, Asia and the Far East, Latin America, and Africa.

■ **THE TRUSTEESHIP COUNCIL** is the principal organ assisting the General Assembly in supervision and administration of trust territories. It comprises member nations administering trust territories, permanent members of the Security Council not administering trust territories, and as many other members (elected to three-year terms by the General Assembly) as are required to provide an equal number of administering and non-administering members.

Originally, 11 territories were placed under the trusteeship system; eight have become independent or joined other independent states. The three still under U.N. trusteeship are: East New Guinea, under Australian administration; Nauru, administered by Australia on behalf of Australia, New Zealand, and the United Kingdom; and the Trust Territory of the Pacific Islands, under U.S. administration.

■ **THE INTERNATIONAL COURT OF JUSTICE** is the principal judicial organ of the United Nations. It sits at The Hague, in the Netherlands. Fifteen judges are elected to nine-year terms by the General Assembly and the Security Council, voting independently. Every U.N. member has automatic access to the Court and is pledged to comply with its decisions. The Court has jurisdiction over all cases specifically referred to it, and over all matters specially provided for in the Charter or in treaties and conventions in force. The Court renders legal opinions on matters referred to it by the General Assembly, Security Council, and specialized agencies authorized by the General Assembly.

## SECRETARIAT

Composed of an international staff, the Secretariat performs administrative functions of the United Nations and operates continuously to service other U.N. organs as well as to administer their programs and policies. The Secretary-General is appointed by the General Assembly, upon recommendation by the Security Council. In addition to functioning as the U.N.'s chief administrative officer, he is responsible for bringing to the attention of the Security Council any situation that in his opinion threatens international peace or security.

**Secretary-General: U Thant (Burma)**
**Office of the Secretary-General**
    Under-Secretary for General Assembly Affairs and Chef de Cabinet: C. V. Narasimhan (India)
    Office of Legal Affairs, Under-Secretary: C. A. Stavropoulos (Greece)
    Office of the Controller, Under-Secretary: B. R. Turner (New Zealand)
    Office of Personnel, Under-Secretary: Sir Alexander MacFarquhar (United Kingdom)
    Under-Secretaries for Special Political Affairs: Ralph J. Bunche (United States), J. Rolz-Bennett (Guatemala)

**Department of Political and Security Council Affairs**
    Under-Secretary: Aleksei E. Nesterenko (U.S.S.R.)
**Department of Economic and Social Affairs**
    Under-Secretary: Philippe de Seynes (France)
**Department of Trusteeship and Non-Self-Governing Territories**
    Officer in charge: Issoufou-Saidou Djernakoye (Niger)
**Office of Conference Services**
    Under-Secretary: Jiri Nosek (Czechoslovakia)
**Office of Public Information**
    Under-Secretary: J. Rolz-Bennett (Guatemala)
**Office of General Services**
    Under-Secretary: David B. Vaughan (United States)

## SECRETARIES-GENERAL

Since its beginning in 1945, the United Nations has had three Secretaries-General. U Thant, the present Secretary-General, is serving his second five-year term.

**Trygve Lie** (1896–   ), a Norwegian lawyer and statesman, was elected the organization's first Secretary-General on February 1, 1946. He had previously led the Norwegian delegation to the United Nations Conference at San Francisco in 1945 and was chairman of the commission that drafted Security Council provisions for the U.N. Charter. In 1950 the General Assembly named him to an additional three-year term, from which he resigned in September, 1952.

**Dag Hammarskjöld** (1905–61), the son of Sweden's World War I Prime Minister, was named to succeed Lie in April, 1953. In September, 1957, he was re-elected for a second five-year term, but died before its completion in a plane crash in the Congo on September 18, 1961.

As Secretary-General, Hammarskjöld worked for resolution of the Suez Canal dispute in 1957 and support of armistice agreements between Israel and the Arab states. After his trip to Peiping in the winter of 1954–55, 15 American fliers held by the Chinese Communists since the end of the Korean War were released. His last major work was with the U.N. assistance mission to the Congo.

**U Thant** (1909–   ), of Burma, was named acting Secretary-General on November 3, 1961. On November 30, 1962, he was appointed Secretary-General. In 1966 Thant announced he would not consider serving another term, but on December 2 of that year he reluctantly accepted his unanimous reappointment.

Confronted with a deteriorating international situation in 1967, the Secretary-General continued to work for world peace. In an effort to find a satisfactory solution to the Vietnamese conflict, he conferred with officials of both the North Vietnamese government and the United States government and proposed a plan designed to lead to negotiations. Neither side seemed prepared to accept his plan, however.

In the Middle East, Thant worked for a settlement of Syrian-Israeli border disputes. After the Arab-Israeli war erupted in June, he campaigned for cessation of hostilities. Although the U.N. effected a cease-fire after six days of fighting, it was unable to come to grips with the underlying causes of the conflict, and Arab-Israeli hostility remained a serious problem.

Born in Pantanaw, Burma, he attended University College in Rangoon, became headmaster of his alma mater, the National High School, and worked as a free-lance journalist. In 1947 he assumed the first in a series of Ministry of Information posts. After serving as an adviser to Burma's prime ministers, he was named Burma's Permanent Representative to the United Nations in 1957.

Secretary-General U Thant

## SPECIALIZED AGENCIES OF THE UNITED NATIONS

The United Nations Charter provides for establishment of agreements between the United Nations and "specialized agencies . . . having wide international responsibilities . . . in economic, social, cultural, educational, health, and related fields." Each agency operating under such an agreement with the United Nations is autonomous, with its own executive and legislative bodies, secretariat, and budget. Each reports annually to the Economic and Social Council. The International Atomic Energy Agency (IAEA), established "under the aegis of the United Nations," reports annually to the General Assembly and, when appropriate, to the Security Council and to the Economic and Social Council.

### International Atomic Energy Agency (IAEA)

Established: July 29, 1957

Purpose: To accelerate and enlarge the contribution of atomic energy to peace, health, and prosperity, and to ensure IAEA assistance is never used to further military aims.

Director: Sigvard Eklund (Sweden)

Headquarters: Kaerntnerring 11, Vienna 1, Austria

### International Labor Organization (ILO)

Established: April 11, 1919 (became a specialized agency of the U.N. in 1946)

Purpose: To contribute to establishment of lasting peace by promoting social justice; to improve labor conditions and living standards through international action; and to promote economic and social stability.

Director: David A. Morse (United States)

Headquarters: 154 Rue de Lausanne, Geneva, Switzerland

### Food and Agriculture Organization of the United Nations (FAO)

Established: October 16, 1945

Purpose: To raise levels of nutrition and standards of living; to improve efficiency of production and distribution of food and agricultural products from farms, forests, and fisheries, thus contributing to an expanding world economy.

Director-General: B. R. Sen (India)

Headquarters: Viale delle Terme di Caracalla, Rome, Italy

### United Nations Educational, Scientific, and Cultural Organization (UNESCO)

Established: November 4, 1946

Purpose: To contribute to peace and security by promoting international collaboration in education, science, and culture in order to further universal respect for justice, the rule of law, human rights, and the fundamental freedoms that are affirmed by the United Nations Charter.

Director-General: René Maheu (France)

Headquarters: UNESCO House, Place de Fontenoy, Paris 7e, France

### World Health Organization (WHO)

Established: April 7, 1948

Purpose: To promote the attainment by all peoples of the best possible level of health. World Health Organization services are advisory and technical.

Director-General: Dr. M. G. Candau (Brazil)

Headquarters: Palais des Nations, Geneva, Switzerland

### International Bank for Reconstruction and Development (WORLD BANK)

Established: December 27, 1945 (by agreement drawn up at Bretton Woods Conference, July, 1944)

Purpose: To assist reconstruction and development of member states by facilitating capital investment; to supplement private investment by providing loans; to promote foreign investment, a balanced growth of international trade, and equilibrium in balances of payments.

President: George D. Woods (United States)

Headquarters: 1818 H Street, N.W., Washington, D.C. 20006

### International Development Association (IDA)

Established: September 24, 1960

Purpose: Under the administration of the World Bank, IDA makes loans to less developed countries, on terms that are more flexible and bear less heavily on the balance of payments than terms of conventional loans among nations.

President: George D. Woods (United States)

Headquarters: 1818 H Street, N.W., Washington, D.C. 20006

### International Finance Corporation (IFC)

Established: July, 1956

Purpose: To further economic development by encouraging growth of private enterprise in member countries, particularly in less developed areas. IFC is permitted to invest in private enterprises, in association with private investors, without government guarantee of repayment, if sufficient private capital is unavailable on reasonable terms. IFC helps to stimulate investment of foreign and domestic capital, and serves as a clearinghouse, bringing together investment opportunities, private capital, and experienced management.

President: George D. Woods (United States)

Headquarters: 1818 H Street, N.W., Washington, D.C. 20006

### International Monetary Fund (FUND)

Established: December 27, 1945

Purpose: To promote international monetary cooperation and expansion of international trade; to promote exchange stability, maintain orderly exchange arrangements, and avoid competitive exchange depreciations; to assist in establishment of a multilateral system of payments between members; and to assist in elimination of foreign exchange restrictions that hamper world trade.

Director: Pierre-Paul Schweitzer (France)

Headquarters: 1818 H Street, N.W., Washington, D.C. 20006

### International Civil Aviation Organization (ICAO)

Established: April 14, 1947

Purpose: To establish international standards and regulations for civil aviation, and to study international civil aviation problems.

ICAO Council President: Walter Binaghi (Argentina)

Secretary-General: Bernard T. Twigt (Netherlands)

Headquarters: International Aviation Building, 1080 University Street, Montreal 3, Quebec

**Universal Postal Union (UPU)**

Established: July 1, 1875 (by the Postal Convention adopted at Berne, October 9, 1874)

Purpose: To form a single postal territory of all member states for reciprocal exchange of correspondence and to promote international collaboration in organization and improvement of postal services. Each member state agrees to transmit the mail of other members by the means used for its own mail.

Director-General: Michel Rahi (United Arab Republic)

Headquarters: Schosshaldenstrasse 46, Berne 15, Switzerland

**International Telecommunication Union (ITU)**

Established: Founded at Paris, 1865 (became a U.N. specialized agency in 1947)

Purpose: To establish international regulations for telegraph, telephone, and radio services, in order to further their development and extend their utilization by the public at the lowest possible rates.

Secretary-General: Mohammed Ezzedine Mili (Tunisia), *interim*

Headquarters: Palais des Nations, Geneva, Switzerland

**World Meteorological Organization (WMO)**

Established: March 23, 1950

Purpose: To promote international cooperation in meteorology, establishment of a world-wide network of meteorological stations, and rapid exchange of weather data; to promote standardization of weather observations and publication of statistics; and to further application of meteorology to aviation, shipping, agriculture, and other activities.

Secretary-General: David A. Davies (U.K.)

Headquarters: Avenue Giuseppe Motta, Geneva, Switzerland

**Intergovernmental Maritime Consultative Organization (IMCO)**

Established: March 17, 1959

Purpose: To promote international cooperation in maritime navigation and to provide machinery for consultation on shipping matters; to encourage removal of discriminatory practices and unnecessary governmental restrictions; and to encourage high standards of navigation and safety. IMCO has special responsibility in matters relating to safety of life at sea, and functions as an advisory body.

Secretary-General: Jean Roullier (France)

Headquarters: Chancery House, London

**General Agreement on Tariffs and Trade (GATT),** drafted in 1946, to which 66 nations are parties, is designed to ease trade barriers and establish rules of fair trade. GATT embodies some of the objectives of the International Trade Organization (ITO), planned when the specialized agencies were set up, but not yet established.

Executive Secretary: Eric Wyndham-White (United Kingdom)

Headquarters: Geneva, Switzerland

WHO/ P.N. Sharma

An elephant transports a World Health Organization (WHO) malaria team in India. Since 1955 when WHO launched its campaign against malaria, incidence of the disease has dropped from 250,000,000 to 140,000,000 cases.

## MEMBERSHIP IN PRINCIPAL UNITED NATIONS BODIES: 1967

**SECURITY COUNCIL:** 15 members: five (*) are designated in the Charter as permanent; ten are elected by the General Assembly for two-year terms, ending December 31 of year indicated.

| | | | |
|---|---|---|---|
| Argentina (1967) | China * | India (1968) | U.S.S.R. * |
| Brazil (1968) | Denmark (1968) | Japan (1967) | United Kingdom * |
| Bulgaria (1967) | Ethiopia (1968) | Mali (1967) | United States * |
| Canada (1968) | France * | Nigeria (1967) | |

**ECONOMIC AND SOCIAL COUNCIL:** 27 members elected by the General Assembly for three-year terms, ending December 31 of year indicated.

| | | | |
|---|---|---|---|
| Belgium (1967) | Guatemala (1967) | Pakistan (1967) | Turkey (1969) |
| Cameroon (1967) | India (1967) | Panama (1968) | U.S.S.R. (1968) |
| Canada (1967) | Iran (1968) | Peru (1967) | United Kingdom (1968) |
| Czechoslovakia (1968) | Kuwait (1969) | Philippines (1968) | United Republic of |
| Dahomey (1967) | Libya (1969) | Romania (1967) | Tanzania (1969) |
| France (1969) | Mexico (1969) | Sierra Leone (1969) | United States (1967) |
| Gabon (1967) | Morocco (1968) | Sweden (1968) | Venezuela (1968) |

**TRUSTEESHIP COUNCIL:** Eight members; four are states administering Trust Territories: three (*) are nonadministering permanent members of the Security Council; one, Liberia, is a nonadministering member elected by the General Assembly to a three-year term, ending December 31, 1968.

| | | | |
|---|---|---|---|
| Australia | France * | New Zealand | United Kingdom |
| China * | Liberia | U.S.S.R. * | United States |

**INTERNATIONAL COURT OF JUSTICE:** 15 members, elected by the General Assembly to nine-year terms ending February 5 of the year indicated. Officers serve three-year terms.

| | |
|---|---|
| President: José Luis Bustamante y Rivero, Peru......(1970) | Luis Padilla Nervo, Mexico......................(1973) |
| Vice President: Vladimir M. Koretsky, U.S.S.R.......(1970) | Isaac Forster, Senegal..............................(1973) |
| Fouad Ammoun, Lebanon.........................(1976) | André Gros, France................................(1973) |
| Cesar Bengzon, Philippines.......................(1976) | Sir Gerald Fitzmaurice, United Kingdom............(1973) |
| Kotaro Tanaka, Japan............................(1970) | Manfred Lachs, Poland............................(1976) |
| Philip C. Jessup, United States...................(1970) | Charles D. Onyeama, Nigeria......................(1976) |
| Gaetano Morelli, Italy.............................(1970) | Sture Petren, Sweden.............................(1976) |
| Sir Muhammad Zafrullah Khan, Pakistan...........(1973) | |

## PRESIDENTS OF THE GENERAL ASSEMBLY

| PRESIDENT | COUNTRY | YEAR | SESSION |
|---|---|---|---|
| Paul-Henri Spaak................. | Belgium..................... | 1946 | First Session |
| Oswaldo Aranha................. | Brazil....................... | 1947 | First Special Session and Second Regular Session |
| José Arce...................... | Argentina................... | 1948 | Second Special Session |
| Herbert V. Evatt................ | Australia.................... | 1948 | Third Session |
| Carlos P. Romulo............... | Philippines.................. | 1949 | Fourth Session |
| Nasrollah Entezam.............. | Iran........................ | 1950 | Fifth Session |
| Luis Padilla Nervo.............. | Mexico..................... | 1951 | Sixth Session |
| Lester B. Pearson.............. | Canada.................... | 1952 | Seventh Session |
| Mme. Vijaya L. Pandit........... | India...................... | 1953 | Eighth Session |
| Eelco N. van Kleffens........... | Netherlands................. | 1954 | Ninth Session |
| José Maza..................... | Chile...................... | 1955 | Tenth Session |
| Rudecindo Ortega.............. | Chile...................... | 1956 | First and Second Emergency Special Sessions |
| Prince Wan Waithayakon........ | Thailand.................... | 1956–57 | Eleventh Session |
| Sir Leslie Munro................ | New Zealand................. | 1957–58 | Twelfth Session and Third Emergency Special Session |
| Charles Malik.................. | Lebanon.................... | 1958–59 | Thirteenth Session |
| Victor Andres Belaunde.......... | Peru....................... | 1959–60 | Fourteenth Session and Fourth Emergency Special Session |
| Frederick Henry Boland.......... | Ireland..................... | 1960–61 | Fifteenth Session and Third Special Session |
| Mongi Slim.................... | Tunisia..................... | 1961–62 | Sixteenth Session |
| Muhammad Zafrulla Khan....... | Pakistan.................... | 1962–63 | Seventeenth Session and Fourth Special Session |
| Charles Sosa-Rodriguez.......... | Venezuela.................. | 1963–64 | Eighteenth Session |
| Alex Quaison-Sackey............ | Ghana..................... | 1964–65 | Nineteenth Session |
| Amintore Fanfani............... | Italy....................... | 1965–66 | Twentieth Session |
| Abdul Rahman Pazhwak.......... | Afghanistan................. | 1966–67 | Twenty-first Session |
| Corneliu Manescu............... | Romania................... | 1967–68 | Twenty-second Session |

# FOCUS ON THE NEWS

## DE GAULLE IN CANADA: LA GRANDE GAFFE

De Gaulle shouting "Vive le Québec Libre"

Paris Match/Pictorial Parade

"After Quebec falls . . ."

©1967 Herblock in the Washington Post

From the onset Canadian officials were skittish about French President Charles de Gaulle's scheduled five-day tour of Canada in July 1967. The crusty French general had been invited along with other chiefs of state to help commemorate the 100th anniversary of Canada's confederation. With a small but vociferous segment of Quebec's French-speaking population clamoring for secession, it seemed unlikely that de Gaulle would strive for detachment.

The first stop was Quebec. The Canadian capital city of Ottawa, where visiting dignitaries are traditionally received, was not scheduled until the last day of de Gaulle's visit. His Navy cruiser steamed into Quebec Harbor flying the French tricolor, although naval protocol requires visiting ships to honor the flag of the host country. For travel through Canada he demanded a French-made Citroën.

The city of Quebec gave the general a tumultuous welcome. Greeted with shouts of "Vive de Gaulle" and "Vive la France," he answered "Vive le Québec," "Vive le Canada Français," "Vive la Nouvelle France" —everything, in fact, except "Vive le Can-

ada." Ottawa fumed, but Prime Minister Lester Pearson remained calm.

From Quebec de Gaulle went on to Montreal. Speaking from the balcony of the city hall he cried out to the crowds below, "Vive le Québec Libre." The words are the literal slogan of the French Quebec separatists.

Many Canadians urged Pearson to order de Gaulle out of the country. However, Pearson was in a delicate position. By rebuking the French president too strenuously he could lose the support of the French-speaking Liberal Party. He deftly shifted the burden back to de Gaulle. In a tersely worded statement Pearson charged that de Gaulle's remarks were "unacceptable to the Canadian government and its people." French officials shot back a reply stating that Pearson's use of the word "unacceptable" was unacceptable to the general. With that de Gaulle cancelled his Ottawa visit and flew back to France on July 26, one day ahead of schedule. In Paris the self-styled "liberator" brushed aside his government's halting efforts to explain his behavior and proclaimed himself the spiritual leader of all "Canadian Frenchmen."

# U.S. FOREIGN RELATIONS: 1967

U.S. foreign relations in 1967 were dominated by the Vietnam war. What had begun only four years before as a limited counterinsurgency operation with 15,000 advisers had escalated into all-out combat involving more than 500,000 U.S. troops and costing $2 billion a month.

As the military and political demands of the war increased, the U.S. Government sought to improve and clarify its position. President Lyndon B. Johnson and Secretary of State Dean Rusk stated repeatedly that while the U.S. wanted to negotiate a settlement, it had both the capacity and the will to continue the struggle until a just solution could be found.

Several times during the year the U.S. sought unsuccessfully to enter into negotiations with Hanoi, most notably in March when Ho Chi Minh, President of North Vietnam, made public and rejected a confidential letter from President Johnson urging "direct talks."

Through its Ambassador to the United Nations, Arthur Goldberg, the U.S. offered to debate the question of Vietnam in the Security Council (a proposal Russia blocked) and also requested the good offices of the U.N. to settle the war.

When U.S. Ambassador to Saigon Henry Cabot Lodge resigned in March, 1967, the White House appointed Ellsworth Bunker, a pragmatic New England businessman-diplomat, to the post. Bunker put pressure on the Saigon government to stop censoring the press and jailing political opponents. The U.S. also did what it could to ensure fair national elections in South Vietnam on September 3. The heavily favored government ticket of Lieutenant General Nguyen Van Thieu and Premier Nguyen Cao Ky emerged victorious from the elections, but a peace candidate, Truong Din Dzu, was a surprisingly strong runner-up.

U.S. handling of the Vietnamese situation was criticized with increasing intensity in 1967 by prominent figures at home and by friendly and hostile powers abroad. In the latter half of the year some Administration spokesmen explained that it was U.S. security that was at stake in Vietnam, not simply the pacification of the country and the assurance of self-determination for the people.

In spite of the Vietnam war, the U.S. continued to seek more cordial relations with the U.S.S.R. in 1967. Soviet Premier Aleksei Kosygin and President Johnson met in Glassboro, N. J., on June 25 and publicly agreed that the two countries had "a special responsibility for restraint." As evidence of their willingness to explore areas of agreement, the two major powers and 15 other nations made steady progress at Geneva on a draft treaty to bar the spread of nuclear weapons; a document should be ready for signing sometime in 1968. Also during 1967 the U.S. Senate approved a new consular treaty that provided for the resumption of consular relations between the U.S. and the U.S.S.R.

While East-West relations appeared to be improving slightly, the U.S. in 1967 was having increasing difficulties with its partners in the North Atlantic Treaty Organization (NATO). France's President Charles de Gaulle, who in 1966 served an eviction notice on NATO's Paris headquarters and withdrew the entire French troop contingent, was as adamant as ever in opposing American dominance of the alliance. Some observers were convinced that de Gaulle planned to quit the political arm of the organization in 1969. Most NATO members opposed de Gaulle's stand, concluding that Western European security must ultimately depend upon close cooperation with the U.S. But even these countries were anxious to assert their independence and reserved the right to be critical of U.S. policy.

In April President Johnson traveled to South America for the first time to meet with Latin American leaders at Punta del Este, Uruguay. The President's theme in his speeches and in informal conversations with other heads of state was that future U.S. aid would only reinforce and build on what the Latin Americans could do for themselves. In a "Declaration of the Presidents of America" all but one of the conferees pledged themselves to create a Latin common market to begin operating in 1970. Under this plan a common currency would be established, tariffs lowered, and capital and labor permitted to move freely from one country to another—all measures heartily endorsed by U.S. policymakers. The meeting was a success from the U.S. standpoint: The President's words about Latin American self-help were well-received, and the Declaration expressed the leaders' desire to solve common problems through common action. But Peru's President Belaunde Terry perhaps summed up the significance of the meeting best when he said: "The documents of this conference are like the score of a symphony. It all depends on how it is played."

The U.S. decided in April to suspend arms shipments to India and Pakistan over the objections of both nations. The intended effects of the move were to ease tensions by preventing another arms race and to divert money in both countries into positive programs. In reality India's greatest enemy in 1967 was not Pakistan or Red China but famine. To combat it, the U.S. sent India 2,000,000 tons of grain, which was barely enough to stave off mass starvation even in a record-harvest year.

The U.S. maintained a watchful stance toward Africa and the Middle East during 1967, and offered its aid and good offices in negotiating a Middle Eastern settlement following the Arab-Israeli war in June.

At the year's end the Vietnam war remained the overriding factor in U.S. foreign affairs and, barring major policy changes in Hanoi or Washington, it appeared likely to be just as important in 1968.

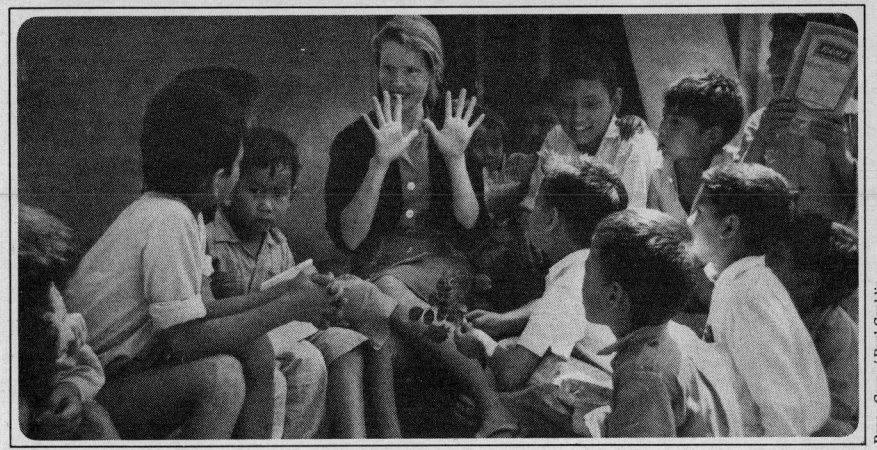

Peace Corps / Paul Conklin

Peace Corps volunteer Barbara J. Wylie (center) is an English teacher in Katmandu, Nepal. As an extra project she conducts classes for untouchable children, who would normally get little or no schooling.

## THE PEACE CORPS: 1967

The Peace Corps, a revolutionary idea in foreign aid, was established by an executive order of President John F. Kennedy on March 1, 1961. A missionary-type program consisting of trained American volunteers who assist interested countries in solving their domestic problems, it was conceived with the objectives of promoting understanding, peace, friendship, goodwill, and prosperity. During its six years of existence the Peace Corps has managed to live up to these objectives. While speaking to Peace Corps volunteers, President Lyndon B. Johnson stated: "I wish we had as many in your outfit as we have in the armed forces. . . . If we had more of you we would have less of them."

For its first year, $40,000,000 was allotted to the Peace Corps. Its requested budget for 1967–68 totals $118,700,000. It is anticipated that a total of 17,750 volunteers will be working in various countries around the world by August 31, 1968.

In 1967 the Peace Corps, with requests for volunteers from nine more areas, planned to be at work in a total of 58 countries and territories. Ceylon, where a 1962–64 program was discontinued by mutual agreement, invited the Peace Corps to return to help increase agricultural production. The other eight new areas added to the Peace Corps program were Gambia, Tonga, Western Samoa, Upper Volta, Lesotho, Paraguay, Fiji, and Dahomey.

Below are listed the number of Peace Corps volunteers assigned to each country as of September, 1967. The figures include members in host countries, in training, and in "hold" status.

| REGION AND COUNTRY | VOLUN-TEERS | REGION AND COUNTRY | VOLUN-TEERS | REGION AND COUNTRY | VOLUN-TEERS |
|---|---|---|---|---|---|
| AFRICA | 3,636 | Uganda | 162 | Guyana | 52 |
| Botswana | 55 | Upper Volta | 59 | Honduras | 143 |
| Cameroon | 94 | EAST ASIA, PACIFIC | 3,213 | Jamaica | 130 |
| Chad | 38 | Malaysia | 871 | Panama | 254 |
| Dahomey | 15 | Philippines | 806 | Paraguay | 34 |
| Ethiopia | 449 | Republic of Korea | 321 | Peru | 355 |
| Gabon | 61 | Thailand | 369 | Uruguay | 55 |
| Gambia | 23 | Tonga | 40 | Venezuela | 390 |
| Ghana | 261 | Trust Territories | 709 | Eastern Caribbean | 102 |
| Ivory Coast | 91 | Western Samoa | 97 | Latin America Regional | 91 |
| Kenya | 321 | LATIN AMERICA | 4,718 | NORTH AFRICA, NEAR EAST, SOUTH ASIA | 2,581 |
| Lesotho | 88 | Bolivia | 360 | Afghanistan | 219 |
| Liberia | 279 | Brazil | 694 | Ceylon | 78 |
| Malawi | 180 | British Honduras | 54 | India | 1,102 |
| Niger | 129 | Chile | 431 | Iran | 358 |
| Nigeria | 373 | Colombia | 718 | Libya | 15 |
| Senegal | 130 | Costa Rica | 149 | Morocco | 91 |
| Sierra Leone | 314 | Dominican Republic | 167 | Nepal | 229 |
| Somalia | 101 | Ecuador | 316 | Tunisia | 248 |
| Tanzania | 303 | El Salvador | 123 | Turkey | 241 |
| Togo | 108 | Guatemala | 100 | | |

## U.S. FOREIGN ASSISTANCE

Foreign-assistance programs originated during World War II and have become important instruments of United States foreign policy. Designed to provide military assistance and to spur economic and social development in underdeveloped nations, the aid is given in three forms: grants (for which no repayment is expected), credits (loans), and other assistance (the sale of farm products for payment in foreign currency). Aid is seldom given to a foreign nation in dollars; rather, most economic assistance involves the financing of U.S. goods and services for specific programs abroad.

Since World War II there have been several acts authorizing aid programs, including the European Recovery Act (Marshall Plan) which provided economic aid to war-damaged European nations. Today most foreign aid is authorized by the Foreign Assistance Act of 1961, and the primary administrator of this assistance is the Agency for International Development (AID).

AID is an arm of the Department of State and is organized into four divisions, with bureaus for the Far East, the Near East and South Asia, Africa and Europe, and Latin America. Its goal is to help the recipients develop their own resources and abilities to attract foreign investment and to secure loans.

AID coordinates both military and economic assistance. The Military Assistance Program provides arms for the military forces of foreign nations, helps to train their personnel, and provides other "supporting" aid that enables the nations to allocate greater percentages of their own resources to military purposes. (Support for United States troops fighting abroad is not included, and its cost is covered by direct appropriation to the Department of Defense.)

Economic assistance is given primarily through development loans. These loans provide for a wide range of projects, including roads, dams, and irrigation. They are repayable in dollars and the terms are usually "soft" —low interest rates and a long period of time for repayment. Technical assistance provides for training of managers and technicians and is usually given in the form of grants.

The Foreign Assistance Act of 1961 also authorizes programs administered by other agencies such as the International Cooperation Administration, the Development Loan Fund, and the Export-Import Bank. Food for Peace and the Peace Corps are other, separately financed foreign aid programs.

## U.S. FOREIGN MILITARY ASSISTANCE PROGRAM
Source: Department of Defense, Office of the Secretary

The figures in the table below are given in millions of dollars. They include expenditures for military construction and the training of military personnel, as well as appropriations for equipment and supplies under the Military Assistance Program.

| COUNTRY | 1950–1967 | 1966 [1] | 1967 [1] |
|---|---|---|---|
| **Europe** | $15,527.6 | $135.6 | $ 96.7 |
| Belgium-Luxembourg | 1,255.3 | 1.0 | — |
| Denmark | 617.6 | 1.2 | 0.1 |
| France | 4,233.4 | — | — |
| Germany | 900.8 | — | — |
| Greece | 1,489.0 | 78.7 | 65.0 |
| Italy | 2,289.7 | — | — |
| Netherlands | 1,219.3 | — | — |
| Norway | 896.5 | 34.5 | 18.2 |
| Portugal | 322.8 | 0.8 | 1.0 |
| Spain | 573.1 | 19.4 | 12.4 |
| United Kingdom | 1,034.5 | — | — |
| Yugoslavia | 695.6 | — | — |
| **Near East** | 4,153.8 | 206.6 | 389.3 |
| Iran | 1,036.8 | 63.3 | 141.6 |
| Iraq | 46.8 | 0.2 | 0.2 |
| Israel | 27.6 | — | — |
| Jordan | 68.2 | 10.1 | 12.6 |
| Lebanon | 29.8 | 4.1 | 21.1 |
| Saudi Arabia | 241.5 | 0.9 | 79.8 |
| Turkey | 2,703.1 | 128.0 | 134.0 |
| **Africa** | 101.9 | 27.5 | 27.9 |
| Congo, Dem. Rep. of | 21.8 | 3.5 | 4.0 |
| Ethiopia | n.a. | 15.0 | n.a. |
| Liberia | 7.2 | n.a. | 0.9 |
| Libya | 31.5 | 2.3 | 19.0 |
| Morocco | 41.4 | 4.6 | 4.0 |
| Tunisia | n.a. | 2.1 | n.a. |
| **Far East** | 9,483.7 | 281.5 | 368.0 |
| Australia | 125.9 | 5.0 | — |

| COUNTRY | 1950–1967 | 1966 [1] | 1967 [1] |
|---|---|---|---|
| Cambodia | $ 87.1 | — | — |
| China (Taiwan) | 2,492.3 | $ 94.1 | $ 100.0 |
| Indochina [2] | 709.6 | — | — |
| Indonesia | 63.6 | — | 0.4 |
| Japan | 898.5 | 1.6 | 0.4 |
| Korea, South | 2,524.9 | 157.0 | 165.0 |
| Malaysia | 23.9 | 1.8 | 20.2 |
| Philippines | 378.6 | 22.0 | 22.0 |
| Thailand | 667.6 | n.a. | 60.0 |
| Vietnam, South | 1,511.7 | n.a. | n.a. |
| **Latin America** | 887.2 | 89.0 | 82.5 |
| Argentina | 71.1 | 12.7 | 15.9 |
| Bolivia | 18.5 | 2.7 | 3.4 |
| Brazil | 271.0 | 16.8 | 29.6 |
| Chile | 96.2 | 10.8 | 5.2 |
| Colombia | 83.0 | 11.6 | 8.1 |
| Cuba | 10.6 | — | — |
| Dominican Republic | 19.2 | 2.2 | 3.1 |
| Ecuador | 37.8 | 2.7 | 3.0 |
| El Salvador | n.a. | 0.9 | — |
| Guatemala | 12.3 | 1.4 | 1.2 |
| Haiti | n.a. | — | — |
| Honduras | n.a. | 1.2 | — |
| Mexico | 7.1 | 0.3 | 0.1 |
| Nicaragua | 10.0 | 1.4 | 1.2 |
| Paraguay | 7.0 | 0.9 | 1.0 |
| Peru | 107.7 | 9.6 | 5.0 |
| Uruguay | 38.9 | 2.5 | 1.5 |
| Venezuela | 96.8 | 11.3 | 4.2 |
| **Total [3]** | $35,371.6 | $1,615.8 | $1,274.8 |

N.A., not available.   [1] Estimates for fiscal year ending June 30.   [2] The figure for Indochina refers to the total U.S. military aid during World War II and after. Indochina no longer exists as a political unit.   [3] Totals reflect U.S. military aid expenditures for all countries receiving military assistance, even those where specific figures are classified information.

## MAJOR U.S. FOREIGN ASSISTANCE: 1945–1966
Source: U.S. Office of Business Economics

The figures below, given in millions of dollars, represent aid dispensed by government agencies such as the Agency for International Development, and under special programs.

| COUNTRY | TOTAL AID |
|---|---|
| **Total U.S. Foreign Aid, 1945–1966......** | **$106,925** |
| **Western Europe.......................** | **27,118** |
| Austria............................. | 1,089 |
| Belgium–Luxembourg................. | 650 |
| Denmark............................ | 263 |
| Finland............................. | 54 |
| France.............................. | 4,142 |
| Germany, West...................... | 2,849 |
| Greece............................. | 1,656 |
| Iceland............................. | 67 |
| Ireland............................. | 129 |
| Italy............................... | 2,793 |
| Netherlands........................ | 828 |
| Norway............................. | 236 |
| Portugal............................ | 162 |
| Spain.............................. | 910 |
| Sweden............................. | 84 |
| Turkey............................. | 1,888 |
| United Kingdom.................... | 6,450 |
| Yugoslavia......................... | 2,009 |
| Other countries and programs........ | 859 |
| **Eastern Europe......................** | **1,606** |
| Albania............................ | 20 |
| Czechoslovakia..................... | 191 |
| Germany, East...................... | 17 |
| Hungary............................ | 22 |
| Poland............................. | 969 |
| U.S.S.R............................ | 387 |
| **Near East...........................** | **12,073** |
| Afghanistan........................ | 285 |
| Ceylon............................. | 94 |
| Cyprus............................. | 20 |
| India.............................. | 5,901 |
| Iran............................... | 687 |
| Iraq............................... | 47 |
| Israel.............................. | 908 |
| Jordan............................. | 525 |
| Lebanon............................ | 86 |
| Nepal.............................. | 99 |
| Pakistan........................... | 2,804 |
| Saudi Arabia....................... | 12 |
| Syria.............................. | 57 |
| Yemen............................. | 44 |
| Other countries and programs........ | 504 |
| **Africa.............................** | **3,731** |
| Algeria............................ | 158 |
| Cameroon.......................... | 20 |
| Congo, Democratic Republic of........ | 277 |
| Dahomey........................... | 8 |
| Ethiopia............................ | 136 |
| Ghana............................. | 127 |
| Guinea............................. | 71 |
| Ivory Coast........................ | 25 |
| Kenya............................. | 50 |
| Liberia............................ | 184 |
| Libya.............................. | 208 |
| Malagasy Republic.................. | 8 |
| Mali............................... | 13 |
| Morocco........................... | 497 |

| COUNTRY | TOTAL AID |
|---|---|
| Nigeria............................. | $    117 |
| Senegal............................ | 17 |
| Sierra Leone....................... | 27 |
| Somalia............................ | 48 |
| South Africa....................... | −85 * |
| Sudan............................. | 85 |
| Tanzania.......................... | 47 |
| Togo.............................. | 10 |
| Tunisia............................ | 430 |
| Uganda............................ | 17 |
| United Arab Republic (Egypt)......... | 1,106 |
| Other countries and programs........ | 129 |
| **Far East and Pacific.................** | **15,499** |
| Australia........................... | 37 |
| Burma............................. | 100 |
| Cambodia.......................... | 256 |
| China (Taiwan)..................... | 2,150 |
| Hong Kong......................... | 39 |
| Indonesia.......................... | 708 |
| Japan............................. | 2,587 |
| Korea, South....................... | 4,037 |
| Laos.............................. | 490 |
| Malaysia.......................... | 35 |
| New Zealand....................... | 25 |
| Philippines......................... | 1,151 |
| Ryukyu Islands..................... | 322 |
| Thailand........................... | 384 |
| Trust Territory of the Pacific Islands... | 134 |
| Vietnam, South..................... | 2,831 |
| Other countries and programs........ | 213 |
| **Western Hemisphere.................** | **6,327** |
| Argentina.......................... | 377 |
| Bolivia............................ | 374 |
| Brazil............................. | 1,892 |
| Canada............................ | −7 * |
| Chile.............................. | 822 |
| Colombia.......................... | 474 |
| Costa Rica......................... | 107 |
| Cuba.............................. | 41 |
| Dominican Republic................. | 224 |
| Ecuador........................... | 144 |
| El Salvador........................ | 73 |
| Guatemala......................... | 165 |
| Guyana............................ | 11 |
| Haiti.............................. | 99 |
| Honduras.......................... | 62 |
| Jamaica........................... | 23 |
| Mexico............................ | 457 |
| Nicaragua.......................... | 78 |
| Panama............................ | 133 |
| Paraguay........................... | 71 |
| Peru.............................. | 282 |
| Surinam........................... | 5 |
| Trinidad and Tobago................. | 41 |
| Uruguay........................... | 64 |
| Venezuela.......................... | 189 |
| Other countries and programs........ | 124 |
| **Other Organizations and Areas........** | **2,595** |

* A negative figure occurs, for example, when returns from repayment of loans exceed expenditures for new grants.

## FOOD FOR PEACE

The Food for Peace Program was initiated in 1954 and utilizes surplus agricultural products. The program provides for sale of farm products for foreign currencies, emergency food relief, donations to private agencies dispensing help abroad, and long-term loans.

# THE COMMUNIST WORLD: 1967

In 1967 it became clear that the Communist world—like Humpty Dumpty after his fall—was unlikely ever again to be put together in one piece. The Communist countries were probably more deeply split apart than ever before in their history. No longer was the split a simple fracture with the adherents of the Soviet Union aligned against the supporters of Communist China. Rather, 1967 was the year of polycentrism—the year when many Communist nations and parties made independent decisions heedless of the approval or disapproval of Moscow or Peking.

Evidence of the growing confusion in the Communist world was abundant in 1967. In the spring Moscow called a meeting of all the European Communist parties, to be held in the Czechoslovak resort of Karlovy Vary. Six European Communist parties—including the ruling parties of Yugoslavia, Romania, and Albania—either refused to take part or refused to sign the final communique.

In Havana in the summer of 1967, the Castro-assembled congress of Latin American revolutionaries passed a resolution denouncing the Soviet Union. Castro and his friends were furious with Moscow and with the Latin American Communist parties supporting Moscow. Castro demanded that Moscow recognize guerrilla warfare as the only approved means of Latin American revolution. He also demanded that Moscow refrain from giving economic aid to and increasing its trade with Latin American countries such as Brazil and Argentina, whose governments Castro wants to overthrow. Moscow simply went on doing as it pleased.

Local Communist parties in North Korea and Japan also made clear during 1967 that they were far from fully satisfied either with Moscow or Peking.

When the Arab-Israeli war broke out in June, 1967, Moscow sought to build Communist unity around condemnation of Israel and support of the Arabs. The Romanians coolly refused and at the U.N. publicly adopted a distinctly different attitude based on genuine neutrality. The Romanians also bluntly refused to follow the Soviet ban against Eastern European recognition of West Germany, and entered into diplomatic relations with Bonn despite the open displeasure of the East German, Polish, and Soviet regimes.

Romania's major role in asserting its independence as a Communist state in 1967 has deep historic roots. Romanians have traditionally thought of themselves as a Latin enclave in Eastern Europe, one threatened by a surrounding flood of Slavs. In particular, the Romanian Communists share with their fellow countrymen a deep bitterness against the Soviet Union for Stalin's seizure of the Romanian areas of Moldavia and Northern Bukovina. Similar but less effective nationalist sentiments in other Eastern European countries also roiled relations with the Soviet Union.

A measure of Moscow's concern with the area was the frequency with which visits were exchanged between Soviet and Eastern European leaders in 1967. East Germany made little secret of its anxiety that its interests might be sold out to West Germany by Moscow and the other East European countries. In Czechoslovakia people took pride in the way their exhibit at Expo 67 overshadowed the exhibits of other Communist countries. Czechoslovak intellectuals simultaneously spoke out more bluntly against Soviet domination and demanded recognition of the great figures of Czechoslovakia's pre-Communist history.

All through Eastern Europe—but notably in Poland—there was a near explosion of public anger at the Soviet-forced all-out support of the Arab states against Israel. There was also resentment at the glorification of the Soviet Union, centered in 1967 around the 50th anniversary of the Russian Revolution.

Almost the only bright feature in Moscow during the anniversary year was the performance of the Soviet economy, which did relatively well. But it was a measure of the nation's continued poverty that the most important economic gain announced in 1967 was the raising of the minimum monthly wage to 60 rubles, equivalent to $16 a week at the official rate of exchange. And 1967 was the year in which the Kremlin publicly lost an astronaut; in which Joseph Stalin's daughter, Svetlana, escaped to the West and denounced Communism; and in which more than $1 billion worth of Soviet arms sent to the Middle East was captured by the Israeli army.

The intense competition for power in the Soviet Politburo continued unchecked during 1967, although it was kept carefully from public view. Thus Premier Kosygin's talks with President Johnson in Glassboro, N.J., were played down in the Soviet press so as to avoid giving him too much personal publicity. The most vivid public sign of the struggle was the demotion of Politburo member Alexander Shelepin, who lost his post as a Communist party secretary and had to take a job heading the impotent Soviet trade union movement.

Soviet-American relations during 1967 suffered from the undeviating Moscow support of North Vietnam and the huge deliveries of rockets, planes, and other Soviet supplies sent to the Communist forces. That the two countries had very different views on the Middle East crisis was an additional irritant. Nevertheless, in 1967 both the U.S. and the U.S.S.R. played major roles in helping conclude the first international treaty on space. And at Geneva the two countries collaborated in presenting a joint text of most of a treaty aimed at preventing proliferation of nuclear weapons. Against this, however, observers had to take account of the reality that by year's end both countries were engaged in a new extension of the arms competition.

## ANGRY GIANT: RED CHINA

Chinese officials chanted Communist slogans from their London legation's steps after clashing with British police on August 29. Earlier, Chinese Red Guards had sacked the British mission in Peking.

The explosion of irrational nationalism and disorder that marked Red China in 1967 had profound international implications. With regard to Vietnam, for example, the Chinese spoke often and loudly about their support for the Vietnamese Communists. But their opposition to any collaboration with the Soviet Union prevented the formation of any united Communist anti-American front on the Vietnam issue.

Throughout 1967 gigantic anti-foreign demonstrations were held in Peking to demonstrate Chinese hatred for assorted foreign powers. The Soviet Embassy in Peking was the target of repeated demonstrations of this sort, and both the Soviet Embassy compound and Soviet diplomatic personnel were attacked and subjected to indignities by Chinese rioters. Other Communist embassies and diplomats received similar treatment.

Western nations also suffered similar treatment, with the British—whose embassy compound was ransacked and partially destroyed —suffering the most. The anger at Britain was born of Chinese resentment at British action to stop a possible Chinese Communist takeover of Hong Kong.

Indonesian-Chinese relations also reached a new low, and diplomatic ties were suspended after the Chinese attacked the Indonesian Embassy in Peking and Indonesian students reciprocated against the Chinese Embassy in Djakarta.

There was renewed fighting on the Chinese-Indian border. China's formerly good relations with Burma were turned into bitter hostility when the Burmese refused to permit adulation of Mao Tse-tung in their country. China withdrew its aid mission in Burma on October 31.

Among the few countries with which the Chinese managed to retain really good relations in 1967 were North Vietnam, Albania, and Pakistan.

# OTHER INTERNATIONAL ORGANIZATIONS

Because the United Nations does not have a sufficient peace force to guarantee protection against aggression, regional agreements have been made for collective security. Smaller countries, by uniting to improve their economic and military position, gain a greater voice in the world political arena. Larger nations join (or instigate) pacts to strengthen the economic and military position of their allies. The organizations resulting from these alliances are not officially affiliated with the United Nations, but their influence may extend into the U.N. through the formation of voting blocs.

Often mutual assistance pacts are difficult to categorize. An economic or military agreement usually has political overtones and vice versa. In general, however, a pact can be classified as either military, political, or economic, although these categories are not necessarily mutually exclusive.

## ECONOMIC ORGANIZATIONS

### ■ COMMON MARKETS

Modern common markets are modeled on the 19th-century German *Zollverein,* or customs union, which dissolved tariff barriers restricting trade among individual German states. The first successful 20th-century common market was the Benelux Customs Union, established in 1948. Since then, common markets have been established in many areas of the world.

Each organization has as its primary goals promotion of economic development and foundation of closer economic links among member nations through the elimination of customs barriers. The following are the principal common-market organizations:

### AFRICAN-MALAGASY COMMON ORGANIZATION (OCAM)

Founded in 1965 in succession to the Afro-Malagasy Union for Economic Cooperation (UAMCE).

*Headquarters:* Yaoundé, Cameroon.

*Members:* Cameroon, Central African Republic, Chad, Congo (Brazzaville), Dahomey, Democratic Republic of the Congo, Gabon, Ivory Coast, Malagasy Republic, Niger, Rwanda, Senegal, Togo, and Upper Volta.

### ARAB COMMON MARKET

The treaty establishing the Arab Common Market, signed in August, 1964, went into effect on January 1, 1965.

*Headquarters:* Cairo, United Arab Republic.

*Members:* Iraq, Jordan, Syria, United Arab Republic.

### ASIAN AND PACIFIC COUNCIL (ASPAC)

Founded on June 16, 1966.

*Headquarters:* Bangkok, Thailand.

*Members:* Australia, Japan, Malaysia, New Zealand, Philippines, Republic of China (Taiwan), South Korea, South Vietnam, and Thailand. Laos attends as an observer nation.

*Purpose and aims:* To promote economic, social, and political cooperation among the non-Communist nations of Asia and the Pacific and to safeguard the national independence of member nations.

*Current status:* At the July, 1967, conference it was decided that ASPAC should avoid a hard anti-Communist line. Members were undecided, however, on the organization's future role.

### ASSOCIATION OF SOUTHEAST ASIAN NATIONS (ASEAN)

The declaration founding ASEAN was signed on August 8, 1967.

*Members:* Indonesia, Malaysia, Philippines, Singapore, and Thailand.

*Current status:* ASEAN will absorb the Association of Southeast Asia, which was disbanded in August, 1967, when ASEAN was formed.

### BENELUX ECONOMIC UNION

The treaty establishing the Benelux Economic Union, signed in February, 1958, went into effect November 1, 1960. The Benelux Economic Union grew out of the Benelux Customs Union established in 1948.

*Headquarters:* Brussels, Belgium.

*Members:* Belgium, Luxembourg, and the Netherlands.

*Purposes and aims:* To ensure the free circulation of persons, goods, capital, and services, and to coordinate the economic policies of member nations; to provide for eventual complete economic union of the member nations.

### CENTRAL AMERICAN COMMON MARKET (CACM)

The treaty establishing CACM was signed in 1958 by all the members except Costa Rica, which ratified it in 1962.

*Headquarters:* Guatemala City, Guatemala.

*Members:* Costa Rica, El Salvador, Guatemala, Honduras, and Nicaragua.

*Current status:* At the Council of American Presidents held in April, 1967, it was decided to work for the inauguration of a Latin American Common Market by 1970. It would be based upon the development of CACM and the Latin American Free Trade Association.

### COUNCIL FOR MUTUAL ECONOMIC ASSISTANCE (COMECON)

Founded in 1949 by representatives of European Communist-bloc nations. A charter modification in 1962 opened membership to non-European countries.

*Headquarters:* Moscow, U.S.S.R.

*Members:* Bulgaria, Czechoslovakia, East Germany, Hungary, Poland, Romania, U.S.S.R., and the Mongolian People's Republic, which was admitted in 1962. The following countries are observers: Cuba, North Korea, North Vietnam, People's Republic of China, and Yugoslavia.

## EUROPEAN ECONOMIC COMMUNITY (EEC or COMMON MARKET)

The treaty establishing the Common Market was signed in March, 1957, and went into effect on January 1, 1958.

*Headquarters:* Brussels, Belgium.

*Members:* Belgium, France, Italy, Luxembourg, the Netherlands, and West Germany. Greece, Turkey, 18 African states, and 13 overseas territories are associated with the Common Market.

During 1967 Great Britain again applied for membership and President de Gaulle of France opposed acceptance, effectively blocking membership. Ireland and Finland also applied for membership, and Sweden and Norway indicated that they intended to apply.

## EUROPEAN FREE TRADE ASSOCIATION (EFTA)

The treaty establishing EFTA was signed in January, 1960, and went into force in May, 1960.

*Headquarters:* Geneva, Switzerland.

*Members:* Austria, Denmark, Norway, Portugal, Sweden, Switzerland, and the United Kingdom. Finland is an associate member.

## LATIN AMERICAN FREE TRADE ASSOCIATION (LAFTA)

Established February, 1960.

*Headquarters:* Montevideo, Uruguay.

*Members:* Argentina, Brazil, Chile, Colombia, Ecuador, Mexico, Paraguay, Peru, Uruguay, and Venezuela.

*Purposes and aims:* Eventual establishment of a South American common market. (See also the entry on the Central American Common Market.)

## ■ OTHER ECONOMIC ORGANIZATIONS
## ALLIANCE FOR PROGRESS (ALIANZA PARA EL PROGRESO)

The treaty founding the Alliance was signed on August 17, 1961, by representatives of all the American republics except Cuba. The program was originally proposed by President John F. Kennedy on March 13, 1961.

*Headquarters:* Washington, D.C.

*Members:* Argentina, Bolivia, Brazil, Chile, Colombia, Costa Rica, Dominican Republic, Ecuador, El Salvador, Guatemala, Haiti, Honduras, Mexico, Nicaragua, Panama, Paraguay, Peru, the United States, Uruguay, and Venezuela.

*Purpose and aims:* To carry out a ten-year program of assistance in solving economic and social problems of Latin America and to improve and strengthen democratic institutions.

At the Council of American Presidents held in April, 1967, at Punta del Este, Uruguay, it was decided that the Alliance for Progress will continue to focus on the financial and economic development of Latin America.

## COLOMBO PLAN

The Colombo Plan went into effect on July 1, 1950. It developed from a proposal by British Commonwealth members for a plan of economic development in southern and southeastern Asia.

*Headquarters:* Colombo, Ceylon.

*Members:* Afghanistan, Australia, Bhutan, Burma, Cambodia, Canada, Ceylon, India, Indonesia, Japan, South Korea, Laos, Malaysia, Maldive Islands, Nepal, New Zealand, Pakistan, Philippines, Thailand, the United Kingdom, the United States, and South Vietnam.

# POLITICAL ORGANIZATIONS

## COMMONWEALTH OF NATIONS

The Commonwealth of Nations is an outgrowth of the British Empire. In 1931 the Statute of Westminster recognized the formal nationhood of Canada, Australia, New Zealand, and South Africa. Since World War II many former British colonies have become independent and most have chosen to remain within the Commonwealth, but with their own forms of government. India, for instance, became a republic with its own chief of state but continued to recognize the British monarch as head of the Commonwealth. This pattern has been followed by many of the new Afro-Asian nations. There is no written constitution for the Commonwealth, but its members are joined by economic, cultural, and political ties and agreements.

*Headquarters:* London, England.

*Members:* Independent members are Australia, Barbados, Botswana, Britain, Canada, Ceylon, Cyprus, Gambia, Ghana, Guyana, India, Jamaica, Kenya, Lesotho, Malawi, Malaysia, Malta, New Zealand, Nigeria, Pakistan, Sierra Leone, Singapore, Tanzania, Trinidad and Tobago, Uganda, and Zambia. States in association with Britain are Antigua, Dominica, Grenada, St. Christopher-Nevis-Anguilla, and St. Lucia. All dependencies of member nations

are part of the Commonwealth. In November, 1965, Rhodesia issued a unilateral declaration of independence from Britain. Britain, however, did not recognize this declaration and still considered that Rhodesia was a self-governing country within the Commonwealth.

## FRENCH COMMUNITY

Established as part of the constitution of the Fifth French Republic, which came into force on October 4, 1958.

*Headquarters:* Paris, France.

*Members:* France, Central African Republic, Chad, Congo (Brazzaville), Gabon, Malagasy Republic, and Senegal. Nonmembers having agreements with France are Algeria, Cameroon, Dahomey, Ivory Coast, Mali, Mauritania, Niger, Togo, and Upper Volta.

## LEAGUE OF ARAB STATES (ARAB LEAGUE)

The covenant establishing the League was signed on March 22, 1945, by the seven founding nations.

*Headquarters:* Cairo, United Arab Republic.

*Members:* Algeria, Iraq, Jordan, Kuwait, Lebanon, Libya, Morocco, Saudi Arabia, Sudan, Syria, Tunisia, the United Arab Republic, and Yemen.

*(continued)*

**MAJOR INTERNATIONAL ORGANIZATIONS** (*continued*)

*Purposes and aims:* The Arab League was established to strengthen ties among Arab states and to coordinate their political activities; to safeguard their independence; and to ensure closer cooperation in political, economic, legal, and social areas.

The Arab-Israeli war of June, 1967, involved members of the league.

**ORGANIZATION OF AFRICAN UNITY (OAU)**
The charter establishing the Organization was signed on May 25, 1963.

*Headquarters:* Addis Ababa, Ethiopia.

*Members:* Algeria, Botswana, Burundi, Cameroon, Central African Republic, Chad, Congo (Brazzaville), Dahomey, Democratic Republic of the Congo, Ethiopia, Gabon, Gambia, Ghana, Guinea, Ivory Coast, Kenya, Lesotho, Liberia, Libya, Malagasy Republic, Malawi, Mali, Mauritania, Morocco, Niger, Nigeria, Rwanda, Senegal, Sierra Leone, Somalia, Sudan, Tanzania, Togo, Tunisia, Uganda, United Arab Republic, Upper Volta, and Zambia.

*Purposes and aims:* To promote the unity and development of Africa, to defend the sovereignty of member nations, and to eradicate colonialism.

## MILITARY ORGANIZATIONS

**CENTRAL TREATY ORGANIZATIONS (CENTO)**
CENTO originated in the Baghdad Pact between Iraq and Turkey that was signed on February 24, 1955. Britain, Pakistan, and Iran joined later in 1955. After Iran's withdrawal in March, 1959, the Baghdad Pact Organization was reorganized as CENTO.

*Headquarters:* Ankara, Turkey.

*Members:* Iran, Pakistan, Turkey, and the United Kingdom. The United States participates as an observer and has virtually all the privileges of full membership.

*Purposes and aims:* To stabilize and reinforce the security of the Middle East, principally by organizing a system of regional military defense, and to establish economic and social cooperation among member states.

During 1967 the U.S.S.R. concluded an arms agreement with Iran and economic and trade agreements with Turkey. These agreements raised doubts about CENTO's effectiveness as a defensive alliance.

**EASTERN EUROPEAN MUTUAL ASSISTANCE TREATY (WARSAW PACT)**
The Warsaw Pact was signed on May 14, 1955.

*Headquarters:* Moscow, U.S.S.R.

*Members:* Albania, Bulgaria, Czechoslovakia, East Germany, Hungary, Poland, Romania, and the U.S.S.R.

*Purposes and aims:* Mutual defense of the members. It is the Soviet bloc's equivalent of the North Atlantic Treaty Organization.

**NORTH ATLANTIC TREATY ORGANIZATION (NATO)**
The treaty establishing NATO was signed on April 4, 1949, and entered into force on August 24, 1949.

The OAU's Liberation Committee has called for the immediate independence of the remaining colonies in Africa.

**ORGANIZATION OF AMERICAN STATES (OAS)**
The charter establishing the OAS was signed on April 30, 1948, and came into force on December 13, 1951.

*Headquarters:* Washington, D.C.

*Members:* Argentina, Bolivia, Brazil, Chile, Colombia, Costa Rica, Dominican Republic, Ecuador, El Salvador, Guatemala, Haiti, Honduras, Mexico, Nicaragua, Panama, Paraguay, Peru, Trinidad and Tobago, the United States, Uruguay, and Venezuela. Cuba is a member, but in January, 1962, representatives of the present government were excluded from participation.

**ORGANIZATION OF CENTRAL AMERICAN STATES (ODECA)**
Founded in 1951.

*Headquarters:* San Salvador, El Salvador.

*Members:* Costa Rica, El Salvador, Guatemala, Honduras, and Nicaragua.

*Purposes and aims:* To strengthen ties among Central American nations through solution of common problems and promotion of economic, social, and cultural development.

*Headquarters:* Brussels, Belgium, with a special group assigned to Washington, D.C.

*Members:* Belgium, Canada, Denmark, France, Greece, Iceland, Italy, Luxembourg, the Netherlands, Norway, Portugal, Turkey, the United Kingdom, the United States, and West Germany.

*Purposes and aims:* NATO was established to provide for the collective defense of the Atlantic Community.

*Current status:* In 1966 France withdrew from NATO's integrated military command, although remaining a member of NATO's Council. At French President de Gaulle's request, virtually all American military forces had been removed from French soil by mid-April, 1967, and the Supreme Headquarters Allied Powers, Europe (SHAPE) had been moved from Paris to Casteau, Belgium. The headquarters of the NATO organization, moved from Paris to Brussels, was officially opened in October, 1967. During October, 14 of the 15 member nations (France not participating) agreed to discuss reorienting NATO as a political rather than a military alliance.

**SOUTHEAST ASIA TREATY ORGANIZATION (SEATO)**
The treaty establishing SEATO was signed on September 8, 1954, and entered into force on February 1, 1955.

*Headquarters:* Bangkok, Thailand.

*Members:* Australia, France, New Zealand, Pakistan, Philippines, Thailand, the United Kingdom, and the United States.

*Purposes and aims:* To guarantee peace in Southeast Asia and the Southwest Pacific and to promote economic, social, and cultural cooperation among the member countries.

# NATIONS OF THE WORLD

## Gazetteer of Countries · Gazetteer of Major Cities

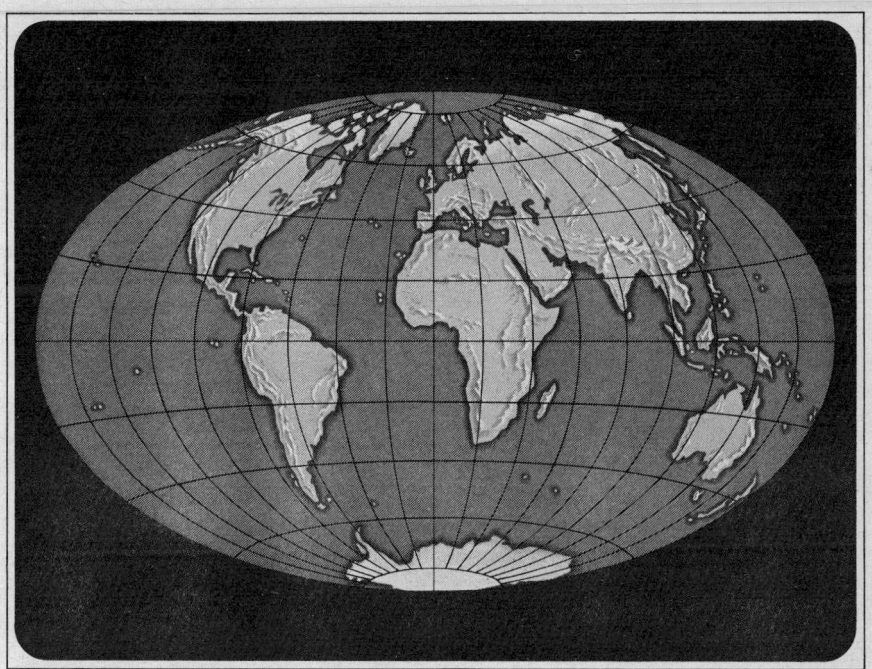

The world in 1967 saw the continued development of new nations, most notably on the African continent, where the need for increasing industrialization has become apparent. In countries lacking local industry, the vacuum has generally been filled by foreign enterprise. Thus, although the African nations export roughly 5 per cent of the world's commodities, their total income is proportionately much lower.

However, there are indications that this unfavorable discrepancy is gradually being reversed. For example, rapidly industrializing Gabon ranks second in per capita income among the African countries. And in Zambia domestic interests are gaining increasing control over the world's second largest copper industry.

A problem of a different order continued to beset Western Europe during 1967, as such highly industrialized countries as Britain and West Germany seemed unable to pull out of their economic slumps. A sharp rise in West German unemployment began in late 1966 and continued throughout much of 1967.

British Prime Minister Harold Wilson continued to be unsuccessful in his effort to gain Britain's admission into the European Economic Community. Success would have done much to cure the country's economic ills, but France's President de Gaulle remained an insurmountable obstacle to Wilson's efforts.

In the Western Hemisphere an inter-American summit conference was held at Punta del Este, Uruguay, in April. The American nations mapped plans for increased cooperation in economic and industrial development. The Communist movement in the underdeveloped American nations appeared to gain little headway, and was in fact set back by a major failure in Bolivia, where Castroite guerrilla leader Ernesto ("Che") Guevera was killed.

The year 1967 was unique in that no new nation gained its independence; the number of sovereign countries thus remained at 136. However, the Federation of South Arabia plans to achieve independence in 1968, and Swaziland, in Africa, seeks sovereignty by 1969.

# AFGHANISTAN

*Official Name:* Kingdom of Afghanistan. *Area:* 250,000 square miles. *Population:* 15,909,000. *Principal Cities* (with populations): Kabul, the capital, 450,000; Kandahar, 110,000; Herat, 75,000. *Flag:* A black, red, and green tricolor, with a white device showing a mosque between two flags and within a wreath. *Monetary Unit:* The afghani of 100 puls (worth two U.S. cents).

**LAND AND PEOPLE.** The landlocked Kingdom of Afghanistan is situated in Southwest Asia and is bordered by the Soviet Union on the north, by West Pakistan on the east and south, by Communist China on the northeast, and by Iran on the west. (See map on page 139.) The country has a series of central mountain ranges running east to west. Four principal river systems with fertile valleys contrast markedly with great stretches of desert in the south.

The Pushtuns represent 60 per cent of the population; minority groups include Tadzhiks (31 per cent of the population), Uzbeks (five per cent), and Hazaras (three per cent). The official languages are Pushto, which is also the national language, and Persian. The state religion is Islam.

**HISTORY.** Historically, Afghanistan has served as a crossroads for conquerors or empire builders. Persian monarchs in the fourth century B.C. were succeeded as rulers by Alexander the Great. After his empire broke up the country was overrun by a series of overlords, including Greeks, Turks, Chinese, and, in the ninth and tenth centuries A.D., Muslims. The invading Mongol hordes of Genghis Khan were followed in the 15th century by the culturally minded Timurids. A brief dominion by the Uzbeks in the early 16th century was succeeded for the next 200 years by Mogul and Persian rule.

Events set in motion by tribal resistance against Persian domination in the early 18th century led to the removal of all foreign influence under the leadership of Ahmad Khan Durani, who became king in 1747. Attempts by his successors to extend their dominion at the expense of British possessions in India led to the First Afghan War of 1838–42. Afghan resistance caused the British to withdraw temporarily, but fear of extending Russian influence brought on the Second Afghan War of 1878–79. A victorious Britain sought to impose a resident system but without great success. Internal unrest was brought to an end by Abdurrahman Khan, who established firm rule and a definite boundary with India.

In 1901 Abdurrahman Khan was succeeded by his son, Habibullah, who sought to promote internal reform in administration and education. Habibullah's third son and successor, Amanullah Khan, declared Afghanistan's independence in 1919. This act brought about the inconclusive Third Afghan War and British recognition of the country's independence. Amanullah's efforts to continue his father's program of reform led to civil war and a reign of terror. His cousin, Sardar Mohammed Nadir Khan, removed a usurper in 1929 and became king, but his reign ended with his assassination in 1933.

Nadir's son, Mohammed Zahir Shah, maintained neutrality during the Second World War and has pursued a neutralist foreign policy in the postwar period. In the 1960s he introduced gradual constitutional reforms.

**GOVERNMENT AND POLITICS.** Afghanistan is a limited constitutional monarchy. In 1963 the King instituted a process to transform the system of absolute monarchy. A liberal constitution, which came into force in August, 1965, accorded sovereignty to a bicameral legislature and excluded members of the royal family from political and judicial office. The lower house of Parliament consists of 216 deputies who are popularly elected; the King, provincial councils, and residents of the provinces each choose a third of the 84 senators in the upper house. The prime minister (Muhammad Hashim Maiwandwal, appointed in October, 1965) is chosen by the King and is responsible to Parliament.

Afghanistan has consistently pursued a nonaligned foreign policy. Her principal foreign policy involvement has been a dispute with Pakistan over a demand for the establishment of an independent state of Pakhtunistan. In 1963 Afghanistan resumed relations with Pakistan, and their association has improved in recent years. President Ayub Khan of Pakistan visited Kabul in 1966. In the same year Abdul Rahman Pashwak, Afghanistan's chief representative at the United Nations, was elected president of the General Assembly.

**ECONOMY.** Most of the people farm and raise livestock for a living. Although only 12 per cent of the land area is cultivated, Afghanistan is self-sufficient in food supply, except for sugar and tea. Although there is great mineral wealth, only coal has been extracted in quantity.

Chief exports are Karakul (Persian lamb) skins and raw cotton. Petroleum products and machinery have to be imported. The trade deficit is about U.S. $50 million a year.

Economic aid is received from both Communist and non-Communist countries. An obstacle to increased exports is the country's landlocked position, but in 1966 an agreement was made with Pakistan to establish a rail link to facilitate transshipment of goods. The United States was to finance the railway.

**EDUCATION.** Over 90 per cent of the population is illiterate, although education is free and theoretically compulsory. Elementary school facilities have been increased in recent years, but only Kabul and the provincial capitals have secondary schools. There are several technical schools, two institutions for teacher's training, and a university.

**ARMED FORCES.** Two years of military service are compulsory for Afghan enlisted men at the age of 20; officers serve one year. The armed forces total 90,000 men and officers.

# ALBANIA

*Official Name:* People's Republic of Albania. *Area:* 11,101 square miles. *Population:* 1,914,000. *Principal Cities* (with populations): Tiranë, the capital, 156,950; Durrës, 74,165; Korçë, 51,680; Shkodër, 47,040. *Flag:* A red field with a centered black two-headed eagle topped by a gold-edged red star. *Monetary Unit:* The lek of 100 quintars (worth 20 U.S. cents).

**LAND AND PEOPLE.** Located on the west coast of the Balkan peninsula, Albania is bounded on the north and east by Yugoslavia, on the southeast and south by Greece, and on the west by the Adriatic Sea. (See map on page 197.) Rugged mountains are characteristic of its terrain, with some peaks rising to 8,500 feet.

Albanians make up 97 per cent of the people; the rest are Greeks, Vlachs, Bulgarians, and Serbs. Islam is the religion of 65 per cent of the population. Most of the remainder is Albanian Orthodox or Roman Catholic.

**HISTORY.** Once part of the kingdom of Illyria and then of the Roman and Byzantine empires, Albania was later invaded by Slavic tribes and was absorbed in the ninth century by Bulgaria. The country became a target of Ottoman Turkish expansion in the late 14th century. The Turks controlled Albania from 1478, when they completed its conquest, until 1912, when the Albanians rebelled and won independence.

Italian, Greek, French, and Serbo-Montenegrin forces occupied the land during World War I. The Albanians eventually expelled all foreign troops and also successfully resisted Yugoslav and Greek encroachments. Ahmed Zogu emerged from Albania's internal political struggle to seize power in 1925. At first he proclaimed a republic with himself as president, but in 1928 he established a monarchy and became King Zog I. He ruled as a dictator until 1939, when the country was again invaded by Italy. German occupation troops replaced the Italians in 1943 but withdrew at the end of 1944, leaving the nation to Communist partisans, whose leader, Enver Hoxha, established a people's republic in 1946.

At the time of the Tito-Cominform schism, Albania sided with Moscow against Yugoslavia. The nation has since followed the hardest of Communist lines. The process of de-Stalinization in the Soviet Union and the growing Soviet rift with China brought about, in 1961, a break in diplomatic relations between the U.S.S.R. and Albania, which has since then been China's only firm European ally.

**GOVERNMENT AND POLITICS.** Albania is a Communist People's Republic. Its constitution vests the legislative power in a unicameral People's Assembly, which is elected every four years from a single list of candidates by universal, direct, and secret suffrage. The Chairman of the Presidium is the titular chief of state, but Enver Hoxha, the Albanian Labor Party Chairman, has exercised the real power. Albania is divided into 27 administrative districts which are governed by People's Councils.

**ECONOMY.** Albanians have the lowest living standard in Europe. There are extensive but largely undeveloped mineral deposits (chromite, bitumen, coal, copper, lignite, iron, nickel). The production of crude petroleum in 1964 totaled 830,000 tons. Albania is also rich in timber, but agriculture remains the most important industry. Despite Chinese-financed five-year plans to increase industrial output, there is little manufacturing aside from some production of processed foods, textiles, and cement. Transportation facilities are also poorly developed. Sino-Albanian trade has grown to the point where China absorbs about half of Albania's exports and supplies 60 per cent of its imports.

**EDUCATION.** Albania's educational system is technically compulsory, but the shortage of classrooms inhibits its enforcement. There are eight institutions of higher education emphasizing technical and professional training, with 12,165 students. The country has a teacher-training college and, since 1957, a university.

**ARMED FORCES.** Albania has an army of 30,000; a navy of 2,800; and an air force of 5,000. Two years of military service is compulsory for men between the ages of 19 and 35.

# ALGERIA

*Official Name:* Democratic and Popular Republic of Algeria. *Area:* 919,592 square miles. *Population:* 12,102,000. *Principal Cities* (with populations): Algiers, the capital, 883,879; Oran, 392,637; Constantine, 223,259; Bône (Annaba), 164,844; Sidi-Bel-Abbés, 105,357. *Flag:* Green and white stripes with a red crescent enclosing a star. *Monetary Unit:* The African dinar (worth 20.41 U.S. cents). *Gross National Product:* $2,630,000,000 (1965). *Average Annual Income per Person:* $225.

**LAND AND PEOPLE.** Algeria, situated in north Africa, has a 620-mile Mediterranean coast. The country is bordered on the east by Tunisia and Libya; on the south and southeast by Niger; on the west and southwest by Mali, Mauritania, and Spanish Sahara; and on the west and northwest by Morocco. (See map on page 111.)

The Atlas Mountains divide Algeria into three zones: the Mediterranean Zone, or the Tell; the Zone of Steppes, or the High Plateau; and the Sahara Zone. The coastal region has a temperate climate with adequate rainfall. Temperatures in that area range from an average high of 85° F. in August to an average low of 49° F. in January. The Tell area is mild, cool, and moist. The Sahara is extremely hot and dry.

Islam is the state religion. About 99 per cent of the population is Muslim, of Arabic or Berber stock. The official languages are Arabic and French.

**HISTORY.** The Berbers were in Algeria before

recorded history, but the country did not gain political cohesion until the 19th century. In the 12th century B.C. the Phoenicians used Algerian ports, and Carthage controlled the area for six centuries. After crushing Carthage, Rome governed the coastal areas and parts of the interior. Islam was introduced into the country by 7th-century Arab invaders. Berber Muslim rulers united Algeria with Morocco and Spain in a great Moorish empire. A 16th-century Turkish pirate, Barbarossa, helped Algiers expel Spanish invaders and then declared himself sultan. Thus, Algiers came under the Ottoman Empire. By the 18th century Algiers had become a haven for pirates.

France invaded Algeria in 1830, and northern Algeria was made an integral part of France in 1848. European settlers took over much of the fertile land. Fierce Berber resistance delayed effective control of the Sahara region until the first decade of the 20th century. In 1944 the French extended citizenship to certain categories of Muslims and, in 1947, created an Algerian assembly and promulgated other political reforms.

In 1954 a group of rebels, the National Liberation Front (F.L.N.), organized a series of uprisings against French rule. The organization's terrorist tactics brought stern French countermeasures. In 1958 a French military junta seized power in Algeria, hoping to prevent negotiation with the rebels. The power seizure caused the downfall of France's Fourth Republic and resulted in Charles de Gaulle's return to power. De Gaulle granted independence to Algeria on July 3, 1962. The O.A.S., a secret army of ultranationalist Europeans, unleashed a campaign of terror in France and Algeria. The movement collapsed after the capture of its leaders.

After independence, a power struggle among F.L.N. leaders was resolved when Ahmed Ben Bella gained control in August, 1962. A new constitution was approved in 1963, and Ben Bella was elected Algeria's first president. In June, 1965, however, he was deposed by a military coup led by Colonel Houari Boumedienne.

**GOVERNMENT AND POLITICS.** Algeria is a one-party socialist democracy that is controlled by the army through the 24-member Council of the Revolution. Boumedienne is president of the Council, the supreme political body. Most opposition has been crushed, and all political parties except the F.L.N. have been outlawed. Algeria's foreign policy is neutralist; its internal policy is socialist.

**ECONOMY.** Unemployment is estimated at 40 per cent, and the economy, hurt by the emigration of most French settlers and reduced French economic aid, has declined.

Some 65 per cent of the population depends on agriculture for a living. The chief crops are wine grapes, citrus fruits, vegetables, wheat, and olives. Sheep are also raised.

The leading industries are construction and public works, food processing, and metal working. Like agriculture, however, industrial output and services have failed to advance beyond their pre-rebellion (1954) levels. The

government's socialist policies have, on the whole, discouraged foreign investment. Political instability, lack of capital, and shortage of skilled manpower have combined to hold back economic growth. Algeria suffers from an unfavorable balance of trade, but income from the vast petroleum and natural gas deposits discovered in the Sahara in 1956 has prevented economic collapse.

**EDUCATION.** There are primary and secondary schools, a university in Algiers, and several institutions for specialized training. In 1954, before the rebellion, the literacy rate was estimated at 19 per cent.

**ARMED FORCES.** Algeria has a modern armed force, estimated at 60,000 in 1965 and mainly Soviet-equipped. There is no compulsory military service.

# ANDORRA

*Official Name:* The Valleys of Andorra. *Area:* 190 square miles. *Population:* 13,000. *Principal City:* Andorra la Vella, the capital. *Flag:* Blue, yellow, and red stripes with a coat of arms in the yellow stripe. *Monetary Units:* Spanish peseta (worth 1.43 U.S. cents) and French franc (worth 20 U.S. cents).

**LAND AND PEOPLE.** Tiny Andorra, situated high in the Pyrenees Mountains on the Spanish-French border, is a picturesque land of gorges and valleys, drained by the Valira River. (See map on page 117.) Winters are severe and summers are either mild or warm, depending on elevation. Its people are almost totally of Catalan stock and are Roman Catholics.

**HISTORY.** Tradition says that Charlemagne granted the Andorrans a charter for their support in his war against the Moors. His grandson made the Spanish count of Urgel overlord in Andorra in the ninth century. The bishop of Urgel and the count of Foix were established as co-princes of Andorra in 1278; the rights of the latter passed to the kings, and later the presidents, of France. In 1793 the revolutionary government of France renounced its claim to Andorra, but Napoleon later reclaimed it at the Andorrans' request.

**GOVERNMENT AND POLITICS.** Andorra has an exceptional form of government, with the president of France and the bishop of Urgel holding equal authority.

Legislation is enacted by the 24-member General Council of the Valleys, which also names administrators. Its members are elected for four-year terms. Although no political parties exist, there are usually two factions in the Council—a liberal group leaning to France, and a conservative one favoring Spain.

**ECONOMY.** Andorra has deposits of iron, lead, aluminum, and marble. There are extensive pine forests. Other major sources of income are tourism and smuggling.

**EDUCATION.** France pays for some French-language schools, while those near Spain are church-supported.

# ARGENTINA

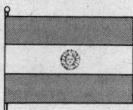

*Official Name:* The Argentine Republic. *Area:* 1,072,069 square miles. *Population:* 22,800,000. *Principal Cities* (with populations): Buenos Aires, the capital, 2,966,816; Rosario, 671,852; Córdoba, 589,153; Matanza, 402,642. *Flag:* A blue, a white, and a blue horizontal stripe; a golden sun in the white stripe has 32 rays. *Monetary Unit:* The peso of 100 centavos (worth 0.28 U.S. cent). *Gross National Product:* $18,840,000,000 (1965). *Average Annual Income per Person:* $765.

**LAND AND PEOPLE.** Argentina, the second largest country in South America, extends 2,295 miles in length to the southern tip of the Western Hemisphere. It is bordered on the north by Bolivia and Paraguay, on the east by Brazil, Uruguay, and the Atlantic Ocean, and on the west by Chile. On the south the archipelago of Tierra del Fuego, the northern part of which belongs to Chile, is separated from the mainland by the Strait of Magellan. (See map on page 75.)

Argentina shares with Chile the majestic mountain peaks of the Andes range. In the east are the fertile plains of the Pampa, home of the Argentine cowboy, the gaucho. To the northeast lie subtropical deltas, dense forests, and grassy savannas; in the north are relatively dry lowlands. South of the Pampa are broad, barren, and uninhabited stretches known as Patagonia, Argentina's still untapped frontier.

The climate is temperate, except for the extreme north, which is subtropical, and the extreme south, which extends toward the Antarctic. Average temperature in Buenos Aires is 61° F. Annual rainfall varies from two inches in the northwest to 37.9 inches around Buenos Aires.

The majority of Argentines (84 per cent) are native born and of European extraction (mostly Spanish and Italian); 13 per cent are European by birth. Three per cent of the population are of indigenous Indian and other non-Caucasian stock. About 93 per cent are Roman Catholic. The language is Spanish.

Argentina is one of the more sparsely populated countries of the world, with an average of only about 20 persons per square mile. However, it is an urbanized country; 40 per cent of the people live in cities of over 100,000.

**HISTORY.** Colonizing Spaniards discovered Argentina in 1516. They considered the region the least interesting in South America because it was a source of less mineral wealth than many neighboring areas. Buenos Aires long remained a muddy, inconspicuous village known only for the occasional smuggling that occurred there.

In the 18th century the Spanish Bourbon kings made Buenos Aires a free port, one of the hubs of its enterprises in the New World. Buenos Aires quickly became an important commercial center and the capital of a viceroyalty that included present-day Argentina, Uruguay, Paraguay, and parts of Bolivia.

In 1810 revolutionists, seeking independence from Spain, overthrew the viceroyalty and set up a governing junta. Buenos Aires became the seat of this agitation for self-government. Other Argentine provinces joined her, and in 1816 an official declaration of independence was made.

Throughout the 19th century Buenos Aires' port duties on exports created strong opposition from rural Argentine cities. Buenos Aires was also distrusted because it preferred materials from Europe which were both cheaper and better than local products. During this period British investments were concentrated in Buenos Aires, to the neglect of interior Argentina. Under dictator Juan Manuel de Rosas (1829–32; 1835–52), Argentina assumed its role as supplier of meat for European dinner tables. Much of the 19th century was taken up with the struggle between the forces that wanted a strong unitary state led by Buenos Aires and those that strove for a confederation of Argentine regions with a certain amount of local autonomy.

Under the forceful leadership of Presidents Mitre and Sarmiento (1862–74), Argentina became a magnet for European immigration and capital. Railroads flourished, telegraph lines multiplied, and the port of Buenos Aires was refurbished. Though Argentina was prospering by the turn of the century, her small ruling oligarchy monopolized power, limited popular participation, and neglected the needs of the middle and lower classes. The Irigoyen administration (1916–22; 1928–30) was a product of the growing mobilization of the urban middle classes and an expression of the new immigrant and commercial strength in political and economic areas.

In the 1930s the military became embroiled in politics and represented the dominant force in the government. A military man, Juan Perón, was elected Argentina's president in 1946, and went on to rule dictatorially for a decade. Perón left his mark on almost every political, economic, educational, and social institution in Argentina. He intervened in the affairs of labor unions, displaced congressmen at will, abolished social clubs, interfered in universities, suspended newspapers, and issued decrees in all areas of life.

Despite his authoritative methods, Perón pursued policies that tended to make income distribution more equitable and to spread purchasing power to the lower classes. He is also credited with extending public works programs and strengthening the labor movement. However, Perón eventually antagonized the Roman Catholic Church, the affluent classes, and the military hierarchy; this community of anti-Perón sentiment toppled him in 1955. Perón fled to Spain, but Peronism remained a force in Argentina.

A series of provisional, military-dominated, and minority governments succeeded each other until the armed forces again took full control in June, 1966.

**GOVERNMENT AND POLITICS.** Argentina is a federal republic whose constitution, dating back to 1853, is closely modeled after that of the United States. However, after the recent military coup, many constitutional guarantees were suspended.

Under Lt. Gen. Juan Onganía, the military has closed the National Congress, abolished political parties, and ruled by decree. The military government has reformed the university structure by ending traditional university autonomy and making the rectors responsible to the Ministry of Education. Student involvement in university administration and national politics is forbidden. Such measures, combined with inadequate professional opportunities, have contributed to the emigration of 10,500 university graduates in the last 15 years.

A Communist-control law prohibits any Communist from holding public office. The military leaders have not announced plans for a return to normal political life. Some members of the government have spoken of a decade of development under the auspices of a military-technocratic cabinet.

**ECONOMY.** The military government has taken a strong hand in guiding Argentina's recuperating economy. Thus, beginning in 1968, annual targets will be fixed for all government corporations, including railways, electricity, gas, petroleum, and steel.

Along with government employees, university faculties and labor union members will be expected to participate in an overall ten-year plan (1968–77) for the country's economic advancement. The plan will be sponsored and supervised by two specially created government agencies, one made up of technicians and economists, and the other, of military personnel.

The announced aim is to minimize Argentina's dependence on beef and grains for income. Emphasis is on developing the industrial potential of Patagonia, known to have 70 per cent of all the nation's oil reserves, 50 per cent of its hydroelectric potential, and 60 per cent of its gas resources.

Another goal is to cut down the number of employees in the state bureaucracies (an estimated 30,000 were relieved in 1967). The outmoded railways, responsible for 60 per cent of Argentina's 1966 budget deficit of $600 million, are prime targets for improvement.

Industry, concentrated in and around Buenos Aires, includes meat packing, food processing, machinery manufacture, leather goods, textiles, and chemicals. Also important are rubber, cement, and metalworking.

Agricultural produce includes corn, flax, citrus fruits, tobacco, cotton, rice, and sugarcane. Argentina accounts for 80 per cent of all wheat produced in Latin America and is the world's largest producer of flaxseed (exported as linseed oil). Argentina's meat products, grains, vegetable oil, fats, and wool earn over 90 per cent of her foreign exchange.

**EDUCATION.** Schooling is compulsory for children from ages 6 to 12. More than 92 per cent of the population is literate.

**ARMED FORCES.** Service in the armed forces is compulsory between the ages of 20 and 22; one year in the army or air force and two in the navy are required. Regular strength of the combined forces is 113,000.

# AUSTRALIA

*Official Name:* Commonwealth of Australia. *Area:* 2,967,741 square miles. *Population:* 11,544,691. *Principal Cities* (with populations): Canberra, the capital, 93,197; Sydney, 2,444,735; Melbourne, 2,108,499; Brisbane, 719,140; Adelaide, 726,930; Perth, 499,494; Hobart, 119,415. *Flag:* A blue field with the red, white, and blue union jack in the upper left and a large white seven-pointed star below it; five smaller white stars on the right represent the Southern Cross. *Monetary Unit:* The dollar of 100 cents (worth U.S. $1.12). *Gross National Product:* U.S. $22,680,000,000 (1965–66). *Average Annual Income per Person:* U.S. $1,590.

**LAND AND PEOPLE.** The island continent of Australia lies southeast of Asia between the Indian and Pacific oceans. Entirely surrounded by water, it is bounded by the Indian Ocean on the west, by the Timor, Arafura, and Coral seas on the north, and by the Pacific Ocean on the east and south. (See map on page 67.)

Over half of Australia's population is concentrated along its eastern and southeastern shores. The majority of the people live in the large cities of the narrow coastal plain—Melbourne, Brisbane, and Sydney; the remainder live in the towns and lush countryside of the Eastern Highlands, or Great Dividing Range. The highlands, averaging 150 miles in width and rarely exceeding 5,000 feet in height, stretch along the entire east coast from Cape York in Queensland to southern Victoria and then emerge from the sea again as the island state of Tasmania. They have a warm, moist climate and contain much of the country's richest farming and grazing land.

West of the highlands are the Central-Eastern Lowlands, which extend from the Gulf of Carpentaria to the Great Australian Bight. Large areas of the lowlands are too dry for farming or ranching, but there are some good grazing ranges in the Great Artesian Basin and in the Murray-Darling Basin. Thousands of acres in the southern lowlands are planted with special varieties of wheat developed for Australia's dry climate.

Nearly all Australians are Caucasian, and more than 95% of them are of British stock. Pure and mixed-blood aborigines now number around 80,000. Since federation, immigration has been restricted almost completely to Caucasians, but laws governing the entry of nonwhites were relaxed in 1966. The official language of Australia is English. Religious freedom is guaranteed by the federal constitution. According to the 1961 census, more than 55% of the people are of various Protestant faiths and 25% are Roman Catholic.

**HISTORY.** Primitive nomadic aborigines were the Australian continent's only inhabitants when Captain James Cook took formal possession of the east coast for Britain in 1770. The first European settlement was a British penal colony established in 1788 at Port Jack-

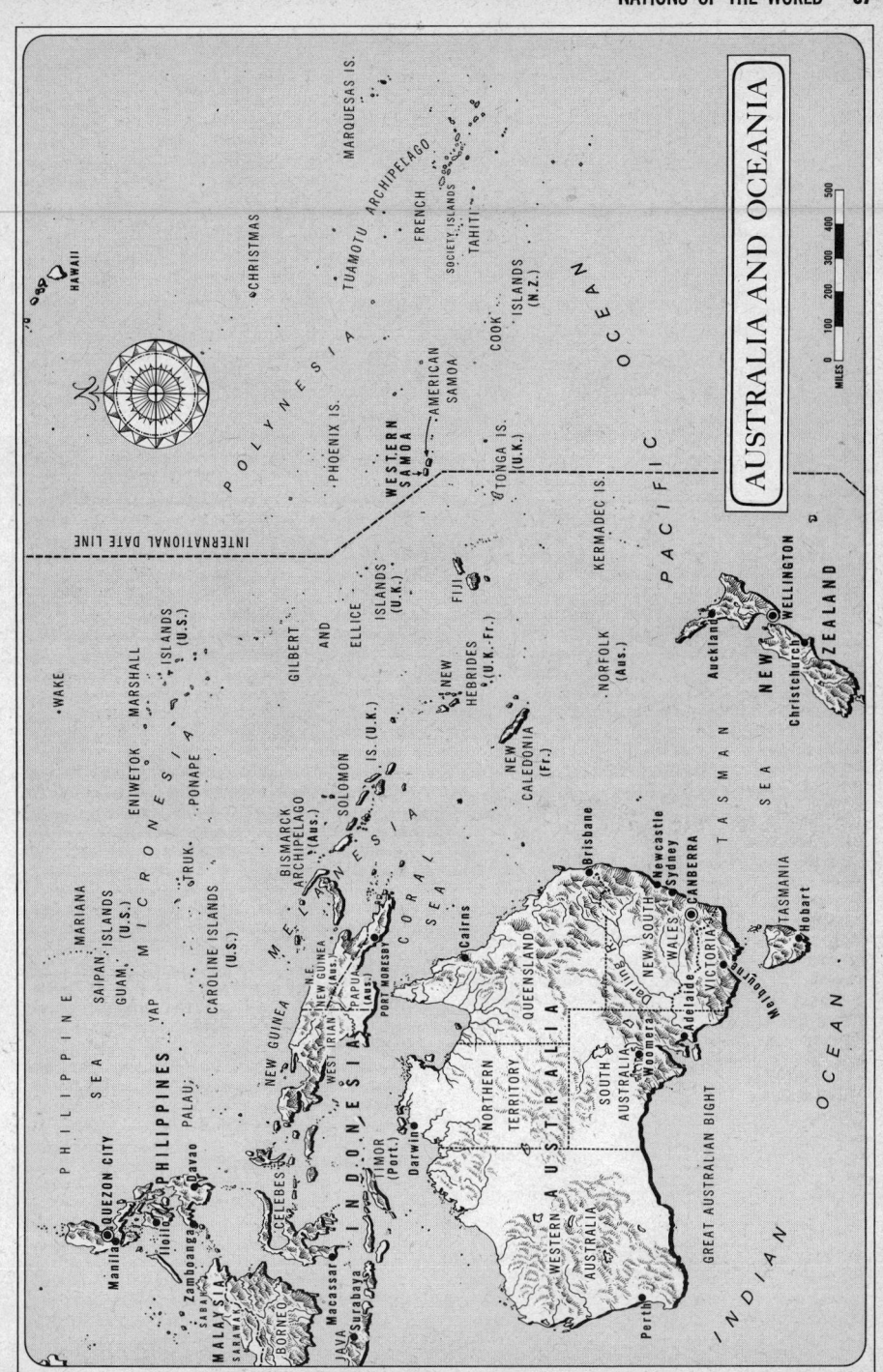

AUSTRALIA AND OCEANIA

MILES
0 100 200 300 400 500

PHILIPPINE SEA

PHILIPPINES

QUEZON CITY
Manila
Iloilo
Zamboanga Davao

MALAYSIA
SABAH
BORNEO
JAVA Macassar
Surabaya
CELEBES
INDONESIA
TIMOR (Port.)
Darwin

MARIANA ISLANDS (U.S.)
SAIPAN
GUAM (U.S.)
YAP
PALAU
CAROLINE ISLANDS (U.S.)

WAKE

MICRONESIA

ENIWETOK
MARSHALL ISLANDS (U.S.)
PONAPE
TRUK

MELANESIA

NEW GUINEA
W. NEW GUINEA (Indon.)
WESTERN IRIAN
N.E. NEW GUINEA (Aus.)
PAPUA (AUS.)
PORT MORESBY

BISMARCK ARCHIPELAGO (Aus.)
SOLOMON IS. (U.K.)

CORAL SEA

Cairns

NORTHERN TERRITORY

QUEENSLAND
Brisbane

WESTERN AUSTRALIA

SOUTH AUSTRALIA
Woomera
Adelaide

NEW SOUTH WALES
Newcastle
Sydney
CANBERRA

VICTORIA
Melbourne

AUSTRALIA

GREAT AUSTRALIAN BIGHT

Perth

INDIAN OCEAN

TASMANIA
Hobart

TASMAN SEA

NEW CALEDONIA (Fr.)

NEW HEBRIDES (U.K.-Fr.)

FIJI

NORFOLK (Aus.)

KERMADEC IS.

NEW ZEALAND
Auckland
WELLINGTON
Christchurch

PACIFIC OCEAN

POLYNESIA

HAWAII

CHRISTMAS

PHOENIX IS.

WESTERN SAMOA

AMERICAN SAMOA

TONGA IS. (U.K.)

COOK ISLANDS (N.Z.)

MARQUESAS IS.

TUAMOTU ARCHIPELAGO
FRENCH
SOCIETY ISLANDS
TAHITI

GILBERT AND ELLICE ISLANDS (U.K.)

INTERNATIONAL DATE LINE

son (now Sydney), and many of the early settlers came as convicts or soldiers. As the numbers of free settlers increased, the practice of transporting convicts was curtailed and finally discontinued altogether in 1868.

A gold strike in Victoria colony in 1851 brought thousands of new settlers, and the population continued to grow rapidly. By 1859 six colonies, including the island of Tasmania, had been organized. Each dealt directly with the mother country.

The colonies were to remain independent for over 40 years, but the advantages of federation eventually became apparent. A constitution drafted in 1898 was approved by the colonists and the British Parliament, and the Commonwealth of Australia came into being in 1901. The parliament of the new federal government met in Melbourne until 1927 when it moved to the permanent federal capital at Canberra.

During World War I, 330,000 Australian volunteers served with distinction overseas, sustaining a higher proportion of casualties (69%) than any other contingent of the combined British forces. In World War II Australia's manpower contribution was proportionate to that of the United States and Britain. Enlistments reached nearly 1,000,000, and casualties totaled 237,000.

Australia began the century as an agricultural country but emerged from World War II as a highly industrial one. In 1945 the government initiated a program to encourage immigration; people were needed to work in the country's rapidly expanding industries. Between 1946 and 1966, 2,506,736 people poured into the country, and the population grew from 7,500,000 to over 11,500,000, an increase of more than 54%.

**GOVERNMENT AND POLITICS.** Under the federation agreement of 1901 Australia is a fully independent, self-governing nation within the British Commonwealth of Nations. The British sovereign is the sovereign of Australia and is represented by a governor general. Executive power is invested formally in the governor general and an executive council but, in practice, it is held by the prime minister and his cabinet. The prime minister represents the political party or coalition with a majority in the House of Representatives.

Legislative power rests in a federal parliament consisting of a Senate and a House of Representatives. The states are entitled to ten senators each but are allotted representatives on the basis of their populations. Each state has a governor, representing the sovereign, and a cabinet responsible to a legislative body. All state legislatures are bicameral with the exception of Queensland.

There is universal suffrage for all Australian citizens over 21, and voting is compulsory. The major political parties are the Liberal Party, the Country Party, and two labor parties, the Australian Labor Party and the Democratic Labor Party. A Liberal-Country coalition has governed the country since 1949 when Robert Menzies became prime minister.

Menzies resigned in January, 1966, and was replaced by Harold E. Holt.

Australia is closely allied with the United States in international affairs, notably in Southeast Asia. Australian troops fighting in Vietnam totaled 6,300 by the summer of 1967.

**ECONOMY.** The greater part of the country is not suitable for heavy settlement, but Australians are working on several projects that will open up interior areas for development. The billion-dollar Snowy Mountains Scheme, for example, involves diverting the headwaters of the Snowy River across the Eastern Highlands, to generate electricity and to increase the water available for irrigation in the vast Murray and Murrumbidgee river valleys.

However limited its arable lands may be, Australia provides all its own basic foodstuffs and produces large surpluses for export. It is also self-supporting in iron, steel, and most minerals. Coal, found in every state, is used to generate nearly three-fourths of the nation's electric power. Nearly $400 million has been invested recently in petroleum exploration and development, and new commercial fields are now yielding over three million barrels annually.

Australia is the world's leading sheep-raising nation, producing annually about 30% of the world's supply of wool. Other important agricultural exports are wheat, mutton, beef, sugarcane, butter, and cheese. Although ranch and farm products make up nearly four-fifths of its exports, Australia is not chiefly an agricultural country. Nearly a third of the total work force is employed at industrial installations of all kinds. These include steel mills, oil refineries, automobile and aircraft factories, paper and textile mills, and food processing plants. At the present time, however, Australians still use most of their industrial output, and manufactured products constitute only about 15% of the country's total exports.

The more than 25,000-mile rail system is government-owned. There are over 558,000 miles of roads, about 40% of which are paved. Eleven airlines handle domestic service and the government's airline, Quantas, flies to most major cities in the world.

**EDUCATION AND HEALTH.** Education is compulsory for a period of from eight to ten years and is free in municipal kindergartens and in state primary, secondary, and technical schools. Australia has 12 universities, two university colleges, seven state agricultural colleges, and many other diploma-granting institutions. Practically the entire population is literate.

Australia has advanced health services, and its death and infant mortality rates are among the lowest in the world. The National Health Act of 1953, with amendments, set up a system of non profit medical insurance organizations to help individuals cover medical costs.

**NATIONAL DEFENSE.** Registration for military service is compulsory for males when they reach the age of 20, but the annual draft call (by lottery) is small. Total strength of the regular forces is 75,000.

## AUSTRALIAN TERRITORIES AND DEPENDENCIES

**THE NORTHERN TERRITORY.** *Area:* 520,280 square miles. *Population:* 37,166. *Capital:* Darwin (population 20,261).

The Northern Territory is bordered on the north by the Timor and Arafura seas and the Gulf of Carpentaria, on the east by Queensland, on the south by South Australia, and on the west by Western Australia.

Most of the interior is a tableland that rises to a maximum elevation of 1,200 feet from the 1,040-mile-long coastline. There are large areas of fine pasture lands, but most of the southern part of the territory is generally dry and sandy. Chief products include gold, beef, peanuts, and pearl shell.

South Australia formally transferred the territory to the federal government in 1911. An administrator, located at Darwin on the northwest coast, governs through a legislative council; all ordinances must be approved by the federal parliament. The territory is represented in the Australian Parliament by one elected member who can vote only on matters affecting the territory.

Ashmore and Cartier islands, situated in the Indian Ocean about 200 miles from Australia's northwest coast, are considered to be part of the Northern Territory.

**AUSTRALIAN CAPITAL TERRITORY.** *Area:* 939 square miles. *Population:* 95,913.

The Capital Territory is bordered on all sides by New South Wales. The land was turned over to the Commonwealth for the seat of government in 1911.

Residents are represented in Parliament by one elected member. The Federal Minister of the Interior is responsible for general administration.

**LORD HOWE ISLAND.** *Area:* 5 square miles. *Population:* 267.

Lord Howe Island, the largest of the 13 islands in the Lord Howe Group, is situated in the Tasman Sea 436 miles northeast of Sydney. It was discovered in 1788. A dependency of New South Wales, the island is constitutionally part of that state.

**TERRITORIES OF PAPUA AND NEW GUINEA.** *Area:* Papua, 86,100 square miles; New Guinea, 92,-160 square miles. *Population:* Papua, 573,411; New Guinea, 1,575,966.

Both territories are situated on the eastern portion of the island of New Guinea, off Australia's northern coast.

Mountains, with peaks to 16,000 feet, run through the center of the 1,800-mile-long island.

Most of the Territory of Papua is on the southeastern part of the island, but about 3,000 square miles is on adjacent islands. The Trust Territory of New Guinea is on the northeastern part; nearly a quarter of its area is in islands. Almost 99 per cent of the people are Papuans.

New Guinea, possibly first sighted by a Portuguese explorer in 1511, was named for its similarity to the Guinea coast of West Africa. In the 19th century parts of the island were occupied by the Dutch, Australians, Germans, and British. The territory was seized by Australian troops in 1914 and placed under Australian civil administration by a League of Nations mandate in 1921. Australia's Papua and New Guinea Act of 1949 placed the Territory of New Guinea under the U.N. trusteeship system. The act also provided that the Trust Territory and the Territory of Papua were to be jointly administered by an Australian parliament.

**CHRISTMAS ISLAND.** *Area:* 52.1 square miles. *Population:* 3,333.

Christmas Island is in the Indian Ocean, about 225 miles south of Java. Sovereignty was transferred to Australia from Singapore in 1958. About 70 per cent of its people are Chinese. The island's only economic activity is phosphate extraction and export.

**TERRITORY OF COCOS (KEELING) ISLAND.** *Area:* 5.4 square miles. *Population:* 674.

The territory, two atolls comprising 27 small coral islands, is in the Indian Ocean, about 1,400 miles south of Ceylon. Cocos Island was discovered in 1609 by Captain William Keeling but remained uninhabited until 1826. It was placed under Australian authority in 1955. Less than a third of the inhabitants are Europeans.

**AUSTRALIAN ANTARCTIC TERRITORY.** *Area:* 2,360,000 square miles.

Australia claimed this section of Antarctica in 1936 and has set up two research and weather bases there.

**TERRITORY OF HEARD AND McDONALD ISLANDS.** The islands, in the Indian Ocean about 2,500 miles southwest of Perth, were transferred to Australia by Britain in 1947. The territory is governed under the laws of the Australian Capital Territory.

**NORFOLK ISLAND.** *Area:* 13.9 square miles. *Population:* 980.

Norfolk Island, situated in the Tasman Sea 1,035 miles east of Sydney, was discovered by Captain James Cook in 1774. It has been a distinct settlement since 1856, and its population includes descendants of the Bounty mutineers. Its pictorial appeal and delightful climate have attracted a large number of tourists to the island.

**NAURU ISLAND.** *Area:* 8.1 square miles. *Population:* 5,561.

Nauru is in the central Pacific, just south of the equator. The oval-shaped coral island was discovered in 1798, taken by Germany 90 years later, and surrendered to Australia in 1914. Since 1947 it has been administered within the U.N. trusteeship system.

A narrow, fertile section circles Nauru, and the inland plateau is rich in high-grade phosphates. About half of the population is Nauruan, and the rest are other Pacific islanders, Chinese, and Europeans.

**MACQUARIE ISLAND.** Macquarie, about 1,000 miles southeast of Hobart, has been a dependency of Tasmania since the 19th century. It is uninhabited except for a federal government weather and research base, established there in 1948.

## AUSTRIA

*Official Name:* Republic of Austria. *Area:* 32,376 square miles. *Population:* 7,290,-000. *Principal Cities* (with populations): Vienna, the capital, 1,627,516; Graz, 237,080; Linz, 195,978; Salzburg, 108,114; Innsbruck, 100,695. *Flag:* Horizontal red, white, and red stripes. *Monetary Unit:* The schilling of 100 groschen (worth 3.9 U.S. cents). *Gross National Product:* $9,190,000,-000 (1965). *Average Annual Income per Person:* $2,000.

**LAND AND PEOPLE.** Austria, a landlocked nation in central Europe, is bordered on the north by West Germany and Czechoslovakia, on the east by Hungary, on the south by Yugoslavia and Italy, and on the west by Liechtenstein and Switzerland. (See map on page 117.)

West and central Austria are mountainous, while the east is hilly. Forests cover much of the land and wildlife is plentiful. The Danube River, flowing through the northeast, is a major traffic route.

German-speaking groups make up 99 per cent of the population. Less than 1 per cent of the population is made up of Croats and Magyars and Slovenes. Roman Catholics comprise 89 per cent of the population, and Lutherans, 6 per cent.

**HISTORY.** From prehistoric times Austria has been a crossroads of Europe. There were many invaders even before Rome conquered the territory between 16 and 9 B.C. From the end of the Roman Empire until 803, when it became part of Charlemagne's empire, it was overrun, devastated, or conquered by neighboring tribes. In the tenth century Austria was added to the Holy Roman Empire.

By 1282 the Austrian lands had come under the control of the House of Hapsburg, and until 1918 its history was closely tied to that of the Hapsburgs. From 1438 they ruled with only one brief interruption until 1806, when the Empire was dissolved by Napoleon.

By the end of the 14th century the Hapsburg territories ranged from the plains north of the Danube to the Adriatic. After the 15th century they formed a kind of multinational empire with the German-speaking lands (in substance, the future Austrian republic) in the center; to the north, east, and west were the Czech, Hungarian, Italian, Polish, Ruthenian, Romanian, Slovak, and Southern Slav territories.

The cultural development of Austria was strongly influenced by both her German ethnic, social, and political composition and by her historic ties to Slavic and Romance peoples and to Magyars (Hungarians). These bonds were strengthened by participation in the struggle between the forces of Reformation and Counter-Reformation in the 16th and 17th centuries; by the defense against the Ottoman Turkish onslaught from the 15th to the 18th century; and by the conflict for supremacy in Germany between Austria and Prussia in the 18th and 19th centuries.

An Austrian empire was officially established in 1804, and by 1815 Austria had become the leading power in the German confederation and in the Holy Alliance. Austria's skillful foreign minister, Prince Clemens von Metternich, became chief arbiter of Europe, but revolutions in Hungary, Bohemia, and Vienna brought an end to the Age of Metternich in 1848. Wars diminished Austria's political influence, and Hungary forced Emperor Francis Joseph to accord it equal rights in a dual monarchy under one ruler. Thus was formed the Austro-Hungarian Empire in 1867.

The assassination by Serbian irredentists of Archduke Francis Ferdinand, the emperor's nephew and heir, triggered World War I and brought about the dissolution of the Austro-Hungarian Empire. Austria was reduced to its German-speaking sections and proclaimed a republic at the war's end. Postwar Austria suffered economic collapse and social and political unrest. The Austrian Nazis assassinated Chancellor Engelbert Dollfuss in 1934 but failed in their attempted coup. In March, 1938, Hitler annexed Austria to the German Reich.

After World War II Austria was divided into occupation zones, but in 1955 it was re-established as an independent nation with the obligation to remain neutral in matters pertaining to Eastern and Western bloc rivalries.

**GOVERNMENT AND POLITICS.** The president, elected by direct popular vote, serves for six years. The 165 members of the Lower House, the Nationalrat, are popularly elected for four-year terms. The 54 members of the Upper House, the Bundesrat, are elected for four years by provincial legislatures. The one-party cabinet is headed by Chancellor Josef Klaus of the People's Party.

In 1945 the federal republic, consisting of nine lands, was re-established according to the Moscow Declaration of the Great Powers of October, 1943. These component parts are Vienna, Lower and Upper Austria, Salzburg, Styria, Carinthia, the Tyrol, Vorarlberg, and Burgenland. Coalition governments ruled Austria until March, 1966, when the moderately conservative People's Party won a parliamentary majority. The Socialists, who had been represented by heads of state since 1945, are now the opposition party, along with the Freedom Party.

**ECONOMY.** Increased European postwar trade, industrial skill of the people, and generous help from the Marshall Plan have put the Austrian economy on a far sounder foundation than at any time between 1918 and 1938. Heavy industry and banking are largely government controlled, while light industry is entirely in private hands.

Industrial production is high, with iron and steel the leading products and chief exports. Other important resources lie in the development of hydroelectric power, transportation, and the oil wells whose operation on a large scale started only after 1945.

Tourist trade, a major source of foreign revenue, ranks among Europe's largest. Agriculture contributes less than ten per cent to the gross national product, but lumber is an important export item.

**EDUCATION AND HEALTH.** Health standards are high, and Vienna is noted for its medical training, research facilities, and outstanding specialists. The literacy rate is nearly 100 per cent. School attendance is compulsory for a minimum of eight years.

**ARMED FORCES.** Austria has universal conscription for men 18 to 50. Its armed forces number over 40,000.

## BARBADOS

*Official Name:* Barbados. *Area:* 166 square miles. *Population:* 255,000. *Principal City* (with population): Bridgetown, the capital, 11,-452. *Flag:* A blue, a gold, and a blue horizontal stripe, with a black trident in the gold stripe. *Monetary Unit:* The East Caribbean dollar (worth 58 U.S. cents). *Gross National Product:* $97,380,000 (1965). *Average Annual Income per Person:* $392.

**LAND AND PEOPLE.** The island of Barbados is on the eastern edge of the Lesser Antilles, with its eastern coast facing the Atlantic Ocean and its western, the Caribbean Sea. The generally flat land rises to a central high point of 1,100 feet; most of it is arable. The climate is temperate, with average temperatures ranging between 75° and 85° F.

Barbados is the most densely populated island in the West Indies. About 95 per cent of the islanders are of African or mixed African and European extraction. Some 70 per cent are of the Anglican faith. English is spoken generally.

**HISTORY.** Barbados was claimed for England by Captain John Powell in 1625 and was first settled in 1627. The slaves who were imported to work the extensive sugar plantations were freed in 1834. However, the plantation owners succeeded in retaining political control of the island until 1937, when their power was broken, largely as a result of the efforts of a Negro attorney, now Sir Grantley Adams. The island achieved independent dominion status within the Commonwealth of Nations on November 30, 1966, after a brief membership in the abortive Federation of the West Indies.

**GOVERNMENT AND POLITICS.** Barbados is a parliamentary democracy. The present prime minister, Errol W. Barrow, head of the Democratic Labour Party, came to power in the pre-independence election of November 30, 1966. The leader of the opposition Barbados Labour Party is Sir Grantley Adams.

**ECONOMY.** Sugar constitutes between 20 and 30 per cent of the island's production and (with molasses) 85 per cent of its exports. Tourism is becoming an increasingly important source of income.

**EDUCATION.** Education is free but not compulsory. Nevertheless, 98 per cent of the adult population is literate.

**ARMED FORCES.** There are no regular military forces on the island.

## BELGIUM

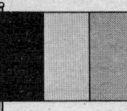

*Official Name:* Kingdom of Belgium. *Area:* 11,781 square miles. *Population:* 9,528,000. *Principal Cities* (with metropolitan populations): Brussels, the capital, 1,100,000; Antwerp, 657,485; Liège, 452,-713; Charleroi, 283,426; Ghent, 232,915. *Flag:* Three vertical stripes of black, yellow, and red. *Monetary Unit:* The franc of 100 centimes (worth 2 U.S. cents). *Gross National Product:* $16,740,000,000 (1965). *Average Annual Income per Person:* $1,447.

**LAND AND PEOPLE.** Belgium, situated in northwestern Europe, is bordered on the north by the Netherlands, on the east by West Germany and Luxembourg, on the south and southwest by France, and on the northwest by the North Sea. The sand dunes and low, level pasturelands of the coastal region give way to a gently rolling plain with many fertile, irrigated valleys. In the southeast are the higher elevations of the densely forested Ardennes region. Two principal rivers, the Scheldt and the Meuse, flow from France into the Netherlands. Belgium's moderate climate is greatly affected by the North Sea; summers are cool and winters are damp and foggy.

Belgium's two principal ethnic groups are the French-speaking Walloons, centered in the south, and the more numerous Dutch-speaking Flemish who predominate in the north. Most Belgians are Roman Catholics, but religious freedom is constitutionally guaranteed.

**HISTORY.** The country now known as Belgium was part of the Roman province of Belgica, and later part of Charlemagne's empire. Under Burgundian rule since the middle of the 14th century, Belgium passed to the Hapsburgs with the marriage of Mary of Burgundy to Maximilian of Austria (1477), and later to the Hapsburg Philip II of Spain when his father, Charles V, divided his kingdom. In 1567 the Low Countries (modern Belgium, Netherlands, and Luxembourg) revolted against King Philip. The northern, predominantly Protestant Netherlands provinces won their independence, but Belgium was reconquered by Spain.

The victorious powers of the Napoleonic Wars again united Belgium with the Netherlands and Luxembourg under Dutch King William I, in order to form a buffer state against France. When the Belgians revolted in 1830, England and France imposed an armistice, dissolved the unitary kingdom and guaranteed Belgium's independence and neutrality, which was finally recognized by King William in 1839.

The new state chose Leopold of Saxe-Coburg as its king. Upon his death in 1865 he was succeeded by his son Leopold II, whose encouragement of rapid industrialization and colonial acquisition brought about prosperity. He established the African Congo as a private colony, but it was transferred to the state in 1908 after reports of misgovernment inspired agitation in Belgium and other European countries.

Albert I, nephew of Leopold II, acceded to the throne in 1909. After World War I Belgium made an end to its status of guaranteed neutrality and entered into a defensive alliance with France. King Albert died in 1934 and was succeeded by his son, Leopold III.

With the increase of tensions caused by the rise of Hitler, Belgium again shifted its foreign policy. It withdrew from the alliance with France in 1936 and declared a policy of independent neutrality. When the Germans invaded Belgium in 1940 King Leopold, as chief of his country's army, surrendered and refused to accompany his government to London. The cabinet declared the surrender illegal. Leopold's unpopularity caused a long political crisis after the liberation of Belgium in 1944; he was barred from returning to the country to resume his royal function. In a popular referendum in 1950, 57.68 per cent of the people voted in favor of the return of the King. However, continued hostility led Leopold to transfer his royal powers to his son Baudouin, who ascended the throne on coming of age, September 7, 1951.

**GOVERNMENT AND POLITICS.** The Belgian government is a constitutional monarchy. The ministry is responsible to Parliament, which is composed of a Chamber of Representatives with 212 members and a Senate of 178 members. Belgium is divided into nine provinces headed by a governor who is appointed by the central government and is assisted by an elected council.

The existence of three major political parties—Christian Social, Socialist, and Freedom and Progress (formerly the Liberal Party)—has usually led to coalition governments and consequent political instability. A center-right coalition government headed by Christian Socialist Paul Vanden Boeynants was in power in late 1967. Representing an alliance of Christian Socialists and Liberals, it was installed in 1966 after a prolonged governmental crisis. The present government is the 17th since 1944.

There have been recurrent controversies between the formerly dominant French-speaking Walloons and the Flemish who are seeking equality for their language. In 1963 the redrawing of a 1962 line which created two separate language areas but left Brussels bilingual failed to satisfy the Flemish.

Since Belgium granted independence to the Congo in 1960, relations with the former colony have constituted its major foreign-policy problem. The seizure of the Belgian mining corporation Union Minière du Haut Katanga in January, 1967, and the rebellion of mercenary troops caused a sharp deterioration in relations. On August 28, 1967, Brussels announced that it would withhold most of its technical assistance of $70,000,000 a year, as well as the services of over 3,500 teachers and administrative personnel, until President Mobutu agreed to give adequate guarantees for the safety of some 40,000 Belgians in the Congo.

**ECONOMY.** With the growth of industry, agriculture has declined in importance in the Belgian economy. Only about six per cent of the working population is engaged in farming, yet it produces four-fifths of the country's needs.

Belgium is highly industrialized. Its economy quickly recovered after World War II and a boom developed. Chief products are iron and steel, textiles, coal, light machinery, and chemical supplies.

After 1965 economic activity declined. A number of uneconomic coal mines had to be closed, and inflation slowed economic development. Belgium has traditionally followed a low-tariff policy and since World War II has strongly supported Western European economic integration.

**EDUCATION.** Education is free and compulsory for all children from 6 to 14 years of age. There is practically no adult illiteracy. Belgium has four major universities: the state universities of Liège (French speaking) and Ghent (Flemish speaking), the bilingual Catholic University of Louvain, and the University of Brussels.

**ARMED FORCES.** One year of military service is compulsory for all able-bodied young men. Belgium's armed forces total about 111,000 officers and men.

# BHUTAN

*Official Name:* Bhután. *Area:* 18,000 square miles. *Population:* 750,000. *Capital:* Thimbu. *Flag:* An orange-yellow field above a crimson one, divided diagonally, with a large white dragon in the center. *Monetary Unit:* Indian rupee (worth 13.3 U.S. cents).

**LAND AND PEOPLE.** Bhutan, a small kingdom in the eastern Himalayan hill area, is bordered on the northwest and the north by Chinese-controlled Tibet, on the east and south by India, and on the southwest by Sikkim. (See map on page 139.) Climate varies with elevation, from the icy 24,000-foot peaks of the Himalayas to the steamy jungles of the southern lowland. Between these extremes lie eight fertile valleys, with irrigated, terraced hillsides and extensive forests.

The three major ethnic groups are Mongoloid Bhotias (or Bhutanese proper), Dukpas of Tibetan descent, and Nepalese. Those of Mongoloid origin are Mahayana Buddhists; the Nepalese are mostly Hindus. The language is Dzohgkha, akin to Tibetan.

**HISTORY.** Bhutan's early history is obscure. Around 1630 a refugee Dukpa Lama from Tibet became the first Dharma Raja, with both spiritual and temporal powers. In recent centuries Bhutan was beset by its neighbors to the south (British India) and by the Tibetans in the north. After a war in 1865 the British annexed part of southern Bhutan and later assumed control of Bhutan's foreign relations. In 1949 India returned the annexed lands and took over control of external affairs. In 1950 China threatened Bhutan's sovereignty, thus causing Bhutan to close its northern border and seek defense guarantees from India.

**GOVERNMENT AND POLITICS.** In 1907 the religious-based political system was abolished and a hereditary monarchy established. A government council selected Sir Ugyen Wangchuk as the country's first maharaja. He was succeeded in 1926 by his son, and in 1952 by his grandson, Jigme Dorji Wangchuk, whose rule has been marked by efforts to modernize the social and economic structure.

The king is, in theory, an absolute monarch who rules with the assistance of a small advisory council. Legislation is enacted in consultation with the Tsongdu, an assembly established by the present ruler in 1954 of village representatives elected by family heads.

**ECONOMY.** Small-scale farming and animal husbandry are the primary occupations. Chief crops are rice, maize, wheat, millet, and oranges. Yaks, cattle, sheep, pigs, and ponies are also raised.

**EDUCATION.** Bhutan's 101 schools offer free education, but the curriculum is limited. The literacy rate is not over 5 per cent.

**ARMED FORCES.** Bhutan has announced plans to introduce compulsory military service for all males between 23 and 50. The present militia, an estimated 8,000–10,000 troops, is being built into a modern army with India's help.

# BOLIVIA

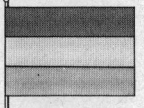

*Official Name:* Republic of Bolivia. *Area:* 424,162 square miles. *Population:* 3,748,000. *Principal Cities* (with populations): La Paz, the actual capital, 366,487; Cochabamba, 95,083; Oruro, 94,336; Santa Cruz, 88,000; Sucre, the official capital, 59,000; Potosí, 58,000; Tarija, 21,000. *Flag:* Three horizontal stripes of red, gold, and green. *Monetary Unit:* The peso boliviano of 100 centavos (worth 8.5 U.S. cents). *Gross National Product:* $792,600,000 (1965). *Average Annual Income per Person:* $128.

**LAND AND PEOPLE.** Bolivia, in the heart of South America, is bordered on the north and east by Brazil, on the southeast by Paraguay, on the south by Argentina, and on the west by Chile and Peru. (See map on page 75.)

The country is divided into three regions. The two bleak Andean ranges that flank a high plateau (Altiplano) stretch along the Chilean border in the west. The valleys (Yungas) scar the eastern slopes of the Andes. The tropical plains (Llanos and Chaco) are in the east. Lake Titicaca, on the border of Bolivia and Peru, is the highest navigable body of water in the world.

Quechua and Aymara Indians, with a few other Indian linguistic groups, comprise over half the population. Spanish is the official language. Ninety-four per cent of the people are Roman Catholic.

**HISTORY.** Pre-Inca ruins, such as those at Tiahuanaco, indicate the existence of a very early Indian civilization in Bolivia. About 1200 A.D. the country came under the benevolent rule of the Incas. The Spanish conquest of the Inca empire, which began in 1532, completed the subjection of the Bolivian region by 1538. The Spanish colonial period was characterized by intensive mining of silver, especially at Potosí, once the largest metropolis in America.

Bolivia, called Upper Peru, was one of the first Spanish colonies to rebel and one of the last to gain freedom. The War of Independence lasted from 1809 to 1824, and when the republic was proclaimed the following year, it was named for its liberator, General Simón Bolívar. For most of its independent life, Bolivia has been torn by factional strife, and most of its rulers have been dictators.

Bolivia has lost much of its territory in wars. In 1879 Chile seized Bolivia's only exit to the ocean, the mineral-rich Desert of Atacama, and in 1903 Brazil took a huge rubber-tree area. From 1932 to 1935 Bolivia fought the bloody Chaco War with Paraguay. Paraguay was frustrated in trying to occupy the petroleum fields of the southeast, but Bolivia lost much land.

The Chaco War created a new generation of young, educated revolutionaries dedicated to social and economic reforms. Organized as the Movement of the National Revolution (MNR), they achieved power by force in 1952 and instituted drastic reforms, giving equality to the Indian masses, introducing land reforms, nationalizing big foreign mining companies, and abolishing the old army. In 1964 the 12-year rule of MNR came to an end when Vice President René Barrientos Ortuño, a product of the new army created after 1952, seized power. He has supported the MNR's social reforms.

**GOVERNMENT AND POLITICS.** Bolivia is officially a constitutional republic and a democracy. It has a centralized form of government, with powers separated into executive, legislative, and judicial branches. The executive and legislative offices, including the presidency, are located in the actual capital, La Paz, but the supreme court resides in the constitutional capital of Sucre. The legislature has a senate of 27 members and a chamber of deputies of 102. The country is divided into nine departments.

The government has had a stormy history. Since independence in 1825, Bolivia has had well over 200 revolutions. Few presidents have finished their terms of office. The present government, under General René Barrientos Ortuño (a U.S.-trained Air Force officer), came to power in a 1964 revolution. After serving as co-president since May, 1965, Barrientos resigned in January, 1966, and organized an election, which he won by a heavy majority.

In 1967 government troops, fighting a tough guerrilla war in the rugged southwest section, killed guerrilla leader Ernesto "Che" Guevara.

**ECONOMY.** Virtually all of Bolivia's income is from mining. Since the Chaco War the country has suffered great economic ills. U.S. aid to Bolivia, which is larger per capita than that to any other Latin American nation, has been a decisive factor in averting economic collapse. In the past few years the economy has slowly and steadily improved. Exports in 1966 totaled $121 million, of which tin accounted for 70 per cent. Imports came to $130 million, most of which were machinery, vehicles, and food. Almost 67 per cent of Bolivia's population depends on agriculture for a livelihood.

**EDUCATION.** Primary education is free and compulsory, with about 525,000 students enrolled in grammar school. Enrollment stands at about 12,000 in the National University Council's seven universities that are distributed among the country's nine departments. The literacy rate is about 37 per cent.

**ARMED FORCES.** Military service is compulsory at the age of 18; armed-forces strength is estimated at between 10,000 and 12,000.

## BOTSWANA

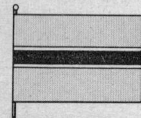

*Official Name:* Republic of Botswana. *Area:* 220,236 square miles. *Population:* 576,000. *Principal Cities* (with populations): Gaberones, the capital, 6,000; Serowe, 34,182; Kanye, 34,045. *Flag:* Wide blue bands separated from a central black band by narrow white stripes. *Monetary Unit:* The rand of 100 cents (worth U.S. $1.40). *Gross National Product:* $35,000,000 (1966). *Average Annual Income per Person:* $67.

**LAND AND PEOPLE.** Botswana, formerly called Bechuanaland, is bordered by South Africa on the east and south, South West Africa on the west and north, and Rhodesia on the east. (See map on page 111.) The Kalahari Desert covers a large part of the south, and the Okavango River forms an extensive swamp in the northwest.

The country is inhabited chiefly by Africans who speak Bantu languages. There are about 4,000 Europeans and 4,000 Asians. Some 14 per cent of the people are Christians; the rest practice traditional tribal religions.

**HISTORY.** Under Khama the Great and other 19th-century chiefs, the Bechuana (Botswana) people sought British protection against the Transvaal Boers. Britain thus established the Bechuanaland Protectorate in 1885. At various times between 1909 and 1955, Bechuanaland was threatened by incorporation into South Africa, but leaders staved off the moves by appeals to the British government. The protectorate achieved full independence in 1966 and was renamed Botswana.

**GOVERNMENT AND POLITICS.** Sir Seretse Khama took office as the first president of the new republic. A cabinet plus a House of Chiefs, composed of tribal leaders, advises the president. Sir Khama's Democratic Party won 28 seats in the National Assembly in 1965.

**ECONOMY.** Botswana's economy is based on cattle, which accounts for 85 per cent of the country's exports. A seven-year drought, which ended in 1966, killed one-fourth of the cattle and necessitated large-scale famine relief. Asbestos, manganese, gold, and silver are the leading mineral resources. Copper and nickel have recently been discovered.

The country has 5,000 miles of roads, and a railway links Botswana to South Africa and Rhodesia. An airline connects with international flights in Johannesburg.

**EDUCATION.** Botswana has 263 schools, including nine at the secondary level. There are two teacher-training colleges and four vocational schools. Education is not compulsory.

**ARMED FORCES.** The country has no army.

## BRAZIL

*Official Name:* Brazil. *Area:* 3,286,473 square miles. *Population:* 87,209,000. *Principal Cities* (with populations): Brasília, the capital, 370,000; São Paulo, 5,835,000; Rio de Janeiro, 4,230,000; Belo Horizonte, 1,152,000; Recife, 1,087,000; Porto Alegre, 919,000; Salvador, 915,000; Fortaleza, 840,000; Belém, 560,000. *Flag:* A green field with a yellow diamond in the center that holds a blue globe with 22 stars (five of which form the Southern Cross) and the motto *Ordem e Progresso.* *Monetary Unit:* The new cruzeiro (worth 37 U.S. cents as of May 1967). *Gross National Product:* $22,201,665,000 (1966). *Average Annual Income per Person:* $265.

**LAND AND PEOPLE.** Occupying almost half the South American continent, Brazil is bordered on the north by French Guiana, Surinam, Guyana, Venezuela, and Colombia; on the west by Peru and Bolivia; on the southwest by Paraguay and Argentina; and on the south by Uruguay. Its Atlantic coastline is 4,603 miles long. (See map on page 75.)

A tropical climate prevails in the Amazon River basin in the north. Over half the country's area consists of highlands between 650 and 3,000 feet above sea level, where the climate is temperate. Brazil's major waterways are the Amazon, which is one of the world's greatest rivers, the Paraná, and the São Francisco.

Over 55 per cent of the population is white, 30 per cent mixed, 12 per cent Negro, and between 1 and 2 per cent Oriental. Descendants of European immigrants predominate in the south, while descendants of African slaves are the principal group in the northeast. The official language is Portuguese. About 94 per cent of the population is Roman Catholic.

**HISTORY.** In 1500 Pedro Álvares Cabral, a Portuguese admiral, claimed the region for his country. In 1532 Martim Afonso de Sousa founded the first colony at São Vincente and introduced sugarcane cultivation. When Brazil became the major source of sugar in the 17th century, many Negro slaves were imported to work the large plantations in the northeast.

Between 1693 and 1700 mineral wealth was discovered in central Brazil, and the region flourished for a century as a major world supplier of gold and diamonds. By 1763 Rio de Janeiro had replaced Salvador as the colony's capital. In 1808, after Napoleon's capture of Lisbon, Portugal's royal family fled to Brazil. Rio became the seat of the Portuguese empire.

King João VI returned home in 1821, leaving his son, Dom Pedro, as regent. In 1822, ac-

SOUTH AMERICA

ceding to widespread demands for liberty, Dom Pedro became Pedro I, emperor of an independent Brazil. His popularity diminished, and in 1831 he abdicated in favor of his son Pedro de Alcântara (Pedro II), who governed until 1889. Pedro II's progressive rule laid the foundation of modern Brazil.

With increasing European immigration, the construction of railways and roads, and the beginning of large-scale coffee production, the southeast region became the center of Brazil's development. Foreign demand for rubber stimulated the growth of such cities as Belém and Manaus. The abolition of slavery in 1888 fanned the sparks of rebellion, and the owners of the large plantations supported the growing republican movement. In 1889 a bloodless revolt established the United States of Brazil, with Manuel Deodoro da Fonseca as first president.

By World War I, with Brazil on the Allied side, the nation had gained in constitutional stability and international recognition. Her rubber monopoly ended, however, with the development of plantations in southeast Asia. She had become the world's leading coffee producer, but falling prices and a worldwide depression created economic and political crises.

In 1930 a revolution brought Getúlio Vargas to the presidency. His regime fostered centralization and industrialization but degenerated into a dictatorship and was overthrown in 1945. Brazil fought on the side of the Allies in World War II. Vargas became president again in 1950, this time by popular vote, but a serious political crisis led to his suicide.

Juscelino Kubitschek, elected president in 1955, initiated heavy construction programs and industrial expansion. He created a new capital, Brasília, out of the country's central wilderness, attempting thereby to encourage development of the interior. During his term rampant inflation undermined the currency, causing most Brazilians intense hardship. Jânio Quadros, elected president in 1960 by the largest plurality vote in Brazil's history, failed to stem the economic crisis and resigned after seven months. João Goulart, the vice-president, took over. His 30-month regime was marked by economic slowdowns, strikes and riots, battles with Congress, and crippling inflation. Goulart turned increasingly leftward in support of "basic reforms," and Brazil's relations with the United States deteriorated.

A military uprising forced Goulart into exile in 1964. Congress elected Marshal Humberto de Alencar Castelo Branco interim president. In 1966 the same Congress elected Marshal Artur da Costa e Silva to a four-year presidential term beginning March 15, 1967.

**GOVERNMENT AND POLITICS.** Brazil consists of 22 states with limited autonomy, a federal district, and four federal territories. Congress is made up of a 66-member Senate and a 409-member Chamber of Deputies. All literate men and women are required to vote.

Accusations of Communism and corruption in past regimes resulted in the expulsion of 55 members of Congress in 1964, the abrogation of civil rights, and the dismissal of thousands of government employees and members of the armed forces. In October, 1965, Castelo Branco dissolved all political parties. A new government party, the National Renovating Alliance (ARENA), was organized in December, along with an opposition party, the Brazilian Democratic Movement. The opposition, however, was reduced to impotence by the government's revolutionary decrees.

**ECONOMY.** The Brazilian economy, formerly based upon one or two products and consequently vulnerable to changing markets and falling prices, is becoming increasingly diversified. Coffee still accounts for about two-fifths of Brazil's export income.

Brazil is self-sufficient in consumer and light capital goods. Heavy capital goods production is increasing rapidly. The populous southern third of the country is becoming urbanized and is developing a modern industrial society, but the 25 million inhabitants of the underdeveloped northeast have not shared in this progress.

Despite Castelo Branco's austerity program, the cost of living rose 84 per cent in 1964, 46 per cent in 1965, 41 per cent in 1966, and 16 per cent during the first half of 1967.

The use of five different gauges has added to the inefficiency of Brazil's mostly government-owned railway system. There are over 877,000 miles of road, but fewer than 9,000 miles are paved. Domestic and international air service is highly developed, and many foreign carriers serve the country. Intracoastal shipping links the ports, and the merchant fleet has a cargo capacity of 1.5 million tons.

**EDUCATION.** Elementary education is by law free and compulsory. School units of all levels exceeded 135,500 in 1966, and there are 35 private and Catholic universities. In many rural areas, however, schools are all but totally lacking. Literacy is estimated at 57.5 per cent.

**ARMED FORCES.** Men over 18 are eligible for the draft. The army comprises some 140,000 men; the navy under 50,000; and the air force nearly 30,000. State paramilitary militia forces total more than 100,000.

## BULGARIA

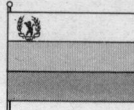

*Official Name:* Bulgarian People's Republic. *Area:* 42,823 square miles. *Population:* 8,258,000. *Principal Cities* (with populations): Sofia, the capital, 800,953; Plovdiv, 222,737; Varna, 180,062; Ruse, 128,-384. *Flag:* Three horizontal stripes of white, green, and red; the national coat of arms is in the left-hand corner of the top stripe. *Monetary Unit:* The lev of 100 stotinki (worth 85.5 U.S. cents). *Average Annual Income per Person:* $687.

**LAND AND PEOPLE.** Bulgaria, situated on the Balkan peninsula, is bordered on the north by Romania, on the east by the Black Sea, on the south by Turkey and Greece, and on the west by Yugoslavia. (See map on page 197.)

The Balkan Mountains cross Bulgaria from

east to west between the Danubian tableland in the north and the Thracian Plain in the south. The Danube flows along Bulgaria's northern boundary, and the Maritsa River drains the Thracian Plain region.

Bulgarians, chiefly of Slavic and Turkic origin, comprise more than 90 per cent of the population. Macedonians, Turks, Armenians, and Gypsies constitute the major ethnic minorities. Bulgarian is spoken by 88 per cent of the population and Turkish by 9.8 per cent.

About 85 per cent of the people belong to the Bulgarian Orthodox Church. There are over 750,000 Muslims.

**HISTORY.** Bulgaria, part of ancient Thrace and Moesia, was settled by Slavic tribes in the sixth century. In 679–80 the Bulgars, a Turkic-speaking people, crossed the Danube, conquered the Slavs, and, after founding the first Bulgarian Empire, gradually merged with the Slavic population. During the next two centuries the Bulgars waged a series of wars against various Slavic groups and the Byzantine Empire. Under the leadership of Krum (802?–814) they expanded and consolidated their state; Krum's forces captured Sofia and killed the Byzantine emperor, Nicephorus I. Under Boris I the Bulgars adopted Christianity (865). The first Bulgarian empire fell in 1018, when it was annexed by Byzantium. The second empire, founded in 1186, lasted until the Ottoman Turks subdued the Bulgars in 1396.

For nearly 500 years the Turks held sway over Bulgaria. In the 19th century the Bulgarian liberation movement culminated in the national revolt of 1876, which was savagely put down by the Turks in the "Bulgarian Massacres." Russia intervened on behalf of her brother Slavs, defeated the Turks, and imposed the Treaty of San Stefano, creating an expanded and hopefully pro-Russian Bulgaria.

Other European powers, particularly Britain and Austria-Hungary, feared Russian penetration into the Balkans. At their insistence, Russia was forced to accept a treaty revision at the Congress of Berlin (1878): northern Bulgaria was made an autonomous principality under Ottoman control, with Alexander of Battenberg as its first prince. Eastern Rumelia, the area south of the Balkan Mountains, was made an autonomous province under Ottoman rule, but Alexander annexed it in 1885. His successor, Prince Ferdinand of Saxe-Coburg-Gotha, who came to power in 1887, proclaimed himself the tsar in 1908.

Bulgaria sided with Germany in World War I. In 1918 the tsar abdicated in favor of his son, Boris III. Bulgaria lost much territory as the result of the peace treaty. After a few years of stability there ensued a decade of political confusion, with violent activity by Macedonian terrorists. A military dictatorship was set up in 1936, with Boris assuming authoritarian powers a year later.

In an effort to regain lost territory, Bulgaria backed the Axis powers in World War II. When Soviet troops entered the country in 1944, Bulgaria tried to sign an armistice with the Western Allies, but the Soviets declared war, and military occupation followed. The coalition government soon came under Communist domination. Moderate or dissident elements were purged; farms were collectivized; industry was nationalized; and a one-party government was installed. In 1950 Bulgaria forced the return to Turkey of 250,000 Bulgarian Turks.

**GOVERNMENT AND POLITICS.** Bulgaria is a Communist People's Republic. In theory supreme power is vested in the National Assembly, whose members are elected directly to four-year terms by universal suffrage and secret ballot. Responsible to and elected by the assembly is its own ruling body, the Presidium (the state's highest organ); all judges, including those of the Supreme Court, are appointed and subject to removal by the assembly. In fact, however, national policy is determined by the Bulgarian Communist Party's Politburo, elected by the party's Central Committee.

Heads of state are the President of the Presidium (Georgi Traikov since 1964) and the First Secretary of the Central Committee (Todor Zhivkov). Since 1948 the Communist Party has ruled as part of the New Fatherland Front, polarized around the Communist Party and its ally, the Agricultural People's Union.

Since 1946 Bulgaria's foreign policy has been marked by close cooperation with the Soviet Union. In 1948 she concluded a 20-year treaty of friendship, cooperation, and mutual assistance with Russia. In 1950 the National Assembly granted Soviet residents in Bulgaria equal rights with its own citizens, including that of holding public office. Bulgaria is a member of Comecon (the Communist regional economic pact) and the Warsaw Pact. Over the past decade the government has achieved a degree of cultural and political independence within the Communist bloc and has increased its contacts with the West.

**ECONOMY.** All economic activity is planned and controlled by the state. Banks are nationalized and foreign trade is a state monopoly. Before World War II Bulgaria was predominantly agricultural; since the war the Communist government has stressed industrialization, especially in engineering and chemical fields.

The leading minerals are coal, iron, copper, lead, zinc, and, on the Black Sea coast, oil. The main agricultural products are grains, grapes, and tobacco; food production accounts for almost a quarter of the national income. Some 80 per cent of Bulgaria's trade is with the Soviet bloc.

Bulgaria's 2,600 miles of railroad are the primary means of transportation; waterways are second in importance. A national airline flies to some foreign cities, and international carriers serve Sofia. There are about 6,200 miles of paved roads.

**EDUCATION.** Education is free and compulsory from the ages of 7 to 16. The literacy rate, 77 per cent in 1946, is now estimated at 93 per cent.

**ARMED FORCES.** Two years' military service is compulsory for men between 19 and 25. The army numbers 125,000 men; the air force, 20,-000; and the navy, 7,000.

## BURMA

*Official Name:* Union of Burma. *Area:* 261,789 square miles. *Population* (est.): 25,000,000. *Principal Cities* (with populations): Rangoon, the capital, 1,-530,000; Mandalay, 322,000; Moulmein, 190,-000. *Flag:* A red field with a blue rectangle in the upper left-hand corner containing a centered white star with smaller stars between its points. *Monetary Unit:* The kyat (worth 21 U.S. cents). *Gross National Product:* $1,760,-000,000 (1965). *Average Annual Income per Person:* $70.

**LAND AND PEOPLE.** A small Southeast Asian country off the main sealanes of the Indian Ocean, Burma is bordered on the north by Tibet, on the east by China, Laos, and Thailand, on the south by the Andaman Sea, and on the west by the Bay of Bengal, East Pakistan, and India.

The country has two distinct land regions: the fertile plains and delta in the south and central area; and the uplands, which form a protective arc of hills across the northern frontiers. (See map on page 243.)

The major rivers—the Irrawaddy, Chindwin, and Salween—flow north to south and are important for transportation. Rainfall is heavy, totaling 100 inches a year in lower Burma and the Rangoon area, and more than 200 inches in upper Burma during the monsoon season. Central Burma's dry zone has 20 to 45 inches of rainfall annually. Most of Burma is forested and rich in animal and plant life.

The population is multiracial, but the overwhelming majority are of Burmese stock, related to the Tibetans. The Burmese live mainly in the plains-delta region and dominate the nation's history and culture. The Karens and Kayahs are the largest of the minorities. There are smaller groups of Shans, Kachins, and Chins living in the hill areas, and of Chinese and Indians in the cities.

More than 100 native languages are spoken in Burma, most of them belonging to the Tibeto-Chinese language group. Burmese is the official language. Eighty-five per cent of the Burmese are Buddhists.

**HISTORY.** Before the British entered Burma in 1824, the people had three periods of political unity: the Pagan Dynasty, from the 11th to 13th centuries, during which the Hinayana Buddhism practiced today was introduced into the country; the 16th century Toungoo Dynasty; and the Konbaung Dynasty during the 18th and 19th centuries. Between dynasties there were wars among competing groups: Burmese, Shans, Mons, and Arakanese.

Conflict between the British and the Burmese for influence over states bordering Burma brought about an Anglo-Burmese war (1824–26), as a result of which the British gained control of part of lower Burma. A second war in 1852 and a third in 1885 ended Burma's independence.

Grafted onto India as a province, Burma was governed from New Delhi. Under British rule the country was administered by a governor and a strong bureaucracy. In 1921 a partially elected Parliament was introduced.

Burma developed a foreign exchange system under British rule and became the world's largest exporter of rice—"the rice bowl of Asia." Little industrialization took place. In the world depression of 1930 Burma suffered heavily from depressed prices and the lack of demand for its products. During this period a strong nationalist movement began among its youth. In 1937 Burma was separated from India and drew up a new constitution which gave it an elected one-house Parliament with responsibility for nearly all subjects.

In 1942 the Japanese, aided by Burmese nationalists, expelled the British from most of Burma. Under the Japanese, the Burmese developed a small national army and in 1943 were given their independence in the Japanese-designed "New Order of Asia." The nationalist movement gained strength during this period, under the leadership of Aung San, U Nu, Ne Win, and Than Tun.

British civil rule was restored in 1946. The next year a Constituent Assembly voted for complete independence outside the Commonwealth of Nations. The same year Aung San was assassinated and U Nu became leader of Burma. The Union of Burma was formed January 4, 1948. U Nu was named premier.

Government clashes with rebellious tribes and native Communist factions have been frequent since independence. Thousands of refugee Nationalist Chinese troops, driven into Burma during the Communist Chinese revolution, caused great social and economic disruption. Post-World War II economic difficulties, plus the difficulties common to all newly independent nations, added to Burma's hardships.

Under these pressures the governing party broke up, and U Nu resigned in favor of a military caretaker government under General Ne Win in 1958. This regime was dissolved in 1960 and U Nu was elected head of the government, but in 1962 a coup d'etat by Ne Win re-established the military regime.

**GOVERNMENT AND POLITICS.** Prior to the present military dictatorship, Burma was a constitutional democracy in which an elected legislature was dominant. The people enjoyed many political and social rights. Under a combined federal and unitary structure, the larger indigenous minorities had separate states. There were popular elections, political parties, and judicial independence.

The military rulers, functioning under a self-chosen Revolutionary Council, swept away the constitutional system and replaced it with a dictatorial one based on their own ideology which they call the "Burmese Way to Socialism." The federal form was kept, but a new, centralized bureaucracy was erected to run the whole nation. The Revolutionary Council, with General Ne Win as Chairman, set up its own political party and banned opposition. It was hoped eventually to create a hierarchy of peasant and worker's councils.

Burmese celebrate Buddhist Festival of the Lights.

**ECONOMY.** When its constitution was in force, Burma had a mixed economy with a healthy private as well as public sector. After the 1962 coup, the whole economic structure was brought under government control, and private interests were driven out. Declines in production, breakdowns in distribution, and the rise of shortages and black marketeering have brought some relaxation in government controls.

Rice remains the dominant crop in this primarily agricultural land, and is its chief export. Timber production—principally of teak—is important; 900 elephants are used to extract and haul the trees. Petroleum and precious stones are among the other resources. A narrow-gauge railway connects major cities.

**EDUCATION.** Schooling is free but not compulsory in primary, secondary, and vocational schools. Plans are under way to institute four years of compulsory schooling in 1969 and to extend it to nine years by 1977.

Burma has 12,000 primary schools with 1,-600,000 pupils and more than 800 secondary schools with 250,000 pupils. The universities of Rangoon and Mandalay have been reorganized into the Arts-Science University and independent degree-giving institutes. University students number about 15,000. Latest available figures give Burma's literacy as 58 per cent of the population over 15 years old.

**ARMED FORCES.** Military service is voluntary. The army has an estimated 49,000 men; the navy, 5,250; and the air force, 900.

# BURUNDI

*Official Name:* Republic of Burundi. *Area:* 10,747 square miles. *Population:* 3,200,000. *Principal Cities* (with populations): Bujumbura, the capital, 75,000; Gitega, 35,000. *Flag:* A white diagonal cross, with red quarters on top and bottom and green quarters to the left and right; the white circle bears three red stars. *Monetary Unit:* The Burundi franc (worth U.S. $1.16). *Gross National Product:* $140,000,000 (1965). *Average Annual Income per Person:* $53.

**LAND AND PEOPLE.** Burundi is a tiny, landlocked country of east-central Africa, bordered on the north by Rwanda, on the east and south by Tanzania, and on the west by Lake Tanganyika and the Democratic Republic of the Congo. (See map on page 111.)

Burundi's plateau country, averaging 5,000–6,500 feet in height, slopes eastward toward Tanzania. The western mountains, which reach 8,000 feet, continue north into Rwanda. Major rivers are the Malagarasi, Ruzizi, Nyakyanda, and the Ruvuvu and Kagera, southernmost sources of the Nile.

Burundi's climate, typical of tropical highlands, is cool in the central plateau and slightly warmer near Lake Tanganyika.

The Bahutu, or Hutu, a Bantu people, make up 84 per cent of the population; the Watutsi, or Tutsi, an unusually tall people of Nilotic origin, comprise 15 per cent; the Batwa, pygmies who were the original settlers of the region, number slightly less than 1 per cent. All three tribes speak a Bantu dialect called Kirundi, but French is the official language. Over 50 per cent of the population are Christians, mainly Roman Catholics; the rest are animists.

**HISTORY.** The pastoral Watutsi, thought to have come from Ethiopia, began to conquer the Bahutu in the 15th century. They established and dominated a feudal kingdom, which was ruled by an absolute monarch called the Mwami. Farming and manual labor were left to the Bahutu.

The first Europeans to explore the Lake Tanganyika region arrived in 1858. Stanley and Livingstone visited Bujumbura in 1871. Burundi was absorbed into German East Africa in 1894. Belgian troops occupied Burundi (then Urundi) along with Rwanda (then Ruanda) in World War I, and in 1923 Belgium received the entire area as a mandate from the League of Nations.

Burundi's transition to self-government was relatively smooth. Political ideas sweeping the rest of Africa began to affect Burundi in the late 1950s. A Bahutu movement emerged, and in early 1961 a dominantly Bahutu national government was hurriedly formed by Belgium out of borough councillors. U.N.-supervised elections in 1961 gave an overwhelming majority to the Uprona party. Burundi declared itself the independent Kingdom of Burundi in 1962.

**GOVERNMENT AND POLITICS.** Since independence, Burundian politics have been marked by continuous conflict between the seven successive governments and the Bahutu-controlled Parliament. Two prime ministers were assassinated in 1965, and, after an abortive coup by Bahutu military elements, almost all the Bahutu political leaders were wiped out by Communist Chinese-influenced Watutsi extremists. In July, 1966, the Mwami, an exile in Switzerland since the 1965 revolt, was deposed by his 19-year-old son, who became Mwami Ntare V; he, in turn, was overthrown by his prime minister, Colonel Michel Micombero, in November, 1966. The new President proclaimed Burundi a republic, which he rules with the aid of a 13-man National Revolutionary Committee.

**ECONOMY.** Agriculture, mostly subsistence farming, is the livelihood of 90 per cent of the people. Coffee is the principal export crop. Cattle, for centuries a Burundian status symbol, are raised in large numbers, but their quality is poor. The economy is dependent on Belgian aid. Burundi has no railways and only a few miles of paved roads. Main access to the outside world is via Lake Tanganyika and by air service to Kinshasa, Lubumbashi, and Nairobi.

**EDUCATION.** There are 1,300 primary, 6 secondary, and 25 technical schools, but nearly 95 per cent of the population is illiterate.

**ARMED FORCES.** Burundi's combined army and police force numbers about 800 men.

# CAMBODIA

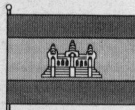

*Official Name:* Kingdom of Cambodia. *Area:* 69,898 square miles. *Population:* 6,250,000. *Principal Cities* (with populations): Phnom Penh, the capital, 400,000; Battambang, 40,000. *Flag:* A center red stripe with the Angkor Wat Pagoda in white, bordered by blue stripes. *Monetary Unit:* The riel of 100 centimes (worth U.S. $2.85). *Gross National Product:* $726,110,000 (1963). *Average Annual Income per Person:* $99.

**LAND AND PEOPLE.** Cambodia is bordered on the west and north by Thailand, on the northeast by Laos, on the east and south by South Vietnam, and on the southwest by the Gulf of Siam. (See map on page 243.)

The border with Thailand is marked by mountains that rise sharply from the Gulf of Siam coast, drop to a plains region, and ascend again in the north. The rest of Cambodia consists of plains and a vast central basin where the Tonle Sap (Great Lake) and the Mekong River are located. During Cambodia's six-month wet season the overflowing Mekong greatly increases the lake's size; as the river drains the basin it leaves behind thick deposits of alluvial soil.

Nearly 85 per cent of all Cambodians are of Khmer descent. Important minority groups include Vietnamese and Chinese. Khmer (Cambodian) is the official language; French is also widely used. Hinayana Buddhism is the state religion, and about 90 per cent of the people are Buddhists.

**HISTORY.** In the first century A.D. the Kingdom of Funan was established in Cambodia. Three centuries later an Indian Brahman took control of Funan; Indian influences shaped the country's customs, alphabet, and legal code. The kingdom that developed from the sixth-century Khmer conquest of Funan reached its peak between the 10th and 14th centuries. A vast and magnificent complex of shrines and temples was built at its capital, Angkor, and the Khmer Empire eventually spread over much of southeast Asia.

For centuries after the empire's fall in the 15th century, Cambodia was attacked by the Thais and the Vietnamese. In the 18th century Siam annexed three of Cambodia's provinces, and the Cochin-China territory was won by the Annamese. Cambodia was saved from total dissolution when France answered the Cambodian king's plea for aid and established a protectorate in 1863. The country later became part of French Indochina.

Nationalist spirit grew in the 1930s. Anti-French sentiment spread during World War II, when Vichy France bowed to Japan's demands for Cambodian bases and Thailand temporarily held part of the territory. Early in 1945 Japan suppressed Cambodia's Vichy administration; at the same time King Norodom Sihanouk, who had become monarch in 1941 at the age of 18, renounced treaties with France.

French authority was re-established when Japan was defeated, but Cambodia gained more self-government. In 1947 it became a constitutional monarchy, and in 1949 it became associated with the French Union. During the French-Indochinese War in 1953 Sihanouk was granted full military control.

Sihanouk abdicated in favor of his parents in 1955, but soon returned as premier. His Popular Social Community Party won all National Assembly seats in that year's election. Cambodia left the French Union that same year, declaring itself a sovereign and independent state. In 1960 Sihanouk was installed as chief of state.

Cambodia has increasingly aligned itself with Communist nations. The country has recognized Communist China and established diplomatic relations with the Communist bloc. In 1963 Cambodia refused all further U.S. economic and military assistance, and in 1965 it broke diplomatic ties with the U.S. In June, 1967, the U.S.S.R. recognized Cambodia's frontiers, an action followed by similar declarations from other Communist countries. But in September, 1967, Sihanouk dismissed two pro-Chinese cabinet ministers and scheduled a national referendum for early 1968, thus indicating a new shift in foreign policy.

**GOVERNMENT AND POLITICS.** The nominal head of Cambodia is the monarch, but actual power rests in the office of chief of state. Parliament, which chooses the chief of state, consists of the 24-member Council of the Kingdom (upper house) and the 82-member National Assembly (lower house).

The Popular Socialist Community Party, founded and headed by Prince Sihanouk, holds all seats in the National Assembly. The only opposition is the pro-Communist Preacheachon Party.

**ECONOMY.** Rice, rubber, and maize are the leading products of the basically agricultural economy; they account for over 90 per cent of the total value of the country's exports. Most of the comparatively small-scale industries have been developed with Communist Chinese and Soviet aid. Government management and nationalization of the economy have grown considerably in recent years.

Increased exports and austerity measures since 1963 have helped Cambodia cope with the loss of U.S. aid, which amounted to nearly $400,000,000 between 1955 and 1963.

Cambodia has a 240-mile long, single-track railway. The highway system totals about 3,200 miles, about half of which is paved. The Mekong River is the key waterway in the complex system of inland water transportation. A new seaport, Sihanoukville, has eliminated dependence on transshipment of goods through South Vietnam.

**EDUCATION.** Some 723,000 students were attending various Cambodian schools in 1964. Attendance is not compulsory, and an estimated 67 per cent of the people over 15 years of age are illiterate. Higher education facilities center about the Buddhist University and four teacher-training colleges.

**ARMED FORCES.** Cambodia's army numbers about 24,350 men. In addition, there are about 1,300 in the air force, 1,200 in the navy, and 150 in the marine corps.

# CAMEROON

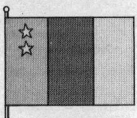

*Official Name:* Federal Republic of Cameroon. *Area:* 183,568 square miles. *Population:* 5,210,000. *Principal Cities* (with populations): Yaoundé, the capital, 98,-000; Douala, 200,000; Kumba, 40,000; Nkongsamba, 39,800; Garoua, 30,000; Victoria-Bota, 15,000; Buea, 3,000. *Flag:* A tricolor of green, red, and yellow vertical stripes with two yellow stars in upper part of green stripe. *Monetary Unit:* CFA franc (worth 0.4 U.S. cent). *Gross National Product:* $670,000,000 (1965). *Average Annual Income per Person:* $110.

**LAND AND PEOPLE.** Cameroon, on Africa's west coast, is bordered on the north and northeast by Chad; on the east by the Central African Republic; on the south by Congo (Brazzaville), Gabon, and Spanish Guinea (Río Muni); on the southwest by the Gulf of Guinea; and on the west by Nigeria. (See map on page 111.)

Southern Cameroon rises eastward from the coastal plains to a densely wooded plateau about 1,000 feet high. In the central interior region is the Adamaoua Plateau, from 2,500 to 4,500 feet above sea level. The two principal rivers are the Benoué and the Sanaga.

Cameroon, with about 150 different ethnic groups, is considered the ethnic crossroads of Africa. Among its people are Bantu, Bamiléké, Kirdi, Ewondo, Fulani, and Pygmies. More than half the people are tribal religionists, 29 per cent are Christians, and 14 per cent are Muslims. French is the principal language of East Cameroon; in West Cameroon the principal language is English.

**HISTORY.** Little is known about Cameroon's history prior to the 19th century. The Portuguese visited the area in the 15th century but made no permanent settlements. Between the 16th and 19th centuries the Cameroon coast was a regular source of supply for the slave trade carried on by Portuguese, Dutch, English, French, German, and later, U.S. interests.

European colonization began when the Germans established a protectorate in 1884. The Germans pushed into the interior, developing plantations and building roads, ports, and railways. Germany lost her protectorate to British and French troops during World War I. In the postwar settlement, the western sections were turned over to Britain; the remainder, about four-fifths of the total territory, was ceded to France. Each of the divided Cameroons was administered by its new government under a League of Nations mandate.

French Cameroon made substantial economic progress after the war, but France expanded the forced-labor system introduced by the Germans and restricted political liberties. The British Cameroons, administered by Britain through neighboring Nigeria, made some progress between the wars, mainly because German owners of plantations had been permitted to buy back their lands in 1924.

In 1946 French Cameroon became a U.N. trust territory and was given a voice in France's National Assembly. A local assembly was established, and political parties became active. The Cameroon People's Union (UPC) demanded reunification of the British and French regions and independence, but it was banned in 1955 after attempting an open revolt. The French Cameroon Assembly voted for full independence in 1957. France and the U.N. concurred, and the Republic of Cameroon came into being on January 1, 1960. Ahmadou Ahidjo was chosen as the first president.

Plebiscites were held in British Cameroons in 1961. The northern region chose to unite with Nigeria; the southern region elected to join with Cameroon, which then became the Federal Republic of Cameroon. The former British region became West Cameroon; the original, larger Republic of Cameroon became East Cameroon.

**GOVERNMENT AND POLITICS.** The federal republic has a president and vice president who are elected for five-year terms. National Assembly members serve five years. Major political parties are President Ahidjo's Cameroon Union and the Kamerun National Democratic Party of John Foncha, federal vice president and premier of West Cameroon. In 1966 the two parties merged as the Cameroon Union.

**ECONOMY.** Ninety per cent of the population is engaged in agriculture, most of which is subsistence farming or production for local markets. The main exports are bananas, cocoa, and coffee; Cameroon is among the world's leading cocoa producers.

Efforts are under way to diversify and improve production, and in recent years cotton, rubber, and oil palm products have been exported in increasing quantities. In addition, a number of small industries, principally to process agricultural products or manufacture items for local consumption, are being developed.

**EDUCATION.** Although education is not compulsory, 55 per cent of the children from 7 to 15 are in school; over 500 students attend the Federal University. The literacy rate is about 15 per cent of the population.

**ARMED FORCES.** Cameroon has a voluntary army of 2,700 men.

# CANADA

*Official Name:* Canada. *Area:* 3,851,809 square miles. *Population:* 20,014-880. *Principal Cities* (with populations): Ottawa, the capital, 290,741; Montreal, 1,222,255; Toronto, 664,584; Vancouver, 410,-375. *Flag:* A red maple leaf on a white field with red bars at each side. *Monetary Unit:* The Canadian dollar (worth U.S. $0.9245). *Gross National Product:* C$57,781,-000,000 (1966). *Average Annual Income per Person:* C$2,151.

LAND AND PEOPLE. The largest country in the Western Hemisphere, Canada is bordered on the north by the Arctic Ocean, on the northeast by Baffin Bay and Davis Strait, on the east by the Atlantic Ocean, on the south by the United States, and on the west by the Pacific Ocean and Alaska.

The land consists of many mountains, vast prairies, fertile lowlands, and Arctic wastes. There are many bays, lakes, rivers, and streams. The country is rich in natural resources, but much of the land is unpopulated and very cold most of the year. The plains areas vary in temperature from subzero lows in the winter to hot summer highs. Rainfall varies from 2.6 inches at Eureka in the Arctic to 107.6 inches at Estevan Point in British Columbia. Less than one-third of the land area is developed, and only about 8 per cent is under cultivation; some 19 per cent is forest land available for commercial exploitation.

By concentrating on the industrial development of natural resources, Canadians have earned a high standard of living. About 44 per cent of the people are of British origin, 30 per cent are of French extraction, and 25 per cent derive from other European groups. There are 220,121 native Indians and Eskimos. The principal religious groups are Anglicans (13 per cent), Roman Catholics (45 per cent), and members of the United Church of Canada (20 per cent).

HISTORY. The Vikings may have visited the northeast coast of North America, but the first recorded landing on what is now Canada was by John Cabot, an Italian-born explorer in the service of Henry VII of England. In 1524 Verrazano explored the coast, and in 1534 Jacques Cartier erected a cross at Gaspé and claimed the land for the King of France. A succession of further visits by British and French explorers was followed with settlements by the Frenchmen Champlain and de Monts at the St. Croix River in New Brunswick (1604) and Port Royal in Nova Scotia (1605). Quebec was founded in 1608. In 1610–11 Henry Hudson explored Hudson's Bay and James Bay, opening the way for the later fur trade of the Hudson's Bay Company chartered by Charles II.

The struggle between the English and French became intense after the British established their first settlement in Nova Scotia in 1623. Port Royal and Quebec were captured by Sir David Kirke in 1628 and 1629, respectively, but were returned to the French in 1632. The French gradually pushed westward in search of furs, following such explorers as Nicolet, La Salle, and Brébeuf. The French settlement in Acadia was captured by an expedition from New England in 1654 but was restored to the French in 1655. The colony of New France, centered on the St. Lawrence River, grew steadily and attained a population of more than 12,000 by 1692. By contrast Acadia at this date had barely 1,000 inhabitants. Newfoundland, with both French and English settlers engaged in the fishing industry, numbered about 4,000.

Warfare among the British and French colonies in North America culminated in the defeat of the French on the Plains of Abraham and the surrender of Quebec in 1759. New France was ceded to the British by the Treaty of Paris in 1763. The Quebec Act of 1774 provided for preservation of the French Canadian language, religion, and culture, and generated a Canadian loyalty to the British crown that lasted through the revolt of the American colonies in the 1770s.

After the American Revolution, British North America became a haven for Americans loyal to England. The Constitutional Act of 1791 created a division between Upper Canada (later Ontario) and Lower Canada (later Quebec), making a total of five colonial units with Nova Scotia, New Brunswick (separated from Nova Scotia in 1784), and Newfoundland. Ile St. Jean was renamed Prince Edward Island in 1798. The population of the colonies by 1800 was less than 500,000.

In the 19th century the British North American colonies took a succession of important steps toward nationhood. Westward expansion was marked by the establishment of the Red River Settlement in 1812 on land obtained from the Hudson's Bay Company. The War of 1812, by identifying the United States as a serious external threat, generated a sense of urgency and common purpose. New staple products such as grain and timber began to replace fur and fish in importance, and new methods of transport were introduced with the construction of canals in the 1820s and railways in the 1830s.

Rebellions in Upper and Lower Canada led to Lord Durham's report (1839) that set forth the principles of responsible government in the colonies, as well as the rationale for an association of free but related nations that later became the British Commonwealth. Upper and Lower Canada were united again in 1841 and a larger union was formed after mid-century.

Following conferences at Charlottetown and Quebec, the British North America Act of 1867 created the Dominion of Canada with the four provinces of Quebec, Ontario, Nova Scotia, and New Brunswick. The Hudson's Bay Company territories in the Northwest were surrendered to Canada in 1869. The province of Manitoba was established in 1870, British Columbia in 1871, Prince Edward Island in

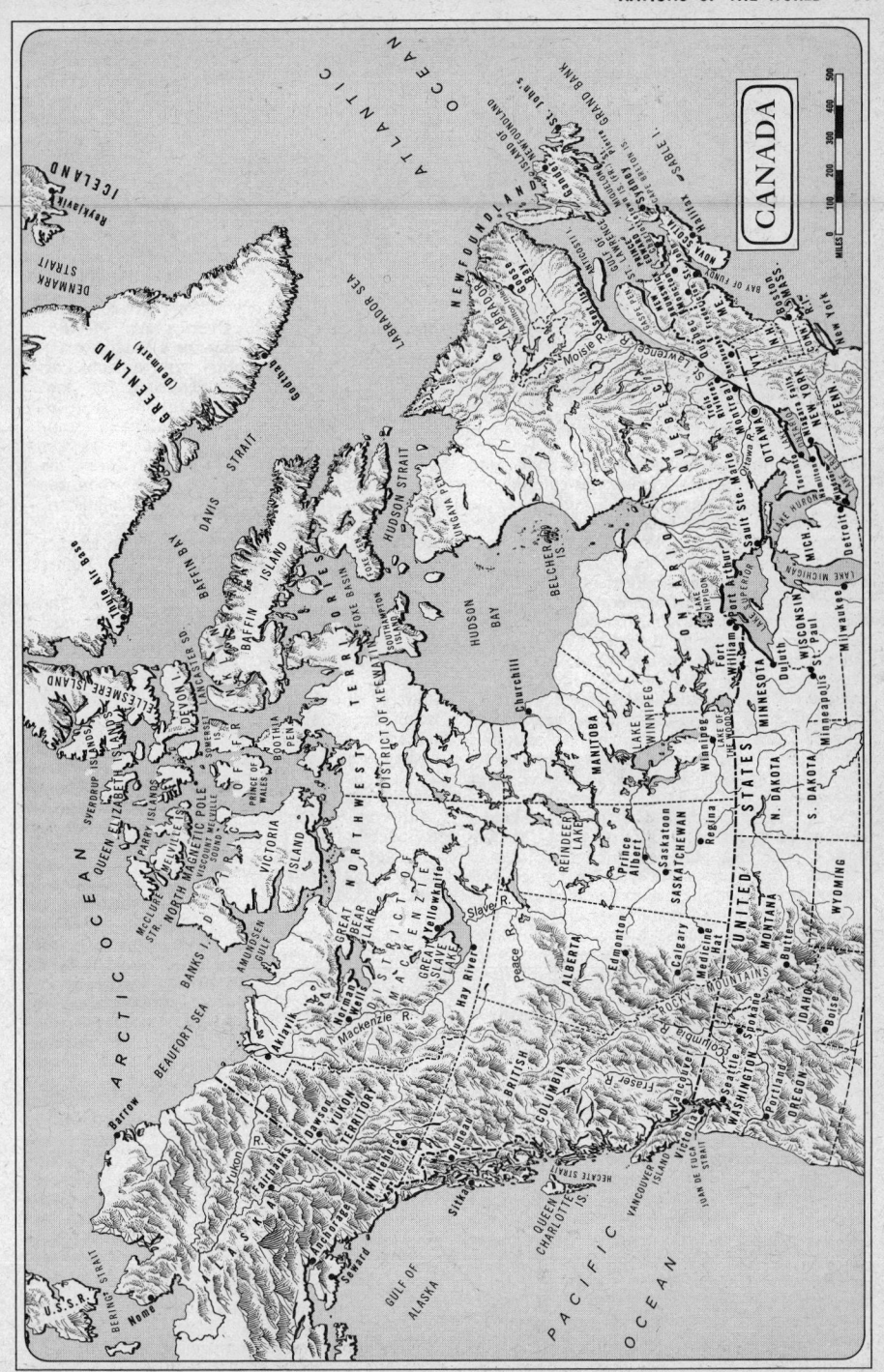

CANADA

Queen Elizabeth visited Ottawa on July 5, 1967.

1873, Alberta and Saskatchewan in 1905, and Newfoundland in 1949. Canada entered the 20th century with more than 5 million people and a railway system linking its coasts.

After Confederation the Canadian government recognized the need to develop all aspects of nationhood. Participation at the side of Britain in the Boer War and in World War I increased national consciousness and demonstrated forcibly the desirability of an independent foreign policy. The Statute of Westminster in 1931 established complete equality of the Canadian Parliament with that of the United Kingdom. Thereafter Canada moved quickly to develop an autonomous role in the world. Significantly, Canada declared war on Germany in 1939 a week after Britain.

Since World War II, Canada has taken a leading part in world affairs as a "middle power." She has played a significant role in postwar organizations such as the United Nations and NATO. She has maintained close relations with her two traditional allies, Britain and the United States, but has also maintained a measure of independence from both. In particular, Canada refused to participate in the Anglo-French invasion of Egypt in 1956 and has refrained from becoming involved with the United States in the Vietnam war.

The most controversial domestic issue in the 1960s has been interpretation of the federal-provincial relationship. Diversity in levels of economic achievement among geographic regions and ethnic groups has created sharp differences of view over such an important policy question as the sharing of tax revenues between the federal and provincial governments. A slow growth rate in the Maritime Provinces and rapid modernization in French Canada have helped to cause interprovincial tensions to mount.

While all responsible provincial leaders advocate preservation of the Canadian union, some sentiment has developed for creation of a separate French-Canadian nation. However, Canadian unity was strengthened in 1967 by means of the celebration of the 100th anniversary of Confederation and the presentation of a successful world's fair, Expo 67, in Montreal. (For information about Expo 67, see page 629.)

**GOVERNMENT AND POLITICS.** Canada is a federation of ten provinces—Newfoundland, Nova Scotia, Prince Edward Island, New Brunswick, Quebec, Ontario, Manitoba, Saskatchewan, Alberta, British Columbia—and two territories —Northwest Territories and Yukon Territory. Elizabeth II of Britain is both queen of Canada and head of the Commonwealth of Nations, of which Canada is a wholly self-governing member.

The Canadian Constitution, as contained in the British North America Act of 1867 with amendments, provides for a federal structure and for parliamentary government. This document has been supplemented by constitutional usages and conventions, such as the cabinet form of government. The governor general is appointed by the queen as her personal representative on the advice of the prime minister of Canada. Acting upon the recommendations of his responsible ministers, the governor general exercises executive functions in the queen's name. D. Roland Michener succeeded the late General Georges P. Vanier as governor general in April, 1967.

The Canadian Parliament consists of the Senate and the House of Commons. Bills must pass both houses and receive royal assent before becoming law. The Senate acts chiefly as a second chamber giving scrutiny to bills initiated in the House. This body has 102 members appointed by the governor general on advice from the prime minister for terms ending when members reach the age of 75. The House of Commons consists of 265 members elected for no more than five years. With rare exceptions, cabinet ministers are members of the House of Commons.

Lester Bowles Pearson, leader of the Liberal Party, was elected prime minister in April, 1963, and reelected in November, 1965. Party representation in the House following the general election of 1965 was as follows: Liberal, 131; Progressive Conservative, 97; New Democratic Party, 21; La Ralliement des Creditistes, 9; Social Credit, 5; and independents, 2. Political philosophy does not differ widely among the major political parties; the Progressive Conservative Party tends to be farthest to the right, and the New Democratic Party to the left.

Premier Robert Stanfield of Nova Scotia succeeded former Prime Minister John Diefenbaker as leader of the Progressive Conservatives in September, 1967.

**ECONOMY.** Canada has the natural resources and hydroelectric power necessary for large-scale industrial development, as well as the world's largest industrial nation as a neighbor to provide markets, investment capital, and technical knowledge. The economic growth rate has fluctuated since the Second World War but has reached a high level in the 1960s. The gross national product increased by 10.9 per cent in 1966.

The rapidly growing industrial sector has provided much of the impetus for economic development. Business spending on plant and equipment increased by 18 per cent in 1966, helping to make possible a 13 per cent gain in labor income. The agricultural sector also has been highly productive. Farm production from about 270 million acres of occupied land has brought near self-sufficiency in many products and increased exports of food grains, which are among the largest in the world. Accrued net income of farm operators from agricultural production totaled more than C$2 billion in 1966. High growth rates have generated certain strains within the economy, notably a rise of 4.6 per cent in the price level during 1966.

A topic of intense controversy in the early 1960s was nonresident ownership and control of domestic industry. In a few areas, such as railways and public utilities, foreign participation has declined during the 20th century. In the three crucial sectors of manufacturing, petroleum and natural gas, and mining and smelting, majority ownership and control have passed outside of Canada, mainly to the United States. Most Canadians recognize the substantial contribution made to their standard of living by investment from abroad, but some critics have expressed deep concern about a potential loss of national autonomy.

A Royal Commission on Taxation submitted a significant report in February, 1967, that may serve as the basis for a complete reform of the Canadian tax structure.

**EDUCATION AND HEALTH.** Over 90 per cent of the population is literate, and all children begin school at the age of 6, although the age of compulsory attendance varies from 13 to 16 in the various provinces. There are 370 institutions of higher learning, among which are the universities of Montreal, British Columbia, Toronto, New Brunswick, and McGill University in Montreal and Carleton University in Ottawa.

Canada has one of the lowest death rates in the world and excellent health facilities and services. The national medicare program will take effect in July 1968.

**ARMED FORCES.** Canada does not have compulsory military service. Unification of the armed forces was begun in 1964, and a universal uniform for all branches was introduced in June, 1967. The military services had 104,972 officers and men at the end of February, 1967.

## CENTRAL AFRICAN REPUBLIC

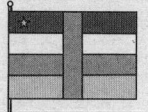

*Official Name:* Central African Republic. *Area:* 240,543 square miles. *Population:* 1,352,000. *Principal Cities* (with populations): Bangui, the capital, 111,266; Bouar, 20,700; Bossangoa, 16,000; Berbérati, 11,000. *Flag:* Four horizontal stripes—blue, white, green, and yellow—crossed by a vertical red stripe. There is a gold star in the upper left on the blue stripe. *Monetary Unit:* The CFA

franc (worth .004 U.S. cent). *Gross National Product:* $122,000,000 (1965). *Average Annual Income per Person:* $90.

**LAND AND PEOPLE.** The landlocked Central African Republic is one of the most remote and least developed regions of Africa. It stretches north to Chad, east to the Sudan, south to the two Congos, and west to Cameroon. (See map on page 111.) The terrain is chiefly rolling plateau, becoming tropical forest in the south and hilly savanna in the north. From October to June the weather is dry and hot; temperatures exceed 110° F. in the daytime and range from 55° to 70° F. at night. From June through September temperatures range from 75° to 110° F., and there are frequent tornadoes and floods. Rainfall is minimal throughout most of the country. The east and northeast are particularly dry, with average annual precipitation of less than ten inches.

The population consists chiefly of Banda, M'Baka, Zandé, and Mandjia-Baya tribesmen. A variety of African languages and dialects are spoken; Sangho serves as the common tongue in all parts of the country, and French is also spoken. About 36 per cent of the people are Muslim, and 9 per cent are Christian; the majority of the population are animists.

**HISTORY.** Little is known of the precolonial period. In 1889 the French established an outpost at Bangui and in 1894 constituted the area between the Ubangi and Shari rivers as a territory. Given administrative structure in 1900, the area was united with Chad in 1905 to form the Ubangi-Shari-Chad Colony. In 1910 the colony became part of French Equatorial Africa. Chad was detached from Ubangi-Shari in 1920.

The first Representative Assembly was created in 1945; a year later Ubangi-Shari began to send representatives to the French Parliament. The Framework Law of 1956 abolished the double electoral college (European and African) and established universal suffrage. The Central African Republic was proclaimed in 1958 as an autonomous state within the French Community. It attained full independence on August 31, 1960.

**GOVERNMENT AND POLITICS.** The president of the republic, Jean-Bedel Bokassa, assumed the office in a military coup d'etat on January 1, 1966. He formed a new cabinet of ten members and on January 4 dissolved the National Assembly. The country is divided into 11 regions, and local government is decentralized.

**ECONOMY.** The economy is almost exclusively agricultural, but the soil is poor and both livestock and people are plagued by tsetse flies. Access to the sea is difficult; the nearest port is nearly 900 miles from the country's border, and there are no railroads. Exports, chiefly coffee, cotton, and diamonds, are therefore unable to compete effectively in world markets and require French subsidization.

Between 1926 and 1930 cotton production was organized by four large commercial concessionaires. The abuses and brutality of the concessionary companies touched off a series of African rebellions between 1928 and 1946 that were suppressed by French troops. In 1946 forced labor was finally abolished.

A National Diamond Office was created in 1967 to organize the collection and foreign sales of diamonds, which represent 43 per cent of the export trade.

**EDUCATION AND HEALTH.** Education is free and school attendance begins at the age of seven. In 1964 there were some 123,000 students, 95 per cent at the primary level. Literacy is estimated at 7 per cent of the population.

In 1961 the republic had 37 physicians and three dentists. Mobile crews treat epidemic diseases, conduct research, and enforce local health regulations.

**ARMED FORCES.** Military service is not compulsory. The republic's armed forces total 500 men, plus 1,500 in the internal security forces.

# CEYLON

*Official Name:* Ceylon. *Area:* 25,332 square miles. *Population:* 11,232,000. *Principal Cities* (with populations): Colombo, the capital, 510,947; Jaffna, 94,248; Moratuwa, 77,632; Kandy, 67,768. *Flag:* A maroon rectangle with yellow finials in each corner, bearing a yellow sword-carrying lion; the rectangle and two stripes of green and orange to the left are bordered in yellow. *Monetary Unit:* The rupee of 100 cents (worth 21 U.S. cents). *Gross National Product:* $1,535,000,000 (1965); *Average Annual Income per Person:* $126.

**LAND AND PEOPLE.** Ceylon, a pear-shaped island off the Indian subcontinent, is bordered on the northeast and east by the Bay of Bengal, on the southeast, south, and southwest by the Indian Ocean, and on the west by the Gulf of Mannar. Its northwest coast is narrowly seperated from India's southeast coast by the shoals of Adam's Bridge and the shallow waters of Palk Strait. (See map on page 139.)

Plains sweep in a broad band from northern Ceylon around the island's coast, bordering the mountains and rugged plateaus in cental and southern Ceylon. The island's highest point is Pidurutalagal (8,291 feet), but most of Ceylon has altitudes of 1,000 feet or less. Rainfall, heaviest in the southwest plains and hills, averages about 90 inches annually.

Sinhalese constitute about 79 per cent of the population; Tamils, 13 per cent; Moors, 7 per cent; others, including Eurasians, Malays, Veddas, and Europeans, about 1 per cent. Sinhalese (the official language), Tamil, and English are spoken.

Some 64 per cent of the people are Buddhists; 20 per cent, Hindus; 9 per cent, Christians; and 7 per cent, Muslims. Deep differences between the predominantly Buddhist Sinhalese and the Hindu Tamil minority have resulted in political strife, riots, and campaigns of civil disobedience by the Tamils.

**HISTORY.** Ceylon was settled in the sixth century B.C. by Sinhalese from northern India. They conquered what were probably the island's most ancient settlers, the Veddas, who survive only as a small group living in the remote interior. In 483 B.C. Vijaya, an Indian prince, established the first Sinhalese kingdom. With the introduction of Buddhism in the third century B.C., Anuradhapura, the Sinhalese capital, became one of the major Buddhist centers of the world.

The early Sinhalese civilization slowly disintegrated as India's Tamils invaded Ceylon. Rajaraja I, ruler of the Tamil kingdom of Chola in southern India, extended his domain to Ceylon in the 11th century, but the Sinhalese soon regained power. In the middle of the 12th century, during the "Golden Age of Lanka," the Sinhalese under King Prakrama Bahu I ruled the whole island, but thereafter they retreated southward before the Tamil invaders.

Arab traders, ancestors of Ceylon's Muslim Moors, were attracted during the 12th and 13th centuries by the island's rich supplies of spices. The first Western occupiers were Portuguese conquerors who established control over part of the coastal area in 1505 and introduced Christianity. All the Sinhalese and Tamil kingdoms fell to the Portuguese except Kandy, which maintained its independence until the 19th century. In the 17th century the Dutch replaced the Portuguese as rulers. They in turn were forced out by the British in 1796.

Kandy, the last free kingdom, was overcome in 1815, and all of Ceylon came under British rule. Coffee, tea, and rubber cultivation were introduced by the British and flourished. Self-government developed by slow stages. In 1948 Ceylon achieved full independence, remaining a dominion in the British Commonwealth of Nations.

Don Stephen Senanayake, Ceylon's first prime minister, held office until his death; his son Dudley succeeded him in 1952. In elections held that year the United National Party (UNP) retained power, but was badly beaten in 1956 by the People's United Front (a coalition of Trotskyite and Buddhist parties) and the Sri Lanka Freedom Party (SLFP), whose leader, S. W. R. D. Bandaranaike, became prime minister. A socialist and "neutralist" of the Nehru pattern, he was assassinated in 1959 by a Buddhist monk. After a brief return to power by Senanayake, new elections in 1960 made Bandaranaike's widow, Sirimavo Bandaranaike, the world's first woman prime minister. During her period in office Sinhalese was declared Ceylon's official language.

The Bandaranaike administrations were marked by strife over Tamil demands for language parity and autonomy; a two-year state of national emergency; increased socialism, including nationalization of schools, the press, and some industries; strained relations with the United States and Britain; and closer ties with the Soviet Union and Communist China. Parliament was dissolved in 1964 when Mrs. Bandaranaike failed to win a vote of confidence.

In 1965 Senanayake returned as prime minister of a pro-Western UNP government, and a significant political and economic shift took place. In 1966 Parliament approved the use by Tamils of their own language in transacting official business.

**GOVERNMENT AND POLITICS.** Ceylon is a fully independent member of the Commonwealth of Nations. The British sovereign is represented by a governor general. The system of government is parliamentary; the prime minister heads a cabinet responsible to Parliament, which consists of a 30-member Senate and a 151-member House of Representatives. The UNP and the SLFP are the leading political parties.

**ECONOMY.** Tea, rubber, and coconut products account for over 90 per cent of total exports. Ceylon, second only to India in tea production, leads the world in tea exports. It is the world's fourth largest rubber producer. Because nearly half its food requirements (mainly rice) and most of its manufactured goods must be imported, an effort is being made to broaden the economy.

Ceylon's socialist policy has reduced foreign investment, but before 1956 and after 1965 the government tried to attract foreign capital. Economic development is slow. U.S. economic aid, suspended in 1963 when American oil properties were expropriated, was resumed in 1966 after settlement of the oil dispute.

There are 12,600 miles of roads which carry motor traffic. The state-owned railroad operates at a loss. Colombo's harbor is a leading Asian seaport. A Ceylonese air line and several international carriers serve the country.

**EDUCATION AND HEALTH.** Elementary schooling is compulsory, and education is free from kindergarten to university levels. There are four universities. The literacy rate is 68 per cent of persons 15 years of age and older.

The government's free health program is hampered by a shortage of hospital beds and of trained medical personnel.

**ARMED FORCES.** Military service is voluntary. The army numbers some 5,200 men; the navy and air force, 3,600.

# CHAD

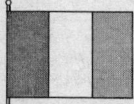

*Official Name:* Republic of Chad. *Area:* 495,000 square miles. *Population:* 3,361,-000. *Principal Cities* (with populations): Fort-Lamy, the capital, 100,000; Fort-Archambault, 30,000; Moundou, 25,000. *Flag:* Vertical blue, yellow, and red bars. *Monetary Unit:* CFA franc (worth 0.4 U.S. cent). *Gross National Product:* $237,000,000 (1966). *Average Annual Income per Person:* $70.

**LAND AND PEOPLE.** Chad is a landlocked country situated in north-central Africa. It is bordered on the north by Libya, on the east by Sudan, on the south by the Central African Republic and Cameroon, on the southwest by Nigeria, and on the west by Niger. (See map on page 111.)

The northern desert region of Chad, merging into the southern Sahara, is a dry, barren land relieved only by occasional oases, with a temperature range from 10° to 122° F. Chad's central area is semi-desert with some tropical trees and grazing land. The savanna country in the south has comparatively moderate temperatures, with a six-month dry season followed by heavy rainfall and frequent flooding. Its grasslands are suited for grazing.

Lake Chad, on the western border, is an outstanding topographic feature—a broad body of water surrounded by huge marshes that shrink toward the lake during the dry season. The lake's depth averages only 3 to 4 feet and some specialists believe that sand blowing from the Sahara is slowly drying it up. The major source of Lake Chad is the country's principal river, the Shari.

Chad has fewer than six persons per square mile. In the north several indigenous Negro tribes have slowly merged with the Arabs who invaded the country centuries ago. Among the Bantu tribes of the south, the largest is the Sara, inhabiting the southwestern valleys. Other tribes are the Fulani, Hausa, Wadai, Massa, and Baguirmi.

The official language is French; Arabic is also spoken. About 45 per cent of the population are Muslims, living in the north; in the south, 50 per cent follow tribal religions (animism), and almost 5 per cent are Christians.

**HISTORY.** In the eighth century peoples from the upper Nile built walled city-states on the eastern shores of Lake Chad. Within two centuries they were infiltrated by Saharan Berbers who forged these states into a centralized kingdom called Kanem, which embraced Islam in 1090. Kanem was later absorbed into the empire of Bornu in what is now Nigeria. Other Muslim states in Chad were Bagirmi, founded in the 16th century, and Waday.

British explorers first entered the area in 1822, but major exploration did not begin until 1853. The French pushed northward into Chad in the 1890s, killing Rabeh, a military adventurer who had devastated the Muslim states (1892–98), and creating the Military Territory of Chad in 1900.

In 1906 Chad was united with Ubangi-Shari (now the Central African Republic), and in 1910 it became a part of French Equatorial Africa. Chad was detached from Ubangi-Shari in 1920 and placed under a French civil administration. In 1958 it became an autonomous state in the French Community and in 1960 gained complete independence. François Tombalbaye was elected Chad's first president.

There are sharp cleavages between the Muslim, Arab-oriented North and the Christian-led but largely animist South. In March, 1963, President Tombalbaye, a Negro Christian, arrested and tried several high officials and former ministers, all Muslims; he alleged that they were fomenting subversion by provoking north against south and were plotting his assassination. Egyptian and Sudanese elements were accused at the trial of helping the plotters.

Nearly 400 people have been killed since late 1965 in disturbances near the Sudanese border. Relations with the Sudan have been strained since that time.

**GOVERNMENT AND POLITICS.** Chad is a republic with a president elected for a seven-year term by an electoral college comprising members of the assembly and local officials. The 85 members of the unicameral National Assembly are elected by universal suffrage for five-year terms.

The Parti Progressiste Tchadien (P.P.T.), headed by President Tombalbaye, has been the only party in Chad since 1962, when all opposition movements were outlawed. In January, 1967, at its first Congress meeting since 1963, the P.P.T. permitted a measure of self-criticism.

**ECONOMY.** Although 95 per cent of the population is engaged in agriculture and related areas, only 5 per cent of the land is under cultivation. Cotton accounts for 80 per cent of Chad's exports; livestock ranks second. Because the country is landlocked, the cost of production and shipment makes cotton unsalable at world prices. France buys it at artificially high prices.

To diversify its agriculture, a program of reclaiming land from Lake Chad has begun. The rich soil of the first 4,900 recovered acres produced 1,800 tons of wheat in the spring of 1966. Chad's Development Plan (1966–70) provides for total expenditures of $190 million.

**EDUCATION.** Education is not compulsory, and the illiteracy rate is estimated at 97 per cent. About 20 per cent of school-age children attend classes, almost all at the primary level.

**ARMED FORCES.** Chad's army totals only 400 men; a battalion of French troops is maintained at Fort-Lamy.

## CHILE

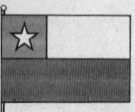

*Official Name:* Republic of Chile. *Area:* 292,256 square miles. *Population:* 8,588,-100. *Principal Cities* (with populations): Santiago, the capital, 2,459,400; Valparaíso, 290,900; Concepción, 174,400; Viña del Mar, 161,600; Talcahuano, 131,400; Antofogasta, 114,600. *Flag:* Horizontal stripes of white and red; in the white stripe is a blue square holding a five-pointed white star. *Monetary Unit:* the escudo of 100 centésimos (worth 21.1 U.S. cents). *Gross National Product:* $4,257,000,000 (1966). *Annual Average Income per Person:* $474.

**LAND AND PEOPLE.** Situated on the southwest coast of South America, the Republic of Chile is bordered on the north by Peru, on the east by Bolivia and Argentina, on the south by Drake Passage, and on the west by the Pacific Ocean. The country is a string-bean shaped strip of land extending from the southernmost tip of the continent 2,650 miles northward; it averages 110 miles in width, reaching 221 miles at its widest point. (See map on page 75.)

Chile, a land of dramatic contrasts, is hemmed by natural frontiers of desert, mountains, and ocean. Its white deserts in the north, especially the Atacama Desert, are among the driest regions in the world and are rich in nitrate, copper, and other mineral deposits. In the east are the immense Andes Mountains; Mount Aconcagua, on the border with Argentina, is 23,080 feet high—the loftiest peak in the western hemisphere. The Andes decrease in height as they run south to Chile's beautiful lake country. About 30 rivers drain into the Pacific from the Andes. To the west, a lower coastal range runs along the ocean.

A hilly central valley, about 600 miles long and 45 miles wide, is the center of Chile's agriculture and industry and the home of 90% of the population. It is a fertile area of vineyards and orchards. Chile's sparsely settled southern zone is mostly mountains, rocky islands, fjords and dense forests, boasting lakes as well as volcanoes and terminating in uninhabited glacial moraine. Much of Chile is subject to earthquakes, many of which have been disastrous.

The north of the country is hot, arid, and practically rainless. The central region enjoys a Mediterranean climate, rainy in winter and dry in summer, with temperatures ranging seasonally from 37° F. to 84° F. The southern region is rainy. Temperatures from north to south range from tropical heat to sub-Antarctic cold.

The population is about 68% mestizo, or mixed Spanish and Indian; 30% European; and 2% pure Indian. Some 84.6% of the people are Roman Catholics; 4.1% are Protestants; and the remainder are Jews, members of the Greek Orthodox Church, and free thinkers.

**HISTORY.** Led by Pedro de Valdivia, the Spanish conquistadores founded Santiago in 1541 and later established other settlements in the central region. During its colonial period, which was marked by savage Indian wars and internal dissension, Chile was essentially a rude and neglected land of pioneers. The governor was appointed by the king of Spain, but was immediately responsible to the viceroy of Peru.

In 1818, after a seven-year war against the Spanish forces, Chilean patriots led by Bernardo O'Higgins won the country's independence. The constitution of 1833, chiefly the work of Diego Portales, paved the way for parliamentary government and lasted until 1925 with few amendments. The years 1841 to 1861 were marked by political reform and material progress. In 1879 Chile won the "War of the Pacific" against Bolivia and Peru, acquiring the northern desert regions with their mineral wealth. The new prosperity brought increased reliance on foreign markets and unbalanced Chile's internal economy.

In 1891 a split in the Chilean aristocracy precipitated a civil war, culminating in the defeat and suicide of President José Manuel Balmaceda. For nearly 35 years thereafter, Congress was virtually omnipotent under a parliamentary regime.

In 1920, when unemployment and political unrest had brought Chile to the verge of revolution, Arturo Alessandri was elected president with the support of the working and middle classes. Ousted by a military coup in 1924, he was recalled in 1925. Alessandri introduced labor reforms and a new constitution strengthening the executive branch of the government. Conservative opposition led to his second ouster and to the military dictatorship of Colonel Carlos Ibáñez, which in turn collapsed in 1931. Following two years of disorder, Alessandri returned to the presidency in 1932 and restored the economy, though at the expense of civil liberties.

In 1938 a "Popular Front" of Democrats, Radicals, Socialists, and Communists carried Pedro Aguirre Cerda into the presidency. Various coalitions of the Center and Left parties held power to the end of the decade. Following a period of industrial progress after World War II, the country suffered serious economic and social maladjustments. The presidential election of 1964 was essentially a contest between the FRAP, a coalition of Socialists and Communists, and the Christian Democratic Party, both of which advocated revolutionary changes. Christian Democrat Eduardo Frei won an impressive victory, emphasizing a "Revolution in Freedom" by democratic rather than totalitarian means. Frei's policies have been moderately socialistic and nationalistic, aiming at greater independence in foreign affairs while maintaining friendly relations with the United States.

**GOVERNMENT AND POLITICS.** The president is popularly elected for a six-year term and cannot succeed himself. The National Congress consists of a Senate of 45 members and a Chamber of Deputies of 147, elected on a proportional basis for eight- and four-year terms, respectively. Suffrage is universal except for illiterates. The major political parties are the Conservatives and Liberals on the Right, united since 1966 as the National Party; the Socialist and Communist Parties on the Left, banded together as the Popular Action Front (FRAP); and the Radical Party and the Christian Democratic Party in the Center. The CDP holds an absolute majority in the Chamber of Deputies—the first party to do so in over 100 years—and despite declining popularity remains the strongest political group in Chile.

**ECONOMY.** As Chile ranks third in world production of copper and mining furnishes almost 80 per cent of her exports, the nation's economy is vulnerable to fluctuations in the international market. Food production and population are precariously balanced. Agriculture is hampered by a land tenure system, and of the 10 per cent of the land fit for cultivation, half lies fallow. Chile spends about one-sixth of her foreign currency on farm products necessary to meet increasing food demands. Insufficient domestic markets and inability to compete in foreign markets have caused industrialization to stagnate since 1946. As a result, Chile is pressing for the economic integration of Latin America.

In recent years Chile has exported about $450 million worth of goods annually and imported $600 million, relying on foreign loans to make up the difference. In 1965–66 there was a reversal of the growing trade imbalance, with an excess of $79 million in export earnings. Raging inflation has plagued Chile since

the last century, although the Frei government has slowed the rate considerably.

The Chilean railway system extends 5,500 miles, with connections to Peru, Bolivia, and Argentina. The 2,200-mile Pan American highway is the country's principal road, and there are two trans-Andine roads to Argentina. Valparaíso is the leading port, and the commercial fleet (over 300,000 tons) totals 102 ships. Air traffic increased from less than 10,000 passengers in 1940 to over 300,000 in 1960. The state-owned Línea Aérea Nacional (LAN) is both domestic and international.

**EDUCATION AND HEALTH.** Education is compulsory between the ages of 7 and 15; about 88 per cent of the population is literate, and this is one of the highest rates in South America. The University of Chile is considered among the best on the continent.

In recent years Chile has spent about 10 per cent of her annual budget on health services, and advancement of health standards has been substantial.

**ARMED FORCES.** Military service is compulsory for all men between the ages of 18 and 45. Recruits are trained for 12 months. Chile's army numbers 21,500 men; the navy 17,000; and the air force 7,210.

## TERRITORIES AND DEPENDENCIES OF CHILE

**EASTER ISLAND.** *Area:* 62.7 square miles. *Population:* 1,000. Easter Island, a volcanic island in the south Pacific about 2,350 miles west of Chile, is noted principally for its hieroglyphics and large monolithic stone heads carved from a soft volcanic stone.

The people are of Polynesian origin and raise yams, taro roots, bananas, potatoes, and sugarcane. The island is governed as a department of Valparaíso province.

**JUAN FERNÁNDEZ.** *Area:* Robinson Crusoe Island, 36 square miles; Alexander Selkirk Island, 21 square miles. *Population:* 900. Robinson Crusoe and Alexander Selkirk islands, about 100 miles apart, are the largest of several volcanic islands in the Juan Fernández group, which is located about 400 miles west of Valparaíso. The people engage in lobster fishing.

The islands are believed to have been discovered by a Spanish explorer, possibly before 1572. The English author Daniel Defoe is generally considered to have based his story of *Robinson Crusoe* on the four-year confinement on Más Atierra (the original name of Robinson Crusoe Island) of the Scottish sailor, Alexander Selkirk.

**CHILEAN ANTARCTIC TERRITORY.** *Area:* 482,625 square miles. *Population:* 200. Chile claimed the Palmer Peninsula section of Antarctica in 1940 and has established four bases there. Parts of the territory also are claimed by Britain and Argentina.

**DIEGO RAMÍREZ ISLANDS.** This group of uninhabited islands is situated 60 miles southwest of Cape Horn.

**SALA Y GOMEZ ISLAND, SAN AMBROSIO ISLAND, AND SAN FELIX ISLAND.** These are small, uninhabited Pacific Ocean possessions of Chile.

# CHINA

*Official Name:* People's Republic of China. *Area:* 3,-691,506 square miles. *Population:* 700,000,000. *Principal Cities* (with estimated populations): Peking, the capital, 4,000,000; Shanghai, 6,900,000; Tientsin, 3,200,000; Shenyang (Mukden), 2,500,-000; Chungking, 2,100,000; Wuhan, 2,100,000; Canton, 1,840,000. *Flag:* A red field with a gold star in the left-hand corner and four smaller gold stars forming an arc on its right. *Monetary Unit:* The yüan (worth 41 U.S. cents). *Gross National Product:* $70 billion (1965). *Average Annual Income per Person:* $100.

**LAND AND PEOPLE.** Mainland China, the world's most populous country and second in size only to the U.S.S.R., is bordered on the north by Mongolia and the U.S.S.R.; on the east by North Korea and the Yellow and East China seas; on the south by the South China Sea, North Vietnam, Laos, Burma, India, Bhutan, Sikkim, and Nepal; and from the southwest to the northwest by India, Pakistan, Afghanistan, and the U.S.S.R. (See map on page 93.) Hainan, China's largest island, is 15 miles off the South China Sea coast.

About a fifth of China, principally in the east, is a region of lowlands. The rest consists of great plateaus, plains, and massive mountains. Serving as natural boundaries are the mountain systems of the Altai in the northwest and the Himalayas in the southwest. The Tien Shan range separates the Tarim and the Dzungarian basins in the far west, while the Kunlun range branches eastward to form the northern border of the Tibetan plateau.

These mountain systems are the major watershed for the country's principal waterways. The mightiest of these is the Yangtze River, over 3,400 miles long, which drains more than 700,-000 square miles of central China. The second longest, the Yellow River, is the principal waterway of northern China, although the Amur on the northeastern border drains much of the Manchurian plain. Main rivers in the south are the Min, Pearl, and headwaters of the Mekong and the Red rivers.

Most of China's climate is temperate, although greatly affected by topography, Siberian air masses, and monsoons. The greatest seasonal extremes occur in northern Manchuria. Rain, falling primarily in the summer, is heavier toward the south. The diverse regions range from areas of tropical abundance to desolate deserts, and from dense coniferous forests to depleted woodlands converted to agriculture.

About 94 per cent of the people are Chinese. Principal ethnic minorities are the Chuang, Uigur, Hue, Yi, Tibetan, Miao, Mongol, Puyi, and Korean. Each group totals more than one million, with the Chuang numbering nearly 7 million.

The minorities are more important than numbers indicate because they inhabit key nuclear-testing regions, which are rich in natural resources, and strategic border areas. Also, these thinly populated areas add up to over half of China's total land area.

A mixture of Confucianism, Buddhism, and Taoism, though officially suppressed, is the religion of most Chinese. There are about 150 million Buddhists, 30 million Taoists, 10 million Muslims, 3 million Roman Catholics, and fewer than one million Protestants. The Chinese Catholics broke away from the Vatican in 1957.

**HISTORY.** The story of the Hsia, traditionally China's first dynasty, is largely legendary, for the recording of history began only during the subsequent Shang dynasty (about 1766–1123 B.C.). The Chou dynasty (about 1122–256 B.C.) ruled during a classical era that produced the philosophers Confucius and Lao-tze as well as material progress and invention. Near the end of its reign it experienced destructive political turmoil.

Before coming to power, the Ch'in dynasty (221–207 B.C.) had already unified the country. It gave China its name and its first emperor, ended feudalism, and centralized the government. Roads, canals, and much of the Great Wall were constructed then. The native Han dynasty (206 B.C.–220 A.D.) was noted for its artistic achievements and territorial expansion.

The Period of the Six Dynasties (220–589) was also one of scientific and cultural advance and of growing Buddhist and Taoist influence. It was, however, marked by internal warfare and invasions by the barbaric Huns and the Turks. Central control dwindled and feudalism re-emerged under the Tsin dynasty.

During the next two dynasties (the Sui, 589–618, and the T'and, 618–907), a brilliant era emerged. The empire was consolidated, good communications and administration evolved, and poetry and sculpture were outstanding. In the T'ang dynasty's later years border control was lost, revolts erupted, and corruption became widespread.

The years from 907 to 960 during the Five Dynasties were ones of great disorder and corruption. Under the Sung dynasty (960–1279) gunpowder for military use, printing, the magnetic compass, and a new literary form, the novel, were developed. Again, however, the north was invaded, and barbarian empires were formed there. The Mongols, under the brilliant, ruthless Genghis Khan, subsequently conquered them and by 1215 had taken North China. Within nine years he had expanded his conquest westward to encompass one of the largest land empires ever ruled by one man.

Genghis' grandson, Kublai Khan, founded the Yüan dynasty and completed the conquest of the Sung. The most noted European traveler of the time to reach the Mongol capital, Cambuluc (present-day Peking), was Marco Polo.

The unpopular Mongols were ousted by the native Ming dynasty in 1368. Art, architecture, and writing continued to flourish, and the empire, at its peak, stretched from Burma to Korea. In the dynasty's early years naval expeditions engaged in conquest and trade, but China soon reverted to the policy of restricting its ships to coastal waters.

European penetration of China began in the early 16th century, and in 1557 the Portuguese established a colony at Macao. The Manchus, meanwhile, were advancing from the north, and they took Peking in 1644. Their dynasty, the Ch'ing, ruled until 1912.

The Manchus adopted Chinese culture and gave China its greatest territorial expansion, but contributed little else. China's vast riches increasingly lured Europe's maritime traders; however, efforts (particularly by Britain) to further liberalize trade relations failed. China refused to import opium, although the drug was brought in with the connivance of corrupt officials. Disputes over this and other issues precipitated the first Opium War (1839–42).

Untouched by an industrial revolution, China was no match for foreign expansionism. In the 19th century she suffered a series of military and political humiliations at the hands of the West. She was forced to open five ports to British trade and residence and to cede Hong Kong.

When, as a result of the second Opium War (1856–60), the British and French joined forces, treaty ports were opened from the Yangtze north to Manchuria. By the end of the century the Ch'ing dynasty was undermined by internal strife and external intervention, including the first Sino-Japanese War (1894–95). China was carved into spheres of foreign influence. The Boxer Rebellion of 1900 marked a desperate popular attempt to eliminate foreign domination.

The "Open Door" policy proposed in 1900 by the United States—all nations were to have equal trade rights in the treaty ports, regardless of their sphere of influence, and China's territorial and administrative integrity was to be guaranteed—was often flouted.

In 1911 a republican revolution planned by Dr. Sun Yat-sen succeeded in forcing the emperor to abdicate. Sun was named provisional president, but resigned soon afterward. His successor's dictatorial rule brought about another revolt led by Sun in 1913. It failed and Sun was exiled.

During World War I Japan increased its demands on China. The reactions of Chinese youth and intellectuals to the repeated humiliations culminated in the May Fourth Movement (1919), which opened a new stage in the rise of Chinese nationalism.

Sun, who had created his Kuomintang Party out of the earlier Revolutionary Alliance, returned to China in 1917. Civil war began between the Kuomintang, centered in the south, and the national government and its war lords in the north. In 1921 the Chinese Communist Party was founded. Sun, now president of a self-proclaimed national government, cooperated with the party and sought aid from the U.S.S.R. Sun died in 1925, but the Kuomintang army went on under Chiang Kai-shek, one of Sun's chief aides, to defeat the central and northern warlords.

Civil war again erupted in 1927 when Chiang ended cooperation with the Communists and executed many of their leaders. Initial victories went to Chiang, and in 1928 his government received foreign recognition. He continued to press the Communists and forced them into the 6,000-mile Long March to the northwest, where they settled in Shensi province in 1935. Many leaders of today's Communist regime are veterans of that march.

Taking advantage of the chaos, Japan occupied Manchuria in 1931 and declared a puppet state there. A shaky truce was reached between Chiang and the Communists in 1937, when Japan extended its hostilities into a full-scale war.

World War II brought Allied aid to Chiang, but peace within the country was as remote as before. Efforts to mediate were futile, and civil war resumed. The Nationalists received U.S. support and supplies, but by 1949 Communist control was so extensive that the Chiang government and supporters fled to the island of Taiwan, their only remaining possession.

The People's Republic was declared by the Communists in September, 1949, and soon won diplomatic recognition from many foreign governments. In 1950 China openly intervened in the Korean War on the side of the North Koreans, and also overran Tibet. In 1962 China engaged in an undeclared border war with India. China also has been sending material aid to North Vietnam and the Vietcong guerrillas in South Vietnam.

**GOVERNMENT AND POLITICS.** Communist China's government is built on a pyramidal structure. The one-house National People's Congress is constitutionally the highest state organ and the sole legislative body. Its deputies (3,040 in the 1964 elections) are elected for four years from provinces, autonomous regions and municipalities, the armed forces, and Chinese residents abroad. Constitutionally required to meet at least once a year, the congress in fact last met in 1958.

A Standing Committee elected by the congress has broad legislative and supervisory powers that include conducting elections and convening the congress. It consists of a chairman, a secretary-general, 18 vice-chairmen, and 96 members.

Also elected by the congress is one national executive, the Chairman of the People's Republic (Liu Shao-chi, since 1959). He has broad appointive powers, commands the armed forces, and presides over the National Defense Council and the Supreme State Conference. (Liu has been vilified by the regime as anti-Maoist, but he has not lost his post, although it is unlikely that he can exercise power.)

The Central Committee, too, is elected by the Congress. It consists of 91 full members and 89 alternates. Its chairman is Mao Tse-tung. This committee in turn elects a Politburo and a Secretariat.

The Politburo, consisting of 17 full and 6 alternate members, makes policy. The Secretariat (10 full and 3 alternate members) is its executive arm.

The most important body of this Central Committee, and perhaps of the nation, is the Standing Committee of the Politburo. Its membership now includes the Chairman of the Central Committee, Mao Tse-tung; Liu Shao-chi, Chairman of the People's Republic; Premier Chou En-lai; Chu Teh, Chairman of the Congress Standing Committee; Lin Piao, Deputy Premier and Minister of Defense; and Teng Hsiao-ping, Deputy Premier and General Secretary of the Party.

The State Council (or cabinet), headed by Premier Chou En-lai and composed of a secretary-general and 15 vice-premiers, is the center of day-to-day government of this vast and complex nation.

There are numerous governmental agencies that administrate departments such as finance, education, agriculture, and so on. A number of quasi-governmental agencies administer specialized institutions such as the People's Bank of China and the Academy of Sciences. Complementing these agencies are many "public bodies" organized for any sort of interest—a writers' federation, a women's federation, and so on.

The Communist Party maintains control of this organizational maze in three fashions: firstly, party committees, established at all administrative levels, issue policy orders and often share in the administration; secondly, a watchdog group, responsible to a party committee, is in every organization; and thirdly, officers of the organizations are either party people or closely supervised by a party adviser.

The socio-political campaigns that lend direction and spiritual aura to the movement are conducted through these many organizations, public meetings, and the extensive use of mass media.

The rural "class enemy" was destroyed in the land reform of 1949–53 that made political allies of those who benefited from expropriation of the land.

China's "Great Proletarian Cultural Revolution," begun in 1966, has convulsed the nation. It is generally described as an attempt by Mao to regain full power and to reverse the trend toward "revisionist" Communism. It is essentially a rebellion against the party establishment and its leader, Chairman of the Republic Liu Shao-chi.

The technique of the revolutionists is to establish "rebel" groups within the multiple existing organizations. Maoist groups in the schools, called the Red Guards, have become the driving force behind the rebellion. In the background, but of great importance, is the People's Liberation Army (PLA). For having indoctrinated the PLA with Maoism, Minister of Defense Lin Piao has risen to prominence as the heir apparent of Mao, displacing Liu Shao-chi.

The "rebel" and Red Guard groups were intended to form alliances with the PLA to establish provisional organs of power called Revolutionary Committees. However, as of August, 1967, such committees as were recognized by Mao had taken power in only four of China's 26 provincial areas and in the metropolitan areas of Peking and Shanghai.

The Red Guards were at first used as shock troops for the revolution. Later, the PLA was called into action, but on occasion was found to be of dubious loyalty to Mao. Armed clashes and rioting in many areas, including those nominally under revolutionary committees, indicate that the revolution may be in danger of collapse.

Chances for success of the Maoists rest upon many factors. The absurdity of applying dialectics to all aspects of society offers a poor alternative to responsible statesmanship within China and abroad. For the individual, Mao gives little more than the promise of unremitting austerity in life and thought. His demands for collective ideology seem to aim at a depersonalized "new man," devoid of intellectualism. The "Cultural Revolution" is directed by a small group that includes few men of eminence, and it has no reliable organized support other than Red Guards and the "rebels."

In Mao's favor is his value as a symbol to the people and his control of mass communications. Also, the radicalism of the revolution may be an attraction for nationalistic Chinese imbued with idealistic fervor. Lastly, the PLA has, on the whole, been an asset for the Maoists.

**ECONOMY.** Centralized economic planning was introduced gradually in China after the revolution of 1949. The First Five Year Plan (1953–57) was carried out with notable success. By 1956 the collectivization of agriculture was complete and industry was either nationalized or forced into partnership with the state.

The Second Five Year Plan (1958–62) was sidetracked by the rural commune movement and by a Maoist campaign called the "Great Leap Forward." In 1958 the rural collectives were merged into much larger communes in which private incentives were virtually abolished. Local governmental functions were incorporated in these communal units, thereby approaching the basic-level social organization envisaged by Mao Tse-tung.

Strenuous peasant opposition and natural disasters created a serious economic setback. By 1964 the communes had been redivided into nearly three times the number of the previous collectives. Some private plots and incentives had been restored, and community control was somewhat decentralized.

The "Great Leap Forward" attempted to accelerate the economy through development of a vast number of small enterprises, substituting human effort and traditional techniques for the materials and technical knowledge that China largely lacks. The wholesale withdrawal of Soviet technical assistance in 1960 further aggravated the economic crisis, which continued through 1962.

The two economic plans concentrated on the development of heavy industry to the neglect of agriculture. However, by 1957 nearly 40 per cent of the net domestic product was still derived from farming, with almost 80 per cent of the people employed in it. The agricultural sector suffers from overpopulation. The cultivated acreage per capita is only 0.38. During 1962–65 more emphasis was placed on agri-

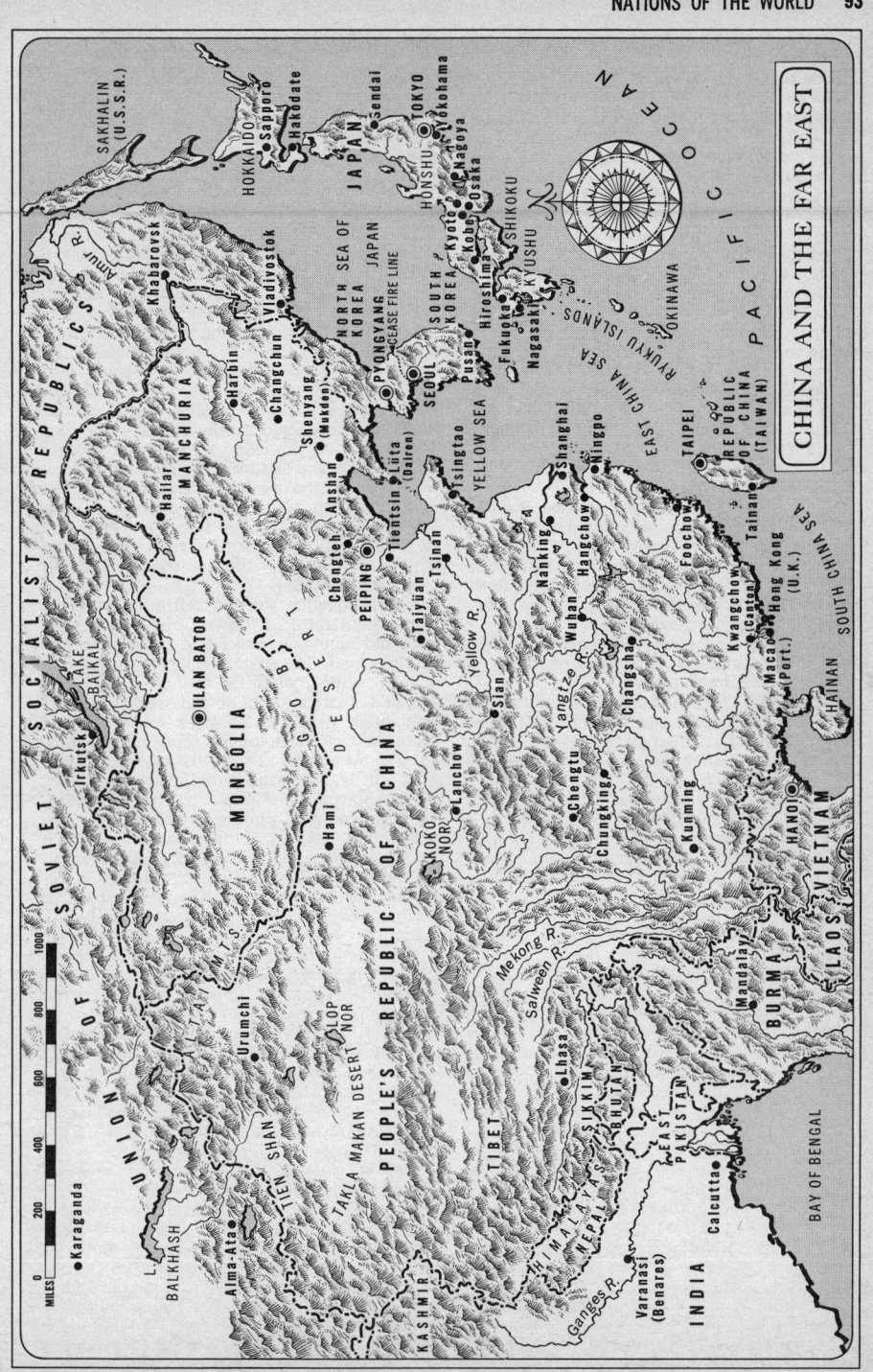

CHINA AND THE FAR EAST

PACIFIC OCEAN

SAKHALIN (U.S.S.R.)

HOKKAIDO
Sapporo
Hakodate
JAPAN
Sendai
TOKYO
Yokohama
HONSHU
Nagoya
Kyoto
Osaka
Kobe
SHIKOKU
Hiroshima
Fukuoka
KYUSHU
Nagasaki

NORTH SEA OF JAPAN
NORTH KOREA
PYONGYANG
CEASE FIRE LINE
SOUTH KOREA
SEOUL
Pusan

RYUKYU ISLANDS
OKINAWA

Amur R.
Khabarovsk
Vladivostok
Changchun
Harbin
MANCHURIA
Hailar
Shenyang (Mukden)
Anshan
Chengteh
PEIPING
Tientsin
Luta (Dairen)
Tsingtao
YELLOW SEA
Tsinan
Taiyuan
Yellow R.
Sian
Lanchow

EAST CHINA SEA
Shanghai
Ningpo
Hangchow
Nanking
Wuhan
Changsha
Foochow
TAIPEI
REPUBLIC OF CHINA (TAIWAN)
Tainan

SOVIET SOCIALIST REPUBLICS

UNION OF SOVIET

Irkutsk
LAKE BAIKAL

ULAN BATOR
MONGOLIA

GOBI DESERT

Hami
KOKO NOR
LOP NOR
Urumchi
ALTAI MTS.
TIEN SHAN
TAKLA MAKAN DESERT

PEOPLE'S REPUBLIC OF CHINA

Chengtu
Chungking
Kunming
Kwangchow (Canton)
Hong Kong (U.K.)
Macao (Port.)
HAINAN
SOUTH CHINA SEA

Karaganda
BALKHASH
L. BALKHASH
Alma-Ata

KASHMIR
TIBET
Lhasa
SIKKIM
BHUTAN
NEPAL
HIMALAYA
EAST PAKISTAN
Calcutta
Varanasi (Benares)
Ganges R.
INDIA
BAY OF BENGAL

Mekong R.
Salween R.
Mandalay
BURMA
LAOS
VIETNAM
HANOI

MILES
0  200  400  600  800  1000

culture and related industry, such as chemical fertilizers.

Industry is handicapped by the small per capita income, the ensuing low rate of voluntary savings, and technological backwardness. The state has tried to increase the rate of investment through forced saving and consumption control, and to improve technology through organized research and the development of industrial designs.

In 1966 China produced about 180 million metric tons of food grains (including potatoes), which was barely comparable to or below the 1957 level. The principal cereals are rice and wheat. Since 1961 China's annual grain imports, mostly wheat, have averaged six million metric tons. Cotton is the principal fiber crop.

China is high in coal and iron-ore reserves. Crude oil production has been sufficient to meet domestic demands since 1965. Steel production totals about 13.2 million tons annually.

In 1966 Chinese imports were estimated as $1.9 billion, while her total exports were about $2.3 billion. The bulk of this trade has been conducted with Free World countries. Prior to 1960 the Soviet Union accounted for 50 per cent of China's trade, and other Communist countries for another 25 per cent. Since then China has reduced her economic dependence on the U.S.S.R. and by 1964 had repaid her indebtedness to the Soviets.

Since 1949 many new industries have been introduced into China. A number of major industrial centers have sprung up.

**EDUCATION.** The "Cultural Revolution" of 1966 brought education to a standstill. Classes were suspended in order to reshape the structure and content of the system, and to free Red Guard students for revolutionary activity. Early in 1967 the schools were ordered to reopen, but students responded poorly.

Political indoctrination is the goal of all Chinese education, with minor attention paid to science. Indications are that professionalism and competence will be sacrificed for the sake of Communist ideology, with a shortened period of education and work programs combined with schooling.

**ARMED FORCES.** China's regular armed force, the People's Liberation Army (PLA), totals about 2.5 million. An estimated 1.3 million serve in the infantry, 150,000–175,000 in the air force, about 135,000 in the navy, and others in special units and supporting services.

There is also an elite Public Security Force of 300,000 officers and men, and a People's Militia of some 60–100 million men.

In addition to military functions, the PLA is important in production and construction activities, such as building railroads. The PLA also has been held up as a model for the new Chinese society, in that it attempts to create the selfless man and to eliminate class distinctions. In May, 1965, military ranks and distinctions in uniforms were abolished.

The Chinese started an intensive nuclear-weapons program in 1957 and exploded their first atomic bomb in October, 1964. A hydrogen bomb was tested in June, 1967.

# CHINA, REPUBLIC OF

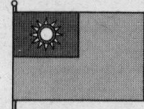

*Official Name:* Republic of China. *Area:* 13,885 square miles. *Population:* 13 million. *Principal Cities* (with populations): Taipei, the capital, 1,135,500; Kaohsiung, 596,092; Tainan, 399,820; Taichung, 364,262. *Flag:* A red field bearing a blue rectangle, upper left, that contains a 12-pointed white sun. *Monetary Unit:* The New Taiwan dollar (worth 2.5 U.S. cents). *Gross National Product:* $3,112,225,000 (1966). *Average Annual Income per Person:* $189.

**LAND AND PEOPLE.** Taiwan, present home of the Republic of China, is an island about 100 miles from the south-China mainland. (See map on page 93.) It measures some 240 miles, north to south, and 85 miles at its greatest width. It is bordered on the north by the East China Sea; on the east by the Pacific Ocean; on the south and southwest by the South China Sea; and on the west by Taiwan Strait. The Pescadores, an island group belonging to Taiwan, lie about 25 miles from the southwest coast. Matsu and Quemoy, two small island groups controlled by the Republic, are just off the mainland coast.

Coastal plains, running north to south in the western third of Taiwan, rise to the foothills and mountain range that occupy the rest of the island. The eastern slope is rugged and sparsely settled, while the western slope is fertile and contains one of the world's highest population densities. Taiwan's rivers all flow from the central mountains, but only the Tanshui, flowing past Taipei, is navigable. Surrounded by water and lying in a monsoon region, subtropical Taiwan has damp, warm summers and mild winters. Crops can be grown year-round except in the colder mountain heights, where snow occasionally falls. Rainfall averages from 50 to 250 inches annually, depending on the region. The island is subject to Pacific typhoons during the summer and early fall.

Taiwanese (descendants of earlier immigrants, chiefly from southeast China) constitute 80 per cent of the population; mainland Chinese (post-World War II refugees and their families), 18 per cent; and aborigines, 2 per cent. Mandarin Chinese is the official language; southern Chinese dialects, including Amoy, Swatow, and Hakka, are also spoken. About 92 per cent of the population is Buddhist, 3 per cent Muslim, 2.2 per cent Roman Catholic, and 2 per cent Protestant.

**HISTORY.** Chinese immigration to Taiwan began as early as the T'ang dynasty (618–907). Heavier migration, beginning in the 17th century, forced the aboriginal inhabitants away from the western plains. The Portuguese (who called the island Formosa, or beautiful), Spanish, and Dutch established commercial interests in the same century. The Dutch built forts on Taiwan between 1624 and 1661 but were driven out by Cheng Ch'eng-kung (Koxinga) in 1662. Migration from the mainland continued, and after the Manchu conquest of the island in 1683, Taiwan was administered as part of China until 1895, when it was ceded to Japan at the end of the Sino-Japanese War. When Japan took over, the islanders declared independence and established a republic. They were able to put up only several months' opposition to the Japanese, but political uprisings continued for decades. The Japanese administration modernized Taiwan's economy and improved transportation but made no effort to colonize the island, using it chiefly to supply food for Japan. After 1937 the Japanese began to build industrial plants, but these were mostly destroyed or heavily damaged by Allied bombing raids during the course of World War II.

The Japanese surrendered Taiwan to the Republic of China in 1945. In 1949 the advancing Communist forces of Mao Tse-tung forced President Chiang Kai-shek's Nationalist government and his remaining armies to flee from the mainland to Taiwan. Communist China's plans to invade the island were blocked in 1950 when President Harry S. Truman sent the U.S. Seventh Fleet to patrol Taiwan Strait. The U.S. Navy screen between the two Chinas was lifted in 1953, but Communist attacks on Nationalist-held offshore islands brought a signed agreement from the United States in 1955 that it would defend Taiwan and the Pescadores.

The U.S. government has emphasized that it did not intend to build up Chiang's armies for an invasion of the People's Republic and has advised Peking that it would not support any Nationalist attempt to land forces on the mainland. Chiang, nonetheless, has been steadfast in his avowal to return and rid China of the Communists, and Taiwan remains a springboard for guerrilla forays on the mainland.

Although Japan renounced all claims to Taiwan in 1951, the island's legal status has become a contentious point in world politics. Strong United States backing and Communist China's continuing aggression have been the main factors enabling Nationalist China to hold its seat in the United Nations. Attempts have been made to give the seat to the vastly more populous People's Republic, or at least to allow both Chinas to be represented. The latter policy has always been sharply rejected by Peking.

**GOVERNMENT AND POLITICS.** In late 1946 an elected National Assembly, boycotted by its Communist members, met in Nanking to draft a new constitution for the Republic of China; it was promulgated on January 1, 1947. The assembly gave President Chiang Kai-shek extraordinary powers to be held until the Communist Revolution ended. It reconvened on Taiwan in 1954, re-elected Chiang, and extended the powers granted him earlier. Chiang was elected to his fourth six-year term in 1966 and was granted extraordinary new powers "to meet the needs during the period of [mainland] Communist rebellion."

The legislative Yuan is the Republic's top law-making body, and tenure of its members has been extended indefinitely pending the "return to the mainland." The Nationalist government is largely controlled by officials who came from the mainland in 1949. The Kuomintang is the government party, and Chiang is its director general. Other political groups are the Young China Party and the China Democratic Socialist Party.

**ECONOMY.** The economic growth rate of Taiwan has been one of the highest in the world as the result of large-scale U.S. aid beginning in 1953. The gross national product (GNP) doubled between 1954 and 1964 and grew another 10 per cent in 1965, the year when direct U.S. aid was terminated. The economy continues to grow at about the same 7 per cent annual rate that it has maintained over the last 15 years.

Industrial production is increasing at about 15 per cent per annum and in 1963 for the first time surpassed agriculture in its contribution to the GNP. The more important industries include food processing, chemicals, textiles, electronics equipment, plywood, cement, glass, and plastics.

Foreign trade has more than tripled since 1955, and foreign investment, including overseas Chinese money, continues to be attracted. Exports and imports are balanced at more than half a billion dollars each. Textiles, chemicals, lumber products, bananas, canned pineapple, sugar, rice, and tea are the chief exports. Imports include tools, ores, metals, manufactures, and raw materials.

As a result of the ten-year land reform program instituted in 1953, 85 per cent of the farmers own the land they cultivate. Although only 25 per cent of Taiwan is suitable for cultivation, most of the people are engaged in agriculture that is more intensive than in any other country except Japan. Rice and sugar are the two most important crops. About 60 per cent of the land is forested, and there are great timber reserves. Taiwan is the world's largest producer of natural camphor.

Some 300 miles of state-owned railroads connect most towns on the island. There are no east-west rail connections, but two cross-island highways have been built. Highways on Taiwan total some 10,000 miles. Intracoastal shipping is important, and the leading ports are Keelung in the north and Kaohsiung in the southwest. The country is served by several airlines.

**EDUCATION AND HEALTH.** Primary education is free and compulsory for children from ages 6 to 12. There are 44 national, provincial, and private universities, colleges, and research institutes. Literacy is estimated at 77 per cent.

Since World War II progress has been made in controlling Taiwan's most serious and prevalent diseases. Purity of drinking water and sanitation are serious problems, but the government has embarked on an islandwide program to improve conditions. There are 8,224 registered physicians in 1965.

**ARMED FORCES.** Conscription is universal, and most men serve two years sometime after the age of 18. There are 400,000 men in the army, 80,000 in the air force, 70,000 in the combined service force, and 50,000 in the navy.

## COLOMBIA

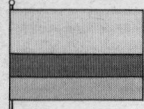

*Official Name:* Republic of Colombia. *Area:* 455,335 square miles. *Population:* 18,068,000. *Principal Cities* (with populations): Bogotá, the capital, 1,697,311; Medellín, 772,887; Cali, 637,929; Barranquilla, 498,301. *Flag:* A tricolor of yellow, blue, and red. *Monetary Unit:* Peso (worth 6.2 U.S. cents). *Gross National Product:* $3,495,000,000 (1966). *Average Annual Income per Person:* $261.

**LAND AND PEOPLE.** Colombia is situated in northwest South America and has coastlines on the Caribbean to the north and the Pacific to the west. Called the "Gateway to South America," the country is bordered on the northwest by Panama, on the northeast by Venezuela, on the southeast by Brazil, and on the south and southwest by Peru and Ecuador. (See map on page 75.)

Just above the Colombia-Ecuador border the Andes Mountains split into three chains. The eastern cordillera forks into two branches as it runs northeastward. The central and western cordilleras roughly parallel the Pacific and run north to the Caribbean lowlands.

Colombia has two major rivers: the Magdalena, which divides the central and eastern cordilleras, and its tributary, the Cauca, which flows between the central and western cordilleras. The rivers converge in the north and empty into the Caribbean.

The climate in Colombia varies with the altitude. In the tropical section (*tierra caliente*), starting at the coast and rising to about 3,400 feet, the temperature averages around 80° F. In the temperate zone (*tierra templada*), from 3,400 to 6,800 feet, the temperature ranges from 63° to 75° F. In the cold country (*tierra fría*), from 6,800 to 10,000 feet, the temperature varies from a high of 60° to a low of 5° F.; above 10,000 feet, the temperature runs from about 55° F. to below zero.

Approximately 58 per cent of Colombia's people are mestizos (of Spanish-Indian ancestry); about 20 per cent are European. There are smaller groups of mulattoes, Negroes, zambos (Indian-Negro), and pure Indians. Roman Catholicism, the national religion, is the faith of about 90 per cent of the people. The language of the country is Spanish.

Colombia is of considerable strategic and political importance to the United States for two reasons: its proximity to the Canal Zone, and the fact that one of four possible routes for the proposed sea-level Atlantic-Pacific Canal would go through the country.

**HISTORY.** When the Spanish explorers came to Colombia in 1499, they found many native tribes, some gold and jewels, but no civilization comparable to that of the Incas, Mayas, or Aztecs. Permanent colonization was begun on the isthmus after 1514, and the settlements at Santa Marta and Cartagena, established between 1525 and 1533, secured Spain's hold on the Colombian coast.

The most noteworthy conqueror-explorer of the period was Gonzalo Jiménez de Quesada, who in 1538 founded Santa Fé de Bogotá (known today as Bogotá) on a high plateau in the Andes. The surrounding region, which was called New Granada, included portions of present-day Panama, Venezuela, Ecuador, and most of Colombia.

New Granada continued as part of Spain's colonial empire until Simón Bolívar decisively defeated the royalists in 1819. He became president of the new republic of Gran Colombia, which included Colombia, Ecuador, Panama, and Venezuela. By 1830, however, Venezuela and Ecuador had declared themselves separate states, and the remaining territory of Gran Colombia became the republic of New Granada. In 1886 the region was given its present name.

Two political parties developed, almost equal in strength: the Conservatives, who stood for a strongly centralized government and close ties between the state and the Roman Catholic Church; and the Liberals, who favored a loose federal government, universal suffrage, and the separation of church and state.

Bitter rivalry between Conservatives and Liberals continued throughout most of the 19th century. There were nearly a hundred insurrections and civil wars up to 1899, when the War of a Thousand Days broke out; 100,000 lives were lost before the Liberals were defeated in 1902.

Some progress was made, however, during the 19th century. Tomás Cipriano de Mosquera, president of New Granada in 1845, sponsored many reforms and advanced economic growth. In 1846 he signed a treaty giving the United States transit rights across the Isthmus of Panama. By 1903 the Colombian government still had not ratified the treaty leasing territory to build the canal. Panama, supported by the United States, revolted and declared its independence. In 1914 Colombia recognized the Republic of Panama in return for rights in the Canal Zone and the payment of indemnity by the United States.

From 1914 until after World War II, Colombia enjoyed political stability, despite growing social unrest and the emergence of a Communist party. Then the basic enmity between Conservatives and Liberals flared up once more. For about a decade the country was torn by factional strife and rule by violence.

In 1953 ultra-conservative Laureano Gómez, who had assumed dictatorial powers in 1950, was overthrown by a military coup led by Gustavo Rojas Pinilla. Rojas brought back a measure of stability by pacifying those regions which were in the hands of rebels, guerrillas and brigands, but met his downfall in 1957 after the church had withdrawn its support. At this time the Conservatives and Liberals made peace and called for a constitutional convention that would allow them to share the national and local government.

**GOVERNMENT AND POLITICS.** The constitutional amendment, approved by popular plebiscite in December, 1957, provided that the Conservative and Liberal parties were to alternate the presidency until 1974 and would share equally in the legislative and judicial branches, regional legislatures, and municipal councils.

Dr. Carlos Lleras Restrepo, a Liberal, was elected president in 1966 for a four-year term. A new political movement, backed by Rojas, emerged at this time as the coalition's chief opposition. It gained nearly 30 per cent of the votes, winning 18 Senate and 37 House seats—enough to thwart, if it wished, the two-thirds majority vote needed to approve legislation.

**ECONOMY.** Colombia is the world's second largest producer of coffee, which accounts for about 69 per cent of the country's foreign exchange earnings. The climate is suitable for a wider variety of crops, but less than 25 per cent of the land is used for agriculture and stock raising; only about 13 per cent of that total is utilized for commercial crops. The country is practically self-sufficient in meeting its food needs.

Although Colombia is primarily an agricultural country, there are extensive and varied mineral resources. The production of petroleum has become increasingly important. In 1965 significant oil discoveries were made near the Ecuadorian border. Exploitation of large coal and iron deposits is growing. Colombian emeralds are world famous; gold, once of major importance to the Spanish conquerors, now makes a significant contribution to export earnings. Colombia is the only country in Latin America known to possess the important strategic metal, platinum.

President Lleras has been trying to re-invigorate the country's economy through land reform and other measures. Manufacturing industries are being rapidly developed and diversified. Large-scale aid from the United States, resumed in late 1965, assisted these efforts. The U.S. is still Colombia's principal market, although European countries have increased their imports in recent years.

**EDUCATION.** Education is compulsory for children from 7 to 14. Literacy is estimated at 62.3 per cent for ages 15 and over.

**ARMED FORCES.** Colombia was the only Latin-American country with a contingent that served continuously in the Korean War. One year of army service is obligatory for men between 18 and 30; from 30 to 45 they serve in the reserves. The armed forces total about 63,000 men.

# CONGO, DEMOCRATIC REPUBLIC OF THE

*Official Name:* Democratic Republic of the Congo. *Area:* 905,562 square miles. *Population:* 15,986,000. *Principal Cities* (with populations): Kinshasa, the capital, 402,492; Lubumbashi, 183,711; Luluabourg, 115,049. *Flag:* A blue field with a yellow star in the upper left corner, crossed diagonally by a yellow-bordered red stripe. *Monetary Unit:* The Zaïre (worth U.S. $2.00). *Gross National Product:* $1,273,000,000 (1965). *Average Annual Income per Person:* $70.

**LAND AND PEOPLE.** Almost six times the size of California, the Congo is the second largest nation in Africa. It derives its name from the Congo River, whose entire course lies within the country's borders. Save for a narrow corridor on the northern bank of the Congo's estuary, the country is landlocked. It is bordered on the north by the Central African Republic and Sudan; on the east by Uganda, Rwanda, Burundi, and Tanzania; on the southeast and south by Zambia and Angola; and on the west by the Atlantic Ocean, the Cabinda enclave of Angola, and the Congo Republic (Brazzaville). (See map on page 111.)

Much of the central Congo River basin area, comprising nearly half the country, is dense rain forest and swamps; the land in the higher regions to the north is savanna or bush country. Southeast of the low central plateau are mountains that rise over 6,000 feet, and to the east the ranges reach a peak of 16,795 feet at the crest of Mount Ruwenzori.

In the lower western and central regions the climate is tropically hot and humid; the climate in the higher eastern elevations is more temperate. South of the equator rains are heavy and frequent from fall to late spring; north of the equator the season of heaviest rainfall is from April to November. The Congo has a rich variety of plant, animal, and fish life.

The people, mostly Bantu, are divided into many groups. There are some Sudanese and smaller groups of Nilotic, Pygmy, and Hamitic peoples. French is the official language for government business. The Lingala, Kiswahili, Tshiluba, and Kikongo languages serve as the major tongue. It is estimated that 33 per cent of the population are Roman Catholic; 7 per cent are Protestant; 10 per cent are members of independent African churches; and the remainder are adherents to tribal religions.

**HISTORY.** Little is known of the Congo prior to the 19th century. It is believed that Pygmies or Bushmen first ruled the Congo basin but were later displaced by Bantu tribes who settled the area and established kingdoms. Some of these attained substantial size, and one, the kingdom of Kongo, gave its name to the river and to the two colonial territories carved from the river basin.

Europe was not markedly concerned with the region's potential until Henry Stanley made his historic trip along the course of the Congo River in 1877. His reports of the Congo's riches sparked the interest of King Leopold II of Belgium. He commissioned Stanley to make further explorations and to negotiate treaties with local leaders. In 1878 the King formed a company to exploit the region, with himself as chief stockholder. The Congress of Berlin in 1885 recognized Leopold's rights in the region, and he became absolute monarch of the Congo Free State. International protests over reported abuse of the Congolese population forced Leopold to cede his private state to Belgium. It became the colony of Belgian Congo in 1908. After World War I the former German territory of Ruanda-Urundi was placed under Belgian Congo administration.

Until 1957 the colony was ruled without a vestige of self-government. In that year popular elections for councilmen were held in some of the larger cities. The flood of nationalism that swept Africa after World War II had some effect in the Congo, and demands for freedom surfaced suddenly in 1959. Riots started in Léopoldville (now Kinshasa), then spread to other parts of the colony. The Belgians first announced a program of gradual transition to self-government but eventually capitulated to persistent Congolese demands and agreed to total independence by June 30, 1960.

Belgium had failed to give the Congolese any political training. Though a few had developed into capable administrators, none had experience on a national level. Instead of national political organizations, there were some 200 political groups, split by personal, tribal, and religious squabbles. The first chief of state elected by the Parliament was Joseph Kasavubu. The Belgians appointed Patrice Lumumba premier, and he became the head of government under the parliamentary system then in effect.

Economic, military, political, and social chaos confronted the nation almost immediately. The gravest challenge to the new government was the announcement by President Moise Tshombe of Katanga, the Congo's richest area, of his province's secession. The loss of Katanga and the emigration of Belgian administrators, medical personnel, teachers, and technicians were staggering blows to the country. Belgium's military forces intervened and the Congo called on the U.N. for assistance in expelling foreign troops and mercenaries. In July, 1960, the U.N. sent in a force to re-establish order.

In September, 1960, Kasavubu dismissed Lumumba, who had Communist backing, for having "plunged the nation into fratricidal war." Colonel Joseph Mobutu, a Kasavubu supporter and new head of the army, consolidated the government's control in mid-September. Lumumba attempted flight but he was captured by the Congolese and was murdered in 1961 in an alleged escape attempt. In death, he became a martyred hero throughout the continent, a symbol of Africa's hopes and frustrations.

After three years of civil strife the central government, with U.N. military aid, regained total control. Katanga was reunited with the country in January, 1963. Meanwhile, self-styled heirs to Lumumba were fomenting rebellion in the eastern part of the country. A Congolese government in exile was formed with headquarters in Brazzaville. In several provinces guerrilla control and savagery increased.

The controversial Tshombe, invited to return from exile in 1964, was sworn in as the Congo's new premier, and a constitution was finally promulgated. Almost immediately Stanleyville (now Kisangani) fell to the rebels, who announced that all the city's whites were being held hostage. At the request of the Congo government, Belgian paratroops, flown into Stanleyville in U.S. planes, were successful in rescuing 1,900 of the hostages. At the same time Congolese forces began to regain much of the territory lost to guerrilla bands. The cost of the rebellion reached terrible proportions: thousands of civilians were estimated to have been murdered by rebel terrorists.

In 1965 President Kasavubu dismissed Tshombe and appointed Evariste Kimba prime minister. Kimba, blocked by Tshombe, was unable to form a government. Mobutu, now a general, became president by military coup. He canceled the scheduled 1966 elections, re-established rule by decree, and later assumed all of Parliament's legislative powers. Kimba and several others accused of plotting Mobutu's death were hanged in Kinshasa's main square before an audience of 100,000.

Mobutu exploited nationalist feeling to build up his personal prestige. He gave the major cities African, rather than European names; he created an impression of radicalism in many of his statements and speeches; and he glorified the memory of Lumumba. His government took a small, though well-publicized step toward "economic independence" by demanding and gaining nominal control over some of the largest foreign corporations operating on Congolese soil, including the largest of all, Union Minière, reorganized under the name Gecomin.

In 1967 European mercenaries formerly employed by Tshombe staged an unsuccessful rebellion in the Congo's eastern provinces. Diplomatic observers speculated that the mercenaries originally intended to take over the provinces in Tshombe's name and await his return from exile in Spain. But Tshombe's kidnapping and subsequent detention in Algeria led the rebels to begin a premature rebellion that was eventually put down by the central government.

**GOVERNMENT AND POLITICS.** The Congo has had three constitutions since becoming independent. The first, voted by the Belgian Parliament, set up a parliamentary system modeled on Belgium's own. The second, adopted by referendum in 1964, was a hybrid of parliamentary and presidential systems, with federalistic features. The present constitution, adopted by referendum in 1967, does away with federalism and concentrates executive power in the hands of a popularly elected president. The legislature, elected directly by all citizens of 18 or over, is unicameral.

General Mobutu reduced the number of provinces to eight, and, under the 1967 constitution, these are now mere administrative units headed by appointees of the central government. The constitution permits only two parties. The MPR (Mouvement Populaire de la Révolution) is sponsored by Mobutu himself. It is doubtful whether adversaries of the regime will dare to take advantage of the President's invitation to organize an opposition party. Presidential elections under the new constitution are not likely to be held for several years.

**ECONOMY.** The Congo is superbly endowed with mineral deposits and natural energy sources, but good farm land is relatively scarce.

Before 1960, exports were roughly balanced between agriculture and mining. Under European control, agriculture was on a plantation basis, and the chief crops—coffee, palm products, and rubber—were grown almost totally for markets abroad. These items, plus cocoa, cotton, timber, and fibers, are still important export crops. Since 1960 the decline in world prices and the breakdown in law and order within the country have produced a drop in the percentage of national income deriving from agricultural export. The vast majority of the Congolese, however, are engaged in subsistence agriculture, which by its very nature remains comparatively resilient.

The Congo's wealth is in its vast mineral resources, accounting for 84% of its 1966 exports. The Congo leads the world in output of industrial diamonds and cobalt. Copper is the most valuable mineral, but many others, including cobalt, zinc, tin, cadmium, and germanium, are being increasingly exploited. The country is far from advanced industrially, but manufactures include a wide range of products, among them cement, gunpowder, explosives, and sulfuric acid.

**EDUCATION.** There are three universities, over 400 libraries, and several museums. The literacy rate is about 15 per cent.

**ARMED FORCES.** There is no compulsory military service, though college graduates can be conscripted for two years into a "Civilian Service." There are about 36,000 men in the armed forces. The army numbers some 35,000; the navy, 200; and the air force, 600.

# CONGO REPUBLIC

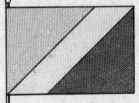

*Official Name:* Republic of Congo. *Area:* 132,046 square miles. *Population:* 850,000. *Principal Cities* (with populations): Brazzaville, 150,000; Pointe Noire, 75,000; Dolisie, 12,000. *Flag:* A diagonal yellow stripe divides a green triangle (left) from a red triangle (right). *Monetary Unit:* The CFA franc (worth 0.4 U.S. cent). *Gross National Product:* $138,000,000 (1965). *Average Annual Income per Person:* $140.

**LAND AND PEOPLE.** The Congo, on the west-central coast of Africa, is bordered on the north by Cameroon and the Central African Republic, on the east and south by the Democratic Republic of the Congo (Kinshasa), on the southwest by the Cabinda enclave and the Atlantic Ocean, and on the west by Gabon. (See map on page 111.)

**HISTORY.** From the little that is known of the early history of the Congo region there is reason to believe that there was a large Congo Empire that reached the peak of its power during the 16th century. In the preceding century the Portuguese became the first European explorers of the coastal areas of the Congo and it was a Portuguese who discovered the mouth of the Congo River in 1484. Beginning in the 17th century French traders, interested in slaves and ivory, began to establish trading centers; by

1785 at least a hundred French ships a year visited the region. With the end of the slave trade, French patrols plied the coastal waters of the area seeking out illegal slave ships. Exploration of the interior also was undertaken by the French beginning in the 1870s. The Congress of Berlin in 1885 gave recognition to French claims in the area and also opened the whole Congo Basin region to the traders of all countries.

The territory first was called French Congo, then later renamed Middle Congo. In 1910 Middle Congo, Gabon, and Ubangi-Shari were administratively established as colonies to form French Equatorial Africa. By 1956 Middle Congo had gained local autonomy and in 1958 the colony's voters approved a referendum making Middle Congo an autonomous republic within the French Community, to be known as the Congo Republic. On August 15, 1960, the Republic became fully independent. Fulbert Youlou was elected first president, with the support of all parties. In 1963 Youlou was toppled by a popular revolt. A provisional government ruled until December, when elections were held for a new constitution. On its approval Alphonse Massemba-Débat was chosen as the new president; he was unopposed.

**GOVERNMENT AND POLITICS.** The president of the Congo Republic is chosen for a five-year term by an electoral college composed of members of the National Assembly and of the regional and municipal councils. Election of the National Assembly is by universal suffrage. The president, who can dissolve the 55-man Assembly, appoints the premier and his cabinet. The president also is assisted by a National Council of the Revolution during the present period, which is described as "consolidation of the revolution." The only political party is the Mouvement National de la Révolution (MNR).

The Brazzaville government describes its foreign policy as "nonaligned," but in fact it has associated itself with the Communist countries on almost all matters of international importance. Because of persistent harassment of official American personnel by the Congolese government, the U.S. Embassy in Brazzaville closed in August, 1965.

**ECONOMY.** Based on the latest national income estimates, made in 1963, the most important sectors of the Congolese economy are transport, commerce, and communications.

The most important Congolese exports are wood and wood products. Beginning in 1969, the exploitation of a large and rich potash deposit near the seaport of Pointe Noire will double Brazzaville's exports and add an estimated 15 per cent to the country's gross domestic product. The country has received relatively large amounts of foreign aid from France, the Common Market, Communist China, and the Soviet Union.

**EDUCATION.** The schools have one of the highest attendance rates in Africa: an estimated 75–80 per cent of school-age children. About 20 per cent of the adult population is literate.

**ARMED FORCES.** Total strength of the Congo's armed forces is 700.

## COSTA RICA

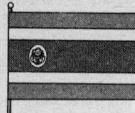

*Official Name:* Republic of Costa Rica. *Area:* 19,575 square miles. *Population:* 1,486,000. *Principal Cities* (with populations): San José, the capital, 101,162; San Sebastián, 23,166; Guadalupe, 21,413. *Flag:* A blue stripe at top and bottom, separated by two white stripes from a broad center red stripe containing the national crest. *Monetary Unit:* The colón (worth 15 U.S. cents). *Gross National Product:* $591,000,000 (1965). *Average Annual Income per Person:* $416.

**LAND AND PEOPLE.** A tiny nation in Central America, Costa Rica is bordered on the north by Nicaragua, on the east by the Carribbean Sea and Panama, and on the south and west by the Pacific Ocean. (See map on page 176.)

Costa Rica lies entirely within the tropical zone, but its climate, flora, and living conditions are all tempered by the altitude. Individual mountain peaks soar more than two miles high and the great majority of Costa Ricans (who like to call themselves Ticos) live at altitudes of 3,000 to 4,000 feet where the climate is springlike throughout the year.

There is a high degree of social, racial, and economic homogeneity among the people, who are mainly rural, Roman Catholic, and of Spanish origin.

**HISTORY.** Costa Rica was discovered and probably named by Columbus during his voyage of 1502. Spain ignored her small colony because of the scarcity of minerals, and the province grew slowly. Settlers turned to farming in the colonial period and set the pattern of peaceful, slow progress. Costa Rica, along with the rest of Central America, separated bloodlessly from Spain in 1821. In 1824 it became a state in the Federal Republic of Central America. When that government failed in 1838, Costa Rica assumed independence.

Since the mid-19th century the country's prosperity has been based on coffee production, and the many small growers have tended to shun the anarchy and civil strife of the neighboring states. An invasion by the American William Walker was put down in 1856 by a united Costa Rican people. Only for three periods (1870–82, 1917–19, and in 1948) has Costa Rica been ruled by forceful dictatorship. The 1890s saw the arrival of the great fruit companies and the construction of a railroad from the Caribbean to San José.

**GOVERNMENT AND POLITICS.** Under the constitution of 1949, José Joaquín Trejos was elected president in 1966 for a term of four years. His party, the National Unification Party, holds 26 of the 57 seats in the unicameral legislature, whose members also serve for four years. The chief opposition comes from the National Liberation Party, led by José Figueres, Costa Rica's president from 1953 to 1958. Other parties include the vigorous Civic Revolutionary Union and the Christian Democratic Party. The Communist Party is outlawed and Communism is very weak.

**ECONOMY.** Costa Rica's great variations in altitude, rainfall, and temperature produce significant diversification of agriculture, which engages about one-half of the working population and accounts for about one-third of the gross domestic product. Satisfactory exploitation of agricultural resources lags, however, because a scarcity of roads has prevented development of almost one-half of the cultivable land. Chief agricultural products are coffee and bananas. Only about 15 per cent of the nation's income is derived from manufacturing, but between 1961 and 1965 this phase of the economy grew at a rate in excess of 11 per cent annually.

**EDUCATION AND HEALTH.** Schooling is free and compulsory for children between the ages of seven and 13. Eighty-four per cent of the adult population is literate.

The principal cities have hospitals, and there are special sanitary units and dispensaries to help meet the needs of the poorer citizens. Sickness and old age insurance, already available for some, is being expanded.

**ARMED FORCES.** There never has been compulsory military service in Costa Rica. The army was abolished in 1948 and replaced by a civil guard, now totaling 1,200 men. A navy of fewer than 50 men performs coast-guard functions. The country has eight police forces totaling about 4,500 men.

## CUBA

*Official Name:* Republic of Cuba. *Area:* 44,218 square miles. *Population:* 7,833,-000. *Principal Cities* (with populations): Havana, the capital, 978,400; Marianao, 230,000; Holguín, 226,000; Santiago de Cuba, 219,800; Camagüey, 162,400. *Flag:* Five horizontal stripes, three blue and two white; the red triangle at the left bears a five-pointed white star. *Monetary Unit:* The peso (worth U.S. $1). *Gross National Product:* $4,284,000,-000 (1965). *Average Annual Income per Person:* $516.

**LAND AND PEOPLE.** Cuba is the largest island in the Caribbean Sea. Its northern coast is about 90 miles south of Key West, Florida, at its nearest point. Jamaica lies about 100 miles below Cuba's southeast coast, and the Windward Passage separates its eastern tip from Haiti. (See map on page 176.)

The island, about 760 miles long, averages 56 to 60 miles in width. Its nearly 2,200-mile-long coast is marked by bays, inlets, coral reefs and cays, and marshes. There are three mountainous regions: the rugged Sierra Maestra in the easternmost province, Oriente, reaching to about 6,500 feet; the lower Sierra de los Órganos in the west; and the Sierra de Trinidad, a large group of hills in central Cuba's region of plains and rolling land. The most important river is the Cauto, in Oriente Province. The mountains are covered by a variety of tropical trees; much of the rest of the land is grassy and palm-studded. There are several small islands, the largest of which is the Isle of Pines off the southeastern coast. The climate is mildly tropical.

Nearly 73 per cent of the population is white, about 15 per cent mulatto, 12 per cent Negro, and less than 1 per cent Oriental. Spanish is the national language. About 84 per cent of the people are Roman Catholic, and there is a small Protestant minority.

**HISTORY.** Discovered by Columbus on his first voyage to America in 1492, Cuba remained under Spanish rule till 1898. During the early colonial period Havana served as the last port visited by ships carrying treasure back to Spain; as a result the capital was often under attack. In 1762 the English captured Havana. Their occupation lasted only a year, but their rule encouraged free trade and gave rise to a spirit of unity among the people. In 1868 Carlos Manuel de Céspedes and other patriots issued a proclamation calling for revolt against Spain. The civil conflict that erupted lasted ten years before being crushed; it was followed by deep bitterness among the people and further attempts at rebellion.

The renowned Cuban patriot and writer, José Martí, formed the Cuban Revolutionary Party while in exile in the United States. As the leading figure in the freedom movement, he kept Cuba's spirit alive. His call to arms in 1895 sparked a new civil war. He was killed in battle the same year, but the revolt continued. The United States was openly sympathetic to the revolutionary cause and for years was at odds with Spain over her Cuban policy. After the U.S. battleship *Maine* was blown up in Havana harbor in 1898, the United States declared war. Spain was defeated by U.S. forces, and Cuban independence was declared. Cuba's constitution was adopted in 1901. In 1902 the republic's first president, Tomás Estrada Palma, was sworn in, and U.S. occupation forces left the island.

Cuba was ostensibly free, but the U.S. government had insisted that it ratify the Platt Amendment, giving the United States the right to intervene in Cuban affairs. In addition, United States companies owned or controlled about half of Cuba's cultivated land, utilities, mines, and other economic resources. In 1906 President Estrada Palma, unable to suppress a revolt by the opposition Liberal Party, called in U.S. troops, and a U.S. military governor took over for the next two years and four months. U.S. Marines also intervened during revolts in 1912 and 1917. In 1921 a U.S. supervisor was imposed on the Cuban government for several years. The Platt Amendment was abrogated by President Franklin D. Roosevelt in 1934.

With the post-World War I economic decline, Cuba fell victim to increasing unemployment and poverty. President Gerardo Machado y Morales, inaugurated in 1925, established dictatorial rule. He was ousted in 1933 by the democratic opposition, which in turn fell victim in 1934 to a coup led by Fulgencio Batista y Zaldívar, then an army sergeant. Batista ruled through puppet presidents, becoming president himself in 1940. He was supported in the election by the Communists, to whom he had handed over control of the trade union movement. After his four-year term he continued to be a powerful political force, although his candidate was defeated in the 1944 election.

In 1952, just before the scheduled election, Batista returned to power through an army coup. In 1953 an abortive raid on an army barracks by a group of young rebels led to about 100 deaths and the imprisonment of the group's leader, Fidel Castro Ruz. In 1954, after a dishonest election, Batista again became president. Castro was released from prison under a general presidential amnesty and left Cuba to organize the so-called 26th of July rebel movement.

In 1956 Castro and a group of supporters, including his lieutenant, Ernesto "Che" Guevara, an Argentine Communist, landed in Oriente Province, went into hiding in the Sierra Maestra, and launched an uprising. The rebellion spread. Batista undermined his own authority by resorting to bloody repression of the rebels. On Jan. 1, 1959, he was forced to flee the country. Within six weeks Castro became premier. Moderate policies in the early months of his regime gave way to increasingly radical measures. By March, 1960, every anti-Communist in the cabinet had resigned or been purged; by the end of the year the government had seized almost all businesses. Most U.S.-owned property, totaling about $1 billion in value, was nationalized, and Cuba was proclaimed a socialist state on May 1, 1961. Diplomatic relations between Cuba and the United States had been broken off four months earlier.

The United States, Cuba's chief customer and supplier, had in the meantime canceled Cuba's sugar quota, and in 1962 the Organization of American States excluded Cuba from membership because of her alignment with the Communist bloc. On April 17, 1961, an invasion force of Cuban exiles, trained and equipped by the U.S., landed at the Bay of Pigs with the intention of launching a rebellion against the Castro government. The invaders were quickly overwhelmed, and many were captured. The United States later exchanged some $35 million worth of pharmaceutical supplies for 1,200 prisoners.

U.S.-Soviet relations sank to a dangerous level when the Soviet Union began to install ballistic missiles on Cuban soil. Faced with a direct and forceful challenge by President John F. Kennedy in October, 1962, the Soviets removed their missiles and jet bombers. Castro remained in control in Cuba and continued to spread subversion throughout Latin America, but with few signs of real success.

Although economically and militarily dependent on the U.S.S.R., Cuba is not an obedient Soviet satellite. Castro has repeatedly criticized the U.S.S.R. and has lashed out at pro-Soviet Latin American Communist parties for their reluctance to join in guerrilla activities. In 1967 Soviet Premier Kosygin went to Cuba in an apparent attempt to iron out differences, but he was met with a cold reception.

In the first years of the Castro regime, an

estimated 240,000 Cubans emigrated to the U.S. and other countries. Since December, 1965, Castro has permitted a daily airlift of Cubans to the United States.

**GOVERNMENT AND POLITICS.** National elections promised by Castro early in his regime have never been held. Osvaldo Dorticós Torrado is nominal president, but all power rests with Castro. Radio and television speeches and mass meetings have replaced parliamentary deliberations. There is no independent judiciary, and political prisoners are subject to summary trial by a revolutionary tribunal. The only political party is the Cuban Communist Party (PCC); Castro is its secretary-general.

**ECONOMY.** Cuba's land and industry are under state control; productivity and the overall economy have fallen below pre-Revolutionary levels. Sugar remains the chief prop of Cuba's economy and the major source of foreign exchange. The government abandoned efforts at agricultural diversification in 1962 after a poor sugar harvest. The Soviet Union has replaced the United States as Cuba's best sugar customer. Agricultural workers are salaried employees of state-owned farms, which constitute over 70 per cent of the cultivated land. Productive norms were set in September, 1966, and a competitive collective brigade system was created to overcome low productivity that Castro blamed on ignorant and inexperienced agricultural directors.

In addition to sugar, crops include coffee and tobacco. Animal raising and fishing also contribute to the national income, two-thirds of which depends directly or indirectly on the sugar industry. Minerals, the third most important export after sugar and tobacco, include nickel, chromite, copper, iron, and manganese.

The chief industries include sugar refining, food processing, and the production of textiles; industrial chemicals; building materials; wood, metal, and leather goods; paints; tires; and liquors. Inability to obtain replacement parts for machinery and transport equipment, mostly American-made prior to Castro, has constituted a technological curb and has been only partially eased by supplies from Soviet-bloc countries and from France, Spain, and England. Immense quantities of technical and financial aid have been pumped into Cuba, principally from Communist countries. Rationing of food, clothing, and manufactured items was extended for another year in July, 1966. The rice ration had already been cut 50 per cent in January of that year because of bitter relations with Communist China. The country's debt to Communist nations is estimated to run into billions.

"Che" Guevara, Cuba's first economic minister, disappeared from general public view early in 1965. He reportedly was killed while working with guerrilla forces in Bolivia in October, 1967.

**EDUCATION AND HEALTH.** Six years of primary education are now compulsory. At least 70 per cent of the population is literate; the government claims the literacy rate to be 96 per cent. The entire educational system is under state control. Agricultural and industrial training have been added to the liberal-arts curriculum.

A great step forward in general health conditions in Cuba was taken at the beginning of the 20th century when Walter Reed, an American army surgeon, led a successful campaign aimed at eliminating yellow fever. Reed undertook the battle against the disease in 1900–01, during the American occupation.

In the 1960s there were nearly 48,000 hospital beds, and Cuba reported having about 5,800 doctors. Sanitary conditions continued to improve, and public health campaigns, such as vaccination against poliomyelitis, were conducted; but malnutrition, parasitic infection, and tuberculosis remained as serious problems.

**ARMED FORCES.** Three years' service in the armed forces is compulsory for all men between the ages of 17 and 45. Women may serve for two years on a voluntary basis. Cuba's regular army numbers 43,000 men; an armed militia of men and women, serving as an internal security force, numbers 250,000; the navy numbers 6,000; and the air force 3,000. The regular armed forces are well equipped by the Soviet Union.

## CYPRUS

*Official Name:* Republic of Cyprus. *Area:* 3,572 square miles. *Population:* 603,000. *Principal Cities* (with populations): Nicosia, the capital, 103,000; Limassol, 47,-000; Famagusta, 38,000; Larnoea, 20,000. *Flag:* A white field bearing an outline map of Cyprus in gold placed above crossed green olive branches. *Monetary Unit:* the Cyprus pound of 1,000 mils (worth U.S. $2.40). *Gross National Product:* $417,000,000 (1966). *Average Annual Income per Person:* $574.

**LAND AND PEOPLE.** Cyprus is an island in the eastern Mediterranean about 44 miles south of Turkey and 65 miles west of Syria. (See map on page 197.) Its commanding position on the approaches to the Suez Canal enhances its strategic value. Two mountain systems dominate much of the island. The Kyrenias run for about 100 miles along the north coast in a series of jagged peaks. In the southwest the Troodos Massif branches out to the northern and southern coasts. The mountains, containing copper and iron pyrites, flank a treeless, low plain that stretches across northcentral Cyprus and is the heart of the island's agricultural and pastoral productivity.

Except during summers, when the coastal areas become more humid and the central plain is hot, a Mediterranean climate of low humidity, sunshine, and pleasant temperatures generally prevails. The wet season is fall and winter, but rain is sporadic. Snow blankets the upper peaks of the Troodos during winter.

Nearly 79 per cent of the population is of Greek descent, and about 18 per cent is Turkish; most of the remainder are Maronites and Armenians. The Greeks belong to the Greek Orthodox Church; the Turks are Muslims.

**HISTORY.** Excavations prove that Cyprus was

inhabited as long ago as 4000 B.C. By 2200 B.C. it was the major source of the ancient world's copper. After 1500 B.C. Greeks began to colonize the island, and Phoenicians began to settle there about 800 B.C. For centuries Cyprus was ruled variously by Egyptian, Persian, Greek, Roman, and Byzantine empires.

Christianity was brought to Cyprus by the apostles Paul and Mark. King Richard I of England took Cyprus from the Byzantine empire in 1191. The island was awarded to Guy of Lusignan, whose dynasty lasted until Cyprus was annexed by Venice in 1489. By 1571 Cyprus was under Ottoman rule, and a large but separate Turkish community developed. At the Congress of Berlin in 1878 the Ottomans placed Cyprus under British administration. Britain annexed the island in 1914 and made it a crown colony in 1925.

The burgeoning Greek Cypriote movement for *enosis*—the union of Cyprus with Greece—became a source of increasing tension, flaring up in 1931 and again in 1954. In 1955 EOKA, an underground Cypriote force led by a Greek ex-army officer, Colonel George Grivas, instituted a reign of terror against the British, opposing Greek Cypriotes, and the Turkish minority. EOKA intensified its campaign in 1956 when the British deported Archbishop Makarios III, the elected head of the Greek Orthodox Church in Cyprus, on grounds of complicity in the terrorism.

Turkey's strong support of the Turkish community further aggravated the situation. The effectiveness of the NATO alliance in the eastern Mediterranean was jeopardized, for both Turkey and Greece are members. At least 2,000 people were killed during the struggle.

In 1959 an agreement was reached by the Greek and Turkish foreign ministers and approved by Greece, Turkey, and Britain. The major provision was the establishment of Cyprus as an independent republic. Makarios, who returned from exile a hero, was elected president in December, 1959, and in August, 1960, the nation's independence was formally declared.

A civil war broke out late in 1963, a few days after President Makarios unilaterally proposed a constitutional revision restricting the rights of the Turkish community. A United Nations peacekeeping force was dispatched in 1964, by which time a far wider war threatened. Greece continued to call for *enosis;* Turkey demanded partition and threatened to intervene militarily. Makarios insisted on total independence and went to Moscow and Cairo for help; Grivas, returning to Cyprus as commander of Greek forces, advocated *enosis* but disapproved of Makarios' dealings with the leftists and split with him. Fighting declined but there was little easing of tension.

Sporadic shootings and bombings resumed in the spring of 1966. U.N. Secretary-General U Thant persuaded Makarios to end the blockade of Nikosia's Turkish Cypriotes. Renewed violence in November, 1967, was answered with a Turkish threat to invade Cyprus. Representatives from the U.N., NATO, and the U.S. took diplomatic action in an effort to avert a war between Greece and Turkey.

**GOVERNMENT AND POLITICS.** Cyprus is an independent republic in the British Commonwealth of Nations. The 1960 constitution provided for a Greek Cypriote president and a Turkish Cypriote vice-president who also had the right of veto. Membership in the cabinet, legislature, and civil service was allocated on a 70% Greek, 30% Turkish basis. Since December, 1963, however, the Turkish members have ceased to attend the House of Representatives. The Greeks have assumed control of the central government and legislature, while the Turks have retreated to urban and rural enclaves, establishing their own independent administration.

**ECONOMY.** Although minerals are major exports, Cyprus remains basically an agricultural country. About 40% of the labor force is engaged in agriculture. Principal crops are grapes, citrus fruits, and cereal grains, but Cyprus produces less than half her food needs. There are many small industries, mostly employing fewer than ten people. Electric power stations have recently been built, and there is a 1,500-mile, all-weather road system. To spur industry and agriculture a five-year plan requiring an investment of about $175 million was adopted in 1962.

**EDUCATION AND HEALTH.** Elementary education is free but not compulsory between ages 6 and 12. The literacy rate is 82%.

Cyprus is without any serious infectious diseases, and the island's natural death rate is one of the lowest in the world.

**ARMED FORCES.** Six month's compulsory conscription was introduced in 1964. By the terms of the Zurich agreement the armed forces are limited to 2,000 men. In November, 1967, however, Greek troops numbered 8,500, and Turkish troops 1,200.

## CZECHOSLOVAKIA

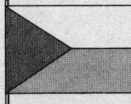

*Official Name:* Czechoslovak Socialist Republic. *Area:* 49,370 square miles. *Population:* 14,272,000. *Principal Cities* (with populations): Prague, the capital, 1,032,000; Brno, 336,000; Bratislava, 280,000; Ostrava, 272,000; Plzeň, 148,000; Košice, 106,000. *Flag:* A blue triangle at the flagstaff over a red and a white stripe. *Monetary Unit:* The koruna (worth 13.5 U.S. cents). *Gross National Product:* $9,200,000,000 (1966). *Average Annual Income per Person:* $1,660.

**LAND AND PEOPLE.** Czechoslovakia, landlocked in central Europe, is bordered on the north by Poland, on the east by the Soviet Union, on the south by Hungary and Austria, on the southwest by West Germany, and on the northwest by East Germany. (See map on page 197.)

The Carpathian Mountains and the Sudetes range in the north form a natural boundary, as do the Erzgebirge (Iron Mountains) in the northwest and the Bohemian Forest in the west. From these northern heights the country slopes to an area of hills, lowlands, and plains. Between Bohemia, the country's western region, and central Moravia and eastern Slovakia is the Moravian Gate, a natural line of north-south travel along the Oder and Morava rivers.

Czechoslovakia's topography creates climatic and seasonal variations, but the weather generally is moderate. Rainfall, occurring chiefly in the spring and summer, averages between 20 and 40 inches over most of the country, but there is more than 50 inches in the mountains of north-central Slovakia. The country's principal rivers—the Danube, the Elbe, the Moldau, and the Oder—are of importance because they give access to the sea.

Ethnically, the population consists of Czechs (65 per cent), Slovaks (29 per cent), Magyars (Hungarians; 4 per cent), and Germans (1 per cent), with a few Poles, Russians, and Ukrainians. The largest church affiliation is Roman Catholic (77 per cent); other groups include the Czechoslovak Church (8 per cent) and Protestants (7 per cent). All churches are under state control. The two major and official languages are Czech and Slovak.

**HISTORY.** Czechoslovakia did not come into being as a unified nation until 1918. The first known settlers of the Czech lands of Bohemia and Moravia were Celts followed in about the first century B.C. by Germanic tribes. Between the first and fifth centuries A.D. Slovak settlers from the east had displaced both the Celtic and Germanic peoples, and in the next century the Slavs had spread into Slovakia. By the ninth century the Czech and Slovak regions had become part of the great empire of Moravia, and Christianity was introduced into the empire. The kingdom of Bohemia emerged under "Good King Wenceslas" in the tenth century but was soon absorbed into the Holy Roman Empire. In centuries following, the lands were governed by a succession of rulers of Bohemia, Hungary, and Austria.

The Czech lands were torn by the religious disputes of the Reformation. In Bohemia the German settlers who had been brought in by the kings tended to remain Catholic, while the Czech majority followed John Huss, one of the earliest of the Protestant reformers. In the early 17th century the quarrel between the Catholic Hapsburg emperor, the champion of the Counter-Reformation, and the Czech nobility led to the Thirty Years War. From this time the country was superficially Germanized, with Czech the language of the peasants.

Toward the end of the 18th century this process began to be reversed. Between 1848 and 1914, the resistance of the Germans, particularly in Bohemia, contributed to the debilitation of the Hapsburg Empire, which finally collapsed during World War I.

On October 28, 1918, the first Czechoslovak Republic came into being. It included formerly Austrian Bohemia and Moravia, which were mainly Czech, and formerly Hungarian Slovakia; Ruthenia, which was mainly Ukrainian, was added in 1919. Thomas G. Masaryk became the first president of the new Czechoslovakian democracy. His disciple, Eduard Benes, succeeded him in 1935, after serving for many years as foreign minister.

The first Czechoslovak Republic enjoyed the benefits of a liberal, democratic constitution, internationally respected leadership, and economic advantages resulting from the fact that most of Austria-Hungary's industries were in territory incorporated into Czechoslovakia. However, serious problems resulted from differences arising among the several ethnic groups. Especially critical was the problem with the large Sudeten German minority living in the border districts of Bohemia. Their demands for union with Germany increased in proportion to Hitler's rising power. In September, 1938, the Munich Pact awarded the Sudetenland to Germany; in March, 1939, Hitler occupied the rest of Bohemia and Moravia, retaining control until Germany's collapse in 1945.

Benes, who had resigned as president in 1938, established a government-in-exile in London during World War II. In 1943 he signed a friendship treaty with the Soviet Union, and in 1945 he entered into an agreement with the Czech Communists. The agreement stipulated that political groups were to be restricted in number between Czech and Slovak parties; the country's foreign policy was to be based solely on the 1943 Soviet treaty; and Czechoslovakia was to be an exclusively Slavic state of two nations, the Czechs and the Slovaks. In the spring of 1945 Benes returned to Prague and resumed the presidency of Czechoslovakia. He approved the socialization of the nation's industries.

Benes' hopes that the second Czechoslovak Republic would be a bridge between western and eastern Europe were destroyed by the Communist coup of 1948, and he resigned in June of that year. Klement Gottwald, the Communist premier, was named president.

**GOVERNMENT AND POLITICS.** A new constitution, adopted in 1960, proclaimed Czechoslovakia a socialist republic. The chief executive of the state is the president, elected for a five-year term by the National Assembly. President Antonin Novotny, now serving his second term, is also First Secretary of the Communist Party. The government is headed by a prime minister, Jozef Lenart.

The National Assembly is a one-chamber legislature of 300 members elected for four-year terms from a single slate of candidates. The assembly is called into session briefly at least twice a year. Although the Communist Party is dominant, there are several non-Communist splinter groups.

**ECONOMY.** Industry accounts for 70 per cent of the national income and agriculture for only 13 per cent. The Communist regime, which controls almost every phase of the nation's economy, has emphasized heavy industry at the expense of consumer goods. The government adopted comprehensive economic reforms in 1965, including decentralization of administrative responsibility and greater profit incentives. In 1966 the gross industrial output rose by 7.4 per cent, manufacturing industries gained by 7.5 per cent, and consumer goods grew by 6.4 per cent over 1965. The productivity of labor continued to lag, however, because of a shortage of workers for industry and because of the tendency of the ruling authorities to favor wage equality.

Farm production in 1966 was about 10 per cent higher than in 1965. Some 20 per cent of the total labor force is engaged in agriculture. About 30 per cent of the land under cultivation is held by state farms and 60 per cent by collective farms. The country must still import some food to meet its requirements. To improve agricultural production the government has increased the rate of capital investment and has initiated reforms similar to those being introduced in industry.

The Czechoslovak economy is heavily dependent on foreign trade. The country imports most of its industrial raw materials and exports a great variety of finished products. In 1966 the value of foreign trade exceeded $5.6 billion for the first time since World War II. About 70 per cent of Czechoslovakia's foreign trade is with member states of the Council of Mutual Economic Assistance (Comecon) and other socialist states. In 1966, however, exchange of goods between Czechoslovakia and Western powers increased by 20.2 per cent over 1965. Among the country's trading partners, West Germany and Britain rank fifth and sixth behind the Soviet Union, East Germany, Poland, and Hungary.

**EDUCATION.** Education is free at all levels, with attendance compulsory for children from 6 to 15. The literacy rate is almost 100 per cent. Charles University in Prague was the first central European university, founded in 1348 by Emperor Charles IV.

**ARMED FORCES.** Universal military service is for two years. The armed forces total about 225,000.

## DAHOMEY

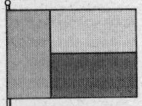

*Official Name:* Republic of Dahomey. *Area:* 43,483 square miles. *Population:* 2,-410,000. *Principal Cities* (with populations): Porto Novo, the capital, 60,000; Cotonou, 86,000; Abomey, 23,000. *Flag:* A yellow and a red horizontal stripe, flanked on the left by a vertical green stripe. *Monetary Unit:* The CFA franc (worth 0.4 U.S. cent). *Gross National Product:* $165,000,000 (1965). *Average Annual Income per Person:* $70.

**LAND AND PEOPLE.** Dahomey, situated in West Africa, is bordered on the north by Niger, on the east by Nigeria, on the south by the Gulf of Guinea, on the west by Togo, and on the northwest by Upper Volta. (See map on page 111.)

Behind the flat, sandy southern coast are lagoons. Farther inland, swampy forests give way to hill country, followed by wooded plateau, and, in the north, by savanna. The Atakora Mountains in the northwest range from 1,500 to above 2,400 feet. Equatorial heat and humidity prevail in the south.

Dahomeyans comprise several ethnic and linguistic groups. The Fon in the south make up about one-third of the population. The remainder are Adja, Aizo, Bariba, Yoruba, Holli, Somba, and Fulani. French (the official language), English, and numerous African dialects are spoken. Some 68 per cent of the people adhere to tribal religions; 15 per cent are Muslims; and the remainder are mostly Christians.

**HISTORY.** Dahomey's earliest known settlers, the Adja, established a kingdom near the coast before the 12th century. It was divided early in the 17th century into four kingdoms: Allada, Abomey (later called Dahomey), Ouidah, and Porto Novo. Portuguese traders were the first Europeans in the area, but as the slave trade grew, other European traders came in increasing numbers.

French influence was established in 1851 when France signed a treaty with Abomey, then the most powerful Adja kingdom. After several attacks by Abomey on coastal trading posts between 1889 and 1891, France retaliated with force and established a protectorate that in 1904 became a territory of French West Africa.

In 1958 Dahomey was made an autonomous state within the French Community, and on August 1, 1960, it declared itself an independent republic. In 1965 General Christophe Soglo took over the government because of the "incapacity of the politicians to govern."

**GOVERNMENT AND POLITICS.** General Soglo suspended the constitution, banned political parties, dissolved municipal councils, and postponed elections. In April, 1967, a military Committee of Vigilance was formed, tightening the army's control over the government, and the civilian National Committee of Renewal was dissolved.

**ECONOMY.** Dahomey's economy is almost totally agricultural. Subsistence farming is of great importance. Since independence the government has operated under chronic deficits. Budget difficulties arose from overexpansion of social services, a 50 per cent increase in the number of civil servants between 1960 and 1965, and agricultural stagnation or decline. France has granted direct budgetary aid (about $3.6 million in 1966), plus additional advances and credits for agricultural development and research. Industry is limited to a few small factories, mostly engaged in processing.

Dahomey's 360 miles of railways are state-owned and run. Of its approximately 3,800 miles of roads, about 10 per cent are paved. A new deepwater harbor, constructed at Cotonou with French aid, can handle a million tons of shipping annually; the port also serves Niger. Domestic air services exist, and the country is served by several foreign carriers.

**EDUCATION.** Education is compulsory between the ages of 6 and 12. In 1966 there were 812 schools, mostly primary. About 25 per cent of school-age children attend school. Adult literacy is estimated at 5 per cent.

**ARMED FORCES.** Military service is not compulsory. There is a 1,000-man army, a 100-man navy, and a 25-man air force. Dahomey can call on French military aid if needed.

# DENMARK

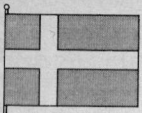

*Official Name:* Kingdom of Denmark. *Area:* 16,619 square miles. *Population:* 4,813,892. *Principal Cities* (with populations): Copenhagen, the capital, 694,479; Aarhus, 118,945; Frederiksberg, 112,211; Odense, 109,681. *Flag:* A white Latin cross on a red field. It is the oldest unchanged and continuously used flag in the world. *Monetary Unit:* The krone of 100 øre (worth 14.48 U.S. cents). *Gross National Product:* $11,118,600,-000 (1966). *Average Annual Income per Person:* $1,799.

**LAND AND PEOPLE.** Denmark consists of the Jutland Peninsula and 500 neighboring islands. (See map on page 117.) The country's only land connection with Europe is its 42-mile southern frontier with Germany. Denmark's 4,600-mile coastline is bordered on the north by the Skagerrak; on the east by the Kattegat, the Øresund, and the Baltic Sea; and on the west by the North Sea.

About 32 per cent of Denmark's total land area is in its islands, a quarter of which are inhabited. The five largest islands are Funen, Lolland, Bornholm, Falster, and Zealand, where Copenhagen is located. The countryside is predominantly rolling flatland; the highest point in Denmark is 568 feet above sea level, and average elevation is about 98 feet.

The population is 98 per cent Danish, and 97 per cent of the population belong to the state-supported Lutheran Church. The official language is Danish.

**HISTORY.** Denmark's historical period began in the ninth century, when Danish Vikings led raids against England and the Continent. The Viking king, Harold Bluetooth—"the Harold who won for himself all Denmark and Norway and made the Danes Christians"—died about 985, and his son Sweyn Forkbeard conquered England. At the height of the Viking era, King Canute the Great, Sweyn's younger son, ruled over an empire that included England, Norway, and Denmark. After his death in 1035 the empire disintegrated.

During the 12th century a feudal social and economic structure emerged in Denmark. The 13th and early 14th centuries were marked by civil war and internal chaos. In 1397 Norway and Sweden were united under Denmark's Queen Margaret, but a Swedish revolt ended the union in 1523. Norway, however, remained united with Denmark until 1814.

The Lutheran movement came into Denmark from Germany in 1536, and the power of the monarchy increased when the king became head of the new church. Wars between the Scandinavian powers for control of the Baltic dominated the 16th and much of the 17th centuries; the wars ended in 1660 with Denmark's total defeat. At this time Frederick III established an absolute monarchy that endured for more than 180 years. Educational and economic reforms were advanced, and the peasantry was slowly emancipated. In 1808 Frederick VI allied himself with Napoleon, and, with Napoleon's defeat, Denmark was forced to cede Norway to Sweden in 1814.

The next half century was one of external battles and internal revolution. In 1830 a nationalist rebellion erupted in Schleswig and Holstein, closely linked duchies on the German border subject to the Danish king. The uprising led to two Prusso-Danish Wars—in 1848 and 1864—and in both cases Denmark was defeated. In 1864 Prussia forced Denmark to cede the two duchies. Meanwhile, the liberal trend within Denmark was making progress. Frederick VII (1848–63) was forced to give up his absolute rule and introduce a constitution guaranteeing legislative representation and civil liberties. Under Christian IX (1863–1906) Denmark became one of the most modern European countries; social reform, expansion of trade, and wider suffrage were achieved.

Although Denmark was neutral during World War I, the Allied blockade of Germany and trade restrictions disrupted its economy. After the war (1920) a plebiscite was held in northern Schleswig, which voted to become part of Denmark. In April, 1940, German troops invaded Denmark and remained until 1945.

Postwar policy has aimed at military security, Scandinavian collaboration, and European economic cooperation. Denmark is currently trying to join the Common Market. Social welfare legislation has been passed that provides for health insurance, social security, old-age pensions, and many other benefits.

**GOVERNMENT AND POLITICS.** The Kingdom of Denmark is a constitutional monarchy with a parliamentary form of government. Under the constitution of 1953 the king and his cabinet exercise executive and administrative power. The cabinet, appointed by the king, is headed by a prime minister who is usually the leader of the majority party in the parliament. Administrative power is shared by the king and the Folketing, a one-chamber parliament with 179 members elected by popular vote to four-year terms.

The king, who must belong to the Lutheran Church, is Frederick IX. The prime minister is Jens Otto Krag, leader of the Social Democratic Party. Since the end of World War II, Denmark has been governed by coalition cabinets headed, except for three years, by the Social Democrats. In 1967 Prime Minister Krag headed a Social Democratic minority cabinet.

**ECONOMY.** Since 1945 industry has replaced agriculture as the greatest contributor to Denmark's gross national product. Leading industries are food processing, shipbuilding, heavy machinery, textiles, furniture, chemicals, and pharmaceuticals. The country imports nearly all its fuel and raw materials.

Although manufacturing's contribution to the gross national product is about double that of agriculture, over 70 per cent of the land is under cultivation. Dairy goods, cattle, hogs, poultry, and grain are the main products, but with a decline of the farm labor force, farmers now favor products requiring fewest laborers.

**EDUCATION.** The literacy rate is close to 100 per cent. Education is free and compulsory for children from 7 to 14. The national library is the largest in Scandinavia.

**ARMED FORCES.** Denmark, a member of NATO, has an army estimated at 49,200 men. There is compulsory military service for males between the ages of 19 and 25.

## DANISH TERRITORIES AND DEPENDENCIES

### GREENLAND

*Official Name:* Greenland. *Area:* 840,000 square miles. *Population:* 40,000. *Capital:* Godthåb (population 5,783). *Languages:* Danish and Greenlandic.

Greenland, the world's largest island, is bordered on the north by the Arctic Ocean, on the east by the Greenland Sea, on the southeast by the Denmark Strait, on the south by the Atlantic Ocean, and on the west by Baffin Bay and Davis Strait.

The ice cap, covering 84 per cent of the island, has an average thickness of nearly 5,000 feet but may be over 14,000 feet thick in some areas.

The bulk of Greenland's population is concentrated along the southwestern coast. Most inhabitants are Greenlanders, people of mixed Eskimo and European ancestry.

Although known by the ancient Greeks, Greenland first was colonized about 982 A.D. by Eric the Red. Modern colonization was begun in 1721 by Hans Egede, a Norwegian missionary. When Denmark lost Norway after the Napoleonic wars, the peace conference delegates apparently overlooked Norway's outlying possessions, so Greenland remained Danish.

Greenland was administered as a colony until 1953, and is now an integral part of Denmark. The island has two elected members in the Danish Folketing. The chief administrative authority on Greenland is the governor, who is responsible to the Danish Ministry for Greenland.

Denmark and the United States have an agreement for the common defense of the island. There is a major U.S. air base at Thule in northern Greenland.

### FAROE ISLANDS

*Official Name:* Faroe Islands. *Area:* 540 square miles. *Population:* 37,000. *Capital:* Thorshavn (population 7,447).

The Faroe Islands lie in the North Atlantic between Scotland's Shetland Islands and Iceland. Eighteen of the 19 islands are inhabited. Strömö, on which the capital, Thorshavn, is located, is the largest island.

Celts were the earliest known inhabitants, but in the eighth century Norsemen settled the Faroes, and they became part of Norway. Christianity was introduced in the 11th century. After the Black Death nearly annihilated the entire population, Norwegians resettled the islands in the 14th and 15th centuries.

Norway and the Faroes came under Danish rule in 1380, and the islands remained Danish

after the Treaty of Kiel (1814) in which Denmark lost Norway. The Faroese parliament proclaimed the islands' independence in 1946 after a plebiscite, but the Danish king dissolved the parliament and a new vote reversed the original proclamation. The islands obtained home rule, however, in 1948.

The popularly elected parliament is the Lagting. Two Faroese members sit in the Danish parliament.

## DOMINICAN REPUBLIC

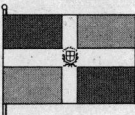

*Official Name:* Dominican Republic. *Area:* 18,816 square miles. *Population:* 3,750,000. *Principal Cities* (with populations): Santo Domingo, the capital, 466,800; Santiago de los Caballeros, 185,000; La Vega, 164,478; San Francisco de Macorís, 107,000. *Flag:* A white cross bearing the national coat of arms divides the flag into four quarters, of which the upper left and lower right are blue and the others red. *Monetary Unit:* the peso of 100 centavos (at par with the U.S. dollar). *Gross National Product:* $960 million. *Average Annual Income per Person:* $190.

**LAND AND PEOPLE.** The republic is situated on the eastern two-thirds of the Caribbean island of Hispaniola. It has a 193-mile border in the west with Haiti; the Atlantic Ocean is on the north; the Mona Passage on its east coast separates it from Puerto Rico; and the Caribbean is on its south shore. (See map on page 76.)

The country has a coastal plain and four nearly parallel east-west mountain chains. The Cibao, the republic's most important valley system, is noted for its immensely fertile black soil; it lies to the north of the Cordillera Central, a mountain range bisecting the country. The climate is mildly tropical and humid. Temperatures range from 72° to 83° F., but the winters are colder in the mountain areas of the interior.

The population is 20 per cent Negro, 15 per cent white, and 65 per cent mulatto. The official language is Spanish. Some 98.2 per cent of the Dominicans adhere to Roman Catholicism, the state religion; 1.4 per cent are Protestants.

**HISTORY.** The bellicose Caribe Indians are believed to have been the island's first inhabitants; they were succeeded by the peaceable, farming Arawaks. Columbus discovered the island in 1492, claimed it for Spain, and named it Las Española (Hispaniola). Santo Domingo was the first European settlement in the Western Hemisphere. The colony grew rapidly for a time, but was eventually ravaged by small pox, pirates, and earthquakes. Within 70 years the population was reduced by half.

In 1697 Spain was forced by the Treaty of Ryswick to cede to France the western third of the island, the area now known as Haiti. The Treaty of Basel, signed in 1795, gave the rest of Hispaniola to France. The Negro leader Toussaint L'Ouverture, who had created a practically autonomous state in Haiti, conquered

Santo Domingo in 1801. The Dominicans, fearful of Negro rule, backed a French force that overcame the Haitian conquerors. With British aid, the Dominicans revolted against French rule in 1809, proclaiming the first Dominican Republic.

The 1814 Treaty of Paris returned the country to Spanish rule. In 1821 a republic was again proclaimed, but was overrun and annexed by Haiti the following year. For 22 years the Dominicans lived under a repressive Haitian occupation. Practically all whites of any position or wealth fled the island. Economic and intellectual life virtually ceased, and implacable racial and cultural hatreds arose between the Dominicans and the Haitians. By 1844 the Dominicans rebelled and drove out the Haitians, and once again the republic became independent.

The following decades were marked by revolts, changes of government, dictatorship, assassination, continued attacks by Haiti, widespread corruption, and a four-year return to Spanish rule. In 1870 the Dominicans approved by plebiscite a treaty negotiated by their president that would have annexed the republic to the United States, but the U.S. Senate refused to ratify it. Economic chaos engendered by constant internal turmoil led the government into bankruptcy, and in 1904 several foreign powers intervened to collect their debts. To forestall such a move, the United States in 1905 took over the administration of Dominican customs. In 1916 the United States occupied the republic and established a military government that ruled till 1924. Customs control was retained until 1941.

From 1930 to 1961 the Dominican Republic was the personal holding of General Rafael Leonidas Trujillo Molina and his relatives. A dictator who crushed resistance by means of murder, imprisonment, economic pressure, and exile, Trujillo was assassinated in 1961.

From 1961 to 1966 the country was ruled chiefly by a series of provisional governments. As the economic situation deteriorated, popular discontent grew. Corrupt elements in the armed forces attempted to continue profitable illicit activities such as smuggling and to maintain the freedom from civilian control that they had enjoyed under Trujillo. The old oligarchy tried to reassume the dominance taken from them by Trujillo, while would-be leaders pursued their personal ambitions.

A freely elected democrat of the moderate left, Juan Bosch, served as president for seven months in 1963, until his overthrow by the military. Early in 1965 civil war broke out between the left-wing forces, including Communists, who were trying to restore Bosch to power, and the right-wing and military elements. Wary of permitting Communist influence to expand in Latin America, President Johnson sent U.S. troops into the republic in April, intervening against the pro-Bosch forces. After another interlude of provisional government, Joaquín Balaguer ran for the presidency, defeating Bosch in an honest election. Balaguer, who had served as president at the time of Trujillo's assassination and had presided over the transition from Trujilloism, took office in 1966.

**GOVERNMENT AND POLITICS.** The president and Parliament are elected for terms of four years. Parliament consists of an upper chamber of 27 members and a lower chamber of 74 members.

President Balaguer, whose Partido Reformista has a majority in the upper chamber, has moved cautiously ahead, using massive U.S. aid in an attempt to revive the country's war-devastated economy. He has managed to survive in office, but has failed to control right-wing political gangsterism and assassinations. Bosch's Partido Revolucionario Dominicano at first played the role of loyal opposition but has become noncooperative. Bosch himself, presumably fearing assassination, took up residence in Spain in 1967, leaving direction of the PRD in younger and more radical hands.

**ECONOMY.** The republic's principal export and source of foreign exchange is sugar. Other crops include coffee, tobacco, and cacao. Minerals contribute importantly to the economy; 74,400 metric tons of bauxite were mined in 1965. Food processing, especially that of sugar, accounts for much of the national industry.

**EDUCATION.** Primary education is free and nominally compulsory from the ages of 6 to 14; literacy is estimated at about 60 per cent.

**ARMED FORCES.** Military service is not compulsory. There are some 12,000 men in the army; 3,830 in the navy; and 3,500 in the air force.

# ECUADOR

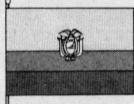

*Official Name:* Republic of Ecuador. *Area:* 104,515 square miles. *Population:* 5,326,000. *Principal Cities* (with populations): Quito, the capital, 450,000; Guayaquil, 600,000. *Flag:* Yellow, blue, and red horizontal stripes with national badge. *Monetary Unit:* The sucre (worth 5.5 U.S. cents). *Gross National Product:* $1,040,000,000. *Average Annual Income per Person:* $181.

**LAND AND PEOPLE.** Ecuador, so named because the equator passes through the country, is bordered on the north by Colombia, on the east and south by Peru, and on the west by the Pacific Ocean. (See map on page 75.) The country also includes the Galápagos Islands.

Plains border Ecuador's coastline. The highlands, formed by two parallel ranges of the Andes, run north-south in mid-country. A sparsely inhabited and largely unexplored jungle area (the Oriente) is in the east. Climate varies with the region. Most of the northern coast is a wet, tropical forest. The southern coastal area, including Guayaquil, is affected by the cold Humboldt current of the Pacific.

Most of the people are either Indian or mestizo. About 10 per cent are Negroes. Another 10 per cent are whites, who constitute the dominant, elite group and are largely of Spanish descent. Ecuador is a Spanish-speaking country. Over 90 per cent of the people are Roman Catholics.

**HISTORY.** Small tribes of Indians first inhabited Ecuador. They were conquered near the end of the 15th century by Incas from the south who ruled until the Spanish conquest in 1534. The Spanish conquerors introduced new crops and domestic animals. They also Christianized the Indians. Native culture declined, and the Indians became an exploited working class, living like slaves.

In the battle of Pichincha in 1822 Ecuador gained independence from Spain and became part of Simón Bolívar's Gran Colombia. When that confederation was dissolved in 1830, Ecuador became a separate, independent nation. Two men, alternating in the presidency, dominated the first 15 years of independence: the country's first president, Conservative Juan José Flores, and the Liberal Vicente Rocafuerte. Bitter struggles between conservative and liberal factions have marked Ecuador's political history since that time.

Flores was exiled in 1845; rival military factions struggled for power during the next 15 years. Ecuador's defeat in a war with Peru and consequent loss of much Amazonian territory brought to power Gabriel García Moreno, a Conservative who dominated political life for another 15 years. In an effort to center national life around the Roman Catholic Church, he gave the church special privileges. He also encouraged education (under church control) and initiated public works projects. In 1876 he was assassinated.

After two decades of political disorder, Liberal Eloy Alfaro became president. Under his leadership the separation of church and state was clearly defined and basic personal freedoms were established. Alfaro was assassinated, but his reforms started a long period of political division, frequent violence, and loss of lands. Liberals continued to dominate Ecuador's politics until World War II. Another brief war with Peru ended in 1942 with the loss of most of the Amazonian territory claimed by Ecuador.

An era of more stable constitutional government began with the election of Galo Plaza Lasso in 1948. He was Ecuador's first freely elected president who served out his full term. He was followed by the Liberal José María Velasco Ibarra, who revived the territorial dispute with Peru, almost bringing the nation to open war in 1955. The Conservative Camilo Ponce was elected in 1956. In 1960 Velasco Ibarra, running as an independent, was again elected. He was forced into exile in 1961 by what he called "a Communist-style coup," and Vice President Carlos Julio Arosemena Monroy assumed the office. In July, 1963, he was deposed by a military junta.

After a short provisional presidency, elections were held in November, 1966, for a Constitutional Assembly, which chose Otto Arosemena Gómez as provisional president until a popular election scheduled for June, 1968.

**GOVERNMENT AND POLITICS.** Ecuador is a republic with a president, a bicameral legislature, and a single national court system. Provincial governors are appointed and hold office at the discretion of the president. Rivalry of interests between the capital, Quito, and the commercial capital, Guayaquil, influences politics.

**ECONOMY.** Agriculture employs about two-thirds of the labor force and provides some 85 per cent of the exports (bananas, cacao, sugar, coffee). Manufacturing accounts for one-fifth of the gross national product. Mining and petroleum production are small but growing. The vast forests have a potentially great economic value.

**EDUCATION.** Education is free and compulsory for all children between 6 and 14. About 68.5 per cent of the population is literate. A program has begun to further adult literacy.

**ARMED FORCES.** Although one year of military training is compulsory for men at age 20, only a small percentage are actually conscripted. The standing army numbers 10,000. There is a navy and air force.

## ECUADORIAN TERRITORIES AND DEPENDENCIES

### GALÁPAGOS ISLANDS

*Official Name:* Galápagos Islands. *Area:* 3,029 square miles. *Population:* 3,000. *Capital:* San Cristóbal.

This cluster of about 60 volcanic islands, scattered over 23,000 square miles of the Pacific, lies on the equator about 650 miles west of Ecuador. Isabela, the largest island, with about half of the total land area of the group, has a 5,500-foot-high volcano. Mountains on some of the other islands rise from 2,000 to 3,000 feet.

The Galápagos are known for their unique animal life. There are 15 species of tortoises, thought to be the oldest living creatures on earth, with a life span of over 200 years. Huge land and sea iguanas and many unusual birds, such as the flightless cormorant, are also found here. The Humboldt Current cools the tropical islands, and the higher elevations have substantial rainfall, creating a dense jungle. The government declared the Galápagos a national park in 1936 to prevent decimation of wildlife.

Early Indians were believed to have traveled by raft to the Galápagos for the excellent fishing. The first Spaniard to visit there was the Bishop of Panama, who drifted off course in 1535 while en route to Peru.

Pirates in the 17th century, and whalers two centuries later, used meat and oil from the tortoises to replenish their ships' supplies. Ecuador's first president claimed the islands in 1832. The English naturalist Charles Darwin visited the Galápagos in 1835, gathering information that later led to his formulation of a theory of evolution. During World War II the United States established a military base there.

Attempts at settlement have been frequent and usually unsuccessful. The dry, low-lying regions of the islands are almost totally without soil. Volcanic soils cultivated at higher elevations became exhausted after one long period of large-scale plantings of sugarcane.

Once under the jurisdiction of the Ministry of Defense, the islands have been administered by a governor since 1959.

# EGYPT (UNITED ARAB REPUBLIC)

*Official Name:* United Arab Republic. *Area:* 386,100 square miles. *Population:* 30,147,000. *Principal Cities* (with populations): Cairo, the capital, 3,518,200; Alexandria, 1,587,700; Giza, 276,200; Port Said, 256,000; Ismailia, 156,300. *Flag:* Red, white and black horizontal stripes with two green stars in the white stripe. *Monetary Unit:* The Egyptian pound of 100 piasters (worth U.S. $2.30). *Gross National Product:* $4,700,000,000 (1965). *Average Annual Income per Person:* $135.

**LAND AND PEOPLE.** Egypt, which occupies the northeast corner of Africa, is bordered on the north by the Mediterranean Sea; on the east by Israel, the Gulf of Aqaba, and the Red Sea; on the south by Sudan; and on the west by Libya. (See map on page 111.)

The northward-flowing Nile River and its fertile valley and delta divide the high desert plateaus of western Egypt from those in the east. Upper Egypt is the name given to the southern region, while that in the north is called Lower Egypt. Lower Egypt, which includes the Nile Delta, is an area of about 8,500 square miles of cropland enriched by silt brought down by the river from the Ethiopian highlands. (An ancient myth held that the Nile's source was in the "Mountains of the Moon.") The productive portion of Upper Egypt consists of a narrow strip of irrigated land about 20 miles wide, reaching from Cairo to the Sudan.

Ninety-nine per cent of the people live in the Nile Valley, whose cliffs in some sections tower as high as 1,800 feet. The annual rise of the Nile is about 22 feet near Cairo, and about 40 feet in its upper regions, in August-October.

Rainfall in Egypt is scanty—six or eight inches a year in parts of the delta; almost none falls in the Libyan and Sinai deserts and some parts of Upper Egypt.

Most of the country is hot, but nighttime temperatures drop sharply. The coastal region is cooled by winds from the Mediterranean. The country has a limited mountainous region in the Sinai peninsula (now held by Israel).

Egyptians, who are a mixture of ancient local peoples and invaders from Asia, Africa, and Europe, make up 96 per cent of the population. Minority groups include Europeans and Indians. Biologically, today's Egypt is one of the youngest nations; nearly two-thirds of the present population is under 30 years of age. Ninety per cent of the people are Muslim; the main religious minority is Coptic Christian. Arabic is the national language; some English and French are spoken.

**HISTORY.** Egypt is one of the oldest nations in the world; the historical record dates back at least 5,000 years. The country already had an advanced civilization when the earliest native dynasty united the kingdoms of Upper and Lower Egypt about 3200 B.C. This and the following dynasties had close links with other Mediterranean lands, such as Crete and Greece, and with peoples on the east of the Sahara Desert. It was in the fourth through sixth dynasties (2613 B.C.–2181 B.C.) that the great pyramids were built.

Egypt fell under Persian control in 525 B.C. Greek rule by the Macedonians under Alexander the Great and the Ptolemy dynasty followed; then came Roman rule. The present culture of Egypt was basically set by the Muslim conquest of 640 that imposed the Islamic religion on the country.

After the breakup of the Abbasid Empire in the ninth century, Egypt was ruled by a long succession of minor local caliphs and sultans. In the 12th century a great Muslim warrior, Saladin—the respected opponent of King Richard I of England during the Third Crusade—established the Ayyubite dynasty. In the 13th century the "slave" dynasty of the Turkish and Circassian Mamelukes (slaves of non-Arabic stock who were used as soldiers) took and held power until the end of the 18th century.

The modern history of Egypt begins with the invasion of the country by Napoleon in 1798. During the disorders which followed the French withdrawal in the early 1800s, a former soldier named Mohammed Ali seized power and massacred the last of the Mamelukes in 1811. Under his rule Egypt began its version of the Western industrial revolution.

In 1882 a nationalist revolt led by Arabi Pasha brought in British troops to protect British interests. Britain remained in effective political control of Egypt until 1919, and made Egypt an independent kingdom in 1922.

In World War II, Egypt, though neutral until the last months, was a crucial base for the Western Alliance in the fighting in North Africa and the Mediterranean. Egypt did not cooperate with the West willingly; it was necessary for the British to threaten force in 1942 to get King Farouk to appoint a government that would support the Allies.

Egypt took the major part in the Arab-Israeli war of 1948, and the humiliating defeat of the Egyptian forces and the suspicions of corruption in their management were among the main reasons for the decay of King Farouk's regime. In 1952 Farouk, last of the dynasty of Mohammed Ali, was exiled after a bloodless military coup. Colonel Gamal Abdel Nasser quickly emerged as the leader of the revolt, but he was not in complete control until he had ousted (November, 1954) General Mohammed Naguib, first president of the new republic established 18 months earlier.

Nasser's ambitious policies, aimed at taking over the leadership of the Arab world, had their most successful moment during the Suez crisis of 1956. Nasser then turned a military defeat at the hands of Britain, France, and Israel into a resounding political victory—and he retained control of the Suez Canal, which he had seized. During this crisis he had the support of Russia, and he benefited by the neutrality of the U.S.

For the next 11 years Nasser was the most powerful and famous figure in the Arab world.

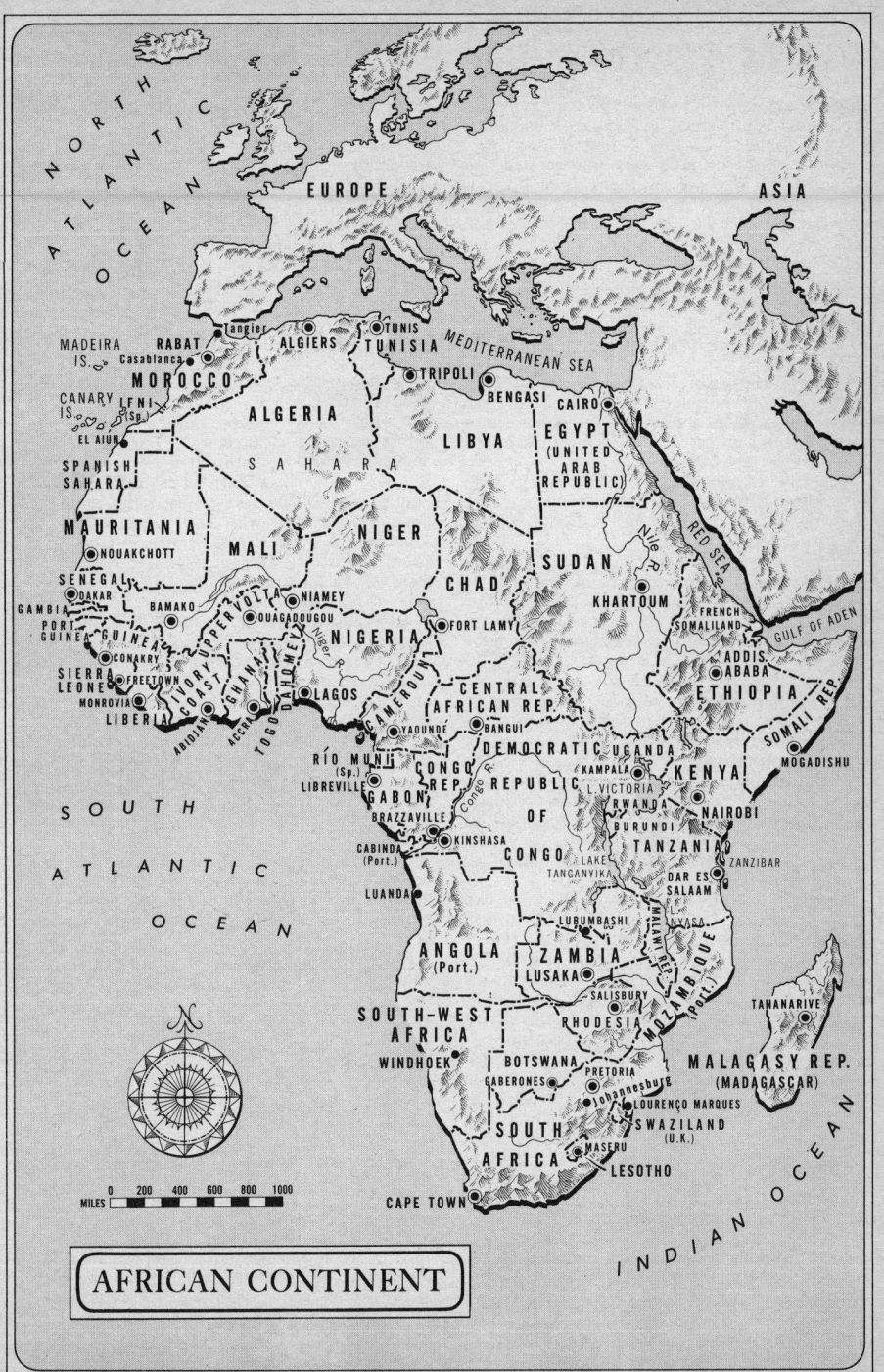

AFRICAN CONTINENT

He sought to expand his influence in February, 1958, by setting up the United Arab Republic (U.A.R.) with neighboring Syria (a federation that has since collapsed). And in 1963 he committed Egyptian troops to support a republican government in Yemen in hopes of extending Egypt's domain.

In the spring of 1967 Nasser requested and obtained the removal of the United Nations peace-keeping force in the area between Egypt and Israel, which he had lost in 1956. He then blockaded the Gulf of Aqaba against Israeli shipping. The result, on June 5, 1967, was the outbreak of a fresh Egyptian-Israeli war. Israel was victorious in a five-day blitz, driving the Egyptians out of the Gaza Strip and the Gulf of Aqaba and occupying the east bank of the Suez Canal.

Nasser's supporters shouted down his offer to resign, and internally he appears to keep strong control. As a result of the defeat, however, Egypt has lost enormous prestige in the Middle East and Africa.

**GOVERNMENT AND POLITICS.** The United Arab Republic is a presidential government based on the rule of one party, the National Union. Other parties are banned.

The constitution adopted in 1964 says that the U.A.R. is a democratic socialist state. The National Assembly is elected by popular vote, although the president may appoint ten members and may dissolve the assembly when he wishes.

Nasser was re-elected to the presidency by the National Assembly and by referendum in March, 1965, for another six-year term. The cabinet, formed in October, 1965, consists of about 30 members.

Egypt is divided into 16 governates, each ruled by a governor appointed by the president. The governor rules with the advice of an elected Provincial Assembly.

There is state control of the press and of all other information services.

**ECONOMY.** Egypt's economy is beset by two great difficulties. One is that it is still largely dependent on one farm crop, cotton. (Communist countries have for political reasons become the main purchasers—55 per cent—of the crop, which makes it hard for the U.A.R. to get a good price.) The other difficulty is Egypt's high rate of population expansion.

Since 1960 the regime has followed a program of rapid industrialization, aimed at setting up steel plants and motor and chemical industries almost exclusively by state action. The Aswan High Dam, which is expected to triple hydroelectric power and to add two million acres to Egypt's cultivable land, is essential to government plans. The dam was estimated to be 80 per cent complete early in 1967.

Seventy per cent of the people work in agriculture. Besides cotton, crops include cereals, rice, sugar, fruits, and onions. Farming accounts for 90 per cent of Egypt's exports and 40 per cent of her income.

The main industries are cotton spinning and weaving, tourist trade, feed processing, industrial chemicals, soap, petroleum products, and cement. Industry is concentrated in Cairo and Alexandria.

Natural resources include petroleum, phosphate, manganese, natron, salt, and iron ore. There are 10,000 miles of highways and 2,600 miles of state-owned railroads.

**EDUCATION.** Schooling is free and compulsory for children aged 6 to 12. Secondary education is also free. Chief universities are Cairo, Alexandria, Ain Shams (in Cairo), and Asyut. The literacy rate is 19.5 per cent. All schools are state-controlled.

**ARMED FORCES.** Service is compulsory at the age of 18. There are 113,000 in the armed forces, plus 50,000 in the National Guard.

# EL SALVADOR

*Official Name:* Republic of El Salvador. *Area:* 8,260 square miles. *Population:* 3,-300,000. *Principal Cities* (with populations): San Salvador, the capital, 350,000; Santa Ana, 100,000. *Flag:* Blue, white, and blue horizontal stripes, with the nation's coat of arms in the white stripe. *Monetary Unit:* The colon (worth 40 U.S. cents). *Gross National Product:* $832,000,000 (1966). *Average Annual Income per Person:* $235.

**LAND AND PEOPLE.** The smallest country in Central America and the most densely populated (about 400 per square mile), El Salvador is bordered on the north and east by Honduras, on the south by the Pacific Ocean, and on the west by Guatemala. (See map on page 176.)

Most of the people live in the central plateau, which runs east-west between volcanic ranges at an average elevation of 2,000 feet above sea level. The rich, porous soil of the plateau is ideal for coffee planting. El Salvador's temperature ranges from 64° to 90° F.

Over 92 per cent of the Salvadorans are Spanish-speaking mestizos; nearly 6 per cent are Indian, and about 2 per cent are white. The population is about 98 per cent Roman Catholic.

**HISTORY.** Before the Spanish Conquest, El Salvador, called Cuscatlan (Land of Jewels), was the home of the Aztec-related Pipil Indians, and probably one of the few Aztec colonies in Central America. When the fortune-hunting Spanish conquistador Pedro de Alvarado conquered El Salvador in 1525, he found few jewels or precious metals. Consequently, during the colonial period the Spanish neglected the area in favor of wealthier territories of the Mayas and Aztecs. El Salvador developed slowly in comparative isolation for nearly 300 years. Most settlers herded livestock and raised subsistence crops.

El Salvador was under Spanish rule until 1821, when it became part of the Mexican empire. When that empire collapsed in the mid-1820s, El Salvador joined the Federal Republic of Central America. This union was dissolved in 1838.

Much of El Salvador's life as a republic has been beset by international rivalries, internal strife, and military dictatorship. One of the longest stable periods in El Salvador's history was between 1931 and 1944 when General Maximiliano Hernández Martínez controlled the government.

Land, tax, and social reforms were almost completely neglected until 1961, when a six-man civilian-military government seized power. The presidential term of Colonel José Julio Rivera (1962–67) was characterized by stabilization of the currency, initiation of an income tax, and some pro-labor legislation. Nevertheless, agitation for further reforms, led by the Christian Democratic Party and the Party of Renovating Action, has increased in recent years. Colonel Fidel Sánchez Hernández became president on July 1, 1967; his program stressed the continuation of mild reforms.

**GOVERNMENT AND POLITICS.** El Salvador is a unitary republic with a unicameral legislative body. The 52 deputies of the assembly and all municipal officials are elected every two years, and the president is elected every five years. President Sánchez is a member of the Party of National Conciliation, a coalition of conservative groups.

**ECONOMY.** Although the most highly industrialized country in Central America, El Salvador has an economy based chiefly on agriculture. Agricultural products, especially coffee and cotton, account for more than 80 per cent of exports. Most of the coffee goes to West Germany and most of the cotton to Japan. The U.S. is the primary supplier of manufactured goods.

One of the most significant trends in El Salvador's international trade in recent years is the increasing importance of the Central American Common Market. Between 1958 and 1965 trade with the four Central American republics increased from $18,600,000 to $87,800,000.

**EDUCATION.** Schools are government-controlled and primary education is compulsory. The literacy rate is about 49 per cent. Over 21 per cent of the 1966 budget was allocated to education. The National University of El Salvador is in San Salvador.

**ARMED FORCES.** There is one-year compulsory military service for men between the ages of 18 and 30. About 6,000 men are in the army, 100 in the navy, and 500 in the air force.

# ETHIOPIA

*Official Name:* Kingdom of Ethiopia. *Area:* 471,776 square miles. *Population:* 22,600,000. *Principal Cities* (with populations): Addis Ababa, the capital, 560,000; Asmara, 131,800; Dessie, 53,000; Diredawa, 40,000; Harar, 40,000. *Flag:* Stripes of green, yellow, and red, with the large Lion of Judah inscribed in yellow. *Monetary Unit:* The Ethiopian dollar of 100 cents (worth 40 U.S. cents). *Gross National Product:* U.S. $982,-000,000 (1964). *Average Annual Income per Person:* $50.

**LAND AND PEOPLE.** Ethiopia is bordered on the north and northeast by the Red Sea and French Somaliland, on the east and southeast by Somalia, on the south by Kenya, and on the west and northwest by Sudan. (See map on page 111.)

It is a land of vivid topographical contrasts, including Africa's third loftiest peak—the 15,158-foot-high Ras Dashan—as well as a region 380 feet below sea level. Dramatically dividing the plateau country that makes up about two-thirds of the land is the Great Rift Valley, Ethiopia's most outstanding physical feature. The Blue Nile forms in Lake Tana, the country's largest lake. Most of the waters that annually flood the Nile flow from Ethiopia. About half the country, principally in the east and south where lands are below 5,500 feet, is in the hot desert zone. Most of the population and the main agricultural areas are in the temperate zone, from 5,500 to 8,000 feet.

There are five major tribal groups. The politically and economically dominant group are the Amhara-Tigrai, about a third of the people. Other groups are the Galla, 40 per cent of the population; the Sidama, 10 per cent; the Somali, 6 per cent; the Shankali, a Negroid group, about 6 per cent; and the Danakil, 5 per cent. Of the 70 or more Semitic-Cushitic languages, Amharic is official and is spoken by almost half of the people. The principal religion is Coptic Christian, and the emperor is titular head of the Ethiopian Orthodox Church. There are also many Muslims.

**HISTORY.** The original settlers of Ethiopia were the Cushites, ancestors of the Galla and Sidama tribal groups. Between the tenth and seventh centuries B.C., Semitic tribes from southern Arabia came to the region; from them descended the Amhara and the Tigrai tribes.

Menelik, the legendary first son of Solomon and the Queen of Sheba, is credited with having founded the Ethiopian Empire about 1000 B.C. The earliest authentic history records that in the first century A.D. Ethiopia was a pagan empire with its capital at Axum, but in the fourth century Christianity was introduced and took hold. Islam's ascendancy in the mid-seventh century was a threat to Ethiopia, and the country soon was surrounded by Muslim territory. About 1260 a new Ethiopian dynasty came to power that allegedly returned the throne to the line of Solomon, and under this dynasty Ethiopian suzerainty was restored over the principalities in the east and south.

In the 16th century the Somalis, with the help of Ottoman Turks, began a holy war for Islam against Ethiopia, and most of the country was overrun. With Portuguese help, the Ethiopians drove them out by 1543. Years of princely rivalry and civil strife followed; wars with the Muslims and the Gallas were frequent. By 1855, authority was centralized under Emperor Theodore II, originally a petty chieftain. He was defeated in 1868; his subsequent suicide led to a resumption of internal strife.

The ras, or prince, of the highland kingdom of Shoa, later to become Menelik II, eventually won control over most of Ethiopia, mainly with the help of Italy, which had begun its penetration of Eritrea in 1869. Menelik signed a treaty with Italy in 1889, only to repudiate it later when Italy claimed the treaty gave it the right to establish a protectorate over Ethiopia. The Italians invaded the country in 1895 but were defeated the next year and forced to acknowledge Ethiopia's independence. During Menelik's reign laws were codified, a railroad was constructed, and the present frontiers were established.

In 1913 Menelik was succeeded by his grandson. When the new emperor embraced the Muslim faith, he was deposed in 1916 by Ras Tafari Makonnen, a Christian and a favorite grandnephew of Menelik II. Afterward Ras Tafari had Menelik's daughter, Judith, crowned empress with himself as regent. In 1928 he became king of Ethiopia. On the death of the empress in 1930 he was crowned emperor and ascended the throne as Haile Selassie I. In 1935 the Italians again invaded the country, with planes and modern weapons, and in 1936 the Emperor was forced to flee to Britain. With British help he returned to the throne in 1941.

A landlocked country for centuries, Ethiopia gained a coastline on the Red Sea in 1952 when Eritrea, with U.N. approval, became a state; in 1962 it became an Ethiopian province.

**GOVERNMENT AND POLITICS.** Ethiopia is an hereditary, constitutional monarchy. Emperor Haile Selassie has designated his eldest and last living son, Asfaw Wossen, as crown prince. The 1955 constitution provided for the lower house of Parliament to be elected by universal suffrage. This was the first time that the people had been granted the right to vote. Selassie has attempted to modernize Ethiopia, but governmental machinery for implementing reforms has been archaic and lethargic.

In February, 1966, the Emperor asked for measures to grant "local self-administration to some of the provinces." The next month, in a warmly received move, he introduced major administrative revisions: nomination by the prime minister of his own appointees subject to imperial approval; a cabinet directly responsible only to the prime minister; and the prime minister and his cabinet responsible to the Emperor and Parliament.

The first government under the new system was formed in April, 1966, with Aklilu Habte-Wolde as prime minister. His domestic policies emphasized land and judicial reforms. Accordingly, the Land Reform Agency was promoted to a ministry, and a new Ministry of Planning and Development was established. The Emperor still holds veto power, and political parties do not exist.

Ethiopia's principal problem in its foreign relations has been the continuing dispute with Somalia over their common border and the territory of Djibouti (French Somaliland or Afar Territory). Sporadic clashes have occurred after a 1964 cease-fire, and the 1967 referendum in Djibouti that confirmed French rule aroused Ethiopian and Somalian counterclaims, although Ethiopia continued to accept French presence in Djibouti.

Another long-standing border problem, with Sudan, was quieted in January, 1967, when border populations were granted permission to farm on both sides, and the two governments agreed to prohibit border subversion. Border incidents recurred in July.

Ethiopia's capital, Addis Ababa, is the seat of the Organization of African Unity (OAU) and the U.N. Economic Commission for Africa (UNECA).

**ECONOMY.** Ethiopia is an agricultural country. Coffee accounts for over half of its export trade, and oil seeds rank second. A campaign to encourage tea production was launched in 1966 in order to diversify exports. The country supplies most of its own food needs, although a severe drought in 1966 caused wheat production to fall from an average 6,000,000 tons a year to 900,000 tons. Agricultural mechanization is almost totally unknown. Livestock provide hides and skins for export. In 1965 Ethiopian exports were valued at $124,000,000 while exports amounted to $126,000,000.

A five-year (1962–67), $1,062,000,000 development plan called for increases in mining, power, and manufacturing. The construction of generating facilities and dams has increased the production of electricity. Industry is primarily concerned with processing agricultural commodities. With the help of foreign aid, a papermill and a synthetic factory are being built, and the World Bank has provided loans in 1967 for an expansion of urban and interurban communications.

**EDUCATION AND HEALTH.** Education is not compulsory, and less than 10 per cent of the people are literate. In 1962 there were 362,000 students, of whom nearly 95 per cent were at the primary level.

Health standards are not high, and in 1961 there were only 230 doctors, or one for every 96,000 people.

**ARMED FORCES.** Military service is voluntary. Army strength is estimated at about 30,000 men with about 10,000 serving in the Imperial Guard. An air force and a navy are being formed.

# FINLAND

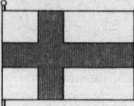

*Official Name:* Republic of Finland. *Area:* 130,119 square miles. *Population:* 4,639,000. *Principal Cities* (with metropolitan populations): Helsinki, the capital, 661,800; Turku, 185,600; Tampere, 184,500; Lahti, 81,500. *Flag:* A blue cross on a white field. *Monetary Unit:* The markka of 100 pennia (worth 32 U.S. cents). *Gross National Product:* $8,119,000,000 (1965). *Average Annual Income per Person:* $1,392.

**LAND AND PEOPLE.** Finland is bordered on the north and west by Norway, on the north and east by the Soviet Union, on the south by the Gulf of Finland and the Baltic Sea, and on the west by the Gulf of Bothnia and Sweden. (See map on page 117.)

The land in the north, where Finland extends above the Arctic Circle and forms part of Lapland, is densely forested and has a generally low mountainous topography. In the central and southern regions the land is mainly low-lying and level with many lakes. The southwest has the densest population.

Temperatures are mild despite the northern location of the country. The average July temperature in southern Finland is 60° F.; in February, the coldest month, temperatures range from 12° to 23° F. Length of daylight varies in northern Finland from 24 hours a day for 60 to 70 days during the summer months to no daylight during the winter months. Southern Finland in the winter has about 6 daylight hours in 24.

Finns comprise 92 per cent of the population; Swedo-Finns, 7 per cent. There are also about 2,000 Lapps and Gypsies. Finnish and Swedish are the official languages. Ninety-seven per cent of the people are Lutherans.

**HISTORY.** The Finns' ancestors came into the country from the south through Estonia and Livonia in the second century A.D. By the eighth century the Finns had taken the country from the Lapps, who retreated northward. A Swedish crusade in the 1150s is traditionally credited with having converted the Finns to Christianity, but relics from graves dating to the 11th and 12th centuries show that part of southwestern Finland had been Christianized before then.

Sweden established control over the land in 1520–40, and Finland became an integral part of the Swedish kingdom. Political, religious, educational, and administrative institutions in Finland developed in ways common to the kingdom as a whole. These institutions remained after 1809, when Russia annexed Finland. Tsar Alexander I joined Finland to the Russian Empire not as a province ruled by St. Petersburg, but as an autonomous Grand Duchy that retained its pre-1809 structure. Thus Finland has been a self-governing nation in which institutional ways established 300 years before have continued almost unchanged.

In 1863 the Finnish legislature (Diet) was called into session for the first time since the Russian annexation. During the next four decades a national system of primary schools was established, secondary schools and universities were expanded, modernization of industry was begun, and growth of the nation's culture was encouraged. Finnish was made an official language, along with Swedish, during this period.

But the Russianization of Finland was a rising threat, particularly after 1900. The 1905 Russian revolution briefly slowed this tide, but by 1914 Finland's constitution and autonomy were dangerously undermined. Russia's 1917 revolution gave the Finns an opportunity to declare their independence, and they did so on December 6, 1917. After a war of independence (which was also a civil war precipitated by domestic radical elements) Finland emerged fully free and adopted a republican constitution on July 17, 1919.

The secret pact (August, 1939) between the Soviet Union and Hitler's Germany gave Russia a free hand in Finland. Moscow then made demands which the Finns could not accept. The winter war of 1939–40 followed. Although the Finns put up amazing resistance against the Soviet invaders, they lost and were forced to cede to Russia a tenth of their land. German troops stationed in Finland's north after the summer of 1940 compromised the country's declared neutrality in World War II. As a cobelligerent of Germany, Finland was again drawn into war with Russia.

Finland's separate war, the Continuation War, began in June, 1941, with an attack on Russia that regained lost territory plus a part of the Soviet republic of Karelia. However, the Soviets mounted a massive offensive against the Finns in June, 1944, that was followed by an armistice three months later. The peace terms of 1940 were re-established, further territory was lost, heavy war indemnities were imposed, and Finnish troops were required to drive out the Germans still in the north.

**GOVERNMENT AND POLITICS.** The president serves a six-year term and is chosen by an electoral college whose members are directly elected. The 200 members of the one-house parliament, the Eduskunta, are directly elected for four-year terms. Everyone 21 and over has the vote. The prime minister and cabinet are responsible to the parliament. The president directs foreign affairs, can dissolve parliament, and is commander-in-chief of the armed forces.

President Urho Kaleva Kekkonen was elected to his second six-year term in 1962. He is a member of the Center Party. The parties in order of strength shown in the 1966 elections are: the Social Democrats, the Center, the People's Democratic League (predominantly Communist), the Conservative Party, the Liberal People's Party, the Social Democratic League (aligned with the Communists), and the Farmer's Party. Gains by the leftist parties ended nonsocialist rule, and a coalition government led by Social Democrats was formed that included Communists.

**ECONOMY.** Finland is the most heavily forested country in Europe, and wood, wood pulp, and paper account for over half of the country's exports. About 8 per cent of the country is agricultural land, mostly in small farms.

The principal industries are wood-processing and food production. Major mineral resources include pyrites, iron, copper, and zinc.

The country has an excellent system of inland waterways, more than 42,000 miles of highways, over 3,400 miles of railroads, and a 1,039,000-ton merchant fleet.

The 1944 armistice and the 1947 peace treaty obliged Finland to pay Russia $300,000,000 in reparations. This sum was later reduced by $75,000,000; payments were completed in 1952.

**EDUCATION.** Finland's educational system includes primary, secondary, and vocational schools. There are also 14 universities. Schooling is compulsory from age 7 to 16. Nearly all of the people are literate.

**ARMED FORCES.** Military service of 240 days is compulsory for males at the age of 19. There are 34,400 men in the army, 4,500 in the navy, and 3,000 in the air force.

# FRANCE

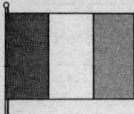

*Official Name:* The French Republic. *Area:* 211,207 square miles. *Population:* 49,440,003. *Principal Cities* (with populations): Paris, the capital, 2,790,091; Marseilles, 778,071; Lyons, 528,535; Nice, 292,958; Toulouse, 323,724; Bordeaux, 249,688; Nantes, 240,028; Strasbourg, 228,971. *Flag:* A blue, a white, and a red vertical stripe. *Monetary Unit:* The franc (worth 20 U.S. cents). *Gross National Product:* $94,139,442,000 (1965). *Average Annual Income per Person:* $1,446.

**LAND AND PEOPLE.** France, which occupies the northwestern corner of the continent of Europe, is bordered on the north by the English Channel, the North Sea, Belgium, Luxembourg, and West Germany; on the east by West Germany, Switzerland, and Italy; on the south by Monaco, the Mediterranean Sea, Spain, and Andorra; and on the west by the Bay of Biscay and the Atlantic Ocean. (See map on page 117.)

The land is varied and rich. In the southwest the Pyrenees rise along the Spanish border. In the east are the rugged peaks of the Alps and the Jura Mountains, and the wooded hills of the Vosges range and the Ardennes plateau. Four major river systems water the country. The Seine rises in the mountainous Central Massif and flows northwest through the Paris Basin to the English Channel; the Loire, also flowing from the Central Massif, courses westward to the Atlantic; the Garonne runs northwest from the Pyrenees to the Atlantic estuary of the Gironde; and the Rhone-Saône system flows from the Alps into the Mediterranean. The Rhine, constituting the Franco-German frontier for more than 100 miles north from Basel, irrigates the Alsatian plain.

The country has three distinct climatic regions. The dry Mediterranean south has hot summers and mild winters. The central and eastern uplands are moist and seasonally varied. The oceanic west and northwest have cool temperatures and considerable rainfall.

The French are a mixture of Mediterranean, Latin, Celtic, and Germanic stock, with a tiny Semitic strain. More than 85 per cent of the people are native-born. The largest of the non-French population groups are Italians, Spaniards, Poles, and North Africans. In addition to French, languages most spoken are Breton, Flemish, Spanish, Catalan, Basque, Italian, and a German dialect. Eighty-three per cent of the people are Roman Catholics; 2 per cent are Protestants; and 15 per cent are Jews or Muslims, or are nonaffiliated.

**HISTORY.** Hundreds of years before Christ, France was a crossroads of migrant agricultural peoples. Conquering Celtic invaders brought a degree of order among the quarreling inhabitants, imposed their language to some extent, and gave the area the name "Gaul."

In the first century B.C. the forces of Rome were called upon to help defend Gaul against marauding tribes. Rome's assistance turned to conquest. A vulgarized Latin tongue took root, and a network of military roads brought some degree of unity. Christianity was introduced at about the same time.

When the Roman Empire weakened in the third century A.D., Gaul was a prey to barbarian invaders. A northern tribe, the Salian Franks, subdued much of the country. After making an alliance with the Roman Catholic Church, Clovis, their tribal leader, extended Frankish rule and Christianity by force of arms in the fifth century. Clovis founded the first great dynasty, the Merovingians. But during the sixth and seventh centuries, royal control of France weakened; Clovis' descendants fought among themselves and destroyed their own authority. Beset by Muslim invaders moving up from Spain, the Franks found leadership and salvation from another family, who were the founders of the Carolingian dynasty in the eighth century.

The greatest of these rulers was Charlemagne. A militant imperialist and ally of the Church, he was crowned Emperor of the Western Roman Empire on Christmas Day in the year 800. Under Charlemagne, France (which then was only a part of a vast Frankish domain) had a basic sort of royal justice, a flourishing industry and commerce—but still no common language or central administration.

Following Charlemagne's death the empire fell apart under the impact of Norse invasions and regional revolts. The Carolingian rulers sank into obscurity.

In 987 a fresh beginning was made with the election of Hugh Capet, Duke of Francia, to the throne. The Capetians, as the new ruling group was known, allied themselves with the Church and the growing urban classes to challenge their powerful vassals and to extend their rule slowly over the whole country.

For more than 300 years the Capetians wore down the feudal forces in France. They disciplined the bishops, created the beginnings of a modern administrative system, crusaded against infidels and heretics, and warded off the English. Their line ended in 1328.

The successors, the Valois kings, almost collapsed under the assault of plague, revolts by nobles, and invasion by the English. In the Hundred Years War (1337–1453) with England, France was devastated and her people starved and butchered. The appearance of Joan of Arc, the reorganization of the royal armies, and English domestic troubles finally turned the tide. By the mid-15th century the Valois triumph was secure.

In the next century the country's rebellious nobles were brought under control, and the Church's influence in civil affairs was curbed. The new rulers also restrained the ambitious commoners who had met with the nobles and clergy in the parliamentary States-General since 1302 in an effort to limit the monarchy's authority. The Valois kings thus established France as a European power.

In the late 1550s this achievement was seriously threatened. The Reformation swept through France, and civil war followed.

# WESTERN EUROPE

MILES
0   100   200   300   400   500

ICELAND
REYKJAVIK

FAEROES

SHETLANDS

ORKNEYS

HEBRIDES

NORTH SEA

U.S.S.R.

FINLAND

GULF OF BOTHNIA

SWEDEN

Trondheim

Tampere

HELSINKI

Turku

NORWAY

Bergen

Uppsala
Örebro
STOCKHOLM

OSLO

Stavanger
Göteborg

LAKE VÄNERN

Norrköping

SCOTLAND
Glasgow    Edinburgh

NORTHERN IRELAND
Belfast

Newcastle

Baltic Sea

Aarhus    COPENHAGEN
Malmö
Odense

DENMARK

U.S.S.R.

IRELAND
DUBLIN
Liverpool    Manchester
Cork    Sheffield

Birmingham
Cardiff    LONDON
Bristol

ENGLAND

NETHER-
LANDS
AMSTERDAM

Hamburg
EAST
GERMANY

BERLIN

WARSAW

Poznan    Lodz
POLAND

Dresden    Wroclaw
Leipzig    PRAGUE    Krakow

Düsseldorf    Essen
Cologne
BELGIUM
BRUSSELS    BONN    WEST
LUXEMBOURG    GERMANY

CZECHOSLOVAKIA

Brno
Linz    Bratislava
Munich    VIENNA    Miskolc
BUDAPEST

ENGLISH CHANNEL

Seine R.

PARIS
Strasbourg

AUSTRIA    HUNGARY
Graz

Nantes

FRANCE
Geneva
Lyons

Zürich
SWITZ. LIECH.
BERN
Turin    Milan
Bologna

Trieste
Danube R.
Zagreb    BELGRADE

Venice
Genoa    Florence
SAN MARINO

YUGOSLAVIA

Sarajevo
Skopje

BAY
OF
BISCAY

Bordeaux

Bilbao    Toulouse
PYRENEES
ANDORRA

Rhône R.
Marseille
MONACO
Nice

ADRIATIC SEA

ALBANIA

CORSICA

ROME
Naples

SARDINIA

Palermo

SICILY

ATLANTIC OCEAN

Oporto
Coimbra
SPAIN
Zaragoza    Barcelona
MADRID

LISBON
PORTUGAL
Valencia
Palma
BALEARIC ISLANDS

Seville
Granada
GIBRALTAR
(U.K.)

MEDITERRANEAN SEA

AFRICA

The struggle exhausted the people and brought chaos with it. A strong central government with a high degree of religious tolerance was now considered necessary to save the nation, and a Protestant, the Bourbon Prince Henry of Navarre, took the throne. Embracing Catholicism himself and granting religious freedom to the Protestants (Huguenots) in the Edict of Nantes (1598), he became the most popular king France ever had. Though the wealthy urban classes enjoyed prestige and power, France was still a feudal monarchy. The assassination of Henry in 1610 left the royal government open to further challenges from both nobles and bourgeoisie.

In this struggle Henry's successors were supported by two great statesmen, Cardinals Mazarin and Richelieu, who were enemies of the nobles, of Protestantism, and of urban democratic tendencies. Guiding France through the perils of the Thirty Years' War (1618–48), they put down internal revolt (the Fronde of 1648–53), continued the colonial enterprise in the New World begun in the previous century, and helped project the Bourbon house in the person of Louis XIV (1643–1715) to the peak of its power and fame.

Louis and his lieutenants held the nobility in check, helped industry expand, and systematically eliminated old provincial, municipal, and religious liberties. Royal control was as absolute as the size of the country and communications permitted. The iron control was tempered, too, by the fact that the government drew on talent from all social levels, and that it encouraged the arts on the grandest scale ever seen. Warlike and authoritarian, Louis made France the greatest of Europe's powers, but he also brought the country to economic ruin and to defeat at the hands of European powers that unified against her.

The reign of Louis XV was marked by opposition at home, the loss of empire abroad (Canada fell to England in 1763), and a dazzling display of art and literature. This was the great age of the Enlightenment, and France was the intellectual capital of Europe.

The French state, however, was insolvent, and the farmers suffered from landlords seeking higher revenues in an expanding economy. The monarchy was finally bankrupted through involvement in the American Revolution. The wealthy bourgeois creditors of the state refused to advance more credit unless they got social and political concessions from the crown. The aristocracy was determined to reverse the trend toward absolute monarchy and to regain their former authority. And the ordinary people of rural France waited for some royal action that would ease their lot.

Nobles and bourgeois joined forces to compel Louis XVI to summon the States-General, which had not met since 1614. Then the struggle for power became more complex. The middle-class representatives of the common people challenged the aristocracy in 1789, rallied a hesitant king temporarily to their side, and within months, following riots against crown and nobility, seized control of the state. They overturned the social and political structure of France, launched the egalitarian creed throughout Europe, reduced the Church to a department of state, and executed the king, who had turned against them and had hoped to be rescued by other European monarchs.

By 1799, after a decade of domestic battles, the epochal French Revolution ended in military dictatorship. Young, brilliant, ambitious General Napoleon Bonaparte seized total power and in 1804 crowned himself emperor of the French. At home he quashed political conflict, regulated the activities of the Church, and consolidated the social and economic effects of the revolution.

The greatest of modern commanders, Napoleon drove from victory to victory over the ancient powers of Europe until he controlled most of the Continent. But neither he nor France could rest—and finally they overreached themselves. The Napoleonic conquests were stripped away by the victory of an allied coalition in 1814. Napoleon returned from exile in 1815 to rally France again, but was routed at Waterloo. Imprisoned on Saint Helena, he died in 1821.

The unpopular Bourbons were restored by allied arms, but the old order never returned. The revolution had given the wealthy middle class an entrenched position. In 1830 Charles X was driven out by the revolt of the middle and lower classes in the cities. His successor, Louis Philippe, was ousted in 1848. A growing working class was created by the rising Industrial Revolution, and a strong current of new reformist thought began to flow.

The Second Republic of 1848 was undermined by clashes between the new French factions and was eliminated entirely by its elected president, Louis Napoleon Bonaparte. Like his uncle, France's new ruler established a dictatorship to end political quarrels and to preserve the social order. Proclaimed emperor in 1852, he presided until 1870.

The regime evolved from authoritarian dictatorship to a form of democracy, but it never silenced its critics. It enriched the industrial and commercial classes, but won no loyalty from them. It always faced hostility among the workers. Its one strength was its great peasant base. Its Achilles' heel was foreign policy. Napoleon expanded the empire in Southeast Asia but was defeated in Mexico. He helped bring about the unification of Italy but was caught up in a war with Germany.

Out of defeat by Germany (1870–71), another republic was born. It accepted severe peace terms, mastered the revolt of the Paris commune, and by 1875 had all but banished the ghost of monarchy. This Third Republic had a conservative and parliamentary government. It improved the schools, extended its empire in Africa and Asia, made an ally of Russia in 1894, and buried its rivalries with Britain in 1904.

Increasingly industrialized, this republic was ruled by the substantial middle classes—with the consent of the peasantry, the collaboration of the trained aristocracy, and the grudging cooperation of the proletariat. But it lived in the expectation of having to go to war. Like much of armed and divided Europe, it took up arms in 1914 hoping to win security. It also hoped to recover the lands of Alsace-Lorraine, surrendered in 1871.

France emerged victorious but exhausted from World War I. Her full recovery was prevented by a series of troubling events: the worldwide depression, the loss of Russia as an ally, disagreements with Britain over policy, the withdrawal of the United States from Europe, and the collapse of Italian and German democracy. The rise of Nazism in Germany undermined her morale. France was drawn into the British effort to check Hitler's Germany in 1939. The consequence was swift and total catastrophe in 1940—the greatest rout of a nation in modern times.

Hoping to save France from complete destruction by Hitler, Parliament granted full powers to Marshal Pétain to treat with the enemy and rebuild the nation. A small rebel Free French movement led by General Charles de Gaulle condemned this legal government at Vichy, won over the loyalty of much of the empire, and fought on with the Allies. After liberation, France was ruled by de Gaulle until he resigned suddenly in 1946 rather than accept a return to parliamentary government.

For 12 years this unstable Fourth Republic struggled to modernize the economy and cope with nationalist movements in the crumbling empire, while it watched French prestige sinking in the world. The regime went under in 1958 when faced with a French Army rebellion in Algeria. Having abandoned Syria, Lebanon, Indochina, Tunisia, and Morocco, the powerful and embittered French Army leadership determined to hold Algeria against a Parliament obviously preparing to negotiate with Algerian rebels demanding independence. To avoid civil war, Paris called de Gaulle from retirement, and the nation gave him a mandate to rule and to prepare a new constitution.

General de Gaulle quickly established a Fifth Republic—governed by decree when it was deemed necessary—and continued the previous regime's development of economic and nuclear power while instituting modest social reforms. He drove forcefully toward the leadership of Western Europe and liquidated the Algerian war, thereby earning popular approval along with the undying hostility of some army officers and former European settlers in Algeria.

Master of the French as no one had been since the Bonapartes, de Gaulle denigrated politicians and cultivated public opinion by state monopoly of radio and TV. The farmers and the bourgeoisie prospered, Parliament languished, the political dialogue stagnated, and the working classes remained bitter and isolated. The regime concentrated on foreign affairs while social and economic problems continued to await solution.

**GOVERNMENT AND POLITICS.** The president (formerly chosen by an electoral college of 80,000 notables) has been elected by popular vote to a seven year term since 1962. He appoints the prime minister and the cabinet, enjoys many special powers, and may dissolve Parliament.

The 482 members of the National Assembly are elected for five years by universal suffrage; the 274 members of the Senate, by indirect suffrage for nine years. Technically, Parliament may overthrow the government and compel new elections. However, its revolts against the Gaullist regime have resulted only in increasing the president's popular support.

Most of the political parties, such as the Radicals, Socialists, Popular Republicans, Independents, or the smaller groups of Left and Right, are objects of voter indifference. Only the Communist Party and the Gaullist Union for the New Republic have much stability. An attempt failed to create a great Federation of the Left to challenge de Gaulle in the 1965 presidential election and the 1967 parliamentary elections.

Thus solidly in power at home, de Gaulle has set out to bind Western Europe to French leadership and nuclear arms. He has encouraged closer relations with West Germany. At the same time he has used his influence in the Common Market to reject British application for membership. He has courted the Soviet Union with a view to reuniting Europe and countering American economic and military influence in the Atlantic community.

By 1967 de Gaulle had removed France from all military participation in NATO and had obtained withdrawal of all NATO installations from French soil. De Gaulle's often stunning political initiatives, seemingly designed to create a powerful, far flung French community, included in 1967 a call for the independence of Canada's largely French Quebec.

**ECONOMY.** France has generally recovered from the economic stresses of two World Wars. Today she is a strong member of the Common Market. But poor housing conditions and wage grievances still embitter much of the working class. Farmers, by demonstrations and violence, have generally obtained the protection and subsidies they demanded.

France ranks high in the production of iron, steel, aluminum, textiles, aircraft, automobiles, petroleum, chemicals, and electrical equipment. Agricultural products include cereals, sugar beets, flax, root crops, and wine. Small farms predominate in France—of 2,000,000 farms, 50 per cent are less than 20 acres and 17 per cent, less than five. Fishing is an important industry. Minerals include principally iron ore, coal, antimony, bauxite, and magnesium.

**EDUCATION.** Education is free and compulsory for children aged 6 to 16. There are 20 universities, of which the University of Paris (founded 1150) is the oldest and largest.

**ARMED FORCES.** Military service of 16 months is compulsory. Total forces number 560,000.

# FRENCH TERRITORIES AND DEPENDENCIES

### FRENCH SOUTHERN AND ANTARCTIC TERRITORIES

*Area:* 2,918 square miles. *Population:* 137.

French Southern and Antarctic Territories consists of: *Karguelen Archipelago* in the South Indian Ocean, a large subantarctic island that rises to about 6,100 feet, and 300 smaller islands; discovered by Yves de Karguelen in 1772, it was not settled until 1949. Research stations, a hospital, and a military camp are located there. *Crozet Archipelago,* five large and 15 small islands in the South Indian Ocean, about 800 miles west of Karguelen. It was discovered in 1772; a meteorological station was built there in 1964. *Saint Paul,* an uninhabited island of less than three square miles in the Indian Ocean, northeast of Karguelen. *New Amsterdam,* about 50 miles north of Saint Paul; it has research stations and a hospital. *Adélie Coast,* on the Antarctic continent, discovered in 1840 by the French navigator Jules Dumont d'Urville. France also has claimed Antarctic land totaling 156,000 square miles.

Islands that had been administered from Madagascar were added to the Territories in 1960: *Europa,* which has a meteorological station; *Juan de Nova,* with an emergency airfield; *Tromelin Island,* with an important meteorological station; and several others. Their total area is about 23 square miles.

## FRENCH GUIANA

*Area:* 35,135 square miles. *Population:* 34,000. *Capital:* Cayenne (population: 18,635). *Language:* French.

Guiana, on the north coast of South America, is bordered on the north by the Atlantic Ocean, on the east and south by Brazil, and on the west by Surinam. Off Guiana's 200-mile-long marshy coast are several islands, including the notorious former penal colony of Devil's Island.

Most of the people are of mixed Caucasian and Negro stock. There are groups of aboriginal Indians, and descendants of freed or fugitive slaves live along the rivers. Roman Catholicism is the predominant faith.

France began to colonize Guiana in 1604, using it as a penal colony and place of exile during the French Revolution. Napoleon III started sending criminals there, but it has not served as a prison colony since 1946. The territory's borders were settled in 1854, and it became an overseas department of France in 1946.

Guiana is administered by a prefect; there is also a General Council elected by universal suffrage. The department is represented in the French Parliament by a senator and a deputy. The Socialist Party of Guiana (PSG) has campaigned for Guianese autonomy.

Agriculture is limited to the coastal region, much of which is swampland. The small acreage under cultivation has been poorly developed and labor is scarce, but the French government is spurring development of new farms.

## GUADELOUPE AND DEPENDENCIES

*Area:* 687 square miles. *Population:* 316,000. *Capital:* Basse-Terre (population: 14,000). *Language:* A French dialect.

Guadeloupe is in the Leeward Islands of the Lesser Antilles, in the eastern Caribbean Sea.

The tropical island, 583 square miles in all, actually is two islands—Basse-Terre and Grande-Terre—separated by a narrow channel, the Rivière Salée. Volcanic Basse-Terre has an active peak, La Soufrière, that erupted in the 18th and 19th centuries. Grande-Terre is a low limestone plain surrounded by a coral reef; its lack of natural streams is in wide contrast to the many found on Basse-Terre that are fed by the 200 to 400 inches of rainfall each year.

Dependencies include the nearby islands of *Marie Galante* (population: 16,300), *Les Saintes* (population: 2,800), *Désirade* (population: 1,600), and *Saint Barthélemy* (population: 2,200), some 75 miles to the northwest. About two-thirds of the island of *Saint Martin* (population: 4,500), lying about 110 miles northeast, is administered by Guadeloupe; the other section, called Saint Maarten, is a Dutch possession.

The dependencies are still inhabited by descendants of the Bretons and Normans who settled there more than 300 years ago. The population of Guadeloupe proper consists mostly of Negroes and a mixture of Negroes and early colonizers. Most of the population is Roman Catholic.

Columbus discovered Guadeloupe in 1493; France started the first permanent colony in 1635. Except for British occupation twice in the 18th century and later during the Napoleonic wars, Guadeloupe has remained a French possession.

Guadeloupe became an overseas department of France in 1946. It is represented in the French Parliament by two senators and three deputies. The administrator of Guadeloupe, an appointed prefect, is aided by an elected General Council.

Agriculture is the basis of the economy, but tourism is growing in value. The chief crops are sugarcane and bananas.

## MARTINIQUE

*Area:* 425 square miles. *Population:* 321,000. *Capital:* Fort-de-France (population: 85,300). *Language:* A French dialect.

Martinique is in the Windward Islands of the Lesser Antilles, in the eastern Caribbean Sea.

Volcanic Mont Pelée (4,583 feet) is the island's highest point; thick, sterile layers of volcanic ash that blanket the land around Pelée make it useless for any sort of growth. The agricultural areas are in the hot valleys and along the coast.

The people are mostly Negro or of mixed stock. The principal religion is Roman Catholicism.

Although discovered by Columbus about 1502, Martinique was first settled in 1635. British occupation came in 1762–63, during the Seven Years War; a second occupation occurred from the time of the French Revolution through the Napoleonic wars (1794–1815).

Martinique has been subject to many disasters, ranging from tidal waves to drought. The eruption of Mont Pelée on May 8, 1902, was one of the worst natural catastrophes of modern times.

The island became an overseas department of France in March, 1946. It is represented in the French Parliament by two senators and three deputies. An appointed prefect administers the island, assisted by a directly elected General Council.

The chief products of the basically agricultural economy are sugar and bananas; the chief exports are sugar and rum. Industry is mainly concerned with the processing of sugar and tropical fruits and the distilling of rum. Coastal fishing also is important. Tourism is a valuable addition to the island's economy.

## SAINT PIERRE AND MIQUELON

*Area:* 93 square miles. *Population:* 5,000. *Capital:* Saint Pierre (population: 4,000). *Language:* A French dialect.

Saint Pierre and Miquelon are located in the Atlantic Ocean a few miles southwest of Newfoundland's Burin Peninsula.

The archipelago consists of eight small islands; the Saint Pierre group, although much smaller than that of Miquelon, has the majority of the population. A low, sandy spit of land connects the northern portion, Miquelon, with the lower part, Langlade. The land is volcanic, rocky, mostly barren, and unfit for agriculture.

The people are descendants of early Basque and French settlers. Most of the population is Roman Catholic.

Jacques Cartier gave the islands their names in 1536. The harbor of Saint Pierre was known to Basque and Breton fishermen by the 16th century, and Basques probably were the first settlers. France officially began colonization in 1604. The islands were taken by the British in 1713, restored to France 50 years later, twice retaken by the British after that, and then finally turned back to France in 1814, with the condition that they should never be fortified.

The islands first gained local autonomy in 1935 and were declared a French overseas territory in 1946. A senator and a deputy represent the islands in the French Parliament. A governor, aided by a privy council, is the administrator; there is also a General Council with elected members. However, France dissolved the General Council in June, 1965, because of economic problems "aggravated by local political rivalries."

Fishing is the mainstay of the territory's economy. Lack of soil for agricultural production makes it necessary to import most food.

There are ferry connections from Cape Breton Island and Newfoundland; an air service operates daily during summer and fall.

## COMORO ISLANDS

*Area:* 838 square miles. *Population:* 220,000. *Capital:* Moroni, Grande Comore (population: 10,000). *Languages:* French and Malagasy. *Monetary Unit:* The CFA franc.

The Comoro Islands are situated in the Mozambique Channel between the east African coast and the island of Madagascar.

The major islands are Grande Comore, the largest and most populous, and Anjouan, Mohéli, and Mayotte. The rich soil produces lush vegetation, including plants used for perfume oils and tropical hardwood and fruit trees.

The people are mostly of Arab, Malagasy (a name given to the people of Madagascar), and

African stock. Most of them are Muslims.

In 1503 the Portuguese discovered the islands and in 1517 the French arrived. Invasions by the Malagasy also took place during the 16th century.

France made a protectorate of the islands in 1886; they were given overseas-territory status and granted administrative autonomy in 1946. In 1958 the Territorial Assembly voted to stay in the French Republic.

A high commissioner represents France. Local government is by a Council of Ministers, responsible to a Territorial Assembly whose members are elected by universal suffrage.

The Comoros have an agricultural economy. The most important products are vanilla, copra, cocoa, coffee, cloves, and essential oils for the perfume industry.

## RÉUNION

*Area:* 969 square miles. *Population:* 397,000. *Capital:* Saint-Denis (population: 75,100). *Other Cities:* Saint-Paul (population: 39,200), Saint-Pierre (population: 38,900). *Monetary Unit:* The CFA franc.

Réunion is in the Indian Ocean, over 400 miles east of the island of Madagascar. The island has one active and nine inactive volcanoes, the highest of which rises to more than 10,000 feet. There are fine growths of tropical hardwoods in the forests near the coast and a widely varied marine life in the surrounding seas. The climate, mostly tropical but pleasant, varies according to the topography.

Most of the people are descendants of French colonists and Negroes, Malays, Indochinese, and Malabar Indians. About 80 per cent are Roman Catholics; most of the rest are Muslims.

The Arabs knew Réunion originally, but it was rediscovered early in the 16th century by Portuguese explorers. Bourbon Island, as Réunion was known until 1793, was settled by the French about 1646, serving first as a penal colony. Coffee cultivation, which was introduced in 1715, brought prosperity, but after 1800 it was replaced in economic importance by sugarcane. Réunion became an overseas department of France in 1947.

Unemployment and concentration of much of the wealth in the hands of a few planters have in the past caused discord among the numerous agricultural workers, and Communist influence is strong.

Réunion has an appointed prefect, a popularly elected General Council, and two senators and three deputies in the French Parliament.

A third Réunion is under intense cultivation, with most of the land planted in sugarcane. Large quantities of tropical fruits are grown, and several plants used to make perfumes are important to the economy.

## FRENCH POLYNESIA

*Area:* 1,544 square miles. *Population:* 88,000. *Capital:* Papeete, Tahiti (population: 20,000). *Languages:* French and Polynesian. *Monetary Unit:* The CFP franc.

French Polynesia's nearly 130 islands dot a

vast area of the South Pacific. For administrative purposes, France has grouped them into five divisions: the *Windward Islands,* including Tahiti and Moorea; the *Leeward Islands,* including Raiatea and Bora-Bora (together these two divisions are known as the *Society Islands*); the *Tuamotu Islands* and the *Gambier Islands* (the Tuamotus comprise two parallel strings of islands stretching for a thousand miles, of which Rangiroa and Fakarava are the most important; the Gambiers, located below the Tuamotus, have Rikitea, on Mangareva, as their chief center); the *Tubuai Islands,* or *Austral Islands,* south of the Society group, including Rururu, Tubuai, Raivavae, Rimatara, and the dependency of Rapa, about 350 miles southeast; and the *Marquesas Islands,* northwest of the Society Islands.

Most of the people are Polynesian and profess the Christian faith.

The Society Islands (named for the British Royal Society and called that since 1769), were discovered and claimed for England in 1767, but a year later French claims were established. France established a protectorate over the islands in 1843; they became a colony in 1880.

Spaniards discovered the Tuamotu Islands in 1606. France's protectorate was proclaimed in 1844, and the islands were annexed to France in 1881. The Gambier Islands, discovered by the British in 1797, were annexed by France in 1881. Tubuai came under French control in 1880.

The fertile, mountainous Marquesas are exceptionally beautiful. The group's southern cluster of islands was found in 1595 by a Spanish navigator; the northern islands, sometimes called the Washington group, were discovered by an American navigator in 1791. Nuku Hiva was claimed for the United States in 1813, but Congress failed to confirm the action. France took possession in 1842, establishing and later abandoning a settlement, then re-established control in 1870.

Known as French Oceania, the islands became an overseas territory of France on January 1, 1947. The name was changed to French Polynesia in 1957.

Polynesia has a French-appointed governor. There is an advisory Council of Government, secretly elected by the Territorial Assembly. Assembly members are directly elected by universal suffrage for five-year terms.

In 1958, when there were indications that certain leftist members of the ruling political party advocated an independent republic, thousands of Tahitians demonstrated in what were probably the world's first pro-colonial riots.

Some political leaders were reported to feel that security restrictions resulting from France's installation of a nuclear-testing site in the territory were a serious block to more self-rule.

A barrier to the further development of agriculture has been the land-tenure system—groups of families owning most of the land.

Among the products of economic value are copra, vanilla, coffee, and phosphate.

Tourism is increasingly promoted and new facilities are being planned or developed to handle the growing flow of visitors.

To protect and preserve the health and racial purity of the Polynesians on Rururu and Rimatara in the Australs, non-natives are forbidden to visit there. The Marquesans have suffered most from the introduction of European diseases; the indigenous population there has dwindled from 20,000 in the 1850s to a mere 4,800 today.

France's nuclear-testing center, on uninhabited Mururoa (720 miles southeast of Tahiti), became operational in 1966. President de Gaulle, while on a world tour, visited the site in September and became the first chief of state known to have seen a nuclear device exploded.

## NEW CALEDONIA

*Area:* 7,202 square miles. *Population:* 91,000. *Capital:* Nouméa (population: 35,000). *Languages:* French and Melanesian. *Monetary Unit:* The CFP franc.

New Caledonia, a South Pacific island, is about 1,200 miles northeast of Sydney, Australia.

Partly circled by coral reefs, it is generally mountainous and covered with vegetation that ranges from bushland to dense forests. Climate is maintained at an enjoyable level all year by the ever-present trade winds.

The Loyalty Islands, largest and most populous of New Caledonia's dependencies, lie 60 miles to the east; others are the Isle of Pines, the barren Huon Islands, the Belep Archipelago, the Chesterfield Islands, and Walpole Island.

Over half the people are of Melanesian stock; 40 per cent, European; 5 per cent, Polynesian; and the rest, Vietnamese and Indonesian. The principal religion is Roman Catholicism.

New Caledonia was visited by a French explorer in 1768, but it was Captain James Cook who gave the island its name a few years later. Other Frenchmen explored there and in 1844 native chiefs acknowledged France's claim. It was annexed by France in 1853 and served as a prison colony from 1864 to 1894. To prevent a Japanese takeover in World War II, U.S. forces occupied the island. In 1946 it became an overseas territory of France.

The territory is headed by a French-appointed governor who is assisted by a Council of Government chosen by the popularly elected Territorial Assembly.

New Caledonia is rich in minerals. It has the world's largest known reserves of nickel, and the high-quality ore accounts for about 90 per cent of its export value. Other important minerals are iron, high-grade chrome, manganese, and cobalt. Copra, coffee, maize, and tropical fruits are the chief crops.

Industries include a nickel refinery, a chemical plant, and some food processing. A dam and hydroelectric plant have been built near Nouméa.

## THE ANGLO-FRENCH CONDOMINIUM OF NEW HEBRIDES

*Area:* 5,700 square miles. *Population:* 68,000. *Capital:* Vila, Efate. *Languages:* French, English, and Melanesian. *Monetary Units:* The CFP franc and the pound sterling.

The New Hebrides are a chain of Pacific islands about 250 miles northeast of New Caledonia and about 500 miles west of Fiji.

Of the twelve principal islands in the group, Espiritu Santo and Malekula are the largest; others of importance are Efate and Pentecost. Three of the larger islands have active volcanoes.

About 7 per cent of the population is European, with the French numerically dominant; most of the remainder are Melanesians. The principal religion is Roman Catholicism.

Espiritu Santo was discovered in 1606 by a Portuguese navigator. In 1774 Captain James Cook named the islands after Scotland's Hebrides. British, Australian, and French planters came during the 19th century. For most of the 19th century there was no government on the islands. In 1887 Britain and France placed the islands under a joint naval commission, and in 1906 the Anglo-French condominium was established.

New Hebrides is jointly administered by two resident commissioners—one British and one French. They serve under the authority of the British and French High Commissioners of the Pacific.

Copra is the chief crop; copra, coffee, and cocoa are the main exports.

### WALLIS AND FUTUNA

*Area:* 77 square miles. *Population:* 8,400. *Capital:* Mata-Utu, Wallis. *Languages:* French and Polynesian. *Monetary Unit:* The CFP franc.

Wallis and Futuna are two small groups of Pacific islands located about 250 miles west of Samoa. Wallis, which was formerly called Uvea, is circled by a coral reef; there are about 20 uninhabited small islets in the lagoon formed by the reef. Futuna and uninhabited Alofi are also of volcanic origin.

Most of the people are Polynesian. Roman Catholic missions have been active on the islands since 1837.

The Futuna group was found by a Dutch explorer in 1617. About 100 years later Wallis was discovered by an English explorer bearing that name.

In 1842 France established a protectorate over the islands, making it permanent by 1888. Wallis and Futuna became a French overseas territory in 1961.

The French administrator of the islands is assisted by a Territorial Council and an elected Territorial Assembly. Local government, however, is still headed by kings—one on Wallis and two on Futuna.

The islands' principal agricultural products are yams, bananas, cassavas, and arrowroot. Copra production and fishing are the main economic activities.

### FRENCH TERRITORY AND THE AFARS AND THE ISSAS (FORMERLY FRENCH SOMALILAND)

*Area:* 8,880 square miles. *Population:* 125,050. *Capital:* Djibouti (population 62,000). *Languages:* French, Arabic, Afar, and Somali. *Monetary Unit:* The Djibouti franc.

This French Overseas Territory in Africa is situated on the Gulf of Aden at the southern entrance to the Red Sea. It is bounded on the east by Babel Mandeb Strait, the Gulf of Aden, and Somalia, and on the south, west, and north by Ethiopia. Its most important ethnic groups are the Afars, who are nomads, and the Issas, who are in the minority except in Djibouti; both groups are adherents of Islam.

The opening of the Suez Canal in 1869 gave importance to Obock, which France had gained in 1862. French expansion southward along the Somali coast and the transfer of the capital to Djibouti in 1892 were prompted by France's military operations in Indochina and Madagascar and by Ethiopia's development. French Somaliland became a colony in 1896, and in 1917 a 486-mile railroad was completed between Djibouti and Addis Ababa.

After World War II, French Somaliland elected representatives to the French Parliament and to a Territorial Assembly. In 1958, 75 per cent of its population voted to remain a French Overseas Territory with limited autonomy. Thousands of Somali immigrants were attracted to Djibouti by its comparatively high living standards, particularly after Somalia had become independent and was united with British Somaliland in 1960.

The Afars carried the vote in favor of continued association with France in a referendum on March 19, 1967. Subsequent rioting by Somalis caused the expulsion of over 8,000 who were not French citizens. Somalia refused to receive many of them and also contested the validity of the referendum vote, but Ethiopia recognized continued French control of the territory as preferable to its annexation by Somalia. France granted the territory a new statute and renamed it the French Territory of the Afars and the Issas in July, 1967, retaining control of its foreign relations, currency, defense and internal order, and communications.

## GABON

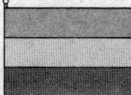

*Official Name:* Gabon Republic. *Area:* 103,346 square miles. *Population:* 468,000. *Principal Cities* (with populations): Libreville, the capital, 45,000; Port Gentil, 25,000. *Flag:* Green, yellow, and blue stripes. *Monetary Unit:* The CFA franc (worth 0.41 U.S. cents). *Gross National Product.* $174,-000,000 (1965). *Average Annual Income per Person:* $297.

LAND AND PEOPLE. Gabon, a republic located on the west coast of Africa, is bordered on the north by Río Muni (also called Spanish Guinea) and Cameroon, on the east and south by the Republic of Congo (Brazzaville), and on the west by the Atlantic Ocean. (See map on page 111.)

The coastal lowlands extend 20 to 125 miles into the interior and adjoin a 60-mile-wide belt of rocky cliffs as high as 2,000 feet. The highest point in the mountainous regions farther inland is over 5,000 feet.

The people of Gabon may be divided into

40 distinct ethnic groups. The Fang group comprises about 30 per cent of the population; the Eshiras, including Bapounous, about 20 per cent. Other leading groups include the Mbede, Bakota, and Omiene. About 40 per cent of the people are Catholic, and 11 per cent are Protestant. Nearly half the people practice ancient tribal religions.

Fifty per cent of the people speak French, the official language. Fang is spoken extensively in northern Gabon, and Bantu languages in other sections of the country.

**HISTORY.** Portuguese exploration began about 1470, followed by British, Dutch, Spanish, and French efforts during the centuries of slave trading. The trade was ended by the Congress of Vienna (1815), but French interests survived when French ships were assigned to stamp out illegal slave traffic. The French occupied the coastal ports, and in 1839 explorer Edouard Baout-Willaumez signed a treaty of peace with "King" Denis of Gabon. Denis, an important African slave trader, turned over part of northern Gabon to France in return for protection. French control expanded, and the colony of Gabon was officially established in 1885. The capital of the new colony (and of the French Congo, which Gabon joined in 1890) was named Libreville because a number of slaves freed from a slave trader settled there in 1849.

Gabon became one of the four territories of French Equatorial Africa in 1910. In 1958, as independence swept Africa, the Gabonese voted to become an autonomous republic within the French Community. The country was proclaimed fully independent from France on August 17, 1960. Leon M'ba, who had served as the first premier, was elected president. In 1964 French troops intervened to prevent the overthrow of M'ba by a military coup.

**GOVERNMENT AND POLITICS.** Gabon amended its constitution in February, 1967. The vice-president, formerly appointed by the president, is now elected. In March President M'ba was reelected to a seven-year term, and Albert Bongo, M'ba's heir apparent, was elected vice-president. The 47 members of the one-house National Assembly were elected to terms of the same length.

**ECONOMY.** Gabon's economic prospects are bright. Timber accounts for 52 per cent of exports; remaining exports consist of manganese, uranium, gold, and oil. Gabon has one of the world's largest deposits of iron ore, and mining is expected to start by 1972 after completion of a 490-mile railroad. The country ranks second among the African states in per capita income (South Africa ranks first).

**EDUCATION AND HEALTH.** An estimated 85 per cent of the children over six years of age attend school; education is theoretically compulsory until age 16. The literacy rate is about 12.4 per cent.

The mission hospital at Lambarene founded by the late Dr. Albert Schweitzer has attracted international attention.

**ARMED FORCES.** There is a 600-man army, 100-man navy, and 50-man air force.

# GAMBIA

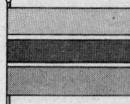

*Official Name:* The Gambia. *Area:* 4,000 square miles (est.). *Population:* 336,000. *Principal Cities* (with populations): Bathurst, the capital, 29,800; Kombo St. Mary, 14,000. *Flag:* Red, blue, and green stripes separated by narrow white stripes. *Monetary Unit:* The Gambian pound of 20 shillings (worth U.S. $2.80). *Gross National Product:* $28,000,000 (1966).

**LAND AND PEOPLE.** Gambia is situated in West Africa, with an Atlantic shoreline of about 50 miles and the rest of the country surrounded by the Republic of Senegal. (See map on page 111.) The Northern upriver boundary is still to be agreed upon. The country extends eastward for about 200 miles from the Atlantic on both sides of the Gambia River.

The Mandingo tribe accounts for 46 per cent of the population. Other tribes are the Fula, Jola, Wolof, and Serahuli. The predominant religion is Islam. The official and commercial language is English; common vernacular dialects are Wolof, Mandinga, and Fula.

**HISTORY.** The Gambia River was discovered in 1456 by Portuguese explorers, and Portugal controlled the region until the late 16th century. Britain and France fought for the territory and the moderately profitable slave trade until the 19th century. After 1815 France regained Saint-Louis and Gorée island, and British dominance was maintained by the merchants who traded on the Gambia River.

The British established the first permanent settlement at Bathurst in 1816. Gambia was administered through a governor-general in Sierra Leone from 1821 to 1843 and from 1866 to 1888. It was a separate colony between 1843 and 1866 and returned to separate Crown Colony status in 1888. Gambia became independent within the Commonwealth of Nations on February 18, 1965.

**GOVERNMENT AND POLITICS.** The British monarch is recognized as sovereign and is represented in Bathurst by a Gambian governor-general. The executive branch is headed by a prime minister and cabinet. Thirty-two members of the one-chamber legislature are elected by universal suffrage, and four are selected by an assembly of tribal chiefs.

The present prime minister is Sir David K. Jawara, who heads the Progressive People's Party.

**ECONOMY.** Gambia is one of Africa's poorest countries, depending entirely upon the production and export of peanuts. Britain contributes extensive financial and economic aid.

There are about 750 miles of roads, but the majority are impassable except in dry weather. The bulk of transportation is by boat, since the Gambia River can be navigated by oceangoing ships as far as 150 miles inland. Bathurst is the principal port.

**EDUCATION.** Literacy is estimated at 10 per cent of the population.

**ARMED FORCES.** Gambia has no army.

# GERMANY, FEDERAL REPUBLIC OF

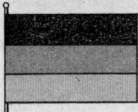

*Official Name:* Federal Republic of Germany. *Area:* 95,928 square miles. *Population:* 59,872,000. *Principal Cities* (with populations): Bonn, the capital, 138,500; West Berlin, 2,785,400; Hamburg, 1,847,300; Munich, 1,235,500; Cologne, 859,800; Essen, 716,000; Düsseldorf, 699,200. *Flag:* Three horizontal black, red, and gold stripes. *Monetary Unit:* The deutsche mark (worth 25 U.S. cents). *Gross National Product:* $119,500,000,000 (1966). *Average Annual Income per Person:* $1,448.

**LAND AND PEOPLE.** West Germany is bordered on the north by the North Sea and Denmark; on the east by the Baltic Sea, East Germany, and Czechoslovakia; on the south by Austria and Switzerland; and on the west by France, Luxembourg, Belgium, and the Netherlands. (See map on page 117.)

The country falls into four geographical zones: wide lowlands extending from the Netherlands to East Germany in the north; the uplands of the central German mountains, stretching from the Rhine to the East German border; the wide valley and gorge of the Rhine; and a region of mountains and plateaus in southern Germany, with the Black Forest in the west and the Bavarian Forest in the east, and in the far south, the Bavarian Alps that form a natural boundary with Switzerland and Austria.

The Rhine River, whose two main tributaries are the Mosel and the Main, empties into the North Sea. To the east are the Ems, Weser, and Elbe rivers, all with important ports on their estuaries. To the south the Danube flows to the east for about 400 miles. Lake Constance, lying on the Swiss and Austrian borders, is the largest lake.

The temperature ranges from below 21° F. in the mountains during the winter to about 68° F. in the valleys during the summer. Rain, falling throughout the year, varies from 20 to 78 inches, depending on the region and altitude. Snow may reach a depth of six feet in some areas during January and February.

Deciduous trees such as oak and beech make up a third of Germany's forests. Heavy spruce growths are found in the mountains, while pine and larch predominate in the sandy lowlands. Deer, wildcats, and martens are among the wildlife. Fish are plentiful in the North Sea and in the rivers. Birds include varieties from both eastern and western Europe.

Almost all the population is German; the only minority group comprises the Danes in Schleswig-Holstein. German is the national language.

About 51 per cent of the people are Protestants; 44 per cent are Roman Catholics. Jews, once a sizable and productive minority in Germany, were decimated in the 1930s and 1940s as a result of Hitler's exterminatory racial policies, and now number less than half of one per cent of the total population.

**HISTORY.** The Teutons and the Cimbri are thought to be among the earliest Germanic tribes. Roman records report their defeat by the general Marius in 102–101 B.C. These tribes, along with the Alemanni, Burgundii, Franks, Lombards, Ostrogoths, and Visigoths, settled in the territory between the Rhine estuary, the Elbe River, and northern Italy. The area on each side of the Rhine was a battleground for these warlike tribes until Charlemagne, the Frankish emperor whose father was the founder of the Carolingian dynasty, extended his sovereignty over most of Germany. He was crowned Emperor of the West in 800 A.D. After his death his empire, including Germany, was divided among his three grandsons.

Powerful feudal princes helped to weaken medieval Germany at a time when it was being invaded by Slavs, Norsemen, and Magyars. Otto I, Saxon king of the Germans, is generally credited with the creation of the Holy Roman Empire; he was crowned its first emperor in Rome in 962. However, ensuing fights among the many feudal states in Germany and the struggle for supremacy between the emperors and the popes made the nation a loose and ineffective federation with little central authority.

The empire was strengthened under the Hohenstaufens, who subdued many of the large duchies. In 1180 Frederick I dismembered Saxony, the last remaining great duchy. His grandson, Frederick II, was king of Sicily, and he also became king of the Germans (1212) and emperor of the Holy Roman Empire (1220–1250). He was one of the outstanding figures of the Middle Ages, but he ruled mostly from Sicily, paying little attention to German problems. By the end of his reign the great days of the German Empire were over, and the French monarchy and Italian city-states had begun their ascendancy.

The weakness of the Holy Roman Empire became particularly evident when Germany found itself the center of the Reformation, the religious schism initiated by Martin Luther. The Catholic emperor could not enforce his own religious policies or halt the conversion to Protestantism of many of the powerful nobles. As a result of religious and political conflicts, the empire was torn by the Thirty Years War (1618–48), at the end of which it was formally dismembered in the Treaty of Westphalia.

In the hundred years following Westphalia, Prussia, under a remarkable line of kings, grew into the only German power that could challenge Austrian pre-eminence. In 1740–42 Frederick the Great defeated Austria, and Prussia joined the ranks of the great European powers.

Napoleon's rise to power in France brought only a temporary halt to the Austro-Prussian rivalry. At the Congress of Vienna (1814–15), the German states were reduced in number, and a national structure was formed through the German Confederation, with Prussia and Austria as the dominant states. Austria, however, gained control of the confederation, and Prince Klemens von Metternich suppressed German nationalism.

In the year 1848 several revolutions were fomented in Germany with the objective of unifying the nation under liberal auspices. After the failure of these efforts, the Prussian monarchy tried its own conservative scheme of unification, but in 1850 Austria decisively and humiliatingly checked Prussian ambitions by threatening war. Negotiations were held between Prussia and Austria, at which Prussia was intimidated into abandoning all plans of unifying Germany.

In 1862 Otto von Bismarck took control of Prussian policy and resolved to eliminate Austrian influence over Germany. He achieved his aim with victory in the Austro-Prussian War (1866). Bismarck went on to win the Franco-Prussian War of 1870–71, and Germany—although still a confederation of lesser principalities and Hanseatic cities—became unified, with William I of Prussia as emperor.

Between 1871 and 1914 the German empire expanded with amazing rapidity. Its economy flourished, and the acquisition of colonies and construction of a navy enhanced its power and prestige. After 1888, however, when William II began his reign, German policy no longer aimed at preserving the peace of Europe, as it had for the preceding 20 years under Bismarck. In 1914 Germany's leaders, fearing isolation and encirclement, seized upon the assassination of the heir to the Austrian throne as an opportune occasion to defeat or at least to divide their country's enemies. Europe was thus plunged into World War I, which ended with Germany's defeat. In November, 1918, William fled to the Netherlands and abdicated, leaving an exhausted Germany to accept a harsh armistice from the Allies.

With the German defeat the Weimar Republic replaced the empire. From its inception the republic was saddled with the Treaty of Versailles (1918), imposed by the victorious Allies. Under the terms of the treaty, Germany lost some of her European territory, was stripped of her overseas possessions, and was required to pay heavy reparations.

For a time the republic weathered the political challenges of right-wing and left-wing extremists and the nearly disastrous inflation of 1923. In the late 1920s it had attained a degree of stability. However, the world-wide depression hit the German economy particularly hard, caused massive unemployment on an unprecedented scale, and led to the undermining of the nation's political institutions. In the ensuing economic and social chaos, Paul von Hindenburg, Germany's president, assumed greater powers and veered ever farther to the right, while the German electorate cast an increasingly larger percentage of its votes for the two extremist parties, the Communists on the left and the National Socialists on the right.

By 1932 Adolf Hitler's National Socialist Party was the largest in the Reichstag, and he became chancellor in January, 1933. Within the year Hitler was granted dictatorial powers; Germany fell completely under the control of the Nazis; and the government launched a campaign to eliminate Jews from German life. The official policy of anti-Semitism culminated during World War II in the "final solution" to the "Jewish problem"—the extermination of over six million Jews in death camps.

In violation of the stipulations of the Versailles Treaty, Hitler remilitarized the Rhineland in 1936, annexed Austria in March, 1938, and took part of Czechoslovakia in September of the same year. In March, 1939, Germany took over Bohemia, Moravia, and Memel, and demanded Danzig and the Polish corridor. World War II began when Germany invaded Poland in September, 1939.

The Nazis enjoyed spectacular successes up to 1942, but the war ended in May, 1945, with Germany's unconditional surrender and many of her cities in ruins. At conferences in Yalta and Potsdam the Allies decided to divide Germany into four occupation zones, with Berlin under four-power control. The U.S.S.R., however, embarked on its own policy, and efforts to govern Germany through the Allied Control Commission collapsed.

In 1948, as a result of decisions reached at a foreign ministers' conference in London, a democratic, federal state was created out of the American, British, and French zones of Germany. A provisional constitution was approved by the Bonn Assembly in May, 1949. Theodor Heuss was elected first president of the Federal Republic in September, 1949, and the new Bundestag chose Konrad Adenauer as the first chancellor. In October the German Democratic Republic was formed in the Soviet Zone (often called East Germany), but Berlin remained divided among the occupying powers.

Having been freed of most Allied restrictions by 1952, West Germany recovered rapidly, and in 1955 the Federal Republic became fully sovereign. Efforts toward reunification with East Germany have been unsuccessful.

Relations between the East and West were critically strained during the Berlin blockade of 1948–49, when East Germany cut off the West's access to the city by land. The Allies mounted an airlift to maintain communications with and transport supplies to Berlin, thus demonstrating their determination to protect the city and West Germany. In 1961, in an effort to stem the tide of escapes by East Germans fleeing to the West, East Germany erected the Berlin Wall and cordoned off the Soviet sector of the city. At least 133 Germans have been killed and 2,000 escape attempts have been thwarted at the east-west border since the wall was built. Over the years the Soviets have tried to force the Western nations to recognize East Germany's sovereignty, but, with the exception of Finland, none has done so.

In May, 1965, despite threats from Egypt and other Arab states and over the opposition of many Israelis, the Federal Republic and Israel exchanged ambassadors. In retaliation, ten of the 13 Arab League members withdrew recognition from West Germany. In February, 1967, Jordan became the first Arab state to resume normal relations with West Germany. After the Arab-Israeli War of June, 1967, Bonn sent aid to various Middle Eastern countries.

The West German government has generally given political and moral support to many policies of the United States. However, the present West German government, under the leadership of Chancellor Kurt Georg Kiesinger, has pursued a policy of increasing independence from its American ally. In 1967 the most significant point of contention between the two nations centered on the issue of European military defense. Despite U.S. opposition, West Germany viewed a cut in its military spending as an economic necessity. In August, 1967, Kiesinger met in Washington with President Johnson in an effort to come to terms with this problem. Although talks between the two leaders failed to resolve the European defense issue, Kiesinger's visit was generally acknowledged to have done much to restore mutual confidence between the two nations.

West Germany has sought increasingly stronger ties with France in recent years. However, important political differences remain between Bonn and Paris. Significant among these has been West Germany's opposition to France's continued efforts to exclude Britain from the European Economic Community.

**GOVERNMENT AND POLITICS.** The Basic Law (constitution) of the Federal Republic of Germany provides that the president is to be elected by a Federal Assembly comprising members of the Bundestag and delegates selected on a proportional basis by the state (*Land*) legislatures. He serves for a five-year term and can be re-elected only once.

The 498 members of the Bundestag, the lower house of parliament, are elected by universal, direct suffrage and secret ballot for four-year terms. The Bundestag in turn elects the chancellor. Cabinet ministers are appointed by the president on the chancellor's recommendation and can be dismissed by him as well. The president is the nominal head of state, but most executive power rests with the chancellor. The considerably less powerful upper house, the Bundesrat, comprises 41 members appointed by the various state governments.

Of the three major political parties in Germany, the most powerful group since the war has been the Christian Democratic Union (CDU). The next most powerful group is the Social Democratic Party (SDP), headed by Willy Brandt. The third group, the Free Democrats (FDP), joined with the CDU to form the coalition governments of Konrad Adenauer and his successor, Ludwig Erhard. The Federal president, Heinrich Lübke, was re-elected in July, 1964; Erhard was re-elected chancellor in October, 1965.

Dissatisfaction with Erhard became widespread, and his cabinet collapsed a year later with the resignation of four FDP members in a budget dispute. In November, 1966, the CDU designated Kurt Georg Kiesinger as Erhard's successor. Kiesinger formed a coalition government composed of CDU and SDP ministers. The tiny and embattled FDP was thus left as the only opposition party in the Bonn parliament. Willy Brandt became foreign minister, and Franz Josef Strauss, leader of the CDU's Bavarian branch, became Finance Minister.

The new government quickly conveyed a sense of energy and purpose, and the electorate rewarded the CDU in several state elections in 1967. The Kiesinger regime pursued a flexible policy in Eastern Europe, establishing diplomatic relations with Romania and trade missions with Czechoslovakia. The government also proved flexible in its dealings with East Germany. The two Germanys seemed to be moving toward closer contacts with each other, at least on purely technical matters, although it is still too early to tell whether there are any grounds for hopes of a rapprochement.

In 1966 and early 1967 the National Democratic Party (NPD), an extreme right-wing group, scored significant successes in local and state elections. Democrats in and outside of Germany were alarmed by the appearance of this violently nationalistic party that had many ex-Nazis among its leaders. In the spring of 1967 the party suffered internal dissensions, and its appeal seemed to diminish.

The architect of postwar Germany, Konrad Adenauer, died in April, 1967, at the age of 91. The new government, based on a coalition he had opposed, pursued policies more independent from Washington's and more adventurous in the East than any he had followed. In the summer of 1967 severe financial difficulties caused Bonn to cut its defense budget, with the probable result that the strength of the army would have to be reduced. Such action by an important NATO ally created tensions between Bonn and Washington and epitomized the independent spirit of the Kiesinger government.

**ECONOMY.** The spectacular postwar recovery of Germany's economy has made the Federal Republic one of the leading industrial powers of the world. In 1966–67 the economy underwent a crisis, including a decline in production. The Kiesinger government responded with new and far-reaching budgetary policies that discouraged savings and emphasized limited deficit spending; these measures were generally expected to stimulate further growth.

Manufacturing and services make up the largest share of the national product. They consist of metallurgical, chemical, textile, automotive, electrical, and consumer-goods industries. Agriculture, forestry, fisheries, and mining are of comparatively less value, although Germany's coal reserves are considered the most important in Western Europe.

The railroads, totaling about 23,000 miles, are mostly operated by the Federal Railways System. There are over 258,125 miles of roads, a third of which are first-class. The important inland-waterways system consists of nearly 3,800 miles of navigable routes. Lufthansa is the government-subsidized airline.

**EDUCATION.** Education is compulsory for all children from the age of 6 to 14 or 15. Almost the entire population is literate, and in 1966 school attendance totaled more than 10 million students.

**ARMED FORCES.** The Federal Republic has a combined armed force strength of 459,600. Eighteen months' military service is compulsory.

## GERMAN DEMOCRATIC REPUBLIC

*Official Name:* German Democratic Republic. *Area:* 41,659 square miles. *Population:* 17,067,000. *Principal Cities* (with populations): East Berlin, the capital, 1,-079,000; Leipzig, 595,203; Dresden, 503,859; Karl-Marx-Stadt (formerly Chemnitz), 293,-549; Halle, 274,402; Magdeburg, 265,141. *Flag:* Black, red, and gold stripes with a centered coat of arms. *Monetary Unit:* The Ostmark (worth 45.3 U.S. cents). *National Income:* $37,600,000,000 (1965). *Average Annual Income per Person:* $2,355.

**LAND AND PEOPLE.** The German Democratic Republic (East Germany) is situated in north-central Europe and is bordered on the north by the Baltic Sea, on the east by Poland, and on the south and west by Czechoslovakia and West Germany. (See map on page 117.)

The sandy Baltic coastland has hills and lakes, and the central region has fertile plains; the Mittelgebirge mountains and heavy forests dominate the southern area. In the southeast the Erzgebirge mountains form a natural frontier with Czechoslovakia. Temperature variations, minimal in the northwest, become more seasonal farther inland, particularly in the southeast. The average annual range is from a winter low of 32° F. to a summer high of 65° F. Rainfall, about 24 inches a year, occurs most frequently during the summer.

The influence of the Slavs, who invaded in medieval times, appears in some parts of the country, but generally the population is homogeneous and predominantly Protestant. The language is German.

**HISTORY.** East Germany and a section of Berlin came under Soviet occupation at the end of World War II. Under the terms of the vaguely worded Potsdam Agreement between the Soviet Union, Britain, and the United States, Germany was to be treated as an economic unit, and a single policy of reparations was to be established. However, these intentions were frustrated in the ensuing disputes between the occupying powers. The U.S.S.R. demanded $10 billion in war indemnities to be extracted from German production, and refused to allow the free flow of goods between the four zones of occupation.

In March, 1948, the U.S.S.R. walked out of the Allied Control Council in protest against Western plans for Germany's future. Later that year the Soviet Union sought to detach West Berlin from Western control by imposing an 11-month blockade of Allied traffic. The, decision to turn the Soviet-occupied zone into a puppet state, the German Democratic Republic (GDR), in October, 1949, followed the creation of the Federal Republic of Germany in the area formerly under Allied occupation. Soviet troops effectively crushed an anti-Communist revolt in East Germany in June, 1953.

The GDR was empowered by treaty with the Soviet Union in September, 1955, to decide its own domestic and foreign policies and to control traffic to and from West Berlin. The country, however, remains responsive to Soviet demands, although recently the GDR has made some independent moves, including attempts to curb Soviet anti-Chinese policies.

In August, 1961, a wall of barbed wire and concrete was erected around the Soviet zone of Berlin to prevent East Germans from escaping to the West. In the next three years the number of political prisoners rose from 10,000 to about 20,000, but several thousand were amnestied on the 15th anniversary of the regime in 1964. The republic still lacks recognition by non-Communist states.

(See article on the Federal Republic of Germany for history up to World War II.)

**GOVERNMENT AND POLITICS.** The GDR is a People's Democracy along the Soviet pattern. It has a unicameral legislature, the Volkskammer (People's Chamber), whose 434 members are elected every four years by citizens aged 18 and up from a single list of candidates preselected by the Socialist Unity (Communist) Party. The chief administrative organ is the 24-man Council of State, but effective power is concentrated in the Politburo of the Socialist Unity Party. The Party's First Secretary, Walter Ulbricht, is also Chairman of the Council of State (President of the Republic) and appoints the prime minister, presently Willi Stoph.

Striving to raise East Germany's political status, the Ulbricht regime has harassed West German positions in West Berlin, utilized Bonn's difficulties with the Arab world to its own advantage, and attempted to gain admission to the United Nations.

**ECONOMY.** The economy is state-controlled, and almost every economic activity in the country has been nationalized. Until the mid-1950s East Germany's postwar recovery was slow—the Soviet Union took some 30 to 50 billion marks in reparations. Recently, however, the country's industrial development has been rapid, and the GDR has become the ninth largest industrial country in the world. Economic success has been partly due to reforms initiated in 1963. Also, greater autonomy was granted to local enterprises, which gave material incentives to workers.

Agriculture, which accounts for nearly 35 per cent of the national income, has fared less well since collectivization (completed in 1960), and food has to be imported to meet national needs. Principal crops are potatoes, beets, and grains. East Germany's mineral wealth is limited; however, the country is the world's leading producer of lignite.

Nearly 50 per cent of the country's trade is with the Soviet Union, and some 10 per cent is with West Germany.

**EDUCATION.** Education is free and compulsory for children to the age of 17. Almost the entire population is literate.

**ARMED FORCES.** Men between 18 and 25 are conscripted for 18-month service. The army has about 131,000 men; the navy, 11,000; the air force, 15,000; the police, 42,500; and the militia, 320,000. About 20 Soviet military divisions are stationed in East Germany.

# GHANA

*Official Name:* Republic of Ghana. *Area:* 91,843 square miles. *Population:* 7,800,000. *Principal Cities* (with populations): Accra, the capital, 491,000; Kumasi, 221,000; Sekondi-Takoradi, 121,000; Tamale, 58,000. *Flag:* A red, a gold, and a green horizontal stripe, with a black star in the gold stripe. *Monetary Unit:* The cedi (worth U.S. $1.40). *Gross National Product:* $1,908,000,000 (1965). *Average Annual Income per Person:* Over $200.

**LAND AND PEOPLE.** Ghana is situated in West Africa and is bordered by Upper Volta on the north, Togo on the east, the Atlantic Ocean on the south, and Upper Volta and Ivory Coast on the west. (See map on page 111.)

A coastal plain parallels the 334-mile shoreline. In the west a forested belt extends north from the coast, verging in the east into the hilly Ashanti region. Farther north is a high, rolling savanna. Ghana's highest point (about 2,900 feet) lies on the Togo border. The climate is mildly tropical.

The population is of Negroid stock, comprising many small tribal groups. Over 50 African languages are spoken, including those of the Ashanti, Ewe, and Moshi-Dagomba groups. English is also spoken.

Some 62 per cent of the population adhere to tribal religions, 24 per cent are Christians, and 14 per cent are Muslims.

**HISTORY.** Ghana has no written history prior to the arrival of the Portuguese in 1471. The name "Ghana" was assumed on independence in the belief that the inhabitants were descended from the Ghana Empire that flourished in the western Sudan from the 4th to the 13th century. After the Portuguese, traders came from several European countries, including Britain. Commerce in gold soon gave way to slave trading, until the British Parliament declared it illegal in 1807. All Europeans except the British gradually withdrew from the area.

During the 19th century the British engaged in a series of wars with the Ashanti Confederation. The coastal region became the Gold Coast Crown Colony in 1874.

The northern territory was made a British protectorate in 1897, and in 1901 Ashanti was annexed. A part of neighboring Togoland, formerly a German colony, was turned over to the British in 1922 under a League of Nations mandate and was administered as part of the Gold Coast.

Africans were admitted into the Gold Coast government in 1942. The Convention People's Party (CPP), founded by Kwame Nkrumah, swept the Legislative Assembly elections in 1951, and for the first time the African majority had a significant voice in its own affairs. In 1957 Ghana became the first Negro African country to pass from colonial status to independence.

In 1960 a constitution was approved making Ghana a republic. Nkrumah, who had stated that he planned a West African Soviet Republic that would include the Gold Coast, was elected president. He was re-elected in 1965, but in 1966, while visiting Peking, he was deposed by a military coup d'etat. The National Liberation Council (NLC), headed by Lieutenant General Joseph A. Ankrah, was formed to rule the country. The NLC resumed relations with Britain, which had been broken by Nkrumah. It shifted from Nkrumah's pro-Communist policies and expelled some Soviet and all Communist Chinese technicians and teachers. Junior officers unsuccessfully attempted a coup against the NLC on April 17, 1967.

**GOVERNMENT AND POLITICS.** Following independence, Nkrumah established total control of the country. A one-party system, censorship, deportation, the death penalty for a long list of offenses, and imprisonment without trial for up to ten years were among devices used to consolidate his power. He was the leading proponent of Pan-Africanism, but found few supporters among other African leaders.

Since coming to power the NLC has established an emergency regime, dissolved parliament, and banned political parties. A return to constitutional government within 18 months was promised, however. In foreign affairs the NLC follows a policy of "absolute neutrality."

**ECONOMY.** The economy is based primarily on agriculture and mining. Ghana is the world's leading producer of cocoa, providing about one-third of the world total; cocoa accounted for 60 per cent of its exports in 1965. Coconuts, palm kernels, palm oil, and lumber are also produced. Important minerals are manganese, diamonds, bauxite, and gold. Since 1959 Ghana has had an annual foreign trade deficit.

The Volta River Dam, primarily a hydroelectric project, has created Volta Lake, the largest artificial body of water in Africa.

Nkrumah's regime left large deficits. Foreign exchange reserves, which stood at $548 million at independence, were exhausted by 1966, while the public debt had risen to $1.1 billion. The NLC has followed a policy of retrenchment, reform, and greater reliance on private investment.

**EDUCATION.** Primary and secondary education are free but not compulsory. There are three universities, and literacy is estimated at 25 per cent. Total school enrollment is 1,196,400.

**ARMED FORCES.** Military service is not compulsory. There is an army of about 7,000 men, and a small navy and air force.

# GREECE

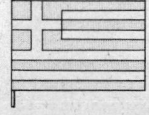

*Official Name:* Kingdom of Hellas. *Area:* 50,944 square miles. *Population:* 8,540,000. *Principal Cities* (with populations): Athens, the capital, 627,564; Salonica, 378,444; Piraeus, 183,877; Patras, 102,244; Heraklion, 69,983. *Flag:* Blue and white horizontal stripes, with a white cross on a blue field in the upper left-hand corner. *Monetary Unit:* The drachma of 100 lepta (worth 3.4 U.S. cents).

*Gross National Product:* $6,347,000,000 (1966). *Average Annual Income:* $738.

**LAND AND PEOPLE.** Greece, the southernmost country of the Balkan peninsula, is bordered on the north by Albania, Yugoslavia, and Bulgaria; on the east by Turkey and the Aegean Sea; on the south by the Mediterranean Sea; and on the west by the Ionian Sea. (See map on page 197.)

Greece is largely a mountainous and heavily wooded country. The Pindus range, running north and south, is the most important. Mount Olympus, home of the gods in Greek mythology, is the highest peak (9,554 feet). Numerous valleys and plains are situated between the mountains. The main rivers are in the north and have their origins in other countries; none of them are navigable.

Southern Greece consists primarily of the Peloponnesian peninsula and a multitude of off-shore islands. Nearly one-fifth of the total land area of Greece comprises 437 islands. The coastline of 9,355 miles, with its hundreds of harbors and bays, encourages navigation, as it has since the earliest stages of Greek civilization. The summers are sunny and dry but not unbearably hot, due to the sea winds. The annual mean temperatures range from 16° to 106° F.

Over 96 per cent of the inhabitants are Greek, but there is a Turkish minority of over 100,000, located primarily in Thrace. Greek Orthodoxy is the established religion, to which 97 per cent of the population adheres.

**HISTORY.** Greece has been known as the cradle of European civilization. Traces of Neolithic man, dating from 4000 B.C., are to be found there. By 1100 B.C. two major civilizations had flourished and vanished. The Minoan civilization was centered on the island of Crete and later influenced the mainland from the south; the Mycenaean civilization, generally less advanced than the Minoan, was centered on the mainland. Beginning about 2000 B.C., successive waves of Greek-speaking Achaeans, an Indo-European people, migrated into the area, mixing with and eventually supplanting the existing cultures.

Greek city-states began to develop about 1000 B.C. By 800 B.C. they were sufficiently well established to become the source of colonization efforts. By 600 B.C. colonies founded from the city-states were to be found on islands in the Ionian, Aegean, and Mediterranean seas, in Asia Minor, on the African Coast, and as far west as France and Spain. Ancient Greek civilization reached its zenith in the fifth century B.C., when Athens was the center of a vast overseas empire. During this century and the next, such prominent persons as the dramatists Aeschylus and Sophocles and the philosophers Socrates, Plato, and Aristotle lived in Athens. After the death of Alexander the Great in 323 B.C. the political disintegration of Greece became marked. By 146 B.C. it had become a province of the new Mediterranean power, the Roman Empire.

After Constantine moved the capital of the empire to Constantinople in 330 A.D., the Grecian influence was felt more strongly. In the ensuing centuries, while Rome languished under barbarian control, Constantinople and Greece were the centers of a thriving Byzantine civilization. In the course of the Fourth Crusade Constantinople was sacked by crusaders en route to the Holy Land (1204). It remained in Western hands until 1261, when it was won back by the Greeks. Constantinople fell to the Turks in 1453, and in 1460 Greece became a Turkish province. The Turks governed the Greeks within their domains through the Orthodox Church and allowed them a relatively large amount of autonomy.

After almost four centuries of subjugation to the Turks, a war of independence was declared by the Greeks in 1821. Supported by Britain, France, and Russia, the revolt was ultimately successful, and in July, 1832, the sultan recognized the independence of Greece. Prince Otto of Bavaria was made king by the three powers who had supported Greek independence. He was overthrown in 1862 and was succeeded by Prince William George of Denmark, who became George I of the Hellenes. In 1864 Britain ceded the Ionian islands to Greece to strengthen the new monarch's position.

The residence of large numbers of Greeks in territories outside the Greek nation gave rise to a belief that those areas should be incorporated into Greece. This so-called "Great Idea" envisioned the restoration of Constantinople as the capital of a nation of all the Hellenes. Appropriately, the King of Greece was called the King of the Hellenes to signify his theoretical jurisdiction over all those who were ethnically Greek but resided in foreign territories. These views led to the Greco-Turkish war of 1897, which was disastrous for the small and as yet weak kingdom of Greece.

At the beginning of the 20th century, the Greeks were fighting with neighboring Slavs and Turks in an effort to reclaim national territory. Following the two Balkan wars (1912 and 1913), Epirus, parts of Thrace and Macedonia, and Crete became part of the Greek state. It was not until 1947, however, that the Dodecanese islands were united with Greece.

Between the two World Wars the major issue in Greece was whether the country should remain a monarchy or become a republic. The population voted for a monarchy in 1920 and for a republic in 1924. King George II, who was dethroned in 1924, returned in 1935, following a plebiscite. On August 4, 1936, the Crown acquiesced to the dictatorship of General Ioannis Metaxas. Although Metaxas had imitated the Nazis in many ways, he headed the resistance movement when Italian Fascists invaded Greece by way of Albania in 1940 and King George II fled the country. The Greek soldiers fought valiantly, but German Nazis and their Bulgarian allies came to the aid of Italy, and by June, 1941, Greece was an occupied country. The occupation ended on October 12, 1944.

Following World War II, five years of civil strife ensued; Communist guerrillas, who were aided by neighboring Communist countries, were finally defeated in 1949. Meanwhile, King George II had returned to Greece in September, 1946, following a plebiscite. He died the next year and was succeeded by his brother, Paul I, who reigned until 1964. Upon his death his son, Constantine II, came to the throne; he married Princess Anne-Marie, the youngest daughter of King Frederick and Queen Ingrid of Denmark, in September, 1964.

**GOVERNMENT AND POLITICS.** Until April 21, 1967, Greece was a constitutional monarchy. On that date a military coup took place and effective control passed into the hands of a military junta, which announced that it was acting to crush a Communist conspiracy. Constantine Kollias, a judge, was appointed prime minister by the junta.

The events which led to the coup began with the 1964 election of George Papandreou (Center Union party) by a majority of 53 per cent, an unprecedented victory in Greek politics. He resigned as prime minister and the Center Union party was ousted by King Constantine in July, 1965. It was succeeded by a series of short-lived governments, amid widespread popular demonstrations in favor of Papandreou.

After the military takeover, plans were announced to revise the constitution, which was to be submitted to a popular referendum. However, the suppression of fundamental constitutional guarantees of civil liberties, the detention of thousands of political prisoners, and other repressive measures, such as censorship of the press, aroused many protests in other parts of the world. The United States government partially suspended military aid to Greece. King Constantine visited President Johnson on September 11, 1967, in an effort to normalize relations between the two countries.

**ECONOMY.** Greece's economy has been undergoing rapid expansion since 1960. In 1966 the value of industrial production surpassed that of agriculture for the first time. Agriculture, which has been considerably bolstered by the government since World War II, accounted for 25 per cent of the nation's income, while industrial production accounted for 29 per cent.

The principal industrial products are aluminum, textiles, electrical appliances, ships, leather goods, and chemicals. Iron ore, pyrites, chromite, and bauxite comprise 75 per cent of mineral exports. Agricultural exports are cotton, fruits, olives, olive oil, and tobacco.

Greece has the world's second-largest merchant shipping fleet. Merchant ships include 1,734 sailing under the Greek flag and an additional 1,014 sailing under the flags of other nations but owned and operated by Greeks.

**EDUCATION.** Education is free and compulsory for all children between the ages of 6 and 14 years. Approximately 86 per cent of the population over 14 is literate. Higher education, available at 12 universities and colleges, is free.

**ARMED FORCES.** All men of 21 years are conscripted for military service for two years. The total armed forces of Greece number over 158,000 officers and men (army, 117,000; navy, 18,000; air force, 23,000).

# GUATEMALA

*Official Name:* Republic of Guatemala. *Area:* 42,042 square miles. *Population:* 4,800,000. *Principal Cities* (with populations): Guatemala City, the capital, 635,000; Quezaltenango, 96,000; Coban, 38,000. *Flag:* A vertical tricolor of blue, white, and blue; the national coat of arms is on the white stripe. *Monetary Unit:* The quetzal (worth U.S. $1). *Gross National Product:* $1,410,000,000 (1965). *Average Annual Income per Person:* $280.

**LAND AND PEOPLE.** Guatemala, the most populous country in Central America, has a 70-mile coastline on the Caribbean and a 220-mile coast on the Pacific. It is bordered on the west and north by Mexico, and on the east by British Honduras, Honduras, and El Salvador. (See map on page 176.)

The topography ranges from a coastal plain (altitude: 300 to 4,500 feet) to a mountainous area in the northwest and southwest; 30 of the mountains are volcanic, and two of them are still active (Mt. Fuego erupted in April, 1966). In the north are the continental divide and the Atlantic lowlands.

Although Guatemala is wholly within the tropical zone, the climate is generally temperate in the rugged highlands in the central and western part of the country. Guatemala City, at an altitude of nearly 5,000 feet, has a year-round springlike climate. The rainy season lasts from June to October, with an average of 50 inches a year in Guatemala City. Few people live in the hot plains along the Pacific shore or in the thickly jungled provinces on the Atlantic side.

About 53 per cent of the people are Indians; 45 per cent are mestizos; and 2 per cent are whites. The population is 90 per cent Catholic. Spanish is the official language.

**HISTORY.** Guatemala was part of the territory occupied by the Mayans, whose influence and power began to decline in the 12th century; Spanish conquistadores completed their downfall by the mid-16th century.

From 1524 to 1821 Central America from Yucatan to Panama was ruled by the Spanish, with Guatemala as the center of government. Indians were converted to Catholicism by missionaries and were forced to work for Spanish overlords. The Church and Spanish Crown, however, protected them from the worst abuses of the landholders. By the mid-18th century Antigua, the capital, was one of the great cities of America, comparable to Mexico City and Lima. Severe earthquakes in 1773 virtually destroyed the city, and the capital was moved to the present site of Guatemala City.

Guatemala won its independence from Spain in 1821, was briefly annexed by Mexico, and then was a member of the Central American Federation until 1838. Independence brought little change until the regime of Justo Rufino Barrios (1873–85), who reduced the power of the Catholic Church, emphasized material improvements, stimulated plantation agriculture, and modernized the educational system.

During the 19th and 20th centuries Guatemala has been under the control of a long line of military dictatorships. Following the revolution of 1944, a reform government under Juan José Arévalo lasted from 1945 until 1951. Communist influence was apparent in the regime of Jacobo Arbenz Guzmán (1951–54). He was overthrown in 1954 by Carlos Castillo Armas, with U.S. aid. Armas was assassinated three years later.

Political turmoil continued until 1966. Military juntas ruled the government, election results were voided, numerous strikes and revolts occurred, and conflict arose with Cuba over the disclosure that anti-Castro Cuban guerrillas had been trained in Guatemala. A state of siege was declared in 1963 to deal with growing terrorism and sabotage by Communist-oriented rebels. Provisional President Enrique Peralta Azurdia suspended the constitution, dissolved congress, canceled all elections, and prohibited all political activities.

A free election was held in March, 1966. Julio César Méndez Montenegro, candidate of the moderately leftist Revolutionary Party, won a plurality and took office on July 1. He restored constitutional guarantees in 1967.

**GOVERNMENT AND POLITICS.** A new constitution, effective in May, 1966, called for a republican form of government and a president elected by popular vote for a four-year term. President Méndez is the first popularly elected president since 1963, when the armed forces took over the government. The 55 members of the one-chamber assembly are also elected by direct popular vote. A cabinet assists the president. Voting is compulsory for literate men and women over age 18.

**ECONOMY.** Guatemala is chiefly an agricultural country. Principal exports are coffee, bananas, and cotton. Government efforts to raise yields of corn have not been successful; the Indians still grow corn in the manner of their ancestors. Forests cover about 60 per cent of the country and are one of the most important natural resources. There are deposits of several minerals; a major nickel ore deposit is being exploited.

Industry is growing, with manufacturing now the second-largest sector of the economy. Industry has been stimulated by the Central American Common Market, and Guatemala has begun to export cloth, tires, chemicals, and small appliances. In 1967 most tariffs were eliminated regarding trade among Central American nations.

Guatemala's transportation network, although improving, is still primitive. The old Inter-American Highway route in the highlands has been replaced by a new, faster highway along the Pacific coast. Guatemala City's Aurora Airport was the first jet air terminal in Central America.

**EDUCATION.** Primary education is compulsory for children aged 7 to 14. About 28 per cent of the people are literate.

**ARMED FORCES.** Armed forces total about 8,000 men.

# GUINEA

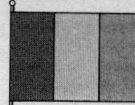

*Official Name:* Republic of Guinea. *Area:* 94,926 square miles. *Population:* 3,42,000. *Principal Cities* (with populations): Conakry, the capital, 150,000; Kankan, 65,-000; Kindia, 50,000. *Flag:* Three vertical red, yellow, and green stripes. *Monetary Unit:* The Guinea franc (worth 0.41 U.S. cents).

**LAND AND PEOPLE.** Guinea, a West African country, is bordered on the north by Portuguese Guinea, Senegal, and Mali, on the east by Mali and Ivory Coast, on the south by Liberia and Sierra Leone, and on the west by the Atlantic Ocean. (See map on page 111.)

The coastal plain rises to a mountainous region called Futa Jallon; interior Guinea is a rolling plain, partly woodland and partly grassy savanna, averaging about 1,000 feet in height. In the forested highlands Mount Nimba rises to some 6,000 feet. The Niger, the Senegal, and the Gambia rivers all rise in the Futa Jallon. The climate is humid and tropical. Temperatures range from 60° to 100° F. and the amount of rainfall has measured as much as 168 inches annually at Conakry.

Of the many ethnic groups forming the population, the most important are the Fulani (Peul), comprising 30 per cent; the Malinke, 15 per cent; the Soussou, 8 per cent; and the Kissi, 5 per cent.

Native languages and French (the official language) are spoken. Approximately 62 per cent of the people are Muslims; 2 per cent are Christians.

**HISTORY.** The medieval empire of Ghana dominated Guinea in ancient times. In the 13th century Ghana was annexed to a Malinke empire, which declined after the 15th century, and the last Malinke emperor was deposed in the 17th century. Portuguese explorers visited the Guinea coast in the 15th century; within two centuries the British, Portuguese, and French were all in competition for trade in the area. The region, however, was never very prominent in the slave trade.

Guinea's modern history began in 1725, following a Muslim holy war. From then until the 19th century, wars and disputes among the area's tribal chiefs threatened the unity of the country. The Treaty of Paris of 1814 secured French rights on the Guinea coast, and in 1849 a French protectorate was declared. Between 1882 and 1911 Guinea's boundaries were settled.

Rejecting an offer of freedom within the French Community, Guinea declared itself a completely independent state in October, 1958, with Sékou Touré as its first president. With no further financial or administrative aid from France, the new nation found itself in a serious predicament. The United States, in fear of disrupting relations with France, ignored Touré's request for aid. Touré—an avowed Marxist, although disclaiming any Communist alignment —turned to the U.S.S.R. and Communist China for aid. Guinea has nevertheless remained non-aligned and has received considerable help from the West, mainly the United States and West Germany.

When Kwame Nkrumah was deposed as President of Ghana early in 1966, Touré granted him political asylum. Touré also announced that henceforth Nkrumah was to be regarded as an honorary president of Guinea.

**GOVERNMENT AND POLITICS.** Guinea's constitution states that the country is a "democratic, secular, and social republic."

The president is elected by universal suffrage for a term of seven years. The National Assembly's members are elected for five-year terms.

The only political party in the country is the Parti Démocratique de Guinée (PDG), and only one list of candidates has appeared in presidential and assembly elections. In 1961 Guinea signed an agreement with Ghana and Mali to foster a Union of African States, but the union has not materialized.

**ECONOMY.** Over 90 per cent of the working population is dependent on agriculture. Rice is the main food crop; bananas, coffee, pineapples, and palm kernels are the leading agricultural exports. Nomads keep small cattle on the interior plateaus.

Mining is economically second in importance to agriculture. Guinea has sizable bauxite reserves which accounted for 80 per cent of Africa's bauxite production in 1964. Alumina is the principal mineral export. Diamonds are the only other significant mineral export, but though reserves exist, their working has been restricted by changes in national policy. There are unworked reserves of iron ore in the Guinea Highlands.

The Conakry-Niger railway (414 miles) is in poor condition. There are 4,725 miles of roads. Conakry is the main deepwater port.

Because of the country's extremely poor economic condition, the government has sought increased foreign aid and private investment. Industries such as tobacco, furniture, bricks, and tiles have been promoted, but some are of doubtful economic value. Much foreign trade is by barter, and the present inconvertibility of the Guinea franc presents problems.

**EDUCATION.** All schools are state-run and free. More than 388,500 children attend primary and secondary classes. The literacy rate is estimated at 70 per cent.

**ARMED FORCES.** Military service is compulsory for all adult males. The armed forces are estimated at 4,800 men.

# GUYANA

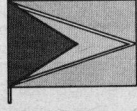

*Area:* 83,000 square miles. *Population:* 662,000. *Principal Cities* (with populations): Georgetown, the capital, 72,964; New Amsterdam, 14,059. *Flag:* Red and yellow triangles separated from the green field by black and white bands. *Monetary Unit:* The Guyana dollar (worth 58.5 U.S. cents). *Gross National Product:* $326,900,000 (1965). *Average Annual Income per Person:* $385.

**LAND AND PEOPLE.** Guyana (formerly British Guiana) is bordered on the east by Surinam, on the south by Brazil, on the west by Brazil and Venzuela, and on the north and northeast by the Atlantic Ocean. (See map on page 75.)

Most of the population lives on the low coastal plain that comprises 4 per cent of the total land area. The plain gives way to a forested, hilly region that leads to mountains and savannas. The climate is subtropical on the coast and tropical inland.

East Indians constitute about 48 per cent of the population and Africans some 33 per cent. About 12 per cent are of mixed blood, 4.5 per cent are Indians, and the rest are Europeans and Chinese. Guyana is the only English-speaking nation on the South American mainland. Christians account for about 57 per cent of the population, Hindus for 34 per cent, and Muslims for 9 per cent.

**HISTORY.** Spaniards charted the Guyana coastline in 1499. By 1620 the Dutch West Indies Company had partially settled the country. The three colonies of Berbice, Demerara, and Essequibo were ceded to Britain in 1814 and united into the colony of British Guiana in 1831. In 1928 it became a Crown colony with limited representative government. Full internal self-government was granted in 1961. Competition between the People's Progressive Party, generally supported by East Indians, and the People's National Congress, generally supported by Negroes, led to outbreaks of violence in 1962 and 1963. This delayed the granting of independence until May 26, 1966.

**GOVERNMENT AND POLITICS.** The constitution provides that the country will become a republic after January 1, 1969. Executive authority is now vested in the British crown and exercised by a governor-general acting on the advice of ministers. The governor-general appoints a prime minister from representatives in the national assembly.

After the last elections (1964) a coalition government was formed under Linden F. S. Burnham, leader of the People's National Congress. Burnham became prime minister. Cheddi B. Jagan's People's Progressive Party, which received 48.5 per cent of the votes, refused to join in shaping the new constitution or in forming the government.

**ECONOMY.** Food growing and processing are the primary industries; there are also rich deposits of bauxite, gold, diamonds, and manganese. Sugar accounts for 38 per cent of exports, bauxite and aluminum for 29 per cent, and rice for 15 per cent. Guyana imports many foodstuffs and all her manufactured goods.

**EDUCATION AND HEALTH.** Education is free and compulsory between the ages of 6 and 14. The literacy rate is 80 per cent. There were 233 doctors registered in 1963, one for every 2,600 people.

**ARMED FORCES.** There is no compulsory military service. Internal security forces are estimated at 1,000 men.

# HAITI

*Official Name:* Republic of Haiti. *Area:* 10,714 square miles. *Population:* 4,485,000. *Principal Cities* (with populations): Port-au-Prince, the capital, 240,000; Cap-Haïtien, 30,000. *Flag:* Black and red bars with a centered white rectangle containing emblems of war grouped around a palm tree. *Monetary Unit:* The gourde (worth 20 U.S. cents). *Gross National Product:* $327,000,000 (1965). *Average Annual Income per Person:* $70.

**LAND AND PEOPLE.** Haiti, occupying the western third of the island of Hispaniola, is bordered on the north by the Atlantic Ocean, on the east by the Dominican Republic, on the south by the Caribbean Sea, and on the west by the Windward Passage. (See map on page 176.) Temperatures in this tropical country range from about 68° to 94° F. The rainy seasons are from April to June and October to November.

Haiti's population, by far the most dense in Latin America, is about 95 per cent Negro and 5 per cent mulatto. The very small white population is nearly all foreign. Although French is the official language, most of the people speak only Creole, a mixture of French, Spanish, African, and English.

The official religion, Roman Catholicism, is practiced by 90 per cent of the people. President Duvalier has expelled from the country most leading Catholic churchmen as well as the Episcopal Bishop of Haiti, alleging political activity. A small minority of the population practice voodooism.

**HISTORY.** The island of Hispaniola, discovered by Christopher Columbus in 1492, was the site of La Navidad, the first Spanish settlement in the New World. Virtually exterminating the Arawak natives by 1533, the Spanish settled mainly on the eastern side in the vicinity of Santo Domingo. The western area became a base for French and English buccaneers, and the French gradually colonized the northern coastal plain. By the Treaty of Ryswick (1697) Spain ceded the western region, present-day Haiti, to the French.

French settlers imported many slaves from Africa and developed the vast sugar plantations that made the island economically important in the 18th century. A complex social structure evolved, with sharp divisions and racial antagonisms between white planters, Creoles (native-born whites), mulattoes, free Negroes, and Negro slaves.

The French Revolution, which began in 1789, sparked Negro demands for emancipation, and in fierce slave rebellions most of the white population was murdered. The white survivors emigrated. In 1792 a French army was sent to crush the revolt but was defeated by a remarkable, self-educated, freed slave, Toussaint L'Ouverture. Agreeing in 1799 to govern for France, L'Ouverture occupied Santo Domingo in the eastern part of the island, abolished slavery, and gave the united island

a new constitution. In 1802, however, France's new ruler, Napoleon Bonaparte, sent his brother-in-law, General Le Clerc, and a large military force to restore French authority on the island and to re-establish slavery. L'Ouverture, captured by treachery, died in a French prison, but the French army was decimated by disease and by clashes with Negro forces led by Jean-Jacques Dessalines. The army withdrew in 1803, and in January, 1804, Dessalines declared the independence of Saint-Domingue and restored its original Indian name, Haiti.

Dessalines ruled as a despot under the title of Emperor Jacques I until his assassination in 1806. The country then divided, with the north ruled autocratically by Henri Christophe, a Negro who had himself proclaimed King Henri I. A more benevolent republic was established in the south and west and was governed by mulatto Alexandre Pétion until his death in 1818. His successor, Jean Pierre Boyer, reunited Haiti following the suicide of King Henri in 1820. The entire island was united in 1822 when Boyer's forces conquered Santo Domingo. A year after Boyer's ouster in 1843, Santo Domingo gained its independence as the Dominican Republic.

Haiti's last emperor was overthrown in 1859, and for decades the republic faced anarchy, with Negroes and mulattoes fighting for power. The country was also burdened by increasingly heavy foreign debts. In 1905 the U.S. took Haiti's customs into receivership, and ten years later the U.S. seized full control of the country. Despite American efforts to improve health and public services, Haiti and most of Latin America bitterly protested the occupation. American forces withdrew in 1934, but financial control was retained by the U.S. until 1941. Since that time Haiti has continued to have revolts, despotic rulers, and clashes with the Dominican Republic.

**GOVERNMENT AND POLITICS.** Officially a republic, Haiti is virtually ruled as a dictatorship. Elected president in 1957, Dr. François Duvalier had the constitution revised to permit his re-election. Dissolving the bicameral legislature in 1961, Duvalier held an election for 58 deputies to a single legislative chamber. He included his own name on each ballot (although the presidential election was not due until 1963), and he was duly declared re-elected for the legislative six-year term. Another revision in 1964 enabled him to be designated president for life. His regime has been marked by economic problems and by terrorist tactics of the secret police.

Haiti and the Dominican Republic have engaged in bitter border clashes. In 1963 the United States broke off relationships with Haiti. President Duvalier, in need of foreign aid and tourist income, has recently attempted to improve foreign relationships.

**ECONOMY.** Most of Haiti's population, 90 per cent agrarian, live at a bare subsistence level. The foremost export is coffee. Foreign aid and tourism used to be principal sources of income. However, when the U.S. broke diplomatic relations in 1963, foreign aid ceased;

relations have been resumed, but only a malaria control project continues.

Haiti's roads are mostly unsuitable for automobiles, and the national railway has ceased operating except in certain sections where it is used to transport sugarcane. Main cities are connected by telegraph, a postal system, and an ineffective telephone system.

**EDUCATION.** The law calls for free and compulsory elementary education in the French language; however, illiteracy stands at about 85 per cent. Government campaigns to reduce illiteracy may improve the situation. Higher education is offered free in many professions at the University of Haiti.

**ARMED FORCES.** Armed forces are estimated at 16,450; about 10,000 of these are in Duvalier's armed civilian militia.

# HONDURAS

*Official Name:* Republic of Honduras. *Area:* 43,281 square miles. *Population:* 2,363,000. *Principal Cities* (with populations): Tegucigalpa, the capital, 180,000; San Pedro Sula, 100,000; La Ceiba, 28,000. *Flag:* Horizontal stripes of blue, white, and blue, with five blue stars in the white stripe. *Monetary Unit:* The lempira of 100 centavos (worth 50 U.S. cents). *Gross National Product:* $504,000,000 (1965). *Average Annual Income per Person:* $194.

**LAND AND PEOPLE.** Honduras is bordered on the north by the Caribbean Sea, on the east and south by Nicaragua and the Gulf of Fonesca on the Pacific Ocean, on the southwest by El Salvador, and on the west by Guatemala. (See map on page 176.) Narrow lowlands along the Gulf of Fonesca and the Caribbean coast fringe this mountainous land, whose southern peaks exceed 8,000 feet.

The climate varies from wet and tropical on the coastal plains to dry and cool in the uplands. Average temperatures range from 88° F. on the coasts to 73° F. in the regions above 2,500 feet. The capital, Tegucigalpa (elevation 3,500 feet), has a continual springlike climate. The wet season is May to November; rainfall averages 100 inches on the northern coast and 30 inches in the south. Principal rivers emptying into the Caribbean are the Ulúa, Aguán, and Patuca. The Choluteca flows to the Pacific.

Most Hondurans (91 per cent) are mestizos, a mixture of European and American Indian stock. The rest of the population is made up of Indians (6 per cent), Negroes or mulattoes (2 per cent), and Spanish (1 per cent). Culture and language are mainly Spanish. Ninety-eight per cent of the people are Roman Catholic.

**HISTORY.** A center of Mayan civilization before 900 A.D., Honduras was discovered by Columbus in 1502 on his fourth voyage to the New World. Attracted by exaggerated tales of gold and silver in Honduras, adventurers made and country's early days a chronicle of revolution and intrigue. Rival Spanish factions from Mexico, Guatemala, and Panama struggled for control of the area. Overland invaders included Hernán Cortés, who in 1524 made an historic march from Mexico to impose his rule on the area. In 1538 Honduras became a part of Spanish-controlled Guatemala.

In 1821 Honduras and the other Central American provinces declared their independence of Spain, but were quickly annexed by the Mexican emperor Agustín de Iturbide. They broke away within a year when Iturbide was overthrown. Honduras joined her neighbors in the United Provinces of Central America, a mutual protective association. This lasted until 1838, when Honduras declared its independence. For decades thereafter, Honduras was embroiled in political battles. Internally, Conservative and Liberal parties fought for control; externally, Honduras was subjected to interference from neighboring states, particularly Guatemala and Nicaragua. American Marines were sent to the country several times between 1912 and 1925 to protect American lives and property.

A Conservative general, Tiburcio Carías Andino, was dictator from 1933 to 1948. His successor, Juan Manuel Gálvez, gave the Hondurans more freedom than they had enjoyed under any earlier ruler. A bloodless revolution deposed President Julio Lozano Díaz in 1956 and brought about new elections and a new constitution in 1957. The Liberal victor, Ramón Villeda Morales, embarked on a program of modernization and agrarian reform. He was overthrown by a military coup in October, 1963—the 136th revolutionary overturn in the history of Honduras. The leader of the revolt, Oswaldo López Arellano, ruled via a military junta until February, 1965; he was elected president in June, 1965, under a new constitution.

**GOVERNMENT AND POLITICS.** Technically a republic, Honduras has had a series of dictatorial governments. A number of constitutions have provided the forms but not the substance of democracy. The present government includes members of the opposition Liberal party, thus avoiding the onus of being called a dictatorship or a one-party state. Communist infiltration continues to beset the country.

Honduras has a one-house legislature, the Congress of Deputies, which is comprised of 58 members chosen for six-year terms by popular vote. The constitution also provides that the president will serve a six-year term. All literate men and women over 18 may vote.

**ECONOMY.** Honduras is a poorly developed, agricultural country. It is a leading producer of bananas, which account for 39 per cent of its exports. In addition, Honduras exports coffee, cotton, lumber, cattle, and minerals.

Industrial and commercial development has been hindered by inadequate road and rail networks. Most of the roads are not paved. The 760 miles of rails link the banana-growing areas with the principal ports. San Pedro Sula is the center of a growing industrial area, but only now is it being connected by road to

Tegucigalpa and other large cities.

**EDUCATION.** Schooling is compulsory and free for children aged 7 to 15. In 1965 there were 3,901 primary schools, 93 secondary schools, and 7 colleges. There is a national university at Tegucigalpa. The United Fruit Company maintains a well-known school that offers boys a three-year course of training in tropical agriculture.

Although the illiteracy rate has decreased in the last decade, it still stands at about 55 per cent.

**ARMED FORCES.** Men between 18 and 55 are subject to eight months of active military training. The size of the army is fixed at 2,500. There are small naval and air units, and a school of military aviation.

# HUNGARY

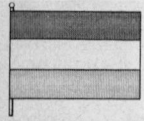

*Official Name:* Hungarian People's Republic. *Area:* 35,915 square miles. *Population:* 10,179,000. *Principal Cities* (with populations): Budapest, the capital, 1,-935,000; Miskolc, 167,000; Debrecen, 146,-000; Pécs 134,000; Szeged, 114,000. *Flag:* A horizontal tri-color of red, white and green. *Monetary Unit:* The forint (officially worth 8.6 U.S. cents; at tourist rate worth 4.3 U.S. cents). *Gross National Product:* $10,300,000,000 (1965). *Annual Average Income per Person:* $1,020.

**LAND AND PEOPLE.** Landlocked Hungary is bordered on the north by Czechoslovakia, on the northeast by the U.S.S.R., on the east by Romania, on the south by Yugoslavia, and on the west by Austria. (See map on page 197.) The Danube River forms over a third of the border with Czechoslovakia, then veers south through Hungary and into Yugoslavia. Plains lie to the east and west of the river. The uplands in the northeast, occupying about a third of the land area, are marked by river valleys and mountains, the highest of which is Kékes in the Mátra range (3,300 feet). Balaton, in west-central Hungary, is the largest lake.

Hungary has a continental climate—hot summers (the average July temperature is 71° F.) and cold winters (the average January temperature is 31° F.). Rainfall averages 25 inches a year, and summer droughts are frequent.

Magyars comprise 96 per cent of Hungary's population. Germans are the largest ethnic minority group. Atheism is the state's goal, and churches are tightly controlled. It is estimated, however, that 67 per cent of the people are Roman Catholics, 27 per cent Protestants, 2.5 per cent Greek Catholics, and 1.5 per cent Jews.

**HISTORY.** Arpad, a semi-legendary chief of the Magyars, brought his people from beyond the Urals about the end of the ninth century A.D., conquered most of Hungary, and founded a dynasty that lasted more than four centuries. In 1001 Hungary was unified as a kingdom under Stephen I. He carried on his father's Christianization efforts and was canonized St.

Stephen in 1083. The crown sent to him by Pope Sylvester II still serves as the holy symbol of Hungary's national existence. Rescued from Hungary in 1944, it remains in the custody of the United States.

Nomadic tribes from Russia began to raid Hungary in the 11th century, but they were later absorbed into the population. In 1222 the lesser nobles, protecting their interests from the many privileges won by a few powerful nobles called the magnates, forced Andrew II to sign the Golden Bull, the "Magna Charta of Hungary." The country fell into anarchy when Andrew III, last of the Arpad line, died in 1301.

Matthias Corvinus, a Hungarian elected king in 1458, restored Hungary to an era of glory. After his death in 1490 the country weakened, and by 1526 it was under Turkish domination.

Hungary split into three regions: the west was controlled by the Hapsburgs, the central plains by the Turks, and the east (Transylvania) by nobles more or less in vassalage to the Turks. At the end of the 17th century the Hapsburg armies expelled the Turks, and the country was reunited under the control of Vienna. Resistance against Austria was led by Francis II Rakoczy, one of Hungary's major national heroes, but by 1711 he had been defeated; the Hungarian Diet later acceded to Hapsburg rule.

Although nationalism was firmly suppressed, it exploded into rebellion in 1848. Louis Kossuth, leader of the rebels, declared Hungary an independent republic in 1849. With Russian assistance, Austria was able to put down the revolt. Following their defeat by the Prussians in 1866, Austria was forced to recognize Hungarian nationalism, and the Austro-Hungarian dual monarchy was created.

After the defeat of the monarchy in World War I, Hungary declared herself an independent republic in January, 1919. Two months later the government surrendered to the Communist dictator Bela Kun. In July of the same year Romanian troops intervened, and Kun fled. In November a new government was established with Admiral Nicholas Horthy de Nagybanya as regent and head of state. His authoritarian regime lasted 25 years.

World War I had cost Hungary two-thirds of her land and half her population. In an ultimately futile effort to regain her ceded territories, Hungary allied herself with the Axis powers. During World War II German troops moved into the country and, in 1944, arrested Horthy. In 1945 a provisional government, formed in Soviet-occupied eastern Hungary, signed an armistice in Moscow. Hungary's last free election, held in November of the same year, gave the anti-Communists a clear majority; the Communists obtained only 17 per cent of the vote.

A Hungarian republic was proclaimed in 1946 with Ferenc Nagy as premier. He was ousted by a Soviet-assisted Communist coup, and the People's Republic came into being on August 20, 1949. With Soviet power fully consolidated, the process began of shaping Hungary into a model Soviet socialist state.

After Stalin's death in 1953 discontent was more openly vented. Premier Imre Nagy was partially successful in relaxing some controls, but two years later he and his cabinet were ousted for "anti-Marxism." In October, 1956, discontent erupted in Budapest. Imre Nagy again became premier. Russian troops intervened, launching armored attacks on Budapest and other Hungarian cities, and Communist rule was forcibly restored under Janos Kadar. Nagy was arrested and executed.

After initial terrorism the Kadar regime undertook to regain some popularity by introducing amnesties and certain liberalizations. There has been an easing of relations between some Western countries and Hungary, but the United States has not resumed diplomatic relations on the ambassadorial level. Kadar voluntarily turned over his premiership to deputy premier Gyula Kallai in 1965, but he retained the all-powerful post of First Secretary of the Hungarian Socialist Workers' (Communist) Party.

**GOVERNMENT AND POLITICS.** Under the constitution of 1949 the one-chamber National Assembly is the highest power in the state. It elects a Presidential Council, which acts as head of state. A council of ministers, headed by a premier, is the principal executive organ. It is elected by, and can be removed by, the assembly. In fact, however, the government and the economic and social life of the country are under the control of the Central Committee of the Socialist Workers' Party.

**ECONOMY.** Though traditionally an agricultural country, Hungary has been industrialized by the Communists. Industry now contributes more to the national income than agriculture. Forced collectivization of farms in 1960–61 led to a decline in crops, and Hungary, once known as the granary of Europe, has recently had to import wheat. Industrial production rose six per cent in 1965, but national income and agricultural production did not meet scheduled levels.

Principal agricultural products are cereal grains, maize, potatoes, and sugar beets. Mineral deposits, chiefly bauxite and coal, are not extensive. Oil sources have been found and tapped. Uranium mining is under Soviet control, with all production going to the U.S.S.R.

Of Hungary's 18,125 miles of roads, about 5,600 are surfaced. There are some 5,600 miles of railways, and the Danube is an important traffic artery. Hungarian Air Lines provides domestic and limited foreign service.

**EDUCATION AND HEALTH.** Education from ages 6 to 16 is compulsory. Primary education is free and the government also contributes most of the cost of secondary and higher education. The literacy rate is 97 per cent of the population. Hungarians receive state insurance, including free medical service. Private practice by doctors is permitted on a restricted basis.

**ARMED FORCES.** Two years' service is compulsory at age 18. Hungary's armed forces were limited by the 1947 peace treaty to 70,000, but latest estimates indicate there are over 100,000. Four Soviet divisions are stationed within the borders of Hungary.

# ICELAND

*Official Name:* Republic of Iceland. *Area:* 39,769 square miles. *Population:* 196,549. *Principal Cities* (with populations): Reykjavik, the capital, 79,000; Akureyri, 9,000. *Flag:* White-bordered red cross on a blue field. *Monetary Unit:* The krona (worth 2.3 U.S. cents). *Gross National Product:* $475,-000,000 (1965). *Average Annual Income per Person:* $1,719.

**LAND AND PEOPLE.** Iceland, an island in the North Atlantic, lies just below the Arctic Circle, 200 miles southeast of Greenland and about 645 miles west of Norway. (See map on page 117.)

The volcanically formed island has a central plateau averaging about 2,000 feet in height and surrounded by mountains; the highest peak rises to about 7,000 feet. In November, 1963, underwater volcanic action created a new island, Surtsey, off the south coast; in a few months it was 600 feet high and a mile long. Iceland's Vatnajokull glacier is the largest in Europe.

The nearby Gulf Stream gives Iceland a relatively mild and humid climate.

More than 99 per cent of the people are of Norwegian descent, and 98 per cent are Lutherans. The language is Icelandic.

**HISTORY.** Norse settlers colonized the island around 850 A.D., and in 930 a judicial and legislative assembly, the Althing, was established. Christianity was introduced in 1000.

Iceland came under Norwegian control in 1262 and became a Danish province in 1381. The island's economy deteriorated after 1602 as a result of economic abuses by Denmark, and it did not recover until the 19th century. In 1874, largely through the efforts of Jon Sigurdsson, an Icelandic statesman, Iceland obtained a constitution and limited home rule. Forty-four years later the country became a sovereign state under the Danish Crown. In 1944, when Denmark was occupied by Germany, the Althing declared Iceland's complete independence.

**GOVERNMENT AND POLITICS.** Iceland is a republic with a parliamentary system of government. The president, primarily a ceremonial official, is elected by popular vote for a four-year term. Executive power is exercised through the prime minister and a six-minister cabinet. President Asgeir Asgeirsson, first elected in 1952, is serving his fourth term. The prime minister is Bjarni Benediktsson of the Independence Party.

The Althing has two chambers with a total of 60 members elected for four years by universal suffrage.

**ECONOMY.** Fishing is Iceland's major industry. Cod and herring account for 90 per cent of the exports.

**EDUCATION.** School is compulsory for children from age 7 to 15. The literacy rate is practically 100 per cent.

**ARMED FORCES.** Iceland has no armed forces.

# INDIA

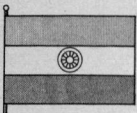

*Official Name:* India. *Area:* 1,262,000 square miles. *Population:* 500,000,000. *Principal Cities* (with populations): New Delhi (including Delhi), the capital, 3,057,000; Bombay, 4,653,700; Calcutta, 3,370,000; Madras 1,988,000; Ahmedabad, 1,386,000; Hyderabad, 1,334,000; Bangalore, 1,040,000. *Flag:* Deep saffron, white, and green stripes, with the Wheel of Asoka in blue on the white stripe. *Monetary Unit:* The rupee (worth 13.21 U.S. cents). *Gross National Product:* $32,500,000,000. *Average Annual Income per Person:* $60.

**LAND AND PEOPLE.** India is bordered on the north by Afghanistan, China, Nepal, Sikkim, and Bhutan; on the east by East Pakistan and Burma; on the south by the Bay of Bengal, the Indian Ocean, and the Arabian Sea; and on the west and northwest by West Pakistan. (See map on page 139.)

In the north the Himalaya Mountains—rising to some of the greatest elevations in the world—serve as a barrier between neighboring Asian countries and India. The area's three great rivers—the Indus, Ganges, and Brahmaputra—start in the Himalayas. The lowlands of India, a trenchlike region stretching eastward for 2,000 miles from the Indus River delta to the delta of the Ganges and the Brahmaputra rivers in India and East Pakistan, contain the world's greatest alluvial plain (420,000 square miles). Centered in the peninsula, and occupying much of it, is the Deccan Plateau, surrounded by hills and mountains that reach to 8,000 feet in the Nilgiri and Gardamon hills of the south. Beyond the Eastern Ghat mountain range are the plains of the Coromandel Coast on the Bay of Bengal.

The peninsular coasts and the Ganges delta are hot and humid. The interior and lowlands vary from damp subtropical to temperate weather. In the far west are the semi-arid steppes and the barren Thar Desert, while in the north the climate changes from near tropical to arctic as the land rises in the Himalayas. Monsoons dominate India's climate.

The ethnic background of the Indian people is extremely complex; however, Indo-European (Aryan) and Dravidian stock form the racial core. There are 20,000,000 or more aborigines, mostly in remote and scattered areas; their racial beginnings are uncertain. Indians speak 14 main languages. Hindi, the official language, is spoken by about 45 per cent of the people; English is also spoken. Some 84 per cent of the people are Hindus, 11 per cent Muslims, and 5 per cent Christians, Sikhs, Buddhists, or Jains.

**HISTORY.** Several millennia before Christ a distinct culture existed in the Indus Valley. About 1500 B.C. the Aryans invaded the country and destroyed or absorbed this civilization, establishing their own in the plains of Punjab and on the upper Ganges. The following 2,000 years saw the unification of the many and diverse cultures of India. The caste system came into being, the pattern of village life evolved, and some distinguished literature was written. The first important Aryan kingdom, Magadha, during the reign of Bimbisara (542–490 B.C.), heard the teachings of Jainism and Buddhism from the mouths of their founders.

Alexander the Great in 327–25 B.C. invaded Gandhara in the northwest, but his armies were overcome by Chandragupta, who founded the Maurya empire. Asoka (273–36 B.C.), one of the greatest of the ancient rulers, unified most of India and established Buddhism as the state religion. After his reign India became a country of small kingdoms, open to invaders from central and western Asia. In the fourth and fifth centuries A.D. the Gupta dynasty ruled the major part of northern India; the dynasty reached its greatest extent with the reign of Samudragupta (about 340–80). In the seventh century King Harsha of Kanauj was temporarily successful in uniting the same area, but after his death the north again became divided, while in the south empires rose and fell.

The Hindu Rajput rulers reached the height of their power from 700 to 1000. Shortly after 1192 the Delhi Sultanate, the first Muslim kingdom, was established, but the Mongol invader Tamerlane captured Delhi in 1398 and brought this regime to an end. A descendant of Tamerlane, Baber, founded the Mogul empire in 1526. Other renowned emperors followed, including Akbar, Shah Hahan (builder of the Taj Mahal), and Aurangzeb. The culture that developed under this rule has seldom been equaled for the magnificence of its works. The Mogul empire reached its greatest extent under Aurangzeb, but after his death it disintegrated. In the 18th century native and foreign forces—Mahrattas, Rajputs, Sikhs, Afghans, French, and British—contended for mastery; the British eventually gained the upper hand.

European contact with India began with the arrival of Vasco da Gama in 1498. The riches of the country attracted traders from England, Holland, Portugal, and France. Seeing India weakened by internal upheaval, the British (the East India Company) and the French proceeded to acquire colonies by force. The company finally eliminated all rivals, and by the mid-19th century Britain had control of most of the territory. British domination and rising internal strife led to the Sepoy Mutiny of 1857, a mutiny of East India Company native troops. The company was dissolved, reforms were introduced, and the Crown afterwards ruled directly through a viceroy. In 1877 Queen Victoria, through the efforts of Prime Minister Disraeli, was crowned Empress of India.

Indian nationalism, social reform movements, and a Hindu renaissance became increasingly powerful forces in the last decades of the 19th century. The spearhead of the nationalist movement was the Indian National Congress. Founded in 1885, the congress originally aimed at economic reform and a greater voice in Britain's India policy, but in the 20th century it became more militant.

During World War I most Indians were

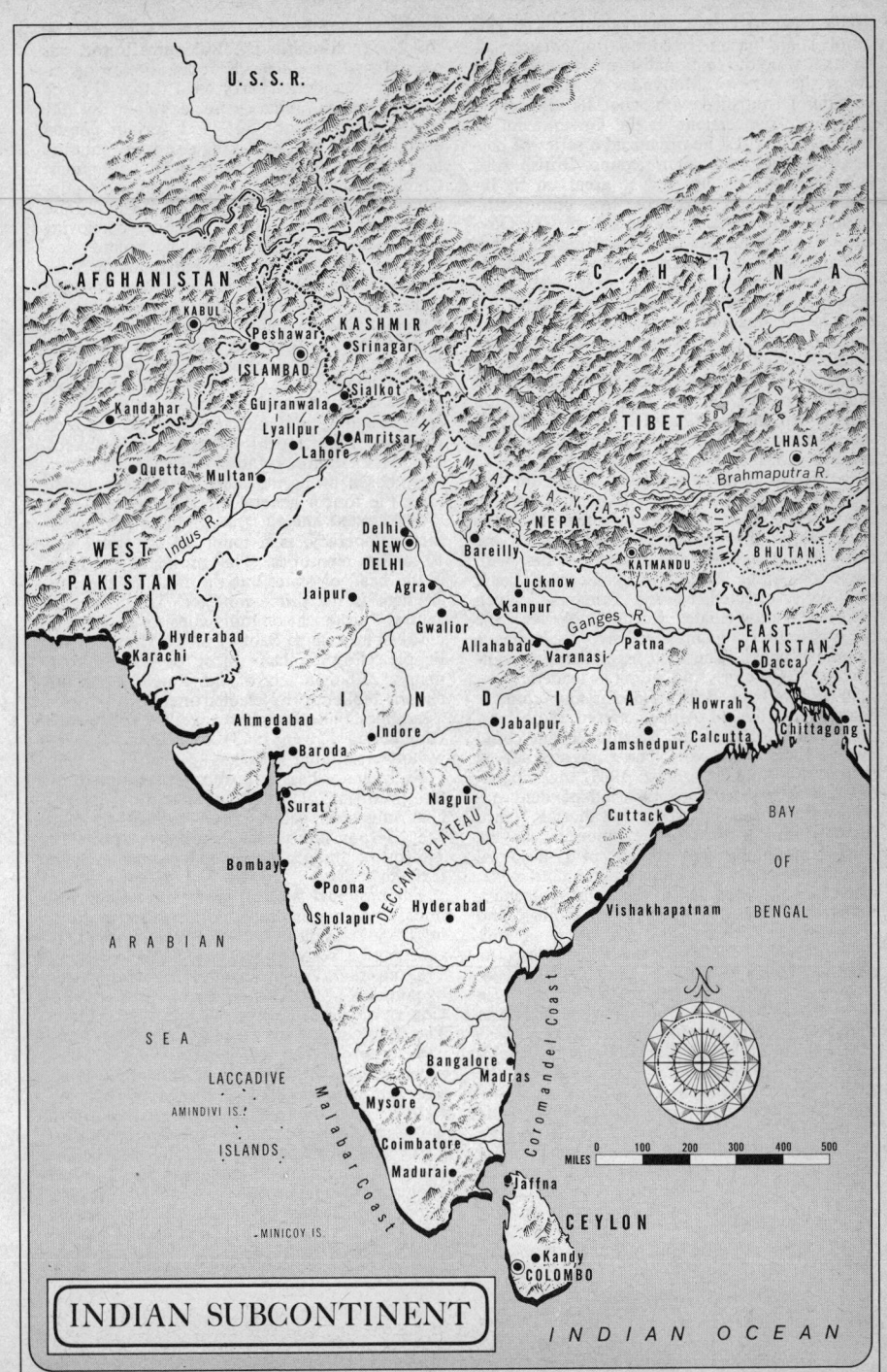

INDIAN SUBCONTINENT

firmly loyal to Britain, many hoping that this stand would hasten freedom. Immediately after the war the nationalist movement came under the sway of Mohandas K. (Mahatma) Gandhi. Dissatisfied with what he considered inadequate concessions in the Government of India Act of 1919, he organized a series of passive resistance campaigns against British rule. His personal standing grew so great among Indians that his very threats of "fasts unto death" brought concessions from the British. The Government of India Act of 1935 proposed a federal status linking the provinces of British India with the many princely states; in addition, provincial legislatures were to be created. Although the federal status was never implemented, the legislatures were created after the elections of 1937, with the Congress winning majorities in most provinces. The demands of Mohammed Ali Jinnah, head of the Muslim League, for the creation of a separate Muslim state balked the Congress' desire for unified action against Britain.

In World War II the British found far less support among the Indians than they had 25 years before. Their placating offer of an interim Indian government autonomous in everything but defense and foreign affairs, with dominion status to follow at the war's end, was flatly rejected by the Congress, which demanded immediate freedom. When the British refused, a massive civil-disobedience campaign began. The British retaliated by outlawing the Congress and jailing its leaders.

In 1946–47 the British Labour Government, headed by Clement Attlee, offered India freedom if the Congress and Muslim League could resolve their differences. The Congress agreed to partition, and in August, 1947, the subcontinent was divided into two independent nations—India and Pakistan. Jawaharlal Nehru became India's first prime minister, having headed an interim government in 1946. Lord Mountbatten was governor-general until 1948, when he was succeeded by C. Rajagopalachari.

Partition caused religious riots, killings, and an enormous crisscrossing migration of millions of people. Gandhi attempted to stop the religious violence, but on January 30, 1948, during a prayer and pacification meeting in New Delhi, he was assassinated by a Hindu who blamed him for India's partition.

Shortly after independence India and Pakistan became involved in the Kashmir dispute. At the time of partition the princely states had been given the option to join either India or Pakistan. More than 500 such states were peacefully integrated into the Indian union before and after partition. Kashmir, however, had hesitated, and infiltrators from Pakistan poured into the state on a massive scale with the intention of forcing union with that country. The Hindu Maharajah of Kashmir decided to join India and requested Indian aid in defending the state. In 1948 India referred the Kashmir question to the United Nations, which effected a cease-fire in 1949.

In 1950 a new constitution went into effect, and India, previously a dominion in the Commonwealth of Nations, became a republic in the Commonwealth. Dr. Rajendra Prasad was elected first president of India. Following independence, Pondicherry and other French possessions in India were acquired by the Indian government. Goa and certain coastal enclaves held by the Portuguese were annexed in 1961. Territorial disputes with Communist China exploded in 1962 when Chinese troops invaded the Ladakh region of Kashmir and the North East Frontier Agency, occupying large sections of land claimed by India.

Nehru died in 1964, and Lal Bahadur Shastri succeeded him as prime minister. In 1965 India and Pakistan clashed in the Rann of Kutch, and renewed infiltration and attacks in Kashmir led to a three-week war. In early 1966 Shastri and Pakistan's president Ayub Khan met at Tashkent, in the Soviet Union, agreed to withdraw their forces to the original cease-fire line, and pledged to seek peace in Kashmir. Shastri died suddenly at Tashkent, and Mrs. Indira Gandhi, Nehru's daughter, was chosen prime minister. She was re-elected after the fourth general elections in 1967.

**GOVERNMENT AND POLITICS.** India, a parliamentary democracy, is a union of 17 states and 10 union territories. The president of India is the head of state, but the head of the government is the prime minister. The bicameral central Parliament of India consists of a Council of State (Rajya Sabha) and a House of the People (Lok Sabha). Most of the approximately 250 members of the Rajya Sabha are chosen indirectly by elected members of state assemblies. The members of the Lok Sabha (numbering 521 in 1967) are elected directly by universal adult suffrage.

Each state has a governor appointed by the president of India, a legislature, and a chief minister, cabinet, and council of ministers responsible to the Legislative Assembly. The main administrative subdivision of a state is the district.

The principal political group, the Indian National Congress, embraces political thought ranging from far right to far left. It held over 70 per cent of the seats in the Lok Sabha until the 1967 elections, when its majority was reduced by some 80 seats. This seemed to mark the beginning of the decline of one-party dominance. The Communist Party is split between pro-Moscow and pro-Peking groups. The main conservative parties are the Swatantra (Freedom) Party and the more militant Jan Sangh (People's Party). Other than the Congress, the two main non-Communist parties are the Praja Socialist Party and the Socialist Party of India. The country's diversity of languages has brought about the reshaping and division of several states along linguistic lines. In non-Hindi-speaking areas, notably in the south, feeling against "Hindi imperialism" is strong. Language riots have frequently occurred, as in Madras in early 1965.

In foreign affairs India has followed a policy of nonalignment, except in relations with Pakistan and, after the Chinese attack of 1962, with Communist China.

## ELECTIONS IN INDIA

| STATES & UNION TERRITORIES | No. OF SEATS | CON | SWA | CPI | CPI(M) | SSP | JS | PSP | REP | IND | OTHER PARTIES | TOTAL DECLARED |
|---|---|---|---|---|---|---|---|---|---|---|---|---|
| STATE VIDHAN SABHA | | | | DATE 23-2-67 | | TIME | 8 P.M. | | | | | |
| ANDHRA PRADESH | 287 | 51 | 14 | 9 | 3 | | 7 | | | 29 | | 22 |
| ASSAM | 126 | 15 | | | | | | | | 2 | 6 | 23 |
| BIHAR | 318 | | | | | | | | | | | |
| GUJARAT | 168 | | 2 | 2 | | | | | | | | |
| HARYANA | 81 | 29 | 2 | | | | 9 | 1 | | 11 | | 52 |
| JAMMU & KASHMIR | 75 | 22 | | | | | | | | | | |
| KERALA | 133 | 15 | | 17 | 52 | 15 | | | | 10 | 12 | 121 |
| MADHYA PRADESH | 298 | 167 | | | | 10 | 77 | 9 | | 22 | | 298 |
| MADRAS | 234 | 27 | 8 | 1 | 5 | 1 | | 4 | | 3 | 18 | 67 |
| MAHARASHTRA | 270 | 4 | | | | | | | 1 | | 1 | 6 |
| MYSORE | 216 | 47 | 7 | 1 | | 1 | 2 | 9 | | 19 | | 86 |
| ORISSA | 140 | | 2 | | | | | | | | | 2 |
| PUNJAB | 104 | 33 | | | 4 | | 1 | 7 | | 5 | 17 | 68 |
| RAJASTHAN | 184 | 66 | 36 | | | 6 | 19 | | | 8 | | 17 |
| UTTAR PRADESH | 425 | 33 | | 2 | | | 4 | | | | | 4 |
| WEST BENGAL | 280 | 104 | 1 | 13 | 17 | 7 | 1 | 6 | | 44 | 51 | 9 |
| | | | | | | | | | | | | |
| GOA, DAMAN & DIU | 30 | | | | | | | | | | | |
| HIMACHAL PRADESH | 60 | 4 | | | | | | | | 2 | | |
| MANIPUR | 30 | 7 | | 1 | | 2 | | | | 2 | | |
| TRIPURA | 30 | 19 | | | | | | | | | | |
| TOTAL | 3487 | 675 | | | | | | | | | | 14 |

India's Prime Minister, Mrs. Indira Gandhi, views results of the February election with dismay. Her Congress Party received the worst setback in its 20-year history, retaining only a slim majority in Parliament.

India's Congress Party, which had maintained firm political control over the nation during 20 years of Indian self-government, suffered severe setbacks in the general elections of February, 1967. The party, headed by Indira Gandhi, India's prime minister, had expected to take some losses, but was unprepared for the shift in public support that took place.

For several weeks after the election there was doubt that Mrs. Gandhi would be able to retain her position as prime minister. As leader of the Congress Party, she was held largely responsible for its severe losses. However, on March 12 the party's parliamentary board voted her return to office. Ironically, her victory was partly due to the fact that many of her opponents within the party had themselves been voted out of office.

As a result of the elections, the states of Madras, Kerala, Orissa, West Bengal, and Bihar were totally won by opposition parties.

Another blow to the Congress Party was its loss of 96 seats in the Lok Sabha (the lower house of Parliament), which left it with a dangerously slim majority of 17 in the 521-member body.

For the time being, at least, one major factor continues to work in favor of the maintenance of central control by the Congress Party: the inability of the opposition to act as a single unit. For example, Kerala is now governed by a Communist coalition, while Orissa is controlled by the right-wing Swaatantra (Freedom) Party. Control of Madras was won by the Dravidian Progressive Federation, which reflects local interests and is largely nonideological.

The immediate effect of the elections has been the creation of a wide gap between the central Indian government and many of the state governments. This political break has seriously strained India's already precarious federal system.

**ECONOMY.** India's most acute problem is over-population; it is the second most populous country in the world. At the present rate of growth, it has been estimated that the population will exceed one billion by the year 2000. The majority of people suffer extreme poverty. Agriculture is still the basis of the economy, but a decline in productivity, several bad crop years, poor distribution, inflation, and growing population have led to famine, food riots, looting, and the need to import vast quantities of grain from abroad. In the last half of 1966 near-famine conditions existed in Bihar and Uttar Pradesh. Since 1962 the United States has authorized shipments of well over $1 billion worth of food.

Nearly 53 per cent of India's total land area is under cultivation. Grains, rice, sugarcane, tea, jute, and cotton are the main crops. Tea is the leading agricultural export. India has more land under irrigation than any country except China. The livestock population is large, for the cow is held sacred by Hindus and the constitution forbids its slaughter.

The country's reserves of high-grade iron ore, coal, bauxite, manganese, chromite, mica, ilmenite, and oil are under-exploited. There is a wide variety of other minerals. In recent years substantial industrial expansion has taken place in steel, cement, and machinery. Textiles, jute products, and food processing constitute important industries.

Despite devaluation of the rupee in June, 1966, exports declined, foreign exchange reserves were further depleted, and the heavy dependence on foreign economic aid continued. The fourth five-year plan, which began in 1966 and placed highest priority on agriculture, was in effect shelved pending drastic reductions and revisions, and an emergency one-year plan was introduced.

India has 36,000 track-miles of government-owned railways—Asia's largest system. Surfaced highways—30 per cent of the country's roads—total about 142,000 miles. Air India is an international service; another airline flies within India and to nearby countries.

**EDUCATION AND HEALTH.** Education is the responsibility of the individual states and varies accordingly; educational opportunities are better in cities than in rural areas. About 78 per cent of those aged 6 to 11 attend school. The literacy rate is 24 per cent of those ten years of age and over.

General health standards are not high. Disastrous epidemics still occur, and dietary deficiencies create a host of diseases. Public health is the responsibility of each state.

**ARMED FORCES.** Service in the armed forces is voluntary. In 1967 there were 950,000 men active in the army, 39,000 in the navy, and 90,000 in the air force.

# INDIAN TERRITORIES AND DEPENDENCIES

## ANDAMAN AND NICOBAR ISLANDS

*Area:* 3,215 square miles. *Population:* 63,548.
*Capital:* Port Blair.

The Andaman and Nicobar Islands, a Union Territory of India, are situated in the Bay of Bengal. Port Blair lies 780 miles southeast of Calcutta and 740 miles east of Madras. The Andaman group consists of five large islands designated the Great Andamans, an island to the south called Little Andaman, and more than 200 islets. The Nicobars, about 75 miles to the south, consist of 19 islands, of which 12 are inhabited. Both groups of islands have hilly terrain and a hot, muggy climate.

The indigenous people of the Adamans are a small Negrito type. Most of the Islanders are Indians, with some Burmese Karennis. The Nicobarese are of Mongoloid stock.

The Andamans were first settled as a penal colony by the British in 1858 and remained as such until 1942, when the Japanese occupied them. The penal colony was abolished when the islands were reoccupied in 1945. Britain settled the Nicobars in 1869.

The president of the Republic of India, acting through a Chief Commissioner and a five-man advisory council, administers the territory. It has one nominated representative in the Indian legislature.

Timber and coconuts are the chief export products. Coffee, rubber, and rice are cultivated. Local industries are lumber and coconut-oil processing. Both island groups have excellent harbors. Port Blair is connected to Madras by mail boat and to Calcutta by boat and air service.

## LACCADIVE, MINICOY, AND AMINDIVI ISLANDS

*Area:* 11 square miles. *Population:* 24,108.

The 20 islands in the group, ten of which are inhabited, are situated in the Arabian Sea some 200 miles west of Kerala. Nearly all the inhabitants are Muslim and speak Malayalam; Mahl is spoken on Minicoy. The islands are centrally administered from Kozhikode, Kerala, with the assistance of a six-man advisory committee. There is a nominated representative in the Indian legislature. Fishing and copra production are important activities.

## SIKKIM

*Area:* 2,818 square miles. *Population:* 176,000.
*Capital:* Gangtok (population 12,000).

Sikkim is bordered on the north and east by Tibet, on the southeast by Bhutan, on the south by India, and on the west by Nepal. The climate of the valleys is tropical; as the Himalayas rise above 8,000 feet, there is a perpetual blanket of snow. About 75 per cent of the people are Nepalese. The original settlers, Lepchas, and the Bhotias, of Tibetan origin, comprise the balance. Tibeto-Burman languages and dialects are widely spoken. Tibetan Buddhism is the state religion, but almost 60 per cent of the people are Hindu.

After the 17th century, rajas of Tibetan descent reigned in Sikkim. Gurkhas from neighboring Nepal invaded several times in the 18th and 19th centuries. Before the middle of the 19th century two cessions of territory were made to Britain, and the British assumed a protectorate over Sikkim. The Chinese, who had held nominal suzerainty over the country, recognized the protectorate in 1890. With British withdrawal from India in 1947 Sikkim became independent, but in 1950 the country signed a treaty giving control of its foreign affairs, communications, and defenses to India. In 1965 Sikkim was threatened with a Chinese invasion, and India now maintains 25,000 or more troops there to keep watch on the border.

Sikkim is an hereditary monarchy. There is no constitution, and the monarch rules by decree, assisted by an Indian Principal Administrative Officer and a 20-man advisory State Council, of whom 14 are elected. The present maharaja, Gyalsay Palden Thondup Namgyal, is trying to introduce elements of representative government.

The country's economy is predominantly agricultural. Potatoes, the main cash crop, and rice, corn, millet, cardamom, and fruits are the principal products. A third of Sikkim is covered by forests.

Transportation, handicapped by the Himalayan terrain, is a major block to development, but India has engaged in the building of strategic roads. There are no airports or railways.

There are about 160 schools in the country, most of them run or aided by the government. Sikkim has a small Palace Guard.

# INDONESIA

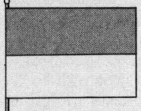

*Official Name:* Republic of Indonesia. *Area:* 735,268 square miles. *Population:* 107,000,000. *Principal Cities* (with populations): Djakarta, the capital, 2,973,052; Surabaja, 1,007,945; Bandung, 972,566; Semarang, 503,153. *Flag:* A horizontal red stripe above a white stripe. *Monetary Unit:* The new rupiah of 100 sen (worth 10 U.S. cents). *Gross National Product:* $10,450,000,000 (1965). *Average Annual Income per Person:* $100.

LAND AND PEOPLE. Indonesia, comprising several large islands and about 3,000 small ones, swings in an arc from west of the Malay Peninsula south and east to New Guinea. Major seas bordering it are the South China Sea, the Pacific Ocean, and the Indian Ocean. (See map on page 243.)

The principal islands are the Greater Sunda Islands, including Sumatra, Java, Kalimantan (occupying three-fourths of the island of Borneo), and Sulawesi (Celebes); the Lesser Sunda Islands, including Bali and Lombok; the Moluccas; and West Irian (western New Guinea).

Central mountain ranges descending to coastal plains typify the terrain of the larger islands. Numerous active and inactive volcanoes, some rising to more than 12,000 feet, are the source of Indonesia's fertile soil. Extensive lowland plains and gently rising, arable mountain foothills are features of Java and Bali. Much of Kalimantan is covered by jungle swamps and comparatively poor soil, while Sulawesi is heavily mountainous. Sparsely settled Sumatra has a swampy east coast and almost impenetrable rain forests inland.

Indonesia's equatorial climate makes the country hot and muggy, with heavy rainfall and gentle winds. The wettest time of year extends over a three-month period, December through February, with the heaviest rains in the mountains, averaging 240 inches annually in some regions. The dry season lasts from June to September.

Ethnic groups on Java, the most densely inhabited island, are Javanese (about 45 per cent of the total population) and Sundanese (about 15 per cent). Smaller groups elsewhere include Achinese, Bataks, and Minangkabaus (Sumatra); Menadonese and Buginese (Sulawesi); Dayaks (Kalimantan); and Ambonese (Moluccas).

More than 250 different languages are spoken in Indonesia, most of them belonging to the Malayo-Polynesian linguistic family. In recent decades Bahasa Indonesian has been successfully introduced as the national language, and is used in schools, public administration, and by mass-communication media. Local ethnic feelings are strong and geographic factors render more difficult the unification of the nation.

Ninety per cent of all Indonesians are nominally Muslim. There are small Christian, Buddhist, and Hindu minorities.

HISTORY. Prehistoric man appeared in Indonesia—on Java, and possibly on Sumatra, Borneo, and several other islands as well—at an early stage in his evolution. Indonesians of today are descended from a Mongoloid people who spread first into Malaya and then invaded the islands at least twice several centuries before the Christian era. Added later to the ethnic strain were Indians who brought Buddhism and their great culture and civilization first to Sumatra and then to Java; by the late 13th century, under the rule of the fabulous Hindu Majapahit empire, they had broadened their control to cover most of the archipelago.

Arab traders brought Muslim influence to Indonesia even before Indian rule had weakened. Conversion to Islam became widespread, but the islands under Islamic control soon broke up into several small, ineffective kingdoms.

Western dominance started in 1511 when the Portuguese landed at Malacca, on the Malayan Peninsula, "in search of Christians and spices" and spread their influence rapidly into the archipelago. By the end of the 16th century the Portuguese grip was broken, and competing Dutch and British trading companies struggled for the immensely profitable trade of the Indies.

By 1623 the Netherlands East India Company was able to establish its monopoly, and for a while its affairs prospered. But eventually mismanagement and corruption prevailed, and in 1790 the Netherlands government revoked the company's charter, assuming full administration of the islands ten years later.

A repressive system of state-controlled exploitation to extract revenue for the Netherlands was enforced until 1877, when liberal attacks on the government in that country led to its abandonment and replacement by private exploitation. This accounts for the strong anti-capitalist bias of earlier generations of Indonesian nationalists, whose historical experience seemed to confirm the Communist argument that imperialism is a manifestation of capitalism.

As the Dutch consolidated their administrative control over the Indonesian archipelago throughout the 19th and 20th centuries, numerous rebellions and local wars occurred, absorbing much of the revenue that could have been used to improve the living standards of the population.

The colonial administration used the prestige and authority of the local aristocrats to help the Dutch rule. While the neutral leaders of the people were corrupted as administrative assistants of the colonial regime, Indonesia had also the misfortune of failing to develop a national business class, as Dutch colonial legislation discriminated in favor of an economically very active Chinese minority.

Early in the 20th century movements for independence began and increased in strength; the most important of these was the Indonesian Nationalist Party, formed in 1927 by Sukarno and Mohammad Hatta.

Japanese occupation of the islands during World War II gave a boost to the nationalists. With Japan's defeat, Sukarno and Hatta in August, 1945, formed a provisional government and battled to keep the Dutch from returning. Chaos, bitter hostilities, and occasional negotiations culminated finally in intervention by the United Nations and concession by the Netherlands in 1949, and independent Indonesia became a reality. Sukarno was elected president in December, 1949, and a few days later the Netherlands recognized his sovereignty. The nation was first established as the United States of Indonesia, a federal republic of 16 states, in a loose union with the Netherlands. That union was subsequently dissolved by Indonesia in 1954.

Almost immediately cracks began to appear in the system as Sukarno changed the government from federal to unitary, with power centralized on Java. First elections for the House of Representatives were held in the fall of 1955 and the growing influence of Communists in Indonesia became apparent. Vice President Hatta, an opponent of Sukarno's growing entanglement with the Communists, resigned and three weeks later, in December, 1956, a military revolt erupted on north and central Sumatra. There had been resentment against Java's hold on the revenues of other islands, and many ranking military leaders had been opposed to Communist influence in government. Soon the rebellion and demands for autonomy spread throughout the outer islands, leaving the central government in firm control only of Java. A state of siege and war was declared throughout the archipelago. In 1960 the army, led by anti-Communist, pro-Indonesian (but not pro-Western) Lt. Gen. Abdul Nasution, strongly denounced the Communists, while on the same day Sukarno indicated that Communist views and his own were not incompatible. By fall nearly three-fourths of the rebels had surrendered under the promise of full amnesty, and in August, 1962, Sukarno announced that internal security had been achieved—at a cost of more than 33,000 lives. However, some fighting continued into 1964.

In the meantime agitation against the Netherlands had increased over control of Netherlands New Guinea (West Irian). Indonesia expelled Dutch nationals and started to expropriate their properties. In 1960 diplomatic relations with the Netherlands were severed and Indonesian troops began their infiltration of West Irian. The Netherlands, under American pressure, turned West Irian over to the United Nations in 1962. The U.N. placed the territory under Indonesia's jurisdiction in May, 1963, with the condition that the Papuans in West Irian be permitted to hold a self-determination plebiscite by 1969.

Sukarno's other major international skirmish was with the British over Malaysia. He fought its formation by openly aiding guerrilla forces on Borneo. "Crush Malaysia" became the official slogan and effort once Malaysia was formed, and when it was admitted to the United Nations, Indonesia walked out (January, 1965).

Indonesia became an arena for the Soviet-Chinese ideological split. Despite vast quantities of Soviet economic and military aid, both Indonesia and the PKI (Communist Party of Indonesia—exceeded in membership only by the Soviet and Chinese parties) moved into the Chinese camp. Relations with the United States, at a low ebb for several years, appeared to be near the breaking point as Indonesia increased its alignment with Communist Chinese policy. After an attempted Communist coup failed (October 1, 1965), warfare erupted between the Indonesian army and members of the PKI. The anti-Communist rioting that swept the country soon turned into a bloodbath. By the time it had ebbed in 1966, the PKI had virtually been eliminated. Estimates of the slaughter placed the toll at between 100,000 and 400,000, but the final figure probably will never be known. Sukarno tried to heal the breach in relations with Communist China, but was thwarted by the military. He replaced Defense Minister Nasution early in 1966; the army, however, soon put their own man in charge—Lt. Gen. Suharto. With troops behind him, Suharto persuaded Sukarno to allow him to act in his behalf. He immediately ordered the army to eliminate all traces of the PKI.

**GOVERNMENT AND POLITICS.** By July, 1966, with the approval of the People's Consultative Assembly, the army's control had been solidified. Sukarno, made president for life in 1963, was stripped of that title and elections were ordered to be held in two years; Sukarno continued as president, but with practically no power. Suharto was named Chairman of the Presidium of a new cabinet and in effect ruled the country. The confrontation with Malaysia was ended. In the fall Indonesia applied for readmission to the U.N., which was approved, effective September 28.

While the Communist Party was outlawed in

March, 1966, it is today a major factor of subversion; its underground leaders have proclaimed their intention to resort to armed revolutionary struggle in accordance with the teachings of Mao Tse-tung. The Suharto government fears that these efforts will be assisted by Communist China, which is viewed today as the major threat to Indonesia's political stability.

**ECONOMY.** Indonesia has a vast wealth of natural resources, but the new ruling body took over a land facing rampant inflation, food shortages, $2.5 billion in foreign debts, and almost no reserves of foreign currency to pay for imports. In September, 1966, eight non-Communist creditor nations (including the United States) agreed to ease Indonesia's debt-repayment schedule; however, substantial aid will be needed to avert national bankruptcy. The reversal of Sukarno's drift to socialism was another step in Indonesia's massive political turnabout. He had fully nationalized or placed control over most foreign-owned business in Indonesia, but the new government has encouraged private business and actively sought direct foreign capital investments.

Indonesia ranks as one of the world's largest producers of tin and rubber. It is the Far East's major producer of petroleum, which along with agricultural products (including rubber) has accounted in the recent past for more than 90 per cent of total exports. Industry, principally consumer goods and the processing of mineral products, is operating below capacity.

Agriculture, particularly subsistence, is of greatest importance to most Indonesians for, along with forestry and fishing, it accounts for more than half the national income and for about 70 per cent of total employment.

**EDUCATION AND HEALTH.** Indonesia has vigorously pushed education. It is compulsory between ages eight and 14. Enrollment in primary, secondary, and higher institutions totaled 11,-279,624 in 1964–65. The government announced that as of January 1, 1965, all Indonesians between 13 and 45 were literate.

The disrupted organization and chaotic conditions of postwar Indonesia added to the country's health problems. A shortage of qualified medical personnel, poor and insufficient housing, substandard sanitation, inadequate water supplies, malnutrition, and starvation have all aggravated the situation.

**ARMED FORCES.** Indonesia has compulsory military service. Current strength of the armed forces is 322,000.

# IRAN

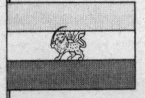

*Official Name:* Iran. *Area:* 636,293 square miles. *Population:* 25,780,000. *Principal Cities* (with populations): Teheran, the capital, 2,317,120; Tabriz, 387,800; Isfahan, 339,900; Meshed, 312,190; Hamadan, 302,190. *Flag:* Three green, white, and red horizontal stripes with a sword-bearing gold lion, the sun rising behind him, centered in the white stripe. *Monetary Unit:* The rial of 100 dinars (worth 1.35 U.S. cents). *Gross National Product:* $6,022,350,000 (1965). *Average Annual Income per Person:* $216.

**LAND AND PEOPLE.** Iran is bordered on the north by the Soviet Union and the Caspian Sea; on the east by Afghanistan and Pakistan; on the south by the Gulf of Oman and the Persian Gulf; and on the west by Iraq and Turkey. (See map on page 151.)

Most of Iran is a plateau averaging 4,000 feet above sea level. Sizable areas are heavily ridged with mountains, including the Elburz range, south of the Caspian coastline, and the larger Zagros Mountains and their extensions, running from north to south. Large sections of the interior are desert. The climate is continental. Heavy snowfall in the mountains is the major source of water for irrigation. Rainfall is generally meager. The Caspian Sea is rich in a variety of fish; its sturgeon provide the world's finest caviar.

Persians, direct descendants of the early Aryans, comprise more than half the population. Groups whose ethnic background is probably similar are the Kurds, the Lurs, and the Bakhtiari. Several other important migratory peoples include the Khamseh, Shahsevans, Arabs, Baluchi, and Turkomans. The official language is Persian; Arabian, Armenian, and various tribal dialects are also spoken. Islam is the state religion. Nearly 95 per cent of the population are Shiite Muslims; the remainder are Christians, Jews, Zoroastrians, and members of other sects.

**HISTORY.** Early settlements in Iran are among the most ancient ever discovered anywhere, and village life is known to have existed in the area about 4,000 years before Christ. Aryan migrations began to spread over the land about 2000 B.C., and nomadic tribes speaking Iranian languages may have moved down from the Caucasus to the Iranian plateau as early as 1500 B.C. The Medes established their domain over a region of what is now western Iran; the Persians controlled an area extending northeast from the Persian Gulf.

The Persian ruler Cyrus the Great overthrew Media's rulers about 550 B.C. He extended his borders to encompass a vast empire that was increased by his dynastic successors, but was toppled by Alexander the Great in 331 B.C. Alexander's empire crumbled after his death, and his successors battled for supremacy. Most of Persia went to Seleucus I, a Syrian king who had been one of Alexander's generals. The Seleucid dynasty tried to follow the Persian pattern of government, but its hold was weak. Parthian rule succeeded the Seleucids. A stronger, more energetic dynasty, the Sassanian, overthrew the Parthians in 226 A.D. and built up a flourishing empire that successfully opposed Rome. Magnificent cities were built, art and architecture reached new heights, and a strong, centralized government developed, based on a class-structured society and the state religion of Zoroastrianism, an ancient Persian faith.

Arab invaders moved into Persia and completed its conquest about 641. Islam became the predominant religion, and the Shiite Muslim sect developed. Turkish invasions and settlement followed in the tenth century. The land then fell to the depradations of the Mongols: Genghis Khan in the 12th century and Tamerlane in the 14th. Order was restored by the Safavid rulers (1499–1736); the Shiite sect's faith became the state religion, and the dynasty reached its peak during the regime of Shah Abbas I (1587–1628). The Safavids were ousted in 1722 by the Afghans, who were soon defeated in turn by the Persians under the despotic Nadir Shah. During its brief reign the Zand dynasty (1750–94) restored order before being overthrown by Aga Mohammed Khan, whose Kajar dynasty lasted until 1925. Persia's borders steadily shrank; land was lost to the Afghans, and in 1813 and 1828 the Caucasian territories were taken by the Russians.

In 1906 the Shah approved the formation of a parliament, or Majlis, and accepted the constitution it enacted. In 1907 an Anglo-Russian pact divided Persia into spheres of influence, but the treaty was annulled at the end of World War I. With the discovery of oil in 1908, Anglo-Russian struggles for domination of Persia intensified. Persia entered the League of Nations as an original member in 1919.

In 1921 a coup d'état directed by a leading army officer, Reza Khan, resulted in virtually a military dictatorship. Four years later Reza Khan deposed the Shah and was himself elected the hereditary ruler, adopting the name Reza Shah Pahlevi. He undertook reforms in all sections of Persian life, revoked the special rights of foreigners, and in 1935 officially changed the country's name to Iran. In the same year Teheran University was opened; in 1937 women were unveiled; and in 1938 the first railroad was built. The ruler's friendly relations with Germany, however, led to the occupation of Iran by British and Russian troops in 1941, and the Shah was forced to abdicate in favor of his son, Mohammed Reza Shah Pahlevi, the present monarch.

In 1945 the Soviets, who occupied northern Iran, sponsored a revolt and formed two People's Republics in their zone, then refused to evacuate their troops. Iran's protest to the U.N. led to the withdrawal of the Soviet troops, but only after the U.S.S.R. had won oil concessions in the area. The rebels surrendered in 1946, and the Iranian Parliament rejected the oil-agreement bargain, despite Soviet threats. The pro-Communist Tudeh Party was abolished in 1949 after one of its members tried to assassinate the Shah.

When militant nationalist Mohammed Mossadegh, leader of the extremist National Front, became premier in 1951, he promptly seized control of the Anglo-Iranian Oil Company. The British retaliated with a blockade that nearly destroyed Iran's oil industry and its economy. The oil problem was settled a few years later by the formation of a consortium of international oil companies.

The Imperial Guard rose against Mossadegh in August, 1953. The revolt was crushed and the Shah fled, but the royalists attempted a second revolt and won. Mossadegh was imprisoned, and Iran moved closer to the West.

In 1961 the Shah implemented his "revolution from the throne," a program calling for the end of serfdom, the breakup of the vast lands held by feudal landlords and powerful Islamic leaders, electoral and administrative reforms, profit-sharing for workers, and measures against government corruption and inefficiency. In 1963 the constitution was altered to give women the vote and to allow them to run for Parliament.

**GOVERNMENT AND POLITICS.** The Iranian Parliament consists of an upper and a lower house, the Senate and the Majlis, respectively. The prime minister, appointed by the Shah, is responsible to Parliament. All Majlis members and half of the Senate are popularly elected; the rest are appointed by the Shah, who may also dissolve either house, as he did in May, 1961, after complaints of election fraud.

Two years of government by decree ended in September, 1963, when new parliamentary elections were held. The elections were deficient by Western standards, but were freer and more democratic than any held earlier in Iran. The new Majlis, though dominated by the Shah's supporters, was the most representative ever elected. Prime Minister Ali Mansur was assassinated in January, 1965.

On October 26, 1967, 26 years after he ascended the throne, Mohammed Reza Shah Pahlevi crowned himself king. He then placed a crown on the head of his wife, Empress Farah, the first crowned queen of Iran.

Iran's ties with Egypt were broken in 1960. Soviet-Iranian relations have improved in recent years, but those with Iraq have not.

**ECONOMY.** Iran's economy, buttressed by more than $1.5 billion in U.S. economic and military aid since World War II, is based on agriculture and oil. Petroleum provides most of the country's foreign currency and government income, while most of the people depend on agriculture and livestock for their living.

The years 1965–66 were marked by increased productivity and bumper crops. Cereal grains, fruits, and vegetables predominate. Sheep are the most important livestock, supplying wool, hides, and food; fishing is also profitable.

Of Iran's extensive mineral deposits, the most important source of wealth is oil, exploited under concessions granted by the government. Petroleum exports totaled nearly $1 billion in the fiscal year ending March 20, 1965. Industry's recent rate of growth may be exceeding that of agriculture.

**EDUCATION.** Education is free in state-run primary schools and universities; there is a small fee for students attending state-run secondary schools. The literacy rate is estimated at 36 per cent. In 1966 the Shah gave the equivalent of a day's arms budget to help UNESCO's fight against illiteracy.

**ARMED FORCES.** Iran's armed forces are equipped by the U.S. The army numbers 170,000 men; the navy, 16,000; and the air force, 10,000.

# IRAQ

*Official Name:* The Republic of Iraq. *Area:* 173,259 square miles. *Population:* 8,-338,000. *Principal Cities* (with metropolitan populations): Baghdad, the capital, 2,124,323; Mosul, 954,157; Basra, 673,623. *Flag:* Three horizontal stripes of red, white, and black, with three green stars on the white stripe. *Monetary Unit:* The Iraqi dinar (worth U.S. $2.80). *Gross National Product:* $1,909,-000,000 (1965). *Average Annual Income per Person:* $193.

**LAND AND PEOPLE.** Iraq is a large, underpopulated Middle Eastern Arab state. It is bordered on the north by Turkey, on the east by Iran, on the southeast by the Persian Gulf and Kuwait, on the south by Saudi Arabia, and on the west by Jordan and Syria. (See map on page 151.)

The country is divided into three geographic regions. The Mesopotamian plain, in the southeast between the great Tigris and Euphrates rivers, is the site of ancient civilizations. The desert and semi-desert uplands in the west correspond roughly to ancient Assyria. The mountains in the northeast, the home of the Kurdish tribes, are part of the Zagros range extending into Iran. The northern climate is temperate, but the plains suffer extreme heat and strong northeasterly winds during the summer. Temperatures may reach 120° F. between May and October. Winters are damp and cool, with temperatures averaging about 50° F.

Arabs comprise about 75 per cent of the population. The largest minority (20 per cent of the people) is the fiercely independent, nomadic Kurds. Other ethnic groups are Persians and Turks. Ninety-four per cent of the people are Muslims; 5 per cent are Christians. The official language is Arabic.

**HISTORY.** Archeological excavations have established that cultures going back at least to 5000 B.C. existed in this region, once known as Mesopotamia. Rich in legend and Biblical history, the country has been called "the cradle of civilization."

The written history of the area began about 3000 B.C. when the Sumerians established city-states in southern Mesopotamia. About 2400 B.C. Sumer was absorbed into a huge empire ruled by Sargon, king of Akkad, a northern region with Semitic culture and language. Later, the area was part of the Babylonian Empire.

Arabs overran Mesopotamia in the seventh century A.D., and Baghdad was made the capital of the Abbasid Caliphate in 762. The fifth caliph, Harun-al-Rashid, is the figure in the stories of the *Thousand and One Nights.*

Mongol conquerors devastated the country in 1258 and again in 1401. Baghdad was captured in 1534 by the Ottoman Turks, and Mesopotamia stayed under Turkish control into the 20th century.

During World War I Britain, with the help of the Sherif of Mecca, gained control of the country, which since 1918 has been known as Iraq. Reciprocally, Britain agreed to demands by the Gran Sherif of Mecca, Hussein ibn Ali, for the formation of independent Arab states. Despite the agreement, the League of Nations established Iraq in 1920 as a mandated territory under British administration. Britain arranged for Feisal I, the son of Hussein, to become king of Iraq. In 1932 the League of Nations mandate was ended, and independent Iraq joined the League of Nations.

A pro-Axis government, briefly in power in 1941, collapsed under British military pressure. In 1955 Iraq, under the veteran pro-Western statesman Nuri es-Said, led Arab opposition to Abdel Nasser's Egypt by joining with Turkey, Iran, Pakistan, and Britain in a defense treaty known as the Middle East Treaty Organization. In July, 1958, General Abdul Karim Kassem overthrew the regime and killed Nuri es-Said and young King Feisal II. Kassem withdrew Iraq from CEATO in 1959 and changed Iraq's pro-Western policy. Disputes with Nasser's Egypt, internal political conflict, and finally a war with the Kurds led to Kassem's downfall in 1963; his regime was overthrown, and he was executed.

The Baathists (Arab unionists who were supported by Egypt and Syria) gained control. However, in 1963 pro-Nasser President Abdul Salam Arif, whom the Baathists had used as a figurehead, led a military coup to oust the Baathist regime. Arif announced that he would aim for "constitutional unity" with Egypt, but despite increased cooperation and consultation between the two countries, no formal federation was formed. In April, 1966, Abdul Salam Arif was succeeded by his more cautious elder brother, Abdul Rahman Arif.

In the aftermath of the Arab defeat by Israel in June, 1967, Iraq joined with three other revolutionary socialist Arab states (Algeria, Syria, and the U.A.R.). Iraq is the most conservative of the four.

**GOVERNMENT AND POLITICS.** Iraq, in a period of transition and uncertainty, has, officially, a "democratic and socialist" government, but the politically powerful army dominates it. President Abdul Rahman Arif was elected for one year on the death of his younger brother, Abdul Salam, in April, 1966, and re-elected in April, 1967. He is a cautious moderate who has tried with some success to improve Iraq's relations with its Turkish and Iranian neighbors while maintaining friendly ties with the revolutionary Arab states led by the U.A.R. On July 10, 1967, following the Arab defeat by Israel, he formed a new government under Lieutenant General Tahir Yahya (who thus became premier for the fourth time), describing it as a government of "war and reconstruction."

Efforts to form governments of national unity, combining all the main civilian elements (Arab Unionists, Baathists, neo-Baathists, and others) have consistently failed, while the Arab Socialist Union, constitutionally Iraq's sole legal political organization, has no real existence. The greatest single achievement of President Arif's regime has been the ending of hostilities with the Kurdish minority which intermittently ravaged northern Iraq between 1961 and 1966.

**ECONOMY.** Iraq has enough land and water to produce all the food it requires, together with a large, exportable surplus. It also has substantial oil revenues for capital development. The potential wealth, however, is largely undeveloped. Drainage and irrigation of the low, salinate plains are difficult. The largest crop is barley, followed by wheat, rice, and dates.

Oil revenues have risen steadily since 1952 to $365,490,000 in 1965. Crude-oil production in 1966 was 5.7 per cent greater than in the previous year, but Iraq suffered losses in revenue due to Syria's closure of its transit pipeline in a dispute with the Iraq Petroleum Company. Other losses were incurred in 1967 when Iraq decided to cut off oil supplies to Western countries that it accused of supporting Israel.

Road, rail, and electric power networks have been extended in recent years. Of the 13,000 miles of highways, less than one-third are paved. The state railways have 1,050 miles of tracks. Basra is the only port; another is under construction at Umm Qasr. There are airports at Baghdad and Basra.

**EDUCATION.** Where schools are available, primary education is free and compulsory. In 1964 there were 4,606 government and private primary schools, 551 secondary schools, 35 vocational schools, and 56 teacher-training schools. There are two universities. The literacy rate is between 15 and 20 per cent.

**ARMED FORCES.** In addition to a 70,000-man army, Iraq has a navy of 1,250 and an air force of 2,500.

# IRELAND

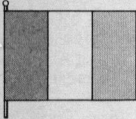

*Official Name:* Irish Republic. *Area:* 27,135 square miles (excluding counties of Northern Ireland). *Population:* 2,881,000. *Principal Cities* (with populations): Dublin, the capital, 647,336; Cork, 125,790; Limerick, 57,338; Waterford, 29,642; Galway, 26,192; Dundalk, 21,510. *Flag:* Three vertical stripes of green, white, and orange. *Monetary Unit:* Irish pound (worth U.S. $2.80). *Gross National Product:* $2,808,706,200 (1965). *Average Annual Income per Person:* $781.

**LAND AND PEOPLE.** The Irish Republic comprises 26 counties of an island off the western coast of Great Britain. It is bordered on the north by the six counties of Northern Ireland, on the east by the Irish Sea, and on the south and west by the Atlantic Ocean. (See map on page 231.)

Coastal highlands and a central plain with lakes, bogs, and hills give a saucer shape to the island, which consists geologically of a limestone plateau. Mild winds from Europe and warm, damp air from the Atlantic Gulf Stream combine to give the country a temperate climate (from a low of 35° F. in winter to a high of 75° F. in summer). Gentle rains average 42 inches a year.

The people comprise a melding of centuries of conquerors and settlers (Celts, Danes, Normans, Scots, Britons). Irish (Gaelic) and English are both recognized as official languages. The population is largely (95 per cent) Roman Catholic.

**HISTORY.** Stone age artifacts and burial chambers of the bronze age indicate that Ireland was inhabited several millenniums before the Christian era. The Gaelic civilization, made up of Celts, Picts, and Érainn, eventually split into five kingdoms. From one of these kingdoms, Connaught, the legendary high kings arose in the second century A.D.; their dynasty continued until 1002.

St. Patrick was captured in Roman Britain and brought to Ireland as a slave about 401. He managed to escape and journeyed to France, where he studied for the priesthood. He returned to Ireland in 432 to teach Christianity.

In the eighth century the Norsemen established seaports in Ireland. In 1170 the first of the Anglo-Norman invaders arrived, inaugurating nearly 800 years of trouble between England and Ireland. Henry II, named overlord of Ireland by Pope Adrian IV, was accepted peacefully when he marched to Dublin the following year. In 1542 Henry VIII added "King of Ireland" to his titles.

To punish Irish rebellion, which had become increasingly bitter after the Reformation, the British confiscated Irish lands and gave them to pro-British Irish and to English Protestants. In the 18th century repeated Irish resistance led to the loss of all legal rights for Irish Catholics. During Oliver Cromwell's rule, the British created bitterness by attempting to confine all native Irish to barren Connaught province.

An independent Protestant parliament was formed in 1782 (although the country was predominantly Roman Catholic), but it was abolished in 1800 when the Act of Union created the United Kingdom of Great Britain and Ireland. The Irish, through their representation in the British Parliament, pressed for home rule, but did not attain it until after World War I. In the middle of the 19th century the country was devastated by a great potato famine; a million Irish died over a five-year period, and 1,600,000 more emigrated.

Sinn Féin, the political arm of the secret Irish Republican Army, instigated the disastrous 1916 Easter Rebellion in Dublin. The British executed 15 rebel leaders, but in the 1919 general elections Sinn Féin won enough seats to set up an independent parliament (Dáil Éireann) in Dublin. They waged successful guerrilla warfare with British forces in Ireland and gained dominion status. The Irish Free State was established in 1922, with six northern (largely Protestant) counties remaining in the United Kingdom as Northern Ireland.

The Sinn Féin divided into conservative and republican groups, and another period of civil war followed. Eamon De Valera's extremists fought for full Republican status for the whole country but were defeated. De Valera boycotted the Dáil until 1927; in 1932 he was elected president. In 1937 a new constitution changed the country's name to Eire, and De

Valera was named prime minister. He held the position until 1948 and twice thereafter, resigning in 1959 to become president. Ireland formally became a republic in 1949.

**GOVERNMENT AND POLITICS.** The president of the Irish Republic is popularly elected for a seven-year term. In 1966 De Valera was reelected for a second term at the age of 83. The parliament consists of the Dáil Éireann (House of Representatives), whose 144 members are elected for five years, and the Seanad Éireann (Senate), comprising 60 members, 43 of whom are elected on a vocational basis, 6 are elected by National and Dublin universities, and 11 are appointed by the prime minister. The prime minister, or taoiseach (John Lynch since November, 1966), is appointed by the president after nomination by the Dáil and is responsible, with his cabinet, to that body.

The leading political parties, Fine Gael (currently in power) and Fianna Fáil, have developed out of the Sinn Féin Party. There is also a moderate Labour Party. All parties have as their common goal the unification of Ireland.

**ECONOMY.** Successive Irish governments have built extensive hydroelectric installations, developed the bogs, erected peat-burning power stations, and encouraged Irish industries with grants and tariff barriers. The country has two successful airlines, and tourist trade has become a major business. Urbanization and economic expansion have caused agriculture to shrink to a quarter of the national income. These trends have reversed the previous steady emigration of young people.

A four-year plan (1959–63), which created some 27,000 new industrial jobs, also attracted foreign investment and doubled industrial exports. Since 1963 Britain's economic difficulties have slowed Ireland's pace of growth, since the bulk of Ireland's trade is still with Britain.

**EDUCATION AND HEALTH.** Education is compulsory for children aged 6 to 14. Elementary education in state schools, normally run by a parish priest, is free. Secondary schools are privately run. Over one million pupils were enrolled in primary, secondary, technical, and university classes in 1963.

Low-income families receive free hospital and medical services; middle-income families pay nominal fees. Treatment for tuberculosis and other infectious diseases is free.

**ARMED FORCES.** Ireland's regular army strength is 12,000, plus a reserve of 13,000. There is a voluntary 300-man navy and 600-man air force.

# ISRAEL

*Official Name:* State of Israel. *Area:* 7,993 square miles. *Population:* 2,629,-000. *Principal Cities* (with populations): Jerusalem, the capital, 187,500; Tel Aviv-Jaffa, 393,800; Haifa, 200,800; Ramat Gan, 100,100. *Flag:* A white field, bearing a blue Star of David between two blue horizontal stripes. *Monetary Unit:* The Israeli pound (worth 34 U.S. cents). *Gross National Product:*

$3,827,040,000 (1966). *Average Annual Income per Person:* $1,080.

**LAND AND PEOPLE.** Located on the Mediterranean coast, Israel is surrounded by Arab nations: Lebanon in the north, Syria in the northeast and east, Jordan in the east, and Egypt in the southwest. (See map on page 151.) The 1967 war (see below) greatly altered Israel's borders and almost doubled the territory under its control. The data in this article is based on the nation's pre-war borders.

Eighty-eight per cent of the people are Jews, about 60 per cent of whom are immigrants from other, mostly European, lands. Muslim Arabs comprise most of the rest of the population. Languages spoken include Hebrew (the official language), Arabic, and English.

**HISTORY.** In the ninth century B.C. scattered Jewish tribes living in Israel (then called Canaan) banded together under the warrior-king Saul to meet the threat of invading Philistines. Political unity was achieved under David, of the Judah tribe, who established the Kingdom of Israel with its political capital at Jerusalem in 1005 B.C. His son and successor, Solomon, built the great Temple and made Jerusalem Israel's cultural and religious capital. After Solomon's death the kingdom was split into two quarrelsome parts, Judah and Israel. Both soon fell to Assyrian conquerors, who banished the Jews from Israel in 722 B.C. In Judah the Assyrians were followed by Egyptians and Babylonians, who exiled the Judaean Jews in 586 B.C. Although soon allowed to return, the Jews were forced from this time onward to bear successive waves of alien conquerors—Persians, Greeks, Seleucids, Romans, Byzantines, Arabs, Crusaders, and Turks.

Zionism, an international movement founded by Theodor Herzl, whose aim was the restoration of Palestine to the Jews, grew rapidly during the late 19th and early 20th centuries. Increasing numbers of European Jews left their homes to settle in Palestine. Toward the end of World War I the region, which since 1516 had been a part of the Ottoman Empire, fell into British hands. Anxious for Jewish help during World War I, England in 1917 issued the Balfour Declaration, promising its support in establishing a national home for the Jewish people. Arabs, who had originally welcomed immigration, grew fearful that they would soon be outnumbered and accused Britain of betraying their trust.

Not wishing further to offend either side, Britain did nothing to implement the declaration. Jewish immigration continued to grow, as did tensions between the new settlers and the indigenous Arabs.

During World War II Zionism suffered a temporary setback when Britain froze immigration and limited land purchases. But after the war Britain was forced to give in to the twin pressures of its own desire to find a haven for Jewish survivors of Nazism and a savage campaign of terrorism by Palestinian Jews. In 1947 the Palestine problem was brought before the United Nations, which agreed to divide Palestine into two independent states, one Jewish

Israel Info. Service

Modern city of Beersheba, Israel

and one Arab, with Jerusalem serving as an international or neutral zone. The plan was accepted by the Jews and on May 14, 1948, they proclaimed Israel's independence. On the same day Egypt, Iraq, Jordan, Lebanon, Syria, and Saudi Arabia attacked Israel and were rapidly defeated. An armistice was concluded in January, 1949, but peace in the Middle East has continued to be elusive ever since. Sporadic border skirmishes have occurred every year, and there have been two more full-scale wars as well. The two most important issues still blocking genuine peace in the area are the resettlement of hundreds of thousands of displaced Arab refugees and adamant Arab refusal to acknowledge Israel's right to exist.

In 1956 Egypt's President Nasser nationalized the Suez Canal, thereby posing a severe threat to Israel's vital shipping. In October Israeli forces quickly overwhelmed Egypt's Sinai region while British and French forces attacked Egypt from the west. Combined pressure from the U.S., the U.N., and the U.S.S.R. forced a quick end to the fighting.

War broke out again in 1967. In May President Nasser of Egypt closed the Gulf of Aqaba to Israeli shipping, demanded that U.N. observer teams leave Egyptian soil, and signed a pact with Jordan putting Jordanian armed forces under Egyptian command. In addition, Syrian war planes had repeatedly violated Israel's airspace. Fearful that the surrounding Arab nations were about to attack and convinced that the blocking of the gulf would cut off shipments of vital commodities such as oil, Israel decided to strike first. On the morning of June 5 the Israeli armed forces launched air and land attacks on Egypt, Jordan, and Syria. Five days later Israeli forces had captured the entire Sinai Peninsula, the west bank of the Jordan, the disputed Gaza strip, and the Syrian heights as far north as Mount Hermon.

Israel has offered to negotiate for all the captured territory except for the old city of Jerusalem (the site of Solomon's Temple) as part of a permanent settlement. But Arab foreign ministers, meeting in August, rejected any negotiations with Israel, and the U.N. was unsuccessful in its attempts to bring the parties together for negotiations. Arab leaders, meeting at Khartoum in early September, agreed to seek a non-military solution with Israel.

**GOVERNMENT AND POLITICS.** Israel's unicameral parliament, the Knesset, holds legislative power. Its 120 members are elected by universal suffrage. The nominal head of state is the president (Zalman Shazar in 1967), chosen by the Knesset to serve for a five-year term. He appoints the prime minister (Levi Eshkol in 1967), who holds executive power.

There are many political parties, but none large enough to win an absolute majority in the Knesset. The leading party, the Mapai Workers' Party, has ruled through coalition governments since the state's inception, mostly with David Ben-Gurion as prime minister. Ben-Gurion, who resigned as premier in 1963, split with his party in 1964 and formed a new party, the Rafi, which was defeated in the 1965 elections. A new coalition government, headed by Eshkol, was sworn into office in January, 1966. In the late spring of 1967 domestic discontent with Eshkol's handling of the mounting Arab threat forced him to appoint to his cabinet several members of the Rafi Party, including the popular General Moshe Dayan as Minister of Defense.

**ECONOMY.** Thanks to wise exploitation of water sources and massive reforestation programs, arable land in Israel has more than doubled since 1948, and agricultural production of such commodities as processed foods, eggs, poultry, cereals, and wine has increased about 16 per cent a year.

The Dead Sea provides potash and other chemical wealth, and deposits of phosphates, copper, glass sands, ceramic clays, and oil are also being exploited. Principal industries are food processing, textiles, chemicals, leather products, plastics, and some heavy manufactures. A three-year plan, intended to cut production costs and make Israeli products more competitive abroad, began in 1966.

Israel has nearly 2,400 miles of main and branch railways. The main ports are Haifa and Ashdod, a man-made deepwater port opened in 1965. Thirteen airlines serve Israel, including its own carrier, El Al.

**EDUCATION AND HEALTH.** Primary education is compulsory and free for all children from 5 to 14. The literacy rate is about 85 per cent of the population. There are several universities, of which the largest is Hebrew University in Jerusalem.

Israel in 1962 had one doctor for every 400 people, the highest proportion of any country in the world.

**NATIONAL DEFENSE.** There is compulsory military service of 26 months for men between 18 and 26, and for 2 years for men from 27 to 29. Unmarried women between 18 and 26 must serve 20 months. Wartime strength of all forces is estimated at 250,000.

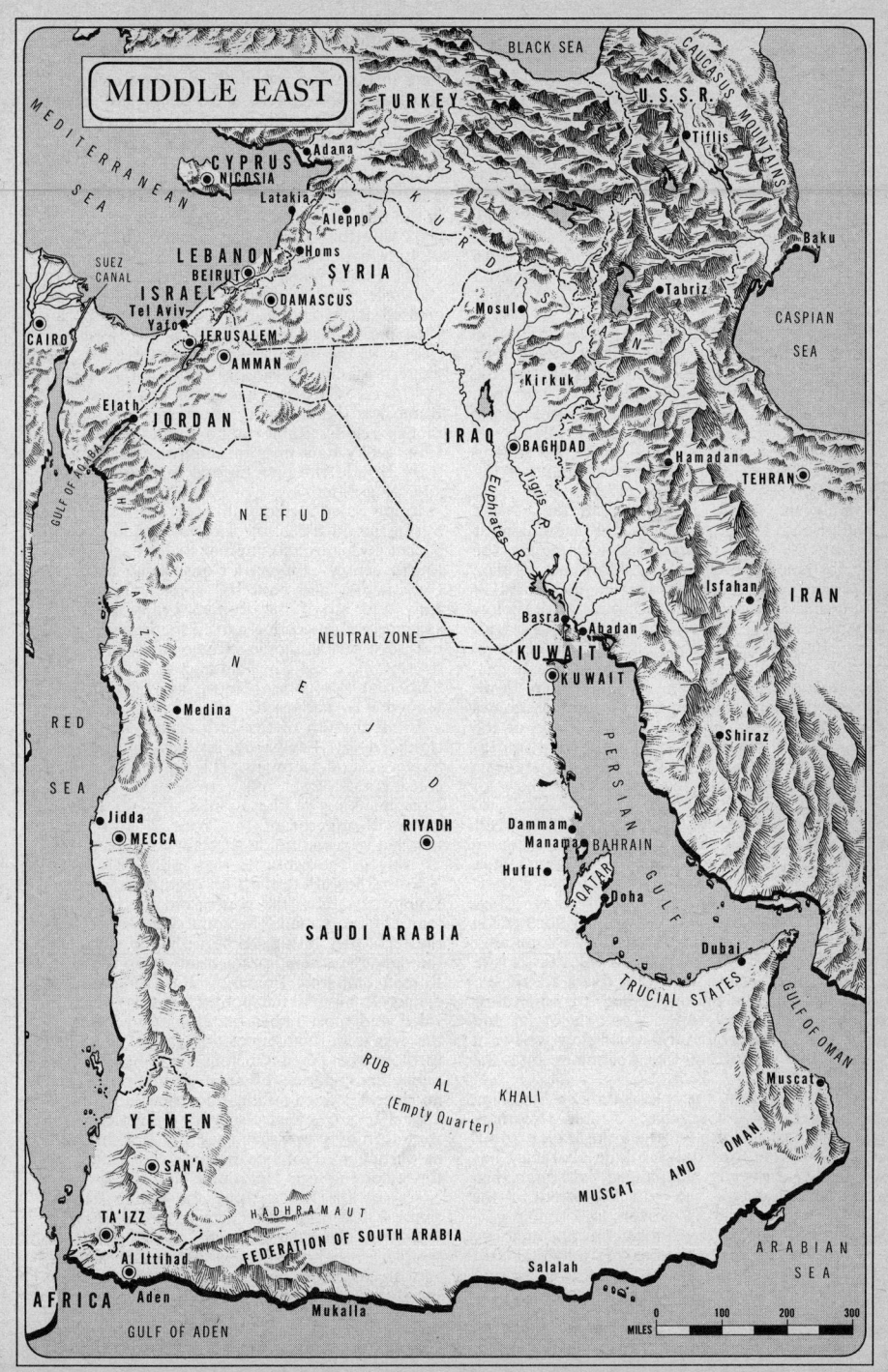

# ITALY

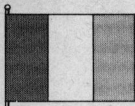

*Official Name:* Republic of Italy. *Area:* 116,303 square miles. *Population:* 51,859,-000. *Principal Cities* (with populations): Rome, the capital, 2,560,000; Milan, 1,-675,000; Naples, 1,245,000; Turin, 1.108,000; Genoa, 848,000; Palermo, 640,000; Bologna, 483,000; Florence, 455,000; Venice, 365,000. *Flag:* Bars of green, white, and red. *Monetary Unit:* The lira of 100 centesimi (worth 0.16 U.S. cent). *Gross National Product:* $56,736,-000,000 (1965). *Average Annual Income per Person:* $883.

**LAND AND PEOPLE.** Italy is bordered on the north by Switzerland and Austria, on the east by Yugoslavia and the Adriatic Sea, on the south by the Ionian and Mediterranean seas, on the west by the Tyrrhenian Sea, and on the northwest by France. The large islands of Sicily and Sardinia in the Mediterranean and Tyrrhenian seas also form integral parts of the country. (See map on page 117.)

Only the Po River valley and the coastal plains and lowlands relieve the mountainous nature of Italy. Alpine ranges dominate the north; among them are the Maritime, Graian, Pennine, and Bergamasque chains, together with the Dolomites and Carnic Alps. Below them lies the great fertile basin of the Po Valley, Italy's agricultural and industrial core. From the valley's lower limits rises the rugged Apennine chain, which runs spinelike down the length of the peninsula and continues across the Strait of Messina, at the toe of the boot-shaped mainland, to cover much of northern Sicily. Sardinia, to the northwest, repeats the craggy terrain characteristic of most of continental Italy. Southern Italy and Sicily together are in the midst of an earthquake belt that has given rise to Europe's three best known active volcanoes: Vesuvius (3,842 feet), Etna (11,122 feet), and Stromboli (3,040 feet).

Italy's largest and most famous lakes—Maggiore, Como, and Garda—are all located in the Alps, although central Italy has a number of fair-sized circular lakes of volcanic origin. The country's most important rivers are the Po and the Adige in the north, both of which flow eastward into the Adriatic, and the Arno and the Tiber in central Italy, which flow westward and southward from the Apennines into the Tyrrhenian.

Many ancient peoples—Italic, Etruscan, Greek, Roman, Germanic, Arabic, Norman, French, and Spanish—formed the Italian populace. For centuries Italy's ethnic character has remained basically unchanged, although historical differences can still be noted in the many Italian dialects spoken in varying geographical regions. The only significant minority groups are the German-speaking inhabitants of the Alto Adige, some Slavs in the area around Trieste, and a few small communities speaking Greek or Albanian in Apulia and Sicily. Roman Catholicism is the religion of almost all of the people.

**HISTORY.** The earliest known settlers—Sabines, Umbrians and Ligurians—took over large areas in the northern part of the peninsula, but were displaced in the ninth century B.C. by the Etruscans. The Greeks and Phoenicians began their expansion in Sicily and the southern part of the peninsula about the eighth century B.C. Rome was the capital of the Latins, lying between the northern and southern settlements. The Romans overthrew the Etruscan kingdom in the fifth century B.C. and, through a series of wars with the Greeks, united almost the whole of Italy by 272 B.C.

The Punic Wars, fought between Rome and Carthage, further strengthened Rome and increased its territories. When the wars began (264 B.C.) Carthage controlled northwest Africa and the islands and commerce of the western Mediterranean. By the time they ended (146 B.C.) Carthage had been destroyed and Rome was the dominant power in the Mediterranean region. Rome found itself transformed from a city-state into an empire that extended from Britain through Europe to North Africa and Asia Minor.

Rome ruled successfully for two centuries, but in the third century was threatened by barbarian invasions and internal strife. Early in the fourth century Emperor Constantine accepted Christianity, and churches spread throughout Italy and all of the Roman Empire. At the same time Constantine moved the imperial capital to Constantinople. Rome was weakened by this move and by subsequent invasions of barbarian Visigoths, Huns, and Ostrogoths. United Italy collapsed.

From the 6th to the 13th century Italy was trampled by bands of invaders—Lombards, Saracens, and Germans. The Lombards gained considerable power, but were defeated by Charlemagne, king of the Franks. In 800 he was crowned emperor of the West, a coronation that led to a multitude of claims to the throne of Italy in the centuries that followed.

From the 10th to the 14th century the various Italian city-states, the popes, and the Holy Roman emperors made the country a web of hostile territories. Struggles between the state and the papacy gathered momentum when the Holy Roman emperor, Frederick II (Hohenstaufen dynasty), battled the pontiff. Towns were divided and most noble families backed one of the two important opposition parties that had formed: the papal Guelphs and the imperial Ghibellines, parties of great strength that had no clearly defined political doctrines nor special appeal to any social class. Autonomous towns were torn by power struggles, but Bologna and, in particular, Florence became the centers of the emerging arts, literature, music, and sciences. By the 16th century the Italian Renaissance was flourishing to a point where its effect was felt throughout much of the civilized world.

Strife in Spain and France brought havoc to the Italian states, although Venice, Genoa, Milan, and Piedmont retained much of their early Renaissance greatness. The disorders of the French Revolution, followed by Napoleon's spreading conquests, did not help Italy's internal problems. Kingdoms grew and fell, and in the early 19th century Napoleon's efforts to unite Italy were a failure. Many underground societies began to form; they were, in part, responsible for the eventual unification of the country. The Congress of Vienna (1814–15) re established the pre-Napoleonic status, and many of the ancient ruling families were restored to power. Naples and Sicily were united in 1816.

Austria's influence in Italian affairs came to the fore at this time, but Prince Metternich and the Holy Alliance (a league formed by Russia, Austria, and Prussia) could not sustain their power in the face of the new nationalism, or *risorgimento,* under such leaders as Giuseppe Mazzini and Count Camillo Cavour. The latter, in 1861, brought most of the states under the rule of Victor Emmanuel II of Savoy. Giuseppe Garibaldi, the Sardinian republican leader, contributed immeasurably to the change taking place within the structure of the united kingdom.

Unemployment and illiteracy dogged Italy in the early 20th century. During World War I the country was at first neutral, but then, promised certain territories and concessions, entered the war on the Allied side. Italy's dissatisfaction with the postwar settlements, plus a severely depressed economy and the resultant unrest of the people, made the road easy for Benito Mussolini's "march on Rome" (1922). His powerful Fascist dictatorship was hailed by most of the Italian lower class, who at first gained much in social welfare, employment, and public works, but lost much in personal freedom.

The open opposition of the League of Nations to the colonial expansion of Fascism after the conquest of Ethiopia (1935–36) slowly led to Italy's isolation and helped to push the government toward closer relations with Nazi Germany. Britain and France drew farther away from Italy when the Fascist government intervened in the Spanish civil war and gave assistance to the nationalists. Another serious international crisis swept the world when Germany annexed Austria (March, 1938), with the tacit consent of Italy. German policy was inevitably directed toward war, and Italy followed the same path. Italy entered hostilities on the side of Germany on June 11, 1940.

Forced to send troops to distant fronts, Italy found itself without sufficient weapons to defend its cities and vast coastline, and without raw materials and a modern industry geared to war. Since Germany could not give much help to its ally, Italy could not withstand the pressures of the war.

The defeats suffered in North Africa and the Soviet Union marked a definite break between the Italian people and the Fascist regime. King Victor Emmanuel took advantage of a vote taken by the Fascist Grand Council on the night of July 24–25, 1943, and ordered Mussolini's arrest. The new government succeeded in concluding an armistice with the Allies, who had already started the invasion of Italy with landings in Sicily. The German retaliatory reaction forced the king and the government to abandon Rome and seek refuge at Brindisi. German forces took control of the whole of northern and central Italy; the peninsula was completely divided and subjected both to German and Allied occupation.

After a successful offensive south of Rome, the Allies entered the capital on June 4, 1944. In April, 1945, the "Italian Social Republic" collapsed, followed by the violent deaths of Mussolini and the leading exponents of the Fascist regime.

Italy passed through a difficult period at the end of World War II because of the immense destruction, hunger, and misery that was the aftermath of the war. Rival political parties cooperated in a spirit of national solidarity, and the task of reconstruction progressed with energy and decision. Much credit is due to those governments led by Alcide De Gasperi (1881–1954), the prime minister of reconstruction.

A peace treaty was signed between Italy and the Allies on February 10, 1947. Under its provisions, formerly Italian Trieste became a free city, the adjacent territory of Istria was given to Yugoslavia, and all African territorial claims were abandoned by Italy.

The leader of the Christian Democratic Party, Alcide De Gasperi, formed his first cabinet in December, 1945. National elections were held in June, 1946, marking the virtual end of the Italian monarchy. The Italian Republic officially came into being on January 1, 1948. National elections were held in April, at which time the country's Communist Party seriously threatened to take control of the government. However, De Gasperi and his Christian Democrats won a decisive victory at the polls, thereby placing Italy firmly in the pro-Western bloc of European nations.

After De Gasperi's last government fell in 1953, there was a chaotic succession of governments, all of which were coalitions of Christian Democrats and other center and left-center parties. However, a gradual tendency toward political stability appears to have taken place since the accession of Aldo Moro to the premiership in 1963. Amintore Fanfani, Moro's long-time rival within the Christian Democratic Party, nearly succeeded in an effort to wrest the party leadership from Moro in early 1966. However, Moro was able to form a new four-party coalition in February, and in March his new government won votes of confidence from both houses of parliament.

Undoubtedly the worst catastrophe to strike Italy since World War II was the floods of the Po and Arno rivers in November, 1966. Venice and Florence were severely damaged, and the death toll was placed at more than 110. Florence, famed since the Renaissance for its art treasures, suffered inestimable damage. Its famed Ponte Vecchio was wrecked, and paintings, frescoes, sculptures, and rare manuscripts were destroyed or damaged at the Uffizi Gallery, the National Library, and many famous churches. Even before the flood waters had subsided, rescue teams went to work salvaging and restoring many of the damaged works of art. Nevertheless, authorities have estimated that years of work and more than $30,000,000 will be needed to complete the task.

**GOVERNMENT AND POLITICS.** Italy has been a parliamentary democracy since the adoption of a new constitution and the establishment of the republic on January 1, 1948.

The head of state is the president, who is elected for a seven-year term by both houses of the legislature. He is empowered to dissolve Parliament (except in the last six months of his term) and to appoint the prime minister, or President of the Council of Ministers. The prime minister, who is the real head of government, selects his own cabinet and is responsible to Parliament, whose support he must retain in order to continue in office.

The two houses of Parliament—the Chamber of Deputies and the Senate—have equal legislative authority. Deputies are elected for five-year terms by universal suffrage on the basis of proportional representation, although the Chamber is now limited to 630 members. Senators are elected for six-year terms by regions on the basis of one senator for every 200,000 people; the present Senate, including six senators appointed for life by the president, has 321 members.

Governments are usually formed by a coalition of parties. The order of political party strength in the Chamber, based on the 1963 elections, is: Christian Democrats; Communists; Socialists; Liberals; Social Democrats; Social Movement, a neo-Fascist group; Monarchists; and Republicans. The present premier, Aldo Moro (Christian Democrat), has been in office since December, 1963. The President is Giuseppe Saragat (Social Democrat).

Italy is divided administratively into 19 regions, several of which (Sicily, Sardinia, Trentino-Alto Adige, Val d'Aosta, and Friuli-Venezia Giulia) have been granted semi-autonomous status.

Since 1945 Italy has pursued a foreign policy of European and Atlantic cooperation as a member of NATO and of the European Common Market. A dispute with Yugoslavia over the city of Trieste was settled in 1954, when Trieste was ceded to Italy. A long-standing quarrel with Austria over the South Tyrol (Alto Adige), a part of Austria ceded to Italy after World War I, remains unsettled. The Italian government has accused the Austrian government of supporting the terrorist activities of the German-speaking population of the area. The rebels claim the government has not given the region the degree of autonomy to which it is entitled. Discussions between the German group and the Italian government have failed to end the terrorism.

**ECONOMY.** World War II created an economic shambles in Italy. However, with the assistance of foreign aid the nation's output soon surpassed prewar levels and the standard of living rose dramatically. Yet despite substantial progress, serious problems remain: the *mezzogiorno* (southern Italy, Sicily, and Sardinia)

are still underdeveloped; unemployment persists; and an inflationary spiral threatens to undermine the gains made by industrial workers over the past ten years.

About a quarter of Italy's work force is engaged in agriculture, and this sector of the economy has made impressive gains in productivity in recent years as the result of doubling the farm acreage under irrigation, increasing mechanization, using fertilizers, and developing specialized cultivation techniques. Wheat, rice, wine (of which Italy is the world's largest producer), olives, olive oil, vegetables, citrus fruits, and almonds are the most important agricultural products. Scientific stock breeding is practiced only in northern Italy, but sheep and goats are raised throughout the mountainous districts, and such famous cheeses as Parmesan, Gorgonzola, Mozzarella, and Pecorino are produced.

Although hampered by a lack of raw materials (Carrara marble, bauxite, sulfur, natural gas, and oil are the only minerals found in the country), Italian industry, concentrated in the Milan-Turin-Genoa triangle, has been expanding steadily for 20 years and now employs more than 8,000,000 people. Iron and steel, petrochemicals, automobiles, motor scooters, rubber products, textiles, machine tools, typewriters, sewing machines, and processed foods (particularly pasta) are the nation's principal products. Italy is also well-known for its fashion and for traditional handicraft products such as Venetian glass, Florentine jewelry, and leatherwork.

Italy's unfavorable balance of trade is largely compensated by a booming tourist industry, which, with 25,000,000 visitors (1966) annually, contributes substantially to the economy. Travel facilities include 37,000 hotels, a national railway system extending over 13,000 miles, and one of the finest highway systems (3,000 miles) in Europe. The merchant marine has about 4,000 ships in service (including a large fleet of luxury liners). The country's airline, Alitalia, regularly links 62 cities in 50 countries.

**EDUCATION AND HEALTH.** Education is free and compulsory for all children from 6 to 14. Financial assistance is given to selected students for higher education. Illiteracy has dropped to 8 per cent of the population, and at least 600,000 illiterates receive yearly instruction through courses of "popular education." The nation has 46 colleges and universities, eight of which were founded before 1400; the oldest is at Bologna.

A social security plan for medical care and disability is provided by the government. A new government program, to be implemented in 1968, will alleviate the shortage of doctors and hospitals in rural areas by integrating the universities and medical schools into the health system.

**ARMED FORCES.** Italy, a member of NATO since 1948, has armed forces totaling 480,000. National military service is compulsory, with 18 months of training required in the army and air force or 24 months in the navy.

# IVORY COAST

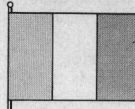

*Official Name:* Ivory Coast. *Area:* 124,503 square miles. *Population:* 4,000,000. *Principal Cities* (with estimated populations): Abidjan, the capital, 400,000; Bouaké, 100,000; Daloa, 40,000; Man, 30,000. *Flag:* A vertical tricolor of orange, white, and green. *Monetary Unit:* The CFA franc of 100 centimes (worth 0.41 U.S. cent). *Gross National Product:* $968,000,000 (1966). *Average Annual Income per Person:* $210.

**LAND AND PEOPLE.** The Ivory Coast is bordered on the north by Mali and Upper Volta, on the east by Ghana, on the south by the Atlantic Ocean, and on the west by Liberia and Guinea. (See map on page 111.)

Most of the Ivory Coast is a huge plateau sloping gently from about 1,400 feet in the north to the ocean on the south. The narrow 315-mile coastline—flat and sandy in the east, with deep lagoons behind it—becomes more indented and rocky in the west. Beyond the coast is a vast forest region occupying nearly one third of the country. In the northwest, mountain ranges reaching 5,000 feet extend into the country from neighboring Guinea.

The five main divisions of the ethnically varied population are the Agni-Ashanti-Baoulé, the Senoufo, the Kru, the Malinke, the Mande, and the Lagoon-dwellers. Over 60 dialects are spoken. About 60 per cent of the people follow traditional tribal cults; 25 per cent are Muslim; and 15 per cent are Christian.

**HISTORY.** Although Portuguese seamen were initially the most active explorers on Africa's west coast, French navigators in the 15th century first braved the Gulf of Guinea's forbidding sand barriers and began the lucrative ivory trade from which the area later derived its name. French missionaries, landing at Assinie in 1687, were the first white settlers. The post was soon abandoned, however, and the Ivory Coast, due to its oppressive climate and coastal intricacies, remained relatively free of European influence (and thereby of the slave trade) until the 19th century.

French development began in earnest in 1842 with the establishment of a protectorate over the coastal area. Thereafter, mostly as the result of private initiative, French influence was carried to the interior, and economic exploitation of the country was vigorously pursued. Additional treaties with local chieftains furthered France's hold, and in 1893 the territory was declared a colony. Complete pacification of the Ivory Coast, however, was not achieved until 1917.

Between World Wars I and II the French built up the country. Yet the colonial administration, based on government by decree, was little changed until the creation of the French Union in 1946, under which political rights were gradually extended to Africans.

Over the next ten years the Parti Démocratique de Côte d'Ivoire (PDCI), under the leadership of Félix Houphouët-Boigny, emerged as the dominant political force; most of its opposition had either been eliminated or absorbed by 1956, the year internal autonomy was granted. The Ivory Coast became a republic within the French Community in 1958, but two years later it withdrew from membership and proclaimed independence (August, 1960). Houphouët-Boigny was elected president in November, 1960, and re-elected in 1965, both times without opposition.

Since independence the economic development of the nation has proceeded rapidly, spurred in large part by the unusually liberal terms offered to foreign investors. The government has adopted a conservative policy with respect to African political affairs and has maintained or developed strong ties with France, the United States, and West Germany.

**GOVERNMENT AND POLITICS.** Executive power is vested exclusively in the president, who is elected by universal suffrage to a five-year term. Cabinet ministers are appointed by the president and are responsible to him. Deputies to the one-chamber National Assembly are elected by universal suffrage for five-year terms. The single political party, the PDCI, has little organized opposition.

**ECONOMY.** The Ivory Coast ranks high among the new African states in annual growth of its gross national product, average per capita income, and industrial expansion. Coffee, cocoa, and timber account for 85 per cent of its exports, but agricultural and industrial diversification has begun. The economy has had a favorable trade balance for nearly 20 years.

A railway connects the capital of Upper Volta to the deepwater port of Abidjan, which also has an international jet airport. The Ivory Coast has over 20,000 miles of roads, of which 570 miles are paved.

**EDUCATION AND HEALTH.** Nearly one-third of the national budget is devoted to education and public health. Illiteracy is widespread, but universal primary education is a major government goal. School attendance has doubled since 1960. A new university at Abidjan was opened in 1964. Most medical services are provided by the government.

**ARMED FORCES.** The armed forces, totaling 6,500 men, are chiefly concerned with the technical training of recruits and with public works projects. A bilateral agreement with France ensures the country's national security.

# JAMAICA

*Official Name:* Jamaica. *Area:* 4,232 square miles. *Population:* 1,839,000. *Principal Cities* (with populations): Kingston, the capital, 123,400; Montego Bay, 26,000; Spanish Town, 16,000. *Flag:* A gold cross, with a green field in the top and bottom quarters, a black field in the left and right quarters. *Monetary Unit:* Jamaica pound (worth U.S. $2.80). *Gross National Product:*

$873,000,000 (1966). *Average Annual Income per Person:* $428.

**LAND AND PEOPLE.** The island of Jamaica lies in the Caribbean, less than 100 miles south of Cuba's southeastern coast. A limestone-based plateau, its average altitude is about 1,500 feet. Alluvial coastal deposits surround a mountainous interior dominated in the east by the Blue Mountains, whose tallest peak rises to 7,402 feet.

The equable climate shows little seasonal change except in rainfall—up to 200 inches a year in some northeastern coastal and mountain regions, and about 33 inches in Kingston. Rainy seasons generally are from May to June and in the month of October.

The majority of the population (76.8 per cent) is of African derivation, with 16.9 per cent of mixed blood. There are also East Indians (1.7 per cent), Europeans (0.8 per cent), and Chinese (0.6 per cent). Jamaicans speak English and are mainly Christians.

**HISTORY.** Jamaica was discovered by Columbus in 1494. It was settled 15 years later by the Spaniards, who introduced the cultivation of sugarcane. The native Arawaks, unused to hard labor and slavery, soon died out, and the Spaniards imported Africans to work the plantations.

At war with Spain, England attacked Spanish possessions in the Caribbean, and, in 1655, took Jamaica. The Spaniards left after freeing their slaves, who took to the hills and harassed the settlers until they were granted land and independence in 1739. Meanwhile the island was a base for pirates who grew rich plundering the Spanish galleons. Port Royal, the capital, acquired a legendary reputation for wickedness but was pushed into the sea by an earthquake in 1692.

The English imported large numbers of African slaves to continue the lucrative business of growing cane. But churchmen and liberals in England were disturbed by the barbarity of the slave trade, and in 1838 slavery was abolished. Most of the former slaves refused to continue working on the estates, and the economy collapsed despite importation of Indian and Chinese laborers.

An administration dominated by planters ignored the hardships of the peasant population. In 1865 a protest march to the Morant Bay Courthouse was met with violence and turned into a riot; its leader, Bogle, and Gordon, a legislator who spoke on behalf of the slaves, were hanged. One result was that Jamaica became a crown colony in 1866. A succession of able governors introduced reforms, but the island never regained its prosperity.

The depression of the 1930s was aggravated by a banana blight and by growing discontent with colonial status. In 1944 Jamaica was granted a new constitution based on universal adult suffrage and a wide measure of self-government. Full internal autonomy was granted in 1953.

In 1958 Jamaica joined with several other British Caribbean possessions in a West Indian Federation. In 1961 Jamaica, now the most prosperous member, voted to withdraw, and the federation collapsed. On August 6, 1962, Jamaica was granted full independence, with Sir Alexander Bustamànte, a Jamaican labor leader, as the first prime minister.

**GOVERNMENT AND POLITICS.** Jamaica is a constitutional monarchy and a member of the British Commonwealth. The Queen is represented by a governor-general, Sir Clifford Campbell, a Jamaican. The bicameral parliament consists of a nominated Senate of 42 members, and a House of Representatives with 45 members elected for five-year terms by universal suffrage. Executive power rests with the cabinet and a prime minister, who is now Hugh Shearer, a trade union leader.

There are two main political parties, the Jamaica Labour Party (JLP) and the People's National Party (PNP), both allied to strong trade unions. The first election since independence was held in February, 1967. The JLP won 33 seats and the PNP, 20.

**ECONOMY.** Bauxite (including alumina) is the largest contributor to the Jamaican economy. The main agricultural exports—sugar, bananas, and citrus fruits—are faced with serious problems. Although they have helped to maintain their earnings of foreign exchange by meeting lower world prices with higher production, there is need for mechanization. Also, prices guaranteed by the United Kingdom are threatened by Britain's possible entry into the European Common Market.

The current adverse balance of trade is largely due to the heavy imports of machinery and construction equipment. New housing and schools are being built with the help of the World Bank and other types of foreign aid.

**EDUCATION AND HEALTH.** The government has a far-reaching health program, including epidemic control and campaigns against special diseases. About 67 per cent of the population over 15 is literate.

**ARMED FORCES.** There is no compulsory military service in Jamaica.

# JAPAN

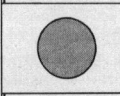

*Official Name:* Nippon. *Area:* 142,722 square miles. *Population:* 99,820,000. *Principal Cities* (with populations): Tokyo, the capital, 11,172,000; Osaka, 3,117,-200; Nagoya, 1,980,300; Yokohama, 1,922,741; Kyoto, 1,392,000; Kobe, 1,237,000; Kitakyushu, 1,049,639. *Flag:* A red sun on a white field. *Monetary Unit:* The yen of 100 sen (worth 0.27 U.S. cent). *Gross National Product:* $97,000,000,000 (1966). *Average Annual Income per Person:* $687.

**LAND AND PEOPLE.** An archipelago off Asia's eastern coast, Japan is bordered by the Sea of Okhotsk to the north, the Pacific Ocean to the east and south, the East China Sea to the southwest, and the Sea of Japan to the west. Stretching in a 1,500-mile-long arc from north to south are four main islands: Hokkaido, Honshu, Shikoku, and Kyushu; and nearly

3,000 smaller islands, mostly tiny islets. (See map on page 93.) Honshu is the principal island, where Tokyo and other large cities and the major industrial areas are located.

Japan's mountainous topography severely restricts living space and leaves only 16 per cent of the total land area available for cultivation. Japan has 192 volcanoes, 40 of them still active. Dormant Mount Fuji (12,395 feet) is the tallest mountain. Japan's rivers are short and swift and of little use for transportation. The country has repeatedly suffered extensive damage from typhoons, earthquakes, and floods.

Descended from the varied peoples of Asia and, in all probability, of the South Pacific region, who entered Japan in a remote, unrecorded past, the present-day Japanese form a remarkably homogenous population. An aboriginal minority, the Ainu, survive in Hokkaido. The physical features of this dwindling race suggest that it is of Caucasian stock. The national language is Japanese. Nearly all Japanese are Shintoists or Buddhists or both; 0.81 per cent are Christians.

**HISTORY.** According to Japanese mythology, Jimmu Tenno, descendant of the sun goddess and ancestor of the present emperor, founded the empire in about 660 B.C. Early in the Christian era the Ainu were being subdued in most parts of Japan; the country was well settled and under the control of the Yamato, a family of clan chieftains. Judging by artifacts brought by the invaders, this family and others must have come from or through Korea, possibly as early as the first century B.C.

Under the cultural influence of early Chinese dynasties, great refinements took place in Japan. Buddhism was introduced in the sixth century A.D., and the upper classes adapted to their own use China's ideographic script, as well as its philosophy, literature, arts, and sciences. Chinese governmental organization was adopted, but with power based on hereditary position rather than merit. The first permanent capital was established at Nara at the beginning of the eighth century, and a new capital was built at Kyoto in 794 on the pattern of China's own capital at that time.

In the 12th century power at Kyoto fell into the hands of the Taira, a military family. They were overthrown by their rivals, the Minamoto, whose leader, Yoritomo, set up a military government in 1192 at Kamakura. For 700 years military governors, usually called shoguns, ruled Japan in the emperor's name. The Mongol invasions of 1274 and 1281 undermined the government's control, and there was almost continual civil war until the end of the 16th century.

Portuguese navigators, arriving in 1542, were the first Europeans seen in Japan. In 1549 St. Francis Xavier introduced Christianity. In the latter half of the century three warrior captains worked to end the civil war and restore internal unity. The first was Nobunaga Oda; at his death the task was completed by Hideyoshi Toyotomi. By 1590 Ieyasu Tokugawa had consolidated the pacification and unification begun by his predecessors. He was appointed shogun in 1603 and established the Tokugawa shogunate that ruled until 1868. Ieyasu's center of government was Edo, the present Tokyo. After Ieyasu's death in 1616, his successors adopted a policy of national isolation, finally enforced in 1639. Japan was closed to the world, except for Dutch and Chinese traders at Nagasaki. Christianity was obliterated. Society became ossified under the ruling lords into four classes: samurai (warriors), peasants, artisans, and merchants.

United States Naval Commodore Matthew C. Perry forced open Japan's doors in 1853, securing a commercial treaty. Other nations followed suit. Fear of foreign influence on the part of many Japanese led to years of turmoil in which the shogunate inevitably lost prestige. A group of samurai finally forced the shogun to abdicate. Ruling power was restored to the emperor in 1868, and the capital was moved from Kyoto to Tokyo. This development was known as the Meiji Restoration. Energetic steps were taken to modernize the country's political, administrative, economic, and social structure. Feudalism was abolished, Western industrial and administrative techniques were introduced, and education was made compulsory. In 1889 the emperor granted a new constitution, after the Prussian model; a bicameral legislature was established, with a civil cabinet headed by a prime minister responsible to the emperor.

Victory in the Sino-Japanese War of 1894–95 gave Formosa and the Pescadores to Japan. After forming an alliance with Britain in 1902, Japan overcame Russia's supposedly invincible power in the Russo-Japanese War of 1904–05 and gained the Liaotung peninsula in Manchuria and the southern half of Sakhalin island. Korea was annexed as a protectorate in 1910. During World War I Japan sided with the Allies and for her support received a mandate over many islands formerly held by Germany. The war caused Japan's economy to boom; at the Washington Naval Conference of 1922, she was recognized as the world's third leading naval power. The catastrophic Tokyo-Yokohama earthquake of 1923 proved only a temporary setback. Universal manhood suffrage was introduced in 1925, and the present emperor, Hirohito, ascended the throne in 1926.

During the economic and social crisis created by the world depression of the 1930s, Japanese nationalism hit a new high. With it came a revival of the earliest mythology of the emperor's divine ancestry and a glorification of the warrior class. Extreme militarist and right-wing nationalist organizations sprang up that were dissatisfied with Japan's pacific attitude toward China. A Japanese-created incident gave the militarists an excuse to overrun all Manchuria in 1931 and to form a puppet state. Criticized for this act, Japan withdrew from the League of Nations in 1933. Militarists organized the assassination of Prime Minister Inukai in 1932 and a coup d'etat in 1936 that failed. In the latter year Japan signed an anti-Comintern pact with Germany and Italy.

Japanese involvement in northern China's economic and political affairs continued from 1932 to 1937. An incident in Peking led to an undeclared war with China. Japan and Russia clashed on the Manchurian border in 1938 and 1939. The defeat of France in 1940 enabled Japan to gain a foothold in French Indo-China.

In December, 1941, Japan suddenly struck at Pearl Harbor and the United States instantly declared war. In the early years of the war Japan gained enormous amounts of territory, extending almost from the borders of Alaska to those of India. But her losses then grew swiftly and steadily and culminated in the atomic bombing of Hiroshima and Nagasaki by the United States in August, 1945.

Japan formally surrendered on September 2. The country was demilitarized and remained occupied by U.S. forces until all conditions of disarmament and control were met by a responsible, nonmilitary government. General Douglas MacArthur was in command, but actual control of internal affairs was left in the hands of the Japanese. A new constitution was adopted.

A sovereign status was achieved when 48 nations signed a peace treaty with Japan in 1951; Japan signed a bilateral security treaty with the United States at the same time. The country recovered full independence in April, 1952, when the peace treaty became effective. In 1956, when the state of war between Japan and the U.S.S.R. officially ended, Japan became a member of the United Nations. The country has progressed to become the most prosperous nation in Asia.

**GOVERNMENT AND POLITICS.** The 1946 constitution states that sovereignty resides with the people and that the emperor is the "symbol of the state and of the unity of the people." Soon after World War II Emperor Hirohito publicly repudiated the attributes of divinity with which folklore, nationalists, and militarists had cloaked him.

Executive power is vested in the prime minister and his cabinet. The prime minister is designated by the Diet (parliament) and must be a member of that body. He and the cabinet are responsible to the Diet, which comprises a House of Representatives, elected for four years, and a House of Councilors, elected for six. Of these two chambers the House of Representatives is the more powerful. The House of Councilors, as the second chamber, cannot reject bills passed up to it by the House of Representatives. All Japanese 20 years old and over have the right to vote.

The ruling Liberal-Democratic Party, now Japan's only conservative party, is broadly pro-Western in outlook and policy. The opposition parties are the Socialists, the Democratic Socialists (a generally centrist party that broke away from the Socialists), the Komei-to (Clean Government Party), and the Communists (now neither pro-Moscow nor pro-Peking but "independent in attitude").

**ECONOMY.** Japan has made a remarkable recovery from the devastation of World War II. The major stimulus to its recuperation was massive American aid. The country expanded at a faster rate than any other in the world, developed an industrial and economic structure similar to that of highly industrialized Western states, and now has the most advanced economy of any Asian nation. A 1965 slowdown in the remarkable rate of growth was followed by recovery in 1966, due to large-scale issuance of government bonds, increased exports, and special procurements rising out of the Vietnam war.

Although agriculture's share in the economy has declined, it is still an important sector. More people work in agriculture than in industry, and every available square foot of land is cultivated. Rice is the main crop; the yield per acre is the world's highest. Most farmers own their own land, and Japan provides most of its food domestically. Fishing is also a major occupation.

The economy, however, is primarily industrial. Japan is the world's leading shipbuilding nation and stands second in sales of electrical products, third in steel production, and fourth in the manufacture of cars and trucks. Bituminous coal, iron pyrites, and limestone are in fair supply, but all other important minerals must be imported. Foreign trade is essential to Japan's existence. Exports were valued at over $10 billion in 1966; nearly one-third of the sum represented exports to the United States. Less than one per cent of the work force is unemployed.

Railroads are the chief form of domestic transportation. Highways, excluding urban roads, total some 90,000 miles. Only a quarter of these are paved, though it is planned to have half of them paved by 1972. Some 370 miles of new highways will be completed in 1968. The merchant fleet, once the world's greatest, was reduced to 17 ships at the end of World War II; today it is the world's fifth largest. Japan Air Lines flies to many parts of the globe, and there is a network of domestic air routes.

**EDUCATION AND HEALTH.** Education is compulsory and free for children from 6 to 15. There are altogether 72 institutions of university rank, including six state universities. Great stress is laid on adult education, particularly in rural regions. Literacy is estimated at close to 100 per cent.

Japan's health insurance laws cover the entire nation, and health examinations are obligatory for all persons over six. Principal causes of death include cancer, heart disease, and cerebral hemorrhage.

**ARMED FORCES.** Service in the armed forces, called "self-defense forces" by the Japanese, is voluntary. The army numbers 185,130 men; the navy, 39,948; the coast guard, 11,187; and the air force, 44,909. The 1952 U.S.-Japan security treaty allowed the United States to maintain armed forces and bases in and around Japan; in a 1960 security treaty the United States and Japan became full-fledged military allies. In 1970 the treaty will be open to abrogation by either nation on a year's notice.

# JORDAN

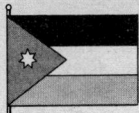

*Official Name:* The Hashemite Kingdom of Jordan. *Area:* 34,820 square miles. *Population:* 1,976,000. *Principal Cities* (with populations): Amman, the capital, 246,475; Jerusalem (the Arab sector prior to the Arab-Israeli war in June, 1967), 60,000; Nablus, 46,000. *Flag:* Black, white, and green with a seven-pointed white star in a red triangle. *Monetary Unit:* The dinar (worth U.S. $2.80). *Gross National Product:* $446,000,000 (1964). *Average Annual Income per Person:* $244.

**LAND AND PEOPLE.** Jordan is bordered by Syria on the north, Iraq on the northeast, Saudi Arabia on the east and south, Israel on the west, and by a small stretch of the Gulf of Aqaba in the southwest. (See map on page 151.)

Western Jordan consists of the Judean and Samarian hills. The low Jordan valley in the north sinks to 1,300 feet below sea level at the Dead Sea, the earth's lowest land point. East of the Jordan River are the Transjordanian hills and plateaus, from which highlands slope toward a cool desert region that covers four-fifths of the area. Most of Jordan is hot and dry between May and October. The remaining months are cool and rainy in the mountain regions, with cool desert conditions in the eastern part of the country.

Jordanians are almost all Arabic-speaking Arabs. Ninety-five per cent are Muslims.

**HISTORY.** The territory west of the Jordan River was once part of ancient Palestine, including the Old City of Jerusalem. Territory to the east covers the Biblical lands of Gilead, Ammon, Bashan, Edom, and Moab. The later Nabataean Kingdom was annexed to the Roman Empire in 106 A.D. Arabs conquered the land in the seventh century A.D. After the Crusades it went to the Mamluks of Egypt, then fell, in the 16th century, to the Ottoman Turks and remained part of their empire until the defeat of the Turks at the end of World War I. In 1916 the Arabs took Palestine from the Turks.

The territory east of the Jordan River became part of the provisional Syrian kingdom of King Feisal I until its overthrow by France in 1920. In the same year the League of Nations gave Britain a mandate over Palestine, and in 1921 Britain recognized Feisal's brother, Abdullah ibn Hussein, as emir of Transjordan. He ruled (despite Zionist protests) under the military and civil supervision of Britain. Abdullah's loyalty in World War II prompted Britain, in 1946, to recognize him as an independent king of the Hashemite Kingdom of Transjordan. Treaties provided for an annual British subsidy and military personnel (the Arab Legion) for Jordan's army.

Anti-Zionist Jordan, a founder-member of the Arab League, joined other League members in 1948 to attack the newly independent Israel. The League's forces failed to destroy Israel, but they defended the Arab-populated uplands of central Palestine, including the Old City of Jerusalem. During the war thousands of Arab refugees from Israel crowded Jordan, creating a major economic problem. After concluding an armistice with Israel in 1949, Abdullah formally annexed the area west of the Jordan River in defiance of other Arab states. Abdullah was assassinated in 1951 by a follower of the former Mufti of Jerusalem. A year later his son, Talal, was deposed by parliament because of mental illness. He was succeeded by his son, King Hussein, the present monarch, who was crowned on May 2, 1953.

Hussein's reign has been a perilous one (his 1962 autobiography was entitled *Uneasy Lies the Head*). In March, 1956, to placate "national-socialists," Hussein dismissed the British chief-of-staff of his army, General John B. Glubb. After the 1956 Suez crisis, Hussein revoked all treaties with Britain, and in 1957 he averted another national-socialist threat by enlisting economic support from the U.S. and Saudi Arabia.

After Israel in 1964 diverted part of the Jordan River for irrigation, Syria and Egypt supported Arab militant organizations in attacking Israel and frequently denounced Hussein's more cautious policy regarding Israel. On May 30, 1967, Hussein signed a military agreement with Egypt, which was committed to encircling Israel. A week later, during a six-day war, the Israelis overran all of Jordan west of the Jordan River (including Arab Jerusalem).

**GOVERNMENT AND POLITICS.** Jordan is a constitutional monarchy. There is a bicameral parliament consisting of a 30-member Council of Notables appointed by the king and a 60-member lower house (Chamber of Deputies) elected by male suffrage. The king rules through a cabinet and a prime minister (Sa'd Jum'a) who are crown-appointed but responsible to parliament.

**ECONOMY.** Agriculture provides the livelihood of most of the people. A seven-year plan (1964–70) has been established to improve farming and increase irrigation. Mining and manufacturing have been increasing. Phosphate is the principal mineral and the major export. Manufacturing is mostly in light industries (food processing, textiles, tobacco, tanneries). A petroleum refining plant and a cement plant are the only heavy industries.

**EDUCATION.** Education is compulsory from age 6 through 12. Higher institutions include the University of Jordan, 7 teacher-training colleges, and 17 agricultural and industrial schools. Literacy in 1961 was about 33 per cent.

**ARMED FORCES.** At the outbreak of the Israel-Arab war it was estimated that Jordan could muster 70,000 to 80,000 men, including regular army forces of about 30,000 (the National Guard militia) and another 5,000 to 10,000 partially trained men of the Palestine Liberation Organization. Before the June war Jordan had several hundred combat vehicles and about 50 aircraft.

# KENYA

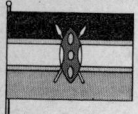

*Official Name:* Republic of Kenya. *Area:* 224,960 square miles. *Population:* 9,643,000. *Principal Cities* (with populations): Nairobi, the capital, 266,794; Mombasa, 179,575; Nakuru, 38,181. *Flag:* Black, red, and green bands separated by white stripes. In the center is a large red, black, and white shield over crossed white spears. *Monetary Unit:* The shilling (worth 14 U.S. cents). *Gross National Product:* $846,-000,000 (1965). *Average Annual Income per Person:* $85.

**LAND AND PEOPLE.** Kenya is bordered by Sudan and Ethiopia on the north, Somalia and the Indian Ocean on the east, Tanzania on the south, and Lake Victoria and Uganda on the west. (See map on page 111.)

The country is noted for its topographical variety. The low-lying coast rises gently to a dry coastal plain that gives way to a high plateau in the southwest (10,000 feet above sea level at some points). Most of the people and economic activity are located in the plateau area. The northern region, containing about 60 per cent of the land mass, is semi-desert; Mount Kenya, with a perpetually snow-clad peak, is in this region. Running north and south across Kenya is the Great Rift Valley, which includes Lake Rudolf, Kenya's largest lake.

Ninety-seven per cent of the population is African and Somali, a people of mixed race from Somaliland. The Bantu Kikuyu tribe is the largest single group. There are small Asian, European, and Arab minorities. Roman Catholicism, Islam, and Protestantism (in that order) account for a majority of the population. Many African languages are spoken, but Swahili is the common language.

**HISTORY.** Throughout the Middle Ages Kenya attracted Indian Ocean trade and was visited by sailors from Asia and Arabia. The Arabs, who came in search of slaves and ivory, stayed to settle the coast. In 1498 Portuguese traders arrived and established trade posts that were finally taken by the Arabs in 1729. From 1740 onward the Arabs ruled the Kenyan coast from a capital on the island of Zanzibar.

During the 19th-century European competition for African colonies, Britain and Germany agreed that Kenya should fall within the British sphere of influence. In 1887 the British East Africa Company leased the Kenyan coast from the Sultan of Zanzibar. The company established some stations but spent much of its assets in quarrels with African tribes and in disputes over German territorial claims. The company was dissolved in 1895; the area of present-day Kenya became a British protectorate.

The great effort of the new official administration was to construct and secure a railway line to Lake Victoria that was regarded as essential to the economic development of Uganda and the strategic protection of the Nile headwaters. A large area of Uganda was transferred to Kenya in 1902.

The administration promoted settlement by Englishmen and white South Africans and, in support of this aim, imposed expropriations and hard labor upon the Africans. The dominant position of the white population was thus strengthened and was further cemented by their participation in the government, which after 1920 was organized as a crown colony.

One of Africa's earliest and most widely known nationalists was Jomo Kenyatta, who as secretary of an association of the Kikuyu tribe, began campaigning in 1928 for land reform and political rights for Africans. Frustration in these ends led the Kikuyu to resort to terrorism, which was carried out beginning in 1952 by a secret organization called the Mau Mau. Savage attacks were made on white settlers and on natives who would not support the Mau Mau. Whites retaliated. By the end of the emergency in 1960, it was estimated that 12,000 people had been killed; only about 35 of them were Europeans. Eighty thousand Mau Mau were imprisoned. Kenyatta, accused and convicted of being a director of the terrorism, was imprisoned from 1954 until 1959.

In the meantime Britain began to prepare Kenya for independence, which was assured in a new constitution negotiated in 1960 in London. Various political parties were formed, the largest of which were the centralist Kenyan African National Union (KANU) under the leadership of Tom Mboya, and the federalist Kenyan African Democratic Union (KADU). Kenyatta became president of KANU in 1961; he was elected to the Legislative Council in 1962 and later that year was appointed to the cabinet.

KANU won control of the legislature in 1963, and in June, when internal self-government came into effect, Kenyatta became the country's first prime minister. Kenya became independent on December 12, 1963.

**GOVERNMENT AND POLITICS.** Kenya is an independent republic in the Commonwealth of Nations. Under the 1963 constitution the head of state was the prime minister, who was leader of the majority party in the two-house National Assembly. Rivalry between the two major parties, KANU and KADU, continued until 1964 when a republican form of government was adopted and KADU dissolved itself. KANU remained as the only major party, and its leader, Kenyatta, continued in office as president of the republic. In the spring of 1966 Kenyatta's vice-president resigned to head a new radical party called the African People's Union. This party has not attained significant size. Early in 1967 the Senate was abolished, leaving Kenya with a unicameral legislature.

President Kenyatta has pursued a pro-Western course in international affairs.

**ECONOMY.** Kenya is primarily an agricultural country, and the wide range of climates makes possible an exceptional variety of crops. Coffee, tea, sisal, maize, wheat, and pyrethrum are grown in the highlands; coconuts, cashew nuts, cotton, sugar, sisal, and maize are grown in the lower altitudes. Although three-fifths of the country is too arid for agriculture, enough is produced so that Kenya can export fruits, flowers, vegetables, meat, and other agricultural products.

After World War II Nairobi became a center of light industry, particularly the processing of agricultural products. However, Tanzania has employed economic sanctions that have retarded industry in Kenya. The East African Development Bank, established in 1967, may help Kenya overcome these difficulties.

Minerals are found in insignificant quantities. A more important natural resource is game, the foundation of a growing tourist industry.

Nairobi's airport is an important terminal for flights from Europe, Asia, and other parts of Africa. Air travel, together with rail, post and telephone services in East Africa, are administered by the East African Common Services Organization, whose headquarters are in Nairobi. Kenya's railroads, the major means of freight transportation, are good.

**EDUCATION.** There is no compulsory education in Kenya. About 1,059,000 children were attending the 5,078 primary schools and 336 secondary schools in 1965. All schools have been fully integrated since 1963. Lack of funds and teachers inhibit the expansion of education. The literacy rate is 33 per cent.

One of the three colleges of the University of East Africa is in Nairobi.

**ARMED FORCES.** In 1964 Kenya signed an agreement allowing the British to use Kenyan military facilities in return for aid in establishing a Kenyan air force and navy and rearming the army. The size of its present forces has not been revealed by the government. There is no compulsory service.

# KOREA, NORTH

*Official Name:* Democratic People's Republic of Korea. *Area:* 46,540 square miles. *Population:* 12,-100,000. *Principal City* (with estimated population): Pyongyang, the capital, 1,000,000. *Flag:* A large red center stripe bordered top and bottom by a thin white stripe, then a wider blue stripe. In the left of the center stripe is a white circle enclosing a red five-pointed star. *Monetary Unit:* The won (worth 83.3 U.S. cents).

**LAND AND PEOPLE.** North Korea is bordered on the north by China, on the far northeast by the U.S.S.R., on the east by the Sea of Japan, on the south by South Korea, and on the west by the Yellow Sea and Korea Bay. (See map on page 93.)

The Korean peninsula is mountainous, with the greatest mass in North Korea. Only about 20 per cent of the entire peninsula is suitable for cultivation, with the south possessing the richer regions. Korea's loftiest peak is Mount Paektu (9,003 feet). Most of the northern boundary is formed by North Korea's two principal rivers, the Yalu and the Tumen. Other main rivers are the Taedong, the Chongchon, and the Imjin.

Almost all of the people are Korean and speak Korean. There are about 50,000 non-Koreans, mostly Chinese. Buddhism is tolerated, but the state discourages any religion.

**HISTORY.** Korea's history (see Korea, South) is regionally inseparable until 1945. With the Japanese defeat at the end of World War II, the 38th parallel was established as an administrative convenience, not as a political dividing line. Americans accepted the surrender of Japanese forces in the south, and Soviet forces did the same in the north.

In 1946 the Soviets established the Communist-dominated Provisional People's Committee, which became the basis for the Democratic People's Republic of Korea in 1948. Kim Il-sung, a veteran of abortive guerrilla activities in Manchuria before he fled to the Soviet Union in 1941, was placed at the helm of the political structure. He has been in power ever since.

The Communists attempted to unify the peninsula by force in 1950. The ensuing Korean War lasted for three years and brought nothing but devastation and misery. In 1967 North Korea increased the number of small-scale raids across the demilitarized zone and intensified espionage operations in South Korea.

**GOVERNMENT AND POLITICS.** The structure of the party and government is very similar to that of the Soviet Union. Sovereignty nominally resides with the Supreme People's Assembly, which is elected every four years. However, the party (130,000 members in 1960) exercises tight control over all aspects of the society. Choe Yong-Kon is president of the Presidium of the Assembly.

The degree of totalitarian control is unsurpassed by any other Communist country today. Although all citizens may vote at 18, elections involve a single slate of Communist-approved candidates. Kim Il-sung is concurrently the premier of the country and the secretary-general of the Korean Worker's Party.

North Korea has attempted to draw maximum benefit from the raging dispute between the Soviet Union and Communist China. While the North Korean Communists share many affinities with the Chinese Communists on disputed points of ideology and revolutionary strategies, Pyongyang has been forced to work closely with Moscow because of economic and defense necessities.

**ECONOMY.** Following the truce agreement at Panmunjom in 1953, North Korea adopted a series of plans to reconstruct the war-torn economy. A three-year plan was inaugurated in 1954 and a five-year plan in 1957. Because the goals of the five-year plan were fulfilled in half the allotted time, the year 1960 was set aside as one of adjustment. A very ambitious seven-year plan, launched in 1961, was postponed in 1967 by three years. The leaders blamed the failure of their third plan on the Vietnam war, which allegedly necessitated further expenditure for defense.

North Korea still suffers from a shortage of labor and food. Since the first economic plan in 1954, the regime has taken advantage of the abundant mineral resources (including coal, iron, and lesser amounts of lead, zinc, tungsten, phosphates, barite, gold, and silver) and has placed primary emphasis on heavy industry (fuels, metals, chemicals, and machinery). As a result, the value of industrial production far exceeds that of agriculture.

Most industry in North Korea has been nationalized since 1954, although about 8 per cent is cooperative and 2 per cent private. All farms are collectivized. About 38 per cent of the working population is engaged in industry and about 44 per cent in farming.

The forests are valuable for their timber and wood pulp used by the paper industry. Fishing, once one of the most important sources of employment, has recovered somewhat since the war.

**EDUCATION.** Education is free and compulsory for those 7 to 15 years of age. The literacy rate is about 90 per cent. Schools of higher education are the Kim Il-sung University, the Kim Chack Technical University, Pyongyang Medical School, and the Academy of Science.

**ARMED FORCES.** North Korea has an army of 280,000 men, a navy of 9,020, and an air force of 20,000. Military service is compulsory at age 17.

## KOREA, SOUTH

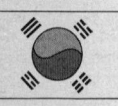

*Official Name:* Republic of Korea. *Area:* 38,004 square miles. *Population:* 29,086,-000. *Principal Cities* (with populations): Seoul, the capital, 3,424,385; Pusan, 1,399,859; Taegu, 787,978; Inchon, 465,158. *Flag:* A white field containing a circular emblem (Chinese yin and yang symbol) that is divided by a curved line into equal halves (red top and blue bottom). At each of the flag's corners is a group of three black parallel lines, divided symbolically. *Monetary Unit:* The won (worth 0.37 U.S. cents). *Gross National Product:* $3,230,000,000 (1965). *Average Annual Income per Person:* $107.

**LAND AND PEOPLE.** South Korea is part of a mountainous peninsula of the Asian mainland that extends southward to the Korea and Cheju straits. On the north is North Korea; on the east, across the Sea of Japan, is Japan; and on the west, across the Yellow Sea, is Communist China. (See map on page 93.)

Almost all the people are Korean and speak Korean, the official language. Of approximately 32,000 non-Koreans, most are Chinese. About 16 per cent of the population are Buddhists; about 5 per cent are Christians (1,300,000 Protestants and 242,000 Roman Catholics).

**HISTORY.** According to Korean legend, Tan'-gun founded Korean civilization about 4,300 years ago. Korea's recorded history began in the 12th century B.C. when a Chinese prince, Ki-tze, founded a colony at Pyongyang. Chinese influence remained until the first century B.C., when three warring tribes (Silla, Koguryo, and Paekche) came into power. Silla conquered its rivals in the seventh century A.D.

In the tenth century a new kingdom, Koryo, overpowered Silla and united the Korean peninsula. Prosperity followed, but in the 13th century the Mongols conquered and devastated the land. They occupied Korea from 1231 to 1260, and the country did not regain national freedom until 1368.

In 1392 the Yi (or Choson) dynasty came to power when Chinese General Yi Sung-Kei seized control of the government. For 200 years thereafter Koreans progressed in spite of internal political strife and Japanese piracies. In 1592 and again in 1598 Japanese Shogun Hideyoshi made unsuccessful attempts to invade Korea. In 1637 Korea fell—not to Japan but to the Manchus of China. Korea became a vassal state, and the Yi dynasty never regained strength. Because of its isolation from the non-Chinese world, Korea became known as the Hermit Kingdom.

However, in 1876 Korea was forced by the Japanese to open her ports to outside trade. Six years later Korea signed a commercial treaty with the United States. In 1895 the Japanese won a war against the Chinese in Korea. Russia tried to acquire Korean territory but was defeated by Japan in 1905. In 1910 Japan formally annexed Korea as a colony.

The Koreans never accepted Japanese domination. In 1919 a government-in-exile was formed in Shanghai under Syngman Rhee. Korea declared war on Japan in 1945, near the end of World War II. Four days later, Russian troops entered the northern part of Korea. A month later, American forces landed in the south. These two countries agreed on a purely administrative dividing line across Korea—the 38th parallel. (See Korea, North.) Efforts toward Korean unification were made at the Moscow Conference (1945) and again by the U.S.-U.S.S.R. Joint Commission on Korea (1946). Neither these attempts nor those of the United Nations were successful.

In 1948 the two separate regimes of North and South Korea were established. Rhee became president of South Korea. U.S. troops were withdrawn by June, 1949; on June 25, 1950, the North Koreans attacked without warning, and the Korean War ensued. An armistice was signed in 1953, but Korea remains divided.

**GOVERNMENT AND POLITICS.** South Korea is a republic. The constitution provides for a president and a one-chamber assembly.

President Rhee served from 1948 to 1960, when charges of election-rigging led to his resignation and subsequent exile. New elections were held, but in less than a year (May 16, 1961) the government was ousted by a military junta. General Chung Hee Park became the political leader. In 1963 he resigned from the military and was elected president. He was re-elected in 1967 amidst a storm of charges of a rigged election.

**ECONOMY.** Agriculture, forestry, and fishing account for over one-third of the gross national product, and manufacturing and construction account for 22 per cent. Only 21 per cent of the land is arable, 80 per cent of which is in grain. Rice is the major crop and most valuable export; barley ranks second. Livestock and poultry are increasing in importance. Progress is being made in the use of scientific farming methods.

The maintenance of a large military force drains one-third of the government's budget, and this is one cause of South Korea's severe imbalance of internal and external payments. U.S. aid to Korea since 1946 has totaled about $4 billion.

**EDUCATION.** Elementary education is compulsory for those 6 to 12 years of age. In 1964 there were 18 teacher-training schools; 110 junior colleges, colleges, and universities; and 863 folk schools to fight adult illiteracy. About 85 per cent of the people are literate.

**ARMED FORCES.** Men may be conscripted at age 20 for two years in the army or three years in the air force and navy. Combined armed forces strength is about 620,000, of whom 560,-000 are in the army.

# KUWAIT

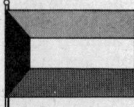

*Official Name:* State of Kuwait. *Area:* 6,178 square miles. *Population:* 467,789. *Principal Cities* (with populations): Kuwait City, 99,633; Hawalli, 64,542; Salmiyah, 38,648. *Flag:* Horizontal green, white and red stripes, with a black trapezoid at the flagstaff. *Monetary Unit:* Kuwaiti dinar of 1,000 fils (worth U.S. $2.80). *Gross National Product:* $1,517,600,000. *Average Annual Income per Person:* $3,076.

**LAND AND PEOPLE.** Kuwait, on the Arabian peninsula, is bordered on the north and west by Iraq, on the east by the Persian Gulf, and on the south by the Neutral Zone region (jointly administered by Kuwait and Saudi Arabia) and by Saudi Arabia. (See map on page 151.) Its capital is a thriving modern city on the shore of Kuwait Bay.

Over 90 per cent of Kuwaiti citizens are Arabs. Non-Kuwaitis, totaling about half the population, are mostly nationals of other Arab countries. The population is 94 per cent Muslim. The official language is Arabic.

**HISTORY.** It is likely that Portuguese sailors and traders, following in the wake of Vasco da Gama, explored the Persian Gulf and established a base where Kuwait City now stands. In the 18th century Arab nomads, familiar with the caravan trade routes of northern Arabia and southern Syria, saw the advantage of sea routes and migrated from northern Arabia to the Gulf coast, where they founded the town of Kuwait. Under the leadership of Sabah Abu Abdullah, who began an emirate there in 1756, and his successors, Kuwait's population grew to several thousand and its prosperity increased greatly.

The British came to Kuwait's aid when it was threatened in the first half of the 19th century by the Wahabi of Arabia, a puritanical Muslim sect that waged holy war against all other forms of Islam. Following a struggle for supremacy by the two great tribal families of the area, the al-Rashids and the Saudis, the latter fled to Kuwait. Emir al-Sabah helped Abdu-l-Aziz ibn Saud regain his territories in central Arabia, which formed the nucleus of modern Saudi Arabia.

In 1897 the emir of Kuwait, fearful that the Turks would extend more than nominal control over his territory, asked the British for protection. An agreement in 1899 made Kuwait a quasi-protectorate of Britain. In 1919 Saudi Arabia invaded Kuwait but was repelled with the help of the British. The Saudis placed a land blockade on Kuwait that lasted 20 years, although in 1922 the two governments established the neutral zones in which they share sovereignty. Britain arranged for a peace treaty between them in 1942.

With the discovery of oil in Kuwait and its development after 1945, Iraq decided in 1952 to review an ancient claim to Kuwait, but it was promptly rejected by the British. By mutual consent the 1899 Britain-Kuwait treaty was revoked in June, 1961, and Kuwait became a fully independent nation. In the face of a new threat of annexation by Iraq, Kuwait received military assistance from Britain and Saudi Arabia. Good relations with Iraq were restored in 1963.

**GOVERNMENT AND POLITICS.** The constitution of November 16, 1962, made Kuwait a constitutionally controlled monarchy, with a hereditary dynasty restricted to the family of al-Sabah. The ruler is vested with full executive power, exercised through a Council of Ministers. Old sheikhly families dominate the executive branch, but the National Assembly, whose 50 members are elected for four-year terms by popular vote, provides a check on arbitrary acts by the ruler and the ruling classes. The present ruler is Sabah al-Salem al-Sabah.

**ECONOMY.** The economy is based on oil. Kuwait's fields have been estimated to hold a quarter of the world's reserves, and the country's gross national product gives the Kuwaitis one of the highest per capita incomes in the world. By 1966 royalties and profits from oil amounted to $5 billion.

Oil concessions are held by the Kuwait National Petroleum Company, owned by the government and Kuwaiti nationals only, and several British, American, and Japanese firms. Kuwait's capital reserves, primarily invested abroad, mostly in London, have been placed by some observers at nearly $2 billion. In 1965 exports amounted to $1,243,000,000, and imports to $377,000.

The Kuwait Fund for the Economic Development of the Arab Countries, established to make loans to other Arab states, was increased in 1966 by 100 per cent to $560 million.

**EDUCATION.** Education, compulsory for an eight-year period, is free from kindergarten through university levels. The Kuwait University was opened in 1967. The literacy rate is 33.9 per cent of the population.

**ARMED FORCES.** Armed forces total about 3,000 men.

## LAOS

*Official Name:* Kingdom of Laos. *Area:* 91,428 square miles. *Population:* 2,700,-000. *Principal Cities* (with populations): Luang Prabang, the capital, 25,000; Vientiane, the administrative capital, 160,000. *Flag:* A red field with a white three-headed elephant. *Monetary Unit:* The kip (worth 0.004 U.S. cent). *Average Annual Income per Person* (estimate): Under $40.

**LAND AND PEOPLE.** Landlocked Laos is bordered on the north by China, on the east by North and South Vietnam, on the south by Cambodia, on the west by Thailand, and on the northwest by Burma. (See map on page 243.)

The country is heavily ridged with mountains, particularly in the north. The Annam range in the east serves as a natural frontier with Vietnam. In the south is the fertile Boloven plateau. Below it are rich, well-watered lowland plains. The Mekong River and its tributaries irrigate much of Laos.

There are two basic racial groups: the Thai (including the predominant Lao) and mountain tribes such as the Kha, Meo, and Yao. Theravada Buddhism, the official faith, is practiced by most lowland Lao; many others practice tribal religions.

**HISTORY.** First settled in the 12th century by refugee Thai tribes from China, Laotian territory was the seat of the Buddhist kingdom of Lan Xang, founded in the mid-14th century. In 1707 the kingdom split into two regions: Luang Prabang in the north, which became subservient to China and Vietnam, and Vientiane in the south, which was annexed by Siam (now Thailand) in 1828. Both regions became parts of a French protectorate in 1893.

France ruled Laos as one of its Indochinese territories until March, 1945, when Japan declared an end to colonial rule. After the Japanese defeat in World War II, Chinese Nationalist troops occupied Laos until French dominance was re-established in 1946. A Franco-Laotian agreement provided for unification of the country's northern and southern kingdoms.

In 1949 Laos became a semi-autonomous state within the French Union. A Communist movement, the Pathet Lao, was created by Prince Souphanouvong in 1950; three years later the Viet Minh (Vietnamese Communists) invaded Laos to assist the Pathet Lao. By December the country was again divided. The international conference at Geneva that ended the Indochina war (1954) brought a cease-fire to Laos, neutralized the country, and called for withdrawal of the Pathet Lao to two northern provinces. Negotiations in 1957 between Laos' premier, Prince Souvanna Phouma, and Prince Souphanouvong led to the formation of a coalition government.

Coups d'etat and a split in the ranks of the military, coupled with an increase in Pathet Lao insurgent activity, threw the country into civil war in 1960. The war—which went badly for the pro-American government forces—ended temporarily in 1962 when the country's three political factions (conservatives, neutralists, and Communists) agreed to a coalition government. The great powers, meeting again at Geneva, agreed to respect the neutrality of Laos. The Pathet Lao renewed fighting in 1963, however.

**GOVERNMENT AND POLITICS.** The nominal head of state is King Savang Vatthana, whose reign began in 1959. The chief of state and premier, reappointed in January, 1967, is Prince Souvanna Phouma, who is backed by a majority of deputies in the National Assembly.

Important sources of political support of the government include the regional military commands, certain families of influence in non-Communist areas, and the majority of the Meo hill tribesmen in Communist-controlled areas.

The Communist Pathet Lao controls about 40 per cent of the country and 25 per cent of the population, but is generally considered too weak to take power without major help from North Vietnam. Its supporters are slowly dwindling in number, and it has actually given up territory while refraining from any major offensive since 1965. Aid from the North Vietnamese has been reduced because of the war in Vietnam.

The most important political development since 1962 has been the disappearance of the neutralist faction, now absorbed by the conservatives. The neutralists' military leader, General Kong Le, went into exile in 1967.

**ECONOMY.** Despite substantial U.S. aid ($55,-000,000 a year, not including military assistance) and international attempts to stabilize the currency, the economy remains underdeveloped.

Farming and livestock raising is at a subsistence level. Rich supplies of commercially valuable timber are not exploited for want of transportation. Industry, limited to light consumer goods, is less developed than in any other Southeast Asian country; most manufactured goods must be imported. Tin mining is important, but other minerals known to be in Laos have not been exploited.

**EDUCATION AND HEALTH.** All children between the ages of 6 and 14 are supposed to attend school, but actually no more than 140,000 students are enrolled in all Laotian schools. Less than 20 per cent of the population is literate.

Malaria and intestinal parasites are the chief health problems of Laos, although other diseases such as tuberculosis and yaws are prevalent. Infant mortality is high.

**ARMED FORCES.** The Laotian armed forces, wholly financed and largely equipped by the United States, number 65,000 men. As many as 5,000 Meo tribesmen, supplied from the air by the U.S., operate behind the lines against the Pathet Lao, whose strength is probably not more than 25,000 men. Aiding the Pathet Lao, however, are an estimated 18,000 to 30,000 North Vietnamese Communists.

# LEBANON

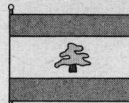

*Official Name:* Republic of Lebanon. *Area:* 4,015 square miles. *Population:* 2,400,-000. *Principal Cities* (with populations): Beirut, the capital, 500,000; Tripoli, 140,000; Saida, 36,000. *Flag:* Red, white, and red, with a green cedar tree in the white stripe. *Monetary Unit:* The Lebanese pound of 100 piasters (worth 33 U.S. cents). *Gross National Product:* $1,120,000,000. *Average Annual Income per Person:* $400.

**LAND AND PEOPLE.** Lebanon, situated on the western edge of the Asian continent, is bordered on the north and east by Syria, on the south by Israel, and on the west by the Mediterranean Sea. (See map on page 151.) The Lebanon Mountains dominate the country; the Anti-Lebanon Range on the east forms much of the boundary with Syria. Between the ranges in the central interior is a fertile plain known as the Bica. Principal rivers are the Litani and Orantes.

The majority of Lebanon's inhabitants are Arabs. Religious groups include Sunni, Shiites, and Druzes (all Muslim), and Greek Orthodox, Maronites, Greek Catholics, and Armenians.

**HISTORY.** Hittite and Aramaean kingdoms occupied the region of Lebanon in ancient times. They were followed by the maritime empire of the Phoenicians that reached the peak of prosperity about 1000 B.C. Persians, Assyrians, Babylonians, Egyptians, and the Greeks under Alexander the Great fought by turns for the area. In time it came under Roman rule along with Syria. A Christian sect, the Maronites, settled there around the 7th century A.D., and while Syria became Muslim, Lebanon remained mainly Christian during the spread of Islam.

After long periods of warfare, Lebanese trade was stimulated by the unification of the Middle East under the Ottoman Empire. Egyptian occupation in 1832 increased tension between the Maronites and the Islamic Druzes who had settled in the south during the 11th century. Fearing annihilation, the Christians called for help from Europe in 1860; European powers forced the Ottomans to grant autonomy to the area, and the province of Mount Lebanon was created in 1864.

After World War I France received a mandate over Lebanon, where tension between Muslims and Christians continued to pose problems. Declared a republic in 1926, the country was promised independence by 1939 in a treaty never ratified by France. Vichy French control was broken during World War II by British and Free French forces. In 1945 Lebanon won its independence and joined the United Nations.

Opposition to policies of President Camille Chamoun led to large-scale rioting in 1958. U.S. military forces, sent at Lebanese request by President Dwight Eisenhower, withdrew soon after the formation of a new government under a compromise presidential candidate.

Lebanon's role in the Arab-Israeli wars of 1948, 1956, and 1967 was minimal, despite its membership in the Arab League.

Lebanon favored the United States stand during the Cuban missile crisis of 1961.

**GOVERNMENT AND POLITICS.** Lebanon is a republic, with a unicameral legislature. Its president, who serves for a term of six years, must be a Maronite Christian; the prime minister, a presidential appointee, must be a Sunni Muslim; and by a similar convention the speaker of the National Assembly is a Shiite and the minister of war a Druze. The foreign minister is usually Greek Orthodox. The size of the assembly is always a multiple of eleven so as to maintain the ratio of six Christians to five Muslims. Political parties are less important than personalities and religious affiliations.

**ECONOMY.** Lebanon benefits greatly from tourism, from its banking and commercial services—especially those it offers the oil-rich countries of the Middle East—and from remittances of foreign capital by Lebanese working abroad.

Capital has been invested to improve agriculture, which has not been very productive. Special emphasis has been placed on the production of fruit, an important export.

Distribution of the national income is fairly even, except among the rural population. Lebanon's standard of living is the highest of any Arab country.

**EDUCATION AND HEALTH.** Lebanon has a literacy rate of 75 per cent. Free primary education was instituted in 1960. Beirut has three excellent universities.

The country has some 100 hospitals and, in 1962, about 1,700 doctors.

**ARMED FORCES.** The Lebanese armed forces total approximately 18,000. Military service is not compulsory.

# LESOTHO

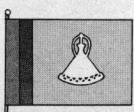

*Official Name:* Kingdom of Lesotho. *Area:* 11,716 square miles. *Population:* 976,000. *Principal Cities* (with populations): Maseru, the capital, 9,000; Leribe, Mafeteng, and Teyateyaneng, each with fewer than 5,000. *Flag:* Stripes of green and red (left), with a white Basuto hat on a blue field. *Monetary Unit:* The South African rand of 100 cents (worth U.S. $1.40). *Gross National Product:* $50,000,000 (1966). *Average Annual Income per Person:* $64.

**LAND AND PEOPLE.** Totally surrounded by the Republic of South Africa, Lesotho (formerly Basutoland) is a rugged, mile-high, plateau country nestled amid the 11,000-foot peaks of the Drakensberg Range. (See map on page 111.) The climate is temperate, with temperature averaging 45° F. in July and 70° F. in January.

The people are Basuto, and they speak English and African dialects. In religion they are mainly Roman Catholic (34 per cent) and French Protestant (22 per cent).

**HISTORY.** The Basuto nation came into being in the 1820s when remnants of clans scattered by Zulu and Matabele invasions united under the strong leadership of Moshoeshoe I. In 1867 the Basuto requested British protection against Boer advances from South Africa, and in 1868 British sovereignty was established. Internal self-government was introduced in 1964; independence was granted on October 4, 1966.

**GOVERNMENT AND POLITICS.** Lesotho is a constitutional monarchy with a bicameral parliament. Moshoeshoe II is the king, and Chief Leabua Jonathan is prime minister.

There are three important political parties: the ruling Nationalist Party, which is conservative; the more radical Pan-African Congress Party; and the small royalist Marematlou Freedom Party. A severe constitutional struggle has developed over the king's desire for more power. The Nationalist Party government has taken a militantly anti-Communist line, refusing aid from and diplomatic relations with Communist states.

**ECONOMY.** Most of the population survives by subsistence farming on the one-fifth of the land that is arable. Not enough is grown to feed the population. About half of the adult labor force works as unskilled migrant laborers in South Africa. Known natural resources are sparse, except for diamonds and hydroelectric capacity. Wool and mohair are chief exports.

All consumer and capital goods, and some agricultural commodities, must be imported, mostly from South Africa. Lesotho is a member of the Rand currency area and of a customs union with South Africa.

**EDUCATION.** The Basuto are among the best-educated Africans. Their literacy rate is 40 per cent. Education is not compulsory. Higher education is provided by what was formerly the Pius II Catholic College at Roma, now independent and non-denominational.

**ARMED FORCES.** The only armed force is a police force of about 900 men.

# LIBERIA

*Official Name:* Republic of Liberia. *Area:* 43,900 square miles. *Population:* 1,016,-443. *Principal Cities* (with populations): Monrovia, the capital, 80,992; Harbel, 31,-730; Buchanan, 11,909; Harper, 7,613. *Flag:* Alternating stripes of red and white, with a blue square containing a white star. *Monetary Unit:* The U.S. dollar. *Gross National Product:* $213,000,000 (1965). *Average Annual Income per Person:* $200.

**LAND AND PEOPLE.** Liberia, situated on the west coast of Africa, is bordered on the north by French Guinea, on the east by the Ivory Coast, on the south and southwest by the Atlantic Ocean, and on the northwest by Sierra Leone. (See map on page 111.) The climate is tropical.

The population is composed chiefly of indigenous Liberians and American-Liberians. The former, living mostly in the interior, include some 30 tribes such as the Kru, Bassa, and Gio; the latter, usually coastal dwellers, are descended from freed American Negro slaves who first colonized Liberia. American-Liberians, a ruling minority elite, control the country although they make up less than 5 per cent of its population. English is the official language. Christianity is the state religion, but many ancient tribal languages and customs have survived.

**HISTORY.** The colony of Liberia was founded by liberated American Negro slaves in 1822. It was intended as an African homeland for American Negroes by the National Colonization Society, a white abolitionist group whose agents governed the area until 1847, when the independent Republic of Liberia was established.

Despite difficulties with the tribal populations at home, pressures for colonization from abroad, and heavy indebtedness to foreign banks, Liberia maintained its independence. Beginning in 1926, in exchange for a U.S. loan, it allowed American investment to develop rubber plantations on Liberian soil and acquired a solid footing for its economy. U.S. and foreign investments multiplied after World War II.

Liberia, a charter member of the United Nations, has always enjoyed warm relations with the United States.

**GOVERNMENT AND POLITICS.** Liberia's constitution and government are modeled after those of the United States. Presidents are elected for an eight-year term; re-election is for four years. Voters must be property owners of Negro blood. The sole political party, the True Whigs, has held power since 1877. Liberia has made great progress under William V. S. Tubman, its president since 1946; he is responsible for many social, political, and economic reforms.

**ECONOMY.** Forestry, fishing, livestock breeding, and agriculture occupy over 80% of the population. Farming is inefficient, and much food must be imported. Since early in the 1960s the mining of iron ore has been the leading industry. Iron and rubber, of which Liberia is a major world producer, together account for 90 per cent of the country's exports and its favorable balance of trade. The railroads, privately owned, serve chiefly to transport iron ore. An important source of capital is the registry of foreign ships under the Liberian flag; the country's merchant fleet, totaling 22,598,000 registered tons, is the world's largest.

The government's "open door" policy has encouraged foreign investments. Liberia is a leader among Africa's developing nations.

**EDUCATION.** In two decades Liberia has reduced its illiteracy rate from 96 to 86 per cent. The largest single budget appropriation in 1966 was for education.

**ARMED FORCES.** The armed forces consist of the National Guard (3,200 men), the Militia (10,000 men) and a Coast Guard. Military service begins at age 16. The United States provides technical assistance.

## LIBYA

*Official Name:* The United Kingdom of Libya. *Area:* 679,701 square miles. *Population:* 1,677,000. *Principal Cities* (with populations): Tripoli, a capital, 213,506; Bengasi, also a capital, 137,295. *Flag:* Red, black, and green, with a white crescent and star. *Monetary Unit:* Libyan pound of 100 piasters (worth U.S. $2.80). *Gross National Product:* $876,000,000 (1965). *Average Annual Income per Person:* $828.

**LAND AND PEOPLE.** Situated on the central African shore of the Mediterranean Sea, Libya consists of a narrow, fertile strip of coastal land and a vast desert hinterland. It is bounded by Egypt and the Sudan on the east, Tunisia and Algeria on the west, the Mediterranean Sea on the north, and Niger and Chad on the south. (See map on page 111.) The nation is divided into the provinces of Tripolitania, Cyrenaica, and Fezzan.

Libya enjoys a moderate climate except in summer, when temperatures soar to over 100° F. on the coast and higher inland. Rainfall is light in all parts of the country. Mountain areas near the coast receive 15 to 20 inches of rain annually, but other sections receive less than six inches. Droughts are frequent.

Most Libyans are of Arab and Berber descent; Arabic is the official language. There is a small percentage of Italians, Greeks, and Jews. Of the 45,000 Italians in the population, most are settled in Tripolitania. Over 95 per cent of Libyans are Muslims.

**HISTORY.** In ancient times Tripolitania and Cyrenaica existed as separate political units. Tripolitania fell under Carthaginian and Roman influences, and Cyrenaica was colonized by the Greeks. United by the Romans in the first century A.D., the provinces were separated again two centuries later, with Tripolitania joining the Western Roman Empire and Cyrenaica joining the Eastern.

In the seventh century A.D. the provinces were invaded by Arabs. Berbers, who comprised most of the existing population, were Islamized, and Arab immigration brought about the dominance of Arab culture and influence. In the 16th century Tripolitania and Cyrenaica fell under Ottoman rule, although administrative autonomy was enjoyed by local rulers.

Ottoman control ended with occupation by Italy in 1911. Under Mussolini, Italian rule was extended to Fezzan, and in 1935 the country was declared the Fourth Shore of Italy. Italian authority, however, was staunchly resisted by a local religious movement known as the Sanusi order. The resistance was crushed for a time, but the movement's leaders recovered their homeland during World War II with the aid of British forces. When the Allied powers disagreed on the future of Libya in the post-war period, the question was referred to the United Nations. In 1949 the U.N. declared Libya ready for independence, and in 1951 independence became a fact with adoption of a constitution.

For a decade following independence the nation depended heavily on foreign economic aid, especially from the United States and Britain. In return for assistance, both powers were granted rights to establish air bases near Tripoli and al-Adem. Meanwhile, the country was developing oil resources and in 1961 began exporting crude oil. No longer dependent on foreign aid, the government pressed for the evacuation of foreign bases. U.S. forces began to withdraw from bases during June 1967.

**GOVERNMENT AND POLITICS.** The Libyan constitution provides for a House of Representatives (91 members) elected on the basis of universal suffrage; an appointed Senate (42 members); and a cabinet appointed by the king (King Idris I, since 1951) but responsible to the House of Representatives. There are no political parties.

**ECONOMY.** Despite increasing oil royalties, Libya is essentially an agricultural country. The principal products, mainly for local consumption, are cereals, dates, almonds, and citrus fruits. Major food exports include olives, peanuts, almonds, and fish.

Oil development accelerated rapidly in 1966, with 15 petroleum companies exploring or producing. Two refineries were built, and several oil pipelines are under construction. Oil royalties in 1966 amounted to over $476,000,000. Plans are being made to use recent gas discoveries for local consumption.

The government has recently undertaken extensive development programs financed by the increasing oil revenues.

**EDUCATION AND HEALTH.** The literacy rate is about 35 per cent. Education is compulsory from age 6 through 12, and public school education is free. The Libyan University was founded in 1956.

Infant mortality remains high; gastroenteritis, trachoma, and tuberculosis are the major health problems. In 1966 the country had 291 doctors.

**ARMED FORCES.** A compulsory military service law has been enacted but not enforced. About 7,000 men are in service.

## LIECHTENSTEIN

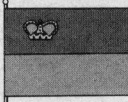

*Official Name:* Principality of Liechtenstein. *Area:* 61.8 square miles. *Population:* 19,304. *Principal Cities* (with populations): Vaduz, the capital, 3,775; Schaan, 3,480; Balzers, 2,464. *Flag:* Blue and red, with a gold crown in the blue stripe. *Monetary Unit:* Swiss franc (worth 23.1 U.S. cents).

**LAND AND PEOPLE.** Situated in western Europe, Liechtenstein is bordered by Austria on the east and Switzerland on the north, south, and west. (See map on page 117.) Warm winds protect the country from temperature extremes.

About 95 per cent of the people are of Germanic origin, with German the leading language. Roman Catholicism claims 92 per cent of the people.

**HISTORY.** The Barony of Schellenberg and the County of Vaduz, founded in 814, were bought by Johann Adam von Liechtenstein in 1699 and 1712. The Holy Roman Emperor joined the two areas to create the Principality of Liechtenstein in 1719.

Following French and Russian invasions during the Napoleonic wars, Liechtenstein joined the German Confederation in 1815. Ties with Austria developed, leading to withdrawal from the Confederation in 1866. After World War I the country aligned itself with Switzerland. Since 1924 Switzerland has controlled the principality's defense, foreign affairs, and customs.

**GOVERNMENT AND POLITICS.** Liechtenstein is a constitutional monarchy ruled since 1938 by Prince Franz Josef II. He may convene and dismiss the 15-member parliament, elected every four years by male voters, and may propose legislation. The Progressive Citizens' Party, the majority political group, and the Fatherland Union hold all parliament seats. The prime minister and his deputy, chosen respectively from the majority and minority parties in parliament, serve six-year terms.

**ECONOMY.** Liechtenstein has become one of the most highly industrialized states in Europe, with 57 per cent of the people working in a variety of light industries. The tourist industry is also important. Postage stamps, yielding $1 million annually, are a leading source of government revenue.

Because of the principality's favorable tax policies, more than 20,000 businesses have incorporated in Liechtenstein since 1921 and have established nominal business headquarters there. A resident of Liechtenstein, however, must serve as a director of each firm.

**EDUCATION AND HEALTH.** Liechtenstein provides free education through age 18, and schooling is compulsory to age 14. The literacy rate is about 98 per cent.

There are ten physicians. Old age, survivors', and health insurance are compulsory.

**ARMED FORCES.** There is no army. The country has a defense agreement with Switzerland.

# LUXEMBOURG

*Official Name:* Grand Duchy of Luxembourg. *Area:* 999 square miles. *Population:* 336,000. *Principal Cities* (with populations): Luxembourg, the capital, 76,500; Esch-Alzette, 30,000. *Flag:* A horizontal tricolor of red, white, and blue. *Monetary Unit:* The Luxembourg franc (worth 2 U.S. cents). *Gross National Product:* $628,000,000 (1965). *Average Annual Income per Person:* $1,497.

**LAND AND PEOPLE.** Luxembourg, a tiny landlocked kingdom in northwest Europe, is bordered on the north and west by Belgium, on the east by Germany, and on the south by France. (See map on page 117.)

The Bon Pays (Good Land) lowlands rise gradually from the Luxembourg-Lorraine iron-mining basin in the southwest to the Ardennes Plateau in the north, reaching maximum altitudes of 800 to 1,200 feet. There are several rivers in the country, draining generally eastward into the Sauer River, which in turn flows into the Moselle River on the eastern border.

About 89 per cent of the population is of mixed Gallo-Germanic background. The population is 94 per cent Roman Catholic. French is the official language; German and Luxembourgeois are also spoken.

**HISTORY.** Luxembourg began as a feudal domain in 963 A.D. In 1308 the Count of Luxembourg became Holy Roman Emperor Henry VII, and in 1354 Luxembourg was raised to a duchy. After 1443 it was ruled at various times by Burgundy, Spain, Austria, and France. In 1482 Luxembourg passed to the House of Hapsburg, and for two centuries it was a part of the Spanish, and later Austrian, Netherlands.

French troops occupied the country in the 1700s, and in 1797 it was formally ceded to France. However, in 1815 the Congress of Vienna made Luxembourg a grand duchy as part of the union with Holland and Belgium in the Kingdom of the Netherlands, and a member of the German Confederation. After Belgium won its independence from the Netherlands, it annexed part of the grand duchy in 1839—the present Belgian province of Luxembourg. Although Luxembourg lost more than half its territory, it gained a large measure of autonomy, although the Dutch ruler remained grand duke. When William III died in 1890, the Dutch throne passed to his daughter Wilhelmina, but the grand duchy went to Duke Adolph of Nassau. The present ruler is Grand Duke Jean, a descendant of Duke Adolph.

**GOVERNMENT AND POLITICS.** Luxembourg is a constitutional monarchy with a bicameral legislature. The 56-member Chamber of Deputies is elected by universal suffrage for five-year terms. The Council of State, 21 members appointed for life by the sovereign, is primarily advisory. The prime minister and his cabinet are also named by the sovereign.

Government since World War II has been by coalition, with the Christian Social Party supplying all the premiers and forming the coalition cabinets. Pierre Werner has been premier since 1959.

**ECONOMY.** Rich iron deposits have made mining and metallurgy Luxembourg's largest industries, accounting for 30 per cent of the national product, 75 per cent of industrial production, and 85 per cent of exports. Luxembourg is the world's eighth largest steel producer.

Mining and manufacturing employ 35.2 per cent of the labor force and account for 47 per cent of the gross national product (GNP). Agriculture employs 15 per cent of the labor force and accounts for 8 per cent of the GNP.

**EDUCATION.** Education is compulsory for children from 6 to 14. The literacy rate is about 97 per cent.

**ARMED FORCES.** Compulsory military service was abolished in 1967. There is a 3,000-man army, committed to NATO.

# MALAGASY REPUBLIC

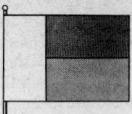

*Official Name:* Malagasy Republic. *Area:* 228,000 square miles. *Population:* 6,335,810. *Principal Cities* (with populations): Tananarive, the capital, 298,813; Majunga, 50,000; Tamatave, 48,000; Tuléar, 40,000; Diégo-Suarez, 39,000; Fianarantsoa, 37,598; Antsirabé, 30,000. *Flag:* A white vertical stripe bordered by horizontal stripes of red and green. *Monetary Unit:* Malagasy franc (worth 0.4 U.S. cents). *Gross National Product:* $578,000,000 (1966). *Average Annual Income per Person:* $145.

**LAND AND PEOPLE.** The Malagasy Republic comprises the world's fourth-largest island, Madagascar, and a few small neighboring islands in the Indian Ocean near the southeast coast of Africa. (See map on page 111.) Madagascar is 980 miles long from north to south, and 360 miles wide at its widest point. The west coast is deeply indented and is bordered by a lowland, which rises in a series of steps to a central plateau, surmounted by Mount Maromokotra in the north and by Mount Tsiafajavona in the Ankaratra Mountains in the center. The climate ranges from sub-tropical to temperate: hot and humid on the coast, hot and dry in the south, and cool in the central highlands.

The Malagasy, a people of mixed Indonesian-African-Arab descent, constitute the vast majority of the population. Historically, they have been subdivided into various groups, the largest of which are the Merina, Betsimisaraka, Betsileo, Tsimihety, Sakalava, Antaisaka, Antandroy, Bara, and Tanala. There are also small foreign communities of French, Chinese, and Asian Indians.

Languages spoken are Malagasy and French. About 30% of the people, especially the Merina and others in central Madagascar, are Christians; about 1.3% are Muslim; and the remaining 68.7% follow tribal religions.

**HISTORY.** People migrated to Madagascar from the southwest Pacific before the Christian era and continued until the 15th century. These immigrants, later known as the Merina, settled mainly in the central highlands. The coastal regions were colonized by immigrants from Africa and Arabia. In the 16th and 17th centuries, the Merina kingdom became the strongest on the island and later ruled over most of Madagascar.

Madagascar came to the attention of Europeans in the 16th century and attracted French and English traders and pirates in the 17th and 18th centuries. In the 19th century King Radama I (reigned 1810–28) allowed English and French missionaries to open churches and schools and they wrote down the Malagasy language. Queen Ranavalona I (reigned 1828–61) expelled the Europeans, but they returned after her death. Dissension between the Merina rulers and the French culminated in the wars of 1883–85 and 1895–96. Madagascar became a French colony in 1896.

Under Merina leadership the Malagasy began agitating for independence during World War I. In 1945–46 the French granted the Malagasy certain financial powers and the right to elect members to an assembly and representatives to the French Parliament. Nationalist agitation increased, however, and in 1947 an armed revolt broke out that was finally crushed by the French in 1949.

Between 60,000 and 90,000 people perished during the conflict, and the nationalist movement was severely disrupted. A peaceful period followed, and in 1960 Madagascar was granted independence under a conservative government that preserved close economic, political, and military ties with France.

**GOVERNMENT AND POLITICS.** Executive power is vested in a president, who is elected by universal suffrage for a seven-year term. Legislative power is exercised by a bicameral parliament: a National Assembly of 107 members elected by popular vote, and a Senate of 54 members, one-third of them appointed by the government, and two-thirds indirectly elected by provincial and local authorities. The country is divided into six administrative provinces.

The dominant political party is the P.S.D. or Social Democratic Party, which favors close ties with France and the West. Its leader is the country's first president, Philibert Tsiranana, who was re-elected to a second term in 1965. Only one important opposition party exists: the A.K.F.M., or Party of the Congress of Independence, which has a more radical socialist program. This party represents mostly the Merina and Betsileo minority. The small Communist Party lacks influence and is split into factions.

**ECONOMY.** The economy is almost completely based on agriculture and is dependent on large-scale aid from France and other European countries.

Exports consist mainly of farm products, with coffee the most important, followed by vanilla, sisal, and sugar. The chief food crop is rice, almost all of which is consumed locally. There is some industry: sugar, meat, hides, sisal, and ores are processed for export; textiles, cigarettes, soap, shoes, beverages, and sacks are manufactured for domestic use.

Mineral resources are diversified, but many are too small to warrant mining. The most important minerals are graphite and mica. Some uranium, gold, chromite, semi-precious stones, iron, and coal are also mined.

**EDUCATION AND HEALTH.** Education is not compulsory. About 47 per cent of school-age children attend school. The literacy rate for ages 14 and over is estimated at 33.5%. A university was opened in 1961 in Tananarive, the capital.

The infant mortality rate is estimated at 676 per thousand. There were 628 doctors in 1966 to take care of the six million-plus population.

**ARMED FORCES.** Military and civic service are compulsory for all citizens over 20. In 1966 there were 3,000 men in the army.

France maintains military bases in the country and, with West Germany, provides training and equipment for the Malagasy forces.

## MALAWI

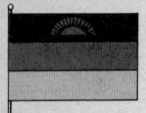

*Official Name:* Republic of Malawi. *Area:* 46,066 square miles. *Population:* 4,042,412. *Principal Cities* (with populations): Zomba, the capital, 19,616; Blantyre-Limbe, 109,795; Lilongwe, 19,176. *Flag:* Black, red, and green, with a red rising sun on the black stripe. *Monetary Unit:* Malawi pound (worth U.S. $2.8065). *Gross National Product:* $163,000,000 (1965). *Average Annual Income per Person:* $49.39.

**LAND AND PEOPLE.** An independent country of southeast Africa, Malawi—formerly Nyasaland —comprises a narrow strip of land bordering on Zambia, Tanzania, and Mozambique. (See map on page 111.)

Lake Nyasa drains southward through southern Malawi. To the west of Lake Nyasa rise the steep escarpments of the Rift Valley. In southern Malawi are the Shire Highlands, surmounted by Mount Zomba and Mount Mlanje.

The climate is tropical. In July (mid-winter) temperatures range from 53° F. to 72° F. In the rainy season (November to April) temperatures range from 65° F. to 80° F. Annual precipitation varies from 30 inches in the central plains to 80 inches in the mountain areas.

The population consists almost entirely of Africans; members of Bantu tribes and Yao and Ngoni groups comprise 99.9 per cent of the total. There are about 7,050 Europeans and 12,000 Asians and Eur-Africans. The official language is English; the African languages are Chinyanja, Chitumbuka (northern provinces), and Yao. About 35 per cent (724,000) of the people are Christian; 30 per cent (500,000) are Muslim. Most of the remaining population practice tribal religions.

**HISTORY.** For several centuries Lake Nyasa attracted Bantu tribes from the northwest. In the early 19th century the Ngoni arrived from the south after the Boer and British northward expansion had dispersed Zulu groups. The Portuguese explored the country in the 17th and 18th centuries, and David Livingstone explored it extensively in 1859. British missionaries arrived in the 19th century, accompanied by Scottish traders who competed in the ivory trade and attempted to counteract the dual ivory and slave trade conducted by the Lake Nyasa Arabs. Britain established the Nyasaland protectorate in 1891.

The first anticolonial demonstration occurred in 1915. John Chilembwe, an American-trained priest, led an armed revolt (partially a religious protest) against the British. The British crushed the rebellion.

In 1953 Nyasaland was forced by the British into the Central African Federation with Northern Rhodesia and Southern Rhodesia. A few social services resulted—post offices and health clinics—but no productive investment. The Nyasaland African Congress (NAC), founded in 1944, opposed the federation. The NAC gained great strength in 1958 when its leaders recalled Dr. Hastings Kamuzu Banda from 40 years' study and work in the United States, Britain, and Ghana.

Banda organized the first major challenge to the federation. The British, faced with rising protests, declared an emergency in 1959. They outlawed the NAC and imprisoned Banda and 1,200 of his followers. Other followers, however, pursued the nationalist movement and built up the Malawi Congress Party, and they persuaded the British to release Banda in 1960. Through negotiations with the British, Nyasaland gained self-government within the federation in 1962, and the federation was dissolved in 1963. Nyasaland became independent as the state of Malawi on July 6, 1964.

**GOVERNMENT AND POLITICS.** Malawi became a republic on July 6, 1966. Governmental powers are vested in President Banda (who is also Minister of External Affairs) and a cabinet of 11 ministers. The legislature consists of a National Assembly of 50 elected members plus a maximum of five other members who are nominated by the president to represent minorities and other special interests. The Malawi Congress Party, which has chosen Banda as its life president, holds all the elected seats in the National Assembly.

A crisis occurred in the party in 1964 when certain senior ministers differed with Banda. An attempted coup was unsuccessful, and Banda was able to resolve dissension within his party. However, he is still faced with considerable opposition from exile groups.

**ECONOMY.** The economy is entirely based on agriculture. Four crops—tea, tobacco, groundnuts, and cotton—account for 90 per cent of exports which, in 1966, amounted to $39,000,-000. Major exports are tea and tobacco.

African farmers recently broke the monopoly of white planters in growing tea. In 1966 tea production increased greatly, as did production of groundnuts. Cotton is usually grown by African tenant farmers; the 1966 crop was drastically cut by drought. Fire-cured tobacco is produced mainly by Africans; the 1966 quota was deliberately cut. Sugarcane has become an important crop. The Blantyre textile mill, completed in 1967, has encouraged industrial investment.

Because of Malawi's dense population (110 per square mile) and lack of industrial jobs, 330,000 men have left Malawi and are working in Rhodesia, South Africa, and Zambia. A 1964–69 development plan to improve northern territory could, however, reverse the exodus of workers.

**EDUCATION AND HEALTH.** Only 6.5 per cent of the African population over 14 was estimated to be literate in 1960. There is no compulsory education. In 1966, 38,000 people completed the eight-year primary course. There are 36 secondary schools, with approximately 8,000 students. The young University of Malawi now has more than 480 students.

The infant mortality rate is estimated at 148 per 1,000.

**ARMED FORCES.** The armed forces, which consist of two infantry battalions (Malawi Rifles), number approximately 800 volunteers.

# MALAYSIA

*Official Name:* Federation of Malaysia. *Area:* 128,429 square miles. *Population:* 9,711,000. *Principal Cities* (with populations): Kuala Lumpur, the capital, 477,000; George Town, 235,000; Ipoh, 127,000; Kuching, 51,000: Jesselton, 22,000. *Flag:* Alternating red and white stripes, one for each constituent state; on a blue field is a gold crescent and a gold star with one point for each state. *Monetary Unit:* The Malaysian dollar (worth 33 U.S. cents). *Gross National Product:* $3,000,000,000 (1966). *Average Annual Income per Person:* $307.

**LAND AND PEOPLE.** Malaysia is composed of the Federation of Malaya, on the Malay Peninsula, and the states of Sabah and Sarawak, in northern Borneo. Malaya is bordered on the east by the South China Sea, on the south by the Strait of Johore, on the west by the Strait of Malacca and the Andaman Sea, and on the north by Thailand. Sarawak and Sabah are bordered on the south by Indonesia's Kalimantan Province; in the west, north, and east are the South China Sea, Pacific Ocean, and Celebes Sea. (See map on page 243.)

Malaysia's climate is equatorial. Its flora and fauna are those of tropical rain forests and jungles, except in the mountainous regions. Malaya consists mostly of swamps and jungles, except for a mountain range in the north. Sabah and Sarawak have alluvial coastal plains that rise to mountain ranges.

Malaysia's population is 45% Malay, 36% Chinese, 9.5% Indian and Pakistani, and 8% aboriginal. In 1967 the controversial National Language Bill made Malay the sole official language in western Malaysia; English is permitted, however, for some government business. Islam is the official religion of the Federation, but Malay has large Hindu, Confucian-Buddhist, and Christian communities. The native population of the Borneo states are mainly animists.

**HISTORY.** The Federation of Malaysia grouping Malaya and the former British colonies of Singapore, Sarawak, and British North Borneo (renamed Sabah shortly after its entry into the Federation) was created in September, 1963. Singapore withdrew from the Federation in August, 1965.

Europeans first arrived on the Malay Peninsula in the 16th century. In 1786 the British East India Company leased the island of Penang; in the 19th century it acquired control over Malacca and Singapore; and all three colonies, known as the Straits Settlements, came under joint Colonial Office administration in 1867. After 1874 British advisers were established in the mainland Malayan sultanates. Early in the 20th century Malaya's rubber and tin industries drew immigrants from China and India. During World War II the Japanese overran the area.

In 1946 Singapore became a crown colony, and the Union of Malaya was formed, uniting Penang and Malacca with the nine Malay states. The Union became the Federation of Malaya in 1948. Communist insurrection erupted the same year, and guerrillas terrorized the countryside until finally brought under control in 1959 with the aid of British troops. In 1957 the Federation of Malaya gained its independence within the Commonwealth of Nations.

Both North Borneo and Sarawak were drawn into the British commercial sphere in the 19th century. North Borneo was exploited by a private commercial company. Sarawak, ceded in 1841 by the Sultan of Brunei to Sir James Brooke, the "white rajah," became the private property of the Brooke family. Both territories enjoyed the protection of the British government, and following Japanese occupation in World War II, both acquired crown colony status.

In 1961 Malaya's Prime Minister Tunku Abdul Rahman, fearing the creation of an independent Singapore controlled by pro-Communist forces, proposed a plan to unite Malaya, Sarawak, North Borneo, and Brunei under the name of Malaysia. With Singapore incorporated as a Malaysian state, Rahman's government could presumably take control over internal security there. The mixed population of the three Borneo states would offset the racial imbalance of predominantly Chinese Singapore, assuring the continued dominance of Rahman's government. President Sukarno of Indonesia was openly hostile to the proposal because he believed Malaysia was a "neo-colonist" creation of the British and an obstacle to the triumph of anti-colonial forces in Asia. Simultaneously the Philippines advanced a territorial claim to Sabah. Indonesian-Filipino opposition persisted even after the creation of Malaysia, without Brunei, in 1963. Premier Sukarno, charging that Sarawak and Sabah had been forced into the union, threatened to "crush Malaysia." Border fighting broke out, and about a thousand pro-Communist Sarawak Chinese entered Kalimantan for guerrilla training by the Indonesian Army. Anti-government riots within the Federation were blamed on Indonesian influence. Malaysia turned to the British for military support.

At the same time acute tensions developed between Rahman's Malay-dominated Alliance government and the predominantly Chinese government of Singapore, headed by Prime Minister Lee Kuan Yew, leader of the democratic socialist People's Action Party (P.A.P.). Conflict also developed over separate plans for industrialization prepared by the two governments. In 1964 the P.A.P. challenged the Alliance in mainland parliamentary elections, arousing Malay fears of future Chinese political domination. Two serious racial riots in Singapore resulted. Abruptly in August, 1965, Rahman decided that only Singapore's expulsion from Malaysia could prevent even graver racial outbreaks. Reluctantly P.A.P. leaders proclaimed an independent Singapore.

Sukarno's gradual political eclipse in 1966 brought a shift in Indonesian foreign policies.

Jakarta's new military leaders dropped the campaign to crush Malaysia, and peaceful relations were resumed through the Bangkok Agreement of 1966. Another year elapsed, however, before full diplomatic relations were restored.

Relations between Malaysia and Singapore remained troubled, however. Each imposed trade and immigration restrictions on the other, and in 1967 the two states adopted separate currencies for the first time. The fact that Singapore joined Malaysia in a Southeast Asian economic association under Indonesian auspices may foreshadow a change in these relations.

Significant states' rights movements developed in Sarawak and Sabah. An ousted minister in Sarawak and a dissident party leader in Sabah both called for increased state autonomy, while avoiding outright separatist claims.

**GOVERNMENT AND POLITICS.** The Federation's constitution is based on that of the Federation of Malaya, adopted in 1957. The heads of the nine Malay states—excluding Malacca and Penang, which are under a governor's rule—choose from among themselves the supreme head of the Malaysian state and his deputy, both of whom serve five-year terms. The bicameral legislature consists of a Senate, elected for a term of six years, and a House of Representatives, elected for a maximum of five years. The head of the Malaysian state may dissolve the house at any time on the advice of his ministers. The prime minister (Tunku Abdul Rahman in 1967) plays a key role in government.

The Alliance Party, a coalition with generally moderate and anti-Communist views, won a large majority in the house in the Federation's first election, held in 1964.

**ECONOMY.** Malaya's economy is based on rubber and tin, which together account for a large percentage of total exports. Agricultural products include rice, food crops, oil palms, tea, and spices. There are deposits of bauxite, iron ore, and other minerals. Sabah exports some rubber, but its chief export is timber. Sarawak, an exporter of rubber, timber, spices, bauxite, and some crude oil, must import a sizable portion of its rice. It has deposits of gold, phosphate, and limestone.

In 1966 a new five-year Malaysian plan for economic development was adopted, calling for diversification of agriculture and of industry to overcome the region's traditional dependence on rubber and tin. The plan will also provide jobs for the rapidly expanding population.

**EDUCATION AND HEALTH.** The literacy rate is 50 per cent in Malaya, where a primary education is compulsory; in the two Borneo states the rate is 25 per cent.

Infant mortality is high; tuberculosis, malaria, dysentery, diphtheria, enteric fever, and yaws are prevalent. The Federation has about 1,200 physicians, most of them in Malaya.

**ARMED FORCES.** There is no compulsory military service in Malaysia. Armed forces total 30,000 men, plus 15,000 territorials and some naval reserves.

## MALDIVE ISLANDS

*Official Name:* The Kingdom of Islands. *Area:* 115 square miles. *Population:* 98,000. *Principal City* (with population): Male, the capital, 11,000. *Flag:* A green rectangle, with a white crescent superimposed on a red field. *Monetary Units:* The lari and bodulari are local copper coins; Indian and Ceylonese coins are accepted.

**LAND AND PEOPLE.** The Maldives, an archipelago of 2,000 coral islands divided into 12 atolls, are situated in the Indian Ocean, southwest of India and Ceylon. (See map on page 139.) The northernmost atoll is about 400 miles from Ceylon. The islands, only 220 of which are inhabited, extend in a north-south line for 600 miles.

The people are primarily of Arabic or Negroid stock, with some Caucasian and Malayan strains. In the southern atolls, where marriage with outsiders is rare, the people are mostly Singhalese. Most Maldivians are Muslims, and speak Maldivian.

**HISTORY.** The Maldives, known to the west since the second century A.D., were converted to Islam in 1153. In the 17th century they came under the protection of Ceylon, which was then under Dutch rule; they retained the same status through the period of British rule over Ceylon and passed under direct British control in 1948.

In 1953 the sultanate was abolished. President Amir Amin Didi proposed progressive social legislation which outraged Muslim conservatives and brought about the restoration of the sultanate the following year.

Since independence, the Maldives' most important foreign policy dispute has been with Britain. Between 1939 and 1946 there was a British Royal Air Force Base on Gan, an island in Addu, the southernmost atoll. In 1956 Britain proposed to reopen the base, over Maldive protests that such a move would violate the island's neutrality. The dispute was resolved in 1960 when the Maldives agreed to allow the British base in exchange for Britain's aid in putting down a separatist movement that included Addu and two other atolls, which were trying to form a United Sudavian Republic. In July, 1965, the reunited Maldives were granted full independence.

**GOVERNMENT AND POLITICS.** The sultan (Al Amir Mohammed Farid Didi I, since 1954) is elected for life. Under the 1932 constitution, a People's Assembly is elected by all literate males over 25. There is a Legislative Council with 54 members, partly elected by the people, partly appointed by the sultan, and partly chosen by the People's Assembly. There are no political parties.

**ECONOMY.** Fish account for 93 per cent of exports. Trade is primarily with Ceylon; most necessities must be imported.

**EDUCATION.** Primary education is compulsory.

**NATIONAL DEFENSE.** There is a militia and a police force.

# MALI

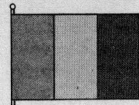

*Official Name:* Republic of Mali. *Area:* 463,948 square miles. *Population:* 4,654,-000. *Principal Cities* (with populations): Bamako, the capital, 130,000; Kayes, 21,-000; Segou, 20,000. *Flag:* Three vertical green, yellow, and red stripes, with a black figure of a man with uplifted arms in the center stripe. *Monetary Unit:* The Mali franc (worth 0.4 U.S. cent). *Gross National Product:* $297,-000,000 (1965). *Average Annual Income per Person:* $66.

**LAND AND PEOPLE.** Mali, a landlocked country in west Africa, is bordered by Senegal, Mauritania, Algeria, Niger, Upper Volta, Ivory Coast, and Guinea. The greater part of the country spreads north, east, and west of the great bend of the Niger River, while a rather small area lies south of the Niger. (See map on page 111.)

The northern half of Mali is occupied by the Sahara Desert. To the south is semi-desert and in the far southwest are savanna lands. The country generally has a hot, dry climate, with rainfall decreasing from an average of 55 inches annually in the extreme south to less than 4 inches in the Sahara.

The population consists almost entirely of Africans belonging to some two dozen tribes, with the Bambara making up about 31 per cent of the total and the Fulani about 10 per cent. Other large groups are Malinke (5 per cent), Songhai (5 per cent), Sarakolé (5 per cent), and Dogon (4 per cent). About 65 per cent of the people are Muslims, 30 per cent follow tribal religions, and 5 per cent are Christians. The official language is French.

**HISTORY.** From the tenth century to the time of the French conquest in the 19th, Mali's history is marked by a succession of large-scale empires. The first known rulers were Berbers from North Africa who settled among the Mande-speaking Soninke in the fourth century and founded the empire of Ghana. In 770 A.D. the Soninke took over the empire. From the tenth century onward gold from this region was a major source of wealth for Moorish Spain and North Africa.

As Islam expanded in the western Sahara, Almoravid Berbers from Mauritania launched a jihad, or holy war, against peoples to the south. In 1076 Abu Bakr overthrew Ghana. Although in 1087 the Soninke recovered their independence for a century, their great empire had been disrupted.

In the 11th century the small Malinke state of Kangaba, south of Ghana, embraced Islam and began to annex nearby kingdoms. The emperor Sundiata Keita conquered Ghana in 1235 and established the Muslim empire of Mali, which became the richest and most powerful of the western Sudanese empires. Under Mansa Musa (1307–32), Mali reached its peak as a center of Muslim trade and learning.

The Songhai controlled the next great Islamic empire, with its center at Gao, until 1591, when the Moroccans defeated the Songhai at Tondibi and became the new rulers. Moroccan control gave way to tribal groups and isolated states in the 17th and 18th centuries.

In the 19th century French military control was extended into the Sudan, in spite of resistance by Islamic groups, and French West Africa was established in 1904. The area known today as Mali eventually became the colony of French Sudan.

After World War II there was competition between the radically nationalist Sudanese Union Party and the Sudanese Progressive Party. By 1958, when France granted autonomy, the Sudanese Union had absorbed its major rival and the smaller, ethnically based parties.

In 1959 the colony, renamed the Sudanese Republic, joined with Senegal in the Mali Federation, which achieved independence in June, 1960. The Federation broke up on August 20, 1960, because of divergences in political and economic interests, as well as ideological and personal differences among Sudanese and Senegalese leaders. Senegal and Sudan became separate republics, Sudan inheriting the historic name of Mali.

**GOVERNMENT AND POLITICS.** Mali is a parliamentary republic. Executive power is vested in a president elected for a five-year term by the 80-member National Assembly, and in a cabinet appointed by the president and responsible to the assembly. The assembly is elected by universal suffrage for a five-year term on a single national list. The government is dominated by Mali's single party, the Sudanese Union. Its secretary-general is Modibo Keita, who is also president of Mali. Pressures from the party's youthful militant wing resulted in a cabinet shake-up in 1966.

**ECONOMY.** The economy depends on livestock herding and agriculture—mainly rice, cotton, millet, and sorghum. Despite a drastic decline since 1960, groundnuts remain the principal export crop and source of foreign exchange.

The most important mineral now being exploited is salt. Known deposits of diamonds, manganese, mineral oil, and phosphates remain untapped because of high transportation costs, and because Mali has limited the investment of foreign private capital.

Mali is an associate member of the European Economic Community and is economically dependent on the subsidized French market. There is also aid from numerous Western and Communist countries. Mali has a cultural and trade agreement with the Soviet Union that provides Soviet teachers for agricultural training.

**EDUCATION AND HEALTH.** Education is free; about 112,000 pupils are enrolled in primary schools, 13,000 in secondary schools, and 1,700 in more advanced schools. Public medical services are available.

**ARMED FORCES.** There is an army of about 3,500 men. Military aid has been provided by France, the Soviet Union, and the United States.

## MALTA

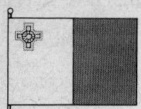

*Official Name:* Malta. *Area:* 122 square miles. *Population:* 317,000. *Principal City* (with population): Valetta, the capital, 17,700. *Flag:* Two vertical white and red stripes, with the George Cross in silver on the white stripe. *Monetary Unit:* The Maltese pound of 20 shillings (worth U.S. $2.80).

**LAND AND PEOPLE.** Three islands—Malta, Gozo, and Comino—and two islets comprise the Maltese archipelago. It is located in the Mediterranean Sea, about 60 miles south of Sicily. (See map on page 117.)

The islands are mainly limestone, and gently hilly. Summers are hot and dry; winters are mild.

Most Maltese are believed to be descended from the Carthaginians. Roman Catholicism is the official religion. Languages are Maltese and English.

**HISTORY.** During its long history Malta has been in many hands. Successive waves of Phoenicians, Greeks, Carthaginians, Romans, Byzantines, and Arabs occupied the island, and in 1091 it was seized by the Normans. In 1530 the Holy Roman Emperor, Charles V, awarded Malta to the Knights of St. John of Jerusalem, who successfully beat off repeated Turkish attacks and ruled the island until 1798. In that year Napoleon seized control, only to surrender Malta to the British two years later.

Thereafter, except for an unsuccessful attempt at self-rule between 1921 and 1936, Malta was ruled by Britain until September 21, 1964, when she received her independence within the British Commonwealth of Nations. During both world wars, Malta served as a vital British naval base. Maltese courage while under siege during World War II was rewarded in 1942 when the George Cross was bestowed on Malta itself—the first time an entire people rather than an individual had been so honored.

**GOVERNMENT AND POLITICS.** The Maltese government is officially headed by the British sovereign with effective power divided between the prime minister (Giorgio B. Olivier) with a cabinet of 7 ministers, and an elected House of Representatives with 50 members. The two major political groups are the Nationalist Party and the Malta Labour Party. Prime Minister Olivier, a member of the controlling Nationalist Party, has held his office since 1962. The most recent elections, held in 1966, gave 28 seats in the House of Representatives to the Nationalists and 22 to the Malta Labour Party.

**ECONOMY.** Malta's economy revolves around the British military forces based on the island under the 1964 independence agreement, but tourism is being encouraged to help make Malta more self-sufficient.

**EDUCATION AND HEALTH.** The literacy rate is 80 per cent of the population; in 1965 there were 75,000 students on the island. A National Insurance Act includes cash benefits for sickness, injury, unemployment, and old age.

## MAURITANIA

*Official Name:* Islamic Republic of Mauritania. *Area:* 419,230 square miles. *Population:* 1,070,000. *Principal Cities* (with populations): Nouakchott, the capital, 15,000; Port-Étienne, 10,000; Aïoun-el-Atrouss, 9,000. *Flag:* A gold star and crescent on a green field. *Monetary Unit:* The CFA franc (worth 0.41 U.S. cent). *Gross National Product:* $127,000,000 (1965).

**LAND AND PEOPLE.** Located in the northwest part of Africa, Mauritania borders on Spanish Sahara, Algeria, Mali, and Senegal. (See map on page 111.) Most of the country is low-lying desert. The Senegal River on the southern border is the only waterway.

The people are largely nomadic or semi-nomadic. There are about 500,000 Moors, 180,000 Tukulor, Sarakole and Fulani, and 2,000 Europeans; the rest are Negro. Arabic is the national language and French the official tongue. Islam is the state religion; 99.9 per cent of the population are Sunni Muslims.

**HISTORY.** Around the fourth century A.D. Berber invasions into the Mauritania area pushed Negro-African inhabitants southward. Islamic influences took over in the seventh century, and 400 years later the area was the base for holy wars in which the Muslims conquered Morocco, Algeria, Spain, and the Ghana Empire. Arabic culture and language were introduced by a Yemenite invasion in the 13th century. Berber resistance against the Arabs ended in the 17th century.

The French began exploring the inland area early in the 19th century. In 1903 the region became a French protectorate, and in 1920 it became part of French West Africa. French rule was largely indirect, with traditional social and political structures hardly disturbed. In 1960 Mauritania gained independence under an elite, French-sponsored party.

**GOVERNMENT AND POLITICS.** Mauritania's 1961 constitution was amended in 1964 to establish a single-party system, which drastically reduced the powers held by the 40 member National Assembly. The current head of state is President Mokhtar Ould Daddah, who is also secretary-general of the Party of the Mauritanian People.

**ECONOMY.** Mauritania's subsistence is based essentially on livestock herding. Most of the livestock, with the exception of camels, is below international marketing standards. There is also some commercial fishing. The economy is augmented by iron and copper mining operations, largely foreign-owned.

**EDUCATION AND HEALTH.** Health standards are considered low. Tuberculosis, sleeping sickness, malaria, trachoma, and leprosy are widespread.

The literacy rate, only 5 per cent a few years ago, has risen to 40 per cent. Education is compulsory from age 6 through 12.

**ARMED FORCES.** At 18 years of age Mauritanian youths undergo military training for 20 months. The permanent defense force consists of about 500 men.

# MEXICO

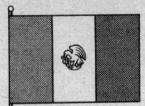

*Official Name:* United States of Mexico. *Area:* 759,529 square miles. *Population:* 45,000,000. *Principal Cities* (with populations): Mexico City, the capital, 3,192,804; Guadalajara, 1,048,351; Monterrey, 821,843; Cuidad Juárez, 385,082; Puebla, 338,690; Mexicali, 288,600. *Flag:* Green, white, and red bars; in the white bar is the national coat of arms—a brown eagle holding a green serpent in its beak (representing an Aztec legend). *Monetary Unit:* The peso of 100 centavos (worth 8 U.S. cents). *Gross National Product:* $19,400,000,000 (1965). *Average Annual Income per Person:* $412.

**LAND AND PEOPLE.** Mexico, the eighth largest country in the world, extends some 2,000 miles south from the border with the United States, between the Pacific Ocean and the Gulf of Mexico, to Guatemala and British Honduras. The Yucatan peninsula juts into the Caribbean Sea from the southeastern tip of the country; the Baja California peninsula extends south from the northwestern border, parallel to the west coast, between the Pacific and the Gulf of California. (See map on page 176.)

The land is dominated by a high central plateau running north and south, enclosed by mountain ranges of the Sierra Madre. The longest river in the country is the Rio Grande. There are good harbors on both the Atlantic and Pacific coasts. Climate ranges from the torrid coastal zones (with temperatures of 77°–80° F. and 51 inches average annual rainfall) to extreme cold in the mountainous regions (17 inches of rain annually). Abundant wildlife includes jaguars, bears, opossums, deer, boars, and monkeys.

Most Mexicans (70 per cent) are mestizos or Indians (28 per cent). Spanish is the predominant language. Indian languages are spoken by about 7 per cent of the people, but the language and other Indian culture traits are disappearing rapidly. About 94 per cent of the people are Roman Catholics.

**HISTORY.** Highly developed Indian civilizations were established in Mexico more than 2,000 years ago, and the country is one of the great archeological treasure-houses of the world. The Maya Indians in the Yucatan peninsula mastered the arts of construction and stone-carving, built cities, developed a calendar, and studied astronomy. The Nahuatl culture, established much later in the central plains, included the Toltecs and the Aztecs.

Descendants of these Indians came under Spanish rule in 1519, when conquistador Hernán Cortés landed at Veracruz and conquered the Indian nation ruled by Montezuma. During the ensuing Spanish colonial period (1519–1821) the territory was called New Spain; its domain stretched from Guatemala to present-day California, New Mexico, and Texas. As European culture transformed Mexico, much of the native culture was modified.

A drive for independence, spurred by political abuses and Indian enslavement, began in 1810 and was led by Miguel Hidalgo, a Mexican priest. Independence from Spain was finally achieved in 1821 under the leadership of Agustín Iturbide and Vicente Guerrero. Iturbide became emperor in 1822, but he was deposed a year later when a republic was established.

Internal political division and dispute among reform groups generated civil strife during the succeeding decades. General Antonio López de Santa Anna emerged as the dominant political figure of the tumultuous 1830s and 1840s. Large national territories were lost in these years. The territory of Texas seceded in 1836 and in 1844 became part of the United States. After the Mexican War (1846–48) Mexico was forced to cede almost half its territory to the U.S.—present-day California, Arizona, and New Mexico, as well as parts of Utah and Colorado.

After the downfall of Santa Anna a reform government was established in 1855. Six years later, during another period of internal disorder, French troops captured the capital and crowned Austrian Archduke Maximilian emperor. His reign was brief. When the French withdrew, the forces of Benito Juárez gained control, and in 1867 Maximilian was executed. Mexico again became a republic.

Porfirio Díaz seized power in 1876 and stifled representative political and governmental institutions. The resultant political peace and public order encouraged economic development and large foreign investment. However, although there was considerable material progress under his absolute rule, the gulf between landowners and peasants widened, and Díaz was overthrown in 1911 during a liberal revolt led by Francisco Madero. Revolutionary control proved unstable. Liberal factions disputed, assassination became an increasingly popular method of settling quarrels, governments were toppled, leaders such as Francisco Villa and Emiliano Zapata rose and fell, and a violent anti-clerical movement persecuted the Church.

A reform constitution was adopted in 1917. But before the reforms could be widely effected, a succession of leaders attempted to bring stability to the political and governmental structure. Most notable of the leaders were Alvaro Obregón and Plutarco Elías Calles. In 1934–40 the liberal regime of Lázaro Cárdenas further consolidated political power and instituted widespread economic and social reform. The programs included land reform, state-assisted economic development, encouragement of labor organizations, and social legislation.

Mexican affairs since 1940 have been marked by political peace and the continuation of highly successful economic policies. Improved communications and education, together with rapid urbanization, have reduced regionalism and promoted national unity. Despite these advances, however, about half the people still live near the subsistence level.

**GOVERNMENT AND POLITICS.** Mexico is a federal republic of 29 states. There is universal suffrage. The president is elected by direct popu-

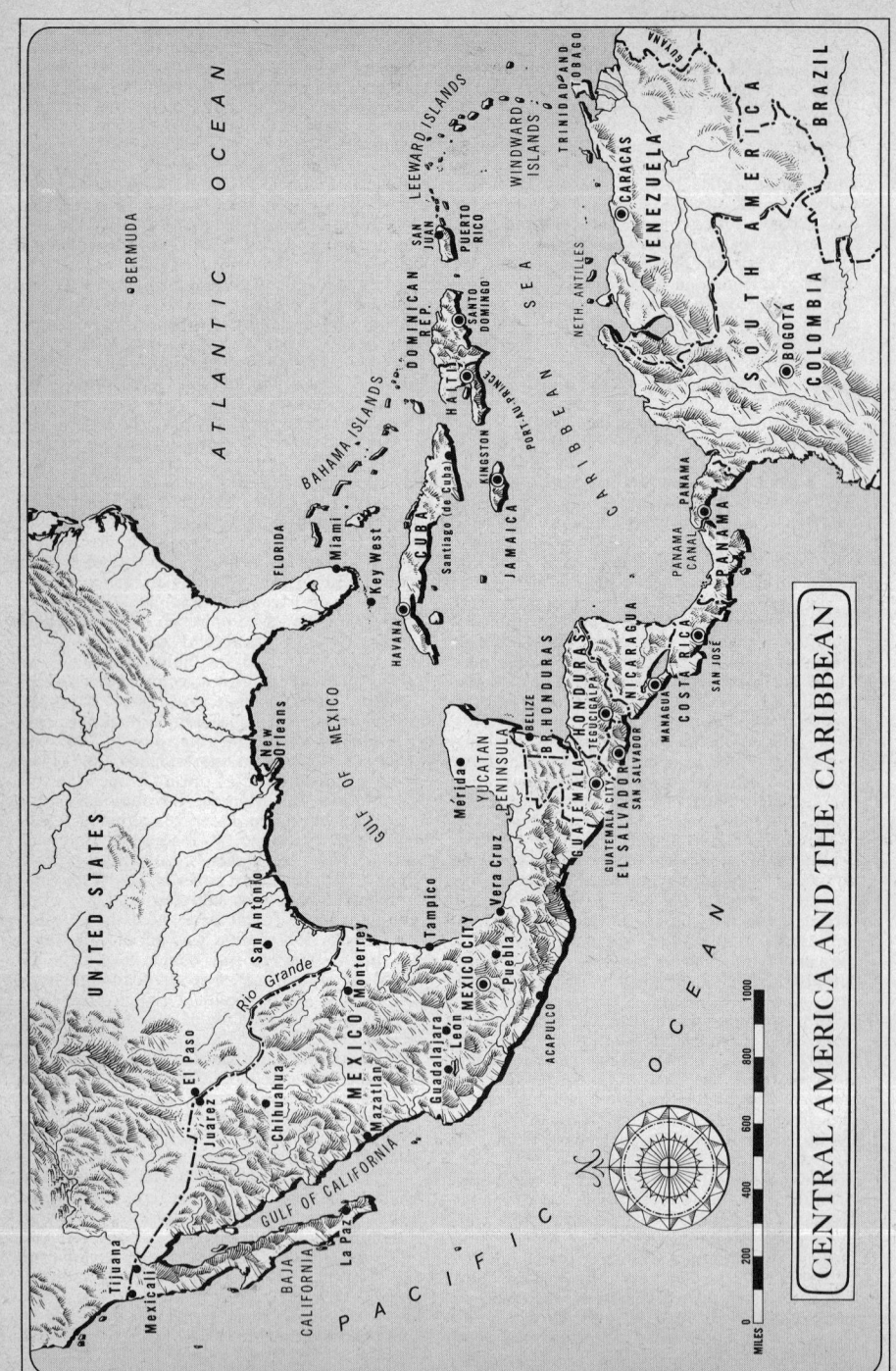

CENTRAL AMERICA AND THE CARIBBEAN

lar vote to a six-year term and may not succeed himself. The bicameral legislature comprises an upper house with two members from each state and the Federal District, and a lower house with one member for each 170,000 citizens.

The power of the states is considerably limited by centralization of authority in the federal government (especially the executive department) and by the political domination of the Institutional Revolutionary Party (PRI). The PRI, which began in the reform movements of the 1920s and 1930s, controls nearly all federal, state, and municipal elective offices. President Gustavo Díaz Ordaz and the great majority of congress are members of the PRI. In the 1964 elections 60 members of the upper house, chosen for six-year terms, were all PRI. The lower chamber has 210 seats held for three-year terms. In 1967, 178 of the seats were contested, and the PRI won 177. Minority parties include the PAN (National Action Party) and the PPS (Popular Socialists).

PRI has emphasized economic development, education, social insurance, and a policy of nonintervention in foreign affairs. Church and state are separate; there is freedom of religion. The armed forces play no overt role in politics.

**ECONOMY.** The Mexican economy is subject to considerable government influence and control. Railroads, petroleum, and electric power industries are government monopolies. In addition, the government exercises extensive control over such major industries as communications, mining, banking, manufacturing, and other fields.

Substantial economic gains have been made over the past 25 years. The government has promoted industrialization, agricultural self-sufficiency, production of export crops, communal and private farming, and national (public and private) ownership or control of subsurface resources and of public utilities. The gross national product has increased at an average rate of 5 per cent annually—the highest in Latin America.

Industrial growth has been particularly striking, with industrial employment increasing faster than population growth. In recent years the government has promoted a shift from the manufacture of consumer products to such items as heavy chemicals, metals, and metal products.

Gains have also been made in agricultural output. Self-sufficiency has been achieved in the production of most fruits, vegetables, and grains, and near self-sufficiency in meat and dairy products. The record is notable because the country has also increased its agricultural exports (principally cotton, sugar, and coffee) while coping with an annual population growth rate of 3.5 per cent—one of the highest in the world.

Foreign trade has risen steadily, reaching $2,706,000,000 in 1965, but leaving an unfavorable trade balance of $414,000,000. The deficit was largely offset by income from tourism. Visitors from the United States alone number over 1,000,000 each year.

Despite this progress, average annual income remains low because few of the economic advances have benefited the peasants, who still account for about half the population. The low average income, in turn, limits the ability of the people to purchase products from the expanded industrial plants.

**EDUCATION.** More than half the Mexican population is literate. Primary schooling is compulsory and free between the ages of 6 and 14. There are 21 autonomous universities and 4 incorporated in the National University at Mexico City.

Mexican painters, sculptors, architects, and writers have contributed to the mainstream of Western art. Colorful Mexican folk art, ceramics, tapestries, and carvings, as well as antiquities unearthed in the Indian ruins, are displayed throughout the world.

**ARMED FORCES.** Mexico has an army of 51,000 men, a navy of 6,200, and an air force of 5,000. A universal military-training program requires all 18-year-old males to serve one year of basic army training.

## MONACO

*Official Name:* Principality of Monaco. *Area:* 0.57 square miles. *Population:* 24,000. *Capital* (with population): Monaco-Ville, 2,-000. *Flag:* Red and white stripes. *Monetary Unit:* Monegasque franc (worth 20.3 U.S. cents).

**LAND AND PEOPLE.** Monaco, the smallest secular state in the world, is bordered on the south by the Mediterranean Sea and on the west, north, and east by France. (See map on page 117.) Rocky cliffs overhang sandy beaches of the Riviera coast, and two peninsulas enclose an excellent harbor. Winters are mild, and summer temperatures are moderated by sea breezes. Rainfall occurs mainly in early winter.

About 57 per cent of the people are French; Italians comprise 18.9 per cent and Monegasques 13.6 per cent. The official language is French. Roman Catholicism is the state religion, but freedom of worship is guaranteed.

**HISTORY.** Monaco was probably settled by Phoenicians. In 1215 the Genoese erected a fortified castle on the site of present-day Monaco, and in 1297 control passed to the Grimaldi family of Genoa. Monaco was a Spanish protectorate from 1524 to 1641, a French protectorate from 1641 to 1793, and a part of metropolitan France from 1793 to 1814. Following Napoleon's defeat, the Treaty of Vienna (1815) established Monaco as a protectorate of Sardinia. In 1861 France annexed the eastern Monegasque cities of Roquebrune and Menton and assumed the protectorate. The Casino at Monte Carlo, opened in 1863, launched development of the principality as a tourist center.

A "tax war" between Monaco and France was settled in 1963. The settlement allowed France to tax French citizens who had resided in Monaco less than five years, and Monaco to tax profits of foreign companies with local headquarters.

**GOVERNMENT AND POLITICS.** Monaco is a constitutional monarchy ruled by Prince Rainier III, a member of the Grimaldi family who became chief of state in 1949. In 1956 Rainier married American actress Grace Kelly. An hereditary monarchy, Monaco would be incorporated into France if the male Grimaldi line were to die out.

The 18-member National Council is elected every four years. The prince selects the minister of state, who is head of the government, from three professional French civil servants proposed by the French president.

**ECONOMY.** Tourism and gambling at the Casino in Monte Carlo are the leading revenue sources. Half the wage earners are employed by the casino corporation (SBM). In recent years Prince Rainier and Aristotle Onassis, prominent Greek shipowner and majority stockholder in SBM, have feuded over control of SBM and over tourist development. Under a recent agreement SBM will return to state ownership, permitting expansion of Casino facilities.

**EDUCATION AND HEALTH.** There is compulsory schooling to age 16. Ninety-nine per cent of the population is literate. Monaco has a hospital and dispensary and 40 physicians.

**ARMED FORCES.** Monaco has a defense agreement with France. About 100 guardsmen are used for ceremonial purposes.

# MONGOLIA

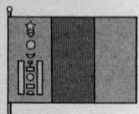

*Official Name:* Mongolian People's Republic. *Area:* 604,247 square miles. *Population:* 1,120,700. *Principal Cities* (with estimated populations): Ulan Bator, the capital, over 200,000; Choibalsan, Sukhe Bator, Kobdo, Darkhan, all probably under 20,000. *Flag:* Three vertical bars of red, blue, and red, with the national emblem in gold. *Monetary Unit:* The tughrik (worth 25 U.S. cents).

**LAND AND PEOPLE.** Mongolia is bordered on the north by the U.S.S.R. and on the east, south, and west by China. (See map on page 93.)

The country, a large plateau of over 600,000 square miles, has an average elevation of 3,000 to 4,000 feet. In the southeast is the vast Gobi Desert, noted for its dinosaur and other fossil remains. The climate is continental, generally dry year-round, with almost snowless and very cold winters.

Forests in the northern mountains, hills, and highland steppes give way gradually to lower steppe grasslands, semidesert country, and barren desert. Animals include bears, deer, panthers, antelopes, wild horses, and marmots. Principal rivers are the Selenga, Orkhon, and Kerulen. The most highly developed and densely populated part of the country follows the valley of the Selenga River northward from Ulan Bator.

Over 75% of the population are Khalkha Mongols; the numerous small minority groups include western Mongols (the Oirats), the Buryat Mongols, and the Kazakhs. A few thousand Russians and Chinese are the main foreign elements. The formerly dominant Lamaist Buddhist religion has been largely eliminated as a force in the country, but some lamas and a few monasteries remain.

**HISTORY.** In the 13th century Genghis Khan established the Mongolian Empire, with its capital at Karakorum. The Mongolian Empire ultimately disintegrated into three factions: the northern Buryat Mongols under Russian domination; the Khalkhas and Oirats in "Outer Mongolia" under the Manchu dynasty of China; and the southern Mongols in "Inner Mongolia" under Peking's control. The overthrow of the Manchus in China in 1911 led to Outer Mongolia's autonomy, with significant Tsarist Russian influence in the country. The 1917 Russian Revolution and near-anarchy in China resulted in a Russian-supported Mongolian "revolutionary" takeover in July, 1921. The Jebtsun Damba Khutukhtu, head of autonomous Mongolia, remained as titular leader until his death in 1924, when the Mongolian People's Republic (MPR) was formally established.

Nationalist China recognized the MPR as independent in 1946, but diplomatic relations began only after the Communist takeover in Peking in 1949. The MPR's unswerving support of the Soviet Union against China has imposed severe limits on Chinese activity and influence in the country.

**GOVERNMENT AND POLITICS.** Yumjagiin Tsedenbal, Prime Minister of the MPR and First Secretary of the ruling Mongolian People's Revolutionary Party, dominates the political leadership. The party's Politburo and Central Committee, along with the government's Great Khural (Parliament) and State ministries, function along lines closely similar to the Soviet system. The Communist party had 48,570 members and candidate-members in 1966.

**ECONOMY.** Tending the total of nearly 24,000,-000 head of sheep and other livestock constitutes the main activity of most Mongols. Most of the herds have been collectivized by the Communists. Grainraising is becoming increasingly important.

There is only light industry, although 1,000,-000 tons of coal are mined annually. The city of Darkhan, north of Ulan Bator in the Selenga Valley, is the scene of recent industrial development. The MPR depends on Soviet economic and technical aid for its industry.

The country belongs to the Communist trade organization, the Council for Economic Mutual Assistance. Most trade is with the U.S.S.R.

**EDUCATION.** Recent health and education improvements have been impressive. The network of schools supply practically universal education at the primary level and significant advanced training at the State University in Ulan Bator. Many Mongols go to the U.S.S.R. for advanced study.

**ARMED FORCES.** The armed forces numbered 80,000 men at the end of World War II, but they have been reduced greatly in recent years.

# MOROCCO

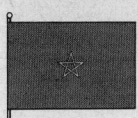

*Official Name:* Kingdom of Morocco. *Area:* 171,834 square miles. *Population:* 13,451,000. *Principal Cities* (with populations): Rabat, the capital, 227,445; Casablanca, 965,277; Marakesh, 243,134; Fez, 216,133; Meknes, 175,943; Tangier, 141,714; Oujda, 128,645. *Flag:* A green five-pointed star bordered in black on a red field. *Monetary Unit:* The dirham of 100 Moroccan francs (worth 19.8 U.S. cents). *Gross National Product:* $2,609,640,000 (1965). *Average Annual Income per Person:* $173.

**LAND AND PEOPLE.** Morocco, in the west of North Africa, is bordered by the Mediterranean Sea on the north, Algeria on the east and southeast, Spanish Sahara on the south, and the Atlantic Ocean on the west and northwest. (See map on page 111.)

The north coastal plain along the Mediterranean Sea includes the Rif Mountains, rising to 8,000 feet above sea level. The Atlas Mountains extend in three parallel ranges from the Atlantic coast in the southwest to Algeria and the Mediterranean Sea in the northeast. South of the Atlas Range is the so-called Anti-Atlas, including volcanic Mount Siroua. In the south and east semi-arid steppes stretch into the Sahara Desert. Rain (about 40 inches annually) and mountain snow make northwestern Morocco the best-watered country of North Africa. The peak rainy seasons are in October, November, and April.

The majority of the people are Berbers or Arabs, with some intermarriage of African Negroes. Arabic is the official language, but Berber, as well as French and Spanish, is also spoken. Almost 98 per cent of the people are Sunni Muslims.

**HISTORY.** Phoenician settlements existed at Melilla, Tangier, and Larache from 1100 B.C. The Romans formed northeast Morocco into the province of Mauritania Tingitana. Arab conquest in the seventh century introduced the religion of Islam. From 1064 to 1269 two great dynasties, the Almoravides and the Almohades, united Morocco and, at times, ruled all North Africa and southern and eastern Spain.

In the early 16th century Spain and Portugal took nearly all Moroccan ports. (Ceuta and Melilla are still Spanish.) The strongly Muslim country, however, retained its independence until the Franco-Spanish occupation of 1912.

From the mid-19th century France, Spain, Britain, Italy, and Germany rivaled one another for influence in Morocco. In 1912 Morocco signed the treaty of Fez. By this agreement, Morocco became a French protectorate, with Spain administering the northern area and the semi-desert province of Tarfaya adjoining the Spanish Sahara. Tangier became a multi-national zone.

Abdelkrim al-Khattabi, a Rifi Berber chief, fought the French and Spanish from 1921 to 1926. He was defeated, but resistance in the Atlas Mountains continued until 1934.

As a French protectorate Morocco was transformed from a medieval state into a modern one. After World War II nationalism grew stronger. Sultan Sidi Mohammed demanded a free Morocco. Although he was deposed in 1953, increasing French difficulties throughout North Africa led to his restoration in 1955, and in 1956 the country gained its independence.

Sidi Mohammed became King Mohammed V, and in 1961 he was succeeded by his son, King Hassan II. A constitution was promulgated in 1962, and a parliament was elected. In 1965, when the government Front for Defense of Constitutional Institutions appeared to be losing its majority, the King declared a state of emergency. He suspended parliament, assumed full executive and legislative powers himself, and promised to streamline the national administration.

In general, Moroccan foreign policy is nonaggressive and Western-oriented. Morocco has had several disputes with neighboring Arab states and also with Syria, Lebanon, Egypt, and the Soviet Union. Relations with France were strained by the 1966 Paris kidnapping of a prominent Moroccan opposition leader; they were further strained in 1967 when a French court placed the responsibility for the kidnapping on the Moroccan Minister of the Interior.

**GOVERNMENT AND POLITICS.** Morocco is officially a constitutional monarchy with a bicameral parliament. The parliament, however, was suspended in 1965, and only in 1967 was a prime minister (Premier Mohammed Benhima) again appointed. By constitution, the House of Representatives is elected for four years by universal adult suffrage; the House of Councilors is chosen for six years. Cabinets are appointed by the king.

The leading political parties are the Istiqlal (Independence) Party, the Front for Defense of Constitutional Institutions, and the National Union of Popular Forces.

**ECONOMY.** Agriculture and mining provide employment for 75 per cent of the population. They also account for about 40 per cent of the national income and supply over 90 per cent of annual exports. Manufacturing is primarily for domestic consumption.

Since independence, Morocco's economy has been hampered by lack of trained personnel and by periodic droughts, but the country is potentially rich in minerals (phosphates, iron ore, manganese, lead, zinc, cobalt) and agricultural products (grains, vegetables, citrus fruits, wine grapes).

Modernization during the protectorate included the development of good ports, roads, railways, schools, and hospitals.

**EDUCATION.** Literacy has been estimated at 13–20 per cent. The number of children receiving primary education rose from 300,000 in 1955 to over 1,000,000 in 1967. There are universities at Rabat and Fez.

**ARMED FORCES.** Armed forces total about 48,000. Eighteen-month compulsory service for men between 25 and 30 was instituted in 1966.

## MUSCAT AND OMAN

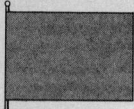

*Official Name:* Sultanate of Muscat and Oman. *Area:* 82,000 square miles. *Population:* 750,000. *Principal Cities* (with populations): Muscat, the capital, 6,200; Matrah, 10,000. *Flag:* A red rectangle. *Monetary Unit:* The Indian rupee of 64 baizas (worth about 21 U.S. cents) and the Maria Theresa dollar or thaler (worth U.S. $1.05).

**LAND AND PEOPLE.** Muscat and Oman, often regarded as separate countries, is a sultanate situated on the southeast corner of the Arabian peninsula. The area is bounded by the Arabian Sea, the Eastern Protectorate states of South Arabia, Saudi Arabia, the Trucial States, and the Gulf of Oman. (See map on page 151.) Muscat includes a coastal strip running along the Gulf of Oman and the Arabian Sea. Oman, mountainous and landlocked, is located between Muscat and the Rub al Khali (Empty Quarter) of Saudi Arabia.

The country generally has a hot desert climate, with temperatures reaching 130° F. Average annual rainfall is less than four inches in the Muscat-Matrah area.

Three-fourths of Muscat's people are Arabs; Indians, Iranians, and Africans comprise the leading minority groups. Oman's population is almost entirely Arab. Arabic and Indian are the chief languages. About half the people belong to the Ibadhi sect of the Muslim faith.

**HISTORY.** In the seventh century A.D. Saudi Arabian traders spread Muslim influence. Starting in the 16th century, the European maritime powers contended for control of the area. The Portuguese conquered the land, using Muscat as a base to control Persian Gulf trade. Local Arabs ejected the Portuguese in the mid-17th century. Brief Iranian rule in the 18th century ended when the present al-bu-Said dynasty came to power in 1844. British influence was established in 1891.

The nation was split in 1954 when the Imam of Oman, a theocratic leader, rebelled against the Muscat sultan; the effort was unsuccessful. A similar revolt beginning in 1957 was quelled by British troops in 1959, and the Imam was forced into exile in Saudi Arabia. The Imam, supported by the Arab states, has brought the issue before the United Nations. No progress has been made toward settling the dispute.

**GOVERNMENT AND POLITICS.** Although associated with the United Kingdom, the country is independently ruled by the Sultan of Muscat, Said ibn Taymur.

**ECONOMY.** The economy, based on agriculture, has improved due to recent oil production. Three coastal oil fields produce over 200,000 barrels daily. A 156-mile oil pipeline from central Oman to a coastal terminal was put in service late in 1967. Exports besides oil include dates, pomegranates, and limes.

The nation's 500-mile interior road system is being improved, and a local airline serves Muscat and points on the western shore of the Persian Gulf.

**EDUCATION AND HEALTH.** The nation has only three modern schools. Education consists of traditional Koranic instruction. Infant mortality is high, and trachoma and tuberculosis are widespread.

**ARMED FORCES.** A 2,000-man army is staffed by volunteers largely under the command of British officers.

## NEPAL

*Official Name:* Nepal. *Area:* 54,362 square miles. *Population:* 10,294,000. *Principal Cities* (with populations): Kathmandu, the capital, 122,500; Patan, 48,800; Biratnagar, 33,300; Bhatagaon, 33,000; Nepalgano, 15,800; Birganj, 10,800. *Flag:* Red, bordered in blue; white stylized moon in the upper triangle and white stylized sun in the lower. *Monetary Unit:* Nepali rupee (worth 0.1316 U.S. cents). *Gross National Product:* $736,000,000 (1965).

**LAND AND PEOPLE.** Nepal dominates the central region of the great Himalayan barrier separating the Indian subcontinent from central Asia. It is bordered on the west, south, and southeast by India, on the east by Sikkim, and on the north by Tibet. (See map on page 139.)

The Terai region in the south is a semitropical area of jungles, swamp, and arable land. Central Nepal is a zone of moderately high elevations, in the middle of which lies the Kathmandu Valley. The Himalaya Mountains in the north include Mount Everest, the world's highest peak. There are three major river systems: the Karnali, Gandaki, and Kosi. The climate is subtropical in the Terai, moderate in the central valleys, and alpine in the Himalayas. Rainfall in the Kathmandu Valley averages 60 inches annually.

The majority of the population are of Indo-Aryan or Paleo-Mongoloid descent. The Ghurkas are a mixture of the two ethnic groups. Bhotians of Tibetan origin are found in the northern border area. The official language is Nepali. Hinduism, the official religion, is the religion of four-fifths of the population, but a substantial minority adhere to Mahayana Buddhism or animism. There is a small Muslim minority.

**HISTORY.** Little is known of Nepal's history prior to 1768 when Prithur Narayan Shah of Ghurka conquered the central valley and established the modern kingdom. An unsuccessful war with Tibet and China (1791–92) closed off expansion to the north, and an even more disastrous war with British India (1814–16) limited Nepal approximately to its present boundaries.

The Shah rulers were reduced to figureheads in 1847 by a noble family, the Ránás, who ruled the country as hereditary prime ministers for more than a century.

In 1951 a rebellion started by the Nepali Congress Party led to the overthrow of the Ráná regime. King Tribhuvan ascended the throne, succeeded in 1955 by King Mahendra Bir Bikram Shah Deva. In a general election held in 1959 under a new constitution, the Nepali Congress Party emerged with a large majority and formed Nepal's first elected government. In 1960 King Mahendra dismissed the government and discarded the constitution. Sporadic rebellions began in 1961. These ended the following year as a direct consequence of the Sino-Indian border war. No effective political challenges to the royal regime have subsequently developed.

**GOVERNMENT AND POLITICS.** Nepal takes pride in being the only independent Hindu monarchy in the world. The 1962 constitution, as amended in 1967, provides for a system of panchayats (councils) organized on a three-tier hierarchical basis: village and town panchayats, district panchayats, and the National Panchayat (parliament). Political parties were banned in 1960. Nepal's foreign policy is based upon nonalignment and equal friendship with both its giant neighbors, China and India.

**ECONOMY.** Nearly 85 per cent of the population is engaged in agriculture, much of it on a subsistence level. Rice is the principal crop in the Terai and lower hill areas and valleys; maize, millet, and potatoes are grown on the higher slopes. Jute, sugar, and tobacco are the main cash crops. A variety of minerals are known to exist, but the country has not been fully surveyed. Industry is limited to the processing of domestic agricultural and forestry products.

Ninety-five per cent of Nepal's foreign trade is with India. The construction of a Kathmandu-Tibet road and a trade treaty with Pakistan have as yet had little economic impact. Nepal accepts foreign aid from the United States, the Soviet Union, China, and India.

There are about 800 miles of motorable roads, one-fourth of which are paved, and two short narrow-gauge railway lines. The Royal Nepal Airlines Corporation serves the interior and connects Kathmandu with several Indian and Pakistani cities.

**EDUCATION AND HEALTH.** There is no compulsory education, and literacy is estimated at 10 per cent. A national school system was instituted in 1954, and Tribhuvan University was opened in 1960. There is a serious shortage of medical personnel and facilities.

**ARMED FORCES.** Nepal has a 10,000-man regular army, backed by about 25,000 reserves. Ghurka soldiers also serve in the British and Indian armies.

# THE NETHERLANDS

*Official Name:* Kingdom of the Netherlands. *Area:* 12,978 square miles. *Population:* 12,455,000. *Principal Cities* (with populations): Amsterdam, the capital, 868,173; Rotterdam, 732,232; The Hague, seat of government, 601,134; Utrecht, 265,432; Eindhoven, 177,002; Haarlem, 172,817. *Flag:* Horizontal red, white, and blue bars. *Monetary Unit:* The guilder (worth 28 U.S. cents). *Gross National Product:* $20,700,000,000 (1966).

*Average Annual Income per Person:* $1,696.

**LAND AND PEOPLE.** The Netherlands is bordered on the west and north by the North Sea, on the east by West Germany, and on the south by Belgium. (See map on page 117.)

The country's terrain is divided into three regions: the barrier dunes; the "polders," or lowlands—land reclaimed from the North Sea and from lakes; and a higher section in the east, reaching its greatest elevation at the Vaalserberg. A considerable portion of the country has come into existence through Dutch ingenuity, for about 20 per cent of the kingdom is below sea level. The Delta project, a massive coastal protection project, is expected to be completed by 1980; the Zuiderzee land reclamation project, another major undertaking, is also scheduled to be finished at that time.

The flora and fauna are generally typical of temperate climes. The country is renowned for its flowers, particularly the cultivated varieties such as tulips and hyacinths.

The languages are Dutch and Frisian. The country is 40.4 per cent Roman Catholic and 37.6 per cent Protestant.

**HISTORY.** The Batavi, the Frisians, and other Germanic and Celtic tribes first settled the marshy Rhine and Meuse delta areas of the Low Countries. Julius Caesar conquered a large part of this territory about 55 B.C., and the tribes eventually entered into an alliance with the Romans, receiving help from them to develop their canals and dikes. With the collapse of Rome, progress generally ceased for centuries.

The dukes of Burgundy extended their control over a greater part of the Low Countries in the 14th and 15th centuries. In 1515 the Hapsburg dynasty's Charles V inherited the Burgundian lands. He abdicated (1555) in favor of his son, Philip II, king of Spain. Philip's suppression of religious freedom, of local and regional autonomies, and attacks on burgeoning Protestantism in the Low Countries evoked fierce resistance. In 1568 the Netherlands' 80-year war of liberation began; it was led by William the Silent, Prince of Orange, founder of the present dynasty and architect of Netherlands' independence.

Under his leadership the seven northern provinces united, first as the Union of Utrecht, later (1581) as the Republic of the United Netherlands, and they continued the fight even after the southern provinces had again succumbed to Spanish rule. It was a struggle that was not resolved until the Peace of Westphalia (1648), ending the Thirty Years' War, recognized the Netherlands Republic as independent.

Meanwhile, the Dutch were laying the foundations for an overseas empire—the Netherlands East Indies, and colonies in North and South America and in South Africa. The 17th century in the Netherlands was its "golden age," but its ranking position as a maritime power brought the country into growing conflict with England. The 18th century was one of internal strife, political struggles, naval wars with England, and the loss of many colonies.

In 1795 French revolutionary troops invaded and founded the Republic of Batavia, which in 1806 became a Napoleonic "Kingdom of Holland." After 1813 the Netherlands resumed its course as a free nation. A union with the southern (Catholic) provinces—now Belgium—under the rule of the House of Orange lasted but 15 years (until 1830); nine years later the Dutch finally had to accept the fact of Belgian independence. During the reign of William I (1815–40), the "Merchant King," the country again became a maritime and trading power and regained many of its lost colonial possessions.

The Netherlands remained neutral in international affairs until World War II, when the country was swiftly occupied by German forces. After prolonged terror and ruthless suppression, including the Nazis' wanton and senseless destruction of Rotterdam and extermination of most of the nation's Jews, the country was liberated in 1945. Queen Wilhelmina, after 58 years of rule, abdicated (1948) in favor of her daughter, Juliana.

Indonesian nationalists in 1945 began their battle for possession of the Netherlands East Indies, Dutch-held for centuries. After four years of periodic fighting and negotiations, the archipelago was ceded to them. In 1962 the Dutch were forced to give up Netherlands New Guinea, now Indonesia's West Irian.

Crown Princess Beatrix, who was married to Prince Claus (formerly Claus von Amsberg of West Germany) on March 10, 1966, gave birth to a son, Prince Alexander, on April 27, 1967. He became the first male in line of succession to the Dutch throne since 1884.

**GOVERNMENT AND POLITICS.** The Kingdom of the Netherlands, a constitutional monarchy, is a sovereign state comprising three autonomous members: the Netherlands, Surinam, and Netherlands Antilles. A Council of Ministers, whose members are appointed by the three components, deals with matters affecting the kingdom as a whole, especially defense and foreign relations. The kingdom's rule is hereditary through lineal descendants of the House of Orange-Nassau.

The Netherlands Parliament has two chambers. Members of the First (upper) Chamber are elected by provincial legislatures; those of the politically more important Second (lower) Chamber are elected by universal suffrage. All eligible voters must by law cast a ballot, but it need not be marked. The main political groups are the Catholic Peoples' Party, the Socialist (Labor) Party, the Liberals, the Anti-Revolutionary Party, and the Christian Historical Union. The present coalition government (Catholic, Liberal, Anti-Revolutionary, and Christian Historical Union) is headed by Premier Petrus J. S. de Jong. National elec-

Twenty per cent of the Netherlands lies below sea level. This section has been reclaimed from the sea.

Netherlands Info. Service

tions were held in February, 1967, after two previously designated premiers had been unable to form a coalition cabinet from the major parties represented in the Dutch lower house.

**ECONOMY.** The Netherlands' geographical location has determined to a considerable degree its economic structure, one based on services, industry, and agriculture. Bolstered by considerable American aid, the country made a remarkable recovery from severe wartime damage, and expansion has continued. Industries, and to some extent agriculture, are concerned with the import of raw materials and the export of processed goods; in 1966 foreign trade reached a record high of nearly $14.8 billion.

Dairying is the chief agricultural activity; the nation is the world's leading exporter of eggs. Agricultural production is being aided by continued land reclamation and increasing scientific research. Fishing adds considerably to the food supply. Natural resources are limited and most raw materials must be imported. The Netherlands is a member of Benelux.

There are nearly 28,000 miles of surfaced roads, an extensive modern railway system, and well-developed inland waterways. KLM, the Royal Dutch Airlines, provides regular service to 66 countries.

**EDUCATION AND HEALTH.** Education is compulsory for children from 6 to 15; there is no illiteracy. The University of Leyden, founded in 1574, is the oldest of the country's 11 institutions of higher learning. There are many excellent libraries and more than 350 museums, several of which are world-renowned.

The country has compulsory sickness insurance and has increasingly stressed preventive care. Community sanitation standards are equal to or above those of most U.S. cities.

**ARMED FORCES.** The Netherlands is a member of NATO. Armed forces total 141,000.

# DUTCH TERRITORIES AND DEPENDENCIES

## SURINAM

*Area:* 55,144 square miles. *Population:* 360,-000. *Principal City* (with population): Paramaribo, the capital, 122,630. *Monetary Unit:* The Surinam guilder (worth 53.7 U.S. cents).

Surinam is bordered on the north by the Atlantic Ocean, on the east by French Guiana, on the south by Brazil, and on the west by Guyana. Most of the interior is covered by virgin forest, but the flat coast is a rich alluvial plain. The average year-round temperature is about 81° F. The population of Surinam is predominantly Creole and East Indian, with sizable minorities of Indonesians, Bush Negroes, and indigenous Indians. Among the variety of religious faiths held by the people are Christianity, Hinduism, and Islam. Almost all the Surinamese speak Dutch.

Surinam, or Dutch Guiana, was explored in the 16th century by the Spanish, who soon left. British, French, and Dutch contested for supremacy until the Treaty of Breda (1667), between Britain and the Netherlands, ceded Surinam to the latter in return for the colony of New Netherland (New York).

Surinam is a component part of the Kingdom of the Netherlands. The governor, assisted by an advisory council, is constitutional head of government. A 36-member Legislative Council is elected by universal suffrage.

Bauxite is Surinam's principal mineral, major export, and leading source of income. Agriculture, concentrating on rice, sugarcane, citrus fruits, coconuts, and bananas, and timber are important economic sectors.

Primary and secondary education is free, and schooling is compulsory for all children between the ages of 7 and 12.

## NETHERLANDS ANTILLES

*Area:* 390 square miles. *Population:* 208,000. *Principal City* (with population): Willemstad, the capital, 43,550. *Monetary Unit:* The Netherlands Antilles guilder (worth 53.7 U.S. cents).

The islands are divided into two groups: the Windward Islands, Curaçao, Aruba, and Bonaire, off the north coast of South America; and the Leeward Islands, St. Maarten (or St. Martin, shared with France), Saba, and St. Eustatius, more than 500 miles to the northeast.

The Windward Islands are volcanic-based, partly coral, semi-arid, and covered with desertlike vegetation. The smaller Leeward Islands are hilly to mountainous and lushly fertile, with adequate rainfall. The Antilles' temperature ranges between 77° and 87° F.

Many nationality groups are represented, but the people are approximately 85 per cent mestizo, a mixture of Negro, Indian, Spanish, and Dutch elements. Almost all are Christians. Literacy is estimated to be at least 95 per cent. The people speak Dutch, Papiamento, and English.

Curaçao, the largest island in the Antilles, was discovered in 1499 by the explorers Alonso de Ojeda and Amerigo Vespucci. Along with Aruba and Bonaire, Curaçao was captured by the Dutch in 1634, and Peter Stuyvesant became Curaçao's first governor. England occupied the island briefly during the Napoleonic Wars but it was restored to the Netherlands in 1816 after Napoleon's defeat.

Netherlands Antilles is a coequal part of the Kingdom of the Netherlands. Its governmental structure is similar to that of Surinam. The legislature is elected by universal suffrage.

Aruba and Curaçao, with some of the world's largest oil refineries, have a prosperous economy largely based on the petroleum industry. The Windward Islands depend on subsistence agriculture and must import much of their food.

The Leeward Islands depend on fishing, boatbuilding, herding, salt-collecting and agriculture.

The Antilles' equable climate and unique blend of Dutch, African, and Spanish cultures draw increasing numbers of tourists annually.

# NEW ZEALAND

*Official Name:* New Zealand. *Area:* 103,736 square miles. *Population:* 2,678,855. *Principal Cities* (with populations): Wellington, the capital, 126,700; Christchurch, 158,800; Auckland, 149,400; Dunedin, 77,500. *Flag:* A blue field with the British Union Jack (left) and four red stars outlined in white. *Monetary Unit:* New Zealand dollar of 100 cents (worth U.S. $1.40). *Gross National Product:* $5,242,000,000 (1965). *Average Annual Income per Person:* $1,690.

**LAND AND PEOPLE.** Situated about 1,200 miles southeast of Australia, New Zealand is bordered by the South Pacific Ocean on the east and the Tasman Sea on the west. (See map on page 67.) It consists of two principal islands, North Island and South Island, separated by Cook Strait; Stewart Island, off the southern tip of South Island; and the Chatham Islands, about 500 miles east of South Island.

A high range of mountains, the Southern Alps, runs the length of South Island and contains several glaciers. The climate is generally moist and temperate; the temperature, from 50° to 58° F. The kauri, rimu, and totara trees are valuable for their wood. Seals and bats are the only indigenous mammals. Distinctive birds are the flightless kiwi and notornis and the kea, a large parrot.

About 92 per cent of New Zealanders are of British stock, with other European and Asiatic groups also represented. Approximately 7 per cent of the population are Maoris, a Polynesian group who speak the Maori language. Elsewhere English is spoken. Some 64 per cent of the people are Protestants; 15 per cent are Catholics; the remaining 21 per cent are of other faiths or nonaffiliated.

**HISTORY.** The race of Polynesians called Maoris came to New Zealand at least as early as 1350 from southeast Asia. When the Dutch explorer Abel J. Tasman discovered the islands in 1642, the unfriendly Maoris prevented him from landing. In 1769 Captain James Cook of England visited the islands, and in the 1790s several small English whaling settlements were established. In the early 19th century whaling, sealing, and a little primitive agriculture were the only activities carried on by the few settlers, some of whom were naval deserters and escaped convicts from Australia.

In 1840 the New Zealand Company organized the first large migration to the islands and established a settlement at Wellington. In that year the Maoris granted sovereignty over New Zealand to the British Crown, in return for a guarantee that they would be allowed full possession of their lands. This promise was not kept, and in 1845–48 and again in 1860–70 bloody Maori uprisings were suppressed by the use of military force.

The first real stimulant to New Zealand's settlement was the discovery of gold on South Island in 1861, and in a short time the population boomed. Development of an export trade in wool and meat products, primarily to Britain, was accelerated by refrigerated ships after 1882 and gave a firm base to the economy.

New Zealand became a dominion in 1907 and was granted full autonomy within the Commonwealth of Nations in 1947. It has continued to maintain close economic and sentimental ties with the mother country. It supported Britain in both world wars and, symbolically, was the last dominion to ratify the Statute of Westminster, passed in 1931 to grant autonomy to members of the Commonwealth. In recent years New Zealand has broadened its international contacts through Commonwealth programs such as the Colombo Plan and through United Nations activities which have included military service in Korea.

Immigration has been restricted for the past decades. Relations with the Maoris, who have four seats in Parliament, are generally good, but there is still some discrimination. In 1962 the New Zealand Council of Tribal Executives was formed, in an attempt to give the Maoris a unified voice.

**GOVERNMENT AND POLITICS.** New Zealand is a self-governing member of the Commonwealth. Queen Elizabeth II is recognized as sovereign of New Zealand and is represented by the governor-general, Sir Arthur Porritt, who was appointed in December, 1966. A prime minister and his cabinet together with the governor-general form the Executive Council, the country's highest executive body. The supreme law-making body is the General Assembly, which includes the governor-general and the House of Representatives, a unicameral parliament. Members of the House are elected every three years by universal suffrage.

The National Party has headed the government since 1960; Keith J. Holyoake is the prime minister. The official opposition is the Labour Party. Major political issues in recent years have been the economy and the government's support of the United States in Vietnam.

In 1962 New Zealand appointed a Parliamentary Commissioner for Investigations, or "ombudsman," to act on citizens' complaints against government officials and departments.

**ECONOMY.** New Zealand has always been heavily dependent upon agriculture for its livelihood, with nearly two-thirds of the total land presently under cultivation. However, as the economy has matured, other sectors have grown in importance. An interindustry study in 1954 revealed that farming contributed 20.7 per cent to the total product, manufacturing 21.6 per cent, and services 45.8 per cent. Principal manufacturing activities are processing of forest and agricultural products, cement, fertilizer, and transport assembly. Mineral resources are minimal and largely undeveloped.

Of great significance is the production of wool, meat, and dairy products, which account for nearly 90 per cent of all exports. New Zealand's supply of foreign exchange depends directly upon the world markets for these commodities. A fall in wool prices and a rise in imports contributed to a serious balance of payments deficit of about $307 million for the year ending in March, 1967. New Zealand's dependence upon agricultural exports may create a problem if its main customer, the United Kingdom, enters the Common Market. Steps taken to assure future markets included a trade agreement with the United Kingdom in June, 1966, to provide for unrestricted entry of New Zealand meat and dairy products until 1972 in exchange for preferences for British goods in the New Zealand market. An agreement with Australia provided that each country would eliminate or reduce duties on imports from the other.

New Zealand has been progressive in its economic philosophy. In 1898 it was the first nation to adopt noncontributory old-age pensions; a social security act was passed in 1938; and in 1941 nationalized medicine was instituted. In addition, New Zealand has pioneered legislation for land division, wage arbitration, workers' compensation, farm price guarantees, and marketing boards. Results have been a high standard of living, low numbers of unemployed, and a relatively small disparity of income among workers.

The 3,300 miles of railroads in New Zealand are state-owned; paved roads total over 57,000 miles. There is both domestic and international air service, with international airports at Auckland, Christchurch, and Wellington.

**HEALTH AND EDUCATION.** The National Health Service provides assistance in paying private medical bills. Hospital services and most drugs are free to residents. There is one physician for every 670 inhabitants.

Education is compulsory for children between 7 and 15. There are special schools for Maori children, but the majority attend public schools. Literacy is almost 100 per cent. New Zealand has six universities.

**ARMED FORCES.** Service in the armed forces is compulsory for men at the age of 20. Men under arms total about 13,000 regulars; reserves number nearly 62,500. An artillery battery and surgical teams have been sent to South Vietnam.

# NEW ZEALAND TERRITORIES AND DEPENDENCIES

## COOK ISLANDS

*Area:* 93 square miles. *Population:* 20,519. *Principal City* (with population): Avarua, 9,-800.

The Cook Islands are situated in the South Pacific and are divided into two groups. The seven Northern Group islands are low-lying, sparsely populated, scattered atolls; those in the Lower Group have fertile soil, are the seat of government, and home for most Cook Islanders. Rarotonga, the largest Cook island, is volcanic. The people are almost all Polynesian and Christian; they speak Maori and English.

Some of the islands were discovered in 1773 by Captain James Cook, others by John Williams 50 years later. They became a British protectorate in 1888 and were annexed to New Zealand in 1901.

The islands' constitution, adopted in 1965, provides for full internal autonomy in association with New Zealand, with the British sovereign recognized as ruler.

Citrus fruits and juices, copra, and tomatoes are the leading exports. All residents are eligible for free medical treatment. Education is compulsory and free for children from 6 to 16; instruction is in English above the second grade.

## NIUE ISLAND

*Area:* 100 square miles. *Population:* 5,145.

Niue, part of the Cook group but separately administered, lies in the Pacific 580 miles northwest of Rarotonga. The people are Polynesian and speak Samoan.

A Resident Commissioner and an Island Assembly are in charge of administration and legislative matters. The soil is fertile, producing copra, sweet potatoes, and bananas. Medical services and education are free.

## TOKELAU ISLANDS

*Area:* 4 square miles. *Population:* 1,835.

The islands, consisting of three atolls, lie about 300 miles north of Western Samoa and are administered from there. Once part of the Gilbert and Ellice Islands colony, they became New Zealand territory in 1926.

The people are Polynesian; they farm for a living and grow coconuts to produce copra, the chief export. Postage stamps also add to the islands' income.

## ROSS DEPENDENCY

*Area:* 160,000 square miles.

This totally ice-covered region of Antarctica, lying between 160° east and 150° west longitude, was placed under New Zealand's jurisdiction in 1923. The region, which has become a whaling center, has a research station.

# NICARAGUA

*Official Name:* Republic of Nicaragua. *Area:* 53,938 square miles. *Population:* 1,715,000. *Principal Cities* (with populations): Managua, the capital, 250,000; León, 50,000; Granada, 30,000; Masaya, 25,-000. *Flag:* Blue, white, and blue, with the coat of arms on the white stripe. *Monetary Unit:* The córdoba of 100 centavos (worth 14.3 U.S. cents). *Gross National Product:* $485,900,000 (1964). *Average Annual Income per Person:* $305.

**LAND AND PEOPLE.** The largest of the Central American republics, Nicaragua lies between the Caribbean Sea and the Pacific Ocean, and is bordered by Honduras on the north and Costa Rica on the south. (See map on page 176.)

Tropical rain forests grow in the sultry lowland plains of the Mosquito Coast, near the Caribbean. Farther inland are large stands of pines that give way to a central plateau broken by mountains. The nation's principal cities, highways, and most of its people are concentrated in a narrow, fertile volcanic belt between lakes Nicaragua and Managua and the Pacific Ocean. The climate is warm and humid. Annual rainfall along the Pacific coast is about 80 inches; Managua, in western Nicaragua, receives 45 inches; the eastern coast has up to 250 inches.

The population is about 68 per cent mestizo, 15 per cent white (European), 9 per cent Negro, and 5 per cent Indian. Spanish is the official language. Ninety-five per cent of the people are Roman Catholics.

**HISTORY.** Columbus, the first European explorer to reach Nicaragua, landed in 1502 on his fourth voyage to the New World. The conquistador Fernández de Córdoba established Spanish cities at León and Granada in 1524. Nicaragua won independence from Spain in 1821 and was then allied briefly with Mexico and later (1825–38) with the Central American Federation.

In 1838 the country became a republic. A century of political instability and civil strife followed. Foreign intervention occurred in the 19th and 20th centuries (partially because of Nicaragua's potential as a site for an interoceanic canal). U.S. Marines were stationed in Nicaragua from 1912 to 1925 and from 1926 to 1933.

Anastasio Somoza emerged as the Nicaraguan strong man and ruled as a dictator from 1936 until his assassination in 1956. A "Somoza dynasty" seemed assured when Luis Somoza was elected to his father's office. He served from 1956 until 1962. In 1963 the official Somoza party, the Nationalist Liberals, elected René Schick as president. He died in office in 1966, and Dr. Lorenzo Guerrero Gutiérrez completed his term. In 1967 Major General Anastasio Somoza, a 1946 West Point graduate and a son of the former dictator, was elected for a five-year term, thus restoring the "dynasty." Luis Somoza died unexpectedly in April, 1967.

**GOVERNMENT AND POLITICS.** The Nicaraguan constitution vests considerable power in the executive branch of the republic and provides for direct popular election of the president and of a bicameral legislature (Senate and Chamber of Deputies).

**ECONOMY.** Political turmoil hampered economic development for years. Since about 1960, however, the economy has increased about 8.9 per cent annually. Rising productivity and development of land for agriculture account for much of the improvement in this country where 58 per cent of the people are farmers or raisers of livestock, and only 12 per cent are engaged in industry.

Major exports are cotton and coffee. Light industry produces mainly consumer goods. Though forests abound, the production of rubber, pine, and hardwoods has been little developed. Gold, silver, and (since 1958) copper represent the principal mineral wealth.

**EDUCATION AND HEALTH.** Education is compulsory for children from 7 to 14. About half of the population over ten is literate. There are two universities.

Health standards are not high, particularly in the rural areas. Poor sanitation and malnutrition cause many deaths. The government has been increasing its health and education expenditures since 1963, and the National Health Institute now provides free medical examinations.

**ARMED FORCES.** The National Guard, numbering about 5,400 men (plus a 4,000-man reserve), performs both police and army duties. The navy includes coast guard patrols. A small air force was formed in 1938. Military service is voluntary.

# NIGER

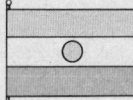

*Official Name:* Republic of Niger. *Area:* 489,189 square miles. *Population:* 3,433,-000. *Principal Cities* (with populations): Niamey, the capital, 41,975; Zinder, 23,-965; Tahoua, 18,415; Maradi, 18,250. *Flag:* Horizontal stripes of orange, white, and green with orange disk representing the sun in center stripe. *Monetary Unit:* CFA franc (worth 0.41 U.S. cent). *Gross National Product:* $250,000,-000.

**LAND AND PEOPLE.** Niger, a landlocked country in central West Africa, is bordered on the north by Algeria and Libya, on the east by Chad, on the south by Nigeria and Dahomey, on the southwest by Upper Volta, and on the west by Mali. (See map on page 111.) Most of northern and central Niger lies within the Sahara Desert, which merges into semi-desert toward the south. The climate is hot and dry; 48 per cent of the land has an average annual rainfall of less than four inches.

The population consists almost entirely of Africans belonging to four principal tribal groups: Hausa (43 per cent); Djerma-Songhai (20 per cent); Peul, or Fulani (14 per cent); and Touareg and other nomads (11 per cent). The other 12 per cent are made up of Europeans and other nonindigenous groups. Muslims comprise 73 per cent of the population, animists (those who follow tribal religions) 26 per cent, and Christians 1 per cent. French is the official language. Other tongues are the tribal Hausa, Tamachek, Djerma, and Peul (Fulani).

**HISTORY.** Because its frontiers lack natural barriers, Niger has had to contend throughout its history with migrations, smuggling, invasions, and secessionist movements. Several important West African empires have been located partly within its borders. From the seventh until the late 19th century portions of Niger successively belonged to the Songhai, Hausa, and Peul empires, and in the 17th century Touareg tribes formed confederations in the north.

European explorers who first reached Niger in the 19th century found a state of chronic warfare and anarchy. French penetration began in the 1890s with the establishment of military posts along the Niger River. Through conquest and treaties with local sultans and Britain, most of the country's present boundaries were set by 1914. After putting down a number of tribal revolts before and during World War I, the military government ended in 1921, when Niger became a colony under civil administration and a territory of the French West Africa federation.

In 1946 a political party was formed, the Parti Progressiste Nigérien (PPN). In 1950 it split into two factions, one led by the pro-French Hamani Diori and Boubou Hama, of the Djerma-Songhai, and the other by the Marxist-oriented Djibo Bakary, a Hausa. In 1958 Bakary formed the Sawaba Party and campaigned for independence from France and union with Northern Nigeria. The PPN, assisted by traditional chiefs and the French administration, ousted him from his position as head of Niger's government council, and he went into exile.

Niger became autonomous in 1958 and in August, 1960, was granted full independence. Diori, twice elected president of Niger, survived an assassination attempt in April, 1965. A serious border dispute with Dahomey was settled in the same year.

**GOVERNMENT AND POLITICS.** Niger is a republic, with executive power vested in a president elected by universal suffrage for a five-year term. Legislative power is vested in a 50-member National Assembly, similarly elected. The only legal political party, the PPN, is led by President Diori.

Niger's main political problems result from internal antagonisms—between "white" nomads and Negro sedentaries, between Djerma-Songhai and Hausa, and between traditional conservatives and Western-educated young radicals. The country's present leaders have maintained its territorial integrity and political stability but have not yet created a nation of its many tribes.

**ECONOMY.** Farming accounts for 64 per cent of the economy but is confined to the extreme south and covers only 2 per cent of the total area. Principal crops are millet, sorghum, beans, and rice, grown for domestic consumption, and peanuts and cotton for export. Animal husbandry—cattle, sheep, goats, and camels—provides 36 per cent of Niger's production, with the export of livestock to Nigeria a major source of cash income. Industry is limited to the processing of meat and a few crops, and the manufacture of cement. The discovery of a sizable uranium deposit in 1967 may promote economic expansion.

Niger's chronically unfavorable trade balance is largely due to poor internal communications, great distance from the nearest seaports (Cotonou in Dahomey and Lagos in Nigeria), and smuggling across the frontiers. Through a Four-Year Plan (1965–68) costing $176 million, the government hopes to increase production and exports by modernizing farming methods and reorganizing commerce.

**EDUCATION AND HEALTH.** Education is not compulsory, and only 10.8 per cent of school-age children attend classes. The literacy rate is 0.9 per cent for ages 15 and over.

The infant mortality rate is 20 per cent. In 1965 the country had 49 doctors.

**ARMED FORCES.** There are about 800 men in the army, which is equipped by France. The country participates in the mutual defense pact of the Afro-Malagasy Common Organization (OCAM).

## NIGERIA

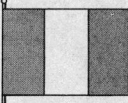

*Official Name:* Federation of Nigeria. *Area:* 356,667 square miles. *Population:* 58,600,000. *Principal Cities* (with populations): Lagos, the capital, 665,246; Ibadan, 627,379; Ogbomosho, 343,279; Mushin, 312,-063. *Flag:* Three vertical bars of green, white, and green. *Monetary Unit:* The Nigerian pound (worth U.S. $2.80). *Gross National Product:* $4,852,000,000 (1965). *Average Annual Income per Person:* $114.

**LAND AND PEOPLE.** Situated on the West Coast of Africa, Nigeria is bordered on the north and northwest by Niger, on the northeast by Lake Chad, on the east by Cameroon, on the south by the Gulf of Guinea, and on the west by Dahomey. (See map on page 111.) Coastal mangrove swamps along the Atlantic coast give way to tropical forests, which ascend to a high savanna plateau reaching 6,000 feet above sea level.

Africa's most populous country, Nigeria is composed of 250 ethnic groups, each with its own language. Three groups are dominant: the Hausa-Fulani (about 25 per cent of the population) in the Northern Region; the Yoruba (23 per cent) in the Western Region; and the Ibo (14 per cent) in the Eastern Region. Each of these groups has the characteristics of a nation. Thus Nigeria is essentially a multinational country with many ethnic minorities.

About 42 per cent of the people are Muslims, 33 per cent follow tribal religions, and 25 per cent are Christians.

**HISTORY.** Nigeria's earliest known culture, Nok, flourished in 500 B.C. However, modern Nigeria's history started about 1,000 years ago with the emergence of diverse empires and kingdoms along the southern fringes of the Sahara and in the tropical forests. Sometime in the first millennium migrants from the northeast established the Yoruba and Edo kingdoms of Oyo and Benin and the spiritual center of Ife.

The sub-Saharan states were founded in the seventh and eighth centuries A.D. by the Zaghawa nomads, thought to be of Berber origin. These states were the forerunners of the Kanem Empire, which was established in the eighth century. Islamic traditions were spread by Kanem's expanding influence and were diffused through the seven Hausa city-states on the savanna fringes of the western Sahara. By the 15th century several of these city-states, including Kano, Zaria, and Katsina, were flourishing centers of culture and commerce.

In the 15th and 16th centuries the Portu-

The New York Times

These Ibo refugees took shelter in a Nigerian school.

On January 15, 1966, the national government was ousted by a military coup attributed to young Ibo officers. The federal prime minister, Sir Abubakr Tafawa Balewa, and the premiers of the Western and Northern Regions were among those murdered. Power was taken from the young mutineers by the army chief of staff, Major General Johnson Aguiyi-Ironsi, himself an Ibo. Northern fears of possible Ibo domination were strengthened by Ironsi's decision in May, 1966, to dissolve the federation in favor of a unitary Republic. Anti-Ibo riots in the north were followed on July 29 by a second army mutiny in which Ironsi was murdered.

The new military leadership was an uneasy coalition between the regions under a Supreme Military Commander, Lt. Col. Yakubu Gowon, who, though a Northerner, was a Christian from a non-Hausa minority group. The second mutiny, however, had strong anti-Ibo overtones, which were sharply accentuated by two outbursts of violence against the Ibo in the north; thousands were massacred in September and October, 1966, and more than a million Ibo were driven out of the north.

On May 30, 1967, the young Ibo leader, Col. Odumegwu Ojukwu, proclaimed the Republic of Biafra (the 29,484-square-mile former Eastern Region) as a separate state. Biafra's secession was resisted by the rest of the country on three grounds: (1) much of the oil wealth of Nigeria lay in Biafra; (2) its 12,000,000 inhabitants included 5,000,000 non-Ibo; (3) its secession would precipitate the total fragmentation of Nigeria. Therefore, in July, 1967, the Nigerian government decided to crush the Biafra secession by force. Federal troops invaded the region and reached Enugu, the capital, in October. Meanwhile, however, the new military regime had itself introduced radical political changes by creating a federation of 12 states in place of the original four regions.

Whatever the outcome of the military conflict, the future of Nigeria probably will remain unsettled for some time to come. Its economy has been severely damaged by the civil war. Its international relations are being transformed, partly because of the refusal of its traditional allies to supply military aid and the subsequent successful appeal to the Soviet bloc for military aircraft.

**GOVERNMENT.** Nigeria is led by a military government under the Chief of State, Yakubu Gowon, who assumed control on August 1, 1966, in an effort to restore national unity in the wake of two rebel coups.

**ECONOMY.** Nigeria is primarily an agricultural country, depending heavily on oil-palm produce, cocoa, peanuts, rubber, and cotton. Over 75 per cent of the people are farmers. In recent years it has become the 12th largest oil producer in the world.

**EDUCATION.** There is no compulsory education. The literacy rate varies from 2 per cent in the North to 16 per cent in the East and 18 per cent in the West.

**ARMED FORCES.** Nigeria has an army of 9,000, a navy of 1,500, and an air force of 1,000.

guese and then the British engaged in commerce and slave trading on the Atlantic coast. (The Hausa city-states, however, were hardly touched by the advent of Western influence; their fortunes were profoundly altered by the Islamic crusade of the Fulani warrior Usman dan Fodio at the beginning of the 19th century.) Exportation of slaves, forbidden by the British in 1807, ended in 1861. In 1883 the Niger Coast Protectorate was declared, and in 1885 the Berlin conference recognized Britain's claim to southern Nigeria. In 1886 the Royal Niger Company was formed to explore the interior; 20 years later the British established their control over the northern and southern areas of Nigeria. In 1914 they were joined to form the unified colony and protectorate of Nigeria.

After World War II the nationalist movement became more intense, receiving strong support mainly from Ibo leadership. In 1954 Nigeria became a federation of three autonomous regions, later increased to four. In 1960 it became an independent member of the Commonwealth of Nations.

Nigeria's success at independence rested on its leaders' capacity to maintain a political system acceptable to each of the three major national groups—the Hausa-Fulani, the Yoruba, and the Ibo—and to the 250 tribal and clan minorities. Regional cultural factors (north versus south) rather than religion (Islam versus Christianity) were the decisive factors. Until 1965 an uneasy political balance was maintained by a coalition in the federal government between the northern Hausa-Fulani and the eastern Ibo, with the Yoruba of the west forming the opposition. But pressure on the Yoruba led to a split in the government of the Western Region, necessitating emergency rule to cope with the subsequent breakdown of law and order.

# NORWAY

*Official Name:* Kingdom of Norway. *Area:* 125,181 square miles. *Population:* 3,753,000. *Principal Cities* (with populations): Oslo, the capital, 486,000; Trondheim, 117,500; Bergen, 117,000. *Flag:* A blue Latin cross bordered in white on a red field. *Monetary Unit:* The krone (worth 14 U.S. cents). *Gross National Product:* $7,000,000,000 (1965). *Average Annual Income per Person:* $1,149.

**LAND AND PEOPLE.** Norway occupies the western and northernmost part of the Scandinavian peninsula. It is bordered on the north by the Arctic Ocean and on the northeast by Finland and the U.S.S.R.; on the east by Sweden; on the south and southwest by the North Sea; and on the west by the Atlantic Ocean. (See map on page 117.) About a third of the country lies within the Arctic Circle. The terrain is mountainous, and the 1,700-mile coastline is deeply marked with fjords, bays, and inlets. There are numerous offshore island chains.

Norway's climate is comparatively mild due to the Gulf Stream. The far north is the land of the midnight sun; daylight is continuous from mid-May to the last of July, and from late November to the end of January the sun does not rise above the horizon.

The population is extremely homogeneous—98.5 per cent of the people are Norwegian-born. There is a Lapp minority of 20,000. The official language, Norwegian, exists in two forms: Riksmål, which is derived from Danish, long the literary language of Norway; and Landsmål. About 96 per cent of the population is Evangelical Lutheran, the state religion.

**HISTORY.** Hunters and fishermen lived in Norway as early as the Stone Age. Earldoms and small kingdoms, which first emerged during the Iron Age, were united in the ninth century by Harold Fairhair (Harold I), Norway's first king. Christianity was introduced by Olaf I (995–1000) and continued by Olaf II, who was ultimately canonized. Olaf II was killed by a peasant army in 1030, and Norway passed under the rule of Canute the Great of England and Denmark.

Magnus I, son of Olaf II, gained the throne in 1035, and in 1046 shared the crown with his uncle, Harold III. A year later Harold became the sole king. Both men played a large part in the complex 11th-century politics and warfare of Denmark and England. The latter half of the 12th century was a period of warfare among contenders to the throne. A strong monarchy was finally established by Sverre. Under his grandson, Haakon IV, Norway reached its medieval zenith, acquiring Iceland, Greenland, the Faeroe Islands, the Shetlands, and the Orkneys. The royal line died out with Haakon V in 1319, and Norway entered into union with Sweden under Magnus VII. Queen Margaret of Denmark united the three Scandinavian kingdoms in the Union of Kalmar (1397), which lasted until Sweden broke away in 1523.

Union between Norway and Denmark lasted until 1814, with Denmark being ascendant.

The Danes granted substantial economic freedom to the Norwegians, and by the 17th century Norway had regained its prosperity. Denmark allied with France during the Napoleonic Wars. After Napoleon's defeat, Denmark was forced to cede Norway to Sweden. Norway failed in an effort to form a separate kingdom, and in 1814 the country was forced by military intervention to accept Swedish rule. However, Norway was officially recognized as an independent kingdom, but in union with Sweden. Tensions existed between the two nations throughout the 19th century. In 1905, when the Norwegian Parliament declared the union dissolved, Norway became totally free.

Norway was neutral in World War I and sought neutrality in World War II. However, Germany invaded in April, 1940, and occupied the country until 1945. King Haakon VII set up a government-in-exile in London. A puppet government was established under Premier Quisling, a Norwegian national whose name has become synonymous with treason.

The postwar period saw rapid economic and industrial recovery and development, as well as the enactment of much progressive legislation. With the death of Haakon VII in 1957, Olav V succeeded to the throne.

**GOVERNMENT AND POLITICS.** Norway is a constitutional monarchy. Executive power is exercised by the king through the prime minister and cabinet. Legislative power is invested in the Storting (Parliament) whose 150 representatives are elected to four-year terms by direct adult suffrage. The 1965 elections brought to an end almost 30 years of unbroken Labor Party rule and installed a coalition of the four non-Socialist parties.

**ECONOMY.** Norway's economy, once based primarily on agriculture and fishing, is now also industrial, with manufacturing and shipping services playing important roles. Forests remain one of the country's most valuable natural resources. Agriculture and livestock raising are limited because less than 4 per cent of the land is cultivable.

Major industries are fish processing, paper and pulp manufacture, electrochemical and electrometallurgical processing, shipbuilding, food processing, textiles, and tourism. The merchant marine brings in about 14 per cent of the national income and this, together with the income from tourism, helps to balance the gap between imports and exports.

**EDUCATION AND HEALTH.** Education is compulsory for children between the ages of 7 and 16, and virtually all Norwegians are literate. There are two universities—one at Oslo and one at Bergen—as well as a technological institute at Trondheim and an agricultural college at Ås.

Health standards are excellent; in 1965 it was reported that there was one doctor for every 1,796 people.

**ARMED FORCES.** Norway's armed forces include 18,000 in the army, 5,200 in the navy, and 4,800 in the air force.

## NORWEGIAN TERRITORIES AND DEPENDENCIES

### SVALBARD

*Area:* 23,950 square miles. *Population:* 3,700.

Svalbard, some 400 miles north of Norway, is a barren archipelago with an Arctic climate. The largest island of the archipelago is West Spitsbergen. About 64 per cent of the population are Russian; the rest are Norwegian.

It is believed that the islands first were found by Norwegians near the end of the 12th century. The Dutch rediscovered them in 1596, and in the 17th century rival claims were made by the Dutch, British, and Norwegians. After that time sovereignty disappeared as an issue until the 20th century, when rich coal deposits were discovered. In 1920 Norway's sovereignty was recognized; five years later, Svalbard officially became part of Norway.

There are six mining camps (three Russian and three Norwegian), but only three are in operation. Oil prospecting has begun, and in mid-1965 a Norwegian and a U.S. oil company each began deep drilling.

Svalbard's governor, responsible to Norway's Minister of Industry, lives at Longyearbyen on West Spitsbergen.

**JAN MAYEN.** Annexed in 1929, it is an island of 145 square miles some 300 miles north of Iceland. It has a meteorological station.

**BOUVET ISLAND.** An uninhabited island of 36 square miles in the South Atlantic, it was made a dependency in 1930.

**PETER I ISLAND.** An uninhabited island of 150 square miles in the Antarctic Ocean, it became a dependency in 1933.

**QUEEN MAUD LAND.** A large sector of the Antarctic continent, it lies between longitude 20° west and 45° east. The area was placed under Norwegian sovereignty in 1939.

## PAKISTAN

*Official Name:* Islamic Republic of Pakistan. *Area:* 365,527 square miles. *Population:* 105,044,000 (excluding Jammu and Kashmir). *Principal Cities* (with populations): Rawalpindi, the temporary capital, 340,175; Karachi, 1,912,598; Lahore, 1,296,477; Dacca, 556,712; Hyderabad, 434,537; Lyalpur, 425,248. *Flag:* A green field with a white crescent and star; there is a white band at the flagstaff. *Monetary Unit:* The rupee (worth 21 U.S. cents). *Gross National Product:* $10,008,364,000 (1965). *Average Annual Income per Person:* $87.

**LAND AND PEOPLE.** Pakistan is divided into two distinct provinces by about 1,000 miles of Indian territory. West Pakistan occupies 310,403 square miles, or nearly six times the area of East Pakistan, and is bordered on the west by Iran, on the northwest and north by Afghanistan, on the northeast by Communist China, on the east and southeast by the disputed territories of Jammu and Kashmir, and on the south by the Arabian Sea. East Pakistan is bordered on the north, east, and west by India, on the southeast by Burma, and on the south by the Bay of Bengal. (See map on page 139.)

West Pakistan rises from the arid wastes of Sind and Baluchistan in the south and west to the forested hills in the north, and then to the soaring heights of the Himalaya Mountains. The Indus River, flowing more than 1,000 miles from Kashmir to the Arabian Sea, irrigates much of the eastern and central region. Temperatures range from as high as 120° F. in the summer to 30° F. or colder in the winter. Rainfall averages from 15 inches a year in the Indus River basin to 60 inches in the northern areas. More than two-thirds of the territory is arid or semi-arid.

With an average of 1,000 persons per square mile, East Pakistan is among the world's most densely populated areas. The climate throughout the year is warm and humid, with heavy rainfall during the monsoon season. There are primeval forests in the southeast. Many river valleys and extensive deltas mark the area. The main rivers include the Ganges, Brahmaputra, and Meghna.

West Pakistanis are mainly of mixed Baluchi, Pathan, and Arab ancestry. East Pakistanis are mostly Bengalis, probably of Dravidian origin. Bengali is the official language of East Pakistan, Urdu that of West Pakistan; English is used in government and commerce. Islam, the official religion, accounts for 88.1 per cent of the population; Hinduism for 10.7 per cent; Christianity for 0.8 per cent and Buddhism for 0.4 per cent.

**HISTORY.** The Indus Valley civilization in the West Pakistan region was displaced in the second millennium B.C. by barbarian Aryan tribesmen from the Asian steppes. About 326 B.C. Alexander the Great invaded and conquered the Punjab, in central West Pakistan. By 305 B.C. Sandracottus had expelled the last of Alexander's successors from Gandhara, a region astride the Indus River, and founded the Maurya Empire, which a century later was converted to Buddhism. The Maurya civilization flourished from the first century A.D., under the strong Kushan king, Kanishka, until the sixth century.

Islam began its spread into the subcontinent in the 8th century, followed by a series of Muslim invaders. The powerful Mogul Empire was at its peak during the 16th century. Europeans first arrived in the late 15th century, and by the 17th century the British East India Company had become dominant. Using Hindu uprisings as justification, the British and French in the mid-18th century fought for control of India. By 1757 Britain had firmly established its hold. Under the British the Hindus gradually assumed positions of leadership.

In the early stages of the struggle for independence, Muslim political leaders were closely associated with the Indian National Congress, a political group founded in 1885. However, the Muslim League, founded in 1906, grew substantially in membership after World War I. Agitation for a separate Muslim state increased in the 1930s under the leadership of Mohammed Iqbal and Mohammed Ali Jinnah.

The Muslim League demanded a separate state composed of those areas of the Indian subcontinent where Muslims were the majority. The Muslim League supported Great Britain during World War II, while the Indian National Congress was split by anti-British factions. Finally, in 1947, Britain agreed to the formation of a separate state, and India and Pakistan came into being as independent countries within the Commonwealth of Nations.

The Muslim-Hindu disputes intensified after independence. States with Hindu majorities but Muslim rulers were forcibly joined to India. Kashmir, a state with a majority of Muslim residents but ruled by a Hindu minority, became the chief point of contention, and fighting over control of Kashmir broke out between Pakistan and India in 1948. The U.N. negotiated a cease-fire the following year, but tension remained high. Pakistani-Indian fighting resumed in September, 1965, and for a while full-scale warfare threatened. A peace accord was finally signed early in 1966.

Elsewhere, Pakistan faced economic and political difficulties. In the early 1950s Afghanistan supported the Pathans' demand for creation of an independent state. Border clashes broke out, and Pakistani-Afghan diplomatic relations were severed; they have since been resumed.

President Iskander Mirza declared martial law in 1958, abrogated the constitution, and gave overall power to Field Marshal Mohammed Ayub Khan, who took the title of president. Ayub Khan, who ruled by decree, instituted a program of land reform and promulgated a new constitution in 1962. Under this constitution elections were held for the National Assembly and the two provincial assemblies. Political parties resumed their activities, and the President himself assumed leadership of the reconstituted Muslim League. Three years later he won re-election, and his party gained a decisive majority in the central legislature and control of both provincial assemblies.

**GOVERNMENT AND POLITICS.** Pakistan's government is a federal republic with a constitution providing for a strong executive. The legislatures are elected for five years by an electoral college, whose members are chosen by means of universal suffrage. In 1967 the National Assembly consisted of 75 men and 3 women from each of the two provinces. The two provincial assemblies each had 150 men and 5 women. The president is also elected for five years by the electoral college, and he in turn appoints the governors.

There are two major political parties. The Pakistan Muslim League (the President's party) controls the legislatures. It is challenged, especially in East Pakistan, by the Combined Opposition. The nation's political stability owes much to the support of the bureaucracy and the armed forces. The government generally respects individual rights, but freedom of the press is at times impaired.

**ECONOMY.** Pakistan's third five-year plan, which set forth ambitious goals in industrial growth, was inaugurated in 1965. Agriculture, however, generates almost half the annual gross national product, and 90 to 95 per cent of foreign exchange earnings are derived from agricultural exports. Some 85 per cent of the people are dependent on farming. Produce includes grains, jute, cotton, tea, sugarcane, wool, and hides and skins. Rice and jute are grown mostly in East Pakistan, wheat and cotton in the West. The country exports 75 per cent of the world's jute and is also a leading cotton exporter. Timber is being rapidly depleted, and soil erosion has become a growing threat in West Pakistan.

Pakistan has about 7,000 miles of railroads; less than a quarter of the mileage is in East Pakistan, where inland waterways are a major means of transportation. Roads total 65,000 miles, including 10,500 miles of all-weather highways. Several foreign airlines service Karachi's airport. Pakistan International Airlines provides internal and foreign service.

**EDUCATION AND HEALTH.** Only about 30 per cent of the children attend primary schools; teachers are largely untrained. Literacy is estimated at about 19 per cent.

Health conditions are generally poor; the infant mortality rate is formidable, with some 25 per cent of the children dying before the age of four. There are fewer than 10,000 physicians, most of whom are in the cities.

**ARMED FORCES.** Military service is voluntary. Although the country's military strength is a closely guarded secret, it is estimated that there are 230,000 men in the army, 8,350 in the navy, and 15,000 in the air force.

# PANAMA

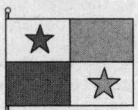

*Official Name:* Republic of Panama. *Area:* 28,576 square miles. *Population:* 1,287,000 (excluding the Canal Zone). *Principal Cities* (with populations): Panama City, the capital, 348,000; Colón, 65,-000. *Flag:* Quarters of blue, red, and white with blue and red stars on the two white quarters. *Monetary Unit:* The Balboa (worth U.S. $1). *Gross National Product:* $646,000,000 (1965). *Average Annual Income per Person:* $425.

**LAND AND PEOPLE.** Panama is located between the Caribbean and the Pacific, on the isthmus linking Central and South America. Colombia is to the east and Costa Rica to the west. (See map on page 176.) Mountains stretch along the coasts, enclosing heavily wooded inland plateaus, valleys, and ridges. Panama has nearly 500 rivers that flow into the Pacific, but only the Tuira is commercially important. There are more than 1,600 offshore islands; the largest, Coiba, is a penal colony. Panama's climate is generally tropical, but higher inland regions are cooler. Rainfall averages 117 inches on the Caribbean coast and 63 inches on the Pacific coast.

About 65 per cent of the people are mestizo or mulatto; 13 per cent are Negro; 11 per cent are white; 10 per cent are Indian; and 1 per cent are Oriental. Spanish is the official language. The country is predominantly Roman Catholic.

**HISTORY.** Panama's history has been shaped by its strategic location between oceans. Bastidas explored eastern Panama in 1501, and Columbus claimed the area for Spain in the following year. In 1513 Balboa crossed the narrow isthmus, becoming the first white man to see the eastern shore of the Pacific. Occupied by Spaniards, Panama served as the route for shipping Inca treasures to Spain in the 16th and 17th centuries. Spanish rule was overthrown in 1821, and Panama voluntarily became a province of Colombia.

The California gold rush in 1849 revived interest in Panama's geographical importance as a route from the Atlantic to the Pacific. The Panama Railroad (completed in 1855) carried gold-rush traffic across the isthmus. However, the value of an interocean canal to eliminate the long sea journey around the tip of South America became increasingly evident. French attempts during the 1880s to build a canal were unsuccessful. The U.S. bought the canal rights from France, but Colombia—still controlling Panamanian territory—demanded higher fees for construction rights than were offered. In 1903, with indirect U.S. support, Panama revolted and declared its independence. The U.S. quickly recognized the new government, and Panama immediately granted the U.S. permission to build the canal (the Hay-Bunau-Varilla Treaty). Construction of the canal began in 1904; it opened in 1914.

The Panama Canal Zone, extending five miles on both sides of the waterway, cuts across the country from Colón to Balboa on the Pacific. U.S. sovereignty over the area has been a persistent issue in Panamanian politics. In treaty revisions of 1939 and 1955 the U.S. accepted certain business and residence limitations and raised its annual rental payments for the Zone to $1,930,000. Rioting by Panamanians in 1964 disrupted relations briefly. The two countries drew up a new treaty in 1967, subject to ratification by their governments.

**GOVERNMENT AND POLITICS.** The Republic of Panama is governed by a president and a 55-member National Assembly elected to 4-year terms by popular vote. Nine provinces are administered by governors appointed by the president. Marco Aurelio Robles of the Liberal Party was elected president in 1964. The major challenge to his coalition government has been to work out a new agreement for control of the Canal Zone.

**ECONOMY.** The economy is centered about the canal, but exports of bananas, shrimp, coffee, sugar, cacao, coconuts, and refined petroleum products are also of major economic importance. Industrial development, particularly cement and cement manufacturing, has been increasing since World War II.

**EDUCATION.** Education is free and compulsory between the ages of 7 and 15. The literacy rate is 76.6 per cent.

**ARMED FORCES.** Panama has a 3,900-man National Guard, but no standing army.

# PARAGUAY

*Official Name:* Republic of Paraguay. *Area:* 157,047 square miles. *Population:* 2,094,000. *Principal Cities* (with populations): Asunción, the capital, 305,000; Encarnación, 19,000; Concepción, 18,200; Villarrica, 15,600. *Flag:* A red, white, and blue horizontal tricolor with the national coat of arms in the center of the white stripe; the reverse side is the Treasury seal. *Monetary Unit:* The guaraní (worth 81 U.S. cents). *Gross National Product:* $459,000,000 (1966). *Average Annual Income per Person:* $175.

**LAND AND PEOPLE.** Situated in central South America, the landlocked Republic of Paraguay is bounded on the south and west by Argentina, on the northeast by Brazil, and on the northwest by Bolivia. (See map on page 75.) The Paraguay and Alto Paraná rivers are important waterways. To the west of the Paraguay River lies the arid, sparsely settled region of the Chaco Boreal; the area to the east is rich in vegetation and is heavily populated. The climate is subtropical; temperatures range from 35° F. in winter to over 100° F. in summer.

The population is 95 per cent mestizo (mixed Spanish and Guaraní Indian). Immigration is encouraged by the government and there are small settlements of Germans, Japanese, and Koreans. The official languages are Spanish and Guaraní. Approximately 92 per cent of the population adhere to Roman Catholicism, the state religion.

**HISTORY.** Spanish conquistadores came to Paraguay in 1524, establishing Asunción in 1537 and intermarrying with the docile Guaraní Indians. Between the 16th and 17th centuries Jesuit missionaries constituted the dominant influence in the country. They instituted a written form of the Guaraní language, thus preserving a tongue that is used by almost all Paraguayans today.

Independence from Spain, peacefully achieved in 1811, was followed by the dictatorships of José Gaspar Rodríguez Francia (1814–40); Carlos Antonio López (1842–62); and López's son, Francisco Solano López (1862–70). In 1865 López plunged his country into war with Brazil, Argentina, and Uruguay. At the war's end in 1870 Paraguay had lost 55,000 square miles of territory and over half her population.

Economic problems and political instability plagued the country thereafter. In 1932 a territorial dispute led to a three-year war with Bolivia. Paraguay emerged victorious, but at a cost of some 40,000 men. Higinio Morínigo established a dictatorship in 1940, but was unseated in 1948. In 1954 General Alfredo Stroessner ousted the legal president, Federico Chávez, and has retained power since that time.

**GOVERNMENT AND POLITICS.** Under the constitution of 1940 Paraguay is a parliamentary republic. Power is concentrated in the president, who must be a Catholic. He appoints a ten-man cabinet and an advisory Council of

State. The president is constitutionally limited to two five-year terms of office, although President Stroessner took office for a third term in 1963. A legislature of 60 members and 60 alternates is elected by proportional representation. Political parties are restricted, and the Communist Party is outlawed.

Since 1940, presidents have suspended constitutional guarantees and ruled by decree. Many Paraguayans have fled the country, and about a third of the population is said to live in exile.

**ECONOMY.** Agriculture accounts for 37 per cent and manufacturing for 17.4 per cent of the gross national product, which has increased about 4 per cent yearly since 1963. Cattle raising is the leading economic activity. Paraguay must import most of her manufactured goods and much of her food.

Paraguay depends primarily on Argentina for access to the seas. To reduce economic ties with Argentina, Paraguay is studying with Brazil the joint development of common water resources. In 1964 Paraguay finished the 475-mile Trans-Chaco road to the Bolivian border and in 1965 completed a highway link with the Brazilian port of Paranagua.

**EDUCATION AND HEALTH.** Education is free and compulsory between the ages of 7 and 14; 68 per cent of the population above the age of 7 is literate.

The Servicio Cooperativo Interamericano, created in 1942, administers public health and welfare programs. Most medical facilities are in cities and towns, although rural hospitals have been built.

**ARMED FORCES.** Military service is compulsory for men over 18. Paraguay's armed forces total 9,100, of whom 7,000 are in the army.

# PERSIAN GULF STATES

*Official Names:* Sheikhdom of Bahrain; Sheikhdom of Qatar; and the Trucial States, consisting of the sheikhdoms of Sharjah, Ras al Khaimah, Umm al Quwain, Ajman, Dubai, Abu Dhabi, and Fujairah. *Areas:* Bahrain, 231 square miles; Qatar, 8,500 square miles; Trucial States, 32,000 square miles. *Populations:* Bahrain, 150,000; Qatar, 55,000; Trucial States, 110,000. *Principal Cities* (with populations): Manama, capital of Bahrain, 62,000; Dubai (Trucial States) 55,000; Muharraq (Bahrain) 32,000; Doha, capital of Qatar, 30,000. *Flags:* Bahrain: a red rectangle with a serrated white stripe; Qatar: a maroon rectangle with a serrated white stripe; Fujairah, Ras al Khaimah, and Sharjah: a white square containing a red square; Abu Dhabi, Ajman, Dubai, and Umm al Quwain: a red rectangle with a white stripe. *Monetary Units:* Persian Gulf rupee (worth 21.1 U.S. cents); Bahrain dinar (worth $2.11).

**LAND AND PEOPLE.** The Persian Gulf States (Bahrain, Qatar, and the seven Trucial States) are British-protected states situated in southeast Arabia. (See map on page 151.) The four islands of the Bahrain archipelago lie between the Saudi Arabian mainland and the west coast of Qatar, a peninsula protruding north into the Persian Gulf. The seven Trucial States line the coast, extending about 400 miles southeast from Qatar. Sand and gravel plains are interspersed with salt flats, and massive sand dunes reach inland to the Saudi Arabian frontier. Humid summer temperatures range from 90° F. to 120° F.; winter temperatures average 60° F.

The population is basically Arab and the language Arabic. The majority of the people are Sunni Muslims, with a minority of Shiite Muslims.

**HISTORY.** After several centuries of independence, Bahrain was ruled by Portugal in the 16th and 17th centuries and by Iran in the 17th and 18th centuries. The Iranians were expelled in 1783 by an Arabian tribe that established the present ruling dynasty. Qatar had an obscure early history. The Trucial States were noted as the Pirate Coast.

From the early 1800s onward, the Persian Gulf States gradually came under British protection. Contact between Arab pirates and Englishmen developed when Britain determined to end the slave trade in the Persian Gulf. Piracy ended in 1853 when all the principal sheikhs signed the Perpetual Maritime Truce, arranged and supervised by Britain. Economic development soared when oil in commercial quantity was discovered in Bahrain and Qatar in the 1930s and in Abu Dhabi in 1962.

**GOVERNMENT AND POLITICS.** Between 1880 and 1916 the sheikhs of the Persian Gulf States concluded treaties of protection with Britain. These treaties committed the British to defend the region and forbade the sheikhs to dispose of parts of their territories to anyone except Britain. The sheikhs (who inherit their sheikhdoms) exercise absolute rule within their domains. The British government, however, handles foreign relations. Also, British political agents act as advisers to the sheikhs and as judges for the British courts.

**ECONOMY.** Oil is the mainstay of the economy of the Persian Gulf States. Oil production in the Trucial State of Abu Dhabi alone totaled 16.2 million tons in 1966. Oil from offshore fields supports Qatar's economy. Also, a large oil refinery is located on Bahrain Island. Pearl fishing, once a major trade, has declined. Agriculture centers on date palm cultivation.

Bahrain and Qatar contain a network of surfaced roads, but the Trucial States are served only by sandy tracks. Ten steamship lines call regularly at Bahrain. International airlines use the Muharraq Airport in Bahrain.

**EDUCATION AND HEALTH.** Illiteracy ranges from an estimated 74 per cent in Bahrain to probably over 95 per cent in Qatar and the Trucial States. Educational facilities are limited, and schooling is not compulsory.

Medical facilities are concentrated in Bahrain and Qatar, which provide free health services. There are also several hospitals in Dubai, Ras al Khaimah, and Buraimi.

**ARMED FORCES.** Britain is responsible for defense, and the Persian Gulf States have no compulsory military service. The Trucial States have a small constabulary force of about 3,000, known as the Trucial Oman Scouts.

# PERU

*Official Name:* Republic of Peru. *Area:* 496,222 square miles. *Population:* 12,385,200. *Principal Cities* (with populations): Lima, the capital, 1,436,231; Callao, 155,953; Arequipa, 135,358; Trujillo, 100,130; Chiclayo, 96,000. *Flag:* Vertical red, white, and red stripes, with the coat of arms centered on the white stripe. *Monetary Unit:* The sol (worth 3 U.S. cents). *Gross National Product:* $4,880,000,000 (1966). *Annual Average Income per Person:* $378.

**LAND AND PEOPLE.** Peru ranges along the west coast of South America and is the third largest country on the continent. It is bordered by Ecuador and Colombia on the north, Brazil and Bolivia on the east, Chile on the south, and the Pacific Ocean on the west. (See map on page 75.)

The Andes Mountains, running roughly parallel to the coastline, form the Peruvian continental divide and split the country into four isolated areas. The eastern slope, known as the Selva (jungle), stretches to the Amazon basin, into which the Marañón, Huallaga, and Ucayali rivers drain Sparsely settled by primitive Indians, it is a hot, humid area of rain forests and jungles.

The sierra (upland plateau) has an average elevation of 13,000 feet. In the western cordillera of the Andes is Huascarán, one of South America's loftiest peaks (22,180 feet). This region, crisscrossed with rivers, contains about one-fourth of the country's total area and about 60 per cent of the population. El Misti, a volcanic peak famous in legend, is in the south. Lake Titicaca, the highest navigable lake in the world, lies on the Bolivian border.

The western Andes descend into a flat desert strip extending about 1,400 miles along the Pacific Coast. Parts of the strip are kept semiarid by the Humboldt (or Peru) Current, while in other sections mountain streams irrigate agricultural areas. The mountain and desert areas are hit periodically by torrential rains and severe earthquakes. Climate varies with altitude: tropical in the lowlands; temperate above 3,000 feet; and cold above 10,000 feet, with snow and bitter frost all year round on the highest peaks.

About 46 per cent of the people are Indian, 43 per cent mestizo, and 11 per cent white. Roman Catholicism, the state religion, is the faith of 95 per cent of the population. Spanish is the official language, but Indian languages are spoken by the Indian population.

**HISTORY.** The Inca empire, with its capital at Cuzco in the Peruvian Andes, controlled territory from Ecuador to Chile for centuries before the coming of the Spanish conquistadores. Drawn by the glittering stores of Inca treasure, Francisco Pizarro conquered the empire in 1533. Peru became the most important Spanish territory in the New World. Lima, established in 1535, was for three centuries the seat of Spanish control over all Hispanic South America except Venezuela.

The Andes yielded such vast wealth, particularly in gold, that Spain did not give up Peru until 1824, when revolutionary forces under José de San Martín and Simón Bolívar won Peruvian independence. From 1826 until 1908 Peru was beset by rigid class structure, political instability, and militarism. The Indians remained subject to an oligarchy of wealthy landowners.

By the turn of the century foreign interest in Peruvian resources, plus local efforts, had developed a more stable economy. Augusto B. Leguía, energetic and able, was president from 1908 to 1912 and seized power again in 1919. Civil strife followed the end of his authoritarian regime in 1930, and liberal reform movements emerged. Attempts to establish a moderate government following World War II failed, and in 1948 a rightist military revolt installed General Manuel Odría as head of the government. The Odría regime brought some economic progress and political stability. Odría submitted to free elections in 1956, and Manuel Prado, a conservative who had been president during World War II, returned to office. Although troubled by civil unrest, the Prado regime achieved considerable economic stability.

In 1962 an election dispute led to military intervention. A military junta ruled until 1963, when elections were held; Fernando Belaúnde Terry was elected president as the candidate of the Christian Democratic and Popular Action parties. However, the American Popular Revolutionary Alliance (APRA) and the Odrista National Union gained control of the Congress, an advantage which they still retain.

**GOVERNMENT AND POLITICS.** The constitution of 1933 established Peru as a republic governed by a president and a bicameral congress. Both are elected to six-year terms by popular vote. Strong executive power is vested in the president, who is prohibited from running for a consecutive term.

There are four major political parties. The APRA controls most of unionized labor and is anti-Communist. President Belaúnde Terry's Popular Action Party represents the moderate left. The Christian Democratic Party is representative of the Christian social movement throughout the hemisphere, and the Odrista National Union is made up of followers of ex-President Odría. The Communist Party, outlawed in 1948, was resurrected as the Revolutionary Labor Party.

The opposition majority in Congress has cut many of the present administration's social reforms and development plans. This has made it difficult for Belaúnde to enact his program of agrarian, tax, and social reforms. However, the government has been able to make strides in low-cost housing, education, and rural (particularly Indian) community development.

**ECONOMY.** Agriculture is the base of Peru's economy. It contributes 25 per cent of the gross national product and is the source of livelihood for half the population. Leading crops are cotton, sugar, and coffee, which are also among the chief exports. Peru is the world's largest producer and exporter of fish meal; other important exports are wool and metals. Mining is the nation's most important industry with copper, lead, zinc, gold, silver, vanadium, and uranium among the leading ores exploited; petroleum production is expanding.

The manufacture of consumer goods comprises 90 per cent of Peru's industrial production. Economic expansion has favored the urbanized Pacific Coast areas, where capital and industry are concentrated. In recent years large capital investments, provided by earnings from mineral resources, have opened the eastern Andean slopes to agriculture and provided irrigation for the western deserts.

**EDUCATION.** Primary education is free and compulsory for children between 6 and 16; secondary education is also free. About 61.1 per cent of the population 15 years and older is literate.

**ARMED FORCES.** Military service for men ages 20 to 25 is compulsory. The army numbers 30,000 men and the navy 7,200 men; there is a separate air force.

# PHILIPPINES

*Official Name:* Republic of the Philippines. *Area:* 116,-000 square miles. *Population:* 33,500,000. *Principal Cities* (with populations): Manila, the administrative capital, 1,350,000; Quezon City, the legal capital, 475,400; Cebu, 296,000; Davao, 265,800. *Flag:* Blue and red bands bordered by a white triangle containing yellow stars and a sun. *Monetary Unit:* The peso (worth 25.7 U.S. cents). *Gross National Product:* $5,700,000,000 (1966). *Average Annual Income per Person:* $143.

**LAND AND PEOPLE.** The Philippine archipelago, consisting of 7,100 islands, stretches some 1,200 miles in a spray of islands from within 40 miles of Taiwan (Formosa) to within 90 miles of Borneo. (See map on page 67.) Most of the islands consist of mountain ranges, valleys and plains, and narrow coastal strips with many coves and bays. Between the two largest islands—Luzon in the north and Mindanao in the south—lie the nine major islands of Cebu, Negros, Bohol, Panay, Leyte, Samar, Masbate, Mindoro, and Palawan, collectively called the Visayas.

Although generally considered to have two clearly defined seasons, dry and wet, various regions experience these seasons at different times of the year, while some areas enjoy fairly even dispersal of rainfall. From June to November typhoons are a seasonal hazard. Temperatures range from the steaming jungle and rain forest to the pine-clad highlands and coolness of the summer capital, Baguio. Taal volcano in southern Luzon, dormant since 1911, erupted destructively in 1965 and is again showing activity, as is the "perfect cone" of Mount Mayon.

The population shows remarkable contrasts. Descendants of the aboriginal Negrito—dark, kinky-haired, and little more than four feet high—still hunt with blowgun and bow and arrows in mountain homes only a few hundred miles from cosmopolitan Manila. Other ancient tribes still cultivate the intricately engineered mountain rice terraces constructed by their ancestors. Within Manila's skyscrapers, Filipinos manage and staff modern and sophisticated commercial and industrial enterprises.

The modern Filipino is mainly of Malay stock, blended in significant proportions with Chinese, Indian, Southeast Asian, and Spanish strains. There are more than 50 ethnic groups speaking some 70 dialects, although more than 80 per cent of the population use the eight major dialects. Tagalog-based Filipino is making progress as a national language. Eighty-four per cent of the people are Roman Catholics.

**HISTORY.** From their autonomous and self-contained *barangay*, or tribal system of political organization, the Filipinos first accepted association during the 13th century with the Indo-Malay empires. The most lasting effect of this relationship was exposure to the missionary zeal of Islam, which swept the region from the Middle East and reached as far as Luzon. It receded somewhat under the pressures of the Christian faith, imported by the Spanish in the 16th century, but survives to the present in Mindanao.

Ferdinand Magellan, in search of spices for Spain, reached the islands in 1521. He was slain during a tribal feud, but one of his vessels went on to circle the earth and report on what was then called the St. Lazarus Islands, renamed the Philippines in honor of Philip II of Spain. In 1564 Miguel López de Legaspi arrived with soldiers of "the cross and the sword," instructed to Christianize the islands and to use force only where necessary. In 20 years he was able to establish control over the major inhabited areas except for Muslim Mindanao and Sulu. Ultimately the new colony was placed under the jurisdiction of the Viceroy of Mexico.

As Spanish and Christian influences became dominant during subsequent centuries, there were frequent uprisings and challenges from other foreign imperial powers. In 1896 an unsuccessful revolt of "Young Filipinos" was led by José Rizal. Although Rizal was executed by Spanish authorities, the revolt became more violent under the leadership of Emilio Aguinaldo. In 1898, when the Spanish-American War broke out, the insurgents accepted U.S. aid, with the expectation of receiving independence at the cessation of hostilities.

When Admiral Dewey destroyed the Spanish fleet in Manila Bay and U.S. forces landed to bring about the surrender of Spanish authorities, Filipinos and Americans regarded each other as friendly allies. However, domestic American pressures, plus doubt that Filipino independence would long survive the threat of outside imperialism, led to the decision to acquire the Philippines (under terms of the Treaty of Paris) and establish U.S. rule, with the prospect of Filipino self-government in the distant future. The Filipinos considered themselves robbed of their independence. Sparked by an accidental clash, fighting took place between Filipinos and Americans for another two years.

Filipinos continued to press vigorously for independence. In 1935 the Tydings-McDuffie Act gave them Commonwealth status, with a ten-year period in which to prepare for final transfer of sovereignty.

On December 8, 1941, Japan launched a surprise attack against the U.S. and Filipino forces on the islands, and within a month Manila had fallen to the Japanese army. U.S. General Douglas MacArthur, in command of some 90,000 American and Filipino troops, was forced to withdraw to Bataan peninsula on Luzon. MacArthur was recalled to the United States, but his forces, commanded by General Jonathan Wainwright, held out against overwhelming odds on Bataan until April 9, 1942—and then on the nearby island of Corregidor until May 6.

On October 20, 1944, a U.S. invasion force, under MacArthur's command, made a landing on the central Philippine island of Leyte. On July 5, 1945, MacArthur announced that all of the Philippines had been liberated from the Japanese.

World War II had disrupted the schedule of Philippine independence from the United States, bringing destruction to the country's economy and serious damage to its social and political institutions. Nevertheless, the Philippines chose to become independent on schedule, and transfer of sovereignty took place on July 4, 1946.

During the Republic's more than two decades of existence, it has survived and crushed an armed Communist insurrection, maintained an orderly transfer of political power by popular vote as provided in its constitution, and has registered slow but steady progress in developing and modernizing its economy.

**GOVERNMENT AND POLITICS.** Executive power is vested in a president, and legislative power in a Senate and House of Representatives. All are elected by literate adults 21 years of age and over. The president and representatives serve for four years and the senators for six. The current president, Ferdinand Marcos, was elected in 1965.

The Nationalist Party and the Liberal Party are the principal political organizations, differing from each other only in terms of personalities. Both profess anti-Communism, continued cooperation with the West—particularly with the United States—and closer ties and cooperation with free Asian neighbors. Elections are held every two years for some congressmen, 8 of the 24 senators, governors of the provinces, and other local officials. The next presidential election will be held in 1969.

**ECONOMY.** The economy is based primarily on agriculture, principally the cultivation of rice and corn for subsistence, and coconut,

sugarcane, abaca (Manila hemp), and pineapples for export. Farms are generally small; about half of them occupy less than five acres. One-third of the farms are worked by tenants, but a land reform program is gradually increasing farmer-ownership and leaseholds.

Fishing for the domestic market is an important industry. Timber and mining have become increasingly important export industries.

Economic growth through industrialization is indicated by the decline of the share of agriculture in the national income from 40 per cent in 1949 to 33 per cent in 1965. Meanwhile, manufacturing has increased from 10 per cent of the national income in 1949 to 18 per cent in 1965. Since 1951 the production indexes of agriculture and mining have almost doubled; the manufacturing index has almost trebled.

**EDUCATION AND HEALTH.** Seven years of schooling is compulsory for all children. About 72 per cent of the population is literate.

The infant mortality rate was estimated at 70.5 per 1,000 in 1964, down from 101.5 per 1,000 in 1950–54. There is one doctor per 1,700 inhabitants. However, medical facilities are concentrated in the Manila area.

**ARMED FORCES.** The Philippines maintains an army of 15,400, a navy of 5,500, and an air force of 8,200. There is compulsory registration of all men at age 20; of these, 4–5,000 men are drafted annually into an inactive reserve.

# POLAND

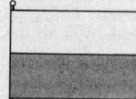

*Official Name:* Polish People's Republic. *Area:* 120,-359 square miles. *Population:* 31,800,000. *Principal Cities* (with populations): Warsaw, the capital, 1,264,-900; Lódź, 747,300; Kraków, 527,800; Wrocław, 497,200; Poznań, 441,700. *Flag:* White and red. *Monetary Unit:* The zloty (worth four U.S. cents). *Gross National Product:* $22,158,-000,000 (1966). *Average Annual Income per Person:* $900.

**LAND AND PEOPLE.** The largest state in eastern Europe, Poland is bordered on the north by the Baltic Sea, on the northeast and east by the U.S.S.R., on the south by Czechoslovakia, and on the west by East Germany. (See map on page 197.) The land is generally low, about nine-tenths of it lying below 1,000 feet. Temperatures range from an average of 60° F. in the summer to 45° F. in the winter. The principal rivers are the Vistula, Oder, Bug, and Warta.

Post-World War II border changes resulted in almost total ethnic homogeneity. Estimates now place the non-Polish population at only 4 per cent. The language spoken is Polish. Approximately 96 per cent of the population is Roman Catholic. There are also Eastern Orthodox, Protestant, and very small Jewish minorities.

**HISTORY.** Slavic tribes in Poland were united about the ninth or tenth century A.D. by the

# EASTERN EUROPE AND ASIA MINOR

NORWAY

SWEDEN

FINLAND

Turku

HELSINKI

STOCKHOLM

Tallinn

ESTONIAN S.S.R.

LAKE LADOGA

Leningrad

Yaroslavl'

URAL MOUNTAINS

Perm'

Dvina R.

Riga

LATVIAN S.S.R.

BALTIC SEA

LITHUANIAN S.S.R.

Vilnius

Volga R. Kazan'

Ufa

MOSCOW

Gor'kiy

POLAND

Minsk

Smolensk

UNION OF SOVIET SOCIALIST REPUBLICS

Kuybyshev

WARSAW

Voronezh

Saratov

CZECHOSLOVAKIA

L'vov

Kiev

Kharkov

Don R.

Volga R.

Volgograd

BUDAPEST

HUNGARY

Cluj

ROMANIA

Timisoara

BELGRADE

YUGOSLAVIA

BUCHAREST

Dnepropetrovsk

Krivoy Rog

Zaporozh'ye

Donets R.

Dnieper R.

Donetsk

Rostov

Volga R.

Astrakhan'

CASPIAN SEA

Odessa

SEA OF AZOV

CRIMEA

CAUCASUS MOUNTAINS

Danube R.

Constanta

Yalta

SOFIA

BULGARIA

Varna

BLACK SEA

TIRANA

Plovdiv

Salonika

Istanbul

BOSPORUS

Sinop

Trabzon

Tiflis

Baku

GREECE

Bursa

ANKARA

MT. ARARAT

Yerevan

Volos

Patras

ATHENS

Smyrna

TURKEY

Adana

KURDISTAN

IRAN

Iraklion

RHODES

CRETE

CYPRUS

NICOSIA

SYRIA

Mosul

MEDITERRANEAN SEA

LEBANON

BEIRUT

DAMASCUS

BAGHDAD

Tigris R.

IRAQ

ISRAEL

A R A B I A

JERUSALEM

AMMAN

JORDAN

Euphrates R.

MILES  0  100  200  300  400  500

Polanie, who began their rule as the Piast dynasty. In 966 Duke Mieszko I, the dynasty's first noteworthy member, adopted Christianity on behalf of his subjects. Otto III, Holy Roman Emperor, granted Poland independence, and in 1025 Boleslaw the Brave, Mieszko's son, was crowned king. Polish expansionism caused almost continuous conflict with neighboring states and Mongol invaders for the next three centuries.

A new dynasty was established in the late 14th century by a Lithuanian grand duke, Wladyslaw Jagiello, who became King Wladyslaw III of Poland. The Polish-Lithuanian union encompassed an empire extending from the Baltic to the Black Sea, and in 1410 was successful in destroying the Poles' most formidable foe, the Teutonic Knights.

The 16th century was Poland's "golden age." Nicholas Copernicus, renowned founder of modern astronomy, was a product of that time. However, during this period the country was being weakened by the *szlachta* (gentry), whose influence rose in direct proportion to the decline of royal authority, and finally the Jagiellonian dynasty was overthrown in 1572. The throne became elective and unanimity rule by Parliament was established. Wars, foreign interference, and internal strife weakened the country, and in 1772 Poland was partitioned by Russia, Austria, and Prussia. Two later partitions, in 1793 and 1795, brought a total loss of sovereignty. Control by foreign powers lasted until World War I.

Allied victory in 1918 brought complete but short-lived independence. In 1939 a Soviet-German pact opened the way for invasion of Poland. The ensuing Nazi march into the country marked the start of World War II. Less than three weeks later the Soviets invaded from the east. Poland was the victim of incredible destruction and genocide. The 6,000,000 death toll included 95 per cent of the country's more than 3,000,000 Jews.

The 1945 Yalta agreement by the Allies pledged free and unrestricted elections in Poland at the end of the war. The Soviets then installed 20,000 Polish Communists to rule the country. Elections were held by the recognized provisional government, but, in 1947, after a campaign of internal terrorism, abetted by the U.S.S.R., the Communists won more than 80 per cent of the votes.

Stalin's death in 1953 initiated an apparent relaxation of Communist tyranny in Poland. After a violent strike and riots at Poznań in 1956 cost many lives, Poland's de-Stalinization became more pronounced than that of any other Soviet satellite. Wladyslaw Gomulka returned to power in 1956 after having been imprisoned in 1951 for "Titoism." He announced his interest in discussing economic aid with the United States, freed the jailed Polish primate Stefan Cardinal Wyszyński, and removed from office Soviet Marshal Konstantin Rokossovsky, then Poland's defense minister.

In recent years, however, the Polish people have experienced a steady loss of freedoms. Church-state relations have deteriorated sharply since a 1956 rapprochement. Cardinal Wyszyński has come under increasingly harsh attack by the government, although the state's continued efforts to isolate and undermine him appear to have had little effect on his massive following. In 1966, even as the Polish people celebrated the millennium of their nation's conversion to Christianity and of its statehood, the Roman Catholic Church was being constantly harassed, and the U.S.S.R. was still attempting to re-orient the country toward the East.

Poland has supported the U.S.S.R. in its rift with Communist China.

**GOVERNMENT AND POLITICS.** Poland is only nominally a people's democracy. A parliamentary facade screens the actual power structure, a self-perpetuating elite within the ruling Communist Polish United Workers' Party (PZPR). Gomulka has been PZPR leader for more than a decade, with Zenon Kliszko as his heir-apparent. The constitution provides for a cabinet (29 members in 1967), which has been headed by Premier Józef Cyrankiewicz since 1954, and for a 17-member Council of State (collective presidency), which has been headed by Edward Ochab since 1964. PZPR officials occupy all key government posts.

The unicameral parliament or *Sejm* has 460 deputies, elected in 1965 to four-year terms. The deputies represent different parties, but all belong to the United Front and support regime policies. Brief biannual sessions of the *Sejm* rubber-stamp PZPR proposals, although a few individual Catholic deputies have recently voted against certain government legislation. There is a pyramidal arrangement of local administrative bodies, with authority ultimately culminating in the Council of State.

**ECONOMY.** A food exporter before 1939, Poland now imports grain from the West and the U.S.S.R. About 85.5 per cent of the arable land remains in private hands—collectivization of farms collapsed over a decade ago. Industry is almost totally state owned or controlled. Principal industries are metals, heavy machinery, food processing, chemicals, and consumer goods. Poland must rely on the U.S.S.R. for much of its industrial raw material. Only a few minerals, including coal, zinc-lead ores, salt, and sulfur, are found in any abundance in the country.

An adverse trade balance ($36,991,000 in 1966) is compounded by a $485,000,000 debt to the United States, primarily for agricultural commodities delivered since 1957. State-owned railways measure more than 16,700 miles. Of the nearly 69,000 miles of roads, less than 43 per cent are improved.

**EDUCATION AND HEALTH.** Primary education is free and compulsory from ages 7 to 14. Literacy was estimated at 95.3 per cent in 1960 and is now claimed to be total. Health services are under government jurisdiction.

**ARMED FORCES.** Military training is universal and compulsory, with induction at age 20. The army numbers 185,000 men; the navy 15,000; the air force 60,000. Internal security forces number 45,000.

# PORTUGAL

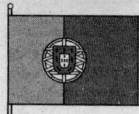

*Official Name:* Republic of Portugal. *Area:* 35,510 square miles. *Population:* 9,218,000. *Principal Cities* (with populations): Lisbon, the capital, 828,500; Porto, 315,000; Coimbra, 46,313; Setúbal, 44,435; Braga, 40,977. *Flag:* Green and red, with the national coat of arms. *Monetary Unit:* The escudo of 100 centavos (worth 4 U.S. cents). *Gross National Product:* $4,000,000,000 (1966). *Average Annual Income per Person:* $368.

**LAND AND PEOPLE.** Portugal occupies about one-sixth of the Iberian peninsula. On the north and east it is bordered by Spain, and on the south and west by the Atlantic Ocean. (See map on page 117.)

Extensive plains are found from the Tagus River south to Cape Saint Vincent, Europe's southwestern tip. Portugal's highest point is the Serra da Estrêla, northeast of Lisbon. The Minho River forms the northern boundary; other rivers of importance are the Douro, Tagus, and Guadiana, all originating in Spain. The weather varies considerably—cool summers and cold, wet, occasionally snowy winters in the north, with a mild, dry Mediterranean climate in the south. The Portuguese are among the most homogeneous peoples in Europe, both ethnically and culturally. About 96 per cent of the population is Roman Catholic.

**HISTORY.** The Romans arrived in western Iberia in the second century B.C. After the initial opposition was overcome, Rome's province of Lusitania thrived. After the Romans, Visigoths controlled the region, until they were defeated in 711 by the Moors who then dominated the peninsula for several centuries.

Modern Portugal began in 1095 with a grant of lands by Alfonso VI of Castile to Henry of Burgundy, who had helped him fight the Moors. In 1185 Portugal became an independent nation; it was consolidated in 1249 when the Moors were evicted from Algarve.

Portugal's era of glory began with the reign of John I (1385–1433). With independence firmly established by defeat of the Castilians in 1385, administrative reforms were introduced and an alliance formed with Britain. John's sons, particularly Henry the Navigator, contributed greatly to the early growth of Portugal's overseas empire. The Madeira and Cape Verde islands were colonized, and explorations of the western coast of Africa laid the basis for a lucrative slave trade, which Portugal dominated for many years. Bartholomew Diaz rounded Africa's southernmost tip in 1488, and Vasco da Gama discovered the sea route to India (1497–99). Further discoveries, including that of Brazil, spread the country's colonial empire.

The decline in Portugal's fortunes from the mid-1500's was given impetus by neglect of the domestic economy, loss of manpower, repression of the Jews, and increasing competition in foreign trade. In 1581, with the forced accession of Philip II of Spain to the Portuguese throne, the "Spanish captivity" began. Independence was re-established in 1640 when John of Braganza was made king. However, the country's involvement in the War of the Spanish Succession, the growth of absolutism, and a disastrous earthquake that destroyed Lisbon (1755) further sapped the country's wealth and power.

Napoleon's forces invaded Portugal in 1807, and the royal family fled to Brazil. French occupation lasted until 1814; King John VI returned to Portugal in 1820. Civil unrest and political corruption led to the overthrow of the Braganza dynasty in 1910, and a republic was declared. But in 1926 General Antonio Carmona seized power. After 1928 Portugal was dominated by Antonio de Oliveira Salazar, who still rules as prime minister. An expert in finance, Salazar placed Portugal on a sounder economic footing, but did little to encourage democracy.

**GOVERNMENT AND POLITICS.** Portugal is a highly centralized (corporative) state with an indirectly elected president whose duties are ceremonial. The parliament consists of an appointed Corporative Chamber and a National Assembly elected by direct suffrage. Political liberties are rigidly curbed, with all parties outlawed except the semi-official National Union. A strict new civil code, introduced in 1966, increased state control over the life and private property of individuals.

In 1961 Portugal's colonies in India were seized by that country. A widespread insurrection in Angola was crushed in 1961, but independence-minded rebel groups have continued to fight sporadically, as they have in Portuguese Guinea and Mozambique. In May, 1966, Prime Minister Salazar announced his refusal to step down as premier despite his advanced age (77), fearing that such a move would be interpreted as a change in Portugal's colonial policy.

**ECONOMY.** Portugal's corporative system calls for governmental supervision over practically all phases of the country's economic life. Emigration (much of which is illegal) has caused a labor shortage.

The local economy is based largely on agriculture, forestry, and fishing. Industry—mostly light manufacturing—includes textiles, cork processing (Portugal is the world's leading producer of cork), leather goods, glass, ceramics, and food processing. Mineral production includes wolfram, copper pyrites, coal, and iron ore. Principal agricultural products include grains, fruits, and wines.

The airports in Lisbon and in the Azores are of major importance in international air traffic. Tourism is growing; there were 1,900,000 visitors in 1966, a 27 per cent increase over 1965.

**EDUCATION.** Education is compulsory and free until age 11. (The age will be raised to 13 in 1970). About 68 per cent of the population is literate.

**ARMED FORCES.** Eighteen months of active military service is compulsory at age 21. Portugal's armed forces total 148,000.

## PORTUGUESE TERRITORIES AND DEPENDENCIES

### ANGOLA

*Area:* 481,351 square miles. *Population:* 5,360,-000. *Capital:* Luanda (population: 238,000).

Angola is bordered on the north by the Democratic Republic of the Congo, on the east by Zambia, on the south by South West Africa, and on the west by the Atlantic Ocean. A small enclave, Cabinda, separate from Angola proper, lies within the Democratic Republic of the Congo. The people are predominantly Bantu.

Angola has been under Portuguese control since the late 15th century, except for a short period of Dutch occupation (1641–48). From 1575 until the end of slavery in 1836, Angola was the major source of slaves for Brazil. A rebellion in 1961 was quickly suppressed, but rebel activity still persists.

Angola is a major earner of foreign exchange for Portugal. The country produces nearly half of Africa's coffee; other exports are diamonds, sisal, corn, and iron ore.

Angola is administered by an appointed governor-general, and is represented in the National Assembly in Lisbon by three elected members.

### CAPE VERDE ISLANDS

*Area:* 1,557 square miles. *Population:* 232,000. *Capital:* Praia.

The Cape Verde Islands consist of ten islands and five islets in the Atlantic, 370 miles west of Dakar. Cape Verdians are mostly mulattoes and Africans.

The islands were discovered in 1456 and were colonized by the end of the 16th century. The islands' principal value is as a refueling station for ships. They are administered by an appointed governor and two local councils.

### MACAO

*Area:* 6 square miles. *Population:* 175,000. *Capital:* Macao City.

Macao, at the mouth of mainland China's Canton River, is located about 35 miles from Hong Kong. It consists of Macao City on Chungshan Island, and two smaller islands—Taipa and Coloane. About 99 per cent of the population is Chinese.

The Portuguese gained possession of Macao in 1557 and established a trading post. Gambling and smuggling are leading occupations.

Macao is governed by an appointed governor who is responsible to Lisbon.

### MOZAMBIQUE

*Area:* 302,227 square miles. *Population:* 7,040,-000. *Capital:* Lourenço Marques (population: 184,000).

Mozambique is bordered on the north by Tanzania, on the east by the Indian Ocean, on the south and southwest by Swaziland and South Africa, on the west by Rhodesia, and on the northwest by Zambia, Malawi, and Lake Nyasa. About 97 per cent of the population is African.

Vasco da Gama visited Mozambique en route to India in 1498, and Portuguese settlements on the coast were established in the 16th century. Mozambique's ports and transportation system are vital for the transshipment of goods to and from several African nations in the interior. The economy is based chiefly on subsistence agriculture.

The governor is appointed by and responsible to Lisbon. There is also a legislative council. The province has three representatives in the Portuguese National Assembly. The Portuguese announced in 1965 that African nationalist forces had been dispersed from Mozambique, but guerrillas continue to infiltrate from Tanzania.

### PORTUGUESE GUINEA

*Area:* 13,948 square miles. *Population:* 529,000. *Capital:* Bissau (population: 47,000).

Portuguese Guinea is bordered on the north by Senegal, on the east and southeast by Guinea, and on the southwest and west by the Atlantic Ocean.

The region was first visited by the Portuguese in 1446–47. It became a source of slaves as early as the 16th century and was a dependency of the Cape Verde Islands until 1879. In the early 1960s a rebellion began; it has not been entirely extinguished.

There is a subsistence agriculture, and some export of oil seeds. The province is administered by a governor responsible to Lisbon.

### SÃO TOMÉ AND PRINCIPE

*Area:* 372 square miles. *Population:* 59,000.

The islands, about 74 miles apart, are located in the Gulf of Guinea, some 125 miles from the west African coast. Tropical agriculture is the basis of the economy. Cocoa is the most valuable crop. São Tomé and Principe are ruled by a Lisbon-appointed governor.

### PORTUGUESE TIMOR

*Area:* 5,763 square miles. *Population:* 560,000. *Capital:* Dili (population: 52,160).

Timor is part of the Lesser Sundra island group in the Malay archipelago, lying between the Celebes Islands and Australia. The people are of Malay and Papuan stock, with some Arab, African, and Chinese strains. The Portuguese arrived in Timor in the mid-1500s. After World War II western Timor, a Dutch possession, became part of Indonesia. The economy is totally agricultural. The governor rules with the help of a consultative council.

## RHODESIA

*Official Name:* Rhodesia. *Area:* 150,332 square miles. *Population:* 4,400,000. *Principal Cities* (with populations): Salisbury, the capital, 324,800; Bulawayo, 225,500; Umtali, 49,000; Gwelo, 38,000. *Flag:* A blue field containing in the upper left corner the Union Jack and in the lower right the Rhodesian badge (a green shield with a gold pick and a red lion between two thistles). *Monetary Unit:* The Rhodesian pound (worth U.S. $2.81). *Gross National Product:* $1,022,-000,000 (1965). *Average Annual Income per Person:* European, $3,404; African, $322.

**LAND AND PEOPLE.** Bordered by Zambia on the north, Mozambique on the east, the Republic of South Africa on the south, and Botswana on the west, Rhodesia (formerly Southern Rhodesia) lies between the Limpopo and Zambezi rivers. (See map on page 111.)

Most of Rhodesia lies above 3,000 feet, and about one-quarter of the country is above 4,000 feet. A broad ridge from 4,000 to more than 5,000 feet high crosses the country from southwest to northeast. A mountainous area along the eastern border rises to 8,251 feet in Mount Inyangani. Except in the lowlands, where warm, humid, tropical conditions prevail, Rhodesia generally has a subtropical climate.

About 94 per cent of the people are indigenous Africans belonging to various Bantu tribes, notably the Mashona and the Matabele. There are small Asian and colored minorities. The rest of the people, some 5.17 per cent of the population, are ethnic Europeans; many are recent immigrants from Great Britain and South Africa. The Africans are subservient to the Europeans, who have exclusive rights to the cities and to half the land, including much of the best farmland. Africans are permitted residence in special quarters within these areas only if they are laborers employed by the Europeans.

The official language is English. The Africans principally speak various Bantu languages and dialects. Most Africans practice tribal religions. A minority of 15 per cent are Christians, as are the vast majority of Europeans.

**HISTORY.** Iron-using farmers settled on the Rhodesian plateau about 2,000 years ago, displacing or absorbing the earlier inhabitants. After the eighth century they started trading gold and ivory to the Arabs on the east coast, and between the 11th and 15th centuries they built the great stone structures of Zimbabwe, near Fort Victoria. In the mid-15th century the Vakaranga, a branch of the Mashona, moved northward and established a state under their ruler, the Monomatapa, which extended over the northern and eastern Rhodesian plateau and over the southern Mozambique lowlands.

At the end of the 17th century the Monomatapas and their Portuguese overlords were overthrown by the Changamires, who ruled the plateau until the massive Zulu emigration from Natal in the early 19th century that led to Matabele rule. In the 1890s the British South Africa Company of Cecil Rhodes, assisted by regular British troops, conquered Mashonaland and Matabeleland. European colonists followed, and in 1923, when the British government took over the area, they were granted internal self-government. Britain retained only veto power over African legislation and control of foreign affairs.

During the late 1940s, African nationalist movements emerged in Northern Rhodesia (now Zambia) and Nyasaland (now Malawi).

The European colonists persuaded Britain to establish, in 1953, the Federation of Rhodesia and Nyasaland, which was effectively and profitably dominated by the European settlers in Southern Rhodesia until 1963. In 1964 Britain allowed the two northern territories to proceed to independence under African majority rule, thus, in effect, isolating the ruling white minority of Southern Rhodesia.

In the 1965 elections the Rhodesia Front, representing white nationalism, won an overwhelming victory. Ian Smith, leader of the Front, was retained as prime minister. In November, 1965, his government issued a Unilateral Declaration of Independence (UDI) from Britain. Supported by the U.N. Security Council, Britain retaliated with economic sanctions, including an oil embargo, but stopped short of military intervention. The nations of the world in general observed the sanctions, but Portugal and South Africa disregarded them and provided Rhodesia with oil and other supplies. By mid-1967 Rhodesia had declared a state of emergency and appeared to be weathering the hardships of ostracism and sanctions. British-Rhodesian discussions had proved fruitless, and Prime Minister Smith talked of republic status for a Rhodesia cut off from Commonwealth ties.

**GOVERNMENT AND POLITICS.** The 1962 constitution provided for a prime minister and a parliament of 65 members, elected under a system designed to ensure that 50 were Europeans and 15 were Africans approved by the Europeans. The franchise was restricted in such a way that virtually all the voters were Europeans. The UDI constitution of 1966 favors the voting roll of white parliamentary seats, as against that of the Africans. Smith appointed a committee to draft a new constitution in 1967. While earlier African nationalist parties have been outlawed, there is a legal African opposition, the United People's Party.

**ECONOMY.** The economy rests on agriculture. The European farms are oriented toward the export market and specialize in tobacco, corn, livestock, and dairying. The African farms grow corn and small grains for subsistence. There is a mining industry, and manufactures include iron, steel, cement, and chemicals.

Exports consist chiefly of tobacco, Rhodesia's main money crop, and asbestos. Chief imports are machinery and textiles.

**EDUCATION AND HEALTH.** Except at the University College at Salisbury, education is racially segregated. It is noncompulsory for Africans—although the government claims that 95 per cent receive a minimum of five years' schooling—and compulsory for Europeans between the ages of 7 and 15. African literacy is estimated at 30 per cent, European at nearly 100 per cent.

There are 39 hospitals, 75 rural clinics, and 65 medical missions. For every 7,300 Rhodesians there is one medical practitioner. Infant mortality among Africans is over five times that among Europeans.

**ARMED FORCES.** There are European-officered army and air forces. Before unilateral independence, the regular army and air force totaled 4,600 men; a territorial force and reserves comprised an additional 7,400 men. Since independence military units and internal police have been considerably expanded.

## ROMANIA

*Official Name:* Socialist Republic of Romania. *Area:* 91,699 square miles. *Population:* 19,143,000. *Principal Cities* (with populations): Bucharest, the capital, 1,-239,458; Cluj, 167,011; Timisoara, 152,230; Brasov, 137,231; Ploesti, 133,711; Constanta, 121,071. *Flag:* Vertical blue, yellow, and red stripes, with the national coat of arms on the yellow stripe. *Monetary Unit:* The leu of 100 bani (worth 16.5 U.S. cents).

**LAND AND PEOPLE.** Romania, a Balkan state in southeastern Europe, is bordered on the north and northeast by the U.S.S.R., on the east by the Black Sea, on the south by Bulgaria, and on the west by Yugoslavia and Hungary. (See map on page 197.)

Romania is a land of great geographical contrasts. Surrounding the central plateau of Transylvania is the chain of Carpathian Mountains, and beyond are three major plateaus: the Moldavian to the east, the Wallachian to the south, and the Dobrijan between the Danube River and the Black Sea.

The climate is moderate. Average January temperatures range from 25° to 32° F. During the summer the highest temperatures are in the Danube Valley (about 75° F.), decreasing toward the higher elevations in the northwest and under the moderating influence of the Black Sea in the southeast. Average rainfall is 40 inches in the mountains and 15 inches in the delta.

Romanians, who are of Latin ancestry, make up 87 per cent of the population; Hungarians and Germans account for most of the rest. The main church is the Romanian Orthodox. The largest religious minorities are the Roman Catholics and the Protestants; there are some Jewish and Muslim communities.

The national language is Romanian. Some Hungarian, German, Ukrainian, and Yiddish are spoken.

**HISTORY.** Most of present-day Romania was in the Roman province of Dacia in the second and third centuries A.D. After Rome withdrew, the area was overrun successively by Goths, Huns, Avars, Slavs, and Mongols, but the local people retained their identity.

By the 13th century the regions of Wallachia, Moldavia, and Transylvania had emerged as distinct entities, although still subjected to the great contending powers of Europe. Transylvania was for several centuries under Hungarian rule; Wallachia and Moldavia became holdings of the Ottoman Empire by the early 15th century. Late in that century Michael the Brave, a prince of Wallachia, led a brief revolt, then conquered the other two principalities. After Michael's assassination in 1601 Moldavia

and Wallachia reverted to Turkish rule, and Transylvania passed to Austrian control. Not until the Congress of Paris (1856) did Moldavia and Wallachia achieve virtual independence from Turkish control.

In 1861 Moldavia and Wallachia united as Romania under Prince Alexander John Cuza. Cuza was cast aside in 1866 in favor of King Carol I of the House of Hohenzollern-Sigmaringen. In 1878, after restoring south Bessarabia to Russia and accepting Dobruja in exchange, Romania became fully independent. Three years later it was recognized as a kingdom.

After World War I, which it entered late on the side of the Allies, Romania acquired Transylvania and the Banat from Hungary, Bukovina from Austria, and, again, Bessarabia from Russia. After the death of King Ferdinand in 1927 Romanian political life became more unstable, and by 1938 the country was virtually a Fascist state under Carol II's royal dictatorship.

In 1940 Marshal Ion Antonescu ousted Carol with the help of the Iron Guard—a militaristic, anti-Semitic, anti-parliamentary organization—and Romania joined the Axis Powers. In August, 1944, Antonescu was overthrown by King Michael, and Romania switched to the Allied side.

After the Soviet advance into the country in 1944–45, a Communist-led coalition headed by Petri Groza came to power. In 1947 Michael was forced to abdicate, and Romania was declared a People's Republic until 1965, when, under a new constitution, the country was called a Socialist Republic.

For several years Romania had been a Soviet satellite, but in the early 1960s the Communist Party leader Gheorge Gheorgiu-Dej began to map an independent course for his country within the Communist orbit. This course has been followed since his death in 1965.

**GOVERNMENT AND POLITICS.** Romania's top policy-making body is the Communist Party Presidium (formerly the Politburo). The party's Secretary-General, Nicolae Ceausescu, is the country's most influential politician.

The supreme administrative organ is the Council of Ministers, whose chairman is the Prime Minister, Ion Gheorghe Maurer. This body is responsible to the Grand National Assembly of 465 deputies elected every four years from a single list of candidates. The President of the Grand National Assembly is Stephen Voitec. Since the failure in 1962 of Russian attempts to persuade Romania to abandon a highly successful plan of industrialization and become a virtual agricultural reserve for the Soviet bloc, the country has pursued an increasingly independent line. A party statement of April, 1964, claimed the right of each Communist country to shape its own political program without interference. Romania's dependence on the Soviet market has lessened as its trade ties with the West have been rapidly expanded. It has established friendly relations with China and Albania, shunned by the rest of the bloc, and remained neutral in the Sino-Soviet dispute.

In January, 1967, Romania shocked its fellow Soviet-bloc countries by giving unconditional recognition to West Germany. It further shook the Communist world by dissociating itself from the anti-Israel measures of its allies following the Arab-Israeli war in June, 1967. In September, 1967, Romania's foreign minister, Corneliu Manescu, became the first representative of a Communist nation to be elected president of the U.N. General Assembly.

**ECONOMY.** Next to the Soviet Union, Romania is Europe's largest producer of petroleum. There are extensive deposits of natural gas, manganese, and other minerals. Since the Communists nationalized industry and collectivized agriculture after World War II, they have been substituting industry for agriculture as the basis of Romania's economy.

With the six-year industrialization plan of 1960, Romania achieved one of the fastest growth rates in Europe. In 1966 she raised industrial production 11.7 per cent. But although forced industrialization and collectivization have sometimes brought agricultural shortages, the grain harvests of 1965 and 1966 reached record levels.

In recent years tourism has been encouraged, and Romania's railways and national highways are being modernized. The state airline serves several European cities.

**EDUCATION.** Schooling is free and compulsory for children aged 7 to 15. In the 1965–66 school year the number of students at all levels reached 3.7 million, nearly one-fifth of the total population. The literacy rate is 87.4 per cent of the population over 14. There are five principal universities.

**ARMED FORCES.** Service is compulsory for about 16 months. Total strength of Romania's armed forces is 325,000.

# RWANDA

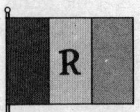

*Official Name:* Republic of Rwanda. *Area:* 10,169 square miles. *Population:* 3,110,000. *Principal Cities* (with populations): Kigali, 10,000; Gisenyi, 7,000; Gitarama, 6,000. *Flag:* Three vertical bars of red, yellow, and green, with a black *R* superimposed on the yellow. *Monetary Unit:* The Rwanda franc (worth 2 U.S. cents). *Gross National Product:* $155,000,000 (1965). *Average Annual Income per Person:* $50.

**LAND AND PEOPLE.** A small country in east-central Africa, Rwanda is bordered on the north by Uganda, on the east by Tanzania, on the south by Burundi, and on the west by the Democratic Republic of the Congo. (See map on page 111.)

The land is mountainous, with elevations ranging from 4,800 feet at Lake Kivu in the west to nearly 15,000-foot peaks in the northwest. In the east is a hilly plateau and marshy lakes. The climate is tropical.

The population consists mostly of Hutu tribesmen, with a dwindling minority of Tutsi and a few Twa, a Pygmy race who originally inhabited the area. About half of the people are Christians, mostly Roman Catholics.

**HISTORY.** The kingdom of Rwanda, one of the oldest in Africa, can be traced back to the 16th century. Under the leadership of a royal clan believed to have originated in Ethiopia, successive waves of Hamitic pastoralists, the Tutsi, conquered the indigenous Bantu tribes, the Hutu, whose customs and traditions they proceeded to assimilate into their own. Traditional Rwanda society was rigidly stratified, with the Tutsi holding a virtual monopoly of power and influence at the expense of the low-caste Hutu. The political system consisted of the *mwami* (king) and a complex hierarchy of army, cattle, and land chiefs.

Following the penetration of European influences in the late 19th century, Rwanda was annexed by Germany and incorporated as a colony into German East Africa. After World War I Rwanda passed into the hands of the Belgians, first as a League of Nations mandate and, after World War II, as a United Nations trusteeship. From about 1916 to 1962 Rwanda and Burundi were administered as a single unit known as Ruanda-Urundi.

Before Rwanda became an independent nation, on July 1, 1962, the country was the scene of violent revolution. Beginning in 1957, Hutu politicians brought increasing pressure to bear upon the European administration to abolish Tutsi supremacy. After riots in November, 1959, Belgian authorities gave their full support to the Hutu against the Tutsi, and in October, 1960, an autonomous, Hutu-dominated provisional government was established. In January, 1961, a Belgian-sponsored coup d'etat led to the proclamation of the Republic. Not until September, 1961, however, was the Republic officially proclaimed, following a UN-sponsored referendum conducted jointly with the legislative elections. Sporadic violence continued; an estimated 200,000 Tutsi have sought asylum in neighboring countries since November, 1959.

**GOVERNMENT AND POLITICS.** Rwanda is a "democratic, social, and sovereign Republic." The President of the Republic is both head of state and head of government. He is elected for a four-year term by universal adult suffrage. Legislative powers are vested in a 47-member National Assembly elected for a four-year term.

In the 1965 presidential and legislative elections, President Gregoire Kayibanda ran unopposed and was elected by a majority of 98 per cent of the registered voters. All of the Assembly delegates but two belong to the governing party, the *MDR Parmehutu.*

**ECONOMY.** Agriculture forms the basis of the economy, although erosion and soil depletion are serious problems. Chief exports are coffee and cassiterite, the source of tin. There is very little industry.

**EDUCATION.** There are very few schools at the secondary and higher level. The University of Butare was founded in 1963.

**ARMED FORCES.** Rwanda has an army of 1,000 men.

## SAN MARINO

*Official Name:* The Most Serene Republic of San Marino. *Area:* 24 square miles. *Population:* 17,000. *Principal City* (with population): San Marino, the capital, 2,-500. *Flag:* Horizontal blue and white stripes, with the national coat of arms superimposed in the center. *Monetary Unit:* Italian currency is used. San Marino also issues its own coins in limited numbers.

**LAND AND PEOPLE.** San Marino, completely surrounded by Italy, is situated near the Adriatic Sea, about 65 miles east of Florence. (See map on page 117.) Most of the enclave lies on the slopes or summit of Mount Titano, each of whose three pinnacles is topped by an old fortification. Most San Marinesi are Roman Catholics and speak Italian.

**HISTORY.** According to legend, San Marino was founded in the fourth century by Marino, a Christian stonecutter from Dalmatia fleeing religious persecution, who was eventually canonized. The independence of San Marino was recognized in 1631 by Pope Urban VIII; it may be the oldest republic in the world.

In 1862 San Marino and Italy signed a customs treaty and a treaty of friendship, which have been renewed periodically. San Marino declared war on Germany in World War I but tried to remain neutral in World War II despite German occupation and heavy fighting during the advance of Allied forces into northern Italy.

**GOVERNMENT AND POLITICS.** The 60 members of the Grand and General Council are elected every five years by popular vote. Before 1960 only heads of families were able to vote, but in that year electoral restrictions were removed, primarily as an anti-Communist move, and women were given the vote (although they still are ineligible for public office). The Grand and General Council selects from its membership a Council of State and two Captains-Regent, appointed every six months.

From 1945 to 1957 a Communist-Socialist coalition ruled San Marino. In 1957 six Council members defected and formed a new coalition with the Christian Democrats that held power until November, 1966, when it split over the issue of mail votes by overseas San Marinesi. The Christian Democrats then formed a new, one-party government.

**ECONOMY.** The economy of San Marino is based on farming, light manufacturing, animal raising, and tourism. The issuance of ornate postage stamps for collectors is a main source of revenue.

**EDUCATION AND HEALTH.** Primary education is compulsory, and illiteracy is rare. There are public health facilities.

**NATIONAL DEFENSE.** There are two ceremonial military organizations (a Noble Guard and a Border Guard) of about 180 men, but in cases of necessity most able-bodied men between the ages of 16 and 55 are called to arms. There is also a 60-man police force.

## SAUDI ARABIA

*Official Name:* Kingdom of Saudi Arabia. *Area:* 870,000 square miles. *Population:* 6,630,000. *Principal Cities* (with populations): Riyad, the capital, 175,000; Hofuf, 200,000; Jidda, 200,000; Mecca, 165,000; Medina, 60,000. *Flag:* Green with the inscription "There is no god but God and Mohammed is His prophet" in white Arabic characters above a white sword. *Monetary Unit:* The riyal of 20 qirsh (worth 20 U.S. cents).

**LAND AND PEOPLE.** Saudi Arabia occupies most of the Arabian peninsula, from the Red Sea and the Gulf of Aqaba in the west, to the Persian Gulf, Qatar, and Trucial States in the east. To the north are Jordan, Iraq, Kuwait, and two small neutral zones; to the southwest, south, and southeast are Yemen, the Federation of South Arabia, and Muscat and Oman. Many boundaries are disputed. (See map on page 151.)

Most of Saudi Arabia is desert. In the west is a fertile coastal plain 10 to 40 miles wide, succeeded by steep mountains that rise to over 9,000 feet near Yemen. The Nejd plateau slopes eastward and is bordered by the great desert areas of Nefud in the north, Dahna and Nefud Dahi in the east, and Rub al Khali in the south. Coastal regions have a high, tropical humidity; the deserts are extremely dry. Temperatures range from 70° to 130° F., with lower temperatures in the mountains. Average annual rainfall is between three and five inches, although some areas have no rain for years.

Most Saudi Arabians are Arab and speak Arabic, the official language of the kingdom. About 66 per cent are nomadic or seminomadic (Bedouin) herders, and 20 per cent are urban dwellers. Almost all of the people are Muslims. Mecca, the birthplace of Islam and its prophet Mohammed, yearly draws about 500,000 Muslims from all over the world.

**HISTORY.** Saudi Arabia was part of the Ottoman Empire for several centuries, although the Turks exercised only nominal control over the desert interior. In the 18th century Mohammed ibn Saud, the local Arab ruler in the central province of Nejd, was converted to a puritan Islamic doctrine by Mohammed ibn Abdul Wahhab. Saud gathered a large Bedouin army in order to spread Wahhabism and to gain control of central and eastern Arabia. His "empire" was defeated by Egypt's Mohammed Ali in the early 19th century, and the ruling Saud dynasty was subsequently expelled by rival chieftains from Riyad.

In 1902 young Abdul Aziz ibn Saud regained control of Nejd, and by 1925 he had annexed the Kingdom of Hejaz. Britain endorsed the independence of the dominions in a 1927 treaty, and Saudi Arabia was proclaimed a unified kingdom in 1932. King Abdul Aziz ibn Saud was succeeded by his son, Saud (ruled 1953–64), who was dethroned by a council of princes. His younger brother, Faisal, became king in 1964.

**GOVERNMENT AND POLITICS.** Saudi Arabia is an absolute monarchy ruled by the House of Saud. The present ruler, King Faisal, is also the prime minister. He is assisted by a cabinet composed of princes and commoners, with Crown Prince Khaled (the king's younger brother) as vice-premier.

Islam, the state religion, provides the basis for political and social institutions. Legislation is based on Islam's holy book, the Koran, and on Islamic tradition (Sunna) in its most puritan and austere Wahhabi version. All courts are served by religious judges. State-supported Committees of Public Morality supervise conformance with religious law. The law forbids, for example, the production, importation, and consumption of alcohol.

Since 1962 Faisal (first as premier, then as king) has supported a ten-point modernization program that calls for the abolition of slavery. In addition, it pledges partial court secularization, administrative improvement, and economic development. Faisal also formed a consultative assembly.

In 1945 Saudi Arabia joined the United Nations and the Arab League, thereby ending isolation. Since the 1960s it has been a leading conservative, peaceful power in the Arab world, stressing Islamic solidarity and opposing the revolutionary expansionism of Nasser's Egypt. In the Yemen civil war, begun in 1962, Saudi Arabia supported Yemen royalists; Egypt supported the Yemen republicans. In early 1967 Egypt gave asylum to the dethroned King Saud and supported his aim to regain power in Saudi Arabia.

The Saudi-Egyptian enmity was temporarily suspended during the brief Arab-Israeli war in June, 1967. The Saudi government, previously friendly towards the West, embargoed exports of oil to the U.S. and Britain. Later, Egypt and Saudi Arabia agreed to cease hostilities in Yemen.

**ECONOMY.** The chief economic asset is the vast oil reserve along the Persian Gulf. Since the 1940s oil has provided over 90 per cent of government revenue ($700,000,000 in 1967). The oil industry employs more than 20,000 people, and the Arabian-American Oil Company (Aramco) produced 2,400,000 barrels of oil a day in 1967. Saudi Arabia is now the third leading oil producer of the Free World.

Saudi Arabia was originally a pastoral land and, to a lesser extent, an agricultural country. Over three-quarters of the people continue to herd camels, sheep, and goats, and to cultivate dates and grains.

**EDUCATION.** Primary education is compulsory from ages 6 through 12. Many schools, a university, and a college for studying subjects related to the petroleum industry have been built recently.

**ARMED FORCES.** Land forces include the regular army (30,000 men), a separate, tribal National Guard ("White Army"), and Royal Guards. A small air force is centered on the American-built base of Dhahran. A $700,000,-000 military modernization program including antiaircraft missile facilities was begun in 1966.

# SENEGAL

*Official Name:* Republic of Senegal. *Area:* 77,240 square miles. *Population* 3,-490,000. *Principal Cities* (with populations): Dakar, the capital, 383,000; Kaolack, 81,600; Thiès, 69,000; Saint-Louis, 58,-000. *Flag:* Three vertical green, gold, and red bars, with a centered green star. *Monetary Unit:* The CFA franc (worth 0.41 U.S. cent).

**LAND AND PEOPLE.** Senegal lies in the westernmost portion of Africa's Atlantic bulge and is bordered on the north by Mauritania, on the east by Mali, and on the south by the Republic of Guinea and Portuguese Guinea. The narrow territory of Gambia extends almost 250 miles into Senegal from the coast. (See map on page 111.)

Most of Senegal consists of savanna with light, low-fertility soil and is hot and dry. Some parts of the north are semi-desert, with 20 inches of annual rainfall; the extreme south is forested, with 40 inches of rain annually. The chief rivers are the Gambia and Senegal.

The Wolof tribe, which makes up 32 per cent of the population, was the most influential during the 19th and 20th centuries. Other tribal groups include the Mandingo, Peul (Fulani), Tucolor, and Serer. There are about 50,000 Europeans, mostly French. The official language is French, but tribal dialects are spoken widely. The people are 80 per cent Muslim and about 10 per cent Christian.

**HISTORY.** In medieval times eastern Senegal was ruled by many kingdoms such as those of Ghana and of Mali. The Almoravids, who eventually conquered Spain, originated there. After the breakup of the Mali Empire in the 14th century a number of small states emerged, among the most important of which were the Wolof kingdoms.

Portuguese traders reached Senegal in the mid-15th century, followed by Dutch, French, and British. European rivalries and the profitable slave trade made the area a center of conflict for centuries, particularly between France and Britain.

After the Napoleonic Wars Britain recognized French claims to the area north of the Gambia River. French designs on the interior were long blocked by the Tucolor empire of El Hadj Omar, which did not fall to French conquest until 1893, although by 1861 the French had absorbed western Senegal. In 1902 Dakar became the administrative center for French West Africa. In the 20th century France expended more funds on Senegal than on any of its other sub-Saharan territories. Until 1958, when it separated from France, Senegal was a model for the policy of assimilation.

Remaining loyal to the Vichy regime in World War II, Senegal repulsed an attempt by the Free French to take Dakar in 1940. After the war the country worked for a viable French Union, but when Guinea defected from the Union in 1958, Senegal became an autonomous member of the French Community. In 1959 the country joined with the Sudanese Republic to form the short-lived Mali Federation.

In 1960 Senegal declared itself an independent republic; it was admitted to the United Nations in that year. A political conflict in 1962 resulted in the imprisonment of Premier Mamadou Dia and the introduction of a new constitution vesting greater power in the presidency, held by Léopold Senghor.

**GOVERNMENT AND POLITICS.** Senegal is a republic, with its president and National Assembly of 80 deputies elected by universal suffrage for a four-year term. The pro-French Senegal Progressive Union, led by President Senghor, has dominated politics under various names since 1951. Several small, radical parties have been circumscribed or outlawed.

**ECONOMY.** The economy is agrarian, with peanuts and by-products providing 90 per cent of export earnings. Much food is imported. The considerable industrial capacity is underutilized. Large foreign-trade and balance-of-payment deficits are regularly offset by French aid and Common Market grants.

**EDUCATION.** Total school enrollment, including technical and university classes, was 235,958 in 1964. The 1961 literacy rate in French for those over 13 was 5.6 per cent. The University of Dakar, founded in 1957, and the headquarters of the Institut Français d'Afrique Noire, a famous center of African studies, are both situated in the capital.

**ARMED FORCES.** Senegal has an army of about 2,500 men. Military aid is supplied by France. Most French forces in Senegal were withdrawn in 1964.

# SIERRA LEONE

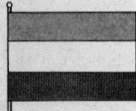

*Area:* 27,698 square miles. *Population:* 2,403,000. *Principal Cities* (with populations): Freetown, the capital, 127,917; Bo, 20,000; Kenema, 10,000; Makeni, 9,000. *Flag:* Green, white, and light blue stripes. *Monetary Unit:* The leone (worth U.S. $1.41). *Gross National Product:* $327,600,000 (1964). *Average Annual Income per Person:* $116.

**LAND AND PEOPLE.** Situated on the west African bulge, with a 210-mile Atlantic coastline, Sierra Leone occupies a roughly circular area bordered by Guinea in the northwest, north, and northeast, and by Liberia in the southeast. (See map on page 111.)

There are three main regions. The peninsula in the extreme west is a hilly area, rising to almost 3,000 feet. The remainder of western Sierra Leone consists of a coastal plain 60 to 100 miles wide. Farther inland the land rises abruptly to a low plateau, with peaks over 6,000 feet in the Lomo Mountains and Tingi Hills. The country has a warm tropical climate with an average temperature of 80° F. and heavy rainfall (125 inches annually).

The Mende and Temne tribes claim the majority of the inhabitants. A small minority of nontribal Africans are Creoles, descendants of freed slaves, mainly from the Americas, who founded the peninsula colony of Freetown. English is the official and commercial language; Krio is the common language spoken by most of the people. About 23 per cent of the population are Muslims and about 4 per cent Christians; the remainder are animists.

**HISTORY.** The coastal area was named Serra Lyoa (later corrupted to Sierra Leone)—meaning "Lion Mountain"—in the 15th century by Portuguese seamen. Between the 16th and 19th centuries the country was raided for slaves. In 1787 British abolitionists, in a plan to return former English and American slaves to Africa, sent a small expedition to Sierra Leone. They were driven away by the local tribal chief, but other expeditions followed. By 1792 nearly all of England's destitute Negroes had been transported to Sierra Leone. They were joined by Negroes from Nova Scotia, former American slaves who had escaped to Canada, and captured Maroons from Jamaica.

In 1808 the colony was taken over by the British government to be used as a naval base. During the next 60 years Sierra Leone received thousands of Africans who had been liberated from slave ships by British patrols.

In the late 19th century the British expanded inland from the colony around Freetown, and in 1896 the interior was declared a protectorate. The two areas later were merged. Sierra Leone became independent in April, 1961.

**GOVERNMENT AND POLITICS.** Until March, 1967, governmental power was vested in a prime minister. A cabinet, responsible to the House of Representatives, was appointed by the governor-general (the British sovereign's representative) with the advice of the prime minister.

Elections on March 17 resulted in a tie between the ruling Sierra Leone People's Party, headed by Sir Albert Margai, and the All People's Congress, led by Siaka Stevens. Later developments gave the All People's Congress a slight edge, and Stevens was appointed prime minister. On March 21, Brigadier David Lansana arrested Stevens and declared martial law. Three days later a group of junior army officers staged a counter coup and announced the formation of an eight-man National Reformation Council, headed by Lt.-Col. Andrew Juxon-Smith. The Council assumed all legislative and executive powers, suspended the constitution, and outlawed political activity.

**ECONOMY.** The economy is based on mining and farming. Eighty per cent of the population is engaged in agriculture, forestry, and livestock raising. The export of minerals, principally diamonds and iron ore, provides the bulk of foreign exchange.

Of 3,500 miles of road, only 250 are paved. There is one railroad of some 360 miles. Freetown is one of the finest natural harbors in the world.

**EDUCATION.** Education is neither compulsory nor free, but the cost is low. There are about 113,000 primary and secondary school students. Sierra Leone has two universities.

**ARMED FORCES.** About 1,850 men are in military service.

## SINGAPORE

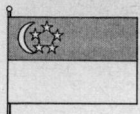

*Official Name:* Republic of Singapore. *Area:* 225 square miles. *Population:* 1,900,000. *Principal City* (with population): Singapore, the capital, 1,820,000.
*Flag:* Two red and white horizontal stripes, with a white crescent and five white stars on the red stripe. *Monetary Unit:* The Singapore dollar of 100 cents (worth 33 U.S. cents).

**LAND AND PEOPLE.** The Republic of Singapore consists of the island of Singapore, off the southern tip of the Malay Peninsula, and several islets in the Indian Ocean. (See map on page 243.) The city of Singapore is at the southern end of the island. There is a rain forest in central Singapore and large mangrove swamps along the coast. Average temperatures range from 74° to 87° F., and rainfall averages 95 inches a year.

Singapore is among the world's most cosmopolitan cities. Although about 75 per cent of the people are Chinese, there are sizable minorities of Malayans, Indians, Pakistanis, Europeans, and Eurasians. There is considerable friction between the Chinese, whose loyalties are often torn between Singapore and their ancestral home, and the minority groups, who are loyal only to Singapore. While most citizens of Singapore are Buddhists, Taoists, and Confucianists, there are large numbers of Muslims, Hindus, and Christians. Malay, Chinese, Tamil, and English are the predominant languages.

**HISTORY.** The earliest known colonizers of Singapore were Sumatrans, who landed on the island in the 11th century. Siamese and Javanese raiders and Chinese merchants soon followed.

In the 18th century Singapore became, nominally, a part of the Dutch colony of Johore. In 1819 Sir Thomas Stamford Raffles replaced the Dutch puppet-sultan with one of his own and thus won Singapore for the British East India Company. In 1824 it was formally ceded to the British, along with Malaya, under an Anglo-Dutch agreement. Under Raffles' enlightened rule, the extensive slave trade was suppressed and Singapore began to develop into a major Asian port. In 1826 it was made a part of the Straits Settlements, with Malacca and Penang.

Singapore was an important British naval base before World War II. In 1941 Japanese forces seized the city after a fierce battle. It was retaken, without fighting, in 1945. In 1946 Singapore was made a Crown Colony, along with the Christmas and Cocos-Keeling islands. It became a separate and self-governing state within the British Commonwealth of Nations in 1959.

In 1963 Singapore joined the Federation of Malaysia, but tensions grew between her Socialist Chinese leaders and the conservative, Malay-dominated federation government. In August, 1965, Malaya forced Singapore's withdrawal from the federation.

**GOVERNMENT AND POLITICS.** Singapore is a fully independent state, headed by a president (Yusof bin Ishak) and a prime minister (Lee Kuan Yew), the leader of the majority party in the popularly elected parliament of 51 members. The cabinet is made up of 14 members, including the prime minister. Political parties are unstable, but tend to be either Communist or anti-Communist. Relations with Malaysia have continued to deteriorate, although agreement was finally reached in August, 1966, over their shared currency, and each country began to issue its own in 1967.

**ECONOMY.** Singapore, the world's fifth largest port, depends almost exclusively on the transshipping of cargo, but is trying to expand native industry. It exports tin and rubber.

**EDUCATION AND HEALTH.** About half the population over 14 is literate. Education from 6 to 12 is free but not compulsory.

The Ministry of Health operates 9 general hospitals, 27 state dispensaries, and 63 maternal and child care centers. Dental care for children and young mothers is provided without charge.

**ARMED FORCES.** Singapore still serves as British military headquarters in Asia, but also supports an infantry brigade of its own.

## SOMALIA

*Official Name:* Somali Republic. *Area:* 251,046 square miles. *Population:* 2,500,000. *Principal Cities* (with populations): Mogadishu, the capital, 141,770; Hargeisa, 50,000; Kisimayu, 30,000; Berbera, 20,000. *Flag:* A light blue field with a white star in the center. *Monetary Unit:* The Somali shilling of 100 cents (worth 14 U.S. cents). *Gross National Product:* $150,000,000 (1965).

**LAND AND PEOPLE.** Somalia occupies the horn of East Africa. It is bordered on the north by the Gulf of Aden, on the east and south by the Indian Ocean, on the west by Kenya and Ethiopia, and on the northwest by French Somaliland. (See map on page 111.) The boundaries with Ethiopia are not accepted by Somalia. Dispute over the boundary with Kenya appeared resolved after an October, 1967, agreement.

The greater part of the country is occupied by the vast Ogaden plateau, mountain bordered in the north, but sloping in the south to a lowland area crossed by the Webi Shebeli and Juba rivers. Most of the country has a warm, dry, tropical climate, modified by altitude. Rainfall is scanty except in the mountains.

The majority of the inhabitants are Somali, divided into two lineages: the nomadic Samaale in the north and central areas, comprising 80 per cent of the total; and the agricultural Sab, a mixture of Negroid, Bantu-speaking, and Galla forebears. Samali, Arabic, English, and Italian are spoken.

The Somali are Muslims and adhere to the Sunni sect. Although Islam is the state religion, freedom of worship is guaranteed.

**HISTORY.** Overseas empires have contended

for control of the horn of East Africa since ancient times. From the 10th to the 15th century the eastern coast was part of the Zenj Empire, which was overthrown by the Portuguese in the 16th century. In the 17th century Muscat and Oman gained control of the coastal towns; in the 19th century their authority passed to the Sultan of Zanzibar.

European occupation of the country began in the late 19th century. A British protectorate was established in the north between 1884 and 1886, and an Italian protectorate in the south in 1889. British rule was constantly threatened by Somali resistance, led by Mohammed Ibn Abdullah Hassan, who was finally defeated in 1920 by British forces.

In 1934–36 Italian Somalia was used as a staging area for the Italian conquest of Ethiopia. During World War II Italian troops briefly occupied British Somaliland, but it, along with Italian Somalia, was reoccupied by the British in 1941. The territory was returned to Italian control in 1950, under a ten-year U.S. trusteeship. In 1954 a portion of British Somaliland was transferred to Ethiopia. Pan-Somali nationalism developed strongly in both the British and Italian sectors, and in 1960 Britain agreed to unification of the two territories in the independent Somali Republic.

In March, 1963, diplomatic relations were broken with Britain, and since 1964 there has been sporadic fighting along the frontiers with Ethiopia and Kenya. During 1965 there were efforts to resolve the disputes peacefully. Somalia has also called for self-determination for French Somaliland, which includes the strategic port of Djibouti, the terminus of the railroad from Ethiopia.

**GOVERNMENT AND POLITICS.** Somalia is a parliamentary democracy. Executive power is vested in a president, assisted by a prime minister and cabinet; legislative power rests with a National Assembly. The president is chosen by the assembly for a six-year term, and is allowed only one consecutive re-election. The assembly, in turn, is elected by universal adult suffrage. The prime minister and cabinet are chosen by the president. The president since June, 1967, has been Abdirashid Ali Shermarke.

**ECONOMY.** The economy is based mainly on subsistence livestock herding, supplemented by small-scale cultivation of corn, sorghum, legumes, sesame, sugarcane, cotton, and bananas.

Soviet aid to Somalia has included construction of a modern port at Berbera and sizable military assistance, the latter being a source of alarm to Somalia's neighbors. Financial and technical assistance are also contributed by Communist China, East Germany, the United Arab Republic, the United States, and the World Bank.

**EDUCATION AND HEALTH.** Education is not compulsory, and the rate of literacy is estimated to be between 2 and 10 per cent. The University Institute of Somalia, in Mogadishu, had 534 students in 1962.

A modern hospital with up-to-date equipment was finished in 1963. Somalia suffers a high incidence of tuberculosis and other pulmonary diseases, malaria, yaws, and intestinal diseases.

**ARMED FORCES.** The Somali army numbers some 5,000 men; the air force, 1,000. There is no navy.

## SOUTH AFRICA

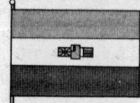

*Official Name:* Republic of South Africa. *Area:* 472,359 square miles. *Population:* 18,298,000. *Principal Cities* (with populations): Johannesburg, 595,083; Cape Town, the legislative capital, 508,341; Durban, 560,010; Pretoria, the administrative capital, 303,684; Bloemfontein, the judicial capital, 112,606. *Flag:* Three horizontal stripes of orange, white, and blue, with small replicas of the flag of the Orange Free State, the old Transvaal Vierkleur banner, and the Union Jack in the white stripe. *Monetary Unit:* The Rand (worth U.S. $1.40). *Gross National Product:* $11,965,000,000 (1966). *Average Annual Income per Person:* $594.

**LAND AND PEOPLE.** The Republic of South Africa, situated at the southern tip of Africa, is bordered on the north by South West Africa, Botswana, and Rhodesia, and on the northeast by Mozambique and Swaziland. (See map on page 111.) Cape Agulhas, at the southwestern tip of the country, marks the division between the Atlantic Ocean on the west and the Indian Ocean on the east and south. In the eastern part of South Africa is the newly independent state of Lesotho.

Most of South Africa is higher than 3,000 feet. In the east the land rises from the coastal lowlands to the Drakensberg Mountains in the east. The western and southern coastal belts are also fertile. In the south are the semi-arid and arid Little Karroo and Great Karroo. In the center and northeast are high grass prairies, the veld. The Orange River and its tributary, the Vaal, flow from the east into the Atlantic. The Limpopo River flows through Mozambique to the Indian Ocean, forming the boundary between South Africa, Botswana, and Rhodesia.

Wild game abounds, and many national parks and reserves have been established to protect indigenous animals from destruction.

The population is 68 per cent African, of whom the largest group is the Bantus; 19 per cent white, of whom three-fifths are Afrikaners, primarily of Dutch descent, and the rest of English stock; 10 per cent Coloreds, of mixed African and white blood; and 3 per cent Asian. Principal languages spoken are Afrikaans, English, and Bantu dialects. Protestants number 57.8 per cent of the population; members of the African separatist churches, 14.4 per cent; animists, 23.7 per cent; and there are small Roman Catholic, Hindu, Muslim, and Jewish minorities.

**HISTORY.** Little is known of the early history of the Hottentots, Bushmen, and other Africans who inhabited southern Africa before the arrival of the Portuguese at the end of the 15th century. The first permanent European settlement was made at Cape Town in 1652 by the Dutch East India Company for the purpose of supplying fresh food and water to ships bound for India. The Dutch—called Boers (farmers) —were soon joined by French and German immigrants. The African inhabitants were used as slave labor. By 1800 there were 15,000 whites, who by then were calling themselves Afrikaners, in Cape Colony.

As a result of the Napoleonic Wars, Britain gained formal possession of the Cape Colony in 1814. In 1820, the first British settlers began arriving, slowly displacing the Boers. After the British abolished slavery in 1833, one-fourth of the Boer population migrated to the interior during 1835–43 and founded the Transvaal and Orange Free State Territories. The Great Trek led to a series of conflicts in which the Boers defeated the Bantu and Zulu tribesmen. The latter were finally crushed at the Battle of Blood River in 1838.

The British annexed Natal in 1843 and, after the discovery of gold and diamonds, the Orange Free State in 1871 and the Transvaal in 1877. Mounting Boer resentment erupted in 1899 into the Boer or South African War, won by the British in 1902.

The Union of South Africa was formed in 1910 from the former crown colonies of Cape of Good Hope, Natal, the Orange River Colony (Orange Free State), and the Transvaal. The long years of fighting left lasting bitterness which persists today, even though the Boers control the country. After the formation of the Union, two political parties emerged. The South African Party, headed by Louis Botha and Jan Christiaan Smuts, hoped that the British and Afrikaner elements would form a white South African nation freely cooperating with Britain. The Nationalists sought to re-establish the Transvaal and Orange Free State as Afrikaner republics. During World War I the Nationalists attempted an unsuccessful coup d'etat to oust the pro-Allied government. Again, in World War II, the Nationalist Party bitterly opposed South Africa's entry into the war on the Allied side.

During these years the ruling whites implemented white-supremacist policies. After World War II, apartheid—the separation or separate development of races—became an official government policy under Nationalist Prime Minister Daniel Malan, whose party won the 1948 elections and has been in power since then. This separatist doctrine was carried a stage further in 1959 with the passage of the Promotion of Bantu Self-Government Act, providing for eight self-governing African states. Of these, the Transkei now has its own parliament.

In 1961 South Africa withdrew from the Commonwealth of Nations because of opposition to its policies and in that same year became a republic. In spite of widespread external criticism and some opposition within the country, South Africa continued its apartheid policies under Prime Minister Hendrik F. Verwoerd, who was murdered by a deranged, white assassin in 1966, and under his successor, Balthazar Johannes Vorster.

**GOVERNMENT AND POLITICS.** For the dominant white minority, South Africa is a parliamentary democracy.

The state president, who serves for seven years, is elected by Parliament. The prime minister (head of government) is the leader of the majority party in Parliament. The Senate has 54 members representing the four provinces and South West Africa; 11 are appointed members, of whom one represents the Coloreds in Cape Province; 43 are elected. In the House of Assembly, 160 representatives are directly elected from South African constituencies, 6 are directly elected from South West Africa, and 4 are elected on a separate roll to represent the interests of the Coloreds in Cape Province. White suffrage is universal above the age of 18. Africans cannot vote in parliamentary elections, and members of Parliament, elected for five-year terms, must be white.

The leading political party is the Nationalist Party, which won 126 seats in the elections of March, 1966. The fact that the United Party, in favor of white leadership but opposed to independent black states within the country's borders, captured only 39 seats reveals the widespread acceptance of apartheid policies. The Progressive Party, opposed to apartheid, won a single seat.

**ECONOMY.** South Africa has the best developed economy of any African state, and its economic growth rate in recent years has been 5 to 7 per cent annually. Although the nation's wealth was built on mining, today manufacturing is the largest single contributor to the national income. Both heavy and light industry, including steel, machinery, chemicals, textiles, tires, paper, and plastics, are highly diversified. The rapid development of manufacturing has given South Africa a self-sustaining economy, but foreign investment capital is still sought to facilitate achievement of the government's projected high growth rate.

South Africa remains the world's leading supplier of gold, diamonds, and platinum. Other important minerals include uranium, coal, asbestos, copper, iron, and manganese. Although only 15 per cent of the land is arable, more than a third of the nation's exports, excluding gold, are agricultural products, mainly wool, fruit, and sugar.

South Africa's transportation network is the best in Africa and is steadily being improved. The country has over 115,000 miles of roads and more than 13,000 miles of railroads. There are well-equipped ports at Durban, Cape Town, Port Elizabeth, and East London.

**EDUCATION.** Education is free and compulsory for white children between 7 and 16, and white literacy is practically 100 per cent. For non-whites education is generally free but not compulsory, and educational standards vary considerably. Nonwhite literacy is estimated at 60 per cent.

**ARMED FORCES.** With certain exceptions and qualifications, nine months' military service is compulsory for men between the ages of 18 and 25. The army totals 16,200 men; the air force 3,000; and the navy 3,000.

## SOUTH ARABIA

*Official Name:* Federation of South Arabia. *Area:* Aden, 73 square miles; Protectorate, 116,967 square miles. *Population:* 1,250,000. *Principal Cities* (with populations): Aden, 99,285; Sheikh Othman, 29,879; Crater, 55,-000; Tawahi, 20,000; Maalla, 20,000. *Monetary Units:* The South Arabian dinar (worth U.S. $2.8175) and the East African shilling (worth 14 U.S. cents).

**LAND AND PEOPLE.** The Federation of South Arabia is scheduled to become an independent nation in 1968. It consists of Aden State and 16 of the 25 territories included in the British Protectorate of South Arabia. Separated from Muscat and Oman on the northeast by Protectorate states, the federation extends southwestward along the Indian Ocean to the junction of the Red Sea and the Gulf of Aden. Its borders with Yemen on the west and with Saudi Arabia on the north are disputed. (See map on page 151.)

Aden itself, a small coastal district, has a superb natural harbor only 100 miles from the entrance to the Red Sea. The remainder of the federation consists of a narrow coastal plain 4 to 40 miles deep, and, farther inland, hills that rise to a mountainous area and then fall away in the north to the desert region of the Rub al Khali (Empty Quarter). The climate is generally mild in the highlands and hot and humid on the coast.

The inhabitants are 98 per cent Arab, and 96 per cent are Muslims. The languages of the federation are Arabic and English.

**HISTORY.** Aden, traditionally an important trading station between east and west, was absorbed into the Arab Caliphate in the 7th century and into the Ottoman Empire in the 16th century. Occupied briefly by the Portuguese, it was captured by the British in 1839. Its strategic importance increased after the opening of the Suez Canal in 1869. By 1914 Yemeni forces had been expelled from the territories north of Aden, and British protectorates had been established over all the minor states of the South Arabian coast.

The Federation of South Arabia was gradually brought into existence between 1959 and 1965. The name was adopted in 1962. Britain imposed the federation on Aden in 1963, hoping to safeguard British military and economic interests there. Britain rejected Yemeni claims on the territory and a U.N. report indicating that many people in the federation favored union with Yemen. The ensuing outbreak of strikes, violence, and terrorism continued in 1967. Aden's citizens are divided between two organizations: the National Liberation Front that favors an independent South Arabia, and the Egyptian-backed Front for the Liberation of Occupied South Yemen.

**GOVERNMENT AND POLITICS.** The federation is headed by a British High Commissioner with exclusive authority over external affairs, defense, and internal security. The legal government collapsed in August, 1967, in advance of Britain's scheduled withdrawal in January, 1968. However, on Sept. 25, 1967, the National Liberation Front and the Front for Liberation of Occupied South Yemen agreed to lay down their arms and cease terrorist activities. Britain then updated its withdrawal plans, scheduling departure by the end of 1967, regardless of whether or not a government was formed.

**ECONOMY.** The bulk of the population relies on livestock herding and farming. Subsistence crops are sorghum, millet, sesame, dates, wheat, barley, and coffee. The federation's economy revolves almost exclusively around Aden, with its major free port, oil refinery, and large British army and air force bases. Aden serves as distribution center for the products of surrounding countries.

**EDUCATION AND HEALTH.** Education is not compulsory, and literacy is estimated at 10 per cent. Virtually all hospitals are situated in Aden.

**ARMED FORCES.** There is a small federal army of 5,000 volunteers, but no compulsory service.

## SOUTH WEST AFRICA

*Official Name:* South West Africa. *Area:* 318,-261 square miles. *Population:* 610,000. *Principal City* (with population): Windhoek, the capital, 48,000. *Flag:* Same as South Africa's. *Monetary Unit:* The rand (worth U.S. $1.40). *Gross National Product:* $299,460,000 (1963). *Average Annual Income per Person:* $390.

**LAND AND PEOPLE.** South West Africa is bordered by South Africa on the south and southeast, Botswana on the east, Angola on the north, and the Atlantic Ocean on the west. (See map on page 111.) Most of South West Africa is mountainous plateau; a long strip of desert runs along the coast. The climate is warm in winter and hot in summer.

The majority of the inhabitants are Bantu. Whites constitute one-seventh of the population and are of Afrikaner (Dutch), German, or English stock. There is also a sizable Colored population of mixed European and African or Malayan descent. Afrikaans, German, and English are spoken, in addition to African dialects.

**HISTORY.** In 1884 Germany claimed a protectorate over South West Africa, but African resistance delayed actual German control until about 1908. South African troops captured the area in 1915, and in 1920 it became a South African mandate under League of Nations supervision. South Africa maintained the mandate after dissolution of the League.

In 1960 Ethiopia and Liberia, on behalf of other independent states of Africa, challenged South Africa's right to administer the territory, charging that the policy of apartheid was illegal. Suit was brought before the International Court of Justice, but in 1966 the court refused to decide the case, claiming that the plaintiffs had no legal interest in the matter. The U.N. General Assembly thereupon adopted a resolution that South Africa had forfeited its rights under the mandate. South Africa rejected the resolution.

**GOVERNMENT AND POLITICS.** The territory is governed by South Africa and administered by a South African administrator, an Executive

Committee, and a Legislative Assembly. Recent statements by South African authorities indicate that some form of self-rule is planned for the future.

**ECONOMY.** Most of the people live by raising cattle and sheep. The major exports are fish and fish products, diamonds, copper, lead, manganese, and zinc.

**EDUCATION.** The white literacy rate is nearly 100 per cent; the nonwhite rate is 30 per cent.

## SPAIN

*Official Name:* The Spanish State. *Area:* 194,883 square miles. *Population:* 31,871,-000. *Principal Cities* (with populations): Madrid, the capital, 2,558,583; Barcelona, 1,696,008; Valencia, 583,151; Seville, 531,571; Zaragoza, 377,412. *Flag:* A yellow, a red, and a yellow horizontal stripe, with the Spanish coat of arms centered on the red stripe. *Monetary Unit:* The peseta of 100 centimos (worth 1.7 U.S. cents). *Gross National Product:* $24,566,000,000 (1966). *Average Annual Income per Person:* $770.

**LAND AND PEOPLE.** Spain is situated on the Iberian Peninsula of western Europe. It is bounded on the north by the Bay of Biscay, the rugged Pyrenees that separate it from France, and the independent republic of Andorra; on the east by the Mediterranean Sea; on the south by the Mediterranean Sea, the British Crown Colony of Gibraltar, the Strait of Gibraltar, and the Atlantic Ocean; and on the west by Portugal and the Atlantic Ocean. (See map on page 117.)

The Balearic Islands (principally Iviza, Majorca, and Minorca) are in the Mediterranean off the east coast. The Canary Islands (divided into two provinces, the larger of which is Las Palmas), lie in the Atlantic west of Morocco.

There are distinct topographical regions in Spain, but the overall aspect is one of mountains (there are six separate ranges), alluvial valleys, grazing lands, a vast central plateau, plains, steep rocky coastlines, and rivers. Most important of the latter are the Ebro, Douro, Tagus, Guadalquivir, and Guadiana. Weather follows the pattern of the land: a cool, humid, northern coastal climate; cold winters and hot summers in the central plateau; and a usually temperate climate in the south, but the thermometer in summer can soar past 100° F.

Spain's people are almost all grouped as Castilians, Basques, Catalans, Galicians, or Andalusians. While Castilian Spanish is the official language, distinctive dialects, such as Basque, Catalan, and Galician, are spoken in the regions inhabited by these groups.

Religious education, controlled by the Roman Catholic Church, begins in the schools. Ninety-nine per cent of the population is Catholic.

**HISTORY.** Evidence of a people who inhabited the Iberian Peninsula in prehistoric times was found in Spain's Altamira caves in 1879. In the ninth century B.C. Phoenician traders reached the country and settled on the southwest coast.

Carthaginians settled on the east coast and the Balearic Islands, where Greeks also planted colonies. In the third century B.C. the Carthaginians conquered most of Iberia, but with Hannibal's defeat by Roman forces they were expelled. By the first century A.D. Roman control was well established, and under the empire the country prospered, grew, and was peaceful.

Christianity was established in the second and third centuries, but hordes of Germanic barbarians began sweeping into the peninsula in 409. In the eighth century Spain was conquered by Muslim Berbers; under Abdu-r-Rahman III (891–961) Muslim Spain reached its apex. The Christian reconquest pushed slowly south, but the Moors did not lose their last stronghold (Granada) until 1492, when it fell to the forces of Ferdinand V and Isabella I, rulers of Castile and Aragon. In that same year Christopher Columbus set out on his first voyage to the west under their patronage.

Spain's "Golden Century" was the 16th, coinciding with the Hapsburg dynasty's accession to the throne. Vast wealth came from the Americas, and Spain ruled the seas and had the strongest military force in Europe. But incessant wars with England, the Netherlands, and France brought about the decline of Spanish power. Spain's deepest humiliation came in 1808 with the forced abdication of King Charles IV and his heir, Napoleon's occupation, and the accession to the country's throne of Joseph Bonaparte. By 1814 British forces under the Duke of Wellington had succeeded in driving out the French armies. Colonial rebellion began the dissolution of most of Spain's overseas empire; the Spanish-American War (1898) completed it.

Spain remained neutral in World War I. Afterward economic and social unrest grew deeper, and with it anticlericalism. A military dictatorship led by Primo de Rivera took over (1923) under the Bourbon king, Alfonso XIII. De Rivera was ousted in 1930, and a republican victory at the polls brought an end to the monarchy (1931). The republic was first led by a moderate liberal regime, but it met increasing opposition from extremes of left and right and fell to a Popular Front (Republicans, Socialists, Communists, and Syndicalists) in 1936. At the same time, however, a military coup was taking shape in Spanish Morocco. General Francisco Franco, in semi-exile on the Canary Islands, took command of the forces in Morocco, most powerful segment of the Spanish Army; he led them in the invasion of Spain, and three years of civil war began.

Internal support for General Franco came from the country's conservative elements, including the Fascist Falange Party, founded in 1933 by the son of ex-dictator de Rivera; the defending Loyalists (Republicans) were backed by the Popular Front and the Basques and Catalans. Franco received substantial aid from Nazi Germany and Fascist Italy; the Loyalists, handicapped by the nonintervention policy of many great powers, received help from an idealistic band of mercenaries and from the Soviet Union. Factionalism split both sides; the Communists used it to gain the upper hand in the Loyalist camp, and Franco managed to hold ascendancy over the army-Fascist rivalries in his ranks. By early 1939, the insurgents and Franco won their revolution and set up a highly authoritarian corporative state that suppressed all internal political opposition.

During World War II Spain clearly favored the Axis Powers, while remaining technically neutral. Such policies made her generally unpopular in the postwar era, and in 1947 she was refused admission to the U.N. The Korean War, however, led the U.S. to sign a pact with Spain permitting establishment of American naval and air bases on Spanish soil (1953). Two years later Spain entered the U.N.

Since 1964 a major goal of Spanish foreign policy has been the recovery of Gibraltar, held by Britain since 1704; but the colony's population voted overwhelmingly to remain British in a referendum in September, 1967.

**GOVERNMENT AND POLITICS.** Although nominally a constitutional monarchy since the referendum of 1947, Spain has been dominated for three decades by the personal rule of its caudillo (chief of state), General Francisco Franco, who appoints his own cabinet. The 564-member Cortes (Parliament), organized on corporate lines, acts on government-presented legislation, and has the power—though seldom exercised—to introduce legislation. Franco controls Spain's only legal political party, the National Movement. The first direct election since 1936 was held on October 10, 1967, to choose 108 deputies to the Cortes from a list of National Movement candidates.

The Press Law of 1966 abolished direct censorship while maintaining tight controls on the press. One result of this measure has been the expression of opposition to the regime, voiced particularly by trade-union members, university students, intellectuals, and the clergy. Illegal "Workers' Commissions" set up within the state-controlled unions have called strikes to support their demands for labor freedom and economic gains.

The constitutional law and accompanying legislation voted by the Cortes in 1967 allow the Cortes and the Council of the Realm the right to select a regent to succeed Franco as chief of state if no agreement can be reached on a person of royal blood to serve as king.

**ECONOMY.** Foreign investments (chiefly from the U.S.) and tourism are partly responsible for nearly a decade of economic progress in Spain. By 1964, however, inflation had begun to plague the economy. The industrial recession of 1967 saw the cost of living rise by an estimated minimum of 10 per cent, the first noticeable surge of unemployment in ten years, and the second increase in a year of the nation's minimum wage, now $1.60 a day.

Agriculture, the basis of Spain's economy, has long been neglected in favor of industry. Food production is low, and as many as 200,-000 farmers annually have migrated to the cities. The need for food imports has further aggravated Spain's foreign trade deficit, esti-mated at some $2 billion for the 1966–67 period. The government's Second Economic Development Plan for the years 1968–72 calls for increased investment and improvement in the area of agriculture.

Leading industries are iron and steel, textiles, chemicals, shipbuilding, and cement.

Spanish hopes of association with the European Common Market remained unrealized in 1967, and Spain, despite her policy of anti-Communism, increased her bilateral trade with the Soviet bloc.

Since 1964 special efforts have been made to improve the country's transportation facilities. Highways, 60 per cent of which are paved, total about 51,600 miles; railways, mostly state-owned, aggregate about 7,000 miles. Iberia Airlines provides domestic and international service.

**EDUCATION.** The literacy rate is 91 per cent. Education is under state control and is free and compulsory at the primary level. There are 13 universities.

**ARMED FORCES.** Spain's armed forces are estimated to total over 220,000 men.

## SPANISH TERRITORIES AND DEPENDENCIES

### IFNI

*Area:* 676 square miles. *Population:* 51,500. *Principal City* (with population): Sidi Ifni, the capital, 13,770.

Ifni is a dry, mountainous province on the west coast of Africa, peopled by Muslim Berbers. Although ceded by Morocco in 1860, Spain did not take it over administratively until 1934. Since 1956 Morocco has demanded its return, and there have been armed clashes between Spanish and Moroccan forces. The province is ruled by a governor-general responsible to Madrid.

Ifni bases its economy on fishing, agriculture, herding, and a few light industries.

### EQUATORIAL GUINEA

*Area:* 10,829 square miles. *Population:* 267,-000. *Principal Cities* (with populations): Santa Isabel, the capital, 37,240; Bata, 27,000.

Equatorial Guinea comprises two provinces: Fernando Po, in the Gulf of Guinea about 20 miles west of Cameroon, with the island of Annobón, about 400 miles to the southwest; and Río Muni, bordered on the north by Cameroon, on the east and south by Gabon, and on the west by the Gulf of Guinea.

Fernando Po is a volcanic island with plentiful rains and several rivers, and is populated by the Bubi (a Bantu people), Nigerians, and descendants of West Indian Maroons and Africans from Sierra Leone who still speak an English Creole. The island was discovered by the Portuguese in 1471 and ceded to Spain in 1778. It became a Spanish province in 1960 under the Treaty of Berlin. The economy is primarily agricultural. Hot and muggy Río Muni is chiefly populated by Africans.

Internal self-government was granted to Equatorial Guinea after the 1964 elections. Spain is represented by a High Commissioner.

## SPANISH SAHARA

*Area:* 102,702 square miles. *Population:* 45,-000. *Principal City* (with population): El Aaiún, the capital, 5,500.

Spanish Sahara is bordered on the north by Morocco, on the northeast by Algeria, on the east and south by Mauritania, and on the west by the Atlantic Ocean. An arid land, inhabited mostly by nomadic Muslim herders, it was organized as a province in 1958.

## CEUTA AND MELILLA

*Area:* 12 square miles. *Population:* 154,000.

These two city enclaves are situated on the Mediterranean coast of Morocco. Ceuta is seven square miles in size, with a population of 76,000; Melilla has an area of five square miles and a population of 81,000. Both encalves are parts of Metropolitan Spain and are fishing ports. Ceuta exports iron ore.

The fortified port of Ceuta was built on the site of a Phoenician colony and may have been the site of one of the ancient Pillars of Hercules. It was seized from the Arabs by Portugal in 1415 and passed into Spanish hands in 1580. Melilla has been Spanish since 1496 and was the site of the initial uprising of the Spanish Civil War in 1936.

# SUDAN

 *Official Name:* The Republic of the Sudan. *Area:* 967,494 square miles. *Population:* 13,940,000. *Principal Cities* (with populations): Khartoum, the capital, 173,-500; Omdurman, 185,380; Port Sudan, 110,000. *Flag:* A blue, a yellow, and a green horizontal stripe. *Monetary Unit:* The Sudanese pound of 100 piasters (worth U.S. $2.88). *Gross National Product:* $1,453,000,000 (1966). *Average Annual Income per Person:* $95.

**LAND AND PEOPLE.** Situated in northeastern Africa, the Sudan is bordered by Egypt on the north; by the Red Sea and Ethiopia on the east; by Kenya, Uganda, and the Republic of the Congo on the south; and by the Central African Republic and Chad on the west. (See map on page 111.)

The Sudan is a vast plain sloping gently from south to north. Through it flow the Nile and its tributaries, playing a preponderant role in Sudanese life. Beyond the rivers, the character of the land changes with the amount of rainfall; undulating desert in the north gives way to savanna grasslands in the central portions and tropical rain forest along the southern frontier.

The Sudan is dominated by the people of the northern provinces, who claim Arab descent and practice Islam. Scattered among them are groups of non-Arabic Muslims, including the Beja of the Red Sea Hills, the Darfur in the west, and the Nubians along the northern Nile Valley. In all, 65 per cent of the population are Muslims. Arabic is the official language.

The southern Sudan is inhabited by four to five million people, speaking African languages and practicing animistic or Christian rites, who have traditionally been associated with the Africans to the south.

**HISTORY.** During the first millennium B.C. Egypt established outposts in the Sudan from which developed the kingdom of Kush. In later centuries, as Egypt itself declined, Kush preserved Egyptian culture. In 350 A.D. it was destroyed by the Aksumites from Ethiopia.

In the sixth century Christian missionaries established states which co-existed with Muslim-Arab Egypt for over 600 years. With Egypt later under the control of non-Arabs, Arab nomads were encouraged to move to Upper Egypt and to pillage along the Sudan frontier. By the end of the 13th century the Arabs had taken over Christian Nubia, settling in the Sudan, where they intermarried and introduced Islam. Farther south the Funj, a people of unknown origin, conquered Christian Alwa, which had dominated central Sudan.

In 1820–21 troops of the Ottoman Viceroy of Egypt, Mohammed Ali, overwhelmed the Funj and established Turco-Egyptian rule throughout most of the northern Sudan. The southern Sudan was conquered during the reign of the Khedive Ismail (1863–79). The area was administered for the Khedive by European officials who combated the slave trade dominating relations among the Arabs, the northern Sudanese, and the Africans of the south.

Increasingly resentful of Turco-Egyptian rule, the Sudanese, under the leadership of Mohammed Ahmed, the Mahdi, revolted; by 1885 they had driven the Egyptians from the Sudan and had established an independent, theocratic Mahdist state. Anglo-Egyptian forces invaded the Sudan and destroyed the Mahdist state in 1898. British officials introduced Western technology, education, and culture.

After World War I Sudanese nationalism developed rapidly in the north. At the same time the differences between the northern and southern Sudan were exacerbated by the exclusion of northern Muslim Sudanese from the south and by the opening of the south to Christian missionaries and English education. In 1955 the southerners revolted and, in the face of continuing efforts by the Sudan government to press Arabization in the south, the revolt remains unsuppressed.

In 1956 Sudanese nationalism was triumphant, and the Sudan was declared an independent republic. Two years later rebellious army officers seized control of the government and suspended the constitution.

**GOVERNMENT AND POLITICS.** A popular revolution in 1964 established civilian rule after six years of military rule. After elections in 1965, the Constituent Assembly was controlled by a coalition cabinet headed by Mohammed Ahmed Mahgoub, who represented the conservative religious brotherhood, the Ansar, and post-World War I nationalists. He was soon challenged by Sayyid Saddiq al-Mahdi, a grandson of the original Mahdi. Oxford-educated, Saddiq attracted the new intelligentsia—workers, students, and civil servants. In July, 1966, he rallied sufficient support to replace the Mahgoub government, but his political victory proved short-lived. Unable to heal a rift with the Ansari, a powerful religious brotherhood founded by his grandfather, Saddiq resigned in May, 1967, and was replaced by a coalition government under Mahgoub.

**ECONOMY.** Sudan's economy is based on cotton-growing south of Khartoum, between the Blue Nile and the White Nile. Cotton accounts for about 70 per cent of the Sudan's foreign exchange. Cultivation of grain crops and the raising of herds of cattle, camels, and sheep provide subsistence for the great majority of Sudanese. Around urban centers industrial complexes have developed, consisting of agricultural processing and light manufacturing.

**EDUCATION.** School enrollment in 1964 was over 570,000, with the nation's literacy rate about 12 per cent of the population 15 years old and over. The University of Khartoum was established in 1956.

**ARMED FORCES.** There is a volunteer army of 20,000.

# SWEDEN

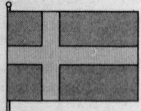

*Official Name:* Kingdom of Sweden. *Area:* 173,665 square miles. *Population:* 7,844,000. *Principal Cities* (with populations): Stockholm, the capital, 793,714; Goteborg, 442,799; Malmo, 255,315; Vasteras, 107,082. *Flag:* A blue field with a yellow cross. *Monetary Unit:* The krona of 100 ore (worth 19.4 U.S. cents). *Gross National Product:* $23,030,000,000 (1966). *Average Annual Income per Person:* $1,110.

**LAND AND PEOPLE.** Sweden, situated on the eastern part of the Scandinavian peninsula, is bordered by Norway on the west; Finland on the northeast; the Gulf of Bothnia and the Baltic Sea on the east and south; and the Sound (Oresund), the Kattegat, and the Skagerrak on the southwest. (See map on page 117.) The largest of its several islands are Gotland and Oland in the Baltic.

The climate varies greatly between the north and the south (15 per cent of the country lies north of the Arctic Circle). The south has a temperate climate with about a two-month winter and four-month summer; winter in the north lasts more than seven months.

The Swedish people, except for a small minority of Finns and Lapps in Lapland, are descended from Germanic-Scandinavian tribes. The established church is Lutheran (with the king as its head), and 94 per cent of the population belong to it.

**HISTORY.** Tacitus, the Roman historian, first mentioned the Swedes (Suiones) about 100 A.D. In the ninth century their semi-legendary chieftain, Rurik, is reputed to have founded Russia, and by the tenth century Swedish influence extended south to the Black Sea. Warfare against Norsemen and Danes went on for centuries. By the 13th century there was a decline in royal power because of the rise of an independent feudal system, and in 1397 all the Scandinavian crowns were united in the Kalmar Union under Queen Margaret of Denmark. The Union ended in 1523 when the Swedes elected Gustavus Vasa to their throne as Gustavus I.

By the time of its involvement in the Thirty Years War (1618–48), Sweden, under Gustavus II Adolphus (1611–32), was the foremost Protestant power on the Continent and had acquired much territory.

The monarchy became absolute during the reign of Charles XI (1660–97). Sweden declined in the 18th century under Charles XII, who involved the country in disastrous wars. When he died the absolute monarchy was abolished.

In the early 19th century Sweden warred with Napoleon I and lost Finland to Russia (1809). Napoleon's brilliant marshal, Jean Baptiste Jules Bernadotte, although an adversary of the Swedes, so impressed them in their negotiations with him that the Riksdag elected him to succeed the childless Charles XIII, who adopted him in 1810. Eight years later Bernadotte ascended the throne as Charles XIV John, and founded a new Swedish dynasty. The last war in Swedish history was fought in 1814, when Bernadotte enforced the Congress of Vienna's award of Norway to Sweden. Norway remained a semi-independent kingdom in union with Sweden until 1905, when the union was peacefully dissolved.

In the 19th century the country made great progress in liberalizing the government and in developing industry. With neutrality as the basis of its foreign policy in the 20th century, Sweden remained militarily uninvolved in both world wars.

Gustavus VI Adolphus, crowned in 1950, is the sixth king in the Bernadotte line.

**GOVERNMENT AND POLITICS.** Sweden, a constitutional monarchy, is in practice a parliamentary democracy. The king is the nominal head of state but exercises no political power. The prime minister, who heads the cabinet, is the real chief of state; his power depends on majority support from the Parliament (Riksdag). Parliament is composed of two houses, each with equal power: the 151 members of the upper house are indirectly elected for eight-year terms by officials of the 19 local governments; the 233 members of the lower house are elected by popular vote for four-year terms. The judicial system is based on a three-tier hierarchy of courts: the lower courts, the intermediate court of appeals, and the supreme court.

The Social Democratic Party, dominant since 1932 (except for a short period in 1963), lost its majority in many local elections in 1966. Tage Erlander has been prime minister since 1946. Other parties are the Conservative, Liberal, Center, Communist, and Citizens' Front.

**ECONOMY.** Economic expansion and a rising standard of living have marked Sweden's continued economic progress. In particular, there has been a substantial acceleration in the growth of production. Her manufacturing plants, 95 per cent privately owned, are among the most modern in the world. Major industries are timber, paper, pulp, machine tools, metalworking, iron and steel, shipbuilding, textiles, fishing, chemicals, and glass manufacture. Water power is plentiful, but Sweden is almost totally lacking in coal and oil, and mineral fuel is therefore one of her chief imports. Although only 10 per cent of the land is under cultivation, modern farming methods produce about 90 per cent of the country's basic foodstuffs.

Highways and railroads (mostly electrified and state-owned) are modern and efficient. Taxation is heavy, largely due to the magnitude of the nation's social welfare system.

**EDUCATION.** Sweden's social legislation is as advanced as any in the world; its educational and cultural level is exceptionally high. Literacy is almost 100 per cent. Schooling, compulsory between the ages of 7 and 16, is free. Higher education is also tuition-free and, in addition, students are given a small monthly study grant. State universities are located at Uppsala (founded in 1477) and Lund, and private universities are at Stockholm and Goteborg.

**ARMED FORCES.** The Swedish army's full strength is 600,000. The navy numbers 12,000 officers and men. Military service is compulsory and starts at age 18.

# SWITZERLAND

*Official Name:* Switzerland. *Area:* 15,941 square miles. *Population:* 5,953,000. *Principal Cities* (with populations): Bern, the capital, 5,-953,000; Zurich, 433,200; Basel, 212,800; Geneva, 169,700. *Flag:* A white cross on a red field. *Monetary Unit:* The Swiss franc of 100 rappen or centimes (worth 23 U.S. cents). *Gross National Product:* $14,-800,000,000 (1966). *Average Annual Income per Person:* $2,057 (1966).

**LAND AND PEOPLE.** Switzerland is bordered on the north by West Germany, in the east by Austria and Liechtenstein, on the south by Italy, and on the west by France. (See map on page 117.)

Two mountain systems occupy most of the country—the Alps in the south and the Jura in the west and northwest. In the central Alps rise the Rhine, the Rhone, and the Ticino rivers. Between the Alps and the Jura, the Midlands, a densely populated plateau with an average altitude of 1,500 feet, stretches from west to east. About 70 per cent of the people speak German. Other languages are French, Italian, and Romansh. The population is 52.7 per cent Protestant and 45.4 per cent Catholic.

**HISTORY.** The Helvetians, who lived on the northern foothills of the Alps, were conquered by the Romans in 58 B.C. After the retreat of the Romans in 401, the area was dominated by a succession of rival neighbors.

In the 9th century the area was part of the Empire of Charlemagne. As the Carolingian Empire fell into decay, the encroachment of the Hapsburg, Zahringer, and Savoy dynasties made the citizens increasingly restive. In 1291 a defensive league against the House of Hapsburg, whose rule reached as far as Lake Lucerne, was formed by the cantons of Uri, Schwyz (from which the country takes its name), and Unterwalden. This commonly marks the beginning of the Swiss confederation.

In the late 14th century, the confederation twice defeated Austria; it then developed into a major military power. In the 15th century the Swiss defeated Charles the Bold of Burgundy and Emperor Maximilian I, who in 1499 gave Switzerland its virtual independence.

By 1513 the confederation had grown to 13 largely autonomous cantons. In 1515 Francis I, king of France, defeated the Swiss mercenaries at Marignano, in northern Italy. But the following year, an "everlasting peace" was negotiated by Francis I and the Swiss. After this treaty of "perpetual alliance," neutrality became a cornerstone of Swiss policy.

Feelings of national unity were almost erased by religious conflicts stemming from the Reformation. The Treaty of Westphalia, which in 1648 ended the Thirty Years War, also recognized Swiss independence.

In 1798 French revolutionary forces invaded Switzerland and after their victory formed the Helvetic Republic. Napoleon's Act of Mediation in 1803 restored the old confederation, subservient to France. In 1815 the Treaty of Paris and the Congress of Vienna guaranteed Switzerland's perpetual neutrality. In the same year the country adopted its present borders.

In 1848 a more liberal constitution was promulgated, and oligarchic rule in the cantons was softened. A new spirit of national unity was diffused, culminating in the Constitution of 1874, under which Switzerland is governed today.

**GOVERNMENT AND POLITICS.** Switzerland is a parliamentary democracy. The supreme legislative authority is vested in a parliament of two chambers: the Standerat (Council of States) and the Nationalrat (National Council). The Council of States is composed of two representatives from each of the 22 cantons. The National Council has 200 seats, distributed in proportion to the population. A joint session of the Federal Assembly elects the executive Federal Council of seven members; the Federal Council is the executive branch of the government. The Federal Assembly names the president and vice president of the Council for one-year terms.

The cantons have sovereignty in all matters not specifically given to the federal government. Women are not allowed to vote in federal elections.

**ECONOMY.** Manufacturing and finance form the backbone of the Swiss economy. Machinery and equipment, chemicals and drugs, watches, textiles, and food are the principal products and the chief exports.

Switzerland imports nearly all its raw materials and fuel. In 1966 exports totaled $3,283 billion, while imports reached $3,932 billion. International banking, insurance, and transportation are also important. Because of unmatched gold backing for its currency and the secrecy accorded to depositors by Swiss banks, there has usually been an influx of money.

Although Switzerland is a member of the European Free Trade Association, its principal trading partners are Common Market countries, especially West Germany and France. A manpower shortage has led to an influx of foreign workers.

The 3,200-mile totally electrified Swiss railway system is one of the best in the world. Freight is carried on the Rhine between Basel and the North Sea. The Swiss have a merchant marine of 31 units (gross tonnage: 182,355). International railroad traffic passes through the St. Gotthard, Simplon, and Lotschberg tunnels. The first automobile passage under the Alps, the Great St. Bernard tunnel, opened in 1964.

**EDUCATION.** Education from ages seven to 15 is free and compulsory. There is 100 per cent literacy. There are seven universities.

**ARMED FORCES.** All able-bodied men between 20 and 50 are in the armed forces. They normally serve four months under arms and 30 years in the reserves. Total strength of the armed forces, including reservists, is 700,000.

# SYRIA

*Official Name:* Syrian Arab Republic. *Area:* 71,498 square miles. *Population:* 5,300,000. *Principal Cities* (with populations): Damascus, the capital, 562,907; Aleppo, 547,030; Homs, 182,020; Hama, 131,-630. *Flag:* Horizontal red, white, and black stripes, with three green stars on the middle stripe. *Monetary Unit:* The Syrian pound of 100 piasters (worth 24 U.S. cents). *Gross National Product:* $1,025,000,000 (1965).

**LAND AND PEOPLE.** Syria is in southwest Asia at the eastern end of the Mediterranean Sea. It is bounded by Turkey on the north, Iraq on the east and southeast, Jordan on the south, Israel on the southwest, and Lebanon on the west. (See map on page 151.)

Northwestern Syria consists of a narrow Mediterranean coastal plain, the Ansariyah highland area (average elevation 4,000 feet); and the Rift Zone (about 3,000 feet lower). Eastward the land rises gradually to a rolling plateau of steppe land (average elevation 1,500 to 2,000 feet) crossed by the Euphrates River, which flows southeastward, and the Khabur River, which flows into the Euphrates from the northeast. The Barada River flows through the Damascus Oasis, a fruit and vegetable growing area and the site of the capital city.

Southern Syria is occupied by the Syrian Desert, a dry wasteland reaching to the mountains in the southwest and passing into steppe land toward the north.

Ninety per cent of the people are Arabs, with Kurds, Armenians, Turkmen, Circassians, and Jews comprising the principal minority groups. With the exception of 212,000 desert nomads, the population is clustered in the areas of heavier rainfall and river irrigation. Arabic is the official language. The major religious groups are Muslims (84.7 per cent), chiefly Sunnites, and Christians (12 per cent).

**HISTORY.** Before World War I, Syria's history embraced a large geographic and cultural area that included all of modern Lebanon, Jordan, and Israel, and parts of northwestern Turkey and southwestern Iraq. Ancient Syria was the home of Amorites, Canaanites, Phoenicians, Arameans, and Hebrews. It was conquered by several waves of foreign invaders—Hittites, Assyrians, Neo-Babylonians, and Persians—and was unified after its conquest by Alexander the Great in 332 B.C. It passed to the Romans in 63 B.C. and to the Byzantine Empire in 395 A.D.

In the seventh century Syria fell to the Arabs, who introduced the Arabic language and Islam. From 661 to 750, under the Damascus Caliphate of the Omayyads, Syria was the center of a vast Islamic domain. Over the next five centuries Syria disintegrated. Seljuk Turks invaded northern Syria in the 11th century. From 1097 onward came the Crusaders, who were not expelled until the late 13th century by the Egyptian Mamelukes. The Mamelukes fell before the Ottoman Turks in 1516.

Syria remained part of the Ottoman Empire until after the Ottoman defeat in World War I, when France gained control under a League of Nations mandate. Full independence was not achieved until after World War II.

After France withdrew its troops in 1946, Syria's history was marked by turbulence in both domestic and international affairs. A war with Israel in 1948 was followed by repeated border incidents. Between 1958 and 1961 Syria was part of the United Arab Republic of Egypt and Syria under the presidency of Gamal Abdel Nasser. The Arab-Israeli war of 1967 resulted in Israel's occupation of Syria's southwest corner, including the city of El Quneitra.

**GOVERNMENT AND POLITICS.** Although the Baath Party regained control of the government in 1963, a long series of power struggles within the party has resulted in extreme political instability. In a 1966 coup led by a radical group, Nureddin Attassi became head of state, with Youssef Zayyen as premier.

**ECONOMY.** Syria is predominantly an agricultural country but has had recent industrial growth. Agricultural development has been limited by primitive farming techniques, poor climate, and the division of land into small plots worked by peasants.

A persistent unfavorable balance of trade has hampered development of natural resources. Exports consist chiefly of raw cotton and textiles. There has been some dispute between Syria and Iraq over royalties from Iraq oil passing through pipelines that cross Syria on the way to the Mediterranean. Economic activities are insufficient to finance development projects. The U.S.S.R. is financing a dam on the upper Euphrates River.

**EDUCATION.** Education is compulsory from ages 6 to 12, with 90 per cent of the primary schools publicly run. Some 35 per cent of the people over 10 years are literate.

**ARMED FORCES.** Two years of military training are required. Some 63,000 men are in uniform.

# TANZANIA

*Official Name:* United Republic of Tanzania. *Area:* 362,820 square miles. *Population:* 10,567,000. *Principal Cities* (with populations): Dar es Salaam, the capital, 198,000; Zanzibar, 72,000; Tanga, 42,000; Mwanza, 21,000. *Flag:* Green, black, and blue diagonal stripes separated by gold bands. *Monetary Unit:* The Tanzanian shilling of 100 cents (worth 14 U.S. cents).

**LAND AND PEOPLE.** Tanzania comprises the former republics of Tanganyika and Zanzibar. It encompasses 361,800 square miles of mainland in eastern Africa and the two offshore islands of Zanzibar and Pemba, lying about 25 miles off the coast. It is bordered on the east by the Indian Ocean; on the south by Zambia, Malawi, and Mozambique; on the west by Rwanda, Burundi, and the Democratic Republic of the Congo; and on the north by Kenya and Uganda. (See map on page 111.)

Most of mainland Tanzania is an infertile plateau, 3,000 to 4,000 feet high, sloping gently to a coastal plain on the east and bisected from north to south by the Great Rift Valley. On the more fertile northern, western, and southern margins of the plateau are Lakes Victoria, Tanganyika, and Nyasa. Mount Kilimanjaro (19,565 feet—the highest mountain in Africa), Mount Meru, and the Usambara Mountains are in the northeast; the Southern Highlands dominate the southwest. The climate is tropical on the coastal plain and moderate in the higher interior. The low-lying islands of Zanzibar and Pemba have a wet and hot climate, tempered by cool sea breezes.

About 99 per cent of the people belong to 123 various African tribes. Some 12 per cent, the largest single group, belong to the Sukuma tribe. Swahili is spoken throughout mainland Tanzania, and is the universal language in Zanzibar. About 44 per cent of the people practice tribal religions; 31 per cent are Muslims; and 25 per cent are Christians.

**HISTORY.** Archeological discoveries at Olduvai Gorge in 1959 suggest that man lived in this area one million years ago. Ancient Greek mariners called the coast Azania. Trade across the Indian Ocean and connections with Arabia, Persia, and China have existed for at least 1,200 years. Zanzibar and various coastal cities, especially Kilwa, were colonized from the Persian Gulf area, probably in the eighth century. With the expansion of Islam several centuries later, a series of autonomous Muslim city-states with a Swahili language and culture were established. They flourished until the 16th century when they were destroyed by the Portuguese. The Portuguese exercised loose control of the coast until the 18th century when they were ousted by Arabs from Oman.

European influence increased in the late 19th century, combating the slave trade and eventually leading to the establishment (in 1890) of a British protectorate in Zanzibar and to German control of Tanganyika. German control was resisted but not removed until the Germans were defeated in World War I. Britain then took over Tanganyika under a League of Nations mandate and, later, under a United Nations trusteeship arrangement.

Nationalism spread rapidly after World War II. On the mainland the Tanganyika African National Union (TANU), headed by Julius Nyerere, led Tanganyika to independence in 1961. The country became independent in December, 1963, but the sultan's government was overthrown the following month, and the Arabs, the politically dominant ethnic group, were ousted. The country's African ethnic majority, led by Abeid Karume of the Afro-Shirazi Party (ASP), took power and guided Zanzibar to a union with Tanganyika. In April, 1964, Karume and President Nyerere signed an agreement creating a united republic to be called Tanzania.

**GOVERNMENT AND POLITICS.** Tanzania became a one-party state in 1965. Nationally, the mainland's TANU and Zanzibar's ASP share power, but in their respective territories each is the only party.

Executive power is vested in a president. Nyerere was nominated in 1965 by a joint conference of TANU and ASP, and he was elected without major opposition. He reappointed Karume first vice-president. There is a National Assembly of up to 204 members, including 52 from Zanzibar who are appointed rather than elected. TANU's National Executive Committee is the major policy-making body. Zanzibar has considerable autonomy under quasi-federal arrangements. There is not yet central control of the army or of immigration policy.

The present Tanzanian government has proclaimed a policy of democratic socialism. Clove plantations were nationalized in Zanzibar in 1964, and many major companies were taken over by the central government in 1967. In its foreign policy Tanzania is a strong advocate of nonalignment. It has accepted foreign aid from China and the Soviet Union, as well as from Britain and the United States. Diplomatic relations with Britain were broken in November, 1965, over the issue of Rhodesia and have not been resumed.

**ECONOMY.** The economy is primarily agricultural, the major export being sisal. Farmers produce for their own needs; fewer than 400,000 adults are wage earners in this subsistence economy. Wildlife resources are extensive, and a series of game parks has been created to encourage tourism.

**EDUCATION.** Education is compulsory only in certain urban centers. About 55 per cent of the children attend primary school. The literacy rate is about 12 per cent. In 1961 the University College of Dar es Salaam opened; together with Makerere College in Uganda and the Royal College in Kenya, it forms the University of East Africa.

**ARMED FORCES.** The People's Defense Forces of Tanzania include the former Tanganyika and Zanzibar forces, which retain their separate identities. The army numbers about 3,000 men. Military service is not compulsory.

## THAILAND

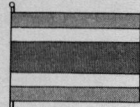

*Official Name:* Thailand. *Area:* 198,455 square miles. *Population:* 31,508,000. *Principal Cities* (with populations): Bangkok, the capital, 1,669,246; Thonburi, 403,828; Chiengmai, 65,736. *Flag:* Red, white, blue (double width), white, and red horizontal stripes. *Monetary Unit:* The baht (worth 4.87 U.S. cents). *Gross National Product:* $3,-854,000,000 (1965). *Average Annual Income per Person:* $102.

**LAND AND PEOPLE.** Situated in southeast Asia, Thailand occupies an irregular area which narrows as it extends down the Malay Peninsula. The country is bounded by Laos on the northeast and east; Cambodia, the Gulf of Thailand, and Malaysia on the south; the Andaman Sea on the southwest; and Burma on the west and northwest. (See map on page 243.)

The country has four main regions. The north is a forest highland area characterized by a series of mountain ranges in the northwest, rising to 8,468 feet in Inthanon Peak. The central plains are a fertile, alluvial lowland based on silt accumulations from the Chao Phraya River, which bisects the plains and flows into the Gulf of Siam. The most fertile section in this region is the Bangkok Delta, known as the rice basket or heartland of the country. To the northeast rises a dry upland area covering almost one-third of the country and ending at the Mekong River on the border with Laos. Peninsular Thailand, reaching to Malaysia, is a mountainous ridge, highest in the Tenasserim Range of Thailand and Burma.

The population is dense and very heavily concentrated in the Bangkok Delta and other fertile areas. The majority (80 per cent) are Thais. The Chinese are an economically important minority of three to four million (10 to 13 per cent) and are concentrated in urban areas. About 800,000 Malays live mainly in the south, and an estimated 250,000 hill people belonging to several tribes live mostly in the isolated areas of the northern hills and mountains. There is also a small but politically significant group of 45,000 refugees from North Vietnam, most of whom live in the northeast area adjacent to Laos.

Over 93 per cent of the people are Hinayana Buddhists. There are Muslim Malays in the south (3.9 per cent), a Christian minority in Bangkok (0.6 per cent), and Confucianists (1.7 per cent). Thai is the language of 97 per cent of the population.

**HISTORY.** The history of Thailand, or Siam, as the kingdom was known before World War II, began with the southward migration along the Chao Phraya of Thai peoples from Yunnan Province in China between the 7th and 13th centuries. They established a kingdom at Sukhothai in the 13th century. In the middle of the 14th century the capital was moved to Ayuthia. In 1767 the Burmese sacked Ayuthia, but General Phya Tak rallied Thai forces and drove the Burmese from the country. In 1782 the new Chakkri dynasty was established with its capital at Bangkok, and has continued to reign to the present time.

Diplomatic and commercial relations with Western Europe were established in the 16th and 17th centuries, and Western influence increased in the 19th century. Modernization began under the enlightened rule of King Mongkut (Rama IV, 1851–68) and his son Chulalongkorn (Rama V, 1868–1910). The Western powers acquired extensive extraterritorial privileges, which they retained until 1937. In 1932 a group of Westernized Thai intellectuals overthrew the absolute monarchy and established a constitutional monarchy, but thereafter effective power passed to a succession of military oligarchies which generally took power through a coup d'etat.

During World War II Japan occupied Thailand, its ally, and helped the Thai annex territory from Cambodia and Burma. After the war Thailand returned these acquisitions and later joined with the United States in the anti-Communist South East Asia Treaty Organization (SEATO), which has had its headquarters in Bangkok since 1954. Substantial U.S. military aid and economic assistance have been given to Thailand, which is fighting pro-Communist insurgency in the northeast and on the Thai-Malaysian border. At present there are 40,000 U.S. troops in Thailand.

**GOVERNMENT AND POLITICS.** Thailand is a constitutional monarchy ruled by a military oligarchy under Field Marshal Thanom Kittikachorn, who is prime minister and minister of defense. The king, Bhumibol Adulyadej (Rama IX), is head of state.

Thailand had several constitutions before 1958, but in that year the constitution was suspended following a military coup d'etat. The military government has functioned under an interim constitution while an appointed constituent assembly has been preparing a new constitution. Occasionally this group acts as a legislative assembly to ratify acts of the government. There are no political parties or elections under the present system.

**ECONOMY.** Thailand is mainly a producer of food products and raw materials, with rice the staple food and principal export. In 1960, 85 per cent of the economically active population 11 years and older were engaged in agriculture, forestry, hunting, and fishing; only 3.4 per cent were in manufacturing. Besides rice, the principal exports are crude rubber and tin ore from peninsular Thailand, teak and other woods from the north, jute, corn, and tapioca. The country relies on imports for manufactured goods, machinery, chemicals, and mineral fuels.

**EDUCATION.** Primary education is free and compulsory for children from 7 to 14. The literacy rate for those 10 years and older is 62 per cent.

**ARMED FORCES.** There is compulsory military service for men at the age of 21. The armed forces total 125,000, excluding the U.S. troops stationed in Thailand in connection with the war in Vietnam.

## TOGO

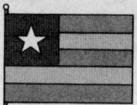

*Official Name:* Republic of Togo. *Area:* 21,853 square miles. *Population:* 1,682,-000. *Principal Cities* (with populations): Lomé, the capital, 92,000; Sokodé, 15,-000. *Flag:* Horizontal green and yellow stripes with a white star centered in a red square, upper left. *Monetary Unit:* The CFA franc (worth .41 U.S. cent).

**LAND AND PEOPLE.** Togo is a narrow West African country some 340 miles long. It is bounded by Upper Volta on the north, Dahomey on the east, the Gulf of Guinea on the south, and Ghana on the west. (See map on page 111.) Owing to coastal sandbars and lagoons, there is no good harbor on its 30-mile coast.

Inland the terrain is hilly, with plateaus descending northward and southward from mountains that bisect the country. The tropical climate has an average rainfall of 40 inches in the north and 70 inches in the south.

The population is a mixture of tribal groups —Negroid in the heavily populated south, Sudanic in the north. The Ewe, occupying the southern third of Togo, make up 18 per cent of the population and are the dominant tribe. Another major tribe is the Kabrai, who comprise about 12 per cent. Animism is the religion of about 75 per cent of the people, Christianity of some 20 per cent, and Islam of 5 per cent. French is the official language, although various tribal dialects are spoken.

**HISTORY.** As a nation Togo has little precolonial history. The colony of Togoland, created by Germany in 1885, consisted of today's Togo in the east and part of the present Ghana in the west. In 1922 the League of Nations divided Togoland into French and British mandates, with Togo going to the French.

The United Nations assumed trusteeship of the territory in 1946. In a 1956 plebiscite the Togolese voted 3 to 1 for autonomy, and in April, 1960, Togo became an independent state.

Sylvanus Olympio, a man of great ability, was president of Togo until his assassination in the military coup of 1963. His successor was Nicolas Grunitzky, a relative by marriage and Olympio's political rival. Appointed by the military, Grunitzky survived various political crises until January, 1967, when he was peacefully ousted by Lieutenant Colonel Etienne Eyadema, who became president on April 16.

**GOVERNMENT AND POLITICS.** Officially a republic, Togo is in fact ruled by a military junta which consists of four army officers and eight civilians, presided over by President Eyadema.

Relationships with neighboring Ghana have been excellent since the fall of President Kwame Nkrumah in February, 1966.

**ECONOMY.** The economy rests primarily upon small-scale subsistence farming. In 1961 exploitation of the sizable phosphate reserves began. Exports of coffee, cocoa, and palm nuts rarely produce a favorable trade balance. The loan burden has grown alarmingly since 1963, despite aid from France and the Ivory Coast.

**EDUCATION.** Primary education is free but not compulsory. There were over 160,500 pupils attending classes in 1965.

**ARMED FORCES.** There is no compulsory military service in Togo; the army numbers about 1,000 men and the navy, 200.

## TIBET

*Official Name:* Tibet Autonomous Region. *Area:* 471,660 square miles. *Population:* 1,300,-000. *Principal Cities* (with populations): Lhasa, the capital, 50,000; Shigatse, 26,000. *Monetary Unit:* The Chinese yuan (worth U.S. $2.46).

**LAND AND PEOPLE.** Tibet, now an integral part of Communist China, lies between Sinkiang, Tsinghai, Szechwan, and Yunnan provinces on the north, and Burma, India, Bhutan, Sikkim, and Nepal on the south. (See map on page 139.)

Tibet consists of a plateau, averaging 13,000 feet in height, between the Himalaya and the Kunlun mountains. The people are mainly of Mongolian stock. The national language is Tibetan. Lamaism, a modified form of early Buddhism, is the state religion.

**HISTORY.** An ancient land, Tibet is known to have been independent in the seventh century A.D. From the 13th to the 18th century it was under Mongolian rule; since 1720 China has claimed suzerainty. The British tried to establish friendly relations with the country in the 18th and 19th centuries, but the Tibetans remained generally aloof from the outside world. In the 19th century Tibet lost Ladakh to Kashmir and was defeated by Nepal. The British detached Sikkim from the country in 1890 and set up trading posts in Tibet. In 1906–07 they recognized Chinese suzerainty over Tibet.

The Tibetans expelled the Chinese in 1912, but in 1913–14 agreed with the British and Chinese to divide the country: part was placed under Chinese rule and the rest remained autonomous. China never ratified the agreement, and increasingly exerted its influence over the whole area. In 1950, after the establishment of Communist China, Chinese troops invaded Tibet and conquered it within a year. In 1956 a Preparatory Committee for the Autonomous Region of Tibet was established with the Dalai Lama as head, but real authority remained with the Chinese.

Sporadic uprisings against Chinese rule culminated in a general revolt in 1959. The Dalai Lama fled to India; the Chinese suppressed the revolt and appointed the Panchen Lama head of the Preparatory Committee. In 1965 the Panchen Lama was replaced by another puppet, and in the same year the Tibet Autonomous Region was formally inaugurated.

**GOVERNMENT.** Before 1950, Tibet was a theocracy under the rule of the Dalai Lama. Although nominally autonomous under Chinese rule, it is now comparable in status to a Chinese province.

**ECONOMY.** Most Tibetans exist by herding or subsistence agriculture. There is some trade with China. Gold deposits have been found, but natural resources are largely untapped.

## TRINIDAD AND TOBAGO

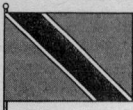

*Official Name:* Trinidad and Tobago. *Area:* 1,980 square miles. *Population:* 1,000,000. *Principal Cities* (with populations): Port of Spain, the capital, 100,000; San Fernando, 40,000. *Flag:* A red field crossed by a white-bordered black stripe. *Monetary Unit:* Trinidad and Tobago dollar (worth 58.5 U.S. cents). *Gross National Product:* $630,-000,000 (1965). *Average Annual Income per Person:* $600.

**LAND AND PEOPLE.** The islands of Trinidad and Tobago, together with 16 offshore islands, lie about 20 miles apart in the Caribbean Sea, off Venezuela's northeast coast. (See map on page 75.)

Trinidad, largest island in the group, has three mountain ranges, which run east to west. Mountains in the northern range rise to more than 3,000 feet; those in the central range rise to over 1,000 feet; the southern range is somewhat lower. Streams drain seaward through gently rolling flatlands between the mountains. There is heavy rainfall between June and December.

Tobago, which is generally more rugged than Trinidad, has a central volcanic core that ascends to more than 1,800 feet. The largest stretch of flatland in Tobago is the southwestern tip.

The population is composed of Negroes (43 per cent), Asiatic Indians (36 per cent), mixed bloods (18 per cent), and whites and Chinese (3 per cent). English is the predominant language. About 65 per cent of the people are Christians; Hindus and Muslims form a large minority (35 per cent).

**HISTORY.** The islands were discovered by Columbus in 1498. Development under Spanish rule lagged because mineral resources were few. During the 17th and 18th centuries cocoa plantations were established with slave labor imported from Africa. In 1783 the Spanish government offered free land grants that attracted many non-Spanish settlers, especially French. Trinidad was captured by a British expedition in 1797; it formally became a crown colony in 1802.

Slaves on Trinidad were emancipated in 1834. To replace them as plantation workers, the British brought more than 150,000 Hindus and Muslims from India to the island as indentured laborers between 1845 and 1917.

Tobago, which became a British crown colony in 1877, was joined with Trinidad in 1889. A drive for self-government began in 1955 under the leadership of Dr. Eric Williams, culminating in full independence within the Commonwealth of Nations in 1962.

**GOVERNMENT AND POLITICS.** The government recognizes the British sovereign as head of the British Commonwealth and her appointed representative (Sir Solomon Hochoy) as governor-general of Trinidad and Tobago. The 1962 constitution provides for election by universal suffrage of a bicameral parliament.

Executive power is vested in the prime minister, Eric Williams, and his cabinet.

There are two leading political parties. The People's National Movement, headed by Prime Minister Williams, has business and urban-Negro support, and the Democratic Labour Party, led by Rudranath Capildeo, has support from the Indian population.

**ECONOMY.** Petroleum and sugar products account for about 80 per cent of the country's exports. Coffee, cocoa, and citrus fruits are important minor exports. About one-fifth of the population is engaged in agriculture.

Efforts are being made to develop varied manufacturing industries and to boost tourism. New hotel developments are planned for both Trinidad and Tobago. To reduce the high rate of population growth, the government has embarked on a comprehensive program of family-planning aid. Unemployment, estimated at 14 per cent, continues to be a serious problem.

**EDUCATION.** Education is compulsory from age 6 through 12, and 82 per cent of the people are literate. The government supports state schools and contributes to the maintenance of private schools.

**ARMED FORCES.** Coast Guard personnel and the Trinidad and Tobago regimental force number about 2,000 men.

## TUNISIA

*Official Name:* Republic of Tunisia. *Area:* 63,378 square miles. *Population:* 4,800,000. *Principal Cities* (with populations): Tunis, the capital, 685,000; Sfax, 67,000; Bizerta, 46,000; Kairouan, 39,-000. *Flag:* A red field with a white disc containing a red crescent and star. *Monetary Unit:* The dinar (worth U.S. $1.92). *Gross National Product:* $945,200,000 (1965). *Average Annual Income per Person:* $178.

**LAND AND PEOPLE.** Tunisia is a small country on the Mediterranean coast of Africa between Algeria in the west and Libya in the southeast. (See map on page 111.)

It is divided into two main regions by the Atlas Mountains, running from west to east. North of the mountains is the relatively well-watered, fertile Tell zone; to the south is a semi-arid plain and plateau that extends into the Sahara Desert. The Tell zone includes the mountainous northwest, with its rocky coastline and cork forests, and the north-central area surrounding the Majarda River Valley, the grain and livestock center of Tunisia. The eastern coastal plain beyond Tunis becomes increasingly arid.

The population is concentrated in the coastal plain. More than a third of the people are city dwellers, and about a fifth live in metropolitan Tunis. About 93 per cent of Tunisians are of Arab stock; 5 per cent are Berber, and 2 per cent are European. Languages are Arabic, French, and Berber. Islam is the state religion; 98 per cent of the people are Muslim.

**HISTORY.** During ancient times Tunisia was

the center of the Carthaginian realm and later, from the mid-second century B.C., of the Roman province of Africa. Occupied by the Vandals in the fifth century A.D. and recovered by the Byzantine empire in the sixth century, the country was finally conquered by the Arabs in the seventh century.

During the Middle Ages it was the center from which Arab power and Islam spread south and west and also north across the Mediterranean. In 1535 Carthage was captured by Holy Roman Emperor Charles V, and the ruling dynasty turned for help to the Turks, who expelled the Spaniards in 1573 and made Tunisia a Turkish province.

During the 17th century Tunisia was ruled by governors from Istanbul. In the 18th century an Ottoman Turk of Cretan origin became hereditary ruler, owing allegiance to the sultan in Istanbul, and his descendants remained in power until 1957.

During the middle of the 19th century Bey Ahmed, an ambitious but extravagant reformer, led the country into bankruptcy and thus provided a pretext for Britain, France, and Italy to assume financial control of Tunisia in 1869. Tunisia was declared a protectorate under French rule in 1881.

Modern Tunisian nationalism stems from the formation first of the Young Tunisian Party in 1907, then of the Destour (Constitutional) Party after World War I, and later of the more activist breakaway Neo-Destour Party during the 1930s. Under the leadership of Habib Bourguiba, Neo-Destour organized the struggle for independence from France, which resulted in the establishment of the republic in 1957.

France did not evacuate its naval base at Bizerta until 1963, two years after an attempted Tunisian blockade had resulted in a French massacre of Tunisian civilians. In May 1964 the Tunisian government nationalized all foreign-owned land. In retaliation, France terminated its export subsidies, withdrew its technical experts, and suspended its financial aid.

A large-scale Tunisian public works program to reduce urban unemployment has received U.S. assistance in the form of surplus grains, which are distributed to the workers partly in lieu of cash.

**GOVERNMENT AND POLITICS.** The 1959 constitution provided for a president as the head of state and government and for a 90-member National Assembly, both elected simultaneously for five-year terms by universal adult suffrage. The assembly is dominated by the ruling party, the Destourian-Socialist, which has some 300,000 members. The party was founded by its present leader, the popular Habib Bourguiba, who has been president of the country since independence. Although President Bourguiba is assisted by his government ministers, he has almost unrestricted power in the formation and execution of policy.

**ECONOMY.** The economy is based primarily on the production of wheat and barley, olive oil, wine, citrus fruits, esparto grass, dates, and cork, and the mining of phosphates and iron,

lead, and zinc ores. Agriculture accounts for about 40 per cent of Tunisian exports and about 25 per cent of the gross national product.

Petroleum in commercial quantities was discovered in 1964. In 1966 an important strike was made at El Borma near the Algerian border. Significant advances in mining include expansion of rock phosphate output by 60 per cent between 1960 and 1966, an increase in iron ore production in Djerissa and Tamera, and development of mercury and fluorspar deposits.

The El Foulader steel mill (90 per cent government owned, but operated by foreign technicians) was built between 1964 and 1966. The plant produced 42,000 tons of steel, or 60 per cent of its rated capacity, in the first year of operation.

**EDUCATION AND HEALTH.** In 1956 the illiteracy rate in the Muslim population ten years of age and over was 84 per cent. In 1966 there were about 741,000 primary and 83,000 postprimary students. Primary education is compulsory. The University of Tunisia, formed in 1960, has over 5,000 students.

There is approximately one physician per 10,000 inhabitants. The infant mortality rate is estimated to be 74 per 1,000.

**ARMED FORCES.** Tunisia has a national army of about 22,500 men, a navy of about 750, and an air force of 1,250.

# TURKEY

*Official Name:* Republic of Turkey. *Area:* 301,380 square miles. *Population:* 32,901,000. *Principal Cities* (with populations): Ankara, the capital, 130,373; Istanbul, 1,750,642; Izmir, 417,418, Adana, 290,515. *Flag:* A white star and crescent on a red field. *Monetary Unit:* The Turkish lira of 100 kurus (worth 11.1 U.S. cents). *Gross National Product:* $8,844,500,000 (1965). *Average Annual Income per Person:* $281.

**LAND AND PEOPLE.** Turkey straddles the Black Sea straits system—the Dardanelles, the Sea of Marmara, and the Bosporus—between Europe and Asia. European Turkey is bounded on the west by Greece and the Aegean Sea, on the north by Bulgaria, and on the northeast by the Black Sea. Southeast of the straits on the Anatolian peninsula lies Asiatic Turkey, which makes up 97 per cent of the country's land mass. It is bordered on the west by the Aegean Sea; on the south by the Mediterranean Sea, Syria, and Iraq; on the east by Iran; and on the northeast by the Soviet Union. (See map on page 197.)

Asiatic Turkey rises from fertile coastal strips into the high, semi-arid Anatolian plateau, enclosed and laced by mountains. The country's highest peak, the famous Mount Ararat (traditional landing place of Noah's Ark), rises to a height of 16,945 feet near the eastern border.

Most Turks have a mixed ancestry. Minority groups in Turkey include the Kurds, Arabs,

Circassians, Greeks, Armenians, and Russians. About 99 per cent of the population are Muslims, and 95 per cent speak Turkish.

**HISTORY.** Turkey was for centuries the bridge between Europe and Asia. It became the meeting point and the battleground of Occidental and Oriental cultures. In the seventh century B.C. Byzantium was established on hills strategically commanding the Bosporus. Since the time of the Peloponnesian Wars, the city has been the goal of conquerors sweeping east and west across the Black Sea straits. Roman legions captured Byzantium in 196 A.D. and established the eastern seat of the Roman government there. The Roman ruler Diocletian partitioned the Empire late in the third century, and in 330 A.D. the Christian Emperor Constantine moved his capital from Rome to Byzantium, which he rebuilt and renamed Constantinople. These events brought about a political and social split between East and West that lasted 1,600 years.

The Byzantine Empire had its golden age during the sixth century under Emperor Justinian. In 1453, the Turks, led by Ottoman Sultan Mohammed II, captured Constantinople. Islam supplanted Christianity, and the Ottoman Empire dominated the Middle East until the early 20th century. At its peak in the 16th century under Sultan Suleiman I, the Empire included Asia Minor, much of the Arabian peninsula, and North Africa, and extended north through the Balkans to the gates of Vienna and east to the Caucasus.

Turkey's modern history began in 1918, with the collapse of the Ottoman Empire. Ottoman forces were drawn into World War I on the German side. In 1915 Allied forces tried to force their way through the Dardanelles and occupy Constantinople, but the attempt failed. After Turkey's surrender in 1918, however, Constantinople was occupied by Allied forces. The treaty of Sèvres (1920) reduced the empire to a minor state. The Black Sea straits were neutralized and occupied by the Allies.

Sultan Mohammed VI, last of the Ottoman rulers, accepted the terms of the Sèvres pact, but a Turkish nationalist resistance movement, led by Mustafa Kemal (later called Kemal Atatürk), rejected the settlement. Establishing a rival government at Ankara, Atatürk declared the sultan deposed (1922) and repulsed an Allied-supported Greek offensive in the west. In 1923 the Treaty of Lausanne established the present Turkish boundaries. Control over the Black Sea straits was restored to the Turkish government in 1936.

A republic, with Kemal Atatürk as president, was proclaimed in 1923. The next year Atatürk exiled members of the Ottoman dynasty and introduced a new constitution that gave all Turkish men the right to vote and that set up a national legislative assembly.

During the next 14 years Atatürk changed Turkey from an oriental sultanate into a Western republic. He abolished Islam as the state religion, replaced Islamic law with European law, and moved the capital from Istanbul (Constantinople) to Ankara.

Former Premier Ismet Inonu became president after Atatürk's death in 1938. Turkey did not declare war on Germany and Japan until 1945; later the same year it joined the United Nations. Atatürk's successors remained in power until 1950, when Celal Bayar, leader of the Democratic Party, won the presidency and appointed Adnan Menderes premier. The Bayar-Menderes regime controlled Turkey for the next decade, which was marked by economic crises brought on by rapid industrialization and subsequent repressive measures.

In May 1960 an army revolt overthrew the elected government, and a military junta took control. Menderes was sentenced to death and hanged in 1961. In the same year, General Cemal Gursel, head of a faction favoring strict adherence to the principles of Atatürk, won the presidency. Gursel died in 1966 and was succeeded as president by General Cevdet Sunay.

A new constitution, adopted in July 1961, provided for a two-house legislature. However, political unrest, marked by unsuccessful army revolts in 1962 and 1963, continued.

Since 1955 Turkey has been embroiled in a dispute with Greece over Cyprus, a Mediterranean island republic 40 miles south of the Turkish coast. Heavy fighting broke out between Greek and Turkish Cypriotes in 1964, and relations between the two countries have been strained. A U.N. peace-keeping force was sent to Cyprus, but the fragile cease-fire there has frequently been broken. Turkey's relations with Greece were further disturbed in 1967 by a shooting fray between Turkish and Greek naval vessels over fishing rights.

**GOVERNMENT AND POLITICS.** The 1961 constitution vests legislative power in a Grand National Assembly, made up of a 184-member Senate, whose members are elected by direct popular vote to six-year terms, and a 450-member National Assembly, whose members are elected by a proportional-representation system to four-year terms. Executive power is vested in the president, who is elected by a joint session of the legislature. The premier is appointed by the president and must win a vote of confidence from the National Assembly.

Prior to the 1960 coup, the main political groups were the Republican People's Party and the Democratic Party. Political activity was banned after the 1960 revolt, the Democratic Party was outlawed, and the New Turkey and Justice parties were formed. Following general elections in October 1965, the Justice Party, headed by Suleyman Demirel, came to power. Premier Demirel has gained political strength by establishing a stable regime.

**ECONOMY.** Turkey is primarily an agricultural and pastoral country, although there has been important industrial development. About half the land is given over to livestock raising; some 25 per cent of the land is arable. The chief crops are cotton, cereals, sugar beets, tobacco, raisins, fruits, nuts, and potatoes. Over 75 per cent of the labor force is engaged in agriculture, and farm products account for 90 per cent of the country's exports. Only about 14 per cent of the land is forested.

Manufacturing accounts for about 15 per cent of the gross national product. Industrial products include textiles, cement, iron and steel, light machinery, industrial chemicals, and glass. Despite a growing trend toward industrialization, the nation continues to rely to some extent on imported machinery and manufactured goods.

**EDUCATION.** Schooling is free at the primary and secondary levels, with primary schooling being compulsory. However, a shortage of teachers and educational facilities prevents many students from attending classes. About half the population is literate. Universities are located at Istanbul, Ankara (site of the newly formed Middle East Technical University), Izmir, and Erzerum.

**ARMED FORCES.** Turkish men are required to serve for two years in the military at the age of 20. The combined strength of the armed forces is 372,000.

# UGANDA

*Official Name:* Uganda. *Area:* 91,133 square miles. *Population:* 7,740,000. *Principal Cities* (with populations): Kampala, the capital, 46,785; Jinja, 29,741; Mbale, 13,569; Entebbe, 10,941; Kabale, 10,919. *Flag:* Six horizontal black, yellow, and red stripes with a crested crane on a white circle in the center. *Monetary Unit:* The Uganda shilling of 100 cents (worth 14 U.S. cents). *Gross National Product:* $658,000,000 (1966). *Average Annual Income per Person:* $17.

**LAND AND PEOPLE.** Uganda lies on the great east-African plateau between Kenya in the east, Sudan in the north, the Democratic Republic of the Congo in the west, and Tanzania and Rwanda in the south. (See map on page 111.)

Although the equator runs through the southern part of the country, the high altitude of most of Uganda (3,500 to 4,500 feet) gives it a pleasant climate throughout the year, with warm days and cool nights. Notably high peaks are Mount Margherita in the Ruwenzori Mountains on the Congo border (16,798 feet) and Mount Elgon on the eastern frontier (14,178 feet).

Over 98 per cent of the people are African. The largest tribes include the Baganda, Iteso, Banyankore, Basoga, and Bakiga; there are also Banyaruanda, migrant workers from Rwanda. Asians, who make up a small Indo-Pakistani community, number 1.1 per cent.

More than half the population is Christian, but there are large Muslim and pagan minorities. The official language is English; most Africans speak either Bantu or Nilotic.

**HISTORY.** Powerful kingdoms began to develop in the lakes area south of the Nile during the late 15th or early 16th centuries, following a large-scale movement into the area of Lwo (Nilotic) peoples from the north who clashed with the earlier Bantu settlers. North and east of the Nile the predominantly Nilotic and Nilo-Hamitic tribes were more loosely organized into clans or smaller units.

Bunyoro was the most powerful of the southern kingdoms until the 19th century, when a succession of able rulers raised Buganda into prominence. The first visitors from outside the region were Arab and Swahili ivory and slave traders, followed soon afterward by European explorers. Egypt, in the meantime, was pursuing a policy of expansion up the Nile.

With the arrival of the first Christian missionaries in 1877, Buganda began to consolidate its position. The British East Africa Company sent its representative there after a treaty between Britain and Germany in 1890 had declared Uganda to be a British sphere of influence. In 1894 Britain established a protectorate over Buganda that was later extended to the rest of Uganda.

Uganda gained its independence in 1962 with a federal constitution that gave considerable autonomy to the kingdom of Buganda and somewhat less to the other kingdoms. In 1963 Kabaka Mutesa of Buganda became Uganda's first president, with Milton Obote as prime minister.

In February, 1966, Obote suspended the constitution, assuming the full powers of government, and the kabaka fled to Britain. Obote suppressed a rebellion in Buganda and introduced a new constitution that abolished the federal system. It was replaced in 1967 by a republican constitution with Obote as president. The kingdoms were abolished.

**GOVERNMENT AND POLITICS.** When Uganda became a federal state in 1963, the post of governor-general was replaced by that of president, to be elected by the National Assembly for a five-year term. A prime minister, chosen from and responsible to the elected assembly, was to be head of government.

The republican constitution of 1967 gave executive power to a president elected by universal suffrage. The National Assembly, also popularly elected, consists of a speaker and 92 members. In 1967 Buganda was divided into four administrative districts to bring its administration into line with that of the rest of the country.

**ECONOMY.** Although Uganda is almost entirely an agricultural country, it has maintained a favorable balance of trade for many years. Cotton was the chief source of wealth until 1955, when coffee took the lead. Sugar and tea have been developed on a smaller scale as plantation crops. Copper in the Ruwenzori area is the only mineral of any value.

**EDUCATION.** The government has encouraged primary education and, more recently, has supported further secondary education. The literacy rate is 25.1 per cent for ages 16 and over. Makerere College in Kampala is a constituent of the University of East Africa.

**ARMED FORCES.** Uganda has two army battalions, with about 2,000 men.

# UNION OF SOVIET SOCIALIST REPUBLICS

*Official Name:* Union of Soviet Socialist Republics. *Area:* 8,649,489 square miles. *Population:* 235,500,-000. *Principal Cities* (with populations): Moscow, the capital, 6,366,000; Leningrad, 3,329,000; Kiev, 1,332,000; Gorki, 1,085,000; Tashkent, 1,092,-000; Kharkov, 1,070,000; Novosibirsk, 1,029,-000. *Flag:* A red field with a gold hammer and sickle and a gold-bordered red star. *Monetary Unit:* The ruble (worth U.S. $1.11). *Gross National Product:* $330 billion. *Average Annual Income per Person:* $917.

**LAND AND PEOPLE.** The U.S.S.R. is the world's largest country, encompassing nearly one-sixth of the earth's inhabited land area. To the west it is bordered in Europe by Norway, Finland, the Baltic Sea, Poland, Czechoslovakia, Hungary, and Romania. It extends across the Asian continent to eastern boundaries on the Bering Sea and the Pacific Ocean. On the south it is bordered by the Black Sea, Turkey, Iran, the Caspian Sea, Afghanistan, China, Mongolia, and North Korea; on the north, by the Arctic Ocean. (See map on page 225.)

The U.S.S.R. extends through 11 time zones and varies widely in terrain, climate, flora, and fauna. The Ural Mountains are usually considered the dividing line between its European and Asian components. The European region is largely a continuation of the great plain that extends across the northern portions of western Europe. East of the Urals are the vast Siberian plains. There are frozen wastelands in the north, many great rivers and thousands of lakes, and deserts in the Asiatic southwest. The Carpathian Mountains fringe the territory in the west; the Caucasus mountains lie between the Black and Caspian seas, and the Pamir, Tien Shan, Altain, and other ranges rise along the southern border.

The climate is generally continental, although Siberian winter temperatures can drop to −90° F., and summer temperatures above 100° F. are not unusual in some regions.

The U.S.S.R. holds within its borders more than 100 nationalities. Russians account for 54.6 per cent of the population, Ukrainians 17.9 per cent. There are smaller percentages of Belorussians, Uzbeks, Tatars, Kazakhs, Azerbaijhanis, Armenians, Georgians, Lithuanians, Latvians, Estonians, Jews, Moldavians, and Chuvashes. The national language is Russian. Ukrainian and Belorussian are also spoken.

Although the state fosters atheism, it is estimated that 15.4 per cent of the population is Russian Orthodox; 6.6 per cent is Muslim; and 6.1 per cent are Old Believers, Evangelical Christian Baptists, Roman Catholics, Lutherans, or Jews.

**HISTORY.** The many lands now collectively called the Soviet Union were for centuries inhabited by myriad ethnic groups. There are indications of settlement as early as the Old Stone Age. Rurik, the almost legendary Swede, is generally credited with founding the Russian state when he led his Varangian tribe into Novgorod in the year 862. The dynasty that sprang from Rurik grew in power, later ruling the duchy of Moscow (Muscovy) and eventually all of Russia.

Saint Vladimir (Vladimir I, about 980–1015), initially a pagan, became the first Christian duke of Kiev and an ardent spreader of the faith. Through his conquest and unification of many Slavic tribes and his victories over Lithuanians, Bulgars, and the Greeks in the Crimea, he is considered the founder of the powerful Kievan state. Under Yaroslav the Wise in the 11th century, Kiev reached a peak of prosperity and culture. By the 13th century it had fallen to the Mongols who, under Batu Khan, created the Golden Horde, an empire of southern and eastern Russia that lasted until 1480.

The principalities of northern Russia gradually came together under Moscow, and its power was solidified in the 14th century by Dmitri Donskoi. Under Ivan III (1462–1505), who drove out the Mongols, and Vasily III (1505–33), many principalities were united or at least dominated by a single power. Ivan IV, better known as "Ivan the Terrible" and the first ruler to be crowned Tsar (Caesar) of all Russia (1547), further enlarged the domain.

After the reign of Boris Godunov (1598–1605) came dynastic upheavals, civil war, and territorial losses to Sweden and Poland. Following the defeat of the Poles the nobleman Michael Romanov was elected tsar (1613), founding the last Russian dynasty. In the early 17th century the country was isolated, ignorant, suspicious of foreigners, and in most respects centuries behind the West. Under serfdom, many of the peasants were virtual slaves. In the latter half of the century Peter the Great (1689–1725) opened the country to Westernization.

After Peter's expansionist and authoritarian policies, it remained for Catherine the Great (1762–96) to make Russia a leading power. With the crushing of the Pugachev Rebellion, a peasant uprising, Catherine became reactionary in her attitude toward social reform, and the privileges of the nobility were left untouched. Under Alexander I (1801–25) more lands were added to the empire. With Napoleon's defeat on Russian soil (1812), Alexander became one of Europe's most powerful rulers.

The spread of liberal ideas among many of the aristocrats and educated bourgeois led to the abortive Decembrist Conspiracy (1825), an attempt to block the accession of Nicholas I. Though unsuccessful, the conspiracy is often viewed as the initial phase of the Russian revolutionary movement. Thereafter, the tsarist regime fluctuated between reaction and reform in response to pressures for change. Similarly, opponents of tsarism resorted to tactics ranging from legal means to terrorism and violence.

After Britain and France defeated Russia in the Crimean War (1854–56), Tsar Alexander II (1855–81) inaugurated a series of

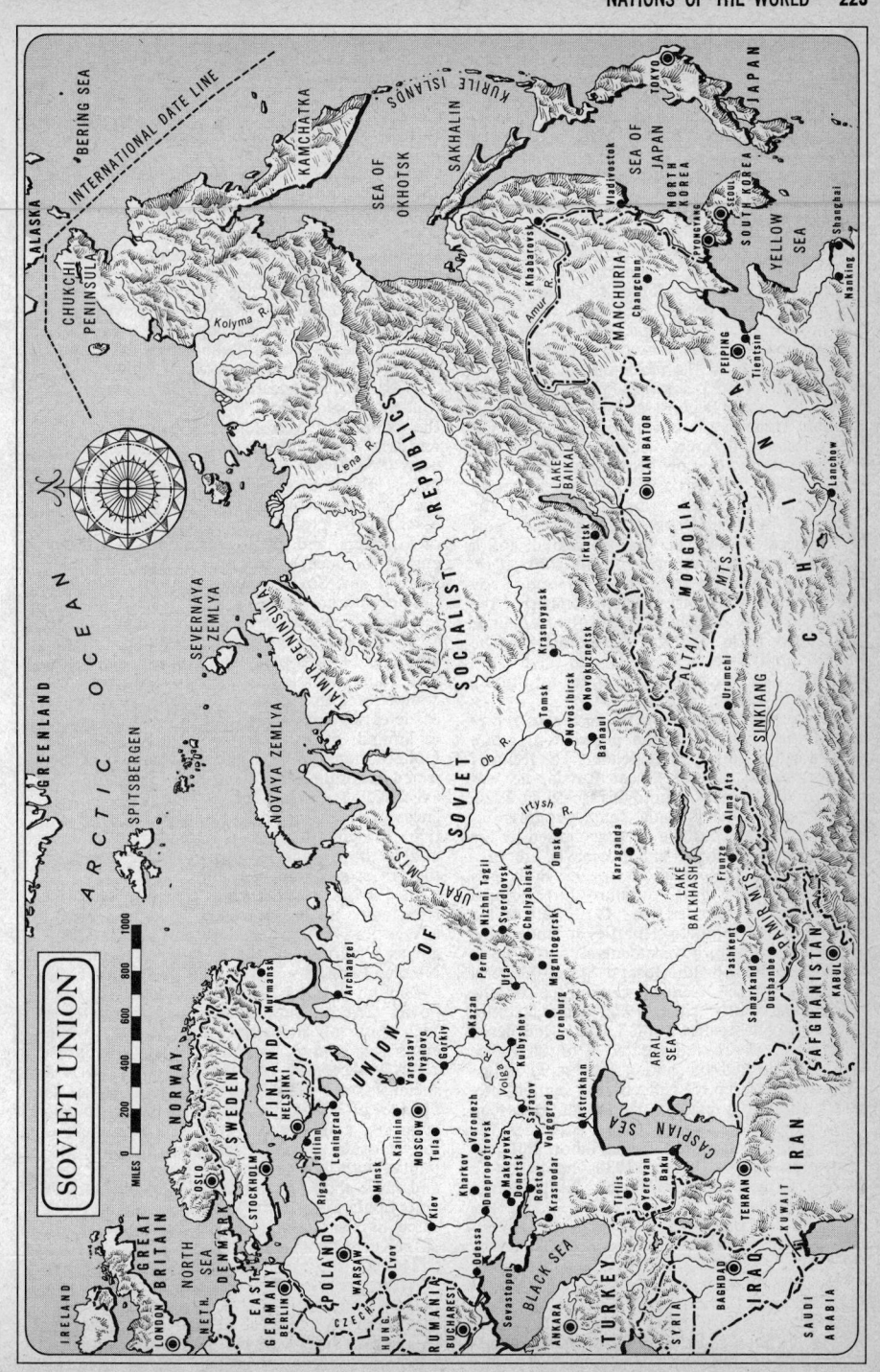

SOVIET UNION

MILES
0   200   400   600   800   1000

IRELAND
GREAT BRITAIN
LONDON
NORTH SEA
NETH.
DENMARK
EAST GERMANY
BERLIN
POLAND
WARSAW
CZECH.
HUNG.
RUMANIA
BUCHAREST
ANKARA
TURKEY
SYRIA
IRAQ
BAGHDAD
SAUDI ARABIA
KUWAIT
IRAN
TEHRAN
AFGHANISTAN
KABUL

GREENLAND
SPITSBERGEN

ARCTIC OCEAN

NORWAY
SWEDEN
OSLO
STOCKHOLM
FINLAND
HELSINKI
Murmansk
Archangel
Leningrad
Tallinn
Riga
Kalinin
MOSCOW
Minsk
Smolensk
Kiev
Kharkov
Voronezh
Dnepropetrovsk
Makeyevka
Donetsk
Odessa
Rostov
Krasnodar
Sevastopol
BLACK SEA
Tiflis
Yerevan
Baku
CASPIAN SEA
Volgograd
Astrakhan
Saratov
Kuibyshev
Kazan
Gorkiy
Yaroslavl
Tula
Volga
Penza
Orenburg
Ufa
Perm
Sverdlovsk
Nizhni Tagil
Chelyabinsk
Magnitogorsk
URAL MTS.
UNION OF
SOVIET SOCIALIST REPUBLICS
ARAL SEA
Tashkent
Samarkand
Dushanbe
Frunze
Alma Ata
LAKE BALKHASH
Karaganda
Omsk
Irtysh R.
Ob R.
Novosibirsk
Barnaul
Tomsk
Krasnoyarsk
Novokuznetsk
ALTAI MTS.
Urumchi
SINKIANG
PAMIR MTS.
MONGOLIA
ULAN BATOR
LAKE BAIKAL
Irkutsk
Lena R.
TAIMYR PENINSULA
NOVAYA ZEMLYA
SEVERNAYA ZEMLYA
Kolyma R.
CHUKCHI PENINSULA
ALASKA
BERING SEA
INTERNATIONAL DATE LINE
KAMCHATKA
SEA OF OKHOTSK
KURILE ISLANDS
SAKHALIN
Vladivostok
Khabarovsk
Amur R.
MANCHURIA
Changchun
CHINA
Lanchow
Nanking
Shanghai
PEIPING
Tientsin
YELLOW SEA
NORTH KOREA
SOUTH KOREA
PYONGYANG
SEOUL
SEA OF JAPAN
JAPAN
TOKYO

reforms: he freed the serfs; established provincial, county, and town self-government on a modest scale; and modernized the judiciary. He also extended the Russian Empire in the Far East. Despite his achievements, he was assassinated by the People's Will, a terrorist group. Alexander III (1881–94) repudiated his father's policies and instituted a period of severe repression. He was followed by Nicholas II, the last tsar. During Nicholas' inept administration, Russia was defeated in the Russo-Japanese War (1904–05). Popular discontent in 1905 assumed the proportions of a revolution, and Nicholas was forced to promulgate a constitution and permit the establishment of a representative parliament, the Duma. The regime, however, was subsequently able to reduce the power of the parliament.

In World War I a poorly prepared Russia joined the battle against the Central Powers. Russian armies suffered massive setbacks and casualties; food grew scarce; inflation was rampant; army morale broke down. Revolution erupted in February, 1917, when troops refused to fire upon crowds milling in the streets of St. Petersburg (Petrograd) as part of a general strike. The Tsar abdicated, and a moderate provisional government took over, headed successively by Prince Georgi Lvov and Alexander Kerensky. In November of the same year the Bolsheviks, led by Vladimir Lenin and Leon Trotsky, seized power. The Royal family was executed, and civil war, arising from attempts at counter-revolution, lasted until 1921.

Though the Communists by no means represented the majority of the population, Lenin was an astute and dynamic leader. The founder of Bolshevism and of Soviet Russia, he was dictator of the nation until his death in 1924. Lenin's government made some progress toward repairing economic damage caused by the revolution, civil strife, and Bolshevik administrative mistakes. Revolution was not limited to the home front: the Communist International (Comintern), founded in 1919, attempted through local Communist parties to undermine Western European governments.

After Lenin's death, Joseph Stalin, General Secretary of the Central Committee of the Communist Party since 1922, won a bitter power struggle against Leon Trotsky (murdered in Mexico, 1940) and created a brutal police state. He pushed the nation into rapid industrialization, forcibly collectivized agriculture, and instituted a massive campaign to spread literacy and education. He also expanded the secret police, censorship, forced labor, and concentration camps. In the 1930s he instituted bloody purges of high officials in the party, state, and army.

The Soviet Union was recognized by a number of European governments in 1924 and by the United States in 1933. It became a member of the League of Nations in 1934. In 1939 the U.S.S.R. signed a nonaggression pact with Nazi Germany and was thus enabled to absorb Latvia, Lithuania, Estonia (political conquests still not recognized by the United States and many other nations), and later the eastern half of Poland. Also in 1939 Russia abrogated a nonaggression pact with Finland, attacking that country and eventually taking a large part of its eastern territory. In 1941 Hitler launched a surprise attack on Russia, inflicting civilian and military losses of 20 million lives and driving the Soviet Union to the Allied side. Following the Allied victory, the U.S.S.R. established Communist governments in eastern European countries liberated by the Red Army. By mid-1948 Poland, Czechoslovakia, Hungary, Romania, Bulgaria, and Albania were Soviet satellites. With the breakup of the wartime alliance, intransigence came to characterize Soviet relations with the West. During the Korean War the U.S.S.R. gave considerable material support to North Korea and Communist China.

With Stalin's death in 1953, Georgi M. Malenkov succeeded to the chairmanship of the Council of Ministers. He resigned in 1955 and was replaced by Nikolai A. Bulganin.

In 1958 Nikita S. Khrushchev, who as Communist Party First Secretary had emerged as the most powerful figure in the U.S.S.R., also assumed the post of Chairman of the Council of Ministers, and the Soviets agreed to a treaty ending the occupation status of Austria. Under Khrushchev, Soviet industrialization continued, but totalitarian controls were relaxed and attempts were made to raise living standards. In 1956 Khrushchev condemned Stalin as a despot who had harmed party and country. He modified Stalin's foreign policy, stressed economic competition and ideological rivalry as a means of defeating capitalism, and in 1963 agreed to a limited nuclear test-ban treaty with the United States. The Chinese Communists rejected de-Stalinization and the "Peaceful Coexistence" formula. Out of Sino-Soviet differences grew an ideological and political schism that divided the world Communist movement and is the primary foreign policy concern of the Soviet government today.

In 1964 Khrushchev was abruptly removed from office, to be succeeded by Leonid Brezhnev as Party First Secretary and Alexei Kosygin as Chairman of the Council of Ministers. Nikolai Podgorny was named president of the Presidium in 1965. Under their leadership the Soviet government has continued to pursue a high rate of industrial development, while emphasizing improvement of living standards.

**GOVERNMENT AND POLITICS.** The U.S.S.R. is a socialist state of workers and peasants. It is formed of 15 Soviet republics based on the country's major ethnic groups. The largest is the Russian Soviet Federated Socialist Republic, with 70 per cent of the total land area and more than half the people. Second largest (in population) is the Ukrainian S.S.R., with some of the Union's richest land and nearly 20 per cent of its people.

Though the government is patterned after Western democracies, there are no checks and balances and little real separation of powers. In theory, the highest legislative body is the bicameral Supreme Soviet, popularly elected by universal suffrage from single lists of Commu-

## RUSSIAN REVOLUTION: 1917

Painting by Soviet artist V. Kuznetzov shows Russian Red Guards storming Petrograd's Winter Palace.

The year 1967 marked the 50th anniversary of the Russian Revolution. It began in March, 1917, with the abdication of Tsar Nicholas II, "Emperor of All the Russias," and ended in November with the coup by the Bolshevik (Communist) Party. Out of the Russian Revolution grew the modern Communist state.

After centuries of oppression and poverty the Russian people finally revolted against their imperial rulers. In March, 1917, angry mobs surged through the streets of Petrograd (formerly St. Petersburg and now Leningrad) demanding higher food rations. The Tsar first tried to quell the riots by force, but his army threatened to mutiny. Nicholas was finally persuaded to abdicate on March 15. His statement, ending three centuries of Romanov rule, concluded with the words: "May the Lord God help Russia."

A provisional government, headed by Alexander Kerensky and composed largely of moderates and liberals, tried unsuccess-

fully to preserve political order. The Bolsheviks, a tiny faction of revolutionary Marxists organized in 1903 by Vladimir Ilyich Lenin, had little voice in the new government. But under the leadership of Lenin and Leon Trotsky, they proceeded to infiltrate the powerful worker's councils or soviets and took control of key soviets in Moscow and Petrograd. On November 7 the Bolsheviks seized power; Red Guards (armed workers) and rebellious troops stormed Petrograd's Winter Palace, seat of the provisional government.

Fifty years later the Russian Revolution stands as one of the most decisive events in modern history. It led to the creation of the totalitarian Communist State, initially ruled by Lenin (until his death in 1924) and later by Joseph Stalin (until 1953). The revolution gave rise to a whole new set of political ideals—revolutionary in their goals, international in their application, and unrelenting in their challenge to democratic society.

nist Party-approved candidates. The organization consists of the 767-member Soviet of the Union, with one deputy for every 300,000 inhabitants, and the 750-member Soviet of Nationalities, with representatives of the various republics, regions, and national areas. It meets twice yearly, but its legislative function is to be a rubber stamp. It elects a Presidium to act for it when it is not in session. The Presidium consists of a chairman (the nominal head of state), 15 vice-chairmen (one for each constituent republic), a secretary, and 20 members. The executive power of state rests with the Council of Ministers, headed by a chairman.

The Communist Party is in control of all levels of government and, thus, of practically every phase of Soviet life. It is the only political party in the country—its hegemony guaranteed by the constitution. Membership in the party is about 12.7 million, or 8 per cent of the adult population. The party's highest organ, theoretically, is its Congress, which meets every four years to formalize broad policies of the party's Politburo (formerly Presidium) and theoretical precepts of the current party line. Major pronouncements, such as Khrushchev's stunning downgrading of Stalin, are usually made at Congress sessions. The Congress elects a Central Committee to act for it between sessions. The Central Committee in turn selects the Party's chief administrative officials, the Secretariat, and the Politburo (formerly Presidium). The Politburo has 11 members and 8 alternating members, and the Secretariat has 11 members. Membership of the Politburo and Secretariat interlock, and supreme in the party is the General Secretary of the Secretariat. Party power passes down from the chief officials, who determine both the membership of the collective bodies and the policies to be supported, as well as who will hold the top posts.

In essence, the two most powerful figures in the party and government are the Chairman of the Council of Ministers or Premier and the First Secretary of the Secretariat, with the latter usually exercising the most power. Sometimes the posts are held jointly, as they were by Khrushchev; other times separately, as by Kosygin and Brezhnev.

**ECONOMY.** Since the Revolution the Soviet economy has changed profoundly. Primarily agricultural before 1917, Russia now has the world's second-highest level of industrial production. This achievement was made possible by forced investment in heavy industry at the expense of agriculture and living standards during the Stalin era. From 1928 to 1964 heavy industry received 87.6 per cent of all new investment channeled into industry.

Since 1928 industry has operated under a series of five-year plans. The entire economy is organized on a basis of state ownership and management. The chief planning organ of the government is the State Planning Committee (Gosplan U.S.S.R.), working directly under the authority of the Council of Ministers. Individual republics also have state planning committees. The system has led to elaborate and often cumbersome bureaucracies. Kosygin

and Brezhnev have introduced changes to give factory managers more decision-making power in order to adjust to fluctuating consumer demands and markets.

Heavy industry still dominates the economy, accounting for 74.8 per cent of total industrial output and employing 15.8 million of the 21.4 million industrial workers. Machinery, tools, chemicals, and petroleum products are among the chief exports, while foodstuffs, certain consumer goods, ores, metals, machine tools, and raw materials such as rubber are chief imports. Recently, with Western help, steps have been taken to quadruple the size of the automobile industry.

Agriculture is the Soviet Union's chief economic problem. Little of the land is of the highest caliber; only 10 per cent is crop land. The government operates a limited number of state farms, but the bulk of the farming population live on collective farms. Several times in recent years Canadian, Australian, and U.S. wheat has been imported to supplement insufficient harvests. The present government has increased agricultural investment, raised farm income, and, by means of reclamation and irrigation, tried to enlarge the area under cultivation. Chief crops include grains and sugar beets; there are also large meat and dairy industries.

The Soviet Union is one of the world's great fishing nations. Catches of fish and seafood increased from 1.8 metric tons in 1952 to 5.2 million in 1964. The country's timber resources are tremendous, for forests cover almost one-third of the land. There are vast deposits of minerals, including manganese, copper, chrome, and iron ore, as well as large petroleum and natural gas resources.

The country depends mainly on rail, air, and inland waterway transportation. The longest railway system in the world, the Trans-Siberian Railroad, stretches 5,787 miles from Moscow to Vladivostok, and construction has begun on a new line to run north of the present route. The total length of railroads in 1961 was 78,915 miles; in addition, there were 64,930 miles of spurs. Domestic air service reaches virtually every part of the country, and Moscow's international airport handles cargo and passenger flights to and from dozens of foreign countries.

**EDUCATION AND HEALTH.** Education is free and compulsory between the ages of 7 and 15, but in most cities pupils attend school until at least 17. There are over 3,000 specialized secondary and technical schools and 756 institutions of higher learning. Literacy is officially claimed to be 98 per cent.

The standards of health are generally high, and scientific institutes have conducted noteworthy research in the medical sciences. Health services are free to citizens, with some private practice by physicians allowed.

**ARMED FORCES.** The Red Army is estimated to have a strength of some 2,200,000 men; the air force and navy, a strength of 500,000 each. Military service begins at age 18 or 19 and continues for two to five years, depending on the branch of service.

# UNITED KINGDOM

*Official Name:* United Kingdom of Great Britain and Northern Ireland. *Area:* 94,214 square miles (England, 50,331; Wales, 8,016; Scotland, 30,411; Northern Ireland, 5,642). *Population:* 54,744,000 (England and Wales, 47,763,000; Scotland, 5,242,000; Northern Ireland, 1,469,000). *Principal Cities* (with populations): London, the capital, 7,948,800; Birmingham, 1,102,660; Glasgow, 1,000,857; Liverpool, 722,010; Manchester, 638,360; Sheffield, 488,950; Edinburgh, 478,800; Belfast, 406,800; Cardiff, 260,170. *Flag:* The Union Jack, a combination of the red-on-white crosses of England's St. George and Ireland's St. Patrick with the white-on-blue cross of Scotland's St. Andrew. *Monetary Unit:* The pound sterling of 20 shillings (worth U.S. $2.80). *Gross National Product:* $90,580,000,000 (1965). *Average Annual Income per Person:* $1,609.

**LAND AND PEOPLE.** Great Britain (England, Wales, and Scotland), which runs some 600 miles from northeast to southwest, is Europe's largest island; its total coastline measures 2,675 miles. The island borders the Atlantic Ocean on the northwest, north, and southwest, and is separated from the Continent by the North Sea, the Strait of Dover, and the English Channel. To the west is Northern Ireland, another part of the United Kingdom; it is bordered on the north by the Atlantic Ocean, on the east by the Irish Sea and the North Channel, and on the south and west by the independent Republic of Ireland (Eire). (See map on page 231.)

Scotland is divided into three major regions: the Northern Highlands, a bleak area of mountain ranges running roughly north to south, and broken by narrow glens and lakes; the Central Lowlands, with the fertile valleys of the rivers Tay, Forth, and Clyde and most of Scotland's cities; and the Southern Uplands, a region of rolling moorland separated from England by the Cheviot Hills. Ben Nevis (4,406 feet), the highest point in the British Isles, is in the Grampian Mountains of northern Scotland. The rocky, barren Hebrides Islands stretch along Scotland's deeply indented west coast; the Orkney and Shetland islands lie off the north coast.

England has three important topographical divisions: the Pennines, an iron and coal-rich region running south from the Scottish border to Derbyshire; the Midlands, a rolling lowland area containing the nation's most industrialized cities; and the Southeastern Plains, which contain the country's richest farmlands. England's chief rivers are the Thames and Severn; also important are the Tyne, Tees, Humber, Ouse, Trent, Mersey, and Avon. Lake Windermere, in the northwest's Lake District, is England's largest. The Isle of Wight lies just off the south coast opposite Southampton; the Scilly Isles are off the Cornish coast southwest of Land's End.

Wales is mountainous, bleak, and almost entirely covered by the Cambrian Mountains.

Northern Ireland contains low-lying plateaus, hills, bogs, and the United Kingdom's largest lake, Lough Neagh.

The temperate climate is due in part to warm currents of the North Atlantic and to rain-bearing southwest winds. Winters are coldest in the mountains. Rainfall averages over 40 inches annually. Fog is a common phenomenon.

The British people are descended from several peoples—Iberians, Picts, Celts, Romans, Anglo-Saxons, Danes, and Norman French—all of whom settled in the area by the 11th century. The Welsh, Scots, and Irish are primarily a Germanic people. English is the common tongue, although Welsh is still heard in some parts of Wales. An estimated two-thirds of the people belong to the Church of England (in Northern Ireland, the Church of Ireland); the Roman Catholic Church has 5,000,000 members, and the Church of Scotland (Presbyterian), 1,250,000.

**HISTORY.** A people called the Iberians are thought to have inhabited Britain during the Stone Age. Sometime before the 6th century B.C. Celtic tribes from northern Europe began a centuries-long series of invasions and occupied the area of present-day England and Wales. Troops under Julius Caesar landed in southern Britain in 55 B.C.; serious colonization began a century later; and by 85 A.D. Rome held all the land to the Clyde, where Hadrian's Wall was put up to keep out the Picts, a warlike Scottish people. The Romans built roads and towns, and introduced Christianity to the Celts.

As their empire declined, the Romans withdrew their legions, and Germanic invaders from northern Europe—Angles, Saxons, and Jutes—took their place in Britain. Driving the Celts west to Wales and Cornwall, they formed the kingdoms of Kent, Essex, Wessex, Sussex, East Anglia, Mercia, and Northumbria in the south and east during the period 500–800 A.D.

Late in the 8th century Denmark began to harass the Anglo-Saxon kingdoms from the sea; in the 860s the Danes invaded the island. They progressively absorbed most of the kingdoms into the Danelaw, or Danish-ruled area. By 1016 Canute, a Dane, was king of England, and Anglo-Saxon rule, except for a brief period (1042–66) under Edward the Confessor, was over.

In 1066 a French duke, William the Conqueror, led the last successful invasion of Britain and became William I (1066–87) of England when his Norman troops beat a force of Anglo-Saxons under Harold at Hastings. William imposed a feudal system of strong central government, further strengthened by such rulers as Henry I (1100–35) and the first of the Plantagenet line, Henry II (1154–89), who began the conquest of Ireland. To protect themselves from the king's great power, the feudal nobles forced King John (1199–1216) to sign the Magna Charta, a document from which the English parliamentary system grew.

Edward I (1272–1307), who completed the conquest of Wales in 1282, set a pattern for

English constitutional government by enlarging Parliament and increasing its powers. In 1296 he conquered Scotland, but the defeat of his son Edward II (1307–27) at Bannockburn by Robert the Bruce in 1314 restored Scottish independence, which England recognized by treaty in 1328. Long-standing English claims to French territory and commercial rivalry with France led Edward III (1327–77) to invade Normandy during the Hundred Years' War (1337–1453). He crushed the French at Crécy in 1346; and ten years later his son, the Black Prince, won a second victory for England at Poitiers.

The war continued under Henry IV (1399–1413), Britain's first ruler of the Lancastrian line. Henry V (1413–22) routed the French at Agincourt (1415) and was acknowledged heir to the throne of France, much of whose territory was then in English hands. After Henry's death the French rallied under Joan of Arc. The French victory at Orleans was the first of a series which, in time, left the English holding only the port of Calais.

Toward the end of the Hundred Years' War the rival families of York and Lancaster began a bloody struggle, the Wars of the Roses (1455–85), for the English throne. Henry Tudor, a Lancastrian, ended the wars by defeating Richard III (1483–85) of York at Bosworth Field in 1485, and founded the Tudor dynasty as Henry VII (1485–1509). Supported by the rising middle class, he cooperated with Parliament and, through the marriages of his daughter and his son, the future Henry VIII (1509–47), formed useful alliances with Scotland and Spain.

Henry VIII, a headstrong ruler, broke with the Pope when denied the right to divorce the first of his six wives, and claimed supreme authority over the Catholic Church in England. But under Henry the Church of England, affected by the Reformation then under way, emerged as Anglican Protestant, rather than Catholic. His eldest daughter, Mary (1553–58), restored Catholicism as the state religion, but supremacy of the Church of England was permanently re-established by another of Henry's daughters, Elizabeth I (1558–1603).

Elizabeth's reign was one of the glories of English history. The defeat of the Spanish Armada made England a major naval power in 1588, a year after the execution of Mary Stuart, Queen of Scots, a Catholic rival for the throne. British diplomacy triumphed; British trade flourished; men of daring such as Sir Walter Raleigh and Sir Francis Drake staked out an overseas empire whose expansion was to continue for three centuries; and men of genius such as William Shakespeare and Francis Bacon brought England to a cultural flowering.

Elizabeth, the last Tudor monarch, was succeeded by James VI of Scotland, the Protestant son of Mary Stuart. Ruling over Scotland and England as James I (1603–25), he established the first North American colonies, at Jamestown and Plymouth. Conflict with Parliament arose from James' belief in the divine right of kings; and his son, Charles I (1625–49), aggravated the conflict until civil war broke out in 1642 between his supporters, the Royalists, and the Puritan partisans of Parliament. Oliver Cromwell led the Puritans to victory, and King Charles was captured and beheaded by parliamentary order in 1649.

England, now a commonwealth, was governed by parliamentary committee until 1653, when Cromwell dismissed Parliament. During his five-year rule as Lord Protector, or dictator, he vigorously pursued the conquest of Ireland without, however, bringing it to completion.

In 1660, two years after Cromwell's death, the monarchy was restored, and the popular reign of Charles II (1660–85), a Stuart, saw a sharp reaction from Puritan austerity, which was replaced by Restoration license. Political and religious strife returned when Charles was succeeded by his brother James II (1685–88), who reasserted the discredited divine right of kings and intrigued to restore Roman Catholicism. James was deposed in 1688, without bloodshed, in the "Glorious Revolution," and his Protestant daughter Mary and her husband, William of Orange, the ruler of Holland, were invited to govern England. The rule of William III (1689–1702) and Mary II (1689–94) ushered in a long period of political stability and virtually completed the structure of English government as it now stands. The Bill of Rights was passed and a two-party system was established in Parliament.

Under Queen Anne (1702–14), the last of the Protestant Stuarts, the Act of Union (1707) created the United Kingdom of Great Britain by uniting Scotland with England and Wales. It gave the Scots parliamentary representation in England, but left Scottish legal and religious patterns intact. (In 1715, and again in 1745, when Bonnie Prince Charlie was defeated at Culloden, the English put down rebellions by Highland Scots who continued to support Stuart claims to rule England.)

Anne's death brought a German cousin, George I (1714–27), the first of the Hanover line, to the throne. Like him, his son and successor George II (1727–60) spoke little English and lacked interest in English affairs. As a result the role of Parliament in government became more important than that of the king, and the prime minister emerged as a key figure. Under George II Britain added to her empire, chiefly at the expense of Bourbon France, and emerged from the Seven Years' War (1756–63) in possession of India and of North America from the Atlantic to the Mississippi River.

King George III (1760–1820) dismissed William Pitt the Elder, the brilliant prime minister largely responsible for Britain's colonial successes, and attempted to impose his own shortsighted views on Parliament. In consequence relations with the American colonies deteriorated; the American Revolution (1775–83) broke out; and all the North American colonies except Canada were lost. Britain nevertheless registered new imperial gains in the Mediterranean and Caribbean, as well as in Africa and Asia, following the defeat of Napoleon at

GREAT BRITAIN AND IRELAND

MILES  0   50   100   150   200

SHETLAND ISLANDS

ORKNEY ISLANDS

ATLANTIC OCEAN

OUTER HEBRIDES

LEWIS

SKYE

Inverness

SCOTLAND

Aberdeen

Dundee

NORTH SEA

FIRTH OF FORTH

Glasgow   Edinburgh

ISLAY

NORTHERN IRELAND

Londonderry

Belfast

Newcastle

Sligo

ISLE OF MAN

ENGLAND

IRISH SEA

IRELAND

Galway

Leeds

Liverpool   Manchester   Sheffield

Shannon R.

DUBLIN

Nottingham

Limerick

Norwich

Leicester

Waterford

ST. GEORGE'S CHANNEL

Birmingham   Coventry

Ipswich

Cork

WALES

Oxford

LONDON

Nottingham

Swansea   Cardiff

Bristol

Thames R.

Kingston   Canterbury

Dover

Southampton

Bournemouth   Portsmouth

ISLES OF SCILLY

Plymouth

Land's End

ISLE OF WIGHT

ENGLISH   CHANNEL

CHANNEL ISLANDS

Le Havre

FRANCE

P. L. A.

**The Port of London.**

Waterloo (1815) by an allied army under the command of the Duke of Wellington.

The beginning of the 19th century saw the British occupied with domestic problems. Ireland, which had never fully accepted British rule, was frequently close to revolt. In 1800 an Act of Union made Ireland part of the United Kingdom. The unpopularity of this measure was slightly mitigated by the Reform of 1829, which gave Catholics throughout the British Isles the right to vote for the first time since the 17th century. Home rule for Ireland, however, was rejected by Parliament in 1886 and 1893.

Other domestic problems stemmed from the Industrial Revolution; begun in the middle of the 18th century, it had given Britain the world's first industrial economy at the cost of profound changes in the lot of the working classes. The enclosure movement, which aimed at more efficient cultivation of the land, drove many farmers to industrial cities such as Birmingham and Manchester; and factory workers were subject to depression, unemployment, and hardship. The first of a series of corrective reforms, in 1832, extended the franchise to the middle classes and made Parliament more truly representative. The following year child labor and factory inspection laws were passed, and slavery was abolished in the colonies. Repeal of the Corn Laws in 1846 was intended to lower the price of grain for ordinary consumers. Benjamin Disraeli's Reform Bill of 1867 extended voting privileges to many factory laborers, and William Gladstone's Reform Bill of 1884 established universal male suffrage and redivided the voting districts along more equitable lines.

Many of these reforms occurred during the long reign of Queen Victoria (1837–1901), which also witnessed the transfer of India from rule by the British East India Company to the British Crown (1859) and the annexation of South Africa after the Boer War (1899–1902). By the end of the 19th century, the globe-girdling British Empire, rich, stable, and prosperous, was at the peak of its power.

The rapid industrialization, growing naval power, and aggressive colonial ambitions of Germany led Britain to ally herself with her traditional enemy, France, in 1904. Ten years later she entered World War I against the empires of Germany and Austro-Hungary. Under Prime Minister David Lloyd George, Britain emerged victorious; to her empire were added formerly German colonies in Africa, and formerly Turkish provinces in the Middle East, given under mandate by the League of Nations.

World War I, a turning point in British history, marked the end of over three centuries of prosperity and expansion. Ireland's bloody rebellion (1916–21) against English rule ended in 1922 with the division of the island into the Irish Free State and Northern Ireland (which remained loyal to the United Kingdom). Postwar Britain was racked by economic upheaval and severe unemployment, which were further aggravated by the worldwide depression beginning in 1929. Industrial difficulties led to the development of a powerful trade union movement and the rise of the Labour Party, which replaced the Liberal Party as the chief rival of the Conservatives.

In 1936 Edward VIII's abdication to marry an American divorcee, an act disapproved of by the Church of England and the cabinet, divided the nation.

Despite the dangers posed by a renascent Nazi Germany, Neville Chamberlain's government adopted a disastrous policy of appeasement, and in 1939 World War II broke out.

The British people rallied under the inspired leadership of Prime Minister Winston Churchill and managed to hold out against almost overwhelming odds. In 1941 the U.S.S.R. and the U.S. entered the conflict as her allies, and Britain again emerged victorious in 1945, but six years of wartime suffering and sacrifice had taken a heavy toll.

Popular demand for radical change marked the return to peace. In July, 1945, the Labour Party, led by Clement Attlee, won an overwhelming electoral victory; its socialist platform pledged the nationalization of basic industries and public utilities and the adoption of a comprehensive social security and national health program.

Churchill returned to power in 1951 but retired in 1955. His successor, Sir Anthony Eden, met political disaster in 1956 when, with France and Israel, he undertook military operations against Egypt for nationalizing the Suez Canal. The Labour Party returned to power in 1964 with Harold Wilson as prime minister.

Postwar Britain has achieved a higher standard of living for the masses at home, but its decline in power and prestige abroad has been dramatic. Over the past 20 years, strong nationalistic pressures have led Britain to grant independence to most of her colonies, and constitutional progress toward autonomy is being made in the remaining territories. Elizabeth II, a member of the House of Windsor and a great-great-granddaughter of Queen Victoria, has been the reigning monarch since the death of her father George VI (1936–52) in 1952.

**GOVERNMENT AND POLITICS.** The United Kingdom is a constitutional monarchy under which the monarch reigns but does not rule. Supreme authority is vested in Parliament, which comprises the monarch, the House of Lords, and the House of Commons, a legislative body elected by universal suffrage. Executive power is exercised by a prime minister appointed by the sovereign on the advice of the majority party in the House of Commons. The Constitution, based on centuries of customs, common law, and parliamentary acts, has never been codified.

The House of Lords, which also functions as the highest court in the land, is composed of archbishops and senior bishops of the Church of England, certain lords of appeal, and hereditary and life peers and peeresses; it can delay, but not prevent, legislation. The prime minister and his cabinet are responsible to the House of Commons, a legislative body elected by universal suffrage for a maximum term of five years, although new elections may be requested by the prime minister at any time. Harold Wilson's present Labour government was returned to office in March, 1966, by an overwhelming majority.

**ECONOMY.** One of the world's most highly industrialized nations, Britain is vitally dependent on its export trade. British industry produces virtually everything, from the heaviest manufactures to light consumer goods, but a scarcity of natural resources obliges Britain to import half her food and most of the raw materials required by industry. Earnings from overseas investment, shipping, tourism, industrial exports, and a variety of commercial and financial services pay for Britain's imports.

In the past 15 years industrial production has expanded steadily and living standards have risen. Serious balance of payment difficulties have frequently resulted from the fact that incomes have risen faster than production, and the pound sterling has weathered a number of crises. A six-month freeze of prices and incomes, imposed in July, 1966, was followed by economic restraint in the first half of 1967. The 12 months following June, 1967, are expected to be a period of continued moderation.

In March, 1966, the British government announced that a decimal system of currency would be adopted in 1971.

In 1966 the British merchant fleet totaled 20.4 gross million tons (vessels of 500 gross tons and over). The state-owned railways had nearly 15,000 route miles, and there were some 201,000 miles of roads. British Overseas Airways Corporation (BOAC) and British European Airways (BEA), both government owned, offer extensive domestic and international routes.

**EDUCATION AND HEALTH.** Britain's non-contributory and almost totally free National Health Service is available to every person in the country.

Education is compulsory and free for children between the ages of 5 and 15. Extensive educational facilities are being expanded. Britain has 42 universities.

**ARMED FORCES.** Britain must maintain considerable forces for national defense and to meet her international obligations under the U.N. Charter and defense agreements with other countries. A continuing review of defense needs is being carried out with a view to stabilizing expenditure. Costs for 1967–68 are estimated at 6.5 per cent of the gross national product. Military service is voluntary.

## UNITED KINGDOM TERRITORIES AND DEPENDENCIES

*Europe*
### CHANNEL ISLANDS

*Area:* 75 square miles. *Population:* 114,000.

Although the Channel Islands, lying in the English Channel near the French coast, are often statistically treated as part of the United Kingdom, they are in fact dependencies. The main islands are Jersey, Guernsey, Alderney, and Sark. The islanders are mostly of Norman descent; Alderney alone is predominantly English. French and English are spoken.

The islands were acquired by the Duke of Normandy in the tenth century and became part of Britain after the Norman Conquest (1066). Despite French efforts to regain the islands in the 14th century and later, they have remained loyal to Britain. In World War II they were occupied by German troops.

The British sovereign is represented in Jersey and Guernsey by lieutenant governors. Voting members of the islands' legislatures are elected by universal suffrage.

The islands ship large quantities of vegetables, fruits, and flowers to the English market. Jersey and Guernsey cattle are noted breeds, kept pure by strict laws.

### ISLE OF MAN

*Area:* 227 square miles. *Population:* 48,150
*Capital:* Douglas (population: 18,837).

The Isle of Man lies in the north Irish Sea midway between Britain and Northern Ireland. It consists of a central mountain mass with low-lying farmlands in the north and south. Manx-speaking people now number fewer than 400, and English is generally spoken. Inhabited since Neolithic times, Man was ruled by the Vikings until about 800, by the Norwegians until 1266, and by the Scots until the 14th century, when it passed to the earls of Salisbury and Derby. It came under the British Crown in the 1820s.

Although a dependency, Man is not subject to the acts of Britain's Parliament. Man's Court of Tynwald is one of the world's oldest legislative bodies.

Dairying, fishing, quarrying, light industry, and agriculture contribute to the economy. Man is well-known as a tourist resort.

## GIBRALTAR

*Area:* 2.5 square miles. *Population* (excluding armed forces): 24,485.

The Rock of Gibraltar, reaching more than 1,400 feet at its highest point, is a peninsula jutting into the Mediterranean from Spain's southwest coast. Most of the people are of Spanish, Portuguese, and Italian descent.

The Moors settled Gibraltar in 711, naming it Jebel-al-Tarik (mount of Tarik). The Spanish took it in 1309, lost it again to the Moors, and regained it in 1462. The English won possession in 1704 and have maintained it since, although besieged a number of times by the Spanish and French. Spain renewed her claim after World War II. Anglo-Spanish talks on Gibraltar's future status were held in 1966, but Spain then announced that she was closing the border to all but pedestrians. Britain's proposal, that the Gibraltar issue be placed before the International Court of Justice, was rejected by Spain. In a referendum on September 10, 1967, the people of Gibraltar voted overwhelmingly to keep their special ties with Britain.

The governor, who also serves as commander in chief, is appointed by the sovereign. He has executive powers and acts on the advice of the Gibraltar Council. There is a large degree of internal self-government.

The economy is based almost wholly on transit trade and the refueling of ships. Some small firms process food and manufacture consumer goods; almost all food must be imported. Tourism, important to the economy, has dropped about 40 per cent as a result of Spain's recent actions impeding traffic to Gibraltar.

## Africa
### BRITISH INDIAN OCEAN TERRITORY

In 1965 the Chagos Archipelago (Oil Islands), the Aldabra and Farquhar groups, and Desroches Islands were formed into a new colony—British Indian Ocean Territory. Chagos lies some 300 miles south of the Kingdom of the Maldives; Aldabra and Farquhar, about 2,000 miles west, are north of Madagascar; the Desroches lie in the Amirantes Islands, a dependency of the Seychelles. The territory is administered by a commissioner resident on Mahé Island in the Seychelles.

## MAURITIUS

*Area:* 720 square miles (including its dependencies, St. Brandon, Agalega, and the Rodrigues Island, in the Indian Ocean). *Population:* 756,472. *Capital:* Port Louis (population: 128,430).

An island in the Indian Ocean about 550 miles east of Madagascar, Mauritius consists of a coastal plain rising to a 2,200-foot plateau bordered by volcanic mountain ranges. The climate is hot and humid. The people are Indo-Mauritians, Sino-Mauritians, Europeans (mainly French), and Chinese. English, French, and Creole are spoken.

Portuguese sailors discovered the island in 1510. It was occupied by the Dutch at intervals from 1638 to 1712. France subsequently claimed the island, but it was captured by the British in 1810.

Mauritius is a Crown Colony. Government is vested in a governor, a Council of Ministers, and a partly elected Legislative Assembly.

Sugar cultivation and export are the basis of the economy. Tea, tobacco, and aloe fibers are also cultivated.

## SAINT HELENA

*Area:* 47 square miles. *Population:* 4,634. *Capital:* Jamestown (population: 1,600).

A mountainous island in the South Atlantic Ocean about 1,200 miles west of Africa, Saint Helena was discovered by the Portuguese in 1502 and claimed by the Dutch in 1633. The British East India Company took the island in 1659. The Dutch attempted to regain it in 1673 but held it less than a year. Napoleon I was exiled on the island after his defeat at Waterloo (1815) until his death in 1821. In 1834 Saint Helena became a Crown Colony.

*Tristan da Cunha* (38 square miles; population: 278), an island 1,500 miles to the southwest, is a dependency of Saint Helena. It was evacuated after a volcanic eruption in 1961, but its people returned in 1963. *Ascension Island* (34 square miles; population 581), a cable station about 700 miles northwest of Saint Helena, and *Gough, Nightingale,* and *Inaccessible islands* (total area: 40 square miles; all uninhabited) are also dependencies of Saint Helena.

## SEYCHELLES

*Area:* 101 square miles. *Population:* 46,472. *Capital:* Port Victoria (population: 11,440).

The Seychelles lie in the Indian Ocean some 1,000 miles east of Tanzania. The principal islands are Mahé, Praslin, LaDigue, and Silouette. The people are of African, Creole, European, Indian, and Chinese stock.

Discovered by the Portuguese in 1505, the Seychelles became a base for pirates until the French settled there in 1768. In 1794 Britain took the islands, which in 1810 became a dependency of the British colony of Mauritius. They became a separate colony in 1903. The British sovereign is represented by a governor; there are also an Executive Council and a partly elected Legislative Council.

Copra is the principal export; cinnamon, patchouli oil, and vanilla are also produced.

There are five government hospitals and three clinics. Primary education is free but not compulsory; literacy in 1960 was 46 per cent.

## SWAZILAND

*Area:* 6,705 square miles. *Population:* 375,000. *Capital:* Mbabane (population: 8,390).

Swaziland is bordered on the north, west, and south by the Transvaal province of the Republic of South Africa and on the east by Mozambique and South Africa's Natal province. The land is a sloping plateau, 500 feet high in the east and 1,500 feet in the west. The people are Swazis, of the Bantu group, and most follow tribal religions.

Driven from their homes in northern Zululand, the Swazis settled the area early in the

19th century. Their independence was guaranteed by Britain in 1881 and by South Africa in 1884. In 1907 the area became a British High Commission Territory.

In April, 1967, under a new constitution, Swaziland became internally self-governing. Britain retains responsibility for external affairs, defense, and internal security. It is expected that Swaziland will become independent not later than the end of 1969.

Agriculture and mining form the base of the economy. Asbestos, sugar, and timber are the chief exports; iron ore is also an important source of income. There are seven hospitals. Primary education is free at government schools, and 23 per cent of the population are literate.

*Americas*
## BAHAMAS

*Area:* 4,400 square miles. *Population:* 140,000. *Capital:* Nassau (population: 83,837).

The Bahamas archipelago consists of some 700 islands, of which 22 are inhabited, in the Atlantic Ocean between Florida and Cuba. New Providence, on which Nassau is located, is the most important but not the largest island; most consist of low coral reefs with lakes and mangrove swamps. The climate is subtropical and mild. Three-quarters of the population is Negro; about 14 per cent are European and 11 per cent are of mixed origin. Most inhabitants are Christians.

Columbus first set foot in the New World on San Salvador (now Watling's Island) in the Bahamas in 1492, but the first settlement was made in the 17th century by Britons from Bermuda. Pirates who used the Bahamas as their base were expelled after 1717.

The Bahamas are an internally self-governing colony with an appointed 15-member Senate and a 33-member House of Assembly elected by universal suffrage.

Tourism is the chief industry and major source of income. Main exports are salt, lumber, crayfish, and tomatoes. The government administers medical care, and education is compulsory from ages 6 to 14.

## BERMUDA

*Area:* 21 square miles. *Population:* 48,000. *Capital:* Hamilton (population: 3,000).

Situated in the Atlantic Ocean some 580 miles east of Cape Hatteras, North Carolina, Bermuda consists of about 300 coral islands, 20 of them inhabited. The climate is mild and humid. About 60 per cent of the population are Negroes; the rest are of European descent. The people are mostly Christians.

Discovered in 1515 by the Spaniard Juan de Bermúdez, the islands were settled in 1609 by a group of Englishmen who had been shipwrecked while on their way to Virginia. The Crown acquired the islands from a chartered company in 1684. A Crown Colony, Bermuda has the oldest British colonial legislature in the world. The Crown-appointed governor is assisted by a 9-member Executive Council. The legislature consists of an appointed Legislative Council of 11 members and a 36-member House of Assembly elected by limited suffrage. Women received the franchise in 1944.

Tourism is the chief industry, and its demands have led to full employment. Bermuda enjoys a higher standard of living than other Caribbean countries. Principal products are pharmaceuticals, essences, lilies, and fruits and vegetables. Medical care is privately administered. Primary education is free and compulsory from ages 7 to 13.

## BRITISH ANTARCTIC TERRITORY
*Area:* 2,040 square miles (excluding Graham Land).

The South Shetland Islands (1,800 square miles), the South Orkney Islands (240 square miles) and Graham Land (the British territory on Palmer Peninsula, Antarctica), formerly administered as part of the Falkland Islands, were created as the separate colony of British Antarctic Territory in 1962.

## BRITISH HONDURAS
*Area:* 8,867 square miles. *Population:* 103,104. *Capital:* Belize (population: 45,572).

British Honduras is bordered on the north by Mexico, on the west and south by Guatemala, and on the east by the Caribbean Sea. The land is generally low and jungle-covered. Rainfall ranges from 69 to 156 inches a year; temperatures vary from 60° to 90° F. Some 60 per cent of the people are of mixed Negro and white stock; 17 per cent are Maya Indians, and 7 per cent are Carib Indians. About half the population is Roman Catholic; most of the remainder are Protestants.

Although Cortés probably marched through the area in 1524–25, the first European settlements were made by British seamen, who founded Belize in the 17th century. In 1798 Britain established dominance, and in 1859 Guatemala yielded her claim to the territory. British Honduras became an independent colony in 1884. Guatemalan claims to the colony were renewed in the 1940s, and in 1963 Guatemala severed diplomatic relations with Britain.

British Honduras became self-governing in 1964, but the governor retains reserve powers so long as the country "is in receipt of budgetary aid" from Britain. There is an 18-member House of Representatives and an 8-member Senate.

Over-exploitation has badly depleted the country's forests, once the basis of the economy, but reforestation has begun. Sugar and citrus fruit now comprise the main exports. Half the country's food requirements are imported.

The level of public health is not high. Education is free and compulsory for children aged 6 to 14 who live near schools. About 90 per cent of the people are literate.

## BRITISH VIRGIN ISLANDS
*Area:* 67 square miles. *Population:* 8,619. *Capital:* Road Town (population: 1,500).

The British Virgin Islands consist of 36 islands and islets in the Caribbean east of Puerto Rico. Almost all the people are of African descent. Britain obtained the islands in 1666. The Crown-appointed administrator is assisted by an Executive Council and a partly elected Legislative Council. Livestock raising, farming, fishing, and tourism all contribute to the economy.

## CAYMAN ISLANDS

*Area:* 100 square miles. *Population:* 7,662. *Capital:* Georgetown (population: 2,573).

The Cayman Islands consist of Grand Cayman, the principal island, Little Cayman, and Cayman Brac; they lie in the Caribbean Sea some 200 miles northwest of Jamaica. About a third of the people are European; a fifth Negro; and the rest of mixed blood. They are Christians.

Although discovered by Columbus in 1503, the islands were never settled by the Spanish. They were colonized by British from Jamaica and were its dependency until 1959. In 1962 they became a separate colony. A Crown-appointed administrator rules with the advice and consent of a Legislative Assembly and Executive Council, both partly elected.

Fishing is the main industry, with tourism increasing in importance. The chief sources of income are tourism and remittances sent back by islanders serving as seamen on foreign ships.

## FALKLAND ISLANDS

*Area:* 4,700 square miles. *Population:* 2,079. *Capital:* Stanley (population: 1,039).

Situated in the South Atlantic some 480 miles northeast of Cape Horn, the Falklands consist of two principal islands, East Falkland and West Falkland. They are mostly hilly moorlands with a cool, rainy, and windy climate. The people are Christians, mainly of British stock.

An English navigator, John Davis, sighted the islands in 1592, but the first settlement was made by the French in 1764 on East Falkland. The British settled West Falkland in 1765, but both colonies were later abandoned. In 1820 Argentina colonized East Falkland. The British recaptured it in 1832–33. Argentina still claims the islands. South Georgia, a whaling settlement 800 miles to the east, and the South Sandwich Islands are administered as part of the colony.

The Falkland Islands are a Crown Colony, with a governor, an Executive Council, and a partly elected Legislative Council of 11 members. The main industry is sheep farming. There are whale-processing plants. Produce includes wool, hides, skins, tallow, meat, fish, and vegetables. Education is free and compulsory for children aged 5 to 14.

## LEEWARD ISLANDS

*Area:* 355 square miles. *Population:* 132,000. *Chief Cities* (with populations): Basseterre, St. Kitts (21,400); St. John's, Antigua (13,000); Charlestown, Nevis (4,000); Plymouth, Montserrat (3,500).

Part of the Lesser Antilles, the Leeward Islands are situated east and southeast of Puerto Rico and north of the Windward Islands. St. Kitts and Montserrat rise to over 3,000 feet; Antigua is mostly rolling land. The people are of mixed African and European stock and are mainly Christian. When discovered by Columbus in 1493, the islands were inhabited by Carib Indians. St. Kitts was settled in 1623, Nevis in 1628, and Antigua and Montserrat in 1632. The French briefly held some of the islands in the late 17th century and again in the late 18th century.

The islands are divided into three territorial units: Antigua, with the dependencies of Redonda and Barbuda; St. Kitts-Nevis-Anguilla; and Montserrat. Each unit has a Crown-appointed administrator, an appointed Executive Council, and a partly elected Legislative Council. Adult suffrage is universal. In February, 1967, Antigua and St. Kitts-Nevis-Anguilla became associated states and attained full internal self-rule. On May 31, 1967, Anguilla declared itself independent. Attempts by the government of St. Kitts to crush the revolt were unsuccessful.

Agriculture is the basis of the economy and principal source of export revenue, but tourism has become increasingly important. Medical and sanitation facilities are poor. Education is generally free and compulsory from ages 5 to 13, and some 88 per cent of the people are literate.

## TURKS AND CAICOS ISLANDS

*Area:* 166 square miles. *Population:* 6,000. *Capital:* Grand Turk (population: 2,346).

Situated east of Cuba and north of Hispaniola, the Turks and Caicos are geographically part of the Bahamas. The most important and the only regularly inhabited of the eight Turk Islands are Grand Turk and Salt Cay; South and North Caicos are the most important of the Caicos group. The climate is temperate. The population is mostly of African descent and mixed blood.

Though discovered by Ponce de León in 1512, the islands were uninhabited until Bermudians arrived to gather salt in 1678. Administered as part of Jamaica until 1962, the islands are governed by a Crown-appointed administrator with the assistance of an assembly and partly-elected Executive Council. Salt, crayfish, sisal, and conch products are exported.

## WINDWARD ISLANDS

*Area:* 826 square miles. *Population:* 341,000. *Chief Cities* (with populations): Saint George's, Grenada (7,300); Castries, Saint Lucia (40,000); Kingstown, Saint Vincent (20,688); Roseau, Dominica (10,400).

Lying southeast of Puerto Rico and south of Trinidad and Tobago, the Windwards are part of the Lesser Antilles. The people are a mixture of European, African, and Carib Indian stock. Discovered by Columbus, the islands were settled by the English in the 17th century. By 1815 disputed French claims to the islands had been resolved in favor of Britain.

The Windwards are divided into four territorial units: Dominica, Grenada, Saint Lucia, and Saint Vincent. They are governed by a Crown-apointed administrator, an appointed Executive Council, and a partly elected Legislative Council. Adult suffrage is universal. In 1967 Dominica, St. Lucia, and Grenada became states in association with Britain, acquiring full responsibility for internal affairs.

Crops are grown for both domestic consumption and export; there are, in addition, fishing and livestock raising.

## Asia and Oceania
### BRUNEI

*Area:* 2,226 square miles. *Population:* 105,876. *Capital:* Brunei (population: 17,317).

The Sultanate of Brunei, lying on the northwest coast of Borneo, is split into two parts. It is bordered by the Malaysian state of Sarawak and the South China Sea. The climate is tropical. Some 55 per cent of the population are Malaysian, more than 25 per cent Chinese, and the remainder Indians, Europeans, and native races. Malay and English are spoken. Islam is the state religion.

Once a powerful state controlling Borneo, Sulu, and some of the Philippine Islands, Brunei lost much of its territory to European colonists in the mid-19th century. Britain in 1888 established a protectorate, which in 1953 became part of the British association of Brunei, North Borneo, and Sarawak. Brunei's first constitution was promulgated in 1959, when Brunei was administratively separated from Sarawak. A revolt against the government for proposing membership in the Federation of Malaysia broke out in 1962 and was suppressed. The Sultanate is a protectorate state in the Commonwealth of Nations, and Britain is responsible for its foreign affairs and defense. In 1965 the 1959 constitution was amended to provide for general elections to the 21-member Legislative Council.

Petroleum is the base of the economy; natural gas, timber, and rubber are exported. The state provides free health care, and there are English, Malay, and Chinese schools. Free education in the Malay language is provided in 83 state schools.

### BRITISH SOLOMON ISLANDS

*Area:* 11,500 square miles. *Population:* 139,730. *Capital:* Honiara (population: 6,684).

The Solomons comprise a 900-mile chain of volcanic islands and atolls in the Southwest Pacific, north of Australia, that begin 300 miles east of New Guinea. With an area of 3,500 square miles, Guadalcanal is the largest of the islands. The larger Solomons are mountainous and heavily forested. Most of the people are Melanesians.

Although discovered by Alvaro de Mandaña in 1567, the islands were not colonized by Europeans until the 18th century. A British protectorate was established in 1893. Other islands became part of the colony in 1898, and Germany ceded the last group in 1900. The Western Pacific High Commissioner is ex-officio president of the protectorate's partly elected Legislative Council. The economy is slowly expanding; principal products are copra, cocoa, and timber.

### FIJI

*Area:* 7,056 square miles. *Population:* 476,727. *Capital:* Suva (population: 60,000).

Fiji comprises some 322 islands—106 of which are inhabited—clustered in the South Pacific about 1,200 miles north of Auckland, New Zealand. The largest islands are Viti Levu (4,010 square miles) and Vanua Levu (2,137 square miles). The smaller islands are of limestone and coral; the larger are mountainous and volcanic. The climate is tropical. About half the people are Indians, 41 per cent Fijians, and the rest Europeans, Eurasians, and Chinese. More than half the people are Christians, although there is a large Hindu minority.

The Fiji Islands were discovered by the Dutch explorer Abel Tasman in 1643. In the 19th century European traders arrived in search of sandalwood. They brought with them diseases that quickly spread and firearms that became weapons used in tribal warfare. Tribal chiefs repeatedly asked the British to intervene. Britain annexed the islands in 1874 and restored order, but the population had been decimated. At the beginning of the 20th century indentured laborers were imported from India; most remained after their contracts ended, and Indians are now the largest ethnic group.

Fiji is administered by a governor in Suva. First elections for an enlarged Legislative Assembly were held in 1966, elected members constituting a majority. There is some light industry, but sugar, tourism, and forestry products are the mainstays of the economy. There are general hospitals and medical facilities, and over 660 schools.

### GILBERT AND ELLICE ISLANDS

*Area:* 369 square miles. *Population:* 48,780. *Capital:* Tarawa (population: 8,439).

The colony comprises 37 coral atolls and islands ranging across more than two million square miles of the south and central Pacific, beginning 2,500 miles northwest of Auckland, New Zealand. It also includes the Phoenix, Line, and Ocean islands; Christmas Island, in the Line group, is the largest (222 square miles) atoll in the Pacific. The Gilbertese are Micronesians; Ellice Islanders are Polynesians.

Although the islands probably were sighted by the Spanish in the mid-16th century, their discovery was first recorded by British naval officers between 1764 and 1824. The islands became a British protectorate in 1892 and a colony in 1915. Under the jurisdiction of the Western Pacific High Commissioner, they are administered by a resident commissioner; each island has a native government. Canton and Enderbury islands (3 square miles), in the Phoenix group, are an Anglo-U.S. condominium. There is no heavy industry. Copra and phosphates are the major exports. Copra production, fishing, and subsistence farming are the leading occupations.

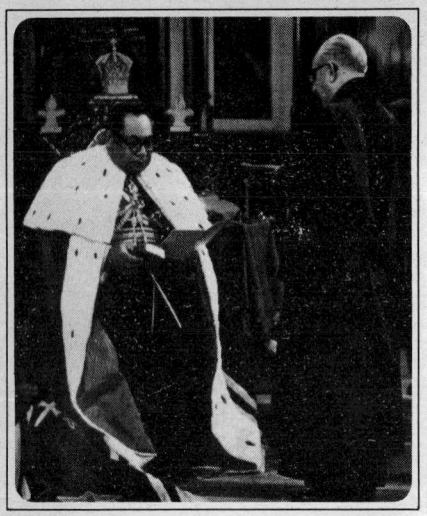

Wide World

Tupou IV is crowned new King of Tonga, July 4, 1967.

## HONG KONG

*Area:* 398 square miles. *Population:* 3,785,300. *Principal City:* Victoria (population: 633,138). *Monetary Unit:* The Hong Kong dollar (worth 17.55 U.S. cents).

Hong Kong lies on the China coast, 91 miles southeast of Canton, and has access to the Pacific. It comprises Hong Kong Island (29 square miles), separated from the mainland peninsula of Kowloon (3.5 square miles) by the harbor, and the New Territories (365.5 square miles), which includes the area between Kowloon and the Communist Chinese border, as well as numerous offshore islands. Hong Kong Harbor is one of the world's busiest. Victoria, the administrative capital, rises sharply from the waterfront and extends halfway up Victoria Peak. Kowloon is a crowded commercial and industrial center. The New Territories are partially under cultivation; however, there are steep hillsides and swamps that have never been developed. The climate is subtropical, and there are occasional typhoons. More than 98 per cent of the people are of Chinese origin. English and Chinese are spoken.

China ceded Hong Kong Island to Britain in 1842 following British occupation during the Opium War. Kowloon became part of the colony in 1860 under terms of the Convention of Peking. In 1898 China leased the New Territories to Britain for 99 years. The Crown Colony is administered by a governor, aided by an Executive Council and a Legislative Council; the latter comprises Europeans, Chinese, and an Indian. In June, 1967, Hong Kong Communists began a violent campaign against the British authorities there.

The colony's location, its deep, sheltered harbor, abundant labor supply, and free-port economy have made it an important center of trade, commerce, and industry. The largest industry is textile manufacturing, but there are

other light and heavy industries, and fishing contributes to the economy. Much food, raw material, and water come from Communist China. A large tourist industry has been developed. The colony has become an international banking center and a leading source of foreign currency for Communist China.

There are 33 hospitals, but maintaining high standards of public health has been made difficult by a steady stream of refugees from mainland China; widespread poverty exists among some elements of the Chinese community. Education is neither free nor compulsory, but there are Chinese, Anglo-Chinese, and English schools, and two universities.

## PITCAIRN ISLAND

*Area:* 2 square miles. *Population:* 107.

Pitcairn is a volcanic, mountainous Pacific island about 1,200 miles southeast of Tahiti. Adamstown is its only village. The island was discovered by the British in 1767 and settled in 1790 by mutineers off H.M.S. *Bounty* and some Tahitian women. Most of the islanders are their descendants. The island came under British jurisdiction in 1898 and was transferred to the control of Fiji, whose governor administers the colony. The chief source of revenue is the sale of postage stamps. The main occupation is subsistence farming.

## TONGA

*Official Name:* Friendly Islands. *Area:* 270 square miles. *Population:* 71,412. *Capital:* Nuku'alofa (population: 9,202).

Tonga is a South Pacific archipelago of over 150 islands. The islands' three most important groups are Tongatapu, Vava'u, and Ha'apai. The climate is semi-tropical. The population is Polynesian; the people are Christians, mostly Methodists.

Tonga's early history has been handed down orally, for its language was not put into written form until the 19th century. Its absolute and hereditary monarchs date back at least to the tenth century. One of the islands was discovered by the Dutch in 1616, and others by Captain James Cook in 1777 and 1779. The kingdom was united before the middle of the 19th century by Taufa'ahau Tupou (George I), who became a Christian in 1831. By 1860 the islanders had been Christianized. A British protectorate was proclaimed over the islands after the signing of a treaty of friendship between Britain and George II, great-grandson of George I Tupou. Tonga remains a hereditary monarchy—the last Polynesian kingdom in Oceania.

Tonga is governed by a British chief commissioner and a Legislative Assembly composed of seven nobles elected by their peers, seven popularly elected members, and seven Crown ministers. The Tongans continue to exercise a high degree of political independence.

Products for export consist almost completely of copra and bananas. There is free medical aid, including dental treatment. Education at the primary level is compulsory and free, and literacy is widespread.

## UPPER VOLTA

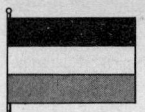

*Official Name:* Republic of Upper Volta. *Area:* 105,869 square miles. *Population:* 4,995,000. *Principal Cities* (with populations): Ouaga-dougou, the capital, 63,000; Bobo-Dioulasso, 55,000. *Flag:* Black, white, and red. *Monetary Unit:* The CFA franc (worth 0.41 U.S. cents).

**LAND AND PEOPLE.** Situated in the west African savanna region, Upper Volta is bounded by Mali on the west and north, Niger on the east, and Dahomey, Togo, Ghana, and the Ivory Coast on the south. (See map on page 111.) It lies on a plateau 650 to 1,000 feet high, slightly inclined toward the south and notched by the valleys of the Black, White, and Red Volta rivers and their tributaries.

Most of the population consists of peasant farmers in the central and southern parts of the country. About half the people belong to the Mossi tribe, one of the Voltaic peoples. French is the official language, and Mossi the principal African language.

**HISTORY.** The early history of Upper Volta is largely that of the Mossi people, whose empire originated sometime around the 13th century. By the 14th and 15th centuries they were raiding the wealthy trading cities on the Niger River and beyond. Stopped by the Songhai kingdom of Gao after the later 15th century, they organized their conquests into the states of Ouagadougou, Yatenga, and Fada-n-Gurma, and they later expanded south and southwest, leading to the establishment of the Dagomba state (in modern Ghana). These states probably profited from the export of gold, kola nuts, and slaves from the forest area in the south to the markets of the north. With the rise of Gonja in the 17th century, direct contact with the forest area was cut off. In the 18th century, the Ashanti expanded northward from the forest at the expense of Dagomba. Nonetheless, the Mossi-Dagomba states survived intact until the late 19th-century European conquest.

French authority was established in 1896. At first Upper Volta was included in the Ivory Coast colony. In 1919 it was detached, to the dismay of French colonists and merchants along the coast, who feared losing a source of migrant labor and a potential market. In 1933 the territory was divided among the Ivory Coast, Niger, and French Sudan colonies. However, the difficulties of effecting a practical merger, together with pressure from the Mossi people, led to its reconstitution as an administrative unit in 1937. At the end of 1947 it was reconstituted as a separate territory, largely because of a new coincidence of interest between the Mossi, who wanted a separate state, and the French, who wanted to halt the spread of an interterritorial nationalist organization, the African Democratic Rally. Upper Volta became autonomous in 1958, after voting in favor of the de Gaulle constitution, and independent on August 5, 1960. Since then it has remained closely aligned with France, which still controls the economy, and it has participated in the French-oriented Afro-Malagasy Common Organization (OCAM).

A crisis in 1961 disrupted relations between Ivory Coast and Upper Volta, and in May of that year President Maurice Yaméogo re-established the customs barriers between the two countries, but abolished those between Upper Volta and Ghana. In July, 1964, after a border dispute with Ghana, the agreement with Ivory Coast was renewed.

In January, 1966, following anti-government riots, the army chief-of-staff, Lieutenant-Colonel Sangoulé Lamizana, seized power. Yaméogo, who had been re-elected several days earlier, was imprisoned. Lamizana suspended the constitution, dissolved the National Assembly, appointed a provisional cabinet, and outlawed all political parties. He announced that he would exercise all legislative and executive powers during an "interim period."

**GOVERNMENT AND POLITICS.** The 1960 constitution provided for a popularly elected president and legislative assembly. There is a one-party system. The dominant organization was the Voltaic Democratic Union, led by Yaméogo. Gen. Sangoulé Lamizana has served as president since the 1966 military coup.

**ECONOMY.** The economy is based on subsistence cultivation of sorghum, millet, peanuts, and other food crops; on livestock herding; and on the export of a portion of the labor force, to work in the Ivory Coast and Ghana. Livestock are the principal resource.

Upper Volta is associated with the European Economic Community (EEC), and it has depended for its economic development on French and EEC aid, tied to purchases in the French and European markets.

**EDUCATION.** Illiteracy is widespread, and only a small proportion of the children are in school.

**NATIONAL DEFENSE.** There is an army of 1,000 men, and police and security forces of 1,835.

## URUGUAY

*Official Name:* Republic of Uruguay. *Area:* 72,153 square miles. *Population:* 2,749,000. *Principal Cities* (with populations): Montevideo, the capital, 1,203,700; Salto, 60,000; Paysandú, 60,000; Rivera, 40,000. *Flag:* Blue stripes on a white field, with a golden sun (symbolic of Uruguayan independence) in upper left. *Monetary Unit:* The peso (worth 1.17 U.S. cents). *Gross National Product:* $324,710,982 (1964). *Average Annual Income per Person:* $107.

**LAND AND PEOPLE.** Uruguay, the smallest country in South America, is situated on the east coast in the southern half of the continent. It is separated from Brazil on the north by the Cuareim and Yaguarón rivers, and from Argentina by the Uruguay River on the west and the Río de la Plata on the south. With the Atlantic Ocean on the southeast, more than half the national boundary is navigable coastline. (See map on page 75.)

The people are predominantly white (89 per cent), of Spanish and Italian origin. About ten per cent of the population are mestizo and about one per cent Negro or mulatto. Two-thirds of the population is Roman Catholic; there are approximately 10,500 Protestants. The official language is Spanish.

**HISTORY.** Spaniards explored the Río de la Plata as early as 1515, but permanent settlement did not occur until 1624. Uruguay's native Charrúa Indians, who strenuously resisted Spanish occupation, had been killed off or absorbed by the 1830s. Portuguese from Brazil fortified the present site of Montevideo in 1717, but later the Spaniards drove them off, and Uruguay became part of the Spanish viceroyalty centered in Argentina. Montevideo was permanently settled in 1726.

A war of independence, led by José Gervasio Artigas, began in 1810. Portuguese forces captured Montevideo in 1820, and for five years Uruguay was part of Brazil. In 1825 the "Thirty-three Immortals," led by Juan Antonio Lavalleja, declared Uruguay's independence, and in 1828 Uruguay was established as an independent buffer state between Brazil and Argentina. A constitution was adopted in 1830, with Fructuoso Rivera as the nation's first president. The 19th century was marked by internal strife, disputes with Brazil and Argentina, and violent changes of government.

José Batlle y Ordóñez, a distinguished, liberal statesman who served two terms as president (1903–07, 1911–15) launched a series of social, economic, and political reforms that were continued by succeeding regimes. Uruguay has achieved political stability and economic progress, despite leftist agitation.

Socially progressive programs, begun in the early 20th century, have grown to include comprehensive labor laws, pension plans, housing for the poor and aged, mother and child care, free education, and care for the deaf, dumb, and blind. Uruguay was the first Latin American country to adopt an eight-hour workday, and one of the first to legalize divorce and to grant woman suffrage.

**GOVERNMENT AND POLITICS.** From 1952 to 1966 Uruguay was governed by a council form of executive organization. In November, 1966, however, the people voted overwhelmingly to return to the presidential system that had been dropped in 1952. After eight years of domination by the conservative Blancos (officially the National Party), Oscar Daniel Gestido, of the liberal Colorados, was elected president for a five-year term. A majority of seats in both legislative chambers also went to the Colorados.

In addition to the presidency, the executive branch includes nine cabinet members and numerous independent agencies or government corporations operating the many social services and economic functions under government control. Legislative power is vested in a Congress, including a Senate of 31 members and a Chamber of Representatives of 99.

**ECONOMY.** The economy is based primarily on the production and processing of livestock and agricultural products. Leading exports are wool, meat and meat products, hides, textiles, and vegetable oils. Manufacturing is limited almost entirely to Montevideo. Railroads and communications are run by the government.

The economy deteriorated badly in the 1960s, with foreign exchange reserves progressively depleted over several years. However, by 1966 a favorable balance of trade had been restored.

**EDUCATION.** Primary education is compulsory for ages 8 through 14. Schooling is free through the secondary level and at the university in Montevideo. The literacy rate is 90.3 per cent of the population over 14 years old.

**ARMED FORCES.** Military service is voluntary. The armed forces total 12,350.

# VATICAN CITY STATE

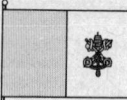

*Official Name:* Vatican City State. *Area:* 0.17 square miles. *Population:* 1,000. *Flag:* Yellow and white; crossed keys of St. Peter under a papal tiara on the white band. *Monetary Unit:* Italian lira (worth 0.161 U.S. cents).

**LAND AND PEOPLE.** Vatican City State is located wholly within Rome, in a somewhat triangular area near the west bank of the Tiber River. The Vatican exercises jurisdiction over a number of churches and palaces in Rome, the areas of the papal villa at Castel Gandolfo, and the Vatican radio station at Santa Maria di Galeria. Latin and Italian are used as the official languages.

**HISTORY.** Vatican City State, the spiritual and governmental center of the Roman Catholic Church, is the remainder of a papal domain that once included large areas of central Italy. Rome was captured from the papacy in 1870 and annexed to the kingdom of Italy. In 1871 the Italian government issued certain papal guarantees. However, Pope Pius IX and his successors refused to recognize these guarantees as a solution to the so-called "Roman Question," and they regarded themselves as "prisoners of the Vatican" until the Lateran accords were signed and ratified in 1929. These accords recognized Vatican City State as independent and sovereign; established the Roman Catholic Church as the state church of Italy; and awarded the Holy See a financial indemnity to compensate for the former Papal States.

The Vatican has been the site of the two most recent ecumenical councils of the Church. The First Vatican Council (1869–70) proclaimed the dogma of papal infallibility in matters of faith and morals. The Second Vatican Council (1962–65) was summoned by Pope John XXIII to modernize aspects of the Church's liturgy, discipline, and organization, and to further Christian unity.

**GOVERNMENT.** Supreme sovereignty over Vatican City State is vested in the Pope, assisted by a Pontifical Commission. The present pontiff, Paul VI (elected in 1963), has played an increasingly important role in world affairs.

**ARMED FORCES.** Colorfully attired Swiss guards constitute a symbolic army.

# VENEZUELA

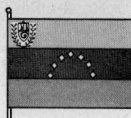

*Official Name:* Republic of Venezuela. *Area:* 352,143 square miles. *Population:* 9,351,602. *Principal Cities* (with populations): Caracas, the capital, 1,551,303; Maracaibo, 589,103; Valencia, 203,177; Barquisimeto, 253,670; Maracay, 172,105. *Flag:* A tricolor of yellow, blue, and red with seven white stars on the blue stripe and the national coat of arms on the yellow stripe. *Monetary Unit:* The bolivar of 100 centimos (worth 22.3 U.S. cents). *Gross National Product:* $7,829,-000,000 (1965). *Average Annual Income per Person:* $760.

**LAND AND PEOPLE.** Venezuela, sixth largest country in South America, lies on the north coast of that continent. It is bordered on the north by the Caribbean Sea, on the south by Brazil and Colombia, on the east by Guyana, and on the west by Colombia. (See map on page 75.)

In northern Venezuela an extension of the Andes runs to the Caribbean coast. More than 1,000 rivers flow through the land; the Orinoco, 1,600 miles long, bisects the country. Navigable for about 700 miles, the river forms a 9,000 square-mile delta and drains four-fifths of the land. South of the Orinoco lie the Guiana Highlands, a vast region of wild, largely unexplored jungles and plateaus constituting half the country's area. Angel Falls, the world's highest, is deep in the highlands. To the west lies Lake Maracaibo with its oil-rich basin.

Venezuela's mountains divide the country into distinct climatic regions. Much is tropical forest or swamp, but many major cities are located at from 1,500 to 7,000 feet above sea level.

About 67 per cent of the people are mestizos (Indian-white), 21 per cent are white, and the rest are Indians and Negroes. The white population, swelled by immigration of Europeans after World War II, is centered in the larger cities. The official language is Spanish. The overwhelming majority of the people are Catholic.

Although its people enjoy the highest per capita income in Latin America, Venezuela exhibits extreme examples of both wealth and poverty.

**HISTORY.** Columbus discovered the Orinoco River in 1498. German adventurers followed, but organization of the country was undertaken by Spain. Caracas was founded in 1567. The country remained a Spanish colony for nearly 300 years.

In 1811 Francisco de Miranda led a revolt against Spanish leaders in a bid for independence. Simón Bolívar completed the struggle in 1821, after bloody campaigns verging on civil race wars nearly erased the white population. Bolívar's dream of a Greater Colombia to include Venezuela was realized briefly, but after his death in 1830 the country became an independent state.

Dictator succeeded dictator throughout the remainder of the century, and the country was weakened by internal strife. Venezuela lost land to the British in 1895 and suffered the shelling, in 1902, of its principal port by a joint British-Italian-German fleet trying to collect debts contracted by earlier dictators.

In 1908, General Juan Vicente Gómez became absolute dictator. Although his regime was tyrannical, he did unify the country for the first time. The discovery of oil in 1921 and the entry of British and American petroleum companies enabled him to lift the nation to solvency.

After Gómez' death in 1935, a military junta took over. A revolution in 1945 brought to power a liberal democratic government headed by Rómulo Betancourt. In 1947 Rómulo Gallegos won a free presidential election, but was ousted nine months later by a military coup. General Carlos Delgado Chalbaud became president and, after his assassination in 1950, was succeeded by Germán Suarez Flámerich. In 1953 Marcos Pérez Jiménez was elected president and under a new constitution assumed complete governmental power. Jiménez was overthrown in 1958 during a revolt supported by liberal elements of the armed forces.

With the fall of Jiménez, democratic processes were restored. Rómulo Betancourt was elected president in 1958, and his government steered a moderate course of economic and social reform. Communist terrorism plagued the country during the early 1960s, but by 1967 the government appeared to have subversive elements under control.

**GOVERNMENT AND POLITICS.** Venezuela is a republic governed by a president and a bicameral National Congress whose members are elected by direct popular vote for five-year terms. Citizens of 18 years of age and over must vote. Although there are executive, legislative, and judicial branches and a theoretical separation of powers, the president traditionally tends to dominate the government.

The strongest political force is the Democratic Action Party (AD) that elected Raúl Leoni to the presidency in 1961. Other parties are the Social Christian Party (COPEI), the Democratic Republic Union (URD), and the Democratic National Front (FND). The Leoni government is a coalition of AD, URD, and some independents. A coalition of leftist parties was formed in 1967 to contest the 1968 elections.

**ECONOMY.** With its abundant reserves of oil and iron ore, Venezuela is one of the richest Latin American countries. The nation produces 3.4 million barrels of crude oil daily, primarily around Lake Maracaibo, and is the world's largest oil exporter. Oil taxes pay about 60 per cent of government revenues and earn 90 per cent of foreign exchange earnings. Iron ore is of small but rising importance. Gold, diamonds, and tropical hardwoods also are exported.

About 44 per cent of the labor force is engaged in agriculture. Coffee and bananas are the leading export crops. Agriculture has benefited recently from improved financing and government marketing support. The government has sponsored one of the most successful agrarian reform programs in Latin America, partly in an effort to reduce rural migration to the cities.

**EDUCATION.** Elementary education is free and compulsory through the primary level. An estimated 84 per cent of the people 15 years of age and over are literate.

**ARMED FORCES.** There is universal military service for all 18-year-old males. Current army strength stands at 15,500; air force, 2,500; navy, 5,000; and national guard, 8,500.

## VIETNAM, NORTH

*Official Name:* Democratic Republic of Vietnam. *Area:* 61,293 square miles. *Population:* 15,903,000. *Principal Cities* (with populations): Hanoi, the capital, formerly 500,000; Haiphong, formerly 185,000 (city populations have been greatly reduced by wartime evacuation). *Flag:* A gold star centered on a red field. *Monetary Unit:* The dong of 10 hào (worth 28.33 U.S. cents).

**LAND AND PEOPLE.** Situated in the northeastern part of the Indochinese peninsula, North Vietnam is bordered on the north by Communist China, on the east by the Gulf of Tonkin and the South China Sea, on the south by South Vietnam, and on the west by Laos. (See map on page 243.)

The delta of the Red River, emptying into the Gulf of Tonkin, is low-lying fertile land. There are highlands in the north and a mountain chain along the western border. The wet season, from July through September, averages from 68 to 160 inches of rain annually.

The North Vietnamese are related ethnically to the Chinese. In addition to ethnic Vietnamese, who account for 85.2 per cent of the population, there are also Chinese, mostly in the cities; tribal peoples of Thai and Chinese stock inhabit the uplands. The national language is Vietnamese. Chinese, Lao and Thai dialects, and French are also spoken. The majority of the people practice religions intermingling Mahayana Buddhism, Taoism, Confucianism, and ancestor worship. In addition, there are approximately 800,000 Roman Catholics.

**HISTORY.** As a result of the Geneva Conference on Indochina, North Vietnam came into being in 1954, created out of Tonkin and the northern region of Annam. The early years of its existence saw the imposition of Communism and the collectivization of farms, the latter reportedly entailing the execution of more than 100,000 farmers. Armed peasant revolts against collectivization in 1956 were suppressed militarily.

In 1959 North Vietnam instigated a campaign of terror and subversion in South Vietnam, hoping to annex that state and unify Vietnam under Communist rule. The southern segment of the Communist Lao Dong Party, which had remained clandestinely active in South Vietnam after 1954, spearheaded the insurgency, which was directed and supplied from the north. The United States helped South Vietnam to defend itself, providing military supplies, technicians, advisers, and, since 1965, fighting men.

As resistance to the insurgency grew, North Vietnam increased its infiltration of soldiers and weapons into the South, thereby provoking U.S. air attacks against her territory. Bombing of North Vietnam has continued since 1965, increasing the cost and difficulty of reinforcing the Viet Cong in the South. As a result of the war, North Vietnam depends heavily on foreign Communist aid for military and other supplies.

(For history prior to 1954, see *Vietnam, South.*)

**GOVERNMENT AND POLITICS.** North Vietnam is ruled by the Communist Lao Dong Party. Its Politburo makes all important policy decisions, which are subsequently endorsed by the party's Central Committee. Although the Politburo is in theory composed of 11 members, one member, General Nguyen Chi Thanh, died in 1967 and has not been replaced, while the 77-year-old chairman, Ho Chi Minh, apparently is little more than a figurehead. Power thus rests with the remaining nine members, who reportedly are divided over the war question.

Although dependent on aid from the U.S.S.R., China, and Eastern Europe, North Vietnam has maintained neutrality in the Sino-Soviet dispute. Nevertheless, she has evinced dissatisfaction and growing apprehension over the disorders in China caused by the Cultural Revolution, for the bulk of her foreign aid is transported via Chinese territory.

**ECONOMY.** North Vietnam's economy is principally agrarian, rice being the most important crop. Production is insufficient to meet domestic needs, and food must be imported. Mineral resources include large coal deposits, tin, tungsten, iron, zinc, gold, phosphates, antimony, manganese, and chromium. Forestry and fishing also contribute to the economy. Some industrialization, including the building of iron and steel works, cotton-spinning mills, and a machine-tools factory, has been effected with foreign Communist aid. Manpower withdrawals necessitated by the war, the evacuation of factories, and bombing damage have hurt the economy.

**EDUCATION AND HEALTH.** There are numerous primary and secondary schools and a university in Hanoi, but the shortage of qualified teachers keeps educational standards low. Thousands of students receive higher education in other Communist countries.

Tropical diseases are endemic, and infant mortality is high. Medical personnel and facilities are grossly inadequate, while low standards of hygiene further exacerbate health problems.

**ARMED FORCES.** Large-scale mobilization in recent years has greatly increased regular armed strength. Actual figures remain secret. Other Communist nations have furnished North Vietnam with massive anti-aircraft defenses, including an extensive radar network and surface-to-air missiles.

SOUTHEAST ASIA

# VIETNAM, SOUTH

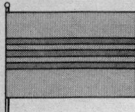

*Official Name:* Republic of Vietnam. *Area:* 65,948 square miles. *Population:* 13,960,000. *Principal Cities* (with populations): Saigon, the capital, 1,336,000; Danang, 121,400; Hué, 103,000. *Flag:* A yellow field with three horizontal red stripes. *Monetary Unit:* The dong (worth 28.33 U.S. cents). *Gross National Product:* $1,171,000,000 (1965). *Average Annual Income per Person:* $60.

**LAND AND PEOPLE.** South Vietnam is bordered on the north by North Vietnam, on the east and south by the South China Sea, and on the west by Cambodia and Laos. (See map on page 243.)

The northern part of the country consists of fertile coastal plains and a plateau leading to the Annamite Mountains, where there are tropical evergreen and pine forests. Cochin China, in the southern part, is a flat plain containing the Mekong Delta, one of the world's best rice-growing areas, in the southeast. Coconut and mangrove forests grow along the coast. Deer, buffalo, wild oxen, elephants, and tigers are found in the uplands.

The South Vietnamese are ethnically related to the Chinese. There are minorities of Chinese and Cambodians, and tribal aborigines live in the high plateaus of central Vietnam.

In addition to the Vietnamese language, Chinese, Lao and Thai dialects, French, and English are spoken. The majority of the population practices religions combining Mahayana Buddhism, Taoism, Confucianism, and ancestor worship. There are some 1.5 million Roman Catholics.

**HISTORY.** The forebears of the modern Vietnamese inhabited a territory extending over the Red River delta and part of southern China. China annexed the region in the second century B.C. and ruled it until about 938 A.D. During this period the Vietnamese became deeply imbued with Chinese culture and learning, still discernible today in every facet of their lives. Independence was re-established by Ngo Quyen and lasted until the early 15th century when, weakened by dynastic disputes, the country was defeated by China and underwent a brief period of Chinese rule. In 1427 Le Loi freed the nation from the Chinese and founded the later Le dynasty, which lasted until 1788.

Between the 11th and 18th centuries the Vietnamese extended their territory southward, absorbing the kingdom of Champa and much of Cambodia in the process, and occupying the southernmost part of modern Vietnam as late as 1780. Early in the 17th century the land was, in effect, split into two hostile kingdoms, with the boundary set at very nearly the present dividing line on the 17th parallel. The Le emperor still exercised nominal control over both halves. National unity was restored in 1802 when Gia-Long, ruler of South Vietnam, conquered the North.

European incursions into Vietnam began when Christian missionaries arrived in the 16th century, soon to be followed by traders. By the 19th century France was dominant in the peninsula. In 1858, using Indochinese mistreatment of Christians as a pretext, the French set out to conquer Annam. By 1884 the province of Cochin China had become a French colony, and Annam (Central Vietnam) and Tonkin (North Vietnam) were French protectorates. By 1893 Vietnam, Laos, and Cambodia had been incorporated into the Indochinese Union.

During World War II the government of French Indochina sided with Vichy France, permitted Japanese military forces to use the territory, and continued to administer Vietnam under Japanese overlordship. Vietnamese Communists and nationalists fled to southern China, where they organized movements designed to end French rule. Under the cover of a popular front (the Viet Minh), the Communists obtained help from the Allies and established guerrilla forces inside North Vietnam.

In 1945, with defeat impending, the Japanese granted independence to the three constituent states of Vietnam. When Japan surrendered to the Allies, Viet Minh guerrillas seized Hanoi, forced the abdication of Emperor Bao Dai, and established the Democratic Republic of Vietnam. Chinese forces occupied North Vietnam and British forces held the South on behalf of the Allies. The returning French landed first in the South, where they undertook reconquest of the area, moving later into the North.

In 1946, with most Vietnamese nationalists rallying to their side, the Viet Minh resorted to military force against the French. The fighting was inconclusive, and in 1949 the French restored Bao Dai as head of state, promising national independence, with the hope that the nationalists would abandon the Viet Minh and come over to Bao Dai's side. France's obvious reluctance to transfer power, however, discredited Bao Dai and failed to effect nationalist defection from the Communists.

In the same year a Communist regime assumed power in neighboring China and thereafter greatly aided the Viet Minh. The war dragged on until 1954, ending with the defeat of French forces at Dien Bien Phu and a peace settlement arrived at by an international conference in Geneva. Vietnam was divided at the 17th parallel, with North Vietnam coming under Communist rule and South Vietnam under nationalist control.

South Vietnam, comprising Cochin China and the southern area of Annam, withdrew from the French Union and asserted its complete sovereignty in 1954. The following year a national referendum deposed absentee Chief of State Bao Dai and created a republic with Ngo Dinh Diem as president. Almost a million refugees came from North Vietnam in 1954–55.

With U.S. aid, South Vietnam made rapid economic and political progress, repairing war damage, undertaking agrarian reforms, and holding parliamentary elections. But government control over the whole territory, as well as advances in the economic, social, and political spheres, were threatened by the Communist campaign of terror, violence, and sabo-

# FOCUS ON THE NEWS

## ELECTIONS IN SOUTH VIETNAM

United Press Int'l.

Nguyen Van Thieu and his wife cast their ballots in South Vietnam's national election, Sept. 3, 1967.

On September 3, 1967, nearly 5,000,000 South Vietnamese elected a chief of state and an upper house. Since the overthrow of President Ngo Dinh Diem in November, 1963, the leadership of the Saigon government had been determined by military coups and power plays. The election, regarded as an important step toward political stability, restored to power the incumbent military junta that had been headed by Air Marshal Nguyen Cao Ky. Lt. Gen. Nguyen Van Thieu was elected president, and Ky was elected vice-president.

The large turnout was especially heartening in view of repeated efforts by Viet Cong terrorists to sabotage the election. Their savage attacks left 55 dead and 267 wounded in 171 incidents. During the days leading up to the elections, Viet Cong terrorists burst into Saigon theaters and intimidated audiences with violent anti-election harangues. Potential voters in a northern province were abducted and threatened with terms of up to one year in "thought-reform" camps. Despite such tactics, 83 per cent of the registered voters turned out to cast a total of approximately 4,700,000 votes. (In contrast, the turnout in the 1964 U.S. Presidential election was 62 per cent.)

There were 11 presidential candidates. Generals Thieu and Ky were expected to draw at least 40 per cent of the votes but received only 34.5 per cent. An impressive 17 per cent went to runner-up Truong Dinh Dzu, a Saigon lawyer. His peace platform stressed two points: a denunciation of the present government and a promise to open immediate negotiations with Hanoi.

The South Vietnamese government invited a team of 22 U.S. observers to witness the elections. There was some criticism of preelection strategy, but the observers were generally agreed that the actual balloting was conducted honestly.

tage which began in 1959. Created and supported by North Vietnam, the Viet Cong (the term means "Vietnamese Communists") struggled to overthrow the government of South Vietnam. To combat the Viet Cong, President Diem introduced draconian security measures which restricted civil liberties and disaffected many of the South Vietnamese people. As terrorism spread, countermeasures became harsher, and resentment against President Diem steadily increased. Following allegations of anti-Buddhist persecution and violent street demonstrations in 1963, the government was overthrown by an army revolt, and Diem was murdered.

Throughout 1964 political instability persisted as government succeeded government, and the Viet Cong made large gains. In the spring of 1965 a military government led by Chief of State General Nguyen Van Thieu and Premier Air Vice Marshal Nguyen Cao Ky assumed office and, over the next two years, worked for the restoration of order and stability. The United States decision of 1965 to participate in the fighting did much to restore South Vietnamese confidence. Political progress recommenced and a new constitution, drafted by an elected assembly, was promulgated.

**GOVERNMENT AND POLITICS.** The violent overthrow of President Diem's government in November, 1963, left successor governments without a popular mandate. To remedy this lack, the military government of General Thieu and Air Vice Marshal Ky held elections in 1966 for a constituent assembly that drafted a new democratic constitution. Hamlet and village councils were also voted into office. In national elections held in September and October, 1967, representatives were elected to the bicameral parliament, Nguyen Van Thieu was elected President, and Nguyen Cao Ky was elected Vice President of the Republic.

**ECONOMY.** Agriculture is the mainstay of the economy, with rice and rubber the chief cash crops. Subsidiary crops include tea, coffee, tobacco, vegetables, fruit, quinine, sugarcane, peanuts, and copra. Fishing is an important contribution to the economy. Light industry, located mostly in and around Saigon, includes textile manufacturing, food processing, the assembling of vehicles, radios, and sewing machines, and the production of cigarettes, mineral water, glass, paper, and sacks. There is no heavy industry. All sectors of the economy have been seriously handicapped by the war.

**EDUCATION AND HEALTH.** Primary and secondary schools are numerous, and there are four universities. Reasonable academic standards are maintained despite wartime difficulties.

Medical facilities and personnel are inadequate, and health standards remain low. Most new doctors are drafted for military service.

**ARMED FORCES.** South Vietnam's armed forces totaled 635,000 men in 1967 and are scheduled to reach 700,000 in 1968. U.S. forces in Vietnam totaled 525,000 men in September, 1967. In addition there are 45,000 South Koreans, 6,700 Australians and New Zealanders, 2,400 Thais, and 2,400 Filipino civil action personnel.

# WESTERN SAMOA

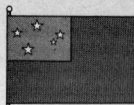

*Area:* 1,133 square miles. *Population:* 130,000. *Principal City* (with population): Apia, the capital, 21,699. *Flag:* A red field with a blue rectangle, upper left, bearing five white stars (representing the Southern Cross). *Monetary Unit:* West Samoan pound (worth U.S. $2.78).

**LAND AND PEOPLE.** Situated in the Pacific Ocean, halfway between Honolulu and Sydney, Western Samoa consists of two principal islands (Savai'i and Upolu) and several small islands, of which only Manono and Apolima are inhabited. Volcanic in origin, the islands are surrounded by coral reefs. The climate is tropical and wet, and the vegetation is lush.

Samoa's predominantly Christian people are of Polynesian origin and speak Samoan and English.

**HISTORY.** The first Europeans to sight the islands were the Dutch in 1772. English missionaries arrived in 1830, in the midst of a long struggle among the native chiefs that ended in 1889 when the kingship was abolished and the islands were divided between the United States (American Samoa) and Germany.

From 1919 to 1946 New Zealand administered Western Samoa as a League of Nations mandate. During this time a Samoan nationalist organization campaigned for independence. Ten years later the islands passed to U.N. trusteeship, while remaining under New Zealand supervision. Cabinet government was introduced in 1959, and on January 1, 1962, following a plebiscite, Western Samoa became independent.

**GOVERNMENT AND POLITICS.** The constitution provides that the office of head of state shall be held jointly by two hereditary rulers of the Typua and Malietoa Royal lines. The Typua ruler died in 1963, and his successor, Malietoa Tanumafili II, holds office for life. Future rulers will be chosen for five-year terms by the 47-member Legislative Assembly, two of whose members are elected by universal suffrage, and the remainder by the matais, or chiefs. Effective executive power is in the hands of the Prime Minister (Fiame Mata'afa Faumuina Mulinu'u II) who is elected by universal suffrage.

Western Samoa has little political contact with the rest of the world. Under a 1962 treaty, New Zealand acts for it in foreign affairs and has continued its economic assistance.

**ECONOMY.** The economy is almost entirely agricultural, with copra, cocoa, and bananas the principal exports. Most food is grown for home consumption.

Tourism has grown in recent years, as the Samoans' desire to protect their way of life has slowly given way to economic necessity.

**EDUCATION AND HEALTH.** There are 33,174 pupils enrolled in primary and secondary schools and an agricultural college. A central hospital is located at Apia, with 15 smaller outstation hospitals scattered among the islands.

# YEMEN

*Official Name:* Yemen Arab Republic. *Area:* 75,290 square miles. *Population:* 5,000,000. *Principal Cities* (with populations): Sana, the capital, 75,000; Taiz, 40,000; Hodeida, 30,000. *Flag:* Red, white, and black with a green star. *Monetary Unit:* The Yemen riyal (worth 95 U.S. cents). *Gross National Product:* $489,000,000 (1965). *Average Annual Income per Person:* Under $100.

**LAND AND PEOPLE.** Yemen, situated in the southwest corner of the Arabian peninsula, is bordered on the west by the Red Sea, on the south by the Federation of South Arabia (Aden and its hinterland), and on the east and north by Saudi Arabia. The boundary between Yemen and Aden is disputed. (See map on page 151.)

The section of Yemen along the Red Sea is a hot, humid, but nearly rainless plain (the Tihamah) 20 to 30 miles wide. Inland, mountains rise above 12,000 feet; summers are temperate, winters are cool, and rainfall is abundant. In the east and northeast the mountains descend to desert areas of Saudi Arabia.

The Yemenis of the central highlands are Arabs, and those of the Tihamah are of Persian-Arab background. Nearly all the people are Muslims, about equally divided between the Zaydi and Shafi sects. Arabic is the principal language.

**HISTORY.** Yemen developed urban culture in ancient times. It was the site of the Minaean state before 2000 B.C. and, later, of the kingdom of Saba (Biblical Sheba). The Sabaeans were succeeded in the first century B.C. by the Himyarites, who gradually spread eastward to the Wadi Hadhramaut (now in South Arabia). The territory was conquered by the Abyssinians in 525 A.D.

Successive invaders then held the territory but could not establish firm control. Persians ruled from 575 to 628, at which time Islam was introduced. Yemen broke away from the Abbasid caliphate, centered in Baghdad, in the mid-eighth century, and from the ninth century onward a number of dynasties established themselves in Sana and other cities. There were two periods of Turkish domination: 1536 to about 1636, and 1849 to 1918. During these periods the imams of Yemen were allowed to retain spiritual authority over the Zaidi sect, from which they came, but they were deprived of temporal authority.

After the Turkish defeat in World War I, Yemen's Imam Yahya, neutral in the conflict, resumed control of the country. He made treaties with several foreign powers, and in 1947 he brought Yemen into the United Nations. Northern and southern boundaries were defined by treaties in 1934 (although the southern boundary is still in dispute), and tribal revolts were put down. Imam Yahya and his successor, Imam Ahmad (1948–62), centralized administration and tried to isolate the country from external influences.

The need for foreign trade and the exodus of many Yemenis to other Muslim lands increased contacts with the outside world and stirred notions of reform. Coups in 1948, 1955, and 1961 failed, but a revolution in 1962 resulted in the overthrow of Imam Muhammed al-Badr. Abdullah al-Sallal, military chief of state who headed the coup, established a republican regime in the place of the feudalistic tribal system. He later became president.

The Imam, who had escaped, organized royalist resistance with the help of Saudi Arabia. The resistance drew support from the north and northeast areas populated by Zaydi tribes. Civil war erupted, with the republicans receiving military support from Nasser's United Arab Republic (U.A.R.). In 1964 a U.N. mission was unable to negotiate a settlement, and a 1965 Egyptian-Saudi peace pact was never implemented. The country thus remains in a state of civil war, with a de facto division of Yemen into the royalist-held north and northeast and the republican-held west and south. In September 1967 the U.A.R. and Saudi Arabia again agreed to implement a cease-fire in Yemen.

**GOVERNMENT AND POLITICS.** Yemen currently has an interim constitution with the president subject to the Republican Council and a 99-member Consultative Assembly, which will prepare the constitution.

Under the presidency of Abdullah al-Sallal, political power in the republic has shifted between pro-Nasser and independent elements. U.A.R. willingness to risk withdrawal of support has varied accordingly. Following the Israeli war in 1967, the U.A.R. proposed withdrawal of the troops to replace forces lost in the war.

**ECONOMY.** The economy rests entirely on agriculture. Terraced civilization is practiced in the highlands where the people grow coffee, qat (a stimulant), grain, fruits, and vegetables. Inhabitants of the coastal plain raise livestock, grain, and cotton.

The republican government has undertaken various development projects, including enlargement of the port at Hodeida and construction of roads between Mokha and Taiz, Sana and Hodeida, and Sana and Taiz. A modern textile plant was recently completed, and a power station, glass factory, and cement factory have been planned. Substantial assistance has been provided to Yemen by the United Arab Republic, Communist China, the Soviet Union, and the United States.

**EDUCATION AND HEALTH.** Education is not compulsory. Only five to ten per cent of the people are literate. There are universities at Sana and Ibb.

The first government efforts to improve health conditions were not made until after the revolution. Major health problems include malnutrition and associated diseases. Malaria and typhus are widespread. There are few physicians.

**ARMED FORCES.** Military service is compulsory. The regular army has a force of about 20,000. There is also a militia of 20,000.

# YUGOSLAVIA

*Official Name:* Socialist Federal Republic of Yugoslavia. *Area:* 98,766 square miles. *Population:* 19,981,000. *Principal Cities* (with populations): Belgrade, the capital, 697,000; Zagreb, 503,000; Skopje, 228,000; Saravejo, 227,000; Ljubljana, 182,000. *Flag:* A red star outlined in gold, superimposed on three horizontal stripes of blue, white, and red. *Monetary Unit:* The new dinar (worth 8 U.S. cents). *Gross National Product:* $6,352,-000,000 (1965). *Average Annual Income per Person:* $294.

**LAND AND PEOPLE.** Yugoslavia lies on the western side of the Balkan peninsula, the Adriatic shore forming its western border. It is bounded on the north by Austria and Hungary, on the northeast by Romania, on the east by Bulgaria, on the south by Greece, on the southwest by Albania, and on the northwest by Italy. (See map on page 197.) Mountains, including the Julian and Dinaric Alps, dominate much of the country, and with the highlands make up 71 per cent of the area. The Pannonian plain extends across the north to the Romanian border. The climate is Mediterranean—mild winters and warm summers—along the Adriatic coast, and continental and alpine inland, with long, cold winters and short, cool summers.

Ethnically, Yugoslavia is one of the most diverse nations in Europe. In the 1961 census, Serbs accounted for 42.1 per cent of the population, Croats for 22.8 per cent, Slovenes for 8.5 per cent, Macedonians for 5.5 per cent, Albanians for 4.9 per cent, Montenegrins for 2.8 per cent, Hungarians for 2.7 per cent, and other groups for 10.7 per cent. Serbo-Croatian, Slovenian, and Macedonian are the languages spoken. The chief religions are Serbian (Eastern) Orthodox, adhered to by 48 per cent of the population; Roman Catholic, adhered to by 36 per cent; and Islam, adhered to by 14 per cent. State relations with the Vatican, broken in 1952, were renewed in 1966.

**HISTORY.** Prior to 1918, the various parts of Yugoslavia (Serbia, Croatia, Bosnia-Herzegovina, Macedonia, Slovenia, and Montenegro) had never been united under one government. Serbia was under Turkish domination from 1371 to 1878. After the Balkan Wars of 1912-13, Serbia acquired Macedonia, an ancient kingdom that had been variously under Bulgarian and Turkish control. Montenegro, under Turkish rule for centuries but never fully subdued, became independent in 1878. Slovenia, passing to Hapsburg rule in 1335, was under their domination until 1918. Croatia was part of Hungary from the 11th to the 16th century, under the Turks until the 19th century, and was Hungarian-controlled at the time of Yugoslavia's creation in 1918. Bosnia and Herzegovina, united from the 15th century, were subjugated by the Turks in 1463 and passed to Austria Hungary in 1908.

In 1914 the Austrian Archduke Francis Ferdinand was assassinated in Sarajevo, Bosnia, a murder that was the final spark needed to touch off World War I. King Peter I of Serbia became the ruler of the new Kingdom of the Serbs, Croats, and Slovenes in 1918, but his son Alexander ruled as regent until Peter's death in 1921. There was dissension from the start. The Serbs demanded—and got—a strong central government which they dominated. In 1928 the Croats set up a separate parliament in Zagreb. Alexander declared a dictatorship in 1929 and changed the kingdom's name to Yugoslavia. In 1931 a new constitution ensured that his party would keep power.

In 1934 Alexander was assassinated. His heir, Peter II, still not of age, succeeded under the regency of Prince Paul. The premier signed a treaty of alliance with the Axis powers in March, 1941. Within two days the government had been overthrown, and the new regime signed a nonaggression pact with the Soviet Union. The Axis, led by Hitler's forces joined by Bulgarians, Hungarians, and Italians, invaded and conquered Yugoslavia within a week. Draja Mikhailovich, a Yugoslav army officer, successfully led initial resistance to Axis armies with his Chetniks. An ardent royalist, he clashed with the partisan forces of Josip Broz, the Communist leader who later changed his name to Tito. Allied support swung to Tito. Mikhailovich was tried for collaboration by the Titoists and executed. By 1944 the Germans had been driven out. Tito became premier in 1945, and the federal republic, comprising Bosnia-Herzegovina, Serbia, Croatia, Slovenia, Montenegro, and Macedonia, was proclaimed. The Communists held power in the new government, and socialization and industrialization began immediately.

In 1948 Yugoslavia was expelled from the Cominform. Tito, elected president in 1953 (and three times since), embarked on a course of "national communism" and received vast amounts of aid from the West. By 1960 there had been a rapprochement with Moscow, and Tito was once again warmly received in Communist circles. The nation, however, has been careful to preserve her independence in foreign affairs and has developed a form of socialism uniquely her own. Significantly, Tito has gone so far as to explore the possibility of affiliation with the Common Market. A relaxation of central political control in the mid-1960s led to demonstrations of Serb-Croat animosity, in late 1966 and early 1967, which were promptly put down.

**GOVERNMENT AND POLITICS.** The Federal Assembly, which sits in Belgrade, consists of five chambers regulating different spheres of national life. Members are elected for terms of four years. A Federal Executive Council, the executive body of the assembly, presides over the gamut of government activities. This political structure is guided by the League of Communists of Yugoslavia, whose 35-member presidium and 11-member executive committee are the supreme policy-making organs of the country. In October, 1966, a major purge and reorganization of the Communist Party leadership took place, with Tito still at the top.

There have been no indications that the League is prepared to yield its leading role in Yugoslavia or even to permit the existence of any organized opposition, as demanded by such outspoken Yugoslavs as Mihajlo Mihajlov and Milovan Djilas.

**ECONOMY.** Since the end of World War II industry has surpassed agriculture as the chief source of income. Yugoslavia suffers from a chronic deficit in its balance of payments, and an economic reform plan was introduced in 1965 to open the economy to full-scale competition on the world market. Chief industries are metal manufacturing, textiles, food processing, and production of electrical energy. Since the early 1950s the trend in management has been away from centralism toward greater autonomy for productive units, even though these remain socially owned. Coal, iron, petroleum, bauxite, copper, lead, and zinc are the leading minerals. Nearly 90 per cent of the agricultural land is privately owned, but holdings are limited to 25 acres. All industry with more than five employees is state-owned.

**EDUCATION.** Education is compulsory between the ages of 7 and 15, and literacy is estimated at 80.3 per cent.

**ARMED FORCES.** Men between the ages of 17 and 50 are subject to compulsory service. In 1967 the army numbered 325,000 men, the navy 27,000, and the air force 20,000.

# ZAMBIA

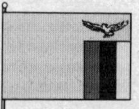

*Official Name:* Republic of Zambia. *Area:* 290,586 square miles. *Population:* 4,000,000. *Principal Cities* (with populations): Lusaka, the capital, 151,418; Kitwe, 146,372; Ndola, 107,320. *Flag:* Green, with a striped swatch of orange, black, and red surmounted by an eagle. *Monetary Unit:* The kwacha of 100 ngwee (worth U.S. $1.40). *Gross National Product:* $850,000,000 (1965). *Average Annual Income per Person:* $175.

**LAND AND PEOPLE.** Zambia, formerly Northern Rhodesia, is a kidney-shaped republic in the heart of Africa surrounded by the Democratic Republic of the Congo, Tanzania, Malawi, Mozambique, Rhodesia, Botswana, South West Africa, and Angola. (See map on page 111.) Most of the country is a plateau of flat, wooded grassland broken by scrub-covered hills and by valleys of the Zambezi and Luangwa rivers. The climate varies; Lusaka, for instance, has temperatures ranging from 39° to 100° F. and about 30 inches of rain annually.

About 98 per cent of the population are Africans who belong to various Bantu-speaking tribes. Europeans number about 79,000. Tribal religions are practiced by 40 per cent of the people. About 45 per cent are Christians.

**HISTORY.** Remains of Stone Age men have been found along Zambia's central plateau, and sophisticated works of iron have been traced to the time of Christ. Around the 15th century immigrants moved into the area from the Congo basin to the north. In the early 19th century Nguni-speaking Africans and Swahili-speaking traders arrived. Commerce in copper and slaves thrived during this period.

Near the end of the 19th century the British South Africa Company, developing the copper resources, occupied and governed the territory. In 1924 it became a British protectorate.

With the rise of African nationalism after World War II, European settlers induced Britain to found the Federation of Rhodesia and Nyasaland, transferring control of the area to settler-dominated Southern Rhodesia. Bitter African opposition ensued, and nearly all the important African leaders were jailed for political activities in 1959–60. The Federation was dissolved at the end of 1963, and Northern Rhodesia proceeded toward independence under African majority rule. Zambia, as the new state was named, became independent as a republic within the Commonwealth on October 24, 1964.

**GOVERNMENT AND POLITICS.** The 1964 constitution provides for a president to be elected by universal adult suffrage at the same time as members of the National Assembly, who must declare their support of a presidential candidate in advance of the election. The National Assembly consists of 75 popularly elected members and up to 5 special members nominated by the president. The only significant political party is the United National Independence Party, headed by Kenneth Kaunda, Zambia's first president. In August, 1967, the National Independence Party nominated him for re-election to a second term. Since there was no opposition, his re-election was assured.

**ECONOMY.** Nearly half of Zambia's wealth derives from mining and refining industries. Copper operations are second largest in the world, after the United States. All the mines are controlled either by the South African-based Anglo-American Corporation or the Roan Selection Trust, a Zambian company that draws financial backing from U.S. and British firms. Zinc, lead, cobalt, vanadium, coal, iron, and amethysts are also mined in significant quantities. Agriculture contributes only nine per cent of the gross national product.

Railways connect Zambia with Rhodesia, Angola, Mozambique, South Africa, and the Congo. Since Britain applied economic sanctions against Rhodesia in late 1965, Zambia has opened roads eastward to the cities of Dar es Salaam and Beira on the Indian Ocean. In May, 1967, President Kaunda reported that Zambia had cut its imports from Rhodesia by 75 per cent since Rhodesia declared its independence from the Commonwealth.

**EDUCATION AND HEALTH.** There is no compulsory education, although much of the population receives some primary schooling. The literacy rate is 28 per cent. The University of Zambia opened in 1966.

Malaria and tuberculosis are major health problems. Health services for Africans are available at clinics.

**ARMED FORCES.** Zambia has a 3,000-man army, an air force contingent of 200, and 600 reservists. Military service is voluntary.

# CITIES OF THE WORLD

## ACCRA

The capital, largest city, and main port of Ghana, Accra (population: 491,000) is situated on the Gulf of Guinea. There are many small industries, chiefly brick and tile manufacturing, canning, and lumber milling.

The original village on the site of Accra was the capital of a native kingdom. In 1657 Fort Christianborg, a Danish military post, was constructed, around which Accra grew into a sizable town under successive Danish, Dutch, and British governments. In 1876 the capital of the British Gold Coast colony was moved from Cape Coast to Accra; the city remained the capital after Ghana became independent in 1957. The completion in 1923 of a railroad linking Accra with the mining and agricultural interior spurred the city's commercial growth. Destroyed by fire in 1894 and badly damaged by an earthquake in 1939, it was rebuilt both times. In February 1966 Accra was the scene of a coup d'etat that ousted President Kwame Nkrumah. A huge statue of Nkrumah, one of the city's landmarks, was subsequently toppled by mobs.

Today Accra is a metropolis in which modern buildings tower over ancient slums. There is an international airport. The University of Ghana is on a hill that overlooks the city.

## ALGIERS

The capital and largest city of Algeria, Algiers (population: 883,879) is situated on the Mediterranean Sea. One of the principal ports of North Africa, the city exports wine, citrus fruits, and iron ore. There are chemical and metallurgical industries.

Algiers was founded by Phoenicians at an unknown but early date. In the second century B.C., it was taken by the Romans. Sacked by the Vandals in the fifth century A.D., Algiers remained uninhabited until rebuilt by Berbers in the tenth century. It fell into Spanish hands in 1511, but seven years later was captured by the pirate Khair ad-Din (Barbarossa), who placed it under Turkish control. For the next 300 years Algiers was the base of Muslim pirates who preyed on European and American shipping in the Mediterranean. In 1815, however, an American naval squadron under Stephen Decatur forced the dey of Algiers to give up his demands for tribute from American shipping.

In 1830 Algiers fell to the French, who built a modern port and brought prosperity to the city. During World War II the city was under the control of the Vichy government until Allied liberation in 1943. In 1958 Algiers was the focal point of a rebellion that caused the collapse of the Fourth Republic and restored Charles de Gaulle as President of France. Revolts in 1959 and 1962, led by French generals, failed to overthrow the de Gaulle government, but throughout 1960 and 1961 Algiers served as headquarters of a rightwing terrorist group, the French Secret Army Organization, which refused to reconcile itself to Algerian independence. There were frequent bombings and assassinations. Algiers nevertheless took its place as the capital of the newly independent republic, a role that it is slated to surrender on completion of a new capital at Rocher Noir.

Life in this ancient North African city is a mixture of Muslim and European elements. The Casbah, a 16th-century fortress, lends its name to the nearby Muslim quarter. Surrounding the former Place de Gouvernement is the historic European section. The southern quarter encloses the government buildings, museums, and shopping district. The Great Mosque, begun in the 11th century, and the National Library are of special interest.

## AMSTERDAM

The constitutional capital and largest city of the Netherlands, Amsterdam (population 869,173) is situated at the juncture of the Amstel and Ij rivers, near the Zuider Zee. It is a major port connected to the North Sea by the Noordzee Kanaal, and one of the world's principal diamond-cutting centers. The city is also an intellectual and artistic capital of Europe.

Founded in the 13th century, Amsterdam prospered as a trade center. In 1578 the city, which had accepted the Protestant Reformation, expelled its Spanish Catholic overlords and joined the insurgent Netherlands provinces. After the ruin of Antwerp and Ghent by the Spanish, an influx of skilled Flemish, Jewish, and French Huguenot refugees came to Amsterdam. The 17th century was Amsterdam's golden age. The city was then the home of the painters Meindert Hobbema and Rembrandt, the philosopher Spinoza, and other leading scholars and intellectuals. In 1609 Henry Hudson sailed for the New World from Amsterdam.

Amsterdam became the capital of the Kingdom of the Netherlands, under Louis Bonaparte, after the French seized it in 1795. It continued as the Dutch capital under the Constitution of 1814, but the seat of government has remained in The Hague. Dutch monarchs are crowned in Amsterdam but rule from The Hague. The city was captured and occupied by the Germans from 1940 to 1945.

Amsterdam is built mostly below sea level, with dikes and retaining walls, a huge network of canals, and countless bridges. Among its cultural treasures are the Rijksmuseum, housing over 3,000 paintings of Dutch, Flemish, and other masters; the Municipal Museum, famous for its Van Gogh collection; the Concertgebouw Orchestra; and the University of Amsterdam, founded in 1632. The Oude Kerk (old church) dates from 1306, and the Nieuwe Kerk (new church) from the 15th to the 17th century. The Dam Palace, built in the 1600s as a city hall, became the royal palace in 1808.

# ATHENS

The capital and largest city of Greece, Athens (population: 627,564) is situated on the Plain of Attica between the Cephissus and Ilissus rivers. Piraeus, a few miles to the southwest on the Saronic Gulf, is Athens' seaport. Most of the nation's industry is centered around Athens; principal manufactures include textiles, machine tools, armaments, steel products, and ships. Aghia Paraskevi, northeast of the city, has facilities for nuclear research.

For a brief period in the fifth century B.C., Athens was the scene of a brilliant flowering of the human spirit that vastly influenced the course of history.

Named for the goddess Athena, the city was probably founded in the second millenium B.C. In the sixth century B.C. the code of laws of Solon was promulgated and, under Cleisthenes, a democracy—the first—was established for the freemen of Athens. Commerce began to grow, but it was not until the Persian Wars (500–449 B.C.) that Athens assumed dominance over most other Greek city-states.

In 445 Pericles arranged a truce between Athens and Sparta and, under his leadership, Athens entered its golden age. Socrates, Aeschylus, Aristophanes, Euripides, and Sophocles lived and wrote here, and Athenian craftsmen built splendid monuments. In 431 B.C., the truce between Athens and Sparta was broken, and the Peloponnesian Wars began. Sparta could not match Athens in the sphere of philosophy and the arts, but it had superior soldiers and decisively defeated its rival by 404 B.C. During the following century Athens was the home of Plato and Aristotle. The Athenians threw off the Spartan yoke early in the fourth century B.C., but, in 338, succumbed to Philip, King of Macedon. In the second century B.C. the city became a minor ally of Rome.

In 395 A.D. Athens was taken by the Visigoths, but for some time it retained the status of a Byzantine provincial capital. In 1458 the Acropolis fell to Ottoman troops. The city subsequently endured nearly four centuries of Turkish rule. Venetians held Athens briefly in 1466. When they again besieged it in 1687–88, the Parthenon, used as a powder store by the Turks, was largely destroyed in a Venetian bombardment.

The history of modern Athens began in 1834 when it was proclaimed the capital of the new Greek kingdom. Otto I, the first King of the Hellenes, rebuilt much of the city. After the fall of the Ottoman Empire (1920), Athens began a period of rapid growth, its population swelled by Greek refugees from Turkey. Athenian citizens suffered great hardships under German occupation (1941–44).

Many monuments of the past are still standing. The Parthenon, on the 260-foot-high Acropolis, was built between 447 and 432 B.C. Sacred to Athena, it contained a huge statue of the goddess, made of gold and ivory. Portions of the marble frieze of the Parthenon (called the Elgin Marbles) are now in the British Museum. At the west end of the Acropolis is the monumental Propylaea. Another temple on the Acropolis, the Erectheum, was a tribute to the deities Athena Polias, Poseidon, and Erectheus. To the northwest is the Areopagus, a hill where St. Paul once preached.

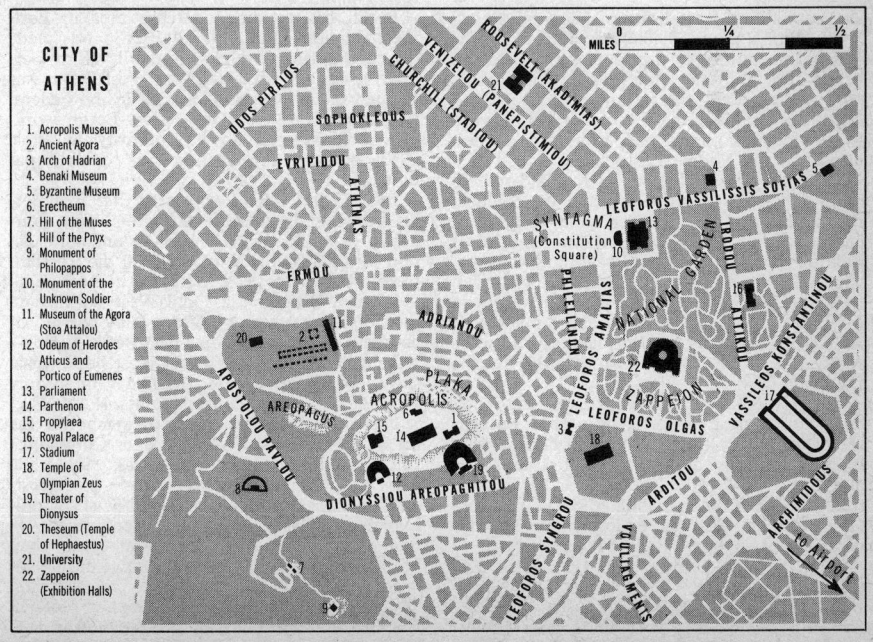

CITY OF ATHENS

1. Acropolis Museum
2. Ancient Agora
3. Arch of Hadrian
4. Benaki Museum
5. Byzantine Museum
6. Erectheum
7. Hill of the Muses
8. Hill of the Pnyx
9. Monument of Philopappos
10. Monument of the Unknown Soldier
11. Museum of the Agora (Stoa Attalou)
12. Odeon of Herodes Atticus and Portico of Eumenes
13. Parliament
14. Parthenon
15. Propylaea
16. Royal Palace
17. Stadium
18. Temple of Olympian Zeus
19. Theater of Dionysus
20. Theseum (Temple of Hephaestus)
21. University
22. Zappeion (Exhibition Halls)

# BANGKOK

The capital, largest city, and principal port of Thailand, Bangkok (population: 1,669,246) is situated on the Chao Phraya River, 15 miles from the Gulf of Siam. It is the commercial, cultural, and communications center of the country, with industries that include oil refining, textiles, and cement. A large export trade is conducted in rice, teak, and rubber.

Not an ancient city by Asian standards, Bangkok was established at the site of a Siamese fort sometime before 1767. It became the capital of the kingdom in 1782. Today it also serves as headquarters of the Southeast Asia Treaty Organization and of the U.N.'s Economic Commission for Asia. Bangkok was modernized in the late 19th century by the construction of wide boulevards and many European-style buildings, but it remains largely a city of criss-crossing canals (the "Venice of the East") teeming with sampans and lined with rickety houses that crowd the water's edge. It is also famous for the glittering pagodas of nearly 400 Buddhist monasteries.

Points of interest include the 18th-century Grand Palace (actually the remains of the old walled town), within which lies the Wat Phra Keo, or Temple of the Emerald Buddha; the Wat Po, Bangkok's largest temple; the Ananta Samakom Palace, in Renaissance style (now the seat of the National Assembly); and Chulalongkorn University. Bangkok's large Chinese colony (about half of the population) is quartered in the southern part of the city.

# BEIRUT

The capital and largest city of Lebanon, Beirut (population: about 500,000) is situated on the Mediterranean Sea at the foot of the Lebanon Mountains. It is the chief seaport and transportation center in the Levant. Due to its strategic location along the route of travel between Europe and southern Asia, it has the busiest airport in the Middle East.

Founded by Phoenicians in the 2nd millennium B.C., Beirut flourished under the Seleucid rulers of Syria and reached great heights of commercial prosperity under Roman control. It eventually passed to the Byzantines, but declined after a severe earthquake in 551. It fell to the Arabs in 635 and to the Crusaders in 1110 (forming a part of the Latin Kingdom of Jerusalem until 1291). It was later ruled by the Mamelukes of Egypt and, from 1517, by the Ottoman Turks.

Beirut was taken by the forces of the rebellious Mohammed Ali of Egypt in 1831, but was restored to the Ottomans in 1840 and held by them until occupied by British and Arab troops at the end of World War I. In 1920 it became the capital of French-mandated Syria and Lebanon, and in 1941 was made capital of an independent Lebanon by the Free French.

The American University of Beirut, founded in 1866, is one of the largest universities in the Middle East. The National Museum features archeological finds dating back 5,000 years.

# BERLIN

Berlin, situated in East Germany on the Spree and Havel rivers, is divided into West Berlin (population: 2,201,835), the de jure capital of the Federal Republic of Germany (although it remains under the occupational authority of the Western Allies), and East Berlin (population: 1,071,462), the capital of the German Democratic Republic. West Berlin, the largest industrial city in Germany, manufactures electrical goods, food products, chemicals, clothing, and machinery.

Two small Germanic villages, Berlin and Kölln, founded in the 12th century, merged in 1307 as Berlin. The city prospered as a trading center and became the seat of the Electors of Brandenburg in 1486. Heavily damaged during the Thirty Years' War (1618–48), Berlin was rebuilt by Frederick William and in 1701 became the capital of the Kingdom of Prussia. As the capital of the German Empire, established in 1871, Berlin developed into one of the world's greatest cities.

During World War II Berlin was damaged extensively by Allied aerial bombing and by concentrated Soviet artillery attack; the city was captured by Marshal Georgi Zhukov on May 2, 1945. Six days later, Germany's unconditional surrender was signed there.

At the end of the war, Berlin, though under joint Allied occupation, was within Soviet-controlled territory. In 1948–49, Soviet authorities closed all of its land access routes through East Germany. During the resulting "Berlin airlift," U.S. and British planes successfully supplied the city with food and other essentials for 11 months.

Berlin has remained a tense area in East-West relations. In 1949 East Berlin was made the capital of the People's Republic (East Germany), and the following year West Berlin was granted the privileges of a state in the Federal Republic (West Germany). East Berlin workers rioted against Soviet authority in June, 1953, but the insurrection was quickly put down by Russian tanks.

In 1955 the U.S.S.R. declared that East Berlin was East German territory and that four-power occupation had ended—a unilateral action rejected by the West. In 1960 the Russians transferred to the East Germans control of all movement between East and West Berlin, and the following year a 12-foot-high barrier of concrete and barbed wire—the "Berlin Wall"—was erected between East and West Berlin; passage between the two sectors is permitted only at 12 heavily guarded checkpoints.

Postwar Berlin has come to symbolize the difference between Western and Communist rule. East Berlin is a drab, joyless city, while West Berlin, aided by heavy infusions of Western funds, has become a prosperous cosmopolitan center. West Berlin has been largely rebuilt since 1945, although the bombed-out shell of the Kaiser Wilhelm Memorial Church has been left as a reminder of war's devastation. The city's best-known monument, Frederick II's Brandenburg Gate, is in East Berlin.

## BOMBAY

The second largest city in India, Bombay (population: 4,653,700) is situated on a consolidated group of seven islets (including Salsette and Bombay) in the Arabian Sea, off the coast of west-central India. The city overlooks a fine, 14-mile-long harbor and is one of the world's great ports, with excellent shipyards. A center of commerce, it serves as the terminus of two of India's railroads. Its industries include textiles, metal manufacturing, and ceramics.

Bombay was already an ancient city when ceded to Portugal in 1534 by the Sultan of Gujarat. In 1661 it came under English rule as part of the dowry of Catherine of Braganza, consort of Charles II, and in 1669 it was leased to the British East India Company. During the 19th century it became one of the world's leading centers of spinning and weaving.

Modern Bombay is a city of great contrasts. Attractive residential sections, such as Malabar Hill, exist side-by-side with some of the most crowded and unhealthy slums in the world. There are many temples in the southern part of the city. Under British rule a number of Indo-Victorian Gothic buildings were constructed, including the post office, the Senate house, Victoria railroad terminus, the clock tower, and the Crawford Market. The 1960s have seen the addition of several commercial and residential skyscrapers.

The University of Bombay has 22 colleges of arts and sciences, and a student body of more than 30,000.

## BRUSSELS

The capital and largest city of Belgium, Brussels (population: 1,100,000) is situated on the Senne River. Especially famed for its lace, the city also manufactures pharmaceuticals, electronic equipment, and machine tools.

In the 10th century Brussels became a major trade center on the route from Bruges and Ghent to Cologne. An important wool industry was established in the 13th century. With the unification of the Low Countries in the 1400s, Brussels was made the capital of Brabant.

After the religious wars of the 16th century, the city remained the capital of the Spanish Netherlands, which later became Belgium. In 1815 it served as headquarters of the Duke of Wellington during his final campaign against Napoleon, which culminated in the battle at the nearby village of Waterloo. From 1815 to 1830 the United Netherlands Parliament sat alternately in The Hague and Brussels, but Brussels was becoming a center of agitation for separation from the north. In 1830 it became the capital of independent Belgium. Brussels was occupied by the Germans in both World Wars.

A city of broad, tree-lined esplanades and well-tended parks, Brussels is a mixture of the old and the new. The Gothic Hotel de Ville (rebuilt according to 15th-century plans) and the Maison du Roi (a 19th-century replacement for the 13th-century Broodhuis) are outstanding structures. The collegiate Church of St. Michael and St. Gudule was completed in the 17th century. Brussels has several academies, museums, and art galleries. The University of Brussels, founded in 1834, includes several schools that were transferred from the University of Louvain. Brussels is the administrative center of the European Common Market.

## BUENOS AIRES

The capital of Argentina, Buenos Aires (population: 3,876,000) is situated on the Rio de la Plata. It is the commercial and industrial center of Argentina.

Buenos Aires was founded in 1536 by the Spanish explorer Pedro de Mendoza, but Indians forced the settlers to flee to Asunción in 1541. A second settlement was made in 1580, and the city prospered through lucrative trading, most of it in contraband goods. Buenos Aires was made a seat of provincial government when the Province of Buenos Aires was separated from the administration of Asunción in 1617. In 1776 it became the capital of the vice-royalty of Río de la Plata.

The British captured Buenos Aires in 1806. It was retaken by the Spanish shortly afterwards, but its citizens soon rebelled against Spanish rule, and in May, 1810, a junta seized power. In 1862 Buenos Aires was made the national capital, and in 1880 it was detached from the Province of Buenos Aires and made a federal district. The city grew enormously during the 19th century, attracting immigrants from all parts of the world.

Buenos Aires is a beautiful, cosmopolitan city of parks, gardens, and modern skyscrapers. There are broad, spacious streets, such as the Avenida de Mayo. José de San Martín, a leader of the Argentine Revolution, is buried in the cathedral (completed in 1804).

## CAIRO

The capital of Egypt and largest city in Africa, Cairo (population: 3,518,200) is situated at the head of the Nile River delta. There are steel mills and iron foundries, cement works, and a motion picture industry. Its bazaars and markets offer gold and silver work, tapestries, and leather products.

Cairo was founded in 969 A.D., long after the age of the Pharaohs and of Roman Egypt, by the general Jauhar of the Fatimite dynasty.

The city was unsuccessfully attacked by Crusaders in the 12th century; a citadel erected by Saladin (about 1179) still stands. Under the rule of the Mamelukes the city flourished from the 13th century to the early 16th century, but its prestige and economy declined after it fell under Ottoman rule in 1517, and it came to be completely overshadowed by Alexandria. After its occupation by Napoleon (1798–1801), Cairo began to revive.

The city was under British rule from 1882 until 1936, when Egypt attained full independence. When Syria and Egypt formed the United Arab Republic (1958), the city became its headquarters. In June, 1967, the airfields outside Cairo were bombed by Israel during the brief Arab-Israeli war.

Cairo's older section is Arabic in character, boasting many mosques and over 500 palaces. Notable mosques are those of Amus (643), Ibn Tulun (ninth century), Hassan (1356), and Kait Bey (15th century). The Mosque of El Azhar (970) and surrounding structures constitute the world's leading center of Koranic studies. Important museums include the Museum of Egyptian Antiquities and the Coptic Museum.

Downtown Cairo is modern, with new buildings and wide streets. On Gezira Island in the Nile is the 19th century palace of Khedive Ismail Pasha. Across the Nile, at Giza, are the Pyramids and the Sphinx.

## CARACAS

The capital and largest city of Venezuela, Caracas (population: 1,551,303) is situated in northern Venezuela, in a mountain valley near the Caribbean Sea.

Founded as Santiago de León de Caracas in 1567 by Spanish explorer Diego de Losada, Caracas, by its strategic location, became the key to the control of Venezuela. Independence from Spain was declared here in 1811, but the insurgents were thwarted by a severe earthquake on March 26, 1812. Bolivar took the city from the Spanish in 1813 but was driven out in 1814. Seven years later, he entered Caracas again in triumph.

The city's explosive growth in the 20th century was triggered by the discovery of Venezuela's oil deposits. Along with prosperity came an almost complete reconstruction of Caracas. Schools, aqueducts, residences, highways, gigantic shopping centers, and factories were built, and slums were torn down. Especially stunning is the futuristic University City. The old town, with its colonial architecture, was

Renaissance buildings of Copenhagen's "inner city"

*Danish Nat'l, Travel Assoc.*

planned by the Spanish; most of the government buildings are in this part of the city.

## COLOMBO

The capital, largest city, and principal port of Ceylon, Colombo (population: 510,947) is situated on the southwestern coast of Ceylon on the Indian Ocean. Exports include rubber, coconut fiber, copra, and tea.

Colombo was a relatively unimportant town until the opening of trade with Europe in the 16th century. The Portuguese constructed a fort here in 1565 and subsequently made the city their headquarters. Colombo later served as the base of Dutch administration and (after 1798) of British rule. When Ceylon was granted independence in 1948, Colombo became its capital.

Today Colombo is a modern city. Its recent expansion has left few traces of the early Portuguese and Dutch settlements.

## COPENHAGEN

The capital and largest city of Denmark, Copenhagen (population: 694,479) is situated on the eastern coast of the island of Zealand and the northern end of Amager Island. It is strategically located on the Oresund (Sound), opposite the coast of Sweden, and has been called the "Gateway to the Baltic." Copenhagen is Denmark's most important commercial center; its port handles over half of the country's trade. Major industries include shipbuilding, machinery, iron foundries, breweries, and chemical works. Royal Copenhagen porcelain is also made here.

Copenhagen was first known as a fishing village (Havn), but by the 11th century it had become an important trade center. After two disastrous military defeats by a coalition of its trade rivals (the cities of the Hanseatic League), it withstood a final assault in 1428, and in 1443 became the capital of Denmark. The 1500s were marked by religious and civil wars, and in 1658–59 the city was besieged by Sweden. In 1801 the British—who feared a Danish alliance with Napoleon—partially destroyed the Danish fleet in Copenhagen Harbor and later bombarded the city itself, with devastating effect. During World War II Copenhagen was occupied by the Germans (1940–45) but escaped damage except to its shipyards.

Copenhagen is a city of parks and boasts many impressive landmarks. Among them are Amalienborg Square, surrounded by four 18th-century palaces, including the residence of the royal family (since 1794); the 17th-century Round Tower; the restored 18th-century Christiansborg Palace, now housing the Danish Parliament; Rosenborg Palace, containing the crown jewels; and the Tivoli, a world-renowned recreation park. Overlooking Langelinie Harbour is the famous statue of *The Little Mermaid* that was inspired by the Hans Christian Andersen fairy tale. Most of the city's wider avenues radiate from Kongens Nytorv, a square dominated by the Charlottenborg castle.

## DJAKARTA

The capital, largest city, and chief seaport of Indonesia, Djakarta (population: 2,906,500) is located in northwest Java at the mouth of the Chiliwung River. It is an important industrial and commercial center, with a large export trade in tea, coffee, rubber, quinine, and minerals. Factories produce textiles, leather goods, chemicals, and iron.

After the Dutch established a fort adjacent to the old Javanese settlement of Djakarta in 1619, the town assumed the name Batavia. It became the main center of trade in the Dutch East Indies during the 1600s, but declined in importance after suffering several native uprisings in the next century. The introduction of plantation cultivation in the 19th century brought the city to a new peak of prosperity. Batavia was occupied by the British in 1811–16 and, during World War II, by the Japanese (1942–45). After Indonesia gained its independence in 1949, the city, under its ancient name, became capital of the Republic.

The old town, built along both sides of the Chiliwung on low swampy ground, contains Chinese and Arabic quarters and several 17th century gates. The modern town, to the south, has important government buildings, the University of Indonesia, and an archeological museum.

## DUBLIN

The capital and largest city of the Irish Republic, Dublin (population: 647,336) is situated on Dublin Bay at the mouth of the River Liffey. It has brewing, distilling, food-processing, and textile industries and is an important trade center.

Dublin was a Norse town from about 840 until 1014, when an Irish force led by Brian Boru captured it. The Danes soon re-established themselves, but were in turn expelled by Richard Strongbow, earl of Pembroke, in 1170. Two years later, Henry II made Dublin the seat of English government in Ireland. Thereafter, Dublin was the chief center of Irish resistance to British rule. In 1209, the population rose and massacred the English inhabitants. In 1647, during the English Civil War, the city surrendered to the Parliamentary forces. Later, in 1689, Dublin was taken from James II by William of Orange. Dublin enjoyed its greatest prosperity during the 1700s but declined after the Act of Union (1800) put an end to the temporarily independent Irish Parliament (1782–1800).

Nationalist insurrections and terrorist activity marked the 19th century. In the early 1900s city life was disrupted by a paralyzing general strike (1913), the unsuccessful Easter Rebellion (1916), the "Black and Tan Wars" against Britain (1919–22), and the civil disturbances that followed the establishment of the Irish Free State in 1922.

Dublin today is a placid city, somewhat somber in appearance, but with many fine Georgian residences and some outstanding public buildings of the 18th century; these include Leinster House, now occupied by the Dail (Parliament), the Bank of Ireland, the Customs House, the Four Courts, and Trinity College (founded in 1591 and containing in its library the celebrated Book of Kells). Dublin Castle, dating back to 1220, was the residence of the lord lieutenants of Ireland during the English administration. Christ's Church and St. Patrick's (where Jonathan Swift served as dean, 1713–45) both date from the 12th century. The National Museum contains an important collection of Irish antiquities.

Modern Dublin has a special place in the history of the arts, having produced the famous Abbey Theater (opened in 1904) and such literary giants as W. B. Yeats and James Joyce.

## GENEVA

The second largest city in Switzerland, Geneva (population: 175,500) stands at the southwest tip of Lake Geneva, at the point at which the Rhone River leaves the lake. It is a banking, administrative, and educational center. Manufactures include watches, jewelry, clothing, metalware, and precision instruments.

Geneva came successively under the rule of Roman Gaul, the Kingdom of the Franks, and Transjurane Burgundy before being incorporated into the Holy Roman Empire in the 11th century. The bishops of Geneva gradually acquired temporal authority over the city, although their rule was later contested by the Dukes of Savoy. Spurred by this competition, the citizenry succeeded in gaining considerable autonomy by 1530. Inspired by the teachings of Guillaume Farel, the city adopted the Reformed faith as the established religion in 1536 and set itself up as an independent republic. Under the theocratic leadership of John Calvin, 16th-century Geneva was a refuge for persecuted Huguenots and became the most powerful Protestant center on the continent. In the 18th century the city was the home of Jean-Jacques Rousseau, Voltaire, and Albert Gallatin.

Annexed by France from 1798 to 1814, Geneva joined the Helvetic Confederation in 1815. In 1864 the International Red Cross established its headquarters here, and in 1920 the city became the seat of the League of Nations. Today Geneva is the permanent home of the U.N.'s International Labor Organization and World Health Organization. The city has been the scene of several high-level international conferences since World War II.

Geneva has many beautiful gardens and promenades along the lakefront. Points of interest in the city include the League of Nations (now United Nations) Palace, the Cathedral of Saint Pierre (12th–13th centuries), the 16th-century town hall, the 18th-century Palace of Justice, and the University of Geneva, founded by Calvin in 1559. In the southeastern part of the city is the celebrated Reformation Monument, with its larger-than-life-sized representations of Calvin, Knox, Guillaume Farel, Theodore Beda, and other Reformation leaders.

## ISTANBUL

The largest city in Turkey, Istanbul, formerly Constantinople (population: 1,750,642), is situated on both the European and Asiatic sides of the Bosporus at its entrance into the Sea of Marmara. Istanbul is the religious, commercial, financial, and transportation hub of Turkey.

Constantinople was founded in 330 A.D. by Roman Emperor Constantine I on the site of ancient Byzantium. It became the largest and most magnificent city of medieval Europe. In 1204 it was taken by Crusaders, who established the short-lived Latin Empire of Constantinople. In 1261 Byzantine Emperor Michael VIII recaptured the city from Baldwin II.

When Sultan Mohammed II took Constantinople in 1453, hundreds of scholars fled to Western Europe, infusing European intellectual life with a new vigor. Meanwhile, Constantinople became the seat of the Ottoman Empire.

An earthquake destroyed Constantinople in 1509. It was rebuilt by Sultan Bajazet II, and in the following years Turkish culture reached its zenith in the metropolis. The Turks built the city that exists today. The Allies occupied Constantinople from 1918 to 1923. In 1922 Sultan Mohammed VI, the last Ottoman ruler, was deposed; the following year the Turkish capital was moved to Ankara. Constantinople was officially renamed Istanbul in 1930.

Istanbul's best-known edifice is the Basilica of Hagia Sophia, the most sublime surviving example of Byzantine architecture. Other treasures include the mosques of Bajazet II, Suleiman I, and Ahmed I, all dating from the 16th and 17th centuries. The Seraglio, formerly the sultan's palace, is now a museum.

## JERUSALEM

An ancient city in Palestine, Jerusalem (population: 297,000) is comprised of the "New City," which is the capital of Israel, and the "Old City," which was, until the time of the Arab-Israeli war of June 1967, under the rule of the Hashemite Kingdom of Jordan.

From the time of the city's capture from the Jebusites by King David (about 1000 B.C.) to its consolidation in 1967 by Israel, Jerusalem has been repeatedly conquered, leveled, and rebuilt; it has been administered by Greeks, Romans, Egyptians, 11th-century Crusaders, and Ottoman Turks. From World War I until the creation of Israel in 1948, the city was under British jurisdiction.

The Old City contains most of the shrines venerated by Christians, Jews, and Muslims. Both Israel and Jordan have been careful to preserve the city's holy places. Among the most sacred are the Christian Church of the Holy Sepulchre; the Jewish Wailing Wall (the last remnant of the temple begun by Herod the Great); and the Mohammedan Dome of the Rock, known as the Mosque of Omar. Among the chief historical landmarks in the New City is the 14th century Citadel, the Palestine Archaeological Museum, the Hebrew University, and the Israeli Knesset (Parliament).

The political status of Jerusalem was being debated late in 1967. The Arab world was insisting that the city be returned to its former, partitioned condition; Israel was adamant that it remain undivided. The placing of the city under international administration was proposed in the United Nations as a possible alternative.

## JOHANNESBURG

The largest city in the Republic of South Africa, Johannesburg (population: 595,083) is situated in the southern Transvaal on the southern slopes of the Witwatersrand. One of the world's principal gold centers, the city is the industrial and transportation hub of South Africa.

Johannesburg was founded as a mining settlement in 1886 after gold was discovered in the Witwatersrand. By 1900 its population had swelled to about 10,000; its industrial growth has been steady ever since. Construction in the city has carefully followed a gridwork street plan. Major streets and avenues are shaded with large trees. Joubert Park has a fine zoo, and there are museums and observatories. The University of the Witwatersrand was founded in 1921.

Since 1956 Johannesburg has been beset by racial problems. The government policy of apartheid (separation of the races) has been particularly disruptive in Johannesburg, owing to the large number of workers from the hinterlands attracted by its industries. The city still has a sizable Bantu (Negro) population, despite increasingly stringent laws restricting their freedom.

## KINSHASA

The capital of the Democratic Republic of the Congo, Kinshasa, formerly Léopoldville (population: 402,492), is situated on Stanley Pool of the Congo River, across from Brazzaville. The nation's largest city, Kinshasa is the hub of transportation on the Congo River between the ocean and Kisangani in the interior. It is the terminus of a railroad from Matadi, and its airport is a major link with the rest of Africa and leading European cities.

Kinshasa was founded in 1887 by Henry M. Stanley, the English explorer and adventurer, and named for King Léopold II of Belgium. It succeeded Boma in 1926 as the capital of the Belgian Congo, and in 1960 became capital of the new republic. Since the Congo's independence it has been a victim of political unrest and economic insecurity. Its modern international airport has often witnessed the departure of streams of refugees to Europe and the arrival of foreign troops.

The newer section of Kinshasa, extending ten miles upriver, has sparkling new buildings surrounded by lush tropical vegetation. The older quarter, in the south, is being rebuilt as rapidly as present conditions will allow. Lovanium University, founded in 1954, and numerous technical and mission schools are here. There is a research center for tropical medicine and a good museum of Africana.

Pan American Airways

A tower of the Houses of Parliament, with its large clock and the famous bell, "Big Ben," stands majestically at the end of a London street.

## LONDON

The capital of the United Kingdom, chief city of the British Commonwealth, and one of the major cities of the world, London (population: 7,948,800) is situated in southern England on the Thames River. Greater London includes portions of the counties of Essex, Kent, Hertfordshire, Middlesex, and Surrey. The oldest section, called "the City," is a one-square-mile area on the north side of the Thames that still serves as the commercial core of London.

The origins of London are unknown, but it predates the arrival of the Romans, who occupied it in 43 A.D. It was sacked and burned by local tribes in 61 and, in the 2nd century, was fortified by the Romans, who surrounded the city with a wall, traces of which can still be seen. In 866, King Alfred refortified London to protect it against the Danes.

In 1066, after the Battle of Hastings, in which William the Conqueror won England, the Saxon inhabitants of London declared themselves independent and forced William to negotiate a settlement with them. London prospered under the rule of Norman and Plantagenet kings. By the time of Elizabeth I, it had come to dominate English commercial life. When the Stuarts acceded to the throne in 1603, a struggle began between the Crown and London, eager to defend its privileges. This eventually expanded into the Puritan Revolution and the English civil wars.

Some 90,000 lives were lost during the Great Plague of 1665 and, in the following year, the Great Fire, which raged for five days, nearly leveled the city. The architectural designs of Sir Christopher Wren played an important part in London's reconstruction.

German aerial attacks during the Battle of Britain in 1940–41 and rockets fired at the city in 1944–45 caused great damage. After the war London was rebuilt, and many ancient monuments were restored. An extensive program of urban renewal is now under way.

Among the outstanding edifices is Buckingham Palace, built in 1703 and the residence of British monarchs since Queen Victoria's ascension in 1837. The Houses of Parliament, formerly a royal palace, were rebuilt (1840–60) after a disastrous fire. The House of Commons was destroyed by German bombs in 1941 and has since been rebuilt. St. Paul's Cathedral, begun in 1675 and completed in 1710, is Wren's greatest monument. Its great dome is one of the most famous landmarks of London.

The Tower of London, begun by William the Conqueror in 1078, was the scene of many executions, including those of Anne Boleyn and Catherine Howard, two of Henry VIII's wives. The Crown jewels are kept here.

Westminster Abbey, probably the most historic spot in England, was built beginning in 1050 on the site of a seventh-century church. In 1245 a long period of reconstruction began. Since William the Conqueror, nearly every English monarch has been crowned in Westminster Abbey, and many of England's famous men are buried there. Westminster Hall, adjoining the Houses of Parliament, was built in 1097. London Bridge (the third structure of that name) is to be replaced by a new span.

Among the museums are the British Museum, established in 1753; the Victoria and Albert Museum, opened in 1852; and the National Gallery, built in 1828.

The names of many of London's streets have become synonymous with the activities carried on there. Bond Street is a shopping center. Fleet Street is the center of English journalism. Threadneedle Street is the home of the Bank of England. Whitehall is lined with government buildings. Downing Street contains the official residence of the prime minister. And Carnaby Street has become identified with modern fashions.

## MADRID

The capital and largest city of Spain, Madrid (population: 2,558,583), is situated on the Manzanares River on a large plateau in New Castile. It is near the geographical center of the Iberian Peninsula. A Moorish fortress occupied the site as early as the 10th century. The town that grew in the shadow of its walls played only a minor role in Castilian history during the Middle Ages, but in 1561 King Philip II made it his capital. In the 18th century Madrid flourished under the Bourbon kings.

In 1808 French troops occupied the city at the beginning of the Peninsular War between France and an alliance of Spain, Great Britain, and Portugal. On May 2, citizens of Madrid rose up against their French captors and fought a fierce battle in the Puerta del Sol, the central square of the city. That night, in reprisal, French Marshal Joachim Murat ordered hundreds of Madrid citizens summarily executed. This event is commemorated in two paintings by Francisco Goya, both in the Prado museum. During the Spanish Civil War, Republican troops under General José Miaja resisted a 29-month siege by the Falange, finally surrendering in March 1939 after severe air and ground bombardment. It was during this siege that the Falangist commander, General Émilio Mola, sent four columns of troops against Madrid and boasted that the city would soon fall to a "fifth column" of insurgents inside the city. The term "fifth column" has come to be a synonym for subversion.

The streets of modern Madrid radiate from the old quarter, which is still the heart of the city. Numerous parks and gardens add to Madrid's beauty. The most noteworthy of these is Buen Retiro Park, laid out in 1631. The Prado, the national Spanish museum of art and sculpture, is one of the finest in Europe. There is a university, founded in 1508 in Alcalá de Henares and transferred here in 1836. The Ciudad Universitaria is a good example of modern Spanish architecture.

## MANILA

The former capital of the Philippines, Manila (population: 1,356,000) is situated on Manila Bay in the southwestern part of Luzon Island. The capital was transferred to suburban Quezon City in 1948, but Manila remains the republic's leading city and principal port. Manufactures include cigars and cigarettes, rubber products, drugs, rope, shoes, and textiles.

The Spanish explorer Miguel López de Legaspi established a fortified colony at Manila in 1571; over the years this settlement was developed by Spanish missionaries. U.S. troops occupied the city during the Spanish-American War following Commodore George Dewey's victory at Manila Bay on May 1, 1898, but Filipino sentiment for independence remained strong. During World War II the city was occupied by the Japanese from 1942 to 1945; much of it was destroyed by American bombardment prior to General MacArthur's victorious return to the city on February 27, 1945. After the Philippines gained independence in 1946, Manila served as the capital for two years.

One of the few historic monuments left standing at the end of the war was the Church of San Augustín, dating from 1606. Since then, a massive rebuilding program has turned Manila into one of Asia's most modern cities. Among the more notable buildings are the Cathedral (reconstructed in 1958), post office, city hall, legislature, and Malacanan Palace. Institutions of higher learning include Santo Tomás University (1611) and the University of the Philippines.

## MEXICO CITY

The capital and largest city of Mexico, Mexico City (population: 3,192,804) is situated in the central part of the republic at an altitude of 7,440 feet. It is the economic, cultural, and transportation hub of the nation.

The Aztec capital of Tenochtitlán was built in the 14th century on an island in Lake Texcoco (now downtown Mexico City). Captured by Spanish conquistador Hernán Cortés in 1519, the city was razed in 1521 and a new capital was created. Mexico City was taken by General Winfield Scott in 1847 during the Mexican War. In 1864, after its capture by French forces, the city became the capital of an empire ruled by the ill-fated Maximilian. Benito Juárez, at the head of patriot troops, retook the city in 1867. After the Revolution of 1910, Mexico City was occupied in 1914–15 by Generals Pancho Villa and Emiliano Zapata. Extensive damage caused by an earthquake in 1957 has since been repaired.

Notable monuments are the National Palace (1692), housing the presidential offices and the National Museum; the Cathedral (1573–1667), oldest church in North America; the Palace of Fine Arts (1905), with murals by Diego Rivera and José Orozco; and Chapultepec Castle (1783–1840). The National University, founded in 1551, is now housed in the strikingly modernistic University City, opened in 1952. Two important museums were completed in recent years: a museum of art in 1964 and a museum of anthropology in 1965. To the south of Mexico City is Xochimilco, famous for its "floating gardens" rooted in canal beds.

## MONTREAL

The largest city in Canada and the world's greatest inland seaport, Montreal (population: 1,222,255) is in southern Quebec on Montreal Island, at the confluence of the Ottawa and St. Lawrence rivers. Industries include food and drink processing, oil refining, shipbuilding, clothing, and the manufacture of aircraft, rail stock, steel, and electrical equipment.

An Indian village named Hochelaga was here when the French explorer Jacques Cartier first discovered the site in 1535. Samuel de Champlain visited the island in 1611, and French settlement followed in 1642 with the founding of Ville-Marie de Montréal by Paul de Chomeday and his small band of Catholic missionaries. Fortified soon afterwards, the town remained in French hands until 1760, when it surrendered to the British at the close of the French and Indian War. Americans briefly occupied the city in 1775–76. Montreal was the focus of French rebellion against the English in the 1830s and 1840s and for this reason lost its position as capital of United Canada (1844–49). The city experienced its greatest growth after completion of the St. Lawrence Seaway in 1959.

Montreal remains predominantly French in population, customs, and appearance. Many old French colonial buildings are in the vicinity of the Place d'Armes. Historic monuments include the Hôtel-Dieu, founded in 1644 and rebuilt in 1861; the Seminary of St. Sulpice (1685); Notre Dame Church (1656; rebuilt

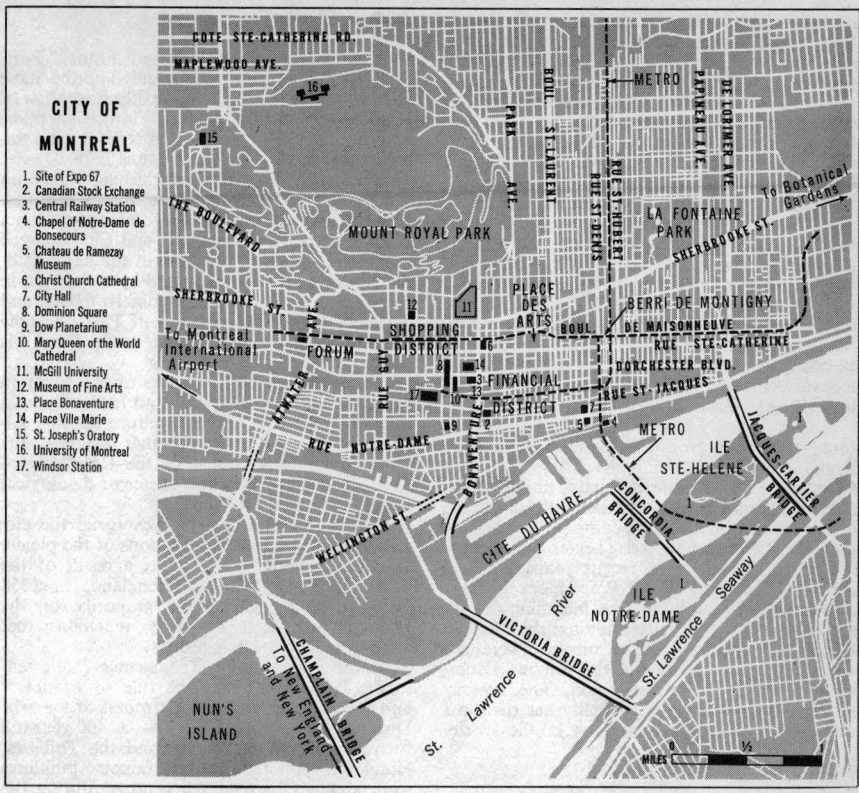

**CITY OF MONTREAL**

1. Site of Expo 67
2. Canadian Stock Exchange
3. Central Railway Station
4. Chapel of Notre-Dame de Bonsecours
5. Chateau de Ramezay Museum
6. Christ Church Cathedral
7. City Hall
8. Dominion Square
9. Dow Planetarium
10. Mary Queen of the World Cathedral
11. McGill University
12. Museum of Fine Arts
13. Place Bonaventure
14. Place Ville Marie
15. St. Joseph's Oratory
16. University of Montreal
17. Windsor Station

1824); and the Château de Ramezay (1705). McGill University and the University of Montreal are located here.

A $2 billion building program, launched in 1962, included an ultra-modern subway system (opened in 1966). In 1967, in celebration of Canada's Centennial of Confederation, Montreal hosted a world's fair—Expo 67. Among its highlights were the U.S. Pavilion, a gigantic geodesic sky-bubble designed by Buckminster Fuller; Habitat 67, a rambling apartment complex containing 158 preassembled units; and West Germany's sprawling steel and plastic-covered tent. (For more information about Expo 67, see page 629.)

## MOSCOW

The capital and largest city of the U.S.S.R., Moscow (population: 6,366,000) is in the central part of the Russian Soviet Federated Socialist Republic, on the Moskva River near its junction with the Moscow Canal. It is the transportation, commercial, and industrial hub of the country. Manufactures include machinery, automobiles, airplanes, chemicals, wood and paper products, textiles, and clothing.

An ancient village, Moscow in the late 13th century became the seat of the grand duchy of Suzdal-Vladimir, later the grand duchy of Moscow. As the grand duchy and the city grew in the 14th and 15th centuries, Moscow gradually took precedence over the other Russian states; the grand duke of Moscow became the ruler of Russia, and the city his capital.

Moscow was ravaged several times in its history, notably by the Tatars in 1381 and 1572. In 1712 the capital of Russia was moved to St. Petersburg, now Leningrad, and remained there until 1918. Moscow was constructed mainly of wood, and had several disastrous fires. The most spectacular was in 1812. Napoleon I in his invasion of Russia entered Moscow on September 14. The next day a great conflagration broke out, raging uncontrolled and nearly destroying the city. Napoleon was forced to evacuate and subsequently lost the greater part of his army on his retreat.

Moscow was rebuilt and in the 1830s became a manufacturing center. Its main growth, however, came after the Bolshevik Revolution: the population doubled between 1926 and 1939. In 1941 Moscow was the target of a German attack; at one point the advancing armies came within 25 miles of the city.

The heart of Moscow is the Kremlin—literally, citadel—built in the 13th century and surrounded by crenelated walls, erected in the 15th century. The walls are topped by 20 towers. Within the Kremlin are numerous churches, such as Uspenski Cathedral, built in the 15th century, and the Blagoveschenski Cathedral, 15th and 16th centuries. In Arkhangelski Cathedral, built between the 14th and 17th centuries, are the tombs of the tsars. The 19th-century Grand Palace (Bolshoi Dvorets) now houses the Supreme Soviet. Adjoining the Kremlin is the new Rossiya (Russia) Hotel.

To the east of the Kremlin is Red Square. Built originally as a market place and a meeting ground for popular assemblies, it is still used for ceremonial purposes. Located here is the gigantic mausoleum of Lenin, whose embalmed body is viewed by thousands each day. South of the Kremlin is the 16th century St. Basil's Cathedral. Each of the cathedral's numerous cupolas, grouped around a central tower, is a different color.

Gorky Street, Moscow's principal thoroughfare, runs north from the Kremlin. It is lined with large modern buildings and stores. Near Gorky Street is Sverdlov Square, one of Moscow's cultural centers, with the Bolshoi (home of the world-famous ballet company) and Maly theaters. The Moscow Art Theater has become renowned, especially in recent years.

Since the end of World War II, several skyscrapers have been built here, including the 32-story Moscow University building, the Moskva Hotel, and the Palace of Culture. There are numerous parks, including the famous Ostankino, Izmailovo, and Sokolniki. The subway system, opened in 1935, probably has the most attractive underground stations in the world.

## NEW DELHI

The capital of India, New Delhi (population 2,369,500, including Delhi) is situated on the right bank of the Jumna River. The city is predominantly an administrative center, but it has some textile mills, printing plants, and factories.

Built between 1912 and 1931, New Delhi replaced the old city of Delhi as the administrative capital of British India in 1931. The largest street is the Raj Path, an east-west thoroughfare leading from the War Memorial Arch to the government house—formerly the British viceroy's palace and now the residence of the Indian president. There are many temples, sports stadiums, and medical institutions. Mahatma Gandhi was assassinated in New Delhi in 1948.

Old Delhi, an ancient city, adjoins New Delhi. It became the capital of the Mogul Empire in 1638. Shah Jehan built high walls around the city, within which he constructed the Red Fort and a palace. The Jama Masjid, or great Mosque, was also built during Jehan's reign. Delhi was plundered by the Persian Nadir Shah in 1739. From 1771 until it was captured by the British in 1803, the city was in the hands of the Hindu Mahrattas. During the Sepoy rebellion of 1857, Delhi was held by the rebels for five months. It was the interim capital of India from 1912 to 1931.

## PARIS

The capital and largest city of France, Paris (population: 2,779,935) is situated on the Seine River. Paris is a city of the world rather than of France alone. For centuries artists, writers, revolutionaries, dreamers, expatriates, and intellectuals have found their home here.

Founded as a small Gallic fishing village on the Île de la Cité in the Seine, it was taken by Julius Caesar in 52 B.C. Several Merovingian kings had their capitals here, and Charlemagne made it a center of learning in the early Middle Ages. Paris was devastated by Norsemen in the ninth century but was quickly rebuilt and fortified. Hugh Capet, count of Paris, became king of France in 987 and made Paris his capital.

The city achieved a measure of prosperity in the 12th and 13th centuries and began to build a reputation as a seat of culture. Under Albertus Magnus and St. Thomas Aquinas, the Sorbonne, now a college of the University of Paris, became the greatest center of theological study in the medieval world.

During the 14th and 15th centuries the city was hard hit by several visitations of the plague and also suffered hardship as a result of the Hundred Years War with England. In 1358 Paris revolted against the authority of the Dauphin—the first of many rebellions that were to mark the city's history.

At the height of the Renaissance (16th century), Paris was under the rule of Francis I and of Marie de Medici, a patroness of the arts. During this era, the Louvre—a 400-year-old fortress-palace—was rebuilt and the Tuileries, Hotel de Ville, and other famous buildings were erected. In the 17th century, during the time of Cardinal Richelieu, Paris achieved preeminence as the intellectual capital of Europe. It was becoming less comfortable, however, as a seat of kings. After another rebellion against royal authority (the Fronde, 1648–53), King Louis XIV moved his entire court to Versailles, a few miles west of the city.

The French revolution began in 1789 when mobs hauled the royal family to Paris and stormed the Bastille. Paris was replanned under Napoleon I, and after the Bourbon Restoration expansion was rapid. Most of modern Paris, with its great boulevards, public buildings, and parks, dates from Napoleon III. The siege of Paris during the Franco-Prussian War of 1870–71 interrupted this era of splendor; however, the work of Napoleon III was continued under the Third Republic.

Shelled by German artillery in World War I, the city escaped capture. In World War II, however, Paris was occupied by the Germans from June 14, 1940, to August 25, 1944, when Allied forces recaptured it. Recent research has revealed that Adolf Hitler planned to destroy the city before abandoning it in 1944; his commander in Paris, however, refused to carry out the orders. In 1961–62 there was turmoil in Paris over the Algerian war.

Paris is divided into two sections by the Seine River. The stately air of the right bank is created by its wide avenues, large, ornate monuments, and fashionable shops. Montmartre, the home of lavish nightclubs, is here. The left bank is the governmental section and the focus of intellectual life. Its most celebrated districts are Montparnasse, noted for its small cafés; the Faubourg Saint-Germain, a haven for both aristocrats and artists; and the Latin Quarter, for centuries a preserve for students.

Two woods stand at opposite ends of Paris, the Bois de Boulogne, with the Longchamp and Auteuil racetracks, and the Bois de Vincennes, dating from the 13th century.

The Arc de Triomphe, commemorating Napoleon's victories, was begun in 1806 and completed 30 years later. At its center is the tomb of France's Unknown Soldier, guarded by an eternal flame. The Arc is situated on the Place de l'Étoile, or Star Place, so called because 12 avenues radiate from it. Among these are such renowned thoroughfares as the Avenue des Champs Élysées, Avenue Foch, and Avenue de Wagram. The Champs Élysées leads to the Place de la Concorde, one of the world's most famous squares. Around the Place are grouped the magnificent formal Jardin des Tuileries, the massive Pont de la Concorde, leading to the left bank, and various imposing buildings. The Louvre is one of the finest museums in the world. Among its treasures are Leonardo da Vinci's *Mona Lisa* and the statues of the *Venus de Milo* and *Nike of Samothrace*.

On the Île de la Cité are the Sainte Chapelle, dating from the 13th century, one of the jewels of Gothic architecture, and Notre Dame. The Panthéon was completed on the site of the former church of Ste. Geneviève in 1781 and now contains the tombs of Voltaire, Rousseau, and other illustrious Frenchmen. The Hôtel des Invalides, completed in 1676 as a hospital for disabled veterans, adjoins the Dôme des Invalides, completed in 1706. To this place, in 1861, were transferred the remains of Napoleon I. One of the city's most famous landmarks is the Eiffel Tower—long the tallest man-made structure in the world—built for the Exposition of 1889 by Gustave Eiffel.

The cleaning of many of the historic buildings in Paris, a project begun in the early 1960s, has given the "City of Light" a sparkling new look.

## PEKING

The capital of the People's Republic of China, Peking (population est., 4,000,000), formerly called Peiping, is situated in northeastern China. It is a transportation and industrial hub. Cotton mills, iron and steel works, railroad repair shops, machine tool factories, and chemicals and plastics industries, as well as governmental offices, are located here.

Several cities have been built on the site of Peking since 723 B.C. The core of the present city is Cambuluc, built by Kublai Khan between 1260 and 1290 A.D. Britain and France seized the city in 1860 and forced the Emperor to cede land within the Imperial City for foreign legations and extracted from him an agree-ment to allow foreign troops to be quartered there. Resentment of this action led to the Boxer Rebellion of 1900. Peking changed hands several times in the battles that followed the Revolution of 1911, and in 1937 it was occupied by the Japanese. The last foreign concession was abolished in 1946.

Peking consists of the outer—or Chinese—city, surrounded by a low rampart, and the inner—or Tatar—city, completely enclosed by the outer city and formerly protected by 50-foot-high crenelated walls. Within the Tatar city is the Forbidden City (now a museum), where the emperors of China formerly resided. Few Westerners had ever been inside the Forbidden City until the end of the Chinese Empire in 1911. At the southern edge of the Forbidden City is the T'ien An Men, the Gate of Heavenly Peace, leading to a huge open area which serves as the Peking equivalent of Moscow's Red Square.

Since the Communist victory in 1949, the face of Peking has changed greatly. Many new structures have been erected, including the 80,-000-seat Peking Workers' Stadium. Rickshas have disappeared, and ancient streets and buildings have been renamed. In 1966 and 1967 the city witnessed numerous mass demonstrations by Mao Tse-tung's Red Guards, one of which (Aug. 22, 1967) culminated in the destruction by fire of the British diplomatic compound.

## PRAGUE

The capital of Czechoslovakia, Prague (population: 1,032,000) is situated on the Moldau River. It is one of the major commercial and cultural cities of Europe. Heavy machinery, machine tools, and automobiles are manufactured.

The growth of the city began when a group of Germans settled here under King Wenceslaus I of Bohemia in 1232. The city prospered and was soon made the capital of Bohemia. During the 14th century reign of Emperor Charles IV, Prague was one of Europe's leading cities, and in the 16th and 17th centuries it became a major center of scientific learning.

The city was occupied by the French in 1742 and by the Prussians two years later. Frederick the Great of Prussia won a significant victory here in 1757 against the Austrian empress, Maria Theresa. She regained the city, however, and under her rule Prague was almost completely rebuilt in baroque and rococo architecture. Prague became the capital of the Czechoslovakian Republic in 1918. It was under German occupation in 1939–45 and was taken by Soviet armies in 1945.

Nestled in the hills around the Moldau, Prague is a handsome city. Among its architectural treasures are the tenth-century Cathedral of St. Vitus, rebuilt in the 14th century. Hradcany Castle, a royal palace until 1918, has since been the residence of the presidents. Also noteworthy are the Waldenstein and Czernin palaces. The residential sections of Prague are predominantly modern. In 1966 the construction of a subway was begun.

## RIO DE JANEIRO

The former capital and second largest city of Brazil, Rio de Janeiro (population: 4,102,000) is situated on Guanabara Bay on the Atlantic Ocean. It is the cultural, financial, commercial, and transportation center of the country. Rio de Janeiro's natural harbor is known for its great beauty. Across the bay lies the city of Niteroi, one of Rio de Janeiro's residential suburbs. Mountain peaks that ring the city include Sugar Loaf, 1,290 feet; Corcovado, 2,310 feet, topped by a gigantic statue of Christ; Tijuca, 3,350 feet; and Gávea, 2,760 feet.

The site was first visited in January 1502 by Portuguese explorers who mistook the bay for the mouth of a river and called the site Rio de Janeiro—River of January. Sacked by the French in 1711, the city was quickly rebuilt and prospered during the 18th century, when it became the country's leading gold-shipping center. In 1763 the city replaced Bahia as the capital of Brazil and served as such until the dedication of the new city of Brazilia in 1960.

Rio de Janeiro is one of the world's most beautiful cities. Its sparkling white beaches are world-renowned, especially the Copacabana, flanked by mosaic-inlaid sidewalks. A Mardi Gras is held here every year. A large-scale modernization of Rio, begun in the early 1900s, is still in progress. Hills have been leveled, tunnels have been bored, and parts of the bay have been reclaimed. The city boasts spacious parks, avenues lined with palm trees, and a gigantic sports stadium.

## ROME

The capital of Italy, Rome (population: 2,560,-000) is situated on both banks of the Tiber River, 17 miles from the Tyrrhenian Sea, in western Italy. A cultural, administrative, and educational center, Rome is often called the "Eternal City" because of its involvement for 27 centuries in the history of the Western world. Today its historical sites, museums, and churches attract over 2,000,000 visitors a year.

Originally built on seven hills, Rome was traditionally believed to have been founded in 753 B.C. by Romulus, the wolf-weaned twin of Remus. In the 5th century B.C. the Roman Republic was established and during the next several centuries came to dominate all of Italy and much of the Mediterranean area. Under the Empire, which succeeded the Republic in the 1st century B.C., extensive building took place. Augustus, the first Emperor, was said to have made Rome a city of marble. Most of the famous ruins visible today date from Roman imperial times.

With the establishment of Christianity as the accepted religion of the Empire in the early 4th century A.D., an era of church building began and some of the ancient pagan temples were converted to Christian use. However, the capital of the Empire was moved to Byzantium (330) and imperial power began to decline in Rome. The western branch of the Empire and the city itself were invaded and sacked by barbarian hordes several times in the 5th century, and, after 476, the Papacy provided the only real authority in the region. In the next 1,000 years Rome was periodically threatened and thrown into chaos by the squabbling of the great Roman families and the ambitious intrigues of the Holy Roman emperors.

The patronage of the Papacy during the Renaissance helped to make Rome a center for art. Today its many museums and galleries are world famous. The Capitoline Museum, built from a design of Michelangelo, houses a renowned collection of Greek and Roman sculpture. St. Peter's Basilica and the Sistine Chapel are perhaps the greatest achievements of Renaissance architecture and art.

During the 19th century the Papal States of central Italy, long ruled by the popes as independent sovereignties, were gradually absorbed and, in 1871, Rome became the capital of the newly united Italy. A treaty between the Papacy and the Italian government in 1929 created Vatican City, an independent state within Rome which serves as the administrative headquarters of the Roman Catholic Church.

Mussolini's regime was responsible for the restoration and beautification of many ancient historical sites and for the moving of Rome University (founded in 1303) to modern quarters in 1932.

Rome was bombed several times in World War II, but on September 11, 1943, it was declared an "open" city. Allied troops arrived on June 11, 1944. Since World War II immigration from rural districts has caused a rapid increase in Rome's population. There has also been an expansion of Rome's industrial parks on the outskirts of the city. From 1963 to 1965 the deliberations of Ecumenical Council Vatican II—the 21st in the history of the Roman Catholic Church—were held in St. Peter's Basilica.

The center of Rome is the Piazza Venezia, with its imposing statue of King Victor Emmanuel II. To the south and southeast are the major ancient Roman ruins, including the Colosseum, the Arch of Constantine, the Palantine Hill, the Roman and Imperial Forums, and the Baths of Caracalla. To the north of the Piazza is the famed Trevi Fountain and the Quirinal Palace, the residence of the President of Italy. Across the Tiber to the West is Vatican City, which includes St. Peter's and the Vatican Museum. Rome has over 300 churches; the most famous are St. Mary Major, St. John Lateran, and St. Paul Outside the Walls. Rome is honeycombed with catacombs; these ancient Christian burial grounds include the burial places of Saints Callistus, Agnes, and Sebastian.

## SAIGON

The capital and largest city of South Vietnam, Saigon (population: 1,336,000) is situated on the right bank of the Saigon River, about 50 miles from the South China Sea. It is linked by a canal to the lower Mekong River. There are many shipyards, food-processing plants, and distilleries. The city's well-equipped port exports rice, dried fish, rubber, and copra —the dried and broken kernel of coconut which yields coconut oil.

When Saigon passed to the Annamese in the 17th century, it was already an ancient Khmer settlement. Little more than a village, it was captured by the French in 1859 and was ceded to them four years later. Under their administration it grew into a city. From 1887 to 1902 Saigon was the capital of Indochina. The Westernized city and its oriental suburb of Cholon were consolidated in 1932. During World War II Saigon was occupied by the Japanese, who used it as a base of operations for attack against other areas of Southeast Asia. After the war the French colonial administration reassumed control, but when Indochina was split into two political entities after the departure of the French in 1954, Saigon became the capital of South Vietnam.

Since the early 1960s when Vietcong guerrillas became increasingly active in South Vietnam, Saigon has seen a great influx of American civilian and military personnel and has experienced many incidents of terrorism. Scores of people have been killed in the bombings of hotels, restaurants, barracks, and transportation facilities, and organized Vietcong military operations have been conducted within a few miles of the capital.

Saigon has the appearance of a European city and is called the "Paris of the East." The city is laid out along rectangular lines, with many tree-shaded boulevards and public gardens. Many of the government buildings, theaters, and churches are distinctly French. Notable buildings include the governor's palace and the cathedral.

## SANTIAGO

The capital and largest city of Chile, Santiago (population: 2,459,400) is situated in the central part of the nation. The intellectual and cultural hub of Chile, Santiago is also an important commercial center.

The city was founded on February 12, 1541, by Pedro de Valdivia, the Spanish conqueror of Chile. He named it Santiago de Nueve Estremadura, or St. James of New Estremadura, after the Spanish province of Estremadura. The city still follows his basic plan, a gridiron pattern of streets.

Misfortune has repeatedly visited Santiago during its 400-year history. Auraucanian Indians rose against the Spaniards in 1541 and almost decimated the settlement. The city was leveled by an earthquake in 1647. It has frequently been the victim of flooding by the Maipocho River. When the Campania Church was destroyed by fire in 1863, about 2,000 persons died.

Despite such catastrophes, Santiago has grown steadily into one of the largest cities of South America. It has spread out beyond its original valley site to the foothills of the Andes, and snowcapped peaks form a backdrop to the city's suburbs.

Some remnants of colonial architecture can be seen, but in the main Santiago is a modern city. There are numerous parks, plazas, and broad avenues, such as Avenida Bernardo O'Higgins, which runs for two miles through the center of the city. The national library, theater, and museum are here, as is the National University, successor institution to the University of San Felipe, established in 1738.

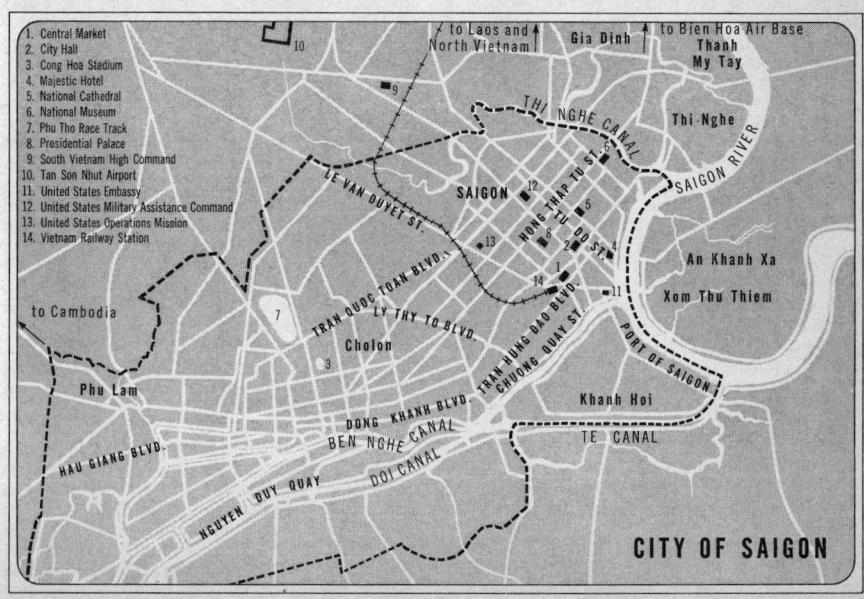

1. Central Market
2. City Hall
3. Cong Hoa Stadium
4. Majestic Hotel
5. National Cathedral
6. National Museum
7. Phu Tho Race Track
8. Presidential Palace
9. South Vietnam High Command
10. Tan Son Nhut Airport
11. United States Embassy
12. United States Military Assistance Command
13. United States Operations Mission
14. Vietnam Railway Station

CITY OF SAIGON

## SYDNEY

The principal port and largest city in Australia, Sydney (population 2,101,000) is situated on the southeastern coast of the continent. It is the capital of the state of New South Wales. Its harbor, one of the finest in the world, is spanned by the Harbor Bridge. Sydney has become the country's leading commercial and industrial center, active in finance, storage, shipping, and manufacturing. It is a major railroad hub and serves as the continent's main air terminal and port of entry.

Sydney's present site was chosen in 1788, shortly after the first British colonists landed. Founded as a penal colony, it was named after Thomas Townshend, Lord Sydney, the British home secretary. Places of interest include the Art Gallery of New South Wales; extensive botanical gardens; the Conservatorium of Music; and the Public Library of New South Wales, containing the world's largest collection of works about Australia. A revolutionary type of new Opera House, collectively seating 5,000 in four separate auditoriums, is being completed. Government House is an outstanding example of Victorian Gothic architecture; other notable architecture includes the two cathedrals, St. Andrew's and St. Mary's.

Sydney enjoys an almost ideal climate, averaging about 340 days of sunshine a year. All water sports are popular; magnificent nearby beaches and resorts include Bondi, Manly, and Avalon. Chartered deep-sea fishing boats put out of port daily, and fishermen are usually to be found strung out along the miles of wharves and piers that line the extensive waterfront. Sports centers in or near Sydney include White City, where international championship tennis matches are played; Warwick Farm, a motor racing site; and six horse and greyhound racing tracks. Koala Park, one of several wildlife sanctuaries, protects wombats, kangaroos, wallabies, koalas, and other animals unique to Australia.

## TOKYO

The capital of Japan, Tokyo (population: 11,050,000) is situated in south-central Honshu (Japan's largest island), on the northwest shore of Tokyo Bay. It has the largest population of any city in the world; the number of residents account for more than 11% of the total population of the Japanese islands. Tokyo is the financial, political, administrative, and cultural center of Japan, and its port is one of the busiest in Asia.

Founded as the village of Yedo in the 12th century and made the capital of a province in 1590, it became, in 1603, the seat of Ieyasu, the first shogun of the Tokugawa line that was to rule Japan for 264 years. After the shogunate was overthrown in 1868, the city became the capital of imperial Japan and was renamed Tokyo.

A disastrous earthquake and fire in 1923 killed 150,000 inhabitants and destroyed half of the city. It was soon rebuilt, and a subway system was added. Badly damaged by air raids in World War II, Tokyo was again rebuilt and is now one of the world's most modern cities, with up-to-date commuter trains and a computerized traffic system, which was installed in 1966. However, traces of Old Tokyo remain, notably the Meiji and Hie shrines; the Sengakuji, Gokokuji, and Sensoji temples; Korakuen, a 17th-century landscaped garden; and Ueno Park. The Ginza is the shopping and entertainment area and Marunouchi the commercial hub.

Tokyo is an internationally known education center. Among its 146 universities and colleges are Keio-Gijuku (1867); Tokyo (1869); Rikkyo, or St. Paul's (1883); Waseda (1882); and Tokyo Women's Medical College (1900). The Imperial Museum and the Museum of Arms are noteworthy cultural institutions.

The famous, earthquake-proof Imperial Hotel, partly designed by Frank Lloyd Wright, is to be replaced by a new structure. Within sight of Tokyo is the symmetrical, snow-capped cone of Fujiyama, a 12,389-foot-high extinct volcano. The city played host to the Olympic Games in 1964.

## VIENNA

The capital and largest city of Austria, Vienna (population: 1,627,516) is situated on the Danube River. It is a focal point of European trade routes and a major port city. Industries that were more important prior to 1914 have included machinery, textiles, and musical and optical instruments.

Occupied successively by Celts, Romans, Franks, Magyars, and other peoples, Vienna became commercially important during the Crusades. In 1282 the Hapsburgs made it their official residence. It was besieged by the Turks in 1529 and again in 1683. In the 18th century —Vienna's most splendid era—at least five famous palaces were built. In the same era Haydn, Mozart, Beethoven, and Schubert composed enduring music here. The city was occupied by Napoleon's forces in 1805–09. Diplomats of many powers attended the Congress of Vienna in 1815 and redrew Europe's boundaries. After the Revolution of 1848, the Ringstrasse, a broad, encircling avenue, replaced the old city wall; many new buildings were added, including the celebrated Vienna Opera House (rebuilt after World War II).

In the late 19th and early 20th centuries, Vienna was one of Europe's major cultural and intellectual centers, attaining particular fame in medicine and psychology. Johannes Brahms, Johann and Richard Strauss, and Arnold Schonberg continued the city's great musical tradition.

With the collapse of Austria-Hungary in 1918, Vienna became the capital of the much smaller Republic of Austria. In 1938 Austria was seized by Nazi Germany. Vienna was captured by Soviet troops in 1945. A peace treaty ended four-power occupation of the city in 1955. U.S. President John F. Kennedy and Soviet Premier Nikita S. Khrushchev conferred here in 1961.

# UNITED STATES

## The Nation • The States • The Cities

U. S. Capitol Building, remodeled many times since George Washington laid the cornerstone in 1793, had its east wing extended in 1961. Plans for refurbishing the west wing are now before Congress.

America in 1967 moved forward on many fronts. The economy advanced, although at a somewhat slower pace; space probes sent back more pictures of the moon's dark side; the cold war eased slightly following the summit meeting at Glassboro, New Jersey, and the announcement in Geneva that the United States and the Soviet Union had tentatively agreed on a plan for limiting the spread of nuclear weapons.

But there were problems as well as progress. With nearly full employment, pockets of urban and rural poverty persisted. Although wages were high and people had money in the bank, inflation continued to be a threat. Capital investment reflected confidence in the long-term future, but experts differed on what the economy would be like in 1968.

The country was divided over what to do about urban riots and the war in Vietnam. Related to both issues were the debate over how to implement civil rights legislation and the slowdown of social welfare measures such as the anti-poverty program. The public was alarmed about the steady increase of crime and violence, and authorities differed about how best to deal with the narcotics problem and the widespread use of hallucinogenic drugs.

It was clear in 1967 that a price must be paid for scientific and technological progress. The country was saddened by the tragedy at Cape Kennedy, where three astronauts burned to death in a space vehicle. A supersonic plane was in the planning stages, but no-one knows how to cope with sonic boom. Government agencies sought solutions to environmental problems, such as air and water pollution.

This section of the *Almanac* contains basic information—historical, political, economic, and geographical—about the nation as a whole, about its states and territories and its major cities.

# OUTLINE OF AMERICAN HISTORY

The North American continent, unknown for thousands of years to European civilization, was first peopled by wandering tribes that came from Asia and over the centuries spread downward across the Western hemisphere. With the exception of an accidental visit by Norsemen about the year 1000, these tribes (later collectively named Indians by Columbus) lived undisturbed until the fifteenth century.

In 1492 Christopher Columbus, sailing under the Spanish flag to seek a western ocean route to the Orient, landed at several islands in the Caribbean. When it was realized that he had discovered a New World, other European countries sent expeditions to explore the Western hemisphere, which soon came to be known as America, after the Italian geographer Amerigo Vespucci. The most important of these voyages for the future of North America were those of John Cabot, who explored the east coast of what is now the United States and claimed the area for England. During the reign of Elizabeth I, English merchants made numerous attempts to establish colonies in North America, but each attempt ended in failure as the colonists, overwhelmed by primitive conditions, were driven back to England.

The first successful English colony was established at Jamestown, Virginia, in 1607. Though beset by famine, disease, Indian harassment, and internal strife, the colony in time flourished. The first settlement in New England was made by the Pilgrims at Plymouth, Massachusetts, in 1620. The Puritans, another religious sect that had broken from the Anglican Church, founded Massachusetts Bay Colony in 1630. The Great Migration from 1630 to 1642 increased the population of New England to about 20,000.

The theocracy established by the Puritans assimilated the Pilgrims and ruled New England in strict accord with scriptural dictates. The Puritans were not democrats, but some democratic attitudes pervaded their theology and eventually passed over into politics. They contributed to the American tradition the intellectuality of their religion, their respect for education (they founded Harvard College in 1636), and their sense of the dignity of work, thrift, and profits.

Another religious sect that made a major contribution to American culture were the Quakers, who settled Pennsylvania after 1681 and made that colony a haven for diverse religious and racial groups.

By 1732 English-dominated settlements stretched from Massachusetts to Georgia. The settlers of the middle and northern colonies were mainly middle-class farmers, tradesmen, and artisans. This range of talents plus the unsuitability of much of the land for large-scale farming made a diversified economy inevitable. Labor was supplied by indentured servants, men without capital who bound themselves to several years of service in exchange for ocean passage, upkeep, and training in a trade.

In the South, along the tidewater strip, the availability of arable land served to disperse the population and make agriculture the basis of the economy. Virginians of the first century, for example, were mostly yeoman farmers; a few were tobacco aristocrats who owned plantations manned by Negro slaves. At first the Negro and the indentured servant were of indistinguishable status. But by 1700 a combination of race prejudice and economic expediency forced the Negro into a legally subservient caste.

The English were enthusiastic in support of their colonies, finding them a solution to overpopulation at home, potentially a market for empire goods, and a source of raw materials and agricultural produce. The New World was considered, by the colonies and England alike, to be an outpost of the realm, both subject to English law and entitled to English liberties. The colonists desired neither independence nor political union. (A Plan of Union devised by Benjamin Franklin in 1754 was rejected by the colonial assemblies.) But they were bound together by their common English language and culture and by the similarities of the colonizing experience.

As part of their own attempt to profit from the New World, the French had circled British North America with a ring of strategically placed forts. Since 1689 a struggle with Britain for the inland West had been slowly developing —a struggle that culminated in the French and Indian War of 1754 to 1763. The French were decisively defeated at the Battle of Quebec and driven out of North America.

The end of that conflict saw the community of interests that tied the colonies and Britain together into a flourishing imperial system begin to break down. Dissension arose from two main sources. First, during the preceding century Parliament had enacted a series of mercantilist Acts of Trade and Navigation, designed to restrict colonial trade for the benefit of the entire imperial economy. These acts, however, had seldom been enforced. Now Britain prepared to embark on a sterner policy.

Second, to protect the colonists from the Indians, the British decided to garrison the backcountry with 10,000 troops. Maintenance of these forces required financing, much of which was expected to come from taxation of the colonies. These new policy aims required greater control over the colonies, but for a part of the world that had been tending increasingly to self-government and self-reliance, controls came too late, and in their cumulative effect would lead to rebellion.

The Stamp Act of 1765, which required that legal documents and newspapers bear a tax stamp, was seen by the already harassed colonists as arbitrary and resulted in a massive protest movement. Resistance organizations were formed and British imports were boycotted. Though Parliament repealed the act in the face of this reaction, the constitutional question of taxation went unresolved. The crisis was renewed in 1767 by the passage and stern enforcement of the Townshend Acts, which placed import duties on glass, lead, paper, paints, and tea. Once more the colonies united in a policy of non-importation and once more Parliament backed down, but not before friction generated by the presence of British troops had erupted into the Boston Massacre of 1770.

To sustain the principle of parliamentary authority, however, a small tax on tea was retained. Refusing to give in, a small band of Bostonians dumped a cargo of British tea into the harbor. This incident, the Boston Tea Party, rallied public opinion against the British. In a spirit of rebellion the colonies began to organize and sent representatives to the first Continental Congress in Philadelphia in 1774.

Hostilities began at Lexington and Concord in April 1775. As the rebellion progressed British authority in the colonies collapsed. Unable to receive redress for their grievances, emboldened by their own show of union, and informed by the natural rights philosophy of the 18th-century Enlightenment, the Continental Congress turned from rebellion to revolution and, in the Declaration of Independence (July 4, 1776), proclaimed the birth of thirteen independent states.

The military phase of the American Revolution lasted for six years. Hampered by inadequate financing, arms, and provisions, the Continental army had to battle not only the superior manpower of the British army, but also Loyalist sentiment and popular indifference. But the Patriots had the advantages of fighting on their own terrain, their tenacity, an alliance with France, and the leadership of General George Washington. These factors prevailed, and in 1781 Lord Cornwallis's surrender at Yorktown virtually ended the fighting. By the Peace of Paris, negotiated by Benjamin Franklin, John Adams, and John Jay, Americans won formal recognition of their independence, and dominion over the territory between the Appalachians and the Mississippi River.

The Americans discovered a basis for permanent union in their struggle to secure independence. Under the Articles of Confederation a loose "league of friendship" was formed in 1781. The Confederation had no national executive or court system, and its legislature had no power to enforce laws. Though chaotic financial conditions prevailed under the Confederation, there was no popular movement for radical change.

In Philadelphia in 1787 a convention called to revise the Articles of Confederation turned instead to the task of writing a constitution to create a stronger union. Led by James Madison and James Wilson, the convention drafted a document distributing authority between the national government and the states. The national government was to consist of three branches: Executive, bicameral Congress, and Supreme Court. The Constitution was to become effective upon ratification by nine states. The arguments for the document were pre-sented in *The Federalist,* a series of essays by Hamilton, Madison, and Jay. By the middle of 1778 the requisite number of states, meeting in conventions, had ratified the Constitution. The major argument against the document was that it did not contain sufficient safeguards for individual rights and liberties. This reservation was answered by the Bill of Rights, which was almost immediately appended to the Constitution as the first ten amendments.

The powers inherent in the Constitution were put to maximum use in the setting up of the national government in 1789. Washington was the obvious and unanimous choice for first President. The first Congress set up the cabinet, the court system, and designated the District of Columbia as the permanent national capital. Alexander Hamilton, the first Secretary of the Treasury, established the Bank of the United States and the national mint, and thus stimulated business enterprise by creating new capital, extending the basis of commercial credit, and laying the foundations for a stable monetary system.

The strong nationalism of the Federalists was opposed with increasing strength in the 1790s by the advocates of state sovereignty and the primacy of individual liberties. From this philosophical breach emerged the party system. With Thomas Jefferson as their rallying point, Madison, James Monroe, and Albert Gallatin organized the Democratic-Republican Party and by 1800 had gathered enough strength to elect Jefferson President. The Federalists never regained national power, but the Jeffersonians did not repeal their program, and the administrations of Jefferson and his successors, Madison and Monroe, successfully reconciled the demands of democracy and nationalism. Jefferson's greatest achievement as President, the purchase of Louisiana from France in 1803, required an exercise of national authority inconsistent with Jefferson's strict construction of constitutional grants of power. Such grand ventures were, however, consistent with the Constitution as expounded by Jefferson's antagonist, Federalist John Marshall, who was Chief Justice of the Supreme Court from 1801–35.

During the first decade of the nineteenth century American shipping was increasingly obstructed by the naval battles of the Napoleonic Wars. Trade was harassed and American seamen were impressed into the British navy. In 1812 Congress declared war on Great Britain. The War of 1812 lasted three years and was fought to an inconclusive result, but it gave to the American people a stronger sense of their common identity and raised their confidence as a nation. The position of the United States in world politics was further enhanced by Andrew Jackson's raid on Florida in 1818, which led to the cession of that territory by Spain the following year. The ultimate expression of the new confidence was the Monroe Doctrine. President James Monroe, fearful that Spain or an ally might seek to recapture the newly independent states of Latin America, warned in 1823 that the United States would

(*continued*)

**OUTLINE OF AMERICAN HISTORY** (*continued*)

resist any such attempt and announced that the New World was henceforth closed to further European colonization.

The period 1820–60 witnessed a rapid expansion in territory and economic development and the triumph of egalitarianism in politics. Public programs supported the building of roads, canals, and especially railroads, which doubled in mileage every five years between 1830 and 1860. Natural resources thus became accessible and the Industrial Revolution began to develop in the eastern cities about 1840, bringing with it the beginning of the factory system. A distinct working class emerged, comprised largely of immigrants from England, Germany, and Ireland.

Because industrialization was centered in the North, it contributed to the development of sectional self-consciousness. Decentralized agriculture remained the basis of the Southern economy. With the invention of the cotton gin in 1793, cotton became the dominant crop and settled the position of slavery as central to the Southern labor system. Intimidated by the rise of militant abolitionism in the North in the 1830s, the Southerner was thrown on the defensive and began to invoke history, science, and religion in the defense of slavery as a positive good.

By 1800 the promise of cheap land had pulled settlement into the Ohio and Mississippi Valleys. The trek gained momentum each decade before 1850. The frontier was a social process as well as a line; it encouraged individual initiative, rough manners, and political democracy.

One man in particular, Andrew Jackson, symbolized the upheaval generated by expanding capitalism, democracy, and the rise of the trans-Appalachian West. For lack of an effective opposition the Democratic-Republican Party had atrophied after the election of James Monroe in 1816. Now revitalized and named the Democratic Party, it elected Jackson President in 1828. Jackson became the hero of the small capitalist by destroying the centralized

Bank of the United States, which had operated to exclude new entrepreneurs from business opportunity; the hero of nationalists by thwarting anti-tariff nullification sentiment in South Carolina; and, as the first Westerner to be elected President, the hero of the rising aspirations of that section. Jackson was succeeded by Martin Van Buren, who had been his political manager. By 1836 the factions opposing the Jacksonians had organized the Whig Party. In 1840 their candidate, William Henry Harrison, captured the Presidency.

Texas, a section of Mexico colonized by American slaveholders, rebelled in 1835 and established its independence the following year. Southern politicians, desiring to add slave territory to the union, demanded its annexation. The demand was met in 1845 by President James K. Polk, who wanted also to acquire the Mexican territory between Texas and the Pacific. Mexico declined to sell the area. Congress, taking advantage of a skirmish on the disputed Texas-Mexico border, declared war on Mexico over the vehement opposition of the Whigs. Defeated in a series of battles by American troops under General Zachary Taylor, and with much of their territory occupied, the Mexicans agreed to the Treaty of Guadalupe Hidalgo in 1848, which transferred the present states of California, Utah, Arizona, and New Mexico to the United States. These acquisitions, together with the settlement of the Oregon boundary by treaty with Britain in 1846, the Gadsden Purchase of 1853, and the acquisition of Alaska from Russia in 1867, established the present boundaries of the continental United States.

The paramount issue raised by the territorial expansion of the 1840s was whether slavery should be permitted to follow the flag. The problem became a crisis in 1850 when California, developing rapidly after gold was discovered in 1849, applied for admission to the union as a free state. Statehood was granted by Congress but only in the context of a major sectional adjustment that became known as the Compromise of 1850. The main features of the adjustment were the partitioning of the remainder of the Mexican cession into the territories of New Mexico and Utah, with ambiguous pronouncements on the permissibility of slavery, and a Federally enforceable fugitive slave law. Passage of these measures was secured by a coalition of Northern Democrats and Southern Whigs.

The decade after 1850, far from realizing the tranquility sought by the compromise, was torn by one irritation after another. Harriet Beecher Stowe's novel, *Uncle Tom's Cabin,* offended the South while bringing home to many Northerners for the first time the abuses of slavery. In two crucial areas, the compromise itself did not work. The Fugitive Slave Act was ignored by Northerners most of the time, but when it was enforced, the return of Negroes to slavery aroused loud protests. The ambiguity of the territorial settlement permitted the reopening of the question of slavery in the territories when Senator Stephen Douglas persuaded Congress to organize the Nebraska Territory on

Andrew Jackson, 7th President of the U.S.

Granger Collection

the principle of popular sovereignty—removing the question of slavery from Congressional dispute by leaving it to the settlers themselves. This action repealed the Missouri Compromise of 1820, which had prohibited slavery north of latitude 36'30". The passions aroused by this legislation solidified the South, destroyed the Whig Party, and gave birth to the Republican Party, which committed itself to opposing the extension of slavery.

Year by year the threat of disunion grew stronger. In the Dred Scott decision (1857), the Supreme Court ruled that Congress had no power to exclude slavery from the territories. In 1859 John Brown attempted to incite a major slave uprising in Virginia and succeeded only in convincing the South that the North would not rest until slavery had been abolished.

The Presidential election of 1860 precipitated the final crisis. The Republican Party nominated Abraham Lincoln of Illinois, who had gained national prominence in a series of debates while attempting to unseat Senator Douglas in 1858. The Democratic Party, unable to resolve the conflicting sectional views of its leaders, split apart, thus insuring Lincoln's election. Unwilling to accept the prospect of Republican rule and weary of being told that slavery was wrong, the South began to secede from the Union.

Lincoln and the Republicans refused to let the South depart peaceably, and the Northern attempt to send supplies to beleaguered Fort Sumter in South Carolina caused the beginning of hostilities in April 1861. Thus began the Civil War, which lasted for four years and ended in the saving of the Union at the cost of a million casualties. Lincoln, who never expected to see the end of slavery in his lifetime, insisted that his primary aim in waging war was to restore the Union. But when he became convinced that freeing the slaves was politically prudent, he acceded to the demands of his more radical advisers and issued an Emancipation Proclamation in 1863.

The North lost several important military battles early in the war—notably at Bull Run, Fredericksburg, and Chancellorsville—and was plagued at first by indecisive military leadership and political wrangling as to the aims of the conflict. The South benefited from its martial spirit and the strategic fact that it had only to stage a holding action to win, but it was weakened at the same time by inadequate political leadership and financial policies and by an obsession with state sovereignty. Eventually the superior resources and manpower of the North were decisive. By 1865 large areas of the South had been laid to waste and in the end Southern morale began to collapse. On April 9, 1865, General Robert E. Lee surrendered to Ulysses S. Grant at Appomattox. Five days later President Lincoln was assassinated in Washington.

The North now faced the issue of the nature of the peace to be dealt out to the South. Lincoln, determined to restore the Union as soon as possible, had devised a conciliatory plan of reconstruction, which his successor,

Andrew Johnson, tried to follow. But Radical Republicans in Congress, led by Thaddeus Stevens and Charles Sumner, were determined to precipitate a social and political revolution in the South by destroying the ascendancy of the planter class and uplifting the Negro. To this end the Radicals established state governments dominated by Northerners and Negroes and supported by a comprehensive system of military rule. Negro rights were supposed to be protected by the 14th amendment to the Constitution, which declared the freedman a citizen of the United States and entitled to the same civil rights as white persons. But in the 1870s reconstruction ended, and the Republicans abandoned the Negro to white Southern authority, the sharecropper economy, and nearly a century of racial segregation.

The years between 1865 and 1900, often called the Gilded Age, are most notable for the expansion of the economy and the identification of problems caused by that expansion. Stimulated by new mining developments in the Rocky Mountains, the completion of a national system of railroads, and the protective tariff, giant corporations (commonly organized as trusts or holding companies) and large banking houses came to dominate the economy. Great fortunes were made by bold entrepreneurs, such as Vanderbilt, Stanford, and Harriman in railroads, Carnegie in iron and steel, Weyerhauser in lumber, Armour and Swift in meat-packing, and Rockefeller in oil. By 1900 the United States was the most highly developed industrial nation in the world. The needs of industry for centralized facilities led to the rapid growth of cities as the laborer followed the factory. Chicago, for example, with 30,000 people in 1840, more than doubled its size every succeeding decade until by 1890 it had a population of over two million.

The urge to expand geographically outlived the American frontier, which disappeared about 1890. An opportunity to extend American influence into the Caribbean arose in 1895 when Cuba revolted against Spain. Three years later a United States ultimatum to Spain to withdraw from Cuba set off the Spanish-American War, which lasted for ten weeks and resulted in the independence of Cuba (though under American tutelage). Spain also ceded Puerto Rico, Guam, and the Philippines to the United States. The war, largely because it involved a far-flung demonstration of the force of the United States navy, raised the United States to the first rank of world powers.

The economic expansion of the Gilded Age had its dark side. The trusts were seen as destructive to the American ideals of individual opportunity and competition. The alliance of the Republican Party and big business created opportunities for corruption, which was particularly rampant during the administration of President Grant (1869–77).

Farmers of the plains, themselves businessmen in the new economy, did not share proportionately in the profits of the new. The farmer was plagued by unsteady prices and

*(continued)*

Granger Collection

President Woodrow Wilson with his wife, Edith

## OUTLINE OF AMERICAN HISTORY (continued)

discriminating, exorbitant freight rates. Agricultural development was largely dependent on borrowed Eastern capital, and as gold appreciated in value it seemed to the farmer that his debt was increasing at the same time.

Immigrants, now coming in a flood and originating more and more from Eastern and Southern Europe, tended to settle in ghettos in the industrial cities of the East and Midwest. They could not afford to travel farther, but because they often lacked required skills, opportunity was not always abundant, and the city slum was born. Economic conditions in general, though expanding over the long term, were subject to unusually marked cyclical fluctuations. Speculation, especially in railroads, went unbounded, and the currency was often unstable. Major financial panics occurred in 1873 and 1893, each followed by several years of harsh economic contraction.

The determination of various groups and individuals to cope with the increasing stress in the social and economic fabric of the nation gave rise to a period that has become known as the Age of Reform. The workingman, organizing into trade and industrial unions, such as the Knights of Labor and the American Federation of Labor, began to develop the strike as an effective bargaining weapon. In the cities urban reformers—notably Jane Addams in Chicago—struggled with the problems of poverty and overcrowding.

The Populist Party arose in the agrarian South and Midwest after 1891 to demand relief from political corruption and low farm prices. The Populists proposed a variety of reforms to make government more democratic and called for the nationalization of railroads and essential communications. Their politics nearly captured the government in 1896 when the Populist hero, William Jennings Bryan, won the Democratic nomination and campaigned on a free-silver platform; but the "Great Commoner" was defeated by the traditional Republicanism of William McKinley.

The Populists were superseded by a more fundamental wave of reform, the progressive movement, which reached deeply into all areas of national life, challenging the value of tradition in literature, philosophy, law, and social relationships in general. During the administrations of Theodore Roosevelt, William Howard Taft, and Woodrow Wilson, the progressives acted to ameliorate the economic excesses of the previous half century. Roosevelt did not want to destroy the trusts, but by threatening a crusade against "malefactors of great wealth," he induced the trusts to accept regulation. Federal control over railroads, initiated by the Interstate Commerce Act of 1887, was extended through the Elkins Act of 1903 and the Hepburn Act of 1906. A Pure Food and Drugs Act was enacted, also in 1906. Roosevelt was succeeded by his chosen heir, Taft, but became dissatisfied with Taft's leadership and sought to capture for himself the 1912 Republican nomination. Defeated by Taft at the convention, Roosevelt and his followers abandoned the Republican Party and entered the campaign under the Progressive banner. Taft and Roosevelt were defeated by the Democratic candidate, Woodrow Wilson.

During the first two years of the Wilson Administration the progressive movement achieved most of its political goals. Wilson secured the first major reduction in tariff duties since the Civil War. The Federal Reserve Act afforded better banking facilities to the South and West by decentralizing the banking system and providing in Federal Reserve notes an elastic currency under government control. The Federal Farm Loan Act made credit available to farmers at low rates of interest. The power of the Federal government to deal with trusts was strengthened by the Clayton Anti-trust Act of 1914.

In Europe in that same year the peace of a century deteriorated into World War I, and Wilson's attention was increasingly turned abroad. Though he urged strict neutrality it was clear that American sympathy lay with the Allies (Britain, France, and Belgium) against the Central Powers, dominated by Germany. German submarine attacks on American shipping eventually made neutrality impossible, and in April 1917 at Wilson's request, Congress declared war. In November 1918, overwhelmed by the Allies and broken by revolt at home, Germany sued for peace. Determined that the postwar world should be made "safe for democracy," Wilson traveled to Europe to participate in the peace negotiations. He insisted that the covenant of a League of Nations be bound up in the terms of the treaty. Returning home he sought to compel Senate ratification of the League by taking his case to the people in a nationwide tour, but the effort broke his health and permanently removed him from active participation in the affairs of his administration. The League was rejected by the Senate.

In 1920 the electorate renounced internationalism in favor of Republican candidate Warren Harding's promise of a "return to normalcy." The political tone of the decade was set by the dictum of Harding's successor, Calvin Coolidge, that "the business of America is business." The progressives had not shared in Republican leadership since the party split in 1912, and without their sensitive ear, the conservative leaders of the party were impervious to the fact that agriculture and labor were not sharing in the general economic advance of the decade. Farm income, for example, declined sporadically through the 1920s. Late in 1929 the economic structure of the nation collapsed into the Great Depression. By 1932, some 12 million workers were unemployed and 5,000 banks had shut their doors.

Unable to give credence to the Republican view that prosperity was "just around the corner," the electorate turned overwhelmingly in 1932 to the Democratic Party and the New Deal of its Presidential nominee, Franklin D. Roosevelt. The depression aligned urban workers, immigrants, farmers, Negroes, and whites in the small towns in a coalition that was to keep the Democrats in office for twenty years.

The ideological legacy of the progressive movement, with its insistence on overhauling rather than abandoning free enterprise, conditioned the direction of Roosevelt's recovery and reform programs. Attempting to improve the condition of all segments of the economy, Roosevelt, with a heavily Democratic Congress, secured minimum wage and maximum hour legislation for the workers, collective bargaining for the trade unionists, parity prices for the farmer, social security for the elderly, and relief and public works for the unemployed. Supported by the New Deal, a new group of labor leaders formed the Congress of Industrial Organizations (C.I.O.), and soon millions of skilled and unskilled workers in basic industries were brought into the ranks of organized labor. But for all of its success in shoring up segments of the economy, the New Deal, rather than ending the depression, succeeded in staging a holding action for capitalism until World War II restored prosperity.

The depression in Europe had contributed to the rise in Germany of the Nazi regime of Adolf Hitler. When Hitler invaded Poland in 1939 the majority of the American people were united in the desire to remain aloof from World War II. But in 1940 as France fell and Britain was besieged, the United States became the "arsenal of democracy," trading destroyers to Britain. The following year Roosevelt inaugurated the Lend-Lease plan, which provided military supplies to Britain and subsequently to the Soviet Union.

On December 7, 1941, the question of the degree of intervention was taken out of American hands when Japan, which for a decade had been subduing Asia, attacked the United States Pacific Fleet at Pearl Harbor. The first year of the war was a disaster for the United States; defeat followed defeat in both the European and Asian theaters, and not until the end of 1942 did the tide of battle begin to turn against the Axis. Pooling their efforts, resources, and manpower, the Allies invaded Italy in 1943, and the following year they

Pearl Harbor, December 7, 1941

National Archives

moved into France at Normandy and began a fierce drive toward Germany. In May 1945 Hitler's government collapsed and the Germans surrendered. To Harry Truman, who succeeded to the Presidency on the death of Roosevelt in 1945, fell the task of leadership as the war effort turned on Japan. Truman's decision to drop the newly developed atomic bomb on Hiroshima led almost immediately to the surrender of the Japanese.

The creation of the United Nations in 1945 reflected the American hope that the world would now achieve the peace and stability that lasted so briefly after World War I. But the coming of the Cold War, with its recurrent crises, confounded that hope and occupied the greater part of the attention of the next four Presidents, Truman, Eisenhower, Kennedy, and Johnson. An "iron curtain" fell across Europe as the Soviet Union set up satellite regimes in its war-occupied territory. The free city of West Berlin, situated inside the Iron Curtain, created a special problem because it provided a haven for refugees and thrived while the rest of East Germany stagnated economically. In 1948 the Soviets temporarily cut off Allied access to Berlin, but this act was frustrated by a massive American airlift. Over the next fifteen years repeated Soviet threats to oust the Americans from Berlin were firmly resisted.

The rest of Europe, devastated by the war, threatened for a time to share the fate of the satellite countries. To counter the danger the Truman Administration secured the cooperation of Europe in forming a mutual security pact, the North Atlantic Treaty Organization. The Truman Doctrine provided economic aid to Greece and Turkey, and the Marshall Plan (named for Secretary of State George C. Marshall), a massive program designed to rehabilitate the economy of western Europe, was inaugurated in 1947. These plans were forerunners of the foreign aid program developed during the administrations of Eisenhower and Kennedy. In later years foreign
(continued)

## GUADALCANAL: 1942

Wide World

On August 7, 1942, troops of the First Marine Division made an amphibious landing on the islands of Guadalcanal and Tulagi. The Japanese were driven from Guadalcanal after many months of bitter fighting.

In the history of America at war, no name brings back more vivid memories than that of Guadalcanal. Twenty-five years after one of the bitterest battles of World War II, the United States Marines returned to the island on August 7, 1967, to honor the small band of American soldiers and their allies who fought off the Japanese for several months in 1942. And on the same day, men now fighting in Vietnam who had taken part in the Guadalcanal landing, met on a hillside near Danang and exchanged memories.

The battle of Guadalcanal was the turning point of the fighting in the Pacific, and the ultimate testing ground for the courage, stamina, and ingenuity of the U.S. Marines. On August 7, 1942, troops of the First Marine Division fought their way up the beaches of Guadalcanal and Tulagi, a nearby island. But they were soon locked in. The jungle hid the retreating Japanese and barred the

Marines; at their rear, enemy planes and warships bombarded cargo vessels attempting to deliver much-needed food and ammunition. With their lifeline impaired, the Marines survived by wresting Japanese supplies.

There were also other enemies—energy-sapping heat and tropical diseases. Exhausted, malnourished, and with 98 per cent of their numbers weakened by malaria, the Marines fought off wave after wave of enemy attackers, while in the surrounding waters the American Navy was devastated from the air. Finally, in November the Allies won control of the sea. On December 9 the battle-weary Marines were taken to Australia for rest and hospitalization.

By February, 1943, fresh troops finally forced the Japanese from the island. Although losses were staggering, the Marines had held Guadalcanal until reinforcements could arrive.

**OUTLINE OF AMERICAN HISTORY** (*continued*)

aid was increasingly directed at developing the economies of countries that became independent as European colonialism declined. In 1961, after Cuba fell under Communist domination, Kennedy inaugurated the Alliance for Progress, aimed at improving the economies of Latin America.

Checked in Europe as that continent recovered and grew strong, the Communist thrust was more successful in Asia. Nationalist China collapsed in 1949 as Communist forces drove Chiang Kai-shek's army from the mainland. When Communist North Korea invaded South Korea with Russian arms in June 1950, Truman, believing that the fate of much of Asia depended on the outcome of the foray, committed American troops to the U.N.'s effort to repel the attack. The military effort achieved its objective of saving South Korea, and an armistice was reached in 1953, but not before Douglas MacArthur, the American field commander, differed with the administration on the scope and conduct of the war, and was relieved of his command by Truman.

The most jarring domestic repercussion of the cold war in the 1950s was the attempt by Senator Joseph McCarthy to capitalize on the frustrations inherent in a long conflict where victory for either side was impossible. Blaming recurrent American setbacks on Communist infiltration of the State Department, he set out on a search for traitors in the government. Because his methods seemed to threaten freedom of speech he was censured by his colleagues in 1954 and fell from influence.

Later in the decade South Vietnam was besieged by guerrilla bands supported by Communist North Vietnam. A long-standing pledge by Eisenhower to aid the people of South Vietnam grew into a program of extensive military aid and advice under Kennedy and then to large-scale participation of American troops in combat under Johnson.

Superimposed on the recurrent crises was the development by the United States and the Soviet Union of large arsenals of nuclear weapons and sophisticated guided missile systems. In 1962 Russia's Khrushchev attempted to install missiles in Cuba and Kennedy blockaded the island. The confrontation seemed to take the world to the edge of nuclear war, but Khrushchev, appearing to realize the peril, withdrew his missiles. The following year Kennedy secured the cooperation of the Soviet Union in the enactment of a limited test-ban treaty, and the Soviet threat in general subsided as the Russians, breaking with China over ideological differences, turned inward to concentrate on domestic development. China, however, became more militant than ever, refusing to agree to the test-ban treaty as it embarked on a nuclear development program.

The space age began in 1957 when the Soviet Union launched the first Earth satellite. The United States, which had been lagging in space science, was jarred from its complacency and stepped up its program, launching manned space capsules early in the 1960s and em-barking on a project designed to land a man on the Moon before 1970.

In domestic politics between 1945 and 1966 successive administrations presided over the continuation of social reforms that had been begun under the New Deal. Though Truman presented to Congress a series of domestic measures (called the Fair Deal) that were even more far-reaching than those of the New Deal, the program was blocked on nearly every front by the development of a conservative coalition in Congress of Republicans and Southern Democrats. The Republican administration of Dwight Eisenhower (1953–61) did not repudiate the New and Fair Deals but instead continued and even expanded them. John Kennedy, elected President in 1960 on the Democratic ticket, asked Congress to pass legislation to aid economically depressed areas and higher education, and to enact a system of health care for the aged under social security. But Kennedy was assassinated in 1963 before the major parts of his program had received Congressional approval, and the task of obtaining final passage was left to his successor, Lyndon Johnson. The efforts by both Kennedy and Johnson to stimulate the economy met with some initial success, but by 1967 the Vietnam war was costing $2 billion a month and corporation profits and personal incomes were below expectation. President Johnson called for new taxes in an attempt to reduce a looming record budget deficit and to curb inflation.

Twenty million American Negroes shared only marginally in America's postwar affluence. For nearly a century, first in the rural South and then increasingly in the ghettos of Northern cities, the Negro had been the object of condescension and abuse—or was ignored altogether. In the 1950s two events precipitated a major civil rights movement. First, the Supreme Court ruled in 1954 that segregation in public schools was unconstitutional. Slowly during the next decade, amid frequent riots and forceful Federal intervention, specific court orders desegregated a number of secondary schools and universities in every Southern state. Second, a Negro bus boycott in Alabama in 1955, protesting segregated seating on transportation facilities, was successful, and inspired a massive nonviolent sit-in movement, designed to desegregate public facilities of all types. The objectives of the sit-in movement were achieved in the Civil Rights Act of 1964. Voting rights, denied to Negroes in the South since Reconstruction, were assured by Federal enforcement in the Civil Rights Act of 1965. But if he had received freedom of movement and the ballot, the Negro, despite anti-poverty programs, still remained at the bottom of the economic stratum. Frustration at the seeming insolubility of this plight erupted into a series of riots in several Northern cities in the 1960s. The Negro movement itself, torn between the advocates of nonviolence and "black power," began to fragment, and by the end of 1967 it was clear that a solution to the Negro problem was nowhere in sight.

# THE CONFEDERACY AND THE CIVIL WAR

On February 4, 1861, delegates from six states of the lower South met in convention at Montgomery, Alabama, to form a Southern republic. South Carolina had seceded from the Union in December 1860, followed, in January 1861, by Mississippi, Florida, Alabama, Georgia, and Louisiana. On February 22, 1862, Jefferson Davis and Alexander Stephens were inaugurated as President and Vice President of the Confederacy at the permanent capital in Richmond, Virginia. By this time, Texas (having seceded in late February 1861), Virginia (in April), North Carolina, Arkansas, and Tennessee (by June) had joined the newly formed nation.

The South had deep faith in its strong position as "Cotton King" of the world and its vital importance to the British cotton industry. This was a fallacy. The British believed that the North would be unable to conquer the South, until they received the news of Gettysburg and Vicksburg. (A paramount factor preventing British recognition of the Confederacy was the military failure of the South at critical times.) Nevertheless, Confederate statesmen had an exaggerated opinion of the value of foreign recognition. The only means by which England or France could effectively have aided the Confederacy were breaking the blockade with force, sending huge supplies, and making large financial loans.

Militarily, the Confederacy had to depend entirely upon its militia and on volunteers. It is highly probable that the typical soldier, Northern or Southern, had no clear idea why he was fighting. Defense of the homeland from invasion was enough of an imperative for many Southerners to volunteer. It was not until the South realized that the war was more than a holiday frolic that a military conscription act was passed in April 1862. This act's greatest weakness was that it permitted a man to avoid the draft by sending a substitute, and a thriving trade developed in securing replacements.

The success of the South in winning its independence had to depend largely on brilliant leadership and the high morale of the people, for the North had a vast preponderance of manpower and economic resources. It is generally believed that the Confederate Army was less than half the size of the Union Army.

A distressing and significant episode in the inner history of the Confederate command was the clash of wills among the officers.

Northern military leadership improved as the war progressed, while the original Southern superiority in personnel declined, for the tremendous attrition of officers was more serious for the South than for the Union.

The broad military policy which President Davis and his advisors adopted was to fight a defensive war. The wisdom of their defensive strategy will always be a subject of debate but it seems to have been basically sound. Although the Confederacy could claim that the immense superiority of the North in economic resources and in manpower made the contest an unequal one, it did not use its own limited military resources to the best advantage.

The inability of the Confederate government to mobilize its resources went far to explain the economic deterioration of the Confederacy. The armies and the civilian population should have been better nourished than they were, for surplus food in some districts was made unavailable by lack of railroad transportation. The war effort of the Confederacy also would have been greatly strengthened if the government had taken control of the vital blockade-running activities early. The government was also remiss on regulating manufacturing and stimulating new industries. Its currency and taxation policies proved disastrous, but reflected the lack of industrial development. All these factors lowered the morale of the people and interfered with the vigorous prosecution of the war.

Lee's surrender to Grant at Appomattox Court House on April 9, 1865, marked the end of the major military conflict. Not until November 6, 1865, was the last flag of the Confederacy furled when the cruiser *Shenandoah* surrendered in Liverpool, England.

Like the French Revolution, the Civil War destroyed the society of the old regime. Not only was there the tragedy of the death of vigorous young men but the traumatic effect on the mind and spirit of the South. The memory of the defeat of the Confederacy has continued long, especially in the rural South. The dying Confederacy passed into the emotional realm of the "Lost Cause."

**From left: Jefferson Davis, Alexander H. Stephens, General Thomas J. (Stonewall) Jackson, and General Robert E. Lee**

## MAJOR BATTLES OF THE CIVIL WAR

| DATE | BATTLE | MILITARY COMMANDERS | | RESULTS |
|------|--------|------|------|---------|
| | | Union | Confederate | |
| **1861** | | | | |
| April 11 | Fort Sumter (South Carolina) | Robert Anderson | P. G. T. Beauregard | First engagement of the war. Union garrison surrendered. |
| July 19 | First Manassas or First Bull Run (Virginia) | Irvin McDowell | Joseph E. Johnston and P. G. T. Beauregard | Victory in war's first major engagement gave Confederates control of Virginia. |
| **1862** | | | | |
| Feb. 15 | Forts Henry and Donelson (Kentucky) | U. S. Grant | S. B. Buckner | Seizure of forts broke Confederate line in Kentucky and opened Tennessee to Union troops. |
| March 9 | Hampton Roads (Virginia) | MONITOR John L. Worden | MERRIMAC (The Virginia) Franklin Buchanan; C. R. Jones | Although neither ironclad was able to defeat the other, the battle began the end of the era of wooden warships. |
| April 6–7 | Shiloh (Tennessee) | U. S. Grant and D. C. Buell | A. S. Johnston and P. G. T. Beauregard | Confederate forces failed to prevent Union move south into Tennessee after Grant's seizure of Forts Henry and Donelson. |
| June 25– July 1 | Seven Days (Virginia) | George B. McClellan | Robert E. Lee | In a series of five battles, Lee and Jackson forced the Union army away from Richmond. |
| Aug. 29–30 | Second Manassas or Second Bull Run (Virginia) | John Pope | Robert E. Lee | Retreat of Union forces left Virginia clear of invaders. |
| Sept. 17 | Antietam (Maryland) | George B. McClellan | Robert E. Lee | Victory for neither side, but the results enabled Lincoln to issue the Emancipation Proclamation. |
| Oct. 8 | Perryville (Kentucky) | D. C. Buell | Braxton Bragg | Despite some success, Confederates retreated into Tennessee, leaving Kentucky under Union control. |
| Dec. 13 | Fredericksburg (Virginia) | A. Burnside | Robert E. Lee | Union drive on Richmond halted by stubborn Confederate defense. |
| Dec. 31– Jan. 1, 1863 | Murfreesboro or Stone River (Tennessee) | W. S. Rosecrans | Braxton Bragg | Although initially victorious, the Confederates lost half of Tennessee to the Union. |
| **1863** | | | | |
| May 2–5 | Chancellorsville (Virginia) | Joseph Hooker | Robert E. Lee | Repulse of Union drive to capture Richmond. |
| May 19– July 4 | Vicksburg (Mississippi) | U. S. Grant | John C. Pemberton | Union victory split the Confederacy in half and gave the North control of the Mississippi River. |
| July 1–4 | Gettysburg (Pennsylvania) | George G. Meade | Robert E. Lee | Farthest advance north by Lee's armies; his repulse marked the turning point of the war. |
| Sept. 19–20 | Chickamauga (Tennessee) | W. S. Rosecrans | Braxton Bragg | Victorious Confederates besieged Union army in Chattanooga. |
| Nov. 23–25 | Chattanooga (Tennessee) | U. S. Grant | Braxton Bragg | End of siege: Confederate forces lost Tennessee and were driven back into Georgia. |
| **1864** | | | | |
| May 5–19 | The Wilderness and Spotsylvania (Virginia) | U. S. Grant | Robert E. Lee | Despite temporary Confederate success, Grant advanced toward Richmond. |
| June 14–17 | Petersburg (I) (Virginia) | U. S. Grant | P. G. T. Beauregard | Beginning of the final siege of Richmond. |
| Aug. 5 | Mobile Bay (Alabama) | David S. Farragut | Franklin Buchanan | Confederate fleet destroyed in the largest naval action of the war. |
| Sept. 2 | Atlanta (Georgia) | W. T. Sherman | John B. Hood | Beginning of Sherman's devastating march through Georgia. |
| Oct. 19 | Cedar Creek (Virginia) | P. H. Sheridan | Jubal Early | Sheridan's cavalry finally cleared the Shenandoah Valley of Confederate forces. |
| Dec. 15–16 | Nashville (Tennessee) | G. H. Thomas | John B. Hood | Union forces effectively destroyed remnants of the Confederate Army in the West. |
| **1865** | | | | |
| April 2 | Petersburg (II) (Virginia) | U. S. Grant | Joseph E. Johnston | Last Confederate retreat left Richmond to Union forces. |
| April 9 | Appomattox | U. S. Grant | Robert E. Lee | Not a battle, not the war's final encounter, but Lee's surrender to Grant formally ended Civil War. |

## HISTORY OF THE AMERICAN FLAG

Left to right: the Great Union Flag; the original Stars and Stripes; the flag of 1794; the flag since 1960

For a century and a half, the American colonies shared Britain's flags, the Union and the red Meteor banners. On January 1, 1776, at a ceremony at George Washington's headquarters near Boston, soldiers of the Continental Army raised the first American flag.

The Great Union Flag was nothing more than the Meteor Flag of Great Britain modified by having six horizontal white stripes imposed on its field, thereby dividing the field into thirteen alternate red and white stripes. These signified the thirteen original colonies, while retention of the British Union in the first canton testified to their continued loyalty—as Americans saw it—to the constitution of the government against which they were fighting. While Congress never formally adopted it, this banner soon became known as the Union Flag, the Grand Union Flag, the Congress Flag, and the Colours of the United Colonies.

On June 14, 1777, in the journal of the Continental Congress was made this entry: "Resolved: that the flag of the United States be made of thirteen stripes, alternate red and white; that the union be thirteen stars, white in a blue field representing a new constellation." Thus was born the Stars and Stripes.

There seems to be sufficient evidence that varying forms of the Stars and Stripes were flown on land at different times and places during the Revolutionary War as national or as regimental standards, even though no such flags were officially delivered to General Washington until 1783.

Nevertheless, the Stars and Stripes seems to have been designed primarily for use at sea, not as a battle flag on land. On a voyage begun on September 30, 1787, and ended on August 6, 1790, Captain Robert Gray in the *Columbia* carried the flag for the first time around the world.

The original flag, with its 13 stripes and 13 stars, remained in use only a few years. On December 26, 1793, after the admission of two new states to the Union, Stephen R. Bradley of Vermont introduced a bill in Congress "for altering the Flag of the United States." It provided, in less than four lines of print, that beginning on May 1, 1795, the Flag of the United States should be "fifteen stripes, alternate red and white, with a union of fifteen stars white in a blue field." This was passed on January 13, 1794.

Peter H. Wendover, Representative to Congress from New York, was responsible for the Flag Act of April 4, 1818, which is still in effect today. This act specified "thirteen horizontal stripes, alternate red and white" and provided that the "union have 20 stars, white on a blue field" and "on the admission of every new state into the Union, one star be added to the union of the flag."

On June 24, 1912, President William Howard Taft issued an executive order in which the relative proportions of the flag and the arrangement of the stars were officially prescribed. Then, by an executive order of President Eisenhower, dated August 21, 1959, a banner with 50 stars became the official flag of the United States on July 4, 1960.

## CONFEDERATE FLAGS

Left to right: the Stars and Bars; the Southern Cross; the second official flag; the final design of March 1865

On March 4, 1861, the Stars and Bars of the Confederate States of America rose over the State Capitol at Montgomery, Alabama. It displayed a red stripe at top and bottom and a white stripe between them. The union in the upper left corner was blue, with a circle of seven white stars representing the states then comprising the infant Confederacy.

At Bull Run, the Confederate flag's great similarity to the Stars and Stripes made distinguishing marks difficult to see in the confusion of battle. A new design by General P. G. T. Beauregard was selected, which became known as the Southern Cross. This flag, although the most familiar of the Confederacy's standards, supplanted the Stars and Bars only on the battlefield. It consisted of a red field, emblazoned with a blue St. Andrew's Cross having 13 white stars representing the states the Confederacy claimed as her own. The cross and the red field were bordered in white.

A final design for a national flag was created, and approved on March 4, 1865. Only one major change was made from the battle flag of 1863. A red bar was added, extending the width of the white field opposite the union.

## DESPERADOES, GAMBLERS, AND LAW MEN OF THE OLD WEST

**William Clarke Quantrill** (1837–65), born in Ohio, became the leader of a band of gunmen in the Kansas-Missouri slavery struggles in the 1850s. After the outbreak of the Civil War he tried unsuccessfully to obtain a commission in the Confederate Army, but even without official sanction styled himself a Confederate guerrilla leader. His exact role in the war is still the subject of controversy. Quantrill's exploits reached their climax on August 21, 1863, when his gang rode into Lawrence, Kansas, sacked the town, and murdered about 150 townspeople. Abandoned by most of his men, Quantrill was shot by Federal troops.

Among the men, and boys, who took their apprenticeship in lawlessness under Quantrill were **Jesse James** (1847–82) and **Cole Younger** (1844–1916). After the dissolution of the Quantrill raiders, the James-Younger gang reorganized and embarked on a highly successful ten-year career. Among other gang members were Jesse's brother **Frank James** (1844–1915), and three of Cole's brothers—**James Younger** (d. 1902), **John Younger** (d. 1874), and **Robert (Bob) Younger** (d. 1889). The first James-Younger crime was a bank holdup in Clay County, Missouri, in 1866. Until 1876 the gang rode unchecked, beginning with banks and later branching out into train robberies. In 1876 the gang attempted to hold up a bank in Northfield, Minnesota. The James brothers and James, Bob, and Cole Younger were captured and sent to prison. The James brothers escaped and began another crime spree, but three years later Jesse James was shot in the back by **Robert Ford**, a member of his gang who sought the rewards offered for Jesse's death or capture. Frank James was captured shortly thereafter, but he was never convicted. He lived out his life peaceably.

John Younger had been shot to death in 1874. Of the three Younger brothers caught at Northfield, Robert died in prison in 1889; James was released and committed suicide in 1902; and Cole, pardoned in 1903, went to Missouri, where he became a member of a Wild West show.

Much romantic lore has grown up around **Belle Starr** (1848?–89), born Myra Belle Shirley. She had a daughter by Cole Younger, but it is categorically untrue that for years she slipped away from his pursuers to ride to her Texas home to see her. They probably saw each other only once or twice after the child was born. Belle married **Sam Starr**, an Indian, in 1880 and moved to Oklahoma—then Indian Territory—where she sheltered several outlaws. She was murdered by an unidentified person in 1889.

Another renowned outlaw band was the Dalton gang—**Grattan, Bill, Bob,** and **Emmett Dalton.** They were reputed to be related to the Youngers and the Jameses, but in reality were not. Grattan (Grat) and Bob were killed in 1892 when they attempted to rob two banks in Coffeyville, Kansas, their boyhood home. Emmett was captured at the same time and sent to

prison, but he was later released. Bill Dalton went to California while his brothers were robbing banks, entered local politics, and returned to Kansas after the Coffeyville debacle. He organized a gang of his own and was shot to death by a Texas Ranger in 1894.

The second generation of Western outlaws had a shorter life. **Billy the Kid** (William H. Bonney, 1859–91) was born in New York City, but moved to Kansas and then New Mexico as a child. By the time he was 16 he had killed several men. In 1878 he joined a local gang involved in cattle wars, killed a sheriff, and became a cattle rustler. Captured and sentenced to death, he escaped but was later shot to death by Sheriff Pat F. Garrett.

Indiana-born **Sam Bass** (1851–78) moved to the West as a child. He became an accomplished holdup man and train robber, operating mainly in Texas and South Dakota. One of his gang informed on him, and he was shot to death by a Texas Ranger as he tried to rob a bank in Round Rock, Texas.

Among the West's leading lawmen was **Wyatt Earp** (1848–1929), who served as United States marshal in Kansas, and later went to Tombstone, Arizona, as a Wells Fargo guard. With his brothers Virgil and Moran and a friend, **"Doc" Holliday,** an Eastern-bred dentist, Earp killed several men in a bloody gunfight at the OK Corral near Tombstone, October 26, 1881. Some historians claim that Earp was little better than a criminal himself, and that the OK Corral slaughter was just an excuse to rid himself of his enemies. Others maintain that he was a staunch lawman. After 1882 Earp traveled widely in the West and became a celebrity in sporting circles.

**Wild Bill Hickok** (James Butler Hickok, 1837–76) was made United States marshal in Abilene, Kansas, in 1871 and acquired a reputation as a sterling marksman. Later he moved to Deadwood, South Dakota, where he was murdered by Jack McCall.

**Bat Masterson** (William Barclay Masterson, 1853–1921) was variously a gambler and buffalo hunter before becoming a law officer in Dodge City, Deadwood, and Tombstone between 1876 and 1885. He acquired a reputation as a gunman and an implacable enemy of desperadoes, but in 1902 returned to New York, where he became a sports writer for the *Morning Telegraph.*

**Roy Bean** (1825?–1903) was born in Kentucky but soon moved West. He rode in a band similar to Quantrill's during the Civil War, and later became a cattle rustler, gambler, and saloon keeper, once being deported from Mexico for rustling. In 1882, however, he settled in Vinegaroon, Texas.

Infatuated with the English actress Lillie Langtry, he renamed the town Langtry, opened the Jersey Lily Saloon, and declared himself justice of the peace. As the "law west of the Pecos," he sold drinks and dispensed justice with his revolver and a Bible always on the table in front of him.

## FAMILIAR AMERICAN SAYINGS

**America first** President Woodrow Wilson (1856–1924) discussed American neutrality in the early days of World War I: "Our whole duty for the present," he declared in 1915, "is summed up in the motto, 'America first' . . . Let us think of America before we think of Europe, in order that America may be fit to be Europe's friend when the day of tested friendship comes."

**A chicken in every pot and a car in every garage** A Republican slogan during the 1928 Presidential campaign, the expression was borrowed from King Henry IV of France (1553–1610), who reputedly declared: "There should be a chicken in every peasant's pot every Sunday."

**Damn the torpedoes! Go ahead!** On August 5, 1864, a Union Navy flotilla commanded by Admiral David Farragut attacked Confederate forces massed at Mobile Bay. The Southerners sank Farragut's lead ship with a torpedo (mine), and the rest of his formation fell back. "Damn the torpedoes!" Farragut bellowed. "Go ahead!" His men obeyed, and 25 Union ships forced the harbor defenses, breaking through a double line of torpedoes to destroy the Confederate fleet and blockade the city.

**Don't fire until you see the whites of their eyes** The order was issued by Colonel William Prescott, American commander at the Battle of Bunker Hill (June 17, 1775), and obeyed by his troops with such precision that the outnumbered colonial militia withstood naval bombardment and two charges by a 3,000-man British force, before they were forced to retreat.

**Don't give up the ship** James Lawrence, commander of the American frigate *Chesapeake*, was mortally wounded in a battle with *H.M.S. Shannon*, off Boston, in 1813. As he lay dying below decks, Lawrence heard the British boarding party coming over the side. "Don't give up the ship," he ordered. "Sink her. Blow her up."

**Fifty-four forty or fight** The slogan was adopted by extremists in the dispute between the United States and Great Britain over extension of the Oregon Territory boundary in the 1840s. The issue figured prominently in the 1844 Presidential election campaign. A boundary at 54°40′ was never accepted, and there was no fight. In 1846, the disputants set the boundary at the forty-ninth parallel. Washington, Idaho, and Oregon now comprise the old Oregon Territory.

**First in war, first in peace** Henry Lee (1756–1818), father of the Confederate general, eulogized George Washington before Congress on December 14, 1799, calling the late President "first in war, first in peace, first in the hearts of his countrymen."

**Go West, young man** Horace Greeley (1811–72), editor of the *New York Tribune* and a booster of the undeveloped West, in 1851 reprinted an editorial entitled "Go West, Young Man," by John L. Soule, editor of the *Terre Haute Express*. In his own editorial, Greeley later added the phrase "Go West, young man, and grow up with the country."

**Hew to the line, let the chips fall where they may** At the 1880 Republican National Convention in Chicago, Senator Roscoe Conkling of New York nominated General Ulysses S. Grant (1822–85) for a third term in the White House, describing his candidate as a man who would "hew to the line of right, and let the chips fall where they may." James A. Garfield of Ohio won the G.O.P. nomination and the election.

**How the other half lives** Jacob August Riis's (1849–1914) account of life in squalid New York City tenements, entitled *How the Other Half Lives* (1890), influenced Theodore Roosevelt, then the city's police commissioner, who mounted a slum clearance campaign. The expression has come to connote rueful recognition of conditions in any class other than that of the person speaking.

**I only regret that I have but one life to lose for my country** Nathan Hale, a 21-year-old Connecticut schoolteacher, commissioned in the Continental Army, volunteered for an espionage mission behind British lines in 1776. Disguised as a Dutch schoolteacher, he was captured attempting to return to the American side, and condemned to death. As he stood on the gallows, his reputed last words were "I only regret that I have but one life to lose for my country."

**Iron Curtain** The expression was first used by Sir Winston Churchill (1874–1965) in a speech at Fulton, Missouri, to describe the impenetrable barriers dividing Communist-bloc nations from the free world. Churchill's address was largely a warning against Soviet expansionist tendencies.

**I would rather be right than be President** Five times a Presidential candidate, and five times defeated, Kentucky-born Henry Clay won re-election to the Senate in 1848, and in 1850 introduced a series of resolutions aimed at averting civil war by healing sectional disputes over slavery. In Senate debate on the measures, Clay was taunted about his unsuccessful attempts to win the Presidency. Convinced of the merit of his proposals, he replied he "would rather be right than be President."

**If this be treason, make the most of it** On May 29, 1765, Patrick Henry rose in the Virginia House of Burgesses to attack the Stamp Act. His speech was interrupted by the outraged Speaker's cry that his address was "Treason!" "If this be treason," Henry replied, "make the most of it."

**I'm from Missouri; you've got to show me** Missouri Congressman Willard Duncan Vandiver referred to his state's "show-me" reputation during an informal Philadelphia speech (c. 1902), in which he challenged a statement made by a preceding speaker. The phrase became Missouri's unofficial state slogan, and has been used widely for "one not easily deceived."

**In a smoke-filled room in some hotel** The phrase was used in connection with Ohio Senator Warren G. Harding's nomination as the Republican Presidential candidate in 1920. Harding's campaign manager, Harry Daugherty, was quoted as saying: "The convention will be deadlocked, and after other candidates have gone their limit, some twelve or fifteen men, worn out and bleary-eyed from lack of sleep, will sit down about two o'clock in the morning around a table in a smoke-filled room in some hotel and decide the nomination. When that time comes, Harding will be selected."

**I've just begun to fight** John Paul Jones (1747–92), Scottish-born naval hero of the American Revolution, encountered two British men-of-war off Flamborough Head, England, on September 23, 1779. In command of the *Bonhomme Richard,* Jones fought a bloody battle with *H.M.S. Serapis.* Both ships were damaged badly, and the British commander asked Jones if he was ready to surrender. "I've just begun to fight," he signaled back. Three hours later, the British commander capitulated, the American crew took command of the *Serapis,* and the *Bonhomme Richard* sank.

**Let's look at the record** Alfred E. Smith (1873–1944), four-term Governor of New York, and Democratic Presidential candidate in 1928, used the slogan extensively in his political campaigns.

**Lunatic fringe** Theodore Roosevelt (1858–1919) reputedly coined the expression in the early 1900s to deride irrational, impractical, or overzealous support of a cause.

**The man in the street** Characterizing the average man who represents the general public, the phrase appears first in the *Memoirs* (c. 1830) of Charles Fulke Greville, ". . . knowing as the man in the street does . . . ." It appears first in America in Ralph Waldo Emerson's essays.

**Millions for defense, but not one cent for tribute** With Franco-American relations strained almost to the point of war, the French government, in 1796, refused to receive the new American minister, Charles Pinckney. A French official suggested that a $250,000 bribe might make Pinckney's reception warmer. In America, word spread that Pinckney had rejected the bribery attempt, declaring "Millions for defense, but not one cent for tribute." However, Pinckney disclaimed the phrase, and *The American Daily Advertiser* credited the statement to Robert Goodloe Harper of South Carolina, who reputedly offered it as one of sixteen toasts drunk at a dinner given by Congress for John Marshall on his return from France.

**My hat is in the ring** In 1912, amateur boxer Theodore Roosevelt declared he would oppose William Howard Taft for the Republican Presidential nomination: "My hat is in the ring. The fight is on, and I am stripped to the buff." Later, Roosevelt more sedately announced he would "accept the nomination if it is tendered."

**One if by land, two if by sea** In Henry Wadsworth Longfellow's (1807–82) poem describing Paul Revere's ride:

". . . If the British march
By land or sea from the town tonight,
Hang a lantern aloft in the belfry arch
Of the North Church tower as a signal light—
One if by land, and two if by sea."

**The only thing we have to fear is fear itself** The United States and Europe were feeling the effects of a depression when Franklin Roosevelt (1882–1945) became President. On March 4, 1933, in his inaugural address, Roosevelt sought to boost national morale with his famous declaration, based on Francis Bacon's words: "Nothing is terrible except fear itself."

**Say it ain't so, Joe** Eight Chicago White Sox team members were suspected of throwing the 1919 World Series to the Cincinnati Reds. Among them was power hitter Joe Jackson, a popular idol who, according to legend, was confronted as he emerged from the hearing room by a tearful newsboy who demanded, "Say it ain't so, Joe."

**The shot heard 'round the world** In his four-stanza *Concord Hymn,* Ralph Waldo Emerson described the first major engagement of the Revolutionary War—the Battle of Concord (April 19, 1775)—in which poorly armed New England farmers successfully defended their ammunition stores against attack by crack British troops:

"And fired the shot heard 'round the world."

**The solid South** A description of the Southern states' unanimous support of the Democratic Party, from Reconstruction days until recent times, the expression is believed to have been used first about 1876 by the Confederate guerrilla raider, General John S. Mosby.

**Speak softly and carry a big stick** In 1901, shortly before he was thrust into the Presidency by the assassination of William McKinley, then Vice President Theodore Roosevelt discussed his approach to foreign policy. "There is a homely adage which runs 'Speak softly and carry a big stick, and you will go far,' " he told a Minneapolis audience. "If the American nation will speak softly, yet build and keep at a pitch of the highest training, a thoroughly efficient Navy, the Monroe Doctrine will go far."

**The Spirit of '76** The title of a painting by Archibald M. Willard, first shown at the 1876 Philadelphia Centennial Exhibition. The painting depicts the artist's vision of the patriotic fervor that gripped American colonists in Revolutionary times.

**There never was a good war or a bad peace** In 1783, Benjamin Franklin helped negotiate the Revolutionary War peace treaty with Great Britain. From Paris, site of the negotiations, he wrote: "May we never see another war. For in my opinion, there never was a good war or a bad peace."

**There's a sucker born every minute** The expression was coined when Phineas Taylor Barnum (1810–91), the showman who exhibited, among other curiosities, Tom Thumb, unabashedly proclaimed his faith in American gullibility.

**These are the times that try men's souls** Thomas Paine (1737–1809) appealed to Patriot fortitude in *The American Crisis* (1776). "These are the times that try men's souls. The summer soldier and the sunshine patriot will, in this crisis, shrink from the service of their country; but he that stands it now deserves the love and thanks of man and woman."

# HISTORIC STRUCTURES

## INDEPENDENCE HALL

Independence Hall, an historic shrine in Philadelphia, was built to house the colonial Pennsylvania Assembly, but achieved its greatest fame as the seat of the American Revolutionary government. Now a national monument, it was begun in 1732, under the supervision of Edmund Wooley.

The Pennsylvania Assembly met in its new building for the first time in 1735. However, construction work continued, and between 1750 and 1753, a steeple and the tower, in which the Liberty Bell was hung, were added.

The Second Continental Congress convened in the State House—lent by Pennsylvania for the occasion—on May 10, 1775. On July 4, 1776, colonial leaders meeting in the same hall signed the Declaration of Independence. A few days later, on the same site, George Washington formally agreed to lead Continental forces against the British.

Another federal convention met in Independence Hall in 1787, and this time emerged with the Constitution.

Philadelphia remained the seat of the American government for a time after the Revolution. However, when Federal legislators shifted the capital, first to New York and later to Washington, the national importance and rec-

Independence Hall, Philadelphia

National Park Service

ognition of Independence Hall declined somewhat, and parts of the building were torn down. The structure's historical significance went largely unnoticed until 1824, when the Marquis de Lafayette visited the hall as a guest of the U.S. Government. In the 19th century, the building was recognized as a shrine of independence. Restoration was begun, and the hall was opened to the public.

Independence Hall is now part of the Independence National Historical Park, established on July 4, 1956.

## THE LIBERTY BELL

The Liberty Bell is an historic relic of the American Revolution, now on display in Independence Hall, Philadelphia. First hung in 1753, the bell was ordered from England by the Pennsylvania Assembly on the fiftieth anniversary of Penn's Charter. It cracked during testing shortly after arrival, was recast at least once by Pass and Stow of Philadelphia, and was finally installed in the State House tower.

The Continental Congress convened in the hall below the tower, and in July 1776, the bell rang out, proclaiming adoption of the Declaration of Independence. In 1777, as British troops converged on Philadelphia, colonial patriots hauled the bell down from the tower, and spirited it off to Allentown, Pennsylvania, where

it remained hidden (probably under the floor of the Zion Reform Church) until 1778.

When the Redcoats had evacuated the city, the bell was rehung. It rang on every ceremonial occasion—notwithstanding another crack and repairs in 1835—until it was cracked irreparably on Washington's Birthday, 1846.

The bell cost about 60 pounds sterling and weighs 2,080 pounds. It is 3 feet from lip to crown; 2 feet 3 inches over the crown; 12 feet in circumference around the lip; 7 feet 6 inches around the crown; 3 inches thick at the lip, and 1¼ inches thick at the top.

Its inscription reads: "Proclaim Liberty throughout all the Land to all the Inhabitants Thereof."

## THE WASHINGTON MONUMENT

Erected in honor of the nation's first President, the Washington Monument is a hollow stone obelisk, rising more than 555 feet above the Washington, D.C., Mall, from a site south of Constitution Avenue and west of 14th Street.

The idea of a monument to Washington was officially approved at the close of the Revolutionary War; yet construction of the present structure was not completed until 1884. In 1783, the Continental Congress endorsed a proposal to honor George Washington with an equestrian statue. However, Washington is believed to have objected to the expense, and the project was dropped.

Federal lawmakers discussed a monument after Washington's death in 1799. However, little was accomplished until 1832–33, when the Washington National Monument Society was formed and began raising funds. The Society's efforts brought financial contributions, as well as gifts of inscribed stone blocks for the obelisk's interior, donated by state and foreign governments, organizations, and private individuals.

A design by John Mills, a 19th-century architect-engineer, was chosen, and on July 4, 1848, the cornerstone was laid. According to contemporary sources, Mills's plan called for a 600-

foot obelisk, rising from a base ringed by a neoclassic Greek colonnade, replete with niches for statues of prominent Americans, and a colossal rendition of Washington driving a battle chariot. Lack of funds caused considerable modification of the design.

Construction on the shaft moved rapidly for a time, then faltered, and finally ground to a halt during the Civil War. The monument stood half-finished until 1876, when Congress appropriated funds to complete construction.

## THE STATUE OF LIBERTY
Source: U.S. National Park Service

This colossal statue at the entrance to New York Harbor, officially entitled the Statue of Liberty Enlightening the World, is possibly the best-known symbol of the United States. Yet it was conceived, designed, and constructed by the French to commemorate the American and French Revolutions and to promote Franco-American amity.

The idea for a monument was originated in 1865 by the French historian Édouard de Laboulaye and a group of friends. They commissioned a young French sculptor, Frédéric Auguste Bartholdi (1834–1904), to explore the possibility of a commemorative statue. As his ship entered New York Harbor, Bartholdi was struck by the idea of a huge statue guarding the entrance to the New World.

De Laboulaye accepted Bartholdi's plan and in 1875 formed the Franco-American Union to raise funds. By 1882, the total cost of the statue, $250,000, had been raised privately in France. The American share in the building of the monument—the cost of the pedestal—remained unfulfilled. Shocked by the languishing fund drive, Joseph Pulitzer, publisher of the New York *World*, began a vigorous campaign for public participation, and by August 1885 $250,000 had been raised for the pedestal, bringing total funds for the monument to $500,000.

Bartholdi, who had begun work before 1875, constructed the statue of copper plates three-thirty-seconds of an inch thick, pressured on to wooden forms and hammered into shape. The statue's steel framework was built by Gustave Eiffel, the engineer who designed the Eiffel Tower. On July 4, 1884, in Paris, the Statue of Liberty was officially presented to Fernando Wood, U.S. minister to France. In 1885 it was dismantled and crated for shipment to the United States. On October 28, 1886, President Grover Cleveland officially dedicated the statue on Bedloe's Island. Bartholdi and De Lesseps, De Laboulaye's successor, were present.

The statue was at first under the jurisdiction of the Lighthouse Board. In 1901 jurisdiction was transferred to the War Department, which administered Fort Wood on Bedloe's Island.

On October 15, 1924, the statue was declared a national monument and placed under the administration of the National Park Service of the Department of the Interior. In 1956 Bedloe's Island, originally named for a Dutch settler, was renamed Liberty Island.

A base, far simpler than the colonnade Mills had envisioned, was completed in 1880. The capstone of the obelisk was set in place late in 1884, and the monument was dedicated on Washington's Birthday, 1885. It was opened to the public in 1888.

Long a capital tourist attraction, the monument contains a mechanical lift, and an inside staircase of nearly 900 steps, leading to an observation room high in the shaft. From the top, there is a panoramic view of the city.

| STATUE'S DIMENSIONS | FEET | INCHES |
|---|---|---|
| Height from base to torch | 151 | 1 |
| Foundation of pedestal to torch | 305 | 1 |
| Heel to top of head | 111 | 1 |
| Length of hand | 16 | 5 |
| Index finger | 8 | 0 |
| Circumference at second joint | 3 | 6 |
| Size of fingernail, 13 x 10 inches | — | — |
| Head from chin to cranium | 17 | 3 |
| Head thickness from ear to ear | 10 | 0 |
| Distance across the eye | 2 | 6 |
| Length of nose | 4 | 6 |
| Right arm, length | 42 | 0 |
| Right arm, greatest thickness | 12 | 0 |
| Thickness of waist | 35 | 0 |
| Width of mouth | 3 | 0 |
| Tablet, length | 23 | 7 |
| Tablet, width | 13 | 7 |
| Tablet, thickness | 2 | 0 |
| Height of granite pedestal | 89 | 0 |
| Height of foundation | 65 | 0 |

Weight of copper used in statue, 200,000 pounds (100 tons).
Weight of steel used in statue, 250,000 pounds (125 tons).
Total weight of statue, 450,000 pounds (225 tons).
Copper sheeting of statue is $\frac{3}{32}$-inch thick.

Two stairways, each of 168 steps, lead to and from an observation platform within the head of the statue; an elevator runs from the pedestal.

Cradled in the statue's left arm is a tablet engraved with the date July 4, 1776, and at its feet are the broken shackles of tyranny. Inside the pedestal is a bronze plaque engraved with a sonnet written in 1883 by the American poet Emma Lazarus (1849–87):

Not like the brazen giant of Greek fame,
With conquering limbs astride from land to land;
Here at our sea-washed, sunset gates shall stand
A mighty woman with a torch, whose flame
Is the imprisoned lightning, and her name
Mother of Exiles. From her beacon-hand
Glows world-wide welcome; her mild eyes command
The air-bridged harbor that twin cities frame.
"Keep ancient lands, your storied pomp!" cries she
With silent lips. "Give me your tired, your poor,
Your huddled masses yearning to breathe free,
The wretched refuse of your teeming shore.
Send these, the homeless, tempest-tost to me,
I lift my lamp beside the golden door!"

Ellis Island, formerly a detention center for aliens entering America, is part of the Statue of Liberty National Monument.

## THE STAR-SPANGLED BANNER

A naval bombardment during the War of 1812 led to the writing of the American national anthem. Francis Scott Key, a successful Washington lawyer, visited the flagship of the British fleet in Chesapeake Bay, accompanying Colonel John S. Skinner on an official mission to secure the release of a prisoner. Detained on board the tender on which they had come out to the flagship, the two watched the bombardment of Fort McHenry on the night of September 13–14, 1814.

Seeing the American flag still aloft at dawn, Key was inspired to write a poem. It was first printed as a broadside and then, on September 20, published in the Baltimore *Patriot*. The next day, the Baltimore *American* also printed it with the title, *Defence of Fort M'Henry*.

On October 19, 1814, the poem was first sung in public, and for the first time given the title, *The Star-Spangled Banner*. As entertainment following a performance in Baltimore of the play, *Count Benyowski*, the words were sung to a tune, *Anacreon in Heaven*, then widely known in America. Key had composed his poem in obvious imitation of it; he borrowed not only the melody but meter and verse form as well.

President Wilson proclaimed *The Star-Spangled Banner* as the national anthem of the United States in 1916, but Congress did not confirm this action until 1931. There is no official act of Congress setting the exact wording of the national anthem, and several versions—differing only in detail—remain in use today.

O say can you see, by the dawn's early light,
What so proudly we hailed at the twilight's last gleaming,
Whose broad stripes and bright stars through the
   perilous fight
O'er the ramparts we watched, were so gallantly
   streaming?
And the rocket's red glare, the bomb bursting in air,
Gave proof through the night that our flag was still
   there,
O say does that star-spangled banner yet wave
O'er the land of the free and the home of the brave?

On the shore dimly seen through the mists of the deep,
Where the foe's haughty host in dread silence reposes,
What is that which the breeze, o'er the towering steep,
As it fitfully blows, half conceals, half discloses?
Now it catches the gleam of the morning's first beam,
In full glory reflected now shines in the stream,
'Tis the star-spangled banner—O long may it wave
O'er the land of the free and the home of the brave!

And where is that band who so vauntingly swore,
That the havoc of war and the battle's confusion
A home and a Country should leave us no more?
Their blood has washed out their foul footsteps' pol-
   lution.
No refuge could save the hireling and slave
From the terror of flight or the gloom of the grave,
And the star-spangled banner in triumph doth wave
O'er the land of the free and the home of the brave.

O thus be it ever when freemen shall stand
Between their loved home and the war's desolation!
Blest with vict'ry and peace may the heaven rescued
   land
Praise the Power that hath made and preserved us a
   nation!
Then conquer we must, when our cause it is just,
And this be our motto "In God is our trust."
And the star-spangled banner in triumph shall wave
O'er the land of the free and the home of the brave.

## THE PLEDGE OF ALLEGIANCE

The Pledge of Allegiance to the flag was written by Francis Bellamy of Mount Morris, New York, for the National Public School Celebration of Columbus Day in 1892. An ordained Baptist minister who had resigned his pastorate to enter the field of journalism, Bellamy was working for *The Youth's Companion*, a journal published in Boston. He had been appointed chairman of a committee to develop a program for the celebration, which marked the 400th anniversary of the discovery of America. The idea for the celebration came from Bellamy's boss, James B. Upham, who was determined to arouse patriotic zeal in young persons.

Bellamy wrote the pledge in two hours on an August evening, and it was published in *The Youth's Companion* on September 8, 1892, and in the official program of the celebration. It was first publicly recited on October 12, 1892, by 4,000 Boston high school students at the Columbus Day ceremonies.

Originally, the pledge read: "I pledge allegiance to my flag and to the Republic for which it stands, one Nation indivisible, with liberty and justice for all." In 1923, at the First National Flag Conference in Washington, D.C.,

the words "my flag" were changed to "the flag of the United States," and the following year, at the Second National Flag Conference, "of America" was added to the phrase. There were no other changes to the pledge until 1954, when "under God" was inserted after "one Nation."

The pledge now reads: "I pledge allegiance to the flag of the United States of America and to the Republic for which it stands, one Nation under God, indivisible, with liberty and justice for all."

Although the pledge became popular throughout the nation, it was not until 1942 that its words were included in Federal legislation about flag use and customs. And it was not until 1945 that the pledge was given official Congressional sanction.

For many years there was controversy over the authorship of the pledge. Members of Upham's family claimed that he had written the words. A committee of historians appointed by the United States Flag Association examined the complaint and in 1939 declared that Bellamy was the author. Further investigation by the Library of Congress in 1957 confirmed this judgment.

# HISTORIC DOCUMENTS

## THE PILGRIMS, THE MAYFLOWER, AND THE COMPACT

The Pilgrims, who were destined to found historic Plymouth colony in the New World, were of humble origin. This band of sturdy English farmers and artisans, pious but nonconformist in belief, had formed in 1606 a religious congregation separate from the Church of England. They soon suffered persecution and in 1608 fled to Holland, where other sects had found religious liberty. The Pilgrims remained in the Netherlands for several years, but finally their leaders, preferring life under the English flag—even at great distance—decided to start anew in North America.

Those members of the congregation who joined the venture obtained from a company of London merchants a loan of several thousand pounds and a grant to set up a colony in Virginia. The Pilgrims were borne from Holland to England on the *Speedwell,* where that vessel joined the *Mayflower,* a ship of 180 tons, for the long and arduous trip to America. The ships set sail in company, but the *Speedwell* proved unseaworthy and both ships returned to port. Many of her passengers and much of her cargo were crowded onto the *Mayflower,* and on September 16, 1620, the *Mayflower* departed on her momentous voyage alone.

She carried, besides officers and crew, about 100 passengers. Although the Pilgrims retained control and were the moving force behind the emigration, they were almost outnumbered by their sailing companions who were neither true Pilgrims nor religious dissenters. The name Pilgrim, however, is given to all those passengers who made the first, memorable crossing on the *Mayflower.*

On November 9, after a two-month trip entailing much hardship, the coast of Cape Cod was sighted and a landing was made near Provincetown, Massachusetts. Exploration of the region began, and on December 21, Plymouth, Massachusetts, was chosen as the site of the permanent settlement, the first colony of New England.

While the small vessel lay at anchor in Provincetown harbor, the Pilgrim leaders, including William Bradford and Miles Standish, facing a wilderness far from the colonial government of Virginia, drew up the famous Mayflower Compact. This constitution provided for government by the will of the majority with the right to frame just and equal laws. And so, in effect, the seed of democratic rule was implanted in the New World.

The text of the Mayflower Compact is here set forth:

IN The Name of God, Amen. We, whose names are underwritten, the Loyal Subjects of our dread Sovereign Lord King James is by the Grace of God, of Great Britain, France, and Ireland, King, Defender of the Faith, &c. Having undertaken for the Glory of God, and Advancement of the Christian Faith, and the Honour of our King and Country, a Voyage to plant the first colony in the northern Parts of Virginia; Do by these Presents, solemnly and mutually in the Presence of God and one another, covenant and combine ourselves together into a civil Body Politick, for our better Ordering and Preservation, and Furtherance of the Ends aforesaid; And by Virtue hereof do enact, constitute, and frame, such just and equal Laws, Ordinances, Acts, Constitutions, and Offices, from time to time, as shall be thought most meet and convenient for the general Good of the Colony; unto which we promise all due Submission and Obedience. In Witness whereof we have hereunto subscribed our names at Cape Cod the eleventh of November, in the Reign of our Sovereign Lord King James of England, France, and Ireland, the eighteenth and of Scotland, the fifty-fourth. Anno Domini, 1620

**Mayflower II,** now moored at Plymouth, Mass.

| | |
|---|---|
| John Carver | Degory Priest |
| William Bradford | Thomas Williams |
| Edward Winslow | Gilbert Winslow |
| William Brewster | Edmund Margeson |
| Isaac Allerton | Peter Browne |
| Miles Standish | Richard Britteridge |
| John Alden | George Soule |
| John Turner | Edward Tilley |
| Francis Eaton | John Tilley |
| James Chilton | Francis Cooke |
| John Crackston | Thomas Rogers |
| John Billington | Thomas Tinker |
| Moses Fletcher | John Rigdale |
| John Goodman | Edward Fuller |
| Samuel Fuller | Richard Clarke |
| Christopher Martin | Richard Gardiner |
| William Mullins | John Allerton |
| William White | Thomas English |
| Richard Warren | Edward Dotey |
| John Howland | Edward Leister. |
| Stephen Hopkins | |

Plimoth Plantation

## DECLARATION OF INDEPENDENCE

IN CONGRESS. JULY 4, 1776.

The unanimous Declaration of the thirteen united States of America.

The Declaration of Independence, one of the great political documents of history, was the formal announcement that separated the Thirteen Colonies from Great Britain and made them into the United States.

Although the colonists had been openly fighting the British, many members of the Continental Congress still sought a compromise. When the fighting developed into the full-scale American Revolution, however, conservatives of the Congress were replaced by new, radical leaders, such as John Hancock, John Adams, and Samuel Adams, who demanded complete independence from the British. On June 7, 1776, Richard Henry Lee of Virginia called for a resolution on independence, and four days later a committee was appointed to draw up a declaration. The actual drafting of the document was entrusted to Thomas Jefferson, who, in setting forth the rights of man and in defending the principle of self-government, created the most eloquent statement of the American creed.

On July 4, 1776, Congress adopted the Declaration of Independence without dissent.

**In Congress, July 4, 1776,**
**The unanimous Declaration of the**
**thirteen united States of America,**

When in the Course of human events, it becomes necessary for one people to dissolve the political bands which have connected them with another, and to assume among the Powers of the earth, the separate and equal station to which the Laws of Nature and of Nature's God entitle them, a decent respect to the opinions of mankind requires that they should declare the causes which impel them to the separation.

We hold these truths to be self-evident, that all men are created equal, that they are endowed by their Creator with certain unalienable Rights, that among these are Life, Liberty and the pursuit of Happiness. That to secure these rights, Governments are instituted among Men, deriving their just powers from the consent of the governed, That whenever any Form of Government becomes destructive of these ends, it is the Right of the People to alter or to abolish it, and to institute new Government, laying its foundation on such principles and organizing its powers in such form, as to them shall seem most likely to effect their Safety and Happiness. Prudence, indeed, will dictate that Governments long established should not be changed for light and transient causes; and accordingly all experience hath shown, that mankind are more disposed to suffer, while evils are sufferable, than to right themselves by abolishing the forms to which they are accustomed. But when a long train of abuses and usurpations, pursuing invariably the same Object evinces a design to reduce them under absolute Despotism, it is their right, it is their duty, to throw off such Government, and to provide new Guards for their future security.—Such has been the patient sufferance of these Colonies; and such is now the necessity which constrains them to alter their former Systems of Government. The history of the present King of Great Britain is a history of repeated injuries and usurpations, all having in direct object the establishment of an absolute Tyranny over these States. To prove this, let Facts be submitted to a candid world.

He has refused his Assent to Laws, the most wholesome and necessary for the public good.

He has forbidden his Governors to pass Laws of immediate and pressing importance, unless suspended in their operation till his Assent should be obtained; and when so suspended, he has utterly neglected to attend to them.

He has refused to pass other Laws for the accommodation of large districts of people, unless those people would relinquish the right of Representation in the Legislature, a right inestimable to them and formidable to tyrants only.

He has called together legislative bodies at places unusual, uncomfortable, and distant from the depository of their Public Records, for the sole purpose of fatiguing them into compliance with his measures.

He has dissolved Representative Houses repeatedly, for opposing with manly firmness his invasions on the rights of the people.

He has refused for a long time, after such dissolutions, to cause others to be elected; whereby the Legislative Powers, incapable of Annihilation, have returned to the People at large for their exercise; the State remaining in the mean time exposed to all the dangers of invasion from without, and convulsions within.

He has endeavoured to prevent the population of these States; for that purpose obstructing the Laws of Naturalization of Foreigners; refusing to pass others to encourage their migration hither, and raising the conditions of new Appropriations of Lands.

He has obstructed the Administration of Justice, by refusing his Assent to Laws for establishing Judiciary Powers.

He has made Judges dependent on his Will alone, for the tenure of their offices, and the amount and payment of their salaries.

He has erected a multitude of New Offices, and sent hither swarms of Officers to harass our People, and eat out their substance.

He has kept among us, in times of peace, Standing Armies without the Consent of our legislature.

He has affected to render the Military independent of and superior to the Civil Power.

He has combined with others to subject us to a jurisdiction foreign to our constitution, and unacknowledged by our laws; giving his Assent to their acts of pretended legislation:

For quartering large bodies of armed troops among us:

For protecting them, by a mock Trial, from Punishment for any Murders which they should commit on the Inhabitants of these States:

For cutting off our Trade with all parts of the world:

For imposing taxes on us without our Consent:

For depriving us in many cases, of the benefits of Trial by Jury:

For transporting us beyond Seas to be tried for pretended offences:

For abolishing the free System of English Laws in a neighbouring Province, establishing therein an Arbitrary government, and enlarging its Boundaries so as to render it at once an example and fit instrument for introducing the same absolute rule into these Colonies:

For taking away our Charters, abolishing our most valuable Laws, and altering fundamentally the Forms of our Governments:

For suspending our own Legislature, and declaring themselves invested with Power to legislate for us in all cases whatsoever.

He has abdicated Government here, by declaring us out of his Protection and waging War against us.

He has plundered our seas, ravaged our Coasts, burnt our towns, and destroyed the lives of our people.

He is at this time transporting large armies of foreign mercenaries to compleat the works of death, desolation and tyranny, already begun with circumstances of Cruelty & perfidy scarcely paralleled in the most barbarous ages, and totally unworthy the Head of a civilized nation.

He has constrained our fellow Citizens taken Captive on the high Seas to bear Arms against their Country, to become the executioners of their friends and Brethren, or to fall themselves by their Hands.

He has excited domestic insurrections amongst us, and has endeavoured to bring on the inhabitants of our frontiers, the merciless Indian Savages, whose known rule of warfare, is an undistinguished destruction of all ages, sexes and conditions.

In every stage of these Oppressions We have Petitioned for Redress in the most humble terms: Our repeated Petitions have been answered only by repeated injury. A Prince, whose character is thus marked by every act which may define a Tyrant, is unfit to be the ruler of a free People.

Nor have We been wanting in attention to our British brethren. We have warned them from time to time of attempts by their legislature to extend an unwarrantable jurisdiction over us. We have reminded them of the circumstances of our emigration and settlement here. We have appealed to their native justice and magnanimity, and we have conjured them by the ties of our common kindred to disavow these usurpations, which, would inevitably interrupt our connections and correspondence. They too have been deaf to the voice of justice and of consanguinity. We must, therefore, acquiesce in the necessity, which denounces our Separation, and hold them, as we hold the rest of mankind, Enemies in War, in Peace Friends.

We, therefore, the Representatives of the united States of America, in General Congress, Assembled, appealing to the Supreme Judge of the world for the rectitude of our intentions, do, in the Name, and by Authority of the good People of these Colonies, solemnly publish and declare, That these United Colonies are, and of Right ought to be Free and Independent States; that they are Absolved from all Allegiance to the British Crown, and that all political connection between them and the State of Great Britain, is and ought to be totally dissolved; and that as Free and Independent States, they have full Power to levy War, conclude Peace, contract Alliances, establish Commerce, and to do all other Acts and Things which Independent States may of right do. And for the support of this Declaration, with a firm reliance on the Protection of Divine Providence, we mutually pledge to each other our Lives, our Fortunes and our sacred Honor.

**John Hancock.**

**New Hampshire**
Josiah Bartlett,
Wm. Whipple,
Matthew Thornton.

**Massachusetts-Bay**
Saml. Adams,
John Adams,
Robt. Treat Paine,
Elbridge Gerry.

**Rhode Island**
Step. Hopkins,
William Ellery.

**Connecticut**
Roger Sherman,
Sam'el Huntington,
Wm. Williams,
Oliver Wolcott.

**Georgia**
Button Gwinnett,
Lyman Hall,
Geo. Walton.

**Maryland**
Samuel Chase,
Wm. Paca,
Thos. Stone,
Charles Carroll
of Carrollton.

**Virginia**
George Wythe,
Richard Henry Lee,
Th. Jefferson,
Benja. Harrison,
Ths. Nelson, Jr.,
Francis Lightfoot Lee,
Carter Braxton.

**New York**
Wm. Floyd,
Phil. Livingston,
Frans. Lewis,
Lewis Morris.

**Pennsylvania**
Robt. Morris,
Benjamin Rush,
Benja. Franklin,
John Morton,
Geo. Clymer,
Jas. Smith,
Geo. Taylor,
James Wilson,
Geo. Ross.

**Delaware**
Caesar Rodney,
Geo. Read,
Tho. M'Kean.

**North Carolina**
Wm. Hooper,
Joseph Hewes,
John Penn.

**South Carolina**
Edward Rutledge,
Thos. Heyward, Junr.,
Thomas Lynch, Junr.,
Arthur Middleton.

**New Jersey**
Richd. Stockton,
Jno. Witherspoon,
Fras. Hopkinson,
John Hart,
Abra. Clark.

## THE CONSTITUTION OF THE UNITED STATES

The Constitution of the United States embodies the fundamental principles upon which the American republic rests. A *living* instrument of government, the Constitution has been kept abreast of the times through the process of amendment, by Federal laws that elaborate its clauses, and by judicial interpretation through the U.S. Supreme Court.

The original Constitution of the Thirteen American States was the Articles of Confederation, ratified in 1781. Although the Articles established a kind of national unity, it did not provide for a strong central government; the individual states still held power.

When it became apparent that government under the Articles was, in the words of George Washington, "little more than the shadow without substance," agitation for a strong Federal government began. This resulted in the Constitutional Convention of 1787, which met in Philadelphia to revise the Articles of Confederation. Instead of revision, the Convention brought forth the new Constitution.

Before this historic event occurred, however, the Convention, presided over by George Washington, was torn by sharp conflict that developed over the apportionment of power under a new government. A rift grew between the smaller states, fighting to retain their power, and the larger states, arguing that power should fall where population lay.

Neither the large states nor the small states would yield, and for a time it seemed that the Convention would break up. Finally, a compromise measure won approval; this measure provided for a lower house to be elected according to population (the House of Representatives) and an upper house to be chosen by the state legislatures (the Senate). (This provision for the Senate held true until 1913, when the 17th Amendment provided for the direct popular election of Senators.)

After the Constitution was issued, the struggle for ratification was bitter, especially over the conferring of new powers on the central government. Alexander Hamilton, John Jay, and James Madison, in a series of newspaper essays now known as the *Federalist Papers*, did much to promote the acceptance of the Constitution. Delaware, on December 7, 1787, became the first state to ratify the new Constitution, and Pennsylvania ratified on December 12, 1787. New Jersey ratified on December 19, 1787; Georgia on January 2, 1788; and Connecticut, seven days later. On February 6, 1788, Massachusetts endorsed the new Constitution, but recommended that a bill of rights be added to protect the states from Federal encroachment on individual liberties. Maryland ratified on April 28, 1788, and South Carolina on May 23, 1788. On June 21, 1788, by a vote of 57 to 46, New Hampshire became the ninth state to ratify but, like Massachusetts, suggested a bill of rights.

By the terms of the Constitution, nine states were sufficient for its establishment among the states so ratifying. But the government could not succeed without the addition of New York and Virginia, neither of which had ratified. On June 25, 1788, Virginia ratified, over many objections. In New York, an attempt to attach conditions to ratification almost succeeded. But on July 26, 1788, New York ratified, with a recommendation that a bill of rights be appended.

With 11 states having thus ratified the Constitution (North Carolina added her ratification on November 21, 1789; Rhode Island did not ratify until May 29, 1790), the Continental Congress—which still functioned at irregular intervals—passed a resolution on September 13, 1788, to put the new Constitution into operation. On March 4, 1789, the first session of the First Congress convened.

### PREAMBLE

We the People of the United States, in Order to form a more perfect Union, establish Justice, insure domestic Tranquility, provide for the common defence, promote the general Welfare, and secure the Blessings of Liberty to ourselves and our Posterity, do ordain and establish this Constitution for the United States of America.

### ARTICLE I

Section 1. All legislative Powers herein granted shall be vested in a Congress of the United States, which shall consist of a Senate and House of Representatives.

Section 2. The House of Representatives shall be composed of Members chosen every second Year by the People of the several States, and the Electors in each State shall have the Qualifications requisite for Electors of the most numerous Branch of the State Legislature.

No Person shall be a Representative who shall not have attained to the Age of twenty five Years, and been seven Years a Citizen of the United States, and who shall not, when elected, be an Inhabitant of that State in which he shall be chosen.

Representatives and direct Taxes shall be apportioned among the several States which may be included within this Union, according to their respective Numbers, [which shall be determined by adding to the whole Number of free Persons, including those bound to Service for a Term of Years, and excluding Indians not taxed, three fifths of all other Persons.] [1] The actual Enumeration shall be made within three Years after the first Meeting of the Congress of the United States, and within every subsequent Term of ten Years, in such Manner as they shall by Law direct. The Number of Representatives shall not exceed one for every thirty Thousand, but each State shall have at Least one Representative; and until such enumeration shall be made, the State of New Hampshire shall be entitled to chuse three, Massachusetts eight, Rhode-Island and Providence Plantations one, Connecticut five, New-York six, New Jersey four, Pennsylvania eight, Delaware one, Maryland six, Virginia ten,

[1] Superseded by the Fourteenth Amendment.

North Carolina five, South Carolina five, and Georgia three.

When vacancies happen in the Representation from any State, the Executive Authority thereof shall issue Writs of Election to fill such Vacancies.

The House of Representatives shall chuse their speaker and other Officers; and shall have the sole Power of Impeachment.

Section 3. The Senate of the United States shall be composed of two Senators from each state, [chosen by the Legislature thereof,][2] for six Years; and each Senator shall have one Vote.

Immediately after they shall be assembled in Consequence of the first Election, they shall be divided as equally as may be into three Classes. The Seats of the Senators of the first Class shall be vacated at the Expiration of the second Year, of the second Class at the Expiration of the fourth Year, and of the thrid Class at the Expiration of the sixth Year, so that one third may be chosen every second Year; [and if Vacancies happen by Resignation, or otherwise, during the Recess of the Legislature of any State, the Executive thereof may make temporary Appointments until the next Meeting of the Legislature, which shall then fill such Vacancies.][3]

No Person shall be a Senator who shall not have attained to the Age of thirty years, and been nine Years a Citizen of the United States, and who shall not, when elected, be an Inhabitant of that State for which he shall be chosen.

The Vice President of the United States shall be President of the Senate, but shall have no Vote, unless they be equally divided.

The Senate shall chuse their other Officers, and also a President pro tempore, in the Absence of the Vice President, or when he shall exercise the Office of President of the United States.

The Senate shall have the sole Power to try all Impeachments. When sitting for that Purpose, they shall be on Oath or Affirmation. When the President of the United States is tried, the Chief Justice shall preside: And no Person shall be convicted without the Concurrence of two thirds of the Members present.

Judgment in Cases of Impeachment shall not extend further than to removal from Office, and disqualification to hold and enjoy any Office of honor, Trust or Profit under the United States: but the Party convicted shall nevertheless be liable and subject to Indictment, Trial, Judgment and Punishment, according to law.

Section 4. The Times, Places and Manner of holding Elections for Senators and Representatives, shall be prescribed in each State by the Legislature thereof; but the Congress may at any time by Law make or alter such Regulations, except as to the Places of chusing Senators.

[The Congress shall assemble at least once in every Year, and such Meeting shall be on the first Monday in December, unless they shall by Law appoint a diffent Day.][4]

Section 5. Each House shall be the Judge of the Elections, Returns and Qualifications of its own Members, and a Majority of each shall constitute a Quorum to do Business; but a smaller Number may adjourn from day to day, and may be authorized to compel the Attendance of absent Members, in such Manner, and under such Penalties as each House may provide.

Each House may determine the Rules of its Proceedings, punish its Members for disorderly Behavior, and, with the Concurrence of two thirds, expel a Member.

Each House shall keep a Journal of its Proceedings, and from time to time publish the same, excepting such Parts as may in their Judgment require Secrecy; and the Yeas and Nays of the Members of either House on any question shall, at the Desire of one fifth of those Present be entered on the Journal.

Neither House, during the Session of Congress, shall, without the Consent of the other, adjourn for more than three days, nor to any other Place than that in which the two Houses shall be sitting.

Section 6. The Senators and Representatives shall receive a Compensation for their Services, to be ascertained by Law, and paid out of the Treasury of the United States. They shall in all Cases, except Treason, Felony and Breach of the Peace, be privileged from Arrest during their Attendance at the Session of their respective Houses, and in going to and returning from the same; and for any Speech or Debate in either House, they shall not be questioned in any other Place.

No Senator or Representative shall, during the Time for which he was elected, be appointed to any civil Office under the Authority of the United States, which shall have been created, or the Emoluments whereof shall have been encreased during such time; and no Person holding any Office under the United States, shall be a Member of either House during his Continuance in Office.

Section 7. All Bills for raising Revenue shall originate in the House of Representatives; but the Senate may propose or concur with Amendments as on other Bills.

Every Bill which shall have passed the House of Representatives and the Senate, shall, before it become a Law, be presented to the President of the United States; If he approve he shall sign it, but if not he shall return it, with his Objections to that House in which it shall have originated, who shall enter the Objections at large on their Journal, and proceed to reconsider it. If after such Reconsideration two thirds of that House shall agree to pass the Bill, it shall be sent together with the Objections, to the other House, by which it shall likewise be reconsidered, and if approved by two thirds of that House, it shall become a Law. But in all such Cases the Votes of both Houses shall be determined by Yeas and Nays, and the Names of the Persons voting for and against the Bill shall be entered on the Journal of each House respectively. If any Bill shall not be returned by the President within ten Days (Sundays excepted) after it shall have been presented to him, the Same shall be a Law, in like Manner as if he had signed it, unless the Congress by their Adjournment prevent its Return, in which Case it shall not be a Law.

Every Order, Resolution, or Vote to which the Concurrence of the Senate and House of Representatives may be necessary (except on a question of Adjournment) shall be presented to the President of the United States; and before the Same shall take Effect, shall be approved by him, or being disapproved by him, shall be repassed by two thirds of the Senate and House of Representatives, according to the Rules and Limitations prescribed in the Case of a Bill.

---

[2] Superseded by the Seventeenth Amendment.  [3] Modified by the Seventeenth Amendment.  [4] Superseded by the Twentieth Amendment.

Section 8. The Congress shall have Power To lay and collect Taxes, Duties, Imposts and Excises, to pay the Debts and provide for the common Defence and general Welfare of the United States; but all Duties, Imposts and Excises shall be uniform throughout the United States;

To Borrow Money on the Credit of the United States;

To regulate Commerce with foreign Nations, and among the several States, and with the Indian Tribes;

To establish an uniform Rule of Naturalization, and uniform Laws on the subject of Bankruptcies throughout the United States;

To coin Money, regulate the Value thereof, and of foreign Coin, and fix the Standard of Weights and Measures;

To provide for the Punishment of counterfeiting the Securities and current Coin of the United States;

To establish Post Offices and post Roads;

To promote the Progress of Science and useful Arts, by securing for limited Times to Authors and Inventors the exclusive Right to their respective Writings and Discoveries;

To constitute Tribunals inferior to the supreme Court;

To define and punish Piracies and Felonies committed on the high Seas, and Offences against the Law of Nations;

To declare War, grant Letters of Marque and Reprisal, and make Rules concerning Captures on Land and Water;

To raise and support Armies, but no Appropriation of Money to that Use shall be for a longer Term than two Years;

To provide and maintain a Navy;

To make Rules for the Government and Regulation of the land and naval Forces;

To provide for calling forth the Militia to execute the Laws of the Union, suppress Insurrections and repel Invasions;

To provide for organizing, arming, and disciplining, the Militia, and for governing such Part of them as may be employed in the Service of the United States, reserving to the States respectively, the Appointment of the Officers, and the Authority of training the Militia according to the discipline prescribed by Congress;

To exercise exclusive Legislation in all Cases whatsoever, over such District (not exceeding ten Miles square) as may, by Cession of particular States, and the Acceptance of Congress, become the Seat of the Government of the United States, and to exercise like Authority over all Places purchased by the Consent of the Legislature of the State in which the Same shall be for the Erection of Forts, Magazines, Arsenals, dock-Yards, and other needful Buildings;—And

To make all Laws which shall be necessary and proper for carrying into Execution the foregoing Powers, and all other Powers vested by this Constitution in the Government of the United States, or in any Department or Officer thereof.

Section 9. The Migration or Importation of such Persons as any of the States now existing shall think proper to admit, shall not be prohibited by the Congress prior to the Year one thousand eight hundred and eight, but a Tax or duty may be imposed on such Importation, not exceeding ten dollars for each Person.

The Privilege of the Writ of Habeas Corpus shall not be suspended, unless when in Cases of Rebellion or Invasion the public Safety may require it.

No Bill of Attainder or ex post facto Law shall be passed.

[No Capitation, or other direct Tax shall be laid, unless in Proportion to the Census or Enumeration herein before directed to be taken.][5]

No Tax or Duty shall be laid on Articles exported from any State.

No Preference shall be given by any Regulation of Commerce or Revenue to the Ports of one State over those of another: nor shall Vessels bound to, or from, one State, be obliged to enter, clear, or pay Duties in another.

No Money shall be drawn from the Treasury, but in Consequence of Appropriations made by Law; and a regular Statement and Account of the Receipts and Expenditures of all public Money shall be published from time to time.

No Title of Nobility shall be granted by the United States: And no Person holding any Office of Profit or Trust under them, shall, without the Consent of the Congress, accept of any present, Emolument, Office, or Title, of any kind whatever, from any King, Prince, or foreign State.

Section 10. No State shall enter into any Treaty, Alliance, or Confederation; grant Letters of Marque and Reprisal; coin Money; emit Bills of Credit; make any Thing but gold and silver Coin a Tender in Payment of Debts; pass any Bill of Attainder, ex post facto Law, or Law impairing the Obligation of Contracts, or grant any Title of Nobility.

No State shall, without the Consent of the Congress, lay any Imposts or Duties on Imports or Exports, except what may be absolutely necessary for executing its inspection Laws: and the net Produce of all Duties and Imposts, laid by any State on Imports or Exports, shall be for the Use of the Treasury of the United States; and all such Laws shall be subject to the Revision and Controul of the Congress.

No State shall, without the Consent of Congress, lay any Duty of Tonnage, keep Troops, or Ships of War in time of Peace, enter into any Agreement or Compact with another State, or with a foreign Power, or engage in War, unless actually invaded, or in such imminent Danger as will not admit of delay.

## ARTICLE II

Section 1. The executive Power shall be vested in a President of the United States of America. He shall hold his Office during the Term of four Years, and, together with the Vice President*, chosen for the same term, be elected, as follows

Each State shall appoint, in such Manner as the Legislature thereof may direct, a Number of Electors, equal to the whole Number of Senators and Representatives to which the State may be entitled in the Congress: but no Senator or Representative, or Person holding an Office of Trust or Profit under the United States, shall be appointed an Elector.

[The Electors shall meet in their respective States, and vote by Ballot for two Persons, of whom one at least shall not be an Inhabitant of the same State with themselves. And they shall make a List of all the Persons voted for, and of the Number of Votes for each; which List they shall sign and certify, and trans-

[5] Modified by the Sixteenth Amendment.      * The Twelfth Amendment defines Vice-Presidential qualifications.

mit sealed to the Seat of the Government of the United States, directed to the President of the Senate. The President of the Senate shall, in the Presence of the Senate and House of Representatives, open all the Certificates, and the Votes shall then be counted. The Person having the greatest Number of Votes shall be the President, if such Number be a Majority of the whole Number of Electors appointed; and if there be more than one who have such Majority, and have an equal Number of Votes, then the House of Representatives shall immediately chuse by Ballot one of them for President; and if no Person have a Majority, then in like Manner chuse the President. But in chusing the President, the Votes shall be taken by States, the Representation from each State having one Vote; A quorum for this Purpose shall consist of a Member or Members from two thirds of the States, and a Majority of all the States shall be necessary to a Choice. In every Case, after the Choice of the President, the Person having the greatest Number of Votes of the Electors shall be the Vice President. But if there should remain two or more who have equal Votes, the Senate shall chuse from them by Ballot the Vice President.][6]

The Congress may determine the Time of chusing the Electors, and the Day on which they shall give their Votes; which Day shall be the same throughout the United States.

No Person except a natural born Citizen, or a Citizen of the United States, at the time of the Adoption of this Constitution, shall be eligible to the Office of President; neither shall any Person be eligible to that Office who shall not have attained to the Age of thirty five Years, and been fourteen Years a Resident within the United States.

[In Case of the Removal of the President from Office, or of his Death, Resignation, or Inability to discharge the Powers and Duties of the said Office, the Same shall devolve on the Vice President, and the Congress may by Law provide for the Case of Removal, Death, Resignation or Inability, both of the President and Vice President, declaring what Officer shall then act as President, and such Officer shall act accordingly, until the Disability be removed, or a President shall be elected.][7]

The President shall, at stated Times, receive for his Services, a Compensation, which shall neither be encreased nor diminished during the Period for which he shall have been elected, and he shall not receive within that Period any other Emolument from the United States, or any of them.

Before he enter on the Execution of his Office, he shall take the following Oath or Affirmation:—"I do solemnly swear (or affirm) that I will faithfully execute the Office of President of the United States, and will to the best of my Ability, preserve, protect and defend the Constitution of the United States."

Section 2. The President shall be Commander in Chief of the Army and Navy of the United States, and of the Militia of the several States, when called into the actual Service of the United States; he may require the Opinion, in writing, of the principal Officer in each of the executive Departments, upon any Subject relating to the Duties of their respective Offices, and he shall have Power to grant Reprieves and Pardons for Offences against the United States, except in Cases of Impeachment.

He shall have Power, by and with the Advice and Consent of the Senate to make Treaties, provided two thirds of the Senators present concur; and he shall nominate, and by and with the Advice and Consent of the Senate, shall appoint Ambassadors, other public Ministers and Consuls, Judges of the supreme Court, and all other Officers of the United States, whose Appointments are not herein otherwise provided for, and which shall be established by Law: but the Congress may by Law vest the Appointment of such inferior Officers, as they think proper, in the President alone, in the Courts of Law, or in the Heads of Departments.

The President shall have Power to fill up all Vacancies that may happen during the Recess of the Senate, by granting Commissions which shall expire at the End of their next Session.

Section 3. He shall from time to time give to the Congress Information of the State of the Union, and recommend to their Consideration such Measures as he shall judge necessary and expedient; he may, on extraordinary Occasions, convene both Houses, or either of them, and in Case of Disagreement between them, with Respect to the Time of Adjournment, he may adjourn them to such Time as he shall think proper; he shall receive Ambassadors and other public Ministers; he shall take Care that the Laws be faithfully executed, and shall Commission all the Officers of the United States.

Section 4. The President, Vice President and all civil Officers of the United States, shall be removed from Office on Impeachment for, and Conviction of, Treason, Bribery, or other High Crimes and Misdemeanors.

## ARTICLE III

Section 1. The judicial Power of the United States, shall be vested in one supreme Court, and in such inferior Courts as the Congress may from time to time ordain and establish. The Judges, both of the supreme and inferior Courts, shall hold their Offices during good Behaviour, and shall, at stated Times, receive for their Services, a Compensation, which shall not be diminished during their Continuance in Office.

Section 2. The judicial Power shall extend to all Cases, in Law and Equity, arising under this Constitution, the Laws of the United States, and Treaties made, or which shall be made, under their Authority;—to all Cases affecting Ambassadors, other public Ministers and Consuls;—to all Cases of admiralty and maritime Jurisdiction;—to Controversies to which the United States shall be a Party;—to Controversies between two or more States; [between a State and Citizens of another State;][8]—between Citizens of different States;—between Citizens of the same State claiming Lands under Grants of different States, and between a State, or the Citizens thereof, and foreign States, Citizens or Subjects.

In all Cases affecting Ambassadors, other public Ministers and Consuls, and those in which a State shall be Party, the Supreme Court shall have original Jurisdiction. In all the other Cases before mentioned, the supreme Court shall have appellate Jurisdiction, both as to Law and Fact, with such Exceptions, and under such Regulations as the Congress shall make.

The Trial of all Crimes, except in Cases of Impeachment, shall be by Jury; and such Trial shall be held in

---

[6] Superseded by the Twelfth Amendment.     [7] Augmented by the Twentieth Amendment.     [8] Modified by the Eleventh Amendment.

the State where the said Crimes shall have been committed; but when not committed within any State, the Trial shall be at such Place or Places as the Congress may by Law have directed.

Section 3. Treason against the United States, shall consist only in levying War against them, or in adhering to their Enemies, giving them Aid and Comfort. No Person shall be convicted of Treason unless on the Testimony of two Witnesses to the same overt Act, or on Confession in open Court.

The Congress shall have Power to declare the Punishment of Treason, but no Attainder of Treason shall work Corruption of Blood, or Forfeiture except during the Life of the Person attainted.

## ARTICLE IV

Section 1. Full Faith and Credit shall be given in each State to the public Acts, Records, and judicial Proceedings of every other State. And the Congress may by general Laws prescribe the Manner in which such Acts, Records and Proceedings shall be proved, and the Effect thereof.

Section 2. The Citizens of each State shall be entitled to all Privileges and Immunities of Citizens in the several States.

A Person charged in any State with Treason, Felony, or other Crime, who shall flee from Justice, and be found in another State, shall on Demand of the executive Authority of the State from which he fled, be delivered up, to be removed to the State having Jurisdiction of the Crime.

No Person held to Service or Labour in one State, under the Laws thereof, escaping into another, shall, in Consequence of any Law or Regulation therein, be discharged from such Service or Labour, but shall be delivered up on Claim of the Party to whom such Service or Labour may be due.

Section 3. New States may be admitted by the Congress into this Union; but no new State shall be formed or erected within the Jurisdiction of any other State; nor any State be formed by the Junction of two or more States, or Parts of States, without the Consent of the Legislatures of the States concerned as well as of the Congress.

The Congress shall have Power to dispose of and make all needful Rules and Regulations respecting the Territory or other Property belonging to the United States; and nothing in this Constitution shall be so construed as to Prejudice any Claims of the United States, or of any particular State.

Section 4. The United States shall guarantee to every State in this Union a Republican Form of Government, and shall protect each of them against Invasion; and on Application of the Legislature, or of the Executive (when the Legislature cannot be convened) against domestic Violence.

## ARTICLE V

The Congress, whenever two thirds of both Houses shall deem it necessary, shall propose Amendments to this Constitution, or, on the Application of the Legislatures of two thirds of the several States, shall call a Convention for proposing Amendments, which, in either Case, shall be valid to all Intents and Purposes, as Part of this Constitution, when ratified by the Legislatures of three fourths of the several States, or by Conventions in three fourths thereof, as the one or the other Mode of Ratification may be proposed by the Congress; Provided that no Amendment which may be made prior to the Year One thousand eight hundred and eight shall in any Manner affect the first and fourth Clauses in the Ninth Section of the first Article; and that no State, without its Consent, shall be deprived of its equal Suffrage in the Senate.

## ARTICLE VI

All Debts contracted and Engagements entered into, before the Adoption of this Constitution, shall be as valid against the United States under this Constitution, as under the Confederation.

This constitution, and the Laws of the United States which shall be made in Pursuance thereof; and all Treaties made, or which shall be made, under the Authority of the United States, shall be the supreme Law of the Land; and the Judges in every State shall be bound thereby, any Thing in the Constitution or Laws of any State to the Contrary notwithstanding.

The Senators and Representatives before mentioned, and the Members of the several State Legislatures, and all executive and judicial Officers, both of the United States and of the several States, shall be bound by Oath or Affirmation, to support this Constitution; but no religious Test shall ever be required as a Qualification to any Office or public Trust under the United States.

## ARTICLE VII

The Ratification of the Conventions of nine States, shall be sufficient for the Establishment of this Constitution between the States so ratifying the Same.

Done in Convention by the Unanimous Consent of the States present the Seventeenth Day of September in the Year of our Lord one thousand seven hundred and Eighty seven and of the Independence of the United States of America the Twelfth in witness whereof We have hereunto subscribed our Names,

G$^o$ Washington—Presid$^t$ and deputy from Virginia

**New Hampshire**
John Langdon
Nicholas Gilman
**Massachusetts**
Nathaniel Gorham
Rufus King
**Connecticut**
W$^m$ Sam$^l$ Johnson
Roger Sherman
**New York**
Alexander Hamilton
**New Jersey**
Wil: Livingston
David Brearley
W$^m$ Paterson.
Jona: Dayton
**Virginia**
John Blair—
James Madison Jr.
**North Carolina**
W$^m$ Blount
Rich$^d$ Dobbs Spaight.
Hu Williamson
**Pennsylvania**
B Franklin
Thomas Mifflin

Rob$^t$ Morris
Geo. Clymer
Tho$^s$ FitzSimons
Jared Ingersoll
James Wilson
Gouv Morris
**South Carolina**
J. Rutledge
Charles Cotesworth Pinckney
Charles Pinckney
Pierce Butler
**Delaware**
Geo: Read
Gunning Bedford jun
John Dickinson
Richard Bassett
Jaco: Broom
**Maryland**
James M$^c$Henry
Dan of St Tho$^s$ Jenifer
Dan$^l$ Carroll
**Georgia**
William Few
Abr Baldwin

# AMENDMENTS

*The first ten amendments were ratified December 15, 1791, and form what is known as the "Bill of Rights".*

### AMENDMENT 1

Congress shall make no law respecting an establishment of religion, or prohibiting the free exercise thereof; or abridging the freedom of speech, or of the press; or the right of the people peaceably to assemble, and to petition the Government for a redress of grievances.

### AMENDMENT 2

A well regulated Militia, being necessary to the security of a free State, the right of the people to keep and bear Arms, shall not be infringed.

### AMENDMENT 3

No Soldier shall, in time of peace be quartered in any house, without the consent of the Owner, nor in time of war, but in a manner to be prescribed by law.

### AMENDMENT 4

The right of the people to be secure in their persons, houses, papers, and effects, against unreasonable searches and seizures, shall not be violated, and no Warrants shall issue, but upon probable cause, supported by Oath or affirmation, and particularly describing the place to be searched, and the persons or things to be seized.

### AMENDMENT 5

No person shall be held to answer for a capital, or otherwise infamous crime, unless on a presentment or indictment of a Grand Jury, except in cases arising in the land or naval forces, or in the Militia, when in actual service in time of War or public danger; nor shall any person be subject for the same offence to be twice put in jeopardy of life or limb; nor shall be compelled in any criminal case to be a witness against himself, nor be deprived of life, liberty, or property, without due process of law; nor shall private property be taken for public use, without just compensation.

### AMENDMENT 6

In all criminal prosecutions, the accused shall enjoy the right to a speedy and public trial, by an impartial jury of the State and district wherein the crime shall have been committed, which district shall have been previously ascertained by law, and to be informed of the nature and cause of the accusation; to be confronted with the witnesses against him; to have compulsory process for obtaining witnesses in his favor, and to have the Assistance of Counsel for his defence.

### AMENDMENT 7

In Suits at common law, where the value in controversy shall exceed twenty dollars, the right of trial by jury shall be preserved, and no fact tried by a jury, shall be otherwise re-examined in any Court of the United States, than according to the rules of the common law.

### AMENDMENT 8

Excessive bail shall not be required, nor excessive fines imposed, nor cruel and unusual punishments inflicted.

### AMENDMENT 9

The enumeration in the Constitution, of certain rights, shall not be construed to deny or disparage others retained by the people.

### AMENDMENT 10

The powers not delegated to the United States by the Constitution, nor prohibited by it to the States, are reserved to the States respectively, or to the people.

### AMENDMENT 11

*(Ratified February 7, 1795)*

The Judicial power of the United States shall not be construed to extend to any suit in law or equity, commenced or prosecuted against one of the United States by Citizens of another State, or by Citizens or Subjects of any Foreign State.

### AMENDMENT 12

*(Ratified July 27, 1804)*

The Electors shall meet in their respective states and vote by ballot for President and Vice-President, one of whom, at least, shall not be an inhabitant of the same state with themselves; they shall name in their ballots the person voted for as President, and in distinct ballots the person voted for as Vice-President, and they shall make distinct lists of all persons voted for as President, and of all persons voted for as Vice-President, and of the number of votes for each, which lists they shall sign and certify, and transmit sealed to the seat of the government of the United States, directed to the President of the Senate;—The President of the Senate shall, in the presence of the Senate and House of Representatives, open all the certificates and the votes shall then be counted;— The person having the greatest number of votes for President, shall be the President, if such number be a majority of the whole number of Electors appointed; and if no person have such majority, then from the persons having the highest numbers not exceeding three on the list of those voted for as President, the House of Representatives shall choose immediately, by ballot, the President. But in choosing the President, the votes shall be taken by states, the representation from each state having one vote; a quorum for this purpose shall consist of a member or members from two-thirds of the states, and a majority of all the states shall be necessary to a choice.

And if the House of Representatives shall not choose a President whenever the right of choice shall devolve upon them, before the fourth day of March next following, then the Vice-President shall act as President, as in the case of the death or other constitutional disability of the President.—The person having the greatest number of votes as Vice-President, shall be the Vice-President, if such number be a majority of the whole number of Electors appointed, and if no person have a majority, then from the two highest numbers on the list, the Senate shall choose the Vice-President; a quorum for the purpose shall consist of two-thirds of the whole number of Senators, and a majority of the whole number shall be necessary to a choice. But no person constitutionally ineligible to the office of President shall be eligible to that of Vice-President of the United States.

## AMENDMENT 13
*(Ratified December 6, 1865)*

Section 1. Neither slavery nor involuntary servitude, except as a punishment for crime whereof the party shall have been duly convicted, shall exist within the United States, or any place subject to their jurisdiction.

Section 2. Congress shall have power to enforce this article by appropriate legislation.

## AMENDMENT 14
*(Ratified July 9, 1868)*

Section 1. All persons born or naturalized in the United States, and subject to the jurisdiction thereof, are citizens of the United States and of the State wherein they reside. No State shall make or enforce any law which shall abridge the privileges or immunities of citizens of the United States, nor shall any State deprive any person of life, liberty, or property, without due process of law; nor deny to any person within its jurisdiction the equal protection of the laws.

Section 2. Representatives shall be apportioned among the several States according to their respective numbers, counting the whole number of persons in each State, excluding Indians not taxed. But when the right to vote at any election for the choice of electors for President and Vice President of the United States, Representatives in Congress, the Executive and Judicial officers of a State, or the members of the Legislature thereof, is denied to any of the male inhabitants of such State, being twenty-one years of age, and citizens of the United States, or in any way abridged, except for participation in rebellion, or other crime, the basis of representation therein shall be reduced in the proportion which the number of such male citizens shall bear to the whole number of male citizens twenty-one years of age in such State.

Section 3. No person shall be a Senator or Representative in Congress, or elector of President and Vice President, or hold any office, civil or military, under the United States, or under any State, who, having previously taken an oath, as a member of Congress, or as an officer of the United States, or as a member of any State legislature, or as an executive or judicial officer of any State, to support the Constitution of the United States, shall have engaged in insurrection or rebellion against the same, or given aid or comfort to the enemies thereof. But Congress may be a vote of two-thirds of each House, remove such disability.

Section 4. The validity of the public debt of the United States, authorized by law, including debts incurred for payment of pensions and bounties for services in suppressing insurrection or rebellion, shall not be questioned. But neither the United States nor any State shall assume or pay any debt or obligation incurred in aid of insurrection or rebellion against the United States, or any claim for the loss or emancipation of any slave; but all such debts, obligations and claims shall be held illegal and void.

Section 5. The Congress shall have power to enforce, by appropriate legislation, the provisions of this article.

## AMENDMENT 15
*(Ratified February 3, 1870)*

Section 1. The right of citizens of the United States to vote shall not be denied or abridged by the United States or by any State on account of race, color, or previous condition of servitude.

Section 2. The Congress shall have power to enforce this article by appropriate legislation.

## AMENDMENT 16
*(Ratified February 3, 1913)*

The Congress shall have power to lay and collect taxes on incomes, from whatever source derived, without apportionment among the several States, and without regard to any census or enumeration.

## AMENDMENT 17
*(Ratified April 8, 1913)*

The Senate of the United States shall be composed of two Senators from each State, elected by the people thereof for six years; and each Senator shall have one vote. The electors in each State shall have the qualifications requisite for electors of the most numerous branch of the State legislatures.

When vacancies happen in the representation of any State in the Senate, the executive authority of such State shall issue writs of election to fill such vacancies: Provided, That the legislature of any State may empower the executive thereof to make temporary appointments until the people fill the vacancies by election as the legislature may direct.

This amendment shall not be so construed as to affect the election or term of any Senator chosen before it becomes valid as part of the Constitution.

## AMENDMENT 18*
*(Ratified January 16, 1919)*

Section 1. After one year from the ratification of this article the manufacture, sale, or transportation of intoxicating liquors within, the importation thereof into, or the exportation thereof from the United States and all territory subject to the jurisdiction thereof for beverage purposes is hereby prohibited.

Section 2. The Congress and the several States shall have concurrent power to enforce this article by appropriate legislation.

Section 3. This article shall be inoperative unless it shall have been ratified as an amendment to the Constitution by the legislatures of the several States, as provided in the Constitution, within seven years from the date of the submission hereof to the States by the Congress.

## AMENDMENT 19
*(Ratified August 18, 1920)*

The right of citizens of the United States to vote shall not be denied or abridged by the United States or by any State on account of sex.

Congress shall have power to enforce this article by appropriate legislation.

## AMENDMENT 20
*(Ratified January 23, 1933)*

Section 1. The terms of the President and Vice-President shall end at noon on the 20th day of January, and the terms of Senators and Representatives at noon on the 3d day of January, of the years in which such terms would have ended if this article had not been ratified; and the terms of their successors shall then begin.

Section 2. The Congress shall assemble at least

* Repealed by the Twenty-first Amendment.

## THE CONTINENTAL CONGRESS
### PLACE OF MEETING AND DATES OF SESSION

**Philadelphia, Pennsylvania**
   From September 5, 1774, to October 26, 1774;
   From May 10, 1775, to December 12, 1776
**Baltimore, Maryland**
   From December 20, 1776, to March 4, 1777
**Philadelphia, Pennsylvania**
   From March 5, 1777, to September 18, 1777
**Lancaster, Pennsylvania**
   September 27, 1777 (one day only)
**York, Pennsylvania**
   From September 30, 1777, to June 27, 1778

**Philadelphia, Pennsylvania**
   From July 2, 1778, to June 21, 1783
**Princeton, New Jersey**
   From June 30, 1783, to November 4, 1783
**Annapolis, Maryland**
   From November 26, 1783, to June 3, 1784
**Trenton, New Jersey**
   From November 1, 1784, to December 24, 1784
**New York, New York** (five sessions)
   From January 11, 1785, to November 4, 1785;
   From November 7, 1785, to November 3, 1786;
   From November 6, 1786, to October 30, 1787;
   From November 5, 1787 to October 21, 1788;
   From November 3, 1788, to March 2, 1789

once in every year, and such meeting shall begin at noon on the 3d day of January, unless they shall by law appoint a different day.

Section 3. If, at the time fixed for the beginning of the term of the President, the President-elect shall have died, the Vice-President-elect shall become President. If a President shall not have been chosen before the time fixed for the beginning of his term, or if the President-elect shall have failed to qualify, then the Vice-President-elect shall act as President until a President shall have qualified; and the Congress may by law provide for the case wherein neither a President-elect nor a Vice-President-elect shall have qualified, declaring who shall then act as President, or the manner in which one who is to act shall be selected, and such person shall act accordingly until a President or Vice-President shall have qualified.

Section 4. The Congress may by law provide for the case of the death of any of the persons from whom the House of Representatives may choose a President whenever the right of choice shall have devolved upon them, and for the case of the death of any of the persons from whom the Senate may choose a Vice-President whenever the right of choice shall have devolved upon them.

Section 5. Sections 1 and 2 shall take effect on the 15th day of October following the ratification of this article.

Section 6. This article shall be inoperative unless it shall have been ratified as an amendment to the Constitution by the legislatures of three-fourths of the several States within seven years from the date of its submission.

### AMENDMENT 21*
(*Ratified December 5, 1933*)

Section 1. The eighteenth article of amendment to the Constitution of the United States is hereby repealed.

Section 2. The transportation or importation into any State, Territory, or possession of the United States for delivery or use therein of intoxicating liquors, in violation of the laws thereof, is hereby prohibited.

Section 3. This article shall be inoperative unless it shall have been ratified as an amendment to the Constitution by conventions in the several States, as provided in the Constitution, within seven years from the date of the submission hereof to the States by the Congress.

\* The only amendment that repealed an amendment.

### AMENDMENT 22
(*Ratified February 27, 1951*)

Section 1. No person shall be elected to the office of the President more than twice, and no person who has held the office of President, or acted as President, for more than two years of a term to which some other person was elected President shall be elected to the office of the President more than once. But this Article shall not apply to any person holding the office of President when this Article was proposed by the Congress, and shall not prevent any person who may be holding the office of President, or acting as President, during the term within which this Article becomes operative from holding the office of President or acting as President during the remainder of such term.

Section 2. This article shall be inoperative unless it shall have been ratified as an amendment to the Constitution by the legislatures of three-fourths of the several States within seven years from the date of its submissions to the States by the Congress.

### AMENDMENT 23
(*Ratified March 29, 1961*)

Section 1. The District constituting the seat of Government of the United States shall appoint in such manner as the Congress may direct:

A number of electors of President and Vice President equal to the whole number of Senators and Representatives in Congress to which the District would be entitled if it were a State, but in no event more than the least populous State; they shall be in addition to those appointed by the States, but they shall be considered, for the purposes of the election of President and Vice President, to be electors appointed by a State; and they shall meet in the District and perform such duties as provided by the Twelfth article of amendment.

Section 2. The Congress shall have power to enforce this article by appropriate legislation.

### AMENDMENT 24
(*Ratified January 23, 1964*)

Section 1. The right of citizens of the United States to vote in any primary or other election for President or Vice President, for electors for President or Vice President, or for Senator or Representative in Congress, shall not be denied or abridged by the United States or any State by reason of failure to pay any poll tax or other tax.

Section 2. The Congress shall have power to enforce this article by appropriate legislation.

## AMENDMENT 25

(*Ratified February 10, 1967*)

Section 1. In case of the removal of the President from office or of his death or resignation, the Vice President shall become President.

Section 2. Whenever there is a vacancy in the office of the Vice President, the President shall nominate a Vice President who shall take office upon confirmation by a majority vote of both houses of Congress.

Section 3. Whenever the President transmits to the President pro tempore of the Senate and the Speaker of the House of Representatives his written declaration that he is unable to discharge the powers and duties of his office, and until he transmits to them a written declaration to the contrary, such powers and duties shall be discharged by the Vice President as Acting President.

Section 4. Whenever the Vice President and a majority of either the principal officers of the executive departments or of such other body as Congress may by law provide, transmit to the President pro tempore of the Senate and the Speaker of the House of Representatives their written declaration that the President is unable to discharge the powers and duties of his office, the Vice President shall immediately assume the powers and duties of the office as Acting President.

Thereafter, when the President transmits to the President pro tempore of the Senate and the Speaker of the House of Representatives his written declaration that no inability exists, he shall resume the powers and duties of his office unless the Vice President and a majority of either the principal officers of the executive department or of such other body as Congress may by law provide, transmit within four days to the President pro tempore of the Senate and the Speaker of the House of Representatives their written declaration that the President is unable to discharge the powers and duties of his office. Thereupon Congress shall decide the issue, assembling within forty-eight hours for that purpose if not in session. If the Congress, within twenty-one days after receipt of the latter written declaration, or, if Congress is not in session, within twenty-one days after Congress is required to assemble, determines by two-thirds vote of both houses that the President is unable to discharge the powers and duties of his office, the Vice President shall continue to discharge the same as Acting President; otherwise, the President shall resume the powers and duties of his office.

---

**AMENDMENT 25** ends more than 175 years of debate over the interpretation of Article II, Section I, Clause 6 of the Constitution, the vague "disability" clause, by defining how the Vice President may become Acting President. It also provides for the appointment of a Vice President if there is a vacancy in that office. Attention was focused on the need for this amendment after President Eisenhower suffered two heart attacks, and following the Kennedy assassination when President Johnson served more than a year without a Vice President. The amendment became part of the Constitution on February 10, 1967, when Nevada became the 38th state to ratify it.

---

## CONSTITUTIONAL AMENDMENTS NOT RATIFIED

During the course of U.S. history, in addition to the 25 amendments that have been ratified by the required three fourths of the states, five other amendments have been submitted to the states but have not been ratified by them. In 1798, of the 12 proposed amendments to the Constitution, articles III–XII were ratified and became the Bill of Rights, the first ten amendments to the Constitution. But the following, proposed articles I and II, were not ratified:

Article I. After the first enumeration required by the first article of the Constitution, there shall be one Representative for every thirty thousand, until the number shall amount to one hundred, after which the proportion shall be so regulated by Congress, that there shall be not less than one hundred Representatives, nor less than one Representative for every forty thousand persons, until the number of Representatives shall amount to two hundred; after which the proportion shall be so regulated by Congress, that there shall not be less than two hundred Representatives, nor more than one Representative for every fifty thousand persons.

Article II. No law varying the compensation for the services of the Senators and Representatives shall take effect, until an election of Representatives shall have intervened.

The 11th Congress, in its second session, proposed the following amendment to the Constitution relating to acceptance by citizens of the United States of titles "of nobility or honour" from any foreign government or ruler:

If any citizen of the United States shall accept, claim, receive or retain any title of nobility or honour, or shall, without the consent of Congress, accept and retain any present pension, office or emolument of any kind whatever, from any emperor, king, prince or foreign power, such person shall cease to be a citizen of the United States, and shall be incapable of holding any office of trust or profit under them, or either of them.

During the second session of the 36th Congress, on March 2, 1861, the following proposed amendment to the Constitution relating to slavery was signed by President James Buchanan, but was not ratified by the states:

No amendment shall be made to the Constitution which will authorize or give to Congress the power to abolish or interfere, within any State, with the domestic institutions thereof, including that of persons held to labor or service by the laws of said State.

In recent times, the only proposed amendment not ratified was a child-labor amendment:

Section 1. The Congress shall have power to limit, regulate, and prohibit the labor of persons under 18 years of age.

Section 2. The power of the several States is unimpaired by this article except that the operation of State laws shall be suspended to the extent necessary to give effect to legislation enacted by the Congress.

## THE GETTYSBURG ADDRESS

On July 1, 1863, Union and Confederate troops met at Gettysburg, Pennsylvania, in one of the major battles of the Civil War. Three days of heavy fighting ended with Southern forces in retreat. Both sides suffered heavy casualties.

On November 19, 1863, the Gettysburg battlefield was dedicated as a national cemetery. Edward Everett, a prominent 19th-century orator, delivered the principal speech. However, the day's immortal words came in President Abraham Lincoln's brief address, in which he made no distinction in honoring Union and Confederate dead, but called upon all Civil War survivors to rededicate themselves to the task of building a strong new nation, based upon the proposition that all men are created equal.

### THE ADDRESS

Four score and seven years ago our fathers brought forth on this continent, a new nation, conceived in Liberty, and dedicated to the proposition that all men are created equal.

Now we are engaged in a great civil war, testing whether that nation or any nation so conceived and so dedicated, can long endure. We are met on a great battle-field of that war. We have come to dedicate a portion of that field, as a final resting place for those who here gave their lives that that nation might live. It is altogether fitting and proper that we should do this.

But, in a larger sense, we can not dedicate—we can not consecrate—we can not hallow—this ground. The brave men, living and dead, who struggled here, have consecrated it, far above our poor power to add or detract. The world will little note, nor long remember what we say here, but it can never forget what they did here. It is for us the living, rather, to be dedicated here to the unfinished work which they who fought here have thus far so nobly advanced. It is rather for us to be here dedicated to the great task remaining before us—that from these honored dead we take increased devotion to that cause for which they gave the last full measure of devotion—that we here highly resolve that these dead shall not have died in vain—that this nation, under God, shall have a new birth of freedom—and that government of the people, by the people, for the people, shall not perish from the earth.

## THE EMANCIPATION PROCLAMATION

On January 1, 1863, President Abraham Lincoln issued the Emancipation Proclamation, which freed slaves in Confederate territory. The President described his act as a "necessary war measure for suppressing" Southern rebellion. His declaration did not affect slave states loyal to the Union, or Confederate territory under Union forces. Southern leaders bitterly denounced the measure as an invitation to Negro insurrection, which, in fact, never occurred.

Lincoln favored gradual, voluntary, compensated emancipation, yet found little support for his position. On September 22, 1862, after the Union Army's bloody, if technical, victory at Antietam, the President issued a preliminary Proclamation, declaring his intent to free Confederate slaves.

Congress had earlier approved antislavery legislation. However, no other U.S. declaration against slavery received such an enthusiastic reception abroad, or in domestic areas where antislavery feeling ran high. Coupled with Union military victories, foreign acceptance of the Emancipation Proclamation crushed Confederate hopes for European aid, and moved the North one step closer to victory.

### BY THE PRESIDENT OF THE UNITED STATES OF AMERICA: A PROCLAMATION.

Whereas on the 22d day of September, A.D. 1862, a proclamation was issued by the President of the United States, containing, among other things, the following, to wit:

"That on the 1st day of January, A.D. 1863, all persons held as slaves within any State or designated part of a State the people whereof shall then be in rebellion against the United States shall be then, thenceforward, and forever free; and the executive government of the United States, including the military and naval authority thereof, will recognize and maintain the freedom of such persons and will do no act or acts to repress such persons, or any of them, in any efforts they may make for their actual freedom.

"That the executive will on the 1st day of January aforesaid, by proclamation, designate the States and parts of States, if any, in which the people thereof, respectively, shall then be in rebellion against the United States; and the fact that any State or the people thereof shall on that day be in good faith represented in the Congress of the United States by members chosen thereto at elections wherein a majority of the qualified voters of such States shall have participated shall, in the absence of strong countervailing testimony, be deemed conclusive evidence that such State and the people thereof are not then in rebellion against the United States."

Now, therefore, I, Abraham Lincoln, President of the United States, by virtue of the power in me vested as Commander-in-Chief of the Army and Navy of the United States in time of actual armed rebellion against the authority and government of the United States, and as a fit and necessary war measure for suppressing said rebellion, do, on this 1st day of January, A.D. 1863, and in accordance with my purpose so to do, publicly proclaimed for the full period of one hundred days from the first day above mentioned, order and designate as the States and parts of States wherein the people thereof, respectively, are this day in rebellion against the United States the following, to wit:

Arkansas, Texas, Louisiana (except the parishes of St. Bernard, Plaquemines, Jefferson, St. John, St. Charles, St. James, Ascension, Assumption, Terrebonne, Lafourche, St. Mary, St. Martin, and Orleans, including the city of New Orleans), Mississippi, Alabama, Florida, Georgia, South Carolina, North Carolina, and Virginia (except the forty-eight counties designated as West Virginia, and also the counties of Berkeley, Accomac, Northhampton, Elizabeth City, York, Princess Anne, and Norfolk, including the cities of Norfolk and Portsmouth), and which excepted parts are for the present left precisely as if this proclamation were not issued.

And by virtue of the power and for the purpose aforesaid, I do order and declare that all persons held as slaves within said designated States and parts of States are, and henceforward shall be, free; and that the Executive Government of the United States, including the military and naval authorities thereof, will recognize and maintain the freedom of said persons.

And I hereby enjoin upon the people so declared to be free to abstain from all violence, unless in necessary self-defense; and I recommend to them that in all cases when allowed, they labor faithfully for reasonable wages.

And I further declare and make known that such persons of suitable condition will be received into the armed service of the United States to garrison forts, positions, stations, and other places, and to man vessels of all sorts in said service.

And upon this act, sincerely believed to be an act of justice, warranted by the Constitution upon military necessity, I invoke the considerate judgment of mankind and the gracious favor of Almighty God.

## THE MONROE DOCTRINE

The Monroe Doctrine, one of the basic tenets of American foreign policy, was first stated by President James Monroe in his annual message to Congress on December 2, 1823. It firmly established the principle that the United States would oppose European intervention in, or further colonization of, the Western Hemisphere. The Doctrine was originally intended to prevent European nations from aiding Spain in a reconquest of the newly independent Latin American republics and to halt Russian expansion along the west coast of North America. In 1904, President Theodore Roosevelt expounded the so-called Roosevelt corollary to the Doctrine, saying that continued disturbances in Latin America might force U.S. intervention. This interpretation was regarded as disguised imperialism by many Latin American countries, and later Presidents have tended to move away from it, with the exception of instances such as the Dominican crisis.

### A SELECTION FROM THE MONROE DOCTRINE

It is only when our rights are invaded or seriously menaced that we resent injuries or make preparation for our defense. With the movements in this hemisphere we are of necessity more immediately connected, and by causes which must be obvious to all enlightened and impartial observers. The political system of the allied powers is essentially different in this respect from that of America. This difference proceeds from that which exists in their respective Governments; and to the defense of our own, which has been achieved by the loss of so much blood and treasure, and matured by the wisdom of their most enlightened citizens, and under which we have enjoyed unexampled felicity, this whole nation is devoted. We owe it, therefore, to candor and to the amicable relations existing between the United States and those powers to declare that we should consider any attempt on their part to extend their system to any portion of this hemisphere as dangerous to our peace and safety.

## THE ATLANTIC CHARTER

The Atlantic Charter was a joint statement of postwar aims and policies issued on August 14, 1941, by President Franklin D. Roosevelt of the United States and Prime Minister Winston Churchill of Great Britain. The statement was drawn up by the two wartime leaders during a series of secret meetings held in August 1941, aboard the American cruiser *Augusta* and the British battleship *Prince of Wales*, in Argentia Bay, off the coast of Newfoundland.

### THE CHARTER

The President of the United States of America and the Prime Minister, Mr. Churchill, representing His Majesty's Government in the United Kingdom, being met together, deem it right to make known certain common principles in the national policies of their respective countries on which they base their hopes for a better future for the world.

First, their countries seek no aggrandizement, territorial or other;

Second, they desire to see no territorial changes that do not accord with the freely expressed wishes of the peoples concerned;

Third, they respect the right of all peoples to choose the form of government under which they will live; and they wish to see sovereign rights and self government restored to those who have been forcibly deprived of them;

Fourth, they will endeavor, with due respect for their existing obligations, to further the enjoyment by all States, great or small, victor or vanquished, of access, on equal terms, to the trade and to the raw materials of the world which are needed for their economic prosperity;

Fifth, they desire to bring about the fullest collaboration between all nations in the economic field with the object of securing, for all, improved labor standards, economic advancement and social security;

Sixth, after the final destruction of the Nazi tyranny, they hope to see established a peace which will afford to all nations the means of dwelling in safety within their own boundaries, and which will afford assurance that all the men in all the lands may live out their lives in freedom from fear and want;

Seventh, such a peace should enable all men to traverse the high seas and oceans without hindrance;

Eighth, they believe that all of the nations of the world, for realistic as well as spiritual reasons must come to the abandonment of the use of force. Since no future peace can be maintained if land, sea or air armaments continue to be employed by nations which threaten, or may threaten, aggression outside of their frontiers, they believe, pending the establishment of a wider and permanent system of general security, that the disarmament of such nations is essential. They will likewise aid and encourage all other practicable measures which will lighten for peace-loving peoples the crushing burden of armaments.

# THE PRESIDENCY

The Presidency of the United States is an institution unique among the nations of the world. No other country demands that its leader perform both the symbolic role of chief of state and at the same time the grueling job of directing its turbulent course in the political fray. Although the Constitution provides for a system of checks and balances, with each branch of the government—Executive, Legislative, and Judicial—acting as a limiting force on the other two, the United States has evolved a system of presidential leadership, in order to bring the governing of the country into a central focus.

Although the President's roles are provided for by the Constitution, they are only incompletely detailed and are constantly being enlarged and elaborated upon. The President is simultaneously chief of state, chief executive, chief legislator, party leader, chief diplomat, and commander-in-chief of the armed forces. The action of the President in any one role materially affects the others, for the President is the mainspring of the governmental system.

The Presidency is what the men who are elected to the office make it. Many factors, including the personality of the man and the circumstances of his time, enter into this process. Nevertheless, as foreign affairs have increasingly dominated the activities of the U.S. government, the President has taken on greater powers.

The only official elected by the American people as a whole, the President is chosen to be some sort of embodiment of the character and purpose of the government. This symbolic role, reinforced by his personality and initiative, may be used to persuade the people and the Congress to adopt his views on how the country should be governed. The manner in which the President exercises this function generally determines the place he occupies in political history. Whether he supplies creative leadership and seeks positively to change the shape of public opinion, or whether he assumes the role of a charismatic leader by inspiring the people to greater heights of action, the man who is elected President assumes the ultimate responsibility for directing the most complex organization in the world today.

## LITTLE-KNOWN FACTS ABOUT U.S. PRESIDENTS

- During Jefferson's Administration, the official dinner table was circular so that all seats were equal in importance.
- After the White House was destroyed by fire during the War of 1812, the Octagon House became the Executive Mansion for President and Mrs. Madison.
- During General Lafayette's visit to the United States in July–August 1825, he left his live alligator in the White House East Room.
- Andrew Jackson, known as the "People's President," spent, during his two Presidential terms, over $50,000 for refurbishing the White House.
- On Washington's Birthday, 1837, President Jackson provided for his guests a huge cheese, weighing 1,400 pounds and measuring 4 feet by 2 feet.
- William Henry Harrison died after having served only one month as President, the result of pneumonia brought on by delivering a two-hour inaugural address in a freezing wind.
- Julia Gardiner Tyler, married to President Tyler while he was in office, established the custom of playing Hail to the Chief whenever the President makes an appearance. (Tyler was the first President to marry while in office.)
- Sarah Polk was her husband's confidential secretary, the first time that a First Lady had ever served in that capacity.
- Abigail Fillmore is responsible for obtaining the first library for the White House. Until 1850, no books were part of the White House furnishings.
- During the visit to Washington of the Prince of Wales (later Edward VII) President Buchanan slept in a hallway in the White House in order that the royal visitor could be put up in decent style.
- President Grant, a life-long lover of horses, had the White House stables enlarged and filled with racing and carriage horses.
- The wife of President Rutherford Hayes was the first First Lady to be college-trained.
- President Hayes was the first President ever to go to the West Coast, visiting all the principal towns from Omaha to San Francisco and traveling as far north as Seattle.
- President William Howard Taft, weighing 332 pounds at his inauguration, got stuck in the White House bathtub and had to have a specially constructed extra-large one installed. The new one comfortably held four average-size men.
- President Wilson, during World War I, had a flock of sheep grazing on the White House grounds.
- Calvin Coolidge was sworn into office by his father, Colonel John Coolidge, a notary public, in the middle of the night, after being notified of the death of President Harding.
- Franklin Delano Roosevelt inaugurated the custom of "Fireside Chats," making widespread use of the radio to keep in close contact with the nation.
- President Truman arose each day at 5:30 A.M. and went for a brisk walk. His impromptu news conferences held during these walks provided good newspaper copy for the enterprising reporters who got up at that hour.
- President Eisenhower added two innovations to the Presidential press conferences by allowing television cameras to be used and reporters to quote him verbatim.

## HOW A PRESIDENT IS ELECTED

The President and Vice President of the United States are elected every four years in the only nationwide election in the United States, the only one that involves all voters regardless of state boundaries. Besides satisfying the constitutional requirements that he be at least 35 years old, a natural-born citizen of the United States, and a resident of the country for 14 years, a candidate must, in effect, win two elections. He must emerge as the successful candidate of his political party's national convention and then win more electoral votes than any one of his opponents.

The national convention, held in the summer of election year, has been the accepted method of selecting a party's Presidential candidate since 1831, when the first real national convention was held by a major political party. The two major parties in the United States, the Republicans and the Democrats, select the number of delegates to attend the convention on different bases, but once the delegates have assembled, the procedure of each convention is essentially the same. Delegates to the conventions are selected according to *state* law, which varies considerably from state to state. About two thirds of the states choose their delegates by committee or state convention; one third use primary elections; and a few use a combination of both methods. Even though they do not have any voice in the final election, Puerto Rico, the Virgin Islands, and the Canal Zone (Democrats only) send delegates to the national conventions.

The chairman of the party's national committee, acting as temporary chairman, calls the convention to order, and a credentials committee seats state and territorial delegations. A permanent chairman is then elected, and the convention votes on a party platform drawn up by a platform committee.

Nominations for the Presidential candidate follow. Most candidates actively seeking endorsement have campaigned in state primaries, and enter the conventions with a base of delegate support. To select a national standard-bearer, the convention chairman calls the roll of states alphabetically: a state may nominate a candidate, or pass to another state. When the nominations are completed, the convention votes, alphabetically by state, until one candidate wins a majority. This may require a number of ballots.

After the Presidential nominee has been selected, the Vice-Presidential candidate is chosen in much the same manner, except that the Presidential candidate usually exerts considerable influence over the choice of his running mate.

Some minor political parties nominate Presidential and Vice-Presidential candidates. However, the principal contest in recent years has been between the Republican and Democratic nominees.

The election campaign may begin immediately after the convention adjourns, although most candidates prefer to rest for a few weeks, but it comes to an end with election day. At this time (the first Tuesday after the first Monday in November), the American voter registers his choice at the polls. Technically the people do not vote directly for the President; they vote for a slate of men known as electors, who in turn select the President. This system of indirect election was devised by the framers of the Constitution to allow a group of qualified men to meet and, without influence by any faction, select the most qualified man to be President. Political changes since 1787 have reduced the importance of this system. In many ways it is today a mere formality. The procedure that is followed begins with the voter choosing the electors on election day. These electors in turn go to their respective state capitals on the first Monday after the second Wednesday in December, where they vote for the candidate of their choice. Although they are not in all states legally bound to vote for the man who received the majority of their state's votes, custom demands that the man who has received the state's popular majority vote is also the choice of the electors. These votes are in turn sent to the nation's capitol, where, upon the convening of Congress, the President of the Senate, in a joint session, opens the ballots, counts the votes, and announces the name of the next President of the United States, who is limited to two terms by the 22nd amendment to the Constitution. The successful candidate is inaugurated on the following January 20th.

If no man wins a majority of the electoral votes for President, the decision goes to the House of Representatives. This body, with each state having one vote, selects a winner from among the top three candidates. This has happened only once, in 1824, when John Quincy Adams was chosen from a group of four candidates. The selection of a Vice President under similar circumstances is made by the Senate's choosing between the top two candidates, again with each state having one vote.

The electoral college system has been criticized for many reasons, but chiefly because it permits the election of a President who has not received a majority of the nation's popular vote. Since the electoral college is composed of as many members as each state has senators and representatives (a total of 538 in 1964), a man needs only 269 votes to become President. These votes may be tallied from states whose total population is less than a majority of the country's popular vote. In the history of the United States, a number of men have become President without having won a majority of the popular vote.

The high stability of our party system can be remarked from the fact that Presidents have been elected only from the Federalist, Democratic-Republican, Democratic, Whig, and Republican ranks. Third parties have generally made a small impression on this firm tradition, though they have had a somewhat greater effect than is generally realized.

## ELECTORAL VOTES

In the election of 1964, the electoral votes to which each state was entitled (listed below) were based on the 1960 census. A state's quota of Representatives varies with population. Because of periodic Congressional reapportionments, many of these totals are likely to change in the future. The national total (538 in 1964) is subject to change as the state totals change.

| STATE | VOTES | STATE | VOTES | STATE | VOTES |
|---|---|---|---|---|---|
| Alabama | 10 | Louisiana | 10 | Ohio | 26 |
| Alaska | 3 | Maine | 4 | Oklahoma | 8 |
| Arizona | 5 | Maryland | 10 | Oregon | 6 |
| Arkansas | 6 | Massachusetts | 14 | Pennsylvania | 29 |
| California | 40 | Michigan | 21 | Rhode Island | 4 |
| Colorado | 6 | Minnesota | 10 | South Carolina | 8 |
| Connecticut | 8 | Mississippi | 7 | South Dakota | 4 |
| Delaware | 3 | Missouri | 12 | Tennessee | 11 |
| Florida | 14 | Montana | 4 | Texas | 25 |
| Georgia | 12 | Nebraska | 5 | Utah | 4 |
| Hawaii | 4 | Nevada | 3 | Vermont | 3 |
| Idaho | 4 | New Hampshire | 4 | Virginia | 12 |
| Illinois | 26 | New Jersey | 17 | Washington | 9 |
| Indiana | 13 | New Mexico | 4 | West Virginia | 7 |
| Iowa | 9 | New York | 43 | Wisconsin | 12 |
| Kansas | 7 | North Carolina | 13 | Wyoming | 3 |
| Kentucky | 9 | North Dakota | 4 | District of Columbia | 3 |

## MINORITY PRESIDENTS

| ELEC-TION | PRESIDENT | PARTY | POPULAR VOTE | ELEC-TION | PRESIDENT | PARTY | POPULAR VOTE |
|---|---|---|---|---|---|---|---|
| 1824 | John Quincy Adams | Independent | 31.89% | 1884 | Grover Cleveland | Democrat | 48.50% |
| 1844 | James K. Polk | Democrat | 49.56 | 1888 | Benjamin Harrison | Republican | 47.81 |
| 1848 | Zachary Taylor | Whig | 47.31 | 1892 | Grover Cleveland | Democrat | 46.04 |
| 1856 | James Buchanan | Democrat | 45.63 | 1912 | Woodrow Wilson | Democrat | 41.85 |
| 1860 | Abraham Lincoln | Republican | 39.79 | 1916 | Woodrow Wilson | Democrat | 49.26 |
| 1876 | Rutherford B. Hayes | Republican | 47.94 | 1948 | Harry S. Truman | Democrat | 49.51 |
| 1880 | James A. Garfield | Republican | 48.32 | 1960 | John F. Kennedy | Democrat | 49.71 |

## INCOMPLETED TERMS OF U.S. PRESIDENTS AND VICE PRESIDENTS

The deaths of seven Presidents have resulted in the Vice-Presidential succession to the office of President. There has never been a Presidential resignation nor has any President been replaced because of inability. The Constitution does not attempt to determine inability. It merely suggests the voluntary resignation of the incapacitated President. During President Dwight Eisenhower's two sicknesses, fruitless attempts were made to provide specific definitions of inability. Eisenhower and Kennedy established informal agreements with their Vice Presidents providing that the Vice President could decide Presidential disability.

The following table lists Presidents and Vice Presidents who died in office, with their terms of service. One Vice President resigned his office. John C. Calhoun, who served one term with President John Quincy Adams and from March 4, 1829, to December 28, 1832, with President Andrew Jackson, resigned to become a U.S. Senator.

| PRESIDENT | TERM | SUCCESSOR |
|---|---|---|
| William Henry Harrison | March 4, 1841—April 4, 1841 | John Tyler |
| Zachary Taylor | March 5, 1849—July 9, 1850 | Millard Fillmore |
| Abraham Lincoln | March 4, 1865—April 15, 1865 (second term) | Andrew Johnson |
| James A. Garfield | March 4, 1881—September 19, 1881 | Chester A. Arthur |
| William McKinley | March 4, 1901—September 14, 1901 (second term) | Theodore Roosevelt |
| Warren G. Harding | March 4, 1921—August 2, 1923 | Calvin Coolidge |
| Franklin D. Roosevelt | January 20, 1945—April 12, 1945 (fourth term) | Harry S. Truman |
| John F. Kennedy | January 20, 1961—November 22, 1963 | Lyndon B. Johnson |

| VICE PRESIDENT | TERM | PRESIDENT |
|---|---|---|
| George Clinton | March 4, 1809—April 20, 1812 (second term) | James Madison |
| Elbridge Gerry | March 4, 1813—November 23, 1814 | James Madison |
| William R. King | March 4, 1853—April 18, 1853 | Franklin Pierce |
| Henry Wilson | March 4, 1873—November 22, 1875 | Ulysses S. Grant |
| Thomas A. Hendricks | March 4, 1885—November 25, 1885 | Grover Cleveland |
| Garret A. Hobart | March 4, 1897—November 21, 1899 | William McKinley |
| James S. Sherman | March 4, 1909—October 30, 1912 | William H. Taft |

J.D. Barnell

## THE WHITE HOUSE

The official residence of the President of the United States is located at 1600 Pennsylvania Avenue in Washington, D.C., and is known as the White House. The first public building to be erected in the nation's capital, its cornerstone was laid on October 13, 1792. The original structure was designed by James Hoban, an Irish architect then living in South Carolina, and was estimated to cost $400,000. Hoban drew mainly on the Palladian architecture of mid-18th century Europe, but his work exhibits freshness in having the main drawing room (today the Blue Room) oval in shape. The French doors of this room served for many years as the principal access to the mansion from the South garden or front.

The first President to reside in the White House was John Adams, who moved in on November 1, 1800. The exact design by Hoban was never fully carried out and successive changes have marked the history of the White House from its very beginning. Funds for construction were raised grudgingly by a nation wary of too much pomp and splendor, by sale of government-owned lands in the District of Columbia, and from contributions by Maryland and Virginia. The first restoration of the White House was begun in 1815 after the interior was gutted during the War of 1812. James Hoban again was responsible for its design and construction. By 1817 the executive mansion was ready for President Monroe to move in.

Contrary to general belief, the original structure was well built, at least by the standards of that day, and was well reconstructed after the fire. Problems arose as the demands of the government caused greater use to be made of the official residence, and larger and larger numbers of people put a strain on the structure and equipment. But not until 1902, during the administration of Theodore Roosevelt, was another alteration of major importance made.

The main floor was reconstructed, and to some extent restored to its original architectural design. Separation of residence and executive offices ended the jumble of domestic and official rooms, making the second floor available for sole use as Presidential living quarters and reestablishing the residential character of the building, a feature that remains true today.

The office functions of the White House are now located in separate wings that are actually independent structures, although connected with the main building. The President's office, the Cabinet Room, and other general offices are located in the West Wing. Originally constructed under Theodore Roosevelt in 1902, this wing was completely rebuilt in 1910, damaged by fire in 1929, and largely rebuilt in 1934. The East Wing, providing additional office space as well as small assembly and conference rooms, was constructed in 1942 during the administration of Franklin D. Roosevelt.

The second major change in the White House occurred in 1927. The first and third stories were made fire-resistant but the second story, of wood construction dating back to 1815, was left untouched. In 1948 an extensive examination revealed the necessity of a thorough renovation of the White House. During this renovation, the White House was closed to visitors and government personnel. President Harry S. Truman established his official residence at Blair House, across the street.

The visitor arriving at the East Gate on the official free tour starts at the ground floor. From there, a major stairway opens into the entrance hall, where portraits of the Presidents are hung. This main hall leads from the State Dining Room on the west to the East Room; the Red, Blue, and Green Rooms open on the right or south side of the hall. The rooms open to visitors are:

*The State Dining Room*—largest except for the East Room, it can seat about 100 in horseshoe and E-shape table arrangement.

*The Red Room*—for many years the First Lady's Reception Room, it was the first of the State Rooms to be refurnished entirely by the Fine Arts Committee for the White House.

*The Blue Room*—considered the most beautiful in the White House, this is the room where the President often receives official guests.

*The Green Room*—used for formal and informal receptions, it has been refurnished as a fashionable parlor of the Federalist period.

*The East Room*—the scene of levees and receptions, weddings and funerals, it is today the first State Room seen by the public visitor on a tour of the White House and the room where guests gather before a great reception or state dinner. Other rooms are open to visitors with a special pass or to invited guests.

The White House has, excluding minor rooms, 12 rooms on the ground floor, 7 rooms on the first floor, 14 rooms on the second floor, and 21 rooms on the third. The house is 168 feet long and, including porticos, 152 feet wide. The grounds of the White House cover an area of about 18½ acres and include the famous Rose Garden.

# PRESIDENTIAL ELECTIONS: 1789–1960

The first four Presidential elections (1789, 1792, 1796, and 1800) were conducted under Article II, Section 1 of the Constitution, which called for the electors to vote for two candidates: the one with the majority of votes was elected President, and the next highest became Vice President.

In the event that no candidate had a majority, the House of Representatives (voting by states, with one vote for each state) was to choose the President from among the five candidates highest on the electoral list. The candidate second to the President in the voting became Vice President.

A tie in the Electoral College in 1800 led to the passage of the Twelfth Amendment, which provides for separate ballots for President and Vice President.

## 1789

| PRESIDENTIAL CANDIDATES | PARTY | ELECTORAL VOTES |
|---|---|---|
| George Washington...... | None | 69 |
| John Adams............ | None | 34 |
| Other candidates........ | None | 35 |
| Votes not cast.......... | — | 4 |

**Nominations:** Washington, the most popular man at the Constitutional Convention, was chosen by the Continental Congress. **Campaign Issues:** In this, the first U.S. Presidential election, party division was at a minimum, for only those who supported the new Constitution took part. **Remarks:** Ten of the 11 states which had recently ratified the Constitution had their state legislatures choose Presidential electors. New York failed to do so. Rhode Island and North Carolina had not yet ratified the Constitution.

## 1792

| PRESIDENTIAL CANDIDATES | PARTY | ELECTORAL VOTES |
|---|---|---|
| George Washington...... | Federalist | 132 |
| John Adams............ | Federalist | 77 |
| George Clinton.......... | Anti-Federalist | 50 |
| Other candidates....... | — | 5 |
| Votes not cast.......... | — | 3 |

**Nominations:** Washington and Adams, the incumbents, received the nomination of those who advocated a strong central government. Clinton was chosen by anti-Administration Congressional leaders. **Campaign Issues:** The fiscal policy and strong centralization advocated by Alexander Hamilton, then Secretary of the Treasury and a staunch Federalist, provided the issues. **Remarks:** Washington's popularity could not be eclipsed, and the Anti-Federalists had hoped to elect Clinton as Vice President.

## 1796

| PRESIDENTIAL CANDIDATES | PARTY | ELECTORAL VOTES |
|---|---|---|
| John Adams............ | Federalist | 71 |
| Thomas Jefferson........ | Dem.-Rep. | 68 |
| Thomas Pinckney....... | Federalist | 59 |
| Aaron Burr............. | Dem.-Rep. | 30 |
| Other candidates........ | — | 48 |

**Nominations:** Congressional leaders of the two parties chose their respective candidates. **Campaign Issues:** Foreign policy dominated the campaign; the Federalists supported closer ties with England, while the Democratic-Republicans sought France's friendship. **Remarks:** Because of a factional split in the Federalist Party—between Hamilton and Adams—many Federalist electors gave their second vote to Jefferson.

## 1800

| PRESIDENTIAL CANDIDATES | PARTY | ELECTORAL VOTES |
|---|---|---|
| Thomas Jefferson........ | Dem.-Rep. | 73 |
| Aaron Burr............. | Dem.-Rep. | 73 |
| John Adams............ | Federalist | 65 |
| Charles C. Pinckney..... | Federalist | 64 |
| John Jay............... | Federalist | 1 |

**Nominations:** Jefferson and Adams were the acknowledged leaders of their respective parties. **Campaign Issues:** Both parties debated an undeclared naval war with France and the Federalist repression of its political opponents through the Alien and Sedition Acts. **Remarks:** Because electoral voting ended in a tie, the House of Representatives decided the contest; on the 36th ballot Jefferson was chosen President.

## 1804

| PRESIDENTIAL CANDIDATES | PARTY | ELECTORAL VOTES | VICE-PRESIDENTIAL CANDIDATES | PARTY | ELECTORAL VOTES |
|---|---|---|---|---|---|
| Thomas Jefferson........ | Dem.-Rep. | 162 | George Clinton.......... | Dem.-Rep. | 162 |
| Charles C. Pinckney..... | Federalist | 14 | Rufus King............. | Federalist | 14 |

**Nominations:** At the first regular political caucuses, the Congressional delegates of both parties unanimously nominated their respective candidates. **Campaign Issues:** Debate centered on the territorial expansion of the United States through the Louisiana Purchase. **Remarks:** This was the first Presidential election carried out under the Twelfth Amendment to the Constitution.

## 1808

| PRESIDENTIAL CANDIDATES | PARTY | ELECTORAL VOTES | VICE-PRESIDENTIAL CANDIDATES | PARTY | ELECTORAL VOTES |
|---|---|---|---|---|---|
| James Madison............ | Dem.-Rep. | 122 | George Clinton........... | Dem.-Rep. | 113 |
| Charles C. Pinckney....... | Federalist | 47 | Rufus King.............. | Federalist | 47 |
| George Clinton........... | Dem.-Rep. | 6 | Other candidates........ | — | 15 |
| Votes not cast............ | — | 1 | Votes not cast........... | — | 1 |

**Nominations:** Congressional caucuses nominated respective party candidates. **Campaign Issues:** Jefferson's Embargo Act. **Remarks:** A faction of the Democratic-Republicans supported Clinton despite Madison's candidacy on the Democratic-Republican ticket.

## 1812

| PRESIDENTIAL CANDIDATES | PARTY | ELECTORAL VOTES | VICE-PRESIDENTIAL CANDIDATES | PARTY | ELECTORAL VOTES |
|---|---|---|---|---|---|
| James Madison............ | Dem.-Rep. | 128 | Elbridge Gerry........... | Dem.-Rep. | 131 |
| DeWitt Clinton............ | Federalist | 89 | Charles J. Ingersoll....... | Federalist | 86 |
| Votes not cast............ | — | 1 | Votes not cast........... | — | 1 |

**Nominations:** A Congressional caucus nominated the Democratic-Republican ticket. **Campaign Issues:** The major issue was the desirability and conduct of the War of 1812. **Remarks:** This was the first Presidential election carried out while the nation was formally at war.

## 1816

| PRESIDENTIAL CANDIDATES | PARTY | ELECTORAL VOTES | VICE-PRESIDENTIAL CANDIDATES | PARTY | ELECTORAL VOTES |
|---|---|---|---|---|---|
| James Monroe............ | Dem.-Rep. | 183 | Daniel D. Tompkins....... | Dem.-Rep. | 183 |
| Rufus King.............. | Federalist | 34 | John E. Howard.......... | Federalist | 22 |
| Votes not cast............ | — | 4 | Other candidates........ | — | 12 |
|  |  |  | Votes not cast........... | — | 4 |

**Nominations:** A Congressional caucus nominated the Democratic-Republican ticket. **Campaign Issues:** There were no real issues because the Democratic-Republican Party had by this time adopted most of the Federalist program. **Remarks:** The Federalist electors voted for King but scattered their votes for Vice President.

## 1820

| PRESIDENTIAL CANDIDATES | PARTY | ELECTORAL VOTES | VICE-PRESIDENTIAL CANDIDATES | PARTY | ELECTORAL VOTES |
|---|---|---|---|---|---|
| James Monroe............ | Dem.-Rep. | 231 | Daniel D. Tompkins....... | Dem.-Rep. | 218 |
| John Quincy Adams....... | Independent | 1 | Other candidates........ | — | 14 |
| Votes not cast............ | — | 3 | Votes not cast........... | — | 3 |

**Nominations:** Poor attendance at the Democratic-Republican Congressional caucus resulted in little opposition to Monroe's bid for a second term. **Campaign Issues:** No issues were debated. **Remarks:** William Plumer of New Hampshire voted against Monroe because he believed only Washington's election should be unanimous.

## 1824 *

| PRESIDENTIAL CANDIDATES | PARTY | ELECTORAL VOTES | POPULAR VOTE | | VICE-PRESIDENTIAL CANDIDATES AND ELECTORAL VOTES | PARTY |
|---|---|---|---|---|---|---|
|  |  |  | Total | Percentage |  |  |
| John Quincy Adams...... | None | 84 | 115,696 | 31.89 | John C. Calhoun..... 182 | None |
| Andrew Jackson......... | None | 99 | 152,933 | 42.16 | Nathan Sanford..... 30 | None |
| William H. Crawford...... | None | 41 | 46,979 | 12.95 | Nathaniel Macon.... 24 | None |
| Henry Clay.............. | None | 37 | 47,136 | 12.99 | Other Candidates.... 25 | — |

**Nominations:** The disintegration of the Democratic-Republican Party led to Presidential nominations by state legislatures; there were several "favorite son" candidates. **Campaign Issues:** The candidates supported domestic improvements and a higher protective tariff. **Remarks:** No candidate received a majority of the electoral vote. The House of Representatives finally chose Adams.

* Before 1824, records of popular vote are all but nonexistent; state legislatures, faced with negligible returns, often chose the Presidential electors.

## 1828

| PRESIDENTIAL CANDIDATES | PARTY | ELECTORAL VOTES | POPULAR VOTE Total | Percentage | VICE-PRESIDENTIAL CANDIDATES AND ELECTORAL VOTES | PARTY |
|---|---|---|---|---|---|---|
| Andrew Jackson..... | Democratic | 178 | 647,292 | 56.04 | John C. Calhoun..... 171 | Democratic |
| John Quincy Adams.. | Natl. Rep. | 83 | 507,730 | 43.96 | Richard Rush....... 83 | Natl. Rep. |
|  |  |  |  |  | William Smith....... 7 | Democratic |

**Nominations:** The Tennessee legislature nominated Jackson for the Presidency. Adams was the incumbent, as was Calhoun, but Calhoun switched to Jackson. **Campaign Issues:** Jackson and his followers charged that the government was in the hands of an "aristocratic minority." **Remarks:** Jackson was the first popular hero; he campaigned for reform.

## 1832

| PRESIDENTIAL CANDIDATES | PARTY | ELECTORAL VOTES | POPULAR VOTE Total | Percentage | VICE-PRESIDENTIAL CANDIDATES AND ELECTORAL VOTES | PARTY |
|---|---|---|---|---|---|---|
| Andrew Jackson..... | Democratic | 219 | 688,242 | 54.50 | Martin Van Buren... 189 | Democratic |
| Henry Clay.......... | Natl. Rep. | 49 | 473,462 | 37.49 | John Sergeant...... 49 | Natl. Rep. |
| John Floyd.......... | Independent | 11 | — | — | Henry Lee.......... 11 | Independent |
| William Wirt........ | Anti-Masonic | 7 | 101,051 | 8.00 | Amos Ellmaker...... 7 | Anti-Masonic |
| Votes not cast....... | — | 2 | — | — | William Wilkins..... 30 | Independent |
|  |  |  |  |  | Votes not cast....... 2 | — |

**Nominations:** The modern political convention system dates from September 26, 1831. Wirt was nominated on the first ballot by the Anti-Masonic Party. The National Republican Party convention met in Baltimore, December 12–15, 1831, and chose Clay and Sergeant. At the Democratic Party convention in Baltimore, May 21–23, 1832, Jackson unanimously received the nomination. The Independents nominated Floyd and Lee. **Campaign Issues:** The Democrats fought the rechartering of the Second Bank of the United States. **Remarks:** The Anti-Masonic Party was the first legitimate third party in the United States.

## 1836

| PRESIDENTIAL CANDIDATES | PARTY | ELECTORAL VOTES | POPULAR VOTE Total | Percentage | VICE-PRESIDENTIAL CANDIDATES AND ELECTORAL VOTES | PARTY |
|---|---|---|---|---|---|---|
| Martin Van Buren.... | Democratic | 170 | 764,198 | 50.93 | Richard M. Johnson.. 147 | Democratic |
| William H. Harrison.. | Whig | 73 | 549,508 | 36.63 | Francis Granger..... 77 | Whig |
| Hugh L. White....... | Whig | 26 | 145,352 | 9.69 | John Tyler.......... 47 | Democratic |
| Daniel Webster...... | Whig | 14 | 41,287 | 2.75 | William Smith....... 23 | Independent |
| W. P. Mangum...... | Independent | 11 | — | — |  |  |

**Nominations:** At the Democratic convention in Baltimore, May 20–22, 1835, Van Buren was nominated unanimously. The Whigs, who held no national convention, nominated several strong sectional candidates. **Campaign Issues:** The campaign centered on Andrew Jackson, his policies, and whether Van Buren should succeed him. **Remarks:** This was the only election in which none of the Vice Presidential candidates received the required majority vote; the House of Representatives chose Johnson over Granger.

## 1840

| PRESIDENTIAL CANDIDATES | PARTY | ELECTORAL VOTES | POPULAR VOTE Total | Percentage | VICE-PRESIDENTIAL CANDIDATES AND ELECTORAL VOTES | PARTY |
|---|---|---|---|---|---|---|
| William H. Harrison.. | Whig | 234 | 1,275,612 | 52.87 | John Tyler.......... 234 | Whig |
| Martin Van Buren.... | Democratic | 60 | 1,130,033 | 46.84 | Richard Johnson..... 48 | Democratic |
| James G. Birney..... | Liberty | — | 7,053 | .29 | Thomas Earle....... — | Liberty |
|  |  |  |  |  | L. W. Tazewell..... 11 | Independent |
|  |  |  |  |  | James K. Polk...... 1 | Democratic |

**Nominations:** The Whigs, convened in Harrisburg, Penn., May 4–5, 1840, chose Harrison and Tyler. The Democrats met in Baltimore, May 5–7, 1840, and chose Van Buren without dissent. The Liberty Party met on April 1, 1840, at Albany and nominated Birney and Earle. **Campaign Issues:** A divided Whig Party, hungry for power, banded together behind the slogan of "Tippecanoe and Tyler too," and campaigned on personalities. **Remarks:** The Liberty Party was the first national political manifestation of the antislavery movement in America.

## 1844

| PRESIDENTIAL CANDIDATES | PARTY | ELECTORAL VOTES | POPULAR VOTE Total | Percentage | VICE-PRESIDENTIAL CANDIDATES |
|---|---|---|---|---|---|
| James K. Polk........ | Democratic | 170 | 1,339,368 | 49.56 | George M. Dallas |
| Henry Clay.......... | Whig | 105 | 1,300,687 | 48.13 | Theodore Frelinghuysen |
| James G. Birney....... | Liberty | | 62,197 | 2.30 | Thomas Morris |

**Nominations:** At the Whig convention in Baltimore, May 1, 1844, Clay was chosen on the first ballot by acclamation; on the third ballot Frelinghuysen received 155 out of 275 votes; his nomination was made unanimous. The Democrats met in Baltimore, May 27–30, 1844, and although Van Buren had a majority of the votes, he could not obtain the necessary two-thirds majority. On the ninth ballot Polk was nominated. Dallas received the Vice-Presidential nomination on the second ballot, after Silas Wright had declined the nomination. The Liberty Party met in Buffalo, New York, on August 30, 1843, and unanimously nominated its candidates, Birney and Morris. **Campaign Issues:** Foreign and domestic issues included the questions of whether Texas should be annexed as a slave state, whether the tariff should be lowered, and what steps should be taken to settle the Oregon dispute with Great Britain favorably. **Remarks:** Polk is often called the first dark horse nominee in American politics.

## 1848

| PRESIDENTIAL CANDIDATES | PARTY | ELECTORAL VOTES | POPULAR VOTE Total | Percentage | VICE-PRESIDENTIAL CANDIDATES |
|---|---|---|---|---|---|
| Zachary Taylor........ | Whig | 163 | 1,362,101 | 47.31 | Millard Fillmore |
| Lewis Cass........... | Democratic | 127 | 1,222,674 | 42.47 | William O. Butler |
| Martin Van Buren..... | Free Soil | — | 291,616 | 10.13 | Charles Francis Adams |

**Nominations:** The Democratic convention in Baltimore, May 22–26, 1848, chose Lewis Cass on the fourth ballot; Butler was chosen on the second ballot with 169 out of 253 votes cast. The Whig convention at Philadelphia, June 7–9, 1848, chose Taylor by a majority vote on the fourth ballot; Fillmore was chosen on the second ballot. The Free Soil Party, in convention at Buffalo, New York, on August 9–10, 1848, nominated Van Buren and Adams unanimously, the former by acclamation. **Campaign Issues:** The major issue concerned the extension of slavery to the territories newly won from Mexico. **Remarks:** The Free Soil Party was less radical than other abolitionist groups in that it did not want to end the institution, but only to prevent its extension to the new territories.

Taylor died on July 9, 1850, and Fillmore succeeded him the following day.

## 1852

| PRESIDENTIAL CANDIDATES | PARTY | ELECTORAL VOTES | POPULAR VOTE Total | Percentage | VICE-PRESIDENTIAL CANDIDATES |
|---|---|---|---|---|---|
| Franklin Pierce........ | Democratic | 254 | 1,609,038 | 50.85 | William R. King |
| Winfield Scott......... | Whig | 42 | 1,386,629 | 43.82 | William A. Graham |
| John P. Hale.......... | Free Soil | — | 156,297 | 4.94 | George Julian |

**Nominations:** At the Whig convention in Baltimore, June 17–20, 1852, Scott received a majority on the 53rd ballot; after a number of candidates declined, Graham was chosen unanimously. At the Democratic convention in Baltimore, June 1–5, 1852, on the 49th ballot Pierce was chosen unanimously; King got a majority on the second ballot. The Free Soil Party met at Pittsburgh, August 11, 1852; the delegates chose Hale and Julian. **Campaign Issues:** Both major political parties were split internally and, for political unity, they sought to avoid the slavery issue; the campaign centered on personalities. **Remarks:** Pierce was a compromise candidate for the Democratic Party, now split between Northern and Southern wings.

## 1856

| PRESIDENTIAL CANDIDATES | PARTY | ELECTORAL VOTES | POPULAR VOTE Total | Percentage | VICE-PRESIDENTIAL CANDIDATES |
|---|---|---|---|---|---|
| James Buchanan...... | Democratic | 174 | 1,839,237 | 45.63 | John C. Breckinridge |
| John C. Frémont...... | Republican | 114 | 1,341,028 | 33.27 | William L. Dayton |
| Millard Fillmore....... | American | 8 | 849,872 | 21.08 | Andrew J. Donelson |

**Nominations:** The Republican convention was held in Philadelphia, June 17–19, 1856. On the first official ballot Frémont got 520 out of 558 votes; Dayton's nomination came on the first ballot. At the Democratic convention in Cincinnati, June 2–6, 1856, Buchanan was chosen on the 17th ballot, receiving over two thirds of the votes cast; the nomination of Breckinridge was unanimous. The American ("Know-Nothing") convention met at Philadelphia, February 22, 1856, and the candidates received majority votes, Fillmore on the second ballot and Donelson on the first ballot. **Campaign Issues:** Slavery in the Kansas-Nebraska territories was the main issue. The Republicans and the Democrats offered a clear choice, each presenting self-determination solutions for the settlers there; the Republicans were the antislavery party. **Remarks:** The American Party was the ballot designation for the "Know-Nothings," an anti-Catholic, anti-foreigners group which ultimately split up over the slavery issue.

## 1860

| PRESIDENTIAL CANDIDATES | PARTY | ELECTORAL VOTES | POPULAR VOTE Total | Percentage | VICE-PRESIDENTIAL CANDIDATES |
|---|---|---|---|---|---|
| Abraham Lincoln.......... | Republican | 180 | 1,867,198 | 39.79 | Hannibal Hamlin |
| Stephen A. Douglas........ | Democratic | 72 | 1,379,434 | 29.40 | Herschel V. Johnson |
| John C. Breckinridge....... | National Democratic | 39 | 854,248 | 18.20 | Joseph Lane |
| John Bell................. | Constitutional Union | 12 | 591,658 | 12.61 | Edward Everett |

**Nominations:** The Democrats met in Charleston, South Carolina, April 23–May 3, 1860. They failed to choose a candidate and many Southerners bolted the party. The convention reassembled in Baltimore on June 18 and met through the 23rd. Finally, after more Southerners had left, Douglas was nominated. The Vice Presidential nominee, Benjamin Fitzpatrick of Alabama, declined the honor and the party national committee chose Johnson. Many of the "bolters," who called themselves National Democrats, met at Baltimore, June 23, 1860, and chose Breckinridge and Lane. The Republicans met May 16–18, 1860, in Chicago. On the third ballot Lincoln received a majority and the nomination was then made unanimous. Hamlin was chosen on the second ballot. The Constitutional Union Party met at Baltimore, May 9–10, 1860, and unanimously chose its candidates. **Campaign Issues:** The campaign centered about the issues of slavery and the status of the Union. **Remarks:** Parts of the South had declared before Lincoln's election that if he became President they would withdraw from the Union. South Carolina, the first to do so, seceded from the Union on December 20, 1860.

## 1864

| PRESIDENTIAL CANDIDATES | PARTY | ELECTORAL VOTES | POPULAR VOTE Total | Percentage | VICE-PRESIDENTIAL CANDIDATES |
|---|---|---|---|---|---|
| Abraham Lincoln.......... | Republican | 212 | 2,219,362 | 55.15 | Andrew Johnson |
| George McClellan.......... | Democratic | 21 | 1,805,063 | 44.85 | George Pendleton |
| Votes not cast............. | — | 1 | — | — | Votes not cast |

**Nominations:** The Republicans, who had been joined by the pro-war Democrats (Johnson was one), met as the National Union Party in Baltimore, June 7–8, 1864. Lincoln on a roll-call vote on the first ballot received all but 22 votes (which went to U. S. Grant), and his nomination was then made unanimous; by the end of the first ballot, after switching had taken place, Johnson had received 494 out of 500 votes and the Vice-Presidential nomination. The Democratic convention met in Chicago, August 29–31, 1864, and McClellan was chosen on the third ballot, and the nomination made unanimous; Pendleton was selected on the first ballot. **Campaign Issues:** The main issue was the conduct of the Civil War. **Remarks:** Because of their secession from the Union, Alabama, Arkansas, Florida, Georgia, Louisiana, Mississippi, North Carolina, South Carolina, Tennessee, Texas, and Virginia did not participate in the national election. Lincoln, who died on April 15, 1865, was succeeded by Johnson on the same day.

## 1868

| PRESIDENTIAL CANDIDATES | PARTY | ELECTORAL VOTES | POPULAR VOTE Total | Percentage | VICE-PRESIDENTIAL CANDIDATES |
|---|---|---|---|---|---|
| Ulysses S. Grant........... | Republican | 214 | 3,013,313 | 52.71 | Schuyler Colfax |
| Horatio Seymour.......... | Democratic | 80 | 2,703,933 | 47.29 | Francis P. Blair, Jr. |

**Nominations:** The Republican convention met in Chicago, May 20–21, 1868, using the name Union-Republican Party, and chose Grant. Colfax was picked on the fifth ballot. The Democratic Party met in New York City, July 4–9, 1868, nominated Seymour on the 22nd ballot, and declared the nomination unanimous. **Campaign Issues:** In this and a number of subsequent elections the Republicans waved the "bloody shirt of the Rebellion" and attempted to label, sometimes successfully, the Democrats as the party of secession. In this election, another paramount issue was the program for the Reconstruction of the Confederate states, with the Republicans in favor of harsh measures. **Remarks:** Because of Reconstruction difficulties, Mississippi, Texas, and Virginia did not participate in the Presidential election.

## 1872

| PRESIDENTIAL CANDIDATES | PARTY | ELECTORAL VOTES | POPULAR VOTE Total | Percentage | VICE-PRESIDENTIAL CANDIDATES | ELECTORAL VOTES |
|---|---|---|---|---|---|---|
| Ulysses S. Grant.......... | Republican | 286 | 3,597,375 | 55.63 | Henry Wilson........ | 286 |
| Horace Greeley........... | Dem., Liberal Rep. | — | 2,833,711 | 43.82 | B. Gratz Brown........ | 47 |
| Thomas A. Hendricks.... | Democratic | 42 | — | — | Other Candidates..... | 19 |
| B. Gratz Brown........... | Dem., Liberal Rep. | 18 | — | — | Votes not cast........ | 14 |
| Other candidates........ | | 3 | — | — | | — |
| Votes not cast........... | | 17 | — | — | | — |

**Nominations:** Liberal Republicans, who had defected from the Republican Party because they were dissatisfied with Grant, met in Cincinnati, May 1, 1872, and nominated Greeley and Brown on the sixth ballot. Democrats, meeting in Baltimore, July 9–10, 1872, accepted Greeley and Brown on the first ballot. The Republican convention at Philadelphia, June 5–6, 1872, chose Grant and Wilson. **Campaign Issues:** Besides the "bloody shirt" and Reconstruction, other important issues were corruption in government and the desirability of issuing paper money, which many debtors, especially among the farmers, thought would aid them. **Remarks:** Greeley died after the election but before the Electoral College met, and his electoral votes went to various opponents. Congress rejected the votes of Arkansas and Louisiana as coming from improperly constituted state governments; it also rejected Georgia's three votes.

## 1876

| PRESIDENTIAL CANDIDATES | PARTY | ELECTORAL VOTES | POPULAR VOTE Total | Percentage | VICE-PRESIDENTIAL CANDIDATES |
|---|---|---|---|---|---|
| Rutherford B. Hayes....... | Republican | 185 | 4,035,924 | 47.94 | William A. Wheeler |
| Samuel J. Tilden.......... | Democratic | 184 | 4,287,670 | 50.93 | Thomas A. Hendricks |
| Peter Cooper.............. | Greenback | — | 82,797 | .98 | Samuel F. Carey |

**Nominations:** The Republican convention at Cincinnati, June 14–16, 1876, nominated Hayes on the seventh ballot; Wheeler was nominated by acclamation. The Democrats, meeting at St. Louis, June 27–29, 1876, nominated Tilden on the second ballot; he received well over two thirds of the votes and the nomination was then made unanimous; Hendricks on a first ballot roll-call vote received the votes of all delegates except eight. The Greenback Party convened in Indianapolis, May 17, 1876, and unanimously chose Cooper and Carey. **Campaign Issues:** The main issues were Reconstruction, corruption in government, and the "bloody shirt." **Remarks:** Tilden came within one electoral vote of winning. An electoral commission composed of eight Republicans and seven Democrats (who voted along party lines) awarded disputed votes to Hayes, who thus won the Presidency by one electoral vote.

## 1880

| PRESIDENTIAL CANDIDATES | PARTY | ELECTORAL VOTES | POPULAR VOTE Total | Percentage | VICE-PRESIDENTIAL CANDIDATES |
|---|---|---|---|---|---|
| James A. Garfield.......... | Republican | 214 | 4,454,433 | 48.32 | Chester A. Arthur |
| Winfield S. Hancock....... | Democratic | 155 | 4,444,976 | 48.21 | William English |
| James B. Weaver.......... | Greenback | — | 308,649 | 3.35 | B. J. Chambers |

**Nominations:** The Republicans met in Chicago, June 2–8, 1880, and on the 36th ballot Garfield received the nomination; Arthur was chosen on the first ballot. The Democrats met at Cincinnati, June 22–24, 1880, and nominated Hancock and English. **Campaign Issues:** There were no real issues; the parties based their campaigns on the personalities of their candidates.

## 1884

| PRESIDENTIAL CANDIDATES | PARTY | ELECTORAL VOTES | POPULAR VOTE Total | Percentage | VICE-PRESIDENTIAL CANDIDATES |
|---|---|---|---|---|---|
| Grover Cleveland.......... | Democratic | 219 | 4,875,971 | 48.50 | Thomas A. Hendricks |
| James G. Blaine........... | Republican | 182 | 4,852,234 | 48.26 | John A. Logan |
| Benjamin F. Butler........ | Greenback | — | 175,066 | 1.74 | A. M. West |
| John P. St. John.......... | Prohibition | — | 150,957 | 1.50 | William Daniel |

**Nominations:** The Republicans met in Chicago, June 3–6, 1884, and Blaine was nominated on the fourth ballot, receiving 541 of 813 votes; Logan was the only candidate presented formally for the Vice-Presidential nomination. The Democrats met in Chicago, July 8–11, 1884, and on the second ballot Cleveland received 683 of 820 votes before the nomination was made unanimous; Hendricks was chosen unanimously. **Campaign Issues:** Corruption in government was allegedly the major issue but, in reality, the campaign was mostly an exercise in personal vitupera-tion. It was argued that Cleveland had fathered an illegitimate child and that Blaine's vote in Congress had been bought a number of times. During this campaign a Blaine supporter in the presence of the candidate accused the Democrats of being the party of "Rum, Romanism, and Rebellion." This statement redounded to the benefit of the Democrats in New York; it is probable that the enraged Irish voters there narrowly gave the state and the election to Cleveland.

## 1888

| PRESIDENTIAL CANDIDATES | PARTY | ELECTORAL VOTES | POPULAR VOTE Total | Percentage | VICE-PRESIDENTIAL CANDIDATES |
|---|---|---|---|---|---|
| Benjamin Harrison........ | Republican | 233 | 5,445,269 | 47.81 | Levi P. Morton |
| Grover Cleveland.......... | Democratic | 168 | 5,540,365 | 48.64 | Allen G. Thurman |
| Clinton B. Fisk............ | Prohibition | — | 250,122 | 2.20 | John A. Brooks |
| Aaron J. Streeter.......... | Union Labor | — | 147,606 | 1.30 | C. E. Cunningham |

**Nominations:** The Democrats met in St. Louis, June 5–7, 1888, and nominated Cleveland by acclamation; Thurman was a unanimous choice on the first roll-call vote. The Republicans met in Chicago, June 19–25, 1888, and on the eighth ballot Harrison received 544 of 830 votes; Morton received 592 votes on the first ballot. **Campaign Issues:** A number of minor activities became major issues. Cleveland had restored the Confederate battle flags to the South, and the Repub-licans made much of this. Also, a Republican politician managed to get the British ambassador to write in a letter that Cleveland would best serve the interests of Great Britain. **Remarks:** The Union Labor Party was an early attempt to form a farmer-labor party.

## 1892

| PRESIDENTIAL CANDIDATES | PARTY | ELECTORAL VOTES | POPULAR VOTE Total | Percentage | VICE-PRESIDENTIAL CANDIDATES |
|---|---|---|---|---|---|
| Grover Cleveland.......... | Democratic | 277 | 5,556,982 | 46.04 | Adlai E. Stevenson |
| Benjamin Harrison........ | Republican | 145 | 5,191,466 | 43.01 | Whitelaw Reid |
| James B. Weaver.......... | Populist | 22 | 1,029,960 | 8.53 | James G. Field |
| John Bidwell.............. | Prohibition | — | 271,111 | 2.25 | James B. Cranfill |

**Nominations:** The Republicans met at Minneapolis, June 7–10, 1892, and Harrison received 535 1/6 votes on the first roll call with 369 1/6 against him; Reid was chosen by acclamation. The Democrats met in Chicago, June 21–23, 1892, and Cleveland received 617 1/3 votes, barely more than the two thirds necessary for the nomination. A motion to make the nomination unanimous was then carried. Stevenson won the nomination for the Vice Presidency on the first roll-call vote. The Populists met in Omaha, July 2–5, 1892, where Weaver won the nomination on the first ballot. **Campaign Issues:** Discontent among farmers became a major issue in this campaign. Another major issue was the tariff; the Democrats favored a lower tariff. **Remarks:** Populist was the popular designation for the People's Party, probably one of the most dynamic and vocal forces of agrarian discontent ever channeled into politics in this country.

## 1896

| PRESIDENTIAL CANDIDATES | PARTY | ELECTORAL VOTES | POPULAR VOTE Total | Percentage | VICE-PRESIDENTIAL CANDIDATES |
|---|---|---|---|---|---|
| William McKinley.......... | Republican | 271 | 7,113,734 | 51.00 | Garret Hobart |
| William J. Bryan.......... | Democratic | 176 | 6,516,722 | 46.72 | { Arthur Sewall<br>{ Thomas E. Watson |
| John M. Palmer........... | Natl. Dem. | — | 135,456 | .97 | Simon Buckner |
| Joshua Levering.......... | Prohibition | — | 131,285 | .94 | Hale Johnson |

**Nominations:** The Republicans met at St. Louis, June 16–18, 1896, and McKinley with 661 1/2 of 907 votes was nominated on the first ballot; Hobart was nominated by roll call. The Democrats met at Chicago, July 7–11, 1896, and Bryan was nominated by acclamation on the fifth ballot with 652 of 768 votes; Sewall achieved the Vice-Presidential nomination on the fifth ballot. The Populists at their St. Louis convention, July 22–25, 1896, accepted Bryan as their Presidential candidate by 1,042 of 1,375 votes; Watson was nominated for Vice President before the Presiden-tial nomination was made. **Campaign Issues:** The Democrats came out for "free and unlimited coinage of silver" which, they argued, by putting more money into circulation, would aid farm debtors. Another important issue was whether there should be American overseas expansion, specifically with respect to Hawaii, which some Americans (there and in the United States) hoped to annex. **Remarks:** The Populists, though accepting Bryan as their standard-bearer, refused Sewall. In some states a fusion of Populists and Democrats took place, but in most of the South the Watson and Bryan ticket was more usual, and this accounts for the Watson vote. The Na-tional Democrats were so-called Gold Democrats, who opposed Bryan's silver programs and who received financial support from Republicans who hoped to split the Democratic vote.

## 1900

| PRESIDENTIAL CANDIDATES | PARTY | ELECTORAL VOTES | POPULAR VOTE Total | Percentage | VICE-PRESIDENTIAL CANDIDATES |
|---|---|---|---|---|---|
| William McKinley.......... | Republican | 292 | 7,219,828 | 51.67 | Theodore Roosevelt |
| William J. Bryan.......... | Democratic | 155 | 6,358,160 | 45.50 | Adlai E. Stevenson |
| John C. Wolley............ | Prohibition | — | 210,200 | 1.50 | Henry B. Metcalf |
| Eugene V. Debs........... | Socialist | — | 95,744 | .69 | Job Harriman |

**Nominations:** The Republicans, meeting in Philadelphia, June 19–21, 1900, made McKinley's nomination unanimous; he received 926 out of 926 votes on the first ballot: Roosevelt did not receive a unanimous vote because one New York delegate did not cast his vote. The Democrats, meeting in Kansas City, Missouri, July 4–6, 1900, chose Bryan unanimously on the first ballot; Stevenson was chosen unanimously after the first roll call. **Campaign Issues:** The silver issue and imperialism. **Remarks:** After being shot on September 6, 1901, McKinley died September 14. Roosevelt succeeded him on the same day.

## 1904

| PRESIDENTIAL CANDIDATES | PARTY | ELECTORAL VOTES | POPULAR VOTE Total | Percentage | VICE-PRESIDENTIAL CANDIDATES |
|---|---|---|---|---|---|
| Theodore Roosevelt........ | Republican | 336 | 7,628,831 | 56.40 | Charles W. Fairbanks |
| Alton B. Parker........... | Democratic | 140 | 5,084,533 | 37.59 | Henry G. Davis |
| Eugene V. Debs........... | Socialist | — | 402,714 | 2.98 | Benjamin Hanford |
| Silas C. Swallow.......... | Prohibition | — | 259,163 | 1.92 | George W. Carroll |

**Nominations:** Republicans met in Chicago, June 21–23, 1904, and chose Roosevelt unanimously on the first roll call, 994 delegates voting for him; Fairbanks was nominated by acclamation. Democrats met at St. Louis, July 6–9, 1904, and on the first ballot Parker received a little over two thirds of the vote and the nomination; Davis won the nomination on the first roll-call vote. **Remarks:** Roosevelt received the largest percentage of the popular vote of any President since tabulation of the vote had begun in 1824; it was to remain a record until 1920.

## 1908

| PRESIDENTIAL CANDIDATES | PARTY | ELECTORAL VOTES | POPULAR VOTE Total | Percentage | VICE-PRESIDENTIAL CANDIDATES |
|---|---|---|---|---|---|
| William H. Taft............ | Republican | 321 | 7,679,114 | 51.57 | James S. Sherman |
| William J. Bryan........... | Democratic | 162 | 6,410,665 | 43.05 | John W. Kern |
| Eugene V. Debs........... | Socialist | — | 420,858 | 2.83 | Benjamin Hanford |
| Eugene W. Chafin.......... | Prohibition | — | 252,704 | 1.70 | Aaron S. Watkins |

**Nominations:** The Republicans met in Chicago, June 16–19, 1908. Of 979 possible votes, Taft received 702 on the first ballot; Sherman received 816 votes on the first roll call. The Democrats, meeting at Denver, July 8–10, 1908, selected Bryan on the first ballot after he received 888 votes of 993; Kern won by acclamation. **Campaign Issues:** The Republicans promised tariff revision, and the Democrats unequivocally said that they would reduce the tariff.

## 1912

| PRESIDENTIAL CANDIDATES | PARTY | ELECTORAL VOTES | POPULAR VOTE Total | Percentage | VICE-PRESIDENTIAL CANDIDATES |
|---|---|---|---|---|---|
| Woodrow Wilson........... | Democratic | 435 | 6,301,254 | 41.85 | Thomas R. Marshall |
| Theodore Roosevelt........ | Progressive | 88 | 4,127,788 | 27.42 | Hiram Johnson |
| William H. Taft............ | Republican | 8 | 3,485,831 | 23.15 | James S. Sherman / Nicholas M. Butler |
| Eugene V. Debs........... | Socialist | — | 901,255 | 5.99 | Emil Seidel |
| Eugene Chafin............. | Prohibition | — | 209,644 | 1.39 | Aaron S. Watkins |

**Nominations:** Republicans met at Chicago, June 18–22, 1912. Taft received 561 votes of 728, but 344 delegates of the 1,078 present did not vote; Sherman was renominated on the first ballot. He died during the campaign and was replaced by Nicholas Murray Butler. Abstainers and other opposition to Taft formed the Progressive ("Bull Moose") Party, which at its convention in Chicago on August 5–7, 1912, nominated Roosevelt and Johnson by acclamation on the first ballot. The Democrats, in Baltimore, June 25–July 2, 1912, on the 46th ballot finally decided on Wilson, giving him all but 96 of the 1,086 votes; Marshall received the nomination on the second ballot.

## 1916

| PRESIDENTIAL CANDIDATES | PARTY | ELECTORAL VOTES | POPULAR VOTE Total | Percentage | VICE-PRESIDENTIAL CANDIDATES |
|---|---|---|---|---|---|
| Woodrow Wilson........... | Democratic | 277 | 9,131,511 | 49.26 | Thomas R. Marshall |
| Charles E. Hughes........ | Republican | 254 | 8,548,935 | 46.12 | Charles W. Fairbanks |
| Allan L. Benson........... | Socialist | — | 585,974 | 3.16 | George R. Kirkpatrick |
| J. Frank Hanly............ | Prohibition | — | 220,505 | 1.19 | Ira Landrith |

**Nominations:** The Republican convention in Chicago, June 7–10, 1916, chose Hughes on the third ballot when he received 949 1/2 votes of 986; Fairbanks received 863 votes on the first roll call. The Democratic convention in St. Louis, June 14–16, 1916, renominated its previous ticket by acclamation, with only one delegate opposed to Wilson. **Campaign Issues:** The question of American neutrality was paramount. Wilson campaigned as the candidate who had kept the country out of war. **Remarks:** Hughes went to bed believing he had won in a close election. When he awakened, the returns from California had finally come in, and they showed Wilson to be the winner.

## 1920

| PRESIDENTIAL CANDIDATES | PARTY | ELECTORAL VOTES | POPULAR VOTE Total | Percentage | VICE-PRESIDENTIAL CANDIDATES |
|---|---|---|---|---|---|
| Warren G. Harding........ | Republican | 404 | 16,153,785 | 60.31 | Calvin Coolidge |
| James M. Cox.............. | Democratic | 127 | 9,147,353 | 34.15 | Franklin D. Roosevelt |
| Eugene V. Debs........... | Socialist | — | 919,801 | 3.43 | Seymour Stedman |
| Parley P. Christensen...... | Farmer-Labor | — | 265,421 | .99 | Max S. Hayes |

**Nominations:** The Republican convention, in Chicago, June 8–12, 1920, selected Harding on the tenth ballot with 692 1/2 votes; Coolidge received 674 1/2 votes on the first ballot. The Democrats, in San Francisco, June 28–July 6, 1920, were deadlocked until the 44th ballot. Cox then received 732 1/2 votes, or 3 1/2 more than the necessary 729, but a motion was carried to make the nomination unanimous; Roosevelt was selected by acclamation. **Campaign Issues:** The Democrats attempted to make the League of Nations an issue. Harding campaigned for a return to "normalcy." **Remarks:** Harding died on August 2, 1923, and was succeeded the following day by Coolidge.

## 1924

| PRESIDENTIAL CANDIDATES | PARTY | ELECTORAL VOTES | POPULAR VOTE Total | Percentage | VICE-PRESIDENTIAL CANDIDATES |
|---|---|---|---|---|---|
| Calvin Coolidge........... | Republican | 382 | 15,725,016 | 54.04 | Charles G. Dawes |
| John W. Davis............. | Democratic | 136 | 8,386,624 | 28.82 | Charles W. Bryan |
| Robert M. LaFollette....... | Progressive | 13 | 4,831,470 | 16.60 | Burton K. Wheeler |

**Nominations:** The Republicans, meeting in Cleveland, June 10–12, 1924, chose Coolidge on the first ballot with 1,065 of 1,109 votes; Dawes was chosen on the third ballot, after Frank Lowden had declined the Vice-Presidential nomination given him on the second ballot. The Democrats met in New York City in the longest of nominating conventions—it lasted from June 24 to July 9, 1924, with 60 candidates nominated for the Presidency. On the 103rd ballot Davis finally received the nomination, which was then made unanimous. Bryan barely received the necessary two-thirds majority. **Campaign Issues:** The main issues were the Harding Administration scandals. **Remarks:** The third party in this campaign was formed as a result of left-wing dissatisfaction with the major candidates as well as with the contemporary social scene. The Conference for Progressive Political Action, which successfully fought Communist attempts to control it, was the backbone of the LaFollette candidacy. Wisconsin was the only state whose electoral vote he won.

## 1928

| PRESIDENTIAL CANDIDATES | PARTY | ELECTORAL VOTES | POPULAR VOTE Total | Percentage | VICE-PRESIDENTIAL CANDIDATES |
|---|---|---|---|---|---|
| Herbert C. Hoover......... | Republican | 444 | 21,430,743 | 58.22 | Charles Curtis |
| Alfred E. Smith........... | Democratic | 87 | 15,016,443 | 40.79 | Joseph T. Robinson |
| Norman M. Thomas........ | Socialist | — | 267,420 | .73 | James Maurer |

**Nominations:** The Republicans met in Kansas City, Missouri, June 12–15, 1928. On the first ballot, Hoover received 837 of 1,089 votes; Curtis on the first roll-call vote received 1,052 of 1,089 votes. The Democrats, convened in Houston, Texas, June 26–29, 1928, chose Smith on the first ballot as he received 849 2/3 of 1,097 1/2 votes, or well over the two-thirds majority; Robinson received the Vice-Presidential nomination on the first ballot. **Campaign Issues:** Issues of importance were Smith's Catholicism, Prohibition, and Federal farm relief.

## 1932

| PRESIDENTIAL CANDIDATES | PARTY | ELECTORAL VOTES | POPULAR VOTE Total | Percentage | VICE-PRESIDENTIAL CANDIDATES |
|---|---|---|---|---|---|
| Franklin D. Roosevelt...... | Democratic | 472 | 22,821,857 | 57.41 | John Nance Garner |
| Herbert C. Hoover......... | Republican | 59 | 15,761,841 | 39.65 | Charles Curtis |
| Norman M. Thomas........ | Socialist | — | 884,781 | 2.23 | James Maurer |

**Nominations:** The Republicans held their convention in Chicago, June 14–16, 1932. On the first ballot Hoover received 1,126 1/2 votes of 1,150; Curtis barely received a majority on the first roll call. The Democrats met in Chicago, June 27–29, 1932. Roosevelt on the fourth ballot received 945 of 1,148 1/2 votes; Garner was unanimously chosen on the first ballot. **Campaign Issues:** The major campaign issues dealt with methods of meeting and alleviating the economic depression that gripped the country. **Remarks:** Roosevelt broke tradition by flying to Chicago to accept the nomination.

## 1936

| PRESIDENTIAL CANDIDATES | PARTY | ELECTORAL VOTES | POPULAR VOTE Total | Percentage | VICE-PRESIDENTIAL CANDIDATES |
|---|---|---|---|---|---|
| Franklin D. Roosevelt...... | Democratic | 523 | 27,751,841 | 60.80 | John Nance Garner |
| Alfred M. Landon.......... | Republican | 8 | 16,679,491 | 36.54 | Frank Knox |
| William Lemke............ | Union | — | 892,390 | 1.96 | Thomas C. O'Brien |

**Nominations:** The Republicans convened in Cleveland, June 9–12, 1936. Landon was the only candidate placed in nomination, although 19 votes went to Senator Borah. Before balloting took place, all others nominated for Vice President withdrew in favor of Knox. The Democrats, meeting in Philadelphia, June 23–27, 1936, renominated Roosevelt and Garner by acclamation. At this convention the Democrats dropped the two-thirds rule. **Campaign Issues:** Nominally the policies of the New Deal were the issues, but the Roosevelt personality dominated the campaign. **Remarks:** Lemke and O'Brien ran as candidates of a party sponsored by a coalition of groups opposed to Roosevelt. Included in this party were the supporters of Dr. Townsend, Father Coughlin, and the then recently assassinated Huey Long, whose organization was headed by Gerald L. K. Smith. Roosevelt won a record-breaking 60.8 per cent of the vote. This record remained until Lyndon Johnson's win in 1964.

## 1940

| PRESIDENTIAL CANDIDATES | PARTY | ELECTORAL VOTES | POPULAR VOTE Total | Percentage | VICE-PRESIDENTIAL CANDIDATES |
|---|---|---|---|---|---|
| Franklin D. Roosevelt...... | Democratic | 449 | 27,243,466 | 54.69 | Henry A. Wallace |
| Wendell L. Willkie......... | Republican | 82 | 22,334,413 | 44.83 | Charles L. McNary |

**Nominations:** The Republicans held their convention in Philadelphia, June 24–28, 1940. On the sixth ballot Willkie received 655 of 1,000 possible votes; on the first ballot McNary received 890 votes. The Democrats met in Chicago, July 15–18, 1940. Roosevelt on the first ballot received 946 13/30 votes and was nominated by acclamation, and Wallace got 626 11/30 out of 1,100. The convention then made their nominations unanimous. **Campaign Issues:** Major campaign issues centered about American neutrality in World War II and the effects of the New Deal social and economic reforms. **Remarks:** Roosevelt broke tradition by running for a third term; this was a target for Republican attacks.

## 1944

| PRESIDENTIAL CANDIDATES | PARTY | ELECTORAL VOTES | POPULAR VOTE Total | Percentage | VICE-PRESIDENTIAL CANDIDATES |
|---|---|---|---|---|---|
| Franklin D. Roosevelt...... | Democratic | 432 | 25,612,474 | 53.39 | Harry S. Truman |
| Thomas E. Dewey......... | Republican | 99 | 22,017,570 | 45.89 | John W. Bricker |

**Nominations:** The Republicans convened in Chicago, June 26–28, 1944. Dewey was the only Presidential candidate nominated and received all but one of the votes cast, that one going to General Douglas MacArthur; Bricker received the nomination unanimously. The Democrats at their convention in Chicago, July 19–21, 1944, gave Roosevelt 1,086 of 1,176 votes on the first ballot. At the end of the second roll call for the Vice-Presidential nomination, Truman was in the lead and most states swung over to him; he received 1,031 of 1,146 votes cast. **Campaign Issues:** The conduct of the war and the preparations for peace were major issues. **Remarks:** Roosevelt died on April 12, 1945, and Harry S. Truman succeeded him on the same day.

## 1948

| PRESIDENTIAL CANDIDATES | PARTY | ELECTORAL VOTES | POPULAR VOTE | | VICE-PRESIDENTIAL CANDIDATES |
|---|---|---|---|---|---|
| | | | Total | Percentage | |
| Harry S. Truman.......... | Democratic | 303 | 24,104,030 | 49.51 | Alben W. Barkley |
| Thomas E. Dewey......... | Republican | 189 | 21,971,004 | 45.13 | Earl Warren |
| J. Strom Thurmond........ | States Rights | 39 | 1,169,032 | 2.40 | Fielding L. Wright |
| Henry A. Wallace.......... | Progressive | — | 1,157,063 | 2.38 | Glenn Taylor |

**Nominations:** The Republicans met in Philadelphia, June 21–25, 1948, and on the third ballot Dewey received a unanimous vote; Warren received the Vice-Presidential nomination by acclamation. The Democrats convened in Philadelphia, July 12–14, 1948. Truman received 947 1/2 votes on the first ballot; Barkley was chosen by acclamation. **Campaign Issues:** Many issues, such as civil rights and the conduct of the Cold War, had split the Democratic Party. During the election campaign Dewey seemed certain to win, but Truman capitalized on issues such as the alleged ineffectiveness of the 80th Congress, which had been controlled by Republicans. **Remarks:** Truman and the Democrats faced defections from members of both wings of the party who hoped either to defeat him or to bring the election into the House of Representatives. The most irreconcilable of the anti-Truman Southerners, who opposed the party's civil rights platform, convened in Birmingham, Alabama, on July 17, 1948, and nominated Thurmond and Wright. Those who considered Truman to be socially conservative and a warmonger met in Philadelphia and formed the Progressive Party, which, infiltrated by Communists, nominated Wallace and Taylor, July 24–27, 1948.

## 1952

| PRESIDENTIAL CANDIDATES | PARTY | ELECTORAL VOTES | POPULAR VOTE | | VICE-PRESIDENTIAL CANDIDATES |
|---|---|---|---|---|---|
| | | | Total | Percentage | |
| Dwight D. Eisenhower...... | Republican | 442 | 33,937,252 | 55.14 | Richard M. Nixon |
| Adlai E. Stevenson........ | Democratic | 89 | 27,314,992 | 44.38 | John J. Sparkman |

**Nominations:** The Republicans met in Chicago, July 7–11, 1952. At the end of the first ballot Eisenhower had 845 of 1,206 votes and his nomination was made unanimous. Nixon was chosen by acclamation. The Democrats held their convention in Chicago, July 21–26, 1952. Stevenson on the third ballot had 617 1/2 votes of 1,228; Sparkman was chosen by acclamation. **Campaign Issues:** Important issues were the conduct of the Korean War, the stalemate in the Cold War, corruption in the Democratic Administration, and the McCarthy charges of Communist infiltration of the Federal government. **Remarks:** Stevenson, who did not seek the nomination, was the first Presidential nominee since Garfield to be drafted.

## 1956

| PRESIDENTIAL CANDIDATES | PARTY | ELECTORAL VOTES | POPULAR VOTE | | VICE-PRESIDENTIAL CANDIDATES |
|---|---|---|---|---|---|
| | | | Total | Percentage | |
| Dwight D. Eisenhower...... | Republican | 457 | 35,589,477 | 57.37 | Richard M. Nixon |
| Adlai E. Stevenson........ | Democratic | 73 | 26,035,504 | 41.97 | Estes Kefauver |
| Walter B. Jones........... | No party | 1 | — | — | — |

**Nominations:** The Democrats met in Chicago, August 13–17, 1956. On the first ballot Stevenson had 905 1/2 of 1,372 votes, and his nomination was made unanimous; Kefauver was chosen on the second ballot. The Republicans, meeting in San Francisco, August 20–23, 1956, renominated Eisenhower and Nixon by acclamation. **Campaign Issues:** The conduct of the Cold War, atomic testing, and Eisenhower's health. **Remarks:** One Alabama elector voted for Jones.

## 1960

| PRESIDENTIAL CANDIDATES | PARTY | ELECTORAL VOTES | POPULAR VOTE | | VICE-PRESIDENTIAL CANDIDATES |
|---|---|---|---|---|---|
| | | | Total | Percentage | |
| John F. Kennedy.......... | Democratic | 303 | 34,221,349 | 49.71 | Lyndon B. Johnson |
| Richard M. Nixon.......... | Republican | 219 | 34,108,647 | 49.55 | Henry Cabot Lodge |
| Harry F. Byrd............. | No party | 15 | 440,298 | .64 | — |

**Nominations:** The Democrats met in Los Angeles, July 11–15, 1960. Kennedy received 806 votes out of 1,521 and was nominated on the first ballot; Johnson was chosen by acclamation. The Republicans, meeting in Chicago, July 25–28, 1960, nominated Nixon on the first ballot by 1,321 to 10; Lodge was chosen unanimously. **Campaign Issues:** The Democrats charged that there was a "missile gap," that American prestige was declining abroad, and that the Soviets had forged ahead militarily. **Remarks:** Unpledged electors in Alabama and Mississippi cast their votes for Byrd. Kennedy, assassinated November 22, 1963, was succeeded on the same day by Johnson.

Wide World

Four front-runners for the Republican Presidential nomination pose at a GOP fund-raising dinner in Washington. From left to right, Ronald Reagan, Richard Nixon, George Romney, and Charles Percy.

## U.S. PRESIDENTIAL ELECTION: 1968

When President Lyndon Johnson routed Barry Goldwater and the Republican party in 1964, it did not seem possible that four years later his chances of re-election might be in doubt. Yet such is the unpredictable nature of politics, that while the Democrats are still favored to win in 1968, the possibility of a GOP upset cannot be discounted.

What caused this drastic change? In 1964 President Johnson swept all but six states and won 486 electoral votes to Goldwater's 52. It was about as overwhelming a mandate as any President has ever received. Add to this the fact that Johnson had assumed the Presidency in 1963 with the reputation of being one of the most astute politicians in the nation's history, and the situation becomes more perplexing.

### THE ISSUES

The President's difficulties can be attributed to two major issues: the Vietnam war and the racial disturbances that many now call the Negro revolution. Two other issues, almost as important to millions of voters, are taxes and farm prices. In addition, a by-product of the racial issue is the problem of George C. Wallace and his Presidential ambitions, however illusory. What effect will the expected third-party campaign of the former Alabama governor have on the election?

Johnson's Vietnam policy, critics charge, has advanced from one of moderation to one of dangerous escalation of the war. By mid-1968 about 525,000 American troops are expected to be in Vietnam. Bombing of North Vietnam has been instituted, intensified, and justified as necessary to win the war, which, at last estimates, was costing the U.S. about $2 billion a month.

In 1967 there was a growing uneasiness in the country regarding the necessity and the morality of such a war. There is also considerable skepticism regarding the war's progress and vast concern about when it will end. The effect of all this on the electorate is the big imponderable of 1968. But one thing is reasonably certain: The Republicans will make the issue of a negotiated peace, as opposed to stepped-up bombing, a factor in the campaign.

The race riots that ravaged so many cities in the summer of 1967, and the prospect that the Negro struggle for economic and social equality will continue in 1968, have hurt President Johnson's image. Whether the Administration can afford to spend more in Vietnam and in attempting to satisfy the demands of the urban Negroes, is a question that increasingly troubles many people. Vice President Hubert H. Humphrey, whom President Johnson has virtually assured of renomination as his running mate, has called for a Marshall Plan for the ghettos. But the real Marshall Plan cost the U.S. a total of $20 billion, and the program President Johnson has talked about to save our deteriorating cities would cost many billions more. Much of the Negro discontent may be caused by the Administration's failure to provide the means to reach the vast objectives it outlines.

Opposition to rising taxes cuts across party lines, and President Johnson's 1967 request for an increased surcharge was no exception. Many Democratic and Republican leaders objected strenuously to the higher tax. If the economy does not remain strong through 1968, and if the predicted budget deficit is not reduced to reasonable proportions, the GOP will have a prime bread-and-butter issue.

The President scored impressive victories in 1964 in the Farm Belt. His chances of repeating this in 1968 are regarded as slim. Low prices and high production costs are plaguing the farmers, and the normally Republican farm states may come back into the fold.

The possible third-party candidacy of George Wallace has dismayed many Democrats and Republicans alike. Democrats are afraid that he will entice away votes both in the South and in the North, where white antagonism has been aroused by the pressures of the civil rights drive. The GOP is worried that Wallace (whose wife, Lurleen, succeeded him as Alabama governor) will attract enough Southern votes so that Republicans will not carry the Southern states that Goldwater carried in 1964.

The threat of a possible peace candidate, such as Dr. Martin Luther King, Jr., has caused concern among Johnson adherents, since the President's chances of being re-elected would be seriously affected. If King should run, and if Wallace should campaign as vigorously as he promises, it is possible neither of the major-party candidates would get the required absolute majority of the electoral college vote. In that event the House of Representatives would have to choose the President.

## THE CANDIDATES

Barring some unforseen catastrophe, the Democratic nomination is President Johnson's for the asking, and his running mate will be Vice President Humphrey. There has been some sentiment among party liberals for Senator Robert F. Kennedy of New York, and there are even groups working in his behalf. Whatever Senator Kennedy's opposition to Johnson's policies, however, he is not expected to endanger his 1972 Presidential hopes by vainly challenging President Johnson in 1968.

There are five potential Republican nominees: Governor Nelson A. Rockefeller of New York; Governor George Romney of Michigan; former Vice President Richard M. Nixon, now a New York resident; Governor Ronald Reagan of California; and Senator Charles H. Percy of Illinois.

Rockefeller has denied vehemently that he is a candidate, and insists that those who so designate him are attempting to divide the party and weaken Romney's chances. The New Yorker has been so adamant in his stand that many GOP moderates are beginning to suspect that he is serious in his support of Romney for the nomination. Still, Rockefeller, while reiterating that he is "not a candidate," has not completely closed the door.

The probable 1968 Democratic ticket is flanked by Mrs. Lyndon Johnson (left) and Mrs. Hubert Humphrey.

Wide World

Governor Romney is the other big hope of the moderate wing of the GOP. He is not as well known nationally as Rockefeller, but he has the virtue of being an attractive and fresh personality. A leader of the Mormon Church and a former president of American Motors, he was elected governor of Michigan in 1962 and re-elected in 1964 and 1966. Romney was among those who fought the Goldwater nomination in 1964 and refused to campaign for him. His views on the major issues are in harmony with Rockefeller's. The unanswered question is: Can their combined strength stave off the conservative wing of the party—something that could not be done in 1964—and win the nomination for one or the other?

The conservatives, for their part, are looking to Richard Nixon, who narrowly lost the Presidency to John F. Kennedy in 1960, and to the rising star of Ronald Reagan. Nixon is well-known nationally, but some Republicans believe that he is perhaps a little too well-known and that the party needs a new face in 1968. Nevertheless, the former Vice President is the first choice of a majority of party conservatives, but if he should falter in the primaries, many conservatives would throw their support to Reagan, a handsome former film actor with a magnetic personal appeal.

Senator Percy is the proverbial dark horse. With a deadlocked convention, the former boy wonder of business (he was elected president of Bell & Howell Company at age 29 in 1949) might be the spearhead of a compromise movement. A moderate, Percy has all the necessary credentials: He is young, personable, a war veteran, and comes from a vital Midwestern state with a large block of electoral votes (26).

The Republicans are convinced that they have a chance to defeat President Johnson—if they can avoid a repetition of the bitter 1964 fight for the nomination. There has been discussion of a Rockefeller-Reagan ticket, or a Romney-Reagan ticket, to assure party unity. Whatever the outcome, President Johnson faces a tough election campaign in 1968.

George Wallace, shown here with his wife, Governor Lurleen Wallace, may head a third-party slate in 1968.

United Press Int'l.

## FACTS ABOUT THE 1964 PRESIDENTIAL ELECTION

■ A total of 70,643,526 Americans voted in the 1964 Presidential election, the greatest turnout in American history. The previous record was established in the 1960 Presidential election, when 68,839,000 Americans went to the polls.
■ Major candidates for President and Vice President: *Democratic:* Lyndon B. Johnson, Texas; Hubert H. Humphrey, Minnesota. *Re-*

*publican:* Barry M. Goldwater, Arizona; William E. Miller, New York.
■ President Lyndon B. Johnson amassed the largest share of any total popular vote ever recorded in the United States. His total of 43,-128,956 votes far exceeded the high of 35,-589,477 votes set by Dwight D. Eisenhower in 1956.

| STATE | POPULAR VOTE | | | PLURAL- ITY | PERCENTAGE† | | ELECTORAL VOTE | |
|---|---|---|---|---|---|---|---|---|
| | Johnson | Goldwater | Other Candi- dates * | | Johnson | Goldwater | Johnson | Goldwater |
| Alabama......... | †† | 479,085 | 210,733 | 268,353 | — | 69.5 | — | 10 |
| Alaska........... | 44,329 | 22,930 | none | 21,399 | 65.9 | 34.1 | 3 | — |
| Arizona.......... | 237,753 | 242,535 | 482 | 4,782 | 49.5 | 50.4 | — | 5 |
| Arkansas........ | 314,197 | 243,264 | 2,965 | 70,933 | 56.1 | 43.4 | 6 | — |
| California........ | 4,171,877 | 2,879,108 | 6,601 | 1,292,769 | 59.1 | 40.8 | 40 | — |
| Colorado......... | 476,024 | 296,767 | 4,195 | 179,257 | 61.3 | 38.2 | 6 | — |
| Connecticut...... | 826,269 | 390,996 | 1,313 | 435,273 | 67.8 | 32.1 | 8 | — |
| Delaware........ | 122,704 | 78,078 | 538 | 44,626 | 60.9 | 38.8 | 3 | — |
| Florida......... | 948,540 | 905,941 | none | 42,599 | 51.1 | 48.9 | 14 | — |
| Georgia.......... | 522,557 | 616,600 | 195 | 94,043 | 45.9 | 54.1 | — | 12 |
| Hawaii.......... | 163,249 | 44,022 | none | 119,227 | 78.8 | 21.2 | 4 | — |
| Idaho........... | 148,920 | 143,557 | none | 5,363 | 50.9 | 49.1 | 4 | — |
| Illinois.......... | 2,796,833 | 1,905,946 | 62 | 890,887 | 59.5 | 40.5 | 26 | — |
| Indiana......... | 1,170,848 | 911,118 | 9,640 | 259,730 | 56.0 | 43.6 | 13 | — |
| Iowa............ | 733,030 | 449,148 | 2,361 | 283,882 | 61.9 | 37.9 | 9 | — |
| Kansas.......... | 464,028 | 386,579 | 7,294 | 77,449 | 54.1 | 45.1 | 7 | — |
| Kentucky........ | 669,659 | 372,977 | 3,469 | 296,682 | 64.0 | 35.7 | 9 | — |
| Louisiana........ | 387,068 | 509,225 | none | 122,157 | 43.2 | 56.8 | — | 10 |
| Maine........... | 262,264 | 118,701 | none | 143,563 | 68.8 | 31.2 | 4 | — |
| Maryland........ | 730,912 | 385,495 | 50 | 345,417 | 65.5 | 34.5 | 10 | — |
| Massachusetts.... | 1,786,422 | 549,727 | 8,649 | 1,236,695 | 76.2 | 23.4 | 14 | — |
| Michigan........ | 2,136,615 | 1,060,152 | 6,335 | 1,076,463 | 66.7 | 33.1 | 21 | — |
| Minnesota....... | 991,117 | 559,624 | 3,721 | 431,493 | 63.8 | 36.0 | 10 | — |
| Mississippi...... | 52,618 | 356,528 | none | 303,910 | 12.9 | 87.1 | — | 7 |
| Missouri......... | 1,164,344 | 653,535 | none | 510,809 | 64.0 | 36.0 | 12 | — |
| Montana......... | 164,246 | 113,032 | 1,350 | 51,214 | 58.9 | 40.6 | 4 | — |
| Nebraska........ | 307,307 | 276,847 | none | 30,460 | 52.6 | 47.4 | 5 | — |
| Nevada.......... | 79,339 | 56,094 | none | 23,245 | 58.6 | 41.4 | 3 | — |
| New Hampshire... | 184,064 | 104,029 | none | 80,035 | 63.9 | 36.1 | 4 | — |
| New Jersey...... | 1,867,671 | 963,843 | 15,256 | 903,828 | 65.6 | 33.9 | 17 | — |
| New Mexico...... | 194,015 | 132,833 | 1,792 | 61,177 | 59.0 | 40.4 | 4 | — |
| New York........ | 4,913,156 | 2,243,559 | 9,488 | 2,669,597 | 68.6 | 31.3 | 43 | — |
| North Carolina.... | 800,139 | 624,844 | none | 715,295 | 56.2 | 43.8 | 13 | — |
| North Dakota..... | 149,784 | 108,207 | 398 | 41,577 | 58.0 | 41.9 | 4 | — |
| Ohio............ | 2,498,331 | 1,470,865 | none | 1,027,466 | 62.9 | 37.1 | 26 | — |
| Oklahoma........ | 519,834 | 412,665 | none | 107,169 | 55.7 | 44.3 | 8 | — |
| Oregon.......... | 501,017 | 282,779 | 2,509 | 218,328 | 63.7 | 36.0 | 6 | — |
| Pennsylvania..... | 3,130,954 | 1,673,657 | 18,079 | 1,457,297 | 64.9 | 34.7 | 29 | — |
| Rhode Island..... | 315,463 | 74,615 | none | 240,848 | 80.9 | 19.1 | 4 | — |
| South Carolina.... | 215,700 | 309,048 | 8 | 93,348 | 41.1 | 58.9 | — | 8 |
| South Dakota..... | 163,010 | 130,108 | none | 32,902 | 55.6 | 44.4 | 4 | — |
| Tennessee....... | 635,047 | 508,965 | 34 | 126,082 | 55.5 | 44.5 | 11 | — |
| Texas........... | 1,663,185 | 958,566 | 5,060 | 704,619 | 63.3 | 36.5 | 25 | — |
| Utah............ | 219,628 | 181,785 | none | 37,843 | 54.7 | 45.3 | 4 | — |
| Vermont......... | 108,127 | 54,942 | 20 | 53,185 | 66.3 | 33.7 | 3 | — |
| Virginia......... | 558,038 | 481,334 | 2,895 | 76,704 | 53.5 | 46.2 | 12 | — |
| Washington...... | 779,699 | 470,366 | 8,309 | 309,333 | 62.0 | 37.4 | 9 | — |
| West Virginia..... | 538,087 | 253,953 | none | 284,134 | 67.9 | 32.1 | 7 | — |
| Wisconsin....... | 1,050,424 | 638,495 | 2,896 | 411,929 | 62.1 | 37.7 | 12 | — |
| Wyoming......... | 80,718 | 61,998 | none | 18,720 | 56.6 | 43.4 | 3 | — |
| District of Columbia....... | 169,796 | 28,801 | none | 140,995 | 85.5 | 14.5 | 3 | — |
| TOTALS:........ | 43,128,956 | 27,177,873 | 336,697 | 15,951,083 | 61.1% | 38.5% | 486 | 52 |

* Other candidates included Eric Haas and Henning A. Blomen, Socialist Labor Party; Clifton DeBerry and Edward Shaw, Socialist Workers Party; Earle H. Munn and Mark Shaw, Prohibition Party; Joseph B. Lightburn and Theodore C. Billings, Constitution Party; John Kasper and J. B. Stoner, National States Party; and Kirby J. Hensley and John O. Hopkins, Universal Party.
† Percentages of total Presidential vote cast, including minor party candidates.     †† Democratic electors were not pledged to Johnson, thus their vote appears under Other Candidates column.

# U.S. PRESIDENTIAL BIOGRAPHIES

## GEORGE WASHINGTON

1st President
1789–1797

The son of a moderately wealthy Virginia planter, George Washington was born on the family estate (now known as Wakefield), on February 22, 1732. His father died in 1743, and George's eldest brother, Lawrence, became head of the family. George displayed an early affinity for basic mathematics, and at the age of 15, was earning small fees from surveying. In 1748, young George helped make an extensive survey of the wilderness country west of the Blue Ridge Mountains.

In 1751–52, he accompanied Lawrence, who was suffering from tuberculosis, to Barbados in an attempt to restore Lawrence's health. There George survived a siege of smallpox and was rendered immune to the disease that was to plague his troops in the Revolution. Lawrence died shortly after returning to his Mount Vernon home. George inherited part of Lawrence's estate, and with it he became a district military adjutant, which made him Major Washington. In this post he was charged with training units of local militia.

Washington first gained public notice in 1753, during the French and Indian Wars, when he was entrusted with dangerous missions. On one occasion he volunteered to deliver a message from Governor Robert Dinwiddie of Virginia to the French in the Ohio country, warning them to leave this territory claimed by the British. Upon returning to Virginia, he was commissioned lieutenant colonel. Washington was then sent back to the area to hold back the French, and in May 1754 he won his first military victory. In 1755, as aide-de-camp to the British General Edward Braddock in the disastrous expedition against Fort Duquesne, Washington established his reputation as a military leader by rallying the survivors and conducting them back in orderly retreat. In 1758, commanding colonial forces supporting British regulars, he distinguished himself anew in the final capture of the French stronghold.

Peace being restored, Washington, not yet 27 years old, retired to private life. A tall, well-built man, he was amiable, just, and immensely vital. In 1759, he married Martha Dandridge Custis, a beautiful, wealthy widow with two children, and settled down to the life of a Virginia gentleman on his plantation, Mount Vernon.

From 1759 to 1774, Washington was a member of the Virginia House of Burgesses, where he became a leader in the opposition to British colonial policy. He served (1774–75) as a delegate to the Continental Congress, and after the American Revolution broke out at Lexington and Concord, he was named, largely through the efforts of John Adams, commander in chief of the Continental forces.

Few military leaders have faced greater difficulties. Washington's troops, unorganized and poorly disciplined, were militia on such short terms of enlistment that during the first years of the war his armies were in a continuous state of disbandment and retraining. Congress, functioning more like an assembly of ambassadors than as representatives of one nation, had little power and failed to provide essential equipment, supplies, and soldiers' pay. To these difficulties were added the jealousies and intrigues of insubordinate officers. Nonetheless, he maintained the field against trained armies of British regulars and German mercenaries.

After his defeat at Germantown, Washington went into winter quarters at Valley Forge. Seldom in military history has any general faced such want and misery as Washington did in the winter of 1777–78. His essential greatness matched every problem, and in the spring he emerged with increased powers from Congress and a well-trained striking force. Three years later, with the surrender of General Charles Cornwallis at Yorktown, where Washington had trapped him, the war ended, and Washington emerged as the most respected man in the country.

In 1783, Washington retired from the army and returned to Mount Vernon. The following year he traveled West to inspect his property holdings there. However, along with other patriots, he grew dissatisfied with the weakness of the government under the Articles of Confederation and he joined a movement determined to reorganize it. In 1787, he presided over the Constitutional Convention, which brought forth the Constitution of the United States, the basis for a new and lasting national government.

After the new government was organized, Washington was unanimously chosen as the first President and took office on April 30, 1789, in New York City.

Washington's own views were Federalist, but in staffing his Administration he was above partisanship. It was mainly his capacity for conciliation that kept the revolution free of terrorism, purges, and arbitrary seizures of power. He brought both Alexander Hamilton and Thomas Jefferson, leaders of opposing factions, into his cabinet. However, the factions persisted, and it was the constant strain put upon him as arbiter and conciliator that led to his refusal to stand for a third term. Washington's poise, prestige, and dignity and the establishment of a formal republican court made the new government respected at home and abroad. Washington demonstrated his strong belief in the nationalism of his office by traveling extensively throughout the nation, meeting local leaders.

The nearly eight years of Washington's Presidency saw the establishment of the basic institutions of our country. Among the precedents set was the interpretation of the "advise and consent" of the Senate as the right of that body to approve or disapprove the President's actions, but never to give him formal advice beforehand. Chief among the vigorously debated issues were taxation and banking policies, the assumption of state debts, and the jurisdiction of Federal courts. In the war between England and France, Washington proclaimed neutrality and urged it as basic U.S. policy in his Farewell Address, warning against "entangling alliances."

During his second administration, his Federalist Party was severely criticized by the Jeffersonians, especially for Jay's Treaty with England.

His *Farewell Address* on September 17, 1796, warned against "permanent alliances" with foreign powers.

In his public life, Washington combined modesty with self-assurance. In his first inaugural address, he acknowledged "deficiencies" in natural endowments and administrative experience. Characteristically, he set about overcoming them by study, just as he had equipped himself for the management of his plantations by studying works on agriculture. In social relations he was hospitable, holding frequent balls and banquets.

Washington died on December 14, 1799, leaving the inspiring heritage of the supreme patriot, above party, special interests, and personalities—the "father of his country." Thomas Jefferson, though disapproving of Washington's Federalist views, paid him this memorable tribute: "His integrity was the most pure, his justice the most flexible, I have ever known. He was, indeed, in every sense of the word, a wise, a good and a great man."

Martha Washington was born in 1731. At the age of 18 she married Daniel Parke Curtis, a wealthy plantation owner, who died in 1757. She married Washington in 1759. Known as a great beauty, Martha Washington had much besides wealth to commend her. She was noted for her common sense, her charm, and her aristocratic graciousness. A devoted wife, she was at her husband's side during the long, bitter winter of Valley Forge. She died in 1802 and was buried beside her husband at Mount Vernon.

## JOHN ADAMS

**2nd President
1797–1801**

Born October 30, 1735, at Quincy, Massachusetts, Adams graduated from Harvard at 20, taught school for a time, and was admitted to the bar in 1758. He was an outspoken opponent of the Stamp Act, and argued vehemently against the principle of taxation without representation. Moving to Boston, the center of revolutionary activity, Adams joined colonial patriots in opposition to oppressive British measures that led to the American Revolution.

Adams was sent to the Continental Congresses, where he distinguished himself as a forceful leader. He proposed George Washington as commander in chief of the Continental troops, helped draft the Declaration of Independence, and was eloquent in its defense. As a diplomat seeking foreign aid for the embattled young nation, he had a thorny career. In 1777, he was appointed Ambassador to France; he accomplished little, quarreled intermittently, and returned home empty-handed. In 1783, however, he returned to France and helped draw up the momentous Treaty of Paris to end the Revolutionary War. As an envoy to Great Britain in 1785, he and his wife, Abigail, were met with ill-concealed British hostility, and soon after Adams asked for his own recall.

In America once more, he was chosen Vice President and served throughout George Washington's administration. Although a Federalist and inclined to "the rich, the well-born, and the able," he feuded with Alexander Hamilton, the Federalist leader. In the 1796 election, Adams succeeded Washington as President by the slim margin of three electoral votes: 71 votes for Adams and 68 votes for Jefferson, who became his Vice President. In Washington, Adams was the first President to reside in the White House.

The Adams Administration was marred by factional intrigues that embittered Adams's life. A man of stubborn integrity, he narrowly averted open war with France, agitated for by Hamilton, and did not wholeheartedly endorse the Alien and Sedition Acts of 1798, sponsored by Hamilton, which were aimed at Jefferson and other critics of the government. He was, however, hated by the Jeffersonians, perhaps unfairly. In the election of 1800, he and Hamilton were both submerged in the tide of Jeffersonian democracy.

After 1801, Adams lived in retirement at Quincy, issuing political statements and writing and receiving letters from Jefferson, his former rival. Their historic correspondence was collected in *The Adams–Jefferson Letters,* published in 1959. By extraordinary coincidence, he and Jefferson died on the same day, Independence Day, July 4, 1826. Adams was buried in the First Unitarian Church of Quincy.

His wife, Abigail Smith Adams, born in 1744, the daughter of a Congregational minister, was a lively and intelligent woman and one of the most distinguished of the First Ladies. Their son, John Quincy Adams, became the sixth President of the United States.

# THOMAS JEFFERSON

3rd President
1801–1809

Like many distinguished men, Thomas Jefferson achieved distinction early. The son of a Virginia planter and scholar, he was born April 13, 1743, at Shadwell, the family estate. His father died when Thomas was 14, and the boy took over management of Shadwell. He graduated from the College of William and Mary at the age of 19, and was admitted to the bar in 1767. Five years later, he married Martha Wayles Skelton, and settled at Monticello, a mansion he had designed himself.

Jefferson was one of the organizers of the Virginia branch of the Committees of Correspondence, the chief medium of revolutionary agitation in the colonies. A brilliantly written pamphlet, "A Summary View of the Rights of British America," called attention to his logic, his knowledge of law, and his literary gifts, and at the Continental Congress of 1775, to which he was a delegate, he was chosen to draft the Declaration of Independence.

In 1776, he returned to Virginia to carry out some of his political and social principles in the newly established state. Serving in its legislature (1776–79) and as its governor (1779–81), he removed feudal vestiges from the landholding system and framed a statute on religious freedom that became a model for the rest of the country. His proposals for public education, public libraries, and a liberal university, though not then adopted, anticipated later developments.

From 1784 to 1789, Jefferson served on special diplomatic assignments and replaced Benjamin Franklin as minister to France. His absence prevented his direct participation in the drafting of the U.S. Constitution, but his pressure from abroad contributed to the addition of the first ten amendments, the Bill of Rights.

In 1790, he was called into George Washington's cabinet as Secretary of State. Jefferson at first subordinated his views to preserve the unity of the new nation, backing Alexander Hamilton, the Secretary of the Treasury, in his trade and banking measures. However, Jefferson soon became convinced that Hamilton and his group —the Federalist Party—sought to establish a monarchy, or at least an oligarchy of wealth. Jefferson went into opposition and began rallying around him like-minded men who began to call themselves Republicans—a group from which the present Democratic Party traces its origin. Jefferson and Hamilton, from being suspicious of each other, became openly antagonistic. President Washington was unable to reconcile them, and in 1793 Jefferson left the cabinet.

Returning to Virginia, Jefferson spent the next two years remodeling his Monticello home and experimenting in scientific agriculture. But he was also active in building up the Republican Party. Receiving its Presidential nomination in 1796, he lost by only three electoral votes to Washington's Vice President, the Federalist John Adams, and as runner-up became, under a constitutional provision then in effect, Adams's Vice President. Jefferson was opposed to Adams's policies, particularly the passage of the repressive Alien and Sedition Acts, aimed at Jefferson and his followers, and participated little in the Administration. Instead, in protest against the Alien and Sedition Acts, he drafted the Kentucky Resolutions, the earliest statement of the states' rights interpretation of the Constitution.

Jefferson's Anti-Federalist Party (by this time called the Democratic-Republicans) kept up its agitation and widened its field of operations, while the Federalists drifted into dissension. In 1800, after Jefferson had been nominated for the Presidency and Aaron Burr for the Vice Presidency, the Democratic-Republicans easily triumphed over John Adams and the Federalists. Aaron Burr, however, received the same number of electoral votes as Jefferson, and the choice of President was left to the House of Representatives. Jefferson was elected after a long deadlock, largely because Hamilton advised Federalist Congressmen to support Jefferson rather than Burr.

As President, Jefferson instituted a republican simplicity in the new capital, cut government expenditures, and sought to curb the growing power of the Supreme Court, where he felt the Federalists were attempting to entrench their philosophy. Jefferson believed that the Federal government should be concerned mostly with foreign affairs, leaving the states free to administer local matters.

The chief foreign problem throughout Jefferson's two administrations was the maintenance of neutrality in the conflict between England and France, both of whom preyed upon American shipping. Seeking to bring pressure by withholding needed goods, Jefferson sponsored acts suspending trade, especially the Embargo Act of 1807. These acts, though they finally became effective, caused loss and suffering to many Americans and aroused such protest that Jefferson relaxed attempts to enforce them. However, the European wars brought a great gain to America in the Louisiana Purchase, by which the United States doubled its territory. In the interest of exploration and settlement, Jefferson sponsored the Lewis and Clark expedition, which blazed the westward pioneer trail.

Retiring in 1809, Jefferson remained active; he kept up a voluminous correspondence with many public figures, including his former adversary, John Adams. He died on July 4, 1826, within a few hours of John Adams, on the fiftieth anniversary of the Declaration of Independence, which both had signed.

A leading figure of the 18th century, Jefferson was rivaled among Americans only by Benjamin Franklin in the range of his interests, the quality of his intellectual contribution, and his faith in human progress.

His curriculum for the University of Virginia, whose buildings he designed and of which he was rector in 1819, made it one of the most advanced institutions of its time. In his epitaph Jefferson specified what he wanted most to be remembered for: "Here was buried Thomas Jefferson, author of the Declaration of American Independence, of the statute of Virginia for religious freedom, and father of the University of Virginia."

## JAMES MADISON

**4th President
1809–1817**

Born March 16, 1751, in Port Conway, Virginia, the son of a planter and magistrate, James Madison graduated from Princeton at 20, then spent four years studying law, constitutional law, and history. Like George Washington and others of the Virginia planter class, he supported the patriots agitating against British colonial administration.

Madison's profound knowledge of government was first proved in 1776 when he helped to draft a constitution for the new state of Virginia. In 1776 and 1777 he was a member of the executive council directing Virginia's participation in the Revolutionary War.

A delegate to the Continental Congress for four years, Madison grew increasingly apprehensive as he watched the Congress flounder under the ineffective Articles of Confederation. After much thought, he became convinced of the necessity for a strong national government, and in 1786 he endorsed the calling of a constitutional convention. In 1787, at the convention, he and Alexander Hamilton became the leading spokesmen for a strong Federal government. Madison's political knowledge and persuasive logic helped secure the Constitution's adoption, and for this he earned the title "father of the Constitution."

Madison fought for the adoption of the Constitution. In his own state he overcame the opposition of Patrick Henry, and in the national ratification campaign his contributions to the brilliant *Federalist Papers,* along with those of Hamilton and John Jay, had a powerful effect. Madison was also instrumental in assuring the passage of the Bill of Rights.

During Washington's administration Madison became a steadfast enemy of Alexander Hamilton and a supporter of Thomas Jefferson. He was author of the Virginia Resolutions, protesting the repressive Alien and Sedition Acts inspired by Hamilton. By asserting the right of individual states to decide on the constitutionality of the acts, these resolutions became the theoretical base for the states' rights doctrine.

His marriage to Martha Wayles Skelton was a happy one, and he did not remarry after her death in 1782. Only two of their six children survived to maturity, Martha Washington Jefferson, who married Thomas Mann Randolph, and Mary Jefferson, who married John Wayles Eppes. Jefferson had been a widower for about 18 years when he entered the White House. Both his daughters served as White House hostesses, with the occasional assistance of Mrs. Dolley Madison, wife of Jefferson's Secretary of State.

When Jefferson won the Presidential election of 1800, Madison became his Secretary of State. In 1808, following the tradition of Washington, Jefferson declined a third term, and Madison became the successful candidate of the Democratic-Republicans.

A small man of uncommanding presence, Madison was not a forceful President. He began his administration by following Jefferson's policy of neutrality toward warring England and France but was finally bullied by the "war hawks," led by John C. Calhoun and Henry Clay, into the indecisive War of 1812 against England. To pay war bills and rehabilitate the national economy, Madison was forced to resort to such Federalist measures as the funding of the national debt, the establishment of a national bank, and a protective tariff.

The war went badly for Madison. New England merchants and industrialists openly opposed American participation in the conflict. And even friends and supporters of the Madison Administration became discouraged by repeated setbacks suffered by American forces.

Madison's reputation dimmed by his flight from Washington before invading British troops in 1814, and he barely won in his bid for reelection. Westward expansion and the promotion of trade and industry had become the dominant themes in American life. Among the events of Madison's second administration were wars and treaties with the Indians, which gave additional millions of acres to American settlers, the opening of steamboat navigation on the Mississippi, and the incorporation of the first gaslight company.

Madison's last years were spent in retirement, his only political participation being unobtrusive advice to President James Monroe. He died on his estate at Montpelier, Virginia, on June 28, 1836.

Madison was forty-three when he married Dolley (Dorothea) Dandridge Payne Todd, a Quaker widow of twenty-six and the daughter of a North Carolina planter. She was the official White House hostess for Thomas Jefferson and for her husband.

An attractive, vivacious, and intelligent woman, Dolley Madison was probably the most popular of America's First Ladies. After her husband's death she was voted an honorary seat in the House of Representatives by a unanimous Congressional resolution.

## JAMES MONROE

5th President
1817–1825

Like three of the four Presidents who preceded him, Monroe was a Virginian. He was born in Westmoreland County on April 28, 1758, the son of a judge. He left the College of William and Mary in 1776 to join the Revolutionary Army, was wounded twice. Cited for bravery, he was promoted to captain by General Washington. When the war ended, Monroe studied law under Thomas Jefferson, and the two became close friends.

Monroe began his political career in 1782, when he was elected to the Virginia legislature. For three years he served in the Continental Congress, where he opposed a centralized Federal government. In his own state of Virginia, Monroe supported Patrick Henry, who fought the adoption of the Constitution.

Under the new government Monroe served in the U.S. Senate, where he proved himself a leading spokesman for Jefferson and the Democratic-Republicans and a militant opponent of George Washington, Alexander Hamilton, and the Federalists.

Monroe carried out several diplomatic missions, including assisting Robert Livingston in the Louisiana Purchase negotiations. From 1811 to 1816 he was President Madison's Secretary of State. In 1816 Monroe obtained the Presidential nomination and was easily elected.

Because of its political calm, the first years of his administration became known as the "era of good feeling." In 1820 Monroe was reelected, receiving all but one electoral vote, which was withheld so that Washington would remain our only President to be the unanimous choice. The good feeling was, however, only apparent; dissensions were seething, and finally erupted in North-South disputes over the extension of slavery into the new states formed from the territories. The conflict was temporarily composed in 1820 by the Missouri Compromise. Maine was admitted as a free state, and Missouri as a slave state, and a boundary was drawn in the Louisiana Purchase territories between future free and slave states.

Among events of Monroe's administration were the establishment in 1817 of Liberia in west Africa as a colony for free American Negroes, with its capital, Monrovia, named in honor of the President; the purchase of Florida from Spain (1819); recognition of the new Latin American republics (1822); and the formulation of the Monroe Doctrine (1823) to cope with the European threat to restore or replace Spain's Latin American empire.

At the end of his term, Monroe retired to his farm in Loudoun County, Virginia, served as regent of the University of Virginia in 1826, and chaired the Virginia Constitutional Convention in 1829. He died on a visit to New York City on July 4, 1831.

His wife was Elizabeth Kortright Monroe, whom he married in 1786 and who bore him a son and two daughters. Having accompanied him on diplomatic missions and at political functions, she proved a polished and highly regarded White House hostess.

## JOHN QUINCY ADAMS

6th President
1825–1829

Born July 11, 1767, in Quincy, Massachusetts, John Quincy Adams was the son of the second President of the United States. He was educated abroad during his father's diplomatic service, and at Harvard. He was admitted to the bar in 1791, and served as minister to the Netherlands under President Washington, and as minister to Prussia during his father's administration. A Federalist, he was elected to the U.S. Senate in 1803, but his independence generated Federalist disapproval, and he resigned in 1808, to become a Democratic-Republican, and later, an independent.

Adams performed some of his most valuable service to the nation in diplomacy. In 1809 he was sent as minister to Russia, where he was held in esteem; and in 1814 he negotiated the Treaty of Ghent which ended the War of 1812. As Secretary of State under President James Monroe, Adams gained renown as the chief architect of the Monroe Doctrine.

In 1824 Adams was a candidate for President, but neither he nor his opponents—Andrew Jackson and Henry Clay—received an electoral majority. The election was decided in the House of Representatives, where Clay supported Adams, making him President.

A high-minded man, with little popular support and no political party, Adams entered upon the Presidency with gloomy prospects. With a frankness rare in politics, however, he assailed political corruption and advocated a professional civil service free of patronage. This alienated politicians, and the one important act passed by Congress with Adams's approval, raising the protective tariff rates, angered the farmers. In 1828, on the Whig ticket, Adams was defeated in his bid for reelection.

After his retirement from the Presidency, Adams rose to his greatest height. In 1830 he ran for Congress, and for seventeen years, until a stroke killed him on February 23, 1848, at the age of eighty, he distinguished himself by his untiring and conscientious service. He opposed the extension of slavery and the war with Mexico; he succeeded in preventing the imposition of "gag rules" in Congressional debate; and he sponsored the advancement of science. The Smithsonian Institution owes its development largely to him.

Although he was regarded as dour and reserved, Adams made the White House a center for cultured and animated social life. In this he was aided by his wife, Louisa Catherine Johnson Adams, herself the daughter of an American diplomat, who was esteemed as a hostess of graciousness and charm. They had been married in London in 1797 and had four children, three sons and a daughter.

# ANDREW JACKSON

7th President
1829–1837

A child of the backwoods, and the first "log cabin" President, Jackson was born March 15, 1767, in Waxhaw Settlement, Carolina,* the son of an immigrant farmer. He was orphaned at 14, served in the Revolutionary Army, and was admitted to the North Carolina bar in 1787. He prospered in law, land speculation, and commercial ventures. Hermitage, his estate, was operated as a slave-holding plantation. Jackson married Rachel Donelson Robards, a divorcée; however, a mistake in the divorce proceedings made it necessary for the couple to be wed in two ceremonies, three years apart. This sometimes made Jackson the butt of slurs, one of which led to a duel in which he killed his opponent.

In 1797 and 1798 he served briefly in Congress, once in the House and once in the Senate. But his reputation in the period before the War of 1812 was founded on his six years' service as a judge of the Tennessee superior court, where he became highly popular.

In 1801 Jackson had been elected major general of the state militia guarding the western frontier, and in the War of 1812 he campaigned against the Creek Indians, who had become allies of the British, crushing them and forcing them to make peace. This brought him the rank of major general in the U.S. Army. In one campaign he captured British strongholds in Florida; in another he was given command of an expedition against a seasoned British army marching on New Orleans. Though outnumbered at the Battle of New Orleans, he gained the victory that made him the military hero of the war.

By this time he had also acquired the reputation for personal toughness, symbolized in his nickname, "Old Hickory." According to some sources, his duels and brawls numbered close to a hundred. A vein of violence marks Jackson's entire career, and he was to be the first President on whom an attempt at assassination was made.

In 1818, ordered to punish the border-raiding Seminole Indians, Jackson captured Pensacola, Florida, and hanged two British subjects accused of inciting the raids. He thus involved the United States in serious trouble with both Spain and Great Britain.

The greatest popular hero of his time, a man of action, and an expansionist, Jackson now stood on the threshold of the White House. He was nominated for the Presidency by one of four factions into which the ruling Democratic-Republican Party had split. He received a plurality of the electoral votes in the election of 1824, but a majority being required, the election was decided in the House of Representatives, where the support of one of the four candidates, Henry Clay, secured the Presidency for another, John Quincy Adams. The Jacksonians were frustrated and angry. In the election of 1828, however, Jackson easily defeated Adams's bid for reelection.

Though personally a man of dignity and integrity, Jackson was viewed by the established families as a dangerous upstart who brought the "rabble" into the White House. Jackson became more and more associated with the movement toward increased popular participation in government and was soon the symbol of a "new democracy."

There was, however, a strong element of authoritarianism in Jackson's rule, and his "kitchen cabinet"—an unofficial group of favorite advisers—was powerful. Party loyalty was intense, and party members were rewarded with government posts in what came to be known as the spoils system, first adopted by Jackson on a large scale.

In the nullification crisis of 1832, when South Carolina declared null and void the Tariff Act of 1832, which favored Northern interests at the expense of the South, Jackson took a strong pro-Union stand. However, he felt that the South had a real grievance and ordered a compromise tariff act. In other respects Jackson supported the doctrine of states' rights, especially when he fought against the Bank of the United States; he finally removed the funds from this national bank and deposited them in chosen state banks.

Jackson could probably have won a third term in 1836, but he chose instead to put his Vice President, Martin Van Buren, a New York machine politician, into the White House. Jackson retired to the Hermitage, but his voice was heard throughout Van Buren's administration. Still feared as a high-handed dictator by his enemies and revered as a forceful democrat by his followers, Jackson died on June 8, 1845, and was buried at the Hermitage.

* His place of birth is disputed between North and South Carolina.

## MARTIN VAN BUREN

**8th President
1837–1841**

Political skill and native intelligence earned Martin Van Buren the nickname "Red Fox." The son of a New York farmer and innkeeper, Van Buren was born December 5, 1782, at Kinderhook. As a boy, he waited on tables in his father's tavern, which was frequented by local politicians. Although Van Buren never attended college, he trained in law offices, and was admitted to the bar in 1803.

Van Buren's first public office was surrogate of Columbia County, New York, to which he was appointed in 1808 by political boss Governor Daniel D. Tompkins. From then on his career was a smooth ascent, eased by his adept use of the spoils system. He became New York state attorney general and state senator.

He served (1821–28) in the U.S. Senate, where his record proved inconsistent on the issues of states' rights and slavery. Van Buren was far more important as a political leader than as a legislator. He became one of the principal figures in a powerful political clique known as the Albany Regency. Van Buren eventually swung his power to the support of Andrew Jackson, and when Jackson became President he rewarded Van Buren with the post of Secretary of State.

Probably the most influential of Jackson's advisers, Van Buren was nominated for Vice President by the Democratic Party in 1832 and was elected to office along with President Jackson. In 1836, supported by Jackson, he was chosen as Democratic candidate for President; there was no well-organized opposition and Van Buren was swept into office.

At that summit Van Buren's career went into reverse. He was defeated in his campaign for reelection in 1840; he was denied renomination as his party's candidate in 1844; and in 1848, running on the antislavery Free Soil Party ticket, he failed to receive a single electoral vote. Bitterly disappointed, he went into retirement at his Lindenwald estate in Kinderhook, where he died on July 24, 1862.

Though, as a Jacksonian Democrat, Van Buren proclaimed himself a champion of the people, no act of his is cited by historians as truly promoting the public welfare. In the panic of 1837, he opposed Federal aid to alleviate distress. However, he resisted the extension of slavery, and his stand against the annexation of Texas probably cost him the Democratic nomination in 1844.

Van Buren's marriage was born of a schoolboy romance. His wife, Hannah Hoes Van Buren, whom he married in 1807, had been his classmate in Kinderhook.

## WILLIAM HENRY HARRISON

**9th President
1841**

Born February 9, 1773, at "Berkeley," Charles City County, Virginia, Harrison was a member of a distinguished family; his father had been one of the signers of the Declaration of Independence. Harrison attended Hampden-Sidney College and studied medicine in Philadelphia. In 1791, he joined the army and began a brilliant career in the Indian campaigns. He resigned his commission seven years later to become Secretary of the Northwest Territory, in which he had served. He became the first Territorial delegate to Congress in 1799, and saw approved his proposal to divide the Territory into Ohio and Indiana.

From 1800 to 1812 Harrison was governor of the Indiana Territory, and negotiated vast land cessions from the Indian tribes. When Indian hostilities arose in 1811, Harrison led an expedition to victory over Tecumseh at Tippecanoe.

In 1816 Harrison left his army command to enter politics. Becoming successively Congressman, state senator, U.S. Senator, and diplomat, his steady rise was halted when Andrew Jackson came to power. A victim of the spoils system, Harrison was once reduced to taking a post as county recorder to support his family.

His political fortunes recovered in 1836, when a group of dissident Whigs nominated him for President. Harrison demonstrated his vote-getting power by securing the largest number of electoral votes among the opponents of the victorious Democratic candidate, Martin Van Buren. In 1840 the Whigs, including Daniel Webster and Henry Clay, nominated Harrison, and John Tyler for Vice President.

Harrison's second and successful campaign—famous for its slogan "Tippecanoe and Tyler too"—is memorable for its demagogy. Copying the tactics of the Jacksonian Democrats, the Whigs billed their military-hero candidate as a log-cabin man whose drink was hard cider, in contrast to Van Buren, portrayed as a dandy who used scent and drank French wines.

The distinguished cabinet Harrison assembled augured well for his administration, but he died exactly a month after his inauguration, the first of our Presidents to die in office.

His wife, Anna Tuthill Symmes Harrison, whom Harrison married in 1795, bore him ten children, eight of whom survived to maturity. Their grandson, Benjamin Harrison, became the 23rd President.

## JOHN TYLER

**10th President
1841–1845**

The first Vice President to succeed to the Presidency, John Tyler became Chief Executive when William Henry Harrison died a month after his inauguration. Tyler was born March 29, 1790, in Charles City County, Virginia. The son of a prominent lawyer-politician, Tyler graduated from the College of William and Mary at 17; was admitted to the bar at 19, and entered politics at 21 as a member of his state legislature. He served in Congress, and as Governor of Virginia before he was elected Vice President, and succeeded Harrison, who died on April 4, 1841, one month after taking office.

Never did a President prove more disappointing to the party that had placed him in office. Tyler, an ex-Democrat and a cultured Virginia gentleman, had been nominated Vice President by the Whigs to attract Southern votes. Once President, however, it became clear that all he had in common with the Whig regulars was his antagonism to Andrew Jackson.

After Tyler had twice vetoed his party's measure to reestablish the national bank, the keystone of the Whig program, his entire cabinet resigned, with the exception of Daniel Webster, his Secretary of State. Webster remained only long enough to complete a treaty fixing our northeast boundary with Canada. Denounced by the Whigs and with few friends among the Democrats, Tyler became a President without a party.

Despite strong opposition, Tyler advanced the annexation of Texas, which had won its independence from Mexico and was applying for admission into the Union. An antislavery bloc in the Senate withheld the votes necessary for ratification of the annexation treaty, but Tyler outmaneuvered them, preparing the way for annexation.

Only a small faction backed his renomination for President in 1844, and he withdrew from the race. He remained in virtual retirement for fourteen years, but served as chancellor of the College of William and Mary from 1859 to 1861.

Tyler was the first President to marry while in office. His first wife, Letitia Christian Tyler, was an invalid when he assumed the Presidency, and she died in 1842. His second wife, Julia Gardiner Tyler, was the daughter of a Senator from New York. She married the President in 1844, and was First Lady during the last eight months of his term. Tyler had seven children by his first wife and seven by his second.

## JAMES KNOX POLK

**11th President
1845–1849**

Born November 2, 1795, near Pineville, North Carolina, Polk was the son of a surveyor and planter. The family moved to Tennessee in 1806; Polk graduated from the University of North Carolina in 1818, and began to practice law in Columbia, Tennessee, two years later. He entered politics as a Jacksonian Democrat, and his fiery campaigning earned him the title "Napoleon of the Stump." He was elected to the Tennessee Legislature, and to Congress, where he served seven consecutive terms, the last two as Speaker of the House.

At the 1844 Democratic convention, a deadlock was broken when Polk, supported by Andrew Jackson, was proposed as the nominee behind whom the opposed factions could unite. The ninth ballot made him the first "dark horse" Presidential candidate.

In the election, Polk, an avowed expansionist, narrowly defeated Henry Clay, the Whig candidate. In office, Polk pushed through the annexation of Texas. He sent a personal emissary, John Slidell, to Mexico. When the Mexican Government refused to receive Slidell, Polk sent troops under General Zachary Taylor into the disputed area. Mexican troops attacked, and Polk proclaimed that war had begun "by act of Mexico."

In the meanwhile he had been negotiating an Oregon border agreement with Great Britain, whose possible intervention in the war with Mexico had been feared. Ignoring his campaign commitments, he accepted the 49th parallel as the boundary line. Polk was then left free to press the Mexican War. A succession of American victories culminated in the capture of the Mexican capital. In the Treaty of Guadalupe Hidalgo (February 2, 1848), Mexico accepted the Texas boundary claims and, for a payment of $15,000,000, ceded what was to become California, New Mexico, Arizona, Nevada, Utah, and parts of Colorado and Wyoming, the largest accession of territory after the Louisiana Purchase. Polk blocked an attempt—the "Wilmot Proviso" attached to an appropriations bill—to exclude slavery from the new acquisitions.

Few Presidents have equaled Polk's record of achievement in attaining stated aims. Under constant harassment in Congress, not only from the Whig opposition but from resentful northern Democrats, Polk's strenuous labors impaired his health. He refused renomination, and died on June 15, 1849, a few months after retirement.

## ZACHARY TAYLOR

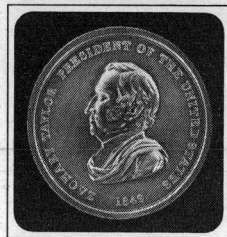

12th President
1849–1850

An outspoken, sometimes defiant army officer who was idolized by his troops and known as "Old Rough and Ready," Zachary Taylor was born November 24, 1784, at Montebello, Virginia, the son of a Revolutionary War colonel. In 1785, the family moved to Kentucky, where Taylor was educated informally. He entered the army in 1808 as a first lieutenant. In 1837, following his victory over the Seminole Indians at Lake Okeechobee, Florida, he was made a brigadier general.

In 1845 he was given command of the army in Texas, and in the Mexican War that followed he was at times defiant to the point of insubordination. The armistice granted by Taylor after his seizure of Monterrey, Mexico, in 1846, created serious friction with President James K. Polk, who thought the terms given the defeated enemy were too lenient. Taylor ignored orders to defend his position in northern Mexico; instead, he led his troops south in February 1847, to defeat numerically superior Mexican forces at Buena Vista. Taylor returned home a national hero, and in 1848 was nominated by the Whig Party as their candidate for President.

As a slaveholder himself, Taylor was conservative in outlook, but he was known to be under the influence of Senator William H. Seward of New York, leader of the antislavery Whigs. Taylor, along with his running mate, Millard Fillmore of New York, campaigned on no apparent platform. Their Democratic opponent, Lewis Cass, was equally neutral, and the 1848 election was referred to as a "contest without an issue." However, the admission of new states—on a free or slave basis—was the unavoidable issue facing his administration.

In his first message to Congress in 1849, the supposedly neutral Taylor began to show a strong, nationalist trend in his policy. Once opposed to the Wilmot Proviso, which held that slavery should never exist in any territory acquired by treaty from Mexico, Taylor indicated that he now favored its principles. His special message to Congress in 1850, calling for admission to statehood of antislavery California, alienated his Southern Whig supporters. Henry Clay offered a series of bills, known collectively as the Compromise of 1850, in an attempt to placate both North and South. Taylor would probably have taken an active part in opposing the Compromise, but he was stricken with cholera and died after having been in office only ten months.

Taylor married Margaret Mackall Smith, the daughter of a Southern planter, in 1810.

## MILLARD FILLMORE

13th President
1850–1853

The son of a pioneer farmer, Fillmore was born at Locke, New York, January 7, 1800. As a youth, he worked at odd jobs to earn a living, and as a result, was largely self-educated. He read law in his spare time and was admitted to the bar in 1823. After practicing briefly in East Aurora, New York, he moved to Buffalo.

Fillmore's political career began with a term in the New York Assembly. He went on to serve four terms in Congress, beginning in 1833. In 1834, he joined the Whig Party, and when the Whigs achieved national power in 1840, Fillmore became prominent. Defeated as the Whig candidate for governor in 1844, he was made controller of New York.

Because of the strong stand Fillmore had taken against the extension of slavery into the territories, Henry Clay backed him for the Vice Presidency on the successful Whig ticket in 1848. His position was intended to offset the supposed proslavery sympathies of the Presidential candidate, General Zachary Taylor.

Taylor died on July 9, 1850, and Fillmore took office the following day. As President, Fillmore sought to preserve the Union, chiefly by conciliating the South. But the nation had become too deeply divided on the slavery issue, and Fillmore's attempt to carry out the Compromise of 1850 alienated both sides. In particular, his strict enforcement of the Fugitive Slave Law of 1850 aroused the wrath of the antislavery wing of the Whig Party.

Apart from the Compromise of 1850, two measures, neither of which he initiated, are associated with Fillmore's administration. One is the dispatch of Commodore Perry to Japan to open its ports to American trade; the other is the reorganization of the postal department to provide cheaper mail rates.

Fillmore lost the support of the Whig convention in 1852, and the Presidential nomination went to General Winfield Scott, exponent of a more radical antislavery program.

Fillmore married twice. He married his first wife, Abigail Powers Fillmore, the daughter of a Baptist clergyman, in 1826. A former schoolteacher and a voracious reader, she provided the White House with its first library. Mrs. Fillmore was too ill to preside at White House functions; she died shortly after the close of Fillmore's administration. In 1858 Fillmore married his second wife, Caroline Carmichael McIntosh, a widow. He died on March 8, 1874.

## FRANKLIN PIERCE

**14th President**
**1853–1857**

Born November 23, 1804, in Hillsboro, New Hampshire, Franklin Pierce was the son of a Revolutionary War general who was twice elected governor of his state. Pierce attended Bowdoin College in Maine. His classmates included Henry Wadsworth Longfellow and Nathaniel Hawthorne; the latter wrote Pierce's campaign biography. Pierce was admitted to the bar in 1827, entered politics as a Jacksonian Democrat, and served for four years as a Congressman. In 1837, at the age of 33, he became one of the youngest men elected to the Senate. In 1842, he resigned his seat because of his wife's ill-health, and returned to law practice in Concord, New Hampshire.

At the outbreak of the war with Mexico, Pierce, a vigorous nationalist, enlisted as a private. He won rapid promotion; he was a brigadier general when the war ended. On his return to civilian life, he continued in political retirement, declining an appointment to the Senate and a nomination for governor.

He resumed political activity in 1850 as a member and president of the New Hampshire Fifth State Constitutional Convention. In 1852 he was a delegate to the national Democratic convention, where he emerged as a dark horse Presidential candidate.

His nomination on the 49th ballot broke a deadlock over the slavery issue. As a Northerner with pro-Southern sympathies, he was considered acceptable to both sides. Pierce went on to defeat the Whig candidate, General Winfield Scott, his commander in the Mexican War.

Believing that conciliation of the South would preserve the Union, he endorsed the Southern doctrine that the constitutional provisions on property rights meant a constitutional guarantee of slavery.

In his expansionist drive Pierce made premature, and consequently unsuccessful, attempts to purchase Alaska from the Russians and to annex Hawaii. Another failure was the Ostend Manifesto, issued by the American ministers to England, France, and Spain, proposing the annexation of Cuba, presumably as a new slave state. Though the Ostend Manifesto was repudiated by the U.S. State Department and in the Senate, it raised storms abroad and at home. Even Pierce's own party was outraged, and his bid for renomination was humiliatingly rejected.

The successful acts of Pierce's administration were the Gadsden Purchase of additional territory on the Mexican border and the ratification of Perry's treaty with Japan.

At the end of his term Pierce toured Europe and returned to private life in Concord. There his opposition to the Civil War and to Lincoln's administration increased his unpopularity, and he died in virtual obscurity on October 8, 1869.

His wife, Jane Means Appleton Pierce, daughter of a president of Bowdoin College, bore him three sons, none of whom survived to maturity. Their last son died two months before Pierce took office.

## JAMES BUCHANAN

**15th President**
**1857–1861**

The son of a merchant farmer, Buchanan was born April 23, 1791, in Cove Gap, Pennsylvania. He graduated from Dickinson College in 1809, was admitted to the bar in 1812, and built up a lucrative law practice in Lancaster, Pennsylvania. With the demise of the Federalist Party, he became a Democrat. He served in both houses of Congress, as Secretary of State, and as minister to England and Russia.

As minister to England he was involved in the notorious Ostend Manifesto, which pressed for the annexation of Cuba as a new slave state. Even the expansionist Administration of Franklin Pierce was forced to disavow it, at home and abroad, and among large groups in the North it left Buchanan permanently discredited.

In 1844, 1848, and 1852, Buchanan was a contender for his party's nomination to the Presidency. Finally, in 1856, he became its candidate and attained the White House, after defeating John C. Frémont, first candidate of the young Republican Party, and Millard Fillmore, candidate of the Whig and American (Know-Nothing) Parties. Buchanan did not win a majority of the popular vote.

To meet the growing crisis between North and South, Buchanan could only propose preservation of the "sacred balance" between them. He avowed personal disapproval of slavery, yet recommended the admission of Kansas as a slave state. He deplored secession, but took no steps to check it by garrisoning Federal forts in the South. He took no action even when a Federal ship was fired on by South Carolina shore batteries. Buchanan's moderate views were disliked and mistrusted by extremists both in the North and in the South.

Buchanan had been engaged to Miss Ann Caroline Coleman of Lancaster, Pennsylvania. After her death in 1819 he remained a bachelor, the first to be elected President and the only one to stay unmarried. He died on June 1, 1868.

## ABRAHAM LINCOLN

**16th President
1861–1865**

Lincoln's father was a farmer, carpenter, and wheelwright, who moved his family from Kentucky to Indiana to Illinois. Abraham was born in a log cabin in Hardin County, Kentucky, on February 12, 1809. His mother died when he was nine, and his father married Sarah Bush Johnston, who proved an affectionate stepmother.

Providing for himself at an early age, Lincoln did handyman jobs, split rails, clerked in a store, carried out land surveys, delivered merchandise downstream on flatboats to New Orleans, and put his hand to other tasks. In 1831, he settled in the little village of New Salem, Illinois, near Springfield. There he became a partner in a grocery store that failed, leaving him burdened with debts. He discharged his debts, which earned him the best known of his many nicknames, "Honest Abe."

Lincoln grew into a tall, gaunt man—his height of six feet four inches, as well as his singularly homely face, drew village comment. Possessed of great physical strength, he often put down bullies. This, along with his talent for pointed story telling, brought him popularity in the frontier villages where he spent his young manhood.

When there was a call for volunteers in the Black Hawk War, Lincoln was chosen captain of the New Salem troop, which, as it happened, never saw service. By 1834, he had gathered such a following that he was elected, as a Whig, to the Illinois legislature, where he achieved prominence. He was admitted to the bar in 1836 and moved to nearby Springfield, where he built up a prosperous practice in a succession of partnerships, the last with William H. Herndon, who later became his biographer.

In 1842, after a troubled courtship, he married Mary Todd of Kentucky, a sister-in-law of the governor of Illinois. It is popularly believed—although discredited by most historians —that the real love of his life was Ann Rutledge, whom he had met in 1835 and who had tragically died the same year.

Lincoln reentered politics in 1847, again as a Whig, and was elected to Congress. There his opposition to the Mexican War cost him the backing of his expansionist-minded constituents, and he withdrew from politics.

In 1855, however, he was goaded out of his retirement by indignation over the Kansas-Nebraska bill, which had favored the extension of slavery and which had been sponsored by the Illinois Democratic Senator, Stephen A. Douglas. Lincoln ran for the Senate on the Whig ticket, but was defeated. The next year he joined the newly formed Republican Party; he was among the candidates for its Vice-Presidential nomination, polling an impressive, though not winning, vote.

In 1858, Lincoln became his party's candidate for U.S. Senator. One of the ringing phrases in his acceptance speech, "A house divided against itself cannot stand," helped to spread his renown. His debates with Douglas, his Democratic opponent, drew nationwide attention to Lincoln, who asserted he was not an abolitionist, but that he regarded slavery as an injustice and an evil, and was adamantly opposed to its extension. Although Douglas won the close election, Lincoln, through his masterful exposition, had made his mark. He was now a potential Presidential candidate for the Republicans.

At the Republican Presidential convention in 1860, William H. Seward was the leading contender, but there was an early swing to Lincoln, who was nominated on the third ballot. With the Democrats split between Northern and Southern wings, Republican victory was inevitable. When it occurred, the South proclaimed Lincoln's election as the end of its place in the Union.

As President, Lincoln was determined both to preserve the Union and to limit slavery. He was willing to tolerate slavery where it existed, but he rejected proposed compromises that might have brought the South back into the Union.

On April 12, 1861, Fort Sumter in South Carolina was bombarded by the Confederates, and the Civil War began. Lincoln became the leader of the people of the North in the greatest crisis and the most tragic experience through which the United States has suffered.

From the beginning, Lincoln faced staggering difficulties. Nonetheless, he attacked the vast problems of the war with vigor and surpassing skill. Lincoln pressed the war forward, but yet, even when prosecuting Southern sympathizers in the North, for which he has been criticized, he sought to temper punishment with mercy. He was beset not only by the difficulties of the war, but by opposition of men on his own side. Radical abolitionists condemned him as weak, and conservatives accused him of dictatorship. In his own cabinet, jealousies and hatreds caused continual friction. In the midst of all this strife Lincoln continued his course, sometimes almost alone, but with wisdom and patience.

The war went against the North at first, and there was a rapid succession of Union commanders in chief. The dubious Northern victory at Antietam in 1862 gave Lincoln the opportunity to make a great stroke in the Emancipation Proclamation, which set Southern slaves free and gave a high moral tone to the Northern cause.

The Proclamation caused renewed enthusiasm for the war, but as it progressed without issue, Lincoln's enemies gathered against him. In 1864, however, after Ulysses S. Grant became commander in chief and William T. Sherman took Atlanta, Lincoln's perseverance seemed vindicated. With victory clearly in sight, his own party, which had been on the point of abandoning him, rallied to Lincoln and he was renominated and reelected.

In his celebrated second inaugural address, Lincoln, the towering figure of the Civil War period, outlined his postwar program. He would show "malice toward none" and grant "charity for all." His policy would be based on peace without conquest, reconstruction without destruction. His dream to restore the Union in harmony was ended on April 14, however, when John Wilkes Booth, a Southern fanatic, assassinated him.

Mary Todd Lincoln served as White House hostess in a simple and quiet manner. Because she had several relatives serving in the Confederate Army, her loyalty to the North was questioned. The Lincolns had four sons, of whom only one, Robert Todd, lived to manhood. One of their sons died at the age of four in Springfield, another in the White House at the age of twelve. His death, and later her husband's assassination while at her side, are said to have affected Mrs. Lincoln's mind. In 1871, the death of her youngest son, Thomas (Tad) Lincoln, caused a collapse, and she was temporarily committed to a private sanitarium. She died in 1882.

## ANDREW JOHNSON

17th President
1865–1869

Abraham Lincoln's successor was born December 29, 1808, at Raleigh, North Carolina. Johnson's father died when he was five; at the age of ten, he was apprenticed to a tailor. In 1826, he moved to Greenville, Tennessee. Johnson's organization of a workingman's political group won him the office of alderman; he was later elected Mayor. Though illiterate, he taught himself to read, and his schoolteacher wife taught him to write and improved his grammar and spelling. Johnson prospered at the tailor's trade and his shop became well known. Many other craftsmen, as well as laborers and small farmers, would meet there to discuss community and general public affairs. The best debater in the community, Johnson was frequently in the public eye, especially as a spokesman on the slavery question. He served in public office as alderman in 1828–30 and mayor of Greenville in 1830–34. He served as a member of the state legislature, as a Congressman, as Governor of Tennessee, and as a U.S. Senator. As U.S. Representative and Senator, Johnson was principally interested in securing legislation to make land in the West available to homesteaders.

Though he had become a slaveowner himself, was a Democrat, and had upheld slavery, Johnson opposed secession and did not resign, as other Southern senators did, when secession began. In 1862 Lincoln appointed him military governor of Tennessee, and by 1864 Johnson had organized a loyal government in that state. For this achievement he was named Lincoln's running mate on the Republican ticket in the campaign of 1864.

Assuming the Presidency on Lincoln's assassination, Johnson reverted to his earlier Democratic Party positions on tariffs, banking, internal improvements, and other issues, in opposition to his nominal party. But the chief issue in his conflict with the "Radical Republicans" in Congress was Reconstruction. He claimed to be following Lincoln's program, though the evidence indicates that Lincoln, while avoiding punitive measures against the South, would have stood firm on Negro civil rights. Johnson, while extending full amnesty to participants in the secession, opposed extension of full civil rights to Negroes and, in general, manifested Southern sympathies.

When Congress passed a succession of acts over his veto, including the Civil Rights Act of 1866, Johnson appealed to the electorate in the Congressional elections of 1866. Baited by mobs and slandered by the press, he struck out at his political enemies in such harsh terms as to do his own cause much harm. The Radical Republicans won, and the conflict between Congress and the President became more acute.

Finally, when Johnson sought to oust Secretary of War Edward M. Stanton, whom he rightly suspected of conspiring with the Congressional leaders, in defiance of the Tenure of Office Act, the Radical Republicans, led by Thaddeus Stevens, brought impeachment charges against him. His first attempt failed, but on February 24, 1868, the House passed a resolution of impeachment. On March 5, the Senate was organized as a court to hear the charges. The vote in the Senate went 35 to 19 against him, one vote short of the required two-thirds majority; thus, the first and, so far, the only move to impeach a President failed.

Despite a series of disappointments that would have deterred a lesser man, Johnson continued his political activity. He sought and failed to win the nomination for President on the Democratic ticket in 1868, for U.S. Senator in 1869, and for Representative in 1872, but in 1874 he was elected to the Senate from Tennessee. He died a few months after reentering the Senate, on July 31, 1875. Although the problems of the postwar South dominated Johnson's administration, there were successes in foreign affairs, notably the purchase in 1867 of Alaska from Russia.

Eliza McCardle and Andrew Johnson were married in 1827, when he was 18 and she was 16; they had three sons and two daughters. Mrs. Johnson was an invalid during her husband's term, and their daughter, Mrs. David Trotter Patterson, served as White House hostess, with another daughter, Mrs. Mary Johnson Stover, sometimes functioning in her place.

## ULYSSES SIMPSON GRANT

18th President
1869–1877

Born Hiram Ulysses Grant on April 27, 1822, in Point Pleasant, Ohio, Grant was the son of a farmer and tanner. His name was changed by clerical error when he applied to West Point in 1839, and Grant accepted the change. He graduated in 1843, served with distinction in the Mexican War, and was promoted twice.

In 1854 Grant was forced to resign from the army because of excessive drinking; he tried farming, real estate, and storekeeping, all without success. The Civil War proved his opportunity. Responding to President Lincoln's call for volunteers, he was given command of a detachment of Illinois trainees. He showed such ability in minor military actions that he was promoted to brigadier general.

After training and mobilizing a force of 17,-000 men, he proposed a bold operation against two Confederate strongholds, Fort Henry and Fort Donelson, on the Tennessee and Cumberland rivers. In this operation—the first major Union victory—he enunciated the terms that brought him the nickname "Unconditional Surrender Grant."

Thereafter his military career was an almost continuous succession of triumphs, the most brilliant being the capture of Vicksburg in 1863, which cleared the Mississippi down to the sea and split the Confederacy in two. Satisfied that he had at last found his general, Lincoln in 1864 put Grant in supreme command of the Union armies.

The collapse of the Confederate armies and the surrender of General Robert E. Lee at Appomattox justified his strategy. Made a full general in 1866, Grant was the first U.S. citizen after George Washington to hold that rank.

A national hero, Grant was the Republican choice in the Presidential election of 1868. He was nominated on the first ballot and elected by a landslide. For his second term his renomination was unanimous and his reelection another landslide.

Grant's Administrations—characterized by bitter politics and notorious corruption—were a national disgrace. His punitive Reconstruction policy gave supremacy to Northern bankers, speculators, and industrialists and encouraged the "carpetbaggers" who moved south to exploit both recently freed Negroes and defeated whites, helping to prolong the sectional division of the country.

Grant allowed himself to become the dupe of the "robber barons" of his time and of the shady politicians associated with them. During his administration, scandals were exposed involving members of his cabinet, his own private secretary, and a number of Congressmen.

In 1880 he sought a third term, but his backers, the "Stalwarts," led by Roscoe Conkling, failed to secure his nomination. Moving to New York City, among his new financier associates, Grant invested his funds in a fraudulent banking firm. When it went bankrupt in 1884, Congress granted him relief by reappointing him general at full pay and later adding retirement pay.

Determined to provide for his family, Grant set to work on his memoirs. Though suffering from cancer of the throat, he kept on indomitably, finishing the two-volume book four days before his death. Grant's memoirs brought his heirs the fortune he had determined to leave them.

He died on July 23, 1885, and lies interred in Grant's Tomb in New York City.

His wife, Julia Dent Grant, daughter of a judge in St. Louis, Missouri, was a reigning belle when Grant, then a young officer, met and won her in 1848. She bore him four children, three sons and a daughter, all of whom survived into maturity. As First Lady, she was admired for her social graces.

## RUTHERFORD BIRCHARD HAYES

19th President
1877–1881

Born October 4, 1822, in Delaware, Ohio, the son of a storekeeper who died the year he was born, Hayes was reared by an uncle. He attended Kenyon College and Harvard Law School, practiced in Lower Sandusky, and in 1849, moved to Cincinnati. In 1852 he married Lucy Webb, daughter of a doctor. From 1857 to 1859, Hayes served as Cincinnati solicitor. On the outbreak of the Civil War, Hayes

volunteered and was commissioned a major. He was wounded four times and rose in rank to major general. Elected to Congress in 1865 as a Republican, he supported the Radical Reconstruction program. In 1867, he was elected governor of Ohio and served three terms. He won the Republican nomination for President in 1876, opposing Samuel J. Tilden, the Democratic candidate.

The election was significant in U.S. history, for it marked the resurgence of the Democrats and the political reentry of the South into the Union. The Republican Party lost heavily in the Congressional elections, and its Presidential candidate, Hayes, received a minority of the popular vote. The tally of electoral votes was disputed but a partisan election commission bestowed the office on Hayes.

Beginning his term under the cloud of the disputed election and facing a hostile Democratic majority in Congress, Hayes could project no far-reaching program, and his Administration, though regarded as honest and efficient, was without effect. His most outstanding act, withdrawal of the last Federal troops from the South, antagonized extremists in his party, and his efforts to reform the civil service angered Republican Party bosses.

Though more esteemed when he left office than when he entered it, Hayes declined renomination and devoted his last years to education and philanthropy. He died in Fremont, Ohio, on January 17, 1893.

Hayes's family life was a happy one, and the White House during his administration was enlivened by his eight children. His wife, Lucy Webb Hayes, was nicknamed "Lemonade Lucy" because she served soft drinks at White House receptions; both she and her husband were total abstainers.

## JAMES ABRAM GARFIELD

20th President
1881

Born November 19, 1831, in Orange, Ohio, the son of a farmer, James Garfield was left fatherless at two, and spent his early years in poverty. He worked as a farmer and carpenter to support his mother, and at 18, entered Hiram College. He went on to Williams College, graduated in 1856, and returned to Hiram, where he became a professor. Garfield was also a lay preacher of the Disciples of Christ. He won a seat in the Ohio Legislature in 1859, and was admitted to the bar a year later.

During the Civil War he began service as an officer of an Ohio volunteer regiment and attained the rank of major general. On his election to Congress in 1863 he resigned from the army to take his seat in the House, which he held until 1880. Garfield was a regular Republican—antislavery in belief—and a staunch advocate of Radical Reconstruction.

Garfield was a dark horse candidate for the Presidential nomination in 1880; top runners at the Republican convention were former President U. S. Grant and James G. Blaine. Up to the 34th ballot Garfield never drew more than two votes, but on the 36th ballot he won the nomination.

Grant and his political sponsor, Roscoe Conkling, were disgruntled. An attempt was made to appease them by giving the Vice-Presidential nomination to Chester Alan Arthur, one of the Stalwarts, as Grant's supporters called themselves. However, they gave only grudging support to Garfield's campaign. One of Garfield's immediate problems, on beginning his administration, was the open break forced by Conkling over the distribution of political spoils.

Garfield was a brilliant orator and a man of integrity and charm. His conflict with Conkling and the political machine remained unresolved, however. An assassin's bullet ended Garfield's life before he could make his personal mark as President.

Shot on July 2, 1881, by Charles Guiteau, a disappointed office seeker who proclaimed himself a Stalwart, Garfield lingered on until September 19, 1881, when he died.

His wife, Lucretia ("Crete") Rudolph Garfield, a farmer's daughter, had been a schoolmate of Garfield's. They were married in 1858 and had seven children, two of whom died in childhood. Mrs. Garfield died in 1918.

## CHESTER ALAN ARTHUR

21st President
1881–1885

A lawyer and teacher, Chester Alan Arthur was born October 5, 1830, at Fairfield, Vermont, the son of a clergyman. He graduated from Union College in 1848, and began teaching while studying law. He was admitted to the bar in 1854, developed a successful practice, and in 1859, married Ellen Herndon of Virginia.

During the Civil War, Arthur, a staunch and loyal Republican, helped organize the New York militia and subsequently served as quartermaster general. In 1871, President Grant rewarded him with the post of collector of the port of New York, a much sought political prize. He administered this office with personal honesty but, in the style of the time, openly dispensed political patronage to members of the powerful New York Republican machine. In 1878, President Hayes, a fellow Republican bent on civil service reform, removed Arthur from office.

At the Republican national convention of 1880, James Garfield was nominated as the Presidential candidate, despite the efforts of the Stalwarts, a clique of New York Republicans, to nominate Grant for a third term. In the interests of party harmony, the convention nominated Arthur, a leading Stalwart, to the Vice Presidency.

Garfield was elected, but soon after his inauguration he was assassinated and Arthur became President. As President, Arthur was stigmatized as a machine politician of dubious integrity and nicknamed the Gentleman Boss for his courtly manners and his taste for fine foods and expensive clothes. Yet, to the dismay of his many political associates. Arthur's Administration proved unexpectedly honest and efficient. He effectively supported the Civil Service Reform Act of 1883, which severely limited the spoils system; fought the passage of the Chinese Exclusion Act; prosecuted corruption in the postal service; and aided the passage of a new protective tariff.

Chiefly because of enemies within his own party, Arthur was denied the Presidential nomination in 1884. He returned to New York City, where he resumed his law practice. He died on November 18, 1886, a little more than a year after leaving office.

His wife, Ellen Lewis Herndon Arthur, born in 1837, died before her husband became President. Arthur's vivacious sister, Mary Arthur McElroy (Mrs. John McElroy of Albany, New York), served as White House hostess during his term.

## GROVER CLEVELAND

**22nd and 24th President
1885–1889, 1893–1897**

The son of a Presbyterian minister, Stephen Grover Cleveland was born March 18, 1837, in Caldwell, New Jersey. The family moved to upstate New York when Cleveland was a child. His father died when he was 16; Cleveland worked in a store in Clinton, and later taught school. He decided to move west as a pioneer, stopped in Buffalo to visit an uncle, and settled there. He clerked in a law office, and was admitted to the bar in 1859.

Cleveland began his political career as a Democrat and, after occupying minor posts, was elected sheriff of Erie County. He was elected mayor of Buffalo in 1882. Known as the "veto mayor," he drove corruption from his administration, and acquired such renown for honesty and efficiency that he was nominated and elected governor of New York the following year.

In 1884 he became the Democratic Presidential candidate, even though he had defied the Tammany Democratic machine and had cooperated with the Republican reform leader, Theodore Roosevelt, in moves to clean up municipal administration in New York City.

The Presidential campaign of 1884 was almost unmatched for vilification. An attack on the Democrats as the party of "Rum, Romanism, and Rebellion" boomeranged. It cost the Republican candidate, James G. Blaine, the Roman Catholic vote. In addition, Cleveland's record as a reformer won him support from the Mugwumps, a reform wing of the Republican Party.

As the first Democratic President since the Civil War, Cleveland faced an unyielding Republican majority in the Senate, whose opposition prevented him from carrying through any formulated policy. Among the few significant acts of his first administration were his appointment of an Interstate Commerce Commission and his part in the passage of the Interstate Commerce Act of 1886. Although he was forced to temper with expediency his own instinct for reform of the civil service, he showed himself adamant against graft, extravagance, and excessive tariff protection.

Renominated in 1888, Cleveland won a plurality of the popular vote, but lost the electoral vote. In the campaign of 1892, however, he regained the White House, the only President to be defeated for reelection, then later reelected.

Cleveland began his second term a popular national figure; at its close he was shunned by his own party and castigated by the Republicans.

Inheriting a financial panic, he forced the repeal of the Sherman Silver Purchase Act and sponsored the issuance of government bonds to protect the gold reserve. By these measures he alienated the Populists, a radical party of that period, and the silver advocates among the Democrats. Determined to prevent interruption of the postal service, he sent Federal troops into Chicago to break the railroad strike of 1894, against the wishes of the Democratic governor of Illinois and the aspirations of organized labor.

He also felt that tendencies toward American imperialism were beginning to grow and, in opposition to this, refused to permit aid to rebel movements in Hawaii and Cuba. Almost the only popular act of Cleveland's second administration was his invocation of the Monroe Doctrine in 1895, which led Great Britain to arbitrate a boundary dispute with Venezuela. His unique style of action was criticized as too just and fair for the majority of his party, and in 1896 the Democrats renounced his politics by nominating William J. Bryan.

Cleveland's personal courage was manifested in the fortitude with which he underwent two major surgical operations in 1893. Stricken by a cancerous growth on his upper jaw, he was, on the advice of friends, operated on in secret to prevent public alarm.

After leaving the White House, Cleveland retired to Princeton, New Jersey, and participated little in public life. In 1901 he became a trustee of Princeton University and occupied a commanding elder statesman position, until his death on June 24, 1908.

At inauguration the second bachelor President after Buchanan, Cleveland did not remain a bachelor. On June 2, 1886, he married his ward, Frances Folsom, daughter of his deceased law partner. The wedding was held in the White House. Mrs. Cleveland officiated at White House functions with poise and skill. Her second child, Esther Cleveland, born in 1893, was the first child of a President to be born in the executive mansion.

## BENJAMIN HARRISON

23rd President
1889–1893

Born August 20, 1833, at North Bend, Ohio, Benjamin Harrison was the son of a Congressman, the grandson of the ninth President of the United States, and a great-grandson of one of the signers of the Declaration of Independence. He graduated from Miami University in Ohio, passed the bar in 1853, and opened his law practice in Cincinnati. In 1854, he moved to Indianapolis, where he became reporter for the Indiana Supreme Court.

When the Civil War broke out, Harrison helped recruit a regiment of volunteers of which he became colonel in 1862. His war record was outstanding, and he attained the rank of brigadier general. After the war, he built up a prosperous practice as a corporation lawyer.

From 1881 to 1887, Harrison served as United States Senator from Indiana. As the Republican Presidential nominee in 1888, he received a majority of the electoral vote, although Grover Cleveland, running for reelection, received a plurality of the popular vote. A factor in the election was a probably calculated exchange of letters between an American citizen and the British minister to Washington,

in which the latter hinted that the reelection of Cleveland was desired by England. This raised a storm of anti-British feeling that aided the Harrison campaign.

A colorless President, Harrison followed the regular Republican line. He supported the McKinley protective tariff and the Disability Pension Act. The outstanding event of his administration was the convening of the first Pan-American Conference in 1889.

The Sherman Anti-Trust Act was passed to counteract popular feeling that the Republicans were the party of Big Business. This proved insufficient, and the Congressional elections of 1890 gave the Democrats control of the House. When he ran for reelection in 1892, Harrison was defeated by Cleveland.

After leaving the White House, Harrison resumed his successful law practice. He also served as counsel for Venezuela in the Venezuelan-British boundary dispute and, in 1899, represented the United States at the Hague Peace Conference. He died in 1901.

His wife, Caroline Lavinia Scott Harrison, daughter of a college professor, was proficient in music and painting and brought cultural distinction to her role as First Lady. When the Daughters of the American Revolution was organized in 1890, she was elected its first president-general. She became ill during the third year of her husband's term and died in the last year. During her illness and after her death, her place as White House hostess was taken by her niece, Mary Scott Lord Dimmick, whom Harrison subsequently married, in 1896.

## WILLIAM McKINLEY

25th President
1897–1901

A schoolteacher, soldier, and lawyer, McKinley was born January 29, 1843, in Niles, Ohio. He graduated from Allegheny College and began teaching. He enlisted as a Union Army private in the Civil War, and rose to the rank of major. After the war, he studied law, passed the bar in 1867, and established a practice in Canton, Ohio. There, he married Ida Saxton, the daughter of a banker.

After serving two years as prosecuting attorney for Stark County, Ohio, McKinley was elected to Congress in 1876, where he remained (except for one term) until 1891. While a member of the House, he sponsored the McKinley Tariff Act, which, though unpopular with some Americans, pleased financial and business interests.

Despite his defeat for reelection to Congress in 1890, McKinley gained and held the backing of Mark Hanna, a powerful Ohio Republican,

who maneuvered McKinley's election as governor in 1892. In 1896, again through Hanna's astute management, McKinley was nominated as the Republican Presidential candidate.

The Republican platform emphasized a higher protective tariff and an expansionist foreign policy. In McKinley's administration, tariffs were raised and Hawaii was finally annexed.

The sinking of the *Maine* in Havana harbor precipitated the war with Spain during McKinley's first term. The Philippines, Guam, and Puerto Rico were acquired with American victory.

In the election of 1900, McKinley won by a sizable margin over Bryan. He was fated to serve only a few months of his second term. Shot by Leon Czolgosz, an anarchist, on September 6, 1901, he died eight days later.

His wife, Ida Saxton McKinley, bore him two daughters, both of whom died in childhood. She was an epileptic, an invalid during her husband's administration, and suffered a seizure at the second inaugural. However, she presided at White House functions, accompanied her husband everywhere, and was with him at the Pan American Exposition in Buffalo, where he was assassinated. She died May 26, 1907.

# THEODORE ROOSEVELT

**26th President
1901–1909**

The "Rough Rider" President was born October 27, 1858, in New York City. The scion of a wealthy and well-established family, Theodore Roosevelt was educated by private tutors, traveled widely, graduated from Harvard in 1880, and entered Columbia Law School. As a youth, Roosevelt's health was poor, and his effort to build up his physical strength by "roughing it" helped to make him a sportsman, hunter, horseman, rancher, and explorer. At the same time, he retained literary and cultural interests.

Throughout his life, however, his major interest was politics, which he entered as a "young insurgent" Republican advocating reforms. Roosevelt served in the New York legislature between 1881 and 1884. At the 1884 Republican presidential convention he opposed the nomination of James G. Blaine because of Blaine's connection with a stock-rigging scandal. This cost him the support of the New York Republican boss, Thomas Collier Platt. When, as a loyal Republican, Roosevelt campaigned for Blaine, he lost the support of the "young insurgents."

Considering his political career over, and bereaved by the deaths of his mother and his wife, Alice Hathaway Lee, in 1884, Roosevelt retired for the next two years to his North Dakota ranch. There he acquired many picturesque Western mannerisms of speech and gesture.

In 1886, Roosevelt was called back to New York City to run for mayor against powerful Democratic candidates. Though he was defeated he attracted so much attention that President Benjamin Harrison appointed him to the Civil Service Commission (1889–95), on which he became the dominant figure. He left to head the New York City Board of Police Commissioners, where his zealous reforms and combative personality offended conservatives and political bosses.

In 1897 President William McKinley appointed him Assistant Secretary of the Navy, in which post, anticipating war with Spain, he was instrumental in placing the navy on a war footing. On the outbreak of the Spanish-American War, he resigned and, with Leonard Wood, organized and led the volunteer cavalry regiment that became known as the "Rough Riders."

When Roosevelt returned from Cuba a military hero, "Boss" Platt, though personally averse to him, supported him for the governorship of New York. Roosevelt won and served from 1899 to 1901. His administration antagonized Platt and the other Republican bosses and in 1900 they decided to dispose of him,

for at least the next four years, by backing his nomination for Vice President. The McKinley-Roosevelt slate was elected, but Roosevelt served as Vice President only a few months; the assassination of McKinley brought Roosevelt into the White House at forty-two, the youngest of our Presidents.

His vivid personality and enthusiasm immediately made him a popular President. His intellectual interests elevated the tone of American politics, although his glorification of military power and force drew considerable criticism.

This was the era of "muckraking" and reform, and Roosevelt embodied the period, coining such phrases as "malefactors of great wealth," strengthening government controls over big business through a reinvigorated Interstate Commerce Commission, directing "trust busting" actions against the more notorious big corporations, and supporting passage of the Meat Inspection Act and the Pure Food and Drugs Act. He also advocated conservation of our forest lands and irrigation of wastelands. By his forceful actions he enhanced and expanded the power of the nation's chief executive.

Roosevelt's "big stick" policy toward Latin America contributed to "anti-Yankee" feeling, particularly his measures against Colombia when it refused him permission to build the Panama Canal on his terms. Backing a revolution in Colombia's Panama province, he immediately recognized the rebel regime, secured from it the desired agreement, and began the construction of the canal. In 1904 he issued a statement interpreting the Monroe Doctrine as a sanction for American intervention in Latin American affairs.

While carrying out this strong policy in the New World, Roosevelt was active in promoting peace in the Old World. Through his mediation, the Russo-Japanese War was ended in 1904 at the Portsmouth peace conference; and the Franco-German dispute over Morocco was negotiated at the Algeciras Conference, averting war though no conclusive agreement was reached. His ardent advocacy of the Hague Tribunal raised hopes for international peace. For these acts Roosevelt was awarded the 1906 Nobel Peace Prize.

At the close of his second term Roosevelt practically chose as his successor William Howard Taft, his Secretary of War, successfully backing him at the 1908 Republican convention and in the ensuing campaign. This accomplished, Roosevelt went off on exploring and big-game expeditions and a triumphant tour of European capitals, where he delivered lectures.

On his return in 1910, Roosevelt reentered active politics. Failing to swing Taft into the courses he favored, he broke with his former protégé. At the 1912 Republican convention, Roosevelt sought the nomination for a third term, and when Taft won the nomination, Roosevelt took the progressive Republicans out of the party, organized them into a new Progressive, or "Bull Moose," Party, and ran as its candidate. This split enabled the Democratic candidate, Woodrow Wilson, to win. Roosevelt came in second, with Taft a poor third.

To the end, Roosevelt spoke out on a wide diversity of subjects and kept the headline writers busy. In addition to politics he engaged in what would have been separate careers for other men—exploration and literature. A former "River of Doubt" in the Brazilian jungle which he traced to its source now bears the name of Rio Roosevelt. His books number close to forty. During World War I, Roosevelt pleaded with President Wilson for permission to organize a volunteer army division in France. His plans for a new group of "Rough

Riders" came to naught, however, in the face of regular army opposition and, so his backers believed, Wilson's reluctance to add to the strength of his 1912 opponent.

On January 6, 1919, Roosevelt died in his sleep, at the age of sixty.

Twice married, Roosevelt lost his first wife, Alice Hathaway Lee Roosevelt, two days after the birth of their daughter, Alice Lee Roosevelt. Roosevelt married his second wife, Edith Kermit Carow, on December 2, 1886. They had five children, four sons and one daughter. All four sons chose an army career; one died in action in World War I and two others died in World War II. As First Lady, Mrs. Roosevelt made the White House the social center of Washington. She died on September 30, 1948, at the age of eighty-seven.

## WILLIAM HOWARD TAFT

**27th President
1909–1913**

An Ohio politician and judge, William Howard Taft was born September 15, 1857, in Cincinnati. His father had served as Secretary of War and Attorney General under President Grant, and as minister to Russia under President Arthur. William Howard Taft graduated from Yale in 1878, and from Cincinnati Law School in 1880, and practiced law briefly before entering public life.

From Cincinnati, where he served successively as assistant prosecutor, assistant county solicitor, and superior court judge, he rose to Federal posts. These included Solicitor General of the United States (1890–92), United States circuit judge (1892–1900), president of the Philippine Commission (1900–01), and Governor of the Philippines (1901–04). President Theodore Roosevelt, his friend, appointed him Secretary of War (1904–08), and entrusted him with special missions to Cuba, Panama, and the Philippines.

A stout, amiable man, deliberate and conservative in temperament, he was the diametric opposite of Theodore Roosevelt. Nonetheless, Roosevelt chose Taft as his successor, and the Republican Party nominated him as its Presidential candidate in the election of 1908, in which Taft defeated William Jennings Bryan.

As President, Taft continued Roosevelt's policies, but the emphasis became more conservative. Republicans who favored dynamic and progressive policies grew increasingly restive, and in 1910, after his return from an African safari, Roosevelt joined their ranks.

Taft sought to conciliate the progressives by approving bills to institute postal savings and the parcel post and by endorsing constitutional amendments authorizing the direct election of Senators and the enactment of an income tax.

This income tax, ratified later in his administration, had been decided upon because government income under the Dingley Tariff had proved inadequate to meet current expenses. An extra session of Congress met to revise this tariff, and this bill became the Paine-Aldrich Act. However, this act failed to reduce duties on imports to the extent expected, but it did mark a distinct step toward a lower scale of import duties, and it opened the door to the free exchange of commerce with the Philippines.

These bids failed, however, to placate the progressives. Led by Theodore Roosevelt, they bolted the Republican Party when it renominated Taft and organized their own Progressive (Bull Moose) Party, with Roosevelt as their candidate. The split gave the election to the Democratic candidate, Woodrow Wilson. Progressivism was the temper of the time, and Taft, labeled a conservative, ran far behind Roosevelt. He received only 8 electoral votes, to 435 for Wilson and 88 for Roosevelt.

In his retirement, Taft taught at Yale. During World War I, he served as co-chairman of the War Labor Conference Board, and he was among the Republicans who advocated our entry into the League of Nations. In 1921 he was appointed Chief Justice of the United States Supreme Court by President Harding, and served until a few weeks before his death on March 8, 1930. (Taft was the only U.S. President who also served on the Supreme Court.)

His wife, Helen Herron Taft, was a daughter of a Cincinnati judge. She was a musician, and her White House musicales were highly regarded. She was ill during part of her husband's administration, and her sister, Mrs. Louise More, presided in her place. Mrs. Taft survived her husband for thirteen years and died on May 22, 1943.

The Tafts' children carried on the distinction of the family. Robert A. Taft became one of the most influential Senators in history; Charles P. Taft became the first layman president of the Federal Council of Churches of Christ in America; their daughter, Mrs. Helen Herron Taft Manning, won note as an educator.

# WOODROW WILSON

**28th President
1913–1921**

The son of a Presbyterian minister, Thomas Woodrow Wilson was born December 28, 1856, in Staunton, Virginia. He graduated from Princeton in 1879, and from the University of Virginia Law School in 1881. He was admitted to the bar in 1882, and practiced law for a year in Atlanta. However, Wilson chose education as his profession, took his Ph.D. at Johns Hopkins University, and held teaching posts at Wesleyan and Bryn Mawr. He joined Princeton's faculty in 1890, as a professor of jurisprudence and political economy. Twelve years later, he became president of the university, a post he held for eight years. An eloquent orator, Wilson was popular with the Princeton student body, and initiated many educational reforms, some of which proved controversial.

Under fire from conservative elements on campus, Wilson resigned, and in 1910 he was nominated and elected Democratic governor of New Jersey. Despite resistance from regular Democrats, Wilson forced progressive policies through the New Jersey legislature: workmen's compensation, the direct primary, simplification of the ballot, creation of a public utilities commission, a corrupt practices act, and regulation of trusts and big business. His gubernatorial record made him a national figure.

At the Democratic national convention of 1912, Wilson, supported by William Jennings Bryan, then dominant in the Democratic Party, won the nomination on the 46th ballot. A split in the Republican Party, which divided into regular Republicans supporting William Howard Taft and progressive Republicans backing Theodore Roosevelt, eased Wilson into the White House.

The beginning of Wilson's tenure was notable for its vigor. Liberal measures, carried out under the slogan "the new freedom," included ratification of the 17th Amendment to the Constitution, instituting direct popular election of U.S. Senators; the Federal Reserve Act, which changed the financial structure of the country; the Keating-Owen Child Labor Act; the Farm Loan Act; the Clayton Anti-Trust Act; the Adamson Eight-Hour Law, reducing the working hours of trainmen; the La Follette Seamen's Act; and a lowered tariff.

Wilson also favored equal rights for women. He welcomed the election in 1916 of America's first Congresswoman, Jeannette Rankin of Montana; he aided the passage of the 19th Amendment, enfranchising women; and he created a precedent by appointing the first woman to a sub-cabinet post, Annette Abbott Adams as Assistant Attorney General. Prohibition did not meet with his favor and he vetoed the Volstead Act; Congress overrode his veto. His foreign policy supported attempts to negotiate anti-war agreements. However, he disappointed many liberals by maintaining the "Big Stick" policy toward Latin America.

But the looming war in Europe, brought on by the rivalry between the Allies and the Central Powers, overshadowed all other foreign problems. Wilson sought to maintain American neutrality, but went further in his warnings to Germany than Secretary of State Bryan considered proper in a neutral. When Wilson insisted on sending a threatening note to Germany after the U-boat sinking of the *Lusitania,* Bryan resigned.

Under the slogan "He kept us out of war," Wilson won reelection in 1916. But with the announcement by Germany that it would resume all-out submarine operations to impose its own blockade against the Allies, Wilson took the United States into the world conflict. Public opinion was behind him when he declared war on Germany on April 6, 1917.

Wilson's conduct of the war was vigorous, and his fiery resolution won international renown. His stated war objectives were to "make the world safe for democracy" and to promote the "ultimate peace of the world." His program for peace was embodied in the famous "fourteen points," calling for open diplomacy in the settlement of international disputes, the adjustment of colonial claims, the self-determination of peoples, and the formation of a "general association of nations" to maintain international justice.

At the Versailles Peace Conference, which he attended in person, he met fierce resistance from Lloyd George, Georges Clemenceau, and other European premiers, who made secret agreements among themselves. Disappointed, Wilson returned to America with what he considered the best treaty obtainable and which was acceptable to him chiefly because it provided for the organization of the League of Nations.

Isolationist feeling in America had grown, however, and the League of Nations was violently attacked by various Senators, and debate was bitter. Despite the agitation of a handful of "unreconcilables," led by Henry Cabot Lodge, the Senate would have ratified the treaty if certain reservations protecting American sovereignty had been incorporated, but Wilson refused to compromise.

Though repudiated at home, Wilson was eulogized abroad. In 1920 he was awarded the Nobel Peace Prize, the second President to receive that honor. He died in Washington on February 3, 1924.

Wilson married twice. His first wife, Ellen Louise Axson Wilson, whom he married in 1885, died during the second year of his first administration. One of her three daughters, Margaret, took over the functions of First Lady until her father's remarriage in 1915. His second wife was Edith Bolling Galt Wilson, a strikingly handsome widow.

## WARREN GAMALIEL HARDING

**29th President
1921–1923**

A lawyer, businessman, and newspaper editor, Warren Gamaliel Harding was born November 2, 1865, in Corsica, Ohio. His father was a country doctor. Harding was educated at Ohio Central College, studied law, and worked as a farmer and insurance man. As editor and part owner of the *Marion* (Ohio) *Star*, he won prominence in local affairs, and soon became active in Republican politics.

Beginning his political career as county auditor, Harding rose to state senator, lieutenant governor, and U.S. Senator from Ohio. He served in the Senate from 1915 to 1921, and although his record was undistinguished, clever maneuvering by his manager, Harry M. Daugherty, brought him the Presidential nomination at the 1920 Republican convention.

Harding's chief campaign issue was disentanglement from European affairs, while his major slogan was "back to normalcy."

Aware of his own limitations, Harding chose to rely on a cabinet of "best minds," but unfortunately he appointed—along with more capable advisers—men who abused his trust. Soon there were scandals over the custodianship of alien property, the sale of government-owned cargo ships, the administration of the Veterans Bureau, the conduct of the Justice Department (which had been Daugherty's reward), and the leasing of naval oil reserves to private oil interests for a bribe by Albert B. Fall, Secretary of the Interior.

Death in San Francisco, on August 2, 1923, on his return from a tour of Alaska, spared Harding the humiliation of witnessing the trials of two of his cabinet members, Fall and Daugherty.

His wife, Florence Kling De Wolfe Harding, was a divorcee, but her marriage to Harding in 1891 took place after the death of her first husband. She was reported to have been chiefly responsible, through her efficient management, for the success of her husband's newspaper, the *Marion Star*. She was active in White House functions, but suffered serious illnesses during her husband's administration. In spite of her ailments, she accompanied the President on his tour of Alaska and was with him in San Francisco when he died.

## CALVIN COOLIDGE

**30th President
1923–1929**

Born July 4, 1872, at Plymouth, Vermont, John Calvin Coolidge was the son of a New England storekeeper and justice of the peace. He graduated from Amherst in 1895, and was admitted to the bar two years later. In many ways the antithesis of the back-slapping politician, Coolidge nonetheless rose swiftly in public life. He held minor offices in Northampton, Massachusetts, where he had practiced law, became a member of the state legislature, then was elected lieutenant governor and governor of Massachusetts.

As governor, he won national prominence for his handling of the Boston police strike, a sensation of the year 1919. Had it not been for the opposition of the influential Senator Lodge, Coolidge would have won the Presidential nomination—instead of Warren G. Harding—at the Republican convention in 1920; Coolidge was named as Vice President. When Harding died in office (1923), Coolidge became President and in 1924 was elected to a full four-year term. Coolidge received 379 electoral votes, John W. Davis, 139, and Robert La Follette, 13.

As President, Coolidge had qualities and a program that appealed to the American of the 1920s, a period of almost wild national prosperity. Spare of words, he was nicknamed "Silent Cal." He was straightforward and honest, and helped liquidate the scandals of the Harding Administration. His program of economy in government administration, tax cuts, and reduction of the national debt, while also supporting flood-control projects, sustained his popularity.

In his cabinet, Coolidge surrounded himself with forceful men, who gave his administration a tone of confidence and strength. Among his cabinet appointees were Herbert Hoover, Secretary of Commerce; Andrew Mellon, Secretary of the Treasury; and Frank B. Kellogg, Secretary of State.

Coolidge probably could have won another Presidential term, but he refused renomination in 1928 in his famous laconic message, "I do not choose to run."

On his retirement Coolidge occupied himself mainly with writing articles for newspapers and magazines and with his autobiography. He died on January 5, 1933.

Grace Anna Goodhue, a graduate of Vermont College, whom Coolidge married in 1905, was highly regarded for her gracious and cultured manner. However, the deaths of the Coolidges' younger son and of the President's father during the Coolidge administration muted and curtailed White House social activities. Mrs. Coolidge survived her husband twenty-four years, and died on July 8, 1957.

# HERBERT CLARK HOOVER

**31st President
1929–1933**

The son of a black-smith, Hoover was born August 10, 1874, in West Branch, Iowa. He graduated from Stanford University in 1895, became a mining engineer, prospector, and businessman, and accumulated a considerable fortune through wide-ranging operations that took him all over the world. Because of his Quaker beliefs, he worked as organizer of relief operations during World War I. His administration of relief agencies attracted world-wide attention, and both major political parties sought his affiliation; he chose the Republicans.

In 1921, Hoover was appointed Secretary of Commerce. He reorganized and expanded the department, sponsored conferences on unemployment, initiated programs to conserve fisheries, and constructed public works, among them Hoover (Boulder) Dam.

When Coolidge declined to run for a third term, he gave his support to Hoover's candidacy and election in 1928. His campaign emphasized the continuation of America's prosperity under Republican administrations. Hoover defeated Alfred E. Smith, the Democratic candidate.

The stock-market crash of 1929 ushered in the Great Depression, which continued throughout Hoover's administration. As countermeasures, Hoover called for an extensive public-works program to restore business and employment. He secured the establishment of the Reconstruction Finance Corporation and other companies; established the Home Loan Bank and expanded the Farm Loan Bank; and supported legislation to relieve states and municipalities unable to bear the burden of the economic crisis. These measures proved ineffective, however, and Hoover's popularity waned. In foreign affairs he faced the problems of Japanese aggression, disarmament, and war debts.

In the Presidential election of 1932, Hoover was overwhelmingly defeated by Franklin D. Roosevelt. In 1946, President Truman appointed him coordinator of food supplies to dozens of countries badly affected by the Second World War. His long life in public service was further extended in 1947–49 and again in 1953–55, when he headed the Hoover Commissions. Hoover died on October 20, 1964, aged 90.

Hoover met his wife, Lou Henry Hoover, at Stanford University, and married her in 1899. She was a charming and friendly White House hostess. She died January 7, 1944.

# FRANKLIN DELANO ROOSEVELT

**32nd President
1933–1945**

Related to 11 former Presidents, Franklin Delano Roosevelt was born into a wealthy, prominent family on January 20, 1882, at Hyde Park, New York. He graduated from Harvard in 1904, and the following year married Eleanor Roosevelt, a distant cousin. Roosevelt graduated from Columbia Law School in 1907, and after practicing for four years, won a Democratic seat in the New York State Legislature. He established himself as leader of the reform Democrats by opposing a Tammany nominee for the U.S. Senate.

In 1912, he vigorously campaigned for Woodrow Wilson, who recognized his abilities and appointed him Assistant Secretary of the Navy. Though he was defeated in the Democratic Senatorial primaries in 1914, Roosevelt remained prominent enough to be chosen as running mate to James M. Cox in the Presidential campaign of 1920. During this period he became associated with the liberal Democrat Alfred E. Smith, at whose insistence, in 1928, he ran for governor of New York, and won though nationally his party went down to defeat.

This was three years after Roosevelt had been stricken with poliomyelitis at his summer estate, Campobello. He had become paralyzed from the waist down. By indomitable efforts he had recovered partial use of his legs, and he never permitted his disability to restrict his activities.

As governor of New York, Roosevelt achieved renown for his honest competence and his program of general welfare. The stock-market crash of 1929 brought with it the Great Depression, against which Governor Roosevelt, advised by a small group of intellectuals and experts, called the Brain Trust, undertook to establish extensive relief measures. At the same time he struck out at corruption in New York City politics, forcing the resignation of Mayor James J. Walker.

Franklin Roosevelt was chosen by the Democratic Party as its Presidential candidate in 1932 to face the Republican Herbert Hoover, whose administration had seen the start of this period of disaster and despair. Roosevelt was elected by a wide margin. He came to the White House at the height of the national economic crisis, and promptly brought new hope to a discouraged nation with his concern for "the little man," to whom he promised a "new deal." Roosevelt buoyantly set out to redeem this promise.

Congress, overwhelmed by the magnitude of the depression and by the forceful personality of Roosevelt, surrendered much power to the

President, who immediately launched a series of emergency measures to reorganize industry and agriculture—under government controls—and to revive the faltering economy by a great expenditure of public funds. Between March 9 and June 16, the famous "hundred days" session, Congress enacted, under Roosevelt's guidance, more decisive legislation than any Congressional session in U.S. history up to that time. This vast and many-faceted New Deal program—which offered greater protection to and benefits for the unemployed and the aged, labor and the farmer—was not undertaken without opposition. Roosevelt's critics accused him of having too many radical schemes of social betterment, and among conservatives he was disparagingly referred to as "that man in the White House." Nonetheless, in 1936 Roosevelt was reelected by an awesome majority over his Republican opponent, Alfred M. Landon, who won the electoral votes of only Maine and Vermont.

The action of the Supreme Court in declaring invalid a number of New Deal measures—notably those creating the National Recovery Administration (NRA) and the Agricultural Adjustment Administration (AAA)—spurred the opponents of Roosevelt and tended to reduce the pace of reform. In 1937, Roosevelt attempted to "pack the court," but failed to reorganize it to his advantage. He failed, too, in attempting to "purge" members of Congress who had opposed New Deal measures. However, the dynamic force of his Administration continued to be exerted.

By 1938, the international skies were black with the shadow of war, and as the power of the Axis nations grew, Roosevelt, by now a world figure, spoke out against aggression and international greed. In 1939, he personally appealed to Hitler and Mussolini for peace. But peace was not to be. After his strenuous efforts to end the domestic crisis, Roosevelt faced the international crises created by the rise of Nazism and Fascism.

Roosevelt was bitterly opposed by isolationist and conservative forces, and in the 1940 Presidential election an acrimonious issue was made of his breaking the third-term tradition. Though Roosevelt's majority was reduced, his vote was large enough to defeat the Republican candidate, Wendell Willkie. The history of Roosevelt's third administration is essentially the history of the United States in World War II.

The Japanese attack on Pearl Harbor finally drew the United States directly into World War II. By a brilliant reorganization of the economy, which multiplied production beyond the most optimistic estimates, the United States was able to overcome initial setbacks and bring irresistible power to bear against the Axis nations. U.S. forces landed in North Africa, and followed with the invasion of Sicily, Italy, and finally Normandy. In the Pacific, U.S. superiority in the air had brought the war to Japan. The turn in the fortunes of war had come, and in the election of 1944, Roosevelt, with Harry S. Truman as his running mate, won an unprecedented fourth term in office.

Roosevelt participated in a series of conferences with Winston Churchill, Joseph Stalin, and other Allied leaders to discuss plans for the dawning postwar world and to lay the foundations of lasting peace through the formation of the United Nations. On April 12, 1945, however, not quite a month before Germany surrendered to the Allies, Franklin Delano Roosevelt suddenly died, and the world mourned.

Eleanor Roosevelt (Anna Eleanor Roosevelt) was born in 1884, the niece of Theodore Roosevelt. As a young woman she had been a volunteer social worker, and she continued her civic activities after her marriage, although she bore six children (five sons and one daughter) and gave her husband substantial assistance in his political career. During her husband's administrations she established a precedent as a First Lady famous in her own right, though not without subjecting herself to controversy and criticism. She traveled widely, making numerous speeches and reporting her observations in the press.

After Roosevelt's death she devoted herself to humanitarian causes, and from 1949 to 1952 she was a U.S. delegate to the United Nations. She died on November 7, 1962.

## HARRY S. TRUMAN

**33rd President
1945–1953**

The son of a farmer and livestock dealer, Truman was born May 8, 1884, in Lamar, Missouri. He began working in a local drugstore at the age of 11, and graduated from high school at 15. He clerked and farmed, and seemed destined for a conventional life, until World War I, when he helped to organize a field artillery unit. A member of the National Guard since 1905, Truman was commissioned a first lieutenant, and finished the war as a major in 1919.

Civilian life again seemed bleak after the failure of a haberdashery business in Kansas City in 1921. However, Truman had attracted the notice of the local Democratic boss, Thomas Pendergast, who eased him into two county judgeships, the first an administrative post, and during this time he studied law.

Elected U.S. Senator from Missouri in 1934, Truman served for ten years as a sometime supporter of President Roosevelt's New Deal. He became a national figure as chairman of the Special Senate Committee to Investigate the National Defense Program (the Truman Committee). His fair and energetic inquiry into inefficiency and bungling on war-production contracts won him wide praise.

At the 1944 Democratic national convention

Truman, acceptable to both conservative Democrats and New Dealers, was named Roosevelt's running mate in his campaign for a fourth term. With the death of Roosevelt on April 12, 1945, Truman became President at a critical time in U.S. history. He was immediately confronted with the problems of ending the Second World War and preparing for the difficulties of postwar readjustment. Germany surrendered in May, and Japan capitulated in September, after Truman authorized the decisive atomic bombing of Hiroshima and Nagasaki.

Renominated in 1948, he upset the public opinion polls, which had forecast his certain defeat by the Republican candidate, Thomas E. Dewey. By his vigorous campaigning he not only countered a nationwide Republican swing, but overcame splits in his own party. On the right, Senator J. Strom Thurmond of South Carolina led a new States Rights ("Dixiecrat") party of Southern Democrats antagonized by Truman's advocacy of civil rights for Negroes. On the left, Henry A. Wallace led "progressive" groups antagonized by Truman's anti-Soviet stand.

In his postwar domestic policy Truman, more or less continuing Roosevelt's New Deal, faced strong Congressional opposition from a coalition of Republicans and Southern Democrats. They overrode his veto of the Labor-Management Relations Act (Taft-Hartley Law); enacted the McCarran-Walter Immigration Bill, which he opposed; withheld support from him in his efforts to initiate a government-sponsored health insurance plan; frustrated his attempts to maintain price controls; and blocked his civil rights program. He managed, however, to force through public housing projects, an increase in the minimum wage, civilian control over nuclear developments, and desegregation of the armed forces.

In foreign affairs, the inability of the United States and the U.S.S.R. to find common ground on which to resolve their international differences, and the threatening advances in 1946–47 of Communism in Europe and the Middle East, had resulted in the Cold War.

Congress backed Truman's foreign policy, which concentrated on the containment of Communism. The establishment of the United Nations was affirmed, and the legislators fully supported the "Truman Doctrine," a program of economic and military assistance to nations threatened by Communism. This was expanded by the European Recovery Program for the reconstruction of the British and European economies, and was supplemented by the Point Four program of technical assistance to underdeveloped nations.

These measures were followed by the formation of the North Atlantic Treaty Organization (NATO), an anti-Communist military alliance. A victory in the Cold War struggle was achieved when the Anglo-American airlift frustrated the Communist Berlin blockade.

The Cold War finally produced a hot war when North Korea attacked her southern neighbor in 1950. The United States seized upon a Russian absence in the Security Council to push through the United Nations a resolution condemning the North Koreans as aggressors. Truman then landed troops at Pusan under the command of General Douglas MacArthur. But an advance to the Yalu River on the Chinese border brought China into the field, and the conflict ended in a stalemate. In 1951 Truman raised a storm of controversy when he relieved MacArthur of his Far Eastern command for insubordination. This, and the charges of Senator Joseph R. McCarthy of Communist infiltration in the Department of State, and the partisan charges that U.S. failure to support General Chiang Kai-shek had lost China to the Communists, shadowed the final years of Truman's administration. It suffered also from the taint of corruption on the part of subordinates, whom Truman defended out of friendship or party loyalty.

Refusing to consider renomination, Truman went into active retirement, giving much time to historical and autobiographical writings and the establishment of the Harry S. Truman Library at Independence, Missouri. He retained his interest in politics, however, and often commented on national issues.

Bess (Elizabeth Virginia) Wallace Truman, who had been a high school classmate and whom Truman married on his return from World War I, was retiring in nature and avoided publicity, but was well regarded as a White House hostess. Their daughter Margaret was a concert singer.

## DWIGHT DAVID EISENHOWER

34th President
1953–1961

The son of a gas company manager, Dwight David Eisenhower (given name: David Dwight Eisenhower) was born on October 14, 1890, in Denison, Texas. When he was a child, his family moved to Abilene, Kansas, where he grew to manhood.

He finished highest in the examination for appointment to West Point or Annapolis but chose the military academy, which he entered when he was 21.

He graduated in 1915 as a second lieutenant in the U.S. Army, and a year later, on July 1, 1916, married Mary (Mamie) Geneva Doud.

In World War I, Eisenhower was commanding officer of a training camp for the new U.S. army tank corps, near Gettysburg, Pennsylvania. After the war he was posted, successively, to the Panama Canal Zone, the office of the Assistant Secretary of War, and from 1935 to 1940, to the Philippines. His performance in the 1941 army maneuvers was impressive and he was assigned to Washington, D.C., as chief of operations.

In World War II, Eisenhower was named U.S. commander of the European theater of operations, and began his spectacular rise as a military leader. He commanded the Americans in the North African landings, and in 1943 became chief of all Allied forces in North Africa. After directing the invasions of Sicily and Italy, he was called to England to be supreme commander of the Allied Expeditionary Force. As such he was largely responsible for the cooperation achieved between the Allied forces in the Normandy invasion and in the momentous battle for the European continent.

In 1944, Eisenhower was made a five-star general and a year later became chief of staff of the U.S. Army. He resigned in 1948 to become president of Columbia University, where he served for two and a half years, prior to his appointment as the supreme commander of the Allied powers in Europe. There he organized the NATO defense forces.

Although he was sought as a U.S. Presidential candidate by both parties from 1948 on, Eisenhower rejected the offers until 1952, when he resigned from the army to be the Republican candidate. An enormously popular figure, he easily defeated his Democratic opponent, Adlai E. Stevenson.

In the White House, Eisenhower followed a middle-of-the-road course. He restricted the role of the Federal government in domestic affairs, but extended social security to millions of self-employed Americans, and increased farm aid. He encouraged business by ending Federal controls on wages, prices, and rents, and by abandoning the excess profits tax on corporations.

In foreign affairs, Eisenhower's administration began auspiciously with the settlement of the Korean War. However, the rising costs of defense obligations abroad frustrated Eisenhower's attempts to reduce the budget. In 1954 he was confronted with charges of Communist subversion in his administration made by the controversial Republican senator, Joseph R. McCarthy. Eisenhower's vacillation in the face of these unsubstantiated accusations drew criticism.

Nevertheless, Eisenhower's personal popularity continued to increase throughout the country, and in the election of 1956 he again won over Adlai E. Stevenson—this time by an even wider margin than in 1952.

In his second term the President promulgated the so-called Eisenhower Doctrine, in which he promised to send military and economic aid to any Middle Eastern nation resisting Communist subversion; in 1958, U.S. Marines were sent to Lebanon under the doctrine.

At home, Eisenhower took steps to revive the economy, after a sharp recession, and attempted to solve the school integration issue in the South. Late in his second term the President was embarrassed by the involvement in a scandal of his confidential aide, Sherman Adams, and by the U-2 espionage flights over the Soviet Union.

During his stay at the White House, Eisenhower suffered several serious illnesses. After leaving Washington, he retired to his farm in Gettysburg, Pennsylvania, but has remained active in politics, campaigning for Republican candidates, writing books, and commenting on national issues.

Mary (Mamie) Geneva Doud Eisenhower, born in 1896, was a reserved and unassuming White House hostess, who avoided unnecessary publicity. The Eisenhowers had two sons, David Dwight, who died when he was 3, and John Sheldon Doud Eisenhower, born in 1923.

## JOHN FITZGERALD KENNEDY

**35th President**
**1961–1963**

Born May 29, 1917, in Brookline, Massachusetts, the son of Joseph P. Kennedy, a prominent businessman who served as U.S. Ambassador to Great Britain for four years, John F. Kennedy acted as his father's secretary in London during 1938, and graduated from Harvard in 1940. He commanded a Navy PT-boat in the Pacific during World War II. In action off the Solomons, his boat was sunk by an enemy destroyer, and young Kennedy was credited with heroism in saving his crew.

His political career began in 1946 when he was elected to Congress as a Democrat from Massachusetts and continued with his reelection in 1948 and 1950. In 1952, despite the landslide for the Republican Presidential candidate,

Dwight D. Eisenhower, Kennedy defeated the incumbent, Henry Cabot Lodge, for the U.S. Senate. In 1954–55 he underwent operations to repair a spinal injury, suffered during the war. Away from the Senate, Kennedy wrote *Profiles in Courage,* for which he won a Pulitzer Prize.

In 1958 Kennedy was overwhelmingly reelected to the Senate, and he began a campaign for the 1960 Democratic Presidential nomination. Several important primary victories in 1960 helped ensure his nomination at the convention; Kennedy chose Lyndon B. Johnson of Texas as his running mate.

Kennedy campaigned against his Republican opponent, Richard M. Nixon, partly on the issue that the country's prestige had declined greatly during the Eisenhower administration. His cause was helped by his performance in a series of television debates with Nixon.

Kennedy won the election in the closest Presidential race of the 20th century, and became at 43 the youngest man ever elected to the White House, and, also, the nation's first Roman Catholic President.

The program of the Kennedy Administration,

called the New Frontier, pressed for Federal aid to education, enlargement of civil rights, aid to economically depressed areas, medical care for the aged, and an accelerated space program. In foreign affairs, principal accomplishments were the establishment of the Peace Corps, the Alliance for Progress with Latin-American countries, and the nuclear test ban treaty. In 1961, when the anti-Castro Cubans' invasion of the Bay of Pigs failed, Kennedy—and the nation— suffered deep humiliation. This was offset in 1962 when the President's firm stand compelled the Soviet Union to dismantle its missile bases in Cuba.

Deeply concerned with American culture, Kennedy did much to foster public interest in literature and the arts. He established several cultural programs, and the White House guest list included distinguished scientists, writers, artists, and musicians.

The march toward a "new frontier" was brutally halted on November 22, 1963, in Dallas, Texas, when Kennedy was shot by Lee Harvey Oswald. The nation and the world mourned his death.

Jacqueline Lee Bouvier, born in 1929, the daughter of a stockbroker, was married to Kennedy in 1953. Mrs. Kennedy as a girl attended several fashionable private schools, made her debut in Newport, Rhode Island, and later studied at Vassar College and the Sorbonne in Paris. As First Lady, Mrs. Kennedy redecorated the White House interior and was known for her charm and command of foreign languages. Widespread admiration was evoked by her courage at the time of her husband's death. The Kennedys had three children, Caroline Bouvier, born in 1957, John Fitzgerald, born in 1960, and Patrick Bouvier, who died soon after birth in 1963.

## LYNDON BAINES JOHNSON

36th President
1963–

The son of a school teacher and legislator, Lyndon B. Johnson was born August 27, 1908, on a farm near Stonewall, Texas. The family moved to Johnson City in 1913, and Johnson graduated from Southwest Texas State College in 1930. He taught high school in Houston for two years, and in 1932 became secretary to a Texas Congressman in Washington. Three years later, Johnson, long an ardent New Deal supporter, was named state director in Texas of the National Youth Administration.

In 1937 he was elected to Congress to fill an unexpired term, and he was reelected to the seat until 1948. Johnson was on active duty in the U.S. Navy in 1941–42, after which he returned to Washington. In 1948 he was elected to the U.S. Senate by a scant 87 votes; the contest was carried to the courts and Johnson's victory was upheld.

Johnson rose quickly in the Senate, becoming Democratic whip in 1951 and minority leader in 1953. In 1954 he was reelected with ease, and when the Democrats gained control of the Senate, Johnson advanced to majority leader, a post he held until 1960. In 1955 Johnson suffered a serious heart attack. As leader of the Senate he was regarded as a powerful and persuasive figure, adroit in legislative matters, conciliatory in attitude, and moderate in policy.

In 1960, after an unsuccessful attempt to gain the Democratic nomination for the Presidency, Johnson accepted the Vice-Presidential nomination on the ticket with John F. Kennedy. By keeping the Southern states within the party, Johnson made a major contribution to the Democrats' narrow victory.

On November 22, 1963, after only 34 months in the White House, Kennedy was assassinated and Lyndon B. Johnson was immediately sworn in as the 36th President. Johnson continued Kennedy's program with notable success, especially in his skillful handling of the Civil Rights Act of 1964 and the Economic Opportunity Act, which declared "war on poverty."

In the 1964 Presidential election Johnson won a landslide victory over Senator Barry M. Goldwater, the Republican candidate. Elected by the largest percentage of the popular vote ever, Johnson strove tirelessly to push his program through Congress, while achieving a national consensus based on his desire to be "President of all the people."

The President—drawing on his years as Senate leader—had spectacular success with his massive domestic program. In a whirlwind of activity he initiated tax cuts, gained passage of the Voting Rights Act of 1965, instituted social security changes incorporating the Medicare plan, secured Federal aid for education, and achieved a new immigration law.

During 1966, Johnson pressed for an end to the fighting in Vietnam, by increasing military pressure on Communist forces, and by spurring intensified diplomatic efforts aimed at bringing the Hanoi Government into negotiations on a settlement of the dispute.

By 1967 Johnson's popularity took a downward turn as the Vietnam war dragged on. The American people, according to major polls, were becoming increasingly dissatisfied with the President's handling of the conflict and were also deeply concerned about urban rioting, rising taxes, and the threat of inflation.

Claudia Alta Taylor Johnson, born in 1912, the daughter of a Texas merchant, is known as Lady Bird. She married Johnson in 1934, and they have two daughters, Lynda Bird, born in 1944, and Luci Baines, born in 1947. On June 21, 1967, Luci Johnson Nugent gave birth to an eight-pound, ten-ounce baby boy. Patrick Lyndon Nugent, the President's first grandchild, was nicknamed "Lyn."

# PRESIDENTS, CABINETS, AND CONGRESSES

## LYNDON BAINES JOHNSON
(36th President)
November 22, 1963–January 20, 1965
January 20, 1965–

**Vice President:**
Hubert H. Humphrey, 1965–
**Secretary of State:**
Dean Rusk, 1963–
**Secretary of the Treasury:**
C. Douglas Dillon, 1963–65
Henry H. Fowler, 1965–
**Secretary of Defense:**
Robert S. McNamara, 1963–
**Attorney General:**
Robert F. Kennedy, 1963–64
Nicholas deB. Katzenbach, 1964–66
Ramsey Clark, 1967–
**Postmaster General:**
John A. Gronouski, 1963–65
Lawrence F. O'Brien, 1965–

**Secretary of the Interior:**
Stewart L. Udall, 1963–
**Secretary of Agriculture:**
Orville L. Freeman, 1963–
**Secretary of Conmerce:**
Luther H. Hodges, 1963–65
John T. Connor, 1965–67
Alexander B. Trowbridge, 1967–
**Secretary of Labor:**
W. Willard Wirtz, 1963–
**Secretary of Health, Education, and Welfare:**
Anthony J. Celebrezze, 1963–65
John W. Gardner, 1965–
**Secretary of Housing and Urban Development:**
Robert C. Weaver, 1965–
**Secretary of Transportation:**
Alan S. Boyd, 1966–

**Congress in Session:**
88th, 89th, 90th

A cabinet officer is not appointed for a fixed term. While it is customary for him to tender his resignation at the time of a change of administration, he remains at the head of his department until a successor is appointed by the new President.

■ **GEORGE WASHINGTON**
(1st President)
April 30, 1789–March 3, 1793
March 4, 1793–March 3, 1797
**Vice President:**
John Adams, 1789–97 [1]
**Secretary of State:**
Thomas Jefferson, 1789–94
Edmund Randolph, 1794–95
Timothy Pickering, 1795–97
**Secretary of the Treasury:**
Alexander Hamilton, 1789–95
Oliver Wolcott, Jr., 1795–97
**Secretary of War:**
Henry Knox, 1789–95
Timothy Pickering, 1795
James McHenry, 1796–97
**Attorney General:[2]**
Edmund Randolph, 1789–94
William Bradford, 1794–95
Charles Lee, 1795–97
**Postmaster General:[2]**
Samuel Osgood, 1789–91
Timothy Pickering, 1791–95
Joseph Habersham, 1795–97
**Congress in Session:**
1st, 2nd, 3rd, 4th

■ **JOHN ADAMS**
(2nd President)
March 4, 1797–March 3, 1801

**Vice President:**
Thomas Jefferson, 1797–1801
**Secretary of State:**
Timothy Pickering, 1797–1800 [3]
John Marshall, 1800–01
**Secretary of the Treasury:**
Oliver Wolcott, Jr., 1797–1801
**Secretary of War:**
James McHenry, 1797–1800
Samuel Dexter, 1800–01
**Attorney General:**
Charles Lee, 1797–1801
**Postmaster General:**
Joseph Habersham, 1797–1801
**Secretary of the Navy:**
Benjamin Stoddert, 1798–1801 [4]
**Congress in Session:**
5th, 6th

■ **THOMAS JEFFERSON**
(3rd President)
March 4, 1801–March 3, 1805
March 4, 1805–March 3, 1809
**Vice President:**
Aaron Burr, 1801–05 [5]
George Clinton, 1805–09
**Secretary of State:**
James Madison, 1801–09
**Secretary of the Treasury:**
Albert Gallatin, 1801–09

**Secretary of War:**
Henry Dearborn, 1801–09
**Attorney General:**
Levi Lincoln, 1801–04
John Breckinridge, 1805–06
Caesar Rodney, 1807–09
**Postmaster General:**
Gideon Granger, 1801–09
**Secretary of the Navy:**
Robert Smith, 1801–09
**Congress in Session:**
7th, 8th, 9th 10th

■ **JAMES MADISON**
(4th President)
March 4, 1809–March 3, 1813
March 4, 1813–March 3, 1817
**Vice President:**
George Clinton, 1809–12
Elbridge Gerry, 1813–14
**Secretary of State:**
Robert Smith, 1809–11
James Monroe, 1811–17
**Secretary of the Treasury:**
Albert Gallatin, 1809–14
William Jones, 1813–14 [6]
George Campbell, 1814
Alexander Dallas, 1814–16
William Crawford, 1816–17

[1] In 1789 and 1792 electors cast votes for two persons, in accordance with the Constitution; the one receiving the most votes became President, the runner-up, Vice-President. Adams received the second most votes and thus became Vice President. [2] Congress created the offices of Attorney General and Postmaster General in 1789, but the Attorney General first became a full-fledged Cabinet member in 1814, the Postmaster General in 1829. [3] He declined to resign when his resignation was requested May 10, 1800, and was dismissed two days later. [4] The U.S. Department of the Navy was established in 1798 by an act of Congress and upon the recommendation of President Adams. It received Cabinet rank under the Secretary of the Navy. [5] Since Jefferson and Burr were tied, the choice was left to the House of Representatives. Jefferson received the votes of ten states, Burr four, making him Vice President. It was not until the election of 1804, after a Constitutional amendment, that electors voted separately for a President and a Vice President. [6] As Secretary of the Navy, William Jones also performed the duties of the Secretary of the Treasury during the extended stay of Albert Gallatin in Europe from April 12, 1813, to February 9, 1814.

**Secretary of War:**
William Eustis, 1809–12
James Monroe, 1813, 1814–15 [7]
John Armstrong, 1813–14
William Crawford, 1815–16
**Attorney General:**
Caesar Rodney, 1809–11
William Pinkney, 1811–14
Richard Rush, 1814–17
**Postmaster General:**
Gideon Granger, 1809–14
Return Meigs, Jr., 1814–17
**Secretary of the Navy:**
Paul Hamilton, 1809–12
William Jones, 1813–14
Benjamin Crowninshield, 1814–17
**Congress in Session:**
11th, 12th, 13th, 14th

■ **JAMES MONROE**
(5th President)
March 4, 1817–March 3, 1821
March 4, 1821–March 3, 1825
**Vice President:**
Daniel Tompkins, 1817–25
**Secretary of State:**
John Quincy Adams, 1817–25
**Secretary of the Treasury:**
William Crawford, 1817–25
**Secretary of War:**
George Graham, 1817
John Calhoun, 1817–25
**Attorney General:**
Richard Rush, 1817 [8]
William Wirt, 1817–25
**Postmaster General:**
Return Meigs, Jr., 1817–23
John McLean, 1823–25
**Secretary of the Navy:**
Benjamin Crowninshield, 1817–18
Smith Thompson, 1818–23
Samuel Southard, 1823–25
**Congress in Session:**
15th, 16th, 17th, 18th

■ **JOHN QUINCY ADAMS**
(6th President)
March 4, 1825–March 3, 1829
**Vice President:**
John Calhoun, 1825–29
**Secretary of State:**
Henry Clay, 1825–29
**Secretary of the Treasury:**
Samuel Southard, 1825 [9]
Richard Rush, 1825–29
**Secretary of War:**
James Barbour, 1825–28
Peter Porter, 1828–29
**Attorney General:**
William Wirt, 1825–29
**Postmaster General:**
John McLean, 1825–29
**Secretary of the Navy:**
Samuel Southard, 1825–29
**Congress in Session:**
19th, 20th

■ **ANDREW JACKSON**
(7th President)
March 4, 1829–March 3, 1833
March 4, 1833–March 3, 1837
**Vice President:**
John Calhoun, 1829–32 [10]
Martin Van Buren, 1833–37
**Secretary of State:**
Martin Van Buren, 1829–31
Edward Livingston, 1831–33
Louis McLane, 1833–34
John Forsyth, 1834–37
**Secretary of the Treasury:**
Samuel Ingham, 1829–31
Louis McLane, 1831–33
Roger Taney, 1833–34
Levi Woodbury, 1834–37
**Secretary of War:**
John Eaton, 1829–31
Lewis Cass, 1831–36 [11]
Benjamin Butler, 1836–37
**Attorney General:**
John Berrien, 1829–31
Roger Taney, 1831–33
Benjamin Butler, 1833–37
**Postmaster General:**
William Barry, 1829–35
Amos Kendall, 1835–37
**Secretary of the Navy:**
John Branch, 1829–31
Levi Woodbury, 1831–34
Mahlon Dickerson, 1834–37
**Congress in Session:**
21st, 22nd, 23rd, 24th

■ **MARTIN VAN BUREN**
(8th President)
March 4, 1837–March 3, 1841
**Vice President:**
Richard Johnson, 1837–41
**Secretary of State:**
John Forsyth, 1837–41
**Secretary of the Treasury:**
Levi Woodbury, 1837–41
**Secretary of War:**
Joel Poinsett, 1837–41
**Attorney General:**
Benjamin Butler, 1837–38
Felix Grundy, 1838–40
Henry Gilpin, 1840–41
**Postmaster General:**
Amos Kendall, 1837–40
John Niles, 1840–41
**Secretary of the Navy:**
Mahlon Dickerson, 1837–38
James Paulding, 1838–41
**Congress in Session:**
25th, 26th

■ **WILLIAM HENRY HARRISON**
(9th President)
March 4, 1841–April 4, 1841
**Vice President:**
John Tyler, 1841
**Secretary of State:**
Daniel Webster, 1841
**Secretary of the Treasury:**
Thomas Ewing, 1841

**Secretary of War:**
John Bell, 1841
**Attorney General:**
John Crittenden, 1841
**Postmaster General:**
Francis Granger, 1841
**Secretary of the Navy:**
George Badger, 1841
**Congress in Session:**
27th

■ **JOHN TYLER**
(10th President)
April 6, 1841–March 3, 1845
**Vice President:**
After the death in office
of President William Henry
Harrison on April 4, 1841,
and Vice President John
Tyler's accession to the
Presidency, the Vice-Presidential office remained vacant, although its duties
were performed by Samuel
Southard and Willie Mangum, the presidents pro
tempore of the Senate.
**Secretary of State:**
Daniel Webster, 1841–43
Abel Upshur, 1843–44 [12]
John Calhoun, 1844–45
**Secretary of the Treasury:**
Thomas Ewing, 1841 [13]
Walter Forward, 1841–43
John Spencer, 1843–44
George Bibb, 1844–45
**Secretary of War:**
John Bell, 1841 [13]
John Spencer, 1841–43
James Porter, 1843–44
Williams Wilkins, 1844–45
**Attorney General:**
John Crittenden, 1841 [13]
Hugh Legaré, 1841–43
John Nelson, 1843–45
**Postmaster General:**
Francis Granger, 1841 [13]
Charles Wickliffe, 1841–45
**Secretary of the Navy:**
George Badger, 1841 [13]
Abel Upshur, 1841–43
David Henshaw, 1843–44
John Mason, 1844–45
**Congress in Session:**
27th, 28th

■ **JAMES KNOX POLK**
(11th President)
March 4, 1845–March 3, 1849
**Vice President:**
George Dallas, 1845–49
**Secretary of State:**
James Buchanan, 1845–49
**Secretary of the Treasury:**
Robert Walker, 1845–49
**Secretary of War:**
William Marcy, 1845–49
(*continued*)

[7] He actually served several short-term appointments during these years.    [8] Held over from the preceding administration, he continued to serve until October 30, 1817.    [9] Although his appointment as Secretary of the Navy was renewed, he assumed the post of the Secretary of the Treasury until his successor took over on August 1, 1825.    [10] He resigned on December 28, 1832, having been elected to the U.S. Senate that month.    [11] Already commissioned Attorney General, he also served as Secretary of War from October 26, 1836, until the end of the administration, receiving his commission to this post on the last day.    [12] He was killed by an explosion on the U.S.S. *Princeton*, after he had served for eight months.    [13] Continued from the preceding administration he remained until the second week of September 1841.

**JAMES KNOX POLK** (*continued*)

Attorney General:
John Mason, 1845–46
Nathan Clifford, 1846–48
Isaac Toucey, 1848–49
Postmaster General:
Cave Johnson, 1845–49
Secretary of the Navy:
George Bancroft, 1845–46
John Mason, 1846–49
Congress in Session:
29th, 30th

■ **ZACHARY TAYLOR**
(12th President)
March 4, 1849–July 9, 1850
Vice President:
Millard Fillmore, 1849–50
Secretary of State:
John Clayton, 1849–50
Secretary of the Treasury:
William Meredith, 1849–50
Secretary of War:
George Crawford, 1849–50
Attorney General:
Reverdy Johnson, 1849–50
Postmaster General:
Jacob Collamer, 1849–50
Secretary of the Navy:
William Preston, 1849–50
Secretary of the Interior:[14]
Thomas Ewing, 1849–50
Congress in Session: 31st

■ **MILLARD FILLMORE**
(13th President)
July 10, 1850–March 3, 1853
Vice President:
After the death in office of
President Zachary Taylor on
July 9, 1850, and Millard
Fillmore's accession to the
Presidency, the office
remained vacant; Vice-
Presidential duties were
handled by William King and
David Atchison, presidents
pro tempore of the Senate.
Secretary of State:
Daniel Webster, 1850–52
Edward Everett, 1852–53
Secretary of the Treasury:
Thomas Corwin, 1850–53
Secretary of War:
Charles Conrad, 1850–53
Attorney General:
John Crittenden, 1850–53
Postmaster General:
Nathan Hall, 1850–52
Samuel Hubbard, 1852–53
Secretary of the Navy:
William Graham, 1850–52
John Kennedy, 1852–53
Secretary of the Interior:
Alexander Stuart, 1850–53
Congress in Session:
31st, 32nd

■ **FRANKLIN PIERCE**
(14th President)
March 4, 1853–March 3, 1857
Vice President:
William King, 1853 [15]
Secretary of State:
William Marcy, 1853–57
Secretary of the Treasury:
James Guthrie, 1853–57
Secretary of the Navy:
Jefferson Davis, 1853–57
Attorney General:
Caleb Cushing, 1853–57
Postmaster General:
James Campbell, 1853–57
Secretary of the Navy:
James Dobbin, 1853–57
Secretary of the Interior:
Robert McClelland, 1853–57
Congress in Session:
33rd, 34th

■ **JAMES BUCHANAN**
(15th President)
March 4, 1857–March 3,
1861
Vice President:
john Breckinridge, 1857–61
Secretary of State:
Lewis Cass, 1857–60
Secretary of the Treasury:
Howell Cobb, 1857–60
Secretary of War:
John Floyd, 1857–61
Attorney General:
Jeremiah Black, 1857–60
Postmaster General:
Aaron Brown, 1857–59
Joseph Holt, 1859–61
Secretary of the Navy:
Issac Toucey, 1857–61
Secretary of the Interior:
Jacob Thompson, 1857–61
Congress in Session:
35th, 36th

■ **ABRAHAM LINCOLN**
(16th President)
March 4, 1861–March 3, 1865
March 4, 1865–April 15, 1865
Vice President:
Hannibal Hamlin, 1861–65
Andrew Johnson, 1865
Secretary of State:
William Seward, 1861–65
Secretary of the Treasury:
Salmon Chase, 1861–64
William Fessenden, 1864–65
Hugh McCulloch, 1865
Secretary of War:
Simon Cameron, 1861–62
Edwin Stanton, 1862–65
Attorney General:
Edward Bates, 1861–64
James Speed, 1864–65
Postmaster General:
Montgomery Blair, 1861–64
William Dennison, 1864–65

Secretary of the Navy:
Gideon Welles, 1861–65
Secretary of the Interior:
Caleb Smith, 1861–63
John Usher, 1863–65
Congress in Session:
37th, 38th, 39th

■ **ANDREW JOHNSON**
(17th President)
April 15, 1865–March 3, 1869
Vice President:
After the assassination of
Abraham Lincoln on April 14,
1865, and Andrew Johnson's
accession to the Presidency,
the office remained vacant;
Vice-Presidential duties
were handled by Lafayette
Foster and Benjamin Wade,
presidents pro tempore
of the Senate.
Secretary of State:
William Seward, 1865–69
Secretary of the Treasury:
Hugh McCulloch, 1865–69
Secretary of War:
Edwin Stanton, 1865–67, 1868 [16]
Ulysses Grant, 1867–68
John Schofield, 1868–69
Attornel General:
James Speed, 1865–66
Henry Stanbery, 1866–68
William Evarts, 1868–69
Postmaster General:
William Dennison, 1865–66
Alexander Randall, 1866–69
Secretary of the Navy:
Gideon Welles, 1865–69
Secretary of the Interior:
James Harlan, 1865–66
Orville Browning, 1866–69
Congress in Session: 39th, 40th

■ **ULYSSES SIMPSON GRANT**
(18th President)
March 4, 1869–March 3, 1873
March 4, 1873–March 3, 1877
Vice President:
Schuyler Colfax, 1869–73
Henry Wilson, 1873–75 [17]
Secretary of State:
Hamilton Fish, 1869–77
Secretary of the Treasury:
George Boutwell, 1869–73
William Richardson, 1873–74
Benjamin Bristow, 1874–76
Lot Morrill, 1876–77
Secretary of War:
John Rawlins, 1869
William Belknap, 1869–76
James Cameron, 1876–77
Attorney General:
Ebenezer Hoar, 1869–70
Amos Akerman, 1870–71
George Williams, 1871–75
Edwards Pierrepont, 1875–76
Alphonso Taft, 1876–77

[14] The U.S. Department of the Interior was organized as an executive department, with Cabinet representation, by an act of Congress in 1849.    [15] Elected Vice President in 1852, he took the oath of office March 4, 1853, in Havana, Cuba, where he had gone for his health; the privilege was extended by a special act of Congress. He died at his plantation in Alabama on April 18, 1853. For the duration of the administration, duties of office were carried out by David Atchison, Lewis Cass, Jesse Bright, Charles Stuart, and James Mason, presidents pro tempore of the Senate.    [16] Suspended August 12, 1867, he was reinstated January 13, 1868, and served until May 26 of that year.    [17] Died in the Capitol Building, Washington, D.C., on November 22, 1875.

**Postmaster General:**
John Creswell, 1869–74
Marshall Jewell, 1874–76
James Tyner, 1876–77
**Secretary of the Navy:**
George Robeson, 1869–77
**Secretary of the Interior:**
Jacob Cox, 1869–70
Columbus Delano, 1870–75
Zachariah Chandler, 1875–77
**Congress in Session:**
41st, 42nd, 43rd, 44th

■ **RUTHERFORD BIRCHARD HAYES**
(19th President)
March 4, 1877–March 3, 1881
**Vice President:**
William Wheeler, 1877–81
**Secretary of State:**
William Evarts, 1877–81
**Secretary of the Treasury:**
John Sherman, 1877–81
**Secretary of War:**
George McCrary, 1877–79
Alexander Ramsey, 1879–81
**Attorney General:**
Charles Devens, 1877–81
**Postmaster General:**
David Key, 1877–80
Horace Maynard, 1880–81
**Secretary of the Navy:**
Richard Thompson, 1877–80
**Secretary of the Interior:**
Carl Schurz, 1877–81
**Congress in Session:**
45th, 46th

■ **JAMES ABRAM GARFIELD**
(20th President)
March 4, 1881–September 19, 1881
**Vice President:**
Chester Arthur, 1881
**Secretary of State:**
James Blaine, 1881
**Secretary of the Treasury:**
William Windom, 1881
**Secretary of War:**
Robert Lincoln, 1881
**Attorney General:**
Wayne MacVeagh, 1881
**Postmaster General:**
Thomas James, 1881
**Secretary of the Navy:**
William Hunt, 1881
**Secretary of the Interior:**
Samuel Kirkwood, 1881
**Congress in Session:**
47th

■ **CHESTER ALAN ARTHUR**
(21st President)
September 20, 1881–March 3, 1885
**Vice President:**
After the death in office of President James A. Garfield on September 19, 1881, and Chester Alan Arthur's accession to the Presidency, this office remained vacant; Vice-

Presidential duties were carried out by Thomas Bayard, David Davis, and George Edmunds, presidents pro tempore of the Senate.
**Secretary of State:**
Frederick Frelinghuysen, 1881–85
**Secretary of the Treasury:**
Charles Folger, 1881–84
Hugh McCulloch, 1884–85
**Secretary of War:**
Robert Lincoln, 1881–85
**Attorney General:**
Benjamin Brewster, 1881–85
**Postmaster General:**
Timothy Howe, 1881–83
Walter Gresham, 1883–84
Frank Hatton, 1884–85
**Secretary of the Navy:**
William Hunt, 1881–82
William Chandler, 1882–85
**Secretary of the Interior:**
Samuel Kirkwood, 1881–82
Henry Teller, 1882–85
**Congress in Session:**
47th, 48th

■ **GROVER CLEVELAND**
(22nd President)
March 4, 1885–March 3, 1889
**Vice President:**
Thomas Hendricks, 1885 [18]
**Secretary of State:**
Thomas Bayard, 1885–89
**Secretary of the Treasury:**
Daniel Manning, 1885–87
Charles Fairchild, 1887–89
**Secretary of War:**
William Endicott, 1885–89
**Attorney General:**
Augustus Garland, 1885–89
**Postmaster General**
William Vilas, 1885–88
Don Dickinson, 1888–89
**Secretary of the Navy:**
William Whitney, 1885–89
**Secretary of the Interior:**
Lucius Lamar, 1885–88
William Vilas, 1888–89
**Secretary of Agriculture[19]:**
Norman Colman, 1889
**Congress in Session:**
49th, 50th

■ **BENJAMIN HARRISON**
(23rd President)
March 4, 1889–March 3, 1893
**Vice President:**
Levi Morton, 1889–93
**Secretary of State:**
James Blaine, 1889–92
John Foster, 1892–93
**Secretary of the Treasury:**
William Windom, 1889–91
Charles Foster, 1891–93
**Secretary of War:**
Redfield Proctor, 1889–91
Stephen Elkins, 1891–93
**Attorney General:**
William Miller, 1889–93

**Postmaster General:**
John Wanamaker, 1889–93
**Secretary of the Navy:**
Benjamin Tracy, 1889–93
**Secretary of the Interior:**
John Noble, 1889–93
**Secretary of Agriculture:**
Jeremiah Rusk, 1889–93
**Congress in Session:**
51st, 52nd

■ **GROVER CLEVELAND**
(24th President)
March 4, 1893–March 3, 1897
**Vice President:**
Adlai Stevenson, 1893–97
**Secretary of State:**
Walter Gresham, 1893–95
Richard Olney, 1895–97
**Secretary of the Treasury:**
John Carlisle, 1893–97
**Secretary of War:**
Daniel Lamont, 1893–97
**Attorney General:**
Richard Olney, 1893–95
Judson Harmon, 1895–97
**Postmaster General:**
Wilson Bissell, 1893–95
William Wilson, 1895–97
**Secretary of the Navy:**
Hilary Herbert, 1893–97
**Secretary of the Interior:**
Hoke Smith, 1893–96
David Francis, 1896–97
**Secretary of Agriculture:**
Julius Morton, 1893–97
**Congress in Session:**
53rd, 54th

■ **WILLIAM McKINLEY**
(25th President)
March 4, 1897–March 3, 1901
March 4, 1901–September 14, 1901
**Vice President:**
Garret Hobart, 1897–99 [20]
Theodore Roosevelt, 1901
**Secretary of State:**
John Sherman, 1897–98
William Day, 1898
John Hay, 1898–1901
**Secretary of the Treasury:**
Lyman Gage, 1897–1901
**Secretary of War:**
Russell Alger, 1897–99
Elihu Root, 1899–1901
**Attorney General:**
Joseph McKenna, 1897–98
John Griggs, 1898–1901
Philander Knox, 1901
**Postmaster General:**
James Gary, 1897–98
Charles Smith, 1889–1901
**Secretary of the Navy:**
John Long, 1897–1901
**Secretary of the Interior:**
Cornelius Bliss, 1897–98
Ethan Hitchcock, 1898–1901
James Wilson, 1897–1901
**Congress in Session:**
55th, 56th, 57th

[18] Died on November 25, 1885.    [19] In 1862, the Department of Agriculture was created with a commissioner at its head. In 1889, President Cleveland gave the department Cabinet status under a Secretary of Agriculture.    [20] Died on November 21, 1899.

■ **THEODORE ROOSEVELT**
(26th President)
September 14, 1901–March 3, 1905
March 4, 1905–March 3, 1909
**Vice President:**
After the death in office of President William McKinley on September 14, 1901, and Vice President Theodore Roosevelt's accession to the Presidency, the Vice-Presidential office remained vacant during Roosevelt's first administration; during this time Vice-Presidential duties were handled by William Frye, who was then president pro tempore of the Senate.
Charles Fairbanks, 1905–09
**Secretary of State:**
John Hay, 1901–05
Elihu Root, 1905–09
**Secretary of the Treasury:**
Leslie Shaw, 1902–07
George Cortelyou, 1907–09
**Secretary of War:**
Elihu Root, 1901–04
William Taft, 1904–08
Luke Wright, 1908–09
**Attorney General:**
Philander Knox, 1901–04
William Moody, 1904–06
Charles Bonaparte, 1906–09
**Postmaster General:**
Henry Payne, 1902–04
Robert Wynne, 1904–05
George Cortelyou, 1905–07
George von L. Meyer, 1907–09
**Secretary of the Navy:**
John Long, 1901–02
William Moody, 1902–04
Paul Morton, 1904–05
Charles Bonaparte, 1905–06
Victor Metcalf, 1906–08
**Secretary of the Interior:**
Ethan Hitchcock, 1901–07
James Garfield, 1907–09
**Secretary of Agriculture:**
James Wilson, 1901–09
**Secretary of Commerce and Labor**[21]:
George Cortelyou, 1903–04
Victor Metcalf, 1904–06
Oscar Straus, 1906–09
**Congress in Session:**
57th, 58th, 59th, 60th

■ **WILLIAM HOWARD TAFT**
(27th President)
March 4, 1909–March 3, 1913
**Vice President:**
James Sherman, 1909–12 [22]
**Secretary of State:**
Philander Knox, 1909–13
**Secretary of the Treasury:**
Franklin MacVeagh, 1909–13
**Secretary of War:**
Jacob Dickinson, 1909–11
Henry Stimson, 1911–13

**Attorney General:**
George Wickersham, 1909–13
**Postmaster General:**
Frank Hitchcock, 1909–13
**Secretary of the Navy:**
George von L. Meyer, 1909–13
**Secretary of the Interior:**
Richard Ballinger, 1909–11
Walter Fisher, 1911–13
**Secretary of Agriculture:**
James Wilson, 1909–13
**Secretary of Commerce and Labor:**
Charles Nagel, 1909–13
**Congress in Session:**
61st, 62nd

■ **WOODROW WILSON**
(28th President)
March 4, 1913–March 3, 1917
March 4, 1917–March 3, 1921
**Vice President:**
Thomas Marshall, 1913–21
**Secretary of State:**
William Jennings Bryan, 1913–15
Robert Lansing, 1915–20
Bainbridge Colby, 1920–21
**Secretary of the Treasury:**
William McAdoo, 1913–18
Carter Glass, 1918–20
David Houston, 1920–21
**Secretary of War:**
Lindley Garrison, 1913–16
Newton Baker, 1916–21
**Attorney General:**
James McReynolds, 1913–14
Thomas Gregory, 1914–19
A. Mitchell Palmer, 1919–21
**Postmaster General:**
Albert Burleson, 1913–21
**Secretary of the Navy:**
Josephus Daniels, 1913–21
**Secretary of the Interior:**
Franklin Lane, 1913–20
John Payne, 1920–21
**Secretary of Agriculture:**
David Houston, 1913–20
Edwin Meredith, 1920–21
**Secretary of Commerce**[21]:
William Redfield, 1913–19
Joshua Alexander, 1919–21
**Secretary of Labor**[21]:
William Wilson, 1913–21
**Congress in Session:**
63rd, 64th, 65th, 66th

■ **WARREN GAMALIEL HARDING**
(29th President)
March 4, 1921–August 2, 1923
**Vice President:**
Calvin Coolidge, 1921–23
**Secretary of State:**
Charles Hughes, 1921–23
**Secretary of the Treasury:**
Andrew Mellon, 1921–23
**Secretary of War:**
John Weeks, 1921–23
**Attorney General:**
Harry Daugherty, 1921–23

**Postmaster General:**
Will Hays, 1921–22
Hubert Work, 1922–23
Harry New, 1923
**Secretary of the Navy:**
Edwin Denby, 1921–23
**Secretary of the Interior:**
Albert Fall, 1921–23
Hubert Work, 1923
**Secretary of Agriculture:**
Henry Wallace, 1921–23
**Secretary of Commerce:**
Herbert Hoover, 1921–23
**Secretary of Labor:**
James Davis, 1921–23
**Congress in Session:**
67th, 68th

■ **CALVIN COOLIDGE**
(30th President)
August 3, 1923–March 3, 1925
March 4, 1925–March 3, 1929
**Vice President:**
After the death in office of President Warren Harding on August 2, 1923, and Calvin Coolidge's accession to the Presidency, the Vice-Presidential office remained vacant during Coolidge's first administration; Vice-Presidential duties were handled by Albert Cummins, president pro tempore of the Senate.
Charles Dawes, 1925–29
**Secretary of State:**
Charles Hughes, 1923–25
Frank Kellogg, 1925–29
**Secretary of the Treasury:**
Andrew Mellon, 1923–29
**Secretary of War:**
John Weeks, 1923–25
Dwight Davis, 1925–29
**Attorney General:**
Harry Daugherty, 1923–24
Harlan Stone, 1924–25
John Sargent, 1925–29
**Postmaster General:**
Harry New, 1923–29
**Secretary of the Navy:**
Edwin Denby, 1923–24
Curtis Wilbur, 1924–29
**Secretary of the Interior:**
Hubert Work, 1923–28
**Secretary of Agriculture:**
Henry Wallace, 1923–24
William Jardine, 1925–29
**Secretary of Commerce:**
Herbert Hoover, 1923–28
William Whiting, 1928–29
**Secretary of Labor:**
James Davis, 1923–29
**Congress in Session:**
68th, 69th, 70th

■ **HERBERT CLARK HOOVER**
(31st President)
March 4, 1929–March 3, 1933
**Vice President:**
Charles Curtis, 1929–33

[21] In February 1903, Congress established the Department of Commerce and Labor with Cabinet status. The Department of Commerce and the Department of Labor became separate executive departments, each with Cabinet representation, by an act of Congress in 1913. [22] Died on October 30 1912, having been renominated Republican candidate for the Vice Presidency.

**Secretary of State:**
Henry Stimson, 1929–33
**Secretary of the Treasury:**
Andrew Mellon, 1929–32
Ogden Mills, 1932–33
**Secretary of War:**
James Good, 1929
Patrick Hurley, 1929–33
**Attorney General:**
James Mitchell, 1929–33
**Postmaster General:**
Walter Brown, 1929–33
**Secretary of the Navy:**
Charles Adams, 1929–33
**Secretary of the Interior:**
Ray Wilbur, 1929–33
**Secretary of Agriculture:**
Arthur Hyde, 1929–33
**Secretary of Commerce:**
Robert Lamont, 1929–32
**Secretary of Labor:**
James Davis, 1929–30
William Doak, 1930–33
**Congress in Session:**
71st, 72nd

■ **FRANKLIN DELANO ROOSEVELT**
(32nd President)
March 4, 1933–January 20, 1937
January 20,1937–January 20,
1941
January 20, 1941–January 20,
1945
January 20, 1945–April 12, 1945
**Vice President:**
John Garner, 1933–41
Henry Wallace, 1941–45
Harry Truman, 1945
**Secretary of State:**
Cordell Hull, 1933–44
Edward Stettinius, 1944–45
**Secretary of the Treasury:**
William Woodin, 1933–34
Henry Morgenthau, Jr., 1934–45
**Secretary of War:**
George Dern, 1933–36
Harry Woodring, 1936–40
Henry Stimson, 1940–45
**Attorney General:**
Homer Cummings, 1933–39
Frank Murphy, 1939–40
Robert Jackson, 1940–41
Francis Biddle, 1941–45
**Postmaster General:**
James Farley, 1933–40
Frank Walker, 1940–45
**Secretary of the Navy:**
Claude Swanson, 1933–39
Charles Edison, 1939–40
Frank Knox, 1940–44
James Forrestal, 1944–45
**Secretary of the Interior:**
Harold Ickes, 1933–45
**Secretary of Agriculture:**
Henry Wallace, 1933–40
Claude Wickard, 1940–45
**Secretary of Commerce:**
Daniel Roper, 1933–38
Harry Hopkins, 1938–40
Jesse Jones, 1940–45
Henry Wallace, 1945

**Secretary of Labor:**
Frances Perkins, 1933–45
**Congress in Session:**
73rd, 74th, 75th, 76th, 77th,
78th, 79th

■ **HARRY S. TRUMAN**
(33rd President)
April 12, 1945–January 20, 1949
January 20, 1949–January 20,
1953
**Vice President:**
After the death in office of
President Franklin Delano
Roosevelt on April 12, 1945,
and Harry Truman's accession
to the Presidency, the Vice-
Presidential office remained
vacant during Truman's first
administration; Vice-Presiden-
tial duties were handled by
Kenneth McKellar and Arthur
Vandenberg, presidents
pro tempore of the Senate.
Alben Barkley, 1949–53
**Secretary of State:**
James Byrnes, 1945–47
George Marshall, 1947–49
Dean Acheson, 1949–53
**Secretary of the Treasury:**
Fred Vinson, 1945–46
John Snyder, 1946–53
**Secretary of Defense[23]:**
James Forrestal, 1947–49
Louis Johnson, 1949–50
George Marshall, 1950–51
Robert Lovett, 1951–53
**Secretary of War[23]:**
Robert Patterson, 1945–47
**Attorney General:**
Tom Clark, 1945–49
J. Howard McGrath, 1949–52
James McGranery, 1952–53
**Postmaster General:**
Robert Hannegan, 1945–47
Jesse Donaldson, 1947–53
**Secretary of the Navy[23]:**
James Forrestal, 1945–47
**Secretary of the Interior:**
Harold Ickes, 1945–46
Julius Krug, 1946–49
Oscar Chapman, 1949–53
**Secretary of Agriculture:**
Clinton Anderson, 1945–48
Charles Brannan, 1948–53
**Secretary of Commerce:**
Henry Wallace, 1945–46
W. Averell Harriman, 1946–48
Charles Sawyer, 1948–53
**Secretary of Labor:**
Lewis Schwellenbach, 1945–48
Maurice Tobin, 1948–53
**Congress in Session:**
79th, 80th, 81st, 82nd

■ **DWIGHT DAVID EISENHOWER**
(34th President)
January 20, 1953–January 20,
1957
January 20, 1957–January 20,
1961

**Vice President:**
Richard M. Nixon, 1953–61
**Secretary of State:**
John Foster Dulles, 1953–59
Christian Herter, 1959–61
**Secretary of the Treasury:**
George Humphrey, 1953–57
Robert Anderson, 1957–61
**Secretary of Defense:**
Charles Wilson, 1953–57
Neil McElroy, 1957–59
Thomas Gates, 1957–61
**Attorney General:**
Herbert Brownell, Jr.,
1953–57
William Rogers, 1957–61
**Postmaster General:**
Arthur Summerfield, 1953–61
**Secretary of the Interior:**
Douglas McKay, 1953–56
Frederick Seaton, 1956–61
**Secretary of Agriculture:**
Ezra Taft Benson, 1953–61
**Secretary of Commerce:**
Sinclair Weeks, 1953–58
Lewis Strauss, 1958–59
Frederick Mueller, 1959–61
**Secretary of Labor:**
Martin Durkin, 1953
James Mitchell, 1953–61
**Secretary of Health, Education,
and Welfare[24]:**
Oveta Culp Hobby, 1953–55
Marion Folsom, 1955–58
Arthur Flemming, 1958–61
**Congress in Session:**
83rd, 84th, 85th, 86th

■ **JOHN FITZGERALD KENNEDY**
(35th President)
January 20, 1961–November 22,
1963
**Vice President:**
Lyndon B. Johnson, 1961–63
**Secretary of State:**
Dean Rusk, 1961–63
**Secretary of the Treasury:**
C. Douglas Dillon, 1961–63
**Secretary of Defense:**
Robert S. McNamara, 1961–63
**Attorney General:**
Robert F. Kennedy, 1961–63
**Postmaster General:**
J. Edward Day, 1961–63
John A. Gronouski, 1963
**Secretary of the Interior:**
Stewart L. Udall, 1961–63
**Secretary of Agriculture:**
Orville L. Freeman, 1961–63
**Secretary of Commerce:**
Luther H. Hodges, 1961–63
**Secretary of Labor:**
Arthur J. Goldberg, 1961–62
W. Willard Wirtz, 1962–63
**Secretary of Health, Education,
and Welfare:**
Abraham A. Ribicoff, 1961–62
Anthony J. Celebrezze,
1962–63
**Congress in Session:**
87th, 88th

[23] In 1947, the War Department was reconstituted as the Department of the Army and, along with the Department of the Navy, became in 1949 a division of the newly formed Department of Defense. [24] In 1953, President Eisenhower formed the Department of Health, Education, and Welfare, whose chief executive officer, the Secretary, has Cabinet rank.

# U.S. EXECUTIVE DEPARTMENTS AND AGENCIES

Source: United States Government Organization Manual

## EXECUTIVE OFFICE OF THE PRESIDENT

This is the official term for a group of individuals and agencies, each charged with assisting the President in carrying out duties that belong distinctly to the Presidency. It was created in 1939 by an Executive Order, and employs, not counting the CIA, over 2,500 people.

President of the U.S.: Lyndon B. Johnson

### THE WHITE HOUSE OFFICE

1600 Pennsylvania Avenue, N.W.
Washington, D.C.

Special Assistants to the President: S. Douglas Cater, Jr.; Joseph A. Califano, Jr.; George E. Christian; Donald F. Hornig; Robert E. Kintner; Walt Whitman Rostow; W. Marvin Watson; Francis M. Bator (Deputy); Miss Betty Furness (Consumer Affairs)

Administrative Assistant to the President: Mike N. Manatos

Special Consultants to the President: John P. Roche; General Maxwell D. Taylor, USA, Ret.

Special Counsel to the President: Harry C. McPherson, Jr.

Legislative Counsel: Harold Barefoot Sanders, Jr.

Adviser for National Capital Affairs: Stephen J. Pollak

Armed Forces Aide to the President: Lt. Col. James U. Cross, U.S. Air Force

Deputy Press Secretary to the President: Robert H. Fleming

Deputy Special Counsels to the President: Clifford L. Alexander, Jr.; Lawrence E. Levinson

Personal Secretary to the President: Mrs. Juanita Duggan Roberts

Press Secretary and Staff Director for the First Lady: Mrs. Elizabeth C. Carpenter

Physician to the President: Vice Admiral George G. Burkley, U.S. Navy Medical Corps

Social Secretary: Mrs. Bess Abell

Executive Assistant to the President: William J. Hopkins

Chief Usher: J. Bernard West

Duties: Serves the President in the performance of his duties. The staff facilitates and maintains communication with the Congress, executive departments and agencies, the press and the general public.

### BUREAU OF THE BUDGET

Executive Office Building
Established: 1921
Director: Charles L. Schultze
Deputy Director: Phillip S. Hughes
Duties: Provides assistance to the President in the preparation and administration of the budget; provides advice on proposed legislation and recommends presidential action on legislative enactments; advises Federal agencies on administrative practices; coordinates government statistical services.

### COUNCIL OF ECONOMIC ADVISERS

Executive Office Building
Established: 1946
Chairman: Gardner Ackley
Duties: Analyzes trends in the national economy; appraises economic programs and policies of the Federal government; recommends to the President policies for economic growth and stability; and assists the President in preparation of economic reports to Congress.

### NATIONAL SECURITY COUNCIL

Executive Office Building
Established: 1947
Members: The President (Lyndon B. Johnson); The Vice President (Hubert H. Humphrey); The Secretary of State (Dean Rusk); The Secretary of Defense (Robert S. McNamara); The Director, Office of Emergency Planning (C. Ferris Bryant)
Officials: Special Assistant to the President (W. W. Rostow); Executive Secretary (Bromley Smith)
Duties: Advises the President on matters of a military and foreign policy nature. Its proceedings are classified top-secret, thereby giving the President a council for discussion of matters concerned with matters of national security.

### CENTRAL INTELLIGENCE AGENCY (CIA)

An operational agency of the National Security Council.
Washington, D.C.
Established: 1947
Director: Richard N. Helms
Deputy Director: Vice Admiral Rufus L. Taylor
Duties: The CIA keeps the National Security Council fully informed on matters pertaining to national security; receives and coordinates intelligence information to assist the President in understanding political and military conditions, particularly those that may affect the national security.

### NATIONAL AERONAUTICS AND SPACE COUNCIL

Executive Office Building
Established: 1958
Chairman: The Vice President (Hubert H. Humphrey)
Members: The Secretary of State (Dean Rusk); The Secretary of Defense (Robert S. McNamara); The Administrator, National Aeronautics and Space Administration (James E. Webb); The Chairman, Atomic Energy Commission (Glenn T. Seaborg)
Executive Secretary: Edward C. Welsh
Duties: Advises the President on the latest developments in space science and assists him in formulating policies pertaining to aeronautical and space activities. (continued)

### OFFICE OF ECONOMIC OPPORTUNITY
1200 Nineteenth Street, N.W.
Established: 1964
Director: Sargent Shriver
Deputy Director: Bertrand M. Harding
*Duties:* Strengthens, supplements, and coordinates Federal efforts to eliminate poverty by opening to everyone the opportunity for education, training, and employment; trains volunteers to work with the poor (VISTA).

### OFFICE OF EMERGENCY PLANNING
Executive Office Building Annex
  (Winder Building)
Established: 1958
Director: Price Daniel
Deputy Director: (vacant)
*Duties:* Advises the President on planning and coordination of policy concerning emergencies, both natural disasters and the consequences of military action; is concerned with the emergency use of resources such as manpower, materials, industry, transportation, and community facilities; plans for emergency government organization, rehabilitation after an enemy attack, and the stockpiling of strategic materials.

## EXECUTIVE DEPARTMENTS

The constitutional basis for the eleven executive departments is found in Article II, Section II of the U.S. Constitution, which states that the President may "require the opinion . . . of the principal officer in each of the executive departments." From this simple phrase have grown eleven major departments, which handle a multitude of executive and administrative duties, as well as provide advice for the President in the execution of his duties.

### DEPARTMENT OF STATE
2201 C Street, N.W.
Established: 1789
Secretary of State: Dean Rusk
Under Secretary: Nicholas de B. Katzenbach
*Functions:* The President is ultimately responsible for United States foreign policy. The State Department, through the Secretary of State, acts as his principal adviser, and has primary responsibility for initiating and implementing foreign policies. It develops policies for American participation in the United Nations and in other international organizations; conducts correspondence with diplomatic and consular representatives of the United States abroad, as well as with the representatives of foreign governments accredited to the United States; issues passports; administers the Peace Corps.

### DEPARTMENT OF THE TREASURY
Fifteenth Street and Pennsylvania Avenue, N.W.
Established: 1789
Secretary of the Treasury: Henry H. Fowler
Under Secretary: Joseph W. Barr
*Functions:* Manages national finances; provides the nation with its coined and printed currency; maintains the credit of the United States; represents the United States in international banking and monetary organizations; collects Federal taxes through the Internal Revenue Service; supervises the Coast Guard, the Bureau of Narcotics, and the Secret Service. The Secretary of the Treasury is required by law to submit periodic reports to Congress on Government fiscal operations, and an annual report on finances.
Treasurer of the United States: (vacant)
Director of the United States Secret Service: James J. Rowley
Commissioner of Internal Revenue: Sheldon S. Cohen

### OFFICE OF SCIENCE AND TECHNOLOGY
Executive Office Building
Established: 1962
Director: Donald F. Hornig
Deputy Director: Dr. Ivan L. Bennet, Jr.
*Duties:* Provides assistance to the President in developing policies and coordinating programs to insure that science and technology are used most effectively in the interests of national security and the general welfare; developed in response to the nation's growing program of scientific research.

### OFFICE OF THE SPECIAL REPRESENTATIVE FOR TRADE NEGOTIATIONS
Executive Office Building
Established: 1963
Special Representative for Trade Negotiations: Christian A. Herter
Deputy Special Representatives: W. Michael Blumenthal; William Matson Roth
*Duties:* Facilitates implementation of the trade agreements program; assists and advises the President on administration of that program; and advises him on nontariff barriers to international trade; especially active in the "Kennedy round" of tariff negotiations.

### DEPARTMENT OF DEFENSE
The Pentagon
Established: 1949
Secretary of Defense: Robert S. McNamara
Deputy Secretary of Defense: Cyrus R. Vance
*Activities:* Provides unified direction, under civilian control, for the Army, Navy (including the Marine and Naval Aviation Corps), and Air Force; maintains and employs armed forces to support and defend the United States Constitution, to insure the security of the United States, its possessions, and areas vital to its interest.
Secretary of the Army: Stanley R. Resor
Secretary of the Navy: Paul H. Nitze
Secretary of the Air Force: Dr. Harold Brown

### DEPARTMENT OF JUSTICE
Constitution Avenue and Tenth Street, N.W.
Established: 1870
Attorney General: Ramsey Clark

*(continued)*

**EXECUTIVE DEPARTMENTS** (continued)

Deputy Attorney General: (vacant)
Solicitor General: Erwin N. Griswold
Activities: Provides the means for enforcement of Federal laws; furnishes legal counsel in Federal cases; construes the laws under which other departments act; conducts Supreme Court suits in which the United States is concerned; supervises Federal penal institutions; investigates and detects violations of Federal laws; represents the Government in legal matters; renders legal advice and opinions to the President and to heads of Executive Departments upon request; directs activities of United States attorneys and marshals.

## POST OFFICE DEPARTMENT
1200 Pennsylvania Avenue, N.W.
Established: 1872
Postmaster General: Lawrence F. O'Brien
Deputy Postmaster General: Frederick C. Belen
Activities: Maintains the United States postal system; operates post offices; processes, dispatches, and delivers mail; implements applicable international postal regulations.

## DEPARTMENT OF THE INTERIOR
C Street, between Eighteenth and Nineteenth Streets, N.W.
Established: 1849
Secretary of the Interior: Stewart L. Udall
Under Secretary: Charles F. Luce
Activities: Formulates and administers programs for the conservation and development of natural resources; supervises public activities of the Bureau of Mines, the Geological Survey, the Bureau of Indian Affairs, the Bureau of Land Management, the National Park Service, the Fish and Wildlife Service, the Bureau of Reclamation, and other offices.

## DEPARTMENT OF AGRICULTURE
Fourteenth Street and Independence Avenue, S.W.
Established: 1862
Secretary of Agriculture: Orville L. Freeman
Under Secretary: John A. Schnittker
Activities: Conducts research on agricultural subjects and makes results available for practical farm application; provides crop supports, commodity standards, grading and marking services, and meat, poultry, and other inspection services; administers the national forests; provides aid in farm soil and water conservation; assists in flood control; directs agricultural attachés abroad; implements the national school-lunch program; administers loans to farmers and to farm organizations.

## DEPARTMENT OF COMMERCE
Fourteenth Street, between Constitution Avenue and E Street, N.W.
Established: 1913
Secretary of Commerce: Alexander B. Trowbridge
Under Secretary: Howard J. Samuels

Activities: Fosters development of domestic and foreign commerce, the manufacturing and shipping industries, and the transportation facilities of the United States; conducts population, agricultural, and other censuses; analyzes and disseminates commercial statistics; compiles nautical and aeronautical charts; establishes weights, measures, and standards; issues patents and registers trademarks.

The Department also supervises issuance of weather information; directs the St. Lawrence Seaway Development Corporation and the Coast and Geodetic Survey; administers Federal redevelopment and highway improvement programs.

## DEPARTMENT OF LABOR
Fourteenth Street and Constitution Avenue, N.W.
Established: 1913
Secretary of Labor: W. Willard Wirtz
Under Secretary: James J. Reynolds
Activities: Administers and enforces statutes designed to promote the welfare of wage earners, improve their working conditions and their opportunities for profitable employment.

## DEPARTMENT OF HEALTH, EDUCATION, AND WELFARE
330 Independence Avenue, S.W.
Established: 1953
Secretary of Health, Education, and Welfare: John W. Gardner
Under Secretary: Wilbur J. Cohen
Activities: Administers and coordinates the work of Federal agencies active in the fields for which it is responsible, among them, the Public Health Service, Office of Education, Social Security Administration; and Federally financed Gallaudet College, Howard University, the American Printing House for the Blind, and St. Elizabeth's Hospital.

## DEPARTMENT OF HOUSING AND URBAN DEVELOPMENT
1626 K Street, N.W.
Established: 1965
Secretary of Housing and Urban Development: Robert C. Weaver
Under Secretary: Robert C. Wood
Activities: Administers housing and urban development programs, including those of the former Housing and Home Finance Agency; deals with problems of housing, mass transportation, urban and suburban development; administers funds, and offers technical assistance to states, cities, and counties.

## DEPARTMENT OF TRANSPORTATION
800 Independence Avenue, S.W.
Established: 1966
Secretary: Alan S. Boyd
Under Secretary: Everett Hutchinson
Activities: Develops national policies to provide fast, safe, efficient, convenient, and economical transportation. Formulates guidelines for the investment of Federal funds in facilities and equipment. Also assures the coordinated administration of the Federal government's transportation programs.

# INDEPENDENT AGENCIES

## ATOMIC ENERGY COMMISSION
Washington, D.C.
Established: 1946
Membership; Five members, appointed by the President with the consent of the Senate.
Chairman: Glenn T. Seaborg
*Activities:* Regulates the control and use of nuclear materials; administers and encourages private participation in programs for atomic research and development, international cooperation in the atomic field, dissemination of scientific and technical information, and production of atomic energy and special nuclear materials; provides for public health and safety in connection with its field of jurisdiction.

## CIVIL AERONAUTICS BOARD
1825 Connecticut Avenue
Established: 1938
Membership: Five members, appointed to six-year terms by the President, with the consent of the Senate.
Chairman: Charles S. Murphy
*Activities:* Regulates economic aspects of United States air carrier operations, and of foreign common carrier operations to and from the United States; participates in establishment and development of international air transportation and establishes rates for the carriage of mail by air carriers.

## EQUAL EMPLOYMENT OPPORTUNITY COMMISSION
1800 G. Street, N.W.
Established: 1965
Membership: Five members, appointed to five-year terms by the President
Chairman: Stephen N. Shulman
*Activities:* Coordinates Federal efforts to end discrimination in employment and to open up new job opportunities for minority group members.

## FARM CREDIT ADMINISTRATION
South Building, Department of Agriculture
Established: 1916
Chairman, Federal Farm Credit Board: J. B. Fuller
*Activities:* Supervises and coordinates a cooperative credit system for agriculture, providing long-term and short-term credits to farmers and their cooperative organizations.

## FEDERAL COMMUNICATIONS COMMISSION
Post Office Department Building
Established: 1934
Membership: Seven members, appointed to seven-year terms by the President.
Chairman: Rosel H. Hyde
*Activities:* Regulates interstate and foreign commerce in communication by radio and wire to make available a rapid, efficient radio communication service at reasonable cost.

## FEDERAL DEPOSIT INSURANCE CORPORATION
550 Seventeenth Street, N.W.
Established: 1933
Membership: The Board of Directors comprises three members. Two are appointed to six-year terms by the President. The Chairman is one of the Presidential appointees. The Comptroller of the Currency serves ex-officio as the third member.
Chairman: K. A. Randall
*Activities:* Insures the deposits of all banks entitled to benefits of insurance under the law, paying depositors of insured banks which close without adequate funds to meet claims against them; acts as a receiver for national banks placed in receivership, and under certain conditions, for state banks placed in receivership; and makes loans to insured banks under certain circumstances.

## FEDERAL MARITIME COMMISSION
1321 H Street, N.W.
Established: 1961
Membership: Five members, appointed to four-year terms by the President.
Chairman: John Harllee
*Activities:* Regulates rates, fares, charges, classifications, tariffs, regulations, and practices of common carriers engaged in maritime commerce within United States jurisdiction, and common carriers engaged in foreign commerce of the United States.

## FEDERAL MEDIATION AND CONCILIATION SERVICE
Department of Labor Building
Established: 1947
Director: William E. Simkin
Membership: The National Labor-Management Panel comprises twelve members appointed by the President, six representing management and six representing labor.
*Activities:* Assists in the solution of labor disputes affecting interstate commerce by offering conciliation and mediation services.

## FEDERAL POWER COMMISSION
General Accounting Office Building, 441 G Street, N.W.
Established: 1930
Membership: Five commissioners, appointed to five-year terms by the President.
Chairman: Lee C. White
*Activities:* Regulates interstate aspects of the electric power and natural gas industries, including issuance of licenses for construction and operation of hydroelectric power projects on Government lands or navigable waters of the United States, issuance of certificates for gas sales to and from interstate pipelines, and construction and operation of pipeline facilities; regulates the rates of interstate wholesale transactions in electric power and natural gas.

## FEDERAL RESERVE SYSTEM
Board of Governors of the Federal Reserve System
Twentieth Street and Constitution Ave., N.W.
Established: 1913
Membership: The Board of Governors has seven members appointed by the President.

(continued)

## INDEPENDENT AGENCIES (*continued*)

Chairman: William McC. Martin, Jr.

*Activities:* Provides for establishment of Federal Reserve Banks to furnish an elastic currency, to afford means of rediscounting commercial paper, and to establish effective supervision of banking in the United States.

## FEDERAL TRADE COMMISSION

Pennsylvania Avenue at Sixth Street, N.W.

Established: 1915

Membership: Five members, appointed to seven-year terms by the President, with the consent of the Senate. Not more than three commissioners may be members of the same political party.

Chairman: Paul Rand Dixon

*Activities:* Promotes fair and free competition in interstate commerce by prevention of price-fixing, boycotts, combinations in restraint of trade, and other unfair practices.

## GENERAL SERVICES ADMINISTRATION

General Services Building, Eighteenth and F Streets, N.W.

Established: 1949

Administrator of General Services: Lawson B. Knott, Jr.

*Activities:* Manages Government property and records, including the construction and operation of buildings, procurement and distribution of supplies, disposal of surplus property, management of traffic and communications, stockpiling of strategic and critical materials, and care of records.

## INTERSTATE COMMERCE COMMISSION

Twelfth Street and Constitution Avenue, N.W.

Established: 1887

Membership: Eleven members, appointed by the President with the consent of the Senate. The members choose a chairman annually.

Chairman: William H. Tucker

*Activities:* Regulates interstate commerce, and foreign import and export commerce to the extent that it takes place in the United States.

## NATIONAL AERONAUTICS AND SPACE ADMINISTRATION

Washington, D.C.

Established: 1958

Administrator: James E. Webb

*Activities:* Conducts research on flight within and outside the Earth's atmosphere; develops, constructs, tests, and operates aeronautical and space vehicles; conducts activities required for exploration of space with manned and unmanned space vehicles.

## NATIONAL LABOR RELATIONS BOARD

1717 Pennsylvania Avenue, N.W.

Established: 1935

Membership: Five members, appointed to four-year terms by the President, with the consent of the Senate.

Chairman: Frank W. McCulloch

*Activities:* Prevents, through a variety of powers, unfair labor practices by either employers or employees.

## SECURITIES AND EXCHANGE COMMISSION

500 N. Capitol Street, N.W.

Established: 1934

Membership: Five members, appointed by the President, with the consent of the Senate, to five-year terms. Not more than three may be members of the same political party.

Chairman: Manuel F. Cohen

*Activities:* Protects the interests of the public and investors against malpractices in securities and financial markets.

## SELECTIVE SERVICE SYSTEM

1724 F Street, N.W.

Established: 1947

Director: Lieutenant General Lewis B. Hershey

*Activities:* Administers examination, classification, induction, and appeal from induction into the armed forces of those persons eligible under the Universal Military Training and Service Act.

## SMALL BUSINESS ADMINISTRATION

1441 L Street, N.W.

Established: 1953

Administrator: Bernard L. Boutin

*Activities:* Aids, counsels, and protects the interests of small business. Presently operates the loan program of the Office of Economic Opportunity.

## TENNESSEE VALLEY AUTHORITY

New Sprankle Building, Knoxville, Tennessee

Woodward Building, Fifteenth and H Streets, N.W., Washington, D.C.

Established: 1933

Membership: Three-member Board of Directors appointed by the President, with the consent of the Senate.

Chairman: Aubrey J. Wagner

*Activities:* Develops the Tennessee River system through construction of a series of dams on the main stream and its principal tributaries; conducts forestry programs; assists in flood control; and is an important supplier of electricity to the surrounding region.

## UNITED STATES ARMS CONTROL AND DISARMAMENT AGENCY

Department of State Building

Established: 1961

Director: William C. Foster

*Activities:* Participates in nuclear-test-ban and general disarmament negotiations at Geneva, and in the United Nations; conducts research on arms control and disarmament and disseminates information to policymakers and the public.

## UNITED STATES INFORMATION AGENCY

1750 Pennsylvania Avenue, N.W.

Established: 1953

Director: Leonard H. Marks

*Activities:* Attempts to generate constructive public support abroad for United States policy through programs of personal contact, radio broadcasting, libraries, book publication, television, exhibits, English-language instruction, etc.

## UNITED STATES TARIFF COMMISSION
E Street and Seventh Street, N.W.
Established: 1916
Chairman: Paul Kaplowitz
*Activities:* Investigates and reports on tariff and foreign trade matters.

## VETERANS ADMINISTRATION
Vermont Avenue and H Street, N.W.
Established: 1930
Administrator of Veterans Affairs: W. J. Driver
*Activities:* Administers laws authorizing benefits for former members of the armed forces, their eligible dependents and beneficiaries.

## COMMISSION OF FINE ARTS
Department of the Interior Building
Established: 1910
Membership: Seven well-qualified judges of the fine arts appointed for four-year terms by the President.
Chairman: William Walton
*Activities:* Advises and assists on matters relating to art, and approves plans for certain designated buildings, monuments, and public works.

## NATIONAL MEDIATION BOARD
1239 Sixteenth Street, N.W.
Established: 1934
Chairman: Francis A. O'Neill, Jr.
*Activities:* Mediates differences between the railroads and airlines on one hand and their employees on the other, and also determines representation disputes among the employees.

## SUBVERSIVE ACTIVITIES CONTROL BOARD
Lafayette Building, 811 Vermont Avenue, N.W.
Established: 1950
Chairman: John W. Mahan
*Activities:* Conducts hearings and determines whether "Communist-front" organizations must register and whether an organization is "Communist-infiltrated."

## EXPORT-IMPORT BANK OF WASHINGTON
811 Vermont Avenue, N.W.
Established: 1934
Chairman and President: Harold F. Linder
*Activities:* Aids in financing and facilitating trade between U.S. and foreign countries.

## FEDERAL HOME LOAN BANK BOARD
101 Indiana Avenue, N.W.
Established: 1955
Chairman: John E. Horne
*Activities:* Provides credit reserve for savings and home-financing institutions.

## NATIONAL SCIENCE FOUNDATION
1800 G Street, N.W.
Established: 1950
Chairman: Dr. Philip Handler
*Purpose:* Strengthens basic research and education in the sciences in the U.S.

## THE AMERICAN NATIONAL RED CROSS
17th and D Streets, N.W.
Established: 1905
Chairman: E. Roland Harriman

*Activities:* Acts as the medium of voluntary relief and communication between the American people and their armed forces; carries on a system of national and international relief; alleviates suffering caused by disasters.

## APPALACHIAN REGIONAL COMMISSION
1666 Connecticut Avenue, N.W.
Established: 1965
Federal Cochairman: Joe W. Fleming II
State Cochairman: Dan K. Moore (Governor of North Carolina)
*Activities:* Administers a broad scope of economic development programs which will contribute to the growth of the region, such as the development of a highway system, land conservation methods, and construction of vocational educational facilities.

## CANAL ZONE GOVERNMENT
312 Pennsylvania Building
Established: 1912—revised 1951
Chairman: Brigadier General W. P. Leber, Governor in Canal Zone
*Activities:* Charged with Civil Government of the Canal Zone.

## UNITED STATES CIVIL SERVICE COMMISSION
1900 E Street, N.W.
Established: 1883
Chairman: John W. Macy, Jr.
*Purpose:* Establishment of a merit system whereby selection for appointment should be made on the basis of demonstrated relative fitness.

## TAX COURT OF THE UNITED STATES
Internal Revenue Building, Twelfth Street and Constitution Avenue, N.W.
Established: 1942
Chief Judge: Norman O. Tietjens
*Activities:* Tries and adjudicates controversies involving the existence of deficiencies in income, excess profits, estate, gift, and personal holding company surtaxes where deficiencies have been determined by the Commissioner of Internal Revenue.

## RAILROAD RETIREMENT BOARD
884 Rush Street, Chicago, Ill.
Washington Liaison Office: Room 444, 425 13th Street
Established: 1935
Chairman: Howard W. Habermeyer
*Purpose:* Administers a retirement system for the payment of retirement and disability annuities to railroad employees, annuities to their spouses, and benefits to their survivors; also seeks to secure reemployment of unemployed railroad workers.

## SMITHSONIAN INSTITUTION
Smithsonian Institution Building, The Mall
Established: 1846
Secretary of the Institution: S. Dillon Ripley
*Activities:* Performs fundamental research, maintains library and museum facilities, engages in programs of national and international cooperative research and training.

# CONGRESS

The legislative branch of the Federal government consists of two houses: the Senate and the House of Representatives. Except for the Senate's exclusive right to ratify treaties and Presidential appointments, and the requirement that money bills must originate in the House, the two are virtually identical in power and function. In addition to making laws, Congress also acts as a watchdog over the Administration, by direct policy-making, investigating, and appointing personnel. Even more important as a control is the power over appropriations.

Many Congressional functions are not really legislative at all but result from the system of "checks and balances." For instance, Congress is the branch of the Federal government concerned with amending the Constitution. It is also responsible for counting the electoral votes and for selecting a President and a Vice President if no one candidate emerges as victor. The judicial process of impeachment also belongs to the houses of Congress.

Congressmen have certain privileges and immunities. Freedom to debate any issue openly on the floor of Congress is guaranteed by the Constitution. They have immunity from arrest while attending sessions and also free use of the mails for official business.

All members of the House of Representatives come up for re-election every two years, along with one third of the Senate. When the newly elected houses convene for the first time, in January of the year following their election, they are known as a Congress and sit until the next one is elected. The 90th Congress, for example, is the ninetieth to convene since the first Congress met in 1789. Most Congresses have two sessions, the second one beginning in January of their second year. Special sessions may be called by the President.

## THE 90TH CONGRESS: 1967

The 90th Congress, with a total of 535 members, convened on January 10, 1967. The average member is 52.1 years old. The average age of a U.S. Senator is 57.7 years, while that of a U.S. Representative is 50.8 years. The youngest Senator is Edward M. Kennedy (D-Mass.), who was 35 in February, 1967. The oldest Senator is Carl Hayden (D-Ariz.), who is 90 and has represented Arizona in either the House or the Senate since it gained statehood in 1912. The youngest Representative is William J. Green (D-Pa.), who was 29 in June, 1967. (Freshmen Republican Representatives Donald W. Riegle, Jr., of Michigan and William A. Steiger of Wisconsin are also 29, but their birthdays occurred earlier in the year.) At 85, Barratt D. O'Hara (D-Ill.) is the oldest Representative.

The youngest Republican Senator is Howard Baker (R-Tenn.), who is 42, about two months younger than Senator John G. Tower (R-Texas). The oldest Republican Senator is George D. Aiken (R-Vt.), who is 75. The oldest Republican Representative is Frances P. Bolton (R-Ohio), who is 81.

Many occupations and professions are represented in the 90th Congress. A total of 470 members have had previous experience in politics and public service; 314 members have been in law, 184 in business and banking, 72 in teaching, 57 in agriculture, 49 in journalism, and 8 in engineering. There are five physicians in Congress: Senator Ernest Gruening (D-Alaska) and Representatives Tim Lee Carter (R-Ky.), Durward G. Hall (R-Mo.), Thomas E. Morgan (D-Penn.), and Henry C. Schadeberg (R-Wis.). Two Representatives were once labor union officials: Joseph E. Karth (D-Minn.) and Joseph G. Minish (D-N.J.). Representative John H. Buchanan, Jr. (R-Ala.) is an ordained Baptist minister, as is former Representative Adam Clayton Powell (D-N.Y.). Most Senators and Representatives have had more than one occupation; 386 members of the 90th Congress are veterans of military service.

Members of the 90th Congress belong to more than 28 religious groups: 109 members are Roman Catholics, 91 are Methodists, 75 are Presbyterians, 65 are Episcopalians, 53 are Baptists, 22 are Congregationalists, 12 are Lutherans, 9 are Mormons, and 7 are Unitarians. Thirty members belong to unspecified Protestant groups. Two members of the House are Greek Orthodox. Sixteen Representatives and two Senators are Jewish. Six members give no religious affiliation.

Twelve women are members of the 90th Congress. Eleven are Representatives and one, Margaret Chase Smith (R-Maine), is a Senator. There are five Negroes in the House and one in the Senate, freshman Senator Edward W. Brooke (R-Mass.), the third Negro Senator and the first to serve since 1881.

There was one vacancy at the beginning of the year. Representative John E. Fogarty (D-R.I.) died on January 10th and was replaced by Robert O. Tiernan (D), who won a special election on March 28th. Two other vacancies occurred later, both in the House. Representative J. Arthur Younger (R-Calif.) who was first elected in 1952, died in June at the age of 74. A special election was scheduled for later in the year to choose his successor. The other vacancy resulted from one of the most controversial situations in the history of the House. In March, 1967, Adam Clayton Powell (D-N.Y.), who had been a Representative since 1944, was denied his seat in the 90th Congress by a 307–116 vote of House members. A special election in Powell's Harlem district returned him to office by an overwhelming majority, but the House once more refused to seat him. Powell fought his exclusion on constitutional grounds, and the issue eventually came before the Supreme Court.

# FOCUS ON THE NEWS

## CONGRESSIONAL ETHICS CRISIS: 1967

Thomas J. Dodd was censured by the Senate.

Adam Clayton Powell was expelled by the House.

During 1967 two major incidents, and at least two minor ones, raised serious questions about the ethical standards and conduct of those serving in the Congress of the United States.

On March 1 the House of Representatives voted 307 to 116 to exclude Adam Clayton Powell, Negro Congressman from the Harlem district of New York, for payroll irregularities and misappropriation of congressional travel funds, amounting to $46,228. Another factor in the House's action was Powell's defiance of New York court orders to pay a libel judgment of $164,000 to Harlem widow Mrs. Esther James.

Powell challenged exclusion in the courts on constitutional grounds. Subsequently, he won a special election – by a margin of nearly 7 to 1–to fill the vacancy for his own House seat, but continued to seek reseating through the courts.

Senator Thomas Dodd of Connecticut was censured by a 92 to 5 vote of his colleagues for diverting to personal use at least $116,000 collected at testimonial dinners to help defray campaign expenses. Dodd insisted that the money was a "tax-free gift" from constituents. The Senate rejected a second charge that Dodd billed both the Senate and private groups for the same travel expenses. Unlike Powell, however,

Dodd retained his Senate seat, his seniority, and his subcommittee chairmanships.

Two other cases during the year involved Senator Edward Long of Missouri, who received fees for referring James Hoffa to legal counsel, and Representative Thaddeus J. Dulski of Buffalo, New York, who accepted $11,000 for personal use from proceeds of a testimonial dinner.

Besides raising moral questions, these cases highlighted the special problems confronting elected representatives who are not independently wealthy. It is virtually impossible nowadays for senators and representatives to live decently, do their jobs effectively, and campaign for re-election without supplementing their official salaries. Part of the solution may lie in the establishment of guidelines specifying when political contributions are acceptable or unacceptable and determining how members of Congress may, or may not, earn extra income.

Congress imposes severe standards on nominees for positions in the executive branch, but does not apply the same standards to its own members. Some reforms are needed, and ethics committees are at work in both houses. As Everett Dirksen, Republican Senate leader, remarked during the debate on Dodd's censure: "... the Senate as an institution is on trial."

# THE SENATE

The upper chamber of the Congress of the United States—originally established as the senior advisory body—today has become merely the "other chamber." The Senate, however, has certain exclusive powers designated by the Constitution: It ratifies treaties and Presidential appointments, tries impeachments, and elects a Vice President if there is no electoral majority. The presiding officer of the Senate is the Vice President of the United States; in his absence his duties are assumed by the president pro tempore. U.S. Senators, two from each state, are elected for six-year terms.

A Senator must be at least 30 years of age, nine years a citizen, and a resident of the state he represents. He receives an annual salary of $30,000. Below is the official Senate roster at the opening of the First Session of the 90th Congress on January 10, 1967. (Dates are those on which the Senators took office.) Changes that occurred during the session are recorded in *The 90th Congress: 1967* on page 352.

**Democrats (D) 64, Republicans (R) 36**
**Vice President:** Hubert H. Humphrey (D-Minn.)
**President Pro Tempore:** Carl Hayden (D-Ariz.)
**Majority Leader:** Mike Mansfield (D-Mont.)
**Majority Whip:** Russell B. Long (D-La.)

**Minority Leader:** Everett McKinley Dirksen (R-Ill.)
**Minority Whip:** Thomas H. Kuchel (R-Calif.)
**Secretary:** J. S. Kimmitt
**Sergeant at Arms:** Robert G. Dunphy
**Chaplain:** Rev. Frederick Brown Harris, D.D.

| | |
|---|---|
| **Alabama** | Lister Hill (D), January 11, 1938 |
| | John J. Sparkman (D), November 6, 1946 |
| **Alaska** | E. L. Bartlett (D), January 3, 1959 |
| | Ernest Gruening (D), January 3, 1959 |
| **Arizona** | Carl Hayden (D), March 4, 1927 |
| | Paul J. Fannin (R), January 3, 1965 |
| **Arkansas** | John L. McClellan (D), January 3, 1943 |
| | J. W. Fulbright (D), January 3, 1945 |
| **California** | Thomas H. Kuchel (R), January 2, 1953 |
| | George Murphy (R) January 1, 1965 |
| **Colorado** | Gordon Allott (R), January 3, 1955 |
| | Peter H. Dominick (R), January 3, 1963 |
| **Connecticut** | Thomas J. Dodd (D), January 3, 1959 |
| | Abraham A. Ribicoff (D), January 3, 1963 |
| **Delaware** | John J. Williams (R), January 3, 1947 |
| | J. Caleb Boggs (R), January 3, 1961 |
| **Florida** | Spessard L. Holland (D), September 25, 1946 |
| | George A. Smathers (D), January 3, 1951 |
| **Georgia** | Richard B. Russell (D), January 12, 1933 |
| | Herman E. Talmadge (D), January 3, 1957 |
| **Hawaii** | Hiram L. Fong (R), August 21, 1959 |
| | Daniel K. Inouye (D), January 3, 1963 |
| **Idaho** | Frank Church (D), January 3, 1957 |
| | Len B. Jordan (R), August 6, 1962 |
| **Illinois** | Everett McKinley Dirksen (R), January 3, 1951 |
| | Charles H. Percy (R), January 3, 1967 |
| **Indiana** | Vance Hartke (D), January 3, 1959 |
| | Birch Bayh (D), January 3, 1963 |
| **Iowa** | Bourke B. Hickenlooper (R), January 3, 1945 |
| | Jack Miller (R), January 3, 1961 |
| **Kansas** | Frank Carlson (R), November 29, 1950 |
| | James B. Pearson (R), January 31, 1962 |
| **Kentucky** | John Sherman Cooper (R), November 7, 1956 |
| | Thruston B. Morton (R), January 3, 1957 |
| **Louisiana** | Allen J. Ellender (D), January 3, 1937 |
| | Russell B. Long (D), December 31, 1948 |
| **Maine** | Margaret Chase Smith (R), January 3, 1949 |
| | Edmund S. Muskie (D), January 3, 1959 |
| **Maryland** | Daniel B. Brewster (D), January 3, 1963 |
| | Joseph D. Tydings (D), January 3, 1965 |
| **Massachusetts** | Edward M. Kennedy (D), November 7, 1962 |
| | Edward W. Brooke (R), January 3, 1967 |
| **Michigan** | Philip A. Hart (D), January 3, 1959 |
| | Robert P. Griffin (R), May 16, 1966 |
| **Minnesota** | Eugene J. McCarthy (D), January 3, 1959 |
| | Walter F. Mondale (D), December 30, 1964 |
| **Mississippi** | James O. Eastland (D), January 3, 1943 |
| | John Stennis (D), November 5, 1947 |
| **Missouri** | Stuart Symington (D), January 3, 1953 |
| | Edward V. Long (D), September 23, 1960 |

| | |
|---|---|
| **Montana** | Mike Mansfield (D), January 3, 1953 |
| | Lee Metcalf (D), January 3, 1961 |
| **Nebraska** | Roman L. Hruska (R), November 8, 1954 |
| | Carl T. Curtis (R), January 1, 1955 |
| **Nevada** | Alan Bible (D), December 2, 1954 |
| | Howard W. Cannon (D), January 3, 1959 |
| **New Hampshire** | Norris Cotton (R), November 8, 1954 |
| | Thomas J. McIntyre (D), November 7, 1962 |
| **New Jersey** | Clifford P. Case (R), January 3, 1955 |
| | Harrison A. Williams, Jr. (D), January 3, 1959 |
| **New Mexico** | Clinton P. Anderson (D), January 3, 1949 |
| | Joseph M. Montoya (D), November 4, 1964 |
| **New York** | Jacob K. Javits (R), January 9, 1957 |
| | Robert F. Kennedy (D), January 3, 1965 |
| **North Carolina** | Sam J. Ervin, Jr. (D), June 5, 1954 |
| | B. Everett Jordan (D), April 19, 1958 |
| **North Dakota** | Milton R. Young (R), March 12, 1945 |
| | Quentin N. Burdick (D), August 8, 1960 |
| **Ohio** | Frank J. Lausche (D), January 3, 1957 |
| | Stephen M. Young (D), January 3, 1959 |
| **Oklahoma** | A. S. Mike Monroney (D), January 3, 1951 |
| | Fred R. Harris (D), November 4, 1964 |
| **Oregon** | Wayne Morse (D), January 3, 1945 |
| | Mark O. Hatfield (R), January 3, 1967 |
| **Pennsylvania** | Joseph S. Clark (D), January 3, 1957 |
| | Hugh Scott (R), January 3, 1959 |
| **Rhode Island** | John O. Pastore (D), December 19, 1950 |
| | Claiborne Pell (D), January 3, 1961 |
| **South Carolina** | Strom Thurmond (R), November 7, 1956 |
| | Ernest F. Hollings (D), November 9, 1966 |
| **South Dakota** | Karl E. Mundt (R), December 31, 1948 |
| | George McGovern (D), January 3, 1963 |
| **Tennessee** | Albert Gore (D), January 3, 1953 |
| | Howard Baker, Jr. (R), January 3, 1967 |
| **Texas** | Ralph W. Yarborough (D), April 29, 1957 |
| | John G. Tower (R), June 15, 1961 |
| **Utah** | Wallace F. Bennett (R), January 3, 1951 |
| | Frank E. Moss (D), January 3, 1959 |
| **Vermont** | George D. Aiken (R), January 10, 1941 |
| | Winston L. Prouty (R), January 3, 1959 |
| **Virginia** | Harry Flood Byrd, Jr. (D), November 12, 1965 |
| | William B. Spong, Jr. (D), December 31, 1966 |
| **Washington** | Warren G. Magnuson (D), December 14, 1944 |
| | Henry M. Jackson (D), January 3, 1953 |
| **West Virginia** | Jennings Randolph (D), November 5, 1958 |
| | Robert C. Byrd (D), January 3, 1959 |
| **Wisconsin** | William Proxmire (D), August 28, 1957 |
| | Gaylord Nelson (D), January 8, 1963 |
| **Wyoming** | Gale W. McGee (D), January 3, 1959 |
| | Clifford P. Hansen (R), January 3, 1967 |

## THE HOUSE OF REPRESENTATIVES

The lower house of Congress was originally intended to represent the people more directly than the Senate. Three powers are delegated exclusively to the House: It originates all bills for raising revenue, elects the President if there is no electoral majority, and impeaches Federal officials. Members receive an annual salary of $30,000, except for the Speaker, who has an annual salary of $43,000 and an expense account of $10,000.

A Representative must be at least 25 years of age, seven years a citizen of the United States, and an inhabitant of the state he represents.

The following list of Representatives is the official roster of the House at the opening of the First Session of the 90th Congress on January 10, 1967. Changes that occurred during the session are recorded in *The 90th Congress: 1967* on page 352.

**Democrats (D) 247, Republicans (R) 187, Vacant 1**

**Speaker:** John W. McCormack (D-Mass.)
**Majority Leader:** Carl Albert (D-Okla.)
**Majority Whip:** Hale Boggs (D-La.)
**Minority Leader:** Gerald R. Ford (R-Mich.)
**Minority Whip:** Leslie C. Arends (R-Ill.)

**Clerk:** W. Pat Jennings
**Sergeant at Arms:** Zeake W. Johnson, Jr.
**Parliamentarian:** Lewis Deschler
**Doorkeeper:** William M. Miller
**Postmaster:** H. H. Morris
**Press Gallery Superintendent:** Richard L. Embly
**Chaplain:** Rev. Edward G. Latch, D.D.

Congressional districts within a state are indicated by numerals, while a Representative-at-Large is shown as AL.

**Alabama**
1. Jack Edwards (R)
2. William L. Dickinson (R)
3. George Andrews (D)
4. Bill Nichols (D)
5. Armistead I. Selden, Jr. (D)
6. John H. Buchanan, Jr. (R)
7. Tom Bevill (D)
8. Robert E. Jones, Jr. (D)
**Alaska**
AL Howard W. Pollock (R)
**Arizona**
1. John J. Rhodes (R)
2. Morris K. Udall (D)
3. Sam Steiger (R)
**Arkansas**
1. E. C. Gathings (D)
2. Wilbur D. Mills (D)
3. John Paul Hammerschmidt (R)
4. David Pryor (D)
**California**
1. Don H. Clausen (R)
2. Harold T. Johnson (D)
3. John E. Moss (D)
4. Robert L. Leggett (D)
5. Phillip Burton (D)
6. William S. Mailliard (R)
7. Jeffery Cohelan (D)
8. George P. Miller (D)
9. Don Edwards (D)
10. Charles S. Gubser (R)
11. J. Arthur Younger (R)
12. Burt L. Talcott (R)
13. Charles M. Teague (R)
14. Jerome R. Waldie (D)
15. John J. McFall (D)
16. B. F. Sisk (D)
17. Cecil R. King (D)
18. Robert B. (Bob) Mathias (R)
19. Chet Holifield (D)
20. H. Allen Smith (R)
21. Augustus F. Hawkins (D)
22. James C. Corman (D)
23. Del Clawson (R)
24. Glenard P. Lipscomb (R)
25. Charles E. Wiggins (R)
26. Thomas M. Rees (D)
27. Ed Reinecke (R)

28. Alphonzo Bell (R)
29. George E. Brown, Jr. (D)
30. Edward R. Roybal (D)
31. Charles H. Wilson (D)
32. Craig Hosmer (R)
33. Jerry L. Pettis (R)
34. Richard T. Hanna (D)
35. James B. Utt (R)
36. Bob Wilson (R)
37. Lionel Van Deerlin (D)
38. John V. Tunney (D)
**Colorado**
1. Byron G. Rogers (D)
2. Donald G. Brotzman (R)
3. Frank E. Evans (D)
4. Wayne N. Aspinall (D)
**Connecticut**
1. Emilio Q. Daddario (D)
2. William L. St. Onge (D)
3. Robert N. Giaimo (D)
4. Donald J. Irwin (D)
5. John S. Monagan (D)
6. Thomas J. Meskill (R)
**Delaware**
AL William V. Roth, Jr. (R)
**Florida**
1. Robert L. F. Sikes (D)
2. Don Fuqua (D)
3. Charles E. Bennett (D)
4. A. Sydney Herlong, Jr. (D)
5. Edward J. Gurney (R)
6. Sam Gibbons (D)
7. James A. Haley (D)
8. William C. Cramer (R)
9. Paul G. Rogers (D)
10. J. Herbert Burke (R)
11. Claude Pepper (D)
12. Dante B. Fascell (D)
**Georgia**
1. G. Elliott Hagan (D)
2. Maston O'Neal (D)
3. Jack Brinkley (D)
4. Benjamin B. Blackburn (R)
5. Fletcher Thompson (R)
6. John J. Flynt, Jr. (D)
7. John W. Davis (D)
8. W. S. (Bill) Stuckey (D)
9. Phil M. Landrum (D)
10. Robert G. Stephens, Jr. (D)

**Hawaii**
AL Spark M. Matsunaga (D)
AL Patsy T. Mink (D)
**Idaho**
1. James A. McClure (R)
2. George V. Hansen (R)
**Illinois**
1. William L. Dawson (D)
2. Barratt O'Hara (D)
3. William T. Murphy (D)
4. Edward J. Derwinski (R)
5. John C. Kluczynski (D)
6. Daniel J. Ronan (D)
7. Frank Annunzio (D)
8. Dan Rostenkowski (D)
9. Sidney R. Yates (D)
10. Harold R. Collier (R)
11. Roman C. Pucinski (D)
12. Robert McClory (R)
13. Donald Rumsfeld (R)
14. John N. Erlenborn (R)
15. Charlotte T. Reid (R)
16. John B. Anderson (R)
17. Leslie C. Arends (R)
18. Robert H. Michel (R)
19. Tom Railsback (R)
20. Paul Findley (R)
21. Kenneth J. Gray (D)
22. William L. Springer (R)
23. George E. Shipley (D)
24. Melvin Price (D)
**Indiana**
1. Ray J. Madden (D)
2. Charles A. Halleck (R)
3. John Brademas (D)
4. E. Ross Adair (R)
5. J. Edward Roush (D)
6. William G. Bray (R)
7. John T. Myers (R)
8. Roger H. Zion (R)
9. Lee H. Hamilton (D)
10. Richard L. Roudebush (R)
11. Andrew Jacobs, Jr. (D)
**Iowa**
1. Fred Schwengel (R)
2. John C. Culver (D)
3. H. R. Gross (R)
4. John Kyl (R)
5. Neal Smith (D)
6. Wiley Mayne (R)

7. William J. Scherle (R)
**Kansas**
1. Robert Dole (R)
2. Chester L. Mize (R)
3. Larry Winn, Jr. (R)
4. Garner E. Shriver (R)
5. Joe Skubitz (R)
**Kentucky**
1. Frank A. Stubblefield (D)
2. William H. Natcher (D)
3. William O. Cowger (R)
4. M. G. (Gene) Snyder (R)
5. Tim Lee Carter (R)
6. John C. Watts (D)
7. Carl D. Perkins (D)
**Louisiana**
1. F. Edward Hébert (D)
2. Hale Boggs (D)
3. Edwin E. Willis (D)
4. Joe D. Waggoner, Jr. (D)
5. Otto E. Passman (D)
6. John R. Rarick (D)
7. Edwin W. Edwards (D)
8. Speedy O. Long (D)
**Maine**
1. Peter N. Kyros (D)
2. William D. Hathaway (D)
**Maryland**
1. Rogers C. B. Morton (R)
2. Clarence D. Long (D)
3. Edward A. Garmatz (D)
4. George H. Fallon (D)
5. Hervey G. Machen (D)
6. Charles McC. Mathias, Jr. (R)
7. Samuel N. Friedel (D)
8. Gilbert Gude (R)
**Massachusetts**
1. Silvio O. Conte (R)
2. Edward P. Boland (D)
3. Philip J. Philbin (D)
4. Harold D. Donohue (D)
5. F. Bradford Morse (R)
6. William H. Bates (R)
7. Torbert H. Macdonald (D)
8. Thomas P. O'Neill, Jr. (D)
9. John W. McCormack (D)
10. Margaret M. Heckler (R)
11. James A. Burke (D)
12. Hastings Keith (R)

*(continued)*

## THE HOUSE OF REPRESENTATIVES (*continued*)

**Michigan**
1. John Conyers, Jr. (D)
2. Marvin L. Esch (R)
3. Garry Brown (R)
4. Edward Hutchinson (R)
5. Gerald R. Ford (R)
6. Charles E. Chamberlain (R)
7. Donald W. Riegle, Jr. (R)
8. James Harvey (R)
9. Guy Vander Jagt (R)
10. Elford A. Cederberg (R)
11. Philip E. Ruppe (R)
12. James G. O'Hara (D)
13. Charles C. Diggs, Jr. (D)
14. Lucien N. Nedzi (D)
15. William D. Ford (D)
16. John D. Dingell (D)
17. Martha W. Griffiths (D)
18. William S. Broomfield (R)
19. Jack H. McDonald (R)

**Minnesota**
1. Albert H. Quie (R)
2. Ancher Nelsen (R)
3. Clark MacGregor (R)
4. Joseph E. Karth (D)
5. Donald M. Fraser (D)
6. John M. Zwach (R)
7. Odin Langen (R)
8. John A. Blatnik (D)

**Mississippi**
1. Thomas G. Abernethy (D)
2. Jamie L. Whitten (D)
3. John Bell Williams (D)
4. G. V. (Sonny) Montgomery (D)
5. William M. Colmer (D)

**Missouri**
1. Frank M. Karsten (D)
2. Thomas B. Curtis (R)
3. Leonor K. Sullivan (D)
4. William J. Randall (D)
5. Richard Bolling (D)
6. W. R. Hull, Jr. (D)
7. Durward G. Hall (R)
8. Richard H. Ichord (D)
9. William L. Hungate (D)
10. Paul C. Jones (D)

**Montana**
1. Arnold Olsen (D)
2. James F. Battin (R)

**Nebraska**
1. Robert V. Denney (R)
2. Glenn Cunningham (R)
3. David T. Martin (R)

**Nevada**
AL Walter S. Baring (D)

**New Hampshire**
1. Louis C. Wyman (R)
2. James C. Cleveland (R)

**New Jersey**
1. John E. Hunt (R)
2. Charles W. Sandman, Jr. (R)
3. James J. Howard (D)
4. Frank Thompson, Jr. (D)
5. Peter H. B. Frelinghuysen (R)
6. William T. Cahill (R)
7. William B. Widnall (R)
8. Charles S. Joelson (D)
9. Henry Helstoski (D)
10. Peter W. Rodino, Jr. (D)
11. Joseph G. Minish (D)

12. Florence P. Dwyer (R)
13. Cornelius E. Gallagher (D)
14. Dominick V. Daniels (D)
15. Edward J. Patten (D)

**New Mexico**
AL Thomas G. Morris (D)
AL E. S. (Johnny) Walker (D)

**New York**
1. Otis G. Pike (D)
2. James R. Grover, Jr. (R)
3. Lester L. Wolff (D)
4. John W. Wydler (R)
5. Herbert Tenzer (D)
6. Seymour Halpern (R)
7. Joseph P. Addabbo (D)
8. Benjamin S. Rosenthal (D)
9. James J. Delaney (D)
10. Emanuel Celler (D)
11. Frank J. Brasco (D)
12. Edna F. Kelly (D)
13. Abraham J. Multer (D)
14. John J. Rooney (D)
15. Hugh L. Carey (D)
16. John M. Murphy (D)
17. Theodore R. Kupferman (R)
18. Adam Clayton Powell (D)
19. Leonard Farbstein (D)
20. William F. Ryan (D)
21. James H. Scheuer (D)
22. Jacob H. Gilbert (D)
23. Jonathan B. Bingham (D)
24. Paul A. Fino (R)
25. Richard L. Ottinger (D)
26. Ogden R. Reid (R)
27. John G. Dow (D)
28. Joseph Y. Resnick (D)
29. Daniel E. Button (R)
30. Carleton J. King (R)
31. Robert C. McEwen (R)
32. Alexander Pirnie (R)
33. Howard W. Robison (R)
34. James M. Hanley (D)
35. Samuel S. Stratton (D)
36. Frank J. Horton (R)
37. Barber B. Conable, Jr. (R)
38. Charles E. Goodell (R)
39. Richard D. McCarthy (D)
40. Henry P. Smith III (R)
41. Thaddeus J. Dulski (D)

**North Carolina**
1. Walter B. Jones (D)
2. L. H. Fountain (D)
3. David N. Henderson (D)
4. James C. Gardner (R)
5. Nick Galifianakis (D)
6. Horace R. Kornegay (D)
7. Alton Lennon (D)
8. Charles Raper Jonas (R)
9. James T. Broyhill (R)
10. Basil L. Whitener (D)
11. Roy A. Taylor (D)

**North Dakota**
1. Mark Andrews (R)
2. Thomas S. Kleppe (R)

**Ohio**
1. Robert Taft, Jr. (R)
2. Donald D. Clancy (R)
3. Charles W. Whalen, Jr (R)
4. William M. McCulloch (R)
5. Delbert L. Latta (R)
6. William H. Harsha (R)
7. Clarence J. Brown, Jr. (R)
8. Jackson E. Betts (R)

9. Thomas L. Ashley (D)
10. Clarence E. Miller (R)
11. J. William Stanton (R)
12. Samuel L. Devine (R)
13. Charles A. Mosher (R)
14. William H. Ayres (R)
15. Chalmers P. Wylie (R)
16. Frank T. Bow (R)
17. John M. Ashbrook (R)
18. Wayne L. Hays (D)
19. Michael J. Kirwan (D)
20. Michael A. Feighan (D)
21. Charles A. Vanik (D)
22. Frances P. Bolton (R)
23. William E. Minshall (R)
24. Donald E. Lukens (R)

**Oklahoma**
1. Page Belcher (R)
2. Ed Edmondson (D)
3. Carl Albert (D)
4. Tom Steed (D)
5. John Jarman (D)
6. James V. Smith (R)

**Oregon**
1. Wendall Wyatt (R)
2. Al Ullman (D)
3. Edith Green (D)
4. John R. Dellenback (R)

**Pennsylvania**
1. William A. Barrett (D)
2. Robert N. C. Nix (D)
3. James A. Byrne (D)
4. Joshua Eilberg (D)
5. William J. Green (D)
6. George M. Rhodes (D)
7. Lawrence G. Williams (R)
8. Edward G. Biester, Jr. (R)
9. G. Robert Watkins (R)
10. Joseph M. McDade (R)
11. Daniel J. Flood (D)
12. J. Irving Whalley (R)
13. Richard S. Schweiker (R)
14. William S. Moorhead (D)
15. Fred B. Rooney (D)
16. Edwin D. Eshleman (R)
17. Herman T. Schneebeli (R)
18. Robert J. Corbett (R)
19. George A. Goodling (R)
20. Elmer J. Holland (D)
21. John H. Dent (D)
22. John P. Saylor (R)
23. Albert W. Johnson (R)
24. Joseph P. Vigorito (D)
25. Frank M. Clark (D)
26. Thomas E. Morgan (D)
27. James G. Fulton (R)

**Rhode Island**
1. Fernand J. St. Germain (D)
2. [Vacant]

**South Carolina**
1. L. Mendel Rivers (D)
2. Albert W. Watson (R)
3. W. J. Bryan Dorn (D)
4. Robert T. Ashmore (D)
5. Tom S. Gettys (D)
6. John L. McMillan (D)

**South Dakota**
1. Ben Reifel (R)
2. E. Y. Berry (R)

**Tennessee**
1. James H. Quillen (R)
2. John J. Duncan (R)
3. W. E. (Bill) Brock III (R)

4. Joe L. Evins (D)
5. Richard Fulton (D)
6. William R. Anderson (D)
7. Ray Blanton (D)
8. Robert A. Everett (D)
9. Dan Kuykendall (R)

**Texas**
1. Wright Patman (D)
2. John Dowdy (D)
3. Joe Pool (D)
4. Ray Roberts (D)
5. Earle Cabell (D)
6. Olin E. Teague (D)
7. George Bush (R)
8. Bob Eckhardt (D)
9. Jack Brooks (D)
10. J. J. Pickle (D)
11. W. R. Poage (D)
12. Jim Wright (D)
13. Graham Purcell (D)
14. John Young (D)
15. Eligio de la Garza (D)
16. Richard White (D)
17. Omar Burleson (D)
18. Robert Price (R)
19. George Mahon (D)
20. Henry B. Gonzalez (D)
21. O. C. Fisher (D)
22. Bob Casey (D)
23. Abraham Kazen, Jr. (D)

**Utah**
1. Laurence J. Burton (R)
2. Sherman P. Lloyd (R)

**Vermont**
AL Robert T. Stafford (R)

**Virginia**
1. Thomas N. Downing (D)
2. Porter Hardy, Jr. (D)
3. David E. Satterfield III (D)
4. Watkins M. Abbitt (D)
5. William M. Tuck (D)
6. Richard H. Poff (R)
7. John O. Marsh, Jr. (D)
8. William Lloyd Scott (R)
9. William C. Wampler (R)
10. Joel T. Broyhill (R)

**Washington**
1. Thomas M. Pelly (R)
2. Lloyd Meeds (D)
3. Julia Butler Hansen (D)
4. Catherine May (R)
5. Thomas S. Foley (D)
6. Floyd V. Hicks (D)
7. Brock Adams (D)

**West Virginia**
1. Arch A. Moore, Jr. (R)
2. Harley O. Staggers (D)
3. John M. Slack, Jr. (D)
4. Ken Hechler (D)
5. James Kee (D)

**Wisconsin**
1. Henry C. Schadeberg (R)
2. Robert Kastenmeier (D)
3. Vernon W. Thomson (R)
4. Clement J. Zablocki (D)
5. Henry S. Reuss (D)
6. William A. Steiger (R)
7. Melvin R. Laird (R)
8. John W. Byrnes (R)
9. Glenn R. Davis (R)
10. Alvin E. O'Konski (R)

**Wyoming**
AL William Henry Harrison (R)

## SPEAKERS OF THE HOUSE OF REPRESENTATIVES

| CONGRESS | SPEAKER | PARTY | CONGRESS | SPEAKER | PARTY |
|---|---|---|---|---|---|
| 1st (1789–91) | Frederick A. C. Muhlenberg | Federalist | 44th (cont.) | Milton Saylor | Democrat |
| 2nd (1791–93) | Jonathan Trumbull | Federalist | | Samuel J. Randall | Democrat |
| 3rd (1793–95) | Frederick A. C. Muhlenberg | Federalist | 45th (1877–79) | Samuel J. Randall | Democrat |
| 4th (1795–97) | Jonathan Dayton | Federalist | 46th (1879–81) | Samuel J. Randall | Democrat |
| 5th (1797–99) | Jonathan Dayton | Federalist | 47th (1881–83) | J. Warren Keifer | Republican |
| | George Dent | Democrat | 48th (1883–85) | John G. Carlisle | Democrat |
| 6th (1799– | | | 49th (1885–87) | John G. Carlisle | Democrat |
| 1801) | Theodore Sedgwick | Federalist | 50th (1887–89) | John G. Carlisle | Democrat |
| 7th (1801–03) | Nathaniel Macon | Democrat | 51st (1889–91) | Thomas B. Reed | Republican |
| 8th (1803–05) | Nathaniel Macon | Democrat | 52nd (1891–93) | Charles F. Crisp | Democrat |
| 9th (1805–07) | Nathaniel Macon | Democrat | 53rd (1893–95) | Charles F. Crisp | Democrat |
| 10th (1807–09) | Joseph B. Varnum | Democrat | 54th (1895–97) | Thomas B. Reed | Republican |
| 11th (1809–11) | Joseph B. Varnum | Democrat | 55th (1897–99) | Thomas B. Reed | Republican |
| 12th (1811–13) | Henry Clay | Whig | 56th (1899– | | |
| 13th (1813–15) | Henry Clay | Whig | 1901) | David B. Henderson | Republican |
| | Langdon Cheves | Democrat | 57th (1901–03) | David B. Henderson | Republican |
| 14th (1815–17) | Henry Clay | Whig | 58th (1903–05) | Joseph G. Cannon | Republican |
| 15th (1817–19) | Henry Clay | Whig | 59th (1905–07) | Joseph G. Cannon | Republican |
| 16th (1819–21) | Henry Clay | Whig | 60th (1907–09) | Joseph G. Cannon | Republican |
| | John W. Taylor | Democrat | 61st (1909–11) | Joseph G. Cannon | Republican |
| 17th (1821–23) | Philip P. Barbour | Democrat | 62nd (1911–13) | Champ Clark | Democrat |
| 18th (1823–25) | Henry Clay | Whig | 63rd (1913–15) | Champ Clark | Democrat |
| 19th (1825–27) | John W. Taylor | Democrat | 64th (1915–17) | Champ Clark | Democrat |
| 20th (1827–29) | Andrew Stevenson | Democrat | 65th (1917–19) | Champ Clark | Democrat |
| 21st (1829–31) | Andrew Stevenson | Democrat | 66th (1919–21) | Frederick H. Gillett | Republican |
| 22nd (1831–33) | Andrew Stevenson | Democrat | 67th (1921–23) | Frederick H. Gillett | Republican |
| 23rd (1833–35) | Andrew Stevenson | Democrat | 68th (1923–25) | Frederick H. Gillett | Republican |
| | John Bell | Whig | 69th (1925–27) | Nicholas Longworth | Republican |
| 24th (1835–37) | James K. Polk | Democrat | 70th (1927–29) | Nicholas Longworth | Republican |
| 25th (1837–39) | James K. Polk | Democrat | 71st (1929–31) | Nicholas Longworth | Republican |
| 26th (1839–41) | Robert M. T. Hunter | Democrat | 72nd (1931–33) | John N. Garner | Democrat |
| 27th (1841–43) | John White | Whig | 73rd (1933–35) | Henry T. Rainey | Democrat |
| 28th (1843–45) | John W. Jones | Democrat | 74th (1935–37) | Joseph W. Byrns | Democrat |
| 29th (1845–47) | John W. Davis | Democrat | | William B. Bankhead | Democrat |
| 30th (1847–49) | Robert C. Winthrop | Whig | 75th (1937–39) | William B. Bankhead | Democrat |
| 31st (1849–51) | Howell Cobb | Democrat | 76th (1939–41) | William B. Bankhead | Democrat |
| 32nd (1851–53) | Linn Boyd | Democrat | | Sam Rayburn | Democrat |
| 33rd (1853–55) | Linn Boyd | Democrat | 77th (1941–43) | Sam Rayburn | Democrat |
| 34th (1855–57) | Nathaniel P. Banks | American | 78th (1943–45) | Sam Rayburn | Democrat |
| 35th (1857–59) | James L. Orr | Democrat | 79th (1945–47) | Sam Rayburn | Democrat |
| 36th (1859–61) | William Pennington | Whig | 80th (1947–49) | Joseph W. Martin, Jr. | Republican |
| 37th (1861–63) | Galusha A. Grow | Republican | 81st (1949–51) | Sam Rayburn | Democrat |
| 38th (1863–65) | Schuyler Colfax | Republican | 82nd (1951–53) | Sam Rayburn | Democrat |
| 39th (1865–67) | Schuyler Colfax | Republican | 83rd (1953–55) | Joseph W. Martin, Jr. | Republican |
| 40th (1867–69) | Schuyler Colfax | Republican | 84th (1955–57) | Sam Rayburn | Democrat |
| | Theodore M. Pomeroy | Republican | 85th (1957–59) | Sam Rayburn | Democrat |
| 41st (1869–71) | James G. Blaine | Republican | 86th (1959–61) | Sam Rayburn | Democrat |
| 42nd (1871–73) | James G. Blaine | Republican | 87th (1961–63) | Sam Rayburn | Democrat |
| 43rd (1873–75) | James G. Blaine | Republican | 88th (1963–65) | John W. McCormack | Democrat |
| 44th (1875–77) | Michael C. Kerr | Democrat | 89th (1965–67) | John W. McCormack | Democrat |
| | Samuel S. Cox | Democrat | 90th (1967–69) | John W. McCormack | Democrat |

First Speaker of the House was Frederick A. C. Muhlenberg (far left). Illinois Representative Joseph G. ("Uncle Joe") Cannon, who held the post for nine years (1903-11) was so tyrannical that House members sharply reduced the Speaker's powers. Sam Rayburn (second from right) holds the record for length of service as Speaker, 17 years. John McCormack is the present Speaker.

# COMMITTEES OF CONGRESS

The fate of legislation introduced in Congress depends to a large extent on what happens to it in House or Senate committees. Before a bill goes back to either house for a vote, the committee can revise it, change it beyond recognition, or simply bottle it up. Committee chairmen, who achieve their positions through seniority, thus have considerable influence in determining which measures will or will not become law, and they can use pressure to get their favorite bills passed. A prestigious chairman gives added weight to his committee. For instance, as chairman of the Senate Foreign Relations Committee, Senator J. William Fulbright of Arkansas has focused national attention on foreign affairs.

A committee's importance is also determined by the kind of legislation it handles. The House Ways and Means Committee and the Senate Finance Committee are responsible for all tax, tariff, and Social Security legislation. The House Rules Committee decides which bills will go to the floor of the House. The House and Senate Appropriations Committees set the pattern for all spending levels, and the House Appropriations Committee is particularly important because it originates all money legislation.

With emphasis in recent years on legislation pertaining to social welfare and individual rights, several other committees have been in the news. Civil rights bills are handled by the House and Senate Judiciary Committees, and "Great Society" matters such as education and poverty go through the House Education and Labor Committee and the Senate Labor and Public Welfare Committee.

The membership by party and the chairmen of the permanent committees of the 90th Congress, First Session, are listed below as of mid-April, 1967. (*D* stands for Democrats, *R* for Republicans.) Any changes that occurred later in the year are recorded in *The 90th Congress: 1967* on page 352.

| COMMITTEE, CHAIRMAN, AND MEMBERSHIP | JURISDICTION | COMMITTEE, CHAIRMAN, AND MEMBERSHIP |
|---|---|---|
| **Senate** | | **House** |
| **Aeronautical and Space Sciences** <br> Clinton P. Anderson (D-N Mex) <br> D-10, R-6 | Nonmilitary scientific research, development, and administration of all matters in the field of space and aeronautical activities | **Science and Astronautics** <br> George P. Miller (D-Calif) <br> D-18, R-13 |
| **Agriculture and Forestry** <br> Allen J. Ellender (D-La) <br> D-10, R-5 | All matters dealing with forestry and agriculture, particularly Federal programs concerned with farm credit and security, crop insurance, soil conservation, and rural electrification | **Agriculture** <br> W. R. Poage (D-Texas) <br> D-20, R-15 |
| **Appropriations** <br> Carl Hayden (D-Ariz) <br> D-17, R-9 | All matters pertaining to the spending of government money | **Appropriations** <br> George H. Mahon (D-Texas) <br> D-30, R-21 |
| **Armed Services** <br> Richard B. Russell (D-Ga) <br> D-12, R-6 | Military affairs, including aeronautical and space activities concerned with weapons systems; conservation of strategic and critical materials, especially petroleum resources | **Armed Service** <br> L. Mendel Rivers (D-SC) <br> D-23, R-17 |
| **Banking and Currency** <br> John J. Sparkman (D-Ala) <br> D-9, R-5 | All financial matters other than taxes and appropriations, particularly those concerned with banking and currency, and including matters pertaining to public and private housing | **Banking and Currency** <br> Wright Patman (D-Texas) <br> D-19, R-14 |
| **Commerce** <br> Warren G. Magnuson (D-Wash) <br> D-12, R-6 | Interstate transportation and communication, inland waterways, civil aeronautics, Weather Bureau, and (House only) foreign commerce, **railroad labor, securities and exchanges, interstate oil compacts, national gas and public health, regulation of interstate transmission of power (except between government protects)** | **Interstate and Foreign Commerce** <br> Harley O. Staggers (D-W Va) <br> D-19, R-14 |
| | Merchant Marine, Coast Guard, Coast and Geodetic Survey, fisheries and wildlife <br> Maintenance and operation of Panama Canal and administration of Canal Zone | **Merchant Marine and Fisheries** <br> Edward A. Garmatz (D-Md) <br> D-19, R-15 |
| **District of Columbia** <br> Alan Bible (D-Nev) <br> D-5, R-3 | Operation of all municipal affairs of the District of Columbia except for the appropriation of money | **District of Columbia** <br> John L. McMillan (D-SC) <br> D-14, R-11 |

| COMMITTEE, CHAIRMAN, AND MEMBERSHIP | JURISDICTION | COMMITTEE, CHAIRMAN, AND MEMBERSHIP |
|---|---|---|
| **Senate** | | **House** |
| **Finance**<br>Russell B. Long (D-La)<br>D-11, R-6 | All matters pertaining to taxes, tariffs, import quotas, and social security<br>Veterans compensation, pensions, armed forces life insurance<br>Rehabilitation, education, medical care, and treatment of veterans, and veterans hospitals | **Ways and Means**<br>Wilbur Mills (D-Ark)<br>D-15, R-10<br>**Veterans Affairs**<br>Olin E. Teague (D-Texas)<br>D-14, R-11 |
| **Foreign Relations**<br>J. W. Fulbright (D-Ark)<br>D-12, R-7 | Relations of the United States with foreign nations and international organizations, including the Red Cross, diplomatic service, United Nations, foreign loans, and (Senate only) treaties | **Foreign Affairs**<br>Thomas E. Morgan (D-Penn)<br>D-21, R-15 |
| **Government Operations**<br>John L. McClellan (D-Ark)<br>D-10, R-5 | All activities concerned with general government and administrative problems, including budgeting and accounting measures, reorganization of the executive branch, and governmental relationships between the Federal government and the states and municipalities, **and (Senate only) between the United States and international organizations to which the United States belongs** | **Government Operations**<br>William L. Dawson (D-Ill)<br>D-20, R-15 |
| **Interior and Insular Affairs**<br>Henry M. Jackson (D-Wash)<br>D-11, R-6 | Public lands, natural resources, and territorial possessions of the United States, and Indian affairs | **Interior and Insular Affairs**<br>Wayne N. Aspinall (D-Colo)<br>D-19, R-14 |
| **Judiciary**<br>James O. Eastland (D-Miss)<br>D-11, R-5 | Activities of Federal courts and judges, civil rights and liberties, constitutional amendments, interstate compacts, immigration and naturalization, apportionment of Representatives, meetings of Congress, and members' attendance. **(Senate only) claims against the U.S. Patent Office; (House only) Presidential succession** | **Judiciary**<br>Emanuel Celler (D-NY)<br>D-20, R-15 |
| **Labor and Public Welfare**<br>Lister Hill (D-Ala)<br>D-10, R-6 | All matters pertaining to education, welfare, and labor; **medical care and veterans affairs (Senate only)** | **Education and Labor**<br>Carl D. Perkins (D-Ky)<br>D-19, R-14 |
| **Post Office and Civil Service**<br>A. S. Mike Monroney (D-Okla)<br>D-8, R-4 | All matters pertaining to the postal and civil services as well as those involving the census and the National Archives | **Post Office and Civil Service**<br>Thaddeus J. Dulski (D-NY)<br>D-15, R-11 |
| **Public Works**<br>Jennings Randolph (D-W Va)<br>D-10, R-6 | Public buildings and roads; flood control, improvement of rivers and harbors; stream pollution; and water power | **Public Works**<br>George H. Fallon (D-Md)<br>D-19, R-15 |
| ——— | Rules and orders of business of the House | **Rules Committee**<br>William M. Colmer (D-Miss)<br>D-10, R-5 |
| **Rules and Administration**<br>B. Everett Jordan (D-NC)<br>D-6, R-3 | General administration of the Senate and management of the Library of Congress and the Smithsonian Institution | ——— |
| ——— | House administration; printing and correction of the Congressional Record; Federal elections; and management of the Library of Congress and the Smithsonian Institution | **House Administration**<br>Omar Burleson (D-Tex)<br>D-14, R-11 |
| **Select Small Business**<br>George A. Smathers (D-Fla)<br>D-11, R-6 | Study and investigation of the problems of small business | **Select Small Business**<br>Joe L. Evins (D-Tenn)<br>D-9, R-6 |
| **Select Standards and Conduct**<br>John C. Stennis (D-Miss)<br>D-3, R-3 | Standards of ethics for members | **Standards of Official Conduct**<br>Melvin Price (D-Ill)<br>D-6, R-6 |
| ——— | Investigation of activities to determine if they are subversive | **Un-American Activities**<br>Edwin E. Willis (D-La)<br>D-5, R-4 |

## HOW A BILL BECOMES A LAW

Bills are introduced, debated, and voted upon in Congress, before they are sent to the President to be signed into law. If Congressional support for a bill is sufficiently strong, it can become a law even over a Presidential veto.

A Senator or Representative sends his bill to the clerk of his house for its first reading. The clerk assigns the bill a title and number. It is then referred to the appropriate committee, which may table the measure, thereby killing it, or consider it. To evaluate a bill, committees may hold hearings, call witnesses, and take testimony from experts and interested parties. A committee may also amend or substantially re-write a bill.

Once approved by committee, the bill goes back to the floor of the house of origin, where it is read aloud by the clerk and opened to debate. Procedural rules limit the length of debates in the House of Representatives. However, the Senate has no such rules. Unless two-thirds of the Senators approve a cloture measure, that body is subject to a filibuster, in which opponents of the bill take the floor and refuse to yield it, hoping by sheer staying power to kill the measure.

When debate ends, the title of the bill is read again, and a voice or roll-call vote is taken. If the bill passes by a majority, it is sent to the other house of Congress, and the debating and voting procedures are repeated. If the other house defeats the bill, it dies. If an amended version of the original is passed, a joint Congressional committee is appointed to adjust the differences.

Once a bill has been approved by both houses, it goes to the President. If he approves the measure, he may sign it, and the bill becomes a law. If he disapproves, he may veto the measure, that is, refuse to sign it and return it to the house of origin together with his objections.

When a bill is returned to Congress, the President's objections are read and debated in the house of origin, and a roll-call vote on the measure is taken. If it passes by a two-thirds majority, the bill is sent to the other house for a vote. If it passes there by a two-thirds majority, the bill becomes a law despite the President's veto. This procedure is called "overriding" a veto.

If for any reason the President wishes neither to sign nor to veto a bill, he may keep it for ten calendar days (excepting Sundays), after which it automatically becomes law. If, however, Congress adjourns during the ten days, the bill is automatically killed. This is known as a "pocket" veto.

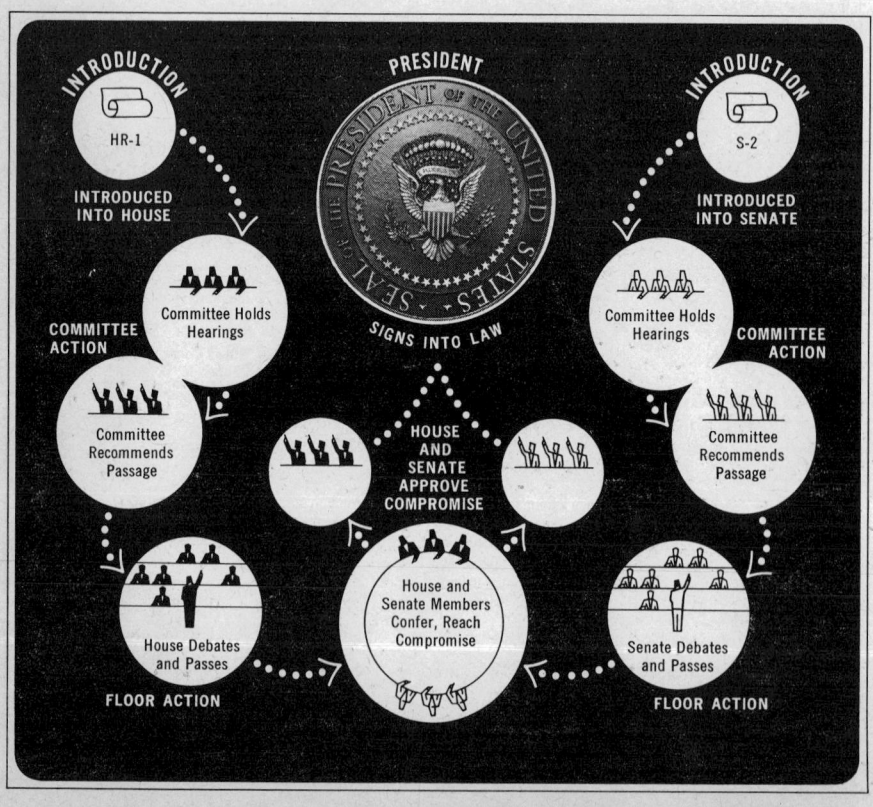

# POLITICAL PARTY STRENGTH IN THE U.S. CONGRESS: 1789–1967

Ad—Administration;  AM—Anti-Masonic;  C—Coalition;  D—Democratic;  DR—Democratic-Republican;  F—Federalist;
J—Jacksonian;  NR—National Republican;  Op—Opposition;  R—Republican;  U—Unionist;  W—Whig.

| CON-GRESS | YEAR | PRESIDENT | SENATE | | | HOUSE | | |
|---|---|---|---|---|---|---|---|---|
| | | | Majority Party | Principal Minority Party | Others | Majority Party | Principal Minority Party | Others |
| 1..... | 1789–1791 | George Washington....... | Ad 17 | Op 9 | 0 | Ad 38 | Op 26 | 0 |
| 2..... | 1791–1793 | George Washington... F | F 16 | DR 13 | 0 | F 37 | DR 33 | 0 |
| 3..... | 1793–1795 | George Washington... F | F 17 | DR 13 | 0 | DR 57 | F 48 | 0 |
| 4..... | 1795–1797 | George Washington... F | F 19 | DR 13 | 0 | F 54 | DR 52 | 0 |
| 5..... | 1797–1799 | John Adams......... F | F 20 | DR 12 | 0 | F 58 | DR 48 | 0 |
| 6..... | 1799–1801 | John Adams......... F | F 19 | DR 13 | 0 | F 64 | DR 42 | 0 |
| 7..... | 1801–1803 | Thomas Jefferson.... DR | DR 18 | F 14 | 0 | DR 69 | F 36 | 0 |
| 8..... | 1803–1805 | Thomas Jefferson.... DR | DR 25 | F 9 | 0 | DR 102 | F 39 | 0 |
| 9..... | 1805–1807 | Thomas Jefferson.... DR | DR 27 | F 7 | 0 | DR 116 | F 25 | 0 |
| 10..... | 1807–1809 | Thomas Jefferson.... DR | DR 28 | F 6 | 0 | DR 118 | F 24 | 0 |
| 11..... | 1809–1811 | James Madison...... DR | DR 28 | F 6 | 0 | DR 94 | F 48 | 0 |
| 12..... | 1811–1813 | James Madison...... DR | DR 30 | F 6 | 0 | DR 108 | F 36 | 0 |
| 13..... | 1813–1815 | James Madison...... DR | DR 27 | F 9 | 0 | DR 112 | F 68 | 0 |
| 14..... | 1815–1817 | James Madison...... DR | DR 25 | F 11 | 0 | DR 117 | F 65 | 0 |
| 15..... | 1817–1819 | James Monroe....... DR | DR 34 | F 10 | 0 | DR 141 | F 42 | 0 |
| 16..... | 1819–1821 | James Monroe....... DR | DR 35 | F 7 | 0 | DR 156 | F 27 | 0 |
| 17..... | 1821–1823 | James Monroe....... DR | DR 44 | F 4 | 0 | DR 158 | F 25 | 0 |
| 18..... | 1823–1825 | James Monroe....... DR | DR 44 | F 4 | 0 | DR 187 | F 26 | 0 |
| 19..... | 1825–1827 | John Quincy Adams.. C | Ad 26 | J 20 | 0 | Ad 105 | J 97 | 0 |
| 20..... | 1827–1829 | John Quincy Adams.. C | J 28 | Ad 20 | 0 | J 119 | Ad 94 | 0 |
| 21..... | 1829–1831 | Andrew Jackson..... D | D 26 | NR 22 | 0 | D 139 | NR 74 | 0 |
| 22..... | 1831–1833 | Andrew Jackson..... D | D 25 | NR 21 | 2 | D 141 | NR 58 | 14 |
| 23..... | 1833–1835 | Andrew Jackson..... D | D 20 | NR 20 | 8 | D 147 | AM 53 | 60 |
| 24..... | 1835–1837 | Andrew Jackson..... D | D 27 | W 25 | 0 | D 145 | W 98 | 0 |
| 25..... | 1837–1839 | Martin Van Buren... D | D 30 | W 18 | 4 | D 108 | W 107 | 24 |
| 26..... | 1839–1841 | Martin Van Buren... D | D 28 | W 22 | 0 | D 124 | W 118 | 0 |
| 27..... | 1841–1843 | William Harrison..... W | | | | | | |
| | | John Tyler.......... W | W 28 | D 22 | 2 | W 133 | D 102 | 6 |
| 28..... | 1843–1845 | John Tyler.......... W | W 28 | D 25 | 1 | D 142 | W 79 | 1 |
| 29..... | 1845–1847 | James Polk......... D | D 31 | W 25 | 0 | D 143 | W 77 | 6 |
| 30..... | 1847–1849 | James Polk......... D | D 36 | W 21 | 1 | W 115 | D 108 | 4 |
| 31..... | 1849–1851 | Zachary Taylor...... W | | | | | | |
| | | Millard Fillmore..... W | D 35 | W 25 | 2 | D 112 | W 109 | 9 |
| 32..... | 1851–1853 | Millard Fillmore..... W | D 35 | W 24 | 3 | D 140 | W 88 | 5 |
| 33..... | 1853–1855 | Franklin Pierce...... D | D 38 | W 22 | 2 | D 159 | W 71 | 4 |
| 34..... | 1855–1857 | Franklin Pierce...... D | D 40 | R 15 | 5 | R 108 | D 83 | 43 |
| 35..... | 1857–1859 | James Buchanan..... D | D 36 | R 20 | 8 | D 118 | R 92 | 26 |
| 36..... | 1859–1861 | James Buchanan..... D | D 36 | R 26 | 4 | R 114 | D 92 | 31 |
| 37..... | 1861–1863 | Abraham Lincoln.... R | R 31 | D 10 | 8 | R 105 | D 43 | 30 |
| 38..... | 1863–1865 | Abraham Lincoln.... R | R 36 | D 9 | 5 | R 102 | D 75 | 9 |
| 39..... | 1865–1867 | Abraham Lincoln.... R | | | | | | |
| | | Andrew Johnson..... R | U 42 | D 10 | 0 | U 149 | D 42 | 0 |
| 40..... | 1867–1869 | Andrew Johnson..... R | R 42 | D 11 | 0 | R 143 | D 49 | 0 |
| 41..... | 1869–1871 | Ulysses S. Grant..... R | R 56 | D 11 | 0 | R 149 | D 63 | 0 |
| 42..... | 1871–1873 | Ulysses S. Grant..... R | R 52 | D 17 | 5 | D 134 | R 104 | 5 |
| 43..... | 1873–1875 | Ulysses S. Grant..... R | R 49 | D 19 | 5 | R 194 | D 92 | 14 |
| 44..... | 1875–1877 | Ulysses S. Grant..... R | R 45 | D 29 | 2 | D 169 | R 109 | 14 |
| 45..... | 1877–1879 | Rutherford Hayes.... R | R 39 | D 36 | 1 | D 153 | R 140 | 0 |
| 46..... | 1879–1881 | Rutherford Hayes.... R | D 42 | R 33 | 1 | D 149 | R 130 | 14 |
| 47..... | 1881–1883 | James Garfield....... R | | | | | | |
| | | Chester Arthur...... R | R 37 | D 37 | 1 | R 147 | D 135 | 11 |
| 48..... | 1883–1885 | Chester Arthur...... R | R 38 | D 36 | 2 | D 197 | R 118 | 10 |
| 49..... | 1885–1887 | Grover Cleveland..... D | R 43 | D 34 | 0 | D 183 | R 140 | 2 |
| 50..... | 1887–1889 | Grover Cleveland..... D | R 39 | D 37 | 0 | D 169 | R 152 | 4 |
| 51..... | 1889–1891 | Benjamin Harrison... R | R 39 | D 37 | 0 | R 166 | D 159 | 0 |
| 52..... | 1891–1893 | Benjamin Harrison... R | R 47 | D 39 | 2 | D 235 | R 88 | 9 |
| 53..... | 1893–1895 | Grover Cleveland..... D | D 44 | R 38 | 3 | D 218 | R 127 | 11 |
| 54..... | 1895–1897 | Grover Cleveland..... D | R 43 | D 39 | 6 | R 244 | D 105 | 7 |
| 55..... | 1897–1899 | William McKinley.... R | R 47 | D 34 | 7 | R 204 | D 113 | 40 |
| 56..... | 1899–1901 | William McKinley.... R | R 53 | D 26 | 8 | R 185 | D 163 | 9 |
| 57..... | 1901–1903 | William McKinley.... R | | | | | | |
| | | Theodore Roosevelt.. R | R 55 | D 31 | 4 | R 197 | D 151 | 9 |
| 58..... | 1903–1905 | Theodore Roosevelt.. R | R 57 | D 33 | 0 | R 208 | D 178 | 0 |
| 59..... | 1905–1907 | Theodore Roosevelt.. R | R 57 | D 33 | 0 | R 250 | D 136 | 0 |
| 60..... | 1907–1909 | Theodore Roosevelt.. R | R 61 | D 31 | 0 | R 222 | D 164 | 0 |

(continued)

| CONGRESS | YEAR | PRESIDENT | SENATE Majority Party | Principal Minority Party | Others | HOUSE Majority Party | Principal Minority Party | Others |
|---|---|---|---|---|---|---|---|---|
| 61..... | 1909–1911 | William H. Taft...... R | R 61 | D 32 | 0 | R 219 | D 172 | 0 |
| 62..... | 1911–1913 | William H. Taft...... R | R 51 | D 41 | 0 | D 228 | R 161 | 1 |
| 63..... | 1913–1915 | Woodrow Wilson..... D | D 51 | R 44 | 1 | D 291 | R 127 | 17 |
| 64..... | 1915–1917 | Woodrow Wilson..... D | D 56 | R 40 | 0 | D 230 | R 196 | 9 |
| 65..... | 1917–1919 | Woodrow Wilson..... D | D 53 | R 42 | 0 | D 216 | R 210 | 6 |
| 66..... | 1919–1921 | Woodrow Wilson..... D | R 49 | D 47 | 0 | R 240 | D 190 | 3 |
| 67..... | 1921–1923 | Warren Harding...... R | R 59 | D 37 | 0 | R 303 | D 131 | 1 |
| 68..... | 1923–1925 | Calvin Coolidge...... R | R 51 | D 43 | 2 | R 225 | D 205 | 5 |
| 69..... | 1925–1927 | Calvin Coolidge...... R | R 56 | D 39 | 1 | R 247 | D 183 | 4 |
| 70..... | 1927–1929 | Calvin Coolidge...... R | R 49 | D 46 | 1 | R 237 | D 195 | 3 |
| 71..... | 1929–1931 | Herbert Hoover...... R | R 56 | D 39 | 1 | R 267 | D 167 | 1 |
| 72..... | 1931–1933 | Herbert Hoover ...... R | R 48 | D 47 | 1 | D 220 | R 214 | 1 |
| 73..... | 1933–1935 | Franklin D. Roosevelt D | D 60 | R 35 | 1 | D 310 | R 117 | 5 |
| 74..... | 1935–1937 | Franklin D. Roosevelt D | D 69 | R 25 | 2 | D 319 | R 103 | 10 |
| 75..... | 1937–1939 | Franklin D. Roosevelt D | D 76 | R 16 | 4 | D 331 | R 89 | 13 |
| 76..... | 1939–1941 | Franklin D. Roosevelt D | D 69 | R 23 | 4 | D 261 | R 164 | 4 |
| 77..... | 1941–1943 | Franklin D. Roosevelt D | D 66 | R 28 | 2 | D 268 | R 162 | 5 |
| 78..... | 1943–1945 | Franklin D. Roosevelt D | D 58 | R 37 | 1 | D 218 | R 208 | 4 |
| 79..... | 1945–1947 | Franklin D. Roosevelt D | | | | | | |
| | | Harry S. Truman.... D | D 56 | R 38 | 1 | D 242 | R 190 | 2 |
| 80..... | 1947–1949 | Harry S. Truman.... D | R 45 | D 51 | 0 | R 188 | D 246 | 1 |
| 81..... | 1949–1951 | Harry S. Truman.... D | D 54 | R 42 | 0 | D 263 | R 171 | 1 |
| 82..... | 1951–1953 | Harry S. Truman.... D | D 49 | R 47 | 0 | D 235 | R 199 | 1 |
| 83..... | 1953–1955 | Dwight D. Eisenhower R | R 48 | D 47 | 1 | R 221 | D 212 | 1 |
| 84..... | 1955–1957 | Dwight D. Eisenhower R | D 48 | R 47 | 1 | D 232 | R 203 | 0 |
| 85..... | 1957–1959 | Dwight D. Eisenhower R | D 49 | R 47 | 0 | D 232 | R 199 | 0 |
| 86..... | 1959–1961 | Dwight D. Eisenhower R | D 62 | R 34 | 0 | D 280 | R 152 | 0 |
| 87..... | 1961–1963 | John F. Kennedy..... D | D 65 | R 35 | 0 | D 261 | R 176 | 0 |
| 88..... | 1963–1965 | John F. Kennedy..... D | | | | | | |
| | | Lyndon B. Johnson... D | D 67 | R 33 | 0 | D 258 | R 177 | 0 |
| 89..... | 1965–1967 | Lyndon B. Johnson... D | D 68 | R 32 | 0 | D 295 | R 140 | 0 |
| 90..... | 1967–1969 | Lyndon B. Johnson... D | D 64 | R 36 | 0 | D 247 | R 186 | 0 |

## LITTLE-KNOWN FACTS ABOUT U.S. CONGRESSES

• The first Congress met in New York City from March 4, 1789, to September 29, 1789.

• The first Congressional act was signed by George Washington on June 1, 1789. It was entitled "An Act to regulate the Time and Manner of administrating certain oaths."

• Theodore Francis Greene of Rhode Island, who died on May 19, 1966, was the oldest man ever to serve in the Senate. He retired in 1960 at the age of 92.

• The first Congresswoman was Jeannette Rankin (R-Montana), elected in 1916. She was also the sole Representative to vote against the entry of the United States into both World War I and World War II, during her only two terms, 1917–19 and 1941–43.

• The first woman Senator was Rebecca Latimer Felton, appointed to an interim term by the Governor of Georgia, October 3, 1922. She attended for only two days before her successor was elected.

• It is a custom, not a law, for Congressmen to be residents of the districts they represent.

• Not until the mid-nineteenth century did the practice of electing Congressmen by districts become established.

• Seating in the House of Representatives originally was arranged on a first-come, first-choice basis, with members living near Washington arriving early, securing the best seats, and keeping them for the duration of the session. In the 29th Congress (1845–47), the custom of drawing lots for seats was begun, with ex-Speakers and one or two members of long service being allowed to select their seats first. In 1914, with House membership at 435, chairs arranged in long benches replaced the former desks and chairs. Now members occupy any vacant chair on their side of the aisle.

• The first Negro Senator was Hiram R. Revels of Mississippi, who was elected in 1870.

• The first Negro Congressman was Joseph Rainey of South Carolina, who was elected in 1870.

• The first Congressional investigation took place in 1792, "to inquire into the causes of the failure of the late expedition under Major General Arthur St. Clair," who had been defeated by Indians in the Northwest Territory.

• Joseph G. Cannon of Illinois had a total, but not continuous, service in the House of Representatives of 50 years, beginning in 1873 —a record that has not been broken.

• Sam Rayburn (D-Texas) holds the record for longest continuous service in the House of Representatives, nearly 49 years at the time of his death on November 16, 1961. During 17 of those years (interrupted by Republican majorities in 1947–49 and 1953–55) he served as Speaker of the House, twice as long as any previous Speaker.

• Thomas J. Dodd of Connecticut was the seventh Senator to be censured (1967) by his colleagues.

• The House has expelled 3 members, censured 17, and denied admission to 4 members-elect.

# U.S. FEDERAL JUDICIARY

Source: Administrative Office of the U.S. Courts

The U.S. Supreme Court, the highest court of the nation, was established by Article 3 of the Constitution. Section 1 of Article 3 provides for vesting the judicial power of the United States in one supreme court and in such inferior courts as Congress establishes.

The Federal judiciary interprets the Federal laws, certain U.S. treaties, and the Constitution. In addition, it has jurisdiction in disputes between states, in maritime cases, in cases involving representatives of other nations, in all controversies in which the Federal government is itself a party, and in legal cases involving citizens of two different states, where an amount of more than $10,000 is involved.

Cases come to the Federal courts along three routes: (1) they may be of such a nature as to start there, (2) they may be removed from a state court, or (3) they may be appealed from a state court. The organization of the Federal courts starts with the U.S. Supreme Court. The nine justices of the Supreme Court are appointed for life by the President, with the approval of the Senate. Below it are the ten U.S. Courts of Appeals (each with jurisdiction over a definite territory) and a Court of Appeals for the District of Columbia. Next are the U.S. District Courts, with 90 Federal judicial districts. There are also U.S. Territorial Judges and courts of special jurisdiction.

---

## JUDICIAL REVIEW

The Constitution of the United States divides the powers of government among three branches, but nowhere does it say which branch should have the final say on what the Constitution means. Although today most people accept without question the right of the Supreme Court (or judicial branch) to determine whether or not a law is constitutional, this power was not assumed by the Court until Chief Justice Marshall did so in the famous 1803 decision in *Marbury* v. *Madison*.

Today the Supreme Court rules on this question, but only after a law has been passed and a case involving the law has been brought before it. There are two major areas in which the Supreme Court may determine constitutionality: cases in which a Federal law is in conflict with the Constitution and cases in which a state law may be in conflict with the supreme law.

---

## FEDERAL IMPEACHMENT

An impeachment is a formal accusation charging a public official with a crime or other serious misconduct. The term is also applied, more loosely, to the trial that follows the accusation.

Under the U.S. Constitution, the "President, Vice President and all civil officers of the United States," but not Congressmen, may be impeached for treason, bribery, or "other high crimes and misdemeanors." Impeachments are voted by the House of Representatives and tried by the Senate sitting as a Court of Impeachment. A two-thirds vote of the Senators present is necessary for conviction. The Chief Justice of the U.S. Supreme Court presides over the Court of Impeachment when a President is tried.

Persons found guilty by the Court of Impeachment may be removed from office and disqualified from holding further office. They are, moreover, subject to subsequent criminal trial for the same offense.

The Senate has sat as a Court of Impeachment in the cases of the following accused officials:

- **William Blount,** a Senator of the United States from Tennessee; charges dismissed for want of Senatorial jurisdiction in 1798–99.
- **John Pickering,** judge of the United States district court for the district of New Hampshire; removed from office in 1803–04.
- **Samuel Chase,** Associate Justice of the Supreme Court of the United States; acquitted in 1804–05.
- **James H. Peck,** judge of the United States district court for the district of Missouri; acquitted in 1830–31.
- **West H. Humphreys,** judge of the United States district court for Tennessee; removed from office in 1862.
- **Andrew Johnson,** President of the United States; acquitted in 1868.
- **William W. Belknap,** Secretary of War; acquitted in 1876.
- **Charles Swayne,** judge of the United States district court for the northern district of Florida; acquitted in 1904–05.
- **Robert W. Archbald,** associate judge, United States Commerce Court; removed from office in 1912–13.
- **George W. English,** judge of the United States district court for the eastern district of Illinois; resigned office November 4, 1926; Court of Impeachment adjourned to December 13, 1926, when, on request of House managers, impeachment proceedings were dismissed.
- **Harold Louderback,** judge of the United States district court for the northern district of California; acquitted in 1933.
- **Halsted L. Ritter,** judge of the United States district court for the southern district of Florida; removed from office in 1936.

## SUPREME COURT OF THE UNITED STATES
Washington, D.C.

**Chief Justice** (Salary: $40,000): Earl Warren of California.
**Associate Justices** (Salaries: $39,500): Hugo L. Black of Alabama; William O. Douglas of Connecticut; John M. Harlan of New York; William J. Brennan, Jr., of New Jersey; Potter Stewart of Ohio; Byron R. White of Colorado; Abe Fortas of Tennessee; Thurgood Marshall of New York.

### ■ U.S. COURTS OF APPEALS
(Salaries: $33,000)
**District of Columbia Circuit:** David L. Bazelon, Chief Judge; John A. Danaher, Warren E. Burger, J. Skelly Wright, Carl McGowan, Edward Allen Tamm, Harold Leventhal, Spottswood W. Robinson, III, all from Washington, D.C.
**First Circuit** (Maine, Massachusetts, New Hampshire, Rhode Island, Puerto Rico): Baily Aldrich, Chief Judge, Boston, Mass.; Edward M. McEntee, Providence, R.I.; Frank M. Coffin, Portland, Me.
**Second Circuit** (Connecticut, New York, Vermont): J. Edward Lumbard, Chief Judge, New York, N.Y.; Sterry R. Waterman, St. Johnsbury, Vt.; Leonard P. Moore, Henry J. Friendly, both from New York, N.Y.; J. Joseph Smith, Hartford, Conn.; Irving R. Kaufman, Paul R. Hays, both from New York, N.Y.; Robert P. Anderson, Hartford, Conn.; Wilfred Feinberg, New York, N.Y.
**Third Circuit** (Delaware, New Jersey, Pennsylvania, Virgin Islands): Austin L. Staley, Chief Judge, Pittsburgh, Penn.; Gerald McLaughlin, Newark, N.J.; Harry E. Kalodner, Philadelphia, Penn.; William Henry Hastie, Philadelphia, Penn.; William F. Smith, Newark, N.J.; Abraham L. Freedman, Philadelphia, Penn.; Collins J. Seitz, Wilmington, Del.; Francis L. Van Dusen, Philadelphia, Penn.
**Fourth Circuit** (Maryland, North Carolina, South Carolina, Virgina, West Virginia): Clement F. Haynsworth, Jr., Chief Judge, Greenville, S.C.; Simon E. Sobeloff, Baltimore, Md.; Herbert S. Boremen, Parkersburg, W. Va.; Albert V. Bryan, Alexandria, Va.; Harrison L. Winter, Baltimore, Md.; J. Braxton Craven, Jr., Shelby, N.C.; John D. Butzner, Jr., Richmond, Va.
**Fifth Circuit** (Alabama, Florida, Georgia, Louisiana, Mississippi, Texas, Canal Zone): John R. Brown, Chief Judge, Houston, Texas; Elbert Parr Tuttle, Atlanta, Ga.; John Minor Wisdom, New Orleans, La.; Walter Pettus Gewin, Tuscaloosa, Ala.; Griffin B. Bell, Atlanta, Ga.; Homer Thornberry, Austin, Texas; James P. Coleman, Aberdeen, Miss.; Irving L. Goldberg, Dallas, Texas; Robert A. Ainsworth, Jr.; New Orleans, La.; John C. Godbold, Montgomery, Ala.; David W. Dyer, Miami, Fla.; Bryan Simpson, Jacksonville, Fla.
**Sixth Circuit** (Kentucky, Michigan, Ohio, Tennessee): Paul C. Weick, Chief Judge, Akron, Ohio; Clifford O'Sullivan, Port Huron, Mich.; Harry Phillips, Nashville, Tenn.; George Clifton Edwards, Jr., Detroit, Mich.; Anthony J. Celebrezze, Cleveland, Ohio; John W. Peck,

Cincinnati, Ohio; Wade Hampton McCree, Jr., Detroit, Mich.; Bert T. Combs, Louisville, Ky.
**Seventh Circuit** (Illinois, Indiana, Wisconsin): John S. Hastings, Chief Judge, Chicago, Ill.; Elmer J. Schnackenberg, Win G. Knoch, Latham Castle, Roger J. Kiley, both from Chicago, Ill.; Thomas E. Fairchild, Milwaukee, Wis.; Walter J. Cummings, Jr., Chicago, Ill.
**Eighth Circuit** (Arkansas, Iowa, Minnesota, Missouri, Nebraska, North Dakota, South Dakota): Charles J. Vogel, Chief Judge, Fargo, N. Dak.; Martin D. Van Oosterhout, Sioux City, Iowa; M. C. Matthes, St. Louis, Mo.; Harry A. Blackmun, Winona, Minn.; Pat Mehaffy, Little Rock, Ark.; Floyd R. Gibson, Kansas City, Mo.; Donald P. Lay, Omaha, Nebr.; Gerald W. Heaney, Duluth, Minn.
**Ninth Circuit** (Arizona, California, Idaho, Montana, Nevada, Oregon, Washington, Alaska, Hawaii, Guam): Richard H. Chambers, Chief Judge, Tucson, Ariz.; Stanley N. Barnes, Los Angeles, Calif.; Frederick G. Hamley, San Francisco, Calif.; Gilbert H. Jertberg, Fresno, Calif.; Charles M. Merrill, M. Oliver Koelsch, both from San Francisco, Calif.; James R. Browning, Great Falls, Mont.; Ben Cushing Duniway, San Francisco, Calif.; Walter Ely, Los Angeles, Calif.
**Tenth Circuit** (Colorado, Kansas, New Mexico, Oklahoma, Utah, Wyoming): Alfred P. Murrah, Chief Judge, Oklahoma City, Okla.; David T. Lewis, Salt Lake City, Utah; Jean S. Breitenstein, Denver, Colo.; Delmas C. Hill, Wichita, Kans.; Oliver Seth, Santa Fe, N. Mex.; John J. Hickey, Cheyenne, Wyo.

### ■ U.S. DISTRICT COURTS
Judges of U.S. District Courts receive yearly salaries of $30,000; the Chief Justice of the District of Columbia gets $30,500.

### ■ U.S. TERRITORIAL JUDGES
The three District Judges serve eight-year terms and receive salaries of $30,000 per year.

### ■ U.S. COURT OF CLAIMS
Washington, D.C. 20005
**Chief Judge:** Wilson Cowen.
**Associate Judges:** Don N. Laramore, James R. Durfee, Oscar H. Davis, Linton M. Collins, Byron G. Skelton, Philip Nichols, Jr. (Salaries: $33,000)

### ■ U.S. COURT OF CUSTOMS AND PATENT APPEALS
Washington, D.C. 20439
**Chief Judge:** Eugene Worley.
**Associate Judges:** Giles S. Rich, Arthur M. Smith, J. L. Almond, Jr. (Salaries: $33,000)

### ■ U.S. CUSTOMS COURT
201 Varick Street, New York, N.Y. 10014
**Chief Judge:** Paul P. Rao.
**Judges:** Morgan Ford, Scovel Richardson, Frederick Landis, James L. Watson, Lindley G. Beckworth. (Salaries: $30,000)

## U.S. SUPREME COURT: 1967

After devoting much of the past 13 years to lowering racial barriers, the U.S. Supreme Court in 1967 marked time in the area of civil rights and concentrated on cases involving the rights of criminal suspects. Ironically, however, on August 30 the Senate confirmed the appointment to the Court of Thurgood Marshall, who as NAACP counsel had led a 23-year legal battle culminating in the historic 1954 school desegregation decision.

Marshall, former U.S. Solicitor General and previously a federal court judge, is the first Negro to serve on the Court. He replaced Justice Tom C. Clark, who retired when his son Ramsey was appointed U.S. Attorney General. Opinions differed as to whether Marshall's appointment would change the alignment of the Court, which had divided 5 to 4 in favor of the liberal wing on many decisions. Although Marshall had been active most of his professional life as a civil rights lawyer, he was considered to be a legal conservative on most other issues.

Many Court decisions in 1967 emphasized the fact that it is not easy to predict how members of the Court will vote in any given case. Justice Clark, long a member of the so-called conservative wing of the Court, last year joined the liberals in overruling legalized wiretapping in New York. Justice Hugo Black, who has generally leaned in the liberal direction, voted to uphold the conviction of Negro civil rights demonstrators in Florida and to give the Georgia legislature the right to elect a governor when no candidate received a majority of the popular vote. Justice White, regarded as a conservative, ruled with the majority in a 5–4 decision declaring unconstitutional California's Proposition 14, which would have abolished the state's fair-housing laws.

In its 177th term the Court moved to curb police powers and to liberalize the rights of criminal suspects. In addition to overturning a New York statute that permitted court-approved electronic eavesdropping, the Court decided that suspects are entitled to counsel at

Justice Tom Clark swearing in his son, Ramsey Clark, as the 66th U.S. Attorney General on March 10, 1967.

Wide World

police lineups. In another decision the Court ruled that youngsters in juvenile court proceedings must be given some of the rights that adults have in criminal trials.

In balancing the rights of criminal suspects against those of law enforcement agencies, the Court faced its first direct confrontation with Congress since the clash over President Roosevelt's New Deal programs. Urban riots and such heinous crimes as the mass murder of nine student nurses in Chicago in 1966 aroused public concern, and Congress considered legislation that would limit the scope of recent Court decisions in favor of more stringent police powers.

Although the Court's position is that without the protection granted by the Bill of Rights there can be no truly democratic process, not all its rulings in 1967 directly benefited criminal suspects. The Court widened the area of evidence admissible in trials and gave the police the right to arrest and search suspects if they had reliable tips from informers. The Court also promised to reconsider at its next session the matter of police eavesdropping and other aids to law enforcement.

The Supreme Court in 1967 no longer appeared to be the catalyst for social and political change that it was ten years ago. In addition to deciding against the civil rights demonstrators in Florida, the Court upheld the 1963 conviction of Dr. Martin Luther King and other civil rights leaders who ignored an Alabama court injunction against marching in Birmingham. The Court was silent on reapportionment, poverty, and separation of church and state, and it refused to become involved in the controversy over the legality of the Vietnam war.

There were, however, some important decisions involving social problems and individual rights. In addition to striking down California's Proposition 14, the Court overturned Virginia's anti-miscegenation law and declared unconstitutional the New York State Regents' loyalty oath. The court also ruled that property owners may refuse to admit health, fire, and other inspectors without search warrants.

Thurgood Marshall, first Negro Supreme Court Justice

United Press Int'l.

## HISTORIC SUPREME COURT DECISIONS

■ **1803** *Marbury* v. *Madison:* William Marbury was appointed a justice of the peace a few weeks before President John Adams's term expired. When the succeeding administration refused to deliver his commission, Marbury petitioned the Supreme Court for a writ of mandamus to compel Secretary of State James Madison to issue a commission. The Court conceded that Marbury was entitled to some redress, but dismissed the case for lack of jurisdiction. Marbury had based his case on the Judiciary Act of 1789, which authorized the Supreme Court to take original jurisdiction over such controversies. Under Article III, Section 2 of the Constitution, Supreme Court jurisdiction over such matters begins at the appellate level. Therefore, the Judiciary Act was void to the extent that it gave the Court powers implicitly denied by the Constitution.

*Significance:* The decision established the principal of "judicial review," whereby the Court has jurisdiction to pass on acts of the legislature.

■ **1819** *McCulloch* v. *Maryland:* Congress chartered a federal bank in 1816 to control unregulated issuances of currency by state banks. Maryland then imposed a tax on notes issued by the U.S. Bank's Baltimore branch. The branch refused to pay, and Maryland sued to collect; at the same time it challenged Congressional authority to charter a bank. The Court ruled that this was within the implied powers of government, that acts of Congress not expressly authorized were valid so long as they remained within the "letter and spirit" of the Constitution. It declared further that federal instrumentalities are not subject to state taxes.

*Significance:* The decision sanctioned "loose," or liberal, interpretation of the Constitution.

■ **1824** *Gibbons* v. *Ogden:* Aaron Ogden, part owner of a steamboat operation monopoly established by New York statute, challenged the right of Thomas Gibbons to operate a rival steamboat service between New Jersey and New York under Federal license. The Court declared the New York statute unconstitutional because it conflicted with Congressional power to regulate commerce.

*Significance:* The decision became the basis for the sweeping exercise of Federal power over commerce, beginning with the Interstate Commerce Act of 1887.

■ **1852** *Cooley* v. *Wardens of the Port of Philadelphia:* The case involved the constitutionality of a Pennsylvania statute regulating navigation in the Port of Philadelphia. Much of the traffic in and out of the harbor was interstate. The question arose as to whether the power to regulate commerce rests exclusively with Congress. In ruling that it did not, the Court noted that some commerce, although technically interstate, is essentially local in character. Federal control is not really necessary, and until it is, states and municipalities are free to act according to local needs.

*Significance:* The decision established the rule that in an area of overlapping jurisdiction

the state may act in the absence of Federal legislation.

■ **1857** *Dred Scott* v. *Sanford:* Dred Scott, a Missouri slave, was at one time taken into free territory, where an Act of Congress (the Missouri Compromise) prohibited slavery. Several years after his return to Missouri, Scott sued for freedom, claiming he had acquired it through residence in free territory. The decision centered on two principals: First, that Scott, being a Negro, was not a U.S. citizen and therefore could not petition Federal courts. Second, that the Missouri Compromise was unconstitutional; slaves were like any other property, the Court said, and under the Fifth Amendment Congress could pass no law depriving citizens of their private property.

*Significance:* The decision, acclaimed in the South and bitterly denounced in the North, brought the nation a step closer to civil war.

■ **1937** *NLRB* v. *Jones & Laughlin Steel Corporation:* In upholding the authority of the National Labor Relations Board to regulate industrial labor relations, the Court ruled that the Federal government has jurisdiction over any dispute that will interfere with interstate commerce. The case grew out of a labor dispute in a Pennsylvania steel plant. Iron ore was shipped into the plant from other states, processed, then shipped to warehouses in Detroit, Memphis, and other cities. A work stoppage in Pennsylvania would directly affect the company's operations in other states. The court ruled that because the manufacturing process was so closely linked to interstate commerce, its control was essential to "protect that commerce from burdens and obstructions."

*Significance:* The decision broadened the definition of interstate commerce to include all activities that would affect its flow, either directly or indirectly.

■ **1954** *Brown* v. *Board of Education of Topeka:* In this case the Supreme Court set aside a Kansas statute authorizing segregation in primary schools. The decision declared that the "separate but equal" doctrine, established in *Plessy* v. *Ferguson* (1896), in fact denied equal protection under the Fourteenth Amendment and was unconstitutional. The verdict directed lower courts to use their authority to implement desegregation of elementary public schools.

*Significance:* This was the first time the Court declared segregation unconstitutional. From the decision evolved a body of legislation and court action aimed at eradicating discrimination in schools, housing, employment, voting, and other areas.

■ **1957** *Roth* v. *United States:* Statutes barring the distribution of obscene or indecent material have generally been upheld as a valid exercise of the state's police power. The decision as to what constitutes obscenity has undergone endless revision by the courts. In an effort to resolve the question, the Court in the Roth case defined obscenity as "that which deals with sex in a manner appealing to prurient interests." This definition continued to be modified until finally the Court ruled in 1966 in the *Fanny Hill* case that a publication must be "utterly without redeeming social value" before it can be labeled obscene.

*Significance:* Concern for freedom of expression has led to an increasing reluctance on the part of the Court to ban literary works on grounds of obscenity.

■ **1961** *Mapp* v. *Ohio:* Despite statutory protection against illegal search and seizure, some states permitted admission of illegally obtained evidence against defendants in criminal trials. The Federal courts uniformly rejected such evidence. In this appeal of an Ohio woman's conviction, the Court ruled that admission of illegally obtained evidence is unconstitutional.

*Significance:* Eliminating a long-standing difference between rules of state and Federal courts, the decision limited state authorities to investigation procedure conforming with provisions of the Fourth Amendment, which specifically prohibits unreasonable searches and seizures.

■ **1962** *Engel* v. *Vitale:* A nondenominational prayer written by the New York State Board of Regents for voluntary recital in the public schools was ruled unconstitutional as a violation of the First Amendment. The Amendment provides that the state "shall make no laws respecting the establishment of religion or prohibiting the free exercise thereof." The opinion stated that by writing the prayer the Board exceeded its authority.

A year later, in *School District of Abbington Township* v. *Schmepp,* the Court banned Bible reading and recitation of the Lord's Prayer in public schools on grounds that it tended to establish a state religion.

*Significance:* In order to maintain a strict separation between church and state, the state may not prescribe any kind of religious exercise for public schools.

■ **1962** *Baker et al.* v. *Carr:* In a decision involving the basic political structure, the Court ruled that Federal courts have the power to review legislative apportionment. As a result of large population shifts, many legislative districts were unevenly drawn and voters were denied the right to "equal protection" guaranteed by the Fourteenth Amendment. The Baker case led to a number of decisions in 1964 calling for reapportionment on a "one man, one vote" basis. Congressional districts, the Court ruled, must be "substantially equal" in population, and both houses of the state legislature must be reapportioned on the basis of population.

*Significance:* Political districts, which often were drawn to favor rural areas, were ordered redrawn to give increased voting strength to city and suburban residents.

■ **1963** *Gideon* v. *Wainright:* The Court unanimously ruled that states must provide free legal counsel to indigent defendants in all criminal cases involving a felony. Previously the obligation to supply counsel applied only in cases involving the death penalty or in cases where the defendant by reason of youth, men-

tal subnormality, or similar disability could not adequately conduct his own defense. The Court held that Clarence Gideon, a Florida resident serving a five-year sentence for burglary, was denied his constitutional right to counsel when his request for a court-appointed lawyer was turned down. A new trial was ordered.

*Significance:* All persons charged with a felony are entitled to court-appointed counsel if they cannot afford to retain a counsel of their own.

■ **1964** *Escobedo* v. *Illinois:* Escobedo was taken into custody as a suspect in a murder case. He was not advised of his right to remain silent; nor was his request to speak to his attorney granted. The Court ruled that such police procedure was unconstitutional on two grounds. First, failure of the police to warn the defendant of his right to remain silent violated the Fifth Amendment. Second, refusal to permit the defendant to consult his attorney violated the right-to-counsel guarantee. The Court ruled that these rights come into effect as soon as the investigation begins to focus on a particular suspect.

*Significance:* The Fifth Amendment privilege against self-incrimination and the Sixth Amendment right to counsel were extended to police interrogations as well as courtroom proceedings.

■ **1964** *New York Times* v. *Sullivan:* The case revolved around a full-page advertisement placed in the *Times* by Dr. Martin Luther King, Jr., and other civil rights leaders. Many statements in the ad—charging that Negroes in Montgomery, Alabama, were being abused —proved false. Sullivan, a Montgomery city official, was subsequently awarded a $500,000 libel judgment. The Court reversed the judgment, ruling that criticism of official conduct cannot be termed libelous without showing actual malice, which is knowledge that the statement was false or reckless disregard for whether or not it was false.

*Significance:* The decision, hailed as a major gain for the news media, gave them greater freedom in reporting the news by limiting their liability for libel.

■ **1966** *Miranda* v. *Arizona:* In one of the most controversial decisions of its history, the Court overturned the conviction of an Arizona man charged with rape and kidnapping, on grounds that his voluntary confession was obtained illegally. The decision, incorporating the principals of the Wainwright and Escobedo cases, invalidated any confessions or incriminating admissions unless the suspect is warned that he may remain silent, that anything he says may be held against him, that he has a right to have a lawyer present, and that if he cannot afford one, he is entitled to court-appointed counsel. If the suspect waives counsel and confesses, there is a "heavy burden" on the prosecution to show a knowing waiver of rights.

*Significance:* The decision has drawn strong criticism from law-enforcement officers, who charge that it will interfere substantially with the administration of criminal justice.

## MEMBERS OF THE U.S. SUPREME COURT

| CHIEF JUSTICES | PLACE OF BIRTH | DATE OF BIRTH | EDUCATION |
|---|---|---|---|
| Jay, John | New York | 1745 | King's College (now Columbia University), grad. 1764 |
| Rutledge, John * | South Carolina | 1739 | Studied law at Middle Temple, London |
| Ellsworth, Oliver | Connecticut | 1745 | College of New Jersey (now Princeton University), grad. 1766. |
| Marshall, John | Virginia | 1755 | Attended College of William and Mary |
| Taney, Roger Brooke | Maryland | 1777 | Dickinson College, Penn., grad. 1795 |
| Chase, Salmon Portland | New Hampshire | 1808 | Dartmouth College, grad. 1826 |
| Waite, Morrison Remick | Connecticut | 1816 | Yale College, grad. 1837 |
| Fuller, Melville Weston | Maine | 1833 | Bowdoin College, grad. 1853; attended Harvard Law School |
| White, Edward Douglass | Louisiana | 1845 | Attended Mount St. Mary's College, Md.; Jesuit College in New Orleans, La.; and Georgetown College, Washington, D.C. |
| Taft, William Howard | Ohio | 1857 | Yale College, grad. 1878; Cincinnati Law School, LL.B. 1880 |
| Hughes, Charles Evans | New York | 1862 | Brown University, Rhode Island, grad. 1881; M.A. 1884; attended Columbia Law School |
| Stone, Harlan Fiske | New Hampshire | 1872 | Amherst College, Mass., grad. 1894; Columbia Law School, LL.B. |
| Vinson, Frederick Moore | Kentucky | 1890 | Centre College, Kentucky, grad. 1909; LL.B. 1911 |
| Warren, Earl | California | 1891 | University of California, LL.B. 1912; J.D. 1914 |
| ASSOCIATE JUSTICES (from 1900) | | | |
| Holmes, Oliver Wendell | Massachusetts | 1841 | Harvard College, grad. 1861; LL.B. 1866 |
| Day, William Rufus | Ohio | 1849 | University of Michigan, grad. 1870 |
| Moody, William Henry | Massachusetts | 1853 | Harvard College, grad. 1876; attended Harvard Law School |
| Lurton, Horace Harmon | Kentucky | 1844 | Attended Douglas University, Chicago (now University of Chicago); Cumberland University, Tenn., LL.B. 1867 |
| Van Devanter, Willis | Indiana | 1859 | Attended Indiana Asbury (now De Pauw) University; Cincinnati Law School, LL.B. 1881 |
| Lamar, Joseph Rucker | Georgia | 1857 | Bethany College, W. Va., grad. 1877; studied law, Washington and Lee University, Va. |
| Pitney, Mahlon | New Jersey | 1858 | College of New Jersey (now Princeton University), grad. 1879. |
| McReynolds, James Clark | Kentucky | 1862 | Vanderbilt University, Tenn., grad. 1882; University of Virginia Law School, LL.B. 1884 |
| Brandeis, Louis Dembitz | Kentucky | 1856 | Harvard Law School, LL.B. 1877 |
| Clarke, John Hessin | Ohio | 1857 | Western Reserve University, Ohio, grad. 1877 |
| Sutherland, George | England | 1862 | Studied law at the University of Michigan |
| Butler, Pierce | Minnesota | 1866 | Carleton College, Minn., grad. 1887 |
| Sanford, Edward Terry | Tennessee | 1865 | University of Tennessee, grad. 1883; Harvard University, M.A. 1889; Harvard Law School, LL.B. 1889 |
| Roberts, Owen Josephus | Pennsylvania | 1875 | University of Pennsylvania, grad. 1895; LL.B. 1898 |
| Cardozo, Benjamin Nathan | New York | 1870 | Columbia University, grad. 1889; M.A. 1890; attended Columbia Law School |
| Black, Hugo Lafayette | Alabama | 1886 | University of Alabama, Law School, LL.B. 1906 |
| Reed, Stanley Forman | Kentucky | 1884 | Kentucky Wesleyan College, grad. 1902; also Yale University, grad. 1906; studied law at Columbia University |
| Frankfurter, Felix | Austria | 1882 | City College of New York, grad. 1902; Harvard Law School, LL.B. 1906 |
| Douglas, William Orville | Minnesota | 1898 | Whitman College, Wash., grad. 1920; Columbia Law School, LL.B. |
| Murphy, Frank | Michigan | 1890 | University of Michigan, LL.B. 1914; studied law at Lincoln's Inn, London, and Trinity College, Dublin |
| Byrnes, James Francis | South Carolina | 1879 | No record of formal education |
| Jackson, Robert Houghwout | New York | 1892 | Attended Albany (N.Y.) Law School |
| Rutledge, Wiley Blount | Kentucky | 1894 | University of Wisconsin, grad. 1914; University of Colorado, LL.B. |
| Burton, Harold Hitz | Massachusetts | 1888 | Bowdoin College, Me., grad. 1909; Harvard Law School, LL.B. 1912 |
| Clark, Thomas Campbell | Texas | 1899 | University of Texas, grad. 1921; LL.B. 1922 |
| Minton, Sherman | Indiana | 1890 | Indiana University, LL.B. 1915 |
| Harlan, John Marshall | Illinois | 1899 | Princeton University, grad. 1920; Rhodes Scholar to Oxford University, 1921–23; New York Law School, LL.B. 1924 |
| Brennan, William Joseph, Jr. | New Jersey | 1906 | University of Pennsylvania, grad. 1928; Harvard Law School, LL.B. 1931 |
| Whittaker, Charles Evans | Kansas | 1901 | University of Kansas City, LL.B. 1924 |
| Stewart, Potter | Michigan | 1915 | Yale University, grad. 1937; attended Cambridge University, England; Yale Law School, LL.B. 1941 |
| White, Byron Raymond | Colorado | 1917 | University of Colorado, grad. 1938; Rhodes Scholar, Oxford, England, 1939; Yale Law School, LL.B. 1946 |
| Goldberg, Arthur J. | Illinois | 1908 | Northwestern University, grad. 1929; J.D. 1930 |
| Fortas, Abe | Tennessee | 1910 | Southwestern College, grad. 1930; Yale Law School, LL.B. 1933. |
| Marshall, Thurgood | Maryland | 1908 | Lincoln University, grad. 1929; Howard University, LL.B. 1933. |

* The U.S. Senate refused to confirm his appointment as Chief Justice.

| APPOINTED BY PRESIDENT | DATE OATH TAKEN | AGE AT OATH | DATE SERVICE ENDED | SERVICE ENDED BY | YEARS OF SERVICE | AGE AT END OF TERM | DATE OF DEATH |
|---|---|---|---|---|---|---|---|
| Washington..... | Oct. 1789 | 44 | June 1795 | resigned | 5 | 49 | May 1829 |
| Washington..... | Aug. 1795 | 55 | Dec. 1795 | rejected | 0 | 56 | June 1800 |
| Washington..... | Mar. 1796 | 50 | Dec. 1800 | resigned | 4 | 55 | Nov. 1807 |
| Adams......... | Feb. 1801 | 45 | July 1835 | death | 34 | 79 | July 1835 |
| Jackson........ | Mar. 1836 | 59 | Oct. 1864 | death | 28 | 87 | Oct. 1864 |
| Lincoln........ | Dec. 1864 | 56 | May 1873 | death | 8 | 65 | May 1873 |
| Grant.......... | Mar. 1874 | 57 | Mar. 1888 | death | 14 | 71 | Mar. 1888 |
| Cleveland...... | Oct. 1888 | 55 | July 1910 | death | 21 | 77 | July 1910 |
| Taft........... | Dec. 1910 | 65 | May 1921 | death | 10 | 75 | May 1921 |
| Harding........ | July 1921 | 63 | Feb. 1930 | retired | 8 | 72 | Mar. 1930 |
| Hoover......... | Feb. 1930 | 67 | June 1941 | retired | 11 | 79 | Aug. 1948 |
| Roosevelt, F.... | July 1941 | 68 | Apr. 1946 | death | 4 | 73 | Apr. 1946 |
| Truman........ | June 1946 | 56 | Sept. 1953 | death | 7 | 63 | Sept. 1953 |
| Eisenhower..... | Oct. 1953 | 62 | — | — | — | — | — |
| Roosevelt, T.... | Dec. 1902 | 61 | Jan. 1932 | retired | 29 | 90 | Mar. 1935 |
| Roosevelt, T.... | Mar. 1903 | 53 | Nov. 1922 | retired | 19 | 73 | July 1923 |
| Roosevelt, T.... | Dec. 1906 | 52 | Nov. 1910 | disabled | 3 | 56 | July 1917 |
| Taft........... | Jan. 1910 | 65 | July 1914 | death | 4 | 70 | July 1914 |
| Taft........... | Jan. 1911 | 51 | June 1937 | retired | 26 | 78 | Feb. 1941 |
| Taft........... | Jan. 1911 | 53 | Jan. 1916 | death | 4 | 58 | Jan. 1916 |
| Taft........... | Mar. 1912 | 54 | Dec. 1922 | disabled | 10 | 64 | Dec. 1924 |
| Wilson......... | Oct. 1914 | 52 | Jan. 1941 | retired | 26 | 78 | Aug. 1946 |
| Wilson......... | June 1916 | 59 | Feb. 1939 | retired | 22 | 82 | Oct. 1941 |
| Wilson......... | Oct. 1916 | 59 | Sept. 1922 | resigned | 5 | 65 | Mar. 1945 |
| Harding........ | Oct. 1922 | 60 | Jan. 1938 | retired | 15 | 75 | July 1942 |
| Harding........ | Jan. 1923 | 56 | Nov. 1939 | death | 16 | 73 | Nov. 1939 |
| Harding........ | Feb. 1923 | 57 | Mar. 1930 | death | 7 | 64 | Mar. 1930 |
| Hoover......... | June 1930 | 55 | July 1945 | resigned | 15 | 70 | May 1955 |
| Hoover......... | Mar. 1932 | 61 | July 1938 | death | 6 | 68 | July 1938 |
| Roosevelt, F.... | Aug. 1937 | 51 | — | — | — | — | — |
| Roosevelt, F.... | Jan. 1938 | 53 | Feb. 1957 | retired | 19 | 72 | — |
| Roosevelt, F.... | Jan. 1939 | 56 | Aug. 1962 | retired | 23 | 79 | Feb. 1965 |
| Roosevelt, F.... | Apr. 1939 | 40 | — | — | — | — | — |
| Roosevelt, F.... | Feb. 1940 | 49 | July 1949 | death | 9 | 59 | July 1949 |
| Roosevelt, F.... | July 1941 | 62 | Oct. 1942 | resigned | 1 | 63 | — |
| Roosevelt, F.... | July 1941 | 49 | Oct. 1954 | death | 13 | 62 | Oct. 1954 |
| Roosevelt, F.... | Feb. 1943 | 48 | Sept. 1949 | death | 6 | 55 | Sept. 1949 |
| Truman........ | Oct. 1945 | 57 | Oct. 1958 | retired | 13 | 70 | Oct. 1964 |
| Truman........ | Aug. 1949 | 49 | June 1967 | retired | 17 | 67 | — |
| Truman........ | Oct. 1949 | 58 | Oct. 1956 | retired | 7 | 65 | Apr. 1965 |
| Eisenhower..... | Mar. 1955 | 55 | — | — | — | — | — |
| Eisenhower..... | Oct. 1956 | 50 | — | — | — | — | — |
| Eisenhower..... | Mar. 1957 | 56 | Apr. 1962 | retired | 5 | 61 | — |
| Eisenhower..... | Oct. 1958 | 43 | — | — | — | — | — |
| Kennedy....... | Apr. 1962 | 44 | — | — | — | — | — |
| Kennedy....... | Oct. 1962 | 54 | July 1965 | resigned | 3 | 57 | — |
| Johnson........ | Oct. 1965 | 55 | — | — | — | — | — |
| Johnson ....... | Oct. 1967 | 59 | — | — | — | — | — |

# DIPLOMATIC REPRESENTATIVES

Official communication between nations is carried out under a system generally accepted in international law. Before two nations can actually have official interchanges, diplomatic recognition—a mutual admission that the government of the other nation is actually the legitimate ruling body—must be established.

Recognition sets the stage for diplomatic relations among nations. Channels of official exchange are protected by the principle of diplomatic immunity, which exempts diplomatic representatives from local jurisdiction so that they may perform their official functions with complete freedom, independence, and security.

The United States adheres to a broad interpretation of diplomatic immunity, emphasizing the inviolability of the diplomatic agent's person and the national advantage that is served by the untrammeled exercise of his functions. At the same time, it considers that a person entitled to diplomatic immunity is not relieved thereby from the obligation to respect U.S. laws. If he performs actions that endanger the safety of the nation, the United States holds that the proper remedy is not to subject him to its jurisdiction but rather to ask for his immediate recall.

In the table of principal diplomatic representatives below, between the United States and a number of foreign nations, a dash (—) indicates no listing by the U.S. Department of State as of May, 1967.

| FROM UNITED STATES TO FOREIGN NATION: | COUNTRY: | FROM FOREIGN NATION TO UNITED STATES: |
|---|---|---|
| Robert G. Neumann | AFGHANISTAN | Abdullah Malikyar |
| John D. Jernegan | ALGERIA | Cherif Guellal |
| Edwin M. Martin | ARGENTINA | Alvaro C. Alsogaray |
| Edward A. Clark | AUSTRALIA | John Keith Waller, C.B.E. |
| Douglas MacArthur II | AUSTRIA | Dr. Ernst Lemberger |
| Turner B. Shelton | BAHAMAS | (British Ambassador) |
| Ridgway B. Knight | BELGIUM | Baron Louis Scheyven |
| George W. Renchard | BERMUDA | (British Ambassador) |
| Douglas Henderson | BOLIVIA | Julio Sanjines-Goytia |
| | BOTSWANA | Zachariah Keodirelang Matthews |
| John W. Tuthill | BRAZIL | Vasco Leitao da Cunha |
| John M. McSweeney | BULGARIA | Dr. Luben Guerassimov |
| Henry A. Byroade | BURMA | U Tun Win |
| | BURUNDI | Terence Nsanze |
| Robert L. Payton | CAMEROON | Joseph N. Owono |
| W. Walton Butterworth | CANADA | A. Edgar Ritchie |
| | CENTRAL AFRICAN REPUBLIC | Michel Gallin-Douathe |
| Cecil B. Lyon | CEYLON | Oliver Weerasinghe, O.B.E. |
| | CHAD | Boukar Abdoul |
| Ralph A. Dungan | CHILE | Radomiro Tomic |
| Walter P. McConaughy | CHINA (Taiwan) | Chow Shu-kai |
| Reynold E. Carlson | COLOMBIA | Dr. Hernán Echavarria |
| | DEMOCRATIC REPUBLIC OF THE CONGO | Cyrille Adoula |
| Clarence A. Boonstra | COSTA RICA | Fernando Ortuño |
| Taylor G. Belcher | CYPRUS | Zenon Rossides |
| Jacob D. Beam | CZECHOSLOVAKIA | Dr. Karel Duda |
| Clinton E. Knox | DAHOMEY | Maxime-Leopold Zollner |
| Mrs. Katharine E. White | DENMARK | Torben Rønne |
| John H. Crimmins | DOMINICAN REPUBLIC | Dr. Hector Garcia-Godoy |
| Wymberley DeR. Coerr | ECUADOR | Gustavo Larrea |
| Raul H. Castro | EL SALVADOR | Ramón de Clairmont-Duenas |
| Edward M. Korry | ETHIOPIA | Tashoma Haile-Mariam |
| Tyler Thompson | FINLAND | Olavi Munkki |
| Charles E. Bohlen | FRANCE | Charles Lucet |
| David M. Bane | GABON | Louis Owanga |
| | THE GAMBIA | (British Ambassador) |
| George C. McGhee | GERMANY | Heinrich Knappstein |
| Franklin H. Williams | GHANA | Abraham Benjamin Bah Kofi |
| Phillips Talbot | GREECE | Alexander A. Matsas |
| John Gordon Mein | GUATEMALA | Dr. Francisco Linares Aranda |
| Robinson McIlvaine | GUINEA | Karim Bangoura |
| Delmar R. Carlson | GUYANA | Sir John Carter, Q.C. |
| Benson E. L. Timmons III | HAITI | Arthur Bonhomme |
| Joseph J. Jova | HONDURAS | Ricardo Midence Soto |
| | HUNGARY | János Radványi |
| Karl F. Rolvaag | ICELAND | Petur Thorsteinsson |
| Chester Bowles | INDIA | Braj Kumar Nehru |
| Marshall Green | INDONESIA | Suwito Kusumowidagdo |
| Armin H. Meyer | IRAN | Hassan Motamedi |

| FROM UNITED STATES TO FOREIGN NATION: | COUNTRY: | FROM FOREIGN NATION TO UNITED STATES: |
|---|---|---|
| Robert C. Strong | IRAQ | Nasir Hani |
| Raymond R. Guest | IRELAND | William P. Fay |
| Walworth Barbour | ISRAEL | Avraham Harman |
| G. Frederick Reinhardt | ITALY | Sergio Fenoaltea |
| George A. Morgan | IVORY COAST | Timothée N' Guetta Ahoua |
| Wilson T. M. Beale, Jr. | JAMAICA | Vivian Courtney Smith |
| U. Alexis Johnson | JAPAN | Ryuji Takeuchi |
| Findley Burns, Jr. | JORDAN | Farhan Shubeilat |
| Glenn W. Ferguson | KENYA | Burudi Nabwera |
| Winthrop G. Brown | KOREA (South) | Hyun Chul Kim |
| Howard R. Cottam | KUWAIT | Talat Al-Ghoussein |
| William H. Sullivan | LAOS | Khamking Souvanlasy |
| Dwight J. Porter | LEBANON | Ibrahim Hussein El-Ahdab |
| Ben H. Brown, Jr. | LIBERIA | S. Edward Peal |
| David D. Newsom | LIBYA | Fathi Abidia |
| Mrs. Patricia R. Harris | LUXEMBOURG | Maurice Steinmetz |
| David S. King | MALAGASY REPUBLIC | Louis Rakotomalala |
| Marshall P. Jones | MALAWI | Joseph M. A. Mseka |
| James D. Bell | MALAYSIA | Tan Sri Ong Yoke Lin |
| C. Robert Moore | MALI | Moussa Léo Keita |
| George J. Feldman | MALTA | Dr. Arvid Pardo |
| Geoffrey W. Lewis | MAURITANIA | Abdallahi Ould Daddah |
| Fulton Freeman | MEXICO | Hugo B. Margáin |
| Henry J. Tasca | MOROCCO | Ahmed Osman |
| Miss Carol C. Laise | NEPAL | Major General Padma Bahadur Khatri |
| William R. Tyler | NETHERLANDS | Carl W. A. Schurmann |
| John F. Henning | NEW ZEALAND | Jack Shepherd |
| Aaron S. Brown | NICARAGUA | Dr. Guillermo Sevilla-Sacasa* |
| Robert J. Ryan | NIGER | Adamou Mayaki |
| Elbert G. Mathews | NIGERIA | N. Ade Martins |
| Margaret J. Tibbetts | NORWAY | Arne Gunneng |
| | PAKISTAN | Agha Hilaly |
| Charles W. Adair, Jr. | PANAMA | Ricardo M. Arias E. |
| William P. Snow | PARAGUAY | Dr. Juan Plate |
| J. Wesley Jones | PERU | Celso Pastor |
| William McC. Blair, Jr. | PHILIPPINES | Dr. José F. Imperial |
| John A. Gronouski | POLAND | Zdzislaw Szewczyk |
| W. Tapley Bennett, Jr. | PORTUGAL | Vasco Vieira Garin |
| Richard H. Davis | ROMANIA | Petre Balăceanu |
| Leo G. Cyr | RWANDA | Celestin Kabanda |
| Hermann F. Eilts | SAUDI ARABIA | Ibrahim Al-Sowayel |
| | SENEGAL | Dr. Ousmane Socé Diop |
| Andrew V. Corry | SIERRA LEONE | Christopher O. E. Cole, O.B.E. |
| Francis J. Galbraith | SINGAPORE | Dr. Wong Lin Ken |
| Raymond L. Thurston | SOMALI REPUBLIC | Ahmed Mohammed Adan |
| William M. Rountree | REPUBLIC OF SOUTH AFRICA | H. L. T. Taswell |
| Angier Biddle Duke | SPAIN | The Marquis de Merry del Val |
| William H. Weatherby | SUDAN | Amin Ahmad Hussein |
| William W. Heath | SWEDEN | Hubert de Besche |
| John S. Hayes | SWITZERLAND | Felix Schnyder |
| Hugh H. Smythe | SYRIAN ARAB REPUBLIC | A. Galeb Kayali |
| John H. Burns | TANZANIA | Chief Michael Lukumbuzya |
| Graham A. Martin | THAILAND | Sukich Nimmanheminda |
| William Witman II | TOGO | Dr. Robert Ajavon |
| Robert G. Miner | TRINIDAD AND TOBAGO | Sir Ellis Emmanuel Innocent Clarke |
| Francis H. Russell | TUNISIA | Rachid Driss |
| Parker T. Hart | TURKEY | Melih Esenbel |
| Henry E. Stebbins | UGANDA | E. Otema Allimadi |
| Llewellyn E. Thompson | U.S.S.R. | Anatoly F. Dobrynin |
| Richard H. Nolte | UNITED ARAB REPUBLIC | Dr. Mostafa Kamel |
| David K. E. Bruce | UNITED KINGDOM | Sir Patrick Dean, G.C.M.G. |
| Arthur J. Goldberg | UNITED NATIONS | — |
| Elliott P. Skinner | UPPER VOLTA | Paul Rouamba |
| Henry A. Hoyt | URUGUAY | Juan Felipe Yriart |
| Maurice M. Bernbaum | VENEZUELA | Dr. Enrique Tejera-Paris |
| Ellsworth Bunker | VIETNAM | Bui Diem |
| George Dolgin | THE WEST INDIES | (British Ambassador) |
| | YEMEN | Abdulaziz Al-Futaih |
| C. Burke Elbrick | YUGOSLAVIA | Dr. Mirko Bruner |
| Robert C. Good | ZAMBIA | Rupiah B. Banda |

*Dr. Sevilla-Sacasa, who presented his credentials July 30, 1943, is dean of the Diplomatic Corps.

# U.S. ARMED FORCES

## U.S. MILITARY FORCES: 1966–1968
Source: Executive Office of the President, U.S. Bureau of the Budget

| | 1966 | 1967* | 1968* | | 1966 | 1967* | 1968* |
|---|---|---|---|---|---|---|---|
| **Strategic forces:** | | | | Antisubmarine warfare | | | |
| Intercontinental ballistic | | | | (ASW) carriers......... | 8 | 8 | 8 |
| missiles (squadrons) | | | | Nuclear attack submarines | 22 | 32 | 44 |
| Minuteman.............. | 17 | 20 | 20 | Other.................... | 328 | 323 | 303 |
| Titan.................... | 6 | 6 | 6 | Amphibious assault ships.... | 159 | 157 | 158 |
| Polaris submarines/missiles.. | 37/592 | 41/656 | 41/656 | Carrier air groups (attack and | | | |
| Straegic bombers (wings): | | | | ASW).................... | 27 | 27 | 27 |
| B-52................... | 13 | 12 | 11 | Marine Corps divisions/ | | | |
| B-58................... | 2 | 2 | 2 | aircraft wings............ | 4/3 | 4/3 | 4/3 |
| Manned fighter | | | | Air Force tactical forces | | | |
| interceptor squadrons... | 33 | 30 | 26 | squadrons............... | 130 | 136 | 135 |
| Interceptor missile squadrons | | | | **Airlift and sealift forces:** | | | |
| (BOMARC)............. | 6 | 6 | 6 | Airlift aircraft (squadrons): | | | |
| Army air defense........... | | | | C-130 through C-141...... | 42 | 44 | 45 |
| missile battalions....... | 18 | 18 | 18 | C-124.................... | 16 | 12 | 8 |
| **General purpose forces** | | | | Troopships, cargo ships, and | | | |
| Army divisions............. | 17 | 17 | 17 | tankers................. | 121 | 124 | 124 |
| Army maneuver battalions... | 191 | 198 | 198 | **Active aircraft inventory:** | | | |
| Army aviation units......... | 160 | 193 | 218 | Army...................... | 8,098 | 9,528 | 11,578 |
| Army special forces groups... | 7 | 7 | 7 | Navy...................... | 8,260 | 8,552 | 8,878 |
| Warships.................. | | | | Air Force................. | 14,196 | 14,230 | 14,012 |
| Attack carriers........... | 15 | 15 | 15 | **Commissioned ships in fleet** | 909 | 941 | 938 |

*Estimated.

## AIRCRAFT OF THE U.S. AIR FORCE: 1957–1968
Source: U.S. Department of Defense

| TYPE OF AIRCRAFT | 1957 | 1958 | 1959 | 1960 | 1961 | 1962 | 1963 | 1964 | 1965 | 1966 | 1967* | 1968* |
|---|---|---|---|---|---|---|---|---|---|---|---|---|
| Total..... | 28,845 | 26,898 | 24,132 | 22,749 | 20,585 | 18,074 | 18,328 | 17,828 | 17,071 | 14,196 | 14,230 | 14,012 |
| Combat.... | 15,881 | 14,880 | 13,122 | 12,750 | 11,455 | 9,442 | 9,490 | NA | NA | NA | NA | NA |
| Transport.. | 4,527 | 4,490 | 4,407 | 4,068 | 3,704 | 3,597 | 3,617 | NA | NA | NA | NA | NA |
| Trainer.... | 7,559 | 6,567 | 5,593 | 5,160 | 4,709 | 4,347 | 4,455 | NA | NA | NA | NA | NA |
| Communi- cations.. | 878 | 961 | 1,010 | 771 | 717 | 688 | 766 | NA | NA | NA | NA | NA |

NA: Not Available for reasons of security.     *Estimated.

## ACTIVE U.S. MILITARY PERSONNEL STRENGTHS: 1965–1968
Source: The Congressional Record

| MILITARY PERSONNEL | JUNE 30, 1965 | AUGUST 31, 1966 | JUNE 30, 1967 | 1968 (Estimated) |
|---|---|---|---|---|
| **ARMY** | 969,066 | 1,267,477 | 1,422,479 | 1,520,000 |
| Officers............... | 112,120 | 119,461 | 140,173 | 154,900 |
| Enlisted Men.......... | 854,929 | 1,144,773 | 1,293,107 | 1,362,000 |
| Cadets................ | 2,017 | 3,243 | 3,018 | 3,100 |
| **NAVY**................. | 671,448 | 745,538 | 749,582 | 762,300 |
| Officers................ | 77,866 | 79,887 | 81,467 | 85,000 |
| Enlisted Men.......... | 588,646 | 660,987 | 666,469 | 673,000 |
| Cadets................ | 4,936 | 4,664 | 5,443 | 4,200 |
| **MARINE CORPS**....... | 190,213 | 274,605 | 285,255 | 294,900 |
| Officers................ | 17,258 | 21,150 | 23,159 | 25,200 |
| Enlisted Men.......... | 172,640 | 253,293 | 259,199 | 269,300 |
| Cadets................ | 315 | 262 | 131 | 400 |
| **AIR FORCE**............ | 824,662 | 896,423 | 897,429 | 887,100 |
| Officers................ | 131,578 | 130,391 | 134,311 | 137,800 |
| Enlisted Men.......... | 690,177 | 762,907 | 760,353 | 745,700 |
| Cadets................ | 2,907 | 3,125 | 2,869 | 3,600 |
| **TOTAL PERSONNEL**.... | 2,655,389 | 3,184,043 | 3,374,808 | 3,464,300 |
| Officers............... | 338,822 | 350,889 | 379,110 | 403,000 |
| Enlisted Men.......... | 2,306,392 | 2,821,860 | 2,979,128 | 3,050,000 |
| Cadets................ | 9,175 | 11,294 | 11,461 | 11,300 |

## U.S. ARMED FORCES IN VIETNAM: 1960–1967
Source: U.S. Department of Defense

| DATE | ARMY | NAVY | MARINE CORPS | AIR FORCE | COAST GUARD | TOTAL U.S. FORCES |
|---|---|---|---|---|---|---|
| December 31, 1960............ | 800 | 15 | 2 | 68 | | 885 |
| December 31, 1961............ | 2,100 | 100 | 5 | 1,000 | | 3,205 |
| December 31, 1962............ | 7,900 | 500 | 500 | 2,400 | | 11,300 |
| December 31, 1963............ | 10,100 | 800 | 800 | 4,600 | | 16,300 |
| December 31, 1964............ | 14,700 | 1,100 | 900 | 6,600 | | 23,300 |
| December 31, 1965............ | 116,800 | 8,400 | 38,200 | 20,600 | 300 | 184,300 |
| December 31, 1966............ | 239,400 | 23,300 | 69,200 | 52,900 | 500 | 385,300 |
| October 5, 1967............... | 299,000 | 29,000 | 75,000 | 56,000 | 1,200 | 460,200 * |

*In addition to the U.S. forces stationed in South Vietnam in 1967, approximately 40,000 men were serving offshore on U.S. ships and 35,000 more (mostly Air Force personnel) were stationed in Thailand.

## U.S. ARMED FORCES IN MAJOR CONFLICTS
Source: U.S. Department of Defense and other sources

Historical statistics for the earlier American wars are unreliable. Here follow, however, scholarly estimates of American forces engaged and battle deaths suffered in those wars. For the Revolutionary War, the number of Americans serving is estimated at from 184,000 to 250,000—battle deaths totaled 4,435; for the War of 1812, 286,730 served and 2,260 deaths were incurred; and for the Mexican War, 78,718 served with 1,733 battle deaths. Statistics on more recent wars are shown in the table.

| PERSONNEL: | | CIVIL WAR [a] | SPANISH AMERICAN WAR | WORLD WAR I | WORLD WAR II | KOREAN WAR |
|---|---|---|---|---|---|---|
| Personnel serving................. | | 2,213,363 | 306,760 | 4,743,826 | [b] 16,353,659 | [c] 5,764,143 |
| Army............................... | | 2,128,948 | [d] 280,564 | [e] 4,057,101 | [f] 11,260,000 | 2,834,000 |
| Navy.............................. | | } 84,415 | 22,875 | 599,051 | 4,183,466 | 1,177,000 |
| Marines........................... | | | 3,321 | 78,839 | 669,100 | 424,000 |
| Air Force........................ | | — | — | — | — | 1,285,000 |
| Coast Guard..................... | | — | — | 8,835 | 241,093 | 44,143 |
| **Average duration of service** | months | 20 | 8 | 12 | 33 | 19 |
| Officers.................. | months | n.a. | 8 | 14 | 39 | 24 |
| Enlisted.................. | months | n.a. | 8 | 12 | 33 | 18 |
| OVERSEAS SERVICE: | | | | | | |
| **Personnel serving..........** | percent | n.a. | [g] 29 | 53 | 73 | [h] 56 |
| Army..................... | percent | — | 29 | [e] 52 | [f] 75 | 66 |
| Navy..................... | percent | n.a. | n.a. | 60 | 87 | [i] 19 |
| Marines.................. | percent | 66 | 56 | 57 | 71 | 39 |
| Air Force................ | percent | — | — | — | — | 39 |
| **Average duration[j]..........** | months | n.a. | 1.5 | [e] 5.5 | [f] 16.2 | 13.4 |
| Army..................... | months | n.a. | [k] 1.5 | 5.5 | 16.0 | 12.5 |
| Navy..................... | months | n.a. | n.a. | n.a. | n.a. | n.a. |
| Marines.................. | months | n.a. | 3.3 | 5.7 | 18.8 | 13.0 |
| Air Force................ | months | — | — | — | — | 17.0 |
| CASUALTIES:[l] | | | | | | |
| **Battle deaths........................** | | 140,414 | 385 | 53,402 | 291,557 | 33,629 |
| Army..................... | | 138,154 | [k] 369 | [e,m] 50,510 | [f] 234,874 | 27,704 |
| Navy..................... | | 2,112 | [n] 10 | 431 | 36,950 | 458 |
| Marines.................. | | 148 | 6 | [m] 2,461 | 19,733 | 4,267 |
| Air Force................ | | — | — | — | — | 1,200 |
| **Wounds not mortal.................** | | 281,881 | 1,662 | 204,002 | 670,846 | 103,284 |
| Army..................... | | 280,040 | 1,594 | [e,m] 193,663 | [f] 565,861 | 77,596 |
| Navy..................... | | 1,710 | 47 | 819 | [o] 37,778 | 1,576 |
| Marines.................. | | 131 | 21 | [m] 9,520 | 67,207 | 23,744 |
| Air Force................ | | — | — | — | — | 368 |

n.a. Not available.    [a] Union forces only. Estimates of the number serving in the Confederate forces range from 600,000 to 1,500,000. There were an estimated 74,524 Confederate deaths in battle.    [b] Covers period December 1, 1941, to December 31, 1946.    [c] Covers period June 25, 1950, to July 27, 1953.    [d] Covers period April 21, to August 13, 1898.    [e] Includes air service.    [f] Includes Army Air Corps.    [g] Based on Army and Marines only.    [h] Excludes Navy. See footnote i.    [i] Covers period July 1950 through January 1955. Represents Far East area only.    [j] During hostilities only.    [k] Covers war personnel who departed from the United States through December 1898.    [l] For periods covered, see footnotes b, c, d, and i.    [m] Includes gassed in action. Army data include casualties in northern Russia to August 25, 1919, and in Siberia to April 1, 1920; Marine data represent casualties in Europe only.    [n] Excludes personnel lost in sinking of the Maine, which occurred two months before hostilities.    [o] Includes casualties incurred in October 1941, due to actions of the enemy forces.

## U.S. MILITARY RANKS AND INSIGNIA

Designation of military rank by insignia first became popular in the 18th century. Before that time, aristocratic dress had distinguished the officer from the common soldier. In the United States, the first rank insignia were devised by General George Washington in 1775; different colored ribbons and cockades were used to denote rank. In 1780 the first of the modern

**ENLISTED PERSONNEL**

### ARMY RANK AND INSIGNIA

| Recruit | Private | Private First Class | Corporal | Sergeant | Staff Sergeant | Sergeant 1st Class | 1st Sgt. / Master Sergeant | Sergeant Major |
|---|---|---|---|---|---|---|---|---|
| | | | Spec. 4 | Spec. 5 | Spec. 6 | Spec. 7 | Spec. 8 | Spec. 9 |

### AIR FORCE RANK AND INSIGNIA

| Airman | Airman Third Class | Airman Second Class | Airman First Class | Staff Sergeant | Technical Sergeant | Master Sergeant | Senior Master Sergeant | Chief Master Sergeant |
|---|---|---|---|---|---|---|---|---|

### MARINE CORPS RANK AND INSIGNIA

| Private | Private First Class | Lance Corporal | Corporal | Sergeant | Staff Sergeant | Gunnery Sergeant | 1st Sgt. / Master Sergeant | Sgt. Maj. / Master Gun.Sgt. |
|---|---|---|---|---|---|---|---|---|

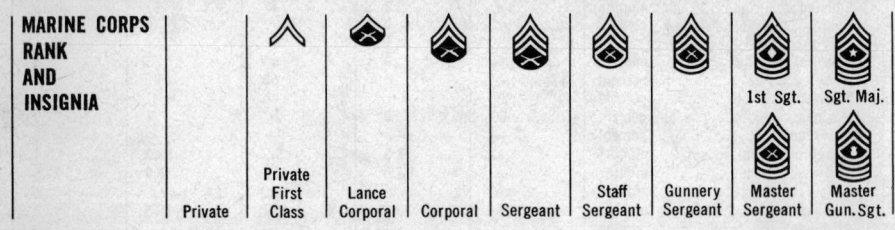

### NAVY RANK AND INSIGNIA

| Seaman Recruit | Seaman Apprentice | Seaman | Petty Officer Third Class | Petty Officer Second Class | Petty Officer First Class | Chief Petty Officer | Senior Chief Petty Officer | Master Chief Petty Officer |
|---|---|---|---|---|---|---|---|---|

**NAVY HAT INSIGNIA**

| Commissioned Officer | Warrant Officer | Chief Petty Officer |
|---|---|---|

**MARINE CORPS HAT INSIGNIA**

| Commissioned Officer (Black) | Warrant Officer (Black) | Enlisted Man (Black) |
|---|---|---|

insignia was adopted—silver stars for general officers.

The chart below contains the insignia for officers and enlisted men in each branch of the U.S. armed forces. When read horizontally, the chart indicates the hierarchy of a particular branch of the service; and a vertical reading shows parallel ranks in all branches.

## COMMISSIONED OFFICERS

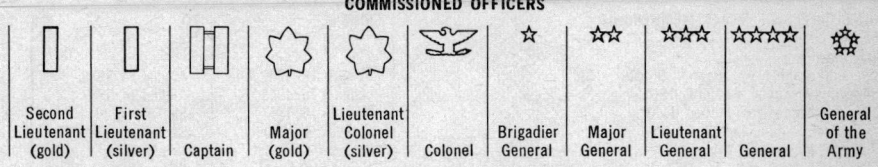

| Second Lieutenant (gold) | First Lieutenant (silver) | Captain | Major (gold) | Lieutenant Colonel (silver) | Colonel | Brigadier General | Major General | Lieutenant General | General | General of the Army |

**ARMY HAT INSIGNIA**

 Commissioned Officer (Gold)    Warrant Officer (Gold)    Enlisted Man (Gold)

**AIR FORCE HAT INSIGNIA**

Commissioned Officer (Silver)   Warrant Officer (Silver)   Enlisted Man (Silver)

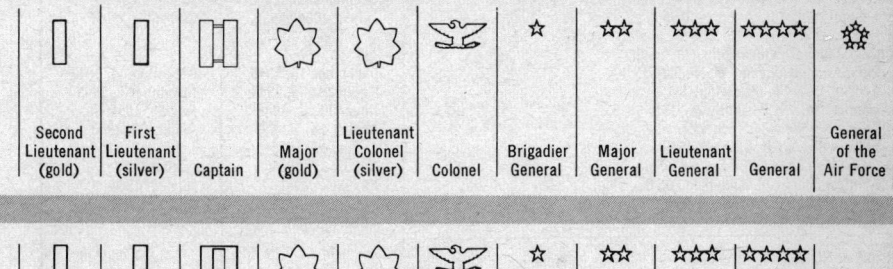

| Second Lieutenant (gold) | First Lieutenant (silver) | Captain | Major (gold) | Lieutenant Colonel (silver) | Colonel | Brigadier General | Major General | Lieutenant General | General | General of the Air Force |

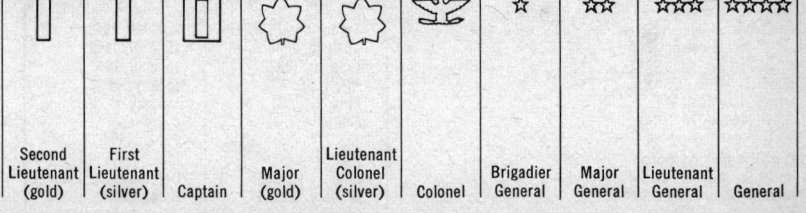

| Second Lieutenant (gold) | First Lieutenant (silver) | Captain | Major (gold) | Lieutenant Colonel (silver) | Colonel | Brigadier General | Major General | Lieutenant General | General |

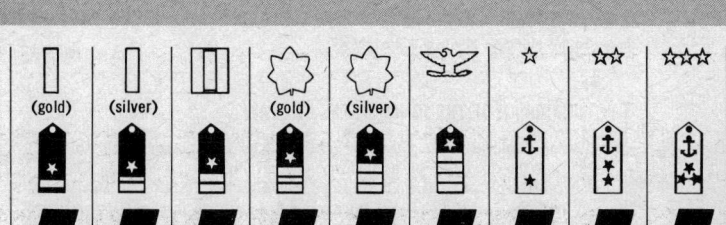

| (gold) | (silver) | | (gold) | (silver) | | | | | | |

  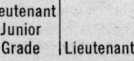         

| Ensign | Lieutenant Junior Grade | Lieutenant | Lieutenant Commander | Commander | Captain | Commodore | Rear Admiral | Vice Admiral | Admiral | Fleet Admiral |

## THE JOINT CHIEFS OF STAFF: 1947–1967
Source: Office of the Secretary of Defense

Established in 1947 as a permanent agency within the Department of Defense, the Joint Chiefs of Staff provides overall military planning for the nation. Its members are the principal military advisers to the President, the National Security Council, and the Secretary of Defense. The four regular members are the chairman; the chief of staff, U.S. Army; the chief of naval operations; and the chief of staff, U.S. Air Force. The U.S. Marine Corps commandant sits as a coequal with the other members on matters that concern the Corps.

| JOINT CHIEFS OF STAFF MEMBERSHIP | FROM | TO |
|---|---|---|
| **Chairman \*** | | |
| General of the Army Omar N. Bradley, USA | August 16, 1949 | August 14, 1953 |
| Admiral Arthur W. Radford, USN | August 15, 1953 | August 14, 1957 |
| General Nathan F. Twining, USAF | August 15, 1957 | September 30, 1960 |
| General Lyman L. Lemnitzer, USA | October 1, 1960 | September 30, 1962 |
| General Maxwell D. Taylor, USA | October 1, 1962 | July 3, 1964 |
| General Earle G. Wheeler, USA | July 6, 1964 | Current |
| **Chief of Staff, U.S. Army** | | |
| General of the Army Dwight D. Eisenhower, USA | November 19, 1945 | February 7, 1948 |
| General Omar N. Bradley, USA | February 17, 1948 | August 15, 1949 |
| General J. Lawton Collins, USA | August 16, 1949 | August 14, 1953 |
| General Matthew B. Ridgway, USA | August 15, 1953 | June 30, 1955 |
| General Maxwell D. Taylor, USA | June 30, 1955 | June 30, 1959 |
| General Lyman L. Lemnitzer, USA | July 1, 1959 | September 30, 1960 |
| General George H. Decker, USA | September 30, 1960 | September 30, 1962 |
| General Earle G. Wheeler, USA | October 1, 1962 | July 3, 1964 |
| General Harold K. Johnson, USA | July 3, 1964 | Current |
| **Chief of Naval Operations** | | |
| Fleet Admiral Chester W. Nimitz, USN | December 15, 1945 | December 15, 1947 |
| Admiral Louis E. Denfield, USN | December 15, 1947 | November 2, 1949 |
| Admiral Forrest P. Sherman, USN | November 2, 1949 | July 22, 1951 |
| Admiral William M. Fechteler, USN | August 16, 1951 | August 17, 1953 |
| Admiral Robert B. Carney, USN | August 17, 1953 | August 16, 1955 |
| Admiral Arleigh A. Burke, USN | August 17, 1955 | August 1, 1961 |
| Admiral George W. Anderson, USN | August 1, 1961 | July 31, 1963 |
| Admiral David L. McDonald, USN | August 1, 1963 | August 1, 1967 |
| Admiral Thomas H. Moorer, USN | August 1, 1967 | Current |
| **Chief of Staff, U.S. Air Force** | | |
| General Carl Spaatz, USAF | September 26, 1947 | April 29, 1948 |
| General Hoyt S. Vandenberg, USAF | April 30, 1948 | June 29, 1953 |
| General Nathan F. Twining, USAF | June 30, 1953 | June 30, 1957 |
| General Thomas D. White, USAF | July 1, 1957 | June 30, 1961 |
| General Curtis E. LeMay, USAF | June 30, 1961 | January 31, 1965 |
| General John P. McConnell, USAF | February 1, 1965 | Current |
| **Commandant of the Marine Corps** | | |
| General Lemuel C. Shepherd, USMC | January 1, 1952 | December 31, 1955 |
| General Randolph McC. Pate, USMC | January 1, 1956 | December 31, 1959 |
| General David M. Shoup, USMC | January 1, 1960 | December 31, 1963 |
| General Wallace M. Greene, Jr., USMC | January 1, 1964 | Current |

\* Position created by a 1949 amendment to the National Security Act of 1947.

U.S. Army

## CHAIRMAN OF THE JOINT CHIEFS OF STAFF

When General Earle Gilmore Wheeler was a teen-ager in Washington he dreamed of a military career. Now he is serving his second term as Chairman of the Joint Chiefs of Staff. At 16 he joined the National Guard, attaining the rank of sergeant. From 1928 to 1932 he attended West Point. He was a divisional chief of staff in Europe in World War II, and became Army deputy chief of operations in 1957. Briefing John F. Kennedy on military matters during the 1960 presidential campaign, General Wheeler so impressed the candidate that, as President, Kennedy named Wheeler Army chief of staff, a command he held until 1964 when he was appointed to the nation's highest military post.

## CURRENT U.S. DRAFT CLASSIFICATIONS

Listed below are the Selective Service classifications, with general descriptions.

**I-A:** Available for military service.

**I-A-O:** Conscientious objector available for non-combatant military service only.

**I-C:** Member of the armed forces, the Environmental Science Services Administration, or the Public Health Service.

**I-D:** Member of a reserve component or a student taking military training.

**I-O:** Conscientious objector available only for noncombatant civilian work contributing to the national health, safety, or interest.

**I-S:** Student deferred by statute until the end of his academic year.

**I-W:** Conscientious objector performing civilian work contributing to the maintenance of the national health, safety, or interest.

**I-Y:** Registrant available for military service only in times of war or national emergency.

**II-A:** Registrant deferred because of civilian occupation (except agriculture and activity in study), or an apprentice.

**II-C:** Registrant deferred because of agricultural occupation.

**II-S:** Registrant deferred because of activity in study.

**III-A:** Registrant with a child or children, or a registrant deferred by reason of extreme hardship to dependents.

**IV-A:** Registrant who has completed service, or a sole surviving son.

**IV-B:** Government official deferred by statute.

**IV-C:** Alien.

**IV-D:** Minister of religion, or a divinity student.

**IV-F:** Registrant not qualified for any military service.

**V-A:** Registrant over the age of liability for military service.

## THE MEDAL OF HONOR

The Medal of Honor, the nation's highest award for valor, was established by the 37th Congress on July 12, 1862. Because the medal is given in the name of Congress, it is often, although inaccurately, referred to as the "Congressional Medal of Honor."

The Medal was originally given only to enlisted men, but the law was amended in 1863 to include officers. In 1918 the criteria for receiving the medal were considerably changed by Congress, and they remain almost the same today.

The President may award and present in the name of Congress a Medal of Honor to a person "who, while a member of the Armed Forces, distinguishes himself conspicuously by gallantry and intrepidity at the risk of his life above and beyond the call of duty while engaged in an action against any enemy of the United States; while engaged in military operations involving conflict with an opposing foreign force; or while serving with friendly foreign forces engaged in an armed conflict against an opposing armed force in which the United States is not a belligerent party."

Medal of Honor recipients can, under certain conditions, obtain free military air transportation. In addition, a veteran who has been awarded the medal for combat in any war is eligible, upon reaching the age of 50, for a special pension of $100 per month.

Since the establishment of the citation over 3,000 Medals of Honor have been awarded: 1,527 for service in the Civil War; 541 in the Indian Wars; 111 in the War with Spain; 87 in the Philippine Insurrection; 60 in the Boxer Rebellion; 56 in the Mexican border conflict; 123 in World War I; 430 in World War II; 131 in the Korean War; and 19 in the Vietnam conflict.

Ten Medals of Honor have been authorized by special acts of Congress: Colonel Charles A. Lindbergh, 1928; Major General Adolphus W. Greely, 1935; to the Unknown American Soldiers of both world wars and Korea; and to those of Belgium, Britain, France, Italy, and Romania after World War I. A list of servicemen who have received the Medal of Honor during the Vietnam conflict (as of Oct. 1, 1967) follows.

| RECIPIENTS | SERVICE | HOMETOWN | DATE AWARDED |
|---|---|---|---|
| Captain Roger H. C. Donlon | USA | Saugerties, N.Y. | December 5, 1964 |
| Staff Sergeant Larry S. Pierce | USA | Wewoka, Okla. | February 24, 1966 |
| Private First Class Milton L. Olive III | USA | Chicago, Ill. | April 21, 1966 |
| First Lieutenant Charles Q. Williams | USA | Charleston, S.C. | June 23, 1966 |
| Construction Mechanic Third Class Marvin G. Shields | USN | Port Townsend, Wash. | September 13, 1966 |
| Sergeant Robert E. O'Malley | USMC | New York, N.Y. | December 6, 1966 |
| Second Lieutenant Walter J. Marm, Jr. | USA | Washington, Penn. | December 19, 1966 |
| Major Bernard F. Fisher | USAF | San Bernardino, Calif. | January 19, 1967 |
| Second Lieutenant Robert J. Hibbs | USA | Omaha, Neb. | January 26, 1967 |
| First Lieutenant Frank S. Reasoner | USMC | Spokane, Wash. | January 31, 1967 |
| Lance Corporal Joe C. Paul | USMC | Williamsburg, Ky. | February 7, 1967 |
| Captain Harvey C. Barnum, Jr. | USMC | Waterbury, Conn. | February 27, 1967 |
| Specialist Six Lawrence Joel | USA | Winston-Salem, N.C. | March 9, 1967 |
| Specialist Four Daniel Fernandez | USA | Albuquerque, N.M. | April 6, 1967 |
| Staff Sergeant Peter S. Connor | USMC | Orange, N.J. | May 2, 1967 |
| Sergeant James W. Robinson | USA | Hinsdale, Ill. | July 12, 1967 |
| Gunnery Sergeant Jimmie E. Howard | USMC | Burlington, Iowa | August 21, 1967 |
| Sergeant Jimmy G. Stewart | USA | Columbus, Ga. | August 24, 1967 |
| Specialist Five David C. Dolby | USA | Oaks, Penn. | September 28, 1967 |

# FOCUS ON THE NEWS

## THE NEW DRAFT LAW

General Lewis B. Hershey, National Director of the Selective Service, confers with President Johnson at the White House on May 3, 1967. Hershey has served as Director since his appointment on July 31, 1941.

On July 1, 1967, President Johnson signed a new draft law extending Selective Service for another four years. It is virtually the same as the old law, and, except for graduate students and conscientious objectors, persons deferrable before remain so now.

Under the new law the first to be drafted will be youths who fail to register for the draft. Most draftees will be from the 19-26 age group, either single men or those married after August 26, 1965. Most fathers will be exempt. The plan to draft 19-year-olds first was postponed for a year.

Most full-time undergraduate students who are satisfactorily pursuing their studies will be deferred until they graduate or reach the age of 24. Class rank will no longer be considered.

Students accepted by a graduate school to pursue a full-time course of study on or before October 1, 1967, will be deferred for one year only. Candidates who have completed one year toward a master's degree will be granted another year to complete their studies; those with one year or more toward their doctorate will be granted deferment up to four additional years. After the spring of 1968, deferments for most beginning graduate students will cease; only students who are studying medicine or dentistry will continue to be deferred.

Local draft boards still determine deferments for Peace Corpsmen and those in VISTA.

The 1967 law, like the old law, requires a conscientious objector to demonstrate that his case rests upon a religious belief.

Potential draftees can still meet their service obligations by enlisting in the National Guard or other reserves as long as they do so *before* they are issued induction orders by their local boards.

# THE SERVICE ACADEMIES

Admission to one of the nation's service academies involves two procedures, *qualification* and *nomination*. Specific details may be obtained from each academy's superintendent but a general statement follows:

**Qualification:** A candidate must be a U.S. citizen, male, single, and between 17 and 22. Rigid physical and educational requirements include completion of a four-year college-preparatory secondary-school education.

**Nomination:** Candidates for the Military, Naval, and Air Force Academies must first be nominated before they can be examined for admission. Nominating authorities include the President, Vice President, Senators, Representatives, and the governing authorities of the District of Columbia, Puerto Rico, the Canal Zone, and other U.S. territories. Appointments are also available to enlisted members of the regular armed services, the reserves, ROTC units, and honor graduates of military and naval schools. Special consideration is often given to sons of deceased war veterans and Congressional Medal of Honor winners.

Unlike the other service academies, there are no Congressional appointments to the U.S. Coast Guard Academy. Candidates who satisfy the basic requirements are eligible to participate in the nationwide examination. Upon attaining a qualifying score on the examination, candidates are given supplementary tests and a personal interview.

## UNITED STATES MILITARY ACADEMY
Source: U.S. Military Academy

**Location:** West Point, New York
**Superintendent:** Major General Donald V. Bennett
**Student Body:** Approximately 3,300 (1967–68)

The United States Military Academy overlooks the Hudson River at West Point, New York, a key fortress during the Revolutionary War. Opened July 4, 1802, under the command of Major Jonathan Williams, the Academy was founded to encourage the study of military arts and sciences. With the growing threat of war with England in 1812, the strength of the Corps of Cadets was increased to 250 by an Act of Congress, with the requirement that cadets be taught "all the duties of a private, a non-commissioned officer, and an officer."

Colonel Sylvanus Thayer, Superintendent of the Academy from 1817 to 1833, demanded excellence of character and knowledge from the cadets. Known as the "Father of the Military Academy," he saw a need for fully trained engineers and made civil engineering courses the core of the curriculum.

After West Point's centennial in 1902, Brigadier General Albert Mills, then Superintendent, liberalized the entire military and academic curriculum, placing heavy stress on proficiency in English. General Douglas MacArthur, who took command after World War I, was particularly interested in the cadets' physical development, and initiated a strenuous program of gymnastic instruction combined with compulsory intramural sports.

Experience gained in World War II and the Korean War led to an extensive analysis of West Point training procedure. As a result, additional emphasis was placed on modern technological advances and the increasingly complex aspects of national security and international relations. Cadets now receive two hours per week of military instruction during the academic year and two months solid military training during the summer.

In March, 1964, President Johnson signed a bill raising the maximum authorized enrollment of the Cadet Corps from 2,529 to 4,417. The full strength of 4,417 is expected to be reached by July, 1971. A ten-year major construction program was begun in 1965, and the barracks, dining hall, and academic facilities will be enlarged to accommodate the increasing numbers.

The four-year course of study at West Point leads to a Bachelor of Science degree and a commission as a second lieutenant in the Regular Army. Cadets in the top 5 per cent of the class may attend graduate school immediately following graduation provided their academic field meets Army requirements. Cadets must serve a minimum of five years as commissioned officers after graduation or the completion of graduate studies.

There is no tuition fee at West Point. A cadet is a member of the Regular Army and receives $151.95 a month with which he buys his uniforms, textbooks, and incidentals. To help pay for these items appointees must deposit $300 before entering the Academy. Meals are paid for by a ration allowance. Cadets receive a month's leave every summer.

Of particular interest to visitors is the Academy's museum containing ordnance and military trophies of historical interest.

## UNITED STATES NAVAL ACADEMY
Source: U.S. Naval Academy

**Location:** Annapolis, Maryland
**Superintendent:** Rear Admiral Draper L. Kauffman
**Student Body:** Approximately 4,000 (1967–68)

The United States Naval Academy was founded in 1845 by Secretary of the Navy George Bancroft, who was dissatisfied with the instruction offered by the four shore schools at New York, Boston, Norfolk, and Philadelphia. Within months he secured Presidential approval; rehabilitated the old buildings at Ford Severn, Maryland, a former army post; and assembled a teaching staff. The Academy opened October 10, 1845, with about 50 midshipmen.

(continued)

**THE SERVICE ACADEMIES** (*continued*)

During the Civil War the Academy was moved to Newport, Rhode Island. Temporary quarters were established aboard the *Constitution* and in the Atlantic House, a resort hotel. The buildings and grounds at Annapolis served as an Army hospital until the Academy returned in 1865. In 1873 the academic program was increased to six years, with the last two years spent at sea. In 1912 a four-year course was established and the two-year sea duty discontinued. A comprehensive building program was begun in 1899. Since then nearly 30 buildings have been constructed, many in the French Renaissance style of architecture. Bancroft Hall, the dormitory, is the largest in the world with eight wings and over 1800 rooms. In 1913 the body of John Paul Jones, "Father of the American Navy," was placed in the crypt of the new chapel.

The purpose of the Navy Academy is to provide properly educated and trained officers. In 1959 the curriculum was extensively revised to meet the demands of the nuclear age and advanced ship technology. The new Intermediate Masters Program enables selected graduates to obtain their Master's degree within seven months of graduation by taking concentrated courses at various American universities.

In addition to the academic program, the Academy has an extensive summer program, including shipboard training with a fleet unit, amphibious warfare training, and flight training indoctrination at Pensacola, Florida.

Midshipmen receive $151.95 a month plus a ration allowance and free medical and dental services. Graduates are awarded a Bachelor of Science degree and a commission as ensign in the Navy or second lieutenant in the Marine Corps.

## UNITED STATES AIR FORCE ACADEMY
Source: U.S. Air Force Academy

**Location:** Near Colorado Springs, Colorado
**Superintendent:** Lieutenant General Thomas S. Moorman
**Student Body:** Approximately 3,250 (1967–68)
The plan for an academy to train officers especially for the Air Force gained impetus after World War II when the importance of aerial warfare became fully recognized. In 1949 Secretary of Defense James Forrestal appointed a board of civilian and military educators to recommend a general system of education for the Army, Navy, and Air Force. The board concluded that the needs of the Air Force could not be met by the expansion of the other service academies and recommended the establishment of an Air Force Academy. After the Korean War, Congress authorized creation of the Academy, and on April 1, 1954, President Eisenhower signed the bill. In June of that year a site eight miles north of Colorado Springs was selected, consisting of approximately 17,900 acres of former ranchland.

Congress appropriated $138,797,000 for construction, including $1,858,000 for temporary quarters at Lowry Air Force Base. Modern buildings of glass, aluminum, steel, granite, and white marble were constructed on mesas extending from the Rampart Range of the Rocky Mountains. About $23,000,000 was spent to furnish and equip the new buildings.

The President appointed Lieutenant General Hubert R. Harmon as the first superintendent. Under his direction a balanced program of science and humanities, designed to meet the challenge of the aerospace age, was organized. On July 11, 1955, the first class of 306 cadets was sworn in. The Academy used quarters at Lowry Air Force Base until the new campus was ready for occupancy in the fall of 1958.

Cadets receive $151.95 a month for books, clothing, and personal items; there are no fees charged for tuition, board, and medical care. The four-year course of study at the Academy leads to a Bachelor of Science degree and a commission as a second lieutenant in the Regular Air Force.

## UNITED STATES COAST GUARD ACADEMY
Source: U.S. Coast Guard Academy

**Location:** New London, Connecticut
**Superintendent:** Rear Admiral Arthur B. Engel
**Student Body:** Approximately 800 (1967–68)
The nation's oldest seagoing service, the U.S. Coast Guard trains future officers at its academy on the Thames River in New London, Connecticut. The Coast Guard was founded by Alexander Hamilton in 1790 as a Revenue Cutter Service to protect the coasts against smugglers and privateers. Today the Coast Guard carries out a variety of missions in the areas of search and rescue, aids to navigation, enforcement of law at sea, and maritime safety and oceanography, as well as some military duties. It was transferred from Treasury Department jurisdiction to the newly established Department of Transportation on April 1, 1967. It is under the Navy Department during time of war.

The first cadets were trained in 1876 on the schooner *Dobbin*, skippered by Captain J. A. Henriques, who served as first superintendent. When the cruise was completed, winter training quarters were established in New Bedford, Massachusetts. The Academy moved to its present Georgian Colonial quarters in 1932, after two previous moves in 1900 and 1910.

The Academy's curriculum is highly diversified because of the variety of responsibilities placed upon Coast Guard officers. Part of the cadet program is conducted at sea aboard the three-masted bark CGC *Eagle*. The four-year course at the Academy leads to a Bachelor of Science degree in engineering. Upon graduation, cadets are commissioned by the President as ensigns and assigned to sea duty aboard one of the larger cutters, buoy tenders, or supply vessels. First-year cadets enter the Academy in late June or early July; this period, known as "swab summer," gives them an opportunity to adjust to military life. Cadets receive $151.95 monthly.

# CRIME IN THE UNITED STATES

## U.S. CRIME RATE RISES IN 1967
Source: U.S. Federal Bureau of Investigation

The crime rate in the United States continued to rise during the first six months of 1967. Law enforcement officials recorded a 17 per cent increase in the number of crimes committed between January and June, 1967, over the number of crimes committed during the same period in 1966.

The 1967 figures show that in both cities and suburban areas with populations of 100,000 people or more, the crime rate increased 18 per cent. Crime in rural areas rose 15 per cent.

There was an increase in every type of crime. Incidence of auto theft rose 19 per cent; burglary and the violent crimes as a group each rose 18 per cent. The number of armed robberies (which comprise more than one-half of all robbery offenses reported to law enforcement agencies in the United States) was up 37 per cent. Residential robberies and residential burglaries increased 12 per cent and 15 per cent respectively.

Crime-rate figures for the first six months of 1967 show a 16 per cent increase in the Southern states over figures for the same period of 1967, a 20 per cent increase in the North Central states, an 18 per cent increase in the Northeastern states, and a 16 per cent increase in the Western states.

According to the *Uniform Crime Reports* issued by the Federal Bureau of Investigation, almost 3,250,000 serious crimes were reported during 1966. This figure represents an increase of 11 per cent over 1965. There were almost two victims of serious crimes per 100 persons in 1966—an increase of 10 per cent over 1965 and 48 per cent over 1960.

During 1966 more than 6,500 murders and 43,500 aggravated assaults were committed with firearms, and over 78,000 armed robberies were reported. Robberies, burglaries, larcenies, and auto thefts accounted for the loss of property valued at more than $1.2 billion.

## CRIME TREND IN THE UNITED STATES
Source: U.S. Federal Bureau of Investigation

Calendar Year 1966 over Calendar Year 1965

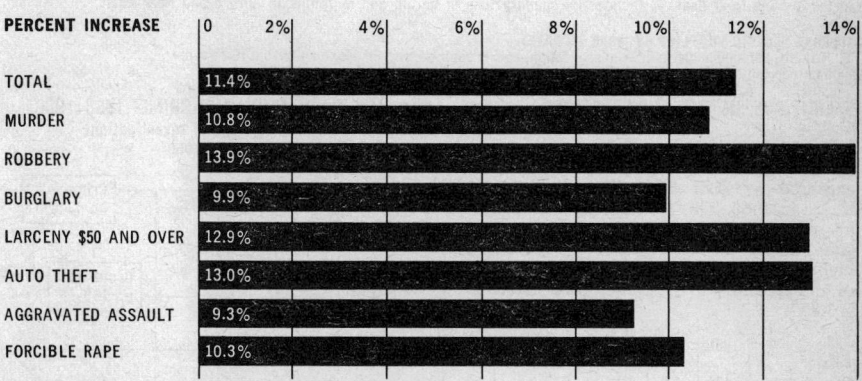

| PERCENT INCREASE | |
| --- | --- |
| TOTAL | 11.4% |
| MURDER | 10.8% |
| ROBBERY | 13.9% |
| BURGLARY | 9.9% |
| LARCENY $50 AND OVER | 12.9% |
| AUTO THEFT | 13.0% |
| AGGRAVATED ASSAULT | 9.3% |
| FORCIBLE RAPE | 10.3% |

## MAJOR CRIMES IN THE UNITED STATES: 1965–1966
Source: Federal Bureau of Investigation

| OFFENSE CHARGED | 1965 TOTAL | NUMBER OF PERSONS ARRESTED (under 18) | (18 and up) | 1966 TOTAL | NUMBER OF PERSONS ARRESTED (under 18) | (18 and up) |
| --- | --- | --- | --- | --- | --- | --- |
| Criminal homicide: | | | | | | |
| Murder and non-negligent manslaughter | 6,447 | 583 | 5,864 | 6,946 | 665 | 6,281 |
| Manslaughter by negligence | 2,445 | 176 | 2,269 | 2,484 | 178 | 2,306 |
| Forcible rape | 9,480 | 1,974 | 7,506 | 10,375 | 2,035 | 8,340 |
| Robbery | 41,049 | 12,369 | 28,680 | 42,995 | 13,536 | 29,459 |
| Aggravated assault | 74,824 | 11,942 | 62,882 | 87,265 | 15,080 | 72,185 |
| Burglary—breaking and entering | 172,008 | 90,519 | 81,489 | 174,133 | 94,968 | 79,165 |
| Larceny—theft | 345,589 | 192,576 | 153,013 | 359,897 | 204,285 | 155,612 |
| Auto theft | 91,904 | 58,448 | 33,456 | 95,776 | 60,607 | 35,169 |
| Total for above offenses | 743,746 | 368,587 | 375,159 | 779,871 | 391,354 | 388,517 |

## NARCOTIC ADDICTION IN THE UNITED STATES: 1900-1966

Source: U.S. Federal Bureau of Narcotics

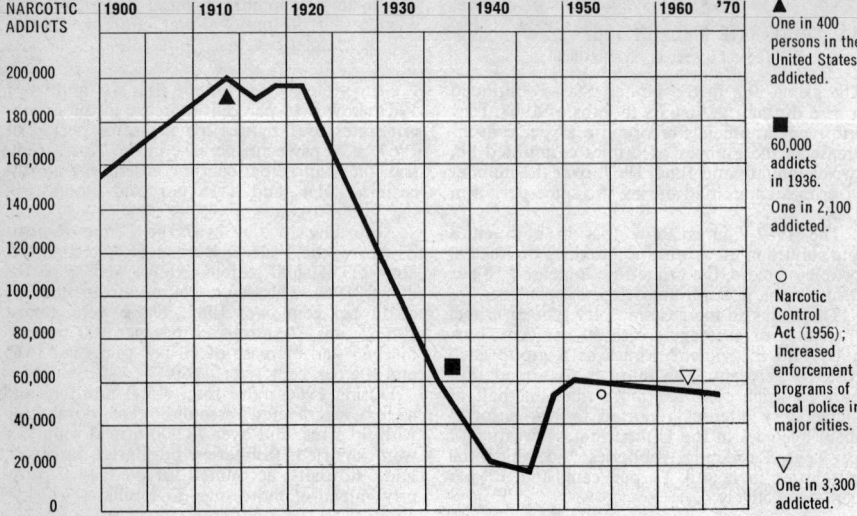

▲ One in 400 persons in the United States addicted.

■ 60,000 addicts in 1936. One in 2,100 addicted.

○ Narcotic Control Act (1956); Increased enforcement programs of local police in major cities.

▽ One in 3,300 addicted.

**ILLEGAL TRAFFIC SUPPLIED BY (1920-1940):**
**1)** Imports from manufacturers in Switzerland, Germany, France (smuggling). **2)** Production of Japanese heroin and morphine factories. **3)** Prescription forgeries and wholesalers' diversion. **4)** Small drugstore larcenies. **5)** India, China, and Near East opium. **6)** Limiting of manufacture to world medical needs puts accent on clandestine factories in Europe and Near East. **7)** Clandestine manufacture of heroin and morphine in Europe and Near East.

**ILLEGAL TRAFFIC SUPPLIED BY (1940 TO DATE):**
**1)** Turkish, Lebanese, Syrian, Chinese, Italian, and French heroin. **2)** Mexican heroin (California).
**3)** Mexican opium. **4)** Drug store robberies, thefts, and prescription forgeries.

## EXECUTIONS IN THE UNITED STATES

A thirty-year-old man, convicted as a murderer by the State of Oklahoma, was the only person executed by civil authorities in the United States in 1966. This year's total was the lowest on record since the U.S. Bureau of Prisons began making an annual survey in 1930. The highest was 199 executions in 1935. The total of all executions in the United States since 1930 is 3,857.

| | 1961 | 1962 | 1963 | 1964 | 1965 | 1966 |
|---|---|---|---|---|---|---|
| **Total executions..** | **42** | **47** | **21** | **15** | **7** | **1** |
| White....... | 20 | 28 | 13 | 8 | 6 | 1 |
| Negro....... | 22 | 19 | 8 | 7 | 1 | — |
| Other....... | — | — | — | — | — | — |
| **Crime committed** | | | | | | |
| MURDER.... | 33 | 41 | 18 | 9 | 7 | 1 |
| White..... | 18 | 26 | 12 | 5 | 6 | 1 |
| Negro..... | 15 | 15 | 6 | 4 | 1 | — |
| Other..... | — | — | — | — | — | — |
| RAPE...... | 8 | 4 | 2 | 6 | — | — |
| White..... | 1 | 2 | — | 3 | — | — |
| Negro..... | 7 | 2 | 2 | 3 | — | — |
| Other..... | — | — | — | — | — | — |
| ALL OTHER OFFENSES... | 1 | 2 | 1 | — | — | — |
| White..... | 1 | — | 1 | — | — | — |
| Negro..... | — | 2 | — | — | — | — |

## U.S. POPULATION AND CRIME: 1960–1966

Source: Federal Bureau of Investigation
Percentage change over 1960

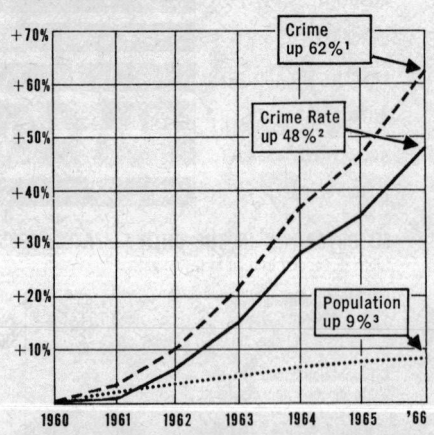

Crime up 62%[1]

Crime Rate up 48%[2]

Population up 9%[3]

[1]The total number of serious crimes reported to law enforcement agencies in 1960 was 2,001,000; in 1966, 3,243,000. [2]The crime rate—offenses per 100,000 population—was 1,115.8 in 1960; 1,656 in 1966. [3]The total U.S. population in 1960 was 179,323,175; in 1966, 195,857,000.

## THE FEDERAL BUREAU OF INVESTIGATION

The Federal Bureau of Investigation (FBI) is a division of the U.S. Department of Justice, with headquarters in Washington, D.C. Directed since 1924 by J. Edgar Hoover, the FBI is responsible for investigating violations of Federal law (except when another agency has specific jurisdiction) and matters of internal security, including espionage, sabotage, treason, and conspiracy against the United States. The Bureau has no power to prosecute. Its function is to investigate and report its findings to the proper authority.

The organization was formed in 1908. At first it handled only special investigations for the Department of Justice. However, its activities increased markedly at the time of World War I, when Congress passed espionage laws and the Selective Service Act; and later, when lawmakers enacted Federal anti-crime legislation.

In the 1930s the FBI mounted a massive assault aimed at smashing underworld gangs and powerful crime syndicates organized during the Prohibition era. The Federal offensive put a host of crime lords behind bars, and crushed a rising tide of organized lawlessness. About this time FBI agents became known in underworld jargon as "G (for Government) Men."

With Nazi aggression threatening wide-scale war in the late 1930s, President Franklin Roosevelt extended FBI jurisdiction to matters of internal American security. Any doubts about the grave threat posed by Axis activity in the United States were dispelled in 1938, when Federal agents uncovered a 33-member Nazi spy ring, directed in this country by a master spy who had been an espionage operative for 40 years.

Early in World War II the FBI organized a national campaign to protect the American defense industry against sabotage. In 1942 Federal agents apprehended eight Nazi saboteurs who had been landed on East Coast beaches with orders to destroy critical U.S. defense installations and generate civil chaos. Federal action against saboteurs inspired American confidence that the national war effort would not be undermined by enemy infiltration. And FBI cooperation with Allied governments resulted in expulsion of more than 14,000 Axis saboteurs from friendly Hemisphere nations.

With the fall of Hitler's Third Reich the Nazi menace abated, only to be replaced with the threat of Communist subversion. Since World War II the FBI has directed much of its attention to Communist activity in the United States. Federal investigations have led to the arrest and conviction of a host of spies, including Julius and Ethel Rosenberg, who were executed in 1953, and Colonel Rudolph Ivanovich Abel, a ranking member of the Soviet espionage network since 1927, who had directed a Red spy ring based in New York. The FBI has also exposed spies and saboteurs protected by diplomatic immunity. Virtually all have been declared persona non grata and expelled from the country.

FBI efforts to control domestic crime have been no less strenuous. Penetration of the shadowy underworld organization, the Cosa Nostra, has given Federal officials new information on organized crime's personnel structure, its scope and method of operation, and its far-reaching connection with underworld and legitimate figures.

The FBI maintains rigid personnel standards, including a special training program mandatory for agents. In addition, the Bureau has developed highly sophisticated techniques of investigation, identification, and communication, all of which are available to local law enforcement agencies.

In fiscal year 1967, 13,032 convictions were obtained in cases handled by the FBI; 97 per cent of the persons brought to trial in FBI cases were convicted; and 15,878 fugitives sought by Federal agents were located, compared with 14,323 apprehended in 1966.

## CAPITAL PUNISHMENT IN THE UNITED STATES: 1967

Among the 50 U.S. states, 13 have abolished the death penalty for most capital crimes, such as murder or forcible rape, while 37 still retain some type of capital punishment. Below is a list of states and their methods of punishment for capital crimes.

| NON-CAPITAL PUNISHMENT Life Imprisonment | CAPITAL PUNISHMENT Electrocution | | Lethal Gas | Hanging | Hanging or Shooting |
|---|---|---|---|---|---|
| Alaska | Alabama | Nebraska | Arizona | Delaware | Utah |
| Hawaii | Arkansas | New Jersey | California | Idaho | |
| Iowa | Connecticut | Ohio | Colorado | Kansas | |
| Maine | Florida | Oklahoma | Maryland | Montana | |
| Michigan | Georgia | Pennsylvania | Mississippi | New Hampshire | |
| Minnesota | Illinois | South Carolina | Missouri | Washington | |
| New York | Indiana | South Dakota | Nevada | | |
| North Dakota | Kentucky | Tennessee | New Mexico | | |
| Oregon | Louisiana | Texas | North Carolina | | |
| Rhode Island | Massachusetts | Virginia | Wyoming | | |
| Vermont | | | | | |
| West Virginia | | | | | |
| Wisconsin | | | | | |

# LAND AND PEOPLE

## OUTSTANDING U.S. GEOGRAPHIC FACTS

Source: National Geographic Society

### UNITED STATES (INCLUDING ALASKA AND HAWAII)

| | | |
|---|---|---|
| Total area for fifty states....... | Land: 3,548,974 square miles\|Water: 66,237 square miles | 3,615,211 square miles |
| Largest state.................... | Alaska................................................. | 586,400 square miles |
| Smallest state................... | Rhode Island.......................................... | 1,214 square miles |
| Largest county.................. | San Bernardino County, California..................... | 20,131 square miles |
| Largest city (in area)*.......... | Los Angeles, California................................ | 454.8 square miles |
| Northernmost town.............. | Barrow, Alaska........................................ | 71°18′ N |
| Southernmost city.............. | Hilo, Island of Hawaii................................. | 19°42′ N |
| Southernmost town............. | Naalehu, Island of Hawaii............................. | 19°4′ N (155°35′ W) |
| Easternmost town.............. | Lubec, Maine.......................................... | 66°59′ W |
| Highest point on Atlantic coast.... | Cadillac Mountain, Mount Desert Island, Maine........... | 1,530 feet |
| Largest and oldest national park.. | Yellowstone National Park (established 1872), Wyoming, Montana, Idaho................................ | 3,472 square miles |
| Largest national monument....... | Katmai National Monument, Alaska...................... | 4,215 square miles |
| Highest waterfall................ | Yosemite Falls—total in three sections:................. | 2,425 feet |
| | Upper Yosemite Fall................................ | 1,430 feet |
| | Cascades in middle section......................... | 675 feet |
| | Lower Yosemite Fall................................ | 320 feet |
| Longest river.................... | Mississippi–Missouri................................... | 3,860 miles |
| Highest mountain................ | Mount McKinley, Alaska................................ | 20,320 feet |
| Lowest point.................... | Death Valley, California................................ | − 282 feet |
| Deepest lake................... | Crater Lake, Oregon................................... | 1,932 feet deep |
| Highest lake................... | Lake Waiau, Hawaii................................... | 13,020 feet |
| Largest inland bay.............. | Chesapeake Bay........................................ | 3,237 square miles |

### THE FORTY-EIGHT STATES

| | | |
|---|---|---|
| Total area for forty-eight states | Land 2,971,494 square miles\|Water 50,893 square miles | 3,022,387 square miles |
| Largest state................... | Texas................................................. | 267,339 square miles |
| Northernmost town.............. | Penasse, Minnesota.................................... | 49°22′ N |
| Southernmost city.............. | Key West, Florida..................................... | 24°33′ N |
| Southernmost mainland town..... | Florida City, Florida................................... | 25°27′ N |
| Highest mountain............... | Mt. Whitney, California................................ | 14,495 feet |

*The 1960 census officially listed Los Angeles as the U.S. city with the largest area—454.8 square miles. However, Oklahoma City claimed an area of 631.168 square miles as of 1963, after some 300 separate annexation ordinances. Further U.S. Census Bureau figures on the area of cities may not be available until the 1970 census.

## HIGHEST U.S. MOUNTAIN PEAKS

| SUMMIT | STATE | RANK | ALTITUDE* | SUMMIT | STATE | RANK | ALTITUDE* |
|---|---|---|---|---|---|---|---|
| Mt. McKinley..... | Alaska | 1 | 20,320 | Blanca Peak...... | Colorado | 24 | 14,317 |
| North Peak...... | Alaska | 2 | 19,470 | Uncompahgre Peak | Colorado | 25 | 14,309 |
| Mt. St. Elias...... | Alaska | 3 | 18,008 | Crestone Peak.... | Colorado | 26 | 14,294 |
| Mt. Foraker...... | Alaska | 4 | 17,400 | Mt. Lincoln....... | Colorado | 27 | 14,286 |
| Mt. Bona........ | Alaska | 5 | 16,500 | Grays Peak....... | Colorado | 28 | 14,270 |
| Mt. Blackburn.... | Alaska | 6 | 16,390 | Mt. Antero....... | Colorado | 29 | 14,269 |
| Mt. Sanford...... | Alaska | 7 | 16,237 | Torreys Peak..... | Colorado | 30 | 14,267 |
| South Buttress... | Alaska | 8 | 15,885 | Castle Peak...... | Colorado | 31 | 14,265 |
| Mt. Vancouver... | Alaska | 9 | 15,700 | Mt. Evans....... | Colorado | 32 | 14,264 |
| Mt. Fairweather.. | Alaska | 10 | 15,300 | Quandary Peak... | Colorado | 33 | 14,264 |
| Mt. Hubbard..... | Alaska | 11 | 15,015 | Longs Peak...... | Colorado | 34 | 14,256 |
| Mt. Bear......... | Alaska | 12 | 14,831 | Mt. Wilson....... | Colorado | 35 | 14,246 |
| East Buttress..... | Alaska | 13 | 14,730 | White Mtn........ | California | 36 | 14,246 |
| Mt. Hunter...... | Alaska | 14 | 14,573 | North Palisade... | California | 37 | 14,242 |
| Mt. Alverstone.... | Alaska | 15 | 14,565 | Mt. Cameron..... | Colorado | 38 | 14,238 |
| Browne Tower.... | Alaska | 16 | 14,530 | Shavano Peak.... | Colorado | 39 | 14,229 |
| Mt. Whitney..... | California | 17 | 14,494 | Mt. Belford...... | Colorado | 40 | 14,197 |
| Mt. Elbert....... | Colorado | 18 | 14,431 | Mt. Princeton.... | Colorado | 41 | 14,197 |
| Mt. Harvard..... | Colorado | 19 | 14,420 | Mt. Yale......... | Colorado | 42 | 14,196 |
| Mt. Massive..... | Colorado | 20 | 14,418 | Crestone Needles | Colorado | 43 | 14,191 |
| Mt. Rainier...... | Washington | 21 | 14,410 | Mt. Bross........ | Colorado | 44 | 14,172 |
| Mt. Williamson... | California | 22 | 14,375 | Kit Carson Mtn... | Colorado | 45 | 14,165 |
| La Plata Peak.... | Colorado | 23 | 14,340 | Mt. Wrangell..... | Alaska | 46 | 14,163 |

* In feet.

## HIGHEST AND LOWEST POINTS IN THE UNITED STATES

Source: U.S. Geological Survey

| STATE | HIGHEST POINT | ALTITUDE[1] | LOWEST POINT | ALTITUDE[1] |
|---|---|---|---|---|
| United States............. | Mount McKinley............ | 20,320 | Death Valley................. | —282 |
| Alabama..................... | Cheaha Mountain............. | 2,407 | Gulf of Mexico............... | (a) |
| Alaska...................... | Mount McKinley............. | 20,320 | Pacific Ocean................ | (a) |
| Arizona..................... | Humphreys Peak............. | 12,633 | Colorado River............... | 70 |
| Arkansas.................... | Magazine Mountain........... | 2,753 | Ouachita River............... | 55 |
| California.................. | Mount Whitney............... | 14,494 | Death Valley................. | —282 |
| Colorado.................... | Mount Elbert................ | 14,431 | Arkansas River............... | 3,350 |
| Connecticut................. | Mount Frissell, on south slope | 2,380 | Long Island Sound........... | (a) |
| Delaware.................... | Ebright Road................ | 442 | Atlantic Ocean............... | (a) |
| Florida..................... | Sec. 30, T6N, R20W, Walton Co.[2] | 345 | Atlantic Ocean............... | (a) |
| Georgia..................... | Brasstown Bald............. | 4,784 | Atlantic Ocean............... | (a) |
| Hawaii...................... | Mauna Kea.................. | 13,796 | Pacific Ocean................ | (a) |
| Idaho....................... | Borah Peak................. | 12,662 | Snake River.................. | 710 |
| Illinois.................... | Charles Mound.............. | 1,235 | Mississippi River............ | 279 |
| Indiana..................... | Franklin T, Wayne Co., Sec. 3, T15N, R1W[2]........ | 1,257 | Ohio River................... | 320 |
| Iowa........................ | T100N, R41W, Osceola Co.[2]... | 1,649 | Mississippi River............ | 480 |
| Kansas...................... | Mount Sunflower, Sec. 12, T12S, R43W, Wallace Co.[2]... | 4,039 | Verdigris River.............. | 680 |
| Kentucky.................... | Black Mountain.............. | 4,145 | Mississippi River............ | 257 |
| Louisiana................... | Driskill Mountain............ | 535 | New Orleans.................. | —5 |
| Maine....................... | Mount Katahdin............. | 5,268 | Atlantic Ocean............... | (a) |
| Maryland.................... | Backbone Mountain........... | 3,360 | Atlantic Ocean............... | (a) |
| Massachusetts............... | Mount Greylock............. | 3,491 | Atlantic Ocean............... | (a) |
| Michigan.................... | Mount Curwood.............. | 1,980 | Lake Erie.................... | 572 |
| Minnesota................... | Eagle Mountain, Cook Co..... | 2,301 | Lake Superior................ | 602 |
| Mississippi................. | Woodall Mountain, near Iuka.. | 806 | Gulf of Mexico............... | (a) |
| Missouri.................... | Taum Sauk Mountain........ | 1,772 | St. Francis River............ | 230 |
| Montana..................... | Granite Peak................ | 12,799 | Kootenai River............... | 1,800 |
| Nebraska.................... | Johnson T, Kimball Co., T12N, R59W[2]........... | 5,424 | Southeast corner of state...... | 840 |
| Nevada...................... | Boundary Peak............... | 13,140 | Colorado River............... | 470 |
| New Hampshire............... | Mount Washington............ | 6,288 | Atlantic Ocean............... | (a) |
| New Jersey.................. | High Point.................. | 1,803 | Atlantic Ocean............... | (a) |
| New Mexico.................. | Wheeler Peak............... | 13,161 | Red Bluff Reservoir.......... | 2,817 |
| New York.................... | Mount Marcy................ | 5,344 | Atlantic Ocean............... | (a) |
| North Carolina............. | Mount Mitchell............. | 6,684 | Atlantic Ocean............... | (a) |
| North Dakota............... | White Butte, Slope Co....... | 3,506 | Red River.................... | 750 |
| Ohio........................ | Campbell Hill............... | 1,550 | Ohio River................... | 433 |
| Oklahoma.................... | Black Mesa.................. | 4,973 | Little River................. | 287 |
| Oregon...................... | Mount Hood................. | 11,235 | Pacific Ocean................ | (a) |
| Pennsylvania................ | Mount Davis................ | 3,213 | Delaware River............... | (a) |
| Rhode Island................ | Jerimoth Hill............... | 812 | Atlantic Ocean............... | (a) |
| South Carolina............. | Sassafras Mountain.......... | 3,560 | Atlantic Ocean............... | (a) |
| South Dakota............... | Harney Peak................ | 7,242 | Big Stone Lake............... | 962 |
| Tennessee................... | Clingmans Dome............. | 6,643 | Mississippi River............ | 182 |
| Texas....................... | Guadalupe Peak............. | 8,751 | Gulf of Mexico............... | (a) |
| Utah........................ | Kings Peak................. | 13,528 | Beaverdam Creek.............. | 2,000 |
| Vermont..................... | Mount Mansfield............. | 4,393 | Lake Champlain............... | 95 |
| Virginia.................... | Mount Rogers............... | 5,729 | Atlantic Ocean............... | (a) |
| Washington.................. | Mount Rainier.............. | 14,410 | Pacific Ocean................ | (a) |
| West Virginia............... | Spruce Knob................ | 4,862 | Potomac River................ | 240 |
| Wisconsin................... | Tim's Hill, Price Co........ | 1,952 | Lake Michigan................ | 581 |
| Wyoming..................... | Gannett Peak............... | 13,785 | Belle Fourche River.......... | 3,100 |
| District of Columbia........ | Tenleytown.................. | 410 | Potomac River................ | (a) |

(a) Sea level.    [1] feet.    [2] "Sec." denotes section; "T," township; "R," range; "N," north; "W," west; "S," south.

## AMERICA'S LOWEST POINT

An area 282 feet below sea level in Death Valley, California, is the lowest point not only in the nation but in the entire Western Hemisphere. Named by gold seekers who barely survived a journey across its arid expanse in 1849, Death Valley is also the nation's hottest and driest spot. The valley's record high temperature is 134° F. in the shade; its average annual rainfall is only 1.78 inches.

National Park Service

## U.S. COAST AND SHORELINE (In Miles)
Source: U.S. Coast and Geodetic Survey

| STATE | GENERAL COASTLINE[1] | TIDAL SHORELINE[2] | STATE | GENERAL COASTLINE[1] | TIDAL SHORELINE[2] |
|---|---|---|---|---|---|
| United States......... | 12,383 | 88,633 | South Carolina........ | 187 | 2,876 |
| Atlantic Coast......... | 2,069 | 28,673 | Virginia.............. | 112 | 3,315 |
| Connecticut.......... | — | 618 | Gulf Coast............ | 1,631 | 17,141 |
| Delaware............. | 28 | 381 | Alabama............. | 53 | 607 |
| Florida.............. | 580 | 3,331 | Florida.............. | 770 | 5,095 |
| Georgia.............. | 100 | 2,344 | Louisiana........... | 397 | 7,721 |
| Maine............... | 228 | 3,478 | Mississippi.......... | 44 | 359 |
| Maryland............ | 31 | 3,190 | Texas............... | 367 | 3,359 |
| Massachusetts....... | 192 | 1,519 | Pacific Coast......... | 7,623 | 40,298 |
| New Hampshire...... | 13 | 131 | Alaska.............. | 5,580 | 31,383 |
| New Jersey.......... | 130 | 1,792 | California........... | 840 | 3,427 |
| New York........... | 127 | 1,850 | Hawaii.............. | 750 | 1,052 |
| North Carolina....... | 301 | 3,375 | Oregon............. | 296 | 1,410 |
| Pennsylvania........ | — | 89 | Washington.......... | 157 | 3,026 |
| Rhode Island........ | 40 | 384 | Arctic Coast, Alaska... | 1,060 | 2,521 |

[1] Figures are lengths of the general outline of the seacoast. Measurements were made with a unit measure of 30 minutes of latitude on charts as near the scale of 1: 1,200,000 as possible.   [2] Shoreline of outer coast, offshore islands, sounds, bays, rivers, and creeks is included to the head of tidewater or to a point where tidal waters narrow to a width of 100 feet.

## U.S. TIDES: 1968
Source: U.S. Coast and Geodetic Survey

Listed below are the average tidal ranges predicted for 1968. "Average range" is the difference in height between average high and low tides. "Spring range" is the average range occurring semi-monthly due to a new or full moon. "Diurnal range" is the difference between average higher high tide and average lower low tide.

| EAST COAST LOCATION | AVERAGE RANGE (in feet) | SPRING RANGE (in feet) | WEST COAST LOCATION | AVERAGE RANGE (in feet) | DIURNAL RANGE (in feet) |
|---|---|---|---|---|---|
| Portland, Maine............... | 9.0 | 10.4 | Seattle, Washington............ | 7.6 | 11.3 |
| Boston, Massachusetts....... | 9.5 | 11.0 | Coos Bay, Oregon............. | 5.6 | 7.3 |
| The Battery, New York City..... | 4.5 | 5.4 | Crescent City, California........ | 5.1 | 6.9 |
| Atlantic City, New Jersey....... | 4.1 | 5.0 | San Francisco, California....... | 4.0 | 5.7 |
| Norfolk, Virginia............. | 2.8 | 3.4 | Santa Barbara, California....... | 3.6 | 5.3 |
| Charlestown, South Carolina.... | 5.2 | 6.1 | Los Angeles, California........ | 3.8 | 5.4 |
| Miami, Florida*............... | 2.0 | 2.4 | San Diego, California.......... | 4.1 | 5.7 |

* Reading at the Causeway (east end); figures are slightly higher at the Harbor Entrance.

## LENGTHS OF MAJOR U.S. RIVERS
All rivers exceeding 500 miles in length

| RIVER | EMPTIES INTO: | LENGTH (in miles) | RIVER | EMPTIES INTO: | LENGTH (in miles) |
|---|---|---|---|---|---|
| Mississippi–Missouri..... | Gulf of Mexico | 3,860 | Tanana................. | Yukon River | 800 |
| Missouri–Red Rock...... | Mississippi River | 2,533 | North Canadian......... | Canadian River | 760 |
| Mississippi............. | Gulf of Mexico | 2,348 | Pecos.................. | Rio Grande | 735 |
| Missouri............... | Mississippi River | 2,315 | Green (Utah-Wyo.)....... | Colorado River | 730 |
| Rio Grande............. | Gulf of Mexico | 1,885 | James (N. Dak.-S. Dak.). | Missouri River | 710 |
| Yukon................. | Bering Sea | 1,800 | White (Ark.-Mo.)....... | Mississippi River | 690 |
| Arkansas.............. | Mississippi River | 1,450 | Cumberland............ | Ohio River | 687 |
| Colorado (U.S.-Mex.).... | Gulf of California | 1,450 | Yellowstone........... | Missouri River | 671 |
| Ohio-Allegheny........ | Mississippi River | 1,306 | Tennessee............. | Ohio River | 652 |
| Columbia.............. | Pacific Ocean | 1,214 | Mobile–Alabama–Coosa.. | Mobile Bay | 639 |
| Mississippi, Upper...... | To mouth of Missouri River | 1,171 | Gila.................. | Colorado River | 630 |
| Snake................. | Columbia River | 1,038 | Milk.................. | Missouri River | 625 |
| Red (Okla.-Texas-La.).... | Mississippi River | 1,018 | North Platte........... | Platte River | 618 |
| Ohio.................. | Mississippi River | 981 | Ouachita.............. | Red River | 605 |
| Canadian.............. | Arkansas River | 906 | Cimarron.............. | Arkansas River | 600 |
| Columbia, Upper........ | To mouth of Snake River | 890 | Little Missouri......... | Missouri River | 560 |
| | | | Kuskokwim............ | Kuskokwim Bay | 550 |
| Brazos............... | Gulf of Mexico | 870 | Red River of the North... | Lake Winnipeg | 545 |
| Tennessee-French Broad.. | Ohio River | 862 | Smoky Hill............ | Kansas River | 540 |
| Colorado (Texas)........ | Matagorda Bay | 840 | Santee–Wateree–Catawba | Atlantic Ocean | 538 |
| | | | Clark Fork–Pend Oreille.. | Columbia River | 505 |

## SELECTED U.S. NATURAL LAKES

Lakes with area of 100 square miles or more

Source: U.S. Geological Survey

| LAKE | LOCATION | AREA | LAKE | LOCATION | AREA |
|---|---|---|---|---|---|
| Lake of the Woods............ | Minnesota and Ontario | 1,485 | Winnebago.................. | Wisconsin | 215 |
| Great Salt [a]................ | Utah | 1,000 [b] | Mille Lacs.................. | Minnesota | 207 |
| Iliamna..................... | Alaska | 1,000 | Flathead................... | Montana | 197 |
| Okeechobee................ | Florida | 700 | Tahoe...................... | California and Nevada | 193 |
| Pontchartrain [a]............. | Louisiana | 625 | Leech...................... | Minnesota | 176 |
| Champlain.................. | New York, Vermont, and Quebec | 490 | Pend Oreille................ | Idaho | 148 |
| St. Clair.................... | Michigan and Ontario | 460 | Ugashik (Upper and Lower).... | Alaska | 147 |
| | | | Upper Klamath.............. | Oregon | 142 |
| Becharof................... | Alaska | 458 | Utah....................... | Utah | 140 |
| Red Lake (Upper and Lower).. | Minnesota | 451 | Yellowstone................. | Wyoming | 137 |
| Salton Sea [a]............... | California | 350 [b] | Moosehead.................. | Maine | 117 |
| Rainy...................... | Minnesota and Ontario | 345 | Tustumena.................. | Alaska | 117 |
| | | | Bear....................... | Idaho and Utah | 110 |
| Teshekpuk.................. | Alaska | 315 | Clark...................... | Alaska | 110 |
| Naknek.................... | Alaska | 242 | Winnibigoshish.............. | Minnesota | 109 |
| | | | Dall....................... | Alaska | 100 |

[a] Salty.  [b] Variable.

## THE GREAT LAKES

Source: Lake Survey, Corps of Engineers, U.S. Army

| DIMEN-SIONS | SUPE-RIOR | MICH-IGAN | HURON | ERIE | ON-TARIO |
|---|---|---|---|---|---|
| Length, in miles | 350 | 307 | 206 | 241 | 193 |
| Breadth, in miles | 160 | 118 [a] | 183 [b] | 57 | 53 |
| Coastline, in miles * | 2,980 | 1,660 | 3,180 [c] | 856 | 726 |
| Surface areas, in sq. mi. | | | | | |
| U.S..... | 20,700 [d] | 22,400 [e] | 9,100 [f] | 4,980 | 3,600 [g] |
| Canada . | 11,100 [d] | | 13,900 [f] | 4,930 | 4,000 [g] |
| Total.... | 31,800 | 22,400 | 23,000 | 9,910 | 7,600 |

*Including islands.  [a] Measured through Green Bay.
[b] Measured through Georgian Bay.  [c] Includes Georgian Bay and North Channel.  [d] Including St. Marys River above Falls.  [e] Lake Michigan, including Green Bay.  [f] Including St. Marys River below Falls, North Channel, and Georgian Bay.  [g] Lake Ontario, including Niagara River and St. Lawrence River to Iroquois Dam.

## LARGEST MAN-MADE U.S. LAKES

Source: National Geographic Society

| LAKE | LOCATION | AREA (in square miles) | MAXI-MUM DEPTH (in feet) |
|---|---|---|---|
| Garrison *...... | North Dakota.... | 609.38 | 200 |
| Fort Peck *.... | Montana........ | 382.81 | 220 |
| Powell......... | Arizona-Utah.... | 252.00 | 580 |
| Kentucky...... | Kentucky-Tenn... | 247.34 | 145 |
| Francis Case... | South Dakota.... | 160.31 | 140 |
| Eufaula *...... | Oklahoma....... | 160.16 | 87 |
| Marion........ | South Carolina... | 157.03 | 35 |
| Texoma....... | Oklahoma-Texas . | 149.06 | 94 |
| F. D. Roosevelt. | Washington...... | 123.44 | 375 |
| Bull Shoals.... | Missouri-Ark..... | 111.31 | 243 |
| Clark Hill *.... | S. Carolina-Georgia | 111.09 | 190 |
| Guntersville.... | Alabama........ | 107.97 | 60 |
| Wheeler..... | Alabama........ | 104.84 | 58 |
| Cumberland.... | Kentucky........ | 78.51 | — |
| John H. Kerr *.. | North Carolina... | 76.4 | 100 |

* Reservoir.

## OZARK NATIONAL SCENIC RIVERWAYS

The nation's first national riverway is an unspoiled stretch of forested river land winding through the Ozark Mountains of Missouri. Incorporated into the National Park System in 1964, the riverway includes 101 miles of the Current River and 39 miles of the Jacks Forks River. Only 175 miles from St. Louis and 250 miles from Kansas City, it is within an easy day's drive for more than 20,000,000 people. Visitors have a unique opportunity to boat and fish, to watch osprey at work, to camp on gravel bars, to explore caves where men of yesterday once lived, to enjoy the Ozarks' renowned fall colors, or perhaps even to just loaf.

National Park Service

## ESTIMATED U.S. POPULATION BY STATES: 1966

Source: U.S. Bureau of the Census

| DIVISION AND STATE | POPULA- TION | Under 18 Years | 18 to 64 Years | 65 Years and over | 18 Years and over | 21 Years and over |
|---|---|---|---|---|---|---|
| **UNITED STATES......** | **195,857,000** | **70,665,000** | **106,736,000** | **18,457,000** | **125,192,000** | **115,348,000** |
| **NEW ENGLAND:** | | | | | | |
| Maine.............. | 983,000 | 357,000 | 515,000 | 111,000 | 626,000 | 575,000 |
| New Hampshire...... | 681,000 | 241,000 | 367,000 | 73,000 | 440,000 | 407,000 |
| Vermont............ | 405,000 | 149,000 | 212,000 | 44,000 | 256,000 | 236,000 |
| Massachusetts....... | 5,383,000 | 1,844,000 | 2,932,000 | 607,000 | 3,539,000 | 3,286,000 |
| Rhode Island........ | 898,000 | 300,000 | 502,000 | 96,000 | 598,000 | 549,000 |
| Connecticut......... | 2,875,000 | 996,000 | 1,610,000 | 269,000 | 1,879,000 | 1,745,000 |
| Total¹............. | 11,224,000 | 3,886,000 | 6,138,000 | 1,200,000 | 7,338,000 | 6,797,000 |
| **MIDDLE ATLANTIC:** | | | | | | |
| New York........... | 18,258,000 | 6,025,000 | 10,339,000 | 1,893,000 | 12,233,000 | 11,410,000 |
| New Jersey.......... | 6,898,000 | 2,342,000 | 3,916,000 | 640,000 | 4,556,000 | 4,228,000 |
| Pennsylvania........ | 11,582,000 | 3,913,000 | 6,471,000 | 1,198,000 | 7,668,000 | 7,123,000 |
| Total¹............. | 36,738,000 | 12,281,000 | 20,726,000 | 3,731,000 | 24,457,000 | 22,761,000 |
| **NORTH CENTRAL:** | | | | | | |
| Ohio............... | 10,305,000 | 3,779,000 | 5,569,000 | 957,000 | 6,526,000 | 6,028,000 |
| Indiana............ | 4,918,000 | 1,818,000 | 2,629,000 | 471,000 | 3,100,000 | 2,861,000 |
| Illinois............ | 10,722,000 | 3,802,000 | 5,861,000 | 1,059,000 | 6,920,000 | 6,427,000 |
| Michigan........... | 8,374,000 | 3,190,000 | 4,471,000 | 713,000 | 5,184,000 | 4,776,000 |
| Wisconsin.......... | 4,161,000 | 1,555,000 | 2,162,000 | 445,000 | 2,606,000 | 2,406,000 |
| Minnesota.......... | 3,576,000 | 1,360,000 | 1,824,000 | 391,000 | 2,215,000 | 2,043,000 |
| Iowa............... | 2,747,000 | 986,000 | 1,417,000 | 345,000 | 1,761,000 | 1,627,000 |
| Missouri........... | 4,408,000 | 1,554,000 | 2,425,000 | 529,000 | 2,954,000 | 2,741,000 |
| North Dakota....... | 650,000 | 252,000 | 335,000 | 62,000 | 398,000 | 362,000 |
| South Dakota........ | 682,000 | 265,000 | 340,000 | 78,000 | 418,000 | 383,000 |
| Nebraska........... | 1,456,000 | 529,000 | 752,000 | 175,000 | 927,000 | 857,000 |
| Kansas............. | 2,250,000 | 800,000 | 1,192,000 | 257,000 | 1,449,000 | 1,337,000 |
| Total¹............. | 54,349,000 | 19,167,000 | 28,977,000 | 5,482,000 | 34,459,000 | 31,847,000 |
| **SOUTH ATLANTIC:** | | | | | | |
| Delaware........... | 512,000 | 195,000 | 277,000 | 40,000 | 317,000 | 292,000 |
| Maryland........... | 3,613,000 | 1,344,000 | 2,009,000 | 261,000 | 2,270,000 | 2,080,000 |
| District of Columbia... | 808,000 | 276,000 | 460,000 | 73,000 | 532,000 | 501,000 |
| Virginia............ | 4,507,000 | 1,643,000 | 2,537,000 | 326,000 | 2,863,000 | 2,602,000 |
| West Virginia........ | 1,794,000 | 636,000 | 975,000 | 183,000 | 1,158,000 | 1,058,000 |
| North Carolina....... | 5,000,000 | 1,856,000 | 2,782,000 | 362,000 | 3,144,000 | 2,847,000 |
| South Carolina....... | 2,586,000 | 1,020,000 | 1,393,000 | 172,000 | 1,566,000 | 1,402,000 |
| Georgia............ | 4,459,000 | 1,703,000 | 2,428,000 | 327,000 | 2,756,000 | 2,500,000 |
| Florida............ | 5,941,000 | 2,045,000 | 3,154,000 | 743,000 | 3,897,000 | 3,616,000 |
| Total¹............. | 29,220,000 | 10,717,000 | 16,015,000 | 2,488,000 | 18,503,000 | 16,900,000 |
| **SOUTH CENTRAL:** | | | | | | |
| Kentucky........... | 3,183,000 | 1,167,000 | 1,703,000 | 314,000 | 2,016,000 | 1,838,000 |
| Tennessee.......... | 3,883,000 | 1,390,000 | 2,150,000 | 342,000 | 2,492,000 | 2,284,000 |
| Alabama............ | 3,517,000 | 1,336,000 | 1,892,000 | 289,000 | 2,181,000 | 1,982,000 |
| Mississippi......... | 2,327,000 | 940,000 | 1,183,000 | 204,000 | 1,387,000 | 1,249,000 |
| Arkansas........... | 1,955,000 | 714,000 | 1,029,000 | 211,000 | 1,241,000 | 1,134,000 |
| Louisiana.......... | 3,603,000 | 1,454,000 | 1,879,000 | 270,000 | 2,149,000 | 1,954,000 |
| Oklahoma........... | 2,458,000 | 843,000 | 1,343,000 | 272,000 | 1,616,000 | 1,488,000 |
| Texas.............. | 10,752,000 | 4,099,000 | 5,774,000 | 878,000 | 6,653,000 | 6,088,000 |
| Total¹............. | 31,678,000 | 11,943,000 | 16,954,000 | 2,780,000 | 19,734,000 | 18,018,000 |
| **MOUNTAIN** | | | | | | |
| Montana............ | 702,000 | 271,000 | 365,000 | 67,000 | 432,000 | 395,000 |
| Idaho.............. | 694,000 | 268,000 | 361,000 | 64,000 | 425,000 | 388,000 |
| Wyoming........... | 329,000 | 126,000 | 174,000 | 29,000 | 203,000 | 186,000 |
| Colorado........... | 1,977,000 | 739,000 | 1,066,000 | 172,000 | 1,238,000 | 1,137,000 |
| New Mexico......... | 1,022,000 | 446,000 | 514,000 | 62,000 | 576,000 | 518,000 |
| Arizona............ | 1,618,000 | 646,000 | 849,000 | 123,000 | 972,000 | 888,000 |
| Utah............... | 1,008,000 | 428,000 | 510,000 | 70,000 | 580,000 | 527,000 |
| Nevada............. | 454,000 | 170,000 | 260,000 | 24,000 | 284,000 | 262,000 |
| Total¹............. | 7,804,000 | 3,094,000 | 4,099,000 | 611,000 | 4,710,000 | 4,301,000 |
| **PACIFIC:** | | | | | | |
| Washington......... | 2,980,000 | 1,062,000 | 1,618,000 | 301,000 | 1,919,000 | 1,759,000 |
| Oregon............ | 1,955,000 | 678,000 | 1,071,000 | 206,000 | 1,276,000 | 1,178,000 |
| California.......... | 18,918,000 | 6,708,000 | 10,599,000 | 1,611,000 | 12,211,000 | 11,266,000 |
| Alaska............. | 272,000 | 119,000 | 146,000 | 7,000 | 152,000 | 135,000 |
| Hawaii............. | 718,000 | 286,000 | 394,000 | 38,000 | 432,000 | 387,000 |
| Total¹............. | 24,843,000 | 8,853,000 | 13,827,000 | 2,163,000 | 15,990,000 | 14,724,000 |

¹ Totals may not equal total of estimated state populations since figures have been independently rounded.

## IMMIGRATION TO THE UNITED STATES: 1820–1966

Source: U.S. Immigration and Naturalization Service

| YEARS | NUMBER OF PERSONS | YEARS | NUMBER OF PERSONS | YEARS | NUMBER OF PERSONS |
|---|---|---|---|---|---|
| 1820–1966........ | 43,614,313 | 1881–1890....... | 5,246,613 | 1951–1960....... | 2,515,479 |
| 1820–1930....... | 151,824 | 1891–1900....... | 3,687,564 | 1961....... | 271,344 |
| 1831–1840....... | 599,125 | 1901–1910....... | 8,795,386 | 1962....... | 283,763 |
| 1841–1850....... | 1,713,251 | 1911–1920....... | 5,735,811 | 1963....... | 306,260 |
| 1851–1860....... | 2,598,214 | 1921–1930....... | 4,107,209 | 1964....... | 292,248 |
| 1861–1870....... | 2,314,824 | 1931–1940....... | 528,431 | 1965....... | 296,697 |
| 1871–1880....... | 2,812,191 | 1941–1950....... | 1,035,039 | 1966....... | 323,040 |

## ALIENS IN THE UNITED STATES

Source: U.S. Department of Justice

A total of 3,668,836 aliens were residing in the United States in 1967. Of this number, 3,210,-768 were permanent residents of the United States and 458,068 were visitors, students, temporary workers, and others in the country for brief stays.

California, with 881,996 aliens—24 per cent of the total—continues to have the largest alien population of any state. New York ranks second, with 661,608. Other states with large alien populations are Texas, Illinois, New Jersey, Florida, Massachusetts, Michigan, Pennsylvania, and Ohio.

Mexican nationals dominate the alien population, with a total of 668,514 permanent residents, and contribute largely to the alien populations of California, Texas, New Mexico, Nevada, and other southwestern states.

Canadians are the second largest group, with 385,367. Nationals of the United Kingdom, Germany, and Italy each number over 200,000; those of Poland and Cuba each total more than 100,000; while Ireland, Japan, and the Philippines have in residence over 50,000 each.

In January of each year aliens are required to report their addresses to the U.S. Immigration and Naturalization Service.

## IMMIGRANTS ADMITTED TO THE UNITED STATES, BY COUNTRY: 1957–1966

Source: U.S. Immigration and Naturalization Service

| Country | Number | Country | Number |
|---|---|---|---|
| ALL COUNTRIES (Total: 1957–1966)...... | 2,879,568 | Syria.................. | 2,342 |
| | | Other Asia....................... | 19,327 |
| Europe.......................... | 1,358,536 | North America.................... | 1,058,906 |
| Austria............................... | 20,098 | Canada........................ | 320,507 |
| Belgium........................... | 10,946 | Mexico.......................... | 399,886 |
| Czechoslovakia.................... | 21,438 | Cuba........................... | 134,669 |
| Denmark.......................... | 13,879 | Dominican Republic.............. | 55,676 |
| Finland............................ | 6,741 | Haiti.......................... | 16,335 |
| France............................. | 39,977 | Jamaica........................ | 16,578 |
| Germany........................... | 289,611 | Other West Indies............... | 25,502 |
| Great Britain...................... | 248,509 | Costa Rica..................... | 13,955 |
| Greece............................ | 44,430 | El Salvador.................... | 12,075 |
| Hungary........................... | 57,282 | Guatemala...................... | 10,022 |
| Ireland............................ | 67,781 | Honduras....................... | 13,052 |
| Italy.............................. | 182,626 | Nicaragua...................... | 12,622 |
| Netherlands........................ | 45,994 | Panama......................... | 17,910 |
| Norway............................ | 22,530 | Other North America............. | 10,117 |
| Poland............................ | 87,760 | South America.................... | 186,762 |
| Portugal........................... | 36,294 | Argentina...................... | 38,401 |
| Romania........................... | 13,140 | Brazil......................... | 17,871 |
| Spain............................. | 19,181 | Chile.......................... | 11,015 |
| Sweden............................ | 20,751 | Colombia....................... | 54,883 |
| Switzerland........................ | 17,961 | Ecuador........................ | 25,992 |
| U.S.S.R. (Europe and Asia)......... | 23,806 | Peru........................... | 17,519 |
| Yugoslavia......................... | 35,243 | Other South America............. | 21,081 |
| Other Europe....................... | 32,558 | Africa........................... | 24,620 |
| Asia............................ | 237,665 | Algeria........................ | 1,596 |
| China (Taiwan)..................... | 52,731 | Morocco........................ | 2,923 |
| Hong Kong......................... | 9,419 | Nigeria........................ | 772 |
| India.............................. | 7,560 | South Africa................... | 3,392 |
| Indonesia.......................... | 18,333 | United Arab Republic (Egypt)..... | 7,895 |
| Iran............................... | 6,019 | Other Africa................... | 8,042 |
| Israel............................. | 13,152 | Oceania.......................... | 12,936 |
| Japan.............................. | 46,739 | Australia...................... | 6,699 |
| Jordan............................. | 7,599 | New Zealand.................... | 2,667 |
| Korea.............................. | 18,150 | Pacific Islands (U.S. adm.).... | 1,329 |
| Lebanon........................... | 4,453 | Other Oceania.................. | 2,241 |
| Philippines........................ | 31,841 | Other countries................. | 143 |

# FINANCE AND TAXES

## U.S. BUDGET: 1967–1968

In his special message to Congress on August 3, 1967, President Johnson told the nation that "no task is more formidable than to try to predict—over 18 months in advance—a budget of around $135 billion and its related revenues for 200,000,000 Americans." Tracing the Federal budget from the time the President submitted it to Congress on the previous January 24 until his special message graphically illustrates the dangers in economic forecasting.

In January the budget for fiscal year 1967–68, which began on July 1, put expenditures at $135 billion and revenues at about $127 billion. The revenue total was predicated on a 6 per cent surcharge on corporate and individual income taxes, scheduled to take effect July 1. Of the estimated expenditures, $75.5 billion was earmarked for defense and the Atomic Energy Commission, and $59.5 billion for civilian programs. The deficit of $8 billion, while high, was considered manageable, because the gross national product—the total of all goods and services—was expected to rise to $787 billion in calendar year 1967.

By mid-year the picture had changed drastically, and for the worse. The Vietnam war was costing $2 billion a month; corporation profits, personal income, and tax yields were lower than the January projections; and the surcharge had still not become effective.

The President therefore offered the country "these hard and inescapable facts":

■ Expenditures probably reaching $143.5 billion.

■ Revenues of $120 billion even with the 6 per cent surcharge.

■ A $23.6 billion deficit, with the possibility that it would hit $28 billion if Congress did not keep a tight rein on spending and if no new taxes were imposed.

President Johnson warned that a deficit of the magnitude of $28 billion "poses a clear and present danger to America's security and economic health." The $8 billion rise in expenditures from the earlier forecast included $4 billion for defense and $2.5 billion for civilian projects. In disclosing the step-up in defense spending, the President also noted that he was dispatching 45,000 more men to Vietnam by mid-1968.

To offset this budget increase, President Johnson requested a 10 per cent, not a 6 per cent surcharge on personal and corporate income taxes, a speed-up on corporate tax collections, and continuation of excise taxes for the immediate future. The tax proposals were expected to add $10 billion in revenues for fiscal year 1967–68. If the necessary steps were taken "to control expenditures," the deficit could be reduced to a "manageable" $15 billion to $18 billion. As the alternative to his program, the President foresaw "a ruinous spiral of inflation" and "brutally higher interest rates."

The first reaction of Congress was one of reluctant acceptance. This later changed to expressions of outright opposition, particularly in the House. Members of the influential House Ways and Means Committee told the Administration that they were not convinced of the need for the surcharge. The American business community, on the other hand, supported the call for the tax increase as necessary to curb dangerous inflationary pressures.

## THE FEDERAL BUDGET DOLLAR
Fiscal Year 1967-68 Estimate

Source: U.S. Bureau of the Budget

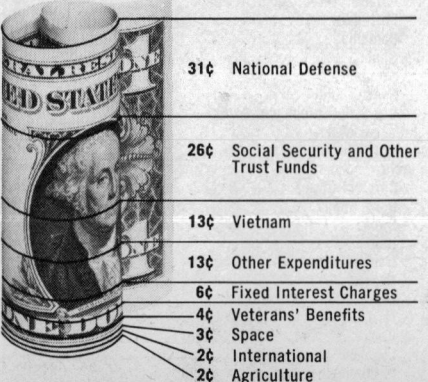

**WHERE IT COMES FROM:**

| | |
|---|---|
| Individual Income Taxes | 42¢ |
| Corporation Income Taxes | 20¢ |
| Employment Taxes | 17¢ |
| Other Revenues | 11¢ |
| Excise Taxes | 8¢ |
| Borrowing | 2¢ |

**WHERE IT GOES:**

| | |
|---|---|
| 31¢ | National Defense |
| 26¢ | Social Security and Other Trust Funds |
| 13¢ | Vietnam |
| 13¢ | Other Expenditures |
| 6¢ | Fixed Interest Charges |
| 4¢ | Veterans' Benefits |
| 3¢ | Space |
| 2¢ | International |
| 2¢ | Agriculture |

## U.S. FEDERAL BUDGET: EXPENDITURES, 1961–1968
Source: U.S. Bureau of the Budget

| BUDGET CATEGORIES | EXPENDITURES (in millions of dollars) | | | | | | | |
|---|---|---|---|---|---|---|---|---|
| | ACTUAL | | | | | | ESTIMATED | |
| | 1961 | 1962 | 1963 | 1964 | 1965 | 1966 | 1967 | 1968 |
| **National defense:** | | | | | | | | |
| Department of Defense—military: | | | | | | | | |
| Military personnel | 12,085 | 13,032 | 13,000 | 14,195 | 14,771 | 16,753 | 20,200 | 21,823 |
| Procurement | 13,095 | 14,532 | 16,632 | 15,351 | 11,839 | 14,339 | 18,465 | 21,632 |
| Operation and maintenance | 10,611 | 11,594 | 11,874 | 11,932 | 12,349 | 14,710 | 18,600 | 19,017 |
| Research and development | 6,131 | 6,319 | 6,376 | 7,021 | 6,236 | 6,259 | 6,700 | 7,200 |
| Military construction, civil defense, etc... | 1,305 | 1,338 | 373 | 1,261 | 978 | 2,349 | 2,985 | 2,628 |
| Subtotal, military | 43,227 | 46,815 | 48,252 | 49,760 | 46,173 | 54,409 | 66,950 | 72,300 |
| Atomic energy | 2,713 | 2,806 | 2,758 | 2,765 | 2,625 | 2,403 | 2,270 | 2,330 |
| Military assistance | 1,449 | 1,390 | 1,721 | 1,485 | 1,229 | 968 | 1,000 | 800 |
| Defense-related activities | 104 | 92 | 24 | 172 | 136 | −62* | 1 | 57 |
| Subtotal | 47,494 | 51,103 | 52,755 | 54,181 | 50,163 | 57,718 | 70,222 | 75,487 |
| **International affairs and finance:** | | | | | | | | |
| Food for Freedom | 1,823 | 1,947 | 2,040 | 2,049 | 1,843 | 1,784 | 1,710 | 1,799 |
| Economic and financial programs: | | | | | | | | |
| Development loans | 258 | 347 | 760 | 768 | 754 | 677 | 710 | 695 |
| Supporting assistance | 1,013 | 618 | 494 | 371 | 387 | 500 | 604 | 680 |
| Alliance for Progress | — | 155 | 260 | 272 | 367 | 459 | 593 | 588 |
| Technical cooperation | 169 | 272 | 245 | 226 | 227 | 224 | 196 | 212 |
| Other | 487 | 738 | 67 | −158* | 359 | 3 | 219 | 229 |
| Conduct of foreign affairs | 216 | 249 | 346 | 297 | 346 | 315 | 335 | 346 |
| Foreign information and exchange activities | 158 | 197 | 201 | 207 | 223 | 227 | 242 | 248 |
| Subtotal | 4,124 | 4,523 | 4,412 | 4,032 | 4,506 | 4,191 | 4,608 | 4,797 |
| **Space research and technology:** | | | | | | | | |
| Manned space flight | 279 | 565 | 1,516 | 2,768 | 3,538 | 4,210 | 3,825 | 3,575 |
| Space science and applications | 249 | 420 | 576 | 754 | 751 | 778 | 770 | 740 |
| Space technology | 87 | 159 | 303 | 432 | 484 | 435 | 450 | 440 |
| Supporting activities | 79 | 82 | 122 | 178 | 262 | 435 | 460 | 435 |
| Aircraft technology | 51 | 31 | 36 | 40 | 58 | 75 | 95 | 110 |
| Subtotal | 744 | 1,257 | 2,552 | 4,171 | 5,093 | 5,933 | 5,600 | 5,300 |
| **Agriculture and agricultural resources:** | | | | | | | | |
| Farm income stabilization | 2,176 | 2,871 | 3,693 | 3,798 | 3,236 | 1,925 | 2,368 | 2,467 |
| Agricultural land and water resources | 347 | 367 | 324 | 324 | 341 | 346 | 379 | 381 |
| Rural electrification and telephone loans... | 301 | 303 | 342 | 342 | 392 | 373 | 259 | 319 |
| Farming and rural housing loans | 349 | 234 | 300 | 251 | 268 | 160 | −532* | −584* |
| Research and other agricultural services.... | 324 | 341 | 391 | 414 | 457 | 503 | 560 | 591 |
| Subtotal | 3,498 | 4,116 | 5,050 | 5,129 | 4,696 | 3,307 | 3,035 | 3,173 |
| **Natural resources:** | | | | | | | | |
| Land, water, and power resources | 1,488 | 1,680 | 1,853 | 1,927 | 2,032 | 2,235 | 2,218 | 2,443 |
| Forests | 331 | 280 | 303 | 332 | 374 | 406 | 463 | 449 |
| Recreational resources | 91 | 94 | 112 | 130 | 134 | 152 | 199 | 246 |
| Minerals | 61 | 68 | 71 | 91 | 105 | 108 | 115 | 140 |
| Fish and wildlife | 73 | 81 | 94 | 105 | 120 | 130 | 134 | 139 |
| General resource surveys and other natural resource activities | 55 | 60 | 73 | 73 | 94 | 89 | 97 | 103 |
| Subtotal | 2,100 | 2,264 | 2,506 | 2,658 | 2,851 | 3,120 | 3,226 | 3,518 |
| **Commerce and transportation:** | | | | | | | | |
| Air transportation | 716 | 781 | 808 | 835 | 875 | 879 | 946 | 890 |
| Water transportation | 569 | 654 | 672 | 658 | 728 | 708 | 757 | 806 |
| Postal service | 914 | 797 | 770 | 578 | 805 | 888 | 1,208 | 544 |
| Advancement of business | 271 | 427 | 366 | 401 | 557 | 193 | 182 | 407 |
| Area and regional development | — | 7 | 101 | 401 | 398 | 156 | 207 | 323 |
| Regulation of business | 67 | 74 | 84 | 91 | 98 | 99 | 103 | 100 |
| Ground transportation | 36 | 33 | 41 | 39 | 39 | 46 | 92 | 19 |
| Subtotal | 2,573 | 2,774 | 2,843 | 3,002 | 3,499 | 2,969 | 3,495 | 3,089 |

*Negative figures show net receipts greater than expenditures.

(*continued*)

**U.S. FEDERAL BUDGET** (*continued*)

| BUDGET CATEGORIES | EXPENDITURES (in millions of dollars) | | | | | | | |
|---|---|---|---|---|---|---|---|---|
| | ACTUAL | | | | | | ESTIMATED | |
| | 1961 | 1962 | 1963 | 1964 | 1965 | 1966 | 1967 | 1968 |
| **Housing and community development:** | | | | | | | | |
| Urban renewal and community facilities.... | 162 | 261 | 222 | 306 | 420 | 446 | 561 | 982 |
| Public housing programs................. | 150 | 163 | 178 | 149 | 230 | 233 | 263 | 282 |
| Aids to private housing:* | | | | | | | | |
| Federal Savings and Loan Insurance Corp. | −35 | −237 | −264 | −248 | −205 | −255 | −130 | −317 |
| Federal National Mortgage Association... | 75 | −123 | −439 | −347 | −540 | −392 | −133 | −82 |
| Federal Housing Administration and other | −84 | 211 | 167 | † | −73 | 241 | 202 | 23 |
| National capital region................... | 51 | 74 | 70 | 59 | 64 | 75 | 127 | 135 |
| Subtotal................... | 320 | 349 | −67 | −80 | −104 | 347 | 890 | 1,023 |
| **Health, labor and welfare:** | | | | | | | | |
| Public assistance................... | 1,918 | 2,087 | 2,361 | 2,506 | 2,544 | 2,797 | 2,942 | 3,036 |
| Health services and research............ | 894 | 1,073 | 1,280 | 1,574 | 1,509 | 1,754 | 2,277 | 2,653 |
| Medicare and medical assistance.......... | 252 | 347 | 427 | 490 | 555 | 770 | 1,988 | 2,113 |
| Economic opportunity programs........... | — | — | — | — | 211 | 1,018 | 1,580 | 1,860 |
| School lunch, special milk, and food stamp | 241 | 275 | 284 | 308 | 299 | 363 | 455 | 540 |
| Labor and manpower.................... | 809 | 591 | 224 | 345 | 464 | 500 | 493 | 526 |
| Vocational rehabilitation, and other........ | 85 | 108 | 140 | 158 | 214 | 373 | 654 | 574 |
| Subtotal................... | 4,200 | 4,481 | 4,715 | 5,381 | 5,797 | 7,574 | 10,389 | 11,304 |
| **Education:** | | | | | | | | |
| Elementary and secondary education....... | 332 | 337 | 392 | 404 | 418 | 1,368 | 1,827 | 2,000 |
| Science education and basic research...... | 143 | 183 | 206 | 310 | 309 | 368 | 395 | 455 |
| Higher education....................... | 286 | 350 | 428 | 383 | 413 | 701 | 451 | −376 |
| Other aid to education.................. | 181 | 207 | 219 | 241 | 405 | 397 | 631 | 737 |
| Subtotal................... | 943 | 1,076 | 1,244 | 1,339 | 1,544 | 2,834 | 3,304 | 2,816 |
| **Veterans benefits and services:** | | | | | | | | |
| Disability and survivors compensation...... | 2,034 | 2,017 | 2,116 | 2,158 | 2,176 | 2,221 | 2,298 | 2,427 |
| Non-service-connected pensions........... | 1,532 | 1,635 | 1,698 | 1,743 | 1,864 | 1,910 | 1,931 | 2,037 |
| Hospitals and medical care.............. | 1,030 | 1,084 | 1,145 | 1,229 | 1,270 | 1,318 | 1,389 | 1,471 |
| Education and training.................. | 237 | 142 | 88 | 59 | 43 | 42 | 366 | 417 |
| Housing loan programs*................. | 312 | 236 | −109 | 44 | −100 | −706 | 144 | −459 |
| Other benefits and services.............. | 268 | 287 | 248 | 259 | 241 | 238 | 266 | 231 |
| Subtotal................... | 5,414 | 5,403 | 5,186 | 5,492 | 5,495 | 5,023 | 6,394 | 6,124 |
| **General government:** | | | | | | | | |
| Tax collection and central fiscal operations.. | 607 | 653 | 715 | 791 | 825 | 864 | 909 | 940 |
| Property and records management......... | 372 | 419 | 444 | 576 | 606 | 585 | 676 | 691 |
| Protective services and alien control...... | 289 | 300 | 323 | 335 | 366 | 385 | 445 | 465 |
| Legislative and judicial functions.......... | 170 | 192 | 194 | 192 | 218 | 238 | 261 | 274 |
| Central personnel management............ | 140 | 153 | 142 | 174 | 174 | 175 | 194 | 197 |
| Territories and possessions, and other..... | 131 | 158 | 160 | 211 | 213 | 216 | 239 | 216 |
| Subtotal................... | 1,709 | 1,875 | 1,979 | 2,280 | 2,402 | 2,464 | 2,725 | 2,781 |
| **Interest**................... | 9,050 | 9,198 | 9,980 | 10,765 | 11,435 | 12,132 | 13,508 | 14,152 |
| **Allowance for:** | | | | | | | | |
| Civilian and military pay increase......... | — | — | — | — | − | — | — | 1,000 |
| Possible shortfall in asset sales........... | — | — | — | — | — | — | — | 750 |
| Contingencies....................... | — | — | — | — | — | — | 100 | 400 |
| Deduct interfund transactions.............. | 654 | 633 | 513 | 664 | 870 | 635 | 766 | 682 |
| **TOTAL U.S. BUDGET EXPENDITURES** | 81,515 | 87,787 | 92,642 | 97,684 | 96,507 | 106,978 | 126,729 | 135,033 |

\* Negative figures show net receipts greater than expenditures.   † Less than $500,000.

## U.S. INTERNAL REVENUES: 1866–1966
Source: U.S. Internal Revenue Service

During the last one hundred years the tax per capita has increased from $8.49 to $654.74. However the cost of collecting these taxes has generally declined and was lowest in 1944 when each $100 in taxes was collected for only 32 cents.

| FISCAL YEAR | COST OF COLLECTING $100 | TAX PER CAPITA | FISCAL YEAR | COST OF COLLECTING $100 | TAX PER CAPITA | FISCAL YEAR | COST OF COLLECTING $100 | TAX PER CAPITA |
|---|---|---|---|---|---|---|---|---|
| 1866 | $2.47 | $8.49 | 1918 | $0.33 | $ 35.38 | 1944 | $0.32 | $288.96 |
| 1871 | 5.30 | 3.50 | 1919 | 0.53 | 36.65 | 1946 | 0.43 | 286.86 |
| 1885 | 3.90 | 1.98 | 1929 | 1.17 | 24.14 | 1952 | 0.42 | 414.00 |
| 1890 | 2.82 | 2.26 | 1930 | 1.13 | 24.68 | 1953 | 0.38 | 436.53 |
| 1900 | 1.58 | 3.88 | 1933 | 1.85 | 12.89 | 1960 | 0.40 | 507.97 |
| 1905 | 2.01 | 2.79 | 1940 | 1.12 | 40.42 | 1965 | 0.52 | 588.14 |
| 1914 | 1.52 | 3.83 | 1943 | 0.44 | 162.55 | 1966 | 0.48 | 654.74 |

## THE U.S. BUDGET AND THE PUBLIC DEBT:* 1789–1968

Source: U.S. Bureau of the Budget

| FISCAL YEAR | U.S. BUDGET RECEIPTS | U.S. BUDGET EXPEND-ITURES | SURPLUS (+) OR DEFICIT (−) | PUBLIC DEBT AT END OF YEAR | FISCAL YEAR | U.S. BUDGET RECEIPTS | U.S. BUDGET EXPEND-ITURES | SURPLUS (+) OR DEFICIT (−) | PUBLIC DEBT AT END OF YEAR |
|---|---|---|---|---|---|---|---|---|---|
| 1789–1849 | 1,160 | 1,090 | +70 | 63 | 1948.... | 41,375 | 32,955 | +8,419 | 252,366 |
| 1850–1899 | 13,895 | 14,932 | −1,037 | 1,437 | 1949.... | 37,663 | 39,474 | −1,811 | 252,798 |
| 1905.... | 544 | 567 | −23 | 1,132 | 1950.... | 36,422 | 39,544 | −3,122 | 257,377 |
| 1910.... | 676 | 694 | −18 | 1,147 | 1951.... | 47,480 | 43,970 | +3,510 | 255,251 |
| 1915.... | 683 | 746 | −63 | 1,191 | 1952.... | 61,287 | 65,303 | −4,017 | 259,151 |
| 1920.... | 6,649 | 6,357 | +291 | 24,299 | 1953.... | 64,671 | 74,120 | −9,449 | 266,123 |
| 1925.... | 3,598 | 2,881 | +717 | 20,516 | 1954.... | 64,420 | 67,537 | −3,117 | 271,341 |
| 1930.... | 4,058 | 3,320 | +738 | 16,185 | 1955.... | 60,209 | 64,389 | −4,180 | 274,418 |
| 1935.... | 3,706 | 6,497 | −2,791 | 32,824 | 1956.... | 67,850 | 66,221 | +1,626 | 272,825 |
| 1936.... | 3,997 | 8,422 | −4,425 | 38,497 | 1957.... | 70,562 | 68,966 | +1,596 | 270,634 |
| 1937.... | 4,956 | 7,733 | −2,777 | 41,089 | 1958.... | 68,550 | 71,369 | −2,819 | 276,444 |
| 1938.... | 5,588 | 6,765 | −1,177 | 42,018 | 1959.... | 67,915 | 80,342 | −12,427 | 284,817 |
| 1939.... | 4,979 | 8,841 | −3,862 | 45,890 | 1960.... | 77,763 | 76,539 | +1,224 | 286,471 |
| 1940.... | 5,137 | 9,055 | −3,918 | 48,497 | 1961.... | 77,659 | 81,515 | −3,856 | 289,211 |
| 1941.... | 7,096 | 13,255 | −6,159 | 55,332 | 1962.... | 81,409 | 87,787 | −6,378 | 298,645 |
| 1942.... | 12,547 | 34,037 | −21,490 | 76,991 | 1963.... | 86,376 | 92,642 | −6,266 | 306,466 |
| 1943.... | 21,947 | 79,368 | −57,420 | 140,796 | 1964.... | 89,459 | 97,684 | −8,226 | 312,526 |
| 1944.... | 43,563 | 94,986 | −51,423 | 202,626 | 1965.... | 93,072 | 96,507 | −3,435 | 317,864 |
| 1945.... | 44,362 | 98,303 | −53,941 | 259,115 | 1966.... | 104,727 | 106,978 | −2,251 | 320,369 |
| 1946.... | 39,650 | 60,326 | −20,676 | 269,898 | 1967.... | 115,794 | 125,732 | −9,938 | 326,733 |
| 1947.... | 39,677 | 38,923 | +754 | 258,376 | 1968 (est) | 126,937 | 135,033 | −8,096 | 335,400 |

*Figures are given in millions of dollars; that is, "000,000" is omitted.

## U.S. TAX COLLECTIONS, BY SOURCE

Selected Fiscal Years, 1929–1968

Source: Tax Foundation and U.S. Treasury Department

| SOURCE | (in millions of dollars) 1929 | 1939 | 1949 | 1959 | 1967 * | 1968 * |
|---|---|---|---|---|---|---|
| Total Internal Revenue Collections........... | $2,939 | $5,182 | $40,463 | $79,798 | $148,327 | $161,472 |
| Income and profits taxes...................... | 2,332 | 2,185 | 29,606 | 58,827 | 104,240 | 115,500 |
| Individual income..................... | 1,096 | 1,029 | 18,052 | 40,735 | 69,325 | 80,800 |
| Corporation income and profits................ | 1,236 | 1,156 | 11,554 | 18,092 | 34,915 | 34,700 |
| Excise taxes.......................... | 540 | 1,768 | 7,580 | 10,760 | 14,130 | 14,118 |
| Manufacturers' excise...................... | 6 | 397 | 1,772 | 3,959 | 5,974 | 5,121 |
| Automobiles.......................... | — | 43 | 333 | 1,039 | 1,580 | 930 |
| Gasoline............................. | — | 207 | 504 | 1,700 | 3,175 | 3,069 |
| Trucks and buses...................... | — | 6 | 137 | 215 | 587 | 510 |
| Tires and tubes....................... | — | 35 | 151 | 279 | 537 | 526 |
| Radios, phonographs, and TV sets [1]...... | — | 5 | 49 | 153 | — | — |
| Parts and accessories for automobiles........ | — | 8 | 120 | 166 | — | — |
| Other............................... | 6 | 94 | 478 | 406 | 95 | 86 |
| Alcoholic beverages...................... | 13 | 588 | 2,211 | 3,002 | 3,996 | 4,203 |
| Tobacco.............................. | 434 | 580 | 1,322 | 1,807 | 2,130 | 2,261 |
| Retailers' excise........................ | — | — | 449 | 356 | 5 | — |
| Documentary stamps and playing cards........... | 64 | 41 | 73 | 134 | 85 | 45 |
| Miscellaneous......................... | 23 | 162 | 1,753 | 1,436 | 1,897 | 2,426 |
| Transportation of property [2]........... | — | — | 337 | 143 | — | 9 |
| General telephone service............... | — | — | 225 | 398 | {1,200 | {1,020 |
| Toll telephone and telegraph messages....... | — | 24 | 311 | 292 | | |
| Transportation of persons [3]............ | — | — | 251 | 227 | 199 | 196 |
| Admissions [4]........................ | 6 | 19 | 435 | 95 | — | — |
| Other............................... | 17 | 119 | 194 | 280 | 498 | 1,201 |
| Undistributed depository receipts and other payments.......................... | — | — | — | 66 | 43 | 62 |
| Estate and gift taxes..................... | 62 | 361 | 797 | 1,353 | 3,001 | 3,130 |
| Employment taxes........................ | — | 740 | 2,476 | 8,854 | 26,956 | 28,724 |
| Customs................................ | 602 | 319 | 384 | 948 | 1,972 | 2,145 |
| Railroad unemployment insurance taxes....... | — | — | 10 | 101 | 145 | 144 |
| TOTAL TAX COLLECTIONS................... | 3,541 | 5,500 | 40,857 | 80,847 | 150,444 | 163,761 |

*Data are preliminary for 1967, estimated for 1968. [1] Repealed as of June 22, 1965. [2] Repealed as of August 1, 1958. [3] Repealed as of November 16, 1962, except on air transportation. [4] Repealed as of December 31 1965.

## INDIVIDUAL FEDERAL INCOME TAX RETURNS

Source: U.S. Internal Revenue Service

Since January 1, 1967, the Federal tax returns of all business and individual taxpayers in the United States have been processed by computers. This new system, called Automatic Data Processing, was installed to enable the Internal Revenue Service to handle the steadily increasing volume of tax returns. It also provides greater assurance that all income is reported, that all deductions are permissible, and that the proper tax is paid.

The system has three major features:

(a) It provides a continuously updated multiple-year digest of each taxpayer's tax history. This is the master file that is maintained on magnetic tape at the National Computer Center in Martinsburg, West Virginia—one for individuals and one for business taxpayers. The file, for example, shows where and when returns were filed, indicates all returns for which the taxpayer is liable, itemizes the amount and status of each liability, records audit status, and provides the additional information that is necessary to administer the Federal tax system.

(b) Each taxpayer is identified in the master file by number. For individuals, the social security number is used; for business taxpayers, the employer identification number.

(c) The system centralizes processing operations in seven regional service centers.

Briefly, the system operates as follows:

Individuals send their tax returns to one of the 58 district offices, where the return is reviewed and remittances deposited. Then the return is forwarded to the Service Center. The Center transcribes information on punch cards, verifies it, converts the data to magnetic tape, and sends it on to the National Computer Center. There all the information received is transferred to the master file. Magnetic tapes are produced from the master file and a variety of output tapes are made, including refund tapes for issuing refund checks and tapes stating notices of tax due.

Most of the tapes produced at the Computer Center are sent back to the Service Center for action. The Service Center then mails delinquency notices and bills to the taxpayer; forwards directories, index listings, and registers to the district offices; and sends delinquent account information to the Collection Division in field offices for collection.

All returns and documents are filed at district offices. While Service Centers do most of the clerical work in connection with returns, district and local offices provide taxpayers with help and assistance in filing their returns.

### GRADUATED INCOME TAX WITHHOLDING

In May, 1966, the President signed into law a new income tax withholding system which should greatly ease the burden of the American taxpayer. Under this graduated withholding system, the employee has withheld from his wages an amount of tax sufficient to meet his tax liability when the time comes to file his Federal tax return.

### WHO MUST FILE FEDERAL INCOME TAX RETURNS

Anyone under 65 years of age (whether single or married) who had a gross income of $600 or more during the year must file a Federal income tax return. Those persons 65 years of age or older on the last day of the tax year who did not have a gross income of $1,200 for the tax year are not required to file Federal returns. They should, however (and this also applies to other individuals who earned less than $600 during the year), file a return and claim their own exemption to obtain a refund of taxes that had been withheld from their earnings. Those American citizens living in a foreign country who earned or had a gross income of $600 or more ($1,200 if 65 or older) must file Federal income tax returns. (A pamphlet, *Tax Guide for U.S. Citizens Abroad,* is available at most U.S. embassies and consulates.) Persons who are self-employed and who had a self-employment income of $400 or more, even though the gross income was under $600, must file Federal tax returns.

A minor is subject to tax on his own earnings even though his parent may, under local law, have the right to them and might actually have received the money. His income is not required to be included in the return of his parent. A minor must file a return if he has a gross income of $600 or more during the year. He is, however, allowed a personal exemption of $600 on his own return regardless of how much money he earned during the year. A dependency exemption is also allowed the parent even though the minor earned more than $600, if the minor is under 19 or is a full-time student, provided that the minor otherwise qualifies as a dependent. A minor who makes less than $600 and whose income tax was withheld from his wages can get his refund by filing Form 1040A, accompanied by the withholding statement (Form W-2). If the minor had income other than from wages subject to withholding, he may be required to file his tax return using Form 1040.

### WHERE TO FILE AND WHEN

Individual Federal income tax returns may be filed with the District Director within the district where you reside at any time after January 1 of the year following the year of earnings, but no later than midnight of April 15, if the calendar year is the basis for these earnings. However, taxpayers may file their returns with their respective Service Centers when refunds are due. If a fiscal year is used, the return is due on or before the 15th day of the fourth month after the close of the fiscal or tax year used. Returns submitted through the mails must be mailed on or before the due date. Payments of all tax liability must be made at the time that the return is filed. Interest at the rate of 6 per cent a year is charged on taxes that are not paid on or before their due date. Such interest is charged even though an extension for filing of a return is authorized. Extensions may be granted under unusual circumstances by application on Form 2688 with the District Director of Internal Revenue, or by letter to the same office. Extensions must be applied for prior to the final due date of filing. U.S. citizens abroad on the final filing date are allowed automatic extensions until June 15; military or naval personnel on duty outside the United States or Puerto Rico are allowed the same extension. Statements that the taxpayer was outside the United States and Puerto Rico on the due date of his return must accompany the return for him to take advantage of this automatic extension.

### FORMS TO USE

Individual income tax returns can be filed through the use of either Form 1040A (short form) or Form 1040.

Form 1040A may be used if the taxpayer uses the cash method of accounting and the calendar year as the basis for his earnings, and if his income was less than $10,000, consisting entirely of wages reported on withholding statements, or of such wages and not more than a total of $200 from other wages, dividends, and interest. The taxpayer using Form 1040A whose income is under $5,000, filing either jointly or separately, may fill out the form and determine his tax from tables furnished, or he may have the District Director determine his tax liability for him. If his income is more than $5,000, the taxpayer must compute his own tax. A joint Form 1040A may be filed only if the combined earnings of husband and wife do not exceed $10,000, and if the above requirements are met.

Form 1040 may be filed by any individual regardless of the source or amount of his income. This form may be used whether the taxpayer takes the ten per cent standard deduction, takes the minimum standard deduction, or itemizes his deductions. If income is solely from salaries and wages, Form 1040 may be used without filing any of the separate schedules.

### OTHER INFORMATION

An income tax return should be complete in every detail for effective processing by the Data Processing Centers. Care should be exercised that every return includes the taxpayer's complete name, social security number, amount of wages from all W-2 forms, total number of personal exemptions, deductions (whether based on the ten per cent standard or the minimum standard deduction, or through itemization), and signature (of both husband and wife if it is a joint return). Any error or omission of the above can result in a delay of the processing of returns and may result in a delay in payment of tax refunds.

### ESTIMATED TAX RETURNS

In some instances individuals are required to file an estimated tax declaration and pay an estimated tax. A person who expects his total tax liability to exceed the amount withheld by $40 or more must declare and pay an estimated tax (1) if he anticipates earnings of $200 or more not subject to withholding; (2) if he is a single person who is the head of a household or a married person or a surviving spouse who expects gross income exceeding $10,000; (3) if he is a single person not heading a household or a married person who is not entitled to file a joint tax declaration and he expects a gross income exceeding $5,000; or (4) if he is married and entitled to file a joint tax declaration, but his income combined with that of his spouse will exceed $10,000. When filing an estimated tax declaration, the taxpayer must be sure to indicate his taxpayer identification number or his social security number.

### WHAT INCOME IS TAXABLE

The following types of income should be included in computing gross income: all wages and salaries, tips and gratuities, annuities, alimony, awards, back pay, bonuses, breach of contract damages, business income, commissions, compensations for personal services, dividends and interest, fees, estate and trust income, gains from sale of property, gambling winnings, hobby income, jury duty fees, partnership income, pensions, prizes, rents, retirement pay, rewards, royalties, severance pay and military pay (derived from active duty or from attending the armed services' academies), lump sum payments upon separation or release to inactive duty (but not including disability severance pay), and re-enlistment bonuses or pay for reserve training. (See Military and Veterans.)

### INCOME NORMALLY NOT TAXABLE

The following are some items that normally are not taxable and should not be reported on the Federal tax return: accident and health insurance proceeds, casualty insurance proceeds (with exceptions; consult *Your Federal Income Tax* booklet), disability and death payments, Federal Employees Compensation Act Payments, gifts, bequests, inheritances, interest on municipal bonds, life insurance proceeds paid because of death, mustering out pay, Railroad Retirement Act pensions, rental allowances of clergymen, certain scholarship and fellowship grants, unemployment compensation, veterans' benefits, workmen's compensation, and cost of living allowances paid to U.S. employees stationed outside of the U.S. Taxpayers should read carefully the detailed explanations in documents issued by the government on taxable and non-taxable income.

### MILITARY AND VETERANS

Payments equal to six months' pay that are made by the United States to beneficiaries of armed forces personnel who died in active service are exempt from tax. Military retirement pay based on age or length of service is taxable. Annuity payments received by widows or children of retired members of the uniformed services under the provisions of the Retired Servicemen's Family Protection Plan are partially taxable. Forfeited pay is not included in income, but fines other than forfeitures, whether or not collected by withholding from pay, may not be excluded or deducted from income. Dislocation allowances paid upon transfer from one post to another are included in gross income, and are therefore taxable. Benefits paid to veterans and their
*(continued)*

## FEDERAL INCOME TAX (*continued*)

families are exempt from tax. These include education and training or subsistence allowances paid to veterans for service-connected and nonservice-connected disabilities, grants to seriously disabled veterans for homes designed for wheelchair living, and grants for motor vehicles to veterans who have lost the use of their limbs. Veterans' insurance proceeds and dividends either to the veteran or to his beneficiaries are not taxable. This includes proceeds of a veteran's endowment policy paid before the death of the veteran. Interest on dividends, however, left on deposit with the Veterans Administration is taxable. Pensions paid to either the veteran or his family are tax exempt.

## MILITARY SERVICE IN VIETNAM

An enlisted man, warrant officer, or commissioned warrant officer need not report compensation when it is received for active service in the armed forces of the United States for any month during any part of which he served in Vietnam or its adjacent waters, or was hospitalized at any place as a result of wounds, disease, or injury incurred in Vietnam and its adjacent waters. A commissioned officer in the armed forces is exempt from income tax on the first $500 of compensation for any month during any part of which he served in Vietnam and its adjacent waters, or was hospitalized at any place as a result of the wounds, disease, or injury incurred in the combat zone.

Servicemen who have not filed returns because of military service in Vietnam have an automatic extension of time for filing. Returns are not due until 180 days after combat zone veterans leave Vietnam. If a serviceman is hospitalized outside the United States as a result of Vietnam service, the due date for returns is 180 days after release from the hospital. No interest or penalties are assessed on returns delayed because of combat service.

## MEDICAL AND DENTAL DEDUCTIONS

Certain medical and dental expenses actually paid for by the taxpayer can be deducted in computing income tax liability. These may be for either the taxpayer, his spouse, or his dependents, and they must be for items for which reimbursement was not made. Such expenses are deductible only to the extent they exceed 3 per cent of the taxpayer's adjusted gross income. These deductions may be made only for the year during which they were actually paid.

## PERSONAL EXEMPTIONS AND DEPENDENTS

Deductions for exemptions may be claimed even though the taxpayer elected to take the 10 per cent standard deduction or the minimum standard deduction. A taxpayer may claim his own exemption, $600, and if he is 65 years of age or over by the end of the tax year, he may claim an additional $600 exemption. If the taxpayer is blind on the last day of the tax year, he may claim another $600 exemption for that year. On joint returns, a husband may claim a personal exemption for his wife, another $600 if she is 65 or older and another $600 if she is blind on the last day of the tax year. When filing a separate return,

a husband may claim the exemption for his wife, but only if she had no gross income and was not the dependent of another taxpayer. If she has income, he may claim his wife's exemption only if she files a joint return with him. In the event that a taxpayer was divorced or legally separated at the end of the tax year, he cannot claim his wife's exemption even though he contributed all of her support. Dependency exemptions may be claimed for children who have $600 or more income if they are under 19 years of age, or older than 19 years of age and are full-time students, provided that at least one-half of their support was supplied by the taxpayer. Under certain conditions dependent exemptions may be allowed for the support of any of the following: a child (a legally adopted child qualifies as a dependent), grandchild, great-grandchild, a stepchild (but not his descendant), a brother or sister, half-brother or half-sister, stepbrother or stepsister, parent, grandparent, or other direct ancestor (but not a foster parent), a stepfather or stepmother, an aunt or uncle, a niece or nephew, and a father-in-law, mother-in-law, son-in-law, daughter-in-law, brother-in-law, or sister-in-law.

An exemption of $600 is allowed for each person qualifying as the taxpayer's dependent. A dependent must: (1) receive over half his total support from the taxpayer (special rules apply to scholarships for study at educational institutions), (2) generally not receive a gross income of $600 or more during the year (not applicable to the taxpayer's child, stepchild, or adopted child under 19, or to a qualified student, except in an armed services' academy, regardless of age), (3) be a member of the taxpayer's household, living with him for the entire year, or be related to the taxpayer in certain degrees, (4) be a citizen or resident of the United States, and (5) not file a joint return. (Rules for claiming dependents contain definitions and exceptions, and should be consulted before filing tax returns.)

## CAPITAL GAINS AND LOSSES

Usually, the tax on capital gains is less than the tax on ordinary income. The deduction for capital losses, however, may be limited.

If the net gains from the sale or exchange of long-term capital assets (those held longer than six months) are greater than the net losses from the sale or exchange of short-term capital assets (those held six months or less), only one-half the excess is subject to tax. The tax on net long-term capital gains cannot exceed 25 per cent of the excess. If the net result of all sales and exchanges of both long-term and short-term capital assets is a loss, not more than $1,000 may be deducted. However, the balance of the loss may be carried over and deducted in succeeding tax years.

## EMPLOYEE DEDUCTIONS

Employees may deduct transportation and traveling expenses, except commuting, which are ordinary and necessary in the performance of their duties. Expenses for entertainment and gifts are sometimes deductible. Meals and lodging are deductible only when the employee travels away from home overnight on business. Deductions must be itemized.

An outside salesman—one who does his selling away from his employer's place of business —is permitted to deduct all expenses incurred in connection with his sales activity, except for meals, whether or not he is away from home. (If an employee's principal duties are service or delivery, he is not considered an outside salesman.)

If an employee is required to use his car exclusively for his work, he may deduct its operational expenses, including the cost of gasoline, oil, repairs, garage rent, insurance, depreciation, interest to purchase the car, taxes, licenses, etc. A standard rate of ten cents a mile for the first 15,000 miles of business use, and seven cents a mile thereafter, may be used to determine deductible costs, in lieu of actual expenses and depreciation. In addition, parking fees and tolls incurred through business use are deductible.

## JOINT RETURNS

Usually, married persons may file a joint return or separate returns. Marital status is determined as of the final day of the tax year. A married taxpayer may owe less if he files a joint return, even though his spouse had no income or deductions. All income, exemptions, and deductions for both persons must be included on a joint return, and it must be signed by both husband and wife.

A taxpayer whose spouse has died during the year is considered to have been married for the entire year, and, if he has not remarried before the close of the tax year, may file a joint return for himself and his deceased spouse. He may be entitled also to surviving spouse benefits for the following two years.

Persons divorced by final decree on or before the last day of the tax year are considered to have been single for the entire year, and may not file a joint return.

## DIVIDENDS

Dividends are distributions of cash, property, services, and accommodations by a corporation to its stockholders. Most are from the cash earnings of the company, and are taxable to the stockholder. Distributions other than cash are included in income to the extent of their fair market value.

The gross amount of dividends must be reported. However, the first $100 of qualified dividends may be excluded from income on both Form 1040 and Form 1040A. To qualify for the exclusion, the dividends must be from fully taxable domestic corporations.

In addition to industrial, mercantile, and commercial corporations, the exclusion and credit apply to dividends on the capital stock of non-exempt cooperatives, stock of the Federal National Mortgage Association, the capital stock of building and loan associations (as distinct from dividends on deposits and withdrawable accounts), and similar organizations.

Some types of corporations whose dividends do not qualify are: foreign corporations, China Trade Act corporations, exempt farmers' cooperatives, real estate investment trusts, corporations doing business in possessions of the United States (under certain conditions), and a corporation that has elected not to be taxed. Husbands and wives are permitted $100 exclusions each, regardless of the type of return filed.

## RETIREMENT INCOME CREDIT

Retired persons, and individuals 65 and older, may be entitled to a tax credit, under certain conditions. The credit is 15 per cent of retirement income received during the year, or 15 per cent of $1,524 (or $2,286 if the alternative joint computation is used), minus social security, certain pensions, annuities, and earned income over certain amounts, whichever is less. Detailed rules pertaining to eligibility should be consulted.

## CASUALTY AND THEFT LOSSES

The first $100 of a casualty or theft loss of nonbusiness property in excess of reimbursement is no longer deductible. The $100 limitation does not apply to casualty or theft loss of business property, or of property held for the production of income.

## TAXES—DEDUCTIBLE AND NOT DEDUCTIBLE

Certain taxes may be deducted on Federal income tax returns as itemized deductions in Part IV, page 2 of Form 1040. Other taxes may be deductible only if they are trade or business expenses or expenses incurred in the production of income. There are other taxes that cannot be deducted either as itemized deduction or as business or income-producing expenses. Some of the deductible taxes are: state, local, or foreign income taxes; real property taxes; personal property taxes; general sales taxes; and state or local gasoline taxes. If the taxpayer is a tenant-shareholder in a cooperative housing, condominium, or apartment corporation, he may deduct his proportionate share of the real estate taxes imposed upon and paid or accrued by the organization on the property. However, if the organization leases the land and building, and if it is required to pay the real estate taxes under the terms of the lease agreement, the taxpayer's share of such taxes is not deductible. Local benefit taxes assessed for the purpose of maintenance or repair or for the purpose of meeting interest charges with respect to such benefits are deductible. If real estate is sold, the deduction for real estate taxes must be apportioned between the buyer and seller according to the number of days in the real property tax year that each held the property. The following taxes are not deductible on a Federal income tax return: Federal income taxes, including taxes withheld by the employer; social security or Railroad Retirement taxes withheld from wages; social security and other employment taxes paid on the wages of domestic help; customs and Federal excise taxes if paid on articles acquired or services rendered for personal or family use (such as those on automobiles, airline tickets, telephone, gasoline, wine, tobacco, and whiskey). Also not deductible are: Federal estate and

(continued)

**FEDERAL INCOME TAX** (continued)

gift taxes, state or local taxes (such as poll or capitation taxes, inheritance, legacy, succession, gift, cigarette and tobacco, or alcoholic beverages taxes), and fees and charges (such as drivers' licenses, auto inspection fees, dog tags, hunting, fishing or marriage licenses, fines, collateral deposits, or charges for utility services for the home). In many of the above instances, there are exceptions to the general rule. Taxpayers may be guided by the instructions that accompany their Federal income tax forms or may obtain clarification from any of the Internal Revenue offices located throughout the country.

## CONTRIBUTIONS

Deductions for contributions may not be made if the taxpayer claims either the ten per cent standard deduction or the minimum standard deduction, or computes his tax by use of a tax table. To be allowable, contributions must actually be paid in cash or property before the close of the tax year whether the cash or accrual method is used. They are deductible only if made without any consideration or benefit coming to the donor. A deduction will not be allowed if any of the net earnings of the organization that receives the contribution inures to the benefit of any private shareholder or individual.

Gifts to individuals are not deductible, nor are gifts made to any of the following; adoption agencies, civic leagues, social clubs and international organizations, Communist organizations, chambers of commerce or other business leagues or organizations, labor unions (dues may be deducted by an employee, but not as contributions), or political parties and candidates. Gifts or amounts expended to influence the general public with respect to legislative matters, elections, or referendums are nondeductible, as are blood donations, tuition or amounts in lieu of tuition, payments to a hospital for care of particular patients or for services rendered to such patients by the hospital (see Medical and Dental Expenses for further provisions).

In general, the deduction for contributions may not exceed 20 per cent of the adjusted gross income (computed without regard to any net operating loss carryback).

However, the taxpayer is allowed an additional deduction of up to ten per cent of his adjusted gross income for contributions paid to churches or conventions or associations of churches; tax-exempt educational organizations with a regular faculty and curriculum and a regular student body attending resident classes; tax-exempt hospitals; organizations directly engaged in continuous medical research in conjunction with such hospitals, and certain organizations operated exclusively to hold and administer property for state and local colleges and universities; a state, a territory, a possession of the United States, any political subdivision of any of the foregoing, the United States, and the District of Columbia, if the contribution is made for exclusively public purposes. A ten per cent deduction is likewise allowed for contributions to an organization exempt as charitable, religious, educational, scientific, or to a literary organization or an organization organized to prevent cruelty to children or animals, if this normally receives a substantial part of its support (aside from income from its religious, charitable, etc., activities) from a governmental unit of the type just described, or from direct or indirect contributions from the general public.

To qualify as this kind of an organization on the basis of public contributions, support must be received from at least a representative number of persons within the community concerned. This excludes contributions to what are generally termed private foundations from qualifying for the additional 10 per cent limitation. Income from unrelated business activities is considered as support from other than governmental and public contributions.

If all of the taxpayer's contributions were made to these special institutions, he may deduct up to 30 per cent of his adjusted gross income.

How to compute: First the taxpayer must total his contributions to these special institutions. If the total is less than 10 per cent of his adjusted gross income, the full amount is deductible. If it is more, he must deduct 10 per cent and add the rest to his contributions to other organizations. If that total is less than 20 per cent of adjusted gross income, he may deduct it all; if it is more, he may deduct 20 per cent of his adjusted gross income.

## CHILD CARE

A woman, whether single, married, widowed, divorced, or deserted, may under certain conditions deduct up to $900 for expenses incurred for the care of children or disabled dependents. A man, however, may deduct these expenses only if he is widowed, divorced, legally separated from his wife, or if his wife is incapacitated or institutionalized. These deductions must be itemized in Part IV, page 2, of Form 1040. It cannot be claimed when using Form 1040A, a tax table, claiming either the 10 per cent standard deduction or the minimum standard deduction. The deduction is limited each year to the amount actually spent, up to $600 for one dependent and $900 for two or more dependents. The expenses are deductible for only two types of dependents: (a) a child under the age of 13, (b) a person who is physically or mentally incapable of caring for himself, regardless of age. The disability may be temporary or permanent. A taxpayer may not deduct expenses for the care of a child after his 13th birthday unless the child is physically or mentally incapable of caring for himself. If the child becomes 13 years of age during the tax year, only the amount paid for his care before he is 13 is deductible. The deductible expenses must be (1) for the care of the dependent, (2) for such care while the taxpayer is gainfully employed or actively seeking gainful employment, and (3) for the purpose of enabling the taxpayer to be gainfully employed or actively seeking gainful employment.

## SICK PAY

A limited amount of sick pay may be excluded from the taxpayer's gross income if he is absent from work because of sickness or injury, if he is paid for the time he was absent under an employer-financed sick pay plan, and if he is absent longer than his waiting period. (An employee may be subject to a 30-day, 7-day, or no waiting period before he can exclude any sick pay, and should consult the Internal Revenue Service document entitled *Sick Pay* for clarification.) If the amount a taxpayer receives during a period of absence because of illness or injury is at a rate of more than 75 per cent of his weekly pay rate for the four weeks immediately preceding his period of absence, he ordinarily will not have a sick pay exclusion for the first 30 calendar days of his absence. The amount of sick pay that can be excluded cannot exceed a weekly rate of $100, or $75 if an exclusion is allowable before 30 days.

## ALIMONY

Alimony or separate maintenance payments paid to a former spouse or a spouse may be deducted if itemized on Form 1040. While these payments are generally deductible by the payer, they are taxable income to the recipient. Child support is not considered alimony and is not deductible by the taxpayer, nor taxable to the recipient.

If the taxpayer is divorced or legally separated from his spouse, alimony or separate maintenance payments are treated as income to the recipient and deductible for the payer provided these payments are (1) required under the terms of the decree of divorce or separation, or a written instrument incident to such decree, (2) paid in discharge of a legal obligation based on the marital relationship, (3) paid after the decree, and (4) are periodic payments. Not deductible as alimony are: lump sum cash settlements required by a decree or agreement, any payment that is not required by the decree or agreement, any payment that does not arise out of the marital relationship that is required by the decree or agreement (such as a repayment of a loan to your wife), any payment made before the decree or agreement, and any payments of so-called alimony accruing before a decree or agreement and paid subsequently.

## INCOME AVERAGING

Certain taxpayers may benefit from a provision that provides for averaging of income. In some cases, persons with fluctuating incomes may be eligible to pay less tax through this income-averaging provision. If the income for a given year exceeds one and one-third times the average annual income for the four preceding years, and the excess is more than $3,000, the taxpayer may be eligible to use this provision in figuring his tax liability.

## DEDUCTIONS

In preparing a tax return on 1967 earnings, it is important that the taxpayer know and understand the provisions which allow him to make legal deductions from his gross income. Such deductions not only reduce the amount of taxable earnings, but also may lower the actual rate of taxation. These include contributions, interest, taxes, medical and dental expenses, child care and disabled dependent care, casualty or theft loss, or alimony payments. In addition, others are allowed if itemized on Form 1040. These are expenditures that are ordinary and necessary for the production or collection of income, for the management of property held for the production of income, or incurred in connection with the determination, collection, or refund of any tax. These expenses must be directly related to the income or income-producing property and the income must be taxable income.

Other itemized deductions include appraisal fees (for establishing the amount of casualty loss), clerical help and office rent incurred in caring for the taxpayer's investment, custodian fees, investment counsel fees, and tax counsel and assistance fees. Documents explaining the limitations of deductions in the above categories may be obtained at any Internal Revenue Service office.

## ADEQUATE RECORDS

It is important that proper records are maintained to prepare correctly the Federal income tax returns. These records, if complete, insure that the taxpayer pays only his proper tax. Paid bills, canceled checks, and other pertinent data that substantiate entries on tax returns should be filed and stored in a safe place so they will be available when needed.

The maintenance of adequate records may help the taxpayer in many ways. He may receive cash or property from many sources. Unless he has records identifying his receipts, he may be unable to substantiate the fact that some of them are from sources that make them non-taxable. Expenses may be overlooked or forgotten when the tax return is prepared unless they were recorded at the time they were incurred or paid. An overlooked item of $25 could cost the taxpayer $3.50 or more in extra tax dollars.

Since many assets are subject to depreciation, it is important that capital expenditures be recorded in a permanent record of some kind. Without a record of the cost and other information concerning such assets, depreciation allowances cannot be determined. If the assets are sold, become fully depreciated, or capital improvements are made to them, only a permanent record will reflect the unrecovered cost. If the taxpayer's records are adequate and they show the date an asset (whether or not it is depreciable) was acquired, what it was used for, and whether it was sold, traded, destroyed, or otherwise disposed of, he may be able to take advantage of the capital gains provisions of the revenue code. He may also be allowed to postpone paying tax on certain gains, or may be allowed to deduct 100 per cent of certain losses that would otherwise not be deductible or deductible only in part. If the taxpayer's income tax return is audited by the Internal Revenue Service, he may be asked to explain the items reported.

(continued)

## FEDERAL INCOME TAX (continued)

Adequate records are always substantiated by sales slips, invoices, receipts, canceled checks, and other documents that are used as evidence of transactions. It is also important that copies of tax returns filed by the taxpayer be maintained as part of his records. These aid in the preparation of future returns and help in making computations if he later files a claim for refund. They may also be helpful to the executor of the taxpayer's estate or to an Internal Revenue agent, if the original return is not available.

### IMPORTANT DATES TO REMEMBER

By January 31, 1968, employers must provide their employees with a Statement of Wages Earned and Tax Withheld (Form W-2) for 1967; January 31—individuals should file an income tax return for 1967 and pay the tax due, if the balance due on their 1967 estimated income tax was not paid earlier in the month; April 15—individuals must file an income tax return for the calendar year 1967. Tax due must be paid in full with the return when filed.

Individuals who are required to do so must file a declaration of estimated income tax for 1968 and pay at least 25 per cent of such tax; June 15—individuals must pay second installment of 1968 estimated income tax; September 15—individuals must pay third installment of 1968 estimated income tax; January 15, 1969—individuals must pay the fourth and final installment of their 1968 estimated income tax.

### TAXPAYER ACCOUNT NUMBERS

All persons who do not have a Social Security number are required by the Internal Revenue Service to obtain a taxpayer account number. Applications for a number may be made on Social Security Form SS-5 or IRS Form 3227.

### DISTRICT DIRECTORS' OFFICES

ALABAMA—Birmingham, Ala., 35203.
ALASKA—Anchorage, Alaska, 99501.
ARIZONA—Phoenix, Ariz., 85025.
ARKANSAS—Little Rock, Ark., 72203.
CALIFORNIA—Los Angeles, 90012; San Francisco, 94102.
COLORADO—Denver, Colo., 80202.
CONNECTICUT—Hartford, Conn., 06115.
DELAWARE—Wilmington, Del., 19801.
DISTRICT OF COLUMBIA—Baltimore, Md., 21202.
FLORIDA—Jacksonville, Fla., 32202.
GEORGIA—Atlanta, Ga., 30303.
HAWAII—Honolulu, Hawaii, 96813.
IDAHO—Boise, Idaho, 83701.
ILLINOIS—Chicago, Ill.; Springfield, Ill.
INDIANA—Indianapolis, Ind., 46204.
IOWA—Des Moines, Iowa, 50309.
KANSAS—Wichita, Kans., 67202.
KENTUCKY—Louisville, Ky., 40202.
LOUISIANA—New Orleans, La., 70130.
MAINE—Augusta, Maine, 04330.
MARYLAND—Baltimore, Md., 21202.
MASSACHUSETTS—Boston, Mass., 02115.
MICHIGAN—Detroit, Mich., 48226.
MINNESOTA—St. Paul, Minn., 55101.
MISSISSIPPI—Jackson, Miss., 39202.
MISSOURI—St. Louis, Mo., 63101.
MONTANA—Helena, Mont., 59601.

NEBRASKA—Omaha, Nebr., 68102.
NEVADA—Reno, Nev., 89505.
NEW HAMPSHIRE—Portsmouth, N.H., 03801.
NEW JERSEY—Newark, N.J., 07102.
NEW MEXICO—Albuquerque, N. Mex., 87101.
NEW YORK—Brooklyn, N.Y., 11201; 120 Church Street, New York, N.Y., 10007; Albany, N.Y., 12210; Buffalo, N.Y., 14202.
NORTH CAROLINA—Greensboro, N.C., 27401.
NORTH DAKOTA—Fargo, N. Dak., 58102.
OHIO—Cleveland, Ohio, 44113; Cincinnati, Ohio, 45202.
OKLAHOMA—Oklahoma City, Okla., 73102.
OREGON—Portland, Oreg., 97232.
PENNSYLVANIA—Philadelphia, Penn.; Pittsburgh, Penn., 15230.
RHODE ISLAND—Providence, R.I., 02907.
SOUTH CAROLINA—Columbia, S.C., 29201.
SOUTH DAKOTA—Aberdeen, S. Dak., 57401.
TENNESSEE—Nashville, Tenn., 37203.
TEXAS—Austin, Texas, 78701; Dallas, Texas, 75201.
UTAH—Salt Lake City, Utah, 84110.
VERMONT—Burlington, Vt., 05401.
VIRGINIA—Richmond, Va., 23240.
WASHINGTON—Tacoma, Wash., 98402.
WEST VIRGINIA—Parkersburg, W. Va., 26102.
WISCONSIN—Milwaukee, Wis., 53202.
WYOMING—Cheyenne, Wyo., 82001.

## U.S. INDIVIDUAL INCOME TAX AT SELECTED INCOME LEVELS *

Source: Compiled by the Tax Foundation from U.S. Treasury Department data

| Standard Deductions | | | Typical Itemized Deductions | | |
|---|---|---|---|---|---|
| ADJUSTED GROSS INCOME (Income year 1967) | TAX: SINGLE PERSON, NO DEPENDENTS | TAX: MARRIED COUPLE, NO DEPENDENTS | ADJUSTED GROSS INCOME (Income year 1967) | TAX: MARRIED COUPLE, NO DEPENDENTS | TAX: MARRIED COUPLE, TWO DEPENDENTS |
| $ 1,000 | $ 14 | $ 0 | $ 5,000 | $ 407 | $ 220 |
| 2,000 | 161 | 56 | 6,000 | 538 | 340 |
| 3,000 | 329 | 200 | 7,500 | 785 | 564 |
| 4,000 | 500 | 354 | 10,000 | 1,204 | 976 |
| 5,000 | 671 | 501 | 12,500 | 1,644 | 1,380 |
| 6,000 | 866 | 658 | 15,000 | 2,111 | 1,847 |
| 7,500 | 1,168 | 915 | 20,000 | 3,158 | 2,858 |
| 10,000 | 1,742 | 1,342 | 25,000 | 4,368 | 4,032 |
| 12,500 | 2,478 | 1,886 | 30,000 | 5,773 | 5,377 |
| 15,000 | 3,334 | 2,460 | 50,000 | 12,843 | 12,267 |
| 17,500 | 4,291 | 3,085 | 75,000 | 21,825 | 21,189 |
| 20,000 | 5,350 | 3,764 | 100,000 | 31,897 | 31,201 |

* Does not include a surtax.

## THE NEW SOCIAL SECURITY LAW
Source: U.S. Social Security Administration

The first U.S. Social Security Law was enacted in 1935 and has been amended several times since. In July, 1965, Congress approved sweeping revisions, including establishment of a medical care and health insurance program (Medicare) for persons 65 and older. Although the Social Security laws and the administrative ground rules are somewhat complex, the principle is simple. During working years, employees, employers, and self-employed persons pay social security tax, at a rate established by law, to the Federal government. When a wage earner retires, becomes disabled, or dies, he (or his family) receives benefit payments designed to replace in part the lost income. Social security covers work in most jobs, businesses, and professions, as well as persons on active duty in the armed forces. Under certain conditions, coverage extends to farm owners and ranchers and their workmen; employees of non-profit organizations, including state and local governments; clergymen; domestics; and Americans working abroad. There are special provisions that apply to work performed by one family member for another.

A wage earner pays social security tax on all earnings covered by the law, regardless of his age, and even though he may be receiving social security benefits at the same time. The employer, however, does not have to match the employee's social security contribution on cash tips received. Taxes are deducted automatically from employee paychecks and are matched by an equal contribution from the employer. Self-employed persons with net earnings of $400 or more must pay a social security self-employment tax at a rate slightly lower than the combined employer-employee assessment.

Social security taxes are collected by the Internal Revenue Service and are credited to special Treasury Department funds: the Federal Old-Age and Survivors Insurance Trust Fund, the Federal Hospital Insurance Trust Fund, the Federal Supplementary Medical Insurance Trust Fund, and the Federal Disability Insurance Trust Fund. They may be used only for payment of benefits and administrative expenses.

### SOCIAL SECURITY TAX RATES

| YEAR | RATE Employer-Employee (each) | Self-Employed |
|---|---|---|
| 1967–68.......... | 4.40 | 6.40 |
| 1969–72.......... | 4.90 | 7.10 |
| 1973–75.......... | 5.40 | 7.55 |
| 1976–79.......... | 5.45 | 7.60 |
| 1980–86.......... | 5.55 | 7.70 |
| 1987 and after.... | 5.65 | 7.80 |

■ AMOUNT OF WORK REQUIRED In order to qualify for benefit payments, a worker must have credit for a certain amount of work under social security. Credits may be earned in employment covered by the law any time after 1936 and in self-employment covered by the law after 1950.

The number of credits required to establish eligibility for benefits depends upon the year in which a man reaches the age of 65 (62 for a woman) or upon the date of death if the wage earner dies before retirement. Detailed information on eligibility requirements, as well as the kind and amount of benefits that may be claimed by a worker and his dependents, can be obtained from local social security offices. In all cases, the amount of the benefit payment will be determined by the Social Security Administration. However, if a claimant believes the decision in his case is incorrect, he may appeal through several channels, as far as the Federal courts.

■ APPLYING FOR BENEFITS Persons claiming benefits must make application through social security offices. The addresses of district offices located in more than 600 cities are listed in telephone directories and can be obtained from any post office. It is especially important that social security offices be informed when a worker dies, becomes disabled, or approaches retirement age. Persons applying for benefits will be required to show proof of age in all cases, as well as other documents pertinent to the type of benefit they wish to claim. Social security workers in district offices will advise claimants which documents they will need before they apply for benefits. It is advisable for persons who have worked under social security to check periodically on the earnings that have been credited to their records. Postcard forms are available at all post offices.

■ RETIREMENT BENEFITS Fully insured workers are eligible to receive full retirement benefits when they reach the age of 65. The amount of the benefit is determined by the worker's average earnings under social security. The maximum amount on which social security tax is paid, and on which average income may be computed, is:

$3,000 a year from 1937 through 1950
$3,600 a year from 1951 through 1954
$4,200 a year from 1955 through 1958
$4,800 a year from 1959 through 1965
$6,600 a year, beginning in 1966

Benefits are payable as early as age 62; however, these will be lower than the payments a beneficiary would receive at the age of 65, since these payments are extended over a longer period of time.

Retired workers' dependents also entitled to benefits are:
● a wife or dependent husband, 62 or older
● a wife, regardless of age, if she has in her care a child who is under 18 or is disabled and who is entitled to benefits on the worker's social security account
● an unmarried child under 18 (under 22, if he is a full-time student)
● an unmarried child who became severely disabled before he reached the age of 18 and has remained so since.

(continued)

The dependent's benefit is one-half the amount of the retiree's monthly payment, except in the case of the wife of a living worker, who receives a reduced amount if she elects to receive benefits before she becomes 65. A wife who is entitled to social security benefits based upon her own earnings and on her husband's will receive no more than the larger of the benefits.

Retired persons may earn up to $1,500 a year without reduction in benefits. However, there is a reduction of one dollar for every two dollars earned between $1,500 and $2,700, and a reduction of one dollar for every dollar earned over $2,700. There are two exceptions to this rule: there is no loss of benefit for any month in which a retired person earns $125 or less in the employ of another person, or performs no substantial work in a business of his own, regardless of the amount he earns during the rest of the year; and there is no reduction in benefits paid in any month to persons 72 or older, regardless of the amount earned.

Income that does not reduce benefits includes royalties received from patents or copyrights obtained before the retired person reached the age of 65, pensions, and interest on savings accounts. Detailed information is available from social security offices.

Social security benefits are not subject to income tax.

■ **DISABILITY PAYMENTS** An insured worker who becomes disabled before reaching the age of 65 generally is eligible to receive benefits equal to the amount of retirement benefit he would receive if he were 65. The disability must have lasted for 12 consecutive months or be expected to last for at least 12 months. Payments may begin for the seventh month of disability. And the worker generally must have credit for at least five years of work under social security

during the ten years prior to becoming disabled in order to qualify for benefits. His dependents generally are entitled to the same benefits they would receive if he were retired.

An insured worker's disabled child is generally entitled to benefits if he is unmarried and became disabled before reaching the age of 18. The disabled child receives 50 per cent of a living parent's benefit or 75 per cent of a deceased parent's benefit, and may, under certain conditions, continue to receive payments as long as he is disabled.

■ **SURVIVORS BENEFITS** If an insured worker dies before reaching retirement age, members of his family generally are entitled to one or more of the following benefits:

● A lump-sum death payment may be made to the widow or widower living in the same household with the worker at the time of his death; otherwise it can be used to pay the worker's burial expenses. The amount is three times the deceased worker's monthly benefit, up to $255.

● A widow or widower, 62 or older, receives 82½ per cent of the deceased worker's benefit. A widow may elect to begin receiving payments at the age of 60; however, these are reduced 5/9 of one per cent for each month the benefit is received before the age of 62 (6⅔ per cent per year).

● Each unmarried child under 18 (under 22 if he is a full-time student) receives 75 per cent of the deceased parent's benefit. An unmarried child who became disabled before reaching the age of 18 generally continues to receive the benefit as long as the disability continues.

● A widow who has in her care children entitled to benefits, receives 75 per cent of her husband's benefit until the youngest child

**EXAMPLES OF MONTHLY CASH BENEFIT PAYMENTS ***

| AVERAGE YEARLY EARNINGS AFTER 1950 | $800 or less | $1,800 | $3,000 | $3,600 | $4,200 | $4,800 | $5,400 | $6,600 |
|---|---|---|---|---|---|---|---|---|
| Retirement at 65 | $ 44.00 | $ 78.20 | $101.70 | $112.40 | $124.20 | $135.90 | $146.00 | $168.00 |
| Disability benefits | 44.00 | 78.20 | 101.70 | 112.40 | 124.20 | 135.90 | 146.00 | 168.00 |
| Retirement at 64 | 41.10 | 73.00 | 95.00 | 105.00 | 116.00 | 126.90 | 136.30 | 156.80 |
| Retirement at 63 | 38.20 | 67.80 | 88.20 | 97.50 | 107.70 | 117.80 | 126.60 | 145.60 |
| Retirement at 62 | 35.20 | 62.60 | 81.40 | 90.00 | 99.40 | 108.80 | 116.80 | 134.40 |
| Wife's benefit at 65 or with child in her care | 22.00 | 39.10 | 50.90 | 56.20 | 62.10 | 68.00 | 73.00 | 84.00 |
| Wife's benefit at 64 | 20.20 | 35.90 | 46.70 | 51.60 | 57.00 | 62.40 | 67.00 | 77.00 |
| Wife's benefit at 63 | 18.40 | 32.60 | 42.50 | 46.90 | 51.80 | 56.70 | 60.90 | 70.00 |
| Wife's benefit at 62 | 16.50 | 29.40 | 38.20 | 42.20 | 46.60 | 51.00 | 54.80 | 63.00 |
| One child of retired or disabled worker | 22.00 | 39.10 | 50.90 | 56.20 | 62.10 | 68.00 | 73.00 | 84.00 |
| Widow age 62 or over | 44.00 | 64.60 | 84.00 | 92.80 | 102.50 | 112.20 | 120.50 | 138.60 |
| Widow at 60, no child | 38.20 | 56.00 | 72.80 | 80.50 | 88.90 | 97.30 | 104.50 | 120.20 |
| Widow under 62 and 1 child | 66.00 | 117.40 | 152.60 | 168.60 | 186.40 | 204.00 | 219.00 | 252.00 |
| Widow under 62 and 2 children | 66.00 | 120.00 | 202.40 | 240.00 | 279.60 | 306.00 | 328.00 | 368.00 |
| One surviving child | 44.00 | 58.70 | 76.30 | 84.30 | 93.20 | 102.00 | 109.50 | 126.00 |
| Two surviving children | 66.00 | 117.40 | 152.60 | 168.60 | 186.40 | 204.00 | 219.00 | 252.00 |
| Maximum family benefit | 66.00 | 120.00 | 202.40 | 240.00 | 280.80 | 309.20 | 328.00 | 368.00 |
| Lump-sum death payment | 132.00 | 234.60 | 255.00 | 255.00 | 255.00 | 255.00 | 255.00 | 255.00 |

* Generally, in figuring average yearly earnings after 1950, five years of low earnings or no earnings can be excluded. The maximum earnings creditable for social security are $3,600 for 1951–1954; $4,200 for 1955–1958; $4,800 for 1959–1965; and $6,600 starting in 1966. Because of this, the benefits shown in the last two columns on the right will not generally be payable for some years to come. When a person is entitled to more than one benefit, the amount actually payable is limited to the largest of the benefits.

reaches the age of 18, or as long as a disabled child entitled to benefits remains in her care.

• Dependent parents each may be eligible to receive 75 per cent of the deceased worker's benefit if they are of retirement age (62 for mother and father) and if they were dependent upon the deceased worker for at least half their support.

If only one parent survives (and meets the above requirements), he receives 82½ per cent of the deceased person's benefit.

Benefits may be reduced slightly to conform to the maximum benefit allowed one family.

Widows who qualify for benefits and remarry after the age of 60 may draw 50 per cent of their former husband's benefit or the benefit to which she is entitled under her present husband's eligibility, whichever is greater.

**Note:** Further amendment to the Social Security Law provides that individuals 72 or older under certain conditions may receive a monthly benefit of $35 without having ever worked under social security. There are also provisions permitting certain divorced wives at 62 or divorced widows at 60 to draw benefits based on their former husband's account under specified conditions. Detailed information on these and other provisions of the law may be obtained from social security offices.

■ **HEALTH INSURANCE (MEDICARE): BASIC PLAN** Social Security amendments enacted in 1965 provide two kinds of health insurance protection for most persons 65 and older. (The exceptions are: Federal employees who are protected under another law; aliens who are not permanent residents of the United States; aliens with less than five years residence in the United States; and persons who have been convicted of subversive activities or are members of subversive organizations.) The basic hospital insurance plan is financed through social security and extends coverage automatically to most persons eligible. Persons who have worked under social security but have never applied for benefits and persons who have never worked under social security should consult local social security offices for detailed information on qualifications and benefits. The basic plan provides the following coverage (except where noted):

**Hospitalization:** Up to 90 days of hospitalization in a participating hospital during any "spell of illness." For health insurance purposes, a "spell of illness" begins on the first day of hospitalization and ends on the 60th consecutive day after hospital or extended care facility treatment ends. The patient pays the first $40 of hospital costs and $10 for each day of hospitalization in excess of 60 days. Subject to these limitations, the insurance covers the cost of a semiprivate room (two to four patients), a private room only if medically necessary (if the patient elects a private room, he pays the difference); board; hospital services except private-duty nursing; the services of interns or residents in approved teaching programs; and prescribed drugs.

A physician must certify that his patient requires hospitalization. The same coverage extends to hospitalization in tuberculosis or psychiatric institutions; however, there is a lifetime limit of 190 days of coverage for treatment in a psychiatric hospital.

**Extended Care Facility:** Up to 100 days in a participating skilled nursing home or similar extended-care facility, after at least three days of hospitalization, provided the requirement for extended care in a nursing home is certified by the attending physician. The patient pays $5 for each day in excess of 20 days, up to the limit of 100 days. Subject to that limitation, insurance covers the cost of a semiprivate room, board, general nursing (but not private-duty nursing), prescribed drugs, and therapy administered by non-physicians who are employees of the Extended Care Facility.

**Home Nursing:** Up to 100 home visits by nurses or therapists of an approved home health agency during a one-year period following the patient's discharge from a hospital or extended-care facility, provided the visits are part of a plan established and reviewed periodically by an attending physician.

**Diagnostic Services:** Eighty per cent of the cost of outpatient diagnostic tests conducted in a hospital (after the patient pays the first $20) for each 20-day period of diagnostic testing. Physicians' fees are not covered.

■ **HEALTH INSURANCE (MEDICARE): VOLUNTARY PLAN** The second part of the health insurance plan is voluntary. Persons wishing to obtain coverage must enroll during certain periods and pay a $3.00 monthly premium, which the Federal government matches. (The rate can be adjusted after 1967 to meet current costs.) Voluntary medical insurance covers 80 per cent of the reasonable charges for the following services, after the patient pays the first $50 (and 20 per cent of the remainder in each calendar year):

• physicians' and surgeons' services

• up to 100 home nursing visits each year (without prior hospitalization), in addition to the 100 visits covered by the basic plan

• many other medical and health services, such as diagnostic tests, surgical dressings and splints, and rental of medical equipment.

Enrollment requirements are specific. Persons must enroll during the seven-month period beginning three months before their 65th birthday. The monthly premium will be deducted automatically from monthly payments of persons receiving social security benefits, railroad retirement benefits, or civil service retirement benefits. Detailed information on the Medicare program can be obtained from social security offices.

■ **WELFARE AID** The 1965 Social Security Law authorized a $400 million increase in annual Federal grants to states for welfare and public assistance programs; established Federal standards covering eligibility of beneficiaries and the extent of benefits; and established the new "Medicaid" program for certain low-income groups. The law further authorized $185 million in grants over a five-year period for establishment of a new health-care program for needy children. Federal funds for aid to crippled children, and maternal and child health services, will be raised to $120 million by 1970.

## VETERANS BENEFITS

Source: U.S. Veterans Administration

Veterans of military service, as well as their dependents and beneficiaries, are entitled to certain Federal benefits. Applicants may consult the Veterans Administration (VA) for detailed information on the nature and amounts of benefits offered, as well as eligibility requirements. There are regional offices in each state, and there are also offices in Puerto Rico and the Philippines.

■ COMPENSATION FOR SERVICE-CONNECTED DISABILITY. Veterans disabled by injury or disease received or aggravated in the line of duty are entitled to monthly payments ranging from $21 to $850. Certain dependents of veterans who are at least 50 per cent disabled are entitled to additional allowances. For disability that occurs during peacetime under non-hazardous conditions, benefits are payable at 80 per cent of wartime rates. Vietnam veterans are considered wartime veterans.

■ MEDICAL CARE. Complete care in VA hospitals, other Federal hospitals, and, in some cases, private hospitals is authorized under a priority system for veterans who: (1) require treatment of service-connected disabilities; (2) have compensable disabilities but require treatment of non-service-connected disabilities; (3) have no service-connected disabilities but require medical treatment (subject to financial need and availability of facilities). Special provisions apply to treatment of mental illness. Other benefits authorized under certain conditions include domiciliary care; outpatient medical and dental treatment in VA field stations or by approved private physicians; fitting and training with prosthetic devices; medical examinations; aid for the blind; and vocational rehabilitation.

■ SOCIAL SECURITY CREDITS. Social Security coverage was extended to armed forces personnel in 1957. However, veterans with 90 days of active service between September 16, 1940, and December 31, 1956, and veterans who served less than 90 days in active service during this period and were discharged because of service-connected disability generally are entitled to gratuitous Social Security wage credits of $160 for each month of duty. The credits are not listed on the individual's Social Security earnings record until he applies for Social Security benefits.

■ EDUCATIONAL ASSISTANCE. Authorized educational training under the GI Bill ended for World War II and Korean veterans in 1956 and 1965 respectively. However, a new GI Bill enacted March 3, 1966, provides educational assistance for all veterans who served 181 days, any part of which came after January 1, 1955. A 1967 amendment to the bill increased the educational allowance and added apprenticeship or on-the-job training, farm cooperative training, and flight training. This includes Vietnam veterans. Monthly educational allowances for full-time training range from $130 for single veterans to $175 for veterans with two dependents, plus $10 for each additional dependent. Proportional allowances are granted for part-time training. Orphans' education assistance provides benefits to children of veterans who died or became totally or permanently disabled while in the line of duty during any one of the following periods: (1) April 21, 1898–July 4, 1902 (July 15, 1903, for those serving in Moro Province, Philippine Islands); (2) April 6, 1917–November 11, 1918 (April 1, 1920, for those serving in Russia); (3) December 7, 1941–December 31, 1946; (4) June 27, 1950–January 31, 1955; or (5) August 5, 1964, to an indefinite future date. Generally, but not always, recipients must be between the ages of 18 and 23. Subject to other requirements, recipients are entitled to monthly benefits up to $110 for 36 months of full-time education or training. Part-time educational assistance allowances are lower.

■ LOANS. The VA is authorized to guarantee or insure loans to veterans of World War II and the Korean War and to their widows if the veteran died of service-connected disabilities received in the line of duty. The VA will guarantee the lender against loss of up to 60 per cent on a maximum of $7,500 on home loans and certain kinds of farm loans; and up to 50 per cent on real estate loans to $4,000 and other types of loans to $2,000. Interest on guaranteed loans may not exceed 5¾ per cent per year on the unpaid balance.

■ EMPLOYMENT PREFERENCE AND RE-EMPLOYMENT RIGHTS. Veterans are entitled to certain preference in obtaining Federal civil service jobs and in referral to appropriate training programs and job openings by state employment offices. Veterans also are entitled to restoration to a former job in private employment or with the Federal government, or to a job of like seniority status and pay, unless in private employment conditions have so changed as to make restoration impossible or unreasonable.

■ DEPENDENCY AND INDEMNITY COMPENSATION (DIC). Payments are authorized for widows, unmarried children under 18, helpless children, children between 18 and 23 who are attending an approved school, and certain parents of a serviceman or veteran who dies on or after January 1, 1957, from a disease or injury incurred or aggravated in the line of duty while on active duty, active duty for training, inactive duty for training, or from a disability otherwise compensable under laws administered by the Veterans Administration. Special provisions apply to survivors of personnel whose deaths occurred before January 1, 1957, and to survivors of wartime veterans who die of non-service-connected causes.

■ BURIAL. A payment of up to $250 is authorized for burial expenses for a wartime veteran or for a peacetime veteran who was receiving compensation for service-connected disability or was discharged or retired for disability incurred in the line of duty. This benefit must be claimed within two years of the veteran's permanent burial or cremation.

## U.S. HOLIDAYS: 1968

Legal holidays that are widely observed throughout the United States are New Year's Day, Washington's Birthday, Memorial or Decoration Day, Independence Day, Labor Day, Veterans' Day, Thanksgiving Day, and Christmas. Each state designates the holidays it will observe, either by legislative enactment or by a proclamation that is made by the governor. Federal "Legal Public Holidays," which are designated by the President and Congress, affect only the District of Columbia and Federal employees throughout the nation.

| DATE | DAY | HOLIDAY | LOCALITY |
|---|---|---|---|
| January 1 | Monday | New Year's Day.............. | Every state, District of Columbia, and all United States territories and possessions |
| January 6 | Saturday | Three Kings' Day............. | Puerto Rico |
| January 8 | Monday | Battle of New Orleans......... | Louisiana |
| January 11 | Thursday | De Hostos's Birthday.......... | Puerto Rico |
| January 19 | Friday | Robert E. Lee's Birthday...... | Alabama, Arkansas, Florida, Georgia, Kentucky, Louisiana, Mississippi, North and South Carolina, Tennessee, Texas |
| | | Lee-Jackson Day............. | Virginia |
| January 26 | Friday | General Douglas MacArthur Day | Arkansas |
| January 30 | Tuesday | Franklin D. Roosevelt's Birthday | Kentucky and Virgin Islands |
| February 12 | Monday | Lincoln's Birthday............ | Every state and the Virgin Islands, except Alabama, District of Columbia, Florida, Georgia, Hawaii, Idaho, Louisiana, Maine, Massachusetts, Mississippi, Nevada, New Hampshire, North Carolina, Oklahoma, Rhode Island, South Carolina, and Virginia |
| February 14 | Wednesday | Admission Day............... | Arizona |
| February 22 | Thursday | Washington's Birthday........ | Every state (except Nevada), District of Columbia, American Samoa, Canal Zone, Guam, Puerto Rico, and Virgin Islands (President's Day in Hawaii) |
| February 27 | Tuesday | Mardi Gras.................. | Alabama and Louisiana * |
| March 2 | Saturday | Texas Independence Day...... | Texas |
| March 5 | Tuesday | Town Meeting Day............ | Vermont |
| March 15 | Friday | Andrew Jackson's Birthday.... | Tennessee |
| March 17 | Sunday | Evacuation Day.............. | Massachusetts (Suffolk County only) |
| March 22 | Friday | Emancipation Day............ | Puerto Rico |
| March 25 | Monday | Maryland Day................ | Maryland |
| March 26 | Tuesday | Kuhio Day................... | Hawaii |
| March 30 | Saturday | Seward's Day................ | Alaska |
| March 31 | Sunday | Transfer Day................. | Virgin Islands |
| April 11 | Thursday | Holy Thursday............... | Virgin Islands |
| April 12 | Friday | Good Friday................. | Alaska, Arkansas, Canal Zone, Connecticut, Delaware, Florida, Guam, Hawaii, Illinois, Indiana, Louisiana, Maryland, Minnesota, New Jersey, North Dakota, Pennsylvania, Puerto Rico, South Carolina, Texas, and Virgin Islands |
| | | Halifax Declaration of Independence Day.......... | North Carolina |
| April 13 | Saturday | Thomas Jefferson's Birthday... | Alabama, Missouri, Nebraska, Oklahoma, and Virginia |
| April 15 | Monday | Easter Monday............... | North Carolina and Virgin Islands |
| April 16 | Tuesday | De Diego's Birthday.......... | Puerto Rico |
| April 19 | Friday | Patriots' Day................. | Maine and Massachusetts |
| April 21 | Sunday | San Jacinto Day............. | Texas |
| April 22 | Monday | Arbor Day................... | Nebraska |
| | | Oklahoma Day............... | Oklahoma |
| | | Fast Day.................... | New Hampshire |
| April 26 | Friday | Confederate Memorial Day..... | Alabama, Florida, Georgia, and Mississippi |
| | | Arbor Day................... | Utah |
| May 4 | Saturday | Rhode Island Independence Day | Rhode Island |
| May 10 | Friday | Confederate Memorial Day..... | North Carolina and South Carolina |
| May 20 | Monday | Mecklenburg Declaration of Independence Day.......... | North Carolina |
| May 29 | Wednesday | John F. Kennedy Day......... | Michigan |
| May 30 | Thursday | Memorial or Decoration Day... | Every state (except Alabama, Georgia, Mississippi, South Carolina, and Texas), District of Columbia, American Samoa, Canal Zone, Guam, Puerto Rico, and Virgin Islands (in Florida, Memorial Day for war veterans; in Idaho, proclamation must be issued by the Governor) |
| June 3 | Monday | Jefferson Davis's Birthday Confederate Memorial Day..... | Alabama, Florida, Georgia, Kentucky, Louisiana, Mississippi, South Carolina, Tennessee, and Texas |

(continued)

* In the parishes of Arcadia, East Baton Rouge, Jefferson, La Fayette, Lafourche, Orleans, Plaquemines, St. Bernard, St. Charles, St. John the Baptist, and Terrebonne, and in all municipalities in which the local authorities declare Mardi Gras a holiday.

## U.S. HOLIDAYS: 1968 (continued)

| DATE | DAY | HOLIDAY | LOCALITY |
|---|---|---|---|
| June 11 | Tuesday | Kamehameha Day........... | Hawaii |
| June 14 | Friday | Flag Day.................... | Pennsylvania |
| June 17 | Monday | Bunker Hill Day............. | Massachusetts (Suffolk County only) |
| June 20 | Thursday | West Virginia Day........... | West Virginia |
| June 22 | Saturday | Organic Act Day............. | Virgin Islands |
| July 4 | Thursday | Independence Day........... | Every state, District of Columbia, and all United States territories and possessions |
| July 13 | Saturday | Nathan B. Forrest's Birthday... | Tennessee |
| July 17 | Wednesday | Muñoz Rivera's Birthday...... | Puerto Rico |
| July 21 | Sunday | Liberation Day.............. | Guam |
| July 24 | Wednesday | Pioneer Day................ | Utah |
| July 25 | Thursday | Constitution Day............ | Puerto Rico |
|  |  | Supplication Day............ | Virgin Islands |
| July 27 | Saturday | Barbosa's Birthday.......... | Puerto Rico |
| August 1 | Thursday | Colorado Day............... | Colorado |
| August 12 | Monday | V.J. Day.................... | Rhode Island |
| August 14 | Wednesday | World War II Victory Day...... | Arkansas |
| August 16 | Friday | Bennington Battle Day........ | Vermont |
| August 30 | Friday | Huey P. Long's Birthday....... | Louisiana |
| September 2 | Monday | Labor Day.................. | Every state, District of Columbia, and all United States territories and possessions |
| September 9 | Monday | Admission Day.............. | California |
| September 12 | Thursday | Defenders' Day............. | Maryland |
| October 5 | Saturday | Missouri Day............... | Missouri |
| October 12 | Saturday | Columbus Day.............. | Every state and Puerto Rico except Alaska, Arizona, Canal Zone, District of Columbia, Guam, Hawaii, Idaho, Maine, Michigan, Mississippi, Nevada, North Carolina, South Carolina, South Dakota, Tennessee, Virginia, Virgin Islands, and Wyoming (Memorial Day in Arkansas, Iowa, Oregon) |
| October 18 | Friday | Alaska Day................. | Alaska |
| October 25 | Friday | Local Thanksgiving Day....... | Virgin Islands |
| October 31 | Thursday | Nevada Day................. | Nevada |
| November 1 | Friday | All Saints' Day.............. | Louisiana |
|  |  | Liberty Day................. | Virgin Islands |
| November 3 | Sunday | Panama Independence Day.... | Canal Zone |
| November 4 | Monday | Will Rogers' Day............. | Oklahoma |
| November 5 | Tuesday | Election Day................ | Every state (except Alabama, Alaska, Connecticut, District of Columbia, Georgia, Idaho, Kansas, Kentucky, Maine, Massachusetts, Minnesota, Mississippi, Nebraska, Nevada, New Mexico, Utah, Vermont, and Wisconsin), Guam, Puerto Rico, and Virgin Islands |
| November 11 | Monday | Veterans' Day.............. | Every state, District of Columbia, American Samoa, Canal Zone, Guam, Puerto Rico, and Virgin Islands |
| November 19 | Tuesday | Discovery Day............... | Puerto Rico |
| November 28 | Thursday | Thanksgiving Day........... | Every state, District of Columbia, and all United States territories and possessions |
| December 25 | Wednesday | Christmas Day.............. | Every state, District of Columbia, and all United States territories and possessions |

## INDEPENDENCE DAY

After approving the resolution of independence on July 2, 1776, the Continental Congress drafted the Declaration of Independence, which was signed on July 4 by John Hancock, president of the Congress, and attested by Charles Thomson. (Other members signed it beginning August 2, 1776.) John Adams wrote to his wife about the momentous event: "It ought to be commemorated as the day of deliverance, by solemn acts of devotion to God Almighty. It ought to be solemnized with pomp and parade, with shows, games, sports, guns, bells, bonfires, and illuminations, from one end of this continent to the other, from this time forevermore."

The custom of celebrating July 4 began in Philadelphia in 1777. Congress was adjourned; a ceremonial dinner was held; there was bell-ringing, bonfires, fireworks. When the requisite nine states had ratified the Constitution in 1788, Philadelphia again led the nation in very special Fourth of July festivities. By the early 1800s Boston, New York, and Washington were having their own observances. Gradually the practice spread as new territories were settled and new states admitted to the Union. Today Americans in every U.S. state and around the world "solemnize with pomp and parade" the birth of the American Republic.

# DIRECTORY OF SOCIETIES, ORGANIZATIONS, AND FOUNDATIONS

**Adult Education Association of the United States of America;** Membership: 4,000 in 23 affiliated groups; Headquarters: 1225 19th Street, N.W., Washington, D.C. 20036

**Alcoholics Anonymous (The General Service Board of A.A., Inc.);** Membership: approx. 350,000 in more than 13,000 affiliated groups; Headquarters: 305 East 45th Street, New York, New York 10017

**American Academy of Political and Social Science;** Membership: 21,577, incl. 6,307 libraries; Headquarters: 3937 Chestnut Street, Philadelphia, Pennsylvania 19104

**American Association for Health, Physical Education, and Recreation;** Membership: 50,000; Headquarters: 1201 16th Street; N.W., Washington, D.C. 20036

**American Association for the Advancement of Science;** Membership: 115,000; Headquarters: 1515 Massachusetts Avenue, N.W., Washington, D.C. 20005

**American Association of University Women;** Membership: over 174,000; Headquarters: 2401 Virginia Avenue, N.W., Washington, D.C. 20037

**American Automobile Association;** Membership: 10,500,000 in 241 clubs in the U.S. and Canada; Headquarters: 1712 G Street, N.W., Washington, D.C. 20006

**American Bankers Association, The;** Membership: 18,300 banks and branches; Headquarters: 90 Park Avenue, New York, New York

**American Bar Association;** Membership: 124,000; Headquarters: 1155 East 60th Street, Chicago, Illinois, 60637

**American Bible Society;** Membership: 450,000; Headquarters: 1865 Broadway, New York, New York 10023

**American Cancer Society, Inc.;** Affiliates: 58 chartered divisions; Headquarters: 219 East 42d Street, New York, New York 10017

**American Chemical Society;** Membership: 107,000; Headquarters: 1155 16th Street, N.W., Washington, D.C. 20006

**American Civil Liberties Union, Inc.;** Membership: 100,000 in 38 affiliated groups; Headquarters: 156 Fifth Avenue, New York, New York 10010

**American Council of Learned Societies;** Membership: 33 professional societies; Headquarters: 345 East 46th Street, New York, New York 10017

**American Council on Education;** Membership: 1,273 colleges and universities and 246 educational organizations; Headquarters: 1785 Massachusetts Avenue, N.W., Washington, D.C. 20036

**American Dental Association;** Membership: 106,328; Headquarters: 211 East Chicago Avenue, Chicago, Illinois 60611

**American Farm Bureau Federation;** Membership: 1,703,908 families; Headquarters: Merchandise Mart Plaza, Chicago, Illinois 60654

**American Federation of Arts, The;** Membership: 3,050; 583 institutions and corporations; Headquarters: 41 East 65th Street, New York, New York 10021

**American Federation of Labor and Congress of Industrial Organizations;** Membership: 14,284,183; Headquarters: 815 16th Street, N.W., Washington, D.C. 20006

**American Field Service;** Membership: 2,800 chapters in 48 states; Headquarters: 313 East 43d Street, New York, New York 10017

**American Friends Service Committee, Inc.;** Headquarters: 160 North 15th Street, Philadelphia, Pennsylvania 19102

**American Geographical Society;** Membership: 3,800; Headquarters: Broadway at 156th Street, New York, New York 10032

**American Heart Association;** Membership: over 70,000 in 54 affiliates and 1,400 other local heart organizations; Headquarters: 44 East 23d Street, New York, New York 10010

**American Historical Association;** Membership: 16,000; Headquarters: 400 A Street, S.E., Washington, D.C. 20003

**American Hospital Association;** Membership: 9,055 persons, 8,990 institutions; Headquarters: 840 North Lake Shore Drive, Chicago, Illinois 60611

**American Institute of Aeronautics and Astronautics;** Membership, 33,000; Headquarters: 1290 Avenue of the Americas, New York, New York 10019

**American Institute of Architects;** Membership: 19,400; Headquarters: 1735 New York Avenue, N.W., Washington, D.C. 20006

**American Institute of Biological Sciences;** Membership: 14,500 members, 44 adherent societies, 2 affiliate societies; Headquarters: 3900 Wisconsin Avenue, N.W., Washington, D.C. 20016

**American Institute of Physics;** Membership: 41,114 in 7 member societies; Headquarters: 335 East 45th Street, New York, New York 10017

**American Jewish Committee;** Membership: 40,000; Headquarters: 165 East 56th Street, New York, New York 10012

**American Jewish Congress;** Membership: 300,000; Headquarters: 15th East 84th Street, New York, New York 10028

**American Legion, The;** Membership: 2,566,333; Headquarters: 700 North Pennsylvania Street, Indianapolis, Indiana 46204

**American Library Association;** Membership: 34,000; Headquarters: 50 East Huron Street, Chicago, Illinois 60611

**American Medical Association;** Membership: 214,691; Headquarters: 535 North Dearborn Street, Chicago, Illinois 60610

**American National Red Cross;** Membership: 30,463,700 in 3,300 chapters; Headquarters: 17th and D Streets, N.W., Washington, D.C. 20006

**American National Theater Academy;** Membership: 3,399; Headquarters: 245 West 52d Street, New York, New York 10022

**American Newspaper Publishers Association;** Membership: 1,008 newspapers; Headquarters: 750 Third Avenue, New York, New York 10017

(continued)

DIRECTORY OF ORGANIZATIONS (*continued*)

**American Nurses' Association;** Membership: 180,000; Headquarters: 10 Columbus Circle, New York, New York 10019

**American Political Science Association;** Membership: 14,000; Headquarters: 1527 New Hampshire Avenue, N.W., Washington, D.C.

**American Psychiatric Association;** Membership: 15,520, 58 district branches in U.S.; Headquarters: 1700 18th Street, N.W., Washington, D.C. 20009

**American Psychological Association;** Membership: 25,800; Headquarters: 1200 17th Street, N.W., Washington, D.C. 20036

**American Society for the Prevention of Cruelty to Animals;** Headquarters: 441 East 92d Street, New York, New York 10028

**American Society of Composers, Authors, and Publishers;** Membership: 9,159 composers and authors, 2,989 publishers; Headquarters: 575 Madison Avenue, New York, New York

**American Youth Hostels, Inc.;** Membership: 31,000 in 25 Councils; Headquarters: 20 West 17th Street, New York, New York 10011

**Ancient Order of Hibernians in America and Ladies Auxiliary;** Membership: 191,000; Headquarters: 248 East 31st Street, Brooklyn, New York 11226

**Arthritis Foundation, The;** Membership: 79 chapters; Headquarters: 1212 Avenue of the Americas, New York, New York 10036

**Associated Councils of the Arts;** Membership: 425 arts councils and individuals; Headquarters: 1564 Broadway, New York, New York

**Association of Better Business Bureaus, International;** Membership: 136 bureaus in U.S., Canada, Israel, Mexico, Puerto Rico, and Venezuela; Headquarters: Chrysler Building, New York, New York 10017

**Association of the Junior Leagues of America, Inc.;** Membership: 97,982 in 213 member leagues; Headquarters: Waldorf-Astoria Hotel, New York, New York 10022

**Avalon Foundation;** Assets: $138,049,000; Headquarters: 713 Park Avenue, New York, New York 10017

**Benevolent and Protective Order of Elks;** Membership: 1,417,435 in 2,091 lodges; Headquarters: 2750 Lake View Avenue, Chicago, Illinois 60614

**Big Brothers of America;** Membership: 20,000 big brothers, 116 member agencies; Headquarters: 341 Suburban Station Building, Philadelphia, Pennsylvania 19103

**B'nai B'rith;** Membership: 500,000 in 4,100 local groups; Headquarters: 1640 Rhode Island Avenue, N.W., Washington, D.C. 20036

**Boy Scouts of America;** Membership: 5,124,656 boys and adults in 142,267 units; Headquarters: New Brunswick, New Jersey 08903

**Boys' Clubs of America;** Membership: 800,000 in 750 clubs; Headquarters: 771 First Avenue, New York, New York 10017

**Brookings Institution, The;** Headquarters: 1775 Massachusetts Avenue, N.W., Washington, D.C. 20036

**Camp Fire Girls, Inc.;** Membership: 600,000; Headquarters: 65 Worth Street, New York, New York 10013

**CARE (Cooperative for American Relief Everywhere, Inc.);** Headquarters: 660 First Avenue, New York, New York 10016

**Carnegie Corporation of New York;** Assets: $325,000,000; Headquarters: 589 Fifth Avenue, New York, New York 10017

**Carnegie Endowment for International Peace;** Assets: $28,374,296.18; Headquarters: United Nations Plaza at 46th Street, New York, New York 10017

**Carnegie Institution of Washington;** Assets: $85,217,612; Headquarters: 1530 P Street, N.W., Washington, D.C. 20005

**Chautauqua Institution;** Headquarters: Chautauqua, New York 14722

**Commonwealth Fund;** Assets: $146,928,366; Headquarters: 1 East 75th Street, New York, New York 10021

**Congress of Racial Equality;** Membership: 100,000; Headquarters: 200 West 135th Street, New York, New York 10030

**Council on Foreign Relations, Inc.;** Membership: 1,500; Headquarters: 58 East 68th Street, New York, New York 10021

**Daughters of the American Revolution (National Society);** Membership: 185,000 in approx. 3,000 chapters; Headquarters: 1776 D Street, N.W., Washington, D.C. 20006

**Democratic National Committee;** Headquarters: 2600 Virginia Avenue, N.W., Washington, D.C. 20037

**Duke Endowment;** Assets: $656,991,592; Headquarters: 30 Rockefeller Plaza, New York, New York 10020

**Engineers Joint Council;** Membership: 17 national engineering societies, 9 associate societies; Headquarters: United Engineering Society Building, 345 East 47th Street, New York, New York 10017

**English-Speaking Union of the U.S.;** Membership: 35,000; Headquarters: 16 East 69th Street, New York, New York 10021

**Field Foundation;** Assets: approx. $43,000,000; Headquarters: 250 Park Avenue, New York, New York 10017

**Ford Foundation;** Book assets: $3,033,507,857 for nine months ending June 30, 1967; Headquarters: 320 East 43d Street, New York, New York 10022

**Foreign Policy Association;** Headquarters: 345 East 46th Street, New York, New York

**4-H Clubs;** Membership: 2,750,000 in 96,000 local clubs; Headquarters: Federal Extension Service, U.S. Department of Agriculture, Washington, D.C. 20250

**Fund for the Advancement of Education;** Headquarters: 477 Madison Avenue, New York, New York 10022

**General Federation of Women's Clubs;** Membership: 11,000,000 in 15,000 affiliated groups; Headquarters: 1734 N Street, N.W., Washington, D.C. 20036

**Girl Scouts of the United States of America;** Membership: 3,594,000 girls and adults; Headquarters: 830 Third Avenue, New York, New York 10022

**Girls Clubs of America;** Membership: 85,000; Headquarters: 133 East 62d Street, New York, New York 10021

**Hadassah;** Membership: 318,000; Headquarters: 65 East 52d Street, New York, New York 10017

**Imperial Council of the A. A. Order of Nobles of the Mystic Shrine;** Membership: 850,907; Headquarters: 323 North Michigan Avenue, Chicago, Illinois 60601

**Independent Order of Odd Fellows;** Membership: 1,287,000; Headquarters: 16 W. Chase Street, Baltimore, Maryland 21201

**Institute of International Education;** Headquarters: 809 United Nations Plaza, New York, New York 10017

**W. K. Kellogg Foundation;** Assets: $344,642,-253; Headquarters: 400 North Avenue, Battle Creek, Michigan 49016

**Kiwanis International;** Membership: 275,000 in 5,500 clubs in U.S., Canada, Western Europe, Mexico, the Far East, the Caribbean, South and Central America, New Zealand, and Australia; Headquarters: 101 East Erie Street, Chicago, Illinois 60611

**Knights of Columbus;** Membership: 1,184,-545; Headquarters: 71 Meadow Street, New Haven, Connecticut 06507

**Kresge Foundation;** Assets: $230,000,000; Headquarters: 211 Fort Street West, Detroit, Michigan 48226

**Samuel H. Kress Foundation;** Assets: $32,665,-364; Headquarters: 221 West 57th Street, New York, New York 10019

**League of Women Voters of the United States;** Membership: 146,000; Headquarters: 1200 17th Street, N.W., Washington, D.C. 20036

**Lions International;** Membership: 837,344 in 21,479 clubs; Headquarters: 209 North Michigan Avenue, Chicago, Illinois 60601

**Loyal Order of Moose;** Membership: 1,061,618 in 3,760 units; Headquarters: Mooseheart, Illinois 60539

**Josiah Macy, Jr., Foundation;** Assets: $44,186,-544; Headquarters: 277 Park Avenue, New York, New York 10017

**Masonic Service Association of the United States;** Membership: most of the Grand Lodges of Masons in the U.S., including many of the approximately 4,000,000 American Masons; Headquarters: 700 10th Street, N.W., Washington, D.C. 20001

**Richard King Mellon Foundation;** Assets: $131,237,868; Headquarters: 525 William Penn Place, Pittsburgh, Pennsylvania 15219

**Milbank Memorial Fund;** Assets: $24,589,548; Headquarters: 40 Wall St., New York, New York 10005

**Modern Language Association of America;** Membership: 25,000; Headquarters: 62 Fifth Avenue, New York, New York 10011

**Modern Woodmen of America;** Membership: 450,000; Headquarters: Seventeenth Street and the Mississippi River, Rock Island, Illinois 61201

**Moody Foundation;** Assets: $242,000,000; Headquarters: 420 National Hotel Building, Galveston, Texas 77550

**Muscular Dystrophy Associations of America;** Membership: 350 chapter affiliates; Headquarters: 1790 Broadway, New York, New York 10019

**National Association for Mental Health, Inc.;** Membership: 50 state and 850 local organizations; Headquarters: 10 Columbus Circle, New York, New York 10019

**National Association for Retarded Children;** Membership: 115,000; Headquarters: 420 Lexington Avenue, New York, New York 10017

**National Association for the Advancement of Colored People;** Membership: 450,000 in 1,800 units; Headquarters: 20 West 40th Street, New York, New York 10018

**National Association of Manufacturers;** Membership: 14,000; Headquarters: 277 Park Avenue, New York, New York 10017

**National Audubon Society;** Membership: 65,715 and 333 affiliated groups; Headquarters: 1130 Fifth Avenue, New York, New York 10028

**National Conference of Christians and Jews, Inc.;** Membership: 200,000 contributors; Headquarters: 43 West 57th St., New York, New York 10019

**National Congress of American Indians;** Membership: 300,000; Headquarters: 1346 Connecticut Ave., N.W., Washington, D.C. 20036

**National Congress of Parents and Teachers;** Membership: 11,029,396 in 44,968 PTAs; Headquarters: 700 North Rush Street, Chicago, Illinois 60611

**National Council of Churches of Christ in the U.S.A.;** Membership: 41,946,590 in 30 constituted bodies; Headquarters: 475 Riverside Drive, New York, New York 10027

**National Council of State Garden Clubs, Inc.;** Membership: 400,000; Headquarters: 4401 Magnolia Avenue, St. Louis, Missouri 63110

**National Education Association of the U.S.;** Membership: 1,028,456 and 8,250 affiliated local associations in 50 states; Headquarters: 1201 16th Street, N.W., Washington, D.C. 20036

**National Farmers Union;** Membership: 250,000 families; Headquarters: 1575 Sherman Street, Denver, Colorado 80201

**National Federation of Business and Professional Women's Clubs, Inc.;** Membership: 178,393 in 3,800 clubs; Headquarters: 2012 Massachusetts Ave., N.W., Washington, D.C. 20036

**National Foundation—March of Dimes, The;** Membership: 3,100 chapters; Headquarters: 800 Second Avenue, New York, New York 10017

**National Grange, The;** Membership: 750,000; Headquarters: 1616 H Street, N.W., Washington, D.C. 20006

**National Industrial Conference Board, Inc.;** Membership: 4,200 subscribing associates; Headquarters: 845 Third Ave., New York, New York 10022

**National Music Council;** Membership: 54 national members representing 1,250,000 individuals; Headquarters: 2109 Broadway, New York, New York 10023

**National Rifle Association of America;** Membership: 825,000; Headquarters: 1600 Rhode Island Avenue, N.W., Washington, D.C.

*(continued)*

DIRECTORY OF ORGANIZATIONS (*continued*)

**National Safety Council;** Membership: 10,500; Headquarters: 425 N. Michigan Avenue, Chicago, Illinois 60611

**National Small Business Association;** Membership: 35,000; Headquarters: 1225 19th Street, N.W., Washington, D.C. 20036

**National Society for Crippled Children and Adults, Inc.;** Membership: 52 state and territorial societies; Headquarters: 2023 West Ogden Avenue, Chicago, Illinois 60612

**National Society for the Prevention of Blindness;** Membership: 95,000; Headquarters: 79 Madison Avenue, New York, New York

**National Tuberculosis Association;** Membership: 1,700 affiliated groups; Headquarters: 1740 Broadway, New York, New York 10019

**National Urban League, Inc.;** Membership: est. 50,000; Headquarters: 55 East 52d Street, New York, New York 10022

**National Wildlife Federation;** Membership: 285,000; Headquarters: 1412 16th Street, N.W., Washington, D.C. 20036

**National Woman's Christian Temperance Union;** Membership: 250,000 in 5,000 local unions; Headquarters: 1730 Chicago Avenue, Evanston, Illinois 60201

**New York Community Trust** (with corporate affiliate Community Funds): Assets: $62,837,556; Headquarters: 230 Park Avenue, New York, New York 10017

**Old Dominion Foundation;** Assets: $101,904,466; Headquarters: 140 East 62d Street, New York, New York 10021

**Order of DeMolay;** Membership: 166,000; Headquarters: 201 East Armour Boulevard, Kansas City, Missouri 64111

**Order of the Eastern Star, General Grand Chapter;** Membership: 3,000,000; Headquarters: 1618 New Hampshire Ave., N.W., Washington, D.C. 20009

**Phelps-Stokes Fund;** Headquarters: 22 East 54th Street, New York, N.Y. 10022

**Photographic Society of America, Inc.;** Membership: approx. 10,000 members and over 1,000 clubs; Headquarters: 2005 Walnut Street, Philadelphia, Pennsylvania 19103

**Planned Parenthood-World Population (Planned Parenthood Federation of America, Inc.);** Membership: 147 affiliated organizations; Headquarters: 515 Madison Avenue, New York, New York 10022

**Republican National Committee;** Headquarters: 1625 I Street, N.W., Washington, D.C. 20006

**Rockefeller Brothers Fund;** Assets: $189,476,288; Headquarters: 30 Rockefeller Plaza, New York, New York 10020

**Rockefeller Foundation;** Assets: $735,035,521; Headquarters: 111 West 50th Street, New York, New York 10020

**Rotary International;** Membership: 621,250 in 12,915 clubs; Headquarters: 1600 Ridge Avenue, Evanston, Illinois 60201

**Russell Sage Foundation:** Assets: $40,080,449; Headquarters: 230 Park Avenue, New York, New York 10017

**Alfred P. Sloan Foundation;** Assets: $309,000,000; Headquarters: 630 Fifth Avenue, New York, New York 10020

**Society of St. Vincent de Paul;** Headquarters: 611 Olive Street, St. Louis, Missouri 63101

**Southern Christian Leadership Conference;** Headquarters: 334 Auburn Avenue, N.E., Atlanta, Georgia 30303

**Tax Institute of America;** Headquarters: 457 Nassau Street, Princeton, New Jersey 08540

**Travelers Aid Association of America;** Membership: 87 local societies; Headquarters: 44 East 23d Street, New York, New York 10010

**Twentieth Century Fund;** Assets: $25,335,000; Headquarters: 41 East 70th Street, New York, New York 10021

**United Cerebral Palsy Associations, Inc.;** Membership: 320 affiliates; Headquarters: 321 West 44th Street, New York, New York

**United Community Funds and Councils of America, Inc.;** Membership: 1,325 communities; represents 2,249 local organizations; Headquarters: 345 East 46th Street, New York, New York 10017

**United Jewish Appeal, Inc.;** Headquarters: 1290 Avenue of the Americas, New York, New York 10014

**United Nations Association of the United States of America;** Membership 44,830; Headquarters: 345 East 46th Street, New York, New York 10017

**United Service Organizations, Inc.;** Membership: 166 U.S.O. clubs, served by 85,000 volunteers; Headquarters: 237 East 52d Street, New York, New York 10022

**United States Catholic Conference;** Membership: 255 bishops, archbishops, and cardinals of the U.S.; Headquarters: 1312 Massachusetts Avenue, Washington, D.C. 20005

**United States Jaycees;** Membership: 290,000 in 6,100 affiliated groups; Headquarters: Box 7, Tulsa, Oklahoma 74102

**United States Steel Foundation, Inc.;** Assets: $12,228,105; Headquarters: 71 Broadway, New York, New York 10006

**Veterans of Foreign Wars of the United States;** Membership: 1,770,000; Headquarters: V.F.W. Building, Broadway at 34th Street, Kansas City, Missouri 64111

**Woodrow Wilson National Fellowship Foundation;** Assets: $9,833,215.74; Headquarters: 32 Nassau Street, Princeton, New Jersey 08540

**Workmen's Circle;** Membership: 60,000; Headquarters: 175 East Broadway, New York, New York 10002

**Young Democratic Clubs of America;** Membership: 950,000; Headquarters: 2600 Virginia Avenue, N.W., Washington, D.C. 20037

**Young Men's Christian Association** (National Council): Membership: 5,183,000 in 1,725 organizations; Headquarters: 291 Broadway, New York, New York 10022

**Young Republican National Federation;** Membership 500,000; Headquarters: 1625 I Street, N.W., Washington, D.C. 20006

**Young Women's Christian Association of the U.S.A.;** Membership: more than 2,000,000; Headquarters: 600 Lexington Avenue, New York, New York 10022

**Zionist Organization of America;** Membership: 100,000 in 600 districts; Headquarters: 145 East 32d Street, New York, New York 10016

# THE STATES

## STATE REAPPORTIONMENT AND REDISTRICTING

The establishment of population-based apportionment for both houses of state legislatures began as a result of the Supreme Court's *Baker v. Carr* ruling in March, 1962. By the end of 1967 every state had taken some action, with only a few states required to make further modifications.

At the time of the *Baker* decision, a survey published by the National Municipal League showed that a majority of the seats in the average state senate could be elected by merely 31 per cent of the electorate, and about 34 per cent could elect a majority in the lower house. The League's 1967 survey disclosed that it now requires approximately 49 per cent to elect control in the average senate and 47 per cent to win in the average house. Further improvement is expected when all states undertake new reapportionments following the 1970 Federal census.

In the following states a court challenge is still pending, or minor adjustments are to be enacted: Arizona, Delaware, Georgia, Kansas, Massachusetts, South Carolina, and Texas. Constitutional changes in apportionment procedures have been made in California, Colorado, Connecticut, Delaware, Maine, Missouri, Montana, Nebraska, New Hampshire, New Jersey, Tennessee, and Wyoming. During 1967 action was begun on changing the constitutions of Hawaii, Iowa, Maryland, New York, Ohio, and Pennsylvania.

Congressional redistricting, closely allied to the reapportionment problem, has taken place under court order, or voluntarily, in 32 states since 1964; a half-dozen others should take action before the 1968 election.

The landmark *Baker* case, which precipitated this reapportionment and redistricting activity, was begun by a group of urban residents in Tennessee who sought to force their state legislature to obey its own state constitution, which it had ignored for 50 years. Similar conditions existed throughout the country.

Once the Federal courts accepted jurisdiction of state apportionment cases, legal action was started regarding congressional redistricting. In early 1964 a ruling in *Wesberry* v. *Sanders* required all congressional districts within a state to be essentially of equal population. In June of that same year the Court held (*Reynolds* v. *Sims*) that both houses of a state legislature must also have equally populated districts.

Thus, while technically different subjects, the legal precedents in state legislative apportionment and congressional districting cases started to have an effect on one another until, early in 1967, the Supreme Court cited criteria for one type of case as binding in the other.

Theoretically, a state's congressional districts have always been equal in population, and most states originally required their legislative districts to be equal. From the admission of Vermont in 1791 to Montana's entry into the Union in 1890, all states based their apportionments on population, as did the original thirteen.

But, as cities began to grow, increasing numbers of Midwestern and Southern states stopped reapportioning every ten years, although their constitutions required it. Other states, primarily in the East and West, passed constitutional amendments changing apportionment formulas.

The past five years has seen rurally led opposition to the Court-initiated "reapportionment revolution" both in Congress and in state legislatures. Senator Everett M. Dirksen of Illinois, Republican minority leader of the U.S. Senate, sponsored an amendment that would allow states to apportion one house on factors other than population. His amendment twice failed (1965 and 1966) to win the necessary two-thirds approval.

Between 1963 and 1967, resolutions calling for a constitutional convention to propose an apportionment amendment were passed and filed with Congress by 28 state legislatures: Alabama, Arkansas, Arizona, Florida, Idaho, Illinois, Indiana, Kansas, Kentucky, Louisiana, Maryland, Minnesota, Mississippi, Missouri, Montana, Nebraska, Nevada, New Mexico, North Carolina, North Dakota, Oklahoma, South Carolina, South Dakota, Tennessee, Texas, Virginia, Washington and Wyoming. Four states—Colorado, Georgia, New Hampshire, and Utah—also passed resolutions, but failed to file them properly.

Of the 32 states taking some kind of action, 27 were malapportioned at the time their resolutions were passed. In addition, the difference in wording among the resolutions, the fact that the states' action spanned four years, and the lack of precedents governing this method of amending the U.S. Constitution, has led to debate in Congress as to whether it will be obligated to call a convention if two-thirds (34) of the states petition for it.

Finally, the apportionment problem has been carried to the local government level. In mid-1967 the Supreme Court ruled on four local government cases. The Court refrained from applying the so-called "one man, one vote" doctrine to that governmental level, but strongly implied that one day it would do so. However, the Court did make it clear, in the case of *Dusch* v. *Davis*, that it would allow greater leeway in structuring local legislative bodies than it would at the state level.

Since the reapportionment upheaval began in 1962, California, Michigan, South Dakota, and Wisconsin have passed laws requiring all local governments to apportion on a population basis. (The Michigan law is being challenged.) Several other states, most notably New York, have had much litigation on the subject.

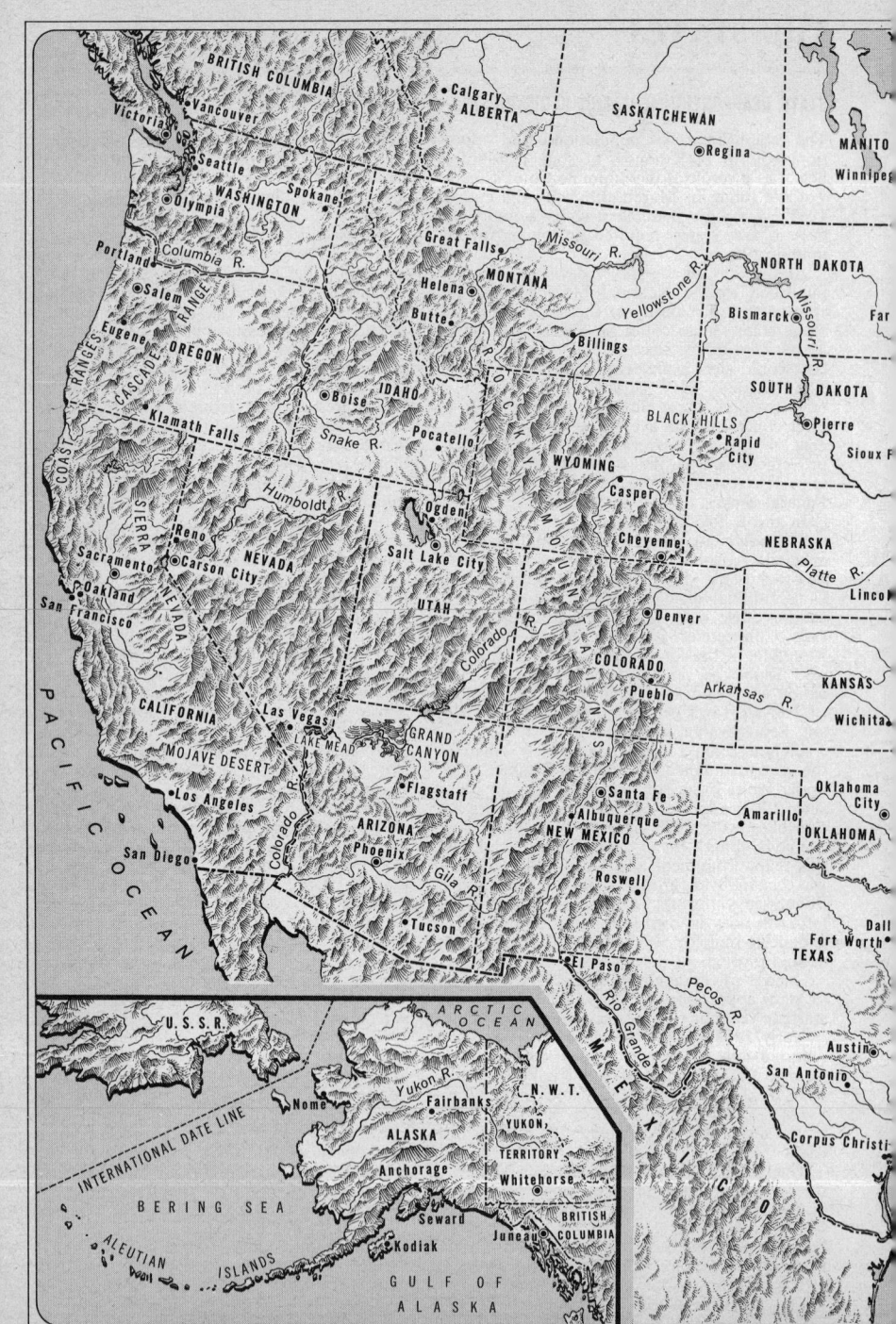

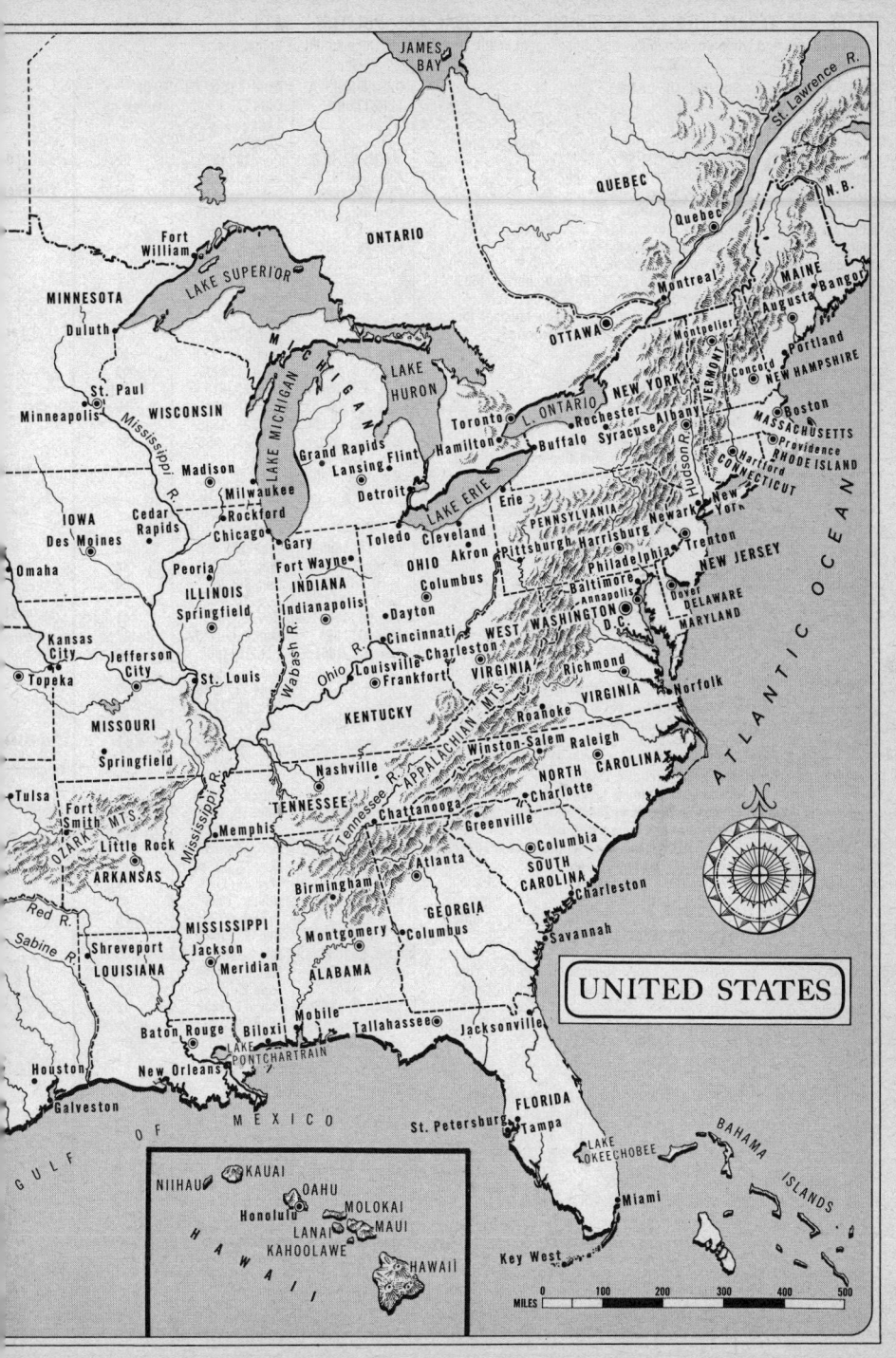

UNITED STATES

## STATES AND TERRITORIES OF THE UNION—HISTORICAL AND POLITICAL DATA

Sources: Council of State Governments; U.S. Department of the Interior; U.S. Department of Commerce.

| STATE OR TERRITORY | SOURCE OF LANDS | ORGANIZED AS TERRITORY | ADMITTED TO UNION Date | Order |
|---|---|---|---|---|
| Alabama......... | Mississippi Territory, 1798 [1]................... | March 3, 1817 | Dec. 14, 1819 | 22 |
| Alaska.......... | Purchased from Russia, 1867................. | Aug. 24, 1912 | Jan. 3, 1959 | 49 |
| Arizona......... | Ceded by Mexico, 1848 [2]..................... | Feb. 24, 1863 | Feb. 14, 1912 | 48 |
| Arkansas........ | Louisiana Purchase, 1803................... | March 2, 1819 | June 15, 1836 | 25 |
| California....... | Ceded by Mexico, 1848.................... | ([3]) | Sept. 9, 1850 | 31 |
| Colorado........ | Louisiana Purchase, 1803 [4]................. | Feb. 28, 1861 | Aug. 1, 1876 | 38 |
| Connecticut...... | Royal charter, 1662 [5]..................... | — | Jan. 9, 1788([6]) | 5 |
| Delaware........ | Swedish charter, 1638; English charter, 1683 [5].... | — | Dec. 7, 1787([6]) | 1 |
| Florida.......... | Ceded by Spain, 1819.................... | March 30, 1822 | March 3, 1845 | 27 |
| Georgia......... | Charter, 1732, from George II to Trustees for Establishing the Colony of Georgia [5]........... | — | Jan. 2, 1788([6]) | 4 |
| Hawaii.......... | Annexed, 1898................... | June 14, 1900 | Aug. 21, 1959 | 50 |
| Idaho........... | Treaty with Britain, 1846.................. | March 4, 1863 | July 3, 1890 | 43 |
| Illinois.......... | Northwest Territory, 1787.................. | Feb. 3, 1809 | Dec. 3, 1818 | 21 |
| Indiana......... | Northwest Territory, 1787.................. | May 7, 1800 | Dec. 11, 1816 | 19 |
| Iowa........... | Louisiana Purchase, 1803.................. | June 12, 1838 | Dec. 28, 1846 | 29 |
| Kansas......... | Louisiana Purchase, 1803 [4].................. | May 30, 1854 | Jan. 29, 1861 | 34 |
| Kentucky........ | Part of Virginia until admitted as state..... | ([3]) | June 1, 1792 | 15 |
| Louisiana........ | Louisiana Purchase, 1803 [7]............... | March 26, 1804 | April 30, 1812 | 18 |
| Maine.......... | Part of Massachusetts until admitted as state.... | ([3]) | March 15, 1820 | 23 |
| Maryland........ | Charter, 1632, from Charles I to Calvert [5]...... | — | April 28, 1788([6]) | 7 |
| Massachusetts.... | Charter to Massachusetts Bay Company, 1629 [5]... | — | Feb. 6, 1788([6]) | 6 |
| Michigan........ | Northwest Territory, 1787.................. | Jan. 11, 1805 | Jan. 26, 1837 | 26 |
| Minnesota....... | Northwest Territory, 1787 [8]................. | March 3, 1849 | May 11, 1858 | 32 |
| Mississippi....... | Mississippi Territory [9]..................... | April 7, 1798 | Dec. 10, 1817 | 20 |
| Missouri........ | Louisiana Purchase, 1803................... | June 4, 1812 | Aug. 10, 1821 | 24 |
| Montana........ | Louisiana Purchase, 1803 [10]................ | May 26, 1864 | Nov. 8, 1889 | 41 |
| Nebraska....... | Louisiana Purchase, 1803................... | May 30, 1854 | March 1, 1867 | 37 |
| Nevada......... | Ceded by Mexico, 1848.................... | March 2, 1861 | Oct. 31, 1864 | 36 |
| New Hampshire... | Grants from Council for New England, 1622 and 1629; made royal province, 1679 [5]........... | — | June 21, 1788([6]) | 9 |
| New Jersey...... | Dutch settlement, 1618; English charter, 1664 [5]... | — | Dec. 18, 1787([6]) | 3 |
| New Mexico..... | Ceded by Mexico, 1848 [2]................... | Sept. 9, 1850 | Jan. 6, 1912 | 47 |
| New York....... | Dutch settlement, 1623; English control, 1664 [5]... | — | July 26, 1788([6]) | 11 |
| North Carolina.... | Charter, 1663, from Charles II [5]............... | — | Nov. 21, 1789([6]) | 12 |
| North Dakota..... | Louisiana Purchase, 1803 [11]................. | March 2, 1861 | Nov. 2, 1889 | 39 |
| Ohio........... | Northwest Territory, 1787.................... | ([3]) | March 1, 1803 | 17 |
| Oklahoma....... | Louisiana Purchase, 1803................... | May 2, 1890 | Nov. 16, 1907 | 46 |
| Oregon......... | Settlement and treaty with Britain, 1846...... | Aug. 14, 1848 | Feb. 14, 1859 | 33 |
| Pennsylvania..... | Grant from Charles II to William Penn, 1681 [5].... | — | Dec. 12, 1787([6]) | 2 |
| Rhode Island..... | Charter, 1663, from Charles II [5]............... | — | May 29, 1790([6]) | 13 |
| South Carolina... | Charter, 1663, from Charles II [5]............... | — | May 23, 1788([6]) | 8 |
| South Dakota.... | Louisiana Purchase, 1803................... | March 2, 1861 | Nov. 2, 1889 | 40 |
| Tennessee....... | Part of North Carolina until admitted as state.... | ([3]) | June 1, 1796 | 16 |
| Texas.......... | Republic of Texas, 1845..................... | ([3]) | Dec. 29, 1845 | 28 |
| Utah........... | Ceded by Mexico, 1848.................... | Sept. 9, 1850 | Jan. 4, 1896 | 45 |
| Vermont........ | From lands of New Hampshire and New York.... | ([3]) | March 4, 1791 | 14 |
| Virginia......... | Charter, 1609, from James I to London Co. [5]..... | — | June 25, 1788([6]) | 10 |
| Washington...... | Oregon Territory, 1848.................... | March 2, 1853 | Nov. 11, 1889 | 42 |
| West Virginia..... | Part of Virginia until admitted as state.......... | ([3]) | June 20, 1863 | 35 |
| Wisconsin........ | Northwest Territory, 1787.................. | April 20, 1836 | May 29, 1848 | 30 |
| Wyoming........ | Louisiana Purchase, 1803 [4],[10]................ | July 25, 1868 | July 10, 1890 | 44 |
| American Samoa.. | By 1899 convention (U.S., U.K., Germany); by cession of certain islands' chiefs, 1900, 1904... | Feb. 20, 1929 | — | — |
| District of Columbia.... | Ceded by Maryland (1788) and by Virginia (1789) | July 16, 1790 | — | — |
| Guam.......... | Ceded by Spain, 1898..................... | Aug. 1, 1950 | — | — |
| Puerto Rico....... | Ceded by Spain, 1898..................... | ([12]) | — | — |
| Virgin Islands.... | Purchased from Denmark, January 17, 1917..... | — | — | — |

[1] By the Treaty of Paris (1783), Britain gave up claim to the 13 original colonies, and to all land within an area extending along the present Canadian border to Lake of the Woods, down the Mississippi River to the 31st parallel, east to the Chattahoochie River, down it to the mouth of the Flint River, east to the source of the St. Mary's River, down it to the ocean. Territory west of the Alleghenies, claimed by various states, was eventually all ceded to the nation. Thus, most of Alabama was acquired by the Treaty of Paris, but the lower part from Spain, 1813.   [2] Part obtained by Gadsden Purchase, 1853.   [3] No territorial status before admission.   [4] Part ceded by Mexico, 1848.   [5] One of original 13 colonies.   [6] Date of ratification of U.S. Constitution.   [7] West Feliciana District (Baton Rouge) acquired from Spain (1810), added to Louisiana,

| GOVERNOR | PARTY | LENGTH OF TERM (in years) | PRESENT TERM BEGAN (January) | RESIDENT POPULATION | | STATE OR TERRITORY |
|---|---|---|---|---|---|---|
| | | | | 1960 Census (in 000s) | 1967 est.[20] (in 000s) | |
| Lurleen Wallace......... | Democrat | 4 | 1967 | 3,267 | 3,540 | .......Alabama |
| Walter J. Hickel......... | Republican | 4 | 1966 [13] | 226 | 273 | .........Alaska |
| Jack Williams........... | Republican | 2 | 1967 | 1,302 | 1,635 | ........Arizona |
| Winthrop Rockefeller..... | Republican | 2 | 1967 | 1,786 | 1,969 | .......Arkansas |
| Ronald Reagan.......... | Republican | 4 | 1967 | 15,717 | 19,163 | ......California |
| John A. Love............ | Republican | 4 | 1967 | 1,754 | 1,975 | ......Colorado |
| John Dempsey........... | Democrat | 4 | 1967 | 2,535 | 2,925 | ....Connecticut |
| Charles L. Terry, Jr....... | Democrat | 4 | 1965 | 446 | 523 | ......Delaware |
| Claude R. Kirk, Jr....... | Republican | 4 | 1967 | 4,952 | 5,996 | .........Florida |
| Lester G. Maddox........ | Democrat | 4 | 1967 | 3,943 | 4,511 | ........Georgia |
| John A. Burns........... | Democrat | 4 | 1966 [13] | 633 | 741 | .........Hawaii |
| Don Samuelson.......... | Republican | 4 | 1967 | 667 | 699 | ..........Idaho |
| Otto Kerner............. | Democrat | 4 | 1965 | 10,081 | 10,894 | .........Illinois |
| Roger D. Branigin........ | Democrat | 4 | 1965 | 4,662 | 4,999 | ........Indiana |
| Harold E. Hughes........ | Democrat | 2 | 1967 | 2,758 | 2,753 | ...........Iowa |
| Robert Docking.......... | Democrat | 2 | 1967 | 2,179 | 2,275 | .........Kansas |
| Edward T. Breathitt...... | Democrat | 4 | 1963 [14] | 3,038 | 3,191 | ......Kentucky |
| John J. McKeithen....... | Democrat | 4 | 1964 [15] | 3,257 | 3,660 | ......Louisiana |
| Kenneth M. Curtis....... | Democrat | 4 | 1967 | 969 | 973 | ...........Maine |
| Spiro T. Agnew.......... | Republican | 4 | 1967 | 3,401 | 3,685 | ......Maryland |
| John A. Volpe.......... | Republican | 4 | 1967 | 5,149 | 5,421 | ..Massachusetts |
| George Romney.......... | Republican | 4 | 1967 | 7,823 | 8,584 | ......Michigan |
| Harold E. LeVander...... | Republican | 4 | 1967 | 3,414 | 3,582 | ......Minnesota |
| Paul B. Johnson......... | Democrat | 4 | 1964 | 2,178 | 2,348 | .....Mississippi |
| Warren E. Hearnes....... | Democrat | 4 | 1965 | 4,320 | 4,605 | ......Missouri |
| Tim Babcock............ | Republican | 4 | 1965 | 675 | 701 | ........Montana |
| Norbert T. Tiemann...... | Republican | 4 | 1967 | 1,411 | 1,435 | ......Nebraska |
| Paul Laxalt............. | Republican | 4 | 1967 | 285 | 444 | .........Nevada |
| John W. King........... | Democrat | 2 | 1967 | 607 | 685 | .New Hampshire |
| Richard J. Hughes........ | Democrat | 4 | 1966 | 6,067 | 7,004 | .....New Jersey |
| David F. Cargo.......... | Republican | 2 | 1967 | 951 | 1,003 | ....New Mexico |
| Nelson A. Rockefeller.... | Republican | 4 | 1967 | 16,782 | 18,335 | ......New York |
| Dan K. Moore........... | Democrat | 4 | 1965 | 4,556 | 5,027 | ..North Carolina |
| William L. Guy.......... | Democrat | 4 | 1965 | 632 | 639 | ...North Dakota |
| James A. Rhodes........ | Republican | 4 | 1967 | 9,706 | 10,462 | ...........Ohio |
| Dewey Bartlett......... | Republican | 4 | 1967 | 2,328 | 2,496 | .....Oklahoma |
| Tom McCall............. | Republican | 4 | 1967 | 1,769 | 1,999 | .........Oregon |
| Raymond P. Shafer...... | Republican | 4 | 1967 | 11,319 | 11,626 | ...Pennsylvania |
| John H. Chafee......... | Republican | 2 | 1967 | 859 | 901 | ...Rhode Island |
| Robert E. McNair........ | Democrat | 4 | 1967 | 2,383 | 2,603 | ..South Carolina |
| Nils A. Boe............. | Republican | 2 | 1967 | 681 | 674 | ...South Dakota |
| Buford Ellington........ | Democrat | 4 | 1967 | 3,567 | 3,888 | ......Tennessee |
| John B. Connally........ | Democrat | 2 | 1967 | 9,580 | 10,783 | ..........Texas |
| Calvin L. Rampton....... | Democrat | 4 | 1965 | 891 | 1,022 | ...........Utah |
| Philip H. Hoff.......... | Democrat | 2 | 1967 | 390 | 416 | ........Vermont |
| Mills E. Godwin, Jr....... | Democrat | 4 | 1966 | 3,967 | 4,533 | ........Virginia |
| Daniel J. Evans.......... | Republican | 4 | 1965 | 2,853 | 3,089 | ......Washington |
| Hulett C. Smith......... | Democrat | 4 | 1965 | 1,860 | 1,798 | ...West Virginia |
| Warren P. Knowles...... | Republican | 2 | 1967 | 3,952 | 4,188 | ......Wisconsin |
| Stanley K. Hathaway..... | Republican | 4 | 1967 | 330 | 315 | ........Wyoming |
| Owen S. Aspinall........ | Democrat | (16) | 1967 | 20 | 27 [21] | American Samoa |
| Walter E. Washington [17]... | Democrat | (16) | 1967 | 764 | 809 | .........District of Columbia |
| Manuel F. L. Guerrero.... | Democrat | 4 | 1967 | 67 | 66 [21] | ..........Guam |
| Roberto Sanchez-Vilella.. | 18 | 4 | 1965 | 2,350 | 2,657 [21] | .....Puerto Rico |
| Ralph M. Paiewonsky.... | Democrat | (16) | (19) | 32 | 46 [21] | ...Virgin Islands |

1812.    [8] Part obtained by Louisiana Purchase, 1803.    [9] See footnote "1"; the lower part of Mississippi was also acquired from Spain, 1813.    [10] Part of land obtained from Oregon Territory, 1848.    [11] The northern part and the Red River Valley acquired by treaty with Britain, 1818.    [12] Became a self-governing commonwealth on July 25, 1952 by compact approved by the U.S. Congress and Puerto Rican voters, as provided in U.S. Public Law 600 of 1950.    [13] State Constitution specifies first Monday in December as Inauguration Day.    [14] December 10, 1963.    [15] May 12, 1964.    [16] Indefinite term.    [17] Commissioner.    [18] Popular Democratic Party.    [19] April 1961.    [20] Provisional estimate as of July 1, 1967, except where noted.    [21] Provisional estimate as of July 1, 1966.

## MAJOR U.S. TERRITORIAL ACQUISITIONS

| DATE | ACQUISITION | AREA (in square miles) | HOW ACQUIRED | ACQUISITION PRICE |
|---|---|---|---|---|
| 1783 | Original Territory.................... | 888,811 | Treaty with Great Britain...... | — |
| 1803 | Louisiana........................... | 827,987 | Purchase from France......... | $15,000,000 |
| 1819 | Florida............................. | 72,101 | Treaty with Spain............ | $5,000,000 |
| 1845 | Texas.............................. | 389,166 | Independent republic annexed | — |
| 1846 | Oregon............................. | 286,541 | Treaty with Great Britain...... | — |
| 1848 | Mexican Cession.................... | 529,189 | Conquest from Mexico........ | $15,000,000 |
| 1853 | Gadsden Purchase.................. | 29,670 | Purchase from Mexico........ | $10,000,000 |
| 1867 | Alaska............................. | 586,400 | Purchase from Russia......... | $7,200,000 |
| 1867 | Midway Islands..................... | 1½ | Occupation.................. | — |
| 1898 | Hawaiian Islands................... | 6,407 | Independent republic annexed | — |
| 1898 | Philippine Islands (Independent, 1946) | 114,400 | Conquest from Spain......... | $20,000,000 |
| 1898 | Puerto Rico........................ | 3,435 | Conquest from Spain......... | — |
| 1898 | Guam.............................. | 212 | Conquest from Spain......... | — |
| 1899 | Wake Island....................... | 3 | Occupation.................. | — |
| 1899 | American Samoa.................... | 76 | Division with Germany and Great Britain.............. | — |
| 1903 | Panama Canal Zone (perpetual lease) | 553 | Treaty with Panama.......... | $10,000,000; annual payment of $450,000 increased to $1,930,000 in 1955 |
| 1916 | Virgin Islands...................... | 133 | Purchase from Denmark...... | $25,000,000 |
| 1947 | Marshall, Caroline, and Marianas islands in the Pacific Ocean........ | 687 | U.N. Trusteeship............. | — |
| 1952 | Ryukyu Islands (U.S. administration) | 848 | Treaty with Japan........... | — |

## GEOGRAPHIC CENTERS OF THE 50 STATES

So many factors are involved that there is no fully satisfactory way to determine a "geographic center," but the U.S. Department of the Interior has made approximations for each state. The geographic center of the U.S. (39° 50' N., 98° 35' W.) is near Lebanon, Kansas.

| STATE | COUNTY | LOCALITY |
|---|---|---|
| Alabama...... | Chilton | 12 miles SW of Clanton. |
| Alaska........ | — | 63°50' N., 152°00' W., 60 miles NW of Mt. McKinley. |
| Arizona....... | Yavapai | 55 miles ESE of Prescott. |
| Arkansas...... | Pulaski | 12 miles NW of Little Rock. |
| California...... | Madera | 35 miles NE of Madera. |
| Colorado...... | Park | 30 miles NW of Pikes Peak. |
| Connecticut... | Hartford | At East Berlin. |
| Delaware..... | Kent | 11 miles S of Dover. |
| District of Columbia.... | — | Near Fourth and L Streets NW. |
| Florida........ | Hernando | 12 miles NNW of Brooksville. |
| Georgia....... | Twiggs | 18 miles SE of Macon. |
| Hawaii........ | Hawaii | 20°15' N., 156°20' W., off Maui Island. |
| Idaho......... | Custer | At Custer, SW of Challis. |
| Illinois........ | Logan | 28 miles NE of Springfield. |
| Indiana....... | Boone | 14 miles NNW of Indianapolis. |
| Iowa.......... | Story | 5 miles NE of Ames. |
| Kansas........ | Barton | 15 miles NE of Great Bend. |
| Kentucky...... | Marion | 3 miles NNW of Lebanon. |
| Louisiana...... | Avoyelles (parish) | 3 miles SE of Marksville. |
| Maine......... | Piscataquis | 18 miles N of Dover. |
| Maryland...... | Prince Georges | 4½ miles NW of Davidsonville. |
| Massachusetts. | Worcester | North part of city of Worcester. |
| Michigan...... | Wexford | 5 miles NNW of Cadillac. |
| Minnesota..... | Crow Wing | 10 miles SW of Brainerd. |
| Mississippi.... | Leake | 9 miles WNW of Carthage. |
| Missouri....... | Miller | 20 miles SW of Jefferson City. |
| Montana...... | Fergus | 12 miles W of Lewistown. |
| Nebraska...... | Custer | 10 miles NW of Broken Bow. |
| Nevada....... | Lander | 24 miles SE of Austin. |
| New Hampshire | Belknap | 3 miles E of Ashland. |
| New Jersey.... | Mercer | 5 miles SE of Trenton. |
| New Mexico... | Torrance | 12 miles SSW of Willard. |
| New York..... | Madison | 6 miles SSE of Oneida. |
| North Carolina | Chatham | 10 miles NW of Sanford. |
| North Dakota.. | Sheridan | 5 miles SW of McClusky. |
| Ohio.......... | Delaware | 25 miles NNE of Columbus. |
| Oklahoma..... | Oklahoma | 8 miles N of Oklahoma City. |
| Oregon........ | Crook | 25 miles SSE of Prineville. |
| Pennsylvania.. | Centre | 2½ miles SW of Bellefonte. |
| Rhode Island.. | Kent | 1 mile SSW of Crompton. |
| South Carolina | Richland | 13 miles SE of Columbia. |
| South Dakota.. | Hughes | 8 miles NE of Pierre. |
| Tennessee..... | Rutherford | 5 m.les NE of Murfreesboro. |
| Texas......... | McCulloch | 15 miles NE of Brady. |
| Utah.......... | Sanpete | 3 miles N of Manti. |
| Vermont...... | Washington | 3 miles E of Roxbury. |
| Virginia....... | Buckingham | 5 miles SW of Buckingham. |
| Washington.... | Chelan | 10 miles WSW of Wenatchee. |
| West Virginia.. | Braxton | 4 miles E of Sutton. |
| Wisconsin..... | Wood | 9 miles SE of Marsfield. |
| Wyoming...... | Fremont | 58 miles ENE of Lander. |

# GAZETTEER OF THE STATES, CAPITAL DISTRICT, AND TERRITORIES

## ALABAMA

*Area:* 51,609 square miles. *Population* (1967 est.): 3,-540,000 (rank: 21st). *Capital:* Montgomery. *State Flower:* Camellia. *Bird:* Yellowhammer. *Motto:* We Dare Defend Our Rights. *Nickname:* Yellowhammer State. *Flag:* Diagonal red cross on a white field.

**LAND AND CLIMATE.** Alabama is bounded on the north by Tennessee, on the east by Georgia, on the south by Florida and the Gulf of Mexico, and on the west by Mississippi. From the Appalachian Mountains in the northeast the land gradually descends to coastal plains, reaching sea level at the Gulf of Mexico. The highest point is Cheaha Mountain (2,407 feet), situated south of Anniston. Principal rivers are the Tennessee, Black Warrior, Tombigbee, Mobile, Alabama, Coosa, and Chattahoochee; chief lakes, largely artificially formed, are Wheeler, Guntersville, Wilson, Martin, and Lewis Smith.

Climatic variations between regions are not great, although light winter snows occur at times in the north. Temperatures range from average January minimums of 33°–43° F. to average summer maximums of 90°–92° F.

**HISTORY.** The first permanent white settlement in Alabama—by the French in the Mobile area—occurred in 1702. England won control of the region in 1763. It came under U.S. jurisdiction following the American Revolution.

The land was mostly wilderness when it became part of the Territory of Mississippi in 1798. Cotton planting was introduced at this time, and settlement was further spurred by Andrew Jackson's decisive defeat of the Creek Indians at Horseshoe Bend in 1814. Alabama became a territory in 1817 and was granted statehood in 1819.

The state was a leader in the secessionist movement that culminated in the Civil War. Montgomery, the present seat of government, also served as the Confederate States' first capital. The harsh military rule imposed after the South's defeat proved more destructive to the state's economy than the war itself.

Coal and iron mining began in Alabama near the end of the 19th century, but cotton long remained the economy's mainstay despite the havoc wreaked by the boll weevil. However, agriculture has been diversified. The growth of industry, particularly since World War II, has transformed the economy into one that is primarily industrial.

Federal-state conflicts over the enforcement of civil rights brought notoriety and bloodshed to Alabama in recent years. However, Negroes have achieved some progress despite the state government's efforts to maintain school segregation. Recent racial violence elsewhere in the nation has tended somewhat to overshadow the impact of the earlier strife in Alabama.

**GOVERNMENT AND FINANCE.** *Governor:* Mrs. Lurleen Wallace (Dem.); *elected:* Nov. 8, 1966; *term:* 4 years; *annual salary:* $25,000. *Senate:* 34 Dem., 1 Rep.; *House of Representatives:* 106 Dem., 0 Rep. Governor Lurleen Wallace succeeded her husband, ex-Governor George C. Wallace, who was prevented by the state's constitution from seeking a second consecutive term. In 1967 she continued his segregationist policies.

*State Finances: Revenue* (fiscal year 1966, including Federal aid): $954 million; *expenditure:* $934 million (chief expenditures: education, 41.5%; highways, 21.8%; public welfare, 13.5%).

**ECONOMY.** *Per Capita Personal Income* (1966): $2,039 (rank: 47th). *Work Force Distribution* (1966): Agriculture, 10.7%; other, 89.3% (manufacturing, government, and trade, in that order, accounted for 70.5% of the nonagricultural payroll). *Leading Industries:* Primary metals, textiles, chemicals, pulp and paper, rubber and metal products. *Chief Agricultural Products:* Beef cattle, cotton, dairy products, forest products, peanuts, corn, soybeans, pecans.

**EDUCATION.** *Elementary and Secondary School Enrollment* (Fall, 1966): Public, 872,711; private (est.), 33,200. *Colleges and Universities:* 81,125.

**RECREATION.** Among Alabama's recreational areas are four national forests, numerous county public lakes, state parks, and Gulf Coast beaches. Points of interest for visitors include Montgomery historic sites, and the Space Orientation Center at the George C. Marshall Space Flight Center in Huntsville.

## ALASKA

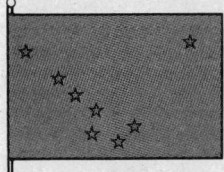

*Area:* 586,400 square miles. *Population* (1967 est.): 273,000 (rank: 50th). *Capital:* Juneau. *State Flower:* Blue Forget-me-not. *Bird:* Alaska Willow Ptarmigan. *Nickname:* Land of the Midnight Sun. *Flag:* Seven gold stars, representing the Big Dipper and Polaris, on a blue field.

**LAND AND CLIMATE.** Alaska, the largest state in the United States, is bounded on the north by the Arctic Ocean, on the east by Canada, on the south by the Pacific Ocean, and on the west by the Bering Sea and Arctic Ocean. Mountain ranges include the east-west Brooks Range in the north, the Alaska and Aleutian ranges, and the Kuskokwim and Wrangell mountains. Mount McKinley (20,320 feet), in the Alaska Range, is the highest peak in North America. Principal rivers are the Yukon and Tanana; chief lakes are Iliamna, Clark, Becharof, and Tustumena. Glaciers, fjords, and forests abound.

Alaska's climate varies widely. A quarter of the state is north of the Arctic Circle and experiences extreme cold. Moderate temperatures prevail in the Panhandle in the southeast and in the Aleutians, an island chain extending westward from the mainland. Average January minimum temperatures range from −23° to 20° F.; average July maximums, from 45° to 72° F.

**HISTORY.** Vitus Bering, a Dane in the service of Russia, first explored Alaska in 1741. Soon Russian fur trappers were exploiting the Aleutian Islands and Alaska proper. The first permanent white settlement was established at Kodiak Island in 1784. The settler's organization grew into the flourishing Russian American Company, and British and American traders began to enter the area.

Declines in the population of fur-bearing sea otters and Russia's defeat in the Crimean War pursuaded Russia to dispose of Alaska. U.S. Secretary of State William H. Seward arranged to buy it for $7.2 million in 1867. Unaware of Alaska's potential, Americans called it "Seward's Folly" or "Seward's Icebox."

American settlement was sparse until 1880, when gold was discovered near Juneau. New discoveries of gold in Canada's Yukon Territory (1896), at Nome (1899), and at Fairbanks (1902) added to the influx of settlers.

In 1906 Juneau succeeded Sitka as the seat of government, and in 1912 Alaska gained territorial status. Fishing gradually replaced mining as the territory's leading industry. By 1916 the Alaska Railroad had linked Anchorage and Fairbanks.

In less than 20 years after World War II, Alaska more than doubled its population, profiting from tourism, oil discoveries, and the building of national defense establishments such as the distant-early-warning (DEW) radar network. In 1959 it became the 49th state.

The Alaskan earthquake of March, 1964, was the severest ever recorded in North America. In August, 1967, during Alaska's centennial year, heavy floods inundated Fairbanks.

**GOVERNMENT AND FINANCE.** *Governor:* Walter J. Hickel (Rep.); *elected:* Nov. 8, 1966; *term:* 4 years; *annual salary:* $27,500. *Senate:* 14 Rep., 6 Dem.; *House of Representatives:* 25 Rep., 15 Dem.

*State Finances: Revenue* (fiscal year 1966, including Federal aid): $199 million; *expenditure:* $203 million (chief expenditures: highways, 33.9%; education, 25.6%; public welfare, 3.4%).

**ECONOMY.** *Per Capita Personal Income* (1966): $3,272 (rank: 9th). *Work Force Distribution* (1966): Agriculture, 1.2%; other, 98.8% (government, trade, and services, in that order, accounted for 68.4% of the nonagricultural payroll). *Leading Industries:* National defense, fishing, mining (petroleum), lumbering, tourism. *Chief Agricultural Products:* Dairy products, vegetables, meat, wool.

**EDUCATION.** *Elementary and Secondary School Enrollment* (Fall, 1966): Public, 61,530; private (est.), 2,500. *Colleges and Universities:* 5,590.

**RECREATION.** Outstanding for camping, fishing, and scenery are Mount McKinley National Park, Tongass and Chugach national forests, and Glacier Bay and Katmai national monuments. The towns of Ketchikan and Sitka feature relics of the Russian period. Alaska is accessible not only by air but via the 1,523-mile Alaska Highway (connecting Fairbanks with Dawson Creek, British Columbia) and the Inside Passage, a scenic interior waterway extending through most of the Alaskan Panhandle.

## ARIZONA

*Area:* 113,909 square miles. *Population* (1967 est.): 1,635,000 (rank: 34th). *Capital:* Phoenix. *State Flower:* Saguaro Cactus. *Bird:* Cactus Wren. *Motto:* *Ditat Deus* (God Enriches). *Nickname:* Grand Canyon State. *Flag:* Copper star, centered on radiating red and yellow stripes and a horizontal blue bar.

**LAND AND CLIMATE.** Arizona is bounded on the north by Utah, on the east by New Mexico, on the south by Mexico, and on the west by California and Nevada. Part of the Colorado River drainage basin, Arizona's topography is marked by mountain ranges (running southeast to northwest across the state), plateaus, chasms (including the Grand Canyon), and deserts. The highest point is Humphreys Peak (12,670 feet) in the San Francisco Mountains. Principal rivers are the Colorado, Little Colorado, Gila, and Verde; chief lakes are Mead (one of the largest reservoirs in the world), Mohave, and Roosevelt.

Arizona's climate is dry and sunny, with temperatures ranging from average January minimums of 15°–37° F. to average summer maximums of 108°–80° F. Precipitation is light.

**HISTORY.** Spaniards were the first Europeans to explore Arizona (1539), finding it inhabited by Pueblo, Zuñi, and other Indians. Colonization began after 1598, with Franciscan and Jesuit missionaries leading the way. Most of the region passed to the United States in 1848 by the Treaty of Guadalupe Hidalgo, which ended the war with Mexico; the rest was acquired in 1853 through the Gadsden Purchase.

Arizona became a separate territory in 1863. Before the Apache wars ended in 1886, mining (copper and silver) and cattle raising had begun to flourish. As sheep grazing increased, range warfare broke out between cattlemen and sheepmen; fighting continued intermittently until 1897.

Arizona became the 48th state in 1912. Since 1940 it has more than tripled its population, due largely to increases in manufacturing activity and to the attractions of its dry climate. Mining has continued to thrive; tourism has become a major industry; and even agriculture has prospered, as large-scale irrigation projects have gradually overcome the natural aridity of the land. A proposal to build two dams that would inundate parts of the Grand Canyon area caused great controversy in 1966.

The Federal Government controls about 71 per cent of the land in Arizona. Indian reservations cover about 28,500 square miles. Of the 15 principal tribes, the Navajos are the most populous, numbering over 50,000.

**GOVERNMENT AND FINANCE.** *Governor:* Jack Williams (Rep.); *elected:* Nov. 8, 1966; *term:* 2 years; *annual salary:* $22,500. *Senate:* 16 Rep., 13 Dem.; *House of Representatives:* 33 Rep., 27 Dem. In 1967, for the first time, an Indian was elected to the legislature.

*State Finances: Revenue* (fiscal year 1966, including Federal aid): $541 million; *expenditure:* $511 million (chief expenditures: education, 40.5%; highways, 22.7%; public welfare, 7%).

**ECONOMY.** *Per Capita Personal Income* (1966): $2,528 (rank: 32nd). *Work Force Distribution* (1966): Agriculture, 7.7%; other, 92.3% (government, trade, manufacturing, and services, in that order, accounted for 79.5% of the nonagricultural payroll). *Leading Industries:* Manufacturing, mining (copper and other nonferrous metals), tourism. *Chief Agricultural Products:* Grains, citrus fruits, vegetables, hay, cotton.

**EDUCATION.** *Elementary and Secondary School Enrollment* (Fall, 1966): Public, 383,239; private (est.), 35,800. *Colleges and Universities:* 73,295.

**RECREATION.** Among Arizona's recreational areas are Grand Canyon and Petrified Forest national parks, eight national forests (covering over 12 million acres), and numerous lakes and reservoirs. Places of special interest include the state's many Indian reservations, Monument Valley, and the Painted Desert. Seventeen national monuments mark such sites as prehistoric Indian cliff dwellings and the ruins of ancient Spanish missions. Remains of the old Wild West, such as Tombstone (with its famous O.K. Corral) and Fort Apache, have also been preserved. "Frontier days" celebrations, Indian tribal ceremonies, and rodeos are typical of the events that draw crowds to various towns.

# ARKANSAS

*Area:* 53,104 square miles. *Population* (1967 est.): 1,969,-000 (rank: 31st). *Capital:* Little Rock. *State Flower:* Apple Blossom. *Bird:* Mockingbird. *Motto: Regnat Populus* (The People Rule). *Nickname:* Land of Opportunity. *Flag:* Star-studded blue and white diamond on a red field.

**LAND AND CLIMATE.** Arkansas is bounded on the north by Missouri; on the east by Missouri,

Tennessee, and Mississippi; on the south by Louisiana; and on the west by Texas and Oklahoma. Rugged highlands, dominated by the Boston and Ouachita mountains, cover most of northwestern Arkansas. The southern and eastern sections consist of flat, low-lying plains. The highest point is Magazine Mountain (2,823 feet) in the Ouachitas. Principal rivers are the Mississippi (marking the eastern border), Arkansas, Ouachita, White, Red, and Saint Francis. Chief lakes are Ouachita, Hamilton, and Norfork; principal reservoirs are Nimrod and Bull Shoals.

The climate is warm, with long summers and short winters. Temperatures range from average January minimums of 29°–35° F. to average summer maximums of 93°–95° F.

**HISTORY.** The Arkansas area was settled by the French and transferred to Spain in 1762. Reacquired by France, it was part of the Louisiana Purchase by the United States in 1803. At first included in the Missouri Territory (1812–19), it became the Arkansas Territory in 1819 and attained statehood in 1836.

A cotton boom that began in 1818 led to the establishment of the plantation system in the southern and eastern sections of Arkansas, while subsistence farming developed in the northwest. Large slaveholders, wielding political power, insisted on secession during the Civil War. After the war small farms replaced plantations throughout the state.

Poverty and race problems have troubled Arkansas since Reconstruction days. The collapse of the cotton market during the drought and depression years of the 1930s had a particularly severe effect, causing a mass migration. Since World War II gradual development of the industrial sector has stimulated the economy.

In 1957 President Eisenhower ordered Federal troops into Little Rock to quell racial disturbances and enforce school desegregation.

**GOVERNMENT AND FINANCE.** *Governor:* Winthrop Rockefeller (Rep.); *elected:* Nov. 8, 1966; *term:* 2 years; *annual salary:* $10,000. *Senate:* 35 Dem., 0 Rep.; *House of Representatives:* 97 Dem., 3 Rep.

Winthrop Rockefeller is the first Republican to be elected governor in Arkansas since Reconstruction times.

*State Finances: Revenue* (fiscal year 1966, including Federal aid): $492 million; *expenditure:* $460 million (chief expenditures: education, 36.3%; highways, 26.95%; public welfare, 15.2%).

**ECONOMY.** *Per Capita Personal Income* (1966): $2,015 (rank: 49th). *Work Force Distribution* (1966): Agriculture, 20.6%; other, 79.4% (manufacturing, trade, government, and services, in that order, accounted for 92% of the nonagricultural payroll). *Leading Industries:* Mining (oil, coal, gas), lumber and wood products, bricks, aluminum, food processing. *Chief Agricultural Products:* Cotton, soybeans, rice.

**EDUCATION.** *Elementary and Secondary School Enrollment* (Fall, 1966): Public, 450,954; private (est.), 13,200. *Colleges and Universities:* 45,583.

**RECREATION.** Hot Springs National Park, with its mineral springs and lakes, is Arkansas's leading resort. Other recreational areas include three national forests and many state parks, wildlife refuges, and artificial lakes featuring boating facilities. Hunting and fishing are excellent in the western highlands.

# CALIFORNIA

CALIFORNIA REPUBLIC

*Area:* 158,693 square miles. *Population* (1967 est.): 19,163,000 (rank: 1st). *Capital:* Sacramento. *State Flower:* Golden Poppy. *Bird:* California Valley Quail. *Motto: Eureka* (I Have Found It). *Nickname:* Golden State. *Flag:* A bear and a red star on a white field, with a red horizontal bar at bottom.

**LAND AND CLIMATE.** California is bounded on the north by Oregon, on the east by Nevada and Arizona, on the south by Mexico, and on the west by the Pacific Ocean. The terrain includes rugged mountains (Coast, Sierra Nevada, and Cascade ranges) with some volcanic cones and glaciers, the Mojave and Colorado deserts (in the southeast), and the fertile Central Valley. In eastern California, Mount Whitney (14,495 feet), the highest U.S. peak outside of Alaska, is within sight of Death Valley, which reaches the nation's lowest elevation (282 feet below sea level). Principal rivers are the Colorado, Sacramento, San Joaquin, and Feather; chief lakes are Tahoe, Mono, Cachuma, Clear, Shasta, Goose, and Salton Sea.

California's climate is one of extremes, with temperature changes of as much as 50 degrees in one day occurring in some areas. Precipitation is greatest in the north, with annual readings of up to 100 inches, and the Pacific coast is notably humid. However, a year may pass in Death Valley without measurable rain. Temperatures range from average January minimums of 9°–47° F. to average summer maximums of 61°–108° F.

**HISTORY.** The first permanent settlement in California was made in 1769 by Spaniards on San Diego Bay. Gradually missions were established along the coast, and Spanish and Mexican settlers (known as Californios) began to develop the area. An American sailing vessel first reached the coast in 1796. In 1839 a Swiss, John Augustus Sutter, established the "Kingdom of New Helvetia" in the Sacramento River Valley. Americans began to arrive overland in significant numbers in 1841, virtually taking possession of the region, and four years later the last Mexican governor was expelled. The short-lived California Republic was established in 1846 by John C. Frémont and his followers. The United States claimed California in 1847 and, by the terms of the Treaty of Guadalupe Hidalgo (1848), Mexico ceded the area officially to the U.S.

With the discovery of gold near Sacramento,

"Forty-niners" swarmed in from all parts of the country, inaugurating a period of lawlessness and wild growth. California acquired statehood in 1850. Soon thousands of Chinese were being imported to help build the transcontinental railroad. Completion of the railroad in 1869 stimulated the state's economy but marked the beginning of a long period of racial trouble, culminating in the Chinese Exclusion Act of 1882. Later the state Alien Land Act (1913) excluded Japanese immigrants. Meanwhile, the verdant Central Valley was being intensively cultivated.

A land boom brought many midwesterners into California after World War I. The 1930s saw an influx of "Okies," farmers driven from their drought-stricken land in Oklahoma and other south-central states. Industrial development during and after World War II increased the already impressive rate of population growth and, in the mid-1960s, California became the most populous state in the Union.

Recent difficulties have included housing shortages, farm-labor troubles, air pollution, and more racial strife. One long-standing problem, that of water, was on its way to partial solution with the inauguration of new irrigation projects. A multibillion-dollar scheme to channel water from northern California to the south is in the planning stage.

**GOVERNMENT AND FINANCE.** *Governor:* Ronald Reagan (Rep.); *elected:* Nov. 8, 1966; *term:* 4 years; *annual salary:* $44,100. *Senate:* 20 Dem., 20 Rep.; *Assembly:* 42 Dem., 38 Rep.

*State Finances: Revenue* (fiscal year 1966, including Federal aid): $7,061 million; *expenditure:* $6,821 million (chief expenditures: education, 27.3%; highways, 16.1%; public welfare, 14.5%).

**ECONOMY.** *Per Capita Personal Income* (1966): $3,449 (rank: 5th). *Work Force Distribution* (1966): Agriculture, 4.6%; other, 95.4% (manufacturing, trade, and government, in that order, accounted for 66.2% of the nonagricultural payroll). *Leading Industries:* Aerospace (electronics, aircraft, missiles, instruments), food processing, mining (petroleum, minerals), tourism. *Chief Agricultural Products:* Cattle, dairy products, poultry, vegetables, fruits, nuts.

**EDUCATION.** *Elementary and Secondary School Enrollment* (Fall, 1966): Public, 4,357,904; private (est.), 434,700. *Colleges and Universities:* 915,260.

**RECREATION.** The recreation areas of California include 120 state parks, of which Mount Tamalpais, Big Basin Redwoods, and Humboldt Redwoods are outstanding. Kings Canyon, Sequoia, Yosemite, and Lassen Volcanic national parks also draw many visitors. There are eight national forests, with a gross area of more than 24 million acres. National monuments of note include Channel Islands, Death Valley, Devils Postpile, Pinnacles, Lava Beds, and Muir Woods. Among the landmarks are 22 old Spanish missions. Of special interest to visitors in the Los Angeles area are Mount Wilson Observatory, Disneyland, and Hollywood. San Francisco's attractions include the Civic Center and Golden Gate Bridge and Park.

# COLORADO

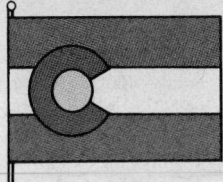

*Area:* 104,247 square miles. *Population* (1967 est.): 1,975,000 (rank: 30th). *Capital:* Denver. *State Flower:* Rocky Mountain Columbine. *Bird:* Lark Bunting. *Motto: Nil Sine Numine* (Nothing Without the Lord). *Nickname:* Centennial State. *Flag:* A red *C* enclosing a gold ball, against blue, white, and blue bars.

**LAND AND CLIMATE.** Colorado is bounded on the north by Wyoming and Nebraska, on the east by Nebraska and Kansas, on the south by Oklahoma and New Mexico, and on the west by Utah. Two-fifths of the state is covered by the Rocky Mountains; to their east are the Great Plains, and to their west is the Colorado Plateau. Mount Elbert (14,431 feet), in the Sawatch Range, is the highest of 50-odd peaks over 14,000 feet. Principal rivers are the Colorado, Rio Grande, South Platte, and Arkansas. Small lakes are numerous.

The climate is generally dry and bracing. Temperatures vary greatly with altitude. Average January minimums range from 1° to 17° F.; average July maximums, from 83° to 93° F.

**HISTORY.** The Colorado area, first claimed by France and Spain in the 18th century, was acquired in part by the Louisiana Purchase (1803) and explored by U.S. Army officers Zebulon Pike (1806), Stephen Long (1819–20), and John Frémont (1842–43). Additional lands came from Mexico in 1848, as a result of the Mexican War, and from Texas in 1850.

Discovery of gold in 1858 near present-day Denver brought the first settlers; rough mining towns sprang up; and Colorado Territory was created in 1861. By the mid-1860s little surface gold remained, but a rich silver lode discovery in 1875 triggered another mining boom.

Meantime, a rail link between Colorado and the East was completed in 1870. The first irrigation canals were dug, cattle ranching and farming began to develop, and lawlessness decreased. Colorado achieved statehood in 1876, three years before the Meeker Massacre ended serious Indian fighting.

Beginning in the 1890s, collapse of the silver market, railway franchise disputes, serious labor strife, and range warfare kept Colorado in turmoil for two decades. Agriculture's importance grew, and silver enjoyed a new boom during World War I. Dam construction in the decades since World War II vastly increased the irrigated acreage (in which Colorado is second only to California) and hydroelectric capacity. In the early 1950s manufacturing passed agriculture as the major industry.

**GOVERNMENT AND FINANCE.** *Governor:* John A. Love (Rep.); *elected:* Nov. 8, 1966; *term:* 4 years; *annual salary:* $20,000. *Senate:* 20 Rep., 15 Dem.; *House of Representatives:* 38 Rep., 27 Dem.

*State Finances:* Revenue (fiscal year 1966, including Federal aid): $646 million; *expenditure:* $589 million (chief expenditures: education, 37.8%; highways, 20.4%; public welfare, 15.8%).

**ECONOMY.** *Per Capita Personal Income* (1966): $2,872 (rank: 21st). *Work Force Distribution* (1966): Agriculture, 7.9%; other, 92.1% (government, trade, services, and manufacturing, in that order, accounted for 79.4% of the nonagricultural payroll). *Leading Industries:* Food processing, military ordnance, machinery, mining (petroleum, natural gas, coal, molybdenum, uranium, copper, lead, zinc, building materials, oil shale), tourism. *Chief Agricultural Products:* Beef cattle, sheep, wheat, hay, sugar beets, vegetables.

**EDUCATION.** *Elementary and Secondary School Enrollment* (Fall, 1966): Public, 498,472; private (est.), 47,900. *Colleges and Universities:* 83,313.

**RECREATION.** Visitors are attracted to Rocky Mountain and Mesa Verde national parks; Dinosaur, Colorado, Black Canyon of the Gunnison, and Great Sand Dunes national monuments; and 12 national forests. Other points of interest include Pikes Peak, Garden of the Gods, and the U.S. Air Force Academy, all near Colorado Springs; the Durango-Silverton narrow gauge rail trip; Central City; and the year-round resort area of Aspen.

# CONNECTICUT

*Area:* 5,009 square miles. *Population* (1967 est.): 2,925,000 (rank: 24th). *Capital:* Hartford. *State Flower:* Mountain Laurel. *Bird:* Robin. *Motto: Qui Transtulit Sustinet* (He Who Transplanted Continues to Sustain). *Nickname:* Constitution State. *Flag:* State seal on a blue field.

**LAND AND CLIMATE.** Connecticut is bounded on the north by Massachusetts, on the east by Rhode Island, on the south by Long Island Sound, and on the west by New York. Gently rolling hills characterize most of the state. The highest point is Mount Frissell (2,380 feet) in the northwest. Principal rivers are the Connecticut, Thames, and Housatonic. There are numerous small natural lakes; the largest body of water, Lake Candlewood, is artificial.

Temperatures range from average January minimums of 18°–23° F. to average maximums of 81°–83° F.

**HISTORY.** Adriaen Block, a Dutch navigator, explored Connecticut's coastal region in 1614 and claimed it for Holland; but Englishmen from nearby Massachusetts Bay Colony made the area's first permanent settlement at present-day Windsor in 1633. In 1639 the colonists drew up the Fundamental Orders, a document that anticipated the U.S. Constitution in calling for government by the people. Granted a Royal charter in 1662, the Connecticut Colony was expanded in 1665 by the addition of neighboring New Haven, a Puritan colony. By their victory in King Philip's War (1676), the colonists ended serious harassment by the Pequot Indians.

By 1766 Connecticut's radicals, angered by British taxes and laws restricting trade, won political power from the Tories, and under Governor Jonathan Trumbull the colony declared its independence from Britain the same year. Its delegates to the Constitutional Convention (1787) devised the Connecticut Compromise, from which the U.S. Congress was derived.

Connecticut acquired its present borders in 1799 after giving up its long-standing claims to other territory, including the Ohio region and part of Pennsylvania. Industrial growth was stimulated by such men as Eli Whitney, who started a factory for the mass production of firearms (1798), and Charles Goodyear, the inventor of the vulcanizing process (1839). After the Civil War, improved transportation and massive immigration further accelerated the growth of industry. By the turn of the century 90 per cent of Connecticut's population was urbanized.

During World War I the state was a leading producer of war materiels. Its economy suffered during the Depression, but prosperity returned in the late 1930s. Industry repeated its key role in war production during World War II. Connecticut's citizens enjoy the highest annual per capita income in the nation.

**GOVERNMENT AND FINANCE.** *Governor:* John N. Dempsey (Dem.); *elected:* Nov. 8, 1966; *term:* 4 years; *annual salary:* $35,000. *Senate:* 25 Dem., 11 Rep.; *House of Representatives:* 117 Dem., 60 Rep.

*State Finances: Revenue* (fiscal year 1966, including Federal aid): $761 million; *expenditure:* $720 million (chief expenditures: education, 25.3%; highways, 25.3%; public welfare, 12.8%).

**ECONOMY.** *Per Capita Personal Income* (1966): $3,678 (rank: 1st). *Work Force Distribution* (1966): Agriculture, 1.6%; other, 98.4% (manufacturing, trade, services, and government, in that order, accounted for 85.4% of the nonagricultural payroll). *Leading Industries:* Transportation equipment (jet engines, helicopters, submarines), machine tools, office machines, silverware, hardware, electrical and electronic machinery, insurance, primary metals, firearms, watches and clocks, hats, chemicals. *Chief Agricultural Products:* Dairy products, poultry, tobacco, fruits.

**EDUCATION.** *Elementary and Secondary School Enrollment* (Fall, 1966): Public, 596,848; private (est.), 123,300. *Colleges and Universities:* 89,591.

**RECREATION.** Connecticut has over 100 state parks and forests, many fine beaches, and facilities for boating, fishing, riding, and skiing. Points of interest include Mystic Seaport; Yale University in New Haven; the Nathan Hale Homestead in South Coventry; the Wadsworth Athenaeum and Mark Twain Memorial in Hartford; the U.S. Coast Guard Academy in New London; the submarine base at Groton; and the Shakespeare Festival Theater in Stratford.

# DELAWARE

*Area:* 2,057 square miles. *Population* (1967 est.): 523,000 (rank: 46th). *Capital:* Dover. *State Flower:* Peach Blossom. *Bird:* Blue Hen Chicken. *Motto:* Liberty and Independence. *Nicknames:* Diamond State; First State. *Flag:* The state seal centered in a yellow diamond on a blue field.

**LAND AND CLIMATE.** Delaware is bounded on the north by Pennsylvania; on the east by New Jersey, Delaware Bay, and the Atlantic Ocean; and on the south and west by Maryland. Most of the state is sandy, marshy coastal plain. Its highest point (442 feet) is at Centerville, near the Pennsylvania border. Principal rivers are the Delaware, Christina, Nanticoke, and Mispillion. There are about 50 small lakes.

Delaware has a temperate, humid climate with cool winters and warm summers. Temperatures range from an average January minimum of 26° F. to an average July maximum of 86° F.

**HISTORY.** The Delaware coast, first explored in 1609 by Henry Hudson, an English navigator acting for the Dutch East India Company, was named in 1610 for Baron De la Warr, governor of the Virginia colony. Swedes made the area's first permanent settlement in 1638 on the site of present-day Wilmington. Delaware passed successively from Sweden to the Netherlands (1655), Britain (1664), and again to the Netherlands (1773), before becoming part of William Penn's Pennsylvania colony (1682).

In 1776, after the start of the American Revolution, Delaware declared its independence. Eleven years later, on December 7, it became the first state to ratify the Constitution.

Industry—based on paper, cloth, and flour, and, after 1802, on the powder mills of Eleuthère du Pont—was centered in the north around Wilmington; the south was solidly agricultural. Farming and industry thrived, aided by the growth of the railroads in the 1850s. Although Delaware remained loyal to the Union during the Civil War, many of its citizens favored the Confederacy.

Fresh waves of immigration swelled the state's population in the 19th and 20th centuries. Hard hit by the depression of the 1930s, Delaware elected a Democratic governor in 1936, its first since 1901. The state's shipyards and factories were important to U.S. war production during World War II. Continuing industrial expansion in the 1950s helped increase its population by 40 per cent within a decade.

Segregation was long practiced in Delaware's public schools, but by the mid-1960s it had been abolished, virtually without incident.

**GOVERNMENT AND FINANCE.** *Governor:* Charles L. Terry, Jr. (Dem.); *elected:* Nov. 3, 1964; *term:* 4 years; *annual salary:* $25,000. *Senate:* 9 Dem., 9 Rep.; *House of Representatives:* 23 Rep., 12 Dem.

*State Finances: Revenue* (fiscal year 1966,

including Federal aid): $210 million; *expenditure:* $209 million (chief expenditures: education, 41.1%; highways, 20.6%; public welfare, 6.2%).

**ECONOMY.** *Per Capita Personal Income* (1966): $3,563 (rank: 2nd). *Work Force Distribution* (1966): Agriculture, 4.4%; other, 95.6% (manufacturing, trade, and government, in that order, accounted for 69.8% of the nonagricultural payroll). *Leading Industries:* Chemicals, food processing, textiles, shipbuilding, leather goods. *Chief Agricultural Products:* Dairy products, poultry, hogs, cattle, truck crops, soybeans, wheat.

Liberal incorporation laws have led many U.S. companies to form corporations in the state. Industry, once confined to the Wilmington area, is now located throughout the state.

**EDUCATION.** *Elementary and Secondary School Enrollment* (Fall, 1966): Public, 112,645; private (est.), 21,000. *Colleges and Universities:* 14,304.

**RECREATION.** Recreation areas include Trap Pond State Park and Redden State Forest. Of interest to visitors are the Henry Francis du Pont Winterthur Museum near Wilmington, and such historic towns as New Castle, Dover, and Lewes. Rehoboth, Bethany, Dewey, and Fenwick Island beaches are popular.

# FLORIDA

*Area:* 58,560 square miles. *Population* (1967 est.): 5,996,000 (rank: 9th). *Capital:* Tallahassee. *State Flower:* Orange Blossom. *Bird:* Mockingbird. *Motto:* In God We Trust. *Nickname:* Sunshine State. *Flag:* State seal and diagonal red bars on a white field.

**LAND AND CLIMATE.** Florida is bounded on the north by Alabama and Georgia, on the east by the Atlantic Ocean, on the south by the Straits of Florida, and on the west by the Gulf of Mexico and Alabama. Hilly central uplands, running north and south, contain the state's highest point (345 feet); they are flanked on the east and west by the broad, low-lying Atlantic and East Gulf coastal plains. The Florida Keys, a series of small islands (many joined by a highway from the mainland), stretch southwesterly from Florida's tip for some 200 miles. Principal rivers include the St. Johns, St. Marys, Apalachicola, Perdido, and Suwannee; chief of the state's 30,000 lakes is Okeechobee, the second largest body of fresh water within the U.S. Much of southern Florida is covered by swampland, such as the 2.5-million-acre Everglades and the Big Cypress Swamp.

**HISTORY.** Juan Ponce de Léon, the Spanish governor of Puerto Rico, claimed the region of Florida for his country in 1513, and Spanish settlement began with the founding of St. Augustine in 1565. Its strategic importance to the rich ship convoys that passed through the Florida straits led England and France to harass Spanish Florida for nearly two centuries. Spain lost the region to England in 1763 as a result of the Seven Years War but recovered it in 1783.

With Spanish permission, Britain used Pensacola as a naval base during the War of 1812; troops under Andrew Jackson took it in 1814. In 1819 Spain officially ceded Florida to the U.S., and American occupation began two years later.

Settlers increased greatly, particularly in the north where the plantation system became entrenched. The southward push brought sharp conflicts with the Indians, but the harsh fighting of the Seminole War (1835–42) did not deter settlement. Florida became a state in 1845.

Although it seceded from the Union in 1861, Florida saw little fighting during the Civil War, and it fared better than many other Southern states during the harsh Reconstruction era. In 1868 it was readmitted to the Union.

In 1881 the near-bankrupt state government sold some four million acres of land for development. Northern capital flowed in; the cultivation of citrus fruits began; and railroads and resorts were built. A huge boom in Florida real estate, begun shortly after World War I, led, before its collapse in 1925, to a great increase in the state's population.

After World War II the Federal government made Cape Canaveral (renamed Cape Kennedy in 1963) a major center for space research, and the first manned U.S. space flights were made from the cape in 1961.

**GOVERNMENT AND FINANCE.** *Governor:* Claude R. Kirk, Jr. (Rep.); *elected:* Nov. 8, 1966; *term:* 4 years; *annual salary:* $27,500. *Senate:* 28 Dem., 20 Rep.; *House of Representatives:* 79 Dem., 40 Rep. In 1967 the U.S. Supreme Court nullified Florida's legislative apportionment law.

*State Finances: Revenue* (fiscal year 1966, including Federal aid): $1,320 million; *expenditure:* $1,207 million (chief expenditures: education, 40.1%; highways, 21.9%; public welfare, 9.5%).

**ECONOMY.** *Per Capita Personal Income* (1966): $2,576 (rank: 31st). *Work Force Distribution* (1966): Agriculture, 6.3%; other, 93.7% (trade, government, and services, in that order, accounted for 62.7% of the nonagricultural payroll). *Leading Industries:* Tourism, manufacturing, agriculture. *Chief Agricultural Products:* Citrus fruits, winter vegetables, beef cattle.

**EDUCATION.** *Elementary and Secondary School Enrollment* (Fall, 1966): Public, 1,260,139; private (est.), 98,700. *Colleges and Universities:* 160,926.

**RECREATION.** Recreation areas include many coastal and inland resort regions; more than 252,000 acres of state parks and forests; three national forests (Ocala, Osceola, and Apalachicola); and Everglades National Park. Among Florida's numerous points of interest are St. Augustine; Marineland; Silver Springs; the Ringling Museums in Sarasota; Cypress Gardens near Winter Haven; and Cape Kennedy and the Kennedy Space Center.

# GEORGIA

*Area:* 58,876 square miles. *Population* (1967 est.): 4,511,000 (rank: 15th). *Capital:* Atlanta. *State Flower:* Cherokee Rose. *Bird:* Brown Thrasher (unofficial). *Motto:* Wisdom, Justice, and Moderation. *Nicknames:* Empire State of the South; Peach State. *Flag:* State seal on a vertical blue bar; Confederate flag to the right.

**LAND AND CLIMATE.** Georgia is bounded on the north by Tennessee and North Carolina, on the east by South Carolina and the Atlantic Ocean, on the south by Florida, and on the west by Alabama. The state's highest point, Brasstown Bald (4,784 feet), is in the mountainous north. Central Georgia has rolling hills. The broad coastal region is gently rolling or flat plain. Principal rivers are the Savannah, Oconee, Chattahoochee, and Ogeechee; chief lakes are Sidney Lanier, Sinclair, Allatoona, and Seminole.

The climate is mild, and temperatures range from average January minimums of 36°–41° F. to average summer maximums of 90°–92° F.

**HISTORY.** The region of Georgia was claimed by Britain as early as 1629. Conflicting claims by Spain dated from the 16th century, but John Oglethorpe, Georgia's founder, defeated the Spanish in the Battle of Bloody Marsh (1742). Georgia, named after George II, became an independent colony in 1732. The colony prospered and was slow to join the agitation for independence from England.

After the Revolution, conflict between Georgia and the Federal government over states' rights led to passage of the 11th Amendment (1798). Further confusion arose when the legislature fraudulently sold state lands to speculators; and, although Georgia set its present boundaries in 1802, Indian claims to much of its territory persisted for years.

Georgia's cotton-based economy prospered. Despite its dependence on slavery, the state was pro-Union in the decades before the Civil War; nevertheless, Georgia seceded in 1861. A major battlefield during the war, the state was the scene of General William T. Sherman's devastating march to the sea. During Reconstruction it was a center of carpetbagger corruption and Ku Klux Klan activity. Readmission to the Union came in 1870. Agriculture after the war was based on sharecropping and tenant farming; rural poverty became commonplace.

After World War I boll weevils ruined the cotton crop, and Georgia's own depression anticipated the national slump of the 1930s by several years. Political and racial strife were commonplace in the post-Depression years, but in 1961 Georgia was the first Deep South state to peacefully desegregate its public schools.

**GOVERNMENT AND FINANCE.** *Governor:* Lester G. Maddox (Dem.); *elected:* Jan. 11, 1967, by the Legislature; *term:* 4 years; *annual salary:* $19,800. *Senate:* 46 Dem., 7 Rep., 1 Ind.; *House of Representatives:* 183 Dem., 21 Rep.

Gubernatorial elections held on Nov. 8, 1966, gave no candidate a majority. The House and Senate jointly designated Maddox by a roll-call vote of 182 to 66.

*State Finances: Revenue* (fiscal year 1966, including Federal aid): $1,058 million; *expenditure:* $964 million (chief expenditures: education, 46%; highways, 19.2%; public welfare, 12.8%).

**ECONOMY.** *Per Capita Personal Income* (1966): $2,311 (rank: 40th). *Work Force Distribution* (1966): Agriculture, 7.8%; other, 92.2% (manufacturing, trade, and government, in that order, accounted for 71.5% of the nonagricultural payroll). *Leading Industries:* Lumbering, mining, textiles, food, apparel, chemicals, paper, transportation equipment. *Chief Agricultural Products:* Cotton, tobacco, peanuts, pecans, peaches, corn, poultry, dairy products.

Agriculture remains the basis of Georgia's economy, but World War II brought much industry to the state.

**EDUCATION.** *Elementary and Secondary School Enrollment* (Fall, 1966): Public, 1,073,707; private (est.), 28,900. *Colleges and Universities:* 91,280.

**RECREATION.** Georgia's numerous state parks and Chattahoochee and Oconee national forests are noteworthy. Points of interest include Okefenokee National Wildlife Refuge, Andersonville, Chickamauga and Chattanooga National Military Park, the Little White House in Warm Springs, and coast resorts such as Sea Island.

# HAWAII

*Area:* 6,424 square miles. *Population* (1967 est.): 741,000 (rank: 40th). *Capital:* Honolulu. *State Flower:* Hibiscus. *Bird:* Hawaiian Goose. *Motto: Ua Mau Ke Ea O Ka Aina I Ka Pono* (The Life of the Land is Perpetuated in Righteousness). *Nickname:* Aloha State. *Flag:* Alternating white, red, and blue bars, with the Union Jack in the upper left.

**LAND AND CLIMATE.** Hawaii is a chain of 122 Pacific islands about 2,400 miles west of California. Eight main islands—from east to west, Hawaii (4,030 square miles), Maui (720 square miles), Kahoolawe, Lanai, Molokai, Oahu (604 square miles), Kauai, and Niihau—account for all but three miles of the state's total area. Fine sandy beaches, rocky coastlines, fertile valleys, jungle, plateau, and rugged mountains characterize the islands, which are volcanic in origin. Mauna Kea (13,796 feet), on the island of Hawaii, is the highest point. Cooling trade winds make the climate ideal. Temperatures, except for variations between coastal and mountainous regions, remain fairly constant throughout the year, averaging 75° F. Average January minimums are 67°–79° F.; average July maximums are 71°–83° F.

**HISTORY.** Polynesians from the southwest Pacific settled Hawaii, probably in the middle of the eighth century. The island chain was discovered in 1778 by Captain James Cook, the English explorer, who named it the Sandwich Islands. At that time each island was ruled by a hereditary chief, but in 1810 Kamehameha, chief of the largest island (Hawaii), became sole ruler.

Agriculture and commerce developed as European and American traders came to Hawaii. Missionaries converted much of the population to Christianity and played a key role in advising King Kamehameha III, who made Hawaii a constitutional monarchy in 1840.

Foreign capital began pouring into the kingdom, and a group of financiers gradually came to control the economy. After 1850 the sugar industry expanded so rapidly that thousands of Orientals were imported to work the fields. Pineapple cultivation began in 1885. American influence won exclusive rights to Pearl Harbor, where a large naval base was built by the U.S. government.

In 1893 Queen Liliuokalani was deposed for resisting constitutional reform, and a provisional government, mainly American-controlled, was formed. When President Grover Cleveland refused to annex the islands, they were declared a republic (1894), with the American Sanford Dole as president. Voluntarily annexed to the U.S. in 1898, Hawaii became a territory in 1900, with Dole as its first governor.

The Japanese attack on Pearl Harbor in 1941 brought the U.S. into World War II. Great economic growth occurred in the postwar years. Hawaii became the 50th state in 1959.

**GOVERNMENT AND FINANCE.** *Governor:* John A. Burns (Dem.); *elected:* Nov. 8, 1966; *term:* 4 years; *annual salary:* $33,500. *Senate:* 15 Dem., 10 Rep.; *House of Representatives:* 39 Dem., 12 Rep.

*State Finances: Revenue* (fiscal year 1966, including Federal aid): $354 million; *expenditure:* $325 million (chief expenditures: education, 40.9%; highways, 8.3%; welfare, 6.2%).

**ECONOMY.** *Per Capita Personal Income* (1966): $3,143 (rank: 13th). *Work Force Distribution* (1966): Agriculture, 7.2%; other 92.8% (government, trade, services, and manufacturing, in that order, accounted for 78.3% of the nonagricultural payroll). *Leading Industries:* Military installations, food processing, tourism. *Chief Agricultural Products:* Sugar, pineapples, beef cattle.

**EDUCATION.** *Elementary and Secondary School Enrollment* (Fall, 1966): Public, 165,789; private (est.): 32,800. *Colleges and Universities:* 22,762.

**RECREATION.** Hawaii Volcanoes National Park and the City of Refuge National Historic Park, both on Hawaii, and Haleakala National Park on Maui draw many visitors. Year-round water sports and fishing are excellent. Points of interest on Oahu include the Polynesian Cultural Center near Laie; the U.S.S. Arizona National Memorial at Pearl Harbor; and, in Honolulu, Iolani Palace (the capitol), the Bishop Museum, and Waikiki Beach.

# IDAHO

*Area:* 83,557 square miles. *Population* (1967 est.): 699,000 (rank: 42nd). *Capital:* Boise. *State Flower:* Syringa. *Bird:* Mountain Bluebird. *Motto: Esto Perpetua* (May Thou Endure Forever!). *Nickname:* Gem State. *Flag:* State seal on a blue field.

**LAND AND CLIMATE.** Idaho is bounded on the north by Canada, on the east by Montana and Wyoming, on the south by Utah and Nevada, and on the west by Oregon and Washington. Most of northern and central Idaho is part of the Rocky Mountain system; southern Idaho is largely plateau country, dominated by the fertile Snake River Plain. Borah Peak (12,662 feet) in the Lost River Range is the state's highest point. Principal rivers are the Snake, Salmon, Clearwater, Payette, and St. Joe, all tributaries of the Columbia River. Chief lakes include Priest, Pend Oreille, Coeur d'Alene, Grays, and Bear.

Warm Pacific air and protective mountain barriers in the north and east make the climate unusually mild. Temperatures range from average January minimums of 3°–24° F. to average July maximums of 88°–90° F.

**HISTORY.** The Idaho region, acquired by the United States in the Louisiana Purchase (1803), was surveyed by the Lewis and Clark expedition in 1805. Indians and fur traders were its chief inhabitants until 1860, when Mormons made the first permanent white settlement at Franklin. Discoveries of gold and silver in 1860–63 drew large numbers of prospectors, mainly from the West Coast, and Idaho Territory was created in 1863.

Intermittent strife with the Indians subsided by 1878. Population increased, and the mining industry boomed with fresh discoveries of gold, silver, and lead in the 1880s. Railroad construction brought more settlers to the area in the 1880s and 1890s, when communities such as Pocatello and American Falls sprang up.

The growth of large sheep and cattle ranches followed Idaho's admission to the Union in 1890. The Reclamation Act of 1902 gave the state direct Federal aid for irrigation projects and began development of its huge hydroelectric potential. Serious labor trouble in the mining industry was climaxed in 1905 by the murder of former Governor Frank Steunenberg, who had used Federal troops to quell the miners.

In 1955 Arco became the first town with atomic-generated electric power, supplied by Idaho's National Reactor Testing Station. Over the past decade the completion of three dams on the Snake River has vastly increased the state's hydroelectric power resources.

**GOVERNMENT AND FINANCE.** *Governor:* Donald Samuelson (Rep.); *elected:* Nov. 8, 1966; *term:* 4 years; *annual salary:* $15,000. *Senate:* 22 Rep., 13 Dem.; *House of Representatives:* 38 Rep., 32 Dem.

*State Finances: Revenue* (fiscal year 1966, including Federal aid): $232 million; *expenditure:* $211 million (chief expenditures: education, 30.3%; highways, 28.9%; public welfare, 8.1%).

**ECONOMY.** *Per Capita Personal Income* (1966): $2,441 (rank: 36th). *Work Force Distribution* (1966): Agriculture, 24.5%; other, 75.5% (trade, government, manufacturing, and services, in that order, accounted for 81% of the nonagricultural payroll). *Leading Industries:* Food processing, mining (silver, lead, zinc, copper, phosphates), forest products, tourism. *Chief Agricultural Products:* Cattle, sheep, wool, dairy products, potatoes, wheat, barley, hay, sugar beets.

**EDUCATION.** *Elementary and Secondary School Enrollment* (Fall, 1966): Public, 174,529; private (est.), 10,200. *Colleges and Universities:* 23,794.

**RECREATION.** Recreation areas include 16 national forests totaling more than 21,500,000 acres (nearly one-third of Idaho is covered by forest), and 19 state parks and recreation areas. Facilities for big-game hunting and fishing, boating, and skiing are excellent. Of special interest are the Hells Canyon-Seven Devils Scenic Area, on both sides of the Snake River; Idaho's famous resort, Sun Valley, in the Sawtooth Mountains; Shoshone Falls, near Twin Falls; and Craters of the Moon National Monument, near Arco. Tourism is now one of the state's leading industries.

# ILLINOIS

*Area:* 56,400 square miles. *Population* (1967 est.): 10,894,000 (rank: 5th). *Capital:* Springfield. *State Flower:* Native Violet. *Bird:* Cardinal. *Motto:* State Sovereignty-National Union. *Nickname:* Prairie State. *Flag:* State seal on a white field.

**LAND AND CLIMATE.** Illinois is bounded on the north by Wisconsin, on the east by Lake Michigan and Indiana, on the southeast by Kentucky, on the southwest by Missouri, and on the west by Missouri and Iowa. Gently rolling plains cover most of the state. The highest point is Charles Mound (1,241 feet) in the north. Principal rivers are the Mississippi, Wabash, Ohio, Illinois, Rock, Sangamon, and Kaskaskia. Chain-O'-Lakes is one of its few large natural lakes; major reservoirs include Crab Orchard, Springfield, and Decatur.

Illinois is ordinarily cold and windy in winter and hot in summer. Temperatures range from average January minimums of 14°–30°F. to average July maximums of 86°–90°F. The state is subject to tornadoes.

**HISTORY.** The French explorers Père Marquette and Louis Jolliet were the first-known white men to traverse Illinois. Marquette established a mission near Utica in 1675. Cahokia, the first permanent settlement, was founded in

1699. In 1763, after the French and Indian Wars, the region was ceded to Britain. During the American Revolution George Rogers Clark captured (1778) the forts of Cahokia and Kaskaskia from the British.

Illinois became part of Northwest Territory in 1800. It was granted separate territorial status in 1809 and statehood in 1818, but frontier conditions prevailed for many years thereafter. The Indian menace was not removed until the defeat of the Sauk and Fox tribes in the Black Hawk War (1832).

By the 1840s industry was burgeoning. Cyrus McCormack began to manufacture farm implements in Chicago in 1847, a canal system linking the Mississippi Valley and the Great Lakes was completed in 1848, and in the 1850s the westward extension of the railroads brought more industry and settlers.

After the Civil War the population of the state swelled with the immigration of foreign laborers to the cities. Chicago was largely destroyed by fire in 1871 but was soon rebuilt and grew into the nation's meat-packing capital and its major grain market. Farmer-labor dissatisfaction marked the last decades of the 19th century, culminating in the bloody Haymarket Square riot in Chicago in 1886 and the violent Pullman strike in 1894.

Under the administration of Governor John P. Altgeld (1893–97), Illinois became a pioneer in the reform movement, but by the 1920s it was more famous for urban corruption and the criminal activities of the Al Capone gang. Illinois's many defense plants played a vital role in World War II, during which University of Chicago scientists produced the first controlled nuclear chain reaction. The state continues to be a leading center of nuclear research as well as the industrial hub of the Midwest.

**GOVERNMENT AND FINANCE.** *Governor:* Otto Kerner (Dem.); *elected:* Nov. 3, 1964; *term:* 4 years; *annual salary:* $30,000. *Senate:* 38 Rep., 20 Dem.; *House of Representatives:* 99 Rep., 78 Dem.

*State Finances: Revenue* (fiscal year 1966, including Federal aid): $2,270 million; *expenditure:* $2,031 million (chief expenditures: education, 35.3%; highways, 20.5%; public welfare, 15.2%).

**ECONOMY.** *Per Capita Personal Income* (1966): $3,511 (rank: 3rd). *Work Force Distribution* (1966): Agriculture, 4.3%; other, 95.7% (manufacturing, trade, services, and government, in that order, accounted for 83.2% of the nonagricultural payroll). *Leading Industries:* Machinery, electrical appliances, iron and steel, metal fabrication, transportation equipment, meat packing, food processing, mining (coal, petroleum), printing. *Chief Agricultural Products:* Corn, oats, wheat, soybeans, hogs, cattle, sheep, dairy products.

**EDUCATION.** *Elementary and Secondary School Enrollment* (Fall, 1966): Public, 2,159,239; private (est.), 590,500. *Colleges and Universities:* 323,522.

**RECREATION.** Illinois's recreation areas include Shawnee National Forest, over 40 state parks, and boating and beach facilities along the shores of Lake Michigan. Points of interest include Dickson Mounds Indian burial ground near Lewiston; the restoration of New Salem, where Lincoln lived as a young man; the Homestead and Mansion House of Joseph Smith in the old Mormon community of Nauvoo; and Lincoln's home and burial place in Springfield. Chicago is noted for its Merchandise Mart and its Union Stockyards, as well as such cultural institutions as the Art Institute, the Field Museum of Natural History, the Museum of Science and Industry, the John G. Shedd Aquarium, and the Adler Planetarium.

# INDIANA

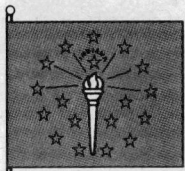

*Area:* 36,291 square miles. *Population* (1967 est.): 4,999,000 (rank: 12th). *Capital:* Indianapolis. *State Flower:* Peony. *Bird:* Cardinal. *Motto:* The Crossroads of America. *Nickname:* Hoosier State. *Flag:* A gold torch and stars on a blue field.

**LAND AND CLIMATE.** Indiana is bounded on the north by Lake Michigan and Michigan, on the east by Ohio, on the southeast and south by Kentucky (separated by the Ohio River), and on the west by Illinois. Nearly two-thirds of the state is covered by level or gently rolling prairie lands, with steep valleys, sharp ridges, and hills in the south. The highest point is in Franklin Township (1,257 feet) in south-central Indiana. Principal rivers are the Wabash, Ohio, White, Kankakee, St. Joseph, and Sugar Creek; chief lakes are Wawasee, Shafer, and Monroe Reservoir.

The climate is generally mild, with occasional extremes of heat and cold. Temperatures range from average January minimums of 18°–26° F. to average summer maximums of 85°–89° F.

**HISTORY.** Indiana, which was inhabited in prehistoric times, was explored by La Salle in the late 1600s and occupied by the French in the early 1700s. The first permanent community developed around Vincennes, which was fortified about 1732. In 1763 the area fell to Britain, but Indian uprisings, especially Pontiac's Rebellion (1763–66), made settlement extremely difficult.

Americans captured Vincennes in 1779 and acquired the whole region as part of the Northwest Territory in 1787. Indiana Territory was organized in 1800. Indian depredations ended soon after the defeat of the Shawnees at Tippecanoe (1811), and statehood was granted in 1816.

During the Civil War Indiana was loyal to the Union, but there was much pro-Confederate sentiment among the many settlers from southern states. After the war manufacturing moved into the state on a large scale. As industry and the railroads grew more powerful, farmers gravitated to the more radical agrarian movements, supporting the Grangers, the Populists, and the Greenback Party.

The struggle between management, labor, and the farmer continued into the 20th century. The socialist Eugene V. Debs was active for many years in the state legislature, and Gary's steelworkers were among the most militant supporters of the national steel strike of 1919. Antilabor sentiment was also strong, with the Ku Klux Klan exercising enormous influence during the 1920s. Since World War II Indiana has prospered on both the industrial and the agricultural front and has become predominantly conservative in its politics.

**GOVERNMENT AND FINANCE.** *Governor:* Roger D. Branigan (Dem.); *elected:* Nov. 3, 1964: *term:* 4 years; *annual salary:* $25,000. *Senate:* 29 Dem., 21 Rep.; *House of Representatives:* 66 Rep., 34 Dem.

*State Finances: Revenue* (fiscal year 1966, including Federal aid): $1,214 million; *expenditure:* $1,108 million (chief expenditures: education, 46.5%; highways, 23.5%; public welfare, 4.7%).

**ECONOMY.** *Per Capita Personal Income* (1966): $3,061 (rank: 14th). *Work Force Distribution* (1966): Agriculture, 8.2%; other, 91.8% (manufacturing, trade, and government, in that order, accounted for 75.3% of the nonagricultural payroll). *Leading Industries:* Steel, aircraft, pharmaceutical and biological products, prefabricated building materials. *Chief Agricultural Products:* Hogs, soybeans, corn.

**EDUCATION.** *Elementary and Secondary School Enrollment* (Fall, 1966): Public, 1,154,927; private (est.), 147,000. *Colleges and Universities:* 153,085.

**RECREATION.** Indiana has one national forest and 32 state parks. Of special interest are the state's prehistoric Indian mounds; the mineral springs at French Lick; Wyandotte Cave, one of the world's largest caverns; and the Indiana Dunes lakeshore area. Indianapolis is noted for its Motor Speedway and its annual Memorial Day 500-mile auto race.

# IOWA

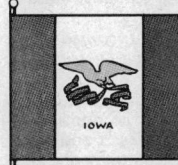

*Area:* 56,290 square miles. *Population* (1967 est.): 2,753,000 (rank: 25th). *Capital:* Des Moines. *State Flower:* Wild Rose. *Bird:* Eastern Goldfinch. *Motto:* Our Liberties We Prize and Our Rights We Will Maintain. *Nickname:* Hawkeye State. *Flag:* Vertical blue, white, and red bars, with an eagle in the larger white bar.

**LAND AND CLIMATE.** Iowa is bounded on the north by Minnesota, on the east by Wisconsin and Illinois (separated by the Mississippi River), on the south by Missouri, and on the west by Nebraska and South Dakota (separated by the Missouri and Big Sioux Rivers).

Except for a hilly northeastern region, the land is chiefly rolling plain. The state's highest point (1,675 feet) is Ocheyedan Mound in the northwest. Among Iowa's numerous rivers, besides those that form its boundaries, are the Iowa, Wapsipinicon, Cedar, and Des Moines.

Lakes include Spirit, Clear, Storm, and West and East Okoboji. Temperatures range from average January minimums of 9°–16° F. to average July maximums of 84°–89° F.

**HISTORY.** White settlement in the region of Iowa in the 17th and 18th centuries was limited to French trading posts. The first permanent settlement, Dubuque, was established in 1788. When the region passed to U.S. control as part of the Louisiana Purchase of 1803, Iowa faced a period of Indian warfare that did not end until the Black Hawk War (1832). By then great numbers of settlers, many of them from New England, were arriving. Iowa Territory was formed in 1838, and eight years later statehood was granted.

Iowa strongly opposed slavery, and many important stations of the Underground Railway, which spirited slaves from the South to freedom, were located on its soil. Having won statehood relatively early, Iowa was spared the bloody warfare over the slavery issue that beset the nearby states of Kansas and Missouri before the Civil War.

In the 1870s the state was swept by the Granger movement and the Populist and Greenback parties, which championed farm interests. By the century's end, however, their radicalism abated, and Iowa became conservatively Republican—a pattern not always followed in recent years.

The state has some of America's best farmland, and its farmers regularly produce 10 per cent of the U.S. food supply. Iowa long typified small-town and rural American life, but industrialization has brought a marked change.

**GOVERNMENT AND FINANCE.** *Governor:* Harold E. Hughes (Dem.); *elected:* Nov. 8, 1966; *term:* 2 years; *annual salary:* $25,000. *Senate:* 32 Dem., 29 Rep.; *House of Representatives:* 89 Rep., 35 Dem.

*State Finances: Revenue* (fiscal year 1966, including Federal aid): $798 million; *expenditure:* $717 million (chief expenditures: education, 32.5%; highways, 28.5%; public welfare, 10.2%).

**ECONOMY:** *Per Capita Personal Income* (1966): $2,931 (rank: 20th). *Work Force Distribution:* (1966): Agriculture, 22.6%; other, 77.4% (manufacturing, trade, and government, in that order, accounted for 68.7% of the nonagricultural payroll). *Leading Industries:* Food processing, meat packing, farm equipment, electronics, metal fabrication. *Chief Agricultural Products:* Corn, soybeans, cattle, hogs, sheep. While Iowa remains in the front rank of agricultural states, its industry has made great strides and now contributes more to income than does farming.

**EDUCATION.** *Elementary and Secondary School Enrollment* (Fall, 1966): Public, 636,285; private (est.), 108,600. *Colleges and Universities:* 94,678.

**RECREATION.** State parks number more than 60. Points of interest for visitors include the Herbert Hoover National Historic Site, the Amana Colonies, Fort Dodge Historical Museum, Effigy Mounds National Monument, and the Des Moines Art Center.

# KANSAS

*Area:* 82,264 square miles. *Population* (1967 est.): 2,275,-000 (rank: 29th). *Capital:* Topeka. *State Flower:* Native Sunflower. *Bird:* Western Meadowlark. *Motto:* Ad Astra Per Aspera (To the Stars Through Difficulties). *Nickname:* Sunflower State. *Flag:* A sunflower over the state seal on a blue field.

**LAND AND CLIMATE.** Kansas is bounded on the north by Nebraska, on the east by Missouri, on the south by Oklahoma, and on the west by Colorado. The High Plains occupy the western third of the state; the central third is made up of prairie land and rolling hills. The eastern third, known as the Osage Plains, is mostly hilly. The highest point in Kansas is Mount Sunflower (4,026 feet). The principal rivers are the Arkansas, Missouri, and Kansas. There are several large reservoirs, but no sizable natural lakes.

The climate is marked by hot summers and cold winters. The January average minimum temperatures range from 14°–22° F.; the July average maximums from 92°–93° F. The average annual precipitation is 40 inches in the southeast and 15 inches in the west.

**HISTORY.** Kansas was within the large Mississippi drainage area claimed by France in the 17th century. A thriving fur trade was developed by the French until the region was ceded to Spain in 1763. Returned to France in 1800, Kansas was acquired by the United States in 1803 as part of the Louisiana Purchase.

Although Kansas was designated Indian territory in 1834, farmers were soon settling on its fertile prairies, army installations were constructed, and in 1854 Kansas became a territory. The first territorial elections, in 1854 and 1855, were won by slavery proponents. In the latter year, an abolitionist group set up a rival, unrecognized government in Topeka, and violence erupted. It continued well into the Civil War, reaching a peak when Confederate raiders burned Lawrence in 1863. "Bleeding Kansas," admitted to the Union as a free state in 1861, was also beset by Indian raids in the west.

In the wake of the Civil War, the state faced fresh troubles. New arrivals included cattlemen and homesteaders, often at odds with each other. Cattle-trailing from ranges in Texas and the Southwest made booming cattle markets of such towns as Abilene and Dodge City, but also attracted gamblers and gunmen. During the era of lawlessness in the cow towns, however, winter wheat was planted on the plains.

By 1900 the cattle drives had ended. Wheat, locally raised meat and dairy cattle, and petroleum (first discovered in 1855) had become mainstays of the economy, and the state was settling into a predominantly agricultural and conservative mold. Kansas prospered during World War I, but suffered during the dust-storm and depression years of the 1930s. Since the beginning of World War II, great increases in manufacturing activity have made industry a greater income producer than agriculture.

**GOVERNMENT AND FINANCE.** *Governor:* Robert Docking (Dem.); *elected:* Nov. 8, 1966; *term:* 2 years; *annual salary:* $20,000. *Senate:* 27 Rep., 12 Dem.; *House of Representatives:* 76 Rep., 49 Dem.

*State Finances: Revenue* (fiscal year 1966, including Federal aid): $589 million; *expenditure:* $541 million (chief expenditures: education, 40.2%; highways, 24.5% public welfare, 10.4%).

**ECONOMY.** *Per Capita Personal Income* (1966): $2,814 (rank: 25th). *Work Force Distribution* (1966): Agriculture, 17.1%; other, 82.9% (trade, government, and manufacturing, in that order, accounted for 66.6% of the nonagricultural payroll). *Leading Industries:* Flour milling, aircraft production, dairy products, meat packing, food processing. *Chief Agricultural Products:* Wheat, corn, alfalfa, grain and forage sorghums, cattle.

**EDUCATION.** *Elementary and Secondary School Enrollment* (Fall, 1966): Public, 515,764; private (est.), 57,100. *Colleges and Universities:* 85,424.

**RECREATION.** Kansas has 49 state parks, featuring facilities for hunting, fishing, and water sports. Places of interest also include Fort Larned National Historic Site, Hollenberg Pony Express Station, Fort Leavenworth, the Eisenhower Center in Abilene, and the restored main street of old Dodge City.

# KENTUCKY

*Area:* 40,395 square miles. *Population* (1967 est.): 3,191,000 (rank: 22nd). *Capital:* Frankfort. *State Flower:* Goldenrod. *Bird:* Cardinal. *Motto:* United We Stand, Divided We Fall. *Nickname:* Bluegrass State. *Flag:* State seal on a blue field.

**LAND AND CLIMATE.** Kentucky is bounded on the north by Illinois, Indiana, and Ohio; on the east by West Virginia and Virginia; on the south by Tennessee; and on the west by Missouri. The highest point is Black Mountain (4,145 feet) in the mountainous eastern section. The Bluegrass region is in north-central Kentucky, north of the hilly Cumberland Plateau. Toward the west the land slopes gradually to the Mississippi, which marks the Missouri border. There are coalfields at the eastern and western ends of the state. Principal rivers are the Kentucky, Ohio, Tennessee, Mississippi, Cumberland, and Licking. The chief lakes are the Kentucky and Cumberland reservoirs.

Temperatures range from average January minimums of 25°–26° F. to average July maximums of 87°–89° F.

**HISTORY.** The first permanent settlement in Kentucky was at Harrodsburg (1774). Boonesboro was founded in the following year by Daniel Boone, who had blazed the Wilderness Road while working for the Transylvania Company. Virginia legislators created Kentucky County in 1776, thus adopting the region as their own, but Kentucky's settlers were soon at odds with the Virginians.

Achieving separate statehood in 1792, Kentucky became the first state west of the Appalachians. Trade along the Ohio and Mississippi rivers increased the pace of settlement in the early 1800s. The importation of slaves, forbidden in 1833, was authorized by the legislature in 1850. More than 200,000 Negroes were subsequently brought into the state, but anti-slavery feeling ran strong, and Kentucky remained in the Union throughout the Civil War.

In the late 19th century Kentucky's over-reliance on a single crop—tobacco—caused agricultural development to languish. Poverty, the race issue, and hostility between farmers and monopolistic tobacco buyers culminated in a decade of open violence (1900–09).

The development of coal mining, particularly during World War I, boosted the economy for a time but eventually brought its own problems in the form of labor unrest in the 1930s and widespread unemployment in the 1950s and 1960s. Gains in prosperity due to increases in manufacturing since World War II (especially in the apparel and chemical industries) have yet to be reflected in the living standards of many Kentuckians.

**GOVERNMENT AND FINANCE.** *Governor:* Edward T. Breathitt (Dem.); *elected:* Nov. 5, 1963; *term:* 4 years; *annual salary:* $18,000. *Senate:* 25 Dem., 12 Rep., 1 vacancy; *House of Representatives:* 63 Dem., 36 Rep., 1 vacancy.

*State Finances: Revenue* (fiscal year 1966, including Federal aid): $795 million; *expenditure:* $790 million (chief expenditures: education, 36.6%; highways, 26.2%; public welfare 13.1%).

**ECONOMY.** *Per Capita Personal Income* (1966): $2,205 (rank: 44th). *Work Force Distribution* (1966): Agriculture, 19.8%; other, 80.2% (manufacturing, trade, and government, in that order, accounted for 66.1% of the nonagricultural payroll). *Leading Industries:* Food products, tobacco, chemicals, machinery, mining. *Chief Agricultural Products:* Tobacco, beef cattle, dairy products.

**EDUCATION.** *Elementary and Secondary School Enrollment* (Fall, 1966): Public, 674,466; private (est.), 99,200. *Colleges and Universities:* 84,692.

**RECREATION.** Kentucky has 23 state parks, including Audubon, Cumberland Falls, Kentucky Dam Village, and Natural Bridge. Nature lovers are also attracted to Cumberland National Forest, the Kentucky Woodlands National Wildlife Refuge, and the Kentucky Lake recreation areas. Places of special interest include Abraham Lincoln's birthplace, near Hodgenville; Cumberland Gap National Historical Park; Mammoth Cave National Park; the thoroughbred horse farms in the "Blue Grass" country around Lexington; and Louisville, site of the famed Churchill Downs race track where the Kentucky Derby is run annually (the first Saturday in May).

## LOUISIANA

*Area:* 48,523 square miles. *Population* (1967 est.): 3,660,000 (rank: 19th). *Capital:* Baton Rouge. *State Flower:* Magnolia. *Bird:* Eastern Brown Pelican. *Motto:* Union, Justice and Confidence. *Nickname:* Pelican State. *Flag:* White pelican on a blue field.

**LAND AND CLIMATE.** Louisiana is bounded on the north by Arkansas, on the east by Mississippi, on the southeast and south by the Gulf of Mexico, and on the west by Texas. Most of Louisiana is part of the predominantly level Gulf coastal plain. There are marshes along the coast, low hills in the north, and rolling alluvial land bordering the Mississippi River. Elevations range from 535 feet (at Driskill Mountain in the north) to five feet below sea level (in the city of New Orleans). Principal rivers, aside from the Mississippi, are the Red, Ouachita, Pearl, Atchafalaya, and Calcasieu. Major lakes are Pontchartrain, Borgne, Grand, Calcasieu, White, and Maurepas.

Louisiana's summers are hot and its winters are mild. The average minimum temperatures in January range from 38° to 44° F.; the average July maximums, from 91° to 94° F.

**HISTORY.** Members of Hernando De Soto's expedition were probably the first Europeans to see the region. In 1682 La Salle claimed for France all lands drained by the Mississippi River. Fur traders and missionaries were the earliest arrivals, and, in the period 1717–20, many more settlers came to the area as a result of the fraudulent Mississippi Scheme, organized by John Law, a Scottish financier operating in Paris. That part of Louisiana lying east of the Mississippi passed to Britain in 1763 and to the United States after the Revolutionary War. The rest of what is now Louisiana (and an immense amount of territory lying to the north and northwest) became American through the Louisiana Purchase in 1803.

Admitted to the Union as a state in 1812, Louisiana developed a plantation economy based on sugar and cotton. New Orleans, successfully defended from British attack by Andrew Jackson in 1815, prospered during the age of the Mississippi steamboat, becoming the nation's second largest port by 1840.

Louisiana's prosperity ended with the Civil War, during most of which Union forces occupied the state. The Reconstruction period was a harsh one, marked by political and economic confusion and graft in high office. The discovery of oil in the early 1900s brightened the prospects for a few Louisiana citizens but failed to relieve the poverty of the many. Under the demagogic rule of Governor Huey P. Long (elected in 1928 and assassinated in 1935), Louisiana made some basic economic progress, at the cost of another orgy of official corruption. A more promising economic revival, with industrial diversification and increases in manufacturing, has occurred since World War II.

**GOVERNMENT AND FINANCE.** *Governor:* John J. McKeithen (Dem.); *elected:* March 3, 1964; *term:* 4 years; *annual salary:* $20,000. *Senate:* 39 Dem., 0 Rep.; *House of Representatives:* 3 Rep., 10 Dem (1 vacancy).

*State Finances: Revenue* (fiscal year 1966, including Federal aid): $1,281 million; *expenditure:* $1,186 million (chief expenditures: education, 36.1%; highways, 19.2% public welfare, 17.6%).

**ECONOMY.** *Per Capita Personal Income* (1966): $2,257 (rank: 42nd). *Work Force Distribution* (1966): Agriculture, 10%; other, 90% (manufacturing, trade, and government, in that order, accounted for 58.3% of the nonagricultural payroll). *Leading Industries:* Petroleum, petrochemicals, agriculture, lumbering, papermaking. *Chief Agricultural Products:* Cotton, rice, sugarcane, corn, soybeans, hay.

**EDUCATION.** *Elementary and Secondary School Enrollment* (Fall, 1966): Public, 820,652; private (est.), 158,000. *Colleges and Universities:* 97,386. Token desegregation of public schools was instituted in New Orleans in 1960. Roman Catholic schools were desegregated in 1962.

**RECREATION.** Among Louisiana's recreation areas are numerous state parks and several historical parks. Of particular interest to visitors is New Orleans, with its old French Quarter and its Mardi Gras carnival preceding Lent; the plantation homes near Natchitoches and New Iberia; the so-called Cajun country; and the resorts along Lake Pontchartrain.

## MAINE

*Area:* 33,215 square miles. *Population* (1967 est.): 973,000 (rank: 38th). *Capital:* Augusta. *State Flower:* Pine Cone and Tassel. *Bird:* Chickadee. *Motto:* Dirigo (I Guide). *Nickname:* Pine Tree State. *Flag:* State seal on a blue field.

**LAND AND CLIMATE.** Maine is bounded on the north and east by Canada, on the south by the Atlantic Ocean, and on the west by New Hampshire and Canada. Inland are wooded hills and mountains; Mount Katahdin (5,268 feet), in the north-central part, is the state's highest point. The rugged, rocky coast with its many offshore islands changes south of Portland to sand beaches. Principal rivers are the St. John, Androscoggin, Kennebec, Penobscot, and St. Croix; among the many lakes are Moosehead and Chesuncook and the Rangeley Lakes.

Maine winters are quite cold and snowy in the north, and warmer and wetter on the coast. Precipitation averages about 42 inches per year. Temperatures range from average January minimums of 1°–12° F. to average July maximums of 75°–80° F.

**HISTORY.** The Maine area, first successfully settled by the British in 1622, was purchased in 1677 by the Massachusetts Bay Colony. Indian attacks, lasting until the end of Queen Anne's War (1702–13), destroyed all but three of the province's settlements; but prosperity was rapidly attained, thanks to the lumbering, shipbuilding, and fishing industries. By the late 18th century feeling against the Crown was strong in Maine. Portland, a center of political agitation, was heavily bombarded by the British during the American Revolution.

Maine began to develop new industries after the Embargo Act (1807) and the War of 1812 impaired its prosperous sea trade. Liberally inclined, the area found its interests increasingly divergent from those of conservative Massachusetts, of which it had been made a district by the Continental Congress prior to the Revolutionary War; and in 1820, as part of the Missouri Compromise, Maine achieved statehood. The Webster-Ashburton Treaty (1842) ended, short of full-scale war, a bitter boundary dispute with neighboring New Brunswick.

Maine became Republican in the 1850s and, strongly opposed to slavery, gave substantial aid in men and money to the Union cause during the Civil War. Except for a brief period in the 1870s and 1880s, it remained strongly Republican until the disruption of traditional voting patterns in the 1960s.

**GOVERNMENT AND FINANCE.** *Governor:* Kenneth M. Curtis (Dem.); *elected:* Nov. 8, 1966; *term:* 4 years; *annual salary:* $20,000. *Senate:* 24 Rep., 10 Dem.; *House of Representatives:* 95 Rep., 56 Dem.

*State Finances: Revenue* (fiscal year 1966, including Federal aid): $283 million; *expenditure:* $255 million (chief expenditures: education, 25.3%; highways, 25.5%; public welfare, 11.1%).

**ECONOMY.** *Per Capita Personal Income* (1966): $2,438 (rank: 37th). *Work Force Distribution* (1966): Agriculture, 8.4%; other, 91.6% (manufacturing, trade, and government, in that order, accounted for 74.8% of the nonagricultural payroll). *Leading Industries:* Pulp and paper, food processing, textiles, lumber, tourism, and mining. *Chief Agricultural Products:* Potatoes, poultry, dairy products, apples, livestock.

To compensate for the damaging decline in the 20th century of its textile manufacturing, Maine has diversified agriculture, added new pulp and paper facilities, and explored promising mineral resources; but the growth of its food-processing industry is considered the most important change in its economy over the last decade.

**EDUCATION.** *Elementary and Secondary School Enrollment* (Fall, 1966): Public, 222,003; private (est.), 38,400. *Colleges and Universities:* 23,757.

**RECREATION.** Maine, known as "vacationland," has 15 state parks, including Baxter and Camden Hills. Among the numerous coastal resorts is Bar Harbor on Mount Desert Island; 40 square miles of the island are included in popular Acadia National Park, the only national park in the northeastern states.

# MARYLAND

*Area:* 10,577 square miles. *Population* (1967 est.): 3,685,-000 (rank: 18th). *Capital:* Annapolis. *State Flower:* Black-eyed Susan. *Bird:* Baltimore Oriole. *Motto: Scuto Bonae Voluntatis Tuae Coronasti Nos* (With the Shield of Thy Goodwill Thou Hast Covered Us). *Nickname:* Old Line State. *Flag:* A geometric black and gold pattern in opposite quarters; red and white crosses in the others.

**LAND AND CLIMATE.** Maryland is bounded on the north by Pennsylvania, on the east by Delaware and the Atlantic Ocean, on the south by Virginia and West Virginia, and on the west by West Virginia. The coastal plain of eastern Maryland is deeply indented by Chesapeake Bay; alternating valleys and ridges in the west rise to the Allegheny Mountains, whose highest point is Backbone Mountain (3,360 feet) near the West Virginia border. Principal rivers are the Potomac, Susquehanna, Patuxent, Choptank, and Elk; chief lakes are Pretty Boy and Loch Raven reservoirs and Deep Creek Lake.

The climate is moderate. Temperatures range from average January minimums of 24°–25° F. to average July maximums of 84°–86° F.

**HISTORY.** Maryland was named for Queen Henrietta Maria, whose husband, Charles I, granted it to George Calvert, 1st Baron Baltimore, in 1632. Calvert's son Cecilius, a Catholic, began to settle it as a haven from religious persecution. In 1655, however, English Puritans took control after two decades of struggle, and anti-Catholic bias continued to the 19th century.

The colony's shipbuilding industry prospered. Strongly anti-Crown during the Revolution, Maryland suffered much destruction from the British in the War of 1812, when the bombardment of Fort Henry, in Baltimore Harbor, inspired Francis Scott Key to write the words of *The Star-Spangled Banner* (1814).

The Baltimore & Ohio Railroad, opened in 1830, helped hasten industrialization of the north, while in the south a plantation economy flourished with the help of slave labor. Loyalties in the state were badly torn at the start of the Civil War, and only prompt occupation by Federal troops prevented Maryland's secession from the Union. A Confederate invasion in 1862 was repulsed at Antietam, one of the bloodiest battles of the war.

Industry resumed its rapid growth after the conflict. Periods of labor trouble followed, but in the 20th century the state has become a leader in labor reform. School integration has been generally accepted.

**GOVERNMENT AND FINANCE.** *Governor:* Spiro T. Agnew (Rep.); *elected:* Nov. 8, 1966; *term:* 4 years; *annual salary:* $15,000. *Senate:* 35 Dem., 8 Rep.; *House of Delegates:* 118 Dem., 24 Rep. A constitutional convention was scheduled for September, 1967.

*State Finances: Revenue* (fiscal year 1966, including Federal aid): $941 million; *expenditure:* $886 million (chief expenditures: education, 31.9%; highways, 19.8%; public welfare, 8.4%).

**ECONOMY.** *Per Capita Personal Income* (1966): $3,220 (rank: 11th). *Work Force Distribution* (1966): Agriculture, 3.3%; other, 96.7% (manufacturing, trade, and government, in that order, accounted for 64.5% of the nonagricultural payroll). *Leading Industries:* Primary metals, food processing, transportation equipment, chemicals, machinery, metal products, clothing. *Chief Agricultural Products:* Poultry, dairy products, tobacco, cattle, hogs, corn, soybeans.

**EDUCATION.** *Elementary and Secondary School Enrollment* (Fall, 1966): Public, 790,928; private (est.), 150,400. *Colleges and Universities:* 103,692.

**RECREATION.** Numerous state parks and forests offer a variety of recreational opportunities. Historic sites include Fort McHenry and Harpers Ferry national monuments, Hampton National Historic Site, and Antietam National Battlefield Site. Also of interest are the U.S. Naval Academy and the State House at Annapolis. Atlantic Ocean and Chesapeake Bay resorts are popular.

# MASSACHUSETTS

*Area:* 8,257 square miles. *Population* (1967 est.): 5,421,-000 (rank: 10th). *Capital:* Boston. *State Flower:* Mayflower. *Bird:* Chickadee. *Motto: Ense Petit Placidam sub Libertate Quietem* (By the Sword She Seeks Peace, but Peace Only Under Liberty). *Nickname:* Bay State. *Flag:* State seal on a white field.

**LAND AND CLIMATE.** Massachusetts is bounded on the north by Vermont and New Hampshire; on the east by the Atlantic Ocean; on the south by the Atlantic Ocean, Rhode Island, and Connecticut; and on the west by New York. The highest point is Mount Greylock (3,491 feet) in the Taconic Mountains on the western border. To the east are, successively, the Berkshire Hills, a high central plateau bisected by the Connecticut Valley, and the coastal lowlands. Principal rivers are the Connecticut, Taunton, Nashua, and Ware; chief inland bodies of water are Quabbin and Wachusett reservoirs and Assawompset Pond.

The Massachusetts climate is variable. Temperatures range from average January minimums of 13°–26° F. to average July maximums of 74°–82° F.

**HISTORY.** In 1620 the Pilgrims, a group of English Puritans seeking religious freedom, arrived on the *Mayflower* and founded Plymouth Colony, the Massachusetts area's first permanent white settlement. Enlarged to include Maine, Massachusetts received its Royal colonial charter in 1691. Pilgrim religious intolerance led to such excesses as witch-hunting, but Pilgrim public schools, and their town meetings, although they were in fact restrictive, helped give shape to American democracy.

In the 17th and 18th centuries fierce Indian attacks ravaged the colony, but by 1750 Massachusetts shipping assured its prosperity. The rising merchant class resented British trade restrictions. Bitterness grew, and such events as the Boston Massacre (1770) and the Boston Tea Party (1773) were preludes to open revolt. Finally, in April, 1775, clashes at Lexington and Concord touched off the American Revolution.

Hard hit when the Embargo Act (1807) and the War of 1812 sharply limited shipping, and unable to compete agriculturally with the western states, Massachusetts turned to manufacturing, and rapidly became the center of the nation's textile industry.

The state constitution was liberalized in 1820, and that same year Maine became a separate state. In the 1830s and 1840s, Massachusetts embarked on an era of religious and social reform and one of the most brilliant intellectual flowerings in American history. A wave of Irish immigration began in the 1840s. After the Civil War, during which the state furnished more than 130,000 troops to the Union, the influx of immigrants (many of Italian origin) continued until well into the 20th century.

A long period of labor unrest and union agitation lasted until after World War I, and public fear of radicalism was dramatized in the Sacco-Vanzetti case (1920–27). Since World War II, electronics have succeeded textiles as the state's most prosperous industry.

**GOVERNMENT AND FINANCE.** *Governor:* John A. Volpe (Rep.); *elected:* Nov. 8, 1966; *term:* 4 years; *annual salary:* $35,000. *Senate:* 26 Dem., 14 Rep.; *House of Representatives:* 168 Dem., 71 Rep., 1 Ind.

*State Finances: Revenue* (fiscal year 1966, including Federal aid): $1,383 million; *expenditure:* $1,302 million (chief expenditures: education, 15.6%; highways, 15.1%; public welfare, 18.5%).

**ECONOMY.** *Per Capita Personal Income* (1966): $3,271 (rank: 10th). *Work Force Distribution* (1966): Agriculture, 1.1%; other, 98.9% (manufacturing, trade, and services, in that order, accounted for 72.1% of the nonagricultural payroll). *Leading Industries:* Printing and publishing, tourism, machinery, footwear, clothing, ordnance, paper and wood pulp, chemicals, electronics. *Chief Agricultural Products:* Dairy products, poultry, nursery stock, vegetables, tobacco, fruits, potatoes.

**EDUCATION.** *Elementary and Secondary School Enrollment* (Fall, 1966): Public, 1,083,141; private (est.), 285,900. *Colleges and Universities:* 232,821.

**RECREATION.** Massachusetts has many state parks, reservations, and beaches. Among its historic sites in the Boston area are Dorchester Heights, Minute Man Historic Park, Bunker Hill Monument, Old North Church, Old State

House, Faneuil Hall, and the U.S.S. *Constitution* and Harvard University (Cambridge). Visitors are also drawn to Cape Cod National Seashore, Provincetown, the islands of Nantucket and Martha's Vineyard, Cape Ann, and the Berkshire Music Festival at Tanglewood.

## MICHIGAN

*Area:* 58,216 square miles. *Population* (1967 est.): 8,584,-000 (rank: 7th). *Capital:* Lansing. *State Flower:* Apple Blossom. *Bird:* Robin. *Motto: Si Quaeris Peninsulam Amoenam Circumspice* (If You Seek a Pleasant Peninsula, Look Around You). *Nickname:* Wolverine State. *Flag:* State seal on a blue field.

**LAND AND CLIMATE.** Michigan's main body is bounded on the north by the Straits of Mackinac and Lake Huron; on the east by lakes Huron and St. Clair, Canada, and Lake Erie; on the south by Ohio and Indiana; and on the west by Lake Michigan. The Upper Peninsula is bounded on the north by Lake Superior; on the east by Canada; on the south by Lake Huron, the Straits of Mackinac, Lake Michigan, and Wisconsin; and on the west by Lake Superior.

Lower Michigan is flat and gently rolling in the south, with tableland in the north; the Upper Peninsula, low-lying and swampy in the east, has rugged mountain country in the west. The state's highest point (2,023 feet) is in the Porcupine Mountains near Lake Superior. Michigan has 36,000 miles of rivers, including the Tahquamenon, Detroit, and Kalamazoo; its inland lakes number more than 11,000.

Climate varies greatly. Temperatures range from average January minimums of 7°–21° F. to average summer maximums of 76°–84° F.

**HISTORY.** The Michigan area was first explored early in the 17th century by the French, who based their fur trade on Mackinac Island and founded Detroit in 1701. Won by Britain at the end of the French and Indian Wars (1763), it was included, after the Revolution, in the Northwest Territory of the United States; but the British, aided by friendly Indians, kept intermittent control of much of Michigan until after the War of 1812.

The influx of Americans grew when, in 1818, the Federal government sold large tracts of land for settlement, and steam navigation began on the Great Lakes. Completion of the Erie Canal (1825) created a water route between the Hudson River and Lake Erie, stimulating Michigan's commerce. Statehood was attained in 1837.

German, Dutch and Irish immigrants swelled the population as roads, railroads, and canals were built; farming prospered and the mining industry began. Strongly Abolitionist, Michigan helped organize the Republican Party and was loyal to it until 1882, when farmers joined forces with labor unions to promote welfare legislation. By 1886 Michigan had child labor laws and a ten-hour work day.

In the 20th century Henry Ford and others introduced automobile manufacturing, and industry boomed. Long and trying labor troubles, often accompanied by violence, continued into the early 1940s, when World War II sparked another period of industrial expansion. In the early 1960s the auto industry suffered from serious unemployment, due in part to automation, but car sales later reached record levels.

In July, 1967, Detroit had the worst racial rioting in the nation's history; over 40 lives were lost and damage exceeded $200 million.

**GOVERNMENT AND FINANCE.** *Governor:* George Romney (Rep.); *elected:* Nov. 8, 1966; *term:* 4 years; *annual salary:* $30,000. *Senate:* 20 Rep., 18 Dem.; *House of Representatives:* 55 Rep., 55 Dem.

*State Finances: Revenue* (fiscal year 1966, including Federal aid): $2,672 million; *expenditure:* $2,413 million (chief expenditures: education, 42.7%; highways, 16.1%; public welfare, 8.8%).

**ECONOMY.** *Per Capita Personal Income* (1966): $3,219 (rank: 12th). *Work Force Distribution* (1966): Agriculture, 5.6%; other, 94.4% (manufacturing, trade, and government, in that order, accounted for 74.8% of the nonagricultural payroll). *Leading Industries:* Motor vehicles and accessories, tourism, and agriculture. *Chief Agricultural Products:* Livestock, dairy products, corn, hay, beans, wheat, fruit.

**EDUCATION.** *Elementary and Secondary School Enrollment* (Fall, 1966): Public, 2,015,000; private (est.), 368,400. *Colleges and Universities:* 295,905.

**RECREATION.** Notable among Michigan's parks and forests are Porcupine Mountains State Park, Isle Royale National Park, and Hiawatha National Forest. Points of interest include historic Fort Mackinac, and Greenfield Village near Dearborn.

## MINNESOTA

*Area:* 84,068 square miles. *Population* (1967 est.): 3,582,-000 (rank: 20th). *Capital:* St. Paul. *State Flower:* Pink and White Lady's-slipper. *Bird:* Common Loon. *Motto: L'Etoile du Nord* (The Star of the North). *Nickname:* Gopher State. *Flag:* State seal and gold stars on a blue field.

**LAND AND CLIMATE.** Minnesota is bounded on the north by Canada, on the east by Lake Superior and Wisconsin, on the south by Iowa, and on the west by South Dakota and North Dakota. Low hills separated by countless lakes and streams typify central Minnesota. Eagle Mountain (2,301 feet), the state's highest point, is in the rugged northeast region. Plains are found in the northwest and south.

Principal rivers are the Mississippi, Red of the North, Minnesota, Rainy, St. Croix, and Cottonwood. Chief lakes are Superior, Lake of the Woods, Itasca (source of the Mississippi River), Upper and Lower Red, Leech, and Mille Lacs. Minnesota has nearly 14,000 lakes.

The climate is subject to great and rapid changes. Temperatures range from average January minimums of −8°–6° F. to average July maximums of 77°–85° F., but readings of −35° F. and 108° F. have been recorded.

**HISTORY.** The Minnesota region passed to Britain after the French and Indian War of 1763. Its eastern part was included by the United States in the Northwest Territory (1787), and the rest was acquired in the Louisiana Purchase (1803). Real effort at settlement started in 1805.

A profitable fur trade begun by early frontiersmen was exploited after 1812 by the American Fur Company. Treaties with the Ojibwa and Sioux Indians in 1848 opened the area for peaceful development. Minnesota became a territory in 1894 and a state in 1858.

Defeat of the bloody Sioux uprising of 1862 brought immigrants, many of them Scandinavian, in increasing numbers. By 1900 railroads stretched west to the Pacific; lumbering had become a major industry; and booming wheat sales made Minnesota prosperous.

Plagued by blizzards and insects, the state's farmers supported the Populists in the 1890s. An alliance, unique in American history, grew up between farm interests and labor unions. The Farmer-Labor Party was a strong political force in the 1920s and 1930s.

**GOVERNMENT AND FINANCE.** *Governor:* Harold LeVander (Rep.); *elected:* Nov. 8, 1966; *term:* 4 years; *annual salary:* $22,500. *Senate:* 67; *House of Representatives,* 135 (nonpartisan election).

*State Finances: Revenue* (fiscal year 1966, including Federal aid): $1,114 million; *expenditure:* $984 million (chief expenditures: education, 41.6%; highways, 23.4%; public welfare, 9.9%).

**ECONOMY.** *Per Capita Personal Income* (1966): $2,871 (rank: 22nd). *Work Force Distribution* (1965): Agriculture, 15.8%; other, 84.2% (manufacturing, trade, and government, in that order, accounted for 66.1% of the nonagricultural payroll). *Leading Industries:* Manufacturing, iron ore and taconite mining, construction, food processing, timber, electrical machinery, electronics. *Chief Agricultural Products:* Dairy products, meat, poultry, soybeans, vegetables, potatoes.

**EDUCATION.** *Elementary and Secondary School Enrollment* (Fall, 1966): Public, 853,138; private (est.), 183,800. *Colleges and Universities:* 126,291.

**RECREATION.** Minnesota has 35 state parks, Chippewa and Superior national forests, and Grand Portage and Pipestone national monuments. Detroit Lakes, a popular resort town, is within 25 miles of 412 lakes. Of interest to visitors are the Institute of Arts, Minnehaha Park, and Tyrone Guthrie Theatre (all in Minneapolis).

# MISSISSIPPI

*Area:* 47,716 square miles. *Population* (1967 est.): 2,348,-000 (rank: 28th). *Capital:* Jackson. *State Flower:* Magnolia. *Bird:* Mockingbird. *Motto: Virtute et Armis* (By Valor and Arms). *Nickname:* Magnolia State. *Flag:* Vertical red, white, and blue bars, with the Confederate flag in the upper left.

**LAND AND CLIMATE.** Mississippi is bounded on the north by Tennessee, on the east by Alabama, on the south by the Gulf of Mexico and Louisiana, and on the west by Louisiana and Arkansas, from which it is separated by the Mississippi River. The state's hilly landscape rises gradually from the Gulf Coast to the northeast, where it reaches a maximum elevation (806 feet) at Woodall Mountain. The fertile, level region in the northwest, between the Mississippi and Yazoo rivers, is known as the Yazoo Basin, or the Delta. Other rivers are the Pearl, Big Black, and Yalobusha. The Mississippi, in its ever-changing course, has left numerous small lakes.

The climate is humid and subtropical during the long summers, and fairly mild during the short winters. The average January minimums range from 37° to 41° F.; average July maximums, from 90° to 93° F.

**HISTORY.** Hernando De Soto's expedition explored the Mississippi region in 1540–41. After La Salle had claimed it for France (1682), Pierre le Moyne, sieur d'Iberville, founded the first permanent colony on Biloxi Bay in 1699. The British acquired the region in 1763 and established a colony near modern Natchez, but this was captured in 1779 by the Spanish, who were not to evacuate the area until 1798, the year that the U.S. Congress organized Mississippi Territory. Cotton planters were soon pouring in, and by 1817, when Mississippi achieved statehood, a plantation economy was developing. Slaves were imported in such large numbers that by 1840 Negroes outnumbered whites in the state.

Mississippi's prosperity was destroyed by the Civil War and has never been restored. The state was readmitted to the Union in 1870, but the newly created sharecropping system kept the economy tied to a single crop (cotton) while exploiting the tenant farmers, both Negro and white, who grew it.

Poverty and the race issue remained a major problem. Segregation has been strictly enforced under the state constitution of 1890 and the "segregation law" of 1904. The 1964 federal Civil Rights Act and subsequent promotion of Negro voter registration have resulted in acts of violence. On the economic front, some progress has been made in persuading northern industries to move to the state. Mississippi, the last state in the U.S. to forbid the sale of liquor, finally repealed prohibition in 1966.

**GOVERNMENT AND FINANCE.** *Governor:* Paul B.

Johnson (Dem.); *elected:* Nov. 5, 1963; *term:* 4 years; *annual salary:* $25,000. *Senate:* 51 Dem., 1 Rep.; *House of Representatives:* 120 Dem., 2 Rep.

In the August, 1967, Democratic gubernatorial primary run-off, John Bell Williams defeated the more moderate John Winter. Negroes failed to win any of the 21 local contests in which they were entered.

*State Finances: Revenue* (fiscal year 1966, including Federal aid): $552 million; *expenditure:* $524 million (chief expenditures; education, 38.9%; highways, 25.8%; public welfare, 13.7%).

**ECONOMY.** *Per Capita Personal Income* (1966): $1,751 (rank: 50th). *Work Force Distribution* (1966): Agriculture, 23.4%; other, 76.6% (manufacturing, government, and trade, in that order, accounted for 72.7% of the nonagricultural payroll). *Leading Industries:* Apparel, lumber and wood products, food processing. *Chief Agricultural Products:* Cotton, poultry and eggs, beef cattle, soybeans, dairy products.

**EDUCATION.** *Elementary and Secondary School Enrollment* (Fall, 1966): Public, 580,470; private (est.), 20,700. *Colleges and Universities:* 61,509.

**RECREATION.** Recreational areas include Gulf Coast resorts and numerous state parks. Places of particular interest are the antebellum homes and gardens of Natchez, Civil War memorials surrounding Vicksburg, and the Old Spanish Trail.

# MISSOURI

*Area:* 69,674 square miles. *Population* (1967 est.): 4,605,-000 (rank: 13th). *Capital:* Jefferson City. *State Flower:* Hawthorn. *Bird:* Bluebird. *Motto:* *Salus Populi Suprema Lex Esto* (Let the Welfare of the People Be the Supreme Law). *Nickname:* Show-Me State. *Flag:* State seal centered on horizontal red, white, and blue bars.

**LAND AND CLIMATE.** Missouri is bounded on the north by Iowa; on the east by Illinois, Kentucky, and Tennessee; on the south by Arkansas; and on the west by Oklahoma, Kansas, and Nebraska. The state offers three distinct types of landscape: the low-lying Mississippi alluvial plain in the extreme southeast; the Ozark Plateau, a region of eroded hills in the south-central and southwestern portions; and the rolling prairies that predominate in the north. The highest point is Taum Sauk (1,772 feet) in the Ozarks. The Missouri River crosses the state from west to east, flowing into the Mississippi, which forms the state's eastern boundary. Other major streams are the Osage, Gasconade, and Grand. Missouri's natural lakes are dwarfed by its several great reservoirs, largest of which is Lake of the Ozarks.

Climatic variations between regions is considerable and abrupt. Temperatures range from average January minimums of 17°–24° F. to average summer maximums of 90°–91° F.

**HISTORY.** French explorers Jolliet and Marquette were the first white men to enter the Missouri region (1673). La Salle, who explored the area in 1682, claimed it for France. French-Canadian lead miners established Ste. Genevieve, the first permanent settlement, in the early 1730s, and in 1764 French fur traders founded St. Louis.

The United States acquired Missouri by the Louisiana Purchase in 1803. In 1812 the Missouri Territory was set up, and in 1821, after considerable controversy, Missouri was admitted to the Union as a slaveholding state under the Missouri Compromise. Slavery proved uneconomical in most areas, however, and Missourians in general remained loyal to the Union in the Civil War.

In the age of railroads that followed the war, Missouri began to develop the mixed agricultural and industrial economy that still sustains it and to profit by its strategic location along the nation's major overland traffic arteries. While some river towns declined, St. Louis—"The Gateway to the Far West"—became a great industrial metropolis. The collapse of farm values in the 1930s caused great hardship, but recovery was bolstered by World War II, during which St. Louis and Kansas City served as major government transportation hubs. In the 1950s and 1960s irrigation, flood control programs, mining (iron and lead), and the development of transportation-equipment manufacture have spurred the economy.

**GOVERNMENT AND FINANCE.** *Governor:* Warren E. Hearnes (Dem.); *elected:* Nov. 3, 1964; *term:* 4 years; *annual salary:* $25,000. *Senate:* 23 Dem., 11 Rep.; *House of Representatives:* 107 Dem., 56 Rep.

*State Finances: Revenue* (fiscal year 1966, including Federal aid): $1,065 million; *expenditure:* $927 million (chief expenditures: education, 35.7%; highways, 25.2%, public welfare, 17.6%).

**ECONOMY.** *Per Capita Personal Income* (1966): $2,845 (rank 23rd). *Work Force Distribution* (1966): Agriculture, 11.8%; other, 88.2% (manufacturing, trade, government, and services, in that order, accounted for 81.4% of the nonagricultural payroll). *Leading Industries:* Food products, shoes, transportation equipment, mining (especially lead). *Chief Agricultural Products:* Corn, beef cattle, soybeans, hogs, cheese, turkeys, hay.

**EDUCATION.** *Elementary and Secondary School Enrollment* (Fall, 1966): Public, 963,830; private (est.), 186,800. *Colleges and Universities:* 143,325.

**RECREATION.** Among Missouri's recreation areas are a number of state parks, Clark and Mark Twain national forests, and the Ozark National Scenic Riverways. Points of special interest include Mark Twain's boyhood home in Hannibal, the Harry S. Truman Library in Independence, and the house where Jesse James was killed, in St. Joseph (a town that is famous as the former eastern terminal of the Pony Express).

## MONTANA

*Area:* 147,138 square miles. *Population* (1967 est.): 701,000 (rank: 41st). *Capital:* Helena. *State Flower:* Bitterroot. *Bird:* Meadowlark. *Motto: Oro y Plata* (Gold and Silver). *Nickname:* Treasure State. *Flag:* State seal on a blue field.

**LAND AND CLIMATE.** Montana is bounded on the north by Canada, on the east by North Dakota and South Dakota, on the south by Wyoming and Idaho, and on the west by Idaho. Western Montana is dominated by the Rocky Mountains, the highest point being Granite Peak (12,799 feet). The Continental Divide meanders through this area, forming a portion of the Idaho border. Eastern Montana is part of the Great Plains. Principal rivers are the Missouri (which has its source in Montana), Yellowstone, Milk, Clark Fork, and Bitterroot. Main lakes include Flathead and Fort Peck Reservoir.

Montana has cold winters and cool summers. Temperatures range from average January minimums of 6°–14° F. to average July maximums of 83°–90° F.

**HISTORY.** Included in the Louisiana Purchase of 1803, the Montana area was then inhabited by the Sioux, Blackfoot, Cheyenne, and Flathead Indians. Lewis and Clark explored the region in 1805–06, and fur trappers and traders followed, but it took a series of gold strikes (1852–64) to produce the first significant influx of settlers.

Congress created Montana Territory in 1864. Cattle were brought from Texas along the Bozeman Trail in 1866, but uprisings by the Sioux made ranching hazardous. In 1876 the Sioux annihilated General George A. Custer's entire force at Little Bighorn. The region was finally pacified in 1881 and towns like Billings and Missoula developed, mining also prospered, as the silver lode at Butte (discovered in 1875) was exploited, and veins of copper were discovered.

Admitted to the Union in 1889, Montana was plagued by industrial strife in the early 1900s. The Great Depression also had severe effects, but these were soon mitigated by federal irrigation projects and the World War II demand for food and metals. The economy was stimulated in the 1950s by an oil boom and in the 1960s by the growth of tourism.

**GOVERNMENT AND FINANCE.** *Governor:* Tim Babcock (Rep.); *elected:* Nov. 3, 1964; *term:* 4 years; *annual salary:* $22,000. *Senate:* 30 Dem., 25 Rep.; *House of Representatives:* 64 Rep., 40 Dem.

*State Finances: Revenue* (fiscal year 1966, including Federal aid): $248 million; *expenditure:* $235 million (chief expenditures: highways, 33.6%; education, 28.9%; public welfare, 6.4%).

**ECONOMY.** *Per Capita Personal Income* (1966): $2,615 (rank: 28th). *Work Force*

*Distribution* (1966): Agriculture, 19.6%; other, 80.4% (government, trade, services, and manufacturing, in that order, accounted for 76.5% of the nonagricultural payroll). *Leading Industries:* Tourism, food processing, cattle and sheep raising, mining (copper, coal, petroleum, natural gas, gold, silver, zinc, manganese), lumbering. *Chief Agricultural Products:* Wheat, barley, hay, sugar beets, potatoes, wool, meat.

**EDUCATION.** *Elementary and Secondary School Enrollment* (Fall, 1966): Public, 167,984; private (est.), 23,000; *Colleges and Universities:* 21,400.

**RECREATION.** Montana's recreation areas include Glacier National Park; part of Yellowstone National Park; 11 national forests; 26 state parks; and numerous areas that offer excellent fishing, hunting, and skiing. Places of special interest include Custer and Big Hole battlefield national monuments and the old mining town of Virginia City. Rodeos and Indian ceremonials are popular in the state.

## NEBRASKA

*Area:* 77,227 square miles. *Population* (1967 est.): 1,435,000 (rank: 35th). *Capital:* Lincoln. *State Flower:* Goldenrod. *Bird:* Western Meadowlark. *Motto:* Equality Before the Law. *Nickname:* Cornhusker State. *Flag:* State seal on a blue field.

**LAND AND CLIMATE.** Nebraska is bounded on the north by South Dakota, on the east by Iowa and Missouri, on the south by Kansas, on the southwest by Colorado, and on the west by Wyoming. Much of Nebraska lies within the Great Plains. The highest elevation (5,340 feet) is near the western border, in an area of high plains and buttes. The grass-covered Sand Hills occupy central Nebraska. Much of the eastern region consists of rolling farmland. The principal rivers are the North Platte, South Platte, and Missouri. There are over 3,000 small lakes.

The state has a harsh climate, with cold winters and hot summers. Average temperatures range from July maximums of 89°–93° F. to January minimums of 7°–16° F.

**HISTORY.** Eighteenth century French fur traders, dealing with the Sioux, Pawnee, and other Indians, were frequent visitors to the Nebraska area, which passed to the United States as part of the Louisiana Purchase in 1803. Westward migration along the Oregon Trail, which followed Nebraska's Platte Valley, was well established by midcentury, and served to spur settlement and trade in the region.

The Nebraska Territory, a vast tract extending to the Canadian border, was created in 1854 by the Kansas-Nebraska Bill. With most of its population concentrated at its eastern fringe, the territory remained pro-Union during the Civil War and, reduced in size to the present boundaries, achieved statehood in 1867. The Homestead Act (1862) and the arrival of the Union Pacific Railroad spurred settlement after the war.

Later in the century Nebraska's farmers, hard hit by droughts, insect plagues, and severe winters, sought solidarity in the Grange, the Farmer's Alliance, and the Populist Party (whose first national convention was held in Omaha in 1892). Nebraskan William Jennings Bryan headed both the Populist and Democratic Presidential tickets in 1896.

Agricultural conditions improved after 1900, but the state suffered severely during the depression of the 1930s. Nebraskans broke new political ground in 1934 by establishing the nation's first one-house legislature with members elected on nonpartisan ballots. Since World War II, the state has acquired some manufacturing industries to balance its economy.

**GOVERNMENT AND FINANCE.** *Governor:* Norbert T. Tieman (Rep.); *elected:* Nov. 8, 1966; *term:* 4 years; *annual salary:* $18,000. *Legislature* (unicameral): 49 members.

*State Finances: Revenue* (fiscal year 1966, including Federal aid): $275 million; *expenditure:* $273 million (chief expenditures: highway, 34.1%; education, 27.8%; public welfare, 12.1%).

**ECONOMY.** *Per Capita Personal Income* (1966): $2,819 (rank: 24th). *Work Force Distribution* (1966): Agriculture, 21.7%; other, 78.3% (trade, government, and manufacturing, in that order, accounted for 63.5% of the nonagricultural payroll). *Leading Industries:* Meat packing, grain products, electrical and farm machinery. *Chief Agricultural Products:* Meat, corn, hay, grain sorghum, wheat, soybeans, sugar beets.

**EDUCATION.** *Elementary and Secondary School Enrollment* (Fall, 1966): Public, 318,819; private (est.), 63,100. *Colleges and Universities:* 51,771.

**RECREATION.** Among the recreation areas in Nebraska are six state parks and the Nebraska National Forest. Of particular interest to visitors are Chimney Rock National Historic Site, Scotts Bluff National Monument, and the re-created pioneer village at Minden.

# NEVADA

*Area:* 110,540 square miles. *Population* (1967 est.): 444,000 (rank: 47th). *Capital:* Carson City. *State Flower:* Sagebrush. *Bird:* Mountain Bluebird. *Motto:* All for Our Country. *Nickname:* Silver State. *Flag:* A blue field with a gold and green insignia in the upper left.

**LAND AND CLIMATE.** Neveda is bounded on the north by Oregon and Idaho, on the east by Utah and Arizona, and on the south and west by California. Located in the heart of the arid Great Basin, most of the state consists of plateau country (averaging 5,500 feet in elevation), broken frequently by mountain ranges rising more than 8,000 feet. The Sierra Nevada forms part of the western border. The state's highest point is Boundary Peak (13,140 feet) in the White Mountains. The Humboldt and Colorado are the only important rivers. Principal natural lakes are Pyramid, Tahoe, and Walker, in the west. Lake Mead, in the southeast, was formed after Hoover Dam was built.

Nevada's climate is dry, with hot summers and cold winters. January average minimums range from 9° to 32° F.; July average maximums, from 86° to 105° F.

**HISTORY.** Apparently the first whites to enter Nevada arrived in the mid-1820s—the American explorer, Jedediah S. Smith, and then Peter S. Ogden, of Canada's Hudson's Bay Company. Kit Carson and John C. Frémont covered much of Nevada (1843–45), and during the 1849 gold rush, large numbers of wagon trains rumbled through on their way to California.

After the Mexican War, the region was ceded to the U.S. (1848), and in 1850 most of present-day Nevada was included in the new Utah Territory. Mormon Station (now Genoa), a trading post for the Mormons, was the first permanent settlement (1851). With the discovery of gold, and the Comstock Lode silver strike in 1859, a flood of miners, promoters, and other fortune-hunters rushed into Nevada from California. Mining camps mushroomed and became raucous centers of lawlessness.

Partly to impose order, Nevada was made a separate territory in 1861. Pro-Union during the Civil War, it gained statehood in 1864, although it did not meet the population requirement. The present boundaries were finally set in 1867, and rail connections with the East were firmly secured in 1869.

Mining still dominated Nevada, and new strikes continued, but with the mining depression of 1882, the industry began to decline. Mining revived early in the 20th century, and still is an important source of income, but the steady growth of gambling (legalized in 1931) and tourism have contributed most to the state's economy in recent years.

**GOVERNMENT AND FINANCE.** *Governor:* Paul Laxalt (Rep.); *elected:* Nov. 8, 1966; *term:* 4 years; *annual salary:* $20,000. *Senate:* 11 Dem., 9 Rep.; *Assembly:* 21 Dem., 19 Rep.

*State Finances: Revenue* (fiscal year 1966, including Federal aid): $180 million; *expenditure:* $177 million (chief expenditures: highways, 32.2%; education, 28.2%; public welfare, 4.5%).

**ECONOMY.** *Per Capita Personal Income* (1966): $3,300 (rank: 7th). *Work Force Distribution* (1966): Agriculture, 2.5%; other, 97.5% (services, trade, and government, in that order, accounted for 76.6% of the nonagricultural payroll). *Leading Industries:* Gambling and tourism; mining and processing of copper, mercury, gold, and silver; chemicals; forest products; electronics; and stone, clay, and glass production. *Chief Agricultural Products:* Livestock, hay, wheat, alfalfa seed, cotton lint.

**EDUCATION.** *Elementary and Secondary School Enrollment* (Fall, 1966): Public, 107,-719; private (est.), 4,400. *Colleges and Universities:* 8,374.

**RECREATION.** Recreation areas include Toiyabe and Humboldt national forests; Lehman Caves National Monument; nine state parks; and many dude ranches. Other places of interest are the Lake Tahoe area, Las Vegas, and Reno; Virginia City, one of the state's most colorful towns; the Ruth Open-Pit Copper Mine, near Ely; and Geyser Basin, near Beowawe. Lake Mead National Recreation Area, near Las Vegas, is famous for its water sports.

## NEW HAMPSHIRE

*Area:* 9,304 square miles. *Population* (1967 est.): 685,000 (rank: 44th). *Capital:* Concord. *State Flower:* Purple Lilac. *Bird:* Purple Finch. *Motto:* Live Free or Die. *Nickname:* Granite State. *Flag:* State seal on a blue field.

**LAND AND CLIMATE.** New Hampshire is bounded on the north by Canada, on the east by Maine and the Atlantic Ocean, on the south by Massachusetts, and on the west by Vermont. It owns the three southernmost offshore Isles of Shoals. The White Mountains in the north are dominated by 6,288-foot Mount Washington, the highest peak in New England. Rolling, lake-filled terrain lies between the mountains and the southeast coastal plains. Major rivers are the Connecticut, Merrimack, Androscoggin, and Saco; Winnipesaukee is the largest lake.

New Hampshire's long, cold winters and brief, mild summers are tempered on the coast by the ocean. Average temperatures range from a January minimum of 11° F. to a July maximum of 83° F.

**HISTORY.** The New Hampshire area was part of the grant made by James I in 1620 to the Council for New England (the former Plymouth Company). The Council, in turn, granted land to John Mason near the Merrimack River in 1622. Mason, who eventually gave the name "New Hampshire" to a 60-mile tract that he owned, is honored by the state as its founder. Religious conflicts between four of the earliest towns in the area (Dover, Portsmouth, Exeter, and Hampton) marred the first decades of settlement. After complex boundary disputes with Massachusetts, New Hampshire was declared a Royal colony (1679), but the two colonies were generally ruled by one governor until their common border was determined in 1741. Many Scotch-Irish came to New Hampshire during the 18th century.

New Hampshire was the first of the original 13 colonies to declare independence from Britain. In June, 1788, it cast the deciding vote for ratification of the U.S. Constitution. Daniel Webster of New Hampshire successfully defended property rights against state abridge-

ment in the famous Dartmouth College case in 1819. In the 1840s abolitionist sentiment initiated the decline of the Democratic Party, which had dominated state politics. Nevertheless, New Hampshire Democrat Franklin Pierce was able to carry the state in his successful bid for the Presidency in 1852.

After the Civil War, urbanization and industrialization steadily increased. Canadian and European immigrants came by the thousands to work in New Hampshire's textile, shoe, and lumber mills. The cities—especially those dependent on one industry—suffered during the depression of the 1930s, but since World War II industry has been diversified. State sweepstakes help to support the schools.

**GOVERNMENT AND FINANCE.** *Governor:* John W. King (Dem.); *elected:* Nov. 8, 1966; *term:* 2 years; *annual salary:* $30,000. *Senate:* 14 Rep., 10 Dem.; *House of Representatives:* 245 Rep., 155 Dem.

*State Finances: Revenue* (fiscal year 1966, including Federal aid): $180 million; *expenditure:* $175 million (chief expenditures: highways, 26.9%; education, 18.3%; public welfare, 7.4%).

**ECONOMY.** *Per Capita Personal Income* (1966); $2,761 (rank: 26th). *Work Force Distribution* (1965): Agriculture, 4.2%; other, 95.8% (manufacturing, trade, and services, in that order, account for 75% of the nonagricultural payroll). *Leading Industries:* Leather and leather goods, electrical products, textiles, machinery. *Chief Agricultural Products:* Apples, milk, eggs.

**EDUCATION.** *Elementary and Secondary School Enrollment* (Fall, 1966): Public, 133,-706; private (est.), 38,300. *Colleges and Universities:* 24,123.

**RECREATION.** New Hampshire has 31 state parks. The White Mountain National Forest covers nearly 725,000 acres. Places of interest include Lake Winnipesaukee, North Conway (a year-round resort center), Portsmouth (an old ship-building town), and several picturesque mountain passes—especially Crawford, Pinkham, and Franconia notches (the last featuring the "Great Stone Face.")

## NEW JERSEY

*Area:* 7,836 square miles. *Population* (1967 est.): 7,004,-000 (rank: 8th). *Capital:* Trenton. *State Flower:* Purple Violet. *Bird:* Eastern Goldfinch. *Motto:* Liberty and Prosperity. *Nickname:* Garden State. *Flag:* State seal on a yellow field.

**LAND AND CLIMATE.** New Jersey is bounded on the north by New York, on the east by New York and the Atlantic Ocean, on the south by Delaware Bay, on the southwest by Delaware, and on the west by Pennsylvania (the latter two separated from New Jersey by the Delaware River). From the Appalachian Highlands in the northwest (highest point: 1,803 feet), the land gradually descends in a south-easterly direction across the Piedmont Plateau to the gently rolling Atlantic Coastal Plain. Principal rivers are the Hudson, Delaware, Passaic, Raritan, and Great Egg Harbor; chief lakes are Hopatcong, Mohawk, Union, and Greenwood.

New Jersey enjoys a temperate climate, with warm summers and moderately cold winters. Temperatures range from average January minimums of 25°–27° F. to average July maximums of 84°–86° F. Precipitation averages 46 inches a year; snowfall varies from an average of 13 inches in the south to 50 inches in the north.

**HISTORY.** First claimed by Henry Hudson as a Dutch possession in 1609, the region of present-day New Jersey was named New Netherland. It became a province in 1623 and annexed neighboring New Sweden colony in the Delaware Valley in 1655.

In 1664 the area was captured by the English, and extensive settlement began. New Jersey was governed jointly with New York from 1702 to 1738.

In June, 1776, the unpopular Royal government was overthrown, and New Jersey declared its independence. Its strategic location made it the scene of heavy fighting during the American Revolution; the battles of Trenton and Princeton were fought in 1776, and Monmouth in 1778. New Jersey became the third state to ratify the Constitution. A 50-year era of economic expansion transformed it from a state of landed gentry to an industrial democracy.

After the Civil War, during which New Jersey fought for the Union, the population and economy continued their upward climb. Political control was seized by special interest groups, but reforms were instituted during the governorship of Woodrow Wilson (1910–12). Later, in 1947, a new constitution helped streamline the state government.

In July, 1967, Newark was the scene of racial rioting rated among the worst in U.S. history; 26 persons were killed, and property damage exceeded $10 million.

**GOVERMENT AND FINANCE.** *Governor:* Richard J. Hughes (Dem.); *re-elected:* Nov. 2, 1965; *term:* 3 years; *annual salary:* $35,000. *Senate:* 19 Dem., 10 Rep.; *General Assembly:* 41 Dem., 19 Rep.

*State Finances: Revenue* (fiscal year 1966, including Federal aid): $1,338 million; *expenditure:* $1,152 million (chief expenditures: education, 25.8%; highways, 19.2%; public welfare, 9.6%).

**ECONOMY.** *Per Capita Personal Income* (1966): $3,414 (rank: 6th). *Work Force Distribution* (1966): Agriculture, 1.2%; other, 98.8% (manufacturing, trade, and services, in that order, accounted for 70.7% of the non-agricultural payroll). *Leading Industries:* Chemicals and pharmaceuticals, machinery, food processing, electronics. *Chief Agricultural Products:* Tomatoes, milk, eggs, asparagus, fruits.

New Jersey, an industrial giant, prospered greatly during World War II. Since the war the growth of scientific research in the fields of chemistry, electronics, and communications has been spectacular.

**EDUCATION.** *Elementary and Secondary School Enrollment* (Fall, 1966): Public, 1,326,000; private (est.), 329,600. *Colleges and Universities:* 139,059.

**RECREATION.** New Jersey's recreation areas include numerous state parks and state forests, and a variety of beach resorts along the Atlantic Shore, such as Asbury Park, Atlantic City (home of the annual Miss America Pageant), and Cape May. Among points of interest for visitors are Washington's headquarters in Morristown National Historical Park, Edison National Historic Site (Thomas A. Edison's home and laboratory) in West Orange, the restored colonial village of Batsto in Wharton Tract State Forest, the Walt Whitman House in Camden, the Grover Cleveland Museum in Caldwell, and Princeton University.

# NEW MEXICO

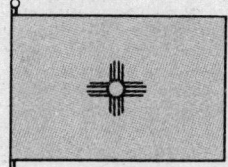

*Area:* 121,666 square miles. *Population* (1967 est.): 1,003,000 (rank: 36th). *Capital:* Santa Fe. *State Flower:* Yucca. *Bird:* Road Runner. *Motto:* Crescit Eundo (It Grows As It Goes). *Nickname:* Land of Enchantment. *Flag:* Stylized red sun on a yellow field.

**LAND AND CLIMATE.** New Mexico is bounded on the north by Colorado, on the east by Oklahoma and Texas, on the south by Texas and Mexico, and on the west by Arizona. Its topography is characterized by high plateaus, rough mesas, deep gorges, rugged mountain ranges, and wide stretches of desert. The mean altitude is 5,700 feet. Wheeler Peak (13,160 feet) in the Sangre de Cristo Mountains is the highest point. Principal rivers are the Rio Grande (which bisects the state), Pecos, San Juan, Canadian, and Gila. New Mexico has few natural lakes. Elephant Butte Reservoir is the largest body of water.

New Mexico's climate is generally warm and dry. Annual precipitation averages only 8.9 inches in the south but is almost three times as great in the north. Snowfall is heavy in the higher mountains. Temperatures range from average January minimums of 13°–28° F. to average July maximums of 80°–97° F.

**HISTORY.** Coronado, in search of gold, led the first full-scale expedition into the New Mexico area in 1540–42; his brutal treatment of the Pueblo Indians turned them against later explorers and missionaries. The first Spanish colony was established in 1598, and Santa Fe was founded about 1610. Spanish rule was interrupted by fierce Indian uprisings (1676 and 1680) and was not restored until 1692.

New Mexico became a Mexican province

after 1821, but American traders soon began pouring in over the Santa Fe Trail. The province was ceded to the U.S. in 1848 by the Treaty of Guadalupe Hidalgo and was enlarged by the Gadsden Purchase in 1853. Before the Territory of New Mexico was freed from Apache and Navajo attacks in 1886, the arrival of the Santa Fe Railroad (1879) had sparked a cattle boom. Mining activity increased after New Mexico entered the Union in 1912. World War II saw the founding of Los Alamos and the explosion of the first atomic bomb near Alamogordo. Albuquerque, the state's largest city, is now a center of nuclear and space research.

**GOVERNMENT AND FINANCE.** *Governor:* David F. Cargo (Rep.); *elected:* Nov. 8, 1966; *term:* 2 years; *annual salary:* $17,500. *Senate:* 25 Dem., 17 Rep.; *House of Representatives:* 45 Dem., 25 Rep.

*State Finances: Revenue* (fiscal year 1966, including Federal aid): $450 million; *expenditure:* $412 million (chief expenditures: education, 47.6%; highways, 24.3%; public welfare, 9%).

**ECONOMY.** *Per Capita Personal Income* (1966): $2,310 (rank: 41st). *Work Force Distribution* (1966): Agriculture, 8.8%; other, 91.2% (government, trade, and services, in that order, accounted for 68.8% of the non-agricultural payroll). *Leading Industries:* Mining (petroleum, natural gas, uranium, potash, copper), chemicals, food processing, ordnance and transportation equipment. *Chief Agricultural Products:* Cattle and sheep, cotton, feed grains, truck crops.

**EDUCATION.** *Elementary and Secondary School Enrollment* (Fall, 1966): Public, 270,562; private (est.), 30,000. *Colleges and Universities:* 32,030.

**RECREATION.** Among New Mexico's national parks and monuments are Carlsbad Caverns National Park, White Sands National Monument (near Alamogordo), and the Aztec Ruins, Bandelier, Chaco Canyon, and Gila Cliff Dwellings national monuments, which preserve vestiges of ancient Indian civilizations. Also attracting visitors are the pueblos at Taos and Acoma, San Miguel Mission and the Governors' Palace in Santa Fe, the Intertribal Indian Ceremonial (in August) at Gallup, and the nuclear science museum in Los Alamos.

# NEW YORK

*Area:* 49,576 square miles. *Population* (1967 est.): 18,335,000 (rank: 2nd). *Capital:* Albany. *State Flower:* Rose. *Bird:* Eastern Bluebird. *Motto: Excelsior* (Higher). *Nickname:* Empire State. *Flag:* State seal on a blue field.

**LAND AND CLIMATE.** New York is bounded on the north by Canada, on the east by Vermont, Massachusetts, and Connecticut, on the south by the Atlantic Ocean, New Jersey, and Pennsylvania, and on the west by Pennsylvania,

Lake Erie, and Canada. The Adirondack Mountains dominate northeastern New York, with Mount Marcy (5,344 feet) the highest point in the state. This mountain system slopes to the lowlands that comprise the Mohawk River and Hudson River valleys and the Lake Ontario plains. Most of the region south of the Mohawk Valley is part of the Allegheny Plateau, which covers more than half the state and merges with the Catskill Mountains in the southeast. Other sections of the plateau are dissected by many river valleys, some of whose streams widen to form long, narrow lakes such as the Finger Lakes in the west. Major lakes include Champlain, Erie, Ontario, Cayuga, Seneca, Chautauqua, Oneida, and George.

New York is subject to extreme seasonal variations. Average January minimums are 18°–26° F.; average July maximums are 81°–88° F.

**HISTORY.** Giovanni da Verrazano is said to have entered New York Bay in 1524. Samuel de Champlain discovered the lake that now bears his name in 1609, and Henry Hudson's voyage in the same year laid the basis for Dutch claims to the lower Hudson Valley. Western New York was then dominated by the various tribes of the Iroquois Confederacy.

The Dutch, having incorporated their claims into the province of New Netherland in 1621, founded Fort Orange (now Albany) in 1624 and New Amsterdam on Manhattan Island in 1626. Meanwhile the English claimed the entire region on the basis of John Cabot's 15th-century explorations. Charles II granted the area to his brother, the duke of York (later James II), and in 1664 an English fleet took New Amsterdam without resistance. New Netherland became the British colonies of New York and New Jersey. Settlement of the western region was slowed by the French and Indian Wars (1689–1763).

The first major Revolutionary War action in New York was the capture of Fort Ticonderoga by the Green Mountain Boys in May, 1775. Although the British were to hold New York City until the war's end, the colony declared its independence. After the new nation was established, New York City served for two years as the national capital (1789–91).

Land speculation in western New York soon grew to spectacular proportions. Many and various industries began to thrive, laying the basis for the diversified economy that still characterizes the state. With the opening of the Erie Canal (1825), and later of the railroad lines running parallel to it, the state became a major east-west commercial route. The port of New York and cities along the canal prospered; New York City became the nation's financial center and its greatest metropolis.

After the Civil War, political corruption, epitomized by the notorious Tweed Ring in New York City, was rampant. Working conditions worsened, especially in New York City's sweat shops, stimulating the growth of labor unions. Political reform began during the brief governorship of Theodore Roosevelt, and governors such as Charles Evans Hughes, Alfred E. Smith, Franklin D. Roosevelt, and Herbert H. Lehman contributed greatly to subsequent reforms. The antiquated, unwieldy state constitution, rewritten by a special constitutional convention, was subject to approval by the state's voters in November, 1967.

**GOVERNMENT AND FINANCE.** *Governor:* Nelson A. Rockefeller (Rep.); *elected:* Nov. 8, 1966; *term:* 4 years; *annual salary:* $50,000. *Senate:* 31 Rep., 25 Dem.; *Assembly:* 80 Dem., 70 Rep.

*State Finances: Revenue* (fiscal year 1966, including Federal aid): $5,730 million; *expenditure:* $5,454 million (chief expenditures: education, 36.4%; public welfare 13.3%; highways, 11%).

**ECONOMY.** *Per Capita Personal Income* (1966): $3,480 (rank: 4th). *Work Force Distribution* (1966): Agriculture, 1.6%; other, 98.4% (manufacturing, trade, and services, in that order, accounted for 66.2% of the nonagricultural payroll). *Leading Industries:* Printing and publishing, food products, mining, machinery, electronics, aircraft. *Chief Agricultural Products:* Milk, poultry, potatoes, apples.

**EDUCATION.** *Elementary and Secondary School Enrollment* (Fall, 1966): Public, 3,248,700; private (est.), 937,100. *Colleges and Universities:* 609,164.

**RECREATION.** In addition to two large forest preserves and several national historic parks and sites, New York has over 75 state parks and a national seashore on Fire Island. Places of great interest include New York City, Niagara Falls, the U.S. Military Academy at West Point, the F. D. Roosevelt home at Hyde Park, Fort Ticonderoga, the Finger Lakes area, the Baseball Hall of Fame (Cooperstown), and Saratoga Springs.

# NORTH CAROLINA

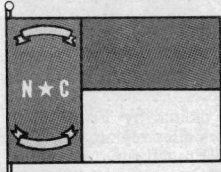

*Area:* 57,712 square miles. *Population* (1967 est.): 5,027,000 (rank: 11th). *Capital:* Raleigh. *State Flower:* Dogwood. *Bird:* Cardinal. *Motto: Esse Quam Videri* (To Be Rather Than to Seem). *Nickname:* Tarheel State. *Flag:* Scrolls and *NC* (separated by a white star) in gold on a blue bar; a red and a white horizontal bar on the right.

**LAND AND CLIMATE.** North Carolina is bounded on the north by Virginia, on the east by the Atlantic Ocean, on the south by South Carolina and Georgia, and on the west by Tennessee. The Blue Ridge and Great Smoky Mountains are in the west. To their east is the hilly piedmont region, which descends to a low coastal plain. The highest point is Mount Mitchell (6,684 feet) in the Black Mountains. Principal rivers are the Neuse, Roanoke, and Yadkin; chief lakes are Chatuge, Fontana, Gaston, Hiwassee, Mattamuskeet, and John H. Kerr Reservoir.

The climate is mild. Temperatures range from average January minimums of 30°–40° F. to average July maximums of 84°–89° F.

**HISTORY.** During the 1580s Sir Walter Raleigh made unsuccessful efforts to colonize the North Carolina region. The first permanent settlements were made by Virginians. After 1691 the province was called North Carolina in honor of King Charles I, and from then until 1711 it was administered by deputy governors from South Carolina.

Despite Indian hostility and a bitter boundary dispute with Virginia, the colony prospered. In 1771 Governor William Tryon brutally suppressed a movement by angry farmers protesting high taxes; Royal authority broke down, and in April, 1776, a provisional government decided to break with England.

The undemocratic state constitution of 1776, created by the planter aristocracy, was replaced in 1835 by a more liberal one. Slavery did not become entrenched in the state until cotton farming began in the 1830s. Abolitionist sentiment was substantial, but North Carolina seceded soon after the Civil War began.

When the state was readmitted to the Union (1868), its plantation economy was in ruins. In the 1880s cigarette-making machines spurred the growth of the tobacco industry. Later, the textile and furniture industries burgeoned.

By 1900, amendments to the liberal Reconstruction constitution assured white supremacy. The 1954 Supreme Court ruling against segregation has been obeyed, however. The nation-wide "sit-in" demonstrations on behalf of integration began in Greensboro in 1960.

**GOVERNMENT AND FINANCE.** *Governor:* Dan K. Moore (Dem.); *elected:* Nov. 3, 1964; *term:* 4 years; *annual salary:* $25,000. *Senate:* 43 Dem., 7 Rep.; *House of Representatives:* 94 Dem., 26 Rep.

*State Finances: Revenue* (fiscal year 1966, including Federal aid): $1,255 million; *expenditure:* $1,127 million (chief expenditures: education, 49.6%; highways, 17.9%; public welfare, 8.5%).

**ECONOMY.** *Per Capita Personal Income* (1966); $2,235 (rank: 43rd). *Work Force Distribution* (1965): Agriculture, 16.9%; other, 83.1% (manufacturing, trade, and government, in that order, account for 74% of the nonagricultural payroll). *Leading Industries:* Textiles, tobacco products, wood products, mining. *Chief Agricultural Products:* Tobacco, cotton, peanuts, corn, soybeans.

**EDUCATION.** *Elementary and Secondary School Enrollment* (Fall, 1966): Public, 1,183,690; private (est.), 21,800. *Colleges and Universities:* 124,088.

**RECREATION.** North Carolina's recreational areas include Cape Hatteras National Seashore; Great Smoky Mountains National Park; Pisgah National Forest; a number of state parks; and many coastal and mountain resorts. Among the state's historic sites are Fort Raleigh on Roanoke Island, site of the first English settlement in America (the famous "lost colony"); Wright Brothers National Memorial at Kitty Hawk; and the Tryon Palace restoration at New Bern, the colonial capital.

## NORTH DAKOTA

*Area:* 70,655 square miles. *Population* (1967 est.): 639,000 (rank: 45th). *Capital:* Bismarck. *State Flower:* Wild Prairie Rose. *Bird:* Western Meadowlark. *Motto:* Liberty and Union, Now and Forever, One and Inseparable. *Nickname:* Flickertail State. *Flag:* Modified U.S. seal on a blue field.

**LAND AND CLIMATE.** North Dakota is bounded on the north by Canada, on the east by Minnesota (separated by the Red River), on the south by South Dakota, and on the west by Montana. Situated in the geographical center of North America, it is characterized by rolling prairies and plains. The highest point is White Butte (3,530 feet) in the southwest. Principal rivers are the Red, Missouri, James, and Sheyenne; chief lakes are Garrison Reservoir, Devils Lake, and Arrowhead.

Climatic variations between regions are considerable. Temperatures range from average January minimums of −4°–0° F. to average July maximums of 82°–86° F.

**HISTORY.** Fur traders from the Hudson's Bay and North West companies were among the first to be drawn to the region of North Dakota. The United States acquired western North Dakota as part of the Louisiana Purchase (1803) and the rest of the area in a convention with Britain (1818). Dakota Territory was formed in 1861 from the present states of North Dakota, South Dakota, Montana, and Wyoming.

Settlement was delayed by the Civil War and the hostility of the Sioux Indians. Following completion of the Northern Pacific Rail Road, emigrants, many of Scandinavian and German origin, poured into the territory and established thriving agricultural communities. North Dakota became the 39th state in 1889, along with South Dakota, the 40th.

The Nonpartisan League, formed by farmers to defend their economic interests, gained control of the legislature in 1919 and strongly influenced the state's politics. North Dakota remains primarily agricultural and sparsely populated.

**GOVERNMENT AND FINANCE.** *Governor:* William L. Guy (Dem.); *elected:* Nov. 3, 1964; *term:* 4 years; *annual salary:* $13,000. *Senate:* 44 Rep., 5 Dem.; *House of Representatives:* 83 Rep., 15 Dem.

*State Finances: Revenue* (fiscal year 1966, including Federal aid): $212 million; *expenditure:* $201 million (chief expenditures: education, 31.2%; highways, 25%; public welfare, 9.8%).

**ECONOMY.** *Per Capita Personal Income* (1966): $2,400 (rank: 38th). *Work Force Distribution* (1966): Agriculture, 32.4%; other, 67.6% (trade, government, and services, in that order, accounted for 73.7% of the nonagricultural payroll). *Leading Industries:* Mining (especially lignite), oil refining, food processing. *Chief Agricultural Products:* Wheat, oats, barley, flax, potatoes, livestock, seeds. South Dakota is the most rural state in the nation, with only 35.2% of its population living in urban areas.

**EDUCATION.** *Elementary and Secondary School Enrollment* (Fall, 1966): Public, 147,575; private (est.), 22,600. *Colleges and Universities:* 23,145.

**RECREATION.** North Dakota has four national forests and ten state parks. Other points of interest are the 2,000-acre International Peace Garden on the Canadian border; Rugby, the geographic center of North America; Snake Creek National Wildlife Refuge; and Theodore Roosevelt National Memorial Park, in the picturesque Badlands.

## OHIO

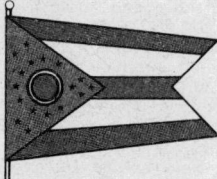

*Area:* 41,222 sq. mi. *Population* (1967 est.): 10,462,000 (rank: 6th). *Capital:* Columbus. *State Flower:* Scarlet Carnation. *Bird:* Cardinal. *Motto:* With God, All Things Are Possible. *Nickname:* Buckeye State. *Flag:* Circle and stars on a blue triangle, with red and white bars at right.

**LAND AND CLIMATE.** Ohio is bordered on the north by the state of Michigan and Lake Erie, on the east by Pennsylvania and West Virginia, on the south by West Virginia and Kentucky (separated by the Ohio River), and on the west by Indiana. In the east the hilly Allegheny Plateau covers almost half the state. Lowlands, beginning on Lake Erie, dominate the central and western region. Principal rivers are the Ohio, Miami, Cuyahoga, Scioto, and Muskingum. Grand Lake is the largest of Ohio's inland bodies of water.

Temperatures range from average January minimums of 14°–28° F. to average summer maximums of 79°–85° F.

**HISTORY.** Conflicting claims by France and Britain to the rich Ohio Valley region and commercial rivalry between French fur traders and those of the Ohio Company (acting for the Virginia Colony) sparked the last of the French and Indian Wars (1754–60). The first Treaty of Paris gave the region to Britain in 1763. To deter Indian uprisings such as Pontiac's Rebellion (1763–66), the British forbade settlement, leaving the area west of the Appalachians to the Indians and to fur traders. Later, the land between the Ohio River and the Great Lakes was included within Canada's boundaries. Britain's prohibition of settlement angered the American colonists.

After the American Revolution the Treaty of Paris of 1783 awarded the region to the United States. The Northwest Ordinance (1787) established a government and resolved claims to the area by Massachusetts, Connecticut, and Virginia that dated from colonial days. Settlers arrived; Marietta became the territory's first permanent settlement in 1788; and General Anthony Wayne's victory at Fallen Timbers in 1794 ended most Indian resistance. Ohio became a territory in 1799 and four years later was admitted to statehood.

With the start of the Ohio canal system in 1825, the economy developed rapidly. Legislation adopted during the Panic of 1837 encouraged railroad building and industrialization. Ohio, predominantly anti-Confederate during the Civil War, contributed much manpower to the Union Army, which was eventually led by Ohioan Ulysses S. Grant. After the war the railroad lines facilitated great industrial expansion. Shipping flourished on the Great Lakes, a vast oil industry grew up around Cleveland, and immigrants began to pour in. The alliance between big business and the state's government was reflected in the political careers of Republican bosses George B. Cox and Mark Hanna.

Ohio has contributed seven presidents to the nation—Ulysses S. Grant, Rutherford B. Hayes, James A. Garfield, Benjamin Harrison, William McKinley, William Howard Taft, and Warren G. Harding—and such notable 20th century statesmen as Senator Robert A. Taft, son of the 27th President.

**GOVERNMENT AND FINANCE.** *Governor:* James A. Rhodes (Rep.); *elected:* Nov. 8, 1966; *term:* 4 years; *annual salary:* $40,000. *Senate:* 20 Rep., 13 Dem.; *House of Representatives:* 62 Rep., 37 Dem.

*State Finances: Revenue* (fiscal year 1966, including Federal aid): $2,668 million; *expenditure:* $2,295 million (chief expenditures: education, 25.7%; highways, 26.2%; public welfare, 10.3%).

**ECONOMY.** *Per Capita Personal Income* (1966): $3,027 (rank: 47th). *Work Force Distribution* (1965): Agriculture, 4.5%; other, 95.5% (manufacturing and government, in that order, accounted for 72.6% of the nonagricultural payroll). *Leading Industries:* Transportation equipment, machinery, primary metals, metals fabrication, rubber and plastic products. *Chief Agricultural Products:* Dairy products, cattle, corn, soybeans. The current economic boom is due, in part, to capital investment in manufacturing and increased traffic on the Great Lakes resulting from the St. Lawrence Seaway, development of dams and locks on the Ohio River, and interstate highway construction.

**EDUCATION.** *Elementary and Secondary School Enrollment* (Fall, 1966): Public, 2,319,985; private (est.), 435,000. *Colleges and Universities:* 294,301.

**RECREATION.** Ohio has nearly 50 state parks, many with facilities for camping and sports. Of interest to visitors are Indian burial mounds such as those in the Mound City Group National Monument and Fort Ancient and Serpent Mound state memorials. Other tourist sites include the homes of such famous Americans as Presidents Ulysses S. Grant (Point Pleasant), William H. Taft (Cincinnati), Rutherford B. Hayes (Fremont), and James A. Garfield (Mentor); and the birthplace of Thomas A. Edison (Milan).

# OKLAHOMA

*Area:* 69,919 square miles. *Population* (1967 est.): 2,496,000 (rank: 27th). *Capital:* Oklahoma City. *State Flower:* Mistletoe. *Bird:* Scissor-tailed Flycatcher. *Motto:* Labor Omnia Vincit (Labor Conquers All Things). *Nickname:* The Sooner State. *Flag:* Symbols of peace and war on a blue field.

**LAND AND CLIMATE.** Oklahoma is bounded on the north by Colorado and Kansas, on the east by Missouri and Arkansas, on the south by Texas (separated by the Red River), and on the west by Texas and New Mexico. The Ozark Plateau and the Ouachita Mountains in eastern Oklahoma are hilly, but most of the state is prairie land that rises gradually from east to west. Black Mesa (4,978 feet), in the northwestern Panhandle region, is Oklahoma's highest point. Principal rivers are the Red, Arkansas, Cimarron, and Canadian. Chief lakes, both natural and man-made, are Texoma, Lake of the Cherokees, and Eufaula and Oologah reservoirs.

Most of the state has hot summers and cool winters. The northwest is drier and colder than the southwest. Precipitation averages 38 inches per year, and temperatures range from average January minimums of 27°–28° F. to average July maximums of 92°–93° F.

**HISTORY.** The Oklahoma region came to the United States in 1803 as part of the Louisiana Purchase. Long the center of a rich and varied Indian culture, the eastern section was designated Indian Territory in 1819, when the government chose it for the resettlement of Indian tribes deported from their homes in the southern United States. After a period of turmoil during the Civil War, in which some Indians were loyal to the Confederacy, deportations to the area were resumed.

Cattle drives across the territory, particularly along the Chisholm Trail, stimulated interest in Oklahoma's grazing land. After the completion of the railroad in 1872, white settlers poured in regardless of U.S. treaties with the Indians settled there. In 1889 the government officially opened up strips of land to cattle ranchers and farmers. Oklahoma Territory was carved out of the western section of Indian Territory in 1890. The Dawes Commission, appointed in 1893, began converting tribal land to private ownership. In 1907, after Indian opposition had been overcome, the two territories were merged into one state.

Meanwhile, Oklahoma found itself in the midst of an oil boom. Agriculture continued to prosper through World War I, but in the 1920s severe drought and improper farming techniques turned some of the state into the Dust Bowl of the 1930s. Thousands of tenant farmers, or "Okies," moved west as migrant laborers. Improved farming methods and large-scale Federal projects, especially since World War II, have improved conditions, and the state has become increasingly urbanized.

**GOVERNMENT AND FINANCE.** *Governor:* Dewey F. Bartlett (Rep.); *elected:* Nov. 8, 1966; *term:* 4 years; *annual salary:* $25,000. *Senate:* 38 Dem., 10 Rep.; *House of Representatives:* 74 Dem., 25 Rep.

*State Finances: Revenue* (fiscal year 1966, including Federal aid): $758 million; *expenditure:* $743 million (chief expenditures: education, 35.9%; highways, 21.7%; public welfare, 23%).

**ECONOMY.** *Per Capita Personal Income* (1966): $2,456 (rank: 35th). *Work Force Distribution* (1966): Agriculture, 15%; other, 85% (government, trade, manufacturing, and services, in that order, accounted for 76.9% of the nonagricultural payroll). *Leading Industries:* Oil refining, meat packing, electronics, mining (petroleum, natural gas, coal, lead, zinc). *Chief Agricultural Products:* Wheat, corn, cotton, sorghums, beef cattle.

**EDUCATION.** *Elementary and Secondary School Enrollment* (Fall, 1966): Public, 598,397; private (est.), 22,400. *Colleges and Universities:* 92,573.

**RECREATION.** Platt National Park, Lake Texoma National Recreation Area, and Ouachita National Forest are noteworthy. Points of special interest include the Philbrook Art Center (Tulsa), the Will Rogers Memorial (Claremore), Fort Sill military center, Indian City (near Anadarko), and the state's many Indian reservations, where traditional ceremonies are held each summer.

# OREGON

**Area:** 96,981 square miles. *Population* (1967 est.): 1,999,000 (rank: 32nd). *Capital:* Salem. *State Flower:* Oregon Grape. *Bird:* Western Meadowlark. *Motto:* The Union. *Nickname:* Beaver State. *Flag:* State seal on a blue field.

**LAND AND CLIMATE.** Oregon is bounded on the north by Washington (separated largely by the Columbia River), on the east by Idaho (partly separated by the Snake River), on the south by Nevada and California, and on the west by the Pacific Ocean. Its Pacific coastal plain adjoins rugged mountainous territory and high plateau land. The highest mountain is Mount Hood (11,245 feet) in the Cascade Range. Principal rivers are the Columbia, Snake, and Willamette; chief lakes are Upper Klamath, Summit, Crater, Abert, and Malheur.

Climatic conditions vary. Winters in the Pacific coastal regions are more humid and milder than inland. Temperatures range from average January minimums of 25°–33° F. to average July maximums of 79°–89° F.

**HISTORY.** British claims to the Oregon area were established in 1778 by Captain James Cook, who was searching for the Northwest Passage. U.S. claims, based on Robert Gray's 1792 voyage up the Columbia River, were enhanced by the success of the government-authorized Lewis and Clark expedition, which arrived at the mouth of the Columbia in 1805. Astoria, a fur-trading post set up in 1811 by John Jacob Astor, was the first permanent settlement.

Domination of the region in the 1820s by the British-owned Hudson's Bay Company was followed in the 1840s by large-scale migrations of American farmers traveling over the Oregon Trail. British resentment of these migrations angered Americans, for whom the annexation of Oregon became a key issue in the Presidential election of 1844. The campaign slogan "Fifty-four Forty or Fight" referred to the boundary claimed at latitude 54.40° north and reflected American readiness to go to war. In 1846 a compromise was reached: The northern boundary was set at latitude 49° north.

Bloody attacks by the Cayuse Indians in 1847 helped spur creation (1848) of the Oregon Territory. Its area reduced by the creation of neighboring Washington Territory (1853), Oregon joined the Union in 1859 but remained virtually unaffected by the Civil War.

The 1861 gold strike, the end to Indian hostility in 1880, and the completion of the transcontinental railroad in 1883 attracted new settlers. Cattle ranchers built up vast holdings, for which sheepherders and homesteaders competed in the late 19th century. The growth of a booming lumber industry, still one of the state's most important, began in the 1890s. Dangerous depletion of Oregon's timber resources led to the creation of government-owned national forests which today cover more than 17 million acres in the state.

**GOVERNMENT AND FINANCE.** *Governor:* Tom McCall (Rep.); *elected:* Nov. 8, 1966; *term:* 4 years; *annual salary:* $23,000. *Senate:* 19 Dem., 11 Rep.; *House of Representatives:* 38 Rep., 22 Dem.

*State Finances: Revenue* (fiscal year 1966, including Federal aid): $757 million; *expenditure:* $690 million (chief expenditures: education, 32.2%; highways, 23.7%; public welfare, 8.6%).

**ECONOMY.** *Per Capita Personal Income* (1966): $2,938 (rank: 18th). *Work Force Distribution* (1966): Agriculture, 10.3%; other, 89.7% (manufacturing, trade, public utilities, construction, and mining, in that order, accounted for 61.5% of the nonagricultural payroll). *Leading Industries:* Forest products, food processing, primary and fabricated metals, machinery. *Chief Agricultural Products:* Cattle, wheat, vegetables, dairy products, fruits, berries, nuts.

**EDUCATION.** *Elementary and Secondary School Enrollment* (Fall, 1966): Public, 474,261; private (est.), 37,800. *Colleges and Universities:* 80,259.

**RECREATION.** Oregon has numerous state parks and the smallest of its 15 national forests encompasses over 600,000 acres. Of added interest are Crater Lake National Park, Mount Hood, Oregon Caves National Monument, Bonneville Dam, and Hells Canyon.

# PENNSYLVANIA

*Area:* 45,333 square miles. *Population* (1967 est.): 11,-626,000 (rank: 3rd). *Capital:* Harrisburg. *Flower:* Mountain Laurel. *Bird:* Ruffed Grouse. *Motto:* Virtue, Liberty and Independence. *Nickname:* Keystone State. *Flag:* State seal and horses on a blue field.

**LAND AND CLIMATE.** Pennsylvania is bounded on the north by New York, on the east by New York and New Jersey, on the southeast by Delaware, on the south by Maryland and West Virginia, on the west by West Virginia and Ohio, and on the northwest by Lake Erie. Low-lying plains in the northwest give way to the low hills and valleys of the Allegheny Plateau. The Appalachian Highlands, parallel mountain ridges and valleys, run from southwest to northeast The highlands gradually descend into the low, rolling hills of the Piedmont Plateau and the flatlands of the Delaware Valley. The highest point is Mount Davis (3,213 feet). Principal rivers are the Delaware, Susquehanna, Allegheny, and Monongahela; chief bodies of water within the state are Wallenpaupack Lake and Pymatunung and Cumberland reservoirs.

Climate varies according to region; winters are cold with heavy snowfall in the northeast, but they are generally milder in the southeast. Temperatures range from average January minimums of 21°–26° F. to average July maximums of 80°–86° F.

**HISTORY.** Pennsylvania came under British control in 1664, after periods of Swedish and Dutch rule. King Charles II, who granted the area to William Penn in 1681, also gave the colony its name. Penn, a Quaker who hoped to make it a haven of political and religious freedom, created a liberal and humane government. He founded Philadelphia, the "City of Brotherly Love," and, in 1682, concluded a treaty with the Delaware Indians that ensured the settlers a long period of peace.

Those who followed Penn were less capable in dealing with the Indians, and the western frontier settlements were under frequent attack; not until 1763 was Indian power broken in that region. The actions of the politically powerful eastern Quakers, and their pacifism, which later aided the Loyalists, caused bitterness in the West.

During the American Revolution, important battles were fought in 1777 on the Brandywine and at Germantown. British forces occupied Philadelphia and Washington's troops spent the cruel winter of 1777–78 at Valley Forge. Philadelphia served from 1790 to 1800 as the new nation's capital. Popular discontent with taxation sparked the Whiskey Rebellion (1794) and Fries's Rebellion (1798), but the economy improved as immigration moved westward. A network of roads, canals, and railroads helped speed industrial development, as did the discovery of oil in 1859.

During the Civil War important battles, such as Lee's defeat at Gettysburg (1863), were fought on Pennsylvania soil. Afterwards, the state emerged as an industrial giant. The great power wielded by such industrialists as Andrew Carnegie, Henry Frick, and Charles Schwab helped to bring on repeated conflicts between capital and labor. One of the bitterest of these, the miners' Homestead Strike of 1892, was led by a secret radical group, the Molly Maguires.

Highlights of the state's political scene since 1900 have been a boss-controlled Republican political machine, the progressive Republicanism of Governor Gifford Pinchot, and a period of reform under Democratic Governor George H. Earle. Both world wars stimulated the state's economy, and it has continued to be one of the nation's industrial leaders.

**GOVERNMENT AND FINANCE.** *Governor:* Raymond P. Shafer (Rep.); *elected:* Nov. 8, 1966; *term:* 4 years; *annual salary:* $45,000. *Senate:* 27 Rep., 22 Dem.; *House of Representatives:* 160 Rep., 97 Dem. In May, 1967, plans for a convention to revise the state constitution were approved by the voters.

*State Finances: Revenue* (fiscal year 1966, including Federal aid): $3,230 million. *Expenditure:* $8.8 million (chief expenditures: education, 32.4%; highways, 19.7%; public welfare, 10.6%).

**ECONOMY.** *Per Capita Personal Income* (1966): $2,951 (rank: 17th). *Work Force Distribution* (1966): Agriculture, 3.2%; other, 96.8% (manufacturing, trade, and services, in that order, accounted for 70.7% of the nonagricultural payroll). *Leading Industries:* Primary metals (including steel), textiles, machinery, chemicals, apparel, mining (coal, petroleum, natural gas, and cobalt). *Chief Agricultural Products:* Dairy products, fruit, poultry, tobacco.

**EDUCATION.** *Elementary and Secondary School Enrollment* (Fall, 1966): Public, 2,211,495; private (est.), 670,400. *Colleges and Universities:* 323,905.

**RECREATION.** Among Pennsylvania's recreational facilities are 75 state parks, the Allegheny National Forest, and the Pocono Mountains resort region. Numerous points of historic interest include Gettysburg National Military Park, Valley Forge State Park, and many notable sites in Philadelphia, including Independence Hall in Independence National Historical Park, which houses the Liberty Bell.

# RHODE ISLAND

*Area:* 1,214 square miles. *Population* (1967 est.): 901,000 (rank: 39th). *Capital:* Providence. *State Flower:* Violet. *Bird:* Rhode Island Red. *Motto:* Hope. *Nickname:* Little Rhody (unofficial). *Flag:* Gold anchors and stars on a white field.

**LAND AND CLIMATE.** Rhode Island is bounded on the north and east by Massachusetts, on the south by the Atlantic Ocean, and on the west by Connecticut. The low-lying Narragansett basin is in the east; rolling upland hills and valleys lie in the west. The state's highest point is Jerimoth Hill (812 feet) in the northwest. Principal rivers are the Sakonnet, Blackstone, and Pawcatuck; major lakes are Scituate Reservoir and Worden Pond.

Rhode Island's climate is temperate. Temperatures range from average January minimums of 21°–26° F. to average July maximums of 76°–81° F.

**HISTORY.** Puritans led by Roger Williams made the first white settlement of the Rhode Island area at Providence in 1636. To forestall encroachment by the Plymouth and Massachusetts colonies, succeeding settlements (Portsmouth, Newport, Warwick) joined forces with Williams, who won them the right by parliamentary patent (1644) to form a government. In 1663, by royal charter of Charles II, the unified Colony of Rhode Island and Providence Plantations was created.

Williams' insistence on complete religious freedom attracted many settlers. Rhode Island suffered greatly during an Indian uprising, King Philip's War (1675–76). Newport prospered, thanks to its trade in rum, molasses, and slaves. Increasingly unpopular British laws in restraint of trade were often ignored. In 1776 Rhode Island, along with the other colonies, declared its independence from Britain.

Rhode Islanders delayed ratifying the Constitution until 1790, out of reluctance to support national import duties. Discontent with the colonial charter by which Rhode Island was still governed led to Dorr's Rebellion (1842) an unsuccessful attempt to establish a new government by force; as a result, a liberalized state constitution was adopted in 1843.

The state was strongly pro-Union during the Civil War; afterwards, a great influx of European immigrants helped make it the most densely populated of the states. Political control was assumed by the affluent textile mill owners, who held it well into the 20th century.

**GOVERNMENT AND FINANCE.** *Governor:* John H. Chaffee (Rep.); *elected:* Nov. 8, 1966; *term:* 2 years; *salary:* $25,000. *Senate:* 35 Dem., 15 Rep.; *House of Representatives:* 67 Dem., 33 Rep.

*State Finances: Revenue* (fiscal year 1966, including Federal aid): $263 million; *expenditure:* $265 million (chief expenditures: education, 25.7%; highways, 17.8%; public welfare, 16.3%).

**ECONOMY.** *Per Capita Personal Income* (1966): $2,980 (rank: 16th). *Work Force Distribution* (1966): Agriculture, 0.9%; other, 99.1% (manufacturing, trade, and services, in that order, accounted for 72.2% of the nonagricultural payroll). *Leading Industries:* Machine tools, jewelry, plastics, electronics. After World War I the state's cotton textile industry, once preeminent, declined in importance. New industries, such as electronics and plastics, have greatly aided the economy.

**EDUCATION.** *Elementary and Secondary School Enrollment* (Fall, 1966): Public, 159,695; pri-

vate (est.), 58,700. *Colleges and Universities:* 35,062.

**RECREATION.** The state has over 8,000 acres of state beaches and parks, as well as two state forests. Points of interest include Roger Williams National Memorial (Providence), Touro Synagogue (Newport), Samuel Slater's Mill (Pawtucket), and the annual music festivals in Newport.

## SOUTH CAROLINA

*Area:* 31,055 square miles. *Population* (1967 est.): 2,603,000 (rank: 26th). *Capital:* Columbia. *State Flower:* Yellow Jessamine. *Bird:* Carolina Wren. *Motto: Animis Opibusque Parati* (Prepared in Mind and Resources). *Nickname:* Palmetto State. *Flag:* White palmetto and crescent on a blue field.

**LAND AND CLIMATE.** South Carolina is bounded on the north and northeast by North Carolina, on the east by the Atlantic Ocean, and on the south and west by Georgia. Its low-lying coastal plain gradually gives way to the piedmont, a rolling plateau. A section of the Blue Ridge Mountains rises in the extreme northwest sector of the state; the highest point is Sassafras Mountain (3,560 feet). Principal rivers are the Pee Dee, Santee, Edisto, and Savannah. Chief lakes are Marion, Moultrie, Catawba, and Murray.

The climate is temperate in the up-country but is humid and subtropical on the plains. Summers are long and hot; winters are short and mild; and rainfall is abundant and well distributed. Temperatures range from average January minimums of 35°–44° F. to average July maximums of 88°–93° F.

**HISTORY.** Charles I of England claimed the region of Carolina (later named after him) in 1629, after sporadic Spanish and French efforts to settle it in the 16th century. A thriving fur trade and rich plantations worked by slaves made the colony prosper, and its capital, Charles Town (now Charleston), soon became the cultural and financial center of the South. In 1713 the southern North Carolina region was separated from North Carolina and was recognized as a royal colony ten years later.

High-handed proclamations by the Crown provoked the colonists, who declared their independence in 1776 and ratified the new Constitution of the United States in May, 1788. As the cotton market became glutted in the 1820s the state's agrarian economy declined. South Carolina's Senator John C. Calhoun spoke eloquently for the entire South in defense of states' rights. The first state to secede from the Union (December, 1860) was South Carolina. In 1861 Confederate artillery fire on Federal troops at Fort Sumter sparked the Civil War.

The state was readmitted to the Union in 1868. Its plantation economy, ruined by the war, gave way to a share-cropping system. In 1890, for the first time, the state's small farmers wrested political control from the planter aristocracy. During the 20th century, and especially since World War II, farming has been diversified and industry has grown rapidly.

School desegregation has been slow, but in 1965 the state pledged compliance with Federal directives. There has been no significant opposition to the growing Negro vote.

**GOVERNMENT AND FINANCE.** *Governor:* Robert E. McNair (Dem.); *elected:* Nov. 8, 1966; *term:* 4 years; *annual salary:* $20,000. *Senate:* 44 Dem., 6 Rep.; *House of Representatives:* 108 Dem., 16 Rep. In March, 1967, the state supreme court limited the size of the Senate to 46 members.

*State Finances: Revenue* (fiscal year 1966, including Federal aid): $594,504 million. *Expenditure:* $528,253 million (chief expenditures: education, 41.7%; highways, 21.5%; public welfare, 7.2%).

**ECONOMY.** *Per Capita Personal Income* (1966): $2,027 (rank: 48th). *Work Force Distribution* (1966): Agriculture, 11.7%; other, 88.3% (manufacturing, trade, and government, in that order, accounted for 74.1% of the nonagricultural payroll). *Leading Industries:* Textiles, wood, pulp, paper products, apparel. *Chief Agricultural Products:* Cotton, tobacco, livestock, corn, peaches.

**EDUCATION.** *Elementary and Secondary School Enrollment* (Fall, 1966): Public, 642,407; private (est.), 16,800. *Colleges and Universities:* 50,162.

**RECREATION.** South Carolina has 20 state parks and two national forests. Points of interest for the visitor include historic Charleston, with its neighboring Middleton, Magnolia, and Cypress gardens; Myrtle Beach, the largest and most popular of the state's many coastal resorts; Cowpens National Battlefield; Fort Sumter; and King's Mountain Military Park.

# SOUTH DAKOTA

*Area:* 77,047 square miles. *Population* (1967 est.): 674,000 (rank: 43rd). *Capital:* Pierre. *State Flower:* Pasqueflower. *Bird:* Ring-necked Pheasant. *Motto:* Under God the People Rule. *Nickname:* The Coyote State. *Flag:* A stylized sun on a blue field.

**LAND AND CLIMATE.** South Dakota is bounded on the north by North Dakota, on the east by Minnesota and Iowa (partly divided by the Red and Big Sioux Rivers), on the south by Nebraska, and on the west by Wyoming and Montana. The state's highest point, Harney Peak (7,242 feet), is located in the Black Hills in the southwest. Principal rivers are the Missouri, which bisects the state from north to south; its tributary, the James; and the Cheyenne. Chief lakes are Big Stone and Traverse.

South Dakota's climate offers wide variations in temperature, ranging from average January minimums of 3°–5° F. to average July maximums of 86°–89° F. In the Black Hills the climatic range is less extreme. Average annual precipitation is about 20 inches.

**HISTORY.** South Dakota came to the United States in 1803 as part of the Louisiana Purchase. The hostility of the Sioux Indians deterred permanent settlement until 1858, when a peace treaty was signed. The Dakota Territory (North and South Dakota and parts of Wyoming and Montana) was created in 1861; its capital was Yankton. The Homestead Act of 1862, the railroad built to Yankton in 1873, and the discovery of gold in the Black Hills in 1874 brought throngs of prospectors, ranchers, and farmers to the area. Lawless mining towns, such as Deadwood and Custer City, sprang up. The Dakota land boom, which took place in the period from 1878 to 1886, more than tripled the area's population.

In 1889 South Dakota was admitted to the Union as the 40th state. Recurring droughts and severe winters, particularly during the 1880s, imperiled agriculture. Efforts by the Populist Party to defend farm interests resulted in the passage (1899) of a legislative amendment —the first such adopted by any state—providing for the referendum and initiative.

A limited prosperity returned in the 1900s, but the state's economy, primarily agrarian, was hard hit by grasshopper plagues, drought, dust storms, and the depression of the 1930s. Agriculture was radically improved after World War II, however, by modern farming methods and by both land reclamation and irrigation projects.

**GOVERNMENT AND FINANCE.** *Governor:* Nils A. Boe (Rep.); *re-elected:* Nov. 8, 1966; *term:* 2 years; *annual salary:* $20,000. *Senate:* 29 Rep., 6 Dem.; *House of Representatives:* 63 Rep., 12 Dem.

*State Finances: Revenue* (fiscal year 1966, including Federal aid): $177 million; *expenditure:* $181 million (chief expenditures: education, 32.0%; highways, 30.9%, public welfare, 9.9%).

**ECONOMY.** *Per Capita Personal Income* (1966): $2,355 (rank: 39th). *Work Force Distribution* (1966): Agriculture, 31.9%; other, 68.1% (government and trade, in that order, accounted for 56.9% of the nonagricultural payroll). *Leading Industries:* Agriculture, tourism, mining. *Chief Agricultural Products:* Beef, pork, dairy products, grains, seeds.

**EDUCATION.** *Elementary and Secondary School Enrollment* (Fall, 1966): Public, 167,861; private (est.), 26,100. *Colleges and Universities:* 25,455.

**RECREATION.** South Dakota has 35 state parks and state recreation areas. Noteworthy tourist areas include Wind Cave National Park, Black Hills and Custer national forests, Jewel Cave National Monument, and Mount Rushmore National Memorial, where the heads of Presidents Washington, Jefferson, Lincoln, and Theodore Roosevelt are carved 60 to 70 feet high on the mountainside.

# TENNESSEE

*Area:* 42,244 square miles. *Population* (1967 est.): 3,888,000 (rank: 17th). *Capital:* Nashville. *State Flower:* Iris. *Bird:* Mockingbird. *Motto:* Agriculture and Commerce. *Nickname:* Volunteer State. *Flag:* White stars in a white-bordered blue circle on a red field, with a narrow white and a blue stripe at the right.

**LAND AND CLIMATE.** Tennessee is bounded on the north by Kentucky and Virginia, on the east by North Carolina, on the south by Georgia, Alabama, and Mississippi, and on the west by Arkansas and Missouri (separated by the Mississippi River). The eastern part of the state contains the Great Smoky and Cumberland mountains; the western part is broad, rolling plain. The highest point is Clingmans Dome (6,642 feet) in the Great Smokies. Principal rivers are the Mississippi, Tennessee, Hiwassee, and Cumberland. Major lakes, or reservoirs, are Watts Bar, Chickamauga, Douglas, Cherokee, Dale Hollow, and Reelfoot.

Climate is generally mild. Temperatures range from average January minimums of 29°–33° F. to average July maximums of from 86° to 92° F.

**HISTORY.** In 1769 the first permanent settlement in the Tennessee area was made by Virginians in the Watauga River valley. Settlers thronged to Tennessee after it joined the Union in 1796; it was the first state to be created out of national territory. By 1829 the economy was prosperous. Tennesseans volunteered for service in the Mexican War (1846–48) in such numbers that the state adopted the "volunteer" nickname.

Pro-Union before the Civil War, the state rejected secession in February, 1861, only to accept it in June. It served as a major theater of military operations and a leading supplier of troops for this conflict. As the first Confederate state readmitted to the Union (March, 1866), Tennessee avoided many of the agonies of Reconstruction.

The postwar years were not without problems. The Ku Klux Klan originated in the state in 1866; small farmers suffered under a farm-tenancy system; agrarian upheaval marked the 1880s; and labor troubles began in the 1890s. In 1925 Tennessee was the site of the famous "monkey trial" of John Scopes, a schoolteacher who violated state law by teaching Darwin's theory of evolution. (In 1967 this law was still in force.)

During World War II Oak Ridge was chosen as one of the sites for developing America's atomic bomb.

**GOVERNMENT AND FINANCE.** *Governor:* Buford Ellington (Dem.); *elected:* Nov. 8, 1966; *term:* 4 years; *annual salary:* 18,500. *Senate:* 25 Dem.; 8 Rep.; *House of Representatives:* 58 Dem.; 41 Rep. The legislature, its authority greatly increased by constitutional amendment, was restructured and fully reapportioned in 1967.

*State Finances: Revenue* (fiscal year 1966, including Federal aid): $859 million. *Expenditure:* $841 million (chief expenditures: education, 37.8%; highways, 30.7%; public welfare, 10.1%).

**ECONOMY.** *Per Capita Personal Income* (1966): $2,199 (rank: 45th). *Work Force Distribution* (1966): Agriculture, 14.3%; other, 85.7% (manufacturing, trade, and government, in that order, accounted for 72% of the nonagricultural payroll). *Leading Industries:* Chemicals, food processing, textiles, apparel, metal products, lumber. *Chief Agricultural Products:* Cotton, livestock, hay, corn, tobacco.

The Tennessee Valley Authority (TVA), created by the Federal government in 1933 to produce inexpensive hydroelectric power, has contributed much to develop the state's industry and water resources.

**EDUCATION.** *Elementary and Secondary School Enrollment* (Fall, 1966): Public, 874,300; private (est.), 34,800. *Colleges and Universities:* 107,087.

**RECREATION.** Greak Smoky Mountains National Park, which Tennessee shares with North Carolina, Cherokee National Forest (covering nearly 600,000 acres), and 20 state parks also offer numerous attraction for visitors. Duck, quail, and fox hunting are popular. Points of interest include Reelfoot Lake; Rock City Gardens on Lookout Mountain, near Chattanooga; Civil War battlefields; and other historic sites.

# TEXAS

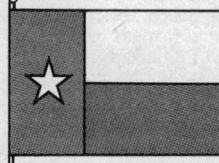

*Area:* 267,339 square miles. *Population* (1967 est.): 10,873,000 (rank: 4th). *Capital:* Austin. *State Flower:* Bluebonnet. *Bird:* Mockingbird. *Motto:* Friendship. *Nickname:* Lone Star State. *Flag:* Lone star on a vertical blue bar with a red and a white bar to the right.

**LAND AND CLIMATE.** Texas is bounded on the north by Oklahoma, on the northeast by Arkansas, on the east by Louisiana, on the south by the Gulf of Mexico and Mexico, and on the west by New Mexico. East Texas and the Gulf Coastal Plain have generally low-lying terrain; West Texas has high, canyon-cut plains. The Rocky Mountains extend into the state's extreme western trans-Pecos region, where Guadalupe Peak (8,751 feet), in the nation's newest (but as yet undeveloped) national park, is the state's highest point. Principal rivers are the Rio Grande (forming the international boundary with Mexico) and the Red, Pecos, Colorado, Brazos, and Trinity rivers. Most of the larger lakes in the state have been created by dams.

Climate varies widely over the state's vast

area. Temperatures range from average January minimums of 33°–60° F. to average July maximums of 77°–84° F. Precipitation is heavier in the east (50 inches) than in the west (10 inches).

**HISTORY.** Spaniards visited Texas in the 16th and 17th centuries, settling at Ysleta (now part of El Paso) about 1681. The growth of French Louisiana spurred the Spanish to settle the region further in the 18th century.

After the Louisiana Purchase (1803) had established a common border between the United States and Texas, American interest in the region led to attempts to dislodge the Spanish. In 1823 newly independent Mexico gave Stephen Austin a grant to settle the area that it had acquired from Spain. Inevitably, Americans and Mexicans clashed over land rights, and in 1836 an American-dominated Texas declared its independence from Mexico. To recover the territory, Mexican troops under General Antonio Lopez de Santa Anna, who wiped out the American garrison at the Alamo in San Antonio before being defeated and captured at San Jacinto.

The independent republic of Texas was then established, with Sam Houston as its first president. Many Texans favored annexation by the United States to solve their economic problems, and, despite opposition by Northern abolitionists, Texas won its statehood in 1845. This annexation precipitated the Mexican War (1846–48). Slaveholding cotton planters led Texas to secede from the Union in 1861, but it was readmitted in 1870.

With the spread of the railroads in the 1870s came a new influx of settlers. During the 19th century powerful cotton and cattle barons dominated the state's economy, and between the small farmers and the big ranchers there was a constant conflict of economic interest. Urbanization and industrialization were hastened by tremendous oil strikes, such as Spindletop in 1901. The Texas oil industry, which managed to expand even during the depression of the 1930s, continues to flourish today. Prosperity was further enhanced during and after World War II by the growth of the aircraft and space industries.

Lyndon B. Johnson, a Texan, became the 36th President of the United States after President John F. Kennedy was assassinated in Dallas on November 22, 1963.

**GOVERNMENT AND FINANCE:** *Governor:* John B. Connally (Dem.); *re-elected:* Nov. 8, 1966; *term:* 2 years; *annual salary:* $25,000. *Senate:* 30 Dem., 1 Rep.; *House of Representatives:* 147 Dem., 3 Rep.

*State Finances: Revenue* (fiscal year 1966, including Federal aid): $2,335 million; *expenditure:* $2,056 million (chief expenditures: education, 42.4%; highways, 22.9%; public welfare, 12.3%).

**ECONOMY.** *Per Capita Personal Income* (1966): $2,511 (rank: 33rd). *Work Force Distribution* (1966): Agriculture, 9%; other, 91% (trade, manufacturing, and government, in that order, accounted for 62.3% of the nonagricultural payroll). *Leading Industries:* Petroleum, manufacturing, aerospace industries, insurance. *Chief Agricultural Products:* Cotton, grain, pecans, fruits, wool, mohair, and livestock.

**EDUCATION.** *Elementary and Secondary School Enrollment* (Fall, 1966): Public, 2,563,083; private (est.), 166,500. *Colleges and Universities:* 320,565.

**RECREATION.** Recreation areas include Big Bend National Park; four national forests; many state parks; and numerous Gulf Coast beach resorts. Other points of interest include the historic Alamo in San Antonio, the state capitol at Austin, the 823,400-acre King Ranch near Kingsville, and the Manned Spacecraft Center at Houston.

## UTAH

*Area:* 84,916 square miles. *Population* (1967 est.): 1,022,000 (rank: 37th). *Capital:* Salt Lake City. *State Flower:* Sego Lily. *Bird:* Seagull. *Motto:* Industry. *Nickname:* Beehive State. *Flag:* State seal on a blue field.

**LAND AND CLIMATE.** Utah is bounded on the north by Idaho, on the northeast by Wyoming, on the east by Colorado, on the south by Arizona, and on the west by Nevada. The Wasatch Range of the Rocky Mountains bisects the state. The highest point is Kings Peak (13,498 ft.), in the Uinta Range in the northeast. Western Utah is largely desert except for Great Salt Lake in the north that covers more than 1,500 square miles. Other lakes include the Bear, Utah, and Sevier. Principal rivers are the Colorado, Green, Sevier, Bear, Fremont, and Escalante.

Utah's climate is dry, with 5 to 40 inches of precipitation annually in various areas. The southwest is usually hot, but northern Utah, where the average yearly snowfall is 50 inches, is cold. Temperature varies widely according to region; it ranges from average January minimums of 5°–20° F. to average maximums of 86°–96° F.

**HISTORY.** Spanish ownership of the Utah region was recognized by the United States in an 1819 treaty with Spain. American fur traders explored the area in the 1820s, when Great Salt Lake was discovered. During the 1840s many westbound wagon trains passed through Utah. In 1847 Brigham Young led a band of his Mormon followers, fleeing persecution, to the Great Salt Lake valley where, despite great hardship, they founded Salt Lake City.

The area, ceded by Spain to Mexico, was re-ceded to the United States in 1848. Utah Territory was created in 1850, with Young as governor; statehood was denied it in 1852 because of Mormon polygamy. The Mormon community long withstood prejudice and hostility among other Americans. By 1857, conflict between Federal and Mormon officials over interpretation of the laws led President Buchanan to remove Young from office and send Federal troops to occupy Utah; there they remained, despite resistance by Mormon guerrillas during the "Utah War," until 1861.

Mormon rights and properties were usurped in the attempt to enforce Congressional antipolygamy acts. The long and bitter conflict ended in 1890 when the Mormon Church renounced polygamy. Property and civil liberties were restored, and in 1896 Utah became a state, although its large area had been reduced by the creation of the separate Nevada, Colorado, and Wyoming territories.

Completion of the Union Pacific Railroad (1869) helped develop the state's mining industry. Non-Mormon settlers came in increasing numbers, and today animosity toward the Mormons is practically nonexistent.

**GOVERNMENT AND FINANCE.** *Governor:* Calvin L. Rampton (Dem.); *elected:* Nov. 3, 1964; *term:* 4 years; *annual salary:* $18,000. *Senate:* 5 Dem., 23 Rep.; *House of Representatives:* 10 Dem., 59 Rep.

*State Finances: Revenue* (fiscal year 1966, including Federal aid): $367 million. *Expenditure:* $374 million (chief expenditures: education, 46.8%; highways, 22.9%; public welfare, 7.8%).

**ECONOMY.** *Per Capita Personal Income* (1966): $2,500 (rank: 34th). *Work Force Distribution* (1965): Agriculture, 7.3%; other, 92.7% (government, trade, and manufacturing, in that order, accounted for 66.3% of the nonagricultural payroll). *Leading Industries:* Mining, agriculture, livestock raising, manufacturing. *Chief Agricultural Products:* Wheat, sugar beets, fruits, animal stock, dairy products.

Since 1960 irrigation facilities have greatly increased. The new Colorado River dam program is expected to boost industrial development in the next decade.

**EDUCATION.** *Elementary and Secondary School Enrollment* (Fall, 1966): Public, 291,829; private (est.), 6,700. *Colleges and Universities:* 62,390.

**RECREATION.** Utah's 15 state parks offer many camping facilities. Three national parks (Bryce Canyon, Zion, and the comparatively undeveloped Canyonlands) and seven national forests are noteworthy. Utah's eight national monuments include the Arches, Rainbow Bridge, Capital Reef, and Dinosaur monuments. The state abounds in deer, and Great Salt Lake offers fine duck hunting. In Salt Lake City the Mormon Tabernacle is open to visitors.

# VERMONT

*Area:* 9,609 square miles. *Population* (1967 est.): 416,000 (rank: 48th). *Capital:* Montpelier. *State Flower:* Red Clover. *Bird:* Hermit Thrush. *Motto:* Freedom and Unity. *Nickname:* Green Mountain State. *Flag:* State seal on a blue field.

**LAND AND CLIMATE.** Vermont is bounded on the north by Canada, on the east by New Hampshire, on the south by Massachusetts, and on the west by New York. The Green Mountains run north and south through Vermont's center; in the northeast are the Granite Hills, and in the southwest the Taconic Mountains run across the border into Massachusetts. Over 100 miles of the state's western border fronts on Lake Champlain. Vermont's highest point is Mount Mansfield (4,393 feet) in the Green Mountains; its principal river is the Connecticut; and its chief lake is Champlain.

Heavy snows are common in winter, with annual falls averaging 70 inches per year. Temperatures range from an average minimum of 9° F. in January to an average summer maximum of 82° F.

**HISTORY.** Samuel de Champlain, who discovered (1609) the lake that now bears his name, was probably the first white man to visit Vermont. The region remained desolate until the British, in 1724, established Fort Dummer (near present-day Brattleboro), the first permanent settlement.

Vermont's early history was marked by disputed claims to the region by New York and New Hampshire and by conflicting land grants issued for its settlement that provoked more than four decades of contention. Ethan Allen organized the Green Mountain Boys to resist New York authority, but that conflict halted when the Revolutionary War broke out. Allen and some of his men captured Fort Ticonderoga (May 1775), while others took Crown Point. The Green Mountain Boys later won an important victory in the Saratoga Campaign at Bennington.

Vermont declared itself a sovereign state in 1777 with a constitution that was unique in establishing universal male suffrage. A bid for recognition as one of the original states was blocked by New York at the Continental Congress. But, in 1791, when the area's land grant quarrels were ended, it was admitted to the Union as the 14th state. The next 20 years saw the greatest population increase in Vermont's entire history.

Strongly abolitionist, Vermont vigorously supported Abraham Lincoln over its native son, candidate Stephen Douglas, in the 1860 Presidential election. Political sentiment in the state was consistently and overwhelmingly Republican until, in 1962, a Democratic governor was elected.

**GOVERNMENT AND FINANCE.** *Governor:* Philip H. Hoff (Dem.); *elected:* Nov. 8, 1966; *term:* 2 years; *annual salary:* $20,000. *Senate:* 8 Dem., 22 Rep.; *House of Representatives:* 51 Dem., 93 Rep., 3 Rep.-Dem., 2 Dem.-Rep., 1 Dem.-Ind.

*State Finances: Revenue* (fiscal year 1966, including Federal aid): $167 million. *Expenditure:* $157 million (chief expenditures: education, 26.8%; highways, 31.2%; public welfare, 8.3%).

**ECONOMY.** *Per Capita Personal Income* (1966): $2,590 (rank: 29th). *Work Force Distribution* (1966): Agriculture, 13.5%; other, 86.5%

(manufacturing, trade, and services, in that order, account for 69.3% of the nonagricultural payroll). *Leading Industries:* Agriculture, granite and marble quarrying, machine tools, plastics. *Chief Agricultural Products:* Milk, beef, maple syrup, eggs and poultry.

**EDUCATION.** *Elementary and Secondary School Enrollment* (Fall, 1966): Public, 87,599; private (est.): 19,400. *Colleges and Universities:* 15,290.

**RECREATION.** Visitors are drawn to the state's many ski areas, including locations at Stowe, Woodstock, Brattleboro, and Mount Snow. Other popular activities are summer hiking in the Green Mountain National Forest and water sports on Lake Champlain. Points of historic interest include the Bennington Battle Monument, the Calvin Coolidge Homestead (Plymouth), and the Chester Arthur House (Fairfield).

# VIRGINIA

*Area:* 40,815 square miles. *Population* (1967 est.): 4,533,000 (rank: 14th). *Capital:* Richmond. *State Flower:* Dogwood. *Bird:* Cardinal. *Motto: Sic Semper Tyrannis* (Thus Ever to Tyrants). *Nickname:* Old Dominion. *Flag:* State seal on a blue field.

**LAND AND CLIMATE.** Virginia is bounded on the north by West Virginia and Maryland, on the east by the Atlantic Ocean, on the south by North Carolina and Tennessee, and on the west by Kentucky and West Virginia.

The piedmont, a rolling plateau, runs northeast and southwest through central Virginia; rising from it, to the west, are the scenic Blue Ridge Mountains, with the state's highest point, Mount Rogers (5,729 feet). The eastern (Tidewater) coastline on Chesapeake Bay is irregular; across the bay, on the Delmarva Peninsula, lies Virginia's Eastern Shore.

The climate is generally mild, ranging from average January minimums of 29°–32° F. and an average July maximum of 88° F. Rainfall averages 45 inches a year.

**HISTORY.** Jamestown, the first permanent English settlement in North America, was founded May 14, 1607, by colonists of the London Company. Disease, starvation, and attacks by the Powhatan Indians almost wiped out the colony, but it survived thanks to such men as Captain John Smith and John Rolfe, whose marriage to Pocahontas, daughter of the Indian chief Powhatan, assured peace for the settlers.

The first legislative body in America, the House of Burgesses, was convened at Jamestown in 1619. The colony's prosperity was enhanced by the development of a rich tobacco strain. Virginia became a Royal colony in 1625, the first in English history. During the 18th century great tobacco plantations, dependent on slave labor, sprang up along Virginia's rivers, and many small farmers, unable to afford slaves, moved farther south, or west to the Shenandoah Valley.

With Massachusetts, Virginia led colonial resistance that culminated in the American Revolution, in which such distinguished Virginians as George Washington, Thomas Jefferson, and James Madison played key roles. Final victory over the British came at Yorktown in 1781.

During the first half of the 19th century the rift grew between the aristocratic eastern planters, who retained political control, and the small farmers in the west. In 1851 a new constitution brought political reforms, such as increased representation for the westerners. As the Civil War neared, many Virginians remained loyal to the Federal government; but despite their efforts, the state seceded from the Union on April 17, 1861. The strongly abolitionist western counties broke away to form a separate state, West Virginia.

Virginia gave the Confederacy such able military leaders as Robert E. Lee and "Stonewall" Jackson. It was also the scene of the South's greatest victories, and of its surrender at Appomattox Courthouse on April 9, 1865. On Jan. 26, 1870, Virginia re-entered the Union.

Bitter political controversy in the 1870s over the state's huge debt ended when a moderate government came to power in 1879. A new constitution in 1902 imposed a poll tax and a literacy test intended to discourage Negro voters. Racial problems, chiefly over public school integration, have marked the 1960s.

**GOVERNMENT AND FINANCE.** *Governor:* Mills E. Godwin (Dem.); *elected:* Nov. 2, 1965; *term:* 4 years; *annual salary:* $30,000. *Senate:* 36 Dem., 4 Rep.; *House of Delegates:* 88 Dem., 11 Rep., 1 Ind.

*State Finances: Revenue* (fiscal year 1966, including Federal aid): $1,085 million. *Expenditure:* $1,037 million (chief expenditures: highways, 32.2%; education, 29.6%; public welfare, 4.1%).

**ECONOMY.** *Per Capita Personal Income* (1966): $2,581 (rank: 30th). *Work Force Distribution* (1966): Agriculture, 9.3%; other, 90.7% (manufacturing, trade, and government, in that order, accounted for 66.5% of the nonagricultural payroll). *Leading Industries:* Chemicals, textiles, food processing, furniture, tobacco processing. *Chief Agricultural Products:* Tobacco, hay, corn, apples, sweet potatoes, peanuts. Natural resources include coal, zinc, stone, gravel, lumber, and fish.

**EDUCATION.** *Elementary and Secondary School Enrollment* (Fall, 1966): Public, 1,003,054; private (est.), 61,400. *Colleges and Universities:* 101,384.

**RECREATION.** Notable recreation areas are Shenandoah National Park, Jefferson and George Washington national forests, Virginia Beach, and the Skyline Drive. Among the state's many points of historic interest are Williamsburg, Mount Vernon, Monticello, Arlington National Cemetery, and Civil War battle sites, such as the Manassas and Richmond National Battlefield parks.

# WASHINGTON

*Area:* 68,192 square miles. *Population* (1967 est.): 3,089,000 (rank: 23rd). *Capital:* Olympia. *Flower:* Western Rhododendron. *Bird:* Willow Goldfinch. *Motto: Alki* (By and By). *Nickname:* Evergreen State. *Flag:* State seal on a green field.

**LAND AND CLIMATE.** Washington is bounded on the north by Canada, on the east by Idaho, on the south by Oregon, and on the west by the Pacific Ocean. The Cascade Range, running north from Oregon, bisects the state; its highest peak is lofty Mt. Rainier (14,410 feet). Eastern Washington consists mainly of the fertile Columbia Plateau (2,500–3,000 feet) and a series of low mountain ranges. Western Washington contains the Puget Sound coastal area, with more than 300 islands, the Olympic Peninsula, and a coastal lowland in the south. Principal rivers are the Columbia, Snake, Yakima, and Spokane. Lake Chelan is the largest of hundreds of natural lakes.

Climatic variations between regions are great. The west is generally cool and wet, and the east often arid. Temperatures range from average January minimums of 18°–37° F. to average July maximums of 84°–89° F.

**HISTORY.** Expeditions searching for the Northwest Passage first sailed along the Washington coast in the mid-1770s. Westward-bound British traders were soon competing for the region's valuable furs with Russians coming from Alaska. The American Robert Gray established U.S. claims (1792) by sailing up the Columbia River, and Lewis and Clark reached the area in 1805; John Jacob Astor's fur-trading post at Astoria was founded in 1811.

Joint Anglo-American occupation of the region was agreed on in 1818, but by 1844 the U.S. desire to annex it has so grown that it became a major issue in the presidential election. In 1846, under threat of war, the British withdrew north to the 49th parallel. In 1853 Washington was detached from Oregon Territory, of which it had been a part for five years. By 1859 an end had been put to Indian attacks against white settlers.

The arrival of the transcontinental railroad in 1883 contributed to the territory's fourfold increase in population by the 1890s. Washington entered the Union in 1889. The Alaskan gold rush of 1897 turned Seattle into a boomtown and launched an era of prosperity that lasted until World War I.

During and after that war, labor-management disputes, especially between the leftist Industrial Workers of the World (I.W.W.) and certain business interests, plagued the state. The industrial buildup of World War II restored prosperity.

**GOVERNMENT AND FINANCE.** *Governor:* Daniel J. Evans (Rep.); *elected:* Nov. 3, 1964; *term:* 4 years; *annual salary:* $32,500. *Senate:* 29 Dem., 20 Rep.; *House of Representatives:* 44 Dem., 55 Rep.

*State Finances: Revenue* (fiscal year 1966, including Federal aid): $1,321 million; *expenditure:* $1,102 million (chief expenditures: education, 37.7%; highways, 18.3%; public welfare, 11%).

**ECONOMY.** *Per Capita Personal Income* (1966): $3,280 (rank: 8th). *Work Force Distribution* (1966): Agriculture, 8.4%; other, 91.6% (manufacturing, trade, and government, in that order, accounted for 69.4% of the nonagricultural payroll). *Leading Industries:* Aircraft manufacturing, lumber and wood products, food processing, paper and allied products, chemicals, shipbuilding. *Chief Agricultural Products:* Wheat, apples, vegetables, barley, hops.

Lumbering was Washington's first major industry, but the aircraft and space industries have been the most notable contributors to economic growth in the past decade.

**EDUCATION.** *Elementary and Secondary School Enrollment* (Fall, 1966): Public, 753,068; private (est.), 62,500. *Colleges and Universities:* 133,138.

**RECREATION.** Mount Rainier and Olympic National Parks offer spectacular scenery. Other tourist attractions include nine national forests (covering almost ten million acres); over 100 state parks of scenic, geologic, or historic interest; rugged mountains; and the magnificent Pacific and Puget Sound coastlines. Some specific points of interest are Grand Coulee Dam, Whitman Mission, Fort Vancouver, and Seattle's Civic Center.

# WEST VIRGINIA

*Area:* 24,181 square miles. *Population* (1967 est.): 1,798,000 (rank: 33rd). *Capital:* Charleston. *Flower:* Big Rhododendron. *Bird:* Cardinal. *Motto: Montani Semper Liberi* (Mountaineers Are Always Free Men). *Nickname:* Mountain State. *Flag:* State seal on a blue-bordered white field.

**LAND AND CLIMATE.** West Virginia is bounded on the north by Pennsylvania and Maryland, on the east by Maryland and Virginia, on the south by Virginia, and on the west by Kentucky and Ohio. The terrain is an irregular complex of rugged mountains and valleys (elevations average 1,500 feet), with a high of 4,860 at Spruce Knob. Principal rivers are the Ohio, which marks the state's northern and western borders, the Monongahela, Potomac, and Kanawha.

The climate is moderate and typical for an inland state. Temperatures range from average January minimums of 26°–28° F. to average July maximums of 85°–88° F. Rainfall averages 33.5 inches annually.

**HISTORY.** In 1716 Alexander Spotswood claimed the Valley of Virginia, west of the

Blue Ridge Mountains, for the British. Colonists began to settle the valley in the 1730s. Settlement of the trans-Allegheny area in the 1750s was opposed by the French, who claimed the entire Ohio Valley until their defeat in the French and Indian War (1754–63). Indian resistance to further settlement was ended by Lord Dunmore's War (1774).

Friction that arose between the tidewater aristocracy in eastern Virginia and frontier settlers in the west increased after the victory of the colonies in the American Revolution. The easterners, controlling the legislature, refused to redress any of the western settlers many grievances. A strong abolitionist feeling, directed against slaveholding eastern Virginians, grew as the western sector developed important coal and steel industries with a corresponding lack of dependence on slave labor. In 1861 western Virginia opposed the state's secession, and, as the Civil War began, requested and received protection by Federal troops. A government was immediately set up, and in 1863 West Virginia was admitted to the Union.

Tremendous industrial expansion, accompanied by upheavals on the labor front followed the Civil War. Bitter and often violent strikes in the coal mines were organized by the United Mine Workers, and the ferment continued in the 20th century, especially during the 1930s. A declining coal industry and widespread unemployment due to automation has resulted in a steady decrease in the state's population since 1950. Great efforts were being made to attract new industries.

**GOVERNMENT AND FINANCE.** *Governor:* Hulett C. Smith (Dem.); *elected:* Nov. 3, 1964; *term:* 4 years; *annual salary:* $25,000. *Senate:* 25 Dem., 9 Rep.; *House of Delegates:* 65 Dem., 35 Rep.

*State Finances: Revenue* (fiscal year 1966, including Federal aid): $563 million; *expenditure:* $556 million (chief expenditures: education 31.7%; highways, 29%; public welfare, 11.3%).

**ECONOMY.** *Per Capita Personal Income* (1966): $2,195 (rank: 46th). *Work Force Distribution* (1966): Agriculture, 7.9%; other, 92.1% (manufacturing, government, and trade, in that order, accounted for 62% of the non-agricultural payroll). *Leading Industries:* Coal, steel, chemicals, natural gas, glass. *Chief Agricultural Products:* Livestock, dairy products, fruits, timber, poultry.

**EDUCATION.** *Elementary and Secondary School Enrollment* (Fall, 1966): Public, 420,964; private (est.), 19,100. *Colleges and Universities:* 49,918.

**RECREATION.** White Sulphur Springs and Berkeley Springs are popular resorts. Harpers Ferry National Park and Monongahela National Forest have facilities for hunting, fishing, camping, and skiing. Among many points of interest are the National Radio Astronomy Center at Green Bank, the Chesapeake and Ohio Canal National Monument at Harpers Ferry, and the Grave Creek Mound, Indian burial site, at Moundsville.

# WISCONSIN

*Area:* 56,154 square miles. *Population* (1967 est.): 4,188,000 (rank: 16th). *Capital:* Madison. *Flower:* Wood Violet. *Bird:* Robin. *Motto:* Forward. *Nickname:* Badger State. *Flag:* State seal on a blue field.

**LAND AND CLIMATE.** Wisconsin is bounded on the north by Lake Superior and the state of Michigan, on the east by Lake Michigan, on the south by Illinois, and on the west by Iowa and Minnesota. Much of its area is rolling plain country; the highest point is Sugarbush Hill (1,951 feet). Principal rivers are the Wisconsin, Menominee, St. Croix, Chippewa, and Mississippi; chief lakes are Winnebago, Wisconsin, Mendota, and Chippewa.

The climate is characterized by rapid changes and extremes of temperature which range from average January minimums of 7°–13° F. to average July maximums of 79°–85° F.

**HISTORY.** Jean Nicolet, a French explorer, crossed the Great Lakes in 1634 to the site of present-day Green Bay, which in time became a major center for the fur trade. The entire region was claimed for France in 1686. At the end of the French and Indian Wars (1763), Wisconsin passed to the British, who held it until well after the American Revolution, when Jay's Treaty (1794) forced their evacuation. Though the British won back the area during the War of 1812, the Treaty of Ghent (1814) restored it to the control of the United States.

Wisconsin was transferred from Illinois Territory to Michigan Territory in 1818. Major settlement of the area, begun in the 1820s, bred much Indian resentment, which reached a climax in the Black Hawk War of 1832.

Wisconsin won territorial status in 1836 and admission to the Union in 1848. Its liberal constitution and rich soil attracted many immigrants, particularly Germans, who established thriving farm communities. The Free Soil Party was popular, but for economic, not abolitionist reasons. Anti-slavery sentiment was strong, however, and the state firmly supported the Union during the Civil War.

Wheat production boomed after the war, greatly stimulating Wisconsin's economy. Important brewing, meat-packing, and lumbering industries began in the second half of the 19th century.

During the governorship of Robert M. La Follette (1901–06), who personified political reform, much progressive legislation was passed. Wisconsin's U.S. Senator Joseph McCarthy was one of the most controversial American political figures in the 1950s.

In 1959 the completion of the Saint Lawrence Seaway and Power Project greatly expanded the state's trade.

Racial rioting in Milwaukee during August, 1967, was rapidly contained.

**GOVERNMENT AND FINANCE.** *Governor:* Warren P. Knowles (Rep.); *elected:* Nov. 8, 1966; *term:* 2 years; *annual salary:* $25,000. *Senate:* 12 Dem., 21 Rep.; *Assembly:* 47 Dem., 53 Rep. In April, 1967, the voters approved a constitutional ammendment extending the term of the governor and other state officials from two to four years.

*State Finances: Revenue* (fiscal year 1966, including Federal aid): $1,281 million; *expenditure:* $1,207 million (chief expenditures: education, 33.2%; highways, 16.3%; public welfare, 7.5%).

**ECONOMY.** *Per Capita Personal Income* (1966): $2,935 (rank: 19th). *Work Force Distribution* (1966): Agriculture, 13.2%; other, 86.8% (manufacturing, trade, and government, in that order, accounted for 72.4% of the nonagricultural payroll). *Leading Industries:* Food processing, paper, beer, automobiles, furniture, machinery. *Chief Agricultural Products:* Dairy products, eggs, hay, vegetables, potatoes, cattle.

**EDUCATION.** *Elementary and Secondary School Enrollment* (Fall, 1966): Public, 890,436; private (est.), 284,500. *Colleges and Universities:* 142,660.

**RECREATION.** Wisconsin has 38 state parks, 2 national forests—Nicolet and Chequamegon—and 9 state forests. Its many lakes and streams offer superb fishing. Points of interest for visitors include the Apostle Islands, the Circus World Museum (Baraboo), the rock formations of the Wisconsin Dells, the University of Wisconsin and the University Arboretum (Madison), and the state capitol building.

# WYOMING

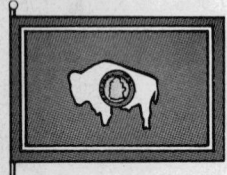

*Area:* 97,914 square miles. *Population* (1967 est.): 315,000 (rank: 49th). *Capital:* Cheyenne. *Flower:* Indian Paint Brush. *Bird:* Meadowlark. *Motto:* Equal Rights. *Nickname:* Equality State. *Flag:* State seal and buffalo on a red-and-white-bordered blue field.

**LAND AND CLIMATE.** Wyoming is bounded on the north by Montana, on the east by South Dakota and Nebraska, on the south by Colorado and Utah, and on the west by Utah, Idaho, and Montana. Among the Rocky Mountain complexes in the state are the Bighorn and the Laramie mountains, the Absaroka Range, and the Wind River Range, which has the state's highest point, Gannett Peak (13,785 ft.). Principal rivers (none navigable) are the Powder, Green, Sweetwater, Yellowstone, and North Platte. Yellowstone Lake is the state's largest (140 square miles).

Climate is generally cool and dry. Temperature changes of as much as 40° may occur in a single day in some regions. Temperatures range from average January minimums of 8°–14° F. to July maximums of 84°–87° F.

**HISTORY.** Wyoming's first inhabitants were Indian tribes such as the Crow, the Sioux, the Arapaho, the Cheyenne, and the formidable Blackfeet. Until 1807, when John Colter became the first American to explore the area, the only whites in the region were some French and Spanish fur traders. A route through the area, pioneered by Americans in 1811, became an important stretch of the Oregon Trail, on which covered wagons moved west. Fort Laramie, established as a fur-trading post in 1834, was the area's first permanent settlement. A gold strike in 1867, the extension of the railroad to Wyoming a year later, and the discovery of vast coal fields drew the first great rush of settlers. Ranching flourished, and cattle were driven from as far away as Texas for shipment east from Wyoming rail towns such as Cheyenne. By 1876 warfare with the Indians finally ended, but fierce range wars between cattlemen and the sheep raisers and homesteaders were common in the 1880s and 1890s.

Wyoming Territory, created in 1868, was admitted to the Union in 1890 despite Congressional distaste for its constitution, which had a then unique provision for women's suffrage. Farming, oil prospecting, and mining grew; in 1900 a copper boom began. After World War I, Wyoming's oil industry acquired great importance, and in 1923 the corrupt handling of leases to government oil reserves at the Teapot Dome field led to a scandal that rocked the administration of President Harding. The oil industry, bolstered by World War II, continues to grow. Uranium deposits were discovered in the 1950s.

**GOVERNMENT AND FINANCE.** *Governor:* Stanley K. Hathaway (Rep.); *elected:* Nov. 8, 1966; *term:* 4 years; *annual salary:* $20,000. *Senate:* 12 Dem., 18 Rep.; *House of Representatives:* 28 Dem., 33 Rep.

*State Finances: Revenue* (fiscal year 1966, including Federal aid): $166 million; *expenditure:* $170 million (chief expenditures: education 36.5%; highways 40.6%; public welfare, 3.5%).

**ECONOMY.** *Per Capita Personal Income* (1966): $2,686 (rank: 27th). *Work Force Distribution* (1966): Agriculture, 14.8%; other, 85.2% (government, trade, and services, in that order, accounted for 62.7% of the nonagricultural payroll). *Leading Industries:* Mining, tourism, food processing, petroleum. *Chief Agricultural Products:* Cattle, sheep, hay, sugar beets, wheat.

**EDUCATION.** *Elementary and Secondary School Enrollment* (Fall, 1966): Public, 84,912; private (est.): 4,400. *Colleges and Universities:* 11,362.

**RECREATION.** Wyoming has two large national parks—Grand Teton and Yellowstone—and ten state parks, including Hot Springs State Park. National forests are the Bighorn, Bridges, and Shoshone. Historic Fort Laramie, Devil's Tower National Monument, and dude ranches, roundups, rodeos, and other reminders of the Old West attract many tourists. Lakes and streams provide excellent fishing, and there is also a good supply of bear, deer, elk, and other game.

# CAPITAL DISTRICT, PUERTO RICO, AND U.S. TERRITORIES

## DISTRICT OF COLUMBIA

*Area:* 69 square miles. *Population* (1967 est.): 810,000. *Commissioner:* Walter E. Washington. *Salary of Commissioner:* $28,500 per year. *Finances* (1965–66): Revenue, $409.0 million; expenditure, $418.2 million. *Leading Industries:* Government, printing and publishing.

The District is situated on the east bank of the Potomac River, coterminous with the city of Washington, bounded on three sides by Maryland and on the southwest by Virginia. It was established by Congress in 1790–91. Its exact site was selected by George Washington, who asked Maj. Pierre L'Enfant to design the city. L'Enfant fell into a dispute with Congress and was dismissed in 1792, but his plan was not entirely abandoned. Maryland and Virginia ceded land for the District, and the capital moved there from Philadelphia in 1800.

In 1878 home rule was ended in the District. From that time until 1967, Congress ran the capital through a three-man board of commissioners—a unique government in that it provided at once the equivalent of local, county, and state services. Residents have had no voice in local government and no elected representative in Congress, but in 1961 they gained the right to vote in presidential elections. (The District has three electoral votes.) Negroes make up about two-thirds of the District's population.

On August 9, 1967, the House of Representatives passed legislation providing for a city government that would include an appointed Commissioner (the equivalent of a mayor), an Assistant Commissioner, and a nine-member Council. In September, Walter E. Washington, a Negro, was sworn in as Commissioner under the new plan; five of the nine Council members appointed by the President were also Negroes. The House voted to allow the city to elect its Board of Education.

## CANAL ZONE

*Area:* 552.8 sq. mi. *Population* (1966): 55,800. *Languages:* Spanish and English. The Canal Zone is a 50-mile-long strip between the Atlantic and Pacific oceans, extending roughly for five miles on either side of the Panama Canal. In 1903 Panama granted the Zone in perpetuity to the United States and authorized construction of the canal across the Isthmus of Panama. Annual payments to Panama for the Zone (which is, in effect, a U.S. reservation) were increased to $1,930,000 in 1965. The governor, a presidential appointee, has headquarters in Balboa, on the Pacific side.

Since 1959, Panamanians have vigorously agitated for a return of the Zone to local control; rioting took place in January, 1964. On June 26, 1967, U.S. and Panamanian negotiators concluded three draft treaties which, if ratified by the two nations, would modify the long-standing bilateral agreements. There were signs, however, that some determined opponents in each country would try to block ratification—although for different reasons.

## COMMONWEALTH OF PUERTO RICO

*Area:* 3,435 sq. mi. *Population* (1966 est.): 2,668,000. *Capital:* San Juan (pop., 1965 est.: 506,000). *Other Cities:* Ponce (pop., 1965 est.: 156,000), Mayagüez (pop., 1965 est.: 88,200). *Governor:* Roberto Sánchez Vilella (Pop. Dem., elected 1965). *Flag:* Three red and two white horizontal stripes; white star in blue triangle at inner edge. *Languages:* Spanish and English.

Puerto Rico, some 950 miles southeast of Miami, is the easternmost island in the Caribbean chain known as the Greater Antilles. It was discovered by Columbus in 1493. Colonization (and extermination of the native Arawak Indians) was begun by Ponce de León in 1508. From 1513 the Spaniards imported Negro slaves to work their plantations. Puerto Rico remained a Spanish colony and was denied self-government for nearly four centuries.

In 1897 the Puerto Ricans, led by Luis Muñoz Rivera, gained some autonomy, but the Spanish-American War broke out a few months later. Spain ceded Puerto Rico to the United States in December, 1898, and it became an unincorporated territory. U.S. citizenship was granted its residents in 1917; the island won the right to its own executive 30 years later; and in 1952 it was granted commonwealth status. Since 1948 Luis Muñoz Marín (son of Muñoz Rivera) and his Popular Democrats have dominated island politics. They have succeeded, with their "Operation Bootstrap" campaign, in attracting much mainland industry to the island and have partially stemmed the heavy tide of emigration to the continental U.S.

The self-governing Commonwealth (including several small outlying islands) now has most of the powers and responsibilities of a state of the Union, but Puerto Rico regulates its own customs and collects its own import duties. Its residents have no vote in U.S. presidential elections and no voting representative in Congress. They pay no U.S. taxes. A plebiscite held in July, 1967, showed that 60 per cent of the voters preferred the commonwealth system to either statehood or independence.

## VIRGIN ISLANDS

*Area:* 132 sq. mi. *Population* (1966): 49,500. *Capital:* Charlotte Amalie (pop., 1960: 12,880), on St. Thomas. *Other Cities:* Christiansted and Frederiksted (both on St. Croix). *Governor* Ralph M. Paiewonsky, a presidential appointee *Language:* English.

The U.S. Virgin Islands are governed as an unincorporated territory. Lying about 75 air miles east of San Juan, Puerto Rico, they consist of three main islands (St. Croix, 82 sq. mi.; St. Thomas, 32 sq. mi.; and St. John, 19 sq. mi.) and some 60 smaller islands, mostly uninhabited.

Tourism is the principal industry. Much of the islands' food is imported, St. Croix being the only island suitable for agriculture. Virgin Islands National Park covers a large part of St. John. About 70 per cent of the population is Negro.

*(continued)*

**VIRGIN ISLANDS** (*continued*)

The islands, discovered and named by Columbus in 1493, remained under Spanish control through most of the 16th century, but in the 1650s France took St. Croix and in 1672 Danish colonists settled on St. Thomas. Denmark occupied St. John in 1684 and bought St. Croix from France in 1733. The United States bought all three islands from Denmark for $25 million in 1917. The islanders were granted U.S. citizenship in 1927; they elect their own unicameral legislature.

**OTHER CARIBBEAN ISLANDS**

*Great Corn* and *Little Corn Islands* (area: 4 sq. mi.) are situated 40 miles off the east coast of Nicaragua. The U.S. obtained them in 1916 through a 99-year lease from Nicaragua, which still administers them.

The two *Swan Islands* (one sq. mi.) lie 125 miles northwest of Honduras. They were acquired by the U.S. in 1863. Honduras also claims sovereignty.

**TRUST TERRITORY OF THE PACIFIC ISLANDS**

The territory consists of the *Carolines*, the *Marianas* (excluding Guam), and the *Marshalls*. Known collectively as Micronesia, they comprise more than 2,000 islands (687 sq. mi.) scattered over 3 million square miles of the western Pacific Ocean. The population (est., 1965: 90,000) is concentrated on about 100 islands. In 1947 the United Nations made the islands a strategic trust territory of the U.S. The people elected their first territorial legislature in 1965. Two of the Marshalls (*Bikini* and *Eniwetok*) served as U.S. testing grounds for nuclear weapons.

**GUAM**

*Area:* 209 sq. mi. *Population* (1964 est.): 72,000. *Capital:* Agana, a tax-free port. *Languages:* Chamorro and English.

Guam is situated in the western Pacific, about 1,400 miles east of Manila. It is an island of volcanic origin, the southernmost and most populous in the Marianas group, and is the largest island between Hawaii and the Philippines. An unincorporated territory, Guam is a major U.S. Pacific military base. Agriculture and work on the base and in the local government support the economy.

Discovered by Ferdinand Magellan in 1521, Guam remained under Spanish control until acquired by the U.S. at the conclusion of the Spanish-American War (1898). It was occupied by Japan on December 11, 1941, and retaken by U.S. forces in July and August, 1944. Its residents were granted citizenship in 1950 and given limited self-government under supervision of the U.S. Department of the Interior.

Guamanians have no vote in U.S. presidential elections and no representative in Congress; their governor is federally appointed. During a stopover in Guam in March, 1967, President Johnson endorsed the proposal that Guamanians be permitted to choose their own governor before 1972. Regular commercial flights between Guam and Tokyo began in 1967.

**AMERICAN SAMOA**

*Area:* 76.1 sq. mi. *Population* (1966 est.): 27,000. *Capital:* Pago Pago, on Tutuila Island. *Languages:* Samoan and English. American Samoa comprises five volcanic islands and two uninhabited coral atolls, about 2,300 miles southwest of Hawaii. The U.S. explorer Charles Wilkes visited these Pacific islands about 1840, and an agreement with Britain and Germany in 1899 acknowledged U.S. rights to them. An unincorporated territory, Samoa was granted limited self-government in 1960. The traditional social structure and native culture of the Polynesian inhabitants have remained largely unchanged.

**OTHER PACIFIC ISLANDS**

The *Ryukyus* are a chain of more than 60 islands stretching southwest from Japan to Taiwan and covering a total land area of 1,803 square miles. Of the total population (1964 est.: 927,000), more than two-thirds reside on *Okinawa*, the largest island, which is the seat of the local Ryukyuan government and the site of a key U.S. military base.

The islands, governed by Japan from 1879, were invaded by American forces on April 1, 1945, and were taken after a bloody three-months' campaign. They were placed under U.S. military administration after World War II. There has been some local agitation for a return of the islands to Japan.

The U.S. military also administers the following islands, held by Japan before World War II: *Marcus Island* (1 sq. mi.), about 1,200 miles southeast of Tokyo; the *Bonins* (30 sq. mi.), 600 miles south-southeast of Tokyo; and the three *Volcano Islands* (11 sq. mi.), 200 miles south of the Bonins. The most important of the Volcano Islands is *Iwo Jima*, captured by U.S. forces in February–March, 1945.

*Wake Island* (3 sq. mi.) is an atoll about 2,300 miles west of Hawaii. Claimed by the U.S. in 1900, it was taken by Japan in December, 1945 (after a valiant defense by a handful of U.S. Marines) and surrendered in September, 1945. It is now administered by the Federal Aviation Agency, which maintains an airfield.

*Midway* (2 sq. mi.) consists of two coral islands some 1,200 miles northwest of Honolulu. It was the site of a U.S. naval and air victory against Japan (June 3–6, 1942). It has an airfield and a cable station.

*Canton* and *Enderbury* islands (27 sq. mi.), 1,600 miles southwest of Hawaii, are administered jointly by the U.S. and Britain under a 1939 agreement. Canton has a population of about 320; Enderbury is uninhabited.

*Johnston* and *Sand* islands (½ sq. mi.) are two parts of a coral atoll, 600 miles southwest of Hawaii. A U.S. naval base was established here in 1941.

Uninhabited islands under U.S. control, lying 1,000 to 1,700 miles south of Hawaii, include *Baker, Howland, Jarvis, Palmyra*, and the smallest of all U.S. territorial possessions, *Kingman Reef*—an isolated atoll measuring 150 by 120 feet at high tide.

## NEGRO VOTER REGISTRATION IN THE SOUTH

Source: Voter Education Project, Southern Regional Council

The total of Negro voters registered in the South by mid-1967 stood in dramatic contrast to that of 11 years ago. The greatest increases have come in those states covered by the Voting Rights Act of 1965. Registration activity in 1967 was somewhat less than in 1966, for the only Southern states with statewide elections were Louisiana, Mississippi, and Virginia.

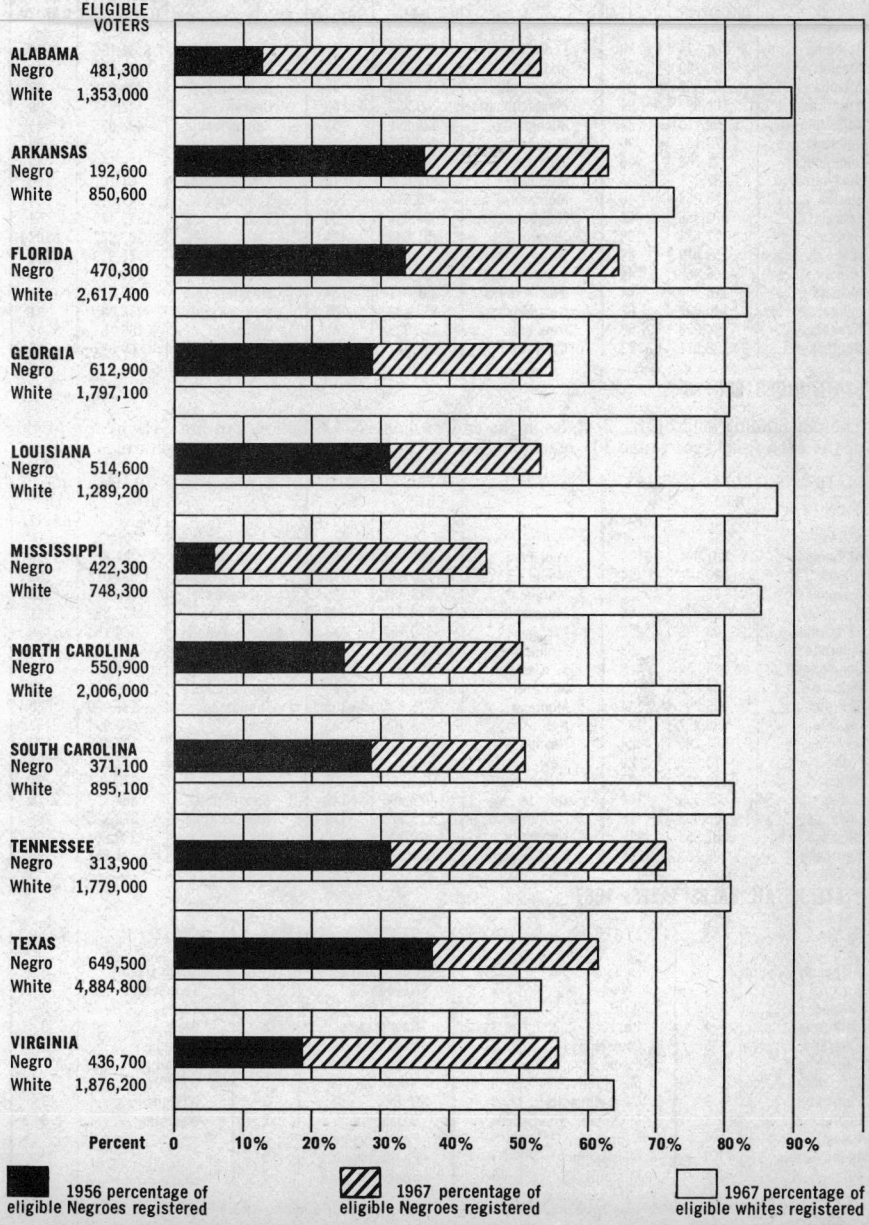

ELIGIBLE VOTERS

| | |
|---|---|
| **ALABAMA** Negro | 481,300 |
| White | 1,353,000 |
| **ARKANSAS** Negro | 192,600 |
| White | 850,600 |
| **FLORIDA** Negro | 470,300 |
| White | 2,617,400 |
| **GEORGIA** Negro | 612,900 |
| White | 1,797,100 |
| **LOUISIANA** Negro | 514,600 |
| White | 1,289,200 |
| **MISSISSIPPI** Negro | 422,300 |
| White | 748,300 |
| **NORTH CAROLINA** Negro | 550,900 |
| White | 2,006,000 |
| **SOUTH CAROLINA** Negro | 371,100 |
| White | 895,100 |
| **TENNESSEE** Negro | 313,900 |
| White | 1,779,000 |
| **TEXAS** Negro | 649,500 |
| White | 4,884,800 |
| **VIRGINIA** Negro | 436,700 |
| White | 1,876,200 |

Percent   0   10%   20%   30%   40%   50%   60%   70%   80%   90%

■ 1956 percentage of eligible Negroes registered
▨ 1967 percentage of eligible Negroes registered
□ 1967 percentage of eligible whites registered

## FEDERAL MONEY GRANTED U.S. STATES

Federal aid to the states includes grants for such programs as highways, health, education, and public welfare. Alaska, on a per capita basis, was the leading aid recipient in 1966.

These Bureau of the Census figures are for the fiscal year ending June 30, 1966, except for Alabama (ending Sept. 30), New York (ending March 31), and Texas (ending Aug. 31).

| STATE | TOTAL AID (000s) | AID PER CAPITA | STATE | TOTAL AID (000s) | AID PER CAPITA | STATE | TOTAL AID (000s) | AID PER CAPITA |
|---|---|---|---|---|---|---|---|---|
| Alabama..... | $ 301,574 | $ 86 | Louisiana.... | $315,658 | $ 88 | North Dakota | $ 52,165 | $ 80 |
| Alaska....... | 96,780 | 356 | Maine....... | 65,866 | 67 | Ohio......... | 475,290 | 46 |
| Arizona..... | 140,352 | 87 | Maryland.... | 147,054 | 41 | Oklahoma.... | 225,175 | 92 |
| Arkansas..... | 163,822 | 84 | Massachusetts | 260,753 | 48 | Oregon...... | 192,777 | 99 |
| California.... | 1,652,270 | 87 | Michigan..... | 425,891 | 51 | Pennsylvania | 498,085 | 43 |
| Colorado..... | 178,132 | 90 | Minnesota.... | 268,595 | 75 | Rhode Island | 52,752 | 59 |
| Connecticut.. | 131,768 | 46 | Mississippi... | 167,344 | 72 | South Carolina | 126,152 | 49 |
| Delaware..... | 37,221 | 73 | Missouri..... | 316,674 | 70 | South Dakota | 61,101 | 90 |
| Florida....... | 273,254 | 46 | Montana..... | 80,614 | 115 | Tennessee.... | 247,918 | 64 |
| Georgia...... | 278,355 | 62 | Nebraska.... | 81,051 | 56 | Texas....... | 575,478 | 54 |
| Hawaii....... | 77,634 | 108 | Nevada...... | 51,830 | 114 | Utah......... | 107,977 | 107 |
| Idaho........ | 58,019 | 84 | New | | | Vermont..... | 49,919 | 123 |
| Illinois....... | 466,468 | 44 | Hampshire | 35,259 | 52 | Virginia..... | 242,350 | 54 |
| Indiana...... | 216,904 | 44 | New Jersey... | 231,671 | 34 | Washington... | 237,615 | 80 |
| Iowa........ | 170,097 | 62 | New Mexico.. | 139,488 | 136 | West Virginia | 162,641 | 91 |
| Kansas..... | 134,928 | 60 | New York.... | 732,093 | 40 | Wisconsin.... | 186,783 | 45 |
| Kentucky.... | 228,516 | 72 | North Carolina | 252,967 | 51 | Wyoming..... | 69,699 | 212 |

## STATE INDEBTEDNESS

The outstanding debt of the 50 states at the end of the 1966 fiscal year (June 30) reached a new high—$29.6 billion. All but $1.1 billion of this amount was of a long-term nature.

| STATE | TOTAL DEBT (000s) | DEBT PER CAPITA | STATE | TOTAL DEBT (000s) | DEBT PER CAPITA | STATE | TOTAL DEBT (000s) | DEBT PER CAPITA |
|---|---|---|---|---|---|---|---|---|
| Alabama..... | $ 501,921 | $143 | Louisiana.... | $ 647,994 | $180 | North Dakota | $ 24,822 | $ 38 |
| Alaska....... | 126,181 | 464 | Maine....... | 160,518 | 163 | Ohio......... | 1,032,018 | 100 |
| Arizona..... | 45,697 | 28 | Maryland.... | 813,431 | 225 | Oklahoma.... | 416,120 | 169 |
| Arkansas..... | 105,927 | 54 | Massachusetts | 1,772,031 | 329 | Oregon...... | 452,558 | 231 |
| California.... | 4,208,793 | 222 | Michigan..... | 949,158 | 113 | Pennsylvania | 1,964,154 | 170 |
| Colorado..... | 123,824 | 63 | Minnesota.... | 322,630 | 90 | Rhode Island | 250,072 | 278 |
| Connecticut.. | 1,234,054 | 429 | Mississippi... | 263,911 | 113 | South Carolina | 238,670 | 92 |
| Delaware..... | 334,452 | 653 | Missouri..... | 137,700 | 31 | South Dakota | 19,021 | 28 |
| Florida....... | 795,005 | 134 | Montana..... | 75,374 | 105 | Tennessee... | 231,060 | 60 |
| Georgia...... | 590,457 | 132 | Nebraska.... | 65,706 | 45 | Texas....... | 609,994 | 57 |
| Hawaii....... | 304,225 | 424 | Nevada...... | 15,942 | 35 | Utah......... | 107,402 | 107 |
| Idaho........ | 15,625 | 23 | New | | | Vermont..... | 77,551 | 191 |
| Illinois....... | 1,150,070 | 107 | Hampshire | 134,300 | 197 | Virginia..... | 276,724 | 61 |
| Indiana...... | 529,566 | 108 | New Jersey... | 1,023,398 | 148 | Washington... | 554,723 | 186 |
| Iowa........ | 70,412 | 26 | New Mexico.. | 125,779 | 123 | West Virginia | 373,225 | 208 |
| Kansas..... | 251,558 | 112 | New York.... | 4,570,701 | 250 | Wisconsin.... | 330,867 | 80 |
| Kentucky.... | 839,263 | 264 | North Carolina | 274,350 | 55 | Wyoming..... | 24,857 | 76 |

## STATE RETAIL SALES TAXES: 1967

| STATE | TAX | STATE | TAX | STATE | TAX | STATE | TAX |
|---|---|---|---|---|---|---|---|
| Alabama....... | 4% | Indiana......... | 2% | Nebraska...... | 2½% | South Dakota... | 3% |
| Arizona........ | 3 | Iowa [2]........ | 3 | Nevada........ | 3 | Tennessee..... | 3 |
| Arkansas....... | 3 | Kansas........ | 3 | New Jersey.... | 3 | Texas........ | 2 |
| California [1].... | 4 | Kentucky....... | 3 | New Mexico.... | 3 | Utah.......... | 3 |
| Colorado....... | 3 | Louisiana...... | 2 | New York...... | 2 | Virginia........ | 3 |
| Connecticut.... | 3½ | Maine......... | 4 | North Carolina.. | 3 | Washington.... | 4½ |
| Dist. of Col.... | 3 | Maryland...... | 3 | North Dakota.. | 3 | West Virginia... | 3 |
| Florida........ | 3 | Massachusetts.. | 3 | Ohio.......... | 3 | Wisconsin...... | 3 |
| Georgia........ | 3 | Michigan...... | 4 | Oklahoma..... | 2 | Wyoming....... | 3 |
| Hawaii........ | 4 | Minnesota...... | 3 | Pennsylvania... | 5 | | |
| Idaho.......... | 3 | Mississippi..... | 3½ | Rhode Island... | 5 | | |
| Illinois......... | 3½ | Missouri....... | 3 | South Carolina.. | 3 | | |

[1] Began Aug. 1, 1967; reduction may take place, depending on school appropriation.     [2] Rose from 2% to 3% Oct. 1, 1967.
(Source: Tax Foundation)

## INDIVIDUAL STATE INCOME TAX RATES AND EXEMPTIONS: 1967

Sources: Custom Clearing House; Tax Foundation

Revenue collected by state governments from all sources in fiscal 1966 totaled $55.2 billion, or 13.1 per cent above the previous year. Their yield from individual income taxes (now imposed by 37 states and the District of Columbia) totaled $4.3 billion—17.2 per cent over fiscal 1965. State government expenditures ($51.0 billion) were 11.8 per cent above 1965.

| STATE | PERSONAL EXEMPTIONS | | | INDIVIDUAL RATES |
|---|---|---|---|---|
| | Single | Married | Dependent | |
| **Ala.** | $1,500 | $3,000 | $ 300 | 1st $ 1,000, 1.5%<br>Next   2,000, 3.0<br>Next   2,000, 4.5<br>Over   5,000, 5.0 |
| **Alaska** | — | — | — | 16% of Federal income tax. |
| **Ariz.** | $1,000 | $2,000 | $ 600 | 1st $ 1,000, 1.3%<br>2nd   1,000, 2.0<br>3rd   1,000, 2.6<br>4th   1,000, 3.3<br>5th   1,000, 4.0<br>6th   1,000, 4.6<br>7th   1,000, 5.3<br>Over  7,000, 5.9 |
| **Ark.** | $17.50[1] | $35.00[1] | $ 6.00[1] | 1st $ 3,000, 1.0%<br>2nd   3,000, 2.0<br>Next   5,000, 3.0<br>Next  14,000, 4.0<br>Over  25,000, 5.0 |
| **Calif.** | $25.00[1] | $50.00[1] | $ 8.00[1] | Not over $2,000 1%<br>$2,001–3,500<br>    $20 plus 2<br>3,501–5,000<br>    $50 plus 3<br>5,001–6,500<br>    $95 plus 4<br>6,501–8,000<br>    $155 plus 5<br>8,001–9,500<br>    $230 plus 6<br>9,501–11,000<br>    $320 plus 7<br>11,001–12,500<br>    $425 plus 8<br>12,501–14,000<br>    $545 plus 9<br>Over $14,000<br>    $680 plus 10 |
| **Colo.** | $ 750 | $1,500 | $ 750 | 1st $ 1,000, 3.0%<br>2nd   1,000, 3.5<br>3rd   1,000, 4.0<br>4th   1,000, 4.5<br>5th   1,000, 5.0<br>6th   1,000, 5.5<br>7th   1,000, 6.0<br>8th   1,000, 6.5<br>9th   1,000, 7.0<br>10th  1,000, 7.5<br>Over 10,000, 8.0<br>Surtax on intangible income over $5,000 2%. |
| **Del.** | $ 600 | $1,200 | $ 600 | 1st $ 1,000, 1.5%<br>2nd   1,000, 2.0<br>3rd   1,000, 3.0<br>4th   1,000, 4.0<br>5th   1,000, 5.0<br>6th   1,000, 6.0<br>Next   2,000, 7.0<br>Next  22,000, 8.0 |
| **Del.** (cont.) | | | | Next 20,000, 9.0<br>Next 50,000, 10.0<br>Over 100,000, 11.0 |
| **D. of C.** | $1,000 | $2,000 | $ 500 | 1st $ 2,000, 2.5%<br>Next   2,000, 3.0<br>Next   2,000, 3.5<br>Next   2,000, 4.0<br>Next   2,000, 4.5<br>Over  10,000, 5.0 |
| **Ga.** | $1,500 | $3,000 | $ 600 | 1st $ 1,000, 1.0%<br>Next   2,000, 2.0<br>Next   2,000, 3.0<br>Next   2,000, 4.0<br>Next   3,000, 5.0<br>Over  10,000, 6.0 |
| **Hawaii** | $ 600 | $1,200 | $ 600 | 1st $  500, 2.25%<br>Next    500, 3.25<br>Next    500, 4.5<br>Next    500, 5.0<br>Next   1,000, 6.5<br>Next   2,000, 7.5<br>Next   5,000, 8.5<br>Next   4,000, 9.5<br>Next   6,000, 10.0<br>Next  10,000, 10.5<br>Over  30,000, 11.0 |
| **Idaho** | $ 600 | $1,200 | $ 600 | 1st $ 1,000, 2.5%<br>2nd   1,000, 5.0<br>3rd   1,000, 6.0<br>4th   1,000, 7.0<br>5th   1,000, 8.0<br>Over   5,000, 9.0<br>Each person (husband and wife filing jointly deemed one person) filing return pays additional $10. |
| **Ind.** | $1,000 | $2,000 | $ 500 | 2% of adjusted gross income. |
| **Iowa** | $15.00[1] | $30.00[1] | $ 7.50[1] | 1st $ 1,000, 0.75%<br>2nd   1,000, 1.5<br>3rd   1,000, 2.25<br>4th   1,000, 3.0<br>5th   1,000, 3.75<br>6th   1,000, 3.75<br>7th   1,000, 3.75<br>8th   1,000, 4.5 |
| **Kans.** | $ 600 | $1,200 | $ 600 | 1st $ 2,000, 2.5%<br>Next   1,000, 3.5<br>Next   2,000, 4.0<br>Next   2,000, 5.0<br>Over   7,000, 6.5 |
| **Ky.** | $20.00[1] | $ 40.00[1] | $20.00[1] | 1st $ 3,000, 2.0%<br>Next   1,000, 3.0<br>Next   1,000, 4.0<br>Next   3,000, 5.0<br>Over   8,000, 6.0 |
| **La.** | $2,500 | $5,000 | $ 400 | 1st $10,000, 2.0%<br>Next  40,000, 4.0<br>Over  50,000, 6.0 |

(continued)    (continued)

[1] From tax.

## STATE INCOME TAX RATES (continued)

| STATE | Single | Married | Dependent | INDIVIDUAL RATES |
|---|---|---|---|---|
| Md. | $800 | $1,600 | $800 | 1st $1,000, 2.0%<br>2nd 1,000, 3.0<br>3rd 1,000, 4.0<br>Over 3,000, 5.0 |
| Mass. | $2,000[1] | Up to $4,000[1] | $400[1] | Interest and dividends, 7.38%<br>Earned income, 3.075%<br>Annuities, 1.845%<br>Capital gains on intangibles, 7.38% |
| Mich. | $1,200 | $2,400 | $1,200 | A tax rate of 2.6% based on Federal definition of personal income, effective Oct. 1, 1967. |
| Minn. | $19.00[2] | $38.00[2] | $19.00[2] | 1st $500, 1.5%<br>2nd 500, 2.0<br>Next 1,000, 3.0<br>Next 1,000, 5.0<br>Next 1,000, 6.0<br>Next 1,000, 7.0<br>Next 2,000, 8.0<br>Next 2,000, 9.0<br>Next 3,500, 10.0<br>Next 7,500, 11.0<br>Over 20,000, 12.0 |
| Miss. | $5,000 | $7,000 | $7,000[3] | 1st $5,000, 2.0%<br>Over 5,000, 3.0 |
| Mo.[4] | $1,200 | $2,400 | $400 | 1st $1,000, 1.0%<br>2nd 1,000, 1.5 (less $5)<br>3rd 1,000, 2.0 (less $15)<br>Next 2,000, 2.5 (less $30)<br>Next 2,000, 3.0 (less $55)<br>Next 2,000, 3.5 (less $90)<br>Over 9,000, 4.0 (less $135) |
| Mont. | $600 | $1,200 | $600 | 1st $1,000, 2.0%<br>2nd 1,000, 3.0<br>Next 2,000, 4.0<br>Next 2,000, 5.0<br>Next 2,000, 6.0<br>Next 2,000, 7.0<br>Next 15,000, 8.0<br>Over 25,000, 10.0 |
| N.H. | $600 | $600 | $600 | 4.25% on income from interest and dividends. |
| N.J. | — | — | — | "Commuters' income tax" is imposed on residents of one "critical area" state (N.J. or N.Y.) on income from sources in other "critical area" state (N.J. or N.Y.). Rates and exemptions identical to those of the N.Y. personal income tax |
| N.Mex. | $600 | $1,200 | $600 | 1st $10,000, 1.5% |
| N.Mex. (con't) | | | | 2nd 10,000, 3.0<br>Next 80,000, 4.5<br>Over 100,000, 6.0 |
| N.Y. | $600 | $1,200 | $600 | 1st $1,000, 2.0%<br>Next 2,000, 3.0<br>Next 2,000, 4.0<br>Next 2,000, 5.0<br>Next 2,000, 6.0<br>Next 2,000, 7.0<br>Next 2,000, 8.0<br>Next 2,000, 9.0<br>Over 15,000, 10.0 |
| N.C. | $1,000 | $2,000 | $300 | 1st $2,000, 3.0%<br>2nd 2,000, 4.0<br>3rd 2,000, 5.0<br>Next 4,000, 6.0<br>Over 10,000, 7.0 |
| N.Dak. | $600 | $1,500 | $600 | 1st $3,000, 1.0%<br>Next 1,000, 2.0<br>Next 1,000, 3.0<br>Next 1,000, 5.0<br>Next 2,000, 7.5<br>Next 7,000, 10.0<br>Over 15,000, 11.0 |
| Okla. | $1,000 | $2,000 | $500 | 1st $1,500, 1.0%<br>2nd 1,500, 2.0<br>3rd 1,500, 3.0<br>4th 1,500, 4.0<br>5th 1,500, 5.0<br>Over 7,500, 6.0 |
| Oreg. | $600 | $1,200 | $600 | 1st $500, 3.0%<br>2nd 500, 4.0<br>3rd 500, 5.0<br>4th 500, 6.0<br>Next 2,000, 7.0<br>Next 2,000, 9.0<br>Over 8,000, 9.5 |
| S.C. | $800 | $1,600 | $800 | 1st $2,000, 2.0<br>2nd 2,000, 3.0<br>3rd 2,000, 4.0<br>4th 2,000, 5.0<br>5th 2,000, 6.0<br>Over 10,000, 7.0 |
| Tenn. | — | — | — | On dividends and interest 6.0%<br>On dividends from corporations 75% of whose property is taxable in state 4.0 |
| Utah | $600 | $1,200 | $600 | 1st $1,000, 2.0%<br>2nd 1,000, 3.0<br>3rd 1,000, 4.0<br>4th 1,000, 5.0<br>5th 1,000, 6.0<br>Over 5,000, 6.5 |
| Vt. | $500 | $1,000 | $500 | 1st $1,000, 2.0%<br>Next 2,000, 4.0<br>Next 2,000, 6.0<br>Over 5,000, 7.5 |
| Va. | $1,000 | $2,000 | $200 | 1st $3,000, 2.0%<br>Next 2,000, 3.0<br>Over 5,000, 5.0 |
| W.Va. | $600 | $1,200 | $600 | 1st $2,000, 1.2%<br>2nd 2,000, 1.3 |

[1] From earned income; from interest, dividends, annuities, and gains, $2,000, if income from all sources does not exceed $2,000 single or $2,500 married. [2] From tax. [3] Head of family. [4] The entire taxable amount of each net income shall be computed at only the one rate in which the income falls.

| STATE | PERSONAL EXEMPTIONS | | | INDIVIDUAL RATES |
|---|---|---|---|---|
| | Single | Married | Dependent | |
| W.Va. (con't) | | | | (plus $24) |
| | | | | 3rd 2,000, 1.6 |
| | | | | (plus $50) |
| | | | | 4th 2,000, 1.8 |
| | | | | (plus $82) |
| | | | | 5th 2,000, 2.0 |
| | | | | (plus $118) |
| | | | | 6th 2,000, 2.3 |
| | | | | (plus $158) |
| | | | | 7th 2,000, 2.6 |
| | | | | (plus $204) |
| | | | | 8th 2,000, 2.8 |
| | | | | (plus $256) |
| | | | | 9th 2,000, 3.0 |
| | | | | (plus $312) |
| | | | | 10th 2,000, 3.1 |
| | | | | (plus $372) |
| | | | | 11th 2,000, 3.4 |
| | | | | (plus $434) |
| | | | | Next 4,000, 3.5 |
| | | | | (plus $502) |
| | | | | Next 6,000, 3.7 |
| | | | | (plus $642) |
| | | | | Next 6,000, 3.9 |
| | | | | (plus $864) |
| | | | | Next 6,000, 4.1 |
| | | | | (plus $1,098) |
| | | | | Next 6,000, 4.3 |
| | | | | (plus $1,344) |
| | | | | Next 10,000, 4.5 |

| STATE | PERSONAL EXEMPTIONS | | | INDIVIDUAL RATES |
|---|---|---|---|---|
| | Single | Married | Dependent | |
| W.Va. (con't) | | | | (plus $1,602) |
| | | | | Next 10,000, 4.7 |
| | | | | (plus $2,052) |
| | | | | Next 10,000, 4.9 |
| | | | | (plus $2,522) |
| | | | | Next 10,000, 5.0 |
| | | | | (plus $3,012) |
| | | | | Next 10,000, 5.2 |
| | | | | (plus $3,512) |
| | | | | Next 50,000, 5.3 |
| | | | | (plus $4,032) |
| | | | | Next 50,000, 5.4 |
| | | | | (plus $6,682) |
| | | | | Over 200,000, 5.5 |
| | | | | (plus $9,382) |
| Wis. | $10.00[1] | $20.00[1] | $10.00[1] | 1st $ 1,000, 2.7 % |
| | | | | 2nd 1,000, 2.95 |
| | | | | 3rd 1,000, 3.2 |
| | | | | 4th 1,000, 4.2 |
| | | | | 5th 1,000, 4.7 |
| | | | | 6th 1,000, 5.2 |
| | | | | 7th 1,000, 5.7 |
| | | | | 8th 1,000, 6.7 |
| | | | | 9th 1,000, 7.2 |
| | | | | 10th 1,000, 7.7 |
| | | | | 11th 1,000, 8.2 |
| | | | | 12th 1,000, 8.7 |
| | | | | 13th 1,000, 9.2 |
| | | | | 14th 1,000, 9.7 |
| | | | | Over 14,000, 10.0 |

[1] From tax.

## STATE CORPORATE INCOME TAXES: 1967 [1]

Source: Tax Foundation

| STATE | RATE |
|---|---|
| Alabama...... | .......... 5.0% |
| Alaska....... | 18% of Federal income tax[2] |
| Arizona....... | 1st $1,000... 1.3% |
| | 2nd 1,000... 2.6 |
| | 3rd 1,000... 3.3 |
| | 4th 1,000... 4.0 |
| | 5th 1,000... 4.6 |
| | 6th 1,000... 5.9 |
| | Over 6,000... 6.6 |
| Arkansas..... | 1st $3,000.. 1.0% |
| | 2nd 3,000.. 2.0 |
| | Next 5,000.. 3.0 |
| | Next 14,000.. 4.0 |
| | Over 25,000.. 5.0 |
| California..... | .......... 7.0% |
| Colorado..... | .......... 5.0% |
| Connecticut[3].. | .......... 5.25% |
| Delaware..... | .......... 5.0% |
| District of Columbia... | .......... 5.0% |
| Georgia....... | .......... 5.0% |
| Hawaii....... | $25,000 or less..... 5.85% |

| STATE | RATE |
|---|---|
| | Over $25,000 ....... 6.435% |
| Idaho[4]....... | .......... 6.0% |
| Indiana[5]..... | .......... 2.0% |
| Iowa......... | $25,000 to 100,000.. 6.0% |
| | Over $100,000 .......... 8.0 |
| Kansas...... | .......... 4.5% |
| Kentucky..... | $25,000 or less.... 5.0% |
| | Over $25,000 7.0 |
| Louisiana..... | .......... 4.0% |
| Maryland[6].... | .......... 5.25% |
| Massachusetts[7] | ......... 6.765% |
| Michigan...... | .......... 1.0% |
| Minnesota[9]..... | .......... 8.5% |
| Mississippi.... | 1st $5,000.. 2.0% |
| | Over 5,000.. 3.0 |
| Missouri...... | .......... 2.0% |
| Montana...... | .......... 5.5% |
| Nebraska..... | 20% of individual income tax rate. |
| New Jersey[8]... | .......... 3.25% |

| STATE | RATE |
|---|---|
| New Mexico... | .......... 3.0% |
| New York[9].... | .......... 5.5% |
| North Carolina | .......... 6.0% |
| North Dakota.. | 1st $ 3,000.. 3.0% |
| | Next 5,000.. 4.0 |
| | Next 7,000.. 5.0 |
| | Over 15,000.. 6.0 |
| Oklahoma..... | .......... 4.0% |
| Oregon........ | .......... 6.0% |
| Pennsylvania.. | .......... 6.0% |
| Rhode Island[10] | .......... 6.0% |
| South Carolina | .......... 5.0% |
| Tennessee..... | .......... 5.0% |
| Utah[11]........ | .......... 6.0% |
| Vermont[12]..... | .......... 5.0% |
| Virginia....... | .......... 5.0% |
| West Virginia[13] | .......... 6.0% |
| Wisconsin..... | 1st $1,000.. 2.0% |
| | 2nd 1,000.. 2.5 |
| | 3rd 1,000.. 3.0 |
| | 4th 1,000.. 4.0 |
| | 5th 1,000.. 5.0 |
| | 6th 1,000.. 6.0 |
| | Over 6,000.. 7.0 |

[1] A special tax on financial institutions levied in all states is based either on net income or, usually, on the value of shares of capital stock. [2] Based on rates in effect Dec. 31, 1963. [3] If tax yield is greater, 2⅝ mills per dollar of asset value, or $30. [4] A license fee of $10 is required. [5] Based on adjusted gross income. [6] Domestic corporations deduct franchise taxes in excess of $25. [7] Tax on net income is supplemented by a levy of $6.15 per $1,000 of tangible property not subject to local taxes, plus 6.765% of net income, or $100, whichever is greater. Interstate corporations not subject to the corporate income tax pay 3.075% of net income. [8] Corporations pay added tax on net worth. [9] Alternative methods of computation are used if tax yield is greater. [10] If yield is greater, 40¢ on each $100 of corporate excess applies. [11] If yield is greater, 1/20 of 1% of the fair value of tangible property applies. [12] Provision made for a tax reduction when general fund surplus occurs. [13] Effective for taxable years starting after June 30, 1967.

## WHAT TIME IS IT?

If, 85 years ago, it had been possible to ask for the time at exactly the same moment in a number of American towns, a confusing variety of answers would have been forthcoming: 12:12 P.M. in New York, noon in Washington, 11:08 A.M. in Memphis, and so on across the nation. Yet each answer would have been correct in the town in which it was given, for "sun time" prevailed throughout much of the world until the 19th century neared its end.

The adoption of standard time in North America stems from the railroads' search for a solution to their chaotic schedules, which were based on at least 100 local time variations. In November, 1883, U.S. and Canadian rail companies agreed to set up zones for each 15 degrees of longitude (the longitude of Greenwich, England, served as the prime meridian),

with uniform time throughout each zone.

Most of the country went along quickly with this orderly system, but Congress did not pass a Standard Time Act until 1917; it also established daylight saving time (from late March to late October), but rural areas opposed this provision and it was repealed in 1919.

However, Congress in 1966 passed the Uniform Time Act, which directed all states to adopt daylight saving time from the last Sunday in April to the last Sunday in October, beginning in 1967. State legislatures could vote to exempt their entire state from daylight saving time. Full implementation of the law has not yet taken place. A few states are submitting a referendum to the voters in 1968 and others, with two time zones in their states, have asked for a realignment of the present zone boundary.

## STANDARD TIME ZONES

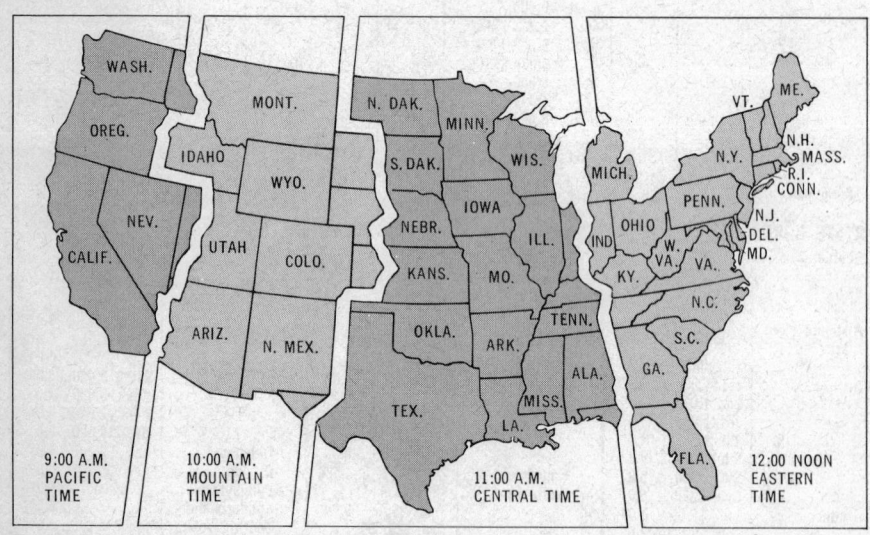

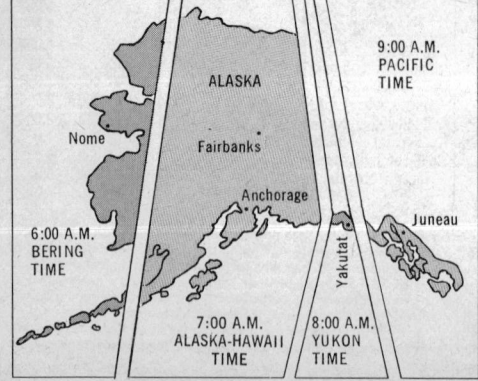

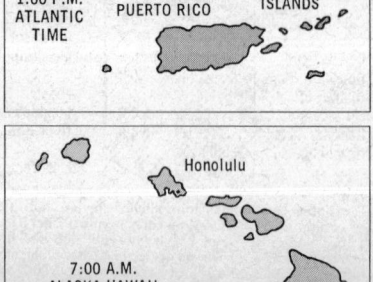

# THE CITIES

Wide World

Fire-bombed buildings burn in the background as a Michigan National Guardsman scans roof-tops for snipers during the week of rioting in Detroit that began on July 23, 1967.

## VIOLENCE IN THE CITIES

The worst city riots in recent U.S. history erupted during the long, hot summer of 1967. About 50 incidents of civil disorder occurred throughout the country. Total fatalities were in the vicinity of 80, with about 3,000 injuries and more than 7,000 arrests. Property damage was estimated at about $750,000,000.

Violence began in the summer of 1964 when the strains on overcrowded and blighted American cities erupted in something more ominous than rising crime rates and relief rolls. That year's ghetto riots were the first of the "long hot summers"—a phrase describing the time and mood of this modern urban turmoil.

In 1965 the major eruption in the Negro community of Watts, Los Angeles, shook the nation: 34 lives were lost and property damage totaled $50,000,000. In 1966 there were 30 minor disturbances across the country.

All this was a prelude to the long hot summer of 1967. The "summer" began early, with police-Negro clashes and vandalism in Chicago, Boston, Cincinnati, Buffalo, Hartford, and Waterloo, Iowa.

Then, on July 12, a group of Negroes gathered at the Fourth Police Precinct in Newark, N.J., to protest the alleged beating of a Negro taxi driver. Tempers flared—and the worst

racial urban outbreak since Watts was under way. Focus of the disturbance was the rundown, teeming Central Ward, home of the most underprivileged of Newark's 200,000 Negroes (half the city's population).

Windows smashed by roving bands left open invitations to looters. Fires tongued through tenements and stores. Snipers fired indiscriminately from tenement roofs. A force of 3,000 National Guardsmen and 375 city and state police was marshalled to break the resistance. After six days of rioting, the toll was 26 dead, 1,200 injured, and 1,316 arrested. Property damage amounted to $15,000,000, mostly to residences and stores in the Central Ward.

Like fireworks tossing sparks, the Newark riot touched off minor disturbances in the surrounding New Jersey towns of Plainfield, where one policeman was killed; New Brunswick; Montclair; and Rahway.

At 4:00 A.M. on July 23 police in Detroit broke up a gathering in a "blind pig" (an illegal drinking and gambling dive), arresting 73 persons. A protesting crowd gathered on 12th street in Detroit's West Side. A firebomb (Molotov cocktail) and several rocks landed near police, and a melee began and spread.

*(continued)*

## VIOLENCE IN THE CITIES (continued)

Looters broke into liquor, clothing, and furniture stores. Plumes of smoke arose, soon to turn blockfronts into walls of flame. Snipers went into action from rooftops. Eight hundred local and state police were soon joined by 1,500 National Guardsmen, and later by 4,700 U.S. paratroopers. When the disorder ended on July 26, the area resembled a ravaged battleground.

The Detroit riot, worst of its kind in U.S. history since the Civil War, lasted four days. The toll was 43 dead, more than 1,000 injured, and 3,500 arrested. Property damage was estimated at $500,000,000. Whole blocks had been leveled by 1,163 fires; 477 buildings had been damaged or destroyed. In the aftermath, political charges were traded between Michigan's Governor Romney and the White House over the timing of the dispatch of Federal troops to the scene.

Detroit's disorder set off lesser riots in the ring of smaller neighboring cities—Flint, Pontiac, Saginaw, Grand Rapids—and across the Ohio border in Toledo.

The riots—as Washington and local officials quickly pointed out—were not expressions of Negro demands for civil rights. Negro leaders joined in the official condemnation of the riots as lawless hoodlumism that needed to be brought swiftly under control. Many of those conspicuous in the riots were known criminals, and more than 300 of the rioters arrested in Detroit had previous criminal records.

Although advocates of "Black Power" harangued Negro crowds before several of the minor riots, the Federal Bureau of Investigation found no evidence of organized political incitement. Its manual on riot handling, subsequently circulated among the nation's police departments, advised on police tactics in mob situations and on counter-sniper procedures, warning against indiscriminate firing. The House of Representatives attached a rider to the 1967 crime bill making it a Federal offense to cross a state line to incite a riot.

The 1967 riots had curiously mixed causes. In some cases, such as in Newark's Central Ward—long a "basic training camp for the poor" from the South and other areas—squalid housing, an enormous problem scarcely improved by the inpouring of Federal slum money in the last five years, was a prime and clear cause. Poor housing, heavy unemployment, and resentment over racial slurs were prime causes of disorder in other areas such as New York's Puerto Rican East Harlem.

In other riot scenes, conditions were much better (as in Detroit, a high-wage town with many well-off Negroes and many "golden-door" opportunities for all non-whites) and the causes were harder to identify. Many of Detroit's underprivileged looked resentfully at those Negroes who had successfully escaped and whose middle-class homes were visible from the slum area. In New Haven's model, slumless city the summer's window-breaking, youthful Negro rioters inspired a headline describing the community as the place "where enough is not enough."

Losses from the riots fell almost exclusively on the Negro sections of the cities involved. Burned dwellings caused already overcrowded families to double up. Many destroyed local stores—mostly small retail shops that had extended credit to nearby residents—were permanently wiped out, since post-riot insurance rates rose so high as to discourage small businessmen. (In Watts only 3 of 40 destroyed businesses have been restored and only 5 new enterprises have located there since the 1965 riots.)

One consequence of the riots was that the House of Representatives drastically revised the Administration's anti-crime bill. The new bill provided strong anti-riot measures which were to be administered by the states.

As for the future of the long, hot summer, three factors must figure in any forecast:

(1) Although slum blight is being attacked in cities across the nation, it will be decades before "pressure-cooker tenements," a primary cause of 1967's riots, are replaced by clean airy dwellings.

(2) Usually riots do not happen twice in the same place. Riots which destroy Negroes' own facilities gain nothing and soon convince the community to put the pressure on disruptive elements. Also, riot-experienced police learn from past disorders how to improve community relations and prevent future riots.

(3) Education and experience are showing more underprivileged Negroes and other minority groups that their rising expectations can, with training, be fulfilled.

New Jersey National Guardsmen stand duty on Newark's riot-torn Springfield Avenue.

Wide World

# FOCUS ON THE NEWS

## URBAN RENEWAL

Prudential Insurance Co.

Boston's $150 million Prudential Center, built on the site of a former railroad yard, was completed in 1965.

At midcentury the world's most prosperous country found that it seriously suffered from an ancient symptom of poverty—the slum. Like a wealthy patient reacting to an unsuspected disease, the United States spent heavily for treatment. Beginning with Congressional passage of the landmark Housing Act of 1949, the United States has financed more than 2,000 urban renewal projects in more than 800 cities.

To this direct assault was added, in 1966, the Demonstration Cities and Metropolitan Development (or Model Cities) Act, designed to put $24,000,000 into the effort initially and far more later. These sums were earmaked for long-range planning of "total environment" (recreational-school-housing) aid to blighted areas. After riots in certain cities in 1967, however, Congress heavily cut back this program in order not to appear to be giving rewards to rioters.

Meantime, mammoth city projects already funded are going forward. Boston is adding to its bold renovation of Scolley Square, Pittsburgh is extending its Golden Triangle, Los Angeles is planning a western Rockefeller Center, and St. Louis is restoring its riverfront. Philadelphia has 80 renewal projects either completed or underway, including the largest residential-industrial renovation of all. New York is pushing its $220,000,000 West Side clean-up. Hartford's Constitution Plaza rehabilitated one of the most blighted areas in the Northeast. New Haven, recipient of more Federal aid per capita than any city, is now virtually slumless.

Is this massive overhaul effective medicine? By evidence from the Department of Housing and Urban Development, which is shifting funds from slum clearance to slum repair to get faster if less thorough improvement, the Model Cities program is proceeding too slowly to be effective in combating fast-spreading urban blight.

## U.S. CITIES: QUICK-REFERENCE INFORMATION

New York, N.Y. leads the list of U.S. cities in every statistical category except average per capita income, where it ranks slightly behind Washington, D.C., and San Francisco, California. "Population" and "Average Per Capita Income" figures, obtained from Sales Manage-

| CITY AND STATE | POPULATION | | CHIEF EXECUTIVE OFFICER | | | |
| | 1966 Estimate | Rank in Nation | Name | Title | Term Ends | Salary |
| --- | --- | --- | --- | --- | --- | --- |
| Akron, Ohio........ | 296,500 | 49 | John S. Ballard | Mayor | Dec. 1967 | $23,500 |
| Albuquerque, N. Mex. | 254,000 | 55 | G. B. Robertson | City Manager | Indefinite | 18,500 |
| Atlanta, Ga......... | 514,100 | 24 | Ivan Allen, Jr. | Mayor | Dec. 1969 | 20,000 |
| Baltimore, Md...... | 926,500 | 7 | Theodore R. McKeldin | Mayor | Nov. 1967 | 25,000 |
| Birmingham, Ala.... | 348,700 | 40 | Albert Boutwell | Mayor | Nov. 1967 | 22,500 |
| Boston, Mass....... | 615,400 | 17 | John F. Collins | Mayor | Dec. 1967 | 20,000 |
| Buffalo, N.Y........ | 480,900 | 28 | Frank A. Sedita | Mayor | Dec. 1969 | 26,000 |
| Charlotte, N.C...... | 254,600 | 54 | W. J. Veeder | City Manager | May 1969 | 26,500 |
| Chicago, Ill........ | 3,543,100 | 2 | Richard J. Daley | Mayor | April 1971 | 35,000 |
| Cincinnati, Ohio.... | 498,600 | 27 | William C. Wichman | City Manager | Indefinite | 35,000 |
| Cleveland, Ohio..... | 816,800 | 9 | Ralph S. Locher | Mayor | Nov. 1967 | 25,000 |
| Columbus, Ohio.... | 558,400 | 20 | M. E. Sensenbrenner | Mayor | Jan. 1968 | 30,000 |
| Dallas, Texas...... | 828,300 | 8 | W. Scott McDonald | City Manager | Indefinite | 28,000 |
| Dayton, Ohio....... | 265,400 | 53 | Graham W. Watt | City Manager | Indefinite | 25,000 |
| Denver, Colo....... | 502,200 | 26 | Thomas G. Currigan | Mayor | June 1971 | 14,000 |
| Des Moines, Iowa... | 206,700 | 66 | Tom Chenoweth | City Manager | Indefinite | 25,750 |
| Detroit, Mich...... | 1,612,100 | 5 | Jerome P. Cavanagh | Mayor | Jan. 1970 | 35,000 |
| El Paso, Texas..... | 325,000 | 43 | Judson F. Williams | Mayor | April 1969 | 9,600 |
| Fort Worth, Texas... | 402,500 | 30 | H. D. McMahan | City Manager | Indefinite | 22,500 |
| Hartford, Conn...... | 162,400 | 84 | Elisha C. Freedman | City Manager | Indefinite | 24,000 |
| Honolulu, Hawaii... | 342,400 | 41 | Neal S. Blaisdell | Mayor | Jan. 1969 | 30,000 |
| Houston, Texas..... | 1,147,400 | 6 | Louie Welch | Mayor | Jan. 1968 | 20,000 |
| Indianapolis, Ind.... | 519,200 | 23 | John Barton | Mayor | Dec. 1967 | 21,200 |
| Jacksonville, Fla.... | 197,300 | 70 | Hans G. Tanzler, Jr. | Mayor | Oct. 1968 | 16,500 |
| Jersey City, N.J..... | 268,000 | 52 | Thomas J. Whelan | Mayor | June 1969 | 30,000 |
| Kansas City, Mo.... | 546,800 | 22 | Carleton F. Sharpe | City Manager | Indefinite | 32,500 |
| Long Beach, Calif... | 380,700 | 35 | John R. Mansell | City Manager | Indefinite | 34,250 |
| Los Angeles, Calif... | 2,796,700 | 3 | Samuel W. Yorty | Mayor | June 1969 | 35,000 |
| Louisville, Ky....... | 390,400 | 31 | Kenneth Schmied | Mayor | Dec. 1969 | 12,000 |
| Memphis, Tenn...... | 614,400 | 18 | William B. Ingram, Jr. | Mayor | Dec. 1967 | 26,500 |
| Miami, Fla......... | 341,900 | 42 | Melvin L. Reese | City Manager | Indefinite | 27,563 |
| Milwaukee, Wis..... | 754,200 | 11 | Henry W. Maier | Mayor | April 1968 | 25,757 |
| Minneapolis, Minn... | 480,400 | 29 | Arthur Naftalin | Mayor | June 1969 | 18,000 |
| Mobile, Ala........ | 232,500 | 59 | Arthur R. Outlaw | Mayor | Oct. 1969 | 15,000 |
| Nashville, Tenn..... | 251,700 | 56 | C. Beverly Briley | Mayor | Aug. 1971 | 25,000 |
| Newark, N.J........ | 387,200 | 32 | Hugh J. Addonizio | Mayor | July 1970 | 35,000 |
| New Haven, Conn... | 150,900 | 91 | Richard C. Lee | Mayor | Dec. 1967 | 25,000 |
| New Orleans, La.... | 663,900 | 16 | Victor H. Schiro | Mayor | May 1970 | 25,000 |
| New York, N.Y...... | 8,025,700 | 1 | John V. Lindsay | Mayor | Dec. 1969 | 50,000 |
| Norfolk, Va......... | 324,500 | 44 | Thomas F. Maxwell | City Manager | Indefinite | 32,500 |
| Oakland, Calif...... | 385,700 | 34 | Jerome Keithley | City Manager | Indefinite | 32,800 |
| Oklahoma City, Okla. | 380,000 | 37 | Robert M. Tinstman | City Manager | Indefinite | 27,500 |
| Omaha, Nebr....... | 351,700 | 39 | A. V. Sorensen | Mayor | May 1969 | 17,500 |
| Philadelphia, Penn. | 2,051,700 | 4 | James H. J. Tate | Mayor | Jan. 1968 | 30,000 |
| Phoenix, Ariz....... | 512,500 | 25 | F. Robert Coop | City Manager | Indefinite | 25,000 |
| Pittsburgh, Penn.... | 555,600 | 21 | Joseph M. Barr | Mayor | Dec. 1969 | 25,000 |
| Portland, Oreg...... | 385,700 | 33 | Terry D. Schrunk | Mayor | Dec. 1968 | 23,500 |
| Providence, R.I..... | 186,100 | 73 | Joseph A. Doorley, Jr. | Mayor | Jan. 1971 | 20,000 |
| Richmond, Va....... | 217,500 | 61 | Horace H. Edwards | City Manager | Indefinite | 31,500 |
| Rochester, N.Y...... | 301,600 | 48 | Seymour Scher | City Manager | Indefinite | 26,500 |
| St. Louis, Mo....... | 696,200 | 14 | A. J. Cervantes | Mayor | April 1969 | 25,000 |
| St. Paul, Minn...... | 314,700 | 47 | Thomas R. Byrne | Mayor | June 1968 | 13,000 |
| Salt Lake City, Utah | 200,400 | 69 | J. Bracken Lee | Mayor | Jan. 1968 | 11,500 |
| San Antonio, Texas | 699,700 | 13 | B. Jack Shelley | City Manager | Indefinite | 27,500 |
| San Diego, Calif..... | 678,400 | 15 | Walter H. Hahn, Jr. | City Manager | Indefinite | 31,824 |
| San Francisco, Calif. | 730,700 | 12 | John F. Shelley | Mayor | Jan. 1968 | 38,365 |
| San Jose, Calif..... | 372,700 | 38 | A. P. Hamann | City Manager | Indefinite | 33,948 |
| Seattle, Wash....... | 574,400 | 19 | J. D. Braman | Mayor | Jan. 1970 | 23,000 |
| Syracuse, N.Y...... | 214,000 | 62 | William F. Walsh | Mayor | Dec. 1969 | 25,000 |
| Tampa, Fla......... | 315,200 | 46 | Dick A. Greco, Jr. | Mayor | Sept. 1971 | 22,500 |
| Toledo, Ohio....... | 380,200 | 36 | John W. Potter | Mayor | Oct. 1967 | 15,000 |
| Tulsa, Okla........ | 316,000 | 45 | J. M. Hewgley, Jr. | Mayor | May 1968 | 20,900 |
| Washington, D.C.... | 809,200 | 10 | Walter E. Washington | Commissioner | Feb. 1969 | 28,500 |
| Wichita, Kans....... | 281,700 | 50 | Russell E. McClure | City Manager | Indefinite | 25,800 |

ment, Inc., were computed in December 1966. "City Finances" data, for the fiscal year 1965–66, was released by the U.S. Department of Commerce. "Chief Executive Officer" and "Assessed Property Valuation" information was supplied by the individual cities in 1967.

| CITY FINANCES | | | ASSESSED PROPERTY VALUATION (in thousands) | AVERAGE PER CAPITA INCOME | CITY AND STATE |
|---|---|---|---|---|---|
| Revenues (in thousands) | Expenditures (in thousands) | Gross Debt (in thousands) | | | |
| $   39,074 | $   43,421 | $   60,723 | $   893,000 | $2,717 | ..........Akron, Ohio |
| 24,829 | 23,282 | 68,722 | 218,081 | 2,432 | ...Albuquerque, N. Mex. |
| 53,113 | 71,164 | 177,115 | 1,411,544 | 2,683 | ...........Atlanta, Ga. |
| 308,111 | 305,863 | 424,913 | 2,954,412 | 2,321 | ........Baltimore, Md. |
| 29,320 | 27,171 | 99,439 | 616,897 | 2,024 | ......Birmingham, Ala. |
| 312,856 | 307,897 | 200,577 | 1,530,752 | 2,403 | ........Boston, Mass. |
| 123,158 | 118,900 | 173,326 | 1,042,849 | 2,471 | .........Buffalo, N.Y. |
| 23,434 | 24,201 | 76,735 | 973,965 | 2,888 | ........Charlotte, N.C. |
| 455,218 | 418,481 | 965,479 | 10,981,953 | 3,101 | ..........Chicago, Ill. |
| 126,280 | 129,990 | 276,298 | 1,645,000 | 2,639 | ........Cincinnati, Ohio |
| 101,340 | 105,334 | 290,549 | 2,894,215 | 2,385 | ........Cleveland, Ohio |
| 48,061 | 56,348 | 161,283 | 1,497,598 | 2,496 | ........Columbus, Ohio |
| 69,592 | 82,650 | 225,234 | 3,127,380 | 3,057 | .........Dallas, Texas |
| 35,246 | 34,499 | 67,861 | 924,339 | 2,605 | .........Dayton, Ohio |
| 95,879 | 93,755 | 191,889 | 1,215,000 | 2,923 | .........Denver, Colo. |
| 20,184 | 19,484 | 20,454 | 343,000 | 3,215 | ......Des Moines, Iowa |
| 291,873 | 260,737 | 525,833 | 4,807,698 | 3,044 | ........Detroit, Mich. |
| 17,666 | 18,343 | 53,739 | 650,000 | 1,908 | .........El Paso, Texas |
| 30,698 | 30,837 | 110,769 | 1,081,444 | 2,411 | .....Fort Worth, Texas |
| 48,543 | 49,467 | 50,185 | 812,746 | 2,956 | ......Hartford, Conn. |
| 89,981 | 90,953 | 205,278 | 2,850,000 | 2,990 | ......Honolulu, Hawaii |
| 93,255 | 109,523 | 330,092 | 3,143,726 | 2,589 | .........Houston, Texas |
| 46,502 | 43,838 | 122,221 | 900,000 | 2,977 | ......Indianapolis, Ind. |
| 19,090 | 31,340 | 176,679 | 998,991 | 1,964 | ......Jacksonville, Fla. |
| 59,794 | 68,354 | 43,904 | 434,801 | 2,429 | .......Jersey City, N.J. |
| 64,479 | 67,850 | 179,683 | 1,188,085 | 2,845 | ......Kansas City, Mo. |
| 67,640 | 59,744 | 36,749 | 1,112,668 | 3,077 | .....Long Beach, Calif. |
| 347,997 | 313,381 | 934,301 | 6,677,425 | 3,254 | .....Los Angeles, Calif. |
| 66,443 | 68,568 | 194,281 | 1,630,983 | 2,499 | ........Louisville, Ky. |
| 109,503 | 119,755 | 483,481 | 1,446,989 | 2,227 | .......Memphis, Tenn. |
| 35,461 | 33,639 | 84,812 | 1,326,686 | 2,246 | ..........Miami, Fla. |
| 119,651 | 114,717 | 224,742 | 2,251,928 | 2,725 | .......Milwaukee, Wis. |
| 56,661 | 55,503 | 61,571 | 401,000 | 3,076 | ...Minneapolis, Minn. |
| 16,892 | 20,626 | 81,009 | 224,637 | 2,203 | ..........Mobile, Ala. |
| 92,642 | 104,593 | 189,649 | 944,291 | 2,368 | ........Nashville, Tenn. |
| 116,295 | 120,434 | 82,319 | 1,380,766 | 2,668 | .........Newark, N.J. |
| 39,342 | 40,666 | 85,976 | 582,009 | 2,698 | ......New Haven, Conn. |
| 73,665 | 81,039 | 163,926 | 1,146,477 | 2,412 | ......New Orleans, La. |
| 3,995,412 | 3,693,993 | 7,696,934 | 32,485,890 | 3,326 | ......New York, N.Y. |
| 68,870 | 67,802 | 126,711 | 508,000 | 2,157 | .........Norfolk, Va. |
| 55,679 | 47,451 | 39,293 | 732,952 | 3,038 | .........Oakland, Calif. |
| 34,128 | 43,427 | 240,748 | 529,910 | 2,585 | ...Oklahoma City, Okla. |
| 26,657 | 27,947 | 37,593 | 2,028,992 | 2,906 | .........Omaha, Nebr. |
| 326,109 | 331,911 | 907,178 | 4,383,357 | 2,496 | ....Philadelphia, Penn. |
| 54,048 | 60,330 | 172,596 | 663,601 | 2,520 | ........Phoenix, Ariz. |
| 80,066 | 81,936 | 133,047 | 1,261,944 | 2,559 | .......Pittsburgh, Penn. |
| 47,442 | 46,645 | 42,346 | 662,281 | 3,058 | .........Portland, Oreg. |
| 49,469 | 44,576 | 66,141 | 603,064 | 2,527 | .......Providence, R.I. |
| 64,260 | 66,510 | 108,718 | 1,001,205 | 2,510 | .........Richmond, Va. |
| 87,604 | 85,811 | 102,765 | 719,729 | 2,853 | ........Rochester, N.Y. |
| 106,882 | 108,008 | 137,854 | 1,700,000 | 2,545 | ..........St. Louis, Mo. |
| 37,920 | 44,800 | 89,617 | 240,656 | 3,036 | .........St. Paul, Minn. |
| 16,897 | 18,049 | 19,950 | 305,378 | 2,716 | ....Salt Lake City, Utah |
| 31,068 | 40,408 | 146,167 | 1,093,427 | 1,847 | ....San Antonio, Texas |
| 65,702 | 62,131 | 106,426 | 1,154,848 | 2,701 | ......San Diego, Calif. |
| 263,456 | 220,402 | 224,740 | 2,164,307 | 3,369 | ....San Francisco, Calif. |
| 38,531 | 38,122 | 68,964 | 742,032 | 2,953 | ......San Jose, Calif. |
| 72,687 | 69,673 | 251,179 | 959,081 | 3,289 | ........Seattle, Wash. |
| 51,420 | 48,791 | 69,793 | 424,468 | 2,781 | ........Syracuse, N.Y. |
| 29,325 | 34,837 | 105,217 | 678,235 | 2,153 | ..........Tampa, Fla. |
| 40,521 | 44,690 | 42,044 | 1,183,947 | 2,667 | ..........Toledo, Ohio |
| 18,820 | 23,649 | 121,573 | 495,776 | 2,830 | ..........Tulsa, Okla. |
| 399,473 | 402,106 | 236,186 | 6,520,331 | 3,367 | ......Washington, D.C. |
| 26,677 | 29,123 | 156,323 | 475,494 | 2,682 | ........Wichita, Kans. |

# GAZETTEER OF U.S. CITIES

## ATLANTA

The state capital, situated in northwestern Georgia near the Appalachian foothills. Elevation: 738 to 1,086 feet.

**HISTORY.** Atlanta, the metropolis of the Southeast, traces its origin to a cabin built by Hardy Ivy in 1833 on Creek Indian land. In 1837 a combine of railroad companies, seeking a rail center, founded the town of Terminus on the site. The town was incorporated as Marthasville in 1843, and two years later the name was changed to Atlanta. In 1847 Atlanta was chartered as a city.

Atlanta was an important Confederate supply depot during the Civil War. On September 1, 1864, after fierce resistance, the city fell to Union General William Tecumseh Sherman; most of the city was burned to the ground before Sherman began his famed march to the sea in November. Rebuilding after the war was rapid, and Atlanta soon developed into an important industrial and transportation center. It became the capital of Georgia *de facto* in 1868, and officially, by popular vote, in 1877. Atlanta was the scene of the Cotton States International Exposition in 1895. A great fire swept the city in 1917, destroying about 2,000 buildings.

**GENERAL.** The Atlanta metropolitan area, the largest in the Southeast, is one of the fastest growing in the country; its population has doubled since 1940. The city annexed 91 more square miles in 1952. The cultural, industrial, transportation, and communications nucleus of Georgia and neighboring states, Atlanta has also emerged in recent years as the financial center for Southeastern industry. The city ranks high in the production of aircraft, chemicals, food products, paper, and textiles. Massive new building projects such as the $18 million Municipal Stadium, home for new major league baseball and football teams, stand as symbols of a new city.

Of historical interest are the capitol and state library, built in 1899; the state archives building, housing a museum; the Cyclorama of the Battle of Atlanta, one of the three largest paintings in the world; Oakland Cemetery for the Civil War dead; and Fort McPherson. Wren's Nest, the former home of Joel Chandler Harris, creator of the Uncle Remus tales, is here. Atlanta is the seat of Emory University, Georgia Institute of Technology, Atlanta University, and Oglethorpe University.

The Atlanta *Constitution*, one of the country's great newspapers, is a leading voice of moderation in the South.

The $12 million Atlanta Memorial Cultural Center was under construction in 1967. The project, containing the High Museum of Art, the Atlanta School of Art, a symphony hall, and a fine arts library, is in memory of the more than 100 members of the Atlanta Art Association who died in a plane crash in 1962.

## BALTIMORE

Situated in northeastern Maryland, near Chesapeake Bay. Elevation: Sea level to 489 feet.

**HISTORY.** The site of Baltimore was first settled in the early 17th century; however, the town was not founded until 1729. Natural harbor facilities soon made the city one of the leading shipping points for tobacco and grain. In 1776, when Philadelphia was occupied by the British, Baltimore was the meeting place of the Continental Congress. Baltimore was incorporated as a city in 1796.

Shipbuilding, one of the city's early industries, received great impetus from the Revolution and the War of 1812; the famous Baltimore clippers were built here in the early 1800s. Baltimore's location near the eastern terminus of the National Road from Cumberland, Maryland, to St. Louis, Missouri, made it a major center of commerce. In 1825, however, after the opening of the Erie Canal in New York State, the city was faced with a rapid loss of trade. To combat this, Baltimore business leaders obtained a charter for the Baltimore & Ohio Railroad. Today the Baltimore & Ohio, one of the country's major rail lines, still operates under its original charter.

Although Maryland remained in the Union during the Civil War, Baltimore's inhabitants sympathized with the Confederacy, and in 1861 they attacked Union troops. After a disastrous fire in 1904, which destroyed about 1,300 buildings, a thoroughly replanned city emerged. In 1912, at the Democratic national convention here, Woodrow Wilson won the nomination for President on the 46th ballot after a dramatic struggle. During both world wars, Baltimore was a strategic supply-shipping and shipbuilding port.

In 1957 the Baltimore Urban Renewal and Housing Agency was established to execute a long-range redevelopment program. The 32-acre Charles Center, a major downtown renewal project, was begun in 1962, and a new civic center was completed the following year. The city's $260 million inner-harbor redevelopment program got under way in 1967. The massive complex will include a World Trade Center and new office, recreational, and housing facilities.

**GENERAL.** Baltimore is the sixth largest city in the country and an important commercial, industrial, and educational center. It is also one of the nation's principal ports for foreign and domestic trade. Shipbuilding, steel manufacturing, food processing, electronics, banking, insurance, and wholesale distributing are the leading industries today.

In Baltimore Harbor is Fort McHenry, whose bombardment by the British during the War of 1812 inspired Francis Scott Key to write *The Star-Spangled Banner*. Also of historical interest are the Maryland Historical Society, which contains the original manuscript of *The Star-Spangled Banner;* the Baltimore Cathedral, the oldest Catholic cathedral in the country; the U.S. frigate *Constellation,* built in Baltimore in 1779; and Westminster Churchyard, where Edgar Allan Poe is buried. Baltimore's 202-foot Washington Monument, erected between 1815 and 1829, is reportedly the first monument built to honor George Washington.

Among the city's fine educational institutions are Johns Hopkins University, and several schools of the University of Maryland.

The Congress of Racial Equality selected Baltimore as a "target city" in 1966 to combat alleged discrimination against Negroes. The city has been the scene of many racial demonstrations in recent years.

## BIRMINGHAM

Situated in north-central Alabama near the southern end of the Appalachian Mountains. Elevation: 496 to 1,060 feet.

**HISTORY.** Birmingham was founded and incorporated in 1871. A decade earlier the rich iron ore, coal, and limestone deposits in the surrounding area were used by Confederate forces to produce cannonballs and rifles.

With the expansion of the railroads and the development of the steel industry in the second half of the nineteenth century, Birmingham emerged as a prosperous industrial city. Its growth was interrupted only by the aftereffects of a money panic in 1900.

**GENERAL.** Birmingham, the "Pittsburgh of the South," is the largest city in Alabama and the leading iron and steel manufacturing center in the South. Other leading industries are the production of fabricated metals, chemicals, textiles, and machinery.

The shooting flames of Birmingham's steel furnaces are a dramatic sight against the nighttime sky. One of the city's oldest landmarks, the Sloss Furnace, built in 1882, is still in operation. Overlooking the city from the summit of Red Mountain is a towering statue of Vulcan, the Roman god of fire. Made entirely of pig iron from the surrounding area, it is one of the largest statues in the world.

The city, famous for its roses and dogwood trees, has many beautiful parks. Cultural attractions include the Birmingham Museum of Art, the Birmingham Symphony Orchestra, the civic ballet, and the annual Festival of Arts. The Arlington Historical Shrine, built in 1842, is one of Alabama's few remaining pre-Civil War homes. Birmingham-Southern College is here, as are the medical and dental schools of the University of Alabama.

A $25 million civic center is under construction on a 23-acre site in the heart of downtown Birmingham. Completion is planned for the city's centennial year in 1971.

## BOSTON

The state capital, situated in eastern Massachusetts on Boston Bay. Elevation: Sea level to 330 feet.

**HISTORY.** Boston was founded in 1630 by a group of Puritan colonists led by John Winthrop. By 1632 the settlement had become the capital of the Massachusetts Bay Colony and an important cultural center. The Boston Public Latin School, founded in 1635, and Harvard College in neighboring Cambridge, founded a year later, were the first American schools. A public library was established in 1653, and in 1704 the first colonial newspaper, the *News-Letter,* was published.

Boston's fine harbor made it one of the chief commercial cities in the colonies. Consequently it became an early focus of opposition to increasingly restrictive measures levied against the colonies by Parliament. The Boston Massacre in 1770 and the Boston Tea Party of 1773 were dramatic preludes to the American Revolution. Many acts of resistance to the British were planned in Faneuil Hall, and on April 19, 1775, the Revolution broke out at Lexington and Concord. The Battle of Bunker Hill was fought nearby in June 1775; Boston remained under siege until the British withdrew in March 1776.

After the war a long era of prosperity began. Ships built here sailed to the major world cities, and fortunes were made in shipping, textiles, and shoes. Boston families such as the Cabots, Lowells, and Lodges made Beacon Hill and Back Bay symbols of wealth and culture; their cultivated taste made Boston the "Athens of America." The influence of these prominent families continued long after the growth of industry and waves of immigration in the 19th century had changed Boston from a farm-surrounded commercial city to an industrial metropolis. Despite its wealth and conservative tendencies, Boston was a center of abolitionism before the Civil War.

In the 20th century New England began losing industry to the South, where labor costs were lower. For many years Boston languished in the memories of its earlier glory, surrounded by signs of poverty and decay. After World War II the newly developed electronics industry gave Boston a new commercial renaissance. Prudential Center, a massive reconstruction of the downtown area, and the new Government Center in Scollay Square reflect the dynamic spirit of the "new Boston."

**GENERAL.** Boston today remains the financial, intellectual, and commercial hub of New England and one of the nation's leading ports. Principal industries are electronics, printing, fishing, food processing, and the production of apparel, shoes, and machinery.

Boston is one of the most history-steeped cities of the nation. Its narrow streets, which run into broad avenues, and its colonial landmarks flanked by modern skyscrapers produce a charming contrast of past and present. Old North Church, South Meeting Hall, the Old State House, Paul Revere's house, King's Chapel, Boston Common, and Faneuil Hall stand as memorials to the Revolution. The oldest lighthouse in the country—Boston Light, erected in 1716—stands in Boston Bay. Also of historical interest are the Massachusetts

Historical Society, founded in 1791; the Boston Athenaeum, founded in 1857; the Mother Church, home of the Christian Science movement; and the State House. Boston's Symphony Orchestra, the New England Conservatory of Music, and the Museum of Fine Arts are monuments of culture. The frigate *Constitution*, built near here in 1797, is berthed in the Naval shipyard.

Boston's educational institutions include Simmons College, Boston University, and Northeastern University. Harvard University, Radcliffe College, and the Massachusetts Institute of Technology are in nearby Cambridge.

In the summer of 1967, Negroes rioted in the Roxbury section of Boston over a welfare department dispute.

Whites and Negroes are currently working together to develop a "model city" plan to rehabilitate about two square miles of slum, in which 80 per cent of the Negroes in the state live. The project will be financed by Federal grants under the new Demonstration Cities program.

## CHICAGO

Situated in northeastern Illinois, on Lake Michigan. Elevation: 577 to 673 feet.

**HISTORY.** Father Marquette and Louis Jolliet first visited the site of Chicago in 1673. Almost a century later Jean Baptiste Point du Sable set up a trading post here, and in 1804 he was succeeded by the first permanent settler, John Kinzie, known as the "father of Chicago." The garrison at nearby Fort Dearborn was massacred by Indians during the War of 1812, in one of the worst tragedies in American history.

After the opening of the Erie Canal in 1825, Chicago became a thriving commercial center for the newly opened settlements in Illinois. It was incorporated as a city in 1837. Development of its harbor for lake traffic brought more settlers and greater prosperity to the city. The first railroads came in the 1840s, and by the 1860s Chicago was a major rail hub. After the Civil War, meat-packing became a leading industry.

In 1871 the great Chicago fire broke out (according to legend it began when Mrs. O'Leary's cow kicked a lantern), killing several hundred people and causing damage estimated at $200 million. Chicago was promptly rebuilt, however, and its many new industries attracted immigrants from all over the world. Labor troubles led to violent episodes such as the Haymarket Square Riot of 1866 and the strikes at nearby Pullman in 1894.

The Columbian Exposition in 1893 was important in the development of American thought and art. Between the end of World War I and the middle 1930s, Chicago was the headquarters of Al Capone and the battleground of rival gangs.

**GENERAL.** The second largest city in the country, Chicago is an important nucleus of transportation, industry, and commerce. It is the world's largest railroad center, a busy airline

Picasso sculpture in front of Chicago's new Civic Center

and highway hub, and the major Great Lakes port. The Union Stockyards and large steel mills, food processing plants, and grain milling facilities are located here. In addition, Chicago produces machinery, electronics equipment, chemicals, clothing, and furniture.

There are many industrial and commercial landmarks, such as the Merchandise Mart, the largest commercial building in the world; the Board of Trade; the Midwest Stock Exchange; and the Water Tower, one of the sole remains of pre-1871 Chicago. Encircling the downtown business district is the Loop, so named because elevated trains and trolleys turn around here for their return trip.

Chicago was an important literary center in the early 20th century. Among writers associated with the city are Carl Sandburg, Theodore Dreiser, Eugene Field, Edgar Lee Masters, James T. Farrell, Ben Hecht, Charles MacArthur, and Nelson Algren. Cultural attractions include the Art Institute of Chicago, the Chicago History Museum, a fine public library, and a theater district on Randolph Street. The Chicago Symphony Orchestra and the Chicago Lyric Opera, organized in 1954, are among the finest in the nation. Adler Planetarium, Soldier Field, and Hull House, the first settlement house in the country, founded in 1889, are here.

In the late 1800s Louis H. Sullivan, D. H. Burnham, and John W. Root established Chicago's architectural reputation. The first skyscraper, designed by William Le Baron Jenney in 1883, was built here, and many of Frank Lloyd Wright's early houses are located in the vicinity. Today Chicago's impressive skyline is still expanding. The cylindrical Marina Towers Apartments and the new 50-story Civic Center building, the city's highest structure, have become new landmarks.

Educational institutions include the University of Chicago and the Illinois Institute of Technology.

## CLEVELAND

Situated in northeastern Ohio, on Lake Erie, at the mouth of the Cuyahoga River. Elevation: 570 to 1,050 feet.

HISTORY. Cleveland was laid out in 1796, in what was then the Northwest Territory, by Moses Cleaveland, a surveyor and ancestor of President Grover Cleveland. A permanent settlement was established by Lorenzo Carter in 1799, and in 1836 Cleveland was chartered as a city.

The completion of the Ohio and Erie Canal in 1832 and the arrival of the railroads in 1851 soon established the city as the most important transshipment point between the interior of Ohio and the eastern markets. During the Civil War, Cleveland was an important station of the underground railroad.

Located near the coal fields of Pennsylvania and accessible, via the Great Lakes, to the iron mines of Minnesota, Cleveland developed into a major ore port and a center of iron and steel production. Also the main refining area for the Pennsylvania oil fields, it was here that John D. Rockefeller founded the Standard Oil Company in 1870.

In the 1930s violence erupted over labor disputes with the steel companies. A newspaper strike in the winter of 1962–63 closed down the city's two major dailies for 129 days.

GENERAL. Cleveland is the metropolis of Ohio and a major Great Lakes port. Besides iron and steel production, its principal industries are the manufacture of electrical equipment, machine tools, automobile parts, and chemicals.

The Cleveland Museum of Art, Western Reserve Historical Society's Museum, The Mall, and Terminal Tower are notable sights. The Cleveland Symphony Orchestra is outstanding, and the Cleveland *Plain Dealer* is one of the leading newspapers in the country. Among the educational institutions are Case Institute of Technology and Western Reserve University.

Cleveland recently inaugurated a comprehensive urban renewal program, including a 163-acre area called Erieview.

In 1967 racial violence flared up in the city's Negro Hough district, which had been the scene of riots a year earlier.

## COLUMBUS

The state capital, situated in central Ohio, on the Scioto River. Elevation: 685 to 893 feet.

HISTORY. Columbus, located at almost the exact geographical center of the state, was laid out as the state capital by the Ohio General Assembly in 1812; however it did not take over government functions from Chillicothe until 1816.

It was incorporated as a borough that same year and as a city in 1834.

Linked with the rest of the country by canals in 1831, the National Road in 1833, and by railroads in 1850, Columbus soon became the chief commercial and transportation center for the surrounding area. During the Civil War, Camp Chase in Columbus was a prison camp for Confederate soldiers. In 1913 over 100 people died and much property was destroyed when the Scioto River flooded parts of the city.

GENERAL. Columbus is the hub of a road and rail network and the chief market for a rich farming region. Principal industries include the production of aircraft, electrical machinery, home appliances, foundry products, automobile parts, and shoes.

The city is the seat of Ohio State University and Battelle Memorial Institute for Industrial Research. Landmarks include the state capitol and office building, the Columbus Gallery of Fine Arts, and the library and museum of the state archeological society. The state fairgrounds are located here.

## DALLAS

Situated in north-central Texas on the Trinity River. Elevation: 390 to 686 feet.

HISTORY. John Neely Bryan, a Tennessee trader, built the first house here in 1841, and three years later he founded a village on the site. In 1858 Dallas was settled by the followers of the French social philosopher Charles Fourier after they abandoned their socialist community, La Réunion, across the river.

A fire in 1860 destroyed most of the town; however rebuilding was rapid. During the Civil War, quartermaster, commissary, and administrative headquarters for the Confederate Army were located here. Chartered as a city in 1871, Dallas soon developed as a major cotton-trading and railroad center, and subsequently as the financial hub of the Southwest. The Texas Centennial Exposition was held here in 1936.

GENERAL. Today Dallas has more millionaires among its residents than any other American city. Banking, insurance, electronics, aerospace, cotton, and oil are the mainstays of the city's well-balanced economy.

Important to the city's active cultural life are the Dallas Little Theater, the Dallas Theater Center, the Dallas Civic Opera, and the Dallas Symphony. There are two fine art museums, the Dallas Museum of Fine Arts and the Dallas Museum for Contemporary Crafts. Fair Park is the scene of the annual Texas State Fair, the largest state fair in the country, and the Cotton Bowl football game.

Also noteworthy are the Hall of State, housing two of the world's largest oil murals; and the new 52-story First National Bank Building, the tallest building west of the Mississippi. Dallas is the seat of the University of Dallas and Dallas Theological Seminary. Southern Methodist University is located in a nearby suburb.

# DENVER

The state capital, situated in north-central Colorado, in the Rocky Mountains. Elevation: 5,130 to 5,470 feet.

**HISTORY.** Denver was settled in 1858, incorporated in 1861, and named the capital of the Colorado Territory in 1867. Although most of the city was destroyed by fire in 1863, it was rapidly rebuilt. In the 1870s and 1880s, rich lodes of silver, gold, and copper were found in the nearby Rocky Mountains, giving rise to an influx of miners and fortune seekers.

Plush opera houses, featuring singers imported from the East to bring culture to the city, were surrounded by makeshift boardinghouses and noisy saloons, such as the famous Silver Dollar. Ornate mansions on the city's fine streets were often owned by illiterate miners who had made fortunes overnight.

As the boom quieted in the 1880s, Denver began its steady growth as a commercial, shipping and food-processing center. A private mint, formed here and purchased by the U.S. Government in 1862, is one of three Federal mints still in operation.

**GENERAL.** Denver is the financial and administrative hub of the Rocky Mountain region, an important commercial and manufacturing center, and a processing point for an extensive agricultural area. The Union Stockyards here rank among the nation's largest.

Situated in the foothills of the Rocky Mountains, the city is flanked by the snow-capped Rockies to the West and the vast expanse of the Great Plains to the East. Denver maintains the largest system of public parks and recreational facilities in the world, and is a major city for winter sports.

The local historical society has kept the city's past alive. Especially noteworthy are the Colorado State Historical Museum, the tomb of Buffalo Bill, and the Cody Museum. Cultural attractions include the Denver Art Museum, the Denver Museum of Natural History. The Denver *Post* is one of the Far West's finest newspapers.

Among the city's educational institutions are the University of Denver and the University of Colorado Medical School.

In 1959, the $35 million Courthouse Square development in downtown Denver was completed. A $30 million stockyard, planned to centralize Denver's extensive cattle-shipping facilities, and the Skyline Urban Renewal Project are presently under development.

# DETROIT

Situated in southeastern Michigan, on the Detroit River, between Lake St. Clair and Lake Erie. Elevation: 573 to 672 feet.

**HISTORY.** Antoine de la Mothe Cadillac, a French officer, founded a fort and settlement at the site of Detroit in 1701. The British gained control of the area in 1760 and thwarted an Indian attack three years later during Pontiac's Rebellion. In 1796 Detroit and its surrounding area passed to the United States, and from 1805 to 1847 it was the territorial and state capital of Michigan. Although Detroit fell to the British for a short time during the War of 1812, it was recaptured by William Henry Harrison in 1813. Two years later it was incorporated as a town, and in 1824 it received its charter as a city.

Accessible to both land and water transportation, Detroit grew steadily during the 1830s. From the middle of the 19th century it was a major shipping, shipbuilding, and manufacturing city. A thriving carriage trade induced Henry Ford to build his first automobile factory here in 1899. The subsequent development of the automobile industry has been responsible for the city's spectacular growth.

Labor strife is a part of Detroit's history, especially in the 1930s when the United Auto Workers and the automobile manufacturers clashed bitterly.

**GENERAL.** Detroit is the nation's third largest industrial city, the world's leading automobile manufacturing center, and a major shipping and railroad hub. Other industries include food processing, and the production of steel, machinery, and chemicals.

The Detroit Symphony Orchestra, the Detroit Institute of Art, the Detroit Historical Museum, and Civic Center are the city's main cultural attractions. Wayne State University and the University of Detroit are located here. On Belle Isle, in the Detroit River, is a park with magnificent gardens, a conservatory, a children's zoo, and an aquarium. The Henry Ford Museum and Greenfield Village, which contains Thomas Edison's laboratory, are located in nearby Dearborn.

In July, 1967, thousands of Negroes rioted throughout most of Detroit. The disorders were sparked by the arrest of about 80 Negroes at an illegal after-hours bar. To quell the disorders, National Guard troops and Army paratroopers were ordered in. This was the first time Federal troops were used to quell riots since the Detroit racial disorders in 1943. After nearly a week of rioting, deaths totaled 43 and property damage was estimated at over $200 million.

# HARTFORD

The state capital, situated in central Connecticut on the west bank of the Connecticut River. Elevation: Sea level to 280 feet.

**HISTORY.** Led by Thomas Hooker, a group of English colonists settled here in 1635 on the site of a Dutch trading post. In 1662, Charles II granted the Connecticut colonies a charter and Hartford was named the capital. The charter was subsequently hidden in a hollow tree in Hartford, the famed "Charter Oak," to prevent its seizure by New England's governor general. In 1689, however, the charter was fully reinstated. In 1784 Hartford was incorporated as a city.

The Hartford Convention met here in 1814 to protest the War of 1812 and the growing power of the Federal government. Hartford and New Haven were joint capitals of Connecticut until 1875.

**GENERAL.** Long known as the insurance capital of the world, Hartford is also a major manufacturing center for such precision equipment as firearms, machine tools, typewriters, and aircraft engines. The Hartford *Courant,* first published in 1764, is the oldest continuously published daily newspaper in the nation.

Interesting landmarks include the Old State House, designed by Charles Bulfinch and built in 1796; the Connecticut State Capitol Building, which houses many historic relics, paintings, and statues; the Wadsworth Athenaeum; and the Harriet Beecher Stowe House. Among the educational institutions here are Trinity College, the University of Hartford, and several branches of the University of Connecticut.

Hartford's Constitution Plaza urban renewal area has brought new life to the city's once blighted downtown business section. The Plaza's handsome office and commercial buildings tower above landscaped walkways and reflecting pools.

Statue of Kamehameha I, draped with leis, stands before Judiciary building in Honolulu's Civic Center.

## HONOLULU

The state capital, situated on the southeastern coast of the island of Oahu, Hawaii. Elevation: Sea level to 951 feet.

**HISTORY.** Polynesians probably migrated here in the eighth century; however, the first European, William Brown, did not enter the harbor until 1793. By 1820 the first Christian missionaries had arrived. Honolulu became the seat of the powerful Kamehameha dynasty, which had succeeded in unifying the country in 1810, and in 1845 it was named the permanent capital of the kingdom of Hawaii.

The city's strategic location halfway between America and Asia and its excellent natural harbor facilities were important factors in its growth. During the 19th century the city was occupied at various times by Russian, British, and French forces. After U.S. annexation of Hawaii in 1898, Honolulu emerged as an important commercial city.

Following the bombing of Pearl Harbor on December 7, 1941, Honolulu became a major staging area for U.S. forces in the Pacific and an important Naval base. When Hawaii became a state in 1959, Honolulu remained the capital.

**GENERAL.** In recent years the rise in tourism, the boom in construction, and the expansion of industry have made Honolulu the commercial and population center of the state. Sugar and pineapple processing continue to be the major industries.

Honolulu lies on a narrow plain between the Koulau Mountains and the sea. The city's natural beauty, mild climate, and exotic mixture of Caucasian, Asiatic, and Polynesian people have made it a popular year-round tourist attraction. Nearby are excellent beaches, including famous Waikiki. Other points of scenic beauty are Punch Bowl and Diamond Head, extinct craters; Koko Head, a coconut-shaped mountain; and Nuuanu Pali, offering the most spectacular view on the island.

Notable institutions are the Honolulu Academy of Arts, which houses part of the Kress collection of Italian Renaissance paintings; the Tennent Art Foundation; and the Bishop Museum, containing exhibits of Polynesia. Kapiolani, the city's largest park, contains a zoo, an aquarium, and Waikiki Shell, home of the Honolulu Symphony Orchestra.

Iolani Palace, the state capitol and former home of Hawaiian kings, is the only royal palace in the United States. Also located here are Honolulu International Center, a 22-acre complex of public buildings, and the University of Hawaii.

## HOUSTON

Situated in southern Texas, on the Gulf Coast plain, near Galveston Bay. Elevation: Sea level to 83 feet.

**HISTORY.** Founded in 1836 by J. K. and A. C. Allen, Houston was named for Sam Houston, hero of the Battle of San Jacinto, by which Texas gained independence from Mexico. It was the capital of the Texas Republic from 1837 to 1839.

Although Houston grew into a prosperous railroad, cotton, and cattle center during the 19th century, its development as a major commercial city did not begin until the completion in 1914 of a ship channel that linked the city with Galveston Bay, making it a deepwater port. The opening of the Gulf Coast oil fields in the 1920s added greatly to the city's prosperity, and during World War II, shipbuilding emerged as a major industry.

**GENERAL.** Houston is the largest city in the South and the largest inland port in the country. It has direct air connection to most of South America and many European cities, and is a major railroad hub. Leading products include petroleum, cotton, steel, and chemicals.

Known as a boom town during World

*Hawaii Visitors Bureau*

War II, Houston's population and industries are still increasing rapidly. To keep pace with the population and business expansion, a network of highways has been constructed through the downtown area and many residential sections. Located south of Houston is the National Aeronautics and Space Administration's Manned Spaceflight Center, headquarters for future flights to the moon and beyond.

A fine symphony orchestra has attracted at various times such permanent conductors as Efrem Kurtz, Leopold Stokowski, Sir Thomas Beecham, and Sir John Barbirolli. Houston has a Museum of Fine Arts, a Museum of Natural Science, a planetarium, and an outstanding system of parks and recreational facilities. The Astrodome, built in 1965 at a cost of $31.6 million, is the only completely enclosed sports arena in the world.

Houston is the seat of Rice University, the University of Houston, and the 164-acre Texas Medical Center, one of the largest and finest in the nation.

## INDIANAPOLIS

The state capital, situated in central Indiana. Elevation: 664 to 845 feet.

**HISTORY.** Indianapolis was settled in 1820, chosen as the state capital in 1825, and incorporated as a city in 1847. Toward the end of the 19th century the discovery of natural spas nearby and the birth of the automobile industry gave impetus to the city's growth. Today it is the largest city without water transportation in the country.

**GENERAL.** Located in a rich agricultural area, Indianapolis is one of the nation's major corn, grain, and livestock markets and the commercial, transportation, and industrial heart of Indiana. Leading industries are food processing, electronics, and the production of heavy machinery and pharmaceuticals.

The homes of Benjamin Harrison, James Whitcomb Riley, and Booth Tarkington are preserved here as historical monuments. The 284.5-foot-high Soldiers and Sailors Monument, completed in 1901, is the second highest monument in the country. Also of interest are the state library and historical building, and the John Herron Art Institute. The American Legion has its national headquarters here. Educational institutions include Butler University and the University of Indiana Medical Center.

Two of the city's important annual events are the Memorial Day 500-mile automobile race, held at the Indianapolis Motor Speedway, and the Indiana State Fair.

A 55-acre renewal development is under way.

## LOS ANGELES

Situated in southern California, on San Pedro Bay, near the Pacific coast. Elevation: Sea level to 5,074 feet.

**HISTORY.** In 1769 a Spanish expedition headed by Gaspar de Portolá visited the site of Los Angeles in search of the "lost" port of Monterey. Twelve years later Spaniards founded El Pueblo de Nuestra Señora la Reina de los Angeles de Porciuncula (the Town of Our Lady the Queen of the Angels of Porciuncula), later shortened to Los Angeles. An important cattle-ranching area, Los Angeles was at various times the seat of Spanish and Mexican government in Alta California, that part of Mexico northwest of the Gulf of California.

In 1846, during the Mexican War, the town was taken by American troops. When California entered the Union four years later, Los Angeles was incorporated as a city.

Two rail lines linked Los Angeles with the Eastern seaboard: the Southern Pacific in 1876 and the Santa Fe in 1885. The discovery of oil in the late 19th century marked the beginning of the city's great commercial growth, which was further stimulated by the completion of the Panama Canal in 1914.

The motion picture industry settled here in the 1920s, followed in later years by radio. Today, with the emergence of television, Los Angeles continues to be the entertainment capital of the West.

**GENERAL.** Los Angeles and its surrounding area comprise one of the nation's leading aircraft and citrus-fruit centers. Other important industries are motion pictures, television, food processing, and the production of machinery and chemicals.

The Los Angeles area consists of dozens of independent municipalities that are incorporated in Los Angeles County, and some of them are completely surrounded by the city of Los Angeles. Thus, for example, a bus route traversing some 15 miles may need as many as six franchises from various local governments. In addition, there is no coordination in municipal planning, since each locality is highly protective of its rights.

When visitors speak of "Los Angeles," they usually refer to other cities within the county rather than Los Angeles itself. The famed beaches of southern California, for instance, form a crescent along the western edge of the city occupied by the municipalities of Malibu, Santa Monica, Venice, Manhattan Beach, Hermosa Beach, Redondo Beach, Long Beach, and Huntington Beach. Hollywood, home of the movie industry, is within the Los Angeles city limits. The central part of the county—Comp-

Los Angeles County Music Center

All-Year Club

ton, Lynwood, Downey, Norwalk, Torrance—is the industrial heart of Los Angeles. Pasadena, located to the east of the main part of Los Angeles, is the home of the Huntington Library and Museum, and the annual Tournament of Roses and the Rose Bowl football game on New Year's Day.

Within easy driving distance of Los Angeles are San Bernardino, Riverside, and the beginning of the southern California desert. Big Bear Lake, near San Bernardino, is a popular vacation spot. The San Fernando Valley, north of Los Angeles proper, is a large residential region, consisting of such communities as Sunland, Tujunga, San Fernando, and Van Nuys.

Los Angeles has many museums, art galleries, libraries, legitimate theaters, and a symphony orchestra. Concerts are given in the huge outdoor Hollywood Bowl. In late 1964 and early 1965 the $33.5 million Music Center and the $11.5 million Los Angeles County Museum of Art were opened.

There are many unusual reminders of the city's Spanish and Indian heritage, such as the Pueblo de Los Angeles State Historical Monument. Contained within this unique area are Olvera Street, the oldest street in Los Angeles; Old Mission Church, the oldest church in the city; and Old Spanish Plaza, the original center of the city.

Major tourist attractions in addition to the beaches, are Disneyland, in nearby Anaheim; Santa Catalina Island, in the Pacific Ocean; Laguna Beach, the art center of southern California; Marineland; and the movie industry, located in Hollywood, Beverly Hills, Culver City, and Universal City.

Los Angeles is the seat of the University of California at Los Angeles, the University of Southern California, and Claremont College.

In August, 1965, more than 30 persons were killed and an area of 45 square miles was devastated when rioting broke out in Watts, the predominantly Negro section of Los Angeles. The combined efforts of city, county, and state police, plus 15,000 National Guard troops, were required to bring the outbreak under control.

## LOUISVILLE

Situated in northwestern Kentucky, on the Ohio River. Elevation: 382 to 761 feet.
**HISTORY.** The site of Louisville was laid out in 1773 by General George Rogers Clark, the explorer and Revolutionary general, and settled six years later. The Virginia legislature established the town of Louisville in 1780, naming it in honor of King Louis XVI of France. General Clark built Fort Nelson here in 1782, which served as the headquarters for his expeditions to the Northwest.

Incorporated as a city in 1828, Louisville was a portage place around the falls of the Ohio River until the opening of the Louisville and Portland canal in 1830. The city subsequently became an important river port for western traffic; its importance as a transportation hub increased with the arrival of the railroads in 1851. During the Civil War Louis-

ville was an important base for Union forces despite a bitter division of loyalty among its citizens.
**GENERAL.** Louisville is one of the most important industrial, financial, shipping, and market points in the South. The largest electrical and Neoprene rubber plants in the world are located here. Other important industries are distilling, tobacco processing, oil refining, and meat-packing.

Major cultural institutions include the J. B. Speed Museum, one of the South's finest art museums; the Filson Club, with a Kentuckian library and museum; the Kentucky Opera Association; the Society for Arts in Louisville; and the Ranch Memorial Planetarium at the University of Louisville. Churchill Downs, the scene of the annual Kentucky Derby, and the new $15 million State Fair Grounds have made the city popular as a tourist spot.

The University of Louisville is here. The Louisville *Courier-Journal* is one of the nation's great newspapers.

## MEMPHIS

Situated in southwestern Tennessee, on the Mississippi River. Elevation: 195 to 335 feet.
**HISTORY.** The French explorer La Salle built Fort Prudhomme on the bluffs of Memphis overlooking the Mississippi River in 1682. For nearly a hundred years the area was involved in the imperial rivalries of Great Britain, France, and Spain. In 1797, the United States built a fort here, and in 1819 the city was laid out. By 1849, the year it was incorporated as a city, Memphis had become an important Mississippi River port with great steamboats, gambling casinos, and glittering wealth.

The prosperous years ended with the fall of the city to Union forces on June 6, 1862. After the Civil War, a series of yellow fever epidemics occurred, during which time almost 25,000 people fled the city. Bankrupt and depopulated, Memphis was forced to surrender its charter to the state in 1879, and existed only as a tax district until it was granted a new charter in 1891.
**GENERAL.** Besides its importance as a river port, Memphis is one of the world's largest markets for cotton and hardwood lumber. Leading products are chemicals, tires, paper, farm equipment, and cottonseed oil.

Cultural attractions include the Memphis Museum and the Brooks Memorial Art Gallery, housing part of the Kress collection of Italian paintings. Also of interest are Confederate Park, containing the ramparts used in defense against Federal gunboats in 1862, and the Memphis Cotton Exchange. Memphis's Beale Street was immortalized by jazz composer W. C. Handy. The Cotton Carnival and the Mid-South Fair are held here annually.

Memphis is the seat of Southwestern at Memphis University, Memphis State University, the medical divisions of the University of Tennessee, and LeMoyne College.

Several large-scale urban redevelopment programs are presently under way.

## MIAMI

Situated in southeastern Florida, on Biscayne Bay at the mouth of the Miami River. Elevation: Sea level to 30 feet.

HISTORY. Miami was founded in 1870 at the site of Fort Dallas, a major Federal installation in the war against the Seminoles. In 1896, the year Miami was incorporated as a city, the financier Henry M. Flagler extended the Florida East Coast Railroad to Miami, built the Royal Palm Hotel, and dredged the city's harbor. This marked the beginning of Miami's development as a resort, and by 1910 the economy was booming.

In the 1920s Miami and the surrounding area were the scene of unchecked land speculation in which fortunes were lost. Despite the destructive effects of huge hurricanes in 1926 and 1935, the city has developed into one of the nation's leading vacation centers.

GENERAL. Miami is the principal gateway to Latin America, and an important rail, air, and shipping point. Also important to the city's economy are aircraft repairing and the manufacture of apparel and metal products.

The greater Miami area is renowned for its luxurious resort hotels and fine beaches. Noteworthy attractions include Bayfront Park, containing an outdoor amphitheater; the Civic Auditorium; the Miami Seaquarium; and Vizcaya, formerly the estate of James Deering and now the Dade County Art Museum. Nearby is Everglades National Park, a preserve for tropical birds and flora.

Of interest to sporting enthusiasts are horse racing at Hialeah, Tropical, and Gulfstream parks, dog racing, jai-alai, deep sea fishing, and the annual Orange Bowl football game.

## MILWAUKEE

Situated in southeastern Wisconsin on Lake Michigan. Elevation: 577 to 799 feet.

HISTORY. French missionaries Marquette and Saint-Cosme and the French explorer La Salle visited the site of Milwaukee in the late 17th century. In 1795 the North West Company established a trading post, and in 1818 Solomon Juneau, an agent of the American Fur Company, settled here and surveyed the site. In 1835 the settlement merged with several neighboring villages to form Milwaukee, and in 1846 the city was incorporated.

Of great importance to the city's economic, political, and cultural development was the arrival of German immigrants after 1848. In the following decades Milwaukee grew as a shipping hub, and became famous for its brewing and meat-packing industries. Milwaukee was an early center of labor unionism. The Knights of Saint Crispin were organized by shoemakers in 1867, and in 1886 the Social Democratic Party was formed here. Milwaukee has had three Socialist mayors since 1910.

With the opening of the St. Lawrence Seaway in 1959 and extensive Federal improvements in its harbor facilities, Milwaukee has become an important Great Lakes port.

GENERAL. Milwaukee is the world's largest beer producer and a major meat-packing center. Other leading products include construction machinery, electrical equipment, diesel and gasoline engines.

Situated on the western shore of Lake Michigan, the city has many beautiful lakeshore drives and parks. Scenic attractions include Whitnall Park, containing every variety of tree and shrub found in the state; Estabrook Park; Mitchell Park's unusual sunken gardens; and the Milwaukee County Zoo. Also notable are the Milwaukee County Museum; the Milwaukee Art Center; the Milwaukee Auditorium and Arena, one of the largest and finest convention and exposition buildings in the country; and the city's world-famous breweries, offering tours to the public.

Marquette University, the University of Wisconsin at Milwaukee, Milwaukee-Downer College, and the Layton School of Art are among the city's educational institutions.

In 1965, on the 119th anniversary of Milwaukee's incorporation, a massive $112 million urban renewal project was inaugurated.

## NEW ORLEANS

Situated in southeastern Louisiana, on the Mississippi River and Lake Pontchartrain. Elevation: 5 feet below sea level to 25 above.

HISTORY. New Orleans, named in honor of the Duke of Orleans, was founded in 1718 by the Sieur de Bienville. Made the seat of French government in Louisiana in 1722, the settlement soon became an important port. By the secret Treaty of Fontainebleau in 1762, it passed to Spain, but the dominating influence on its cultural and economic development remained French.

Returned to France in 1803, the city came under U.S. jurisdiction at the time of the Louisiana Purchase, the same year. An important stopover on the southern routes to the West, New Orleans flourished as a cotton and slave-trade center. After the Battle of New Orleans on January 8, 1815, the city's prosperity reached unparalleled heights. During this era of spectacular wealth, New Orleans evolved a gay, glamorous way of life, strongly influenced by its large Creole population. It was the capital of Louisiana until 1852, and again from 1865 to 1880.

The city's golden age ended with its capture during the Civil War by Admiral David Farragut in 1862 and subsequent occupation by Union troops under General Benjamin Butler, followed by the hard years of the Reconstruction. Not until the end of World War I, when oil was discovered in Louisiana and sugar and cotton became commercially important once again, did New Orleans regain its former prosperity. A space-age rocket production plant, completed in the 1960s, has been a major development in the city's economic life.

GENERAL. Today New Orleans is the nation's second largest port and a major nucleus of industry, petroleum production, finance, and trade. The largest sugar refinery in the world is located here. Other important industries are aerospace, shipbuilding, and tourism.

New Orleans is both an Old World city and a part of the American South. The Vieux Carré (French Quarter), which comprised the original settlement, is a popular tourist attraction. Among the interesting sites here are Royal Street (Rue Royale), the French Market on Decatur Street, and the Cabildo, built in 1795, formerly the headquarters of the Spanish governor and now the home of the Louisiana State Museum. Dixieland jazz was born in the famous night clubs on Bourbon and Basin streets.

Other landmarks include the Isaac Delgado Museum of Art; the Hibernia Tower, the highest point in the city; and the new International Trade Center. The Lake Pontchartrain Causeway completed in 1956 is the longest overwater highway bridge in the world.

The colorful Mardi Gras celebration, held every winter, is one of the most popular festivals in the country. The city's annual Mid-Winter Sports Carnival is climaxed by the Sugar Bowl football game on New Year's Day.

Among the city's educational institutions are Tulane and Loyola universities, and the medical center of Louisiana State University.

The Port of New Orleans is being improved and expanded under a ten-year $133 million program.

## NEW YORK

Situated in southeastern New York State, on the Hudson and East rivers, Long Island Sound, and the Atlantic Ocean. Elevation: Sea level to 410 feet.

HISTORY. In 1524 Giovanni da Verrazano, a Florentine, became the first European to visit what is now New York. Henry Hudson, in 1609, sailed his ship *Half Moon* through New York Bay and up the Hudson River as far as Albany. Hudson's explorations led to the first permanent European settlements, and in 1625 the colony of New Netherland was established. Its capital, New Amsterdam, was situated at the southern tip of Manhattan Island. In 1626 Peter Minuit of the Dutch West India Company bought the entire island from its Indian inhabitants for the equivalent of $24 in trinkets and beads. In 1664 the city was seized by the English for the Duke of York, for whom it was renamed. It was again under Dutch control for a brief period in 1673–74.

Kings College, now Columbia University, was founded in 1754. In the succeeding years New York became a center of opposition to British policy. In 1775 the revolutionary Sons of Liberty forced Governor William Tryon and the British colonial government to flee the city. Several battles were fought in New York and the surrounding area in the first year of the Revolutionary War. The British, under General William Howe, recaptured the city in 1776, and it remained under their control throughout the war.

New York was the nation's first capital, from 1789 to 1790; here George Washington was inaugurated for his first term and gave his Farewell Address. Until 1797 the city was also the capital of New York State. Banks and stock exchanges were formed, and commerce began to grow. By 1790 it was the largest city in the country. In the early years there was fierce commercial competition among New York, Boston, and Philadelphia. In 1825, however, the Erie Canal opened water navigation from Lake Erie to the Hudson River. It gave a tremendous impetus to New York's growth, and allowed it to far outdistance its rivals. Seven years later the New York and Harlem Railroad stretched its first tracks northward along the Hudson, the first component of the giant New York Central System. By 1840, New York was the largest port in the country.

About this time immigration began in earnest —first by the Irish, and in succeeding decades by Italians, Germans, Scandinavians, Chinese, Spanish, middle Europeans, Middle Easterners, and Englishmen. It was with Irish immigrants that Tammany Hall, the New York County Democratic machine, built its power. William Marcy Tweed (1823–78), one of the most powerful political bosses in the nation's history, and his Tammany associates defrauded New York City of more than $20 million.

During these decades, New York had been expanding northward from the tip of Manhattan. By 1874 the entire island was included in New York City, and in that year the city crossed the Harlem River, to the north, and annexed parts of Westchester County. In 1898 New York assumed its present form. The Bronx, north of the Harlem River, was made a separate borough. New York annexed the independent City of Brooklyn and Queens County, both on the western end of Long Island, and Staten Island, close to the New Jersey shore, to become Greater New York. Each borough is also a county (Manhattan is New York County, Staten Island is Richmond County, Queens and the Bronx are counties with the same names, Brooklyn is Kings County), with its own government, subordinate to the city government.

The Flatiron Building, built in 1902 and still standing, was the first New York skyscraper. The first subway was constructed in 1904, and the first of numerous bridges began to span the rivers enclosing Manhattan Island. Today the most notable bridges are the George Washington, linking Manhattan with New Jersey; the Williamsburg, Brooklyn, and Manhattan, between Manhattan and Brooklyn; the Queensboro, between Manhattan and Queens; the Triboro, between Manhattan, Queens, and the Bronx; the Bronx-Whitestone and the Throgs Neck, between Queens and the Bronx; and the Verrazano-Narrows, opened in 1964, linking Staten Island with Brooklyn. This bridge, the longest suspension span in the world, was the first vehicular link between Staten Island and the rest of New York City.

New York is also linked by many tunnels. The principal ones are the Holland and Lincoln, between Manhattan and New Jersey; the Brooklyn-Battery, between the southern tip of

The New York Times

Drum-shaped Madison Square Garden, completed in 1967

Manhattan and Brooklyn; and the Queens-Midtown, between Manhattan and Queens.

Within the city limits are the world's financial headquarters, one of the two principal theater districts in the world, and the headquarters of some of the world's largest corporations. New York's street names have become symbols for industries, nationalities, and conditions of affluence: Wall Street, Seventh Avenue, Broadway, Mott Street, Sutton Place, Fifth Avenue, Madison Avenue, and Park Avenue.

Educational institutions include Columbia, New York, and Fordham universities, the City University of New York, and Cooper Union.

The Empire State Building, the world's tallest building, the United Nations Headquarters, the Pan Am Building, the Seagram Building, Lever House, the Chrysler Building, Chase Manhattan Plaza, and others enhance the famous New York skyline.

The new 22,000-seat Madison Square Garden, built on the former site of Pennsylvania Station, was completed in 1967. A $575 million World Trade Center is being sponsored by the Port of New York Authority. The center's two 110-story towers, to be constructed on a 16-acre site in downtown New York, are scheduled for completion in 1970.

## PHILADELPHIA

Situated in southeastern Pennsylvania, at the confluence of the Delaware and Schuylkill rivers. Elevation: Sea level to 441 feet.

**HISTORY.** The site of Philadelphia was originally settled by Swedes in the early 17th century. In 1682, William Penn founded a Quaker settlement here, naming it Philadelphia—from the Greek, meaning "Brotherly Love." The city's cultural and commercial growth was rapid, and by the time of the Revolution it was one of the two leading colonial cities. The First Continental Congress met in Carpenter's

Hall in 1774, and Independence Hall witnessed the meeting of the Second Continental Congress the following year and the signing of the Declaration of Independence on July 4, 1776.

The U.S. capital was located here in 1777 and 1778, except for a brief period of British occupation, and again from 1790 to 1800. During these years, two momentous events in the nation's history occurred here: the adoption of the Articles of Confederation in 1778 and the drafting of the United States Constitution in 1787. Philadelphia was also the seat of the Pennsylvania government until 1799.

In the early 19th century Philadelphia was the country's leading financial city, and the site of both Banks of the United States—the first from 1791 to 1811, and the second from 1816 to 1836.

Philadelphia was an important focus of the abolitionist movement long before the outbreak of the Civil War. In 1833 William Lloyd Garrison organized the American Anti-Slavery Society here, and during the war the city was a major station of the underground railroad.

In 1876 the Centennial Exposition marking the 100th anniversary of American Independence was held here.

**GENERAL.** While growing into one of the nation's principal cities, Philadelphia carefully nurtured its traditional culture. Among the notable institutions here are the Pennsylvania Academy of Fine Arts, the American Philosophical Society, the Franklin Institute and the Fels Planetarium, the Philadelphia Museum of Art, the Rodin Museum, the Academy of Natural Science, and the University of Pennsylvania Museum. The Philadelphia Symphony Orchestra is one of the finest in the country.

In Independence National Historical Park are Independence Hall, where the Liberty Bell is housed; Carpenter's Hall; and Congress Hall. Also of historical interest are Old Swedes' (Gloria Dei) Church, the oldest church in the city; Elfreth's Alley, one of the nation's oldest streets; and the Betsy Ross House. One of the three remaining U.S. mints is here. Fairmount Park, one of the largest in the world, contains many historic monuments and the country's oldest zoo.

Philadelphia has many fine educational institutions, among them the University of Pennsylvania, Temple University, Drexel Institute of Technology, the Curtis Institute of Music, the Pennsylvania Academy of Fine Arts, Hahnemann Medical College, and Jefferson Medical College.

The city continues to be an important commercial and manufacturing center. Leading industries include printing and publishing, shipbuilding, oil refining, and the manufacture of machinery, chemicals, and textiles.

In the 1950s a far-sighted urban renewal program was initiated; as part of this program many public buildings of historical importance and fine 18th-century homes have been restored. In downtown Philadelphia the new Penn Center was constructed. A major renovation of the waterfront, estimated to cost $120 million over a 12-year period, is under way.

# PHOENIX

The state capital, situated in south-central Arizona on the Salt River. Elevation: 1,058 to 1,160 feet.

**HISTORY.** Phoenix, situated in an area of ancient Indian civilization, was probably visited by the Spanish explorers Cabeza de Vaca in 1536, Marcos de Niza in 1539, and Vasquez de Coronado in 1540, but it was not permanently settled until 1867. The city was incorporated in 1881 and succeeded Prescott as the territorial capital eight years later. When Arizona entered the Union in 1912, Phoenix was designated the state capital.

The completion of the Roosevelt Dam in 1911, the first successful large-scale irrigation project in the country, made possible the production of citrus fruits, dates, and other agricultural products in the desert climate. Rich mineral deposits have also brought prosperity to the area. Since World War II the population has expanded rapidly and the city has annexed over 150 square miles.

**GENERAL.** Phoenix rests on a stretch of flat desert surrounded by majestic mountains and lush irrigated fields. It has become a winter retreat and health resort, owing to its warm, dry climate. Electronics has emerged as an important industry.

The Phoenix Symphony, the Phoenix Art Museum, South Mountain Park, and the Desert Botanical Gardens are notable. The Heard Museum and the Pueblo Grande Museum contain excellent archeological exhibits of Indian handcrafts. Taliesin West, the architectural school of the late Frank Lloyd Wright, is located in Phoenix, as are several of the houses he designed.

# PITTSBURGH

Situated in southwestern Pennsylvania, where the Allegheny and Monongahela rivers meet to form the Ohio. Elevation: 710 to 1,370 feet.

**HISTORY.** A French military installation, Fort Duquesne, was built here in the 18th century but passed to British control and was renamed Fort Pitt, in honor of William Pitt, then Prime Minister of England. The fort withstood numerous attacks during Pontiac's Rebellion in 1763, and in the ensuing years a village grew up nearby.

With the opening of the Northwest Territory after the American Revolution, the village became an important trading center; its growth was further stimulated in 1795 after Anthony Wayne made peaceful settlements with the Indian tribes. Pittsburgh was chartered as a city in 1816, and with the completion of the Pennsylvania Canal in 1837 and the rail lines in 1851, industrial and commercial development moved ahead rapidly. The world's first cable suspension bridge was constructed here in 1847.

Pittsburgh was a center of the national labor movement in the late 19th century. In 1881 the Federation of Organized Trades and Labor Unions of the United States and Canada was formed here, later to be known as the American Federation of Labor. A disastrous flood in 1936, in which the rivers converging at Pittsburgh rose 46 feet, inundated most of the business district. During World War II Pittsburgh was an important shipbuilding center. The Pittsburgh Bicentennial was observed in 1958 and 1959.

**GENERAL.** Pittsburgh, situated near massive deposits of raw materials, is the leading iron and steel producing center in the world. In addition, the city has made its wealth by manufacturing glass, machinery, and electrical equipment, and processing coal. In the late 19th century, the American industrialists Andrew Carnegie, Andrew Mellon, and Henry Frick amassed great fortunes here.

The main commercial district is the Golden Triangle, where the Allegheny and Monongahela rivers meet to form the Ohio River. A unique redevelopment program began in the 1940s to eradicate the blight caused by industry. The program has been eminently successful in the rebuilding of the downtown area and the controlling of smoke emitted by the industrial complexes.

Pittsburgh is known for its fine park system. City landmarks include the Carnegie Museum and the Carnegie Library; the Phipps Conservatory; the Buhl Planetarium and Institute of Popular Science; and the Zoological Gardens, containing an underground zoo of nocturnal animals. There is a memorial to Stephen C. Foster, the American songwriter, who was born here.

The city is the seat of Carnegie Institute of Technology, the University of Pittsburgh, and Chatham College.

# PORTLAND

Situated in northwestern Oregon, on the Willamette River, near its confluence with the Columbia. Elevation: Sea level to 1,073 feet.

**HISTORY.** Founded in 1845 and incorporated in 1851, Portland expanded rapidly. The establishment of the salmon industry after the Civil War and the arrival of the first railroad in 1883 gave further impetus to the city's growth. A disastrous fire destroyed part of the city in 1873, but rebuilding was rapid.

From 1897 to 1900 Portland was a supply base for the Alaskan gold rush, and in 1905 it was the site of the Lewis and Clark Centennial Exposition. During World War II Portland emerged as a major shipbuilding port.

**GENERAL.** Today Portland is the largest city in Oregon and a major deep-water port. Ocean-going vessels travel 85 miles up the Columbia River from the Pacific Ocean to reach the city's piers. It is a leading exporting point for wheat, wool, and lumber, and ranks high as a producer of chemicals, wood products, aluminum, machinery, and canned foods.

Portland's scenic setting near the Cascade Mountains and snow-capped Mount Hood (altitude 11,245 feet) is enhanced by the city's magnificent rose gardens and parks.

Cultural attractions include the Museum of

Art, the Oregon Historical Society, the Oregon Museum of Science and Industry, and a symphony orchestra.

Portland is the seat of Lewis and Clark University, Reed College, the University of Portland, Portland State College, and the University of Oregon medical school.

## ST. LOUIS

Situated in eastern Missouri, on the Mississippi River. Elevation: 385 to 614 feet.

**HISTORY.** In 1763 the French fur trader Pierre Laclede chose the site of St. Louis for a fur-trading post, and the following year he sent René Auguste Chouteau to build it. The French settlement that developed here, named St. Louis in honor of Louis IX of France, withstood an attack by the British in 1780 during the American Revolution. The area passed to the United States as part of the Louisiana Purchase of 1803, and St. Louis soon became an important point of embarkation for exploratory, military, and scientific expeditions to the West. The famed Lewis and Clark expedition started out from St. Louis in 1804.

St. Louis grew rapidly after the War of 1812 with the arrival of European immigrants. It developed into a market point for the West and was incorporated as a city in 1823. The city subsequently became one of the nation's leading river ports. In 1849 St. Louis was swept by a disastrous fire and a cholera epidemic, but recovery was rapid. Industry burgeoned after the Civil War, as did freight handling. The famous Louisiana Purchase Exposition was held here in 1904. In the 1950s a massive urban renewal program was launched.

**GENERAL.** Today St. Louis is a market for furs, livestock, grain, and farm produce; a banking and wholesale center; and a railroad hub second only to Chicago. Aircraft, leather goods, beer, machinery, and electrical equipment compose a large part of the city's industrial output.

Interesting landmarks include the Old Courthouse, the scene of the Dred Scott case; Forest Park; the Missouri Botanical Garden; the Municipal Opera; the St. Louis Art Museum; the McDonnell Planetarium; Busch Memorial Stadium; and Gaslight Square.

The St. Louis *Post-Dispatch* is one of the country's leading newspapers. Among the city's educational institutions are St. Louis University and Washington University. Many great Americans are associated with St. Louis: Mark Twain, Joseph Pulitzer, Eugene Field, and Charles Lindbergh, whose historic flight in *The Spirit of St. Louis* was sponsored by St. Louis businessmen.

The city's new 50,000-seat Busch Memorial Sports Stadium was completed in 1966. In 1967 the Jefferson National Expansion Memorial, a $30 million project of the National Park Service, was dedicated. The 630-foot Gateway Arch, the tallest monument in the country, was constructed as part of the Memorial and stands as a symbol of St. Louis, the gateway to the West.

## SALT LAKE CITY

The state capital, situated in north-central Utah, southeast of the Great Salt Lake. Elevation: 4,208 to 8,000 feet.

**HISTORY.** Led by Brigham Young, a group of Mormons seeking refuge from religious persecution in the East founded Salt Lake City in 1847. The settlers transformed the dry, desert area into irrigated farm land, built a gigantic temple (requiring nearly fifty years to complete), and established the city as the center of the Mormon religion.

During the California gold rush of 1849, Salt Lake City prospered as a supply point for miners en route to the West Coast. In 1869 the city was connected to the first transcontinental railroad, the Union Pacific. The railroads helped to break down the city's isolation and brought more non-Mormons. Expansion continued, and when Utah entered the Union in 1896, Salt Lake City became its capital. In 1947 the city celebrated its centennial.

**GENERAL.** Today Salt Lake City is an important air and rail hub and a distribution point for a rich agricultural and mining area. Manufacturing, communications, and defense projects are also important to the economy.

Salt Lake City lies at the foot of the beautiful Wasatch Mountains. Temple Square, in the heart of the city, contains the most important buildings of the Mormon Church: the Mormon Temple, an imposing building of gray granite; and the Tabernacle, housing one of the largest organs in the world. Other reminders of the city's heritage are the Pioneer Memorial Building, and the Beehive House, former home of Brigham Young.

The Utah Museum of Fine Arts, the Utah Historical Society, the Salt Lake Art Center, and the Hansen Planetarium are monuments of culture. The magnificent Utah State Capitol contains noted works of art and many interesting exhibits. Salt Lake City is the seat of the University of Utah and Westminster College; Brigham Young University is nearby.

## SAN FRANCISCO

Situated in western California, on a peninsula between the Pacific Ocean and San Francisco Bay. Elevation: Sea level to 934 feet.

**HISTORY.** Sir Francis Drake, sailing under the English flag on a voyage around the world, arrived in the San Francisco Bay area in 1579. A mission and fort, named Yerba Buena, the place of the good herb, were founded in 1776 at a site chosen by Juan Bautista de Anza. In 1846, during the Mexican War, the village was taken for the United States by Commodore John D. Sloat, and renamed San Francisco the following year.

In 1848, gold was discovered in the Sierra Nevada and the California gold rush was launched. The heavy influx of miners and fortune seekers brought an era of lawlessness. Gambling casinos, saloons, and brothels covered the waterfront area, known as the Barbary Coast, and municipal corruption was rampant.

Incensed at the laxity of law enforcement, a group of citizens banded together as vigilantes to bring their own law and order to the brawling town. During this period, San Francisco acquired a cosmopolitan atmosphere, with immigrants arriving from all parts of the world, including China. After the gold rush the foundations of commerce and industry were firmly established. The city was linked with the East by Pony Express in 1860 and by railroads in 1869.

The disastrous earthquake and fire, the single most important event in San Francisco's history, occurred in 1906 when the San Andreas Fault, a long crack in the earth's surface on which the city is built, suddenly settled. The city was almost completely destroyed, but it was quickly rebuilt and its growth continued unchecked.

The Panama-Pacific Exposition was held in 1915 to celebrate the opening of the Panama Canal. By 1939, the year of the Golden Gate International Exposition, San Francisco had become the leading industrial and commercial center on the Pacific Coast. The United Nations charter was drafted here in 1945.

**GENERAL.** The financial center of the West, San Francisco, together with the Bay area, is also the largest port of the West Coast. Principal industries include food processing, printing and publishing, shipbuilding, and the manufacture of textiles and wood products.

Set on steep hills overlooking the Golden Gate, which separates the Pacific Ocean from San Francisco and San Pablo Bays, San Francisco is a picturesque city of lovely vistas, graceful bridges, ornate mansions, imposing public buildings, and unusual districts.

Cable cars, preserved as a national historic landmark, still run up and down steep streets lined with town houses and interesting shops. Telegraph Hill, from which communication with vessels at sea was once maintained, is topped by Coit Tower. Also well known are Twin Peaks, Nob Hill, and Russian Hill. The North Beach section is popular with beatniks.

Of interest to visitors are the Embarcadero and Fisherman's Wharf, along the Bay; Chinatown; Golden Gate Park, which contains a planetarium, a museum of natural history, an aquarium, and flower gardens; Fleishacker zoo; the Presidio, a major Army installation; Mission Dolores; and the civic center.

The San Francisco-Oakland Bay Bridge, connecting the two cities on either side of the Bay, was completed in 1936. In 1937, the Golden Gate Bridge linked San Francisco with Marin County to the north. Until the completion of New York's Verrazano-Narrows Bridge in 1964, the Golden Gate was the longest single-span suspension bridge in the world.

Notable cultural institutions are the San Francisco Museum of Art, the Palace of the Legion of Honor, the M. H. De Young Memorial Museum, and the War Memorial Opera House. San Francisco State College, the University of San Francisco, Stanford University's school of medicine, and several schools of the University of California are located here.

Space Needle towers over Seattle's former fair grounds.

Seattle Chamber of Commerce

## SEATTLE

Situated in northwestern Washington, between Lake Washington and Puget Sound. Elevation: Sea level to 520 feet.

**HISTORY.** Seattle began as a small lumber settlement in 1851. The town was plotted in 1853 and named for Chief Seattle of the Duwamish and Suquamish Indians. Although incorporated in 1869, Seattle remained a small lumber town until it was made the terminus of the Great Northern Railroad in 1893. A huge fire destroyed the downtown area in 1898, but recovery was rapid. The city burgeoned under the impetus of the Alaskan gold rush in 1897 and the opening of the Panama Canal in 1914.

Long a center of the radical labor movement, Seattle was the scene of a general strike by the International Workers of the World in 1919. During World War II the city's aircraft industry boomed, and in the past twenty years Seattle has emerged as a major industrial center.

**GENERAL.** Seattle is the principal city of the Pacific Northwest and the main link between the continental United States and Alaska. It is also an important port for the Far Eastern trade and a major commercial fishing port. Leading industries include aerospace, heavy manufacturing, shipbuilding and repairing, and lumber production.

Seattle is situated on seven hills between Lake Washington and Puget Sound, and is surrounded by the majestic beauty of the Cascade and Olympic Mountains, Mount Baker, and snow-capped Mount Rainier. There are four lakes and 45 parks within the city.

Notable attractions are the Seattle Center, former site of the Century 21 Exposition, held in 1962; the Seattle Art Museum; Pioneer Square; the Undersea Gardens; the Museum of History and Industry; and the International Center, containing many unusual shops and restaurants. Educational institutions include the University of Washington, Seattle University, and Seattle Pacific College.

Hydrofoil service between Seattle and Victoria, British Columbia, began in 1966.

## WASHINGTON, D.C.

See *District of Columbia* on page 455.

## LARGEST U.S. METROPOLITAN AREAS

A metropolitan area, officially termed a "standard metropolitan statistical area" by the U.S. Bureau of the Census, is a group of counties or municipalities socially and economically integrated with a large central city. The metropolitan area of Philadelphia, for example, includes the city of Philadelphia and surrounding towns in Bucks, Chester, Delaware,

and Montgomery counties in Pennsylvania and some towns in Burlington, Camden, and Gloucester counties in New Jersey.

Between 1960 and 1965 the population of metropolitan areas has increased by about 2.4 million, or roughly 2 per cent. The largest increase was registered by the Los Angeles-Long Beach area, with a gain of 727,000.

| METROPOLITAN AREA | POPULATION 1965 | RANK 1965 | RANK 1960 |
|---|---|---|---|
| New York, N.Y............ | 11,366,000 | 1 | 1 |
| Los Angeles–Long Beach, Calif................... | 6,765,000 | 2 | 3 |
| Chicago, Ill............... | 6,689,000 | 3 | 2 |
| Philadelphia, Penn.–N.J.... | 4,664,000 | 4 | 4 |
| Detroit, Mich............. | 3,987,000 | 5 | 5 |
| Boston, Mass............. | 3,205,000 | 6 | 6 |
| San Francisco–Oakland, Calif................... | 2,918,000 | 7 | 7 |
| Washington, D.C.–Md.–Va.. | 2,408,000 | 8 | 10 |
| Pittsburgh, Penn......... | 2,372,000 | 9 | 8 |
| St. Louis, Mo.–Ill........ | 2,249,000 | 10 | 9 |
| Cleveland, Ohio........... | 2,000,000 | 11 | 11 |
| Baltimore, Md............ | 1,854,000 | 12 | 12 |
| Newark, N.J............. | 1,851,000 | 13 | 13 |
| Houston, Texas........... | 1,696,000 | 14 | 15 |
| Minneapolis–St. Paul, Minn. | 1,612,000 | 15 | 14 |
| Cincinnati, Ohio–Ky.–Ind... | 1,347,000 | 16 | 17 |
| Buffalo, N.Y............. | 1,320,000 | 17 | 16 |
| Paterson–Clifton–Passaic, N.J................... | 1,307,000 | 18 | 19 |
| Dallas, Texas............. | 1,289,000 | 19 | 22 |

| METROPOLITAN AREA | POPULATION 1965 | RANK 1965 | RANK 1960 |
|---|---|---|---|
| Milwaukee, Wis........... | 1,275,000 | 20 | 18 |
| Atlanta, Ga.............. | 1,216,000 | 21 | 24 |
| Kansas City, Mo.–Kans.... | 1,183,000 | 22 | 21 |
| Seattle–Everett, Wash...... | 1,179,000 | 23 | 20 |
| San Diego, Calif.......... | 1,136,000 | 24 | 23 |
| Anaheim–Santa Ana– Garden Grove, Calif...... | 1,107,000 | 25 | 38 |
| Denver, Colo............. | 1,073,000 | 26 | 26 |
| Miami, Fla............... | 1,061,000 | 27 | 25 |
| New Orleans, La.......... | 1,027,000 | 28 | 28 |
| San Bernardino–Riverside– Ontario, Calif.......... | 1,026,000 | 29 | 30 |
| Indianapolis, Ind......... | 984,000 | 30 | 27 |
| Portland, Oreg.–Wash..... | 897,000 | 31 | 29 |
| San Jose, Calif........... | 885,000 | 32 | 45 |
| Tampa–St. Petersburg, Fla. | 873,000 | 33 | 31 |
| Columbus, Ohio.......... | 847,000 | 34 | 32 |
| Phoenix, Ariz............ | 818,000 | 35 | 41 |
| San Antonio, Texas....... | 808,000 | 36 | 37 |
| Rochester, N.Y........... | 804,000 | 37 | 33 |
| Dayton, Ohio............. | 791,000 | 38 | 34 |
| Louisville, Ky.–Ind........ | 771,000 | 39 | 35 |

## LATITUDE AND LONGITUDE OF U.S. CITIES

Latitude and longitude, measured in degrees (°) and minutes ('), are used to find position on the globe. Lines of latitude run parallel with the equator, whereas lines of longitude

are drawn through the poles, and are measured from the Greenwich meridian. The following data was released by the U.S. Coast and Geodetic Survey.

| CITY AND STATE | LATITUDE | LONGITUDE |
|---|---|---|
| Albuquerque, New Mexico.. | 35°05' | 106°39' |
| Anchorage, Alaska......... | 61°10' | 149°55' |
| Atlanta, Georgia........... | 33°45' | 84°24' |
| Baltimore, Maryland....... | 39°17' | 76°37' |
| Billings, Montana.......... | 45°47' | 108°30' |
| Birmingham, Alabama..... | 33°31' | 86°49' |
| Bismarck, North Dakota.... | 46°48' | 100°47' |
| Boise, Idaho.............. | 43°37' | 116°12' |
| Boston, Massachusetts..... | 42°21' | 71°03' |
| Burlington, Vermont....... | 44°28' | 73°14' |
| Charleston, West Virginia... | 38°21' | 81°37' |
| Charlotte, North Carolina... | 35°14' | 80°51' |
| Cheyenne, Wyoming....... | 41°08' | 104°49' |
| Chicago, Illinois........... | 41°52' | 87°38' |
| Cleveland, Ohio........... | 41°30' | 81°42' |
| Columbia, South Carolina... | 34°00' | 81°02' |
| Columbus, Ohio........... | 39°58' | 83°00' |
| Dallas, Texas............. | 32°47' | 96°48' |
| Denver, Colorado.......... | 39°45' | 104°59' |
| Des Moines, Iowa.......... | 41°35' | 93°37' |
| Detroit, Michigan.......... | 42°20' | 83°03' |
| Fargo, North Dakota....... | 46°53' | 96°47' |
| Hartford, Connecticut...... | 41°45' | 72°42' |
| Honolulu, Hawaii.......... | 21°19' | 157°50' |
| Houston, Texas........... | 29°45' | 95°22' |
| Indianapolis, Indiana...... | 39°46' | 86°10' |
| Jackson, Mississippi....... | 32°17' | 90°11' |
| Little Rock, Arkansas...... | 34°45' | 92°17' |

| CITY AND STATE | LATITUDE | LONGITUDE |
|---|---|---|
| Los Angeles, California..... | 34°03' | 118°14' |
| Louisville, Kentucky....... | 38°14' | 85°45' |
| Manchester, New Hampshire | 42°59' | 71°28' |
| Memphis, Tennessee....... | 35°09' | 90°03' |
| Miami, Florida............ | 25°47' | 80°12' |
| Milwaukee, Wisconsin...... | 43°02' | 87°54' |
| Minneapolis, Minnesota.... | 44°58' | 93°15' |
| Newark, New Jersey....... | 40°44' | 74°10' |
| New Orleans, Louisiana.... | 29°57' | 90°04' |
| New York, New York...... | 40°45' | 73°59' |
| Oklahoma City, Oklahoma.. | 35°28' | 97°31' |
| Omaha, Nebraska......... | 41°16' | 95°56' |
| Philadelphia, Pennsylvania | 39°57' | 75°09' |
| Phoenix, Arizona.......... | 33°27' | 112°04' |
| Pittsburgh, Pennsylvania... | 40°26' | 80°00' |
| Portland, Maine........... | 43°39' | 70°15' |
| Portland, Oregon.......... | 45°31' | 122°41' |
| Providence, Rhode Island... | 41°50' | 71°25' |
| Reno, Nevada............. | 39°31' | 119°49' |
| Richmond, Virginia........ | 37°32' | 77°26' |
| Saint Louis, Missouri...... | 38°38' | 90°12' |
| Salt Lake City, Utah....... | 40°45' | 111°53' |
| San Francisco, California... | 37°47' | 122°25' |
| Seattle, Washington....... | 47°37' | 122°20' |
| Sioux Falls, South Dakota.. | 43°34' | 96°42' |
| Washington, D.C........... | 38°54' | 77°01' |
| Wichita, Kansas........... | 37°41' | 97°20' |
| Wilmington, Delaware...... | 39°45' | 75°33' |

## INTERESTING FACTS ABOUT U.S. CITIES

Old State House, Little Rock

- Little Rock, Arkansas, is unique in having three capitol buildings: the Territorial Restoration, the Old State House, and the State Capitol.
- The nation's first commercial radio broadcast took place in Pittsburgh on November 2, 1920, when KDKA reported the returns of the Harding-Cox election.
- During the Civil War, Jackson, Mississippi, was nicknamed Chimneyville because Union forces burned so many buildings.
- Santa Fe, New Mexico, founded by the Spanish in 1609, is the oldest capital city in the United States and the nation's second oldest city.
- The $31.6 million Astrodome in Houston is the world's only completely enclosed major sports arena. It is covered by a gigantic steel and transparent plastic "bubble" with a span of 642 feet.

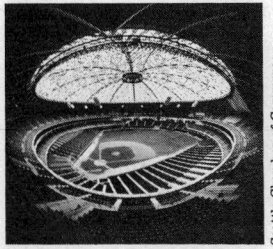

Fish-eye view of Astrodome

- The nation's first skyscraper, the Home Insurance Building, was built in Chicago in 1885. Designed by William LeBaron Jenney, it rose to a height of ten stories.
- San Francisco's Chinatown is the largest Chinese community outside the Orient.

- Boise, Idaho, has one of the world's largest colonies of Basques. Originally from northern Spain, they drifted into Idaho as sheepherders.
- Built on the ruins of a prehistoric Indian city, Phoenix, Arizona, was named for the mythical bird which was consumed by flames and then arose again from its own ashes.
- The world's largest privately-owned business and entertainment complex is Rockefeller Center in New York City. Radio City Music Hall, located here, is the largest indoor theater, with a seating capacity of 6,200.

New York's Rockefeller Center

- The nation's first zoo was the Zoological Gardens in Philadelphia, which opened on July 1, 1874.
- San Francisco's Lombard Street, known as "the world's crookedest street," changes direction ten times in one block as it meanders down Russian Hill.
- Hartford and New Haven were joint capitals of Connecticut until 1875.
- Portland, Oregon, was named by flipping a coin because in 1845 its founders, Francis Pettygrove of Portland, Maine, and Amos Lovejoy of Boston, Massachusetts, could not agree on a name. Pettygrove won.
- New York City was the nation's first capital, from 1789 to 1790; here George Washington was inaugurated for his first term and gave his Farewell Address.

- In 1848, when the first crops of the Mormon settlers in Salt Lake City, Utah, were being devoured by swarms of crickets, sea gulls arrived in time to wipe out the insects and save part of the harvest. Today, a monument to the gulls stands in the city.
- The only royal palace in the United States is Iolani Palace in Honolulu, former home of the Kamehameha dynasty and now the state capitol building.

Iolani Palace in Honolulu

- Oklahoma City was settled almost overnight by 10,000 people when the territory was opened to homesteaders in 1889. Today it is the country's largest city in land area, covering 631 square miles.
- The new 630-foot Gateway Arch in St. Louis is the tallest monument in the country. The arch, which commemorates the opening of the West after the Louisiana Purchase, is 75 feet higher than the Washington Monument.
- Saint Augustine, Florida, founded on September 8, 1565, by Spanish explorer Pedro Menéndez de Avilés, is the nation's oldest city.
- The Parthenon in Nashville, containing casts of the Elgin Marbles, is the only full-sized replica of the original structure on the Acropolis in Athens, Greece.

Nashville's Parthenon

## POPULATIONS OF MAJOR U.S. URBAN PLACES WITH ZIP CODES

An "urban place" is the name applied by the U.S. Bureau of the Census to any concentration of population. The following table includes all urban places of 25,000 or more inhabitants, according to the last official census in 1960. An asterisk (*) indicates a city has more than one ZIP Code. Consult local postmaster for specific ZIP Code within that city.

| URBAN PLACE | 1960 | 1950 | AREA (in square miles) | ZIP CODE NUMBERS |
|---|---|---|---|---|
| **ALABAMA** | | | | |
| Anniston......... | 33,657 | 31,066 | 10.3 | 36201 |
| Bessemer........ | 33,054 | 28,445 | 7.1 | 35020 |
| Birmingham...... | 340,887 | 326,037 | 74.5 | 35203 * |
| Decatur......... | 29,217 | 19,974 | 20.0 | 35601 |
| Dothan.......... | 31,440 | 21,584 | 49.0 | 36301 |
| Florence........ | 31,649 | 23,879 | 11.6 | 35630 |
| Gadsden......... | 58,088 | 55,725 | 30.7 | 35902 * |
| Huntsville....... | 72,365 | 16,437 | 50.7 | 35804 * |
| Mobile.......... | 202,779 | 129,009 | 152.9 | 36601 * |
| Montgomery..... | 134,393 | 106,525 | 31.8 | 36104 * |
| Phenix City...... | 27,630 | 23,305 | 20.0 | 36867 |
| Prichard........ | 47,371 | 19,014 | 10.5 | 36610 |
| Selma.......... | 28,385 | 22,840 | 12.8 | 36701 |
| Tuscaloosa...... | 63,370 | 46,396 | 21.0 | 35401 |
| **ALASKA** | | | | |
| Anchorage....... | 44,237 | 11,254 | 12.5 | 99502 * |
| **ARIZONA** | | | | |
| Mesa........... | 33,772 | 16,790 | 14.7 | 85201 |
| Phoenix......... | 439,170 | 106,818 | 187.4 | 85026 * |
| Tucson.......... | 212,892 | 45,454 | 70.9 | 85702 * |
| **ARKANSAS** | | | | |
| El Dorado........ | 25,292 | 23,076 | 7.6 | 71730 |
| Fort Smith....... | 52,991 | 47,942 | 24.7 | 72901 |
| Hot Springs...... | 28,337 | 29,307 | 9.4 | 71901 |
| Little Rock...... | 107,813 | 102,213 | 28.3 | 72201 * |
| North Little Rock.. | 58,032 | 44,097 | 19.9 | 72114 * |
| Pine Bluff....... | 44,037 | 37,162 | 9.4 | 71601 |
| **CALIFORNIA** | | | | |
| Alameda........ | 63,855 | 64,430 | 8.6 | 94501 |
| Alhambra....... | 54,807 | 51,359 | 7.6 | 91802 * |
| Altadena........ | 40,568 | 36,348 | 8.6 | 91001 |
| Anaheim........ | 104,184 | 14,556 | 24.8 | 92803 * |
| Arcadia......... | 41,005 | 23,066 | 11.2 | 91006 |
| Arden-Arcade.... | 73,352 | — | 6.2 | 95825 |
| Bakersfield...... | 56,848 | 34,784 | 16.0 | 93302 * |
| Baldwin Park..... | 33,951 | — | 5.9 | 91706 |
| Bellflower....... | 45,909 | — | 6.0 | 90706 |
| Bell Gardens..... | 26,467 | — | 2.5 | 90202 |
| Berkeley........ | 111,268 | 113,805 | 9.7 | 94704 * |
| Beverly Hills..... | 30,817 | 29,032 | 5.7 | 90213 * |
| Buena Park...... | 46,401 | — | 9.5 | 90620 |
| Burbank........ | 90,155 | 78,577 | 16.9 | 91503 * |
| Carson......... | 38,059 | — | 8.4 | 90744 |
| Castro Valley.... | 37,120 | — | 6.4 | 94546 |
| Chula Vista...... | 42,034 | 15,927 | 8.9 | 92010 * |
| Compton........ | 71,812 | 47,991 | 8.2 | 90221 * |
| Concord........ | 36,208 | 6,953 | 8.0 | 94520 * |
| Costa Mesa...... | 37,550 | 11,844 | 12.1 | 92626 * |
| Culver City...... | 32,163 | 19,720 | 4.3 | 90230 |
| Daly City........ | 44,791 | 15,191 | 4.2 | 94015 * |
| Downey......... | 82,505 | — | 12.7 | 90241 * |
| East Los Angeles.. | 104,270 | 81,664 | 7.9 | 90022 |
| El Cajon........ | 37,618 | 5,600 | 9.8 | 92020 * |
| El Cerrito........ | 25,437 | 18,011 | 4.0 | 94530 |
| Eureka......... | 28,137 | 23,058 | 10.0 | 95501 |
| Florence-Graham.. | 38,164 | — | 1.6 | 90001 |
| Fremont........ | 43,790 | — | 87.0 | 94536 * |
| Fresno.......... | 133,929 | 91,669 | 28.6 | 93721 * |
| Fullerton........ | 56,180 | 13,958 | 21.4 | 92631 * |
| Gardena........ | 35,943 | 14,405 | 4.2 | 90247 * |
| Garden Grove.... | 84,238 | 3,762 | 16.2 | 92640 * |
| Glendale........ | 119,442 | 95,702 | 29.3 | 91209 * |
| Hawthorne....... | 33,035 | 16,316 | 4.0 | 90250 |

| URBAN PLACE | 1960 | 1950 | AREA (in square miles) | ZIP CODE NUMBERS |
|---|---|---|---|---|
| Hayward......... | 72,700 | 14,272 | 27.6 | 94541 * |
| Huntington Park... | 29,920 | 29,450 | 2.8 | 90255 |
| Inglewood....... | 63,390 | 46,185 | 8.4 | 90306 * |
| La Habra........ | 25,136 | 4,961 | 5.5 | 90631 |
| Lakewood....... | 67,126 | — | 7.1 | 90714 * |
| La Mesa........ | 30,441 | 10,946 | 6.4 | 92041 |
| Lancaster....... | 26,012 | 3,594 | 11.3 | 93534 |
| Lennox.......... | 31,224 | — | 2.4 | 90304 |
| Long Beach...... | 344,168 | 250,767 | 45.9 | 90801 * |
| Los Angeles...... | 2,479,015 | 1,970,358 | 454.8 | 90052 * |
| Lynwood........ | 31,614 | 25,823 | 3.8 | 90262 |
| Manhattan Beach.. | 33,934 | 17,330 | 3.9 | 90266 |
| Menlo Park...... | 26,957 | 13,587 | 8.4 | 94025 |
| Modesto........ | 36,585 | 17,389 | 9.6 | 95350 * |
| Monrovia....... | 27,079 | 20,186 | 13.6 | 91016 |
| Montebello...... | 32,097 | 21,735 | 8.1 | 90640 |
| Monterey Park.... | 37,821 | 20,395 | 8.0 | 91754 |
| Mountain View... | 30,889 | 6,563 | 8.3 | 94040 |
| National City..... | 32,771 | 21,199 | 5.6 | 92050 |
| Newport Beach.... | 26,564 | 12,120 | 8.8 | 92660 * |
| Norwalk........ | 88,739 | — | 9.2 | 90650 |
| Oakland........ | 367,548 | 384,575 | 53.0 | 94615 * |
| Ontario......... | 46,617 | 22,872 | 17.8 | 91761 * |
| Orange......... | 26,444 | 10,027 | 8.8 | 92666 * |
| Oxnard......... | 40,265 | 21,567 | 6.4 | 93030 |
| Palo Alto........ | 52,287 | 25,475 | 21.7 | 94302 * |
| Paramount...... | 27,249 | — | 4.3 | 90723 |
| Pasadena....... | 116,407 | 104,577 | 22.6 | 91109 * |
| Pico Rivera...... | 49,150 | — | 7.8 | 90660 |
| Pomona........ | 67,157 | 35,405 | 18.4 | 91766 * |
| Redlands....... | 26,829 | 18,429 | 19.5 | 92373 |
| Redondo Beach.... | 46,986 | 25,226 | 6.0 | 90277 * |
| Redwood City.... | 46,290 | 25,544 | 19.2 | 94064 * |
| Richmond....... | 71,854 | 99,545 | 28.6 | 94802 * |
| Riverside........ | 84,332 | 46,764 | 40.6 | 92502 * |
| Sacramento..... | 191,667 | 137,572 | 45.1 | 95813 * |
| Salinas......... | 28,957 | 13,917 | 8.6 | 93901 |
| San Bernardino.... | 91,922 | 63,058 | 25.3 | 92403 * |
| San Bruno....... | 29,063 | 12,478 | 5.6 | 94066 |
| San Buenaventura.. | 29,114 | 16,534 | 7.1 | 93001 |
| San Diego....... | 573,224 | 334,387 | 192.4 | 92101 * |
| San Francisco.... | 740,316 | 775,357 | 47.6 | 94101 * |
| San Jose........ | 204,196 | 95,280 | 54.5 | 95125 * |
| San Leandro..... | 65,962 | 27,542 | 14.6 | 94577 * |
| San Mateo...... | 69,870 | 41,782 | 9.8 | 94402 * |
| Santa Ana...... | 100,350 | 45,533 | 21.3 | 92702 * |
| Santa Barbara.... | 58,768 | 44,854 | 19.7 | 93102 * |
| Santa Clara..... | 58,880 | 11,702 | 11.3 | 95050 * |
| Santa Cruz...... | 25,596 | 21,970 | 9.5 | 95060 |
| Santa Monica..... | 83,249 | 71,595 | 8.0 | 90406 * |
| Santa Rosa...... | 31,027 | 17,902 | 11.7 | 95402 * |
| South Gate...... | 53,831 | 51,116 | 7.5 | 90280 |
| South San Francisco | 39,418 | 19,351 | 6.8 | 94080 |
| South San Gabriel.. | 26,213 | — | 3.9 | 91777 |
| Stockton........ | 86,321 | 70,853 | 22.9 | 95204 * |
| Sunnyvale....... | 52,898 | 9,829 | 16.5 | 94086 * |
| Temple City..... | 31,838 | — | 5.1 | 91780 |
| Torrance........ | 100,991 | 22,241 | 20.0 | 90510 * |
| Vallejo......... | 60,877 | 26,038 | 13.3 | 94590 |
| West Covina..... | 50,645 | 4,499 | 12.6 | 91790 |
| West Hollywood.... | 28,820 | — | 1.9 | — |
| Westminster..... | 25,750 | 3,131 | 8.5 | 92683 |
| Whittier......... | 33,663 | 23,433 | 5.8 | 90605 * |

| URBAN PLACE | 1960 | 1950 | AREA (in square miles) | ZIP CODE NUMBERS |
|---|---|---|---|---|
| **COLORADO** | | | | |
| Aurora........... | 48,548 | 11,421 | 9.0 | 80010 |
| Boulder.......... | 37,718 | 19,999 | 7.1 | 80302 |
| Colorado Springs.. | 70,194 | 45,472 | 16.7 | 80901 * |
| Denver.......... | 493,887 | 415,786 | 71.0 | 80202 * |
| Englewood....... | 33,398 | 16,869 | 5.7 | 80110 |
| Fort Collins...... | 25,027 | 14,937 | 6.1 | 80521 |
| Greeley.......... | 26,314 | 20,354 | 5.0 | 80631 |
| Pueblo.......... | 91,181 | 63,685 | 17.0 | 81001 * |
| **CONNECTICUT** | | | | |
| Bridgeport....... | 156,748 | 158,709 | 17.9 | 06602 * |
| Bristol.......... | 45,499 | 35,961 | 26.6 | 06010 |
| East Hartford..... | 43,977 | 29,933 | 18.2 | 06108 |
| Enfield.......... | 31,464 | 15,464 | 33.2 | 06030 |
| Fairfield......... | 46,183 | 30,489 | 29.9 | 06430 |
| Greenwich........ | 53,793 | 40,835 | 47.6 | 06830 |
| Hamden.......... | 41,056 | 29,715 | 24.8 | 06514 |
| Hartford......... | 162,178 | 177,397 | 17.4 | 06101 * |
| Manchester....... | 42,102 | 34,116 | 27.5 | 06040 |
| Meriden......... | 51,850 | 44,088 | 23.5 | 06450 |
| Middletown....... | 33,250 | 29,711 | 45.0 | 06457 |
| Milford.......... | 41,662 | — | 23.6 | 06460 |
| New Britain...... | 82,201 | 73,726 | 13.7 | 06050 * |
| New Haven....... | 152,048 | 164,443 | 17.9 | 06510 * |
| New London...... | 34,182 | 30,551 | 6.1 | 06320 |
| Norwalk......... | 67,775 | 49,460 | 24.7 | 06856 * |
| Norwich......... | 38,506 | 23,429 | 29.3 | 06360 |
| Stamford........ | 92,713 | 74,293 | 38.4 | 06904 * |
| Stratford........ | 45,012 | 33,428 | 18.5 | 06497 |
| Torrington....... | 30,045 | 27,820 | 39.6 | 06790 |
| Wallingford...... | 29,920 | 16,976 | 41.6 | 06492 |
| Waterbury....... | 107,130 | 104,477 | 27.6 | 06701 * |
| West Hartford..... | 62,382 | 44,402 | 21.2 | 06107 |
| West Haven...... | 43,002 | 32,010 | 10.9 | 06516 |
| **DELAWARE** | | | | |
| Wilmington........ | 95,827 | 110,356 | 15.8 | 19899 * |
| **DISTRICT OF COLUMBIA** | | | | |
| Washington....... | 763,956 | 802,178 | 61.4 | 20013 * |
| **FLORIDA** | | | | |
| Brownsville...... | 38,417 | — | 10.5 | 32505 |
| Clearwater...... | 34,653 | 15,581 | 10.3 | 33515 * |
| Coral Gables...... | 34,793 | 19,837 | 12.3 | 33134 |
| Daytona Beach.... | 37,395 | 30,187 | 14.0 | 32015 * |
| Fort Lauderdale... | 83,648 | 36,328 | 21.5 | 33310 * |
| Fort Pierce...... | 25,256 | 13,502 | 10.2 | 33450 |
| Gainesville....... | 29,701 | 26,861 | 6.5 | 32601 |
| Hialeah.......... | 66,972 | 19,676 | 13.4 | 33010 * |
| Hollywood........ | 35,237 | 14,351 | 17.9 | 33022 * |
| Jacksonville...... | 201,030 | 204,517 | 30.2 | 32201 * |
| Key West........ | 33,956 | 26,433 | 4.4 | 33040 |
| Lakeland........ | 41,350 | 30,851 | 11.9 | 33802 * |
| Miami........... | 291,688 | 249,276 | 34.2 | 33101 * |
| Miami Beach..... | 63,145 | 46,282 | 7.2 | 33139 |
| North Miami..... | 28,708 | 10,734 | 5.8 | 33161 |
| Orlando......... | 88,135 | 52,367 | 21.1 | 32802 * |
| Panama City...... | 33,275 | 25,814 | 11.6 | 32401 |
| Pensacola........ | 56,752 | 43,479 | 20.1 | 32502 * |
| St. Petersburg.... | 181,298 | 96,738 | 54.0 | 33730 * |
| Sarasota......... | 34,083 | 18,896 | 14.9 | 33578 * |
| Tallahassee....... | 48,174 | 27,237 | 15.2 | 32302 * |
| Tampa.......... | 274,970 | 124,681 | 85.0 | 33602 * |
| West Palm Beach. | 56,208 | 43,162 | 18.7 | 33401 * |
| **GEORGIA** | | | | |
| Albany.......... | 55,890 | 31,155 | 23.0 | 31702 * |
| Athens.......... | 31,355 | 28,180 | 9.8 | 30601 |
| Atlanta.......... | 487,455 | 331,314 | 128.2 | 30304 * |
| Augusta......... | 70,626 | 71,508 | 15.0 | 30901 * |
| Columbus........ | 116,779 | 79,611 | 26.4 | 31902 * |
| East Point........ | 35,633 | 21,080 | 11.1 | 30044 |
| Macon........... | 69,764 | 70,252 | 15.0 | 31201 * |

| URBAN PLACE | 1960 | 1950 | AREA (in square miles) | ZIP CODE NUMBERS |
|---|---|---|---|---|
| Marietta......... | 25,565 | 20,687 | 8.1 | 30060 |
| Rome............ | 32,226 | 29,615 | 10.4 | 30161 |
| Savannah........ | 149,245 | 119,638 | 41.5 | 31401 * |
| Valdosta......... | 30,652 | 20,046 | 10.7 | 31601 |
| **HAWAII** | | | | |
| Hilo............. | 25,966 | 27,198 | 292.4 | 96720 |
| Honolulu......... | 294,194 | 248,034 | 83.9 | 96813 * |
| Kailua-Lanikai.... | 25,622 | 7,740 | 5.4 | 96734 |
| **IDAHO** | | | | |
| Boise............ | 34,481 | 34,393 | 10.3 | 83707 * |
| Idaho Falls....... | 33,161 | 19,218 | 8.0 | 83401 |
| Pocatello........ | 28,534 | 26,131 | 7.5 | 83201 |
| **ILLINOIS** | | | | |
| Alton............ | 43,047 | 32,550 | 9.8 | 62002 |
| Arlington Heights. | 27,878 | 8,768 | 6.1 | 60004 * |
| Aurora.......... | 63,715 | 50,576 | 10.8 | 60507 * |
| Belleville........ | 37,264 | 32,721 | 8.5 | 62220 |
| Berwyn.......... | 54,224 | 51,280 | 3.8 | 60402 |
| Bloomington...... | 36,271 | 34,163 | 7.2 | 61701 |
| Calumet City..... | 25,000 | 15,799 | 9.0 | 60409 |
| Champaign....... | 49,583 | 39,563 | 6.3 | 61820 |
| Chicago.......... | 3,550,404 | 3,620,962 | 224.2 | 60607 * |
| Chicago Heights... | 34,331 | 24,551 | 7.1 | 60411 |
| Cicero........... | 69,130 | 67,544 | 5.8 | 60650 |
| Danville......... | 41,856 | 37,864 | 10.0 | 61832 |
| Decatur......... | 78,004 | 66,269 | 19.7 | 62525 * |
| Des Plaines...... | 34,886 | 14,994 | 7.9 | 60016 * |
| East St. Louis..... | 81,712 | 82,295 | 13.8 | 62201 * |
| Elgin........... | 49,447 | 44,223 | 9.0 | 60120 |
| Elmhurst........ | 36,991 | 21,273 | 6.4 | 60126 |
| Evanston........ | 79,283 | 73,641 | 8.2 | 60204 * |
| Freeport........ | 26,628 | 22,467 | 5.0 | 61032 |
| Galesburg....... | 37,243 | 31,425 | 8.8 | 61401 |
| Granite City...... | 40,073 | 29,465 | 7.4 | 62040 |
| Harvey.......... | 29,071 | 20,683 | 5.0 | 60426 |
| Highland Park.... | 25,532 | 16,808 | 12.2 | 60035 |
| Joliet........... | 66,780 | 51,601 | 14.2 | 60431 * |
| Kankakee........ | 27,666 | 25,856 | 6.9 | 60901 |
| Maywood........ | 27,330 | 27,473 | 2.8 | 60153 |
| Moline.......... | 42,705 | 37,397 | 9.2 | 61265 |
| Oak Lawn........ | 27,471 | 8,751 | 6.5 | 60453 |
| Oak Park........ | 61,093 | 63,529 | 4.7 | 60301 * |
| Park Forest...... | 29,993 | 8,138 | 4.2 | 60466 |
| Park Ridge....... | 32,659 | 16,602 | 6.4 | 60068 |
| Pekin........... | 28,146 | 21,858 | 6.6 | 61554 |
| Peoria.......... | 103,162 | 111,856 | 15.2 | 61601 * |
| Quincy.......... | 43,793 | 41,450 | 7.7 | 62301 |
| Rockford......... | 126,706 | 92,927 | 26.0 | 61101 * |
| Rock Island...... | 51,863 | 48,710 | 10.9 | 61201 |
| Skokie........... | 59,364 | 14,832 | 10.1 | 60076 |
| Springfield....... | 83,271 | 81,628 | 21.4 | 62701 * |
| Urbana.......... | 27,294 | 22,834 | 5.0 | 61801 |
| Waukegan....... | 55,719 | 38,946 | 11.1 | 60085 |
| Wilmette........ | 28,268 | 18,162 | 5.3 | 60091 |
| **INDIANA** | | | | |
| Anderson........ | 49,061 | 46,820 | 10.4 | 46011 * |
| Bloomington...... | 31,357 | 28,163 | 5.3 | 47401 |
| East Chicago..... | 57,669 | 54,263 | 11.5 | 46312 |
| Elkhart.......... | 40,274 | 35,646 | 10.8 | 46514 |
| Evansville....... | 141,543 | 128,636 | 32.0 | 47708 * |
| Fort Wayne..... | 161,776 | 133,607 | 36.8 | 46802 * |
| Gary........... | 178,320 | 133,911 | 41.6 | 46401 * |
| Hammond........ | 111,698 | 87,594 | 23.5 | 46320 * |
| Indianapolis..... | 476,258 | 427,173 | 71.2 | 46206 * |
| Kokomo......... | 47,197 | 38,672 | 8.3 | 46901 |
| Lafayette........ | 42,330 | 35,568 | 6.5 | |
| Marion......... | 37,854 | 30,081 | 7.8 | 46952 |
| Michigan City..... | 36,653 | 28,395 | 19.5 | 46360 |
| Mishawaka....... | 33,361 | 32,913 | 7.1 | 46544 |
| Muncie.......... | 68,603 | 58,479 | 12.3 | 47302 * |

| URBAN PLACE | 1960 | 1950 | AREA (in square miles) | ZIP CODE NUMBERS |
|---|---|---|---|---|
| New Albany | 37,812 | 29,346 | 10.7 | 47150 |
| Richmond | 44,149 | 39,539 | 11.6 | 47374 |
| South Bend | 132,445 | 115,911 | 23.8 | 46624 * |
| Terre Haute | 72,500 | 64,214 | 24.7 | 47808 * |
| **IOWA** | | | | |
| Ames | 27,003 | 22,898 | 8.5 | 50010 |
| Burlington | 32,430 | 30,613 | 12.0 | 52601 |
| Cedar Rapids | 92,035 | 72,296 | 33.0 | 52401 * |
| Clinton | 33,589 | 30,379 | 11.0 | 52771 |
| Council Bluffs | 55,641 | 45,429 | 16.0 | 51501 |
| Davenport | 88,981 | 74,549 | 46.7 | 52802 * |
| Des Moines | 208,982 | 177,965 | 64.5 | 50318 * |
| Dubuque | 56,606 | 49,671 | 13.6 | 52001 |
| Fort Dodge | 28,399 | 25,115 | 6.7 | 50501 |
| Iowa City | 33,443 | 27,212 | 8.0 | 52240 |
| Mason City | 30,642 | 27,980 | 12.6 | 50401 |
| Ottumwa | 33,871 | 33,631 | 11.6 | 52501 |
| Sioux City | 89,159 | 83,991 | 49.4 | 51101 * |
| Waterloo | 71,755 | 65,198 | 33.8 | 50701 * |
| **KANSAS** | | | | |
| Hutchinson | 37,574 | 33,575 | 10.9 | 67501 |
| Kansas City | 121,901 | 129,553 | 40.6 | 66110 * |
| Lawrence | 32,858 | 23,351 | 8.1 | 66044 |
| Prairie Village | 25,356 | — | 4.6 | 66208 * |
| Salina | 43,202 | 26,176 | 8.2 | 67401 |
| Topeka | 119,484 | 78,791 | 36.1 | 66603 * |
| Wichita | 254,698 | 168,279 | 51.9 | 67202 * |
| **KENTUCKY** | | | | |
| Ashland | 31,283 | 31,131 | 8.0 | 41101 |
| Bowling Green | 28,338 | 18,347 | 7.0 | 42101 |
| Covington | 60,376 | 64,452 | 7.0 | 41011 * |
| Lexington | 62,810 | 55,534 | 13.0 | 40507 * |
| Louisville | 390,639 | 369,129 | 57.1 | 40201 * |
| Newport | 30,070 | 31,044 | 3.2 | 41071 * |
| Owensboro | 42,471 | 33,651 | 6.3 | 42301 |
| Paducah | 34,479 | 32,828 | 9.7 | 42001 |
| **LOUISIANA** | | | | |
| Alexandria | 40,279 | 34,913 | 9.9 | 71301 |
| Baton Rouge | 152,419 | 125,629 | 31.0 | 70821 * |
| Bossier City | 32,776 | 15,470 | 11.0 | 71010 |
| Lafayette | 40,400 | 33,541 | 7.0 | 70501 |
| Lake Charles | 63,392 | 41,272 | 16.3 | 70601 |
| Monroe | 52,219 | 38,572 | 18.1 | 71201 |
| New Iberia | 29,062 | 16,467 | 7.4 | 70560 |
| New Orleans | 627,525 | 570,445 | 198.8 | 70113 * |
| Shreveport | 164,372 | 127,206 | 36.0 | 71102 * |
| **MAINE** | | | | |
| Bangor | 38,912 | 31,558 | 35.4 | 04401 |
| Lewiston | 40,804 | 40,974 | 35.0 | 04240 |
| Portland | 72,566 | 77,634 | 21.6 | 04101 * |
| **MARYLAND** | | | | |
| Baltimore | 939,024 | 949,708 | 79.0 | 21233 * |
| Bethesda | 56,527 | — | 14.3 | 20014 |
| Catonsville | 37,372 | — | 6.2 | 21228 |
| Cumberland | 33,415 | 37,679 | 7.9 | 21502 |
| Dundalk | 82,428 | — | 10.6 | 21222 |
| Essex | 35,205 | — | 5.7 | 21221 |
| Hagerstown | 36,660 | 36,260 | 7.2 | 21740 |
| Parkville-Carney | 27,236 | — | 6.1 | 21234 |
| Rockville | 26,090 | 6,934 | 7.0 | 20850 * |
| Silver Spring | 66,348 | — | 9.3 | 20907 * |
| Wheaton | 54,635 | — | 9.2 | 20902 |
| **MASSACHUSETTS** | | | | |
| Arlington | 49,953 | 44,353 | 5.1 | 02174 |
| Attleboro | 27,118 | 23,809 | 27.3 | 02703 |
| Belmont | 28,715 | 27,381 | 4.6 | 02178 |
| Beverly | 36,108 | 28,884 | 15.1 | 01915 |
| Boston | 697,197 | 801,444 | 47.8 | 02109 * |
| Braintree | 31,069 | 23,161 | 14.3 | 02184 |
| Brockton | 72,813 | 62,860 | 21.5 | 02403 * |

| URBAN PLACE | 1960 | 1950 | AREA (in square miles) | ZIP CODE NUMBERS |
|---|---|---|---|---|
| Brookline | 54,044 | 57,589 | 6.8 | 02146 |
| Cambridge | 107,716 | 120,740 | 6.3 | 02138 |
| Chelsea | 33,749 | 38,912 | 2.4 | 02150 |
| Chicopee | 61,553 | 49,211 | 18.4 | 01020 * |
| Everett | 43,544 | 45,982 | 3.3 | 02149 |
| Fall River | 99,942 | 111,963 | 33.9 | 02722 * |
| Fitchburg | 43,021 | 42,691 | 27.4 | 01420 |
| Framingham | 44,526 | 28,086 | 24.1 | 01701 |
| Gloucester | 25,789 | 25,167 | 24.7 | 01930 |
| Haverhill | 46,346 | 47,280 | 32.0 | 01830 |
| Holyoke | 52,689 | 54,661 | 22.8 | 01040 |
| Lawrence | 70,933 | 80,536 | 7.2 | 01842 * |
| Leominster | 27,929 | 24,075 | 29.5 | 01453 |
| Lexington | 27,691 | 17,335 | 16.5 | 02173 |
| Lowell | 92,107 | 97,249 | 13.1 | 01853 * |
| Lynn | 94,478 | 99,738 | 10.4 | 01901 * |
| Malden | 57,676 | 59,804 | 4.8 | 02148 |
| Medford | 64,971 | 66,113 | 8.1 | 02155 |
| Melrose | 29,619 | 26,988 | 4.8 | 02176 |
| Methuen | 28,114 | 24,477 | 22.5 | 01844 |
| Milton | 26,375 | 22,395 | 12.9 | 02186 |
| Natick | 28,831 | 19,838 | 15.1 | 01760 |
| Needham | 25,793 | 16,313 | 12.5 | 02192 |
| New Bedford | 102,477 | 109,189 | 19.1 | 02741 * |
| Newton | 92,384 | 81,994 | 17.3 | 02158 |
| Northampton | 30,058 | 29,063 | 35.0 | 01060 |
| Peabody | 32,202 | 22,645 | 17.0 | 01960 |
| Pittsfield | 57,879 | 53,348 | 40.9 | 01201 |
| Quincy | 87,409 | 83,835 | 16.8 | 02169 |
| Revere | 40,080 | 36,763 | 5.6 | 02151 |
| Salem | 39,211 | 41,880 | 8.0 | 01970 |
| Somerville | 94,697 | 102,351 | 4.1 | 02143 |
| Springfield | 174,463 | 162,399 | 33.1 | 01101 * |
| Taunton | 41,132 | 40,109 | 11.9 | 02780 |
| Waltham | 55,413 | 47,187 | 13.6 | 02154 |
| Watertown | 39,092 | 37,329 | 4.2 | 02172 |
| Wellesley | 26,071 | 20,549 | 9.9 | 02181 |
| Westfield | 26,302 | 20,962 | 46.3 | 01085 |
| Weymouth | 48,177 | 32,690 | 17.7 | 02188 |
| Woburn | 31,214 | 20,492 | 12.6 | 01801 |
| Worcester | 186,587 | 203,486 | 37.0 | 01601 * |
| **MICHIGAN** | | | | |
| Allen Park | 37,052 | 12,329 | 7.4 | 48101 |
| Ann Arbor | 67,340 | 48,251 | 13.7 | 48106 * |
| Battle Creek | 44,169 | 48,666 | 12.4 | 49016 * |
| Bay City | 53,604 | 52,523 | 9.6 | 48706 |
| Birmingham | 25,525 | 15,467 | 4.8 | 48012 * |
| Dearborn | 112,007 | 94,994 | 25.3 | 48120 * |
| Detroit | 1,670,144 | 1,849,568 | 139.6 | 48233 * |
| East Detroit | 45,756 | 21,461 | 5.0 | 48021 |
| East Lansing | 30,198 | 20,325 | 8.5 | 48823 |
| Ferndale | 31,347 | 29,675 | 4.0 | 48220 |
| Flint | 196,940 | 163,143 | 29.9 | 48502 * |
| Garden City | 38,017 | 9,012 | 5.7 | 48135 |
| Grand Rapids | 177,313 | 176,515 | 24.4 | 49501 * |
| Hamtramck | 34,137 | 43,355 | 2.1 | 48212 |
| Hazel Park | 25,631 | 17,770 | 2.8 | 48030 |
| Highland Park | 38,063 | 46,393 | 3.0 | 48203 |
| Inkster | 39,097 | 16,728 | 6.9 | 48141 |
| Jackson | 50,720 | 51,088 | 10.5 | 49201 * |
| Kalamazoo | 82,089 | 57,704 | 24.1 | 49001 * |
| Lansing | 107,807 | 92,129 | 21.2 | 48924 * |
| Lincoln Park | 53,933 | 29,310 | 5.9 | 48146 |
| Livonia | 66,702 | 17,534 | 35.9 | 48150 * |
| Madison Heights | 33,343 | — | 7.4 | 48071 |
| Midland | 27,779 | 14,285 | 23.5 | 48640 |
| Muskegon | 46,485 | 48,429 | 9.2 | 49440 * |
| Oak Park | 36,632 | 5,267 | 5.5 | 48237 |
| Pontiac | 82,233 | 73,681 | 19.8 | 48053 * |
| Port Huron | 36,084 | 35,725 | 7.5 | 48060 |

| URBAN PLACE | 1960 | 1950 | AREA (in square miles) | ZIP CODE NUMBERS |
|---|---|---|---|---|
| Roseville | 50,195 | 15,816 | 9.5 | 48066 |
| Royal Oak | 80,612 | 46,898 | 12.0 | 48067 * |
| Saginaw | 98,265 | 92,918 | 16.6 | 48605 * |
| St. Clair Shores | 76,657 | 19,823 | 10.5 | 48083 * |
| Southfield | 31,501 | — | 26.6 | 48075 |
| Southgate | 29,404 | — | 6.9 | 48192 |
| Warren | 89,246 | 727 | 34.5 | 48089 * |
| Wyandotte | 43,519 | 36,846 | 5.2 | 48192 |
| Wyoming | 45,829 | — | 22.2 | 49509 |
| **MINNESOTA** | | | | |
| Austin | 27,908 | 23,100 | 4.8 | 55912 |
| Bloomington | 50,498 | — | 3.6 | 55420 |
| Duluth | 106,884 | 104,511 | 62.6 | 55801 * |
| Edina | 28,501 | 9,744 | 16.5 | 55424 |
| Minneapolis | 482,872 | 521,718 | 56.5 | 55401 * |
| Minnetonka | 25,037 | — | 28.2 | 55343 |
| Richfield | 42,523 | 17,502 | 9.5 | 55423 |
| Rochester | 40,663 | 29,885 | 8.4 | 55901 |
| St. Cloud | 33,815 | 28,410 | 9.4 | 56301 |
| St. Louis Park | 43,310 | 22,644 | 10.0 | 55426 |
| St. Paul | 313,411 | 311,349 | 52.2 | 55101 * |
| **MISSISSIPPI** | | | | |
| Biloxi | 44,053 | 37,425 | 6.0 | 39530 * |
| Greenville | 41,502 | 29,936 | 7.3 | 38701 |
| Gulfport | 30,204 | 22,659 | 15.4 | 39501 |
| Hattiesburg | 34,989 | 29,474 | 12.9 | 39401 |
| Jackson | 144,422 | 98,271 | 46.5 | 39205 * |
| Laurel | 27,889 | 25,038 | 11.9 | 39440 |
| Meridian | 49,374 | 41,893 | 24.0 | 39301 |
| Vicksburg | 29,143 | 27,948 | 10.2 | 39180 |
| **MISSOURI** | | | | |
| Columbia | 36,650 | 31,974 | 10.9 | 65201 |
| Florissant | 38,166 | 3,737 | 4.4 | 63031 * |
| Independence | 62,328 | 36,936 | 13.8 | 64051 * |
| Jefferson City | 28,228 | 25,099 | 9.9 | 65101 |
| Joplin | 38,958 | 38,711 | 20.0 | 64801 |
| Kansas City | 475,539 | 456,622 | 129.8 | 64108 * |
| Kirkwood | 29,421 | 18,640 | 8.3 | 63122 |
| St. Joseph | 79,673 | 78,588 | 27.7 | 64501 * |
| St. Louis | 750,026 | 856,796 | 61.0 | 63155 * |
| Springfield | 95,865 | 66,731 | 34.7 | 65801 |
| University City | 51,249 | 39,892 | 4.5 | 63130 |
| Webster Groves | 28,990 | 23,390 | 5.6 | 63119 |
| **MONTANA** | | | | |
| Billings | 52,851 | 31,834 | 9.3 | 59101 * |
| Butte | 27,877 | 33,251 | 5.1 | 59701 |
| Great Falls | 55,357 | 39,214 | 11.4 | 59401 |
| Missoula | 27,090 | 22,485 | 5.5 | 59801 |
| **NEBRASKA** | | | | |
| Grand Island | 25,742 | 22,682 | 5.4 | 68801 |
| Lincoln | 128,521 | 98,884 | 25.4 | 68501 * |
| Omaha | 301,598 | 251,117 | 51.2 | 68108 * |
| **NEVADA** | | | | |
| Las Vegas | 64,405 | 24,624 | 24.7 | 89114 * |
| Reno | 51,470 | 32,497 | 11.8 | 89501 * |
| **NEW HAMPSHIRE** | | | | |
| Concord | 28,991 | 27,988 | 64.1 | 03301 |
| Manchester | 88,282 | 82,732 | 32.0 | 03101 * |
| Nashua | 39,096 | 34,669 | 31.3 | 03060 |
| Portsmouth | 25,833 | 18,830 | 15.2 | 03801 |
| **NEW JERSEY** | | | | |
| Atlantic City | 59,544 | 61,657 | 11.5 | 08401 * |
| Bayonne | 74,215 | 77,203 | 7.5 | 07002 |
| Belleville | 35,005 | 32,019 | 3.2 | 07109 |
| Bergenfield | 27,203 | 17,647 | 3.8 | 07621 |
| Bloomfield | 51,867 | 49,307 | 5.4 | 07003 |
| Camden | 117,159 | 124,555 | 8.7 | 08101 * |
| Clifton | 82,084 | 64,511 | 11.7 | 07015 * |
| Cranford | 26,424 | 18,602 | 5.0 | 07016 |
| Delaware | 31,522 | 10,358 | 24.4 | 07833 |
| East Orange | 77,259 | 79,340 | 4.0 | 07019 * |
| Edison | 44,799 | 16,348 | 31.0 | 08817 * |
| Elizabeth | 107,698 | 112,817 | 11.7 | 07207 * |
| Englewood | 26,057 | 23,145 | 4.9 | 07631 * |
| Ewing | 26,628 | 16,840 | 15.4 | — |
| Fair Lawn | 36,421 | 23,885 | 5.3 | 07410 |
| Garfield | 29,253 | 27,550 | 2.2 | 07026 |
| Hackensack | 30,521 | 29,219 | 4.6 | 07602 * |
| Hamilton | 65,035 | 41,156 | 40.3 | — |
| Hoboken | 48,441 | 50,676 | 1.3 | 07030 |
| Irvington | 59,379 | 59,201 | 3.1 | 07111 |
| Jersey City | 276,101 | 299,017 | 13.0 | 07303 * |
| Kearny | 37,472 | 39,952 | 8.9 | 07032 |
| Linden | 39,931 | 30,644 | 11.1 | 07036 |
| Long Branch | 26,228 | 23,090 | 5.1 | 07740 |
| Middletown | 39,675 | 16,203 | 54.9 | 07748 |
| Montclair | 43,129 | 43,927 | 6.2 | 07042 * |
| Newark | 405,220 | 438,776 | 23.6 | 07102 * |
| New Brunswick | 40,139 | 38,811 | 5.0 | 08901 * |
| New Hanover | 28,528 | 18,168 | 24.4 | — |
| North Bergen | 42,387 | 41,560 | 5.6 | 07047 |
| Nutley | 29,513 | 26,992 | 3.5 | 07110 |
| Orange | 35,789 | 38,037 | 2.2 | 07050 * |
| Parsippany-Troy Hills | 25,557 | 15,290 | 23.7 | 07054 |
| Passaic | 53,963 | 57,702 | 3.1 | 07055 |
| Paterson | 143,663 | 139,336 | 8.4 | 07510 * |
| Pennsauken | 33,771 | 22,767 | 10.4 | 08110 |
| Perth Amboy | 38,007 | 41,330 | 4.4 | 08861 * |
| Plainfield | 45,330 | 42,366 | 6.0 | 07061 * |
| Rahway | 27,699 | 21,290 | 4.1 | 07065 * |
| Ridgewood | 25,391 | 17,481 | 6.2 | 07451 * |
| Teaneck | 42,085 | 33,772 | 6.1 | 07666 |
| Trenton | 114,167 | 128,009 | 7.4 | 08608 * |
| Union City | 52,180 | 55,537 | 1.3 | 07087 |
| Union (Union County) | 51,499 | 38,004 | 9.2 | 07083 |
| Vineland | 37,685 | 8,155 | 68.0 | 08360 |
| Wayne | 29,353 | 11,822 | 25.3 | 07470 |
| Westfield | 31,447 | 21,243 | 6.3 | 07090 |
| West New York | 35,547 | 37,683 | 1.1 | 07093 |
| West Orange | 39,895 | 28,605 | 11.1 | 07052 |
| Woodbridge | 78,846 | 35,758 | 24.1 | 07095 |
| **NEW MEXICO** | | | | |
| Albuquerque | 201,189 | 96,815 | 56.2 | 87101 * |
| Carlsbad | 25,541 | 17,975 | 7.4 | 88220 |
| Hobbs | 26,275 | 13,875 | 10.8 | 88240 |
| Las Cruces | 29,367 | 12,325 | 9.0 | 88001 |
| Roswell | 39,593 | 25,738 | 13.3 | 88201 |
| Santa Fe | 33,394 | 27,998 | 26.0 | 87501 |
| **NEW YORK** | | | | |
| Albany | 129,726 | 134,995 | 19.0 | 12207 * |
| Amsterdam | 28,772 | 32,240 | 6.0 | 12010 |
| Auburn | 35,249 | 36,722 | 8.4 | 13021 |
| Baldwin | 30,204 | — | 4.1 | 11510 |
| Binghamton | 75,941 | 80,674 | 10.9 | 13902 * |
| Buffalo | 532,759 | 580,132 | 39.4 | 14240 * |
| Cheektowaga-Northwest | 52,362 | — | 6.3 | 14225 |
| East Meadow | 46,036 | — | 6.7 | 11554 |
| Eggertsville | 44,807 | — | 10.9 | 14226 |
| Elmira | 46,517 | 49,716 | 7.0 | 14901 * |
| Elmont | 30,138 | — | 3.2 | 11003 |
| Franklin Square | 32,483 | — | 2.8 | 11010 |
| Freeport | 34,419 | 24,680 | 4.6 | 11520 |
| Hempstead | 34,641 | 29,135 | 3.8 | 11551 * |
| Hicksville | 50,405 | — | 6.7 | 11802 * |
| Ithaca | 28,799 | 29,257 | 6.0 | 14850 |
| Jamestown | 41,818 | 43,354 | 9.5 | 14701 |
| Kingston | 29,260 | 28,817 | 7.4 | 12401 |

| URBAN PLACE | 1960 | 1950 | AREA (in square miles) | ZIP CODE NUMBERS |
|---|---|---|---|---|
| Lackawanna...... | 29,564 | 27,658 | 5.7 | 14218 |
| Levittown........ | 65,276 | — | 6.6 | 11756 |
| Lockport......... | 26,443 | 25,133 | 8.2 | 14094 |
| Long Beach...... | 26,473 | 15,586 | 2.1 | 11561 |
| Massapequa...... | 32,900 | — | 5.4 | 11758 |
| Mount Vernon.... | 76,010 | 71,899 | 4.1 | 10551 * |
| Newburgh........ | 30,979 | 31,956 | 3.7 | 12550 |
| New Rochelle.... | 76,812 | 59,725 | 10.7 | 10802 * |
| New York City... | 7,781,984 | 7,891,957 | 315.1 | 10001 * |
| Niagara Falls..... | 102,394 | 90,872 | 13.5 | 14302 * |
| North Tonawanda. | 34,757 | 24,731 | 10.5 | 14120 |
| Oceanside........ | 30,448 | — | 5.0 | 11572 |
| Plainview........ | 27,710 | — | 3.6 | 11803 |
| Poughkeepsie..... | 38,330 | 41,023 | 4.8 | 12601 * |
| Rochester........ | 318,611 | 332,488 | 36.4 | 14603 * |
| Rockville Centre.. | 26,355 | 22,362 | 3.3 | 11570 * |
| Rome............ | 51,646 | 41,682 | 77.1 | 13440 |
| Schenectady..... | 81,682 | 91,785 | 10.3 | 12305 * |
| Syracuse........ | 216,038 | 220,583 | 25.0 | 13201 * |
| Tonawanda..... | 83,771 | 14,617 | 17.6 | 14150 |
| Troy............ | 67,492 | 72,311 | 9.3 | 12180 * |
| Utica........... | 100,410 | 101,531 | 17.0 | 13503 * |
| Valley Stream.... | 38,629 | 26,854 | 3.6 | 11580 * |
| Wantagh....... | 34,172 | — | 5.5 | 11793 |
| Watertown....... | 33,306 | 34,350 | 8.8 | 13601 |
| White Plains...... | 50,485 | 43,466 | 9.4 | 10602 * |
| Yonkers......... | 190,634 | 152,798 | 18.3 | 10701 * |
| **NORTH CAROLINA** | | | | |
| Asheville........ | 60,192 | 53,000 | 24.0 | 28801 * |
| Burlington....... | 33,199 | 24,560 | 12.3 | 27215 |
| Charlotte........ | 201,564 | 134,042 | 64.8 | 28202 * |
| Durham......... | 78,302 | 71,311 | 22.0 | 27701 * |
| Fayetteville...... | 47,106 | 34,715 | 13.0 | 28302 * |
| Gastonia........ | 37,276 | 23,069 | 10.2 | 28052 |
| Goldsboro....... | 28,873 | 21,454 | 7.1 | 27530 |
| Greensboro...... | 119,574 | 74,389 | 48.6 | 27420 * |
| High Point...... | 62,063 | 39,973 | 30.3 | 27260 * |
| Kannapolis...... | 34,647 | 28,448 | 27.6 | 28081 |
| Raleigh......... | 93,931 | 65,679 | 33.5 | 27602 * |
| Rocky Mount..... | 32,147 | 27,697 | 9.7 | 27801 |
| Wilmington...... | 44,013 | 45,043 | 8.1 | 28401 |
| Wilson.......... | 28,753 | 23,010 | 7.0 | 27893 |
| Winston-Salem... | 111,135 | 87,811 | 31.1 | 27102 * |
| **NORTH DAKOTA** | | | | |
| Bismarck........ | 27,670 | 18,640 | 8.9 | 58501 |
| Fargo........... | 46,662 | 38,256 | 9.0 | 58102 |
| Grand Forks...... | 34,451 | 26,836 | 5.7 | 58201 |
| Minot.......... | 30,604 | 22,032 | 7.1 | 58701 |
| **OHIO** | | | | |
| Akron.......... | 290,351 | 274,605 | 53.9 | 44309 * |
| Alliance......... | 28,362 | 26,161 | 5.9 | 44601 |
| Barberton....... | 33,805 | 27,820 | 7.8 | 44203 |
| Canton......... | 113,631 | 116,912 | 14.3 | 44701 * |
| Cincinnati....... | 502,550 | 503,998 | 77.3 | 45202 * |
| Cleveland....... | 876,050 | 914,808 | 81.2 | 44101 * |
| Cleveland Heights. | 61,813 | 59,141 | 8.2 | 44118 |
| Columbus....... | 471,316 | 375,901 | 89.0 | 43216 * |
| Cuyahoga Falls... | 47,922 | 29,195 | 8.7 | 44222 * |
| Dayton......... | 262,332 | 243,872 | 33.6 | 45401 * |
| East Cleveland.... | 37,991 | 40,047 | 3.0 | 44112 |
| Elyria.......... | 43,782 | 30,307 | 14.3 | 44035 |
| Euclid.......... | 62,998 | 41,396 | 9.8 | 44117 |
| Findlay......... | 30,344 | 23,845 | 8.7 | 45840 |
| Garfield Heights... | 38,455 | 21,662 | 7.5 | 44125 |
| Hamilton........ | 72,354 | 57,951 | 12.2 | 45012 * |
| Kettering........ | 54,462 | — | 19.1 | 45429 |
| Lakewood....... | 66,154 | 68,071 | 5.6 | 44107 |
| Lancaster....... | 29,916 | 24,180 | 6.5 | 43130 |
| Lima........... | 51,037 | 50,246 | 8.3 | 45801 * |

| URBAN PLACE | 1960 | 1950 | AREA (in square miles) | ZIP CODE NUMBERS |
|---|---|---|---|---|
| Lorain........... | 68,932 | 51,202 | 18.0 | 44052 * |
| Mansfield........ | 47,325 | 43,564 | 9.7 | 44901 * |
| Maple Heights.... | 31,667 | 15,586 | 5.0 | 44137 |
| Marion.......... | 37,079 | 33,817 | 6.1 | 43302 |
| Massillon........ | 31,236 | 29,594 | 7.4 | 44646 |
| Middletown...... | 42,115 | 33,695 | 14.3 | 45042 |
| Newark.......... | 41,790 | 34,275 | 11.5 | 43055 |
| Norwood........ | 34,580 | 35,001 | 3.2 | 45212 |
| Parma.......... | 82,845 | 28,897 | 19.7 | 44129 |
| Portsmouth....... | 33,637 | 36,798 | 10.5 | 45662 |
| Sandusky........ | 31,989 | 29,375 | 7.4 | 44870 |
| Shaker Heights... | 36,460 | 28,222 | 6 5 | 44120 |
| South Euclid..... | 27,569 | 15,432 | 4.7 | 44121 |
| Springfield....... | 82,723 | 78,508 | 15.7 | 45501 * |
| Steubenville..... | 32,495 | 35,872 | 5.8 | 43952 |
| Toledo.......... | 318,003 | 303,616 | 48.2 | 43601 * |
| Upper Arlington... | 28,486 | 9,024 | 7.4 | 43221 |
| Warren......... | 59,648 | 49,856 | 10.9 | 44481 * |
| Youngstown...... | 166,689 | 168,330 | 33.2 | 44501 * |
| Zanesville....... | 39,077 | 40,517 | 7.9 | 43701 |
| **OKLAHOMA** | | | | |
| Bartlesville...... | 27,893 | 19,228 | 5.6 | 74003 |
| Enid............ | 38,859 | 36,017 | 9.9 | 73701 |
| Lawton.......... | 61,697 | 34,757 | 12.0 | 73501 |
| Midwest City..... | 36,058 | 10,166 | 24.0 | 73110 |
| Muskogee....... | 38,059 | 37,289 | 12.6 | 74401 |
| Norman......... | 33,412 | 27,006 | 10.1 | 73069 |
| Oklahoma City.... | 324,253 | 243,504 | 321.5 | 73125 * |
| Tulsa........... | 261,685 | 182,740 | 47.8 | 74101 * |
| **OREGON** | | | | |
| Eugene.......... | 50,977 | 35,879 | 14.5 | 97401 * |
| Portland......... | 372,676 | 373,628 | 67.2 | 97208 * |
| Salem.......... | 49,142 | 43,140 | 12.9 | 97308 * |
| **PENNSYLVANIA** | | | | |
| Abington........ | 55,831 | 28,988 | 16.3 | 19001 |
| Aliquippa........ | 26,369 | 26,132 | 4.4 | 15001 |
| Allentown........ | 108,347 | 106,756 | 17.6 | 18101 * |
| Altoona......... | 69,407 | 77,177 | 9.0 | 16603 * |
| Bethlehem....... | 75,408 | 66,340 | 19.0 | 18016 * |
| Bristol.......... | 59,298 | 12,184 | 16.9 | 19007 |
| Cheltenham...... | 35,990 | 22,854 | 9.0 | 19012 |
| Chester......... | 63,658 | 66,039 | 4.4 | 19013 |
| Easton.......... | 31,955 | 35,632 | 3.7 | 18042 |
| Erie............ | 138,440 | 130,803 | 18.8 | |
| Falls............ | 29,082 | 3,540 | 27.2 | 18615 |
| Harrisburg....... | 79,697 | 89,544 | 7.6 | 17105 * |
| Haverford....... | 54,019 | 39,641 | 10.0 | 19041 |
| Hazleton........ | 32,056 | 35,491 | 6.0 | 18201 |
| Hempfield....... | 29,704 | 22,463 | 84.4 | — |
| Johnstown....... | 53,949 | 63,232 | 5.6 | 15901 * |
| Lancaster....... | 61,055 | 63,774 | 7.3 | 17604 * |
| Lebanon........ | 30,045 | 28,156 | 4.3 | 17042 |
| Lower Merion.... | 59,420 | 48,745 | 24.0 | 19066 |
| McKeesport...... | 45,489 | 51,502 | 5.1 | 15130 |
| Middletown...... | 26,894 | 4,987 | 20.7 | 17057 |
| Millcreek........ | 28,441 | 17,037 | 35.6 | 17060 |
| Mount Lebanon.. | 35,361 | 26,604 | 6.4 | 15228 |
| New Castle...... | 44,790 | 48,834 | 9.3 | 16101 |
| Norristown...... | 38,925 | 38,126 | 3.5 | 19401 * |
| Penn Hills....... | 51,512 | 25,280 | 20.7 | 15235 |
| Philadelphia..... | 2,002,512 | 2,071,605 | 127.2 | 19104 * |
| Pittsburgh....... | 604,332 | 676,806 | 54.1 | 15219 |
| Pottstown....... | 26,144 | 22,589 | 5.0 | 19464 * |
| Reading......... | 98,177 | 109,320 | 9.6 | 19603 * |
| Ridley.......... | 35,738 | 17,212 | 5.5 | — |
| Ross........... | 25,952 | 15,744 | 13.8 | — |
| Scranton........ | 111,443 | 125,536 | 25.3 | 18503 * |
| Sharon......... | 25,267 | 26,454 | 3.8 | 16146 |
| Springfield....... | 26,733 | 10,917 | 6.9 | 19064 |
| Upper Darby..... | 93,158 | 84,951 | 8.5 | 19082 |

| URBAN PLACE | 1960 | 1950 | AREA (in square miles) | ZIP CODE NUMBERS | URBAN PLACE | 1960 | 1950 | AREA (in square miles) | ZIP CODE NUMBERS |
|---|---|---|---|---|---|---|---|---|---|
| West Mifflin | 27,289 | 17,985 | 16.0 | 15122 | Texas City | 32,065 | 16,620 | 45.0 | 77590 |
| Wilkes-Barre | 63,551 | 76,826 | 6.9 | 18701 * | Tyler | 51,230 | 38,968 | 18.3 | 75701 |
| Wilkinsburg | 30,066 | 31,418 | 2.2 | 15221 | Victoria | 33,047 | 16,126 | 12.2 | 77901 |
| Williamsport | 41,967 | 45,047 | 8.3 | 17701 | Waco | 97,808 | 84,706 | 37.3 | 76701 * |
| York | 54,504 | 59,953 | 4.7 | 17405 * | Wichita Falls | 101,724 | 68,042 | 37.3 | 76307 * |
| **RHODE ISLAND** | | | | | **UTAH** | | | | |
| Cranston | 66,766 | 55,060 | 28.7 | 02910 | Ogden | 70,197 | 57,112 | 18.9 | 84401 * |
| East Providence | 41,955 | 35,871 | 13.8 | 02914 | Provo | 36,047 | 28,937 | 19.2 | 84601 |
| Newport | 47,049 | 37,564 | 7.3 | 02840 | Salt Lake City | 189,454 | 182,121 | 56.1 | 84101 * |
| Pawtucket | 81,001 | 81,436 | 8.6 | 02860 * | **VERMONT** | | | | |
| Providence | 207,498 | 248,674 | 17.9 | 02904 * | Burlington | 35,531 | 33,155 | 16.1 | 05401 |
| Warwick | 68,504 | 43,028 | 36.3 | 02887 | **VIRGINIA** | | | | |
| Woonsocket | 47,080 | 50,211 | 8.6 | 02895 | Alexandria | 91,023 | 61,787 | 15.0 | 22313 * |
| **SOUTH CAROLINA** | | | | | Arlington County | 163,401 | 135,449 | 24.0 | 22210 * |
| | | | | | Charlottesville | 29,427 | 25,969 | 6.0 | 22901 |
| Anderson | 41,316 | 19,770 | 17.9 | 29621 | Danville | 46,577 | 35,066 | 14.0 | 24541 |
| Charleston | 65,925 | 70,174 | 5.1 | 29401 * | Hampton | 89,258 | 5,966 | 57.0 | 23369 * |
| Columbia | 97,433 | 86,914 | 18.4 | 29201 * | Lynchburg | 54,790 | 47,727 | 23.0 | 24505 * |
| Greenville | 66,188 | 58,161 | 24.3 | 29602 * | Newport News | 113,662 | 42,358 | 75.0 | 23607 * |
| Rock Hill | 29,404 | 24,502 | 9.6 | 29730 | Norfolk | 304,869 | 213,513 | 50.0 | 23501 * |
| Spartanburg | 44,352 | 36,795 | 15.8 | 29301 * | Petersburg | 36,750 | 35,054 | 8.0 | 23803 |
| **SOUTH DAKOTA** | | | | | Portsmouth | 144,773 | 80,039 | 18.0 | 23705 * |
| Rapid City | 42,399 | 25,310 | 15.7 | 57701 | Richmond | 219,958 | 230,310 | 37.0 | 23219 * |
| Sioux Falls | 65,466 | 52,696 | 17.0 | 57101 * | Roanoke | 97,110 | 91,921 | 26.0 | 24001 * |
| **TENNESSEE** | | | | | **WASHINGTON** | | | | |
| Chattanooga | 130,009 | 131,041 | 36.7 | 37401 * | Bellingham | 34,683 | 34,112 | 22.0 | 98225 |
| Inglewood | 26,527 | — | 8.4 | 37329 | Bremerton | 28,922 | 27,678 | 4.6 | 98310 |
| Jackson | 34,376 | 30,207 | 7.9 | 38301 | Everett | 40,304 | 33,849 | 11.9 | 98201 |
| Johnson City | 31,187 | 27,864 | 10.9 | 37601 | Seattle | 557,087 | 467,591 | 88.5 | 98101 * |
| Kingsport | 26,314 | 19,571 | 6.5 | 37660 | Spokane | 181,608 | 161,721 | 43.0 | 99210 * |
| Knoxville | 111,827 | 124,769 | 25.4 | 37901 * | Tacoma | 147,979 | 143,673 | 47.5 | 98402 * |
| Memphis | 497,524 | 396,000 | 128.2 | 38101 * | Vancouver | 32,464 | 41,664 | 10.1 | 98660 |
| Nashville | 170,874 | 174,307 | 29.0 | 37202 * | Yakima | 43,284 | 38,486 | 9.1 | 98901 |
| Oak Ridge | 27,169 | 30,229 | 86.0 | 37830 | **WEST VIRGINIA** | | | | |
| **TEXAS** | | | | | Charleston | 85,796 | 73,501 | 28.4 | 25301 * |
| Abilene | 90,368 | 45,570 | 62.5 | 79604 * | Clarksburg | 28,112 | 32,014 | 4.7 | 26301 |
| Amarillo | 137,969 | 74,246 | 54.8 | 79107 * | Fairmont | 27,477 | 29,346 | 7.6 | 26554 |
| Arlington | 44,775 | 7,692 | 24.0 | 76010 | Huntington | 83,627 | 86,353 | 14.0 | 25701 * |
| Austin | 186,545 | 132,459 | 49.4 | 78701 * | Parkersburg | 44,797 | 29,684 | 13.1 | 26101 |
| Baytown | 28,159 | 22,983 | 17.9 | 77520 | Weirton | 28,201 | 24,005 | 18.6 | 26062 |
| Beaumont | 119,175 | 94,014 | 70.8 | 77704 * | Wheeling | 53,400 | 58,891 | 10.8 | 26003 |
| Big Spring | 31,230 | 17,286 | 10.5 | 79720 | **WISCONSIN** | | | | |
| Brownsville | 48,040 | 36,066 | 15.7 | 78520 | Appleton | 48,411 | 34,010 | 9.6 | 54911 |
| Bryan | 27,542 | 18,102 | 16.6 | 77801 | Beloit | 32,846 | 29,590 | 6.6 | 53511 |
| Corpus Christi | 167,690 | 108,287 | 37.8 | 78403 * | Eau Claire | 37,987 | 36,058 | 17.9 | 54701 |
| Dallas | 679,684 | 434,462 | 279.9 | 75221 * | Fond du Lac | 32,719 | 29,936 | 6.9 | 54935 |
| Denton | 26,844 | 21,372 | 9.5 | 76201 | Green Bay | 62,888 | 52,735 | 19.3 | 54301 * |
| El Paso | 276,687 | 130,485 | 114.6 | 79910 * | Janesville | 35,164 | 24,899 | 11.7 | 53545 |
| Fort Worth | 356,268 | 278,778 | 140.5 | 76101 * | Kenosha | 67,899 | 54,368 | 10.1 | 53140 |
| Galveston | 67,175 | 66,568 | 84.2 | 77550 | La Crosse | 47,575 | 47,535 | 13.0 | 54601 |
| Garland | 38,501 | 10,571 | 19.2 | 75040 | Madison | 126,706 | 96,056 | 35.7 | 53703 * |
| Grand Prairie | 30,386 | 14,594 | 14.9 | 75050 | Manitowoc | 32,275 | 27,598 | 10.3 | 54220 |
| Harlingen | 41,207 | 23,229 | 31.0 | 78550 | Milwaukee | 741,324 | 637,392 | 91.1 | 53202 * |
| Houston | 938,219 | 596,163 | 328.1 | 77002 * | Oshkosh | 45,110 | 41,084 | 8.8 | 54901 |
| Irving | 45,985 | 2,621 | 20.8 | 75060 | Racine | 89,144 | 71,193 | 11.2 | 53401 * |
| Kingsville | 25,297 | 16,898 | 5.3 | 78363 | Sheboygan | 45,747 | 42,365 | 7.6 | 53081 |
| Laredo | 60,678 | 51,910 | 13.5 | 78040 | Superior | 33,563 | 35,325 | 36.6 | 54880 |
| Longview | 40,050 | 24,502 | 19.4 | 75601 | Waukesha | 30,004 | 21,233 | 5.8 | 53186 |
| Lubbock | 128,691 | 71,747 | 75.0 | 79408 * | Wausau | 31,943 | 30,414 | 8.0 | 54401 |
| McAllen | 32,728 | 20,067 | 9.5 | 78501 | Wauwatosa | 56,923 | 33,324 | 13.1 | 53213 |
| Mesquite | 27,526 | 1,696 | 21.2 | 75149 | West Allis | 68,157 | 42,959 | 11.4 | 53214 |
| Midland | 62,625 | 21,713 | 22.9 | 79701 | **WYOMING** | | | | |
| Odessa | 80,338 | 29,495 | 15.7 | 79760 | Casper | 38,930 | 23,673 | 6.8 | 82601 |
| Orange | 25,605 | 21,174 | 7.6 | 77630 | Cheyenne | 43,505 | 31,935 | 10.5 | 82001 |
| Pasadena | 58,737 | 22,483 | 22.0 | 77501 | **PUERTO RICO** | | | | |
| Port Arthur | 66,676 | 57,530 | 45.7 | 77640 | Arecibo | 28,828 | 28,659 | 5.7 | 00612 |
| San Angelo | 58,815 | 52,093 | 29.7 | 76901 | Caguas | 32,015 | 33,759 | 2.6 | 00625 |
| San Antonio | 587,718 | 408,442 | 160.5 | 78205 * | Mayagüez | 50,147 | 58,944 | 2.6 | 00708 |
| Temple | 30,419 | 25,467 | 19.2 | 76501 | Ponce | 114,286 | 99,492 | 12.7 | 00731 |
| Texarkana | 30,218 | 24,753 | 15.9 | 75501 | San Juan | 432,377 | 224,767 | 29.9 | 00936 * |

## TEMPERATURES IN U.S. CITIES

Average monthly temperatures in American cities vary from a low of 8.7° F. in Duluth, Minnesota in January, to a high of 89.8° F. in Phoenix, Arizona, in July. The table below shows average monthly Fahrenheit temperatures in selected American cities. Data was compiled by the U.S. Weather Bureau over a 30-year period, from 1931 through 1960.

| CITY AND STATE | Jan. | Feb. | Mar. | Apr. | May | June | July | Aug. | Sept. | Oct. | Nov. | Dec. | ANNUAL |
|---|---|---|---|---|---|---|---|---|---|---|---|---|---|
| Albany, N.Y. | 22.7° | 23.7° | 33.0° | 46.2° | 57.9° | 67.3° | 72.1° | 70.0° | 61.6° | 50.8° | 39.1° | 26.5° | 47.6° |
| Albuquerque, N.Mex. | 35.0 | 39.9 | 45.8 | 55.7 | 65.1 | 74.9 | 78.5 | 76.2 | 70.0 | 58.0 | 43.6 | 37.0 | 56.6 |
| Atlanta, Ga. | 44.8 | 46.5 | 51.9 | 61.0 | 69.6 | 76.8 | 78.8 | 78.4 | 73.1 | 62.7 | 51.1 | 44.1 | 61.6 |
| Atlantic City, N.J. | 34.8 | 34.7 | 41.1 | 51.0 | 61.3 | 70.0 | 75.1 | 73.7 | 67.2 | 57.2 | 46.7 | 36.6 | 54.1 |
| Baltimore, Md. | 37.3 | 37.8 | 44.7 | 55.7 | 66.1 | 74.7 | 79.1 | 77.3 | 70.6 | 60.0 | 48.8 | 39.0 | 57.6 |
| Bismarck, N. Dak. | 9.9 | 13.5 | 26.2 | 43.5 | 55.9 | 64.5 | 71.7 | 69.3 | 58.7 | 46.7 | 28.9 | 17.8 | 42.2 |
| Boise, Idaho | 29.1 | 34.5 | 41.7 | 50.4 | 58.2 | 65.8 | 75.2 | 72.1 | 62.7 | 51.6 | 38.6 | 32.2 | 51.0 |
| Boston, Mass. | 29.9 | 30.3 | 37.7 | 47.9 | 58.8 | 67.8 | 73.7 | 71.7 | 65.3 | 55.0 | 44.9 | 33.3 | 51.4 |
| Buffalo, N.Y. | 24.5 | 24.1 | 31.5 | 43.5 | 54.8 | 64.8 | 69.8 | 68.4 | 61.4 | 50.8 | 39.1 | 27.7 | 46.7 |
| Burlington, Vt. | 16.2 | 17.4 | 26.7 | 41.2 | 53.8 | 64.2 | 69.0 | 66.7 | 58.4 | 47.6 | 35.3 | 21.5 | 43.2 |
| Charleston, W. Va. | 36.6 | 37.5 | 44.4 | 55.3 | 64.8 | 72.0 | 74.9 | 73.8 | 68.2 | 57.3 | 45.3 | 37.1 | 55.6 |
| Charlotte, N.C. | 42.7 | 44.2 | 50.0 | 60.3 | 69.0 | 77.1 | 79.2 | 78.7 | 72.9 | 62.5 | 50.4 | 42.7 | 60.8 |
| Cheyenne, Wyo. | 25.4 | 27.3 | 32.4 | 42.6 | 52.9 | 63.0 | 70.0 | 67.7 | 58.6 | 47.5 | 34.2 | 29.5 | 45.9 |
| Chicago, Ill. | 26.0 | 27.7 | 36.3 | 49.0 | 60.0 | 70.5 | 75.6 | 74.2 | 66.1 | 55.1 | 39.9 | 29.1 | 50.8 |
| Cincinnati, Ohio | 35.5 | 36.8 | 44.3 | 55.7 | 65.8 | 75.3 | 78.8 | 77.4 | 70.6 | 59.5 | 46.4 | 37.2 | 56.9 |
| Cleveland, Ohio | 27.6 | 27.6 | 35.4 | 46.6 | 57.5 | 67.2 | 71.5 | 69.9 | 63.4 | 52.8 | 40.4 | 29.9 | 49.2 |
| Columbia, S.C. | 46.9 | 48.4 | 54.4 | 63.6 | 72.2 | 79.7 | 81.6 | 80.5 | 75.3 | 64.7 | 53.7 | 46.4 | 64.0 |
| Columbus, Ohio | 29.9 | 31.1 | 38.9 | 50.8 | 61.5 | 70.8 | 74.8 | 73.2 | 65.9 | 54.2 | 41.2 | 31.5 | 52.0 |
| Concord, N.H. | 21.2 | 22.7 | 31.7 | 43.8 | 55.5 | 64.5 | 69.6 | 67.4 | 59.3 | 48.7 | 37.6 | 25.0 | 45.6 |
| Dallas, Texas | 45.9 | 49.5 | 56.1 | 65.0 | 72.9 | 81.3 | 84.9 | 85.0 | 77.9 | 67.8 | 54.9 | 48.1 | 65.8 |
| Des Moines, Iowa | 20.8 | 24.4 | 35.5 | 50.4 | 62.3 | 72.4 | 77.5 | 75.0 | 66.4 | 54.2 | 37.4 | 25.5 | 50.2 |
| Denver, Colo. | 28.5 | 31.5 | 36.4 | 46.4 | 56.2 | 66.5 | 72.9 | 71.5 | 63.0 | 51.4 | 37.7 | 31.6 | 49.5 |
| Detroit, Mich. | 26.9 | 27.2 | 34.8 | 47.6 | 59.0 | 69.7 | 74.4 | 72.8 | 65.1 | 53.8 | 40.4 | 29.9 | 50.1 |
| Duluth, Minn. | 8.7 | 10.8 | 21.3 | 37.0 | 49.2 | 58.8 | 65.5 | 63.8 | 54.2 | 44.6 | 27.3 | 14.0 | 37.9 |
| El Paso, Texas | 42.9 | 49.1 | 54.9 | 63.4 | 71.9 | 81.0 | 81.9 | 80.4 | 74.5 | 64.4 | 51.2 | 44.1 | 63.3 |
| Great Falls, Mont. | 22.1 | 23.8 | 30.7 | 43.6 | 53.0 | 59.9 | 69.4 | 66.8 | 57.4 | 47.5 | 34.3 | 27.3 | 44.7 |
| Hartford, Conn. | 27.4 | 28.5 | 36.7 | 48.2 | 59.1 | 67.9 | 72.8 | 70.8 | 63.0 | 52.9 | 41.8 | 30.2 | 49.9 |
| Honolulu, Hawaii | 72.5 | 72.4 | 72.8 | 74.2 | 75.9 | 77.9 | 78.8 | 79.4 | 79.2 | 78.2 | 75.9 | 73.6 | 75.9 |
| Houston, Texas | 54.6 | 57.1 | 62.4 | 69.3 | 76.2 | 82.2 | 83.9 | 84.1 | 79.8 | 72.4 | 61.6 | 56.5 | 70.0 |
| Indianapolis, Ind. | 29.1 | 31.1 | 38.9 | 50.8 | 61.4 | 71.1 | 75.2 | 73.7 | 66.5 | 55.4 | 40.9 | 31.1 | 52.1 |
| Jackson, Miss. | 48.0 | 50.7 | 56.4 | 64.4 | 72.5 | 79.4 | 81.6 | 81.3 | 76.2 | 66.5 | 54.9 | 49.0 | 65.1 |
| Jacksonville, Fla. | 55.9 | 57.5 | 62.2 | 68.7 | 75.8 | 80.8 | 82.6 | 82.3 | 79.4 | 71.0 | 61.7 | 56.1 | 69.5 |
| Juneau, Alaska | 25.1 | 26.8 | 30.4 | 38.0 | 45.6 | 52.3 | 55.3 | 54.1 | 48.9 | 41.6 | 34.3 | 28.4 | 40.1 |
| Kansas City, Mo. | 31.7 | 35.8 | 43.3 | 55.7 | 65.6 | 75.9 | 81.5 | 79.8 | 71.3 | 60.2 | 44.6 | 35.8 | 56.8 |
| Little Rock, Ark. | 40.6 | 44.4 | 51.8 | 62.4 | 70.5 | 78.9 | 81.9 | 81.3 | 74.3 | 63.1 | 49.5 | 41.9 | 61.7 |
| Louisville, Ky. | 35.0 | 35.8 | 43.3 | 54.8 | 64.4 | 73.4 | 77.6 | 76.2 | 69.5 | 57.9 | 44.7 | 36.3 | 55.7 |
| Los Angeles, Calif. | 55.8 | 57.1 | 59.4 | 61.8 | 64.4 | 68.0 | 73.0 | 73.1 | 71.9 | 67.4 | 62.7 | 58.2 | 64.4 |
| Memphis, Tenn. | 41.5 | 44.1 | 51.1 | 61.4 | 70.3 | 78.5 | 81.3 | 80.5 | 73.9 | 63.1 | 50.1 | 42.5 | 61.5 |
| Miami, Fla. | 66.9 | 67.9 | 70.5 | 74.2 | 77.6 | 80.8 | 81.8 | 82.3 | 81.3 | 77.8 | 72.4 | 68.1 | 75.1 |
| Milwaukee, Wis. | 20.6 | 22.4 | 31.0 | 43.6 | 53.4 | 63.3 | 68.7 | 67.8 | 60.3 | 50.0 | 35.8 | 24.6 | 45.1 |
| Minneapolis, Minn. | 12.4 | 15.7 | 27.4 | 44.3 | 57.3 | 66.8 | 72.3 | 70.0 | 60.4 | 48.9 | 31.2 | 18.1 | 43.7 |
| Mobile, Ala. | 53.0 | 55.2 | 60.3 | 67.6 | 75.6 | 81.5 | 82.6 | 82.1 | 77.9 | 69.9 | 58.9 | 54.1 | 68.2 |
| Nashville, Tenn. | 39.9 | 42.0 | 49.1 | 59.6 | 68.6 | 77.4 | 80.2 | 79.2 | 72.8 | 61.5 | 48.5 | 41.4 | 60.0 |
| New Orleans, La. | 55.5 | 57.7 | 62.1 | 68.9 | 75.7 | 81.1 | 82.6 | 82.5 | 78.9 | 71.1 | 61.0 | 56.6 | 69.5 |
| New York, N.Y. | 32.2 | 33.4 | 40.5 | 51.4 | 62.4 | 71.4 | 76.8 | 75.1 | 68.5 | 58.3 | 47.0 | 35.9 | 54.5 |
| Norfolk, Va. | 41.2 | 41.6 | 48.0 | 58.0 | 67.5 | 75.6 | 78.8 | 77.5 | 72.6 | 62.0 | 51.4 | 42.5 | 59.7 |
| Omaha, Nebr. | 22.3 | 26.5 | 36.9 | 51.7 | 63.0 | 73.1 | 78.5 | 76.2 | 66.9 | 55.7 | 38.9 | 28.2 | 51.5 |
| Oklahoma City, Okla. | 37.0 | 41.3 | 48.5 | 59.9 | 68.4 | 78.0 | 82.5 | 82.8 | 73.8 | 62.9 | 48.4 | 40.3 | 60.3 |
| Philadelphia, Penn. | 32.3 | 33.2 | 41.0 | 52.0 | 62.6 | 71.0 | 75.6 | 73.6 | 66.7 | 55.7 | 44.3 | 33.9 | 53.5 |
| Phoenix, Ariz. | 49.7 | 53.5 | 59.0 | 67.2 | 75.0 | 83.6 | 89.8 | 87.5 | 82.8 | 70.7 | 58.1 | 51.6 | 69.0 |
| Pittsburgh, Penn. | 28.9 | 29.2 | 36.8 | 49.0 | 59.8 | 68.4 | 72.1 | 70.8 | 64.2 | 53.1 | 40.8 | 30.7 | 50.3 |
| Portland, Maine | 21.8 | 22.8 | 31.4 | 42.5 | 53.0 | 62.1 | 68.1 | 66.8 | 58.7 | 48.6 | 38.1 | 25.8 | 45.0 |
| Providence, R.I. | 29.2 | 29.7 | 37.0 | 47.2 | 57.5 | 66.2 | 72.1 | 70.5 | 63.2 | 53.2 | 43.0 | 32.0 | 50.1 |
| Richmond, Va. | 38.7 | 39.9 | 47.7 | 58.1 | 67.0 | 75.1 | 78.1 | 76.0 | 70.2 | 58.7 | 48.5 | 39.7 | 58.1 |
| Sacramento, Calif. | 46.4 | 50.5 | 54.2 | 59.3 | 64.2 | 70.0 | 74.0 | 72.8 | 71.4 | 63.7 | 54.3 | 47.3 | 60.7 |
| St. Louis, Mo. | 31.9 | 34.7 | 42.6 | 54.9 | 64.2 | 74.1 | 78.1 | 76.8 | 69.5 | 58.4 | 44.1 | 34.8 | 55.3 |
| Salt Lake City, Utah | 27.2 | 32.5 | 40.4 | 49.9 | 58.9 | 67.4 | 76.9 | 74.5 | 64.4 | 51.7 | 36.7 | 30.1 | 50.9 |
| San Francisco, Calif. | 50.7 | 53.0 | 54.7 | 55.7 | 57.4 | 59.1 | 58.8 | 59.4 | 62.0 | 61.4 | 57.4 | 52.5 | 56.8 |
| San Juan, P.R. | 75.1 | 75.1 | 76.0 | 77.0 | 78.8 | 79.9 | 80.1 | 80.8 | 80.7 | 80.2 | 78.6 | 76.7 | 78.3 |
| Sault Ste. Marie, Mich | 15.8 | 15.7 | 23.8 | 38.0 | 49.6 | 59.0 | 64.6 | 64.0 | 55.8 | 46.3 | 33.3 | 20.9 | 40.6 |
| Seattle, Wash. | 41.2 | 43.6 | 46.4 | 51.8 | 57.4 | 61.4 | 65.6 | 65.0 | 61.2 | 54.4 | 46.9 | 43.8 | 53.2 |
| Sioux Falls, S. Dak. | 15.2 | 19.1 | 30.1 | 45.9 | 58.3 | 68.1 | 74.3 | 71.8 | 61.8 | 50.3 | 32.6 | 21.1 | 45.7 |
| Spokane, Wash. | 25.3 | 30.0 | 38.1 | 47.3 | 56.2 | 61.9 | 70.5 | 68.0 | 60.9 | 49.1 | 35.7 | 30.1 | 47.8 |
| Wichita, Kans. | 32.0 | 36.3 | 44.5 | 56.7 | 66.0 | 76.5 | 80.9 | 80.8 | 71.3 | 59.9 | 44.4 | 35.8 | 57.1 |
| Washington, D.C. | 36.9 | 37.8 | 44.8 | 55.7 | 65.8 | 74.2 | 78.2 | 76.5 | 69.7 | 59.0 | 47.7 | 38.1 | 57.0 |
| Wilmington, Del. | 33.4 | 33.8 | 41.3 | 52.1 | 62.7 | 71.4 | 76.0 | 74.3 | 67.6 | 56.6 | 45.4 | 35.1 | 54.1 |

## RECORD TEMPERATURES IN U.S. CITIES

The highest temperature ever recorded in the United States was 134° F. at Death Valley, California in July 1913; the record low, −78° F., was set at Fort Yukon, Alaska, in January 1934. Temperatures listed below were compiled by the U.S. Weather Bureau.

| CITY AND STATE | RECORD TEMPERATURE Highest | Lowest | CITY AND STATE | RECORD TEMPERATURE Highest | Lowest |
|---|---|---|---|---|---|
| Albuquerque, N. Mex......... | 103° F. | −7° F. | Los Angeles, Calif............ | 110° F. | 28° F. |
| Atlanta, Ga................. | 98° | −3° | Memphis, Tenn.............. | 106° | −13° |
| Baltimore, Md.............. | 107° | −7° | Miami, Fla................. | 98° | 32° |
| Bismarck, N. Dak........... | 108° | −38° | Milwaukee, Wis............ | 98° | −24° |
| Boise, Idaho............... | 111° | −17° | Minneapolis–St. Paul, Minn... | 99° | −32° |
| Boston, Mass.............. | 100° | −12° | Mobile, Ala................ | 100° | 8° |
| Buffalo, N.Y............... | 94° | −20° | Nashville, Tenn............ | 107° | −15° |
| Burlington, Vt............. | 101° | −30° | New Orleans, La............ | 97° | 17° |
| Charleston, W. Va......... | 102° | −12° | New York, N.Y............. | 106° | −15° |
| Charlotte, N.C............. | 100° | 2° | Omaha, Nebr............... | 107° | −15° |
| Cheyenne, Wyo............ | 96° | −27° | Oklahoma City, Okla........ | 107° | −4° |
| Chicago, Ill............... | 104° | −15° | Philadelphia, Penn......... | 100° | −5° |
| Cleveland, Ohio........... | 93° | −19° | Phoenix, Ariz.............. | 114° | 20° |
| Columbia, S.C............. | 107° | 4° | Pittsburgh, Penn........... | 95° | −18° |
| Concord, N.H............. | 100° | −37° | Portland, Maine........... | 100° | −39° |
| Dallas, Texas............. | 107° | 8° | Portland, Oreg............ | 105° | −3° |
| Des Moines, Iowa......... | 100° | −22° | Providence, R.I............ | 97° | −9° |
| Denver, Colo.............. | 100° | −25° | Reno, Nev................. | 104° | −16° |
| Detroit, Mich............. | 105° | −16° | Richmond, Va.............. | 104° | −12° |
| Great Falls, Mont......... | 106° | −36° | St. Louis, Mo.............. | 105° | −11° |
| Hartford, Conn............ | 101° | −26° | Salt Lake City, Utah........ | 107° | −18° |
| Honolulu, Hawaii.......... | 88° | 57° | San Francisco, Calif........ | 101° | 30° |
| Houston, Texas........... | 106° | 17° | San Juan, P.R.............. | 94° | 60° |
| Indianapolis, Ind......... | 97° | −18° | Seattle, Wash............. | 99° | 10° |
| Jackson, Miss............. | 100° | −1° | Sioux Falls, S. Dak........ | 108° | −31° |
| Juneau, Alaska............ | 84° | −21° | Washington, D.C........... | 100° | 3° |
| Little Rock, Ark........... | 108° | −4° | Wichita, Kans............. | 113° | −12° |
| Louisville, Ky.............. | 101° | −20° | Wilmington, Del............ | 102° | −4° |

## PRECIPITATION AND WIND SPEED IN U.S. CITIES

Source: U.S. Weather Bureau

| CITY AND STATE | ANNUAL AVERAGES Rainfall (in inches) | Snow and Sleet (in inches) | Wind Speed (in m.p.h.) | CITY AND STATE | ANNUAL AVERAGES Rainfall (in inches) | Snow and Sleet (in inches) | Wind Speed (in m.p.h.) |
|---|---|---|---|---|---|---|---|
| Albuquerque, N.Mex. | 8.13 | 10.1 | 8.9 | Los Angeles, Calif.. | 14.68 | Trace | 6.2 |
| Atlanta, Ga........ | 47.14 | 1.7 | 9.5 | Memphis, Tenn.... | 49.73 | 5.5 | 9.3 |
| Baltimore, Md...... | 44.21 | 22.7 | 9.9 | Miami, Fla......... | 59.76 | 0.0 | 8.9 |
| Bismarck, N. Dak... | 15.15 | 35.9 | 10.9 | Milwaukee, Wis.... | 29.51 | 42.8 | 12.1 |
| Boise, Idaho...... | 11.43 | 20.4 | 9.1 | Minneapolis– | | | |
| Boston, Mass...... | 42.77 | 40.4 | 13.1 | St. Paul, Minn... | 24.78 | 41.5 | 10.8 |
| Buffalo, N.Y...... | 35.65 | 103.5 | 12.8 | Mobile, Ala........ | 68.13 | 0.5 | 9.7 |
| Burlington, Vt..... | 33.21 | 69.3 | 9.0 | Nashville, Tenn.... | 45.15 | 10.7 | 7.6 |
| Charleston, W. Va.. | 44.43 | 26.1 | 6.6 | New Orleans, La... | 62.96 | 0.1 | 6.9 |
| Charlotte, N.C.... | 43.38 | 4.4 | 7.7 | New York, N.Y..... | 42.37 | 29.7 | 9.6 |
| Cheyenne, Wyo.... | 15.06 | 55.5 | 12.6 | Omaha, Nebr...... | 27.56 | 32.7 | 11.3 |
| Chicago, Ill....... | 33.18 | 37.0 | 10.1 | Oklahoma City, Okla. | 30.82 | 9.3 | 13.8 |
| Cleveland, Ohio... | 35.35 | 51.2 | 11.1 | Philadelphia, Penn. | 42.48 | 20.0 | 9.6 |
| Columbia, S.C.... | 46.82 | 1.2 | 6.9 | Phoenix, Ariz...... | 7.20 | Trace | 5.4 |
| Concord, N.H...... | 38.80 | 61.3 | 6.7 | Pittsburgh, Penn... | 36.14 | 43.8 | 9.5 |
| Dallas, Texas...... | 34.55 | 2.0 | 10.9 | Portland, Maine... | 42.85 | 71.7 | 9.0 |
| Des Moines, Iowa.. | 30.37 | 33.8 | 11.5 | Portland, Oreg.... | 42.37 | 9.0 | 7.7 |
| Denver, Colo....... | 14.81 | 59.1 | 9.6 | Providence, R.I.... | 42.13 | 39.3 | 11.2 |
| Detroit, Mich...... | 30.95 | 31.5 | 10.1 | Reno, Nev........ | 7.15 | 23.9 | 6.4 |
| El Paso, Texas..... | 7.89 | 4.5 | 10.4 | Richmond, Va..... | 44.21 | 13.1 | 7.7 |
| Great Falls, Mont.. | 14.07 | 53.3 | 13.7 | St. Louis, Mo..... | 35.31 | 17.2 | 9.3 |
| Hartford, Conn.... | 42.92 | 52.8 | 9.3 | Salt Lake City, Utah | 13.90 | 52.0 | 8.8 |
| Honolulu, Hawaii.. | 21.89 | 0.0 | 11.9 | San Francisco, Calif. | 20.78 | Trace | 8.7 |
| Houston, Texas.... | 45.26 | 0.4 | 11.1 | San Juan, P.R..... | 60.36 | 0.0 | 8.2 |
| Indianapolis, Ind... | 39.25 | 19.0 | 10.2 | Seattle, Wash...... | 34.10 | 8.1 | 10.2 |
| Jackson, Miss..... | 49.33 | 2.3 | 6.5 | Sioux Falls, S. Dak. | 25.16 | 42.6 | 11.0 |
| Juneau, Alaska.... | 54.62 | 94.9 | 8.4 | Washington, D.C... | 40.78 | 16.4 | 9.6 |
| Little Rock, Ark.... | 48.66 | 5.2 | 8.3 | Wichita, Kans...... | 28.41 | 16.6 | 13.0 |
| Louisville, Ky...... | 41.32 | 15.4 | 8.3 | Wilmington, Del.... | 44.56 | 21.2 | 8.8 |

## OCCURRENCE OF FROST IN U.S. CITIES

The latest spring frost was recorded on June 25 at Reno, Nevada; the earliest autumn frost on August 22 at Sault Ste. Marie, Michigan.

The following data on record dates of frost occurrence was compiled over a 30-year period by the U.S. Weather Bureau.

| CITY AND STATE | ELEVATION OF WEATHER STATION (in feet) | SPRING FROST DATE | | FALL FROST DATE | |
|---|---|---|---|---|---|
| | | Average | Latest on record | Average | Earliest on record |
| Albany, N.Y. | 19 | April 27 | May 20 | October 13 | September 23 |
| Albuquerque, N. Mex. | 5,310 | April 16 | May 18 | October 29 | October 11 |
| Atlanta, Ga. | 1,054 | March 20 | April 15 | November 19 | October 24 |
| Baltimore, Md. | 146 | March 28 | April 16 | November 17 | October 20 |
| Bismarck, N. Dak. | 1,650 | May 11 | May 30 | September 24 | September 6 |
| Boise, Idaho | 2,842 | April 29 | May 23 | October 16 | September 20 |
| Boston, Mass. | 15 | April 16 | May 19 | October 25 | September 26 |
| Buffalo, N.Y. | 693 | April 30 | May 24 | October 25 | September 23 |
| Burlington, Vt. | 331 | May 8 | May 23 | October 3 | September 13 |
| Charleston, W. Va. | 950 | April 18 | May 11 | October 28 | September 29 |
| Charlotte, N.C. | 727 | March 21 | April 16 | November 15 | October 15 |
| Cheyenne, Wyo. | 6,131 | May 20 | June 18 | September 27 | September 5 |
| Chicago, Ill. | 610 | April 19 | May 13 | October 28 | September 25 |
| Cincinnati, Ohio | 761 | April 15 | May 25 | October 25 | September 28 |
| Cleveland, Ohio | 787 | April 21 | May 14 | November 2 | September 29 |
| Columbia, S.C. | 217 | March 14 | April 13 | November 21 | November 1 |
| Columbus, Ohio | 815 | April 17 | May 9 | October 30 | October 7 |
| Concord, N.H. | 339 | May 11 | May 26 | September 30 | September 13 |
| Dallas, Texas | 487 | March 18 | April 15 | November 22 | October 27 |
| Des Moines, Iowa | 807 | April 20 | May 11 | October 19 | September 28 |
| Denver, Colo. | 5,221 | May 2 | May 28 | October 14 | September 18 |
| Detroit, Mich. | 619 | April 25 | May 12 | October 23 | September 29 |
| El Paso, Texas | 3,920 | March 13 | April 11 | November 11 | October 31 |
| Great Falls, Mont. | 3,664 | May 14 | June 8 | September 26 | September 7 |
| Hartford, Conn. | 169 | April 22 | May 10 | October 19 | September 27 |
| Houston, Texas | 41 | February 5 | March 26 | December 11 | October 25 |
| Indianapolis, Ind. | 718 | April 17 | May 11 | October 27 | October 1 |
| Jackson, Miss. | 305 | March 10 | April 13 | November 13 | October 17 |
| Jacksonville, Fla. | 18 | February 6 | May 14 | December 16 | November 9 |
| Juneau, Alaska | 15 | April 27 | June 8 | October 19 | September 22 |
| Kansas City, Mo. | 741 | April 5 | April 17 | October 31 | October 6 |
| Little Rock, Ark. | 257 | March 16 | April 13 | November 15 | October 23 |
| Louisville, Ky. | 457 | April 1 | April 19 | November 7 | October 15 |
| Los Angeles, Calif. | 312 | — | January 21 | — | December 9 |
| Memphis, Tenn. | 263 | March 20 | April 15 | November 12 | October 17 |
| Miami, Fla. | 8 | — | February 6 | — | — |
| Milwaukee, Wis. | 672 | April 20 | May 9 | October 25 | September 24 |
| Minneapolis, Minn. | 830 | April 30 | May 24 | October 13 | September 18 |
| Mobile, Ala. | 10 | February 17 | March 20 | December 12 | November 15 |
| Nashville, Tenn. | 577 | March 28 | April 19 | November 7 | October 17 |
| New Orleans, La. | 9 | February 15 | March 20 | December 3 | November 13 |
| New York, N.Y. | 10 | April 7 | April 24 | November 12 | October 19 |
| Norfolk, Va. | 26 | March 18 | April 14 | November 27 | November 7 |
| Omaha, Nebr. | 978 | April 14 | May 11 | October 19 | September 24 |
| Oklahoma City, Okla. | 1,254 | March 28 | April 17 | November 7 | October 23 |
| Philadelphia, Penn. | 26 | March 30 | April 20 | November 17 | October 19 |
| Phoenix, Ariz. | 1,083 | January 27 | March 2 | December 11 | November 4 |
| Pittsburgh, Penn. | 749 | April 16 | May 4 | November 3 | October 10 |
| Portland, Maine | 61 | April 29 | May 30 | October 15 | September 17 |
| Portland, Oreg. | 30 | February 25 | May 4 | December 1 | October 30 |
| Providence, R.I. | 55 | April 13 | April 24 | October 27 | October 3 |
| Reno, Nev. | 4,397 | May 14 | June 25 | October 2 | August 30 |
| Richmond, Va. | 162 | April 2 | April 20 | November 8 | October 21 |
| Sacramento, Calif. | 25 | January 24 | March 14 | December 11 | November 4 |
| St. Louis, Mo. | 465 | April 2 | May 2 | November 8 | October 14 |
| Salt Lake City, Utah | 4,260 | April 12 | April 30 | November 1 | September 25 |
| San Francisco, Calif. | 52 | — | January 21 | — | December 11 |
| Sault Ste. Marie, Mich. | 721 | May 18 | June 8 | October 3 | August 22 |
| Seattle, Wash. | 14 | February 23 | April 3 | December 1 | October 19 |
| Sioux Falls, S. Dak. | 1,420 | May 5 | May 29 | October 3 | September 12 |
| Spokane, Wash. | 2,357 | April 20 | May 16 | October 12 | September 18 |
| Washington, D.C. | 72 | April 10 | May 12 | October 28 | October 2 |
| Wichita, Kans. | 1,321 | April 5 | April 21 | November 1 | September 27 |
| Wilmington, Del. | 73 | April 18 | May 9 | October 26 | September 27 |

# NATIONAL AND WORLD ECONOMY

## U. S. Business, Labor, Agriculture • Other National Economies • Foreign Trade

Harnessing the power potential of the Niagara River are New York's Robert Moses Niagara Power Plant (left) and Canada's Sir Adam Beck Generating Station (right). Such complexes help fill the growing demand for electricity.

State of New York Power Authority

## U.S. ECONOMY: 1967

For the American economy the year 1967 was one of realistic readjustment as the prosperous nation paused after an overheated 1966 and before a potentially overheated 1968. Moreover, as a direct result of the turbulent growth of the previous year, the Johnson Administration chose to use fiscal as well as monetary policy changes to restrain demand and to stabilize the growth rate throughout 1967.

Halfway through 1965 the nation suddenly realized that it was at war, economically as well as politically. For the following nine months the economy—already growing dynamically at over 4 per cent per year—was pressed by tremendous demands for greater plant capacity, for skilled workers, and, finally, for money and credit. The growth rate rose to over 5½ per cent; plant use grew to 92 per cent of capacity;

and skilled labor demanded higher wages.

The Federal Reserve Board, the nation's central bank, used credit control to dampen excessive demand by raising the interest rates. Using monetary policy alone to control demand, however, had serious consequences: the nation's construction industry came to a virtual standstill, and a near-panic seized the money and credit markets as interest rates broke 40-year-old record highs. Also, as bonds became more attractive investments than stocks, the stock market took a nose dive.

As 1967 began, the signs of recession were in the wind. When the economy had begun to slow down, wholesale inventories had accumulated to near-record levels—usually the prelude to a slump in production and employment. Clearly, the economic boom was ending. *(continued)*

## U.S. ECONOMY: 1967 *(continued)*

Worse yet, a feeling of general apprehension about the war in Vietnam and the direction in which that war, swept the country in early 1967. As the result of a massive wholesale inventory, consumer savings began to rise from an expected 5 per cent to over 7 per cent, and this lack of spending served to exaggerate the inventory problem.

But the expected recession failed to take place. In late November, 1966, the Federal Reserve Board completely reversed its stand and liberalized credit. Almost immediately, the major banks cut their prime lending rates, and a sigh of relief was nearly audible in the money markets and along Wall Street. The government also gave the economy a quick shot in the arm, not only by maintaining defense spending at high levels, but by releasing previously withheld highway construction funds. Both actions, while not of great economic significance in themselves, had a profoundly salutary psychological effect.

Finally, in mid-March, 1967, consumer savings began to drop as confidence in the economy was restored. And, with this resumption in spending, inventories began to dwindle. In six months the national inventory accumulation rate dropped from $20 billion annually to less than $5 billion a year.

As industry placed new orders for capital equipment, production began to increase. Almost overnight an inventory drag on the economy turned into an inventory push.

Prices felt the push first. During 1966 the economy was characterized by "demand-pull" inflation; excessive demand for goods and services in the wholesale markets "pulled" up the cost of both labor and materials. But with a huge wholesale inventory to liquidate quickly, businesses, in general, could not pass on their 1966 cost increases to the consumer. However, as inventories dropped, consumer prices responded to the pressure and were expected to keep on rising through the winter of 1967–68.

But price increases began to erode wage gains, setting off an intensification of the wage-price spiral and pushing settlements over 5 per cent on the average. The settlement of the auto strike was expected to set a precedent for large wage increases throughout industry in 1968 and perhaps make collective bargaining in the steel industry even more costly than had been previously anticipated. With its eyes on the record corporate profits of the 1960–66 period, labor was clearly bargaining successfully for high settlements.

As the signs continued to point to the beginning of yet another period of inflationary growth, President Johnson called for a 10 per cent increase in taxes to be imposed as a surcharge on both corporate and individual income taxes for 1967. In addition, increased Federal spending, both domestically and for Vietnam, by late summer threatened "a budget deficit of a size that poses a clear and present danger to America's security and economic health," the President said in a special message to Congress.

Even with this added tax, it seemed likely that the deficit for fiscal year 1968 would be between $14 and $18 billion, Johnson said. In 1966 the Administration had also asked for a tax increase but then deferred it, partly on the grounds that raising taxes in a Congressional election year is bad politics. However, Washington apparently discovered that low taxes accompanied by demand-pull inflation and sky-high interest rates aren't good politics, either.

Gardner Ackley, Chairman of the President's Council of Economic Advisers, felt that by the end of the year the economy would have revitalized to the extent that a tax increase would not stifle continued growth.

As U.S. military, political, and economic commitments to Vietnam continued to rise, the Johnson Administration has maintained that the country could afford guns and butter simultaneously, without sacrificing either economic goals or political aspirations for peace in Vietnam. However, during 1967, as it continued to increase the size of armaments, the Administration found it necessary to call for increased taxes—a move that emphasized the economic impact of the war in Vietnam.

## GROSS NATIONAL PRODUCT, 1961-1967 (In billions of current dollars)
Source: U.S. Department of Commerce, Office of Business Economics

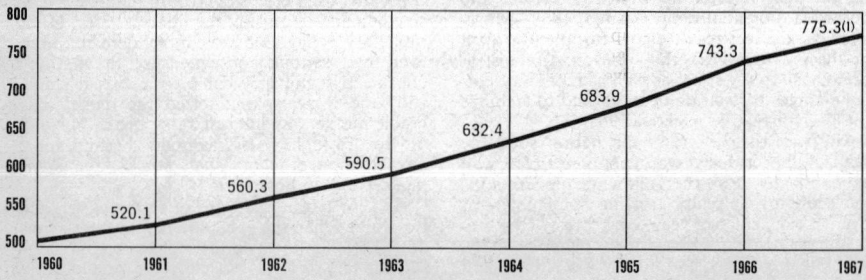

1 Seasonally adjusted at annual rate; figures are for 2nd quarter of year, preliminary.

## "THE DEATH OF WAGE-PRICE GUIDELINES"

Gardner Ackley (right) outlines his stand at a Senate-House Economic Committee hearing.

"And this time you'll have to do it without guidelines!"

It only takes such simple pursuits as buying groceries or going to a movie to be acutely aware that inflation is a fact of life today. Its effect is felt daily, but what of its cause? And what has been done to alleviate it?

First, the cause. Wages rise as new labor contracts go into force. Next, wholesale prices go up to compensate. Higher wholesale costs, in turn, pass to the consumer (many of them union workers themselves) as higher retail prices. Then bargaining begins for yet another boost to "offset the rising cost of living." This is the wage-price spiral —the enemy of price stability.

The President's Council of Economic Advisors in 1962 came up with the now-controversial wage-price guidelines, which they intended as an objective administration standard to use in determining if a specific labor settlement might be inflationary in its effect on the national economy.

Perhaps the most important reason for the apparent failure of the guideposts was that they were devised for application in an economy unlike ours in the past few years— one that by mid-1965 was working at near capacity, then suddenly was overheated by the excessive demands of war production.

Gardner Ackley, now Chairman of the President's Council of Economic Advisors, explained it this way: "The economic pressures that emerged in 1965 and 1966 imposed severe strains on the system. Rising demand, particularly the surge that followed mid-1965, was bound to and did sharply raise prices of many raw materials and farm products, at least until production could expand adequately."

The guidelines also lost what restraining influence they might have had because they repeatedly were violated by powerful unions. With the inflationary settlement of the 1966 airline machinists' strike, the guidelines were effectively buried.

Are the guideposts really dead? Apparently so, at least for the present, despite Ackley's statement that something like the present guideposts will be with us for a long time to come." For, in the absence of "voluntary restraint" on the part of both unions and management, or unless outright wage-price controls are imposed, inflation may be an ever-present companion to consumers for a long time to come.

## UNITED STATES CURRENCY

Although paper money was used early in U.S. history, the first issued under American authority (the Continental Congress), called Continental currency, had its birth in 1775. Its value became so small, however, that "not worth a Continental" became a common saying during the American Revolution.

Congress enacted laws (in 1777, 1785, and 1786) to establish a Mint and authorize coinage, but their implementation was deferred. An abortive first issue took place in 1788 when a few hundred thousand cents were struck for the government, but because of the depreciation of copper coins and their sudden rejection by the public in 1789, most did not enter circulation for a number of years.

The Act of April 2, 1792, which established a national system of coinage, authorized the following coins: gold eagles (each valued at $10), half eagles, and quarter eagles; silver dollars, half dollars, quarter dollars, dimes (each valued at one-tenth of a silver dollar), and half dimes; and copper cents and half cents.

When the Mint Act was before Congress, debate raged over the design of the proposed coins. The original bill provided that the head of the President would appear on the obverse. Patterns for a Washington-head half dollar were submitted, but the House of Representatives attacked it as "monarchical," and in the end a Liberty head was substituted.

Although regular Mint operations did not get under way until 1793, a special issue of 1,500 half dimes was struck in July, 1792, from silver deposited by President Washington. It has always been believed that the Liberty head on this issue is a portrait of Martha Washington.

Many changes in the laws governing coinage, and in the coins themselves, have been made over the years. Gold coins no longer are issued, nor are half dimes or half cents. At various times, odd denominations were issued: 1851–73, a silver three-cent piece; 1854–89, a gold three-dollar coin; 1864–73, a silver three-cent piece; 1865–89, a nickel three-cent coin; 1875–78, a twenty-cent piece. From 1873 to 1883 the Mint also struck a special coin known as the "trade dollar." Although intended only for use in the Orient (to compete with the popular Mexican peso), it entered domestic circulation because of a legislative error. Trade dollars were so abused by speculators and brokers that they were demonetized, something no other U.S. coin has ever suffered.

U.S. coins are presently minted in the following denominations: half dollar (50 cents); quarter dollar (25 cents); ten cents (dime); five cents (nickel); and one cent (penny). The only silver coin now issued is the half dollar. Quarters and dimes presently consist of a copper core sandwiched between two layers of 75 per cent copper and 25 per cent nickel. The terms "penny" and "nickel" although incorrect, have long been sanctioned by usage. But the copper-nickel cents of 1857–58 and the three-cent pieces of 1865–89 also were called nickels in their day. Today's nickel, last of the current

coins to be authorized (1866), is the only one that has never changed its composition.

The government's inability to maintain a bimetallic coinage was painfully evident by the early 1800s. A general decline in the market value of silver had caused the gold dollar to be undervalued, and gold coins were seldom found in circulation. In 1804 the Mint suspended issuance of gold eagles and silver dollars. Most of the dollars were sent to the West Indies, where they were at par value with the heavier Spanish "pieces of eight." The Spanish coins then were sent to the U.S. Mint for recoinage into dollars that, in turn, went back to the West Indies for a repeat of the cycle.

Except for copper cents and half cents, the only coin issued in any quantity in the early 19th century was the half dollar. For the Mint's first three decades, the number of half dimes, dimes, and quarters issued was less than one for every person in the nation. The Mint Act of 1834 reversed the situation by overvaluing gold. Silver coins virtually disappeared by 1849, but they returned in 1853 after their intrinsic value had been reduced. With the issuance of paper money during the Civil War, however, they were largely exported to Canada and South America, while gold coins were hoarded at home. Neither were seen in circulation between 1861 and 1876, and fractional notes, ranging in value from three to fifty cents, were issued in their place.

With the exception of Treasury notes issued in 1815 to aid the sagging war economy, there was no Federal paper currency until the Civil War. The first issuance (1861) only provided notes worth five, ten, and twenty dollars, but in 1862 a new law allowed denominations of from one to 1,000 dollars.

During the last quarter of the 19th century, legislation was passed, despite political controversy, that insured better regulation of the coinage. An 1879 act allowed the unlimited redemption of coins so that excessive issues, or the sudden dumping of hoarded or exported coins, no longer would glut the channels of trade. Laws passed in 1873, 1878, and 1889 eliminated useless denominations, and the repeal of the free coinage of silver (1900) irrevocably established a single gold standard.

Paper currency presently issued includes gold certificates and U.S. notes issued by the Treasury, and notes issued by Federal Reserve Banks under government auspices. Silver certificates (recently discontinued) are now being retired and will not be redeemable in silver after June 8, 1968. Gold certificates (Series of 1934) in denominations of $100, $1,000, $10,000 and $100,000, are issued only to Federal Reserve Banks under certain credits established with the Treasurer of the United States and do not appear in circulation. U.S. Notes, received on any account by the U.S. Treasurer, are re-issued mainly in the $5 denomination. A reserve in gold is held in the Treasury against these notes and Treasury notes of 1890.

Federal Reserve notes, the most common

## INTERESTING FACTS ABOUT AMERICAN COINS

● **The Most Valuable U. S. Coin:** The highest price ever paid for any U. S. coin — $46,000—was for a 1913 Liberty head "nickel." Only five were made, and all were originally owned by a former U. S. Mint employee. However, since no 1913 Liberty five-cent coins are accounted for in Mint records, nor any dies for striking them, their issue is believed to have been unauthorized.

● **Confederate Coinage:** In April, 1861, the Confederate government took over the Mint branch at New Orleans, intending to strike its own coins. Four half-dollar patterns were made, but for want of bullion the project was abandoned. Two of the four pattern half dollars have been located during the past few years, showing signs of considerable circulation.

● **A Slightly Late Commemorative Coin:** The Mint issued a half dollar in 1936 to commemorate "the 50th anniversary of Cincinnati, Ohio, as a center of music, and its contribution to the art of music for the past fifty years." The coin depicted Stephen Foster, who had established a music club in Cincinnati in the late 1840s and had published several of his songs (including *Oh, Susanna*) during the few years he lived there. But this commemoration was somewhat behind schedule, for the event generally recognized as having started Cincinnati's musical growth occurred 63 years before the 50th anniversary coin was issued, and in 1936 Stephen Foster had been dead for 72 years.

● **Indian Head Coin:** Various Indian heads have appeared on U. S. coins, but only two really qualify as such. The first, designed by Bela Pratt for the quarter eagle and half eagle of 1908, proved unpopular and has been described as sickly and emaciated. The other, by James Fraser for the 1913 five-cent piece, is a composite of three Indian chiefs: Iron Tail, Two Moons, and John Tree. The "Indians" on the cent (1859-1909) and on the eagle (1907-33) are actually classical heads in Indian headdress.

● **An Illegal Quarter:** William G. McAdoo, then Secretary of the Treasury, asked Congress in 1917 for legislation to permit a slight change of design in the quarter dollar adopted the previous year. The arrangement of the devices on opposite sides was said to prevent stacking the coins properly. Congress complied but prohibited any changes in the designs themselves. Nevertheless, when the new coins appeared, the beautiful but bold Liberty figure was found to be dressed in a mailed vest that reached almost to her neck. This flagrantly illegal coinage was continued through 1930.

Half dollar-Foster: Chase Manhattan Bank, 1913 Liberty Head: A. E. Bebee, 1913 Indian Head: A. E. Bebee.

---

type of U.S. paper currency, are issued in denominations of $1, $5, $10, $20, $50, $100, $500, $1,000, $5,000, and $10,000, and are retired according to currency demands. Large denominations are printed only when required. Until 1965, Federal Reserve Banks had to maintain a reserve in gold certificates, or gold-certificate credits, of at least 25 per cent of these notes. The Act of May 12, 1933, as amended, declared all U.S. coins and currencies theretofore or thereafter coined or issued to be legal tender for all debts, public and private, public charges, taxes, duties, and dues.

The U.S. Treasury Department's Mints are in Philadelphia, Denver, and San Francisco (the latter has not issued any coins since 1955). The Treasury's Bureau of Engraving and Printing in Washington manufactures U.S. paper currency and securities.

Determination of designs used on paper currency, including the selection of portraits, is a responsibility of the Secretary of the Treasury. Portraits on paper currency must be those of deceased statesmen whose place in American history are well known. Selection of designs for regular coinage is made by the Director of the Mint, with the approval of the Secretary of the Treasury; the advice of the Federal Commission of Fine Arts is also solicited. Congress, in a few cases, has prescribed a coin design, such as the Washington bicentennial 25-cent piece, issued since 1932.

The John F. Kennedy 50-cent piece, approved December 30, 1963, and released March 24, 1964, was the sixth "portrait" coin to be used as coinage. Presidential portraits are on all coins now being minted.

"In God We Trust" first appeared on a U.S. coin in 1864; heightened religious sentiment during the Civil War was mainly responsible for its use. Salmon P. Chase, then Treasury Secretary, authorized use of a motto on November 20, 1861. The now-familiar form was finally selected, but its use has occasionally been interrupted, and it has not been used on all coins of all series. It first appeared on a new two-cent piece in 1864. A law passed in 1955 provided that "In God We Trust" appear on all U.S. paper currency and coins, and in 1965 it officially became the U.S. motto.

The Great Seal of the Treasury, imprinted on the face of U.S. paper money and official Treasury documents, is older than the Consti- (continued)

**UNITED STATES CURRENCY** (*continued*)

tution. The design includes a shield on which appear the scales of justice, a key (emblem of official authority), and 13 stars (representing the original states). A Latin inscription circling the shield reads *Thesaur. Amer. Septent Sigil.* (for *Thesauri Americae Septentrionalis Sigillum*), meaning "The Seal of the Treasury of North America."

The Great Seal of the United States was adopted by the Continental Congress in 1782 and by the U.S. government in 1789. Both sides of the seal are reproduced on the U.S. $1 bill. The face shows an American bald eagle with wings spread and talons clutching an olive branch (symbol of peace) and a cluster of 13 arrows (the mark of might). In its beak the eagle grasps a ribbon with the motto *E Pluribus Unum*—Out of Many, One—in reference to the Union of the 13 states. Above the eagle's head are 13 silver stars, and its breast is protected by a plate shield of 13 stripes.

The seal's reverse side shows an unfinished pyramid of 13 steps surmounted by an aureole of light through which an eye is visible (symbolic of the eternal eye of God). The motto *Annuit Coeptis*—He Has Smiled on Our Undertaking—is imprinted above the eye. Carved into the base of the pyramid are the Roman numerals MDCCLXXVI (1776), and below it is the motto *Novus Ordo Seclorum*—New Order of the Ages. Both mottoes on the reverse side of the seal were adopted from lines written by the Roman poet Vergil.

The origin of the dollar sign ($) has been variously explained; the most widely accepted reason is that it evolved from the Mexican or Spanish "Ps" for pesos, or piastres, or pieces of eight. The theory, based on a study of old manuscripts, is that the "S" gradually came to be written over the "P," developing a close approximation of the $ mark. It was widely used before the U.S. dollar was adopted in 1875.

United States currency of the size now in use—a finished note is approximately 2.61 inches by 6.14 inches, with a thickness of 0.0043 inch—was first issued in July, 1929, replacing larger notes. New notes will stack 233 to one inch.

When paper currency becomes unfit for general use, it is withdrawn from circulation, completely destroyed by incineration, and replaced by new notes. One-dollar bills, which generally last about 18 months, make up the bulk of the currency that has to be retired in this manner. More than a billion one-dollar bills are in circulation. Worn and unfit coins are withdrawn and returned to the mints, where they are melted and the metal reused.

Mutilated U.S. paper currency with at least three-fifths of the original proportion remaining will be exchanged at full face value. Fragments less than that but clearly more than two-fifths are not exchangeable unless accompanied by satisfactory proof that the missing portions have been totally destroyed.

Printed reproductions of U.S. and foreign paper money are permissible for numismatic, educational, historical, and newsworthy purposes, but the illustrations must be in black and white and must be less than three-fourths or more than one and one-half times the actual size of the currency bill.

The gold dollar is the standard U.S. unit of value, and the Secretary of the Treasury is required to maintain all forms of money issued or coined by the U.S. at parity with the gold dollar. However, the government does not issue any gold coins, does not allow the hoarding of gold, and issues gold certificates only to Federal Reserve Banks. At least in these respects the present U.S. monetary system (sometimes described as a "gold bullion standard" or a "modified gold standard") is different from the gold standard system in operation prior to April, 1933.

## DESIGNS ON U.S. PAPER CURRENCY

| DENOMINATION | FACE | REVERSE | DENOMINATION | FACE | REVERSE |
|---|---|---|---|---|---|
| **Silver Certificates** | | | **Federal Reserve Notes** (*continued*) | | |
| $1 | Washington | Face and reverse of Great Seal of the United States | $5 | Lincoln | Lincoln Memorial |
| | | | $10 | Hamilton | U.S. Treasury Building |
| | | | $20 | Jackson | White House |
| $5 | Lincoln | Lincoln Memorial | $50 | Grant | U.S. Capitol |
| $10 | Hamilton | U.S. Treasury Building | $100 | Franklin | Independence Hall |
| **U.S. Notes** | | | $500 | McKinley | Ornate Five Hundred |
| $2 | Jefferson | Monticello | $1,000 | Cleveland | Ornate One Thousand |
| $5 | Lincoln | Lincoln Memorial | $5,000 | Madison | Ornate Five Thousand |
| **Federal Reserve Notes** | | | $10,000 | Chase | Ornate Ten Thousand |
| $1 | Washington | Face and reverse of Great Seal of the United States | **Gold Certificate** | | |
| | | | $100,000 | Wilson | Ornate One Hundred Thousand |

## PERSONAL INCOME: RANK OF THE STATES

Connecticut, where the per capita personal income in 1966 was 25% above the national average, ranked as the richest U.S. state, according to preliminary data from the U.S. Department of Commerce. Alaska and Hawaii were not included in the U.S. averages prior to 1960.

| RANK IN 1966 | STATE | PER CAPITA INCOME (in current dollars) | | | RANK IN 1966 | STATE | PER CAPITA INCOME (in current dollars) | | |
|---|---|---|---|---|---|---|---|---|---|
| | | 1966 | 1950 | 1929 | | | 1966 | 1950 | 1929 |
| 1 | Connecticut........ | $3,678 | $1,873 | $1,029 | 27 | Wyoming.......... | $2,686 | $1,668 | $677 |
| 2 | Delaware.......... | 3,563 | 2,107 | 1,017 | 28 | Montana.......... | 2,615 | 1,622 | 595 |
| 3 | Illinois............ | 3,511 | 1,825 | 957 | 29 | Vermont.......... | 2,590 | 1,145 | 627 |
| 4 | New York......... | 3,480 | 1,871 | 1,159 | 30 | Virginia.......... | 2,581 | 1,228 | 435 |
| 5 | California......... | 3,449 | 1,851 | 995 | 31 | Florida............ | 2,576 | 1,281 | 521 |
| 6 | New Jersey........ | 3,414 | 1,834 | 931 | 32 | Arizona........... | 2,528 | 1,329 | 591 |
| 7 | Nevada........... | 3,330 | 2,021 | 878 | 33 | Texas............. | 2,511 | 1,349 | 478 |
| 8 | Washington....... | 3,280 | 1,672 | 750 | 34 | Utah............. | 2,500 | 1,307 | 559 |
| 9 | Alaska............ | 3,272 | 2,384 | — | 35 | Oklahoma......... | 2,456 | 1,144 | 454 |
| 10 | Massachusetts..... | 3,271 | 1,638 | 913 | 36 | Idaho............. | 2,441 | 1,293 | 503 |
| 11 | Maryland.......... | 3,220 | 1,602 | 777 | 37 | Maine............. | 2,438 | 1,184 | 601 |
| 12 | Michigan.......... | 3,219 | 1,699 | 793 | 38 | North Dakota...... | 2,400 | 1,264 | 375 |
| 13 | Hawaii............ | 3,143 | 1,386 | — | 39 | South Dakota...... | 2,355 | 1,242 | 417 |
| 14 | Indiana........... | 3,061 | 1,513 | 612 | 40 | Georgia........... | 2,311 | 1,025 | 350 |
| 15 | Ohio.............. | 3,027 | 1,622 | 781 | 41 | New Mexico........ | 2,310 | 1,176 | 407 |
| 16 | Rhode Island...... | 2,980 | 1,623 | 871 | 42 | Louisiana......... | 2,257 | 1,120 | 415 |
| 17 | Pennsylvania...... | 2,951 | 1,540 | 775 | 43 | North Carolina..... | 2,235 | 1,031 | 334 |
| 18 | Oregon........... | 2,938 | 1,585 | 683 | 44 | Kentucky.......... | 2,205 | 997 | 391 |
| 19 | Wisconsin......... | 2,935 | 1,475 | 682 | 45 | Tennessee......... | 2,199 | 1,000 | 377 |
| 20 | Iowa............. | 2,931 | 1,496 | 577 | 46 | West Virginia...... | 2,195 | 1,065 | 462 |
| 21 | Colorado.......... | 2,872 | 1,487 | 637 | 47 | Alabama........... | 2,039 | 879 | 324 |
| 22 | Minnesota......... | 2,871 | 1,410 | 598 | 48 | South Carolina..... | 2,027 | 893 | 270 |
| 23 | Missouri.......... | 2,845 | 1,431 | 628 | 49 | Arkansas.......... | 2,015 | 841 | 305 |
| 24 | Nebraska.......... | 2,819 | 1,490 | 590 | 50 | Mississippi........ | 1,751 | 755 | 285 |
| 25 | Kansas........... | 2,814 | 1,444 | 535 | | | | | |
| 26 | New Hampshire.... | 2,761 | 1,322 | 690 | | United States Average..... | $2,940 | $1,496 | $703 |

## DISPOSABLE PERSONAL INCOME: 1966 [1]
Source: U.S. Department of Commerce

After paying their taxes, Americans in 1966 had nearly $509 billion left in personal income. It is interesting to note that expenditures for private education and research and for religious and welfare activities totaled less than those for alcoholic beverages.

| PERSONAL CONSUMPTION EXPENDITURES | $466.0 |
|---|---|
| Food........................... | 93.0 |
| Alcoholic beverages........................ | 13.7 |
| Tobacco products......................... | 8.7 |
| Clothing, accessories, and jewelry | 48.4 |
| Personal care........................... | 8.2 |
| Housing.............................. | 67.1 |
| Household operation...................... | 66.7 |
| Medical care expenses.................... | 31.3 |
| Personal business....................... | 24.0 |
| Transportation.......................... | 59.6 |
| Recreation............................ | 28.7 |
| Private education and research............. | 6.7 |
| Religious and welfare activities............. | 6.5 |
| Foreign travel and other (net)............. | 3.4 |
| PERSONAL SAVINGS....................... | 29.8 |
| INTEREST PAID BY CONSUMERS............ | 12.4 |
| PERSONAL TRANSFER PAYMENTS TO FOREIGNERS.............................. | .6 |

## U.S. GROSS NATIONAL PRODUCT [1]
Source: U.S. Department of Commerce

| | 1964 | 1965 | 1966 | 1967 [2] |
|---|---|---|---|---|
| Gross national product...... | 632.4 | 683.9 | 743.3 | 775.3 |
| Personal consumption expenditures............. | 401.2 | 433.1 | 465.9 | 488.9 |
| Durable goods........... | 59.2 | 66.0 | 70.3 | 72.1 |
| Nondurable goods........ | 178.7 | 191.2 | 207.5 | 216.6 |
| Services................ | 163.3 | 175.9 | 188.1 | 200.2 |
| Gross private domestic investment............... | 94.0 | 107.4 | 118.0 | 106.1 |
| Fixed investment........ | 88.2 | 98.0 | 104.6 | 104.0 |
| Nonresidential.......... | 61.1 | 71.1 | 80.2 | 81.3 |
| Structures......... | 21.2 | 25.1 | 27.9 | 26.3 |
| Durable equipment... | 39.9 | 46.0 | 52.3 | 55.0 |
| Residential structures... | 27.1 | 27.0 | 24.4 | 22.7 |
| Nonfarm........... | 26.6 | 26.4 | 23.8 | 22.1 |
| Farm.............. | .5 | .5 | .5 | .6 |
| Change in business inventories............. | 5.8 | 9.4 | 13.4 | 2.1 |
| Nonfarm............. | 6.4 | 8.4 | 13.7 | 2.2 |
| Farm................ | —.6 | 1.0 | —.3 | —.1 |
| Net exports of goods and services................. | 8.5 | 6.9 | 5.1 | 5.2 |
| Exports.............. | 37.1 | 39.1 | 43.0 | 44.8 |
| Imports.............. | 28.6 | 32.2 | 37.9 | 39.6 |
| Government purchases of goods and services......... | 128.7 | 136.4 | 154.3 | 175.2 |
| Federal.............. | 65.2 | 66.8 | 77.0 | 89.5 |
| National defense....... | 50.0 | 50.1 | 60.5 | 72.6 |
| Other.............. | 15.2 | 16.7 | 16.5 | 16.9 |
| State and local.......... | 63.5 | 69.6 | 77.2 | 85.6 |

[1] In billions of current dollars.    [2] 2nd quarter 1967, preliminary; seasonally adjusted at annual rate.

# A NATION OF CAPITALISTS

## U.S. CORPORATIONS AND THEIR STOCKHOLDERS
Source: New York Stock Exchange

It was recently estimated by the New York Stock Exchange that some 22 million Americans owned shares of stock—more than three times the number of individual shareowners in 1952.

Other highlights of the NYSE survey are some interesting facts about the average investor: a median age of 49; a median household income of $9,500 (the median income of all families in the United States for 1966

was $7,400); and over half of the adult shareowners were women.

Buying by financial institutions reached a new level in 1966, but activity by individuals accounted for more than 43% of the Exchange's volume. Investment for long-term purposes still dominated individual purchases, although a much higher percentage of the public engaged in short-term trading than in 1965.

| CORPORATION | 1966 | RANK | 1962 | RANK |
|---|---|---|---|---|
| American Telephone & Telegraph..... | 3,000,000 | 1 | 2,049,000 | 1 |
| General Motors.... | 1,313,000 | 2 | 842,000 | 2 |
| Standard Oil (N.J.) | 728,000 | 3 | 715,000 | 3 |
| General Electric.... | 515,000 | 4 | 442,000 | 4 |
| General Telephone & Electronics.... | 416,000 | 5 | 283,000 | 5 |
| Ford Motor........ | 401,000 | 6 | 234,000 | 7 |
| U.S. Steel......... | 335,000 | 7 | 280,000 | 6 |
| Radio Corporation of America...... | 305,000 | 8 | 156,000 | 19 |
| International Business Machines........ | 281,000 | 9 | 170,000 | 14 |
| Bethlehem Steel.... | 245,000 | 10 | 228,000 | 8 |
| Sears Roebuck.... | 244,000 | 11 | 160,000 | 17 |
| E.I. du Pont de Nemours........ | 238,000 | 12 | 211,000 | 10 |
| Standard Oil of California....... | 211,000 | 13 | 172,000 | 12 |
| Texaco............ | 208,000 | 14 | 155,000 | 21 |
| Mobil Oil......... | 208,000 | 15 | 227,000 | 9 |
| Consolidated Edison........... | 200,000 | 16 | 169,000 | 15 |
| Columbia Gas System ........ | 190,000 | 17 | 204,000 | 11 |
| Westinghouse Electric........ | 187,000 | 18 | 160,000 | 16 |
| Pacific Gas & Elec... | 184,000 | 19 | 147,000 | 23 |
| Tenneco.......... | 182,000 | 20 | | |
| Standard Oil (Indiana)........ | 174,000 | 21 | 172,000 | 12 |
| Sperry Rand...... | 174,000 | 22 | 172,000 | 13 |
| Commonwealth Edison.......... | 169,000 | 23 | 150,000 | 22 |
| Gulf Oil........... | 162,000 | 24 | 131,000 | 26 |

## DIVIDEND STALWARTS: 1966

The common stocks of nearly 200 American companies traded on the New York Stock Exchange have paid cash dividends for 35 to 100

years. The year noted below is that in which quarterly dividend payments began; the yield is the annual dividend yield per share.

| COMPANY | YEAR | YIELD | COMPANY | YEAR | YIELD |
|---|---|---|---|---|---|
| Abbott Laboratories................. | 1929 | 2.1% | Burroughs Corp.................... | 1906 | 0.8% |
| Abex Corporation.................. | 1904 | 4.8 | Carolina Telephone & Telegraph Co. | 1900 | 2.3[1] |
| Air Reduction Co., Inc.............. | 1917 | 3.3[1] | Carpenter Steel Co................. | 1908 | 4.0[1] |
| Allied Chemical Corp.............. | 1921 | 5.0[1] | Carriers & General Corp............ | 1930 | 3.8[1] |
| Amerada Petroleum Corp........... | 1922 | 3.7[1] | Castle & Cooke, Inc............... | 1928 | 3.0[1] |
| American Bakeries Co.............. | 1925 | 3.9 | Central Aguirre Sugar Co........... | 1916 | —[2] |
| American Can Co................ | 1923 | 3.8 | Central Hudson Gas & Elec. Corp.... | 1903 | 4.6[2] |
| American Electric Power Co., Inc.... | 1910 | 3.8[1] | Central Illinois Light Co............ | 1921 | 4.2[1] |
| American Home Products Corp...... | 1926 | 1.7[1] | Chase Manhattan Bank.............. | 1918 | 3.5[1] |
| American Investment Co........... | 1931 | 6.2 | Chesebrough-Pond's, Inc........... | 1919 | 2.0[1] |
| American Machine & Foundry Co.... | 1927 | 4.4 | C.I.T Financial Corp............... | 1924 | 5.5 |
| American Natural Gas Co.......... | 1904 | 4 8[1] | Cleveland Elec. Illuminating Co...... | 1912 | 4.3[1] |
| American News Co.............. | 1864 | 3.7 | Clevite Corp...................... | 1922 | 4.7 |
| American Sterilizer Co............ | 1914 | 1.7 | Cluett, Peabody Co., Inc........... | 1924 | 4.4 |
| American Telephone & Telegraph Co. | 1882 | 3.9 | Coca-Cola Co..................... | 1921 | 1.6[1] |
| American Tobacco Co ............. | 1921 | 5.6 | Columbia Broadcasting System, Inc. | 1931 | 2.1[1] |
| Anchor Hocking Glass Corp........ | 1928 | 2.9 | Combustion Engineering, Inc........ | 1912 | 2.6[1] |
| Archer-Daniels-Midland Co.......... | 1931 | 3.6 | Commonwealth Edison Co........... | 1890 | 4.2[1] |
| Associates Investment Co.......... | 1920 | 6.1 | Consolidated Edison Co. of N.Y., Inc. | 1892 | 5.4 |
| Atlantic Richfield Co.............. | 1927 | 2.8 | Continental Can Co., Inc........... | 1923 | 3.5[1] |
| Baltimore Gas & Electric Co........ | 1911 | 4 9[1] | Cornwood Corp.................... | 1903 | 4.4[1] |
| Beech-Nut Life Savers, Inc......... | 1903 | 3.0 | Corn Products Co.................. | 1919 | 4.0[1] |
| Bemis Co., Inc................... | 1931 | 3.4 | Corning Glass Works............... | 1922 | 1.1[1] |
| Beneficial Finance Co............. | 1929 | 5.2 | Dentists' Supply Co. of New York... | 1923 | 4.9 |
| Borden Co...................... | 1924 | 3.5 | Detroit Edison Co................. | 1909 | 4.7 |
| Boston Edison Co................. | 1892 | 4.7[1] | Dictaphone Corp.................. | 1926 | 2.3 |
| Brown Shoe Co., Inc.............. | 1923 | 3.4[1] | Dr. Pepper Co.................... | 1930 | 2.0[1] |

| COMPANY | YEAR | YIELD | COMPANY | YEAR | YIELD |
|---|---|---|---|---|---|
| Dome Mines, Ltd. | 1920 | 1.7% | New England Tel. & Tel. Co. | 1886 | 5.4% |
| Dominick Fund, Inc. | 1930 | 2.1 | Norfolk & Western Railway Co. | 1910 | 6.1 |
| Dow Chemical Co. | 1912 | 2.6[1] | Norwich Pharmacal Co. | 1925 | 1.7 |
| Duke Power Co. | 1926 | 3.3 | Olin Mathieson Chemical Corp. | 1926 | 2.5[1] |
| E.I. du Pont de Nemours & Co. | 1905 | 3.8 | Orange & Rockland Utilities, Inc. | 1914 | 3.7[1] |
| Duquesne Light Co. | 1913 | 5.1[1] | Otis Elevator Co. | 1911 | 4.3 |
| Eastern Utilities Associates | 1928 | 5.1[1] | Owens-Illinois Inc. | 1907 | 2.6 |
| Eastman Kodak Co. | 1902 | 1.6[1] | Pacific Gas & Electric Co. | 1919 | 3.8[1] |
| ESB Incorporated | 1900 | 3.7[1] | Pacific Lighting Corp. | 1909 | 5.4[1] |
| Fafnir Bearing Co. | 1913 | 4.8 | Pacific Tel. & Tel. Co. | 1925 | 4.6 |
| Family Finance Corp. | 1929 | 6.4 | Parke, Davis & Co. | 1897 | 5.2 |
| Federated Department Stores, Inc. | 1931 | 2.6 | J. C. Penney Co. | 1930 | 2.8[1] |
| Firestone Tire & Rubber Co. | 1924 | 3.0[1] | Pennsalt Chemicals Corp. | 1913 | 2.1 |
| First National Stores, Inc. | 1914 | —[2] | Pennzoil Company | 1926 | 1.2 |
| Foxboro Co. | 1916 | 1.4[1] | Peoples Drug Stores, Inc. | 1927 | 6.0 |
| Freeport Sulphur Co. | 1927 | 2.1[1] | Philadelphia Electric Co. | 1913 | 4.7[1] |
| Garlock Inc. | 1906 | 3.4 | Pillsbury Co. | 1927 | 3.2 |
| General Cigar Co., Inc. | 1909 | 5.8 | Pittsburgh Plate Glass Co. | 1899 | 4.4 |
| General Electric Co. | 1899 | 3.0 | Plough, Inc. | 1931 | 1.1[1] |
| General Foods Corp. | 1922 | 2.9[1] | Potomac Electric Power Co. | 1920 | 5.1[1] |
| General Mills, Inc. | 1928 | 2.1[1] | Procter & Gamble Co. | 1898 | 2.4[1] |
| General Motors Corp. | 1923 | 5.3 | Public Service Elec. & Gas Co. | 1920 | 4.4[1] |
| Genesco Inc. | 1932 | 4.6[1] | Pullman Inc. | 1867 | 5.4 |
| W. T. Grant Co. | 1917 | 3.8 | Quaker Oats Co. | 1922 | 3.2 |
| Great American Insurance Co. | 1919 | 4.5[1] | Raybestos-Manhattan, Inc. | 1898 | 5.3 |
| Great Atlantic & Pacific Tea Co., Inc. | 1920 | 5.3[1] | Rex Chainbelt Inc. | 1922 | 3.4[1] |
| Great Northern Paper Co. | 1910 | 2.5[1] | R. J. Reynolds Tobacco Co. | 1901 | 5.1 |
| Walter E. Heller & Co. | 1921 | 4.6 | Richardson-Merrell Inc. | 1925 | 1.5 |
| Helme Products, Inc. | 1912 | 3.8 | Riegel Paper Corp. | 1897 | 4.1[1] |
| Hercules Inc. | 1913 | 2.7 | Safeway Stores, Inc. | 1927 | 4.8[1] |
| Hershey Chocolate Corp. | 1930 | 4.1 | San Diego Gas & Electric Co. | 1909 | 4.0[1] |
| Hobart Manufacturing Co. | 1906 | 2.4[1] | Scott Paper Co. | 1926 | 3.7 |
| Household Finance Corp. | 1926 | 3.8 | Sherwin-Williams Co. | 1922 | 4.4[1] |
| Houston Lighting & Power Co. | 1922 | 2.3 | Shoe Corp. of America | 1930 | 6.4 |
| Ingersoll-Rand Co. | 1919 | 4.5 | Singer Co. | 1890 | 3.4 |
| Interco Inc. | 1913 | 3.4[1] | Southern California Edison Co. | 1910 | 3.4[1] |
| International Business Machines Corp. | 1916 | 0.9 | Standard Oil Co. of California | 1912 | 4.4[1] |
| International Harvester Co. | 1910 | 4.6 | Standard Oil Co. (Indiana) | 1913 | 3.1[1] |
| International Salt Co. | 1929 | 4.5 | Standard Pressed Steel Co. | 1930 | 1.3[1] |
| Iowa Power & Light Co. | 1916 | 5.1[1] | Stanley Works | 1895 | 3.6 |
| Island Creek Coal Co. | 1912 | 3.1[1] | Stauffer Chemical Co. | 1915 | 3.7[1] |
| Jewel Companies, Inc. | 1928 | 4.0[1] | Sterling Drug, Inc. | 1913 | 1.8[1] |
| Johnson Service Company | 1901 | 3.5[1] | Sun Oil Co. | 1912 | 1.4[1] |
| Joy Manufacturing Co. | 1929 | 4.0 | Tampa Electric Co. | 1911 | 2.1 |
| Keebler Co. | 1928 | 3.1 | Texaco Inc. | 1903 | 3.7[1] |
| Kroger Co. | 1910 | 5.7 | Texas Gulf Sulphur Co. | 1921 | 0.3 |
| Lehman Corp. | 1930 | 2.0 | Texas Utilities Co. | 1919 | 2.7[1] |
| Liggett & Myers Tobacco Co. | 1912 | 7.0 | Time, Inc. | 1930 | 2.4 |
| Lily-Tulip Cup Corp. | 1929 | 3.6[1] | Timken Roller Bearing Co. | 1921 | 5.0 |
| P. Lorillard Co. | 1932 | 4.3 | Toledo Edison Co. | 1922 | 3.7[1] |
| Ludlow Corp. | 1886 | 3.5 | Torrington Co. | 1898 | 4.3 |
| MacAndrews & Forbes Co. | 1908 | 4.9 | Union Carbide Corp. | 1918 | 3.9 |
| R. H. Macy & Co., Inc. | 1927 | 2.6[1] | Union Electric Co. | 1918 | 4.9[1] |
| May Department Stores Co. | 1911 | 5.0 | Union Oil Co. of California | 1916 | 2.1 |
| McCall Corp. | 1926 | 1.3[1] | Union Pacific R.R. Co. | 1907 | 4.8 |
| McIntyre Porcupine Mines, Ltd. | 1924 | 3.4 | Union Tank Car Co. | 1919 | 3.5 |
| McQuay-Norris Manufacturing Co. | 1927 | 5.9 | United Elastic Corp | 1927 | 5.3 |
| Melville Shoes Corp. | 1917 | 2.5[1] | United Engineering & Foundry Co | 1902 | 5.7 |
| Mesta Machine Co. | 1927 | —[2] | United Shoe Machinery Corp | 1899 | 3.8[1] |
| Miles Laboratories, Inc. | 1929 | 2.7 | United States Gypsum Co. | 1919 | 4.8 |
| Minnesota Mining & Mfg. Co. | 1916 | 1.5[1] | U.S. Pipe & Foundry Co. | 1926 | 6.3 |
| Monsanto Co. | 1928 | 3.6[1] | U.S. Playing Card Co. | 1896 | 4.2[1] |
| Philip Morris, Inc. | 1928 | 3.0 | U.S. Tobacco Co. | 1918 | 4.9 |
| Mountain States Tel. & Tel. Co. | 1911 | 4.6[1] | Universal Leaf Tobacco Co., Inc. | 1927 | 5.1 |
| G. C. Murphy Co. | 1928 | 5.4 | Upjohn Co. | 1921 | 2.6[1] |
| Nalco Chemical Co. | 1928 | 1.3[1] | Washington Gas Light Co. | 1885 | 5.3[1] |
| National Biscuit Co. | 1899 | 4.3[1] | Waukesha Motor Co. | 1927 | 4.8 |
| National Dairy Products Corp. | 1924 | 3.9 | West Virginia Pulp & Paper Co. | 1895 | 4.4[1] |
| National Fuel Gas Co. | 1903 | 5.6[1] | Westinghouse Air Brake Co. | 1894 | 4.7 |
| National Lead Co. | 1906 | 5.3 | Whirlpool Corp. | 1929 | 3.8 |
| National-Standard Co. | 1922 | 3.5[1] | F. W. Woolworth Co. | 1912 | 3.6 |
| National Steel Corp. | 1908 | 5.6 | Wm. Wrigley, Jr. Co. | 1911 | 5.0 |

[1] = Dividend rate increased since July 1, 1966.    [2] = Dividend rate decreased since July 1, 1966.

## LARGEST U.S. BUSINESSES: 1966
Source: Fortune Magazine

| INDUSTRIALS | NET SALES |
|---|---|
| 1. General Motors | $20,208,505,000 |
| 2. Ford Motor | 12,240,048,000 |
| 3. Standard Oil (N.J.) | 12,191,405,000 |
| 4. General Electric | 7,177,256,000 |
| 5. Chrysler | 5,649,505,000 |
| 6. Mobil Oil | 5,253,909,000 |
| 7. Texaco | 4,427,321,000 |
| 8. U.S. Steel | 4,355,412,000 |
| 9. International Business Machines | 4,247,706,000 |
| 10. Gulf Oil | 3,781,837,000 |
| 11. Western Electric | 3,623,601,000 |
| 12. Du Pont (E.I.) de Nemours | 3,185,142,000 |
| 13. Swift | 2,970,466,000 |
| 14. Shell Oil | 2,789,805,000 |
| 15. Standard Oil (Ind.) | 2,708,531,000 |
| 16. Standard Oil of California | 2,698,295,000 |
| 17. Bethlehem Steel | 2,669,437,000 |
| 18. International Harvester | 2,583,035,000 |
| 19. Westinghouse Electric | 2,581,415,000 |
| 20. Radio Corporation of America | 2,548,814,000 |
| 21. Goodyear Tire and Rubber | 2,475,665,000 |
| 22. General Telephone & Electronics | 2,390,503,000 |

| MERCHANDISING FIRMS | SALES |
|---|---|
| 1. Sears, Roebuck | $6,804,894,000 |
| 2. Great Atlantic & Pacific | 5,475,259,000 |
| 3. Safeway Stores | 3,345,187,000 |
| 4. Kroger | 2,659,983,000 |
| 5. J. C. Penney | 2,549,362,000 |
| 6. Montgomery Ward | 1,894,123,000 |
| 7. F. W. Woolworth | 1,573,470,000 |
| 8. Federated Department Stores | 1,412,026,000 |
| 9. Acme Markets | 1,253,748,000 |
| 10. Food Fair Stores | 1,204,520,000 |
| 11. National Tea | 1,190,495,000 |
| 12. S. S. Kresge | 1,102,688,000 |
| 13. Spartans Industries | 1,085,386,000 |
| 14. Jewel Companies | 1,060,137,000 |
| 15. Allied Stores | 1,030,428,000 |
| 16. Mays Department Stores | 983,693,000 |
| 17. Winn-Dixie Stores | 982,459,000 |
| 18. W. T. Grant | 923,047,000 |
| 19. Grand Union | 836,242,000 |
| 20. Rapid-American | 755,085,000 |
| 21. R. H. Macy | 719,207,000 |

| COMMERCIAL BANKS | ASSETS |
|---|---|
| 1. Bank of America | $18,213,176,000 |
| 2. Chase Manhattan Bank | 15,775,549,000 |
| 3. First National City Bank | 15,065,547,000 |
| 4. Morgan Guaranty Trust of New York | 7,863,688,000 |
| 5. Manufacturers Hanover Trust | 7,728,672,000 |
| 6. Chemical Bank New York Trust | 7,277,321,000 |
| 7. Bankers Trust | 5,945,066,000 |
| 8. Continental Illinois National Bank | 5,609,459,000 |
| 9. Security First National Bank | 5,088,143,000 |
| 10. First National Bank of Chicago | 4,941,165,000 |
| 11. Wells Fargo Bank | 4,204,572,000 |
| 12 Crocker-Citizens National Bank | 3,950,206,000 |
| 13 Irving Trust | 3,801,602,000 |
| 14. United California Bank | 3,637,401,000 |
| 15. Mellon National Bank & Trust | 3,560,135,000 |
| 16. National Bank of Detroit | 3,210,815,000 |
| 17. First National Bank of Boston | 2,933,916,000 |
| 18. Cleveland Trust | 2,099,648,000 |
| 19. Franklin National Bank | 1,924,896,000 |
| 20. First Pennsylvania Banking & Trust | 1,806,567,000 |
| 21. Philadelphia National Bank | 1,685,803,000 |

| TRANSPORTATION COMPANIES | OPERATING REVENUES |
|---|---|
| 1. Pennsylvania Railroad | $1,093,901,000 |
| 2. Southern Pacific | 1,040,782,000 |
| 3. United Air Lines | 856,903,000 |
| 4. Pan American World Airways | 840,967,000 |
| 5. Chesapeake & Ohio Railway | 827,908,000 |
| 6. New York Central Railroad | 817,856,000 |
| 7. Atchison, Topeka & Santa Fe Rwy. | 767,237,000 |
| 8. American Airlines | 727,712,000 |
| 9. Trans World Airlines | 681,632,000 |
| 10. Union Pacific Railroad | 617,067,000 |
| 11. Norfolk & Western Railway | 613,985,000 |
| 12. Greyhound | 520,529,000 |
| 13. Eastern Air Lines | 500,989,000 |
| 14. Southern Railway | 474,368,000 |
| 15. Missouri Pacific Railroad | 441,430,000 |
| 16. Delta Air Lines | 373,568,000 |
| 17. Chicago, Burlington & Quincy Railroad | 347,011,000 |
| 18. Chicago & North Western Railway | 315,883,000 |
| 19. Northwest Airlines | 311,319,000 |
| 20. Consolidated Freightways | 304,676,000 |
| 21. Illinois Central Industries | 295,989,000 |

| LIFE INSURANCE COMPANIES | ASSETS |
|---|---|
| 1. Prudential | $23,594,698,000 |
| 2. Metropolitan | 23,511,678,000 |
| 3. Equitable Life Assurance | 12,575,680,000 |
| 4. New York Life | 9,169,101,000 |
| 5. John Hancock Mutual | 8,379,785,000 |
| 6. Aetna | 5,828,815,000 |
| 7. Northwestern Mutual | 5,229,009,000 |
| 8. Travelers | 3,938,281,000 |
| 9. Connecticut General | 3,634,854,000 |
| 10. Massachusetts Mutual | 3,436,446,000 |
| 11. Mutual of New York | 3,317,996,000 |
| 12. New England Life | 2,981,323,000 |
| 13. Mutual Benefit | 2,256,598,000 |
| 14. Connecticut Mutual | 2,249,875,000 |
| 15. Penn Mutual | 2,203,119,000 |
| 16. Lincoln National Life | 1,992,493,000 |
| 17. Bankers Life | 1,585,882,000 |
| 18. Western & Southern | 1,510,899,000 |
| 19. Teachers Insurance & Annuity | 1,401,156,000 |
| 20. National Life & Accident | 1,373,938,000 |
| 21. Continental Assurance | 1,281,785,000 |

| UTILITIES | ASSETS |
|---|---|
| 1. American Telephone & Telegraph | $35,218,280,000 |
| 2. Consolidated Edison | 3,528,061,000 |
| 3. Pacific Gas & Electric | 3,457,998,000 |
| 4. Commonwealth Edison | 2,269,180,000 |
| 5. Southern California Edison | 2,245,270,000 |
| 6. Southern Company | 2,121,998,000 |
| 7. American Electric Power | 1,987,520,000 |
| 8. Public Service Electric & Gas | 1,830,796,000 |
| 9. Columbia Gas System | 1,612,807,000 |
| 10. El Paso Natural Gas | 1,561,535,000 |
| 11. Consumers Power | 1,380,143,000 |
| 12. General Public Utilities | 1,364,943,000 |
| 13. Philadelphia Electric | 1,313,636,000 |
| 14. Niagara Mohawk Power | 1,293,130,000 |
| 15. American Natural Gas | 1,246,726,000 |
| 16. Middle South Utilities | 1,232,634,000 |
| 17. Detroit Edison | 1,230,415,000 |
| 18. Texas Utilities | 1,185,059,000 |
| 19. Texas Eastern Transmission | 1,171,091,000 |
| 20. Virginia Electric & Power | 1,068,859,000 |
| 21. Consolidated Natural Gas | 997,321,000 |

## U.S. STEEL INDUSTRY PROFITS: 1948–1966
Source: American Iron and Steel Institute

Steel industry profits, after taxes, in 1966 surpassed those of the previous year, and for the second time since the record-breaking year of 1957, were above the $1 billion mark.

| YEAR | PROFITS AFTER TAX | DEPRECIATION AND DEPLETION | CASH FLOW | YEAR | PROFITS AFTER TAX | DEPRECIATION AND DEPLETION | CASH FLOW |
|---|---|---|---|---|---|---|---|
| 1966 | $1,075,800,000 | $1,171,900,000 | $2,247,700,000 | 1956 | $1,113,000,000 | $748,000,000 | $1,861,000,000 |
| 1965 | 1,069,300,000 | 1,102,100,000 | 2,171,400,000 | 1955 | 1,099,000,000 | 737,000,000 | 1,836,000,000 |
| 1964 | 992,000,000 | 1,061,000,000 | 2,053,000,000 | 1954 | 637,000,000 | 670,000,000 | 1,307,000,000 |
| 1963 | 782,000,000 | 996,000,000 | 1,778,000,000 | 1953 | 735,000,000 | 614,000,000 | 1,349,000,000 |
| 1962 | 566,000,000 | 929,000,000 | 1,495,000,000 | 1952 | 541,000,000 | 450,000,000 | 991,000,000 |
| 1961 | 690,000,000 | 739,000,000 | 1,429,000,000 | 1951 | 682,000,000 | 374,000,000 | 1,056,000,000 |
| 1960 | 811,000,000 | 698,000,000 | 1,509,000,000 | 1950 | 767,000,000 | 327,000,000 | 1,094,000,000 |
| 1959 | 831,000,000 | 665,000,000 | 1,496,000,000 | 1949 | 529,000,000 | 278,000,000 | 807,000,000 |
| 1958 | 788,000,000 | 673,000,000 | 1,461,000,000 | 1948 | 541,000,000 | 302,000,000 | 843,000,000 |
| 1957 | 1,132,000,000 | 766,000,000 | 1,898,000,000 | | | | |

## U.S. PASSENGER CAR PRODUCTION BY MAKES: 1961–1966

The number of passenger cars coming off the factory assembly lines from 1961 through 1966 are shown below in a report issued by the Automobile Manufacturers Association. Production of the Chrysler Corporation's DeSoto line was discontinued in 1960.

| MANUFACTURER | 1961 | 1962 | 1963 | 1964 | 1965 | 1966 |
|---|---|---|---|---|---|---|
| AMERICAN MOTORS CORPORATION..... | 372,485 | 454,784 | 480,365 | 393,863 | 346,367 | 279,225 |
| CHECKER MOTORS CORPORATION...... | 5,683 | 8,026 | 7,231 | 6,310 | 6,136 | 5,761 |
| CHRYSLER CORPORATION.............. | 648,670 | 716,809 | 1,047,722 | 1,242,162 | 1,467,553 | 1,445,616 |
| Plymouth............................ | 310,445 | 331,079 | 496,412 | 571,339 | 679,539 | 640,450 |
| Dodge.............................. | 220,779 | 251,722 | 421,301 | 505,094 | 547,531 | 532,026 |
| Chrysler............................ | 117,446 | 134,008 | 130,009 | 165,729 | 240,483 | 273,140 |
| FORD MOTOR COMPANY............... | 1,689,940 | 1,935,203 | 1,963,869 | 2,145,943 | 2,565,776 | 2,425,442 |
| Ford............................... | 1,345,124 | 1,565,928 | 1,638,066 | 1,787,535 | 2,164,902 | 2,038,415 |
| Mercury............................ | 311,636 | 335,446 | 292,086 | 320,658 | 355,404 | 334,858 |
| Lincoln............................ | 33,180 | 33,829 | 33,717 | 37,750 | 45,470 | 52,169 |
| GENERAL MOTORS CORPORATION...... | 2,726,577 | 3,741,538 | 4,077,272 | 3,956,637 | 4,949,395 | 4,448,668 |
| Chevrolet.......................... | 1,604,820 | 2,161,409 | 2,303,315 | 2,114,718 | 2,587,509 | 2,202,792 |
| Pontiac............................ | 360,336 | 547,350 | 625,268 | 693,634 | 860,652 | 481,591 |
| Oldsmobile......................... | 321,838 | 458,359 | 504,555 | 510,931 | 650,801 | 594,069 |
| Buick.............................. | 291,285 | 415,892 | 479,399 | 482,731 | 653,838 | 580,421 |
| Cadillac........................... | 148,298 | 158,528 | 164,735 | 154,623 | 196,595 | 205,001 |
| STUDEBAKER CORPORATION........... | 78,664 | 86,974 | 67,918 | 577 | — | — |
| **Total Passenger Cars**................. | 5,522,019 | 6,943,334 | 7,644,377 | 7,745,492 | 9,335,227 | 8,604,712 |

## U.S. IMPORTS OF PASSENGER CARS

The introduction in 1960 of U.S.-made compacts caused only a temporary decrease in the import of new foreign cars, according to the Automobile Manufacturers Association.

| YEAR | CARS | YEAR | CARS | YEAR | CARS | YEAR | CARS |
|---|---|---|---|---|---|---|---|
| 1955......... | 57,115 | 1958...... | 430,808 | 1961........ | 279,437 | 1964....... | 536,705 |
| 1956......... | 107,675 | 1959...... | 668,070 | 1962........ | 375,187 | 1965....... | 559,430 |
| 1957........ | 259,343 | 1960...... | 444,474 | 1963....... | 409,024 | 1966....... | 913,207 |

## U.S. PASSENGER CAR IMPORTS, BY COUNTRY OF ORIGIN: 1966
Source: U.S. Department of Commerce

Americans in 1966 imported more than three times as many new passenger cars from West Germany as they did from its nearest competitor, Canada.

| EXPORTING COUNTRY | NUMBER OF NEW PASSENGER CARS | TOTAL VALUE | EXPORTING COUNTRY | NUMBER OF NEW PASSENGER CARS | TOTAL VALUE |
|---|---|---|---|---|---|
| West Germany.. | 527,137 | $591,938,926 | France......... | 33,122 | $30,169,513 |
| Canada......... | 165,645 | 370,617,494 | Italy........... | 14,110 | 18,096,577 |
| United Kingdom. | 81,870 | 114,549,091 | Venezuela ..... | 380 | 434,244 |
| Sweden........ | 56,050 | 56,230,830 | Belgium........ | 117 | 408,788 |
| Japan.......... | 34,362 | 53,892,182 | Other.......... | 144 | 193,956 |

## THE BANK CREDIT CARD BOOM

For a while last year nearly every mail delivery would bring another bank credit card, or so it seemed. Did it mean that the long-predicted "cashless society" was actually here at last?

No, not quite. But the discovery that consumer credit, plus modern computers, could be made to pay brought hundreds of major banks (as well as many minor ones) rushing into the consumer credit card business in 1967.

"Bank credit cards hold both promise and pitfalls for banks," said Federal Deposit Insurance Corporation Chairman Kenneth A. Randall. The promise, of course, is profits. Bank credit cards are usually free to customers, for the banks make their money on a charge to cardholders (usually 1½ per cent on any unpaid balance after 30 days) and on a 3 to 5 per cent discount charge to merchants.

Among the pitfalls, of course, is fraud. Chicago banks still are smarting from an un-

precedented abuse of credit cards during late 1966 and early 1967. Several major banks launched new plans, mailing cards to everyone on hastily collected mailing lists; some families were amazed to receive as many as a dozen. Partly as a result of this mismanagement, a major bank in Chicago reported that its 1967 second-quarter profits dropped a full 9 per cent as a result of the "fraudulent use of the cards."

The Federal Reserve Board formed a task force in March, 1967, to study the problems and the national policy implications of this rapid credit development. An interim report in August stated that 627 banks had either a credit card system or a similar credit operation, with total receivables of over $800 million, or nearly one-fifth of the $5 billion outstanding under all consumer credit card plans. Several hundred additional banks served as local agents for the credit card plans of other banks.

## U.S. ELECTRIC ENERGY PRODUCTION: 1966
Source: Federal Power Commission

Nearly 65 per cent of the fuel-produced electric energy in the U.S. in 1966 came from coal. Hydroelectric power output was up slightly, but its share of the total declined. Private utilities generated more than 75 per cent of the nation's electric energy during the year.

| ENERGY SOURCE | 1966 [1] | 1965 [1] | FUEL CONSUMED | 1966 | 1965 |
|---|---|---|---|---|---|
| Fuel—Coal | 613.2 | 570.9 | Coal | | |
| Oil | 79.0 | 64.8 | (millions of tons) | 266.4 | 244.8 |
| Natural Gas | 251.0 | 221.6 | Oil | | |
| Nuclear | 5.5 | 3.7 | (millions of barrels) | 140.9 | 115.2 |
| Hydroelectric | 194.5 | 193.9 | Natural gas | | |
| TOTAL | 1,143.7 [2] | 1,055.3 [2] | (billions of cubic feet) | 2,608.8 | 2,321.1 |

[1] Billions of kilowatt hours.  [2] Includes minor production from geothermal sources, wood, and waste.

## OPERATIONAL U.S. CENTRAL STATION NUCLEAR POWER PLANTS: 1967 [1]
Source: Atomic Industrial Forum

| REACTOR | LOCATION | NET PLANT CAPACITY [2] | BECAME OPERATIONAL |
|---|---|---|---|
| **Boiling Water Reactors:** | | | |
| Humboldt Bay Power Plant | Humboldt Bay, California | 68,000 | 1963 |
| Dresden Nuclear Power Station I | Morris, Illinois | 200,000 | 1959 |
| Big Rock Point Nuclear Power Plant | Big Rock Point, Michigan | 72,000 | 1962 |
| Elk River Reactor | Elk River, Minnesota | 20,000 | 1962 |
| BONUS (Boiling Nuclear Superheat Reactor) | Punta Higuera, Puerto Rico | 16,500 | 1963 |
| Pathfinder Atomic Power Plant | Sioux Falls, South Dakota | 54,000 | 1964 |
| **Pressurized Water Reactors:** | | | |
| San Onofre Nuclear Generating Station | San Clemente, California | 428,000 | 1967 |
| Yankee Nuclear Power Station | Rowe, Massachusetts | 185,000 | 1960 |
| Indian Point Station I | Buchanan, New York | 200,000 | 1962 |
| Shippingport Atomic Power Station | Shippingport, Pennsylvania | 90,000 | 1957 |
| Connecticut Yankee Atomic Power Station | Haddam Neck, Connecticut | 562,000 | 1967 |
| **Fast Breeder Reactor:** | | | |
| Enrico Fermi Atomic Power Plant | Lagoona Beach, Michigan | 60,000 | 1963 |
| **Organic Cooled Reactor:** | | | |
| Piqua Nuclear Power Facility | Piqua, Ohio | 11,000 | 1963 |
| **High Temperature Gas Cooled Reactor:** | | | |
| Peach Bottom Atomic Power Station I | Peach Bottom, Pennsylvania | 40,000 | 1967 |
| **Heavy Water Reactor:** | | | |
| Carolinas-Virginia Tube Reactor | Parr, South Carolina | 16,000 | 1963 |
| **Graphite Reactor:** | | | |
| Hanford | Richland, Washington | 776,000 | 1965 |

[1] As of September 1.  [2] In kilowatts of electricity.

# LABOR

## TOP-PAYING U.S. OCCUPATIONS

According to a study published in 1965 by the U.S. Department of Labor (based on data from the 1960 Census), medicine, dentistry, and law ranked among the highest paying occupations in the United States. Annual median earnings, median schooling, and the percentage of women are given for the top 83 of the 321 occupations covered in the study.

| OCCUPATION | EARNINGS | SCHOOLING | WOMEN |
|---|---|---|---|
| Physicians | $14,561 | 17.5 | 6.8% |
| Managers, self-employed—banking and other finance | 12,757 | 14.3 | 5.2 |
| Dentists | 11,858 | 17.3 | 2.3 |
| Professors and instructors—medical sciences | 11,666 | 17.5 | 17.2 |
| Lawyers and judges | 10,587 | 17.4 | 3.5 |
| Airplane pilots and navigators | 10,274 | 13.5 | .6 |
| Osteopaths | 10,128 | 17.3 | 12.0 |
| College presidents and deans | 9,704 | 17.4 | 23.0 |
| Managers, self-employed—insurance and real estate | 9,410 | 12.9 | 13.2 |
| Managers, salaried—manufacturing | 9,090 | 13.1 | 6.7 |
| Physicists | 9,043 | 17.2 | 4.2 |
| Aeronautical engineers | 9,018 | 16.3 | 1.6 |
| Veterinarians | 8,882 | 17.4 | 2.1 |
| Chemical engineers | 8,810 | 16.7 | .9 |
| Sales engineers | 8,694 | 16.1 | .3 |
| Architects | 8,651 | 16.8 | 2.5 |
| Economists | 8,649 | 16.8 | 14.5 |
| Electrical engineers | 8,553 | 16.2 | .8 |
| Metallurgical engineers and metallurgists | 8,534 | 16.3 | 1.0 |
| Geologists and geophysicists | 8,409 | 16.9 | 2.3 |
| Optometrists | 8,404 | 17.0 | 4.2 |
| Mining engineers | 8,359 | 16.5 | .3 |
| Mechanical engineers | 8,355 | 16.1 | .3 |
| Managers, salaried—business services | 8,340 | 14.6 | 21.1 |
| Managers, salaried—insurance and real estate | 8,231 | 13.7 | 17.2 |
| Engineers, technical | 8,062 | 16.0 | .8 |
| Professors and instructors—agricultural sciences | 7,918 | 17.4 | — |
| Managers, salaried—communications and utilities | 7,916 | 12.8 | 10.9 |
| Professors and instructors—engineering | 7,841 | 17.4 | 2.2 |
| Public relations men and publicity writers | 7,826 | 16.1 | 23.1 |
| Professors and instructors—psychology | 7,811 | 17.5 | 21.2 |
| Mathematicians | 7,780 | 17.1 | 26.5 |
| Managers, self-employed—manufacturing | 7,736 | 12.3 | 6.9 |
| Psychologists | 7,726 | 17.5 | 31.1 |
| Industrial engineers | 7,673 | 15.2 | 2.1 |
| Managers, salaried—construction | 7,632 | 12.4 | 3.4 |
| Civil engineers | 7,606 | 16.1 | .6 |
| Locomotive engineers | 7,586 | 9.8 | .2 |
| Professors and instructors—social sciences | 7,510 | 17.5 | 29.9 |
| Personnel and labor relations workers | 7,490 | 15.9 | 30.9 |
| Managers, self-employed—wholesale trade | 7,465 | 12.3 | 5.1 |
| Professors and instructors—economics | 7,447 | 17.5 | 6.6 |
| Managers, salaried—banking and other finance | 7,439 | 13.7 | 12.7 |
| Professors and instructors—biological sciences | 7,410 | 17.5 | 16.5 |
| Managers, self-employed—business services | 7,399 | 12.9 | 15.8 |
| Professors and instructors—physics | 7,373 | 17.3 | 3.8 |
| Managers, salaried—transportation | 7,351 | 12.4 | 4.5 |
| Natural scientists—miscellaneous | 7,351 | 16.5 | 9.8 |
| Professors and instructors—chemistry | 7,340 | 17.4 | 12.1 |
| Managers, salaried—wholesale trade | 7,339 | 12.7 | 7.0 |
| Professors and instructors—geology and geophysics | 7,319 | 17.4 | 2.6 |
| Designers | 7,296 | 13.8 | 18.3 |
| Managers (non-farm)—officials, societies, unions, etc. | 7,187 | 12.1 | 10.1 |
| Railroad conductors | 7,179 | 10.5 | .3 |
| Pharmacists | 7,176 | 16.2 | 7.7 |
| Foremen—communications, utilities, sanitary services | 7,147 | 12.0 | 1.8 |
| Chemists | 7,120 | 16.6 | 8.6 |
| Officer pilots, pursers, and engineers—ship | 7,119 | 10.5 | .5 |
| Sales workers—stock and bond salesmen | 7,118 | 14.5 | 6.4 |
| Electrotypers and stereotypers | 7,042 | 11.7 | .8 |
| Photoengravers and lithographers | 7,026 | 12.2 | 5.2 |

(*continued*)

| OCCUPATIONS (continued) | EARNINGS | SCHOOLING | WOMEN |
|---|---|---|---|
| Statisticians and actuaries | $7,015 | 16.1 | 30.6% |
| Foremen—manufacturing | 6,932 | 11.8 | 7.7 |
| Professors and instructors—subject not specified | 6,883 | 17.4 | 24.1 |
| Purchasing agents and buyers | 6,839 | 12.9 | 9.4 |
| Managers, self-employed—communications and utilities | 6,835 | 12.3 | 7.9 |
| Editors and reporters | 6,832 | 16.0 | 37.2 |
| Managers, salaried—not elsewhere classified | 6,737 | 13.5 | 31.1 |
| Salesmen and sales clerks—manufacturing | 6,725 | 12.8 | 10.4 |
| Managers (non-farm)—store buyers and department heads | 6,691 | 12.6 | 23.0 |
| Authors | 6,676 | 15.6 | 25.4 |
| Accountants and auditors | 6,591 | 15.3 | 16.8 |
| Managers, salaried—furniture and housefurnishings | 6,546 | 12.6 | 10.6 |
| Managers, self-employed—construction | 6,540 | 11.9 | 1.3 |
| Pattern and model makers (except paper) | 6,525 | 12.0 | 1.7 |
| Toolmakers; die makers and setters | 6,503 | 11.7 | .6 |
| Managers, self-employed—transportation | 6,460 | 11.3 | 6.0 |
| Officials and administrators—public administration | 6,449 | 12.9 | 19.1 |
| Foremen—transportation (except railroad) | 6,427 | 11.0 | 1.1 |
| Professors and instructors—mathematics | 6,418 | 17.4 | 15.8 |
| Professional, technical, and kindred workers—not elsewhere classified | 6,402 | 15.6 | 20.4 |
| Biological scientists | 6,383 | 17.2 | 26.7 |
| Professors and instructors—nonscientific subjects | 6,356 | 17.4 | 30.8 |

## AVERAGE WEEKLY HOURS AND EARNINGS IN MANUFACTURING: 1967

Workers in durable goods industries generally worked longer hours and received higher earnings in early 1967 than did their counterparts in nondurable goods industries, according to the U.S. Department of Labor. Durable goods industries—those producing goods whose usefulness continues for several years—had average earnings of $119.09 for 40.9 hours worked weekly; workers in nondurable goods industries averaged $105.02 for 40.2 hours per week.

| INDUSTRIES | EARNINGS | HOURS |
|---|---|---|
| **Durable Goods** | | |
| Transportation equipment | $115.08 | 41.3 |
| Metal forging, casting, smelting, and refining | 122.84 | 40.9 |
| Machinery | 110.80 | 42.5 |
| Fabricated metal products | 134.73 | 41.5 |
| Instruments, photographic equipment, and clocks | 92.04 | 41.1 |
| Stone, clay, and glass products | 135.38 | 41.7 |
| Electrical equipment | 141.25 | 40.0 |
| Furniture and fixtures | 117.59 | 39.9 |
| Miscellaneous manufacturing (luxury items, toys, musical instruments, etc.) | 91.57 | 39.5 |
| Lumber and wood products, except furniture | 92.17 | 40.8 |
| **Nondurable Goods** | | |
| Petroleum and related products | 109.71 | 43.2 |
| Chemicals and allied products | 155.09 | 41.7 |
| Printing and publishing | 128.85 | 38.4 |
| Paper and allied products | 125.18 | 42.7 |
| Rubber and plastic products | 78.66 | 41.4 |
| Food and kindred products | 94.25 | 41.1 |
| Tobacco products | 82.42 | 39.6 |
| Textile mill products | 72.11 | 40.6 |
| Leather and leather products | 82.66 | 38.0 |
| Wearing apparel | 121.27 | 35.7 |

## CIVILIAN EMPLOYMENT AND UNEMPLOYMENT *
Source: U.S. Department of Labor

| YEAR | LABOR FORCE (000s) | EMPLOYED (000s) | UNEMPLOYED (000s) | Percent of Labor Force | YEAR | LABOR FORCE (000s) | EMPLOYED (000s) | UNEMPLOYED (000s) | Percent of Labor Force |
|---|---|---|---|---|---|---|---|---|---|
| 1966 | 75,770 | 72,895 | 2,875 | 3.8 | 1957 | 66,929 | 64,071 | 2,859 | 4.3 |
| 1965 | 74,455 | 71,088 | 3,366 | 4.5 | 1956 | 66,552 | 63,802 | 2,750 | 4.1 |
| 1964 | 73,091 | 69,305 | 3,786 | 5.2 | 1954 | 63,643 | 60,110 | 3,532 | 5.5 |
| 1963 | 71,833 | 67,762 | 4,070 | 5.7 | 1952 | 62,138 | 60,254 | 1,883 | 3.0 |
| 1962 | 70,614 | 66,702 | 3,911 | 5.5 | 1950 | 62,208 | 58,920 | 3,288 | 5.3 |
| 1961 | 70,459 | 65,746 | 4,714 | 6.7 | 1945 | 53,860 | 52,820 | 1,040 | 1.9 |
| 1960 | 69,628 | 65,778 | 3,852 | 5.5 | 1940 | 55,640 | 47,520 | 8,120 | 14.6 |
| 1959 | 68,369 | 64,630 | 3,740 | 5.5 | 1933 | 51,590 | 38,760 | 12,830 | 24.9 |
| 1958 | 67,639 | 63,036 | 4,602 | 6.8 | 1929 | 49,180 | 47,630 | 1,550 | 3.2 |

* Data prior to 1950 for persons 14 years of age and over; for 16 years and over since then.

## WORKTIME REQUIRED TO BUY GOODS AND SERVICES

When the Bureau of Labor Statistics, U.S. Department of Labor, made its most recent study of the worktime required to buy goods and services (September 1965), American production workers in manufacturing were earning an average of $2.63 hourly, including overtime. The following list, selected from the BLS report, is based on prices prevailing at that time. It took a worker 28 weeks to buy a new eight-cylinder, four-door sedan; eight minutes for a pack of cigarettes; 21 minutes to buy his wife a pair of nylons; 13 minutes to buy a pound of ground beef; and three hours and 28 minutes to pay for a house visit by a physician.

| GOODS | AVERAGE RETAIL PRICE | WORKTIME REQUIRED |
|---|---|---|
| Automobile, new 8-cylinder, 4-door sedan with automatic transmission (Chevrolet, Ford, or Plymouth) | — | approximately 28 weeks |
| Automobile, new 6-cylinder compact 4-door sedan with automatic transmission (Chevrolet, Ford, Plymouth, or Rambler) | — | approximately 23 weeks |
| Automobile, 4-year-old used Chevrolet or Ford (1961 model) | — | approximately 10 weeks |
| Automobile tires, size 7.50 x 15 | $ 29.90 | 9 hours, 51 minutes |
| Beer, six 12-ounce cans or bottles | 1.13 | 26 minutes |
| Butter, one pound, 92 score | .76 | 18 minutes |
| Carpet, square yard of tufted nylon broadloom | 7.66 | 2 hours, 55 minutes |
| Chicken (ready to cook), one pound | .40 | 10 minutes |
| Cigarettes, pack of 20 | .31 | 8 minutes |
| Cigarettes, carton of 200 | 2.76 | 1 hour, 3 minutes |
| Coffee, one pound can | .83 | 19 minutes |
| Cooking stove, semi-deluxe gas stove, 36"–38" long | 192.37 | 73 hours, 9 minutes |
| Detergent, 20 ounces of granules or flakes | .33 | 8 minutes |
| Eggs, one dozen large Grade A | .56 | 13 minutes |
| Gasoline, one gallon premium | .36 | 9 minutes |
| Ham (whole or smoked), one pound | .71 | 17 minutes |
| Hamburger, one pound ground beef | .53 | 13 minutes |
| Milk, one quart fresh | .24 | 6 minutes |
| Motion picture admission, one adult | 1.26 | 29 minutes |
| Pants, man's cotton (for work) | 3.85 | 1 hour, 28 minutes |
| Paper napkins, box or package of 80 | .15 | 4 minutes |
| Penicillin prescription, 12 tablets | 2.32 | 53 minutes |
| Potatoes, one pound | .07 | 2 minutes |
| Radio, 4-tube table model | 17.40 | 6 hours, 38 minutes |
| Refrigerator freezer, 2-door unit with total capacity of 11.5 to 14.5 cubic feet and freezer capacity 85 to 120 pounds of frozen food | 252.61 | 96 hours, 3 minutes |
| Sheet, percale, 81 x 108 inches | 3.08 | 1 hour, 11 minutes |
| Shirt, man's business broadcloth | 4.56 | 1 hour, 45 minutes |
| Shoes, man's high work shoes with composition sole | 10.98 | 4 hours, 11 minutes |
| Shoes, man's oxford street shoes with calf uppers, leather sole | 17.32 | 6 hours, 36 minutes |
| Skirt, woman's wool | 6.16 | 2 hours, 21 minutes |
| Slip, woman's nylon, tricot, plain | 4.00 | 1 hour, 32 minutes |
| Sneakers, boy's oxford tennis shoes | 5.26 | 2 hours |
| Socks, man's cotton, argyle knit | .85 | 20 minutes |
| Steak, round, one pound best grade | 1.10 | 26 minutes |
| Stockings, one pair nylon | .91 | 21 minutes |
| Sugar, one pound | .12 | 3 minutes |
| Television set, 19-inch portable | 149.63 | 56 hours, 54 minutes |
| Toothpaste, one ounce | .16 | 4 minutes |
| Tuna (canned), 6½ ounces | .32 | 8 minutes |
| Undershorts, boy's | .70 | 17 minutes |
| Vacuum cleaner, electric | 46.04 | 17 hours, 31 minutes |
| Washing machine, electric, automatic | 211.02 | 80 hours, 15 minutes |
| Whiskey, ⅕ gallon spirit blended | 4.66 | 1 hour, 47 minutes |

| SERVICES | AVERAGE COST | WORKTIME REQUIRED |
|---|---|---|
| Bus fare, one | .24 | 6 minutes |
| Dentist, extraction | 7.43 | 2 hours, 50 minutes |
| Dentist, filling | 6.11 | 2 hours, 20 minutes |
| Dry cleaning, man's 2-piece suit, cash and carry | 1.36 | 32 minutes |
| Electricity, 250 kilowatt hours | 7.41 | 2 hours, 50 minutes |
| Gas, 25 therms | 4.08 | 1 hour, 34 minutes |
| Haircut, man's | 1.99 | 46 minutes |
| Hospital, semi-private room, per day | 26.86 | 10 hours, 13 minutes |
| Laundry service, 10-pound bundle, finished | 2.31 | 53 minutes |
| Permanent wave | 13.02 | 4 hours, 58 minutes |
| Physician, house visit | 9.09 | 3 hours, 28 minutes |

## U.S. INDUSTRIAL EMPLOYMENT: 1929–1966

Significant changes have occurred in the U.S. labor market since 1929. All non-agricultural industry divisions, except mining, have had substantial employment growth, some at a phenomenal rate. U.S. government employment, for example, has grown nearly fivefold in the past 37 years. The totals in this U.S. Department of Labor table are given in thousands.

| YEAR | TOTAL WAGE AND SALARY WORKERS | MANUFACTURING | MINING | CONSTRUCTION | TRANSPORTATION AND PUBLIC UTILITIES | WHOLESALE AND RETAIL TRADE | FINANCE, INSURANCE, AND REAL ESTATE | SERVICE AND MISCELLANEOUS | FEDERAL GOVERNMENT | STATE AND LOCAL GOVERNMENTS |
|---|---|---|---|---|---|---|---|---|---|---|
| 1929 | 31,339 | 10,702 | 1,087 | 1,497 | 3,916 | 6,123 | 1,509 | 3,440 | 533 | 2,532 |
| 1930 | 29,424 | 9,562 | 1,009 | 1,372 | 3,685 | 5,797 | 1,475 | 3,376 | 526 | 2,622 |
| 1931 | 26,649 | 8,170 | 873 | 1,214 | 3,254 | 5,284 | 1,407 | 3,183 | 560 | 2,704 |
| 1932 | 23,628 | 6,931 | 731 | 970 | 2,816 | 4,683 | 1,341 | 2,931 | 559 | 2,666 |
| 1933 | 23,711 | 7,397 | 744 | 809 | 2,672 | 4,755 | 1,295 | 2,873 | 565 | 2,601 |
| 1934 | 25,953 | 8,501 | 883 | 862 | 2,750 | 5,281 | 1,319 | 3,058 | 652 | 2,647 |
| 1935 | 27,053 | 9,069 | 897 | 912 | 2,786 | 5,431 | 1,335 | 3,142 | 753 | 2,728 |
| 1936 | 29,082 | 9,827 | 946 | 1,145 | 2,973 | 5,809 | 1,388 | 3,326 | 826 | 2,842 |
| 1937 | 31,026 | 10,794 | 1,015 | 1,112 | 3,134 | 6,265 | 1,432 | 3,518 | 833 | 2,923 |
| 1938 | 29,209 | 9,440 | 891 | 1,055 | 2,863 | 6,179 | 1,425 | 3,473 | 829 | 3,054 |
| 1939 | 30,618 | 10,279 | 854 | 1,150 | 2,936 | 6,426 | 1,462 | 3,517 | 905 | 3,090 |
| 1940 | 32,376 | 10,985 | 925 | 1,294 | 3,038 | 6,750 | 1,502 | 3,681 | 996 | 3,206 |
| 1941 | 36,554 | 13,192 | 957 | 1,790 | 3,274 | 7,210 | 1,549 | 3,921 | 1,340 | 3,320 |
| 1942 | 40,125 | 15,280 | 992 | 2,170 | 3,460 | 7,118 | 1,538 | 4,084 | 2,213 | 3,270 |
| 1943 | 42,452 | 17,602 | 925 | 1,567 | 3,647 | 6,982 | 1,502 | 4,148 | 2,905 | 3,174 |
| 1944 | 41,883 | 17,328 | 892 | 1,094 | 3,829 | 7,058 | 1,476 | 4,163 | 2,928 | 3,116 |
| 1945 | 40,394 | 15,524 | 836 | 1,132 | 3,906 | 7,314 | 1,497 | 4,241 | 2,808 | 3,137 |
| 1946 | 41,674 | 14,703 | 862 | 1,661 | 4,061 | 8,376 | 1,697 | 4,719 | 2,254 | 3,341 |
| 1947 | 43,881 | 15,545 | 955 | 1,982 | 4,166 | 8,955 | 1,754 | 5,050 | 1,892 | 3,582 |
| 1948 | 44,891 | 15,582 | 994 | 2,169 | 4,189 | 9,272 | 1,829 | 5,206 | 1,863 | 3,787 |
| 1949 | 43,778 | 14,441 | 930 | 2,165 | 4,001 | 9,264 | 1,857 | 5,264 | 1,908 | 3,948 |
| 1950 | 45,222 | 15,241 | 901 | 2,333 | 4,034 | 9,386 | 1,919 | 5,382 | 1,928 | 4,098 |
| 1951 | 47,849 | 16,393 | 929 | 2,603 | 4,226 | 9,742 | 1,991 | 5,576 | 2,302 | 4,087 |
| 1952 | 48,825 | 16,632 | 898 | 2,634 | 4,248 | 10,004 | 2,069 | 5,730 | 2,420 | 4,188 |
| 1953 | 50,232 | 17,549 | 866 | 2,623 | 4,290 | 10,247 | 2,146 | 5,867 | 2,305 | 4,340 |
| 1954 | 49,022 | 16,314 | 791 | 2,612 | 4,084 | 10,235 | 2,234 | 6,002 | 2,188 | 4,563 |
| 1955 | 50,675 | 16,882 | 792 | 2,802 | 4,141 | 10,535 | 2,335 | 6,274 | 2,187 | 4,727 |
| 1956 | 52,408 | 17,243 | 822 | 2,999 | 4,244 | 10,858 | 2,429 | 6,536 | 2,209 | 5,069 |
| 1957 | 52,894 | 17,174 | 828 | 2,923 | 4,241 | 10,886 | 2,477 | 6,749 | 2,217 | 5,399 |
| 1958 | 51,363 | 15,945 | 751 | 2,778 | 3,976 | 10,750 | 2,519 | 6,806 | 2,191 | 5,648 |
| 1959 | 53,313 | 16,675 | 732 | 2,960 | 4,011 | 11,127 | 2,594 | 7,130 | 2,233 | 5,850 |
| 1960 | 54,234 | 16,796 | 712 | 2,885 | 4,004 | 11,391 | 2,669 | 7,423 | 2,270 | 6,083 |
| 1961 | 54,042 | 16,326 | 672 | 2,816 | 3,903 | 11,337 | 2,731 | 7,664 | 2,279 | 6,315 |
| 1962 | 55,596 | 16,853 | 650 | 2,902 | 3,906 | 11,566 | 2,800 | 8,028 | 2,340 | 6,550 |
| 1963 | 56,702 | 16,995 | 635 | 2,963 | 3,903 | 11,778 | 2,877 | 8,325 | 2,358 | 6,868 |
| 1964 | 58,332 | 17,274 | 634 | 3,050 | 3,951 | 12,160 | 2,957 | 8,709 | 2,348 | 7,249 |
| 1965 | 60,770 | 18,032 | 632 | 3,181 | 4,033 | 12,683 | 3,019 | 9,098 | 2,378 | 7,713 |
| 1966 | 63,864 | 19,081 | 628 | 3,281 | 4,137 | 13,220 | 3,086 | 9,582 | 2,565 | 8,284 |

## U.S. LABOR STRIKES: 1965–1966

Wage changes were the leading issue in strikes beginning in 1966, and were responsible for nearly half of all man-days idle during the year, according to the U.S. Department of Labor.

| MAJOR ISSUES | NUMBER OF STRIKES 1966 | 1965 | WORKERS INVOLVED 1966 | 1965 | MAN-DAYS IDLE 1966 | 1965 |
|---|---|---|---|---|---|---|
| General wage changes.............. | 1,913 | 1,597 | 937,000 | 659,000 | 15,100,000 | 12,000,000 |
| Supplementary benefits............. | 71 | 114 | 36,000 | 50,000 | 802,000 | 711,000 |
| Wage adjustments.................. | 272 | 198 | 139,000 | 98,000 | 1,910,000 | 594,000 |
| Hours of work..................... | 5 | 14 | 2,000 | 15,000 | 93,000 | 510,000 |
| Other contractual matters........... | 38 | 60 | 10,000 | 19,000 | 171,000 | 251,000 |
| Union organization and security...... | 597 | 594 | 130,000 | 154,000 | 3,160,000 | 2,980,000 |
| Job security....................... | 180 | 203 | 201,000 | 145,000 | 1,500,000 | 3,630,000 |
| Plant administration................ | 683 | 589 | 362,000 | 287,000 | 1,850,000 | 1,890,000 |
| Other working conditions............ | 96 | 67 | 61,000 | 31,000 | 362,000 | 298,000 |
| Inter-union or intra-union matters.... | 516 | 475 | 80,000 | 81,000 | 446,000 | 438,000 |
| Not reported...................... | 34 | 52 | 4,000 | 9,000 | 24,000 | 32,000 |
| Total........... | 4,405 | 3,963 | 1,960,000 | 1,550,000 | 25,400,000 | 23,300,000 |

## TEN PRINCIPAL U.S. UNIONS: 1966
Source: U.S. Department of Labor

| UNION | AFFILIATION | MEMBERSHIP |
|---|---|---|
| International Brotherhood of Teamsters.......................... | Independent | 1,651,240 |
| Automobile Workers of America................................ | AFL-CIO | 1,402,700 |
| United Steel Workers of America............................... | AFL-CIO | 1,068,000 |
| International Brotherhood of Electrical Workers................. | AFL-CIO | 875,000 |
| International Association of Machinists and Aerospace Workers... | AFL-CIO | 836,163 |
| United Brotherhood of Carpenters and Joiners of America........ | AFL-CIO | 800,000 |
| Laborers International Union of North America.................. | AFL-CIO | 474,529 |
| International Ladies' Garment Workers Union................... | AFL-CIO | 455,164 |
| United Mine Workers of America (1965; 1966 total not available)... | Independent | 450,000 |
| Hotel and Restaurant Employees and Bartenders International Union........ | AFL-CIO | 449,974 |

## STRIKES IN THE UNITED STATES: 1933–1966
Source: U.S. Department of Labor

| YEAR | STRIKES Number | Average Duration (in days) | WORKERS INVOLVED Number | % of Total Employed in U.S. | YEAR | STRIKES Number | Average Duration (in days) | WORKERS INVOLVED Number | % of Total Employed in U.S. |
|---|---|---|---|---|---|---|---|---|---|
| 1933 | 1,695 | 16.9 | 1,170,000 | 6.3 | 1950 | 4,843 | 19.2 | 2,410,000 | 6.9 |
| 1934 | 1,856 | 19.5 | 1,470,000 | 7.2 | 1951 | 4,737 | 17.4 | 2,220,000 | 5.5 |
| 1935 | 2,014 | 23.8 | 1,120,000 | 5.2 | 1952 | 5,117 | 19.6 | 3,540,000 | 8.8 |
| 1936 | 2,172 | 23.3 | 789,000 | 3.1 | 1953 | 5,091 | 20.3 | 2,400,000 | 5.6 |
| 1937 | 4,740 | 20.3 | 1,860,000 | 7.2 | 1954 | 3,468 | 22.5 | 1,530,000 | 3.7 |
| 1938 | 2,772 | 23.6 | 688,000 | 2.8 | 1955 | 4,320 | 18.5 | 2,650,000 | 6.2 |
| 1939 | 2,613 | 23.4 | 1,170,000 | 4.7 | 1956 | 3,825 | 18.9 | 1,900,000 | 4.3 |
| 1940 | 2,508 | 20.9 | 577,000 | 2.3 | 1957 | 3,673 | 19.2 | 1,390,000 | 3.1 |
| 1941 | 4,288 | 18.3 | 2,360,000 | 8.4 | 1958 | 3,694 | 19.7 | 2,060,000 | 4.8 |
| 1942 | 2,968 | 11.7 | 840,000 | 2.8 | 1959 | 3,708 | 24.6 | 1,880,000 | 4.3 |
| 1943 | 3,752 | 5.0 | 1,980,000 | 6.9 | 1960 | 3,333 | 23.4 | 1,320,000 | 3.0 |
| 1944 | 4,956 | 5.6 | 2,120,000 | 7.0 | 1961 | 3,367 | 23.7 | 1,450,000 | 3.2 |
| 1945 | 4,750 | 9.9 | 3,470,000 | 12.2 | 1962 | 3,614 | 24.6 | 1,230,000 | 2.7 |
| 1946 | 4,985 | 24.2 | 4,600,000 | 14.5 | 1963 | 3,362 | 23.0 | 941,000 | 2.0 |
| 1947 | 3,693 | 25.6 | 2,170,000 | 6.5 | 1964 | 3,655 | 22.9 | 1,640,000 | 3.4 |
| 1948 | 3,419 | 21.8 | 1,960,000 | 5.5 | 1965 | 3,963 | 25.0 | 1,550,000 | 3.1 |
| 1949 | 3,606 | 22.5 | 3,030,000 | 9.0 | 1966 | 4,405 | 22.2 | 1,960,000 | 3.7 |

## THE AUTOMOBILE INDUSTRY STRIKE: 1967

At midnight on September 7, 1967, the nation's second largest labor union and its second largest motor vehicle manufacturer went to war.

As United Automobile Workers' picket lines formed outside Ford Motor Company's 101 plants in 25 states and Canada, the union and Ford fired heavy salvos by press release.

U.A.W. President Walter Reuther had demanded pay and fringe benefit boosts approximating 6 per cent yearly, or 90 cents an hour over the three-year life of the contract. Ford, in turn, offered the union a package equal to about 60 cents an hour over three years. The U.A.W. said this was only about a 3.2 per cent annual increase. The difference between the offer and the demand was $100,000,000.

An agreement was reached on October 22. Reuther called it "the most substantial contract ever negotiated in any corporation in the industrial field in the United States." Ford officials termed the accord "a realistic one." Its provisions include a 5% yearly hike in wage and fringe benefits, cost-of-living increases adding nearly 2 per cent annually for the last two years, a 30¢ hourly increase for skilled workers, and guaranteed annual income.

The time-tested strategy of the U.A.W. is to pick out and corner the one company among the industry's "Big Three"—General Motors, Ford, and Chrysler—that in their judgment can least afford a lengthy walkout. A single company will succumb more easily to a fast, high settlement, thus setting a precedent for still higher returns when the union faces the other companies across the bargaining table. Chrysler probably could not have withstood much of a strike, and mighty General Motors might have weathered one only too well. So, to almost no one's surprise, Reuther chose Ford.

For Ford, strategically struck when production of 1968 models was just getting under way, the walkout unavoidably meant a sales slump. For dealers, the first weeks of a new model year without cars placed them in a hazardous competitive disadvantage. For unions, it meant that their 1968 bargaining base, partly as a result of an inevitably higher settlement in the auto industry, was going to be a package of 6 per cent or more. For the nation, the strike was expected to merely slow the economy slightly during the fall and winter of 1967–68. The President's Council of Economic Advisers hopefully forecast that any slowdown would quickly be followed by a surge of activity in both the auto industry and the economy in general early in the new year.

# AGRICULTURE

Farming is the nation's single biggest industry, according to studies made by the U.S. Department of Agriculture:

● Farming employs 5.2 million workers, more than the combined employment in transportation, public utilities, and the motor vehicles industries. And, three out of every ten jobs in private industry are related to agriculture.

● Agriculture's assets total $230 billion, equal to about two-thirds of the value of the current assets of all U.S. corporations, or about 60% of the market value of all corporation stocks on the New York Stock Exchange.

● Some 3,252,000 U.S. farms realized a gross farm income in 1966 of more than $49.7 billion: 1,413,000 farms sold less than $2,500 worth of products; 356,000 had sales of $2,500 to $4,999; 446,000 sold products valued from $5,000 to $9,999; 510,000 had sales between $10,000 and $19,999; and, of the 527,000 realizing $20,000 or more, 36% grossed $40,000 and over.

Farmers spend over $33 billion a year for goods and services to produce crops and livestock, and another $12 billion a year for food, clothing, drugs, furniture, appliances, and the like. Farmers' purchases include:

● $4.6 billion in new tractors and other motor vehicles, machinery, and equipment.

● $3.4 billion for fuel, lubricants and maintenance of machinery and motor vehicles.

● $1.9 billion for fertilizer and lime.

● 28–30 billion kilowatt-hours of electricity—more than is needed annually by Baltimore, Chicago, Boston, Detroit, Houston, and Washington, D.C.

● 5 million tons of steel in the form of farm machinery, trucks, cars, fencing, and building materials.

● One hour of farm labor produces more than six times as much food and other crops as it did in 1919–21; crop production is 80 per cent higher per acre; output per breeding animal has doubled.

● Productivity of the average farm worker since the 1950–1959 period has increased by 6 per cent a year.

● Output per man-hour in nonagricultural industry has increased by 3 per cent a year.

● One farm worker produces food, fiber, and other commodities for himself and 38 others.

The farmer is a major taxpayer, too. In 1964, farm real estate taxes totaled $1.7 billion; tax on personal property on farms was about one-third of a billion dollars; Federal and state income taxes paid by the farm population totaled $1.5 billion; net taxes paid by farmers on motor fuels were $320 million; motor vehicle license fees and taxes paid by farmers were about $180 million; sales taxes paid by farmers totaled about $350 million.

Of the farmer's produce, each American consumes annually 214 pounds of meat, 527 pounds of fruit and vegetables, and 603 pounds of dairy products. In return, the farmer receives 40 cents for each dollar spent on food, or about 3 cents for the wheat in a loaf of bread, and 12 cents for a quart of milk.

## NET INCOME PER U.S. FARM

Source: U.S. Department of Agriculture

| STATE AND REGION | 1966 | 1965 | 1964 | STATE AND REGION | 1966 | 1965 | 1964 |
|---|---|---|---|---|---|---|---|
| **North Atlantic** | **$5,146** | **$4,444** | **$3,708** | West Virginia | $ 967 | $ 935 | $ 851 |
| Maine | 6,020 | 8,191 | 4,795 | North Carolina | 3,691 | 2,980 | 3,209 |
| New Hampshire | 2,240 | 1,711 | 1,354 | South Carolina | 3,307 | 2,769 | 2,578 |
| Vermont | 4,692 | 3,828 | 3,196 | Georgia | 5,155 | 4,530 | 3,666 |
| Massachusetts | 5,535 | 5,062 | 4,428 | Florida | 11,330 | 11,411 | 11,734 |
| Rhode Island | 3,816 | 3,500 | 3,034 | **South Central** | **3,956** | **3,288** | **3,060** |
| Connecticut | 8,918 | 5,973 | 5,131 | Kentucky | 2,482 | 2,400 | 2,917 |
| New York | 5,561 | 4,719 | 4,170 | Tennessee | 1,903 | 1,921 | 1,750 |
| New Jersey | 8,801 | 6,069 | 5,132 | Alabama | 2,879 | 2,802 | 2,539 |
| Pennsylvania | 4,110 | 3,356 | 2,931 | Mississippi | 4,155 | 3,547 | 3,171 |
| **East North Central** | **5,243** | **4,022** | **3,618** | Arkansas | 5,451 | 4,649 | 4,714 |
| Ohio | 4,260 | 3,128 | 2,884 | Louisiana | 4,643 | 3,328 | 3,372 |
| Indiana | 5,236 | 4,255 | 3,398 | Oklahoma | 4,001 | 3,387 | 2,022 |
| Illinois | 7,462 | 5,392 | 5,309 | Texas | 6,070 | 4,463 | 3,998 |
| Michigan | 3,717 | 2,958 | 2,683 | **Western** | **7,677** | **5,995** | **5,916** |
| Wisconsin | 4,970 | 4,002 | 3,435 | Montana | 6,980 | 4,768 | 3,990 |
| **West North Central** | **5,714** | **4,559** | **3,902** | Idaho | 5,390 | 4,574 | 3,750 |
| Minnesota | 4,699 | 3,868 | 3,393 | Wyoming | 6,589 | 3,606 | 2,828 |
| Iowa | 7,344 | 6,301 | 5,124 | Colorado | 4,863 | 3,407 | 4,477 |
| Missouri | 3,790 | 3,298 | 2,548 | New Mexico | 8,689 | 6,004 | 5,897 |
| North Dakota | 6,569 | 5,430 | 3,351 | Arizona | 22,826 | 21,457 | 17,192 |
| South Dakota | 6,529 | 5,206 | 4,093 | Utah | 3,210 | 2,205 | 1,504 |
| Nebraska | 6,710 | 4,903 | 4,958 | Nevada | 7,499 | 3,877 | 905 |
| Kansas | 6,036 | 3,619 | 4,048 | Washington | 5,818 | 4,416 | 3,611 |
| **South Atlantic** | **4,151** | **3,702** | **3,549** | Oregon | 4,000 | 3,292 | 2,329 |
| Delaware | 7,530 | 7,507 | 5,501 | California | 12,461 | 9,853 | 11,128 |
| Maryland | 4,508 | 4,496 | 3,258 | | | | |
| Virginia | 2,367 | 2,390 | 2,253 | **United States** | **5,049** | **4,109** | **3,747** |

## LEADING U.S. CROPS: ACRES HARVESTED AND TOTAL PRODUCTION *

| CROP | UNIT | ACRES HARVESTED (in 000s) | | | TOTAL PRODUCTION (in 000s) | | |
|------|------|------|------|------|------|------|------|
| | | 1966 | 1965 | 1960–64 Average | 1966 | 1965 | 1960–64 Average |
| Barley....... | Bushels | 10,227 | 9,144 | 12,078 | 389,557 | 392,279 | 405,613 |
| Beans....... | Hundredweight | 1,519 | 1,484 | 1,397 | 20,271 | 16,457 | 18,476 |
| Corn, grain... | Bushels | 56,888 | 55,332 | 59,876 | 4,103,323 | 4,084,342 | 3,722,911 |
| Cotton....... | Bales | 9,595 | 13,615 | 14,956 | 9,627 | 14,956 | 14,795 |
| Flaxseed..... | Bushels | 2,627 | 2,775 | 2,932 | 23,871 | 35,402 | 28,050 |
| Hay......... | Tons | 65,192 | 67,684 | 67,211 | 120,863 | 125,356 | 118,638 |
| Oats......... | Bushels | 17,848 | 18,479 | 22,784 | 798,089 | 926,851 | 998,722 |
| Potatoes..... | Hundredweight | 1,479 | 1,403 | 1,382 | 300,940 | 289,783 | 265,773 |
| Rice......... | Hundredweight | 1,967 | 1,793 | 1,703 | 85,060 | 76,281 | 63,654 |
| Rye......... | Bushels | 1,283 | 1,469 | 1,699 | 27,921 | 33,223 | 32,559 |
| Sorghum..... | Bushels | 12,837 | 13,029 | 12,645 | 720,415 | 672,698 | 537,127 |
| Soybeans.... | Bushels | 36,644 | 34,449 | 27,535 | 931,491 | 845,608 | 660,582 |
| Wheat....... | Bushels | 49,843 | 49,560 | 48,481 | 1,310,642 | 1,315,613 | 1,221,844 |

## U.S. CROP YIELD *

| CROP | UNIT | YIELD PER ACRE | | | CROP | UNIT | YIELD PER ACRE | | |
|------|------|------|------|------|------|------|------|------|------|
| | | 1966 | 1965 | 1950–54 | | | 1966 | 1965 | 1950–54 |
| Barley..... | Bushels | 38.1 | 42.9 | 27.8 | Potatoes... | Hundredweight | 203.0 | 207.0 | 151.0 |
| Corn, | | | | | Rice....... | Pounds | 4,324.0 | 4,255.0 | 2,411.0 |
| grain.... | Bushels | 72.1 | 73.8 | 39.4 | Sorghum | | | | |
| Cotton..... | Pounds | 482.0 | 526.0 | 297.0 | grain.... | Bushels | 56.1 | 51.6 | 19.4 |
| Flaxseed... | Bushels | 9.1 | 12.8 | 8.7 | Soybeans.. | Bushels | 25.4 | 24.5 | 20.3 |
| Hay....... | Tons | 1.85 | 1.85 | 1.43 | Sugarbeets | Tons | 17.4 | 16.8 | 15.5 |
| Oats....... | Bushels | 44.7 | 50.2 | 33.9 | Tobacco.... | Pounds | 1,894.0 | 1,898.0 | 1,292.0 |
| Peanuts.... | Pounds | 1,691.0 | 1,661.0 | 889.0 | Wheat...... | Bushels | 26.3 | 26.5 | 17.3 |

## LEADING U.S. CROPS, BY VALUE *

| CROP | VALUE OF TOTAL PRODUCTION | | CROP | VALUE OF TOTAL PRODUCTION | |
|------|------|------|------|------|------|
| | 1966 | 1965 | | 1966 | 1965 |
| Corn for grain..... | $5,285,313,000 | $4,731,871,000 | Potatoes.......... | $625,439,000 | $730,750,000 |
| Hay............... | 2,890,553,000 | 2,913,418,000 | Oats.............. | 539,009,000 | 585,453,000 |
| Soybeans......... | 2,582,795,000 | 2,151,305,000 | Oranges.......... | 421,384,000 | 339,148,000 |
| Wheat............ | 2,142,237,000 | 1,774,537,000 | Barley............ | 407,603,000 | 395,389,000 |
| Cotton, lint and seed........... | 1,251,634,000 | 2,390,500,000 | Rice.............. | 405,369,000 | 376,227,000 |
| Tobacco.......... | 1,254,394,000 | 1,206,734,000 | Tomatoes, fresh and processing.. | 353,393,000 | 359,774,000 |
| Sorghum grain.... | 746,166,000 | 667,967,000 | Peanuts.......... | 271,190,000 | 272,248,000 |

## LIVESTOCK AND POULTRY ON U.S. FARMS AND RANCHES *

| YEAR (as of January 1) | CATTLE AND CALVES | SHEEP AND LAMBS | HOGS AND PIGS | CHICKENS |
|------|------|------|------|------|
| 1961............ | 97,700,000 | 32,725,000 | 55,560,000 | 366,082,000 |
| 1962............ | 100,369,000 | 30,969,000 | 56,619,000 | 377,392,000 |
| 1963............ | 104,488,000 | 29,176,000 | 57,993,000 | 375,575,000 |
| 1964............ | 107,903,000 | 27,116,000 | 56,757,000 | 382,262,000 |
| 1965............ | 109,000,000 | 25,127,000 | 50,792,000 | 394,118,000 |
| 1966............ | 108,862,000 | 24,734,000 | 47,414,000 | 393,019,000 |
| 1967............ | 108,491,000 | 23,727,000 | 51,035,000 | 427,619,000 |
| Value, 1967.... | $16,151,486,000 | $469,635,000 | $1,719,575,000 | $511,798,000 |

## LEADING U.S. BEEF CATTLE STATES: JANUARY 1, 1967 *

| RANK | STATE | NUMBER OF HEAD | RANK | STATE | NUMBER OF HEAD | RANK | STATE | NUMBER OF HEAD |
|------|------|------|------|------|------|------|------|------|
| 1..... | Texas....... | 10,146,000 | 7.... | South Dakota | 3,986,000 | 13.... | Mississippi.. | 2,030,000 |
| 2..... | Iowa........ | 6,403,000 | 8.... | California... | 3,520,000 | 14.... | North Dakota | 1,999,000 |
| 3..... | Nebraska.... | 6,077,000 | 9.... | Illinois...... | 2,946,000 | 15.... | Kentucky.... | 1,913,000 |
| 4..... | Kansas.... | 5,149,000 | 10.... | Colorado.... | 2,872,000 | 16.... | Tennessee... | 1,724,000 |
| 5..... | Oklahoma... | 4,037,000 | 11.... | Montana.... | 2,786,000 | 17.... | Florida...... | 1,636,000 |
| 6..... | Missouri..... | 4,020,000 | 12.... | Minnesota... | 2,145,000 | 18.... | Alabama.... | 1,604,000 |

* Source: U.S. Department of Agriculture

# WORLD ECONOMY

## LARGEST CORPORATIONS IN THE WORLD

When assets are used to measure a corporation's size, those of the American Telephone and Telegraph Company—$35.2 billion at the end of 1966—put it far in front of the nearest U.S. or foreign runner-up. A.T.&T. also ranked first on the basis of income, with a 1966 net of nearly $2 billion. Another U.S. company, General Motors, easily took the top spot in annual sales—a net of $20.2 billion in 1966. Royal Dutch/Shell held its lead among foreign industrial corporations—in sales, assets, and net profits.

Sales of foreign companies increased substantially, but earnings, particularly for many Western European businesses, were far below the profit advances made in 1964 and 1965.

## LARGEST FOREIGN INDUSTRIAL COMPANIES: 1966

The corporations in the following list, ranked in size by sales, are the top 50 from *Fortune* magazine's 1967 directory of "The 200 Largest Industrials Outside the U.S."

| COMPANY | HEADQUARTERS | INDUSTRY | SALES |
|---|---|---|---|
| Royal Dutch/Shell | Netherlands-Britain | Petroleum prod., natural gas, chemicals | $7,711,432,000 |
| Unilever | Britain-Netherlands | Food, detergents, paper, chemicals | 5,300,733,000 |
| British Petroleum | Britain | Petroleum products | 2,543,240,000 |
| Volkswagenwerk | Germany | Automobiles | 2,499,500,000 |
| ICI (Imperial Chemical Industries) | Britain | Chemicals | 2,478,560,000 |
| National Coal Board | Britain | Coal | 2,338,095,000 |
| Philips' Gloeilampenfabrieken | Netherlands | Electrical equip., electronics, chemicals | 2,228,959,000 |
| Montecatini Edison | Italy | Chemicals, synthetic fibers | 1,998,400,000 |
| Siemens | Germany | Electrical equipment | 1,957,750,000 |
| Nestlé | Switzerland | Food products | 1,702,950,000 |
| August Thyssen-Hütte | Germany | Iron and steel | 1,694,581,000 |
| Fiat | Italy | Automobiles, tractors, aircraft, engines | 1,678,710,000 |
| Daimler-Benz | Germany | Automobiles | 1,475,000,000 |
| British Motor | Britain | Automobiles | 1,472,674,000 |
| Farbwerke Hoechst | Germany | Chemicals, pharmaceuticals | 1,456,750,000 |
| Renault | France | Automobiles, tractors | 1,427,721,000 |
| Farbenfabriken Bayer | Germany | Chemicals, pharmaceuticals | 1,385,075,000 |
| Hitachi | Japan | Electrical equipment, appliances, machinery | 1,366,569,000 |
| Mitsubishi Heavy Industries | Japan | Machinery, autos, shipbuilding, aircraft | 1,268,403,000 |
| Fried. Krupp | Germany | Iron & steel, eng., mach., electrical equipment | 1,243,750,000 |
| British-American Tobacco | Britain | Tobacco | 1,225,980,000 |
| AEG-Telefunken | Germany | Electrical equipment | 1,215,250,000 |
| BASF (Badische Anilin- & Soda-Fabrik) | Germany | Chemicals | 1,176,750,000 |
| Yawata Iron & Steel | Japan | Iron and steel | 1,157,190,000 |
| Cie Française des Pétroles | France | Petroleum products | 1,140,000,000 |
| Rhône-Poulenc | France | Textiles, chemicals | 1,107,081,000 |
| ENI (Ente Nazionale Idrocarburi) | Italy | Petroleum products, eng., textiles, machinery | 1,099,040,000 |
| Società Finanziaria Siderurgica | Italy | Iron and steel | 1,094,794,000 |
| Gutehoffnungshütte | Germany | Machinery, engines, metal products | 1,078,000,000 |
| Rheinische Stahlwerke | Germany | Iron & steel, machinery, eng., coal | 1,075,000,000 |
| Hawker Siddeley | Britain | Aircraft, missiles, engines, eng. | 1,074,657,000 |
| Mannesmann | Germany | Tubes, machinery, iron & steel, coal | 1,018,750,000 |
| Guest, Keen & Nettlefolds | Britain | Iron and steel, engineering | 998,432,000 |
| Hoesch | Germany | Iron and steel, coal | 996,203,000 |
| Courtaulds | Britain | Fibers, textiles, chemicals | 978,628,000 |
| Dunlop | Britain | Rubber products | 974,400,000 |
| Matsushita Electric Industrial | Japan | Electrical equipment, appliances | 961,689,000 |
| Fuji Iron & Steel | Japan | Iron and steel | 953,664,000 |
| Peugeot | France | Automobiles | 934,507,000 |
| Toyota Motor | Japan | Automobiles | 929,925,000 |
| Alcan Aluminium | Canada | Aluminum | 923,418,000 |
| Nissan Motor | Japan | Automobiles | 921,400,000 |
| Charbonnages de France | France | Coal, electricity, chemicals | 894,459,000 |
| Salzgitter | Germany | Iron and steel, machinery, coal | 892,875,000 |
| Tokyo Shibaura Electric | Japan | Electrical equipment | 892,553,000 |
| Citroën | France | Automobiles | 887,409,000 |
| Schneider | France | Iron & steel, mach., electrical equipment | 879,876,000 |
| Metallgesellschaft | Germany | Nonferrous metals, chemicals, engines | 879,750,000 |
| ARBED | Luxembourg | Iron and steel | 862,400,000 |
| Massey-Ferguson | Canada | Farm equipment, engines, machinery | 862,213,000 |

## WORLD ECONOMIC SUMMARY: 1960–1965
Source: United Nations *Statistical Yearbook*

Corresponding to a general yearly rise in world population, there has been an annual increase in total world production, consumption, and trade. The following record gives totals for production of selected major commodities, consumption, and external trade in recent years.

| ITEM | UNIT | 1960 | 1961 | 1962 | 1963 | 1964 | 1965 |
|---|---|---|---|---|---|---|---|
| POPULATION | Millions | 3,010.0 | 3,055.0 | 3,117.0 | 3,176.0 | 3,234.0 | 3,295.0 |
| AGRICULTURE, FORESTRY, FISHING PRODUCTION: | | | | | | | |
| Barley | Million MT [1] | 86.9 | 81.3 | 97.9 | 100.4 | 107.7 | 101.7 |
| Cocoa beans | Million MT | 1.2 | 1.1 | 1.2 | 1.2 | 1.5 | 1.3 |
| Coffee | Million MT | 3.9 | 4.3 | 4.1 | 4.0 | 3.1 | 4.7 |
| Corn (maize) | Million MT | 213.1 | 214.9 | 220.0 | 224.7 | 225.9 | 231.6 |
| Cotton | Million MT | 10.7 | 10.2 | 10.9 | 11.4 | 11.9 | 12.1 |
| Cottonseed | Million MT | 19.9 | 19.0 | 20.3 | 21.3 | 22.0 | 22.4 |
| Linseed (flaxseed) | Million MT | 3.2 | 3.2 | 3.5 | 3.4 | 3.4 | 3.6 |
| Livestock | | | | | | | |
| Cattle | Million head | 949.6 | 967.2 | 979.5 | 992.0 | 1,012.4 | — |
| Pigs | Million head | 532.4 | 550.6 | 555.1 | 537.0 | 560.0 | — |
| Sheep | Million head | 997.3 | 1,001.0 | 1,003.3 | 1,006.8 | 1,011.5 | — |
| Horses | Million head | 75.7 | 64.8 | 63.8 | 62.7 | 63.6 | — |
| Milk (cow, goat, etc.) | Million MT | 343.0 | 348.8 | 352.5 | 351.4 | 355.9 | 370.1 |
| Oats | Million MT | 58.3 | 50.5 | 50.3 | 47.5 | 44.8 | 46.8 |
| Peanuts (groundnuts) [2] | Million MT | 13.9 | 14.2 | 14.5 | 15.0 | 16.3 | 15.3 |
| Potatoes | Million MT | 282.7 | 279.8 | 263.2 | 280.3 | 293.3 | 273.9 |
| Rice | Million MT | 235.9 | 239.5 | 240.5 | 249.6 | 259.8 | 248.7 |
| Rye | Million MT | 37.3 | 35.5 | 35.0 | 30.4 | 32.8 | 35.4 |
| Soybeans | Million MT | 27.3 | 31.1 | 30.7 | 31.6 | 32.6 | 36.5 |
| Tobacco | Million MT | 3.6 | 3.4 | 3.9 | 4.3 | 4.5 | 4.1 |
| Wheat | Million MT | 242.8 | 227.8 | 257.3 | 239.1 | 275.0 | 260.5 |
| Wool | Million MT | 2.5 | 2.6 | 2.6 | 2.6 | 2.6 | 2.6 |
| Roundwood | Million cu. ft. | 67,062.6 | 66,674.1 | 67,451.1 | 68,086.7 | 70,523.4 | 71,017.8 |
| Rubber (natural) | Million MT | 2.0 | 2.1 | 2.2 | 2.1 | 2.3 | 2.4 |
| Fish catches | Million MT | 39.5 | 43.0 | 46.4 | 47.6 | 52.0 | 52.4 |
| MINING PRODUCTION: | | | | | | | |
| Bauxite [2] | Million MT | 25.1 | 25.9 | 27.7 | 26.9 | 29.9 | 34.1 |
| Coal | Million MT | 1,986.1 | 1,811.8 | 1,857.3 | 1,928.3 | 1,997.1 | 2,045.9 |
| Lignite | Million MT | 639.1 | 662.3 | 684.2 | 718.7 | 749.4 | 745.0 |
| Copper ore [2] | Million MT | 3.8 | 3.9 | 4.0 | 4.1 | 4.2 | 4.4 |
| Iron ore | Million MT | 232.2 | 233.2 | 242.6 | 253.6 | 286.1 | 305.1 |
| Nickel ore [2] | Thousand MT | 282.0 | 300.0 | 282.0 | 282.0 | 311.0 | 343.0 |
| Tin concentrates [2] | Thousand MT | 138.7 | 138.7 | 143.9 | 143.6 | 149.6 | 154.6 |
| Petroleum (crude) [2] | Million bbls | 1,053.9 | 1,121.9 | 1,216.1 | 1,305.1 | 1,409.5 | 1,511.4 |
| MANUFACTURING PRODUCTION: | | | | | | | |
| Meat | Million MT | 61.4 | 63.4 | 65.8 | 67.7 | 67.1 | — |
| Sugar | Million MT | 51.0 | 53.5 | 50.2 | 50.8 | 57.9 | 62.4 |
| Wine | Million US gal. | 6,445.8 | 5,917.5 | 7,528.9 | 6,736.4 | 7,449.7 | 7,581.7 |
| Cigarettes | Billions | 1,845.0 | 1,927.0 | 2,039.0 | 2,112.0 | 2,160.0 | 2,322.0 |
| Rayon and acetate yarns | Thousand MT | 1,131.0 | 1,135.0 | 1,203.0 | 1,235.0 | 1,332.0 | 1,370.0 |
| Noncellulosic yarns | Thousand MT | 420.0 | 500.0 | 640.0 | 775.0 | 975.0 | 1,115.0 |
| Lumber (sawn) | Million cu. ft. | 11,911.6 | 11,784.7 | 11,953.0 | 12,346.4 | 12,900.5 | 13,063.6 |
| Wood pulp | Million MT | 59.6 | 62.6 | 65.1 | 69.7 | 75.4 | 78.1 |
| Newsprint | Million MT | 14.0 | 14.4 | 14.6 | 15.1 | 16.4 | 16.8 |
| Paper (all other) | Million MT | 35.2 | 37.2 | 38.5 | 41.2 | 43.9 | 46.0 |
| Nitrogenous fertilizers | Million MT | 10.9 | 12.0 | 13.2 | 15.0 | 16.8 | 19.3 |
| Petroleum products [1] | Million MT | 833.3 | 884.8 | 956.7 | 1,036.7 | 1,121.6 | 1,205.9 |
| Cement | Million MT | 317.0 | 333.0 | 358.0 | 378.0 | 415.0 | 433.0 |
| Pig iron and ferro-alloys | Million MT | 231.3 | 241.3 | 250.3 | 264.3 | 299.5 | 316.5 |
| Crude steel | Million MT | 327.6 | 341.3 | 350.1 | 374.8 | 424.0 | 443.3 |
| Aluminum | Million MT | 3.7 | 3.6 | 4.0 | 4.4 | 4.9 | 5.2 |
| Merchant vessels [2] | Million GRT [3] | 8.4 | 7.9 | 8.4 | 8.5 | 10.3 | 12.2 |
| Electric energy | Billion KWH [4] | 2,303.6 | 2,434.0 | 2,635.9 | 2,846.9 | 3,109.3 | 3,339.7 |
| CONSUMPTION: | | | | | | | |
| Cotton | Million MT | 10.2 | 10.0 | 9.8 | 10.3 | 10.9 | 11.1 |
| Wool | Million MT | 1.5 | 1.5 | 1.5 | 1.5 | 1.5 | 1.5 |
| Rubber (all types) | Million MT | 3.6 | 3.6 | 4.0 | 4.2 | 4.7 | 4.9 |
| Phosphatic fertilizers | Million MT | 10.0 | 10.4 | 11.1 | 12.2 | 13.6 | 14.5 |
| Nitrogenous fertilizers | Million MT | 10.3 | 11.0 | 12.4 | 14.1 | 15.3 | 17.6 |
| EXTERNAL TRADE: | | | | | | | |
| Imports | Billion US $ | 135.3 | 140.9 | 149.5 | 162.1 | 181.5 | 196.8 |
| Exports | Billion US $ | 128.0 | 134.0 | 141.6 | 154.0 | 172.4 | 186.3 |

[1] Metric tons.    [2] Excludes U.S.S.R.    [3] Gross registered tons.    [4] Kilowatt-hours.

## FOREIGN MONEY AND ITS VALUE [1]

Source: Manufacturers Hanover Trust Company

| COUNTRY | CURRENCY | CONSISTING OF | U.S VALUE |
|---|---|---|---|
| Aden | Dinar | 1,000 Fils | $2.817 |
| Afghanistan[2] | Afghani | 100 Puls | .022 |
| Albania[2] | Lek | 100 Qintar | .20 |
| Algeria | Dinar | 100 Centimes | .204 |
| Angola | Escudo | 100 Centavos | .035 |
| Argentina | Peso | 100 Centavos | .003[3] |
| Australia | Dollar | 100 Cents | 1.115[3] |
| Austria | Schilling | 100 Groschen | .039 |
| Bahamas | Dollar | 100 Cents | .982 |
| Bahrain | Dinar | 1,000 Fils | 2.11 |
| Barbados | Dollar | 100 Cents | .585 |
| Belgium | Franc | 100 Centimes | .02 |
| Bermuda | Pound | 20 Shillings | 2.80 |
| Bolivia | Peso | 100 Centavos | .085 |
| Botswana | Rand | 100 Cents | 1.394[5] |
| Brazil | New Cruzeiro | 100 Centavos | .372[3] |
| British Honduras | Dollar | 100 Cents | .704 |
| Brunei | Dollar | 100 Cents | .33 |
| Bulgaria | Lev | 100 Stotinki | .855 |
| Burma | Kyat | 100 Pyas | .212 |
| Cambodia | Riel | 100 Sen | .029 |
| Cameroon | Franc | 100 Centimes | .004 |
| Canada | Dollar | 100 Cents | .929[3] |
| Cent. African Rep. | Franc | 100 Centimes | .004 |
| Ceylon | Rupee | 100 Cents | .209[3] |
| Chad | Franc | 100 Centimes | .004 |
| Chile | Escudo | 100 Centesimos | .173[3] |
| China (Taiwan) | NT Dollar | 100 Cents | .025 |
| Colombia | Peso | 100 Centavos | .062[3] |
| Congo (Kinshasa) | Franc | 100 Centimes | .007 |
| Congo, Rep. of[3] | Franc | 100 Centimes | .004 |
| Costa Rica[2] | Colon | 100 Centimos | .151 |
| Cuba | Peso | 100 Centavos | 1.00 |
| Cyprus | Pound | 1,000 Mils | 2.81 |
| Czechoslovakia | Crown | 100 Hellers | .14 |
| Dahomey | Franc | 100 Centimes | .004 |
| Denmark | Krone | 100 Ore | .144[3] |
| Dominica | Dollar | 100 Cents | .585 |
| Domincan Rep. | Peso | 100 Centavos | 1.00 |
| Dubai | Gulf Riyal | 100 Dirhams | .21 |
| Ecuador[2] | Sucre | 100 Centavos | .056 |
| Egypt (UAR) | Pound | 100 Piasters | 2.31 |
| El Salvador | Colon | 100 Centavos | .40 |
| Ethiopia | Dollar | 100 Cents | .40 |
| Fiji Islands | Pound | 20 Shillings | 2.527 |
| Finland | Markka | 100 Pennis | .311[3] |
| France | Franc | 100 Centimes | .205[3] |
| Gabon | Franc | 100 Centimes | .004 |
| Gambia | Pound | 20 Shillings | 2.807 |
| Germany, West | Mark | 100 Pfennig | .252[3] |
| Ghana | Cedi | 100 Pesewas | 1.40 |
| Gibraltar | Pound | 20 Shillings | 2.807 |
| Greece | Drachma | 100 Lepta | .034 |
| Guadeloupe | Franc | 100 Centimes | .203 |
| Guatemala[2] | Quetzal | 100 Centavos | 1.00 |
| Guiana, French | Franc | 100 Centimes | .203 |
| Guinea | Franc | 100 Centimes | .004 |
| Guyana | Dollar | 100 Cents | .585 |
| Haiti | Gourde | 100 Centimes | .20 |
| Honduras | Lempira | 100 Centavos | .50 |
| Hong Kong | Dollar | 100 Cents | .174 |
| Hungary | Florint | 100 Fillers | .086 |
| Iceland | Krona | 100 Aurar | .023 |
| India | Rupee | 100 Paise | .133[3] |
| Indonesia[2] | New Rupiah | 100 Sen | .10 |
| Iran | Rial | 100 Dinars | $ .014 |
| Iraq | Dinar | 1,000 Fils | 2.805 |
| Ireland | Pound | 20 Shillings | 2.785[3] |
| Israel | Pound | 100 Agorot | .34 |
| Italy | Lira | 100 Centesimi | .002[3] |
| Ivory Coast | Franc | 100 Centimes | .004 |
| Jamaica | Pound | 20 Shillings | 2 80 |
| Japan | Yen | 100 Sen | .003[3] |
| Jordan | Dinar | 1,000 Fils | 2.805 |
| Kenya | Shilling | 100 Cents | .14 |
| Korea, South | Won | 100 Chon | .004 |
| Kuwait | Dinar | 1,000 Fils | 2.80 |
| Laos | Kip | 100 At | .004 |
| Lebanon[4] | Pound | 100 Piasters | .323 |
| Leeward Islands[5] | Dollar | 100 Cents | .59 |
| Lesotho | Rand | 100 Cents | 1.394[5] |
| Liberia | U.S. Dollar | 100 Cents | 1.00 |
| Libya | Pound | 1,000 Milliemes | 2.81 |
| Liechtenstein | Franc | 100 Centimes | .232 |
| Luxembourg | Franc | 100 Centimes | .02 |
| Macao | Pataca | 100 Avos | .179 |
| Madagascar | Franc | 100 Centimes | .004 |
| Malawi | Pound | 20 Shillings | 2.807 |
| Malaysia | Dollar | 100 Cents | .325[3] |
| Mali | Franc | 100 Centimes | .004 |
| Malta | Pound | 20 Shillings | 2.807 |
| Martinique | Franc | 100 Centimes | .203 |
| Mauritania | Franc | 100 Centimes | .004 |
| Mauritius | Rupee | 100 Cents | .21 |
| Mexico | Peso | 100 Centavos | .08[3] |
| Monaco | Franc | 100 Centimes | .203 |
| Morocco | Dirham | 100 Moroccan Francs | .20 |
| Mozambique | Escudo | 100 Centavos | .035 |
| Nepal | Rupee | 100 Pice | .132 |
| Netherlands | Guilder | 100 Cents | .278[3] |
| Neth. Antilles | Guilder | 100 Cents | .535 |
| New Caledonia | Franc | 100 Centimes | .011 |
| New Guinea | Dollar | 100 Cents | 1.119 |
| New Hebrides | Franc | 100 Centimes | .011 |
| New Zealand | Dollar[6] | 100 Cents | 1.388[3] |
| Nicaragua[2] | Cordoba | 100 Centavos | .143 |
| Niger | Franc | 100 Centimes | .004 |
| Nigeria | Pound | 20 Shillings | 2.816 |
| Norway | Krone | 100 Øre | .139[3] |
| Oceania (French) | Franc | 100 Centimes | .011 |
| Pakistan | Rupee | 100 Paisa | .21[3] |
| Panama | Balboa | 100 Centesimos | 1.00 |
| Paraguay | Guarani | 100 Centimos | .008 |
| Peru | Sol | 100 Centavos | .038 |
| Philippines | Peso | 100 Centavos | .257 |
| Poland | Zloty | 100 Grosze | .25 |
| Portugal | Escudo | 100 Centavos | .035 |
| Portuguese Guinea | Escudo | 100 Centavos | .035 |
| Puerto Rico | U.S. Dollar | 100 Cents | 1.00 |
| Qatar | Gulf Rupee | 100 Paise | .211 |
| Rhodesia | Pound | 20 Shillings | 2.807 |
| Romania | Leu | 100 Bani | .167 |
| Saudi Arabia | Riyal | 20 Gurshes | .224 |
| Senegal | Franc | 100 Centimes | .004 |
| Sierra Leone | Leone | 100 Cents | 1.41 |
| Somalia | So. Shilling | 100 Centesimi | .141 |
| South Africa (Rep.) | Rand | 100 Cents | 1.394 |
| Spain | Peseta | 100 Centimos | .017[3] |
| Sudan | Pound | 100 Piasters | 2.885 |
| Surinam | Guilder | 100 Cents | .538 |

[1] As of May 1, 1967, unless otherwise noted.   [2] Official rate.   [3] As of Sept. 11, 1967.   [4] Free rate.   [5] St. Kitts, Antigua, Nevis, Montserrat.   [6] Replaced Pound July 10, 1967.

| COUNTRY | CURRENCY | CONSISTING OF | U.S. VALUE | COUNTRY | CURRENCY | CONSISTING OF | U.S. VALUE |
|---|---|---|---|---|---|---|---|
| Swaziland....... | Rand...... | 100 Cents | $1.394 | Uganda.......... | Shilling... | 100 Cents | $ .14 |
| Sweden.......... | Krona.... | 100 Øre | .194[1] | U.S.S.R.......... | Ruble..... | 100 Kopecks | 1.11 |
| Switzerland...... | Franc..... | 100 Centimes | .231[1] | United Kingdom.. | Pound.... | 20 Shillings | 2.785[1] |
| Syria............ | Pound.... | 100 Piasters | .241 | Upper Volta...... | Franc..... | 100 Centimes | .004 |
| Tanzania........ | Shilling... | 100 Cents | .14 | Uruguay......... | Peso...... | 100 Centesimos | .008[1] |
| Thailand......... | Baht..... | 100 Satang | .049 | Venezuela........ | Bolivar.... | 100 Centimos | .223[1] |
| Togo............ | Franc..... | 100 Centimes | .004 | Vietnam, South... | Piaster.... | 100 Cents | .009 |
| Tonga Islands.... | Pound.... | 20 Shillings | 2.24 | Western Samoa... | N.Z. Dollar | 100 Cents | 1.387[1] |
| Trinidad & Tobago | Dollar..... | 100 Cents | .59 | Windward Islands[3] | Dollar..... | 100 Cents | .59 |
| Tunisia.......... | Dinar..... | 1.000 Mill. | 1.92 | Yugoslavia[2]...... | Dinar..... | 100 Paras | .08 |
| Turkey[2]......... | Pound.... | 100 Piasters | .111 | Zambia.......... | Pound.... | 20 Shillings | 2.807 |

[1] As of Sept. 11, 1967.    [2] Free rate.    [3] Grenada, St. Lucia, St. Vincent.

## WORLD COMMERCE, BY REGION AND COUNTRY: 1965

Source: United Nations *Statistical Yearbook*

| Region and Country | Exports (million U.S. $) | Imports (million U.S. $) | Region and Country | Exports (million U.S. $) | Imports (million U.S. $) | Region and Country | Exports (million U.S. $) | Imports (million U.S. $) |
|---|---|---|---|---|---|---|---|---|
| NORTH AMERICA | | | Ireland......... | 627 | 1,040 | Niger.......... | 25 | 38 |
| Canada........ | 8,107 | 7,986 | Italy........... | 7,188 | 7,347 | Nigeria......... | 751 | 771 |
| United States[1].. | 27,057 | 21,347 | Malta.......... | 24 | 98 | Rhodesia........ | 442 | 335 |
| LATIN AMERICA | | | Netherlands.... | 6.393 | 7,472 | Senegal........ | 128 | 164 |
| Argentina...... | 1,493 | 1,200 | Norway........ | 1,443 | 2,210 | Sierra Leone.... | 176 | 108 |
| Bolivia........ | 107 | 122 | Portugal........ | 576 | 924 | South Africa.... | 1,468 | 2,453 |
| Brazil.......... | 1,596 | 1,096 | Spain.......... | 964 | 3,025 | Sudan......... | 196 | 208 |
| Chile.......... | 688 | 604 | Sweden........ | 3,968 | 4,375 | Tanzania[5]...... | 187 | 152 |
| Colombia...... | 539 | 454 | Switzerland..... | 2,959 | 3,696 | Togo.......... | 27 | 45 |
| Costa Rica..... | 112 | 178 | Turkey......... | 459 | 577 | Tunisia........ | 120 | 245 |
| Cuba.......... | 686 | 865 | United Kingdom | 13,227 | 15,654 | Uganda[5]....... | 179 | 114 |
| Dominican Rep. | 123 | 92 | Yugoslavia..... | 1,091 | 1,288 | Upper Volta..... | —[2] | —[2] |
| Ecuador....... | —[2] | 152 | Other.......... | 30 | 50 | Zambia........ | 532 | 295 |
| El Salvador..... | 189 | 201 | EASTERN EUROPE | | | Other Africa.... | 116 | 188 |
| Guatemala..... | 187 | 229 | Albania........ | —[2] | —[2] | ASIA | | |
| Haiti.......... | 36 | 36 | Bulgaria........ | 1,179 | 1,178 | Aden.......... | 190 | 301 |
| Honduras...... | 129 | 122 | Czechoslovakia.. | 2,689 | 2,672 | Brunei......... | 64 | 36 |
| Mexico........ | 1,146 | 1,560 | Germany, East[3] | 2,776 | 2,546 | Burma......... | 226 | 247 |
| Nicaragua..... | 160 | 149 | Hungary........ | 1,510 | 1,521 | Cambodia...... | 105 | 103 |
| Panama....... | 78 | 190 | Poland......... | 2,228 | 2,340 | Ceylon......... | 409 | 310 |
| Paraguay...... | 57 | 44 | Romania....... | 1,102 | 1,077 | China, mainland; N. Korea; N. Vietnam; Mongolia[6].... | 2,000 | 2,200 |
| Peru.......... | 669 | 719 | U.S.S.R........ | 8,166 | 8,053 | | | |
| Uruguay....... | 191 | 151 | AFRICA | | | | | |
| Venezuela...... | 2,784 | 1,201 | Algeria......... | —[2] | —[2] | China, Rep. of... | 450 | 556 |
| CARIBBEAN AND REST OF AMERICA | | | Angola......... | 200 | 195 | Cyprus......... | 71 | 148 |
| | | | Cameroon...... | 139 | 152 | Hong Kong..... | 1,143 | 1,569 |
| | | | Cent. Afr. Rep.[4] | 26 | 28 | India.......... | 1,688 | 2,811 |
| Bahamas....... | 19 | 105 | Chad[4]......... | 27 | 31 | Indonesia...... | —[2] | —[2] |
| Barbados...... | 38 | 68 | Congo Rep.[4].... | 47 | 65 | Iraq........... | 882 | 450 |
| Bermuda...... | 54 | 57 | Congo, Dem. Rep. of....... | 329 | 320 | Israel......... | 406 | 814 |
| Guadeloupe.... | 38 | 85 | | | | Japan......... | 8,452 | 8,170 |
| Guyana....... | 97 | 104 | Dahomey...... | 14 | 34 | Jordan......... | 25 | 157 |
| Jamaica........ | 212 | 295 | Egypt (UAR).... | 605 | 934 | Korea, South... | 175 | 450 |
| Martinique..... | 40 | 92 | Ethiopia........ | 117 | 151 | Laos.......... | 1 | 33 |
| Neth. Antilles... | 603 | 616 | Gabon[4]........ | 96 | 62 | Lebanon....... | —[2] | —[2] |
| Surinam........ | 58 | 95 | Gambia........ | 14 | 16 | Malaysia....... | 1,256 | 1,120 |
| Trinidad, Tobago | 402 | 475 | Ghana......... | 291 | 448 | Pakistan....... | 528 | 1,043 |
| Other......... | 127 | 156 | Guinea......... | —[2] | —[2] | Philippines..... | 768 | 894 |
| WESTERN EUROPE | | | Ivory Coast.... | 277 | 237 | Ryukyu Is....... | 84 | 235 |
| Austria........ | 1,600 | 2,101 | Kenya[5]........ | 145 | 249 | Singapore...... | 981 | 1,243 |
| Belgium-Luxem. | 6,382 | 6,374 | Liberia........ | —[2] | 111 | Syria.......... | 168 | 212 |
| Denmark....... | 2,320 | 2,822 | Libya......... | 797 | 320 | Thailand....... | 627 | 726 |
| Finland........ | 1,427 | 1,646 | Madagascar..... | 92 | 138 | Vietnam, South | 36 | 357 |
| France........ | 10,051 | 10,339 | Malawi........ | —[2] | 57 | OCEANIA | | |
| Germany, West.. | 17,892 | 17,472 | Mali.......... | 16 | 43 | Australia....... | 2,922 | 3,315 |
| Greece........ | 328 | 1,134 | Mauritania...... | —[2] | —[2] | New Zealand.... | 1,006 | 1,052 |
| Iceland........ | 129 | 137 | Morocco....... | 430 | 451 | Other Oceania... | 220 | 430 |
| | | | Mozambique.... | 108 | 174 | WORLD TOTAL | 186,300 | 196,800 |

[1] See page 517 for 1966 data.    [2] Not available.    [3] Excludes trade with West Germany.    [4] Equatorial Customs Union; trade between members excluded.    [5] Excludes trade between Kenya, Uganda, and former Tanganyika.    [6] Excludes trade with one another.

## LENDING RATES IN WORLD MONEY CENTERS

Interest on short-term loans in 1966 ranged from a low of 4.5 per cent in Portugal to a high of 10.5 per cent in Turkey, according to the First National City Bank of New York.

| MAJOR MONEY CENTERS | PER CENT 1966 | PER CENT 1962 | OTHER MONEY CENTERS | PER CENT 1966 | PER CENT 1962 |
|---|---|---|---|---|---|
| Belgium | 7.00 | 5.75–7.00 | Australia | 6.75–7.25 | 6.00–6.50 |
| Canada | 6.00 | 5.50 | Austria | 7.50–8.50 | 7.50–8.00 |
| France | 5.35 | 5.50–6.50 | Denmark | 8.50–9.00 | 8.50–9.00 |
| Germany, West | 6.75 | 5.75–6.25 | Finland | 7.00–8.00 | 7.00–7.50 |
| Japan | 5.475 | 7.30 | Greece | 8.50 | 7.00–9.00 |
| Italy | 7.50 | 7.125 | Ireland | 7.25 | 7.00 |
| Netherlands | 6.00–6.50 | 5.25 | Norway | 5.75–6.25 | 5.75–6.25 |
| Sweden | 7.25–7.75 | 7.25 | Portugal | 4.50 | 5.00 |
| Switzerland | 5.25–6.00 | 4.50 | Turkey | 9.00–10.50 | 9.00 |
| United Kingdom | 6.75–7.00 | 6.50–7.00 | South Africa | 7.00 | 6.50 |
| United States | 5.50 | 4.50 | Spain | 7.50 | 6.50 |

## WORLD MOTOR VEHICLE PRODUCTION

Source: Automobile Manufacturers Association

| 1965 | TOTAL PRODUC-TION | PASSENGER CARS | TRUCKS AND BUSES | 1964 | TOTAL PRODUC-TION | PASSENGER CARS | TRUCKS AND BUSES |
|---|---|---|---|---|---|---|---|
| United States | 11,137,830 | 9,355,227 | 1,802,603 | United States | 9,307,860 | 7,745,492 | 1,562,368 |
| West Germany | 2,976,477 | 2,440,448 | 536,029 | West Germany | 2,909,657 | 2,650,183 | 259,474 |
| United Kingdom | 2,177,261 | 1,722,045 | 455,216 | United Kingdom | 2,332,376 | 1,867,640 | 464,736 |
| Japan | 1,875,614 | 696,176 | 1,179,438 | Japan | 1,702,469 | 579,660 | 1,122,809 |
| France | 1,616,153 | 1,373,969 | 242,184 | France | 1,582,129 | 1,321,081 | 261,048 |
| Italy | 1,175,548 | 1,103,932 | 71,616 | Italy | 1,090,078 | 1,028,930 | 61,148 |
| Canada | 854,876 | 710,111 | 144,765 | Canada | 670,582 | 560,392 | 110,190 |
| U.S.S.R. | 616,000 | 196,000 | 420,000 | U.S.S.R. | 603,100 | 185,200 | 417,900 |
| Australia | 407,596 | 334,953 | 72,643 | Australia | 411,750 | 340,614 | 71,136 |
| Spain | 225,462 | 159,145 | 66,317 | Sweden | 184,018 | 160,106 | 23,912 |
| Sweden | 205,717 | 181,755 | 23,962 | Brazil | 183,735 | 97,768 | 85,967 |
| Argentina | 194,536 | 133,734 | 60,802 | Spain | 178,128 | 119,327 | 58,801 |
| Brazil | 185,155 | 103,471 | 81,684 | Argentina | 166,483 | 115,857 | 50,626 |
| Belgium | 166,954 | 161,846 | 4,748 | East Germany | 112,500 | 90,000 | 22,500 |
| East Germany | 110,000 | 95,000 | 15,000 | India | 67,135 | 23,227 | 43,908 |
| All others | 341,980 | 204,102 | 137,878 | All others | 225,002 | 129,078 | 95,924 |
| TOTAL | 24,266,799 | 18,951,914 | 5,314,885 | TOTAL | 21,727,002 | 16,734,646 | 4,992,356 |

## LEADING CRUDE OIL PRODUCING NATIONS

The U.S. retained its position as the world's leading crude oil producer in 1966, according to figures from the U.S. Bureau of Mines. Totals show average daily production in barrels.

| COUNTRY | 1966 | 1965 | 1964 | COUNTRY | 1966 | 1965 | 1964 |
|---|---|---|---|---|---|---|---|
| United States | 8,326,025 | 7,804,000 | 7,676,000 | West Germany | 153,053 | 156,000 | 151,400 |
| U.S.S.R. | 5,275,315 | 4,893,000 | 4,439,200 | Trinidad | 152,338 | 134,000 | 137,500 |
| Venezuela | 3,371,134 | 3,473,000 | 3,375,000 | Egypt (U.A.R.) | 118,624 | 120,000 | 120,000 |
| Saudi Arabia | 2,392,737 | 2,025,000 | 1,700,000 | Brazil | 116,303 | 94,000 | 91,000 |
| Kuwait | 2,275,444 | 2,170,000 | 2,135,000 | Brunei | 95,813 | 80,391 | 72,000 |
| Iran | 2,113,217 | 1,886,000 | 1,656,000 | India | 95,372 | 61,771 | 47,500 |
| Libya | 1,506,647 | 1,220,000 | 950,000 | Bulgaria | 77,623 | 4,558 | — |
| Iraq | 1,387,958 | 1,321,000 | 1,250,000 | Peru | 63,088 | 63,000 | 58,200 |
| Canada | 878,372 | 809,000 | 765,000 | Bahrain | 61,701 | 57,000 | 48,600 |
| Algeria | 704,394 | 560,000 | 570,000 | France | 58,234 | 59,000 | 56,000 |
| Indonesia | 454,892 | 490,000 | 470,000 | Austria | 46,480 | 54,000 | 48,700 |
| Neutral Zone (Saudi Arabia-Kuwait) | 420,328 | 362,000 | 352,000 | Netherlands | 44,182 | 44,000 | 42,500 |
| Nigeria | 417,616 | 269,000 | 91,000 | Yugoslavia | 43,043 | 42,000 | 36,800 |
| Abu Dhabi (Trucial States) | 359,667 | 282,000 | 195,000 | Hungary | 35,646 | 38,000 | 37,600 |
| Mexico | 331,585 | 323,000 | 340,000 | Turkey | 36,296 | 29,000 | 16,500 |
| Qatar | 289,833 | 229,000 | 200,000 | Chile | 34,052 | 35,000 | 38,000 |
| Argentina | 287,028 | 269,000 | 273,000 | Italy (Sicily) | 29,071 | 37,043 | 46,000 |
| Romania | 259,717 | 257,000 | 249,600 | Gabon | 28,881 | 25,000 | 20,300 |
| Mainland China | 200,000 | 157,534 | 115,000 | Albania | 16,000 | 15,000 | 14,600 |
| Colombia | 196,005 | 201,000 | 166,000 | Bolivia | 15,828 | 9,197 | — |
| | | | | Japan | 14,603 | 11,767 | 15,500 |
| | | | | Angola | 12,464 | 15,000 | 16,000 |

# FOREIGN TRADE

The United States in 1966 exported nearly $5 billion more in goods than it imported, according to the U.S. Department of Commerce. Exports were nearly $3 billion more than the total in 1965, while imports exceeded the 1965 figure by more than $4 billion.

| COUNTRY AND AREA | U.S. EXPORTS (in 000s) | U.S. IMPORTS (in 000s) |
|---|---|---|
| NORTH AMERICA..... | $8,901,000 | $8,043,000 |
| Bahamas........... | 133,000 | 24,000 |
| Barbados.......... | 11,000 | 2,000 |
| Bermuda........... | 49,000 | 3,000 |
| Canada............ | 6,636,000 | 6,125,000 |
| Costa Rica......... | 62,000 | 60,000 |
| Dominican Republic.. | 87,000 | 128,000 |
| El Salvador........ | 69,000 | 44,000 |
| Guatemala......... | 89,000 | 82,000 |
| Haiti.............. | 22,000 | 19,000 |
| Honduras.......... | 68,000 | 85,000 |
| Jamaica........... | 115,000 | 133,000 |
| Leeward and Windward Islands. | 18,000 | 2,000 |
| Mexico............ | 1,179,000 | 750,000 |
| Netherlands Antilles. | 72,000 | 304,000 |
| Nicaragua......... | 71,000 | 31,000 |
| Panama Republic.... | 138,000 | 68,000 |
| Trinidad and Tobago. | 59,000 | 163,000 |
| Other............. | 22,000 | 18,000 |
| SOUTH AMERICA..... | 2,465,000 | 2,785,000 |
| Argentina......... | 240,000 | 149,000 |
| Bolivia........... | 46,000 | 28,000 |
| Brazil............ | 566,000 | 600,000 |
| Chile............. | 250,000 | 229,000 |
| Colombia.......... | 283,000 | 245,000 |
| Ecuador........... | 80,000 | 94,000 |
| Guyana........... | 25,000 | 29,000 |
| Paraguay.......... | 19,000 | 13,000 |
| Peru.............. | 305,000 | 311,000 |
| Surinam........... | 32,000 | 50,000 |
| Uruguay........... | 23,000 | 30,000 |
| Venezuela......... | 595,000 | 1,002,000 |
| Other............. | 1,000 | 5,000 |
| EUROPE........... | 9,603,000 | 7,864,000 |
| Austria........... | 55,000 | 80,000 |
| Belgium and Luxembourg..... | 686,000 | 567,000 |
| Bulgaria.......... | 4,000 | 3,000 |
| Czechoslovakia...... | 37,000 | 28,000 |
| Denmark.......... | 181,000 | 202,000 |
| Finland........... | 64,000 | 97,000 |
| France............ | 991,000 | 698,000 |
| Germany, East..... | 25,000 | 8,000 |
| Germany, West...... | 1,577,000 | 1,797,000 |
| Gibraltar.......... | 1,000 | [1] |
| Greece........... | 137,000 | 51,000 |
| Hungary.......... | 10,000 | 3,000 |
| Iceland........... | 20,000 | 20,000 |
| Ireland........... | 86,000 | 94,000 |
| Italy (and Trieste)... | 887,000 | 743,000 |
| Netherlands........ | 1,191,000 | 320,000 |
| Norway........... | 144,000 | 129,000 |
| Poland (and Danzig). | 53,000 | 83,000 |
| Portugal.......... | 64,000 | 75,000 |
| Romania.......... | 27,000 | 5,000 |
| Spain............. | 512,000 | 163,000 |
| Sweden........... | 357,000 | 300,000 |
| Switzerland........ | 410,000 | 388,000 |
| Turkey............ | 178,000 | 96,000 |
| Soviet Union....... | 42,000 | 49,000 |
| United Kingdom..... | 1,683,000 | 1,786,000 |

| COUNTRY AND AREA | U.S. EXPORTS (in 000s) | U.S. IMPORTS (in 000s) |
|---|---|---|
| Yugoslavia.......... | $ 173,000 | $ 74,000 |
| Other.............. | 9,000 | 5,000 |
| ASIA................ | 6,003,000 | 5,279,000 |
| Afghanistan......... | 14,000 | 14,000 |
| Burma............. | 24,000 | 3,000 |
| Ceylon............. | 16,000 | 33,000 |
| China (Taiwan)..... | 180,000 | 117,000 |
| Hong Kong......... | 228,000 | 416,000 |
| India.............. | 929,000 | 327,000 |
| Indonesia.......... | 60,000 | 179,000 |
| Iran............... | 183,000 | 115,000 |
| Iraq............... | 44,000 | 21,000 |
| Israel and.......... | 188,000 | 77,000 |
| Japan............. | 2,332,000 | 2,964,000 |
| Jordan............. | 28,000 | [1] |
| Korea, South....... | 229,000 | 85,000 |
| Kuwait............ | 89,000 | 29,000 |
| Laos............... | 9,000 | 1,000 |
| Lebanon........... | 83,000 | 9,000 |
| Malaysia........... | 45,000 | 177,000 |
| Pakistan........... | 239,000 | 68,000 |
| Philippines......... | 342,000 | 398,000 |
| Saudi Arabia....... | 139,000 | 96,000 |
| Syria.............. | 20,000 | 5,000 |
| Thailand........... | 128,000 | 76,000 |
| Vietnam........... | 311,000 | [2] |
| Other............. | 143,000 | 68,000 |
| OCEANIA.......... | 779,000 | 594,000 |
| Australia.......... | 643,000 | 395,000 |
| New Zealand and Western Samoa... | 110,000 | 180,000 |
| Other............. | 26,000 | 19,000 |
| AFRICA............. | 1,326,000 | 978,000 |
| Algeria............ | 67,000 | 3,000 |
| Angola............ | 17,000 | 53,000 |
| Cameroon.......... | 6,000 | 28,000 |
| Central African Rep.. | 1,000 | 11,000 |
| Congo (Kinshasa)... | 57,000 | 45,000 |
| Egypt (U.A.R.)..... | 189,000 | 18,000 |
| Ethiopia........... | 16,000 | 45,000 |
| Gabon............. | 5,000 | 12,000 |
| Ghana............. | 53,000 | 46,000 |
| Guinea............ | 11,000 | 12,000 |
| Ivory Coast........ | 23,000 | 65,000 |
| Kenya............. | 28,000 | 21,000 |
| Liberia............ | 38,000 | 59,000 |
| Libya............. | 58,000 | 57,000 |
| Madagascar........ | 4,000 | 23,000 |
| Malawi, Zambia, and Rhodesia..... | 46,000 | 13,000 |
| Morocco........... | 56,000 | 10,000 |
| Mozambique........ | 14,000 | 10,000 |
| Nigeria............ | 103,000 | 52,000 |
| Sierra Leone........ | 5,000 | 14,000 |
| South Africa........ | 401,000 | 251,000 |
| Sudan............. | 14,000 | 6,000 |
| Tanzania.......... | 8,000 | 17,000 |
| Tunisia............ | 43,000 | 3,000 |
| Uganda........... | 2,000 | 57,000 |
| Other............. | 62,000 | 48,000 |
| TOTAL............. | $30,336,000 | $25,550,000 |

[1] Less than $500,000.     [2] Not applicable.

## U.S. EXPORTS AND IMPORTS: 1950–1966

Source: U.S. Department of Commerce

| YEAR | U.S. EXPORTS (in millions of dollars) | | | | | U.S. IMPORTS (in millions of dollars) | EXCESS OF IMPORTS (in millions of dollars) |
| | Total | Military Grant-aid | Excluding Military Grant-aid | Domestic Merchandise | Reexports of Foreign Merchandise | | |
|---|---|---|---|---|---|---|---|
| 1966 | $30,336 | $ 941 | $29,395 | $29,899 | $437 | $25,550 | $3,845 |
| 1965 | 27,478 | 779 | 26,699 | 27,135 | 343 | 21,366 | 5,333 |
| 1964 | 26,489 | 818 | 25,671 | 26,136 | 352 | 18,684 | 6,987 |
| 1963 | 23,351 | 920 | 22,431 | 23,066 | 285 | 17,142 | 5,289 |
| 1962 | 21,672 | 727 | 20,945 | 21,403 | 269 | 16,389 | 4,556 |
| 1961 | 20,962 | 810 | 20,152 | 20,717 | 245 | 14,713 | 5,439 |
| 1960 | 20,558 | 949 | 19,609 | 20,358 | 200 | 15,017 | 4,592 |
| 1959 | 17,633 | 1,227 | 16,406 | 17,449 | 184 | 15,627 | 779 |
| 1958 | 17,916 | 1,543 | 16,373 | 17,751 | 165 | 13,255 | 3,118 |
| 1957 | 20,862 | 1,355 | 19,507 | 20,682 | 180 | 13,255 | 6,252 |
| 1956 | 19,095 | 1,757 | 17,338 | 18,945 | 150 | 12,774 | 4,564 |
| 1955 | 15,550 | 1,256 | 14,294 | 15,422 | 128 | 11,491 | 2,803 |
| 1954 | 15,110 | 2,255 | 12,855 | 14,981 | 129 | 10,292 | 2,563 |
| 1953 | 15,774 | 3,511 | 12,263 | 15,652 | 122 | 10,914 | 1,349 |
| 1952 | 15,201 | 1,997 | 13,204 | 15,049 | 152 | 10,753 | 2,451 |
| 1951 | 15,032 | 1,065 | 13,967 | 14,879 | 153 | 10,998 | 2,969 |
| 1950 | 10,275 | 282 | 9,993 | 10,142 | 133 | 8,874 | 1,119 |

## THE KENNEDY ROUND: 1967

During the last week of the Kennedy Round tariff meetings in Geneva, Switzerland, shirt-sleeved delegates held all-night sessions to avert a threatened collapse of their four years of work. Their long efforts to achieve an accord culminated on May 15, when 54 of the free world's industrial nations agreed to make tariff reductions (averaging about 35 per cent overall) on 60,000 products worth more than $40 billion in global trade. This historic tariff-cutting pact directly affects more than 80 per cent of today's foreign commerce operations by, among others, the United States, Britain, and Europe's six Common Market nations (Belgium, France, West Germany, Italy, Luxembourg, and the Netherlands).

The multi-nation agreement also signified the end of most of the 5 per cent nuisance tariffs between the United States and Canada.

Kennedy Round negotiators reach final accord at Geneva.

The Kennedy Round was by far the most significant of the six international tariff discussions held since World War II. The chief U.S. representative, Ambassador William Roth, noted at the conclusion of the talks that the agreement, for all intents and purposes, makes tariffs little more than a "nuisance" in international trade, rather than an obstacle.

Consider the Kennedy Round's main results:
- Inclusion for the first time of agricultural products; a minimum world export price for wheat of about $1.75 a bushel.
- A world wheat program for underdeveloped nations that will give them 4,500,000 metric tons annually for the next three years, with the U.S. supplying nearly 43 per cent of the total.
- The first agreement to protect nations from foreign companies "dumping" goods abroad at less than cost.
- Tariff reductions that will cut thousands of duties in dozens of countries by 50 per cent or more. The specific impact of the agreement on the individual was difficult to determine. The cuts will be made over a five-year period, and the share of savings that will eventually be passed on to the consumers in each nation is an unknown factor.

U.S. reaction was predictable: Farmers cheered the prospect of new overseas markets; the chemical industry complained that they were being exposed to foreign competition.

Despite its commercial and economic impact, the Kennedy Round may be considered most important by future historians for what it averted. If the talks had failed—and near the end of the conference that likelihood was quite real—the United States might well have returned to the high-tariff days of the 1930s, while the Common Market erected walls to protect itself from U.S. and British imports. Politically, the agreement was a huge plus, for freer trade may contribute much to a lessening of international tensions.

## U.S. SHARE OF WORLD TRADE: 1948–1966
Source: United Nations *Statistical Yearbook*

The decline in the United States' share of the world export market that began after 1948, its peak year, continued in 1966. U.S. import trade recovered somewhat from its 1964 low.

| YEAR | TOTAL WORLD EXPORTS | U.S. EXPORTS | PER CENT OF TOTAL | YEAR | TOTAL WORLD IMPORTS | U.S. IMPORTS | PER CENT OF TOTAL |
|---|---|---|---|---|---|---|---|
| 1966 | $201,710,000,000 | $30,015,000,000 | 14.8 | 1966 | $212,700,000,000 | $25,473,000,000 | 12.0 |
| 1965 | 186,300,000,000 | 27,057,000,000 | 14.5 | 1965 | 196,800,000,000 | 21,347,000,000 | 10.8 |
| 1964 | 172,400,000,000 | 26,280,000,000 | 15.2 | 1964 | 181,500,000,000 | 18,666,000,000 | 10.3 |
| 1963 | 154,000,000,000 | 23,104,000,000 | 15.0 | 1963 | 162,100,000,000 | 17,072,000,000 | 10.5 |
| 1962 | 141,600,000,000 | 21,446,000,000 | 15.1 | 1962 | 149,500,000,000 | 16,316,000,000 | 10.9 |
| 1961 | 134,000,000,000 | 20,791,000,000 | 15.5 | 1961 | 140,900,000,000 | 14,703,000,000 | 10.4 |
| 1960 | 128,000,000,000 | 20,412,000,000 | 15.9 | 1960 | 135,300,000,000 | 15,071,000,000 | 11.1 |
| 1959 | 115,600,000,000 | 17,472,000,000 | 15.1 | 1959 | 121,300,000,000 | 15,478,000,000 | 12.8 |
| 1958 | 108,000,000,000 | 17,755,000,000 | 16.4 | 1958 | 114,000,000,000 | 13,298,000,000 | 11.7 |
| 1957 | 112,000,000,000 | 20,694,000,000 | 18.5 | 1957 | 119,900,000,000 | 13,388,000,000 | 11.2 |
| 1956 | 103,800,000,000 | 18,952,000,000 | 18.3 | 1956 | 108,600,000,000 | 12,803,000,000 | 11.8 |
| 1953 | 82,600,000,000 | 15,661,000,000 | 19.0 | 1953 | 84,200,000,000 | 10,915,000,000 | 13.0 |
| 1948 | 57,500,000,000 | 12,545,000,000 | 21.8 | 1948 | 63,600,000,000 | 7,183,000,000 | 11.3 |

## LEADING COMMODITIES IN U.S. FOREIGN TRADE

Transactions not included in this U.S. Department of Commerce list of the leading commodities involved in American foreign trade are: exports of war material; shipments abroad valued at $100 or less; low-value shipments into the country; and the return of U.S. goods.

| COMMODITY GROUP | EXPORTS (in millions) 1966 | 1965 | IMPORTS (in millions) 1966 | 1965 |
|---|---|---|---|---|
| Non-electrical machinery | $5,747 | $5,243 | $1,677 | $1,160 |
| Textiles, clothing, and all other manufactured goods | 5,256 | 4,814 | 8,636 | 7,521 |
| Food and live animals | 4,567 | 4,003 | 3,948 | 3,460 |
| Transport equipment | 3,162 | 2,706 | 2,135 | 1,148 |
| Inedible crude materials, except fuels | 3,072 | 2,856 | 3,266 | 3,047 |
| Chemicals | 2,676 | 2,402 | 957 | 769 |
| Electrical apparatus | 1,899 | 1,660 | 1,016 | 640 |
| Mineral fuels and related materials | 978 | 947 | 2,262 | 2,222 |
| Beverages and tobacco | 624 | 517 | 642 | 553 |
| Animal and vegetable oils and fats | 356 | 472 | 146 | 116 |

## FREE WORLD TRADE WITH COMMUNIST NATIONS
Source: Organisation for Economic Co-operation and Development

| TRADING COUNTRY | EASTERN EUROPE[1] Value of Exports to:[2] 1966 | 1965 | Value of Imports from:[2] 1966 | 1965 | MAINLAND CHINA Value of Exports to:[2] 1966 | 1965 | Value of Imports from:[2] 1966 | 1965 |
|---|---|---|---|---|---|---|---|---|
| Austria | $24.81 | $23.61 | $22.32 | $21.19 | $ 0.39 | $ 0.14 | $ 0.77 | $ 0.41 |
| Belgium-Luxembourg | 11.26 | 9.07 | 12.03 | 10.83 | 1.69 | 1.41 | 1.28 | 1.18 |
| Canada | 30.78 | 24.20 | 4.36 | 3.44 | 14.25 | 8.11 | 1.59 | 1.11 |
| Denmark | 8.48 | 8.47 | 10.78 | 9.86 | 0.21 | 0.17 | 0.98 | 0.88 |
| France | 36.28 | 28.95 | 31.45 | 24.32 | 7.70 | 5.01 | 4.49 | 3.64 |
| Germany, West | 73.74 | 60.58 | 65.48 | 58.97 | 10.79 | 6.58 | 7.71 | 6.06 |
| Greece | 9.49 | 7.35 | 10.43 | 10.53 | — | — | 0.05 | 0.01 |
| Iceland | 1.50 | 1.24 | 1.50 | 1.83 | — | — | 0.01 | 0.01 |
| Ireland | 0.12 | 0.37 | 1.36 | 1.44 | — | — | 0.17 | 0.10 |
| Italy | 44.53 | 39.46 | 56.41 | 48.44 | 5.22 | 4.70 | 4.71 | 3.20 |
| Japan | 36.06 | 20.27 | 29.21 | 23.05 | 26.26 | 20.42 | 25.32 | 18.73 |
| Netherlands | 11.47 | 10.41 | 13.52 | 13.47 | 1.35 | 1.58 | 2.52 | 2.12 |
| Norway | 4.76 | 5.66 | 6.07 | 5.76 | 0.44 | 0.43 | 0.41 | 0.40 |
| Portugal | 0.67 | 0.52 | 1.09 | 0.96 | — | — | 0.02 | 0.02 |
| Spain | 5.06 | 2.34 | 4.13 | 6.00 | — | — | 0.30 | 0.15 |
| Sweden | 14.86 | 14.10 | 18.12 | 15.89 | 2.06 | 1.14 | 1.20 | 1.26 |
| Switzerland | 10.99 | 8.98 | 9.21 | 7.61 | 1.75 | 1.51 | 1.34 | 1.05 |
| Turkey | 6.47 | 6.03 | 7.43 | 5.15 | — | 0.19 | 0.01 | — |
| United Kingdom | 41.45 | 31.66 | 59.37 | 54.77 | 6.03 | 4.16 | 7.89 | 6.94 |
| United States | 30.91 | 24.00 | 20.09 | 16.56 | — | — | 0.01 | 0.04 |
| TOTAL | 403.69 | 327.27 | 384.36 | 340.07 | 78.14 | 55.55 | 60.78 | 47.31 |

[1] Includes Yugoslavia.  [2] Value given in millions of U.S. dollars.

# GLOSSARY OF ECONOMY

**Antitrust laws:** A body of U.S. laws, also called antimonopoly laws, designed to encourage competition and prevent the undesirable concentration of economic power. Major antitrust laws are: the Sherman Act (1890); the Clayton Act (1914); the Federal Trade Commission Act (1914); the Robinson-Patman amendment to the Clayton Act (1936); and the Celler–Kefauver merger amendment to the Clayton Act (1950).

**Arbitration:** A procedure for settling a labor dispute. Both union and management agree in advance to abide by the decisions of some impartial person or board.

**Assessed valuation:** Value placed upon property, usually real estate, for the purpose of determining the amount of tax to be levied upon it. Frequently the assessed valuation of property is considerably below its real, or market, value.

**Assets:** Anything of material value belonging to a person or business firm. The term includes not only property but intangibles, such as rights, privileges, and franchises.

**Audit:** An examination by an accountant of the financial books of a person or business firm to determine whether there are errors, fraud, or improprieties.

**Automation:** The technical processes by which electronic or automated devices replace human labor in routine decision-making.

**Balance of international payments:** Popularly called the balance of payments, it determines a nation's international financial position. All nations transact business with other nations—trade in goods and services, direct investments in foreign business, tourism, and the like. If a nation's total outflow of currency exceeds its foreign earnings, the result is an unfavorable balance of payments. The debtor nation then suffers a drain of gold, which weakens its financial position.

**Balance of trade:** The difference between the total value of a nation's exports and imports in international trade. A "favorable balance" is frequently used to describe an excess of exports; an "unfavorable balance," an excess of imports. Balance of trade constitutes part of the total balance of international payments.

**Bankruptcy:** Proceedings under which the property of an insolvent debtor may be distributed among his creditors under court supervision.

**Bears:** Market speculators who gain by a decline in the price of a commodity or stock.

**Big Board:** Popular term for the New York Stock Exchange.

**Blue chip:** A high-quality stock issue, popular for its continuity of earnings and dividends.

**Bonds:** Securities issued by a corporate or government body, by which that body pays interest semi-annually to the purchaser, the principal redeemable at face value on a set maturity date.

**Broker:** An agent who handles on a commission basis the public's orders to buy and sell securities.

**Budget:** A statement of expected revenues and contemplated expenditures for a specified period of time, usually a year.

**Bulls:** Market speculators who gain by a rise in the price of a commodity or stock.

**Business cycle:** A type of fluctuation, of greater or less intensity, found in the free enterprise system. A cycle consists of prosperity, followed by depression, and then another period of prosperity. A complete business cycle may stretch over many years.

**Buyers' market:** A market in which goods are so plentiful that the buyer holds the advantage.

**Capital:** All economic goods that yield income or services. Land, producer goods (such as machinery), and consumer goods are capital. In a business sense, capital may also refer to the investment in a business or to its net worth.

**Capital gains tax:** A tax on the gain arising from the sale of a capital asset, usually real estate or securities.

**Capitalism:** An economic system characterized by the private ownership of property and the production of goods for private profit. Capitalism, or the free enterprise system, stresses the freedom of individual economic initiative.

**Cartel:** Any international combine or agreement between domestic and foreign monopoly groups fixing prices and dividing market territory.

**Closed shop:** An agreement between union and management under which both old and new employees must be members of the union.

**Collective bargaining:** The negotiation of a labor contract between union and employer.

**Common stock:** Stock shares that represent a part ownership in everything a corporation owns. If a company has also issued preferred stock, the preferred has prior claim to dividends and, in the event of liquidation, assets. Because common stockholders assume the greater risk, they generally obtain the greater reward of dividends and capital gains.

**Consumer goods:** Goods used by, or destined for use by, families and individuals for household and other personal purposes.

**Consumer price index:** A measure of the time-to-time fluctuations in consumer prices. It can be thought of as the rising or lowering cost of maintaining the same standard of living.

**Cooperatives:** Voluntary societies or associations formed to supply needs through mutual action.

**Corporation:** A form of organization chartered by the Federal or state governments by which a group of individuals is enabled to conduct business as a separate legal entity. The most common form is the joint stock corporation, which is organized for the profit of its shareholders. Shareholders, who are the owners of the corporation, elect its management. A corporation's most distinctive characteristic is limited liability; thus, individual shareholders are not legally responsible for the corporation's debts.

**Curb Exchange:** A popular term for the American Stock Exchange.

**Deficits:** Deficits are the amounts by which total expenses exceed total income. In public finance, deficits are the amounts by which government expenditures exceed revenues.

**Depreciation:** The gradual reduction in the worth of property as a result of wear and tear, natural causes, or obsolescence.

**Depression:** The contraction phase of a business cycle. It is characterized by an unusually low level of business activity and high unemployment.

**Devaluation:** A deliberate step undertaken by a government to reduce the foreign exchange value of its currency. This places the country in an improved international trading position.

**Discount rate:** The interest rate charged by Federal Reserve Banks to member banks, computed on an annual percentage basis. This rate affects in turn the interest rate banks charge to loan customers.

**Dividend:** The payment, usually derived from earnings, made to holders of shares in a corporation. Preferred-stock dividends are usually fixed. Common-stock dividends may vary considerably, depending on a company's earnings and the amount of funds the directors decide to keep in the business.

**Durable goods:** Generally, goods such as machinery, passenger cars, homes, furniture, and refrigerators, whose continuous serviceability is likely to exceed three years.

**Duty:** A tax imposed on the importation, exportation, or consumption of goods. It usually means a customs duty.

**Escalator clause:** A clause in a collective bargaining agreement providing for automatic wage increases or decreases periodically in proportion to changes in the cost of living as measured by an appropriate index.

**Estate tax:** A tax levied directly upon the estate of a deceased person. This differs from an inheritance tax in that the latter is levied upon the beneficiaries of such an estate.

**Excess profits tax:** A tax applied to profits in excess of a rate of return on capital or investment defined as "normal." In the United States, an excess profits tax on corporations was employed during 1917–21, 1940–45, and 1950–53.

**Excise tax:** A tax on certain items of domestic consumption, such as beer, cigarettes, automobile tires, and services.

**Fiscal policy:** The financial policy of a government concerning regulation of revenue and expenditure procedures, such as taxes, public works projects, defense spending. Changes in fiscal policy are made to stabilize the national economy, to reduce inflation, or to effect increases in personal and corporate income.

**Fiscal year:** Any 12 consecutive months used as a period for financial accounts. The fiscal year of the Federal government runs from July 1 through June 30.

**f.o.b.:** Free on board. Cost of a commodity reckoned without the transportation and any other costs incurred from the point of origin or some other specified point. In domestic trade, this generally refers to price at the factory, processing plant, or warehouse.

**Foreign exchange market:** The market where foreign currencies are bought and sold and the daily trading price in terms of dollars is set. It

is not a specific place but a series of trades, mainly conducted at banks.

**Free trade:** A policy of permitting goods and services to move across national boundaries without payment of tariffs or other duties, or being subject to other types of controls that are used primarily to reduce trade.

**Fringe benefits:** General term used to describe extra benefits (for example, pensions, insurance, vacations, and paid holidays) received by workers in addition to regular wages for time actually spent on the job.

**Full employment:** A condition that exists when the number of job vacancies is at least as great as the number of people seeking work. Since some unemployment exists at all times, full employment is said to exist when the number of job seekers does not exceed three to four per cent of the total labor force.

**Gold standard:** A country is said to be "on the gold standard" when the standard unit of its currency is defined by law as a fixed quantity of gold and when its currency is freely convertible at home or abroad into that quantity of gold. Most countries have sharply modified versions of the gold standard. Nowadays, the principal use of gold is limited to the settlement of international payments.

**Gross National Product** (GNP): The total value of all goods and services produced by a nation's economy. GNP is the broadest available measure of the rate of economic activity and reflects a country's economic strength.

**Inflation:** An economic state characterized by a rapid rise in the prices of commodities and services and the consequent sharp decrease in purchasing power of a currency.

**Inheritance tax:** A tax levied on the beneficiaries of an estate.

**Injunction, labor:** A court order restraining employees or unions from acting in any manner that the court considers illegal. Violation of an injunction is a contempt of court and punishable by fine or imprisonment.

**Installment credit:** Credit extended to consumers by retailers or financial institutions usually to purchase cars, appliances, and other durable goods. It is usually repayable in three years or less by a pre-arranged schedule.

**Laissez-faire:** An economic system in which government intervention is held to an absolute minimum. It is the counterpart to the political philosophy which holds that government is best that governs least.

**Margin:** The down payment required when a customer buys a security on credit. Under Federal Reserve regulations, the margin requirement has ranged from 40 to 100 per cent. It currently is about 70 per cent.

**Monopoly:** A situation in which a company—or a group of companies, acting singly or together—has the power to control prices or exclude competitors from a market. Such a combination is called a trust and is subject to antitrust laws.

**Most-favored-nation clause:** A trade arrangement between two countries by which they agree to extend to each other the benefit of any concessions made to any other country.

(continued)

## GLOSSARY OF ECONOMY (continued)

**Mutual fund:** A company that uses its capital to invest in other companies. Its shares are not listed on any exchange, and its capital is not fixed—increasing as people buy more shares.

**Nationalization:** The transfer of the ownership of privately owned property or businesses to the government in response to governmental order or legislation. The former owners may or may not be compensated.

**Nondurable goods:** Goods whose serviceability is generally limited to less than three years.

**Official exchange rate:** Rate or rates at which the monetary authorities of a country will buy and sell the domestic currency in exchange for foreign currency.

**Open shop:** A company in which no individual has to be a union member in order to secure or retain employment, even though a union contract may be in effect.

**Overhead:** Business expenses not chargeable to a particular part of the work or product, such as rent, taxes, depreciation, insurance, office and accounting costs.

**Over the counter:** Generally, the market for thousands of companies too new or too small to warrant listing on a national exchange. Trading is not done in any one place but is arranged among dealers over the telephone.

**Parity:** In agriculture, financial assistance given to farmers through government-sponsored price-support programs. The programs were initiated to reduce the instability of farm prices and to raise farm income. Parity prices, or the prices that the government will pay for certain crops, are based on the prices paid for agricultural products during the period 1910–14, when farmers enjoyed prosperity. Since the price offered by the government is generally higher than that on the open market, considerable government purchases occur, resulting in large government-held farm surpluses.

**Par value:** The nominal value printed on the face of a stock certificate. It may or may not be related to actual or market value. In international trade, the value of a currency expressed as so many ounces of gold or so many U.S. dollars.

**Personal income:** Income received by individuals, unincorporated businesses, and nonprofit institutions from all sources. Personal income includes the total of wage and salary receipts, rental income, interest, and dividends.

**Planned economy:** A fully developed planned economy, such as is found in Communist nations, is one in which the allocation of land, labor, and capital is based on governmental decision. It is the opposite of a laissez-faire economy.

**Price discrimination:** An illegal pricing process under which an individual seller charges different customers different prices for the same product sold at the same time and under the same conditions. The buyer paying the higher price is said to suffer "price discrimination."

**Price fixing:** An agreement by companies setting the price they will charge for a product. Such an agreement violates the Sherman Act and the Federal Trade Commission Act.

**Progressive tax:** A tax with rates that increase as the amount of income increases. The personal income tax is the most common example.

**Purchasing power of the dollar:** A measurement of the quantity of commodities and services that can be purchased with a dollar in a given period as compared with another period.

**Reciprocal trade agreements:** Agreements between nations setting forth the terms for the mutual exchange of goods and services. They concern tariffs, import and export quotas, bounties or taxes on foreign trade, and the like. The aim of the agreements is to increase trade between two countries.

**Right-to-work laws:** Legislation enacted by U.S. states that forbids making membership in a union a condition for getting or holding a job. It is directed against the closed shop principle.

**Sellers' market:** A market in which goods are so scarce that the seller can increase the price of a product or service without materially affecting the volume of sales.

**Services:** When work is performed by businesses or individuals on behalf of other persons, no goods or commodities being transferred, the firms or individuals so engaged are said to be providing "services." Service organizations include financial firms, most areas of government, and the utilities supplying electricity, gas, and telephone service. Examples of individuals engaged in providing services are doctors, bankers, barbers, and auto mechanics.

**Stock:** Evidence of ownership in a corporation. Legally, it represents a contract stating the terms under which the corporation accepts capital from the stockholders. Stocks exist in many varieties, of which the two predominant types are preferred and common stock.

**Subsidy:** Financial aid extended by a government to private enterprise (in the form of direct payments, tax exemptions or reductions, or the sale of goods or services at prices which are below cost or market value) when it is considered to be in the public interest.

**Surtax:** An additional tax levied on top of the basic or "normal" tax.

**Tariff:** A schedule of duties imposed by a government on commodities imported or exported. For the United States, it refers to the tax on imports since there is no duty on exports. It is mainly used to protect domestic industry from foreign competition.

**Technological unemployment:** Unemployment resulting from the displacement of men by machinery, such as in automation, or by the introduction of more efficient methods of production.

**Ticker:** The instrument that prints prices and volume of security transactions in cities throughout the United States within minutes after a trade occurs on the floor of an exchange. The names of stocks are expressed in symbols.

**Unfair labor practice:** A practice by an employer, employee, or union, that violates provisions of the National Labor Relations Act or of similar state laws that regulate relationships among the parties.

**Union shop:** All employees hired by a company must either be members of a specified union or become and remain members of the union or lose their jobs.

# WORLD HISTORY

## World Leaders · Chronology of Historical Events

© National Geographic Society

Man's history may have begun nearly 2.5 million years ago in East Africa. Findings by anthropologist Dr. Louis S. B. Leakey at Olduvai Gorge (**above**), Tanzania, included possible remains of man's ancestors.

History may be seen in terms of man's efforts to translate his ideals into reality. His nearest, albeit imperfect, approaches to this elusive goal stand out as the golden ages of his span on earth. Now, in the last decades of the 20th century, man stands at the threshold of the greatest of all possible golden ages. But at the same time, the ideals of modern man are higher than those of any period in the past, and thus the disparity between the practical and the ideal remains vast.

Such concepts as equality for all men and an end to all wars would have been scoffed at during even the most advanced stages of the great civilizations of the past. But the demands of today's complex civilization make these ideals not merely reasonable, but unarguable.

Our science is on the verge of solving the mystery of life; it has already perfected the methods of universal destruction. Our technology has shown us the possibility of giving all men the benefits of life once reserved for the privileged few; we are still groping after the methods of distributing this wealth equitably. Our law expresses our recognition of the dignity inherent in all men; we are still painfully learning that the law applies to men of all races.

It is only in solving these problems that our civilization will fulfill its great potential. Then man will know of starvation in India, as well as in rural Mississippi, but only as remote events of history—much as we now know of the black death that ravaged Europe centuries ago. And chaos and destruction, whether in places as distant as the jungles of Vietnam or as near as the ghettos of Detroit and Newark, will be nothing more than dark memories of an imperfect past.

This section of the *Almanac* is a compact record of man's ideals and actions from the dawn of history to the present day.

# FOCUS ON THE PAST

## 1917: THE UNITED STATES ENTERS WORLD WAR I

Troops of the Second Battalion, 16th U.S. Infantry, marched in Paris on July 4, 1917, as French citizens lined the streets to cheer American participation in World War I.

On April 6, 1917, the U.S. Congress responded to a request by President Woodrow Wilson and declared war on Germany. Thus, the United States joined the side of Britain, France, and Russia in history's first global conflict. This step marked the end of America's isolationist policy and signaled the start of its role as a world power.

Throughout 1916 President Wilson had struggled to maintain U.S. neutrality, while at the same time attempting to play the part of world peacemaker. Believing that the only lasting European peace would be one without victory for either side, he tried unsuccessfully to initiate peace talks between the Allied and the Axis powers.

However, the sympathies of the United States had been increasingly on the Allies' side since the war's outset. In May, 1915, a German submarine had torpedoed Britain's *Lusitania* off the Irish coast; the resulting deaths of over 100 American passengers had set off a strong wave of anti-German sentiment in the United States. In following years many American merchant ships were sunk by the Germans. On Feb. 1, 1917, Germany began unrestricted submarine warfare against all merchant shipping, belligerent or neutral, in an attempt to cut off all U.S. aid to the Allies and to break the stalemate on the Western Front. This meant that the United States was already at war in the Atlantic theater. Wilson was forced to abandon all hopes of U.S. neutrality.

In August, 1917, the U.S. Rainbow (42d) Division was organized from National Guard units of 26 states and the District of Columbia. By early December, all of the components of this 26,265-man outfit had arrived in France. Before the war ended, 2,057,675 U.S. troops were sent to France; about 1 million of these men saw active combat.

## SEVEN ANCIENT WONDERS OF THE WORLD

The Seven Wonders of the World, renowned works of ancient art and engineering, were so named by travel writers of the Hellenistic period, 4th–1st centuries B.C., who wished to entertain and astound Greek tourists of the time. The oldest extant list of the Wonders is that of the 2nd-century writer, Antipater of Sidon.

■ **THE PYRAMIDS OF EGYPT.** The largest of the pyramids is that of the Pharaoh Cheops, or Khufu. Situated at Giza, near modern Cairo, the Great Pyramid was constructed about 2680 B.C. and is the most ancient and only surviving Wonder of the World. It is a solid mass of limestone blocks covering 13 acres, and it originally measured 755 feet across each base line and reached a height of 481 feet. It was adorned with a highly polished stone facing, which was destroyed by an earthquake in A.D. 1301.

■ **THE MAUSOLEUM AT HALICARNASSUS.** The tomb of Mausolus of Caria, Persian satrap in Asia Minor, has given the name *mausoleum* to all subsequent grandiose tombs. The original Mausoleum, erected about 352 B.C. by the satrap's wife, Artemisia, was a magnificent white marble structure, supported by 36 Ionic columns and richly embellished with the works of two great Greek sculptors, Scopas and Praxiteles. The tomb was demolished by earthquake before the 15th century and its marble reused. Some of its sculpture was recovered, however, and is now in the British Museum. The ancient site of Halicarnassus is 95 miles south of Izmir, Turkey.

■ **THE GREAT TEMPLE OF ARTEMIS AT EPHESUS.** The worship of Artemis, an earth goddess of Asia Minor, centered on the town of Ephesus, where was built, in about 550 B.C., a great temple. Supported by 96 marble columns, the temple, handsomely decorated with sculpture, measured 360 feet in length and 180 feet in width. Pilgrims from all parts of the Mediterranean world bore gifts of gold, silver, and ivory to Ephesus, and the wealth of the temple became legendary. Under Roman rule, the temple was renamed for the goddess Diana. It was burned in the 4th century B.C., rebuilt, then utterly destroyed by the barbarian Goths in A.D. 262. The site of Ephesus is 35 miles southeast of Izmir, Turkey.

■ **THE HANGING GARDENS OF BABYLON.** During the reign of Nebuchadnezzar II in the 6th century B.C., Babylon was the greatest city of the ancient world. This splendid capital of Mesopotamia, defended by concentric walls 11 miles in circuit, was famous for its processional way, its Ishtar Gate, and its ziggurats, or terraced towers. The Hanging Gardens, however, were Nebuchadnezzar's most wondrous achievement. Rising in terraces to a height of 335 feet, the gardens, each of which covered an area of some four acres, nourished trees, flowers, and vegetables. The site of Babylon, some 55 miles south of modern Baghdad, is partly excavated; only remnants of its great walls remain.

■ **THE COLOSSUS OF RHODES.** The Colossus was a massive bronze statue of the Sun god, Helios, who was worshiped in Rhodes. Reaching a height of about 105 feet, and built wholly or in part by Chares of Lindus about 285 B.C., the statue was located on a promontory overlooking the harbor of Rhodes—not astride the harbor as reported in medieval legend. The Colossus was toppled by an earthquake about 244 B.C. and lay in ruins until the Saracens took Rhodes in A.D. 653, and the ruins were sold.

■ **THE OLYMPIAN ZEUS.** Olympia, the scene of the first Olympic games, was from earliest times a center of worship of Zeus. Here was erected a great temple, which was famous for a colossal ivory and gold-encrusted statue carved by the Greek sculptor Phidias between 437 and 425 B.C. The temple, with its celebrated statue, was destroyed by Vandals or plundering Goths. On ancient Greek coins, the Olympian Zeus is pictured as a majestic bearded figure, seated upon a highly ornamented throne.

■ **THE PHAROS, OR LIGHTHOUSE, AT ALEXANDRIA.** Completed about 280 B.C. by Ptolemy II, Greek King of Egypt, the Lighthouse was situated on a small peninsula extending into the Mediterranean Sea from Alexandria. It was a towering structure, between 200 and 600 feet high, and with its beacon fires burning atop was said to be visible from a distance of 42 miles. The Lighthouse was demolished by an earthquake in the 14th century.

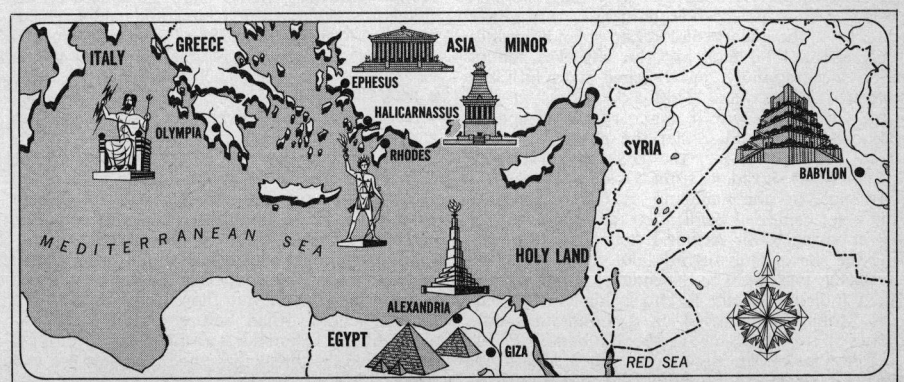

## VANISHED CITIES

■ **ANGKOR:** Situated in northwestern Cambodia, Angkor was for 550 years the capital of the Khmer Empire. In the 12th century A.D., about 200 years after the city was founded, King Suryavarman II directed the building of Angkor Wat (Angkor Temple), one of the world's largest and most imposing religious edifices. Impressive as is the architecture of Angkor Wat, it is surpassed by the extensive bas-reliefs depicting the life of Vishnu and Krishna and historical events in the reign of Suryavarman II.

Angkor was sacked in 1177 and Angkor Wat fell into ruins. King Suryavarman VII a few years later established a new capital, Angkor Thom (Great Angkor), a few miles from the original temple. The architecture of Angkor Thom is superb, and there is also an abundance of bas-reliefs and exquisite sculpture.

After raids by Thais in the 14th and 15th centuries, the Khmer capital was moved to Pnon Penh, Cambodia, and the Khmer Empire declined. Angkor was gradually overtaken by jungle. Rediscovered accidentally in 1861, it was excavated and restored in the early 20th century by the French.

■ **ATLANTIS:** The Greek island of Thera in the Aegean Sea, 70 miles north of Crete, has proven to be the site of an ancient Minoan city destroyed by a volcano in 1500 B.C. Discoveries made in 1966 and 1967 support the theory that the city was the fabled Atlantis. Findings indicate that the Minoan city probably encompassed the entirety of Thera, as well as smaller islands nearby and an adjacent area that is now covered by the sea. The city had a population of about 30,000 and contained two- and three-story houses. The absence of human skeletons and gold among the ruins indicates that the inhabitants had some warning of the volcanic eruption and fled before the city was destroyed.

■ **CNOSSUS:** Cnossus, on the northern coast of the island of Crete near modern Candia, was settled long before 3000 B.C. For a time it was the center of the civilization that became the basis of European culture. The great flowering of Cnossus, the center of Minoan culture, a name derived from the legendary Minos, King of Crete, began between 2000 B.C. and 1800 B.C., when a huge palace was built. An earthquake destroyed the palace and other splendid buildings about 1500 B.C., but the city was rebuilt even more grandly and reached its zenith between 1500 B.C. and 1400 B.C. It was at this time that the labyrinth, home of the legendary Minotaur, was built under the palace.

In about 1400 B.C. the city was destroyed, probably by invaders from Greece. Thereafter, Mycenae, on the mainland of Greece, became the chief center of civilization, and Cnossus lost its importance. Sir Arthur Evans began excavating the site of Cnossus in 1900.

■ **MACHU PICCHU:** The legendary home of the Inca Indians, Machu Picchu is high in the Andes Mountains, situated on a mountain saddle between two peaks above the Urubamba River.

Little is known of Machu Picchu's history. Spanish explorers probably did not know of its existence. The architecture is massive and austere, and the city, carved out of stone, seems to have been fortified. Machu Picchu is the only large pre-Columbian city found virtually intact. A temple at the site was a center of Peruvian sun worship, and here were discovered human skulls showing signs of trepanning, or brain surgery. The Incas of Machu Picchu were also adept at using metal plates to replace injured body members. Machu Picchu was abandoned when the Incas migrated to Cuzco.

Discovered by the American explorer and archeologist Hiram Bingham in 1911, Machu Picchu is 50 miles northwest of, and easily accessible from, Cuzco.

■ **MOHENJO-DARO:** Mohenjo-Daro, the ruins of which are in Sind, West Pakistan, was one of two great centers of the Indus Valley civilization, which flourished from the third millennium B.C. to about 1500 B.C. The city was apparently a thriving commercial center in a fertile farming area. Fortified hill citadels, with residential palaces, granaries, and baths, were built near the city. The city itself had well-planned streets, lined with spacious houses often of two stories. The structures were apparently bare of ornaments. A well-developed drainage system included stone sewers and reservoirs to collect rainwater. There were several great baths, apparently used for ceremonial ablutions.

The origins of Mohenjo-Daro are unknown. About 1500 B.C. it fell to invaders, probably Aryans, and was abandoned. Harappa, about 400 miles away, seems to have undergone the same growth and history.

The site of Harappa was first discovered in 1820. In 1922, large-scale excavations began at Mohenjo-Daro under Sir John Hubert Marshall.

■ **PAGAN:** An ancient capital of Burma, Pagan is one of the archeological gems of Asia. It was founded in 849 A.D., and in the 11th century became the capital of King Anawratha, who introduced Buddhism into upper Burma. During his reign, thousands of Buddhist shrines and temples were built at Pagan.

The surviving ruins, covering 40 square miles and extending for several miles along the shore of the Irrawaddy River, show influences of architectural styles from China and India. Occupied by Mongols in 1287, Pagan was sacked and burned by the Shans in 1299. Today it is a village of fewer than 3,000 inhabitants.

■ **POMPEII:** An ancient city in Italy, Pompeii was occupied successively by various peoples and was finally conquered by Romans in the 1st century B.C. Because of its situation on the Tyrrhenian Sea near modern Naples, it soon became a resort for wealthy Romans. There were lavish villas, amphitheaters, temples, public baths, and a forum, all Roman in style.

An earthquake destroyed much of Pompeii and the neighboring cities of Herculaneum and Stabiae in 63 A.D., but they were rebuilt even more splendidly than before. In 79 A.D., however, Mount Vesuvius, a mile away, erupted and buried the three cities under volcanic ash and stone.

Gradually forgotten, Pompeii was accidentally rediscovered in 1748, excavated, and slowly restored. The deep layers of volcanic debris protected its painted frescoes and ornaments from corrosion, and they remain vivid. The habits and manners of Roman life have been revealed in great detail at Pompeii, and the ruins have yielded important examples of Roman art.

■ **TEOTIHUACÁN:** The world's largest pyramids, after the Pyramid of Khufu (Cheops) in Egypt, are located at the Toltec ceremonial center at Teotihuacán, the most ordered pre-Columbian site yet discovered in America. In addition to the Pyramid of the Sun, now eroded to a height of 216 feet, and the Pyramid of the Moon, there is a smaller pyramid to the deity of rain and agriculture. A large temple is thought to be a shrine to the Toltec warrior-god Quetzalcoatl. These structures were probably built between the 1st and 2nd centuries A.D.

Teotihuacán's people were agricultural and sophisticated in astronomy, art, and architecture.

The site, 30 miles northwest of Mexico City, was abandoned about A.D. 900 for unknown reasons.

■ **TROY:** An ancient city of Asia Minor, Troy was the scene of the Trojan War and of the Homeric epics, and the home of Helen of Troy. The first city of Troy was built in about 2300 B.C.; because of fire, conquest, and earthquakes, nine successive cities were built on the site.

Troy became an important and thriving commercial center and was a city of great splendor by 1200 B.C., when the Homeric city came into being. The city was well populated and wealthy and had paved streets and a ring of walls and towers. Destroyed by Greeks in the Trojan War, it was abandoned but reoccupied by Greeks in 700 B.C. The ninth and last city of Troy was captured and destroyed by Romans in 85 B.C. Rebuilt a few years later, it was an important center until its final abandonment in A.D. 300.

In the late 19th century, the German archeologist Heinrich Schliemann uncovered remains of all nine cities. The site of Troy is near Hissarlik, four miles from the mouth of the Dardanelles.

■ **UR:** An ancient seat of Sumerian culture in Mesopotamia, Ur is identified in the Bible as the home of Abraham, progenitor of the Jews and founder of Judaism. The city was built on the banks of the Euphrates River and was an important commercial center before 2500 B.C. A huge ziggurat, or pyramid-like temple tower, dates from the 21st century B.C., as does an inscription recently identified as part of a code of law antedating by three centuries the code of Hammurabi (18th century B.C.), King of Babylonia and a great ancient lawgiver.

Ur was conquered, destroyed, and rebuilt many times during its history. About the middle of the 6th century B.C., it began declining and never regained its grandeur.

Inscriptions connecting the site with Biblical Ur were found in the 19th century, but not until Sir Charles Leonard Woolley excavated the area from 1922 to 1934 was the history of Ur reconstructed. It is situated a few miles from Nasiriyeh in southern Iraq.

■ **ZIMBABWE:** The extensive ruins at Zimbabwe in Southern Rhodesia were once thought to be the Biblical Ophir, a region of immense wealth and the site of King Solomon's mines. It was rediscovered by Europeans in the 1870s, and in subsequent years thousands of barren holes were dug in a fruitless search for gold.

The city, built by Negro tribes, was probably first settled in the 9th century. Its surviving structures show great engineering skill, but the architecture is unique, unrelated to any other African style. Included in the 70 acres of ruins are a massive wall, a fortress, dwellings, and a building thought to be a temple. Zimbabwe is a few miles southwest of Fort Victoria.

Remains of ancient Minoan city, found in 1967 on Greek Island of Thera, are linked to fabled Atlantis.

James W. Mavor Jr.

## STATESMEN AND MILITARY LEADERS OF CLASSICAL HISTORY

**Lucius Tarquinius Priscus,** 7th century B.C., Etruscan king who defeated the tribes of Italy and established Etruscan dominance.

**Draco,** 7th century B.C., Athenian statesman, proverbial for a harsh code of law.

**Solon,** 6th century B.C., Athenian statesman; known as a lawgiver, he considerably softened the code of Draco and extended Athenian democracy.

**Pisistratus,** 605(?)–527 B.C., Athenian statesman, famous as a patron of the arts.

**Darius I,** d. 486 B.C., king of Persia who consolidated Persian power and began the Persian War against the Greeks. The Athenians, under **Miltiades** (d. 489 B.C.), won a stunning victory over superior Persian forces at Marathon, 490 B.C. Darius' son, **Xerxes I** (d. 465 B.C.), succeeded him and pursued the war. He defeated the Spartan general **Leonidas** at Thermopylae, 480 B.C., after the Greeks had been betrayed. In the same year, however, the Athenian admiral **Themistocles** (d. 460 B.C.) defeated Persian naval forces at Salamis, ending Xerxes' dreams of conquering Greece.

**Pericles,** 495(?)–429 B.C., Athenian statesman identified with the Golden Age of Athens, a period of magnificent flowering of culture and democracy. A popular leader in Athens, he carried out many democratic reforms. Under his leadership, the Delian League, an anti-Persian alliance, reached the height of its power.

**Alcibiades,** 450(?)–404 B.C., Athenian statesman and general. Brilliant but dissolute, he led Athenian forces against Sparta in the Peloponnesian War (431–404 B.C.). The war ended when the Spartan statesman and admiral **Lysander** (d. 395 B.C.) crushed the Athenian forces in 404 B.C. and forced Athens to surrender.

**Dionysius the Elder,** 430(?)–367 B.C., Greek ruler of Syracuse in Sicily, known for the high level of culture attained under his patronage. Many liberal reforms, such as the distribution of land to the poor and the enfranchisement of the serfs, were enacted under his rule.

**Demosthenes,** 384(?)–322 B.C., Greek statesman and orator who attempted to arouse the Greeks to the danger of invasion by **Philip II** (382–326 B.C.), King of Macedonia, a region in northern Greece. Philip conquered Greece, 338 B.C., and established Macedonian hegemony.

**Alexander the Great,** 356–323 B.C., King of Macedonia. The son and successor of Philip II, he conquered most of the then-known Western world. At his death, his empire was divided between two of his generals, **Ptolemy Soter** (d. 284 B.C.), founder in Egypt of the Ptolemaic dynasty which endured until 44 B.C., and **Seleucus Nicator** (d. 280 B.C.), who founded the Seleucid dynasty which brought Hellenic culture to most of Asia Minor and Syria. Later, the Ptolemaic and Seleucid dynasties struggled for control of Egypt and Syria.

**Hannibal,** 247–182 B.C., ruler of Carthage in North Africa. Staunch opponent of Rome, he crossed the Alps and invaded Italy. Harassed but never decisively engaged by the Roman general **Fabius Cunctator** (d. 203 B.C.), Hannibal won a series of brilliant tactical victories but was not able to capture Rome. He was defeated at Zama, 202 B.C., by **Scipio Africanus Major** (234?–183 B.C.). **Cato the Elder** (234–129 B.C.) also implacably opposed the existence of Carthage. **Scipio Africanus Minor** (185?–129 B.C.), adopted grandson of the victor of Zama, led a Roman naval force in the destruction of Carthage, 147 B.C., thus ending the Punic Wars.

**Tiberius Sempronius Gracchus,** d. 133 B.C., Roman statesman, who, with his brother **Caius Sempronius Gracchus** (d. 121 B.C.), effected liberal reforms. The reforms were suppressed by the aristocratic party.

**Lucius Cornelius Sulla,** 138–78 B.C., Roman general and statesman. A member of the aristocratic party, he was opposed by **Caius Marius** (157?–86 B.C.) of the popular party. Warfare between the two parties erupted, and in 88 B.C. Sulla marched into Rome and defeated Marius. Sulla ruled Rome brutally. Among his lieutenants were **Quintus Lutatius Catulus** (d. 87 B.C.) and **Marcus Linius Crassus** (d. 53 B.C.), who crushed a slaves' revolt led by **Spartacus,** 71 B.C. During this period, the republic was profoundly shaken by conflicts between leaders of the aristocratic and popular parties.

**Julius Caesar,** 102(?)–44 B.C., Roman statesman and general. Even though of noble birth, he was of the democratic party. Caesar supported **Catiline** (108?–62 B.C.), who tried to win control of Rome by force from **Cicero** (106–43 B.C.); Catiline was put to death. Meanwhile, Caesar's military conquests had won him great popularity, and, overcoming the opposition of Cicero and **Cato the Younger** (95–46 B.C.), he became dictator of Rome by destroying the aristocratic oligarchy. His chief military antagonist, **Pompey** (106–48 B.C.), was murdered in Egypt after losing to Caesar. Caesar's rule was brief, and after his assassination by a group of conspirators, Rome degenerated into chaos. **Marcus Junius Brutus** (85?–42 B.C.), one of the assassins of Caesar, was defeated at Philippi, 42 B.C., by Augustus, Caesar's grandnephew. One of Caesar's supporters, **Marc Antony** (83?–30 B.C.), ruled for five years as a member of the Second Triumvirate, but later went to Egypt, where he became Cleopatra's lover. He was allied with Augustus, but soon the alliance dissolved and Antony committed suicide after his defeat at Actium, 31 B.C., by Augustus.

**Augustus** (original name Caius Julius Octavianus), 63 B.C.–A.D. 14, Roman statesman. After Antony's defeat, Augustus was the sole ruler of Rome. A strong leader, he reformed the laws, rebuilt Roman tradition, and brought back constitutional rule. At first he adhered to republican principles, but the weakened Senate willingly abdicated its power, and the republic was ended. Augustus became in fact, and later in title, the first emperor of Rome.

# ROMAN EMPERORS

Octavian, the grandnephew and adopted son of Julius Caesar, was the founder of the Roman imperial system. He became emperor in 27 B.C., called himself Augustus, and possessed hitherto unknown military and governmental powers. At the death of Theodosius the Great in 395, the Empire was divided into East and West, never again to be reunited. The large-scale barbarian invasions of the fifth century caused the Empire in the West to crumble, and in 476, Odoacer, a German captain, entered Rome and forced the emperor, Romulus Augustus, to abdicate.

| REIGN | EMPEROR | REIGN | EMPEROR | REIGN | EMPEROR |
|---|---|---|---|---|---|
| 27 B.C.– 14 A.D. | Augustus | 238....... | Balbinus | 360–363... | Julian the Apostate |
| 14–37..... | Tiberius | 238....... | Pupienus Maximus | 363–364... | Jovian |
| 37–41..... | Caligula | 238–244... | Gordina III Pius | 364–375... | Valentinian I |
| 41–54..... | Claudius | 244–249... | Philip the Arab | 364–378... | Valens |
| 54–68..... | Nero | 249–251... | Decius | 367–383... | Gratian |
| 68–69..... | Galba | 251....... | Hostilianus | 383–388... | Magnus Maximus |
| 69........ | Otho | 251–253... | Gallus | 375–392... | Valentinian II |
| 69........ | Vitellius | 253....... | Aemilianus | 392–394... | Eugenius |
| 69–79..... | Vespasian | 253–260... | Valerian | 378–395... | Theodosius I the Great |
| 79–81..... | Titus | 253–268... | Gallienus | | |
| 81–96..... | Domitian | 268–270... | Claudius II Gothicus | **Emperors in the East** | |
| 96–98..... | Nerva | 270–275... | Aurelian | 395–408... | Arcadius |
| 98–117... | Trajan | 275–276... | Tacitus | 408–450... | Theodosius II |
| 117–138... | Hadrian | 276....... | Florianus | 450–457... | Marcian |
| 138–161... | Antoninus Pius | 276–282... | Probus | 457–475... | Leo I |
| 161–180... | Marcus Aurelius | 282–283... | Carus | 474....... | Leo II |
| 161–169... | Lucius Verus | 283–285... | Carinus | | |
| 180–192... | Commodus | 283–284... | Numerianus | **Emperors in the West** | |
| 193....... | Pertinax | 284–305... | Diocletian | 395–423... | Honorius |
| 193....... | Didius Julianus | 286–305... | Maximian | 410–411... | Maximus |
| 193–211... | Septimius Severus | 293–306... | Constantius I Chlorus | 421....... | Constantius III |
| 211–217... | Caracalla | 293–311... | Galerius | 425–455... | Valentinian III |
| 211–212... | Geta | 308–313... | Maximin | 455....... | Petronius Maximus |
| 217–218... | Macrinus | 311–323... | Licinius | 455–456... | Avitus |
| 218–222... | Heliogabalus | 306–321... | Maxentius | 457–461... | Majorian |
| 222–235... | Alexander Severus | 306–337... | Constantine I the Great | 461–465... | Libius Severus |
| 235–238... | Maximinus Thrax | 337–340... | Constantine II | 467–472... | Anthemius |
| 238....... | Gordian I Africanus | 337–350... | Constans | 472–473... | Olybius |
| 238....... | Gordian II | 337–361... | Constantius II | 473–474... | Glycerius |
| | | 350–353... | Magnetius | 474–475... | Julius Nepos |
| | | | | 475–476... | Romulus Augustus |

# HOLY ROMAN EMPERORS

On Christmas Day in the year 800, Pope Leo III crowned Charlemagne Emperor of the West, thus breaking ties with the Byzantine Empire in Constantinople and reviving in the West a concept of empire that had been dead since the fall of Rome. But the Carolingian Empire fell into decay gradually after the death of Charlemagne in 814, and by 888 it had become divided into the three fairly distinct units of France, Germany, and Italy. After more than half a century of instability, the vigorous assertion of royal authority by Otto I, King of Germany, served as an important unifying influence over the former Carolingian Empire. In 962, Pope John XII crowned Otto emperor with the right to approve or reject papal elections, a power that Charlemagne had never possessed. Hence, 962 is regarded as the beginning of the Holy Roman Empire, which endured for more than eight hundred years, until the death of Francis II in 1806.

**■ Saxon Dynasty**
Otto I....................962–73
Otto II.................973–83
Otto III...............983–1002
Henry II...............1002–24

**■ Franconian Dynasty**
Conrad II...............1024–39
Henry III..............1039–56
Henry IV...............1056–1106
Henry V................1106–25
Lothair II (of Saxony)
  King ............1125–33
  Emperor .............1133–37

**■ Hohenstaufen Dynasty**
Conrad III.............1138–52
Frederick I (Barbarossa)...1152–90
Henry VI...............1190–97

Philip of Swabia, 1198–1208 ⎫ Rivals
Otto IV (Welf), 1198–1215 ⎭
Frederick II.............1212–50
Conrad IV..............1250–54

**■ Interregnum, 1254–73**

**■ Various Dynasties**
Rudolf I (Hapsburg).......1273–91
Adolf (Nassau)...........1292–98
Albert I (Hapsburg).....1298–1308
Henry VII (Luxemburg)...1308–13
Ludwig IV (Wittelsbach)..1314–47
Charles IV (Luxemburg)...1347–78
Wenceslas (Luxemburg)..1378–1400
Rupert (Wittelsbach)....1400–10
Sigismund (Luxemburg)...1410–37

**■ Hapsburg Dynasty**
Albert II.................1438–39

Frederick III.............1440–93
Maximilian I..........1493–1519
Charles V..............1519–56
Ferdinand I...........1556–64
Maximilian II..........1564–76
Rudolf II..............1576–1612
Matthias ..............1612–19
Ferdinand II...........1619–37
Ferdinand III..........1637–57
Leopold I.............1658–1705
Joseph I..............1705–11
Charles VI.............1711–40

**■ Interregnum, 1740–42**
Charles VII (Wittelsbach)..1742–45
Francis I..............1745–65
Joseph II..............1765–90
Leopold II.............1790–92
Francis II.............1792–1806

# KINGS, QUEENS, AND DYNASTIES

King Baudouin
(Belgium)

King Frederick IX
(Denmark)

Queen Elizabeth II
(Great Britain)

King Constantine II
(Greece)

Prince Jean
(Luxembourg)

Queen Juliana
(Netherlands)

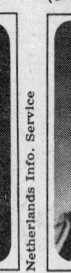
King Olav V
(Norway)

King Gustavus Adolphus
(Sweden)

## BELGIUM

### ■ House of Coburg
| | |
|---|---|
| Leopold I | 1831–65 |
| Leopold II | 1865–1909 |
| Albert I | 1909–34 |
| Leopold III | 1934–51 [1] |
| Baudouin | 1951– |

## DENMARK

### ■ Waldemarian Dynasty
| | |
|---|---|
| Waldemar the Great | 1157–82 |
| Knut VI | 1182–1202 |
| Waldemar II | 1202–41 |
| Eric Plowpenny | 1241–50 |
| Abel | 1250–52 |
| Christopher | 1252–59 |
| Eric V | 1259–86 |
| Eric VI | 1286–1319 |
| Christopher II | 1320–32 [2] |
| Waldemar IV | 1340–75 |
| Olaf | 1376–87 [3] |
| Margaret of Denmark | 1387–1412 [4] |
| Eric | 1412–39 [4] |
| Christopher | 1439–48 [4] |
| Christian of Oldenburg | 1448–81 [4] |
| John | 1481–1513 [4] |
| Christian II | 1513–23 [4] |
| Frederick I | 1523–33 [5] |
| Christian III | 1533–59 |

| | |
|---|---|
| Frederick II | 1559–88 |

### ■ House of Oldenburg
| | |
|---|---|
| Christian IV | 1588–1648 |
| Frederick III | 1648–70 |
| Christian V | 1670–99 |
| Frederick IV | 1699–1730 |
| Christian VI | 1730–46 |
| Frederick V | 1746–66 |
| Christian VII | 1766–1808 |
| Frederick VI | 1808–39 |
| Christian VIII | 1839–48 |
| Frederick VII | 1848–63 |
| Christian IX | 1863–1906 |
| Frederick VIII | 1906–12 |
| Christian X | 1912–47 |
| Frederick IX | 1947– |

## FRANCE

### ■ The Carolingian Dynasty
| | |
|---|---|
| Pepin, Mayor of the Palace | 714 |
| Charles Martel, Mayor of the Palace | 715–41 |
| Pepin I, Mayor of the Palace | 741 |
| King | 751–68 |
| Charlemagne, King | 768–814 |
| Emperor | 800–14 |
| Louis the Pious, Emperor | 814–40 |
| WEST FRANCIA | |
| Charles the Bald, King | 840–77 |
| Emperor | 875 |
| Louis II, King | 877–79 |

| | |
|---|---|
| Louis III, King | 879–82 |
| Carloman, King | 879–84 |
| MIDDLE KINGDOMS | |
| Lothair, Emperor | 840–55 |
| Louis (Italy), Emperor | 855–75 |
| Charles (Provence), King | 855–63 |
| Lothair II (Lorraine), King | 855–69 |
| EAST FRANCIA | |
| Ludwig, King | 840–76 |
| Carloman, King | 876–80 |
| Ludwig, King | 876–82 |
| Charles the Fat, Emperor | 876–87 |

### ■ Capetian Kings
| | |
|---|---|
| Hugh Capet | 987–96 |
| Robert II | 996–1031 |
| Henry I | 1031–60 |
| Philip I | 1060–1108 |
| Louis VI | 1108–37 |
| Louis VII | 1137–80 |
| Philip II (Augustus) | 1180–1223 |
| Louis VIII | 1223–26 |
| Louis IX | 1226–70 |
| Philip III | 1270–85 |
| Philip IV | 1285–1314 |
| Louis X | 1314–16 |
| Philip V | 1316–22 |
| Charles IV | 1322–28 |

### ■ House of Valois
| | |
|---|---|
| Philip VI | 1328–50 |
| John | 1350–64 |
| Charles V | 1364–80 |
| Charles VI | 1380–1422 |

1. Leopold III abdicated in 1951. 2. A period of anarchy followed the death of Christopher II, 1332–40. 3. King of Denmark and Norway after 1380. 4. Ruler of Denmark, Norway, and Sweden. 5. Norway remained under Danish rule until 1815.

## FRANCE (continued)

Charles VII..............1422–61
Louis XI................1461–83
Charles VIII............1483–98
Louis XII..............1498–1515
Francis I...............1515–47
Henry II...............1547–59
Francis II..............1559–60
Charles IX..............1560–74
Henry III..............1574–89

■ **Bourbon Dynasty**
Henry IV...............1589–1610
Louis XIII.............1610–43
Louis XIV.............1643–1715
Louis XV...............1715–74
Louis XVI..............1774–92
■ **First Republic, 1792–99**
■ **Napoleon Bonaparte,**
   **First Consul, 1799–1804**
■ **Napoleon I, Emperor, 1804–14**
■ **Bourbon Restoration**
Louis XVIII............1814–24
Charles X..............1824–30
Louis Philippe.........1830–48
■ **Second Republic, 1848–52**
■ **Napoleon III, Emperor, 1852–70**
■ **Third Republic, 1870–1940**
■ **Pétain regime, 1940–44**
■ **Provisional government, 1944–46**
■ **Fourth Republic, 1946–59**
■ **Fifth Republic, 1959–**

## GREECE

■ **Danish House**
Otto I.................1832–62 [1]
George I...............1863–1913
Constantine I..........1913–17
Alexander I............1917–20
Constantine I..........1920–22 [2]
George II..............1922–23
■ **Greek Republic 1924–35**
George II..............1935–47 [3]
Paul I.................1947–64
Constantine II.........1964– [4]

## ITALY

■ **House of Savoy** [5]
Emmanuel Philibert.....1553–80
Charles Emmanuel I.....1580–1630
Victor Ammadeus I......1630–37
Charles Emmanuel II....1637–75
Victor Ammadeus II.....1675–1730
Charles Emmanuel III...1730–73
Victor Ammadeus III....1773–96
Charles Emmanuel IV....1796–1802
Victor Emmanuel I......1802–21
Charles Felix..........1821–31

■ **House of Savoy-Carignan**
Charles Albert.........1831–49
■ **Kings of Italy** [5]
Victor Emmanuel II......1849–78
Humbert I..............1878–1900 [6]
Victor Emmanuel III.... 1900–46 [7]
Humbert II.............1946 [8]
■ **Italian Republic, 1946–**

## LIECHTENSTEIN

Prince Johann II.......1858–1929
Prince Franz I.........1929–1938
Prince Franz Josef.....1938–

## LUXEMBOURG

Duke Adolf of Nassau...1890–1912
Marie Adelaide.........1912–1919
Grand Duchess Charlotte.1919–1961
Prince Jean............1961–

## THE NETHERLANDS

■ **Houses of Orange and Nassau**
William I (the Silent)....1581–84 [9]
Maurice of Nassau......1584–1625
Frederick Henry........1625–47
William II..............1647–50
John de Witt...........1650–72 [10]
William III............1672–1702 [11]
John William...........1702–11
William IV.............1711–51
William V..............1751–95
■ **The Batavian Republic,**
   **1795–1806**
■ **French King of the Netherlands**
   **Louis Bonaparte, 1806–10**
■ **Kingdom of Holland incorporated**
   **into France, 1810–13**
■ **The Dutch Royal House**
William I...............1813–40
William II..............1840–49
William III.............1849–90
Wilhelmina ............1890–1948 [12]
Juliana.................1948–

## NORWAY

■ **Norwegian Royal House**
Haakon VII.............1905–57
Olav V.................1957–

## PORTUGAL

■ **Burgundian Dynasty**
Alfonso Henriques......1139–85
Sancho I...............1185–1211
Alfonso II.............1211–23

Sancho II..............1223–45
Alfonso III............1245–79
Diniz..................1279–1325
Alfonso IV.............1325–57
Pedro I................1357–67
Ferdinand I............1367–83
■ **Avis Dynasty**
John I .........  1385–1433 [13]
Edward I...............1433–38
Alfonso V..............1438–81
John II................1481–95
Emanuel I..............1495–1521
John III...............1521–57
Sebastian I............1557–78
Henry .................1578–80 [14]
■ **House of Braganza**
John IV................1640–56
Alfonso VI.............1656–67
Pedro II...............1667–1706
John V.................1706–50
Joseph I...............1750–77
■ **House of Coburg-Braganza**
Maria I and Pedro III....1777–86
Maria I................1786–1816
John VI................1816–26
Pedro IV ..............1826 [15]
Maria II...............1826–28
Miguel ................1828–33 [16]
Maria II...............1833–53
Pedro V................1853–61
Louis I................1861–89
Carlos I...............1889–1908
Manuel II .............1908–10
■ **Portuguese Republic, 1910–28**
■ **Portuguese Corporative State**
Antonio Salazar........1928–

## PRUSSIA AND GERMANY

■ **Hohenzollern Dynasty**
Frederick I............1701–13 [17]
Frederick William I.....1713–40 [17]
Frederick II
   (the Great).........1740–86 [17]
Frederick William II...1786–97 [17]
Frederick William III.1797–1840 [17]
Frederick William IV....1840–61 [17]
William I (German Emperor
   after 1871)..........1861–88 [17]
Frederick III..........1888
William II.............1888–1918
■ **Weimar Republic, 1918–33**
■ **Third Reich (Nazi Dictatorship),**
   **1933–45**
■ **Allied occupation, 1945–52**
■ **Division into Federal Republic of**
   **Germany (West) and German**
   **Democratic Republic (East), 1949–**
   (continued)

1. Greece was part of the Ottoman Empire from 1453 to 1829. Otto I was deposed in 1862.   2. After Alexander's death in 1920, a plebiscite was held that restored Constantine I to the throne.   3. A plebiscite in 1935 called for the restoration of the monarchy and George II returned to the throne.   4. In 1965 the Princess Alexia was born to King Constantine and Queen Anne-Marie.   5. Savoy rulers were regional Italian nobility until Victor Emmanuel II.   6. Assassinated in 1900.   7. Abdicated in 1946. Under the Fascist regime, from 1922 to 1943, he was king in name only.   8. Ruled from May to June, 1946. 9. Spain ruled the Netherlands from 1504 to 1581.   10. John de Witt, statesman and diplomat, virtually ruled Holland after the death of William II in 1650.   11. William III ruled as king of England and Scotland from 1689 to 1702. His death brought to an end the direct line of the House of Orange.   12. Queen Wilhelmina abdicated in 1948 in favor of her daughter, Juliana.   13. Established by John I, an illegitimate son of Pedro I, after leading a revolt that drove the Burgundian regent out of Portugal.   14. Spain assumed rule of Portugal from 1580 to 1640.   15. Emperor of Brazil from 1826 to 1831. 16. A coup d'etat by Miguel forced Maria off the throne of Portugal. She was restored in 1833.   17. Kings of Prussia.

KINGS, QUEENS, AND DYNASTIES (*continued*)

## RUSSIA

**■ Early Rulers**
Ivan III (the Great).....1462–1505
Basil III................1505–33
Ivan IV (the Terrible).....1533–84
Theodore I..............1584–98
Boris Godunov......1598–1605
Theodore II..............1605
Basil IV................1606–10
**■ Romanov Dynasty**
Michael................1613–45
Alexius................1645–76
Theodore III.............1676–82
Ivan V and Peter I......1682–89 [1]
Peter I (the Great)......1689–1725
Catherine I............1725–27
Peter II...............1727–30
Anna..................1730–40
Ivan VI................1740–41
Elizabeth..............1741–62
Peter III..............1762
Catherine II (the Great)...1762–96
Paul..................1796–1801
Alexander I............1801–25
Nicholas I.............1825–55
Alexander II............1855–81
Alexander III...........1881–94
Nicholas II...........1894–1917
**■ Kerensky (Provisional Government), 1917**
**■ The Bolshevik Revolution, 1917**
**■ Soviet Republic, 1917–**

## SPAIN

**■ Houses of Aragon and Castile**
Ferdinand II of Aragon and
  Isabella of Castile..1479–1504 [2]
Ferdinand II and
  Philip I.........1504–06 [2]
Ferdinand II and
  Charles I........1506–16 [2]
**■ The Spanish Hapsburgs**
Charles I (as Holy Roman
  Emperor, Charles V)...1516–56
Philip II............1556–98
Philip III..........1598–1621
Philip IV...........1621–65
Charles II..........1665–1700
**■ The Spanish Bourbons**
Philip V............1700–46
Ferdinand VI........1746–59
Charles III.........1759–88
Charles IV..........1788–1808
**■ French King of Spain**
Joseph Bonaparte......1808–13
**■ Bourbon Restoration**
Ferdinand VII........1813–33
Isabella II..........1833–68
**■ House of Savoy**
Amadeo I............1868–73 [3]
**■ The First Spanish Republic, 1873–75**
**■ Bourbon Restoration**
Alfonso XII..........1875–85
Alfonso XIII........1886–1931 [4]

**■ Spanish Republic, 1931–39**
**■ Spanish Corporate State**
Francisco Franco........1939–

## SWEDEN

**■ House of Vasa**
Gustavus I..............1523–60
Eric XIV...............1560–68
John III................1568–92
Sigismund .............1592–99 [5]
Charles IX.............1604–11
Gustavus Adolphus.......1611–32
Christina..............1632–54
Charles X..............1654–60
Charles XI.............1660–97
Charles XII...........1697–1718
Ulrica Eleonora........1718–20
Frederick I............1720–51
Adolphus Frederick......1751–71
Gustavus III...........1771–92
Gustavus IV
  Adolphus..........1792–1809
Charles XIII.........1809–18 [6]
**■ House of Bernadotte**
Charles XIV...........1818–44
Oscar I...............1844–59
Charles XV............1859–72
Oscar II.............1872–1907
Gustavus V...........1907–50
Gustavus VI
  Adolphus..........1950–

1. Joint tsars under the regency of Sophia Alekseyevna.   2. Joint rulers of Aragon and Castile   3. Amadeo abdicated in 1873.   4. King Alfonso was tried by the Spanish Cortes, found guilty of high treason, and forbidden to return to Spain. The royal property was confiscated.   5. King of Poland from 1587 to 1632.   6. Union of Norway and Sweden from 1814 to 1905.

## RULERS OF BRITAIN

The chronology of British rulers begins with Egbert, King of Wessex. By his death in 839, Egbert had united the other English kingdoms under his overlordship, and is considered the first king of England. Succeeding rulers are listed below by dynasty and the years of their reign.

**■ Saxons and Danes**
Egbert ................827–839
Ethelwulf ............839–858
Ethelbald ............858–860
Ethelbert ............858–866
Ethelred .............866–871
Alfred the Great ........871–901
Edward the Elder.......901–925
Athelstan .............925–940
Edmund ..............940–946
Edred ...............946–955
Edwy ...............955–959
Edgar ...............959–975
Edward the Martyr.......975–978
Ethelred II.............978–1016
Edmund Ironside...........1016
Canute the Dane.......1016–1035
Harold I.............1035–1040
Hardicanute ..........1040–1042
Edward the Confessor..1042–1066
Harold II................1066
**■ Norman**
William I............1066–1087
William II...........1087–1100
Henry I .............1100–1135
Stephen ............1135–1154

**■ Plantagenet**
Henry II...............1154–1189
Richard I.............1189–1199
John ...............1199–1216
Henry III............1216–1272
Edward I.............1272–1307
Edward II............1307–1327
Edward III...........1327–1377
Richard II...........1377–1399
**■ Lancaster**
Henry IV.............1399–1413
Henry V .............1413–1422
Henry VI....1422–1461, 1470–1471
**■ York**
Edward IV...1461–1470, 1471–1483
Edward V .............1483
Richard III..........1483–1485
**■ Tudor**
Henry VII............1485–1509
Henry VIII...........1509–1547
Edward VI............1547–1553
Jane (14 days).........1553
Mary I ..............1553–1558
Elizabeth I..........1558–1603
**■ Stuart**
James I .............1603–1625
Charles I............1625–1649

**■ Commonwealth**
Oliver Cromwell........1653–1658
Richard Cromwell.......1658–1659
**■ Stuart Restoration**
Charles II...........1660–1685
James II.............1685–1688
**■ Orange**
William III...........1689–1702
  and Mary II........1689–1694
**■ Stuart**
Anne ...............1702–1714
**■ Hanover**
George I.............1714–1727
George II............1727–1760
George III...........1760–1820
  (Regency........1811–1820)
George IV............1820–1830
William IV...........1830–1837
Victoria.............1837–1901
**■ Saxe-Coburg-Gotha**
Edward VII...........1901–1910
**■ Windsor**
George V ............1910–1936
Edward VIII (325 days)......1936
George VI............1936–1952
Elizabeth II.........1952–

# PRIME MINISTERS OF GREAT BRITAIN

| PRIME MINISTER | PARTY | MINISTRY | PRIME MINISTER | PARTY | MINISTRY |
|---|---|---|---|---|---|
| Sir Robert Walpole | Whig | 1721–42 | Earl Russell **† | Liberal | 1865–66 |
| Lord John Carteret | | | Earl of Derby *** | Conservative | 1866–68 |
| (Earl of Wilmington) | Whig | 1742–43 | Benjamin Disraeli * | Conservative | 1868 (Feb. to Dec.) |
| Henry Pelham | Whig | 1743–54 | | | |
| Duke of Newcastle * | Whig | 1754–56 | William E. Gladstone * | Liberal | 1868–74 |
| Duke of Devonshire | Whig | 1756–57 | Benjamin Disraeli ** | Conservative | 1874–80 |
| Duke of Newcastle ** | Whig | 1757–61 | William E. Gladstone ** | Liberal | 1880–85 |
| Earl of Bute | Tory | 1761–63 | Marquis of Salisbury * | Conservative | 1885–86 |
| George Grenville | Whig | 1763–65 | William E. Gladstone *** | Liberal | 1886 (Feb. to July) |
| Marquis of Rockingham * | Whig | 1765–66 | | | |
| Earl of Chatham | Whig | 1766–67 | Marquis of Salisbury ** | Conservative | 1886–92 |
| Duke of Grafton | Whig | 1767–70 | William E. Gladstone **** | Liberal | 1892–94 |
| Lord Frederick North | Tory | 1770–82 | Earl of Rosebery | Liberal | 1894–95 |
| Marquis of Rockingham ** | Whig | 1782 (Mar. to July) | Marquis of Salisbury *** | Conservative | 1895–1902 |
| | | | Arthur J. Balfour | Conservative | 1902–05 |
| Earl of Shelburne | Whig | 1782–83 | Sir Henry Campbell- | | |
| Duke of Portland * | Coalition | 1783 (Apr. to Dec.) | Bannerman | Liberal | 1905–08 |
| | | | Herbert H. Asquith * | Liberal | 1908–15 |
| William Pitt * | Tory | 1783–1801 | Herbert H. Asquith ** | Coalition | 1915–16 |
| Henry Addington | Tory | 1801–04 | David Lloyd George * | Coalition | 1916–19 |
| William Pitt ** | Tory | 1804–06 | David Lloyd George ** | Coalition | 1919–22 |
| Lord William Grenville | Whig | 1806–07 | Andrew Bonar Law | Conservative | 1922–23 |
| Duke of Portland ** | Tory | 1807–09 | Stanley Baldwin * | Conservative | 1923–24 |
| Spencer Perceval | Tory | 1809–12 | James Ramsay MacDonald * | Labour | 1924 (Jan. to Nov.) |
| Earl of Liverpool | Tory | 1812–27 | | | |
| George Canning | Tory | 1827 (Apr. to Aug.) | Stanley Baldwin ** | Conservative | 1924–29 |
| | | | James Ramsay MacDonald ** | Labour | 1929–31 |
| Viscount Goderich | Tory | 1827–28 | James Ramsay MacDonald *** | Coalition | 1931–35 |
| Duke of Wellington | Tory | 1828–30 | | | |
| Earl Grey | Whig | 1830–34 | Stanley Baldwin *** | Coalition | 1935–37 |
| Viscount Melbourne * | Whig | 1834 (July to Nov.) | Neville Chamberlain | Conservative | 1937–40 |
| | | | Winston S. Churchill * | Coalition | 1940–45 |
| Sir Robert Peel * | Tory | 1834–35 | Winston S. Churchill ** | Conservative | 1945 (May to July) |
| Viscount Melbourne ** | Whig | 1835–41 | | | |
| Sir Robert Peel ** | Tory | 1841–46 | Clement R. Attlee | Labour | 1945–51 |
| Lord John Russell *† | Whig | 1846–52 | Sir Winston S. Churchill *** | Conservative | 1951–55 |
| Earl of Derby * | Tory | 1852 (Feb. to Dec.) | Sir Anthony Eden | Conservative | 1955–57 |
| | | | Harold Macmillan | Conservative | 1957–63 |
| Earl of Aberdeen | Coalition | 1852–55 | Sir Alec Frederick | | |
| Viscount Palmerston * | Liberal | 1855–58 | Douglas-Home | Conservative | 1963–64 |
| Earl of Derby ** | Conservative | 1858–59 | Harold Wilson | Labour | 1964– |
| Viscount Palmerston ** | Liberal | 1859–65 | | | |

\* First Ministry.   \*\* Second Ministry.   \*\*\* Third Ministry.   \*\*\*\* Fourth Ministry.   † Lord John Russell, later Earl Russell, sat in the House of Commons during his first ministry, and in the House of Lords during his second ministry.

Britain's House of Commons in Session. **Inserts:** Prime Ministers Walpole (left) and Wilson (right)

## EUROPE

**3000 BC**

**3000 B.C.** Danube valley culture: Stone Age people settled along the banks of the great rivers of Europe.

**2800–1100 B.C.** Minoan civilization of Crete: a high civilization, centered in Cnossus, and noted for its palaces and art work. Mycenaean civilization: Greek-speaking peoples settled on the Greek mainland; competed with the Minoans for control of the eastern Mediterranean.

**2500–1100 B.C.** Megalithic culture of Europe: among its remains are dolmens—large stone monuments—probably serving a ritual use.

**2500–1200 B.C.** Barbarian Celts, ruled by Druids, a priestly class, and armed with iron weapons and mounted on horses, began invasions of western Europe.

**2500–2000 B.C.** Illyrians, and other peoples, settled Italy.

**1850 B.C.** Stonehenge built: megalithic monument on Salisbury Plain, England; used for religious purposes.

Impressive and mysterious ruins of Stonehenge (AERO PICTORIAL LTD.)

**3000 B.C.** Indians, having crossed the Bering Strait many centuries before, settled in North and South America. Chipped flint points found near Folsom, New Mexico, in association with the remains of extinct mammals, such as the camel and mastodon, indicate the distinct antiquity of Indians.

Centuries-old Folsom point
(AMERICAN MUS. OF NAT. HIST.)

**2000 B.C.** Indians domesticated animals and cultivated manioc, maize, beans, and squash; preparatory step before the rise of high Indian civilizations.

**1500 BC**

**1200 B.C.** Trojan Wars: Greeks conquered Troy in Asia Minor.

**1100–950 B.C.** Dorian invasions of Greece: conquered Mycenaean civilization and destroyed Cnossus, center of the Minoans.

**1000 B.C.** Teutonic tribes conquered northern Europe; Latin tribes settled in Italy.

**900–400 B.C.** Etruscan people, probably from Asia Minor, migrated to Italy and created a high civilization.

**850–600 B.C.** Homeric Greece: Greeks founded colonies on almost all Mediterranean shores.

**753 B.C.** Traditional date for founding of Rome by Romulus and Remus.

**750–509 B.C.** Etruscans conquered Romans and ruled as kings.

**736–630 B.C.** Rise of Sparta on Greek mainland.

**700 B.C.** Celtic invasion of Spain and France.

Romulus and Remus, traditional founders of Rome, suckled by a she-wolf
(CAPITOLE MUS., ROGER-VIOLLET)

Chavin Jaguar-god sculpture
(UNIV. OF PENN. MUSEUM)

**700–200 B.C.** Chavin de Huantar, Peru: chief ceremonial center of the earliest civilization in South America; the Chavin built large temples with painted sculpture of symbolic character, and designed ceramics, gold objects, and textiles.

## WEST ASIA

**4000–2000 B.C.** Sumerians in Mesopotamia created a flourishing civilization, possibly earliest in world; Ur was a leading Sumerian city.

Egyptian scale of the dead
(METROPOLITAN MUS. OF ART)

**3200–2200 B.C.** Old Kingdom of Egypt: unification of Upper and Lower Egypt by the legendary Menes.

**2400–2200 B.C.** Semitic conquest of Mesopotamia: Sargon created an empire.

**2100–1786 B.C.** Middle Kingdom of Egypt: civilization reached a new splendor.

**2000–1700 B.C.** Wanderings of Hebrews.

**1900–1600 B.C.** Babylonian dynasty of Mesopotamia.

**1600–1200 B.C.** Hittite Empire of Asia Minor: a chief power in West Asia.

**1570–1085 B.C.** New Kingdom of Egypt: cultural and territorial zenith of ancient Egypt.

**1468 B.C.** Battle of Megiddo: Egyptian conquest of Syria and part of Mesopotamia.

**1301–1234 B.C.** Ramses II, ruler of Egypt; Moses led exodus of Hebrews.

**1250 B.C.** Phoenician civilization flourished in Syria and Lebanon.

**1020–1004 B.C.** Saul, King of Israel.

**1000–774 B.C.** Maritime supremacy of Phoenicians established.

**972–932 B.C.** Solomon ruled Israel; later, it was divided into the Kingdom of Israel and the Kingdom of Judah.

**931–722 B.C.** Kingdom of Israel.

**931–586 B.C.** Kingdom of Judah.

**910–606 B.C.** Assyrian Empire in Mesopotamia; founded after conquest of Babylonia.

**774–625 B.C.** Phoenicia ruled by Assyria.

**670 B.C.** Conquest of Egypt by Assyrians.

## EAST ASIA

**3000 B.C.** Stone Age villages existed in the valley of Yellow River of China.

**3000–1500 B.C.** Indus valley civilization of India; cities of Harappa and Mohenjo-Daro attained high level of culture; houses, often two-storied and spacious, lined the city streets.

**1523–1027 B.C.** Shang dynasty of China, first recorded in Chinese history: the Shang had a complex civilization of farmers and craftsmen, with a priestly class, nobles, and a priest-king.

Shang ornamental bronze vessel
(METROPOLITAN MUS. OF ART)

**1500 B.C.** Barbarian Aryans from the steppes of central Asia invaded India, destroyed Indus valley civilization.

**1027–256 B.C.** Chou dynasty of China: the philosophers Confucius, Lao-tze, and Mencius lived.

**1000–500 B.C.** Rise of caste system in India; the original basis of caste may have been racial.

Sacred bull: Indus valley seal
(PAKISTAN INTL. AIRLINES)

## AFRICA

**3000 B.C.** Remnants of an ancient Saharan culture, probably founded in 6000 B.C., as evidenced by the Tasilli Frescoes; these rock murals, located in southeast Algeria, indicate an early Negro pastoral civilization.

Tasilli Frescoes: Pastoral scene
(DOCUMENT MISSION LHOTE)

**1200–200 B.C.** Nok culture of Nigeria: advanced Negro civilization with a remarkable tradition of terra cotta sculpture.

**800–586 B.C.** Phoenicians founded Carthage in North Africa; Carthage became a flourishing trade center.

Expressive Nok sculpture
(COURTESY BRITISH MUSEUM)

## EUROPE

## THE AMERICAS

**650 BC**

**600–300 B.C.** Teutonic tribes broke up into various groups and invaded western Europe: the Alemanni settled on the upper Rhine, the Franks and Saxons settled between the Weser and the Elbe, and the Thuringians settled south of the Saxons.

**594–560 B.C.** Solon, the law-giver, introduced judicial reforms into Athens, a Greek city-state; abolished serfdom, gave power to propertied classes, established a qualified democracy.

**509 B.C.** Traditional date for founding of the Roman Republic.

**508 B.C.** Age of Democracy in Athens: every citizen given right to vote.

**500–300 B.C.** Classical Greek civilization.

**500–449 B.C.** Greek-Persian Wars: caused by commercial rivalry between Athens and Persia; resulted in Athens becoming leading city-state of Greece.

**457–429 B.C.** Age of Pericles: Golden Age of Athens; sculpture, philosophy, and painting flourished; Parthenon built on the Acropolis.

**431–404 B.C.** Peloponnesian War: caused by rivalry between Sparta and Athens; resulted in Spartan victory and subsequent control of Greece.

**404–371 B.C.** Spartan hegemony of Greece.

**400–270 B.C.** Rome conquered Italy: defeated Etruscans, Samnites, and Greek colonists.

**359–336 B.C.** Reign of Philip II of Macedon; conquered Thrace, Thebes, and Athens, and attempted to unite Greece; Demosthenes, greatest of Greek orators, denounced Philip.

**336–323 B.C.** Reign of Alexander the Great of Macedon, son of Philip II; conquered Greece and most of west Asia and invaded India; first of the great European conquerors.

**323 B.C.** Hellenistic civilization began: Greek influence spread over the Mediterranean world.

**300 B.C.** Roman expansion: the city of Rome became a major power in the Mediterranean world.

**264–241 B.C.** First Punic War: Carthage, in North Africa, warred against Roman occupation of Sicily.

**227 B.C.** Sardinia and Corsica became Roman provinces.

**218–201 B.C.** Second Punic War: Hannibal, the Carthaginian leader, invaded Italy.

**149–146 B.C.** Third Punic War: Romans destroyed Carthage.

**146 B.C.** Greek mainland conquered by Rome.

**88–82 B.C.** Civil War in Rome.

**60 B.C.** First Triumvirate: Caesar, Pompey, and Crassus ruled Rome.

**46–44 B.C.** Rule of Julius Caesar in Rome: reorganized the conquered provinces, reformed land tenure, and reduced taxes; territories ruled by Rome included Gaul, Italy, part of Illyria, Macedonia, Greece, Asia Minor, Egypt, and part of North Africa.

**44 B.C.** Assassination of Julius Caesar.

**43–31 B.C.** Second Triumvirate in Rome: Antony, Lepidus, and Octavian.

**31 B.C.** Battle of Actium: Octavian, Caesar's nephew, defeated Antony and Cleopatra and became Augustus, first Roman emperor; Egypt became a Roman province.

**14 B.C.–192 A.D.** *Pax Romana:* 200 years of peace in Roman Empire.

**500 B.C.–1150 A.D.** Olmec culture of Mexico: highly developed agricultural civilization; famous for huge sculptured heads, carved out of basalt, and sometimes weighing over 20 tons.

Gigantic Olmec head
(AMERICAN MUS. OF NAT. HIST.)

**100 B.C.–1550 A.D.** Zapotec Indians of Mexico: established a great religious center at Mitla and a magnificent city at Monte Albán, where a high civilization flourished.

Monte Albán: Zapotec center
(AMERICAN MUS. OF NAT. HIST.)

**1 AD**

**1 A.D.** Beginning of the Christian era.

**34–60** Missionary journeys of St. Paul.

**43–407** Roman rule in Britain.

**64** Fire destroyed most of Rome: Nero blamed Christians.

**96–180** "The Five Good Emperors": Nerva, Trajan, Hadrian, Antonius Pius, and Marcus Aurelius; great public works undertaken and the Empire was enlarged.

**1 A.D.** Mayan culture long in existence; possibly an offshoot of Olmec civilization.

## WEST ASIA

**625–539 B.C.** Chaldean Empire of Mesopotamia.

**612 B.C.** Fall of Nineveh, Assyrian capital, to Medes, Chaldeans, and Scythians.

**606 B.C.** Battle of Carchemish: end of Assyrian Empire.

**559–330 B.C.** Persian Empire founded by Cyrus the Great; included vast areas of west Asia.

**538 B.C.** Persian conquest of Babylon; return of Hebrews to Jerusalem.

**525 B.C.** Conquest of Egypt by Persians.

**490 B.C.** First Persian expedition to Greece under Darius I.

**480–479 B.C.** Second Persian expedition to Greece under Xerxes.

**332 B.C.** Conquest of Phoenicia, Palestine, and Egypt by Alexander the Great.

Greek coin: Alexander the Great
(OTTO P. WENGER BERN)

**323 B.C.** Egypt under Ptolemies, a Greek dynasty.

**300–50 B.C.** Alexandria, Egypt, the intellectual center and fountainhead of Hellenistic world.

**250 B.C.–226 A.D.** Parthian Empire: successor to Persian Empire.

**167 B.C.** Revolt of Hebrew Maccabees against Antiochus IV, king of Syria, who tried to Hellenize Palestine.

**150 B.C.** Rome turned its imperial ambition to west Asia.

**47–30 B.C.** Reign of Cleopatra in Egypt.

**31 B.C.** Annexation of Egypt to Roman Empire.

**6 B.C.–41 A.D.** Palestine under rule of Romans.

**6 or 4 B.C.** Birth of Jesus in Bethlehem.

**30 A.D.** Crucifixion of Jesus in Jerusalem.

**70** Revolt in Jerusalem suppressed by Titus.

**98–117** Mesopotamia and Assyria became Roman provinces.

## EAST ASIA

**563–483 B.C.** Gautama Buddha preached in India.

**551–479 B.C.** Confucius taught in China.

**327–326 B.C.** Alexander the Great and his Greek troops entered India.

**325–298 B.C.** Chandragupta Maurya, founder of the Maurya dynasty, united India.

**269–232 B.C.** Reign of Emperor Asoka the Great in India; Buddhism became state religion.

**221–207 B.C.** Ch'in dynasty of China: began construction of Great Wall; first dynasty to unify country.

**202 B.C.–220 A.D.** Han dynasty of China: noted for long peaceful rule, expansionist policies, and great artistic achievement; Buddhism introduced into China.

Great Wall of China
(AMERICAN MUS. OF NAT. HIST.)

**60 A.D.** Kushan kings of Gandhara in West Pakistan: established an empire extending from central Asia to India; a famous school of Buddhist sculpture developed under the Kushans.

## AFRICA

**650 B.C.–650 A.D.** The flourishing Kingdom of Axum in Ethiopia: palaces, temples, and carved stone obelisks built.

Obelisk of the Kingdom of Axum
(CALVERT-STEARNS)

**350 B.C.** Meroe, capital of Nubia, fell to Ethiopians and was abandoned; extensive archaeological remains.

Ruins of Meroe (SUDAN EMBASSY)

100

100–476 Barbarian invasions: Goths, Vandals, and Huns invaded various parts of the Roman Empire.

101–07 Dacian Wars: Roman Empire extended north of Danube.

113–17 Parthian Wars: Armenia and Assyria became provinces of Roman Empire.

117–38 Reign of the Emperor Hadrian: the Roman Empire at its greatest extent.

161–80 Marcus Aurelius: "philosopher king" ruled Roman Empire.

192–284 Barracks emperors: rule of the Roman Empire by the army.

284–305 Reign of Diocletian: Roman Empire divided into eastern and western regions, each under separate rule.

306–37 Reign of Constantine the Great: first Christian emperor; built his capital at Constantinople (now Istanbul); Constantinople became center of Eastern Roman Empire.

337–476 Decline of the Roman Empire: barbaric tribes overran much of western and central Europe.

400–50 Goths invaded Italy, Spain, and Gaul.

400 End of Eastern Roman Empire: succeeded by the Byzantine Empire.

407 Roman armies evacuated Britain: Jutes, Angles, and Saxons overran Britain.

450 Attila and his Huns ravaged eastern Europe.

455 Alaric led Visigoths in sack of Rome.

476 End of Western Roman Empire: Romulus Augustus, last Roman emperor in the West.

481–511 Clovis led the Franks to victory over the Burgundians and Visigoths and established the Frankish kingdom.

497 Ostrogoth kingdom of Italy established by Theodoric.

500

527–65 Justinian the Great, Byzantine emperor: conquered the Vandals of North Africa, Visigoths of Spain, and the Ostrogoths of Italy.

568 Lombards invaded and settled northern Italy.

698 Moslem Arabs took Carthage, ending Byzantine rule in North Africa.

711–15 Moslem conquest of Spain.

712–44 Franks destroyed Lombard kingdom of Italy.

715–41 Charles Martel, ruler of Frankish kingdom: for the next two centuries, Franks were dominant power in Europe.

732 Battle of Tours: Moslem sweep into Europe checked by Charles Martel.

756–1031 Omayyad Dynasty of Cordova: ruled Moslem Spain.

768–814 Charlemagne, king of the Franks: leading ruler of medieval times; extended Frankish kingdom; France, Italy, and Germany under his control.

800 Charlemagne crowned Roman emperor by Pope Leo III.

827–78 North African Moslems conquered Sicily and Malta.

843 Treaty of Verdun: Frankish Empire divided into three separate states; formed basis for modern Germany, France, and Italy.

850 Feudalism developed in western Europe.

867–1025 Macedonian dynasty ruled Byzantine Empire; new period of splendor.

822 Kiev became Russian capital.

912–61 Under Moslems, Cordova emerged as greatest intellectual center of Europe.

920–42 Byzantine Empire extended its power to the Euphrates and Tigris rivers in Mesopotamia.

962 Founding of Holy Roman Empire by Otto the Great; conquered north and central Italy.

987–1328 Capetian line established in France by Hugh Capet; gradual growth of French royal power.

## THE AMERICAS

317–889 A.D. Classic period of Mayan civilization of south Mexico, much of Guatemala, and extreme west Honduras: a flourishing culture, well advanced in art and science; developed an original system of writing.

Mayan sculpture
(AMERICAN MUS. OF NAT. HIST.)

700–1200 Toltec civilization of Mexico flourished; probably built the great pyramids at Teotihuacán; Toltecs formed a warrior aristocracy; succeeded by the Aztecs.

Aztec death mask
(COURTESY BRITISH MUSEUM)

## WEST ASIA

Constantine the Great
(METROPOLITAN MUS. OF ART)

**226–40** Ardashir I founded Sassanian dynasty; reunited Persia.
**232** Sassanian-Roman War: Sassanians became major power.
**258–60** Sassanians, under Shapur I, took Asian territory from Rome and held Roman emperor Valerian a prisoner.
**330** Constantinople founded by Roman emperor Constantine; the Byzantine Empire, ruled from Constantinople, became successor to the Roman Empire in Asia Minor.

**531–79** Reign of Khosru I, illustrious Sassanian king.
**570** Birth of Mohammed, Prophet of Islam, in Mecca.

Anointing of Mohammed
(COURTESY UNIV. OF EDINBURGH)

**622** Traditional date of Mohammed's flight, or hegira, from Mecca to Medina; marked beginning of the Moslem Era.
**633–42** Islam expanded: Moslem Arabs invaded Persia, Syria, Palestine, and Egypt.
**661–750** Islam under the Omayyads: centered in Damascus.
**750–1258** Islam under the Abbasid caliphate: centered in Baghdad; Moslem empire at its zenith.

## EAST ASIA

**100** Traditional date for beginning of Japanese state.
**317–589** China divided between Northern and Southern dynasties.
**320–544** Gupta dynasty united India after five centuries of war and chaos; the Golden Age of Hindu art and literature.

Sculpture of Hindu god, Brahma
(METROPOLITAN MUS. OF ART)

**550** Cambodians founded Khmer Empire in area roughly corresponding to modern Laos and Cambodia.
**552** Introduction of Buddhism into Japan.
**585–608** Reconstruction of Great Wall of China as defense against the Turks and Mongols of central Asia.
**606–47** Reign of Harsha in India: India enjoyed a renaissance of Hindu art and letters.
**618–906** T'ang dynasty: Korea came under Chinese rule, and the Chinese army swept into Mongolia, Nepal, Tibet, and Turkestan; Golden Age of medieval China, an era of brilliance.
**712** Moslem Arabs devastated much of northwestern India.
**800–1600** Feudalism in Japan; rise of Samurai military class.
**889–1434** Golden Age of Khmer civilization; capital at Angkor; ruled over modern Thailand, Cambodia, South Vietnam, and Laos; great strides in art and learning.
**960–1279** Sung dynasty in China: period of scholarly studies and artistic progress.

## AFRICA

**320–50 A.D.** Christianity introduced in Kingdom of Axum.

Ethiopian host of angels
(CALVERT-STEARNS)

**700** Islam arrived and prospered in Africa.
**800–1000** Arab colonies founded on Madagascar and in Zanzibar; Arab expeditions into the African interior for slaves.
**990–1750** Great Zimbabwe civilization of modern Southern Rhodesia; highly developed Negro culture; massive stone buildings erected.

Wall of Great Zimbabwe
(EWING GALLOWAY)

## EUROPE

## THE AMERICAS

**1000**

1014–16 Byzantine Emperor Basil II wiped out Bulgarian army and incorporated Bulgaria into the Empire.

1020 Armenia annexed to Byzantine Empire.

1024–1125 Franconian house ruled in Germany; dawn of a great imperial age.

1054 Final schism between Rome and Constantinople resulted in two distinct faiths: Roman Catholicism and Greek Orthodoxy.

1066 Battle of Hastings in England: William the Conqueror and Norman troops conquered Harold, king of the Anglo-Saxons; end of Anglo-Saxon rule.

1072–1109 Toledo taken from Moslems by Alfonso VI, king of Castile and Leon.

1095–99 First Crusade declared by Pope Urban II: papal dominance of Crusade signified new prestige of papacy.

1147–49 Second Crusade: led by Conrad III of Germany and Louis VII of France.

1152–90 Frederick Barbarossa, medieval German king, ruled Germany and considered himself heir to the tradition of Constantine, Justinian, and Charlemagne; took Poland and Bavaria, destroyed Milan, and conquered Rome.

1154–1399 Plantagenet kings ruled England.

1176 Frederick Barbarossa defeated at Battle of Legnano by Lombard League: first major defeat of feudal cavalry by infantry.

1187–93 Third Crusade: led by Frederick Barbarossa, Richard I of England, and Philip II of France.

Norsemen reach Vinland
( GRANGER COLLECTION )

1000 Leif Ericsson discovered part of North American coast.

1003–06 Thorfinn Karlsefni, with a party of three ships, left Greenland to spend three years in America.

1050 Machu Picchu, immense fortress city in Peru, was inhabited.

1100–1521 Aztec civilization of Mexico: established capital at Tenochtitlán (now Mexico City) and grew into a powerful political and cultural force; in 1519, their empire included an estimated 5,000,000 people; destroyed by Hernán Cortés.

**1200**

1202–04 Fourth Crusade: led by French.

1209 Albigensian Crusade proclaimed by Pope Innocent III against heretics in southern France.

1213–76 James I of Aragon drove Moslems out of Aragon.

1215 Magna Carta: basis of modern English constitution; asserted supremacy of law over the king.

1217–21 Fifth Crusade: led by Pelasius, papal legate.

1223 Mongol invasion of Russia.

1226–29 Teutonic Knights overran Prussia.

1226–70 "Golden age of medieval France" under King Louis IX.

1228–29 Sixth Crusade: led by Frederick II.

1236–63 Alexander Nevsky ruled Russia: united the country.

1237–42 Mongols invaded and defeated Poland and Bulgaria, and settled on lower Volga where a Tartar, or Mongol, state was organized under the name of Golden Horde.

1242 Alexander Nevsky defeated Teutonic Knights at Battle of Lake Peipus.

1248–54 Seventh Crusade: led by King Louis IX of France.

1263 Teutonic Knights became military and commercial power.

1270 Eighth Crusade: attack on Tunis; death of Louis IX.

1273–91 Rudolph I founded Hapsburg dynasty in Austria.

1289 Venice rose as a maritime power.

1300–1600 The Renaissance: marked the close of the Middle Ages in Europe and the beginning of modern times; the greatest flowering of art in European history.

1309–77 Avignon Papacy, "the Babylonian captivity": political chaos in Italy led to residence in France of seven popes.

1325–41 Ivan I, Grand Duke of Russia: vassal of the Mongols.

1326–59 Arrival of the Ottoman Turks in eastern Europe.

1337–1453 Hundred Years War: caused by King Edward III of England, who claimed France; English were defeated.

1344 Establishment of the Hanseatic Leauge; association of German towns in a trade monopoly.

1346–55 Stephen Dushan: emperor of Serbs, Greeks, Bulgars, and Albanians.

1200–1533 Inca Empire, with a population of 6,000,000 to 8,000,000, centered at Cuzco, Peru: tribe gradually established hegemony over neighboring peoples; a splendid civilization, noted for its efficient organization and rich cities. It dominated the Andean area from Quito, Ecuador, to Río Maule, Chile; Empire destroyed by Francisco Pizarro.

Last of Inca emperors
(AMERICAN MUS. OF NAT. HIST.)

## WEST ASIA

**1071—84** Seljuk Turks from central Asia established in Asia Minor after defeating Byzantines and Arabs.

**1095—99** First Crusade: Christians invaded Palestine and established Kingdom of Jerusalem.

**1147—49** Second Crusade: defeated at Damascus.

**1164—93** Saladin defeated Crusaders and recaptured Jerusalem.

**1187—93** Third Crusade: failed to reconquer Jerusalem.

Crusaders in the Holy Land (CULVER)

## EAST ASIA

Towers of Angkor Wat
(EWING GALLOWAY)

**1050** Pagan, Burma, became the seat of King Anawratha, who introduced Buddhism into Burma.

**1190—1294** Jenghiz Khan created Mongol Empire in central Asia; Mongol hordes swept into east Europe and west Asia.

**1192—1333** Kamakura period in Japan; rule of military warriors.

## AFRICA

**1000—1240** Height of Negro Kingdom of Ghana: extended from Atlantic coast to Timbuktu; known as "the land of gold."

**1054** Beginning of Islamic conquest of West Africa under the Almoravides, Moslem Berber tribes.

**1100—1264** Songhay Kingdom, with capital at Timbuktu, dominated West Africa.

**1147—59** Almohades, fierce Berber Moslems, ruled Morocco, conquered other parts of North Africa, and established Berber hegemony.

---

**1202—04** Fourth Crusade: Crusaders, turning away from Islamic Syria, attacked Christian Constantinople and sacked Byzantine territories.

**1217—21** Fifth Crusade: Crusaders failed in Egypt.

**1219—21** Mongol legions of central Asia conquered Turkestan; a new and powerful force in west Asia.

**1228—29** Sixth Crusade: Crusaders concluded treaty with Turkish sultan; established free access to Jerusalem.

**1245—53** Mongols ravaged Mesopotamia and Armenia.

**1248—54** Seventh Crusade: Crusaders massacred in Egypt.

**1258** Capture and sack of Baghdad by Mongols; the Mongol hordes devastated the surrounding territories.

**1270** Further Mongol advances checked in Egypt.
Eighth Crusade: Crusaders attacked Tunis, were finally turned back.

**1290—1326** Rise of the Ottoman Turks: under Osman I, traditional founder of the Ottoman dynasty.

**1206** Moslems captured Delhi: Delhi Sultanate first Moslem kingdom of India.

**1271—92** Marco Polo left Venice; visited China and other parts of east Asia.

**1279—1368** Yüan (Mongol) dynasty of China founded by Kublai Khan, grandson of Jenghiz.

**1336—92** Civil wars convulsed Japan; Kamakura regime collapsed.

Kublai Khan (BROWN BROTHERS)

**1269** End of Berber Empire in North Africa.

**1300—1500** Height of Ife, holy city of Nigeria, where artistic sculpture was produced.

**1307—32** Mandingo Empire ruled West Africa; displaced the Kingdom of Ghana and the Songhay Empire.

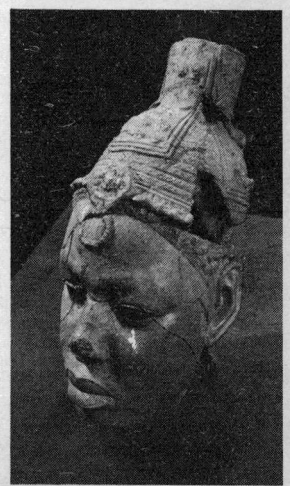

Royal Ife head (FRANK WILLETT)

## EUROPE

**1350**  **1361–87** Series of wars between Denmark and Hanseatic League for control of trade.

**1378–1417** Great Western Schism: division of papacy, Rome and France fought for control.

**1386–1572** Under Jagiello dynasty, Lithuania and Poland united; golden age of Polish culture and power.

**1389** Battle of Kossovo: Serbia became a vassal of Turks; decisive event in Balkan history.

**1391–1453** Ottoman Turks conquered Byzantine lands, and, in 1453, captured Constantinople; Byzantine Empire ended.

**1399–1461** House of Lancaster ruled in England.

**1413–22** Henry V brought England to first rank among European powers.

**1419–36** Hussite religious wars in Bohemia.

**1434–94** Domination of the Medici in Florence, made it center of Italian Renaissance.

**1437** John Hunyadi, frontier lord in Hungary, defeated Turks.

**1455–85** Wars of the Roses in England for the throne; ended feudalism in England.

**1461–83** France became a nation under rule of Louis XI.

**1462–1505** Ivan the Great, first national sovereign of Russia, took title of Tsar and adopted Byzantine court ceremonials.

**1463–79** First great war between Turks and Venetians.

**1469** Union of Aragon and Castile in Spain; strengthened by marriage of Ferdinand and Isabella.

**1478** Inquisition established in Spain: period of terror.

**1485–1603** Henry VII of England founded the house of Tudor.

**1492** Spanish took Granada from Moslem Moors.

**1492–1648** Discovery and exploration of the New World: new wealth and new conflicts of trade.

**1495–1559** Italian Wars: wars among Venice, Milan, Florence, Papal States, and Naples.

**1499–1516** Successful wars of Turks against Venetians.

**1500**  **1503** Peace between Russia and Lithuania: brought new territories to Russia.

**1509–47** Henry VIII, king of England.

**1517** Martin Luther opened the Protestant Reformation.

**1519–56** Charles V, Holy Roman Emperor, inherited Spain, Sardinia, Sicily, Naples, the Netherlands, and Hapsburg lands in central Europe.

**1519** Beginning of Reformation in Switzerland under Ulrich Zwingli.

**1533–84** Reign of Tsar Ivan the Terrible in Russia: expanded Russian frontiers on the east and on the west.

**1534** Act of Supremacy: beginning of English Reformation.

**1534** Founding of the Jesuit order by St. Ignatius of Loyola; chief force in the Roman Catholic Counter-Reformation.

**1537** End of trade monopoly of Hanseatic League in Scandinavia.

**1541–64** John Calvin founded Calvinism; Protestantism spread over north Europe.

**1541–1688** Hungary became vassal state of Turks.

**1545–63** Council of Trent: brought about sweeping internal reform of the Roman Catholic Church.

**1556–98** Philip II of Spain: Hapsburg power at its zenith.

**1557–82** Livonian War: Russians invaded Poland.

**1558–1603** Queen Elizabeth I reigned in England: the Elizabethan Age marked English expansion and a great flowering of literature.

**1562–98** Religious wars in France: Huguenots (French Protestants) persecuted.

**1563–81** The Netherlands revolted against Spanish domination and gained independence.

**1563** Establishment of the Church of England.

**1569** Union of Lublin: merged Lithuania and Poland.

## THE AMERICAS

Landing of Columbus   (CULVER)

**1492** First voyage of Christopher Columbus: reached Canary Islands, Bahamas, Cuba, Santo Domingo, and the West Indies.

**1497** John Cabot of England arrived in North America.

**1501** Amerigo Vespucci, under the flag of Portugal, explored south along Brazilian coast.

**1511** Spanish gained a foothold in Cuba, conquered Puerto Rico, founded San Juan, and settled Jamaica.

**1518–1609** English, French, Portuguese, and Spanish exploration of the New World.

**1519–1600** The Spanish Conquistadores: Hernán Cortés of Spain conquered Mexico; Pedro de Alvarado invaded Guatemala; Francisco Pizarro subjugated Inca Empire of Peru.

**1530–32** Portuguese colonized Brazil.

**1534–41** Voyages of Jacques Cartier, French navigator: explored and discovered St. Lawrence River, stopped at sites of Quebec and Montreal.

**1565** Portuguese founded Rio de Janeiro.

## WEST ASIA

**1369–1405** Tamerlane, Mongol leader, conquered Persia and Mesopotamia, and defeated Ottoman Turks at Angora (now Ankara), Turkey.

**1391–1425** Byzantine Empire, formerly of great extent, reduced to the city of Constantinople by Ottoman Turks.

**1453** Ottoman Turks captured Constantinople; end of Byzantine Empire.

St. Sophia, church of Constantinople
(EWING GALLOWAY)

Suleiman the Magnificent    (CULVER)

**1520–66** Suleiman the Magnificent ruled over Ottoman Empire: his reign marked the greatest flowering of Turkish literature, art, and architecture.

## EAST ASIA

**1368–1644** Ming dynasty founded in China; Mongols driven out, Chinese rule restored.

**1392–1910** Yi dynasty in Korea, with capital at Seoul, remained loyal and subservient to China.

**1398** Sack of Delhi by Tamerlane; desolation of Delhi Sultanate.

**1498** Portuguese explorer Vasco da Gama landed at Calicut, India.

Vasco da Gama    (ROGER-VIOLLET)

**1510** Portuguese conquered Goa in India.

**1526** Mogul Empire of India—to become the most splendid in Indian history—founded by Baber, remote descendant of Tamerlane and Jenghiz Kahn.

**1549–52** Saint Francis Xavier introduced Christianity into Japan.

**1557** Portuguese settled in Macao; began trade with China.

**1560–1605** Akbar, the greatest Mogul emperor, ruled in India; his court attracted many European traders.

Mogul architecture
(INDIA TOURIST OFFICE)

## AFRICA

**1350–1897** Ife ruler established in Benin, Nigeria; Benin grew into a great city, the seat of a royal court; famous for bronze sculpture.

**1400** Baluba Kingdom emerged in Congo.

**1433–44** Portuguese arrived in Africa; the search for gold and the trade in slaves began.

**1450–1800** Kingdom of the Congo covered a vast territory and prospered.

**1471** Portuguese traders in West Africa built forts to discourage other European traders.

**1483** The king of the Congo struck an alliance with the Portuguese, agreed to export slaves, and was baptized King John.

**1487** Portuguese reached Timbuktu.

**1488** Bartolomew Dias, Portuguese explorer, rounded Cape of Good Hope.

**1493–1529** Songhay Empire, resurgent under Askia Mohammed, defeated Mandingos.

**1503–07** Portuguese colonized Mozambique.

**1513–17** Hausa states, an alliance of Moslems in Nigeria, conquered by Songhay Empire; Negroes replaced Arabs, formed Hausa Confederation, and carried on trade.

Portuguese soldiers in Africa
(COURTESY BRITISH MUSEUM)

## EUROPE

## THE AMERICAS

Pilgrims landing at Plymouth

(CULVER)

**1570**

**1571** Battle of Lepanto: Austrian and Holy League forces defeated Ottoman Turks in greatest naval battle since Actium; marked beginning of Ottoman decline.

**1572** Saint Bartholomew's Day Massacre: killing of French Protestants by Catherine de' Medici.

**1575–81** Stephen Bathory, Polish leader, ousted Russians from Polish territories.

**1588** War between England and Spain: the Spanish Armada destroyed.

**1589–1792** Bourbon House ruled France.

**1598** Edict of Nantes: French Huguenots received equal rights with Catholics.

**1610–43** French royal authority consolidated by Louis XIII.

**1613** Michael Romanov elected tsar of Russia; founded Romanov dynasty.

**1618–48** Thirty Years War: conflict between Catholic and Protestant Europe; last of the great religious wars; devastated Germany.

**1640–49** Puritan revolution in England.

**1645–64** Venetians and Turks warred: Ottoman power further declined.

**1643–1715** Age of Louis XIV in France: royal absolutism reached new peak; French power and culture on the rise.

**1648** Peace of Westphalia: ended Thirty Years War.

**1649–60** England's King Charles I beheaded; commonwealth form of government set up under Oliver Cromwell.

**1652–78** Series of Anglo-French and Anglo-Dutch wars for supremacy of the seas.

**1654–1807** Economic and social decline of Portugal and Spain.

**1659** Peace of Pyrenees: ended Spanish power in Europe and made France supreme on the Continent.

**1660** Stuart restoration in England: accession of Charles II.

**1682–1725** Peter the Great attempted to "Westernize" Russia.

**1683** Turkish siege of Vienna repulsed.

**1685** Edict of Nantes revoked: French Protestants persecuted.

**1688–97** War between France and the Grand Alliance of Sweden, Spain, Bavaria, Saxony, England, Holland: decline of French power.

**1580** Buenos Aires founded by Juan de Garay, a Spanish conquistador.

**1603–15** Samuel de Champlain, French explorer, founded Quebec.

**1607** Founding of Jamestown by English; first permanent English settlement in America; led by John Smith.

**1620** Pilgrims arrived at Plymouth, Massachusetts.

**1625–64** French settled West Indies.

**1630** Massachusetts Bay colony established by the Puritans.

**1672** Jacques Marquette and Louis Jolliet explored the Mississippi.

**1700**

**1700–21** Great Northern War: Russia, Poland, and Denmark opposed Swedish supremacy in the Baltic; Russia, under Peter the Great, emerged as a European power.

**1700–46** Philip V, first Bourbon king, recognized by England and Holland as king of Spain.

**1701–1918** Hohenzollern kings ruled Prussia and Germany.

**1701–14** War of the Spanish Succession: resulted in permanent separation of thrones of France and Spain; further deterioration of French power.

**1707** Great Britain formed by union of England and Scotland.

**1714–1901** House of Hanover ruled in England.

**1715–89** Age of Enlightenment: high point in the mainstream of European thought.

**1733–35** War of Polish Succession: Russia and Austria defeated Spain and placed Augustus III on Polish throne.

**1740–86** Frederick the Great, king of Prussia; Prussia rose to greatness under his rule.

**1750–1878** Russo-Turkish Wars: Russia, in a series of wars, drove Turkey from the Crimea and much of Slavic Europe.

**1756–63** Seven Years War: England and France in colonial wars; France lost Canada and India; England became the world's major colonial power.

**1721–1825** Wars of independence in South America: nationalistic wars with Spain.

**1754–60** French and Indian Wars in North America; on the Plains of Abraham in Quebec, Canada, the British general, James Wolfe, defeated the French under Montcalm and ended the Wars; the British gained supremacy in Canada.

Death of General Wolfe

(GRANGER COLLECTION)

## WEST ASIA

**1571** Ottoman Turks defeated at Battle of Lepanto by Christian naval forces: the Ottoman Empire in decline.

**1598** Abbas I, shah of Persia, built the imperial mosque in Isfahan, one of the masterpieces of world architecture.

Victorious Christians at Lepanto
(CULVER)

**1724** Russia and Turkey, by treaty, dismembered Persia.

**1736–47** Nadir Shah, Persian ruler, conquered Afghanistan, defeated Turks; last of the great Asian conquerors.

**1750–94** Zand dynasty in Persia: period of peace and prosperity.

Nadir Shah, King of Persia (CULVER)

## EAST ASIA

**1571** Spanish founded Manila, colonized Philippines.

**1600** British East India Company chartered for trade in India.

**1603–1867** Tokugawa period in Japan: system of feudalism prevailed; Spanish and Dutch traders arrived.

**1622–51** Under Iemitsu, Christianity suppressed in Japan and a policy of national isolation followed.

**1630–48** Taj Mahal in India, one of the most beautiful buildings in the world, built by Mogul emperor Shah Jehan after the death of his favorite wife.

**1641** Dutch captured Malacca and for next century and a half dominated East Indies.

**1644–1912** Ch'ing dynasty founded in China by Manchus of Siberia; Korea became so isolated it was known as the "hermit kingdom."

**1650–1818** Mahratta Confederacy of India arose, helped bring about fall of Mogul Empire, and remained as most powerful force in India until conquered by the British.

**1659–1707** Mogul Empire reached its greatest territorial extent in India.

**1690** The British, their power in India on the rise, founded Calcutta.

Prime minister in court of Ch'ien Lung (METROPOLITAN MUS. OF ART)

**1735–96** Under Emperor Ch'ien Lung, China reached its greatest territorial extent.

**1751** Chinese invasion of Tibet.

**1757** Traditional date of founding of British rule in India, under Robert Clive.

**1758–1824** Modern Burmese state born with capital at Rangoon.

## AFRICA

**1571–1603** Height of Kanem, or Bornu, Empire, around Lake Chad.

**1590–1618** Moroccans defeated Songhays and controlled much of West Africa.

**1652** Founding of Capetown by Dutch.

**1660** Rise of Bambara Kingdom in Niger.

**1697–1893** Ashanti Kingdom in West Africa; noted for high-quality gold work.

Ashanti gold-weight
(MUSEUM OF PRIMITIVE ART)

**1713** Asiento Treaty: under its terms, British government monopolized slave trade to Latin America.

European ivory-buyer
(AMERICAN MUS. OF NAT. HIST.)

## EUROPE

**1760** | 1760–1820 Rule of George III in England.
1760–1860 Industrial revolution in England; England industrialized.
1762–96 Catherine the Great ruled Russia.
1775–83 The War of the American Revolution.
1789–99 French Revolution: monarchy overthrown; Paris became center of European liberal thought.
1799 Coup d'état of Napoleon Bonaparte in France.
1799–1815 Napoleonic conquests made France most powerful country on the Continent.

**1800** | 1800–1900 Rise of socialism in Europe in reaction to shameful industrial conditions.
1801 United Kingdom formed by union of Great Britain and Ireland.
1804–14 Napoleon I, emperor of France.
1806 End of Holy Roman Empire: imperial title renounced by Francis II.
1810 Kingdom of Holland incorporated into French empire.
1812 French invasion of Russia: Napoleon led disastrous campaign.
1814–24 Napoleon abdicated; Louis XVIII, king of France.
1814–15 Congress of Vienna: monarchies re-established in Europe; revolutionary fervor suppressed.
1815 Battle of Waterloo: Napoleon escaped from Elba and defeated by British and Prussian armies.
1821–30 Greek War of Independence against Turks: ended with Greek independence.
1830–31 Polish insurrection suppressed by Russia: beginning of "Russification" of Poland.
1831–65 Leopold I, ruler of Belgium.
1833–71 Unification of Germany.
1837–1901 Victoria, Queen of England: period of great industrial expansion and increased prosperity.
1848 Revolutions in France, Germany, Hungary, and Bohemia; publication of Karl Marx's *Communist Manifesto.*
1848–1916 Francis Joseph, Emperor of Austria; became ruler of the Austro-Hungarian Empire in 1867.
1852–70 Napoleon III, emperor of the Second French Empire.
1854–56 Crimean War: Britain and France checked Russian expansion.
1855–81 Alexander II, Tsar of Russia.
1858 Formation of Rumania.
1859–70 Risorgimento in Italy: period of cultural nationalism and political unification led by Italian patriot and soldier, Giuseppe Garibaldi.
1861 Emancipation of Russian serfs by Tsar Alexander II.
1862–90 Otto von Bismarck, premier and chancellor of Germany, created German Empire.
1864–1905 Russia expanded in Poland, Balkans, and central Asia.

## THE AMERICAS

1775–83 American Revolution.
1776 Declaration of Independence signed in Philadelphia.
1788 U.S. Constitution ratified.
1789 George Washington became first U.S. President.
1791 Canada Act: Canada divided into Upper Canada (chiefly English) and Lower Canada (predominantly French).

1801–06 Toussaint L'Ouverture, Haitian Negro patriot, liberated Santo Domingo from the French and governed the island.
1803 Louisiana Purchase.
1806 Henri Christophe, Haitian revolutionary, elected president of Haitian republic.
1810 Beginning of Mexican revolution for independence from Spain.
1811 Paraguay gained independence.
1811–13 Venezuela, led by Francisco de Miranda, achieved independence.
1812 War of 1812 between United States and Great Britain.
1816 Argentina attained independence.
1818 Chile gained independence under José de San Martín.
1818–23 Bernardo O'Higgins, Chilean revolutionist, ruled Chile.
1819–30 Simón Bolívar, the Liberator, led patriots to victory over Spanish and became president of Greater Colombia (modern Colombia, Venezuela, Ecuador, and Panama).
1821 Independence won in Mexico.
1822 Independence for Brazil and Peru.
1823 Monroe Doctrine.
1825 Bolivia became independent.
1837–40 Upper and Lower Canada united.
1846–48 The Mexican War: between United States (and Texas) and Mexico.
1861–65 Civil War in the United States.
1862 The Emancipation Proclamation.
1862–67 Maximilian and Carlotta, Austrian royalty, backed by French troops, attempted to rule Mexico; overthrown by Benito Juárez; Juárez, an Indian, became Mexican national hero.

Napoleon returning to Paris from Elba    (BROWN BROTHERS)

## WEST ASIA

**1798–1801** Napoleon Bonaparte undertook occupation of Egypt; driven out by combined British and Turkish forces.

**1811–49** Mohammed Ali, ruler of Egypt, extended Egyptian power to the Persian Gulf.
**1839–49** Series of Afghan-British wars.

Crimean War   (BROWN BROTHERS)

**1854–56** Crimean War: Britain and France aided Turkey; forced Russian concessions.
**1856** British declared war on Persia and forced Persians to evacuate Afghanistan.
**1859–69** Suez Canal built.

Suez Canal: 19th century
(BROWN BROTHERS)

## EAST ASIA

**1782** Rama I founded modern Siamese dynasty, with its capital at Bangkok.
**1786** British East India Company leased the island of Penang in Malaya; ultimate British domination of the Malay Peninsula had begun.
**1798** Ceylon became territory of British crown.

Sir T. Stamford Raffles
(BROWN BROTHERS)

**1819** Founding of Singapore by Sir T. Stamford Raffles.
**1824–88** Series of British-Burmese wars led to the annexation of Burma by British, who made it a dependency of India.
**1839–42** Opium War: provoked, waged, and won by British against China; British obtained commercial concessions and established colonies.
**1848–65** Taiping Rebellion in China further weakened Ch'ing (Manchu) dynasty.
**1854** Opening of Japanese trade with West.
**1857–58** Sepoy Rebellion, or Great Mutiny, in India against the British; first serious revolt of Indians against foreign rule.

Truce in Taiping Rebellion   (CULVER)

## AFRICA

**1787** British acquired Sierra Leone from tribal chiefs.
**1795–96** Mungo Park, great British explorer, explored Gambia and reached the Niger.
**1798–1801** Portuguese, French, Spanish, Danes, Dutch, and Swedes all held posts along West African coasts and engaged in slave trade.

**1807–11** Britain abolished the slave trade.
**1808** Sierra Leone became a British crown colony and Gambia was put under its government.
**1814** Treaty of Paris: British secured possession of the Cape of Good Hope.
**1815** France, Spain, and Portugal abolished slave trade.
**1821** Sierra Leone, Gold Coast, and Gambia joined as British West Africa.
**1830** French troops took Algiers.
**1835–37** The Great Boer Trek to Transvaal, Zululand, and Natal.
**1840–70** Dr. David Livingstone carried on explorations of central Africa: his reports created interest in the "Dàrk Continent" and its natural resources.
**1842** British and Boers fought a short war in Natal over land claims; resulted in British annexation of Natal.
**1847** Republic of Liberia established: founded as a haven for freed American slaves.

Dr. David Livingstone
(N. Y. PUBLIC LIBRARY)

## EUROPE

**1867** Austro-Hungarian Empire founded: Austria and Hungary united to repress rising aspirations of their national minorities.

**1868–94** The British statesmen Benjamin Disraeli, an imperialist, and William Gladstone, an anti-imperialist, vied for control of the prime ministry.

William Gladstone        Benjamin Disraeli

(BROWN BROTHERS)

**1870–71** Franco-Prussian War: German invasion of France; Third French Republic formed and endured until 1940.

**1870–1914** European imperialism at its peak; industrial prosperity; social and economic abuses gave rise to labor movements and Marxism.

**1871** The Paris Commune: Paris, a revolutionary center, set up its own government and warred with the national government of France.

**1875** Charles Stewart Parnell, Irish nationalist leader, elected to British Parliament; first to press for Irish independence.

**1878** Congress of Berlin: division of much of the Ottoman Empire between Austria, Russia, and Britain.

**1881** Assassination of Alexander II of Russia.

**1882** Triple Alliance between Germany, Austria-Hungary, and Italy.

**1894–1906** The Dreyfus Affair: Capt. Alfred Dreyfus, a French military officer, was unjustly convicted of treason by a court-martial and sentenced to Devils Island, but was eventually pardoned; the case marked the end of French army influence in government.

**1903** Split between Bolsheviks and Mensheviks of the Russian Social Democratic Labor Party; Bolsheviks, the more radical wing, became modern Communists.

**1904** Triple Entente between Britain and France, later joined by Russia; offset Triple Alliance threat.

**1908** Austria proclaimed annexation of Bosnia and Herzegovina.

## THE AMERICAS

**1865–70** Argentina and Paraguay waged boundary war.

**1867** British North America Act: the Canadian confederation founded.

United States purchased Alaska from Russia.

**1868–78** Cuba struggled for independence from Spain.

**1876–1911** Porfirio Díaz, president of Mexico: established order by force of arms; invited foreign capital; peons in virtual bondage.

**1879–84** War of the Pacific: Chile, Bolivia, and Peru in a territorial dispute; resulted in Bolivia's loss of access to sea.

**1889** Republic of Brazil established.

**1895** Cuban revolt with José Martí as leader.

**1898** Spanish-American War: the sinking of the *Maine* in Havana harbor led the United States to declare war; United States defeated Spain; end of waning Spanish control in Latin America.

Sinking of the Maine

(BROWN BROTHERS)

**1899** Cuba became an independent republic.

Haiti, virtually bankrupt, in a state of political anarchy.

**1901** President William McKinley assassinated by an anarchist; Theodore Roosevelt became President.

**1903** Panama gained independence from Colombia through a revolution backed by the United States.

## WEST ASIA

**1870** Turkish government permitted European Jews to colonize Palestine.

**1878** Congress of Berlin: Cyprus, formerly a Turkish possession, placed under British administration.

**1888** Suez Canal Convention: declared canal open and free to merchant and war vessels, outlawed blockades or acts of aggression within the confines of the canal zone.

**1892** British took over Trucial Oman, a region of eastern Arabia, and forbade the local sheiks any treaty-making powers.

**1894–1915** Armenians in Turkey persecuted and massacred, victimized by an extermination plan put into action by Sultan Abdu-I-Hamid II.

**1896** The Young Turks, a new national force, arose in Turkey.

Ibn Saud     (CULVER)

## EAST ASIA

Emperor Meiji Mutsuhito

(BROWN BROTHERS)

**1868–1912** Meiji period in Japan: feudalism abolished, foreign trade prospered, industrialization and military conscription introduced.

**1887** France forced union of Vietnam and Cambodia, naming it Indo-China; Laos later added to union.

**1889** New constitution granted by emperor of Japan; supreme authority vested in emperor.

**1894–95** Sino-Japanese War: marked real emergence of imperial Japan; acquisition of Formosa (Taiwan) and the Pescadores from China.

**1895** British formed Malay Federation as protectorate.

**1898** Philippines ceded to the United States by Spain.

**1898–1900** Boxer Rebellion in China; Boxers, a secret society called, in Chinese, the harmonious fists, tried to suppress foreign influence; defeated by combined forces of England, Russia, Germany, France, Japan, and United States.

**1899** Open Door policy forced on China: equal trade rights in China for all nations.

## AFRICA

**1867–71** Discovery of diamonds in South Africa; Kimberley became center of diamond industry; diamond rush began.

**1871** British annexed Orange Free State.

**1873–74** British conquered Ashanti Kingdom of West Africa.

**1876** Leopold II of Belgium set up organization to exploit the Congo.

**1877** British annexed Transvaal.

**1879** Zulu War: Zulus, who resented the English, rebelled against their rule; the British won a decisive victory at Ulundi.

**1880** Founding of Brazzaville in the Congo by French.

**1881** Treaty of Bardo: Tunis accepted status as French protectorate.

**1885** Germans proclaimed protectorate over Tanganyika.

**1885–97** Prolonged wars of British in Nyasaland against Arab slave traders.

**1886** Gold rush to the Witwatersrand in southern Transvaal.

**1889–1911** Treaty of Uccialli: Italians derived a claim to a protectorate over Ethiopia; later repudiated by Ethiopia.

**1889** Germany gave up its claim of Uganda to Britain.

**1890–97** Cecil Rhodes, British diamond tycoon, became leading figure in South Africa.

**1893** British established protectorate over Ashanti Kingdom of West Africa and Nyasaland in central Africa.

**1896** Treaty of Addis Ababa: ended with Battle of Adua, where Italian forces were devastated by Ethiopians, forcing Italian withdrawal from Ethiopia.

**1898–99** French possessions in West Africa joined as French West Africa.

**1899** Nigeria became a British protectorate.

**1899–1902** Boer War: British defeated Boers in south Africa.

---

**1901–32** Ibn Saud slowly conquered Arabia; it became Saudi Arabia.

**1901** Discovery of oil in Persia led to intense struggle for power between England and Russia.

**1907** Anglo-Russian agreement divided Persia into two spheres of influence.

**1904–05** Russo-Japanese War: Japan defeated Russia and gained recognition as a world power.

**1909** Mahatma Gandhi, great Indian leader, led non-violent demonstrations against British.

**1904** International protest against Belgian abuses in the Congo.

**1908** Belgium annexed Congo Free State.

**1909** Germany received economic concessions in Morocco from French.

## EUROPE

**1911** Tripolitan War: fought between Italy and Turkey; Italy gained control of Tripoli.

**1912–13** The Balkan Wars: Bulgaria, Serbia, and Greece fought Turkey for control of the Balkans.

**1914–18** Assassination of Archduke Francis Ferdinand at Sarajevo by a Serbian nationalist; World War I began; Triple Entente of France, Russia, and England fought Central Powers (Germany, Austria-Hungary, and Turkey).

**1917** United States entered World War I on the side of the Triple Entente.

Bolshevik Revolution in Russia: Vladimir Lenin led Bolsheviks; overthrew provisional government.

Lenin addressing his Bolshevik followers　(BROWN BROTHERS)

**1918** Kingdom of Yugoslavia proclaimed.
Austro-Hungarian Empire dissolved.

**1918–20** Civil war in Russia: Bolshevik Party renamed Communist Party.

**1918–19** German Republic proclaimed; Weimar Constitution adopted.

**1919** Treaty of Versailles: ended World War I; treaty negotiated by Woodrow Wilson for the United States, Georges Clemenceau for France, David Lloyd George for England, and Vittorio Orlando for Italy.

**1920** League of Nations formed.

**1922** Russia became the Union of Soviet Socialist Republics, the first Communist state in the world.

**1922–33** Benito Mussolini, leader of the Fascist Party, rose to power in Italy.

**1924** Death of Lenin in Russia: power struggle ensued.

**1925** Albania proclaimed a republic.

**1927–53** Joseph Stalin assumed dictatorship in U.S.S.R.

**1928** Five-Year Plan inaugurated in U.S.S.R.; peasants who refused to join collective farms under the new order were killed or sent as forced laborers to Siberia; more than five million peasant households "liquidated."

**1929** Lateran Treaties: creation of independent state of Vatican City in Rome.

## THE AMERICAS

**1910–20** Revolution in Mexico against President Díaz: led by Francisco Madero; after Madero's assassination, the revolution was pressed forward by Emiliano Zapata, Francisco Villa, and Venustiano Carranza.

**1914** Panama Canal opened.

**1916–24** U.S. military occupation of Dominican Republic.

**1916** Denmark ceded Danish West Indies to United States.

**1917** United States entered World War I.

Doughboys in World War I

(NATIONAL ARCHIVES)

**1919** New constitution in Uruguay disestablished Roman Catholic Church and curtailed powers of the president.

**1929–34** Great Depression in the United States; brought about by stock-market crash of 1929; period of wholesale poverty and tragedy; 16 million Americans unemployed.

Dust Bowl of the 1930s

(LIBRARY OF CONGRESS)

# WEST ASIA

Lawrence of Arabia    (CULVER)

**1914–18** World War I: British declared a protectorate over Egypt; initiated Mesopotamian campaign; Lawrence in Arabia; Turks repulsed two British attempts to invade Dardanelles.

Kemal Ataturk (TURKISH INFO. OFFICE)

**1920–38** Kemal Ataturk, founder of modern Turkey, proclaimed Turkish republic (1923) and abolished the Islamic caliphate.
**1922** End of British protectorate over Egypt.

Reza Shah Pahlevi (BROWN BROTHERS)

**1925–41** Reza Shah Pahlevi came to power in Persia.
**1925** Damascus and Aleppo united to form modern state of Syria.

# EAST ASIA

**1910** Japanese annexed Korea.
**1911** Revolution in China, led by Sun Yat-sen, forced the abdication of the Manchu emperor.
**1912** Sun Yat-sen became first president of new Chinese Republic.
**1916** Gandhi supported British in World War I in hope of hastening India's freedom.
**1917** Civil War in China: Kuomintang, the party of the Republic under Sun Yat-sen, established its own government in Canton; fought northern war lords.
**1918–22** Japanese troops occupied Siberia.
**1919** Amritsar Massacre: Indian nationalists killed and wounded when fired upon by British troops.
**1921–23** Chinese Communist party founded, formally allied with Kuomintang.
**1926** Chiang Kai-shek led Kuomintang army northward to victory against war lords; after victory, broke with Communists.

Mao Tse-tung    Chiang Kai-shek
(WIDE WORLD)

**1927** Chiang drove Communists from Shanghai and executed many leaders; Communists resigned from Kuomintang and long civil war ensued.
**1928–49** Chiang established Nationalist government at Nanking and received foreign recognition.
**1929** Jawaharlal Nehru, supported by Gandhi, elected president of the Indian National Congress, largest political party in India.

# AFRICA

**1910** Union of South Africa established; comprised the former British colonies of Cape of Good Hope and Natal, Orange Free State, and Transvaal; Louis Botha, former Boer general, became its first prime minister.
**1912** Major European powers completed partition of Africa: only Ethiopia and Liberia remained independent.
**1914** French and British forces conquered German colonies of Togoland and Cameroons in World War I.
**1920** British mandate over German East Africa went into effect: territory became Tanganyika; Kenya formed.

Cecil Rhodes    (BROWN BROTHERS)

**1923** Rhodesia, a region named for Cecil Rhodes, was divided into Northern and Southern Rhodesia and placed under British administration.
**1924–26** Abd-el-Krim, leader of the Riff tribes of Morocco, waged a successful war against combined French and Spanish troops in Morocco.
**1926** Firestone company purchased a million acres in Liberia for rubber plantations; the company extended medical and educational services to Liberians.
Boundary established between South African trust territory of South West Africa and Portuguese territory of Angola.
**1928** Treaty between South Africa and Portugal signed; regulated problems of transport and labor recruitment between Angola and South Africa.
Twenty-year friendship treaty signed between Italy and Ethiopia; was later violated when Italy attacked Ethiopia.

## EUROPE

**1930**

**1930–35** Worldwide economic depression; many European nations on verge of bankruptcy; inflation rampant; extremist political parties gained adherents.

**1931** British Commonwealth of Nations formed.

The Spanish Republic proclaimed.

**1933** The democratic Weimar Republic fell in Germany.

**1933–45** Adolph Hitler, leader of the Nazis, became chancellor of Germany and formed the brutal Third Reich; concentration camps set up throughout Germany for the extermination of Jews and other groups.

**1935–36** Germany began to rearm in violation of the Treaty of Versailles; German storm troopers occupied the Rhineland.

**1936–37** Purge trials in U.S.S.R.: Stalin removed his enemies.

**1936–39** Spanish Civil War: Republican forces, backed by Communist Russia, and Falangist forces, supported by Nazi Germany and Fascist Italy, fought bloody civil war; Gen. Francisco Franco rose to power.

**1937** Rome-Berlin-Tokyo Axis formed: aggressive pact led to World War II.

**1938** Munich Pacts dismembered Czechoslovakia; Germany absorbed Austria.

**1939** League of Nations collapsed in the face of growing European hostilities.

U.S.S.R. concluded nonaggression treaty with Germany.

Italian invasion and conquest of Albania; German invasion of Poland.

Soviet forces marched into Poland, which was divided between Nazi Germany and U.S.S.R.; U.S.S.R. took over Lithuania, Latvia, and Estonia.

**1939–40** Finnish-Russian War: Finland checked Soviet expansion.

**1939–45** World War II: global conflict, caused by totalitarian regimes in Germany, Italy, and Japan.

**1932–35** Chaco War: Bolivia and Paraguay waged war over the Chaco, a disputed plain; Paraguay won major part of Chaco.

**1933–39** Franklin Roosevelt's New Deal in United States.

New Deal: National Recovery Act
(BROWN BROTHERS)

**1935–40** Dictatorships arose in Latin America.

**1938** Mexican government nationalized foreign oil companies.

**1940**

Benito Mussolini and Adolph Hitler          (WIDE WORLD)

**1940–45** Winston Churchill, prime minister of England, and Franklin Roosevelt led Allies.

**1945** World War II ended.

San Francisco conference formed United Nations.

**1945–46** Nuremberg trials: international tribunal tried Nazi military and civilian leaders for war crimes.

**1945–50** Poland, Rumania, and Bulgaria fell under Communist control.

**1941–45** United States in World War II; on Dec. 7, 1941, Japanese bombed Pearl Harbor and U.S. declared war; Nazi Germany and Fascist Italy declared war on the U.S.; defeat of German army and atomic bombing of Hiroshima and Nagasaki concluded war.

**1945–55** Juan Perón regime in Argentina.

Atomic explosion: Nagasaki
(U.S. AIR FORCE)

## WEST ASIA

**1930–48** Struggle for independence from British rule in Palestine.
**1935** Persia officially became Iran.
**1936–52** Farouk, king of Egypt.

King Farouk    (BROWN BROTHERS)

**1941** Mohammed Reza Shah Pahlevi became Shah of Iran.
**1943** Cairo Conference: guaranteed territorial independence of Iran.

Allied conference: Roosevelt, de Gaulle, Churchill

(FRANKLIN D. ROOSEVELT LIB.)

**1945** Lebanon became independent.
Arab League: association of Arab countries formed chiefly to oppose a Jewish state in Palestine.
**1946** Kingdom of Jordan proclaimed.

## EAST ASIA

Mahatma Gandhi    (PICTORIAL PARADE)

**1931** Japanese occupied Manchuria and set up puppet state.
Mao Tse-tung elected chairman of Soviet Republic of China.
**1932–37** Japanese penetrated northern China.
**1934** Communists forced on the Long March to the northwest by Chiang; settled in Yenan.
**1937–45** Sino-Japanese War between Japan and China: became part of World War II.
**1937** Burma separated from India and given self-government.
**1939** Long fasts by Gandhi compelled several Indian states to grant democratic reforms.

**1940** Japanese established puppet government in Nanking and signed military alliance pact with Germany and Italy.
**1941–45** Japanese bombed Pearl Harbor, captured Singapore and other Pacific possessions; World War II underway.
**1945** Atomic bombs dropped on Hiroshima and Nagasaki by United States; Japan capitulated; end of World War II and beginning of Atomic Age.
Indo-Chinese nationalists demanded independence from France.
Korea divided between American and Russian occupation zones.
**1946** U.S. granted Philippines independence.
**1947** British leave India; India (Hindu) and Pakistan (Moslem) became independent countries; Jawaharlal Nehru, Prime Minister of India, and Mahomed Ali Jinnah, Governor-General of Pakistan; following partition, mass religious riots exceeded all bounds and millions of Hindus and Moslems were murdered.
Burma became independent.

## AFRICA

**1930** Haile Selassie I, Emperor of Ethiopia.
**1935–42** Italian invasion and conquest of Ethiopia.

Haile Selassie    (PICTORIAL PARADE)

**1945–65** Postwar independence movement in Africa; many new African nations born and European domination of the continent ended.

Surging African nationalism

(WIDE WORLD)

**1946** India broke diplomatic relations with Union of South Africa for mistreatment of its Indian minority.

## EUROPE

**1948**

**1948** The Cold War was fully developed; the Western nations opposed the expansionist aims of the Soviet Union.
**1948–49** Berlin Blockade: Soviet Union failed to isolate Berlin.
**1948** Communist coups in Hungary and Czechoslovakia.
**1949** German partition: West Germany, democratic government; East Germany, Communist regime.
North Atlantic Treaty Organization: for mutual military assistance against Communist aggression in Europe.

American airlift defeats Berlin Blockade   (GERMAN INFO. CENTER)

**1950**

**1953** Josip Broz Tito became president of Communist Yugoslavia.
Death of Joseph Stalin.
**1956** Uprising in Hungary was ruthlessly quelled by Soviets.
**1957** Common Market (European Economic Community) was formed in Europe.
**1958** Fifth Republic was proclaimed in France under Gen. Charles de Gaulle.
**1958–64** Nikita Khrushchev became undisputed leader of the U.S.S.R.

Hungarian freedom-fighters demolish Stalin statue   (WIDE WORLD)

## THE AMERICAS

**1948** Harry S. Truman elected President in an upset victory; initiated social legislation and, in foreign affairs, continued his military and economic aid program to halt Communist expansion in the Cold War; Truman a leader in the formation of NATO.
Organization of American States (OAS) created for hemispheric mutual help and protection.
**1949** Former U.S. State Department official Alger Hiss convicted of perjury after being linked with confessed former Communist Whittaker Chambers. U.S. Senate ratified NATO treaty by vote of 82 to 13.

Fidel Castro   (WIDE WORLD)

**1952–58** Fulgencio Batista seized power in Cuba.
**1954** Gen. Alfredo Stroessner engineered successful coup in Paraguay.
**1957** François Duvalier elected president of Haiti; maintained power by reign of terror.
**1959–61** Fidel Castro forced Batista from Cuba; took over country; publicly proclaimed loyalty to Communism; diplomatic relations with U.S. severed.

## WEST ASIA

David Ben-Gurion    (WIDE WORLD)

**1948** State of Israel, created from ancient Palestine, achieved independence after bitter struggle; led by David Ben-Gurion.

**1948–49** Israeli forces defeated armies of Arab League.

**1951–53** Iran nationalized its oil industry; British outraged, blocked oil exports.

**1952** Gamal Abdel Nasser deposed King Farouk, ruled Egypt; new voice among Arabs.

**1956** Suez crisis: Nasser nationalized Suez Canal; Anglo-French and Israeli forces invaded Egypt; withdrew at U.N. request.

**1958** U.S. forces temporarily occupied Lebanon. British paratroopers landed in Jordan to protect king from pro-Nasser factions.

Gamal Abdel Nasser

(PICTORIAL PARADE)

## EAST ASIA

**1948** Gandhi assassinated by a Hindu fanatic. Division of Korea formalized when two separate regimes were established on either side of 38th parallel: North Korea (Democratic People's Republic of Korea), South Korea (Republic of Korea). Communist insurrection, which was to last for more than a decade, began in Malaya.

Indonesians celebrate independence

(WIDE WORLD)

**1949** Indonesian nationalists, led by Sukarno, defeated Dutch and received independence.

**1950** Mao Tse-tung defeated Chiang Kai-shek and established Communist regime in China; Chiang established Nationalist government on Taiwan (Formosa).

**1950–53** Korean War: instigated by North Korean invasion of South Korea; United Nations forces, comprised largely of United States troops, intervened.

**1951** Tibet conquered by Communist China.

**1954** Battle of Dienbienphu: last French stand in Indo-China; end of French control; Vietnam divided at 17th parallel, and Ho Chi Minh became president of North Vietnam. Laos and Cambodia recognized as independent nations.

**1957** Beginning of Chinese-Indian border wars. Federation of Malaya became an independent state.

**1959** Uprising in Tibet suppressed by Communist Chinese.

**1959–61** Communist Pathet Lao forces overran almost half of Laos.

## AFRICA

**1948** Apartheid policy of racial segregation took hold in South Africa under D. F. Malan: as officially stated, the aim of apartheid was to perpetuate the domination of the white minority in South Africa.

Bantu reserve:
South African apartheid

Mau-Mau terrorists enter prison camp

(UNITED PRESS INTL.)

**1952–60** Mau-Mau terrorized British in Kenya.

**1956** Tunisian independence from France.

**1958–62** A revolt of Algerians against French rulers led to independence.

## EUROPE

**1960 1960** Charles de Gaulle dominated the Common Market and threatened the existence of NATO.

The European Free Trade Association formed by European nations excluded from Common Market.

**1961** East Germany constructed the Berlin wall.

**1963** Pope John XXIII died; Giovanni Battista Cardinal Montini elected Pope as Paul VI.

Chancellor Konrad Adenauer of West Germany retired; succeeded by Ludwig Erhard.

**1964** France recognized Communist China.

Harold Wilson became prime minister of Great Britain.

Khrushchev ousted from Soviet leadership, replaced by Leonid Brezhnev and Alexi Kosygin.

Soviet leaders: Mikoyan, Brezhnev, Khrushchev before the storm

(WIDE WORLD)

**1965** Charles de Gaulle of France reelected by slim majority.

**1965–66** Differences grew between some Eastern European countries and the U.S.S.R.

**1966** Harold Wilson's Labour Party won large Parliamentry majority in English elections.

France requested removal of NATO troops from country.

Kurt Georg Kiesinger became chancellor of West Germany.

Belgian Premier Paul Van Den Boeynants and NATO commander, General Lyman Lemnitzer at new NATO headquarters, Casteau, Belgium.

(WIDE WORLD)

**1967** New NATO military headquarters established at Casteau, Belgium.

Great Britain intensified efforts to gain entrance into European Common Market.

## THE AMERICAS

**1961** Bay of Pigs: U.S.-trained Cuban exiles' attempt at invasion of Cuba ended in disaster.

**1962** United States forced Soviet missiles out of Cuba.

**1963** President John F. Kennedy assassinated in Dallas. Texas.

John F. Kennedy lies in state

(WIDE WORLD)

**1964** Lyndon B. Johnson overwhelmingly defeated Barry M. Goldwater for U.S. presidency.

Riots in Panama against U.S.

**1965** U.S. marines landed in Dominican Republic.

Medicare and War on Poverty, bills enacted.

Detroit: after the riot

(WIDE WORLD)

Pope Paul VI spoke before United Nations on world peace.

Race riots killed 34 in Los Angeles suburb of Watts.

**1966** Guyana, formerly British Guiana, became independent.

**1967** Inter-American summit conference held at Punta del Este, Uruguay, mapped plans for increased economic cooperation among American nations.

Race riots ravaged Newark, Detroit, and other U.S. cities; death toll included 26 in Newark and 43 in Detroit.

## WEST ASIA

**1960** Nasser accepted Soviet aid in building up armaments.
Cyprus given independence following bloody conflict.

**1961** Kuwait independence.

**1961–63** Iraq attempted to annex small oil-rich Kuwait.

**1962** Kurdish tribes in northern Iraq staged revolts.
Yemen monarchy overthrown; civil war between royalists and revolutionaries.

**1963** Federation of South Arabia formed as British protectorate.

**1964** Cyprus crisis: Turkish and Greek Cypriots clashed; dispute settled by U.N. intervention.

Archbishop Makarios inspects Greek Cypriot fighters.   (WIDE WORLD)

**1965** West Germany established diplomatic relations with Israel. Most Arab nations severed ties with West Germany.

**1965–66** Aswan dam project ahead of schedule in Egypt.

**1967** Arab-Israeli war: six-day war followed U.A.R. President Nasser's closing of Gulf of Aqaba to Israeli shipping; Israel defeated Arab forces, occupied Sinai peninsula and Jerusalem.

Israeli troops invade Sinai.

(PICTORIAL PARADE)

## EAST ASIA

**1961** India forcibly annexed Goa, Damão, and Diu.
Laotian cease-fire secured at Geneva Conference.

**1962** Formation of Federation of Malaysia.

**1962–65** Series of coup d'etats in South Vietnam. Intervention by United States military forces.

**1963** Open split between China and the U.S.S.R.

**1964** China set off her first nuclear explosion.
Peiping government recognized by France.
Jawaharlal Nehru, first prime minister of India, died; succeeded by Lal Bahadur Shastri.

**1965** Indonesia left the U.N.
Singapore became independent. Strongman Nguyen Cao Ky became premier of South Vietnam. India–Pakistan conflict.

**1966** India's Prime Minister Shastri died; former Prime Minister Nehru's daughter, Indria Gandhi, elected to replace him.
Estimated 300,000 killed in Indonesian anti-Communist purge. President Sukarno lost right to life-time presidency, with General Suharto assuming power. U.S. planes bombed Hanoi and Haiphong areas in Vietnam. Communist China exploded atomic warhead carried by guided missile.

**1967** Widespread internal struggles developed in Communist China between pro and anti-Maoist factions.

U.S. GI aids Vietnamese civilian.

(WIDE WORLD)

U.S. intensified bombing of industrial centers in North Vietnam.
In South Vietnam's first national election, Nguyen Van Thieu became president, and Nguyen Cao Ky vice president. U.S. troop increase to 525,000 authorized for Vietnam duty.

## AFRICA

**1960–63** Belgian Congo given independence; entire Congo in tribal war and anarchy.

**1960** The West and the Communist powers, including China, competed for new alignments among the African nations.

**1961** Dag Hammarskjöld, U.N. secretary-general, killed in plane crash in Northern Rhodesia.
Union of South Africa left the British Commonwealth.

**1963** Jomo Kenyatta became Kenya's first prime minister.

**1964** Tanzania, the united state of Tanganyika and Zanzibar, formed; Julius K. Nyerere became first president.
Nyasaland became independent as Malawi, and Northern Rhodesia achieved independence as Zambia.
Moise Tshombe, former head of secessionist Katanga province, named Congolese premier.

**1965** Mohammed Ben Bella, Algerian premier, overthrown by Col. Houari Boumédienne.
Joseph Mobutu became President of the Democratic Republic of the Congo, deposing former President Joseph Kasavubu.

Joseph Mobutu of the Congo

(UNITED PRESS INT'L.)

Former British colony, The Gambia, achieved independence. Rhodesia unilaterally declared independence of Great Britain.

**1966** President Kwame Nkrumah deposed in Ghana.
Nigerian army officers took over government in bloody coup.

**1967** Congolese ex-premier Moise Tshombe held in custody in Algeria as Congo, demanding his death, sought his extradition; Congolese troops engaged rebel forces in Kisangani and Bukavu. Eastern Province of Nigeria seceded, becoming Republic of Biafra; Nigerian troops invaded area.

## WORLD STATESMEN, POLITICAL FIGURES, AND MILITARY LEADERS

**Abd-el Krim,** 1882?–1963, Moroccan soldier and nationalist leader

**Abdu-l-Hamid II,** 1842–1918, Ottoman sultan

**Abdullah,** 1882–1951, King of Jordan

**Abdu-r-Rhaman I,** d. 788 A.D., Emir of Cordoba

**Aga Khan,** 1877–1957, Moslem statesman

**Akbar,** 1542–1605, Mogul emperor

**Alaric I,** 370?–410 A.D., Visigoth ruler

**Alba, Fernando Álvarez de Toledo, Duque de,** 1508–82, Spanish general

**Albuquerque, Alfonso de,** 1453–1515, Portuguese admiral

**Allenby, Sir Edmund,** 1861–1936, British general

**Almeida, Antonio José de,** 1866–1929, Portuguese statesman

**Amherst, Jeffrey, Baron Amherst,** 1717–97, British general

**Andrassy, Count Julius,** 1823–90, Hungarian statesman

**Antiochus III (the Great),** d. 187 B.C., ruler of Syria

**Antonescu, Ion,** 1882–1946, Romanian soldier and statesman

**Apponyi, Count Albert,** 1846–1933, Hungarian statesman

**Ariovistus,** 1st century B.C., Germanic chieftain

**Asoka,** d. 232 B.C., Indian emperor

**Asquith, Herbert Henry, Earl of Oxford and Asquith,** 1852–1928, British statesman

**Atahualpa,** d. 1533, Inca leader

**Ataturk, Kemal,** 1881–1938, Turkish statesman and founder of modern Turkey

**Attila,** d. 453 A.D., leader of the Huns

**Aurangzeb,** 1618–1707, Mogul emperor

**Avellaneda, Nicolás,** 1837–85, Argentine statesman

**Averescu, Alexander,** 1859–1938, Romanian general and statesman

**Badoglio, Pietro,** 1871–1956, Italian general

**Baldwin, Robert,** 1804–58, Canadian statesman

**Baldwin, Stanley,** 1867–1947, British statesman

**Bajazet I,** 1347–1403, Ottoman sultan

**Bajazet II,** 1481–1512, Ottoman sultan

**Balfour, Arthur James,** 1848–1930, British statesman

**Baranov, Aleksandr Andreyevich,** 1747–1819, Russian colonizer

**Baring, Alexander, Baron Ashburton,** 1774–1848, British statesman

**Baring, Evelyn, Earl of Cromer,** 1841–1917, British statesman and diplomat

**Belisarius,** 505?–565 A.D., Byzantine general

**Beneš, Eduard,** 1889–1948, Czechoslovakian statesman

**Bennett, Richard Bedford,** 1870–1947, Canadian political leader

**Bentinck, Lord William Cavendish,** 1774–1839, British statesman

**Bernadotte, Count Folke,** 1895–1948, Swedish statesman

**Bevan, Aneurin,** 1897–1960, British statesman

**Bevin, Ernest,** 1881–1951, British political leader

**Bismarck, Otto von,** 1815–98, German statesman who was instrumental in creating a united Germany

**Blücher, Gebhard Leberecht von,** 1742–1819, Prussian general

**Blum, Léon,** 1872–1950, French political leader

**Boabdil,** d. 1538, Moorish ruler of Granada

**Bolívar, Simón,** 1783–1830, South American soldier and statesman

**Bonaparte, Joseph,** 1768–1844, French statesman

**Bonaparte, Louis,** 1778–1846, French statesman

**Bonaparte, Lucien,** 1775–1840, French statesman

**Borden, Sir Robert Laird,** 1854–1937, Canadian statesman

**Botha, Louis,** 1862–1919, South African statesman

**Bouillon, Godfrey de,** 1058?–1100, French soldier and Crusade leader

**Bourbon, Charles, Duc de,** 1490–1527, French general

**Bourbon, Louis I de, Prince de Condé,** 1530–69, French statesman

**Braddock, Edward,** 1695–1755, British general

**Branting, Hjalmar,** 1860–1925, Swedish political leader

**Brian Boru,** 940?–1014, Irish king

**Briand, Aristide,** 1862–1932, French statesman

**Brooke, Sir James,** 1803–68, British rajah of Sarawak

**Bruce, James, Earl of Elgin and Kincardine,** 1766–1841, British diplomat

**Bruce, Robert,** 1274–1329, Scottish king

**Brudenell, James Thomas, Earl of Cardigan,** 1797–1868, British general

**Brunhilde,** 534?–613 A.D., Visigoth princess

**Bryce, James, Viscount Bryce,** 1838–1922, British statesman

**Buchan, John, Baron Tweedsmuir,** 1875–1940, British statesman and author

**Bülow, Bernhard, Fürst von,** 1849–1929, German statesman

**Burgoyne, John,** 1722–92, English general

**Burke, Edmund,** 1729–97, British statesman and political writer

**Cadogan, William, Earl Cadogan,** 1675–1726, English general and diplomat

**Campbell, Colin, Baron Clyde,** 1792–1863, British general

**Campbell-Bannerman, Sir Henry,** 1836–1908, British statesman

**Canaris, Constantine,** 1790–1877, Greek patriot

**Canaris, Wilhelm,** 1887–1945, German admiral

**Canning, Charles John, Earl Canning,** 1812–62, British statesman

**Canning, George,** 1770–1827, British statesman

**Carnot, Hippolyte,** 1801–88, French statesman

**Carranza, Venustiano,** 1859–1920, Mexican statesman

**Carteret, John, Earl Granville,** 1690–1763, British statesman

**Cavendish, Stephen Compton, Earl of Devonshire,** 1833–1908, British statesman

**Cavendish, Victor, Earl of Devonshire,** 1868–1938, British statesman

**Cavendish, William, Duke of Newcastle,** 1593?–1676, English soldier and diplomat

**Cavour, Count Camilio Benso di,** 1810–61, Italian statesman

**Cecil, Edgar, Viscount Cecil of Chelwood,** 1864–1958, British statesman and winner of the Nobel Peace Prize in 1937

Cecil, Robert, Marquess of Salisbury, 1563–1612, English statesman

Cecil, Robert Gascoyne, Marquess of Salisbury, 1830–1903, British statesman

Cecil, William, Baron Burghley, 1520–98, English statesman

Chamberlain, Sir Austen, 1863–1937, British statesman

Chamberlain, Joseph, 1836–1914, British statesman

Chamberlain, Neville, 1869–1940, British statesman

Chang Tso-lin, 1873–1928, Chinese general

Chateaubriand, François René, Vicomte, 1768–1848, French statesman

Christophe, Henri, 1767–1820, ruler of Haiti

Churchill, John, Duke of Marlborough, 1650–1722, English soldier and statesman

Churchill, Sir Winston Leonard Spencer, 1874–1965, British statesman and soldier

Chu Yüan-chang, d. 1398, Chinese emperor

Clausewitz, Karl von, 1780–1831, Prussian general and military theoretician

Clemenceau, Georges, 1841–1929, French statesman

Cleopatra, 69–30 B.C., Queen of Egypt

Clinton, Sir Henry, 1738?–95, British general

Clive, Robert, Baron Clive of Passey, 1725–74, British statesman

Cobden, Richard, 1804–65, British statesman

Codrington, Sir Edward, 1770–1851, British admiral

Coke, Sir Edward, 1552–1634, English jurist

Colbert, Jean, 1619–83, French statesman

Collins, Michael, 1890–1922, Irish patriot

Comnenus, Alexius, 1048–1118, Byzantine emperor

Cornwallis, Charles, Marquess Cornwallis, 1738–1805, British statesman and general

Cortés, Hernán, 1485–1547, Spanish soldier

Corvinus, Matthias, 1443?–90, King of Hungary and Bohemia

Cripps, Sir Stafford, 1889–1952, British statesman

Cromwell, Oliver, 1599–1658, English statesman and general

Cromwell, Thomas, 1485?–1540, English soldier

Curzon, George Nathaniel, Marquess Curzon of Keddleston, 1859–1925, British statesman

Dalberg, Emmerich Joseph, 1773–1833, French statesman

Dalberg, Karl Theodor, Freiherr von, 1744–1817, German statesman

Danton, Georges Jacques, 1759–94, French revolutionist

Deak, Francis, 1803–76, Hungarian statesman

Deakin, Alfred, 1856–1919, Australian statesman

Deschanel, Paul Eugène Louis, 1855–1922, French statesman

Desmoulins, Camille Benoit, 1760–94, French revolutionist

Dessalines, Jean Jacques, 1758?–1806, Emperor of Haiti

Diaz, Porfirio, 1830–1915, Mexican statesman

Disraeli, Benjamin, Earl of Beaconsfield, 1804–81, British statesman

Doumergue, Gaston, 1863–1937, French statesman

Drake, Sir Francis, 1540?–96, English admiral

Dreyfus, Alfred, 1859–1935, French army officer

Dudley, Robert, Earl of Leicester, 1532?–88, English courtier

Ebert, Friedrich, 1871–1925, German statesman

Emmet, Robert, 1778–1803, Irish revolutionist

Erskine, Thomas, Baron Erskine, 1750–1823, British jurist

Esperey, Louis Félix Franchet d', 1856–1942, French general

Fallières, Armand, 1841–1931, French statesman

Farnese, Alessandro, Duke of Parma and Piacenza, 1545–92, Spanish general and diplomat

Farouk I, 1920–65, King of Egypt

Faure, Félix, 1841–99, French statesman

Feuerbach, Paul Johann Anselm von, 1775–1833, German jurist

Fisher, Andrew, 1862–1928, Australian statesman

Fisher, John Arbuthnot, Baron Fisher, 1841–1920, British admiral

Foch, Ferdinand, 1851–1929, French general

Foix, Gaston de, 1489–1512, French general

Fonseca, Manuel Deodoro da, 1827–92, Brazilian statesman

Forbes, John, 1710–59, British general

Forster, William Edward, 1818–86, British statesman

Fouché, Joseph, 1759?–1820, French revolutionist and politician

Fouquet, Nicolas, 1615–80, French statesman

Fox, Charles James, 1749–1806, British statesman

French, John, 1852–1925, British general

Gage, Thomas, 1721–87, English general

Gaitskell, Hugh Todd Naylor, 1903–63, British statesman

Gallieni, Joseph Simon, 1849–1916, French general

Gambetta, Léon, 1838–82, French statesman

Gandhi, Mohandas Karamchand, 1869–1948, Indian political leader

Garibaldi, Giuseppe, 1807–82, Italian soldier and patriot

Gasperi, Alcide de, 1881–1954, Italian statesman

Giraud, Henri Honoré, 1879–1949, French general

Gladstone, William Ewart, 1809–98, British statesman

Glendower, Owen, 1359?–1416?, Welsh leader

Gneisenau, August, Graf Neithardt von, 1760–1831, Prussian general

Goebbels, Paul Josef, 1897–1945, German Nazi leader

Goering, Herman Wilhelm, 1893–1946, German Nazi leader

Gordon, Charles George, 1833–85, British general

Grasse, François Joseph Paul, Comte de, 1722–88, French admiral

Grenville, Sir Richard, 1542?–91, English admiral

Grey, Charles, Earl Grey, 1764–1845, British statesman

Grey, Edward, Viscount Grey of Fallodon, 1862–1933, British statesman

Griffith, Arthur, 1872–1922, Irish statesman

Grouchy, Emmanuel, Marquis de, 1766–1847, French general                         (continued)

**WORLD LEADERS** (*continued*)

**Guesclin, Bertrand du,** 1320?–80, French general

**Guiscard, Robert,** 1015?–85, Norman-French soldier

**Guise, François de Lorraine, Duc de,** 1519–63, French general

**Guise, Henri de Lorraine, Duc de,** 1614–64, French general

**Guizot, François,** 1787–1874, French statesman

**Haig, Douglas, Earl Haig,** 1861–1928, British soldier

**Haldane, Richard Burdon, Viscount Haldane of Cloan,** 1856–1928, British statesman

**Hammarskjöld, Dag,** 1905–61, Swedish statesman, Secretary-General of the United Nations

**Hammurabi,** 1792–1750 B.C., King of Babylonia

**Hardenberg, Karl August, Fürst von,** 1750–1822, Prussian statesman

**Hardie, James Keir,** 1856–1915, British labor leader

**Harley, Robert, Earl of Oxford,** 1661–1724, English statesman

**Harun-al-Rashid,** 764?–809 A.D., Caliph of Islam

**Hastings, Warren,** 1732–1818, British statesman

**Havelock, Sir Henry,** 1795–1857, British general

**Hepburn, Mitchell Frederick,** 1869–1953, Canadian political leader

**Heraclius I,** 575?–641 A.D., Byzantine emperor

**Herriot, Édouard,** 1872–1957, French statesman

**Hindenburg, Paul von,** 1847–1934, German soldier and statesman

**Hitler, Adolf,** 1889–1945, German dictator

**Hofer, Andreas,** 1767–1810, Austrian patriot

**Hohenlohe-Schillingfürst, Chlodwig Karl Viktor, Fürst zu,** 1819–1901, German statesman

**Horthy de Nagybanya, Nicolas,** 1868–1957, Hungarian statesman

**Howard, Charles, Earl of Nottingham,** 1536–1624, English admiral

**Howard, Thomas, fourth Duke of Norfolk,** 1536–72, English general

**Howe, Richard, Earl Howe,** 1726–99, British admiral

**Howe, William, Viscount Howe,** 1729–1814, British general

**Hughes, William Morris,** 1864–1952, Australian statesman and labor leader

**Humphrey, Duke of Gloucester,** 1391–1447, English soldier and statesman

**Hunyadi, Janos,** 1385?–1456, Hungarian patriot

**Ibn Saud,** 1888?–1953, first king of Saudi Arabia

**Irene,** 752–803 A.D., Byzantine empress

**Ironside, William Edward, Baron Ironside,** 1880–1959, British general

**Isaacs, Sir Isaac Alfred,** 1855–1948, Australian jurist and statesman

**Ito, Prince Hirobumi,** 1841–1909, Japanese statesman

**Iturbide, Agustín de,** 1783–1824, Mexican revolutionist

**Jameson, Sir Leander Starr,** 1853–1917, British statesman

**Jaurès, Jean,** 1859–1914, French political leader

**Jehangir,** 1569–1627, Mogul emperor

**Jenghiz Khan,** 1167?–1227, Mongol conqueror

**Jinnah, Mahomed Ali,** 1876–1948, Pakistani statesman

**Joan of Arc,** 1412?–31, French religious and military leader

**Joffre, Joseph Jacques Césaire,** 1852–1931, French general

**John of Austria,** 1629–79, Spanish general and statesman

**John of Gaunt, Duke of Lancaster,** 1340–99, English soldier

**Johnson, Sir William,** 1715–74, British soldier

**Juárez, Benito,** 1806–72, Mexican statesman

**Kalb, Johann,** 1721–80, German soldier in the American Revolution

**Kalinin, Mikhail Ivanovich,** 1875–1946, Russian revolutionist

**Karolyi, Count Michael,** 1875–1955, Hungarian statesman

**Kassem, Abdul Karim,** 1914–63, Iraqui general and political leader

**Keitel, Wilhelm,** 1882–1946, German general

**Kesselring, Albert,** 1885–1960, German general

**Keyes, Sir Roger,** 1872–1945, British admiral

**King, William Lyon Mackenzie,** 1874–1950, Canadian statesman

**Kitchener, Horatio Herbert, Earl Kitchener of Khartoum,** 1850–1916, British general

**Kléber, Jean Baptiste,** 1753–1800, French general

**Kosciusko, Thaddeus,** 1746–1817, Polish soldier in the American Revolution

**Kossuth, Louis,** 1802–94, Hungarian patriot

**Kropotkin, Peter,** 1842–1921, Russian revolutionist

**Kruger, Stephanus Johannes Paulus,** 1825–1904, Boer statesman

**Kublai Khan,** 1215?–94, Mongol emperor

**Kutuzov, Mikhail Ilarionovich, Prince of Smolensk,** 1745–1813, Russian soldier

**Lafayette, Marie Jean P. G. du Motier, Marquis de,** 1757–1834, French statesman, and soldier in the American Revolution

**La Fontaine, Sir Louis Hippolyte,** 1807–64, Canadian statesman

**Lamb, Willam, Viscount Melbourne,** 1779–1848, British statesman

**Laval, Pierre,** 1883–1945, French political leader

**Lavalle, Juan,** 1797–1841, Argentine general

**Law, Andrew Bonar,** 1858–1923, British statesman

**Lawrence, Thomas Edward,** 1888–1935, British soldier and adventurer

**Lebrun, Albert,** 1871–1950, French statesman

**Leclerc, Jacques Philippe,** 1902–47, French general

**Lenin, Vladimir Ilyich,** 1870–1924, Russian revolutionist and statesman

**Lerma, Francisco Gómez de Sandoval y Rojas, Duque de,** 1532?–1623, Spanish statesman

**Liebknecht, Karl,** 1871–1919, German political leader

**Liebknecht, Wilhelm,** 1826–1900, German political leader

**Littleton, Sir Thomas,** 1422?–81, English jurist

**Litvinov, Maxim Maximovich,** 1876–1951, Russian statesman

**Lloyd George, David, Earl Lloyd George of Dwyfor,** 1863–1945, British statesman

**L'Ouverture, François Dominique Toussaint,** 1744?–1803, Haitian patriot

**Ludendorff, Erich,** 1865–1937, German general

**Lvov, Prince Georgi Yevgenyevich,** 1861–1925, Russian statesman

**Lyautey, Louis Hubert Gonzalve,** 1854–1934, French general

**Lytton, Victor Alexander, Earl of Lytton,** 1871–1947, British diplomat

**Macdonald, Sir John Alexander,** 1815–91, Canadian statesman

**MacDonald, Ramsay,** 1866–1937, British political leader

**Machado, Gerardo,** 1871–1939, Cuban political leader

**Mackenzie, Alexander,** 1822–92, Canadian statesman

**Madero, Francisco Indalecio,** 1873–1913, Mexican statesman

**Magsaysay, Ramon,** 1907–57, Filipino statesman

**Manfred,** 1232?–66, Sicilian king

**Mannerheim, Baron Carl Gustav Emil,** 1867–1951, Finnish general and statesman

**Marat, Jean Paul,** 1743–93, French revolutionist

**Marat, Joachim,** 1767–1815, French general

**Martí, José,** 1853–95, Cuban patriot

**Masaryk, Jan,** 1886–1948, Czechoslovakian statesman

**Masaryk, Thomas Garrigue,** 1850–1937, Czechoslovakian statesman

**Matsudaira, Tsuneo,** 1877–1949, Japanese statesman

**Matsukata, Prince Masoyochi,** 1835–1924, Japanese statesman

**Mazarin, Jules,** 1602–61, French statesman and cardinal

**Mazzini, Giovanni,** 1805–72, Italian patriot

**Medici, Cosimo de',** 1389–1464, Italian statesman

**Medici, Giovanni de',** 1498–1526, Italian soldier

**Medici, Lorenzo de',** 1449–92, Italian statesman

**Meighen, Arthur,** 1874–1960, Canadian statesman

**Metaxas, John,** 1871–1941, Greek soldier and statesman

**Metternich, Clemens Wenzel Nepomuk Lothar, Fürst von,** 1773–1859, Austrian statesman

**Millerand, Alexandre,** 1859–1943, French statesman

**Milner, Alfred, Viscount Milner,** 1854–1925, British statesman

**Mirabeau, Gabriel Honoré Riquetti, Comte de,** 1749–91, French statesman

**Miranda, Francisco de,** 1750–1816, Venezuelan revolutionist

**Mitre, Bartolomé,** 1821–1906, Argentine statesman

**Mohammed Ahmed Mahdi,** 1844–85, Moslem religious leader and soldier

**Mohammed Ali,** 1872–1925, Shah of Iran

**Moltke, Helmuth Karl Bernhard, Count von,** 1800–91, German general

**Montagu, Charles, Earl of Halifax,** 1661–1715, English statesman

**Montcalm, Louis Joseph de,** 1712–59, French general

**Montezuma,** 1480?–1520, Aztec emperor

**Montfort, Simon de,** 1160?–1218, Anglo-French general

**Montfort, Simon de,** 1208?–65, English soldier

**Morgan, Sir Henry,** 1635?–88, English pirate

**Mussolini, Benito,** 1883–1945, Italian dictator

**Nadir Shah,** 1688–1747, Iranian ruler

**Napier, Sir Charles James,** 1782–1853, British general

**Napoleon I,** 1769–1821, French emperor

**Nehru, Jawaharlal,** 1889–1964, Indian statesman

**Nelson, Horatio, Viscount Nelson,** 1758–1805, British admiral

**Nevsky, Alexander,** 1220–63, Russian leader

**Ney, Michel,** 1769–1815, French general

**Obregón, Álvaro,** 1880–1928, Mexican statesman

**O'Connell, Daniel,** 1775–1847, Irish nationalist

**O'Connor, Feargus,** 1794–1855, Irish patriot

**O'Connor, Thomas Power,** 1848–1929, Irish political leader

**Odoacer,** 435?–93 A.D., German chieftain

**Oglethorpe, James Edward,** 1696–1785, English general

**O'Higgins, Bernardo,** 1776–1842, Chilean revolutionist

**Oldenbarneveldt, Johann van,** 1547–1619, Dutch statesman

**Ollivier, Émile,** 1825–1913, French statesman

**Orlando, Vittorio Emmanuele,** 1860–1952, Italian statesman

**Orléans, Louis Philippe Joseph, Duc d',** 1747–93, French statesman

**Osmeña, Sergio,** 1878–1961, Filipino statesman

**Oyama, Iwao,** 1842–1916, Japanese general

**Pahlevi, Reza Shah,** 1877–1944, Shah of Iran

**Pangalos, Theodore,** 1878–1952, Greek soldier

**Parnell, Charles Stewart,** 1846–91, Irish statesman

**Pasha, Essad,** 1863–1920, Albanian dictator

**Pasha, Ismail,** 1830–95, Egyptian statesman

**Pasha, Tewfik,** 1852–92, Egyptian statesman

**Peel, Sir Robert,** 1788–1850, British statesman

**Périer, Casimir Pierre,** 1777–1832, French statesman

**Pétain, Henri Philippe,** 1856–1951, French general

**Pilsudski, Joseph,** 1867–1935, Polish soldier and statesman

**Pitt, William, Earl of Chatham,** 1708–78, British statesman

**Pitt, William,** 1759–1806, British statesman

**Pizarro, Francisco,** 1476?–1541, Spanish conquistador

**Plunkett, Sir Horace,** 1854–1932, Irish statesman

**Poincaré, Raymond,** 1860–1934, French statesman

**Potemkin, Grigori Aleksandrovich,** 1739–91, Russian general

**Primo de Rivera, Miguel,** 1870–1930, Spanish soldier and diplomat

**Pulaski, Casimir,** 1748?–79, Polish soldier in the American Revolution

**Quezon, Manuel Luis,** 1878–1944, Filipino statesman

**Quiroga, Juan Facundo,** 1790–1835, Argentine statesman

**Raeder, Erich,** 1876–1960, German admiral

**Raglan, Fitzroy James Henry Somerset, Baron Raglan,** 1788–1855, British general

**Raleigh, Sir Walter,** 1552?–1618, English statesman

**Ramsay, James Andrew Broun, Marquess of Dalhousie,** 1812–60, British statesman

**Rasputin, Grigori Yefimovich,** 1872–1916, Russian monk

**Rathenau, Walter,** 1867–1922, German statesman

(*continued*)

**WORLD LEADERS** (*continued*)

**Rhodes, Cecil John,** 1853–1902, South African statesman

**Rizal, José Mercado,** 1861–91, Filipino patriot

**Richelieu, Armand Jean du Plessis, Duc de,** 1585–1642, French statesman and cardinal

**Roberts, Frederick Sleigh, Earl of Kandahar and Waterford,** 1832–1914, British general

**Robespierre, Maximilien,** 1758–94, French revolutionist

**Rochambeau, Jean de Vimeur, Comte de,** 1725–1807, French general in the American Revolution

**Rodney, George Brydges, Baron Rodney,** 1719–92, British admiral

**Rohan, Henri, Duc de,** 1579–1638, French general

**Rommel, Erwin,** 1891–1944, German general

**Rundstedt, Karl Rudolf Gerd von,** 1875–1953, German general

**Russell, John, Earl Russell,** 1792–1878, British statesman

**Saint John, Henry, Viscount Bolingbroke,** 1678–1751, British statesman

**Saladin,** 1137?–93, Moslem ruler and general

**San Martín, José de,** 1778–1850, South American revolutionist

**Santa Anna, Antonio Lopéz de,** 1794–1876, Mexican soldier

**Santander, Francisco de Paula,** 1792–1840, Colombian revolutionist

**Saxe, Maurice, Comte de,** 1696–1750, French general

**Schlieffen, Alfred, Graf von,** 1833–1913, German general

**Séchelles, Marie Jean Hérault de,** 1759–94, French revolutionist

**Sforza, Count Carlo,** 1872–1952, Italian statesman

**Sharett, Moshe,** 1884–1965, Israeli statesman

**Shih Hwang-ti,** d. 210 B.C., Chinese emperor

**Smith, Donald Alexander, Baron Strathcona and Mount Royal,** 1820–1914, Canadian financier and political leader

**Smuts, Jan Christian,** 1870–1950, South African statesman

**Snowden, Philip, Viscount Snowden,** 1864–1937, British political leader

**Soult, Nicolas Jean de Dieu,** 1769–1851, French general

**Stalin, Josef Vissarionovich,** 1879–1953, Russian dictator

**Stambuliski, Alexander,** 1879–1923, Bulgarian statesman

**Stanley, Edward George, Earl of Derby,** 1799–1869, British statesman

**Steuben, Friedrich Wilhelm, Baron von,** 1730–94, Prussian soldier in the American Revolution

**Stolypin, Piotr Arkadevich,** 1863–1911, Russian statesman

**Stuart, James, Earl of Murray,** 1531–70, Scottish statesman

**Sturluson, Snorri,** 1178–1241, Icelandic ruler

**Stuyvesant, Peter,** 1610?–72, Dutch colonial administrator

**Sucre, Antonio José de,** 1795–1830, South American revolutionist

**Suleiman I (the Magnificent),** 1520–66, Ottoman ruler

**Sun Yat-sen,** 1866–1925, Chinese statesman

**Talleyrand-Périgord, Charles Maurice de,** 1754–1838, French statesman

**Tamerlane,** 1336?–1405, Mongol conqueror

**Taro, Prince Katsura,** 1847–1913, Japanese statesman

**Temple, Henry John, Viscount Palmerston,** 1784–1865, English statesman

**Theodoric the Great,** 454?–526 A.D., Ostrogoth ruler

**Thiers, Adolphe,** 1797–1877, French statesman

**Thomas, David Alfred, Viscount Rhonda,** 1856–1918, British poitical leader

**Thomson, Charles Edward Poulett, Baron Sydenham,** 1799–1841, British statesman

**Tirpitz, Alfred von,** 1849–1930, German admiral

**Tolly, Mikhail Barclay de,** 1761–1818, Russian general

**Tromp, Maarten Harpertzoon,** 1597–1653, Dutch admiral

**Trotsky, Leon,** 1879–1940, Russian revolutionist

**Trujillo Molina, Rafael Leonidas,** 1897–1961, Dominican dictator

**Tserklaes, Johannes, Count of Tilly,** 1559–1632, Bulgarian soldier

**Tupper, Sir Charles,** 1821–1915, Canadian statesman

**Turgot, Anne Robert Jacques,** 1727–81, French statesman

**Ubico, Jorge,** 1878–1946, Guatemalan dictator

**Vargas, Getúlio Dornelles,** 1883–1954, Brazilian statesman

**Venizelos, Eleutherios,** 1864–1936, Greek statesman

**Vercingetorix,** d. 46 B.C., Gallic chieftain

**Villiers, George William Frederick, Earl of Clarendon,** 1800–70, British statesman

**Vishinsky, Andrei Yanuarievich,** 1883–1954, Russian diplomat

**Waldensee, Alfred, Graf von,** 1832–1904, German general

**Wallenstein, Albrecht Wenzel Eusebius von,** 1583–1634, German soldier

**Walpole, Robert, Earl of Orford,** 1676–1745, British statesman

**Wavell, Archibald Percival, Earl Wavell,** 1883–1950, British general and statesman

**Webster, Richard, Viscount Alverstone,** 1842–1915, British jurist

**Weizmann, Chaim,** 1874–1952, Israeli statesman and scientist

**Wellesley, Arthur, Duke of Wellington,** 1769–1852, British general and statesman

**Wilberforce, William,** 1759–1833, British statesman

**Witte, Count Sergei Yulievich,** 1849–1915, Russian statesman

**Wolfe, James,** 1727–59, British soldier

**Wood, Edward, Earl Halifax,** 1881–1959, British diplomat and statesman

**Yamamoto, Count Gombei,** 1852–1933, Japanese admiral

**Yamamoto, Isoroku,** 1884–1943, Japanese admiral

**Yamashita, Tomoyuki,** 1888–1946, Japanese general

**Ypsilanti, Alexander,** 1792–1828, Greek soldier

**Yüan Shih-kai,** 1859–1912, Chinese statesman

**Zaïmis, Alexander,** 1855–1936, Greek statesman

# FIRSTS IN THE WORLD

The first use of *gunpowder* in Western warfare allegedly occurred at the Battle of Bannockburn in Scotland in 1314.

The *printing press* was first brought to North America by Juan Pablas of Spain, who set it up in Mexico City in 1539.

The word *"nicotine"* is derived from the name of Jean Nicot, French ambassador to Portugal, who helped in bringing the *tobacco* plant from the Americas to Europe in 1558.

The introduction of the practice of *smoking* to Europe is ascribed to Sir Walter Raleigh. His last wish before going to the scaffold in 1618 was to smoke a pipe.

The first *English colony* in America was Jamestown, Virginia.

The first known *brain surgery* in the world is accredited to two Hindu surgeons who operated on the skull of a Hindu king in 927. The surgeons used the drug *Samohini* as an anesthetic. The results of the operation are unknown.

*"America"* as a geographical designation was first used by Martin H. Waldseemüller in his *Cosmographiae Introductio,* published in April 1507. Giovanni Mateo, in 1506, made the first *map of the New World.*

The first *newspaper advertisement* in America appeared May 1, 1704, in the Boston *News-Letter.* Three ads were set in a four-inch column, with the word "Advertisement" above them. One was for a plantation, another offered a reward for the capture of a thief, and the third was a notice of the loss of two anvils.

The first successful *artificial heart* was developed at the Rockefeller Institute in New York City in 1935 by Dr. Alexis Carrel, assisted by Colonel Charles A. Lindbergh.

The first *North Pole flight* was made by Lieutenant Commander Richard Evelyn Byrd, U.S.N. and Floyd Bennett on May 9, 1926. In the *Josephine Ford,* a triple-engine Fokker monoplane, they flew from King's Bay, Spitzbergen, to the Pole and back nonstop. The flight covered 1,545 miles in 15 hours and 30 minutes.

The *Bachelor of Arts degree* was first conferred by European universities sometime in the 13th century. It took from four to six years to obtain a B.A. In the United States, the first Bachelor of Arts degree was conferred upon nine graduates of Harvard College, Cambridge, Massachusetts, on September 23, 1642.

The first known *battleship* was the *Rolf Krake,* designed for the Danish Navy by Capt. C. P. Coles of England in 1860. The first American battleship of importance was the *U.S.S. Maine,* authorized by an Act of Congress in 1886 and launched in 1890. A "mysterious" explosion in Havana Harbor, Cuba, destroyed her on February 15, 1898.

Joseph and Jacques Montgolfier, French inventors, developed the first practical *air balloon* in 1783. They sent up a large linen bag inflated with hot air at Annonay, near Lyons, France. The flight lasted ten minutes and covered more than a mile.

The first *child born of colonial parents* in America was Virginia Dare in 1587. The daughter of Ananias Dare and Eleanor White Dare, she was born at Roanoke Island, North Carolina.

The term *"boycott"* was derived from the name of Captain Charles Boycott, a ruthless land agent in County Mayo, Ireland, who was the victim of the first boycott.

The first *stock exchange* in the world was established in Antwerp between 1297 and 1353. The Amsterdam bourse, the European term for stock exchange, dates from after 1602. The first stock exchange in the United States was the New York Stock Exchange (1817).

The first building known as a *skyscraper* was a ten-story steel-skeleton building erected by the Home Insurance Company of New York at La Salle and Adams streets in Chicago, Illinois. Designed by Major William Le Baron Jenney, it was completed in the fall of 1885.

The first *telegraph line* in the world was established in 1794 and extended from Lille to Paris.

The first *newspaper cartoon* was "Join or Die," designed by Benjamin Franklin and published in Philadelphia, Pennsylvania, in his newspaper, the *Pennsylvania Gazette,* on May 9, 1754. Franklin's cartoon depicted a snake cut up into segments, each representing a colony.

The first *Roman Catholic priest to serve in Congress* was Gabriel Richard, 56 years old, who served as a Delegate from Michigan Territory in the Eighteenth Congress from March 4, 1823, to March 3, 1825.

The first *circus* in America was owned by John Bill Ricketts and was known as Ricketts' Circus. It first performed in 1792.

The first *university* in the world was the University of Salerno, said to have been founded in the ninth century.

The first *women's college* in America was Mount Holyoke Seminary, South Hadley, Massachusetts, chartered in 1836. Its first principal was Mary Lyon, who served until 1849.

The first *Congresswoman* elected to the House of Representatives was Jeannette Rankin. She was elected as a Republican by Montana and served from 1917 to 1919, and again from 1941 to 1943.

*Daylight Saving Time,* sponsored by the National Daylight Saving Association, was first put into operation in the United States on Easter Sunday, March 31, 1918.

The first *Doctor of Philosophy degrees* awarded in America were conferred in 1861 upon three Yale University students.

Probably the world's first *dictionary* was published by Hu Shin of China, in 150 B.C. It contained 10,000 characters. The first European dictionary was one in Italian published by the *Academia della Crusca* in 1626. The first dictionary published in the United States was *The Royal Standard English Dictionary, the First American Dictionary,* by William Perry, lecturer at the Academy at Edinburgh, Scotland. It was printed in 1788 in Worcester, Massachusetts.

The first *general* in the U.S. Army was George Washington, appointed June 15, 1775, by the Second Continental Congress. Washington's

(continued)

**FIRSTS IN THE WORLD** (continued)

salary was $500 a month, including expenses.
The first *electrocution* of a human being in
America was that of William Kemmler, alias
John Hart, on August 6, 1890, at Auburn Prison,
Auburn, New York. The electric chair used was
invented by Dr. Alphonse David Rockwell.

The first *gasoline automobile* in the world was
the Panhard, and it incorporated many of the
features of modern cars. It appeared in 1894.

The first *woman governor* of a state was
Nellie T. Ross, inaugurated governor of Wyoming to fill the unexpired term of her husband,
William Bradford Ross, on January 5, 1925.
Miriam Amanda ("Ma") Ferguson of Texas
was inaugurated governor of Texas on January
10, 1925.

The first *Labor Day* holiday occurred in 1869
when the Knights of Labor, an organization in
Philadelphia, Pennsylvania, took the day off. It
became an annual holiday in 1884 when the
American Federation of Labor resolved in convention at Chicago, Illinois, "that the first Monday in September be set aside as a laborer's
national holiday."

The first *Father's Day* celebration was sponsored by the Ministerial Association and the
YMCA of Spokane, Washington, on June 19,
1910. The idea originated with Mrs. John Bruce
Dodd of Spokane.

The first *Mother's Day* was suggested by Miss
Anna Jarvis of Philadelphia, Pennsylvania, in
1907. Mother's Day received national recognition May 12, 1914.

The *lightning rod* was invented in 1749 by
Benjamin Franklin, who installed it on his home
in Philadelphia, Pennsylvania.

The first *medical college* in the United States
was the College of Philadelphia, Department of
Medicine, now the University of Pennsylvania
School of Medicine, first established in Philadelphia, Pennsylvania, in 1765.

The first *moving pictures* in color were shown
by Thomas Alva Edison in 1895 at the Cotton
States Exposition in Atlanta, Georgia. One of
the pictures was "Annabelle, the Dancer." The
film was hand-colored at West Orange, New
Jersey, in 1894.

The first *newspapers* in the world were circulated in German towns during the 15th century.
The news sheets were sent out in the form of
letters. The first English newspaper was *A Cur-
rant of Newes*, published by Nathaniel Battler
in June 1622. The first newspaper in the United
States was *The Present State of the New English
Affairs*, a broadside, published in 1689 by Samuel
Green in Cambridge, Massachusetts.

The first development of *hydroelectric power*
in the world was at Niagara Falls, New York,
in 1877.

The first *Nobel Prize* awarded to an American
was granted to President Theodore Roosevelt in
1906 for his service in the cause of world peace.

The first *novel* published in America was *The
Power of Sympathy or the Triumph of Nature
Founded in Truth*, dedicated to "the young
ladies of America." The author used the nom de
plume "Philenia." It was printed in two volumes
in 1789 in Boston, Massachusetts.

The first *novel* to win the Pulitzer Prize in letters was *His Family* by Ernest Poole, published
in 1917 by the Macmillan Company, New York
City.

The first *patent* granted by the U.S. government
was issued to Samuel Hopkins of Vermont on
July 31, 1790, for the process of making a
fertilizer. The document bore the signatures of
George Washington, President; Thomas Jefferson, Secretary of State; and Edmund Randolph,
Attorney General.

The first *magazine* published in America was
*The American Magazine, or a Monthly View
of the Political State of the British Colonies*. Its
first issue probably appeared February 13, 1741,
in Philadelphia, Pennsylvania, about three days
before Benjamin Franklin's *The General Magazine and Historical Chronicle for All British
Plantations in America*.

The first *news photographer* in America was
Mathew Brady of New York City, who followed
the Union Army and photographed it in action.
He took more than 7,000 pictures, 2,000 of
which were purchased by the Federal government for $25,000.

The *safety pin* was invented by Walter Hunt of
New York City, who received a patent for it in
1849.

The first U.S. *Presidential Mansion* was at No.
1 Cherry Street, the Franklin House, in New
York City, occupied by President and Mrs.
George Washington from 1789 to 1790. It
originally was the home of Samuel Osgood.

The first *prison* constructed in America was
built in 1676 in Nantucket, Massachusetts.

The first *railroad* for commercial and passenger
use in the United States was the Baltimore and
Ohio Railroad Company, incorporated in Maryland in 1827.

The first regular *transatlantic service* was initiated in 1818 by the Black Ball Line of England. The company used fast sailing ships between New York and Liverpool.

The first known *soap* to float was manufactured
in 1878 by the Procter & Gamble Company,
Cincinnati, Ohio. Until 1879 it was known as
"White Soap." Its name was then changed to
"Ivory Soap."

The first *spa* known to the Western world was
the mineral springs in Spa, Belgium. The first
spa in America opened in 1756 in Berkeley
Springs, West Virginia, and was visited by
George Washington.

The first *submarine* actually used in combat was
the *American Turtle*, built by David Bushnell
of Saybrook, Connecticut, in 1776.

The first *atomic-powered submarine* was the
*Nautilus*, built by the Electric Boat Company,
a division of the General Dynamics Corporation,
Groton, Connecticut. It was commissioned in
1954 and tested under nuclear power in 1955.

The first underground *subway* in the world was
opened in London in 1863. The first city in the
United States to build a subway was Boston, in
1895.

*The first Indian to serve as Vice President of the
United States* was Charles Curtis of Kansas, who
served under President Herbert C. Hoover, from
1929 to 1933. Curtis was of Shawnee descent.

## CHRONOLOGY OF HISTORIC ASSASSINATIONS

**Julius Caesar,** *Roman statesman and general:* his dictatorial powers had aroused great resentment and on March 15, 44 B.C., he was stabbed to death in the Roman senate by Cimber, Brutus, Cassius, Casca, and others.

**Caligula,** *Roman emperor:* said to be insane, he was assassinated by an officer of the Praetorian Guard in 41 A.D.

**Claudius I,** *Roman emperor:* he was poisoned in 54 A.D. by his fourth wife, Agrippina, after he promised the crown to Nero, her son by a former marriage.

**Saint Thomas à Becket,** *Archbishop of Canterbury:* he was murdered in Canterbury cathedral by a band of armed men. King Henry II, Becket's close friend for many years, was indirectly responsible for the martyr's death on December 19, 1170.

**Alessandro de' Medici,** *Duke of Florence:* he was stabbed to death by a hired assassin of Lorenzo de' Medici on January 5, 1537.

**Lord Henry Darnley,** *a claimant to the throne of England and husband of Mary Queen of Scots:* he was strangled in Edinburgh on February 10, 1567. Details of his murder remain an historical mystery.

**William the Silent (William of Orange),** *Dutch statesman and principal founder of Dutch independence:* he was assassinated at Delft on July 10, 1584, by a French Roman Catholic fanatic.

**Henry III,** *King of France:* a weak, debauched, and unscrupulous king, he was stabbed to death in 1589 by Jacques Clément, a French Dominican monk who thought Henry a threat to Catholicism.

**Christopher Marlowe,** *English dramatist and poet:* he was killed in 1593 in a barroom brawl by a drinking companion. His death may have been carefully plotted since Marlowe was known to have been a government agent.

**Henry IV,** *King of France and of Navarre:* he was stabbed to death by François Ravaillac, a religious fanatic, on May 14, 1610, just as he was preparing for war against the Spanish and Austrian Hapsburgs.

**Wallenstein (Albrecht Wenzel Eusebius von Waldstein),** *a general in the Thirty Years War and later a German noble:* he was accused of treason, and murdered on February 25, 1634.

**James Sharp,** *Scottish archbishop:* he was intensely hated for his persecution of non-Episcopalians. On May 3, 1679, he was beaten to death by his enemies.

**Peter III,** *Tsar of Russia:* he was forced to abdicate by his wife (later Empress Catherine II), and a few days later, on July 17, 1762, his guards, led by Aleksey Orlov, assassinated him.

**Gustavus III,** *King of Sweden:* he was assassinated at a masked ball on March 29, 1792, by a representative of the nobles who resented the king's absolute power.

**Jean Paul Marat,** *a French revolutionist:* he indirectly caused the September massacres of 1792 in France. On July 13, 1793, he was stabbed to death by Charlotte Corday, who believed that Marat was the evil genius of France.

**Jean Baptiste Kléber,** *French general:* he was left in command of Cairo when Napoleon returned to France and subsequently defeated the Turks at Heliopolis. On June 14, 1800, he was assassinated by a Turkish fanatic in Cairo.

**Paul I,** *Tsar of Russia:* his apparent insanity led to an attempt by the nobles to force his abdication. When the effort failed, the conspirators strangled him on March 24, 1801.

**Abraham Lincoln,** *16th President of the United States:* he was shot by a Southern fanatic, John Wilkes Booth, while attending a performance at Ford's Theater on April 14, 1865.

**Abdu-l-Aziz,** *Ottoman sultan:* he was overthrown by a member of the liberal opposition party and a few days later, on June 4, 1876, he died, apparently by an assassin's hand.

**Alexander II,** *Tsar of Russia:* he was assassinated on March 13, 1881, by a member of The People's Will, a Russian terrorist group.

**James Abram Garfield,** *20th President of the United States:* he was constantly harassed by office seekers and met his death through one of them. On July 2, 1881, he was shot by Charles J. Guiteau. Garfield died in September 1881.

**Nasr-ed-Din,** *Shah of Iran:* he was assassinated by one of his subjects, Mullah Reza, on May 1, 1896.

**Elizabeth,** *Empress of Austria and Queen of Hungary:* she was assassinated in 1898 by the Italian anarchist Luccheni, in Geneva.

**Humbert I,** *King of Italy:* he escaped two attempts on his life but fell victim to the third. He was killed by Gaetano Bresci in 1900.

**William McKinley,** *25th President of the United States:* on the day after addressing the Pan-American Exposition at Buffalo, New York, he was shot down by an anarchist, Leon Czolgosz, September 6, 1901. He died eight days later.

**Alexander,** *King of Serbia:* on June 11 or 10, 1903, he and his Queen, Draga, were assassinated by a clique of officers.

**Carlos I,** *King of Portugal:* he gained notoriety by his extravagance and licentiousness. Discontent grew and on February 1, 1908, the King and Crown Prince were assassinated in the streets of Lisbon.

**Prince Hirobumi Ito,** *Japanese statesman, Prime Minister of Japan:* he forced an agreement in 1905 making Korea a virtual protectorate of Japan and became resident general there. He was assassinated October 26, 1909, by a Korean.

**Piotr Arkadevich Stolypin,** *Russian statesman and premier:* he sought to suppress revolutionary movements in Russia. He was assassinated by a terrorist on September 14, 1911.

**Francisco I. Madero,** *Mexican statesman and President of Mexico:* he was shot at the order of General Victoriano Huerta, commander of the government's forces, on February 23, 1913.

**George I,** *King of Greece:* he was assassinated shortly before the outbreak of the second Balkan War, on March 18, 1913.

**Francis Ferdinand,** *Austrian archduke and heir apparent to the throne of Austria-Hungary:* he and his wife were assassinated by Gavrilo Princip, a Serbian nationalist, at Sarajevo on

(continued)

## HISTORIC ASSASSINATIONS (*continued*)

June 28, 1914. His death was the occasion for the Austrian ultimatum to Serbia which led to World War I.

**Jean L. Jaurès,** *French Socialist leader and historian:* he advocated arbitration instead of war and on July 31, 1914, he was assassinated by a fanatic patriot.

**Grigori Y. Rasputin,** *Russian monk:* he was a notorious figure in the court of Nicholas II and hated for his patronage and immorality. He was killed in December 1916 by conspirators, some of whom belonged to the highest nobility.

**Emiliano Zapata,** *Mexican revolutionist:* he was assassinated in 1919 by agents of President Venustiano Carranza.

**Sir Henry Hughes Wilson,** *British Field Marshal:* he was killed by Irish terrorists in London on June 22, 1922.

**Walter Rathenau,** *German industrialist, social theorist, and statesman, foreign minister of Germany:* he was assassinated by nationalist fanatics on June 24, 1922.

**Francisco Villa (Pancho Villa),** *Mexican revolutionist:* he was assassinated on July 20, 1923.

**Michael Collins,** *Irish revolutionary leader:* he was assassinated by Sinn Fein irregulars on August 22, 1922, near Brandon in County Cork.

**Giacomo Matteotti,** *Italian Socialist leader and anti-Fascist:* he was murdered by Fascist hirelings on June 10, 1924.

**Álvaro Obregón,** *President of Mexico:* he was involved in a long and bitter quarrel with the Church and on July 17, 1928, shortly before taking office for another term, he was assassinated by a Roman Catholic fanatic.

**Sergei Mironovich Kirov,** *Russian Communist leader:* he was murdered in 1934 by Leonid Nikolayev at the instance of Joseph Stalin.

**Ernst Roehm,** *German National Socialist leader and rival of Hitler:* he was murdered in the "blood purge" of June 30, 1934.

**Engelbert Dollfuss,** *Austrian statesman and Chancellor:* he aligned himself with Austrian fascists. On July 25, 1934, Dollfuss was brutally assassinated by Austrian Nazis.

**Alexander,** *King of Yugoslavia;* and **Jean Louis Barthou,** *French foreign minister:* both were killed at Marseilles during the king's state visit to France on October 9, 1934, by a member of a Croatian terrorist organization.

**Huey P. Long,** *Governor of Louisiana and U.S. Senator from Louisiana:* he was assassinated on September 8, 1935, by Dr. Carl A. Weiss, who was immediately slain by Long's bodyguards.

**Leon Trotsky,** *Russian revolutionist:* exiled from Russia in 1929, he finally settled in Mexico City in 1937, where he was assassinated on August 21, 1940, by Spanish-born Ramón Mercader, an agent of Joseph Stalin.

**Jean François Darlan,** *French admiral and commander of the French navy:* he assumed control over French Africa and exercised authoritarian rule there until he was assassinated by a French anti-fascist at Algiers, December 24, 1942.

**Lord Moyne (Walter Edward Guinness),** *British High Commissioner to the Middle East:* he was assassinated in Cairo by two Israeli terrorists on November 6, 1944.

**Ahmed Maher Pasha,** *Premier of Egypt:* he was assassinated on February 24, 1945, after announcing Egypt's declaration of war against the Axis powers.

**Gualberto Villarroel,** *President of Bolivia:* he was killed and his regime overthrown by rebellious workers, soldiers, and students on July 21, 1946.

**U Aung San,** *Premier of Burma:* he and five members of his provisional government were assassinated by political opponents on July 19, 1947.

**Mohandas Karamchand Gandhi,** *Indian political leader:* he was shot January 30, 1948, while holding a prayer and pacification meeting at New Delhi, by Natheram Jodre, a Hindu who blamed Gandhi for the partition of India.

**Count Folke Bernadotte,** *Swedish internationalist and United Nations mediator in Palestine:* he was assassinated by Israeli terrorists on September 17, 1948.

**Jorge E. Gaitán,** *Colombian liberal leader:* his assassination in 1948 provoked riots in Bogotá.

**Abdullah (Abdullah ibn Husein),** *King of Jordan:* he was assassinated in Jerusalem, July 20, 1951.

**Liaquat Ali Khan,** *Indian political leader and first prime minister of Pakistan:* he was assassinated on October 16, 1951, by Said Akbar, a Moslem fanatic.

**José Antonio Rémon,** *President of Panama:* he was shot down by machine-gun fire while at a race track in Panama on January 2, 1955.

**Anastasio Somoza,** *President of Nicaragua:* his dictatorial rule ended when he was shot down on September 21, 1956, and died eight days later.

**Carlos Armas,** *President of Guatemala:* he was shot and killed by one of his personal guards in Guatemala City, July 26, 1957.

**Feisal II,** *King of Iraq:* he was killed on July 14, 1958, when a revolution led by Abdul Karim Kassem overthrew the Iraqi monarchy.

**Solomon Bandaranaike,** *Prime Minister of Ceylon:* he was assassinated by Buddhist extremists on September 25, 1959.

**Rafael L. Trujillo,** *dictator and President of the Dominican Republic:* he was assassinated on May 30, 1961.

**Patrice Lumumba,** *Prime Minister of the Republic of the Congo:* he was dismissed by President Kasavubu and placed under house arrest. He escaped, was recaptured, and, in January 1961, flown to Katanga. In February of that year it was announced that he had been killed.

**Mohammed Khemisti,** *Algerian foreign minister:* he was shot, and died on May 5, 1963.

**Ngo Dinh Diem,** *President of the Republic of Vietnam:* he was assassinated in a military coup d'etat on November 1–2, 1963.

**John F. Kennedy,** *35th President of the United States:* he was shot down by Lee Harvey Oswald on November 22, 1963, in Dallas, Texas.

**Pierre Ngendandumwe,** *Premier of Burundi:* he was assassinated on January 15, 1965, by unknown murderers.

**Hassan Ali Mansour,** *Premier of Iran:* he was killed on January 26, 1965, by a Moslem fanatic.

**Hendrik F. Verwoerd,** *Prime Minister of South Africa:* he was stabbed to death in Parliament on September 6, 1966, by Dimitri Stifianos.

# DISASTERS

## Earthquakes and Avalanches · Storms · Aircraft Rail, and Marine Disasters · Fires and Explosions

Hurricane Beulah's winds washed these two shrimp boats aground at Port Isabel, Texas, Sept. 20, 1967.

*United Press Int'l.*

## MAJOR DISASTERS: 1967

Throughout history the forces of nature and human error have persisted as the causes of disasters. In 1967, fires, storms, floods, and earthquakes left their dreaded marks on various parts of the world. The year's greatest disaster directly attributable to man was the fire that crippled the U.S. Navy's aircraft carrier *Forrestal* (see next page).

Although most of 1967's hurricanes remained comfortably far out at sea, Hurricane Beulah raged through the West Indies in mid-September with winds up to 140 miles per hour, and then struck Southern Texas, where it caused heavy flooding.

On August 15 the Chena River in Alaska peaked at seven feet above flood level, inundating the city of Fairbanks. About 7,000 residents were evacuated to high ground at the nearby University of Alaska, and another 4,000 were moved to Anchorage, 260 miles to the south. Damage to Fairbanks was extensive, and major rehabilitation efforts were begun immediately after the flood subsided so that the city could be back on its feet before the start of the deep winter freeze (see photograph on page 574).

Another major disaster on the North American continent was the series of forest fires that ravaged the Pacific Northwest in August and September (see page 580).

A devastating series of earthquakes occurred in Turkey during late July. Destruction wracked six provinces from the Black Sea to the Aegean coast. Hardest hit was the small city of Adapazari, about 80 miles southeast of Istanbul. Roughly one-quarter of the city was heavily damaged by tremors on July 22. A total of 213 people were killed in the Turkish quakes.

## FIRE ON THE FORRESTAL

United Press Int'l.

Fire and explosions crippled the U.S. aircraft carrier **Forrestal**, on duty off the coast of Vietnam, July 29, 1967. The ship's 83-plane air wing was destroyed, and 129 men were killed or missing.

It was 10:53 A.M. on July 29, 1967, and the giant aircraft carrier *Forrestal*, on duty in the Gulf of Tonkin, had just swung into the wind. Its flight deck was crowded with planes, engines idling, preparing for their 11:00 A.M. takeoff for strikes against North Vietnam. Suddenly there was an explosion, followed by a chain of blasts. Before anybody knew what had happened, the entire four-acre flight deck was engulfed in flames.

An A-4 Skyhawk had experienced what is called an extreme "wet start"—a short burst of flame from the exhaust as the engine is started. The flame leaped several yards, igniting a missile carried by an adjacent plane. The missile went off, slamming into the fuel tank of a third plane. The highly volatile jet fuel began splashing across the deck and burst into flame, thus starting a chain reaction. In a few seconds, bombs and rockets burst into balls of fire and chunks of shrap-

nel. Planes disintegrated, and crewmen disappeared behind walls of fire.

The ship's rescue crew responded immediately, manning fire hoses and carrying the wounded to safety. Members of all sections of the crew soon joined in the rescue operation, performing what the *Forrestal's* skipper, Captain John Beling, called acts of outstanding bravery.

But flames were burning through six of the ship's ten decks, and exploding bombs were making huge craters in the flight deck. The *Forrestal's* 83-plane air wing was wiped out, 129 men were dead or missing, and hundreds more were wounded.

Forced to leave its battle station, the *Forrestal* made its way to the U.S. base at Subic Bay in the Philippines to undergo extensive repairs.

The disaster was the worst in U.S. Naval history since the end of World War II.

# WORLD EARTHQUAKES AND AVALANCHES

Great earthquakes usually begin with slight tremors, rapidly take the form of one or more violent jolts, and end in vibrations of gradually diminishing force. They are most commonly caused by the shock given the Earth's surface when a fault occurs; a fault is a rupture in the Earth's crust due to subterranean strain.

The source of an earthquake is called the focus and it is commonly located at some distance below the surface of the land; the point on the surface directly above the focus is called the epicenter, the area of greatest devastation.

The intensity of an earthquake is measured by the Richter scale. The scale, named for Charles F. Richter of the California Institute of Technology, is a measure of the energy of an earthquake at its source. The scale is logarithmic, so that, for example, a recording of 7 signifies a disturbance 10 times as powerful as a recording of 6. The Good Friday earthquake of 1964 in Alaska was the most violent in North America, with a scale value of 8.3. Earthquakes with a Richter value of 6 or more are commonly considered major in proportion. There are perhaps as many as 10,000 earthquakes a year on Earth, of which about 50 are of great magnitude.

The scientific study of earthquakes is called seismology; instruments used to detect and record seismic disturbances are known as seismographs or seismometers. When tremors of the Earth occur, the pendulum or the magnet of the seismograph, because of inertia, remains still as the Earth moves beneath; the force of the tremor is accurately recorded on a graph.

Efforts to develop a system that might give warning of coming earthquakes are particularly widespread among seismologists in the United States and Japan. Sensitive instruments—called strain seismometers—have been developed to measure the accumulating strain in the Earth's crust—a strain that might produce a subterranean rupture and a resultant earthquake.

| DATE | PLACE | DEATHS * | EXPLANATION |
|---|---|---|---|
| 365, July 21 | Mediterranean area................ | 1,000 | Earthquake induced tidal wave. |
| 526, May 20 | Antioch, Syria.................... | 250,000 | Earthquake. |
| 546, Aug. 15– Sept. 23 | Constantinople, Thrace, Nicomedia, Bithynia.......................... | — | Recurring earthquakes caused heavy damage and loss of life; Nicomedia almost leveled. |
| 550, Oct. 6–16 | Constantinople, Thrace............ | — | Earthquakes destroyed many historic buildings. |
| 551, July 9 | Beirut, Syria....................... | — | Destroyed by earthquake. |
| 856, Dec. | Corinth, Greece.................... | 45,000 | Earthquake. |
| 936 | Constantinople.................... | — | Destroyed by earthquake. |
| 1268 | Cilicia, Asia Minor................ | 60,000 | Earthquake. |
| 1290, Sept. 27 | Chihli, China...................... | 100,000 | Earthquake. |
| 1293, May 20 | Kamakura, Japan.................. | 30,000 | Earthquake. |
| 1531, Jan. 26 | Lisbon, Portugal................... | 30,000 | Earthquake. |
| 1556, Jan. 24 | Shensi, China..................... | 800,000 | Earthquake. |
| 1667 | Shemakha, East Azerbaijan......... | 80,000 | Earthquake. |
| 1703, Dec. 30 | Tokyo, Japan...................... | 200,000 | Earthquake. |
| 1737, Oct. 11 | Calcutta, India.................... | 300,000 | Earthquake. |
| 1755, June 7 | Northern Persia.................... | 40,000 | Earthquake. |
| 1755, Nov. 1 | Lisbon, Portugal................... | 60,000 | Earthquake destroyed most of city. |
| 1783, Feb. 4 | Southern Italy and Sicily........... | 60,000– 100,000 | Wide-ranging earthquake; Messina ravaged. |
| 1797, Feb. 4 | Cuzco, Peru, and Quito, Ecuador.... | 40,000 | Earthquakes destroyed cities. |
| 1811, Dec. 6–1812, Jan. 23, Feb. 7 | North American continent......... | — | Earthquake, greatest on continent, felt on more than a 2-million-square-mile area. |
| 1822, Sept. 5 | Aleppo, Syria..................... | 22,000 | Earthquake. |
| 1828, Dec. 28 | Honshu, Japan.................... | 30,000 | Earthquake. |
| 1868, Aug. 13–16 | Peru and Ecuador................. | 25,000 | Earthquakes razed towns in southern Peru and northern Ecuador; loss of $300 million. |
| 1875, May 16 | Venezuela and Colombia........... | 16,000 | Earthquakes. |
| 1884, Apr. 22 | Colchester, England................ | — | Earthquake destroyed city. |
| 1896 | Sanriku Coast, Japan.............. | 28,000 | Earthquakes and tidal wave destroyed 6,000 houses. |
| 1896, Aug. 16 | Ecuador and Peru................. | 70,000 | Earthquake. |
| 1897, June 12 | Assam, India...................... | 1,542 | Earthquake. |
| 1906, Apr. 16 | Chile, principally Santiago and Valparaiso...................... | 5,000 | Earthquake; $100 million loss. |
| 1906, Apr. 18 | San Francisco, California.......... | 700 | Earthquake followed by fire; $500 million loss. |
| 1908, Dec. 28 | Southern Italy and Sicily........... | 96,000 | Earthquake. |
| 1915, Jan. 13 | Central Italy...................... | 30,000 | Earthquake. |
| 1920, Dec. 16 | Kansu, China..................... | 180,000 | Earthquake destroyed ten cities. |
| 1923, Sept. 1 | Yokohama and Tokyo, Japan........ | 200,000 | Earthquake destroyed all of Yokohama and half of Tokyo. |
| 1932, Dec. 26 | Kansu, China..................... | 70,000 | Earthquakes. |
| 1933, Mar. 10 | Long Beach, California............. | 115 | Earthquake; loss of about $40 million. |
| 1935, May 31 | Quetta, Baluchistan, India......... | 50,000 | Earthquake. |
| 1939, Jan. 24 | Chile............................. | 30,000 | Earthquake. |
| 1939, Dec. 27 | Anatolia, Turkey.................. | 45,000 | Series of earthquakes followed by floods. |
| 1946, Dec. 21 | Southern Japan................... | 1,000 | Strong subterranean earthquake and six tidal waves wrecked 60,000 square miles. |

* Estimated.

(continued)

## EARTHQUAKES AND AVALANCHES (*continued*)

| DATE | PLACE | DEATHS * | EXPLANATION |
|---|---|---|---|
| 1948, June 28 | Honshu, Japan.................... | 3,200 | Earthquake followed by fire destroyed most of Fukai and surrounding towns. |
| 1949, Aug. 5 | Ecuador......................... | 6,000 | Earthquake heavily damaged 50 towns; 100,000 homeless; $20 million loss. |
| 1950, Aug. 15 | Assam, India..................... | 1,500 | Earthquake and widespread flooding. |
| 1953, Feb. 12 | Eastern Iran..................... | 1,100 | Earthquake destroyed town of Trud. |
| 1953, Mar. 18 | Northwestern Turkey............. | 1,200 | Earthquake; 50,000 homeless. |
| 1954, Sept. 9–12 | Algeria.......................... | 1,600 | Earthquake destroyed most of Orléansville. |
| 1956, June 10–17 | Northern Afghanistan............ | 2,000 | Series of earthquakes. |
| 1957, July 2 | Iran............................. | 1,500 | Earthquakes along shores of Caspian Sea. |
| 1957, Dec. 13, 15–17 | Western Iran..................... | 1,400 | Earthquakes. |
| 1960, Feb. 29 and Mar. 1 | Agadir, Morocco.................. | 20,000 | Earthquake, tidal wave, and fire destroyed most of port. |
| 1960, May 21–29 | Chile............................ | 5,700 | Earthquake and resulting tidal waves in southern coastal areas. |
| 1962, Jan. 10 | Peru............................ | 2,000 | Avalanche on Huascarán, extinct volcano. |
| 1962, Sept. 1 | Northwestern Iran............... | 12,403 | Earthquake. |
| 1963, July 26 | Skoplje, Yugoslavia.............. | 1,011 | Earthquake destroyed most of city. |
| 1964, Mar. 27 | Alaska.......................... | 114 | Earthquake caused property damage estimated at $750 million; entire downtown area of Anchorage leveled. |
| 1965, Mar. 28 | Near Santiago, Chile............. | 400 | Earthquake. |
| 1965, Aug. 30 | Saas-Fee, Switzerland........... | 107 | Avalanche. |
| 1966, Jan. 11–13 | Rio de Janeiro, Brazil........... | 300 | Landslide caused by record rain |
| 1966, Feb. 5 | Greece, Eurytania district......... | 1 | Three earthquakes; 10 villages destroyed; 4,500 homeless. |
| 1966, Mar. 7 | Ankara, Turkey.................. | 15 | Earthquakes. |
| 1966, Mar. 19 | Uganda......................... | 79 | Earthquake. |
| 1966, May 15 | Tashkent, U.S.S.R............... | 10 | Earthquakes. |
| 1966, May 22 | Léopoldville, The Congo......... | 90 | Earth tremors. |
| 1966, Aug. 19 | Mus, Erzurum, Bingol Provinces, Turkey...................... | 3,000 | Earthquake; 1,000,000 homeless. |
| 1966, Oct. 17 | Lima and Callao, Peru........... | 100 | Earthquake; hundreds hurt; heavy damage. |
| 1966, Oct. 21 | Aberfan, Wales.................. | 131 | Avalanche of coal waste engulfed schoolhouse, farm, and 13 homes, killing mostly children. |
| 1967, Feb. 9 | Colombia........................ | 100 | Earthquake; worst in 50 years. |
| 1967, Mar. 19 | Caraguatatuba, Brazil........... | 160 | Landslide caused by flood. |
| 1967, July 22 | Turkey.......................... | 213 | Three earthquakes east of Istanbul. |
| 1967, July 31 | Venezuela....................... | 110 | Earthquake extending from Andes to Caribbean Sea. |

## MAJOR VOLCANIC ERUPTIONS

| DATE | PLACE | DEATHS * | REMARKS |
|---|---|---|---|
| 79 A.D., Aug. 24–26 | Pompeii and Herculaneum, Italy... | 2,000 | Mount Vesuvius erupted; destroyed both towns. |
| 1631, Dec. 16 | Italy............................ | 4,000 | Mount Vesuvius erupted; destroyed 15 towns. |
| 1693, Jan. 11 | Sicily........................... | 60,000 | Mount Etna erupted and either partially or wholly destroyed 40 towns. |
| 1772............ | Java............................ | 3,000 | Volcano blew up and lost about 4,000 feet in height. |
| 1783............ | Iceland......................... | 9,000 | Mount Hekla erupted; 20 villages obliterated by lava and many more flooded by water. |
| 1815............ | Java............................ | 12,000 | Tamboro exploded, followed by violent whirlwinds and tidal waves. |
| 1882............ | Java............................ | 4,000 | Galingoon erupted twice, four days apart, followed by a violent earthquake; 100 villages devastated. |
| 1883, Aug. 26–28 | East Indies ..................... | 35,000 | Krakatoa erupted; most of the islands destroyed; Java and Sumatra heavily damaged by tidal wave. |
| 1902, Apr. 8 | Guatemala....................... | 1,000 | Santa Maria erupted. |
| 1902, May 8 | Martinique, West Indies......... | 40,000 | Mount Pelée erupted, wiping out the city of St. Pierre. |
| 1906, Apr. | Italy............................ | — | A series of eruptions by Mount Vesuvius destroyed several towns. |
| 1919 | Java............................ | 5,000 | Mount Kelud erupted; 100 villages destroyed. |
| 1951, Jan. 18–21 | New Guinea..................... | 3,000 | Mount Lamington erupted. |
| 1963, Mar. 20 | Bali............................ | 1,500 | Mount Agung erupted, leaving 85,000 homeless. |
| 1964, Mar. and Apr. | Chile............................ | — | Villarrica erupted, routing 30,000 persons and causing heavy damage. |
| 1965, Sept. 28. | Philippines..................... | 500 | Mt. Taal, on Luzon, erupted for the first time in 54 years. |
| 1966, Apr. 28 | Java............................ | 150 | Mount Kelut erupted; nine villages destroyed. |
| 1966, Aug. 12 | Sangi Island, Indonesia.......... | 28 | Mount Awu erupted. |

* Estimated.

## TORNADOES

A tornado is a violently rotating column of air several hundred yards in diameter, nearly always visible as a funnel-shaped cloud associated with a severe thunderstorm. As the tornado moves along with its parent cloud, the funnel occasionally dips to the ground, leaving almost complete destruction in its path. The rotating winds of the column have been estimated at 300 miles per hour, or greater, and the upward velocities may exceed 150 miles per hour.

Some tornadoes form within tropical cyclones, but by far the greater number in the United States occur within lines or groups of severe thunderstorms that develop when a cool, dry westerly air current moves over a southerly current of warm, moist air. This situation is most prevalent in the late spring and early summer in the midwestern part of the country. When tornado outbreaks are considered likely, the Weather Bureau broadcasts a *tornado watch* by radio and television to alert the public. When

a tornado has actually been sighted or detected by radar, a *tornado warning* is issued.

On hearing a tornado warning, persons in the path of the storm should immediately seek safety. In open country, attempt to escape by running or driving at right angles to the tornado's path; if there is no time for escape, lie flat in the nearest depression, such as a ditch or ravine. In cities or towns, the basement and interior hallways of office buildings or schools, or the southwest corner of a home basement, offer the best protection. Stay away from windows, and avoid auditoriums and gymnasiums with large, poorly supported roofs.

Although the exact mechanism producing tornadoes is not known, modern techniques of observing clouds and other weather elements are revealing in great detail the conditions under which they form. An especially promising research tool is radar, by which the motion within tornado-producing clouds can be observed.

## TORNADOES IN THE UNITED STATES

In April, 1967, the midwestern U.S. was hit by an unusually severe series of tornadoes that took 54 lives in Illinois, Indiana, Kansas, Missouri, Iowa, and Michigan. Hardest hit were the northern Illinois communities of Oak Lawn, a Chicago suburb, and Belvidere, about 65 miles northwest of Chicago.

Twenty persons were killed in Belvidere, many of them teen-agers leaving the town high school. The buses they were boarding were lifted into the air by a tornado funnel and smashed to pieces. In Oak Lawn, 32 persons were killed and about 100 injured when a tornado swept through a shopping center, a bus terminal, and a trailer park. Although Chicago escaped direct tornado strikes, it suffered heavy wind damage and scattered power blackouts. Weathermen counted 44 separate tornado funnels in the Illinois storm. Less severe tornadoes hit Barring-

ton and Lake Zurich in Illinois, and Grandville and Wyoming in Michigan. More than 1,500 injuries were reported in the six-state area.

In May, members of the National Severe Storms Laboratory, a research unit of the U.S. Weather Bureau, began intensive tornado study at a center in Norman, Oklahoma. Norman is located in the middle of an area that has more tornadoes than any other place in the world. Operating with an $860,000 annual budget, the laboratory has five radar sets, two airplanes, and special photographic equipment, with which the researchers hope to learn more about the many factors that combine to cause tornadoes. Several research institutes, working with the Norman group, are developing tornado-origin theories, to be tested at the center. The Norman laboratory will also attempt to discover presently unknown factors contributing to the origin of tornadoes.

## TORNADOES, FLOODS, AND TROPICAL STORMS IN THE UNITED STATES: 1931–1966

| PERIOD OR YEAR | DISASTROUS TORNADOES | | | | MAJOR FLOODS | | NORTH ATLANTIC TROPICAL STORMS AND HURRICANES | | |
|---|---|---|---|---|---|---|---|---|---|
| | Number of tornadoes | Total lives lost | Most lives lost in a single tornado | No. with major property loss | Total lives lost | Property loss (in millions of dollars) | Total | Hurricanes only | Lives lost in U.S. |
| 1931–35 | 830 | 909 | 37 | 15 | 368 | 187 | 21 | 12 | 494 |
| 1936–40 | 787 | 916 | 216 | 17 | 607 | 879 | 21 | 8 | 663 |
| 1941–45 | 727 | 980 | 100 | 39 | 346 | 605 | 20 | 11 | 105 |
| 1946–50 | 902 | 813 | 169 | 50 | 306 | 843 | 22 | 12 | 79 |
| 1951–55 | 2,087 | 940 | 116 | 80 | 502 | 2,507 | 18 | 9 | 416 |
| 1956–60 | 3,168 | 445 | 44 | 80 | 228 | 877 | 20 | 7 | 507 |
| 1956 | 532 | 83 | 25 | 25 | 42 | 65 | 2 | 1 | 21 |
| 1957 | 864 | 191 | 44 | 29 | 82 | 360 | 5 | 1 | 395 |
| 1958 | 565 | 66 | 19 | 9 | 47 | 218 | 1 | 0 | 2 |
| 1959 | 589 | 58 | 21 | 5 | 25 | 141 | 7 | 3 | 24 |
| 1960 | 618 | 47 | 16 | 12 | 32 | 93 | 5 | 2 | 65 |
| 1961 | 683 | 51 | 16 | 22 | 52 | 154 | 3 | 2 | 46 |
| 1962 | 658 | 28 | 17 | 10 | 19 | 75 | 1 | 0 | 4 |
| 1963 | 461 | 31 | 5 | 16 | 39 | 176 | 1 | 1 | 11 |
| 1964 | 713 | 75 | 22 | 22 | 73 | 650 | 6 | 4 | 49 |
| 1965 | 898 | 299 | 44 | 39 | 97 | 450 | 6 | 4 | 75 |
| 1966 | 570 | 105 | 58 | 79 | 57 | 150 | 11 | 7 | 54 |

## WORLD CYCLONES, HURRICANES, AND TYPHOONS

The following list of natural disasters excludes those that have occurred in the United States. (For records of the number of U.S. tornadoes and hurricanes and the extent of their damage, consult pages 571 and 573.) Due to the widespread damage and confusion following these disasters, the number of deaths and amounts of property damage are usually estimated figures.

| DATE | PLACE | DEATHS | REMARKS |
|---|---|---|---|
| 1703, Nov. 26–27 | England | 8,000 | Hurricane |
| 1864, Oct. 5 | Calcutta, India | 70,000 | Much of city stripped by cyclone |
| 1876, Oct. 31 | Bakarganj, India | 200,000 | Storm waters inundated city |
| 1881, Oct. 8 | Indochina | 300,000 | Typhoon and tidal wave |
| 1882, June 5 | Bombay, India | 100,000 | Cyclone and tidal wave |
| 1906, Sept. 18 | Hong Kong | 10,000 | Typhoon |
| 1926, Oct. 20 | Havana, Cuba | 600 | Hurricane struck city and suburbs |
| 1930, Sept. 3 | Santo Domingo, Dominican Republic | 2,000 | Hurricane |
| 1934, Sept. 21 | Honshu, Japan | 4,000 | Typhoon caused property damage of $50 million |
| 1935, Oct. 21 | Haiti | 2,000 | Storm |
| 1942, Oct 16 | Bengal, India | 40,000 | Cyclone |
| 1947, Sept. 15–19 | Honshu, Japan | 1,000 | Typhoon and flood |
| 1949, Oct. 27 | Southeastern coast of India | 1,000 | Cyclone |
| 1949, Oct. 31– Nov. 2 | Philippine Islands | 1,000 | Typhoon |
| 1951, Dec. 9–10 | Philippine Islands | 569 | Typhoon left 60,000 homeless |
| 1952, Oct. 22 | Philippine Islands | 431 | Southern Luzon hit by typhoon |
| 1953, Jan. 31– Feb. 1 | England and the Lowlands | 2,100 | Storm and high tides |
| 1953, Sept. 26 | Vietnam | 1,000 | Typhoon and resulting floods devastated cultivated areas |
| 1954, Sept. 26 | Northern Japan | 1,218 | Typhoon caused train ferry to capsize in Tsugaru Strait |
| 1954, Oct. 12 | Southwestern Haiti | 410 | Hurricane left 250,000 homeless |
| 1955, Sept. 19 | Tampico, Mexico | 238 | Hurricane |
| 1955, Sept. 22–28 | British West Indies and Mexico | 550 | Hurricane hit Lesser Antilles and Yucatán Peninsula |
| 1956, Aug. 1 | China | 2,161 | Typhoon devastated Hopeh and Honan provinces |
| 1958, Sept. 27–28 | Japan | 679 | Typhoon Ida struck central Honshu |
| 1958, Oct. 30– Nov. 5 | East Pakistan | 500 | Storms |
| 1959, Aug. 20 | China | 720 | Typhoon struck coast of Fukien Province |
| 1959, Sept. 17–19 | South Korea | 669 | Typhoon |
| 1959, Sept. 26–27 | Japan | 4,464 | Typhoon struck central Honshu |
| 1959, Oct. 27–28 | Mexico | 1,452 | Hurricane, flood, and mud slides devastated states of Jalisco and Colima on Pacific Coast |
| 1960, Oct. 10, 31 | East Pakistan | 6,000 | Two cyclones struck Bay of Bengal area; tidal waves followed each |
| 1961, May 9 | East Pakistan | 2,000 | Typhoon and tidal waves |
| 1961, Sept. 16–17 | Japan | 185 | Typhoon struck Honshu and other islands |
| 1961, Oct. 31 | British Honduras | 250 | Hurricane devastated towns, including Belize |
| 1961, Nov. 14 | Southern Mexico | 330 | Hurricane |
| 1962, Aug. 9 | Philippine Islands | 155 | Typhoon |
| 1962, Sept. 1 | Hong Kong | 171 | Typhoon |
| 1962, Oct. 27 | Thailand | 769 | Storm |
| 1964, June 13–14 | West Pakistan | 250 | High winds and floods ruined hundreds of homes, killed 60,000 cattle |
| 1964, Aug. 14 | South Korea | 69 | Week of torrential rains caused floods and landslides |
| 1964, Aug. 22 | Caribbean Sea | 138 | Hurricane Cleo swept through Guadeloupe and Haiti |
| 1964, Sept. 5 | Kwangtung Province, China | 700 | Typhoon |
| 1964, Dec. 22 | Ceylon | 650 | Cyclone hit east coast, principally the port of Trincomalee |
| 1965, May 12 | Barisal district, East Pakistan | 12,000 | Cyclone and tidal wave |
| 1965, June 10–19 | Japan, China, and western North Pacific | 75 | Typhoon Dinah left over 30,000 homeless; $12 million damage |
| 1965, Sept. 10–18 | Japan | 93 | Typhoon Trix left 190,000 homeless |
| 1965, Oct. 1–9 | Northern Mariana Islands | 208 | Typhoon Carmen carried 150 mph winds; islands almost 80 per cent destroyed |
| 1965, Dec. 15 | Karachi, Pakistan | 1,000 | Cyclone and tidal wave |
| 1966, Jan. 9–13 | Rio de Janeiro, Brazil | 405 | Worst recorded rainstorm in Rio's history; floods and landslides left 50,000 homeless |
| 1966, June 6–7 | Cuba, Honduras | 73 | Rare June hurricane brought heavy rains and mud floods |
| 1966, Sept. 25 | Japan | 174 | Typhoons Ida and Helen struck Japan with winds up to 202 mph; Tokyo heavily damaged. |
| 1966, Sept. 25– Oct. 11 | Dominican Republic, Haiti, Cuba, Florida, and Mexico | 223 | Hurricane Inez carried 135–145 mph winds |
| 1967, July 9 | Japan | 347 | Typhoon Billie struck Honshu and Kyushu; landslides and floods destroyed 2,000 homes. |

# MAJOR U.S. HURRICANES SINCE 1900

Source: U.S. Weather Bureau

| DATE | DEVASTATED AREAS | DEATHS | ESTIMATED DAMAGE (In millions) | REMARKS |
|---|---|---|---|---|
| 1900, Aug. 27– Sept 15 | Texas | 6,000 | 25 | Principal damage and most loss of life caused by storm tide that inundated Galveston Island. |
| 1909, Sept. 14–21 | Louisiana and Mississippi | 350 | 2 | Wide extent of Louisiana coast inundated. |
| 1915, Aug. 5–25 | Texas and Louisiana | 275 | 25 | Twelve-foot storm tide inundated Galveston to a depth of five to six feet. |
| 1915, Sept. 22– Oct. 1 | Middle Gulf Coast | 275 | 25 | Ninety per cent of buildings destroyed over a large area of Louisiana south of New Orleans. |
| 1919, Sept. 2–15 | Florida, Louisiana, and Texas | 287 | 25 | Hurricane severe both in Florida and in Texas; over 500 casualties in ships lost at sea. |
| 1926, Sept. 11–22 | Florida and Alabama | 243 | 225 | Very severe in the Miami area and from Pensacola into southern Alabama. |
| 1928, Sept. 6–20 | Southern Florida | 1,836 | 25 | Wind-driven waters of Lake Okeechobee overflowed into populated areas. |
| 1935, Aug. 29– Sept. 10 | Southern Florida | 408 | 25 | "Labor Day Storm." Barometer reading of 26.35 inches on Long Key is lowest on record in the Western Hemisphere. |
| 1938, Sept. 10–22 | Long Island, New York; southern New England | 600 | 225 | Very heavy wind and storm damage in most of New England. |
| 1940, Aug. 5–15 | Georgia and the Carolinas | 50 | 2 | Heavy flooding in the Southeastern states as far as Tennessee from hurricane-induced rains. |
| 1944, Sept. 9–16 | North Carolina to New England | 46 | 225 | Heavy damage. |
| 1944, Oct. 12–23 | Florida | 18 | 225 | Warnings and evacuation prevented heavier casualties. |
| 1947, Sept. 4–21 | Florida and Middle Gulf Coast | 51 | 225 | Wind and water damage heavy on east coast of Florida and in Louisiana and Mississippi. |
| 1954, Aug. 25–31 Carol | North Carolina to New England | 60 | 225 | Property losses greatest of any single storm up to this date. |
| 1954, Sept. 2–14 Edna | New Jersey to New England | 21 | 25 | Heavy damage in New England. |
| 1954, Oct. 5–18 Hazel | South Carolina to New York | 95 | 225 | Heavy damage in exposed North Carolina shore areas; storm retained destructive intensity through Middle Atlantic states. |
| 1955, Aug. 3–14 Connie | North Carolina | 25 | 225 | Heavy rainfall from North Carolina to New England, varying from six inches to over 12 inches on western Long Island. |
| 1955, Aug. 7–21 Diane | North Carolina to New England | 184 | 550 | Heavy rainfall with near-maximum runoff caused severe floods throughout the Northeast; damage exceeded any prior storm on record. |
| 1955, Sept. 10–23 Ione | North Carolina | 7 | 225 | Third hurricane in eastern North Carolina within five weeks. |
| 1956, Sept. 21–30 Flossy | Louisiana to northern Florida | 15 | 25 | Damage over area from New Orleans and mouth of Mississippi eastward to western Florida. |
| 1957, June 25–28 Audrey | Texas to Alabama | 390 | 225 | Storm surge over 12 feet caused inundation of flat Louisiana coast by Gulf waters as far as 25 miles inland in some places; off-shore oil installations heavily damaged. |
| 1960, Aug. 29– Sept. 13 Donna | Florida to New England | 50 | 225 | Record amount of damage in Florida; winds estimated near 140 mph. with gusts 175–180 mph on central Florida Keys. |
| 1961, Sept. 3–15 Carla | Texas | 46 | 225 | Largest and most intense Gulf Coast hurricane in many years; severe damage along wide expanse of Texas coast. |
| 1964, Sept. 8–9 Dora | St. Augustine and Jacksonville, Florida; and Brunswick, Georgia | 6 | 240 | First hurricane to enter northeastern Florida during this century. |
| 1964, Oct. 2–3 Hilda | Louisiana, the Carolinas, and Georgia | 10 | 100 | Entire Louisiana coastal area evacuated (150,000 people); six closely associated tornadoes took 27 lives. |
| 1965, Sept. 7–11 Betsy | Florida coast and Louisiana | 100 | 1000 | Struck Miami and devastated New Orleans and Plaquemines Parish. |
| 1966, June 9 Alma | Florida and Georgia | 7 | 5 | Extensive crop damage caused by 100 mph winds and heavy rainfall; 100,000 evacuated. |
| 1967, Sept. 8–25 Beulah | Texas | 10 | 1000 | Severe flooding and side-tornadoes; third most devastating storm in Texas history. |

## PRINCIPAL WORLD FLOODS

| DATE | PLACE | DEATHS * | EXPLANATION |
|------|-------|----------|-------------|
| 1228 | Holland................................... | 100,000 | Sea flood in Friesland. |
| 1642 | China..................................... | 300,000 | Kaifeng seawall destroyed. |
| 1787 | Eastern India............................ | 10,000 | Storm drove seawater inland 20 miles. |
| 1887 | Honan, China............................. | 900,000 | Yellow River overflowed. |
| 1889 | Johnstown, Pennsylvania................. | 2,000 | Flood. |
| 1900 | Galveston, Texas......................... | 6,000 | Tidal wave. |
| 1903 | Heppner, Oregon......................... | 247 | Flood destroyed town of Heppner. |
| 1911 | China..................................... | 100,000 | Yangtze River overflowed. |
| 1913 | Ohio and Indiana......................... | 730 | Ohio and Indiana rivers flooded. |
| 1928 | Santa Paula, California................... | 450 | Collapse of St. Francis Dam. |
| 1939 | China..................................... | 1 million | Floods in north; extensive drownings and starvation. |
| 1947 | Honshu Island, Japan.................... | 2,000 | Flooding after typhoon. |
| 1948 | Southern Turkey......................... | 100 | Dikes burst on two rivers. |
| 1948 | Foochow, China.......................... | 1,000 | Flood. |
| 1950 | Southern and eastern China............. | 500 | Flooding left 1 million homeless. |
| 1951 | Manchuria................................ | 1,800 | Flood. |
| 1953 | Northwest Europe, principally the Netherlands | 1,794 | Storm and floods devastated North Sea coastal areas. |
| 1954 | Iran....................................... | 2,000 | Flash flood. |
| 1955 | Oregon and northern California.......... | 74 | Rains and flooding; $150 million in damages. |
| 1955 | Pakistan and India....................... | 1,700 | Flood. |
| 1956 | China..................................... | 2,000 | Three provinces flooded after typhoon. |
| 1957 | Kyushu Island, Japan..................... | 513 | Flood. |
| 1957 | Ceylon.................................... | 300 | Flood. |
| 1959 | Western Mexico.......................... | 2,000 | Flood. |
| 1959 | Frejus, France............................ | 412 | Collapse of dam and flood. |
| 1960 | East Pakistan............................ | 10,000 | Tidal wave. |
| 1962 | German North Sea Coast................. | 343 | Flood. |
| 1963 | Barcelona, Spain......................... | 445 | Flash flood, west and north of city. |
| 1963 | Northern Italy............................ | 2,000 | Vaiont Dam collapsed |
| 1963 | Haiti...................................... | 500 | Flood. |
| 1964 | New Delhi and Macheria, India........... | 85 | Flood. |
| 1965 | South Korea.............................. | 94 | Flood; 190,000 homeless. |
| 1965 | Italy...................................... | 90 | Floods after torrential rains. |
| 1966 | Texas..................................... | 37 | Floods caused $50–$500 million damage. |
| 1966 | Arno Valley, Italy......................... | 112 | Arno River overflowed; Florence, Naples, Rome, Venice hit; art treasures lost in Florence. |
| 1967 | Brazil..................................... | 600 | Heavy rains in Rio de Janeiro and San Paulo states. |
| 1967 | Brazil..................................... | 119 | Heavy rains in Guanabara State.    * Estimated. |

Worst flood in the history of Fairbanks, Alaska, left more than 14,000 homeless in August 1967.

Wide World

# WORLD AIRCRAFT DISASTERS

The following chart, prepared from statistical information supplied primarily by the Civil Aeronautics Board and *The New York Times,* includes disasters with fatalities estimated at above 30. Exceptions are made for disasters that have been of national or international significance, such as the crash on September 18, 1961, in which Dag Hammarskjöld died, for memorable ones from the early days of aviation, and for those that occurred in late 1967.

| DATE | AIRCRAFT | DEATHS | EXPLANATION |
|---|---|---|---|
| 1921, Aug. 24 | English dirigible R-38 (U.S. ZR-2).... | 62 | Broke in two over Hull, England |
| 1922, Feb. 21 | U.S. dirigible ROMA............... | 34 | Exploded over Hampton, Virginia |
| 1923, Dec. 21 | French dirigible DIXMUDE......... | 52 | Vanished over Mediterranean Sea or Sahara Desert |
| 1925, Sept. 3 | U.S. dirigible SHENANDOAH....... | 14 | Broke apart over Caldwell, Ohio |
| 1930, Oct. 5 | English dirigible R-101........... | 47 | Crashed near Beauvais, France |
| 1933, Apr. 4 | U.S. dirigible AKRON II........... | 73 | Crashed off New Jersey coast |
| 1935, May 18 | Soviet dirigible MAXIM GORKY.... | 49 | Collided with a small plane over Moscow |
| 1937, May 6 | German zeppelin HINDENBURG .... | 36 | Burned at mooring in Lakehurst, New Jersey |
| 1938, July 24 | Military stunt plane............... | 53 | Crashed into grandstand in Bogotá, Colombia |
| 1938, Aug. 24 | Two airplanes.................... | 58 | Collided and crashed, setting fire to iron foundry in Tokyo, Japan |
| 1944, Aug. 23 | U.S. bomber.................... | 76 | Crashed into school and burst into flames in Freckleton, England |
| 1945, July 28 | U.S. bomber.................... | 13 | Crashed into Empire State Building between 78th and 79th floors in New York City |
| 1946, Dec. 25 | Three Chinese airliners............ | 71 | Crashed separately in fog near Shanghai, China |
| 1947, Feb. 15 | Colombian DC-4.................. | 53 | Crashed into Mount Tablazo in Colombia |
| 1947, May 29 | U.S. airliner.................... | 43 | Crashed at takeoff at La Guardia Airport, New York City |
| 1947, May 30 | Airliner....................... | 53 | Crashed near Port Deposit, Maryland |
| 1947, June 13 | Airliner, DC-4.................. | 50 | Crashed into mountain and exploded near Leesburg, Virginia |
| 1947, Oct. 24 | Airliner, DC-6.................. | 52 | Crashed into hillside in Bryce Canyon, Utah |
| 1948, Apr. 15 | U.S. airliner................... | 50 | Crashed at Shannon Airport, Ireland |
| 1948, Aug. 1 | French flying boat............... | 53 | Crashed off coast of West Africa |
| 1949, June 7 | C-46 twin-engine airplane......... | 53 | Crashed off coast of Puerto Rico |
| 1949, Nov. 1 | P-38 fighter and DC-4 airliner...... | 55 | Collided above airport in Washington, D.C. |
| 1950, Mar. 12 | English airliner................. | 80 | Crashed near Cardiff, Wales |
| 1950, June 24 | Airliner...................... | 58 | Exploded and fell into Lake Michigan |
| 1950, Aug. 31 | U.S. Constellation.............. | 55 | Crashed near Cairo, Egypt |
| 1950, Nov. 13 | Canadian airliner............... | 58 | Crashed on mountain near Grenoble, France |
| 1951, Mar. 23 | U.S. Air Force transport......... | 53 | Crashed in ocean off Irish coast |
| 1951, June 30 | Airliner...................... | 50 | Crashed northwest of Denver, Colorado |
| 1951, Aug. 24 | Airliner...................... | 50 | Crashed near Decoto, California |
| 1951, Dec. 16 | Nonscheduled airliner............ | 56 | Crashed after takeoff into Elizabeth River, New Jersey |
| 1952, Jan. 22 | U.S. Convair.................. | 30 | Crashed in Elizabeth, New Jersey |
| 1952, Feb. 11 | U.S. DC-6.................... | 33 | Crashed in Elizabeth, New Jersey |
| 1952, Mar. 27 | Two Soviet planes.............. | 70 | Collided over Tula Airport, Moscow |
| 1952, Apr. 11 | U.S. DC-4.................... | 52 | Crashed in harbor in San Juan, Puerto Rico |
| 1952, Apr. 29 | U.S. Stratocruiser.............. | 50 | Crashed in Brazilian jungle |
| 1952, Nov. 23 | U.S. Air Force plane............ | 52 | Crashed near Elmendorf Air Force Base, Alaska |
| 1952, Dec. 20 | U.S. Air Force plane............ | 87 | Crashed and burned after takeoff at Larson Air Force Base, Moses Lake, Washington |
| 1953, June 18 | U.S. Air Force Globemaster........ | 129 | Crashed near Tokyo, Japan |
| 1953, July 11 | U.S. DC-6B................... | 58 | Crashed into sea east of Wake Island |
| 1955, Mar. 22 | U.S. Navy plane................ | 66 | Crashed into cliff near Honolulu, Hawaii |
| 1955, Aug. 11 | Two U.S. Flying Boxcars.......... | 66 | Mid-air collision near Edelweiler, Germany |
| 1955, Oct. 6 | Airliner, DC-4................. | 66 | Crashed in mountains near Laramie, Wyoming |
| 1955, Nov. 1 | U.S. DC-6B................... | 44 | Sabotaged; exploded near Longmont, Colorado |
| 1956, Feb. 18 | English airplane................ | 50 | Crashed on Malta |
| 1956, June 20 | Venezuelan airliner.............. | 74 | Crashed in Atlantic 40 miles south of New York |
| 1956, June 30 | Two airliners.................. | 128 | Collided over Grand Canyon, Arizona |
| 1956, Oct. 10 | U.S. Air Force transport.......... | 59 | Disappeared north of Azores |
| 1956, Dec. 9 | Canadian airliner............... | 62 | Crashed in mountains near Vancouver, British Columbia |
| 1957, Mar. 21 | U.S. Air Force plane............ | 67 | Crashed in ocean 250 miles from Tokyo, Japan |
| 1957, July 16 | Dutch airliner................. | 57 | Crashed into sea off coast of New Guinea |
| 1957, Aug. 11 | Chartered Canadian airliner........ | 79 | Crashed near Quebec, Canada |
| 1957, Dec. 8 | Argentine airliner.............. | 62 | Crashed near Bolívar, Argentina |
| 1958, May 18 | Belgian airliner................ | 65 | Crashed in Casablanca, Morocco |
| 1958, Aug. 14 | Dutch airliner................. | 99 | Crashed in ocean west of Ireland |
| 1958, Oct. 17 | Soviet jet airliner.............. | 75 | Crashed in Kanash, U.S.S.R. |
| 1959, Feb. 3 | U.S. turboprop airliner........... | 65 | Crashed into East River, New York City |
| 1959, June 26 | U.S. luxury airliner............. | 68 | Exploded near Milan, Italy |
| 1959, Sept. 24 | French airliner................. | 54 | Crashed in Bordeaux, France |
| 1960, Jan. 18 | U.S. jet-propelled airliner......... | 50 | Crashed near Holdcroft, Virginia |

*(continued)*

**WORLD AIRCRAFT DISASTERS** (*continued*)

| DATE | AIRCRAFT | DEATHS* | EXPLANATION |
|---|---|---|---|
| 1960, Feb. 25 | U.S. Navy plane and Brazilian airliner | 61 | Collided over Rio de Janeiro |
| 1960, Mar. 17 | Turboprop airliner | 63 | Mid-air explosion over Tell City, Indiana |
| 1960, Aug. 29 | French airliner | 63 | Crashed into sea near Dakar, Senegal |
| 1960, Sept. 19 | U.S. airliner | 78 | Mid-air explosion over Agaña, Guam |
| 1960, Oct. 4 | U.S. Electra | 62 | Crashed into harbor at takeoff in Boston, Massachusetts |
| 1960, Dec. 16 | U.S. DC-8 and U.S. Super-Constellation | 134 | Collided over New York City |
| 1960, Dec. 17 | U.S. Air Force transport | 50 | Crashed into crowded street in Munich, Germany |
| 1961, Feb. 15 | Belgian jet airliner | 73 | Crashed near Berg, Belgium |
| 1961, May 10 | French airliner | 79 | Crashed in Ghadames, Libya |
| 1961, July 12 | Czech airliner | 72 | Crashed near Casablanca, Morocco |
| 1961, Sept. 1 | U.S. Constellation | 78 | Crashed after takeoff in Chicago, Illinois |
| 1961, Sept. 10 | U.S. charter plane | 83 | Crashed in Shannon, Ireland |
| 1961, Sept. 12 | French jet airliner | 73 | Crashed near Rabat, Morocco |
| 1961, Sept. 18 | U.N. airplane | 12 | Crashed near Ndola, Northern Rhodesia |
| 1961, Nov. 8 | U.S. charter plane | 77 | Crashed in Richmond, Virginia |
| 1962, Mar. 1 | U.S. B-707 | 95 | Exploded as it crashed into Jamaica Bay, New York |
| 1962, Mar. 4 | English DC-7 | 111 | Crashed in jungle near Douala, Cameroun |
| 1962, Mar. 16 | U.S. Super-Constellation | 107 | Crashed into western Pacific Ocean |
| 1962, June 3 | French B-707 | 130 | Crashed at takeoff in Paris, France |
| 1962, June 22 | French B-707 | 113 | Crashed near Guadeloupe, West Indies |
| 1962, July 7 | Italian DC-8 | 94 | Crashed near Bombay, India |
| 1962, Nov. 27 | Brazilian jet airliner | 97 | Crashed and burned in Lima, Peru |
| 1962, Dec. 14 | Brazilian airliner | 50 | Crashed in Amazon jungle clearing |
| 1963, Feb. 1 | Viscount and Turkish Air Force plane | 95 | Collided over Ankara, Turkey |
| 1963, June 3 | U.S. military chartered airliner | 101 | Crashed in Pacific Ocean off British Columbia |
| 1963, July 28 | U.A R. jet airliner | 62 | Crashed into sea off Bombay, India |
| 1963, Sept. 2 | Swiss jet airliner | 80 | Crashed after takeoff in Zurich, Switzerland |
| 1963, Nov. 29 | Canadian airliner | 118 | Crashed after takeoff in Montreal, Canada |
| 1963, Dec. 8 | U.S. jet airliner | 82 | Crashed near Elkton, Maryland |
| 1964, Feb. 25 | U.S. DC-8 | 58 | Crashed in Lake Pontchartrain, Louisiana |
| 1964, Feb. 26 | English Britannia | 83 | Crashed near Innsbruck, Austria |
| 1964, Mar. 1 | U.S. Constellation | 85 | Crashed near Lake Tahoe, California |
| 1964, May 11 | U.S. military C-135 transport | 75 | Crashed at Clark Air Force Base, the Philippines |
| 1964, June 20 | Chinese Nationalist Civil Air Patrol plane | 53 | Crashed near Fengyuan, Taiwan |
| 1964, Oct. 2 | South African DC-6 | 80 | Crashed southeast of Granada, Spain |
| 1964, Nov. 23 | U.S. B-707 | 44 | Skidded into pavement roller on takeoff near Rome, Italy |
| 1965, Feb. 6 | Chilean DC-6B | 87 | Crashed in the Andes |
| 1965, Feb. 8 | U.S. DC-7B | 84 | Plunged into Atlantic Ocean near Kennedy Airport |
| 1965, Mar. 31 | Spanish jet airliner | 50 | Crashed in Strait of Gibraltar |
| 1965, May 20 | Pakistani jet airliner | 119 | Crashed near Cairo, Egypt |
| 1965, June 25 | U.S. Air Force transport | 84 | Crashed into mountains near Los Angeles, California |
| 1965, July 8 | Canadian DC-6B | 52 | Crashed in British Columbia |
| 1965, Nov. 8 | U.S. B-727 | 58 | Crashed during landing near Cincinnati, Ohio |
| 1965, Dec. 11 | U.S. Air Force transport C-123 | 85 | Crashed into mountain north of Nhatrang, South Vietnam |
| 1966, Jan. 17 | U.S. B-52 and U.S. KC-135 tanker | 7 | Collided during refueling, dropping four unarmed nuclear devices in Spain |
| 1966, Jan. 24 | Indian B-707 | 117 | Crashed into Mont Blanc, France |
| 1966, Jan. 28 | German Convair Metropolitan | 46 | Crashed during landing at Bonn, Germany |
| 1966, Feb. 4 | Japanese B-727 | 133 | Plunged into Tokyo Bay during landing |
| 1966, Feb. 17 | Soviet TU-114 | 48 | Crashed on takeoff from Moscow |
| 1966, Mar. 4 | Canadian DC-8 | 64 | Crashed during landing at Tokyo's International Airport |
| 1966, Mar. 5 | British B-707 | 124 | Caught fire above Mount Fuji and crashed on slopes |
| 1966, Apr. 22 | U.S. Lockheed Electra | 82 | Crashed near Ardmore, Oklahoma |
| 1966, Sept. 1 | British turboprop | 95 | Crashed during landing in Belgrade, Yugoslavia |
| 1966, Nov. 24 | TABSO Airways, Ilyushin-18 | 82 | Crashed at Bratislava, Czechoslovakia |
| 1966, Dec. 24 | Flying Tiger CL-44 | 111 | Cargo flight crashed at Danang, Vietnam |
| 1967, Mar. 30 | U.S. airliner, DC-8 | 18 | Crashed into motel near New Orleans airport; six crewmen, nine motel guests killed |
| 1967, Apr. 8 | South Korean Airforce C-47 | 55 | Crashed at Seoul, Korea, killing 41 on ground |
| 1967, Apr. 20 | Swiss jetliner | 126 | Crashed while landing at Nicosia, Cyprus |
| 1967, June 3 | British DC-6 | 88 | Crashed into Mount Canigou in French Pyrenees |
| 1967, June 4 | British DC-4 | 72 | Crashed at Stockport, England |
| 1967, June 17 | U.S. C-130 transport plane | 34 | Crashed upon landing in South Vietnam |
| 1967, July 19 | U.S. jetliner, Boeing 727 | 82 | Struck by private plane over Hendersonville, N.C.; among dead was U.S. Secretary of the Navy-designate J. T. McNaughton |
| 1967, Aug. 17 | U.S. B-25 converted bomber | 17 | Skydivers drowned in Lake Erie after carrier plane strayed off course, dropping them over water |
| 1967, Oct. 12 | BEA Comet | 66 | Crashed off southwest coast of Turkey |

* Estimated

# WORLD MARINE DISASTERS

| DATE | CRAFT | DEATHS * | EXPLANATION |
|---|---|---|---|
| 1831, July 19 | LADY SHERBROOKE, immigrant vessel | 263 | Sank off Cape May, New Jersey. |
| 1833, May 11 | LADY OF THE LAKE | 215 | Struck iceberg while bound for Quebec. |
| 1850, Mar. 29 | ROYAL ADELAIDE | 400 | Wrecked off Margate, England. |
| 1852, Mar. 26 | BIRKENHEAD, troopship | 454 | Wrecked; bound for Cape of Good Hope. |
| 1853, Sept. 29 | ANNIE JANE, immigrant vessel | 348 | Wrecked off Scotland. |
| 1854, Mar. | CITY OF GLASGOW | 450 | Vanished; bound for Philadelphia from Liverpool. |
| 1854, Sept. 27 | ARCTIC | 322 | Sank in collision near Grand Banks, off Newfoundland. |
| 1857, Sept. 12 | CENTRAL AMERICA | 400 | Sank in storm; bound for New York from Havana. |
| 1858, Sept. 13 | AUSTRIA | 471 | Burned on Hamburg–New York run. |
| 1859, Apr. 27 | POMONA | 386 | Wrecked off Ireland. |
| 1859, Oct. 25 | ROYAL CHARTER | 450 | Wrecked in Irish Sea. |
| 1860, Sept. 8 | LADY ELGIN, excursion steamer | 300 | Collided with lumber ship on Lake Michigan. |
| 1865, Apr. 27 | SULTANA, river steamer | 1,450 | Exploded and sank in Memphis, Tennessee. |
| 1867, Oct. 29 | RHONE and WYE, mail boats, many small vessels | 1,000 | Wrecked in storm; St. Thomas, West Indies. |
| 1870, Sept. 17 | CAPTAIN, English warship | 472 | Foundered off Finistère, France. |
| 1873, Apr. 1 | ATLANTIC, English steamer | 547 | Wrecked off Nova Scotia. |
| 1878, Sept. 3 | PRINCESS ALICE, English steamer | 700 | Collided and sank in Thames. |
| 1890, Sept. 19 | ERTOGRUL, Turkish frigate | 540 | Burned off Japanese coast. |
| 1891, Mar. 17 | UTOPIA, British steamer | 574 | Collided and sank off Gibraltar. |
| 1895, Mar. 14 | REINA REGENTA, Spanish cruiser | 400 | Foundered in the Atlantic near Gibraltar. |
| 1898, Feb. 15 | MAINE, U.S. battleship | 264 | Blown up in Havana Harbor. |
| 1898, July 4 | LA BOURGOGNE and the CROMARTYSHIRE | 560 | Collided near Sable Island off Nova Scotia. |
| 1904, June 15 | GENERAL SLOCUM | 1,000 | Burned in East River, New York. |
| 1904, June 28 | NORGE | 600 | Wrecked on Rockall Reef off Scotland. |
| 1912, Mar. 5 | PRINCIPE DE ASTURIAS | 500 | Wrecked on rocks. |
| 1912, Apr. 15 | TITANIC | 1,502 | Struck iceberg and sank in the North Atlantic. |
| 1912, Sept. 28 | KICHEMARU | 1,000 | Sank off coast of Japan. |
| 1914, May 29 | EMPRESS OF IRELAND | 1,024 | Collided with Norwegian collier in St. Lawrence River and sank. |
| 1915, May 7 | LUSITANIA | 1,195 | Sunk by German submarine off coast of Ireland. |
| 1915, June 24 | EASTLAND, excursion steamer | 812 | Capsized in Chicago River, Illinois. |
| 1916, Aug. 29 | HSIN YU | 1,000 | Sank off coast of China. |
| 1917, July 9 | VANGUARD, English warship | 800 | Blown up at Scapa Flow dock off northern Scotland. |
| 1918, Apr. 25 | KIANG KWAN | 500 | Collided and sank off Hankow, China. |
| 1918, July 12 | KAWACHI, Japanese battleship | 500 | Exploded in Tokayama Bay, Japan. |
| 1919, Jan. 17 | CHAONIA | 460 | Wrecked in Strait of Messina, between Sicly and Italy. |
| 1921, Mar. 18 | HONG KONG | 1,000 | Wrecked on rocks off Swatow in South China Sea. |
| 1926, Oct. 16 | Chinese troopship | 1,200 | Exploded in Yangtze River, China. |
| 1928, Nov. 12 | VESTRIS | 113 | Foundered off the Virginia Capes. |
| 1931, June 14 | French excursion steamer | 450 | Overturned in storm off St. Nazaire, in Bay of Biscay. |
| 1934, Sept. 8 | MORRO CASTLE | 137 | Burned off coast of New Jersey; beached at Asbury Park. |
| 1942, Oct. 2 | QUEEN MARY and CURAÇAO | 338 | Liner rammed and sank British cruiser. |
| 1942, Oct. 26 | Jewish refugee ship | 200 | Wrecked in Sea of Marmara, Turkey. |
| 1944, Dec. 17–18 | U.S. Third Fleet: three destroyers capsized, six or seven other ships damaged, 146 aircraft destroyed | 800 | Wrecked during typhoon in Philippine Sea. |
| 1945, Apr. 9 | U.S. Liberty ship | 360 | Exploded in harbor at Bari, Italy. |
| 1946, Aug. 2 | VITYA | 295 | Sank in Lake Nyasa, Tanganyika. |
| 1947, Jan. 19 | HIMARA | 392 | Hit mine and sank off Athens, Greece. |
| 1947, July 17 | RAMDAS, coastal steamer | 550 | Sank off Bombay, India. |
| 1948, Jan. 19 | CAUTIN | 150 | Sank in Imperial River, Chile. |
| 1948, Jan. 28 | JOO MARU, freighter | 250 | Hit mine and sank in Inland Sea, Japan. |
| 1948, Feb. 28 | Steamer | 160 | Sank during pirate attack near Amoy, China. |
| 1948, June 11 | KJOEBENHAVN, Danish passenger liner | 140 | Hit mine and sank off coast of Jutland. |
| 1948, Dec. 3 | Steamer | 1,140 | Exploded and sank south of Shanghai. |
| 1949, Jan. 27 | Chinese liner and collier | 600 | Collided and sank off south coast of China. |
| 1949, Sept. 17 | NORONIC, Great Lakes liner | 130 | Burned at pier in Toronto, Canada. |
| 1950, Jan. 12 | TRUCULENT, English submarine | 65 | Rammed by Swedish tanker in Thames Estuary. |
| 1951, Apr. 16 | AFFRAY, English submarine | 75 | Sank off Isle of Wight, near southern England. |
| 1952, Apr. 26 | HOBSON, U.S. destroyer-minesweeper, and WASP, aircraft carrier | 176 | Collided; HOBSON sank in Atlantic Ocean. |
| 1953, Jan. 9 | South Korean passenger liner | 249 | Sank in heavy seas off Pusan, South Korea. |
| 1953, Jan. 31 | Ferry | 132 | Sank in storm off Donaghadee, Northern Ireland. |
| 1953, Aug. 1 | MONIQUE | 120 | Vanished near New Caledonia in the South Pacific. |
| 1954, May 26 | BENNINGTON, U.S. aircraft carrier | 103 | Exploded and burned off Quonset Point, Rhode Island. |

* Estimated

(continued)

## WORLD MARINE DISASTERS (*continued*)

| DATE | CRAFT | DEATHS * | EXPLANATION |
|---|---|---|---|
| 1954, Sept. 26 | TOYA MARU, Japanese ferry....... | 1,172 | Sank in Tsugaru Strait, Japan. |
| 1956, June 3 | Pakistani liner..................... | 199 | Wrecked in storm in the Bay of Bengal. |
| 1956, July 26 | ANDREA DORIA and STOCKHOLM.. | 50 | Collided; ANDREA DORIA sank off Massachusetts coast. |
| 1957, Apr. 10 | Two pilgrimage boats.............. | 150 | Sank in Godavari River, India. |
| 1957, July 14 | Soviet ship........................ | 270 | Ran aground in storm in Caspian Sea. |
| 1958, Jan. 26 | Japanese ferry.................... | 170 | Vanished in Inland Sea. |
| 1958, Mar. 1 | Turkish ferry..................... | 238 | Sank near Istanbul, in Sea of Marmara. |
| 1959, May 8 | Nile River excursion boat.......... | 150 | Sank north of Cairo, Egypt. |
| 1960, Dec. 19 | CONSTELLATION, U.S. aircraft carrier (under construction)....... | 50 | Burned in Brooklyn Navy Yard. |
| 1961, Apr. 8 | DARA, English liner................ | 212 | Burned in Persian Gulf. |
| 1961, July 8 | SAVE............................. | 259 | Ran aground and exploded in Mozambique. |
| 1961, Sept. 3 | VENCEDOR, excursion ship........ | 150 | Sank near Buenaventura, Colombia. |
| 1963, Apr. 10 | THRESHER, U.S. nuclear submarine | 129 | Sank in North Atlantic. |
| 1963, May 4 | Motor launch..................... | 206 | Sank in Upper Nile. |
| 1963, Aug. 17 | MIDORI MARU, Japanese ferry..... | 128 | Sank in East China Sea. |
| 1963, Dec. 23 | LAKONIA, Greek liner............. | 155 | Sank after fire, north of Madeira Island, Atlantic Ocean. |
| 1964, Feb. 11 | VOYAGER, destroyer, and MELBOURNE, aircraft carrier..... | 85 | Collided; VOYAGER sank near Ulladulla, Australia. |
| 1964, Nov. 26 | SHALOM, Israeli liner, and STOLT DAGALI, Norwegian tanker....... | 19 | Collided off New Jersey coast; tanker sank. |
| 1965, Feb. 11 | Four fishing trawlers.............. | 100 | Sank in Bering Sea. |
| 1965, May 24 | African ferry..................... | 150 | Capsized in Shire River, Malawi. |
| 1965, Nov. 13 | YARMOUTH CASTLE, Panamanian cruise ship..................... | 90 | Caught fire and sank in the Caribbean. |
| 1966, Jan. 30 | Pakistani passenger launch and steamer...................... | 80 | Collided at Chandpur Port, East Pakistan. |
| 1966, Feb. 2 | Indonesian freighter.............. | 89 | Sank near Belawan. |
| 1966, June 16 | ALVA CAPE, tanker.............. | 33 | Collided with another tanker in New York harbor. |
| 1966, Oct. 26 | Indian vessel.................... | 100 | Sank in Kosie River, eastern India. |
| 1966, Oct. 26 | ORISKANY, U.S. aircraft carrier..... | 43 | Damaged by fire in Gulf of Tonkin. |
| 1966, Dec. 8 | HERAKLION, Greek ferry.......... | 217 | Sank in storm in Sea of Crete. |
| 1967, Mar. 18 | TORREY CANYON, U.S. tanker...... | 1 | Ran aground and broke up off English coast; 118,000 tons of oil polluted beaches and killed wildlife. |
| 1967, June 8 | LIBERTY, U.S. communications vessel | 34 | Attacked by Israeli aircraft in Mediterranean Sea during Arab-Israeli war. |
| 1967, July 29 | FORRESTAL, U.S. aircraft carrier.... | 129 | Crippled by fire off Vietnam; worst U.S. Naval disaster since WW II. |
| 1967, Oct. 9 | PANOCEANIC FAITH, U.S. freighter | 35 | Sank 870 miles southwest of Kodiak Island, Alaska. |
| 1967, Oct. 21 | ELATH, Israeli destroyer........... | 47 | Sunk by Egyptian missiles near Port Said. |

## WORLD RAIL DISASTERS

| DATE | PLACE | DEATHS* | EXPLANATION |
|---|---|---|---|
| 1856, July 17 | Near Philadelphia, Pennsylvania.... | 66 | Train wrecked. |
| 1857, Mar. 17 | Near Hamilton, Ontario, Canada..... | 60 | Train derailed on bridge over Desjardins Canal. |
| 1864, July 15 | Near Lackawaxen, Pennsylvania..... | 65 | Two trains collided. |
| 1867, Dec. 19 | Angola, New York................. | 44 | Two rear cars of passenger train fell off bridge and burned. |
| 1876, Dec. 29 | Ashtabula, Ohio................... | 92 | Bridge collapsed in snowstorm. |
| 1879, Dec. 28 | Dundee, Scotland................. | 78 | Train fell from Tay Bridge. |
| 1880, Aug. 11 | Mays Landing, New Jersey.......... | 40 | Train wrecked. |
| 1881, June 24 | Cuautla, Mexico................... | 200 | Train fell into river. |
| 1882, July 13 | Near Tchnery, Russia............... | 150 | Train derailed. |
| 1887, Aug. 10 | Chatsworth, Illinois............... | 81 | Train wrecked as burning bridge collapsed. |
| 1888, Oct. 10 | Mud Run, Pennsylvania............ | 62 | Locomotive hit standing excursion train. |
| 1889, June 12 | Near Armagh, Ireland............. | 80 | Train collision. |
| 1891, June 14 | Near Basel, Switzerland............ | 100 | Train collision. |
| 1896, July 30 | Atlantic City, New Jersey.......... | 60 | Train wrecked. |
| 1903, Dec. 23 | Laurel Run, Pennsylvania.......... | 78 | Train wrecked. |
| 1904, Aug. 7 | Eden, Colorado................... | 96 | Train wrecked. |
| 1904, Sept. 24 | New Market, Tennessee........... | 56 | Train wrecked. |
| 1906, Dec. 30 | Washington, D.C................. | 53 | Train wrecked. |
| 1910, Mar. 1 | Wellington, Washington........... | 96 | Avalanche threw two trains into canyon. |
| 1910, Mar. 21 | Green Mountain, Iowa............. | 55 | Passenger train wrecked. |
| 1915, May 22 | Quintinshill, near Gretna, Scotland.. | 228 | Troop train collided with local train; express train crashed into wreckage. |
| 1917, Dec. 12 | Modane, France.................. | 550 | Troop train derailed near entrance of Mont Cénis tunnel. |

* Estimated.

| DATE | PLACE | DEATHS * | EXPLANATION |
|------|-------|----------|-------------|
| 1918, June 22 | Ivanhoe, Indiana.................. | 68 | Train rammed circus train. |
| 1918, July 9 | Near Nashville, Tennessee.......... | 98 | Two trains collided head-on. |
| 1918, Nov. 1 | Brooklyn, New York............... | 92 | Five-car train of Brooklyn rapid transit line derailed. |
| 1925, June 16 | Hackettstown, New Jersey......... | 50 | Passenger train derailed at highway crossing. |
| 1937, July 16 | Near Patna, India................. | 107 | Delhi-Calcutta Express derailed. |
| 1938, June 19 | Saugus, Montana.................. | 47 | Flood-weakened bridge collapsed under crack passenger train. |
| 1938, Dec. 19 | Babacena, Minas Gerais, Brazil...... | 90 | Freight and passenger trains collided head-on. |
| 1938, Dec. 25 | Near Kishinev, Romania............ | 100 | Passenger trains collided. |
| 1939, Dec. 22 | Near Magdeburg, Germany......... | 132 | Two express trains collided. |
| 1939, Dec. 22 | Near Friedrichshafen, Germany..... | 99 | Train wrecked. |
| 1940, Jan. 29 | Osaka, Japan..................... | 200 | Passenger trains collided and burned. |
| 1940, July 31 | Cuyahoga Falls, Ohio.............. | 43 | Suburban passenger train collided with freight train. |
| 1943, Sept. 6 | Philadelphia, Pennsylvania........ | 79 | Nine cars of Congressional Limited derailed. |
| 1943, Dec. 16 | Lumberton, North Carolina........ | 72 | Two streamliners collided. |
| 1944, Jan. 16 | León Province, Spain.............. | 500 | Train wrecked inside tunnel. |
| 1944, Mar. 2 | Salerno, Italy.................... | 521 | Train stalled in tunnel; mass suffocation. |
| 1944, Dec. 31 | Near Ogden, Utah................ | 50 | Two sections of the Pacific Limited wrecked. |
| 1945, Feb. 1 | Cazadero, Mexico................. | 100 | Train with religious pilgrims hit by freight train. |
| 1946, Mar. 20 | Near Aracaju, Brazil.............. | 185 | Train wrecked. |
| 1946, Apr. 25 | Naperville, Illinois............... | 45 | Train collision. |
| 1947, Aug. 3 | Sumatra, East Indies.............. | 400 | Train wrecked. |
| 1948, Mar. 31 | Osaka, Japan..................... | 70 | Express hit electric train. |
| 1949, Apr. 28 | Near Johannesburg, South Africa.... | 73 | Three trains collided. |
| 1949, Oct. 22 | Nowy Dwor, Poland............... | 200 | Danzig-Warsaw Express derailed. |
| 1950, Apr. 6 | Near Tanguá, Brazil.............. | 108 | Train fell into flooded Indios River. |
| 1950, May 7 | Bihar State, India................ | 81 | Punjab mail train crashed near Jasidih; possibly sabotaged. |
| 1950, Nov. 22 | Richmond Hill, New York.......... | 79 | Train collided with standing commuter train. |
| 1951, Feb. 6 | Woodbridge, New Jersey.......... | 85 | Commuter train fell through temporary overpass. |
| 1951, June 7 | Near Rio de Janeiro, Brazil........ | 54 | Train and gasoline truck collided at grade crossing. |
| 1952, Mar. 4 | Near Rio de Janeiro, Brazil........ | 119 | Two passenger trains collided. |
| 1952, July 9 | Near Rzepin, Poland.............. | 160 | Train wrecked. |
| 1952, Oct. 8 | Harrow, England................. | 112 | Commuter train hit by two express trains. |
| 1953, Dec. 24 | Near Wairoa, New Zealand........ | 155 | Wellington-Auckland Express fell into stream. |
| 1954, Jan. 21 | North of Karachi, Pakistan........ | 60 | Mail express wrecked. |
| 1954, Jan. 31 | Near Seoul, South Korea........... | 56 | Train crashed. |
| 1954, Sept. 2 | Northern Negros Island, the Philippines.................. | 55 | Logging train wrecked on bridge. |
| 1954, Sept. 28 | East of Hyderabad, India........... | 137 | Express fell from flood-damaged bridge. |
| 1955, Apr. 3 | Near Guadalajara, Mexico......... | 300 | Train fell into canyon. |
| 1956, Sept. 2 | Near Secunderabad, India......... | 121 | Two coaches fell into river as bridge collapsed. |
| 1956, Nov. 23 | Marudaiyar River, India........... | 143 | Express train plunged down river embankment. |
| 1957, Sept. 1 | Jamaica, British West Indies....... | 178 | Train pitched into ravine. |
| 1957, Sept. 29 | Near Montgomery, West Pakistan.... | 250 | Express crashed into standing oil train. |
| 1957, Oct. 20 | Near Istanbul, Turkey............. | 89 | Two trains collided at high speed. |
| 1957, Dec. 4 | Near London, England............ | 92 | Commuter trains collided. |
| 1958, Mar. 7 | Santa Cruz, Brazil................ | 67 | Three commuter trains collided. |
| 1958, May 8 | Near Rio de Janeiro, Brazil........ | 128 | Two trains collided head-on. |
| 1958, Sept. 15 | Newark Bay, Bayonne, New Jersey.. | 48 | Train plunged through lift bridge. |
| 1959, May 28 | Java, Indonesia.................. | 92 | Train plunged into ravine. |
| 1959, June 5 | São Paulo, Brazil................. | 60 | Two trains collided head-on. |
| 1960, May 15 | Leipzig, East Germany............ | 59 | Local train and express collided. |
| 1960, Nov. 14 | Pardubice, Czechoslovakia......... | 110 | Two passenger trains collided. |
| 1961, Dec. 23 | Cantanzaro, Italy................. | 69 | Train car plummeted into gorge. |
| 1962, Jan. 8 | Woerden, Netherlands............ | 91 | Passenger trains collided. |
| 1962, May 3 | Tokyo, Japan.................... | 163 | Two commuter trains collided with a freight train. |
| 1962, May 31 | Voghera, Italy................... | 63 | Passenger train collided with a freight train. |
| 1962, July 21 | Dumraon, India.................. | 69 | Passenger train and freight train collided. |
| 1964, Jan. 4 | Jajinci, Yugoslavia............... | 66 | Commuter train hit stalled passenger train. |
| 1964, Feb. 1 | Altamirano, Argentina............ | 70 | Express rammed stalled freight train. |
| 1964, July 26 | Oporto, Portugal................. | 94 | Train wrecked. |
| 1965, Oct. 5 | Near Durban, South Africa........ | 100 | Passenger train derailed. |
| 1965, Dec. 9 | Burma.......................... | 76 | Two trains collided head-on near Tungoo. |
| 1966, Apr. 20 | Lumding, India.................. | 55 | Passenger train exploded; suspected sabotage. |
| 1966, June 13 | Bombay, India................... | 60 | Two suburban trains collided. |
| 1967, July 6 | Langenweddingen, East Germany.... | 82 | Train collided with gasoline truck, causing explosion; most persons killed were children. |
| 1967, July 6 | Korat, Thailand.................. | 43 | Train hit crowded bus near station; country's worst rail disaster. |

* Estimated.

# FOCUS ON THE NEWS

## FOREST FIRES IN THE NORTHWEST

Wilde World

Flames move up Johnson Ridge in Washington's Snoqualmie National Forest during August 1967. About 850 men battled the blaze which destroyed more than 4,000 acres of timber before it was contained.

Vast timber areas in the western United States and Canada were destroyed in August and early September, 1967, when drought, dry lightning, and human carelessness combined to set off hundreds of forest fires. Major blazes raged in Idaho, Montana, Oregon, Washington, California, and British Columbia. Dry lightning (lightning unaccompanied by rainstorms) was said to have caused the great majority of the fires. However, in late August large sections of the Pacific Northwest were placed off limits to campers in order to reduce the possibility of fires caused by carelessness.

Hardest hit was the heavily forested Idaho panhandle. On August 30 President Johnson declared Idaho a major disaster area. The destruction in Montana included about 8,500 acres of timber in Glacier National Park. Oregon's most serious fire was in the area overlooking the Snake River Canyon,

on the Idaho state line, where more than 400 men battled a blaze that ultimately destroyed 1,100 acres. Large fires in Washington were confined to the northeastern section of the state.

The worst forest fire in the history of British Columbia claimed tens of thousands of acres in the area of Lake Sushwap. A squad of more than 1,000 men was needed to bring the blaze under control.

In California, the town of Three Rivers, near Sequoia National Park, was threatened for several days by a major fire that was finally halted at the community's outskirts. Smaller blazes destroyed homes in southern California's San Fernando Valley.

By early September the epidemic of forest fires had abated. However, well over 100,000 acres of timber had been destroyed, and the area's wildlife had suffered inestimable losses.

## WORLD'S MOST DEVASTATING FIRES AND EXPLOSIONS

| DATE | PLACE | DEATHS * | EXPLANATION |
|------|-------|----------|-------------|
| 1666, Sept. 2–6 | London, England | — | Fire destroyed many public buildings, 89 churches, and over 13,200 houses; 200,000 homeless. |
| 1835, Dec. 16 | New York, New York | — | Nearly 700 buildings burned; about a $20 million loss. |
| 1836, Feb. 14 | St. Petersburg, Russia | 700 | Theater fire. |
| 1842, May 5–7 | Hamburg, Germany | 100 | More than 4,000 buildings lost; property damage about $35 million. |
| 1845, Apr. 10 | Pittsburgh, Pennsylvania | — | 1,000 buildings destroyed in fire; a $6 million loss. |
| 1846, June 12 | Quebec, Canada | 200 | Theater fire. |
| 1851, May 4 | St. Louis, Missouri | — | Much of city burned; a $15 million loss. |
| 1863, Dec. 8 | Santiago, Chile | 2,000 | Church of the Compania burns while filled with worshipers. |
| 1866, July 4 | Portland, Maine | — | City almost totally destroyed by fire; a $10 million loss. |
| 1866, Oct. 13 | Quebec, Canada | — | 2,500 buildings burned. |
| 1871, Oct. 8–9 | Chicago, Illinois | 250 | 3½ square miles devastated by fire; 17,450 buildings lost; 100,000 homeless; about a $200 million loss. |
| 1871, Oct. 8–14 | Michigan and Wisconsin | 1,000 | Great forest fire, after three months drought, devastated large area, including town of Pestigo, Wisconsin. |
| 1872, Nov. 9–11 | Boston, Massachusetts | — | More than 600 buildings ruined in fire; about a $75 million loss. |
| 1876, Dec. 5 | Brooklyn, New York | 295 | Conway's theater fire. |
| 1877, June 20 | St. John, New Brunswick, Canada | 100 | Fire; about a $12,500,000 property loss. |
| 1881, Dec. 8 | Vienna, Austria | 640 | Ring Theater fire. |
| 1883, Jan. 13 | Berdichev, Russia | 270 | Theater fire. |
| 1887, May 25 | Paris, France | 200 | Opéra Comique fire. |
| 1887, Sept. 4 | Exeter, England | 200 | Theater fire. |
| 1888, May 25 | Oporto, Portugal | 200 | Baquet Theater fire. |
| 1889, June 6 | Seattle and Spokane, Washington | — | Fire loss in each city about $10 million. |
| 1894, Sept. 1 | Hinckley, Minnesota | 418 | 160,000 forest acres burned; loss at $25 million. |
| 1897, May 4 | Paris, France | 150 | Fire at charity bazaar. |
| 1899, Mar. 17 | New York, New York | 45 | Windsor Hotel fire. |
| 1900, Apr. 26 | Hull and Ottawa, Canada | — | Fire losses ot $10 million. |
| 1900, June 30 | Hoboken, New Jersey | 300 | Pier burned; property damage, $4,627,000. |
| 1902, Sept. 20 | Birmingham, Alabama | 115 | Church fire. |
| 1903, Dec. 30 | Chicago, Illinois | 639 | Iroquois Theater fire. |
| 1904, Feb. 7–8 | Baltimore, Maryland | — | 140 acres, encompassing 75 city blocks, destroyed by fire; an $85 million loss. |
| 1906, Mar. 10 | Courrières, France | 1,060 | Mine explosion. |
| 1906, Apr. 18 | San Francisco, California | 700 | Following earthquake, fire devastated four square miles; property damage about $500 million. |
| 1908, Jan. 13 | Bovertown, Pennsylvania | 100 | Motion picture machine exploded; Rhoades Opera House burned. |
| 1908, Mar. 4 | Collinwood, Ohio | 161 | School fire. |
| 1908, Apr. 12 | Chelsea, Massachusetts | — | Destroyed by fire; a $17 million loss. |
| 1909, Feb. 15 | Acapulco, Mexico | 250 | Flores Theater fire. |
| 1911, Mar. 25 | New York, New York | 145 | Triangle Shirtwaist Factory fire. |
| 1913, Mar. 7 | Baltimore, Maryland | 55 | Dynamite exploded in harbor. |
| 1914, June 25–26 | Salem, Massachusetts | — | 1700 buildings burned; a $14 million loss. |
| 1916, July 30 | Jersey City, New Jersey | — | German war sabotage caused Black Tom Island explosion, with $22 million loss. |
| 1917, Apr. 10 | Eddystone, Pennsylvania | 133 | Munitions plant explosion. |
| 1917, Dec. 6 | Halifax, Nova Scotia | 1,500 | Explosion of war material caused fire; 20,000 homeless; a $35 million loss. |
| 1918, Oct. 4–5 | Morgan Station, New Jersey | 64 | Gillespie Loading Co. explosion. |
| 1918, Oct. 13–15 | Minnesota and Wisconsin | 1,000 | Forest fires; a loss of $100 million. |
| 1919, June 20 | San Juan, Puerto Rico | 150 | Mayaguez Theater fire. |
| 1921, Sept. 21 | Oppau, Germany | 600 | Ammonium nitrate plant exploded. |
| 1922, Sept. 13 | Smyrna, Turkey | — | City almost totally destroyed by fire; 100,000 homeless; financial loss about $100 million; great loss of life. |
| 1929, May 15 | Cleveland, Ohio | 125 | Poisonous fumes generated from burning X-ray film caused mass suffocation at Crile Hospital Clinic. |
| 1930, Apr. 21 | Columbus, Ohio | 317 | Convicts burned to death as fire swept through four cellblocks of Ohio State Penitentiary. |
| 1934, Mar. 22 | Hakodate, Japan | 1,500 | Fire destroyed largest city north of Tokyo. |
| 1934, May 19 | Chicago, Illinois | — | Union Stockyards burned; a $10 million loss. |
| 1934, Sept. 22 | Wrexham, Wales | 265 | Coal mine explosion. |
| 1937, Feb. 13 | Antung, Manchuria | 658 | Theater fire. |
| 1937, Mar. 18 | New London, Texas | 413 | Schoolhouse destroyed by natural gas explosion. |

* Estimated.

| DATE | PLACE | DEATHS * | EXPLANATION |
|------|-------|----------|-------------|
| 1938, Nov. 12–16 | Changsha, China | 2,000 | Fire leveled city. |
| 1939, Mar. 1 | Osaka, Japan | 500 | Explosion of munitions dump destroyed village in Osaka district; thousands homeless. |
| 1939, July 10 | Peñaranda de Bracamonte, Spain | 100 | Town demolished by munitions factory explosion. |
| 1939, Nov. 14 | Lagunillas, Venezuela | 500 | Oil town built on Lake Maracaibo destroyed by fire. |
| 1940, Apr. 23 | Natchez, Mississippi | 198 | Dance hall fire. |
| 1941, May 31 | Jersey City, New Jersey | — | Eight square blocks of waterfront ruined by fire; a $25 million loss. |
| 1941, June 8 | Smederevo, Yugoslavia | 1,000 | Explosion of ammunition plant; most of town destroyed. |
| 1942, Apr. 26 | Honkeiko Colliery, Manchuria | 1,549 | Worst mine disaster in history. |
| 1942, May 1 | Tessenderlo, Belgium | 250 | Chemical works explosion. |
| 1942, Nov. 28 | Boston, Massachusetts | 493 | Cocoanut Grove nightclub fire. |
| 1942, Dec. 13 | St. John's, Newfoundland | 100 | Knights of Columbus Hostel fire panic. |
| 1943, May 7 | Sandoná, Colombia | 103 | Municipal Palace demolished by fire. |
| 1944, Apr. 14 | Bombay, India | 128 | Ship's fire caused explosion in ammunition dump. |
| 1944, July 6 | Hartford, Connecticut | 165 | Audience panicked in circus "Big Top" fire. |
| 1944, July 17 | Port Chicago, California | 300 | Two ammunition dump explosions. |
| 1944, Oct. 20 | Cleveland, Ohio | 121 | Liquid gas tanks exploded; fire raged through 50-block area; 1,000 homeless; property damage at $10 million |
| 1946, June 5 | Chicago, Illinois | 60 | LaSalle Hotel fire. |
| 1946, Dec. 7 | Atlanta, Georgia | 120 | Winecoff Hotel fire. |
| 1947, Mar. 25 | Centralia, Illinois | 111 | Coal mine explosion. |
| 1947, Apr. 16 | Texas City, Texas | 468 | Explosion of French ship GRANDCAMP ruined most of city. |
| 1947, Aug. 20 | Cádiz, Spain | 400 | Shipyard explosion. |
| 1947, Oct. 25 | Bar Harbor, Maine | — | Statewide disaster area as a result of forest fire; large part of Bar Harbor destroyed; estimated loss at $30 million. |
| 1948, Mar. 9 | Tsingtao, China | 200 | Ammunition storehouse exploded. |
| 1948, July 28 | Ludwigshafen, Germany | 200 | I. G. Farben Company wrecked by explosions and fire; loss at $15 million. |
| 1948, Sept. 22 | Hong Kong | 135 | Fire and chemical explosion in warehouse. |
| 1949, Sept. 4 | Chungking, China | 1,700 | Central part of city burned; 100,000 homeless. |
| 1951, May 13 | Kano, Nigeria | 100 | Movie house burned. |
| 1951, Dec. 21 | West Frankfort, Illinois | 119 | Coal mine explosion. |
| 1955, Feb. 17 | Near Yokohama, Japan | 97 | Home for aged women burned. |
| 1956, Aug. 7 | Cali, Colombia | 1,100 | Seven trucks carrying dynamite exploded. |
| 1956, Aug. 8 | Marcinelle, Belgium | 263 | Coal mine fires. |
| 1957, Feb. 17 | Warrenton, Missouri | 72 | Home for aged burned. |
| 1958, Feb. 19 | Near Asansol, India | 180 | Coal mine explosion. |
| 1958, June 23 | Santo Amaro, Brazil | 100 | Fireworks explosion. |
| 1958, Dec. 1 | Chicago, Illinois | 93 | Parochial school fire. |
| 1958, Dec. 16 | Bogotá, Colombia | 84 | Department store fire. |
| 1960, Jan. 21 | Coalbrook, South Africa | 437 | Coal mine cave-ins and explosion. |
| 1960, Feb. 22 | Zwickau, East Germany | 123 | Explosion in Karl Marx Mine. |
| 1960, Mar. 4 | Havana, Cuba | 75 | French munition ship exploded. |
| 1960, July 14 | Guatemala City, Guatemala | 200 | Hospital for insane swept by fire. |
| 1960, Nov. 13 | Amude, Syria | 152 | Movie house fire. |
| 1961, July 8 | Dolna Suce, Czechoslovakia | 108 | Coal mine gas explosion. |
| 1961, Dec. 17 | Niteroi, Brazil | 323 | Circus tent fire. |
| 1962, Feb. 7 | Saar, Germany | 299 | Coal mine explosion. |
| 1963, May 4 | Diourbel, Senegal | 64 | Theater fire. |
| 1963, Oct. 31 | Indianapolis, Indiana | 73 | Explosion at State Fair coliseum. |
| 1963, Nov. 23 | Fitchville, Ohio | 63 | Fire burned rest home. |
| 1964, July 23 | Bone, Algeria | 100 | Explosion aboard Egyptian munitions ship STAR OF ALEXANDRIA. |
| 1964, Aug. 24 | Atlatahuca, Mexico | 45 | Fireworks explosion. |
| 1965, Mar. 1 | Montreal, Canada | 23 | Apartment house explosion. |
| 1965, May 17 | Rhondda Valley, Wales | 31 | Mine explosion. |
| 1965, May 26 | Bihar, India | 400 | Mine disaster. |
| 1965, June 1 | Fukuoka, Japan | 236 | Mine disaster. |
| 1965, June 8 | Kakanj, Yugoslavia | 108 | Mine disaster. |
| 1965, Aug. 9 | Searcy, Arkansas | 53 | Explosion in a Titan II missile silo. |
| 1966, Jan. 28 | Boston, Massachusetts | 12 | Explosion and fire in two hotels; 50 injured. |
| 1966, Feb. 8 | Iloilo, Philippines | 18 | Fire left 10,000 homeless. |
| 1966, Apr. 26 | Amraoti, India | 32 | Explosion in cotton seed oil mill. |
| 1966, Oct. 17 | New York, N.Y. | 12 | Firemen killed when floor collapsed in burning building; worst disaster in New York Fire Department's history. |
| 1967, July 16 | Jay, Florida | 38 | Convicts burned in prison work-camp barracks. |
| 1967, Aug.–Sept. | Montana, Idaho, Oregon, Washington, British Columbia, California | — | Massive forest fires. |

* Estimated.

# AMERICAN HOME AND FAMILY

## The American Woman · The Family · The Kitchen · Marriages and Divorces

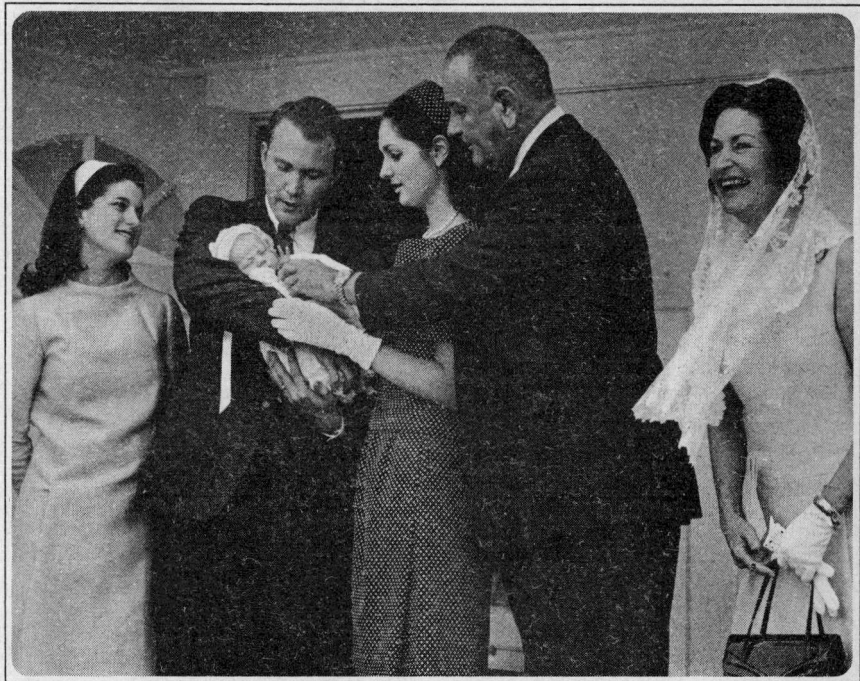

The Nation's First Family admires its newest member. Left to Right: Luci Johnson Nugent and husband Patrick Nugent, who holds their infant son Patrick Lyndon, Lynda Bird Johnson, the President, and Mrs. Johnson.

### THE AMERICAN WOMAN: 1968

The American woman stands at the threshold of a new era. Modern appliances have lightened her work load, giving her more free time than ever before. Social legislation has given her equal rights with men and equal opportunities for employment. She may marry or not, early or late; she may have as many children as she wants, when she wants; she may work full-time, part-time, or not at all.

Today 46 per cent of all American women between the ages of 18 and 64 are employed; the time is coming when only one woman in 20 will have gone through life without ever working. Women first streamed into the labor force in large numbers during World War II, when the male labor force was greatly depleted by the war effort. Since then they have made valuable contributions in such fields as science, medicine, welfare, education, and literature. Some have

gone into politics; others have championed social reform. President Johnson, speaking on feminine achievement, has noted: "Women have been on the forefront of nearly every great social reform that we have had in America."

But the American woman's most important role is still that of homemaker and mother. As a homemaker, she must be skilled in such diverse fields as interior decorating, home maintenance, child psychology, nutrition, health, and budget planning.

In her role as a mother, the American woman takes on her greatest responsibility and exerts her most significant influence. As a creator of social values, she is virtually a creator of the future. The love and training she gives her child will go far in shaping the role he is to play in the succeeding generation—as a member of society as well as an individual.

# THE AMERICAN WOMAN

Photos from Eleanor Lambert

Three designs by winners of the 1967 Coty American Fashion Critics' Awards: Rudi Gernreich's off-beat cape and tunic; Oscar de la Renta's elegant evening dress; and a lumber jacket suit by Donald Brooks.

## FASHION: 1967

Fashions in 1967 underwent a dizzying succession of changes. The girl who ushered in the new year in a silver vinyl "miniskirt" was likely to have switched by September to a demure velvet pageboy suit.

Hemlines fluctuated like an uneasy stock market. Twiggy, the puckish English model who took the fashion world by storm, introduced the "micro-mini," an abbreviated version of the miniskirt worn seven or eight inches above the knee. In the fall the mid-calf skirt—promptly dubbed the "midi," or "maxi"—made a strong showing after several earlier starts by such well-known designers as Marc Bohan. (His calf-length "soldier" coats were shown over miniskirts the previous season.) For the most part, hemlines fell around the knee, varying one or two inches above for younger wearers.

● **The Look:** Fashion drew on a far-ranging assortment of periods, places, and things. Perhaps the strongest single influence was Russian. It appeared everywhere—in long "maxi-coats" cuffed in fox or sable, in cossack tunics and blouses, and even in hairdos looped in peasant braids. The military look was also popular, with coats, capes, and doughboy jackets displaying an abundance of brass buttons and epaulets. For evening there were caftans from the Middle East, lounging pajamas in exotic African prints, and romantic black velvets framed in lace in the Edwardian tradition.

A major revival of 1967 was the belt. Variations of Dior's chain hung low on the hips; wide swatches of crushed leather cinched the waist; skinny leather straps lent shape to the popular cardigan coat. Hardware was another big item. Sportswear flashed shiny brass and steel studs, bolts, grippers, and locks; huge industrial zippers took the place of buttons.

● **Coats and Suits:** Coats tended to curve into the figure from narrow armholes, then curve out again at the hips. A favorite shape was the "pyramid," a dramatic extension of the A-line. "Fun furs" were younger and wilder than ever; rabbit, sheared and stenciled, masqueraded as everything from antelope to zebra. Suits often came with a matching vest or jerkin. Short dirndls replaced A-line skirts, while the equestrian hacking jacket inspired suits with a long, lean look. The continuing popularity of the pantsuit (both long and short) led inevitably to the pants-dress, usually a straight little shift ending in a flip of culottes.

● **Dresses:** Dress favorites included the tent, the T-shirt dress, the coat dress, the crocheted baby dress, and the halter dress. The "little black dress" made a spirited comeback after being relegated to the back of the closet for two years by the Courrège white and the Cardin pastels.

● **Sportswear:** Another classic that reappeared was the Scottish tartan. Kilts were especially popular, but the Highland hues carried over to coats, slacks, and jumpers. Sweaters were frequently trimmed with shoulder buttons or self-belts. "Maxi-sweaters," long shetland pullovers that stretched below the hips, were featured in college collections.

- **Paper Fashions:** The paper trade, which began as a sales gimmick in 1966, boomed in 1967. Paper boutiques cropped up everywhere, with a ream of offerings from bedroom slippers to evening dresses. One enterprising manufacturer, quick to grasp the trend, came out with paper bathing suits. Topping off the disposable wardrobe was papier-mâché jewelry, brightly lacquered in such shades as hot pink, citron yellow, and poison green.
- **Accessories:** Hats returned as brightly colored scarves slipped back around the neck. The general look was casual—perky berets, wide-brimmed floppy hats (or stiff-brimmed and tied under the chin), fur cossack hats, and visored deerslayer caps.

## BEAUTY HINTS: 1967

Beauty editors in 1967 emphasized the natural glowing look, heightened by translucent foundations, rosy skin toners, sheer face powders, and pale, glossy lipsticks. The effect was a fragile luster by day, a glowing luminescence by night. In summer the paler tones deepened to a tawny glow, a look characterized by one authority as "instant Acapulco."

Powder bases were lighter and sheerer with only the slightest hint of color. Powders were often transparent, playing up the natural color of the skin. Lipsticks came in glossy tones of pink and bronze. One major cosmetic house attempted to revive the vibrant reds, but the paler tones continued to be the most popular. Eyes were dark and dramatic, often underscored by an extra set of lashes; the English model, Twiggy, started a fad with lower lashes sketched beneath the eye. Eye shadows were muted, often highlighted with white. Hairstyles ranged from the very short feather cut to the long, thick fall, regally shaped and frequently curled.

- **Eye Makeup:** Eye makeup that is carefully applied lights up the eyes and gives the illusion of greater depth. Here's how to do it: Apply white eye shadow in two strips, one just below the eyebrow, the other across the lid. Then smudge a soft halo of colored shadow in the hollow between the eyebrows and the lid. A trick the models use is to draw a thin line across the curve of the eyesocket, just where the lid begins; use liquid eyeliner or an eyebrow pencil or dry cake powder, whichever is easiest. Finish up with eyeliner traced along the base of the lids and mascara brushed over the lashes. For eyelashes that are on the skimpy side, there are special mascaras containing tiny particles of silk which cling to the lashes for added thickness and length.

Eyebrows look best if they follow a natural line, paralleling the brow bone as closely as possible. Unnaturally extended or arched eyebrows look harsh and artificial. Dry cake powder in brown, gray, or auburn may give better results than a black pencil. To apply the powder, draw a tiny dot on the brow, directly above the outer edge of the iris. (This is where the

Shoes were low and chunky, squared off at the end or softly rounded. The favorite was a sturdy little pump buckled or chained across the vamp; sling backs and Mary Janes appeared in bright patents for day, silver kid for evening. Boots went thigh-high in skintight stretch leather or vinyl.

Hosiery departments bloomed in a profusion of colors, patterns, and textures. There were pale string stockings for spring and dark, slinky stockings for fall. For evening there were silver-threaded sheers or lacy, textured tights. College girls favored knee socks.

Handbags continued to be on the small side, often suspended from shoulder chains. For summer, wooden-beaded bags appeared alongside the traditional straw bag. For fall, there were bright patent leather bags.

brow should arch.) Starting at this point, make short feathery strokes backward to the beginning of the brow; then return to the dot, and lightly sketch in the rest of the brow. Gently smooth the brows into place and you are finished.

- **Lipstick:** To make old lipsticks easier to apply, shave off the ends with a razor blade, cutting diagonally to make a sharp point.
- **Steam Facial:** Healthy, glowing skin is a must for today's "translucent look," and a steam facial is one of the best ways to achieve it. Steam mist opens and cleanses the pores. Circulation is stimulated and the complexion takes on a new and radiant tone. Give yourself a facial. You can easily have steam treatment at home by using an electric frying pan. It should be filled with about half an inch of water and set at 400°. Cleanse your face thoroughly with cream while the water is heating. When the water begins to steam, lean over the pan, letting the steam bathe your face. Steam for about five minutes; then splash on cold water to close the pores. Finish up with a facial mask or cleansing grains.

If you do not have an electric frying pan, turn on the hot water faucet full force and lean over the basin, using a towel to form a tent over you and the steam. *Never use a teakettle* —the steam is concentrated and could burn. For the full salon effect there is a facial sauna designed for home use. It comes with the cleanser, freshener, moisturizer, and emollient that are generally used in professional skin treatment.

- **Hair Care:** The new emphasis on thickness and the old injunction against teasing your hair call for hairdos with extra body. You can achieve this by using stale beer as a setting lotion; it dries without aroma or stickiness and gives greater body than plain water. To apply, pour the beer into an atomizer and spray it on as needed.
- **Patent Shine:** To keep patent leather sleek and shiny, clean it with ordinary window cleaner. Simply spray on the cleaner and then polish to a high luster. Never use shoe polish— it will destroy the shine.

# ETIQUETTE AND PROTOCOL

Forms of etiquette and protocol date back to the beginnings of history. The world's major civilizations, no less than the most primitive tribes, established and observed rules of social conduct among their members. The rigidity of the forms varied, and the rules changed with the lives of the people. Codes of social behavior have been influenced by shifting mores and customs, by geography, by technological progress and inventions, even by legislation, politics, and war. However, most basic forms of etiquette and protocol remain rooted in the simple principles of courtesy, common sense, and respect for fellow human beings.

Contemporary social codes have evolved to meet the needs of modern men living in a highly mobile, increasingly complex society. In the mid-twentieth-century world of shrinking distances, jet travel, and greatly expanded technical facilities, the importance of effective communication among men becomes increasingly apparent. The manner in which men write and speak to each other, in both business and society, frequently determines the way in which their messages are received.

This article deals generally with some of the basic, commonly accepted forms of communication among contemporary men and women. Under certain circumstances, rules of social behavior may be qualified by exceptions or modifications. And special forms frequently apply in special situations. More detailed information may be found in books dealing extensively with the subject of etiquette and protocol. Two such works are: *Emily Post's Etiquette, The Blue Book of Social Usage,* revised by Elizabeth L. Post (Funk & Wagnalls Company, Inc., New York), and *Amy Vanderbilt's New Complete Book of Etiquette,* by Amy Vanderbilt (Doubleday & Company, Inc., Garden City, New York).

## ■ INVITATIONS AND REPLIES

Formal invitations are issued for weddings, formal dinners, debuts, formal dances, and official functions. Engraved on a white card, or handwritten (never typed) on plain stationery, the formal invitation is extended in the third person, following a stylized format (see examples below). It should be sent about two to three weeks ahead of time. The courtesy of a reply is requested by the inclusion of *R.s.v.p.* (from the French, *Répondez s'il vous plaît,* "Respond if you please") in the lower left-hand corner of the invitation. If the address to which the reply is to be sent is other than the address given in the invitation, it is written below *R.s.v.p.* Informal invitations, which are used much more frequently than formal invitations in the United States, are issued for informal or semi-formal dinners, cocktail parties, dances, *(continued)*

Mr. and Mrs. Thomas Hendricks
request the pleasure of your company
at dinner
on
Thursday, June the twelfth
at seven o'clock
21 East Fiftieth Street
R.s.v.p.

**Engraved Formal Invitation**

Mr. and Mrs. Thomas Hendricks
request the pleasure of
Mr. and Mrs. John Hall's
Company at dinner
on Thursday, June the twelfth
at seven o'clock
21 East Fiftieth Street
R.S.V.P.

**Handwritten Formal Invitation**

## FORMAL INVITATIONS AND REPLIES

Mr. and Mrs. John Hall
accept with pleasure
the kind invitation of
Mr. and Mrs. Thomas Hendricks
for dinner
on Thursday, the twelfth of June
at seven o'clock

**Acceptance of a Formal Invitation**

Mr. and Mrs. John Hall
regret that they are unable to accept
the kind invitation of
Mr. and Mrs. Thomas Hendricks
for Thursday, the twelfth of June

**Regrets to a Formal Invitation**

luncheons, teas, etc. Informal invitations may be written in the second person on visiting cards or informals, as well as on printed or plain stationery. They may also be extended in person or by telephone. Unless black tie, or some other special form of dress, is specified, guests should assume that street dress will be appropriate. *R.s.v.p.* may be used if desired. A practice gaining increasing acceptance is that of using *R.s.v.p.* followed by *Regrets Only* and a telephone number, to indicate that a reply is expected only from those persons who will be unable to attend. This form, however, is never used on a formal invitation.

### ■ ACCEPTANCES AND REGRETS

The form of an invitation determines the form of the reply. When the invitation carries the notation *R.s.v.p.*, a reply is mandatory and should be sent promptly.

Formal acceptances and regrets are handwritten in the third person on plain stationery, following a stylized format (see examples on page 586). The date and hour indicated on the invitation are repeated in the acceptance; the date only in regrets. Acceptances and regrets are addressed to both the host and hostess.

Strictly speaking, a reply to an informal invitation is required only when the invitation carries the notation *R.s.v.p.* However, it is always considered correct and courteous to acknowledge the invitation in some manner. Informal replies, like their formal counterparts, must follow the form of the invitation. If written, the reply may be sent on a visiting card, on an informal, or on printed or plain stationery. Informal replies may also be telephoned or delivered in person.

### ■ INTRODUCTIONS

In most instances, younger people are introduced to their elders. However, a man usually is introduced to a woman, even if she is much younger than he. A woman is introduced to a man only if he is the head of a government, a member of a royal family, a clergyman, a governor, or a mayor.

Introductions should be short and direct, and both names should be pronounced clearly: "Mr. Jones, Mr. Smith," "Mrs. Thomas, this is Mr. Richardson," "Father Harris, may I present Mrs. Jones." Generally, "How do you do" or "Very nice to meet you" is sufficient acknowledgment.

In the United States, men shake hands as they are introduced, and stand when they are introduced to a woman. The woman may remain seated as men or other women are introduced to her. However, she stands when she is introduced to an older person or to a person of some distinction. A hostess always rises and goes forward to greet her guests, usually shaking hands with each one as he arrives and departs. Although a woman generally extends her hand first, she never refuses to shake hands if a gentleman takes the initiative.

Guests arriving at a large gathering, such as a reception or a cocktail party, need be introduced only to the persons nearest them; they are expected to introduce themselves to other guests as they move through the group.

It is usually correct—and often a great help —to add a polite word or two about one or both of the persons being introduced. Thus, it would be quite proper to say, "Mrs. Street, this is my daughter, Sarah," or "Mr. Michaels, I would like you to meet Mr. Gardner, our house guest," or "May I present my brother-in-law, Henry Slater," or "Mrs. Courtney, this is my son, Jim," (then to Jim) "Mrs. Courtney is a member of our fund-raising committee."

Rarely, if ever, is it correct to introduce one person to another simply as "my friend," since in most instances this implies that one person is less a friend than the other.

### ■ THE TELEPHONE

Since the telephone is used extensively today for the conduct of social and business affairs that were formerly transacted by invitation or by letter, correct use of this medium is essential. The caller must always identify himself fully to the person who answers the telephone.

When a social call is made to a private home, the name of the caller generally is sufficient: "This is Mrs. Jones. Is Mrs. Thomas at home, please?" If the person called is not available, the caller should leave his name and, if appropriate, an indication of the reason for his call: "Please tell Mrs. Thomas that Mrs. Jones called about her dinner party on Thursday. I will call her again this evening"; or "Please ask Mrs. Thomas to call me at her convenience."

Identification is equally important in business calls. Reaching a secretary, the caller should identify himself and the concern he represents: "This is James Smith of the Acme Sales Corporation. Is Mr. Johnson in, please?" Again, if the person is not available, the caller should leave a message indicating the reason for his call.

If the caller reaches an answering service, he should leave his name, address, and telephone number, as well as an indication of the reason for his call.

### ■ THE OFFICE

If observance of accepted amenities is important in social life, it is doubly so in business.

An office is, first of all, a place of business. Personal problems and personal relationships have no place in the nine-to-five world of commerce and industry. Business professionals do not use their offices for the conduct of extensive personal discussions or private telephone calls. Rather, they arrive on time to conduct the day's affairs with a minimum of confusion and a maximum of dispatch, relegating personal business to non-working hours. Needless to say, discretion is mandatory for all employees; there are few surer ways of losing a job than by discussing confidential business matters outside one's office.

An employer sets the tone for his entire place of business. Since employees quite naturally follow the example of their employer, he should be courteous and pleasant, and at the same time, efficient and impersonal.

## U.S. FAMILY INCOME RISES

Approximately 800,000 American families took a giant step in 1966. Their income edged over the $3,000 mark—and out of what the Administration defines as the "poverty bracket."

At the higher end of the scale, the number of families with incomes of $10,000 or more increased by 2.5 million, according to a U.S. Census Bureau report.

The median income increased from $6,957 to $7,436, a 7 per cent jump from 1965 and a 55 per cent increase over 1956. Prices also rose, however, meaning that the increase in purchasing power was only 4 per cent. The median income is the exact middle income for the 48.9 million American families. That is, half are above and half below that level.

In the lower level, 7.0 million families, or 14.0 per cent, received incomes under $3,000,

compared with 16.5 per cent in 1965. Almost 26 per cent had incomes below $3,000 in 1956.

Some 14.5 million families had incomes of $10,000 or more in 1966. This represented 30 per cent, compared with 25 per cent in 1965 and fewer than 8 per cent in 1956.

More than one out of every 10 families had incomes of at least $15,000, compared with one out of every 50 in 1956. The largest single percentage of American families, 20.4 per cent, were in the $10,000 to $15,000 category.

Median income of non-white families was $4,628, compared with $7,722 for whites. Over 30 per cent of non-white families were below the poverty line, with 12 per cent of white families in that category. Only 12.2 per cent of non-white families had incomes above $10,000, compared with 31.6 per cent of white families.

## FAMILY INCOME IN THE UNITED STATES: 1961–1966

Source: U.S. Bureau of the Census

| FAMILY INCOME | 1966 | 1965 | 1964 | 1963 | 1962 | 1961 |
|---|---|---|---|---|---|---|
| Under $1,000 | 2.3% | 2.9% | 3.2% | 3.8% | 4.2% | 5.0% |
| $1,000 to $1,999 | 5.4 | 6.0 | 6.3 | 6.8 | 7.4 | 7.7 |
| $2,000 to $2,999 | 6.6 | 7.2 | 8.1 | 7.9 | 8.3 | 8.7 |
| $3,000 to $3,999 | 6.8 | 7.7 | 8.4 | 8.7 | 9.2 | 9.4 |
| $4,000 to $4,999 | 7.1 | 7.9 | 8.6 | 9.0 | 9.9 | 10.5 |
| $5,000 to $5,999 | 8.4 | 9.3 | 9.9 | 11.1 | 11.5 | 11.7 |
| $6,000 to $6,999 | 9.4 | 9.5 | 9.9 | 10.2 | 10.9 | 10.2 |
| $7,000 to $7,999 | 9.3 | 9.7 | 9.3 | 9.1 | 8.6 | 9.1 |
| $8,000 to $9,999 | 15.1 | 14.5 | 13.9 | 13.4 | 12.3 | 11.6 |
| $10,000 to $14,999 | 20.4 | 17.7 | 16.2 | 14.5 | 12.8 | 11.3 |
| $15,000 to $24,999 | 7.5 | 6.2 | 5.2 | 4.4 | 4.0 | 3.6 |
| $25,000 and over | 1.7 | 1.4 | 1.1 | 1.0 | 0.9 | 1.1 |
| **Median Family Income** | **$7,436** | **$6,957** | **$6,569** | **$6,249** | **$5,956** | **$5,737** |
| **Total Number of Families** | 48,922,000 | 48,279,000 | 47,835,000 | 47,436,000 | 46,998,000 | 46,341,000 |

## THE AMERICAN HOUSEWIFE AND THE MAN AROUND THE HOUSE

Is the American wife, or the American male, worth more around the house? Economists for the Chase Manhattan Bank have attempted to settle the argument through a comparison of 12 of the tasks a husband and wife are each called upon to perform daily, the number of hours they spend on them—and the going rate of pay for these jobs on the labor market.

If the American housewife complains that she spends 99.6 hours per week in work around the house, the American male can argue that

out of his 39 hours of "leisure" per week, he spends 24 of them on household chores. Husbands about to use this statistical weapon should remember, however, that the economists value a wife's various chores at $159.34 per week, while his task, from bartending to balancing checkbooks, would bring in a paltry $51.01 per week.

The comparative studies in the following table should do much to continue the battle between the sexes.

| WIFE'S JOBS | HOURS PER WEEK | RATE PER HR. | VALUE PER WEEK | HUSBAND'S JOBS | HOURS PER WEEK | RATE PER HR. | VALUE PER WEEK |
|---|---|---|---|---|---|---|---|
| Nursemaid | 44.5 | $1.25 | $55.63 | Lawn mower | 3½ | $1.55 | $5.43 |
| Dietitian | 1.2 | 2.50 | 3.00 | Night watchman | 1¼ | 1.96 | 2.45 |
| Food buyer | 3.3 | 1.50 | 4.95 | Garbage man | ¾ | 2.77 | 2.08 |
| Cook | 13.1 | 2.50 | 32.75 | Chauffeur | 4 | 2.20 | 8.80 |
| Dishwasher | 6.2 | 1.50 | 9.30 | Accountant | 1 | 3.00 | 3.00 |
| Housekeeper | 17.5 | 1.50 | 26.25 | General handyman | 1½ | 1.80 | 2.70 |
| Laundress | 5.9 | 1.90 | 11.21 | Fashion consultant | ½ | 2.00 | 1.00 |
| Seamstress | 1.3 | 2.50 | 3.25 | Bartender | 1 | 2.01 | 2.01 |
| Practical nurse | .6 | 2.00 | 1.20 | | | (with tips) | |
| Maintenance man | 1.7 | 2.25 | 3.83 | Barbecue chef | 2½ | 1.81 | 4.53 |
| Gardener | 2.3 | 1.55 | 3.57 | Youth counselor | 2 | 4.00 | 8.00 |
| Chauffeur | 2.0 | 2.20 | 4.40 | Maintenance man | 3½ | 2.25 | 7.88 |
| | | | | Assistant shopper | 2½ | 1.25 | 3.13 |
| **Total** | 99.6 | — | $159.34 | **Total** | 24 | — | $51.01 |
| | | | ($8,285.68 a year) | | | | ($2,652.52 a year) |

# 1967 AVERAGE RETAIL PRICES OF FOOD

Estimated retail prices of individual foods (excluding sales taxes) for urban United States as of July 1967 are given in the table below. This food price index is derived from U.S. Department of Labor studies of chain and independent retail food stores in 39 standard metropolitan areas and 17 smaller cities selected to represent all urban areas of the United States.

| FOOD | UNIT | PRICE |
|---|---|---|
| **Cereals and Bakery Products** | | |
| Flour, white............... | 5 lb. | 60.5¢ |
| Cornflakes................. | 12 oz. | 31.5 |
| Bread, white.............. | 1 lb. | 22.4 |
| Bread, whole wheat...... | 1 lb. | 29.7 |
| **Meats, Poultry, and Fish** | | |
| Steak, round.............. | 1 lb. | 109.8 |
| Steak, sirloin............. | 1 lb. | 118.8 |
| Steak, porterhouse........ | 1 lb. | 138.5 |
| Rib roast................. | 1 lb. | 94.1 |
| Hamburger................ | 1 lb. | 54.8 |
| Beef liver................ | 1 lb. | 61.2 |
| Veal cutlets.............. | 1 lb. | 163.0 |
| Pork chops............... | 1 lb. | 104.7 |
| Pork loin roast........... | 1 lb. | 74.6 |
| Pork sausage............. | 1 lb. | 65.4 |
| Ham, whole............... | 1 lb. | 69.7 |
| Bacon.................... | 1 lb. | 90.1 |
| Lamb chops.............. | 1 lb. | 161.8 |
| Frankfurters.............. | 1 lb. | 70.8 |
| Ham, canned.............. | 1 lb. | 107.3 |
| Frying chicken............ | 1 lb. | 38.8 |
| Chicken breasts........... | 1 lb. | 68.5 |
| Turkey................... | 1 lb. | 48.7 |
| Shrimp, frozen............ | 10 oz. | 86.1 |
| Tuna fish................. | 6½-oz. can | 34.6 |
| Sardines................. | 4-oz. can | 14.9 |

| FOOD | UNIT | PRICE |
|---|---|---|
| **Dairy Products** | | |
| Milk, fresh................ | ½ gal. | 51.5 |
| Milk, evaporated.......... | 14½-oz. can | 16.9 |
| Ice cream................. | ½ gal. | 82.7 |
| Butter.................... | 1 lb. | 84.0 |
| **Fresh Fruits and Vegetables** | | |
| Apples.................... | 1 lb. | 23.7 |
| Bananas................... | 1 lb. | 15.9 |
| Oranges.................. | 1 doz. | 74.5 |
| Grapefruit................ | each | 14.7 |
| Potatoes.................. | 10 lb. | 80.0 |
| Carrots................... | 1 lb. | 16.3 |
| Lettuce................... | head | 38.4 |
| Tomatoes................. | 1 lb. | 42.3 |
| **Other Home Foods** | | |
| Eggs, Grade A, large........ | 1 doz. | 44.9 |
| Margarine................. | 1 lb. | 28.6 |
| Sugar.................... | 5 lb. | 61.5 |
| **Non-alcoholic Beverages** | | |
| Coffee.................... | 1-lb. can | 77.5 |
| Coffee, instant............ | 6 oz. | 89.2 |
| Tea bags.................. | pkg. of 48 | 61.4 |
| **Prepared and Partially Prepared Foods** | | |
| Spaghetti................. | 15¼-oz. can | 16.4 |
| Potatoes, french fried, frozen | 9 oz. | 15.6 |
| Baby foods................ | 4½ oz. | 10.4 |

# HOW AMERICANS SPEND THEIR MONEY

The following chart, released by the Department of Commerce, gives personal consumption figures in millions of dollars for 12 main types of expenditures, and major subdivisions.

| GOODS AND SERVICES | 1965 | 1966 |
|---|---|---|
| **Clothing, jewelry**............. | $ 43,502 | $ 48,406 |
| Clothing, including cleaning..... | 34,389 | 38,033 |
| Jewelry and watches........... | 2,838 | 3,283 |
| Shoes, including repair......... | 5,681 | 6,373 |
| **Food and tobacco**.............. | 107,352 | 115,446 |
| Alcoholic beverages........... | 12,955 | 13,705 |
| Food only.................... | 98,952 | 106,677 |
| Tobacco..................... | 8,400 | 8,769 |
| **Foreign travel**................ | 3,150 | 3,384 |
| **Household operation**.......... | 61,793 | 66,658 |
| China and kitchenware........ | 2,524 | 2,774 |
| Domestic service............. | 3,964 | 4,028 |
| Furniture and furnishings...... | 16,531 | 18,166 |
| Household appliances.......... | 6,023 | 6,764 |
| Household supplies........... | 4,230 | 4,497 |
| Stationery.................. | 1,423 | 1,628 |
| Telephone and telegraph....... | 6,453 | 6,929 |
| Utilities.................... | 17,860 | 18,907 |
| **Housing**...................... | 63,649 | 67,135 |
| Farmhouses................. | 2,289 | 2,308 |
| Owner-occupied nonfarm....... | 41,725 | 44,087 |
| Tenant-occupied nonfarm...... | 17,578 | 18,529 |
| **Medical care**.................. | 28,266 | 31,250 |
| Dentists.................... | 2,835 | 3,043 |
| Drugs and drug products...... | 5,888 | 6,635 |
| Health insurance............. | 1,960 | 2,110 |
| Physicians.................. | 7,713 | 8,281 |
| Private hospitals............. | 8,488 | 9,650 |
| **Personal business**............. | 21,818 | 23,992 |
| Bank service charges......... | 1,394 | 1,514 |

| GOODS AND SERVICES | 1965 | 1966 |
|---|---|---|
| **Personal business** (cont.) | | |
| Brokerage charges............. | $ 1,950 | $ 2,465 |
| Funeral expenses............. | 1,755 | 1,830 |
| Legal services................. | 2,631 | 2,850 |
| Life insurance handling........ | 5,193 | 5,628 |
| **Personal care**................. | 7,690 | 8,215 |
| Barbershops, beauty parlors.... | 3,367 | 3,525 |
| Toilet articles................. | 4,323 | 4,690 |
| **Private education, research**.... | 5,916 | 6,667 |
| Higher education.............. | 2,856 | 3,372 |
| Elementary and secondary schools..................... | 1,837 | 1,905 |
| **Recreation**.................... | 26,386 | 28,673 |
| Books and maps.............. | 2,049 | 2,350 |
| Magazines, newspapers........ | 2,844 | 2,995 |
| Radio, television, music........ | 6,110 | 6,902 |
| Spectator amusements........ | 1,811 | 1,846 |
| Toys, sport equipment, boats, pleasure aircraft............. | 6,393 | 7,054 |
| **Religious and welfare activities** | 5,972 | 6,475 |
| **Transportation**................. | 57,608 | 59,645 |
| Automobile insurance.......... | 2,291 | 2,560 |
| Automobile maintenance, rental | 6,080 | 6,555 |
| Gasoline and oil.............. | 15,094 | 16,220 |
| New and used cars............ | 26,763 | 26,280 |
| Parts and tires............... | 3,155 | 3,534 |
| Intercity airlines, buses, railways | 1,781 | 1,961 |
| Local buses, railways, taxis..... | 2,017 | 2,077 |
| **TOTAL**...................... | 433,102 | 465,946 |

# THE KITCHEN

## A FOOD PLAN FOR GOOD NUTRITION

In a plan suggested by the U.S. Department of Agriculture for a well-balanced and nutritious diet, quantities of various foods for a week are listed. There is no absolute scale but plans vary from family to family. When a range is given, unless otherwise noted, the smaller quantity is for younger children, for adults over 55, or for pregnant women.

| KINDS OF FOOD | FOR CHILDREN 1 TO 6 YEARS | FOR CHILDREN 7 TO 12 YEARS | FOR GIRLS 13 TO 19 YEARS | FOR BOYS 13 TO 19 YEARS | FOR WOMEN All ages | Pregnant and nursing | FOR MEN, ALL AGES |
|---|---|---|---|---|---|---|---|
| Milk, cheese, ice cream...... | 6 quarts | 6–6½ quarts | 7 quarts | 7 quarts | 3½ quarts | 7–10 quarts | 3½ quarts |
| Meat, poultry, fish[1] | 1½–2 pounds | 3–4 pounds | 4½ pounds | 5–5½ pounds | 4–4½ pounds | 4–5 pounds | 5–5½ pounds |
| Eggs............. | 6 eggs | 7 eggs | 7 eggs | 7 eggs | 6 eggs | 7 eggs | 7 eggs |
| Dry beans and peas, nuts...... | 1 ounce | 2–4 ounces | 2 ounces | 4–6 ounces | 2 ounces | 2 ounces | 2–4 ounces |
| Grain products Whole-grain, enriched, or restored....... | 1–1½ pounds | 2–3 pounds | 2½–3 pounds[2] | 4–5 pounds | 2–2½ pounds | 2–3 pounds | 3–4 pounds |
| Citrus fruits, tomatoes....... | 1½–2 pounds | 2½ pounds | 2½ pounds | 3 pounds | 2½ pounds | 3½–5 pounds | 2½–3 pounds |
| Dark-green and deep-yellow vegetables..... | ¼ pound | ½–¾ pound | ¾ pound | ¾ pound | ¾ pound | 1½ pounds | ¾ pound |
| Potatoes......... | ½–1 pound | 1½–2½ pounds | 2 pounds | 3–4 pounds | 1–1½ pounds | 1½–3 pounds | 2–3 pounds |
| Other vegetables and fruits...... | 3½ pounds | 5½ pounds | 6 pounds | 7 pounds | 4–6 pounds | 6–6½ pounds | 5–7 pounds |
| Fats, oils......... | ¼–⅓ pound | ½–¾ pound | ¾ pound | 1–1¼ pounds | ½ pound | ½–¾ pound | ¾–1 pound |
| Sugars, sweets.... | ¼–⅔ pound d | ¾ pound | ¾ pound | 1–1¼ pounds | ½–1 pound | ¾ pound | 1–1½ pounds |

[1] To meet the iron allowance needed by children 1 to 6 years, girls 13 to 19, and pregnant and nursing women, include weekly 1 large or 2 small servings of liver or other organ meats.  [2] The larger quantity is for the younger girls.

## FOOD VALUES

Source: U.S. Department of Agriculture

| KIND OF FOOD | SIZE OF SERVING | PER CENT OF DAILY REQUIREMENT | | | | B Vitamins | | | | |
|---|---|---|---|---|---|---|---|---|---|---|
| | | Protein | Calcium | Iron | Vitamin A value | Thiamine | Riboflavin | Niacin | | Vitamin C |
| Milk.............. | 1 cup | 10% | 40% | — | 10% | 10% | 20% | — | | — |
| Cheese, cheddar..... | 1 ounce | 10% | 30% | — | 10% | — | 10% | — | | — |
| Meat, poultry, fish ... | 2 ounces | 20% | — | 20% | 10% | 10% | 10% | 20% | | — |
| Eggs.............. | 1 large egg | 10% | — | 10% | 10% | — | 10% | — | | — |
| Dry beans and peas, nuts......... | ¾ cup cooked beans | 20% | 10% | 30% | — | 10% | 10% | 10% | | — |
| Grain products...... | 2 slices bread | 10% | 10% | 10% | — | 10% | 10% | 10% | | — |
| Citrus fruits......... | ½ cup | — | — | — | — | — | — | — | | 50% |
| Other fruits......... | ½ cup | — | — | 10% | 10% | — | — | — | | 10% |
| Tomatoes, tomato juice............. | ½ cup | — | — | 10% | 30% | — | — | 10% | | 30% |
| Dark-green and deep-yellow vegetables.. | ½ cup | — | 10% | 10% | 50% | — | 10% | — | | 40% |
| Sweet potatoes...... | 1 medium | — | 10% | 10% | 50% | 10% | 10% | 10% | | 30% |
| Light-green vegetables ........ | ½ cup | — | 10% | 10% | 10% | — | — | — | | 20% |
| Potatoes............ | 1 medium | — | — | 10% | — | 10% | — | 10% | | 30% |
| Other vegetables.... | ½ cup | — | — | 10% | — | — | — | — | | 10% |
| Butter, margarine.... | 1 table-spoon | — | — | — | 10% | — | — | — | | — |
| Other fats........... | 2 table-spoons | — | — | — | — | — | — | — | | — |

# CALORIE CHART

The "calorie" is basically a unit of measure of heat. It is defined as the amount of heat required to raise the temperature of one kilogram of water one degree centigrade. The calorie is used as the unit for expressing the heat-producing or energy-producing value of food. For the average adult American, energy is expended at the following rates: 19.4 calories per minute for running; 11.2 calories per minute for swimming; 8.2 calories per minute for bicycle riding; 5.2 calories per minute for walking; and 1.3 calories per minute for reclining. Energy values in excess of those expended for bodily activities are stored in the body as fat.

| AVERAGE SERVING | CALORIE COUNT |
|---|---|
| **Breads and Cereals** | |
| white bread (1 slice) | 64 |
| whole wheat bread (1 slice) | 55 |
| roll, hard (1) | 160 |
| roll, soft (1) | 115 |
| waffle (1) | 240 |
| doughnut (1) | 136 |
| macaroni with cheese (1 cup) | 464 |
| rice (1 cup) | 201 |
| **Beverages** | |
| cocoa, made with milk (1 cup) | 235 |
| coffee or tea (plain) | 0 |
| carbonated beverages (8 oz.) | 85 |
| milk, whole (1 cup) | 166 |
| milk, skim (1 cup) | 87 |
| chocolate malted milk (2 cups) | 562 |
| ice-cream soda | 400 |
| whiskey (100-proof, jigger) | 125 |
| table wines (3 oz.) | 75 |
| beer (8 oz.) | 100 |
| **Dairy Foods** | |
| butter (1 tbs.) | 100 |
| cheese, cheddar (1 oz.) | 113 |
| cheese, cottage (1 cup) | 215 |
| cream, light (1 tbs.) | 30 |
| cream, whipped unsweetened (1 tbs.) | 25 |
| cream, sour (1 tbs.) | 55 |
| half and half (1 tbs.) | 20 |
| egg (1 medium size) | 77 |
| **Desserts** | |
| pie, apple (4 in. sector) | 345 |
| pie, custard (4 in. sector) | 280 |
| pie, mince (4 in. sector) | 365 |
| pie, lemon meringue (4 in. sector) | 302 |
| cupcake, iced (1 medium) | 185 |
| cake, angel food (2 in. sector) | 108 |
| cake, layer (2 in. sector) | 410 |
| brownie (3" by 2" by 2") | 295 |
| eclair, chocolate | 300 |
| ice cream, plain (1/7 of a quart) | 167 |
| sherbet (1/2 cup) | 118 |
| vanilla pudding (1 cup) | 275 |
| **Snacks** | |
| bacon and tomato sandwich | 290 |
| ham and cheese sandwich | 360 |
| hamburger on a bun | 492 |
| hot dog on a bun | 300 |
| liverwurst sandwich (2 slices) | 350 |
| peanut butter sandwich | 220 |
| cheese sandwich | 333 |
| chocolate nut sundae with whipped cream | 350 |
| cashews (1 oz.) | 164 |
| peanuts, chopped (1 tbs.) | 50 |
| pecans, chopped (1 tbs.) | 52 |
| pretzels (5 small sticks) | 20 |
| fudge (1 oz.) | 116 |
| chocolate creams (1 oz.) | 110 |
| chocolate milkshake (12 oz.) | 520 |
| marshmallows (3) | 90 |

| AVERAGE SERVING | CALORIE COUNT |
|---|---|
| **Fruits** | |
| apple, raw (medium size) | 76 |
| banana, raw (medium size) | 88 |
| cantaloupe (1/2) | 37 |
| cherries (1/2 cup) | 60 |
| fruit cocktail, canned (1/2 cup) | 100 |
| grapefruit (1/2 small) | 49 |
| orange, raw (medium size) | 70 |
| peach, raw (medium size) | 46 |
| pear, raw (medium size) | 95 |
| pineapple, canned (1 large slice) | 95 |
| **Fruit Juices** | |
| grapefruit, fresh (1 cup) | 87 |
| orange, fresh (1 cup) | 108 |
| pineapple, canned (1 cup) | 121 |
| tomato, canned (1 cup) | 50 |
| **Meat, Fish, and Poultry** | |
| beef, roast (4 oz.) | 300 |
| beef, sirloin steak (3 oz.) | 257 |
| lamb chop (3 oz.) | 356 |
| pork chop (3 oz.) | 284 |
| ham (3 oz.) | 339 |
| bacon (2 strips) | 97 |
| veal chop (3 oz.) | 193 |
| liver (4 oz.) | 240 |
| chicken, broiled (1/2 small) | 300 |
| chicken, canned, boned (3 oz.) | 169 |
| turkey (4 oz.) | 300 |
| tuna (3 oz.) | 169 |
| lobster, whole (1/2 pound) | 150 |
| mackerel (3 oz.) | 200 |
| clams, raw (3 oz.) | 65 |
| **Soups** | |
| bouillon, broth, and consommé (1 cup) | 30 |
| chicken noodle (1 cup) | 65 |
| cream of mushroom (1 cup) | 200 |
| minestrone (1 cup) | 105 |
| tomato (1 cup) | 90 |
| **Miscellaneous** | |
| catchup or chili sauce (1 oz.) | 30 |
| mayonnaise (1 tbs.) | 92 |
| French dressing (1 tbs.) | 59 |
| assorted jams (1 tbs.) | 55 |
| sugar (1 tbs.) | 48 |
| gravy (2 tbs.) | 35 |
| white sauce (1/4 cup) | 110 |
| **Vegetables** | |
| asparagus (1 cup) | 36 |
| beets (1 cup) | 68 |
| broccoli (1 cup) | 44 |
| carrots (1 cup) | 44 |
| corn (1 cup) | 140 |
| mushrooms (1 cup) | 30 |
| peas (1 cup) | 111 |
| potatoes, mashed (1 cup) | 159 |
| potatoes, pan-fried (1 cup) | 460 |
| spinach (1 cup) | 46 |
| sweet potato, baked (medium size) | 183 |
| tomato, raw (medium size) | 30 |
| turnips (1 cup) | 40 |

## FAVORITE RECIPES

A good collection of recipes is an essential part of every woman's kitchen. The collection of recipes below has been selected from a listing of all-time favorites featured in the 30th anniversary issue of *Woman's Day** (September, 1967). The following group includes an assortment of delicious and economical recipes for main dishes and desserts.

### SWEDISH MEATBALLS

| | |
|---|---|
| 1 pound ground lean beef | 1 teaspoon salt |
| ½ pound of lean pork and of veal, ground | 3 tablespoons flour |
| | 2 cups meat stock or consommé |
| 1 cup dry, stale bread crumbs | Pinch of grated lemon rind |
| 1 cup milk | 1 cup dairy sour cream |
| 1 onion, minced | Chopped dill or parsley |
| Butter | Cooked noodles |
| 2 eggs, beaten | |
| Dash of nutmeg and of pepper | |

Blend meat, crumbs, and milk. Sauté onion in 1 tablespoon butter and add to meat with eggs and seasonings. Mix with hands to get even texture; roll in small balls. Brown in 2 tablespoons butter. Remove meatballs. To pan juices, add flour and stock to make gravy. Stir until hot. Check seasoning and add lemon rind. (Gravy should not be too thick at this point.) Return meatballs to gravy and simmer over low heat 1 hour. Remove meatballs to serving dish with slotted spoon. Stir sour cream into gravy and heat. Pour over meat; add dill. Serve with noodles. Makes 6 to 8 servings.

### BAKED SPICY CORNED BEEF

| | |
|---|---|
| 4- to 6-pound corned brisket of beef | 1 stalk celery with leaves, sliced |
| 2 tablespoons pickling spice | 1 carrot, sliced |
| 1 orange, sliced | ⅓ cup packed brown sugar |
| 1 onion, sliced | 1 tablespoon prepared mustard |

Cover corned beef with water and soak ½ hour, or longer if deeply corned. Place a large sheet of heavy foil on a shallow pan. Take corned beef from water and pat dry to remove any salt on surface. Put in center of foil and pour ¼ cup fresh water over top. Sprinkle with the spice and arrange orange slices and vegetables over and around meat. Bring long ends of foil up over meat and seal with a light double fold. Seal other ends, turning them up so liquid cannot run out. Bake in slow oven (300° F.) 4 hours. Cool slightly, unwrap, and put in shallow pan. Spread with brown sugar mixed with mustard. Bake in moderate oven (375° F.) 20 minutes, or until glazed. Makes 8 to 10 servings.

### SCALLOPED CHICKEN SUPREME

| | |
|---|---|
| 3 tablespoons butter or margarine | 1 cup sliced cooked mushrooms |
| 3 tablespoons flour | ½ cup slivered blanched almonds |
| 2 cups chicken broth | |
| 1 cup milk | 1 can (4 ounces) pimientos, chopped |
| Salt and pepper | |
| 3 cups cooked rice | Soft bread crumbs |
| 3 cups diced cooked chicken | |

Melt butter in saucepan and blend in flour. Add chicken broth, milk, and salt and pepper to taste.

Cook, stirring, until slightly thickened. Butter a 2-quart casserole. Spread 1½ cups rice evenly over the bottom. Top rice with 1½ cups chicken, ½ cup mushrooms, ¼ cup almonds, and ½ can pimientos. Carefully pour in half the sauce. Repeat the layers, except the pimientos, and add remaining sauce. Sprinkle lightly with crumbs. Decorate with pimientos. Bake in moderate oven (350° F.) 45 minutes. Makes 6 servings. Good with a creamy mushroom sauce.

### FLOUNDER FILLETS SUPREME

| | |
|---|---|
| 1½ cups water | ¼ cup butter |
| 1 onion, sliced | 2 tablespoons flour |
| ½ lemon, sliced | ½ cup milk |
| 1 bay leaf | ½ cup dry white wine or sherry |
| Few celery leaves | |
| Salt and pepper | 1 egg, beaten |
| Flounder fillets, 1 pound | |

Put first 5 ingredients in skillet. Add salt and pepper to taste. Bring to boil. Add fish and reduce heat, simmering gently 5 minutes. Remove fish to shallow broiler-proof baking dish. Melt 2 tablespoons butter and blend in flour. Gradually add milk and ½ cup fish liquid and cook until thickened, stirring constantly. Add wine and bring to boil. Add remaining butter and pour slowly over beaten egg, stirring. Pour over fish and brown lightly under broiler. Makes 4 servings.

### FILIPINO CHICKEN

| | |
|---|---|
| 1 frying chicken (about 3 pounds) cut up | ½ teaspoon pepper |
| | 1 teaspoon ginger |
| ⅓ cup soy sauce | Flour |
| Juice of 1 lemon | ¼ cup fat |
| 1 teaspoon poultry seasoning | 2 onions, cut in half |
| | 1 cup boiling water |

Wash chicken and put in bowl. Combine soy sauce, lemon juice, and seasonings. Pour over chicken and allow to stand at least ½ hour. Lift chicken from sauce, roll in flour, and brown in hot fat. Place chicken, sauce, and remaining ingredients in covered roaster or casserole. Bake at 350° F. 45 minutes, or until chicken is tender. Makes 4 servings.

### STUFFED SOLE FILLETS

| | |
|---|---|
| 6 large or 12 small (2 pounds) sole fillets | 6 slices bread, cubed |
| | 2 pimientos, minced |
| Melted butter or margarine | 2 green onions, chopped, or 1 small onion, minced |
| Chopped parsley | |
| 2 carrots, peeled and shredded | Salt and pepper |
| | Paprika |

Mix ¼ cup melted butter, 2 tablespoons parsley, and remaining ingredients, except paprika. Divide mixture onto fillets and roll up from small end, securing with toothpicks. Put in baking dish and brush with melted butter. Bake at 375° F. 30 minutes. Sprinkle with parsley and paprika. Makes 6 servings.

## CHILI CON CARNE

1 cup dried pinto beans
3 pounds lean beef
¼ cup olive oil
1 bay leaf
2 tablespoons chili powder
1 tablespoon salt
4 cloves garlic, minced
1 teaspoon crushed cumin seed
1 teaspoon oregano
3 tablespoons paprika
3 tablespoons cornmeal
1 tablespoon flour

Cover washed beans with 4 cups water. Bring to boil and boil 2 minutes. Cover and let stand 1 hour, then cook until tender. Drain. Meanwhile, cut meat in ½-inch cubes and sear in hot oil. Add 6 cups water, cover, bring to boil and simmer 1 hour. Add bay leaf and next 6 ingredients. Simmer ½ hour. Blend cornmeal, flour, and cold water to make a paste. Stir into mixture; simmer 5 minutes. Add beans and heat. Makes 6 servings.

## NEAPOLITAN-STYLE MEATBALLS AND SPAGHETTI

1 pound round steak, ground
½ pound of lean pork and of veal, ground
2 cloves garlic
1 cup fine dry bread crumbs
1 egg, beaten
Salt and pepper
Olive oil
2 medium onions, chopped
2 cans condensed tomato soup
2 cans (6 or 7 ounces each) tomato paste
2 cans (1 pound each) tomatoes
1 can (32 ounces) Italian-style tomatoes
1 pound thin spaghetti
Grated Parmesan cheese

Mix meat, 1 minced clove garlic, crumbs, egg, 2 teaspoons salt, and ¼ teaspoon pepper. Shape in balls about the size of a walnut. Heat 2 tablespoons oil in large kettle and brown onion lightly. Remove onion. Add more oil to kettle and brown meatballs on all sides. Add onion, 1 clove garlic, and remaining ingredients, except last 2. Simmer, stirring occasionally, 8 to 12 hours, or until thick. Uncover last few hours. Season to taste. Serve on cooked spaghetti and sprinkle generously with grated Parmesan cheese. Makes 10 servings.

## MIRACLE ROAST OF BEEF

This is beef cooked to perfection, rare all the way through. Roast beef in very slow oven (200° F.), allowing about 1 hour per pound. To reheat, wrap in foil and roast for same length of time.

## RED DEVIL'S-FOOD CAKE

¾ cup butter or margarine, softened
2 cups sugar
2⅔ cups sifted cake flour
1½ teaspoons baking powder
¾ teaspoon of soda and of salt
1⅓ cups milk
3 eggs
3 squares unsweetened chocolate, melted and cooled
1½ teaspoons red food coloring
1 teaspoon vanilla extract

Cream butter. Sift dry ingredients into butter. Add 1 cup milk and mix until flour is dampened. Beat 2 minutes. Add remaining milk and remaining ingredients. Beat 2 minutes. Pour into three 8-inch layer pans lined on the bottom with waxed paper. Bake in a moderate oven (350° F.) 30 to 35 minutes. Cool and frost as desired.

## SOUTHERN PECAN PIE

½ cup sugar
1 cup dark corn syrup
¼ teaspoon salt
1 tablespoon flour
2 eggs
1 teaspoon vanilla extract
1¼ cups pecan halves
Unbaked 9-inch pie shell

Beat together sugar, syrup, salt, flour, and eggs. Add vanilla, butter, and pecans. Pour into pie shell. Turn up rounded side of some pecans. (For a brown crust, brush edges with evaporated milk before baking.) Bake at 300° F. for 1 hour or until set. Cool.

## FRESH-FRUIT COMPOTE

1 cup sugar
2 cups water
1 lemon, sliced
4 firm peaches, peeled and halved
4 pears, peeled, cored, and halved
4 plums (see note)
8 apricots

Put first 3 ingredients in saucepan. Bring to boil and simmer 5 minutes. Add peaches and pears; cover and simmer 5 minutes. Prick skins of plums and add with apricots to mixture. Cover and simmer 5 minutes, or until all fruit is tender. Cool, then chill. Makes 8 servings. **Note:** If purple plums are used, cook separately in a little syrup and add to compote just before serving.

## DOUBLE-FROSTED BROWNIES

5 squares unsweetened chocolate
½ cup butter or margarine
2 eggs
1 cup sugar
½ cup all-purpose flour
¼ teaspoon salt
1 teaspoon vanilla extract
½ cup chopped nuts
Frosting

Melt 2 squares chocolate with the butter. Beat eggs, add sugar, and mix well. Stir in chocolate mixture. Mix flour and salt and blend into first mixture. Add vanilla and nuts and spread in greased 11 × 7 × 1½-inch baking pan. Bake at 350° F. 20 to 25 minutes. Cool in pan, then frost. Melt remaining chocolate and spread on frosting. Put in refrigerator to harden. When set, cut in small squares. **Frosting:** Put 1½ cups sugar, ⅓ cup butter, and ½ cup medium cream in heavy saucepan. Bring to boil and cook until a small amount of mixture forms a soft ball when dropped in very cold water (236° F. on a candy thermometer). Set in pan of cold water until cool. Add 1 teaspoon vanilla and beat until creamy and of spreading consistency.

## LEMON MERINGUE PIE

Sugar
Salt
6 tablespoons cornstarch
2 cups boiling water
Grated rind of 1 lemon
¼ cup butter
3 eggs, separated
Lemon juice
Baked 9-inch pie shell

Mix 1¼ cups sugar, ⅛ teaspoon salt, and the cornstarch. Add water and lemon rind. Cook until thickened, stirring. Then simmer 10 minutes. Add butter but do not stir. Gradually stir into egg yolks mixed with ½ cup lemon juice. Strain into pie shell and bake at 400° F. 10 minutes. Add ⅛ teaspoon salt and 1 teaspoon lemon juice to egg whites and beat until stiff. Pile lightly on pie and spread to edge. Bake at 350° F. for 18 minutes. Cool.

## EQUIVALENT COOKING MEASURES

| UNITS | FLUID DRAMS | TEA-SPOON-FULS | TABLE-SPOON-FULS | FLUID OUNCES | ¼ CUP-FULS | GILLS (½ cup-fuls) | CUP-FULS | LIQUID PINTS | LIQUID QUARTS | LITERS |
|---|---|---|---|---|---|---|---|---|---|---|
| 1 fluid dram equals | 1 | ¾ | ¼ | ⅛ | ¹⁄₁₆ | ¹⁄₃₂ | ¹⁄₆₄ | ¹⁄₁₂₈ | ¹⁄₂₅₆ | 0.004 |
| 1 teaspoonful equals | 1⅓ | 1 | ⅓ | ⅙ | ¹⁄₁₂ | ¹⁄₂₄ | ¹⁄₄₈ | ¹⁄₉₆ | ¹⁄₁₉₂ | 0.005 |
| 1 tablespoonful equals.......... | 4 | 3 | 1 | ½ | ¼ | ⅛ | ¹⁄₁₆ | ¹⁄₃₂ | ¹⁄₆₄ | 0.015 |
| 1 fluid ounce equals | 8 | 6 | 2 | 1 | ½ | ¼ | ⅛ | ¹⁄₁₆ | ¹⁄₃₂ | 0.030 |
| ¼ cupful equals.... | 16 | 12 | 4 | 2 | 1 | ½ | ¼ | ⅛ | ¹⁄₁₆ | 0.059 |
| 1 gill (½ cupful) equals.......... | 32 | 24 | 8 | 4 | 2 | 1 | ½ | ¼ | ⅛ | 0.118 |
| 1 cupful equals.... | 64 | 48 | 16 | 8 | 4 | 2 | 1 | ½ | ¼ | 0.237 |
| 1 liquid pint equals | 128 | 96 | 32 | 16 | 8 | 4 | 2 | 1 | ½ | 0.473 |
| 1 liquid quart equals | 256 | 192 | 64 | 32 | 16 | 8 | 4 | 2 | 1 | 0.946 |
| 1 liter equals...... | 270 | 203 | 67.6 | 33.8 | 16.9 | 8.45 | 4.23 | 2.11 | 1.06 | 1.000 |

## TIMETABLE FOR ROASTING MEATS
Source: U.S. Department of Agriculture

| KIND AND CUT OF MEAT | READY-TO-COOK WEIGHT | APPROXIMATE ROASTING TIME AT 325° F. | INTERNAL TEMPERATURE OF MEAT WHEN DONE |
|---|---|---|---|
| **Beef** | | | |
| Standing rib: | | | |
| Rare.................... | 6 to 8 pounds | 2 to 2½ hours | 140° F. |
| Medium.................................. | 6 to 8 | 2½ to 3 | 160 |
| Well done................................ | 6 to 8 | 3⅓ to 4½ | 170 |
| Rolled rib: | | | |
| Rare.................................... | 4 to 6 | 2 to 3 | 140 |
| Medium.................................. | 4 to 6 | 2½ to 3¼ | 160 |
| Well done................................ | 4 to 6 | 3 to 4 | 170 |
| Rolled rump.............................. | 5 | 3 to 3¼ | 160 to 170 |
| Sirloin tip............................... | 3 | 2 to 2¼ | 160 to 170 |
| **Veal** | | | |
| Leg..................................... | 5 to 8 | 2½ to 3½ | 170 to 180 |
| Loin.................................... | 5 | 3 | 170 to 180 |
| Rolled shoulder.......................... | 3 to 5 | 3 to 3½ | 170 to 180 |
| **Lamb** | | | |
| Leg..................................... | 6 to 7 | 3¼ to 4 | 180 |
| Shoulder................................ | 3 to 6 | 2¼ to 3¼ | 180 |
| Rolled shoulder.......................... | 3 to 5 | 2½ to 3 | 180 |
| **Pork** | | | |
| Loin.................................... | 3 to 5 | 3 to 4 | 185 |
| Shoulder................................ | 5 to 8 | 3½ to 5 | 185 |
| Ham, whole.............................. | 10 to 14 | 5½ to 6 | 185 |
| Ham, half............................... | 6 | 4 | 185 |
| Spareribs................................ | 3 | 2 | 185 |
| Picnic shoulder.......................... | 6 | 3½ | 170 |

## GUIDE FOR ROASTING POULTRY
Source: U.S. Department of Agriculture

| KIND OF BIRD | READY-TO-COOK WEIGHT (pounds) | LARGE BREADCRUMBS FOR STUFFING (quarts) | ROASTING TIME AT 325° F. FOR STUFFED, CHILLED BIRD (hours) |
|---|---|---|---|
| **Chicken:** Broilers or fryers........................... | 1½ to 2½ | ¼ to ½ | 1¼ to 2 |
| Roasters..................................... | 2½ to 4½ | ½ to 1¼ | 2 to 3½ |
| Capons...................................... | 4 to 8 | 1¼ to 1¾ | 3 to 5 |
| **Duck**.................................................. | 3 to 5 | ½ to 1 | 2½ to 3 |
| **Goose**................................................. | 4 to 8 | ¾ to 1½ | 2¾ to 3½ |
| | 8 to 14 | 1½ to 2½ | 3½ to 5 |
| **Turkey:** Fryers or roasters (very young birds)............. | 4 to 8 | 1 to 2 | 3 to 4½ |
| Roasters (fully grown birds)..................... | 6 to 12 | 2 to 3 | 3½ to 5 |
| | 12 to 16 | 3 to 4 | 5 to 6 |
| | 16 to 20 | 4 to 5 | 6 to 7½ |
| | 20 to 24 | 5 to 6 | 7½ to 9 |

## CALORIES AND WEIGHT

The human body needs energy for growth and work; this energy is provided by food in the form of calories. The weight of an adult man or woman reflects the extent to which he or she balances the intake of energy in food with the expenditure of energy in activity and growth. Weight will stay the same when the number of calories brought into the body by food equals the number of calories used by the body. Similarly, the body loses weight when it receives fewer calories from food than it uses, and gains weight when it receives more than it uses.

Weight can be controlled, therefore, by regulating either the amount of food eaten, or the extent of physical activity, or both, so that the balance of calories is in the desired direction. The chart below will provide a guide to what weights are desirable at given heights.

## DESIRABLE WEIGHTS

Source: U.S. Department of Health, Education, and Welfare, and U.S. Office of Education

**Men age 25 and over**
Weight in pounds according to frame (in indoor clothing).

| HEIGHT (WITH SHOES ON) Feet | Inches | SLENDER FRAME | MEDIUM FRAME | LARGE FRAME |
|---|---|---|---|---|
| 5 | 2 | 112–120 | 118–129 | 126–141 |
| 5 | 3 | 115–123 | 121–133 | 129–144 |
| 5 | 4 | 118–126 | 124–136 | 132–148 |
| 5 | 5 | 121–129 | 127–139 | 135–152 |
| 5 | 6 | 124–133 | 130–143 | 138–156 |
| 5 | 7 | 128–137 | 134–147 | 142–161 |
| 5 | 8 | 132–141 | 138–152 | 147–166 |
| 5 | 9 | 136–145 | 142–156 | 151–170 |
| 5 | 10 | 140–150 | 146–160 | 155–174 |
| 5 | 11 | 144–154 | 150–165 | 159–179 |
| 6 | 0 | 148–158 | 154–170 | 164–184 |
| 6 | 1 | 152–162 | 158–175 | 168–189 |
| 6 | 2 | 156–167 | 162–180 | 173–194 |
| 6 | 3 | 160–171 | 167–185 | 178–199 |
| 6 | 4 | 164–175 | 172–190 | 182–204 |

**Women age 25 and over \***
Weight in pounds according to frame (in indoor clothing).

| HEIGHT (WITH SHOES ON) Feet | Inches | SLENDER FRAME | MEDIUM FRAME | LARGE FRAME |
|---|---|---|---|---|
| 4 | 10 | 92–98 | 96–107 | 104–119 |
| 4 | 11 | 94–101 | 98–110 | 106–122 |
| 5 | 0 | 96–104 | 101–113 | 109–125 |
| 5 | 1 | 99–107 | 104–116 | 112–128 |
| 5 | 2 | 102–110 | 107–119 | 115–131 |
| 5 | 3 | 105–113 | 110–122 | 118–134 |
| 5 | 4 | 108–116 | 113–126 | 121–138 |
| 5 | 5 | 111–119 | 116–130 | 125–142 |
| 5 | 6 | 114–123 | 120–135 | 129–146 |
| 5 | 7 | 118–127 | 124–139 | 133–150 |
| 5 | 8 | 122–131 | 128–143 | 137–154 |
| 5 | 9 | 126–135 | 132–147 | 141–158 |
| 5 | 10 | 130–140 | 136–151 | 145–163 |
| 5 | 11 | 134–144 | 140–155 | 149–168 |
| 6 | 0 | 138–148 | 144–159 | 153–173 |

**Boys between 10 and 18 years**
In schoolroom clothing, without shoes.

| HEIGHT (in inches) | AVERAGE WEIGHT IN POUNDS FOR EACH SPECIFIED AGE AND WEIGHT | | | | | | | |
|---|---|---|---|---|---|---|---|---|
| | 10–11 yrs. | 11–12 yrs. | 12–13 yrs. | 13–14 yrs. | 14–15 yrs. | 15–16 yrs. | 16–17 yrs. | 17–18 yrs. |
| 52 | 64 | 64 | 64 | — | — | — | — | — |
| 53 | 67 | 68 | 68 | — | — | — | — | — |
| 54 | 70 | 71 | 71 | 72 | — | — | — | — |
| 55 | 73 | 74 | 74 | 74 | — | — | — | — |
| 56 | 77 | 77 | 78 | 78 | 80 | — | — | — |
| 57 | 81 | 81 | 82 | 83 | 83 | — | — | — |
| 58 | 84 | 85 | 85 | 86 | 87 | — | — | — |
| 59 | 88 | 89 | 89 | 90 | 90 | 90 | — | — |
| 60 | 92 | 92 | 93 | 94 | 95 | 96 | — | — |
| 61 | 95 | 96 | 97 | 99 | 100 | 103 | 106 | — |
| 62 | 100 | 101 | 102 | 103 | 104 | 107 | 111 | 116 |
| 63 | 105 | 106 | 107 | 108 | 110 | 113 | 118 | 123 |
| 64 | — | 109 | 111 | 113 | 115 | 117 | 121 | 126 |
| 65 | — | 114 | 117 | 118 | 120 | 122 | 127 | 131 |
| 66 | — | — | 119 | 122 | 125 | 128 | 132 | 136 |
| 67 | — | — | 124 | 128 | 130 | 134 | 136 | 139 |
| 68 | — | — | — | 134 | 134 | 137 | 141 | 143 |
| 69 | — | — | — | 137 | 139 | 143 | 146 | 149 |
| 70 | — | — | — | 143 | 144 | 145 | 148 | 151 |
| 71 | — | — | — | 148 | 150 | 151 | 152 | 154 |
| 72 | — | — | — | — | 153 | 155 | 156 | 158 |
| 73 | — | — | — | — | 157 | 160 | 162 | 164 |
| 74 | — | — | — | — | 160 | 164 | 168 | 170 |

**Girls between 10 and 18 years**
In schoolroom clothing, without shoes.

| HEIGHT (in inches) | AVERAGE WEIGHT IN POUNDS FOR EACH SPECIFIED AGE AND HEIGHT | | | | | | | |
|---|---|---|---|---|---|---|---|---|
| | 10–11 yrs. | 11–12 yrs. | 12–13 yrs. | 13–14 yrs. | 14–15 yrs. | 15–16 yrs. | 16–17 yrs. | 17–18 yrs. |
| 49 | 56 | — | — | — | — | — | — | — |
| 50 | 61 | 62 | — | — | — | — | — | — |
| 51 | 63 | 65 | — | — | — | — | — | — |
| 52 | 65 | 67 | — | — | — | — | — | — |
| 53 | 68 | 69 | 71 | — | — | — | — | — |
| 54 | 71 | 71 | 73 | — | — | — | — | — |
| 55 | 74 | 75 | 77 | 78 | — | — | — | — |
| 56 | 78 | 79 | 81 | 83 | — | — | — | — |
| 57 | 82 | 82 | 84 | 88 | 92 | — | — | — |
| 58 | 86 | 86 | 88 | 93 | 96 | 101 | — | — |
| 59 | 90 | 90 | 92 | 96 | 100 | 103 | 104 | — |
| 60 | 95 | 95 | 97 | 101 | 105 | 108 | 109 | 111 |
| 61 | 99 | 100 | 101 | 105 | 108 | 112 | 113 | 116 |
| 62 | 104 | 105 | 106 | 109 | 113 | 115 | 117 | 118 |
| 63 | — | 110 | 110 | 112 | 116 | 117 | 119 | 120 |
| 64 | — | 114 | 115 | 117 | 119 | 120 | 122 | 123 |
| 65 | — | 118 | 120 | 121 | 122 | 123 | 125 | 126 |
| 66 | — | — | 124 | 124 | 125 | 128 | 129 | 130 |
| 67 | — | — | 128 | 130 | 131 | 133 | 133 | 135 |
| 68 | — | — | 131 | 133 | 135 | 136 | 138 | 138 |
| 69 | — | — | — | 135 | 137 | 138 | 140 | 142 |
| 70 | — | — | — | 136 | 138 | 140 | 142 | 144 |
| 71 | — | — | — | 138 | 140 | 142 | 144 | 145 |

**\* For girls between 18 and 25, subtract one pound for each year under 25.**

# EMERGENCY FIRST AID

The guides laid down by the American Medical Association for emergency first aid—the immediate and temporary care given to a victim of accident or illness—are simple and concise, and when followed accurately, without panic, can be lifesaving measures. The cardinal rules are: prevent heavy loss of blood; maintain breathing; prevent further injury; prevent shock; and, as soon as possible, send for a doctor.

Since heavy loss of blood can cause death within three to five minutes, act immediately. Place a clean pad—or, if one is not available, your hand and fingers—over the wound and apply direct pressure. Hold the pad in place with a strong bandage, raise the bleeding area higher than the rest of the body, and keep the victim lying down. Instructions emphasize that a tourniquet should not be used to control bleeding except for an amputated, mangled, or crushed arm or leg.

Manual lifesaving action to maintain breathing is often vital in many emergency situations, including electric shock, drowning, choking, poisoning, and gas or smoke inhalation. Artificial respiration, the process of forcing air into and from the lungs of the victim, should be started at once when breathing stops or lips, tongue, and fingernails turn blue. The recommended method is mouth-to-mouth or mouth-to-nose rescue breathing. However, if for any reason it is impossible to use this process, the manual system may be employed.

● When applying mouth-to-mouth breathing to a child victim follow the procedures outlined below:
(1) put the child in a face-up position, check his mouth and throat for obstructions, tilt his head backward and lift his lower jaw so that the tongue will not fall back and block the air passage; keep the child in this position
(2) take a deep breath, place your mouth over the child's mouth *and* nose, and blow gently until his chest rises and his lungs expand
(3) remove your mouth, and as soon as the child exhales, repeat the procedure
(4) continue at the rate of 15 times per minute, and, when possible, place your hand over the child's stomach, using moderate pressure to keep it from becoming inflated.

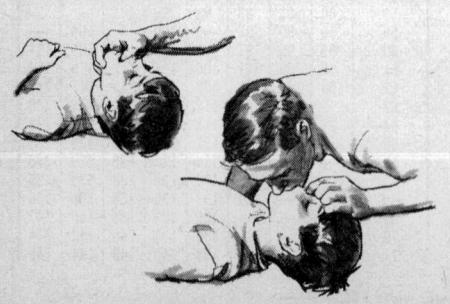

● If an adult is involved:
(1) place the victim halfway between a face-up and a side position, check for obstructions in mouth and throat, lift his neck, tilt his head back, and pull his chin upward
(2) take a deep breath, place your mouth over the victim's mouth *or* nose and blow until his chest rises. If mouth-to-nose breathing is used, keep the victim's mouth sealed with your thumb, and be sure that your lips do not close the victim's nostrils. In mouth-to-mouth breathing, seal your lips around the victim's mouth and close his nostrils with your thumb and finger
(3) remove your mouth, permit the victim to exhale, and then repeat at the rate of 15 times per minute.

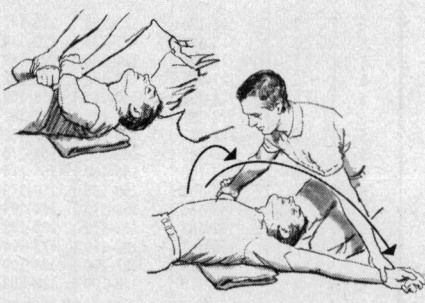

● In the manual method of artificial respiration follow this procedure:
(1) place the victim in a face-up position, put something under his shoulders to raise them, and allow his head to drop backward
(2) kneel above the victim's head and grasp his arms at the wrists, crossing and pressing his wrists against his lower chest
(3) pull the arms upward, outward, and backward as far as possible and repeat 15 times per minute. If another person is present, he should tilt the victim's head backward so that his jaw juts forward.

In all methods, persistence is often the essential factor in the success of artificial respiration, for the victim may not immediately respond to treatment.

A condition that usually accompanies severe injury or emotional upset is shock, which can be recognized by symptoms such as cold and clammy skin, beads of perspiration, a pale face, a feeling of chilliness, nausea or vomiting, and shallow breathing. Corrective measures are: correct the cause if possible; keep the victim lying down; keep his air passages open (turn his head to the side if he vomits); raise his legs if no bones are broken and keep his head lower than his body; keep the victim warm; if he is able to swallow, give him fluids, such as water, tea, or coffee, but never alcoholic beverages, and do not introduce fluids if the victim is unconscious, semiconscious, or has a suspected abdominal injury.

## EMERGENCY COUNTERDOSES *

In an accident involving poison or an overdose of drugs, proper emergency measures can save a life. Following are procedures recommended by the Poison Control Branch of the U.S. Department of Health, Education, and Welfare.

**FIRST**
- Send for a doctor immediately.
- Keep the patient warm.

- While waiting for your doctor, determine if the patient has swallowed a poison or an overdose of medication.
- If the patient is conscious, administer the proper counterdose listed below.
- Do *not* force any liquids on the patient if he is unconscious. And do *not* induce vomiting if the patient is having convulsions.

---

**TO FIND THE CORRECT COUNTERDOSE:** In the list below, you will find the type of poison or overdose that the victim has taken. The number next to each substance refers to the proper counterdose bearing the same number in the section below.

### Poisons

| | |
|---|---|
| Acids | 18 |
| Bichloride of mercury | 6 |
| Camphor | 1 |
| Carbon monoxide inhalation | 16 |
| Chlorine bleach | 8 |
| Disinfectant | |
|   with chlorine | 8 |
|   with carbolic acid | 12 |
| Food poisoning | 11 |
| Furniture polish | 17 |
| Gasoline, kerosene | 17 |
| Household ammonia | 10 |

### Insect and rat poisons

| | |
|---|---|
|   with arsenic | 2 |
|   with sodium fluoride | 14 |
|   with phosphorus | 5 |
|   with DDT | 11 |
|   with strychnine | 15 |
| Iodine tincture | 4 |
| Lye | 10 |
| Mushrooms | 11 |
| Oil of wintergreen | 9 |
| Pine oil | 17 |
| Rubbing alcohol | 9 |
| Turpentine | 17 |
| Washing soda | 10 |

### Overdoses

| | |
|---|---|
| Alcohol | 9 |
| Aspirin | 9 |
| Barbiturates | 3 |
| Belladonna | 15 |
| Bromides | 11 |
| Codeine | 13 |
| Headache and cold compounds | 9 |
| Iron compounds | 7 |
| Morphine, opium | 13 |
| Paregoric | 13 |
| Pep medicines | 2 |
| Sleeping medicines | 3 |

### 1
Induce vomiting with
Finger in throat, or
Teaspoonful of mustard in half glass of water, or
Syrup of ipecac, or
3 teaspoons of salt in warm water.

### 2
Give glass of milk, or give "universal antidote" (obtain from drug store and keep on hand at home).
Induce vomiting. (See #1)

### 3
Induce vomiting. (See #1)
Give 2 tablespoons Epsom salt in 2 glasses of water.
Then give large quantities of hot coffee or strong tea (instant or regular).

### 4
Give 2 oz. thick starch paste. Mix cornstarch (or flour) with water.
Then give 2 oz. salt in quart of warm water. Drink until vomit fluid is clear.
Finally, give glass of milk.

### 5
Induce vomiting. (See #1)
Then give 4 oz. mineral oil. Positively do NOT give vegetable or animal oil.
4 oz. hydrogen peroxide.
1 tablespoon sodium bicarbonate in quart of warm water.

### 6
Give glass of milk or universal antidote. (See #2)
Induce vomiting. (See #1)
Give 1 oz. of Epsom salt in a pint of water.

### 7
Induce vomiting. (See #1)
2 teaspoons of sodium bicarbonate in a glass of warm water.
Give glass of milk.

### 8
Give patient one or two glasses of milk.

### 9
Give glass of milk.
Induce vomiting. (See #1)
Tablespoon sodium bicarbonate in quart of warm water.

### 10
Give 2 tablespoons vinegar in 2 glasses of water.
Give white of 2 raw eggs or 2 ounces of olive oil.
Do NOT induce vomiting!

### 11
Induce vomiting. (See #1)
Give 2 tablespoons Epsom salt in 2 glasses of water.

### 12
Induce vomiting. (See #1)
Then give 2 ounces of castor oil.
Next give glass of milk or whites of 2 raw eggs.

### 13
Give glass of milk or universal antidote. (See #2)
2 tablespoons Epsom salt in 2 glasses of water.
Keep patient awake.

### 14
Give 2 tablespoons of milk of magnesia.
Give glass of milk.
Induce vomiting. (See #1)

### 15
Give glass of milk or universal antidote. (See #2)
Induce vomiting. (See #1)
Give artificial respiration.
Keep patient quiet.

### 16
Carry victim into fresh air.
Make patient lie down.

### 17
Give water or milk.
Give 2 oz. vegetable oil.
Do NOT induce vomiting!

### 18
Give 1 oz. milk of magnesia in large quantity of water.
Do NOT induce vomiting!

## MARRIAGES IN THE UNITED STATES BY GEOGRAPHIC AREA: 1964–1966

The year 1966 saw a 3.2 per cent increase over 1965 in marriages across the country, according to this chart released by the Metropolitan Life Insurance Company. The largest increase for any state in 1966 was Massachusetts' 14.4 per cent gain from 35,391 marriages in 1965 to 40,485 in 1966. Decreases in marriages (denoted by a minus sign) for 1966 occurred in New Hampshire, Rhode Island, New York, North Dakota, Maryland, West Virginia, Georgia, Tennessee, New Mexico, and Hawaii. Figures are given for total marriages in each of the 50 states from 1964 to 1966, along with percentage changes from year to year.

| AREA OF OCCURRENCE | NUMBER | | | PER CENT CHANGE | |
| --- | --- | --- | --- | --- | --- |
| | 1966* | 1965 | 1964 | 1965 TO 1966 | 1964 TO 1965 |
| United States | 1,858,827 | 1,801,977 | 1,725,221 | 3.2 | 4.4 |
| New England | 89,707 | 84,025 | 81,963 | 6.8 | 2.5 |
| Maine | 8,983 | 8,726 | 8,269 | 2.9 | 5.5 |
| New Hampshire | 8,909 | 8,988 | 8,461 | −0.9 | 6.2 |
| Vermont | 3,860 | 3,646 | 3,303 | 5.9 | 10.4 |
| Massachusetts | 40,485 | 35,391 | 35,772 | 14.4 | −1.1 |
| Rhode Island | 6,122 | 6,321 | 6,103 | −3.1 | 3.6 |
| Connecticut | 21,348 | 20,953 | 20,055 | 1.9 | 4.5 |
| Middle Atlantic | 264,666 | 263,823 | 257,074 | 0.3 | 2.6 |
| New York | 136,463 | 137,355 | 134,782 | −0.6 | 1.9 |
| New Jersey | 46,966 | 46,281 | 45,632 | 1.5 | 1.4 |
| Pennsylvania | 81,237 | 80,187 | 76,660 | 1.3 | 4.6 |
| East North Central | 346,826 | 340,021 | 320,688 | 2.0 | 6.0 |
| Ohio | 80,794 | 78,982 | 74,979 | 2.3 | 5.3 |
| Indiana | 51,825 | 49,732 | 47,066 | 4.2 | 5.7 |
| Illinois | 101,820 | 101,650 | 97,900 | 0.2 | 3.8 |
| Michigan | 83,903 | 81,247 | 73,911 | 3.3 | 9.9 |
| Wisconsin | 28,484 | 28,410 | 26,832 | 0.3 | 5.9 |
| West North Central | 135,300 | 131,346 | 127,716 | 2.9 | 2.9 |
| Minnesota | 26,566 | 26,472 | 25,453 | 0.4 | 4.0 |
| Iowa | 21,130 | 20,247 | 20,232 | 4.4 | 0.1 |
| Missouri | 42,597 | 40,600 | 39,100 | 4.9 | 3.8 |
| North Dakota | 4,740 | 4,939 | 4,675 | −4.0 | 5.6 |
| South Dakota | 8,517 | 8,317 | 8,055 | 2.4 | 3.3 |
| Nebraska | 12,390 | 12,069 | 11,920 | 2.7 | 1.3 |
| Kansas | 19,360 | 18,806 | 18,281 | 2.9 | 2.9 |
| South Atlantic | 319,831 | 312,073 | 300,639 | 2.5 | 3.8 |
| Delaware | 3,160 | 3,105 | 2,918 | 1.8 | 6.4 |
| Maryland | 46,925 | 47,345 | 45,331 | −0.9 | 4.4 |
| District of Columbia | 9,548 | 9,541 | 9,109 | 0.1 | 4.7 |
| Virginia | 46,819 | 45,976 | 43,504 | 1.8 | 5.7 |
| West Virginia | 14,011 | 14,167 | 13,879 | −1.1 | 2.1 |
| North Carolina | 43,482 | 40,667 | 36,790 | 6.9 | 10.5 |
| South Carolina | 48,959 | 46,336 | 44,204 | 5.7 | 4.8 |
| Georgia | 54,502 | 55,537 | 60,228 | −1.9 | −7.8 |
| Florida | 52,425 | 49,399 | 44,676 | 6.1 | 10.6 |
| East South Central | 133,283 | 132,092 | 124,250 | 0.9 | 6.3 |
| Kentucky | 28,402 | 28,340 | 27,353 | 0.2 | 3.6 |
| Tennessee | 39,673 | 40,054 | 36,874 | −1.0 | 8.6 |
| Alabama | 41,732 | 40,355 | 37,239 | 3.4 | 8.4 |
| Mississippi | 23,476 | 23,343 | 22,784 | 0.6 | 2.5 |
| West South Central | 201,186 | 193,146 | 185,698 | 4.2 | 4.0 |
| Arkansas | 20,600 | 20,000 | 20,600 | 3.0 | −2.9 |
| Louisiana | 30,694 | 28,972 | 27,086 | 5.9 | 7.0 |
| Oklahoma | 33,786 | 32,574 | 31,112 | 3.7 | 4.7 |
| Texas | 116,106 | 111,600 | 106,900 | 4.0 | 4.4 |
| Mountain | 167,183 | 156,977 | 148,940 | 6.5 | 5.4 |
| Montana | 4,914 | 4,688 | 4,556 | 4.8 | 2.9 |
| Idaho | 17,129 | 15,864 | 14,019 | 8.0 | 13.2 |
| Wyoming | 3,696 | 3,608 | 3,607 | 2.4 | ‡ |
| Colorado | 19,849 | 18,721 | 18,400 | 6.0 | 1.7 |
| New Mexico | 12,138 | 12,223 | 12,285 | −0.7 | −0.5 |
| Arizona | 13,499 | 12,113 | 11,716 | 11.4 | 3.4 |
| Utah | 9,623 | 8,736 | 8,463 | 10.2 | 3.2 |
| Nevada | 86,335 | 81,024 | 75,894 | 6.6 | 6.8 |
| Pacific | 200,845 | 188,370 | 178,253 | 6.6 | 5.7 |
| Washington | 34,560 | 30,564 | 28,884 | 13.1 | 5.8 |
| Oregon | 13,981 | 13,252 | 12,297 | 5.5 | 7.8 |
| California | 144,086 | 136,090 | 129,104 | 5.9 | 5.4 |
| Alaska | 2,426 | 2,393 | 2,178 | 1.4 | 9.9 |
| Hawaii | 5,792 | 6,071 | 5,790 | −4.6 | 4.9 |

* Provisional.    ‡ Less than 0.05.

## 1966 MARRIAGE LAWS, BY STATE

Source: U.S. Department of Labor, Women's Bureau

| STATE OR OTHER JURISDICTION | AGE AT WHICH MARRIAGE CAN BE CONTRACTED WITH PARENTAL CONSENT | | AGE BELOW WHICH PARENTAL CONSENT IS REQUIRED | | COMMON-LAW MARRIAGE | MEDICAL EXAMINATION REQUIRED | WAITING PERIOD BEFORE LICENSE* |
|---|---|---|---|---|---|---|---|
| | Male | Female | Male | Female | | | |
| Alabama | 17(a) | 14(a) | 21 | 18 | Yes | (b) | — |
| Alaska | 18(c) | 16(c) | 21 | 18 | No | (b) | 3 days |
| Arizona | 18(c) | 16(c) | 21 | 18 | No | (b) | — |
| Arkansas | 18(c) | 16(c) | 21 | 18 | No | (b) | 3 days |
| California | 18(a,d) | 16(a,d) | 21 | 18 | No | (b) | — |
| Colorado | 16(d) | 16(d) | 21 | 18 | Yes | (b) | — |
| Connecticut | 16(d) | 16(d) | 21 | 21 | No | (b) | 4 days |
| Delaware | 18(c) | 16(c) | 21 | 18 | No | (b) | — |
| Florida | 18(a,c) | 16(a,c) | 21 | 21 | Yes | (b) | 3 days |
| Georgia | 18(c,e) | 16(c,e) | 19(e) | 19(e) | Yes | (b) | 3 days(f) |
| Hawaii | 18 | 16(d) | 20 | 20 | No | (b) | 3 days |
| Idaho | 15 | 15(d) | 18 | 18 | Yes | (b) | — |
| Illinois | 18 | 16 | 21 | 18 | No | (b) | — |
| Indiana | 18(c) | 16(c) | 21 | 18 | No | (b) | 3 days |
| Iowa | 18(c) | 16(c) | 21 | 18 | Yes | (b) | 3 days |
| Kansas | 18(d) | 16(d) | 21 | 18 | Yes | (b,g) | 3 days |
| Kentucky | 18(a,c) | 16(a,c) | 21 | 21 | No | (b) | 3 days |
| Louisiana | 18(d) | 16(d) | 21 | 21 | No | (b) | — |
| Maine | 16(d) | 16(d) | 21 | 18 | No | (b) | 5 days |
| Maryland | 18(c) | 16(c) | 21 | 18 | No | — | 48 hours |
| Massachusetts | 18(d) | 16(d) | 21 | 18 | No | (b) | 3 days |
| Michigan | (i) | 16(c) | 18 | 18 | No | (b) | 3 days |
| Minnesota | 18(a) | 16(j) | 21 | 18 | No | — | 5 days |
| Mississippi | 17(d) | 15(d) | 21 | 21 | No | (b) | 3 days |
| Missouri | 15(d) | 15(d) | 21 | 18 | No | (b) | 3 days |
| Montana | 18(d) | 16(d) | 21 | 18 | Yes | (b) | 5 days |
| Nebraska | 18(c) | 16(c) | 21 | 21 | No | (b) | — |
| Nevada | 18(a,d) | 16(a,d) | 21 | 18 | No | — | — |
| New Hampshire | (k) | (k) | 20 | 18 | No | (b) | 5 days |
| New Jersey | 18(d) | 16(d) | 21 | 18 | No | (b) | 72 hours |
| New Mexico | 18(c) | 16(c) | 21 | 18 | No | (b) | — |
| New York | 16 | 14(d) | 21 | 18 | No | (b) | — |
| North Carolina | 16 | 16(c) | 18 | 18 | No | (m) | (n) |
| North Dakota | 18 | 15 | 21 | 18 | No | (o) | — |
| Ohio | 18(c) | 16(c) | 21 | 21 | Yes | (b) | 5 days |
| Oklahoma | 18(c) | 15(c) | 21 | 18 | Yes | (b) | 72 hours(p) |
| Oregon | 18(j) | 15(j) | 21 | 18 | No | (r) | 7 days |
| Pennsylvania | 16(d) | 16(d) | 21 | 21 | Yes | (b) | 3 days |
| Rhode Island | 18(d) | 16(d) | 21 | 21 | Yes | (s) | — |
| South Carolina | 16(c) | 14(c) | 18 | 18 | Yes | — | 24 hours |
| South Dakota | 18(c) | 16(c) | 21 | 18 | No | (b) | — |
| Tennessee | 16(d) | 16(d) | 21 | 21 | No | (b) | 3 days(t) |
| Texas | 16 | 14 | 21 | 18 | Yes | (b) | 3 days(p) |
| Utah | 16(a) | 14(a) | 21 | 18 | No | (b) | — |
| Vermont | 18(d) | 16(d) | 21 | 18 | No | (b) | — |
| Virginia | 18(a,c) | 16(a,c) | 21 | 21 | No | (b) | — |
| Washington | 17(d) | 17(d) | 21 | 18 | No | (o) | 3 days |
| West Virginia | 18(a) | 16(a) | 21 | 21 | No | (b) | 3 days |
| Wisconsin | 18 | 16 | 21 | 18 | No | (b) | 5 days |
| Wyoming | 18 | 16 | 21 | 21 | No | (b) | — |
| District of Columbia | 18(a) | 16(a) | 21 | 18 | Yes | — | 3 days |

* Five states also require a waiting period after the issuance of a license: Delaware (24 hours for residents and 96 hours for nonresidents); Louisiana (72 hours); New York (24 hours); Rhode Island (if female is nonresident, must complete and sign license five days prior to marriage); Vermont (5 days).    a Parental consent is not required if minor was previously married. b Venereal diseases (blood test).    c Statute establishes procedure whereby younger parties may obtain license in case of pregnancy or birth of a child.    d In special circumstances, statute establishes procedure whereby younger parties may obtain license.    e If parties are under 19, proof of age and consent of parents in person required. If parent is ill, affidavits by parent and physician required.    f Unless parties are 21 years or more, or female is pregnant, or applicants are parents of child born out of wedlock.    g Feeblemindedness.    i No provision in law for parental consent for males.    j Parental consent and permission of judge required.    k Below age of consent parties need parental consent and permission of judge. m Uncontrolled epileptic attacks, idiocy, imbecility, mental defectiveness, unsound mind, infectious tuberculosis, and venereal diseases.    n Forty-eight hours if both are nonresidents.    o Feeblemindedness, imbecility, insanity, chronic alcoholism, and venereal diseases. (Also in Washington, advanced tuberculosis.)    p If one or both parties are below the age for marriage without parental consent.    r Venereal diseases, feeblemindedness, mental illness, drug addiction, and chronic alcoholism. s Infectious tuberculosis and venereal diseases.    t Does not apply when parties are over 21 years of age.

## 1966 DIVORCE LAWS, BY STATES

Source: U.S. Department of Labor, Women's Bureau

| STATE OR OTHER JURISDICTION | RESIDENCE REQUIRED FOR DIVORCE | GROUNDS FOR DIVORCE (a) | | | | | | |
|---|---|---|---|---|---|---|---|---|
| | | Cruelty | Desertion | Alcoholism | Impotency | Non-support | Insanity (from commit-ment) | Pregnancy at marriage |
| Alabama | (b) | Yes | 1 year | Yes | Yes | Yes(c) | 5 years | Yes |
| Alaska | 1 year | Yes | 1 year | Yes | Yes | Yes | 18 months | No |
| Arizona | 1 year | Yes | 1 year | Yes | Yes | Yes | No | Yes |
| Arkansas | 2 months | Yes | 1 year | Yes | Yes | Yes(h) | 3 years | No |
| California | 1 year | Yes | 1 year | Yes | No | Yes | 3 years | No |
| Colorado | 1 year(j) | Yes | 1 year | Yes | Yes | Yes | 3 years | No |
| Connecticut | 3 years(j) | Yes | 3 years | Yes | No | No | 5 years | No |
| Delaware | 2 years(j) | Yes | 2 years | Yes | No | Yes | 5 years | No |
| Florida | 6 months | Yes | 1 year | Yes | Yes | No | No | No |
| Georgia | 6 months | Yes | 1 year | Yes | Yes | No | 2 years | Yes |
| Hawaii | 2 years | Yes | 6 months | Yes | No | Yes | 3 years | No |
| Idaho | 6 weeks | Yes | 1 year | Yes | No | Yes | 6 years | No |
| Illinois | 1 year(j) | Yes | 1 year | Yes | Yes | No | No | No |
| Indiana | 1 year(r) | Yes | 2 years | Yes | Yes | Yes | 5 years | No |
| Iowa | 1 year | Yes | 2 years | Yes | No | No | No | Yes(t) |
| Kansas | 1 year(u) | Yes | 1 year | Yes | No | Yes | 5 years | No |
| Kentucky | 1 year | Yes | 1 year | Yes(v) | Yes | No | 5 years | Yes |
| Louisiana | (y) | No | No | No | No | No | No | No |
| Maine | 6 months(j) | Yes | 3 years | Yes | Yes | Yes | No | No |
| Maryland | 1 year(ab) | No | 18 months | No | Yes | No | 3 years | No |
| Massachusetts | 5 years(j) | Yes | 3 years | Yes | Yes | Yes | No | No |
| Michigan | 1 year(j) | Yes | 2 years | Yes | Yes | Yes | No | No |
| Minnesota | 1 year(j) | Yes | 1 year | Yes | Yes | No | 5 years | No |
| Mississippi | 1 year | Yes | 1 year | Yes | Yes | No | 3 years | Yes |
| Missouri | 1 year(j) | Yes | 1 year | Yes | Yes | No | No | Yes |
| Montana | 1 year | Yes | 1 year | Yes | No | Yes | 5 years | No |
| Nebraska | 2 years(j) | Yes | 2 years | Yes | Yes | Yes | 5 years | No |
| Nevada | 6 weeks(j) | Yes | 1 year | Yes | Yes | Yes | 2 years | No |
| New Hampshire | 1 year(j) | Yes | 2 years | Yes | Yes | Yes | No | No |
| New Jersey | 2 years(j) | Yes | 2 years | No | No | No | No | No |
| New Mexico | 1 year | Yes | Yes | Yes | Yes | Yes | 5 years | Yes |
| New York | 1 year | Yes | 2 years | No | No | No | No | No |
| North Carolina | 6 months | No | No | No | Yes | No | 5 years | Yes |
| North Dakota | 1 year(r) | Yes | 1 year | Yes | No | Yes(h) | 5 years | No |
| Ohio | 1 year | Yes | No | Yes | Yes | Yes | No | No |
| Oklahoma | 6 months(u) | Yes | 1 year | Yes | Yes | Yes | 5 years | Yes |
| Oregon | 1 year | Yes | 1 year | Yes | Yes | No | 2 years | No |
| Pennsylvania | 1 year | Yes | 2 years | No | Yes | No | No | No |
| Rhode Island | 2 years | Yes | 5 years(aj) | Yes | Yes | Yes | No | No |
| South Carolina | 1 year | Yes | 1 year | Yes | No | No | No | No |
| South Dakota | 1 year(j) | Yes | 1 year | Yes | No | Yes | 5 years | No |
| Tennessee | 1 year | Yes | 1 year | Yes | Yes | Yes | No | Yes |
| Texas | 12 months | Yes | 3 years | No | No | No | 5 years | No |
| Utah | 3 months | Yes | 1 year | Yes | Yes | Yes | Yes | No |
| Vermont | 6 months(ap) | No | 3 years | No | No | Yes | 5 years | No |
| Virginia | 1 year | No | 1 year | No | Yes | No | No | Yes |
| Washington | 1 year | Yes | 1 year | Yes | Yes | Yes | 2 years | No |
| West Virginia | 2 years(j) | Yes | 1 year | Yes | No | No | No | No |
| Wisconsin | 2 years | Yes | 1 year | Yes | No | Yes | No | No |
| Wyoming | 60 days(j) | Yes | 1 year | Yes | Yes | Yes | 2 years | Yes |
| District of Columbia Washington, D.C. | 1 year | No | 1 year | No | No | No | No | No |

[a] Adultery is grounds for divorce in all 50 states. [b] No specific period, except 1 year when ground is desertion or defendant is nonresident or 2 years if wife sues husband for nonsupport. [c] To wife, living separate and apart from husband, as resident of the state for 2 years before suit and without support from him during such time. [d] Crime against nature. [e] Except to each other. [f] Incompatibility. [g] Crime before marriage. [h] Also to husband in certain circumstances. [i] Final decree is not entered until 1 year after interlocutory decree. [j] Under certain circumstances a lesser period of time may be required. [k] Female under 16, male under 18, complaining party under age of consent at time of marriage has not confirmed the marriage after reaching such age. [l] In the discretion of the court. [m] Habitual violent and ungovernable temper. [n] Defendant obtained divorce from plaintiff in another state. [o] Mental incapacity. [p] Under decree of separate maintenance. [q] Loathsome disease. [r] Five years if on ground of insanity. [s] Two years where service on defendant is only by publication. [t] Unless at time of marriage husband had an illegitimate child living which fact was not known to wife. [u] Five years if on ground of insanity and insane spouse is in out-of-state institution. [v] If on part of the husband, accompanied by wasting of husband's estate to the detriment of the wife and children. [w] Joining religious sect disbelieving in marriage. [x] Unchaste behavior on part of wife after marriage. [y] No statutory requirement for adultery or felony conviction; 2 years when ground is separation. [aa] When divorce is granted on ground of adultery, guilty party cannot marry the accomplice in adultery during lifetime of former spouse. [ab] No specific period required, ex-

## GROUNDS FOR DIVORCE (continued)

| Bigamy | Separation or absence | Felony conviction or imprisonment | Drug addiction | Fraud, force, or duress | Infamous crime | Other | PERIOD BEFORE PARTIES MAY REMARRY AFTER FINAL DECREE | |
|---|---|---|---|---|---|---|---|---|
| | | | | | | | Plaintiff | Defendant |
| No | No | Yes | Yes | No | No | (d) | 60 days(e) | 60 days(e) |
| No | No | Yes | Yes | No | No | (f) | No | No |
| No | 5 years | Yes | No | No | Yes | (g) | 1 year | 1 year |
| Yes | 3 years | Yes | No | No | Yes | No | No | No |
| No | No | Yes | No | No | No | (i) | No | (i) |
| No | 3 years | Yes | Yes | No | No | No | No | No |
| No | 7 years | Yes | No | Yes | Yes | No | No | No |
| Yes | 3 years | Yes | No | No | No | (k) | 3 months(l) | 3 months(l) |
| Yes | No | No | Yes | No | No | (m,n) | No | No |
| No | No | Yes | No | Yes | No | (o) | (l) | (l) |
| No | 2 years(p) | Yes | Yes | No | No | No | (i) | (i) |
| No | 5 years | Yes | No | No | No | No | No | No |
| Yes | No | Yes | No | No | Yes | (q) | No | No |
| No | No | Yes | No | No | Yes | (s) | No | No |
| No | No | Yes | No | No | No | No | 1 year(e,l) | 1 year(e,l) |
| No | No | Yes | No | No | No | No | 60 days | 60 days |
| No | 5 years | Yes | No | Yes | No | (q,w,x) | No | No |
| No | 2 years | Yes | No | No | No | No | wife, 10 months | wife, 10 months(aa) |
| No | No | No | Yes | No | No | No | No | No |
| No | 18 months | Yes | No | No | No | (ac) | No | No |
| No | No | Yes | Yes | No | No | No | No | No |
| No | No | Yes | No | No | No | (n) | No | (ad) |
| No | 2 years(p) | Yes | No | No | No | No | 6 months | 6 months |
| Yes | No | Yes | Yes | No | No | (o) | No | (ae) |
| Yes | No | Yes | No | No | Yes | (g,af) | No | No |
| No | No | Yes | No | No | No | No | 6 months | 6 months |
| No | No | Yes | No | No | No | No | 6 months | 6 months |
| No | 3 years | Yes | No | No | Yes | No | No | No |
| No | 2 years | Yes | No | No | No | (w,ag) | No | No |
| No | No | No | No | No | No | (f) | 3 months(l) | 3 months(l) |
| No | 2 years(p) | Yes | No | No | No | No | No | No |
| No | 1 year | Yes | No | No | No | (d) | No | No |
| No | No | Yes | Yes | No | No | No | (l) | (l) |
| Yes | 1 year | Yes | No | Yes | No | (n) | (ah) | No |
| No | No | Yes | No | Yes | No | (f,n) | 6 months | 6 months |
| No | No | Yes | No | No | No | No | 6 months | 6 months |
| Yes | No | Yes | No | Yes | No | (ai) | No | (aa) |
| No | 10 years | No | Yes | No | No | (ak,al) | 6 months | 6 months |
| No | No | No | Yes | No | No | No | No | No |
| No | No | Yes | No | No | No | No | No | (am) |
| Yes | 2 years(an) | Yes | No | No | Yes | (ai) | No | (aa) |
| No | 7 years | Yes | No | No | No | No | (ao) | (ao) |
| No | 3 years(p) | Yes | No | No | No | No | 3 months(l) | 3 months(l) |
| No | 3 years | Yes | No | No | No | (aq) | 6 months(l) | 2 years(l) |
| No | 2 years | Yes | No | No | Yes | (d,ar) | (as) | (as) |
| No | 2 years | Yes | No | Yes | No | (at) | 6 months | 6 months |
| No | No | Yes | Yes | No | No | No | 60 days | 60 days(au) |
| No | 5 years | Yes | No | No | No | No | 1 year | 1 year |
| No | 2 years | Yes | No | No | Yes | (g,af) | No | No |
| No | 1 year | Yes | No | No | No | No | 6 months | 6 months |

cept 1 year if cause occurred out of state and 2 years if on ground of insanity. ad Not more than 2 years in court's discretion. ae When divorce is granted on ground of adultery, court may prohibit remarriage. After 1 year court may remove disability upon satisfactory evidence of reformation. af Husband a vagrant. ag Wife's absence out of state for 10 years without husband's consent. ah When husband is entitled to a divorce and alimony or child support from husband is granted, the decree may be delayed until security is entered for payment. ai Incapable of procreation. aj Or a lesser time in court's discretion. ak Void or voidable marriage. al Gross misbehavior or wickedness, loss of citizenship rights of one party due to crime, presumption of death. am When divorce is for adultery, guilty party cannot remarry except to the innocent person, until the death of the other. an To husband for wife's refusal to move with him to this state without reasonable cause, and willfully absenting herself from him for 2 years. ao When divorce is granted on ground of cruelty, neither party may remarry for 12 months except each other. ap One year before final hearing, and 2 years if on ground of insanity. aq Intolerable severity. ar Wife a prostitute prior to marriage. as When divorce is granted on ground of adultery, court may decree the guilty party cannot remarry. After 6 months the court may remove disability for good cause. Remarriage of either party is forbidden pending appeal. at Want of legal age or sufficient understanding. au In court's discretion, guilty party may be prohibited from remarrying for a period not to exceed 1 year.

ac Any cause which renders marriage null and void from the beginning.

## U.S. MARRIAGES AND MARRIAGE RATES, BY MONTH: 1965–1966

June continued in 1966 to be the most popular month for marriages in the United States. The 1966 total for June of 230,000 was greater than the 226,000 for 1965. This chart, compiled by the U.S. Public Health Service, gives figures for total marriages each month, as well as for the rate of marriages monthly and annually per 1,000 population.

| MONTH | NUMBER 1965 | 1966 | RATE 1965 | 1966 | MONTH | NUMBER 1965 | 1966 | RATE 1965 | 1966 |
|---|---|---|---|---|---|---|---|---|---|
| January | 102,000 | 105,000 | 6.2 | 6.4 | August | 193,000 | 198,000 | 11.7 | 11.9 |
| February | 121,000 | 121,000 | 8.2 | 8.1 | September | 166,000 | 171,000 | 10.4 | 10.6 |
| March | 115,000 | 113,000 | 7.0 | 6.8 | October | 139,000 | 143,000 | 8.4 | 8.6 |
| April | 125,000 | 140,000 | 7.8 | 8.7 | November | 139,000 | 146,000 | 8.7 | 9.1 |
| May | 137,000 | 139,000 | 8.3 | 8.3 | December | 160,000 | 172,000 | 9.7 | 10.3 |
| June | 226,000 | 230,000 | 14.2 | 14.3 | | | | | |
| July | 166,000 | 166,000 | 10.1 | 10.0 | **Total Marriages** | **1,789,000** | **1,844,000** | **9.2** | **9.4** |

## MEDIAN AGE OF AMERICANS AT FIRST MARRIAGE: 1910—1966
Source: U.S. Bureau of the Census

| YEAR | MALE | FEMALE | YEAR | MALE | FEMALE | YEAR | MALE | FEMALE | YEAR | MALE | FEMALE |
|---|---|---|---|---|---|---|---|---|---|---|---|
| 1966 | 22.8 | 20.5 | 1960 | 22.8 | 20.3 | 1954 | 23.0 | 20.3 | 1948 | 23.3 | 20.4 |
| 1965 | 22.8 | 20.6 | 1959 | 22.5 | 20.2 | 1953 | 22.8 | 20.2 | 1947 | 23.7 | 20.5 |
| 1964 | 23.1 | 20.5 | 1958 | 22.6 | 20.2 | 1952 | 23.0 | 20.2 | 1940 | 24.3 | 21.5 |
| 1963 | 22.8 | 20.5 | 1957 | 22.6 | 20.3 | 1951 | 22.9 | 20.4 | 1930 | 24.3 | 21.3 |
| 1962 | 22.7 | 20.3 | 1956 | 22.5 | 20.1 | 1950 | 22.8 | 20.3 | 1920 | 24.6 | 21.2 |
| 1961 | 22.8 | 20.3 | 1955 | 22.6 | 20.2 | 1949 | 22.7 | 20.3 | 1910 | 25.1 | 21.6 |

## U.S. MARRIAGES AND DIVORCES: 1921–1966
Source: U.S. Public Health Service

| YEAR | MARRIAGES Number | Rate* | DIVORCES Number | Rate* | YEAR | MARRIAGES Number | Rate* | DIVORCES Number | Rate* |
|---|---|---|---|---|---|---|---|---|---|
| 1921 | 1,163,863 | 10.7 | 159,580 | 1.5 | 1944 | 1,452,394 | 10.9 | 400,000 | 2.9 |
| 1922 | 1,134,151 | 10.3 | 148,815 | 1.4 | 1945 | 1,612,992 | 12.2 | 485,000 | 3.5 |
| 1923 | 1,229,784 | 11.0 | 165,096 | 1.5 | 1946 | 2,291,045 | 16.4 | 610,000 | 4.3 |
| 1924 | 1,184,574 | 10.4 | 170,952 | 1.5 | 1947 | 1,991,878 | 13.9 | 483,000 | 3.4 |
| 1925 | 1,188,334 | 10.3 | 175,449 | 1.5 | 1948 | 1,811,155 | 12.4 | 408,000 | 2.8 |
| 1926 | 1,202,574 | 10.2 | 184,678 | 1.6 | 1949 | 1,579,798 | 10.6 | 397,000 | 2.7 |
| 1927 | 1,201,053 | 10.1 | 196,292 | 1.6 | 1950 | 1,667,231 | 11.1 | 385,144 | 2.6 |
| 1928 | 1,182,497 | 9.8 | 200,176 | 1.7 | 1951 | 1,594,694 | 10.4 | 381,000 | 2.5 |
| 1929 | 1,232,559 | 10.1 | 205,876 | 1.7 | 1952 | 1,539,318 | 9.9 | 392,000 | 2.5 |
| 1930 | 1,126,856 | 9.2 | 195,961 | 1.6 | 1953 | 1,546,000 | 9.8 | 390,000 | 2.5 |
| 1931 | 1,060,914 | 8.6 | 188,003 | 1.5 | 1954 | 1,490,000 | 9.2 | 379,000 | 2.4 |
| 1932 | 981,903 | 7.9 | 164,241 | 1.3 | 1955 | 1,531,000 | 9.3 | 377,000 | 2.3 |
| 1933 | 1,098,000 | 8.7 | 165,000 | 1.3 | 1956 | 1,585,000 | 9.5 | 382,000 | 2.3 |
| 1934 | 1,302,000 | 10.3 | 204,000 | 1.6 | 1957 | 1,518,000 | 8.9 | 381,000 | 2.2 |
| 1935 | 1,327,000 | 10.4 | 218,000 | 1.7 | 1958 | 1,451,000 | 8.4 | 368,000 | 2.1 |
| 1936 | 1,369,000 | 10.7 | 236,000 | 1.8 | 1959 | 1,494,000 | 8.5 | 395,000 | 2.2 |
| 1937 | 1,451,296 | 11.3 | 249,000 | 1.9 | 1960 | 1,523,000 | 8.5 | 393,000 | 2.2 |
| 1938 | 1,330,780 | 10.3 | 244,000 | 1.9 | 1961 | 1,548,000 | 8.5 | 414,000 | 2.3 |
| 1939 | 1,403,633 | 10.7 | 251,000 | 1.9 | 1962 | 1,577,000 | 8.5 | 413,000 | 2.2 |
| 1940 | 1,595,879 | 12.1 | 264,000 | 2.0 | 1963 | 1,651,000 | 8.8 | 428,000 | 2.2 |
| 1941 | 1,695,999 | 12.7 | 293,000 | 2.2 | 1964 | 1,720,000 | 9.0 | 445,000 | 2.3 |
| 1942 | 1,772,132 | 13.2 | 321,000 | 2.4 | 1965 | 1,789,000 | 9.2 | 481,000 | 2.5 |
| 1943 | 1,577,050 | 11.7 | 359,000 | 2.6 | 1966 | 1,844,000 | 9.4 | 494,000 | 2.5 |

* Per 1,000 population.

## WEDDING ANNIVERSARY GIFTS

| ANNIVERSARY | GIFT | ANNIVERSARY | GIFT | ANNIVERSARY | GIFT |
|---|---|---|---|---|---|
| 1 | Paper or Plastics | 9 | Pottery | 25 | Silver |
| 2 | Calico or Cotton | 10 | Tin or Aluminum | 30 | Pearl |
| 3 | Leather | 11 | Steel | 35 | Coral or Jade |
| 4 | Silk | 12 | Linen | 40 | Ruby |
| 5 | Wood | 13 | Lace | 45 | Sapphire |
| 6 | Iron | 14 | Ivory | 50 | Gold |
| 7 | Copper or Wool | 15 | Crystal or Glass | 55 | Emerald |
| 8 | Electrical appliances | 20 | China | 60 | Diamond |

# RELIGION AND PHILOSOPHY

## World Religions • U.S. Religious Bodies • Famous Philosophers

Pictorial Parade

In search for Church unity, Pope Paul and Patriarch Athengoras, leader of the Eastern Orthodox Church, pray together at the Church of St. George in Istanbul, Turkey, during Pope's historic visit in July 1967.

### ECUMENICAL MOVEMENT: 1967

The movement toward ecumenism in Christendom began to take new shape in 1967. It has grown into a genuine movement cutting vigorously across the organizational lines of church circles.

Almost every Christian church body has become aware of the strong appeal that ecumenism holds for the average man. Denominations that showed little interest during the movement's early stages—particularly those known as "fundamentalist" or "evangelical"—began to reassess their attitudes. Instead of their former aloofness, they began to consider attempts to influence ecumenism in directions more acceptable to themselves—and perhaps more productive for Christendom as a whole.

Church groups long identified with ecumenical endeavors through interdenominational associations have begun to acknowledge that the

ecumenical movement cannot be tied exclusively to any one organizational form if it is to accomplish its purpose. Rather, it must transcend such organizations as the World Council of Churches and the national and international federations and alliances of churches formed in the past on various confessional or interconfessional lines.

Talks between Roman Catholics and Protestant and Orthodox denominations received great impetus from the Second Vatican Council, which explicitly encouraged such conversations. During 1967 interdenominational dialogues took place at all levels, from international meetings of ecclesiastical delegations to parish meetings conducted exclusively by laymen.

Conversations were begun on the highest level, in January at Gazada, Italy, between *(continued)*

Wide World

Rt. Rev. James Pike (left), former Episcopal Bishop of California, confers with Dr. Eugene Carson Blake, General Secretary of the World Council of Churches, at the **Pacem in Terris** Conference in Geneva in May, 1967.

representatives of the Anglican Communion and of the Holy See. These meetings resulted from an agreement reached between Pope Paul VI and the Archbishop of Canterbury, the Most Rev. Arthur Michael Ramsey, in March, 1966. Although the talks began in an atmosphere of near euphoria, they were continued later in the year in a more realistic mood, as it became apparent that great problems must be overcome if genuine understanding is to be achieved between Christian groups long separated by differences in doctrine, tradition, practical church life, and history.

Similar conversations on the international level were mapped out by delegations of the Lutheran World Federation and the Holy See. Subjects planned for a coming series of discussions are "The Nature of the Christian Gospel" and "The Theology of Marriage." The latter subject will include reference to the practical problems presented by "mixed marriages" (where one party to a marriage is Roman Catholic and the other Lutheran).

Roman Catholics, Protestants, Anglicans, and Orthodox Christians participated in various ways and places during the Week of Prayer for Christian Unity, January 18–25, 1967. In Ireland, during the same week, 100 citizens representing various denominations took part in an ecumenical conference on Christian marriage—a significant event in view of the history of this predominantly Roman Catholic country.

Lutherans and other Protestant denominations throughout the world observed the 450th Anniversary of the Lutheran Reformation (commemorating Martin Luther's posting of the 95 Theses on the door of the Castle Church at Wittenberg, Saxony, October 31, 1517). Roman Catholic dignitaries took part in some of the Reformation observances.

In April the World Council of Churches and the Lutheran World Federation completed a five-year series of joint discussions at Bad Schauenburg, Germany. Reformed and Lutheran theologians from 11 European countries participated.

Conversations among Protestant bodies—some designed to promote church unions as well as Christian unity—took place in the United States, England, New Zealand, Canada, and Australia. In Canada the Board of Colleges and Secondary Schools of the United Church of Canada approved a plan whereby training of clergy for the nation's Protestant and Roman Catholic churches could be carried on at five major ecumenical centers. The plan also has strong Roman Catholic support. In Australia a merger took place between the country's two major Lutheran bodies.

A Christian Council was formed in the New Hebrides to further the unity of Christian churches there. Roman Catholics, Anglicans, Presbyterians, and members of the Churches of Christ Mission participated in the council. In New Zealand 150 official representatives of five denominations committed their churches "to seek a basis of union and ways of common action." The five denominations represented were the Associated Churches of Christ, the Congregational Union, and the Methodist, Presbyterian, and Anglican churches.

During 1967 several new approaches took place between the Roman Catholic Church and the Eastern Orthodox Church as an outgrowth of the Second Vatican Council. An indication of increasing cooperation between the two churches was their mutual removal of excommunications, which date back a thousand years. Pope Paul VI went to Istanbul for a personal meeting with Patriarch Athenagoras, generally recognized as the prime spokesman for Eastern Orthodoxy. The visit was returned in October when Patriarch Athenagoras visited Pope Paul at the Vatican and pledged continued efforts to end the thousand-year-old schism between their churches.

In June more than 40 liturgical specialists from Europe and North America met at Driebergen, Holland, to found *Societas Liturgica*, a new organization for international liturgical exchange between Roman Catholic, Orthodox, Lutheran, and Reformed theologians.

Thus 1967 marked the beginning of the age of dialogue between Christians, many of whose ancestors had not talked to each other for four-and-a-half centuries. The new conversations have indicated that wide agreement exists in some areas—perhaps wider agreement than had been generally recognized. At the same time, areas in which disagreement persists may be given sharper definition as the conversations proceed. Hopefully, agreement that can be understood and disagreement that can be discussed will be the products of the new ecumenicity. The major Christian churches are showing signs of willingness to seek accord without resorting to hiding differences that actually exist, or compromising deep theological convictions. The mood is conciliatory, and fortunately it appears to be divorced from the sentimentality that characterized some earlier ecumenical endeavors.

# MAJOR WORLD RELIGIONS

One of the most fundamental beliefs underlying the destiny or existence of man, wherever or whenever he has lived, is religion. Man's awareness of God, or of some supernatural power or powers, has given rise to the belief in a sacred, transcendent order, which deals with the inexplicable or unpredictable elements of human experience in the world or beyond it. The practice of religion is rooted in the inner, often mystical, experience of the believer.

Modern world religions are commonly classified according to the number of gods worshiped within a religion. Thus, Judaism, Christianity, and Islam are monotheistic religions, each having one God, while Hinduism, Buddhism (in some branches), Taoism, Confucianism, and Shintoism are polytheistic, each with many gods.

## JUDAISM

The oldest monotheistic faith in the world, and one of the oldest religions of any kind, is Judaism. There are about 13,121,000 Jews in the world, including 6,579,000 in the Americas, 3,919,000 in Europe, and 2,143,000 in Israel. The remainder are scattered in Jewish communities throughout the world. The word Jew is derived from the Latin *Judaeus*, from the Hebrew *Yehudhi*, signifying a member of the ancient kingdom of Judah. Christianity and Islam are inextricably joined with Judaism because the basic beliefs of Judaism are fundamental to the two younger faiths.

The complex of law, prophecy, and tradition known as Judaism has its basis in two works—the Old Testament (particularly the Torah, or first five books) and the Talmud, a collection of later teachings and interpretation. The creed of Judaism is flexible. It is the sum of the experiences of the Jews over 3,500 years, beginning with the patriarch Abraham.

Abraham, who is considered to have lived around 1500 B.C., is regarded as the founder of Judaism because of his covenant with God that he and his descendants would carry the Biblical message to all men. The covenant is commemorated in the rite of circumcision. The followers of Abraham consolidated the religion and received new revelations. Moses, among the greatest of Jews, freed his people from bondage in Egypt in the 13th century B.C. and received the Ten Commandments and the Torah as a constitution for the new nation. The basic prayer of Judaism, called the Sh'ma, begins: "Hear, O Israel, the Lord our God, the Lord is one." Its principal day, the Sabbath, is from sunset Friday to sunset Saturday.

In the United States, Jewish congregations are classified as Orthodox, Conservative, or Reform, depending upon their adherence to dietary laws and religious customs. Orthodox Jews over the world are divided into a number of sects grouped around various spiritual leaders and regional or historical traditions.

Jewish holidays include *Pesach* (Passover), celebrating the Exodus; *Shabuoth* (Pentecost); *Rosh Hashanah* (New Year); and *Yom Kippur* (Day of Atonement).

## CHRISTIANITY

Although it continues from the Judaic tradition, Christianity actually begins with Jesus of Nazareth, or Jesus Christ, who lived from about 5 B.C. to A.D. 30. (The month, day, and year of Jesus' birth are unknown. Most authorities place his birth in or about 5 B.C.) The name Jesus Christ is of Greek derivation from the Hebrew *Joshua,* meaning the Savior, and *Messiah,* or the Anointed. The primary sources for the life of Jesus are the four Gospels of Matthew, Mark, Luke, and John and the Epistles of the New Testament. Jesus was born of Mary, wife of Joseph, a carpenter of Nazareth, who had brought his wife to Bethlehem, his family home, for a Roman tax census.

Today there are about one billion Christians in the world, concentrated mainly in Europe, the Americas, and such countries as Lebanon and Ethiopia, but also including Christian communities in every nation. The Christian population includes about 575 million Roman Catholics, 224 million Protestants, and 142 million Eastern Orthodox believers.

The Christian article of faith is that Jesus was the son of God, that he came to save the world and was crucified, that he was resurrected and will come again on the world's last day to judge mankind. The primary commandment of Jesus was to believe in God and to love Him. Jesus also insisted on the virtue of meekness, assistance to the poor and unfortunate, and adherence to the principle expressed in the Golden Rule: "Thou shalt love thy neighbor as thyself." The foundation of Christianity is the New Testament, which recounts the life and teachings of Jesus and the works and doctrines of his early followers, notably St. Paul.

There are many differences among the various Christian groups, based primarily on whether later church tradition or the Bible alone is to have authority, whether good works or faith defines the Christian, and whether churches are to be controlled by a hierarchy or by the believers themselves. With the increasing influence of the ecumenical movement through interfaith organizations, however, Christians are coming to find large areas of agreement where before there had been discord. A number of Protestant denominations have merged in the last 20 years and more mergers are expected. Cooperation among Protestant groups and Catholics and Jews has greatly increased during the 1960s.

The largest Christian body is the Roman Catholic Church, although the Roman rite is only one of many in the Catholic Church. Its members acknowledge the supreme jurisdiction of the Pope, the Bishop of Rome, who is considered Christ's vicar and the successor of St. Peter. The Roman rite of the Church, by far the largest, is practiced in Europe and the Americas.

*(continued)*

**MAJOR WORLD RELIGIONS** (*continued*)

Other rites within the Catholic Church are the Alexandrian, the Antiochene, the Chaldean, the Armenian, and the Byzantine.

The Protestant churches are the products of the Reformation of the 16th century, although the Anglican church was in existence before that time. There are hundreds of Protestant churches, fragmented by national or doctrinal differences or schisms.

The term Protestant derives from the formal *protestatio* issued in 1529 by the Lutheran rulers in the Holy Roman Empire against the repressive Diet of Speyer. It became the general term for all who argued against the Papal claim of universal supremacy. The principal early forms of Protestantism were: Calvinism, from which sprang the Presbyterian and Reformed traditions; Lutheranism; and the Anglican church. From the Anglican came the Baptists, the Methodists, and a number of smaller movements such as the Quakers, Puritans, and Congregationalists. Methodism has been the fountainhead of many denominations, including many separate Methodist churches and also most of the Pentecostal groups. There are also some churches with separate prophetic traditions, such as the Latter-Day Saints (Mormons) and Christian Scientists, and some that seek to find a common base for all religions, such as the Unitarians and the Bahai.

The third great Christian group is the Eastern Orthodox. These ancient churches were formed after disputes with Rome, arising mainly from the splitting of the old Roman Empire into a Western half—centered on Rome—and an Eastern half—with Constantinople as its capital. The 15 Orthodox churches consist of the four ancient Eastern patriarchates—Constantinople, Alexandria, Antioch, and Jerusalem—and the national churches of Moscow, Georgia, Serbia, Romania, Bulgaria, Cyprus, Greece, Sinai, Albania, Poland, and Czechoslovakia. The Patriarch of Constantinople is first in honor among all the Orthodox leaders, and most of the churches consider him the spiritual leader of Eastern Orthodoxy.

Orthodoxy is characterized by a concern with the other world and with personal development in this one. It finds its way in contemplation rather than action. Christ is conceived of as the Risen Christ rather than—as in the West—the Crucified Christ.

## ISLAM

Islam, an Arabic word meaning "submission to, or being at peace with, God," was founded by Mohammed, who was born in Mecca (now in Saudi Arabia) and who lived from about 570 to 632 A.D. Estimates put the number of Moslems at 466 million, which makes Islam the second largest of the world's religions. The principal Moslem areas are the Middle East, North Africa, and western Asia, particularly Egypt, Morocco, Iran, Iraq, Syria, Jordan, Saudi Arabia, Turkey, Pakistan, Afghanistan, and parts of the Soviet Union in Asia. There are also large Islamic communities in the Philippines, Indonesia, and Malaysia. The religion is making great missionary gains—probably surpassing Christianity—in Africa.

Among Moslems, Mohammed is regarded as the "Seal of the Prophets," the last in a line that includes Adam, Noah, Abraham, Moses, and Jesus. His teachings are compiled in the Koran, the word of God. This holy book is supplemented by the Sunna, a compendium of later traditions. These books are reinforced by the principle of Ijma—the belief that the majority of Islam cannot agree in an error.

The moral precepts of Mohammed extend to all areas of secular and civil life. The Islamic article of faith, however, is a simple one: "There is no god but God (Allah), and Mohammed is His Prophet." Any man who one time in his life says the article of faith with complete belief and understanding is considered a Moslem. There are, in addition, four other duties of the follower of Islam: recitation of prayers; observance of Ramadan (a month-long period of fasting and self-examination); giving of alms; and, if possible, a pilgrimage, or hajj, to Mecca. Moslems pray five times daily—at dawn, noon, mid-afternoon, dusk, and night. The prayers, which consist of praise of Allah rather than requests for intercession or favors, are accompanied by traditional postures and ablutions. The main service at midday on Friday is usually held in the mosque.

Islam does not look upon Jews or Christians as pagans, and generally has allowed adherents of those two earlier faiths to keep their own religions after conquest. Islam, soon after its birth, spread in tremendous waves over much of the known world; Moslem armies came within 100 miles of the gates of Paris and conquered large areas of India. An early dispute over Mohammed's successor, called the Caliph, or the deputy, led to the split of Islam into Sunnites and Shiites; adherents of the Shia belief are mainly located in Iran. Wahabi, a third group, was originally a reform movement of the 18th century.

## HINDUISM

The religion of the vast majority of the people of India is Hinduism, the world's oldest religious faith. It has about 350 million adherents in India and in Indian communities overseas. Hinduism is the supreme example of polytheism. Its principal gods—Brahma, Siva, and Vishnu—represent various aspects of the world and are concerned both with good and with evil. The religion, which has grown gradually over the last 5,000 years, has not given birth to any widely held ethical system. Many aspects of Indian life and culture, such as the caste system, have their base in Hinduism, however. A Hindu believes that his caste, or social position, is determined by his actions, or *Karma*, in his present life. If he leads a good life, he will be reborn into a superior caste. However, if his soul achieves perfection he will be saved from continual rebirth and death.

The principal holy book is the Veda, a collection of hymns and incantations of great antiquity; some are believed to date from the arrival of the Aryans in India about 1500 B.C. Later commentaries, such as the *Brahamanas* and the *Upanishads,* provide the sources of the various schools of Indian philosophy and are concerned with mysticism and intuitive examination of the spirit. Much of the emphasis of Hinduism is on worship and ceremonials, including pilgrimages. In the so-called Higher Hinduism, worship is looked upon as an entry to ultimate truth. Hinduism played an influential role in the formation of Buddhism.

## BUDDHISM

Buddhism is based on the teachings of the Indian, or Nepalese, prince Siddhartha Gautama, who lived from about 563 to 483 B.C. After meditating under a bo tree in Buddh Gaya, he achieved enlightenment and came to be called the Buddha, the enlightened one. In the years following, he preached in India a system of philosophy and ethics that only temporarily took hold in his homeland, but which, in the centuries that followed, found wide currency in other parts of Asia. Today there are about 160 million Buddhists, chiefly in Ceylon, China, Korea, Japan, and Southeast Asia.

The Buddha taught that the way beyond human sorrow and suffering was a middle path between human striving and spiritual contemplation. His ethical system is based on compassion and elimination of self-interest. Buddhist theology accepts the rebirth of persons through the transmigration of souls to different bodies. One object of Buddhist life is to achieve *Nirvana,* a state of blissful detachment from the world through which the cycle of rebirth stops.

Buddhism spread rapidly from India, particularly under the Emperor Asoka, who died in 232 B.C. Early Buddhism was close to Hinduism, but later it developed separately, eventually splitting into a number of branches. The principal branches are: Mahayana Buddhism, found in China, Korea, and Japan, which stresses salvation and contemplation; and Hinayana, as practiced in Southeast Asia, which preserves the monastic tradition of the early believers. The form of Buddhism known as Zen is a Japanese type of Mahayana that stresses introspection, self-examination, and gentleness. The Lamaism of Tibet is a combination of Buddhism and the primitive beliefs of the region.

## TAOISM

The religion known as Taoism is derived from a philosophy that arose in China around the 6th century B.C. Current estimates put the number of Taoists in mainland China and on Taiwan at about 50 million; the estimates are problematic, however, since the Red Chinese have proscribed the religion.

The book of the Taoists is the *Tao-te ching,* attributed to Lao-tze, the legendary Chinese philosopher. However, since Lao-tze probably lived in the 6th century B.C. and the book in its known form is from the 3rd century B.C., it is thought that the *Tao-te ching* is a later clarification of the founder's thought. *Tao* in Chinese means path, and the basis of early Taoism is the allowance of the affairs of men to take the path of nature. For Taoists, the ideal government would be the one that governed least. The religion stressed quietism, contemplation, and the elimination of all striving and strong passions.

Taoism reached its height around the 6th century A.D. Thereafter, it took on many aspects of Confucianism and Buddhism and became concerned with emotional satisfaction, magic, and mystical guarantees of immortality. Among the most powerful of the Taoist gods is the Emperor of the Eastern Mountains. In its latest development, Taoism provided the basis for many secret societies.

## CONFUCIANISM

The religion founded by Confucius, or K'ung Fu-tse, is based on a system of ethical rules for the proper management of human affairs. Estimates of the number of Confucians in mainland China and on Taiwan are as high as 343 million, but these figures, like those for Taoists, are extremely high, since they are based on pre-Communist estimates. In China, before the rise of Communism, all families had at least one religion, and many people espoused elements of all three major Chinese religions—Taoism, Confucianism, and Buddhism. Since the establishment of the Red Chinese government, however, religions have been suppressed and places of worship destroyed.

Confucius lived in the 6th century B.C., probably from 550 to 480. His Analects, together with the later writings of Mencius, the 4th-century Chinese sage, form the basis of Confucianism. Confucius taught that the chief ethic was benevolence, and thus he believed in altruism and cherished filial piety. One of his prime precepts was "treat inferiors with propriety." In later years, the philosophy of Confucius grew into a religion, with a chief god, Shang-Ti, who caused natural calamities when displeased with the rulers, and in which Confucius himself came to be venerated as a deity.

## SHINTO

The origins of this ancient religion are lost in antiquity, since until the 5th century A.D. the Shinto tradition was oral, and no written documents exist. In Japan today, however, a modified form of the religion survives among 53 million believers.

Shinto is a set of rituals and customs involving pilgrimages, festivals, and worship of a great host of gods. It grew through the centuries from a primitive nature worship and was later influenced by Buddhism, which arrived from China and Korea. Participation in Shinto rites is generally thought to bring good fortune, but the religion has no ethical or moral system except an emphasis on ceremonial life and bodily cleanliness.

The deity having the most exalted position is the sun goddess, known as the Ruler of Heaven. From about the 7th century, the emperor of Japan was considered the chief Shinto priest and had the immortal status of a deity. In the late 19th century, a state form of Shinto was organized which was used to glorify the militaristic philosophy of the government. After World War II, this was disbanded and Emperor Hirohito disavowed his divinity.

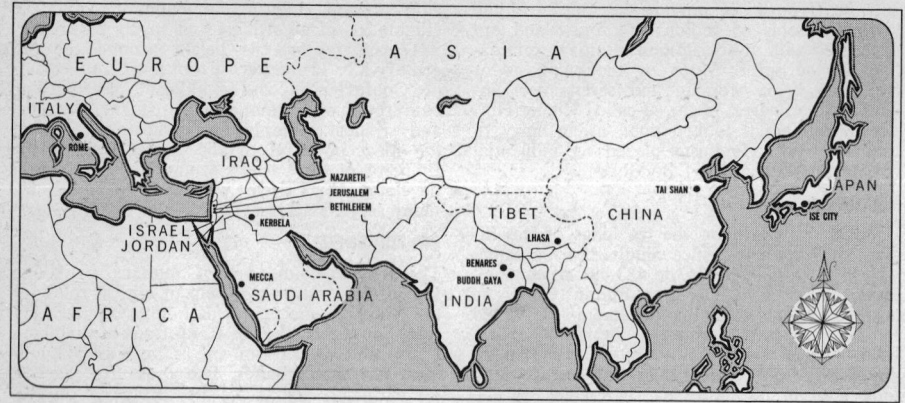

# HOLY PLACES OF THE WORLD

## WESTERN RELIGIONS

■ **BETHLEHEM,** ancient town of Palestine, now under Jordanian rule. As the birthplace of Jesus, it is one of the major shrines of the Christian world. The Church of the Nativity there is shared by monks of the Greek, Latin, and Armenian rites; the grotto beneath the church is said to hold the manger in which Jesus was born. Jews also revere the town as the birthplace of Benjamin, the scene of the Book of Ruth, and the home of David.

■ **NAZARETH,** town of Galilee, now in Israel. As the home of Jesus, it is a great place of Christian pilgrimage.

■ **JERUSALEM,** famous city of Palestine, occupied in 1967 by Israeli forces. Under the name of Zion, it figures prominently in Jewish and Christian literature as the residence of the Messiah. A sacred city for Jews, Christians, and Moslems, it contains numerous shrines, churches, and mosques. The most notable structures are: the Wailing Wall, sacred to Jews as the only remaining wall of the great Temple of Solomon; the Church of the Holy Sepulcher, built on the supposed site of Jesus' tomb; and the Mosque of Omar, or the Dome of the Rock, holy to Moslems as the place where Mohammed began his spiritual journey to heaven.

■ **ROME,** capital of Italy, the spiritual center of Roman Catholicism. Called the Eternal City, it is sacred as the residence of the Pope, as the scene of the early Christian struggle, and as the place of martyrdom of Saints Peter and Paul. Catholics come to Rome in great numbers, visiting its innumerable churches and shrines.

## EASTERN RELIGIONS

■ **MECCA,** city in western Saudi Arabia, near the Red Sea. As the birthplace of Mohammed, the Prophet, it is the most sacred city of Islam. *The Hegira,* or the flight of Mohammed from Mecca to the town of Medina in 622, marks the beginning of the Moslem era; Islamic calendars be-

gin with that year. At the center of Mecca is the Haram, a great mosque, which encloses the Kaaba, the most sacred sanctuary of Islam. Thousands of Moslems from all over the world visit Mecca each year, usually in early April. Unbelievers are banned from the city.

■ **KERBELA,** city in southwestern Iraq, on the edge of the Syrian Desert. It is the place of the martyrdom of Husein, grandson of Mohammed the Prophet, and the greatest goal of pilgrimage for Moslems of the Shia belief. During the fall, thousands of Shiites visit the tomb of Husein.

■ **BENARES,** city in northeast India, also called Varanasi. Situated on the sacred Ganges River, the city is holy chiefly to Hindus. Every year thousands of pilgrims visit the city to bathe in its waters, and thus to cleanse themselves of sin. Benares is especially sacred to Siva, a major Hindu god, and the Golden Temple there is dedicated to the deity. Near Benares is Sarnath, where the Buddha first preached.

■ **BUDDH GAYA,** village in northeast India. The site of the pipal, or bo, tree, under which the Buddha received enlightenment, the village is sacred to Buddhists and is a place of pilgrimage. Buddh Gaya is studded with temple remains.

■ **LHASA,** capital of Tibet, often called the Forbidden City. The center of the Lamaist religion —a type of Buddhism—the city has the magnificent Potala, in which formerly resided the Dalai Lama, spiritual head of the religion. Since the Chinese Communist occupation in 1951, pilgrimages to the city have been disrupted.

■ **MT. TAI** or **TAI SHAN,** mountain in east China, the most sacred place in China. On its peak are numerous Taoist and Buddhist shrines, and for many centuries it was the goal of pilgrimage. After the rise of the Communist regime, pilgrimage to the mountain was proscribed.

■ **ISE CITY,** city in south Honshu, Japan, also called Uji-yamada. One of the most ancient centers of the Shinto religion, it is dedicated to the divine ancestress of the imperial family.

# PROMINENT BIBLICAL PERSONS

## OLD TESTAMENT

**Aaron:** older brother of Moses, he often acted as spokesman for Moses both in Egypt and during the Exodus. Moses annointed him the first head of the Israelite priesthood (*Exodus 29*).

**Abel:** a herdsman and son of Adam and Eve, he was murdered by his brother Cain, after God accepted Abel's offering and rejected Cain's (*Genesis 4:1–8*).

**Abner:** general of Saul's army who championed the cause of Saul's son, Ish-bosheth, as king, after Saul's death. He eventually went over to David's camp, but was murdered by jealous followers of David (*2 Samuel 3:20–39*).

**Abraham:** the first patriarch of the Hebrew people, who, in obedience to God's command, led his family from Mesopotamia to Canaan. God made a covenant or pact with Abraham, that if he obeyed God, he and his descendants would become a great and blessed nation (*Genesis 13; 17*).

**Absalom:** a favorite son of David who led a revolt against his father and was killed in battle. David bitterly mourned his death (*2 Samuel 18*).

**Adam:** the first man, he and his wife Eve were created by God in His own image (*Genesis 1:27–28*). For eating of the tree of knowledge against God's command, he and Eve were expelled from the Garden of Eden (*Genesis 3*).

**Ahab:** king of Israel, who was denounced by the Prophet Elijah because he fostered the worship of pagan gods at the urging of his wife, Queen Jezebel (*I Kings 16:29–22:40*).

**Bathsheba:** the beautiful wife of Uriah, she was the mistress of David, who sent her husband to his death in battle. David later married her. Among their children was Solomon (*2 Samuel 11:1–12:25*).

**Cain:** eldest son of Adam and Eve and a farmer, he became the first murderer in the Bible when he killed his brother Abel (*Genesis 4:1–15*).

**Cyrus the Great:** founder of the Persian Empire, he allowed the exiled Judeans to return to Jerusalem, rebuild the city, and re-establish their country as a province of his empire (*Isaiah 44: 28–45:1–7; Ezra 1:1–4*).

**Daniel:** hero of the Book of Daniel, he is presented as spending most of his life in high positions in the royal court of Babylon. Because he refused to worship pagan gods, he was thrown into a den of lions from which God rescued him (*Daniel 6*).

**David:** king of Israel, who united all Israel and made Jerusalem his capital (*II Samuel 5:6–10*). He was reputed to be a great musician and many of the psalms are attributed to him. As a young man he slew the Philistine giant, Goliath (*I Samuel 17:4–52*).

**Delilah:** Philistine courtesan and mistress of Samson, who discovered the secret of his strength (*Judges 16*).

**Elijah:** the first great prophet of Israel, he denounced the introduction of idol worshiping by King Ahab and his wife Jezebel. He helped to cause their eventual downfall (*I Kings 17–22*).

**Esau:** son of Isaac and Rebecca whom his younger brother Jacob tricked out of his inheritance as the firstborn son (*Genesis 25:19–34; 27*).

**Esther:** a beautiful Jewish maiden, she was chosen to be the wife of King Ahashuerus of Persia. At the risk of her life she interceded with the King, saved the lives of her countrymen, and had her cousin Mordecai made prime minister (*Esther*).

**Eve:** the first woman, she was created from Adam's rib. Tempted by the serpent, she persuaded Adam to disobey God's command and was exiled from the Garden of Eden with him (*Genesis 2:21–3:24*).

**Ezekiel:** major prophet and priest, he preached to the exiles in Babylon and foretold that they would be restored to their land if they remained faithful to God (*Ezekiel*).

**Ezra:** Jewish priest and scribe who, with the permission of Persian King Artaxeres I, led back a group of his countrymen from Babylonian exile, and, with Nehemiah, led a religious reformation (*Ezra, Nehemiah*).

**Hagar:** Egyptian maidservant of Sarah, Abraham's wife, she bore Ishmael, and together with her son was dismissed after the birth of Isaac (*Genesis 16; 21:8–21*).

**Isaac:** son of Abraham, whom God commanded Abraham to sacrifice but sent an angel to stay his hand at the last moment (*Genesis 22*). Isaac became patriarch after Abraham's death and married Rebecca, who bore him Esau and Jacob.

**Isaiah:** great prophet of Judah, he stressed the holiness of God and a consciousness of man's sinfulness. He also foretold the coming of the Messiah king who would save Israel (*Isaiah*).

**Jacob:** son of Isaac, he succeeded him as patriarch. Through deceit he obtained Issac's paternal blessing which was intended for his firstborn son, Esau. The twelve tribes of Israel were named after his sons (*Genesis 27:1–41*).

**Jeremiah:** a major prophet who, during the time of Babylonian invasion, warned the Judeans of their impending defeat and exile which was God's punishment for their corruption (*Jeremiah*).

**Jezebel:** the Phoenician wife of King Ahab of Israel, she tried to introduce the worship of pagan gods into Israel (*I Kings 16 to 22*).

**Job:** a wealthy farmer who, despite the loss of his family and fortune, still trusted in God (*Job*).

**Jonah:** an Israelite prophet who, as the main character of the Book of Jonah, tried to escape God's command to preach to the wicked city of Nineveh, but was thrown into the sea, swallowed by a large fish, and delivered to Nineveh, where he successfully preached and converted the people (*Jonah*).

**Jonathan:** Saul's son and close friend of David, he died with his father in battle (*2 Samuel 4*).

**Joseph:** young son of Jacob, he was sold into slavery in Egypt by his jealous brothers but rose to be vice-regent of the Pharoah. During a famine Joseph arranged for his father and *(continued)*

**PROMINENT BIBLICAL PERSONS** (*continued*)

brothers to come to Egypt and gave them the land of Goshen to live in (*Genesis 30 to 47*).

**Joshua:** a warrior and spy during the Exodus, he was chosen by God to succeed Moses as leader of the Israelites (*Deuteronomy 31:14–16*). He led the conquest of Canaan and apportioned the land among the Israelite tribes (*Joshua 14–19*).

**Lot:** a nephew of Abraham, he accompanied him from Mesopotamia and settled in Sodom. Warned of the impending destruction of Sodom, he escaped, but his wife, contrary to God's command, looked back on the city and was turned into a pillar of salt (*Genesis 14:17–20*).

**Melchizedek:** priest and king of Salem (later called Jerusalem), he conferred God's blessing upon Abraham (*Genesis 14:17–20*).

**Miriam:** she was the sister of Moses and Aaron, and was the first prophetess of the Israelites during the Exodus (*Exodus 15:20–21*). She was stricken with leprosy for joining Aaron in criticizing Moses for his marriage to an Ethiopian woman. Moses asked God to heal her, and He did so (*Numbers 12*).

**Moses:** first lawgiver of the Israelites and first spokesman of God to His people, Moses guided the Israelites to the border of Canaan, the "promised land." On Mt. Sinai, Moses received a set of laws, including the Ten Commandments (*Exodus 20:2–17*).

**Nathan:** a prophet and advisor to King David, he rebuked the King for his affair with Bathsheba and David's arranging for her husband Uriah to be killed in battle (*2 Samuel 12:1–25*). He also helped Solomon to gain the throne (*I Kings 1:8–53*).

**Nebuchadnezzar:** King of Babylonia, he destroyed Jerusalem and plundered the Temple. According to the Book of Daniel he sent three young Judeans—Shadrack, Meshach, and Abednego—into a fiery furnace because they believed in God; when they emerged unscathed the King was convinced of God's power (*Daniel 3*).

**Noah:** a Hebrew patriarch who resisted the evil of his time and was chosen by God to build an ark, on board which he brought his family and a male and female of every living thing and rode out the flood which God sent upon the earth. After the flood Noah and his descendants repopulated the earth (*Genesis 6:5–10*).

**Rachel:** daughter of Laban, who used her to exploit Jacob. Jacob worked seven years for her hand, only to find that he had been tricked into marrying her elder sister Leah. He worked another seven years for Rachel (*Genesis 28:15–30*), who bore him Joseph and Benjamin.

**Rebecca:** wife of Issac and mother of Esau and Jacob, she favored Jacob and suggested the ruse whereby he gained his father's blessing intended for his brother Esau (*Genesis 27:7–13*).

**Ruth:** Naomi, Ruth's mother-in-law, took her home to Bethlehem from Ruth's native country, Moab, where their husbands had died. The destitute women survived on remnants gathered after the reapers. Befriended by Boaz, the land-owner, Ruth later married him. David was numbered among their descendants (*Ruth*).

**Samson:** military chieftain of the Israelites and renowned for his strength, he was lured into a love affair by Delilah, a Philistine, and was tricked into revealing the secret of his strength. He pulled down the pillars of the Temple in which he was held captive, killing himself and his captors (*Judges 13–16*).

**Samuel:** last of the "judges" or military chieftains, Samuel was also a priest and prophet who annointed both Saul and David, Saul's successor, as kings of Israel (*I Samuel 12; 16:3*).

**Sarah:** wife of Abraham who became the mother of Isaac after many years of barrenness, as God had promised (*Genesis 21:1–3*).

**Saul:** the first king of Israel, Saul was a great warrior whose brilliant career was ruined by his brashness, jealousy, and finally, by madness (*I Samuel 1 to 31*).

**Solomon:** son of David and Bathsheba, he succeeded his father as king (*I Kings 3*). Renowned for his wealth and wisdom he built the Temple to God in Jerusalem. After his death the Kingdom of Israel was divided (*Kings 11:40–12:25*).

**Zerubabel:** appointed governor of Jerusalem by King Cyrus of Persia, he returned there and completed the rebuilding of the Temple (*Ezra 1:1; 5:14; Haggai 1:12–2:4*).

## NEW TESTAMENT

**Andrew:** brother of the apostle Peter, he was a disciple of John the Baptist before becoming the first Apostle of Jesus (*John 1:40–42*).

**Anna:** aged prophetess of the tribe of Ahser, she hailed the baby Jesus in the Temple as a sign of the coming deliverance of Jerusalem (*Luke: 2:36–38*).

**Annas:** priest of Jerusalem and father-in-law of the High Priest Caiaphas, he was the first to interrogate Jesus after His arrest (*John 18:12–14*).

**Barabbas:** convicted thief, seditionist, and murderer, he was spared from death when the people called for his release in preference to that of Jesus (*Matthew 27:12–22*).

**Barnabas:** a generous member of the early Jerusalem church, he convinced the Apostles to accept Paul, the former persecutor, as one of their number (*Acts 9:26–28*). He accompanied Paul on his first missionary journey.

**Bartholomew:** he appears only in the New Testament lists of the Apostles (*Mark 3:18; Matthew 10:3; Luke 6:14; Acts 1:13*).

**Caiaphas:** High Priest of Jerusalem and son-in-law of Annas, he plotted the arrest of Jesus, presided over His trial before the Jewish council, condemned and delivered Him to Pontius Pilate for execution (*Matthew 26:57–68; 27:1*).

**Cornelius:** a Roman centurion converted by Peter, his conversion pointed up that the Gentiles had a rightful place in the Church and in the mission of the Apostles (*Acts 10:1–11:18*).

**Elizabeth:** wife of Zacharias and mother of John the Baptist, she was the cousin of Mary, the mother of Jesus (*Luke 1:36*).

**Gamaliel:** Pharisee scholar and teacher, he urged his brethren to tolerate the teachings of the Apostles, in case their claim of being sent by God were true (*Acts 5:33–39*).

**Herod the Great:** King of Judah and founder of the Herodian dynasty, he ordered the slaughter of all the male children in Bethlehem in a vain attempt to do away with the future King of the Jews whose birth had been related to him by the three wise men (*Matthew 22:16–18*).

**James the Greater:** older brother of the Apostle John, James was a fisherman who, with his brother, joined Jesus on the shores of the Sea of Galilee (*Mark 1:16–20*). Christ chose him and Peter and John to be present at important events (*Mark 5:37; 13:3; Matthew 17:1*).

**James the Less:** traditionally identified with James the son of Cleophas (*Mark 16:1; John 19:25*), he played a very important role in the affairs of the early Church at Jerusalem (*Acts 12:17; 15:13–23; 21:18*).

**John:** author of the Gospel which bears his name and younger brother of James the Greater, with whom he shared the zeal and impetuosity that earned them both the name "Boanerges," or Sons of Thunder (*Mark 1:16–20*). John was Jesus' most trusted disciple and was present at the Transfiguration (*Mark 9:2*), the agony in the Garden of Gethsemene (*Mark: 14:33*), and alone among the disciples was present at the Crucifixion (*John 19:26*).

**John the Baptist:** son of Zacharias and Elizabeth, cousin of Jesus, he announced that the Messiah would soon come. He baptized Jesus in the Jordan River (*Mark 9:1–9*). He lived for several years as a hermit in the desert before emerging to preach repentance and to baptize. John was beheaded by Herod because he reproved Herod's marriage to his own sister-in-law as contrary to Jewish law (*Mark 6:14–29*).

**Joseph:** husband of Mary, the mother of Jesus (*Matthew 1:16; Luke 3:23*), he was a carpenter who lived in Nazareth. Mary went with him to Bethlehem to register for the census, and Jesus was born there (*Luke 2:4–6*).

**Joseph of Arimathea:** wealthy and faithful disciple of Jesus, he obtained the permission of Pontius Pilate to bury Jesus (*Mark 15:42–47*).

**Judas Iscariot:** he betrayed Jesus to His enemies among the Jewish leaders. He served as treasurer for the other disciples (*John 12:6*). The New Testament gives two accounts of his death: *Matthew 27:1–3* relates that Judas hung himself after returning the 30 pieces of silver he had received for the betrayal; *Acts 1:18–19* reports his death as occurring after he had bought a field with his ill-gotten gains.

**Jude:** also called Judas, he was possibly the brother of James the Less (*Luke 6:16; Acts 1:13*) and may have written the Epistle of St. Jude.

**Lazarus:** a friend of Jesus and brother of Mary and Martha of Bethany, he died and was restored to life by Jesus (*Mark 15:42–47*).

**Luke:** a learned physician, he traveled with Paul on some of his missionary journeys and was with him during his final captivity in Rome. He is the author of the Gospel bearing his name and the Acts of the Apostles.

**Mark:** cousin of Barnabas, he accompanied Paul and Barnabas on their first missionary journey but deserted them at Perga (*Acts 13:13*). He was again associated with Paul during the latter's final imprisonment in Rome.

**Mary Magdalene:** a woman from the village of Magdala, she was cured by Jesus of an unknown malady (*Luke 8:2*) and in gratitude joined His followers, helping to care for Him and the Apostles. After the Crucifixion she was the first person to visit the tomb of Jesus (*John 20:1–2*). In art and literature, she has been traditionally identified as the repentant prostitute, the sinful woman who washed Jesus' feet (*Luke 7:36–50*).

**Mary, the Virgin:** while Mary was betrothed to Joseph, the Angel of God announced to her that she would become the mother of the Messiah, the Son of God (*Luke 1:26–35; 2:21*).

**Matthew:** also called Levi, he was a tax collector before joining the followers of Jesus (*Matthew 9:9*). Matthew is probably the author of the Gospel bearing his name.

**Matthias:** a follower of Jesus but not one of the original Twelve Apostles, he was chosen by lot to replace Judas Iscariot after Judas' death (*Acts 1:23–26*).

**Nicodemus:** a Pharisee and a prominent Jewish leader, he secretly visited Jesus when He came to Jerusalem and was greatly impressed by Him (*John 3:1–15*). He saw to it that Jesus was properly buried after the Crucifixion (*John 19:39*).

**Paul:** born in Tarsus and educated as a Pharisee, Paul's original name was Saul. While on the way to Damascus to continue his persecution of the Christians, Jesus appeared to him and struck him blind. After three days in Damascus, Ananias, a trusted disciple, came to him, restored his sight, and baptized him (*Acts 9:1–20*). Paul devoted the rest of his life to the preaching of the Gospel to the Gentiles in the Middle East, Asia Minor, and finally in Rome itself, where in 67 or 68 A.D. he was beheaded. He wrote many letters to those churches which he had established during his travels.

**Peter:** brother and fellow-fisherman of the Apostle Andrew, Peter became the leader of the Apostles, often acting as their spokesman in discussions with Jesus. Like Andrew, Peter had been a disciple of John the Baptist. Jesus changed Peter's name from Simon to Peter (rock) (*John 1:35–42*). Despite his three-time denial of Him following His arrest, Jesus appeared to Peter first among the Apostles after His Resurrection (*Luke 24:34*). Like Paul, Peter traveled through many countries, preaching the Gospel.

**Philip:** a fisherman, he was among the first of the Apostles to join Jesus (*John 1:43–44*).

**Pontius Pilate:** Roman governor of Judah, he presided at the trial of Jesus and reluctantly sentenced Him to be crucified when the Jewish mob opposed releasing Him instead of Barabbas (*John 18:28–19:22*).

**Salome:** daughter of Queen Herodias, she danced so pleasingly that King Herod offered to grant her anything she wished. Upon her mother's instructions she requested and got the head of John the Baptist on a silver platter (*Mark 6:27–29*).

**Simeon:** an aged and devout Jew who had been told by God that he would live to see the Messiah. He proclaimed the Baby Jesus to be the Messiah as soon as he saw Him in His mother's arms (*Luke 19:1–10*).

**Simon of Cyrene:** a Greek-speaking Jew, he was forced by the Romans to carry the cross of Jesus when Jesus collapsed beneath its weight on the road to Golgatha (*Luke 23:26*).

**PROMINENT BIBLICAL PERSONS** (*continued*)

**Simon the Zealot:** a little-known Apostle, he had belonged to the fiercely nationalistic Jewish organization called the Zealots, who opposed Roman rule.

**Stephen:** a Greek-speaking Jew and deacon of the church at Jerusalem, he became the first Christian martyr when he was stoned to death by a Jewish mob angered by his recriminations against them (*Acts 6:5–7, 2:1–60*).

**Thomas:** he was slow to believe Jesus' teachings. Even after the Resurrection he doubted that Jesus had appeared again until he had touched Jesus' wounds from the crucifixion (*John 20:19–29*).

**Timothy:** Paul's traveling companion on several of his journeys, he received two letters of instruction from Paul.

**Titus:** a Gentile converted by Paul, he traveled with Paul on several of his journeys. Paul put him in charge of the Church on the island of Crete.

**Zacchaeus:** chief tax collector of Jericho, he met Jesus and promised to give one-half of his wealth to the poor and to restore fourfold any money he had collected dishonestly (*Luke 19:1–10*).

# FAMOUS CHRISTIAN SAINTS

Here follows a partial list of those renowned Christian thinkers, poets, missionaries, and reformers who were influential in the early development, diffusion, and preservation of Western civilization.

**Saint Albert the Great,** 1206(?)–1280, born in Germany. He was known as the "Universal Doctor" for his many treatises on philosophy and science.

**Saint Ambrose of Camaldoli,** 1385–1439, born in Italy. He was a great scholar and theologian.

**Saint Anselm of Canterbury,** 1033(?)–1109, born in Italy. He is called the "father of scholasticism" for his philosophical writings.

**Saint Anthony,** 251(?)–356(?), born in Egypt. He formed the earliest recluse communities and is therefore regarded as the founder of Christian monasticism.

**Saint Augustine,** 354–430, born in North Africa. He was one of the outstanding intellects of Western history, especially famous for his works *Confessions* and the *City of God.*

**Saint Basil the Great,** 330(?)–379, born in Asia Minor. He was a great theologian.

**Saint Bede the Venerable,** 673(?)–735, born in England. One of the most learned men of his day, he is famous for the *Ecclesiastical History of the English Nation.*

**Saint Benedict of Nursia,** 480(?)–547(?), born in Italy. He was the founder of the Benedictine monastic order.

**Saint Bernard of Clairvaux,** 1090(?)–1153, born in France. A theologian and mystic, he helped found the Cistercian monastic order.

**Saint Bonaventure,** 1221–74, born in Italy. He is regarded as one of the greatest theologians and philosophers of the Middle Ages.

**Saint Boniface,** 680(?)–754, born in England. Known as the Apostle of Germany, he established many monasteries in northern Europe.

**Saint Catherine of Siena,** 1347–80, born in Italy. A noted mystic, she was one of the major religious figures of the Middle Ages.

**Saint Columba,** 521(?)–597, born in Ireland. He was famous as a missionary in Britain.

**Saint Cyril of Alexandria,** 376(?)–444, born in Egypt. Known as the "Great Cyril," he was a distinguished theologian.

**Saints Cyril** (d.869) **and Methodius** (d.885), brothers born in Greece. They are often called the Apostles to the Slavs. The Cyrillic alphabet, used in Slavic nations, is ascribed to Saint Cyril.

**Saint Dominic,** 1170(?)–1221, born in Spain. He was the founder of the Dominican order.

**Saint Francis of Assisi,** 1181(?)–1226, born in Italy. One of the greatest of Christian saints, he was the founder of the Franciscan order.

**Saint Francis Xavier,** 1506–52, born in Spain. He was a major missionary in the Far East.

**Saint Ignatius of Loyola,** 1491(?)–1556, born in Spain. A missionary, he founded the Jesuit order.

**Saint Isidore of Seville,** 560(?)–636, born in Spain. He was the most distinguished scholar of his time.

**Saint Jerome,** 340(?)–420(?), born in Dalmatia. He translated the Bible into Latin.

**Saint John Chrysostom,** 347(?)–407, born in Antioch. He was an orator and noted scholar.

**Saint John Damascene,** 676(?)–749, born in Damascus. He was a great poet and theologian.

**Saint John of the Cross,** 1542–91, born in Spain. A Christian mystic, he is regarded as Spain's finest lyric poet.

**Saint Nicholas,** fourth-century bishop of Myra in Lycia, Asia Minor. Regarded as the patron of children, sailors, and captives, he is today popularly known as Santa Claus.

**Saint Paul,** d.67(?), born in Tarsus, Asia Minor. He was the greatest Christian missionary and was famous for his work in Greece and Rome.

**Saint Peter Canisius,** 1521–97, born in Germany. A missionary in central Europe, he was also a literary figure.

**Saint Peter Claver,** 1581–1654, born in Spain. He is called the Apostle of the Negroes for his work among the African slaves of South America.

**Saint Teresa of Avila,** 1515–82, born in Spain. She is one of the most famous Christian mystics.

**Saint Thomas Aquinas,** 1225–74, born in Italy. One of the greatest intellects of Western history, and founder of the official Roman Catholic philosophy, he wrote the *Summa Theologica.*

**Saint Thomas More,** 1478–1535, born in England. He is regarded as the "ideal Christian" and is noted for his philosophic tract, *Utopia.*

**Saint Thomas of Canterbury** (Thomas à Becket), 1118–70, born in England. He was a defender of the Church and a Christian martyr.

**Saint Valentine,** b.270(?). A Roman martyr priest, he is widely known as the patron of lovers. His feast day, February 14, is celebrated as Valentine's Day.

**Saint Vincent Ferrer,** 1350(?)–1419, born in Spain. He was a noted missionary and theologian.

# PHILOSOPHERS, THEOLOGIANS, AND CHURCHMEN

**Thales,** 7th–6th centuries B.C., Greek philosopher

**Zoroaster,** 628–551 B.C., Persian prophet

**Parmenides,** 6th century B.C., Greek philosopher

**Anaximander,** 6th century B.C., Greek philosopher

**Anaxagoras,** 5th century B.C., Greek philosopher

**Protagoras,** 5th century B.C., Greek philosopher

**Zeno of Elea,** 5th century B.C., Greek philosopher

**Socrates,** 469–399 B.C., Greek philosopher

**Diogenes,** 412?–323 B.C., Greek philosopher

**Democritus,** 5th–4th centuries B.C., Greek philosopher

**Plato,** 5th–4th centuries B.C., Greek philosopher

**Heraclitus,** 5th–4th centuries B.C., Greek philosopher

**Aristotle,** 384–322 B.C., Greek philosopher

**Epicurus,** 341–270 B.C., Greek philosopher

**Zeno of Citrium,** 4th–3rd centuries B.C., Greek philosopher

**Seneca,** 3 B.C.?–A.D. 65, Roman philosopher

**Philo Judaeus,** 1st century, Jewish philosopher

**Epictetus,** 1st–2nd centuries, Greek philosopher

**Clement of Alexandria,** 3rd century, Greek theologian

**Origen,** 3rd century, Egyptian philosopher

**Plotinus,** 205?–270, Egyptian-Roman philosopher

**Arius,** 256?–336, Lybian theologian

**Nestorius,** 5th century, Middle Eastern theologian and heretic

**Boethius,** 455?–525, Roman philosopher

**Avicenna,** 980–1037, Moorish philosopher and physician

**Berengard of Tours,** 1000–88(?), French theologian

**Peter the Hermit,** 1050?–1115, French monk, preacher, and Crusader

**Peter Abelard,** 1079–1142, French philosopher

**William of Champeaux,** d. 1121, French scholastic philosopher

**Bernard of Cluny,** 12th century, Anglo-French monk

**Peter Lombard,** 12th century, Italian theologian

**John of Salisbury,** 1110?–1180, English scholastic philosopher

**Averroës,** 1126–98, Moorish philosopher

**William of Occam,** 14th century, English scholastic philosopher

**John Wyclif,** 1328?–84, English ecclesiastical reformer

**Gerard Groote,** 1340–84, Dutch ecclesiastical reformer

**John Huss,** 1369?–1415, Czechoslovakian religious reformer

**Thomas à Kempis,** 1380?–1471, German devotional writer

**Girolamo Savonarola,** 1452–98, Italian Catholic reformer

**Miles Coverdale,** 1458–1569, English translator of the Bible into English

**Thomas Wolsey,** 1473?–1530, English statesman and prelate

**Martin Luther,** 1483–1546, German Protestant reformer, founder of Lutheranism

**Huldreich Zwingli,** 1484–1531, Swiss Protestant reformer

**Hugh Latimer,** 1485?–1555, English bishop and martyr

**Thomas Cranmer,** 1489–1556, English churchman

**William Tyndale,** 1494?–1536, English Biblical translator and martyr

**Philip Melanchthon,** 1497–1560, German theologian

**Nicholas Ridley,** 1500?–55, English ecclesiastical reformer

**Matthew Parker,** 1504–75, English prelate

**John Calvin,** 1509–64, French theologian, founder of Calvinism

**Luis Molina,** 1535–1600, Spanish theologian

**Giordano Bruno,** 1548–1600, Italian philosopher

**Richard Hooker,** 1554?–1600, English theologian

**Jacobus Arminius,** 1560–1609, Dutch theologian

**Francis Bacon,** 1561–1626, English philosopher

**William Laud,** 1573–1645, English churchman

**James Ussher,** 1581?–1656, Irish prelate

**Cornelis Jansen,** 1585–1638, Dutch theologian

**Thomas Hobbes,** 1588–1679, English philosopher

**René Descartes,** 1596–1650, French philosopher

**Jeremy Taylor,** 1613–67, English churchman and theologian

**John Biddle,** 1615–62, founder of English Unitarianism

**Blaise Pascal,** 1623–62, French philosopher and mathematician

**Baruch Spinoza,** 1632–77, Dutch-Jewish philosopher

**John Locke,** 1632–1704, English philosopher

**Increase Mather,** 1639–1723, American Puritan clergyman

**Pierre Bayle,** 1647–1706, French philosopher

**Gottfried Wilhelm von Leibniz,** 1646–1716, German philosopher and mathematician

**Cotton Mather,** 1663–1728, American clergyman

**Isaac Watts,** 1674–1748, English theologian and hymnologist

**George Berkeley,** 1685–1753, Anglo-Irish philosopher and clergyman

**Emanuel Swedenborg,** 1688–1772, Swedish theologian

**Jonathan Edwards,** 1703–58, American theologian and preacher

**John Wesley,** 1703–91, founder of Methodism

**David Hume,** 1711–76, Scottish philosopher and historian

**Jean Jacques Rousseau,** 1712–78, French philosopher

**Jean le Rond d'Alembert,** 1717–83, French mathematician and philosopher

**Immanuel Kant,** 1724–1804, German philosopher

**Jeremy Bentham,** 1748–1832, English philosopher

**Johann Gottlieb Fichte,** 1762–1814, German philosopher

**Thomas Robert Malthus,** 1766–1834, English economist

**Friedrich Daniel Ernst Schleiermacher,** 1768–1834, German theologian

**Georg Wilhelm Friedrich Hegel,** 1770–1831, German philosopher

**David Ricardo,** 1772–1823, English political economist

**Friedrich Wilhelm Joseph von Schelling,** 1775–1854, German philosopher

**Johann Friedrich Herbart,** 1776–1841, German philosopher and educator (*continued*)

**PHILOSOPHERS AND CHURCHMEN** (*continued*)

**Arthur Schopenhauer,** 1788–1860, German philosopher

**Auguste Comte,** 1798–1857, French philosopher

**Brigham Young,** 1801–77, American Mormon leader

**John Henry Newman,** 1801–90, English cardinal and philosopher

**Ralph Waldo Emerson,** 1803–82, American writer and theologian

**Joseph Smith,** 1805–44, American founder of Mormonism

**John Stuart Mill,** 1806–73, English philosopher and economist

**Sören Kierkegaard,** 1813–55, Danish philosopher

**Rudolph Hermann Lotze,** 1817–81, German philosopher and psychologist

**Karl Marx,** 1818–83, German social and economic philosopher

**Herbert Spencer,** 1820–1903, English philosopher

**Charles Sanders Peirce,** 1839–1914, American philosopher

**Eduard von Hartmann,** 1842–1906, German philosopher

**William James,** 1842–1910, American philosopher

**Friedrich Wilhelm Nietzsche,** 1844–1900, German philosopher

**Josiah Royce,** 1855–1916, American philosopher

**Thorstein Veblen,** 1857–1929, American economic and social philosopher

**Edmund Husserl,** 1859–1938, German philosopher

**Henri Bergson,** 1859–1941, French philosopher

**John Dewey,** 1859–1952, American philosopher and educator

**William Ralph Inge,** 1860–1954, English theologian

**Alfred North Whitehead,** 1861–1947, English philosopher and mathematician

**George Santayana,** 1863–1952, American philosopher

**Bertrand A. W. Russell, Earl Russell,** 1872–, English philosopher and mathematician

**George Edward Moore,** 1873–1958, English philosopher

**Ernst Cassirer,** 1874–1945, German philosopher

**Stephen Samuel Wise,** 1874–1949, American Jewish reformer and Zionist leader

**Albert Schweitzer,** 1875–1965, French theologian and philosopher

**Martin Buber,** 1878–1965, Jewish philosopher

**Nicolai Hartmann,** 1882–1950, German philosopher

**Jacques Maritain,** 1882–, French philosopher

**Karl Jaspers,** 1883–, German philosopher

**Étienne Gilson,** 1884–, French philosopher

**Karl Barth,** 1886–, Swiss theologian

**Paul Johannes Tillich,** 1886–1965, German-American theologian

**Ludwig Joseph Johann Wittgenstein,** 1889–1951, Austrian philosopher

**Martin Heidegger,** 1889–, German philosopher

**Reinhold Niebuhr,** 1892–, American theologian

**Helmut Richard Niebuhr,** 1894–1962, American theologian

**Willem Adolph Visser't Hooft,** 1900–, Dutch church leader

Jews observe Rosh ha-Shanah at Jerusalem's Wailing Wall, after Israel seized Old City in June 1967.

Wide World

# POPES, THE PAPACY, AND VATICAN CITY

As head of the Roman Catholic Church, the Pope is the Bishop of Rome and therefore, according to Roman Catholic belief, successor to Saint Peter, its first bishop, and to the sacred seat of government, the Holy See. Thus, the Pope claims to be the supreme shepherd of all Christians and the representative (vicar or vicegerent) of Christ. The Roman Catholic Church further holds the doctrine of papal infallibility; that is, God will not permit the Pope to make an error in a solemn official declaration concerning a matter of faith or morals.

The Pope is elected to the papacy, the office of the Pope, by the college of cardinals meeting in high and secret conclave 15 to 18 days after the death of the pontiff. The Pope resides in Rome, of which a small portion, Vatican City, has been since 1929 politically independent and under his rule.

In the list of popes that follows, the date of election, not consecration, is given. The dates for the 1st and 2nd centuries are approximations. Antipopes, uncanonical and illegitimate claimants to the papacy, are indicated in italics.

## THE POPES

### ■ 1ST CENTURY

Saint Peter ............d.67
Saint Linus ...........67–76
Saint Cletus or
   Anacletus .........76–88
Saint Clement I .......88–97

### ■ 2ND CENTURY

Saint Evaristus ......97–105
Saint Alexander I ....105–115
Saint Sixtus I ........115–125
Saint Telesphorus ...125–136
Saint Hyginus ......136–140
Saint Pius I ........140–155
Saint Anicetus ......155–166
Saint Soter .........166–175
Saint Eleutherius ....175–189
Saint Victor I ......189–199

### ■ 3RD CENTURY

Saint Zephyrinus ..199(?)–217
Saint Callistus I ......217–22
*Saint Hippolytus .....217–35*
Saint Urban I .......222–30
Saint Pontian ......230–35
Saint Anterus ......235–36
Saint Fabian ........236–50
Saint Cornelius ....251–53
*Novatian* ...............*251*
Saint Lucius I ......253–54
Saint Stephen I ......254–57
Saint Sixtus II ......257–58
Saint Dionysius ......259–68
Saint Felix I ........269–74
Saint Eutychian ......275–83
Saint Caius .........283–96

### ■ 4TH CENTURY

Saint Marcellinus ....296–304
Saint Marcellus I ....308–09
Saint Eusebius .... 309 or 310
Saint Miltiades or
   Melchiades ........311–14
Saint Sylvester I ......314–35
Saint Marcus .........336
Saint Julius I ......337–52
Liberius ............352–66
*Felix II* ..............*355–65*

Saint Damasus I .....366–84
*Ursinus* .............*366–67*
Saint Siricius .......384–99

### ■ 5TH CENTURY

Saint Anastasius I ....399–401
Saint Innocent I .....401–17
Saint Zosimus ......417–18
Saint Boniface I ......418–22
*Eulalius* ..............*418–19*
Saint Celestine I ......422–32
Saint Sixtus III ......432–40
Saint Leo I ..........440–61
Saint Hilarius .......461–68
Saint Simplicius .....468–83
Saint Felix III (II) * ..483–92
Saint Gelasius I ......492–96
Anastasius II .......496–98

### ■ 6TH CENTURY

Saint Symmachus ....498–514
*Lawrence* ........*498, 501–05*
Saint Hormisdas ......514–23
Saint John I ........523–26
Saint Felix IV (III) ...526–30
Boniface II ..........530–32
*Dioscurus* ...............*530*
John II .............535–35
Saint Agapetus I ......535–36
Saint Silverius ......536–37
Vigilius ..........537(?)–555
Pelagius I ..........556–61
John III ............561–74
Benedict I .........575–79
Pelagius II ........579–90
Saint Gregory I .....590–604

### ■ 7TH CENTURY

Sabinianus .........604–06
Boniface III ...........607
Saint Boniface IV ....608–15
Saint Deusdedit or
   Adeodatus I ......615–18
Boniface V .........619–25
Honorius I .........625–38
Severinus ............640
John IV .............640–42
Theodore I .........642–49
Saint Martin I ......649–55
Saint Eugene I .......654–57

Saint Vitalian ........657–72
Adeodatus II ......672–76
Donus ............676–78
Saint Agatho .......678–81
Saint Leo II ........682–83
Saint Benedict II ....684–85
John V .............685–86
Conon .............686–87
*Theodore* .............*687*
*Paschal* ..............*687*
Saint Sergius I ....687–701

### ■ 8TH CENTURY

John VI ...........701–05
John VII ..........705–07
Sisinnius ............708
Constantine .......708–15
Saint Gregory II .....715–31
Saint Gregory III ...731–41
Saint Zacharias ......741–52
Stephen II .........752
  (never consecrated)
Stephen II (III) .....752–57
Saint Paul I .......757–67
*Constantine* ..........*767–69*
*Philip* .................*768*
Stephen III (IV) ...768–72
Adrian I ...........772–95

### ■ 9TH CENTURY

Saint Leo III .......795–816
Stephen IV (V) .....816–17
Saint Paschal I ......817–24
Eugene II .........824–27
Valentine ............827
Gregory IV ........827–44
*John* ................*844*
Sergius II .........844–47
Saint Leo IV ......847–55
Benedict III .......855–58
*Anastasius* ............*855*
Saint Nicholas I ....858–67
Adrian II .........867–72
John VIII .........872–82
Marinus I .........882–84
Saint Adrian III ....884–85
Stephen V (VI) ....885–91
Formosus ........891–96
Boniface VI ..........896
             (continued)

* The presence of antipopes on the papal list often changes the numbering of popes; thus, Saint Felix III, 483–92, is actually Saint Felix II, as shown in parentheses, because Felix II, 355–65, was an antipope.

**THE POPES** (*continued*)

| | |
|---|---|
| Stephen VI (VII) | 896–97 |
| Romanus | 897 |
| Theodore II | 897 |
| John IX | 898–900 |

■ **10TH CENTURY**

| | |
|---|---|
| Benedict IV | 900–03 |
| Leo V | 903 |
| *Christopher* | *903–04* |
| Sergius III | 904–11 |
| Anastasius III | 911–13 |
| Lando | 913–14 |
| John X | 914–28 |
| Leo VI | 928 |
| Stephen VII (VIII) | 928–31 |
| John XI | 931–35 |
| Leo VII | 936–39 |
| Stephen VIII (IX) | 939–42 |
| Marinus II | 942–46 |
| Agapetus II | 946–55 |
| John XII* | 955–64 |
| Leo VIII* | 963–65 |
| Benedict V* | 964–66 |
| John XIII | 965–72 |
| Benedict VI | 973–74 |
| *Boniface VII* | *974, 984–85* |
| Benedict VII | 974–83 |
| John XIV | 983–84 |
| John XV | 985–96 |
| Gregory V | 996–99 |
| *John XVI* | *987–98* |

■ **11TH CENTURY**

| | |
|---|---|
| Sylvester II | 999–1003 |
| John XVII | 1003 |
| John XVIII | 1004–09 |
| Sergius IV | 1009–12 |
| Benedict VIII | 1012–24 |
| *Gregory* | *1012* |
| John XIX | 1024–32 |
| Benedict IX† | 1032–44, 1045, 1047–48 |
| Sylvester III† | 1045 |
| Gregory VI† | 1045–46 |
| Clement II† | 1046–47 |
| Damasus II | 1048 |
| Saint Leo IX | 1049–54 |
| Victor II | 1055–57 |
| Stephen IX (X) | 1057–58 |
| *Benedict X* | *1058–59* |
| Nicholas II | 1059–61 |
| Alexander II | 1061–73 |
| *Honorius II* | *1061–72* |
| Saint Gregory VII | 1073–85 |
| *Clement III* | *1080–1100* |
| Victor III | 1086–87 |
| Urban II | 1088–99 |

■ **12TH CENTURY**

| | |
|---|---|
| Paschal II | 1099–1118 |
| *Theodoric* | *1100* |
| *Albert* | *1102* |
| *Sylvester IV* | *1105–11* |
| Gelasius II | 1118–19 |
| *Gregory VIII* | *1118–21* |

| | |
|---|---|
| Callistus II | 1119–24 |
| Honorius II | 1124–30 |
| *Celestine II* | *1124* |
| Innocent II | 1130–43 |
| *Anacletus II* | *1130–38* |
| Victor IV | 1138 |
| Celestine II | 1143–44 |
| Lucius II | 1144–45 |
| Eugene III | 1145–53 |
| Anastasius IV | 1153–54 |
| Adrian IV | 1154–59 |
| Alexander III | 1159–81 |
| *Victor IV* | *1159–64* |
| *Paschal III* | *1164–68* |
| *Callistus III* | *1168–78* |
| *Innocent III* | *1179–80* |
| Lucius III | 1181–85 |
| Urban III | 1185–87 |
| Gregory VIII | 1187 |
| Clement III | 1187–91 |
| Celestine III | 1191–98 |

■ **13TH CENTURY**

| | |
|---|---|
| Innocent III | 1198–1216 |
| Honorius III | 1216–27 |
| Gregory IX | 1227–41 |
| Celestine IV | 1241 |
| Innocent IV | 1243–54 |
| Alexander IV | 1254–61 |
| Urban IV | 1261–64 |
| Clement IV | 1265–68 |
| Gregory X | 1271–76 |
| Innocent V | 1276 |
| Adrian V | 1276 |
| John XXI | 1276–77 |
| Nicholas III | 1277–80 |
| Martin IV | 1281–85 |
| Honorius IV | 1285–87 |
| Nicholas IV | 1288–92 |
| Saint Celestine V | 1294 |
| Boniface VIII | 1294–1303 |

■ **14TH CENTURY**

| | |
|---|---|
| Benedict XI | 1303–04 |
| Clement V | 1305–14 |
| John XXII | 1316–34 |
| *Nicholas V* | *1328–30* |
| Benedict XII | 1334–42 |
| Clement VI | 1342–52 |
| Innocent VI | 1352–62 |
| Urban V | 1362–70 |
| Gregory XI | 1370–78 |
| Urban VI | 1378–89 |
| *Clement VII* | *1378–94* |
| Boniface IX | 1389–1404 |

■ **15TH CENTURY**

| | |
|---|---|
| *Benedict XIII* | *1394–1423* |
| Innocent VII | 1404–06 |
| Gregory XII | 1406–15 |
| *Alexander V* | *1409–10* |
| *John XXIII* | *1410–15* |
| Martin V | 1417–31 |
| *Clement VIII* | *1423–29* |
| Benedict XIV | 1425–30 |
| Eugene IV | 1431–47 |

| | |
|---|---|
| *Felix V* | *1439–49* |
| Nicholas V | 1447–55 |
| Callistus III | 1455–58 |
| Pius II | 1458–64 |
| Paul II | 1464–71 |
| Sixtus IV | 1471–84 |
| Innocent VIII | 1484–92 |
| Alexander VI | 1492–1503 |

■ **16TH CENTURY**

| | |
|---|---|
| Pius III | 1503 |
| Julius II | 1503–13 |
| Leo X | 1513–21 |
| Adrian VI | 1522–23 |
| Clement VII | 1523–34 |
| Paul III | 1534–49 |
| Julius III | 1550–55 |
| Marcellus II | 1555 |
| Paul IV | 1555–59 |
| Pius IV | 1559–65 |
| Saint Pius V | 1566–72 |
| Gregory XIII | 1572–85 |
| Sixtus V | 1585–90 |
| Urban VII | 1590 |
| Gregory XIV | 1590–91 |
| Innocent IX | 1591 |
| Clement VIII | 1592–1605 |

■ **17TH CENTURY**

| | |
|---|---|
| Leo XI | 1605 |
| Paul V | 1605–21 |
| Gregory XV | 1621–23 |
| Urban VIII | 1623–44 |
| Innocent X | 1644–55 |
| Alexander VII | 1655–67 |
| Clement IX | 1667–69 |
| Clement X | 1670–76 |
| Innocent XI | 1676–89 |
| Alexander VIII | 1689–91 |
| Innocent XII | 1691–1700 |

■ **18TH CENTURY**

| | |
|---|---|
| Clement XI | 1700–21 |
| Innocent XIII | 1721–24 |
| Benedict XIII | 1724–30 |
| Clement XII | 1730–40 |
| Benedict XIV | 1740–58 |
| Clement XIII | 1758–69 |
| Clement XIV | 1769–74 |
| Pius VI | 1775–99 |

■ **19TH CENTURY**

| | |
|---|---|
| Pius VII | 1800–23 |
| Leo XII | 1823–29 |
| Pius VIII | 1829–30 |
| Gregory XVI | 1831–46 |
| Pius IX | 1846–78 |
| Leo XIII | 1878–1903 |

■ **20TH CENTURY**

| | |
|---|---|
| Saint Pius X | 1903–14 |
| Benedict XV | 1914–22 |
| Pius XI | 1922–39 |
| Pius XII | 1939–58 |
| John XXIII | 1958–63 |
| Paul VI | 1963– |

* John XII was deposed in 963 by a Church council. If this deposition was invalid, Leo was an antipope. If the deposition was valid, however, Leo was the legitimate pope and Benedict an antipope.   † Benedict IX was deposed on three different occasions (in 1044, 1046, and in 1048). If the depositions were illegitimate, Sylvester III, Gregory VI, and Clement II were antipopes.

## NATIONAL COUNCIL OF CHURCHES

The National Council of the Churches of Christ in the United States of America, a federation of 34 Protestant and Eastern Orthodox denominations, was founded in 1950. Its purpose is to advance programs and policies of common concern to the constituent denominations, which embrace a total of somewhat more than 40 million members, and to increase cooperation among denominations through its own institutions and through local and state councils of churches. The NCC, as it is called, is the principal instrument of the ecumenical movement in the United States, a movement that seeks to unite Protestant and Eastern Orthodox churches and ultimately all Christians.

The council is the successor to the Federal Council of Churches, which was founded in 1908. Its membership includes most of the major Protestant and Eastern Orthodox denominations; the notable exceptions are the Southern Baptist Convention, the Lutheran Church-Missouri Synod, and all of the Pentecostal and theologically fundamentalist churches.

The council has four major divisions: the Division of Christian Life and Mission, which is concerned with domestic churches; the Division of Christian Education, which publishes Sunday School material for all Protestant churches and conducts other programs; the Division of Overseas Ministries, which coordinates missionary work and maintains missionaries of its own; and the Division of Christian Unity, which seeks to forward the ecumenical movement.

The council has no juridical authority over the member denominations, nor can it speak for them either singly or as a whole. Its persuasive powers as an overall Protestant spokesman, however, have been considerable, particularly in the fields of social action and influencing legislation.

A number of local churches, particularly in the South, have withdrawn—or have threatened to withdraw—from their member denominations because they disagree with the social and theological stands of the council. Much of the controversy is centered on the council's Commission on Religion and Race, an agency formed in 1963 to bring the churches into more active participation in the civil rights movement in America.

The headquarters of the NCC are at 475 Riverside Drive, New York 27, New York. It also maintains a Washington, D.C., office. The general secretary—the chief administrative officer—is the Rev. Dr. R. H. Edwin Espy. The president is Bishop Reuben H. Mueller of the Evangelical United Brethren Church.

All of the members of the National Council in the United States are members of the World Council of Churches.

## WORLD COUNCIL OF CHURCHES

The World Council of Churches, an ecumenical agency for 223 Protestant and Eastern Orthodox churches in most of the nations of the world, was founded in Amsterdam, the Netherlands, in 1948. It is an outgrowth of various movements seeking to establish common theological and ecclesiastical ground for church unity. The Council's ultimate goal is to establish complete unity among the world's Christians.

Most of the World Council's activities are on the level of theology and communication. It has done much to bring Christian churches together for discussion, and from its conferences have come notable advances in the ecumenical movement. Perhaps most significant was the beginning in 1965 of conversations between the World Council and the Roman Catholic Church, which is not a member of the group. These conversations led in 1966 to the coordination of relief activities for the victims of famine in India and Africa. Similar action has also taken place in Vietnam. The council also conducts some missionary and publication programs.

All of the members of the National Council of Churches in the United States are members of the World Council.

The offices of the agency are at 150 Route de Ferney, Geneva, Switzerland. The General Secretary is the Rev. Dr. Eugene Carson Blake, who was elected in 1966. The American office is at 475 Riverside Drive, New York, New York 10027. There is a six-member presidency elected at each general assembly; the next will be held in 1968.

## RISING CHURCH MEMBERSHIP

Church membership in the United States has risen from an estimated 16 per cent of the population in 1850 to 64.3 per cent in 1965. The numbers of persons listed as members of all faiths has risen from 54,576,346 in 1926 to 124,682,422 in 1965.

The table below summarizes church membership in the United States between 1850 and 1965. The figures represent the percentages of the estimated American population listed on the membership rolls of organized religious bodies in a given year, as compiled for the 1967 *Yearbook of American Churches*.

Prior to the 1926 Census of Religious Bodies, however, methods of reporting church membership varied. Some organizations carried on membership rolls only the names of heads of families; wives and children were not listed. Other religious bodies carried the names of all baptized persons, children as well as adults. Therefore, figures given for the years 1850–1920 have been compiled on a basis different from those given for the years 1930–65.

**Church Membership As Percentage of Population**

| YEAR | PER CENT | YEAR | PER CENT |
|------|----------|------|----------|
| 1850 | 16 | 1920 | 43 |
| 1860 | 23 | 1930 | 47 |
| 1870 | 18 | 1940 | 49 |
| 1880 | 20 | 1950 | 57 |
| 1890 | 22 | 1955 | 61 |
| 1900 | 36 | 1960 | 63.6 |
| 1910 | 43 | 1965 | 64.3 |

**RELIGIOUS GROUPS IN THE UNITED STATES**
Source: Yearbook of American Churches, 1967

| RELIGIOUS GROUP | CHURCHES | MEMBERS | CLERGY |
|---|---|---|---|
| Buddhists........................................................ | 93 | 92,000 | 130 |
| Old Catholic, Polish National Catholic, and Armenian Churches......... | 321 | 483,901 | 335 |
| Eastern Churches............................................... | 1,529 | 3,172,163 | 1,948 |
| Jewish Congregations (includes Orthodox, Conservative, and Reform)... | 4,079 | 5,600,000 | 5,190 |
| Roman Catholics................................................ | 23,668 | 46,246,175 | 59,491 |
| Protestants...................................................... | 296,406 | 69,088,183 | 335,461 |
| Totals.......................................................... | 326,096 | 124,682,422 | 402,555 |

# RELIGIOUS BODIES IN THE UNITED STATES

Membership: 85,000 or more
Source: Yearbook of American Churches, 1967

**African Methodist Episcopal Church:** Began in 1787 in Philadelphia when persons in St. George Methodist Episcopal Church withdrew as a protest against color segregation. Churches: 5,878; Membership: 1,166,301; President of Bishops' Council: Bishop Carey A. Gibbs, Allen University, Columbia, South Carolina.

**African Methodist Episcopal Zion Church:** An independent body, having withdrawn from the John Street Methodist Church of New York City in 1796. Churches: 5,289; Membership: 789,000; Secretary, Board of Bishops: Felix S. Anderson, 741 South 44 St., Louisville, Ky.

**American Baptist Association:** A fellowship of regular and independent missionary Baptist churches distributed throughout the United States, with its greatest strength in the South. Formed in 1905. Churches: 3,227; Membership: 726,112; Headquarters: 214 East Broad Street, Texarkana, Arkansas-Texas.

**American Baptist Convention:** Formerly known as the Northern Baptist Convention; changed its name to American Baptist Convention in 1950. First organized in 1907. Churches: 6,164; Membership: 1,557,633; National Offices: Valley Forge, Pennsylvania.

**The American Carpatho-Russian Orthodox Greek Catholic Church:** A self-governing diocese in communion with the Ecumenical Patriarchate of Constantinople (Istanbul). The late Patriarch Benjamin I canonized the Diocese in 1938 in the name of the Orthodox Church of Christ. Churches: 69; Membership: 104,000; Headquarters: Johnstown, Pennsylvania.

**The American Lutheran Church:** Organized in 1960, the American Lutheran Church, combines the following four bodies: American Lutheran Church (ALC), The Evangelical Lutheran Church (ELC), United Evangelical Lutheran Church (UELC), and The Lutheran Free Church (LFC). The union brought together, for the first time this century, major Lutheran church bodies of different national heritage—German (ALC), Norwegian (ELC), Danish (UELC). Churches: 4,909; Membership: 2,569,150; Headquarters: 422 South 5th Street, Minneapolis, Minnesota.

**Armenian Church, Diocese of America, Diocese of California:** American branch of the Ancient Church of Armenia, established in 1889. The organization is under the jurisdiction of the Holy See of Etchmiadzin, Armenia, U.S.S.R. Churches: 43; Membership: 132,000; Primate: Bishop Torkom Manoogian, 630 Second Avenue, New York, New York.

**Assemblies of God:** A Pentecostal, evangelical, missionary denomination that grew out of the spiritual revivals of the early 1900s. Composed of self-governing churches located in every U.S. state and in 75 countries of the world. Founding meeting held in 1914. Churches: 8,506; Membership: 576,058; Headquarters: 1445 Boonville Avenue, Springfield, Missouri.

**Baptist General Conference:** This body was formerly known as the Swedish General Conference of America; it has operated as a general conference since 1879. Churches: 650; Membership: 95,000; Headquarters: 5750 North Ashland Avenue, Chicago, Illinois.

**Buddhist Churches of America:** Organized in 1914 as the Buddhist Mission of North America, this body was incorporated in 1942 under the present name and represents the Jodo Shinshu Sect of Buddhism in this country. It believes in salvation by faith in the Wisdom and Compassion of Amida Buddha. Churches: 82; Membership: 100,000; Headquarters: 1710 Octavia Street, San Francisco, California.

**Christian Churches (Disciples of Christ), International Convention:** In the revival period of the early 19th century, a movement under Thomas Campbell and his son, Alexander, resulted in the establishment of a fellowship called "Christians" or "Disciples." The plea of this movement is for the reunion of the church on the basis of a return to New Testament faith and order. It is congregational in government. Churches: 8,066; Membership: 1,894,927; Headquarters: 221 Ohmer Avenue, P.O. Box 19136, Indianapolis, Indiana.

**Christian Methodist Episcopal Church:** In 1870, the General Conference of the M.E. Church, South, approved the request of its Negro membership for the formation of a separate ecclesiastical body, the Colored Methodist Episcopal Church. In 1954, the name was changed to the Christian Methodist Episcopal Church, which became the official name in 1956. Churches: 2,523; Membership: 444,493; Secretary: Reverend A. R. Davis, 6432 South Green Street, Apartment 1, Chicago, Illinois.

**Christian Reformed Church:** Founded by a group of Dutch Calvinists who dissented from the Reformed Church in America in 1857. Their doctrines are the Heidelberg Catechism, the Canons of Dort, and the Belgic Confession. Churches: 629; Membership: 275,530; Stated Clerk: Dr. R. J. Danhof, 2850 Kalamazoo Avenue, S.E., Grand Rapids, Michigan.

**Church of Christ, Scientist:** A religion founded by Mary Baker Eddy in 1879 to reinstate the healing power of original Christianity. As defined by Mrs. Eddy, her religion is the scientific system of divine healing. The denomination is represented by The Mother Church, The First Church of Christ, Scientist, in Boston, Massachusetts, and its more than 3,200 branches throughout the world. Publishes numerous periodicals but is most famous for *The Christian Science Monitor*. *Note:* The membership of the Church of Christ, Scientist, is not given. There is a prohibition in this church's manual forbidding the numbering of people and the reporting of such statistics for publication. Headquarters: 107 Falmouth Street, Boston, Massachusetts.

**Church of God (Anderson, Indiana):** One of the largest of the groups that have taken the name Church of God. Originated about 1880 and emphasizes Christian unity. Churches: 2,287; Membership: 143,231; Executive Secretary: Charles V. Weber, Box 2420, Anderson, Indiana.

**Church of God (Cleveland, Tennessee):** One of the large groups that use the name Church of God. Originally organized in 1886 in Monroe County, Tennessee, under the name Christian Union, it was reorganized in 1902 as the Holiness Church and in 1907 under the name Church of God. Its doctrine is fundamental and pentecostal; its government is central. Churches: 3,575; Membership: 205,465; Headquarters: 922–1080 Montgomery Avenue, Cleveland, Tennessee.

**The Church of God in Christ:** Organized in Arkansas in 1895 by C. P. Jones and C. H. Mason, who believed there was no salvation without holiness, it was incorporated in 1897. Churches: 4,500; Membership: 425,500; Headquarters: 958 Mason Street, Memphis, Tennessee.

**Church of Jesus Christ of Latter-Day Saints (Mormons):** Organized in 1830, at Fayette, New York, by Joseph Smith. Members consider the Bible, the Book of Mormon, Doctrine and Covenants, and the Pearl of Great Price to be the Word of God. Their belief is summed up in 13 Articles of Faith written by Joseph Smith. Membership is worldwide. Churches: 6,075; Membership: 2,480,899; Headquarters: 47 East Souh Temple Street, Salt Lake City, Utah.

**Church of the Brethren:** German pietists, under the leadership of Peter Becker, entered the American colonies in 1719 and settled in Germantown, Pennsylvania. They believe in the New Testament and hold to the principles of reconciliation, non-violence, the simple life, servanthood, and the expression of religion through the good life. Churches: 1,056; Membership: 191,402; Headquarters: Church of the Brethren General Offices, Elgin, Illinois.

**Church of the Nazarene:** Organized in Texas in 1908. In general accord with the early doctrines of Methodism, it emphasizes entire sanctification as a second definite work of grace. Churches: 4,926; Membership: 363,585; Headquarters: 6401 The Paseo, Kansas City, Missouri.

**Churches of Christ:** This body is made up of a large group of churches reported with Disciples of Christ until the Religious Census of 1906. They are strictly congregational and have no organization larger than the local congregation. Churches: 18,500; Membership: 2,350,000.

**Congregational Christian Churches, National Association of:** Organized in 1955 by a number of representatives of Congregational Christian Churches that wished to continue as such and not to enter the United Church of Christ. It has no doctrinal requirements. Churches: 300; Membership: 110,000; Officer: Executive Secretary: Reverend A. Vaughan Abercrombie, 176 West Wisconsin Avenue, Milwaukee, Wisconsin.

**Conservative Baptist Association of America:** Formed in 1947, at Atlantic City, New Jersey. The Old and New Testaments are regarded as the divinely inspired Word of God and are therefore infallible and of supreme authority. Each local church is independent and autonomous and free from ecclesiastical or political authority. Churches: 1,500; Membership: 500,000; President: Dr. Lester Thompson; Headquarters: Wheaton, Ill.

**The Evangelical Lutheran Synodical Conference of North America:** Organized in 1872 by groups that held to the stricter doctrines of the Lutheran Church and to closer adherence to the historical confessions. Comprises the following bodies: (1) *The Lutheran Church—Missouri Synod*, the largest constituent part of the Synodical Conference, organized in 1847, holds to an unwavering confessionalism, and is the leader in the conservative group among the Lutherans. Churches: 5,979; Membership: 2,816,883; Headquarters: The Lutheran Building, 210 North Broadway, St. Louis, Missouri; (2) *Synod of Evangelical Lutheran Churches*, a constituent part of the Synodical Conference, organized in 1902. Churches: 65; Membership: 21,656; and (3) *Missions of the Lutheran Synodical Conference*. The Synodical Conference has limited its activities to mission work in Nigeria and Ghana.

**The Evangelical United Brethren Church:** Originated in Johnstown, Pennsylvania, in 1946, with the union of the Evangelical Church and the Church of the United Brethren in Christ. Both these former communions had their beginnings in Pennsylvania in the evangelistic movement of the early 19th century. Church is Arminian in doctrine and Methodistic in government. Churches: 4,084; Membership: 746,099; Headquarters: Administrative Office Building, 601 West Riverview Avenue, Dayton, Ohio.

**Federated Churches:** A Federated Church is a congregation in which two or more denominational units conduct local affairs in common but maintain their separate denominational affiliation. Churches: 508; Membership: 88,411.

**Free Will Baptists:** A body of Arminian Baptists, organized in the South in 1727 by Paul Palmer and in the North in 1787 by Benjamin Randall. Embraces churches in 38 U.S. states, Africa, Brazil, Uruguay, Central America, Mexico, Japan, and India. Churches: 2,109; Membership: 178,450; Headquarters: 1134 Murfreesboro Road, Nashville, Tennessee.

*(continued)*

**RELIGIOUS BODIES IN THE U.S.** (*continued*)

**The General Association of Regular Baptist Churches:** Founded in 1932 by a group of churches that had withdrawn from the Northern Baptist Convention (now the American Baptist Convention) because of doctrinal differences. Its Confession of Faith, which it requires all churches to subscribe to, is essentially the historic New Hampshire Confession of Faith. Churches: 1,264; Membership: 175,250; Headquarters: 1800 Oakton Blvd., Des Plaines, Illinois.

**Greek Orthodox Archdiocese of North and South America:** A body of Greek-speaking Orthodox Christians with parishes in the United States, Canada, and South America. These are under the Ecumenical Patriarchate of Constantinople (Istanbul). Churches: 443; Membership: 1,770,000; Headquarters: 10 East 79th Street, New York, New York.

**Independent Fundamental Churches of America:** Organized in 1930, at Cicero, Illinois, by representatives of various independent churches. Churches: 872; Membership: 106,572; Headquarters: 145 N. Washington St., Wheaton, Ill. 60187

**International Church of the Foursquare Gospel:** An evangelistic missionary body organized by Aimee Semple McPherson in 1927. Churches: 2,508; Membership: 180,039; Headquarters: Angelus Temple, 1100 Glendale Blvd., Los Angeles, California.

**International General Assembly of Spiritualists:** Organized in 1936 for the purpose of chartering Spiritualist churches. Churches: 209; Membership: 164,072; Headquarters: 1915 Omohundro Avenue, Norfolk, Virginia.

**Jehovah's Witnesses:** Jehovah's witnesses adhere to the worship of Almighty God revealed in His Bible as Jehovah. They are primitive Christians and remain consistently neutral toward any nationalistic interests. They use the Watch Tower Bible and Tract Society of Pennsylvania, the Watchtower Bible and Tract Society of New York, the International Bible Students Association, and other corporations in their worldwide preaching activity, and they preach to all regardless of denomination. Their *Yearbook* shows them active during 1966 in 199 countries of the world, where there are approximately 1,118,665 such ministers preaching. There are now 5,242 congregations in continental United States, with 318,559 members (ministers), and 24,910 worldwide congregations. Headquarters: 124 Columbia Heights, Brooklyn, New York 11201.

**Jewish Congregations:** Jews arrived in the American colonies before 1650. The first congregation was recorded in 1654, in New York City, and was called the Shearith Israel (Remnant of Israel). It was founded by Jews who had fled from the Inquisition in Portuguese Brazil. Congregations: 4,079; Membership: 5,600,000.

**Lutheran Church in America:** Organized in 1962 by the consolidation of the American Evangelical Lutheran Church, founded in 1874; the Augustana Evangelical Lutheran Church, formed in 1860; the Finnish Evangelical Lutheran Church, organized in 1890; and the United Lutheran Church in America, founded in 1918. Churches: 5,883; Membership: 3,156,118; Headquarters: 231 Madison Avenue, New York, New York.

**The Methodist Church:** The present organization began in 1939, with the unification of three branches of Methodism—the Methodist Episcopal Church; the Methodist Episcopal Church, South; and the Methodist Protestant Church. All three of the uniting churches were in unbroken historical connection with Methodism in America. The 1948 General Conference adopted a resolution stating that the Christmas Conference of 1784 be regarded as the date on which the organized Methodist Church was founded as an ecclesiastical organization. The Methodist movement began in England with John and Charles Wesley, leaders of an evangelical revival, and was carried to America in 1760 by Methodist emigrants from Ireland. Churches: 39,050; Membership: 10,310,619; Council of Bishops, President: Bishop Donald H. Tippett, P.O. Box 467, San Francisco, California.

**National Baptist Convention of America:** Organized in 1880. Churches: 11,398; Membership: 2,668,799; President: Dr. C. D. Pettaway, 714 West 10th Street, Little Rock, Arkansas.

**National Baptist Convention, U.S.A., Inc.:** The parent convention of Negro Baptists, to be distinguished from the National Baptist Convention of America, which is usually referred to as the "unincorporated" body. Churches: 26,000; Membership: 5,500,000; President: Reverend J. H. Jackson, 3101 South Parkway, Chicago, Illinois.

**National Primitive Baptist Convention in the U.S.A.:** Organized in 1907. Churches: 1,880; Membership: 768,800; Headquarters: 2116 Clinton Avenue, West Huntsville, Alabama.

**North American Baptist Association:** A group of regular Baptist churches organized in 1950 in Little Rock, Arkansas. In theology these churches are evangelical, missionary, fundamental, and in the main premillennial. Churches: 2,000; Membership: 250,000; President: Dr. E. Harold Henderson, Lubbock, Texas.

**North American Old Roman Catholic Church:** A body identical with Roman Catholicism in most of its worship and discipline, with differences in doctrine. Membership: 88,788; Primate: The Most Reverend John E. Schweikert, Oak Lawn, Illinois.

**Pentecostal Church of God of America, Inc.:** Organized in 1919 at Chicago, Illinois. Churches: 958; Membership: 115,000; Headquarters: 312-316 Joplin Street, Joplin, Missouri.

**Polish National Catholic Church of America:** After a long period of dissatisfaction with Roman Catholic administration and ideology, this body separated from the parent church and in 1897 formed a distinct unit. Churches: 162; Membership: 282,411; Headquarters: 529 East Locust Street, Scranton, Pennsylvania.

**Presbyterian Church in the U.S.:** A branch of the Presbyterian Church, established in 1861. Churches: 4,008; Membership: 950,139; Moderator: Rev. Frank H. Caldwell, Office of General Assembly, 341 Ponce de Leon Avenue, N.E., Atlanta 8, Georgia.

**Progressive National Baptist Convention, Inc.:** Formed in 1961. Churches: 650; Membership: 521,581; President: Dr. G. C. Taylor, 833 Marcy Ave., Brooklyn, N.Y.

**The Protestant Episcopal Church:** Entered the American colonies with the earliest settlers (Jamestown, Virginia, 1607) as the Church of England. Became autonomous and adopted its present name in 1789. An integral part of the world-wide Anglican Communion. Churches: 7,595; Membership: 3,584,613; Headquarters: 815 Second Avenue, New York, New York.

**Reformed Church in America:** Established by the earliest Dutch settlers of New York as the Reformed Protestant Dutch Church in 1628. Evangelical in theology and Presbyterian in government. Churches located in 26 states. Churches: 934; Membership: 233,020; Headquarters: 475 Riverside Drive, New York, New York.

**Reorganized Church of Jesus Christ of Latter Day Saints:** A division among the Latter-Day Saints occurred after the death of Joseph Smith in 1844. His son, Joseph Smith, Jr. became presiding officer of this group. Churches: 1,200; Membership: 194,188; Headquarters: The Auditorium, Independence, Missouri.

**The Roman Catholic Church:** The largest single body of Christians in the United States, it is under the spiritual leadership of His Holiness Pope Paul VI. Its history in the American colonies began in Maryland in 1634. Churches: 23,668; Membership: 46,246,175.

**Russian Orthodox Catholic Church in America Patriarchal Exarchate:** This autonomous body is the direct canonical successor of the Orthodox Catholic mission established in Alaska by the Russian Orthodox Church in 1793, and is under the spiritual jurisdiction of His Holiness the Patriarch of Moscow and All Russia. In 1962, a Western Rite Orthodox administration was established. Churches: 67; Membership: 152,973; Exarch: Most Reverend Metropolitan John Wendland, 15 East 97th Street, New York, N.Y.

**The Russian Orthodox Greek Catholic Church of America:** This church entered Alaska in 1792 before the territory's purchase by the United States. In 1872, the headquarters were moved to San Francisco and, in 1905, to New York. Churches: 397; Membership: 600,000; Headquarters: 59 East 2nd Street, New York, New York.

**The Salvation Army:** An evangelistic organization with a military government, first set up by General William Booth (1829–1912) in England in 1865 and introduced into America in 1880. Churches: 1,220; Membership: 292,713; National Headquarters: 120–130 West 14th Street, New York, New York.

**Seventh-Day Adventists:** A Protestant body formally organized in 1863. Stressing the imminence of the Second Advent of Christ, the Seventh-Day Adventists take the Bible as their sole rule of faith and practice, are fundamentally evangelical, and hold to the inspiration of the Scriptures. Their two cardinal points of faith are: belief in the imminent, premillennial personal and visible return of Christ; and observance of the seventh day as the Sabbath. Churches: 3,339; Membership: 391,014; Headquarters: 6840 Eastern Avenue, N.W., Washington, D.C.

**Religious Society of Friends:** Originated in England in the 17th century under George Fox. Commonly called Quakers, the Friends regard church sacraments as unessential to Christian life. The accomplishments in the cause of international understanding achieved by the American Friends Service Committee, organized in 1917, are widely recognized. Two of the largest Quaker groups in America are the Friends United Meeting and the Friends General Conference. The **Friends United Meeting** (formerly the Five Years Meeting of Friends) was formed in 1902. Churches: 487; Membership: 70,167; Clerk: Byron Haworth, 902 Fairway, High Point, N.C. The **Friends General Conference** was organized in 1900. Churches: 314; Membership: 32,462; Headquarters: 1520 Race Street, Philadelphia, Pennsylvania.

**Southern Baptist Convention:** In 1845, Southern Baptists withdrew from the General Missionary Convention over the question of slavery and other matters and formed the Southern Baptist Convention. Churches: 33,949; Membership: 10,952,463; Offices: 460 James Robertson Parkway, Nashville, Tennessee 37219.

**Syrian Antiochian Orthodox Church:** A division of the Orthodox Church under the jurisdiction of the Patriarch of Antioch. A member of the Standing Conference of Canonical Orthodox Bishops in America. Churches: 80; Membership: 110,000; Headquarters: 239 85th Street, Brooklyn, N.Y.

**Unitarian Universalist Association:** The consolidated body of the former American Unitarian Association and the Universalist Church of America formed in 1961. The Unitarian movement arose in Congregationalism in the 18th century, producing the American Unitarian Association in 1825. The philosophy of Universalism originated with the doctrine of universal salvation and was brought to America in the 18th century. Universalists were first formally organized in the 1770s. Churches: 1,044; Membership: 166,622; Headquarters: 25 Beacon Street, Boston, Mass.

**United Church of Christ:** A union of the Evangelical and Reformed Church and the General Council of the Congregational Christian Churches, formed in 1957. Churches: 6,947; Membership: 2,063,481; Headquarters: 297 Park Avenue South, New York, New York.

**The United Free Will Baptist Church:** Set up its organization in 1870. Churches: 836; Membership: 100,000; Headquarters: Kinston College, 1000 University Street, Kinston, North Carolina.

**United Pentecostal Church, Inc.:** Consists of the Pentecostal Church, Inc., and the Pentecostal Assemblies of Jesus Christ, which merged in 1945 at St. Louis, Missouri. Churches: 2,000; Membership: 125,000; Headquarters: 3645 South Grand Boulevard, St. Louis, Missouri.

**The United Presbyterian Church in the United States of America:** In 1958, The United Presbyterian Church of North America and The Presbyterian Church in the United States of America merged to form the new denomination, The United Presbyterian Church in the United States of America. The Presbyterian Church in the United States of America dated from the first presbytery, organized in Philadelphia in 1706. The United Presbyterian Church of North America was formed in 1858. Churches: 9,002; Membership: 3,298,583; Office: 510 Witherspoon Building, Philadelphia, Pennsylvania.

**Wisconsin Evangelical Lutheran Synod:** Organized in Wisconsin in 1850. Churches: 908; Membership: 367,959; President: Rev. Oscar Naumann, 3512 West North Avenue, Milwaukee, Wisconsin.

## ANNUAL FINANCIAL REPORT OF SOME U.S. RELIGIOUS BODIES

Compiled from the *Yearbook of American Churches, 1967,* the following list does not include some religious groups, such as Roman Catholic and Jewish, which do not compile a general financial report.

| RELIGIOUS BODY | TOTAL CONTRIBUTIONS | PER MEMBER CONTRIBUTIONS | PER MEMBER FOREIGN MISSIONS |
|---|---|---|---|
| **Baptist:** American Convention | $104,699,557 | $ 69.99 | $ 1.98 |
| North American General Conference | 6,425,120 | 120.44 | 6.00 |
| Seventh Day General Conference | 386,564 | 67.46 | 4.18 |
| Southern Convention | 591,587,981 | 55.80 | 2.21 |
| **Brethren:** Brethren in Christ | 1,976,840 | 210.80 | 18.93 |
| Brethren Church (Ashland, Ohio) | 1,436,842 | 80.22 | 6.37 |
| Church of the Brethren | 15,221,162 | 76.08 | 1.60 |
| **Christian and Missionary Alliance** | 5,000,000 | No Report | 40.00 |
| **Church of the Nazarene** | 56,016,446 | 160.38 | 12.89 |
| **Church of God (Anderson, Indiana)** | 21,732,533 | 155.75 | 3.92 |
| **Churches of God in North America** | 2,940,116 | 80.99 | 2.27 |
| **Christian (Disciples of Christ)** | 102,102,840 | 86.44 | 2.27 |
| **Evangelical Congregational** | 2,688,056 | 89.25 | 5.75 |
| **Evangelical Covenant Church of America** | 13,059,923 | 201.81 | 11.21 |
| **Evangelical Free Church of America** | 11,133,816 | 247.30 | 46.99 |
| **Evangelical United Brethren** | 56,552,783 | 76.34 | .39 |
| **Friends:** Ohio Yearly Meeting | 1,136,519 | 179.40 | 16.12 |
| **Lutheran:** The American Lutheran Church | 143,687,165 | 83.83 | 2.04 |
| Lutheran Church in America | 170,012,096 | 76.35 | 2.57 |
| Missouri Synod | 184,658,337 | 103.90 | 2.33 |
| Evangelical Synod | 871,100 | 88.79 | .31 |
| Synod of Evangelical | 1,482,640 | 96.06 | No Report |
| Wisconsin Synod | 19,568,979 | 80.24 | 2.05 |
| **Mennonite:** Evangelical | 509,644 | 201.36 | 39.80 |
| General Conference | 4,913,639 | 137.83 | 16.41 |
| **Methodist:** African Methodist Episcopal | 3,014,922 | 4.88 | .22 |
| Free | 19,198,629 | 358.17 | 17.59 |
| Methodist Church | 608,841,881 | 59.09 | 1.75 |
| Wesleyan | 10,917,613 | 282.00 | 13.94 |
| **Moravian:** Unity of the Brethren | 299,661 | 61.14 | 1.93 |
| Northern Province | 2,868,694 | 103.54 | 4.98 |
| **Pentecostal Holiness** | 8,240,426 | 133.91 | 4.69 |
| **Pilgrim Holiness** | 7,054,236 | 233.70 | 13.21 |
| **Presbyterian:** Associate Reformed | 1,421,894 | 52.63 | 5.21 |
| Cumberland | 5,227,136 | 65.15 | 2.54 |
| Orthodox | 1,562,561 | 193.70 | 19.60 |
| U.S. | 108,269,579 | 114.61 | 4.52 |
| United, U.S.A. | 304,833,435 | 92.29 | 3.29 |
| **Protestant Episcopal** | 175,374,777 | 76.66 | 1.96 |
| **Reformed Church in America** | 29,174,103 | 126.44 | 6.56 |
| **United Brethren in Christ** | 2,976,977 | 141.09 | No Report |
| **United Church of Christ** | 169,208,042 | 75.94 | 1.82 |

## THE FIRST CATHOLIC COLLEGE TO BECOME A SECULAR INSTITUTION

In January, 1967, Webster College, a Roman Catholic school for women in Webster Groves, Missouri, was transformed into a secular institution. Its board of directors, which had been composed entirely of members of the religious order of the Sisters of Loretto, was replaced by a group of laymen. Thus, for the first time in the U.S., a Roman Catholic college relinquished its authority to secular directorship.

The individual most responsible for the change was Jacqueline Grennan, who had been a member of the Sisters of Loretto for 18 years. She decided that she could best ". . . live as a responsible human being" by renouncing her vows. Her act of leaving the order had the approval of Joseph Cardinal Ritter, who was, until his death in June, head of the Archdiocese of St. Louis.

Miss Grennan was asked to stay on as Webster's president. Although accepting the request, she acted immediately to sever official connections between the Church and the college. She explained her move by stating that it was her ". . . personal conviction that the very nature of higher education is opposed to juridical control by the Church." Regarding her own future, she stated her belief that a cloistered life is not valid for those dedicated women who are in the public forum.

The unprecedented relinquishment of Church authority in this instance appeared to indicate a shift away from what many liberal Catholics have sometimes felt to be excessive paternalism on the part of the Catholic hierarchy. Certainly reflected is increasing Church acceptance of the freedom of inquiry in education, and a stronger spirit of liberalism in accordance with the sentiments expressed at Ecumenical Council Vatican II.

## U.S. ROMAN CATHOLIC HIERARCHY

There are 29 Roman Catholic archbishops in the United States, appointed by the Pope. Seven archbishops are cardinals (*), designated by the Pope.

**Anchorage, Alaska:** Most Rev. Joseph T. Ryan, Archbishop. *Jurisdiction:* Third Judicial Division of Alaska.

**Atlanta, Ga.:** Most Rev. Paul J. Hallinan, Archbishop. *Jurisdiction:* Georgia, South Carolina, North Carolina, and eastern Florida.

***Baltimore, Md.:** His Eminence Lawrence J. Cardinal Shehan, Archbishop. *Jurisdiction:* Maryland (except five counties), Delaware, Virginia, and West Virginia.

***Boston, Mass.:** His Eminence Richard Cardinal Cushing, Archbishop. *Jurisdiction:* Massachusetts, Maine, New Hampshire, and Vermont.

***Chicago, Ill.:** His Eminence John Patrick Cardinal Cody, Archbishop. *Jurisdiction:* Illinois.

**Cincinnati, Ohio:** Most Rev. Karl J. Alter, Archbishop. *Jurisdiction:* Ohio.

**Denver, Colo.:** Most Rev. Urban J. Vehr, Archbishop. *Jurisdiction:* Colorado and Wyoming.

**Detroit, Mich.:** Most Rev. John F. Dearden, Archbishop. *Jurisdiction:* Michigan.

**Dubuque, Iowa:** Most Rev. James J. Byrne, Archbishop. *Jurisdiction:* Iowa.

**Hartford, Conn.:** Most Rev. Henry J. O'Brien, Archbishop. *Jurisdiction:* Connecticut and Rhode Island.

**Indianapolis, Ind.:** Most Rev. Paul C. Schulte, Archbishop. *Jurisdiction:* Indiana.

**Kansas City, Kans.:** Most Rev. Edward J. Hunkeler, Archbishop. *Jurisdiction:* Kansas.

***Los Angeles, Calif.:** His Eminence James Francis Cardinal McIntyre, Archbishop. *Jurisdiction:* Southern California and Arizona (except five counties).

**Louisville, Ky.:** Most Rev. John A. Floersh, Archbishop. *Jurisdiction:* Kentucky and Tennessee.

**Milwaukee, Wis.:** Most Rev. William E. Cousins, Archbishop. *Jurisdiction:* Wisconsin.

**Newark, N.J.:** Most Rev. Thomas A. Boland, Archbishop. *Jurisdiction:* New Jersey.

**New Orleans, La.:** Most Rev. Philip M. Hannan, Archbishop. *Jurisdiction:* Louisiana, Arkansas, western Florida, Alabama, Mississippi.

***New York, N.Y.:** His Eminence Francis Cardinal Spellman, Archbishop, and the Most Rev. John J. Maguire, Archbishop. *Jurisdiction:* New York.

**Omaha, Nebr.:** Most Rev. Gerald T. Bergan, Archbishop. *Jurisdiction:* Nebraska.

***Philadelphia, Penn.:** His Eminence John J. Cardinal Krol, Archbishop. *Jurisdiction:* Pennsylvania.

**Philadelphia, Penn.:** (Byzantine Rite) Most Rev. Ambrose Senyshyn, Metropolitan. *Jurisdiction:* All Ukraine Catholics of the U.S.

**Portland, Oreg.:** Most Rev. Robert J. Dwyer, Archbishop. *Jurisdiction:* Oregon, Idaho, Montana.

**St. Louis, Mo.:** See vacant. Most Rev. George Gottwald, administrator. *Jurisdiction:* Missouri.

**St. Paul, Minn.:** Most Rev. Leo Binz, Archbishop. *Jurisdiction:* Minnesota and the Dakotas.

**San Antonio, Tex.:** Most Rev. Robert E. Lucey, Archbishop. *Jurisdiction:* Texas (except El Paso) and Oklahoma.

**San Francisco, Calif.:** Most Rev. Joseph T. McGucken, Archbishop. *Jurisdiction:* Northern California, Nevada, Utah, and Hawaii.

**Santa Fe, N. Mex.:** Most Rev. James Peter Davis, Archbishop. *Jurisdiction:* New Mexico, northern Arizona, and El Paso, Texas.

**Seattle, Wash.:** Most Rev. Thomas A. Connolly, Archbishop. *Jurisdiction:* Washington and Alaska.

***Washington, D.C.:** His Eminence Patrick A. Cardinal O'Boyle, Archbishop. *Jurisdiction:* Washington, part of Maryland, Virgin Islands.

## METHODIST BISHOPS IN THE UNITED STATES: 1967

Ralph T. Alton, Madison, Wisconsin
L. Scott Allen, Waveland, Mississippi
Newell S. Booth, Harrisburg, Pennsylvania
Kenneth W. Copeland, Lincoln, Nebraska
Fred Pierce Corson, Philadelphia, Pennsylvania
F. Gerald Ensley, Columbus, Ohio
H. Ellis Finger, Jr., Nashville, Tennessee
Eugene M. Frank, St. Louis, Missouri
Paul V. Galloway, Little Rock, Arkansas
Paul N. Garber, Raleigh, North Carolina
Edwin R. Garrison, Aberdeen, South Dakota
Charles F. Golden, Nashville, Tennessee
W. Kenneth Goodson, Birmingham, Alabama
Walter C. Gum, Richmond, Virginia
Paul Hardin, Jr., Columbia, South Carolina
James W. Henley, Lakeland, Florida
Fred G. Holloway, Charleston, West Virginia
Earl G. Hunt, Jr., Charlotte, North Carolina
Francis E. Kearns, Canton, Ohio
Gerald Kennedy, Los Angeles, California
Dwight E. Loder, Detroit, Michigan
John Wesley Lord, Washington, D.C.
Edgar A. Love, Atlanta, Georgia
Paul E. Martin, Houston, Texas

James K. Mathews, Boston, Massachusetts
Noah W. Moore, Jr., Houston, Texas
T. Otto Nall, Minneapolis, Minnesota
Frederick B. Newell, Pittsburgh, Pennsylvania
Everett W. Palmer, Seattle, Washington
Edward J. Pendergrass, Jackson, Mississippi
Glenn R. Phillips, Portland, Oregon
W. Kenneth Pope, Dallas, Texas
Thomas Pryor, Chicago, Illinois
Richard C. Raines, Indianapolis, Indiana
Roy H. Short, Louisville, Kentucky
Eugene Slater, San Antonio, Texas
John Owen Smith, Atlanta, Georgia
W. Angie Smith, Oklahoma City, Oklahoma
W. McFerrin Stowe, Topeka, Kansas
R. Marvin Stuart, Denver, Colorado
Prince A. Taylor, Jr., Princeton, New Jersey
James S. Thomas, Des Moines, Iowa
Donald H. Tippett, San Francisco, California
Aubrey G. Walton, New Orleans, Louisiana
William Ralph Ward, Jr., Syracuse, New York
Lance Webb, Springfield, Illinois
Hazen G. Werner, New York, New York
Lloyd C. Wicke, New York, New York

## PROTESTANT EPISCOPAL BISHOPS IN THE UNITED STATES: 1967

Key: PB—Presiding Bishop; D—Diocesan Bishop; C—Coadjutor Bishop; S—Suffragan Bishop; EC—Executive Council

John M. Allin (D) Mississippi
Scott F. Bailey (S) Texas
Alfred L. Banyard (D) New Jersey
William P. Barnds (S) Dallas, Texas
George W. Barrett (D) Rochester, New York
Lane W. Barton (D) Eastern Oregon
Stephen F. Bayne, Jr. (EC) Overseas Dept.
Charles E. Bennison (D) Western Michigan
Roger W. Blanchard (D) Southern Ohio
Francis E. I. Bloy (D) Los Angeles, California
Charles F. Boynton (S) New York, New York
William H. Brady (D) Fond du Lac, Wisconsin
Allen W. Brown (D) Albany, New York
Robert R. Brown (D) Arkansas
John M. Burgess (S) Massachusetts
Gerald F. Burrill (D) Chicago, Illinois
Nelson M. Burroughs (D) Ohio
John H. Burt (C) Ohio
Harvey D. Butterfield (D) Vermont
George L. Cadigan (D) Missouri
Wilburn C. Campbell (D) West Virginia
James W. F. Carman (D) Oregon
Charles C. J. Carpenter (D) Alabama
Albert A. Chambers (D) Springfield, Illinois
Samuel B. Chilton (S) Virginia
Randolph R. Claiborne, Jr. (D) Atlanta, Georgia
Ned Cole, Jr. (C) Central New York
Daniel Corrigan (EC) Home Department
John P. Craine (D) Indianapolis, Indiana
William F. Creighton (D) Washington, D.C.
William Crittenden (D) Erie, Pennsylvania
Archie H. Crowley (S) Michigan
Ivol I. Curtis (D) Olympia, Washington
William Davidson (D) Western Kansas
Robert L. De Witt (D) Pennsylvania
R. Earl Dicus (S) West Texas
Harry L. Doll (D) Maryland
Horace W. B. Donegan (D) New York, N.Y.
James L. Duncan (S) South Florida
Richard S. M. Emrich (D) Michigan
John H. Esquirol (S) Connecticut
Norman L. Foote (D) Idaho
Thomas A. Fraser, Jr. (D) North Carolina
William F. Gates, Jr. (S) Tennessee
Conrad H. Gesner (D) South Dakota
Robert F. Gibson, Jr. (D) Virginia
F. Percy Goddard (S) Texas
William J. Gordon, Jr. (D) Alaska
Walter H. Gray (D) Connecticut
Hal R. Gross (S) Oregon
George P. Gunn (D) Southern Virginia
Clarence W. Haden, Jr. (D) Northern California
Charles F. Hall (D) New Hampshire
Robert B. Hall (C) Virginia
Donald H. V. Hallock (D) Milwaukee, Wis.
William L. Hargrave (S) South Florida
John Joseph M. Harte (D) Arizona
Robert M. Hatch (D) Western Massachusetts
M. George Henry (D) Western North Carolina
John S. Higgins (D) Rhode Island
Walter M. Higley (D) Central New York
John E. Hines (PB, EC)
Earl M. Honaman (S) Harrisburg, Pennsylvania
William W. Horstick (D) Eau Claire, Wisconsin
James W. Hunter (D) Wyoming

J. Warren Hutchens (S) Connecticut
Everett H. Jones (D) West Texas
Girault M. Jones (D) Louisiana
Christoph Keller, Jr. (C) Arkansas
Hamilton H. Kellogg (D) Minnesota
Harry S. Kennedy (D) Honolulu, Hawaii
Charles J. Kinsolving III (D) N. Mex. and SW
  Texas
Walter C. Klein (D) Northern Indiana
Frederic C. Lawrence (S) Massachusetts
Arnold M. Lewis (S) Armed Forces
F. William Lickfield (D) Quincy, Illinois
Oliver L. Loring (D) Maine
Henry I. Loutitt (D) South Florida
Charles W. MacLean (S) Long Island
C. Gresham Marmion (D) Kentucky
William H. Marmion (D) Southwestern Virginia
Richard B. Martin (S) Long Island, N.Y.
C. Avery Mason (D) Dallas, Texas
George T. Masuda (D) North Dakota
Theodore H. McCrea (S) Dallas, Texas
Edward McNair (S) Northern California
Philip F. McNairy (D) Minnesota
George M. Millard (S) California
Joseph S. Minnis (D) Colorado
James W. Montgomery (C) Chicago, Illinois
William R. Moody (D) Lexington, Kentucky
Paul Moore, Jr. (S) Washington, D.C.
William M. Moore (S) North Carolina
J. Brooke Mosley (D) Delaware
George M. Murray (C) Alabama
C. Kilmer Myers (D) California
Iveson B. Noland (C) Louisiana
Lyman C. Ogilby (C) South Dakota
Austin Pardue (D) Pittsburgh, Pennsylvania
Charles B. Persell, Jr. (S) Albany, New York
John A. Pinckney (D) Upper South Carolina
Chilton Powell (D) Oklahoma
Frederick W. Putnam, Jr. (S) Oklahoma
George H. Quarterman (D) Northwest Texas
George E. Rath (S) Newark, New Jersey
Russell T. Rauscher (D) Nebraska
J. Milton Richardson (D) Texas
David S. Rose (C) Southern Virginia
Robert C. Rusack (S) Los Angeles, California
William E. Sanders (C) Tennessee
Lauriston L. Scaife (D) Western New York
George R. Selway (D) Northern Michigan
Jonathan G. Sherman (D) Long Island
Gordon V. Smith (D) Iowa
Robert R. Spears, Jr. (S) West Missouri
Leland Stark (D) Newark, New Jersey
Chandler W. Sterling (D) Montana
Dean T. Stevenson (D) Harrisburg, Pennsylvania
Anson P. Stokes, Jr. (D) Massachusetts
Albert R. Stuart (D) Georgia
George A. Taylor (D) Easton, Maryland
Gray Temple (D) South Carolina
Edwin B. Thayer (S) Colorado
William S. Thomas (S) Pittsburgh, Penn.
Edward C. Turner (D) Kansas
John VanderHorst (D) Tennessee
Albert W. Van Duzer (S) New Jersey
Sumner F. D. Walters (D) San Joaquin, Calif.
Frederick J. Warnecke (D) Bethlehem, Penn.

**PROTESTANT EPISCOPAL BISHOPS** (*continued*)

Richard S. Watson (D) Utah
Edward R. Welles (D) West Missouri
E. Hamilton West (D) Florida
J. Stuart Wetmore (S) New York, New York

Milton L. Wood (S) Atlanta, Georgia
Thomas H. Wright (D) East Carolina
William G. Wright (D) Nevada
John R. Wyatt (D) Spokane, Washington

## MAJOR RELIGIOUS HOLIDAYS: 1968
### PROTESTANT EPISCOPAL

| DATE | HOLIDAY | DATE | HOLIDAY | DATE | HOLIDAY |
|---|---|---|---|---|---|
| January 1..... | The Holy Name | May 1........ | St. Philip and | September 21.. | St. Matthew |
| January 6..... | The Epiphany | | St. James | September 29.. | St. Michael and |
| January 25.... | The Conversion of | May 19....... | Rogation Sunday | | All Angels |
| | St. Paul | May 23....... | Ascension Day | October 18.... | St. Luke |
| February 2.... | The Purification of | June 2........ | Whitsunday | October 28.... | St. Simon and St. Jude |
| | St. Mary the Virgin | June 9........ | Trinity Sunday | November 1.... | All Saints' Day |
| February 24... | St. Matthias | June 11....... | St. Barnabas | November 28.. | Thanksgiving Day |
| February 28... | Ash Wednesday | June 24....... | Nativity of St. John | November 30.. | St. Andrew |
| March 25...... | The Annunciation | | the Baptist | December 1... | Advent Sunday |
| April 7........ | Palm Sunday | June 29....... | St. Peter and St. Paul | December 21.. | St. Thomas |
| April 11....... | Maundy Thursday | July 4........ | Independence Day | December 25.. | Christmas Day |
| April 12....... | Good Friday | July 25....... | St. James | December 26.. | St. Stephen |
| April 13....... | Easter Even | August 6...... | The Transfiguration | December 27.. | St. John the Evangelist |
| April 14....... | Easter Day | August 24..... | St. Bartholomew | December 28.. | The Holy Innocents |

### ROMAN CATHOLIC

| DATE | HOLIDAY | DATE | HOLIDAY | DATE | HOLIDAY |
|---|---|---|---|---|---|
| January 1..... | Octave of Nativity * | April 14....... | Easter Sunday * | August 15..... | The Assumption * |
| February 28... | Ash Wednesday | May 23....... | The Ascension * | November 1.... | All Saints' Day |
| April 7........ | Palm Sunday | June 2........ | Pentecost | December 8... | The Immaculate |
| April 11....... | Holy Thursday | June 13....... | Corpus Christi * | | Conception * |
| April 12....... | Good Friday | June 29....... | Martyrdom of Saints | December 25.. | Christmas * |
| April 13....... | Holy Saturday | | Peter and Paul ** | | |

### JEWISH (Jewish Years: 5728–5729)

| DATE | HOLIDAY | DATE | HOLIDAY |
|---|---|---|---|
| March 14, 1968 (Adar 14, 5728)...... | Purim | October 2, 1968 (Tishri 10, 5729)..... | Yom Kippur |
| April 13, 1968 (Nisan 15, 5728)...... | Pesach | October 7, 1968 (Tishri 15, 5729)..... | Sukkoth |
| June 2, 1968 (Sivan 6, 5728)......... | Shavuoth | October 14, 1968 (Tishri 22, 5729).... | Shemini Atzeret |
| September 23–24, 1968 (Tishri 1, 5729) | Rosh Hashanah | December 16–23, 1968 (Kislev 25, 5729) | Hanukkah |

### EASTERN ORTHODOX

| DATE | HOLIDAY |
|---|---|
| January 1 ††..................... | The Circumcision of Jesus Christ; the Feast of St. Basil; New Year's Day |
| January 6 ††..................... | The Epiphany; The Baptism of Jesus Christ; the Sanctification of the Waters |
| January 7 ††..................... | The Feast of St. John the Baptist |
| January 30 ††.................... | The Feast of the Three Hierarchs: St. Basil, St. Gregory, and St. John Chrysostom |
| March 4......................... | Beginning of Easter Lenten Period |
| March 25 ††...................... | The Annunciation of the Blessed Virgin Mary |
| April 14......................... | Palm Sunday |
| April 15–21...................... | Holy Easter Week of the Passion |
| April 19......................... | Great Friday, The Burial of Jesus Christ |
| April 21......................... | Easter Sunday, The Resurrection of Jesus Christ |
| May 30.......................... | The Ascension |
| June 9.......................... | Pentecost Sunday |
| June 29 ††....................... | The Feast of Saints Peter and Paul, Apostles of Jesus Christ |
| June 30 ††....................... | The Feast of the Twelve Apostles of Jesus Christ |
| August 6 ††...................... | The Transfiguration of the Savior |
| August 15 ††..................... | The Dormition of the Virgin Mary (Repose or Falling Asleep of the Blessed Virgin Mary) |
| August 29 ††..................... | The Commemoration of the Beheading of St. John the Baptist |
| September 1 ††................... | The Beginning of the Church Year |
| September 14 ††.................. | The Elevation of the Holy Cross |

(continued)

* Holy Day of Obligation in the United States.   ** Holy Day of Obligation outside the United States.   † Movable holidays' dependent on the date of Easter, calculated on a special calendar. Note: In 1966 the Eastern and Western Easters were celebrated on the same date, April 10. This occurs every few years, but not in a fixed pattern. When the two Easters are not celebrated together, the Eastern always follows the Western. The Orthodox Easter was set by the Council of Nicaea (325 A.D.) which decreed that it would follow on the first Sunday after the first full moon after the first day of Spring, but always after the Jewish Passover, to maintain the Biblical sequence of events.   †† Celebrated every year on this date in accordance with the Gregorian Calendar, now generally observed by the Greek Orthodox Churches. However, some Eastern Orthodox Churches, which still adhere to the old Julian Calendar, observe this holiday 13 days later.

**RELIGIOUS HOLIDAYS** (*continued*)

| DATE | HOLIDAY |
|------|---------|
| October 23 †† | The Feast of St. James (Iakovos) |
| November 15 †† | The Beginning of the Advent Period (Christmas Lent) |
| November 21 †† | The Presentation of the Blessed Virgin Mary |
| November 30 †† | The Feast of St. Andrew, Founder of the Ecumenical Patriarchate of Constantinople |
| December 25 †† | The Holy Nativity (Christmas), The Birth of Jesus Christ |

†† Some Eastern Orthodox Churches, which still adhere to the old Julian Calendar, observe this holiday 13 days later.

**Islamic (Islamic Year: 1387–88; 1968 A.D.)**

| DATE | HOLIDAY |
|------|---------|
| January 1, 1968 (Monday, Shawal 1, 1387) | Idul-Fitr—The Feast celebrating the end of Fasting |
| March 8, 1968 (Friday, Zul-Hijjah 9, 1387) | Waqfat 'Arafat—The Pilgrimage Day |
| March 9, 1968 (Saturday, Zul-Hijjah 10, 1387) | Idul-Adha—The Feast of Sacrifice |
| March 30, 1968 (Saturday, Muharram 1, 1388) | The New Year Day |
| April 8, 1968 (Monday, Muharram 10, 1388) | The 'Ashura Day |
| June 8, 1968 (Saturday, Rabi' Al-Awal 12, 1388) | The Birthday of the Prophet |
| October 19, 1968 (Saturday, Rajab 27, 1388) | Isra' and Mi'raj |
| November 6, 1968 (Wednesday, Sha'ban 15, 1388) | The Middle of Sha'ban |
| November 21, 1968 (Thursday, Ramadan 1, 1388) | Beginning of the Fasting Month |
| December 17, 1968 (Tuesday, Ramadan 27, 1388) | The Night of al-Qadr, Anniversary of the beginning of the Koranic revelation |
| December 20, 1968 (Friday, Ramadan 30, 1388) | End of the Fasting Month |
| December 21, 1968 (Saturday, Shawal 1, 1388) | Idul-Fitr—The Feast celebrating the end of Fasting |

## GREAT THOUGHTS

Before God, there is neither Greek nor barbarian, neither rich nor poor, and the slave is as good as his master, for by birth all men are free; they are citizens of the universal commonwealth which embraces all the world, brethren of one family, and children of God.

> —Lord Acton, English historian, *The History of Freedom in Antiquity* (1877).

Those who won our independence believed that the final end of the state was to make men free to develop their faculties; and that in its government the deliberative forces should prevail over the arbitrary. They believed that freedom to think as you will and to speak as you think are means indispensable to the discovery and spread of political truth; that without free speech and assembly discussion would be futile; that with them, discussion affords ordinarily adequate protection against the dissemination of noxious doctrine; that the greatest menace to freedom is an inert people; that public discussion is a political duty; and that this should be a fundamental principle of the American government.

> —Louis D. Brandeis, U.S. Supreme Court justice, concurring opinion in *Whitney* v. *California* (1927).

If there be a country . . . where knowledge cannot be diffused without perils of mob law and statute law; where speech is not free; where the post-office is violated . . . ; where public debts and private debts outside of the State are repudiated; where liberty is attacked in the primary institution of social life; where the position of the white woman is injuriously affected by the outlawry of the black woman; where the arts, such as they have, are all imported, having no indigenous life; where the laborer is not secured in the earnings of his own hands; that country is, in all these respects, not civil, but barbarous.

> —Ralph Waldo Emerson, American essayist, *Civilization* (1862).

Knowledge for the sake of knowledge, so far from having anything aristocratic or sublime about it (as some believe), would be an idiotic pastime for idiots . . . ; in reality there is no such thing, it is intrinsically impossible and the stimulus ceases with the failure of the material itself and of the end of knowledge. Those intellectuals who see salvation in the withdrawal of the artist or the thinker from the world around him, in his deliberate non-participation in vulgar practical contests . . . do without knowing it compass the death of the intellect.

> —Benedetto Croce, Italian historian, *History as the Story of Liberty* (1941).

What is the meaning of human life, or for that matter, of the life of any creature? To know an answer to this question means to be religious. . . . The man who regards his own life and that of his fellow creatures as meaningless is not merely unhappy but hardly fit for life.

> —Albert Einstein, German-American scientist, in *The New York Times*, 1955.

History teaches that among the men who have overturned the liberties of republics, the greatest number have begun their career by paying an obsequious court to the people; commencing demagogues, and ending tyrants.

> —Alexander Hamilton, American statesman, *The Federalist Papers* (1787).

Let no one . . . be superior to the others: never one above the other. This is the formula of equality. Men cannot be brothers if they are not humble. It is pride, no matter how legitimate it may seem to be, which provokes tensions and struggles for prestige, for predominance, colonialism, egoism . . . Mankind must put an end to war or war will put an end to mankind . . . Peace, it is peace which must guide the destinies of peoples and of all mankind.

> —Pope Paul VI, in speech to the U.N. (1965).

# TRAVEL AND TRANSPORTATION

## International Travel · Domestic Travel · Private and Commercial Transportation

Electric trains such as this one carry Japanese commuters between Tokyo and Osaka at speeds as high as 125 miles per hour. Studies in high-speed interurban transportation are under way in the U.S.

### TRAVEL: 1967

The announcement by the Cunard Line that it had sold the *Queen Mary* to the City of Long Beach, California, and that the *Queen Elizabeth* would soon follow it to the block, seemed to mark more poignantly than any other event the decline of steamships on the Atlantic. The *Queen Mary,* with the three black-and-red stacks that made her such a familiar sight at Southampton and New York, embarked on her nostalgic farewell cruise from Manhattan. Her place will eventually be taken by Cunard's 58,000-ton liner, the *Queen Elizabeth II,* which is under construction in Scotland.

The ship will reflect the changes that have come to ships on the transatlantic route: She will be largely a classless ship; her restaurants will be on the upper decks; her staterooms will have large windows; she will have drive-on, drive-off room for 80 cars. She will also have

what is called a "functional funnel," and her profile will be radically different from ships that have for more than a century nestled along the quays of the North River.

With the last great moan of the *Mary's* horn still echoing across the waters, sensitive ears could also pick up a new, and to some an ominous sound—the unmistakable sonic boom of supersonic aircraft. Since the award of the United States contract to Boeing, and in light of the progress being made by the Russians and the Anglo-French Concorde, the supersonic era seemed to be just beyond the next cloud bank, and getting closer. Boom-fretters noted that the so-called "boom carpet" will extend to a width of 70 miles, thus creating problems for ships at sea as well as for families home asleep in the midlands.

*[continued]*

**TRAVEL: 1967** (*continued*)

But long before the supersonics fly off to detonate the blue yonder, the airline industry will be rolling out its jumbo jets capable of disgorging hundreds of passengers at one time—figures have been placed between 350 and 500 people, depending upon the airplane. The prospect, so soon to be a realization, spurred emergency meetings of travel officials in cities from Puerto Rico to Hawaii. After all, the current traffic patterns at places like New York's John F. Kennedy Airport and Los Angeles International are already creating monster tie-ups both in the air and on the ground.

Hours of tedious circling in the air, often leading to missed plane connections, were only two of the discomforts suffered by passengers. One could only wonder how the problem will be compounded if the passenger loads of the jumbo jets are increased three-fold over the current Boeing 707s and DC-8s.

Such widely disparate reasons as the acute traffic snarls on the ground and the unique requirements of the war in Vietnam were responsible for the advent of the commercial, passenger-carrying helicopter. Choppers were flying regular schedules between San Francisco Airport and outlying suburbs in the Bay Area. In Southern California they were connecting places like Van Nuys, Newport Beach, Whittier, and Anaheim with Los Angeles Airport, making such a celebrated destination as Disneyland a mere 16 minute ride from the air terminal. And nowhere was the helicopter more sophisticated than in New York, where a fleet of fast copters were ferrying passengers between three airports and a number of heliports, among them the nest atop the Pan Am Building, 60 floors above Manhattan's sidewalks.

Although scarcely apparent from a look at the nation's trains, especially the short-run routes along the Eastern seaboard, there seemed to be an awakening on the rails. The monorail appeared consistently and attractively, first at Disneyland and then at Seattle where, as a leftover from the fair, it became a part of the city. Tokyo had rushed its monorail into existence for the Olympics, but unfortunately its track, which begins downtown, stops just short of the airport. In 1967 the Pennsylvania Railroad and Budd Company (manufacturers of railroad cars and locomotives) tried out a new high-speed train that could whiz between New York and Washington at speeds as high as 150 miles an hour. Budd is now making 50 such cars for the Pennsylvania Railroad.

There seemed no help in store for the commuter, however, unless one could take hope from the hovercraft, the jet-propelled boat which rides above the water on a cushion of air. It was tried out at Expo 67 in Montreal last summer, and presumably it could adapt itself to commuter services in the New York and San Francisco bay areas.

The United Nations, taking official cognizance of the world of travel and its potential possibilities for spreading peace, ordained 1967 as International Tourist Year. That lofty intention hardly deterred the outbreaks that occurred in the Middle East and the Far East which had severe effects on tourism. The short-lived Arab-Israeli war, coming as it did early in June, put a damper on summer travel to the Middle East; riots in Hong Kong also deterred some Far Eastern tourists. Travel agents were hard put to rearrange summer itineraries. A junta takeover of Greece and the imposition by the new military rulers of censorship and controls was a further deterrent.

When the dust cleared, the situation in Greece was quiet, Beirut was empty of tourists, and Egypt was off limits to American travelers and its tourism was at a dead standstill. Israel, on the other hand, had assumed control of all of Jerusalem with its many holy places, as well as Bethlehem, and could look forward to vastly increased tourism in the future if it held its gains and if the military situation remained quiet. Until peace negotiations could be started, Israel was even operating sight-seeing flights over the Sinai battlefields.

If there was invisible international amity, it showed up not in the home territory of the world's nations, but on the banks of the St. Lawrence in Canada. Here the Canadian government was host to Expo 67, judged by almost all who saw it as one of the best world's fairs in memory. The loftiness of purpose and of spirit, rising above pure commercialism, was infectious from the start. Word-of-mouth accolades spread quickly, and new travel patterns were set which will benefit Canadian tourism for years to come. Canada took on a new posture and importance; and Montreal, with its shining skyscrapers, its fascinating underground city, its fine hotels and excellent French restaurants, assumed a new rank among the world's cities. The Expo fairgrounds were slated to become a permanent exhibition ground in which the original theme of the fair, Man and His World, is to be perpetually pursued.

Ever seeking new adventures abroad, man looked ahead in 1967 to the Pacific. This, as President Johnson and others had proclaimed, is the beginning of the Pacific era. The airlines thought so, too, and nearly a score of them filed for new routes that would stretch the sky lanes into once-remote corners of the Pacific and to the far ports of Asia.

While awarding the right to fly to such exotic stations, the nation also recognized the problem of its transportation complex at home. A Department of Transportation was created, with a new Secretary added to the President's Cabinet. The first appointee to the position was Alan Boyd, formerly of the Civil Aeronautics Board. His jobs included relieving congestion on the nation's highways, probing for reasons for the 50,000 traffic deaths a year, trying to halt the decline of the railroads, assisting the airports and their terminals prepare for the giant new planes; and, in short, bringing some order from the uncoordinated chaos that threatens the transportation systems of the nation. However awesome the challenge, the formation of the Department of Transportation seemed to sound the most hopeful note in the field of travel and transportation in 1967.

## EXPO 67: THE BIGGEST FAIR YET

Many nations sent exhibits to Montreal in 1967 to celebrate Canada's 100th anniversary of Confederation.

Canada's Expo 67, a wonderland of architectural fancy whose displays of past glories and future promises told of "Man and His World," opened April 28, 1967, and closed October 29, 1967, two days later than its originally scheduled ending. The unprecedented two-day extension had been granted by the International Bureau of Exhibitions, the worldwide governing body for fairs, because Expo was such an overwhelming success. More than 50,000,000 persons attended, making it the world's most visited fair. Many critics found it the most imaginative display in world's fair history.

Sixty-two nations exhibited at Expo. The U.S.'s 20-story "bubble" and the U.S.S.R.'s glass-walled pavilion both emphasized space explorations; the U.S. also portrayed the American creative arts. The British pavilion had a six-minute "ride" across 3,000 years of British history from Stonehenge to the Industrial Revolution. Emphasis in the Czechoslovakian exhibit was on cinematic effects, with one theater simultaneously showing 150 different images on as many screens.

One of the exhibits built to be a permanent part of the fairgrounds was Habitat, a prototype residential complex for urban living that is expected to be a major architectural influence in the 1970s. A museum, which had 200 works of art from around the world, will also remain open permanently.

Cultural events abounded during Expo and ranged from the circus to the opera. Several of the world's leading symphonies and major ballet companies performed. Sir Laurence Olivier and Jean-Louis Barrault, respectively, headed theater troupes from Britain and France.

The $1 billion Expo 67 was, as Canadian Prime Minister Lester Pearson said, "the fulfillment of one of the most daring acts of faith in Canadian enterprise and ability."

# INTERNATIONAL TRAVEL

## INTERNATIONAL TRAVEL CALENDAR: 1968

Americans going abroad in 1968 will have no trouble keeping busy for the year is crammed with interesting and exciting events all around the world. Globetrotters can bid at Leningrad's fur auction in January, help celebrate the Queen's birthday in the Netherlands in April, and look over the new cars at the Paris International Automobile Show in October. Sports fans can enjoy the unusual every month, starting with the world bobsledding championships in January and ending with Canadian football in December. Whatever your tastes, the following list will help you get the most fun out of your trip. Dates vary; check your travel agent or the tourist office of the country you plan to visit for exact information.

### JANUARY

**Australia Day,** Sydney and all Australia
**Balinese Temple Festivals** (all year long), Bali, Indonesia
**Chinese New Year** (Year of the Monkey), Hong Kong, Singapore, and Taiwan
**Cruft's Dog Show,** London, England
**Fasching Carnival,** Munich and all West Germany
**Fasching Carnival,** Vienna and all Austria
**Fiesta of Quiapo,** Manila, Philippines
**"Green Week,"** Berlin, Germany
**Indian Republic Day,** New Delhi and all India
**International Boat Show,** London, England
**International Fur Auction** (also July and October), Leningrad, U.S.S.R.
**Monte Carlo Automobile Rally,** ends Monte Carlo, Monaco
**Quebec Winter Carnival,** Quebec City, Canada
**South African Grand Prix Auto Race,** Johannesburg, South Africa
**World Bobsledding Championships,** St. Moritz, Switzerland

### FEBRUARY

**Anglo-American Pancake Race** (with Liberal, Kansas), Olney, England
**Calypso Carnival King's Coronation,** Port-of-Spain, Trinidad, British West Indies
**Carnival Time,** Rio de Janeiro, Brazil
**European Figure Skating Championships,** Genoa, Italy
**Fastnacht Carnival,** Basle, Locarno, and Lucerne, Switzerland
**German Alpine Ski Championships,** Garmisch-Partenkirchen, West Germany
**International Frankfurt Fair,** Frankfurt, West Germany
**International Toy Fair,** Nuremberg, West Germany
**"Jour Des Diables" Parade,** Martinique, French West Indies
**Lapp Fair,** Jokkmokk, Sweden
**Mardi Gras Carnival,** Binche, Belgium
**Mardi Gras Carnival,** Nice, France
**Tenth Winter Olympic Games,** Grenoble, France
**Winter Festival,** Malaga, Spain
**World Speed Ice Skating Championships,** Oslo, Norway
**World Tobogganing Championships,** Davos, Switzerland

### MARCH

**College Weeks,** Bermuda
**"Fallas De San Jose,"** Valencia, Spain
**"Golden Shears" Sheepshearing Contest,** Masterton, New Zealand
**Holmenkollen Ski Week,** Oslo, Norway
**International Spring Trade Fair,** Vienna, Austria
**Japanese Doll Festival,** Tokyo, Japan
**Miami-Nassau Ocean Yacht Race,** Nassau, Bahamas
**"Moomba" Festival and Parade,** Melbourne, Australia
**National Horse and Cattle Show,** Lahore, Pakistan
**No-Ruz (New Year's) Celebrations,** Teheran and all Iran
**Oxford-Cambridge Boat Race,** River Thames, Putney, England
**St. Patrick's Day Observance,** Dublin, Ireland
**Vasa Cross-Country Ski Race,** Mora, Sweden

### APRIL

**Anzac Remembrance Day,** Sydney and Melbourne, Australia
**Cherry Blossom Festival,** Tokyo, Kyoto, and Osaka, Japan
**East African Motor Safari,** Nairobi, Kenya
**Easter "Explosion of the Cart" Spectacle,** Florence, Italy
**Easter Sunday Services,** St. Peter's Cathedral, Rome, Italy
**Easter Week Celebrations,** Seville, Granada, and Malaga, Spain
**Emperor's Birthday Observance,** Tokyo and all Japan
**Grand National Horse Race,** Fairyhouse, Dublin, Ireland
**Grand National Steeplechase,** Aintree, Liverpool, England
**International Spring Trade Fair,** Zagreb, Yugoslavia
**International Trade Fair,** Brussels, Belgium
**Osaka International Festival of Music,** Osaka, Japan
**Queen's Birthday Observance,** The Hague and all the Netherlands
**Seville Spring Fair and Bullfights,** Seville, Spain
**Shakespeare Drama Season,** Stratford-on-Avon, England
**Tulip Time Festival,** Haarlem, the Netherlands
**Walpurgis Night Celebrations,** Finland and Sweden

### MAY

**Budapest Trade Fair,** Budapest, Hungary
**Chelsea Flower Show,** London, England
**Coral Sea Week Observance,** Sydney, Australia
**Dragon Boat Festival,** Hong Kong, Singapore, and Taiwan
**Ethiopian Liberation Day,** Addis Ababa and all Ethiopia
**Feast of St. Isidro,** Madrid, Spain
**Festival of Bergama,** Izmir, Turkey
**Glyndebourne Opera Festival,** Glyndebourne, England
**Grand Prix Auto Race,** Monte Carlo, Monaco
**International Festival of Music,** Bergen, Norway
**International Film Festival,** Cannes, France
**International Labor Day,** Moscow and all U.S.S.R.
**International Trade Fair,** Luxembourg City, Luxembourg
**International Trade Fair,** Valencia, Spain
**Israeli Independence Day,** Jerusalem and all Israel
**Lord Buddha's Birthday Observance,** Nepal (birthplace)
**"Mille Miglia" Auto Race,** Brescia, Italy
**Moroccan Folklore Festival,** Marrakesh, Morocco
**Pilgrimage of the Gypsies** (also October), Saintes Maries de la Mer, France
**Pilgrimage to Our Lady of Fatima,** Fatima, Portugal
**Prague Spring Music Festival,** Prague, Czechoslovakia
**Procession of the Holy Blood,** Bruges, Belgium
**World Plowing Championship,** Christchurch, New Zealand

### JUNE

**Allied "D-Day" Commemoration,** Utah Beach, Normandy, France
**Corpus Christi Day Celebration,** Mexico City, Mexico
**Derby and Oaks Horse Races,** Epsom, England
**Epidaurus Drama Festival,** Epidaurus, Greece
**Festival of Two Worlds,** Spoleto, Italy
**"Grand Prix de Paris" Horse Race,** Longchamps, Paris, France

Henley Royal Regatta, Henley-on-Thames, England
International Music Festival, Strasbourg, France
International Tuna Tournament, Nassau, Bahamas
La Biennale Art Exhibition, Venice, Italy
Le Mans 24-Hour Auto Race, Le Mans, France
Medieval-style Football Game, Florence, Italy
Midsummer Eve Celebrations, Denmark and all Scandinavian
   countries
Queen's Birthday Observances, Jamaica and all British West
   Indies
Queen's Birthday "Trooping of the Colour," London,
   England
Royal Ascot Horse Race, Ascot, England
Sibelius Music Festival, Helsinki, Finland
Stratford Shakespeare Festival, Stratford, Ontario,
   Canada
"Tour de France" Bicycle Race, throughout France
Varna Summer Music Festival, Varna, Bulgaria
Viking Festival, Frederickssund, Denmark
Wimbledon Lawn Tennis Championships, London, England

## JULY

Athens Drama Festival, Athens, Greece
Baalbek Music Festival, Baalbek, Lebanon
Bastille Day Celebrations, Paris and all France
Cowes Week Yachting Regatta, Isle of Wight, England
Dominion Day Observance, Ottawa and all Canada
Egyptian Revolution Day Observance, Cairo and all United
   Arab Republic
Feast of the Hungry Ghosts, Hong Kong, Singapore, and
   Taiwan
Feast of the Lanterns, Nikko and all Japan
Festival of the Sacred Tooth, Kandy, Ceylon
General Patton Remembrance Day, Ettelbruck, Luxembourg
Hans Christian Andersen Festival, Odense, Denmark
International Film Festival, Locarno, Switzerland
International Music and Drama Festival, Caesarea, Israel
International Music Eisteddfod, Llangollen, Wales
International Music Festival, Aix-en-Provence, France
Iraqi Republic Day, Baghdad and all Iraq
July Handicap Horse Race, Durban, South Africa
Munich Opera Festival, Munich, West Germany
National Folklore Festival, Mamaia, Romania
"Palio" Medieval-style Horse Race (also August), Siena,
   Italy
Richard Wagner Festival, Bayreuth, West Germany
"Running of the Bulls" Fiesta, Pamplona, Spain
Salzburg Festival of Music, Salzburg, Austria
Summer Festivals of Drama, Dubrovnik and Split, Yugoslavia
U.S. Independence Day Celebration, Rebild, Denmark
"William Tell" Open Air Drama, Interlaken, Switzerland

## AUGUST

August Bullfight Festival, Malaga and San Sebastian,
   Spain
Edinburgh Music Festival, Edinburgh, Scotland
Independence Day Celebration, Jamaica, British West Indies
Indian Independence Day, New Delhi and all India
International Damascus Fair, Damascus, Syria
International Fall Fair, Frankfurt, West Germany
International Music Festival, Lucerne, Switzerland
International Peace Festival, Hiroshima, Japan
International Trade Fair, Izmir, Turkey
Korean Liberation Day, Seoul and all South Korea
Malaysian National Day, Kuala Lumpur and all Malaysia
Nile Flood Festival, Cairo, U.A.R.
Open Air Theatre, Rome and Verona, Italy

## SEPTEMBER

"Autumn in Warsaw" Festival, Warsaw, Poland
Beethoven Festival, Bonn, West Germany
Festival of the Cedars, Ehden, Lebanon

Frankfurt Book Fair, Frankfurt, West Germany
Gondoliers Regatta, Venice, Italy
"Human Chess Game," Marostica, Italy
International Trade Fair, Salonika, Greece
International Wine Fair, Ljubljana, Yugoslavia
Mexican Independence Day, Mexico City and all Mexico
National Day Regatta, Valetta, Malta
New Wine Festival, Daphne, Greece
Oktoberfest Beer Festival, Munich, West Germany
Scandinavian Design Cavalcade, Copenhagen, Denmark
Stockholm Festival of Music, Stockholm, Sweden

## OCTOBER

Arch of Triumph Grand Prix Horse Race, Longchamps, Paris,
   France
"Double Tenth" National Day, Tapei and all Taiwan
Fall Wine Festival, Lugano and Neuchatel, Switzerland
Gastronomical Fair, Dijon, France
"Gran Premio Nacional" Horse Race, Buenos Aires,
   Argentina
Hindu "Dussehra" Fete, Mysore, India
International Automobile Show, Turin, Italy
International Motor Show, London, England
Leif Ericson Discovery Day, Reykjavik, Iceland
New Wine Festival, Neustadt, West Germany
Nineteenth Olympic Games, Mexico City and Acapulco,
   Mexico
Paris International Automobile Show, Paris, France
Scandinavia Design Cavalcade, Helsinki, Stockholm, and
   Oslo
Tunis International Fair, Tunis, Tunisia
Turkish Republic Day, Ankara and all Turkey

## NOVEMBER

Bullfighting Season Opening, Mexico City, Mexico
Cambodian Water Festival, Phnom Penh, Cambodia
Children's Shrine Day (Shicho-go-san), Tokyo and all
   Japan
Festival of Lights (Diwali), New Delhi and all India
Independence Day Celebration, Barbados, British West
   Indies
Independence Day Fiesta, Cartagena, Colombia
Independence Day Horse Race, Panama City, Panama
Invitation Tennis Championships, Bermuda
"Les Trois Glorieuses" Wine Festival, Beaune, France
Macao Grand Prix Auto Race, Macao
Melbourne Cup Horse Race, Melbourne, Australia
Royal Smithfield Livestock Show, London, England
Thai Elephant Roundup, Surin, Thailand

## DECEMBER

Christmas Eve Observance, Church of the Nativity,
   Bethlehem, Israeli-occupied Jordan
Columbus Discovery Day, Haiti
Day of Our Lady of Guadalupe, Mexico City and all
   Mexico
Feast of Lights (Chanukah), Tel Aviv, Israel
Grey Cup Football Classic, Ottawa, Ontario, Canada
King's Birthday Observance, Bangkok and all Thailand
Lord Mayor's Procession, London, England
Mar del Plata Week, Mar del Plata, Argentina
Nobel Prize Ceremonies, Stockholm and Oslo
"Nuts Day" Fair (Battle of the Bulge), Bastogne, Belgium
Opera Season Opening, Milan, Naples, and Rome, Italy
Rizal Commemoration Day, Manila, Philippines
St. Lucia's Day Yuletide Observance, Stockholm and all
   Sweden
St. Nicholas Day Yuletide Observance, The Hague and all
   the Netherlands
Santon Christmas Creche Fair, Marseilles, France
Sydney-Hobart Ocean Yacht Race, Sydney, Australia

## HOW TO OBTAIN A U.S. PASSPORT
Source: Passport Office, U.S. Department of State

A passport may be issued only to a U.S. citizen or to a person owing allegiance to this country. It serves as proof of citizenship when abroad and identifies the bearer as entitled to the protection granted U.S. travelers. Some countries require that visas issued by their consulates be stamped in a passport, but many have eliminated this requirement or issue tourist cards for visitors making a short stay. A U.S. passport is valid for travel to all countries except Albania, Mainland China, Cuba, North Korea, and North Vietnam. A U.S. passport is not required for travel by an American citizen to any territory or waters subject to U.S. jurisdiction, including the Canal Zone.

All passport applications must be executed in person before a Department of State passport agent, or before a clerk of a Federal or state court having naturalization jurisdiction. Documents and personal identification are required.

Applicants for a first passport must submit either an official birth certificate, a baptismal certificate, or a certified copy of a baptismal certificate. When this evidence is unobtainable, census records, affidavits from persons having personal knowledge of applicant's birth, or other secondary proof will be accepted. Proof of this type, however, must be accompanied by a notice from appropriate authorities stating that no birth record exists. All documents establishing citizenship by birth must include the place and date of birth, the seal of office, and the signature of the person before whom they were executed. A naturalized citizen must submit his certificate of naturalization with his application.

If citizenship is acquired through parental naturalization or by birth abroad to U.S. citizens, the citizenship certificate issued by the Immigration and Naturalization Service must be submitted. If unavailable, and the claim is based on birth abroad, the applicant must submit a Department of State Consular Report of Birth or his foreign birth certificate, evidence of the U.S. citizenship of parents, and an affidavit from his parents showing the times and places of residence here and abroad. When citizenship is acquired through parents' naturalization, their naturalization certificates, the applicant's foreign birth certificate, and evidence of admission to the United States for permanent residence are needed. If an applicant has held, or been included in, a previous U.S. passport, it will be accepted as proof of citizenship in applying for a new one.

Documents submitted for required personal identification must bear the signature and physical description or photograph of the applicant. Accepted are: previous U.S. passport; naturalization certificate; driver's license; government, industrial, or business identification. If unable to establish identity by any of these means, the applicant must have a witness who has known him at least two years and who is a citizen.

Two duplicate, front-view, head-and-shoulders photographs, from 2½ to 3 inches square and signed by the applicant, must also be submitted.

Photographs can be black and white or in color, but cannot be black-and-white photographs that have been tinted. They must have been taken within the previous two years and must bear a good likeness. Snapshots and Polaroid or vending-machine prints are unacceptable. When a wife or children are included in the passport, a group photograph is preferred.

Passports, initially good for three years, can be renewed for an additional two years, but never are valid for more than five years from date of issue. Renewal applications, together with the passport and $5 renewal fee, can be submitted in person or by mail to any Passport Office. If expiration occurs while abroad, it may be renewed by a U.S. consular officer. The old passport is returned with the renewed one. The fee for a new passport, including execution, is $10. If the application is executed before a state Clerk of Court the fee is $11.

On request of the holder, a passport can be amended to show a married name, to correct the description, or to add or exclude a spouse or children. A person can be included in or removed from a passport only once. An Application for Amendment of Passport form is required and must be executed before a Clerk of Court or passport agent.

Loss of a valid passport is serious and should be reported immediately to the Passport Office, U.S. State Department, in Washington or, if lost while abroad, to the nearest U.S. consulate. Deliberate mutilation or alteration of a passport is forbidden.

A vaccination certificate proving smallpox immunity, issued within the previous three years, is required for entry into the United States. Great inconvenience and delay on return to this country may be caused by the lack of the necessary inoculation certificate.

---

## DO'S AND DON'TS FOR EVERY TRAVELER
Source: U.S. Department of State

**DO** sign your passport on page two. It is not valid unless signed by the bearer.

**DO** fill in the information required on the inside front cover. In case of accident, it may be necessary to contact next of kin.

**DO** register your passport if you must mail it while abroad.

**DO** check the validity of your passport before you travel.

**DO** check the visa requirements of the countries you plan to visit.

**DON'T** lend your passport for use by anyone or use it as collateral or pledge.

**DON'T** alter or insert any information or entry in the passport.

**DON'T** tamper with the passport picture.

**DON'T** pack your passport in your luggage. When traveling, keep it readily available but safe.

**DON'T** tear or substitute pages in your passport.

# TOURIST DOCUMENTS FOR FOREIGN TRAVEL

**Explanation of Terms Used in the Table:** *Visas* for most countries may be obtained from their consulates, which are located in most major U.S. cities. Visas for Communist countries may be obtained only through their embassies in Washington, D.C. Travel agents will obtain visas and all other necessary documents for their clients. *Tourist card*—obtained from consulates (or travel agents) in lieu of a visa, it is proof that the traveler is a tourist. *Doctor's letter* (*Health certificate*)—from a local physician stating that the traveler has no communicable diseases. This letter should not be confused with the yellow World Health Organization form, which is an inoculation record. *Letter of financial responsibility*—from a local bank stating that the traveler has funds deposited therein. The dollar amount is not generally specified. *Letter of introduction*—proof of identity and of monetary responsibility, usually obtained from a travel agent. *Picture*—a passport-size, front view, head-and-shoulders photograph (2½ to 3 inches square). *Police certificate*—from a local chief of police stating that the traveler has no criminal record. *Proof of citizenship* (*or nationality*)—birth certificate; voter's registration; automobile license; etc.

| COUNTRY | PAPERS |
|---|---|
| AFGHANISTAN | Passport, visa, 3 pictures, no fee, letter of introduction, valid 6 months from date of issue |
| ALGERIA | Passport, visa valid for 3 months, $3.07 fee, 5 pictures |
| ANGOLA | Passport, visa, $3.65 fee |
| ANTIGUA | Proof of citizenship, ticket to leave |
| ARGENTINA | Passport, no visa up to 90 days |
| AUSTRALIA | Passport, visa, no fee, valid up to 4 years, return or onward ticket |
| AUSTRIA | Passport, no visa for 3 months |
| BAHAMAS | Proof of citizenship or some means of identification, ticket to leave |
| BARBADOS | Proof of citizenship, ticket to leave |
| BELGIUM | Passport, no visa for 3 months |
| BERMUDA | Proof of citizenship, ticket to leave |
| BOLIVIA | Passport or tourist card, no fee |
| BRAZIL | Passport, no visa for 3 months, onward ticket |
| BRITISH HONDURAS | Proof of citizenship, ticket to leave |
| BULGARIA | Passport, no visa for stays exceeding 24 hours |
| BURMA | Passport, transit visa valid for 24 hours, 2 pictures, $2.10 fee, or entry visa valid up to 6 months, 7 pictures, $6.30 fee, letter of reference |
| CAMBODIA | Passport, visa, 3 pictures, visa for next country, $4.30 fee, valid 3 months |
| CANADA | Proof of citizenship |
| CEYLON | Passport, no visa for 30 days, ticket to leave |
| CHAD | Passport, visa, 3 pictures, visa for next country, $6.25 fee, round-trip or onward ticket |
| CHILE | Passport, tourist card on arrival, valid 3 months |
| CHINA (Taiwan) | Passport, visa valid for 4 years for multiple entry for stay up to 30 days, return ticket |
| COLOMBIA | Proof of nationality or passport, tourist card, no fee, 2 pictures, valid for 90 days of multiple entry within 4 years, return ticket |
| CONGO (Brazzaville) | Passport, visa, 2 pictures, visa valid 2 days to 2 months, $5 fee |
| CONGO, Dem. Rep. of | Passport, visa, $5 fee, 3 pictures, police certificate, round-trip ticket, letter of financial responsibility |
| COSTA RICA | Passport or proof of nationality, tourist card for 30 days, $2 fee for 30 days, entry to be within 90 days of issue |
| CYPRUS | Passport, no visa up to 3 months |
| CZECHOSLOVAKIA | Passport, visa, $4 fee, 2 pictures |
| DAHOMEY | Passport, visa, 2 pictures, visa for next country, round-trip or onward ticket, police certificate |
| DENMARK | Passport, no visa for 3 months |
| DOMINICAN REPUBLIC | Tourist card, ticket to leave |
| ECUADOR | Passport or proof of nationality, tourist card, $2 fee, valid 90 to 180 days, 2 pictures, proof of trip from transportation company or return ticket |
| EL SALVADOR | Proof of nationality, tourist card valid 90 days from day of issue, $2 fee, entry within 90 days of issue |
| ETHIOPIA | Passport, visa on landing, $4 fee, or visa here, 2 pictures, $3.20 fee |
| FIJI | Passport, no visa up to 4 months, ticket to leave |
| FINLAND | Passport, no visa for 3 months |
| FRANCE | Passport, no visa for 3 months |
| FRENCH GUIANA | Passport, no visa for 3 months |
| GABON | Passport, visa, 3 pictures, $10 fee, visa for next country, round-trip or onward ticket |
| GAMBIA | Passport, visa valid for entry within 6 months, $2.20 fee, ticket to leave |
| GERMANY, EAST | Passport, visa |
| GERMANY, WEST | Passport, no visa |
| GHANA | Passport, visa valid 3 months from date of issue, 3 pictures, $2 fee, letter from transportation company, onward ticket |
| GIBRALTAR | No visa for 30 days |
| GREAT BRITAIN | Passport, no visa |
| GREECE | Passport, no visa for 2 months |
| GUADELOUPE | Proof of citizenship for stay of 10 days or less, or passport and ticket to leave |
| GUATEMALA | Passport or other proof of citizenship, tourist card for 6 months, to be used within 60 days of issue, $3 fee |
| GUINEA | Passport, visa valid for 3 months, $5 fee, 3 pictures, return ticket |
| GUYANA | Proof of citizenship, no visa for up to 90 days |

(continued)

**TOURIST DOCUMENTS FOR FOREIGN TRAVEL** (*continued*)

| COUNTRY | PAPERS |
|---|---|
| HAITI | Passport or proof of citizenship for tourist card issued on arrival, $2 fee, valid for 30 days of multiple entry within 2 years, return ticket |
| HONDURAS | Passport, visa valid for 90 days |
| HONG KONG | Passport, no visa up to 14 days, onward ticket confirmed within 14 days or tourist visa, no fee, 3 pictures, valid for 3 entries within 3 months |
| HUNGARY | Passport, visa, $4.50 fee, 2 pictures |
| ICELAND | Passport, no visa for 3 months |
| INDIA | Passport, $2.10 fee, 3 pictures, valid for 3 entries within 3 months; tourists entering Nepal or Ceylon need double-entry for India |
| INDONESIA | Passport, visa, 3 pictures, valid 30 days, extendable locally for 30 days more, $3.30 fee per person and $2.20 per passport, proof of transportation in and out of country, letter from travel agent that traveler is bona fide tourist, visa valid 6 months from issuance |
| IRAN | Passport, visa, 3 pictures |
| IRAQ | Passport and visa; either transit visa good for 1-week stay, no fee, or visa for longer stay, letter from transportation company listing all countries visited on trip, 2 pictures |
| IRELAND | Passport, no visa |
| ISRAEL | Passport, no visa for 3 months, extendable locally up to 1 year |
| ITALY | Passport, no visa for 3 months |
| JAMAICA | Proof of citizenship, return ticket and sufficient funds |
| JAPAN | Passport, visa, no fee, valid 4 years for multiple entry for stay of 60 days |
| JORDAN | Passport, visa, 1 picture, valid 1 year for multiple entry |
| KENYA | Passport, visa, $3.20 fee, valid for multiple entry for up to 6-month stay, onward ticket |
| KUWAIT | Passport, visa, $2.80 fee, valid for stay of up to 1 month, proof of onward transportation |
| LAOS | Passport, visa valid up to 3 months, $2.50 fee, 3 pictures |
| LEBANON | Passport, visa; either transit visa, $2.50 fee, valid for one entry and stay of up to 15 days, or entrance visa, 1 picture, $5 fee, valid for 2 entries within 6 months |
| LIBERIA | Passport, visa, $2 fee, 2 pictures, police certificate |
| LIBYA | Passport, visa, $2.80 fee, valid 3 months for 30-day stay, 2 pictures |
| LUXEMBOURG | Passport, no visa |
| MACAO | Passport, visa, $3.65 fee |
| MALAGASY REPUBLIC | Passport, visa, 2 pictures, $2.05 fee, letter of recommendation, round-trip or onward ticket |
| MALAYSIA | Passport, no visa |
| MALTA | No visa for 2 months |
| MARTINIQUE | Proof of citizenship for 10 days or less, or passport and ticket to leave |
| MAURITANIA | Passport, visa; either transit visa, valid 3 days, 2 pictures, $2.50 fee, or visa valid up to 3 months, $4.12 fee, 2 pictures, onward ticket |
| MEXICO | Proof of citizenship for tourist card, valid 6 months |
| MONACO | Passport, no visa for 3 months |
| MONGOLIA | Passport, visa, 2 pictures, $9.60 fee, valid for time of trip |
| MOROCCO | Passport, no visa for 3 months |
| MOZAMBIQUE | Passport, visa, $3.65 fee, prior entry authorization required |
| NEPAL | Passport, visa, $1 fee, 2 pictures |
| NETHERLANDS | Passport, no visa for 3 months |
| NETHERLANDS ANTILLES | Proof of citizenship, ticket to leave |
| NEW GUINEA | Passport, visa, 2 pictures, $3.30 fee |
| NEW ZEALAND | Passport, visa, no fee, valid for up to 6 months, round-trip ticket |
| NICARAGUA | Passport, visa for 30 days, no fee, 2 pictures. For U.S.-born citizens, proof of citizenship for tourist card valid up to 60 days, issued by airline |
| NIGER | Passport, visa for stay over 24 hours, 2 pictures, no fee for 1-week stay but fee ranging from $3.15 to $16.50 for stays of up to 1 year, onward ticket |
| NIGERIA | Passport, visa valid for entry within 3 months for stay up to 28 days, $2 fee, round-trip ticket |
| NORWAY | Passport, no visa for 3 months |
| PAKISTAN | Passport, visa, no fee for 2-week transit visa, visa for next country, onward transportation; or tourist visa, no fee, good for multiple entry within 4 years, financial guarantee needed for stays over 14 days |
| PANAMA | Proof of citizenship for tourist card, $2 fee, valid 30 days, extendable 60 days, return ticket |
| PARAGUAY | Passport, no visa up to 3 months |
| PERU | Passport, tourist card from transportation company, $2 fee, valid 90 days, extendable 90 more days, for $6.50 |
| PHILIPPINES | Passport, visa, 1 picture, valid 3 months for stay up to 59 days, transportation and visa for next country, letter from travel agent |
| POLAND | Passport, visa, $4 fee, 4 pictures ($9.90 fee for visit to relatives) |
| PORTUGAL | Passport, no visa for 60 days (visa needed for all overseas possessions, except Madeira, $4.77 fee for single passport) |
| RHODESIA | Passport, visa, onward ticket |
| ROMANIA | Passport, visa, no fee, 2 pictures |
| SAMOA, NEW ZEALAND | Passport, visa, no fee, for stay up to 72 hours |
| SAMOA, AMERICAN | No visa required for 30 days |
| SAUDI ARABIA | Passport, visa, 1 picture, letter from church, $4.44 fee |
| SIERRA LEONE | Passport, visa, $2 fee, 1 picture, valid for entry within 3 months |
| SINGAPORE | No visa required |

| COUNTRY | PAPERS |
|---|---|
| SOMALIA | Passport, visa, $5 fee, 2 pictures |
| SOUTH AFRICA | Passport, visa, no fee |
| SOUTH KOREA | Passport, visa, no fee for stay up to 15 days, extendable locally 15 days more, or visa, no fee for longer stay, air ticket or letter from travel agent confirming purchase of ticket |
| SOUTH VIETNAM | Passport, transit visa, $2.75 fee, valid 3 months for up to 2 weeks, or entry visa, $5.60 fee, 2 pictures, for one-month stay, valid 3 months |
| SOVIET UNION | Passport, visa, no fee, valid for time of trip, 3 pictures |
| SPAIN | Passport, no visa for 6 months |
| SUDAN | Passport, transit visa 3 days, 3 pictures, $1.45 fee; or entry visa valid up to 3 months, 3 pictures, $4.30 fee, bank reference, ticket to leave |
| SURINAM | Passport, no visa for 30 days |
| SWEDEN | Passport, no visa for 3 months |
| SWITZERLAND | Passport, no visa for 3 months |
| SYRIA | Passport, visa, 2 pictures, $2.23 fee, valid 6 months for stay of 3 months |
| TAHITI | Passport, no visa for stay up to 10 days, visa for longer visit, valid 4 months, return ticket |
| TANZANIA | Passport, visa valid for 6 months, 2 pictures, $3.15 fee |
| THAILAND | Passport, no visa |
| TRINIDAD AND TOBAGO | Proof of citizenship for visit up to 6 months, return ticket |
| TUNISIA | Passport, no visa for 4 months |
| TURKEY | Passport, no visa for 3 months |
| UGANDA | Passport, visa, $2.00 fee, valid for multiple entry within 1 year for up to 2-month stay |
| UNITED ARAB REPUBLIC (EGYPT) | Passport, visa, 2 pictures plus $2 contribution to save Nubian monuments |
| UPPER VOLTA | Passport, visa, 2 pictures, no fee |
| URUGUAY | Passport, no visa for 3 months |
| VENEZUELA | Passport or proof of citizenship for tourist card, valid 30 days, 4 pictures, return ticket |
| YEMEN | Passport, visa, 3 pictures, $3.85 fee |
| YUGOSLAVIA | Passport, visa valid 6 months for one-month stay, or visa at border; or 12-entry-and-exit visa, valid 1 year |
| ZAMBIA | Passport, visa, onward ticket |

## IMMUNIZATIONS REQUIRED OR RECOMMENDED FOR FOREIGN TRAVEL
Source: U.S. Public Health Service

Vaccination certificates required by countries are related not only to the health conditions prevailing in the country from which the traveler originally departs, but also to conditions in countries in which he disembarks during his journey. Vaccinations should be obtained several weeks in advance of leaving the United States since it takes time to develop immunity after vaccinations; also, vaccination certificates become valid only at the end of a period that varies from six to twelve days, according to the disease. The only valid documents for proof of vaccination are the International Certificates of Vaccination. Failure to produce these certificates may subject the traveler to great inconvenience.

**Smallpox:** Evidence of vaccination within three years is required by most countries at the time of arrival. The countries of western Europe, under normal conditions, do not have this requirement, but many require a valid certificate if the traveler is arriving from an infected area. A valid certificate is *always* required for entry or re-entry into the United States from countries other than Canada and a few other nearby places. Smallpox is found in Asia and Africa and in parts of South America.

**Yellow Fever:** Travelers who, within six days (nine days for Ceylon, India, and Pakistan) of their arrival in yellow-fever receptive countries, have come from or passed through an area considered as infected with yellow fever by the country of arrival, are required to present a valid certificate of vaccination against yellow fever. The vaccination certificate is valid for six years. Today yellow fever is found in the tropical jungles of the Americas and in Africa.

**Cholera:** Vaccination against cholera is generally required by countries when a traveler has passed through or come from an area in which the disease is present. The vaccination certificate is valid for six months.

**Typhoid and Paratyphoid fever:** Inoculations are recommended for foreign travel as a personal and public health precaution, with an annual booster if the traveler is still in the infected area.

**Tetanus:** Inoculations are recommended as a protection in case of accident in foreign lands. A booster dose should be taken every five years.

**Typhus:** Inoculations are recommended for travelers to eastern Europe, Africa, Asia, the Andean region of South America, and Mexico. A further dose should be taken every 6 to 12 months for those living in the infected area.

**Diphtheria:** Immunization is recommended for all children, 15 years or under, not already immune. Diphtheria is more prevalent in most foreign countries than in the United States.

**Plague:** Immunization is not required by any country for entrance. If, however, a journey is planned to the interior regions of Asia, Africa, or Latin America, immunization is recommended. A booster dose should be taken at three-month intervals when the traveler is remaining in a known plague area.

**Poliomyelitis:** This vaccination is recommended for all international travel.

**Malaria:** Suppressive medication should be initiated before traveling into infected areas, and be continued while in these areas and for several weeks after leaving them.

## CUSTOMS CHARGES
Source: U.S. Commissioner of Customs

Because customs charges are highly complex and voluminous, none of the duty rates listed here should be considered final by the traveler; they serve only as a guide. All per cent charges listed here are on the retail cost of the article ad valorem.

| ARTICLE | DUTY |
|---|---|
| Antiques | |
| Items at least 100 years old when entered...... | none |
| Art | |
| Paintings, drawings, sculptures............... | none |
| Etchings, engravings, woodcuts, original proofs | none |
| Cameras and photographic equipment | |
| Still cameras—over $10 each.................. | 15.0% |
| Motion picture cameras | |
| 8 mm, valued under $50..................... | 15.0% |
| 8 mm, valued over $50..................... | 12.0% |
| Equipment | |
| Light meters............................. | 9.0% |
| Lenses.................................. | 25.0% |
| Flash-lighting apparatus.................. | 11.5% |
| Range finders............................ | 25.0% |
| Leather cases............................ | 20.0% |
| China cups and saucers | |
| Bone.................................... | 35.0% |
| Non-bone, other than tableware............. | 45.0% |
| Tableware............................... | 36–60% |
| Cigarette lighters—pocket.................... | 45.0% |
| Dolls...................................... | 35.0% |
| Foods and delicacies | |
| Candy containing chocolate or cocoa......... | 10–14% |
| Caviar................................... | none |
| Cookies, biscuits, cakes................... | 6.5% |
| Cheese | |
| Swiss.................................... | 16.0% |
| Roquefort................................ | 12–20% |
| Gouda-Edam.............................. | 15.0% |
| Small jewelry articles | |
| Valued not over $1.50 each, of silver........... | 55.0% |
| Valued over $1.50, of silver and other precious metals............................. | 24.0% |
| Gems | |
| Diamonds, cut but not set, not over ½ carat.... | 8.0% |
| Diamonds, cut but not set, over ½ carat....... | 10.0% |
| Lace—shawls, scarfs........................ | 42.5% |
| Leather goods | |
| Belts.................................... | 17.5% |
| Handbags, reptile leather.................... | 17.5% |
| Handbags, other leathers.................... | 20.0% |

| ARTICLE | DUTY |
|---|---|
| Leather goods (cont'd) | |
| Luggage, reptile leather...................... | 17.5% |
| Luggage, other leathers...................... | 20.0% |
| Wallets, key cases, coin purses, reptile leather.. | 14.0% |
| Wallets, key cases, coin purses, other leathers... | 16.0% |
| Pearls | |
| Natural pearls, temporarily strung............. | 3.0% |
| Natural pearls, permanently strung............ | 24.0% |
| Cultured pearls, temporarily strung............ | 5.0% |
| Cultured pearls, permanently strung............ | 55.0% |
| Phonograph records............................ | 10.0% |
| Radios...................................... | 12.5% |
| Tablecloths and napkins, not ornamented | |
| Damask, cotton............................ | 17.5% |
| Damask, other vegetable fibers............... | 10.0% |
| Television sets............................... | 10.0% |
| Toys........................................ | 35.0% |

### Customs Charges on Alcoholic Beverages

Up to one quart (or one gallon from the Virgin Islands) of alcoholic beverages per adult may be brought into the United States free of duty and internal revenue tax. Any amount in excess of this limitation is subject to the following duties and Internal Revenue taxes per gallon:

| BEVERAGE | INTERNAL REVENUE TAX | DUTY |
|---|---|---|
| Brandy.................. | $10.50 | $1.25 to $5.00 |
| Gin....................... | 10.50 | $1.00 |
| Liqueurs.................. | 10.50 | $1.00 |
| Rum...................... | 10.50 | $1.75 |
| Whiskey | | |
| Scotch.................. | 10.50 | $1.02 |
| Irish................... | 10.50 | $1.02 |
| Other................... | 10.50 | $1.25 |
| Wine | | |
| Sparkling............... | $2.40 to $3.40 | $1.50 |
| Still................... | $.17 to $2.25 | $.37½ to $1.00 |

## CUSTOMS HINTS FOR U.S. TOURISTS
Source: U.S. Commissioner of Customs

**Customs exemptions:** With few exceptions, returning U.S. residents are granted a $100 exemption after a stay abroad of at least 48 hours. This means you may bring back articles valued up to $100 (retail price) free of duty (subject to the limitations on liquor and cigars) if they are for your personal use and are properly declared at Customs. If you are returning from the U.S. Virgin Islands, America Samoa, or Guam, you may receive a customs exemption of $200, based on the fair retail value of the articles in the country where acquired, provided that not more than $100 of this exemption is applied to merchandise obtained elsewhere than in these islands. The U.S. Virgin Islands are also excepted from the 48-hour minimum time requirement.

**Liquor and cigars:** Not more than one quart of alcoholic beverages (for each person 21 years of age or older) nor more than 100 cigars may be included in your exemption. Additional quantities may be imported but will be subject to duties and internal revenue taxes. There is no limitation on the number of cigarettes for your personal use.

**Articles in excess of your exemption:** You may import articles in excess of your exemption, but you will be required to pay duty on any article not entitled to free entry.

**Time limit:** A period of 30 days must elapse after the use of the exemption, in whole or in part, before it may be claimed again. Otherwise, you may bring with you into the United States free of duty and tax articles totaling $10 or less.

**Customs declaration forms:** You must declare all articles acquired abroad. In addition to articles for your personal use, you must declare (1) any article you are bringing home for another person at his request, (2) any article you intend to sell or use in your business, and (3) any alterations or repairs to articles taken abroad.

**Oral declaration permissible in some cases:** At Canadian or Mexican border ports you may make your declaration orally if: (1) you are entitled to the $100 exemption and the total value of all articles you acquired abroad (including alterations and repairs) is not more than $100 and all articles are exempt from duty; (2) all articles are for your personal or household use and not for sale; and (3) no more than one quart of alcoholic beverages nor more than 100 cigars are included.

**Family declaration:** The head of a family may make a joint declaration for all members residing in the same household and returning with him to the United States as a group. For example, a family of four may jointly bring in articles free of duty valued up to $400 on one declaration, and it does not matter if the articles acquired by one member of the family exceed his $100 exemption. With the exception of the restriction on alcoholic beverages, children are entitled to the same exemption as adults when they are returning to the United States.

**Value of articles brought back:** You must declare the prices actually paid. If you cannot furnish dependable information, Customs may assign its own value. To declare the wrong price may cause delay as well as the assessment of penalties. If the article was not purchased, declare the fair value in the country of origin.

**Articles sent home:** Merchandise acquired abroad may be sent home by you or by the store where purchased. However, it cannot be included within your exemption. Packages may be sent home by mail, express, or freight. Mail shipments are more convenient and less costly because they arrive in your home post office. Packages shipped home by express or freight before you return (with no prior arrangement in the United States for acceptance by a broker or agent) will be placed in storage by Customs after five days. This storage is at the expense and risk of the owner. If the articles are not claimed within one year (either by the owner or his agent), they will be sold. Packages shipped by mail before you return will be held by the post office for 30 days and, if not claimed, will then be returned to the sender as being undeliverable.

**Personal belongings sent home:** Personal belongings taken abroad, such as worn clothing, may be sent home by mail before you return and receive free entry if a statement is enclosed in the package explaining the articles were taken out of the United States as personal effects and are being returned without having been altered or repaired while abroad.

**Household effects:** Furniture, carpets, dishes, linens, books, pictures, and other similar household furnishings may be imported into the United States free of duty if: (1) they are not imported for another person; (2) they are not imported for sale; and (3) they have been used by the resident for at least one year, or were used abroad not less than one year by a family of which the importer was a resident member for not less than one year during such period of use.

**Gifts:** Gifts accompanying you at the time of your return are considered for your personal use and may be included within your exemption—both those given you by others before you left, and those you intend to give to others after you arrive. While abroad you may send gifts valued at $10 or less to persons in the United States without payment of duty and taxes. You may send as many gifts as you desire, provided the total value of gift packages or shipments received by one person in one day does not exceed $10. Write GIFT ENCLOSED and the value in large letters on the outside of the package. Alcoholic beverages and tobacco products are not included in this privilege, nor are perfumes valued at more than $1.

**Automobiles, boats, airplanes:** Automobiles, boats, planes, or other vehicles taken abroad for noncommercial use may be returned duty free by proving to the Customs officer they were taken out of the United States.

**Certificate of registration:** Foreign-made articles are dutiable upon each importation into the United States unless entitled to free entry as personal or household effects taken by you out of the United States and returned. If you believe you will have difficulty proving that you took abroad any valuable article of foreign manufacture, such as a camera or watch, you may register it at any customhouse before you leave the United States.

**Prohibited and restricted articles:** When a law prohibits entry of an article into the United States, the Customs officer cannot permit you to have it. Examples are narcotics, drugs containing narcotics, obscene articles and publications, and lottery tickets.

**Fruits, vegetables, plants, and meat:** The U.S. Department of Agriculture is responsible for preventing the entry of injurious insect pests and plant diseases into this country from foreign lands. The Bureau of Customs cooperates with the Department of Agriculture in enforcing special regulations affecting the importation of fruits, vegetables, plants, and plant products.

**Pets:** The entry of pets (cats, dogs, monkeys, and psittacine birds such as parakeets and parrots) is subject to the regulations of the U.S. Public Health Service.

**Merchandise prohibited by foreign assets control regulations:** The importation as well as the purchase abroad of all goods originating in Mainland China, North Korea, or North Vietnam is prohibited without a U.S. Treasury Department license. In addition, the importation of all goods of Cuban origin or containing Cuban components is likewise prohibited. Licenses are generally not available to be used for tourist purchases.

**Gold coins:** The Treasury Department prohibits the importation of gold bullion or gold coins except under license. Gold-coin jewelry is restricted and may be imported only if it meets certain requirements. Gold-coin jewelry and gold coins taken out of the United States cannot be returned without special authorization.

## AIRLINE DISTANCES BETWEEN PRINCIPAL CITIES OF THE WORLD
Source: USAF Aeronautical Chart and Information Center

| | Bangkok | Berlin | Cairo | Capetown | Caracas | Chicago | Hong Kong | Honolulu | Istanbul | Lima | London | Madrid | Melbourne |
|---|---|---|---|---|---|---|---|---|---|---|---|---|---|
| Accra, Ghana | 6,849 | 3,330 | 2,672 | 2,974 | 4,576 | 5,836 | 7,614 | 10,052 | 3,038 | 5,420 | 3,169 | 2,412 | 9,325 |
| Amsterdam, Netherlands | 5,707 | 360 | 2,014 | 5,997 | 4,882 | 4,117 | 5,772 | 7,253 | 1,372 | 6,537 | 222 | 921 | 10,286 |
| Anchorage, Alaska | 6,022 | 4,544 | 6,116 | 10,478 | 5,353 | 2,858 | 5,072 | 2,778 | 5,387 | 6,385 | 4,490 | 5,181 | 7,728 |
| Athens, Greece | 4,929 | 1,121 | 670 | 4,957 | 5,814 | 5,447 | 5,316 | 8,353 | 351 | 7,312 | 1,488 | 1,474 | 9,296 |
| Auckland, New Zealand | 4,644 | 9,994 | 8,825 | 6,573 | 9,619 | 9,507 | 4,625 | 5,346 | 9,202 | 7,989 | 10,569 | 10,883 | 159 |
| Baghdad, Iraq | 3,756 | 2,029 | 797 | 4,924 | 7,019 | 6,430 | 4,259 | 8,399 | 1,006 | 8,487 | 2,546 | 2,675 | 8,104 |
| Bangkok, Thailand | 4,271 | 5,351 | 4,521 | 6,300 | 10,558 | 8,568 | 1,076 | 6,610 | 4,648 | 12,240 | 5,929 | 6,333 | 4,579 |
| Beirut, Lebanon | 5,072 | 1,689 | 340 | 4,793 | 6,519 | 6,096 | 4,756 | 8,536 | 614 | 7,971 | 2,150 | 2,190 | 8,579 |
| Belgrade, Yugoslavia | 5,351 | 623 | 1,147 | 5,418 | 5,586 | 4,999 | 5,326 | 7,881 | 499 | 7,169 | 1,053 | 1,262 | 9,578 |
| Berlin, Germany | 1,869 | — | 1,760 | 5,958 | 5,241 | 4,414 | 5,443 | 7,322 | 1,075 | 6,893 | 580 | 1,162 | 9,928 |
| Bombay, India | 10,490 | 3,914 | 2,716 | 5,102 | 9,034 | 8,065 | 2,679 | 8,035 | 2,999 | 10,389 | 4,478 | 4,689 | 6,101 |
| Buenos Aires, Argentina | 4,521 | 7,394 | 7,360 | 4,284 | 3,155 | 5,582 | 11,477 | 7,553 | 7,608 | 1,945 | 6,907 | 6,235 | 7,218 |
| Cairo, Egypt | 6,300 | 1,767 | — | 4,510 | 6,336 | 6,116 | 5,056 | 8,817 | 740 | 7,725 | 2,158 | 2,069 | 8,700 |
| Capetown, South Africa | 10,558 | 5,958 | 4,510 | — | 6,360 | 8,489 | 7,376 | 11,534 | 5,203 | 6,073 | 5,988 | 5,305 | 6,428 |
| Caracas, Venezuela | 8,568 | 5,241 | 6,336 | 6,360 | — | 2,500 | 10,170 | 6,023 | 6,049 | 1,699 | 4,662 | 4,351 | 9,702 |
| Chicago, Illinois | 5,360 | 4,414 | 6,116 | 8,489 | 2,500 | — | 7,797 | 4,255 | 5,484 | 3,771 | 3,960 | 4,191 | 9,666 |
| Copenhagen, Denmark | 8,409 | 222 | 1,963 | 6,179 | 5,214 | 4,262 | 5,391 | 7,100 | 1,251 | 6,886 | 595 | 1,289 | 9,935 |
| Denver, Colorado | 5,304 | 5,092 | 6,846 | 9,330 | 3,078 | 919 | 7,475 | 3,346 | 6,164 | 3,986 | 4,701 | 5,028 | 8,755 |
| Frankfort, West Germany | 4,903 | 49 | 1,729 | 5,943 | 5,289 | 4,460 | 5,402 | 7,340 | 1,031 | 6,939 | 628 | 1,193 | 9,881 |
| Helsinki, Finland | 1,050 | 689 | 2,068 | 6,490 | 5,658 | 4,442 | 4,867 | 6,818 | 1,330 | 7,348 | 1,134 | 1,835 | 9,447 |
| Hong Kong | 1,102 | 5,443 | 5,056 | 7,376 | 10,170 | 7,797 | — | 5,557 | 4,989 | 11,415 | 5,986 | 6,555 | 4,604 |
| Honolulu, Hawaii | 1,076 | 7,322 | 8,817 | 11,534 | 6,023 | 4,255 | 5,557 | — | 8,117 | 5,943 | 7,241 | 7,873 | 5,501 |
| Houston, Texas | 6,610 | 5,337 | 7,004 | 8,607 | 2,261 | 941 | 8,348 | 3,902 | 6,400 | 3,122 | 4,860 | 5,013 | 8,978 |
| Istanbul, Turkey | 9,260 | 1,075 | 740 | 5,203 | 6,049 | 5,484 | 4,988 | 8,117 | — | 7,593 | 1,551 | 1,701 | 9,100 |
| Karachi, Pakistan | 4,648 | 3,364 | 2,221 | 5,153 | 8,501 | 7,563 | 2,976 | 8,059 | 2,456 | 9,943 | 3,928 | 4,151 | 6,646 |
| Keflavik, Iceland | 2,305 | 1,505 | 3,267 | 7,107 | 4,269 | 2,941 | 6,044 | 6,085 | 2,577 | 5,964 | 1,187 | 1,802 | 10,552 |
| Leningrad, U.S.S.R. | 4,718 | 825 | 2,033 | 6,500 | 5,842 | 4,589 | 4,687 | 6,816 | 1,305 | 7,533 | 1,307 | 1,985 | 9,263 |
| Léopoldville, Congo | 5,974 | 3,915 | 2,617 | 2,046 | 5,752 | 7,085 | 6,903 | 11,178 | 3,240 | 6,322 | 3,951 | 3,305 | 8,111 |
| Lima, Peru | 12,240 | 6,893 | 7,725 | 6,073 | 1,699 | 3,771 | 11,415 | 5,943 | 7,593 | — | 6,316 | 5,907 | 8,051 |
| Lisbon, Portugal | 6,650 | 1,441 | 2,351 | 5,301 | 4,040 | 4,000 | 6,861 | 7,834 | 2,015 | 5,590 | 988 | 317 | 11,049 |
| London, England | 5,929 | 580 | 2,158 | 5,988 | 4,662 | 3,960 | 5,986 | 7,241 | 1,550 | 6,316 | — | 785 | 10,507 |
| Madrid, Spain | 6,333 | 1,162 | 2,068 | 5,305 | 4,351 | 4,191 | 6,555 | 7,873 | 1,701 | 5,907 | 785 | — | 10,765 |
| Melbourne, Australia | 4,579 | 9,928 | 8,700 | 6,428 | 9,702 | 9,666 | 4,604 | 5,501 | 9,100 | 8,051 | 10,507 | 10,765 | — |
| Mexico City, Mexico | 9,792 | 6,054 | 7,676 | 8,515 | 2,234 | 1,688 | 8,789 | 3,790 | 7,106 | 2,635 | 5,557 | 5,642 | 8,420 |
| Montreal, Canada | 8,337 | 3,740 | 5,403 | 7,920 | 2,443 | 746 | 7,735 | 4,919 | 4,797 | 3,966 | 3,256 | 3,449 | 10,390 |
| Moscow, U.S.S.R. | 4,393 | 1,001 | 1,769 | 6,276 | 6,176 | 4,984 | 4,442 | 7,049 | 1,087 | 7,854 | 1,556 | 2,139 | 8,965 |
| Nairobi, Kenya | 4,480 | 3,947 | 2,217 | 2,543 | 7,179 | 8,012 | 5,446 | 10,739 | 2,957 | 7,821 | 4,229 | 3,839 | 7,159 |
| New Delhi, India | 1,811 | 3,598 | 2,752 | 5,769 | 8,836 | 7,485 | 2,339 | 7,413 | 2,837 | 10,429 | 4,177 | 4,527 | 6,339 |
| New York, New York | 8,668 | 3,979 | 5,597 | 7,800 | 2,124 | 714 | 8,061 | 4,969 | 5,022 | 3,634 | 3,472 | 3,595 | 10,352 |
| Oslo, Norway | 5,394 | 522 | 2,242 | 6,477 | 5,167 | 4,050 | 5,342 | 6,800 | 1,517 | 6,856 | 717 | 1,485 | 9,934 |
| Panama City, Panama | 10,870 | 5,856 | 7,117 | 7,020 | 867 | 2,321 | 10,089 | 5,254 | 6,756 | 1,453 | 5,284 | 5,080 | 9,026 |
| Paris, France | 5,876 | 549 | 1,972 | 5,781 | 4,735 | 4,144 | 5,991 | 7,452 | 1,400 | 6,366 | 214 | 652 | 10,441 |
| Peking, China | 2,026 | 4,600 | 4,686 | 8,034 | 8,977 | 6,624 | 1,195 | 5,084 | 4,407 | 10,365 | 5,088 | 5,759 | 5,632 |
| Rabat, Morocco | 6,651 | 1,623 | 2,230 | 4,954 | 4,110 | 4,281 | 6,954 | 8,177 | 2,007 | 5,589 | 1,253 | 473 | 10,856 |
| Rio de Janeiro, Brazil | 9,987 | 6,206 | 6,152 | 3,772 | 2,804 | 5,288 | 11,001 | 8,294 | 6,378 | 2,351 | 5,751 | 5,044 | 8,217 |
| Rome, Italy | 5,492 | 735 | 1,304 | 5,230 | 5,198 | 4,822 | 5,773 | 8,039 | 852 | 6,748 | 892 | 848 | 9,940 |
| Saigon, South Vietnam | 466 | 5,770 | 4,986 | 6,534 | 10,905 | 8,695 | 937 | 6,302 | 5,101 | 12,179 | 6,345 | 6,779 | 4,168 |
| San Francisco, California | 7,929 | 5,673 | 7,436 | 10,247 | 3,907 | 1,860 | 6,903 | 2,396 | 6,711 | 4,515 | 5,369 | 5,805 | 7,850 |
| Santiago, Chile | 10,967 | 7,771 | 7,967 | 4,946 | 3,032 | 5,294 | 11,614 | 6,860 | 8,135 | 1,527 | 7,240 | 6,638 | 7,016 |
| Seattle, Washington | 7,454 | 5,059 | 6,809 | 10,205 | 4,095 | 1,736 | 6,480 | 2,681 | 6,076 | 4,961 | 4,798 | 5,302 | 8,176 |
| Shanghai, China | 1,796 | 5,230 | 5,187 | 8,061 | 9,508 | 7,070 | 760 | 4,947 | 4,975 | 10,665 | 5,727 | 6,386 | 4,990 |
| Shannon, Ireland | 6,255 | 939 | 2,534 | 6,187 | 4,303 | 3,582 | 6,245 | 7,006 | 1,937 | 5,991 | 387 | 884 | 10,825 |
| Singapore | 887 | 6,167 | 5,142 | 6,006 | 11,408 | 9,375 | 1,607 | 6,728 | 5,378 | 11,688 | 6,747 | 7,079 | 3,766 |
| St. Louis, Missouri | 8,762 | 4,675 | 6,369 | 8,549 | 2,414 | 264 | 7,949 | 4,133 | 5,744 | 3,588 | 4,215 | 4,425 | 9,475 |
| Stockholm, Sweden | 5,141 | 505 | 2,084 | 6,422 | 5,422 | 4,287 | 5,114 | 6,873 | 1,346 | 7,108 | 891 | 1,612 | 9,693 |
| Teheran, Iran | 3,391 | 2,183 | 1,220 | 5,240 | 7,322 | 6,501 | 3,844 | 8,072 | 1,273 | 8,850 | 2,739 | 2,974 | 7,837 |
| Tokyo, Japan | 2,864 | 5,556 | 5,937 | 9,154 | 8,812 | 6,312 | 1,791 | 3,860 | 5,573 | 9,628 | 5,955 | 6,703 | 5,069 |
| Vienna, Austria | 5,252 | 323 | 1,454 | 5,655 | 5,373 | 4,696 | 5,431 | 7,632 | 791 | 6,989 | 766 | 1,124 | 9,802 |
| Warsaw, Poland | 5,032 | 321 | 1,588 | 5,933 | 5,562 | 4,679 | 5,146 | 7,367 | 857 | 7,212 | 901 | 1,424 | 9,608 |
| Washington, D.C. | 8,806 | 4,181 | 5,799 | 7,891 | 2,051 | 598 | 8,156 | 4,839 | 5,225 | 3,503 | 3,675 | 3,793 | 10,174 |

| Mexico City | Montreal | Moscow | Nairobi | New Delhi | New York | Paris | Peking | Rio de Janeiro | Rome | San Francisco | Singapore | Stockholm | Teheran | Tokyo | Vienna | Warsaw |
|---|---|---|---|---|---|---|---|---|---|---|---|---|---|---|---|---|
| 6,677 | 5,145 | 4,037 | 2,603 | 5,278 | 5,125 | 2,987 | 7,358 | 3,500 | 2,624 | 7,687 | 7,183 | 3,834 | 3,874 | 8,594 | 3,100 | 3,440 |
| 5,735 | 3,425 | 4,336 | 4,136 | 3,958 | 3,653 | 270 | 4,890 | 5,937 | 807 | 5,465 | 6,526 | 700 | 2,532 | 5,787 | 581 | 681 |
| 3,776 | 3,132 | 4,364 | 8,286 | 5,708 | 3,373 | 4,697 | 3,997 | 8,145 | 5,263 | 2,004 | 6,677 | 4,101 | 5,654 | 3,462 | 4,855 | 4,600 |
| 4,736 | 8,579 | 1,387 | 2,827 | 3,120 | 4,937 | 1,305 | 4,756 | 6,029 | 654 | 6,792 | 5,628 | 1,498 | 1,538 | 5,924 | 800 | 995 |
| 10,231 | 9,578 | 9,017 | 7,315 | 6,419 | 10,193 | 10,519 | 5,626 | 8,259 | 10,048 | 7,691 | 3,847 | 9,731 | 7,934 | 5,016 | 9,886 | 9,676 |
| 5,768 | 9,928 | 1,583 | 2,430 | 1,966 | 6,007 | 2,404 | 3,925 | 6,938 | 1,836 | 7,466 | 4,427 | 2,164 | 431 | 5,199 | 1,780 | 1,751 |
| 8,337 | 8,337 | 4,393 | 4,480 | 1,811 | 8,668 | 5,876 | 2,026 | 9,987 | 5,493 | 7,929 | 887 | 5,141 | 3,391 | 2,864 | 5,252 | 5,032 |
| 7,707 | 5,404 | 1,513 | 2,419 | 2,479 | 5,621 | 1,986 | 4,352 | 6,478 | 1,368 | 7,301 | 4,935 | 1,930 | 913 | 5,598 | 1,401 | 1,459 |
| 6,610 | 4,305 | 1,065 | 3,328 | 3,270 | 4,525 | 901 | 4,633 | 6,145 | 448 | 6,296 | 5,832 | 1,010 | 1,741 | 5,720 | 308 | 515 |
| 6,054 | 3,740 | 1,001 | 3,947 | 3,598 | 3,979 | 549 | 4,600 | 6,206 | 735 | 5,673 | 6,167 | 505 | 2,183 | 5,556 | 323 | 321 |
| 9,738 | 7,524 | 3,132 | 2,811 | 722 | 7,811 | 4,366 | 2,953 | 8,334 | 3,845 | 8,406 | 2,426 | 3,879 | 1,743 | 4,195 | 3,724 | 3,601 |
| 4,579 | 5,597 | 8,369 | 6,478 | 9,822 | 5,279 | 6,857 | 11,994 | 1,230 | 6,925 | 6,454 | 9,870 | 7,798 | 8,565 | 11,410 | 7,333 | 7,655 |
| 7,676 | 5,403 | 1,769 | 2,217 | 2,752 | 5,597 | 1,972 | 4,686 | 6,152 | 1,304 | 7,436 | 5,142 | 2,084 | 1,220 | 5,937 | 1,454 | 1,588 |
| 8,515 | 7,920 | 6,276 | 2,543 | 5,769 | 7,800 | 5,781 | 8,034 | 3,772 | 5,230 | 10,247 | 6,006 | 6,422 | 5,240 | 9,154 | 5,655 | 5,933 |
| 2,234 | 2,443 | 6,176 | 7,179 | 8,837 | 2,124 | 4,735 | 8,977 | 2,804 | 5,198 | 3,907 | 11,408 | 5,422 | 7,322 | 8,812 | 5,373 | 5,562 |
| 1,688 | 746 | 4,984 | 8,012 | 7,485 | 714 | 4,144 | 6,624 | 5,288 | 4,822 | 1,860 | 9,375 | 4,287 | 6,501 | 6,312 | 4,696 | 4,679 |
| 5,918 | 3,605 | 970 | 4,156 | 3,639 | 3,857 | 642 | 4,503 | 6,321 | 952 | 5,473 | 6,195 | 325 | 2,286 | 5,414 | 539 | 417 |
| 1,438 | 1,638 | 5,501 | 8,867 | 7,730 | 1,631 | 4,899 | 6,385 | 5,865 | 5,587 | 552 | 9,079 | 4,878 | 7,033 | 5,814 | 5,395 | 5,321 |
| 6,101 | 3,787 | 961 | 3,914 | 3,550 | 4,027 | 589 | 4,567 | 6,236 | 728 | 5,709 | 6,119 | 502 | 2,134 | 5,533 | 295 | 273 |
| 6,126 | 3,844 | 554 | 4,282 | 3,247 | 4,125 | 1,191 | 3,955 | 6,871 | 1,369 | 5,435 | 5,759 | 248 | 2,062 | 4,872 | 895 | 568 |
| 8,789 | 7,735 | 4,442 | 5,446 | 2,339 | 8,061 | 5,991 | 1,195 | 11,001 | 5,773 | 6,903 | 1,607 | 5,114 | 3,844 | 1,791 | 5,431 | 5,146 |
| 3,790 | 4,919 | 7,049 | 10,739 | 7,413 | 4,968 | 7,452 | 5,084 | 8,294 | 8,039 | 2,396 | 6,728 | 6,873 | 8,072 | 3,860 | 7,632 | 7,367 |
| 749 | 1,604 | 5,925 | 8,745 | 8,387 | 1,418 | 5,035 | 7,243 | 5,015 | 5,701 | 1,647 | 9,953 | 5,226 | 7,441 | 6,684 | 5,609 | 5,609 |
| 7,106 | 4,797 | 1,087 | 2,957 | 2,837 | 5,022 | 1,400 | 4,407 | 6,378 | 852 | 6,711 | 5,378 | 1,346 | 1,273 | 5,573 | 791 | 857 |
| 9,248 | 6,996 | 2,600 | 2,707 | 677 | 7,277 | 3,817 | 3,020 | 8,082 | 3,305 | 8,077 | 2,941 | 3,340 | 1,193 | 4,312 | 3,175 | 3,052 |
| 4,614 | 2,317 | 2,082 | 5,404 | 4,749 | 2,597 | 1,401 | 4,951 | 6,090 | 2,067 | 4,196 | 7,181 | 1,351 | 3,568 | 5,496 | 1,812 | 1,744 |
| 6,275 | 4,005 | 395 | 4,233 | 3,069 | 4,290 | 1,350 | 3,789 | 7,028 | 1,460 | 5,523 | 5,575 | 430 | 1,925 | 4,732 | 985 | 641 |
| 7,915 | 6,377 | 4,327 | 1,505 | 4,692 | 6,377 | 3,742 | 7,002 | 4,104 | 3,185 | 8,919 | 6,131 | 4,388 | 3,611 | 8,307 | 3,618 | 3,910 |
| 2,635 | 3,966 | 7,854 | 7,821 | 10,429 | 3,634 | 6,366 | 10,365 | 2,351 | 6,748 | 4,515 | 11,688 | 7,109 | 8,850 | 9,628 | 6,989 | 7,212 |
| 5,935 | 3,255 | 2,433 | 4,012 | 4,844 | 3,377 | 904 | 6,040 | 4,777 | 1,162 | 5,678 | 7,393 | 1,862 | 3,288 | 6,943 | 1,432 | 1,720 |
| 5,557 | 3,256 | 1,556 | 4,229 | 4,177 | 3,472 | 214 | 5,088 | 5,751 | 892 | 5,369 | 6,747 | 891 | 2,739 | 5,955 | 766 | 901 |
| 5,642 | 3,449 | 2,139 | 3,839 | 4,527 | 3,595 | 652 | 5,759 | 5,044 | 848 | 5,805 | 7,079 | 1,612 | 2,974 | 6,703 | 1,124 | 1,424 |
| 8,420 | 10,390 | 8,965 | 7,159 | 6,339 | 10,352 | 10,441 | 5,632 | 8,217 | 9,940 | 7,850 | 3,766 | 9,693 | 7,837 | 5,069 | 9,802 | 9,608 |
| — | 2,314 | 6,670 | 9,217 | 9,118 | 2,086 | 5,723 | 7,771 | 4,769 | 6,373 | 1,889 | 10,330 | 5,964 | 8,181 | 7,035 | 6,315 | 6,334 |
| 2,314 | — | 4,396 | 7,266 | 7,012 | 332 | 3,432 | 6,541 | 5,082 | 4,102 | 2,544 | 9,206 | 3,666 | 5,879 | 6,470 | 4,006 | 4,021 |
| 6,670 | 4,396 | — | 3,928 | 2,702 | 4,679 | 1,549 | 3,627 | 7,162 | 1,477 | 5,883 | 5,236 | 764 | 1,534 | 4,663 | 1,039 | 715 |
| 9,217 | 7,266 | 3,928 | — | 3,371 | 7,365 | 4,019 | 5,720 | 5,555 | 3,339 | 9,597 | 4,635 | 4,299 | 2,709 | 6,996 | 3,625 | 3,800 |
| 9,118 | 7,012 | 2,702 | 3,371 | — | 7,319 | 4,102 | 2,349 | 8,746 | 3,684 | 7,690 | 2,573 | 3,466 | 1,583 | 3,637 | 3,466 | 3,277 |
| 2,086 | 332 | 4,679 | 7,365 | 7,319 | — | 3,637 | 6,866 | 4,805 | 4,293 | 2,573 | 9,538 | 3,938 | 6,140 | 6,756 | 4,232 | 4,270 |
| 5,722 | 3,418 | 1,023 | 4,445 | 3,725 | 3,686 | 837 | 4,394 | 6,462 | 1,248 | 5,195 | 6,249 | 260 | 2,461 | 5,238 | 839 | 661 |
| 1,496 | 2,542 | 6,719 | 8,042 | 9,422 | 2,212 | 5,388 | 8,939 | 3,296 | 5,916 | 3,326 | 11,692 | 5,956 | 8,011 | 8,441 | 6,031 | 6,174 |
| 5,723 | 3,432 | 1,549 | 4,019 | 4,102 | 3,637 | — | 5,137 | 5,680 | 688 | 5,578 | 6,675 | 963 | 2,624 | 6,053 | 643 | 853 |
| 7,771 | 6,541 | 3,627 | 5,720 | 2,349 | 6,866 | 5,137 | — | 10,777 | 5,075 | 5,934 | 2,753 | 4,197 | 3,496 | 1,305 | 4,663 | 4,340 |
| 5,611 | 3,536 | 2,579 | 3,733 | 4,840 | 3,636 | 1,125 | 6,205 | 4,588 | 1,183 | 5,994 | 7,348 | 2,084 | 3,262 | 7,174 | 1,545 | 1,866 |
| 4,769 | 5,082 | 7,162 | 5,555 | 8,746 | 4,805 | 5,680 | 10,777 | — | 5,704 | 6,621 | 9,775 | 6,637 | 7,367 | 11,534 | 6,123 | 6,453 |
| 6,373 | 4,102 | 1,477 | 3,339 | 3,683 | 4,293 | 688 | 5,075 | 5,704 | — | 6,258 | 6,231 | 1,229 | 2,126 | 6,139 | 476 | 819 |
| 9,717 | 8,557 | 4,797 | 4,873 | 2,268 | 8,888 | 6,303 | 2,072 | 10,290 | 5,942 | 7,829 | 682 | 5,534 | 3,850 | 2,688 | 5,686 | 5,453 |
| 1,889 | 2,544 | 5,883 | 9,597 | 7,690 | 2,573 | 5,578 | 5,934 | 6,621 | 6,258 | — | 8,449 | 5,371 | 7,362 | 5,148 | 5,992 | 5,854 |
| 4,093 | 5,436 | 8,769 | 7,180 | 10,518 | 5,106 | 7,223 | 11,859 | 1,820 | 7,390 | 5,925 | 10,189 | 8,120 | 9,185 | 10,711 | 7,760 | 8,059 |
| 2,339 | 2,288 | 5,217 | 9,005 | 7,046 | 2,408 | 5,011 | 5,431 | 6,889 | 5,679 | 679 | 8,074 | 4,731 | 6,685 | 4,792 | 5,381 | 5,221 |
| 8,032 | 7,066 | 4,248 | 5,950 | 2,646 | 7,384 | 5,771 | 644 | 11,339 | 5,679 | 6,149 | 2,362 | 4,836 | 3,973 | 1,096 | 5,280 | 4,963 |
| 5,171 | 2,873 | 1,863 | 4,563 | 4,529 | 3,086 | 562 | 5,288 | 5,596 | 1,247 | 5,040 | 7,089 | 1,135 | 3,117 | 6,063 | 1,152 | 1,257 |
| 10,330 | 9,206 | 5,236 | 4,635 | 2,573 | 9,538 | 6,675 | 2,753 | 10,777 | 6,231 | 8,449 | — | 5,992 | 4,105 | 3,303 | 6,039 | 5,846 |
| 1,425 | 977 | 5,248 | 8,230 | 7,736 | 877 | 4,397 | 6,791 | 5,217 | 5,073 | 1,744 | 9,544 | 4,551 | 6,766 | 6,407 | 4,955 | 4,942 |
| 5,964 | 3,666 | 764 | 4,299 | 3,466 | 3,938 | 963 | 4,197 | 6,637 | 1,229 | 5,371 | 5,992 | — | 2,217 | 5,091 | 771 | 503 |
| 8,181 | 5,879 | 1,534 | 2,709 | 1,583 | 6,140 | 2,624 | 3,496 | 7,367 | 2,126 | 7,362 | 4,105 | 2,217 | — | 4,774 | 1,982 | 1,877 |
| 7,035 | 6,470 | 4,663 | 6,996 | 3,637 | 6,756 | 6,053 | 1,305 | 11,534 | 6,139 | 5,148 | 3,303 | 5,091 | 4,774 | — | 5,688 | 5,346 |
| 6,315 | 4,006 | 1,039 | 3,625 | 3,466 | 4,232 | 643 | 4,663 | 6,123 | 476 | 5,992 | 6,039 | 771 | 1,982 | 5,688 | — | 346 |
| 6,334 | 4,021 | 715 | 3,800 | 3,277 | 4,270 | 853 | 4,340 | 6,453 | 819 | 5,854 | 5,846 | 503 | 1,877 | 5,346 | 346 | — |
| 1,883 | 489 | 4,872 | 7,550 | 7,500 | 203 | 3,840 | 6,964 | 4,782 | 4,495 | 2,444 | 9,666 | 4,134 | 6,339 | 6,791 | 4,435 | 4,471 |

# DOMESTIC TRAVEL

## TRAVEL CALENDAR: 1968

Beauty pageants and dog-sled contests . . . summer festivals and winter carnivals . . . rodeos, 500-mile automobile races, and a national marbles tournament: tourists in America can see all these and more this year. For exact dates of the year's highlights summarized in the following listing, consult your travel agent or state tourist office.

### JANUARY
**Rose Bowl Parade and Football Game,** Pasadena, Calif.
**Orange Bowl Festival and Football Game,** Miami, Fla.
**Sugar Bowl Festival and Football Game,** New Orleans, La.
**Cotton Bowl Festival and Football Game,** Dallas, Texas.
**Mummers Parade,** Philadelphia, Penn.
**Three Kings Festival,** San Juan, Puerto Rico, and St. Thomas, Virgin Islands.
**Greek Cross Day,** Tarpon Springs, Fla.
**Narcissus Festival and Chinese New Year,** Honolulu, Hawaii.
**Stephen Foster Week,** White Springs, Fla.

### FEBRUARY
**Fur Rendezvous and Sled Dog Races,** Anchorage, Alaska.
**Parada del Sol,** Scottsdale, Ariz.
**Anglo-American Pancake Race,** Liberal, Kans. (with Olney, England).
**Mardi Gras Carnival,** New Orleans, La., Biloxi, Miss., and Mobile, Ala.
**Dartmouth Winter Carnival,** Hanover, N.H.
**Gasparilla Pirate Carnival,** Tampa, Fla.
**National Boat Show,** New York, N.Y.
**National Date Festival,** Indio, Calif.
**Edison Pageant of Light,** Fort Myers, Fla.
**International Beauty Pageant,** Long Beach, Calif.
**World Sled Dog Championship,** Laconia, N.H.
**North American Winter Festival,** Lake Placid, N.Y.
**Daytona "500" Auto Race,** Daytona Beach, Fla.

### MARCH
**Hernando De Soto Day,** Bradentown, Fla.
**Old Homes Pilgrimage,** Natchez and Vicksburg, Mississippi

**St. Patrick's Day Celebration,** New York, N.Y., and Boston, Mass.
**Historic Homes Tour,** Charleston, S.C.
**Open Surfing Championship,** San Juan, Puerto Rico.
**National Orange Show,** San Bernadino, Calif.
**Old Island Days,** Key West, Fla.
**Island Shrimp Festival,** Fort Myers, Fla.
**Home and Garden Tour,** Savannah, Ga.
**Transfer Day,** St. Thomas, Virgin Islands.
**Spring Fiesta,** New Orleans, La.
**Championship Rodeo,** Phoenix, Ariz.

### APRIL
**Dogwood and Arts Festival,** Knoxville, Tenn.
**Holiday in Dixie,** Shreveport, La.
**South Carolina Spring Festival,** Columbia, S.C.
**Spring Wildflower Pilgrimage,** Gatlinburg, Tenn.
**National Cherry Blossom Festival,** Washington, D.C.
**Easter Sunday Promenade,** Atlantic City, N.J.
**Easter Sunrise Services,** Grand Canyon, Ariz., and Hollywood Bowl, Los Angeles, Calif.
**White House Easter Monday Egg Roll,** Washington, D.C.
**North Carolina Azalea Festival,** Wilmington, N.C.
**Masters Golf Tournament,** Augusta, Ga.
**National Championship Stock Car Race,** Atlanta, Ga.
**Patriots' Day,** Boston and Concord, Mass.
**Oklahoma '89ers Day,** Guthrie, Okla.
**Virginia Garden Week,** Richmond and all Va.
**National Trout Festival,** Kalkaska, Mich.
**Grand Prix Auto Endurance Race,** W. Palm Beach, Fla.
**Daffodil Festival,** Tacoma, Wash.
**Festival of States,** St. Petersburg, Fla.
**Hemisfair Exposition Opening,** San Antonio, Texas.
**Kentucky Derby Festival,** Louisville, Ky.
**Shenandoah Apple Blossom Festival,** Winchester, Va.
**Flag Day,** Pago Pago, American Samoa.

### MAY
**Kentucky Derby,** Churchill Downs, Louisville, Ky.
**Apple Blossom Festival,** Wenatchee, Wash.
**Preakness Horse Race,** Pimlico, Baltimore, Md.
**Indianapolis "500" Festival and Auto Race,** Indianapolis, Ind.
**Pablo Casals Music Festival,** San Juan, Puerto Rico.
**Lei Day Celebration,** Honolulu, Hawaii.
**Cotton Carnival,** Memphis, Tenn.
**Jumping Frog Jubilee,** Angels Camp, Calif.
**Helldorado and Rodeo,** Las Vegas, Nev.
**Tulip Time Festival,** Pella, Iowa, and Holland, Mich.
**Miss U.S.A. Beauty Pageant,** Miami Beach, Fla.
**Mountain Laurel Festival,** Pineville, Ky.
**Golden Spike Railroad Ceremony,** Promontory, Utah.

### JUNE
**American Shakespeare Festival,** Stratford, Conn.
**Fiesta of Five Flags,** Pensacola, Fla.
**Sun Fun Festival,** Myrtle Beach, S.C.
**National Musical Camp,** Interlochen, Mich.

The Tournament of Roses, Pasadena, California

King Kamehameha Day Pageant, Honolulu, Hawaii.
National Marbles Tournament, Wildwood, N.J.
"Unto These Hills" Outdoor Drama, Cherokee, N.C.
Summer Jubilee, Washington, D.C.
Nebraskaland Days, Lincoln, Neb.
Yale-Harvard Crew Race, New London, Conn.
Berkshire Music Festival, Lenox, Mass.
Belmont Stakes Horserace, Aqueduct, New York, N.Y.
"Custer's Last Stand" Outdoor Drama, Hardin, Mont.
"The Common Glory" Outdoor Drama, Williamsburg, Va.
Jazz Festival, Newport, R.I.
Rose Festival, Portland, Oreg.
"The Lost Colony" Outdoor Drama, Manteo, N.C.
Aspen Music Festival, Aspen, Colo.
Black Hills Passion Play, Spearfish, S. Dak.
Blessing of the Fleet, Provincetown and Gloucester, Mass.
P. T. Barnum Festival, Bridgeport, Conn.
Old Milwaukee Days and Circus Parade, Milwaukee, Wis.
"Legend of Daniel Boone" Drama, Harrodsburg, Ky.
Midnight Sun Festival, Nome, Alaska.
Pawnee Indian Powwow, Pawnee, Okla.
National Old Time Fiddlers Contest, Weiser, Idaho.
"Cross and Sword" Outdoor Drama, St. Augustine, Fla.
June Week, Naval Academy, Annapolis, Md.
"Honey in the Rock" Outdoor Drama, Beckley, W. Va.
Old Time Whalers Festival, Sag Harbor, N.Y.
"Singing on the Mountain" Songfest, Linville, N.C.
Delmarva Chicken Festival, Dover, Del.

## JULY
Pennsylvania Dutch Folk Festival, Kutztown, Pa.
Aquatennial Show, Minneapolis, Minn.
Log-Rolling and Lumberjack Championship, Hayward, Wis.
Southwest All-Indian Powwow, Flagstaff, Ariz.
American Indian Exposition, Anadarko, Okla.
Cheyenne Frontier Days, Cheyenne, Wyo.
Tom Sawyer Days, Hannibal, Mo.
Miss Universe Pageant, Miami Beach, Fla.
Old Windjammer Days, Boothbay Harbor, Maine.
World Championship Hydroplane Races, Detroit, Mich.
Utah Days of '47 Pageant, Salt Lake City, Utah.
Wild Pony Round-up, Chincoteague, Va.
Pike's Peak Auto Climb, Colorado Springs, Colo.
Music at the Vineyards, Saratoga, Calif.
Old Homes Tour, Litchfield, Conn.
National Cherry Festival, Traverse City, Mich.
Yachting Race Week, Marblehead, Mass.
Thoroughbred Racing Meet, Saratoga Springs, N.Y.
Liberation Day, Island of Guam.
Golden Days Celebration, Fairbanks, Alaska.
All-Indian Rodeo, Browning, Mont.
"Teddy Roosevelt Rides Again" Drama, Medora, N. Dak.
Frontier Days, Prescott, Ariz.
Timber Carnival, Albany, Oreg.

## AUGUST
All-American Soap-Box Derby, Akron, Ohio.
"Abe Lincoln in Illinois" Drama, New Salem, Ill.
Hambletonian Harness Race, Du Quoin, Ill.
Inter-Tribal Indian Ceremonial, Gallup, N. Mex.
Old Spanish Days Fiesta, Santa Barbara, Calif.
Gold Rush Days of '76, Deadwood, S. Dak.
Deep Sea Fishing Rodeo, Mobile, Ala.
Hula Festival, Honolulu, Hawaii.
Beautiful Baby Parade, Ocean City, N.J.
Little League World Series, Williamsport, Penn.
Maryland Clam Festival, Annapolis, Md.
Classic Car Exhibition, Cypress Gardens, Fla.

Pennsylvania Dutch Days, Hershey, Penn.
Days in Spain Festival, St. Augustine, Fla.
All-American Indian Days, Sheridan, Wyo.
Outdoor Art Festival, Mystic, Conn.
Shrimp Festival, Morgan City, La.
College All-Star Football Game, Chicago, Ill.
Schweizer Fest, Tell City, Ind.
Camel Races, Virginia City, Nev.
Mormon Pageant, Palmyra, N.Y.

## SEPTEMBER
Miss America Pageant, Atlantic City, N.J.
Tennessee Walking Horse Contest, Shelbyville, Tenn.
Pendleton Rodeo Roundup, Pendleton, Oreg.
Monterey Jazz Festival, Monterey, Calif.
"Wilhelm Tell" Outdoor Drama, New Glarus, Wis.
Midwest Oldtimers Reunion, Mt. Pleasant, Iowa.
President's Cup Regatta, Washington, D.C.
Atlantic Tuna Tournament, Galilee, R.I.
Old Car Festival, Dearborn, Mich.
Fall Foliage Festival, North Adams, Mass.
Striped Bass Derby, Martha's Vineyard, Mass.
Cherokee Strip Celebration, Perry, Okla.
Ak-Sar-Ben Championship Rodeo, Omaha, Nebr.
Oldtimers Sourdough Celebration, Skagway, Alaska.
Fiesta de Santa Fe, Santa Fe, N. Mex.
Ohio Swiss Festival, Sugarcreek, Ohio.

## OCTOBER
National Tobacco Festival, Richmond, Va.
Cherokee Indian Fair, Cherokee, N.C.
Aloha Week, Honolulu, Hawaii.
Alaska Day Festival, Sitka and all Alaska.
Oktoberfest, La Crosse, Wis.
Pumpkin Show, Circleville, Ohio.
Ozark Folk Festival, Eureka Springs, Ark.
National "500" Auto Race, Charlotte, N.C.
United Nations Day, New York, N.Y. and worldwide.
Grand Prix Auto Race, Watkins Glen, N.Y.
Fall Foliage Festival, Bennington, Vt. and Warner, N.H.
Grape Harvest Festival, Naples, N.Y.
National Horse Show, Madison Sq. Garden, N.Y.
Veiled Prophet Parade, St. Louis, Mo.

## NOVEMBER
Pilgrims Progress Thanksgiving Pageant, Plymouth, Mass.
Thanksgiving Day Parades, New York, N.Y., and Philadelphia, Penn.
Death Valley Encampment, Death Valley, Calif.
Carolinas Carousel Parade, Charlotte, N.C.
International Horse Race, Laurel, Md.
Veterans Day Ceremony, Arlington Cemetery, Washington, D.C.
Swamp Buggy Derby, Naples, Fla.
Army-Navy Football Game, Philadelphia, Penn.
International Livestock Exposition, Chicago, Ill.

## DECEMBER
Pearl Harbor Commemoration Day, Honolulu, Hawaii.
Wright Brothers Day, Kitty Hawk, N.C.
International Surfing Championship, Makaha Beach, Honolulu, Hawaii.
Southwestern Sun Carnival, El Paso, Texas.
Christmas Water Pageant, Long Beach, Calif.
Old Christmas Festivities, Williamsburg, Va.
"Light of the World" Christmas Pageant, Minden, Neb.
National Christmas Pageant, Washington, D.C.
Los Posadas Christmas Observance, Tucson, Ariz.

## U.S. PRESIDENTIAL HOMES
Source: American Automobile Association

### GEORGE WASHINGTON

*George Washington Birthplace National Monument,* 38 miles east of Fredericksburg, Virginia. Open 8 A.M. to 5 P.M. daily. Admission: 25¢.
Washington was born here in 1732. The estate, called Wakefield, has no original buildings, but the reconstruction has been done to period.
*Mount Vernon,* 16 miles south of Washington, D.C. Open 9 A.M. to 5 P.M. daily, March–September; 9 A.M. to 4 P.M. daily, October–February. Adults: 75¢; children under 12 free, if with adult.
Washington lived on this spacious estate in Virginia most of his life. Many relics, including the bed in which he died, are on display. He and his wife, Martha, are buried here.

### JOHN ADAMS AND JOHN QUINCY ADAMS

*John Adams House,* 133 Franklin Street, Quincy, Massachusetts. Open 10 A.M. to 5 P.M. Tuesday–Sunday, April 19–September 30. Adults: 30¢; children: 15¢.
The 2nd President, John Adams, was born here. The house, built in 1681, has many family relics.
*John Quincy Adams House,* 141 Franklin Street, Quincy, has the same hours and fees as the John Adams House. Combination ticket for both houses: adults, 50¢; children, 25¢.
It is the birthplace of John Quincy Adams, the 6th President.
*Adams National Historic Site,* 135 Adams Street, Quincy. Open 9 A.M. to 5 P.M. daily, April 19–November 10. Adults: 50¢; children under 16 free, if with adult.
Four generations of the Adams family, including two Presidents, lived here from 1788 to 1927. Original furnishings are still in the house.

### THOMAS JEFFERSON

*Monticello,* three miles from Charlottesville, Virginia. Open 8–5 daily. Admission: $1.
Built by Jefferson, it was his home for 54 years. Its beauty and elegant furnishings make it one of the most impressive estates in Virginia.

### JAMES MADISON

*Montpelier,* five miles west of Orange, Virginia, is not open to the public, but the graves of James and Dolley Madison, situated on the estate, may be visited.

### JAMES MONROE

*Ash Lawn,* five miles southeast of Charlottesville, Virginia. Open 7 A.M. to 7 P.M. daily. Admission: 75¢.
Designed and built for Monroe by Thomas Jefferson, it is well restored and furnished.

### ANDREW JACKSON

*The Hermitage,* 13 miles east of Nashville, Tennessee. Open 8 A.M. to 5 P.M. daily, April–September; 8–4 daily, October–March; closed Christmas. Adults: 75¢; children under 12, 25¢.
The furnishings and fixtures are in place as Jackson left them. He and Rachel Jackson are buried in the garden.

### MARTIN VAN BUREN

*Lindenwald,* 2½ miles south of Kinderhook, New York. Privately owned; it may be seen by appointment only.
Built in 1797, it was Van Buren's residence.

### WILLIAM HENRY HARRISON AND BENJAMIN HARRISON

*Berkeley,* 6½ miles west of Charles City, Virginia. Open Monday–Saturday 8 A.M. to 5 P.M.; Sundays 9–5. Adults: $1.25; children, 60¢.
This outstanding plantation, home of two Presidents, has been restored and furnished.

### JOHN TYLER

*Sherwood Forest,* 4½ miles east of Charles City, Virginia. Open 9 A.M. to 5 P.M. Monday–Saturday. Adults: $1; children under 12, 60¢.
An enormous house with fine interiors.

### ZACHARY TAYLOR

*Baton Rouge, Louisiana.* A marker on the grounds of the State Capitol shows the site of Taylor's home from 1840 to 1848.

### FRANKLIN PIERCE

*Franklin Pierce Homestead,* northwest of Hillsboro, New Hampshire. Open 9:30 A.M. to 5 P.M. daily, May–October. Admission: 50¢.
Built in 1804, it has unusual stenciled and papered walls and period furniture.

### JAMES BUCHANAN

*Wheatland,* 1½ miles west of Lancaster, Pennsylvania, on Marietta Avenue. Open 9 A.M. to 4:30 P.M. Monday–Saturday; 10 A.M. to 4:30 P.M. Sundays; March 15–November 30. Adults: 75¢; children under 12, free.
Home of the 15th President.

### ABRAHAM LINCOLN

*Abraham Lincoln Birthplace National Historic Site,* three miles south of Hodgenville, Kentucky. Open 8 A.M. to 4:45 P.M. daily, September–May; 8 A.M. to 6:45 P.M. daily, June–August; closed Christmas. Free.
The log cabin where Lincoln was born is enshrined in a granite memorial on part of his father's original farm.
*Lincoln Home,* 8th and Jackson Streets, Springfield, Illinois. Open 9 A.M. to 6 P.M. daily, late April to late October; 9 A.M. to 5 P.M. daily at other times. Closed some holidays. Free.
The only house Lincoln ever owned, it has many original furnishings.

### ANDREW JOHNSON

*Andrew Johnson National Historic Site,* Greenville, Tennessee. Open 9–5, November–April; 8–5, May–October.
The site includes the tailor shop where Johnson worked, his restored home, and his grave.

### ULYSSES S. GRANT

*Grant's Cottage,* Mount McGregor, New York. Open 9 A.M. to 5 P.M. Monday–Saturday; 1
(continued)

## PRESIDENTIAL HOMES (continued)

P.M. to 5 P.M. Sundays. Closed some holidays. The cottage where Grant died in near-poverty has some of his clothing and other furnishings. *Grant's Birthplace,* Point Pleasant, Ohio. Open 9:30 A.M. to 5 P.M. Tuesday–Sunday, April through October. Adults: 15¢; children: 10¢. The house where Grant was born has been carefully restored.

### RUTHERFORD B. HAYES

*Hayes State Memorial,* Fremont, Ohio. Open 9 A.M. to 5 P.M. Monday–Saturday; 1:30 P.M. to 5 P.M. Sundays and holidays. Free. The home is closed to the public, but the memorial building has family mementos.

### JAMES A. GARFIELD

*Lawnfield,* Mentor, Ohio. Open 9 A.M. to 5 P.M. Tuesday–Saturday; 1 P.M. to 5 P.M. Sundays and holidays; May–October. Adults: 50¢; children: 15¢. The house has many personal belongings and books. Garfield's campaign office and a replica of his birthplace are also on the grounds.

### GROVER CLEVELAND

*Grover Cleveland Museum,* Bloomfield Avenue, Caldwell, New Jersey. Open 10 A.M. to 12 noon, 1 P.M. to 5 P.M., Tuesday–Saturday; 2 P.M. to 5 P.M. Sundays. Admission: 25¢. The birthplace of Cleveland is now a museum.

### THEODORE ROOSEVELT

*Theodore Roosevelt Birthplace National Historic Site,* 28 East 20th Street, New York, N.Y. Open 9 A.M. to 4:30 P.M. daily; closed holidays. Adults: 25¢; children under 12, free. Two museum rooms have relics reflecting Roosevelt's varied interests. *Sagamore Hill National Historic Site,* three miles east of Oyster Bay, New York. Open 10 A.M. to 5 P.M. daily. Adults: 50¢; children under 12 free, if with adult. Closed some holidays. This was Roosevelt's home until his death.

### WOODROW WILSON

*Birthplace,* Coalter and Frederick streets, Staunton, Virginia. Open 9–5 daily. Adults: $1; children 10 to 16, 35¢; under 10, free. Now a national shrine, it has period furniture and mementos of the Wilson family.

### WARREN G. HARDING

*President Harding Home and Museum,* 380 Mount Vernon Avenue, Marion, Ohio. Open 10 A.M. to 5:30 P.M. Monday–Saturday; 1 P.M. to 6 P.M. Sundays. Adults: 50¢; children 6–18, 25¢.

### CALVIN COOLIDGE

*Calvin Coolidge Home,* Plymouth, Vermont. Open 9:30 A.M. to 6 P.M. daily, mid-May to mid-October. Adults: 50¢; children under 15 free, if with adult. Coolidge was reared, lived, and took his Presidential oath here. It is kept as it was in 1923.

### HERBERT HOOVER

*Birthplace of Herbert Hoover,* West Branch, Iowa. Open 9 A.M. to 4:30 P.M. Monday–Saturday. Sundays, 10 A.M. to 5 P.M., June 1–September 15; thereafter, 2 P.M. to 5 P.M. through May 31. Closed some holidays. Free. The cottage where Hoover was born and a replica of his father's blacksmith shop are here.

### FRANKLIN D. ROOSEVELT

*Franklin D. Roosevelt National Historic Site,* two miles south of Hyde Park, New York. Open 9 A.M. to 5 P.M. daily, except Christmas. Adults: 50¢; children under 16 free, if with adult. No charge to visit grounds and graves only. The Hudson Valley home of the Roosevelts, where Franklin and Eleanor Roosevelt are buried.

### HARRY S. TRUMAN

*Harry S. Truman Birthplace Memorial Shrine,* Truman Avenue and 11th Street, Lamar, Missouri. Open 10 A.M. to 4 P.M. Tuesday–Saturday; Sundays, 12 noon to 6 P.M., May 30–Labor Day; thereafter, 12 noon to 5 P.M., same days, through May 29. Closed some holidays. The birthplace of former President Truman has been restored and opened to the public.

### DWIGHT D. EISENHOWER

*Birthplace of President Dwight D. Eisenhower,* Lamar Avenue and Day Street, Denison, Texas. Open 8 A.M. to 6:30 P.M. daily, June 1–Labor Day; rest of the year, 10 A.M. to 5 P.M. Tuesday–Sunday. Adults: 25¢; children: 10¢. A two-story frame house, it has been restored as it was at the time of Eisenhower's birth.

### JOHN F. KENNEDY

*Birthplace,* 83 Beales Street, Brookline, Massachusetts. Established by an act of Congress in 1967 as a National Historical Site.

### LYNDON B. JOHNSON

*Boyhood Home,* Johnson City, Texas. Open 10 A.M. to 4 P.M. Fridays, Saturdays, Mondays; noon to 4 P.M. Sundays. The house where President Johnson spent part of his boyhood was opened to the public in 1965.

Sagamore Hill, Theodore Roosevelt's Long Island Home

National Park Service

## THE NATIONAL PARK SYSTEM: 1966

The National Park Service, an agency of the Department of the Interior, is charged by an act of Congress with administering a system of parks and other areas "for the benefit and enjoyment of the people" and with preserving "the scenery and the natural and historic objects and the wildlife therein in such a manner as will leave them unimpaired for the enjoyment of future generations." Areas included in the National Park System are listed below.

| TYPE OF AREA AND STATE | DURATION OF SEASON | ACRES | DESCRIPTION |
|---|---|---|---|
| **National Parks** | — | 13,903,786 | **33 parks in 23 states.** |
| Acadia, Maine | 5/30–10/1 | 41,634 | An unusual combination of mountains, cliffs, ocean surf, and varied natural life. |
| Big Bend, Texas | All year | 708,221 | Spectacular scenery and odd geological forms in the last great wilderness of Texas. |
| Bryce Canyon, Utah | 4/1–10/15 | 36,010 | Colorful and oddly shaped eroded formations. |
| Canyonlands, Utah | All year | 257,640 | Includes high plateaus and low basin lands in a remote and wild area of the Southwest. |
| Carlsbad Caverns, New Mexico | All year | 46,753 | The caverns, in a picturesque semi-desert area, contain huge and magnificent underground chambers. |
| Crater Lake, Oregon | 6/1–9/30 | 160,290 | Includes a deep lake surrounded by high lava cliffs. |
| Everglades, Florida | All year | 1,400,533 | A vast, subtropical wilderness famed for its rare birds, lush flora, and abundant game fish. |
| Glacier, Montana | 6/1–10/15 | 1,013,129 | Beautiful mountains with numerous glaciers and lakes. The Going to the Sun Road has exceptional views. |
| Grand Canyon, Arizona | All year | 673,575 | Its glowing colors, spectacular size, shapes, and geological importance are unequaled anywhere in the world. |
| Grand Teton, Wyoming | 5/1–9/30 | 310,350 | Majestic alpine scenery of a type rare in this country. Glaciers, canyons, and lakes add to its appeal. |
| Great Smoky Mountains— North Carolina and Tennessee | All year | 512,674 | Masses of blooms, vast forests, and recreational facilities make this the most popular park. |
| Guadalupe Mountains, Texas | All year | 77,518 | Contains the most extensive fossil reefs in the world. |
| Haleakala, Hawaii | All year | 26,403 | An inactive volcano on Maui Island, with one of the largest craters on earth. There is a highway to the summit. |
| Hawaii Volcanoes, Hawaii | All year | 220,345 | Two active volcanoes, giant tree-fern growths, rain forests, and rare plants and birds. |
| Hot Springs, Arkansas | All year | 1,035 | A health resort and recreational center in the Ouachita Mountains. |
| Isle Royale, Michigan | 6/15–9/6 | 539,347 | A densely forested island wilderness. It also is a wildlife sanctuary with excellent fishing. |
| Kings Canyon, California | All year | 460,331 | Situated on the western slope of the Sierra Nevada, it includes some of the most beautiful mountain wilderness in America. |
| Lassen Volcanic, California | 6/1–9/30 | 106,934 | This mountainous country was the scene of the most recent volcanic activity on the U.S. mainland, in 1914–21. |
| Mammoth Cave, Kentucky | All year | 51,354 | A series of underground passages and beautiful limestone formations in domed chambers as high as 192 feet. |
| Mesa Verde, Colorado | 4/15–10/15 | 52,074 | The well-preserved cliff dwellings in this large canyon-filled mesa are of great archaeological importance. |
| Mount McKinley, Alaska | 6/1–9/10 | 1,939,493 | More than 3,000 square miles of primitive, breathtaking country, including North America's tallest mountain. |
| Mount Rainier, Washington | All year | 241,983 | Distinctive features are Mount Rainier, huge glaciers, alpine meadows, and wild flower fields. |
| Olympic, Washington | 5/30–9/5 | 896,599 | Known for its abundant wildlife and rain forests, it covers a diverse area from glacier-clad Mount Olympus to the Pacific Ocean. |
| Petrified Forest, Arizona | All year | 94,189 | Petrified trees, millions of years old, the brilliant hues of the Painted Desert, and many fossil formations. |
| Platt, Oklahoma | 5/1–9/30 | 912 | Verdant country, including many waterfalls and mineral springs. |
| Rocky Mountain, Colorado | All year | 262,324 | One of the highest regions in the United States, containing grand mountain scenery, glaciers, cliffs, and gorges. |
| Sequoia, California | All year | 386,863 | Giant Sequoia trees, many varieties of wild life, and towering Mount Whitney are among its many assets. |
| Shenandoah, Virginia | 4/1–10/31 | 212,304 | It extends along the crest of the Blue Ridge Mountains in one of the East's most beautiful and historic regions. |
| Virgin Islands, U.S. Virgin Islands | All year | 15,150 | Submerged offshore lands, beaches, valleys, mountains, unusual forests, and birds are found in this tropical park. |
| Wind Cave, South Dakota | 4/1–10/31 | 28,059 | The cave, underneath a section of the scenic Black Hills, has a variety of unusual crystal formations. |
| Yellowstone—Idaho, Montana, and Wyoming | 5/1–10/31 | 2,221,773 | The first, and largest, national park. It is a broad, elevated |

**NATIONAL PARK SYSTEM** (*continued*)

| TYPE OF AREA AND STATE | SEASON | ACRES | DESCRIPTION |
|---|---|---|---|
| | | | volcanic plateau with mountain peaks and thousands of geysers and steam springs. |
| Yosemite, California......... | All year | 760,951 | An outstanding mountain and valley region on the western slope of the Sierra Nevada. |
| Zion, Utah................. | 4/1–11/30 | 147,035 | Includes Zion Canyon, a spectacular, multicolored gorge, set in a strangely colored dramatic desert and canyon country. |

| TYPE OF AREA AND STATE | ACRES | TYPE OF AREA AND STATE | ACRES |
|---|---|---|---|
| **National Historical Parks**................ | **44,418** | Grand Portage, Minnesota................ | 770.00 |
| Appomattox Court House, Virginia........ | 972.01 | Gran Quivira, New Mexico.............. | 610.94 |
| Chalmette, Louisiana.................... | 135.61 | Great Sand Dunes, Colorado............. | 36,740.32 |
| City of Refuge, Hawaii.................. | 181.85 | Homestead, Nebraska.................... | 162.73 |
| Colonial, Virginia...................... | 9,430.00 | Hovenweep, Utah–Colorado.............. | 505.43 |
| Cumberland Gap, Kentucky–Tennessee– | | Jewel Cave, South Dakota.............. | 1,274.56 |
| Virginia............................ | 20,169.38 | Joshua Tree, California................. | 557,992.42 |
| George Rogers Clark, Indiana........... | 17.00 | Katmai, Alaska....................... | 2,697,590.00 |
| Harpers Ferry, West Virginia–Maryland.... | 1,530.00 | Lava Beds, California.................. | 46,238.69 |
| Independence, Pennsylvania............. | 21.84 | Lehman Caves, Nevada................. | 640.00 |
| Minute Man, Massachusetts............. | 750.00 | Montezuma Castle, Arizona............. | 842.09 |
| Morristown, New Jersey................. | 957.96 | Mound City Group, Ohio............... | 67.50 |
| Nez Perce, Idaho...................... | 3,000.00 | Muir Woods, California................ | 502.90 |
| San Juan Island, Washington........... | 1,751.99 | Natural Bridges, Utah................. | 7,600.00 |
| Saratoga, New York.................... | 5,500.00 | Navajo, Arizona...................... | 360.00 |
| **National Monuments**................. | **9,066,914** | Ocmulgee, Georgia.................... | 683.48 |
| Agate Fossil Beds, Nebraska............ | 2,995.19 | Oregon Caves, Oregon................. | 480.00 |
| Alibates Flint Quarries and Texas | | Organ Pipe Cactus, Arizona............. | 330,874.25 |
| Panhandle Culture, Texas.............. | 500.00 | Pecos, New Mexico.................... | 340.90 |
| Arches, Utah.......................... | 34,009.94 | Perry's Victory, Ohio.................. | 21.44 |
| Aztec Ruins, New Mexico................ | 27.14 | Pinnacles, California.................. | 14,497.77 |
| Badlands, South Dakota................ | 111,529.82 | Pipe Spring, Arizona.................. | 40.00 |
| Bandelier, New Mexico................. | 29,661.20 | Pipestone, Minnesota.................. | 282.58 |
| Black Canyon of the Gunnison, Colorado... | 13,682.62 | Rainbow Bridge, Utah................. | 160.00 |
| Booker T. Washington, Virginia.......... | 217.93 | Russell Cave, Alabama................. | 310.45 |
| Buck Island Reef, Virgin Islands........ | 850.00 | Saguaro, Arizona..................... | 78,644.00 |
| Cabrillo, California..................... | 80.50 | Saint Croix, Maine.................... | 28.30 |
| Canyon de Chelly, Arizona.............. | 83,840.00 | Scotts Bluff, Nebraska................. | 3,084.00 |
| Capitol Reef, Utah..................... | 39,172.63 | Sitka, Alaska......................... | 54.33 |
| Capulin Mountain, New Mexico........... | 775.42 | Statue of Liberty, New York............ | 58.38 |
| Casa Grande Ruins, Arizona............. | 472.50 | Sunset Crater, Arizona................ | 3,040.00 |
| Castillo de San Marcos, Florida......... | 21.58 | Timpanogos Cave, Utah................ | 250.00 |
| Castle Clinton, New York................ | 1.00 | Tonto, Arizona....................... | 1,120.00 |
| Cedar Breaks, Utah.................... | 6,154.60 | Tumacacori, Arizona.................. | 10.15 |
| Chaco Canyon, New Mexico............. | 21,509.40 | Tuzigoot, Arizona.................... | 42.67 |
| Channel Islands, California............. | 18,166.68 | Walnut Canyon, Arizona............... | 1,879.46 |
| Chesapeake and Ohio Canal, | | White Sands, New Mexico.............. | 146,535.34 |
| Maryland–West Virginia............... | 4,477.47 | Wupatki, Arizona.................... | 35,232.84 |
| Chiricahua, Arizona.................... | 10,645.90 | Yucca House, Colorado................ | 9.60 |
| Colorado, Colorado.................... | 17,362.26 | **National Military Parks**.................. | **31,938** |
| Craters of the Moon, Idaho............. | 53,545.05 | Chickamauga and Chattanooga, | |
| Custer Battlefield, Montana............. | 765.34 | Georgia–Tennessee................. | 8,190.39 |
| Death Valley, California–Nevada......... | 1,907,760.00 | Fort Donelson, Tennessee.............. | 600.00 |
| Devils Postpile, California.............. | 798.46 | Fredericksburg, Virginia............... | 3,672.15 |
| Devils Tower, Wyoming................. | 1,346.91 | Gettysburg, Pennsylvania.............. | 3,671.77 |
| Dinosaur, Colorado–Utah................ | 206,233.55 | Guilford Courthouse, North Carolina....... | 224.00 |
| Effigy Mounds, Iowa................... | 1,467.50 | Horseshoe Bend, Alabama.............. | 2,040.00 |
| El Morro, New Mexico.................. | 1,278.72 | Kings Mountain, South Carolina......... | 3,950.00 |
| Fort Frederica, Georgia................ | 250.00 | Moores Creek, North Carolina.......... | 49.68 |
| Fort Jefferson, Florida................. | 47,125.00 | Pea Ridge, Arkansas.................. | 4,283.40 |
| Fort Matanzas, Florida................. | 298.51 | Shiloh, Tennessee.................... | 3,515.46 |
| Fort McHenry, Maryland................ | 43.26 | Vicksburg, Mississippi................. | 1,740.78 |
| Fort Pulaski, Georgia.................. | 5,516.62 | **National Memorial Park** | |
| Fort Sumter, South Carolina............ | 21.15 | Theodore Roosevelt, North Dakota........ | 70,436.00 |
| Fort Union, New Mexico................ | 720.60 | **National Battlefields**...................... | **4,229** |
| George Washington Birthplace, Virginia.... | 393.68 | Big Hole, Montana.................... | 666.00 |
| George Washington Carver, Missouri....... | 210.00 | Fort Necessity, Pennsylvania........... | 500.00 |
| Gila Cliff Dwellings, New Mexico.......... | 533.13 | Petersburg, Virginia.................. | 2,731.00 |
| Glacier Bay, Alaska.................... | 2,274,595.00 | Stones River, Tennessee............... | 330.86 |
| Grand Canyon, Arizona................. | 198,280.00 | | (*continued*) |

**NATIONAL PARK SYSTEM** (*continued*)

| TYPE OF AREA AND STATE | ACRES |
|---|---|
| Tupelo, Mississippi | 1.50 |
| **National Battlefield Parks** | **9,268** |
| Kennesaw Mountain, Georgia | 3,682.62 |
| Manassas, Virginia | 3,108.87 |
| Richmond, Virginia | 746.56 |
| Wilson's Creek, Missouri | 1,730.00 |
| **National Battlefield Sites** | **786** |
| Antietam, Maryland | 783.63 |
| Brices Cross Roads, Mississippi | 1.00 |
| Cowpens, South Carolina | 1.24 |
| **National Historic Sites** | **8,502** |
| Abraham Lincoln Birthplace, Kentucky | 116.50 |
| Adams, Massachusetts | 4.77 |
| Allegheny Portage Railroad, Pennsylvania | 950.00 |
| Andrew Johnson, Tennessee | 16.68 |
| Ansley Wilcox House, New York | 1.00 |
| Bent's Old Fort, Colorado | 178.00 |
| Chicago Portage, Illinois | 91.20 |
| Chimney Rock, Nebraska | 83.36 |
| Christiansted, Virgin Islands | 27.15 |
| Dorchester Heights, Massachusetts | 5.43 |
| Edison, New Jersey | 20.46 |
| Fort Bowie, Arizona | 900.00 |
| Fort Davis, Texas | 460.00 |
| Fort Laramie, Wyoming | 585.63 |
| Fort Larned, Kansas | 750.00 |
| Fort Raleigh, North Carolina | 159.66 |
| Fort Scott, Kansas | 24.00 |
| Fort Smith, Arkansas | 18.58 |
| Fort Union Trading Post, North Dakota–Montana | 380.00 |
| Fort Vancouver, Washington | 90.00 |
| Gloria Dei Church, Pennsylvania | 3.43 |
| Golden Spike, Utah | 1,542.00 |
| Hampton, Maryland | 45.42 |
| Herbert Hoover, Iowa | 200.00 |
| Home of Franklin D. Roosevelt, New York | 187.69 |
| Hopewell Village, Pennsylvania | 848.06 |
| Hubbell Trading Post, Arizona | 156.00 |
| Jamestown, Virginia | 20.63 |
| Jefferson National Expansion Memorial, Missouri | 85.46 |
| John F. Kennedy Birthplace, Massachusetts | 0.09 |
| John Muir, California | 9.00 |
| McLoughlin House, Oregon | 0.63 |
| Sagamore Hill, New York | 85.00 |
| Saint Gaudens, New Hampshire | 86.00 |
| Saint Paul's Church, New York | 6.09 |
| St. Thomas, Virgin Islands | 1.66 |
| Salem Maritime, Massachusetts | 10.73 |
| San Jose Mission, Texas | 4.13 |
| San Juan, Puerto Rico | 37.73 |
| Theodore Roosevelt Birthplace, New York | 0.11 |
| Touro Synagogue, Rhode Island | 0.23 |
| Vanderbilt Mansion, New York | 211.65 |
| Whitman Mission, Washington | 98.15 |
| **National Memorials** | **5,642** |
| Arkansas Post, Arkansas | 220.60 |
| Chamizal, Texas | 55.00 |
| Coronado, Arizona | 2,834.16 |
| Custis–Lee Mansion, Virginia | 3.47 |
| DeSoto, Florida | 30.00 |
| Federal Hall, New York | 0.45 |
| Fort Caroline, Florida | 119.51 |
| Fort Clatsop, Oregon | 124.97 |
| General Grant, New York | 0.76 |
| Hamilton Grange, New York | 0.71 |
| House Where Lincoln Died, District of Columbia | 0.05 |
| Johnstown Flood, Pennsylvania | 55.00 |

| TYPE OF AREA AND STATE | ACRES |
|---|---|
| Lincoln Boyhood, Indiana | 200.00 |
| Lincoln Memorial, District of Columbia | 163.63 |
| Lincoln Museum, District of Columbia | 0.18 |
| Mount Rushmore, South Dakota | 1,278.45 |
| Roger Williams, Rhode Island | 5.00 |
| Thomas Jefferson, District of Columbia | 18.36 |
| Washington Monument, District of Columbia | 106.01 |
| Wright Brothers, North Carolina | 425.40 |
| **National Cemeteries** | **220** |
| Antietam, Maryland | 11.36 |
| Battleground, District of Columbia | 1.03 |
| Fort Donelson, Tennessee | 15.34 |
| Fredericksburg, Virginia | 12.00 |
| Gettysburg, Pennsylvania | 20.58 |
| Poplar Grove, Virginia | 8.72 |
| Shiloh, Tennessee | 10.25 |
| Stones River, Tennessee | 20.09 |
| Vicksburg, Mississippi | 117.85 |
| Yorktown, Virginia | 2.91 |
| **National Seashores** | **345,557** |
| Assateague Island, Maryland–Virginia | 30,182.00 |
| Cape Cod, Massachusetts | 44,600.00 |
| Cape Hatteras, North Carolina | 28,500.00 |
| Cape Lookout, North Carolina | 24,500.00 |
| Fire Island, New York | 19,311.00 |
| Padre Island, Texas | 133,918.23 |
| Point Reyes, California | 64,546.00 |
| **National Capital Parks** | |
| National Capital Parks, Maryland–Virginia–District of Columbia | 7,973.23 |
| **National Parkways** | **125,231** |
| Baltimore–Washington Parkway, Maryland | 2,489.53 |
| Blue Ridge, North Carolina–Virginia | 69,655.68 |
| George Washington Memorial, Virginia–Maryland | 7,057.58 |
| Natchez Trace, Tennessee–Alabama–Mississippi | 45,297.51 |
| Suitland Parkway, Maryland, District of Columbia | 730.58 |
| **White House** | |
| White House, District of Columbia | 18.07 |
| **National Lakeshores** | **75,721** |
| Indiana Dunes, Indiana | 8,721.00 |
| Pictured Rocks, Michigan | 67,000.00 |
| **National Scenic Riverways** | |
| Ozark, Missouri | 85,000.00 |
| **Other Parks** | **25,691** |
| Catoctin Mountain, Maryland | 5,765.60 |
| Piscataway, Maryland | 1,152.00 |
| Prince William Forest, Virginia | 18,638.62 |
| Wolf Trap Farm, Virginia | 135.00 |
| **National Recreation Areas** | **3,666,376** |
| Amistad, Texas | 65,000.00 |
| Arbuckle, Oklahoma | 8,851.00 |
| Bighorn, Wyoming–Montana | 63,300.00 |
| Coulee Dam, Washington | 98,500.00 |
| Curecanti, Colorado | 41,103.00 |
| Delaware Water Gap, Pennsylvania–New Jersey | 46,375.00 |
| Flaming Gorge, Utah–Wyoming | 108,400.00 |
| Glen Canyon, Arizona–Utah | 1,196,545.00 |
| Lake Mead, Arizona–Nevada | 1,936,978.00 |
| Sanford, Texas | 41,097.00 |
| Shadow Mountain, Colorado | 18,240.00 |
| Whiskeytown–Shasta–Trinity, California | 41,987.00 |
| **International Park** | |
| Roosevelt Campobello, New Brunswick, Canada | 10.50 |
| **National Scientific Reserve** | |
| Ice Age, Wisconsin | 32,500.00 |

## CAMPING IN THE NATIONAL PARKS

The National Parks are meant to be used—and more and more Americans are using them every year. In 1966, parks and other areas administered by the National Park Service enjoyed a bumper crop of over 133,000,000 visitors—an all-time record.

Camping is becoming an increasingly popular means of enjoying the scenic wonders and recreational facilities offered by the U.S. Park System. Thanks to lightweight equipment, ready-to-eat foods, and other conveniences available today, camping is no longer synonymous with "roughing it." With a minimum of expense and effort, nearly everyone can now enjoy the special satisfactions of living close to nature, whether it be for a single weekend or an entire summer.

The following table summarizes camping facilities provided in National Parks; for detailed information, write to the Superintendant of the specific park. Many Park System areas besides the parks themselves offer camping facilities. Useful information on all classes of areas is available from the Bureau of Outdoor Recreation, U.S. Department of the Interior, Washington, D.C. 20240.

National Park Service

Yosemite Falls, Yosemite National Park

| NATIONAL PARK | SEASON | LIMIT OF STAY (DAYS) | CAMPGROUND TYPE * | NUMBER OF CAMPSITES | WATER AND FLUSH TOILETS | SANITARY STATION | TRAILS | CAMPFIRE PROGRAM | SWIMMING | BOATING | FISHING | RIDING | SKIING |
|---|---|---|---|---|---|---|---|---|---|---|---|---|---|
| Acadia | May 1–Oct. 15 | 14 | C | 583 | Yes | Yes | Yes | Yes | Yes | Yes | Yes | Yes | No |
| Big Bend | All Year | 15 | A,C | 162 | Yes | Yes | Yes | Yes | No | No | No | Yes | No |
| Bryce Canyon | Easter–Sept. 15 | 14 | A,C | 216 | Yes | No | Yes | Yes | No | No | No | Yes | No |
| Canyon Lands | All Year | 14 | B | 23 | No | No | Yes | Yes | No | No | No | No | No |
| Crater Lake | June 1–Sept. 15 | 14 | A | 290 | Yes | Yes | Yes | Yes | No | No | Yes | No | Yes |
| Everglades | All Year | 14 | A,B | 356 | Yes | Yes | Yes | Yes | Yes | Yes | Yes | No | No |
| Glacier | June 1–Sept. 30 | 14 | A,B | 1,300 | Yes | Yes | Yes | Yes | Yes | Yes | Yes | Yes | No |
| Grand Canyon | All Year | 14 | A,B,C | 513 | Yes | Yes | Yes | Yes | No | No | Yes | Yes | No |
| Grand Teton | May 25–Sept. 10 | 14 | A,B,C | 968 | Yes | Yes | Yes | Yes | Yes | Yes | Yes | Yes | Yes |
| Great Smoky Mountains | All Year | 14 | A,B,C | 1,522 | Yes | Yes | Yes | Yes | No | Yes | Yes | Yes | No |
| Haleakala | All Year | — | A | 5 | Yes | No | Yes | No | No | No | No | No | No |
| Hawaii Volcanos | All Year | — | A,B,C | 27 | No | No | Yes | No | No | No | No | No | No |
| Hot Springs | All Year | 30 | A | 57 | Yes | Yes | Yes | Yes | No | No | No | No | No |
| Isle Royale | May–October | 14 | A,B | 135 | No | No | Yes | Yes | No | Yes | Yes | No | No |
| Kings Canyon | May 1–Oct. 15 | 14 | A | 865 | Yes | No | No | No | No | No | Yes | Yes | No |
| Lassen Volcanic | May 1–Sept. 15 | 14 | A,B | 545 | Yes | Yes | Yes | Yes | Yes | Yes | Yes | Yes | Yes |
| Mammoth Cave | All Year | 14 | A,B,C | 229 | Yes | Yes | Yes | No | Yes | Yes | Yes | No | No |
| Mesa Verde | Apr.–Oct. 1 | 14 | A,C | 492 | Yes | Yes | Yes | Yes | No | No | Yes | Yes | No |
| Mount McKinley | June 1–Sept. 10 | | A,B | 99 | Yes | No | Yes | Yes | No | No | Yes | No | No |
| Mount Ranier | May–October | 14 | A,B,C | 776 | Yes | No | Yes | Yes | No | No | Yes | No | Yes |
| Olympic | All Year | 14 | A | 964 | Yes | Yes | Yes | Yes | Yes | Yes | Yes | No | Yes |
| Platt | All Year | 14 | A | 206 | Yes | Yes | Yes | Yes | No | Yes | Yes | Yes | No |
| Rocky Mountain | All Year | 14 | A,B,C | 1,127 | Yes | Yes | Yes | Yes | No | No | Yes | Yes | Yes |
| Sequoia | All Year | 14 | A,B,C | 848 | Yes | Yes | Yes | Yes | Yes | No | Yes | Yes | Yes |
| Shenandoah | All Year | 14 | A,B | 534 | Yes | Yes | Yes | Yes | No | No | Yes | Yes | No |
| Virgin Islands | All Year | 30 | A,B | 41 | No | No | Yes | Yes | Yes | Yes | Yes | No | No |
| Wind Cave | May 19–Sept. 20 | 14 | A | 100 | Yes | No | No | Yes | No | No | No | No | No |
| Yellow Stone | All Year | 30 | A,B | 2,617 | Yes | Yes | Yes | Yes | No | Yes | Yes | Yes | Yes |
| Yosemite | All Year | 30 | A,B,C | 3,389 | Yes | Yes | Yes | Yes | Yes | Yes | Yes | Yes | Yes |
| Zion | All Year | 14 | A | 485 | Yes | Yes | Yes | Yes | No | No | Yes | Yes | No |

\* Campground types are as follows: Type A—parking space, tent site, fireplace, bench-table; Type B—range from primitive to slightly less than Type A; Type C—for use by organized groups.

# PRIVATE AND COMMERCIAL TRANSPORTATION

## HOW TO STAY ALIVE ON THE HIGHWAY

When Americans take to the highway, they often act like lemmings migrating into the sea. Motor-vehicle deaths in the United States are the leading cause of accidental deaths for all age groups under 75 years.

Although car manufacturers are equipping their new models with safety devices, the burden of avoiding accidents rests with the individual driver. He must adjust his driving to suit the conditions he encounters: for city street, country lane, or superhighway; for sunshine or blizzard; for night or day; and for the season of the year. Above all, the National Safety Council warns, he must drive defensively. That is, he must drive in such a way as to *prevent* accidents by anticipating the wrong actions of other drivers.

Causes of vehicular accidents can be divided into two categories. *Improper driving techniques* includes speeding, failure to yield the right-of-way, passing a stop sign, disregarding a signal, driving left of center, improperly overtaking another car, making an improper turn, and following a car too closely. The second category is the *condition of the driver,* which comprises inattention, drowsiness or falling asleep, drinking, and the influence of drugs such as patent cold remedies, many of which dull the driver's senses.

Traffic accidents can be prevented. Following are some pointers from professional drivers and from the National Safety Council. Knowing what to do in an emergency or, better still, driving so as to prevent emergencies can mean the difference between life and death.

An automobile is a mechanical device that needs care and maintenance. Check it regularly to keep it in excellent condition. If you cannot do it yourself, take your car to a reliable mechanic.

● Make certain that brakes work properly. Have them adjusted regularly and relined when necessary. The brake pedal should not go down too far, and the car should not pull to one side when you stop. Be certain the parking brake holds on an incline.

● Check headlights, taillights, stoplights, and turn signals. Be sure that low beams and high beams on headlights are working.

● Check the entire steering system, not just the steering wheel. If you have power steering, learn what to do if the drive belt breaks or the motor stalls.

● Check wheel balance and tire wear. Make sure you have correct air pressure in your tires and that they have good tread. The smoother the tires, the less skid control.

● Be certain that windows are clean inside as well as out. A filmed windshield and rear window cut visibility to a dangerous degree, particularly at night. Replace windshield wipers if they do not work properly, and provide windshield washer solvent.

● Be certain that seat belts hold properly and that buckles are not damaged. Always fasten your seat belt.

Driving for "two" requires extra concentration, but a good defensive driver will be aware of what other drivers may do.

● Maintain at least one vehicle length between you and the vehicle in front of you for every 10 miles per hour for speeds up to 50. A greater distance is required for speeds over 50, or in poor weather, or under bad road conditions. If the car in front is maintaining the proper following distance, don't pass and cut in.

● When approaching any intersection, marked or unmarked—and whether or not you have the right-of-way—never assume the other driver will yield to you. Take your foot off the gas and be ready to brake.

● If you drink, don't drive. Nearly 50 per cent of all fatal traffic accidents involve a driver who has been drinking.

Tips from professional drivers can make a difference in your driving technique.

● Sit up straight in the driver's seat, four to eight inches from the wheel.

● Lock your doors. If an accident occurs, you are safer inside the car.

● Watch not only the car directly in front, but the car ahead of that one. Trouble can be spotted sooner.

● Dim the instrument-panel lights at night. Glare tires the eyes and reduces vision.

● Keep your car moving, or get it off the road. Never stop on the highway except for stop signs or in prescribed stopping areas. If there are no such areas, always pull your car completely off the road.

● On crowded roads or streets, avoid left turns whenever possible. Turn right—around the block —to go left.

● In a skid, turn the steering wheel in the direction in which the rear end is skidding.

● If you have a blowout, grip the steering wheel firmly so it cannot be wrenched from your hands. Don't jam on the brakes, but take your foot off the gas until the car has slowed down enough to use the brakes safely.

● If you must leave a car with children in it, even for a moment, turn off the engine and remove the ignition keys.

Today's straight, nearly endless superhighways stretching across the nation require certain extra precautions.

● Pick your lane and stay with it. Don't weave in and out.

● Drive within a 25 per cent range of the speed of traffic. If most cars are doing 60, you should not drop below 45. Change speed level every 20 minutes so as not to dull your reactions. At night drive 10 miles per hour slower than during daylight.

● Avoid "highway hypnosis." Take a break after several hours of constant driving.

Remember at all times to obey the law, especially the speed limits. Use caution, common sense, and courtesy.

# FOCUS ON THE NEWS

## A NEW CABINET POST

Wide World

Alan S. Boyd, accompanied by his wife, is sworn in as America's first Secretary of Transportation.

Transportation plays a vital role in the economic growth of America—it accounts for $1 out of every $5 of the gross national product. Yet until the new Cabinet-level Department of Transportation (DOT) was established on October 14, 1966, the United States had no comprehensive transportation policy and no policy-maker who could determine one. Now it has both.

The first Secretary of the new department is Alan Stevenson Boyd, who will have jurisdiction over nearly 100,000 employees—making it the fourth largest department in the executive branch—and a budget of $6 billion. Broadly, his department's goals are faster movement of goods and people, fewer accidents, less congestion, and better cooperation among government groups handling transportation matters.

The DOT comprises 31 formerly separate agencies and bureaus, including the Federal Aviation Agency, Bureau of Public Roads,

Coast Guard, Great Lakes Pilotage Administration, Alaska Railroad, St. Lawrence Seaway, and the transportation offices formerly under the Commerce Department.

Economic regulatory functions will not be performed by the DOT. These will remain with the Interstate Commerce Commission and the Civil Aeronautics Board. However, the department will absorb the functions of the ICC relating to safety laws affecting railroads and motor carriers.

The objectives of the department are: (1) to make transportation more efficient and economical; (2) to improve safety; (3) to foster research that would help technological progress; and (4) to alleviate some of the irritating effects of transportation on the daily lives of Americans. To accomplish the last objective, the DOT must deal with the problems created by 97,000,000 automobiles, 1,500,000 miles of paved roads, and 97,000 aircraft.

## PASSENGER VEHICLE LAWS: 1967

The following table contains the latest information on legislative limits and specifications for driving in all 50 states and in the District of Columbia. In some cases, the minimum driving age is lower if the applicant has completed a driver-education course. A financial responsibility law covering potential liability from bodily injury and property damage is mandatory in most states.

| STATE OR OTHER JURISDICTION | NEW LICENSE PLATES CAN BE USED ON | MINIMUM DRIVING AGE | LICENSE RENEWAL | FINANCIAL RESPONSIBILITY LAW | GASOLINE TAX (per gallon) | HIGHWAY SPEED LIMITS* (miles per hour) |
|---|---|---|---|---|---|---|
| Alabama....... | October 1 | 16 | 2 years | yes | .07 | (a) 60, (b) 70 |
| Alaska........ | February 15 | 16 | 3 years | yes | .08 | (a) 50 |
| Arizona........ | January 2 | 16 | 3 years | yes | .07 | (a) 65 |
| Arkansas...... | January 1 | 14 | annually | yes | .07½ | (a) 60 |
| California...... | January 1 | 16 | 4 years(c) | yes | .07 | (a) 65 |
| Colorado....... | January 1 | 16 | 3 years | yes | .06 | (a) 60 |
| Connecticut.... | (d) | 16 | 2 years | yes | .06 | (a) 70(e) |
| Delaware...... | (f) | 16 | 2 years | yes | .07 | (a) 60 |
| District of Columbia.... | March 1 | 18(g) | 3 years(h) | yes | .07 | (i) |
| Florida........ | February 1 | 16(j) | 2 years | yes | .07 | (a) 65, (b)(k) 70 |
| Georgia........ | January 1 | 16 | 1 or 5 years(l) | yes | .06½ | (a) 60 |
| Hawaii........ | January 3 | 15 | until revoked | yes | .08½ | (a) 45 |
| Idaho......... | December 1 | 16 | 3 years | yes | .06 | (a) 60, (b) 70 |
| Illinois........ | December 1 | 16 | 3 years | yes | .05 | (a) 65 |
| Indiana........ | January 2 | 16½(j) | 2 years | yes | .06 | (a) 65, (b)(k) 70 |
| Iowa.......... | December 1 | 16(j) | 2 years | yes | .07 | (a) 70, (b) 75 |
| Kansas........ | January 1 | 16(j) | 2 years | yes | .05 | (a)(i), (b) 75, (k) 80 |
| Kentucky...... | December 29 | 16 | 2 years | yes | .07 | (a) 60 |
| Louisiana...... | December 1 | 15 | 2 years | yes | .07 | (a) 60–65 |
| Maine........ | December 25 | 15 | 2 years | yes | .07 | (a) 45 |
| Maryland...... | March 1 | 16 | 2 years | yes | .07 | (a) 50 |
| Massachusetts.. | January 1 | 16(j) | 2 years | no | .06½ | (a) 50 |
| Michigan...... | (m) | 16(j) | 3 years | yes | .06 | (a) 65 |
| Minnesota..... | November 15 | 18(j) | 4 years | yes | .06 | (a) 65 |
| Mississippi..... | November 1 | 15 | 1 or 2 years(l) | yes | .07 | (a) 65 |
| Missouri...... | (d) | 16 | 3 years | yes | .05 | (a) 65 |
| Montana....... | (d) | 15 | 2 years | yes | .06 | (i) |
| Nebraska...... | January 1 | 21(j) | 2 years | yes | .07½ | (a) 65, (b) 75 |
| Nevada....... | December 1 | 16 | 5 years | yes | .06 | (i) |
| New Hampshire | March 1 | 16 | 2 years | yes | .07 | (a) 60, (k) 70 |
| New Jersey.... | (d) | 17 | 1 or 3 years(l) | yes | .06 | (a) 50, (k) 60 |
| New Mexico.... | December 15 | 18 | 2 years | yes | .06 | (a) 60 |
| New York...... | January 1 | 18(j) | 3 years | yes | .06 | (a) 50, (k) 65 |
| North Carolina | January 1 | 16 | 4 years(n) | yes | .07¼ | (a) 55–65 |
| North Dakota... | October 20 | 16(j) | 2 years | yes | .06 | (a) 65, (b) 70 |
| Ohio.......... | March 1 | 16 | 3 years | yes | .07 | (a) 60, (b)(k) 70 |
| Oklahoma...... | December 11 | 16 | 2 years | yes | .06½ | (a) 65 |
| Oregon........ | (d) | 16 | 2 years | yes | .06 | (a) 55 |
| Pennsylvania... | March 15 | 16 | 2 years | yes | .07 | (a) 55–60 |
| Rhode Island... | March 1 | 16 | 2 years | no | .07 | (a) 50 |
| South Carolina | September 7 | 16(j) | 4 years | yes | .07 | (a) 60, (b) 70 |
| South Dakota.. | January 1 | 16(j) | 4 years | yes | .06 | (a) 70 |
| Tennessee..... | March 1 | 16 | 2 years | yes | .07 | (a) 65 |
| Texas......... | February 1 | 16(j) | 2 years | yes | .05 | (a) 70 |
| Utah.......... | December 15 | 17(j) | 3 or 5 years | yes | .06 | (o) |
| Vermont....... | January 1 | 18(j) | annually | yes | .06½ | (a) 50 |
| Virginia....... | March 15 | 18(j) | 3 years | yes | .07 | (a) 55, (b) 65 |
| Washington.... | January 2 | 16 | 2 years | yes | .07½ | (a) 60, (b) 70 |
| West Virginia... | June 1 | 16 | 4 years | yes | .07 | (a) 55 |
| Wisconsin...... | (d) | 16 | 2 years | yes | .07 | (a) 65 |
| Wyoming....... | (d) | 16 | 3 years | yes | .05 | (a) 65 |

**EXPLANATION OF FOOTNOTES USED IN TABLE:** (*) Speed limits apply to daytime driving on highways and generally reflect the major statewide rules. (a) Regular highway. (b) Interstate highway. (c) Original license renewable after three years. (d) When issued. (e) Absolute maximum on superhighways, parkways, and expressways. (f) Three months before current registration expires. (g) Mandatory uninsured motorist coverage. (In California, subject to waiver by motorist.) (h) Special tests required for renewal of licenses of drivers over 65. (i) The law requires reasonable and prudent driving. (j) Law includes specific provisions for licensing younger drivers. (k) Turnpike. (l) Optional. (m) Discretion of the secretary of state. (n) Complete re-examination of all drivers for renewal. (o) As posted.

## THE 1967 MOBIL ECONOMY RUN

Each year many different makes and models of American automobiles compete in a coast-to-coast trip to test fuel consumption. Under the sponsorship of Mobil Oil Corporation, the entrants drive along a route similar to that encountered by average car owners, including stretches of expressways, city streets, and country roads. The 1967 run began in Los Angeles, ran through Tahoe, Salt Lake City, Denver, Omaha, and Chicago, and ended in Detroit for a total distance of 2,886 miles. Results of the run are given in the following table.

| | MILES PER GALLON | | MILES PER GALLON | | MILES PER GALLON |
|---|---|---|---|---|---|
| **Compact Six-Cylinder Cars** | | **Low-Price Standard-Size Eight-Cylinder Cars** | | Chevy II 100........... | 20.58 |
| Plymouth Valiant........ | 24.57 | Chevrolet Impala SS.... | 19.29 | Camaro................ | 19.28 |
| Dodge Dart 170......... | 24.30 | Ford Custom 500........ | 19.26 | **Intermediate-Size** | |
| Ford Falcon 170......... | 24.07 | Plymouth Fury II........ | 19.15 | **Six-Cylinder** | |
| Ford Mustang........... | 24.04 | Chevrolet Bel Air....... | 18.65 | **Cars** | |
| Rambler American 220... | 23.37 | **Luxury Cars** | | Mercury Capri.......... | 23.29 |
| Corvair Monza.......... | 22.83 | Chrysler 300............ | 17.59 | Plymouth Belvedere I... | 22.30 |
| Chevy II 100............ | 22.53 | Buick Electra 225....... | 17.00 | Buick Special V6........ | 21.92 |
| Camaro................ | 22.37 | Toronado.............. | 16.48 | Chevelle DIx........... | 21.46 |
| **Intermediate-Size** | | Oldsmobile 98.......... | 15.94 | Oldsmobile F-85........ | 20.04 |
| **Eight-Cylinder Cars** | | Cadillac Calais.......... | 15.62 | **Medium-Price** | |
| Plymouth Belvedere II... | 20.01 | Thunderbird............ | 15.26 | **Standard-Size** | |
| Mercury Caliente....... | 19.81 | **Compact Eight-Cylinder** | | **Eight-Cylinder** | |
| Buick Special V8........ | 19.72 | **Cars** | | **Cars** | |
| Dodge Coronet DIx...... | 18.99 | Plymouth Barracuda..... | 22.32 | Buick Le Sabre 400..... | 18.74 |
| Ford Fairlane 500....... | 18.89 | Dodge Dart............. | 21.13 | Oldsmobile Delmont 88.. | 18.52 |
| Chevrolet Malibu....... | 18.60 | Mercury Cougar......... | 20.99 | Pontiac Catalina........ | 18.19 |
| Oldsmobile Cutlass...... | 17.06 | Ford Mustang 2+2...... | 20.73 | Dodge Polara 318....... | 17.94 |
| | | | | Mercury Monterey....... | 16.68 |

## TRAVEL FATALITY RATES

Automobiles continued in 1966 to be the most dangerous type of transportation, according to figures released by the National Safety Council. The passenger fatality rate per 100 million passenger miles ranged from a high of 2.5 for cars (passenger automobiles and taxis) to a low of 0.09 for planes (domestic scheduled commercial airliners). Figures for buses and for commercial passenger trains are also included in the table below, which covers the years 1945–66, as well as 1936 and 1940.

| YEAR | CARS | BUSES | TRAINS | PLANES |
|---|---|---|---|---|
| 1966 | 2.5 | 0.20 | 0.16 | 0.09 |
| 1965 | 2.4 | 0.16 | 0.07 | 0.38 |
| 1964 | 2.4 | 0.12 | 0.05 | 0.14 |
| 1963 | 2.3 | 0.23 | 0.07 | 0.10 |
| 1962 | 2.3 | 0.11 | 0.14 | 0.30 |
| 1961 | 2.1 | 0.19 | 0.10 | 0.40 |
| 1960 | 2.2 | 0.13 | 0.16 | 1.00 |
| 1959 | 2.3 | 0.21 | 0.05 | 0.70 |
| 1958 | 2.3 | 0.17 | 0.27 | 0.40 |
| 1957 | 2.6 | 0.19 | 0.07 | 0.10 |
| 1956 | 2.7 | 0.16 | 0.20 | 0.60 |
| 1955 | 2.7 | 0.18 | 0.07 | 0.80 |
| 1954 | 2.7 | 0.11 | 0.08 | 0.10 |
| 1953 | 2.9 | 0.18 | 0.16 | 0.60 |
| 1952 | 3.0 | 0.21 | 0.04 | 0.40 |
| 1951 | 3.0 | 0.24 | 0.43 | 1.30 |
| 1950 | 2.9 | 0.18 | 0.58 | 1.10 |
| 1949 | 2.7 | 0.20 | 0.08 | 1.30 |
| 1948 | 2.1 | 0.18 | 0.13 | 1.30 |
| 1947 | 2.3 | 0.21 | 0.16 | 3.20 |
| 1946 | 2.5 | 0.19 | 0.18 | 1.20 |
| 1945 | 2.9 | 0.17 | 0.16 | 2.20 |
| 1940 | 3.5 | — | 0.34 | 3.00 |
| 1936 | 4.5 | — | 0.09 | 10.00 |

REGULATORY SIGNS

STOP YIELD SPEED LIMIT 50 SPEED ZONE AHEAD

NO LEFT TURN | NO U TURN | KEEP → RIGHT | DO NOT ENTER

ONE WAY → | 2 HR PARKING 8:30 AM TO 5:30 PM | WALK ON LEFT FACING TRAFFIC | CROSS ON WALK SIGNAL ONLY

WARNING SIGNS

MERGING TRAFFIC | R R

GUIDE SIGNS

(STATE) US 40 | INTERSTATE STATE 75 | NEWTON 5 MIAMI 27 | 56 SOUTH Metropolis EXIT ½ MI

## U.S. ROAD MILEAGE CHART

Source: American Automobile Association

| | Albuquerque, N. Mex. | Atlanta, Georgia | Bismarck, N. Dak. | Boston, Mass. | Chicago, Illinois | Cleveland, Ohio | Dallas, Texas | Detroit, Michigan | Denver, Colorado | Helena, Montana | Houston, Texas | Las Vegas, Nevada | Los Angeles, Calif. | Memphis, Tennessee |
|---|---|---|---|---|---|---|---|---|---|---|---|---|---|---|
| Albuquerque, N. Mex... | — | 1441 | 1145 | 2399 | 1381 | 1622 | 651 | 1594 | 452 | 1259 | 943 | 585 | 835 | 1039 |
| Atlanta, Ga............ | 1441 | — | 1580 | 1068 | 709 | 723 | 814 | 731 | 1534 | 2221 | 897 | 2026 | 2276 | 403 |
| Baltimore, Md........ | 2003 | 672 | 1565 | 396 | 694 | 360 | 1332 | 518 | 1617 | 2158 | 1405 | 2563 | 2838 | 964 |
| Birmingham, Ala..... | 1286 | 155 | 1551 | 1223 | 663 | 731 | 659 | 759 | 1379 | 2137 | 742 | 1871 | 2121 | 248 |
| Bismarck, N. Dak..... | 1145 | 1580 | — | 1858 | 871 | 1220 | 1352 | 1143 | 793 | 651 | 1595 | 1590 | 1809 | 1303 |
| Boise, Idaho......... | 1289 | 2348 | 1145 | 2730 | 1743 | 2092 | 1637 | 2015 | 907 | 545 | 1933 | 692 | 900 | 2616 |
| Boston, Mass......... | 2399 | 1068 | 1858 | — | 980 | 651 | 1728 | 735 | 2025 | 2486 | 1965 | 2873 | 3162 | 1360 |
| Buffalo, N.Y......... | 1810 | 975 | 1395 | 463 | 524 | 188 | 1427 | 247 | 1562 | 1988 | 1549 | 2410 | 2699 | 958 |
| Charleston, W. Va..... | 1676 | 519 | 1378 | 788 | 487 | 268 | 1154 | 362 | 1372 | 2080 | 1321 | 2261 | 2511 | 637 |
| Charlotte, N.C....... | 1678 | 261 | 1658 | 807 | 785 | 568 | 1015 | 662 | 1707 | 2386 | 1190 | 2263 | 2513 | 639 |
| Cheyenne, Wyo........ | 555 | 1580 | 690 | 1967 | 980 | 1329 | 932 | 1252 | 101 | 704 | 1175 | 906 | 1195 | 1334 |
| Chicago, Ill........ | 1381 | 709 | 871 | 980 | — | 349 | 1006 | 272 | 1038 | 1464 | 1173 | 1886 | 2175 | 541 |
| Cincinnati, Ohio..... | 1425 | 469 | 1167 | 863 | 296 | 254 | 985 | 262 | 1161 | 1869 | 1107 | 2010 | 2260 | 511 |
| Cleveland, Ohio...... | 1622 | 723 | 1220 | 651 | 349 | — | 1139 | 167 | 1351 | 1813 | 1361 | 2235 | 2457 | 765 |
| Columbia, S.C........ | 1662 | 220 | 1707 | 908 | 836 | 664 | 1043 | 758 | 1749 | 2485 | 1109 | 2241 | 2526 | 623 |
| Columbus, Ohio....... | 1496 | 580 | 1214 | 761 | 322 | 149 | 1093 | 188 | 1225 | 1777 | 1215 | 2081 | 2331 | 619 |
| Dallas, Texas........ | 651 | 814 | 1352 | 1728 | 1006 | 1139 | — | 1278 | 800 | 1607 | 243 | 1236 | 1486 | 474 |
| Denver, Colo......... | 452 | 1534 | 793 | 2025 | 1038 | 1351 | 800 | 1323 | — | 807 | 1043 | 841 | 1202 | 1131 |
| Des Moines, Iowa..... | 1102 | 952 | 692 | 1333 | 347 | 696 | 736 | 619 | 691 | 1269 | 979 | 1539 | 1828 | 620 |
| Detroit, Mich........ | 1594 | 731 | 1143 | 735 | 272 | 167 | 1278 | — | 1323 | 1736 | 1307 | 2158 | 2447 | 716 |
| Fort Worth, Texas.... | 626 | 847 | 1222 | 1761 | 1039 | 1272 | 33 | 1311 | 775 | 1582 | 272 | 1342 | 1468 | 507 |
| Grand Canyon, Ariz.... | 430 | 1857 | 1576 | 2189 | 1821 | 2134 | 1067 | 2106 | 783 | 1015 | 1279 | 287 | 537 | 1455 |
| Hartford, Conn....... | 2298 | 967 | 1784 | 101 | 913 | 677 | 1753 | 661 | 1951 | 2377 | 1864 | 2807 | 3096 | 1259 |
| Helena, Mont......... | 1259 | 2221 | 651 | 2486 | 1464 | 1813 | 1607 | 1736 | 807 | — | 1984 | 940 | 1229 | 1806 |
| Houston, Texas....... | 943 | 897 | 1595 | 1965 | 1173 | 1361 | 243 | 1307 | 1043 | 1984 | — | 1501 | 1566 | 591 |
| Indianapolis, Ind.... | 1322 | 565 | 1057 | 935 | 188 | 302 | 928 | 272 | 1051 | 1650 | 1035 | 1907 | 2196 | 444 |
| Jackson, Miss........ | 1066 | 399 | 1512 | 1467 | 752 | 936 | 415 | 1003 | 1244 | 1980 | 469 | 1651 | 1901 | 209 |
| Kansas City, Mo...... | 893 | 851 | 865 | 1429 | 503 | 794 | 527 | 766 | 644 | 1340 | 770 | 1496 | 1728 | 466 |
| Las Vegas, Nev....... | 585 | 2026 | 1519 | 2873 | 1886 | 2235 | 1236 | 2158 | 841 | 940 | 1501 | — | 292 | 1624 |
| Little Rock, Ark..... | 900 | 542 | 1273 | 1499 | 671 | 893 | 335 | 865 | 992 | 1799 | 452 | 1485 | 1735 | 144 |
| Los Angeles, Calif.... | 835 | 2276 | 1809 | 3162 | 2175 | 2457 | 1486 | 2447 | 1202 | 1229 | 1566 | 292 | — | 1874 |
| Louisville, Ky....... | 1348 | 451 | 1171 | 971 | 300 | 362 | 892 | 370 | 1168 | 1764 | 999 | 1933 | 2183 | 381 |
| Memphis, Tenn........ | 1039 | 403 | 1303 | 1360 | 541 | 765 | 474 | 716 | 1131 | 1806 | 591 | 1624 | 1874 | — |
| Miami, Fla.......... | 2039 | 675 | 1257 | 1540 | 1384 | 1346 | 1346 | 1407 | 2182 | 2896 | 1288 | 2674 | 2832 | 1022 |
| Milwaukee, Wis....... | 1461 | 797 | 774 | 1075 | 88 | 437 | 1127 | 360 | 1050 | 1367 | 1211 | 1911 | 2187 | 629 |
| Minn.-St. Paul, Minn... | 1274 | 1134 | 437 | 1405 | 425 | 774 | 991 | 697 | 916 | 1036 | 1234 | 1729 | 2018 | 863 |
| Montreal, Quebec..... | 2209 | 1289 | 1495 | 327 | 865 | 587 | 1871 | 593 | 1916 | 2146 | 1900 | 2751 | 3040 | 1309 |
| New Orleans, La...... | 1141 | 512 | 1733 | 1580 | 943 | 1108 | 490 | 1116 | 1280 | 2087 | 385 | 1726 | 1976 | 386 |
| New York, N.Y........ | 2191 | 860 | 1721 | 208 | 850 | 507 | 1646 | 636 | 1833 | 2314 | 1593 | 2736 | 3025 | 1152 |
| Norfolk, Va......... | 1973 | 580 | 1783 | 535 | 889 | 557 | 1314 | 767 | 1777 | 2323 | 1496 | 2558 | 2808 | 959 |
| Oklahoma City, Okla... | 531 | 891 | 1013 | 1726 | 830 | 1071 | 211 | 1295 | 618 | 1446 | 454 | 1136 | 1386 | 488 |
| Omaha, Nebr......... | 910 | 1063 | 626 | 1472 | 486 | 835 | 699 | 758 | 552 | 1171 | 942 | 1400 | 1689 | 678 |
| Philadelphia, Penn... | 2074 | 768 | 1646 | 301 | 756 | 426 | 1576 | 580 | 1763 | 2220 | 1501 | 2684 | 2919 | 1060 |
| Phoenix, Ariz....... | 459 | 1876 | 1604 | 2834 | 1751 | 2057 | 1040 | 2029 | 826 | 1257 | 1163 | 338 | 399 | 1474 |
| Portland, Maine..... | 2333 | 1173 | 1919 | 109 | 1048 | 712 | 1833 | 796 | 2086 | 2415 | 1976 | 2934 | 3223 | 1465 |
| Portland, Oreg...... | 1604 | 2804 | 1344 | 2745 | 2156 | 2545 | 2090 | 2429 | 1340 | 693 | 2386 | 1019 | 1001 | 2469 |
| Providence, R.I...... | 2370 | 1039 | 1833 | 44 | 982 | 680 | 1825 | 730 | 2072 | 2481 | 1772 | 2868 | 3103 | 1331 |
| Rapid City, S. Dak..... | 858 | 1599 | 387 | 1994 | 909 | 1271 | 1235 | 1279 | 406 | 643 | 1405 | 1132 | 1421 | 1267 |
| Richmond, Va........ | 1880 | 561 | 1689 | 540 | 798 | 443 | 1323 | 673 | 1683 | 2391 | 1458 | 2473 | 2713 | 844 |
| Saint John, N.B...... | 2669 | 1540 | 2039 | 436 | 1385 | 1049 | 2170 | 1133 | 2423 | 2667 | 2407 | 3271 | 3504 | 1816 |
| St. Louis, Mo........ | 1081 | 565 | 999 | 1196 | 300 | 541 | 676 | 515 | 901 | 1627 | 821 | 1686 | 1916 | 301 |
| Salt Lake City, Utah... | 913 | 2045 | 1073 | 2427 | 1440 | 1789 | 1270 | 1712 | 530 | 494 | 1537 | 441 | 735 | 1619 |
| San Antonio, Texas... | 728 | 1016 | 1579 | 2099 | 1271 | 1536 | 274 | 1552 | 965 | 1853 | 169 | 1310 | 1379 | 739 |
| San Francisco, Calif.... | 1156 | 2592 | 1832 | 3186 | 2299 | 2548 | 1807 | 2471 | 1270 | 1198 | 2019 | 596 | 415 | 2195 |
| Seattle, Wash........ | 1805 | 2884 | 1244 | 3098 | 2141 | 2608 | 2153 | 2531 | 1403 | 638 | 2449 | 1208 | 1177 | 2532 |
| Toronto, Ont........ | 1832 | 969 | 1324 | 563 | 510 | 288 | 1497 | 241 | 1561 | 1952 | 1545 | 2896 | 2685 | 954 |
| Vancouver, B.C....... | 1948 | 3001 | 1380 | 2761 | 2193 | 2542 | 2296 | 2465 | 1412 | 729 | 2642 | 1351 | 1320 | 2638 |
| Washington, D.C...... | 1864 | 665 | 1569 | 435 | 691 | 368 | 1399 | 522 | 1709 | 2123 | 1413 | 2425 | 2799 | 925 |
| Wichita, Kans........ | 674 | 1024 | 870 | 1667 | 705 | 1012 | 385 | 986 | 515 | 1322 | 628 | 1259 | 1509 | 554 |
| Yellowstone Park, Wyo. | 979 | 1963 | 558 | 2336 | 1440 | 1645 | 1327 | 1621 | 571 | 183 | 1570 | 781 | 1070 | 168 |

| Miami, Florida | Milwaukee, Wisconsin | Minn.-St. Paul, Minn. | New Orleans, La. | New York, New York | Omaha, Nebraska | Philadelphia, Penn. | Phoenix, Arizona | Portland, Oregon | St. Louis, Missouri | Salt Lake City, Utah | San Francisco, Calif. | Seattle, Washington | Washington, D.C. | |
|---|---|---|---|---|---|---|---|---|---|---|---|---|---|---|
| 2039 | 1461 | 1274 | 1141 | 2191 | 910 | 2074 | 459 | 1604 | 1081 | 913 | 1156 | 1805 | 1864 | Albuquerque, N. Mex. |
| 675 | 797 | 1134 | 512 | 860 | 1063 | 768 | 1876 | 2804 | 565 | 2045 | 2592 | 2884 | 665 | Atlanta, Ga. |
| 1144 | 782 | 1128 | 1020 | 194 | 1156 | 96 | 2418 | 2881 | 807 | 2107 | 2878 | 2770 | 39 | Baltimore, Md. |
| 803 | 751 | 1088 | 357 | 851 | 926 | 759 | 1699 | 2716 | 548 | 1890 | 2443 | 2779 | 747 | Birmingham, Ala. |
| 1257 | 774 | 437 | 1733 | 1721 | 626 | 1646 | 1604 | 1344 | 999 | 1073 | 1832 | 1244 | 1569 | Bismarck, N. Dak. |
| 3066 | 1755 | 1454 | 2167 | 2593 | 1257 | 2345 | 1030 | 453 | 1754 | 376 | 653 | 510 | 2439 | Boise, Idaho |
| 1540 | 1075 | 1405 | 1580 | 208 | 1472 | 301 | 2834 | 2745 | 1196 | 2427 | 3186 | 3098 | 435 | Boston, Mass. |
| 1434 | 611 | 962 | 1392 | 384 | 1010 | 393 | 2245 | 2687 | 729 | 1964 | 2723 | 2600 | 407 | Buffalo, N.Y. |
| 1043 | 575 | 912 | 936 | 580 | 911 | 488 | 2111 | 2624 | 533 | 1862 | 2627 | 2687 | 367 | Charleston, W. Va. |
| 745 | 873 | 1220 | 773 | 599 | 1198 | 507 | 2113 | 2966 | 759 | 2218 | 2834 | 3029 | 407 | Charlotte, N.C. |
| 2255 | 1052 | 858 | 1383 | 1830 | 494 | 1724 | 929 | 1216 | 938 | 460 | 1219 | 1279 | 1661 | Cheyenne, Wyo. |
| 1384 | 88 | 425 | 943 | 850 | 486 | 756 | 1751 | 2156 | 300 | 1440 | 2299 | 2141 | 691 | Chicago, Ill. |
| 1271 | 384 | 721 | 854 | 665 | 700 | 585 | 1860 | 2413 | 344 | 1657 | 2416 | 2476 | 491 | Cincinnati, Ohio |
| 1346 | 437 | 774 | 1108 | 507 | 835 | 426 | 2507 | 2545 | 541 | 1789 | 2548 | 2608 | 368 | Cleveland, Ohio |
| 757 | 924 | 1270 | 727 | 700 | 1249 | 608 | 2097 | 2966 | 736 | 2960 | 3019 | 3021 | 454 | Columbia, S.C. |
| 1226 | 401 | 738 | 962 | 553 | 764 | 483 | 1931 | 2477 | 415 | 1721 | 2480 | 2389 | 389 | Columbus, Ohio |
| 1346 | 1127 | 991 | 490 | 1646 | 699 | 1576 | 1040 | 2090 | 676 | 1270 | 1807 | 2153 | 1399 | Dallas, Texas |
| 2182 | 1050 | 916 | 1280 | 1833 | 552 | 1763 | 826 | 1340 | 901 | 530 | 1270 | 1403 | 1709 | Denver, Colo. |
| 1627 | 352 | 255 | 1070 | 1161 | 139 | 1091 | 1517 | 1849 | 358 | 1093 | 1852 | 1881 | 1032 | Des Moines, Iowa |
| 1407 | 360 | 697 | 1116 | 636 | 758 | 580 | 2029 | 2429 | 515 | 1712 | 2471 | 2531 | 522 | Detroit, Mich. |
| 1379 | 1455 | 1024 | 523 | 1673 | 697 | 1609 | 1064 | 2065 | 739 | 1236 | 1714 | 2128 | 1432 | Fort Worth, Texas |
| 2505 | 1833 | 1804 | 1557 | 2207 | 1380 | 2515 | 242 | 1350 | 1497 | 391 | 858 | 1413 | 2380 | Grand Canyon, Ariz. |
| 1439 | 1001 | 1338 | 1479 | 116 | 1399 | 200 | 2591 | 3070 | 1075 | 2353 | 3112 | 2989 | 334 | Hartford, Conn. |
| 2896 | 1367 | 1036 | 2087 | 2314 | 1171 | 2220 | 1257 | 693 | 1627 | 494 | 1198 | 638 | 2123 | Helena, Mont. |
| 1288 | 1211 | 1234 | 385 | 1593 | 942 | 1501 | 1163 | 2386 | 821 | 1537 | 2019 | 2449 | 1413 | Houston, Texas |
| 1274 | 274 | 611 | 844 | 727 | 591 | 657 | 1757 | 2303 | 241 | 1547 | 2306 | 2262 | 599 | Indianapolis, Ind. |
| 931 | 840 | 1072 | 181 | 1095 | 881 | 1203 | 1443 | 1545 | 510 | 1716 | 2232 | 2608 | 1013 | Jackson, Miss. |
| 1526 | 568 | 464 | 868 | 1221 | 212 | 1151 | 1346 | 1984 | 257 | 1155 | 1914 | 2047 | 1051 | Kansas City, Mo. |
| 2674 | 1911 | 1729 | 1726 | 2736 | 1400 | 2684 | 338 | 1019 | 1686 | 441 | 595 | 1208 | 2425 | Las Vegas, Nev. |
| 1190 | 759 | 836 | 461 | 1320 | 620 | 1255 | 1335 | 2332 | 361 | 1480 | 2506 | 2395 | 1064 | Little Rock, Ark. |
| 2832 | 2187 | 2018 | 1976 | 3025 | 1689 | 2919 | 399 | 1001 | 1916 | 736 | 415 | 1177 | 2799 | Los Angeles, Calif. |
| 1126 | 388 | 725 | 751 | 773 | 736 | 693 | 1783 | 2484 | 266 | 1679 | 2438 | 2547 | 626 | Louisville, Ky. |
| 1022 | 629 | 863 | 386 | 1152 | 678 | 1060 | 1474 | 2469 | 301 | 1619 | 2195 | 2532 | 925 | Memphis, Tenn. |
| — | 1472 | 1818 | 899 | 1332 | 1738 | 1224 | 2411 | 3519 | 1269 | 2607 | 3270 | 3582 | 1075 | Miami, Fla. |
| 1472 | — | 337 | 938 | 938 | 364 | 844 | 1876 | 2085 | 388 | 1512 | 2223 | 2004 | 786 | Milwaukee, Wis. |
| 1818 | 337 | — | 1275 | 1284 | 374 | 1190 | 1742 | 1723 | 562 | 1283 | 2141 | 1642 | 1132 | Minn.-St. Paul, Minn. |
| 1689 | 955 | 1161 | 1581 | 374 | 1351 | 465 | 2681 | 2816 | 1165 | 2305 | 3099 | 2735 | 600 | Montreal, Quebec |
| 899 | 938 | 1275 | — | 1208 | 1080 | 1116 | 1548 | 2620 | 701 | 1801 | 2297 | 2683 | 1116 | New Orleans, La. |
| 1332 | 938 | 1284 | 1208 | — | 1300 | 93 | 2474 | 3007 | 968 | 2290 | 3049 | 2926 | 233 | New York, N.Y. |
| 994 | 977 | 1323 | 1111 | 327 | 1307 | 251 | 2375 | 3016 | 942 | 2273 | 3047 | 3092 | 195 | Norfolk, Va. |
| 1518 | 975 | 824 | 674 | 1780 | 419 | 1428 | 986 | 1958 | 506 | 1106 | 1707 | 2021 | 1307 | Oklahoma City, Okla. |
| 1738 | 364 | 374 | 1080 | 1300 | — | 1230 | 1378 | 1910 | 469 | 954 | 1713 | 1773 | 1167 | Omaha, Nebr. |
| 1224 | 844 | 1190 | 1116 | 93 | 1230 | — | 2534 | 2798 | 898 | 2184 | 2943 | 2832 | 185 | Philadelphia, Penn. |
| 2411 | 1876 | 1742 | 1548 | 2474 | 1378 | 2534 | — | 1357 | 1529 | 778 | 827 | 1531 | 2399 | Phoenix, Ariz. |
| 1645 | 1136 | 1430 | 1591 | 313 | 1534 | 409 | 2769 | 3085 | 1253 | 2488 | 3241 | 3004 | 567 | Portland, Maine |
| 3519 | 2085 | 1723 | 2620 | 3007 | 1910 | 2798 | 1357 | — | 2241 | 829 | 698 | 176 | 2863 | Portland, Oreg. |
| 1558 | 1090 | 1386 | 1387 | 184 | 1468 | 272 | 2653 | 3174 | 1107 | 2472 | 3181 | 3061 | 406 | Providence, R.I. |
| 2274 | 858 | 563 | 1613 | 1790 | 549 | 1696 | 1232 | 1278 | 1005 | 686 | 1444 | 1254 | 1638 | Rapid City, S. Dak. |
| 1006 | 886 | 1232 | 1073 | 332 | 1222 | 240 | 2323 | 2935 | 844 | 2179 | 2938 | 2994 | 109 | Richmond, Va. |
| 1982 | 1473 | 1705 | 1928 | 616 | 1871 | 769 | 3314 | 3501 | 1590 | 1825 | 3584 | 3420 | 877 | Saint John, N.B. |
| 1269 | 388 | 562 | 701 | 968 | 469 | 898 | 1516 | 2241 | — | 1412 | 2171 | 2259 | 836 | St. Louis, Mo. |
| 2607 | 1512 | 1283 | 1801 | 2290 | 954 | 2184 | 778 | 829 | 1412 | — | 759 | 889 | 2120 | Salt Lake City, Utah |
| 1484 | 1818 | 1265 | 581 | 1898 | 994 | 1799 | 976 | 2312 | 971 | 1426 | 1803 | 2315 | 1630 | San Antonio, Texas |
| 3270 | 2223 | 2141 | 2297 | 3049 | 1713 | 2943 | 827 | 698 | 2171 | 759 | — | 865 | 2885 | San Francisco, Calif. |
| 3582 | 2004 | 1642 | 2683 | 2926 | 1773 | 2832 | 1531 | 176 | 2254 | 889 | 865 | — | 2741 | Seattle, Wash. |
| 1534 | 598 | 990 | 1354 | 484 | 996 | 493 | 2267 | 2645 | 751 | 1950 | 2707 | 2504 | 507 | Toronto, Ont. |
| 3677 | 2121 | 1759 | 2704 | 3043 | 1916 | 2975 | 1674 | 319 | 2376 | 1032 | 1011 | 143 | 2790 | Vancouver, B.C. |
| 1075 | 786 | 1132 | 1116 | 233 | 1167 | 135 | 2399 | 2863 | 836 | 2120 | 2885 | 2741 | — | Washington, D.C. |
| 1603 | 859 | 703 | 818 | 1439 | 314 | 1369 | 1109 | 1855 | 467 | 1003 | 1770 | 1918 | 1306 | Wichita, Kans. |
| 2638 | 1338 | 960 | 1807 | 2146 | 965 | 2110 | 1098 | 839 | 1369 | 366 | 1039 | 775 | 2184 | Yellowstone Park, Wyo. |

## THE SUPERTANKERS: A NEW SUPERHEADACHE?

United Press Int'l.

The **Torrey Canyon**, pouring forth oil, lies battered and broken on England's Seven Stones Reef.

Giant sea-going tankers are the cheapest way to transport crude oil from those lands that are rich in this natural resource to those nations that require it for their complex technologies. When one of these tankers has an accident—as did the *Torrey Canyon* when it went aground near England on March 18, 1967—and spills its cargo into the ocean, oil will pollute the sea for miles around, ruin any beaches it washes upon, and ravage marine and bird life over a wide area.

The *Torrey Canyon,* a Liberian-registered, American-owned, and British-leased tanker, was on its way from the Persian Gulf with 118,000 tons of crude oil when it foundered on Seven Stones Reef near the Scilly Isles, just off England's southwest coast. Before the ship was destroyed by bombing ten days later—the only means of ending the calamity —its cargo of oil, ranging from a shiny film to a foot-and-a-half-thick blanket, had polluted more than 100 miles of English and French beaches, contaminated or perhaps destroyed oyster and mussel beds, and asphyxiated untold numbers of sea birds.

Following the disaster, nations began to look for safeguards against future spillages. A study ordered by President Johnson to determine means of coping with any such misfortune recommended designating oil tanker routes and policing tanker movements within dangerous waters; designing tankers to provide greater protection against oil spillage; intensifying research to improve salvage, control, and destruction of spilled oil; and stockpiling materials and equipment at strategic points to enable quick isolation and cleanup of spillages.

The problem could become more acute in the future, for bigger ships are on the way, including several with capacities ranging upwards of 275,000 tons. Safeguards must be found not only for the ships and their cargoes, but also for the sea itself.

## INTERNATIONAL AVIATION RECORDS

Source: The National Aeronautic Association, Washington, D.C., which is the American representative of the Fédération Aeronautique Internationale (FAI), a world governing body for aeronautical records. It was founded in 1905, and now has 56 member countries.

### WORLD AIRPLANE RECORDS

| | | | | | | |
|---|---|---|---|---|---|---|
| Distance in a Straight Line * | U.S.A. | 12,532.28 miles | Altitude in Horizontal Sustained Flight | U.S.A. | 80,257.86 feet |
| Distance Over a Closed Circuit † | U.S.A. | 11,336.92 miles | Speed Over a Straight Course ‡ | U.S.A. | 2,070.101 mph |
| Altitude | U.S.A. | 314,750 feet | Speed Over a Closed Circuit | U.S.A. | 1,688.889 mph |

|  |  |  |  |
|---|---|---|---|
| Jan. 11, 1962... | **Distance in a Straight Line**.................................... Major Clyde P. Evely, USAF, Boeing B52-H Kadena, Okinawa, to Madrid, Spain | U.S.A. | 12,532.28 miles |
| June 6–7, 1962.. | **Distance Over a Closed Circuit**.............................. Captain William Stevenson, USAF, Boeing B52-H Seymour-Johnson, North Carolina—Kindley, Bermuda—Sondrestrom, Greenland—Anchorage, Alaska—March AFB, California—Key West, Florida—Seymour-Johnson, North Carolina | U.S.A. | 11,336.92 miles |
| July 17, 1962... | **Altitude**................................................. Major Robert M. White, USAF, North American X-15-1 (NASA Aircraft) Edwards Air Force Base, California | U.S.A. | 314,750 feet |
| May 1, 1965.... | **Altitude in Horizontal Flight**.............................. Colonel R. L. Stephens, USAF, YF-12A Jet Edwards Air Force Base, California | U.S.A. | 80,257.86 feet |
| May 1, 1965.... | **Speed Over a Straight Course**............................ Colonel R. L. Stephens, USAF, YF-12A Jet Edwards Air Force Base, California | U.S.A. | 2,070.101 mph |
| May 1, 1965.... | **Speed Over a Closed Circuit**.............................. Major Walter F. Daniel, USAF, YF-12A Jet Edwards Air Force Base, California | U.S.A. | 1,688.889 mph |

### WORLD PROPELLER-DRIVEN AIRPLANE RECORDS (MALE)

|  |  |  |  |
|---|---|---|---|
| Sept. 29, 1946... | **Distance in a Straight Line**................................. Commander T. D. Davies, USN, Lockheed P2V-1 monoplane Pearce Field, Perth, Australia, to Port Columbus, Columbus, Ohio | U.S.A. | 11,235.6 miles |
| Aug. 1, 1947.... | **Distance in a Closed Circuit**............................... Lt. Col. O. F. Lassiter, USAF, Boeing B-29 monoplane, #44-84061 McDill Field, Tampa, Florida | U.S.A. | 8,854.3 miles |
| Oct. 22, 1938... | **Altitude**................................................. Mario Pezzi, Caproni 161 Biplane Montecelio, Italy | Italy | 56,046 feet |
| April 26, 1939... | **Speed Over a Three Kilometer Course**...................... Fritz Wendel, Messerschmitt B. F. 109 R Augsburg, Germany | Germany | 469.220 mph |
| April 19, 1951... | **Speed Over a 15/25 Kilometer Course** ..................... Miss Jacqueline Cochran, North American P-51 low-wing monoplane Near Indio, California | U.S.A. | 464.374 mph |
| June 2–7, 1966.. | **Speed Around the World**................................. Robert and Joan Wallick, Beechcraft Baron C55 Manila–Tokyo–Midway–Honolulu–Seattle–Boston–Santa Maria–Athens–Damascus–Bombay–Singapore–Manila Distance: 23,129.29 miles Time: 5 days, 6 hours, 17 minutes, 10 seconds | U.S.A. | 186.53 mph |

### WORLD PROPELLER-DRIVEN AIRPLANE RECORDS (FEMALE)

|  |  |  |  |
|---|---|---|---|
| April 10, 1966... | **Distance In a Straight Line**................................ Geraldine L. Mock, Cessna Super Skylane Honolulu, Hawaii to Columbus, Ohio | U.S.A. | 4,515.93 miles |
| June 23, 1936... | **Altitude**................................................. Mrs. Maryse Hilsz, Potez 506 Biplane Villacoublay | France | 46,949 feet |
| Dec. 12, 1947... | **Speed Over a Three Kilometer Course**...................... Miss Jacqueline Cochran, North American F-51 Thermal, California | U.S.A. | 412.002 mph |
| March 19– April 18, 1964 | **Speed Around the World**................................. Geraldine L. Mock, Cessna 180 Columbus–Bermuda–Santa Maria, Azores–Casablanca–Bone–Tripoli– Cairo–Dhahran–Karachi–New Delhi–Calcutta–Bangkok–Manila–Guam– Wake Island–Honolulu–Oakland–Tucson–El Paso–Bowling Green– Columbus Distance: 37,347.09 kilometers (23,206.37 miles) Elapsed time: 29 days, 11 hours, 59 minutes, 38 seconds | U.S.A. | 32.777 mph |

(*continued*)

* Nonstop flight with no refueling.   † The aircraft must complete the circuit by returning to the starting point.   ‡ A record flight is made over a 15/25 kilometer course at unrestricted altitude.

**INTERNATIONAL AVIATION RECORDS** (*continued*)

### WORLD HELICOPTER RECORDS (WITHOUT PAYLOAD)

| | | | |
|---|---|---|---|
| April 6–7, 1966.. | Distance in a Straight Line............................<br>Robert G. Ferry, Hughes YOH 6A helicopter<br>Culver City, California, to Daytona Beach, Florida | U.S.A. | 2,213.04 miles |
| Sept. 18, 1964... | Distance in a Closed Circuit..........................<br>Major John A. Johnston, USA, Bell UH-1D helicopter<br>Edwards Air Force Base, California | U.S.A. | 1,615.742 miles |
| June 13, 1958... | Altitude..................................................<br>Jean Boulet, S.E. 3150/022 "Alouette" F-ZWVB helicopter<br>Bretigny sur Orge, France | France | 36,037 feet |
| July 19, 1963... | Speed Over a Three Kilometer Course...............<br>Jean Boulet, "Superfrelon" SA 3210/01 helicopter<br>Istres Airport, France | France | 212.029 mph |
| July 23, 1963... | Speed Over a 15/25 Kilometer Course...............<br>Jean Boulet, "Superfrelon" SA 3210/01 helicopter<br>Istres Airport, France | France | 217.77 mph |

### WORLD (MANNED) BALLOON RECORDS

**Less than 250 cubic meters**

| | | | |
|---|---|---|---|
| July 24, 1960... | Altitude..................................................<br>Donald L. Piccard, "D. Piccard S 10 Holiday" balloon<br>Lake Calhoun, Minneapolis | U.S.A. | 3,740 feet |

**Between 250 and 400 cubic meters**

| | | | |
|---|---|---|---|
| May 3, 1953.... | Duration..................................................<br>Audouin Dollfus, "Zodiac" F. AIJA balloon<br>Senlis to Cheverny, France | France | 4 hours |
| May 3, 1953.... | Distance..................................................<br>Audouin Dollfus, "Zodiac" F. AIJA balloon<br>Senlis to Cheverny, France | France | 129.631 miles |
| Aug. 24, 1962... | Altitude..................................................<br>Donald L. Piccard, Raven Industries "Sioux City Sue"<br>Sioux City, Iowa | U.S.A. | 17,747 feet |

**Between 1,200 and 1,600 cubic meters**

| | | | |
|---|---|---|---|
| March 13, 1941. | Duration..................................................<br>Boris Nevernov, URSS-VR 73 balloon<br>Dolgoproudnaia to Novosibirski, Russia | U.S.S.R. | 69 hours,<br>20 min. |
| March 13, 1941. | Distance..................................................<br>Boris Nevernov, URSS-VR 73 balloon<br>Dolgoproudnaia to Novosibirski, Russia | U.S.S.R. | 1,719.21 miles |
| May 10, 1964.... | Altitude..................................................<br>Tracy Barnes, Barnes 14-A balloon<br>Rosemount, Minnesota | U.S.A. | 38,650 feet |

## COMMERCIAL AVIATION RECORDS

### RECORD SPEEDS ON COMMERCIAL AIR ROUTES

| | | | |
|---|---|---|---|
| Sept. 6, 1962.... | Chicago/Mexico City.................................<br>Captain D. W. Ledbetter, Boeing 720B<br>Elapsed time: 3 hours 10 minutes 6.3 seconds | U.S.A.<br>American<br>Airlines, Inc. | 534.15 mph |
| Oct. 23, 1954... | Havana/Madrid........................................<br>Captain R. de la Pena Moulie, Lockheed Super Constellation L-1049E<br>Elapsed time: 15 hours 20 minutes | Spain<br>Iberia<br>Air Lines | 304.7 mph |
| Apr. 30, 1960... | London/Athens.........................................<br>Captain P. Ioanides, Comet DH-106-4B (SXDAK)<br>Elapsed time: 3 hours 13 minutes 42 seconds | Greece<br>Olympic<br>Airways | 506.29 mph |
| July 28, 1953... | London/Copenhagen..................................<br>Captain R. F. Noden, Vickers Viscount G-AMOA<br>Elapsed time: 2 hours 1 minute 53 seconds | England<br>British<br>European<br>Airways Corp. | 299.46 mph |
| Jan. 2, 1962.... | London/Karachi........................................<br>Captain M. T. Baig, Boeing 720B<br>Elapsed time: 6 hours 43 minutes 51 seconds | Pakistan<br>Pakistan<br>International<br>Airlines | 583.3 mph |
| June 5, 1962.... | London/Miami..........................................<br>Captain G. N. Henderson, Captain P. Wilson, Boeing 707/465<br>Elapsed time: 13 hours 46 minutes 38 seconds | England<br>Cunard Eagle<br>Airways | 321.02 mph |

**RECORD SPEEDS ON COMMERCIAL AIR ROUTES** (*continued*)

| | | | |
|---|---|---|---|
| Dec. 8, 1961.... | Los Angeles/New York........................................... | U.S.A. | 636.8 mph |
| | Captain William Miller, Boeing 707B-123 | American | |
| | Elapsed time: 3 hours 52 minutes 43 seconds | Airlines, Inc. | |
| May 6, 1962.... | Miami/London................................................. | England | 419.94 mph |
| | Captain P. Wilson, Captain M. Gudmundsson, Boeing 707/465 | Cunard Eagle | |
| | Elapsed time: 10 hours 31 minutes 55 seconds | Airways | |
| May 28, 1960.... | Montreal/London.............................................. | Canada | 565.29 mph |
| | Captain R. M. Smith, Douglas DC-8-40 Series, CF-TJC | Trans-Canada | |
| | Elapsed time: 5 hours 44 minutes 42 seconds | Air Lines | |
| June 2, 1963.... | New York/Bergen.............................................. | Norway | 533.13 mph |
| | Captain B. Bjornstad, Douglas DC-8 | Scandinavian | |
| | Elapsed time: 6 hours 32 minutes 20 seconds | Airlines | |
| | | Systems | |
| Nov. 26, 1954... | New York/Madrid............................................. | Spain | 379.624 mph |
| | Captain C. I. Batida, Lockheed Super Constellation L-1049E | Iberia | |
| | Elapsed time: 9 hours 29 minutes | Air Lines | |
| June 3, 1960.... | New York/San Francisco....................................... | Australia | 510.092 mph |
| | Captain A. Yates, Boeing 707-138 VH-EBE | Qantas Empire | |
| | Elapsed time: 5 hours 3 minutes 48.35 seconds | Airways | |
| May 17, 1960... | Paris/Athens................................................. | Greece | 515.737 mph |
| | Panajotis Kyratatos, Comet DH-106 Mark 48 | Olympic | |
| | Elapsed time: 2 hours 39 minutes 29 seconds | Airways | |

## BUSIEST U.S. AIRPORTS

Based on the total number of aircraft arrivals and departures, Chicago's O'Hare International Airport was the busiest U.S. airport in 1965.

The following list of 30 major airports, by rank order of their total itinerant operations, was compiled by the Federal Aviation Agency.

| RANK | AIRPORT | OPERATIONS | RANK | AIRPORT | OPERATIONS |
|---|---|---|---|---|---|
| 1 | O'Hare International (Chicago, Illinois)....................... | 562,607 | 15 | Logan International (Boston, Massachusetts)................ | 241,588 |
| 2 | John F. Kennedy International (New York, New York)......... | 438,670 | 16 | Sky Harbor Municipal (Phoenix, Arizona)....................... | 239,210 |
| 3 | Los Angeles International (California)................... | 406,359 | 17 | Houston International (Texas)...... | 239,001 |
| 4 | Opa Locka (Florida)............... | 357,849 | 18 | Newark Municipal (New Jersey).... | 237,588 |
| 5 | Stapleton International (Denver, Colorado)..................... | 325,697 | 19 | Philadelphia International (Pennsylvania).................. | 228,245 |
| 6 | Dallas Love Field (Dallas, Texas).. | 316,210 | 20 | Honolulu International (Hawaii).... | 224,471 |
| 7 | Washington National (District of Columbia)..................... | 311,819 | 21 | Kansas City Municipal (Missouri)... | 223,110 |
| 8 | La Guardia (New York, New York).. | 300,562 | 22 | Detroit Metropolitan (Romulus, Michigan).................... | 222,392 |
| 9 | Lambert Field (St. Louis, Missouri) | 299,869 | 23 | Cleveland–Hopkins (Cleveland, Ohio) | 216,832 |
| 10 | Atlanta Municipal (Georgia)....... | 294,220 | 24 | Fort Lauderdale (Florida).......... | 215,743 |
| 11 | San Francisco International (California).................... | 288,641 | 25 | Port Columbus (Columbus, Ohio)... | 201,941 |
| 12 | Van Nuys (California)............. | 275,207 | 26 | San Jose (California).............. | 195,078 |
| 13 | Miami International (Florida)...... | 254,978 | 27 | Wold Chamberlain (Minneapolis, Minnesota)................... | 188,117 |
| 14 | Long Beach Municipal (California).. | 245,127 | 28 | Memphis Metropolitan (Tennessee) | 186,687 |
| | | | 29 | Wichita Municipal (Kansas)....... | 180,314 |
| | | | 30 | Tulsa International (Oklahoma).... | 177,596 |

## FASTEST PASSENGER-TRAIN RUNS

These ten high-speed runs are the fastest for scheduled passenger trains in service on United States railroads. Times are measured from start to stop.

| TRAIN AND RAILROAD | FROM | TO | MILES | TIME (min.) | SPEED (mph) |
|---|---|---|---|---|---|
| Morning Zephyr, Burlington.................... | Aurora, Ill........... | Rochelle, Ill......... | 42.5 | 33 | 82.3 |
| Super Chief–El Capitan, Sante Fe............. | Garden City, Kans..... | Lamar, Colo.......... | 99.9 | 73 | 82.1 |
| City of New Orleans, Illinois Central........... | Champaign, Ill........ | Mattoon, Ill......... | 44.6 | 33 | 81.1 |
| Chief, Santa Fe.............................. | St. John, Kans........ | Hutchinson, Kans..... | 48.0 | 36 | 80.0 |
| City of New Orleans, Illinois Central........... | Effingham, Ill........ | Centralia, Ill....... | 53.2 | 40 | 79.8 |
| Grand Canyon, Santa Fe...................... | Gallup, N. Mex........ | Holbrook, N. Mex..... | 94.9 | 72 | 79.1 |
| Morning Hiawatha, Milwaukee................. | Tomah, Wis........... | Portage, Wis......... | 61.9 | 47 | 79.0 |
| Morning Zephyr–Empire Builder, Burlington.... | Prairie du Chien, Wis. | La Crosse, Wis........ | 57.7 | 44 | 78.7 |
| Panama Limited, Illinois Central............... | Champaign, Ill........ | Mattoon, Ill......... | 44.6 | 34 | 78.7 |
| Fast Mail, Santa Fe.......................... | Gallup, N. Mex........ | Holbrook, N. Mex..... | 94.9 | 73 | 78.0 |

## U.S. AND CANADIAN DOMESTIC AIRLINE DISTANCES (In Statute Miles)

This table shows airport-to-airport mileages via airline routes, computed in miles along a Great Circle track (the shortest distance between two points on the Earth). These mileages are based on the official mileage charts prepared by the Civil Aeronautics Board.

| | Albuquerque, N.Mex. | Atlanta, Ga. | Billings, Mont. | Boston, Mass. | Charleston, S.C. | Chicago, Ill. | Cincinnati, Ohio | Cleveland, Ohio | Dallas, Texas | Denver, Colo. | Detroit, Mich. | Houston, Texas | Los Angeles, Calif. | Memphis, Tenn. |
|---|---|---|---|---|---|---|---|---|---|---|---|---|---|---|
| Albuquerque, N. Mex... | — | 1305 | 799 | 1982 | 1522 | 1123 | 1238 | 1438 | 584 | 341 | 1340 | 798 | 676 | 830 |
| Atlanta, Ga............ | 1305 | — | 1604 | 946 | 260 | 607 | 374 | 556 | 721 | 1185 | 596 | 697 | 1966 | 332 |
| Billings, Mont......... | 799 | 1604 | — | 1897 | 1852 | 1098 | 1347 | 1371 | 1114 | 458 | 1267 | 1355 | 1101 | 1317 |
| Birmingham, Ala...... | 1189 | 134 | 1529 | 1050 | 394 | 574 | 409 | 635 | 587 | 1138 | 633 | 572 | 1832 | 212 |
| Boston, Mass......... | 1982 | 946 | 1897 | — | 825 | 865 | 750 | 561 | 1564 | 1766 | 630 | 1613 | 2610 | 1146 |
| Buffalo, N.Y.......... | 1591 | 713 | 1515 | 394 | 741 | 473 | 412 | 191 | 1218 | 1365 | 239 | 1302 | 2208 | 816 |
| Charleston, S.C....... | 1522 | 260 | 1852 | 825 | — | 754 | 533 | 600 | 981 | 1553 | 705 | 957 | 2226 | 592 |
| Charlotte, N.C........ | 1343 | 227 | 1683 | 729 | 169 | 585 | 364 | 431 | 936 | 1384 | 536 | 924 | 2181 | 513 |
| Chicago, Ill.......... | 1123 | 607 | 1098 | 865 | 754 | — | 265 | 316 | 795 | 901 | 224 | 940 | 1746 | 481 |
| Cincinnati, Ohio...... | 1238 | 374 | 1347 | 750 | 533 | 265 | — | 221 | 806 | 1089 | 228 | 890 | 1900 | 404 |
| Cleveland, Ohio...... | 1438 | 556 | 1371 | 561 | 600 | 316 | 221 | — | 1027 | 1216 | 105 | 1128 | 2053 | 625 |
| Columbus, Ohio...... | 1353 | 489 | 1382 | 640 | 608 | 297 | 115 | 114 | 921 | 1118 | 160 | 1005 | 2001 | 519 |
| Dallas, Texas........ | 584 | 721 | 1114 | 1564 | 981 | 795 | 806 | 1027 | — | 656 | 980 | 241 | 1245 | 423 |
| Denver, Colo......... | 341 | 1185 | 458 | 1766 | 1553 | 901 | 1089 | 1216 | 656 | — | 1126 | 897 | 849 | 926 |
| Detroit, Mich........ | 1340 | 596 | 1267 | 630 | 705 | 224 | 228 | 105 | 980 | 1126 | — | 1093 | 1969 | 607 |
| El Paso, Texas....... | 224 | 1284 | 1023 | 2128 | 1544 | 1259 | 1334 | 1514 | 563 | 565 | 1459 | 679 | 712 | 986 |
| Fort Worth, Texas..... | 573 | 733 | 1128 | 1575 | 993 | 804 | 818 | 1039 | 12 | 668 | 992 | 243 | 1234 | 434 |
| Houston, Texas....... | 798 | 697 | 1355 | 1613 | 957 | 940 | 890 | 1128 | 241 | 897 | 1093 | — | 1391 | 486 |
| Indianapolis, Ind..... | 1169 | 432 | 1260 | 820 | 618 | 179 | 98 | 261 | 777 | 1000 | 225 | 868 | 1821 | 382 |
| Jacksonville, Fla...... | 1537 | 277 | 1881 | 1020 | 196 | 857 | 622 | 761 | 953 | 1508 | 866 | 819 | 2198 | 582 |
| Kansas City, Mo...... | 721 | 711 | 938 | 1264 | 971 | 404 | 537 | 692 | 452 | 552 | 619 | 669 | 1368 | 379 |
| Los Angeles, Calif.... | 676 | 1966 | 1101 | 2610 | 2226 | 1746 | 1900 | 2053 | 1245 | 849 | 1969 | 1391 | — | 1533 |
| Louisville, Ky........ | 1185 | 321 | 1374 | 831 | 507 | 288 | 84 | 305 | 726 | 1036 | 304 | 823 | 1846 | 320 |
| Memphis, Tenn........ | 830 | 332 | 1317 | 1146 | 592 | 481 | 404 | 625 | 423 | 926 | 607 | 486 | 1533 | — |
| Miami, Fla........... | 1696 | 598 | 2192 | 1261 | 491 | 1202 | 953 | 1084 | 1112 | 1768 | 1153 | 987 | 2356 | 877 |
| Milwaukee, Wis........ | 1205 | 674 | 1045 | 858 | 826 | 67 | 331 | 329 | 877 | 909 | 228 | 1022 | 1758 | 563 |
| Minn.-St. Paul, Minn... | 1035 | 942 | 748 | 1149 | 1104 | 350 | 599 | 623 | 858 | 694 | 519 | 1075 | 1543 | 749 |
| Montreal, Que......... | 1865 | 1046 | 1795 | 254 | 944 | 742 | 745 | 509 | 1508 | 1654 | 528 | 1621 | 2488 | 1135 |
| Nashville, Tenn....... | 1030 | 213 | 1393 | 948 | 473 | 397 | 232 | 453 | 622 | 1055 | 460 | 671 | 1797 | 200 |
| New Orleans, La...... | 1021 | 427 | 1551 | 1370 | 687 | 829 | 731 | 956 | 437 | 1093 | 959 | 303 | 1681 | 352 |
| New York, N.Y........ | 1795 | 760 | 1776 | 186 | 639 | 740 | 589 | 424 | 1384 | 1638 | 508 | 1430 | 2474 | 965 |
| Norfolk, Va.......... | 1645 | 516 | 1825 | 481 | 352 | 744 | 508 | 437 | 1218 | 1578 | 558 | 1213 | 2328 | 795 |
| Oklahoma City, Okla... | 478 | 684 | 959 | 1520 | 944 | 692 | 770 | 950 | 181 | 501 | 895 | 422 | 1181 | 352 |
| Omaha, Nebr.......... | 826 | 876 | 838 | 1282 | 1139 | 417 | 682 | 731 | 617 | 485 | 641 | 380 | 1330 | 544 |
| Ottawa, Ont.......... | 1732 | 1000 | 1699 | 320 | 899 | 656 | 634 | 413 | 1412 | 1558 | 432 | 1596 | 2401 | 1038 |
| Philadelphia, Penn..... | 1756 | 667 | 1529 | 279 | 553 | 678 | 521 | 363 | 1296 | 1578 | 464 | 1340 | 2402 | 876 |
| Pittsburgh, Penn...... | 1485 | 527 | 1478 | 495 | 535 | 414 | 257 | 107 | 1062 | 1312 | 212 | 1135 | 2137 | 656 |
| Portland, Oreg........ | 1160 | 2249 | 680 | 2576 | 2512 | 1752 | 2017 | 2059 | 1642 | 986 | 1946 | 1883 | 838 | 1917 |
| Raleigh, N.C.......... | 1538 | 355 | 1807 | 616 | 218 | 663 | 421 | 478 | 1060 | 1461 | 540 | 1052 | 2241 | 637 |
| St. Louis, Mo......... | 930 | 485 | 1119 | 1049 | 745 | 256 | 308 | 488 | 547 | 781 | 433 | 691 | 1591 | 257 |
| Salt Lake City, Utah... | 528 | 1643 | 457 | 2114 | 1903 | 1249 | 1469 | 1565 | 1036 | 380 | 1473 | 1277 | 591 | 1306 |
| San Diego, Calif...... | 632 | 1903 | 1136 | 2614 | 2163 | 1749 | 1895 | 2056 | 1182 | 894 | 1968 | 1313 | 109 | 1605 |
| San Francisco, Calif.... | 901 | 2069 | 1058 | 2712 | 2329 | 1847 | 2044 | 2163 | 1477 | 956 | 2071 | 1672 | 340 | 1737 |
| Seattle, Wash......... | 1219 | 2204 | 664 | 2548 | 2464 | 1721 | 1986 | 2022 | 1675 | 1019 | 1918 | 1916 | 957 | 1950 |
| Tampa, Fla........... | 1510 | 410 | 1993 | 1188 | 372 | 1017 | 777 | 931 | 926 | 1582 | 990 | 783 | 2170 | 673 |
| Toronto, Ont.......... | 1546 | 782 | 1528 | 463 | 810 | 430 | 408 | 187 | 1186 | 1332 | 206 | 1299 | 2175 | 812 |
| Tulsa, Okla........... | 579 | 697 | 1019 | 1409 | 957 | 584 | 659 | 839 | 238 | 561 | 784 | 454 | 1282 | 365 |
| Vancouver, B.C........ | 1347 | 2332 | 585 | 2541 | 2592 | 1850 | 2114 | 2150 | 1803 | 1147 | 2046 | 2044 | 1085 | 2078 |
| Washington, D.C....... | 1628 | 547 | 1682 | 399 | 445 | 612 | 411 | 310 | 1183 | 1488 | 415 | 1220 | 2310 | 762 |
| Winnipeg, Man........ | 1281 | 1373 | 737 | 1397 | 1498 | 744 | 993 | 1017 | 1224 | 940 | 913 | 1469 | 1530 | 1143 |

## FEDERAL-AID AIRPORT PROGRAM

In August, 1967, the Federal Aviation Agency announced the allocation of nearly $70,200,000 in Federal funds, to be matched by funds from local communities, to construct or improve 386 public commercial airports in the 50 states, Puerto Rico, and the Virgin Islands. The program, boiled down from a record 778 requests from local sponsors seeking over $339,000,000 in Federal matching funds, emphasizes projects considered most urgent to the national system of

| Miami, Fla. | Milwaukee, Wis. | Minn.-St. Paul, Minn. | New Orleans, La. | New York, N.Y. | Oklahoma City, Okla. | Omaha, Nebr. | Philadelphia, Penn. | Portland, Oreg. | St. Louis, Mo. | Salt Lake City, Utah | San Francisco, Calif. | Seattle, Wash. | Washington, D.C. | |
|---|---|---|---|---|---|---|---|---|---|---|---|---|---|---|
| 1696 | 1205 | 1035 | 1021 | 1795 | 478 | 826 | 1756 | 1160 | 930 | 528 | 901 | 1219 | 1628 | Albuquerque, N. Mex. |
| 598 | 674 | 942 | 427 | 760 | 684 | 876 | 667 | 2249 | 485 | 1643 | 2069 | 2204 | 547 | Atlanta, Ga. |
| 2192 | 1045 | 748 | 1551 | 1776 | 959 | 838 | 1529 | 680 | 1119 | 457 | 1058 | 664 | 1682 | Billings, Mont. |
| 665 | 656 | 905 | 322 | 866 | 564 | 756 | 774 | 2129 | 413 | 1518 | 2064 | 2162 | 654 | Birmingham, Ala. |
| 1261 | 858 | 1149 | 1370 | 186 | 1520 | 1282 | 279 | 2576 | 1049 | 2114 | 2712 | 2548 | 399 | Boston, Mass. |
| 1202 | 467 | 758 | 1113 | 301 | 1141 | 890 | 279 | 2185 | 679 | 1722 | 2320 | 2157 | 296 | Buffalo, N.Y. |
| 491 | 836 | 1104 | 687 | 639 | 944 | 1139 | 553 | 2512 | 745 | 1903 | 2329 | 2464 | 445 | Charleston, S.C. |
| 665 | 720 | 935 | 654 | 532 | 865 | 987 | 449 | 2360 | 593 | 1754 | 2296 | 2343 | 331 | Charlotte, N.C. |
| 1202 | 67 | 350 | 829 | 740 | 692 | 417 | 678 | 1752 | 256 | 1249 | 1847 | 1721 | 612 | Chicago, Ill. |
| 953 | 331 | 599 | 731 | 589 | 770 | 682 | 521 | 2017 | 308 | 1469 | 2044 | 1986 | 411 | Cincinnati, Ohio |
| 1084 | 329 | 623 | 956 | 424 | 950 | 731 | 363 | 2059 | 488 | 1565 | 2163 | 2022 | 310 | Cleveland, Ohio |
| 993 | 351 | 634 | 849 | 482 | 866 | 708 | 406 | 2036 | 410 | 1498 | 2074 | 2018 | 322 | Columbus, Ohio |
| 1112 | 877 | 858 | 437 | 1384 | 181 | 617 | 1296 | 1642 | 547 | 1036 | 1477 | 1675 | 1183 | Dallas, Texas |
| 1768 | 909 | 694 | 1093 | 1638 | 501 | 485 | 1578 | 986 | 781 | 380 | 956 | 1019 | 1488 | Denver, Colo. |
| 1153 | 228 | 519 | 959 | 508 | 895 | 641 | 464 | 1946 | 433 | 1473 | 2071 | 1918 | 415 | Detroit, Mich. |
| 1666 | 1341 | 1259 | 982 | 1947 | 615 | 1050 | 1844 | 1395 | 1026 | 752 | 993 | 1443 | 1745 | El Paso, Texas |
| 1122 | 886 | 863 | 447 | 1395 | 181 | 622 | 1314 | 1654 | 556 | 1048 | 1467 | 1687 | 1194 | Fort Worth, Texas |
| 987 | 1022 | 1075 | 303 | 1430 | 422 | 380 | 1340 | 1883 | 691 | 1277 | 1672 | 1916 | 1220 | Houston, Texas |
| 1030 | 244 | 512 | 749 | 633 | 693 | 606 | 587 | 1914 | 230 | 1380 | 1966 | 1896 | 498 | Indianapolis, Ind. |
| 330 | 939 | 1207 | 516 | 834 | 934 | 1126 | 743 | 2499 | 762 | 1893 | 2430 | 2527 | 640 | Jacksonville, Fla. |
| 1256 | 485 | 406 | 731 | 1109 | 306 | 165 | 1035 | 1538 | 229 | 932 | 1507 | 1571 | 944 | Kansas City, Mo. |
| 2356 | 1758 | 1543 | 1681 | 2474 | 1181 | 1330 | 2402 | 838 | 1591 | 591 | 340 | 957 | 2310 | Los Angeles, Calif. |
| 914 | 353 | 621 | 651 | 661 | 717 | 629 | 593 | 2022 | 255 | 1491 | 1991 | 2005 | 473 | Louisville, Ky. |
| 877 | 563 | 749 | 352 | 965 | 352 | 544 | 876 | 1917 | 257 | 1306 | 1737 | 1950 | 762 | Memphis, Tenn. |
| — | 1263 | 1531 | 675 | 1093 | 1293 | 1421 | 1017 | 2754 | 1073 | 2148 | 2589 | 2787 | 922 | Miami, Fla. |
| 1263 | — | 297 | 911 | 746 | 774 | 429 | 692 | 1724 | 323 | 1289 | 1865 | 1696 | 635 | Milwaukee, Wis. |
| 1531 | 297 | — | 1099 | 1028 | 712 | 283 | 981 | 1427 | 492 | 991 | 1590 | 1399 | 931 | Minn.-St. Paul, Minn. |
| 1320 | 756 | 1102 | 1435 | 333 | 1423 | 1166 | 426 | 2504 | 961 | 2010 | 2608 | 2446 | 499 | Montreal, Que. |
| 811 | 479 | 747 | 499 | 767 | 616 | 648 | 676 | 2021 | 274 | 1435 | 1981 | 2074 | 562 | Nashville, Tenn. |
| 675 | 911 | 1099 | — | 1184 | 618 | 896 | 1091 | 2079 | 607 | 1473 | 1914 | 2112 | 971 | New Orleans, La. |
| 1093 | 746 | 1028 | 1184 | — | 1345 | 1154 | 93 | 2454 | 893 | 1982 | 2587 | 2421 | 213 | New York, N.Y. |
| 804 | 763 | 1074 | 944 | 291 | 1147 | 1161 | 214 | 2496 | 797 | 1958 | 2586 | 2476 | 143 | Norfolk, Va. |
| 1293 | 774 | 712 | 618 | 1345 | — | 471 | 1276 | 1487 | 462 | 881 | 1385 | 1520 | 1158 | Oklahoma City, Okla. |
| 1421 | 429 | 283 | 896 | 1154 | 471 | — | 1093 | 1471 | 376 | 839 | 1434 | 1504 | 1024 | Omaha, Nebr. |
| 1376 | 660 | 1006 | 1369 | 329 | 1327 | 1073 | 384 | 2378 | 865 | 1905 | 2503 | 2350 | 454 | Ottawa, Ont. |
| 1017 | 692 | 981 | 1091 | 93 | 1276 | 1093 | — | 2408 | 814 | 1927 | 2525 | 2380 | 120 | Philadelphia, Penn. |
| 1016 | 433 | 730 | 922 | 339 | 1011 | 827 | 267 | 2155 | 555 | 1661 | 2259 | 2129 | 204 | Pittsburgh, Penn. |
| 2754 | 1724 | 1427 | 2079 | 2454 | 1487 | 1471 | 2408 | — | 1767 | 632 | 552 | 129 | 2364 | Portland, Oreg. |
| 709 | 730 | 1020 | 783 | 459 | 1062 | 1031 | 339 | 2415 | 655 | 1805 | 2380 | 2384 | 228 | Raleigh, N.C. |
| 1073 | 323 | 492 | 607 | 893 | 462 | 376 | 814 | 1767 | — | 1161 | 1736 | 1800 | 719 | St. Louis, Mo. |
| 2148 | 1289 | 991 | 1473 | 1982 | 881 | 839 | 1927 | 632 | 1161 | — | 601 | 691 | 1858 | Salt Lake City, Utah |
| 2300 | 1803 | 1588 | 1616 | 2471 | 1136 | 1379 | 2427 | 944 | 1582 | 626 | 449 | 1063 | 2285 | San Diego, Calif. |
| 2589 | 1865 | 1590 | 1914 | 2587 | 1385 | 1434 | 2525 | 552 | 1736 | 601 | — | 680 | 2443 | San Francisco, Calif. |
| 2787 | 1696 | 1399 | 2112 | 2421 | 1520 | 1504 | 2380 | 129 | 1800 | 691 | 680 | — | 2333 | Seattle, Wash. |
| 204 | 1083 | 1351 | 489 | 1009 | 1107 | 1217 | 924 | 2568 | 874 | 1962 | 2403 | 2601 | 817 | Tampa, Fla. |
| 1271 | 434 | 780 | 1143 | 367 | 1101 | 847 | 348 | 2182 | 639 | 1688 | 2286 | 2124 | 365 | Toronto, Ont. |
| 1242 | 666 | 621 | 557 | 1235 | 111 | 834 | 1169 | 1547 | 351 | 941 | 1466 | 1580 | 1049 | Tulsa, Okla. |
| 2915 | 1824 | 1527 | 2207 | 2445 | 1648 | 1632 | 2508 | 257 | 1928 | 819 | 800 | 128 | 2458 | Vancouver, B.C. |
| 922 | 635 | 931 | 971 | 213 | 1158 | 1024 | 120 | 2364 | 719 | 1858 | 2443 | 2333 | — | Washington, D.C. |
| 1925 | 691 | 394 | 1493 | 1301 | 1106 | 677 | 1375 | 1421 | 886 | 1194 | 1795 | 1401 | 1325 | Winnipeg, Man. |

airports. Included in the program are runway extensions to accommodate larger aircraft; construction of new runways to increase the safety and efficiency of operations; the development of a more extensive system of air taxi services; and the upgrading of 50 locations to allow them to handle traffic diverted from congested major airports. More than $6,000,000 of the money is earmarked for the construction of 38 new public airports.

## SEA DISTANCES BETWEEN MAJOR WORLD PORTS (IN STATUTE MILES)

| MAJOR WORLD PORTS | BOMBAY | BUENOS AIRES | CAPE TOWN | COLOMBO | GIBRALTAR | HAMBURG | HONOLULU | ISTANBUL | LE HAVRE | LISBON |
|---|---|---|---|---|---|---|---|---|---|---|
| Bombay, India.......... | — | 9,601 | 5,317 | 1,042 | 5,639 | 7,552 | 9,631 | 4,412 | 7,024 | 6,036 |
| Buenos Aires, Argentina..... | 9,601 | — | 4,300 | 9,415 | 6,074 | 7,622 | 8,744 | 8,488 | 7,074 | 6,148 |
| Cape Town, South Africa...... | 5,317 | 4,300 | — | 5,070 | 5,982 | 7,388 | 11,948 | 7,137 | 6,861 | 5,904 |
| Colombo, Ceylon............ | 1,042 | 9,415 | 5,070 | — | 6,227 | 8,090 | 8,594 | 4,920 | 7,563 | 6,577 |
| Gibraltar................. | 5,639 | 6,074 | 5,982 | 6,227 | — | 1,863 | 10,433 | 2,094 | 1,336 | 350 |
| Hamburg, West Germany...... | 7,552 | 7,622 | 7,388 | 8,090 | 1,863 | — | 11,283 | 3,939 | 588 | 1,543 |
| Honolulu, Hawaii............ | 9,631 | 8,744 | 11,948 | 8,594 | 10,433 | 11,283 | — | 12,510 | 10,757 | 10,363 |
| Istanbul, Turkey............ | 4,412 | 8,488 | 7,137 | 4,920 | 2,094 | 3,939 | 12,510 | — | 3,421 | 2,430 |
| Le Havre, France............ | 7,024 | 7,074 | 6,861 | 7,563 | 1,336 | 588 | 10,757 | 3,421 | — | 1,017 |
| Lisbon, Portugal............ | 6,036 | 6,148 | 5,904 | 6,577 | 350 | 1,543 | 10,363 | 2,430 | 1,017 | — |
| Liverpool, England.......... | 7,156 | 7,178 | 7,001 | 7,717 | 1,490 | 1,083 | 10,682 | 3,543 | 587 | 1,148 |
| Manila, Philippines.......... | 4,361 | 12,128 | 7,821 | 3,399 | 9,641 | 16,678 | 5,591 | 8,245 | 10,856 | 9,867 |
| Melbourne, Australia........ | 6,365 | 8,477 | 6,998 | 5,380 | 11,257 | 13,066 | 5,691 | 9,928 | 12,540 | 11,551 |
| New Orleans, Louisiana...... | 10,927 | 7,233 | 9,382 | 11,489 | 5,271 | 5,935 | 7,046 | 7,384 | 5,315 | 5,377 |
| New York, New York........ | 9,413 | 6,752 | 7,804 | 9,941 | 3,685 | 4,166 | 7,718 | 5,767 | 3,640 | 3,403 |
| Panama Canal Zone......... | 14,921 | 6,311 | 7,417 | 13,919 | 5,038 | 5,888 | 5,388 | 7,115 | 5,363 | 4,826 |
| Port Said, Egypt........... | 3,506 | 8,259 | 6,212 | 4,003 | 2,217 | 4,058 | 12,604 | 925 | 3,521 | 2,532 |
| Rio de Janeiro, Brazil........ | 8,998 | 1,324 | 3,764 | 8,839 | 4,816 | 6,354 | 9,875 | 6,897 | 5,820 | 4,852 |
| San Francisco, California...... | 11,247 | 10,062 | 11,154 | 10,289 | 8,775 | 9,625 | 2,405 | 10,884 | 9,095 | 8,737 |
| Singapore, Malaysia......... | 2,807 | 10,782 | 6,502 | 1,818 | 8,008 | 9,838 | 6,772 | 6,700 | 9,312 | 8,323 |
| Valparaiso, Chile........... | 11,356 | 3,181 | 6,977 | 11,073 | 9,006 | 8,900 | 6,816 | 11,020 | 8,347 | 7,975 |
| Wellington, New Zealand...... | 7,961 | 6,956 | 8,393 | 7,058 | 12,847 | 13,758 | 4,730 | 11,540 | 12,801 | 12,459 |
| Yokohama, Japan........... | 6,155 | 13,921 | 9,614 | 5,151 | 11,353 | 14,734 | 3,906 | 10,037 | 12,649 | 11,660 |

## RECORD TRANSATLANTIC SHIP CROSSINGS

The times shown are for the passage between various points on the coast of Europe and New York Harbor. The record set by the *S.S. United States* in its 1952 voyage from Bishop Head Lighthouse to Ambrose Lightship remains unsurpassed by any other passenger vessel.

| SHIP | FROM | TO | YEAR | TIME Days | Hours | Minutes | AVERAGE SPEED (in knots) |
|---|---|---|---|---|---|---|---|
| Deutschland........ | Southampton...... | New York.......... | 1900 | 5 | 11 | 54 | 23.15 |
| Deutschland........ | Eddystone Light.... | New York.......... | 1900 | 5 | 7 | 38 | 23.51 |
| Rex............. | Gibraltar.......... | New York.......... | 1933 | 4 | 13 | 58 | 28.92 |
| Normandie......... | Bishop Head....... | Ambrose.......... | 1935 | 4 | 3 | 14 | 29.94 |
| Normandie......... | Ambrose.......... | Bishop Head...... | 1935 | 4 | 3 | 28 | 30.31 |
| Queen Mary........ | Bishop Head....... | Ambrose.......... | 1936 | 4 | | 27 | 30.14 |
| Queen Mary........ | Ambrose.......... | Bishop Head...... | 1936 | 3 | 23 | 57 | 30.63 |
| Normandie......... | Bishop Head....... | Ambrose.......... | 1937 | 3 | 23 | 2 | 30.58 |
| Normandie......... | Ambrose.......... | Bishop Head...... | 1937 | 4 | | 6 | 30.99 |
| Normandie......... | Ambrose.......... | Bishop Head...... | 1937 | 3 | 22 | 7 | 31.20 |
| Queen Mary........ | Bishop Head....... | Ambrose.......... | 1938 | 3 | 21 | 48 | 30.99 |
| Queen Mary........ | Ambrose.......... | Bishop Head...... | 1938 | 3 | 20 | 42 | 31.69 |
| United States........ | Ambrose.......... | Bishop Head...... | 1952 | 3 | 10 | 40 | 35.59 |
| United States........ | Bishop Head....... | Ambrose.......... | 1952 | 3 | 12 | 12 | 34.51 |

## WORLD'S LARGEST PASSENGER LINERS

Source: Lloyd's Register of Shipping

| NAME | COUNTRY OF REGISTRY | YEAR COMPLETED | PASSENGER CAPACITY | GROSS REGISTERED TONS | OVER-ALL LENGTH | EXTREME WIDTH |
|---|---|---|---|---|---|---|
| Queen Elizabeth..... | United Kingdom..... | 1940 | 2,083 | 82,998 | 1,031' | 118' 7'' |
| Queen Mary......... | United Kingdom..... | 1936 | 2,022 | 81,237 | 1,019' 6'' | 118' 7'' |
| France............. | France............. | 1961 | 2,033 | 66,348 | 1,035' 2'' | 110' 11'' |
| United States....... | United States....... | 1952 | 1,930 | 50,924 | 990' | 101' 7'' |
| Raffaello........... | Italy............. | 1963 | 1,775 | 45,933 | 904' 7'' | 101' 10'' |
| Michelangelo........ | Italy............. | 1963 | 1,775 | 45,911 | 904' 11'' | 101' 10'' |
| Canberra........... | United Kingdom..... | 1961 | 2,400 | 45,733 | 818' 6'' | 102' 6'' |
| Oriana............. | United Kingdom..... | 1960 | 2,216 | 41,915 | 804' | 97' 2'' |
| Rotterdam.......... | Netherlands........ | 1959 | 1,499 | 38,621 | 748' 7'' | 94' 2'' |
| Windsor Castle...... | United Kingdom..... | 1960 | 848 | 37,647 | 783' 1'' | 92' 6'' |

| LIVERPOOL | MANILA | MELBOURNE | NEW ORLEANS | NEW YORK | PANAMA CANAL ZONE | PORT SAID | RIO DE JANEIRO | SAN FRANCISCO | SINGAPORE | VALPARAISO | WELLINGTON | YOKOHAMA |
|---|---|---|---|---|---|---|---|---|---|---|---|---|
| 7,156 | 4,361 | 6,365 | 10,927 | 9,413 | 14,921 | 3,506 | 8,998 | 11,247 | 2,807 | 11,356 | 7,961 | 6,155 |
| 7,178 | 12,128 | 8,477 | 7,232 | 6,752 | 6,311 | 8,259 | 1,324 | 10,062 | 10,782 | 3,181 | 6,956 | 13,921 |
| 7,001 | 7,821 | 6,998 | 9,382 | 7,814 | 7,417 | 6,212 | 3,769 | 11,154 | 6,502 | 6,977 | 8,393 | 9,614 |
| 7,717 | 3,399 | 5,380 | 11,489 | 9,941 | 13,919 | 4,003 | 8,839 | 10,289 | 1,818 | 11,073 | 7,058 | 5,151 |
| 1,490 | 9,641 | 11,257 | 5,271 | 3,685 | 5,038 | 2,217 | 4,816 | 8,775 | 8,008 | 9,006 | 12,847 | 11,353 |
| 1,083 | 16,678 | 13,066 | 5,935 | 4,166 | 5,888 | 4,058 | 6,354 | 9,625 | 9,838 | 8,900 | 13,758 | 14,734 |
| 10,682 | 5,591 | 5,691 | 7,046 | 7,718 | 5,388 | 12,604 | 9,875 | 2,405 | 6,772 | 6,816 | 4,730 | 3,906 |
| 3,543 | 8,245 | 9,928 | 7,384 | 5,767 | 7,115 | 925 | 6,897 | 10,884 | 6,700 | 11,020 | 11,540 | 10,037 |
| 587 | 10,856 | 12,540 | 5,315 | 3,640 | 5,363 | 3,521 | 5,820 | 9,095 | 9,312 | 8,347 | 12,801 | 12,649 |
| 1,148 | 9,867 | 11,551 | 5,377 | 3,403 | 4,826 | 2,532 | 4,852 | 8,737 | 8,323 | 7,975 | 12,459 | 11,660 |
| — | 11,111 | 12,764 | 5,266 | 3,659 | 5,287 | 3,652 | 5,932 | 9,024 | 9,490 | 8,299 | 12,778 | 13,399 |
| 11,111 | — | 5,214 | 12,414 | 13,086 | 10,776 | 7,335 | 11,524 | 7,164 | 1,530 | 11,166 | 5,572 | 2,022 |
| 12,764 | 5,214 | — | 10,780 | 11,452 | 9,116 | 9,040 | 9,416 | 8,011 | 4,396 | 7,222 | 1,737 | 5,606 |
| 5,266 | 12,414 | 10,780 | — | 1,970 | 1,658 | 7,498 | 5,965 | 5,287 | 13,207 | 4,663 | 9,133 | 10,489 |
| 3,659 | 13,086 | 11,452 | 1,970 | — | 2,321 | 5,919 | 5,493 | 6,074 | 11,693 | 5,335 | 9,814 | 11,169 |
| 5,287 | 10,776 | 9,116 | 1,658 | 2,321 | — | 7,217 | 5,058 | 3,737 | 12,081 | 3,008 | 7,481 | 8,834 |
| 3,652 | 7,335 | 9,040 | 7,498 | 5,919 | 7,217 | — | 7,006 | 10,986 | 5,771 | 10,225 | 10,630 | 9,128 |
| 5,932 | 11,524 | 9,416 | 5,965 | 5,493 | 5,058 | 7,006 | — | 8,794 | 10,179 | 4,191 | 7,861 | 13,317 |
| 9,024 | 7,164 | 8,011 | 5,287 | 6,074 | 3,737 | 10,986 | 8,794 | — | 8,456 | 5,919 | 6,785 | 5,216 |
| 9,490 | 1,530 | 4,396 | 13,207 | 11,693 | 12,081 | 5,771 | 10,179 | 8,456 | — | 12,534 | 5,992 | 3,322 |
| 8,299 | 11,166 | 7,222 | 4,663 | 5,335 | 3,008 | 10,225 | 4,191 | 5,919 | 12,534 | — | 5,799 | 10,672 |
| 12,778 | 5,572 | 1,737 | 9,133 | 9,814 | 7,481 | 10,630 | 7,861 | 6,785 | 5,992 | 5,799 | — | 6,223 |
| 13,399 | 2,022 | 5,606 | 10,489 | 11,169 | 8,834 | 9,128 | 13,317 | 5,216 | 3,322 | 10,672 | 6,223 | — |

## LEADING MERCHANT FLEETS OF THE WORLD

A continuing downward trend in the size of the privately owned American merchant fleet has reduced United States maritime strength to below the pre-World War II level. According to figures released by the American Merchant Marine Institute, the size of the American fleet has declined about 26 per cent since 1951, while the world fleet has steadily increased—to a 62 per cent gain over 1951. During the same period, the cargo-carrying capacity, or deadweight tonnage, of the United States fleet decreased by 2.7 per cent, while that of the world fleet rose by 156 per cent. A country-by-country comparison of the total number of ships and the total tonnage of the world's leading merchant fleets in 1951 and 1966 is given below.

| 1966 RANK | COUNTRY OF REGISTRY | SHIPS | TONNAGE | 1951 RANK | COUNTRY OF REGISTRY | SHIPS | TONNAGE |
|---|---|---|---|---|---|---|---|
| 1 | United Kingdom | 2,005 | 26,123,000 | 1 | United Kingdom | 2,580 | 22,154,000 |
| 2 | Liberia | 1,406 | 33,703,000 | 2 | United States | 1,264 | 15,180,000 |
| 3 | U.S.S.R. (estimated) | 1,360 | 9,811,000 | 3 | Norway | 965 | 8,021,000 |
| 4 | Japan | 1,353 | 18,048,000 | 4 | Sweden | 556 | 2,844,000 |
| 5 | Norway | 1,342 | 23,791,000 | 5 | France | 534 | 3,826,000 |
| 6 | United States | 955 | 14,766,000 | 6 | Panama | 530 | 5,306,000 |
| 7 | Greece | 933 | 10,132,000 | 7 | Netherlands | 501 | 3,773,000 |
| 8 | Germany, West | 853 | 7,415,000 | 8 | U.S.S.R. (estimated) | 465 | 1,898,000 |
| 9 | Italy | 577 | 7,020,000 | 9 | Italy | 459 | 3,747,000 |
| 10 | Panama | 559 | 7,059,000 | 10 | Japan | 411 | 2,529,000 |
| 11 | France | 536 | 6,535,000 | 11 | Denmark | 308 | 1,746,000 |
| 12 | Netherlands | 478 | 5,997,000 | 12 | Spain | 268 | 1,296,000 |
| 13 | Sweden | 432 | 5,841,000 | 13 | West Germany | 219 | 1,004,000 |
| 14 | Denmark | 338 | 3,696,000 | 14 | Greece | 213 | 1,822,000 |
| 15 | Spain | 328 | 2,141,000 | 15 | Finland | 183 | 743,000 |
| 16 | Finland | 228 | 1,385,000 | 16 | Brazil | 170 | 852,000 |
| 17 | Brazil | 226 | 1,594,000 | 17 | China, Mainland (estimated) | 146 | 580,000 |
| 18 | India | 213 | 2,513,000 | 18 | Canada | 134 | 875,000 |
| 19 | China (Mainland) (estimated) | 180 | 1,023,000 | 19 | Argentina | 133 | 1,073,000 |
| 20 | Yugoslavia | 179 | 1,510,000 | 20 | Turkey | 111 | 524,000 |
| 21 | Poland (estimated) | 173 | 1,383,000 | 21 | India | 82 | 589,000 |
| 22 | Argentina | 157 | 1,432,000 | 22 | Belgium | 80 | 600,000 |
| 23 | Lebanon | 146 | 1,143,000 | 23 | Liberia | 62 | 1,019,000 |
| 24 | China (Taiwan) | 118 | 1,037,000 | 24 | Poland (estimated) | 53 | 276,000 |
| 25 | Australia | 105 | 785,000 | 25 | Yugoslavia | 51 | 345,000 |

## TRAFFIC THROUGH THE PANAMA CANAL: 1966

Ships flying the Liberian flag carried the greatest amount of cargo through the Panama Canal in fiscal 1966. The following list, released by the Panama Canal Company, includes all transiting commercial vessels over 300 tons Panama Canal measurement, except those measured by displacement tonnage. Total displacement tonnage for fiscal 1966 was 218,092.

| NATION OF REGISTRY | TONS OF CARGO | NUMBER OF TRANSITS | GROSS TONNAGE | TOLLS | NATION OF REGISTRY | TONS OF CARGO | NUMBER OF TRANSITS | GROSS TONNAGE | TOLLS |
|---|---|---|---|---|---|---|---|---|---|
| Liberia...... | 16,145,359 | 1,242 | 14,364,770 | $ 9,751,243 | South Korea | 154,167 | 27 | 208,658 | $135,171 |
| Norway..... | 14,157,203 | 1,499 | 15,346,153 | 10,387,299 | Cuba....... | 115,764 | 11 | 105,650 | 69,771 |
| Great Britain | 9,366,894 | 1,308 | 12,854,882 | 8,351,338 | Nicaragua... | 105,524 | 76 | 186,132 | 167,602 |
| United States | 9,351,465 | 1,555 | 15,092,063 | 10,373,403 | Lebanon.... | 95,934 | 11 | 76,772 | 52,091 |
| Japan....... | 5,729,947 | 806 | 7,062,864 | 4,693,975 | Honduras... | 87,335 | 149 | 244,904 | 130,929 |
| Greece...... | 4,702,589 | 472 | 4,608,160 | 3,120,300 | Cyprus...... | 71,813 | 8 | 55,704 | 39,730 |
| Germany.... | 3,912,554 | 1,223 | 5,888,906 | 5,053,167 | Ecuador..... | 66,905 | 34 | 234,696 | 162,789 |
| Netherlands | 2,634,550 | 587 | 3,459,802 | 2,301,961 | Switzerland | 53,959 | 73 | 143,210 | 109,151 |
| Panama..... | 2,564,283 | 533 | 3,375,159 | 2,200,356 | Mexico...... | 50,539 | 47 | 87,448 | 57,321 |
| Sweden..... | 2,437,067 | 398 | 3,626,018 | 2,316,806 | Bulgaria.... | 40,482 | 3 | 32,323 | 24,062 |
| Denmark.... | 2,082,272 | 377 | 2,688,489 | 2,034,844 | Portugal.... | 40,311 | 2 | 28,636 | 20,211 |
| Italy........ | 1,292,892 | 206 | 2,066,486 | 1,363,472 | Czechoslovakia | 25,000 | 1 | 16,623 | 6,440 |
| China | | | | | Kuwait..... | 24,773 | 2 | 19,965 | 12,827 |
| (Taiwan).. | 1,053,115 | 132 | 1,095,977 | 732,570 | Spain....... | 18,419 | 7 | 27,494 | 17,859 |
| France...... | 870,496 | 255 | 1,566,644 | 1,084,118 | Haiti........ | 14,716 | 2 | 13,935 | 10,333 |
| Chile....... | 808,349 | 113 | 956,552 | 654,316 | Poland...... | 13,194 | 2 | 18,565 | 12,417 |
| Peru....... | 600,633 | 117 | 583,498 | 388,121 | Indonesia... | 2,710 | 1 | 6,866 | 6,087 |
| Israel....... | 587,974 | 95 | 692,836 | 489,580 | Venezuela... | 2,436 | 6 | 3,804 | 3,019 |
| India....... | 519,911 | 25 | 399,005 | 264,960 | South Africa | — | 1 | 16,405 | 8,178 |
| Colombia.... | 441,987 | 227 | 1,241,841 | 994,572 | New Zealand | — | 2 | 9,090 | 4,790 |
| Philippines.. | 416,010 | 89 | 896,133 | 560,412 | Pakistan.... | — | 1 | 5,368 | 3,558 |
| U.S.S.R..... | 283,492 | 34 | 282,568 | 173,101 | | | | | |
| Finland..... | 216,199 | 48 | 283,418 | 213,015 | **Totals** | | | | |
| Yugoslavia.. | 195,399 | 20 | 181,635 | 141,620 | Fiscal 1966.. | 81,703,514 | 11,925 | 100,762,225 | $69,095,129 |
| Ireland..... | 193,043 | 24 | 183,757 | 114,816 | Fiscal 1965.. | 76,573,071 | 11,834 | 95,924,123 | 65,442,633 |
| Belgium.... | 155,850 | 69 | 422,361 | 273,428 | Fiscal 1964.. | 70,555,090 | 11,808 | 89,829,766 | 61,098,312 |

Japan's 1,122-foot **Idemitsu Maru,** the world's largest ship

# EDUCATION

## Statistical Highlights • Scholarships and Loans • Fraternities and Sororities • College Guide

Students watch closed-circuit television in their classroom. There is little doubt that the new technology will play an increasingly important role in the schools of the future.

### U.S. EDUCATION: 1967

News of the year in education was dominated, in large part, by forces and events outside the traditional agencies of the educational establishment. The civil rights movement and the problems of the disadvantaged, for instance, continued to play a major role in reshaping the nation's thinking about the nature and function of education in contemporary society. The giant combines of electronics companies and publishing houses, formed in recent years to prepare instructional materials for the education market, made fundamental re-evaluations of their programs and objectives. And among the events that made news within the more traditional areas of education were the dramatic changes in the thinking of Catholics about the role of their colleges and universities, and the nationwide debate about how to make higher education available to all who can benefit from it.

The bright vision of the electronic classroom in which instruction would be individualized for each child by computer-controlled devices, grew somewhat hazy during 1967. The difficulties of preparing instructional materials that could be used effectively in the sophisticated electronic equipment available became clearer and the problems presented by a fragmented market composed of 25,000 separate school systems loomed larger. There remained little doubt that eventually computer-controlled instruction would play a major role in the nation's classrooms, and some firms continued to expand. But a number of the giants, such as International Business Machines Corporation and General Learning Corporation (a creation of General Electric and Time, Inc.) were convinced that the electronic revolution in the classroom is still some years off. [continued]

A dominant theme that continued to be sounded at every level of education in 1967 was the necessity of providing effective education for the disadvantaged members of American society. But the situation was different than in preceding years. As school opened, the more radical groups in the civil rights movement had grown impatient with the necessarily slow process of education and had turned to other avenues of social change.

Three events during the year had special significance for education of the disadvantaged. First, the House of Representatives went on record as favoring strict enforcement of the Civil Rights Act of 1964 equally in the North and the South. In the past, the act had been aimed primarily at officially enforced segregation in the South. Second, Judge J. Skelly Wright of the District of Columbia Court of Appeals for the first time affirmed the responsibility of local boards for seeking racial balance in the schools. Third, Negro demands for greater control over ghetto schools was met by the formation of three experimental school districts in New York City where a substantial degree of control was delegated to local school boards composed of parents, community leaders, and staff members.

The changing temper of Catholic education in the wake of Ecumenical Council Vatican II was demonstrated when a number of leading Church-related universities announced that they were divesting themselves of ecclesiastical control. St. Louis University and Notre Dame, for example, turned over ownership of the institutions to mixed boards of trustees in which laymen were in the majority. Provision was usually made, however, for the president to remain a member of the founding order. Meanwhile, Webster College in St. Louis renounced all ties to the Sisters of Loretto and became completely secular in ownership and control.

Debate on financing public higher education was touched off when California's new governor, Ronald Reagan, proposed that tuition be charged at the traditionally tuition-free University of California—and the university's regents refused to accept the proposal. However, in New York, where tuition of about $400 is charged at the state university and state colleges, a constitutional convention voted to establish "a system of free higher education for the benefit of all the people." Meanwhile, a panel of Presidential advisers called for the creation of an educational opportunity bank that would permit students to borrow the full cost of their college education and repay it out of their future earnings over a period of 40 years. To date, debate on the issue indicates wide awareness of a pressing problem but does not yet point to how it will be resolved nationwide.

## U.S. PUBLIC SCHOOL STATISTICAL HIGHLIGHTS: 1965–1967

Total expenditures for the nation's public schools reached a new high of $27.8 billion in 1966–67, an increase of $2.4 billion (9.3 per cent) over the preceding fiscal year. From 1956–57 through 1966–67 the expenditures for public elementary and secondary schools increased 131.4 per cent. During the same period the average number of pupils in daily attendance rose 37.9 per cent, and expenditures per pupil rose 82.5 per cent. Rising teacher salaries and an increasing number of men teachers were other significant trends.

The estimates below, prepared by the National Education Association, include projected pupil enrollment, teacher salaries, and expenditures.

| | 1966–67 | 1965–66 | PER CENT CHANGE |
|---|---|---|---|
| **TOTAL SCHOOL DISTRICTS**................. | 23,335 | 26,561 | —12.1 |
| **TOTAL PUPIL ENROLLMENT**................. | 42,986,514 | 42,018,433 | +2.3 |
| Elementary school........................... | 27,122,540 | 26,635,520 | +1.8 |
| Secondary school........................... | 15,863,974 | 15,382,913 | +3.1 |
| Pupils in daily attendance..................... | 39,805,427 | 38,904,661 | +2.3 |
| Number of high school graduates.............. | 2,421,666 | 2,358,859 | +2.7 |
| **TOTAL CLASSROOM TEACHERS**.............. | 1,759,236 | 1,696,562 | +3.7 |
| Elementary school........................... | 996,031 | 962,403 | +3.5 |
| Secondary school........................... | 763,205 | 734,159 | +4.0 |
| Men teachers................................ | 557,310 | 535,294 | +4.1 |
| Women teachers............................. | 1,201,926 | 1,161,268 | +3.5 |
| **AVERAGE ANNUAL SALARIES**................ | | | |
| Elementary school teachers.................... | $6,609 | $6,279 | +5.3 |
| Secondary school teachers.................... | $7,095 | $6,761 | +4.9 |
| **TOTAL REVENUE AND NONREVENUE RECEIPTS** | $30,194,908,000 | $27,974,203,000 | +7.9 |
| Revenue receipts by source................... | 26,821,486,000 | 24,819,832,000 | +8.1 |
| Federal.................................... | 2,148,908,000 | 1,914,759,000 | +12.2 |
| State...................................... | 10,689,559,000 | 9,734,866,000 | +9.8 |
| Local, intermediate, and other................ | 13,983,019,000 | 13,170,207,000 | +6.2 |
| Nonrevenue receipts......................... | 3,373,422,000 | 3,154,371,000 | +6.9 |
| **TOTAL EXPENDITURES**...................... | $27,762,098,000 | $25,391,254,000 | +9.3 |
| Elementary and secondary day schools.......... | 22,434,237,000 | 20,429,086,000 | +9.8 |
| Other programs operated by local school districts............................... | 862,218,000 | 700,569,000 | +23.1 |
| Capital outlay............................... | 3,553,110,000 | 3,416,065,000 | +4.0 |
| **Current expenditures for elementary and secondary schools per pupil**................. | $564 | $525 | +7.4 |

# FOCUS ON THE NEWS

## TEACHER STRIKES

Wide World

Many teachers began the 1967-68 school year not in classrooms but in picket lines.

Wide World

Students at some strike-closed schools staged demonstrations urging their teachers to return.

The growing militancy of teachers hit a new high as back-to-school time came in September, 1967. A wave of teacher strikes kept classrooms closed in communities from Florida to Michigan. The strikes reflected not only widespread teacher dissatisfaction with salaries and teaching conditions; they indicated continuing competition for the allegiance of teachers between the small town and rural-oriented National Education Association (NEA), with more than 1,000,000 members, and the urban-oriented, 140,000-member American Federation of Teachers (AFT), an AFL-CIO affiliate.

As the academic year began, teachers in scattered districts in Florida closed the schools by withholding their services. The Florida Education Association, state arm of the NEA, threatened school officials with a statewide walkout of teachers if demands for higher pay and general improvement of the school system and teaching facilities were not met. The United Federation of Teachers, New York City's AFT affiliate, demanded not only higher pay and more adequate conditions for teaching, but also a direct voice in determining educational policy, especially in the inner-city schools.

Meanwhile, the Michigan Education Association and the Michigan Federation of Teachers, each representing teachers in a number of communities, closed the schools in more than 30 school districts in the state.

A new tactic was introduced by both the Florida Education Association and the United Federation of Teachers in New York City in their "cold war" with school and state officials. To avoid the penalties imposed by state laws forbidding strikes by public employees, they substituted for traditional strike techniques the threat of mass resignations by teachers. Written resignations were collected from member teachers by the organizations, which then held them to use when they became necessary. UFT teachers in New York resigned en masse in September to enforce their demands.

Reactions to the teachers' militant drive for higher pay and improved education varied widely across the country. Similarly, the reasons given for their determination to move into picket lines instead of classrooms ranged from charges of a purely selfish preoccupation with money to selfless devotion to the welfare of children—and there was evidence to support both views.

At year's end it was not clear where the new aggressiveness of the nation's teachers would lead, but there seemed little doubt that kindly Mr. Chips was dead.

## ELEMENTARY AND SECONDARY EDUCATION ACT

The Elementary and Secondary Education Act of 1965 provides funds for improving the education of needy children in all 50 states and in the outlying areas of American Samoa, Guam, Puerto Rico, the Virgin Islands, and the U.S. Trust Territories of the Pacific. The table below lists 1968 estimated allotments.

Assistance for Educationally Deprived Children allocates funds for schools in areas with families that have low annual per capita incomes. Money has also been provided for administration of this program.

Grants to States for School Library Mate-

rials provide books for both public and private school students.

The Supplementary Centers and Services provision allocates funds for supplementary educational and cultural programs and innovative projects in elementary and secondary education.

Funds are also available for strengthening state departments of education, the agencies that determine educational needs and create programs to meet them.

There are also provisions allocating money for handicapped children and for educational research and training.

| STATE | ASSISTANCE FOR EDUCATIONALLY DEPRIVED CHILDREN | STATE ADMINISTRATION | GRANTS TO STATES FOR SCHOOL LIBRARY MATERIALS | SUPPLEMENTARY CENTERS AND SERVICES | STRENGTHENING STATE DEPARTMENTS OF EDUCATION |
|---|---|---|---|---|---|
| United States.... | $1,158,507,209 | $12,240,791 | $102,439,024 | $234,146,341 | $24,781,750 |
| Alabama......... | 41,592,572 | 415,926 | 1,865,150 | 4,371,000 | 498,942 |
| Alaska.......... | 1,756,956 | 75,000 | 131,829 | 526,726 | 128,127 |
| Arizona......... | 8,882,769 | 88,828 | 862,745 | 2,091,004 | 275,190 |
| Arkansas........ | 26,010,246 | 260,103 | 955,631 | 2,445,818 | 306,145 |
| California....... | 73,849,950 | 738,500 | 9,867,333 | 21,218,545 | 2,092,128 |
| Colorado........ | 8,585,172 | 85,852 | 1,124,907 | 2,499,713 | 327,866 |
| Connecticut...... | 8,509,146 | 85,091 | 1,482,689 | 3,402,935 | 372,837 |
| Delaware........ | 2,022,296 | 75,000 | 275,363 | 792,987 | 151,493 |
| District of Columbia | 5,642,037 | 75,000 | 356,480 | 1,050,857 | 167,035 |
| Florida......... | 33,099,374 | 330,994 | 2,797,668 | 6,727,003 | 676,047 |
| Georgia......... | 45,366,305 | 453,663 | 2,270,121 | 5,404,550 | 590,823 |
| Hawaii.......... | 2,251,656 | 75,000 | 408,868 | 1,051,451 | 175,787 |
| Idaho........... | 3,199,302 | 75,000 | 380,332 | 1,039,388 | 179,782 |
| Illinois.......... | 46,858,813 | 468,588 | 5,661,346 | 12,314,817 | 1,087,053 |
| Indiana......... | 16,915,974 | 169,160 | 2,680,494 | 5,923,052 | 627,952 |
| Iowa........... | 15,414,565 | 154,145 | 1,533,619 | 3,394,927 | 390,865 |
| Kansas.......... | 9,992,513 | 99,925 | 1,179,451 | 2,804,615 | 335,771 |
| Kentucky........ | 33,736,392 | 337,364 | 1,592,875 | 3,914,671 | 408,319 |
| Louisiana........ | 37,398,616 | 373,986 | 2,014,914 | 4,534,697 | 475,145 |
| Maine........... | 4,711,801 | 75,000 | 536,135 | 1,336,345 | 201,484 |
| Maryland........ | 14,569,292 | 145,693 | 1,938,069 | 4,336,025 | 461,557 |
| Massachusetts.... | 14,814,866 | 148,149 | 2,818,673 | 6,195,703 | 595,136 |
| Michigan........ | 32,086,667 | 320,867 | 4,907,103 | 10,141,093 | 1,021,117 |
| Minnesota....... | 20,159,871 | 201,599 | 2,097,857 | 4,430,590 | 481,766 |
| Mississippi...... | 40,195,350 | 401,954 | 1,237,729 | 3,030,230 | 365,350 |
| Missouri......... | 25,321,803 | 253,218 | 2,368,994 | 5,279,259 | 540,595 |
| Montana......... | 3,548,792 | 75,000 | 393,211 | 1,042,926 | 176,790 |
| Nebraska........ | 7,751,029 | 77,510 | 786,320 | 1,882,882 | 245,742 |
| Nevada......... | 890,231 | 75,000 | 230,838 | 697,128 | 149,242 |
| New Hampshire... | 1,684,163 | 75,000 | 354,137 | 969,601 | 161,121 |
| New Jersey...... | 24,047,443 | 240,474 | 3,408,660 | 7,804,539 | 706,154 |
| New Mexico...... | 9,927,903 | 99,279 | 618,817 | 1,473,463 | 223,682 |
| New York....... | 114,027,374 | 1,140,274 | 8,618,005 | 20,115,247 | 1,585,078 |
| North Carolina.... | 58,859,338 | 588,593 | 2,481,943 | 6,027,947 | 641,100 |
| North Dakota..... | 5,202,448 | 75,000 | 350,368 | 984,343 | 167,461 |
| Ohio........... | 34,779,157 | 347,792 | 5,672,147 | 12,215,835 | 1,160,535 |
| Oklahoma........ | 17,356,626 | 173,566 | 1,278,138 | 2,969,448 | 373,545 |
| Oregon.......... | 7,452,202 | 75,000 | 1,054,265 | 2,439,605 | 316,799 |
| Pennsylvania..... | 48,152,478 | 481,525 | 5,933,438 | 13,255,526 | 1,110,940 |
| Rhode Island..... | 3,552,875 | 75,000 | 449,646 | 1,191,867 | 173,001 |
| South Carolina.... | 35,407,861 | 354,079 | 1,357,219 | 3,308,339 | 393,663 |
| South Dakota..... | 5,967,504 | 75,000 | 399,340 | 1,019,665 | 176,734 |
| Tennessee........ | 40,057,222 | 400,572 | 1,871,716 | 4,659,708 | 499,669 |
| Texas........... | 82,085,382 | 820,854 | 5,619,847 | 12,738,335 | 1,271,662 |
| Utah............ | 2,967,185 | 75,000 | 614,631 | 1,448,469 | 233,404 |
| Vermont......... | 2,020,035 | 75,000 | 220,297 | 668,595 | 140,044 |
| Virginia......... | 32,870,257 | 328,703 | 2,191,569 | 5,342,920 | 558,526 |
| Washington....... | 10,603,489 | 106,035 | 1,679,146 | 3,651,294 | 444,250 |
| West Virginia..... | 18,449,552 | 184,496 | 906,033 | 2,321,503 | 292,435 |
| Wisconsin........ | 16,343,417 | 163,434 | 2,419,037 | 5,064,673 | 507,045 |
| Wyoming......... | 1,558,942 | 75,000 | 183,881 | 594,482 | 138,816 |
| Outlying areas... | 28,962,000 | 290,000 | 2,560,976 | 5,853,659 | 505,750 |

## THE HIGHER EDUCATION ACT

The Higher Education Act of 1965 provides funds for programs related to higher education in all 50 states and the outlying areas of American Samoa, Guam, Puerto Rico, Virgin Islands, and U.S. Trust Territories of the Pacific. Estimated 1968 allotments are listed below.

The Grants to States for Community Service aid college and university projects dealing with community problems such as employment, youth opportunities, health, and land use.

Student Assistance Opportunity Grants assist academically deserving students who are otherwise unable to finance a college education.

Funds are allotted to participating institutions which then choose the recipients.

Student Assistance Work-Study Allotments are used to create jobs for students, preferably from low-income families, who are working to finance their educations.

Two programs authorize grants for improving and remodeling educational facilities and for purchasing TV equipment for educational use.

Other programs provide funds to improve college and university library resources and to strengthen developing institutions through scholar exchanges and other programs.

| STATE | GRANTS TO STATES FOR COMMUNITY SERVICE | OPPORTUNITY GRANTS FOR DESERVING STUDENTS | STUDENT ASSISTANCE WORK-STUDY PROGRAMS | IMPROVEMENT OF UNDERGRADUATE INSTRUCTIONAL EQUIPMENT | IMPROVEMENT OF UNDERGRADUATE INSTRUCTIONAL TV EQUIPMENT |
|---|---|---|---|---|---|
| United States.... | $16,240,587 | $57,705,356 | $137,102,000 | $12,891,231 | $1,487,448 |
| Alabama......... | 300,402 | 823,220 | 3,402,550 | 193,668 | 22,347 |
| Alaska.......... | 115,349 | 24,798 | 110,856 | 6,882 | 794 |
| Arizona......... | 190,543 | 653,620 | 1,267,322 | 159,303 | 18,382 |
| Arkansas........ | 211,584 | 550,654 | 2,070,215 | 127,683 | 14,733 |
| California....... | 1,157,945 | 5,828,613 | 10,940,382 | 1,450,104 | 167,319 |
| Colorado........ | 212,043 | 847,633 | 1,541,683 | 174,365 | 20,119 |
| Connecticut...... | 262,690 | 722,741 | 1,462,549 | 147,353 | 17,002 |
| Delaware........ | 128,916 | 110,472 | 283,348 | 22,164 | 2,557 |
| District of Columbia | 146,105 | 490,281 | 675,945 | 99,897 | 11,526 |
| Florida......... | 433,199 | 1,375,325 | 3,735,748 | 330,296 | 38,111 |
| Georgia......... | 352,428 | 979,601 | 3,817,886 | 226,270 | 26,108 |
| Hawaii.......... | 140,816 | 204,554 | 464,133 | 43,142 | 4,978 |
| Idaho.......... | 139,839 | 241,091 | 535,156 | 55,071 | 6,354 |
| Illinois......... | 711,726 | 2,859,729 | 6,121,921 | 588,086 | 67,856 |
| Indiana......... | 381,287 | 1,610,258 | 3,257,861 | 335,874 | 38,755 |
| Iowa........... | 258,551 | 1,125,440 | 2,343,101 | 229,325 | 26,460 |
| Kansas......... | 229,232 | 984,500 | 1,743,307 | 207,355 | 23,926 |
| Kentucky........ | 282,408 | 902,617 | 2,901,947 | 210,391 | 24,276 |
| Louisiana........ | 304,656 | 1,084,608 | 3,420,112 | 249,146 | 28,748 |
| Maine.......... | 156,683 | 233,334 | 685,469 | 56,399 | 6,507 |
| Maryland........ | 303,161 | 857,344 | 2,081,373 | 188,796 | 21,785 |
| Massachusetts.... | 408,191 | 2,136,959 | 3,564,572 | 437,154 | 50,440 |
| Michigan........ | 578,125 | 2,627,077 | 5,327,980 | 578,607 | 66,763 |
| Minnesota....... | 304,771 | 1,375,088 | 2,849,556 | 293,104 | 33,820 |
| Mississippi...... | 232,739 | 694,658 | 2,875,132 | 163,685 | 18,886 |
| Missouri........ | 358,234 | 1,481,800 | 3,371,160 | 311,137 | 35,900 |
| Montana........ | 140,414 | 261,256 | 555,812 | 54,234 | 6,258 |
| Nebraska....... | 183,874 | 558,234 | 1,196,954 | 120,263 | 13,876 |
| Nevada......... | 124,950 | 67,687 | 175,589 | 13,563 | 1,565 |
| New Hampshire... | 138,689 | 241,743 | 444,257 | 51,759 | 5,973 |
| New Jersey...... | 489,824 | 1,025,243 | 3,036,691 | 227,465 | 26,246 |
| New Mexico...... | 158,292 | 310,006 | 867,005 | 73,910 | 8,528 |
| New York........ | 1,140,872 | 4,571,739 | 9,805,851 | 1,040,626 | 120,071 |
| North Carolina.... | 383,701 | 1,374,555 | 4,898,921 | 317,314 | 36,613 |
| North Dakota..... | 137,482 | 285,194 | 633,909 | 61,709 | 7,120 |
| Ohio............ | 688,731 | 2,816,176 | 6,245,743 | 610,733 | 70,469 |
| Oklahoma........ | 240,730 | 990,215 | 2,191,336 | 229,566 | 26,488 |
| Oregon.......... | 211,411 | 765,379 | 1,417,072 | 164,245 | 18,951 |
| Pennsylvania..... | 765,880 | 2,915,484 | 7,183,823 | 639,488 | 73,787 |
| Rhode Island..... | 151,221 | 328,912 | 613,613 | 74,064 | 8,546 |
| South Carolina.... | 246,593 | 549,499 | 2,623,976 | 130,542 | 15,063 |
| South Dakota..... | 139,437 | 278,770 | 677,459 | 62,211 | 7,178 |
| Tennessee........ | 321,327 | 1,186,079 | 3,616,437 | 276,667 | 31,923 |
| Texas........... | 708,852 | 3,192,861 | 8,448,098 | 728,084 | 84,010 |
| Utah........... | 157,143 | 698,256 | 984,959 | 152,737 | 17,623 |
| Vermont......... | 123,225 | 183,991 | 339,590 | 39,778 | 4,590 |
| Virginia......... | 354,095 | 942,707 | 3,190,184 | 221,728 | 25,584 |
| Washington....... | 270,911 | 1,207,871 | 2,181,966 | 251,586 | 29,029 |
| West Virginia..... | 204,340 | 550,284 | 1,763,312 | 127,359 | 14,696 |
| Wisconsin........ | 337,999 | 1,453,301 | 2,905,393 | 310,579 | 35,836 |
| Wyoming........ | 118,971 | 123,899 | 252,786 | 25,764 | 2,973 |
| Outlying areas... | 259,413 | 394,644 | 2,798,000 | 108,769 | 12,552 |

## EDUCATION AND EMPLOYMENT: 1966

This Department of Labor survey of Americans employed in major occupational fields gives a breakdown of male and female workers for each level of school begun or completed.

| OCCUPATION AND SEX | TOTAL EMPLOYED | EDUCATIONAL LEVEL | | | | |
|---|---|---|---|---|---|---|
| | | None | Elementary | High School | College | Graduate |
| **BOTH SEXES, all occupations** | 69,312,000 | .5% | 21.4% | 55.1% | 18.4% | 4.6% |
| Professional and technical workers | 9,353,000 | — | 1.4 | 21.5 | 49.0 | 28.0 |
| Farmers and farm managers | 2,044,000 | 1.1 | 52.6 | 39.9 | 6.0 | .3 |
| Managers, proprietors, except farm | 7,329,000 | .2 | 12.6 | 49.8 | 32.8 | 4.7 |
| Clerical workers | 11,229,000 | .1 | 5.5 | 73.3 | 20.4 | .8 |
| Sales workers | 4,223,000 | .2 | 11.4 | 61.6 | 25.3 | 1.4 |
| Craftsmen and foremen | 9,042,000 | .2 | 26.5 | 64.4 | 8.6 | .3 |
| Operatives | 13,397,000 | .8 | 32.7 | 61.6 | 4.6 | .2 |
| Service workers | 8,505,000 | .8 | 33.5 | 57.8 | 7.7 | .2 |
| Farm laborers and foremen | 1,168,000 | 5.1 | 50.9 | 39.3 | 4.7 | — |
| Laborers, except farm and mine | 3,022,000 | 1.9 | 44.0 | 49.7 | 4.1 | .2 |
| **MALE, all occupations** | 44,760,000 | .6 | 23.6 | 51.9 | 18.5 | 5.4 |
| Professional and technical workers | 5,833,000 | — | 1.7 | 20.8 | 44.8 | 32.6 |
| Medical and other health workers | 626,000 | — | 1.3 | 9.6 | 18.7 | 70.4 |
| Teachers, except college | 655,000 | — | .3 | 4.9 | 47.9 | 46.9 |
| Other | 4,552,000 | — | 2.0 | 24.6 | 48.0 | 25.4 |
| Farmers and farm managers | 1,918,000 | 1.0 | 53.1 | 40.2 | 5.4 | .3 |
| Managers, proprietors, except farm | 6,200,000 | .2 | 12.5 | 47.9 | 34.4 | 5.0 |
| Salaried workers | 3,943,000 | .1 | 6.5 | 45.9 | 41.0 | 6.5 |
| Self-employed retail workers | 953,000 | .7 | 25.6 | 51.8 | 20.5 | 1.4 |
| Self-employed non-retail workers | 1,304,000 | — | 21.2 | 51.2 | 24.6 | 2.9 |
| Clerical workers | 3,285,000 | .1 | 10.2 | 62.8 | 25.3 | 1.6 |
| Retail and other sales workers | 2,519,000 | .2 | 10.6 | 51.5 | 35.4 | 2.3 |
| Craftsmen and foremen | 8,784,000 | .2 | 26.7 | 64.2 | 8.6 | .3 |
| Carpenters | 833,000 | .2 | 36.4 | 58.4 | 4.8 | .2 |
| Construction craftsmen, except carpenters | 1,841,000 | .2 | 30.0 | 62.8 | 6.9 | — |
| Mechanics and repairmen | 2,131,000 | .1 | 26.7 | 65.9 | 7.2 | .2 |
| Metal craftsmen, except mechanics | 1,099,000 | .2 | 23.9 | 68.9 | 6.9 | .2 |
| Other craftsmen | 1,651,000 | .3 | 23.9 | 64.0 | 11.0 | .8 |
| Other foremen | 1,229,000 | — | 21.9 | 63.0 | 14.4 | .7 |
| Operatives | 9,454,000 | .8 | 31.6 | 62.3 | 5.0 | .3 |
| Drivers and deliverymen | 2,420,000 | .4 | 33.7 | 60.3 | 5.4 | .2 |
| Other operatives | 7,034,000 | .9 | 30.9 | 62.9 | 4.9 | .3 |
| Durable goods manufacturing | 3,494,000 | .7 | 28.6 | 65.6 | 4.9 | .3 |
| Nondurable goods manufacturing | 1,650,000 | 1.0 | 35.0 | 59.4 | 4.3 | .2 |
| Other industries | 1,890,000 | 1.3 | 31.6 | 61.3 | 5.5 | .3 |
| Service workers | 3,034,000 | .8 | 31.5 | 56.0 | 11.4 | .4 |
| Protective service | 849,000 | — | 18.8 | 67.2 | 13.7 | .2 |
| Other, including private household | 2,185,000 | 1.1 | 36.4 | 51.6 | 10.4 | .5 |
| Farm laborers and foremen | 808,000 | 7.4 | 55.7 | 33.2 | 3.7 | — |
| Laborers, except farm and mine | 2,925,000 | 2.0 | 44.6 | 49.1 | 4.2 | .2 |
| **FEMALE, all occupations** | 24,552,000 | .4 | 17.3 | 61.1 | 18.0 | 3.3 |
| Professional and technical workers | 3,520,000 | — | 1.0 | 22.7 | 55.9 | 20.3 |
| Medical and other health workers | 912,000 | — | 1.0 | 41.9 | 49.3 | 7.9 |
| Teachers, except college | 1,493,000 | — | .4 | 5.3 | 69.3 | 25.0 |
| Other | 1,115,000 | — | 2.0 | 30.4 | 43.5 | 24.1 |
| Managers, except farm | 1,129,000 | .2 | 12.7 | 60.1 | 24.0 | 2.9 |
| Salaried workers | 721,000 | — | 8.6 | 63.9 | 24.1 | 3.3 |
| Self-employed workers | 408,000 | .5 | 20.1 | 53.5 | 23.8 | 2.2 |
| Clerical workers | 7,944,000 | * | 3.5 | 77.6 | 18.4 | .4 |
| Stenographers, typists, and secretaries | 2,883,000 | .1 | .9 | 77.4 | 21.5 | .2 |
| Other clerical workers | 5,061,000 | — | 5.1 | 77.6 | 16.7 | .5 |
| Sales workers | 1,704,000 | .2 | 12.6 | 76.6 | 10.4 | .2 |
| Craftsmen and foremen | 258,000 | — | 18.2 | 72.5 | 9.3 | — |
| Operatives | 3,943,000 | .9 | 35.3 | 59.9 | 3.6 | .2 |
| Durable goods manufacturing | 1,149,000 | .4 | 26.1 | 69.6 | 3.8 | — |
| Nondurable goods manufacturing | 2,017,000 | 1.1 | 41.5 | 55.1 | 1.9 | .3 |
| Other industries, drivers, deliverymen | 777,000 | .9 | 33.0 | 58.5 | 7.7 | — |
| Private household workers | 1,658,000 | 1.9 | 50.5 | 44.2 | 3.3 | .2 |
| Service workers, except private household | 3,813,000 | .4 | 27.6 | 64.9 | 6.8 | .2 |
| Waitresses, cooks, and bartenders | 1,241,000 | .2 | 27.4 | 67.3 | 5.2 | — |
| Other service workers | 2,572,000 | .5 | 27.8 | 63.8 | 7.6 | .2 |
| Farmers, farm managers, laborers | 486,000 | .4 | 41.6 | 48.8 | 9.1 | .2 |
| Laborers, except farm and mine | 97,000 | ** | ** | ** | ** | ** |

* Less than 0.05%.    ** This figure not broken down since base is less than 100,000.

# COLLEGE SCHOLARSHIPS AND LOANS

## HOW TO GET A SCHOLARSHIP

The tremendous rise in the cost of a college education has prompted expansion of U.S. scholarship and loan programs, and it is now possible for most promising students to advance their education to the college level. Many students are confused about the types of financial aid available.

According to current usage, a *scholarship* is a grant to a student requiring no repayment or return of service. A *loan,* however, requires repayment in either cash or services, usually fulfilled after college. Often there is a small interest charge. A *grant* is a stipend given an undergraduate or graduate student for research performed under the supervision of the university; and a *scholarship loan* is financial assistance advanced to the student but canceled, either in part or in full, upon completion of services to the granting agency.

Scholarships can be obtained from three main sources: colleges and universities; nonacademic organizations such as foundations, corporations, business organizations, labor unions, service clubs, religious groups, and civic, fraternal, and professional organizations; and Federal, state, and local governments.

In general, most scholarship awards are based on the high school academic and extracurricular record; the recommendation of the school principal or adviser regarding potential and character; and scores and ranking on the College Entrance Examination Board Aptitude and Achievement Tests and/or the National Merit Scholarship Qualifying Test. These factors, together with the extent of financial need, determine the amount of the scholarship. Some scholarships cover full tuition and expenses, but many give only partial coverage.

**College Scholarship Service:** Associated with the College Entrance Examination Board, this service aids participating colleges and national scholarship competitions in determining the financial need of applicants. A Parents' Confidential Statement is completed by the student's parents and sent to the College Scholarship Service. The form, containing pertinent information about the family's financial status, is carefully evaluated. Copies are then forwarded to the colleges that the applicant has selected or the competition that the student is entering, where the final decisions are made.

Forms are available at high schools and colleges. They may also be obtained from the College Scholarship Service, Box 176, Princeton, N.J. 08540; or Box 1025, Berkeley, Calif. 94701; or Box 881, Evanston, Ill. 60204. The cost of the service to the parents is $2.50 for the first copy and $2 for each additional copy.

Below are descriptions of some of the available scholarships and loans. High school guidance counselors or college financial aid officers can provide further information.

## MAJOR NATIONAL SCHOLARSHIP PROGRAMS

**National Merit Scholarship Corporation:** In 1968, 2,900 scholarships will be awarded by the National Merit Scholarship Corporation to high school seniors. A total of 2,400 students will receive scholarships ranging from $250 to $1,500 per year, depending on financial need. In addition, for the first time, 500 students will receive single National Merit $1,000 Scholarships. All scholarship winners may enroll in the school of their choice.

Finalists are picked on the basis of their performance on the National Merit Scholarship Qualifying Test and the Scholastic Aptitude Test. The winners are then chosen from this group on the basis of such qualities as leadership, extracurricular activities, and academic potential. Some of the sponsors have their own particular criteria for selecting their winners from the finalists.

Grants from the Ford Foundation and the Carnegie Corporation helped to establish this nonprofit organization in 1955. Today there are about 350 participating sponsors, including foundations, business organizations, schools, and individuals.

**General Motors Scholarship Program:** General Motors awards about 300 four-year scholarships annually. These range from $200 to $2,000 per year. To be eligible, a student must apply to one of the over 200 approved colleges and must specify interest in the program. The college makes the final selection.

## FEDERAL SCHOLARSHIPS

In 1965 the U.S. Government enacted the Higher Education Act, part of which provides for scholarships known as Educational Opportunity Grants. High school seniors or undergraduates of exceptional need who have academic or creative potential are eligible for these awards.

Grants range from $200 to $1,000 a year, depending upon the college tuition and the amount that the family can afford to contribute. The award can be no more than one-half of the total financial aid given to the student, including such assistance as loans and individual scholarships. The college makes the final student selection based on its own scholarship procedures. The estimated Federal appropriation for 1968 is $140,000,000. The program will be reviewed after June 30, 1968.

For further information on the program, write to the U.S. Department of Health, Education, and Welfare, Office of Education, Washington, D.C. 20202.

## MAJOR STATE SCHOLARSHIPS *

**California.** About 7,200 scholarships (1,800 for new winners) per year for state colleges. From $300 to $1,500. State Scholarship Commission, 520 Capitol Mall, Sacramento, Calif.

**Hawaii.** 256 full-tuition scholarships for state residents to the University of Hawaii, renewable for three years. Scholarship Commission, University of Hawaii, Honolulu, Hawaii.

**Illinois.** About 3,000 scholarships, $300 to $1,000, renewable for three years. State Scholarship Commission, Box 607, Deerfield, Ill.

**Indiana.** Scholarships of $100 to $800 to two students from each of the 92 counties; hundreds of awards given "at large." State Scholarship Commission of Indiana, State Office Building, 100 North Senate Ave., Indianapolis, Ind.

**Iowa.** State College of Iowa offers 500 $280 scholarships, renewable every year for three years. University of Iowa awards Merit Scholarships of $340. Contact these institutions for further information.

**Kansas.** 200 scholarships up to $500 or full tuition for Kansas colleges. State Department of Public Instruction, Topeka, Kansas.

**Maryland.** To be used in Maryland institutions, based on statewide competitive examination: 171 General State Tuition Scholarships with maximum value of $2,000 for all four years; many Legislative (Senatorial) Scholarships to $1,500 per year. Apply at your high school, college of your choice, or State Scholarship Board, 301 West Preston St., Baltimore, Md.

**Massachusetts.** About 1,500 one-quarter to full-tuition scholarships for regionally accredited institutions. About 30 special education awards of $500 to those planning to teach mentally retarded children. Board of Higher Education, 182 Tremont St., Boston, Mass.

**Nebraska.** 300 Regents scholarships awarded annually at the University of Nebraska: 100 full-tuition, four-year awards for top scorers, 200 first-year $204 awards to top scorers by geographic distribution. Contact the University.

**New Jersey.** Competitive scholarships for about 5,000 high school graduates. Some may be used out of state. Awards of $500 or full-tuition renewable for three years. N.J. State Scholarship Commission, N.J. State Department of Education, P.O. Box 2019, Trenton, N.J.

**New York.** (1) Regents College Scholarships: Awarded to 18,843 students annually, allocated on a county basis. Students must attend an approved college in New York State. Range from $250 to $1,000 a year, for four years. (2) Scholar Incentive Program: Assists about 120,000 New York students attending colleges in the state, providing $100, $200, or $500 per year, according to financial ability. Regents Examination and Scholarship Center, State Educational Department, Albany, N.Y.

**Pennsylvania.** Various awards, up to $1,200 per year, based on need. Pennsylvania Higher Education Assistance, Towne House, Harrisburg, Penn.

\* High school graduates interested in a teaching career are offered a variety of state scholarships.

## OTHER SCHOLARSHIPS

**Aluminum Corporation of America Scholarship Fund:** Almost 150 awards, ranging from $250 to $625, at 31 specified schools in the U.S. Also, $2,500 plus $500 resident fee to children of employees. Alcoa Foundation, Aluminum Corp. of America, 1501 Alcoa Bldg., Pittsburgh, Penn.

**American Baptist Student Aid Fund:** Scholarships of varying amounts, applicable to any accredited college in the U.S. High school seniors must be nominated by their pastor. American Baptist Board of Education and Publication, Valley Forge, Penn. 19481.

**Elks National Foundation:** About 75 awards to freshmen, sophomores, and juniors, ranging between $800 and $1,500. Available to high school seniors and undergraduates. Contact local Elk lodges or Elks National Foundation, 2750 Lake View Avenue, Chicago, Ill. 60614.

**Kennecott Copper Corporation:** 26 renewable one-year scholarships of $1,000 for students studying engineering, chemistry, or geology at 23 selected schools. Kennecott Copper Corporation, 161 East 42nd Street, New York, N.Y.

**Lockheed Leadership Fund:** 15 scholarships for engineering or subjects applicable to aircraft industry, covering full tuition and fees plus $500 for personal expenses. Lockheed Leadership Fund, P.O. Box 551, Burbank, Calif. 91503.

**National Honor Society Scholarships:** For members of National Honor Society. Scholarships range from $100 to $6,000. Contact high school principal or National Association of Secondary School Principals, 1201 Sixteenth Street, N.W., Washington, D.C. 20036.

**National Methodist Scholarships:** Approximately 500 scholarships in amounts up to $500 per year are available to students of Methodist faith who attend accredited Methodist colleges and universities. Write Department of Student Loans and Scholarships, P.O. Box 871, Nashville, Tenn. 37202.

**National Presbyterian College Scholarships:** About 50 scholarships, up to $1,200, for members of the United Presbyterian Church entering any of the 45 church-related colleges. Office of Educational Loans and Scholarships, United Presbyterian Church in the U.S.A., 425 Witherspoon Building, Philadelphia, Penn. 19107.

**National Scholarship Service and Fund for Negro Students:** About 150 supplementary scholarships (renewable) up to $600 for Negro students. Director, School-College Relations, National Scholarship Service and Fund for Negro Students, 6 East 82nd Street, New York, N.Y.

**Procter and Gamble Fund:** 47 four-year scholarships, two-thirds of which are for study in liberal arts (including ten at women's colleges) and for study in engineering and technical areas. Selection is made by participating colleges. The Procter and Gamble Scholarship Program, P.O. Box 599, Cincinnati, Ohio 45201.

**Pulitzer Free Scholarship Committee:** Ten four-year scholarships at $250 per year. Male New York high school students receive free tuition at Columbia only, but may attend other colleges or universities. Pulitzer Free Scholarship Committee, 105 Low Library, Columbia University, New York, N.Y. 10027.

**Radio Corporation of America:** Over 30 scholarships for $800 per year for undergraduates studying in a variety of fields in selected colleges. RCA Education Committee, Radio Corporation of America, Camden, N.J. 08101.

**Sears, Roebuck Foundation:** About 500 scholarships to students interested in agriculture and 135 in home economics. Also, City Scholarship Program of about 500 awards averaging $300 to graduating high school seniors in some 85 selected U.S. cities. Contact land-grant college in respective state and ask for information on Sears, Roebuck Foundation Agricultural Scholarship and Home Economics Scholarship programs, or write Director of Education Pro-

grams, The Sears Roebuck Foundation, 333 West Arthington Street, Chicago, Ill. 60607.

**Science Clubs of America:** Five scholarships from $3,000 to $7,000, and 35 at $250 each. To qualify, students must write a report on a science project. Science Clubs of America, 1719 N Street, N.W., Washington, D.C. 20036.

**Sloan National Scholarships:** About 140 awards between $200 and $2,500 given to male high school graduates. Financial need is not a determining factor. Alfred P. Sloan Foundation, Inc., 630 Fifth Avenue, New York, N.Y. 10020.

**Uniroyal, Inc.:** Scholarships of varying amounts to science students. Uniroyal, Inc., 1230 Avenue of the Americas, New York, N.Y. 10020.

**Westinghouse Educational Foundation:** Science Talent Search scholarships for exceptional students: One top award is $10,000, 39 range from $250 to $8,000. 4-H Club program scholarships, $400 for one year. University Relations, Educational Center, Westinghouse Electric Corporation, Pittsburgh, Penn. 15221.

## LOAN PROGRAMS

**Guaranteed Student Loans:** The Higher Education Act of 1965 authorized support for federal, state, and private nonprofit programs which would insure loans to students in institutions of higher education. Under the agreement the Federal Government pays all interest charges on loans up to 6 per cent while the student is in school, and up to half the interest thereafter, if the adjusted income of his family is less than $15,000 per year. The student may borrow up to $1,000 per year and is not required to start repayment until after completion of his studies.

Many state governments have the authority to guarantee those loans which are made by lending institutions in their states. Lending institutions include banks, credit unions, savings and loan associations, and insurance companies. The terms of repayment vary from place to place. In order to apply for a state-guaranteed loan, contact a bank participating in the program.

The United Student Aid Funds (U.S.A.F.) is a private nonprofit organization that endorses loans made by nearly 9,000 lending institutions to deserving college students. This organization, in accordance with the Higher Education Act, lets students borrow up to $1,000 per year to a maximum of $5,000, under a program similar to the state government above. Since many states are not authorized to guarantee loans, students in these states may borrow under the endorsement of the U.S.A.F. The borrower must start repayment within ten months after termination of his studies. Application is made to the college; the money is obtained from a participating bank.

**National Defense Student Loans:** These loans are authorized under provisions of the National Defense Education Act of 1958 and are made available by annual appropriations of Congress. The educational institutions that participate in the program are in charge of administering the loans and selecting the recipients. The institutions provide 10 per cent of the funds for these loans and the government 90 per cent. A needy undergraduate student may borrow up to $1,000 per year to a total of $5,000. The usual interest is 3 per cent after nine months; students have ten years to repay. Repayment must begin nine months after studies are completed, except in cases where a student has good reason, such as continued full or part-time study, or entering the Armed Forces or the Peace Corps. If the borrower becomes a full-time teacher in a public school or institution of higher education, up to one-half of the loan may be canceled, at the rate of 10 per cent a year up to 50 per cent. Teachers in hardship areas receive credit for 15 per cent annually and can pay back the loan in seven years.

Application for the National Defense Student Loans should be made directly to the school in which the student is interested, provided it is accredited. Eligibility is based on the financial need of the student, and special consideration is given to superior students.

**Educational Loans from Banks:** Parents can obtain loans for their children's education from commercial banks. Decisions are based on the credit of the parents. Plans vary, but these loans usually are larger than student loans, have shorter maturity and higher interest rates.

## COLLEGE WORK-STUDY PROGRAMS

The Federal Government helps to pay the basic rate for student jobs on campus or with nonprofit agencies off campus. The pay is $1.25 per hour in most cases, and students may work up to 15 hours a week during the school term

and up to 40 hours during the summer. The students must have great financial need and acceptable academic standing. Many colleges have their own student work plans with jobs available to qualified students.

## RISING COST OF U.S. EDUCATION

The figures below, released by the Life Insurance Agency Management Association, show how annual undergraduate college costs have increased since the 1960–61 academic year.

| INSTITUTION | 1960–61 COSTS | 1967–68 COSTS | INCREASE |
|---|---|---|---|
| **Women's Colleges** | | | |
| Bennington College, Vermont | $2,950 | $3,850 | 31% |
| Sarah Lawrence College, New York | 2,810 | 3,636 | 29 |
| Wheaton College, Massachusetts | 2,500 | 3,310 | 32 |
| Sweet Briar College, Virginia | 2,400 | 3,140 | 31 |
| Mills College, California | 2,450 | 2,985 | 22 |
| Barnard College, New York | 2,275 | 2,950 | 30 |
| **Men's Colleges** | | | |
| Harvard College, Massachusetts | 2,570 | 3,170 | 23 |
| Princeton University, New Jersey | 2,560 | 3,110 | 21 |
| Columbia College, New York | 2,460 | 3,050 | 24 |
| Haverford College, Pennsylvania | 2,250 | 3,010 | 34 |
| Amherst College, Massachusetts | 1,880 | 2,950 | 57 |
| California Institute of Technology, California | 2,201 | 2,883 | 31 |
| **Coeducational Colleges** | | | |
| New York University, New York | 2,360 | 3,395 | 44 |
| University of Chicago, Illinois | 1,995 | 3,330 | 67 |
| Brandeis University, Massachusetts | 2,330 | 3,130 | 34 |
| Cornell University, New York | 2,530 | 3,100 | 23 |
| Stanford University, California | 1,890 | 2,910 | 54 |

## COLLEGE AND UNIVERSITY ENDOWMENTS OVER $20,000,000: 1966
Source: Council for Financial Aid to Education

| INSTITUTION | ENDOWMENT | INSTITUTION | ENDOWMENT |
|---|---|---|---|
| **Major Private Universities** | | **Private Women's Colleges** | |
| Harvard University | $602,909,289 | Wellesley College | $ 68,466,232 |
| Yale University | 396,553,955 | Smith College | 43,389,149 |
| Columbia University | 196,323,669 | Vassar College | 42,337,105 |
| Stanford University | 184,922,426 | Bryn Mawr College | 27,705,134 |
| Chicago, University of | 181,438,787 | Mount Holyoke College | 27,657,737 |
| Cornell University | 163,345,814 | Radcliffe College | 20,715,800 |
| Northwestern University | 146,046,613 | **Private Coeducational Colleges** | |
| Princeton University | 136,904,689 | Oberlin College | 60,455,702 |
| Johns Hopkins University | 116,611,916 | Berea College | 38,116,310 |
| Pennsylvania, University of | 103,000,000 | Hampton Institute | 31,363,341 |
| Dartmouth College | 99,960,173 | Swarthmore College | 25,658,906 |
| Rochester, University of | 89,413,441 | Creighton University | 22,586,957 |
| Rice University | 87,959,337 | Butler University | 22,300,000 |
| Western Reserve University | 81,428,401 | Macalester College | 21,529,257 |
| Pittsburgh, University of | 73,158,984 | Lawrence University | 20,548,079 |
| New York University | 71,542,097 | **Professional and Specialized Schools** | |
| Vanderbilt University | 71,145,231 | Mass. Institute of Technology | 222,055,000 |
| Washington Univ. (St. Louis, Mo.) | 68,535,313 | Rockefeller University | 90,637,683 |
| Notre Dame, University of | 62,865,412 | Calif. Institute of Technology | 78,722,000 |
| Duke University | 61,268,801 | Carnegie Instit. of Technology | 59,929,748 |
| Emory University | 58,557,697 | Rensselaer Polytechnic Instit. | 50,263,992 |
| Brown University | 50,647,287 | Case Institute of Technology | 29,930,003 |
| Boston College | 42,496,168 | Union Theological Seminary | 24,298,468 |
| St. Louis University | 41,795,793 | Rochester Instit. of Technology | 20,537,132 |
| Syracuse University | 36,766,556 | **Public Institutions** | |
| Tulane University | 32,753,907 | Texas, University of | 488,889,339 |
| Texas Christian University | 27,000,000 | California, University of | 190,789,000 |
| Southern California, University of | 25,102,542 | Minnesota, University of | 74,850,108 |
| Loyola University | 23,377,854 | Delaware, University of | 65,495,283 |
| Fordham University | 20,943,413 | Washington, University of | |
| Tufts University | 20,473,271 | (Seattle, Washington) | 52,347,195 |
| Northeastern University | 20,187,401 | Michigan, University of | 46,539,612 |
| **Private Men's Colleges** | | Washington State University | |
| Wesleyan University | 86,460,243 | (Pullman, Washington) | 39,914,155 |
| Amherst College | 53,020,193 | Wisconsin, University of | 34,964,807 |
| Williams College | 42,713,386 | Rutgers—State Univ. of N.J. | 23,281,045 |
| Providence College | 31,659,734 | Oklahoma, University of | 22,312,166 |
| Lehigh University | 29,658,985 | Ohio State University | 21,208,050 |
| Bowdoin College | 25,757,159 | **Municipal Colleges and Universities** | |
| Lafayette College | 24,434,849 | Cincinnati, University of | 27,350,858 |

## FINANCIAL GIFTS TO U.S. COLLEGES AND UNIVERSITIES

Bequests, foundation grants, and private and corporate gifts to institutions of higher learning in 1965–66 fell off 8.7 per cent from the record totals of 1964–65. According to a survey of 50 U.S. colleges and universities conducted by the John Price Jones Company, an institutional fund-raising concern, a total of $447,- 982,000 was received, or $42,625,000 less than the previous fiscal year. Since the 1964–65 figures reflect some unusually large gifts, the drop was not considered indicative of a downward trend. The colleges and universities listed below are arranged according to the size of the gifts received in 1965–66.

| INSTITUTION | 1965–66 | 1964–65 | INSTITUTION | 1965–66 | 1964–65 |
|---|---|---|---|---|---|
| Harvard University | $44,464,000 | $51,063,000 | Oberlin College | $4,472,000 | $3,893,000 |
| Mass. Institute of Technology | 40,740,000 | 23,420,000 | Vassar College | 4,197,000 | 5,084,000 |
| California, University of | 34,615,000 | 24,465,000 | Lehigh University | 3,655,000 | 3,742,000 |
| Yale University | 27,050,000 | 22,670,000 | Carnegie Inst. of Technology | 3,364,000 | 5,275,000 |
| Chicago, University of | 26,412,000 | 14,269,000 | Middlebury College | 3,355,000 | 3,354,000 |
| New York University | 25,043,000 | 23,731,000 | Bowdoin College | 3,291,000 | 3,306,000 |
| Cornell University | 24,984,000 | 29,795,000 | Ohio State University | 3,046,000 | 2,279,000 |
| Pennsylvania, University of | 23,494,000 | 17,667,000 | Beloit College | 2,987,000 | 1,989,000 |
| Stanford University | 21,217,000 | 26,613,000 | Lafayette College | 2,821,000 | 3,228,000 |
| Columbia University | 18,815,000 | 29,794,000 | Trinity College (Conn.) | 2,780,000 | 1,743,000 |
| Johns Hopkins University | 12,578,000 | 9,930,000 | Wellesley College | 2,501,000 | 3,756,000 |
| Northwestern University | 11,748,000 | 9,913,000 | Radcliffe College | 2,374,000 | 3,401,000 |
| Minnesota, University of | 10,323,000 | 9,234,000 | Bryn Mawr College | 2,287,000 | 5,823,000 |
| Princeton University | 9,729,000 | 53,203,000 | Carleton College | 1,899,000 | 1,338,000 |
| Texas, University of | 8,731,000 | 9,135,000 | Mount Holyoke College | 1,788,000 | 5,682,000 |
| Brown University | 6,856,000 | 8,423,000 | Stevens Inst. of Technology | 1,785,000 | 4,044,000 |
| Dartmouth College | 6,614,000 | 9,930,000 | Colby College | 1,556,000 | 2,865,000 |
| Western Reserve University | 6,548,000 | 3,757,000 | Goucher College | 1,414,000 | 697,000 |
| Illinois, University of | 6,440,000 | 5,787,000 | Iowa, University of | 1,405,000 | 3,787,000 |
| Williams College | 5,962,000 | 6,520,000 | Antioch College | 1,316,000 | 2,344,000 |
| Smith College | 5,905,000 | 9,449,000 | Barnard College | 1,199,000 | 1,398,000 |
| Cincinnati, University of | 5,541,000 | 4,717,000 | Wabash College | 981,000 | 1,703,000 |
| Rutgers—State Univ. of N.J. | 4,776,000 | 3,311,000 | Bucknell University | 749,000 | 1,763,000 |

## PUPIL RETENTION RATES: 1957-1969

Source: U.S. Department of Health, Education, and Welfare

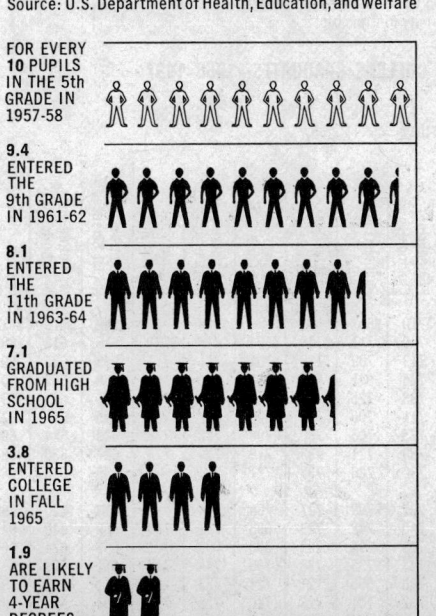

FOR EVERY 10 PUPILS IN THE 5th GRADE IN 1957-58

9.4 ENTERED THE 9th GRADE IN 1961-62

8.1 ENTERED THE 11th GRADE IN 1963-64

7.1 GRADUATED FROM HIGH SCHOOL IN 1965

3.8 ENTERED COLLEGE IN FALL 1965

1.9 ARE LIKELY TO EARN 4-YEAR DEGREES IN 1969

## U.S. SCHOOL ENROLLMENTS: 1930-1970

Source: U.S. Department of Health, Education, and Welfare

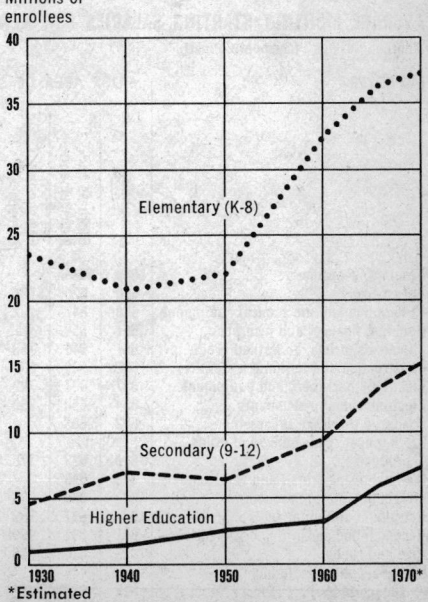

Millions of enrollees

Elementary (K-8)

Secondary (9-12)

Higher Education

1930  1940  1950  1960  1970*
*Estimated

## FOREIGN STUDENTS IN THE UNITED STATES: 1966–1967

Source: Institute of International Education

| COUNTRIES WITH MOST FOREIGN STUDENTS IN THE UNITED STATES | Number of Students | % of Total Foreign Students | U.S. UNIVERSITIES WITH THE HIGHEST FOREIGN-STUDENT ENROLLMENT | Total Enrollment | No. of Foreign Students | % of Total Enrollment |
|---|---|---|---|---|---|---|
| Canada................. | 12,117 | 12.1 | University of California....... | 87,033 | 5,787 | 6.6 |
| India................... | 7,518 | 7.5 | New York University.......... | 40,711 | 2,646 | 6.5 |
| China (Taiwan)*......... | 6,721 | 6.7 | Columbia University.......... | 25,346 | 2,565 | 10.1 |
| Iran................... | 4,346 | 4.3 | University of Wisconsin....... | 51,207 | 1,838 | 3.6 |
| Japan................. | 3,768 | 3.8 | University of Illinois......... | 42,537 | 1,647 | 3.9 |
| Hong Kong............. | 3,578 | 3.6 | University of Michigan........ | 36,063 | 1,546 | 4.3 |
| Korea................. | 3,218 | 3.2 | Howard University............ | 8,548 | 1,502 | 17.6 |
| United Kingdom........ | 3,118 | 3.1 | University of Minnesota....... | 43,997 | 1,337 | 3.0 |
| Philippines............ | 2,679 | 2.7 | Harvard University........... | 14,986 | 1,266 | 8.4 |
| Cuba................. | 2,627 | 2.6 | Wayne State University....... | 30,832 | 1,235 | 4.0 |

* Includes many students who reside in countries other than the Republic of China (Taiwan).

## U.S. STUDENTS ABROAD: 1965–1966

Source: Institute of International Education

| FOREIGN COUNTRIES WITH MOST U.S. STUDENTS | NUMBER OF U.S. STUDENTS | FOREIGN INSTITUTIONS WITH LARGEST NUMBER OF U.S. STUDENTS | NUMBER OF U.S. STUDENTS |
|---|---|---|---|
| France...................... | 4,223 | University of Paris...................... | 1,964 |
| Mexico...................... | 3,434 | University of the Americas, Mexico City............. | 1,634 |
| Canada...................... | 3,146 | Interamerican University, | |
| Germany.................... | 2,392 | Saltillo, Mexico....................... | 1,450 |
| United Kingdom.............. | 2,040 | University of Madrid.................... | 937 |
| Italy....................... | 1,504 | University of London.................... | 752 |
| Spain...................... | 1,182 | McGill University, Montreal.............. | 743 |
| Japan...................... | 1,003 | University of Bologna................... | 632 |
| Philippines................. | 737 | University of the Philippines............ | 603 |
| Switzerland................. | 643 | University of Munich.................... | 523 |
| Belgium.................... | 594 | Sophia University, Tokyo................ | 516 |
| Austria.................... | 559 | University of Toronto................... | 459 |
| Vatican City State.......... | 497 | Italian University for Foreigners........ | 448 |
| Israel..................... | 406 | University of Grenoble.................. | 442 |

## AVERAGE MONTHLY STARTING SALARIES FOR NEW COLLEGE GRADUATES: 1966–1967

Source: College Placement Council

| EMPLOYER | Accounting | Business and Management | Engineering-Aerospace | Engineering-Chemical | Engineering-Civil | Engineering-Electrical | Engineering-Industrial | Engineering-Mechanical | Engineering-Metallurgical | Humanities and Social Sciences | Marketing and Distribution | Physics, Chemistry, Mathematics |
|---|---|---|---|---|---|---|---|---|---|---|---|---|
| Accounting–public................. | $646 | $639 | — | $710 | $657 | — | — | $725 | — | $549 | $619 | $675 |
| Aerospace....................... | 660 | 620 | $724 | 720 | 711 | $728 | $694 | 717 | $721 | 616 | 618 | 698 |
| Automotive and mechanical equipment | 628 | 647 | 722 | 713 | 709 | 718 | 704 | 711 | 717 | 625 | 625 | 698 |
| Banking, finance, and insurance...... | 561 | 558 | — | 725 | 641 | 648 | 575 | 593 | — | 568 | 559 | 604 |
| Chemicals, drugs, and allied products | 651 | 646 | 758 | 733 | 725 | 739 | 726 | 734 | 718 | 621 | 613 | 691 |
| Construction and building materials... | 622 | 628 | 697 | 711 | 700 | 719 | 706 | 712 | 706 | 625 | 611 | 677 |
| Electrical machinery and equipment... | 637 | 637 | 722 | 725 | 708 | 730 | 708 | 722 | 728 | 629 | 624 | 698 |
| Electronics and instruments.......... | 634 | 650 | 730 | 730 | 721 | 733 | 719 | 729 | 727 | 627 | 630 | 694 |
| Food and beverage processing........ | 602 | 603 | — | 730 | 726 | 737 | 721 | 737 | — | 595 | 586 | 663 |
| Glass, paper, packaging, and allied products... | 620 | 623 | 775 | 731 | 709 | 727 | 708 | 724 | 710 | 613 | 620 | 694 |
| Merchandising (retail and wholesale).. | 568 | 543 | — | 740 | 748 | 729 | 695 | 711 | 700 | 550 | 540 | 647 |
| Metals and metal products........... | 633 | 646 | 703 | 708 | 694 | 700 | 693 | 699 | 701 | 633 | 624 | 667 |
| Petroleum and other fuels........... | 630 | 621 | 758 | 743 | 733 | 738 | 736 | 744 | 717 | 611 | 609 | 697 |
| Research and consulting organizations | 661 | 691 | 690 | 730 | 695 | 721 | 724 | 722 | 729 | 511 | 589 | 697 |
| Tire and rubber.................... | 633 | 610 | 735 | 732 | 701 | 728 | 710 | 722 | 720 | 583 | 590 | 698 |
| Utilities–public (including transportation)................... | 612 | 626 | 718 | 691 | 687 | 710 | 690 | 705 | 741 | 600 | 590 | 676 |

# FOCUS ON THE NEWS

## NATIONAL STUDENT ASSOCIATION AND THE CIA

American students paraded at the Communist-sponsored World Youth Festival held at Vienna in 1959. CIA-supported delegates took the lead in challenging Communist propaganda and fighting Communism.

The education world was shocked during the spring of 1967 when *Ramparts* magazine disclosed that the National Student Association (NSA) had been subsidized since 1952 by the Central Intelligence Agency (CIA). NSA, an association of student-government organizations on more than 300 college campuses, had a liberal, socially conscious reputation that seemed to make it an unlikely candidate for funds from the super-secret national agency. Yet, as the story emerged on the nation's front pages, it became clear that for a number of years a major part of NSA's support came from private foundations acting as channels for CIA funds.

Involvement of NSA with CIA subsidies grew out of the U.S.S.R.'s active effort immediately after World War II to organize and influence the world student movement. In 1946, for instance, Communist delegations gained firm control of the first World Student Congress, which met in Prague. Continuing funds were made available by Iron Curtain countries for world youth festivals, rallies, international conferences, and forums. However, American students lacking adequate financing from either public or private sources, were at a serious disadvantage in making heard the voice of the free world. NSA reportedly filled this vacuum with considerable success after 1952.

After the story broke, the major question was whether NSA would be able to survive the disclosure. All doubts were resolved by the time of the organization's annual congress in August 1967. Only one college had resigned from NSA, and an additional 30 had joined. Still unresolved, however, was the question of whether an open society such as exists in the U.S. can survive if its supposedly free institutions are supported secretly by government funds.

# U.S. COLLEGE FRATERNITIES AND SORORITIES

The first fraternities in the United States were founded in the late 1700s, and during the next century they gained widespread popularity among men on college campuses. Today, most fraternities are "collegiate" or "general" organizations, although there are also professional and honor societies. Six interfraternity organizations have been established to coordinate the activities of their member fraternities. The collegiate fraternities encourage scholarship and the participation of members in campus activities; most also sponsor community-service projects. In the tradition of secret societies, they usually have Greek-letter names and utilize cryptic hand signs and other rituals.

A chapter includes all the undergraduate members at a school; many maintain fraternity houses in which members may live during the school year. Those groups composed of women are usually called sororities. Alumni associations are formed by members who have graduated. Below is a list, compiled from a *Reader's Digest Almanac* survey, of the larger national collegiate fraternities:

| FRATERNITY (and Year Founded) | COLLEGE CHAPTERS | ALUMNI ASSOC. | MEMBERS College | MEMBERS Alumni | NATIONAL HEADQUARTERS |
|---|---|---|---|---|---|
| Acacia (1904)................ | 53 | 13 | 1,654 | 24,321 | 1611 Chicago Ave., Evanston, Ill. |
| Alpha Chi Rho (1895)....... | 28 | 37 | 1,000 | 9,000 | 1 Maiden Lane, New York, N.Y. |
| Alpha Delta Gamma (1924).. | 15 | 7 | 550 | 5,050 | P.O. Box 54321, Los Angeles, Calif. |
| Alpha Delta Phi (1832)...... | 30 | 35 | 1,583 | 31,260 | 125 East 50 St., New York, N.Y. |
| Alpha Epsilon Pi (1913)..... | 92 | 38 | 5,000 | 25,000 | 7730 Carondelet Ave., St. Louis, Mo. |
| Alpha Gamma Rho (1904)... | 42 | 59 | 2,222 | 21,247 | 323 Cornell Ave., Des Plaines, Ill. |
| Alpha Kappa Lambda (1914) | 35 | 12 | 1,560 | 6,100 | 4700 College Ave., Fort Collins, Col. |
| Alpha Phi Alpha (1906)..... | 135 | 202 | 2,020 | 5,088 | 4432 South Parkway, Chicago, Ill. |
| Alpha Phi Delta (1914)...... | 22[1] | 14[1] | — | 7,200[2] | 1459 Woodruff Ave., Pittsburgh, Penn. |
| Alpha Sigma Phi (1845)..... | 59 | 30 | 2,496 | 31,985 | 24 West William St., Delaware, Ohio |
| Alpha Tau Omega (1865).... | 128 | 90 | 6,450 | 88,303 | 107 East Green St., Champaign, Ill. |
| Beta Sigma Psi (1925)...... | 13 | 16 | 427 | 1,878 | 60 Progress Parkway, Maryland Heights, Mo. |
| Beta Sigma Rho (1910)..... | 10 | 8 | 400 | 4,200 | 250 Broadway, New York, N.Y. |
| Beta Theta Pi (1839)........ | 103 | 115 | 5,800 | 70,000 | 208 East High St., Oxford, Ohio |
| Chi Phi (1854)............. | 38 | 49 | 369 | 21,844 | 3330 Peachtree Rd., N.E., Atlanta, Ga. |
| Chi Psi (1841)............. | 26 | — | 11,000 | 14,008 | 1705 Washtenaw Ave., Ann Arbor, Mich. |
| Delta Chi (1890)............ | 50 | 18 | — | 28,099[2] | 16 South Clinton St., Iowa City, Iowa |
| Delta Kappa Epsilon (1844).. | 42 | 42 | 2,300 | 23,000 | 50 Vanderbilt Ave., New York, N.Y. |
| Delta Phi (1827)........... | 15[1] | — | — | 7,000[2] | 331 Madison Ave., New York, N.Y. |
| Delta Psi (1847)............ | 9[1] | — | — | 4,776[2] | 16 East 64 Street, New York, N.Y. |
| Delta Sigma Phi (1899)...... | 109 | 27 | 4,059 | 39,808 | 1445 Steele St., Denver, Col. |
| Delta Tau Delta (1858)...... | 97 | 89 | 5,784 | 53,000 | 3665 Washington Blvd., Indianapolis, Ind. |
| Delta Upsilon (1834)....... | 82 | 69 | 4,000 | 66,000 | 271 Madison Ave., New York, N.Y. |
| Farmhouse (1905)........... | 22 | 24 | 908 | 6,885 | 424 South Sixth Ave., La Grange, Ill. |
| Kappa Alpha Order (1865)... | 87 | 65 | 6,283 | 54,202 | 1252 West Peachtree St., Atlanta, Ga. |
| Kappa Alpha Psi (1911)..... | 127 | 150 | 5,000 | 35,000 | 2320 North Broad St., Philadelphia, Penn. |
| Kappa Alpha Society (1825).. | 10 | 9 | 456 | 3,982 | 1 Elk St., Albany, N.Y. |
| Kappa Delta Rho (1905)..... | 20 | 20 | 600 | 9,600 | 481 North Dean St., Englewood, N.J. |
| Kappa Sigma (1869)........ | 152 | 100 | 10,400 | 94,163 | Box 5066, Charlottesville, Va. |
| Lambda Chi Alpha (1909)... | 173 | 89 | 12,000 | 88,000 | 3434 Washington Blvd., Indianapolis, Ind. |
| Omega Psi Phi (1911)....... | 96 | 207 | 5,000 | 27,000 | 2714 Georgia Ave., N.W., Washington, D.C. |
| Phi Beta Sigma (1914)...... | 82 | 133 | 1,800 | 21,701 | 1105 Prospect Pl., Brooklyn, N.Y. |
| Phi Delta Theta (1848)...... | 134 | 150 | 7,500 | 107,026 | 2 South Campus Ave., Oxford, Ohio |
| Phi Epsilon Pi (1904)....... | 54 | 44 | 3,000 | 24,000 | 1015 Lewis Tower Bldg., Philadelphia, Penn. |
| Phi Gamma Delta (1848).... | 94 | 150 | 5,500 | 56,000 | 1757 North St., N.W., Washington, D.C. |
| Phi Kappa Psi (1852)....... | 73 | 78 | 3,404 | 33,152 | 1940 East Sixth St., Cleveland, Ohio |
| Phi Kappa Sigma (1850)..... | 45 | 31 | 1,882 | 22,973 | 335 South 16 St., Philadelphia, Penn. |
| Phi Kappa Tau (1906)....... | 78 | 78 | 3,750 | 29,000 | 15 North Campus Ave., Oxford, Ohio |
| Phi Kappa Theta (1889)..... | 55 | 20 | 2,500 | 23,000 | Suite 400, 544 Main St., Worcester, Mass. |
| Phi Lambda Chi (1924)...... | 5 | 3 | 285 | 2,707 | 1301 No. Garfield, Sand Springs, Okla. |
| Phi Mu Delta (1918)........ | 13 | 15 | 600 | 8,000 | 450 Murry Hill Dr., Lancaster, Penn. |
| Phi Sigma Delta (1909)..... | 49 | 15 | 2,234 | 16,379 | 120 East 34 St., New York, N.Y. |
| Phi Sigma Epsilon (1910).... | 44 | 30 | 2,420 | 16,683 | 2829 No. Pennsylvania St., Indianapolis, Ind. |
| Phi Sigma Kappa (1873).... | 88 | 72 | 3,100 | 36,600 | 2528 Garrett Rd., Drexel Hill, Penn. |
| Pi Kappa Alpha (1868)...... | 138 | 52 | 5,439 | 64,665 | 577 University Blvd., Memphis, Tenn. |
| Pi Kappa Phi (1904)........ | 57 | 30 | 1,870 | 23,200 | 1924 Vail Ave., Charlotte, N.C. |
| Pi Lambda Phi (1895)....... | 45 | 40 | 1,750 | 19,750 | 125 West 43 St., New York, N.Y. |
| Psi Upsilon (1833)......... | 27 | 49 | 1,327 | 18,050 | 4 West 43 St., New York, N.Y. |
| Sigma Alpha Epsilon (1856).. | 159 | 105 | 9,000 | 100,000 | 1856 Sheridan Rd., Evanston, Ill. |
| Sigma Alpha Mu (1909)..... | 64 | 47 | 2,110 | 26,450 | 250 West 57 St., New York, N.Y. |
| Sigma Chi (1855)........... | 144 | 162 | 7,500 | 82,500 | 1714 Hinman Ave., Evanston, Ill. |
| Sigma Nu (1869)........... | 140 | 108 | 7,160 | 76,600 | 9 Lewis St., (Box 1869), Lexington, Va. |
| Sigma Phi (1827)........... | 10 | 11 | 250 | 4,200 | 25 Broadway, New York, N.Y. |

| FRATERNITY (and Year Founded) | COLLEGE CHAPTERS | ALUMNI ASSOC. | MEMBERS College | Alumni | NATIONAL HEADQUARTERS |
|---|---|---|---|---|---|
| Sigma Phi Epsilon (1901).... | 166 | 106 | 10,000 | 60,000 | 5800 Chamberlayne Rd., Richmond, Va. |
| Sigma Pi (1897)............. | 88 | 29 | 4,686 | 21,089 | County Highway 225S, Vincennes, Ind. |
| Sigma Tau Gamma (1920)... | 62 | 15 | 3,124 | 25,551 | 23 No. Gore Ave., St. Louis, Mo. |
| Tau Delta Phi (1910)........ | 32 | 21 | 1,602 | 11,315 | 171 Madison Ave., New York, N.Y. |
| Tau Epsilon Phi (1910)...... | 71 | 36 | 4,000 | 19,000 | 250 Fifth Avenue, New York, N.Y. |
| Tau Kappa Epsilon (1899)... | 236 | 53 | 9,902 | 61,845 | 3755 Washington Blvd., Indianapolis, Ind. |
| Theta Chi (1856)........... | 138 | 62 | 5,520 | 58,307 | 436 Broad St. Bank Bldg., Trenton, N.J. |
| Theta Delta Chi (1847)...... | 32 | 49 | 1,600 | 15,200 | Hotel Biltmore, New York, N.Y. |
| Theta Xi (1864)............. | 73 | 48 | 2,900 | 30,553 | 9974 Old Olive Street Rd., St. Louis, Mo. |
| Triangle (1907)............. | 27 | 27 | 1,079 | 9,989 | Box 1336, Evanston, Ill. |
| Zeta Beta Tau (1898)....... | 75 | 52 | 4,500 | 28,000 | The Statler-Hilton, New York, N.Y. |
| Zeta Psi (1847)............. | 38 | 45 | 3,218 | 20,611 | Beverly Hotel, 125 E. 50 St., New York, N.Y. |

| SORORITY (and Year Founded) | COLLEGE CHAPTERS | ALUMNAE ASSOC. | MEMBERS College | Alumnae | NATIONAL HEADQUARTERS |
|---|---|---|---|---|---|
| Alpha Chi Omega (1885).... | 107 | 82 | 6,200 | 56,000 | 3445 Washington Blvd., Indianapolis, Ind. |
| Alpha Delta Pi (1851)...... | 120 | 361 | 8,600 | 58,400 | 1386 Ponce de Leon Ave., N.E., Atlanta, Ga. |
| Alpha Epsilon Phi (1909).... | 57 | 47 | 2,900 | 22,000 | 3600 Forbes St. #204, Pittsburgh, Penn. |
| Alpha Gamma Delta (1904).. | 90 | 225 | 4,440 | 41,800 | 3444 Washington Blvd., Indianapolis, Ind. |
| Alpha Kappa Alpha (1908)... | 107 | 206 | 5,000 | 35,000 | 5211 South Greenwood Ave., Chicago, Ill. |
| Alpha Omicron Pi (1897).... | 87 | 191 | 3,651 | 37,038 | Suite 109, 3000 Meadows Pkwy., Indianapolis, Ind. |
| Alpha Phi (1872)........... | 90 | 215 | 5,500 | 40,000 | 634 Foster St., Evanston, Ill. |
| Alpha Sigma Alpha (1901)... | 47 | 117 | 2,482 | 20,781 | 1201 East Walnut, Springfield, Mo. |
| Alpha Sigma Tau (1899)..... | 30 | 30 | 1,274 | 9,417 | 6200 Hoffman, St. Louis, Mo. |
| Alpha Xi Delta (1893)....... | 112 | 175 | 7,613 | 41,248 | 3447 N. Washington Blvd., Indianapolis, Ind. |
| Chi Omega (1895)........ | 146[1] | 302[1] | — | 92,411[2] | 2245 Grandin Rd., Cincinnati, Ohio |
| Delta Delta Delta (1888)..... | 110 | 330 | 7,000 | 65,000 | 6 North Michigan Ave., Chicago, Ill. |
| Delta Gamma (1873)........ | 93 | 267 | 5,778 | 59,344 | 3250 Riverside Drive, Columbus, Ohio |
| Delta Phi Epsilon (1917).... | 35 | 40 | 1,000 | 10,000 | 41-25 Kissena Blvd., Flushing, N.Y. |
| Delta Sigma Theta (1913)... | 105 | 211 | 2,000 | 43,000 | 1814 M St., N.W., Washington, D.C. |
| Delta Zeta (1902)........... | 173 | 272 | 9,242 | 53,318 | 3561 N. Pennsylvania St., Indianapolis, Ind. |
| Gamma Phi Beta (1874)...... | 82 | 209 | 3,535 | 44,300 | 630 Green Bay Rd., Box 186, Kenilworth, Ill. |
| Iota Alpha Pi (1903)........ | 13 | 13 | 375 | 5,925 | 81 East Beverly Pkwy., Valley Stream, N.Y. |
| Kappa Alpha Theta (1870)... | 93 | 309 | 6,949 | 63,225 | 1580 Sherman Ave., Suite 342, Evanston, Ill. |
| Kappa Delta (1897)......... | 105 | 356 | 6,575 | 54,682 | 900 Landers Bldg., Springfield, Missouri |
| Kappa Kappa Gamma (1870) | 94 | 363 | 6,600 | 17,326 | 530 East Town St., Columbus, Ohio |
| Phi Mu (1852)............. | 98 | 180 | 4,827 | 43,173 | 22 North Front St., Memphis, Tenn. |
| Phi Sigma Sigma (1913)..... | 30 | 31 | 1,391 | 13,247 | 161 Madeira Ave., Coral Gables, Fla. |
| Pi Beta Phi (1867).......... | 111 | 342 | 8,500 | 73,628 | 112 South Hanley Rd., St. Louis, Mo. |
| Sigma Delta Tau (1917)..... | 51 | 49 | 2,959 | 13,351 | 630 Green Bay Rd., Kenilworth, Ill. |
| Sigma Gamma Rho (1922)... | 45 | 81 | 449 | 1,454 | 2515 Ethel St., Indianapolis, Ind. |
| Sigma Kappa (1874)........ | 104 | 165 | 5,000 | 39,500 | 3433 Washington Blvd., Indianapolis, Ind. |
| Sigma Sigma Sigma (1898).. | 65 | 130 | 3,000 | 28,861 | Walton House, Drawer 466, Woodstock, Va. |
| Theta Phi Alpha (1912)...... | 17 | 20 | 800 | 7,200 | 3738 Clifton Ave., Cincinnati, Ohio |
| Zeta Phi Beta (1920)....... | 85 | 165 | 4,500 | 15,000 | 1734 New Hampshire Ave., N.W., Washington, D.C. |
| Zeta Tau Alpha (1898)...... | 110 | 224 | 5,800 | 45,687 | 708 Church St., Evanston, Ill. |

[1] Figure pertains to 1966 or an earlier year.   [2] Total figure of all college and alumni fraternity members; figure pertains to 1966 or an earlier year.

## HONOR FRATERNITIES

Membership in honor fraternities is based upon overall academic achievement, leadership, or distinguished scholarship in a specific area. Phi Beta Kappa is the oldest and most prestigious of the honor societies. It was founded in 1776 at the College of William and Mary in Williamsburg, Virginia. Students are elected to the society by their school chapter, composed of faculty members. Election is based upon an outstanding academic record and usually occurs during a student's senior year. Other honor societies include Sigma Xi, whose members are chosen for achievements in scientific research, Blue Key, a recognition society for men who have made outstanding contributions to their university, and the National Collegiate Players for achievement in the field of drama. Several honor fraternities publish important journals in their fields of interest.

## PROFESSIONAL FRATERNITIES

Members of professional fraternities are chosen from among college and university students and teachers with common professional goals or academic interests. The main purpose of these groups is educational, and many regularly publish journals with articles pertaining to the organization's field of interest. Some groups also maintain fraternity houses for their members. The first professional fraternity, the Kappa Lamda Society of Aesculapius, was founded in 1819 by medical students at Transylvania College in Lexington, Kentucky. Today there are professional fraternities for members of many professions and academic disciplines, including Phi Chi in the field of medicine, Phi Delta Phi for law, Sigma Tau Delta for English, Sigma Delta Chi for journalism, Kappa Phi Kappa for education, and Phi Mu Alpha for music.

© Ezra Stoller Assoc.

Beinecke Rare Book and Manuscript Library, Yale University

## LEADING U.S. UNIVERSITY LIBRARIES

Source: U.S. Office of Education

| UNIVERSITY | VOLUMES * | UNIVERSITY | VOLUMES * | UNIVERSITY | VOLUMES * |
|---|---|---|---|---|---|
| 1. Harvard | 7,445,072 | 8. Stanford | 2,560,220 | 16. Ohio State University | 1,748,943 |
| 2. Yale | 4,826,148 | 9. University of Chicago | 2,406,142 | 17. Duke University | 1,716,855 |
| 3. University of Illinois | 3,888,983 | 10. University of Minnesota | 2,371,529 | 18. Northwestern University | 1,709,172 |
| 4. Columbia | 3,569,565 | 11. U.C.L.A. | 2,197,175 | 19. University of Wisconsin | 1,635,754 |
| 5. University of Michigan | 3,376,076 | 12. University of Pennsylvania | 1,894,480 | 20. New York University | 1,535,583 |
| 6. University of California | 3,113,024 | 13. University of Texas | 1,794,367 | 21. Johns Hopkins | 1,399,700 |
| 7. Cornell | 2,725,624 | 14. Indiana University | 1,771,900 | 22. University of Washington | 1,390,636 |
| | | 15. Princeton | 1,769,699 | | |

* Total number as of June 30, 1965.

## PRESIDENTIAL LIBRARIES

Source: U.S. National Archives and Records Service

Although there are two other Presidential libraries—the Rutherford B. Hayes Library and the Warren G. Harding Library, both in Ohio —only the following libraries are Federally administered institutions.

**HERBERT HOOVER LIBRARY,** in West Branch, Iowa. Open 9 A.M. to 4:30 P.M. weekdays, 2 P.M. to 5 P.M. Sundays, and 10 A.M. to 5 P.M. on Sundays during the summer. Closed on some holidays. Admission: 50¢ (children free).

Located in Hoover Park, it was dedicated in 1962 and contains Presidential and other papers and mementos of Hoover's long career in public service.

**FRANKLIN D. ROOSEVELT LIBRARY,** south of Hyde Park, Dutchess County, New York. Open 9 A.M. to 5 P.M. Tuesday through Sunday; and Monday through Sunday, June 1 to September 15. Closed Christmas. Admission: 50¢ (children free).

Opened in 1941, it holds a collection of Presidential and other papers, mementos, and more than 33,000 books and 91,000 photographs.

**HARRY S. TRUMAN LIBRARY,** in Independence, Missouri. Open weekdays 9 A.M. to 4:30 P.M., 2 P.M. to 5 P.M. on Sundays, and 10 A.M. to 5 P.M. on summer Sundays. Closed on some holidays. Admission: 50¢ (children free).

Opened in 1957, it holds the Presidential papers and historical documents of the Truman Administration, as well as various mementos.

**DWIGHT D. EISENHOWER LIBRARY,** in Abilene, Kansas, on Southeast Fourth Street. Open daily 9 A.M. to 5 P.M. Closed Christmas. Admission: free.

A part of the Eisenhower family home, it houses the Eisenhower papers and related materials. It was opened in 1961.

**JOHN F. KENNEDY LIBRARY,** to be constructed in Cambridge, Massachusetts, on land adjacent to Harvard University. It will be a repository of papers and memorabilia relating to the Kennedy Administration.

**LYNDON B. JOHNSON LIBRARY,** under construction on the Austin campus of the University of Texas. It will house papers and memorabilia.

# U.S. COLLEGES AND UNIVERSITIES: 1967–1968

Following is a list of regionally accredited four-year colleges with enrollments of at least 100 students during the academic year 1967–68, and universities with academic undergraduate schools. Information was provided by the institutions in a survey conducted by the *Reader's Digest Almanac*, or was taken from the most recent available sources. For further information write to the Admissions Office of the institution itself. **Abbreviations:** Under the column headed TYPE: (M) is Men, (W) is Women, (MW) stands for coed. The subheadings under ENROLLMENT: (U) is Undergraduate, (G) is Graduate. The

subheadings under TUITION AND FEES: (R) is Resident of the state or city, (NR) is Non-Resident; (NE) stands for Not Enrolled, which means that nonresidents are not accepted by the institution. Under the heading ROOM AND BOARD: (NA) means that these accommodations are Not Available. Amounts under COMP-(REHENSIVE) FEE include tuition, room and board, and other fees. (NI) in any column means that No Information was available when the *Almanac* went to press.

The organizations that CONTROL the various institutions are abbreviated as follows:

AB—American Baptist Convention
AC—Advent Christian
AG—Assemblies of God
AMA—American Missionary Association
AME—African Methodist Episcopal
AMEZ—African Methodist Episcopal Zion
BGC—Baptist General Conference
C—Congregational
CB—Church of the Brethren
CG—Church of God
CMA—Christian and Missionary Alliance
CME—Christian Methodist Episcopal
CN—Church of the Nazarene
CR—Christian Reformed
DC—Disciples of Christ
ER—Evangelical and Reformed
EUB—Evangelical United Brethren
Fed—Federal Government
GCNJ—General Church of the New Jerusalem
I—Interdenominational

J—Jewish
L—Lutheran
LDS—Church of Jesus Christ of Latter-day Saints
M—Methodist
MCA—Moravian Church in America
Mn—Mennonite
NB—National Baptist Convention
NPE—Northern Pacific Evangelist
P—Presbyterian
PE—Protestant Episcopal
Pvt.—Privately owned, nonsectarian
Q—Quaker
RC—Roman Catholic
RFC—Reformed Church
RLDS—Reorganized Church of Jesus Christ of Latter Day Saints
SB—Southern Baptist Convention
SDA—Seventh-day Adventists
UBC—United Brethren Church
UCC—United Church of Christ

| NAME AND LOCATION | TYPE | CON-TROL | ENROLLMENT | | TUITION & FEES | | ROOM, | COMP. |
| | | | U | G | R | NR | BOARD | FEE |
|---|---|---|---|---|---|---|---|---|
| Abilene Christian College, Abilene, Texas | MW | Pvt. | 2,590 | 232 | 870 | 870 | 675 | — |
| Adams State College, Alamosa, Colorado | MW | State | 2,250 | 175 | 333 | 730 | 765 | — |
| Adelphi University, Garden City, New York | MW | Pvt. | 4,300 | 3,000 | 1,950 | 1,950 | 1,100 | — |
| Adrian College, Adrian, Michigan | MW | Pvt. | 1,550 | — | 1,216 | 1,216 | 780 | — |
| Agnes Scott College, Decatur, Georgia | W | P | 745 | — | 1,435 | 1,435 | 1,000 | — |
| Air Force Institute of Technology, Dayton, Ohio | M | Fed. | 91 | 552 | Free | Free | Free | — |
| Akron, University of, Akron, Ohio | MW | City | 9,503 | 1,326 | 204 | 480 | 900 | — |
| Alabama, University of, Tuscaloosa, Alabama | MW | State | 10,525 | 2,125 | 350 | 700 | 700 | — |
| Alabama A&M College, Normal, Alabama | MW | State | 1,690 | 90 | 280 | 330 | 520 | — |
| Alabama College, Montevallo, Alabama | MW | State | 23,00 | 300 | 290 | 500 | 551 | — |
| Alabama State College, Montgomery, Alabama | MW | State | 1,600 | NI | 265 | 415 | 635 | — |
| Alaska, University of, College, Alaska | MW | State | 1,746 | 133 | 252 | 552 | 1,148 | — |
| Alaska Methodist University, Anchorage, Alaska | MW | M | 425 | — | 1,040 | 1,040 | 950 | — |
| Albany State College, Albany, Georgia | MW | State | 1,557 | — | 315 | 645 | 573 | — |
| Albertus Magnus College, New Haven, Connecticut | W | RC | 775 | — | — | — | — | 2,200 |
| Albion College, Albion, Michigan | MW | M | 1,657 | — | — | — | — | 2,420 |
| Albright College, Reading, Pennsylvania | MW | EUB | 1,150 | — | 1,750 | 1,750 | 850 | — |
| Albuquerque, University of, Albuquerque, New Mexico | MW | RC | 1,211 | — | 1,000 | 1,000 | 850 | — |
| Alcorn A&M College, Lorman, Mississippi | MW | State | 2,200 | — | 310 | 560 | 340 | — |
| Alderson-Broaddus College, Philippi, West Virginia | MW | AB | 775 | — | 1,700 | 1,700 | 700 | — |
| Alfred University, Alfred, New York | MW | Pvt. | 1,757 | 220 | 1,700 | 1,700 | 950 | — |
| Allegheny College, Meadville, Pennsylvania | MW | Pvt. | 1,500 | 15 | 1,613 | 1,613 | 825 | — |
| Alliance College, Cambridge Springs, Pennsylvania | MW | Pvt. | 600 | — | 1,080 | 1,080 | 750 | — |
| Alma College, Alma, Michigan | MW | P | 1,111 | — | 1,250 | 1,250 | 875 | — |
| Alverno College, Milwaukee, Wisconsin | W | RC | 1,400 | — | 700 | 700 | 840 | — |
| American International College, Springfield, Massachusetts | MW | Pvt. | 1,740 | 210 | 1,506 | 1,506 | 916 | — |
| American University, Washington, D.C. | MW | M | 7,000 | 7,000 | 1,710 | 1,710 | 980 | — |
| Amherst College, Amherst, Massachusetts | M | Pvt. | 1,211 | — | 2,003 | 2,003 | 975 | — |
| Anderson College, Anderson, Indiana | MW | CG | 1,400 | 75 | 990 | 990 | 710 | — |

| NAME AND LOCATION | TYPE | CON-TROL | ENROLLMENT U | G | TUITION & FEES R | NR | ROOM, BOARD | COMP. FEE |
|---|---|---|---|---|---|---|---|---|
| Andrews University, Berrien Springs, Michigan.......... | MW | SDA | 1,600 | 550 | 1,131 | 1,131 | 930 | — |
| Angelo State College, San Angelo, Texas................ | MW | State | 2,400 | — | 165 | 465 | 650 | — |
| Anna Maria College for Women, Paxton, Massachusetts... | W | RC | 600 | — | 900 | 900 | 950 | — |
| Annhurst College, Woodstock, Connecticut.............. | W | Pvt. | 400 | — | 1,200 | 1,200 | 1,000 | — |
| Antioch College, Yellow Springs, Ohio................. | MW | Pvt. | 1,850 | 100 | 1,942 | 1,942 | 628 | — |
| Appalachian State Teachers College, Boone, North Carolina | MW | State | 4,200 | 350 | 325 | 580 | 396 | — |
| Aquinas College, Grand Rapids, Michigan.............. | MW | RC | 1,100 | — | 980 | 980 | 850 | — |
| Arizona, University of, Tucson, Arizona................ | MW | State | 17,000 | 3,700 | 304 | 840 | 735 | — |
| Arizona State University, Tempe, Arizona.............. | MW | State | 17,046 | 2,002 | 341 | 1,156 | 886 | — |
| Arkansas, University of, Fayetteville, Arkansas......... | MW | State | 8,831 | 1,142 | 260 | 660 | 800 | — |
| Arkansas A&M and Normal College, Pine Bluff, Arkansas | MW | State | 3,225 | — | 200 | 470 | 544 | — |
| Arkansas A&M College, College Heights, Arkansas....... | MW | State | 1,750 | — | 200 | 470 | 575 | — |
| Arkansas College, Batesville, Arkansas................ | MW | P | 350 | — | 1,000 | 1,000 | 900 | — |
| Arkansas Polytechnic College, Russellville, Arkansas..... | MW | State | 2,400 | — | 210 | 480 | 640 | — |
| Arkansas State College, Conway, Arkansas............. | MW | State | 3,000 | 500 | 204 | 474 | 640 | — |
| Armstrong College, Berkeley, California............... | MW | Pvt. | 524 | 31 | 900 | 900 | 1,050 | — |
| Armstrong State College, Savannah, Georgia............ | MW | State | 1,700 | — | 285 | 615 | NA | — |
| Art Center College of Design, Los Angeles, California..... | MW | Pvt. | 675 | 7 | 1,040 | 1,040 | 880 | — |
| Art Institute of Chicago, School of the, Chicago, Illinois... | MW | Pvt. | 592 | 92 | 1,210 | 1,210 | NA | — |
| Asbury College, Wilmore, Kentucky................... | MW | Pvt. | 1,060 | — | 987 | 987 | 465 | — |
| Ashland College, Ashland, Ohio....................... | MW | Pvt. | 1,950 | — | 1,580 | 1,580 | 900 | — |
| Assumption College, Worcester, Massachusetts.......... | MW | RC | 600 | 300 | 1,325 | 1,325 | 900 | — |
| The Athenaeum of Ohio, Norwood, Ohio................ | M | RC | 388 | 182 | — | — | — | 1,200 |
| Athens College, Athens, Alabama..................... | MW | M | 1,100 | — | 800 | 800 | 830 | — |
| Atlanta University, Atlanta, Georgia................... | MW | Pvt. | 693 | 260 | 750 | 750 | 450 | — |
| Atlantic Christian College, Wilson, North Carolina........ | MW | DC | 1,500 | — | 865 | 865 | 600 | — |
| Atlantic Union College, South Lancaster, Massachusetts... | MW | SDA | 901 | — | 1,162 | 1,162 | 600 | — |
| Auburn University, Auburn, Alabama.................. | MW | State | 11,400 | 1,100 | 300 | 600 | 645 | — |
| Augsburg College, Minneapolis, Minnesota............. | MW | L | 1,725 | — | 1,330 | 1,330 | 770 | — |
| Augusta College, Augusta, Georgia.................... | MW | State | 2,500 | — | 380 | 820 | NA | — |
| Augustana College, Rock Island, Illinois............... | MW | L | 1,940 | — | 1,350 | 1,350 | 1,000 | — |
| Augustana College, Sioux Falls, South Dakota........... | MW | L | 2,007 | — | 1,150 | 1,150 | 600 | — |
| Aurora College, Aurora, Illinois...................... | MW | AC | 875 | — | 1,310 | 1,310 | 820 | — |
| Austin College, Sherman, Texas...................... | MW | P | 950 | 43 | 1,500 | 1,500 | 850 | — |
| Austin Peay State College, Clarksville, Tennessee........ | MW | State | 2,400 | 60 | 165 | 390 | 750 | — |
| Avila College, Kansas City, Missouri.................. | W | RC | 400 | — | 800 | 800 | 900 | — |
| Azusa Pacific College, Azusa, California................ | MW | Pvt. | 775 | 50 | 1,150 | 1,150 | 800 | — |
| Babson Institute of Business Administration, Babson Park, Massachusetts................................... | M | Pvt. | 800 | 70 | 1,730 | 1,730 | 950 | — |
| Baker University, Baldwin, Kansas.................... | MW | M | 1,011 | — | 940 | 940 | 800 | — |
| Baldwin-Wallace College, Berea, Ohio................. | MW | M | 2,800 | — | 1,693 | 1,693 | 870 | — |
| Ball State University, Muncie, Indiana................. | MW | State | 10,621 | 2,008 | 330 | 600 | 900 | — |
| Barat College, Lake Forest, Illinois................... | W | RC | 600 | — | 1,100 | 1,100 | 1,200 | — |
| Barber-Scotia College, Concord, North Carolina.......... | MW | P | 400 | — | 504 | 504 | 495 | — |
| Bard College, Annandale-on-Hudson, New York.......... | MW | Pvt. | 600 | — | — | — | — | 3,250 |
| Barnard College (of Columbia University), New York, New York........................................ | W | Pvt. | 1,825 | — | 1,800 | 1,800 | 1,150 | — |
| Barrington College, Barrington, Rhode Island........... | MW | Pvt. | 714 | — | 1,390 | 1,390 | 800 | — |
| Barry College, Miami, Florida........................ | MW | RC | 614 | 269 | 900 | 900 | 1,050 | — |
| Bates College, Lewiston, Maine...................... | MW | Pvt. | 975 | — | 1,800 | 1,800 | 850 | — |
| Baylor University, Waco, Texas....................... | MW | SB | 6,335 | 541 | 820 | 820 | 740 | — |
| Beaver College, Glenside, Pennsylvania................ | W | Pvt. | 750 | — | 1,772 | 1,772 | 1,100 | — |
| Belhaven College, Jackson, Mississippi................. | MW | P | 560 | — | 950 | 950 | 700 | — |
| Bellarmine College, Louisville, Kentucky............... | M | RC | 1,550 | — | 990 | 1,150 | 840 | — |
| Belmont Abbey College, Belmont, North Carolina........ | M | RC | 776 | — | 820 | 820 | 870 | — |
| Belmont College, Nashville, Tennessee................. | MW | SB | 1,300 | — | 610 | 610 | 500 | — |
| Beloit College, Beloit, Wisconsin..................... | MW | Pvt. | 1,150 | — | — | — | — | 3,000 |
| Bemidji State College, Bemidji, Minnesota............. | MW | State | 3,800 | — | 310 | 454 | 690 | — |
| Benedict College, Columbia, South Carolina............ | MW | AB | 1,100 | — | 340 | 340 | 363 | — |
| Bennett College, Greensboro, North Carolina........... | W | M | 660 | — | 776 | 776 | 644 | — |
| Bennington College, Bennington, Vermont.............. | W | Pvt. | 430 | 3 | 2,700 | 2,700 | 1,150 | — |
| Bentley College of Accounting and Finance, Boston, Massachusetts................................... | MW | Pvt. | 4,111 | — | 1,270 | 1,270 | 1,000 | — |
| Berea College, Berea, Kentucky...................... | MW | Pvt. | 1,492 | — | 118 | 118 | 512 | — |
| Berry College, Mount Berry, Georgia.................. | MW | Pvt. | 1,250 | — | 978 | 978 | 840 | — |
| Bethany Bible College, Santa Cruz, California........... | MW | AG | 455 | — | 774 | 774 | 648 | — |
| Bethany College, Lindsborg, Kansas.................. | MW | L | 500 | — | 970 | 970 | 720 | — |
| Bethany College, Bethany, West Virginia............... | MW | Pvt. | 1,150 | — | 1,620 | 1,620 | 900 | — |
| Bethany Nazarene College, Bethany, Oklahoma.......... | MW | CN | 1,850 | 50 | 800 | 800 | 550 | — |
| Bethel College, North Newton, Kansas................. | MW | Mn | 625 | — | 1,050 | 1,050 | 695 | — |
| Bethel College, St. Paul, Minnesota................... | MW | BGC | 1,000 | — | 1,125 | 1,125 | 675 | — |
| Bethel College, McKenzie, Tennessee.................. | MW | Pvt. | 800 | — | 840 | 840 | 672 | — |

| NAME AND LOCATION | TYPE | CON-TROL | ENROLLMENT U | ENROLLMENT G | TUITION & FEES R | TUITION & FEES NR | ROOM, BOARD | COMP. FEE |
|---|---|---|---|---|---|---|---|---|
| Bethune Cookman College, Daytona Beach, Florida....... | MW | Pvt. | 1,120 | — | 900 | 900 | 600 | — |
| Biola College, La Mirada, California.................... | MW | I | 1,193 | — | 1,100 | 1,100 | 725 | — |
| Birmingham-Southern College, Birmingham, Alabama.... | MW | M | 1,050 | — | 900 | 900 | 865 | — |
| Bishop College, Dallas, Texas.......................... | MW | AB | 1,976 | — | 850 | 850 | 750 | — |
| Black Hills State College, Spearfish, South Dakota....... | MW | State | 3,356 | 234 | 356 | 656 | 594 | — |
| Blackburn College, Carlinville, Illinois.................. | MW | P | 500 | — | 900 | 900 | 350 | — |
| Bloomfield College, Bloomfield, New Jersey.......... | MW | P | 1,222 | — | 1,180 | 1,180 | 850 | — |
| Bloomsburg State College, Bloomsburg, Pennsylvania..... | MW | State | 3,300 | 250 | 300 | 690 | 648 | — |
| Blue Mountain College, Blue Mountain, Mississippi....... | W | SB | 400 | — | 530 | 530 | 550 | — |
| Bluefield State College, Bluefield, West Virginia........ | MW | State | 1,397 | — | 150 | 450 | NI | — |
| Bluffton College, Bluffton, Ohio...................... | MW | Mn | 663 | — | 1,225 | 1,225 | 800 | — |
| Boston College, Chestnut Hill, Massachusetts........... | MW | RC | 6,215 | 1,841 | 1,600 | 1,600 | 1,050 | — |
| Boston University, Boston, Massachusetts.............. | MW | Pvt. | 12,177 | 2,910 | 1,650 | 1,650 | 1,081 | — |
| Bowdoin College, Brunswick, Maine................... | M | Pvt. | 925 | 10 | 2,000 | 2,000 | 1,050 | — |
| Bowie State College, Bowie, Maryland................. | MW | State | 550 | — | Free | 450 | 312 | — |
| Bowling Green State University, Bowling Green, Ohio..... | MW | State | 11,000 | 1,000 | 540 | 1,090 | 850 | — |
| Bradley University, Peoria, Illinois.................... | MW | Pvt. | 5,100 | 950 | 1,300 | 1,300 | 450 | — |
| Brandeis University, Waltham, Massachusetts........... | MW | Pvt. | 1,950 | 650 | 2,050 | 2,050 | 1,100 | — |
| Brenau College, Gainesville, Georgia.................. | W | Pvt. | 625 | — | 800 | 800 | 1,000 | — |
| Brescia College, Owensboro, Kentucky................. | MW | RC | 1,100 | — | 640 | 640 | 775 | — |
| Brevard Engineering College, Melbourne, Florida......... | MW | Pvt. | 500 | 275 | 675 | 675 | 300 | — |
| Briar Cliff College, Sioux City, Iowa.................. | MW | RC | 932 | — | 795 | 795 | 770 | — |
| Briarcliff College, Briarcliff Manor, New York........... | W | Pvt. | 700 | — | — | — | — | 3,150 |
| Bridgeport, University of, Bridgeport, Connecticut........ | MW | Pvt. | 6,812 | 1,714 | 1,200 | 1,200 | 1,000 | — |
| Bridgewater College, Bridgewater, Virginia.............. | MW | CB | 925 | — | 1,260 | 1,260 | 740 | — |
| Brigham Young University, Provo, Utah................ | MW | LDS | 20,028 | 1,923 | 400 | 650 | 650 | — |
| Brooks Inst. of Photography, Santa Barbara, California... | MW | Pvt. | 315 | — | 1,650 | 1,650 | NA | — |
| Brown University, Providence, Rhode Island............. | MW | Pvt. | 3,600 | 1,300 | 2,000 | 2,000 | 1,080 | — |
| Bryant College, Providence, Rhode Island.............. | MW | Pvt. | 1,900 | — | 1,124 | 1,124 | 875 | — |
| Bryn Mawr College, Bryn Mawr, Pennsylvania.......... | W | Pvt. | 775 | 373 | 1,850 | 1,850 | 1,200 | — |
| Bucknell University, Lewisburg, Pennsylvania........... | MW | Pvt. | 2,500 | 200 | 1,900 | 1,900 | 850 | — |
| Buena Vista College, Storm Lake, Iowa................ | MW | P | 900 | — | 1,200 | 1,200 | 750 | — |
| Butler University, Indianapolis, Indiana................ | MW | Pvt. | 2,866 | 1,414 | 1,250 | 1,250 | 890 | — |
| Cabrini College, Radnor, Pennsylvania................ | W | RC | 320 | — | 1,100 | 1,100 | 1,000 | — |
| Caldwell College for Women, Caldwell, New Jersey...... | W | RC | 700 | — | 1,070 | 1,070 | 1,000 | — |
| California, University of, at Berkeley, California.......... | MW | State | 16,862 | 10,101 | 243 | 1,224 | 930 | — |
| at Davis, California................................ | MW | State | 6,300 | 1,468 | 244 | 1,225 | 920 | — |
| at Irvine, California............................... | MW | State | 2,300 | 300 | 240 | 1,200 | 990 | — |
| at Los Angeles, California (UCLA)................... | MW | State | 17,622 | 10,366 | 240 | 1,222 | 920 | — |
| at Riverside, California............................ | MW | State | 2,970 | 912 | 260 | 1,240 | 940 | — |
| at San Diego, La Jolla, California................... | MW | State | 2,000 | 1,000 | 219 | 1,200 | 920 | — |
| at Santa Barbara, California....................... | MW | State | 9,700 | 1,053 | 267 | 1,248 | 920 | — |
| at Santa Cruz, California.......................... | MW | State | 1,825 | 75 | 267 | 1,298 | 1,035 | — |
| College of Medicine, Los Angeles, California......... | MW | State | 293 | 383 | 495 | 1,225 | NI | — |
| California Baptist College, Riverside, California.......... | MW | SB | 600 | — | 870 | 870 | 690 | — |
| California College of Arts & Crafts, Oakland, California.... | MW | Pvt. | 950 | 75 | 980 | 980 | 940 | — |
| California Institute of Technology, Pasadena, California... | M | Pvt. | 717 | 778 | 2,008 | 2,008 | 1,030 | — |
| California Lutheran College, Thousand Oaks, California... | MW | L | 1,119 | — | — | — | — | 2,295 |
| California State College, Clarion, Pennsylvania......... | MW | State | 4,322 | 344 | 290 | 680 | 544 | — |
| California State College, at Dominguez Hills, California.... | MW | State | 128 | — | 128 | 928 | NA | — |
| at Fullerton, California............................ | MW | State | 8,900 | NI | 120 | 720 | 1,060 | — |
| at Hayward, California............................. | MW | State | 5,030 | 1,270 | 110 | 560 | NA | — |
| at Long Beach, California.......................... | MW | State | 11,065 | 19 | 115 | 715 | 860 | 975 |
| at Los Angeles, California......................... | MW | State | 7,000 | 13,000 | 120 | 840 | NA | — |
| at San Bernardino, California...................... | MW | State | 275 | — | 80 | 680 | NA | — |
| California State Polytechnic College, Pomona, California... | MW | State | 5,000 | NA | 90 | 690 | 804 | — |
| California State Polytechnic College, San Luis Obispo, California..................................... | MW | State | 7,900 | 400 | 127 | 847 | 849 | — |
| California Western University, San Diego, California...... | MW | M | 1,800 | NI | 1,470 | 1,470 | 900 | — |
| Calvin College, Grand Rapids, Michigan................ | MW | CR | 3,500 | — | 970 | 970 | 825 | — |
| Cambellsville College, Cambellsville, Kentucky.......... | MW | SB | 1,079 | — | 530 | 530 | 550 | — |
| Campbell College, Buie's Creek, North Carolina......... | MW | SB | 2,300 | — | 810 | 860 | 575 | — |
| Canisius College, Buffalo, New York................... | MW | RC | 2,800 | 700 | 1,310 | 1,310 | 1,100 | — |
| Capital University, Columbus, Ohio................... | MW | L | 1,755 | 143 | 1,200 | 1,200 | 550 | — |
| Cardinal Cushing College, Brookline, Massachusetts...... | W | RC | 350 | — | 1,000 | 1,000 | 1,000 | — |
| Cardinal Glennon College, St. Louis, Missouri........... | M | RC | 250 | — | 675 | 675 | 600 | — |
| Cardinal Stritch College, Milwaukee, Wisconsin......... | W | RC | 513 | 100 | 680 | 680 | 850 | — |
| Carleton College, Northfield, Minnesota............... | MW | Pvt. | 1,350 | — | — | — | — | 2,800 |
| Carnegie University, Pittsburgh, Pennsylvania........... | MW | Pvt. | 3,074 | 1,074 | 1,950 | 1,950 | 1,200 | — |
| Carroll College, Helena, Montana.................... | MW | RC | 975 | — | 950 | 950 | 800 | — |
| Carroll College, Waukesha, Wisconsin................. | MW | P | 1,100 | — | 1,490 | 1,490 | 900 | — |
| Carson-Newman College, Jefferson City, Tennessee....... | MW | SB | 1,710 | — | 737 | 837 | 575 | — |

| NAME AND LOCATION | TYPE | CONTROL | ENROLLMENT U | G | TUITION & FEES R | NR | ROOM, BOARD | COMP. FEE |
|---|---|---|---|---|---|---|---|---|
| Carthage College, Kenosha, Wisconsin | MW | L | 1,400 | — | 1,400 | 1,400 | 850 | — |
| Cascade College, Portland, Oregon | MW | NPE | 305 | — | 900 | 900 | 600 | — |
| Case Western Reserve University, Cleveland, Ohio | MW | Pvt. | 6,000 | 5,500 | 1,800 | 1,800 | 1,050 | — |
| Castleton State College, Castleton, Vermont | MW | State | 846 | — | 346 | 846 | 714 | — |
| Catawba College, Salisbury, North Carolina | MW | UCC | 998 | — | 885 | 885 | 695 | — |
| Catherine Spalding College, Louisville, Kentucky | MW | RC | 1,600 | 250 | 810 | 810 | 850 | — |
| Catholic University of America, Washington, D.C. | MW | RC | 2,500 | 4,000 | 1,630 | 1,630 | 1,000 | — |
| Catholic University of Puerto Rico, Ponce, Puerto Rico | MW | RC | 6,000 | 100 | 600 | 600 | 580 | — |
| Cedar Crest College, Allentown, Pennsylvania | W | UCC | 655 | — | 1,585 | 1,585 | 1,100 | — |
| Centenary College of Louisiana, Shreveport, Louisiana | MW | M | 1,900 | — | 850 | 850 | 750 | — |
| Central College, Pella, Iowa | MW | RfC | 1,070 | — | 1,130 | 1,130 | 730 | — |
| Central Connecticut State College, New Britain, Connecticut | MW | State | 4,925 | — | 165 | 165 | 630 | — |
| Central Methodist College, Fayette, Missouri | MW | M | 950 | — | — | — | — | 1,650 |
| Central Michigan University, Mt. Pleasant, Michigan | MW | State | 9,450 | 1,000 | 300 | 600 | 830 | — |
| Central Missouri State College, Warrensburg, Missouri | MW | State | 9,530 | NI | 220 | 440 | 660 | — |
| Central State College, Edmond, Oklahoma | MW | State | 6,966 | 1,410 | 200 | 400 | 500 | — |
| Central State University, Wilberforce, Ohio | MW | State | 2,025 | 500 | 346 | 716 | 774 | — |
| Central Washington State College, Ellensburg, Washington | MW | State | 5,400 | 200 | 264 | 471 | 643 | — |
| Centre College of Kentucky, Danville, Kentucky | MW | P | 750 | — | 1,475 | 1,475 | 875 | — |
| Chadron State College, Chadron, Nebraska | MW | State | 1,760 | 260 | 270 | 420 | 696 | — |
| Chamonade College of Honolulu, Honolulu, Hawaii | MW | RC | 668 | — | 800 | 800 | 800 | — |
| Chapman College, Orange, California | MW | DC | 2,000 | 700 | 1,290 | 1,290 | 800 | — |
| Charleston, College of, Charleston, South Carolina | MW | Pvt. | 500 | — | 1,200 | 1,200 | 1,000 | — |
| Chatham College, Pittsburgh, Pennsylvania | W | Pvt. | 650 | — | 1,900 | 1,900 | 1,050 | — |
| Chattanooga, University of, Chattanooga, Tennessee | MW | Pvt. | 1,805 | 237 | 900 | 900 | 750 | — |
| Chestnut Hill College, Philadelphia, Pennsylvania | W | RC | 648 | — | 1,300 | 1,300 | 1,000 | — |
| Cheyney State College, Cheyney, Pennsylvania | MW | State | 1,688 | — | 281 | 640 | 612 | — |
| Chicago, University of, Chicago, Illinois | MW | Pvt. | 3,500 | 7,000 | 1,980 | 1,980 | 1,350 | — |
| Chicago State College, Chicago, Illinois | MW | State | 3,100 | 3,000 | 240 | 495 | NA | — |
| Chico State College, Chico, California | MW | State | 6,077 | 908 | 144 | 720 | 912 | — |
| Christian Brothers College, Memphis, Tennessee | M | RC | 1,053 | — | 975 | 975 | 900 | — |
| Church College of Hawaii, Laie, Oahu, Hawaii | MW | LDS | 949 | — | 490 | 490 | 630 | — |
| Cincinnati, University of, Cincinnati, Ohio | MW | City | 24,795 | 3,372 | 933 | 993 | 975 | — |
| The Citadel, Charleston, South Carolina | M | State | 2,000 | — | — | — | — | 1977R 2527NR |
| Claflin College, Orangeburg, South Carolina | MW | M | 700 | — | 651 | 651 | 495 | — |
| Claremont Colleges & University Center: | | | | | | | | |
| Claremont Men's College, Claremont, California | M | Pvt. | 720 | — | 1,780 | 1,780 | 1,000 | — |
| Harvey Mudd College, Claremont, California | MW | Pvt. | 297 | — | 2,000 | 2,000 | 1,050 | — |
| Pitzer College, Claremont, California | W | Pvt. | 600 | — | 1,775 | 1,775 | 1,250 | — |
| Pomona College, Claremont, California | MW | Pvt. | 1,200 | — | 1,700 | 1,700 | 1,150 | — |
| Scripps College, Claremont, California | W | Pvt. | 500 | — | — | — | — | 2,975 |
| Clarion State College, Clarion, Pennsylvania | MW | State | 3,215 | 50 | 300 | 640 | 612 | — |
| Clark College, Atlanta, Georgia | MW | Pvt. | 1,007 | — | 908 | 908 | 603 | — |
| Clark University, Worcester, Massachusetts | MW | Pvt. | 1,250 | 350 | 1,900 | 1,900 | 1,000 | — |
| Clarke College, Dubuque, Iowa | W | RC | 1,020 | — | — | — | — | 1,800 |
| Clarkson College of Technology, Potsdam, New York | MW | Pvt. | 2,150 | 100 | 1,900 | 1,900 | 875 | — |
| Clemson University, Clemson, South Carolina | MW | State | 5,400 | 372 | 496 | 996 | 761 | — |
| Cleveland State University, Cleveland, Ohio | MW | State | 8,000 | 100 | 495 | 990 | 990 | — |
| Coe College, Cedar Rapids, Iowa | MW | Pvt. | 1,044 | — | 1,580 | 1,580 | 900 | — |
| Coker College for Women, Hartsville, South Carolina | W | Pvt. | 350 | — | 1,115 | 1,115 | 775 | — |
| Colby College, Waterville, Maine | MW | Pvt. | 1,500 | — | 1,850 | 1,850 | 900 | — |
| Colgate University, Hamilton, New York | M | Pvt. | 1,850 | 100 | 2,100 | 2,100 | 1,100 | — |
| Colorado, University of, Boulder, Colorado | MW | State | 12,785 | 2,896 | 372 | 1,220 | 850 | — |
| Colorado College, Colorado Springs, Colorado | MW | Pvt. | 1,500 | — | 1,710 | 1,710 | 900 | — |
| Colorado School of Mines, Golden, Colorado | MW | State | 1,211 | 138 | 396 | 896 | 810 | — |
| Colorado State College, Greeley, Colorado | MW | State | 6,334 | 1,203 | 293 | 690 | 855 | — |
| Colorado State University, Fort Collins, Colorado | MW | State | 11,049 | 1,652 | 342 | 1,119 | 900 | — |
| Columbia College, Columbia, South Carolina | W | M | 825 | — | 1,040 | 1,100 | 935 | — |
| Columbia Union College, Takoma Park, Maryland | MW | SDA | 1,100 | — | 1,170 | 1,170 | 650 | — |
| Columbia University, New York, New York | MW | Pvt. | 8,356 | 20,092 | 1,950 | 1,950 | 1,100 | — |
| Concord College, Athens, West Virginia | MW | State | 2,000 | — | 210 | 660 | 686 | — |
| Concordia College, Moorhead, Minnesota | MW | L | 2,400 | — | 1,118 | 1,118 | 710 | — |
| Concordia Teachers College, River Forest, Illinois | MW | L | 1,400 | 60 | 635 | 635 | 720 | — |
| Concordia Teachers College, Seward, Nebraska | MW | L | 1,300 | — | 747 | 747 | 620 | — |
| Connecticut, University of, Storrs, Connecticut | MW | State | 11,000 | 5,615 | 202 | 602 | 800 | — |
| Connecticut College, New London, Connecticut | W | Pvt. | 1,394 | 49 | 2,030 | 2,030 | 1,120 | — |
| Converse College, Spartanburg, South Carolina | W | Pvt. | 742 | 48 | — | — | NA | 2,800 |
| Cooper Union, New York, New York | MW | Pvt. | 1,230 | 50 | 100 | 100 | NA | — |
| Coppin State College, Baltimore, Maryland | MW | State | 805 | — | 255 | 505 | NA | — |
| Cornell College, Mount Vernon, Iowa | MW | M | 1,000 | — | 1,860 | 1,860 | 890 | — |

| NAME AND LOCATION | TYPE | CON-TROL | ENROLLMENT U | G | TUITION & FEES R | NR | ROOM, BOARD | COMP. FEE |
|---|---|---|---|---|---|---|---|---|
| Cornell University, Ithaca, New York | MW | Pvt. / State | 9,900 | 4,400 | 2,050 | 2,050 | 1,050 | — |
| Creighton University, Omaha, Nebraska | MW | RC | 3,689 | 391 | 1,070 | 1,070 | 950 | — |
| Culver-Stockton College, Canton, Missouri | MW | DC | 863 | — | 1,190 | 1,190 | 780 | — |
| Cumberland College, Williamsburg, Kentucky | MW | SB | 1,529 | — | 470 | 470 | 380 | — |
| Dakota Wesleyan University, Mitchell, South Dakota | MW | M | 850 | — | 705 | 705 | 670 | — |
| Dallas, University of, Dallas, Texas | MW | RC | 900 | 28 | 770 | 770 | 700 | — |
| Dana College, Blair, Nebraska | MW | L | 1,219 | — | 980 | 980 | 700 | — |
| Danbury State College, Danbury, Connecticut | MW | State | 1,700 | 427 | 200 | 200 | 630 | — |
| Dartmouth College, Hanover, New Hampshire | M | Pvt. | 3,084 | 524 | 2,075 | 2,075 | 1,032 | — |
| David Lipscomb College, Nashville, Tennessee | MW | UCC | 1,773 | — | 900 | 900 | 825 | — |
| Davidson College, Davidson, North Carolina | M | P | 1,000 | — | 1,495 | 1,495 | 645 | — |
| Davis and Elkins College, Elkins, West Virginia | MW | P | 825 | — | 1,400 | 1,400 | 1,000 | — |
| Dayton, University of, Dayton, Ohio | MW | RC | 8,922 | 1,007 | 1,027 | 1,027 | 800 | — |
| Defiance College, Defiance, Ohio | MW | UCC | 1,000 | — | 1,350 | 1,350 | 850 | — |
| Delaware, University of, Newark, Delaware | MW | State | 6,500 | 1,900 | 350 | 820 | 1120R 1605NR | — |
| Delaware State College, Dover, Delaware | MW | State | 915 | — | 288 | 638 | 525 | — |
| Delaware Valley College of Science and Agriculture, Doyleston, Pennsylvania | M | Pvt. | 820 | — | 1,229 | 1,229 | 810 | — |
| Delta State College, Cleveland, Mississippi | MW | State | 2,191 | — | 695 | 995 | incl. | — |
| Denison University, Granville, Ohio | MW | Pvt. | 1,825 | — | 1,800 | 1,800 | 960 | — |
| Denver, University of, Denver, Colorado | MW | M | 5,715 | 2,458 | 1,500 | 1,500 | 900 | — |
| De Paul University, Chicago, Illinois | MW | RC | 3,280 | 6,500 | 1,095 | 1,095 | NA | — |
| De Pauw University, Greencastle, Indiana | MW | M | 2,400 | 40 | 1,750 | 1,750 | 1,000 | — |
| Detroit, University of, Detroit, Michigan | MW | RC | 7,174 | 1,452 | 1,150 | 1,150 | 840 | — |
| Detroit Institute of Technology, Detroit, Michigan | MW | Pvt. | 2,000 | 375 | 840 | 840 | NA | — |
| Dickinson College, Carlisle, Pennsylvania | MW | M | 1,500 | — | 2,037 | 2,037 | 950 | — |
| Dickinson State College, Dickinson, North Dakota | MW | State | 1,600 | — | 345 | 669 | 513 | — |
| Dillard University, New Orleans, Louisiana | MW | Pvt. | 1,000 | — | 800 | 800 | 700 | — |
| District of Columbia Teachers College, Washington, D.C. | MW | State | 1,200 | 900 | 90 | 954 | NA | — |
| Doane College, Crete, Nebraska | MW | C | 750 | — | 1,220 | 1,220 | 780 | — |
| Dominican College, Racine, Wisconsin | MW | RC | 650 | — | 860 | 860 | 825 | — |
| Dominican College of San Rafael, San Rafael, California | MW | RC | 542 | 270 | 850 | 850 | 1,100 | — |
| Drake University, Des Moines, Iowa | MW | Pvt. | 6,310 | 1,140 | 1,200 | 1,200 | 880 | — |
| Drew University, Madison, New Jersey | MW | M | 1,050 | 420 | 1,750 | 1,750 | 925 | — |
| Drexel Institute of Technology, Philadelphia, Pennsylvania | MW | Pvt. | 8,096 | 2,553 | 1,350 | 1,350 | 1,005 | — |
| Drury College, Springfield, Missouri | MW | Pvt. | 1,200 | 250 | 1,100 | 1,100 | 700 | — |
| Dubuque, University of, Dubuque, Iowa | MW | P | 821 | 207 | 1,282 | 1,282 | 870 | — |
| Duchesne College of the Sacred Heart, Omaha, Nebraska | W | RC | 380 | — | 825 | 825 | 975 | — |
| Duke University, Durham, North Carolina | MW | Pvt. | 4,400 | 3,050 | 1,637 | 1,637 | 1,000 | — |
| Dunbarton College of the Holy Cross, Washington, D.C. | W | RC | 485 | — | 1,320 | 1,320 | 1,200 | — |
| Duquesne University, Pittsburgh, Pennsylvania | MW | RC | 4,920 | 1,844 | 1,400 | 1,400 | 870 | — |
| D'Youville College, Buffalo, New York | W | RC | 1,200 | — | 1,295 | 1,295 | 1,100 | — |
| Earlham College, Richmond, Indiana | MW | Q | 1,100 | — | 1,830 | 1,830 | 900 | — |
| East Carolina College, Greenville, North Carolina | MW | State | 8,296 | 624 | 279 | 531 | 672 | — |
| East Central State College, Ada, Oklahoma | MW | State | 2,750 | 150 | 301 | 664 | 650 | — |
| East Stroudsburg State College, East Stroudsburg, Pennsylvania | MW | State | 2,200 | 200 | 300 | 650 | 612 | — |
| East Tennessee State University, Johnson City, Tennessee | MW | State | 8,066 | 545 | 225 | 600 | 720 | — |
| East Texas Baptist College, Marshall, Texas | MW | SB | 663 | — | 665 | 665 | 540 | — |
| East Texas State University, Commerce, Texas | MW | State | 5,330 | — | 194 | 394 | 550 | — |
| Eastern Baptist College, St. Davids, Pennsylvania | MW | AB | 520 | — | 1,460 | 1,460 | 900 | — |
| Eastern Baptist Theological Seminary, Philadelphia, Pennsylvania | MW | AB | 192 | 187 | 355 | 355 | 698 | — |
| Eastern Illinois University, Charleston, Illinois | MW | State | 5,427 | 360 | 233 | 404 | 800 | — |
| Eastern Kentucky University, Richmond, Kentucky | MW | State | 8,000 | 500 | 245 | 585 | 700 | — |
| Eastern Mennonite College, Harrisonburg, Virginia | MW | Mn | 875 | — | 1,050 | 1,050 | 690 | — |
| Eastern Michigan University, Ypsilanti, Michigan | MW | State | 11,000 | 3,000 | 330 | 630 | 800 | — |
| Eastern Montana College, Billings, Montana | MW | State | 2,800 | 200 | 330 | 937 | 785 | — |
| Eastern Nazarene College, Quincy, Massachusetts | MW | CN | 865 | — | 1,085 | 1,085 | 645 | — |
| Eastern New Mexico University, Portales, New Mexico | MW | State | 3,600 | 400 | 340 | 760 | 715 | — |
| Eastern Oregon College, La Grande, Oregon | MW | State | 1,550 | 70 | 333 | 633 | 787 | — |
| Eastern Washington State College, Cheney, Washington | MW | State | 4,550 | 400 | 264 | 471 | 720 | — |
| Edgewood College of the Sacred Heart, Madison, Wisconsin | W | RC | 756 | — | 700 | 700 | 1,000 | — |
| Edinboro State College, Edinboro, Pennsylvania | MW | State | 3,500 | 500 | 285 | 675 | 650 | — |
| Elizabeth City State College, Elizabeth, North Carolina | MW | State | 993 | — | 305 | 505 | 485 | — |
| Elizabethtown College, Elizabethtown, Pennsylvania | MW | CB | 1,359 | — | 1,415 | 1,415 | 780 | — |
| Elmhurst College, Elmhurst, Illinois | MW | UCC | 1,300 | — | 1,370 | 1,370 | 930 | — |
| Elmira College, Elmira, New York | W | Pvt. | 1,136 | 600 | 1,875 | 1,875 | 1,000 | — |
| Elon College, Elon College, North Carolina | MW | UCC | 1,450 | — | 900 | 900 | 650 | — |
| Emerson College, Boston, Massachusetts | MW | Pvt. | 1,050 | 50 | 1,774 | 1,774 | 1,000 | — |

| NAME AND LOCATION | TYPE | CON-TROL | ENROLLMENT U | ENROLLMENT G | TUITION & FEES R | TUITION & FEES NR | ROOM. BOARD | COMP. FEE |
|---|---|---|---|---|---|---|---|---|
| Emmanuel College, Boston, Massachusetts.............. | W | RC | 1,350 | 85 | 1,200 | 1,200 | 1,200 | — |
| Emory and Henry College, Emory, Virginia............... | MW | M | 850 | — | 1,000 | 1,000 | 750 | — |
| Emory University, Atlanta and Oxford, Georgia........... | MW | M | 2,200 | 2,615 | 1,403 | 1,403 | 900 | — |
| Emporia, the College of, Emporia, Kansas............... | MW | P | 1,025 | — | 870 | 870 | 800 | — |
| Erskine College, Due West, South Carolina.............. | MW | P | 722 | — | 1,110 | 1,110 | 580 | — |
| Eureka College, Eureka, Illinois....................... | MW | DC | 535 | — | 1,300 | 1,300 | 840 | — |
| Evangel College, Springfield, Missouri................. | MW | AG | 820 | — | 948 | 948 | 650 | — |
| Evansville, University of, Evansville, Indiana........... | MW | M | 4,700 | 200 | 864 | 864 | 765 | — |
| Fairfield University, Fairfield, Connecticut............. | MW | RC | 1,768 | 1,000 | 1,400 | 1,400 | 1,000 | — |
| Fairleigh Dickinson University, Rutherford, Teaneck, and Madison, New Jersey............................... | MW | Pvt. | 15,876 | 2,379 | 1,370 | 1,370 | 1,135 | — |
| Fairmont State College, Fairmont, West Virginia.......... | MW | State | 2,500 | — | 219 | 669 | 760 | — |
| Farmington State College, Farmington, Maine............ | MW | State | 800 | 150 | 250 | 350 | 708 | — |
| Fayetteville State College, Fayetteville, North Carolina.... | MW | State | 1,142 | — | 100 | 300 | 459 | — |
| Ferris State College, Big Rapids, Michigan.............. | MW | State | 7,465 | — | 285 | 600 | 846 | — |
| Finch College, New York, New York.................... | W | Pvt. | 425 | — | 2.250 | 2,250 | 1,650 | — |
| Findlay College, Findlay, Ohio........................ | MW | CG | 1,320 | — | 1,200 | 1,200 | 800 | — |
| Fisk University, Nashville, Tennessee.................. | MW | Pvt. | 1,100 | 39 | 838 | 838 | 665 | — |
| Florence State College, Florence, Alabama.............. | MW | State | 3,000 | 100 | 280 | 430 | 610 | — |
| Florida, University of, Gainesville, Florida.............. | MW | State | 15,600 | 3,700 | 300 | 700 | 600 | — |
| Florida A&M University, Tallahassee, Florida............ | MW | State | 3,550 | 450 | 312 | 762 | 472 | — |
| Florida Institute of Technology, Melbourne, Florida....... | MW | Pvt. | 578 | 275 | 900 | 900 | NI | — |
| Florida Memorial College, St. Augustine, Florida........ | MW | AB | 483 | 84 | 760 | 760 | 450 | — |
| Florida Presbyterian College, St. Petersburg, Florida...... | MW | P | 980 | — | — | — | — | 2,460 |
| Florida Southern College, Lakeland, Florida............. | MW | M | 1,410 | — | — | — | — | 1,180 |
| Florida State University, Tallahassee, Florida........... | MW | State | 13,300 | 2,000 | 333 | 783 | 864 | — |
| Fontbonne College, St. Louis, Missouri................. | W | RC | 953 | — | 1,350 | 1,350 | 1,000 | — |
| Fordham University, Bronx, New York................... | MW | RC | 6,336 | 2,274 | 1,500 | 1,500 | 450R | — |
| Fort Hays Kansas State College, Hays, Kansas........... | MW | State | 4,453 | 511 | 243 | 508 | 700 | — |
| Fort Lewis College, Durango, Colorado................. | MW | State | 1,600 | — | 495 | 1,095 | 1,110 | — |
| Fort Valley State College, Fort Valley, Georgia........... | MW | State | 1,622 | 102 | 315 | 431 | 570 | — |
| Fort Wright College of the Holy Names, Spokane, Washington......................................... | W | RC | 343 | 86 | 850 | 850 | 800 | — |
| Francis T. Nicholls State College, Thibodaux, Louisiana... | MW | State | 2,902 | 284 | 164 | 762 | 644 | — |
| Franklin College, Franklin, Indiana.................... | MW | AB | 682 | — | 1,440 | 1,440 | 890 | — |
| Franklin and Marshall College, Lancaster, Pennsylvania... | M | UCC | 1,650 | 15 | 1,900 | 1,900 | 930 | — |
| Fresno State College, Fresno, California................ | MW | State | 8,000 | 1,500 | 132 | 852 | 831 | — |
| Friends University, Wichita, Kansas................... | MW | Q | 871 | — | 800 | 800 | 700 | — |
| Frostburg State College, Frostburg, Maryland........... | MW | State | 1,800 | — | 310 | 560 | 675 | — |
| Furman University, Greenville, South Carolina........... | MW | SB | 1,500 | 17 | 1,012 | 1,012 | 1,025 | — |
| Gallaudet College, Washington, D.C................... | MW | Pvt. | 650 | 50 | 590 | 590 | 775 | — |
| Gannon College, Erie, Pennsylvania................... | M | RC | 2,800 | 145 | 839 | 839 | 850 | — |
| General Beadle State College, Madison, South Dakota.... | MW | State | 1,100 | — | 364 | 700 | 550 | — |
| General Motors Institute, Flint, Michigan.............. | MW | Pvt. | 2,800 | — | 774 | 774 | 1,350 | — |
| Geneva College, Beaver Falls, Pennsylvania............. | MW | P | 1,300 | — | 1,238 | 1,238 | 742 | — |
| George Fox College, Newberg, Oregon................. | MW | Q | 376 | — | 1,140 | 1,140 | 795 | — |
| George Peabody College for Teachers, Nashville, Tennessee | MW | Pvt. | 1,600 | 600 | 1,315 | 1,315 | 1,000 | — |
| George Washington University, Washington, D.C......... | MW | Pvt. | 4,500 | 7,000 | 1,675 | 1,675 | 1,150 | — |
| George Williams College, Downers Grove, Illinois....... | MW | Pvt. | 680 | 100 | 1,160 | 1,160 | 897 | — |
| Georgetown College, Georgetown, Kentucky............ | MW | SB | 1,400 | — | 1,640 | 1,640 | 750 | — |
| Georgetown University, Washington, D.C............... | MW | RC | 4,100 | 3,600 | 1,800 | 1,800 | 1,060 | — |
| Georgia, University of, Athens, Georgia................ | MW | State | 13,700 | 2,300 | 333 | 753 | 725 | — |
| Georgia, Women's College of, Milledgeville, Georgia..... | W | State | 1,300 | 250 | 351 | 681 | 600 | — |
| Georgia Institute of Technology, Atlanta, Georgia......... | MW | State | 6,421 | 106 | 375 | 1,065 | 1,225 | — |
| Georgia Southern College, Statesboro, Georgia.......... | MW | State | 4,100 | 250 | 303 | 633 | 570 | — |
| Georgia State College, Atlanta, Georgia................ | MW | State | 8,500 | 1,000 | 375 | 834 | 1,200 | — |
| Georgian Court College, Lakewood, New Jersey.......... | W | RC | 610 | — | 1,235 | 1,235 | 1,100 | — |
| Gettysburg College, Gettysburg, Pennsylvania........... | MW | L | 1,880 | — | 1,700 | 1,700 | 810 | — |
| Glassboro State College, Glassboro, New Jersey.......... | MW | State | 3,400 | 1,500 | 274 | — | 818 | — |
| Glenville State College, Glenville, West Virginia......... | MW | State | 1,700 | — | 201 | 651 | 668 | — |
| Goddard College, Plainfield, Vermont.................. | MW | Pvt. | 741 | — | 2,276 | 2,276 | 900 | — |
| Golden Gate College, San Francisco, California.......... | MW | Pvt. | 900 | 675 | 642 | 642 | 1,000 | — |
| Gonzaga University, Spokane, Washington.............. | MW | RC | 2,203 | 300 | 1,100 | 1,100 | 800 | — |
| Good Counsel College, White Plains, New York.......... | W | RC | 536 | — | 1,100 | 1 100 | 1,050 | — |
| Gordon College, Wenham, Massachusetts............... | MW | Pvt. | 634 | 225 | 1,110 | 1,110 | 600 | — |
| Gorham State College, Gorham, Maine................. | MW | State | 1,150 | 600 | 165 | 265 | 708 | — |
| Goshen College, Goshen, Indiana..................... | MW | Mn | 1,100 | 35 | 1,225 | 1,225 | 670 | — |
| Goucher College, Baltimore, Maryland................. | W | Pvt. | 1,025 | 25 | 1,663 | 1,663 | 1,350 | — |
| Graceland College, Lamoni, Iowa..................... | MW | LDS | 1,200 | — | 1,020 | 1,020 | 750 | — |
| Grambling College, Grambling, Louisiana............... | MW | State | 4,200 | — | 172 | 772 | 419 | — |
| Great Falls, College of, Great Falls, Montana............ | MW | RC | 900 | — | 1,000 | 1,000 | 700 | — |
| Greensboro College, Greensboro, North Carolina.......... | MW | M | 700 | — | 980 | 980 | 670 | — |

| NAME AND LOCATION | TYPE | CON-TROL | ENROLLMENT U | G | TUITION & FEES R | NR | ROOM, BOARD | COMP. FEE |
|---|---|---|---|---|---|---|---|---|
| Greenville College, Greenville, Illinois | MW | M | 718 | — | 980 | 980 | 820 | — |
| Grinnell College, Grinnell, Iowa | MW | Pvt. | 1,185 | — | 2,040 | 2,040 | 860 | — |
| Grove City College, Grove City, Pennsylvania | MW | P | 1,981 | — | 800 | 800 | 825 | — |
| Guam, College of, Agana, Guam | MW | State | 1,000 | 50 | 180 | 325 | NA | — |
| Guilford College, Greensboro, North Carolina | MW | Q | 1,575 | 5 | 1,035 | 1,035 | 660 | — |
| Gustavus Adolphus College, St. Peter, Minnesota | MW | L | 1 775 | — | — | — | — | 2,200 |
| Gwynedd-Mercy College, Gwynedd Valley, Pennsylvania | W | Pvt. | 1,085 | — | 1,000 | 1,000 | 1,300 | — |
| Hamilton College, Clinton, New York | M | Pvt. | 832 | — | 1,775 | 1,775 | 1,000 | — |
| Hamline University, St. Paul, Minnesota | MW | M | 1,250 | — | 1,330 | 1,330 | 870 | — |
| Hampden-Sydney College, Hampden-Sydney, Virginia | M | P | 571 | — | 1,400 | 1,400 | 700 | — |
| Hampton Institute, Hampton, Virginia | MW | Pvt. | 2,150 | 250 | 900 | 900 | 600 | — |
| Hanover College, Hanover, Indiana | MW | P | 1,050 | — | 1,395 | 1,395 | 670 | — |
| Harding College, Searcy, Arkansas | MW | UCC | 1,900 | 30 | 816 | 816 | 620 | — |
| Hardin-Simmons University, Abilene, Texas | MW | SB | 1,363 | 472 | 750 | 750 | 680 | — |
| Harris Teachers College, St. Louis, Missouri | MW | State | 1,100 | — | 150 | NE | NA | — |
| Hartford, University of, Hartford, Connecticut | MW | Pvt. | 2,100 | 1,250 | 1,200 | 1,200 | 1,100 | — |
| Hartwick College, Oneonta, New York | MW | L | 1,500 | — | 1,525 | 1,525 | 900 | — |
| Harvard University, Cambridge, Massachusetts | M | Pvt. | 4,900 | 7,100 | 1,760 | 1,760 | 1,130 | — |
| Hastings College, Hastings, Nebraska | MW | P | 750 | — | 1,250 | 1,250 | 760 | — |
| Haverford College, Haverford, Pennsylvania | M | Q | 590 | — | 2,110 | 2,110 | 900 | — |
| Hawaii, University of, Honolulu, Hawaii | MW | State | 12,321 | 3,720 | 232 | 232 | 1,080 | — |
| Hebrew Teachers College, Brookline, Massachusetts | MW | Pvt. | 135 | 18 | 300 | 300 | NA | — |
| Heidelberg College, Tiffin, Ohio | MW | UCC | 1,200 | — | 1,500 | 1,500 | 845 | — |
| Henderson State Teachers College, Arkadelphia, Arkansas | MW | State | 3,200 | 500 | 200 | 470 | 600 | — |
| Hendrix College, Conway, Arkansas | MW | M | 830 | — | 826 | 826 | 700 | — |
| High Point College, High Point, North Carolina | MW | M | 1,350 | — | 819 | 869 | 630 | — |
| Hillsdale College, Hillsdale, Michigan | MW | Pvt. | 1,050 | — | 1,494 | 1,494 | 890 | — |
| Hiram College, Hiram, Ohio | MW | Pvt. | 1,100 | — | 1,775 | 1,775 | 860 | — |
| Hobart & William Smith Colleges, Geneva, New York | MW | PE | 1,500 | — | 1,900 | 1,900 | 1,050 | — |
| Hofstra University, Hempstead, New York | MW | Pvt. | 5,520 | 3,010 | 1,700 | 1,700 | 1,150 | — |
| Hollins College, Hollins College, Virginia | W | Pvt. | 950 | 15 | — | — | — | 3,050 |
| Holy Cross, College of the, Worcester, Mass. | M | RC | 2,500 | — | 1,700 | 1,700 | 1,130 | — |
| Holy Family College, Philadelphia, Pennsylvania | W | RC | 627 | — | 1,000 | 1,000 | 800 | — |
| Holy Family College, Manitowoc, Wisconsin | W | RC | 564 | — | 557 | 557 | 600 | — |
| Holy Names, College of the, Oakland, California | W | RC | 600 | — | 1,050 | 1,050 | 1,100 | — |
| Hood College, Frederick, Maryland | W | Pvt. | 750 | — | 1,648 | 1,648 | 1,100 | — |
| Hope College, Holland, Michigan | MW | RFC | 1,875 | — | 1,060 | 1,060 | 850 | — |
| Houghton College, Houghton, New York | MW | M | 1,137 | — | 1,195 | 1,195 | 770 | — |
| Houston, University of, Houston, Texas | MW | State | 17,673 | 2,313 | 202 | 502 | 810 | — |
| Howard Payne College, Brownwood, Texas | MW | SB | 1,111 | 88 | 776 | 776 | 775 | — |
| Howard University, Washington, D.C. | MW | Pvt. | 7,826 | 3,336 | 750 | 750 | 812 | — |
| Humboldt State College, Arcata, California | MW | State | 2,750 | NI | 115 | 835 | 918 | — |
| Humphreys College, Stockton, California | MW | Pvt. | 375 | — | 1,055 | 1,055 | NA | — |
| Huntingdon College, Montgomery, Alabama | MW | M | 1,150 | — | 750 | 750 | 750 | — |
| Huntington College, Huntington, Indiana | MW | UBC | 500 | — | 1,010 | 1,010 | 720 | — |
| Huron College, Huron, South Dakota | MW | P | 667 | — | 846 | 846 | 680 | — |
| Huston-Tillotson College, Austin, Texas | MW | Pvt. | 825 | — | 670 | 670 | 567 | — |
| Idaho, the College of, Caldwell, Idaho | MW | P | 835 | 40 | 1,305 | 1,305 | 805 | — |
| Idaho, University of, Moscow, Idaho | MW | State | 5,761 | 527 | 210 | 710 | 790 | — |
| Idaho State University, Pocatello, Idaho | MW | State | 4,259 | 204 | 280 | 640 | 750 | — |
| Illinois, University of, Urbana, Illinois | MW | State | 22,040 | 7,685 | 220 | 800 | 840 | — |
| Illinois College, Jacksonville, Illinois | MW | Pvt. | 875 | — | 1,060 | 1,060 | 850 | — |
| Illinois Institute of Technology, Chicago, Illinois | MW | Pvt. | 2,300 | 600 | 1,600 | 1,600 | 900 | — |
| Illinois State University, Normal, Illinois | MW | State | 9,600 | 1,100 | 225 | 600 | 940 | — |
| Illinois Teachers College, South Chicago, Illinois | MW | State | 3,000 | 1,400 | 200 | 412 | — | — |
| Illinois Wesleyan University, Bloomington, Illinois | MW | M | 1,550 | — | 1,625 | 1,625 | 920 | — |
| Immaculata College, Immaculata, Pennsylvania | W | RC | 1,000 | — | 1,200 | 1,200 | 1,000 | — |
| Immaculate Conception Seminary, Conception, Missouri | M | RC | 444 | — | 550 | 550 | 600 | — |
| Immaculate Heart College, Los Angeles, California | W | RC | 825 | 350 | 1,230 | 1,230 | 985 | — |
| Incarnate Word College, San Antonio, Texas | W | RC | 900 | — | 870 | 870 | 915 | — |
| Indiana Central College, Indianapolis, Indiana | MW | EUB | 1,025 | 125 | 1,120 | 1,120 | 700 | — |
| Indiana Institute of Technology, Fort Wayne, Indiana | MW | Pvt. | 1,300 | — | 1,050 | 1,050 | 1,070 | — |
| Indiana Northern University, Gas City, Indiana | MW | Pvt. | 200 | 15 | 775 | 775 | 1,050 | — |
| Indiana State University, Terre Haute, Indiana | MW | State | 10,190 | 1,150 | 300 | 600 | 882 | — |
| Indiana University, Bloomington, Indiana | MW | State | 31,946 | 12,705 | 360 | 980 | 885 | — |
| Indiana University of Pennsylvania, Indiana, Pennsylvania | MW | State | 6,700 | 1,000 | 420 | 620 | 712 | — |
| Inter-American University of Puerto Rico, San German, Puerto Rico | MW | Pvt. | 4,080 | 1,500 | 650 | 650 | 580 | — |
| Iona College, New Rochelle, New York | M | RC | 2,400 | 600 | 1,200 | 1,200 | NA | — |
| Iowa, University of, Iowa City, Iowa | MW | State | 13,500 | 4,500 | 340 | 930 | 915 | — |
| Iowa State University of Science and Technology, Ames, Iowa | MW | State | 13,977 | 2,523 | 345 | 930 | 735 | — |

| NAME AND LOCATION | TYPE | CONTROL | ENROLLMENT U | G | TUITION & FEES R | NR | ROOM, BOARD | COMP. FEE |
|---|---|---|---|---|---|---|---|---|
| Iowa Wesleyan College, Mt. Pleasant, Iowa | MW | M | 1,000 | — | 1,200 | 1,200 | 800 | — |
| Ithaca College, Ithaca, New York | MW | Pvt. | 3,300 | 60 | 1,885 | 1,885 | 513 | — |
| Jackson State College, Jackson, Mississippi | MW | State | 2,600 | 180 | 258 | 600 | 492 | — |
| Jacksonville State College, Jacksonville, Alabama | MW | State | 4,179 | 76 | 260 | 410 | 567 | — |
| Jacksonville University, Jacksonville, Florida | MW | Pvt. | 2,600 | 100 | 1,025 | 1,025 | 850 | — |
| Jamestown College, Jamestown, North Dakota | MW | P | 650 | — | 1,250 | 1,250 | 850 | — |
| Jersey City State College, Jersey City, New Jersey | MW | State | 5,000 | 1,000 | 246 | NA | 738 | — |
| Jewish Theological Seminary, New York, New York | MW | J | 440 | 193 | 500 | 500 | 680 | — |
| John Brown University, Siloam Springs, Arkansas | MW | Pvt. | 700 | — | 830 | 830 | 820 | — |
| John Carroll University, Cleveland, Ohio | MW | RC | 3,800 | 800 | 1,210 | 1,210 | 900 | — |
| Johns Hopkins University, Baltimore, Maryland | MW | Pvt. | 1,780 | 1,500 | 2,000 | 2,000 | 900 | — |
| Johnson C. Smith University, Charlotte, North Carolina | MW | P | 1,181 | — | 810 | 810 | 690 | — |
| Johnson State College, Johnson, Vermont | MW | State | 496 | — | 360 | 860 | 865 | — |
| Judson College, Marion, Alabama | W | SB | 450 | — | 725 | 725 | 800 | — |
| Juilliard School of Music, New York, New York | MW | Pvt. | 600 | 125 | 1,270 | 1,270 | NA | — |
| Juniata College, Huntingdon, Pennsylvania | MW | Pvt. | 1,100 | — | 1,500 | 1,500 | 850 | — |
| Kalamazoo College, Kalamazoo, Michigan | MW | AB | 1,240 | 54 | 1,335 | 1,335 | 1,125 | — |
| Kansas, University of, Lawrence, Kansas | MW | State | 15,500 | 3,444 | 332 | 792 | 800 | — |
| Kansas City Art Institute, Kansas City, Missouri | MW | Pvt. | 515 | — | 1,080 | 1,080 | 950 | — |
| Kansas State College, Pittsburg, Kansas | MW | State | 5,340 | 660 | 242 | 507 | 700 | — |
| Kansas State Teachers College, Emporia, Kansas | MW | State | 5,850 | 1,100 | 237 | 500 | 750 | — |
| Kansas State University, Manhattan, Kansas | MW | State | 20,854 | 3,956 | 320 | 780 | 700 | — |
| Kansas Wesleyan University, Salina, Kansas | MW | M | 780 | — | — | — | — | 1,825 |
| Kearney State College, Kearney, Nebraska | MW | State | 4,400 | 124 | 270 | 420 | 696 | — |
| Kent State University, Kent, Ohio | MW | State | 19,465 | 2,560 | 510 | 960 | 789 | — |
| Kentucky, University of, Lexington, Kentucky | MW | State | 10,000 | 3,000 | 250 | 820 | 850 | — |
| Kentucky State College, Frankfort, Kentucky | MW | State | 1,700 | — | 240 | 580 | 443 | — |
| Kentucky Wesleyan College, Owensboro, Kentucky | MW | M | 1,000 | — | 840 | 990 | 750 | — |
| Kenyon College, Gambier, Ohio | M | PE | 820 | — | 1,875 | 1,875 | 800 | — |
| Keuka College, Keuka Park, New York | W | AB | 830 | — | — | — | — | 2,500 |
| King College, Bristol, Tennessee | MW | P | 288 | — | 1,092 | 1,092 | 630 | — |
| King's College, Wilkes-Barre, Pennsylvania | M | Pvt. | 1,750 | — | 1,200 | 1,200 | 900 | — |
| Knox College, Galesburg, Illinois | MW | Pvt. | 1,365 | — | — | — | — | 3,015 |
| Knoxville College, Knoxville, Tennessee | MW | P | 1,000 | — | 581 | 581 | 625 | — |
| Kutztown State College, Kutztown, Pennsylvania | MW | State | 3,500 | 500 | 250 | 600 | 648 | — |
| Ladycliff College, Highland Falls, New York | W | Pvt. | 578 | — | 1,007 | 1,007 | 1,050 | — |
| Lafayette College, Easton, Pennsylvania | M | Pvt. | 1,780 | — | 2,455 | 2,455 | 920 | — |
| La Grange College, La Grange, Georgia | MW | M | 600 | — | 900 | 900 | 600 | — |
| Lake Erie College, Painesville, Ohio | W | Pvt. | 600 | — | — | — | — | 3,000 |
| Lake Forest College, Lake Forest, Illinois | MW | P | 1,200 | — | — | — | — | 3,000 |
| Lake Michigan College, Benton Harbor, Michigan | MW | C'nty | 2,050 | — | 240 | 390 | NA | — |
| Lakeland College, Sheboygan, Wisconsin | MW | UCC | 670 | — | 1,176 | 1,176 | 915 | — |
| Lamar State College of Technology, Beaumont, Texas | MW | State | 9,477 | 354 | 100 | 400 | 720 | — |
| Lambuth College, Jackson, Tennessee | MW | M | 925 | — | 950 | 950 | 580 | — |
| Lander College, Greenwood, South Carolina | MW | State | 579 | — | 730 | 730 | 520 | — |
| Langston University, Langston, Oklahoma | MW | State | 1,550 | — | 329 | 705 | 586 | — |
| La Salle College, Philadelphia, Pennsylvania | M | RC | 5,998 | — | 1,150 | 1,150 | 900 | — |
| La Verne College, La Verne, California | MW | EUB | 710 | — | 1,370 | 1,370 | 840 | — |
| Lawrence University, Appleton, Wisconsin | MW | Pvt. | 1,240 | — | — | — | — | 2,525 |
| Lebanon Valley College, Annville, Pennsylvania | MW | EUB | 1,370 | — | 1,600 | 1,600 | 900 | — |
| Lee College, Cleveland, Tennessee | MW | CG | 1,100 | — | 600 | 600 | 600 | — |
| Lehigh University, Bethlehem, Pennsylvania | M | Pvt. | 3,100 | 1,750 | 1,800 | 1,800 | 930 | — |
| Le Moyne College, Syracuse, New York | MW | RC | 1,450 | — | 1,400 | 1,400 | 950 | — |
| Le Moyne College, Memphis, Tennessee | MW | M | 677 | — | 560 | 560 | NA | — |
| Lenoir-Rhyne College, Hickory, North Carolina | MW | L | 1,260 | — | 765 | 765 | 600 | — |
| Lesley College, Cambridge, Massachusetts | W | Pvt. | 549 | 60 | 1,790 | 1,790 | 1,000 | — |
| Lewis College, Lockport, Illinois | M | RC | 1,450 | — | 969 | 969 | 900 | — |
| Lewis and Clark College, Portland, Oregon | MW | P | 1,600 | 250 | — | — | — | 2,550 |
| Lewis-Clark Normal School, Lewiston, Idaho | MW | State | 465 | — | Free | 390 | — | — |
| Limestone College, Gaffney, South Carolina | W | Pvt. | 655 | — | 870 | 870 | 1,015 | — |
| Lincoln Memorial University, Harrogate, Tennessee | MW | Pvt. | 636 | — | 930 | 930 | 765 | — |
| Lincoln University, Jefferson City, Missouri | MW | State | 1,582 | 42 | Free | 100 | 500 | — |
| Lincoln University, Lincoln University, Pennsylvania | MW | Pvt. | 930 | — | 820 | 820 | 690 | — |
| Lindenwood College, St. Charles, Missouri | W | P | 824 | — | — | — | — | 2,535 |
| Linfield College, McMinnville, Oregon | MW | AB | 1,200 | 35 | 1,200 | 1,200 | 820 | — |
| Little Rock University, Little Rock, Arkansas | MW | Pvt. | 3,300 | — | 565 | 565 | NA | — |
| Livingston State College, Livingston, Alabama | MW | State | 1,500 | 60 | 330 | 480 | 560 | — |
| Livingstone College, Salisbury, North Carolina | MW | AMEZ | 795 | — | 697 | 697 | 553 | — |
| Lock Haven State College, Lock Haven, Pennsylvania | MW | State | 1,925 | — | 275 | 650 | 612 | — |
| Loma Linda University, Riverside, California | MW | SDA | 1,500 | 150 | — | — | — | 2,000 |
| Long Island University, Brooklyn Center, Brooklyn, New York | MW | Pvt. | 5,640 | NI | 1,730 | 1,730 | 900 | — |

| NAME AND LOCATION | TYPE | CON-TROL | ENROLLMENT U | G | TUITION & FEES R | NR | ROOM, BOARD | COMP. FEE |
|---|---|---|---|---|---|---|---|---|
| Brooklyn College of Pharmacy, Brooklyn, New York... | MW | Pvt. | 500 | 120 | 1,250 | 1,250 | 1,000 | — |
| C. W. Post College, Brookville, New York.............. | MW | Pvt. | 7,500 | NI | 1,450 | 1,450 | 1,000 | — |
| Southampton College, Southampton, New York....... | MW | Pvt. | 800 | NI | 1,500 | 1,500 | 950 | — |
| Longwood College, Farmville, Virginia.................. | W | State | 1,650 | 45 | 365 | 685 | 720 | — |
| Loras College, Dubuque, Iowa.......................... | M | RC | 1,650 | — | 895 | 895 | 900 | — |
| Loretto Heights College, Denver, Colorado............... | W | RC | 985 | 35 | — | — | — | 2,500 |
| Louisiana College, Pineville, Louisiana................. | MW | SB | 1,275 | — | 620 | 620 | 570 | — |
| Louisiana Polytechnic Institute, Ruston, Louisiana........ | MW | State | 7,427 | 519 | 169 | 750 | 624 | — |
| Louisiana State University and A&M College System | | | | | | | | |
| at Baton Rouge, Louisiana.......................... | MW | State | 23,505 | 3,928 | 220 | 620 | 745 | — |
| at New Orleans, Louisiana.......................... | MW | State | 5,851 | 475 | 140 | 540 | NA | — |
| Medical Center at New Orleans, Louisiana............ | MW | State | 626 | 70 | 600 | 1,600 | 312Rm | — |
| Louisville, University of, Louisville, Kentucky............ | MW | State | 6,800 | 2,000 | 1,200 | 1,800 | 380 | — |
| Lowell Technological Institute, Lowell, Massachusetts..... | MW | State | 2,395 | 75 | 249 | 649 | 700 | — |
| Loyola College, Baltimore, Maryland..................... | M | RC | 2,226 | 709 | 1,100 | 1,100 | 1,000 | — |
| Loyola University, Chicago, Illinois..................... | MW | RC | 11,757 | 5,000 | 1,230 | 1,230 | 950 | — |
| Loyola University of Los Angeles, Los Angeles, California.. | M | RC | 1,582 | 907 | 1,340 | 1,340 | 930 | — |
| Loyola University of New Orleans, New Orleans, Louisiana | MW | RC | 2,912 | 1,123 | 1,200 | 1,200 | 1,000 | — |
| Luther College, Decorah, Iowa......................... | MW | L | 2,050 | — | — | — | — | 1,412 |
| Lycoming College, Williamsport, Pennsylvania........... | MW | M | 1,400 | — | 1,550 | 1,550 | 900 | — |
| Lynchburg College, Lynchburg, Virginia................. | MW | DC | 1,500 | — | 1,336 | 1,336 | 780 | — |
| Lyndon State College, Lyndonville, Vermont............. | MW | State | 471 | — | 364 | 864 | 865 | — |
| Macalester College, St. Paul, Minnesota................. | MW | P | 1,858 | 7 | 1,534 | 1,534 | 900 | — |
| MacMurray College, Jacksonville, Illinois................ | MW | M | 1,050 | — | 1,730 | 1,730 | 865 | — |
| McMurry College, Abilene, Texas....................... | MW | M | 1,600 | — | 700 | 700 | 660 | — |
| McNeese State College, Lake Charles, Louisiana........ | MW | State | 4,015 | 337 | 170 | 770 | 640 | — |
| McPherson College, McPherson, Kansas................. | MW | CB | 840 | — | 900 | 900 | 750 | — |
| Madison College, Harrisonburg, Virginia................ | MW | State | 2,500 | 200 | 406 | 796 | 495 | — |
| Madonna College, Livonia, Michigan.................... | W | RC | 608 | — | 600 | 600 | 800 | — |
| Maine, University of, Orono and Portland, Maine........ | MW | State | 6,906 | 573 | 400 | 1,000 | 850 | — |
| Malone College, Canton, Ohio......................... | MW | Pvt. | 1,000 | — | 850 | 850 | 650 | — |
| Manchester College, North Manchester, Indiana.......... | MW | CB | 1,450 | — | 1,200 | 1,200 | 690 | — |
| Manhattan College, New York, New York................ | M | RC | 3,600 | 93 | 1,400 | 1,400 | 1,050 | — |
| Manhattan School of Music, New York, New York........ | MW | Pvt. | 467 | 146 | 1,225 | 1,225 | NA | — |
| Manhattanville College, Purchase, New York............. | W | RC | 1,100 | 200 | 1,900 | 1,900 | 1,000 | — |
| Mankato State College, Mankato, Minnesota............. | MW | State | 9,172 | 1,176 | 285 | 460 | 720 | — |
| Mansfield State College, Mansfield, Pennsylvania......... | MW | State | 1,935 | — | 363 | 728 | 594 | — |
| Marian College, Indianapolis, Indiana................... | MW | RC | 1,067 | — | 880 | 880 | 750 | — |
| Marian College of Fond du Lac, Fond du Lac, Wisconsin... | W | RC | 600 | — | 575 | 575 | 650 | — |
| Marietta College, Marietta, Ohio....................... | MW | Pvt. | 1,806 | — | 1,450 | 1,450 | 850 | — |
| Marillac College, St. Louis, Missouri.................... | W | RC | 530 | — | 300 | 300 | 1,000 | — |
| Marion College, Marion, Indiana....................... | MW | M | 730 | — | 559 | 559 | 690 | — |
| Marist College, Poughkeepsie, New York................ | M | RC | 1,700 | — | 1,050 | 1,050 | 1,000 | — |
| Marlboro College, Marlboro, Vermont................... | MW | Pvt. | 170 | — | 1,875 | 1,875 | 990 | — |
| Marquette University, Milwaukee, Wisconsin............. | MW | RC | 9,055 | 1,305 | 1,250 | 1,250 | 800 | — |
| Mars Hill College, Mars Hill, North Carolina............. | MW | SB | 1,375 | — | 850 | 850 | 600 | — |
| Marshall University, Huntington, West Virginia........... | MW | State | 6,700 | 950 | 230 | 680 | 700 | — |
| Mary Baldwin College, Staunton, Virginia................ | W | P | 705 | — | — | — | — | 2,734 |
| Mary Hardin-Baylor College, Belton, Texas.............. | MW | SB | 1,140 | 200 | 450 | 450 | 650 | — |
| Mary Manse College, Toledo, Ohio..................... | W | RC | 725 | 700 | 760 | 760 | 790 | — |
| Mary Rogers College, Maryknoll, New York.............. | W | RC | 240 | — | 600 | 600 | 900 | — |
| Marycrest College, Davenport, Iowa.................... | W | RC | 1,009 | — | 860 | 860 | 850 | — |
| Marygrove College, Detroit, Michigan................... | W | RC | 1,000 | 200 | — | — | — | 2,025 |
| Maryknoll College, Glen Ellyn, Illinois.................. | M | RC | 300 | — | — | — | — | 1,098 |
| Maryland, University of, College Park, Maryland.......... | MW | State | 24,000 | 6,000 | 366 | 766 | 800 | — |
| Maryland State College, Princess Anne, Maryland........ | MW | State | 800 | — | 220 | 370 | 445 | — |
| Marylhurst College, Marylhurst, Oregon................. | W | RC | 810 | — | 990 | 990 | 810 | — |
| Marymount College, Palos Verdes Estates, California..... | W | RC | 425 | — | 1,050 | 1,050 | 1,100 | — |
| Marymount College, Salina, Kansas.................... | W | RC | 575 | — | 835 | 835 | 810 | — |
| Marymount College, Tarrytown, New York............... | W | RC | 1,054 | — | 1,535 | 1,535 | 1,200 | — |
| Marymount Manhattan College, New York, New York..... | W | RC | 570 | — | 1,140 | 1,140 | 1,000 | — |
| Maryville College, Maryville, Tennessee................. | MW | P | 875 | — | 970 | 970 | 780 | — |
| Maryville College of the Sacred Heart, St. Louis, Missouri.. | W | RC | 500 | — | 1,300 | 1,300 | 1,300 | — |
| Marywood College, Scranton, Pennsylvania.............. | W | RC | 1,420 | — | 1,150 | 1,150 | 950 | — |
| Massachusetts, University of, at Amherst, Massachusetts.. | MW | State | 11,340 | NI | 336 | 736 | 798 | — |
| at Boston, Massachusetts........................... | MW | State | 2,600 | NI | 280 | 680 | NA | — |
| Massachusetts College of Art, Boston, Mass............. | MW | State | 510 | 105 | 225 | 625 | NI | — |
| Massachusetts Institute of Technology, Cambridge, Massachusetts.................................... | MW | Pvt. | 3,857 | 3,710 | 2,040 | 2,040 | 960 | — |
| Massachusetts State College System at Boston, Massachusetts................................ | MW | State | 4,050 | 2,100 | 230 | 630 | NA | — |
| at Bridgewater, Massachusetts...................... | MW | State | 3,590 | — | 230 | 630 | 800 | — |

| NAME AND LOCATION | TYPE | CON-TROL | ENROLLMENT U | G | TUITION & FEES R | NR | ROOM, BOARD | COMP. FEE |
|---|---|---|---|---|---|---|---|---|
| at Fitchburg, Massachusetts | MW | State | 1,700 | 200 | 230 | 630 | 600 | — |
| at Framingham, Massachusetts | MW | State | 1,350 | 1,000 | 250 | 650 | 512 | — |
| at Lowell, Massachusetts | MW | State | 1,475 | — | 235 | 635 | 675 | — |
| at North Adams, Massachusetts | MW | State | 620 | 240 | 230 | 630 | 540 | — |
| at Salem, Massachusetts | MW | State | 3,400 | 2,200 | 260 | 660 | 600 | — |
| at Westfield, Massachusetts | MW | State | 1,107 | NI | 230 | 630 | NI | — |
| at Worcester, Massachusetts | MW | State | 1,976 | NI | 230 | 630 | NI | — |
| Mayville State College, Mayville, North Dakota | MW | State | 850 | — | 390 | 614 | 544 | — |
| Memphis State University, Memphis, Tennessee | MW | State | 12,881 | 1,305 | 235 | 460 | 880 | — |
| Menlo Park College, Menlo Park, California | M | Pvt. | 510 | — | 1,500 | 1,500 | 1,200 | — |
| Mercer University, Macon, Georgia | MW | SB | 1,600 | 100 | 1,200 | 1,200 | 720 | — |
| Mercy College of Detroit, Detroit, Michigan | MW | RC | 1,200 | — | 918 | 918 | 1,160 | — |
| Mercyhurst College, Erie, Pennsylvania | W | RC | 625 | — | 1,100 | 1,100 | 900 | — |
| Meredith College, Raleigh, North Carolina | W | SB | 850 | — | 1,000 | 1,000 | 800 | — |
| Merrimack College, North Andover, Massachusetts | MW | Pvt. | 1,700 | — | 1,388 | 1,388 | 1,000 | — |
| Messiah College, Grantham, Pennsylvania | MW | Pvt. | 430 | — | 1,222 | 1,222 | 664 | — |
| Methodist College, Fayetteville, North Carolina | MW | M | 990 | — | 800 | 800 | 800 | — |
| Miami, University of, Coral Gables, Florida | MW | Pvt. | 9,100 | 4,197 | 1,494 | 1,494 | 1,040 | — |
| Miami University, Oxford, Ohio | MW | Pvt. | 10,150 | 850 | 520 | 1,020 | 850 | — |
| Michigan, University of, Ann Arbor, Michigan | MW | State | 20,974 | 14,276 | 350 | 1,100 | 1,000 | — |
| Michigan State University, East Lansing, Michigan | MW | State | 31,263 | 8,000 | 472 | 1,360 | 1,160 | — |
| Oakland University of Michigan State University, Rochester, Michigan | MW | State | 3,400 | 250 | 500 | 1,200 | 920 | — |
| Michigan Technological University, Houghton, Michigan | MW | State | 4,223 | 197 | 300 | 750 | 700 | — |
| Middle Tennessee State University, Murfreesboro, Tennessee | MW | State | 5,307 | 454 | 218 | 600 | 825 | — |
| Middlebury College, Middlebury, Vermont | MW | Pvt. | 1,383 | 12 | 1,784 | 1,784 | 900 | — |
| Midland Lutheran College, Fremont, Nebraska | MW | L | 850 | — | 985 | 985 | 690 | — |
| Midwestern University, Wichita Falls, Texas | MW | State | 3,396 | 230 | 150 | 450 | 780 | — |
| Millersville State College, Millersville, Pennsylvania | MW | State | 3,400 | 500 | 294 | 634 | 648 | — |
| Milligan College, Milligan College, Tennessee | MW | Pvt. | 839 | — | 600 | 600 | 700 | — |
| Millikan University, Decatur, Illinois | MW | P | 1,450 | 50 | 1,429 | 1,429 | 900 | — |
| Mills College, Oakland, California | W | Pvt. | 720 | 50 | 1,755 | 1,755 | 1,230 | — |
| Mills College of Education, New York, New York | W | Pvt. | 500 | — | 2,056 | 2,056 | 1,200 | — |
| Millsaps College, Jackson, Mississippi | MW | M | 925 | — | 1,000 | 1,000 | 650 | — |
| Minnesota, University of, Minneapolis, Minnesota | MW | State | 37,345 | 6,652 | 475 | 940 | 820 | — |
| Minneapolis School of Art, Minneapolis, Minnesota | MW | Pvt. | 385 | — | 920 | 920 | 800 | — |
| Minot State College, Minot, North Dakota | MW | State | 2,300 | NI | 306 | 576 | 510 | — |
| Misericordia, College, Dallas, Pennsylvania | W | RC | 1,315 | — | 900 | 900 | 900 | — |
| Mississippi, University of, University, Mississippi | MW | State | 6,950 | 978 | 350 | 800 | 400 | — |
| Mississippi College, Clinton, Mississippi | MW | SB | 1,993 | 374 | 700 | 700 | 600 | — |
| Mississippi State College for Women, Columbus, Mississippi | W | State | 2,640 | 86 | 355 | 670 | 615 | — |
| Mississippi State University, State College, Mississippi | MW | State | 8,000 | 2,000 | 342 | 792 | 700 | — |
| Missouri, University of, Columbia, Missouri | MW | State | 12,803 | NI | 250 | 600 | 770 | — |
| at Kansas City, Missouri | MW | State | 6,104 | 1,787 | 375 | 875 | 850 | — |
| at Rolla, Missouri | MW | State | 3,527 | 511 | 330 | 830 | 850 | — |
| at St. Louis, Missouri | MW | State | 4,658 | 334 | 165 | 500 | NA | — |
| Missouri Valley College, Marshall, Missouri | MW | P | 930 | — | 960 | 960 | 837 | — |
| Monmouth College, Monmouth, Illinois | MW | P | 1,249 | — | 1,740 | 1,740 | 860 | — |
| Monmouth College, West Long Branch, New Jersey | MW | Pvt. | 4,800 | — | 1,224 | 1,224 | 900 | — |
| Montana, University of, Missoula, Montana | MW | State | 5,400 | 666 | 359 | 967 | 775 | — |
| Montana College of Mineral Science & Technology, Butte, Montana | MW | State | 600 | 30 | 265 | 873 | 715 | — |
| Montana State University, Bozeman, Montana | MW | State | 5,774 | 492 | 390 | 998 | 774 | — |
| Montclair State College, Upper Montclair, New Jersey | MW | State | 4,000 | 1,191 | 250 | NA | 818 | — |
| Moore College of Art, Philadelphia, Pennsylvania | W | Pvt. | 500 | — | 1,550 | 1,550 | 1,200 | — |
| Moorhead State College, Moorhead, Minnesota | MW | State | 4,250 | 150 | 300 | 444 | 690 | — |
| Moravian College, Bethlehem, Pennsylvania | MW | MCA | 1,150 | — | — | — | — | 2,578 |
| Morehead State University, Morehead, Kentucky | MW | State | 5,350 | 650 | 240 | 580 | 700 | — |
| Morehouse College, Atlanta, Georgia | M | Pvt. | 898 | — | 885 | 885 | 720 | — |
| Morgan State College, Baltimore, Maryland | MW | State | 3,375 | NI | 260 | 460 | 808 | — |
| Morningside College, Sioux City, Iowa | MW | M | 1,525 | — | 1,231 | 1,231 | 730 | — |
| Morris Brown College, Atlanta, Georgia | MW | Pvt. | 1,200 | — | 950 | 950 | 585 | — |
| Morris Harvey College, Charleston, West Virginia | MW | Pvt. | 1,756 | — | 700 | 1,300 | 850 | — |
| Mount Angel College, Mt. Angel, Oregon | MW | Pvt. | 400 | — | 950 | 950 | 750 | — |
| Mount Angel Seminary, St. Benedict, Oregon | M | RC | 100 | 47 | 535 | 535 | 700 | — |
| Mount Holyoke College, South Hadley, Massachusetts | W | Pvt. | 1,720 | — | 1,850 | 1,850 | 1,200 | — |
| Mount Marty College, Yankton, South Dakota | W | RC | 447 | — | 646 | 646 | 650 | — |
| Mount Mary College, Milwaukee, Wisconsin | W | RC | 950 | — | 785 | 785 | 800 | — |
| Mount Mercy College, Cedar Rapids, Iowa | W | RC | 630 | — | 640 | 640 | 900 | — |
| Mount Mercy College, Pittsburgh, Pennsylvania | W | RC | 1,492 | — | 1,250 | 1,250 | 1,050 | — |
| Mount Saint Agnes College, Baltimore, Maryland | W | RC | 450 | — | 1,000 | 1,000 | 1,100 | — |

| NAME AND LOCATION | TYPE | CONTROL | ENROLLMENT U | G | TUITION & FEES R | NR | ROOM, BOARD | COMP. FEE |
|---|---|---|---|---|---|---|---|---|
| Mount Saint Joseph on the Ohio, College of, Cincinnati, Ohio | W | RC | 1,100 | — | — | — | — | 1,950 |
| Mount Saint Mary College, Hooksett, New Hampshire..... | W | RC | 325 | — | 1,250 | 1,250 | 1,000 | — |
| Mount Saint Mary's College, Los Angeles, California...... | W | RC | 1,266 | — | 1,102 | 1,102 | 1,100 | — |
| Mount Saint Mary's College, Emmitsburg, Maryland...... | M | RC | 850 | — | 1,025 | 1,025 | 1,000 | — |
| Mount Saint Scholastica College, Atchison, Kansas....... | W | RC | 660 | — | 660 | 660 | 800 | — |
| Mount Saint Vincent, College of, Riverdale, New York.... | W | RC | 990 | — | 1,400 | 1,400 | 1,100 | — |
| Mount Union College, Alliance, Ohio................... | MW | M | 1,230 | — | 1,630 | 1,630 | 775 | — |
| Muhlenberg College, Allentown, Pennsylvania........... | MW | L | 1,475 | — | 1,600 | 1,600 | 890 | — |
| Mundelein College, Chicago, Illinois................... | W | RC | 1,200 | — | 1,010 | 1,010 | 920 | — |
| Murray State University, Murray, Kentucky............. | MW | State | 6,500 | 700 | 240 | 580 | 640 | — |
| Muskingum College, New Concord, Ohio............... | MW | P | 1,404 | — | 1,560 | 1,560 | 840 | — |
| Nasson College, Springvale, Maine.................... | MW | Pvt. | 810 | — | 1,700 | 1,700 | 950 | — |
| National College of Education, Evanston, Illinois........ | MW | Pvt. | 600 | 600 | 1,755 | 1,755 | 1,000 | — |
| Nazareth College, Kalamazoo, Michigan................ | W | RC | 500 | — | 880 | 880 | 850 | — |
| Nazareth College of Kentucky, Nazareth, Kentucky....... | W | RC | 450 | — | — | — | — | 1,545 |
| Nazareth College of Rochester, Rochester, New York..... | W | RC | 1,175 | — | 1,300 | 1,300 | 980 | — |
| Nebraska, University of, Lincoln, Nebraska............. | MW | State | 14,500 | 4,300 | 334 | 860 | 800 | — |
| Nebraska Wesleyan University, Lincoln, Nebraska....... | MW | Pvt. | 1,450 | — | 1,100 | 1,100 | 775 | — |
| Nevada, University of, Reno, Nevada.................. | MW | State | 4,685 | 571 | 350 | 950 | 900 | — |
| New Church, Academy of the, Bryn Athyn, Pennsylvania.. | MW | GCNJ | 111 | 2 | 475 | 475 | 725 | — |
| New England Conservatory of Music, Boston, Massachusetts | MW | Pvt. | 1,900 | NI | 1,250 | 1,250 | NI | — |
| New Hampshire, University of, Durham, New Hampshire.. | MW | State | 5,700 | 800 | 538 | 1,433 | 780 | — |
| Keene State College (of U. of N.H.), Keene, New Hampshire | MW | State | 1,600 | 30 | 460 | 860 | 750 | — |
| New Haven College, West Haven, Connecticut........... | MW | Pvt. | 2,987 | — | 1,040 | 1,040 | — | — |
| New Mexico, University of, Albuquerque, New Mexico.... | MW | State | 9,700 | 3,500 | 408 | 918 | 804 | — |
| New Mexico Highlands University, Las Vegas, New Mexico | MW | State | 1,700 | 250 | 315 | 735 | 750 | — |
| New Mexico Institute of Mining & Technology, Socorro, New Mexico...... | MW | State | 439 | 69 | 204 | 565 | 700 | — |
| New Mexico State University, Las Cruces, New Mexico.... | MW | State | 5,160 | 955 | 415 | 915 | 950 | — |
| New Rochelle, College of, New Rochelle, New York....... | W | RC | 920 | — | 1,615 | 1,615 | 1,200 | — |
| New York, City University of, Brooklyn College, Brooklyn, New York............... | MW | City | 18,693 | 4,646 | 37 | 437 | NA | — |
| City College, New York, New York................ | MW | City | 22,151 | 8,331 | 37 | 437 | NA | — |
| Hunter College, New York, New York.............. | MW | City | 20,413 | 5,225 | 30 | 430 | NA | — |
| Queens College, Flushing, New York.............. | MW | City | 18,537 | 3,758 | 34 | 434 | NA | — |
| New York, State University of, at Albany, New York...... | MW | State | 4,825 | 250 | 425 | 625 | 760 | — |
| at Binghamton, New York (including Harpur College).. | MW | State | 2,200 | 154 | 425 | 625 | 828 | — |
| at Buffalo, New York............................ | MW | State | 14,669 | 5,208 | 500 | 700 | 900 | — |
| at Stony Brook, New York........................ | MW | State | 4,400 | 650 | 500 | 700 | 825 | — |
| Downstate Medical Center, Brooklyn, New York....... | MW | State | 800 | 65 | 800 | 1,000 | NA | — |
| Upstate Medical Center, Syracuse, New York......... | MW | State | 112 | 460 | 845 | 1,045 | NA | — |
| State University College, Brockport, New York....... | MW | State | 3,750 | 100 | 600 | 800 | 877 | — |
| State University College, Buffalo, New York.......... | MW | State | 5,028 | 1,311 | 507 | 707 | 715 | — |
| State University College, Cortland, New York........ | MW | State | 3,400 | 75 | 425 | 525 | 855 | — |
| State University College, Fredonia, New York........ | MW | State | 3,100 | 300 | 553 | 753 | 895 | — |
| State University College, Geneseo, New York........ | MW | State | 2,545 | 77 | 425 | 625 | 800 | — |
| State University College, New Paltz, New York....... | MW | State | 3,330 | 916 | 425 | 625 | 785 | — |
| State University College, Oneonta, New York........ | MW | State | 3,295 | 861 | 500 | 700 | 820 | — |
| State University College, Oswego, New York......... | MW | State | 3,805 | 500 | 527 | 727 | 893 | — |
| State University College, Plattsburgh, New York...... | MW | State | 2,525 | 648 | 425 | 625 | 825 | — |
| State University College, Potsdam, New York........ | MW | State | 2,600 | 340 | 400 | 600 | 950 | — |
| College of Agriculture at Cornell University, Ithaca, New York | MW | State | 2,100 | 850 | 676 | 1,076 | 1,000 | — |
| College of Ceramics at Alfred University, Alfred, New York | MW | State | 450 | 57 | 475 | 675 | 850 | — |
| College of Forestry at Syracuse University, Syracuse, New York | MW | State | 1,000 | 172 | 425 | 625 | 937 | — |
| College of Home Economics at Cornell University, Ithaca, New York | W | State | 800 | 135 | 625 | 1,035 | 1,000 | — |
| Maritime College at Fort Schuyler, Bronx, New York... | M | State | 700 | — | 475 | 475 | 930 | — |
| School of Industrial and Labor Relations at Cornell University, Ithaca, New York | MW | State | 420 | 76 | 600 | 1,000 | 1,000 | — |
| New York University, New York, New York.............. | MW | Pvt. | 11,595 | 19,894 | 2,000 | 2,000 | 1,395 | — |
| Newark College of Engineering, Newark, New Jersey..... | MW | State | 3,800 | 960 | 440 | 826 | NA | — |
| Newark State College, Union, New Jersey.............. | MW | State | 5,200 | 1,111 | 254 | 544 | 818 | — |
| Newberry College, Newberry, South Carolina........... | MW | L | 839 | — | 925 | 925 | 660 | — |
| Newton College of the Sacred Heart, Newton, Massachusetts | W | RC | 800 | — | 1,635 | 1,635 | 1,000 | — |
| Niagara University, Niagara Falls, New York............ | MW | RC | 2,400 | 300 | 1,349 | 1,349 | 900 | — |
| Nichols College of Business Administration, Dudley, Massachusetts...... | M | Pvt. | 670 | — | 1,100 | 1,100 | 1,150 | — |
| North Carolina A&T College, Greensboro, North Carolina.. | MW | State | 3,960 | 300 | 383 | 635 | 537 | — |

| NAME AND LOCATION | TYPE | CON-TROL | ENROLLMENT U | G | TUITION & FEES R | NR | ROOM, BOARD | COMP. FEE |
|---|---|---|---|---|---|---|---|---|
| North Carolina College at Durham, Durham, North Carolina | MW | State | 2,915 | 311 | 276 | 626 | 530 | — |
| North Carolina, University of, at Chapel Hill, North Carolina | MW | State | 10,200 | 4,800 | 326 | 751 | 817 | — |
| at Charlotte, North Carolina......................... | MW | State | 1,850 | — | 300 | 725 | NA | — |
| at Greensboro, North Carolina....................... | MW | State | 4,200 | 900 | 414 | 839 | 595 | — |
| at Raleigh, North Carolina........................... | MW | State | 8,516 | 2,134 | 357 | 782 | 766 | — |
| North Carolina Wesleyan, Rocky Mount, North Carolina... | MW | M | 675 | — | 775 | 775 | 800 | — |
| North Central College, Naperville, Illinois............... | MW | EUB | 900 | — | 1,450 | 1,450 | 900 | — |
| North Dakota, University of, at Ellendale, North Dakota... | MW | State | 500 | — | 274 | 598 | 525 | — |
| at Grand Forks, North Dakota........................ | MW | State | 5,520 | 1,044 | 360 | 804 | 670 | — |
| North Dakota State University, Fargo, North Dakota..... | MW | State | 5,400 | 600 | 360 | 804 | 705 | — |
| North Georgia College, Dahlonega, Georgia.............. | MW | State | 1,200 | — | 304 | 639 | 648 | — |
| North Park College, Chicago, Illinois.................... | MW | Pvt. | 1,239 | — | 1,200 | 1,200 | 840 | — |
| North Texas State University, Denton, Texas............ | MW | State | 13,314 | 2,749 | 175 | 375 | 648 | — |
| Northeast Louisiana State College, Monroe, Louisiana..... | MW | State | 6,452 | 599 | 148 | 748 | 664 | — |
| Northeast Missouri State Teachers College, Kirksville, Missouri........................................ | MW | State | 5,320 | NI | 157 | 358 | 666 | — |
| Northeastern Illinois State College, Chicago, Illinois...... | MW | State | 2,798 | 1,810 | 240 | 495 | NA | — |
| Northeastern State College, Tahlequah, Oklahoma........ | MW | State | 4,677 | 403 | 184 | 424 | 584 | — |
| Northeastern University, Boston, Massachusetts.......... | MW | Pvt. | 27,000 | 6,000 | 1,405 | 1,405 | 1,188 | — |
| Northern Arizona University, Flagstaff, Arizona.......... | MW | State | 6,500 | 350 | 272 | 867 | 700 | — |
| Northern Illinois University, DeKalb, Illinois............. | MW | State | 13,750 | 3,000 | 258 | 428 | 888 | — |
| Northern Iowa, University of, Cedar Falls, Iowa.......... | MW | State | 6,780 | 638 | 306 | 606 | 724 | — |
| Northern Michigan University, Marquette, Michigan...... | MW | State | 5,850 | 165 | 300 | 600 | 848 | — |
| Northern Montana College, Havre, Montana.............. | MW | State | 1,288 | — | 343 | 951 | 787 | — |
| Northern State College, Aberdeen, South Dakota......... | MW | State | 2,720 | NI | 489 | 951 | 715 | — |
| Northland College, Ashland, Wisconsin.................. | MW | UCC | 764 | — | 1,236 | 1,236 | 720 | — |
| Northrop Institute of Technology, Inglewood, California... | MW | Pvt. | 1,950 | — | 955 | 955 | 1,012 | — |
| Northwest Christian College, Eugene, Oregon............ | MW | DC | 425 | — | 570 | 570 | 750 | — |
| Northwest Missouri State College, Maryville, Missouri.... | MW | State | 4,000 | 300 | 220 | 440 | 670 | — |
| Northwest Nazarene College, Nampa, Idaho.............. | MW | CN | 1,116 | — | 883 | 883 | 795 | — |
| Northwestern College, Orange City, Iowa................ | MW | Pvt. | 530 | — | 985 | 985 | 345 | — |
| Northwestern State College of Louisiana, Natchitoches, Louisiana........................................ | MW | State | 4,427 | 776 | 77 | 677 | 600 | — |
| Northwestern State College, Alva, Oklahoma............. | MW | State | 1,997 | 171 | 294 | 670 | 576 | — |
| Northwestern University, Evanston, Illinois.............. | MW | Pvt. | 11,207 | 5,962 | 1,860 | 1,860 | 1,000 | — |
| Norwich University, Northfield, Vermont................. | MW | Pvt. | 1,294 | — | — | — | — | 2,530 |
| Notre Dame, College of, Belmont, California............. | W | RC | 450 | 100 | 975 | 975 | 1,100 | — |
| Notre Dame, University of, Notre Dame, Indiana......... | M | RC | 6,038 | 1,387 | 1,950 | 1,950 | 850 | — |
| Notre Dame College, St. Louis, Missouri................. | W | RC | 427 | — | Free | Free | Free | — |
| Notre Dame College, Cleveland, Ohio.................... | W | RC | 619 | — | 900 | 900 | 880 | — |
| Notre Dame of Maryland, College of, Baltimore, Maryland | W | RC | 800 | — | 1,200 | 1,200 | 1,200 | — |
| Notre Dame College of Staten Island, Staten Island, New York............................................ | W | RC | 500 | — | 1,200 | 1,200 | NA | — |
| Notre Dame Seminary, New Orleans, Louisiana........... | M | RC | 141 | — | — | — | — | 900 |
| Nyack Missionary College, Nyack, New York.............. | MW | CMA | 610 | — | 910 | 910 | 750 | — |
| Oakwood College, Huntsville, Alabama.................. | MW | Pvt. | 435 | — | 990 | 990 | 577 | — |
| Oberlin College, Oberlin, Ohio......................... | MW | Pvt. | 2,575 | 55 | 1,859 | 1,859 | 1,060 | — |
| Occidental College, Los Angeles, California.............. | MW | Pvt. | 1,591 | NI | 1,550 | 1,550 | 990 | — |
| Oglethorpe College, Atlanta, Georgia................... | MW | Pvt. | 1,000 | — | 1,178 | 1,178 | 920 | — |
| Ohio Northern University, Ada, Ohio.................... | MW | M | 2,409 | — | 1,380 | 1,380 | 879 | — |
| Ohio State University, Columbus, Ohio.................. | MW | State | 42,000 | 8,282 | 450 | 1,008 | 875 | — |
| Ohio University, Athens, Ohio.......................... | MW | State | 19,350 | 1,650 | 512 | 1,007 | 795 | — |
| Ohio Wesleyan University, Delaware, Ohio............... | MW | M | 2,450 | — | 1,700 | 1,700 | 900 | — |
| Oklahoma, University of, Norman, Oklahoma............. | MW | State | 14,195 | 4,000 | 224 | 576 | 650 | — |
| Oklahoma Baptist University, Shawnee, Oklahoma........ | MW | SB | 1,500 | — | 670 | 670 | 630 | — |
| Oklahoma Christian College, Oklahoma City, Oklahoma... | MW | Pvt. | 1,000 | — | 850 | 850 | 600 | — |
| Oklahoma City University, Oklahoma City, Oklahoma..... | MW | M | 2,175 | 663 | 750 | 750 | 660 | — |
| Oklahoma College of Liberal Arts, Chickasha, Oklahoma.. | MW | State | 1,007 | — | 262 | 591 | 610 | — |
| Oklahoma State University, Stillwater, Oklahoma........ | MW | State | 13,939 | 2,071 | 288 | 776 | 650 | — |
| Old Dominion College, Norfolk, Virginia................. | MW | State | 8,303 | 477 | 400 | 600 | 1,100 | — |
| Olivet College, Olivet, Michigan....................... | MW | UCC | 750 | — | — | — | — | 2,000 |
| Olivet Nazarene College, Kankakee, Illinois.............. | MW | CN | 1,659 | 23 | 900 | 900 | 720 | — |
| Omaha, Municipal University of, Omaha, Nebraska....... | MW | City | 7,400 | 700 | 540 | 840 | NA | — |
| Oregon, University of, Eugene and Portland, Oregon...... | MW | State | 10,537 | 3,674 | 369 | 999 | 790 | — |
| Oregon College of Education, Monmouth, Oregon......... | MW | State | 2,400 | NI | 333 | 672 | 793 | — |
| Oregon State University, Corvallis, Oregon.............. | MW | State | 11,500 | 2,000 | 369 | 999 | 787 | — |
| Ottawa University, Ottawa, Kansas..................... | MW | AB | 1,028 | — | — | — | — | 1,800 |
| Otterbein College, Westerville, Ohio.................... | MW | EUB | 1,400 | — | — | — | — | 1,405 |
| Ouachita Baptist University, Arkadelphia, Arkansas...... | MW | SB | 1,800 | 35 | 375 | 375 | 348 | — |
| Our Lady of Cincinnati College, Cincinnati, Ohio......... | W | RC | 1,200 | — | 1,000 | 1,000 | 930 | — |
| Our Lady of the Elms, College of, Chicopee, Massachusetts | W | RC | 660 | — | 900 | 900 | 800 | — |
| Our Lady of the Lake College, San Antonio, Texas........ | W | RC | 1,977 | 664 | 750 | 750 | 840 | — |

| NAME AND LOCATION | TYPE | CON-TROL | ENROLLMENT U | G | TUITION & FEES R | NR | ROOM, BOARD | COMP. FEE |
|---|---|---|---|---|---|---|---|---|
| Our Lady of Mercy, College of, Burlingame, California.... | W | RC | 121 | — | 1,035 | 1,035 | 1,000 | — |
| Ozarks, College of the, Clarksville, Arkansas............. | MW | P | 500 | — | 325 | 325 | 510 | — |
| Ozarks, School of the, Point Lookout, Missouri........... | MW | P | 691 | — | 675 | 675 | 597 | — |
| Pace College, New York and Pleasantville, New York..... | MW | Pvt. | 8,200 | 800 | 1,354 | 1,354 | NA | — |
| Pacific, University of the, Stockton, California............ | MW | M | 2,672 | 568 | 1,718 | 1,718 | 535 | — |
| Pacific College, Fresno, California....................... | MW | Mn | 270 | — | 740 | 740 | 700 | — |
| Pacific Lutheran University, Tacoma, Washington......... | MW | L | 2,065 | 750 | 1,220 | 1,220 | 800 | — |
| Pacific Union College, Angwin, California................ | MW | SDA | 1,600 | 150 | 1,215 | 1,215 | 765 | — |
| Pacific University, Forest Grove, Oregon................. | MW | C | 1,050 | 25 | 1,341 | 1,341 | 790 | — |
| Paine College, Augusta, Georgia........................ | MW | M | 750 | — | 650 | 650 | 600 | — |
| Pan American College, Edinburg, Texas.................. | MW | State | 3,358 | — | 186 | 486 | 684 | — |
| Panhandle A&M College, Goodwell, Oklahoma........... | MW | State | 1,024 | — | 234 | 530 | 540 | — |
| Park College, Parkville, Missouri....................... | MW | P | 665 | — | 1,230 | 1,230 | 920 | — |
| Pasadena College, Pasadena, California.................. | MW | CN | 1,400 | — | 1,020 | 1,020 | 670 | — |
| Paterson State College, Wayne, New Jersey............. | MW | State | 3,000 | 1,550 | 244 | — | 818 | — |
| Peabody Institute of the City of Baltimore, Baltimore, Maryland................................................ | MW | Pvt. | 421 | 50 | 1,200 | 1,200 | NA | — |
| Pembroke College (of Brown University), Providence, Rhode Island........................................... | W | Pvt. | 1,000 | — | 2,000 | 2,000 | 1,080 | — |
| Pembroke State College, Pembroke, North Carolina..... | MW | State | 1,410 | — | 222 | 577 | 360 | — |
| Pennsylvania, University of, Philadelphia, Pennsylvania... | MW | Pvt. | 9,802 | 8,291 | 1,950 | 1,950 | 1,000 | — |
| Pennsylvania State University, University Park, Pennsylvania............................................ | MW | State | 25,543 | 10,118 | 450 | 1,050 | 825 | — |
| Pepperdine College, Los Angeles, California............. | MW | Pvt. | 1,400 | 200 | 1,280 | 1,280 | 880 | — |
| Peru State College, Peru, Nebraska..................... | MW | State | 1,200 | — | 340 | 620 | 668 | — |
| Pfeiffer College. Misenheimer, North Carolina........... | MW | M | 900 | — | — | — | — | 1,830 |
| Philadelphia College of Art, Philadelphia, Pennsylvania... | MW | Pvt. | 1,500 | — | 1,450 | 1,450 | 1,200 | — |
| Philadelphia College of Pharmacy & Science, Philadelphia, Pennsylvania......................................... | MW | Pvt. | 747 | 105 | — | — | — | 1,185 |
| Philadelphia College of Textiles and Science, Philadelphia, Pennsylvania.......................................... | MW | Pvt. | 1,511 | — | — | — | — | 1,050 |
| Philander Smith College, Little Rock, Arkansas.......... | MW | M | 592 | — | 489 | 489 | 559 | — |
| Phillips University, Enid, Oklahoma..................... | MW | DC | 1,150 | 135 | 930 | 930 | 650 | — |
| Piedmont College, Demorest, Georgia................... | MW | Pvt. | 420 | — | 1,030 | 1,030 | 810 | — |
| Pittsburgh, University of, Pittsburgh, Pennsylvania....... | MW | Pvt. | 14,309 | 6,629 | 550 | 1,400 | 920 | — |
| Plymouth State College, Plymouth, New Hampshire...... | MW | State | 1,500 | Nl | 377 | 800 | 750 | — |
| PMC Colleges, Chester, Pennsylvania................... | MW | Pvt. | 1,615 | — | 1,600 | 1,600 | 1,010 | — |
| Polytechnic Institute of Brooklyn, Brooklyn, New York.... | MW | Pvt. | 2,800 | 3,000 | 1,900 | 1,900 | 800 | — |
| Portland, University of, Portland, Oregon................ | MW | RC | 1,553 | 303 | 1,100 | 1,100 | 800 | — |
| Portland State College, Portland, Oregon................ | MW | State | 8,452 | 1,239 | 379 | 1,009 | NA | — |
| Prairie View A&M College, Prairie View, Texas.......... | MW | State | 3,600 | 450 | 162 | 462 | 525 | — |
| Pratt Institute, Brooklyn, New York..................... | MW | Pvt. | 3,250 | 700 | 1,805 | 1,805 | 1,000 | — |
| Presbyterian College, Clinton, South Carolina........... | MW | P | 710 | — | 1,080 | 1,080 | 720 | — |
| Princeton University, Princeton, New Jersey............. | M | Pvt. | 3,200 | 1,520 | 1,950 | 1,950 | 1,160 | — |
| Principia College, Elsah, Illinois........................ | MW | Pvt. | 695 | — | — | — | — | 3,138 |
| Providence College, Providence, Rhode Island........... | M | RC | 2,700 | 400 | 1,300 | 1,300 | 900 | — |
| Puerto Rico, University of, Rio Piedras, Puerto Rico...... | MW | State | 28,659 | 2,456 | 405 | 405 | 523 | — |
| Puget Sound, University of, Tacoma, Washington........ | MW | M | 2,741 | 220 | 1,235 | 1,235 | 800 | — |
| Purdue University, Lafayette, Indiana................... | MW | State | 17,600 | 5,050 | 330 | 950 | 945 | — |
| Queens College, Charlotte, North Carolina.............. | W | P | 845 | — | 1,100 | 1,100 | 1,400 | — |
| Quincy College, Quincy, Illinois........................ | MW | RC | 1,500 | — | 1,020 | 1,020 | 800 | — |
| Quinnipiac College, Hamden, Connecticut............... | MW | Pvt. | 2,200 | — | 1,095 | 1,095 | 1,040 | — |
| Radcliffe College (of Harvard University), Cambridge, Massachusetts.......................................... | W | Pvt. | 1,200 | — | 2,000 | 2,000 | 1,240 | — |
| Radford College, Radford, Virginia...................... | W | State | 2,700 | — | 345 | 345 | 597 | — |
| Randolph-Macon College, Ashland, Virginia............. | M | M | 850 | — | — | — | — | 2,200 |
| Randolph-Macon Women's College, Lynchburg, Virginia... | W | M | 875 | — | — | — | — | 2,700 |
| Redlands, University of, Redlands, California............ | MW | Pvt. | 1,492 | 367 | 1,635 | 1,635 | 900 | — |
| Reed College, Portland, Oregon........................ | MW | Pvt. | 950 | 127 | 2,102 | 2,102 | 790 | — |
| Regis College, Denver, Colorado........................ | MW | RC | 920 | — | 1,030 | 1,030 | 950 | — |
| Regis College, Weston, Massachusetts.................. | W | RC | 1,174 | — | 1,300 | 1,300 | 1,100 | — |
| Rensselaer Polytechnic Institute, Troy, New York....... | MW | Pvt. | 3,555 | 1,060 | 2,135 | 2,135 | 850 | — |
| Rhode Island, University of, Kingston, Rhode Island...... | MW | State | 5,078 | 1,158 | 345 | 945 | 780 | — |
| Rhode Island College, Providence, Rhode Island......... | MW | State | 2,536 | 1,773 | 245 | 695 | 845 | — |
| Rhode Island School of Design, Providence, Rhode Island. | MW | Pvt. | 892 | 45 | 1,750 | 1,750 | 950 | — |
| Rice University, Houston, Texas........................ | MW | Pvt. | 2,077 | 689 | 1,243 | 1,243 | 1,010 | — |
| Richmond, University of, Richmond, Virginia............ | MW | SB | 4,412 | 605 | 1,000 | 1,000 | 750 | — |
| Richmond Professional Institute, Richmond, Virginia..... | MW | State | 5,530 | 3,000 | 444 | 644 | 790 | — |
| Ricker College, Houlton, Maine......................... | MW | AB | 494 | — | 1,500 | 1,500 | 800 | — |
| Rider College, Trenton, New Jersey..................... | MW | Pvt. | 5,250 | 350 | 1,149 | 1,149 | 950 | — |
| Ripon College, Ripon, Wisconsin........................ | MW | Pvt. | 1,000 | — | — | — | — | 2,800 |
| Rivier College, Nashua, New Hampshire................. | W | RC | 640 | 79 | 1,050 | 1,050 | 850 | — |

| NAME AND LOCATION | TYPE | CON-TROL | ENROLLMENT U | ENROLLMENT G | TUITION & FEES R | TUITION & FEES NR | ROOM, BOARD | COMP. FEE |
|---|---|---|---|---|---|---|---|---|
| Roanoke College, Salem, Virginia | MW | L | 970 | — | — | — | — | 2,250 |
| Roberts Wesleyan College, North Chili, New York | MW | M | 710 | — | 1,125 | 1,125 | 650 | — |
| Rochester Institute of Technology, Rochester, New York | MW | Pvt. | 13,500 | 150 | 1,600 | 1,600 | 1,260 | — |
| Rochester, University of, Rochester, New York | MW | Pvt. | 3,460 | 1,482 | 2,035 | 2,035 | 995 | — |
| Rockford College, Rockford, Illinois | MW | Pvt. | 470 | 44 | 1,400 | 1,400 | 1,000 | — |
| Rockhurst College, Kansas City, Missouri | M | RC | 975 | — | 1,000 | 1,000 | 875 | — |
| Rocky Mountain College, Billings, Montana | MW | UCC, M, P | 530 | — | 1,000 | 1,000 | 750 | — |
| Rollins College, Winter Park, Florida | MW | Pvt. | 1,000 | 40 | — | — | — | 2,675 |
| Roosevelt University, Chicago, Illinois | MW | Pvt. | 5,500 | 2,000 | 993 | 993 | NA | — |
| Rosary College, River Forest, Illinois | W | RC | 850 | — | 1,000 | 1,000 | 1,050 | — |
| Rosary Hill College, Buffalo, New York | W | RC | 1,250 | — | 1,200 | 1,200 | 1,100 | — |
| Rose Polytechnic Institute, Terre Haute, Indiana | M | Pvt. | 925 | 25 | 1,500 | 1,500 | 800 | — |
| Rosemont College, Rosemont, Pennsylvania | W | RC | 650 | — | — | — | — | 2,400 |
| Russell Sage College, Troy, New York | W | Pvt. | 1,300 | 75 | 1,525 | 1,525 | 1,100 | — |
| Rutgers, The State University of New Jersey, Camden, New Brunswick, and Newark, New Jersey | MW | State | 22,448 | 6,403 | 528 | 764 | 900 | — |
| Sacramento State College, Sacramento, California | MW | State | 8,400 | 3,300 | 118 | 838 | 800 | — |
| Sacred Heart, College of the, Santurce, Puerto Rico | W | RC | 316 | — | — | — | — | 1,300 |
| Sacred Heart Dominican College, Houston, Texas | W | RC | 460 | — | 650 | 650 | 880 | — |
| Sacred Heart Seminary, Detroit, Michigan | M | RC | 225 | — | 485 | 685 | 600 | — |
| St. Ambrose College, Davenport, Iowa | M | RC | 1,400 | — | 1,087 | 1,087 | 850 | — |
| St. Andrews Presbyterian College, Laurinburg, North Carolina | MW | P | 960 | — | 1,510 | 1,510 | 885 | — |
| St. Anselm's College, Manchester, New Hampshire | M | RC | 1,418 | — | 1,450 | 1,450 | 800 | — |
| St. Augustine's College, Raleigh, North Carolina | MW | PE | 766 | — | 925 | 925 | 550 | — |
| St. Benedict, College of, Saint Joseph, Minnesota | W | RC | 500 | — | 1,100 | 1,100 | 800 | — |
| St. Benedict's College, Atchison, Kansas | M | RC | 1,000 | — | 900 | 900 | 700 | — |
| St. Bernard College, St. Bernard, Alabama | MW | RC | 800 | — | 800 | 800 | 800 | — |
| St. Bonaventure University, St. Bonaventure, New York | MW | RC | 1,950 | 419 | 1,300 | 1,300 | 950 | — |
| St. Catherine, College of, St. Paul, Minnesota | W | RC | 1,350 | — | 1,110 | 1,110 | 765 | — |
| St. Cloud State College, St. Cloud, Minnesota | MW | State | 7,900 | 100 | 300 | 444 | 690 | — |
| St. Edward's University, Austin, Texas | MW | RC | 864 | — | 753 | 753 | 820 | — |
| St. Elizabeth, College of, Convent Station, New Jersey | W | RC | 946 | — | 1,220 | 1,220 | 1,110 | — |
| St Francis, College of, Joliet, Illinois | W | RC | 960 | — | 600 | 600 | 550 | — |
| St. Francis College, Biddeford, Maine | MW | RC | 550 | — | 1,400 | 1,400 | 1,000 | — |
| St. Francis College, Brooklyn, New York | M | RC | 2,300 | — | 1,350 | 1,350 | NA | — |
| St. Francis College, Fort Wayne, Indiana | MW | RC | 850 | 825 | 610 | 610 | 1,000 | — |
| St. Francis College, Loretto, Pennsylvania | MW | RC | 1,596 | 59 | 1,170 | 1,170 | 900 | — |
| St. John's College, Cleveland, Ohio | W | RC | 650 | 130 | 830 | 685 | 870 | — |
| St. John's College, Annapolis, Maryland, and Santa Fe, New Mexico | MW | Pvt. | 490 | 31 | 1,970 | 1,970 | 1,050 | — |
| St. John's College, Camarillo, California | M | RC | 260 | 120 | 700 | 700 | — | — |
| St. John's University, Collegeville, Minnesota | M | RC | 1,373 | 20 | 1,150 | 1,150 | 790 | — |
| St. John's University, Brooklyn and Jamaica, New York | MW | RC | 13,050 | 6,000 | 1,400 | 1,400 | NA | — |
| St. John Fisher College, Rochester, New York | M | RC | 1,100 | — | 1,300 | 1,300 | 1,000 | — |
| St. Joseph College, West Hartford, Connecticut | W | RC | 575 | 315 | 1,225 | 1,225 | 1,000 | — |
| St. Joseph College, Emmitsburg, Maryland | W | RC | 640 | — | 1,390 | 1,390 | 1,000 | — |
| St. Joseph's College, Rensselaer, Indiana | M | RC | 1,400 | — | 1,320 | 1,320 | 900 | — |
| St. Joseph's College, North Windham, Maine | W | RC | 230 | — | 975 | 975 | 1,000 | — |
| St. Joseph's College, Philadelphia, Pennsylvania | M | RC | 1,791 | 227 | 1,125 | 1,125 | 400 | — |
| St. Joseph's College for Women, Brooklyn, New York | W | RC | 649 | — | — | — | — | 1,050 |
| St. Lawrence University, Canton, New York | MW | Pvt. | 1,800 | 100 | 1,950 | 1,950 | 1,030 | — |
| St. Louis University, St. Louis, Missouri | MW | RC | 8,800 | 3,000 | 1,400 | 1,400 | 900 | — |
| St. Martin's College, Olympia, Washington | MW | RC | 750 | 5 | 1,010 | 1,010 | 830 | — |
| St. Mary, The College of, Omaha, Nebraska | W | RC | 638 | — | 775 | 775 | 850 | — |
| St. Mary College, Xavier, Kansas | W | RC | 602 | 2 | 800 | 800 | 750 | — |
| St. Mary of the Plains College, Dodge City, Kansas | MW | RC | 784 | — | 770 | 770 | 800 | — |
| St. Mary of the Springs, College of, Columbus, Ohio | MW | RC | 1,030 | — | 900 | 900 | 900 | — |
| St. Mary of the Woods College, St. Mary of the Woods, Indiana | W | RC | 643 | — | 1,100 | 1,100 | 800 | — |
| St. Mary's College, Notre Dame, Indiana | W | RC | 1,250 | — | 1,400 | 1,400 | 1,000 | — |
| St. Mary's College, Winona, Minnesota | M | RC | 1,050 | 40 | 1,060 | 1,060 | 850 | — |
| St. Mary's College of California, St. Mary's College, California | M | RC | 1,000 | 20 | 1,175 | 1,175 | 990 | — |
| St. Mary's Dominican College, New Orleans, Louisiana | W | RC | 563 | — | 1,000 | 1,000 | 940 | — |
| St. Mary's Seminary and University, Baltimore, Maryland | M | RC | 800 | 400 | 450 | 450 | 750 | — |
| St. Mary's University, San Antonio, Texas | MW | RC | 3,000 | 600 | 800 | 800 | 850 | — |
| St. Meinrad College, St. Meinrad, Indiana | M | RC | 300 | — | 600 | 600 | 870 | — |
| St. Michael's College, Winooski, Vermont | M | RC | 1,266 | 120 | 1,450 | 1,450 | 850 | — |
| St. Norbert College, West De Pere, Wisconsin | MW | RC | 1,700 | — | 1,100 | 1,100 | 900 | — |

| NAME AND LOCATION | TYPE | CON-TROL | ENROLLMENT U | ENROLLMENT G | TUITION & FEES R | TUITION & FEES NR | ROOM, BOARD | COMP. FEE |
|---|---|---|---|---|---|---|---|---|
| St. Olaf College, Northfield, Minnesota.............. | MW | L | 2,500 | — | — | — | — | 2,400 |
| St. Paul's College, Lawrenceville, Virginia.............. | MW | PE | 520 | — | 773 | 773 | 560 | — |
| St. Peter's College, Jersey City, New Jersey.......... | MW | RC | 3,300 | — | 1,165 | 1,165 | NA | — |
| St. Procopius College, Lisle, Illinois................. | M | RC | 800 | — | 950 | 950 | 800 | — |
| St Rose, College of, Albany, New York.............. | W | RC | 800 | — | 1,146 | 1,146 | 900 | — |
| St. Scholastica, College of, Duluth, Minnesota........ | W | RC | 570 | — | 813 | 813 | 520 | — |
| St. Teresa, College of, Winona, Minnesota........... | W | RC | 1,400 | — | 1,100 | 1,100 | 850 | — |
| St. Thomas, College of, St. Paul, Minnesota.......... | W | RC | 1,900 | 275 | 1,200 | 1,200 | 975 | — |
| St. Thomas, University of, Houston, Texas........... | MW | RC | 1,050 | — | 850 | 850 | 550 | — |
| St. Vincent College, Latrobe, Pennsylvania.......... | M | RC | 993 | 131 | 1,100 | 1,100 | 700 | — |
| St. Xavier College, Chicago, Illinois................. | MW | RC | 1,018 | 69 | 1,210 | 1,210 | 900 | — |
| Salem College, Winston-Salem, North Carolina........ | W | MCA | 600 | — | — | — | — | 2,700 |
| Salem College, Salem, West Virginia................ | MW | Pvt. | 1,549 | — | — | — | — | 2,000 |
| Salisbury State College, Salisbury, Maryland.......... | MW | State | 630 | 100 | 275 | 525 | 675 | — |
| Salve Regina College, Newport, Rhode Island......... | W | RC | 844 | — | 1,100 | 1,100 | 900 | — |
| Sam Houston State College, Huntsville, Texas........ | MW | State | 8,183 | 750 | 168 | 468 | 700 | — |
| Samford University, Birmingham, Alabama............ | MW | SB | 2,631 | 178 | 832 | 928 | 680 | — |
| San Diego State College, San Diego, California........ | MW | State | 14,900 | 4,200 | 123 | 843 | 875 | — |
| San Diego, University of, College for Women, San Diego, California........................................ | W | RC | 625 | 61 | 1,050 | 1,050 | 650 | — |
| San Diego, University of, College for Men, San Diego, California........................................ | M | RC | 450 | 47 | 1,050 | 1,050 | 900 | — |
| San Fernando Valley State College, Northridge, California | MW | State | 12,300 | 2,850 | 100 | 720 | 740 | — |
| San Francisco, University of, San Francisco, California.... | MW | RC | 5,107 | 799 | 1,072 | 1,072 | 1,000 | — |
| San Francisco Art Institute, San Francisco, California..... | MW | Pvt. | 400 | NI | — | — | NA | 1,200 |
| San Francisco College for Women, San Francisco, California | W | RC | 484 | 38 | 900 | 900 | 1,200 | — |
| San Francisco State College, San Francisco, California.... | MW | State | 15,000 | 5,000 | 96 | 696 | 880 | — |
| San Jose State College, San Jose, California.......... | MW | State | 17,000 | 6,000 | 128 | 638 | 700 | — |
| Santa Clara, University of, Santa Clara, California........ | MW | RC | 2,631 | 1,488 | 1,410 | 1,410 | 1,005 | — |
| Sante Fe, College of, Santa Fe, New Mexico.......... | MW | RC | 1,300 | — | 850 | 850 | 840 | — |
| Sarah Lawrence College, Bronxville, New York........... | W | Pvt. | 623 | 16 | 2,350 | 2,350 | 1,200 | — |
| Savannah State College, Savannah, Georgia.............. | MW | State | 1,601 | — | 321 | 651 | 651 | — |
| Scranton, University of, Scranton, Pennsylvania........ | M | RC | 2,000 | 800 | 1,170 | 1,170 | 800 | — |
| Seattle Pacific College, Seattle, Washington.......... | MW | M | 1,982 | 494 | 1,118 | 1,118 | 750 | — |
| Seattle University, Seattle, Washington................ | MW | RC | 3,200 | 400 | 1,170 | 1,170 | 870 | — |
| Seton Hall University, South Orange, New Jersey........ | MW | RC | 7,512 | 2,288 | 1,260 | 1,260 | 900 | — |
| Seton-Hill College, Greensburg, Pennsylvania......... | W | RC | 700 | — | 1,150 | 1,150 | 1,000 | — |
| Shaw University, Raleigh, North Carolina................ | MW | AB | 1,000 | — | 1,050 | 1,050 | 720 | — |
| Shepherd College, Shepherdstown, West Virginia........ | MW | State | 1,376 | — | 206 | 656 | 742 | — |
| Shimer College, Mt. Carroll, Illinois................. | MW | PE | 519 | — | 1,790 | 1,790 | 930 | — |
| Shippensburg State College, Shippensburg, Pennsylvania | MW | State | 3,100 | 400 | 300 | 685 | 612 | — |
| Shorter College, Rome, Georgia................... | MW | SB | 726 | — | 739 | 739 | 750 | — |
| Siena, St. Bernadine of, College, Loudonville, New York.. | M | RC | 1,700 | 285 | 1,050 | 1,050 | 2,230 | — |
| Siena College, Memphis, Tennessee.................... | W | RC | 310 | — | 850 | 850 | 800 | — |
| Siena Heights College, Adrian, Michigan................ | W | RC | 725 | 78 | 700 | 700 | 750 | — |
| Simmons College, Boston, Massachusetts.............. | W | Pvt. | 1,442 | 625 | 1,680 | 1,680 | 1,000 | — |
| Simpson College, Indianola, Iowa...................... | MW | M | 910 | — | 1,340 | 1,340 | 800 | — |
| Sioux Falls College, Sioux Falls, South Dakota........... | MW | AB | 1,700 | — | 830 | 830 | 620 | — |
| Skidmore College, Saratoga Springs, New York.......... | W | Pvt. | 1,600 | — | 1,900 | 1,900 | 1,250 | — |
| Slippery Rock State College, Slippery Rock, Pennsylvania | MW | State | 3,600 | 385 | 321 | 641 | 612 | — |
| Smith College, Northampton, Massachusetts............. | W | Pvt. | 2,326 | 123 | — | — | — | 3,100 |
| Sonoma State College, Rohnert Park, California.......... | MW | State | 1,400 | 500 | 100 | 700 | 900 | — |
| South, University of the, Sewanee, Tennessee........... | M | PE | 837 | 65 | 1,680 | 1,680 | 770 | — |
| South Carolina, University of, Columbia, South Carolina... | MW | State | 8,486 | 1,000 | 825 | 1,375 | 676 | — |
| South Carolina State College, Orangeburg, South Carolina | MW | State | 1,500 | 563 | 385 | 615 | 530 | — |
| South Dakota, University of, Vermillion, South Dakota.... | MW | State | 3,900 | 500 | 459 | 955 | 700 | — |
| South Dakota School of Mines & Technology, Rapid City, South Dakota.................................... | MW | State | 1,200 | 80 | 445 | 802 | 674 | — |
| South Dakota State University, Brookings, South Dakota.. | MW | State | 4,574 | 439 | 391 | 918 | 700 | — |
| South Florida, University of, Tampa, Florida............ | MW | State | 10,200 | 100 | 300 | 750 | 867 | — |
| Southeast Missouri State College, Cape Girardeau, Missouri | MW | State | 5,571 | 402 | 160 | 440 | 650 | — |
| Southeastern Louisiana College, Hammond, Louisiana.... | MW | State | 5,400 | 200 | 184 | 784 | 614 | — |
| Southeastern Massachusetts Technological Institute, North Dartmouth, Massachusetts........................ | MW | State | 2,600 | 24 | 255 | 655 | NA | — |
| Southeastern State College, Durant, Oklahoma........... | MW | State | 2,610 | 500 | 175 | 423 | 520 | — |
| Southern California, University of, University Park, California...................................... | MW | Pvt. | 8,500 | 10,000 | 1,524 | 1,524 | 1,100 | — |
| Southern California College, Costa Mesa, California....... | MW | AG | 400 | — | 900 | 900 | 540 | — |
| Southern Colorado State College, Pueblo, Colorado...... | MW | State | 5,609 | — | 107 | 190 | 695 | — |
| Southern Connecticut State College, New Haven, Connecticut.................................... | MW | State | 4,780 | 2,400 | 165 | 265 | 630 | — |

| NAME AND LOCATION | TYPE | CONTROL | ENROLLMENT | | TUITION & FEES | | ROOM, BOARD | COMP. FEE |
|---|---|---|---|---|---|---|---|---|
| | | | U | G | R | NR | | |
| Southern Illinois University, Carbondale, Illinois......... | MW | State | 21,772 | 3,979 | 241 | 631 | 795 | — |
| Southern Methodist University, Dallas, Texas............ | MW | M | 7,311 | 1,625 | 1,252 | 1,252 | 900 | — |
| Southern Missionary College, Collegedale, Tennessee..... | MW | SDA | 1,202 | — | 1,095 | 1,095 | 750 | — |
| Southern Mississippi, University of, Hattiesburg, Mississippi | MW | State | 6,600 | 1,000 | 312 | 642 | 507 | — |
| Southern Oregon College, Ashland, Oregon............... | MW | State | 3,800 | 200 | 333 | 633 | 800 | — |
| Southern State College, Magnolia, Arkansas............. | MW | State | 2,789 | — | 200 | 470 | 600 | — |
| Southern State College, Springfield, South Dakota........ | MW | State | 873 | — | 359 | 695 | 616 | — |
| Southern University and A&M College, Scotlandville, Louisiana............................................ | MW | State | 8,304 | 1,252 | 42 | 642 | 510 | — |
| Southwest Baptist College, Bolivar, Missouri........... | MW | SB | 1,178 | — | 345 | 345 | 590 | — |
| Southwest Missouri State College, Springfield, Missouri... | MW | State | 6,200 | 100 | 200 | 480 | 740 | — |
| Southwest Texas State College, San Marcos, Texas....... | MW | State | 5,794 | 311 | 170 | 470 | 772 | — |
| Southwestern at Memphis, Memphis, Tennessee......... | MW | P | 1,050 | — | 1,300 | 1,300 | 850 | — |
| Southwestern College, Winfield, Kansas................ | MW | Pvt. | 750 | — | — | — | — | 1,550 |
| Southwestern Louisiana, University of, Lafayette, Louisiana | MW | State | 9,000 | 500 | 182 | 600 | 680 | — |
| Southwestern State College, Weatherford, Oklahoma..... | MW | State | 4,170 | — | 218 | 514 | 572 | — |
| Southwestern University, Georgetown, Texas............ | MW | M | 800 | — | 1,050 | 1,050 | 675 | — |
| Spelman College, Atlanta, Georgia..................... | W | Pvt. | 850 | — | 825 | 825 | 675 | — |
| Spring Arbor College, Spring Arbor, Michigan........... | MW | M | 620 | — | 1,000 | 1,000 | 800 | — |
| Spring Hill College, Mobile, Alabama.................. | MW | RC | 1,000 | — | 1,000 | 1,000 | 900 | — |
| Springfield College, Springfield, Massachusetts.......... | MW | Pvt. | 1,550 | 250 | 1,834 | 1,834 | 820 | — |
| Stanford University, Stanford, California................ | MW | Pvt. | 5,925 | 5,645 | 1,770 | 1,770 | 1,120 | — |
| Stanislaus State College, Turlock, California............ | MW | State | 1,025 | 300 | 110 | 310 | NA | — |
| Stephen F. Austin State College, Nacogdoches, Texas..... | MW | State | 4,286 | NI | 176 | 176 | 570 | — |
| Stephens College, Columbia, Missouri.................. | W | Pvt. | 1,900 | — | — | — | — | 2,900 |
| Sterling College, Sterling, Kansas..................... | MW | P | 650 | — | 900 | 900 | 710 | — |
| Stetson University, Deland and St. Petersburg, Florida.... | MW | SB | 1,750 | 350 | 1,400 | 1,400 | 850 | — |
| Steubenville, College of, Steubenville, Ohio............. | MW | RC | 1,100 | — | 1,200 | 1,200 | 900 | — |
| Stevens Institute of Technology, Hoboken, New Jersey.... | MW | Pvt. | 1,225 | 1,255 | 1,800 | 1,800 | 920 | — |
| Stillman College, Tuscaloosa, Alabama................. | MW | P | 700 | — | 600 | 600 | 625 | — |
| Stonehill College, North Easton, Massachusetts.......... | MW | RC | 1,225 | — | 1,240 | 1,240 | 950 | — |
| Stout State University, Menomonie, Wisconsin........... | MW | State | 3,141 | 111 | 326 | 742 | 724 | — |
| Suffolk University, Boston, Massachusetts.............. | MW | Pvt. | 1,705 | 143 | 1,025 | 1,025 | NA | — |
| Sul Ross State College, Alpine, Texas.................. | MW | State | 1,641 | 150 | 184 | 500 | 650 | — |
| Sulpician Seminary of the Northwest, Kenmore, Washington | M | RC | 100 | 110 | — | — | — | 1,100 |
| Susquehanna University, Selinsgrove, Pennsylvania...... | MW | L | 1,150 | — | 1,322 | 1,322 | 830 | — |
| Swarthmore College, Swarthmore, Pennsylvania......... | MW | Q | 1,010 | 1 | 1,950 | 1,950 | 950 | — |
| Sweet Briar College, Sweet Briar, Virginia.............. | W | Pvt. | 715 | — | — | — | — | 3,100 |
| Syracuse University, Syracuse, New York............... | MW | Pvt. | 9,826 | 7,833 | 1,900 | 1,900 | 1,030 | — |
| Utica College of Syracuse University, Utica, New York | MW | Pvt. | 3,445 | 600 | 1,330 | 1,330 | 1,000 | — |
| Tabor College, Hillsboro, Kansas...................... | MW | Mn | 400 | — | 860 | 860 | NI | — |
| Talladega College, Talladega, Alabama................. | MW | AMA | 450 | — | 675 | 675 | 550 | — |
| Tampa, University of, Tampa, Florida................... | MW | Pvt. | 2,224 | — | 1,100 | 1,100 | 1,000 | — |
| Tarkio College, Tarkio, Missouri...................... | MW | P | 750 | — | 1,840 | 1,840 | 1,260 | — |
| Tarleton State College, Stephenville, Texas............. | MW | State | 2,013 | — | 163 | 463 | 600 | — |
| Taylor University........................... | MW | M | 1,251 | — | 1,240 | 1,240 | 860 | — |
| Temple Buell College, Denver, Colorado................ | W | Pvt. | 1,100 | — | — | — | — | 2,964 |
| Temple University, Philadelphia, Pennsylvania.......... | MW | Pvt. | 20,000 | 6,470 | 450 | 1,350 | 1,350 | — |
| Tennessee, University of, Knoxville, Tennessee.......... | MW | State | 22,783 | 3,806 | 315 | 585 | 900 | — |
| Tennessee A&I State University, Nashville, Tennessee.... | MW | State | 5,434 | 180 | 165 | 330 | 440 | — |
| Tennessee Technological University, Cookeville, Tennessee | MW | State | 5,250 | 240 | 186 | 411 | 675 | — |
| Tennessee Wesleyan College, Athens, Tennessee........ | MW | M | 880 | — | 750 | 750 | 650 | — |
| Texas, University of, Austin, Texas.................... | MW | State | 23,038 | 4,307 | 144 | 444 | 900 | — |
| at Arlington, Texas............................ | MW | State | 11,513 | NI | 87 | 237 | — | — |
| at El Paso, Texas............................. | MW | State | 8,113 | 1,500 | 152 | 452 | 760 | — |
| Texas A&M University, College Station, Texas.......... | M | State | 9,191 | 2,357 | 223 | 523 | 616 | — |
| Texas Christian University, Fort Worth, Texas........... | MW | DC | 6,383 | 957 | 939 | 939 | 650 | — |
| Texas College, Tyler, Texas.......................... | MW | CME | 489 | — | 697 | 697 | 638 | — |
| Texas College of Art & Industries, Kingsville, Texas...... | MW | State | 4,584 | 322 | 146 | 446 | 700 | — |
| Texas Lutheran College, Sequin, Texas................. | MW | L | 799 | — | — | — | — | 1,500 |
| Texas Southern University, Houston, Texas............. | MW | State | 4,198 | 371 | 153 | 353 | 505 | — |
| Texas Technological College, Lubbock, Texas........... | MW | State | 17,406 | 2,054 | 200 | 500 | 837 | — |
| Texas Wesleyan College, Fort Worth, Texas............ | MW | M | 2,200 | — | 762 | 762 | 675 | — |
| Texas Women's University, Denton, Texas.............. | W | State | 4,580 | 50 | 179 | 379 | 656 | — |
| Thiel College, Greenville, Pennsylvania................ | MW | L | 1,251 | — | — | — | — | 2,150 |
| Tift College, Forsyth, Georgia........................ | W | SB | 460 | — | — | — | — | 1,215 |
| Toledo, University of, Toledo, Ohio................... | MW | City | 10,405 | 1,189 | 600 | 1,100 | 860 | — |
| Tougaloo College, Tougaloo, Mississippi............... | MW | Pvt. | 682 | — | 811 | 811 | 575 | — |
| Towson State College, Baltimore, Maryland............. | MW | State | 3,800 | 517 | 300 | 550 | 685 | — |
| Transylvania College, Lexington, Kentucky............. | MW | DC | 850 | — | 1,350 | 1,350 | 825 | — |
| Trenton State College, Trenton, New Jersey............ | MW | State | 6,170 | 1,500 | 382 | NE | 818 | — |
| Trinity College, Hartford, Connecticut.................. | M | Pvt. | 1,399 | 490 | 2,000 | 2,000 | 850 | — |

| NAME AND LOCATION | TYPE | CON-TROL | ENROLLMENT U | G | TUITION & FEES R | NR | ROOM, BOARD | COMP. FEE |
|---|---|---|---|---|---|---|---|---|
| Trinity College, Burlington, Vermont | W | RC | 446 | — | 845 | 845 | 900 | — |
| Trinity College, Washington, D.C. | W | RC | 900 | — | 1,476 | 1,476 | 1,200 | — |
| Trinity University, San Antonio, Texas | MW | P | 2,276 | 517 | 1,455 | 1,455 | 990 | — |
| Tri-State College, Angola, Indiana | MW | Pvt. | 1,900 | — | 1,100 | 1,100 | 840 | — |
| Troy State College, Troy, Alabama | MW | State | 2,900 | 80 | 276 | 426 | 600 | — |
| Tufts University, Medford, Massachusetts | MW | Pvt. | 3,171 | 1,748 | 1,900 | 1,900 | 1,010 | — |
| Tulane University, New Orleans, Louisiana | MW | Pvt. | 5,284 | 2,955 | 1,702 | 1,702 | 1,000 | — |
| Tulsa, University of, Tulsa, Oklahoma | MW | P | 4,000 | 2,113 | 675 | 675 | 725 | — |
| Tusculum College, Greeneville, Tennessee | MW | P | 561 | — | 1,025 | 1,025 | 775 | — |
| Tuskegee Institute, Tuskegee Institute, Alabama | MW | Pvt. | 2,549 | 153 | 700 | 700 | 650 | — |
| Union College, Barbourville, Kentucky | MW | M | 875 | 50 | 1,146 | 1,146 | 680 | — |
| Union College, Lincoln, Nebraska | MW | SDA | 1,202 | — | — | — | — | 1,700 |
| Union College and University, Schenectady and Albany, New York | M | Pvt. | 1,660 | 25 | 1,833 | 1,833 | 1,015 | — |
| Union University, Jackson, Tennessee | MW | M | 900 | — | 685 | 685 | 640 | — |
| United States Air Force Academy, Colorado Springs, Colorado | M | Fed. | 3,286 | — | Free | Free | Free | — |
| United States Coast Guard Academy, New London, Connecticut | M | Fed. | 800 | — | Free | Free | Free | — |
| United States Merchant Marine Academy, Kings Point, New York | M | Fed. | 990 | — | Free | Free | Free | — |
| United States Military Academy, West Point, New York | M | Fed. | 3,200 | — | Free | Free | Free | — |
| United States Naval Academy, Annapolis, Maryland | M | Fed. | 4,000 | — | Free | Free | Free | — |
| Upper Iowa College, Fayette, Iowa | MW | Pvt. | 1,055 | — | 1,100 | 1,100 | 770 | — |
| Upsala College, East Orange, New Jersey | MW | L | 1,600 | — | 1,526 | 1,526 | 850 | — |
| Ursinus College, Collegeville, Pennsylvania | MW | UCC | 1,100 | — | 1,440 | 1,440 | 900 | — |
| Ursuline College, Louisville, Kentucky | W | RC | 550 | — | 960 | 960 | 980 | — |
| Ursuline College for Women, Cleveland, Ohio | W | RC | 500 | — | 750 | 750 | 825 | — |
| Utah, University of, Salt Lake City, Utah | MW | State | 39,311 | 9,361 | 375 | 690 | 768 | — |
| Utah State University, Logan, Utah | MW | State | 7,132 | 982 | 282 | 639 | 726 | — |
| Valdosta State College, Valdosta, Georgia | MW | State | 2,200 | 15 | 315 | 645 | 591 | — |
| Valley City State College, Valley City, North Dakota | MW | State | 1,350 | — | 279 | 603 | 576 | — |
| Valparaiso University, Valparaiso, Indiana | MW | L | 3,800 | 220 | 1,250 | 1,250 | 925 | — |
| Vanderbilt University, Nashville, Tennessee | MW | Pvt. | 3,566 | 1,768 | 1,505 | 1,505 | 1,040 | — |
| Vassar College, Poughkeepsie, New York | W | Pvt. | 1,650 | 15 | 1,840 | 1,840 | 1,300 | — |
| Vermont, University of, Burlington, Vermont | MW | State | 4,431 | 450 | 678 | 1,878 | 870 | — |
| Villa Madonna College, Covington, Kentucky | MW | RC | 1,837 | — | 880 | 880 | 900 | — |
| Villa Maria College, Erie, Pennsylvania | W | RC | 811 | 106 | 500 | 500 | 275 | — |
| Villanova University, Villanova, Pennsylvania | MW | RC | 5,000 | 50 | 1,500 | 1,500 | 1,000 | — |
| Virginia, University of, Charlottesville, Virginia | MW | State | 4,740 | 2,070 | 452 | 1,037 | 1,005 | — |
| Mary Washington College, Fredericksburg, Virginia | W | State | 2,000 | — | 607 | 677 | 593 | — |
| Virginia Military Institute, Lexington, Virginia | M | State | 1,213 | — | 545 | 1,120 | 600 | 2,300 |
| Virginia Polytechnic Institute | MW | State | 8,340 | 712 | 420 | 840 | 756 | — |
| Virginia State College, Petersburg, Virginia | MW | State | 2,100 | 200 | 534 | 744 | 511 | — |
| Virginia Union University, Richmond, Virginia | MW | AB | 1,450 | — | 780 | 780 | 600 | — |
| Viterbo College, La Crosse, Wisconsin | MW | RC | 600 | — | 650 | 650 | 250 | — |
| Wabash College, Crawfordsville, Indiana | M | Pvt. | 889 | — | 1,750 | 1,750 | 825 | — |
| Wagner College, Staten Island, New York | MW | L | 2,400 | 400 | 1,650 | 1,650 | 1,000 | — |
| Wake Forest University, Winston-Salem, North Carolina | MW | SB | 2,305 | 715 | 1,150 | 1,150 | 750 | — |
| Walla Walla College, College Place, Washington | MW | SDA | 1,660 | 40 | 1,200 | 1,200 | 540 | — |
| Walsh College, Canton, Ohio | M | RC | 900 | — | 916 | 916 | 800 | — |
| Wartburg College, Waverly, Iowa | MW | L | 1,350 | — | 1,000 | 1,000 | 700 | — |
| Washburn University of Topeka, Topeka, Kansas | MW | City | 4,020 | 320 | 410 | 620 | 792 | — |
| Washington, University of, Seattle, Washington | MW | State | 22,000 | 4,049 | 345 | 825 | 810 | — |
| Washington and Jefferson College, Washington, Pennsylvania | M | Pvt. | 800 | — | 1,626 | 1,626 | 925 | — |
| Washington and Lee University, Lexington, Virginia | M | Pvt. | 1,200 | 200 | 1,600 | 1,600 | 800 | — |
| Washington College, Chestertown, Maryland | MW | Pvt. | 624 | — | 1,556 | 1,556 | 900 | — |
| Washington State University, Pullman, Washington | MW | State | 9,750 | 1,350 | 345 | 825 | 850 | — |
| Washington University, St. Louis, Missouri | MW | Pvt. | 3,700 | 3,100 | 1,900 | 1,900 | 1,125 | — |
| Wayland Baptist College, Plainview, Texas | MW | SB | 750 | — | 590 | 590 | 580 | — |
| Wayne State College, Wayne, Nebraska | MW | State | 2,550 | 150 | 270 | 420 | 580 | — |
| Wayne State University, Detroit, Michigan | MW | State | 15,000 | 7,104 | 312 | 750 | 756 | — |
| Waynesburg College, Waynesburg, Pennsylvania | MW | P | 1,035 | — | 1,350 | 1,350 | 820 | — |
| Weber State College, Ogden, Utah | MW | State | 8,200 | — | 315 | 705 | 675 | — |
| Webster College, St. Louis, Missouri | MW | Pvt. | 1,000 | 300 | 1,280 | 1,280 | 1,090 | — |
| Wellesley College, Wellesley, Massachusetts | W | Pvt. | 1,783 | — | — | — | — | 3,100 |
| Wells College, Aurora, New York | W | Pvt. | 652 | — | — | — | — | 3,100 |
| Wesleyan College, Macon, Georgia | W | M | 700 | — | 1,315 | 1,315 | 775 | — |
| Wesleyan University, Middletown, Connecticut | M | Pvt. | 1,275 | 1,493 | 1,955 | 1,955 | 1,105 | — |
| West Chester State College, West Chester, Pennsylvania | MW | State | 4,877 | 1,062 | 290 | 680 | 612 | — |
| West Coast University, Los Angeles, California | MW | Pvt. | 1,100 | 250 | 600 | 600 | NA | — |

| NAME AND LOCATION | TYPE | CON-TROL | ENROLLMENT U | G | TUITION & FEES R | NR | ROOM, BOARD | COMP. FEE |
|---|---|---|---|---|---|---|---|---|
| West Texas State University, Canyon, Texas............ | MW | State | 5,254 | 903 | 178 | 478 | 628 | — |
| West Virginia Institute of Technology, Montgomery, West Virginia....................................... | MW | State | 2,104 | — | 219 | 669 | 704 | — |
| West Virginia State College, Institute, West Virginia...... | MW | State | 3,350 | — | 382 | 682 | 648 | — |
| West Virginia University, Morgantown, West Virginia...... | MW | State | 10,000 | 2,500 | 280 | 910 | 830 | — |
| West Virginia Wesleyan College, Buckhannon, West Virginia | MW | M | 1,700 | — | 1,330 | 1,330 | 900 | — |
| Western Carolina University, Cullowhee, North Carolina... | MW | State | 3,592 | 325 | 360 | 612 | 516 | — |
| Western College for Women, Oxford, Ohio............. | W | Pvt. | 550 | — | 1,660 | 1,660 | 1,125 | — |
| Western Illinois University, Macomb, Illinois............ | MW | State | 6,868 | 337 | 235 | 406 | 774 | — |
| Western Kentucky State University, Bowling Green, Kentucky.................................... | MW | State | 7,106 | 577 | 175 | 375 | 600 | — |
| Western Maryland College, Westminster, Maryland........ | MW | M | 850 | 500 | 1,375 | 1,375 | 850 | — |
| Western Michigan University, Kalamazoo, Michigan........ | MW | State | 14,600 | 2,450 | 370 | 800 | 825 | — |
| Western Montana College, Dillon, Montana............. | MW | State | 855 | 54 | 353 | 893 | 672 | — |
| Western New England College, Springfield, Massachusetts | MW | Pvt. | 1,888 | 438 | 1,210 | 1,210 | 460 | — |
| Western New Mexico University, Silver City, New Mexico.. | MW | State | 1,160 | 120 | 247 | 607 | 795 | — |
| Western Reserve University (see Case Western Reserve) | | | | | | | | |
| Western State College of Colorado, Gunnison, Colorado... | MW | State | 2,635 | 125 | 342 | 742 | 754 | — |
| Western Washington State College, Bellingham, Washington | MW | State | 5,900 | 250 | 264 | 471 | 745 | — |
| Westmar College, Le Mars, Iowa...................... | MW | EUB | 1,100 | — | 1,100 | 1,100 | 680 | — |
| Westminster College, Fulton, Missouri................. | M | P | 700 | — | 1,600 | 1,600 | 900 | — |
| Westminster College, New Wilmington, Pennsylvania..... | MW | P | 1,427 | 540 | 1,250 | 1,250 | 778 | — |
| Westminster College, Salt Lake City, Utah.............. | MW | UCC | 657 | — | 749 | 749 | 750 | — |
| Westmont College, Santa Barbara, California............ | MW | Pvt. | 700 | — | 1,539 | 1,539 | 981 | — |
| Wheaton College, Wheaton, Illinois.................... | MW | Pvt. | 1,750 | 100 | 1,420 | 1,420 | 800 | — |
| Wheaton College, Norton, Massachusetts................ | W | Pvt. | 1,120 | — | — | — | — | 3,300 |
| Wheeling College, Wheeling, West Virginia.............. | MW | RC | 1,250 | 800 | — | 1,250 | 1,000 | — |
| Wheelock College, Boston, Massachusetts............... | W | Pvt. | 511 | 74 | 1,700 | 1,700 | 1,000 | — |
| Whitman College, Walla Walla, Washington.............. | MW | Pvt. | 1,025 | — | 1,500 | 1,500 | 810 | — |
| Whittier College, Whittier, California................... | MW | Q | 2,004 | 104 | — | — | — | 2,100 |
| Whitworth College, Spokane, Washington............... | MW | P | 1,595 | 315 | 1,225 | 1,225 | 750 | — |
| Wichita State University, Wichita, Kansas............... | MW | State | 9,800 | 1,700 | 312 | 775 | 725 | — |
| Wilberforce University, Wilberforce, Ohio............... | MW | AME | 800 | — | 880 | 880 | 690 | — |
| Wiley College, Marshall, Texas....................... | MW | M | 650 | — | 779 | 779 | 720 | — |
| Wilkes College, Wilkes-Barre, Pennsylvania............. | MW | Pvt. | 2,400 | 90 | 1,050 | 1,050 | 1,050 | — |
| Willamette University, Salem, Oregon.................. | MW | M | 1,222 | 6 | 1,228 | 1,228 | 800 | — |
| William and Mary, College of, Williamsburg, Virginia...... | MW | State | 3,376 | 744 | 446 | 1,010 | 800 | — |
| William Carey College, Hattiesburg, Mississippi.......... | MW | SB | 900 | — | 714 | 714 | 610 | — |
| William Jewell College, Liberty, Missouri............... | MW | SB | 1,012 | — | 1,150 | 1,150 | 800 | — |
| William Penn College, Oskaloosa, Iowa................. | MW | Q | 925 | — | 1,045 | 1,045 | 920 | — |
| William Woods College, Fulton, Mississippi.............. | W | Pvt. | 720 | — | — | — | — | 2,550 |
| Williams College, Williamstown, Massachusetts.......... | M | Pvt. | 1,230 | 40 | 1,900 | 1,900 | 1,050 | — |
| Willimantic State College, Willimantic, Connecticut....... | MW | State | 850 | 50 | 195 | 195 | 630 | — |
| Wilmington College, Wilmington, Ohio................. | MW | Q | 925 | — | 1,231 | 1,231 | 780 | — |
| Wilson College, Chambersburg, Pennsylvania............ | W | P | 672 | — | 1,800 | 1,800 | 1,100 | — |
| Windham College, Putney, Vermont.................... | MW | Pvt. | 700 | 80 | 1,700 | 1,700 | 950 | — |
| Winona State College, Winona, Minnesota.............. | MW | State | 3,100 | 400 | 300 | 444 | 660 | — |
| Winston-Salem State College, Winston-Salem, North Carolina...................................... | MW | State | 1,450 | — | 280 | 480 | 592 | — |
| Winthrop College, Rock Hill, South Carolina............ | W | State | 3,057 | 123 | 327 | 852 | 575 | — |
| Wisconsin, University of, Madison, Wisconsin........... | MW | State | 22,900 | 10,100 | 325 | 1,050 | 920 | — |
| at Milwaukee, Wisconsin......................... | MW | State | 12,000 | 2,300 | 325 | 1,050 | 850 | — |
| Wisconsin State University System at Eau Claire, Wisconsin | MW | State | 5,800 | 300 | 238 | 654 | 680 | — |
| at La Crosse, Wisconsin.......................... | MW | State | 5,000 | 250 | 350 | 690 | 600 | — |
| at Oshkosh, Wisconsin........................... | MW | State | 8,950 | 350 | 322 | 738 | 760 | — |
| at Platteville, Wisconsin.......................... | MW | State | 4,300 | 100 | 336 | 752 | 638 | — |
| at River Falls, Wisconsin.......................... | MW | State | 3,800 | 250 | 319 | 735 | 630 | — |
| at Stevens Point, Wisconsin....................... | MW | State | 5,800 | 200 | 322 | 738 | 740 | — |
| at Superior, Wisconsin........................... | MW | State | 1,982 | 30 | 332 | 748 | 670 | — |
| at Whitewater, Wisconsin......................... | MW | State | 8,200 | 80 | 318 | 734 | 710 | — |
| Wittenberg University, Springfield, Ohio................ | MW | Pvt. | 2,325 | 125 | 1,731 | 1,731 | 927 | — |
| Wofford College, Spartanburg, South Carolina........... | M | Pvt. | 1,018 | — | — | — | — | 1,990 |
| Woodbury College, Los Angeles, California.............. | MW | Pvt. | 2,181 | — | 810 | 810 | 810 | — |
| Wooster, the College of, Wooster, Ohio................ | MW | P | 1,500 | 3 | 1,833 | 1,833 | 900 | — |
| Worcester Polytechnic Institute, Worcester, Massachusetts | M | Pvt. | 1,510 | 199 | 1,800 | 1,800 | 1,000 | — |
| Wyoming, University of, Laramie, Wyoming............. | MW | State | 6,700 | 1,079 | 345 | 961 | 830 | — |
| Xavier University, Cincinnati, Ohio.................... | M | RC | 3,296 | 2,462 | 1,200 | 1,200 | 990 | — |
| Xavier University of Louisiana, New Orleans, Louisiana... | MW | RC | 1,140 | 60 | 832 | 832 | 658 | — |
| Yale University, New Haven, Connecticut............... | M | Pvt. | 4,080 | 4,306 | 1,950 | 1,950 | 1,050 | — |
| Yankton College, Yankton, South Dakota............... | MW | C | 670 | — | 980 | 980 | 750 | — |
| Yeshiva University, New York, New York................ | MW | J | 2,823 | 2,693 | 1,595 | 1,595 | 1,320 | — |
| Youngstown State University, Youngstown, Ohio......... | MW | State | 13,800 | 50 | 450 | 675 | 850 | — |

# SCIENCE AND TECHNOLOGY

## Scientific Progress • History • Inventions • Units and Standards • Mathematics

A space communications system undergoes tests at NASA's Manned Spacecraft Center, Houston, Texas.

Lockheed Electronics

## A NATION GEARED TO CHANGE

Science and technology both promote change and help us adjust to it. They change national needs: Medical science gave us longer lives — and led to Medicare. They change our vocabulary. How many parents heard their teachers say "retro-rocket," "microclimate," or "R&D"? Science and technology change society, permitting fewer work-hours and greater incomes — then add spice to our new leisure time with finer

hi-fi's, global TV hook-ups, purrier sports cars, and a host of other gadgets.

In 1967 Secretary of Commerce John Connor recalled that more than 100 years ago Frenchman Alexis de Toqueville had written that Americans "sought the immediate and practical results of the sciences." Said Connor, "Technological change is part of our American heritage — and a major element in our visions."

# SCIENCE PROGRESS: 1967

In 1967, science and technology continued to exercise a major influence on the American economy and society, but signs of change were visible. A proposed proton accelerator, with a record price tag of $375,000,000, is a case in point.

More than 200 communities in 46 states sought to provide a home for the giant instrument, whose operation will require a staff of 2,000 and an annual budget of $60,000,000. The winner was Weston, Illinois, a quiet farming community of less than 400 inhabitants located 30 miles southwest of Chicago.

Congress soon began to have second thoughts. The failure of Illinois to pass an open-housing bill, plus rising costs in Vietnam, caused many congressmen to question the wisdom of proceeding with the program. The decade-long romance between science and government may be cooling off somewhat; in any event, scientists can no longer count on blank checks from Uncle Sam.

## ASTRONOMY

The year 1967 opened with a new addition to the Sun's family—a 32d satellite. The satellite's mother planet is Saturn, which has nine other known satellites. The new one, Saturn's tenth, is closest to the planet and just outside Saturn's rings. Ordinarily, the brilliance of the rings masks the satellite, but once every 14½ years the thin rings are seen edgewise from Earth and seem to disappear. This occurred in December, 1966, and a month later French astronomer Audoin Dollfuss spotted the new object on photographs taken in December. As the first satellite out from Saturn and the last of its family to be discovered, it was named Janus after the two-faced Roman god of beginnings. Its orbital period, easy to measure, is 18 hours. Its diameter, less easy to measure, may be as much as 300 miles.

Other noteworthy astronomical firsts occurred in 1967. The heat emitted by the scattered dust in the inner regions of the Solar system has been measured for the first time. The data was gathered during a total solar eclipse in November, 1966, as seen from a 13,000-foot vantage point in the Bolivian Andes. Heat emission could be detected within 17,000,000 miles of the Sun, indicating that the dust cloud that gives rise to the so-called "zodiacal light" is Sun-centered rather than Earth-centered. The Earth is bombarded by this dust in the form of micrometeorites—as much as 2,500 tons per day, according to S. Fred Singer of the U.S. Department of Interior. Radioactive aluminum-26 detected in deep-sea sediments may have originated in this dust.

Far beyond the solar system lies the Crab Nebula, the remnant of a vast star explosion (a "supernova") that took place 900 years ago. Radio emissions from the Crab Nebula have now been analyzed with such precision that a "radio map" has been prepared showing radio intensity at every point. In the course of a supernova explosion, a star shrinks to a tiny white-hot object of enormous density, a "white dwarf." However, some astronomers think that before it reaches this stage it passes through an even hotter stage, radiating in the ultraviolet range.

But such "ultraviolet dwarfs" have not been detected. Why not? Richard Stothers of the Goddard Institute for Space Studies, taking new factors into account, calculated that the ultraviolet stage does not last more than 400,000 years. This is too brief a time, astronomically speaking, to make it likely that astronomers would catch any visible star in that stage.

The center of the Milky Way galaxy (of which our Solar system is part) cannot be seen by ordinary telescopes. Its brilliant light is scattered by vast dust clouds flying between it and Earth. However, the relatively long waves of infrared light are much less scattered. Using infrared detectors in conjunction with optical telescopes, astronomers at the California Institute of Technology now report the detection of the very core of the galaxy. It has an apparent diameter of 30 seconds of arc (one-sixteenth the diameter of the full Moon) and lies in the constellation Sagittarius. The core emits energy equivalent to that of 3,000,000 stars like our Sun.

## PHYSICS

Physicists in 1967 continued to probe the edges of the physical world. A record low temperature was reached—less than a millionth of a degree above absolute zero (−459.69° F.). In addition, slightly less frigid temperatures were reached for extended periods of time by remarkably simple devices. The isotope helium-3 was forced in and out of solution in helium-4 and in this way a temperature of 0.2 degrees Kelvin or absolute scale was reached and maintained.

The world of super-frigid temperatures saw another kind of record as well. Superconductivity (complete lack of resistance to an electric current) is a phenomenon associated with temperatures near absolute zero. No substance had been found to be superconductive at temperatures higher than 18 degrees absolute. In 1967, however, physicists at Bell Telephone Laboratories discovered a mixture of niobium-aluminum alloy and niobium-termanium alloy that remained superconductive at 20 degrees absolute. This holds out the hope of superconductivity at liquid hydrogen temperatures, rather than at the lower —and harder to maintain—temperatures of liquid helium.

Year by year, physical measurements grow more precise. The value of $g$ (the acceleration of an object in free fall under standard conditions on the Earth's surface) was set at 9.801018 meters per second by the National Bureau of Standards. Scientists at Brookhaven National Laboratory, studying collisions of subatomic particles, verified that the speed of light remained an upper limit for the transmission of any conceivable signal. And this was true even over ultra-short distances as small as 1/1000 the diameter of a proton. No physicist had really doubted this, but it was reassuring to get definite evidence.

Perhaps the most exciting recent theory in physics involves the manner in which the numerous baryons (subatomic particles as heavy as, or heavier than, the proton) may be grouped into families according to symmetrical arrangements of their properties. The best known such theory is the "SU (3)" principle propounded by Murray Gell-Mann. It predicts, among other things, certain values for the internal magnetism of the various baryons. The internal magnetism of the sigma-plus particle was actually measured at Vanderbilt University, and the measurement, reported in 1967, closely matched the prediction.

The laser, that remarkable maker of "coherent light" (light with all its waves identical in size and direction), continues to make news. Extremely short bursts of laser light, one-trillionth of a second in duration, were found by physicists at the University of California to be absorbed by atoms of certain substances. The atoms then quickly remit the laser bursts in the original direction. Such bursts of coherent light can thus pass through material that is ordinarily opaque to light. For sheer laser intensity, Korad Corporation at Santa Monica set a new record. Five synthetic rubies set in a row produced bursts of light with a peak power of one million kilowatts —five times more powerful than previous lasers of this type.

## CHEMISTRY

Larger and larger quantities of man-made elements are being produced. At Oak Ridge National Laboratory, 1/250,000 of a gram of einsteinium (element 99) was prepared. This was too little to see, but it represents a record quantity. It will be used for the preparation of new isotopes of still more complex atoms of fermium, mendelevium, and nobelium—the elements 100, 101, and 102, respectively.

New molecules also made headlines. Olin Mathieson Chemical Corporation announced in 1967 the preparation of a new type of plastic, a "polycarboranesiloxane." Its molecules contain boron and silicon atoms in their chain, as well as the usual carbon atoms. The plastic remains flexible for long periods at temperatures from 800° F. down to −80° F.

Metals can now be modified by a new technique called "metalliding," devised by Newell Cook at General Electric. In this process, elements like boron or silicon are dissolved in molten fluorides. Then, under the influence of an electric current, boron or silicon can be made to "drift" into metals placed with them. The metal molybdenum, for instance, is not in itself extraordinarily hard; but once small boron atoms are introduced by metalliding, molybdenum becomes almost diamond-hard.

## BIOCHEMISTRY

Biochemists continue to explore the workings of the genes. Why are there different types of cells in the body if all cells have identical sets of genes? French geneticists Jacob, Monod, and Lwoff suggested that there were repressor substances that "turned off" one particular gene (or group of genes) in one kind of cell, but another gene in another kind of cell.

The three Frenchmen won a Nobel Prize for the suggestion in 1965. In 1967 the theory took concrete form when Walter Gilbert and Benno Muller-Hill of Harvard actually isolated such repressor substances from a common species of bacteria. They proved to be protein molecules.

The detailed structure of protein molecules, those infinitely versatile building blocks of life, is being revealed with increasing ease. Biochemists at Polytechnic Institute of Brooklyn worked out the detailed three-dimensional structure of the important enzyme, ribonuclease. It is the fourth protein thus analyzed.

A newer mystery—the circadian rhythms by which creatures have alternating day-and-night cycles of activity and inactivity—is being explored at the molecular level. An enzyme called transaminase has been found to be four times more active at its daily peak than at its 24-hour low. Correspondingly, the amino acids with which transaminase is involved also show daily high and low concentrations in the blood.

Finally, a possible clue to the agony of migraine headaches has been uncovered. The presence in the blood of a certain chemical compound, tyramine, can cause such headaches. An inherited deficiency of an enzyme may cause tyramine to accumulate at times—and a migraine strikes.

## BIOLOGY

Life's persistence and rugged versatility continues to surprise scientists. Fish capable of living on very little oxygen have been discovered in Lake Tanganyika in Africa. Before this discovery, scientists had placed the lower limit of oxygen for active fish life at 2.9 parts per million. But the Lake Tanganyika fish have been found swimming vigorously where the oxygen is only 0.6 ppm.

This ability of living things to "make do" in unfavorable environments was put to use in 1967. Bacteria that can live on certain inorganic salts have been set to work on low-grade copper sulfide ores from which miners cannot profitably extract copper. By the time the bacteria are finished, useful concentrations of copper sulfate have been formed. Five hundred tons of copper were produced in this fashion in Australia.

Man's folly, however, is ever a formidable threat to the versatility of life. Biologists have now mournfully concluded that the Atlantic salmon is headed irretrievably for extinction in U.S. rivers because of pollution. And Brookhaven National Laboratories report that birds and fish along the south shore of Long Island are carrying a DDT load of near-fatal size.

Amid the woeful tales of dwindling numbers and threatened species, it is pleasant to report two unusual biological finds in 1967. First, a pair of "dibblers," a type of rat-sized carnivorous marsupial thought to have become extinct about 1890, were discovered near Albany, Western Australia. And second, the first albino gorilla ever known—a baby—was found in Rio Muni, a patch of Spanish-owned territory on Africa's west coast. The gorilla now resides in the Barcelona zoo, where it will receive as much tender loving care as the most pampered human infant.

## THE COMPUTER REVOLUTION

Psychiatrists tell us that the things we poke most fun at may be the things of which we are most afraid. If so, we must be scared stiff of the computer. Computer cartoons have never been more popular. One sample: A first-day-at-school youngster offers a shiny apple to an equally shiny computer teaching machine. In another, a bewildered computer attendant reports to his equally bewildered boss: "It says it wants four weeks vacation with pay."

Such jokes mirror the doubts that many people feel about what is now widely called the "computer revolution." Will the computer push me out of a job because it can work better and faster than I? Can computers think? If so, how much control will they exercise?

Much of our deep suspicion of the computer arises from the air of mystery that surrounds it, the notion that it is a kind of super "something" only understood by electronic geniuses. This is nonsense.

In a very basic way a computer resembles a wheel, a lever, or a ramp. Like these things, it is a machine. And a machine is simply something that allows man to work faster, more easily, or more conveniently than he would be able to work unaided.

Of course, the computer is a very special machine because the work it helps us do is of a special kind—problem solving. Very often the problem involves numerical calculations. In fact, the modern computer evolved from a long line of calculating machines, stretching back about 3,300 years to the abacus.

But the computer can also solve problems by storing, analyzing, and rearranging all sorts of information. The name it goes by most often in the business community is a good indication of its functions: "data processing machine." It can add a million numbers on request. But it also can (and does) arrange "perfect dates" between lonely young men and women by matching applicants on the basis of age, height, interests, personality, and so on.

The most awesome thing about a modern computer is its speed. In seconds it can solve equations that would take a mathematician hundreds of hours to unravel. It can execute 10,-000,000 steps per second. By contrast, a human brain cell can "switch" on and off a mere 200 times per second.

The computer is also enormously flexible. It can store vast quantities of information and then logically process the stored knowledge in order to solve problems, even fantastically complex problems involving thousands of steps.

Nevertheless, the computer is quite stupid! It works its wonders by performing a very few elementary functions: It can do arithmetic; it can also rearrange and compare numbers and then go on to a predetermined next step on the basis of the comparison. How can these simple tasks add up to the impressive talents of the computer?

Every bit of information the computer handles is coded into one of the simplest "languages" ever invented—the binary notation. All numbers, letters, and symbols are reduced to combinations of two digits—0 and 1. The computer needs only enough "intelligence" to tell whether an electric current is *on* (1) or *off* (0). This is why the digital computer (there are other, less important, types) can work so fast. Each decision is a simple "yes" or "no" made at the speed of an electronic pulse. And that is very fast indeed. So fast that it more than makes up for the fact that it takes many more zeros and ones to code a number or a message than there were characters in the original. (For example, one simple word might be coded as a sequence of dozens of zeros and ones.)

When information is coded it is fed into the computer *input*, either on a keyboard or else on punched cards, magnetic tape, or other means. It may be processed immediately or stored in the computer's memory section.

This coded information is useless by itself. If the computer is not given a complete, precise set of instructions, called the "program," it will either come up with the wrong answers or with no answers at all. In industry jargon, the program is "software" as opposed to the "hardware"—the computer itself. Right now the software end of the $6-billion-a-year computer business is hampered by a shortage of programmers.

What does the programmer do? He is the man (or woman) who turns a big pile of expensive parts into an instrument of limitless value by properly talking to it. He must prepare each program in a form that will be "readable" by the computer.

This is not easy. The programmer must analyze a problem thoroughly, then prepare a sequence of computer steps that omits nothing. A large inventory-control system might require a

Tiny doughnut-shaped iron cores, each threaded with four hair-thin wires, make up a computer's "memory."

General Electric

**THE COMPUTER REVOLUTION** (*continued*)

program of 60,000 steps or more! Furthermore, the programmer must be familiar with FORTRAN, ALGOL, COBOL, and other special computer languages. (These languages are used to avoid the tedium of coding directly into binary notation. The computer itself has been pre-programmed to translate these into binary code.)

Mistakes in this business can be very costly. A few years ago a programmer left out a hyphen in the flight program of a rocket that was to have been the first U.S. spacecraft to fly by Venus. Result: The rocket, worth almost $20,000,000, would not fly correctly and had to be destroyed. A similar error not long ago sent 200 New York State Reservists marching off to active duty in Wisconsin, where they had no business whatsoever.

No wonder, then, that trained programmers are worth their weight in—computers. Some 100,000 programmers are now busy sweet-talking the 40,000 computers in the U.S., but at least 50,000 more are needed. Programming is one of the best-paid technical careers around. Trained beginners can start at $7,000 a year and earn $15,000 within five years, even without a college degree. Top-notch programmers make $22,000 and more. Experts predict we will have 85,000 computers by 1975, so the "programmer gap" is likely to become wider, not narrower.

Even though the computer revolution is creating thousands of jobs for programmers, won't it do away with many more? Haven't we heard stories about computer-directed machines that do the work formerly performed by 70 assembly-line workers? Yes. Jobs are lost where computer techniques have led to automation. But the computer will eventually replace these jobs by creating brand-new industries such as the information industry. Expected to bring in $2.5 billion by 1975, this business will supply on request information from vast memory stores—even to private homes.

Computers are presently helping people fill more, and better, jobs. In July, 1967, the U.S. Department of Labor began an expanded program to match workers with available job openings by using data processing equipment. And in the personnel offices of many companies, computers help employees get promoted to better jobs by keeping track of their skills.

Most people are unaware of just how many fields the computer has already invaded. Here's a random sample of computer applications in 1967:

- **Publishing:** The Rockland County (N.Y.) Telephone Directory was printed by computer.
- **Crime:** New York City's Police Department became the first to be hooked up to the computerized FBI national data bank of criminal information in Washington, D.C.
- **Textiles:** A computerized drawing board reduced necktie design time from 200 hours to 20 minutes.
- **Education:** While teaching machines continued to make headway, a commercial firm offered a computer service to find scholarships for persons about to enter college.
- **Labor:** Unions turned to computers to spot

*Honeywell E.D.P.*

A computerized Braille printer turns out material 100 times faster than conventional machines.

areas ripe for unionization drives and to bolster their bargaining positions by keeping a nation-wide check on labor contracts.
- **Sociology:** Plans were made to feed enough data to a computer to enable it to predict the next outbreak of racial violence.
- **The Arts:** Computers continued to compose unlistenable music and meaningless poetry.

The last item helps answer a disturbing question: Can computers think creatively, in the human sense? The answer is "not yet." The computer is still a machine that simply follows the orders men give it. Whether computers might learn to think in the future is the subject of hot debate among experts.

Other developments are more predictable, if we look far enough ahead. Banks will become so computerized that we may have a truly "checkless-cashless" society. Most forms of transportation will be handled by computers. And you may even be able to connect your own mind to a central memory bank.

Does all this hold the risk of too much centralization, too much control? Some observers think so. They are concerned, for example, about the chance that the government will compile fact sheets on each of us in a national electronic data center. Such a system, they say, might threaten individual privacy and even lead to a "Big Brother" society.

Regarding this, a report prepared for the United Nations International Year for Human Rights (1968) noted: "There is a grave danger that actual decisions will no longer be in the hands of duly elected representatives . . . but instead in the hands of those who feed data to the computers."

A frightening prospect? Yes. But it must be faced now, for the computer is surely here to stay. Like every other tool man has used, from fire on down, it will control our destinies exactly to the extent we let it.

## THE LASER: SCIENCE'S BRIGHT NEW TOOL

*Riddle:* If, on peril of death, you had to plot the path of a subterranean tunnel between New York City and Washington, D.C., remove a tumor without losing a drop of blood, patch a tattered retina in your eye, and fight a guerilla enemy, what *one* device would you choose?

*Answer:* The laser, a precocious scientific upstart celebrating its tenth birthday in 1968.

The laser, meaning "*l*ight *a*mplification by *s*timulated *e*mission of *r*adiation," is a way of harnessing the vast energies of light. The device was first described in 1958 by Nobel Prize winners Dr. Charles H. Townes and Dr. Arthur L. Schawlow, then of Bell Laboratories. In 1960 the first working laser was built by Dr. Theodore H. Maiman (then at Hughes Aircraft) around a man-made ruby crystal. Immediately, hundreds of uses were proposed for the device, and many U.S. companies were eager to jump on the "laser bandwagon." Applications, however, came more slowly than many hoped. It became a standing joke to refer to the laser as "a solution in search of a problem."

Today, all this has changed. "In the laser field," according to co-discoverer Townes, "we have begun to catch up with our dreams." Laser light is now produced not just by ruby crystals but by a host of other solid materials, as well as by gases, liquids, and semi-conductors. And lasers are finding a seeming endless array of applications.

What is a laser? Essentially, it is nothing but everyday light—specially treated light, to be sure, but light just the same. Ordinary light, from a flashlight or household bulb, spreads in all directions in an uncoordinated maze of random waves and frequencies. The fact that light does travel in waves makes the laser possible.

Working in much the same way as commercial neon display signs, lasing materials such as Maiman's ruby crystal are made to give off light by a powerful electric field. The laser components magnify the energy of this light by passing it

back and forth between silvered mirrors—millions of times in a few thousandths of a second. Furthermore, the light waves have become all the same size, or wavelength, and so instead of dispersing in all directions they stay in a narrow beam. Each time this narrow beam is reflected back through the lasing material it joins forces with a new beam. Surging upward in intensity, the waves remain in perfect step like an ever-growing column of soldiers. When this tamed energy is released, it shoots out in a perfectly straight, needle-thin line, neither wandering nor thickening more than a fraction of an inch over distances of many miles.

A tiny laser "spotlight" can detect fingerprints or remove a birthmark or tattoo. Totally unleashed, it can pierce through solid rock, burn plate metal, and light up the moon or the ocean depths. But such awesome energy can also burn out a careless operator's eye or serve as a swift and silent death ray.

The unwavering accuracy of laser beams has created a revolution in many industries that depend upon precise measurements and alignments. In 1966, lasers were used to drill hairline holes in diamond dies, marking the laser's first application to mass-production techniques. Since then, laser beams have been used to align the paths of both bridges and tunnels; to maintain the critical microscopic tolerances required for space-age components; and to weld not only fine electronic wires but even detached retinas in the human eye. Also, lasers may soon be contributing to air safety. The U.S. Weather Bureau believes that lasers might replace radar as the best means of checking on cloud height, air turbulence, and other atmospheric conditions. Installed at major airfields, "laser ceilometers" would determine cloud structures down to an altitude of 50 feet—all along the approach path of an incoming airliner.

Depending on the lasing material, energy from any portion of the electromagnetic spectrum (not just visible light) can be produced. When they are designed to produce infrared or ultraviolet light, lasers may be used to illuminate, to heat, and even to kill living tissue, whether healthy or diseased. Ultraviolet lasers have removed tumors, creating the completely new field of bloodless laser surgery.

Infrared lasers are now being evaluated in Vietnam in a variety of military applications including nighttime vision and tracking; and laser range-finding units are serving on helicopters, tanks, jeeps, and even on the backs of footsoldiers. Indeed, the U.S. military has emerged as the greatest buyer of laser hardware.

The second largest buyer is probably the communications industry. Voice communication by laser was first attempted in the Gemini space program. Today, variable pulsing of a single laser beam can carry more than 100,000,000 telephone messages—simultaneously. Some manufacturers predict that by 1970 lasers will be a billion-dollar industry—a long way from the scientific toy dreamed up by Townes and Schawlow a mere ten years ago.

A laser device developed by Lockheed Electronics Co. projects light beams in any of ten colors.

Lockheed Electronics

## THEORIES OF RELATIVITY

The theories of special relativity and general relativity, both created by Albert Einstein (1879–1955), deal with the application of the laws of nature to moving things. The distinction between the theories lies in the kinds of moving things they deal with.

The special theory concerns objects and observers that move with uniform speed in straight lines and have no motion with respect to each other. Such movements are called inertial motions. A person traveling in an inertial system of uniformly moving things makes all observations with respect to that inertial frame of reference. He cannot detect the motion of his system, since he is moving along with it at the same velocity. Einstein showed what changes would have to be made if the laws of physics were to appear the same in all inertial systems.

Isaac Newton had shown that mechanical laws apply equally to all elements of an inertial system. Einstein showed that if the laws of electromagnetism were to be the same in all inertial systems, the speed of light must be invariant. That is, if one group of persons measures the velocity of light in a particular inertial system, all other observers who are in uniform motion with respect to the first group will obtain the same value for the speed of light.

While this concept may not seem important, it has had important consequences in the formulation of the foundations of modern physics. Some of the consequences of special relativity theory seem, at first, to defy reason. For example, consider two observers, one on the Earth and one moving by him at great speed. Each has a kilogram weight, a yardstick, and a clock. Each, if he attempts to measure the weight, length, and speed of the other's standards, will find that the weight seems greater, the clock slower, and the yardstick shorter. As the speed nears the speed of light, the mass apparently approaches infinity, the clock seems to stop, the yardstick to have no length. We say "apparently" because each observer detects these changes in the other's standards, but sees no variation in his own. Thus we may not say that "Time slows down as you approach the speed of light" but that the measurement of time in moving systems becomes complicated.

Nor are those consequences of special relativity merely curiosities of the nature of atoms and galaxies, in whose realms the Einstein theory applies more than it does in that of the physical world whose proportions humans are most familiar with. The phenomenon of time dilation, for instance, has been observed in experiments with atom smashers, as has the phenomenon of growing mass with increasing velocity.

One consequence of the principle that the mass of an object varies with its speed has been a growing understanding of why the Sun and other stars burn and the knowledge to make nuclear reactors and weapons. Observation of the effects of motion on mass, which special relativity predicted, led to the famous Einstein equation, $E = mc^2$, where E is energy, m is mass, and c is the velocity of light.

The theory of general relativity has not had as much of an impact on human life as the theory of special relativity has had, for its consequences are more applicable to astronomy and cosmology. General relativity applies not just to inertial systems but to non-inertial ones as well, and holds that the laws of nature apply equally to both inertial and non-inertial observers.

This theory has had its greatest impact on understanding gravitation. What Einstein did was to show that a non-inertial observer—that is, one that is undergoing acceleration of some sort, such as spinning—cannot distinguish between the effects of his acceleration and those of gravity. This led Einstein to conclude that inertial forces come from gravitation, a concept known as the principle of equivalence.

Einstein's theory predicts that light will be bent by gravity. Thus the results of any measurements carried out over long distances will be affected by the gravitational field in space. Thus the measurements will indicate a "bent space," or a "non-Euclidian" geometry.

Einstein was able to make predictions concerning physical phenomena that his general relativity theory accounted for but Newtonian physics did not. For example, Einstein predicted that starlight would be deflected by the Sun's gravitational field as it passed by on its way to Earth. He also predicted that the frequency of vibration of light would be affected by gravity. Both of these predictions have been largely confirmed, although experiments are still in progress to substantiate them completely. Moreover, Einstein's general relativity theory accounted for the observation that the point of Mercury's orbit nearest the Sun moved eastward faster than Newton's theory had predicted.

Finally, latest observations of the universe make it appear likely that further support for the general relativity theory will come from confirmation of the curvature of space, which the theory predicted, and from the victory of the relativistic "Big Bang" theory of the instantaneous creation of the universe over the non-relativistic, so-called Steady State theory of continuous creation.

The last years of Einstein's life were spent in an exciting attempt to develop relativity into a unified field theory. Matter is affected by, or "interacts" according to, many kinds of fields. The unified field theory was an attempt to derive the properties of both the gravitational and electromagnetic fields from the same starting point; i.e., a unified field theory would not postulate two separate sets of field equations, one for gravity and one for electricity, but would exhibit them both as aspects of one field. Such a theory would also have to predict the ratios of mass to charge for the fundamental particles.

The attempt was never successful. Indeed, it could not have been, for during Einstein's lifetime two additional equally disconnected nuclear interactions, and some thirty more fundamental particles, were discovered. Thus a unified field theory, while still the goal of fundamental physics, remains a very distant goal today.

# SCIENCE HISTORY

## THE CHEMICAL ELEMENTS

| SYMBOL, NAME, AND ATOMIC NUMBER | | ATOMIC WEIGHT | DISCOVERY |
|---|---|---|---|
| H | Hydrogen | 1 | 1.008 | 1766 H. Cavendish, Great Britain |
| He | Helium | 2 | 4.003 | 1868 In the sun. P. Janssen, France; J. N. Lockyer, Great Britain |
| | | | | 1895 On earth. W. Ramsay, Great Britain |
| Li | Lithium | 3 | 6.940 | 1817 J. A. Arfvedson, Sweden |
| Be | Beryllium | 4 | 9.013 | 1798 L. N. Vauquelin, France |
| B | Boron | 5 | 10.82 | 1808 J. L. Gay-Lussac & L. J. Thenard, France; H. Davy, Great Britain |
| C | Carbon | 6 | 12.011 | — Ancient |
| N | Nitrogen | 7 | 14.008 | 1772 D. Rutherford, Great Britain |
| O | Oxygen | 8 | 16.000 | 1774 J. Priestly, Great Britain; K. W. Scheele, Sweden |
| F | Fluorine | 9 | 19.00 | 1886 H. Moissan, France |
| Ne | Neon | 10 | 20.183 | 1898 W. Ramsay, M. W. Travers, Great Britain |
| Na | Sodium | 11 | 22.991 | 1807 H. Davy, Great Britain |
| Mg | Magnesium | 12 | 24.32 | 1808 H. Davy, Great Britain |
| Al | Aluminum | 13 | 26.98 | 1827 F. Wohler, Germany |
| Si | Silicon | 14 | 28.09 | 1823 J. J. Berzelius, Sweden |
| P | Phosphorus | 15 | 30.975 | 1669 H. Brand, Germany |
| S | Sulfur | 16 | 32.006 | — Ancient |
| Cl | Chlorine | 17 | 35.457 | 1774 K. W. Scheele, Sweden |
| A | Argon | 18 | 39.944 | 1894 W. Ramsay, J. Rayleigh, Great Britain |
| K | Potassium | 19 | 39.100 | 1807 H. Davy, Great Britain |
| Ca | Calcium | 20 | 40.08 | 1808 H. Davy, Great Britain |
| Sc | Scandium | 21 | 44.96 | 1879 L. F. Nilson, Sweden |
| Ti | Titanium | 22 | 47.90 | 1791 W. Gregor, Great Britain |
| V | Vanadium | 23 | 50.95 | 1830 N. G. Sefström, Sweden |
| Cr | Chromium | 24 | 52.01 | 1797 L. N. Vauquelin, France |
| Mn | Manganese | 25 | 54.94 | 1774 K. W. Scheele & J. G. Gahn, Sweden |
| Fe | Iron | 26 | 55.85 | — Ancient |
| Co | Cobalt | 27 | 58.94 | 1735 G. Brandt, Sweden |
| Ni | Nickel | 28 | 58.71 | 1751 A. F. Cronstedt, Sweden |
| Cu | Copper | 29 | 63.54 | — Ancient |
| Zn | Zinc | 30 | 65.38 | — Medieval |
| Ga | Gallium | 31 | 69.72 | 1875 P. de Boisbaudran, France |
| Ge | Germanium | 32 | 72.60 | 1886 C. A. Winkler, Germany |
| As | Arsenic | 33 | 74.92 | — Medieval |
| Se | Selenium | 34 | 78.96 | 1818 J. J. Berzelius, Sweden |
| Br | Bromine | 35 | 79.916 | 1826 A. J. Balard, France |
| Kr | Krypton | 36 | 83.80 | 1898 W. Ramsay, M. W. Travers, Great Britain |
| Rb | Rubidium | 37 | 85.48 | 1861 R. W. Bunsen, G. R. Kirchoff, Germany |
| Sr | Strontium | 38 | 87.63 | 1808 H. Davy, Great Britain |
| Y | Yttrium | 39 | 88.91 | 1794 J. Gadolin, Finland |
| Zr | Zirconium | 40 | 91.22 | 1789 M. H. Klaproth, Germany |
| Nb | Niobium | 41 | 92.91 | 1801 C. Hatchett, Great Britain |
| Mo | Molybdenum | 42 | 95.95 | 1778 K. W. Scheele, Sweden |
| Tc | Technetium | 43 | 99* | 1937 E. Segre, C. Perrier, Italy |
| Ru | Ruthenium | 44 | 101.1 | 1844 K. Klaus, Estonia |
| Rh | Rhodium | 45 | 102.91 | 1803 W. H. Wollaston, Great Britain |
| Pd | Palladium | 46 | 106.4 | 1803 W. H. Wollaston, Great Britain |
| Ag | Silver | 47 | 107.880 | — Ancient |
| Cd | Cadmium | 48 | 112.41 | 1817 F. Stromeyer, Germany |
| In | Indium | 49 | 114.82 | 1863 F. Reich, H. T. Richter, Germany |
| Sn | Tin | 50 | 118.70 | — Ancient |
| Sb | Antimony | 51 | 121.76 | — Ancient |
| Te | Tellurium | 52 | 127.61 | 1782 F. J. M. von Reichenstein, Austria |
| I | Iodine | 53 | 126.91 | 1811 B. Courtois, France |
| Xe | Xenon | 54 | 131.30 | 1898 W. Ramsay, M. W. Travers, Great Britain |
| Cs | Cesium | 55 | 132.91 | 1860 R. Bunsen, G. R. Kirchoff, Germany |
| Ba | Barium | 56 | 137.36 | 1808 H. Davy, Great Britain |
| La | Lanthanum | 57 | 138.92 | 1839 C. G. Mosander, Sweden |
| Ce | Cerium | 58 | 140.13 | 1803 J. J. Berzelius, W. Hinsinger, Sweden, M. H. Klaproth, Germany |
| Pr | Praseodymium | 59 | 140.91 | 1885 C. A. von Welsbach, Austria |
| Nd | Neodymium | 60 | 144.27 | 1885 C. A. von Welsbach, Austria |
| Pm | Promethium | 61 | 147* | 1947 J. A. Marinsky, L. E. Glendenin, C. D. Coryell, U.S. |
| Sm | Samarium | 62 | 150.35 | 1879 P. de Boisbaudran, France |
| Eu | Europium | 63 | 152.0 | 1896 E. A. Damarçay, France |
| Gd | Gadolinium | 64 | 157.26 | 1880 J. C. de Marignac, Switzerland |
| Tb | Terbium | 65 | 158.93 | 1843 C. G. Mosander, Sweden |

| SYMBOL, NAME, AND ATOMIC NUMBER | | | ATOMIC WEIGHT | DISCOVERY | |
|---|---|---|---|---|---|
| Dy | Dysprosium | 66 | 162.51 | 1886 | P. de Boisbaudran, France |
| Ho | Holmium | 67 | 164.94 | 1879 | P. T. Cleve, Sweden |
| Er | Erbium | 68 | 167.27 | 1843 | C. G. Mosander, Sweden |
| Tm | Thulium | 69 | 168.94 | 1879 | P. T. Cleve, Sweden |
| Yb | Ytterbium | 70 | 173.04 | 1878 | J. de Marignac, Switzerland |
| Lu | Lutetium | 71 | 174.99 | 1906 | G. Urbain, France |
| Hf | Hafnium | 72 | 178.50 | 1923 | G. von Hevesy, Sweden; D. Coster, Netherlands |
| Ta | Tantalum | 73 | 180.95 | 1802 | A. G. Ekeberg, Sweden |
| W | Tungsten | 74 | 183.86 | 1783 | J. J. d'Elhuyar, F. D'Elhuyar, Spain |
| Re | Rhenium | 75 | 186.22 | 1925 | W. Noddack, I. E. Tacke, Germany |
| Os | Osmium | 76 | 190.2 | 1803 | S. Tennant, Great Britain |
| Ir | Iridium | 77 | 192.2 | 1803 | S. Tennant, Great Britain |
| Pt | Platinum | 78 | 195.09 | 1735 | A. De Ulloa, Spain |
| Au | Gold | 79 | 197.0 | — | Ancient |
| Hg | Mercury | 80 | 200.61 | — | Ancient |
| Tl | Thallium | 81 | 204.39 | 1861 | W. Crookes, Great Britain |
| Pb | Lead | 82 | 207.21 | — | Ancient |
| Bi | Bismuth | 83 | 208.99 | — | Medieval |
| Po | Polonium | 84 | 210 | 1898 | M. Curie, P. Curie, France |
| At | Astatine | 85 | 210* | 1940 | E. G. Segre, D. R. Corson, K. R. MacKenzie, U.S. |
| Rn | Radon | 86 | 222 | 1900 | F. E. Dorn, Germany |
| Fr | Francium | 87 | 223* | 1939 | M. Perey, France |
| Ra | Radium | 88 | 226.05 | 1892 | M. Curie, P. Curie, France |
| Ac | Actinium | 89 | 227.0 | 1899 | A. L. Debierne, France |
| Th | Thorium | 90 | 232.05 | 1828 | J. J. Berzelius, Sweden |
| Pa | Protactinium | 91 | 231 | 1913 | J. Cranston, F. Soddy, Great Britain |
| U | Uranium | 92 | 238.07 | 1789 | M. H. Klaproth, Germany |
| Np | Neptunium | 93 | 237* | 1940 | E. McMillan, P. Abelson, U.S. |
| Pu | Plutonium | 94 | 242* | 1940 | G. T. Seaborg, E. M. McMillan, A. C. Wahl, J. W. Kennedy, U.S. |
| Am | Americium | 95 | 243* | 1944 | G. T. Seaborg, R. A. James, L. O. Morgan, A. Chiorso, U.S. |
| Cm | Curium | 96 | 247* | 1944 | G. T. Seaborg, R. A. James, A. Ghiorso, U.S. |
| Bk | Berkelium | 97 | 249* | 1949 | S. G. Thompson, A. Ghiorso, G. T. Seaborg, U.S. |
| Cf | Californium | 98 | 251* | 1950 | S. G. Thompson, K. Street, A. Ghiorso, G. T. Seaborg, U.S. |
| E | Einsteinium | 99 | 254* | 1952 | A. Ghiorso et al., U.S. |
| Fm | Fermium | 100 | 253* | 1953 | A. Ghiorso et al., U.S. |
| Mv | Mendelevium | 101 | 258* | 1955 | A. Ghiorso, B. Harvey, G. Choppin, S. G. Thompson, G. T. Seaborg, U.S. |
| No | Nobelium | 102 | 253* | 1957 | International team of British, Swedish, U.S. physicists |
| Lw | Lawrencium | 103 | 257* | 1958 | A. Ghiorso, A. E. Larsh, R. M. Latimer, T. Sikkeland, U.S. |
| | Kurchatovium(?) | 104 | | 1965? | G. N. Flerov et al., Russia (claim disputed) |

* Most stable isotope

## THE HUMAN ELEMENTS

Consider the human body as a collection of chemical elements—and you are in for some surprises. The element titanium, for example, is used in the "skins" of spacecraft and supersonic jets because of the metal's ability to withstand tremendous temperature extremes. But titanium in our bodies? Yes. Biochemists believe titanium occurs in every cell of our bodies—perhaps only a few atoms of it, but it is there nevertheless. Arsenic, long dreaded as a poison, is also present throughout our bodies. This is a case of a little being quite enough, for too much arsenic is as deadly as it ever was.

Aluminum, calcium, carbon, chlorine, chromium, cobalt, copper, hydrogen, iodine, iron, manganese, molybdenum, nickel, nitrogen, oxygen, phosphorus, selenium, zinc, and many more—the list of "human elements" includes members of every family of elements except those made in atom smashers.

What are these elements doing in our bodies? Who needs them? Part of the answer is that all cells need a watery environment in order to live, function, and reproduce. Water, of course, is $H_2O$—two atoms of hydrogen bound to one atom of oxygen. Roughly 70 per cent of our body weight is water. If we include the hydrogen and oxygen not found as water, this means (since the element oxygen is some 16 times heavier than the element hydrogen) that approximately 65 per cent of our body weight is oxygen and 10 per cent is hydrogen. Oxygen, hydrogen, and carbon (18 per cent by weight) are the three most abundant elements in our bodies. Others include nitrogen (3 per cent), calcium (1.5 per cent), and phosphorus (1 per cent).

But cells require not just plain water, but salty water. This is where a host of other chemical elements come in, as mineral salts dissolved in the blood and passed on to the cells. Salts of iron supply hemoglobin for rich blood. Calcium salts are necessary for good teeth and bones. Manganese salts seem to play a part in bone development. In chickens, copper salts are necessary for the development of healthy hearts; the same may be true for human beings. How do we get such elements as copper, manganese, titanium, or zinc? Rest assured—a well-balanced diet contains all the elements you need.

Albert Einstein (1879-1955)

## GREAT MEN OF SCIENCE AND MATHEMATICS

**Archimedes,** 287–212 B.C., Greek mathematician and physicist: father of scientific mechanics.

**Aristotle,** 384–322 B.C., Greek philosopher: father of objective science.

**Svante August Arrhenius,** 1859–1927, Swedish chemist: originated the theory of chemical ionization.

**Roger Bacon,** 1214–94(?), English philosopher and scientist: pioneered in controlled experiments and accurate observation of phenomena.

**Jöns Jakob Berzelius,** 1779–1848, Swedish chemist: compiled a table of chemical elements arranged by atomic weights and discovered several new elements.

**Niels Henrik David Bohr,** 1885–1962, Danish physicist: furthered the study of nuclear physics.

**Robert Boyle,** 1627–91, Anglo-Irish chemist: first to distinguish between chemical compounds and elements, defined nature of chemical reactions.

**Louis Victor de Broglie,** 1892–, French physicist: inventor of wave mechanics.

**Stanislao Cannizzaro,** 1826–1910, Italian chemist: furthered the classification of elements.

**Georg Cantor,** 1845–1918, German mathematician: developed the set theory, basis of the new mathematics.

**Henry Cavendish,** 1731–1810, English physicist and chemist: discovered hydrogen.

**Nicholas Copernicus,** 1473–1543, Polish astronomer: described the Sun as the center of a great system with the Earth revolving about it, the foundation for modern astronomy.

**Francis H. C. Crick,** 1916–, British scientist: furthered knowledge of heredity and the function of DNA.

**Pierre Curie,** 1859–1906, and **Marie Slodowska Curie,** 1867–1934, French chemists and physicists: pioneered in the study of radioactivity, discovered radium.

**Georges L. F. C. D. Cuvier,** 1769–1832, French naturalist: pioneered in comparative anatomy and paleontology.

**John Dalton,** 1766–1844, English scientist: formulated concept of atomic weights of chemical elements.

**Charles Robert Darwin,** 1809–82, English naturalist: propounded the classic theory of human evolution.

**Sir Humphry Davy,** 1778–1829, English chemist and physicist: pioneered in electrochemistry, the study of electricity generated by chemical change.

**René Descartes,** 1596–1650, French philosopher, mathematician, and scientist: proponent of scientific proof and method; developed analytical geometry.

**Theodosius Dobzhansky,** 1900–, American geneticist: advanced the basic knowledge of genetics and human evolution.

**Albert Einstein,** 1879–1955, German-American physicist: changed the conception of the physical world with his theories of relativity.

**Euclid,** 4th century B.C., Greek mathematician: founder of geometry.

**Michael Faraday,** 1791–1867, English scientist: built the first dynamo, based on the principle of electromagnetic inductance.

**Pierre de Fermat,** 1601–51, French mathematician: introduced theory of mathematical probability.

**Enrico Fermi,** 1901–54, Italian-American physicist: achieved the first atomic chain reaction; helped develop the atomic and hydrogen bombs.

**Leonardo Fibonacci,** 12th–13th century A.D., Italian mathematician: introduced Arabic numbers into Europe.

**Emil Fischer,** 1852–1919, German chemist: advanced the field of organic chemistry.

**Benjamin Franklin,** 1706–90, American statesman and scientist: proved that lightning is a discharge of electricity.

**Galileo Galilei,** 1564–1642, Italian physicist, astronomer, and mathematician: discovered many principles of motion, and increased understanding of celestial phenomena.

**Joseph Louis Gay-Lussac,** 1778–1850, French chemist and physicist: performed fundamental experiments on gases.

**Josiah Willard Gibbs,** 1839–1903, American mathematician and physicist: founder of physical chemistry and thermodynamics.

**Donald Arthur Glaser,** 1926–, American physicist: advanced the study of subatomic physics.

**Robert Hutchings Goddard,** 1882–1945, American physicist: laid the groundwork for modern rocketry.

**Werner Heisenberg,** 1901–, German physicist: founder of the study of subatomic particles.

**Hermann L. F. von Helmholtz,** 1821–94, German scientist: formulated law of the conservation of energy.

**Heinrich Rudolf Hertz,** 1857–94, German physicist: discovered radio waves.

**Jacobus Hendricus van't Hoff,** 1852–1911, Dutch physical chemist: pioneered in stereochemistry, the study of internal molecular structure.

**James Hutton,** 1726–97, Scottish geologist; founded modern geology.

**Thomas Henry Huxley,** 1825–95, English biologist: helped propagate Charles Darwin's theory of evolution.

**James Prescott Joule,** 1818–89, English physicist: determined the relationship between heat and mechanical energy.

**Theodor von Karman,** 1881–1963, Hungarian-American scientist: developed theories of aerodynamics.

**William Thomson Kelvin,** 1824–1907, British mathematician and chemist: formulated an absolute scale of temperature.

**Gustav Robert Kirchhoff,** 1824–87, German physicist: founder of spectroscopy, the analysis of elements by studying their color scale.

**Jean B. P. A. de Monet de Lamarck,** 1744–1829, French naturalist: proposed a theory of evolution based on acquired characteristics.

**Johann Heinrich Lambert,** 1728–77, German-French scientist and mathematician: helped develop trigonometry.

**Lev Davidovich Landau,** 1908–, Russian physicist: pioneered in low-temperature physics and the mathematical theory of gases.

**Antoine Laurent Lavoisier,** 1743–94, French chemist and physicist: founder of modern chemistry.

**Ernest Orlando Lawrence,** 1901–58, American physicist: invented the cyclotron, or atom smasher.

**Tsung-Dao Lee,** 1926–, Chinese-American physicist: contributed to the study of astrophysics.

**Gottfried Wilhelm von Leibniz,** 1646–1716, German philosopher and mathematician: developed calculus (independently of Newton).

**Carolus Linnaeus,** 1707–78, Swedish botanist: first to classify plants, founder of modern botany.

**Nikolai Ivanovich Lobachevsky,** 1793–1856, Russian mathematician: pioneered in non-Euclidean geometry.

**Hendrick Antoon Lorentz,** 1853–1928, Dutch physicist: postulated the existence of electrons.

**James Clerk Maxwell,** 1831–79, Scottish physicist: developed kinetic theory of gases.

**Gregor Johann Mendel,** 1822–84, Austrian monk: developed theory of heredity and founded the science of genetics.

**Dmitri Ivanovich Mendelejeff,** 1834–1907, Russian chemist: formulated periodic law of chemical elements.

**Albert Abraham Michelson,** 1852–1931, American physicist: first to measure accurately the speed of light.

**Henry Gwyn Jeffreys Moseley,** 1887–1915, English physicist: advanced the knowledge of chemical elements.

**Sir Isaac Newton,** 1642–1727, English physicist and mathematician: formulated the fundamental laws of gravity and motion; developed calculus (independently of Leibniz).

**Hans Christian Oersted,** 1777–1851, Danish physicist: established relationship between electricity and magnetism.

**J. Robert Oppenheimer,** 1904–, American physicist: directed the development of the first atomic bomb.

**Wilhelm Ostwald,** 1853–1932, German physical chemist: investigated catalysis and the rates of chemical reaction.

**Linus Carl Pauling,** 1901–, American chemist: studied the structure of molecules.

**Max Planck,** 1858–1947, German physicist: first modern physicist, formulated the quantum theory of energy.

Sir Isaac Newton (1642-1727)

Granger Collection

**Joseph Priestley,** 1733–1804, English theologian and scientist: discovered oxygen.

**Pythagoras,** 6th century B.C., Greek philosopher: earliest of the mathematicians.

**Isidor Isaac Rabi,** 1898–, American physicist: furthered the study of nuclear physics.

**Wilhelm Conrad Roentgen,** 1843–1923, German physicist: discovered X rays.

**Bertrand Arthur William Russell,** 1872–, English mathematician and philosopher: co-author of *Principia Mathematica.*

**Ernest Rutherford,** 1871–1937, British physicist: built the first nuclear reactor.

**Karl Wilhelm Scheele,** 1742–86, Swedish chemist: discovered several new chemical elements.

**Theodor Schwann,** 1810–82, German physiologist and histologist: discovered that cells are the fundamental physiological unit of plant and animal life.

**Thales,** 6th century B.C., Greek philosopher: pioneered the scientific method of observation.

**Joseph John Thomson,** 1856–1940, English physicist: discovered the electron and founded subatomic physics.

**Charles Hard Townes,** 1915–, American physicist: developed the laser-maser principle.

**Alessandro Volta,** 1745–1827, Italian physicist: began modern study of electricity.

**James Dewey Watson,** 1928–, American biologist: studied the nature and function of DNA.

**Alfred North Whitehead,** 1861–1947, English mathematician and philosopher: co-author of *Principia Mathematica,* a landmark in symbolic logic.

**Norbert Wiener,** 1894–1964, American mathematician: devised mathematical theory of cybernetics, which led to electronic automation.

**Maurice H. F. Wilkins,** 1916–, Irish biophysicist: first to explain the structure of deoxyribonucleic acid (DNA), of supreme importance in the study of genetics.

**Friedrich Wöhler,** 1800–82, German chemist: first to synthesize organic compounds from inorganic material.

# PATENTS AND INVENTIONS

## THE PATENT SYSTEM

A patent is issued by the U.S. Government's Patent Office to inventors, or their heirs or persons designated by the inventors, giving them exclusive rights to exclude others from making, using, or selling the invention in the United States. Patents are valid for 17 years and may not be renewed. According to law, patents may be granted for "any new and useful process, machine, manufacture, or composition of matter, or any new and useful improvement thereof." This includes virtually everything made or processed by man, but there are two specific exclusions: inventions "useful solely in the utilization of special nuclear material or atomic energy for atomic weapons," and so-called perpetual motion machines. Ideas, suggestions, methods of doing business, and machines that do not operate may not be patented.

Inventions must meet the test of newness before being patented. Processes of inventions that were in use, or known, either in the United States or in a foreign country before the applicant invented his machine are not granted patents. Also excluded are inventions that have been described in print or are in public use or for sale in the United States more than a year before the date of patent application. When two or more applications for identical inventions are received, or when an applicant claims an invention for which a patent has been issued, the Patent Office begins proceedings to determine who has the prior rights.

Application for a patent must be made by the inventor himself. If two or more persons collaborated in the invention, all must apply. If the inventor is dead or mentally ill, his guardian or his estate may apply for the patent. Applicants must submit to the Commissioner of Patents a petition and specifications for the invention and a $65 fee plus $1 for each specification over 20. The specifications must include a description of the process of making and using the invention.

After a patent examiner studies the application, he either grants the patent—in which case the applicant must pay a $100 fee plus $1 for each specification over 20—or he rejects the claim. The inventor may then amend the petition and submit it again within six months. If the patent is still denied, the inventor may appeal to the Board of Appeals in the Patent Office and, subsequently, to the Court of Customs and Patent Appeals, or he may bring civil action against the Commissioner of Patents in the U.S. District Court for the District of Columbia.

A patent is a negative right. It does not necessarily give the inventor the right to manufacture his invention; thus a patented invention may not be manufactured, sold, or used if it violates any Federal or local law. Owners of patents may license others to manufacture the invention. Basically, a patent is a guarantee that the inventor will have the right to any

financial gain that is derived in any manner from his invention.

Anyone who manufactures, sells, or uses a patented invention without permission of the patent owner has violated the law. Patent infringement suits are heard in Federal courts and may be heard eventually by the U.S. Supreme Court. Since a patent is personal property, it may be sold, transferred, or bequeathed, either in its entirety or in part, and it may also be mortgaged.

Patented articles must be marked with the word "Patent" and the patent number in order to be protected. The phrases "Patent Applied For" and "Patent Pending" mean only that an application has been made for a patent, and they have no legal effect but to establish priority. So-called patent medicines are in fact not patented.

Patents may also be granted to industrial designs. These patents protect only the appearance of an article. They are valid for 3½ years for a fee of $10, 7 years for $15, or 14 years for $30, at the option of the applicant. Also covered by patents, for 17 years, are distinct and new varieties of plants that have been created or discovered.

Forty-four countries have signed an agreement specifying that they will give to citizens of other countries the same rights regarding patents that their own citizens have.

The Commissioner of Patents may order an invention held secret if publication would harm the national security or defense.

Copies of patent laws, the rules of practice in the Patent Office in patent cases, and general information may be obtained from the Superintendent of Documents, Government Printing Office, Washington, D.C.

The right to grant patents is derived from Article I, Section 8 of the Constitution. At first, the patent functions were administered by the Department of State. In 1802, the Patent Office was organized as a separate Federal bureau and the Superintendent of Patents was appointed. The patent law was revised in 1836 and the chief official was called the Commissioner of Patents; the title is still used.

In 1892, the Patent Office was transferred from the Department of State to the Department of the Interior, and in 1925 to the Department of Commerce, under whose jurisdiction it is today. Although the first patent was issued in 1790, the Patent Office did not start numbering patents until 1836. Patent No. 1 was issued to Senator John Ruggles of Maine on July 13, 1836.

In 1965, the Patent Office marked the 175th anniversary of the first patent law, signed by President George Washington on April 10, 1790. The office had issued 3,295,142 patents as of 1966, and continues to grant about 1,000 patents a week.

# CHRONOLOGY OF GREAT INVENTIONS

The origins of many great inventions are shrouded in the far distant past. The inventors of writing and of the wheel and the first fire-maker will forever remain anonymous. And subsequent development of innovations such as the clock, the windmill, the cannon, and the concrete arch must properly be attributed to civilizations, rather than to individuals. Inventions, which advance man's material and technological welfare, are often the product of many people, from many places. Here follows an abbreviated list of some major inventions:

**Navigational astrolabe**
2nd century B.C.: Hipparchus (Greece)
**Lever**
3rd century B.C.: Archimedes
   (Greece)
**Abacus**
1st century A.D.: Indians
**Concrete arch**
2nd century A.D.: Romans
**Aqueduct-fed reservoirs**
2nd century A.D.: Romans
**Four-wheeled carriage**
3rd century A.D.: Romans
**Hydraulic power station**
3rd century A.D.: Romans
**Saddle stirrups**
6th century A.D.: Avars
**Windmill**
7th century A.D.: Persians
**Porcelain**
8th century A.D.: Chinese
**Mechanical clock**
8th century A.D.: Chinese
**Mariner's compass**
9th century A.D.: Arabs
**Gunpowder**
9th century A.D.: Chinese
**Iron horseshoe**
10th century A.D.: Europeans
**Ship rudder**
12th century A.D.: Normans
**Cannon**
1320 (?): Germans
**Movable-type printing press**
1455: Johann Gutenberg (Germany)
**Anti-friction roller bearings**
1496 (?): Leonardo da Vinci (Italy)
**Railed car**
1550: Germans
**Compound microscope**
1590: Hans and Zacharias Janssen
   (Netherlands)
**Thermometer**
1593: Galileo Galilei (Italy)
**Simple telescope**
1608: Hans Lippershey (Netherlands)
**Refracting telescope**
1609: Galileo Galilei (Italy)
**Micrometer**
1636: William Gascoigne (Great Britain)
**Simple adding machine**
1642: Blaise Pascal (France)
**Barometer**
1643: Evangelista Torricelli (Italy)
**Air pump**
1650: Otto von Guericke (Germany)
**Pendulum clock**
1657: Christian Huygens
   (Netherlands)
**Simple pressure cooker**
1675: Denis Papin (France)
**Simple electric generator**
1681: Otto von Guericke (Germany)
**Piston steam engine**
1712: Thomas Newcomen (Great Britain)

**Improved thermometer**
1714: Gabriel D. Fahrenheit (Germany)
**Chronometer**
1735: John Harrison (Great Britain)
**Lightning conductor**
1752: Benjamin Franklin (United States)
**Spinning jenny**
1764: James Hargreaves (Great Britain)
**Condenser steam engine**
1769: James Watt (Scotland)
**Spinning frame**
1769: Sir Richard Arkwright
   (Great Britain)
**Steam-driven car**
1769: Nicolas Cugnot (France)
**Steamship**
1775: J. C. Perier (France)
**Submarine**
1776: David Bushnell (United States);
   improved in 1900 by J. P. Holland and
   Simon Lake (United States)
**Spinning mule**
1779: Samuel Crompton (Great Britain)
**Bifocal lens**
1780: Benjamin Franklin (United States)
**Gas balloon**
1783: Jacques Montgolfier (France)
**Oil lamp**
1783: Pierre Argand (France)
**Power loom**
1785: Edmund Cartwright (Great Britain)
**Self-winding watch**
1791: Abraham-Louis Breguet (France),
   featured a rocker pedometer action
**Gas lighting**
1792: William Murdock (Scotland)
**Cotton gin**
1792: Eli Whitney (United States)
**Lithography**
1796: Aloys Senefelder (Bohemia)
**Parachute**
1797: André-Jacques Garnerin (France)
**Locomotive**
1804: Richard Trevithick (Great Britain)
**Torpedo**
1805: Robert Fulton (United States)
**Commercial steamship**
1807: Robert Fulton (United States)
**Food canning**
1809: Nicolas Appert (France)
**Miner's safety lamp**
1815: Humphry Davy (Great Britain)
**Dental plate**
1817: Anthony A. Planston
   (United States)
**Stethoscope**
1819: René Laennec (France)
**Waterproof rubber**
1819: Charles Macintosh (Scotland)
**Type-setting machine**
1822: William Church (United States)
**Electromagnet**
1824: William Sturgeon (Great Britain);
   improved in 1831 by Joseph Henry
   (United States)

**Cement**
1824: Joseph Aspdin (Great Britain)
**Photography on metal**
1826: J. Nicéphore Niepce (France)
**Friction match**
1827: John Walker (Great Britain)
**Braille printing**
1829: Louis Braille (France)
**Reaping machine**
1831: Cyrus McCormick (United States)
**Electrical telegraph**
1832: Samuel F. B. Morse (U. S.)
**Mechanical refrigeration**
1834: Jacob Perkins (United States)
**Photography on paper**
1835: William H. F. Talbot (Great Britain)
**Revolver**
1835: Samuel Colt (United States)
**Electroplating**
1836: Warren De La Rue (Great Britain)
**Screw propeller**
1836: John Stevens (Great Britain)
**Telegraph code**
1837: Samuel F. B. Morse (United
   States), with Alfred Vail (United States)
**Bicycle**
1839: Kirkpatrick MacMillan (Scotland)
**Daguerreotype**
1839: Louis J. M. Daguerre (France)
**Vulcanized rubber**
1841: Charles Goodyear (United States)
**Nitroglycerine**
1846: Ascanio Sobrero (Italy)
**Sewing machine**
1846: Elias Howe (United States)
**Rotary printing**
1846: Richard Hoe (United States)
**Rubber tires**
1847: Thomas Hancock (Great Britain)
**Safety pin**
1849: William Hunt (United States)
**Elevator**
1852: Elisha G. Otis (United States)
**Nonrigid airship**
1852: Henri Giffard (France)
**Glider**
1853: Sir George Cayley (Great Britain)
**Dynamo**
1854: Ernst Werner von Siemens
   (Germany)
**Bunsen burner**
1855: Robert W. von Bunsen (Germany)
**Safety match**
1855: J. E. Lundstrom (Sweden)
**Steel production**
1855: Henry Bessemer (Great Britain)
**Burglar alarm**
1858: Edwin T. Holmes (United States)
**Railway sleeping coach**
1859: George M. Pullman (United States)
**Oil well**
1859: Edwin L. Drake (United States)
**Repeating rifle**
1860: O. F. Winchester (United States)
   *(continued)*

**GREAT INVENTIONS** (*continued*)

**Linoleum**
1860: Frederick Walton (Great Britain)
**Cylinder lock**
1860: Linus Yale (United States)
**Celluloid**
1861: Alexander Parkes (Great Britain);
improved in 1873 by John W. Hyatt
(United States)
**Dynamite**
1862: Alfred B. Nobel (Sweden)
**Machine gun**
1862: Richard J. Gatling (United States)
**Margarine**
1863: Hippolyte Mège-Mouries (France)
**Commercial typewriter**
1868: Christopher Sholes
(United States)
**Railway car coupling**
1868: Eli H. Janney (United States)
**Westinghouse air brake**
1869: George Westinghouse
(United States)
**Barbed wire**
1873: Joseph F. Glidden (United States)
**Direct-current electric motor**
1873: Zénobe Gramme (Belgium)
**Carpet sweeper**
1876: Melville R. Bissell (United States)
**Microphone**
1876: Alexander G. Bell (United States)
**Carburetor**
1876: Gottlieb Daimler (Germany);
carburetor spray, 1893, Charles E.
Duryea (United States)
**Telephone**
1876: Alexander G. Bell (United States)
**Electric welder**
1877: Elisha Thompson (United States)
**Carbon filament lamp**
1878: Joseph W. Swan (United States)
**Phonograph**
1878: Thomas A. Edison (United States)
**Engraving (half-tone process)**
1878: Frederick E. Ives (United States)
**Cash register**
1879: James Ritty (United States)
**Electric lamp**
1879: Thomas A. Edison (United States)
**Arc lamp**
1879: C. F. Brush (United States)
**Evaporated milk**
1880: John B. Meyenberg (United States)
**Electric flatiron**
1882: H. W. Seeley (United States)
**Fountain pen**
1884: Lewis E. Waterman (United States)
**High-speed internal combustion
engine**
1885: Gottlieb Daimler (Germany)
**Motorcycle**
1885: Gottlieb Daimler (Germany)
**Commercial adding machine**
1885: William Burroughs (United States)
**Linotype machine**
1886: Ottmar Mergenthaler (Germany)
**Automobile**
1887: Gottlieb Daimler (Germany)
**Ballpoint pen**
1888: John J. Loud (United States)
**Alternating-current electric motor**
1888: Nikola Tesla (United States)
**Kodak camera**
1888: George Eastman (United States)

**Pneumatic hammer**
1890: Charles B. King (United States)
**Zipper**
1891: Whitcomb L. Judson
(United States)
**Color photography**
1891: Gabriel Lippmann (France)
**Farm tractor**
1892: John Froelich (United States)
**Addressograph**
1893: J. S Duncan (United States)
**Motion pictures**
1893: Thomas A. Edison (United States)
**Ship turbine**
1894: Charles Parsons (Great Britain)
**Wireless telegraphy**
1894: Guglielmo Marconi (Italy)
**Radio**
1895: Guglielmo Marconi (Italy)
**Pneumatic automobile tire**
1895: André Michelin (France)
**Diesel engine**
1895: Rudolf Diesel (Germany)
**X ray**
1895: Wilhelm Roentgen (Germany)
**Safety razor**
1895: King C. Gillette (United States)
**Cellophane**
1900: J. E. Brandenberger (Switzerland)
**Rigid airship**
1900: Graf Ferdinand von Zeppelin
(Germany)
**Caterpillar tractor**
1900: Benjamin Holt (United States)
**Radio telegraphy, transatlantic**
1901: Guglielmo Marconi (Italy)
**Airplane**
1903: Orville and Wilbur Wright (United
States)
**Radio tube diode**
1904: John A. Fleming (Great Britain)
**Electric washing machine**
1907: Hurley Machine Company (United
States)
**Outboard engine**
1909: Ole Evinrude (United States)
**Bakelite**
1909: Leo H. Baekeland (United States)
**Helicopter**
1909: Igor Sikorsky (United States)
**Rayon**
1910: American Viscose Company
(United States)
**Gyrocompass**
1911: Elmer A. Sperry (United States)
**Air conditioning**
1911: Willis H. Carrier (United States)
**Hydroplane**
1911: Glenn H. Curtiss (United States)
**Self-starter (internal
combustion engine)**
1911: Charles F. Kettering
(United States)
**Stainless steel**
1913: Harry Brearley (Great Britain)
**Geiger counter**
1913: Hans Geiger (Germany)
**Armored tank**
1914: Ernest Swinton (Great Britain)
**Tungsten filament**
1915: Irving Langmuir (United States)
**Neon lamp**
1915: Georges Claude (France)

**Motor scooter**
1919: Greville Bradshaw (Great Britain)
**Rockets**
1920s: Robert H. Goddard (United
States); Hermann Oberth (Germany);
Konstantin E. Tsiolkovsky (U.S.S.R.)
**Autogiro**
1920: Juan de la Cierva (Spain)
**Radar**
1922: Albert H. Taylor and Leo C. Young
(United States)
**Wind tunnel**
1923: Max M. Munk (United States)
**Talking film**
1926: Warner Bros. (United States)
**Television**
1926: John L. Baird (Scotland)
**Automatic pilot (airplane)**
1929: William Green (United States)
**Loudspeaker**
1930: Lee de Forest (United States)
**Electric razor**
1931: Jacob Schick (United States)
**Cyclotron**
1931: Ernest O. Lawrence (United States)
**Frequency modulation (FM)**
1933: Edwin H. Armstrong (United States)
**Technicolor**
1933: D. F. Comstock, H. T. Kalmus, and
W. B. Westcott (United States)
**Launderette**
1934: J. F. Cantrell (United States)
**Parking meter**
1935: Carlton C. Magee (United States)
**Jet engine**
1937: Frank Whittle (Great Britain)
**Nylon**
1937: Wallace H. Carothers (United States)
**Electronic computer**
1937: Howard Aiken (United States)
**Xerography**
1937: Chester Carlson (United States)
**Electron microscope**
1939: Vladimir K. Zworykin (United States)
**Atomic pile, self-sustaining nuclear
chain reaction**
1943: Enrico Fermi and staff (United States)
**Atomic bomb**
1945: International team of scientists
(United States)
**Monorail**
1946: Axel L. Wenner-Gren (Sweden)
**Long-playing record**
1948: Peter Goldmark (United States)
**Transistor**
1948: John Bardeen, William Shockley, and
Walter Brattain (United States)
**Polaroid Land camera**
1950s: Edwin Land (United States)
**Nuclear-powered submarine
(Nautilus)**
1955: U.S. government scientists
**Space flight (Sputnik)**
1957: U.S.S.R. scientists
**Nuclear-powered surface ship**
1959: U.S.S.R. scientists
**Nuclear-powered merchant ship
(Savannah)**
1959: U.S. scientists
**Laser-Maser**
1960: Charles H. Townes (United States)
**Commercial communications satellite**
1965: U.S. scientists

## A BIZARRE NEW WEAPON FOR VIETNAM

U.S. Army

Light enough to be carried on an infantryman's back, the Army's new "people sniffer" can detect humans up to 300 yards away. American patrols in Vietnam began carrying the devices in 1967.

An American soldier cannot always see the enemy in Vietnam, nor hear him, and he certainly doesn't want to get close enough to touch him. So how does he find the Vietcong before the Vietcong finds him? General Electric Company, working with the U. S. Army's Limited Warfare Laboratory, has come up with an answer: Smell him. The enemy-smelling device is known officially as the "Manpack Personnel Detector," and more commonly as the "people sniffer."

The infantry model of the sniffer is light enough to be carried by one soldier. It consists of an air sampler attached to the soldier's rifle barrel, which is connected by hose to a tank on the soldier's back; a pair of earphones connect to the tank. On patrol, the soldier points his rifle at a suspicious spot. If anybody is hiding there, the earphones emit a high-pitched beeping sound, alerting the soldier.

How does it work? The air sampler picks up chemical particles (such as ammonia) released into the air by human perspiration. The presence of such particles is detected in the chamber in the backpack, where they cause a fog. The fog, in turn, causes the earphones to chirp excitedly. If the wind is blowing toward the sniffer, it can detect persons up to 300 yards away. A larger, more advanced model is being used on helicopters.

What about peaceful uses of sniffers? Just as telescopes give men "super eyes," the sniffer principle could lead to a whole array of "super noses"—for example, a burglar alarm, or a fire alarm that would go off at the first whiff of smoke, or a device to sniff out small quantities of potentially dangerous air pollutants. These developments have led to a new branch of physical science—the science of smell, or *olfactronics*.

# UNITS AND STANDARDS

## WEIGHTS AND MEASURES
Source: National Bureau of Standards

The expression "weights and measures" is used here in its basic sense, referring to measurements such as length, mass, and capacity. It is essential to keep in mind the distinction between the terms "units" and "standards" of measurement. A **unit** is a value or quantity in terms of which other values and quantities are expressed. A unit is fixed by definition and is independent of such physical conditions as temperature. Examples are the yard, the pound, the gallon, the meter, the liter, and the gram. A **standard** is a physical embodiment of a unit. It is not independent of physical conditions, and it is a true embodiment of the unit only under specified conditions. For example, a yard standard has a length of one yard when at some definite temperature. It might have a different length if the temperature was varied.

The National Bureau of Standards, a branch of the U.S. Department of Commerce, was established in 1901. It provides fundamental measurement standards for science and industry and certifies the value of weights and measures. The Bureau is the custodian of the primary standard of length in the United States—the U.S. Prototype Meter 27, a 90% platinum, 10% iridium bar. Also in its care is the basic standard of mass, or weight—the U.S. Prototype Kilogram 20, another platinum-iridium standard. The national standards of length and mass are kept in a vault, fully protected by a special glass door and an alarm system. All measurements made with these standards are conducted in special air-conditioned laboratories, maintained at set temperatures, to which the standards are removed when measurements or comparisons are made. Extreme care is taken to prevent any damage to the standards in handling.

The origins of weights and measures go back to primitive man in prehistoric times. Units of length may have been the earliest measures. These were derived from the limbs of the human body and included such standards as the length of the foot, the width of the palm, and the length of the forearm. Units of weights included weights of kernels of grain and weights of shells. At a much later date, physical standards were made and deposited for safekeeping in a temple or other place of security.

The development of units of weights and measures has been investigated in considerable detail, and a number of books have been written on the subject. It is possible to give here, somewhat sketchily, the story of only a few units.

One of the earliest units was the **foot**. This was first the length of the human foot without further specification or modification; then, the length of the foot of various chiefs of tribes. Later, by gradual evolution, it was the foot as used in succession by the Egyptians, Greeks, and Romans, brought to Britain by the Romans, modified with the passing of time, and finally defined as one-third of a yard.

An important unit of length used by many ancient peoples was the **cubit**, originally defined as the distance from the point of the elbow to the end of the middle finger. This unit was about 18 inches long.

The **inch** was originally a thumb's breadth. In the Roman system it was defined as 1/12 of a foot and was introduced into Britain during Roman occupation.

The **mile** was defined by the Romans as 1,000 paces or double steps, the pace being equal to five Roman feet. This Roman mile of 5,000 Roman feet was introduced into Britain, became 5,000 English feet, and in the 16th century was changed to 5,280 feet.

The **yard** as a unit of length is apparently of much later origin than the units previously discussed. There is an old tradition, often stated as a fact, that Henry I of England decreed that the yard should thenceforth be the distance from the tip of his nose to the end of his thumb.

One of the earliest units of weight is the **grain**, originally the weight of a grain of wheat or a seed native to some locality.

The Roman **pound** (libra) was the hundredth part of an older weight, the talent, which is believed originally to have been the weight of an Egyptian royal cubic foot of water. The Roman pound was divided into 12 ounces of 437 grains each. This system was introduced into Britain where the pound was increased so as to have 16 of the original ounces. This pound became known as the avoirdupois pound, the word avoirdupois meaning "goods of weight." The pound, which in England had long been used for mint purposes and called the troy pound, consisted of 5,760 grains (12 ounces of 480 grains each). Sometime prior to A.D. 1600, the avoirdupois pound was increased by eight grains so that it would consist of 7,000 grains instead of 6,992 grains, and thus the number of grains in the avoirdupois pound would have a more simple ratio to the number of grains in the troy pound, which, since it was used for mint purposes, it was considered advisable to keep unchanged.

That the **ton** was the weight of a certain volume of some material is highly probable. Among the Anglo-Saxons it may have been the weight of a quantity of wheat in 32 bushels; that is, in one chaldron.

The **stone** was an early unit of weight in the British Isles. It is still used to a considerable extent in Great Britain, now generally being equal to 14 pounds. Thus, 8 stone = 1 hundredweight = 112 pounds; 20 hundredweights = 1 ton = 2,240 pounds. This ton is commonly referred to as the long ton in the United States.

The **metric system**, the international system of weights and measures, was established by international treaty in 1875 and is now either obligatory or permissive in every civilized country of the world; its use is permitted in the United States. In the metric system the fundamental units are the meter and the gram. The other units of length and mass, as well as all units of area, volume, and capacity, are derived from these two fundamental units.

At the International Bureau of Weights and Measures, established at Sèvres, a suburb of Paris, France, are kept the International Prototype Meter and the International Prototype Kilogram—platinum-iridium bars—many secondary standards of all sorts, and equipment for comparing standards and making precision measurements.

The U.S. standards of length and mass are known in terms of the standard bars deposited at the International Bureau. The only legal relationship between the metric system and the one used in the United States is the equivalence 1 meter = 39.37 inches, which was established by an act of Congress in July 1866. Thus, the yard is defined as follows: 1 yard = 0.9144 meter. The inch is therefore exactly equal to 25.4 millimeters.

In 1960 the world adopted a wavelength of light as the new, exact standard of the meter. Meter bars, however, continue in use for most types of measurements.

In the metric system, designations of multiples and subdivisions of any unit may be arrived at by combining with the name of the unit the prefixes **deka, hecto,** and **kilo,** meaning, respectively, 10, 100, and 1,000, and **deci, centi,** and **milli,** meaning, respectively, one-tenth, one-hundredth, and one-thousandth.

In certain cases, particularly in scientific usage, it becomes convenient to provide for multiples larger than 1,000 and for subdivisions smaller than one-thousandth. Accordingly, the following prefixes have been introduced, and these are now generally recognized:

| | |
|---|---|
| tera, meaning $10^{12}$ | pico, meaning $10^{-12}$ |
| giga, meaning $10^{9}$ | nano, meaning $10^{-9}$ |
| mega, meaning $10^{6}$ | micro, meaning $10^{-6}$ |
| kilo, meaning $10^{3}$ | milli, meaning $10^{-3}$ |
| hecto, meaning $10^{2}$ | centi, meaning $10^{-2}$ |
| deka, meaning $10^{1}$ | deci, meaning $10^{-1}$ |

Thus a kilometer is 1,000 meters and a megameter is 1,000,000, while a millimeter is 0.001 meter and a micrometer is 0.000001 meter. These prefixes are appropriately applied to all kinds of units and retain their significance as in kilowatts, picofarads, megacycles, and microinches.

## TABLES OF UNITED STATES CUSTOMARY WEIGHTS AND MEASURES

### ■ LINEAR MEASURE

| | |
|---|---|
| 12 inches (in.) | = 1 foot (ft.) |
| 3 feet | = 1 yard (yd.) |
| 5½ yards | = 1 rod (rd.), pole, or perch (16½ ft.) |
| 40 rods | = 1 furlong (fur.) = 220 yards = 660 feet |
| 8 furlongs | = 1 statute mile (mi.) = 1,760 yards = 5,280 feet |
| 3 miles | = 1 league = 5,280 yards = 15,-840 feet |
| 5,280 feet | = 1 statute or land mile |
| 6,076.11549 feet | = 1 international nautical mile |

### ■ AREA MEASURE

Squares and cubes of units are sometimes abbreviated by using "superior" figures. For example, ft² means square foot, and ft³ means cubic foot.

| | |
|---|---|
| 144 square inches | = 1 square foot (sq. ft.) |
| 9 square feet | = 1 square yard (sq. yd.) = 1,296 square inches |
| 30¼ square yards | = 1 square rod (sq. rd.) = 272¼ square feet |
| 160 square rods | = 1 acre = 4,840 square yards = 43,560 square feet |
| 640 acres | = 1 square mile (sq. mi.) |
| 1 mile square | = 1 section (of land) |
| 6 miles square | = 1 township = 36 sections = 36 square miles |

### ■ CUBIC MEASURE

| | |
|---|---|
| 1,728 cubic inches (cu. in.) | = 1 cubic foot (cu. ft.) |
| 27 cubic feet | = 1 cubic yard (cu. yd.) |

### ■ LIQUID MEASURE

When necessary to distinguish the liquid pint or quart from the dry pint or quart, the word "liquid" or the abbreviation "liq." should be used in combination with the name or abbreviation of the liquid unit.

| | |
|---|---|
| 4 gills (gi.) | = 1 pint (pt.) (= 28.875 cubic inches) |
| 2 pints | = 1 quart (qt.) (= 57.75 cubic inches) |
| 4 quarts | = 1 gallon (gal.) (= 231 cubic inches) = 8 pints = 32 gills |

### ■ APOTHECARIES' FLUID MEASURE

| | |
|---|---|
| 60 minims (min.) | = 1 fluid dram (fl. dr.) (= 0.2256 cubic inch) |
| 8 fluid drams | = 1 fluid ounce (fl. oz.) (= 1.8047 cubic inches) |
| 16 fluid ounces | = 1 pint (pt.) (= 28.875 cubic inches) = 128 fluid drams |
| 2 pints | = 1 quart (qt.) (= 57.75 cubic inches) = 32 fluid ounces = 256 fluid drams |
| 4 quarts | = 1 gallon (gal.) (= 231 cubic inches) = 128 fluid ounces = 1,024 fluid drams |

### ■ DRY MEASURE

When necessary to distinguish the dry pint or quart from the liquid pint or quart, the word "dry" should be used in combination with the name or abbreviation of the dry unit.

| | |
|---|---|
| 2 pints (pt.) | = 1 quart (qt.) (= 67.2006 cubic inches) |
| 8 quarts | = 1 peck (pk.) (= 537.605 cubic inches) = 16 pints |
| 4 pecks | = 1 bushel (bu.) (= 2,150.42 cubic inches) = 32 quarts |

### ■ AVOIRDUPOIS WEIGHT

When necessary to distinguish the avoirdupois dram from the apothecaries' dram, or to distinguish the avoirdupois dram or ounce from the fluid dram or ounce, or to distinguish the avoirdupois ounce or pound from the troy or apothecaries' ounce or pound, the word "avoirdupois"

(continued)

**WEIGHTS AND MEASURES** (*continued*)

or the abbreviation "avdp." should be used in combination with the name or abbreviation of the avoirdupois unit.

(The "grain" is the same in avoirdupois, troy, and apothecaries' weights.)

| | | |
|---|---|---|
| 27 11/32 grains | = 1 dram (dr.) | |
| 16 drams | = 1 ounce (oz.) = 437½ grains | |
| 16 ounces | = 1 pound (lb.) = 256 drams = 7,000 grains | |
| 100 pounds | = 1 hundredweight (cwt.)* | |
| 20 hundredweights | = 1 ton (tn.) = 2,000 pounds* | |

In "gross" or "long" measure, the following values are recognized:

| | |
|---|---|
| 112 pounds | = 1 gross or long hundred-weight* |
| 20 gross or long hundredweights | = 1 gross or long ton = 2,240 pounds* |

### ■ GUNTER'S OR SURVEYOR'S CHAIN MEASURE

7.92 inches (in.) = 1 link (li.)

| | |
|---|---|
| 100 links | = 1 chain (ch.) = 4 rods = 66 ft. |
| 80 chains | = 1 statute mile (mi.) = 320 rods = 5,280 feet |

### ■ TROY WEIGHT

| | |
|---|---|
| 24 grains | = 1 pennyweight (dwt.) |
| 20 pennyweights | = 1 ounce troy (oz. t.) = 480 grains |
| 12 ounces troy | = 1 pound troy (lb. t.) = 240 pennyweights = 5,760 grains |

### ■ APOTHECARIES' WEIGHT

| | |
|---|---|
| 20 grains | = scruple (s. ap.) |
| 3 scruples | = 1 dram apothecaries' (dr. ap.) = 60 grains |
| 8 drams, apothecaries' | = 1 ounce apothecaries' (oz. ap.) = 24 scruples = 480 grains |
| 12 ounces, apothecaries' | = 1 pound apothecaries' (lb. ap.) = 96 drams apothecaries' = 288 scruples = 5,760 grains |

* When the terms "hundredweight" and "ton" are used unmodified, they are commonly understood to mean the 100-pound hundredweight and the 2,000-pound ton, respectively; these units may be designated "net" or "short" when necessary to distinguish them from the corresponding units in gross or long measure.

## TABLES OF METRIC WEIGHTS AND MEASURES

### ■ WEIGHT

| | |
|---|---|
| 10 milligrams (mg.) | = 1 centigram (cg.) |
| 10 centigrams | = 1 decigram (dg.) = 100 milligrams |
| 10 decigrams | = 1 gram (g.) = 1,000 milligrams |
| 10 grams | = 1 dekagram (dkg.) |
| 10 dekagrams | = 1 hectogram (hg.) = 100 grams |
| 10 hectograms | = 1 kilogram (kg.) = 1,000 grams |
| 1,000 kilograms | = 1 metric ton (t.) |

### ■ VOLUME MEASURE

| | |
|---|---|
| 10 milliliters (ml.) | = 1 centiliter (cl.) |
| 10 centiliters | = 1 deciliter (dl.) = 100 milliliters |
| 10 deciliters | = 1 liter* (l.) = 1,000 milliliters |
| 10 liters | = 1 dekaliter (dkl.) |
| 10 dekaliters | = 1 hectoliter (hl.) = 100 liters |
| 10 hectoliters | = 1 kiloliter (kl.) = 1,000 liters |

### ■ LINEAR MEASURE

| | |
|---|---|
| 10 millimeters (mm.) | = 1 centimeter (cm.) |
| 10 centimeters | = 1 decimeter (dm.) = 100 millimeters |
| 10 decimeters | = 1 meter (m.) = 1,000 millimeters |
| 10 meters | = 1 dekameter (dkm.) |

| | |
|---|---|
| 10 dekameters | = 1 hectometer (hm.) = 100 meters |
| 10 hectometers | = 1 kilometer (km.) = 1,000 meters |

### ■ AREA MEASURE

| | |
|---|---|
| 100 square millimeters ($mm^2$) | = 1 square centimeter ($cm^2$) |
| 10,000 square centimeters | = 1 square meter ($m^2$) = 1,000,000 square millimeters |
| 100 square meters | = 1 are (a.) |
| 100 ares | = 1 hectare (ha.) = 10,000 square meters |
| 100 hectares | = 1 square kilometer ($km^2$) = 1,000,000 square meters |

### ■ CUBIC MEASURE

| | |
|---|---|
| 1,000 cubic millimeters ($mm^3$) | = 1 cubic centimeter ($cm^3$) |
| 1,000 cubic centimeters | = 1 cubic decimeter ($dm^3$) = 1,000,000 cubic millimeters |
| 1,000 cubic decimeters | = 1 cubic meter ($m^3$) = 1 stere = 1,000,000 cubic centimeters = 1,000,000,000 cubic millimeters |

* The liter is defined as the volume occupied, under standard conditions, by a quantity of pure water having a mass of 1 kilogram. This volume is very nearly equal to 1,000 cubic centimeters or 1 cubic decimeter, the actual metric equivalent is, 1 liter = 1.000028 cubic decimeters. Thus the milliliter and the liter are larger than the cubic centimeter and the cubic decimeter, respectively, by 28 parts in 1,000,000.

## APOTHECARIES' MEASURE

The term "apothecary" was applied to shop-keepers and warehousemen until the Middle Ages, when it came to mean one who prepared and sold drugs. The term is still in use in parts of the British Isles. The terms "apothecaries' measure" and "apothecaries' weight" refer, respectively, to the units of liquid measure and the measurements of grains and ounces used by pharmacists in the preparation of medical prescriptions. British apothecaries' measure, for example, divides one fluid ounce into eight fluid drachms, 24 fluid scruples, or 480 minims.

## TABLES OF EQUIVALENTS

The name of a unit enclosed in brackets [1 hand], indicates (1) that the unit is not in current use in the United States, or (2) that the unit is believed to be based on "custom and usage" rather than on formal definition. Equivalents involving decimals are, in most instances, rounded off to the third decimal place except where exact equivalents are so designated.

### ■ LENGTHS

| | |
|---|---|
| 1 Angstrom (A.) | 0.1 millimicron (exactly) |
| | 0.0001 micron (exactly) |
| | 0.0000001 millimeter (exactly) |
| | 0.000000004 inch |
| 1 cable's length | 120 fathoms |
| | 720 feet |
| | 219.456 meters (exactly) |
| 1 centimeter (cm.) | 0.3937 inch |
| 1 chain (ch.) (Gunter's or surveyor's) | 66 feet |
| | 20.1168 meters (exactly) |
| 1 chain (Ramden's or engineer's) | 100 feet |
| | 30.48 meters (exactly) |
| 1 decimeter (dm.) | 3.937 inches |
| 1 dekameter (dkm.) | 32,808 feet |
| 1 fathom | 6 feet |
| | 1.8288 meters (exactly) |
| 1 foot (ft.) | 0.3048 meters (exactly) |
| 1 furlong (fur.) | 10 chains (surveyor's) |
| | 660 feet |
| | 220 yards |
| | ⅛ statute mile |
| | 201.168 meters |
| [1 hand] | 4 inches |
| 1 inch (in.) | 2.54 centimeters (exactly) |
| 1 kilometer (km.) | 0.621 mile |
| 1 league | 3 statute miles |
| | 4.828 kilometers |
| 1 link (li.) (Gunter's or surveyor's) | 7.92 inches |
| | 0.201 meter |
| 1 link (li.) (engineer's) | 1 foot |
| | 0.305 meter |
| 1 meter (m.) | 39.37 inches |
| | 1.093 yards |
| 1 micron (μ [the Greek letter mu]) | 0.001 millimeter (exactly) |
| | 0.00003937 inch |
| 1 mil | 0.001 inch (exactly) |
| | 0.0254 millimeter (exactly) |
| 1 mile (mi.) (statute or land) | 5,280 feet |
| | 1.609 kilometers |
| 1 mile (mi.) (nautical, international, and new U.S. value) | 1.852 kilometers (exactly) |
| | 1.150779 statute miles |
| | 6,076.11549 feet |
| 1 millimeter (mm.) | 0.03937 inch |
| 1 millimicron (mμ [the English letter $m$ in combination with the Greek letter mu]) | 0.001 micron (exactly) |
| | 0.00000003937 inch (exactly) |
| 1 point (typography) | 0.013837 inch (exactly) |
| | 0.351 millimeter |
| 1 rod (rd.), pole, or perch | 16½ feet |
| | 5½ yards |
| | 5.029 meters |
| 1 yard (yd.) | 0.9144 meter (exactly) |

### ■ AREAS OR SURFACES

| | |
|---|---|
| 1 acre | 43,560 square feet |
| | 4,840 square yards |
| | 0.405 hectare |
| 1 are (a.) | 119.599 square yards |
| | 0.025 acre |
| 1 hectare (ha.) | 2.471 acres |
| [1 square (building)] | 100 square feet |
| 1 square centimeter (cm²) | 0.155 square inch |
| 1 square decimeter (dm²) | 15.500 square inches |
| 1 square foot (sq. ft.) | 929.030 square centimeters |
| 1 square inch (sq. in.) | 6.452 square centimeters |
| 1 square kilometer (km²) | 247.105 acres |
| | 0.386 square mile |
| 1 square meter (m²) | 1.196 square yards |
| | 10.764 square feet |
| 1 square mile (sq. mi.) | 258.999 hectares |
| 1 square millimeter (mm²) | 0.002 square inch |
| 1 square rod (sq. rd.), sq. pole, or sq. perch | 25.293 square meters |
| 1 square yard (sq. yd.) | 0.836 square meter |

### ■ CAPACITIES OR VOLUMES

| | |
|---|---|
| 1 barrel (bbl.), liquid | 31 to 42 gallons* |
| 1 barrel (bbl.), standard, for fruits, vegetables, and other dry commodities except cranberries | 7,056 cubic inches |
| | 105 dry quarts |
| | 3.281 bushels, struck measure |
| 1 barrel (bbl.), standard, cranberry | 5,826 cubic inches |
| | 86 45/64 dry quarts |
| | 2.709 bushels, struck measure |

*(continued)*

*There are a variety of "barrels," established by law or usage. For example, Federal taxes on fermented liquors are based on a barrel of 31 gallons; many state laws fix the "barrel for liquids" at 31½ gallons; one state fixes a 36-gallon barrel for cistern measurement; Federal law recognizes a 40-gallon barrel for "proof spirits"; by custom, 42 gallons comprise a barrel of crude oil or petroleum products for statistical purposes, and this equivalent is recognized "for liquids" by four states.

**TABLE OF EQUIVALENTS** (*continued*)

| | |
|---|---|
| 1 bushel (bu.) (U.S.) (struck measure) | 2,150.42 cubic inches (exactly)<br>35.238 liters |
| [1 bushel, heaped (U.S.)] | 2,747.715 cubic inches<br>1.278 bushels, struck measure* |
| [1 bushel (bu.) (British Imperial) (struck measure)] | 1.032 U.S. bushels, struck measure<br>2,219.36 cubic inches |
| 1 cord (cd.) (firewood) | 128 cubic feet |
| 1 cubic centimeter (cm³) | 0.061 cubic inch |
| 1 cubic decimeter (dm³) | 61.023 cubic inches |
| 1 cubic foot (cu. ft.) | 7.481 gallons<br>28.317 cubic decimeters |
| 1 cubic inch (cu. in.) | 0.554 fluid ounce<br>4.433 fluid drams<br>16.387 cubic centimeters |
| 1 cubic meter (m³) | 1.308 cubic yards |
| 1 cubic yard (cu. yd.) | 0.765 cubic meter |
| 1 cup, measuring | 8 fluid ounces<br>½ liquid pint |
| 1 dekaliter (dkl.) | 2.642 gallons<br>1.135 pecks |
| 1 dram, fluid (or liquid) (fl. dr.) (U.S.) | ⅛ fluid ounce<br>0.226 cubic inch<br>3.697 milliliters |
| [1 dram, fluid (fl. dr.) (British)] | 0.217 cubic inch<br>0.961 U.S. fluid dram<br>3.552 milliliters |
| 1 gallon (gal.) (U.S.) | 231 cubic inches<br>3.785 liters<br>0.833 British gallon<br>128 U.S. fluid ounces |
| [1 gallon (gal.) (British Imperial)] | 277.42 cubic inches<br>1.201 U.S. gallons<br>4.546 liters<br>160 British fluid ounces |
| 1 gill (gi.) | 7.219 cubic inches<br>4 fluid ounces<br>0.118 liter |
| 1 hectoliter (hl.) | 26.418 gallons<br>2.838 bushels |
| 1 liter | 1.057 liquid quarts<br>0.908 dry quart<br>61.025 cubic inches |
| 1 milliliter (ml.) | 0.271 fluid dram<br>16.231 minims<br>0.061 cubic inch |
| 1 ounce, fluid (or liquid) (fl. oz.) (U.S.) | 1.805 cubic inches<br>29.573 milliliters<br>1.041 British fluid ounces |
| [1 ounce, fluid (fl. oz.) (British)] | 0.961 U.S. fluid ounce<br>1.734 cubic inches<br>28.412 milliliters |
| 1 peck (pk.) | 8.810 liters |
| 1 pint (pt.), dry | 33.600 cubic inches<br>0.551 liter |
| 1 pint (pt.) liquid | 28.875 cubic inches (exactly)<br>0.473 liter |
| 1 quart (qt.), dry (U.S.) | 67.201 cubic inches<br>1.101 liters<br>0.969 British quart |
| 1 quart (qt.), liquid (U.S.) | 57.75 cubic inches (exactly)<br>0.946 liter<br>0.833 British quart |
| [1 quart (qt.) (British)] | 69.354 cubic inches<br>1.032 U.S. dry quarts<br>1.201 U.S. liquid quarts |
| 1 tablespoon | 3 teaspoons<br>4 fluid drams<br>½ fluid ounce |
| 1 teaspoon | ⅓ tablespoon<br>1 1/3 fluid drams |

■ **WEIGHTS OR MASSES**

| | |
|---|---|
| 1 assay ton† (AT) | 29.167 grams |
| 1 carat (c.) | 200 milligrams<br>3.086 grains |
| 1 dram, apothecaries' (dr. ap.) | 60 grains<br>3.888 grains |
| 1 dram, avoirdupois (dr. avdp.) | 27 11/32 (= 27.344) grains<br>1.772 grams |
| gamma, *see* microgram | |
| 1 grain | 64.799 milligrams |
| 1 gram (g.) | 15.432 grains<br>0.035 ounce, avoirdupois |
| 1 hundredweight, gross or long** (gross cwt.) | 112 pounds<br>50.802 kilograms |
| 1 hundredweight, net or short (cwt. or net cwt.) | 100 pounds<br>45.359 kilograms |
| 1 kilogram (kg.) | 2.205 pounds |
| 1 microgram (γ [the Greek letter gamma]) | 0.000001 gram (exactly) |
| 1 milligram (mg.) | 0.015 grain |
| 1 ounce, avoirdupois (oz. avdp.) | 437.5 grains (exactly)<br>0.911 troy or apothecaries' ounce<br>28.350 grams |
| 1 ounce, troy or apothecaries' (oz. t. or oz. ap.) | 480 grains<br>1.097 avoirdupois ounces<br>31.103 grams |
| 1 pennyweight (dwt.) | 1.555 grams |
| 1 pound, avoirdupois (lb. avdp.) | 7,000 grains<br>1.215 troy or apothecaries' pounds<br>453.59237 grams (exactly) |
| 1 pound, troy or apothecaries' (lb. t. or lb. ap.) | 5,760 grains<br>0.823 avoirdupois pound<br>373.242 grams |
| 1 scruple (s. ap.) | 20 grains<br>1.296 grams |
| 1 ton, gross or long** (gross tn.) | 2,240 pounds<br>1.12 net tons (exactly)<br>1.016 metric tons |
| 1 ton, metric (t.) | 2,204.623 pounds<br>0.984 gross ton<br>1.102 net tons |
| 1 ton, net or short (tn. or net tn.) | 2,000 pounds<br>0.893 gross ton<br>0.907 metric ton |

* Frequently recognized as 1¼ bushels, struck measure.    † Used in assaying. The assay ton bears the same relation to the milligram that a ton of 2,000 pounds avoirdupois bears to the ounce troy; hence the weight in milligrams of precious metal obtained from one assay ton of ore gives directly the number of troy ounces to the net ton.    ** The gross or long ton and hundredweight are used commercially in the United States to only a limited extent, usually in restricted industrial fields. These units are the same as the British "ton" and "hundredweight."

## MISCELLANEOUS UNITS OF MEASUREMENT

**Acre:** Originally, the area a yoke of oxen could plow in one day. The modern standard is 43,560 square feet. Although usually rectangular, an acre may be of any irregular shape.

**Ampere:** The unit of electrical current produced by a pressure of one volt across a resistance of one ohm.

**Bale:** A large, closely pressed bundle of some commodity. In practice, various items are standardized; for example, a bale of cotton weighs 500 pounds gross or 480 pounds net.

**Barleycorn:** Early English unit used as a measure of shoe sizes and equal to ⅓ inch. A size 11 shoe is ⅓ inch longer than a size 10. Thirty-nine "round and dry" barleycorns equal a size 13, normally the largest size.

**Board Foot:** In the lumber industry the volume of a one-inch thick, one-foot square board, rough sawn. Retail lumber, planed and sanded, is priced by the board foot, although as much as ⅜ inch of the thickness is lost to shavings and sawdust.

**BTU:** British thermal unit, equal to 252 calories. It is the amount of heat needed to increase the temperature of one pound of pure water by one degree Fahrenheit.

**Calorie:** Amount of heat needed to increase the temperature of one gram of pure water by one degree Centigrade. Weight-watchers use the *Great Calorie*, a measure of heat-energy in foods, equal to 1,000 regular calories.

**Carat:** Unit of weight used for precious stones and equal to 0.2 gram. The carat (karat) is also used to indicate purity of gold alloys, on a scale of 24: 14 carats means 14 parts gold to 10 parts alloy.

**Decibel:** Unit of relative loudness in acoustics. One decibel is about the smallest amount of change detectable to the human ear. Doubling the intensity of a sound raises its level by about three decibels.

**Denier:** Unit of fineness applied to silk, nylon, and rayon yarn, especially with hosiery, where a length of 9,000 meters of yarn weighs one gram. Sheer stockings are usually 15 denier; "service (business) sheer" are normally 30 denier.

**Ell:** An ancient, rarely used measure of length for cloth. Its length varies from country to country; in England it is 45 inches, whereas the Scotch ell is about 37 inches.

**Fifth:** Popular liquor bottle size equal to 1/5 of a U.S. gallon. It is the same as the British "Reputed Quart." Larger sizes include the *magnum* (2/5 gallon) and the *jeroboam* (4/5 gallon), which are often used to bottle wines, especially champagne.

**Hertz:** Modern unit in electronics, equivalent to and replacing the former, more familiar expression "cycles per second." It was named after the German physicist Heinrich R. Hertz (1857–1894), and is usually abbreviated as "*hz.*" Although not a new term, it was only recently adopted as the official unit for radio, radar, and other electromagnetic wave frequencies.

**Hogshead:** A large cask or barrel of variable measure both in weight and volume. It ranges from 52 to 140 gallons, depending on the country, for liquids such as beer. In the U.S., the weight is approximately 1,000 pounds for tobacco.

**Horsepower:** Standard theoretical unit of the rate of work, or power. It is equal to lifting 550 pounds one foot in one second (originally by horse) as applied to automobile and airplane engines. Also, 746 watts of electrical power.

**Jigger:** From 1 to 1½ fluid ounces. Originally two mouthfuls (½ ounce each) and equal to one handful. Two handfuls, or jiggers, equal one jack; two jacks equal a gill (jill).

**Kilowatt-hour:** Basic unit of home electric bills. It is equal to consumption of 1,000 watts of power over a period of one hour.

**Knot:** Rate of speed of one nautical mile (6,076.12 feet) per hour. This is the standard measure of speed for ships, aircraft, and water and air currents.

**League:** An ancient unit equivalent to an hour's walk. Modern value varies from three to four land miles (three in England).

**Line:** Equal to 1/40 inch for measuring the diameter of buttons. In newspaper advertising, a unit generally known as an *agate* line and equal to approximately 5½ points (about 1/12 inch) in height and a column wide.

**Ohm:** The unit of electrical resistance resulting when a circuit carrying one volt produces a current of one ampere.

**Pica:** In printing, a size of type equal to 12 points, or about 1/6 inch.

**Point:** The standard unit of type size, equal to about 1/72 inch.

**Quintal:** A unit of weight of variable value. It is equal to 101.4 pounds in Spain and most of Latin America, and 220.46 pounds in the metric system.

**Quire:** Either 24 or 25 sheets of paper of uniform size and quality, equal to 1/20 of a ream.

**Ream:** Twenty quire or 480 uniform sheets of paper, except newsprint or book paper (equal to 500 sheets), or a "perfect ream" of 516.

**Roentgen:** The dosage unit of radiation exposure produced by X-rays and gamma rays. The *Rem* (roentgen-equivalent man) is an equivalent unit for exposure to all kinds of radiation (X-ray and gamma ray, alpha, beta, and neutron). It applies to biological effects only.

**Talent:** An ancient unit of coin and weight equal to about 3,600 shekels as a weight, and about 3,000 shekels as silver or gold revenue. The Hebrew gold shekel, valued at about $10.88, probably weighed about 252⅔ grains, or slightly less than half an ounce.

**Township:** A land survey unit equal to 36 square miles—6 miles on a side. Divided into 36 smaller units known as *sections*, it is one of the chief divisions of a public-land survey—especially in oil-producing states.

**Tuffet:** An old English unit equal to two pecks or half a bushel.

**Volt:** In electricity, the unit of electromotive force, or pressure, produced by a current of one ampere over a resistance of one ohm.

**Watt:** The unit of electrical power produced by a current of one ampere at a pressure of one volt.

## TEMPERATURE CONVERSION TABLE *
Source: Ever Ready Thermometer Company

The numbers in boldface type in the center column—the key to the table—refer to the temperature in either centigrade or Fahrenheit degrees. Thus, for example, 30° in the center column, if chosen to represent 30° Fahrenheit, will convert to −1.1° centigrade, the figure found to the left of the column. If, on the other hand, it is made to represent 30° centigrade, it will convert to 86.0° Fahrenheit, the figure to the right of the column.

For degrees of temperature not included in this table, the following formulas will furnish the necessary conversion:

$$F° = \frac{9}{5} C° + 32 \quad \text{or} \quad C° = \frac{5}{9}(F° - 32)$$

| DEGREES C. | DEGREES | DEGREES F. | DEGREES C. | DEGREES | DEGREES F. | DEGREES C. | DEGREES | DEGREES F. |
|---|---|---|---|---|---|---|---|---|
| −34.4 | **−30** | −22.0 | −9.4 | **+15** | +59.0 | +15.6 | **+60** | +140.0 |
| −33.9 | **−29** | −20.2 | −8.9 | **+16** | +60.8 | +16.1 | **+61** | +141.8 |
| −33.3 | **−28** | −18.4 | −8.3 | **+17** | +62.6 | +16.7 | **+62** | +143.6 |
| −32.8 | **−27** | −16.6 | −7.8 | **+18** | +64.4 | +17.2 | **+63** | +145.4 |
| −32.2 | **−26** | −14.8 | −7.2 | **+19** | +66.2 | +17.8 | **+64** | +147.2 |
| −31.7 | **−25** | −13.0 | −6.7 | **+20** | +68.0 | +18.3 | **+65** | +149.0 |
| −31.1 | **−24** | −11.2 | −6.1 | **+21** | +69.8 | +18.9 | **+66** | +150.8 |
| −30.6 | **−23** | −9.4 | −5.5 | **+22** | +71.6 | +19.4 | **+67** | +152.6 |
| −30.0 | **−22** | −7.6 | −5.0 | **+23** | +73.4 | +20.0 | **+68** | +154.4 |
| −29.4 | **−21** | −5.8 | −4.4 | **+24** | +75.2 | +20.6 | **+69** | +156.2 |
| −28.9 | **−20** | −4.0 | −3.9 | **+25** | +77.0 | +21.1 | **+70** | +158.0 |
| −28.3 | **−19** | −2.2 | −3.3 | **+26** | +78.8 | +21.7 | **+71** | +159.8 |
| −27.8 | **−18** | −0.4 | −2.8 | **+27** | +80.6 | +22.2 | **+72** | +161.6 |
| −27.2 | **−17** | +1.4 | −2.2 | **+28** | +82.4 | +22.8 | **+73** | +163.4 |
| −26.7 | **−16** | +3.2 | −1.7 | **+29** | +84.2 | +23.3 | **+74** | +165.2 |
| −26.1 | **−15** | +5.0 | −1.1 | **+30** | +86.0 | +23.9 | **+75** | +167.0 |
| −25.6 | **−14** | +6.8 | −0.6 | **+31** | +87.8 | +24.4 | **+76** | +168.8 |
| −25.0 | **−13** | +8.6 | .0 | **+32** | +89.6 | +25.0 | **+77** | +170.6 |
| −24.4 | **−12** | +10.4 | +0.6 | **+33** | +91.4 | +25.6 | **+78** | +172.4 |
| −23.9 | **−11** | +12.2 | +1.1 | **+34** | +93.2 | +26.1 | **+79** | +174.2 |
| −23.3 | **−10** | +14.0 | +1.7 | **+35** | +95.0 | +26.7 | **+80** | +176.0 |
| −22.8 | **−9** | +15.8 | +2.2 | **+36** | +96.8 | +27.2 | **+81** | +177.8 |
| −22.2 | **−8** | +17.6 | +2.8 | **+37** | +98.6 | +27.8 | **+82** | +179.6 |
| −21.7 | **−7** | +19.4 | +3.3 | **+38** | +100.4 | +28.3 | **+83** | +181.4 |
| −21.1 | **−6** | +21.2 | +3.9 | **+39** | +102.2 | +28.9 | **+84** | +183.2 |
| −20.6 | **−5** | +23.0 | +4.4 | **+40** | +104.0 | +29.4 | **+85** | +185.0 |
| −20.0 | **−4** | +24.8 | +5.0 | **+41** | +105.8 | +30.0 | **+86** | +186.8 |
| −19.4 | **−3** | +26.6 | +5.5 | **+42** | +107.6 | +30.6 | **+87** | +188.6 |
| −18.9 | **−2** | +28.4 | +6.1 | **+43** | +109.4 | +31.1 | **+88** | +190.4 |
| −18.3 | **−1** | +30.2 | +6.7 | **+44** | +111.2 | +31.7 | **+89** | +192.2 |
| −17.8 | **0** | +32.0 | +7.2 | **+45** | +113.0 | +32.2 | **+90** | +194.0 |
| −17.2 | **+1** | +33.8 | +7.8 | **+46** | +114.8 | +32.8 | **+91** | +195.8 |
| −16.7 | **+2** | +35.6 | +8.3 | **+47** | +116.6 | +33.3 | **+92** | +197.6 |
| −16.1 | **+3** | +37.4 | +8.9 | **+48** | +118.4 | +33.9 | **+93** | +199.4 |
| −15.6 | **+4** | +39.2 | +9.4 | **+49** | +120.2 | +34.4 | **+94** | +201.2 |
| −15.0 | **+5** | +41.0 | +10.0 | **+50** | +122.0 | +35.0 | **+95** | +203.0 |
| −14.4 | **+6** | +42.8 | +10.6 | **+51** | +123.8 | +35.6 | **+96** | +204.8 |
| −13.9 | **+7** | +44.6 | +11.1 | **+52** | +125.6 | +36.1 | **+97** | +206.6 |
| −13.3 | **+8** | +46.4 | +11.7 | **+53** | +127.4 | +36.7 | **+98** | +208.4 |
| −12.8 | **+9** | +48.2 | +12.2 | **+54** | +129.2 | +37.2 | **+99** | +210.2 |
| −12.2 | **+10** | +50.0 | +12.8 | **+55** | +131.0 | +37.8 | **+100** | +212.0 |
| −11.7 | **+11** | +51.8 | +13.3 | **+56** | +132.8 | +38.3 | **+101** | +213.8 |
| −11.1 | **+12** | +53.6 | +13.9 | **+57** | +134.6 | +38.9 | **+102** | +215.6 |
| −10.6 | **+13** | +55.4 | +14.4 | **+58** | +136.4 | +39.4 | **+103** | +217.4 |
| −10.0 | **+14** | +57.2 | +15.0 | **+59** | +138.2 | +40.0 | **+104** | +219.2 |

* Absolute zero is −273.16° C. or −459.69° F.

## KELVIN SCALE

In the late 19th century, the British physicist William T. Kelvin conceived a temperature scale based on thermodynamic laws. Known also as the absolute scale, Kelvin's system has become the fundamental temperature scale used in scientific measurement. Absolute temperatures are used in formulas derived from the laws governing the behavior of gases, which expand and contract in volume at high and low temperatures. According to the kinetic molecular theory, absolute zero is the point at which the molecules of substances have no heat energy. Absolute zero, −273.16° on the centigrade scale, is 0° Kelvin. Thus, degrees Kelvin are equivalent to degrees centigrade plus 273.16. The freezing point of water, 0° centigrade and 32° Fahrenheit, is 273.16° Kelvin. The conversion formula is simply K° = C° + 273.16.

# MATHEMATICS

## NAMES FOR LARGE NUMBERS

| The names for the large numbers in the decimal system are used differently in the French and U.S. systems, and the British and German systems. | NAME | EQUIVALENTS French and U.S. systems | Number of zeros | EQUIVALENTS British and German systems | Number of zeros |
|---|---|---|---|---|---|
| | million........ | 1000 thousands........ | 6 | 1000 thousands............... | 6 |
| | milliard........ | 1000 millions......... | 9 | 1000 millions............... | 9 |
| | billion.......... | 1000 millions......... (usual U.S. term) | 9 | 1,000,000 millions................ (1,000,000,000,000) | 12 |
| | trillion......... | 1000 billions or........ 1,000,000 millions (1,000,000,000,000) | 12 | 1,000,000 billions or............... 1,000,000 million millions (1,000,000,000,000,000,000) | 18 |
| | quadrillion...... | 1000 trillions........ | 15 | 1,000,000 trillions.............. | 24 |
| | quintillion...... | 1000 quadrillions....... | 18 | 1,000,000 quadrillions.............. | 30 |
| | sextillion....... | 1000 quintillions....... | 21 | 1,000,000 quintillions.............. | 36 |
| | septillion....... | 1000 sextillions....... | 24 | 1,000,000 sextillions............. | 42 |
| | octillion........ | 1000 septillions....... | 27 | 1,000,000 septillions ............. | 48 |
| | nonillion........ | 1000 octillions......... | 30 | 1,000,000 octillions.................. | 54 |
| | decillion........ | 1000 nonillions........ | 33 | 1,000,000 nonillions.............. | 60 |
| | undecillion..... | 1000 decillions......... | 36 | 1,000,000 decillions.............. | 66 |
| | duodecillion.... | 1000 undecillions........ | 39 | 1,000,000 undecillions............. | 72 |
| | tredecillion..... | 1000 duodecillions...... | 42 | 1,000,000 duodecillions............. | 78 |
| | quattuordecillion | 1000 tredecillions...... | 45 | 1,000,000 tredecillions.............. | 84 |
| | quindecillion.... | 1000 quattuordecillions | 48 | 1,000,000 quattuordecillions.......... | 90 |
| | sexdecillion.... | 1000 quindecillions...... | 51 | 1,000,000 quindecillions............. | 96 |
| | septendecillion.. | 1000 sexdecillions...... | 54 | 1,000,000 sexdecillions............. | 102 |
| | octodecillion.... | 1000 septendecillions... | 57 | 1,000,000 septendecillions........... | 108 |
| | novemdecillion.. | 1000 octodecillions...... | 60 | 1,000,000 octodecillions............. | 114 |
| | vigintillion...... | 1000 novemdecillions... | 63 | 1,000,000 novemdecillions.......... | 120 |

## ROMAN NUMERALS

| | | | | | | | |
|---|---|---|---|---|---|---|---|
| I......... | 1 | IX ..... | 9 | XVII.... | 17 | LXX... | 70 |
| II........ | 2 | X ..... | 10 | XVIII.... | 18 | LXXX.. | 80 |
| III....... | 3 | XI...... | 11 | XIX.... | 19 | XC.... | 90 |
| IV....... | 4 | XII...... | 12 | XX.... | 20 | C..... | 100 |
| V........ | 5 | XIII..... | 13 | XXX.... | 30 | D..... | 500 |
| VI....... | 6 | XIV..... | 14 | XL.... | 40 | M..... | 1000 |
| VII...... | 7 | XV..... | 15 | L...... | 50 | $\overline{V}$..... | 5000 |
| VIII...... | 8 | XVI..... | 16 | LX.... | 60 | $\overline{X}$.... | 10,000 |

The Roman numerals I, V, X, L, C, D, and M represent the Arabic numerals 1, 5, 10, 50, 100, 500, and 1,000, respectively. Repeating the letter I, X, C, or M repeats its value: II=2; XXX=30. The letters V, L, and D are never repeated. One or more letters placed after one of greater value adds to that letter: CL=150; CLX=160; CLXV=165; CLXVIII=168. A single letter placed before one of greater value subtracts from that letter: CM=900; CMXL= 940; CMXLIV=944. A dash line over a numeral multiples the value by 1,000: $\overline{X}$=10,000; $\overline{CC}$=200,000; CMXLIV=$\overline{944,000}$.

**HISTORY OF ROMAN NUMERALS.** For almost 2,000 years, Roman numerals comprised the principal numerical system in Europe, largely because of the immensity of the Roman Empire and the inherent simplicity of the Roman numeral system itself. Their exact origin is still a matter of speculation. The system itself closely resembles that of the earlier Greek Attic numerals, differing only in detail.

The numeral I represents one digit of the hand. A spread hand with the fingers held together and the thumb apart is believed to have been the origin of the numeral V. The numeral X would then be a double V, standing for two hands. The numerals C and M are believed to be adaptations of Greek letters, as they were originally written Θ and Φ. The later forms of C and M may have been either adaptations of the original symbols or the first letters of the Latin words for 100 (centum) and 1,000 (mille). L and D may have come from the bisection of the original symbols for 100 and 1,000.

## DECIMAL EQUIVALENTS OF FRACTIONS

| | | |
|---|---|---|
| 1/64 = .015625 | 1/3 = .33 | 11/16 = .6857 |
| 1/32 = .03125 | 3/8 = .375 | 7/10 = .70 |
| 1/16 = .0625 | 2/5 = .40 | 3/4 = .75 |
| 1/8 = .125 | 7/16 = .4375 | 4/5 = .80 |
| 1/7 = .1429 | 1/2 = .50 | 13/16 = .8125 |
| 1/6 = .1667 | 9/16 = .5625 | 5/6 = .8333 |
| 3/16 = .1875 | 3/5 = .60 | 6/7 = .8571 |
| 1/4 = .25 | 5/8 = .625 | 7/8 = .875 |
| 3/10 = .30 | 2/3 = .6667 | 15/16 = .9375 |

## PER CENTS AS FRACTIONS

| | | | |
|---|---|---|---|
| 5% = 0.05 = 1/20 | | 40% = 0.40 = 2/5 | |
| 8⅓% = 0.08⅓ = 1/12 | | 50% = 0.50 = 1/2 | |
| 10% = 0.10 = 1/10 | | 58⅓% = 0.58⅓ = 7/12 | |
| 12½% = 0.125 = 1/8 | | 60% = 0.60 = 3/5 | |
| 16⅔% = 0.16⅔ = 1/6 | | 62½% = 0.625 = 5/8 | |
| 20% = 0.20 = 1/5 | | 75% = 0.75 = 3/4 | |
| 25% = 0.25 = 1/4 | | 80% = 0.80 = 4/5 | |
| 33⅓% = 0.33⅓ = 1/3 | | 83⅓% = 0.83⅓ = 5/6 | |
| 37½% = 0.375 = 3/8 | | 87½% = 0.875 = 7/8 | |

## MULTIPLICATION TABLE

| | 2 | 3 | 4 | 5 | 6 | 7 | 8 | 9 | 10 | 11 | 12 | 13 | 14 | 15 | 16 | 17 | 18 | 19 | 20 | |
|---|---|---|---|---|---|---|---|---|---|---|---|---|---|---|---|---|---|---|---|---|
| 2 | 4 | 6 | 8 | 10 | 12 | 14 | 16 | 18 | 20 | 22 | 24 | 26 | 28 | 30 | 32 | 34 | 36 | 38 | 40 | 2 |
| 3 | 6 | 9 | 12 | 15 | 18 | 21 | 24 | 27 | 30 | 33 | 36 | 39 | 42 | 45 | 48 | 51 | 54 | 57 | 60 | 3 |
| 4 | 8 | 12 | 16 | 20 | 24 | 28 | 32 | 36 | 40 | 44 | 48 | 52 | 56 | 60 | 64 | 68 | 72 | 76 | 80 | 4 |
| 5 | 10 | 15 | 20 | 25 | 30 | 35 | 40 | 45 | 50 | 55 | 60 | 65 | 70 | 75 | 80 | 85 | 90 | 95 | 100 | 5 |
| 6 | 12 | 18 | 24 | 30 | 36 | 42 | 48 | 54 | 60 | 66 | 72 | 78 | 84 | 90 | 96 | 102 | 108 | 114 | 120 | 6 |
| 7 | 14 | 21 | 28 | 35 | 42 | 49 | 56 | 63 | 70 | 77 | 84 | 91 | 98 | 105 | 112 | 119 | 126 | 133 | 140 | 7 |
| 8 | 16 | 24 | 32 | 40 | 48 | 56 | 64 | 72 | 80 | 88 | 96 | 104 | 112 | 120 | 128 | 136 | 144 | 152 | 160 | 8 |
| 9 | 18 | 27 | 36 | 45 | 54 | 63 | 72 | 81 | 90 | 99 | 108 | 117 | 126 | 135 | 144 | 153 | 162 | 171 | 180 | 9 |
| 10 | 20 | 30 | 40 | 50 | 60 | 70 | 80 | 90 | 100 | 110 | 120 | 130 | 140 | 150 | 160 | 170 | 180 | 190 | 200 | 10 |
| 11 | 22 | 33 | 44 | 55 | 66 | 77 | 88 | 99 | 110 | 121 | 132 | 143 | 154 | 165 | 176 | 187 | 198 | 209 | 220 | 11 |
| 12 | 24 | 36 | 48 | 60 | 72 | 84 | 96 | 108 | 120 | 132 | 144 | 156 | 168 | 180 | 192 | 204 | 216 | 228 | 240 | 12 |
| 13 | 26 | 39 | 52 | 65 | 78 | 91 | 104 | 117 | 130 | 143 | 156 | 169 | 182 | 195 | 208 | 221 | 234 | 247 | 260 | 13 |
| 14 | 28 | 42 | 56 | 70 | 84 | 98 | 112 | 126 | 140 | 154 | 168 | 182 | 196 | 210 | 224 | 238 | 252 | 266 | 280 | 14 |
| 15 | 30 | 45 | 60 | 75 | 90 | 105 | 120 | 135 | 150 | 165 | 180 | 195 | 210 | 225 | 240 | 255 | 270 | 285 | 300 | 15 |
| 16 | 32 | 48 | 64 | 80 | 96 | 112 | 128 | 144 | 160 | 176 | 192 | 208 | 224 | 240 | 256 | 272 | 288 | 304 | 320 | 16 |
| 17 | 34 | 51 | 68 | 85 | 102 | 119 | 136 | 153 | 170 | 187 | 204 | 221 | 238 | 255 | 272 | 289 | 306 | 323 | 340 | 17 |
| 18 | 36 | 54 | 72 | 90 | 108 | 126 | 144 | 162 | 180 | 198 | 216 | 234 | 252 | 270 | 288 | 306 | 324 | 342 | 360 | 18 |
| 19 | 38 | 57 | 76 | 95 | 114 | 133 | 152 | 171 | 190 | 209 | 228 | 247 | 266 | 285 | 304 | 323 | 342 | 361 | 380 | 19 |
| 20 | 40 | 60 | 80 | 100 | 120 | 140 | 160 | 180 | 200 | 220 | 240 | 260 | 280 | 300 | 320 | 340 | 360 | 380 | 400 | 20 |

## COMMON AREA FORMULAS

| FIGURE | FORMULA | MEANING OF LETTERS |
|---|---|---|
| Rectangle........ | $A = ab$ | $a$ = base, $b$ = height |
| Square.......... | $A = a^2$ | $a$ = one side |
| Triangle........ | $A = \dfrac{ab}{2}$ | $a$ = base, $b$ = height |
| Parallelogram.... | $A = ab$ | $a$ = base, $b$ = height |
| Regular pentagon | $A = 1.720a^2$ | $a$ = one side |
| Regular hexagon | $A = 2.598a^2$ | $a$ = one side |
| Regular octagon.. | $A = 4.828a^2$ | $a$ = one side |
| Circle.......... | $A = \pi r^2$ | $\pi = 3.1416$, $r$ = radius |

## COMMON VOLUME FORMULAS

| FIGURE | FORMULA | MEANING OF LETTERS |
|---|---|---|
| Cube........... | $V = a^3$ | $a$ = one side |
| Pyramid........ | $V = \dfrac{ah}{3}$ | $a$ = area of base, $h$ = height |
| Cylinder........ | $V = \pi r^2 h$ | $\pi = 3.1416$, $h$ = height, $r$ = radius of the base |
| Cone........... | $V = \dfrac{\pi r^2 h}{3}$ | $\pi = 3.1416$, $r$ = radius of the base, $h$ = height |
| Sphere........ | $V = \dfrac{4\pi r^3}{3}$ | $\pi = 3.1416$, $r$ = radius |

## MULTIPLES OF $\pi$

| No. | Value | No. | Value |
|---|---|---|---|
| $\pi$ | 3.1416 | $\dfrac{1}{\pi}$ | 0.3183 |
| $2\pi$ | 6.2832 | $\frac{1}{2}\pi$ | 1.5708 |
| $3\pi$ | 9.4248 | $\frac{1}{3}\pi$ | 1.0472 |
| $4\pi$ | 12.5664 | $\frac{1}{4}\pi$ | 0.7854 |
| $5\pi$ | 15.7080 | $\frac{1}{5}\pi$ | 0.6283 |
| $6\pi$ | 18.8496 | $\frac{1}{6}\pi$ | 0.5236 |
| $7\pi$ | 21.9912 | $\frac{1}{7}\pi$ | 0.4488 |
| $8\pi$ | 25.1328 | $\frac{1}{8}\pi$ | 0.3927 |
| $9\pi$ | 28.2744 | $\frac{1}{9}\pi$ | 0.3491 |
| $\pi^2$ | 9.8696 | $\sqrt{\pi}$ | 1.7725 |

## THE GEOMETRY OF REGULAR POLYGONS

| No. of Sides | Polygon | Area | Radius of Circumscribed Circle | Radius of Inscribed Circle | Side if Radius of Circumscribed Circle = 1 |
|---|---|---|---|---|---|
| | | | if Length of Side = 1 | | |
| 3 | triangle | 0.433013 | 0.5773 | 0.2887 | 1.7321 |
| 4 | square | 1 | 0.7071 | 0.5000 | 1.4142 |
| 5 | pentagon | 1.720477 | 0.8056 | 0.6882 | 1.1756 |
| 6 | hexagon | 2.598076 | 1 | 0.8660 | 1 |
| 7 | heptagon | 3.633912 | 1.1524 | 1.0383 | 0.8677 |
| 8 | octagon | 4.828427 | 1.3066 | 1.2071 | 0.7653 |
| 9 | nonagon | 6.181824 | 1.4619 | 1.3737 | 0.6840 |
| 10 | decagon | 7.694209 | 1.6180 | 1.5388 | 0.6180 |

## POWERS OF 10

$$10^1 = 10$$
$$10^2 = 100$$
$$10^3 = 1000$$
$$10^4 = 10,000$$
$$10^5 = 100,000$$
$$10^6 = 1,000,000$$
$$10^7 = 10,000,000$$
$$10^{-1} = 0.1$$
$$10^{-2} = 0.01$$
$$10^{-3} = 0.001$$
$$10^{-4} = 0.0001$$
$$10^{-5} = 0.00001$$
$$10^{-6} = 0.000001$$
$$10^{-7} = 0.0000001$$

## SQUARES, SQUARE ROOTS, CUBES, AND CUBE ROOTS

| NO. | SQUARE | CUBE | SQUARE ROOT | CUBE ROOT | NO. | SQUARE | CUBE | SQUARE ROOT | CUBE ROOT |
|---|---|---|---|---|---|---|---|---|---|
| 1...... | 1 | 1 | 1.000 | 1.000 | 14...... | 196 | 2744 | 3.741 | 2.410 |
| 2...... | 4 | 8 | 1.414 | 1.259 | 15...... | 225 | 3375 | 3.873 | 2.466 |
| 3...... | 9 | 27 | 1.732 | 1.442 | 16...... | 256 | 4096 | 4.000 | 2.519 |
| 4...... | 16 | 64 | 2.000 | 1.587 | 17...... | 289 | 4913 | 4.123 | 2.571 |
| 5...... | 25 | 125 | 2.236 | 1.710 | 18...... | 324 | 5832 | 4.242 | 2.620 |
| 6...... | 36 | 216 | 2.449 | 1.817 | 19...... | 361 | 6859 | 4.358 | 2.668 |
| 7...... | 49 | 343 | 2.645 | 1.913 | 20...... | 400 | 8000 | 4.472 | 2.714 |
| 8...... | 64 | 512 | 2.828 | 2.000 | 21...... | 441 | 9261 | 4.582 | 2.758 |
| 9...... | 81 | 729 | 3.000 | 2.080 | 22...... | 484 | 10648 | 4.690 | 2.802 |
| 10...... | 100 | 1000 | 3.162 | 2.154 | 23...... | 529 | 12167 | 4.795 | 2.843 |
| 11...... | 121 | 1331 | 3.316 | 2.224 | 24...... | 576 | 13824 | 4.899 | 2.884 |
| 12...... | 144 | 1728 | 3.464 | 2.289 | 25...... | 625 | 15625 | 5.000 | 2.924 |
| 13...... | 169 | 2197 | 3.605 | 2.351 | 26...... | 676 | 17576 | 5.099 | 2.962 |

# MEDICINE AND PUBLIC HEALTH

## Medical Advances · Vital Statistics · Public Health · Medical Terms and Definitions

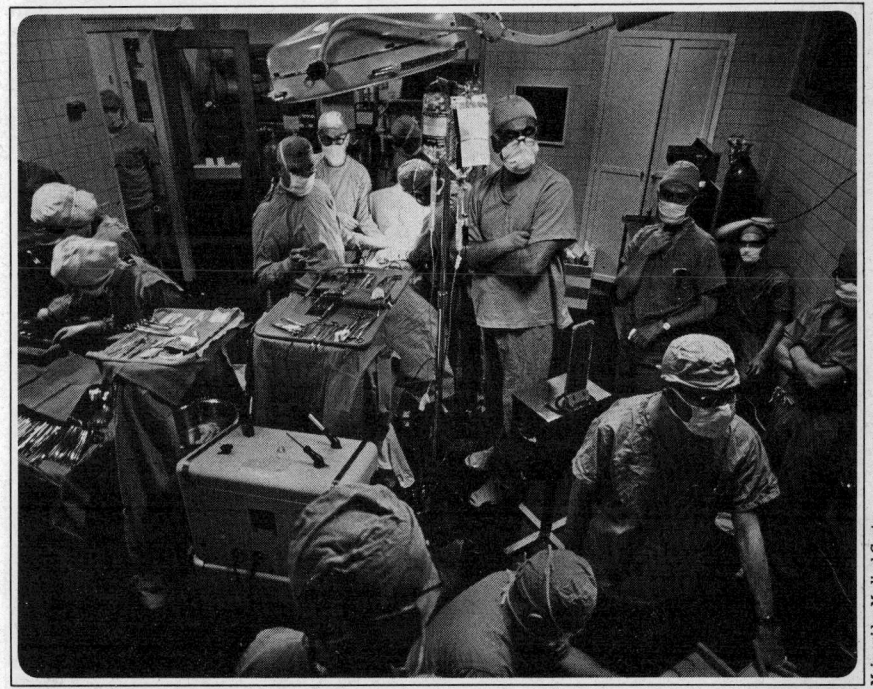

*Maimonides Medical Center*

Surgeons are using an array of new lifesaving tools. Doctors Adrian (left, at operating table) and Arthur Kantrowitz (center, with arms folded) invented an artificial heart to aid patients with severe heart failure.

## MEDICAL ADVANCES: 1967

The most significant development in U.S. medicine in 1967 may well have been the creation of a nationwide system of Regional Medical Programs. These programs, sponsored by the National Institutes of Health of the U.S. Public Health Service, represent an all-out attack on the three diseases that kill 71 out of every 100 Americans: heart disease, cancer, and stroke. The regional programs are planned by local doctors, nurses, and hospital and public health officials who know specific medical needs of their region.

In addition to this nationwide public health effort, there were other important medical developments in 1967.

**Alcoholism.** A report issued by the National Institute of Mental Health cited new facts and attitudes about alcoholics and strongly attacked "myths" about alcoholism. According to the report, about 80,000,000 Americans drink at least occasionally, and only one in 18 of these, or about 4,500,000, can be called alcoholics. The report challenged the myth of a "rising rate of alcoholism" in the United States: "It is impossible to determine if the rate of alcoholism is increasing, decreasing, or remaining steady."

**Smoking.** A new Public Health Service booklet, *The Health Consequences of Smoking*, presents a strong case that "cigarette smoking can cause death from coronary heart disease." It also cites studies that show smokers miss significantly more work-days than nonsmokers. These grim findings are added to the Surgeon General's 1964 report, that smoking causes lung cancer and that smokers, in general, die younger.

**Vaccines and Virus Diseases.** In the next few years new vaccines should be available against

*(continued)*

diseases such as German measles (rubella), syphilis, streptococcus infections, and many varieties of the common cold.

However, the ultimate weapon against all viruses may turn out to be a protein substance called *interferon*, which humans and other animals produce naturally to fight disease. Late in 1967 a team at the Merck Institute for Therapeutic Research, led by Dr. Maurice R. Hilleman, found a way of stimulating interferon production in mice. Still to be answered: Could the same technique work for man?

**Retarded Children.** Two studies reported in 1967 represent landmarks in our understanding of retarded children. In one study Drs. Mavis B. Stoch and Patrick M. Smythe of Capetown, South Africa, presented the first concrete evidence that malnutrition in early childhood causes mental retardation. The 11-year study of a group of Capetown slum children, gravely undernourished since birth, showed the children to have lower IQs, smaller heads, and less brain-body coordination. The second study, by doctors at Johns Hopkins Hospital in Baltimore, showed that a child's physical growth can be severely stunted by growing up in a family environment marred by "marital discord, alcoholism, promiscuity, divorce, emotional immaturity, and other forms of instability." The average IQ of the 13 "dwarf" children was a subnormal 75.

**Birth Control.** One type of "low-dose" oral contraceptive—containing one-tenth as much of the hormone progesterone as pills now in use, and no estrogen at all—is being tested by Population Council (New York) scientists. A second research group at the Population Council, led by Drs. Harry Rudel and Sheldon J. Segal, is working on birth-control capsules that could be planted under the skin and achieve effective contraception for up to 20 years. Finally, promising results with a "morning-after" pill were reported by Dr. John McLean Morris of Yale University Medical School.

**Organ Transplants.** Until the last few years the chances of successfully transplanting a vital organ of one person to the body of another were very poor. The problem is immunological rejection: Our bodies have built-in defense mechanisms that will reject and destroy any foreign tissue. During 1967 doctors at a Duke University seminar on organ transplants reported that about 65 per cent of all kidney transplants are now successful at least through the first year after the operation; the success rate is even higher with kidney transplants between identical twins. And at the annual meeting of the American College of Surgeons, Dr. Richard R. Lower of the Medical College of Virginia reported success in transplanting a heart from one dog to another; the dog with the new heart was still alive and wagging after a year. The increasing success of organ transplants is attributed to two factors: more careful selection and matching of the donor and recipient, and a new anti-rejection serum called anti-lymphocyte globulin.

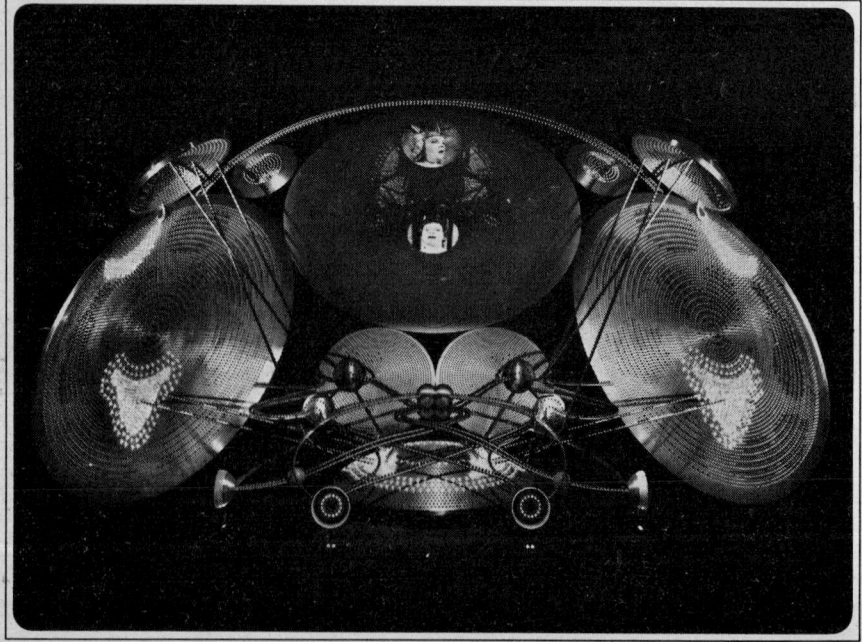

© Ezra Stoller

The Upjohn Company's schematic model of the human brain symbolically demonstrates how we receive, recognize, and memorize sights and sounds.

## Rx FOR SLOW LEARNERS: A TALKING TYPEWRITER

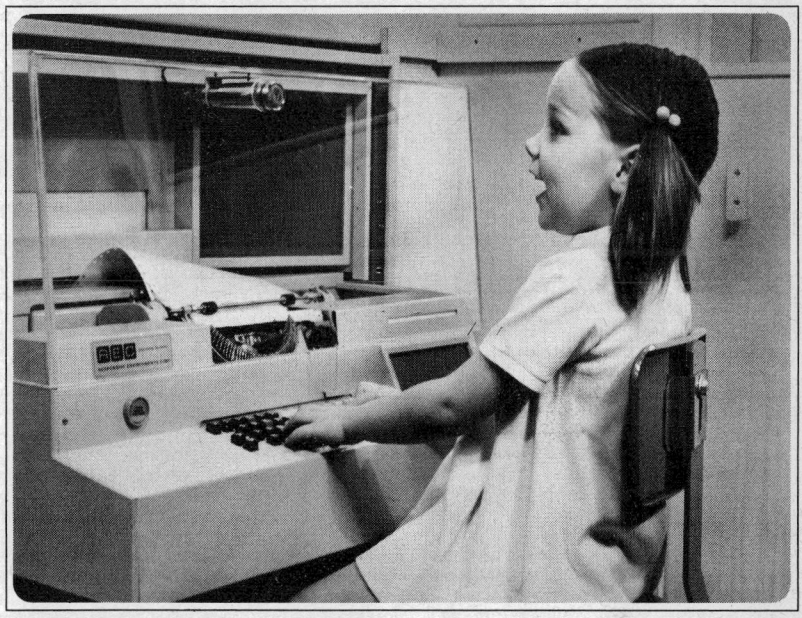

A pre-school child laughs in delight as the "Talking Typewriter" speaks the letter she has just pressed.

*Case History:* Bobby X was five years old and "too severely retarded" to even attend special classes. His next step seemed certain: an institution. Bobby is now seven. He is reading at better than a fourth-grade level and waiting to enter his local school.

Bobby is typical of a growing number of children and adults — normal and retarded — who are being helped to read, write, and speak by a patient electronic teacher, the "Talking Typewriter" of the Responsive Environments Corporation.

Here's how it works for a nonreader such as Bobby. The child enters a soundproof booth and finds what looks like an ordinary typewriter. He presses a key and instantly a voice speaks: "D." Simultaneously, a jumbo-size "D" appears behind the keyboard.

After several such "play" sessions, the child may be ready for his first real challenge: spelling. A simple word such as "dog" appears on a screen, and the type-writer speaks and spells the word. Then the typewriter asks the child to find the first letter of the word. At this point, all the letters on the keyboard become blocked except "D." If he presses the correct letter, the voice encourages him to go on; if not, the instructions are repeated.

At the heart of the typewriter is a computer that can be programmed for almost any teaching task — a foreign language, remedial reading, geography, math. Will it make teachers obsolete? Hardly. But it could free them from much routine work.

And what about pupils? Does the typewriter become a kind of mechanical slave driver? Not according to one story from England. A slow-reading youngster had been progressing beautifully until one day the typewriter gave him some instructions he did not quite understand. He scratched his head, looked the typewriter straight in the face, and asked, "Pardon?"

## SLEEP: "TURNED OFF" OR "TUNED UP"?

"A good, solid eight hours sleep" is prescribed for everything from exhaustion and chicken pox to heartache. Yet what exactly happens during those eight hours? Do our brains and bodies simply need to be "turned off," like an overheated engine, for a third of our lives? And what about dreams—did Freud tell us all we need to know about them?

In the past 15 years, scientists have found that sleep, like our waking day, is a time of turmoil and adjustment for brain and body. Worldwide investigation into the mysteries of sleep was sparked by publication in the 1950s of a scientific paper by two University of Chicago physiologists, Eugene Aserinsky and Nathaniel Kleitman. They studied something almost everyone has observed—the fact that people's eyes flutter rapidly from time to time as they sleep. Although early researchers assumed that the eye movements meant a person was dreaming, it has since been found that the "REM" (Rapid Eye Movement) sleep is not always associated with dreaming.

"Sleep laboratories" have now been established in many countries. Using an electroencephalograph, an instrument that makes pictures (EEG's) of brain-wave patterns, scientists have discovered a characteristic four-stage "sleep cycle." As a person begins to fall asleep, his brain waves show a regular pattern. As he passes into Stage I of true sleep, the waves become small, irregular, and compressed, and breathing and heartbeat begin to slow down. After a few minutes the person moves into Stage II, when the brain waves change again, showing periodic bursts of activity. The person may have been soundly asleep for ten minutes but can still be awakened easily. Then the sleeper moves into Stage III, during which the waves are large and slow. Temperature and blood pressure drop, and about half an hour after first falling asleep, the subject enters Stage IV. This is the phase of deepest sleep.

After about 20 minutes of deep sleep the brain waves of Stage I reappear. But now begin eye movements that register as sharply increased electrical activity on the EEG. This is REM sleep. If the sleeper is awakened at this point, he will usually report a dream. REM sleep lasts for about ten minutes. It is a time of frenzied inner activity: Flow of blood to the brain increases, metabolism quickens, and adrenalin shoots into the blood. Then the eye movements diminish, and the sleeper enters Stage I again to repeat the whole cycle. REM periods occur about five times during the night, becoming longer as morning approaches.

A person's sleep pattern usually stays the same, night after night. However, the pattern changes with the intake of sedatives, excessive alcohol, or drugs. Age, severe fatigue or stress, and mental illness may also alter the pattern.

It is now known that normal adults dream several times throughout the night. Individuals born with vision, then blinded by injury or disease, "see" in their dreams. Persons blind since birth do not see in their dreams, but dream in sound and touch; they also have REM periods. The person mute since birth will move his fingers in "language" signs during dreams.

Studies are being made on the effects of depriving subjects of the various sleep phases. For example, sleepers have been awakened as soon as their eyes began to move. This deprives them of REM sleep. When a REM-deprived subject is allowed uninterrupted sleep the next night, he invariably "makes up" the loss with more frequent and active REM periods.

A recent discovery marks a new stage in sleep research. Scientists found that about half a newborn baby's sleep is of the REM type. This indicates that dreams do not cause REM sleep, even though they are related to it.

What, then, is the function of REM sleep? Some scientists believe that in the case of a newborn baby it may prepare the brain to dream later on. Or perhaps, even before an infant can see or remember, he is developing the brain patterns for seeing and remembering.

In adults the role of REM sleep may be to give frequent stimulation of the higher brain centers during sleep. This would keep the central nervous system in a state of readiness so that it could react quickly, upon awakening, to any emergency. Thus REM may be nature's way of keeping the brain "tuned up" for action.

## OF RATS AND MEN

For every human being on Earth, there is a rat. And each rat is a gnawing, scampering house of pestilence. Rats are notorious as carriers of the plague, which spreads from rats to man via the rat flea. But plague is not the only rat-spread disease; outbreaks of trichinosis, rat-bite fever, murine typhus, and salmonellosis all strike where rats go unchecked. Besides causing diseases, rats eat or contaminate vast quantities of food—33,000,000 tons a year of rice and cereals alone. Will killing off rats somehow upset part of nature's balance? No. "People who suppose rats are in some way necessary to humanity are utterly mistaken," says the World Health Organization. There is, however, one good kind of rat—the specially bred, germ-free one behind bars in a medical research laboratory. There, for a change, the rat is helping to alleviate human misery instead of causing it.

## REPORTED CASES OF VENEREAL DISEASE IN THE UNITED STATES: 1941-1966*

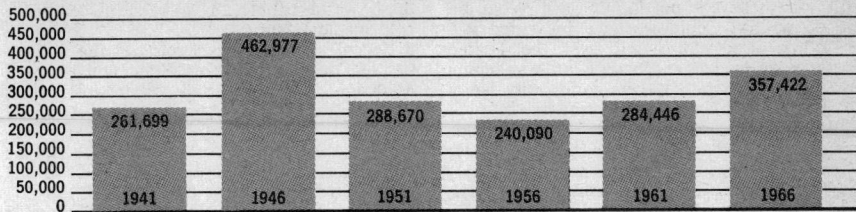

CASES PER YEAR

*Includes syphilis and gonorrhea. (Source: U.S. Public Health Service.)

## VD: AGAIN A GROWING PROBLEM

Venereal disease is back as a major public health problem. After falling off sharply with the advent of penicillin in the late 1940s, incidence of both syphilis and gonorrhea is now rising, particularly among teen-agers and young adults. This upsurge has been attributed by many authorities to false confidence: Educational programs were cut back when it seemed that antibiotics had "conquered" the diseases.

Syphilis is caused by one of a group of microorganisms called spirochetes, and is usually transmitted by sexual contact with an infected person. The first sign of the disease is usually a painless sore (chancre) that develops at the point of infection three or four weeks after contracting the disease. Even without treatment, this sore disappears in about a week. Three to six weeks later a skin rash may develop, sometimes accompanied by sore throat, fever, or headache. These symptoms may also disappear without treatment. Then the microorganisms often seem to vanish from the body, only to reappear—perhaps as much as twenty years later—as the cause of blindness, heart disease, crippling, insanity, or death.

Gonorrhea, caused by a bacterium called gonococcus, is also usually transmitted by sexual contact with an infected person. If untreated, it can cause blindness, crippling, arthritis, or sterility. It rarely causes death.

Although the diseases are not hereditary, babies may be born blind to women who are victims of gonorrhea. Syphilis, passed from mother to child during pregnancy, may cause infants to be born crippled or dead.

In the late 1930s sulfa drugs were used with some effectiveness against venereal diseases. Then penicillin arrived—with startling results. In the U.S. reported cases of syphilis in its early stages dropped from a high of 106,539 in 1947, to 6,251 ten years later. Cases of gonorrhea dropped from a reported 400,639 in 1947, to 216,476 in 1957. The nation began to consider the problem solved. Federal and state spending for VD-education programs was drastically cut. But by 1958 VD's downward trend had been reversed.

Now, according to the National Communicable Disease Center of the Public Health Service, venereal disease has reached epidemic proportions in nearly all metropolitan areas. In adults, gonorrhea is the leading bacterial infection. Figures for 1966 show 22,473 reported cases of syphilis in its early stages and 334,949 cases of gonorrhea. The situation is even more serious than these figures indicate: Actual syphilis infection, for example, is considered to be four times the *reported* figure.

Alarmingly, teen-agers account for most of the rise. In 1964 and 1965 syphilis among U.S. teen-agers rose 12.4 per cent while the overall national incidence remained constant. And in 1965 the rate of infection per 100,000 in the 15–19 group for syphilis *and* gonorrhea was more than double the rate for all age groups combined. Recent data show that one out of about every 250 teen-age boys and girls is infected with gonorrhea.

The problem is not confined to the United States. England and Japan report a rising VD rate among their young persons, and VD is increasing among U.S. troops in Vietnam.

Medical researchers continue the fight against venereal diseases. A new antibiotic, cephaloridine, has shown good results in treating gonorrhea, especially strains of the disease that have proved resistant to penicillin. Scientists at Baylor University are engaged in a three-year research program for a syphilis vaccine.

Yet even medical researchers stress that "miracle cures" alone cannot solve the problem. A strong educational program is needed to teach the public—especially the young—the dangers of the disease and how to avoid it. The National Congress of Parents and Teachers adopted a resolution in 1966 advocating public school courses in VD education "at least by the eighth grade." The VD-education program in Los Angeles schools has shown dramatic results. Since 1963, when courses began, the incidence of infectious syphilis in that city's teen-agers has plummeted by 58 per cent.

A further "must" in combating VD is the prompt reporting of all cases to public health authorities, followed by an immediate effort to track down all persons who may have been infected by known carriers.

In 1967 U.S. health authorities requested that Congress appropriate $17,500,000 for programs against both gonorrhea and syphilis.

## THE DRUG DILEMMA

"I never thought it could happen here. . . I still don't believe it, not in our town. What did we do wrong? Could we have prevented it?"

"It" is drug abuse. All over the United States, civic leaders and parents are awakening to the harsh fact that their community has a drug-abuse problem—or soon may have.

What drugs are involved? There are four main types: *hallucinogens* (marijuana, LSD); *stimulants* (cocaine, benzedrine, dexedrine); *depressants or sedatives* (Nembutal, Amatyl, and "tranquilizers" such as Miltown and Librium); and *narcotics* (heroin, morphine, opium).

There are really two drug problems: legal and medical. An outspoken minority believes drugs such as LSD and marijuana should be legalized. Why jail a person for possessing or using marijuana, they ask, when somebody who possesses and drinks alcohol (which they claim is far more unhealthy) risks no legal action whatsoever?

The trouble with such reasoning, critics answer, is that it assumes anybody who takes drugs can manage them; in other words, that all who experiment with drugs are mature, level-headed adults who would never let a drug get the better of them. This is just not the case, according to public health authorities. Increasingly, drugs are coming into the hands of adolescents; and no group is more likely to turn drug use into drug abuse. A California doctor recently reported that 40 to 50 per cent of the students at some Los Angeles high schools have taken LSD. In Great Neck, N.Y., a survey showed that 10 per cent had experimented with LSD or marijuana.

What is meant by "drug abuse"? One definition of a drug abuser is a person whose health or judgment is habitually affected by drugs. But drug abuse can also be a one-time proposition: The drugs are usually used because they are mind-warpers—they make us feel different than we would if we had not taken them. But a little of a certain drug may be too much for some people, and the mind-warping could take the form of severe depression or even maniacal behavior.

Any type of drug abuse is a potential medical problem. Heroin is perhaps the most dangerous drug. Extremely addictive, its hypodermic-riddled addicts are usually hooked for life. Even "glue-sniffing," which gives many 10- to 15-year-olds a taste for more powerful mind-warpers, can have grave medical consequences, although glue is not a true drug and sniffing it is not addictive. Adolescents who sniff the fumes of solvents such as glue, paint thinner, and lighter fluid—to get a half-hour's "high"—risk suffocation and possible damage to vital internal organs. Moreover, if a glue-sniffer happens to have a genetic blood-cell defect called sickle-celling, he risks severe anemia.

Extravagant claims are being made for the self-enriching, "mind-expanding" effects of LSD and other hallucinogens such as STP (a new "super, long-lasting LSD") and DMT (which has milder effects than LSD). Against these warm tributes have been placed some cold medical facts:

■ Recent studies by geneticists at the University of Oregon, New York State University of Medicine (Buffalo), and other institutions show that LSD may damage and disrupt the chromosomes and genes. Even these early findings, says one New York doctor, "should be a warning to women not to take LSD during pregnancy." Research is continuing.

■ A five-year-old girl swallowed an LSD-loaded sugar cube that had been left in the refrigerator by her uncle. There followed, for this "apparently normal, bright girl," nine months of excruciating mental torture: "feelings of agitation, panic, depression, distortion" and horrible dreams and visions ("they stole my mommy and cut her in half"). Within five days after taking the LSD cube, the girl's IQ dropped from 125 to 94. Although the girl has now apparently returned to normal, she is still being closely watched by her doctors. Reason: Many people who take LSD—even once—have experienced panic feelings and hallucinations as much as two years after their last use of LSD.

■ Perhaps the most dangerous drug now used by some teenagers is Methedrine. Dubbed "speed" by the "hippies," Methedrine is a stimulant rather than an LSD-type hallucinogen. Continued use invites complete mental and physical breakdown. The hippies themselves warn: "Speed kills."

What can be done? Most public health authorities believe "scare tactics" simply will not work on today's youth. According to Dr. David E. Smith, Director of the Alcoholic and Drug Abuse Screening Unit at San Francisco General Hospital, "Using drug misinformation to scare young people actually increases their drug experimentation because they feel they must find out the truth first hand."

Earlier in the year, doctors at the 1967 meeting of the American College Health Association discussed the almost "epidemic" use of LSD in California. Several speakers observed that "preaching" the evils of drugs had little effect on college and high-school users of LSD and marijuana—especially when the preaching was done by parents who drank alcohol, inhaled nicotine, and swallowed tranquilizer pills. One speaker, Dr. Duke Fisher of the Neuropsychiatric Institute of the University of California (Los Angeles) commented: "I feel it is extremely important that information as to the knowable effects of hallucinogenic drugs should be made available to students in high schools, colleges, and universities. There is a great deal of attraction to anything that is forbidden. The more that LSD and the other hallucinogenic drugs are freely discussed, the less forbidden they will be. Those of us who want to be of service to students and young people must stop merely cursing the drug and start looking for ways to provide information and assistance to the young people who are so attracted to it."

## LONGEVITY

Tales of human longevity have intrigued mankind since the Biblical days of Methuselah and Isaac, and during historic times hundreds of claims have been put forth of people living well into their second century. Two Englishmen, Henry Jenkins and Thomas Parr, were reported to have lived for 169 and 152 years respectively. Parr, whose death date in 1935, but not his birth date, is a recorded fact, is reputed to have had a son who carried on the tradition by dying at the age of 127 years. According to some accounts, Katherine, the Countess of Desmond, died at 140; Drakenberg of Norway, at 146; and the French butcher Gascogne, at 120. Elizabeth Durieux, the Frenchwoman credited with subsisting on little other than 40 cups of coffee a day, was said to have reached the age of 114.

Research into the records of the past, however, has largely dissipated the claims, and the most famed centenarians have been reduced to the status of legendary characters. Of the 1,712 centenarians from 66 A.D. to 1799 listed by James Easton, not one claim has been proved acceptable or authentic.

Some of the allegations were advanced legitimately, with inaccuracies attributed to faulty memories or records; some were conscious exaggerations. Other claims arose when father and son or brothers had the same name. Although life expectancy has steadily risen throughout most of the world (in the United States, for example, from less than 35 years in the early 1760s to 70.2 years in 1964), individuals who pass their 110th birthday are extremely rare.

## EXPECTATION OF LIFE IN THE UNITED STATES

The white female at birth has a greater life expectancy, 74.7 years, than either the nonwhite female, the white male, or the nonwhite male.

As age increases, however, the life expectancy of both male and female nonwhites increases beyond that of their white counterparts.

| AGE | WHITE Male | Female | NONWHITE Male | Female | AGE | WHITE Male | Female | NONWHITE Male | Female |
|---|---|---|---|---|---|---|---|---|---|
| 0 | 67.6 | 74.7 | 61.1 | 67.4 | 43 | 29.0 | 34.7 | 26.0 | 30.4 |
| 1 | 68.3 | 75.1 | 62.9 | 68.9 | 44 | 28.2 | 33.8 | 25.3 | 29.6 |
| 2 | 67.4 | 74.2 | 62.1 | 68.0 | 45 | 27.3 | 32.9 | 24.5 | 28.8 |
| 3 | 66.5 | 73.2 | 61.2 | 67.1 | 46 | 26.5 | 32.0 | 23.8 | 28.0 |
| 4 | 65.5 | 72.3 | 60.2 | 66.2 | 47 | 25.6 | 31.1 | 23.1 | 27.3 |
| 5 | 64.5 | 71.3 | 59.3 | 65.3 | 48 | 24.8 | 30.3 | 22.4 | 26.5 |
| 6 | 63.6 | 70.3 | 58.4 | 64.3 | 49 | 24.0 | 29.4 | 21.7 | 25.7 |
| 7 | 62.6 | 69.3 | 57.4 | 63.3 | 50 | 23.2 | 28.5 | 21.0 | 25.0 |
| 8 | 61.7 | 68.4 | 56.4 | 62.4 | 51 | 22.4 | 27.6 | 20.4 | 24.2 |
| 9 | 60.7 | 67.4 | 55.5 | 61.4 | 52 | 21.6 | 26.8 | 19.7 | 23.5 |
| 10 | 59.7 | 66.4 | 54.5 | 60.4 | 53 | 20.8 | 25.9 | 19.1 | 22.8 |
| 11 | 58.7 | 65.4 | 53.5 | 59.5 | 54 | 20.1 | 25.1 | 18.5 | 22.1 |
| 12 | 57.7 | 64.4 | 52.6 | 58.5 | 55 | 19.4 | 24.2 | 17.9 | 21.4 |
| 13 | 56.8 | 63.5 | 51.6 | 57.5 | 56 | 18.7 | 23.4 | 17.3 | 20.7 |
| 14 | 55.8 | 62.5 | 50.6 | 56.5 | 57 | 18.0 | 22.6 | 16.7 | 20.1 |
| 15 | 54.8 | 61.5 | 49.7 | 55.5 | 58 | 17.3 | 21.8 | 16.1 | 19.4 |
| 16 | 53.9 | 60.5 | 48.7 | 54.6 | 59 | 16.6 | 21.0 | 15.6 | 18.8 |
| 17 | 52.9 | 59.5 | 47.8 | 53.6 | 60 | 16.0 | 20.1 | 15.1 | 18.2 |
| 18 | 52.0 | 58.6 | 46.9 | 52.7 | 61 | 15.3 | 19.4 | 14.5 | 17.6 |
| 19 | 51.1 | 57.6 | 46.0 | 51.7 | 62 | 14.7 | 18.6 | 14.0 | 17.0 |
| 20 | 50.2 | 56.6 | 45.1 | 50.8 | 63 | 14.1 | 17.8 | 13.5 | 16.5 |
| 21 | 49.3 | 55.7 | 44.2 | 49.8 | 64 | 13.5 | 17.0 | 13.0 | 15.9 |
| 22 | 48.3 | 54.7 | 43.3 | 48.9 | 65 | 12.9 | 16.3 | 12.6 | 15.5 |
| 23 | 47.4 | 53.7 | 42.4 | 47.9 | 66 | 12.4 | 15.5 | 12.2 | 15.0 |
| 24 | 46.5 | 52.8 | 41.6 | 47.0 | 67 | 11.8 | 14.8 | 11.9 | 14.6 |
| 25 | 45.6 | 51.8 | 40.7 | 46.1 | 68 | 11.3 | 14.1 | 11.7 | 14.3 |
| 26 | 44.7 | 50.9 | 39.8 | 45.1 | 69 | 10.8 | 13.4 | 11.5 | 13.9 |
| 27 | 43.7 | 49.9 | 39.0 | 44.2 | 70 | 10.3 | 12.8 | 11.2 | 13.5 |
| 28 | 42.8 | 48.9 | 38.1 | 43.3 | 71 | 9.8 | 12.1 | 11.0 | 13.1 |
| 29 | 41.9 | 48.0 | 37.3 | 42.4 | 72 | 9.4 | 11.5 | 10.7 | 12.7 |
| 30 | 40.9 | 47.0 | 36.4 | 41.5 | 73 | 8.9 | 10.8 | 10.4 | 12.2 |
| 31 | 40.0 | 46.0 | 35.6 | 40.6 | 74 | 8.5 | 10.2 | 10.1 | 11.7 |
| 32 | 39.1 | 45.1 | 34.8 | 39.7 | 75 | 8.0 | 9.6 | 9.8 | 11.2 |
| 33 | 38.1 | 44.1 | 33.9 | 38.8 | 76 | 7.6 | 9.0 | 9.5 | 10.8 |
| 34 | 37.2 | 43.2 | 33.1 | 37.9 | 77 | 7.2 | 8.5 | 9.2 | 10.3 |
| 35 | 36.3 | 42.2 | 32.3 | 37.1 | 78 | 6.8 | 7.9 | 8.9 | 9.9 |
| 36 | 35.3 | 41.3 | 31.5 | 36.2 | 79 | 6.4 | 7.4 | 8.6 | 9.5 |
| 37 | 34.4 | 40.3 | 30.7 | 35.4 | 80 | 6.0 | 6.9 | 8.3 | 9.0 |
| 38 | 33.5 | 39.4 | 29.9 | 34.5 | 81 | 5.6 | 6.4 | 8.0 | 8.6 |
| 39 | 32.6 | 38.4 | 29.1 | 33.7 | 82 | 5.3 | 6.0 | 7.6 | 8.1 |
| 40 | 31.7 | 37.5 | 28.3 | 32.8 | 83 | 4.9 | 5.5 | 7.2 | 7.6 |
| 41 | 30.8 | 36.6 | 27.5 | 32.0 | 84 | 4.6 | 5.1 | 6.8 | 7.2 |
| 42 | 29.9 | 35.7 | 26.8 | 31.2 | 85 | 4.3 | 4.7 | 6.5 | 6.8 |

## THE GROWTH OF THE AMERICAN LIFE-SPAN: 1900-1965
Source: U.S. Public Health Service

| YEAR | LIFE SPAN (in yrs.) | YEAR | LIFE SPAN (in yrs.) | YEAR | LIFE SPAN (in yrs.) | YEAR | LIFE SPAN (in yrs.) | YEAR | LIFE SPAN (in yrs.) |
|---|---|---|---|---|---|---|---|---|---|
| 1965.... | 70.2 | 1956.... | 69.6 | 1947.... | 66.8 | 1938.... | 63.5 | 1929.... | 57.1 |
| 1964.... | 70.2 | 1955.... | 69.5 | 1946.... | 66.7 | 1937.... | 60.0 | 1928.... | 56.8 |
| 1963.... | 69.9 | 1954.... | 69.6 | 1945.... | 65.9 | 1936.... | 58.5 | 1927.... | 60.4 |
| 1962.... | 70.0 | 1953.... | 68.8 | 1944.... | 65.2 | 1935.... | 61.7 | 1926.... | 56.7 |
| 1961.... | 70.2 | 1952.... | 68.6 | 1943.... | 63.3 | 1934.... | 61.1 | 1925.... | 59.0 |
| 1960.... | 69.7 | 1951.... | 68.4 | 1942.... | 66.2 | 1933.... | 63.3 | 1920.... | 54.1 |
| 1959.... | 69.9 | 1950.... | 68.2 | 1941.... | 64.8 | 1932.... | 62.1 | 1915.... | 54.5 |
| 1958.... | 69.4 | 1949.... | 68.0 | 1940.... | 62.9 | 1931.... | 61.1 | 1910.... | 50.0 |
| 1957.... | 69.3 | 1948.... | 67.2 | 1939.... | 63.7 | 1930.... | 59.7 | 1900.... | 47.3 |

## LIFE EXPECTANCY AT AGE 45 IN SELECTED COUNTRIES

The average male American at age 45 can expect to live another 27.1 years, while the average Congolese at 45 has a life expectancy of only 18.5 years, according to this record prepared by the Metropolitan Life Insurance Company. Figures based on the most recent census reports for men and women in selected countries are as follows.

| COUNTRY | MEN | WOMEN | COUNTRY | MEN | WOMEN | COUNTRY | MEN | WOMEN |
|---|---|---|---|---|---|---|---|---|
| Argentina...... | 24.2 | 28.2 | England........ | 26.9 | 31.9 | Netherlands.... | 30.1 | 32.7 |
| Australia....... | 27.2 | 31.4 | Finland........ | 25.4 | 30.4 | New Zealand.... | 28.3 | 32.0 |
| Austria......... | 26.4 | 30.6 | France........ | 26.9 | 32.5 | Norway........ | 31.0 | 33.1 |
| Belgium........ | 26.5 | 29.8 | Germany, West.. | 27.4 | 31.5 | Philippines.... | 27.6 | 28.6 |
| Bulgaria........ | 28.8 | 31.2 | Greece......... | 29.5 | 31.9 | Poland......... | 27.6 | 31.5 |
| Canada........ | 28.5 | 32.8 | Greenland..... | 22.0 | 22.8 | Portugal....... | 27.5 | 31.6 |
| Ceylon......... | 28.7 | 29.3 | Guatemala...... | 23.6 | 23.6 | Puerto Rico..... | 30.2 | 33.5 |
| Chile.......... | 23.8 | 27.4 | Hungary........ | 27.2 | 30.2 | Scotland...... | 25.6 | 30.4 |
| Colombia...... | 21.3 | 23.0 | India.......... | 19.2 | 19.9 | Spain.......... | 28.4 | 31.8 |
| Congo......... | 18.5 | 20.3 | Ireland........ | 27.0 | 28.9 | Sweden........ | 29.9 | 32.9 |
| Costa Rica..... | 25.6 | 27.2 | Israel.......... | 30.0 | 31.2 | Switzerland..... | 27.5 | 30.5 |
| Cyprus........ | 28.8 | 32.7 | Italy.......... | 28.1 | 31.2 | Thailand....... | 22.2 | 24.9 |
| Czechoslovakia.. | 27.5 | 31.4 | Jamaica........ | 24.8 | 27.6 | Trinidad....... | 23.8 | 26.0 |
| Denmark....... | 29.7 | 32.0 | Japan.......... | 27.4 | 31.3 | United States... | 27.1 | 32.5 |
| Ecuador........ | 25.0 | 27.9 | Luxembourg..... | 26.2 | 29.0 | U.S.S.R....... | 28.0 | 33.4 |
| Egypt.......... | 26.4 | 30.6 | Malta.......... | 26.8 | 29.3 | Venezuela...... | 26.1 | 28.5 |
| El Salvador..... | 24.9 | 26.0 | Mexico......... | 27.3 | 29.9 | Yugoslavia...... | 27.4 | 30.1 |

## LEADING CAUSES OF DEATH AMONG AMERICANS
Source: U.S. Public Health Service

Diseases of the heart and circulatory system remain the leading cause of death in the United States, killing an estimated 1,017,550 of the estimated 1,869,000 people who died in the U.S. in 1966. In the table the death rate means the number of people dying from one cause out of every 100,000 people living in the U.S. The 1966 rates are provisional.

| CAUSE OF DEATH | 1966 RATE | 1965 RATE | CAUSE OF DEATH | 1966 RATE | 1965 RATE |
|---|---|---|---|---|---|
| **Diseases of the cardiovascular system** | 519.5 | 510.9 | Cirrhosis of the liver.................. | 13.5 | 12.8 |
| Diseases of the heart................. | 375.1 | 367.4 | Senility and ill-defined causes........ | 12.8 | 12.1 |
| Stroke........................... | 104.6 | 103.7 | Kidney disorders...................... | 11.0 | 11.3 |
| General arteriosclerosis............. | 19.5 | 19.7 | Suicide.............................. | 10.3 | 11.1 |
| Other diseases of circulatory system... | 20.3 | 20.1 | Congenital malformations............. | 9.3 | 10.1 |
| **Cancer**.............................. | 154.8 | 153.5 | Ulcer of the stomach and duodenum.. | 5.2 | 5.4 |
| Malignant growths................... | 139.8 | 138.9 | Hernia and intestinal obstruction..... | 5.0 | 5.2 |
| Leukemia, blood and lymph cancers... | 15.0 | 14.8 | Homicide............................ | 5.7 | 5.5 |
| **Accidents**.......................... | 57.3 | 55.7 | Tuberculosis......................... | 3.9 | 4.1 |
| Motor vehicle accidents.............. | 27.2 | 25.4 | Gastritis, duodenitis, enteritis, | | |
| Accidents in the home............... | 12.6 | 12.4 | and colitis....................... | 3.3 | 4.1 |
| Other accidents...................... | 17.5 | 17.9 | Benign growths...................... | 2.4 | 2.6 |
| **Bronchopulmonic diseases**........... | 50.9 | 48.6 | Disorders of gall bladder and bile duct | 2.3 | 2.4 |
| Pneumonia......................... | 31.2 | 30.8 | Asthma............................. | 2.2 | 2.3 |
| Bronchitis.......................... | 3.4 | 3.0 | Anemias............................ | 1.9 | 1.8 |
| Other bronchopulmonic diseases...... | 16.3 | 14.9 | Hyperplasia of the prostate........... | 1.5 | 1.8 |
| **Diseases of early infancy**............ | 26.1 | 28.6 | Syphilis............................. | 1.3 | 1.3 |
| **Diabetes**............................ | 18.1 | 17.1 | All other causes..................... | 35.5 | 35.4 |

## MORTALITY RATES IN THE UNITED STATES
Source: U.S. Public Health Service

The following table indicates the probability of dying at any specified age up to 84. Thus, in any sample group of 1,000 white male Americans aged 55, 15 will die in the course of a year, while death will reach only 7 white females of the same age. Rates for nonwhite Americans aged 55 are about 23 males per 1,000 and 15 females per 1,000.

| AGE (in years) | RATE PER 1,000 White Male | White Female | Nonwhite Male | Nonwhite Female | AGE (in years) | RATE PER 1,000 White Male | White Female | Nonwhite Male | Nonwhite Female |
|---|---|---|---|---|---|---|---|---|---|
| 0–1 | 24.2 | 18.3 | 44.2 | 36.0 | 42–43 | 4.1 | 2.3 | 9.3 | 6.3 |
| 1–2 | 1.3 | 1.1 | 2.8 | 2.6 | 43–44 | 4.5 | 2.6 | 9.9 | 6.8 |
| 2–3 | 0.9 | 0.8 | 1.6 | 1.4 | 44–45 | 5.0 | 2.8 | 10.6 | 7.1 |
| 3–4 | 0.7 | 0.6 | 1.2 | 0.9 | 45–46 | 5.5 | 3.1 | 11.4 | 7.5 |
| 4–5 | 0.6 | 0.5 | 1.0 | 0.8 | 46–47 | 6.0 | 3.4 | 12.1 | 8.0 |
| 5–6 | 0.7 | 0.4 | 1.0 | 0.7 | 47–48 | 6.7 | 3.7 | 13.0 | 8.5 |
| 6–7 | 0.7 | 0.4 | 0.8 | 0.6 | 48–49 | 7.5 | 4.0 | 14.0 | 9.1 |
| 7–8 | 0.4 | 0.3 | 0.6 | 0.5 | 49–50 | 8.3 | 4.4 | 15.1 | 9.8 |
| 8–9 | 0.4 | 0.3 | 0.5 | 0.4 | 50–51 | 9.3 | 4.8 | 16.2 | 10.6 |
| 9–10 | 0.3 | 0.3 | 0.5 | 0.4 | 51–52 | 10.2 | 5.1 | 17.4 | 11.4 |
| 10–11 | 0.3 | 0.2 | 0.5 | 0.4 | 52–53 | 11.3 | 5.6 | 18.7 | 12.3 |
| 11–12 | 0.4 | 0.2 | 0.5 | 0.4 | 53–54 | 12.5 | 6.0 | 20.0 | 13.2 |
| 12–13 | 0.4 | 0.3 | 0.6 | 0.4 | 54–55 | 13.7 | 6.5 | 21.5 | 14.2 |
| 13–14 | 0.6 | 0.3 | 0.8 | 0.4 | 55–56 | 15.0 | 7.0 | 23.1 | 15.2 |
| 14–15 | 0.8 | 0.4 | 1.0 | 0.5 | 56–57 | 16.4 | 7.6 | 24.8 | 16.4 |
| 15–16 | 1.0 | 0.4 | 1.2 | 0.6 | 57–58 | 17.9 | 8.2 | 26.5 | 17.7 |
| 16–17 | 1.2 | 0.5 | 1.4 | 0.7 | 58–59 | 19.5 | 8.9 | 28.0 | 19.2 |
| 17–18 | 1.4 | 0.5 | 1.7 | 0.8 | 59–60 | 21.1 | 9.6 | 29.6 | 20.8 |
| 18–19 | 1.5 | 0.6 | 1.9 | 0.9 | 60–61 | 22.8 | 10.3 | 30.8 | 22.5 |
| 19–20 | 1.6 | 0.6 | 2.2 | 1.0 | 61–62 | 24.6 | 11.2 | 32.3 | 24.1 |
| 20–21 | 1.6 | 0.6 | 2.4 | 1.0 | 62–63 | 26.6 | 12.2 | 34.8 | 26.4 |
| 21–22 | 1.7 | 0.6 | 2.7 | 1.1 | 63–64 | 29.0 | 13.5 | 38.9 | 29.2 |
| 22–23 | 1.8 | 0.6 | 2.9 | 1.2 | 64–65 | 31.6 | 15.0 | 44.1 | 32.6 |
| 23–24 | 1.8 | 0.6 | 3.1 | 1.4 | 65–66 | 34.5 | 16.7 | 50.4 | 36.4 |
| 24–25 | 1.7 | 0.7 | 3.3 | 1.5 | 66–67 | 37.5 | 18.6 | 56.8 | 40.2 |
| 25–26 | 1.6 | 0.7 | 3.6 | 1.6 | 67–68 | 40.6 | 20.5 | 62.0 | 43.0 |
| 26–27 | 1.6 | 0.7 | 3.8 | 1.8 | 68–69 | 43.8 | 22.5 | 64.7 | 44.2 |
| 27–28 | 1.5 | 0.7 | 4.0 | 1.9 | 69–70 | 47.0 | 24.6 | 65.3 | 43.9 |
| 28–29 | 1.5 | 0.7 | 4.1 | 2.1 | 70–71 | 50.4 | 26.9 | 64.7 | 42.9 |
| 29–30 | 1.6 | 0.8 | 4.2 | 2.3 | 71–72 | 54.1 | 29.4 | 64.2 | 42.0 |
| 30–31 | 1.6 | 0.9 | 4 3 | 2.5 | 72–73 | 58.0 | 32.4 | 64.1 | 41.8 |
| 31–32 | 1.7 | 0.9 | 4.5 | 2.8 | 73–74 | 62.1 | 35.9 | 65.5 | 43.0 |
| 32–33 | 1.8 | 1.0 | 4.7 | 3.0 | 74–75 | 66.5 | 39.9 | 68.3 | 45.4 |
| 33–34 | 1.9 | 1.1 | 5.0 | 3.3 | 75–76 | 71.3 | 44.3 | 71.6 | 48.4 |
| 34–35 | 2.0 | 1.2 | 5.4 | 3.5 | 76–77 | 76.4 | 49.2 | 74.8 | 51.4 |
| 35–36 | 2.2 | 1.3 | 5.9 | 3.8 | 77–78 | 82.1 | 54.5 | 77.2 | 54.1 |
| 36–37 | 2.3 | 1.4 | 6.4 | 4.1 | 78–79 | 88.3 | 60.2 | 78.3 | 56.2 |
| 37–38 | 2.6 | 1.5 | 6.9 | 4.4 | 79–80 | 95.2 | 66.6 | 78.4 | 58.0 |
| 38–39 | 2.8 | 1.6 | 7.3 | 4.8 | 80–81 | 102.9 | 73.7 | 77.9 | 59.8 |
| 39–40 | 3.0 | 1.8 | 7.8 | 5.1 | 81–82 | 111.4 | 81.9 | 77.8 | 62.4 |
| 40–41 | 3.3 | 1.9 | 8.2 | 5.5 | 82–83 | 121.1 | 91.6 | 79.5 | 66.5 |
| 41–42 | 3.7 | 2.1 | 8.7 | 6.0 | 83–84 | 132.0 | 103.2 | 85.0 | 73.4 |

## U.S. DEATH RATES, BY MONTH: 1956–1965
Source: U.S. Public Health Service

| MONTH | 1966 (est.) | 1965 | 1964 | 1963 | 1962 | 1961 | 1960 | 1959 | 1958 | 1957 |
|---|---|---|---|---|---|---|---|---|---|---|
| Annual Rate.. | 9.5 | 9.4 | 9.4 | 9.6 | 9.5 | 9.3 | 9.5 | 9.4 | 9.5 | 9.6 |
| January....... | 10.3 | 10.1 | 10.2 | 10.4 | 10.4 | 10.0 | 10.8 | 10.2 | 10.7 | 10.1 |
| February...... | 10.2 | 10.4 | 9.8 | 11.2 | 10.3 | 9.8 | 11.2 | 9.7 | 11.1 | 9.6 |
| March........ | 9.9 | 10.1 | 9.9 | 11.1 | 10.0 | 9.4 | 10.2 | 9.8 | 10.1 | 9.7 |
| April......... | 10.1 | 9.5 | 9.5 | 9.6 | 9.6 | 9.4 | 9.3 | 9.7 | 9.5 | 9.4 |
| May.......... | 9.5 | 9.2 | 9.3 | 9.1 | 9.3 | 9.1 | 9.1 | 9.3 | 9.1 | 9.1 |
| June.......... | 9.3 | 9.1 | 9.2 | 9.3 | 8.9 | 9.0 | 9.0 | 9.1 | 9.0 | 9.4 |
| July.......... | 9.7 | 8.9 | 9.4 | 9.0 | 8.8 | 8.9 | 8.7 | 8.8 | 8.7 | 9.1 |
| August........ | 8.8 | 8.7 | 8.6 | 8.5 | 8.8 | 8.6 | 8.5 | 8.8 | 8.5 | 8.5 |
| September.... | 8.7 | 8.8 | 8.8 | 8.7 | 8.7 | 8.8 | 8.6 | 8.6 | 8.6 | 8.8 |
| October....... | 9.2 | 9.3 | 9.1 | 9.0 | 9.2 | 9.2 | 9.2 | 8.9 | 9.1 | 10.2 |
| November..... | 9.2 | 9.5 | 9.3 | 9.3 | 9.5 | 9.4 | 9.4 | 9.5 | 9.3 | 10.5 |
| December..... | 9.7 | 9.9 | 9.8 | 10.3 | 10.1 | 10.0 | 10.1 | 9.8 | 10.1 | 10.2 |

## PIONEERS OF MEDICINE

**Abulcasis,** 11th century, Arabic physician; first known practitioner of dentistry.

**Alfred Adler,** 1870–1937, Austrian psychiatrist; founded school of psychology.

**Arístides Agramonte,** 1869–1931, Cuban physician and pathologist; studied pathological aspects of yellow fever.

**F. H. Albee,** 1876–1945, American surgeon; developed practical bone-grafting technique.

**Leopold Augenbrugger,** 1722–1809, Viennese physician; first used percussion in diagnosing chest diseases.

**Frederick G. Banting,** 1891–1941, and **Charles H. Best,** 1899–, Canadian endocrinologists; isolated insulin from the pancreas and used it in treating diabetes.

**Emil Adolph von Behring,** 1854–1917, German physician; pioneered in serum therapy and the use of antitoxins.

**Claude Bernard,** 1813–78, French physician; a founder of modern experimental medicine; investigated biochemistry of body.

**Alfred Blalock,** 1899–1964, American surgeon; developed operation for treatment of congenital heart conditions in infants.

**Hans Burger,** 1873–1941, German neuropsychiatrist; developed electroencephalograph, which measures electric waves emitted by the brain.

**Alexis Carrel,** 1873–1944, American surgeon; pioneered in transplanting organs.

**Harvey Cushing,** 1869–1939, American surgeon; developed many important techniques of brain surgery.

**John Staige Davis,** 1872–1946, American surgeon; pioneered in plastic surgery using skin grafts.

**George F. Dick,** 1881–, and **Gladys Dick,** 1881–, American physicians; isolated the germ causing scarlet fever and devised a test to determine susceptibility to the disease.

**Paul Ehrlich,** 1854–1915, Germain bacteriologist; discovered drugs for the treatment of syphilis.

**Willem Einthoven,** 1860–1927, Dutch physician; developed electrocardiogram, which measures electric waves emitted by the heart.

**Pierre Fauchard,** 1678–1761, French physician and dentist; raised dentistry from a trade to a profession.

**Carlos Juan Finlay,** 1833–1915, Cuban physician; identified mosquito that carries yellow fever.

**Sir Alexander Fleming,** 1881–1955, Scottish bacteriologist; discovered penicillin.

**Sigmund Freud,** 1856–1939, Austrian psychiatrist; developed a new theory of mental disorders; founder of psychoanalysis.

**Galen,** 2nd century A.D., Greek physician; first to systematize medical knowledge.

**William Harvey,** 1578–1657, English physician; first described the circulation of the blood.

**Sir Frederick G. Hopkins,** 1861–1947, English biochemist; identified vitamins as a vital element in food.

**Hippocrates,** 5th century B.C., Greek physician; the "father of medicine," the first to base medical treatment on scientific observation.

**Charles Huggins,** 1901–, American physician; discovered that growth of cancer in the prostate is stimulated by male hormones.

**Chevalier Jackson,** 1865–1958, American laryngologist; perfected technique for removing objects from respiratory tract and esophagus.

**Edward Jenner,** 1749–1823, English physician; developed vaccination against smallpox.

**Carl Gustav Jung,** 1875–1961, Swiss psychiatrist; founded school of analytical psychology.

**Shibasaburo Kitasato,** 1852–1931, Japanese physician; discovered the infectious agent that spreads bubonic plague.

**Edwin Klebs,** 1834–1913, German-American pathologist; described the diphtheria and typhoid bacilli.

**Robert Koch,** 1843–1910, German bacteriologist; discovered microorganisms causing anthrax and tuberculosis.

**René Théophile Hyacinthe Laënnec,** 1781–1826, French physician; invented the stethoscope.

**Anthony van Leeuwenhoek,** 1632–1723, Dutch student of anatomy; developed the first useful compound microscope.

**Joseph Lister,** 1827–1912, English surgeon; introduced antisepsis into surgery.

**John J. R. Macleod,** 1876–1935, Scottish physiologist; discovered insulin and its application to the treatment of diabetes.

**Maimonides,** 1135–1204, Jewish physician; wrote important treatises on medicine.

**William James Mayo,** 1861–1939, and **Charles Horace Mayo,** 1865–1939, American surgeons; established internationally known Mayo Clinic in Rochester, Minnesota.

**Karl Augustus Menninger,** 1893–, and **William Claire Menninger,** 1899–1966, American psychiatrists; founded Menninger Clinic in Topeka, Kansas.

**Élie Metchnikoff,** 1845–1916, Russian biologist; discovered that white blood cells destroy bacteria.

**Egas Moniz,** 1874–1955, Portuguese neurologist; developed prefrontal lobotomy as a surgical treatment of severe mental illness.

**William T. G. Morton,** 1819–68, American dentist and physician; first to use ether as a surgical anesthetic.

**Auguste Nelaton,** 1807–73, French surgeon; devised probe for locating bullets inside the body.

**Florence Nightingale,** 1820–1910, English nurse; founder of modern nursing.

**Hideyo Noguchi,** 1876–1928, Japanese bacteriologist; developed skin test for the diagnosis of syphilis.

**George Nicholas Papanicolaou,** 1883–1962, American physician and physiologist; devised the "pap" smear test for cancer detection.

**Philippus Aureolus Paracelsus,** 1493(?)–1541, Swiss physician; introduced the use of chemicals as treatment for specific illnesses.

**Amboise Paré,** 1510(?)–90, French surgeon; introduced the use of artificial limbs.

**Louis Pasteur,** 1822–95, French chemist; first proved that bacteria cause disease.

**Ivan Petrovich Pavlov,** 1849–1936, Russian physiologist and psychologist; pioneered in the field of conditioned physical reflexes.

**Walter Reed,** 1851–1902, American physician; helped discover the cause of yellow fever.

**Howard Taylor Ricketts,** 1871–1910, American pathologist; identified the microorganisms of the genus *Rickettsia,* various kinds of which cause such infectious diseases as Rocky Mountain spotted fever and typhus.

**Sir Ronald Ross,** 1857–1932, English physician; isolated the organism causing malaria and conducted research into African sleeping sickness.

**Benjamin Rush,** 1745(?)–1813, American physician; an early student of epidemics.

**Howard Rusk,** 1901–, American physician; pioneered in physical rehabilitation.

**Albert Sabin,** 1906–, American physician; developed live-virus vaccine against poliomyelitis.

**Jonas Salk,** 1914–, American physician; developed killed-virus vaccine against poliomyelitis.

**Béla Schick,** 1877–, American pediatrician; devised test for determining susceptibility to diphtheria.

**Ignaz Philipp Semmelweis,** 1818–65, Hungarian physician; his antiseptic methods greatly reduced death from childbed fever and proved the value of hospital cleanliness.

**James M. Sims,** 1813–83, American gynecologist; developed several gynecological operative procedures and instruments.

**John Snow,** 1813–58, English physician; studied epidemiology and proved that the cholera organism is carried by water.

**Wendell M. Stanley,** 1904–, American biochemist; pioneered in virus research.

**Harry Stack Sullivan,** 1892–1942, American psychiatrist; contributed to the development of psychoanalysis.

**Thomas Sydenham,** 1624–84, English physician; one of founders of modern clinical medicine.

**Andreas Vesalius,** 1514–64, Flemish anatomist; wrote the first comprehensive textbook on human anatomy.

**Rudolf Virchow,** 1821–1902, German pathologist; founder of cellular pathology.

**Selman A. Waksman,** 1888–, American microbiologist; discovered streptomycin and its value in treating tuberculosis.

**August von Wassermann,** 1866–1925, German physiologist and bacteriologist; developed blood test for the diagnosis of syphilis.

## MAJOR DRUG ADVANCES

**800 B.C.:** Ethyl alcohol, used as an anesthetic.

**1550 (?)A.D.:** Digitalis, heart stimulant.

**1796:** Smallpox vaccine.

**1799:** Nitrous oxide, anesthetic.

**1805:** Morphine, narcotic analgesic.

**1811:** Iodine, an anti-infective.

**1820:** Quinine hydrochloride, for malaria.

**1831:** Chloroform, as anesthetic.

**1832:** Codeine, weak analgesic.

**1842:** Ether, as anesthetic.

**1867:** Phenol, earliest disinfectant.

**1869:** Chloral hydrate, first synthetic soporific.

**1876:** Salicin and salicylates, for rheumatism.

**1884:** Cocaine, as local anesthetic.

**1890:** Diphtheria antitoxin.

**1892:** Tetanus antitoxin.

**1893:** Aspirin, an analgesic for mild pain.

**1901:** Adrenaline, a heart and cardiovascular stimulant.

**1903:** Phenobarbitone, a hypnotic sedative and anticonvulsant.

**1905:** Novocain, local anesthetic.

**1905:** Magnesium sulphate, injected for tetanus, strychnine poisoning, and convulsive disorders.

**1909:** Typhus vaccine.

**1910:** Salvarsan, for syphilis.

**1913:** Meningococcus antitoxin.

**1914:** Chaulmoogra oil for leprosy.

**1915:** Sodium hypochlorite, antiseptic for wounds.

**1919:** Mercurochrome, antiseptic.

**1920:** Iodides, for the prevention of goiter.

**1921:** Bismuth, for syphilis.

**1922:** Insulin, for the control of diabetes.

**1922:** Tryparsamid, for African sleeping sickness and for neurosyphilis.

**1923:** Stovarsol, for amoebic dysentery.

**1924:** Serum for scarlet fever.

**1927:** Liver extract for pernicious anemia.

**1928:** Penicillin, major antibiotic for a broad range of infections.

**1928:** Vitamin C, for scurvy.

**1930:** Atebrin, antimalarial.

**1933:** Immune globulins, anti-infectives.

**1933:** ACTH, active against arthritis.

**1934:** Vitamin K, for jaundice.

**1935:** Pentothal, intravenous anesthetic.

**1937:** Sulfanilamide, sulfa drug active against a wide range of infections; sulfone, a derivative used to arrest leprosy.

**1939:** Nicotinic acid, for treatment of pellagra.

**1939:** Pethidine hydrochloride, a narcotic analgesic particularly useful in childbirth.

**1941:** Sulfadiazine, a bactericide.

**1942:** Demerol, synthetic pain-killing drug.

**1942:** Tyrothricin, a bactericide.

**1943:** LSD-25, a hallucinogen.

**1946:** Pyribenzamine, an antihistamine.

**1946:** Cortisone, for a host of maladies.

**1947:** Chloromycetin, an antibiotic.

**1948:** Streptomycin, an antibiotic.

**1948:** Aureomycin, an antibiotic.

**1948:** Bacitracin, an antibiotic.

**1948:** Vitamin B-12, for pernicious anemia.

**1949:** Dramamine, antinauseant.

**1950:** Mustargen, used in cancer treatment.

**1951:** Neomycin, for treatment of cirrhosis.

**1952:** Isoniazid, for oral or intramuscular treatment of tuberculosis.

**1953:** Reserpine, tranquilizing sedative for treatment of mental disorders.

**1953:** Salk vaccine, for polio immunization.

**1953:** Pro-Banthine, for treatment of heart blockage.

**1954:** Thorazine, tranquilizer.

**1954:** Coumarin sodium, an anticoagulant for heart and liver disease.

**1955:** Prednisone, a cortical hormone; more potent than cortisone.

**1956:** Cytomel, used to treat thyroid disorders.

**1957:** Diuril, for congestive heart failure.

**1957:** Leukeran, used in cancer therapy.

**1957:** Enovid, for menstrual disorders and birth control.

**1957:** Indoklon, antishock and antidepressant; replaces electric shock therapy for acute depression.

**1957:** Darvon, a non-narcotic analgesic.

**1957:** Orinase, a synthetic substitute for insulin used in diabetes control.

**1959:** Thio Tepa, pain-killing drug.

**1959:** Sabin vaccine, against polio.

**1960:** Nicalex, cholesterol-reducing agent.

**1960:** Brevital sodium, general anesthetic.

**1963:** Measles vaccine.

**1963:** DMSO, experimental pain-killing, anti-inflammatory penetrant.

**1963:** Marboran, smallpox preventive.

**1963:** Valium, tranquilizer useful in treatment of cerebral palsy.

**1964:** Provest and Ortho-Novum, oral contraceptive pills.

**1964:** Nalidixic acid, against kidney infection.

**1964:** Norpramin, oral, fast-acting antidepressant.

**1964:** Ceporin, reaction-free antibiotic.

**1964:** Gentamicin, against the staphylococcus germ.

**1964:** Perganol, experimental fertility drug.

**1964:** Keflin, broad-spectrum antibiotic.

**1965:** Improved tetanus antitoxin.

**1965:** Tegopen, antibiotic against staphylococcus bacteria.

**1967:** Symmetrel, antiviral agent effective against an influenza virus.

# PUBLIC HEALTH

## OUR WATER: HEALTHIER, BUT NOT YET WELL

Public concern over water pollution continued to rise during 1967. Numerous national magazines and newspapers carried articles on the dangers of contaminated water. Outbreaks of hepatitis and the threat of typhoid fever were mentioned. Water pollution, the articles said, was getting progressively and rapidly worse. Is the picture really so dismal?

The answer, in many areas, is a loud "Yes." Certain types of industrial and agricultural chemicals have been increasing in concentration in the nation's waterways. For example, fertilizer nutrients—nitrogen and phosphorus—are not removed from domestic and industrial sewage by usual treatment processes. Particularly in still waters, such as lakes and estuaries, high nitrogen and phosphorous levels may stimulate the growth of aquatic plants to such an extent that they impair water quality. Also, in many localities industries have simply not met their responsibilities: There is not less but more industrial pollution.

In one area, however, there has been progress. Through the efforts of state and interstate agencies, assisted by Federal grants, there are now only a few locations where municipal sewage in raw form pours into our rivers. The quality of such major waterways as the Delaware, the Ohio, and the Potomac has improved significantly over the past 10 or 15 years. What accounts for our success in cleaning up (at least partially) these rivers? One factor is simply that more people are noticing water pollution. Dead fish, floating sewage, and excessive aquatic plants have become more visible and less tolerable as more people become water-recreation enthusiasts—boat owners, water skiers, snorkelers, fishermen, and campers.

Thus, some of the grossest forms of pollution are beginning to be dealt with across the country. Now the question arises: How much more water quality does the nation want?

If further control of water pollution could be accomplished at small cost, there might not be any debate whatsoever. However, studies have shown that costs rise spectacularly if complete control is the goal. It has been calculated that completely eliminating waste discharges from the nation's streams, lakes, and estuaries might cost about $20 billion per year, or about the amount that the nation spends for primary and secondary education.

How can high water quality be achieved at the least cost? One of the main problems resulting from the discharge of organic waste such as domestic sewage is that the dissolved oxygen of waterways is reduced; if the oxygen level drops too low, fish die. Studies have shown that oxygen can be introduced into rivers through the use of compressed air and various other techniques at a cost considerably lower than that involved in achieving very high-level waste treatment.

Another way of reducing the costs of pollution-control is by the watershed or river-basin approach. This is far more efficient than attacking the problem at specific points of waste discharge. One example of watershed management is reservoir storage; clean water is released during normally low flow periods to literally "flush out" and dilute pollutants. However, setting up a program for an entire river basin often becomes a prickly political problem: River basins usually span state lines and take in many municipalities, and Federal, state, and local governments do not always agree on methods and goals.

Undoubtedly, Congress, the Administration, industry, and conservation groups will continue to debate how best to achieve control of industrial waste discharge. Particularly large amounts of pollutants come from the pulp and paper, food products, petroleum refining, steel, and chemical industries. There is considerable support in Congress for various bills that would provide subsidies in the form of tax write-offs or grants to industry for waste treatment.

But the Council of Economic Advisers, the Bureau of the Budget, and other government agencies say that controlling water pollution is a necessary cost of business and should be borne by the industry and its customers. These agencies propose an "effluent tax"—a charge on factory or mill in proportion to the quantity and type of its waste discharge. This proposal has provoked much discussion.

U.S. Dept. of Interior

The scene is Lake Michigan. Despite the warning sign, bathers still wet their feet.

# FOCUS ON THE NEWS

## THE AIR WE BREATHE—JUST DIRTY

"The threat to health, in my opinion, constitutes the primary impulse for the control of air pollution in the United States."

These words by William H. Stewart, Surgeon General of the U.S. Public Health Service, remind us, if we need reminding, that our polluted air is not only disgusting but also deadly. Severe air pollution multiplies the death rate, as it did in the little Pennsylvania industrial town of Donora in 1948; as it did in London in 1952; as it did in New York City in 1953 and 1962; as it inevitably will again.

Air pollution is linked to a number of respiratory diseases and afflictions. Deaths from emphysema, a progressive breakdown of the lungs' air sacs, have increased more than five times since 1950. Cigarette smoking—a kind of do-it-yourself air pollution—has often been blamed for this rise; but non-smoking emphysema patients also show marked improvement when they are protected from "natural" air pollution. Lung cancer is another disease where both smoking *and* air pollution have been implicated. The incidence of chronic bronchitis, asthma, pneumonia, and the common cold also rises as air pollution gets worse.

What maddens public health workers is that something can be done about air pollu-

Smog in Los Angeles

United Press Int'l.

tion. As the framers of the Air Quality Act of 1967 put it: "No one has the right to use the atmosphere as a garbage dump."

In the following list, 65 U.S. cities are ranked by the Public Health Service according to the severity of their air pollution.

1. New York, N.Y.
2. Chicago, Ill.
3. Philadelphia, Pa.
4. Los Angeles-Long Beach, Calif.
5. Cleveland, Ohio
6. Pittsburgh, Pa.
7. Boston, Mass.
8. Newark, N.J.
9. Detroit, Mich.
10. St. Louis, Mo.
11. Gary-Hammond-East Chicago, Ind.
12. Akron, Ohio
13. Baltimore, Md.
14. Indianapolis, Ind.
15. Wilmington, Del.
16. Louisville, Ky.
17. Jersey City, N.J.
18. Washington, D.C.
19. Cincinnati, Ohio
20. Milwaukee, Wis.
21. Paterson-Clifton-Passaic, N.J.

22. Canton, Ohio
23. Youngstown-Warren, Ohio
24. Toledo, Ohio
25. Kansas City, Mo.-Kansas City, Kans.
26. Dayton, Ohio
27. Denver, Colo.
28. Bridgeport, Conn.
29. Providence-Pawtucket, R.I.
30. Buffalo, N.Y.
31. Birmingham, Ala.
32. Minneapolis-St. Paul, Minn.
33. Hartford, Conn.
34. Nashville, Tenn.
35. San Francisco-Oakland, Calif.
36. Seattle, Wash.
37. Lawrence-Haverhill, Mass.
38. New Haven, Conn.
39. York, Pa.
40. Springfield-Chicopee-Holyoke, Mass.
41. Allentown-Bethlehem-Easton, Pa.

42. Worcester, Mass.
43. Houston, Tex.
44. Chattanooga, Tenn.
45. Memphis, Tenn.
46. Columbus, Ohio
47. Richmond, Va.
48. San Jose, Calif.
49. Portland, Ore.
50. Syracuse, N.Y.
51. Atlanta, Ga.
52. Grand Rapids, Mich.
53. Rochester, N.Y.
54. Reading, Pa.
55. Albany-Schenectady-Troy, N.Y.
56. Lancaster, Pa.
57. Dallas, Tex.
58. Flint, Mich.
59. New Orleans, La.
60. Fort Worth, Tex.
61. San Diego, Calif.
62. Utica-Rome, N.Y.
63. Miami, Fla.
64. Wichita, Kans.
65. High Point-Greensboro, N.C.

## U.S. HOSPITAL FACTS: 1966
Source: American Hospital Association

Latest statistics concerning U.S. hospitals show some surprising changes from the preceding year (1965). In most states, total hospital births declined. A notable exception was Texas, which showed an increase of 44,386 births in 1966. Thirty-seven more hospitals were added in the 50 states and the District of Columbia in 1966, with New York accounting for 17 of the total. While the number of hospital beds declined by nearly 25,000, the number of hospital personnel increased nearly 8 per cent, for a total staff increase of 153,599.

| STATE | NUMBER OF HOSPITALS | BEDS | ANNUAL ADMISSIONS | AVERAGE DAILY OCCUPANCY | BIRTHS | PERSONNEL | TOTAL EXPENSES (in thousands) |
|---|---|---|---|---|---|---|---|
| Alabama | 144 | 27,273 | 512,512 | 23,336 | 55,088 | 31,518 | $ 189,375 |
| Alaska | 26 | 2,006 | 41,999 | 1,313 | 5,999 | 2,709 | 24,468 |
| Arizona | 80 | 9,256 | 241,731 | 7,382 | 28,874 | 14,759 | 103,326 |
| Arkansas | 85 | 13,811 | 339,682 | 10,483 | 27,507 | 16,562 | 97,352 |
| California | 638 | 140,020 | 2,673,038 | 115,394 | 335,427 | 189,460 | 1,527,924 |
| Colorado | 90 | 15,877 | 370,710 | 12,367 | 34,134 | 27,242 | 175,402 |
| Connecticut | 68 | 26,059 | 382,775 | 21,958 | 52,180 | 32,851 | 248,641 |
| Delaware | 16 | 6,109 | 90,443 | 5,283 | 9,962 | 7,872 | 52,252 |
| District of Columbia | 21 | 15,423 | 193,351 | 13,480 | 29,468 | 19,877 | 163,685 |
| Florida | 179 | 39,053 | 873,531 | 32,187 | 94,213 | 55,719 | 354,321 |
| Georgia | 150 | 31,935 | 654,641 | 28,015 | 76,001 | 39,588 | 225,399 |
| Hawaii | 33 | 6,096 | 95,418 | 4,756 | 13,368 | 7,331 | 52,189 |
| Idaho | 53 | 3,727 | 104,500 | 2,546 | 11,731 | 5,082 | 31,372 |
| Illinois | 325 | 106,906 | 1,683,011 | 89,172 | 194,535 | 126,687 | 901,871 |
| Indiana | 139 | 38,635 | 682,875 | 33,071 | 91,545 | 46,443 | 294,434 |
| Iowa | 138 | 20,454 | 460,338 | 15,434 | 43,702 | 28,212 | 175,943 |
| Kansas | 163 | 18,627 | 373,437 | 14,393 | 33,744 | 25,931 | 153,415 |
| Kentucky | 141 | 23,423 | 502,540 | 18,806 | 54,852 | 30,220 | 174,963 |
| Louisiana | 144 | 26,689 | 574,544 | 20,433 | 71,396 | 32,868 | 198,269 |
| Maine | 59 | 9,630 | 147,123 | 7,748 | 17,020 | 10,759 | 63,271 |
| Maryland | 86 | 33,476 | 428,734 | 28,593 | 63,350 | 44,285 | 291,426 |
| Massachusetts | 201 | 64,524 | 864,884 | 53,798 | 102,105 | 85,283 | 580,675 |
| Michigan | 260 | 73,702 | 1,176,681 | 64,242 | 139,811 | 90,941 | 656,255 |
| Minnesota | 205 | 35,377 | 633,507 | 28,168 | 62,138 | 42,943 | 300,506 |
| Mississippi | 106 | 16,288 | 313,977 | 13,113 | 28,484 | 16,990 | 97,267 |
| Missouri | 145 | 40,483 | 704,444 | 33,871 | 70,122 | 51,943 | 330,536 |
| Montana | 64 | 4,388 | 134,894 | 3,065 | 11,586 | 6,678 | 41,345 |
| Nebraska | 118 | 12,692 | 251,081 | 10,181 | 25,301 | 17,558 | 100,123 |
| Nevada | 22 | 2,566 | 62,522 | 1,998 | 14,581 | 3,561 | 27,108 |
| New Hampshire | 36 | 6,473 | 102,444 | 5,351 | 11,508 | 7,044 | 45,117 |
| New Jersey | 141 | 54,933 | 833,630 | 46,216 | 135,954 | 64,376 | 437,151 |
| New Mexico | 58 | 5,922 | 154,179 | 4,535 | 19,274 | 8,754 | 53,462 |
| New York | 440 | 210,038 | 2,493,063 | 187,572 | 329,438 | 251,028 | 1,822,601 |
| North Carolina | 166 | 35,906 | 743,478 | 28,870 | 80,349 | 43,590 | 258,450 |
| North Dakota | 65 | 6,340 | 132,715 | 4,829 | 11,989 | 7,362 | 47,771 |
| Ohio | 255 | 81,456 | 1,422,314 | 70,127 | 177,337 | 105,231 | 693,982 |
| Oklahoma | 141 | 15,875 | 368,329 | 12,312 | 34,244 | 21,757 | 127,584 |
| Oregon | 87 | 15,736 | 289,043 | 11,568 | 28,243 | 17,601 | 119,150 |
| Pennsylvania | 322 | 120,771 | 1,680,209 | 103,103 | 190,574 | 135,476 | 868,473 |
| Rhode Island | 25 | 9,419 | 128,157 | 8,386 | 16,097 | 12,036 | 84,553 |
| South Carolina | 79 | 17,937 | 362,122 | 14,566 | 39,805 | 19,383 | 111,716 |
| South Dakota | 61 | 6,339 | 119,710 | 4,791 | 11,374 | 7,573 | 45,600 |
| Tennessee | 160 | 31,899 | 644,371 | 26,861 | 64,895 | 42,348 | 239,780 |
| Texas | 565 | 72,459 | 1,694,120 | 56,468 | 172,711 | 98,862 | 625,992 |
| Utah | 41 | 4,685 | 145,783 | 3,534 | 21,470 | 8,306 | 53,163 |
| Vermont | 31 | 4,894 | 71,391 | 3,844 | 7,322 | 5,208 | 33,151 |
| Virginia | 127 | 37,603 | 592,111 | 32,196 | 74,345 | 42,010 | 251,977 |
| Washington | 135 | 19,077 | 481,223 | 13,903 | 48,623 | 28,087 | 196,702 |
| West Virginia | 91 | 17,101 | 337,430 | 13,483 | 27,498 | 19,252 | 117,966 |
| Wisconsin | 201 | 35,405 | 725,010 | 28,398 | 78,118 | 44,734 | 307,169 |
| Wyoming | 34 | 3,885 | 61,223 | 2,992 | 5,721 | 4,052 | 23,801 |
| U.S. Total | 7,160 | 1,678,658 | 29,150,978 | 1,398,491 | 3,385,113 | 2,105,942 | $14,198,424 |
| U.S.—Associated Areas | | | | | | | |
| American Samoa | 1 | 175 | 4,952 | 108 | 831 | 285 | 1,106 |
| Canal Zone | 4 | 913 | 10,846 | 611 | 1,392 | 1,180 | 10,833 |
| Guam | 2 | 672 | 10,309 | 405 | 2,576 | 822 | 7,268 |
| Marshall Islands | 1 | 21 | 617 | 9 | 40 | 45 | 149 |
| Puerto Rico | 59 | 9,860 | 206,547 | 7,896 | 36,062 | 14,106 | 65,807 |
| Virgin Islands | 3 | 220 | 7,712 | 181 | 1,999 | 668 | 3,178 |

# MEDICAL TERMS AND DEFINITIONS

## MAJOR DISEASES AND DISORDERS

**Arthritis:** The general name for a group of diseases affecting the joints. Most serious is the chronic disorder *rheumatoid arthritis,* which erodes the cartilage on the surfaces of the bones at the joints, causing stiffness and acute pain; its specific cause is unknown. Crippling deformities can sometimes be prevented by physiotherapy and medication. *Osteoarthritis,* also called degenerative joint disease, is part of the aging process and in most cases produces mild symptoms. (These disorders are often popularly referred to as "rheumatism.")

**Atherosclerosis:** A disease that causes the arteries to narrow and harden, impeding circulation and increasing the danger of *thrombosis* (formation of blood clots). Atherosclerosis is the underlying cause of most heart attacks (*coronary thromboses*) and strokes (*cerebral thromboses*). It is sometimes called "hardening of the arteries," and although the precise cause is unknown, it is common among people who eat a rich diet. Emotional stress and production of sex hormones may also be involved, as well as individual metabolic differences that affect fat and cholesterol deposits on artery walls. *Hypertension,* or high blood pressure, is related to atherosclerosis.

**Botulism:** An extremely dangerous infection caused by toxic bacteria that grow in improperly canned, bottled, and preserved foods. Symptoms are vomiting, diarrhea, and impaired vision. Sometimes referred to as "food poisoning," it requires immediate attention.

**Bubonic Plague:** Highly contagious and dangerous infection, causing death in 60–90 per cent of untreated cases. A bacterial disease, "the plague" is carried by rats and transmitted to humans by fleas. High fever, swelling of the groin and armpits, and black spots are symptoms. Modern treatment is based on streptomycin.

**Cancer:** A disease characterized by abnormal cell growth causing the formation of a malignant mass of tissue (*tumor*) that damages other cells by crowding them and depriving them of nutrients. Localized tumors can be treated or removed, but when diseased cells get into the blood stream and spread through the body (*metastasis*), cancer becomes increasingly hard to control. The specific cause is not known, but research shows that some chemicals are contributing factors. *Leukemia* (cancer of the blood) may be caused by a virus. Cure of cancer is often possible if detection is made early enough.

**Chicken Pox:** A mild, highly contagious virus infection of childhood, characterized by the appearance of a rash after symptoms of headache, loss of appetite, and fever. There is no specific cure. Treatment consists of bed rest and medicines to relieve itching. One infection usually confers lifetime immunity.

**Cirrhosis:** Chronic inflammation of the liver characterized by deterioration of the cells and thickening of the tissue. Cirrhosis is often associated with heavy intake of alcohol. It may also be a consequence of *hepatitis.* Symptoms of cirrhosis include swollen abdomen and ankles, weight loss, and indigestion, as well as jaundice (yellow tinge to eyes and skin). Treatment consists of a high protein diet, Vitamin B, transfusions for blood loss, and elimination of alcohol from the diet.

**Common Cold:** The most widespread of the infectious diseases, caused by at least 20 different viruses affecting the upper respiratory tract. Symptoms vary, but they usually include stuffed head, running nose, sneezing, and lowered energy. Antibiotics are not a cure, but they are prescribed to prevent complications.

**Cystic Fibrosis:** A hereditary disease of childhood associated with a defective pancreas (also known as *fibrocystic disease* or *mucoviscidosis*). Lungs and other respiratory passages become clogged with a thick mucus, causing severe breathing difficulties. The risk of secondary respiratory infection is extremely high. Cystic fibrosis occurs in about one out of every 1,000 live births; over 95 per cent die within seven years. Symptoms may be alleviated by breathing aids and mucus removal, and the risk of secondary infection can be reduced by antibiotics. However, there is no cure; nor do investigators know the exact nature of the hereditary defect.

**Diabetes:** A noncontagious glandular disease caused by the body's failure to produce enough insulin, the hormone that controls sugar metabolism. Symptoms may include excessive urination, constant thirst, and weight loss. Diabetes can be detected by laboratory tests and controlled by insulin injections, or, in mild cases, by medicines taken orally.

**Emphysema:** An increasingly widespread respiratory disorder of middle age. The air sacs in the lungs become inflated, causing impaired breathing and consequent heart strain. Symptoms include persistent cough and short breath. Contributing factors are cigarette smoking and air pollution. There is no cure, but medicines can ease discomfort.

**Encephalitis:** An inflammation of the tissues of the brain and of the *meninges* (coverings of the brain), also known as "sleeping sickness." There are three forms: direct virus infection; as a complication following measles; or through contact with a toxic substance such as lead. The epidemic (virus-caused) form of the disease, which may attack the spine as well as the brain, is *encephalomyelitis.* Symptoms include fever, headache, stiff neck, and in acute cases, drowsiness and delirium. Scientists are now working on an immunizing vaccine. Bed rest and pain-relief drugs are prescribed.

**Epilepsy:** A disorder of the nervous system char-
*(continued)*

**MAJOR DISEASES AND DISORDERS** (*continued*)

acterized by convulsive seizures. *Petit mal* (minor seizure) lasts a few seconds, during which there may be twitching of the eyes and mouth and momentary lapse of attention. *Grand mal* (major seizure) causes the victim to fall unconscious, often foaming at the mouth and shaking violently. Such attacks are usually preceded by a warning sensation called an *aura*. Frequency of seizures varies from several a day to one a year. There is no cure, but medicines can reduce the severity of seizures.

**German Measles:** A contagious virus infection accompanied by swelling of the lymph glands at the back of the neck and a three-day rash. It is also called *rubella*. German measles rarely causes complications, and simple bed rest is the usual treatment for children. However, if the disease occurs in women during early pregnancy, the risk of miscarriage or birth of a defective child is great. At present, gamma globulin is administered to pregnant women who are exposed to, or contract, German measles.

**Gonorrhea:** A dangerous and highly contagious bacterial infection of the genito-urinary organs transmitted commonly, but not always, during sexual intercourse. Symptoms include pain during urination and a pus discharge. Penicillin and sulfa drugs provide effective treatment in many cases.

**Gout:** A noncommunicable metabolic disorder in which excess uric acid, normally expelled in the urine, is passed into the blood stream and deposited in the joints and tissues, causing inflammation, swelling, and acute pain. Most gout cases are males over 30, and the big toe is the area usually affected. The specific cause is unknown. Cortisone and specific gout drugs, as well as diet supervision, are part of the treatment.

**Hepatitis:** An extremely contagious virus infection of the liver transmitted through contact with infected feces, polluted water, or food, or by blood transfusions from an unsuspected carrier. Hepatitis lasts from six to eight weeks and begins with nausea, fever, and a marked yellow tinge to skin and eyes (jaundice). In early stages of the disease, gamma globulin is effective as a treatment.

**Hernia:** The abnormal protrusion of an organ or part of an organ through the tissue wall that surrounds it. "Rupture" is an incorrect designation, since a hernia does not involve any tearing of tissue. The disorder is almost exclusively male and usually results from excessive pressure on the abdominal muscles caused by lifting, coughing, or accidental pressure. The greatest danger connected with hernia is *strangulation*, which can occur when the wall through which an organ protrudes tries to close behind it, cutting off blood supply to the organ. Hernias are corrected by surgery.

**Influenza:** An infectious disease of the respiratory system caused by various strains of virus, and frequently leading to pneumonia or acute ear infection. Symptoms include fever, chills, headache, sore throat, and muscle pain. There is no all-purpose cure, but both antibiotics and a "flu" vaccine are effective against certain strains.

**Kidney Disorders:** *Nephritis* (*Bright's disease*) is an inflammation of the kidney capillaries caused by streptococcus infection elsewhere in the body. Destruction of the capillaries results in scar tissue, which, in turn, affects proper functioning of the kidney. *Nephrosis* is a special form of nephritis in which the kidneys fail to control the water content of the blood, causing the body to swell with excess liquid. *Kidney stones* result from a metabolic disorder that causes calcium deposits or salt crystals to form in the kidney, sometimes resulting in severe pain. They cannot be dissolved by any known medicine and must be removed surgically. *Uremia* is a highly dangerous condition caused by any of the above, or by diabetes, high blood pressure, or an overdose of Vitamin D, in which case the kidneys can no longer remove urea and other waste products from the blood. Antibiotics as well as surgery are used to treat most kidney disorders.

**Malaria:** A severe protozoan infectious disease —chiefly tropical—transmitted by the anopheles mosquito. Symptoms occur every second or third day in cycles of chills followed by very high fever. The preferred medicine is still quinine, although synthetic drugs are being developed to fight new strains of malaria.

**Measles:** A contagious virus disease of childhood. Although usually not serious, secondary complications can cause permanent physical and mental disabilities, or even death. Fever, sensitivity to light, and rash are symptoms. Gamma globulin lessens the effect of the disease. A preventive vaccine that confers lifetime immunity is now being routinely administered, and, with public cooperation, measles could be all but eradicated in the U.S.

**Meningitis:** A viral or bacterial inflammation of the *meninges* (membrane that covers the brain and spinal cord), causing violent headaches, vomiting, and sometimes convulsions and delirium. Treatment with sulfa drugs and antibiotics is usually successful.

**Mononucleosis:** An infection probably caused by a virus that affects white blood cells and results in swelling of the lymph glands, chronic fatigue, and fever. The disease usually attacks persons 10–35 years old, and it is especially common in crowded student quarters. No specific cure exists. Bed rest for a month is recommended. Mononucleosis is also called *glandular fever* or *"kissing disease"* because it is often transmitted between males and females by kissing.

**Multiple Sclerosis:** A disease of the nervous system in which hardened patches appear in parts of the brain and spinal cord, causing impaired speech or vision, loss of fine muscle coordination, and possible paralysis. No means of prevention or cure are known. Physiotherapy is used to prevent muscle deterioration.

**Mumps:** A communicable disease, usually of childhood, affecting the glands that supply saliva to the mouth. These glands, located in front of the ears, become swollen and painful, causing discomfort in opening the mouth, chewing, and swallowing. The disease, which confers lifetime immunity, sometimes shows mild symptoms or none at all. However, it can cause permanent sexual damage when contracted by post-puberty males.

**Muscular Dystrophy:** A group of related disorders of unknown origin that cause the muscles to weaken and deteriorate. Through a loss of protein, healthy muscle fibers are replaced by fat and connective tissue until the muscles themselves become useless, thus incapacitating the victim. The most common type is *pseudohypertrophic muscular dystrophy*, which is hereditary. It is carried by normal women who pass it on only to their male children. Neither pain nor mental deterioration accompanies the disease. There is no cure at present.

**Pneumonia:** An acute infectious lung disease caused by viruses or, more frequently, by pneumococcus bacteria. When one lung is affected, the disease is called *lobar* pneumonia; when both are involved, *double* pneumonia. The infection causes the air spaces in the lungs to become clogged. Symptoms are sharp chest pains, chills, rapid pulse, labored breathing, and high fever. Sulfa drugs, antibiotics, and sometimes oxygen are used in treatment. Prompt diagnosis is extremely important.

**Poliomyelitis:** An acute, contagious disease, also called *infantile paralysis*, caused by one of three viruses that attack the central nervous system and impair muscle control, usually of the legs. *Bulbar* polio affects the breathing and swallowing muscles. There is no cure for polio, but vaccines have practically wiped out the disease in the U.S.

**Pyorrhea:** A noncontagious inflammation of the tissues that line the bony socket of a tooth, and of the socket itself, resulting in bleeding gums, pus flow, and eventual tooth loss. The disease may be caused by incorrect bite (malocclusion), faulty dentures, improper oral hygiene, or general ill health. *Gingivitis*, the general term for gum inflammation, is usually caused by the accumulation of food particles between teeth and gums and can lead to tooth decay and pyorrhea.

**Rheumatic Fever:** A disease that affects the body's connective tissue. It is a secondary infection usually resulting from streptococcus bacteria in the throat or ear. It is most common among children, and its symptoms are often mistakenly called "growing pains." A serious aftereffect is permanent damage called "heart murmur," caused by scar tissue in a heart valve. Treatment for the disease includes prolonged bed rest, antibiotics, and ACTH. A streptococcus vaccine is under development.

**Salmonellosis:** A gastro-intestinal disease caused by any of a number of bacteria of the *Salmonella* genus. Many animals harbor these bacteria, and human beings are constantly exposed to infection by eating contaminated food such as pork, beef, lamb, and particularly poultry products. Severity of the disease depends upon the number and type of salmonella bacteria swallowed. Symptoms are nausea, vomiting, diarrhea, and fever. Rarely fatal for adults, the disease is dangerous for infants and the aged. ("Salmonella" was named, not for the fish, but for a pathologist, D. E. Salmon.)

**Scarlet Fever:** A contagious disease of childhood that has mild or serious effects; it is caused by streptococcus bacteria and produces varied symptoms. If not promptly treated with antibiotics, it can lead to pneumonia, rheumatic fever, or kidney complications. A vaccine giving partial immunity is administered to children.

**Syphilis:** A contagious bacterial disease transmitted in sexual intercourse. It is not inherited but can be transmitted by an infected woman to her unborn child. If unchecked by antibiotics in its early stage, it can eventually attack the central nervous system.

**Tetanus:** A disease caused by bacillary infection spread by animal and human feces. Also known as "lockjaw" because of its first characteristic symptom, it produces muscle spasms and convulsions. It can be largely prevented by immunization with a toxoid.

**Tuberculosis:** A chronic and communicable disease (popularly called "consumption") that attacks the lungs and other parts of the body, excluding the heart, brain, and liver. The tubercle bacillus is transmitted by infected sputum, contaminated utensils, or unpasteurized dairy products from tubercular cows. Typical early symptoms include cough, weight loss, fatigue, and fever. The disease is now effectively treated with streptomycin, isoniazid, and PAS (para-aminosalicylic acid).

**Typhoid Fever:** A bacterial infection transmitted by contaminated water, milk, and food (especially shellfish), by healthy people who are "carriers" and handle food, and by flies that have been in contact with the body wastes of carriers. Infection enters the body through the intestines, multiplies in the blood stream, and causes fever, severe cramps, and diarrhea. Its outbreak has been increasingly prevented by improved sanitation. An immunizing vaccine is recommended when traveling to places lacking modern sanitation.

**Ulcer:** Most commonly refers to *peptic ulcer,* a condition in which an open sore occurs in the inside wall of the digestive tract in, or close to, the stomach. Two types of peptic ulcer are the *gastric* ulcer in the stomach and the *duodenal* ulcer in the small intestine. The precise cause is unknown, but ulcers are connected with the presence of excess acid or gastric juice in the stomach. Emotional stress can increase the damaging secretions. Proper diet, easing of tensions, and elimination of smoking and alcohol are commonly recommended.

**Undulant Fever:** Common name for *brucellosis,* a bacterial disease transmitted by the meat and milk products from infected cattle, goats, and pigs. Raw infected goat's milk causes a variety of undulant fever known as *Malta Fever.* Symptoms can persist for years, either intermittently or continuously, and include weakness, weight loss, muscle pains, chills, and fever. Antibiotics, bed rest, and vitamins usually bring about recovery in a few months. Spread of the disease is checked by herd inspection and milk pasteurization.

## GLOSSARY OF MEDICAL TERMS

**Abscess:** A collection of pus in any area of the body where tissues have broken down because of injury or bacterial infection; usually accompanied by redness and swelling.

**Allergy:** An unusual or exaggerated reaction of the body to substances or "allergens" (for example, pollens and certain foods) that normally have no undesirable effect on most human beings.

**Amnesia:** Loss of memory resulting from disturbance to parts of the brain by injury, disease, alcoholism, or emotional shock.

**Analgesic:** Any chemical substance that relieves pain without affecting consciousness.

**Androgens:** The male sex hormones that determine masculine characteristics. The two most important are androsterone and testosterone.

**Anemia:** A deficiency in the quality or quantity of the blood, usually caused by a decrease in red blood cells. Anemia is a symptom of a disease or disorder rather than a disease itself. Acute anemia, caused by massive bleeding, can result in *shock,* and generally requires an immediate *transfusion.*

**Aneurysm:** An abnormal widening of the wall of an artery, forming a pulsating sac, and usually accompanied by pain caused by excessive pressure. Aneurysms may result from syphilis, hardening of the arteries, and other disorders.

**Angina Pectoris:** Acute chest pain caused by insufficient coronary circulation.

**Antibiotic:** Any one of a large group of substances derived from microorganisms and fungi. They inhibit or destroy organisms that cause disease. Two widely used antibiotics are penicillin and aureomycin.

**Antibody:** Any substance produced by the body to counteract disease-causing *bacteria* or other *antigens.*

**Antigen:** Any substance causing the production of antibodies. Disease "germs" are antigens.

**Ascorbic Acid:** Another name for Vitamin C, contained in citrus fruits, tomatoes, and some vegetables; essential for many body functions.

**Astigmatism:** A defect of the eye, in which some of the rays of light from an object do not focus on the retina at the back of the eye, resulting in blurred vision.

**Auscultation:** The act of listening to sounds within the body, such as chest *rales* or the fetal heartbeat during pregnancy. It is usually done with a *stethoscope.*

**Autonomic:** The involuntary activities of the body, such as the functions of the heart, glands, and stomach. The autonomic nervous system regulates the functions of these organs.

**Bacteria:** One-celled microorganisms ranging from the harmless and beneficial (such as those that help in bloodclotting) to the harmful, *toxin*-producing ones (such as *staphylococci* and *streptococci*).

**Barbiturates:** A group of derivatives of barbituric acid, used as sedatives or sleeping pills and likely to be habit-forming.

**Basal Metabolism Test:** A method of measuring the body's rate of oxygen intake and heat discharge. Basal metabolism rates vary from individual to individual and reflect the functioning of the *thyroid gland.* Metabolism is the process by which the body changes oxygen and food into energy (heat). Basal refers to the state of the body at rest but not asleep.

**Biopsy:** A clinical procedure in which samples of tissue are removed from the body for microscopic examination in order to diagnose a number of diseases such as cancer.

**Blood Types:** There are four main types of whole blood: O, A, B, and AB. The Rh factor is also significant. These classifications are based on differences found in the red blood cells and *plasma.* The same blood types are found everywhere in the world and are not related to sex, skin color, or age. Before transfusions, blood types must be determined since only O-type blood can be given to all; otherwise, blood types must be matched.

**Blue Baby:** An infant born with a heart disorder that causes an abnormal amount of oxygen-lacking blood to circulate in the body, thus giving the skin a blue appearance.

**Calorie:** A unit of measurement for the energy value of foods. One calorie approximately equals the amount of heat needed to raise one pound of water by 4° F.

**Carcinogen:** A cancer-causing substance.

**Cardiac:** Pertaining to the heart.

**Caries:** Bacterial decay of a tooth or bone.

**Cataract:** A disorder of the eye's lens that produces cloudy vision. It can be corrected by surgery.

**Catatonia:** A condition characterized by muscular rigidity. It is usually a symptom of *schizophrenia.*

**Cathartic:** A medicine used to stimulate intestinal action and produce a bowel movement. It is stronger than a laxative. Castor oil is a common cathartic.

**Catheter:** A flexible tube inserted into a body cavity for examination and drainage, or for injecting fluids or oxygen; frequently used for draining urine from the bladder.

**Cell:** The fundamental structural unit of all plant and animal life.

**Cerebral:** Pertaining to the cerebrum, the upper anterior part of the brain which is believed to control all conscious thought.

**Chancre:** A hard type of sore usually associated with syphilis.

**Cholesterol:** A substance found in varying amounts in all fats and oils, and the main material in gallstones. A high cholesterol diet may be one cause of heart ailments.

**Chromosome.** The part of the *cell* that contains the hereditary genes.

**Climacteric:** The stage of life characterized by definite bodily changes in women when they can no longer bear children, and in men when their physical vigor declines. The female climacteric is called the menopause.

**Coagulant:** Any substance that speeds up the clotting of the blood.

**Colostomy:** A surgical procedure in which an

artificial opening is made on the surface of the abdomen to permit bowel evacuation after the rectum has been removed because of cancer.

**Complex:** In psychoanalysis, a group of related feelings, desires, and memories that dominate the personality and, if repressed, can lead to abnormal behavior.

**Conditioned Reflex:** A reaction, automatic once learned, to a particular stimulus.

**Cystoscope:** An instrument consisting of a hollow tube with a light at one end, used to examine the interior of the bladder.

**Delirium:** A temporary mental disturbance, accompanied by *hallucinations,* agitation, and incoherence, that can be brought on by a high fever, shock, injury, or an overdose of drugs. The delirium caused by heavy alcohol intake and lack of food is called "delirium tremens," or simply "the D.T.'s."

**Dermatologist:** A doctor who specializes in disorders of the skin, scalp, and hair. He also frequently treats allergies.

**Diuretic:** Any substance that increases the secretion of urine.

**Drug:** In medical terms, the word applies to any substance—natural or synthetic—used to treat a physical or mental disorder, to relieve symptoms, or to replace a deficiency in the body.

**Drug Resistance:** The capacity of microbes to develop immunity to drugs that previously affected them.

**Electrocardiograph:** An instrument for recording the electric current produced by the action of the heart muscle. The resulting electrocardiogram, or ECG—usually a wave pattern traced on paper—is used in diagnosing heart ailments.

**Electroencephalograph:** An instrument for recording electrical impulses in the brain (brain waves), used in diagnosing epilepsy and other brain disorders, as well as in sleep and dream research. The record itself is commonly referred to as an EEG.

**Embolism:** An obstruction in a blood vessel caused by a loose blood clot, air bubble, or other material that blocks circulation.

**Endocrine:** Applied to the glands that regulate body activities by the secretion of *hormones* directly into the blood system.

**Enzymes:** Protein substances produced by living *cells.* They start, stop, speed up, or slow down specific metabolic activities.

**Epithelial:** Pertaining to the cells forming the outer layer of skin tissue and the lining of the hollow organs such as the nose.

**Estrogens:** The female *hormones* responsible for regulating female sex functions.

**Fluoridation:** The addition of fluoride salts to drinking water for the purpose of reducing tooth decay.

**Fluoroscope:** An X-ray device for observing bones and certain internal *organs* by the shadows they cast on a fluorescent screen.

**Gamma Globulin:** The portion of whole blood that contains the most *antibodies.*

**Gangrene:** The rotting away of body tissues that is caused by failure of blood circulation. Gangrene may set in after wounds, frostbite, or infections.

**Gastric:** Pertaining to the stomach.

**Genes:** The complex protein molecules within the chromosomes of reproductive cells. They transmit specific hereditary characteristics from parents to children.

**Geriatrics:** The branch of medicine that specializes in the problems of old age.

**Hallucination:** Imagined experience unrelated to reality as commonly perceived through the senses.

**Hallucinogen:** Any substance that produces *hallucinations.*

**Hemophilia:** A hereditary disorder in which the blood fails to clot.

**Hepatic:** Pertaining to the liver.

**Hormones:** Chemical substances secreted by the endocrine glands. Hormones specifically influence the activities of other body *organs.*

**Hypertension:** High blood pressure.

**Hypochondriac:** A person excessively concerned with his health, who frequently exaggerates trivial symptoms or suffers from imaginary ailments; a type of *neurosis.*

**Hysterectomy:** Surgical removal of the *uterus.*

**Immunization:** A procedure for protecting a person against disease by inducing the production of *antibodies* or by directly introducing antibodies, usually through *inoculation.* A person may acquire natural immunity to a disease after contracting that disease and recovering from it.

**Inoculation:** The procedure—usually by injection—used to immunize a person against an infectious disease, also called vaccination.

**Internist:** A medical specialist who diagnoses and treats disorders and diseases that do not require surgery.

**Lumbar:** Pertaining to the loins, the part of the body on either side of the spine between the lower ribs and the hip bones.

**Mastectomy:** The surgical removal of breast tissue, usually to treat a tumor.

**Microbe:** A microscopic organism, especially one of the *bacteria* that cause disease; popularly called "germs."

**Migraine:** A severe, recurrent headache sometimes accompanied by nausea; its cause is not known, although emotional factors seem to be involved.

**Mutation:** Alteration of the *chromosomes* of an organism so that hereditary characteristics are affected, usually in an undesirable way.

**Neurosis:** An emotional disturbance produced by unresolved and unconscious conflicts, often accompanied by anxiety and depression.

**Niacin:** One of the family of B *vitamins.* Also called nicotinic acid amine, it is contained in yeast, liver, and peanuts. Severe niacin deficiency results in pellagra.

**Ophthalmologist:** A physician who specializes in treating eye disorders.

**Organ:** Any part or structure of the body that forms a distinct entity and is adapted for a specific function or functions.

**Pap Test:** A quick, simple, and painless test used to check for cancer of the cervix or uterus before any symptoms are visible. The American Cancer Society suggests that women over 30 have a Pap test once a year.

*(continued)*

**GLOSSARY OF MEDICAL TERMS** (*continued*)

**Paranoia:** A mental disorder characterized by delusions of persecution or power.

**Pediatrician:** A doctor who specializes in the care of children from birth to puberty.

**Peristaltic Action:** The muscular movement of a body organ, especially of the alimentary canal or digestive tract, in which the substance passing through the organ is gradually moved to a point of expulsion.

**pH:** The symbol used to indicate the relative acidity or alkalinity in the body.

**PKU:** Abbreviation for a congenital disease in infant body metabolism that, if untreated, results in mental retardation and other serious disorders. PKU can be detected immediately after birth by a simple blood test.

**Placebo:** Any harmless substance given to humor a patient; also used in research to check on the effectiveness of drugs.

**Plasma:** The fluid part of whole blood after the red corpuscles have been removed. In transfusions of plasma, blood types do not have to be determined.

**Pleural:** Pertaining to the membrane that covers the lungs and folds back on the *thorax* and diaphragm.

**Psychiatrist:** A physician who specializes in *psychiatry.*

**Psychiatry:** The treatment of mental illness and personality disorders.

**Psychoanalyst:** A *psychiatrist* who treats mental illness and severe emotional disturbances by the technique developed by Freud, involving the systematic analysis of unconscious factors such as those revealed in dreams, free association, and memory lapses.

**Psychosis:** A severe mental disorder often involving the disintegration of the personality.

**Psychosomatic:** Relating generally to the mutual dependence of the mind (psyche) and the body (soma), and specifically to physical illnesses that appear to have emotional causes, such as ulcers and *migraine* headaches.

**Psychotherapy:** The attempt to cure mental illness or severe emotional disturbance by techniques based on verbal communication between the *psychiatrist* and the patient.

**Rale:** A sound in the chest in addition to that made by natural breathing, heard by *auscultation* and indicating the presence and stage of a respiratory disorder.

**Rh Factor:** An inherited substance found in the red blood cells of most people, whose blood is called Rh positive. When the substance is absent, the blood is called Rh negative. The Rh negative person should never receive an Rh positive *transfusion,* since the mingling of different blood cells may cause serious complications.

**Schizophrenia:** Mental illness characterized by delusions, retreat from reality, and a possible deterioration of personality. Formerly called "dementia praecox."

**Shock:** So-called "primary shock" is associated with a temporary reduction of blood supply to the brain and is similar to "feeling faint"; it may be brought on by pain, the sight of blood, and other frightening events. True medical shock, or secondary shock, may follow (by some hours) extensive surgery, severe injury, or heavy bleeding. "Secondary shock" is caused by a collapse of normal blood circulation, which, in turn, may lead to failure of vital organs. A *transfusion* is often the recommended treatment.

**Shock Therapy:** A treatment for mental illness in which electric current or insulin is administered to produce temporary unconsciousness and to relieve the symptoms causing distress.

**Staphylococcus:** Any of a group of *bacteria,* usually found on the surface of the skin, that causes infection in cuts and boils.

**Stethoscope:** An apparatus used to listen for sounds from the interior of the body.

**Streptococcus:** Any of a group of *bacteria* that invade the bloodstream and cause such diseases as "strep" throat and scarlet fever.

**Thiamine:** Another name for Vitamin B-1. It is found in pork, whole grain cereals, and rice, and is also synthesized chemically. A thiamine deficiency causes beriberi.

**Thorax:** The part of the body between the neck and the abdomen, enclosed by the ribs, and containing the lungs and heart; the chest.

**Thrombosis:** Local blood clot in the heart or blood vessels causing an obstruction in circulation.

**Thyroid Gland:** A two-lobed *endocrine* gland situated in front of the *trachea* and secreting thyroxin, the *hormone* that regulates metabolism and growth.

**Toxin:** Any disease-causing, poisonous compounds produced by animal, plant, or bacterial organisms.

**Toxoid:** A vaccine or, more specifically, a *toxin* administered in a form or amount which, while causing (at most) mild symptoms of a disease, stimulates production of antibodies against that disease and confers immunity.

**Trachea:** The body passage made of membrane and cartilage by which air passes from the larynx to the bronchi and the lungs; commonly called the windpipe.

**Transfusion:** The transfer of blood (either whole blood or blood *plasma*) from one person to the veins or arteries of another.

**Trauma:** Any injury caused to an organ by a blow, impact, or wound; in *psychiatry,* a grave emotional shock that may have a lasting effect on the personality.

**Uterus:** The female organ in which the young develop before birth; the womb.

**Vaccine:** Any preparation containing *bacteria* or *viruses* that have been treated to give immunity against specific diseases when introduced into the body.

**Virus:** Any of a group of disease-causing agents too small to be seen under a microscope.

**Vitamin:** Any of a group of substances found in minute amounts in foods and essential for health.

**WHO:** The abbreviation for World Health Organization, the health agency of the United Nations. It conducts worldwide campaigns to wipe out diseases, coordinates international medical research, and issues warnings of the outbreaks of diseases.

# COMMUNICATIONS

**Newspapers and Magazines · Language Explosion ·
Business Writing · TV · Telephones · Postal Data**

Television pictures that are relayed into this network control room from communications satellites orbiting the globe and from land lines crossing the nation make it possible for home viewers to be witnesses to world history.

## COMMUNICATIONS: 1967

Educational television (ETV), the Hot Line, and a nationwide strike were among the major U.S. communications developments in 1967.

● President Johnson proposed the creation of a Federal corporation, using Federal funds but free of government control, to develop an educational network to broadcast TV classroom instruction. Both the Ford Foundation and the Communications Satellite Corporation had proposed similar plans for such a network.

● The Hot Line teletype between the Kremlin and the White House was used in an emergency for the first time when President Johnson and Premier Kosygin employed it to discuss the world crisis caused by the Arab-Israeli war.

● For the first time in its history the 18,000-member AFL-CIO American Federation of Television and Radio Artists struck the three major radio and TV networks on March 29.

Millions of viewers saw Huntley without Brinkley during the ten-day walkout when NBC's David Brinkley joined other striking newscasters but Chet Huntley did not. The networks kept operating by showing previously taped programs and using executives as performers and newsmen.

● The FCC (Federal Communications Commission) ruled that stations broadcasting cigarette commercials would have to provide "a significant amount of time" for presentation of the opposite position because "smoking may be a hazard to the smoker's health."

● U.S. Attorney General Ramsey Clark ordered a drastic curtailment of bugging and wiretapping by Federal agencies. His order forbids such electronic eavesdropping except in investigations involving national security and in cases where one of the parties has given his consent.

# FOCUS ON THE NEWS

## OBITUARY OF A NEWSPAPER

**The World Journal Tribune's** city room was empty and quiet on May 5, 1967—the day of the New York newspaper's final edition (front page shown above). The paper quit publishing because of high production costs.

In May, 1967, New York City's newest newspaper, the *World Journal Tribune,* closed its doors forever after a brief, unhappy, eight-months life. About 2,600 staff members and other employees lost their jobs, and the nation's largest city was left with only three major dailies—*The Times* and the *Daily News,* competing in the morning, and the *Post,* now with the afternoon to itself.

The *World Journal Tribune,* formed in 1966 from a merger of Scripps-Howard's *World-Telegram and Sun,* Hearst's *Journal-American,* and John Hay Whitney's *Herald Tribune,* had an uphill battle from the start. Severance pay under the old union contracts had cost the three merging papers $7,000,-000, and the new paper was struck by a printer's union on the day of its birth. Not until September 12, 1966—20 weeks after its announced date—did the first issue appear.

Once under way, the *WJT* quickly gained a remarkably high circulation—almost 700,-000 daily and 900,000 on Sundays. But it did not gain enough advertising from New York's local retailers; this, combined with high operating costs, brought a loss of over $22,000 a day. Later, new negotiations between the city's ten newspaper unions and its dailies resulted in a settlement with the flourishing *Daily News* that raised wages almost 25 per cent over a three-year period and greatly increased severance pay. The fledgling *WJT* was asked for a similiar contract, but its three owners claimed that this would add over $3,000,000 annually to their projected $8,000,000-a-year deficit, and they shut down the *WJT.*

The short history of the *World Journal Tribune* was but the latest in a series of births, mergers, and deaths that have reduced the number of New York City newspapers from 15 in 1900 to only 3 today.

## NEW YORK CITY NEWSPAPERS OF GENERAL CIRCULATION, 1900-67

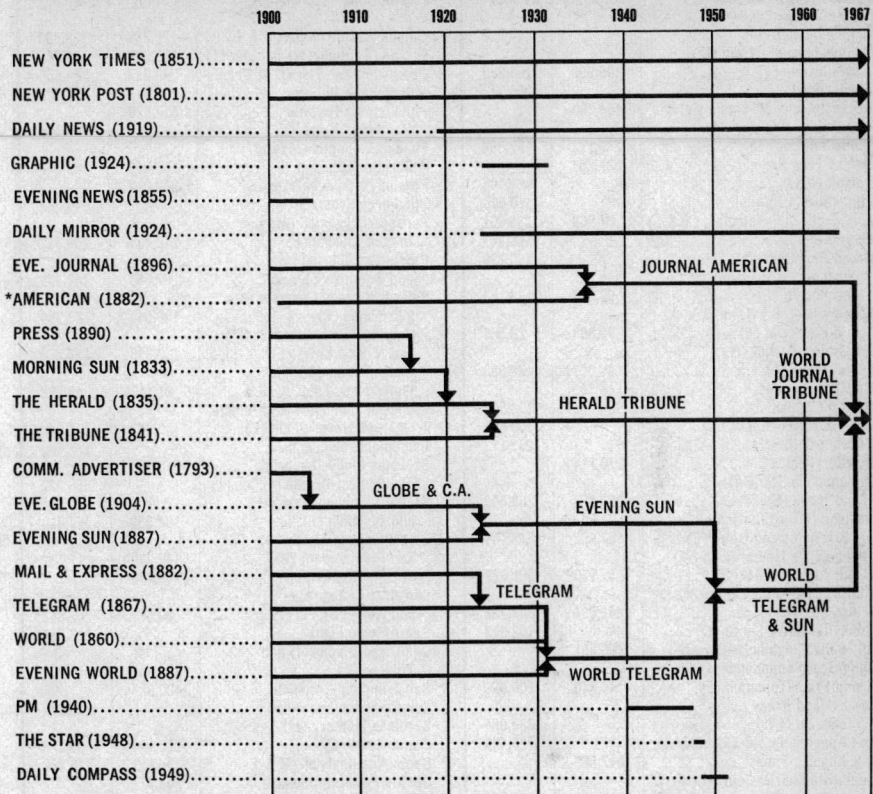

*Founded 1882 as Morning Journal. Name changed in 1901

## U.S. DAILY NEWSPAPERS: CIRCULATION LEADERS

Source: Audit Bureau of Circulations (ABC); Editor & Publisher

| NEWSPAPER (M) Morning   (E) Evening | CIRCULATION [1] Morning | CIRCULATION [1] Evening | NEWSPAPER (M) Morning   (E) Evening | CIRCULATION [1] Morning | CIRCULATION [1] Evening |
|---|---|---|---|---|---|
| Akron Beacon Journal.......... | | 172,451 | Courier (M) and Post (E)..... | 66,084 | 39,966 |
| Albany Times-Union (M) and Knickerbocker News (E)..... | 71,450 | 55,651 | Charlotte Observer (M) and News (E)............... | 174,954 | 63,079 |
| Allentown (Pa.) Call (M) and Chronicle (E)............ | 86,167 | 24,154 | Chicago's American............ | | 439,360 |
| Atlanta Constitution (M) and Journal (E)............. | 199,197 | 247,912 | Chicago Sun-Times (M) and News (E)................ | 547,381 | 466,424 |
| Baltimore News American...... | | 216,453 | Chicago Tribune............... | 832,146 | |
| Baltimore Sun (M & E)......... | 187,635 | 208,722 | Christian Science Monitor..... | | 192,399 |
| Bergen Record (N.J.).......... | | 142,268 | Cincinnati Enquirer.......... | 194,009 | |
| Birmingham News............. | | 177,626 | Cincinnati Post & Times-Star... | | 244,646 |
| Boston Globe (M & E)......... | 234,103 | 139,270 | Cleveland Plain Dealer......... | 377,089 | |
| Boston Herald (M) and Traveler (E)................ | 158,711 | 138,114 | Cleveland Press............... | | 381,708 |
| Boston Record American...... | 418,266 | | Columbia (S.C.) State (M) and Record (E)............ | 99,665 | 30,167 |
| Buffalo Courier-Express........ | 159,704 | | Columbus (O.) Citizen-Journal.. | 112,447 | |
| Buffalo News................. | | 281,557 | Columbus Dispatch............ | | 218,493 |
| Camden (N.J.) Courier Press.... | | 104,520 | Corpus Christi Caller (M) and Times (E)............. | 67.545 | 35,926 |
| Charleston (S.C.) News & | | | Dallas News.................. | 227,725 | |

[1] ABC Publisher's statement; period ending Sept. 30, 1966, unless otherwise noted.          *(continued)*

**U.S. DAILY NEWSPAPERS** (continued)

| NEWSPAPER (M) Morning (E) Evening | CIRCULATION[1] Morning | Evening |
|---|---|---|
| Dallas Times Herald .......... | | 204,552 |
| Dayton Journal Herald (M) and News (E) ............. | 105,996 | 158,860 |
| Denver Post ................. | | 255,372 |
| Denver, Rocky Mountain News .. | 194,360 | |
| Des Moines Register (M) and Tribune (E) ............. | 237,172 | 117,582 |
| Detroit Free Press ............ | 537,203 | |
| Detroit News ................. | | 684,705 |
| Flint (Mich.) Journal .......... | | 110,879 |
| Fort Worth Star-Telegram (M & E) | 97,968 | 133,061 |
| Fresno Bee ................... | | 114,441 |
| Grand Rapids Press ........... | | 130,139 |
| Greensboro (N.C.) News (M) and Record (E) ............. | 92,207 | 33,163 |
| Greenville (S.C.) News (M) and Piedmont (E) ........... | 91,058 | 23,585 |
| Harrisburg Patriot (M) and News (E) ................ | 45,099 | 74,638 |
| Hartford Courant ............. | 143,345 | |
| Hartford Times ............... | | 133,803 |
| Honolulu Star-Bulletin ........ | | 109,865 |
| Houston Chronicle ............ | | 273,112[2] |
| Houston Post ................. | 270,214[2] | |
| Indianapolis Star (M) and News (E) ................ | 228,852 | 201,503 |
| Jackson (Miss.) Clarion-Ledger (M) and News (E).... | 57,697 | 48,659 |
| Jacksonville Times-Union (M) and Journal (E) ............. | 52,920[3] | 201,688[3] |
| Kansas City (Mo.) Times (M) and Star (E) .............. | 341,634 | 337,733 |
| Knoxville News-Sentinel ....... | | 103,313 |
| Little Rock, Arkansas Gazette ... | 106,851 | |
| Long Beach Independent (M) and Press-Telegram (E) ...... | 46,340 | 106,969 |
| Long Island Press (Jamaica, N.Y.) ............ | | 339,064 |
| Los Angeles Herald-Examiner ... | | 726,424 |
| Los Angeles Times ............ | 847,869 | |
| Louisville Courier-Journal (M) and Times (E) ............. | 227,903 | 171,625 |
| Memphis Commercial Appeal (M) and Press-Scimitar (E) ....... | 221,857 | 135,792 |
| Miami Herald ................. | 359,959[3] | |
| Miami News .................. | | 110,118[3] |
| Milwaukee Sentinel (M) and Journal (E) ................ | 168,242 | 366,398 |
| Minneapolis Tribune (M) and Star (E) .............. | 234,045 | 281,008 |
| Mobile Register (M) and Press (E) | 43,456 | 65,646 |
| Nashville Tennessean ......... | 141,822 | |
| New Haven Journal-Courier (M) and Register (E) ........... | 31,850 | 104,472 |
| New Orleans Times-Picayune (M) and States-Item (E) ....... | 194,073 | 137,843 |
| New York Daily News .......... | 2,122,982 | |
| New York Post ............... | | 380,764 |
| New York Times .............. | 762,239 | |
| N.Y. World Journal Telegram ... | | 674,986[4] |
| Newark News ................. | | 279,446 |
| Newark Star-Ledger ........... | 248,096 | |
| Newsday (Garden City, N.Y.).... | | 413,933 |
| Norfolk Virginian-Pilot (M) and Ledger-Star (E) ........ | 125,892 | 106,095 |
| Oakland Tribune .............. | | 224,986 |
| Oklahoma City Oklahoman (M) and Times (E) ............. | 170,709 | 116,379 |
| Omaha World-Herald (M & E)... | 126,888 | 128,350 |
| Orlando Sentinel (M) and Star (E) | 111,066[3] | 32,285[3] |
| Peoria Journal-Star (M & E).... | 40,117 | 64,855 |
| Philadelphia Bulletin ........... | | 670,123 |
| Philadelphia Inquirer .......... | 517,229 | |
| Philadelphia News ............. | | 245,468 |
| Phoenix Republic (M) and Gazette (E) ................. | 152,066 | 89,142 |
| Pittsburgh Post-Gazette ........ | 249,080 | |
| Pittsburgh Press .............. | | 345,762 |
| Portland Oregonian (M) and Oregon Journal (E) .......... | 249,487 | 150,532 |
| Providence Journal (M) and Bulletin (E) ............. | 67,050 | 147,171 |
| Raleigh News & Observer (M) and Times (E) .............. | 130,044 | 23,964 |
| Richmond Times-Dispatch (M) and News-Leader (E) ........ | 150,376 | 127,280 |
| Roanoke Times (M) and World-News (E) ............. | 61,447 | 48,298 |
| Rochester Democrat & Chronicle (M) and Times-Union (E)..... | 140,943 | 141,641 |
| Sacramento Bee .............. | | 176,080 |
| St. Louis Globe-Democrat....... | 318,459 | |
| St. Louis Post-Dispatch ........ | | 356,722 |
| St. Paul Pioneer Press (M) and Dispatch (E) ............. | 102,538 | 127,818 |
| St. Petersburg Times (M) and Independent (E) ......... | 142,048[3] | 19,582[3] |
| Salt Lake City Tribune ......... | 109,738 | |
| San Antonio Express (M) and News (E) ................ | 80,610 | 61,842 |
| San Antonio Light ............. | | 116,011 |
| San Diego Union (M) and Tribune (E) ............... | 124,899 | 115,608 |
| San Francisco Chronicle........ | 490,027 | |
| San Francisco Examiner........ | | 220,058 |
| San Jose Mercury (M) and News (E) ................ | 118,194 | 69,173 |
| Santa Ana Register (M & E).... | 36,199 | 76,426 |
| Seattle Post-Intelligencer....... | 204,777 | |
| Seattle Times................. | | 237,048 |
| South Bend Tribune........... | | 120,390 |
| Spokane Spokesman-Review (M) and Chronicle (E)............. | 86,814 | 70,324 |
| Springfield (Mass.) Union (M) and News (E).............. | 78,948[5] | 98,376[5] |
| Syracuse Herald-Journal....... | | 132,647 |
| Tampa Tribune (M) and Times (E)............. | 162,100[3] | 40,245[3] |
| Toledo Times (M) and Blade (E) | 31,551 | 181,514 |
| Tulsa World.................. | 110,782 | |
| Wall Street Journal Eastern edition............... | 435,094 | |
| Midwestern edition......... | 296,093 | |
| Southwestern edition........ | 87,270 | |
| Pacific Coast edition......... | 170,986 | |
| Washington News............. | | 225,416 |
| Washington Post.............. | 440,762 | |
| Washington Star.............. | | 306,201 |
| Wichita Eagle (M) and Beacon (E)................. | 127,557 | 68,122 |
| Wilmington (Del.) News (M) and Journal (E)............. | 42,933 | 86,943 |
| Winston-Salem Journal (M) and Twin-City Sentinel (E)....... | 75,435 | 43,302 |
| Worcester Telegram (M) and Gazette (E)............... | 62,326 | 94,356 |

[1] ABC Publisher's statement, period ending Sept. 30, 1966, unless otherwise noted. [2] ABC, March 31, 1966. [3] Average for 1966. [4] Average, Oct. 1–Dec. 31, 1966. (See story on page 742). [5] Publisher's statement, Sept. 30, 1966.

## U.S. MAGAZINES: CIRCULATION LEADERS

Source: Audit Bureau of Circulations; Magazine Publishers Association

| MAGAZINE | CIRCULATION * | MAGAZINE | CIRCULATION * |
|---|---|---|---|
| Reader's Digest | 17,222,440 | Young Catholic Messenger | 612,778 |
| TV Guide | 11,508,767 | Flower & Garden Magazine | 608,244 |
| McCall's | 8,585,574 | True Confessions | 604,378 |
| Look | 7,731,177 | Catholic Digest | 600,231 |
| Family Circle | 7,512,516 | Simplicity Fashion Magazine | 598,666 |
| Life | 7,408,123 | Lion Magazine | 582,221 |
| Woman's Day | 7,158,582 | Pageant | 557,153 |
| Better Homes & Gardens | 7,055,967 | Lutheran | 540,319 |
| Ladies' Home Journal | 6,824,478 | Motor Trend | 522,332 |
| Saturday Evening Post | 6,696,050 | Business Week | 519,497 |
| Good Housekeeping | 5,624,772 | McCall's Pattern Fashions & Home Decr. | 500,059 |
| National Geographic | 5,044,802 | Motion Picture | 497,737 |
| Redbook | 4,334,342 | National Observer | 484,741 |
| Playboy | 3,923,266 | New Yorker | 471,865 |
| Scholastic Magazines | 3,770,836 | Capper's Weekly | 464,819 |
| American Home | 3,482,397 | Saturday Review | 463,138 |
| Time | 3,466,326 | Hairdo | 458,454 |
| Farm Journal | 3,022,929 | Fortune | 454,312 |
| American Legion Magazine | 2,517,729 | Forbes | 445,137 |
| True | 2,462,750 | Farmer-Stockman | 430,124 |
| Boy's Life | 2,422,033 | Vogue (inc. Vanity Fair) | 437,373 |
| True Story | 2,290,729 | Popular Photography | 429,302 |
| Parent's Magazine & Better | | Family Handyman | 429,177 |
| Homemaking | 2,023,916 | Harper's Bazaar (inc. Jr. Bazaar) | 422,681 |
| Newsweek | 1,965,095 | Rotarian | 419,560 |
| U.S. News & World Report | 1,522,813 | Scientific American | 415,004 |
| Popular Mechanics | 1,486,185 | Christian Herald | 400,068 |
| Workbasket | 1,463,854 | Flower Grower | 400,060 |
| Popular Science Monthly | 1,404,104 | Westways | 392,886 |
| Elks Magazine | 1,399,286 | Popular Electronics | 385,246 |
| Outdoor Life | 1,397,897 | Car & Driver | 384,869 |
| Argosy | 1,389,765 | Coronet | 382,422 |
| Mechanix Illustrated | 1,389,685 | True Romance | 339,211 |
| Seventeen | 1,384,357 | Movie Mirror | 335,922 |
| Field & Stream | 1,380,766 | Popular Gardening & Living Outdoors | 333,602 |
| Sports Afield | 1,336,730 | Golf (inc. Golfing) | 330,275 |
| Successful Farming | 1,330,991 | Jet | 329,911 |
| Glamour | 1,321,792 | Stag | 326,357 |
| V.F.W. Magazine | 1,298,664 | Southern Living | 319,645 |
| Scouting | 1,286,482 | True Experience | 318,818 |
| Progressive Farmer | 1,267,354 | Workbench | 317,349 |
| House & Garden | 1,256,829 | True Love | 315,033 |
| Sports Illustrated | 1,211,802 | Vogue Pattern Book | 304,693 |
| Newstime | 1,191,787 | Science & Mechanics | 301,696 |
| Photoplay | 1,148,290 | Personal Romances | 301,368 |
| Columbia | 1,142,059 | Extension | 301,317 |
| Grit | 1,064,585 | Atlantic Monthly | 291,303 |
| Presbyterian Life | 1,060,724 | Golf Digest | 288,905 |
| Esquire | 1,035,337 | Male | 283,997 |
| Holiday | 1,029,277 | Electronics Illustrated | 282,681 |
| House Beautiful | 1,026,708 | Gourmet | 280,052 |
| American Girl | 1,003,932 | Sign | 277,226 |
| Co-Ed | 970,702 | Kiwanis Magazine | 277,096 |
| Ebony | 946,115 | Harper's Magazine | 276,638 |
| Cosmopolitan | 895,666 | Flying | 263,876 |
| National Enquirer | 893,758 | Road & Track | 263,854 |
| TV Radio Mirror | 891,594 | Grade Teacher | 260,997 |
| Sunset | 833,065 | Lady's Circle | 253,950 |
| Nation's Business | 800,178 | Modern Photography | 252,547 |
| Modern Screen | 795,718 | Instructor | 244,972 |
| Sport | 792,666 | Cue | 242,046 |
| Ingenue | 783,739 | Real Confessions | 242,020 |
| Our Sunday Visitor | 760,414 | Official Detective Stories | 239,381 |
| Modern Romances | 756,254 | Presbyterian Survey | 239,001 |
| 'Teen | 744,539 | Improvement Era | 236,043 |
| Hot Rod Magazine | 701,123 | TV & Movie Screen | 234,270 |
| Mademoiselle | 676,692 | Intimate Story | 228,181 |
| Together | 616,325 | Bride's Magazine | 227,936 |

*Total net paid average for the six months ending December 31, 1966.

## THE LANGUAGE EXPLOSION

English is one of the world's most flexible languages—one that is constantly being enhanced. Since Americans are generally receptive to fresh ideas and improved ways of doing things, they are particularly adept at augmenting their mother tongue by adding new words and giving new meanings to old ones.

When a word that has taken on new meaning—or a newly coined word—wins acceptance, it soon gains nationwide vogue. Television, radio, magazines, newspapers, and movies quickly see to that, and specialized jargon that had its genesis on a college campus, in a laboratory, or in Greenwich Village soon finds its way into the speech of millions. Some are fad words doomed to a short life-span, but many become a permanent part of the American vocabulary.

A sampling of the new words or word combinations that have evolved in the 1960s is listed below. Many of them have to do with space exploration (soft landing, splashdown); the Vietnam war (defoliation, dove); science and technology (cryogenics, microminiaturize); social tremors (freedom ride, teach-in); and a changing way of life (retirement village, discotheque). Others were known before the 1960s to a few specialists or to small groups, but they have gained currency only in the past decade.

**Acoustical cloud**—a panel hung from an auditorium ceiling to reflect or direct sound.

**A-frame**—a dwelling whose main supporting frame is in the form of an *A*.

**Afterburner**—a device that gives extra thrust to a jet engine by burning its exhaust gases.

**Angry young man**—one whose play, book, or painting criticizes established society and tradition.

**Animal**—a sloppy or uncouth person.

**Antidepressant**—any of various drugs used to relieve mental depression.

**Antigravity**—a hypothetical force that would cancel gravity or make positive and negative particles of matter repel instead of attract each other.

**Antimatter**—particles of matter similar to common particles but having charges opposite to them.

**A-OK**—perfect; great; A-1.

**Astrodome**—a stadium with a movable dome-like roof, such as that in Houston, Texas.

**Automatic data processing**—the processing of information by computers.

**Beach buggy**—a motor vehicle, usually old or lightweight, with oversized tires for driving on the sand.

**Black power**—political and economic power for the American Negro.

**Boss**—the best or most exciting person or thing in any field; wonderful.

**Brain drain**—an excessive flow of highly educated or skilled people from one nation to another, especially from England to the U.S.

**Bringdown**—a critical or insulting remark; anything that deflates one's ego or enthusiasm.

**Bug**—a hidden listening device; to irritate.

**Camp**—the conscious use of artificial, exaggerated, or affected mannerisms or styles of dress, decoration, speech, etc.

**Celestial guidance**—an automatic guidance system in a missile or spacecraft that uses celestial bodies as points of reference.

**Charlie**—a Vietcong soldier or the Vietcong.

**Core curriculum**—a curriculum in which the subjects are correlated to a central theme.

**Counterinsurgency**—a means of combating guerrilla warfare and terrorism.

**Cryogenics**—a science dealing with the effects of extremely low temperatures on the physical properties of matter.

**Defoliation**—destroying or inhibiting growth (usually by chemical means) in an area of jungle or forest used by guerrilla forces or enemy troops as a hiding place.

**Discotheque**—a modern cabaret, especially one in which customers dance to recorded rock-and-roll music.

**Dolce vita**—the sweet life; a life full of self-indulgence and expensive pleasures.

**Dove**—a person who favors U.S. withdrawal from or a lessening of the war in Vietnam.

**Downrange**—in the direction of the target toward which a rocket is launched.

**Ecumenical**—in the liberal or modern spirit of Christian unity, as exemplified by the Ecumenical Council of the Roman Catholic Church.

**Escalation**—an increase in the scope or intensity of something, as of a war.

**Eurodollars**—U.S. dollars deposited in European banks to finance trade and serve as international credit.

**Extra-vehicular activity**—tasks performed by astronauts outside their spacecraft.

**Exurb**—a community smaller and farther from a city than a suburb.

**Fall**—a woman's long artificial hairpiece for adding to or blending with her own hair.

**Fastback**—a car whose back slants in an unbroken line from the roof to the rear bumper.

**Folk rock**—popular music combining rock-and-roll rhythm with folk-song tempo and lyrics.

**Freak out**—to withdraw from normal rational behavior, either permanently or for short periods.

**Freedom ride**—a trip, usually by bus, to a segregated area by persons seeking to promote integration of public places.

**Freeze dry**—to preserve food, blood plasma, etc., by using a combination high-vacuum and low-temperature process.

**Frug**—a popular dance derived from the twist.

**Geodesic dome**—a lightweight, globelike structure combining the strength of a tetrahedron and a dome (as the U.S. building at Expo 67).

**Go ape**—to become so excited as to lose control of oneself (teen-age use).

**Go-go dancer**—a girl employed as an entertainer to dance for patrons at a discotheque or bar.

**Grass**—marijuana.

**G-suit**—a flying suit that exerts pressure so that blood will not collect below the heart when a pilot is subjected to extremely high acceleration.

**Hallucinogen**—a hallucination-producing drug or chemical, such as LSD.

**Hangup**—a preoccupation, fixation, or psychological block.

**Happening**—an entertainment or gathering in which the audience comes to perform a spontaneous part, serving also as performers.

**Hard news**—serious news of national or international importance, as opposed to local news, human interest items, etc.

**Hardware**—military weapons; computers and the equipment used with them.

**Hawk**—a person who strongly supports U.S. involvement in the Vietnam war.

**High rise**—an apartment or office building with many floors; a skyscraper.

**Hippie**—a young person who rebels against adult society and values by refusing to live, dress, or act in the traditional manner.

**Hot Line**—a direct teletype link (initially established between the White House and the Kremlin) for use in preventing an accidental war.

**Hully gully**—a shuffling variety of the frug.

**Ion propulsion**—a hypothetical type of ultra-high-speed propulsion for spacecraft, using a stream of positive ions and negative electrons as a propelling exhaust.

**Isometric exercise**—any exercise that pits one part of the body against another or against an immovable object.

**Kook**—a peculiar or eccentric person; a "character."

**Laser beam**—a beam of amplified light-frequency radiations.

**LSD**—lysergic acid diethylamide; a strongly hallucinogenic, psychedelic drug.

**Megalopolis**—a large, crowded urban area, especially one composed of a series of large adjoining cities whose suburbs overlap.

**Microminiaturize**—electronic components built on a scale smaller than subminiature.

**Mod**—a style of dress, originated in London and popular with U.S. students, in which unconventional designs, patterns, and bright colors are used.

**Multimedia**—the simultaneous use of various media (movies, slides, flashing lights, sound, etc.) combined to flood the senses.

**Napalm**—a highly flammable, sticky, jellied substance used in incendiary bombs.

**New math**—a system for teaching mathematics and set theory that reveals basic arithmetical relations and sequences, currently used in most U.S. schools.

**New wave**—a movement in European filmmaking that emphasizes aesthetic pictorial qualities and psychological reality over plot and characters.

**Op art**—an abstract art style in which lines, shapes, and colors are organized to produce optical illusions.

**Overachiever**—a student whose school work is better than his aptitude or IQ tests indicate it should be.

**Paramedic**—an armed-forces doctor or medical corpsman trained to parachute into remote or dangerous areas to give medical assistance.

**Payola**—any bribe, payoff, or graft; originally, a bribe paid to disc jockeys by singers, recording companies, etc., to promote their records.

**Pep pill**—any amphetamine pill.

**The Pill**—an oral contraceptive.

**Pop art**—a realistic rendering of objects seen in everyday life that uses art techniques derived from comic strips, posters, etc.

**Psychedelic**—a mental state of unreality, and a calm but vivid awareness and acceptance of everything, as caused by LSD or other drugs.

**Putdown**—a humiliating remark or act that deflates someone's ego; a "bringdown."

**Quark**—one of three types of hypothetical elementary particles said by some physicists to be the basis of all matter in the universe.

**Quasar**—any one of various similar celestial bodies from 5 to 10 billion light years away that are a highly powerful source of radio energy.

**Ressentiment**—a cynical or defeatist attitude based on the belief that we live in a hostile, indifferent, or godless universe.

**Retirement village**—a specially built community for retired persons.

**Soft landing**—the landing intact of a spacecraft on a satellite or planet.

**Softwear**—the nonelectric, nonmechanical devices or materials used with a computer, such as the written program or flow charts.

**Solid-state**—containing electronic components, such as transistors, that control current without the use of such elements as heated filaments and vacuum gaps.

**Splashdown**—the landing of a spacecraft on water.

**Supertanker**—a giant oil tanker, especially one with a capacity of over 75,000 tons.

**Swinger**—an active person whose tastes in dress, music, and entertainment are in the latest mode.

**Teach-in**—a protest demonstration of uninterrupted lectures, speeches, or classes staged on a campus by students to gain recognition of their alleged rights or grievances.

**Teeny bopper**—a teen-ager completely enmeshed in the youthful fads of dress, rock-and-roll, and hippie attitudes.

**Throughput**—the amount of material or information processed in a given period of time, as by a computer.

**Trip**—an instance of being under the influence of a drug, particularly LSD.

**Tuned in**—aware of or sympathetic to modern attitudes and fads.

**Underachiever**—a student whose school work is poorer than his aptitude or IQ tests indicate it should be.

**Up tight**—being thoroughly modern, aware, and calm; nervous or neurotic—having a "hangup."

**Vertical mobility**—the ability to move from one economic or social level to a higher one.

**Zap**—to destroy, kill, or defeat an enemy.

## BUSINESS WRITING: LETTERS AND RÉSUMÉS

A business letter or résumé should be typed (single space) on one side of a sheet of 8½-by-11-inch white bond paper. Keep at least a one-inch margin on the left and right of the paper, and at least a 1½-inch margin above and below the centered letter or résumé.

### HOW TO WRITE A RÉSUMÉ

A résumé should look like this:

```
                                        John Doe
                                        128 North Elm St.
                                        Mayesville, Ohio  20267
                                        Telephone:  STerling 3-2078


     RÉSUMÉ


     Business Experience:  May, 1964 to present--Salesman for Metropolitan
     Auto Distributors, Cleveland, Ohio.  Call on and service over 200
     accounts in Cleveland, Mayesville, and Columbus, selling a line of
     over 250 separate items from five automotive manufacturers.  Received
     the Mayesville and Columbus territories after having increased sales
     in Cleveland by 60%.  In June, 1967, delivered talk before the annual
     American Automobile Parts Association meeting, in Chicago, on "Increasing
     Sales in Metropolitan Areas."  Average income over the past three years:
     over $9,000.

     (Continue to list your earlier jobs here.)



     Education:  September, 1952 to June, 1954--University of Michigan;
     majored in Liberal Arts; attended two special classes in business
     administration.  Member University of Michigan Sport's Car Rally Club.

     Personal Data:  Born November 11, 1929; Detroit, Michigan.  Married.
     Three children.

     References:  Mr. Joseph Hopett, Manager, Detroit Auto Parts, Co.,
     (One or two other references here)
```

Give your home address and home or business telephone. Do not include the name and address of the company to which you are submitting your résumé; this will be in the short covering letter accompanying it.

A résumé should be complete but brief—preferably on one page. Essentially, it should contain four types of information: past jobs, education, personal data, and the names and addresses of two or three personal references.

List each job you have had, with the present or last one at the top. In composing your résumé try not to use the word "I." It is also unnecessary to write complete sentences; a telegraphic style is acceptable. For example, use "Employed March 1963 to . . ." instead of "I was employed from March 1963 to. . . ." Be specific: give the month and year you were employed and when and why you left (such as "left for better position"); each position; exact title or job description; the name and address of each firm that hired you; and a brief statement telling exactly what you did. Include any special on-the-job accomplishments or added responsibilities given to you.

Information on education should cover the name of your high school and college (if any), the relevant dates, and when you graduated. Mention any specific scholastic or extracurricular activities that might have a bearing on the work you are seeking.

Personal data should note when and where you were born; your marital status; and number of dependents, if any. Men should briefly mention their military service (dates, branch, duties, and final rank) or draft status.

Finally, list the names and addresses of two or three references. Do not give people for whom you are working unless they know that you are actively seeking another position.

The letter with your résumé should tell how you heard of the job and anything else of specific interest to the prospective employer, such as a willingness to relocate, if necessary. End by saying, "I look forward to an interview at your convenience."

## THE STYLE OF A BUSINESS LETTER

```
                                        128 North Elm St.
                                        Mayesville, Ohio  20267

                                            (Date)

   Mr. Richard Roe
   Personnel Manager
   Universal Auto Sales Co., Inc.
   1428 Wilshire Blvd.
   Los Angeles, California  30225

   Dear Mr. Roe:

                    (The body of the letter here)



                                        Sincerely yours,


                                            (Signature)

                                            John Doe
```

If you are writing an official letter on your company's letterhead, do not put your address at the top right as in the sample letter above. Do, however, put your business title below your typed name at the bottom of the letter.

Abbreviations such as *St., Ave., Blvd., Co., Corp.,* or *Inc.* may be used, but spell out the state name in an address. The block style (unindented lines in the address, and paragraphs, without indentation) is widely accepted today.

## COMMONLY MISSPELLED WORDS

| | | | | |
|---|---|---|---|---|
| accommodate | changeable | existence | occasion | receipt |
| accuracy | coming | extremely | occur | receive |
| accustomed | commit | fascinate | occurrence | recognize |
| acknowledgment | conscious | forty | parliament | recommend |
| acquaintance | correspondence | grammar | permanent | relevant |
| advertisement | decision | immediately | permissible | restaurant |
| apparent | description | incidentally | pleasant | rhythm |
| appearance | desirable | irresistible | possess | separate |
| argument | develop | jewelry | preceding | similar |
| athletic | disappoint | laboratory | preference | stopped |
| beginning | dissatisfied | maintenance | preferred | succeed |
| believe | ecstasy | miscellaneous | privilege | surprise |
| benefit | embarrassed | mischievous | probably | tragedy |
| bicycle | equipped | misspell | procedure | transferred |
| calendar | evidently | mortgage | proceeds | weird |
| campaign | exaggerate | necessity | professor | wholly |

## ABBREVIATIONS IN COMMON USE

**AA** = Alcoholics Anonymous
**AAA** = American Automobile Association
**AAU** = Amateur Athletic Union
**ABM** = Anti-Ballistic Missile
**A.D.** = *Anno Domini* (in the year of our Lord)
**AEC** = Atomic Energy Commission
**AFL-CIO** = American Federation of Labor and Congress of Industrial Organizations
**AL** = American Legion
**A.M.** = *Ante Meridiem* (before noon)
**AMA** = American Medical Association
**APO** = Army Post Office
**ASCAP** = American Society of Composers, Authors, and Publishers
**AWOL** = Absent Without Leave
**BA** = Bachelor of Arts
**B.C.** = Before Christ
**BS** = Bachelor of Science
**CAB** = Civil Aeronautics Board
**CARE** = Co-operative for American Remittances to Everywhere
**CIA** = Central Intelligence Agency
**CO** = Commanding officer
**COD** = Cash on delivery; collect on delivery
**CORE** = Congress of Racial Equality
**CPA** = Certified Public Accountant
**D** = Democrat; Democratic
**DAR** = Daughters of the American Revolution
**DEW** = Distant Early Warning
**DOA** = Dead on Arrival
**e.g.** = *exempli gratia* (for example)
**ESP** = Extra-Sensory Perception
**ETA** = Estimated Time of Arrival
**Etc.** = *Et cetera* (and so forth)
**ETV** = Educational Television
**FAA** = Federal Aviation Agency
**FBI** = Federal Bureau of Investigation
**FCC** = Federal Communications Commission
**FDA** = Food and Drug Administration
**FDIC** = Federal Deposit Insurance Corporation
**FHA** = Federal Housing Administration
**FOB** = Free on Board
**FPO** = Fleet Post Office
**FTC** = Federal Trade Commission
**GHQ** = General headquarters
**GI** = Government Issue; Gastro-Intestinal
**GMT** = Greenwich Mean Time
**GOP** = Grand Old Party (Republican)
**GP** = General Practitioner
**GPO** = General Post Office; Government Printing Office
**HMS** = Her Majesty's Ship
**Ibid.** = *Ibidem* (in the same place)
**ICBM** = Intercontinental Ballistic Missile
**ICC** = Interstate Commerce Commission
**ID** = Identification
**i.e.** = *id est* (that is)
**ILGWU** = International Ladies Garment Workers Union
**IQ** = Intelligence Quotient
**IRS** = Internal Revenue Service
**KKK** = Ku Klux Klan
**KO** = Knockout
**KP** = Kitchen Police
**Kwh** = Kilowatt hour
**LSD** = Lysergic Acid Diethylamide
**LTD.** = Limited
**MA** = Master of Arts
**MP** = Member of Parliament; Military Police
**MS** = Master of Science
**NAACP** = National Association for the Advancement of Colored People
**NAM** = National Association of Manufacturers
**NASA** = National Aeronautics and Space Administration
**NATO** = North Atlantic Treaty Organization
**NBA** = National Boxing Association
**NCAA** = National Collegiate Athletic Association
**NLRB** = National Labor Relations Board
**OAS** = Organization of American States
**OD** = Officer of the Day; Olive Drab
**PAL** = Police Athletic League
**PGA** = Professional Golfers' Association
**PhD** = Doctor of Philosophy
**P.M.** = *Post Meridiem* (after noon)
**PR** = Public Relations
**PS** = *Post Scriptum* (postscript)
**PTA** = Parent-Teachers' Association
**PX** = Post Exchange
**R** = Republican
**R&D** = Research and Development
**Re.** = Regarding
**RFD** = Rural Free Delivery
**R.I.P.** = *Requiescat in Pace* (may he (she) rest in peace)
**RSVP** = *Répondez s'il vous plaît* (please reply)
**SAC** = Strategic Air Command
**SAM** = Surface-to-Air Missile
**SEATO** = Southeast Asia Treaty Organization
**SEC** = Securities and Exchange Commission
**SNCC** = Student Non-Violent Coordinating Committee
**SPCA** = Society for the Prevention of Cruelty to Animals
**SST** = Supersonic Transport
**TD** = Touchdown
**TKO** = Technical Knockout
**UFO** = Unidentified Flying Object
**UNESCO** = United Nations Educational, Scientific, and Cultural Organization
**UNICEF** = United Nations International Children's Emergency Fund
**USA** = United States of America; U.S. Army
**USAF** = U.S. Air Force
**USCG** = U.S. Coast Guard
**USMC** = U.S. Marine Corps
**USN** = U.S. Navy
**USO** = United Service Organization
**USS** = United States Ship
**VA** = Veterans Administration
**VC** = Vietcong
**VFW** = Veterans of Foreign Wars
**VIP** = Very Important Person
**V/STOL** = Vertical and Short Takeoff and Landing (airplane)
**WASP** = White Anglo-Saxon Protestant
**WCTU** = Women's Christian Temperance Union
**YMCA** = Young Men's Christian Association
**YMHA** = Young Men's Hebrew Association

# WORLD RADIO AND TELEVISION SETS

Sources: U.S. Information Agency; Television Factbook; Radio Advertising Bureau

| COUNTRY | RADIOS [1] | TV SETS [2] |
|---|---|---|
| **AFRICA** | 16,627,000 | 779,700 |
| Algeria | 1,900,000 | 150,000 |
| Angola | 100,000 | [3] |
| Burundi | 30,000 | [3] |
| Cameroun | 200,000 | [3] |
| Central African Republic | 30,000 | [3] |
| Congo (Brazzaville) | 50,000 | 400 |
| Congo, Dem. Rep. of | 200,000 | 500 |
| Dahomey | 35,000 | [3] |
| Egypt (UAR) | 5,000,000 | 450,000 |
| Ethiopia | 200,000 | 5,000 |
| Gabon | 36,000 | 950 |
| Ghana | 500,000 | 900 |
| Guinea | 75,000 | [3] |
| Ivory Coast | 75,000 | 2,000 |
| Kenya | 500,000 | 9,900 |
| Liberia | 130,000 | 3,000 |
| Libya | 190,000 | 5,000 |
| Malagasy Republic | 260,000 | [3] |
| Mali | 50,000 | [3] |
| Mauritius | 80,000 | 8,000 |
| Morocco | 700,000 | 30,000 |
| Niger | 40,000 | [3] |
| Nigeria | 1,000,000 | 30,000 |
| Rhodesia | 150,000 | 45,000 |
| Rwanda | 20,000 | [3] |
| Senegal | 220,000 | 100 |
| Sierra Leone | 370,000 | 2,000 |
| Somali Republic | 113,000 | [3] |
| South Africa | 3,100,000 | [3] |
| Sudan | 300,000 | 10,000 |
| Tanzania | 150,000 | [3] |
| Togo | 23,000 | [3] |
| Tunisia | 400,000 | 5,400 |
| Uganda | 200,000 | 5,800 |
| Upper Volta | 50,000 | 250 |
| Zambia | 100,000 | 15,500 |
| Other | 50,000 | [3] |
| **NORTH AMERICA** | 251,378,000 | 83,835,000 |
| Antigua | [3] | 1,500 |
| Barbados | 43,000 | 7,000 |
| Bermuda | 25,000 | 15,000 |
| Canada | 12,000,000 | 5,700,000 |
| Costa Rica | 300,000 | 65,000 |
| Cuba | 1,300,000 | 500,000 |
| Dominican Republic | 400,000 | 65,000 |
| El Salvador | 950,000 | 35,000 |
| Guatemala | 280,000 | 60,000 |
| Haiti | 140,000 | 5,500 |
| Honduras | 235,000 | 8,000 |
| Jamaica | 290,000 | 30,000 |
| Mexico | 4,500,000 | 1,800,000 |
| Neth. Antilles | 105,000 | 17,000 |
| Nicaragua | 200,000 | 19,000 |
| Panama | 480,000 | 77,000 |
| Puerto Rico | [3] | 300,000 |
| Trinidad, Tobago | 130,000 | 30,000 |
| United States | 230,000,000 | 75,100,000 |
| **SOUTH AMERICA** | 30,410,000 | 8,677,500 |
| Argentina | 7,200,000 | 1,600,000 |
| Bolivia | 750,000 | [3] |
| Brazil | 10,000,000 | 5,500,000 |
| Chile | 2,500,000 | 90,000 |
| Colombia | 4,000,000 | 400,000 |
| Ecuador | 650,000 | 50,000 |
| Paraguay | 350,000 | 12,500 |
| Peru | 1,700,000 | 275,000 |
| Uruguay | 660,000 | 200,000 |
| Venezuela | 2,600,000 | 550,000 |
| **ASIA** | 67,595,000 | 20,635,100 |
| Afghanistan | 300,000 | [3] |
| Burma | 330,000 | [3] |
| Cambodia | 400,000 | 6,000 |
| Ceylon | 420,000 | [3] |
| China (mainland) | 5,500,000 | 100,000 |
| China (Taiwan) | 1,400,000 | 75,000 |
| Cyprus | 135,000 | 22,000 |
| Hong Kong | 750,000 | 65,000 |
| India | 5,000,000 | 3,600 |
| Indonesia | 2,700,000 | 46,000 |
| Iran | 2,200,000 | 110,000 |
| Iraq | 1,000,000 | 175,000 |
| Israel | 620,000 | 30,000 |
| Japan | 33,000,000 | 19,000,000 |
| Jordan | 260,000 | 10,000 |
| Korea, North | 160,000 | [3] |
| Korea, South | 1,500,000 | 70,000 |
| Kuwait | 150,000 | 80,000 |
| Laos | 70,000 | [3] |
| Lebanon | 325,000 | 165,000 |
| Malaysia | 690,000 | 80,000 |
| Mongolia | 100,000 | [3] |
| Pakistan | 1,100,000 | 20,000 |
| Philippines | 2,000,000 | 190,000 |
| Saudi Arabia | 300,000 | 30,000 |
| Singapore | 250,000 | 76,000 |
| Syria | 1,000,000 | 70,000 |
| Thailand | 2,500,000 | 210,000 |
| Turkey | 2,600,000 | 1,500 |
| Vietnam, South | 500,000 | [3] |
| **EUROPE** | 167,363,000 | 80,959,700 |
| Albania | 60,000 | 1,000 |
| Austria | 2,300,000 | 890,000 |
| Belgium | 4,000,000 | 1,700,000 |
| Bulgaria | 1,400,000 | 180,000 |
| Czechoslovakia | 3,300,000 | 2,800,000 |
| Denmark | 1,700,000 | 1,145,000 |
| Finland | 1,800,000 | 850,000 |
| France | 19,000,000 | 7,196,000 |
| Germany, East | 6,000,000 | 3,600,000 |
| Germany, West | 20,000,000 | 12,500,000 |
| Gibraltar | 5,000 | 5,700 |
| Greece | 1,400,000 | 6,000 |
| Hungary | 2,500,000 | 830,000 |
| Iceland | 100,000 | 15,000 |
| Ireland | 600,000 | 390,000 |
| Italy | 11,000,000 | 6,670,000 |
| Luxembourg | 150,000 | 35,000 |
| Malta | 35,000 | 35,000 |
| Monaco | 7,000 | 15,000 |
| Netherlands | 3,600,000 | 2,250,000 |
| Norway | 1,800,000 | 595,000 |
| Poland | 4,600,000 | 2,500,000 |
| Portugal | 1,500,000 | 186,000 |
| Romania | 1,900,000 | 450,000 |
| Spain | 8,000,000 | 2,075,000 |
| Sweden | 3,100,000 | 2,200,000 |
| Switzerland | 2,700,000 | 800,000 |
| United Kingdom | 25,000,000 | 15,200,000 |
| U.S.S.R. | 37,000,000 | 15,000,000 |
| Yugoslavia | 2,800,000 | 850,000 |
| Other | 6,000 | [3] |
| **OCEANIA** | 9,056,000 | 3,173,000 |
| Australia | 7,600,000 | 2,700,000 |
| Fiji Islands | 35,000 | [3] |
| New Caledonia | 10,000 | 3,000 |
| New Zealand | 1,400,000 | 470,000 |
| Other | 11,000 | [3] |

[1] Estimated as of Dec. 31, 1965.   [2] Estimated as of Jan. 1, 1967.   [3] Not available or none.

## U.S. BROADCASTING STATIONS: 1958–1967 [1]
Source: Federal Communications Commission

| YEAR [2] | AM RADIO | | FM RADIO | | TELEVISION | | NONCOMMERCIAL TV | |
|---|---|---|---|---|---|---|---|---|
| | Authorized | On the air | Authorized | On the air | Authorized | On the air | Authorized | On the air |
| 1958..... | 3,256 | 3,156 | 590 | 537 | 657 | 492 | 53 | 32 |
| 1959..... | 3,401 | 3,287 | 695 | 578 | 666 | 509 | 59 | 43 |
| 1960..... | 3,487 | 3,416 | 838 | 678 | 668 | 517 | 64 | 47 |
| 1961..... | 3,627 | 3,507 | 1,018 | 821 | 624 | 530 | 67 | 54 |
| 1962..... | 3,788 | 3,653 | 1,128 | 960 | 642 | 545 | 79 | 59 |
| 1963..... | 3,834 | 3,770 | 1,218 | 1,081 | 647 | 556 | 91 | 70 |
| 1964..... | 3,994 | 3,897 | 1,249 | 1,146 | 655 | 563 | 107 | 79 |
| 1965..... | 4,040 | 3,972 | 1,468 | 1,270 | 661 | 572 | 118 | 89 |
| 1966..... | 4,129 | 4,004 | 1,657 | 1,393 | 688 | 589 | 63 | 58 |
| 1967..... | 4,185 | 4,085 | 1,854 | 1,560 | 776 [3] | 616 [3] | 193 [3] | 136 [3] |

[1] Includes Puerto Rico, Virgin Islands, and Guam.    [2] As of January 1.    [3] As of June 30.

## TELEPHONE AREA CODES FOR THE UNITED STATES
Source: American Telephone and Telegraph Company

There is no toll charge for getting a listed telephone number for any point in the United States. Just dial the proper area code, then 555-1212, to reach the information operator.

| STATE OR PROVINCE | AREA CODE | AREA COVERED (with chief city) | STATE OR PROVINCE | AREA CODE | AREA COVERED (with chief city) | STATE OR PROVINCE | AREA CODE | AREA COVERED (with chief city) |
|---|---|---|---|---|---|---|---|---|
| Alabama | 205 | Entire state | | 712 | West (Council Bluffs) | N.C. | 704 | West (Charlotte) |
| Alaska | 907 | Entire state | | | | | 919 | East (Raleigh) |
| Arizona | 602 | Entire state | Kansas | 913 | North (Topeka) | N. Dak. | 701 | Entire state |
| Arkansas | 501 | Entire state | | 316 | South (Wichita) | Ohio | 419 | N.W. (Toledo) |
| Calif. | 707 | N.W. (Santa Rosa) | Kentucky | 502 | West (Louisville) | | 513 | S.W. (Cincinnati) |
| | 415 | San Francisco area | | 606 | East (Covington) | | 216 | N.E. (Cleveland) |
| | 408 | W. Central (San Jose) | La. | 318 | West and Central (Shreveport) | | 614 | S.E. (Columbus) |
| | 805 | S.W. Central (Bakersfield) | | 504 | S.E. (New Orleans) | Oklahoma | 405 | W. Central and South (Oklahoma City) |
| | 213 | Los Angeles area | Maine | 207 | Entire state | | | |
| | 916 | N.E. (Sacramento) | Maryland | 301 | Entire state | | 918 | N.E. (Tulsa) |
| | 209 | Central (Fresno) | Mass. | 413 | West (Springfield) | Oregon | 503 | Entire state |
| | 714 | E. Central, S. to Mexico (San Diego) | | 617 | East (Boston) | Penn. | 412 | S.W. (Pittsburgh) |
| | | | Michigan | 906 | Upper Peninsula (Escanaba) | | 814 | N.W. and W. Central (Altoona) |
| Colorado | 303 | Entire state | | 616 | West (Grand Rapids) | | 717 | N.E. and Central (Harrisburg) |
| Conn. | 203 | Entire state | | 517 | Central (Lansing) | | | |
| Del. | 302 | Entire state | | 313 | East (Detroit) | | 215 | S.E. (Philadelphia) |
| D.C. | 202 | Entire area | Minn. | 218 | North (Duluth) | R.I. | 401 | Entire state |
| Florida | 904 | North and West (Jacksonville) | | 612 | Central (Minneapolis) | S.C. | 803 | Entire state |
| | | | | | | S. Dak. | 605 | Entire state |
| | 813 | W. Central and S.W. (St. Petersburg) | | 507 | South (Rochester) | Tenn. | 901 | West (Memphis) |
| | | | Miss. | 601 | Entire state | | 615 | Central and East (Nashville) |
| | 305 | E. Central and S.E. (Miami) | Missouri | 816 | North and N.W. (Kansas City) | Texas | 806 | N.W. (Amarillo) |
| | | | | 417 | S.W. (Springfield) | | 915 | S.W. and W. Central (Sweetwater) |
| Georgia | 404 | North (Atlanta) | | 314 | East (St. Louis) | | | |
| | 912 | South (Savannah) | Montana | 406 | Entire state | | | |
| Hawaii | 808 | Entire state | Nebraska | 308 | W. and Central (North Platte) | | 817 | N. Central (Fort Worth) |
| Idaho | 208 | Entire state | | | | | | |
| Illinois | 815 | N.W. to E. Central (Rockford) | | 402 | East (Omaha) | | 512 | S. Central (San Antonio) |
| | 312 | Chicago area | Nevada | 702 | Entire state | | 214 | N.E. (Dallas) |
| | 309 | N.W. Central (Peoria) | N.H. | 603 | Entire state | | 713 | S.E. (Houston) |
| | 217 | Central (Springfield) | N.J. | 201 | North (Newark) | Utah | 801 | Entire state |
| | | | | 609 | South (Trenton) | Vermont | 802 | Entire state |
| | | | N. Mex. | 505 | Entire state | Virginia | 703 | Entire state |
| | 618 | South (Centralia) | N.Y. | 716 | West (Buffalo) | Wash. | 206 | West (Seattle) |
| Indiana | 219 | North (South Bend) | | 315 | N. Central (Syracuse) | | 509 | Central and East (Spokane) |
| | 317 | Central (Springfield) | | 607 | S. Central (Binghamton) | W.Va. | 304 | Entire state |
| | 812 | South (Evansville) | | 518 | N.E. and E. Central (Albany) | Wis. | 715 | North (Eau Claire) |
| Iowa | 319 | East (Dubuque) | | 914 | S.E. (White Plains) | | 608 | S.W. (Madison) |
| | 515 | Central (Des Moines) | | 212 | New York City | | 414 | East (Milwaukee) |
| | | | | 516 | Long Island | Wyoming | 307 | Entire state |

## COMPARISON OF ADVERTISING EXPENDITURES: 1950 AND 1966

Source: Printers' Ink

| MEDIUM | EXPENDITURES (in millions) | | PER CENT OF TOTAL | | MEDIUM | EXPENDITURES (in millions) | | PER CENT OF TOTAL | |
|---|---|---|---|---|---|---|---|---|---|
| | 1966 | 1950 | 1966 | 1950 | | 1966 | 1950 | 1966 | 1950 |
| **Grand Total....** | **$16,601** | **$5,710** | **100.0** | **100.0** | **Magazines......** | **$1,291** | **$ 515** | **7.8** | **9.0** |
| National...... | 10,116 | 3,257 | 60.9 | 57.0 | Weeklies...... | 658 | 261 | 4.0 | 4.6 |
| Local......... | 6,485 | 2,453 | 39.1 | 43.0 | Women's...... | 280 | 129 | 1.7 | 2.3 |
| **Newspapers....** | **4,895** | **2,076** | **29.5** | **36.3** | Monthlies..... | 316 | 88 | 1.9 | 1.5 |
| National...... | 975 | 533 | 5.9 | 9.3 | Farm, national | 37 | 37 | 0.2 | 0.6 |
| Local......... | 3,920 | 1,542 | 23.6 | 27.0 | **Farm papers....** | **34** | **21** | **0.2** | **0.4** |
| **Radio.........** | **1,001** | **605** | **6.0** | **10.6** | **Direct mail.....** | **2,454** | **803** | **14.8** | **14.1** |
| Network...... | 65 | 196 | 0.4 | 3.4 | **Business papers** | **712** | **251** | **4.3** | **4.4** |
| Spot.......... | 294 | 136 | 1.8 | 2.4 | **Outdoor........** | **178** | **143** | **1.1** | **2.5** |
| Local......... | 642 | 273 | 3.8 | 4.8 | National...... | 118 | 96 | 0.7 | 1.7 |
| **Television......** | **2,784** | **171** | **16.7** | **3.0** | Local......... | 60 | 46 | 0.4 | 0.8 |
| Network...... | 1,385 | 85 | 8.3 | 1.5 | **Miscellaneous..** | **3,253** | **1,125** | **19.6** | **19.7** |
| Spot.......... | 931 | 31 | 5.6 | 0.5 | National...... | 1,892 | 610 | 11.4 | 10.7 |
| Local......... | 468 | 55 | 2.8 | 1.0 | Local......... | 1,362 | 515 | 8.2 | 9.0 |

## ACTIVE CORPORATIONS: ADVERTISING COSTS COMPARED WITH RECEIPTS

Source: Internal Revenue Service; *Statistics of Income, 1964, Corporation Income Tax Returns.*

| INDUSTRY | RECEIPTS (in millions) | ADVERTISING COSTS Amount (in millions) | % of Receipts | INDUSTRY | RECEIPTS (in millions) | ADVERTISING COSTS Amount (in millions) | % of Receipts |
|---|---|---|---|---|---|---|---|
| **Manufacturing.....** | **$453,157** | **$6,065** | **1.5** | **Retail Trade.......** | **$ 168,017** | **$ 2,668** | **1.6** |
| Food, incl. beverages....... | 66,691 | 1,820 | 2.6 | Food stores....... | 39,338 | 520 | 1.3 |
| Tobacco mfrs...... | 5,406 | 328 | 6.1 | Gen. merchandise stores.......... | 33,924 | 940 | 2.8 |
| Furniture and fixtures.......... | 5,674 | 62 | 1.1 | All other.......... | 98,527 | 1,254 | 1.3 |
| Chemicals and allied prods..... | 34,468 | 1,507 | 4.4 | **Wholesale Trade...** | **157,538** | **759** | **0.5** |
| Scientific instr.; photo equipment | 7,212 | 196 | 2.7 | **Finance, Insurance, and Real Estate..** | **101,297** | **814** | **0.8** |
| Motor vehicles and equipment.. | 35,531 | 230 | 0.6 | **Services...........** | **32,487** | **609** | **1.9** |
| All other.......... | 298,175 | 2,462 | 0.8 | Personal.......... | 4,364 | 66 | 1.5 |
| **Transportation.....** | **79,450** | **413** | **0.5** | Business.......... | 10,949 | 206 | 1.9 |
| | | | | All other.......... | 17,173 | 337 | 2.0 |
| | | | | **All Other Industry..** | **67,538** | **147** | **0.2** |
| | | | | **TOTAL..............** | **$1,062,986** | **$12,058** | **1.1** |

## MORSE CODE

Morse code is an arbitrary but standard set of signals (dots and dashes) used in telegraphy. Samuel F. B. Morse (1791–1872) devised it in 1835, although other scientists—such as the American Joseph Henry, and the Englishmen Sir Charles Wheatstone and Sir W. F. Cooke— invented similar systems. The international (or continental) Morse code, generally used in wireless telegraphy, is a simplified form of the American Morse, which differs from the international in 11 letters, in all the numerals except the numeral 4, and in the punctuation code.

**International Morse**

```
A  ·—            T  —
B  —···          U  ··—
C  —·—·          V  ···—
D  —··           W  ·——
E  ·             X  —··—
F  ··—·          Y  —·——
G  ——·           Z  ——··
H  ····          1  ·————
I  ··            2  ··———
J  ·———          3  ···——
K  —·—           4  ····—
L  ·—··          5  ·····
M  ——            6  —····
N  —·            7  ——···
O  ———           8  ———··
P  ·——·          9  ————·
Q  ——·—          0  —————
R  ·—·           Period  ·—·—·—
S  ···           Comma   ·—·—··
```

**American Morse**

```
A  ·—            T  —
B  —···          U  ··—
C  ·· ·          V  ···—
D  —··           W  ·——
E  ·             X  ·—··
F  ·—·           Y  ·· ··
G  ——·           Z  ··· ·
H  ····          1  ·——·
I  ··            2  ··—··
J  —·—·          3  ···—·
K  —·—           4  ····—
L  ——— (= 5 dots) 5  ———
M  ——            6  ······
N  —·            7  ——··
O  · ·           8  —····
P  ·····         9  —··—
Q  ··—·          0  ————— (= 7 dots)
R  · ···         Period  ·—·—··
S  ···           Comma   —·—·——
```

## U.S. POSTAL INFORMATION
Source: U.S. Post Office

■ **FIRST-CLASS MAIL** includes letters, postal cards, postcards, sealed or unsealed airmail not exceeding eight ounces, all matter wholly or partly in writing (except authorized additions to second, third, and fourth class mail), and matter closed against inspection. Weight limits are the same as those of fourth-class mail.

■ **DOMESTIC AIRMAIL** is carried by air and by the fastest connecting surface carriers and given the most expeditious dispatch and delivery.

■ **SECOND-CLASS MAIL** includes all newspapers, periodicals, and magazines marked as second-class mail. Rates for single copies mailed by the general public, sample copies mailed by publishers in excess of ten per cent allowance, and copies mailed to persons not included in subscription lists are four cents for the first two ounces and one cent for each additional ounce. There is no weight limit.

For special rates for nonprofit organizations and for publishers and news agents, consult local post office.

■ **THIRD-CLASS MAIL** consists of mailable matter that is not mailed or required to be mailed as first-class mail, not entered as second-class mail, and is less than 16 ounces in weight. The single-piece rate is four cents for the first two ounces or fraction, plus two cents for each additional ounce or fraction.

Circulars and printed matter are considered third-class mail. Loose enclosures relating exclusively to the book or catalogue that they accompany may be enclosed and mailed at the third-class bulk rate. Third-class mail must be prepared so that it can be easily examined. For special rates for nonprofit organizations, consult local post office.

■ **FOURTH-CLASS MAIL (PARCEL POST)** includes merchandise, printed matter, mailable live animals, and all other matter not included in first-, second-, or third-class mail. Each addressed piece must weigh 16 ounces or more, but not in excess of 40 pounds if mailed from one first-class post office to another. When mailed to or from a second-, third-, or fourth-class post office, the weight limit is 70 pounds. It must be wrapped or packaged so that it can be easily examined.

■ **EDUCATIONAL MATERIALS.** A special fourth-class postage rate of ten cents for the first pound or fraction and five cents for each additional pound or fraction is provided for the following: bound books with no advertising; 16-millimeter films; printed music; manuscripts for books, magazine articles, and music; and other educational matter. The identification statement, *Special Fourth Class Rate—Educational Material,* must be placed on the address side of the package.

■ **LIBRARY RATE.** A special library rate applies to items conspicuously marked *Library Rate* and items that show nonprofit associations and organizations in the address or return address.

■ **AIR PARCEL POST.** Mail of all classes, except that which may be damaged by low temperatures or high altitudes, is accepted for air shipment. It may weigh from 8 ounces up to 70 pounds and is limited to 100 inches combined in length and girth.

■ **REGISTRY.** The registry of mail provides added protection and gives evidence of mailing and delivery. All mailable matter prepaid with postage at the first-class or airmail rate may be registered. The sender is required to enter the full value of mail matter presented for registration.

■ **INSURANCE.** Third- and fourth-class domestic mail or airmail that contains third- or fourth-class matter may be insured against loss, rifling, or damage. The mail must bear the complete names and addresses of sender and addressee.

■ **C.O.D. SERVICE.** A sender may mail an article for which he has not been paid and have the price and the cost of the postage collected from the addressee when the article is delivered. The amount collected is returned to the sender by a postal money order.

Fees include insurance against loss, rifling, or damage and failure to receive the amount collected from the addressee. Fees and postage must be prepaid. For further information, consult local post office.

■ **SPECIAL DELIVERY MAIL** provides expeditious transportation and immediate delivery to the address indicated during prescribed hours. Payment of a special-delivery fee does not insure safety of delivery or provide for the payment of indemnity. Money or other valuables sent special delivery should be registered also. Insured, certified, and C.O.D. mail may be sent special delivery.

■ **CERTIFIED MAIL** service provides for a receipt to the sender and a record of delivery at the office of address. No record is kept at the office at which it is mailed, and it is handled in the ordinary mail without insurance coverage. Any mailable matter of no intrinsic value on which postage at the first-class rate has been paid will be accepted as certified mail.

■ **MONEY ORDERS.** For safe transmission of money, domestic money orders are available at all post offices, branches, and stations in the United States and its possessions, except for certain offices in Alaska. The maximum amount for a single money order is $100. International money orders (up to $100 for a single order, payable abroad in local currency) can also be purchased, but they are not available for all countries. Consult local post office for details.

■ **SPECIAL HANDLING** service is available for fourth-class mail only, including that which is insured or sent C.O.D. It provides the most expeditious handling, dispatch, and transportation available but does not provide for special delivery. It is delivered as parcel post and is ordinarily delivered on regular scheduled trips.

■ **INTERNATIONAL AIRMAIL RATES** are 15 cents per half ounce to Western Hemisphere nations, except Canada and Mexico, which are 8 cents; 20 cents per half ounce to Europe (except the U.S.S.R.) and North Africa; 25 cents per half ounce elsewhere.

# THE EARTH

## Our Planet Earth · Natural Features · Weather · Life on Earth · Man-Made Features

Sigurgeir Jonasson

Illuminated by the glare of lightning discharges, a towering pillar of ash and steam heralds the birth of Surtsey, a volcanic island off the coast of Iceland.

## THE EARTH SCIENCES: 1967

In several different ways we all may have aged more, in the past year, than we ever thought we would. A Russian geologist, V. I. Baranov, after carefully studying the ratios of the various lead isotopes in Earth's crust, now suggests that the Earth is at least 6 billion years old, perhaps even older. Earlier estimates had put our planet's age at 4.5 to 4.8 billion years.

The birth of life itself is being pushed further and further back. Scientists from Ames Research Center (Mountain View, Calif.) have discovered traces of 22 kinds of amino acids in a rock formation in South Africa. (Amino acids are the basic building blocks of all life on Earth.) These acids, 3.1 billion years old, are the oldest amino acids ever found—yet they are similar to amino acids found in living organisms today.

An unusual form of life, discovered in 1967, also hints that Earth's childhood was "livelier" than we suspected. The discovery was made in an unlikely spot—a place near Harlech Castle in Wales which, for centuries, had been used as an outdoor latrine. Sanford Siegel of Union Carbide Research Institute, coming across the spot, wondered what kind of life, if any, might be found in surroundings so chemically unusual. (Urine, as it decomposes in the ground, liberates ammonia, a gas that is not found free in the environment.) Sure enough, Siegel located microscopic organisms that not only tolerated ammonia but, as he discovered in the laboratory, actually *required* its presence. This represented the first time such ammonia-requiring organisms have been found. Geochemists have long suspected that the Earth's primeval atmosphere contained ammonia, as well as other gases poisonous to present life. *(continued)*

**THE EARTH SCIENCES: 1967** (*continued*)

The new creatures may therefore be remnants of forms of life which were dominant on our planet some few billion years ago.

But where had these microorganisms been hiding for the past few billion years? Siegel has a theory to explain this. The spot where they were found happens to be in an area where pre-Cambrian rocks—the oldest on Earth—come to the surface. The creatures, Siegel thinks, may have existed in the rocks in a spore, or "suspended animation," state until exactly the right conditions came their way. Then, and only then, did they become active again.

Man, also, may have been on Earth much longer than scientists had thought. Somewhere in the distant past, our ancestral stalk of ape-like creatures gave off two branches: One branch was "Hominidae"—creatures whose further development eventually led to man; the other branch led to the present apes. The oldest Hominidae fossil previously discovered had been dated at 14,000,000 years. Now, however, anthropologist Louis Leakey has discovered bits of bones in East Africa that seem to be of hominid nature. These are 20,000,000 years old.

Out of the line of the Hominidae eventually evolved creatures that could be considered varieties of man, creatures that stood on two legs and had a distinctly human set of teeth. A few years ago Leakey caused a splash by finding fossils of such early men that were 1,750,000 years old, nearly doubling the previously supposed duration of man's stay on Earth. Now that record is broken, too. An armbone was discovered in 1965 near Lake Rudolf in Kenya by Bryan Patterson of Harvard. Careful calculations (computer-aided) have now shown the bone to be distinctly man-like. Isotope-ratio measurements show that the rock in which it was found is 2,500,000 years old.

In lesser ways, too, age records were broken. Radiocarbon datings show man to have been in Australia as long as 31,000 years ago—considerably longer than had been previously thought.

But not only age records are being broken. The deepest known submarine canyon has been discovered southwest of Australia. It is 20 miles wide and cuts down 6,000 feet below the ocean floor—a veritable underwater Grand Canyon. And one other addition for the book of records: The ocean current passing through Drake Passage (between the tip of South America and Antarctica) has been found to be unexpectedly immense. The Lamont Geological Observatory of Columbia University estimates its volume at 200,000,000 cubic meters per second, or more than twice that of the Gulf Stream.

NASA

**This photo snapped by Lunar Orbiter 5 shows how the Earth looks from 215,000 miles away.**

# FOCUS ON THE NEWS

## THE GREAT – BUT UNKNOWN – LAKES

General Dynamics

In "Operation Submich" the 17.7-foot, 5.7-ton Star II explored the depths of Lake Michigan.

In June, 1967, *Star II*, a two-man submarine, plunged 912 feet beneath the choppy surface of Lake Michigan—setting a new depth record for fresh-water dives, and signaling an awakening scientific interest in the Great Lakes. Since the 1950s research subs have probed the ocean deeps, but fresh-water environments such as the Great Lakes are largely unexplored.

What are scientists looking for in the Great Lakes? Many things: Clues from deep rock formations as to how the lake basins were formed and how they may change; clues to the behavior and travels of fish species; knowledge of lake-bottom plants and the nature of lake-bottom ooze. Such information, scientists hope, will help combat the already dangerous—and ever-worsening—pollution of the Great Lakes.

What is it like at the bottom of Lake Michigan? A reporter who dove in *Star II* described "a fantastic journey – all green,

silent, and seemingly motionless." Visibility at the bottom was near zero because of a dense "snow"—bits and pieces of decaying plants and animals sinking down from above. The bottom itself, said the reporter, was milky in color, and the water was "a dirty river green."

Before *Star II*'s two-week mission, scientists at the University of Michigan's Great Lakes Research Division had used underwater cameras, as well as recording and sampling instruments lowered from surface ships, to study the lakes. And scuba-diving scientists had finned along the lakes' shallower reaches. But only a "submersible" such as *Star II* allows men to visit the deeper troughs. Built by General Dynamics' Electric Boat Division, *Star II* has a 12-mile range and a speed of 4.5 knots. Its equipment includes an external mechanical claw to snare lake-bottom rocks, a video tape recorder, and several cameras.

# OUR PLANET EARTH

## ORIGIN OF THE EARTH

Over 5,000 years ago men started wondering where the hills, rivers, Sun, Moon, and stars came from. Several different stories of the origin developed: The Babylonians thought that dry land rose up from endless water; the Greeks considered that battles between the gods started everything; the Judeo-Christian story of Genesis starts with Jehovah creating light, then matter, then man.

Until 1600 or later, men in the Western world thought that a flat Earth at the center of the universe was created by God for man, and that Sun, Moon, planets, and stars were created for man's convenience, all moving around the Earth. The motions of five bright planets ("wanderers" among the fixed stars in the sky) caused difficulties in this picture because they made a loop every now and then.

These motions could not be accurately predicted until it was recognized that planets are in orbits around the Sun, along with the Earth. The nine planets we now know all go around the Sun in the same direction, and their elliptical orbits are almost in the same plane. All modern ideas of the Earth's origin refer to this "solar system."

As early as 1755 the German philosopher Kant speculated that the Earth and planets had condensed from a rotating nebula of hot gas as it contracted to form the Sun. Other nebulae that look as if they are rotating had been seen with telescopes by that time. This "nebular hypothesis" was elaborated by the French mathematical astronomer LaPlace, and by physicists in Germany and England, who calculated that the Sun could be no more than 10 or 20 million years old if its energy came from such contraction. Then geologists found radioactive rocks and measured their ages as about two *billion* years.

About 1900 a second hypothesis had been put forward by Chamberlin and Moulton of the University of Chicago. They supposed that another star passed by chance close to the Sun and pulled out material that cooled and later coagulated to form the planets. This theory would make the Earth and solar system most unusual, because the close passage of two stars is very unlikely. Anyway, in 1936 it was proved impossible to pull matter out of the Sun that would condense into planets in orbits around the Sun.

The current theory proposed by a German physicist, von Weizächer, and an American astronomer, Kuiper, makes it seem likely that the solar system originated about six billion years ago from a great cloud of gas and dust. Eddies in the cloud condensed to form compact masses, which in turn attracted additional gas and dust through mutual gravitation. This continual process of accumulating matter created a large central mass which, because of its intense pressure and temperature, produced light, heat, and other radiation through nuclear reaction. Smaller bodies condensed from the cloud to form the Earth and other planets and their satellites. The gas cloud around the primitive Earth probably created water vapor, which condensed to form the seas when the Earth had cooled sufficiently.

## AGE OF THE EARTH

Around 1900, scientists attempted to calculate the age of the Earth by determining the length of time required for the Earth to cool to its present temperature from an assumed initially molten state. A cooling time of 50 million years was estimated. It was soon realized that this age was much too short because the heat produced in rocks by the radioactive elements—uranium, thorium, and potassium—profoundly alters the Earth's heat balance (the relation between the heat radiating from the Earth's interior and the heat coming in from the Sun).

Another estimate of the Earth's age was based on the age of the oceans. The total amount of salt in the oceans was divided by the annual input into the oceans of salt from rivers. This estimate, 100 million years, is also too small. Some salt is returned from sedimentary deposits on land, scientists found, and the present erosion rate is high because of the many mountain belts now existing.

Rocks can now be dated by such radioactivity as the decay of uranium to lead at a known rate. The oldest rocks known range between 3.1 and 3.3 billion years old. The Earth should be still older because the earliest rocks probably have been converted into sediments by erosion or remelted into younger igneous rocks.

The currently accepted age estimate is determined from radioactive dating of lead isotopes. Isotopes are similar species of a given element which differ in relative weight. When the element uranium decays radioactively, it produces two isotopes of relative weights 206 and 207. Natural lead has a relative weight of 204. Thus the ratios of lead-206 to lead-204 and of lead-207 to lead-204 is a measure of the original quantity of uranium. The age of the Earth is obtained by calculating the time required for the original uranium to decay into the current ratios of lead isotopes. This ratio is the same as the lead-isotope ratios found today in several meteorites. The meteorites have such small amounts of uranium compared with lead that their lead-isotope ratios have not changed materially in billions of years. Results of this analysis give an estimated age of at least six billion years for the Earth.

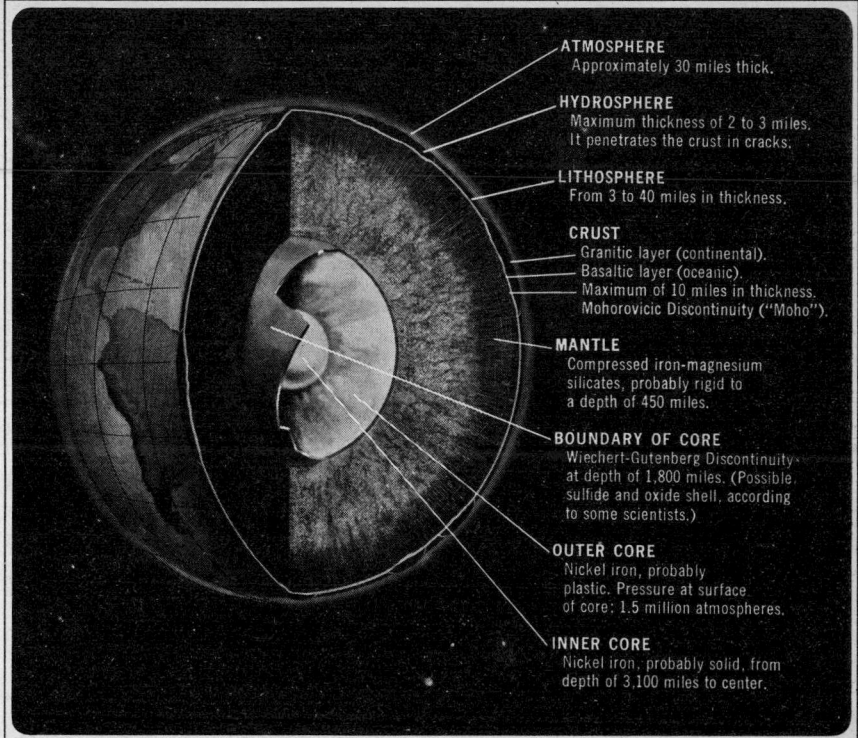

ATMOSPHERE
Approximately 30 miles thick.

HYDROSPHERE
Maximum thickness of 2 to 3 miles.
It penetrates the crust in cracks.

LITHOSPHERE
From 3 to 40 miles in thickness.

CRUST
Granitic layer (continental).
Basaltic layer (oceanic).
Maximum of 10 miles in thickness.
Mohorovicic Discontinuity ("Moho").

MANTLE
Compressed iron-magnesium
silicates, probably rigid to
a depth of 450 miles.

BOUNDARY OF CORE
Wiechert-Gutenberg Discontinuity
at depth of 1,800 miles. (Possible
sulfide and oxide shell, according
to some scientists.)

OUTER CORE
Nickel iron, probably
plastic. Pressure at surface
of core: 1.5 million atmospheres.

INNER CORE
Nickel iron, probably solid, from
depth of 3,100 miles to center.

## THE WHOLE EARTH

A photograph of the Earth taken from near the moon by the U.S. Lunar Orbiter in 1966 shows the Earth as a sphere. Accurate measurements, however, reveal that the Earth has an overall shape that deviates from the spherical in several ways. The greatest deviations are a polar flattening and an equatorial bulge due to the Earth's rotation on its axis. The Earth is an oblate spheroid, that is, a sphere slightly flattened at the poles. The polar diameter (7,898.98 miles) is about 27 miles less than the equatorial diameter (7,926.68 miles).

More accurate measurements made during the International Geophysical Year of 1957–58 revealed that the Earth deviates from an oblate spheroid by being slightly pear shaped. Computations based on satellite orbits show further irregularities, including four points that are higher than they should be for a rounded body. The Earth's equatorial circumference is 24,902 miles. It has a volume of $3.825 \times 10^{22}$ (3 followed by 22 places before the decimal point) cubic feet and a mass of $6.595 \times 10^{21}$ tons. Its average density, therefore, is about 345 pounds per cubic foot. The density of surface rocks is about 169 pounds per cubic foot.

Seismology, the study of waves generated by earthquakes, shows the Earth to consist of several layers that differ in composition. At the center is a very dense inner core believed to be chiefly iron and nickel. An outer liquid core of the same material surrounds this inner core. Next is a plastic zone of less dense material composed largely of iron and magnesium silicates, known as the mantle. The mantle is 1,800 miles thick and it is surrounded by a thin, low-density outer layer (3 to 40 miles thick) called the crust or lithosphere. Water on the Earth forms a partial shell known as the hydrosphere and the envelope of air called the atmosphere surrounds the planet.

Of the 92 naturally occurring elements, 8 account for over 98 per cent of the composition of the Earth's crust. The chief constituents of crustal rocks in percentage by weight are: oxygen, 46.5; silicon, 28.0; aluminum, 8.0; iron, 5.0; and calcium, sodium, potassium, and magnesium each between 2.1 and 3.6 per cent. The hydrosphere is composed mainly of oxygen and hydrogen, but sea water contains minor dissolved amounts of almost every element. The atmosphere consists of 75.5 per cent nitrogen and 23.2 per cent oxygen with other minor constituents, such as water vapor, argon, and carbon dioxide. In the Earth as a whole, iron is estimated to be the most abundant element. Hydrogen and helium make up less than 1 per cent of the Earth's composition.

## EARTH MOTIONS

The Earth has many motions, although from our point of view on its surface the bright objects in the sky—Sun and Moon, stars and planets—seem to be moving, while we seem to be at rest. The fact that the Earth is moving at all is realized not by any sensation of motion but by observations of changes in the sky resulting from these motions. On the one hand, the rotation of the Earth, spinning on its axis, produces alternating periods of daylight and darkness. On the other, the revolution of the Earth in its elliptical course around the Sun, with the inclination of the Earth's axis of rotation, produces the seasons and the apparent motion of the Sun's daily path north and south in the sky through the course of the year.

Both the Earth's rotation and its revolution take place at very great velocities. A point on the Earth's equator, for example, spins from west to east through a distance of 24,900 miles (the Earth's circumference) in 24 hours at a velocity of about 17.4 miles a minute or 1,044 miles an hour. Only the best of military jet planes exceed this velocity in our atmosphere, although spacecraft orbiting the Earth have a velocity of some 17,500 miles an hour. The velocity at the surface from the Earth's rotation diminishes from the equator toward the poles, since less distance is covered in the same time. A mere mile from either pole, the velocity has decreased to a crawl of a quarter of a mile an hour, and the distance traveled to only six miles a day. The Earth's rotation also produces the Coriolis effect, which is involved in the movement of ocean currents and the circulation of winds in the atmosphere. Under the Coriolis effect, in the Northern Hemisphere freely moving objects appear to veer to the right of the observer, and they seem to veer to the left in the Southern Hemisphere.

In its annual elliptical orbit of the Sun, the Earth carries all of us on a space journey of some 600 million miles at a velocity of about 18.5 miles a second, or 66,000 miles an hour. Early in January, the Earth comes closest to the Sun (perihelion), within about 91.4 million miles, and in July the Earth is farthest from the Sun (aphelion), at a distance of about 94.5 million miles. The mean distance between Earth and Sun has recently been calculated very accurately at 92,956,000 miles with the assistance of radar telescopes. As the Earth moves in its orbit around the Sun in the plane of the ecliptic, the Sun appears to move along the ecliptic day by day, passing through the constellations of the zodiac.

## THE SEASONS: 1968

Seasons are the divisions of the year determined by the relative lengths of day and night and by the average amount of heat received from the Sun. At the Equator there is little seasonal change, but in the temperate zones there are four well-defined divisions. Because the plane of the Earth's Equator is inclined to the ecliptic by an angle of 23½°, the Earth's axis is correspondingly inclined and remains directed toward the same point in space. It is this inclination which gives rise to the seasons.

The two points where the celestial equator and the ecliptic intersect are called the vernal (or spring) equinox and the autumnal equinox. Midway between the equinoxes are the winter solstice and the summer solstice.

Equinoxes are simply the places occupied by the Sun each year when day and night are theoretically equal throughout the world, and when the sun rises exactly in the east and sets exactly in the west. Solstices represent the standing still of the Sun and are the places where the Sun attains its greatest northern and southern declination. Application of the words "summer" and "winter" to the solstices, and "spring" and "fall" to the equinoxes, are correct only for the northern hemisphere. For the southern hemisphere the words must be reversed.

The beginning of spring in the northern hemisphere is marked by the vernal equinox, which will occur in 1968 not on the usual March 21, but on March 20 at 8:22 A.M. (EST). This one-day shift of the first day of spring is caused by the addition of leap-year day, February 29. Time of the vernal equinox is the exact instant the Sun crosses the Equator on its northward journey in the sky.

In ancient times the spring equinox was known as the "First Point of Aries," for it was then located in the constellation Aries. Since then, however, the equinoxes and solstices have shifted westward by 30°. This movement, called precession of the equinoxes, has resulted in the migration of the vernal equinox from Aries to the constellation of Pisces.

The summer solstice, which will occur in 1968 on June 21 at 3:13 A.M. (EST), is the instant the Sun is farthest north of the celestial equator. This marks the beginning of summer in the northern hemisphere. The summer solstice is now located in Gemini, but 2,000 years ago it was located in Cancer. The circle of latitude which marks the limit of the Sun's northward swing is still called the Tropic of Cancer, although it more properly might be called the Tropic of Gemini.

The autumnal equinox, located in the constellation of Virgo, marks the beginning of fall or autumn in the northern hemisphere and will occur in 1968 on September 22 at 6:26 P.M. (EST).

The winter solstice, when the Sun is farthest south of the celestial equator, will occur in 1968 on December 21 at 2:00 P.M. (EST), and will signal the beginning of winter in the northern hemisphere. Although the circle of latitude marking the Sun's most southerly limit is called the Tropic of Capricorn, the solstice is actually located in Sagittarius.

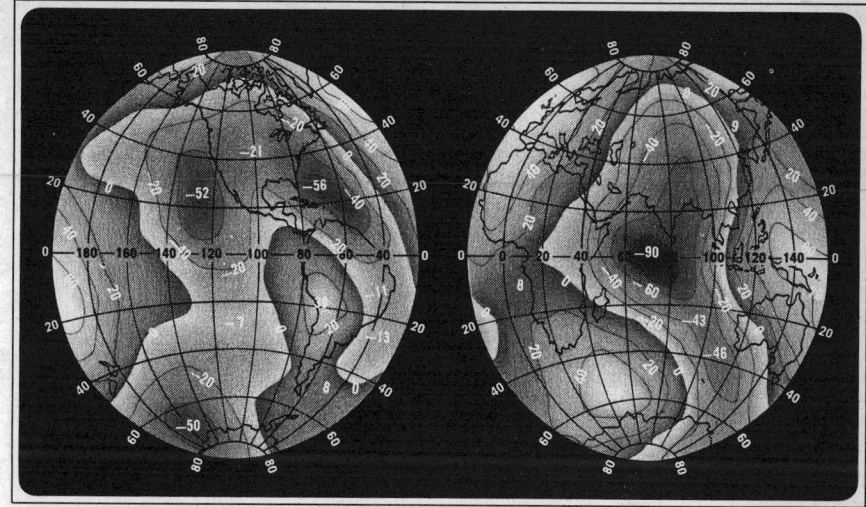

Bumps and hollows in the Earth. Contour lines show meters above and below (−) a water surface.

## THE GRAVITATIONAL FIELD AND SHAPE OF THE EARTH

An accurate description of the Earth's field of gravitational attraction has challenged scientists since Isaac Newton discovered the law of gravity in the seventeenth century. A precise description is vital to the prediction of the motion of such objects near the Earth as ballistic missiles, artificial Earth satellites and space probes, and the Moon. In addition, the location of points on the Earth's surface is most conveniently measured with reference to the local gravity field.

If the density distribution inside the Earth were known, then the external gravity field could be calculated directly from Newton's inverse-square law of gravitation. Alternately, if the strength of gravity could be measured to sufficient accuracy over a large percentage of the Earth's surface, the external field could also be reliably calculated. Unfortunately, scientists do not know enough yet about the details of the Earth's internal density, nor do they have good enough global surface-gravity measurements to permit an exact description of the field from these sources alone.

It is only since artificial satellites have been placed in orbit of the Earth that a truly accurate description of the Earth's gravity field has become available. A single satellite in orbit can be thought of as a high-altitude, world wide gravity probe. Newton first showed that if the Earth were exactly spherical, then the paths of all otherwise undisturbed satellites such as the Moon would be perfect ellipses. Long-term observations of many close-to-Earth satellites have revealed that their paths deviate considerably from unchanging ellipses. After subtracting all other known effects on the satellites' motion, these deviations reveal the extent to which the Earth's mass distribution or gravity field is not spherically symmetric. They can also be directly related to the geoid, the shape that would be assumed by an undisturbed water surface covering the Earth. The best reference surface of the geoid, as determined mainly from observations of satellites, is a near-sphere, flattened at the poles by only 1 part in 298.25 due to the Earth's rotation. The equatorial radius of this reference spheroid is 6,378.155 kilometers (3,964.069 miles). The very small deviation in meters of the sea-level surface from this near-sphere is indicated in the map below.

The minus (−) numbers represent hollows in the surface, and the positive numbers represent bumps, falling below (−) or rising above the overall sea level surface of the Earth. The numbers are meters above or below this surface. (One meter is 3.28 feet.) You will note a hollow of −52 meters in the Pacific Ocean off the west coast of North America, for example, and a bump of 39 meters on the west coast of South America. Similarly, there is a hollow of some 40 meters in the Indian Ocean south of India and a bump of 40 meters across western Europe and northwestern Africa. The Earth seems to be shaped more like a potato than a pear.

Reliable data on the variation of the Moon from a perfect sphere will be available soon from observations of the lunar orbiters of the United States and Russia. The polar flattening of some of the planets has been determined from changes in the motion of their natural satellites as well as visual observations of their disks. The polar flattening of Mars is 1 part in 75 as compared with the Earth's 1 part in 298.25. The polar flattening of the rapidly rotating giant planets is much greater: Jupiter's polar flattening is 1 part in 15.2, Saturn's 1 part in 10.2, Uranus' 1 part in 14, and Neptune's 1 part in 59.

## MAGNETIC FIELD OF THE EARTH

In the year 1600 William Gilbert, Queen Elizabeth's physician, placed a number of small magnetized needles at different points around a sphere-shaped piece of natural magnet and observed that each needle took a different dip, or inclination, with respect to the magnetic sphere. From this experiment he inferred that "the earth globe itself is a great magnet." He also connected the inclination effect with the dip of a perfectly balanced magnet, observed and first measured in London in 1576 by Robert Norman. Gilbert thought that the Earth's magnetism would be constant, but not long after his death it was found that the compass direction in 1635 certainly differed from the value measured in 1580. This was the first indication of the minor variations of geomagnetism. These have no regular timing; they are not global or planetary phenomena, like the Earth's magnetism, but are regional and far more rapid than changes in the crust. This points to a source below the crust.

The mathematical theory of a spherical magnet enables us to infer the strength and direction of the Earth's field above and below the surface, up or down to levels where electric currents flow. At any point just above the core, for example, the strength of the field is about six times that at the Earth's surface immediately above that point. The lines of magnetic force above the core lie nearly in a north and south plane through the magnetic axis, whose ends are not the same as the magnetic poles. The poles are at 75.5° N., 100.5° W., and 66.6° S., 111° E. In the core the field lines are partly wrapped around the axis.

The discovery that the Earth has a liquid core led the way to the most probable theory of the Earth's magnetism—by electric currents flowing in the core, induced as in a dynamo by a slow circulation of the liquid. This flow, with changing eddies in it that are probably the cause of the secular variation, may be due to unequal radioactive heating by the decay of somewhat irregularly distributed uranium there. Studies of rock magnetism and ocean-bed sediments indicate that the Earth's field has been reversed more than four times in the last 2,000,000 years.

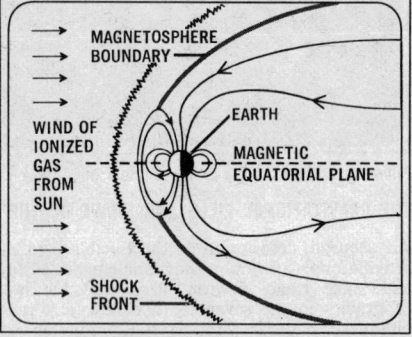

Enclosure and distortion of the geomagnetic field by the solar wind of hydrogen atoms, broken up into protons and electrons.

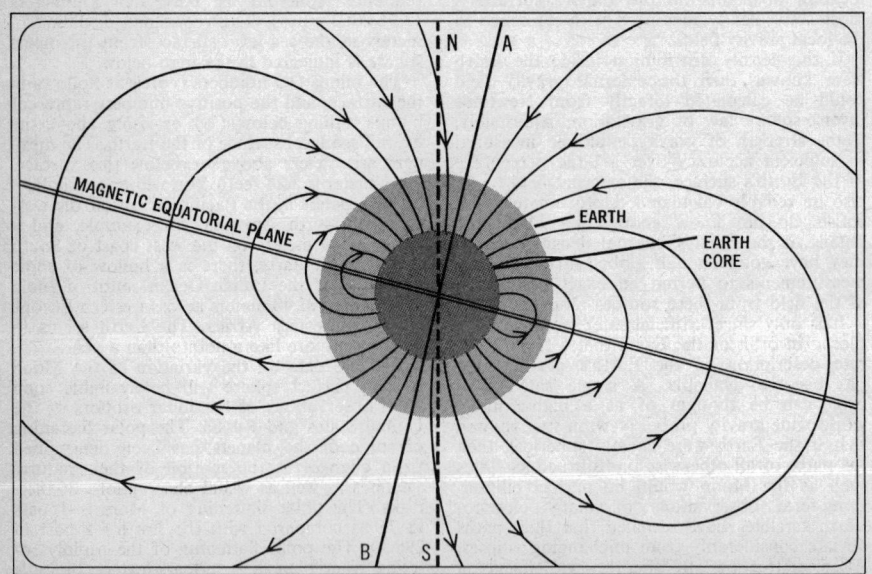

The Earth's lines of magnetic force from the surface of the core, where the geomagnetic field is generated, to about 15,000 miles from the Earth's center. NS is the geographic axis of rotation and AB is the Earth's dipole magnetic axis.

## EARTH CHANGES

Great convulsions of the Earth's crust have taken place in our time as well as in ancient geologic times. Quick snaps and heaves of an earthquake raise hundreds of square miles of land up and down inches to tens of feet, and to and fro inches to hundreds of feet. Molten rock erupts in regular burps totaling several cubic miles per year from the 500 active volcanoes of the world. In contrast, mountains have arisen ever so slowly to heights of five miles and even continents are believed by some to have drifted thousands of miles very gradually.

Earthquakes, occurring at the rate of 10,000 annually, arise mainly from the shock of the natural breaking of strained rock. The adjustment may start at depths as great as 400 miles. This catastrophic release of stored pulling energy involves a momentary loss of cohesion, and a crack develops rapidly, at almost the speed of sound. The broken rocks slide against each other along the crack. However, the manner in which friction is overcome at the high temperatures in the Earth is not as yet well understood. Sometimes the cracks extend to the surface of the Earth and the permanent shifts observed are called faults.

Some volcanic eruptions occur quietly, in Hawaii for example, with lava (molten rock) flowing out of a crater or a crack and over the surrounding countryside as a sheet. Other volcanoes explode with a force equal to 1-100 megatons of TNT, blanketing the countryside with ash and debris. The explosive agent is believed to be mainly steam dissolved in the molten rock under the high pressures at great depths. The molten rock originates at depths of 25 to 35 miles, usually heralded by earthquakes, and rises along cracks at the rate of about 300 feet per day to the surface. Release of gas in bubbles occurs as the molten rock rises in the crack and the pressure is reduced. Expansion of the bubbles thereafter takes place rapidly and the molten rock froths with explosive force. In one explosion at Tamboro, East Indies, in 1815, some 35 cubic miles of molten rock and debris were blown out, a cube over three miles on each side.

Mountains arise in belts as the result of the slow changing of the soft materials deposited by streams in the great troughs of the Earth. These sedimentary rocks, folded and faulted, are of relatively low density, and are buoyed up by the lower crust of higher density. Mountain chains are thickened portions of a less dense portion of the crust. Mountain building involves millions of years. The delicate balance of densities of rocks is maintained throughout geologic time as erosion proceeds.

A few scientists believe that the continents of today were once joined together, that they broke and drifted apart. They cite the close fit of the east coastline of South America with the west coastline of Africa and the similarity of some of the geological features of those continents. Continental drifting may have begun as early as the formative stages of the Earth's crust four billion years ago or as late as 150 million years ago, the age of the oldest rocks in the ocean basins.

The supercontinent, often called Gondwanaland, may have heaved and cracked in response to the same great forces of circulating currents in the Earth's mantle that are believed to produce the spreading ocean basins. Then the broken blocks of continents may have drifted apart (arrows), at a speed of less than an inch a year, to reach their present positions. Whether the continents were formed in this way, or by growing from an original nucleus, is still an unsolved problem.

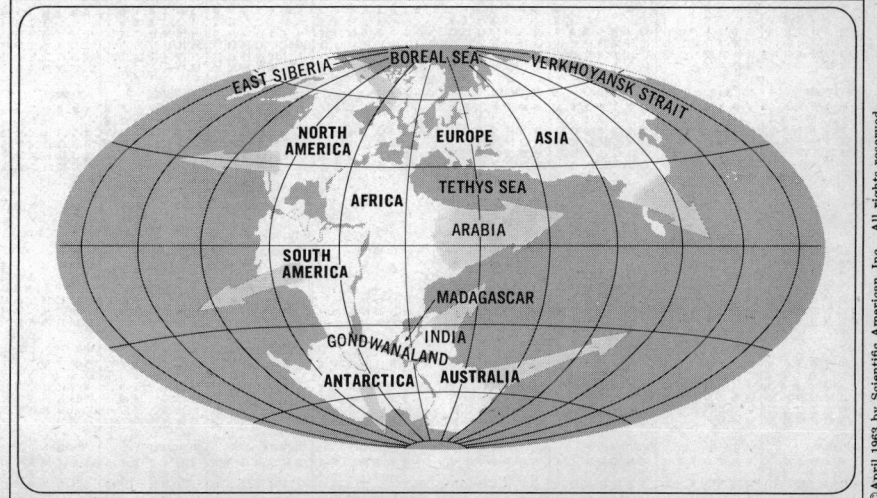

This supercontinent may have broken into the seven continents, which then drifted to their present positions.

## PAST AND FUTURE CALENDARS: 1800 TO 1999

**DIRECTIONS:**
Choose the year you want in the key at left. The number opposite the year is the number of the calendar to use for that year.

| Year | Cal. | Year | Cal. | Year | Cal. | Year | Cal. | Year | Cal. |
|---|---|---|---|---|---|---|---|---|---|
| 1800 | 4 | 1840 | 11 | 1880 | 12 | 1920 | 12 | 1960 | 13 |
| 1801 | 5 | 1841 | 6 | 1881 | 7 | 1921 | 7 | 1961 | 1 |
| 1802 | 6 | 1842 | 7 | 1882 | 1 | 1922 | 1 | 1962 | 2 |
| 1803 | 7 | 1843 | 1 | 1883 | 2 | 1923 | 2 | 1963 | 3 |
| 1804 | 8 | 1844 | 9 | 1884 | 10 | 1924 | 10 | 1964 | 11 |
| 1805 | 3 | 1845 | 4 | 1885 | 5 | 1925 | 5 | 1965 | 6 |
| 1806 | 4 | 1846 | 5 | 1886 | 6 | 1926 | 6 | 1966 | 7 |
| 1807 | 5 | 1847 | 6 | 1887 | 7 | 1927 | 7 | 1967 | 1 |
| 1808 | 13 | 1848 | 14 | 1888 | 8 | 1928 | 8 | 1968 | 9 |
| 1809 | 1 | 1849 | 2 | 1889 | 3 | 1929 | 3 | 1969 | 4 |
| 1810 | 2 | 1850 | 3 | 1890 | 4 | 1930 | 4 | 1970 | 5 |
| 1811 | 3 | 1851 | 4 | 1891 | 5 | 1931 | 5 | 1971 | 6 |
| 1812 | 11 | 1852 | 12 | 1892 | 13 | 1932 | 13 | 1972 | 14 |
| 1813 | 6 | 1853 | 7 | 1893 | 1 | 1933 | 1 | 1973 | 2 |
| 1814 | 7 | 1854 | 1 | 1894 | 2 | 1934 | 2 | 1974 | 3 |
| 1815 | 1 | 1855 | 2 | 1895 | 3 | 1935 | 3 | 1975 | 4 |
| 1816 | 9 | 1856 | 10 | 1896 | 11 | 1936 | 11 | 1976 | 12 |
| 1817 | 4 | 1857 | 5 | 1897 | 6 | 1937 | 6 | 1977 | 7 |
| 1818 | 5 | 1858 | 6 | 1898 | 7 | 1938 | 7 | 1978 | 1 |
| 1819 | 6 | 1859 | 7 | 1899 | 1 | 1939 | 1 | 1979 | 2 |
| 1820 | 14 | 1860 | 8 | 1900 | 2 | 1940 | 9 | 1980 | 10 |
| 1821 | 2 | 1861 | 3 | 1901 | 3 | 1941 | 4 | 1981 | 5 |
| 1822 | 3 | 1862 | 4 | 1902 | 4 | 1942 | 5 | 1982 | 6 |
| 1823 | 4 | 1863 | 5 | 1903 | 5 | 1943 | 6 | 1983 | 7 |
| 1824 | 12 | 1864 | 13 | 1904 | 13 | 1944 | 14 | 1984 | 8 |
| 1825 | 7 | 1865 | 1 | 1905 | 1 | 1945 | 2 | 1985 | 3 |
| 1826 | 1 | 1866 | 2 | 1906 | 2 | 1946 | 3 | 1986 | 4 |
| 1827 | 2 | 1867 | 3 | 1907 | 3 | 1947 | 4 | 1987 | 5 |
| 1828 | 10 | 1868 | 11 | 1908 | 11 | 1948 | 12 | 1988 | 13 |
| 1829 | 5 | 1869 | 6 | 1909 | 6 | 1949 | 7 | 1989 | 1 |
| 1830 | 6 | 1870 | 7 | 1910 | 7 | 1950 | 1 | 1990 | 2 |
| 1831 | 7 | 1871 | 1 | 1911 | 1 | 1951 | 2 | 1991 | 3 |
| 1832 | 8 | 1872 | 9 | 1912 | 9 | 1952 | 10 | 1992 | 11 |
| 1833 | 3 | 1873 | 4 | 1913 | 4 | 1953 | 5 | 1993 | 6 |
| 1834 | 4 | 1874 | 5 | 1914 | 5 | 1954 | 6 | 1994 | 7 |
| 1835 | 5 | 1875 | 6 | 1915 | 6 | 1955 | 7 | 1995 | 1 |
| 1836 | 13 | 1876 | 14 | 1916 | 14 | 1956 | 8 | 1996 | 9 |
| 1837 | 1 | 1877 | 2 | 1917 | 2 | 1957 | 3 | 1997 | 4 |
| 1838 | 2 | 1878 | 3 | 1918 | 3 | 1958 | 4 | 1998 | 5 |
| 1839 | 3 | 1879 | 4 | 1919 | 4 | 1959 | 5 | 1999 | 6 |

### 1

**JANUARY**

| S | M | T | W | T | F | S |
|---|---|---|---|---|---|---|
| 1 | 2 | 3 | 4 | 5 | 6 | 7 |
| 8 | 9 | 10 | 11 | 12 | 13 | 14 |
| 15 | 16 | 17 | 18 | 19 | 20 | 21 |
| 22 | 23 | 24 | 25 | 26 | 27 | 28 |
| 29 | 30 | 31 | | | | |

**FEBRUARY**

| S | M | T | W | T | F | S |
|---|---|---|---|---|---|---|
| | | | 1 | 2 | 3 | 4 |
| 5 | 6 | 7 | 8 | 9 | 10 | 11 |
| 12 | 13 | 14 | 15 | 16 | 17 | 18 |
| 19 | 20 | 21 | 22 | 23 | 24 | 25 |
| 26 | 27 | 28 | | | | |

**MARCH**

| S | M | T | W | T | F | S |
|---|---|---|---|---|---|---|
| | | | 1 | 2 | 3 | 4 |
| 5 | 6 | 7 | 8 | 9 | 10 | 11 |
| 12 | 13 | 14 | 15 | 16 | 17 | 18 |
| 19 | 20 | 21 | 22 | 23 | 24 | 25 |
| 26 | 27 | 28 | 29 | 30 | 31 | |

**APRIL**

| S | M | T | W | T | F | S |
|---|---|---|---|---|---|---|
| | | | | | | 1 |
| 2 | 3 | 4 | 5 | 6 | 7 | 8 |
| 9 | 10 | 11 | 12 | 13 | 14 | 15 |
| 16 | 17 | 18 | 19 | 20 | 21 | 22 |
| 23 | 24 | 25 | 26 | 27 | 28 | 29 |
| 30 | | | | | | |

**MAY**

| S | M | T | W | T | F | S |
|---|---|---|---|---|---|---|
| | 1 | 2 | 3 | 4 | 5 | 6 |
| 7 | 8 | 9 | 10 | 11 | 12 | 13 |
| 14 | 15 | 16 | 17 | 18 | 19 | 20 |
| 21 | 22 | 23 | 24 | 25 | 26 | 27 |
| 28 | 29 | 30 | 31 | | | |

**JUNE**

| S | M | T | W | T | F | S |
|---|---|---|---|---|---|---|
| | | | | 1 | 2 | 3 |
| 4 | 5 | 6 | 7 | 8 | 9 | 10 |
| 11 | 12 | 13 | 14 | 15 | 16 | 17 |
| 18 | 19 | 20 | 21 | 22 | 23 | 24 |
| 25 | 26 | 27 | 28 | 29 | 30 | |

**JULY**

| S | M | T | W | T | F | S |
|---|---|---|---|---|---|---|
| | | | | | | 1 |
| 2 | 3 | 4 | 5 | 6 | 7 | 8 |
| 9 | 10 | 11 | 12 | 13 | 14 | 15 |
| 16 | 17 | 18 | 19 | 20 | 21 | 22 |
| 23 | 24 | 25 | 26 | 27 | 28 | 29 |
| 30 | 31 | | | | | |

**AUGUST**

| S | M | T | W | T | F | S |
|---|---|---|---|---|---|---|
| | | 1 | 2 | 3 | 4 | 5 |
| 6 | 7 | 8 | 9 | 10 | 11 | 12 |
| 13 | 14 | 15 | 16 | 17 | 18 | 19 |
| 20 | 21 | 22 | 23 | 24 | 25 | 26 |
| 27 | 28 | 29 | 30 | 31 | | |

**SEPTEMBER**

| S | M | T | W | T | F | S |
|---|---|---|---|---|---|---|
| | | | | | 1 | 2 |
| 3 | 4 | 5 | 6 | 7 | 8 | 9 |
| 10 | 11 | 12 | 13 | 14 | 15 | 16 |
| 17 | 18 | 19 | 20 | 21 | 22 | 23 |
| 24 | 25 | 26 | 27 | 28 | 29 | 30 |

**OCTOBER**

| S | M | T | W | T | F | S |
|---|---|---|---|---|---|---|
| 1 | 2 | 3 | 4 | 5 | 6 | 7 |
| 8 | 9 | 10 | 11 | 12 | 13 | 14 |
| 15 | 16 | 17 | 18 | 19 | 20 | 21 |
| 22 | 23 | 24 | 25 | 26 | 27 | 28 |
| 29 | 30 | 31 | | | | |

**NOVEMBER**

| S | M | T | W | T | F | S |
|---|---|---|---|---|---|---|
| | | | 1 | 2 | 3 | 4 |
| 5 | 6 | 7 | 8 | 9 | 10 | 11 |
| 12 | 13 | 14 | 15 | 16 | 17 | 18 |
| 19 | 20 | 21 | 22 | 23 | 24 | 25 |
| 26 | 27 | 28 | 29 | 30 | | |

**DECEMBER**

| S | M | T | W | T | F | S |
|---|---|---|---|---|---|---|
| | | | | | 1 | 2 |
| 3 | 4 | 5 | 6 | 7 | 8 | 9 |
| 10 | 11 | 12 | 13 | 14 | 15 | 16 |
| 17 | 18 | 19 | 20 | 21 | 22 | 23 |
| 24 | 25 | 26 | 27 | 28 | 29 | 30 |
| 31 | | | | | | |

### 4

**JANUARY**

| S | M | T | W | T | F | S |
|---|---|---|---|---|---|---|
| | | | 1 | 2 | 3 | 4 |
| 5 | 6 | 7 | 8 | 9 | 10 | 11 |
| 12 | 13 | 14 | 15 | 16 | 17 | 18 |
| 19 | 20 | 21 | 22 | 23 | 24 | 25 |
| 26 | 27 | 28 | 29 | 30 | 31 | |

**FEBRUARY**

| S | M | T | W | T | F | S |
|---|---|---|---|---|---|---|
| | | | | | | 1 |
| 2 | 3 | 4 | 5 | 6 | 7 | 8 |
| 9 | 10 | 11 | 12 | 13 | 14 | 15 |
| 16 | 17 | 18 | 19 | 20 | 21 | 22 |
| 23 | 24 | 25 | 26 | 27 | 28 | |

**MARCH**

| S | M | T | W | T | F | S |
|---|---|---|---|---|---|---|
| | | | | | | 1 |
| 2 | 3 | 4 | 5 | 6 | 7 | 8 |
| 9 | 10 | 11 | 12 | 13 | 14 | 15 |
| 16 | 17 | 18 | 19 | 20 | 21 | 22 |
| 23 | 24 | 25 | 26 | 27 | 28 | 29 |
| 30 | 31 | | | | | |

**APRIL**

| S | M | T | W | T | F | S |
|---|---|---|---|---|---|---|
| | | 1 | 2 | 3 | 4 | 5 |
| 6 | 7 | 8 | 9 | 10 | 11 | 12 |
| 13 | 14 | 15 | 16 | 17 | 18 | 19 |
| 20 | 21 | 22 | 23 | 24 | 25 | 26 |
| 27 | 28 | 29 | 30 | | | |

**MAY**

| S | M | T | W | T | F | S |
|---|---|---|---|---|---|---|
| | | | | 1 | 2 | 3 |
| 4 | 5 | 6 | 7 | 8 | 9 | 10 |
| 11 | 12 | 13 | 14 | 15 | 16 | 17 |
| 18 | 19 | 20 | 21 | 22 | 23 | 24 |
| 25 | 26 | 27 | 28 | 29 | 30 | 31 |

**JUNE**

| S | M | T | W | T | F | S |
|---|---|---|---|---|---|---|
| 1 | 2 | 3 | 4 | 5 | 6 | 7 |
| 8 | 9 | 10 | 11 | 12 | 13 | 14 |
| 15 | 16 | 17 | 18 | 19 | 20 | 21 |
| 22 | 23 | 24 | 25 | 26 | 27 | 28 |
| 29 | 30 | | | | | |

**JULY**

| S | M | T | W | T | F | S |
|---|---|---|---|---|---|---|
| | | 1 | 2 | 3 | 4 | 5 |
| 6 | 7 | 8 | 9 | 10 | 11 | 12 |
| 13 | 14 | 15 | 16 | 17 | 18 | 19 |
| 20 | 21 | 22 | 23 | 24 | 25 | 26 |
| 27 | 28 | 29 | 30 | 31 | | |

**AUGUST**

| S | M | T | W | T | F | S |
|---|---|---|---|---|---|---|
| | | | | | 1 | 2 |
| 3 | 4 | 5 | 6 | 7 | 8 | 9 |
| 10 | 11 | 12 | 13 | 14 | 15 | 16 |
| 17 | 18 | 19 | 20 | 21 | 22 | 23 |
| 24 | 25 | 26 | 27 | 28 | 29 | 30 |
| 31 | | | | | | |

**SEPTEMBER**

| S | M | T | W | T | F | S |
|---|---|---|---|---|---|---|
| | 1 | 2 | 3 | 4 | 5 | 6 |
| 7 | 8 | 9 | 10 | 11 | 12 | 13 |
| 14 | 15 | 16 | 17 | 18 | 19 | 20 |
| 21 | 22 | 23 | 24 | 25 | 26 | 27 |
| 28 | 29 | 30 | | | | |

**OCTOBER**

| S | M | T | W | T | F | S |
|---|---|---|---|---|---|---|
| | | | 1 | 2 | 3 | 4 |
| 5 | 6 | 7 | 8 | 9 | 10 | 11 |
| 12 | 13 | 14 | 15 | 16 | 17 | 18 |
| 19 | 20 | 21 | 22 | 23 | 24 | 25 |
| 26 | 27 | 28 | 29 | 30 | 31 | |

**NOVEMBER**

| S | M | T | W | T | F | S |
|---|---|---|---|---|---|---|
| | | | | | | 1 |
| 2 | 3 | 4 | 5 | 6 | 7 | 8 |
| 9 | 10 | 11 | 12 | 13 | 14 | 15 |
| 16 | 17 | 18 | 19 | 20 | 21 | 22 |
| 23 | 24 | 25 | 26 | 27 | 28 | 29 |
| 30 | | | | | | |

**DECEMBER**

| S | M | T | W | T | F | S |
|---|---|---|---|---|---|---|
| | 1 | 2 | 3 | 4 | 5 | 6 |
| 7 | 8 | 9 | 10 | 11 | 12 | 13 |
| 14 | 15 | 16 | 17 | 18 | 19 | 20 |
| 21 | 22 | 23 | 24 | 25 | 26 | 27 |
| 28 | 29 | 30 | 31 | | | |

### 7

**JANUARY**

| S | M | T | W | T | F | S |
|---|---|---|---|---|---|---|
| | | | | | | 1 |
| 2 | 3 | 4 | 5 | 6 | 7 | 8 |
| 9 | 10 | 11 | 12 | 13 | 14 | 15 |
| 16 | 17 | 18 | 19 | 20 | 21 | 22 |
| 23 | 24 | 25 | 26 | 27 | 28 | 29 |
| 30 | 31 | | | | | |

**FEBRUARY**

| S | M | T | W | T | F | S |
|---|---|---|---|---|---|---|
| | | 1 | 2 | 3 | 4 | 5 |
| 6 | 7 | 8 | 9 | 10 | 11 | 12 |
| 13 | 14 | 15 | 16 | 17 | 18 | 19 |
| 20 | 21 | 22 | 23 | 24 | 25 | 26 |
| 27 | 28 | | | | | |

**MARCH**

| S | M | T | W | T | F | S |
|---|---|---|---|---|---|---|
| | | 1 | 2 | 3 | 4 | 5 |
| 6 | 7 | 8 | 9 | 10 | 11 | 12 |
| 13 | 14 | 15 | 16 | 17 | 18 | 19 |
| 20 | 21 | 22 | 23 | 24 | 25 | 26 |
| 27 | 28 | 29 | 30 | 31 | | |

**APRIL**

| S | M | T | W | T | F | S |
|---|---|---|---|---|---|---|
| | | | | | 1 | 2 |
| 3 | 4 | 5 | 6 | 7 | 8 | 9 |
| 10 | 11 | 12 | 13 | 14 | 15 | 16 |
| 17 | 18 | 19 | 20 | 21 | 22 | 23 |
| 24 | 25 | 26 | 27 | 28 | 29 | 30 |

**MAY**

| S | M | T | W | T | F | S |
|---|---|---|---|---|---|---|
| 1 | 2 | 3 | 4 | 5 | 6 | 7 |
| 8 | 9 | 10 | 11 | 12 | 13 | 14 |
| 15 | 16 | 17 | 18 | 19 | 20 | 21 |
| 22 | 23 | 24 | 25 | 26 | 27 | 28 |
| 29 | 30 | 31 | | | | |

**JUNE**

| S | M | T | W | T | F | S |
|---|---|---|---|---|---|---|
| | | | 1 | 2 | 3 | 4 |
| 5 | 6 | 7 | 8 | 9 | 10 | 11 |
| 12 | 13 | 14 | 15 | 16 | 17 | 18 |
| 19 | 20 | 21 | 22 | 23 | 24 | 25 |
| 26 | 27 | 28 | 29 | 30 | | |

**JULY**

| S | M | T | W | T | F | S |
|---|---|---|---|---|---|---|
| | | | | | 1 | 2 |
| 3 | 4 | 5 | 6 | 7 | 8 | 9 |
| 10 | 11 | 12 | 13 | 14 | 15 | 16 |
| 17 | 18 | 19 | 20 | 21 | 22 | 23 |
| 24 | 25 | 26 | 27 | 28 | 29 | 30 |
| 31 | | | | | | |

**AUGUST**

| S | M | T | W | T | F | S |
|---|---|---|---|---|---|---|
| | 1 | 2 | 3 | 4 | 5 | 6 |
| 7 | 8 | 9 | 10 | 11 | 12 | 13 |
| 14 | 15 | 16 | 17 | 18 | 19 | 20 |
| 21 | 22 | 23 | 24 | 25 | 26 | 27 |
| 28 | 29 | 30 | 31 | | | |

**SEPTEMBER**

| S | M | T | W | T | F | S |
|---|---|---|---|---|---|---|
| | | | | 1 | 2 | 3 |
| 4 | 5 | 6 | 7 | 8 | 9 | 10 |
| 11 | 12 | 13 | 14 | 15 | 16 | 17 |
| 18 | 19 | 20 | 21 | 22 | 23 | 24 |
| 25 | 26 | 27 | 28 | 29 | 30 | |

**OCTOBER**

| S | M | T | W | T | F | S |
|---|---|---|---|---|---|---|
| | | | | | | 1 |
| 2 | 3 | 4 | 5 | 6 | 7 | 8 |
| 9 | 10 | 11 | 12 | 13 | 14 | 15 |
| 16 | 17 | 18 | 19 | 20 | 21 | 22 |
| 23 | 24 | 25 | 26 | 27 | 28 | 29 |
| 30 | 31 | | | | | |

**NOVEMBER**

| S | M | T | W | T | F | S |
|---|---|---|---|---|---|---|
| | | 1 | 2 | 3 | 4 | 5 |
| 6 | 7 | 8 | 9 | 10 | 11 | 12 |
| 13 | 14 | 15 | 16 | 17 | 18 | 19 |
| 20 | 21 | 22 | 23 | 24 | 25 | 26 |
| 27 | 28 | 29 | 30 | | | |

**DECEMBER**

| S | M | T | W | T | F | S |
|---|---|---|---|---|---|---|
| | | | | 1 | 2 | 3 |
| 4 | 5 | 6 | 7 | 8 | 9 | 10 |
| 11 | 12 | 13 | 14 | 15 | 16 | 17 |
| 18 | 19 | 20 | 21 | 22 | 23 | 24 |
| 25 | 26 | 27 | 28 | 29 | 30 | 31 |

### 8

**JANUARY**

| S | M | T | W | T | F | S |
|---|---|---|---|---|---|---|
| 1 | 2 | 3 | 4 | 5 | 6 | 7 |
| 8 | 9 | 10 | 11 | 12 | 13 | 14 |
| 15 | 16 | 17 | 18 | 19 | 20 | 21 |
| 22 | 23 | 24 | 25 | 26 | 27 | 28 |
| 29 | 30 | 31 | | | | |

**FEBRUARY**

| S | M | T | W | T | F | S |
|---|---|---|---|---|---|---|
| | | | 1 | 2 | 3 | 4 |
| 5 | 6 | 7 | 8 | 9 | 10 | 11 |
| 12 | 13 | 14 | 15 | 16 | 17 | 18 |
| 19 | 20 | 21 | 22 | 23 | 24 | 25 |
| 26 | 27 | 28 | 29 | | | |

**MARCH**

| S | M | T | W | T | F | S |
|---|---|---|---|---|---|---|
| | | | | 1 | 2 | 3 |
| 4 | 5 | 6 | 7 | 8 | 9 | 10 |
| 11 | 12 | 13 | 14 | 15 | 16 | 17 |
| 18 | 19 | 20 | 21 | 22 | 23 | 24 |
| 25 | 26 | 27 | 28 | 29 | 30 | 31 |

**APRIL**

| S | M | T | W | T | F | S |
|---|---|---|---|---|---|---|
| 1 | 2 | 3 | 4 | 5 | 6 | 7 |
| 8 | 9 | 10 | 11 | 12 | 13 | 14 |
| 15 | 16 | 17 | 18 | 19 | 20 | 21 |
| 22 | 23 | 24 | 25 | 26 | 27 | 28 |
| 29 | 30 | | | | | |

**MAY**

| S | M | T | W | T | F | S |
|---|---|---|---|---|---|---|
| | | 1 | 2 | 3 | 4 | 5 |
| 6 | 7 | 8 | 9 | 10 | 11 | 12 |
| 13 | 14 | 15 | 16 | 17 | 18 | 19 |
| 20 | 21 | 22 | 23 | 24 | 25 | 26 |
| 27 | 28 | 29 | 30 | 31 | | |

**JUNE**

| S | M | T | W | T | F | S |
|---|---|---|---|---|---|---|
| | | | | | 1 | 2 |
| 3 | 4 | 5 | 6 | 7 | 8 | 9 |
| 10 | 11 | 12 | 13 | 14 | 15 | 16 |
| 17 | 18 | 19 | 20 | 21 | 22 | 23 |
| 24 | 25 | 26 | 27 | 28 | 29 | 30 |

**JULY**

| S | M | T | W | T | F | S |
|---|---|---|---|---|---|---|
| 1 | 2 | 3 | 4 | 5 | 6 | 7 |
| 8 | 9 | 10 | 11 | 12 | 13 | 14 |
| 15 | 16 | 17 | 18 | 19 | 20 | 21 |
| 22 | 23 | 24 | 25 | 26 | 27 | 28 |
| 29 | 30 | 31 | | | | |

**AUGUST**

| S | M | T | W | T | F | S |
|---|---|---|---|---|---|---|
| | | | 1 | 2 | 3 | 4 |
| 5 | 6 | 7 | 8 | 9 | 10 | 11 |
| 12 | 13 | 14 | 15 | 16 | 17 | 18 |
| 19 | 20 | 21 | 22 | 23 | 24 | 25 |
| 26 | 27 | 28 | 29 | 30 | 31 | |

**SEPTEMBER**

| S | M | T | W | T | F | S |
|---|---|---|---|---|---|---|
| | | | | | | 1 |
| 2 | 3 | 4 | 5 | 6 | 7 | 8 |
| 9 | 10 | 11 | 12 | 13 | 14 | 15 |
| 16 | 17 | 18 | 19 | 20 | 21 | 22 |
| 23 | 24 | 25 | 26 | 27 | 28 | 29 |
| 30 | | | | | | |

**OCTOBER**

| S | M | T | W | T | F | S |
|---|---|---|---|---|---|---|
| | 1 | 2 | 3 | 4 | 5 | 6 |
| 7 | 8 | 9 | 10 | 11 | 12 | 13 |
| 14 | 15 | 16 | 17 | 18 | 19 | 20 |
| 21 | 22 | 23 | 24 | 25 | 26 | 27 |
| 28 | 29 | 30 | 31 | | | |

**NOVEMBER**

| S | M | T | W | T | F | S |
|---|---|---|---|---|---|---|
| | | | | 1 | 2 | 3 |
| 4 | 5 | 6 | 7 | 8 | 9 | 10 |
| 11 | 12 | 13 | 14 | 15 | 16 | 17 |
| 18 | 19 | 20 | 21 | 22 | 23 | 24 |
| 25 | 26 | 27 | 28 | 29 | 30 | |

**DECEMBER**

| S | M | T | W | T | F | S |
|---|---|---|---|---|---|---|
| | | | | | | 1 |
| 2 | 3 | 4 | 5 | 6 | 7 | 8 |
| 9 | 10 | 11 | 12 | 13 | 14 | 15 |
| 16 | 17 | 18 | 19 | 20 | 21 | 22 |
| 23 | 24 | 25 | 26 | 27 | 28 | 29 |
| 30 | 31 | | | | | |

### 11

**JANUARY**

| S | M | T | W | T | F | S |
|---|---|---|---|---|---|---|
| | | | 1 | 2 | 3 | 4 |
| 5 | 6 | 7 | 8 | 9 | 10 | 11 |
| 12 | 13 | 14 | 15 | 16 | 17 | 18 |
| 19 | 20 | 21 | 22 | 23 | 24 | 25 |
| 26 | 27 | 28 | 29 | 30 | 31 | |

**FEBRUARY**

| S | M | T | W | T | F | S |
|---|---|---|---|---|---|---|
| | | | | | | 1 |
| 2 | 3 | 4 | 5 | 6 | 7 | 8 |
| 9 | 10 | 11 | 12 | 13 | 14 | 15 |
| 16 | 17 | 18 | 19 | 20 | 21 | 22 |
| 23 | 24 | 25 | 26 | 27 | 28 | 29 |

**MARCH**

| S | M | T | W | T | F | S |
|---|---|---|---|---|---|---|
| 1 | 2 | 3 | 4 | 5 | 6 | 7 |
| 8 | 9 | 10 | 11 | 12 | 13 | 14 |
| 15 | 16 | 17 | 18 | 19 | 20 | 21 |
| 22 | 23 | 24 | 25 | 26 | 27 | 28 |
| 29 | 30 | 31 | | | | |

**APRIL**

| S | M | T | W | T | F | S |
|---|---|---|---|---|---|---|
| | | | 1 | 2 | 3 | 4 |
| 5 | 6 | 7 | 8 | 9 | 10 | 11 |
| 12 | 13 | 14 | 15 | 16 | 17 | 18 |
| 19 | 20 | 21 | 22 | 23 | 24 | 25 |
| 26 | 27 | 28 | 29 | 30 | | |

**MAY**

| S | M | T | W | T | F | S |
|---|---|---|---|---|---|---|
| | | | | | 1 | 2 |
| 3 | 4 | 5 | 6 | 7 | 8 | 9 |
| 10 | 11 | 12 | 13 | 14 | 15 | 16 |
| 17 | 18 | 19 | 20 | 21 | 22 | 23 |
| 24 | 25 | 26 | 27 | 28 | 29 | 30 |
| 31 | | | | | | |

**JUNE**

| S | M | T | W | T | F | S |
|---|---|---|---|---|---|---|
| | 1 | 2 | 3 | 4 | 5 | 6 |
| 7 | 8 | 9 | 10 | 11 | 12 | 13 |
| 14 | 15 | 16 | 17 | 18 | 19 | 20 |
| 21 | 22 | 23 | 24 | 25 | 26 | 27 |
| 28 | 29 | 30 | | | | |

**JULY**

| S | M | T | W | T | F | S |
|---|---|---|---|---|---|---|
| | | | 1 | 2 | 3 | 4 |
| 5 | 6 | 7 | 8 | 9 | 10 | 11 |
| 12 | 13 | 14 | 15 | 16 | 17 | 18 |
| 19 | 20 | 21 | 22 | 23 | 24 | 25 |
| 26 | 27 | 28 | 29 | 30 | 31 | |

**AUGUST**

| S | M | T | W | T | F | S |
|---|---|---|---|---|---|---|
| | | | | | | 1 |
| 2 | 3 | 4 | 5 | 6 | 7 | 8 |
| 9 | 10 | 11 | 12 | 13 | 14 | 15 |
| 16 | 17 | 18 | 19 | 20 | 21 | 22 |
| 23 | 24 | 25 | 26 | 27 | 28 | 29 |
| 30 | 31 | | | | | |

**SEPTEMBER**

| S | M | T | W | T | F | S |
|---|---|---|---|---|---|---|
| | | 1 | 2 | 3 | 4 | 5 |
| 6 | 7 | 8 | 9 | 10 | 11 | 12 |
| 13 | 14 | 15 | 16 | 17 | 18 | 19 |
| 20 | 21 | 22 | 23 | 24 | 25 | 26 |
| 27 | 28 | 29 | 30 | | | |

**OCTOBER**

| S | M | T | W | T | F | S |
|---|---|---|---|---|---|---|
| | | | | 1 | 2 | 3 |
| 4 | 5 | 6 | 7 | 8 | 9 | 10 |
| 11 | 12 | 13 | 14 | 15 | 16 | 17 |
| 18 | 19 | 20 | 21 | 22 | 23 | 24 |
| 25 | 26 | 27 | 28 | 29 | 30 | 31 |

**NOVEMBER**

| S | M | T | W | T | F | S |
|---|---|---|---|---|---|---|
| 1 | 2 | 3 | 4 | 5 | 6 | 7 |
| 8 | 9 | 10 | 11 | 12 | 13 | 14 |
| 15 | 16 | 17 | 18 | 19 | 20 | 21 |
| 22 | 23 | 24 | 25 | 26 | 27 | 28 |
| 29 | 30 | | | | | |

**DECEMBER**

| S | M | T | W | T | F | S |
|---|---|---|---|---|---|---|
| | | 1 | 2 | 3 | 4 | 5 |
| 6 | 7 | 8 | 9 | 10 | 11 | 12 |
| 13 | 14 | 15 | 16 | 17 | 18 | 19 |
| 20 | 21 | 22 | 23 | 24 | 25 | 26 |
| 27 | 28 | 29 | 30 | 31 | | |

### 12

**JANUARY**

| S | M | T | W | T | F | S |
|---|---|---|---|---|---|---|
| | | | | 1 | 2 | 3 |
| 4 | 5 | 6 | 7 | 8 | 9 | 10 |
| 11 | 12 | 13 | 14 | 15 | 16 | 17 |
| 18 | 19 | 20 | 21 | 22 | 23 | 24 |
| 25 | 26 | 27 | 28 | 29 | 30 | 31 |

**FEBRUARY**

| S | M | T | W | T | F | S |
|---|---|---|---|---|---|---|
| 1 | 2 | 3 | 4 | 5 | 6 | 7 |
| 8 | 9 | 10 | 11 | 12 | 13 | 14 |
| 15 | 16 | 17 | 18 | 19 | 20 | 21 |
| 22 | 23 | 24 | 25 | 26 | 27 | 28 |
| 29 | | | | | | |

**MARCH**

| S | M | T | W | T | F | S |
|---|---|---|---|---|---|---|
| | 1 | 2 | 3 | 4 | 5 | 6 |
| 7 | 8 | 9 | 10 | 11 | 12 | 13 |
| 14 | 15 | 16 | 17 | 18 | 19 | 20 |
| 21 | 22 | 23 | 24 | 25 | 26 | 27 |
| 28 | 29 | 30 | 31 | | | |

**APRIL**

| S | M | T | W | T | F | S |
|---|---|---|---|---|---|---|
| | | | | 1 | 2 | 3 |
| 4 | 5 | 6 | 7 | 8 | 9 | 10 |
| 11 | 12 | 13 | 14 | 15 | 16 | 17 |
| 18 | 19 | 20 | 21 | 22 | 23 | 24 |
| 25 | 26 | 27 | 28 | 29 | 30 | |

**MAY**

| S | M | T | W | T | F | S |
|---|---|---|---|---|---|---|
| | | | | | | 1 |
| 2 | 3 | 4 | 5 | 6 | 7 | 8 |
| 9 | 10 | 11 | 12 | 13 | 14 | 15 |
| 16 | 17 | 18 | 19 | 20 | 21 | 22 |
| 23 | 24 | 25 | 26 | 27 | 28 | 29 |
| 30 | 31 | | | | | |

**JUNE**

| S | M | T | W | T | F | S |
|---|---|---|---|---|---|---|
| | | 1 | 2 | 3 | 4 | 5 |
| 6 | 7 | 8 | 9 | 10 | 11 | 12 |
| 13 | 14 | 15 | 16 | 17 | 18 | 19 |
| 20 | 21 | 22 | 23 | 24 | 25 | 26 |
| 27 | 28 | 29 | 30 | | | |

**JULY**

| S | M | T | W | T | F | S |
|---|---|---|---|---|---|---|
| | | | | 1 | 2 | 3 |
| 4 | 5 | 6 | 7 | 8 | 9 | 10 |
| 11 | 12 | 13 | 14 | 15 | 16 | 17 |
| 18 | 19 | 20 | 21 | 22 | 23 | 24 |
| 25 | 26 | 27 | 28 | 29 | 30 | 31 |

**AUGUST**

| S | M | T | W | T | F | S |
|---|---|---|---|---|---|---|
| 1 | 2 | 3 | 4 | 5 | 6 | 7 |
| 8 | 9 | 10 | 11 | 12 | 13 | 14 |
| 15 | 16 | 17 | 18 | 19 | 20 | 21 |
| 22 | 23 | 24 | 25 | 26 | 27 | 28 |
| 29 | 30 | 31 | | | | |

**SEPTEMBER**

| S | M | T | W | T | F | S |
|---|---|---|---|---|---|---|
| | | | 1 | 2 | 3 | 4 |
| 5 | 6 | 7 | 8 | 9 | 10 | 11 |
| 12 | 13 | 14 | 15 | 16 | 17 | 18 |
| 19 | 20 | 21 | 22 | 23 | 24 | 25 |
| 26 | 27 | 28 | 29 | 30 | | |

**OCTOBER**

| S | M | T | W | T | F | S |
|---|---|---|---|---|---|---|
| | | | | | 1 | 2 |
| 3 | 4 | 5 | 6 | 7 | 8 | 9 |
| 10 | 11 | 12 | 13 | 14 | 15 | 16 |
| 17 | 18 | 19 | 20 | 21 | 22 | 23 |
| 24 | 25 | 26 | 27 | 28 | 29 | 30 |
| 31 | | | | | | |

**NOVEMBER**

| S | M | T | W | T | F | S |
|---|---|---|---|---|---|---|
| | 1 | 2 | 3 | 4 | 5 | 6 |
| 7 | 8 | 9 | 10 | 11 | 12 | 13 |
| 14 | 15 | 16 | 17 | 18 | 19 | 20 |
| 21 | 22 | 23 | 24 | 25 | 26 | 27 |
| 28 | 29 | 30 | | | | |

**DECEMBER**

| S | M | T | W | T | F | S |
|---|---|---|---|---|---|---|
| | | | 1 | 2 | 3 | 4 |
| 5 | 6 | 7 | 8 | 9 | 10 | 11 |
| 12 | 13 | 14 | 15 | 16 | 17 | 18 |
| 19 | 20 | 21 | 22 | 23 | 24 | 25 |
| 26 | 27 | 28 | 29 | 30 | 31 | |

## 2

```
JANUARY               FEBRUARY              MARCH                 APRIL
 S  M  T  W  T  F  S    S  M  T  W  T  F  S    S  M  T  W  T  F  S    S  M  T  W  T  F  S
       1  2  3  4  5  6             1  2  3             1  2  3       1  2  3  4  5  6  7
 7  8  9 10 11 12 13    4  5  6  7  8  9 10    4  5  6  7  8  9 10    8  9 10 11 12 13 14
14 15 16 17 18 19 20   11 12 13 14 15 16 17   11 12 13 14 15 16 17   15 16 17 18 19 20 21
21 22 23 24 25 26 27   18 19 20 21 22 23 24   18 19 20 21 22 23 24   22 23 24 25 26 27 28
28 29 30 31            25 26 27 28            25 26 27 28 29 30 31   29 30

MAY                   JUNE                  JULY                  AUGUST
 S  M  T  W  T  F  S    S  M  T  W  T  F  S    S  M  T  W  T  F  S    S  M  T  W  T  F  S
       1  2  3  4  5                1  2       1  2  3  4  5  6  7             1  2  3  4
 6  7  8  9 10 11 12    3  4  5  6  7  8  9    8  9 10 11 12 13 14    5  6  7  8  9 10 11
13 14 15 16 17 18 19   10 11 12 13 14 15 16   15 16 17 18 19 20 21   12 13 14 15 16 17 18
20 21 22 23 24 25 26   17 18 19 20 21 22 23   22 23 24 25 26 27 28   19 20 21 22 23 24 25
27 28 29 30 31         24 25 26 27 28 29 30   29 30 31               26 27 28 29 30 31

SEPTEMBER             OCTOBER               NOVEMBER              DECEMBER
 S  M  T  W  T  F  S    S  M  T  W  T  F  S    S  M  T  W  T  F  S    S  M  T  W  T  F  S
                   1       1  2  3  4  5  6             1  2  3                      1
 2  3  4  5  6  7  8    7  8  9 10 11 12 13    4  5  6  7  8  9 10    2  3  4  5  6  7  8
 9 10 11 12 13 14 15   14 15 16 17 18 19 20   11 12 13 14 15 16 17    9 10 11 12 13 14 15
16 17 18 19 20 21 22   21 22 23 24 25 26 27   18 19 20 21 22 23 24   16 17 18 19 20 21 22
23 24 25 26 27 28 29   28 29 30 31            25 26 27 28 29 30      23 24 25 26 27 28 29
30                                                                  30 31
```

## 3

```
JANUARY               FEBRUARY              MARCH                 APRIL
 S  M  T  W  T  F  S    S  M  T  W  T  F  S    S  M  T  W  T  F  S    S  M  T  W  T  F  S
          1  2  3  4  5             1  2                1  2             1  2  3  4  5  6
 6  7  8  9 10 11 12    3  4  5  6  7  8  9    3  4  5  6  7  8  9    7  8  9 10 11 12 13
13 14 15 16 17 18 19   10 11 12 13 14 15 16   10 11 12 13 14 15 16   14 15 16 17 18 19 20
20 21 22 23 24 25 26   17 18 19 20 21 22 23   17 18 19 20 21 22 23   21 22 23 24 25 26 27
27 28 29 30 31         24 25 26 27 28         24 25 26 27 28 29 30   28 29 30
                                              31

MAY                   JUNE                  JULY                  AUGUST
 S  M  T  W  T  F  S    S  M  T  W  T  F  S    S  M  T  W  T  F  S    S  M  T  W  T  F  S
             1  2  3  4                   1             1  2  3  4  5  6             1  2  3
 5  6  7  8  9 10 11    2  3  4  5  6  7  8    7  8  9 10 11 12 13    4  5  6  7  8  9 10
12 13 14 15 16 17 18    9 10 11 12 13 14 15   14 15 16 17 18 19 20   11 12 13 14 15 16 17
19 20 21 22 23 24 25   16 17 18 19 20 21 22   21 22 23 24 25 26 27   18 19 20 21 22 23 24
26 27 28 29 30 31      23 24 25 26 27 28 29   28 29 30 31            25 26 27 28 29 30 31
                       30

SEPTEMBER             OCTOBER               NOVEMBER              DECEMBER
 S  M  T  W  T  F  S    S  M  T  W  T  F  S    S  M  T  W  T  F  S    S  M  T  W  T  F  S
 1  2  3  4  5  6  7             1  2  3  4  5                1  2    1  2  3  4  5  6  7
 8  9 10 11 12 13 14    6  7  8  9 10 11 12    3  4  5  6  7  8  9    8  9 10 11 12 13 14
15 16 17 18 19 20 21   13 14 15 16 17 18 19   10 11 12 13 14 15 16   15 16 17 18 19 20 21
22 23 24 25 26 27 28   20 21 22 23 24 25 26   17 18 19 20 21 22 23   22 23 24 25 26 27 28
29 30                  27 28 29 30 31         24 25 26 27 28 29 30   29 30 31
```

## 5

```
JANUARY               FEBRUARY              MARCH                 APRIL
 S  M  T  W  T  F  S    S  M  T  W  T  F  S    S  M  T  W  T  F  S    S  M  T  W  T  F  S
                1  2  3  1  2  3  4  5  6  7    1  2  3  4  5  6  7             1  2  3  4
 4  5  6  7  8  9 10    8  9 10 11 12 13 14    8  9 10 11 12 13 14    5  6  7  8  9 10 11
11 12 13 14 15 16 17   15 16 17 18 19 20 21   15 16 17 18 19 20 21   12 13 14 15 16 17 18
18 19 20 21 22 23 24   22 23 24 25 26 27 28   22 23 24 25 26 27 28   19 20 21 22 23 24 25
25 26 27 28 29 30 31                          29 30 31               26 27 28 29 30

MAY                   JUNE                  JULY                  AUGUST
 S  M  T  W  T  F  S    S  M  T  W  T  F  S    S  M  T  W  T  F  S    S  M  T  W  T  F  S
                1  2    1  2  3  4  5  6                1  2  3  4                      1
 3  4  5  6  7  8  9    7  8  9 10 11 12 13    5  6  7  8  9 10 11    2  3  4  5  6  7  8
10 11 12 13 14 15 16   14 15 16 17 18 19 20   12 13 14 15 16 17 18    9 10 11 12 13 14 15
17 18 19 20 21 22 23   21 22 23 24 25 26 27   19 20 21 22 23 24 25   16 17 18 19 20 21 22
24 25 26 27 28 29 30   28 29 30               26 27 28 29 30 31      23 24 25 26 27 28 29
31                                                                  30 31

SEPTEMBER             OCTOBER               NOVEMBER              DECEMBER
 S  M  T  W  T  F  S    S  M  T  W  T  F  S    S  M  T  W  T  F  S    S  M  T  W  T  F  S
       1  2  3  4  5             1  2  3    1  2  3  4  5  6  7             1  2  3  4  5
 6  7  8  9 10 11 12    4  5  6  7  8  9 10    8  9 10 11 12 13 14    6  7  8  9 10 11 12
13 14 15 16 17 18 19   11 12 13 14 15 16 17   15 16 17 18 19 20 21   13 14 15 16 17 18 19
20 21 22 23 24 25 26   18 19 20 21 22 23 24   22 23 24 25 26 27 28   20 21 22 23 24 25 26
27 28 29 30            25 26 27 28 29 30 31   29 30                  27 28 29 30 31
```

## 6

```
JANUARY               FEBRUARY              MARCH                 APRIL
 S  M  T  W  T  F  S    S  M  T  W  T  F  S    S  M  T  W  T  F  S    S  M  T  W  T  F  S
                   1  2          1  2  3  4  5  6             1  2  3  4  5  6             1  2  3
 3  4  5  6  7  8  9    7  8  9 10 11 12 13    7  8  9 10 11 12 13    4  5  6  7  8  9 10
10 11 12 13 14 15 16   14 15 16 17 18 19 20   14 15 16 17 18 19 20   11 12 13 14 15 16 17
17 18 19 20 21 22 23   21 22 23 24 25 26 27   21 22 23 24 25 26 27   18 19 20 21 22 23 24
24 25 26 27 28 29 30   28                     28 29 30 31            25 26 27 28 29 30
31

MAY                   JUNE                  JULY                  AUGUST
 S  M  T  W  T  F  S    S  M  T  W  T  F  S    S  M  T  W  T  F  S    S  M  T  W  T  F  S
                   1       1  2  3  4  5             1  2  3    1  2  3  4  5  6  7
 2  3  4  5  6  7  8    6  7  8  9 10 11 12    4  5  6  7  8  9 10    8  9 10 11 12 13 14
 9 10 11 12 13 14 15   13 14 15 16 17 18 19   11 12 13 14 15 16 17   15 16 17 18 19 20 21
16 17 18 19 20 21 22   20 21 22 23 24 25 26   18 19 20 21 22 23 24   22 23 24 25 26 27 28
23 24 25 26 27 28 29   27 28 29 30            25 26 27 28 29 30 31   29 30 31
30 31

SEPTEMBER             OCTOBER               NOVEMBER              DECEMBER
 S  M  T  W  T  F  S    S  M  T  W  T  F  S    S  M  T  W  T  F  S    S  M  T  W  T  F  S
       1  2  3  4             1  2          1  2  3  4  5  6                1  2  3  4
 5  6  7  8  9 10 11    3  4  5  6  7  8  9    7  8  9 10 11 12 13    5  6  7  8  9 10 11
12 13 14 15 16 17 18   10 11 12 13 14 15 16   14 15 16 17 18 19 20   12 13 14 15 16 17 18
19 20 21 22 23 24 25   17 18 19 20 21 22 23   21 22 23 24 25 26 27   19 20 21 22 23 24 25
26 27 28 29 30         24 25 26 27 28 29 30   28 29 30               26 27 28 29 30 31
                       31
```

## 9

```
JANUARY               FEBRUARY              MARCH                 APRIL
 S  M  T  W  T  F  S    S  M  T  W  T  F  S    S  M  T  W  T  F  S    S  M  T  W  T  F  S
       1  2  3  4  5  6             1  2  3                1  2       1  2  3  4  5  6
 7  8  9 10 11 12 13    4  5  6  7  8  9 10    3  4  5  6  7  8  9    7  8  9 10 11 12 13
14 15 16 17 18 19 20   11 12 13 14 15 16 17   10 11 12 13 14 15 16   14 15 16 17 18 19 20
21 22 23 24 25 26 27   18 19 20 21 22 23 24   17 18 19 20 21 22 23   21 22 23 24 25 26 27
28 29 30 31            25 26 27 28 29         24 25 26 27 28 29 30   28 29 30
                                              31

MAY                   JUNE                  JULY                  AUGUST
 S  M  T  W  T  F  S    S  M  T  W  T  F  S    S  M  T  W  T  F  S    S  M  T  W  T  F  S
          1  2  3  4                   1       1  2  3  4  5  6                1  2  3
 5  6  7  8  9 10 11    2  3  4  5  6  7  8    7  8  9 10 11 12 13    4  5  6  7  8  9 10
12 13 14 15 16 17 18    9 10 11 12 13 14 15   14 15 16 17 18 19 20   11 12 13 14 15 16 17
19 20 21 22 23 24 25   16 17 18 19 20 21 22   21 22 23 24 25 26 27   18 19 20 21 22 23 24
26 27 28 29 30 31      23 24 25 26 27 28 29   28 29 30 31            25 26 27 28 29 30 31
                       30

SEPTEMBER             OCTOBER               NOVEMBER              DECEMBER
 S  M  T  W  T  F  S    S  M  T  W  T  F  S    S  M  T  W  T  F  S    S  M  T  W  T  F  S
 1  2  3  4  5  6  7             1  2  3  4  5                1  2    1  2  3  4  5  6  7
 8  9 10 11 12 13 14    6  7  8  9 10 11 12    3  4  5  6  7  8  9    8  9 10 11 12 13 14
15 16 17 18 19 20 21   13 14 15 16 17 18 19   10 11 12 13 14 15 16   15 16 17 18 19 20 21
22 23 24 25 26 27 28   20 21 22 23 24 25 26   17 18 19 20 21 22 23   22 23 24 25 26 27 28
29 30                  27 28 29 30 31         24 25 26 27 28 29 30   29 30 31
```

## 10

```
JANUARY               FEBRUARY              MARCH                 APRIL
 S  M  T  W  T  F  S    S  M  T  W  T  F  S    S  M  T  W  T  F  S    S  M  T  W  T  F  S
          1  2  3  4  5             1  2                   1             1  2  3  4  5
 6  7  8  9 10 11 12    3  4  5  6  7  8  9    2  3  4  5  6  7  8    6  7  8  9 10 11 12
13 14 15 16 17 18 19   10 11 12 13 14 15 16    9 10 11 12 13 14 15   13 14 15 16 17 18 19
20 21 22 23 24 25 26   17 18 19 20 21 22 23   16 17 18 19 20 21 22   20 21 22 23 24 25 26
27 28 29 30 31         24 25 26 27 28 29      23 24 25 26 27 28 29   27 28 29 30
                                              30 31

MAY                   JUNE                  JULY                  AUGUST
 S  M  T  W  T  F  S    S  M  T  W  T  F  S    S  M  T  W  T  F  S    S  M  T  W  T  F  S
             1  2  3    1  2  3  4  5  6  7             1  2  3  4  5                   1  2
 4  5  6  7  8  9 10    8  9 10 11 12 13 14    6  7  8  9 10 11 12    3  4  5  6  7  8  9
11 12 13 14 15 16 17   15 16 17 18 19 20 21   13 14 15 16 17 18 19   10 11 12 13 14 15 16
18 19 20 21 22 23 24   22 23 24 25 26 27 28   20 21 22 23 24 25 26   17 18 19 20 21 22 23
25 26 27 28 29 30 31   29 30                  27 28 29 30 31         24 25 26 27 28 29 30
                                                                    31

SEPTEMBER             OCTOBER               NOVEMBER              DECEMBER
 S  M  T  W  T  F  S    S  M  T  W  T  F  S    S  M  T  W  T  F  S    S  M  T  W  T  F  S
    1  2  3  4  5  6             1  2  3  4                      1       1  2  3  4  5  6
 7  8  9 10 11 12 13    5  6  7  8  9 10 11    2  3  4  5  6  7  8    7  8  9 10 11 12 13
14 15 16 17 18 19 20   12 13 14 15 16 17 18    9 10 11 12 13 14 15   14 15 16 17 18 19 20
21 22 23 24 25 26 27   19 20 21 22 23 24 25   16 17 18 19 20 21 22   21 22 23 24 25 26 27
28 29 30               26 27 28 29 30 31      23 24 25 26 27 28 29   28 29 30 31
                                              30
```

## 13

```
JANUARY               FEBRUARY              MARCH                 APRIL
 S  M  T  W  T  F  S    S  M  T  W  T  F  S    S  M  T  W  T  F  S    S  M  T  W  T  F  S
                   1  2          1  2  3  4  5  6             1  2  3  4  5                1  2
 3  4  5  6  7  8  9    7  8  9 10 11 12 13    6  7  8  9 10 11 12    3  4  5  6  7  8  9
10 11 12 13 14 15 16   14 15 16 17 18 19 20   13 14 15 16 17 18 19   10 11 12 13 14 15 16
17 18 19 20 21 22 23   21 22 23 24 25 26 27   20 21 22 23 24 25 26   17 18 19 20 21 22 23
24 25 26 27 28 29 30   28 29                  27 28 29 30 31         24 25 26 27 28 29 30
31

MAY                   JUNE                  JULY                  AUGUST
 S  M  T  W  T  F  S    S  M  T  W  T  F  S    S  M  T  W  T  F  S    S  M  T  W  T  F  S
 1  2  3  4  5  6  7             1  2  3  4                   1  2    1  2  3  4  5  6
 8  9 10 11 12 13 14    5  6  7  8  9 10 11    3  4  5  6  7  8  9    7  8  9 10 11 12 13
15 16 17 18 19 20 21   12 13 14 15 16 17 18   10 11 12 13 14 15 16   14 15 16 17 18 19 20
22 23 24 25 26 27 28   19 20 21 22 23 24 25   17 18 19 20 21 22 23   21 22 23 24 25 26 27
29 30 31               26 27 28 29 30         24 25 26 27 28 29 30   28 29 30 31
                                              31

SEPTEMBER             OCTOBER               NOVEMBER              DECEMBER
 S  M  T  W  T  F  S    S  M  T  W  T  F  S    S  M  T  W  T  F  S    S  M  T  W  T  F  S
          1  2  3                      1       1  2  3  4  5             1  2  3
 4  5  6  7  8  9 10    2  3  4  5  6  7  8    6  7  8  9 10 11 12    4  5  6  7  8  9 10
11 12 13 14 15 16 17    9 10 11 12 13 14 15   13 14 15 16 17 18 19   11 12 13 14 15 16 17
18 19 20 21 22 23 24   16 17 18 19 20 21 22   20 21 22 23 24 25 26   18 19 20 21 22 23 24
25 26 27 28 29 30      23 24 25 26 27 28 29   27 28 29 30            25 26 27 28 29 30 31
                       30 31
```

## 14

```
JANUARY               FEBRUARY              MARCH                 APRIL
 S  M  T  W  T  F  S    S  M  T  W  T  F  S    S  M  T  W  T  F  S    S  M  T  W  T  F  S
                      1    1  2  3  4  5             1  2  3  4                      1
 2  3  4  5  6  7  8    6  7  8  9 10 11 12    5  6  7  8  9 10 11    2  3  4  5  6  7  8
 9 10 11 12 13 14 15   13 14 15 16 17 18 19   12 13 14 15 16 17 18    9 10 11 12 13 14 15
16 17 18 19 20 21 22   20 21 22 23 24 25 26   19 20 21 22 23 24 25   16 17 18 19 20 21 22
23 24 25 26 27 28 29   27 28 29              26 27 28 29 30 31       23 24 25 26 27 28 29
30 31                                                               30

MAY                   JUNE                  JULY                  AUGUST
 S  M  T  W  T  F  S    S  M  T  W  T  F  S    S  M  T  W  T  F  S    S  M  T  W  T  F  S
 1  2  3  4  5  6             1  2  3                      1             1  2  3  4  5
 7  8  9 10 11 12 13    4  5  6  7  8  9 10    2  3  4  5  6  7  8    6  7  8  9 10 11 12
14 15 16 17 18 19 20   11 12 13 14 15 16 17    9 10 11 12 13 14 15   13 14 15 16 17 18 19
21 22 23 24 25 26 27   18 19 20 21 22 23 24   16 17 18 19 20 21 22   20 21 22 23 24 25 26
28 29 30 31            25 26 27 28 29 30      23 24 25 26 27 28 29   27 28 29 30 31
                                              30 31

SEPTEMBER             OCTOBER               NOVEMBER              DECEMBER
 S  M  T  W  T  F  S    S  M  T  W  T  F  S    S  M  T  W  T  F  S    S  M  T  W  T  F  S
             1  2    1  2  3  4  5  6  7                1  2  3  4                1  2
 3  4  5  6  7  8  9    8  9 10 11 12 13 14    5  6  7  8  9 10 11    3  4  5  6  7  8  9
10 11 12 13 14 15 16   15 16 17 18 19 20 21   12 13 14 15 16 17 18   10 11 12 13 14 15 16
17 18 19 20 21 22 23   22 23 24 25 26 27 28   19 20 21 22 23 24 25   17 18 19 20 21 22 23
24 25 26 27 28 29 30   29 30 31               26 27 28 29 30         24 25 26 27 28 29 30
                                                                    31
```

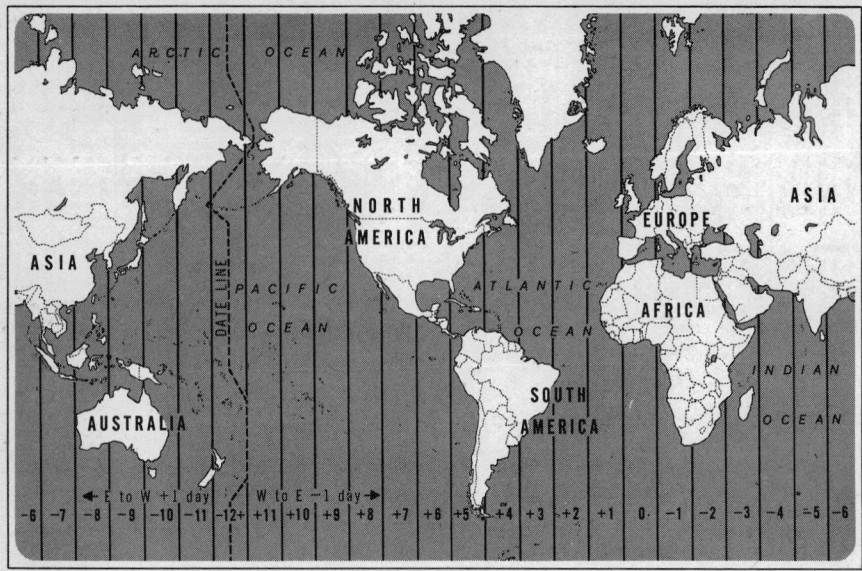

Time zones of the world: Hours are added as indicated west of the zero zone of Greenwich Mean Time, and hours are subtracted east of the zero zone, to the International Date Line.

## FOREIGN CITIES: STANDARD TIME DIFFERENCES

Source: Pan American Airways and Trans World Airlines

When it is 12 noon in New York (Eastern Standard Time), the standard time in foreign cities is as follows (* = following day):

| CITY | TIME | CITY | TIME | CITY | TIME |
|---|---|---|---|---|---|
| Amsterdam......... | 6:00 p.m. | Frobisher.......... | 1:00 p.m. | Nome.............. | 6:00 a.m. |
| Anchorage......... | 7:00 a.m. | Gander........... | 1:30 p.m. | Noumea.......... | 4:00 a.m.* |
| Athens............ | 7:00 p.m. | Geneva........... | 6:00 p.m. | Okinawa......... | 2:00 a.m.* |
| Auckland.......... | 5:00 a.m.* | Glasgow.......... | 5:00 p.m. | Oslo.............. | 6:00 p.m. |
| Azores............ | 3:00 p.m. | Greenwich........ | 5:00 p.m. | Paris.............. | 6:00 p.m. |
| Baghdad.......... | 8:00 p.m. | Guam............ | 3:00 a.m.* | Rangoon.......... | 11:30 p.m. |
| Bangkok.......... | 12:00 | Guatemala City..... | 11:00 a.m. | Recife............ | 2:00 p.m. |
|  | Midnight | Halifax............ | 1:00 p.m. | Reykjavik......... | 4:00 p.m. |
| Barcelona......... | 6:00 p.m. | Havana........... | 12:00 Noon | Rio de Janeiro..... | 2:00 p.m. |
| Basra............. | 8:00 p.m. | Helsinki.......... | 7:00 p.m. | Rome............. | 6:00 p.m. |
| Beirut............ | 7:00 p.m. | Hong Kong........ | 1:00 a.m.* | Saigon........... | 12:00 |
| Belfast........... | 5:00 p.m. | Honolulu.......... | 7:00 a.m. |  | Midnight |
| Berlin............ | 6:00 p.m. | Istanbul.......... | 7:00 p.m. | Samoa........... | 6:00 a.m. |
| Bermuda.......... | 1:00 p.m. | Jerusalem......... | 7:00 p.m. | San Juan......... | 1:00 p.m. |
| Bogotá........... | 12:00 Noon | Johannesburg...... | 7:00 p.m. | Santiago.......... | 1:00 p.m. |
| Bombay.......... | 10:30 p.m. | Juneau........... | 9:00 a.m. | Shanghai......... | 1:00 a.m.* |
| Brussels.......... | 6:00 p.m. | Karachi........... | 10:00 p.m. | Shannon.......... | 5:00 p.m. |
| Bucharest......... | 7:00 p.m. | Keflavik.......... | 4:00 p.m. | Singapore........ | 12:30 a.m.* |
| Buenos Aires....... | 2:00 p.m. | Ketchikan......... | 9:00 a.m. | Stockholm........ | 6:00 p.m. |
| Cairo............. | 7:00 p.m. | Kinshasa......... | 6:00 p.m. | Suva............. | 5:00 a.m.* |
| Calcutta.......... | 10:30 p.m. | La Paz........... | 1:00 p.m. | Sydney........... | 3:00 a.m.* |
| Calgary........... | 10:00 a.m. | Leningrad......... | 8:00 p.m. | Tahiti............ | 7:00 a.m. |
| Canton........... | 1:00 a.m.* | Lima............. | 12:00 Noon | Teheran.......... | 8:30 p.m. |
| Capetown......... | 7:00 p.m. | Lisbon........... | 5:00 p.m. | Tokyo............ | 2:00 a.m.* |
| Caracas.......... | 12:30 p.m. | London........... | 5:00 p.m. | Toronto.......... | 12:00 Noon |
| Copenhagen....... | 6:00 p.m. | Madrid........... | 6:00 p.m. | Valparaiso........ | 1:00 p.m. |
| Dakar............ | 5:00 p.m. | Manila........... | 1:00 a.m.* | Vancouver........ | 9:00 a.m. |
| Damascus......... | 7:00 p.m. | Melbourne........ | 3:00 a.m.* | Vienna........... | 6:00 p.m. |
| Delhi............ | 10:30 p.m. | Mexico........... | 11:00 a.m. | Wake............ | 5:00 a.m.* |
| Dhahran.......... | 9:00 p.m. | Midway.......... | 6:00 a.m. | Warsaw.......... | 6:00 p.m. |
| Djakarta.......... | 12:30 a.m.* | Monrovia......... | 4:00 p.m. | Whitehorse....... | 8:00 a.m. |
| Dublin........... | 5:00 p.m. | Montevideo....... | 2:00 p.m. | Winnipeg......... | 11:00 a.m. |
| Fairbanks......... | 7:00 a.m. | Montreal.......... | 12:00 Noon | Yokohama........ | 2:00 a.m.* |
| Frankfurt......... | 6:00 p.m. | Moscow.......... | 8:00 p.m. | Zurich............ | 6:00 p.m. |

## LOCATION ON THE EARTH

If we look at a terrestrial globe we see that the Equator is not the only line marked on it. There are other lines parallel to the Equator and still others passing through the poles and crossing the Equator at right angles. These imaginary lines, used to pinpoint the position of any place on the globe, are based on the fact that all circles are divided into 360 degrees (°), each degree into 60 minutes ('), and each minute into 60 seconds (").

The Equator lies midway between the North and South Poles, so that from any part of the Earth to either pole is one-quarter around the Earth, or 90°. On either side of the Equator are parallel circles that divide the distance to the poles into 90 equal parts. These circles are called parallels of latitude, and the distance between successive circles is one degree of latitude, or about 69 miles. North latitude is measured from the Equator toward the North Pole; south latitude is measured toward the South Pole.

Latitude, however, is not sufficient to define the exact position of a place, for it only defines distance from the Equator. We must also specify the position of the place as so many degrees east or west of a reference line which is perpendicular to the Equator.

Thus a second series of great circles, 180 in number, has been drawn about the Earth. Each circle crosses the Equator and passes through both poles. The half of each great circle which extends from one pole to the other is called a meridian of longitude. Since each circle consists of two meridians—one on each side of the globe—the 180 great circles comprise a total of 360 meridians. The meridian that passes through the transit instrument of the Royal Observatory at Greenwich, England, has been designated as 0° longitude, or the prime meridian. (The half of the great circle opposite the prime meridian is the meridian of 180° longitude.) Therefore, any place on Earth can be specified as being so many degrees of longitude east or west of the prime meridian.

At the Equator, meridians are about 69 miles apart. As one approaches the poles, however, the distance between two successive meridians decreases. Thus, the length of a degree of longitude is not constant, but varies from about 69 miles at the Equator to zero at the poles.

## LATITUDE AND LONGITUDE OF FOREIGN CITIES

Source: U.S. Naval Oceanographic Office and Others

| CITY AND COUNTRY | LATITUDE Deg. Min. | LONGITUDE Deg. Min. | CITY AND COUNTRY | LATITUDE Deg. Min. | LONGITUDE Deg. Min. |
|---|---|---|---|---|---|
| Aberdeen, Scotland | 57 09 N | 2 05 W | Casablanca, Morocco | 33 37 N | 7 36 W |
| Acapulco, Mexico | 16 51 N | 99 56 W | Colombo, Ceylon | 6 57 N | 79 51 E |
| Accra, Ghana | 5 31 N | 0 12 W | Colón, Panama | 9 22 N | 79 55 W |
| Addis Ababa, Ethiopia | 9 02 N | 38 47 E | Copenhagen, Denmark | 55 42 N | 12 36 E |
| Alexandria, Egypt | 31 11 N | 29 51 E | Dakar, Senegal | 14 41 N | 17 26 W |
| Algiers, Algeria | 36 47 N | 3 04 E | Dar es Salaam, Tanganyika.. | 6 50 S | 39 18 E |
| Amsterdam, Netherlands.... | 52 23 N | 4 54 E | Darwin, Australia | 12 29 S | 130 50 E |
| Antwerp, Belgium | 51 14 N | 4 24 E | Djakarta, Indonesia | 6 06 S | 106 53 E |
| Apia, Samoa | 13 49 S | 171 46 W | Djibouti, French Somaliland. | 11 37 N | 43 08 E |
| Asunción, Paraguay | 25 16 S | 57 41 W | Dublin, Ireland | 53 21 N | 6 13 W |
| Athens, Greece | 37 58 N | 23 43 E | Dubrovnik, Yugoslavia | 42 38 N | 18 07 E |
| Auckland, New Zealand | 36 50 S | 174 47 E | Fort de France, Martinique.. | 14 36 N | 61 04 W |
| Bangkok, Thailand | 13 45 N | 100 30 E | Freetown, Sierra Leone | 8 30 N | 13 14 W |
| Barcelona, Spain | 41 22 N | 2 11 E | Genoa, Italy | 44 24 N | 8 55 E |
| Basra, Iraq | 30 32 N | 47 51 E | Georgetown, Guyana | 6 49 N | 58 10 W |
| Beirut, Lebanon | 33 54 N | 35 31 E | Guayaquil, Ecuador | 2 12 S | 79 53 W |
| Belfast, Northern Ireland.... | 54 37 N | 5 54 W | Haifa, Israel | 32 49 N | 35 00 E |
| Belgrade, Yugoslavia | 44 48 N | 20 28 E | Haiphong, North Vietnam... | 20 52 N | 106 41 E |
| Belize, British Honduras.... | 17 28 N | 88 11 W | Halifax, Canada | 44 39 N | 63 34 W |
| Berbera, Somalia | 10 27 N | 45 01 E | Hamilton, Bermuda | 32 18 N | 64 47 W |
| Bergen, Norway | 60 24 N | 5 19 E | Havana, Cuba | 23 08 N | 82 21 W |
| Berlin, Germany | 52 31 N | 13 25 E | Helsinki, Finland | 60 09 N | 24 56 E |
| Bizerte, Tunisia | 37 14 N | 9 51 E | Hiroshima, Japan | 34 21 N | 132 28 E |
| Bogotá, Colombia | 4 36 N | 74 05 W | Hong Kong | 22 17 N | 114 10 E |
| Bombay, India | 18 56 N | 72 51 E | Inchon, South Korea | 37 28 N | 126 37 E |
| Bremen, Germany | 53 07 N | 8 45 E | Istanbul, Turkey | 41 01 N | 28 59 E |
| Bridgetown, Barbados | 13 05 N | 59 37 W | Jerusalem, Israel-Jordan.... | 31 47 N | 35 13 E |
| Brisbane, Australia | 27 28 S | 153 04 E | Johannesburg, South Africa.. | 26 11 S | 28 03 E |
| Brunei, Borneo | 4 60 N | 115 08 E | Kabul, Afghanistan | 34 30 N | 69 13 E |
| Bucharest, Romania | 44 25 N | 26 06 E | Karachi, Pakistan | 24 49 N | 66 58 E |
| Budapest, Hungary | 47 30 N | 19 20 E | Kingston, Jamaica | 17 58 N | 76 47 W |
| Buenos Aires, Argentina.... | 34 35 S | 58 22 W | Lagos, Nigeria | 6 27 N | 3 23 E |
| Cairo, Egypt | 30 31 N | 31 15 E | Le Havre, France | 49 29 N | 0 06 E |
| Calcutta, India | 22 33 N | 88 19 E | Leningrad, U.S.S.R. | 59 55 N | 30 15 E |
| Canton, China | 23 07 N | 113 16 E | Lisbon, Portugal | 38 42 N | 9 08 W |
| Cape Town, South Africa.... | 33 54 S | 18 26 E | Liverpool, England | 53 27 N | 3 01 W |
| Cardiff, Wales | 51 27 N | 3 10 W | Lomé, Togo | 6 07 N | 1 14 E |

| CITY AND COUNTRY | LATITUDE Deg. Min. ° ' | LONGITUDE Deg. Min. ° ' | CITY AND COUNTRY | LATITUDE Deg. Min. ° ' | LONGITUDE Deg. Min. ° ' |
|---|---|---|---|---|---|
| London, England........... | 51 30 N | 0 01 E | Reykjavik, Iceland......... | 64 09 N | 21 56 W |
| Madrid, Spain............. | 40 25 N | 3 40 W | Riga, Latvia............... | 56 58 N | 24 06 E |
| Malacca, Malaysia......... | 2 10 N | 102 14 E | Rio de Janeiro, Brazil....... | 22 54 S | 43 11 W |
| Manila, Philippines........ | 14 35 N | 120 58 E | Rome, Italy............... | 41 54 N | 12 30 E |
| Maracaibo, Venezuela...... | 10 38 N | 71 37 W | Saigon, South Vietnam...... | 10 47 N | 106 42 E |
| Marseilles, France......... | 43 19 N | 5 21 E | Salonika, Greece........... | 40 38 N | 22 56 E |
| Mecca, Saudi Arabia....... | 21 25 N | 39 49 E | Santo Domingo, | | |
| Melbourne, Australia....... | 37 49 S | 144 56 E |   Dominican Republic...... | 18 28 N | 69 53 W |
| Mexico City, Mexico....... | 19 26 N | 99 07 W | Shanghai, China........... | 31 14 N | 121 30 E |
| Mombasa, Kenya........... | 4 04 S | 39 41 E | Singapore................. | 1 17 N | 103 50 E |
| Monrovia, Liberia.......... | 6 20 N | 10 49 W | Stockholm, Sweden......... | 59 20 N | 18 05 E |
| Montevideo, Uruguay....... | 34 55 S | 56 14 W | Strait of Gibraltar......... | 35 57 N | 5 45 W |
| Montreal, Canada......... | 45 30 N | 73 33 W | Suva, Fiji................. | 18 08 S | 178 25 E |
| Moscow, U.S.S.R......... | 55 45 N | 37 34 E | Sydney, Australia.......... | 33 52 S | 151 13 E |
| Murmansk, U.S.S.R........ | 68 59 N | 33 03 E | Tananarive, Malagasy....... | 18 52 S | 47 35 E |
| Nairobi, Kenya............ | 1 16 S | 36 52 E | Tangier, Morocco.......... | 35 47 N | 5 48 W |
| Naples, Italy.............. | 40 50 N | 14 16 E | Teheran, Iran............. | 35 40 N | 51 25 E |
| Nassau, Bahamas.......... | 25 05 N | 77 20 W | Tokyo, Japan.............. | 35 38 N | 139 46 E |
| Odessa, U.S.S.R.......... | 46 30 N | 30 45 E | Tunis, Tunisia............. | 36 48 N | 10 12 E |
| Oslo, Norway............. | 59 54 N | 10 44 E | Venice, Italy.............. | 45 26 N | 12 18 E |
| Ottawa, Canada.......... | 45 24 N | 75 42 W | Veracruz, Mexico.......... | 19 12 N | 96 08 W |
| Paris, France............. | 48 50 N | 2 20 E | Vienna, Austria............ | 48 14 N | 16 20 E |
| Pnom Penh, Cambodia..... | 11 33 N | 104 51 E | Vladivostok, U.S.S.R....... | 43 07 N | 131 53 E |
| Port Moresby, New Guinea.... | 9 29 S | 147 09 E | Warsaw, Poland........... | 52 15 N | 21 00 E |
| Prague, Czechoslovakia.... | 50 05 N | 14 25 E | Windsor, Canada.......... | 45 00 N | 64 09 W |
| Quebec, Canada........... | 46 49 N | 71 12 W | Zanzibar, Tanzania........ | 6 10 S | 39 11 E |
| Rangoon, Burma.......... | 16 46 N | 96 10 E | Zurich, Switzerland......... | 47 22 N | 8 22 E |

## LANDMARKS IN WORLD EXPLORATION

Many significant achievements of exploration are detailed in the following table. The B.C. dates reflect an expert consensus, but many of these dates are subject to revision. The nations named sponsored the explorations. The explorations are listed in chronological order.

| EXPLORER | NATION | ACHIEVEMENT | CHRONOLOGY |
|---|---|---|---|
| **Great Circumnavigations of the Earth** | | | |
| Ferdinand Magellan........ | Portugal | His expedition was the first to sail around the world. Magellan died before completion of the journey....... | 1519–1522 |
| Francis Drake............. | England | First Englishman to circumnavigate the earth........... | 1577–1580 |
| Louis Antoine de Bougainville | France | Conducted major explorations.......................... | 1767–1769 |
| James Cook............... | England | Conducted major explorations.......................... | 1768–1771 |
| Charles Wilkes........... | United States | Conducted major explorations.......................... | 1838–1842 |
| TRITON (nuclear submarine) | United States | Underwater circumnavigation of earth................. | 1960 |
| **Explorers of the Ancient Mediterranean World** | | | |
| Minoans.................. | Crete | Explored entire Mediterranean world................. | 2000–1400 B.C. |
| Phoenicians............... | Phoenicia | Explored Mediterranean and ventured past Gibraltar as far as England........................... | 600 B.C. |
| Hekataios of Miletus........ | Greece | Explored Mediterranean region, Spain, and North Africa. | 500 B.C. |
| Herodotus................. | Greece | Traveled mostly in eastern Mediterranean region, Italy, and in Asia Minor.......................... | 424 B.C. |
| Pytheas of Massilia......... | Greece | Sailed north out of Gibraltar past Scotland until ice blocked his way........................... | 330 B.C. |
| Decimus Junius Brutus...... | Rome | Explored Spain, Duero River.......................... | 138 B.C. |
| Eudoxus of Cyzicus......... | Egypt | Explored coast of Africa and Arabian Sea............. | 130 B.C. |
| Julius Caesar............... | Rome | Explored (while warring in western Europe) France, Germany, and Great Britain....................... | 58–52 B.C. |
| Strabo.................... | Greece | Explored Roman world, Europe, North Africa, and western Asia........................... | 40 B.C. |
| Gnaeus Julius Agricola...... | Rome | Explored Scottish Highlands.......................... | A.D. 83 (?) |
| **New World** | | | |
| Leif Ericsson............... | Norway | Sailed to North American continent................... | A.D. 1000 (?) |
| Christopher Columbus....... | Spain | Discovered and explored West Indies on several expeditions to North and South America............ | 1492, 1495, 1498, 1502 |
| John and Sebastian Cabot... | England | Explored coastline of North America, Labrador to Hatteras....................................... | 1497–1498 |

| EXPLORER | NATION | ACHIEVEMENT | CHRONOLOGY |
|---|---|---|---|
| Alonso de Ojeda | Spain | Explored northeast coast of South America, reached Guyana and Haiti | 1499 |
| Vicente Pinzón | Spain | Explored Caribbean shore; mouth of the Amazon River, Brazil | 1499–1500 |
| Pedro Alvarez Cabral | Portugal | Discovered Brazilian coast | 1500 |
| Amerigo Vespucci | Portugal | Explored South American coast | 1501–1503 |
| Vasco Núñez de Balboa | Spain | Discovered Pacific Ocean | 1513 |
| Juan Ponce de León | Spain | Discovered Florida | 1513 |
| Hernando Cortés | Spain | Conquered and explored Mexico | 1519–1521 |
| Ferdinand Magellan | Spain | Discovered Straits of Magellan, Tierra del Fuego | 1519–1522 |
| Giovanni da Verrazano | France | Explored Atlantic coast, New York Harbor | 1524 |
| Nikolas Federmann | Germany | Explored interior of Venezuela | 1530–1532 |
| Alfonso de Sonza | Portugal | Discovered and explored the Rio de Janeiro River | 1531 |
| Francisco Pizarro | Spain | Conquered and explored Peru | 1532–1533 |
| Jacques Cartier | France | Discovered and explored Gulf of St. Lawrence and St. Lawrence River | 1534 |
| Pedro de Mendoza | Spain | Explored Argentina; founded Buenos Aires | 1536 |
| Álvar Núñez, Cabeza de Vaca | Spain | Explored Texas coast and southwest America | 1536 |
| Gonzalo Jiménez de Quesada | Spain | Explored Colombian Andes region; founded Bogotá | 1536–1538 |
| Francisco de Ulloa | Spain | Explored California coast, proving Lower California a peninsula | 1539 |
| Hernando de Soto | Spain | Explored southeast America | 1539–1541 |
| Francisco Coronado | Spain | Explored American southwest; discovered Grand Canyon | 1540 |
| Pedro de Valdivia | Spain | Conquered and explored Chile; founded Santiago | 1540–1541 |
| Francisco de Orellana | Spain | Discovered and explored Amazon River | 1541 |
| Pedro Menendez | Spain | Founded St. Augustine, Florida | 1565 |
| Francis Drake | England | Explored northwest coast of America | 1577–1580 |
| Walter Raleigh | England | Explored Guyana; discovered Orinoco River | 1595 |
| Juan de Oñate | Spain | Explored New Mexico and American Great Plains | 1598, 1601 |
| Samuel de Champlain | France | Explored Canadian interior and Lake Champlain; founded Quebec | 1603–1604 |
| John Smith | England | Explored Atlantic coast, North America | 1607 |
| Henry Hudson | Netherlands | Explored Hudson River, Hudson Bay region | 1609–1610 |
| Willem Schouten | Netherlands | Discovered and named Cape Horn, South America | 1616 |
| Jean Nicolet | France | Explored Old Northwest, Michigan, and Wisconsin | 1634 |
| Robert Cavalier La Salle | France | Explored Great Lakes and Mississippi Delta | 1669–1682 |
| Louis Jolliet and Jacques Marquette | France | Explored Mississippi River to its delta | 1673 |
| Antoine de la Mothe Cadillac | France | Explored Upper Mississippi Valley; founded Detroit | 1701 |
| Pierre de la Vérendrye | Canada | Explored Canadian Great Plains; discovered Red River | 1731–1741 |
| James Cook | England | Surveyed St. Lawrence River, coasts of Labrador and Newfoundland | 1759–1767 |
| Samuel Hearne | England | Explored and surveyed Northwest Territory; discovered Great Slave Lake, Canada | 1769–1772, 1785 |
| Daniel Boone | United States | Explored Kentucky and surrounding regions | 1770–1784 |
| Alexander Mackenzie | Canada | Explored Canadian west and crossed North American continent | 1793 |
| Alexander von Humboldt | Germany | Explored Venezuela, Colombia, and Ecuador | 1799–1804 |
| Meriwether Lewis and William Clark | United States | Explored Missouri and Columbia rivers; crossed North American continent | 1803–1806 |
| Zebulon M. Pike | United States | Expedition through American southwest; sighted Pikes Peak | 1806–1807 |
| John Colter | United States | Discovered Yellowstone Park | 1807 |
| James Bowie | United States | Explored Louisiana and American west | 1820 (?) |
| James Bridger | United States | Discovered Great Salt Lake, Utah | 1825 |
| Jedediah Strongsmith | United States | Explored Great Basin, Rocky Mountains, and Pacific northwest | 1826 |
| Benjamin Bonneville | United States | Explored Rocky Mountains and California | 1832–1836 |
| Joseph R. Walker | United States | Discovered Yosemite Valley | 1833 |
| John C. Frémont and Kit Carson | United States | Explored Rocky Mountains and Pacific coast | 1842–1845 |
| Hiram Bingham | United States | Discovered and explored Machu Picchu, ancient Peruvian city | 1911–1912 |

## Polar Explorations

| | | | |
|---|---|---|---|
| Martin Frobisher | England | Discovered Frobisher Bay, Canadian Northwest Territory; explored straits north of St. Lawrence River | 1576 |
| John Davis | England | Discovered Davis Strait, Falkland Islands | 1585, 1592 |
| Willem Barents and Jacob van Heemskerck | Netherlands | Discovered Spitsbergen, Arctic Ocean | 1596 |
| William Baffin | England | Discovered Baffin Bay, Arctic region | 1616 |

*(continued)*

## LANDMARKS IN WORLD EXPLORATION (*continued*)

| EXPLORER | NATION | ACHIEVEMENT | CHRONOLOGY |
|---|---|---|---|
| Vitus Bering............... | Russia | Proved Asia and America separate continents by sailing through Bering Strait............................ | 1728 |
| James Cook................ | England | Discovered Cook Island, Arctic region................ | 1775 |
| Nathaniel B. Palmer....... | United States | Discovered South Orkney Islands, Palmer Land, Antarctica.................................... | 1820–1821 |
| John Franklin.............. | England | Explored northern Canada and Arctic region; died searching for Northwest Passage............... | 1819–1822, 1825–1827, 1845 |
| Thaddeus Bellinghausen..... | Russia | Discovered Peter I and Alexander I islands, in Antarctica.................................... | 1819–1821 |
| Ferdinand von Wrangel...... | Russia | Completed survey of Siberian Arctic coast............. | 1820–1823 |
| William E. Parry........... | England | Attempted to find Northwest Passage; attempted to reach North Pole...................... | 1820–1827 |
| James Weddell............. | England | Discovered Weddell Sea, Antarctica.................. | 1823 |
| John Biscoe................ | England | Discovered Enderby Land, Antarctica................. | 1830 |
| James Clark Ross.......... | Scotland | Located North Magnetic Pole; discovered Ross Ice Shelf; explored Antarctica..................... | 1831, 1839, 1843 |
| John Balleny............... | England | Discovered Balleny Islands; first to discover land south of Australia and New Zealand.................. | 1839 |
| Dumont d'Urville........... | France | Discovered Adélie Coast, Antarctica................. | 1840 |
| Nils A. E. Nordenskjöld..... | Sweden | First to sail Northeast Passage to Asia............... | 1878–1880 |
| Fridtjof Nansen............. | Norway | First to explore ice fields of Greenland; attempted to reach North Pole.................... | 1888, 1895 |
| Robert A. Bartlett.......... | United States | Explorations in Greenland, Alaska, Siberia, and Labrador.................................... | 1897–1935 |
| Carsten E. Borchgrevink..... | Norway | First party to winter in Antarctica; explored and mapped Ross Sea.................... | 1899 |
| William S. Bruce........... | Scotland | Explored Weddell Sea and discovered Coats Land....... | 1902–1904 |
| Knud J. V. Rasmussen....... | Denmark | Numerous Arctic explorations..................... | 1902–1932 |
| Jean B. Charcot............ | France | Discovered Charcot Island, Antarctica; also explored Arctic region.................... | 1903–1907, 1908–1910 |
| Vilhjalmur Stefansson....... | Canada | Two expeditions to Mackenzie River delta; longest Polar exploration in the Canadian Arctic region........ | 1906–1907, 1908–1912; 1913–1918 |
| Frederick A. Cook.......... | United States | Attempted to reach North Pole; probably failed........ | 1907–1909 |
| Douglas Mawson............ | Australia | Led three Australian Antarctic expeditions; reached South Magnetic Pole...................... | 1907–1931, 1909 |
| Robert E. Peary........... | United States | First to reach North Pole...................... | 1909 |
| Roald Amundsen........... | Norway | First to reach South Pole; flew across North Pole....... | 1911–1926 |
| Wilhelm Filchner........... | Germany | Discovered Luitpold Coast and Filchner Ice Shelf, Antarctica............................ | 1911–1912 |
| Donald B. MacMillan....... | United States | Explored Labrador, Greenland, and Baffin Island........ | 1913, 1937, 1948 |
| Lincoln Ellsworth........... | United States | Flights to Polar regions by airplane and airship......... | 1925–1926 |
| Umberto Nobile............ | Italy | Flew over North Pole in airship...................... | 1926 |
| Richard E. Byrd............ | United States | Flew over North Pole; flew over South Pole; led several Antarctic expeditions; established Little America on Bay of Whales; led extensive Antarctic exploration.... | 1926; 1929; 1928–1956; 1929; 1946 |
| Valeri Chkalov and Mikhail Gromov.......... | U.S.S.R. | Nonstop trans-polar flight from Moscow to U.S........ | 1937 |
| Finn Ronne................ | United States | Explored and mapped Edith Ronne Land, Antarctica.... | 1946–1948 |
| Edmund Hillary and Vivian Fuchs............. | England | First completely overland crossing of Antarctica........ | 1955–1958 |
| International Geophysical Year | 12 countries | Antarctic research................................ | 1957–1958 |
| U.S. Navy.................. | United States | Nuclear submarine NAUTILUS crossed North Pole under Arctic Ice Pack............................ | 1958 |
| U.S. Navy.................. | United States | Nuclear submarine SKATE surfaced at North Pole...... | 1959 |
| U.S. Navy.................. | United States | Nuclear submarine SARGO traveled under Arctic Ice Pack to and around North Pole...................... | 1960 |
| U.S. Navy.................. | United States | Nuclear submarine SEADRAGON made first east-west underwater transit through the Northwest Passage.... | 1960 |
| New Zealand expedition..... | New Zealand | Intensive survey and exploration of Oates Land, Northern Victoria Land, and Balleny Islands......... | 1964 |
| Ninth Soviet Antarctic expedition................ | U.S.S.R. | Made geodetic study of the ice cap surface............ | 1964 |
| Argentine Antarctic Institute | Argentina | Continued work in Antarctica in biology and geology.... | 1964 |
| U.S. Navy under Rear Admiral James R. Reedy.......... | United States | Operation Deep Freeze, Antarctic research and exploration.................................. | 1964–1965 |

| EXPLORER | NATION | ACHIEVEMENT | CHRONOLOGY |
|---|---|---|---|
| **Africa** | | | |
| Hanno | Carthage | Explored Africa as far south as Sierra Leone | 470 B.C. |
| Idrisi | Sicily | Traveled extensively in Spain, Africa, and Asia Minor | A.D. 1140 (?) |
| Bartholomew Diaz | Portugal | Discovered South Africa and the Cape of Good Hope | 1488 |
| Leo Africanus | Morocco | Explored the Sudan region | 1508–1515 |
| Pedro Páez | Spain | Discovered source of the Blue Nile River in northwest Ethiopia | 1618 |
| Mungo Park | England | Explored Niger River and interior of West Africa | 1795–1797, 1805 |
| Hugh Clapperton and Dixon Denham | Scotland | Explored Sudan, Nigeria, and West Africa | 1822–1827 |
| René Caillié | France | Reached Timbuktu | 1827 |
| David Livingstone | Scotland | Discovered source of Zambezi River, Victoria Falls, Lake Ngami, Lake Nyasa, and Lake Bangweulu in Central Africa | 1841–1871 |
| Heinrich Barth | Germany | Scientific expeditions into the Sahara and the Sudan in Africa | 1845–1855 |
| Richard Burton and John H. Speke | England | Discovered Lake Tanganyika | 1858 |
| Samuel Baker | England | Discovered Lake Albert and Murchison Falls; explored Nile tributaries in Ethiopia | 1861–1864 |
| Gustav Nachtigal | Germany | Explored central Sahara region | 1869 |
| Henry Morton Stanley | England-America | Explored Congo River, source to mouth | 1874–1889 |
| Pierre de Brazza | France | Explored southern and western Africa; founded Brazzaville, Congo | 1875–1883 |
| Emin Pasha (Eduard Schnitzer) | Germany | Explored Central Africa | 1878–1890 |
| Louis Gentil | France | Explored unpenetrated parts of Morocco and Atlas Mountains | 1902 |
| Leo Frobenius | Germany | Twelve major explorations of Africa | 1904–1935 |
| Martin E. Johnson and Osa Johnson | United States | Explored many parts of Africa | 1921, 1924–1929 |
| **Asia and the Pacific** | | | |
| Xenophon | Greece | Explored Persia during military retreat of the "Ten Thousand" Greek mercenaries | 401 B.C. |
| Ctesias | Greece | Explored India | 400 B.C. |
| Alexander the Great | Greece | While warring in Asia, explored deserts of Arabia, mountains of Afghanistan, India, and Indus River to the Indian Ocean | 333–325 B.C. |
| Megasthenes | Greece | Surveyed in northern India; explored Ceylon and Tibet. | 302 B.C. |
| Hippalus | Rome | Sailed to Malabar Coast, southwest India | 100 B.C. |
| Fa Hsien | China | Explored Central Asia, India, and Ceylon | A.D. 400 |
| Hsuan-Tsang | China | Traveled to India across Central Asia | 629–645 |
| Ibn Rosteh | Arabia | Traveled to southeast Asia, Malaya, and Indonesia | 900 |
| Toi-Kai-Rakan | Polynesia | Explored and settled New Zealand | 1150 (?) |
| Benjamin of Tudela | Spain | Traveled to Mesopotamia, Persia, and China | 1159–1173 |
| Giovanni de Piano Carpini | Italy | Traveled through Central Asia to Mongolia | 1245 |
| Marco Polo | Italy | Traveled to China and throughout Asia | 1275–1292 |
| Ibn Batuta | Morocco | Explored Middle East, India, Ceylon, and Sumatra | 1325–1353 |
| Vasco da Gama | Portugal | Discovered sea route to India | 1498 |
| Saint Francis Xavier | Portugal | Traveled to Goa, the Malay Peninsula, the Moluccas, and Japan | 1541–1552 |
| Fernão Mendes Pinto | Portugal | Explored Asiatic waters, Japan | 1546 |
| Abel Tasman | Netherlands | Discovered Tasmania and rediscovered New Zealand | 1642 |
| Louis Antoine de Bougainville | France | Visited Pacific Islands and rediscovered the Solomon Islands | 1767–1769 |
| James Cook | England | Discovered Australia, New Caledonia, and the Sandwich Islands | 1772–1775 |
| Jean de Galaup, Count of La Pérouse | France | Discovered La Pérouse Strait between Sakhalin Island and Korea | 1787 |
| George Vancouver | England | Explored New Zealand and discovered Vancouver Island, British Columbia | 1791–1794 |
| George Bass | England | Discovered Bass Strait on Australian coast | 1795–1798 |
| Évariste R. Huc | France | Explored China, Mongolia, and Tibet | 1839–1844 |
| John Stuart | England | Crossed and explored central Australia | 1860–1862 |
| Robert O'Hara Burke | Ireland | First to cross Australia, north to south | 1860 |
| Nikolai Przhevalsky | Russia | Explored Mongolia, Gobi Desert, and Tibet | 1870–1873 |
| Roy Chapman Andrews | United States | Explored Korea, Tibet, and Gobi Desert | 1911–1930 |
| Gertrude Bell | England | Explored Arabian Desert | 1913–1914 |
| Harry St. John Bridges Philby | England | Traveled to Arabia; first European to visit the Nejd | 1917 |
| Thor Heyerdahl | Norway | Pacific exploration | 1947 |

# NATURAL FEATURES OF THE EARTH

A globe turned upside down and viewed from the South Pacific reveals mostly oceans. In fact over 70 per cent of the Earth's surface is covered by water. Still, many adventurers of old sailed over the seas to find whatever lay beyond the horizon, as described in "Landmarks of World Exploration." What a thrill it must have been to explore new continents, to discover new rivers, or to climb high mountains that men had never seen before! Over the centuries, these explorers filled in our knowledge of the Americas, "Darkest" Africa, Asia, Australia, and the polar regions of the Earth.

Many of the features of the Earth these men discovered will be found in the pages that follow: its continents and islands, its vast oceans and lakes, its mighty mountains and rivers, and its waterfalls, deserts, and volcanoes.

Although some men now venture into space, others are continuing to explore Antarctica, to map the ridges, plains, and canyons of the ocean floors, and to drill deep into the Earth's crust. However much we know about the natural features of the Earth, there will always be even more to learn.

## EARTH'S EXTREMES
Source: National Geographic Society

| | |
|---|---|
| Wettest spot....... | Mt. Waialeale, Hawaii; annual rain average, 471 inches (one-year record, Cherrapunji, India: 1,042 inches in 1861) |
| Driest spot........ | Atacama Desert, Chile; rainfall barely measurable |
| Coldest spot....... | Vostok, Antarctica; −127° F. recorded in 1960 |
| Hottest spot....... | Al'Aziziyah, Libya; 136° F. recorded in 1922 |
| Northernmost town | Ny Alesund, Spitsbergen, Norway |
| Southernmost town | Puerto Williams, Chile |
| Highest town...... | Aucanquilcha, Chile; 17,500 feet |
| Lowest town....... | Villages along the Dead Sea; 1,286 feet below sea level |
| Largest gorge...... | Grand Canyon, Colorado River, Arizona; 217 miles long, 4–13 miles wide, 1 mile deep |
| Deepest gorge..... | Hells Canyon, Snake River, Idaho; 7,900 feet deep |
| Strongest surface wind.......... | 231 mph; recorded in 1934 at Mount Washington, New Hampshire |
| Greatest tides...... | Bay of Fundy, Nova Scotia; 53 feet |
| Biggest meteor crater........... | Deep Bay, Canada; 2 miles wide |

## THE CONTINENTS
Source: National Geographic Society

| NAME | AREA (in square miles) | PER CENT OF WORLD'S LAND | HIGHEST POINT (in feet) | LOWEST POINT (in feet) | HIGHEST RECORDED TEMPERATURE | LOWEST RECORDED TEMPERATURE |
|---|---|---|---|---|---|---|
| Asia.......... | 16,900,000 | 29.4 | Mount Everest (29,028), Nepal-Tibet | Dead Sea (1,296 below sea level), Israel-Jordan | Jacobabad, Pakistan 127.1° F. | Oymyakon, U.S.S.R. −89.9° F. |
| Africa......... | 11,500,000 | 20.0 | Mount Kibo (19,340), a peak of Kilimanjaro, Tanganyika | Qattara Depression (436 below sea level), Egypt | Al'Aziziyah, Libya 136.0° F. | Semrir, Morocco −11.4° F. |
| North America.. | 8,440,000 | 14.7 | Mount McKinley (20,320), Alaska | Death Valley (282 below sea level), California | Death Valley, California 134.0° F. | Snag, Yukon −81.0° F. |
| South America.. | 6,800,000 | 11.8 | Mount Aconcagua (22,834), Argentina | Salinas Grandes (131 below sea level), Peninsula Valdés, Argentina | Rivadavia, Argentina 120.0° F. | Colonia Sarmiento, Argentina −27.4° F. |
| Europe........ | 3,750,000 | 6.5 | Mount El'brus (18,481), U.S.S.R. | Caspian Sea (92 below sea level), U.S.S.R.-Iran | Seville, Spain 122.0° F. | Ust' Shchugor, U.S.S.R. −67.0° F. |
| Australia...... | 2,945,000 | 5.1 | Mount Kosciusko (7,316), New South Wales | Lake Eyre (39 below sea level), South Australia | Cloncurry, Queensland 127.5° F. | Charlotte Pass, New South Wales, −8.0° F. |
| Antarctica..... | 5,500,000 | 9.5 | Vinson Massif (16,860, est.) | Unknown | Palmer Peninsula 58.3° F. | Vostok −127.0° F. |

## U.S. OCEANOGRAPHIC PROGRAM

For the past ten years the U.S. outer space program—with its astronauts and walks in space—has captured headlines. The next ten years, however, should see so-called "inner space" programs capture not just headlines but new resources of food, fuels, and metals. When, in 1966, President Johnson signed into law the Marine Resources and Engineering Development Act (Public Law 89-454), the United States in effect planted its flag on a piece of the Earth's last and richest frontier—the oceans. On this frontier, government, research institutions, and private industry are joining in a partnership to unlock the oceans' treasure-houses.

What treasures do the oceans hold?

**Food:** Even using present fishing methods, the seas could feed an expanding world population for decades. New "sea farming" methods could increase manyfold the oceans' food yields. Even now the U.S. makes a high-protein fish flour for use in undernourished areas.

**Water:** Improved desalting technology could make unlimited fresh water available.

**Minerals:** Vast deposits of gold, silver, copper, sulfur, zinc, and many other materials lie at the ocean bottoms.

**Fuels and Energy:** Offshore oil wells now provide over 15 per cent (5,000,000 barrels per day) of the world's petroleum, and off-shore output will increase four to five times in the next decade. Another possible source of energy is to use the oceans as a massive heat engine by capitalizing on the temperature difference between the surface and the colder depths. The available "thermopower" is enormous.

**Drugs:** Many of our miracle drugs have come from land microorganisms; many more may be derived from sea microbes.

Practical benefits could also follow in several other areas. Among them:

**Weather Forecasting:** A worldwide network of unmanned ocean buoys, transmitting weather data, could make global forecasting possible.

**Defense:** Submarines have long been plagued by the tricks sound plays underwater. The U.S. Navy is investigating underwater communications.

**Construction:** More knowledge of ocean bottoms, currents, and waves could prevent collapse of docks and jetties. Also, actual under-sea projects, such as the laying of pipelines—and, eventually, undersea research stations—would benefit.

The ocean's promise has spurred development of a host of new research tools. Perhaps the most glamorous are the "submersibles," or research submarines. In 1968 there were some 30 of these subs built or abuilding in the U.S. They ranged from the top-secret, nuclear-powered NR-1 being constructed by General Dynamics for the U.S. Navy, to the tiny *Star I*, which can plumb a maximum depth of only 200 feet. Oddly, submersibles have much in common with spacecraft. Design problems are similar: How do you cram all the necessary equipment into a restricted space? And how do you protect occupants from a totally hostile environment? From this standpoint, it was a logical step for an astronaut, Commander Scott Carpenter, to join the U.S. "Man in the Sea" program.

Above-ocean research is carried on, too, with a whole array of equipment: radio-transmitting buoys, both stationary and free-floating; lonely Texas Towers far out on the continental shelves; airplanes; balloons; and specially equipped surface vessels.

In tapping the oceans' riches, where do you start? The answer, according to the director of Scripps Institution of Oceanography: "I'm sure the continental shelves will be explored and developed first, the deep oceans later." The world's continental shelves comprise about 11,000,000 square miles (roughly the area of Africa) and are of course shallower and more accessible than the ocean depths.

## OCEANS AND SEAS

The principal features of Earth's major oceans and seas are given in this table. All told, they cover about 71 per cent, or 139,434,000 square miles, of the Earth's total area, leaving less than a third in land. Water covers about 61 per cent of the surface of the Northern Hemisphere and about 81 per cent of the Southern Hemisphere.

| OCEAN | AREA (in square miles) | PER CENT OF WORLD'S WATER | GREATEST DEPTH (in feet) |
|---|---|---|---|
| Pacific | 63,800,000 | 45.8 | Mariana Trench, off the Mariana Islands, in the Central Pacific, 36,198 |
| Atlantic | 31,830,000 | 22.8 | Puerto Rico Trench, off Puerto Rico, 27,498 |
| Indian | 28,360,000 | 20.6 | Diamantina Depth, off Australia, 26,400 |
| Arctic | 5,440,000 | 3.9 | Unnamed location, 17,880 |

| SEA | AREA (in square miles) | AVERAGE DEPTH (in feet) |
|---|---|---|
| Caribbean Sea | 1,063,340 | 8,172 |
| Mediterranean Sea | 966,757 | 4,878 |
| Bering Sea | 875,753 | 4,714 |
| Gulf of Mexico | 595,760 | 4,961 |
| Sea of Okhotsk | 589,807 | 2,749 |
| East China Sea | 482,317 | 617 |
| Hudson Bay | 475,792 | 420 |
| Sea of Japan | 389,074 | 4,429 |
| Andaman Sea | 307,954 | 2,854 |
| North Sea | 222,124 | 308 |
| Black Sea | 178,378 | 3,610 |
| Red Sea | 169,073 | 1,611 |
| Baltic Sea | 163,050 | 189 |

## MAJOR WORLD ISLANDS

Source: National Geographic Society

Islands are bodies of land surrounded by water. All continents thus are islands in the strict sense of the word; they differ from other islands only in size. The largest islands in the world are: Greenland (840,000 sq. mi.); New Guinea (317,000); Borneo (287,400); Madagascar (229,812); Baffin (183,810); Sumatra (182,-860); Honshu (88,000); and Great Britain (84,186).

*Islands in minor waters:* Manhattan—22.24 square miles, Staten Island—57 square miles, and Governors Island—173 acres (New York City); Isle Royale—209.9 square miles, Lake Superior (U.S.); Manitoulin—1,068 square miles, Lake Huron (Canada); Penang—110 square miles, Strait of Malacca (Malaysia); Singapore—220 square miles, Singapore Strait.

*Atolls* are coral-formed islands surrounding lagoons. Some typical examples: Bikini (U.S.), lagoon—280 square miles, land—2.87 square miles; Canton (U.S., Britain), lagoon—20 square miles, land—4.3 square miles; Christmas (U.S., Britain), lagoon—89 square miles, land —184 square miles.

| NAME | AREA (in sq. miles) | NAME | AREA (in sq. miles) | NAME | AREA (in sq. miles) |
|---|---|---|---|---|---|
| **ARCTIC OCEAN** | | **BALTIC SEA** | | Hong Kong (Great Britain) | 32 |
| **Canadian** | | Alands (Finland) | 572 | Iwo Jima (U.S.) | 7.8 |
| Axel Heiberg | 15,779 | Bornholm (Denmark) | 217 | Japan | 142,727 |
| Baffin | 183,810 | Gotland (Sweden) | 1,220 | Hokkaido | 30,077 |
| Banks | 23,230 | **CARIBBEAN SEA** | | Honshu | 88,000 |
| Devon | 20,861 | Antigua (Great Britain) | 108 | Kyushu | 13,768 |
| Ellesmere | 82,119 | Barbados | 170 | Shikoku | 6,857 |
| Melville | 16,369 | Cuba | 43,038 | Kodiak (U.S.) | 5,363 |
| Prince of Wales | 12,830 | Isle of Pines | 1,180 | **Marianas (U.S.** | |
| Southampton | 15,700 | Dominica (Great Britain) | 305 | Trust Territory) | 366 |
| Victoria | 81,930 | Guadeloupe (France) | 687 | excluding Guam | 154 |
| **U.S.S.R.** | | Hispaniola (Haiti and | | Guam | 212 |
| Franz Josef Land | 6,400 | Dominican Republic) | 29,530 | Marquesas (France) | 492 |
| Novaya Zemlya | 31,900 | Jamaica | 4,232 | **Marshalls (U.S.** | |
| Wrangel | 2,800 | Martinique (France) | 425 | Trust Territory) | 69.8 |
| **Norwegian** | | Puerto Rico (U.S.) | 3,435 | New Caledonia (France) | 7,202 |
| Svalbard | 24,100 | Trinidad | 1864 | **New Guinea** | |
| Nordaust Landet | 5,792 | Virgins (U.S.) | 133 | (Indonesia-Australia) | 317,000 |
| Vest Spitsbergen | 15,251 | **INDIAN OCEAN** | | New Hebrides (Great | |
| **ATLANTIC OCEAN** | | Andamans (India) | 2,508 | Britain-France) | 5,700 |
| **British Isles** | | Ceylon | 25,332 | New Zealand | 103,736 |
| Great Britain, mainland | 84,186 | Madagascar (Malagasy | | North | 44,281 |
| Hebrides | 2,662 | Republic) | 229,812 | South | 58,093 |
| Ireland | 32,598 | Mauritius (Great Britain) | 720 | **Okinawa (U.S.** | |
| Man | 227 | Pemba (Tanzania) | 380 | Administration) | 463 |
| Orkneys | 375 | Réunion (France) | 969 | Philippines | 115,707 |
| Shetlands | 549 | Seychelles (Great | | Leyte | 2,416 |
| Skye | 670 | Britain) | 156 | Luzon | 46,636 |
| **Other Atlantic Islands** | | Zanzibar (Tanzania) | 640 | Mindanao | 39,191 |
| Anticosti (Canada) | 3,043 | **Persian Gulf** | | Mindoro | 3,891 |
| Azores (Portugal) | 888 | Bahrain | 231 | Negros | 5,041 |
| Bahamas (Great Britain) | 4,400 | **MEDITERRANEAN SEA** | | Palawan | 5,693 |
| Bermudas | | Balearics (Spain) | 1,936 | Panay | 4,047 |
| (Great Britain) | 20.46 | Corfu (Greece) | 246 | Samar | 5,309 |
| Canaries (Spain) | 2,808 | Corsica (France) | 3,367 | Quemoy (Formosa) | 50 |
| Cape Breton (Canada) | 3,970 | Crete (Greece) | 3,207 | Sakhalin (U.S.S.R.) | 28,597 |
| Cape Verde (Portugal) | 1,557 | Cyprus | 3,572 | **Samoa** | 1,173 |
| Faeroes (Denmark) | 540 | Elba (Italy) | 87.4 | American Samoa | 76 |
| Falklands (Great Britain) | 4,618 | Malta | 95 | Western Samoa | 1,097 |
| Greenland (Denmark) | 840,000 | Rhodes (Greece) | 545 | Tahiti (France) | 402 |
| Iceland | 39,768 | Sardinia (Italy) | 9,194 | Tasmania (Australia) | 24,330 |
| Long Island (New York) | 1,723 | Sicily (Italy) | 9,817 | Vancouver (Canada) | 12,408 |
| Madeiras (Portugal) | 308 | **PACIFIC OCEAN** | | Viti Levu (Fiji) | 4,053 |
| Marajó (Brazil) | 1,553 | Aleutians (U.S.) | 6,821 | **East Indies** | |
| Martha's Vineyard | | Carolines (U.S. | | Bali (Indonesia) | 2,269 |
| (Massachusetts) | 108.7 | Trust Territory) | 463 | Borneo (Indonesia- | |
| Nantucket | | Formosa (Taiwan) | 13,885 | Malaysia-Great Britain) | 287,400 |
| (Massachusetts) | 57 | Galápagos (Ecuador) | 2,868 | Celebes (Indonesia) | 72,987 |
| Newfoundland (Canada) | 42,734 | Guadalcanal | | Java (Indonesia) | 48,763 |
| Prince Edward (Canada) | 2,184 | (Great Britain) | 1,130 | Moluccas (Indonesia) | 28,767 |
| South Georgia | | Hainan (China) | 13,000 | New Britain (Australia) | 14,600 |
| (Great Britain) | 1,470 | Hawaiian (U.S.) | 6,424 | New Ireland (Australia) | 3,340 |
| Tierra del Fuego (Chile | | Hawaii | 4,030 | Sumatra (Indonesia) | 182,860 |
| and Argentina) | 18,800 | Oahu | 604 | Timor | 13,071 |

## MAJOR FOREIGN RIVERS
Source: National Geographic Society

Rivers play a significant role in both the Earth's hydrologic (water) cycle and its petrogenic (rock) cycle, emptying water from the land into the oceans and gradually wearing away the land in their drainage systems and carrying sediments to the sea. Moreover, rivers have offered most convenient paths for exploration and then courses for transportation and commerce to follow, and civilizations based on agriculture have always flourished along fertile river valleys. The flood and flow of many river systems are now controlled by dams and reservoirs for the more efficient use of the water.

The longest rivers of the world, in miles, are: the Nile (4,145), Africa; the Amazon (3,900), South America; the Mississippi-Missouri-Red Rock (3,710), United States; the Ob'-Irtysh (3,460), Siberia; the Yangtze (3,400), China; the Huang or Yellow (3,000), China; the Congo (2,718), Africa; the Amur (2,700), Siberia; the Lena (2,680), Siberia; the Mackenzie-Peace (2,635), Canada; the Mekong (2,600), Southeast Asia; the Niger (2,600), Africa; the

Sunset on the Amazon River

Wide World

Paraná (2,500), South America; the Murray-Darling (2,310), Australia; and the Volga (2,290), East Europe.

The Angara is the only outlet of Lake Baykal, U.S.S.R., and drops 1,140 feet in 1,150 miles. The source of the St. Lawrence River is in Minnesota.

| RIVER | EMPTIES INTO | LENGTH (In miles) | RIVER | EMPTIES INTO | LENGTH (In miles) |
|---|---|---|---|---|---|
| Albany | James Bay | 610 | Oder | Baltic Sea | 535 |
| Amazon | Atlantic Ocean | 3,900 | Orange | Atlantic Ocean | 1,300 |
| Amu | Aral Sea | 1,600 | Orinoco | Atlantic Ocean | 1,700 |
| Amur | Tatar Strait | 2,700 | Ottawa | St. Lawrence River | 696 |
| Angara | Yenisey | 1,150 | Paraguay | Paraná River | 1,500 |
| Athabasca | Lake Athabasca | 765 | Paraná | Río de la Plata | 2,500 |
| Back | Chantrey Inlet of Arctic Ocean | 605 | Peace | Slave River | 1,195 |
| Brahmaputra | Bay of Bengal | 1,800 | Pilcomayo | Paraguay River | 1,000 |
| Bug | Dnieper River | 500 | Purus | Amazon River | 2,000 |
| Bug | Wisla River | 450 | Rhine | North Sea | 820 |
| Churchill | Hudson Bay | 1,000 | Rhone | Gulf of Lion | 500 |
| Congo | Atlantic Ocean | 2,718 | Rio Grande | Gulf of Mexico | 1,885 |
| Danube | Black Sea | 1,770 | Rio Theodore Roosevelt (River of Doubt) | Madeira River | 950 |
| Dnieper | Black Sea | 1,420 | Saguenay | St. Lawrence River | 475 |
| Dniester | Black Sea | 880 | St. John | Bay of Fundy | 418 |
| Don | Sea of Azov | 1,210 | St. Lawrence | Gulf of St. Lawrence | 1,900 |
| Drava | Danube River | 450 | Salween | Gulf of Martaban | 1,750 |
| Dvina, Northern | White Sea | 800 | São Francisco | Atlantic Ocean | 1,800 |
| Ebro | Mediterranean | 577 | Saskatchewan | Lake Winnipeg | 1,205 |
| Elbe | North Sea | 724 | Seine | English Channel | 482 |
| Euphrates | Persian Gulf | 1,700 | Si | South China Sea | 1,250 |
| Fraser | Strait of Georgia | 850 | Sungari | Amur River | 1,150 |
| Gambia | Atlantic Ocean | 700 | Syr | Aral Sea | 1,850 |
| Ganges | Bay of Bengal | 1,560 | Tajo, Tagus | Atlantic Ocean | 565 |
| Huang (or Yellow) | Yellow Sea | 3,000 | Tigris | Euphrates | 1,150 |
| Indus | Arabian Sea | 1,900 | Tisza | Danube River | 800 |
| Irrawaddy | Bay of Bengal | 1,250 | Tocantins | Pará River | 1,640 |
| Lena | Laptev Sea | 2,680 | Ural | Caspian Sea | 1,570 |
| Loire | Bay of Biscay | 625 | Uruguay | Río de la Plata | 1,000 |
| Mackenzie-Peace | Beaufort Sea | 2,635 | Usumacinta | Gulf of Mexico | 690 |
| Madeira | Amazon River | 2,100 | Volga | Caspian Sea | 2,290 |
| Magdalena | Caribbean Sea | 1,000 | Weser | North Sea | 500 |
| Mekong | South China Sea | 2,600 | Wisla | Bay of Danzig | 665 |
| Meuse | North Sea | 575 | Yangtze | East China Sea | 3,400 |
| Murray-Darling | Lake Alexandrina | 2,310 | Yapura | Amazon River | 1,500 |
| Negro | Amazon | 1,400 | Yellow (or Huang) | Yellow Sea | 3,000 |
| Nelson | Hudson Bay | 1,600 | Yenisey | Kara Sea | 2,080 |
| Niger | Gulf of Guinea | 2,600 | Yukon | Bering Sea | 1,979 |
| Nile | Mediterranean | 4,145 | Zambezi | Indian Ocean | 1,600 |
| Ob'-Irtysh | Gulf of Ob | 3,460 | | | |

## FAMOUS WATERFALLS

Source: National Geographic Society

There are tens of thousands of waterfalls scattered over the Earth, hundreds of them of considerable magnitude. The highest waterfalls in the world are: Angel (Venezuela), 3,212 feet; Tugela (Republic of South Africa), 3,110 feet; Yosemite (California), 2,425 feet; Cuquenán (Venezuela), 2,000 feet; and Sutherland (New Zealand), 1,904 feet.

On the basis of annual flow combined with considerable height, Guaira, between Brazil and Paraguay, is the world's greatest waterfall; its estimated annual flow is 470,000 cusecs (cubic feet per second). A greater volume of water passes over Stanley Falls, in the Democratic Republic of the Congo, but not one of its seven falls, spread over a distance of 60 miles, is higher than ten feet.

The estimated annual flows of other great waterfalls are: Niagara (Canada and United States), 212,200 cusecs; Paulo Afonso (Brazil), 100,000; Urubupunga (Brazil), 97,000; Iguazú (Argentina and Brazil), 61,660; Patos-Maribondo (Brazil), 53,000; Victoria (Zambia and Southern Rhodesia), 38,430; Grand (Labrador), 30,000 to 40,000; and Kaieteur (Guyana), 23,400.

| LOCATION AND NAME | HEIGHT ** (in feet) | LOCATION AND NAME | HEIGHT ** (in feet) | LOCATION AND NAME | HEIGHT ** (in feet) |
|---|---|---|---|---|---|
| **AFRICA** | | **France** | | Ribbon * | 1,612 |
| **Angola** | | Pyrenees Glaciers | | Silver Strand | 1,170 |
| Duque de Braganca.... | 344 | Gavarnie | 1,385 | Vernal | 317 |
| Ruacana | 406 | **Great Britain** | | Yosemite * | 2,425 |
| **Ethiopia** | | Scotland | | Colorado | |
| Baratieri | 459 | Glomach | 370 | Seven | 266 |
| Fincha | 508 | **Italy** | | Georgia | |
| **Zambia** | | Tosa or Toce | 470 | Tallulah † | 251 |
| Chirombo | 880 | **Norway** | | Idaho | |
| **Zambia and** | | Kjelfossen *† | 2,600 | Shoshone * | 195 |
| **Southern Rhodesia** | | Eastern Mardöla | 1,696 | New York | |
| Victoria * | 355 | Western Mardöla | 1,535 | Taughannock | 215 |
| **Zambia and Tanganyika** | | Skjeggedal | 525 | Oregon | |
| **(Tanzania)** | | Skykkje | 820 | Multnomah † | 620 |
| Kalambo * | 705 | Vettis | 1,214 | Tennessee | |
| **Republic of** | | Vöring | 597 | Fall Creek | 256 |
| **South Africa** | | **Sweden** | | Washington | |
| Basutoland | | Handöl † | 345 | Fairy Falls | 700 |
| Maletsunyane | 630 | Harsprang † | 245 | Palouse | 198 |
| Cape Province | | **Switzerland** | | Sluiskin | 300 |
| Aughrabies or | | Cascade de Giétroz †.. | 1,640 | Wisconsin | |
| King George * | 450 | Diesbach † | 394 | Manitou | 165 |
| Natal | | Giessbach † | 1,312 | Wyoming | |
| Howick | 365 | Iffigen | 394 | Yellowstone National | |
| Tugela † | 3,110 | Reichenbach † | 656 | Park | |
| | | Simmen † | 459 | Yellowstone (upper) | 109 |
| **ASIA** | | Stäuber | 590 | Yellowstone (lower) | 308 |
| **India** | | Staubbach | 984 | **Mexico** | |
| Cauvery * | 299 | Trümmelbach † | 1,312 | El Salto | 218 |
| Gersoppa * | 830 | | | | |
| **Japan** | | **NORTH AMERICA** | | **SOUTH AMERICA** | |
| Kegon * | 330 | **Canada** | | **Argentina–Brazil** | |
| Yudaki | 335 | British Columbia | | Iguazú | 237 |
| | | Takakkaw † | 1,650 | **Brazil** | |
| **AUSTRALASIA** | | Panther | 600 | Glass | 1,325 |
| **Australia** | | Labrador | | Herval | 400 |
| New South Wales | | Grand | 245 | Patos–Maribondo | 115 |
| Wentworth † | 518 | Mackenzie District | | Paulo Afonso | 275 |
| Wollomombi | 1,100 | Virginia | 315 | Urubupunga | 40 |
| Queensland | | Quebec | | **Brazil–Paraguay** | |
| Tully | 550 | Montmorency | 273 | Guaira or Sete Quedas | 130 |
| **New Zealand** | | **Canada–United States** | | **Guyana** | |
| Bowen † | 540 | Ontario–New York | | Kaieteur | 741 |
| Helena | 890 | Niagara | 167 | King Edward VIII | 840 |
| Stirling | 505 | **United States** | | King George VI | 1,600 |
| Sutherland † | 1,904 | Arizona | | **Colombia** | |
| | | Mooney | 220 | Tequendama | 427 |
| **EUROPE** | | California | | Catarata de Candelas.. | 984 |
| **Austria** | | Feather | 640 | **Venezuela** | |
| Gastein (lower) | 280 | Illilouette | 370 | Angel † | 3,212 |
| Krimml | 1,250 | Nevada | 594 | Cuquenán | 2,000 |

* Falls that diminish greatly seasonally, in one or more leaps.   † Falls consisting of more than one leap.   ** Height means total drop whether

## LARGEST LAKES OF THE WORLD
Source: National Geographic Society

A lake is a body of water surrounded by land. Although some lakes may be called seas, they are actually lakes by this definition. The Caspian Sea is bounded by the Soviet Union and Iran and is fed by eight rivers, of which the Volga is the largest.

| LAKE | CONTINENT | AREA (in sq. miles) | LENGTH (in miles) | MAX. DEPTH (in ft.) | LAKE | CONTINENT | AREA (in sq. miles) | LENGTH (in miles) | MAX. DEPTH (in ft.) |
|---|---|---|---|---|---|---|---|---|---|
| Caspian Sea | Asia-Europe | 143,550 | 760 | 3,215 | Nicaragua... | No. Amer... | 3,100 | 100 | 230 |
| Superior.... | No. Amer... | 31,820 | 350 | 1,333 | Rudolf...... | Africa...... | 2,473 | 154 | 240 |
| Victoria.... | Africa...... | 26,828 | 225 | 265 | Reindeer.... | No. Amer... | 2,465 | 143 | — |
| Aral Sea.... | Asia....... | 25,300 | 280 | 223 | Issyk Kul... | Asia....... | 2,355 | 115 | 2,303 |
| Huron...... | No. Amer... | 23,010 | 206 | 750 | Torrens..... | Australia... | 2,230 | 130 | — |
| Michigan.... | No. Amer... | 22,400 | 307 | 923 | Vänern..... | Europe..... | 2,141 | 90 | 321 |
| Tanganyika | Africa...... | 12,700 | 450 | 4,708 | Winnipegosis | No. Amer... | 2,105 | 141 | 38 |
| Great Bear.. | No. Amer... | 12,275 | 232 | 270 | Albert...... | Africa...... | 2,075 | 100 | 54 |
| Baykal...... | Asia....... | 11,780 | 385 | 5,315 | Kariba...... | Africa...... | 2,050 | 160 | 295 |
| Nyasa...... | Africa...... | 11,430 | 360 | 2,226 | Nettilling.... | No. Amer... | 1,956 | 67 | — |
| Great Slave | No. Amer... | 10,980 | 298 | 2,015 | Nipigon..... | No. Amer... | 1,870 | 72 | 540 |
| Erie........ | No. Amer... | 9,910 | 241 | 210 | Gairdner.... | Australia... | 1,840 | 90 | — |
| Winnipeg.... | No. Amer... | 9,464 | 266 | 60 | Manitoba.... | No. Amer... | 1,817 | 140 | 12 |
| Ontario..... | No. Amer... | 7,600 | 193 | 802 | Urmia...... | Asia....... | 1,815 | 90 | 49 |
| Ladoga..... | Europe..... | 6,835 | 120 | 738 | Mweru...... | Africa...... | 1,770 | 76 | 84 |
| Balkhash.... | Asia....... | 6,720 | 300 | 85 | Kyoga...... | Africa...... | 1,710 | 50 | 25 |
| Chad...... | Africa...... | 6,300 | 175 | 24 | Khanka..... | Asia....... | 1,700 | 55 | 33 |
| Maracaibo... | So. Amer... | 6,300 | 100 | 102 | Lake of the Woods | No. Amer... | 1,695 | 72 | 69 |
| Onega...... | Europe..... | 3,710 | 145 | 361 | Koko (Tsing) | Asia....... | 1,625 | 68 | 125 |
| Eyre........ | Australia... | 3,700 | 115 | — | Dubawnt.... | No. Amer... | 1,600 | 69 | — |
| Titicaca..... | So. Amer... | 3,200 | 110 | 1,002 | Great Salt... | No. Amer... | 1,500 | 75 | 48 |
| Athabasca... | No. Amer... | 3,120 | 208 | 407 | | | | | |

## HIGHEST MOUNTAIN PEAKS OF THE WORLD
Source: National Geographic Society

Mountain peaks are formed by the differential lifting and then wearing away of land masses by weathering and erosion. The Himalayas, the loftiest mountain range in the world, culminate in Mount Everest, the highest peak in the world. The highest peaks in Europe lie in the Caucasus, a mountain range in the U.S.S.R. that divides Europe and Asia. In western Europe, the highest peaks are the Alps, located in Switzerland, Italy, and France.

| NAME | LOCATION | FEET | NAME | LOCATION | FEET |
|---|---|---|---|---|---|
| **Highest Peaks in North America** | | | **North America** (cont.) | | |
| McKinley............ | Alaska............. | 20,320 | Harvard............ | Colorado.......... | 14,420 |
| Logan.............. | Canada............ | 19,850 | Rainier............ | Washington........ | 14,410 |
| North.............. | Alaska............. | 19,470 | Massive............ | Colorado.......... | 14,404 |
| Citlaltepec (Orizaba).. | Mexico............ | 18,700 | | | |
| St. Elias........... | Alaska-Canada...... | 18,008 | **Highest Peaks in South America** | | |
| Popocatepetl........ | Mexico............ | 17,887 | Aconcagua.......... | Argentina.......... | 22,834 |
| Foraker............ | Alaska............. | 17,400 | Bonete............ | Argentina.......... | 22,546 |
| Iztaccihuatl........ | Mexico............ | 17,343 | Ojos del Salado...... | Argentina-Chile..... | 22,539 |
| Lucania............ | Canada............ | 17,147 | Tupungato.......... | Argentina-Chile..... | 22,310 |
| King............... | Canada............ | 17,130 | Pissis............. | Argentina.......... | 22,241 |
| Blackburn.......... | Alaska............. | 16,523 | Mercedario......... | Argentina.......... | 22,211 |
| Steele............. | Canada............ | 16,440 | Huascarán.......... | Peru.............. | 22,205 |
| Bona.............. | Alaska............. | 16,420 | Tocorpuri.......... | Bolivia-Chile....... | 22,162 |
| Sanford............ | Alaska............. | 16,208 | Llullaillaco......... | Argentina-Chile..... | 22,057 |
| Wood.............. | Canada............ | 15,885 | El Libertador....... | Argentina.......... | 22,047 |
| Vancouver.......... | Alaska-Canada...... | 15,700 | Cachi............. | Argentina.......... | 22,047 |
| Fairweather........ | Alaska............. | 15,300 | Yerupaja........... | Peru.............. | 21,758 |
| Zinantecatl (Toluca).. | Mexico............ | 15,016 | Lincancaur......... | Argentina-Chile..... | 21,719 |
| Hubbard........... | Alaska-Canada...... | 14,950 | Galán............. | Argentina.......... | 21,654 |
| Bear.............. | Alaska............. | 14,850 | El Muerto.......... | Argentina-Chile..... | 21,457 |
| Walsh............. | Canada............ | 14,780 | Sajama............ | Bolivia............ | 21,391 |
| Matlalcueyetl....... | Mexico............ | 14,636 | Nacimiento......... | Argentina.......... | 21,302 |
| Hunter............. | Alaska............. | 14,573 | Illimani........... | Bolivia............ | 21,201 |
| Browne Tower....... | Alaska............. | 14,530 | Coropuna.......... | Peru.............. | 21,079 |
| Alverstone......... | Alaska-Canada...... | 14,500 | Laudo............. | Argentina.......... | 20,997 |
| Whitney........... | California.......... | 14,495 | Auzangate......... | Peru.............. | 20,944 |
| Elbert............. | Colorado.......... | 14,431 | | | |

(continued)

## HIGHEST MOUNTAIN PEAKS (continued)

| NAME | LOCATION | FEET | NAME | LOCATION | FEET |
|---|---|---|---|---|---|
| Toro | Argentina-Chile | 20,932 | Chamlang | Nepal | 24,012 |
| Ancohuma | Bolivia | 20,873 | Kabru | Nepal-Sikkim | 24,002 |
| Tres Cruces | Argentina-Chile | 20,853 | Alung Gangri | Tibet | 24,000 |
| Huandoy | Peru | 20,852 | Chomo Lhari | Tibet-Bhutan | 23,997 |
| Parinacota | Bolivia-Chile | 20,768 | Baltoro Kangri | Kashmir | 23,990 |
| Tórtolas | Argentina-Chile | 20,745 | Muz Tagh | Sinkiang | 23,890 |
| Ampato | Peru | 20,702 | Mana | India | 23,860 |
| Cóndor | Argentina | 20,669 | Baruntse | Nepal | 23,688 |
| Salcantay | Peru | 20,574 | Nepal Peak | Nepal-Sikkim | 23,458 |
| Chimborazo | Ecuador | 20,561 | Pumori | Nepal-Tibet | 23,442 |
| Huancarhuas | Peru | 20,531 | Gauri Sankar | Nepal-Tibet | 23,440 |
| | | | Badrinath | India | 23,420 |

### Highest Peaks in Asia

| NAME | LOCATION | FEET |
|---|---|---|
| | | |
| Everest | Nepal-Tibet | 29,028 |
| K2 (Godwin-Austen) | Kashmir | 28,250 |
| Kanchenjunga | Nepal-Sikkim | 28,208 |
| Lhotse I | Nepal-Tibet | 27,923 |
| Makalu I | Nepal-Tibet | 27,824 |
| Lhotse II | Nepal-Tibet | 27,560 |
| Dhaulagiri | Nepal | 26,810 |
| Manaslu I | Nepal | 26,760 |
| Cho Oyu | Nepal-Tibet | 26,750 |
| Nanga Parbat | Kashmir | 26,660 |
| Annapurna | Nepal | 26,504 |
| Gasherbrum | Kashmir | 26,470 |
| Broad | Kashmir | 26,400 |
| Gosainthan | Tibet | 26,291 |
| Annapurna II | Nepal | 26,041 |
| Disteghil | Kashmir | 25,868 |
| Himalchuli | Nepal | 25,801 |
| Nuptse | Nepal-Tibet | 25,726 |
| Masherbrum | Kashmir | 25,660 |
| Nanda Devi | India | 25,645 |
| Chomo Lonzo | Nepal-Tibet | 25,640 |
| Rakaposhi | Kashmir | 25,550 |
| Kamet | India-Tibet | 25,447 |
| Namcha Barwa | Tibet | 25,445 |
| Gurla Mandhata | Tibet | 25,355 |
| Ulugh Muz Tagh | Tibet-China | 25,340 |
| Kungur | Sinkiang (China) | 25,325 |
| Tirich Mir | Pakistan | 25,230 |
| Makalu II | Nepal-Tibet | 25,130 |
| Minya Konka | China | 24,900 |
| Kula Gangri | Tibet-Bhutan | 24,784 |
| Changtse | Nepal-Tibet | 24,780 |
| Muztagh Ata | Sinkiang (China) | 24,757 |
| Skyang Kangri | Kashmir | 24,750 |
| Communism Peak | U.S.S.R. | 24,590 |
| Jongsong Peak | Nepal-Sikkim | 24,472 |
| Pobedy Peak | China-U.S.S.R. | 24,406 |
| Haramosh Peak | Pakistan | 24,272 |
| Sia Kangri | Kashmir | 24,350 |
| Istoro Nal | Pakistan | 24,240 |
| Tent Peak | Nepal-Sikkim | 24,088 |

(continuing right column of Asia peaks)

| NAME | LOCATION | FEET |
|---|---|---|
| Nunkun | Kashmir | 23,410 |
| Lenin Peak | U.S.S.R. | 23,405 |
| Pyramid Peak | Nepal-Sikkim | 23,400 |
| Api | Nepal | 23,399 |
| Trisul | India | 23,360 |

### Highest Peaks in Africa

| NAME | LOCATION | FEET |
|---|---|---|
| Kilimanjaro (two peaks) | Tanganyika | |
| Mt. Kibo | | 19,340 |
| Mt. Mawenzi | | 16,896 |
| Kenya | Kenya | 17,058 |
| Ruwenzori | Uganda–Republic of the Congo | 16,763 |
| Ras Dashan | Ethiopia | 15,158 |
| Meru | Tanganyika | 14,979 |
| Buahit | Ethiopia | 14,797 |
| Karisimbi | Rwanda–Republic of the Congo | 14,787 |

### Highest Peaks in Australia, Australasia, and Antarctica

| NAME | LOCATION | FEET |
|---|---|---|
| Vinson Massif | Antarctica | 16,860† |
| Carstensz | New Guinea | 16,500 |
| Tyree | Antarctica | 16,290 |
| Idenburg | New Guinea | 15,748 |
| Wilhelmina | New Guinea | 15,585 |
| Juliana | New Guinea | 15,420 |
| Wilhelm | New Guinea | 15,400 |
| Kirkpatrick | Antarctica | 14,800 |
| Markham | Antarctica | 14,270 |
| Andrew Jackson | Antarctica | 13,750 |
| Fridtjof Nansen | Antarctica | 13,700 |
| Miller | Antarctica | 13,600 |
| Kinabalu | Malaysia | 13,455 |
| Wade | Antarctica | 13,350 |
| Kerintji | Sumatra | 12,484 |
| Erebus | Antarctica | 12,450 |
| Cook | New Zealand | 12,349 |
| Hawkes | Antarctica | 12,000 |
| Habermehl | Antarctica | 10,830 |
| Ulmer | Antarctica | 9,100 |
| Kosciusko | Australia | 7,316 |

† Estimated.

### Highest Peaks in Europe

| NAME | FEET | NAME | FEET | NAME | FEET |
|---|---|---|---|---|---|
| **The Caucasus** | | Täschhorn | 14,733 | Strahlhorn | 13,747 |
| El'brus | 18,481 | Matterhorn | 14,690 | Dent d'Hérens | 13,686 |
| Shkara | 17,064 | Dent Blanche | 14,293 | Breithorn | 13,665 |
| Dykh Tau | 17,054 | Nadelhorn | 14,196 | Bishorn | 13,645 |
| Kashtan Tau | 16,877 | Grand Combin | 14,154 | Jungfrau | 13,642 |
| Dzhangi Tau | 16,565 | Lenzspitze | 14,088 | Ecrins | 13,461 |
| Kazbek | 16,558 | Finsteraarhorn | 14,022 | Mönch | 13,448 |
| | | Castor | 13,865 | Pollux | 13,422 |
| **The Alps** | | Zinalrothorn | 13,849 | Schreckhorn | 13,379 |
| Mont Blanc | 15,771 | Hohberghorn | 13,842 | Ober Gabelhorn | 13,330 |
| Monte Rosa | 15,203 | Alphubelhorn | 13,799 | Gran Paradiso | 13,323 |
| Dom | 14,913 | Rimpfischhorn | 13,776 | Bernina | 13,284 |
| Weisshorn | 14,782 | Aletschhorn | 13,763 | Fiescherhorn | 13,283 |

# NOTABLE FEATS OF MOUNTAINEERING

| YEAR | ACHIEVEMENT |
|------|-------------|
| 1786...... | Dr. Michel G. Paccard and Jacques Balmat, Alpine climbers, made the first ascent of Mont Blanc. |
| 1787...... | Horace Bénédict de Saussure made the third ascent of Mont Blanc after inspiring previous attempts. |
| 1802...... | Ramond de Carbonnières explored the Pyrenees, making the first ascent of Mont Perdu. |
| 1811, 1812 | The brothers Johann and Hieronymus Meyer, Alpine climbers, made the first and second ascents of the Jungfrau and later made the first ascent of the Finsteraarhorn. |
| 1855...... | Charles Hudson, Alpine climber, made the first ascent of Monte Rosa and the first guideless ascent of Mont Blanc; killed in the Matterhorn disaster of 1865. |
| 1856–1911 | Thomas George Bonney, mountaineer and geologist, made about 110 Alpine ascents. |
| 1859...... | John Tyndall, Alpine climber, spent 20 hours on the summit of Mont Blanc carrying out scientific work. |
| 1865...... | Edward Whymper first conquered the Matterhorn, in the Alps; in 1880, he climbed Chimborazo and, in 1897, Aconcagua and Tupungato, all in Andes. |
| 1865–95... | William A. B. Coolidge made more than 1,500 Alpine ascents. |
| 1868...... | Douglas W. Freshfield first conquered the peaks of El'brus and Kazbek, in Caucasus. |
| 1870...... | Leslie Stephen and Melchior Anderegg, Alpine climbers, made the first ascents of the Alphubelhorn and the Blumlisalphorn; Stephen also climbed the Schreckhorn. |
| 1871...... | Lucy Walker became the first woman to ascend the Matterhorn. |
| 1878...... | Thomas Clinton Dent, Alpine climber, made the first ascent of the Aiguillé du Dru after 18 unsuccessful attempts. |
| 1880s..... | William Cecil Slingsby made several first ascents of Norwegian mountains  He also made many ascents of mountains in England's lake district and in Scotland. |
| 1891, 1894 | Sven Hedin climbed Demavend in Persia and later scaled Muztagh Ata in the Himalayas to a record height. |
| 1892....... | Martin Conway led the first major expedition to the Karakoram mountains in Kashmir and there ascended Pioneer Peak. |
| 1894, 1897 | Duke of the Abruzzi climbed the Matterhorn with Albert Frederick Mummery and John Norman Collie. Three years later he made the first ascent of Mount St. Elias, Alaska, and in 1906 he led the first major mountaineering expedition to the Ruwenzori of Africa. |
| 1895...... | Albert Frederick Mummery made the first attempt on Nanga Parbat in the Himalayas with Charles Granville Bruce and John Norman Collie. He also made seven ascents of the Matterhorn. |
| 1901...... | James Outram made the first ascent of Mount Assiniboine, in Canadian Rockies. |
| 1907...... | Tom George Longstaff was the first to climb Trisul, in Himalayas. |
| 1921...... | George Leigh Mallory, a member of the first expedition to reconnoiter Mount Everest, disappeared in the 1924 attempt to climb the mountain. It was he who remarked that men attempted to climb Mount Everest "because it is there." |

| YEAR | ACHIEVEMENT |
|------|-------------|
| 1931, 1951– 1952.... | Eric Shipton reached the summit of Kamet in the Himalayas, then the highest mountain climbed. Later he led expeditions that confirmed a southern route to the summit of Everest. |
| 1932...... | Terris Moore made the first ascent of Minya Konka in Sikang Province, China. |
| 1935...... | John Hunt climbed K36 in the Karakoram and in the following year made the first ascent of the south face of Kolahoi, Kashmir. He planned the successful 1953 Everest expedition. |
| 1935...... | Harold William Tilman, in Africa, climbed Mount Kenya, Mount Kilimanjaro, and the Ruwenzori. He took part in the Anglo-American expedition to Nanda Devi, in Himalayas. |
| 1950...... | Louis Lachenal, Maurice Herzog, and Lionel Terray made the first ascent of Annapurna, in Himalayas. |
| 1951...... | Tenzing Norkay climbed the east peak of Nanda Devi with a French expedition. |
| 1953...... | Edmund Hillary and Tenzing Norkay made the historic first ascent of Mount Everest, in Himalayas, the highest mountain in the world. |
| 1953...... | Dr. Charles Evans, deputy leader of the Everest expedition and a member of the first assault party, reached the south summit of Mount Everest with Tom Bourdillon. |
| 1953...... | Herman Buhl made the solitary and unparalleled first ascent of Nanga Parbat. |
| 1954...... | Ardito Desio led 11 expeditions, the most important being the conquest of K2, in Himalayas, the second highest mountain in the world. He was accompanied by Lino Lacedelli and Achille Compagnoni. |
| 1954...... | Edmund Hillary climbed Baruntse, in Himalayas. |
| 1956...... | Joe Brown and John M. Hartog reached the summit of the Muztagh Tower, in the Himalayas. |
| 1956...... | Ernst Reiss and Fritz Luchsinger conquered Lhotse I, in Himalayas. |
| 1961...... | An Italian team scaled the south face of Mount McKinley, Alaska. |
| 1961...... | A German-Austrian team made the first winter ascent of the north face of Mount Eiger, in the Alps. |
| 1963...... | Paul Etter and three Swiss climbers scaled and then made the dangerous descent of the mile-high north face of Mount Eiger. |
| 1963...... | Members of an American expedition, led by Norman B. Dyhrenfurth, sponsored by the National Geographic Society, made successful climbs of Mount Everest. |
| 1965...... | Members of an Indian team scaled Mount Everest four times in May. |
| 1965...... | Yvette Vaucher, a Swiss mountain climber, became the first woman to climb the sheer north wall of the Matterhorn. |
| 1966...... | German team scaled sheer north face of the Eiger in the Swiss Alps. |
| 1966...... | Nicholas B. Clinche and 10-man American team climbed the Vinson Massif in Antarctica—the last highest point on a continent to be climbed. |

## GREAT VOLCANOES OF THE WORLD
Source: National Geographic Society

More than 500,000 square miles of the Earth's surface has been scarred, within historical time, by molten lava, rocks, cinders, ash, or gases expelled by volcanoes. Although many volcanoes can be recognized by their graceful, cone-shaped mountains—such as the revered Fuji of Japan—others lack prominent cones and are typified by sluggish lava flows emerging from long cracks, or fissures, as in Hawaii.

About 600 active and 10,000 inactive or dormant volcanoes are found along three belts, closely matching the earthquake regions of the world. The circum-Pacific belt, or "ring of fire," includes the Pacific coasts of North and South America as well as Asia. The second belt extends from the Mediterranean to the East Indies. The third lies along the crest of the world's longest mountain chain—the mid-ocean ridge connecting the major oceans of the world.

Volcanic activity is deceptively sporadic—brief periods of outgassing or eruption, followed by unpredictably longer periods of dormancy. History tragically reveals that many societies have been devastated by presumably extinct volcanoes. The classic eruption of Vesuvius, burying Pompeii in 79 A.D., is but one example.

Recent investigation of such dormant volcanoes—sleeping giants—in the state of Washington has raised concern for the hazards presented by Mt. Rainier and neighboring Mts. Shasta, Hood, and St. Helens. The latter erupted about 450 years ago; Mt. Rainier, still steaming from time to time, has a consistent record of eruption every 500 to 1,000 years. A typical eruption of Rainier, statistically overdue, might not be too great, but the resulting floods and avalanches caused by its debris and melted glaciers would indeed be devastating.

Washington State's Mt. Rainier

*National Park Service*

The floor of the Pacific Ocean is dotted with many lava cones that are completely submerged. When they erupt, shock waves are created in the ocean, causing great tidal waves called *tsunami*. The islands of New Guinea, New Zealand, and most of their attendant small islands are built from volcanoes that have grown from the ocean floor.

From the smallest cinder cone measuring less than 100 feet high, to the gigantic shield volcanoes of the Pacific that rise as much as five miles from the ocean floor, volcanoes aid in shaping the face of the Earth—and the destinies of its peoples.

Key to letters: (E) Last eruption, with year in parentheses; (R) Rumbling; (St) Steaming; (D) Dormant.

| NAME | LOCATION | HEIGHT (in feet) | NAME | LOCATION | HEIGHT (in feet) |
|---|---|---|---|---|---|
| **Africa** | | | Tolbachik (E-1941)...... | U.S.S.R. | 12,080 |
| Kibo (Kilimanjaro) (D)... | Tanganyika (Tanzania) | 19,340 | Semeru (E-1960)........ | Indonesia | 12,060 |
| | | | Ichinskiy (St)........... | U.S.S.R. | 11,880 |
| Cameroun Mt. (E-1959).. | Cameroun | 13,350 | Kronotskaya (D)........ | U S.S.R. | 11,575 |
| Nyiragongo (E-1948)..... | Republic of the Congo | 11,385 | Koryakskaya (E-1957).... | U.S.S.R. | 11,339 |
| | | | Slamat (E-1953)......... | Indonesia | 11,247 |
| Nyamlagira (E-1958)...... | Republic of the Congo | 10,028 | Raung (St)............. | Indonesia | 10,932 |
| | | | Shiveluchskaya (D)...... | U.S.S.R. | 10,771 |
| Fogo (E-1951)........... | Cape Verde Islands | 9,281 | Dempo (St)............. | Indonesia | 10,364 |
| | | | Welirang (D)........... | Indonesia | 10,354 |
| Tristan da Cunha (E-1961) | South Atlantic Ocean | 6,760 | Agung (E-1964)........ | Indonesia | 10,308 |
| | | | Sundoro (D)............ | Indonesia | 10,285 |
| San Juan (D)........... | La Palma, Canary Islands | 2,612 | Tjareme (E-1938)........ | Indonesia | 10,098 |
| | | | Gede (E-1949)........... | Indonesia | 9,705 |
| **Antarctica** | | | Apo (D)................ | Philippines | 9,690 |
| Erebus (St)............. | | 12,450 | Merapi (E-1962)........ | Indonesia | 9,551 |
| **Asia and Australasia** | | | Bezymyannaya (E-1961).. | U.S.S.R. | 9,514 |
| Klyuchevskaya (E-1962).. | U.S.S.R. | 15,584 | Marapi (D)............. | Indonesia | 9,485 |
| Kerintji (St)............. | Indonesia | 12,484 | Tambora (D)............ | Indonesia | 9,353 |
| Fuji (D)................ | Japan | 12,388 | Ruapehu (E-1950)....... | New Zealand | 9,175 |
| Rindjani (E-1964)........ | Indonesia | 12,224 | Peuëtsagoë (D).......... | Indonesia | 9,121 |
| | | | Avachinskaya (St)....... | U.S.S.R. | 9,026 |

| NAME | LOCATION | HEIGHT (in feet) |
|---|---|---|
| Balbi (D) | Solomons | 9,000 |
| Papandajan (St) | Indonesia | 8,602 |
| Guereudong (E-1924) | Indonesia | 8,497 |
| Asama (E-1961) | Japan | 8,340 |
| Mayon (E-1947) | Philippines | 8,284 |
| Sumbing (E-1926) | Indonesia | 8,225 |
| Tandikat (E-1924) | Indonesia | 8,166 |
| Yake Dake (E-1962) | Japan | 8,064 |
| Sinabung (St) | Indonesia | 7,913 |
| Bromo (St) | Indonesia | 7,848 |
| Idjen (D) | Indonesia | 7,828 |
| Ulawun (D) | New Britain | 7,532 |
| Ngauruhoe (E-1956) | New Zealand | 7,515 |
| Guntur (D) | Indonesia | 7,379 |
| Bamus (D) | New Britain | 7,338 |
| Galunggung (E-1920) | Indonesia | 7,113 |
| Amburombu (E-1924) | Indonesia | 7,051 |
| Sorikmarapi (E-1917) | Indonesia | 7,037 |
| Petarangan (E-1939) | Indonesia | 7,005 |
| Sibajak (St) | Indonesia | 6,870 |
| Tokachi (E-1962) | Japan | 6,813 |
| Tangkubanperahu (R) | Indonesia | 6,637 |
| Bagana (St) | Solomons | 6,560 |
| Tongariro (E-1950) | New Zealand | 6,458 |
| Sangeang (E-1953) | Indonesia | 6,394 |
| Kaba (E-1941) | Indonesia | 6,358 |
| Awu (E-1931) | Indonesia | 6,102 |
| Soputan (E-1947) | Indonesia | 5,994 |
| Siau (E-1949) | Indonesia | 5,853 |
| Kelud (E-1966) | Indonesia | 5,679 |
| Batur (E-1963) | Indonesia | 5,636 |
| Belerang (St) | Indonesia | 5,636 |
| Ternate (E-1938) | Indonesia | 5,627 |
| Hibok Hibok (E-1960) | Philippines | 5,619 |
| Lewotobi Perampuan (E-1935) | Indonesia | 5,591 |
| Kirishima (St) | Japan | 5,577 |
| Mutu (D) | Indonesia | 5,545 |
| Lamongan (St) | Indonesia | 5,482 |
| Boleng (E-1950) | Indonesia | 5,443 |
| Gamkonora (E-1949) | Indonesia | 5,364 |
| Aso (E-1958) | Japan | 5,223 |
| Lewotobi Lakilaki (E-1940) | Indonesia | 5,217 |
| Lokon (D) | Indonesia | 5,184 |
| Bulusan (E-1962) | Philippines | 5,115 |
| Sarycheva (E-1960) | Kuril Islands, U.S.S.R. | 4,960 |
| Meakan (E-1959) | Japan | 4,931 |
| Ibu (D) | Indonesia | 4,921 |
| Karymskaya (E-1963) | U.S.S.R. | 4,869 |
| Lopevi (E-1960) | New Hebrides | 4,755 |
| Ambrim (E-1951) | New Hebrides | 4,376 |
| Mahawu (D) | Indonesia | 4,367 |
| Long Island (E-1953) | Bismarck Archipelago | 4,278 |
| Manam (E-1960) | Bismarck Archipelago, New Guinea | 4,265 |
| Tongkoko (D) | Indonesia | 3,770 |
| Werung (E-1948) | Indonesia | 3,678 |
| Langla (E-1961) | New Britain | 3,586 |
| Dukono (E-1950) | Indonesia | 3,566 |
| Lamington (E-1951) | New Guinea | 3,500 |
| Minami (E-1963) | Japan | 3,478 |
| Yasur (R) | New Hebrides | 3,420 |
| Lolobau (D) | Bismarck Archipelago | 3,058 |
| Asuncion (St) | Marianas | 2,923 |
| Paloë (E-1964) | Indonesia | 2,871 |
| Sirung (E-1947) | Indonesia | 2,828 |

| NAME | LOCATION | HEIGHT (in feet) |
|---|---|---|
| **Mid-Pacific** | | |
| Mauna Loa (E-1950) | Hawaii | 13,680 |
| Kilauea (E-1963) | Hawaii | 4,090 |
| **Europe** | | |
| Etna (E-1966) | Sicily, Italy | 10,705 |
| Askja (E-1961) | Iceland | 4,954 |
| Hekla (St) | Iceland | 4,892 |
| Vesuvius (St) | Italy | 4,190 |
| Stromboli (E-1966) | Lipari Islands, Italy | 3,038 |
| **North America** | | |
| Popocatepetl (St) | Mexico | 17,887 |
| Wrangell (St) | Alaska | 14,005 |
| Colima (E-1962) | Mexico | 13,993 |
| Spurr (E-1953) | Alaska | 11,069 |
| Torbert (E-1953) | Alaska | 10,600 |
| Lassen (D) | California | 10,457 |
| Redoubt (E-1966) | Alaska | 10,197 |
| Iliamna (St) | Alaska | 10,092 |
| Shishaldin (St) | Aleutians | 9,387 |
| Veniaminof (D) | Alaska | 8,225 |
| Pavlof (E-1950) | Alaska | 8,215 |
| Griggs (St) | Alaska | 7,600 |
| Paricutín (D) | Mexico | 7,451 |
| Mageik (St) | Alaska | 7,244 |
| Douglas (St) | Alaska | 7,064 |
| Chiginagak (D) | Alaska | 7,031 |
| Katmai (E-1962) | Alaska | 6,715 |
| Kukak (St) | Alaska | 6,700 |
| Makushin (D) | Aleutians | 6,680 |
| Pogromni (E-1964) | Aleutians | 6,568 |
| Martin (E-1960) | Alaska | 6,100 |
| Trident (E-1963) | Alaska | 6,010 |
| Tanaga (D) | Aleutians | 5,925 |
| Great Sitkin (St) | Aleutians | 5,710 |
| Cleveland (E-1944) | Aleutians | 5,675 |
| Gareloi (D) | Aleutians | 5,334 |
| Korovin (D) | Aleutians | 4,852 |
| Kanaga (D) | Aleutians | 4,416 |
| Aniakchak (D) | Alaska | 4,275 |
| Akutan (E-1952) | Aleutians | 4,275 |
| Kiska (E-1962) | Aleutians | 4,004 |
| **Central America and Caribbean** | | |
| Tajumulco (R) | Guatemala | 13,812 |
| Tacaná (R) | Guatemala | 13,333 |
| Acatenango (R) | Guatemala | 12,992 |
| Fuego (E-1962) | Guatemala | 12,582 |
| Santa Maria (R) | Guatemala | 12,362 |
| Atitlan (R) | Guatemala | 11,565 |
| Irazú (E-1964) | Costa Rica | 11,260 |
| San Pedro (R) | Guatemala | 9,921 |
| Poás (St) | Costa Rica | 8,930 |
| Pacaya (E-1961) | Guatemala | 8,346 |
| Izalco (E-1957) | El Salvador | 7,828 |
| San Miguel (St) | El Salvador | 6,994 |
| Ometepe (Concepción) (E-1957) | Nicaragua | 5,106 |
| **South America** | | |
| Guallatiri (E-1959) | Chile | 19,882 |
| Lascar (E-1951) | Chile | 19,652 |
| Cotopaxi (St) | Ecuador | 19,347 |
| Misti (D) | Peru | 19,031 |
| Tupungatito (E-1959) | Chile | 18,504 |
| Sangay (E-1946) | Ecuador | 17,159 |
| Tungurahua (R) | Ecuador | 16,512 |
| Cotacachi (E-1955) | Ecuador | 16,197 |
| Pichincha (D) | Ecuador | 15,712 |
| Purace (E-1950) | Colombia | 15,604 |
| Lautaro (St) | Chile | 11,090 |
| Llaima (E-1955) | Chile | 10,239 |
| Villarrica (E-1964) | Chile | 9,318 |

## PRINCIPAL DESERTS OF THE WORLD

Once simply used for an uninhabited—"deserted"—place, the term *desert* is now commonly applied to regions characterized by meager rainfall, scanty vegetation, and limited human use. However, of the three types of deserts commonly recognized, only a few *tropical* deserts, such as the Libyan part of the Sahara, resemble the popular image of a hot, dry, sandy expanse. *Middle latitude* deserts lie in the "rainshadow" of a mountain barrier (as deserts in the southwestern U.S.), or deep within the moisture-starved interiors of continents (the Gobi). *Polar* deserts occur because moisture is "locked up" as ice and snow.

SATOUR

Kalahari Desert, South West Africa

| DESERT | LOCATION | APPROXIMATE SIZE | REMARKS |
|---|---|---|---|
| Atacama | Northern Chile | 600 miles long | An area of rich nitrate and copper deposits. |
| Black Rock | Humboldt and Pershing counties, Nevada | An area of 1,000 square miles | A barren plain practically devoid of vegetation; from its surface, alkaline dust is blown into vast clouds by the summer winds. |
| Colorado | Arid region of southeastern California | 200 miles long; maximum width of 50 miles | The soil of its Imperial Valley is highly productive when irrigated. |
| Dasht i Kavîr | Iran, from the Caspian Sea to the Persian Gulf | 300 miles long; 100 miles wide | Saline swamps and dry salt areas. |
| Death Valley | Eastern California and southwestern Nevada | 2,936 square miles | Yielded much borax in the 19th century. |
| Kara Kum | Asiatic Russia | 110,000 square miles | The Kara Kum has a number of "old river beds" which may have been either channels or tributaries of the Amu and other rivers. |
| Kizil-Kum | Asiatic Russia, in the Kazakhstan, U.S.S.R. | 370 by 220 miles | The surface is characterized by stationary sands with sparse vegetation. |
| Negev | Southern Israel | 4,700 square miles | Barren expanses of sand, now dotted with prosperous farms, orchards, and towns. King Solomon's mines and the Dead Sea are here. |
| Namib | Southwest Africa | 800 miles long, 30–100 miles wide | Long, narrow desert plain along Atlantic coast. |
| Sahara | North Africa; on the west the desert extends to the Atlantic Coast | Over 3,000,000 square miles | Nomadic herding is still an important activity in the desert, but in recent years there has been petroleum extraction. The Libyan and Nubian deserts are part of the Sahara. |
| Gobi | Extends 1,500 miles from Manchuria to Sinkiang Province, China | 500,000 square miles | Many paleontological finds, including dinosaur eggs, have been made here. |
| Syrian | Occupies the whole of northern Arabia above lat. 30° N | —— | The oasis of Jauf has extensive palm groves and a population of more than 10,000. |
| The Nufud | Arabia; a short distance south of Jauf | An average width of 200 miles | During the spring season it is the habitat of Bedouins. |
| Rub al-Khali (Empty Quarter) | Southern Arabia | 300,000 square miles | Practically unexplored; it may contain large tracts of hard gravel or limestone deposits. |
| Great Australian | Much of central and western Australia | —— | Primitive Bushmen live in this area, which Australians prefer to call "Sparselands." |
| Kalahari | South Africa; the Orange River marks its southern limit | 120,000 square miles | Hottentots and Bushmen inhabit the area. |
| Mohave | Southern California; northeast of Los Angeles extends into Mohave County, Arizona | 15,000 square miles | Needles, on the Arizona-California boundary, is one of the hottest towns in the United States. |
| Painted Desert | Coconino and Navajo counties in northern Arizona | 200 miles long and from 15 to 30 miles wide | Within the desert are seven Hopi villages. The Painted Desert is so called because of its coloring, caused by centuries of erosion exposing brilliantly colored rock formations. |
| Taklamakan | Central Asia, in the Chinese province of Sinkiang | 125,000 square miles | Ancient trade routes cross this desert, and there are reports of buried cities. The Chinese exploded their first atomic bomb here in 1964. |
| Thar (Indian) | Northwestern India, between the Gulf of Cutch and the Arabian Sea on the south | 100,000 square miles | Camel caravans still traverse the desert. Parts of the Thar are disputed between India and Pakistan. |

## TEKTITES: MYSTERY MATTER FROM OUTER SPACE

If somebody tried to sell you a rock from the Moon, Mars, or points beyond, chances are you would direct him to the nearest police station.

It could be a rash decision. Many scientists believe that we may have a vast amount of "outer space," or extraterrestrial, material right here on Earth. One example of such material: curious glassy objects called "tektites," some of which may have been shed by the Moon.

Usually about the size of ordinary gravel, tektites are found in widely separated regions of the world known as "strewnfields." Their chemical makeup resembles nothing else on Earth, but the most intriguing aspect of these tektites is the fact that most are "aerodynamically sculpted"—their surfaces are etched and pitted from friction with the atmosphere (a process called *ablation*). Thus, whatever their origin, tektites reached the Earth only after a fiery, high-speed journey through our atmosphere. The ablation surfaces of many tektites have been artificially duplicated in wind tunnels; these artificial tektites are remarkably similar to the real thing.

"Microtektites," so called because of their small size, have been found in great quantity on the floors of the Indian and western Pacific oceans. This miniscule variety has been linked to the cataclysmic disintegration of a cosmic body that was about a mile in diameter and may have weighed as much as one billion tons. Its arrival on Earth, about 700,000 years ago, apparently coincided with a reversal of the Earth's magnetic poles. Drs. Bruce Heezen and Billy Glass of the Lamont Geological Observatory in New York suspect that the apparent relationship of the microtektites to that long-ago magnetic flip-over is not merely accidental. But what causes a magnetic pole reversal (an event that has occurred several times previously in the geologic past) remains a mystery. Nor can scientists predict when—if ever—the Earth will do another magnetic somersault.

A preliminary chemical analysis of a portion of the Moon's surfaces, relayed by Surveyor V in late September, 1967, ruled out the possibility that tektites had originated there. This historic analysis indicated that the Sea of Tranquility, and probably most of the Moon's other "seas," are composed of basalt—the most common volcanic rock

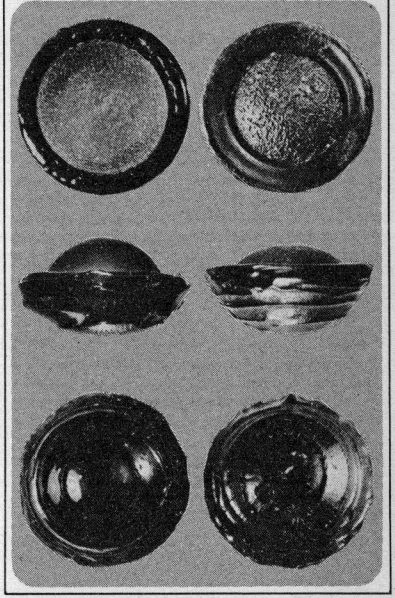

Natural tektites (left) bear a strong resemblance to those produced in a wind tunnel (right).

Ames Research Center

on the Earth's surface. This was a setback to proponents of the lunar origin of tektites, but a boost to those who have felt that other extraterrestrial material has come from the Moon. For example, Dr. Michael Duke of the United States Geological Survey had earlier suggested that the type of meteorites called *basaltic achondrites* had a lunar origin. Future flights in the Surveyor series may help to refine these still tentative scientific opinions.

In the meantime, the search goes on for the extraterrestrial source of the puzzling tektites. Although they are quite rare in the United States, it is possible that new ones could turn up almost anywhere. Each new finding becomes an important piece of evidence in the unsolved mystery. The final solution to the riddle may well provide new insights into the origin of the Earth, the Moon, and the more remote outposts of the solar system.

# WEATHER

The weather reflects changes in the state of the Earth's atmosphere. The properties of the atmosphere that essentially determine weather are its temperature or energy distribution; its composition, including variable amounts of water vapor; and the air's motions, which transport heat and moisture and largely control condensation. Condensation of water vapor in the atmosphere is most frequently caused by upward motion of the air. As it moves up it is brought into regions of lower pressure and cooled by expansion to its dew-point temperature, at which it condenses.

The atmosphere may be regarded as a giant heat engine, powered by radiant energy from the Sun. Because the Earth is a sphere, it receives most radiation around the equator where the Sun's rays strike the surface directly. Since air is relatively transparent to solar radiation, most of the energy not reflected by clouds passes through the atmosphere to be absorbed at the Earth's surface. The temperature differences thus set up between the equatorial and polar regions, and between the Earth's surface and the air above it, result in convection, a process familiar to anyone who has opened a window at both bottom and top to cool an overheated room. If the Earth did not rotate, heated air would rise at the equator, flow poleward aloft, cool and sink near the poles, and return along the Earth's surface to the equator. However, the air currents set up by convection are turned by the Earth's rotation, so that they flow more nearly along the parallels to the equator than across them. The air drifting poleward cools by radiation to space and sinks near latitude 30 degrees. Part of this sinking air supplies the trade winds and another part the prevailing westerlies of middle latitudes, as shown in the chart of the Earth's general air circulation.

One of the consequences of this circulation is that warm, moist air from the tropics is brought next to cooler, drier air at middle latitudes, creating a boundary of sharp temperature contrast called the polar front (see chart). This collision of air masses of different temperature and moisture is unstable. Disturbances in the flow of the wind on either side of the polar front develop into cyclones, which move in an easterly direction as the familiar low-pressure areas seen on the daily weather map. As a large cyclonic disturbance develops, the warm air rises and is carried away by strong winds aloft, resulting in low pressure. Surface air flows inward toward the low-pressure center. This air is turned aside by the Earth's rotation so that the winds blow, in the Northern Hemisphere, in a counterclockwise direction around the center. The sinking cold air mass, contributing to high pressure, flows outward from a center and consequently develops rotation in the opposite or clockwise direction, producing the anticyclone that usually accompanies a cyclone.

The weather of middle and high latitudes, like the United States, is dominated largely by the cyclones and anticyclones that develop and travel along the polar front, which shifts northward and southward with changes in the circulation of the air and with the seasons. In midsummer, the average location of the polar front, and of the associated cyclone tracks, is north of the United States-Canadian border, but in midwinter its average position is as far south as the Gulf of Mexico. Typical weather changes are brought by the passage of a cyclone, with its warm and cold fronts. Layer or stratus clouds are produced as the warm, moist air mass glides upward over the warm-front surface. These clouds usually yield steady rain or snow. Vertically developed or cumulus clouds form in the warm air mass, or at the advancing edges of the cold front where the air is forced abruptly upward. These produce showers or may develop into thunderstorms. Tornadoes occur most frequently within lines of severe thunderstorms, called squall lines, that develop in spring and early summer when cold, dry polar air aloft overruns a current of warm, moist tropical air somewhat in advance of a cold front.

In summer and early fall, occasional tropical cyclones or hurricanes affect the eastern United States. Tropical cyclones may form in the intertropical convergence zone (see chart) created by the trade winds of the two hemispheres, or within disturbances in the trade winds known as easterly waves. Drifting westward and northward, Atlantic hurricanes gradually recurve eastward as they enter the region of prevailing westerlies. Land and water contrasts produce sea breezes in coastal areas. Other topographic features such as mountain ranges introduce many variations in the weather patterns associated with traveling disturbances.

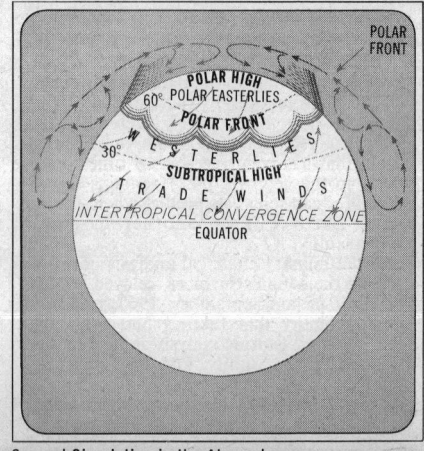

General Circulation in the Atmosphere

## WEATHER FORECASTING

The traditionally subjective "art" of weather forecasting has become increasingly an objective science. Since the 1940s, weathermen have been learning to approximate the atmosphere mathematically, translating the subjective vocabulary about the weather into the objective language of electronic computers. A new technology—one that uses artificial earth satellites, weather radar, automated weather stations, high-speed communications systems, and increasing computer applications—is producing a quantity and coverage of weather information unknown to weathermen ten years ago.

The fundamental physical laws governing atmospheric occurrences were formulated in the 19th century as complex mathematical formulas that expressed atmospheric motions, but their practical use needed today's electronic computers. As computers have improved, so have man's analyses of the atmosphere. Mathematical weather prediction models now in routine daily use are so complex that they tax the speed and capacity of the largest available electronic computers. Using information gathered from a worldwide network of weather balloon observations of pressure, temperature, wind, and moisture, supplemented by data from airborne and satellite-borne instruments, electronic computers calculate the pressure and wind flow for the entire northern hemisphere from the Earth's surface to 100,000 feet. Computer-driven plotting machines draw weather maps, from which surface and intermediate-altitude conditions can be determined.

Local weather forecasts are dependent on these computer forecasts and are refined by the addition of data on the surface and upper air, radar data, and other data gathered from a dense network of stations within 1,000 to 2,000 miles of the forecast area. Because the weather is so dependent on geography and terrain, each community has its special weather features with which the mathematical model and the computer have been unable to cope as yet. The forecaster, well trained in the science of meteorology and familiar with local terrain and geography, is required to tailor weather forecasts to local needs.

To make our weather forecasts more useful, new methods of communicating weather information are being introduced. A good example is the probability forecast, recently added to precipitation forecasts in many parts of the United States. These are based on comparisons of present weather patterns with similar patterns in the past, which relate the likelihood of rain or snow mathematically. Probability forecasting is proving useful because it clearly states the uncertainty in the weather forecasts.

Again, weathermen are using the improved computer-prepared basic forecasts of wind, pressure, and temperature to provide specialized weather services—services tailored to interpret expected weather conditions in terms of their effects on particular activities. Marine, agriculture, and aviation forecasts are examples of this. Investigations in the laboratory and the field are also improving the understanding of severe storms.

Theoretically, it should be possible to refine our knowledge of the atmosphere to a point where reliable prediction can be obtained for several weeks in advance. The practical possibilities of accurate long-range weather forecasts will depend on our ability to obtain adequate observations from the entire globe. The weather satellite now offers hope of acquiring such observations and the nations of the world have joined in a vast new effort to establish a World Weather Watch whose objective is exactly that. It will also be necessary to understand the interactions between the atmosphere and ocean and to treat them as indivisible.

Research in changing and controlling weather has increased substantially in the past several years. There is a growing confidence on the part of many scientists that certain types of weather modification are feasible. Already fogs are being dissipated as part of the operational routine of some airlines. There is growing evidence that we may, under certain conditions, increase rain or snow. Severe storms such as hurricanes are being explored and used as natural laboratories for the testing of ideas for changing weather. Only time and extensive systematic scientific research will fully tell in what ways we can beneficially affect the weather.

## BEAUFORT SCALE

In 1806, a British naval officer named Sir Francis Beaufort created a scale of numbers to indicate wind strength from a calm to a hurricane. The World Meteorological Organization (WMO) adopted this Beaufort scale for use by all its members in 1949. The following table correlates the scale (often given in F or Force numbers, such as Force 12 for a hurricane) with terms describing the wind strength and a series of increasing wind velocities.

| SCALE AND DESCRIPTION | VELOCITY (in miles per hour) | SCALE AND DESCRIPTION | VELOCITY (in miles per hour) | SCALE AND DESCRIPTION | VELOCITY (in miles per hour) |
|---|---|---|---|---|---|
| 0 Calm | Less than 1 | 5 Fresh breeze | 19 to 24 | 9 Strong gale | 47 to 54 |
| 1 Light air | 1 to 3 | 6 Strong breeze | 25 to 31 | 10 Storm | 55 to 63 |
| 2 Light breeze | 4 to 7 | 7 Near gale | 32 to 38 | 11 Violent storm | 64 to 72 |
| 3 Gentle breeze | 8 to 12 | 8 Gale | 39 to 46 | 12 Hurricane | 73 and over |
| 4 Moderate breeze | 13 to 18 | | | | |

# LIFE ON EARTH

## EMERGENCE OF LIFE

Fossil signs and other evidence indicate that life began on this Earth between two and three billion years ago. During that period the first primitive life, probably a single-celled form, evolved and incorporated features of greater complexity and power. With the development of bipeds and of a complex brain, this life reached a stage of evolution at which it began, only within the past few thousand years, to ask of itself the question of its own origin.

In the nineteenth century the controversy waxed hot over the concept of spontaneous generation or life coming into being spontaneously. Louis Pasteur showed that the kinds of experiments that others had used to demonstrate spontaneous generation were faulty. Pasteur's experiments have been cited as having disproved the concept of spontaneous generation, but what they really showed was that other experiments had not demonstrated spontaneous generation. In his later years Pasteur indicated that spontaneous generation was not to be regarded as an impossibility. In the late 1920s, A. I. Oparin, a Russian biochemist, first presented his theory explaining how, by the principles of organic chemistry, life might have originated on the Earth.

In the 1950s the first experiments to test the ideas of Oparin and others were performed. The first experiments showing that inorganic materials could be converted to organic materials under conditions that might have existed on the primitive Earth were those of Melvin Calvin and his associates at the University of California at Berkeley. Calvin submitted gases, carbon dioxide, and water to the high energy radiation of an atom smasher and found that organic compounds like formaldehyde and formic acid were formed. Two years later, Stanley Miller, a graduate student working with Dr. Harold Urey, passed electric sparks into a mixture of gases of the type that Oparin supposed were present on the primitive Earth and obtained in the reaction mixture four of the 18 to 20 amino acids, the building blocks of the proteins essential to life. Some of the compounds based on nitrogen that go to make up elements in the cell nucleus have also been formed under comparable conditions. Methods by which the sugars might have arisen spontaneously on the primitive Earth have also been demonstrated in the laboratory. Harada and Fox showed in 1963 how the passage of gases, such as are found in volcanoes, through tubes containing the silica common in the crust of the Earth would yield on heating to volcanic temperatures most of the amino acids that are found in protein.

Earlier, in 1958, experiments in the laboratory of Dr. Sidney Fox had demonstrated that all of the amino acids common to protein could simultaneously be condensed to yield substances having molecular weights of the size of small protein molecules. While much effort has gone into the artificial preparation of complex molecules like those of the proteins of contemporary organisms, this process of appropriately heating amino acids together gave, by an exceedingly simple means, compounds that were in turn also quite finely structured. The contemporary Earth has many regions that are similar to those used in such laboratory experiments, that is, areas in which the temperature exceeds the boiling point of water. This temperature is sufficient to bring about the condensation and also to carry the reaction out under nearly dry conditions.

Fox has termed these compounds proteinoids. They are not identical to the highly evolved protein molecules of today, but they appear to be sufficiently like them to serve as suitable materials for investigation (and models) of primitive protein. By simple processes of heating, it has been shown how the units of the nitrogen compounds could also have been condensed to form a primitive kind of DNA and RNA, key compounds in the cell.

A principal question standing in the way of an adequate theory of spontaneous generation has been that of how the complex unit that is recognized as the unit of life, the cell, could have come into existence. Experiments with the proteinoid material have shown that the possibility here is even simpler than the one that might have led to the first precellular protein. By simple addition of water to the proteinoid, preferably while the proteinoid is hot, the compound assembles itself into microscopic units that have a striking number of the properties found in contemporary cells. This includes the ability to stain Gram-negative or Gram-positive, ability to grow buds in a way reminiscent of yeast cells, the possibility of division into two particles, and the formation of selective boundary layers, like cell walls. The first laboratory demonstration of the self-organization of matter in this manner was reported by Oparin. He worked with coacervate droplets, the product of interaction of gelatin and gum arabic in water. Such droplets also have a number of cell-like properties. The tiny proteinoid sphere is of unique interest for the reason that it arises from material that is entirely synthetic whereas the coacervate droplets are made from biological compounds.

With the help of such experiments, a theory of spontaneous generation of forerunners of the first cell is now relatively complete in outline. Chemical and geological studies indicate that the formation of proteinoid and of microscopic cell-like particles must have occurred innumerable times on the primitive Earth. The exact degree, however, to which the tiny proteinoid spheres resemble primordial forerunners of the contemporary cell may yield to investigation only with great difficulty.

## DR. LEAKEY'S SEARCH FOR MAN'S BEGINNINGS

Olduvai Gorge cuts a 300-feet deep, 35-mile-long swath along the southeastern corner of East Africa's game-rich Serengeti Plain. Until a few years ago this gorge was one of the least-visited places on Earth. Hot, dusty, all but waterless for most of the year, Olduvai Gorge would hardly make any tourist's list of the world's most thrilling spots.

Except for one thing: The walls of the gorge cut, as through a layer cake, through millions of years of geological history, exposing innumerable fossils of prehistoric animals and men. Here primitive men lived and died. Here gigantic sheep and pigs and pygmy giraffes had a moment in the sun before fading into the long night of extinction. And here, since 1931, a "large, bronzed, stooped, rumpled man with a kind face," crawling on his hands and knees and picking up pebbles and bone fragments, has helped to rewrite the biography of man. The man is Dr. Louis S. B. Leakey.

During his 37 years at Olduvai, Dr. Leakey has found the remains of about 20 prehistoric individuals—a worn tooth of one, a fragment of bone of another. From these bits and pieces he has fleshed out four possible members of man's family tree:
• The oldest of Dr. Leakey's "man" fossils is *Kenyapithecus africanus*, 20,000,000 years old. Although some authorities do not think this creature belongs on man's family tree, Dr. Leakey points to a jaw that is "beginning" to be human.
• Then comes *Kenyapithecus wickeri*, age about 14,000,000 years. In at least one respect this creature had moved a long way toward modern man: Its facial muscles and bones appeared to have evolved toward a structure that would permit human speech.
• It is a leap of over 10,000,000 years to *Zinjanthropus* or "Nutcracker man," a 1,750,000-year-old near-man. Discovered by Dr. Leakey's wife in 1959, this fossil first made Dr. Leakey's work famous. *Zinjanthropus* had huge teeth and a massive "nutcracker" jaw that Dr. Leakey believes had been adapted to a diet of bark, roots, and nuts. Nutcracker man's proper name is *Australopithecus boisei*.
• Finally, there is *Homo habilis,* the nearest thing to modern man Dr. Leakey has yet discovered. *H. habilis,* meaning "able man" or "man with ability," may be one of our direct ancestors. At 2,000,000 years "able

Dr. Louis Leakey examines the skull of **Zinjanthropus** (right) in comparison with that of a chimpanzee.

Armand Denis/ © Nat. Geo. Soc.

man" is older than "nutcracker man," but, he nevertheless had a bigger brain, could probably talk, and was a meat-eater. Dr. Leakey believes that "able man's" superior endowments enabled him to survive, while "nutcracker man" became extinct.

Dr. Leakey was born in Kenya, and at age 13 was initiated into Africa's Kikuyu tribe. He believes that part of his success as a fossil hunter stems from two things the Kikuyus taught him as a boy: patience and observation. "In Africa," he says, "a torn leaf, a paw print, a bush that rustles when there is no breeze, a sudden quiet—these are signals that can spell the difference between life and death." The same heightened sense of observation, Dr. Leakey has learned, leads to the discovery of fossils: "Everything tells you something—a glint of white on the face of a cliff, an odd-shaped pebble. You find a stone that doesn't belong to the area. Perhaps it comes from 40 miles away. It must have been carried to the site. And this tells you something about the hunting range of the men who carried it."

In the nearly three decades that he poked about East Africa without turning up anything that shed much light on man's beginnings, Dr. Leakey remembered often what the Kikuyu elders told boys of his age over and over again: "Be patient, be careful, don't hurry. Try again and again."

## OUR VANISHING WILDLIFE

When explorers first came to North America they found a wilderness community of great size and diversity that stretched across a continent. Wild animals existed in staggering profusion and variety. But today much of the wildlife is in danger of being wiped out forever.

In a few brief centuries man has torn apart the fabric of this country—hacked down the forests, plowed up the long-grass prairie, filled in or drained the swamps, dug into and blasted away at the mountains, polluted the streams, and brought water to change the desert.

Already the official label "extinct" has been applied to nearly 50 species of American wildlife. These range from the great auk and passenger pigeon—notorious examples of how the mindless slaughter by early explorers and settlers erased once-abundant creatures—to several of the hoofed mammals whose western relatives just managed to survive the wholesale killing. Eastern races of elk and bison, for example, once ranged all along the Atlantic coast.

Over the past three years some first steps have been taken in official recognition of the urgency of protecting wilderness and endangered species—primarily the Wilderness Act of 1964 and the Endangered Species Preservation Act of 1966. Under the latter the Secretary of the Interior has the authority to make official designations of endangered species.

But it is up to Congress and conservationists, both government and private groups, to accelerate the legal action necessary to extend protection to the remaining undesignated wilderness areas that shelter wildlife.

This will not be easy. While these laws and a heightened public awareness have slowed the destruction of wild areas, the process of insuring their preservation under the Wilderness Act will be slow. Over a ten-year period, government lands will be surveyed to determine additional areas worthy of the wilderness designation. However, authorization must be preceded by public hearings, and it requires Congressional approval. Nor does the Act automatically protect the lands from intrusions by mining and grazing interests. And it does not cover privately owned property.

Under the 1966 Act an initial list of 78 endangered species had been published, including 14 mammals, 36 birds, 6 reptiles and amphibians, and 22 fish.

Today, the most publicized and carefully counted of the endangered species is the whooping crane, a large, graceful white bird whose numbers hover precariously around 50. The crane's natural tall-grass prairie habitat is long since gone, and its winter refuge area and breeding grounds are confined to a tiny coastal prairie in Texas. As the birds migrate each year from summer quarters in a remote part of Canada, they are carefully counted and guarded by conservationists. Their future is indeed doubtful, since breeding them in captivity has proved difficult. Even if, as is proposed, several more 5,000-acre preserves are acquired, it may be too late.

Time probably has run out, too, for our largest land bird, the California condor. This vulture-like brown bird with a nine-foot wingspread once ranged all across the Far West from Oregon to Baja California. Now the surviving condors have retreated to a few mountainous parts of California, their numbers reduced to near 40. They are further periled by their low breeding rate—only one egg every other year—and the fact that they range widely for food. This makes them a tempting target for hunters, and five of the spectacular birds have died this way in recent years. Now, most of their nesting sites are in national forest areas, and stiff laws against shooting them have been enacted.

Probably the rarest small mammal in all of North America is the black-footed ferret. A large weasel with black feet and face mask, it once ranged the plains and foothills from Canada to Arizona. Apparently it never existed in large numbers, and the widespread destruction of prairie dogs, its main food, has left it on the edge of extinction. Though they occasionally are sighted, no one knows how many survive.

The tiny and delicate Florida key deer, unlike its thriving white-tailed relative, is the victim of man's invasion. Occupation of the Florida keys, plus hunting and natural disasters, have reduced its numbers to only a few hundred. There are two other man-made hazards: death from automobiles and from eating cigarette butts thrown out along the highways. These animals may be saved by a three-way program of Federal acquisition of more land for them, continued strict protection from hunters, and breeding them in captivity.

Heavy poaching and destruction or deterioration of its water habitat has brought the American alligator to a low point. But prospects for its survival could be bright. It is now protected in every state and thrives in captivity. One conservationist has suggested that the alligator could be saved simply by outlawing the making of shoes, handbags, and other items out of its skin.

In this gloomy picture there is an occasional bright story. The highlight of 1967 was the discovery, in Texas, of five to ten breeding pairs of ivory-billed woodpeckers—the first confirmed sighting of this rare bird since 1950. It was believed extinct, or nearly so, because the hardwood forest that yielded its insect diet was destroyed. Now, it seems, the bird may be adapting to the insect supply of the more plentiful slash-pine areas.

But the number of birds and animals able to adapt similarly must necessarily be small. And their real hope for survival is for *man* to adapt—to change from a destroyer to a protector—before it is too late. Otherwise, urbanized peoples will finally find themselves restricted to contact with the infinitely adaptable fauna that has followed man from place to place over the centuries—the house mouse, the Norway rat, the house sparrow, the starling, and the pigeon.

## GESTATION PERIODS OF VARIOUS MAMMALS

| ANIMAL | GESTATION PERIOD | AVERAGE IN LITTER | ANIMAL | GESTATION PERIOD | AVERAGE IN LITTER |
|---|---|---|---|---|---|
| Baboon | 6 months | 1 | Kangaroo | 38–40 days | 1 |
| Badger | 6 months | 2 | Lion | 108 days | 4 |
| Beaver | 4 months | 2–6 | Mink | 6 weeks | 4–8 |
| Camel | 315–389 days | 1 | Moose | 8 months | 1–3 |
| Cat | 9 weeks | 1–6 | Mouse | 24 days | 1–9 |
| Cow | 280 days | 1–2 | Orangutan | 9 months | 1 |
| Chimpanzee | 9 months | 1 | Pig | 113 days | 4–6 |
| Coyote | 2 months | 6 | Polar bear | 9 months | 2 |
| Dog | 61 days | 1–4 | Porcupine | 7 weeks | 1–3 |
| Dolphin | 1 year | 1 | Rabbit | 1 month | 4 |
| Donkey | 9 months | 1 | Raccoon | 9 weeks | 4–5 |
| Duckbill platypus | 15 days | 2 | Rat | 7 weeks | 6–14 |
| Elephant | 21 months | 1 | Rhinoceros | 18 months | 1 |
| Fox | 51 days | 4–10 | Sheep | 148 days | 2 |
| Gibbon | 7 months | 1 | Skunk | 50 days | 4–8 |
| Giraffe | 14–15 months | 1 | Squirrel | 1 month | 4 |
| Goat | 151 days | 1 | Tiger | 100 days | 2–4 |
| Gorilla | 9 months | 1–2 | Weasel | 7 months | 6–12 |
| Hippopotamus | 8–9 months | 1 | Wolf | 2 months | 6 |
| Horse | 330 days | 1 | Zebra | 13 months | 1 |

## LIFE-SPAN OF ANIMALS

Facts and figures on the natural life-span of wild animals differ greatly. The list that follows, compiled from the authoritative records of zoos, aviaries, and aquariums, reflects the maximum age ever achieved by the animals while in captivity.

### MAXIMUM AGE IN YEARS

| | | | | | | | |
|---|---|---|---|---|---|---|---|
| 180 | Giant tortoise | 45 | Baboon | 25 | Camel | 17 | Goat |
| 138 | Eastern box turtle | 37 | Chimpanzee | 25 | Tiger | 16 | Bullfrog |
| 100 | Sea anemone | 36 | Toad | 25 | Zebra | 16 | Cheetah |
| 84 | Elephant | 35 | Domestic pigeon | 23 | Domestic cat | 16 | Jackal |
| 80 | Freshwater oyster | 33 | Polar bear | 23 | Leopard | 16 | Kangaroo |
| 68 | Owl | 31 | Grizzly bear | 22 | Domestic dog | 15 | Pronghorn antelope |
| 56 | Alligator | 30 | Badger | 22 | Jaguar | 15 | Ram |
| 55 | Eagle | 30 | Dolphin | 20 | Cougar | 15 | Reindeer |
| 51 | Pelican | 30 | Lion | 20 | Cow | 15 | Timber wolf |
| 50 | Blue whale | 29 | Cobra | 20 | Moose | 15 | Duck |
| 50 | Domestic horse | 28 | Giraffe | 20 | Rattlesnake | 14 | Coyote |
| 50 | Giant salamander | 28 | Gorilla | 20 | Sheep | 14 | Chicken |
| 50 | Rhinoceros | 26.5 | Orangutan | 20 | White-tailed deer | 13 | Rabbit |
| 46 | Jackass | 25 | Black bear | 19 | Beaver | 10 | Pig |

## SPEEDS OF ANIMALS

(In miles per hour)

| | | | | | | | |
|---|---|---|---|---|---|---|---|
| 180 | Peregrine falcon | 35 | Flying fish | 45 | Kangaroo | 23 | Salmon |
| 120 | Golden eagle | 35 | Rhinoceros | 43 | Saluki | 22.8 | Blue whale |
| 94.3 | Racing pigeon | 35 | Whippet | 40 | Coyote | 22 | Moose |
| 75 | Cheetah | 35 | Wolf | 40 | Zebra | 22 | Wren |
| 68 | Sailfish | 32 | Giraffe | 40 | Killer whale | 20 | Monarch butterfly |
| 65 | Jaguar | 32 | Guano bat | 40 | Emu | 18 | Race-runner lizard |
| 60 | African lion | 30 | Blackbird | 40 | White-tailed deer | 16 | Flying frog |
| 60 | American antelope | 30 | Red fox | 38 | Swallow | 15 | Black mamba |
| 60 | Mallard duck | 28 | Gray heron | 37.8 | Greyhound | 13.3 | Hornet |
| 50 | Starling | 27 | Cuckoo | 37 | Dolphin | 12 | Wasp |
| 45 | California jackrabbit | 24.5 | Elephant | 36 | Dragonfly | 11 | Wild boar |

## FASTEST MAMMAL

The cheetah, speediest of mammals, has been clocked at between 70 and 80 m.p.h. in short bursts, and can average over 50 m.p.h. for 500 yards. In India cheetahs are trained for use in hunting.

American Mus. of Nat. Hist.

# MAN-MADE FEATURES ON EARTH

## WORLD'S MAJOR ENGINEERING FEATS

Source: National Geographic Society

| STRUCTURE | LOCATION AND FEATURES | STRUCTURE | LOCATION AND FEATURES |
|---|---|---|---|
| Longest rail tunnel ..... | Simplon, Switzerland-Italy; 12.3 miles. | Longest single bridge span . | Verrazano-Narrows, New York; 4,260 feet. |
| Longest road tunnel ..... | Mont Blanc, France-Italy; 7.5 miles. | Highest bridge. | Royal Gorge, Colorado; 1,053 feet above water. |
| Tallest dam ... | Grande Dixence, Switzerland; 932 feet | Deepest mine.. | Gold mine, Boksburg, South Africa; 11,003 feet. |
| Biggest dam .. | Fort Peck, Missouri River, Montana; 125,628,000 cubic yards of material used. | Deepest well.. | Oil well, Pecos, Texas; 25,340 feet. |
| Tallest building | Empire State, New York, New York; 1,250 feet (with TV tower, 1,472 feet). | Great Pyramid of Cheops... | 481 feet high, 755 feet square at the base; built of 2,300,000 blocks weighing 2½ tons each. |
| Largest building .... | Pentagon, Washington, D.C.; 6.3 million square feet of floor space. | Great Wall of China ...... | 1,500 miles long; it averages 25 feet in height, 15 feet in width at the top, and 25 feet at the base. |
| Tallest structure.... | TV tower, Fargo, North Dakota; 2,063 feet. | | |

## WORLD'S TALLEST STRUCTURES

| FEET HIGH | BUILDINGS | NO. OF STORIES | LOCATION | FEET HIGH | BUILDINGS | NO. OF STORIES | LOCATION |
|---|---|---|---|---|---|---|---|
| 1,250* | Empire State...... | 102 | New York City | 700 | Metropolitan Life.. | 50 | New York City |
| 1,046 | Chrysler.......... | 77 | New York City | 697 | 500 Fifth Avenue.. | 60 | New York City |
| 950 | 60 Wall Street..... | 67 | New York City | 687 | Chemical Bank New York Trust. | 50 | New York City |
| 900 | Bank of Manhattan...... | 71 | New York City | 686 | 1277 Park Avenue. | 50 | New York City |
| 850 | RCA............ | 70 | New York City | 680 | Chanin........... | 56 | New York City |
| 813 | Chase Manhattan.. | 60 | New York City | 673 | Lincoln.......... | 53 | New York City |
| 808 | Pan Am.......... | 59 | New York City | 662 | Civic Center...... | 31 | Chicago, Illinois |
| 792 | Woolworth........ | 60 | New York City | 654 | Irving Trust...... | 50 | New York City |
| 787 | Moscow State University...... | 28 | Moscow, U.S.S.R. | 625 | Waldorf-Astoria... | 47 | New York City |
| | | | | 620 | 10 East 40th Street | 48 | New York City |
| | | | | 616 | General Electric... | 50 | New York City |
| 756* | Palace of Culture and Science..... | 33 | Warsaw, Poland | 615 | New York Life.... | 40 | New York City |
| 750 | Prudential Tower.. | 52 | Boston, Mass. | 612 | Singer........... | 47 | New York City |
| 741 | City Bank Farmers Trust.......... | 57 | New York City | 604 | Canadian Imperial Bank of Commerce...... | 43 | Montreal, Canada |
| 708 | Terminal Tower... | 48 | Cleveland, Ohio | | | | |
| 707 | Union Carbide.... | 52 | New York City | 601* | Prudential........ | 41 | Chicago, Illinois |

* Without TV tower.

| FEET HIGH | TOWERS | LOCATION | FEET HIGH | TOWERS | LOCATION |
|---|---|---|---|---|---|
| 2,063 | KTHI-TV......... | Blanchard, North Dakota | 1,638 | WPSD-TV........ | Paducah, Kentucky |
| 2,060 | KXJB-TV......... | Valley City, North Dakota | 1,619 | WGAN-TV....... | Portland, Maine |
| 2,000 | KETS-TV......... | Little Rock, Arkansas | 1,610 | KSWS-TV........ | Roswell, New Mexico |
| 2,000 | KTIV-TV......... | Sioux City, Iowa | 1,572 | WKY-TV......... | Oklahoma City, Oklahoma |
| 2,000 | WACB-TV........ | Albany, Georgia | 1,544 | KOVR-TV........ | Walnut Grove, California |
| 2,000 | WEAU-TV........ | Eau Claire, Wisconsin | 1,312 | Peking Radio Mast. | Peking, China |
| 1,999 | WLBT-TV........ | Jackson, Mississippi | 1,296 | Das Fernsehturm.. | Stuttgart, Germany |
| 1,994 | WECT-TV........ | Wilmington, North Carolina | 1,212 | Thule Radio Mast.. | Thule, Greenland |
| 1,985 | KSOO-TV........ | Sioux Falls, Iowa | 1,092 | Tokyo TV Tower... | Tokyo, Japan |
| 1,926 | KCRG-TV........ | Cedar Rapids, Iowa | 1,079 | WITI-TV......... | Milwaukee, Wisconsin |
| 1,909 | KTUL-TV......... | Tulsa, Oklahoma | 1,066 | Leningrad TV Mast | Leningrad, U.S.S.R. |
| 1,898 | KSLA-TV......... | Shreveport, Louisiana | 1,052 | Eiffel Tower...... | Paris, France |
| 1,836 | KBIM-TV......... | Roswell, New Mexico | 1,006 | Lakibegg Broadcasting Tower- | Lakibegg. Hungary |
| 1,749 | WTVM-WRBL Mast | Columbus, Georgia | | | |
| 1,749 | WBIR-TV......... | Knoxville, Tennessee | 1,000 | TV Masts......... | Black Hill and Durris, Scotland |
| 1,676 | KFVS-TV......... | Cape Girardeau, Missouri | | | |

## TALL MAN-MADE STRUCTURES

| The tallest structure in the world: KTHI-TV TOWER, near Fargo, N. Dak., 2,063 feet high. | The tallest building in the world: THE EMPIRE STATE BUILDING, New York City, 1,250 feet high; 1,472 feet high with television tower. | EIFFEL TOWER, Paris, France, 984 feet high; 1,056 feet high with television tower. | THE GATEWAY ARCH, St. Louis, Missouri, 630 feet high. | THE WASHINGTON MONUMENT, Washington, D.C., 555 feet high. | THE GREAT PYRAMID of Cheops, near Cairo, Egypt, 481 feet high. | STATUE OF LIBERTY, New York Harbor, 302 feet high. |
|---|---|---|---|---|---|---|

## MAJOR WORLD TUNNELS

| LENGTH (in miles) | NAME | LOCATION | YEAR OPENED |
|---|---|---|---|
| **Vehicular** | | | |
| 7.2 | Mt. Blanc[1] | France–Italy | 1965 |
| 3.4 | Great St. Bernhard | Italy–Switzerland | 1964 |
| 3.1 | Viella | Pobla de Segur–Viella, Spain | 1948 |
| 2.2 | Queensway Road | Liverpool, England | 1934 |
| 2.1 | Kanmon | Yamaguchi–Fukuoka, Japan | 1944 |
| 1.8 | Lincoln | New York–New Jersey | 1937 |
| 1.8 | Holland | New York–New Jersey | 1927 |
| 1.7 | Brooklyn-Battery | Brooklyn–Manhattan, New York | 1950 |
| 1.6 | Salang | Afghanistan–U.S.S.R. | 1964 |
| 1.5 | Reboucas | Rio de Janeiro, Brazil | 1967 |
| 1.3 | Queens-Midtown | Queens–Manhattan, New York | 1940 |
| 1.2 | Liberty Tubes | Pittsburgh, Pennsylvania | 1923 |
| 1.2 | Baltimore Harbor | Baltimore, Maryland | 1957 |
| 1.1 | Sumner | Boston, Massachusetts | 1934 |
| 1.1 | Caracas-Laguaira Highway | Caracas, Venezuela | 1953 |
| 1.0 | Detroit International | Detroit, Michigan–Windsor, Ontario | 1930 |
| 1.0 (2) | Chesapeake Bay Bridge-Tunnel[2] | Chesapeake Bay, Virginia | 1964 |
| **Railroad** | | | |
| 12.3 | Simplon | Switzerland–Italy | 1905 |
| 11.7 | New York City Extension | New Jersey–Long Island | 1910 |
| 11.5 | Apennine | Florence, Italy | 1934 |
| 9.3 | St. Gotthard | Andermatt, Switzerland | 1881 |
| 9.1 | Lötschberg | Bern–Brig, Switzerland | 1911 |
| 9.0 | Mount Royal | Montreal, Canada | 1916 |
| 8.5 | Mont Cénis | France–Italy | 1871 |
| 8.0 | Hex | Hex River, South Africa | — |
| 7.8 | New Cascade | Cascade Mountains, Washington | 1928 |

*(continued)*

[1] This tunnel, running under Mt. Blanc, represents a monumental engineering feat; it took six years to build. [2] The 17.7-mile Chesapeake Bay Bridge-Tunnel includes two one-mile tunnels, as well as bridges and causeways.

**MAJOR WORLD TUNNELS** (*continued*)

| LENGTH (in miles) | NAME | LOCATION | YEAR OPENED |
|---|---|---|---|
| 7.0 | Vosges | Vosges, France | 1940 |
| 6.4 | Arlberg | Austria (Alps) | 1884 |
| 6.1 | Moffat | James Peak, Colorado | 1928 |
| 6.1 | Shimizu | Gunma–Migata, Japan | 1930 |
| 5.5 | Rimutaka | Wellington, New Zealand | 1955 |
| 5.3 | Ricken | Switzerland (Alps) | 1910 |
| 5.3 | Tauern | Austria (Alps) | 1909 |
| 5.3 | Grenchenberg | Switzerland (Alps) | 1915 |
| 5.3 | Connaught | British Columbia, Canada | 1916 |
| 5.0 | Transandine | Chile–Argentina | 1911 |
| 4.85 | Tanna | Shizuoka, Japan | 1932 |
| 4.7 | Hoosac | Hoosac Mountains, Massachusetts | 1875 |
| 4.47 | Jungfrau | Switzerland (Alps) | 1912 |
| 4.4 | Severn River | England–Wales | 1886 |
| 3.8 | Mont d'Or | France–Switzerland | 1915 |
| 3.3 | Gravehals | Oslo–Bergen, Norway | 1909 |
| 2.9 | Sasago | Tokyo, Japan | 1902 |
| 2.1 | Mersey | Liverpool, England | 1886 |

**Ship Tunnel**

| | | | |
|---|---|---|---|
| 4.5 | Rove | Rhone Canal, France | 1927 |

## MAJOR WORLD SHIP CANALS

| NAME | LOCATION | YEAR OPENED | LENGTH (in miles) | MINIMUM WIDTH OF CHANNELS (in feet) | MINIMUM DEPTH (in feet) | LOCKS |
|---|---|---|---|---|---|---|
| Albert | Belgium: Meuse River near Liège to Sheldt River near Antwerp | 1939 | 76.0 | 53 | 16½ | 6 |
| Amsterdam-Rhine | The Netherlands: Amsterdam to Tiel | 1952 | 44.0 | 164 | 41 | 3 |
| Cape Cod | U.S.A.: Buzzards Bay to Cape Cod Bay | 1914 | 7.6 | 250 | 28 | 0 |
| Corinth | Greece: Gulf of Corinth to Gulf of Aegina | 1893 | 4.0 | 72 | 26¼ | 0 |
| Kiel | Germany: North Sea to Baltic Sea | 1895 | 61.0 | 145 | 37 | 4 |
| Manchester | England: Mersey Estuary to City of Manchester | 1894 | 35.5 | 120 | 28 | 4 |
| Moscow-Volga | U.S.S.R.: Moscow to Volga River | 1937 | 80.0 | 145 | 20 | 13 |
| Panama | Panama: Atlantic Ocean to Pacific Ocean | 1914 | 51.2 | 300 | 40 | 12 |
| St. Lawrence Seaway | U.S.A.-Canada: Atlantic Ocean to Great Lakes System | 1959 | 2,687.0 | 450 | 27 | 20 |
| Welland | (Canada) | 1932 | 28.0 | 310 | 27 | 8 |
| Sault Ste. Marie | (Canada) | 1895 | 1.4 | 150 | 27 | 1 |
| Sault Ste. Marie | (U.S.A.) | 1896 | 1.6 | 100 | 27 | 1 |
| Suez | Egypt: Mediterranean Sea to Gulf of Suez | 1869 | 104.25 | 500 | 37 | 0 |

## MAJOR BRIDGES OF THE WORLD
### Suspension Bridges

| SPAN (in feet) | BRIDGE | LOCATION | WATERWAY | YEAR OPENED |
|---|---|---|---|---|
| 4,260 | Verrazano-Narrows | Brooklyn to Staten Island, New York | Entrance to New York Bay | 1965 |
| 4,200 | Golden Gate | San Francisco to Marin County, California | Entrance to San Francisco Bay | 1937 |
| 3,800 | Mackinac | Michigan | Straits of Mackinac | 1957 |
| 3,500 | George Washington | New York City to Fort Lee, New Jersey | Hudson River | 1931 |
| 3,323 | Salazar | Lisbon, Portugal | Tagus River | 1966 |
| 3,300 | Firth of Forth | Scotland | Firth of Forth | 1964 |
| 3,240 | Severn | Bristol, England to Cardiff, Wales | Severn River | 1966 |
| 2,800 | Narrows | Tacoma, Washington | Puget Sound | 1951 |
| 2,336 | Angustora | Guayana, Venezuela | Orinoco River | 1967 |
| 2,310 | Transbay | San Francisco to Oakland, California | San Francisco Bay | 1936 |

| SPAN (in feet) | BRIDGE | LOCATION | WATERWAY | YEAR OPENED |
|---|---|---|---|---|
| 2,300.... | Bronx-Whitestone.... | Bronx to Whitestone, Queens, New York.... | East River............. | 1939 |
| 2,150.... | Delaware Memorial... | Wilmington, Delaware..................... | Delaware River......... | 1951 |
| 2,150.... | Seaway Skyway...... | Ogdensburg, New York, to Prescott, Ontario, Canada.................................. | St. Lawrence River..... | 1960 |
| 2,000.... | Walt Whitman........ | South Philadelphia, Pennsylvania........... | Delaware River......... | 1957 |
| 1,995.... | Tancarville.......... | Tancarville, France...................... | Seine River........... | 1959 |
| 1,850.... | Ambassador......... | Detroit, Michigan, to Windsor, Canada ..... | Detroit River.......... | 1929 |
| 1,800.... | Throgs Neck......... | Bronx to Queens, New York............... | East River............. | 1961 |
| 1,750.... | Benjamin Franklin.... | Philadelphia, Pennsylvania, to Camden, N.J.. | Delaware River......... | 1926 |
| 1,640.... | Rhine............... | Kleve to Emmerich, West Germany........ | Rhine River........... | 1966 |
| 1,632.... | Bear Mountain....... | Bear Mountain to Peekskill, New York...... | Hudson River.......... | 1924 |
| 1,600.... | Chesapeake Bay...... | Sandy Point, Maryland.................... | Chesapeake Bay........ | 1952 |
| 1,600.... | Williamsburg......... | Manhattan to Brooklyn, New York......... | East River............. | 1903 |
| 1,595.... | Brooklyn............. | Manhattan to Brooklyn, New York......... | East River............. | 1883 |
| 1,550.... | Lions Gate.......... | Vancouver, British Columbia.............. | Vancouver Harbor...... | 1939 |
| 1,500.... | Mid-Hudson.......... | Poughkeepsie to Highland, New York....... | Hudson River.......... | 1930 |
| 1,470.... | Manhattan........... | Manhattan to Brooklyn, New York......... | East River............. | 1909 |
| 1,447.... | Angus L. McDonald... | Halifax, Nova Scotia..................... | Halifax Harbor........ | 1954 |
| 1,380.... | Triborough.......... | Manhattan-Queens-Bronx, New York...... | East River............. | 1936 |
| 1,370.... | Nya Älvorgsbron..... | Göteborg, Sweden........................ | Göta River............. | 1966 |

### Cantilever Bridges

| | | | | |
|---|---|---|---|---|
| 1,800.... | Quebec............. | Quebec, Canada........................ | St. Lawrence River.... | 1917 |
| 1,700.... | Firth of Forth........ | Inch-Garvier to Queensferry, Scotland...... | Firth of Forth.......... | 1889 |
| 1,575.... | Greater New Orleans.. | New Orleans to Algiers, Louisiana........... | Mississippi River...... | 1958 |
| 1,500.... | Howrah............. | Calcutta to Howrah, India................ | Hooghly River......... | 1943 |
| 1,400.... | Transbay (East Bay).. | San Francisco to Oakland, California........ | San Francisco Bay...... | 1936 |
| 1,212.... | Tappan Zee.......... | Tarrytown, New York..................... | Hudson River.......... | 1955 |
| 1,200.... | Longview............ | Longview, Washington.................... | Columbia River........ | 1930 |
| 1,182.... | Queensboro.......... | Manhattan to Queens, New York........... | East River............. | 1909 |
| 1,100.... | Second Narrows...... | British Columbia........................ | Burrard Inlet.......... | 1960 |
| 1,100.... | Carquinez Strait..... | Crockett to Vallejo, California............. | Carquinez Strait....... | 1927 |
| 1,097.... | Harbor Bridge........ | Montreal, Canada....................... | St. Lawrence River..... | 1930 |
| 1,070.... | Richmond-San Rafael. | Richmond, California..................... | San Francisco Bay...... | 1956 |
| 1,060.... | Maysville........... | Maysville, Kentucky, to Aberdeen, Ohio..... | Ohio River............ | 1931 |
| 1,050.... | Cooper River........ | Charleston, South Carolina................ | Cooper River.......... | 1929 |
| 1,000.... | Newburgh-Beacon.... | Newburgh to Beacon, N.Y................. | Hudson River.......... | 1963 |
| 963.... | East St. Louis....... | East St. Louis, Illinois.................... | Mississippi River....... | 1950 |

### Continuous Truss Bridges

| | | | | |
|---|---|---|---|---|
| 1,350.... | S. N. Pearman....... | Charleston, South Carolina................ | Cooper River........... | 1966 |
| 1,232.... | Astoria.............. | Astoria, Oregon, to Point Ellice, Washington.. | Columbia River........ | 1966 |
| 1,088.... | Commodore Point.... | Jacksonville, Florida..................... | St. Johns River........ | 1967 |
| 856.... | Sava River.......... | Belgrade, Yugoslavia..................... | Sava River............ | 1956 |

### Concrete Arch Spans

| | | | | |
|---|---|---|---|---|
| 1,000.... | Gladesville.......... | Sydney, Australia....................... | Parramatta River....... | 1964 |
| 994.... | Brazil-Paraguay...... | Foz do Iguaçu, Brazil.................... | Paraná River.......... | 1961 |
| 866.... | Sandö.............. | Kranfors, Sweden....................... | Angerman River........ | 1943 |
| 645.... | Esla................ | Northwestern Spain...................... | Esla River............. | 1940 |
| 612.... | Plougastel.......... | Brest, France........................... | Elorn River............ | 1929 |

### Floating Bridges

| | | | | |
|---|---|---|---|---|
| 6,560.... | Lake Washington..... | Seattle, Washington...................... | Lake Washington....... | 1940 |
| 6,500.... | Hood Canal......... | Puget Sound, Washington................. | Puget Sound.......... | 1961 |

### Steel Arch Bridges

| | | | | |
|---|---|---|---|---|
| 1,652.... | Kill van Kull........ | Port Richmond, New York, to Bayonne, N.J.. | Kill van Kull.......... | 1931 |
| 1,650.... | Sydney Harbor....... | Sydney, Australia....................... | Sydney Harbor......... | 1932 |
| 1,247.... | Orlik Reservoir...... | Czechoslovakia......................... | Orlik Reservoir........ | 1966 |
| 1,128.... | Thatcher Ferry...... | Balboa, Panama Canal Zone............... | Panama Canal......... | 1962 |
| 1,082.... | Runcorn-Widnes...... | Runcorn to Widnes, England............... | Mersey River.......... | 1961 |
| 1,080.... | Birchenough........ | Umtali to Fort Victoria, Rhodesia.......... | Sabi River............ | 1935 |
| 1,042.... | Nagasaki-Sasebo..... | Nagasaki, Japan........................ | Sasebo Bay........... | 1955 |
| 1,028.... | Glen Canyon......... | Arizona............................... | Colorado River........ | 1959 |
| 1,000.... | Lewiston-Queenston.. | Lewiston, New York, to Queenston, Ontario.. | Niagara River Gorge.... | 1962 |
| 977½.... | Hell Gate Arch...... | Queens to Bronx, New York............... | East River............. | 1917 |
| 950.... | Rainbow............ | Niagara Falls, New York.................. | Niagara River......... | 1941 |
| 912.... | Askero Fjord........ | Bohuslän, Sweden...................... | Askero Fjord.......... | 1960 |
| 838.... | Duisberg-Rheinhausen | Duisberg to Rheinhausen, Germany......... | Rhine River........... | 1951 |
| 806.... | Lincoln Trail........ | Cannelton, Indiana...................... | Ohio River............ | 1966 |
| 805.... | Volta River.......... | Akosombo, Ghana....................... | Volta River........... | 1956 |
| 800.... | Henry Hudson....... | Manhattan to Bronx, New York............. | Harlem River.......... | 1936 |

## DAMS, MAN-MADE LAKES, AND HYDROELECTRIC PLANTS
Source: Department of the Interior

### World's Highest Dams

| NAME | HEIGHT (in feet) | YEAR COMPLETED |
|---|---|---|
| 1. Nurek, U.S.S.R. | 1,017 E | UC |
| 2. Inguri, U.S.S.R. | 988 C | UC |
| 3. Grande Dixence, Switzerland | 932 C | 1962 |
| 4. Vaiont, Italy | 858 C | 1961 |
| 5. Mica, Canada | 800 E | UC |
| 6. Mauvoisin, Switzerland | 777 C | 1958 |
| 7. Sayansk, U.S.S.R. | 774 C | UC |
| 8. Oroville, U.S.A. | 770 E | UC |
| 9. Chirkey, U.S.S.R. | 764 C | UC |
| 10. Contra, Switzerland | 754 C | 1965 |
| 11. Bhakra, India | 740 C | 1963 |
| 12. Hoover, U.S.A. | 726 C | 1936 |
| 13. Mratinje, Yugoslavia | 721 C | UC |
| 14. Glen Canyon, U.S.A. | 710 C | 1964 |
| 15. Toktogul, U.S.S.R. | 705 C | UC |
| 16. Manicouagan No. 5, Canada | 703 C | 1967 |
| 17. Dworshak, U.S.A. | 693 C | UC |
| 18. Luzzone, Switzerland | 682 C | 1963 |
| 19. Keban, Turkey | 672 E | UC |
| 20. Pahlevi, Iran | 668 C | 1963 |
| 21. Bullards Bar, U.S.A. | 645 C | UC |
| 22. Almendra, Spain | 623 C | UC |
| 23. Kurobe No. 4, Japan | 610 C | 1964 |
| 24. Melones, U.S.A. | 608 E | UC |
| 25. Mossyrock, U.S.A. | 605 C | UC |

### World's Largest Dams

| NAME | VOLUME* (in cu. yds.) | YEAR COMPLETED |
|---|---|---|
| 1. Fort Peck, U.S.A. | 125,600,000 | 1940 |
| 2. Mangia, Pakistan | 108,300,000 | 1967 |
| 3. Oahe, U.S.A. | 92,000,000 | 1963 |
| 4. South Saskatchewan, Canada | 86,300,000 | 1966 |
| 5. Oroville, U.S.A. | 80,300,000 | UC |
| 6. San Luis, U.S.A. | 78,000,000 | 1967 |
| 7. Nurek, U.S.S.R. | 75,900,000 | UC |
| 8. Nagajunasagar, India | 73,600,000 | 1966 |
| 9. Garrison, U.S.A. | 66,500,000 | 1956 |
| 10. Kiev, U.S.S.R. | 58,000,000 | 1964 |
| 11. Gorky, U.S.S.R. | 58,000,000 | 1955 |
| 12. Portage Mountain, Canada | 56,700,000 | UC |
| 13. Sadd-El-Aali (High Dam), U.A.R. | 56,300,000 | UC |
| 14. Cochiti, U.S.A. | 53,000,000 | UC |
| 15. Fort Randall, U.S.A. | 50,200,000 | 1956 |
| 16. Kanev, U.S.S.R | 49,500,000 | UC |
| 17. Kakhovka, U.S.S.R. | 46,600,000 | 1955 |
| 18. Tsimlyansk, U.S.S.R. | 44,300,000 | 1952 |
| 19. Volga-V. I. Lenin, U.S.S.R. | 44,300,000 | 1955 |
| 20. Beas, India | 44,200,000 | UC |
| 21. Castaic, U.S.A. | 42,600,000 | UC |
| 22. Jari, Pakistan | 42,000,000 | 1967 |
| 23. Mica, Canada | 40,000,000 | UC |
| 24. Kremenchug, U.S.S.R. | 36,300,000 | 1961 |
| 25. Saratov, U.S.S.R. | 34,500,000 | UC |

### World's Greatest Man-Made Lakes

| NAME | CAPACITY (in acre-feet) | YEAR COMPLETED |
|---|---|---|
| 1. Owen Falls, Uganda | 166,000,000 | 1954 |
| 2. Bratsk, U.S.S.R. | 137,200,000 | 1964 |
| 3. Kariba, Rhodesia-Zambia | 130,000,000 | 1959 |
| 4. Sadd-El-Aali (High Dam), U.A.R. | 125,600,000 | UC |
| 5. Akosombo, Ghana | 120,000,000 | 1965 |
| 6. Manicouagan No. 5, Canada | 115,000,000 | 1967 |
| 7. Krasnoyarsk, U.S.S.R. | 59,400,000 | UC |
| 8. Portage Mountain, Canada | 57,000,000 | UC |
| 9. Sanmen Hsia, China | 52,700,000 | 1962 |
| 10. Ust-Ilim, U.S.S.R. | 48,100,000 | UC |
| 11. Volga-V. I. Lenin, U.S.S.R. | 47,000,000 | 1955 |
| 12. Bukhtarma, U.S.S.R. | 43,000,000 | 1960 |
| 13. Tankiangkow, China | 41,800,000 | 1962 |
| 14. Irkutsk, U.S.S.R. | 37,300,000 | 1956 |
| 15. Hoover, U.S.A. | 31,250,000 | 1936 |
| 16. Sunda, Congo | 28,375,000 | 1961 |
| 17. Volga-22nd Cong., U.S.S.R. | 27,200,000 | 1958 |
| 18. Glen Canyon, U.S.A. | 27,000,000 | 1964 |
| 19. Zeyskaya, U.S.S.R. | 26,000,000 | UC |
| 20. Valerio Trujano, Mexico | 26,000,000 | 1964 |
| 21. Keban, Turkey | 24,700,000 | UC |
| 22. Garrison, U.S.A. | 24,400,000 | 1956 |
| 23. Iroquois, U.S.A.-Canada | 24,300,000 | 1959 |
| 24. Oahe, U.S.A. | 23,600,000 | 1963 |
| 25. Rybinsk-Sheksna, U.S.S.R. | 20,600,000 | 1941 |

### World's Largest Hydroelectric Plants

| NAME AND DATE OF INITIAL OPERATION | INSTALLED CAPACITY (in mgwts) Ultimate | Present |
|---|---|---|
| 1. Sayansk, U.S.S.R. (UC) | 6,300 | — |
| 2. Krasnoyarsk, U.S.S.R. (1967) | 6,000 | 5,000 |
| 3. Grand Coulee, U.S.A. (1941) | 5,574 | 1,974 |
| 4. Bratsk, U.S.S.R. (1961) | 4,500 | 4,500 |
| 5. Sukhovo, U.S.S.R. (UC) | 4,500 | — |
| 6. Churchill Falls, Canada (UC) | 4,500 | — |
| 7. Ust-Illimsk, U.S.S.R. (UC) | 4,329 | 720 |
| 8. Kettle Rapids, Canada (UC) | 3,240 | 1,018 |
| 9. Ilha Solteira, Brazil (UC) | 3,200 | — |
| 10. John Day, U.S.A. (UC) | 2,700 | 2,160 |
| 11. Nurek, U.S.S.R. (UC) | 2,700 | — |
| 12. Volga-22nd Congress, U.S.S.R. (1958) | 2,543 | 2,543 |
| 13. Portage Mountain, Canada (UC) | 2,300 | 1,150 |
| 14. Iron Gate, Romania-Yugoslavia (UC) | 2,160 | — |
| 15. Volga-V. I. Lenin, U.S.S.R. (1955) | 2,100 | 2,100 |
| 16. Sadd-El-Aali (High Dam), U.A.R (1967) | 2,100 | 1,750 |
| 17. Mica, Canada (UC) | 2,000 | — |
| 18. Robert Moses Niagara, U.S.A. (1961) | 1,950 | 1,950 |
| 19. St. Lawrence Power Dam, Canada-U.S.A. (1958) | 1,880 | 1,880 |
| 20. Guri, Venezuela (1967) | 1,757 | 527 |
| 21. Dalles, U.S.A. (1957) | 1,743 | 1,119 |
| 22. Chief Joseph, U.S.A. (1956) | 1,728 | 1,024 |
| 23. Kemano, Canada (1954) | 1,670 | 835 |
| 24. Beauharnois, Canada (1951) | 1,641 | 1,586 |
| 25. Inguri, U.S.S.R. (UC) | 1,600 | — |

C = Concrete. E = Earth. UC= Under Construction. — = Information not available.   *Based on total volume of structure.

# THE UNIVERSE

## The Cosmos · Solar System · The Moon · The Stars

Galaxy NGC 5128, in the constellation Centaurus, emits intense radio signals.

Mt. Wilson & Palomar Observatories

The mysterious quasars continued to disturb and fascinate astronomers in 1967. Are they enormously distant, enormously luminous objects? Indeed, one observation in 1967 claimed record distance. Quasar PKS-0237-23 was found to have a "red shift" indicating a possible speed of recession of 153,000 miles a second. This would mean a distance of well over 8 billion light-years from the Earth.

Yet such distances are not universally accepted. Quasars vary from year to year in the amount of light and radio waves they emit, and such variations seem to indicate small size. It is difficult to explain the facts by assuming both very small sizes *and* very great distances.

What is the answer? W. H. McCrea of the University of Sussex in England suggests that quasars are extremely young galaxies that contain a few enormously luminous stars and many nonluminous conglomerates of gas and dust. Eclipses of the bright stars by dark bodies may produce the observed light variation even at enormous distances. But 1967 saw no decision in this controversy.

Nor was agreement reached in another controversy. Robert Dicke of Princeton University has closely measured the sun's shape and, in 1967, reported that it has a slightly elliptical cross section. The effect that this would have on the motion of the planet Mercury would explain what previously had been explained by Einstein's theory of general relativity. If Dicke is right, then Einstein is wrong. Basic views of gravitation may have to be reconsidered.

However, if the Sun is elliptical, as Dicke proposes, its central regions must be whirling far more rapidly than its outermost layers. What effect might this internal spin have on the Sun? Some astronomers say that the Sun could not be stable under such circumstances and that it therefore cannot have an elliptical cross section. Only new data will settle the controversy.

# THE COSMOS

Two centuries ago the renowned philosopher Immanuel Kant surmised that some of the hazy patches of celestial light might be other Milky Way systems like our own. And he was right. Not many such luminous spots are known to casual observers. Among them, however, is the Andromeda Nebula—a northern galaxy visible to the unaided eye. In the far south are the Magellanic Star Clouds, which are now recognized as nearby irregular galaxies of high importance to those who search the cosmic spaces beyond our Milky Way.

The Andromeda Nebula with its trillions of stars is the best-known spiral galaxy. But only the most powerful telescopes can record its individual super giant stars and its star clusters. The distance is about two million light-years. (A light-year is a unit of distance some 6,000,000,000,000 [six trillion] miles long.)

The Shapley-Ames catalogue of the brightest galaxies records but a little more than a thousand over the whole sky. Much more penetrating reaches into space show that more than a million galaxies are recorded on Harvard, Lick, and Mount Wilson photographs. The 200-inch Hale telescope on Palomar Mountain, if used for census-taking, could photograph ten thousand million galaxies.

The Harvard survey of faint galaxies has explored a volume of space extending about 100,000,000 light years from the Earth. This survey has recorded 1,500 galaxies shining through the bowl of the Big Dipper, a region encompassing less than one per cent of the total sky area.

Nearly a thousand galaxies have been measured for velocity, with a most remarkable result: With very few exceptions they appear to be receding from our own. Moreover, the speed of recession appears to increase with increasing distance from the Milky Way. This means that the entire universe of galaxies is expanding. The velocities are tremendous—some of them approaching the velocity of light.

Studies of the distribution of galaxies meet with one basic difficulty: There is a good deal of interstellar smog in space. This irregularly cuts down the observed brightness and distance of stars and galaxies, especially for those objects observed near the plane of the Milky Way, where the interstellar dust is concentrated. This smog makes it impossible to measure accurately the distances of Milky Way objects.

Our own galaxy—the Milky Way system—is a giant in luminosity and in size. So also is its twin, the Andromeda spiral. Both are in rotation, and both are members of a loose cluster of galaxies, which includes at least four irregular galaxies. It may be that the small irregular type will turn out to be the most common.

So far as the Earth's location inside the "home" galaxy is concerned, a study of the distribution of globular star clusters, and of a type of variable star called Cepheid, has shown that it is far off center. The clusters appear to be concentrated in the star clouds of the southern Milky Way in the constellations Sagittarius, Ophiuchus, and Centaurus. The direction from the Earth to the center of the Milky Way is quite accurately known, but not the distance. The best value now available is 27,000 light-years; the thickness of the Milky Way is about one-fifth as much.

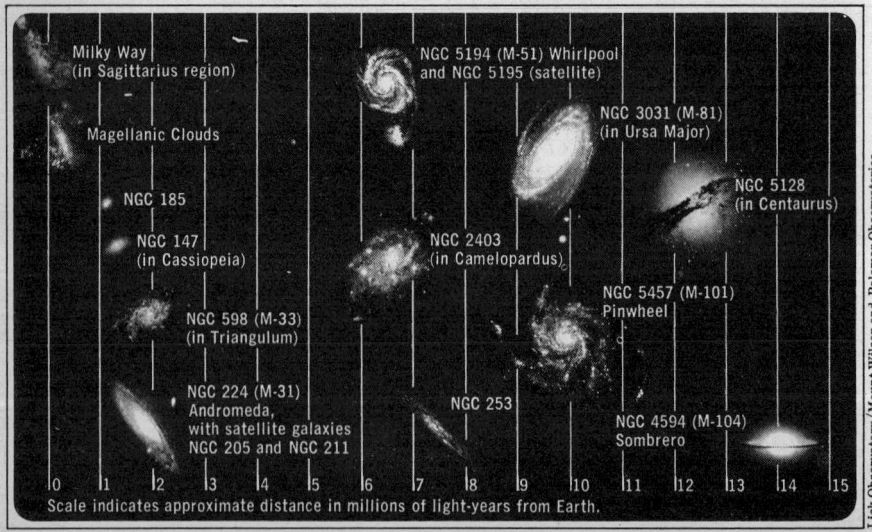

Milky Way (in Sagittarius region)

Magellanic Clouds

NGC 185

NGC 147 (in Cassiopeia)

NGC 598 (M-33) (in Triangulum)

NGC 224 (M-31) Andromeda, with satellite galaxies NGC 205 and NGC 211

NGC 5194 (M-51) Whirlpool and NGC 5195 (satellite)

NGC 3031 (M-81) (in Ursa Major)

NGC 5128 (in Centaurus)

NGC 2403 (in Camelopardus)

NGC 5457 (M-101) Pinwheel

NGC 253

NGC 4594 (M-104) Sombrero

0  1  2  3  4  5  6  7  8  9  10  11  12  13  14  15
Scale indicates approximate distance in millions of light-years from Earth.

Lick Observatory/Mount Wilson and Palomar Observatories

Galaxies in the vicinity of the Milky Way

## A SYMMETRICAL UNIVERSE?

Some scientists believe a ball of antimatter gouged the crater and leveled the forests at Tungaska, Siberia, in 1908. Such a meteorite may have come from an "antimatter universe."

Is the observable universe perhaps "two universes?" Does it consist of both matter and antimatter? Would this help explain the strange quasi-stellar objects called quasars?

An ordinary hydrogen atom consists of a *proton* orbited by an *electron*. Physicists have discovered that both protons and electrons have "antiparticles," which have the same properties except for opposite charges. The positively charged antiparticle of the (negative) electron is called the *positron;* the negatively charged antiparticle of the (positive) proton is called the *antiproton.*

A positron plus an antiproton can form an "antihydrogen" atom. Thus, there may be "antiatoms" of all kinds, which may build up "antimatter" with the same properties as ordinary matter. However, if a piece of matter and a piece of antimatter are brought together, the electrons will annihilate the positrons and the protons will annihilate the antiprotons. Result: Equal amounts of matter and antimatter will simply disappear, or rather — when joining — be transformed into radiation. An enormous quantity of energy is released in this process — some thousand times that of a hydrogen bomb of similar mass.

Before the idea of antimatter it had to be assumed that all heavenly bodies consisted of ordinary matter. Now, however, it is not certain whether stars consist of matter or antimatter. Also, some meteors might consist of antimatter, although no final proof has yet been found.

Suppose the universe did consist half of matter and half of antimatter? Such a symmetry would imply that matter and antimatter, mixing in certain regions of the universe, would release enormous quantities of energy. Matter-antimatter annihilation might provide the immense energy of quasars.

## BIRTH OF THE UNIVERSE

The building blocks of the universe are galaxies, huge aggregates of stars, gas, and cosmic dust. We live in the Milky Way Galaxy, in which the Sun is but one of hundreds of billions of stars. Beyond our Milky Way, billions of galaxies are within the reach of our telescopes out to several billions of light-years. The distant galaxies are rushing away from us; the farther away the galaxies are, the faster they recede from us. Some are moving away from us with speeds of many thousands of miles per second. The universe appears to be expanding.

Those are the observed facts. The question is, how did the universe get started, or has it always been here? The Steady-State theory of the universe holds that there was no beginning and will be no end. This theory must hold that there is a continuous creation of matter and formation of new galaxies, otherwise the expansion of the universe leads to increasing distances between galaxies, thus violating the basic idea of the theory.

Although it is very attractive to many people, the Steady-State theory has been virtually abandoned. No observations support it, and several argue strongly against it, one being the crowding of radio galaxies in the distant reaches of space.

Two basic theories of the nature of the universe remain: the Big-Bang and the Oscillating theories. The former theory, generally associated with the physicist George Gamow, assumes that the observed expansion resulted from a cosmic explosion some ten or more billion years ago. The galaxies are considered as fragments of this explosion. What caused the explosion and what came before it remain unanswered questions.

The oscillating universe, which alternately expands and contracts like a great cosmic in-and-out breathing, in periods of many tens of billions of years, avoids the difficulties of both the Steady-State and Big-Bang theories. According to this theory, the universe is evolutionary and changing, yet has no beginning or end. If the oscillating theory is valid, we are now in a relatively early stage of the current cycle of cosmic expansion.

Which theory of the universe is correct? More observations are needed before any of the theories can be proved. Many of these observations can best be made from telescopes in orbit or on the Moon, where atmospheric and man-made interference to optical and radio telescopes is absent. These theories and other new ones will be developed and matched against observed facts, as we go on learning more about the universe.

## INTERSTELLAR SPACE

Astronomers and cosmic ray physicists study a multitude of events that arise from the interactions between four principal constituents of the space that lies between the stars.

The ordinary matter in space consists of gas, mostly hydrogen and helium, and small "dust" particles less than one ten-thousandth of an inch in diameter. Most of this matter is clumped together into "clouds." A typical cloud may contain 1,000 times the mass of our Sun, and its density may be about 150 atoms per cubic inch, about ten times the average value for interstellar space near the Sun.

Starlight in interstellar space interacts with the matter in several ways. The most important way is by ionization, or breaking up atoms into the ions and electrons of which they are composed, especially within a few light-years of very hot stars. This causes strong pressure differences in the gas and sets the clouds into rapid motion.

Interstellar space also contains very energetic particles, or cosmic rays, and magnetic fields along which the cosmic ray particles travel in a spiral motion. The magnetic fields move with the matter in space. This allows energy to be pumped through the magnetic field into the cosmic rays.

## ORIGIN OF STARS

Very young, hot, massive stars are observed to lie in space in regions where the interstellar gas and dust is very dense. One such region is the Orion Nebula.

There is a general theory of star formation that shows that interstellar matter can collapse to form stars only when a cloud is sufficiently massive, or sufficiently dense, that the gravitational forces tending to pull the matter together can become stronger than the opposing forces, such as heat and magnetic fields, which tend to expand the clouds. During the collapse of a cloud it is evident that the gas must break up into many smaller pieces, since the observed result is an "association" of young stars having approximately the mass of an interstellar cloud. These associations are usually observed to be expanding, and their stars to be scattering in space, although occasionally the stars remain gravitationally bound together as a star cluster. The associations are thought to disrupt when the new stars become hot and ionize the uncondensed gas from the original interstellar cloud. This gas then expands out of the association, and the remaining stars are no longer gravitationally bound together.

The interstellar clouds are believed to have a small amount of spinning motion. As the clouds collapse, their rate of spin and also the spin of their fragments must increase. This will cause much of the matter in a cloud fragment to flatten into a spinning disk. Most modern theories of the origin of the solar system require the planets to form from a primitive disklike solar nebula of this type.

## THE CONSTELLATIONS

When you look up on a clear night at the stars, many of them appear to be clustered in groups, called constellations. Ancient observers gave 48 constellations names suggested by the patterns of their stars. Usually the stars forming these apparent groups are entirely unrelated and are located at greatly varying distances, although all the stars visible to the naked eye are in our own Milky Way Galaxy.

Modern astronomers recognize 88 constellations, including most of the ancient ones. Their strict boundaries were established by the International Astronomical Union in 1928. They are used as reference areas for locating, naming, and classifying the stars, and for roughly fixing the positions of comets, meteors, and other celestial bodies viewed in the sky. The table names the constellations. Those marked with an asterisk (*) are not visible from mid-northern latitudes.

| LATIN NAME AND ABBREVIATION | ENGLISH VERSION | LATIN NAME AND ABBREVIATION | ENGLISH VERSION |
| --- | --- | --- | --- |
| Andromeda...................And | Chained Maiden | Lacerta......................Lac | Lizard |
| Antlia........................Ant | Air Pump | Leo...........................Leo | Lion |
| Apus*.......................Aps | Bird of Paradise | Leo Minor....................LMi | Small Lion |
| Aquarius.....................Aqr | Water Bearer | Lepus........................Lep | Hare |
| Aquila.......................Aql | Eagle | Libra.........................Lib | Scales |
| Ara*........................Ara | Altar | Lupus*......................Lup | Wolf |
| Aries........................Ari | Ram | Lynx.........................Lyn | Lynx |
| Auriga.......................Aur | Charioteer | Lyra..........................Lyr | Lyre |
| Boötes.......................Boo | Herdsman | Mensa*......................Men | Table (Mountain) |
| Caelum......................Cae | Chisel | Microscopium................Mic | Microscope |
| Camelopardus...............Cam | Giraffe | Monoceros...................Mon | Unicorn |
| Cancer......................Cnc | Crab | Musca*......................Mus | Fly |
| Canes Venatici..............CVn | Hunting Dogs | Norma*......................Nor | Square |
| Canis Major.................CMa | Great Dog | Octans*......................Oct | Octant |
| Canis Minor.................CMi | Small Dog | Ophiuchus...................Oph | Serpent Bearer |
| Capricornus.................Cap | Goat | Orion.........................Ori | Orion |
| Carina*.....................Car | Keel | Pavo*.......................Pav | Peacock |
| Cassiopeia..................Cas | Lady in Chair | Pegasus......................Peg | Pegasus |
| Centaurus*..................Cen | Centaur | Perseus......................Per | Perseus |
| Cepheus.....................Cep | Cepheus | Phoenix*....................Phe | Phoenix |
| Cetus........................Cet | Whale | Pictor*.......................Pic | Easel |
| Chamaeleon*................Cha | Chameleon | Pisces........................Psc | Fishes |
| Circinus*....................Cir | Compasses | Piscis Austrinus.............PsA | Southern Fish |
| Columba.....................Col | Dove | Puppis.......................Pup | Poop (Stern) |
| Coma Berenices.............Com | Berenice's Hair | Pyxis.........................Pyx | Ship's Compass |
| Corona Australis.............CrA | Southern Crown | Reticulum*...................Ret | Net |
| Corona Borealis.............CrB | Northern Crown | Sagitta.......................Sge | Arrow |
| Corvus.......................Crv | Crow | Sagittarius...................Sgr | Archer |
| Crater.......................Crt | Cup | Scorpius......................Sco | Scorpion |
| Crux*.......................Cru | Southern Cross | Sculptor......................Scl | Sculptor |
| Cygnus......................Cyg | Swan | Scutum.......................Sct | Shield |
| Delphinus....................Del | Dolphin | Serpens......................Ser | Serpent |
| Dorado*.....................Dor | Swordfish | Sextans......................Sex | Sextant |
| Draco........................Dra | Dragon | Taurus.......................Tau | Bull |
| Equuleus....................Equ | Little Horse | Telescopium..................Tel | Telescope |
| Eridanus.....................Eri | Eridanus | Triangulum...................Tri | Triangle |
| Fornax.......................For | Furnace | Triangulum Australe*.........TrA | Southern Triangle |
| Gemini......................Gem | Twins | Tucana*.....................Tuc | Toucan |
| Grus*.......................Gru | Crane | Ursa Major...................UMa | Great Bear |
| Hercules.....................Her | Hercules | Ursa Minor...................UMi | Small Bear |
| Horologium*.................Hor | Clock | Vela*........................Vel | Sails |
| Hydra........................Hya | Sea Serpent | Virgo.........................Vir | Virgin |
| Hydrus*.....................Hyi | Small Sea Serpent | Volans*......................Vol | Flying Fish |
| Indus*.......................Ind | Indian | Vulpecula.................... Vul | Fox |

**THE ZODIAC:** An imaginary circular band in the sky, the zodiac is determined by the apparent annual path followed by the Sun as the Earth revolves around it. This band is separated into 12 divisions, one for each month of the year, with each occupied by a constellation. Ancient astrologers claimed that the positions of the zodiac controlled the destinies of men, and used a horoscope, or map of the heavenly bodies, to forecast the future. The 12 constellations or divisions in order along the zodiac and their traditional signs are:

♈ ARIES, the Ram      ♋ CANCER, the Crab      ♎ LIBRA, the Scales      ♑ CAPRICORNUS, the Goat

♉ TAURUS, the Bull    ♌ LEO, the Lion         ♏ SCORPIUS, the Scorpion  ♒ AQUARIUS, the Water Bearer

♊ GEMINI, the Twins   ♍ VIRGO, the Virgin     ♐ SAGITTARIUS, the Archer ♓ PISCES, the Fishes

## THE STARS

Our Sun is but one of a countless number of other suns, or stars, in the universe. The sky map shows the apparent patterns, or constellations, that many of the brightest stars make in the northern and southern skies.

Perhaps 2,000 stars can be observed with the unaided eye. Early in the 17th century Galileo turned his small telescope to the Milky Way and discovered that it was not a celestial cloud but consisted of multitudes of stars. Astronomers now estimate that the Milky Way and other galaxies each contain over 100 billion stars, and there are billions of galaxies in the observable universe.

Many of the names of the brighter stars were derived from myths and ancient usage. Stars are identified by a Greek letter (alpha, beta, gamma, etc.) and by the Latin genitive of their constellation. Thus, in the constellation Taurus the Bull, Aldebaran, the brightest star, is called Alpha Tauri, and the second brightest, El Nath, is Beta Tauri.

Because they are so distant, even in the most powerful telescopes stars are seen only as points of light, never as disks like our Sun. However, these points of light have told astronomers about stellar distances, stellar temperatures, the rotation and proper motions of stars, and even the birth, development, and death of stars. Stars range in size from red giants like Betelgeuse of the constellation Orion, which would extend out to the Earth if substituted for our Sun, to spectacular dwarfs like Procyon B of the constellation Canis Minor, which is so dense that a cubic inch of its substance weighs 200 tons.

Wobbles have been found in the motions of several nearby stars, like Barnard's Star. The wobbles may be caused by large dark companions or by a number of smaller bodies, like the planets around our Sun. There may be millions of such solar systems in our Milky Way Galaxy alone and untold numbers in the galaxies beyond our own.

With the design of new equipment like radio telescopes, and the raising of instruments in balloons and satellites above the interference of the Earth's atmosphere, strange new stellar bodies have been discovered radiating in the far infrared and ultraviolet temperature ranges. In addition to these are the quasars (quasi-stellar radio sources), first discovered as strong sources of radio waves and then identified with visible objects. Although there are many theories about quasars, none are acceptable as yet.

## HOW TO FIND STARS AND CONSTELLATIONS

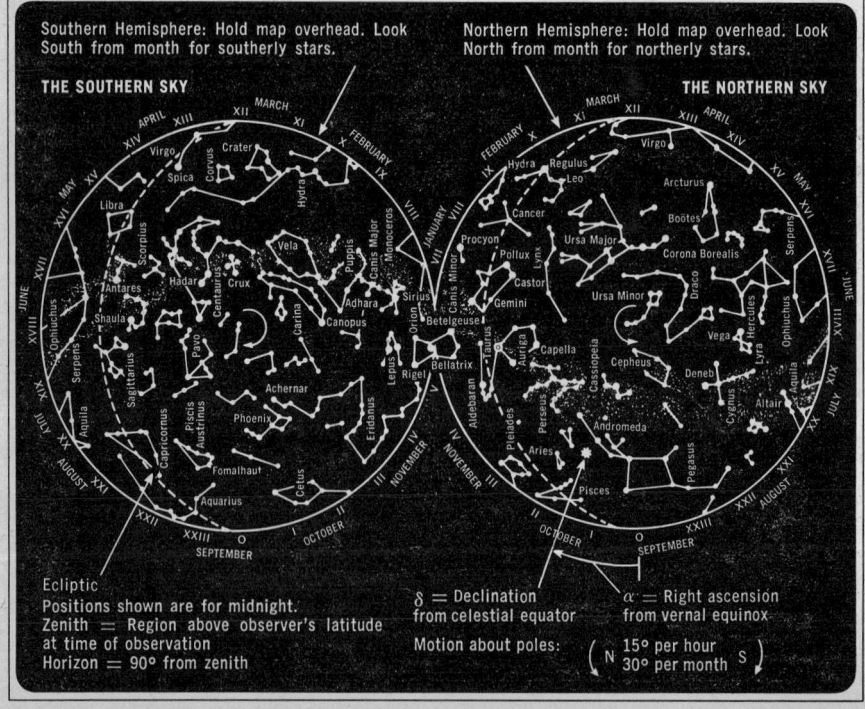

Southern Hemisphere: Hold map overhead. Look South from month for southerly stars.

Northern Hemisphere: Hold map overhead. Look North from month for northerly stars.

THE SOUTHERN SKY

THE NORTHERN SKY

Ecliptic
Positions shown are for midnight.
Zenith = Region above observer's latitude at time of observation
Horizon = 90° from zenith

δ = Declination from celestial equator

Motion about poles:

α = Right ascension from vernal equinox

( N   15° per hour
      30° per month   S )

## DISTANCES OF THE STARS

On Earth we live some 93 million miles away from the nearest star, our Sun. Light from the Sun takes over eight minutes to reach the Earth, even though light travels at some 186,300 miles a second. Other distances in our solar system are so immense that astronomers use the Astronomical Unit (A.U.) to measure them. One A.U. is the average Earth-Sun distance. The Sun's gravitational influence extends over 100,000 A.U.s.

The A.U. is too small a unit, however, to measure the distances to stars other than our Sun. The nearest star is a double star named Rigel Kent (Alpha Centauri A) and a companion. This is 4.31 light-years distant, as shown in the table below. The unit of a light-year (the distance light travels in a year) is about six trillion miles. The table shows some 40 other stars known to be located within a distance of 17 light-years. Also indicated are the spectral type of these stars and their luminosity, or brightness.

Beyond these closest stars lie the billions of other stars in our Milky Way Galaxy, which is a great thin disk about 90,000 light-years in diameter. The nearest galaxies are the Magellanic Clouds, at a distance of about 170,000 light-years. The great Andromeda Galaxy, also a member of our Local Group of galaxies, is over two million light-years away.

| STAR | SPEC-TRAL TYPE | DISTANCE IN LIGHT-YEARS | BRIGHT-NESS (Sun = 1.0) | STAR | SPEC-TRAL TYPE | DISTANCE IN LIGHT-YEARS | BRIGHT-NESS (Sun = 1.0) |
|---|---|---|---|---|---|---|---|
| Sun............ | G2 | — | 1.0 | Kapteyn's........ | M0 | 13.0 | 0.0025 |
| Alpha Cen A *.... | G2 | 4.3 | 1.0 | Kruger 60 *...... | M3 | 13.1 | 0.0013 |
| Barnard's........ | M5 | 6.0 | 0.0004 | Ross 614 *....... | M5 | 13.1 | 0.00052 |
| Wolf 359........ | M6 | 7.7 | 0.000017 | BD-12°4523..... | M4 | 13.4 | 0.0013 |
| Luyten 726-8 *... | M6 | 7.9 | 0.00004 | Van Maanen's.... | F5 | 13.8 | 0.00016 |
| Lalande 21185 *.. | M2 | 8.2 | 0.0048 | Wolf 424 *....... | M6 | 14.6 | 0.00014 |
| Sirius *.......... | A1 | 8.7 | 23.0 | Groombridge | | | |
| Ross 154........ | M5 | 9.3 | 0.00036 | 1618.... | M0 | 14.7 | 0.03 |
| Ross 248........ | M6 | 10.3 | 0.0001 | CD-37°15492..... | M3 | 14.9 | 0.0058 |
| Epsilon Eri....... | K2 | 10.8 | 0.25 | CD-46°11540..... | M4 | 15.3 | 0.0023 |
| Ross 128........ | M5 | 10.9 | 0.0003 | BD+20°2465 *... | M4 | 15.4 | 0.0028 |
| 61 Cygni........ | K5 | 11.1 | 0.052 | CD-44°11909..... | M5 | 15.6 | 0.00058 |
| Luyten 789-6..... | M6 | 11.2 | 0.00012 | CD-49°13515..... | M3 | 15.6 | 0.0044 |
| Procyon *....... | F5 | 11.3 | 5.8 | AOe 17415-6..... | M3 | 15.8 | 0.004 |
| Epsilon Ind...... | K5 | 11.4 | 0.12 | Ross 780........ | M5 | 15.8 | 0.0014 |
| Sigma 2398A..... | M4 | 11.6 | 0.0028 | Lalande 25372.... | M2 | 15.9 | 0.0063 |
| Groombridge 34 * | M2 | 11.7 | 0.0058 | CC 658 | white | | |
| Tau Ceti........ | G8 | 11.8 | 0.36 | | dwarf | 16.0 | 0.0008 |
| Lacaille 9352..... | M2 | 11.9 | 0.013 | 70 Oph*........ | K0 | 16.4 | 0.4 |
| Luyten+5°1668... | M4 | 12.4 | 0.001 | Altair........... | A7 | 16.5 | 8.3 |
| Lacaille 8760..... | M0 | 12.8 | 0.028 | BD+43°4305..... | M5 | 16.5 | 0.0016 |

* These stars are binary or larger multiples, that is, they have one or more smaller stars associated with them, some of which have not yet been seen.

## STAR COLOR AND TEMPERATURE

The floods of radiation given off by stars range the whole electromagnetic spectrum from gamma rays and X rays through light and heat to radio waves. These radiations come from nuclear-fusion reactions maintained by the great pressures and temperatures deep within the stars. The calculated temperature of the center of the Sun is about 25 million degrees Fahrenheit. At such extremes, hydrogen atoms will fuse into helium atoms with a loss in total mass and the release of tremendous quantities of energy.

Stars vary greatly in color and temperature as well as in size. Astronomers analyze the radiations from stars with many instruments, including the spectroscope, which divides light into a color spectrum. The spectra of stars indicate their temperatures. The standard spectral classification of stars is given in the capital letters in the following table, with the color and approximate surface temperatures of stars in these classes. The stars that fall into inter-mediate positions are indicated by a range of numbers from 1 to 10 with each letter. Our Sun, for example, has the spectral classification of G2 and a surface temperature of about 10,440 degrees Fahrenheit.

| SPECTRAL CLASSIFICATION | COLOR SCALE | STAR SURFACE TEMPERATURE (° Fahrenheit) |
|---|---|---|
| O.............. | Blue........... | 63,000 |
| B.............. | Bluish......... | 45,000 |
| A.............. | White......... | 19,800 |
| F.............. | Yellowish....... | 13,500 |
| G Dwarf........ | Yellow......... | 10,440 |
| G Giant........ | Yellow......... | 9,540 |
| K Dwarf........ | Orange......... | 8,820 |
| K Giant........ | Orange......... | 7,200 |
| M Dwarf........ | Orange-red..... | 6,120 |
| M Giant........ | Orange-red..... | 5,400 |
| S.............. | Red........... | 4,680 |
| N.............. | Red........... | 4,680 |
| R.............. | Red........... | 4,140 |

## THE BRIGHTEST STARS

In the second century A.D., Ptolemy, the Greek astronomer, made the first significant attempt to classify the stars by their brightness. According to his system, all the stars that can be seen with the naked eye fall into six groups of brightness, called apparent magnitudes. The first positive (+) magnitude stars are the very brightest, and the sixth positive magnitude stars are the faintest. The planet Uranus is near the limit of naked-eye visibility with a magnitude of +5.5.

With the use of the telescope, photographic plates, and other equipment, fainter stars of much higher apparent magnitude can be seen. Ptolemy's scale of decreasing visible brightness has been extended to over +20. Stars of magnitude +23 have recorded their dim images on photographic plates made with large telescopes. On the present magnitude scale, a difference of one magnitude represents a difference in brightness of 2.512 times. Therefore, a celestial body of magnitude +1 appears to be about +2.5 times brighter than one of magnitude +2.

For the measurement of the luminosity of brighter bodies like our Sun and nearby planets, the magnitude scale has been extended into negative (−) magnitudes. The higher negative magnitudes represent greater brightness. Thus the Sun has an apparent magnitude of −26.78 as shown in the table, the full Moon −12.7, Venus at its brightest −4.2, and Jupiter −2.5. The brightest star is Sirius, with a magnitude of −1.41. The estimated magnitude of the supernova explosion that created the Crab Nebula in 1054 A.D. was −6 at its height.

Since a small but bright star at a great distance appears approximately as bright as a nearby but cooler one, an absolute magnitude scale has also been devised. The absolute brightness of a star is the numerical value it would have if it were seen at a set distance from the Earth. The distance that has been chosen is ten parsecs. One parsec is equal to 3.262 light-years, or about 19 trillion miles.

The following table lists all those stars that have an apparent magnitude brighter than magnitude +1. The lower the value of their magnitude, the brighter they appear to be in the sky.

| PROPER NAME OF STAR | GREEK LETTER AND CONSTELLATION | APPARENT MAGNITUDE | ABSOLUTE MAGNITUDE | DISTANCE IN LIGHT-YEARS |
|---|---|---|---|---|
| Sun | Sun | −26.73 | 4.84 | — |
| Sirius | Alpha Canis Majoris | −1.42 | 1.45 | 8.7 |
| Canopus | Alpha Carinae | −0.72 | −3.1 | 98 |
| Arcturus | Alpha Boötis | −0.06 | −0.3 | 36 |
| Vega | Alpha Lyrae | 0.04 | 0.5 | 26.5 |
| Capella | Alpha Aurigae | 0.05 | −0.6 | 45 |
| Rigel | Beta Orionis | 0.14* | −7.1 | 900 |
| Rigel Kent | Alpha Centauri A | 0.01 | 4.39 | 4.3 |
| Procyon | Alpha Canis Minoris | 0.37 | 2.7 | 11.3 |
| Betelgeuse | Alpha Orionis | 0.41* | −5.6 | 520 |
| Achernar | Alpha Eridani | 0.51 | −2.3 | 118 |
| Hadar | Beta Centauri AB | 0.63 | −5.2 | 490 |
| Altair | Alpha Aquilae | 0.77 | 2.2 | 16.5 |
| Aldebaran | Alpha Tauri | 0.86* | −0.7 | 68 |
| Acrux | Alpha Crucis | 1.39 | −3.9 | 370 |
| Antares | Alpha Scorpii | 0.92* | −5.1 | 520 |
| Spica | Alpha Virginis | 0.91* | −3.3 | 220 |
| Pollux | Beta Cominorum | 1.16 | 1.0 | 35 |
| Fomalhaut | Alpha Picis Australis | 1.19 | 2.0 | 22.6 |

* Variable star

## VARIABLE AND EXPLODING STARS

Changes in the brightness of the many different kinds of variable stars have taught astronomers a great deal about the nature, evolution, and distances of stars, and even about events going on within them. Some pulsating variables, whose light brightens and dims regularly, are caused by the passage of companions in front of the brighter stars, or by the relations of several stars orbiting in a complex system. The radiation of other stars may vary because of changes in their outer layers.

Explosive variables are stars that suddenly brighten by many magnitudes. They are called novas, or new stars, because they suddenly become so bright. Their light may increase in intensity by a million times in a day or two. Then they decrease slowly to about their orig-

inal magnitude. Novas may be stars that have reached an unbalanced state in which they blow off large portions of their substance in cataclysmic explosions. Novas have been known to recur from one to three times.

Supernovas, which show much greater variations in intensity, may be stars tearing themselves to bits. Only a few supernovas have been recorded in the Milky Way Galaxy. In 1054 A.D., for example, the Chinese recorded a bright new star, which was probably a supernova that exploded to form the Crab Nebula, in which the debris is still shooting outward at great velocities. In 1572, the Danish astronomer Tycho Brahe reported a strange bright object that may have been a nova or a supernova, and in 1604 Kepler observed another.

# FOCUS ON THE NEWS

## VISITORS TO VENUS

Soviet Venus IV space probe ejected "piggyback" sphere that soft-landed on surface of Venus.

United States' Mariner 5, following Venus IV by a day, flew within 2,480 miles of Venus.

Utilizing a timely break in space and time called a "launch window," the U.S.S.R. and the United States sent separate probes to Venus in June, 1967. On October 18 the Soviet probe, Venus IV, startled the world by accomplishing the first soft-landing on another planet. After a few hours of successful transmission, the Soviet capsule fell silent, a victim no doubt of the searing heat. The next day, October 19, the U.S. probe, Mariner 5, completed a successful fly-by of Venus and several hours of transmission; no landing attempt was made.

For many generations the planet Venus has been referred to as a nearly identical twin of the Earth. With 80 per cent of Earth's mass, 95 per cent of its diameter, and nearly the same force of gravity, Venus was thought to be a close facsimile—capable of supporting life and with an average global climate comparable to the balmy Caribbean.

Mariner 2, the first successful interplanetary fly-by, revealed in 1962 that Venus, with surface readings as high as 800° F (hot enough to melt lead), was uninhabitable. It was suggested, however, that its atmosphere might possess enough oxygen, nitrogen, and water vapor to support hypothetical organ-isms kept aloft by gas bags—kind of airborne "Portuguese Men-of-War."

The results from the two most recent excursions were both revealing and confusing. Preliminary data confirmed the hostile heat of the planet, but in a probable range from 104° F to 536° F. Venus IV found the atmospheric pressure to be from 15 to 22 times that at sea level on Earth. While Venus IV did not detect any magnetic field, Mariner 5 did sense weak magnetic activity. The Russian probe found the atmosphere to be about 90 per cent carbon dioxide. Mariner 5 gave a lower figure, 75 to 85 per cent, and also reported some hydrogen. The virtual absence of nitrogen, comprising about 80 per cent of Earth's atmosphere, was totally unexpected. It rules out the possibility of life and poses some serious problems to students of planetary evolution: How, scientists must now ask, did Venus become so different from Earth?

Debate on the differing Soviet and U.S. findings will likely continue for quite some time. New theories of planetary evolution may be forthcoming. Thus, while Venus has lost much of her charm, tantalizing mysteries remain beneath her turbulent clouds.

## ASTRONOMICAL TELESCOPES

Astronomical telescopes are of two types, refractors and reflectors. The refractor uses a lens to collect the light from a distant object and to bring it to a focus, while a reflector uses a concave mirror for this purpose. Because of the failure of a lens to bring all colors to the same focus, practically all large astronomical telescopes constructed in the last half century are of the reflector type.

Visual observations are rarely made with modern astronomical telescopes. The photographic plate can record objects much fainter than the eye can see. The plate also provides a permanent record which can be referred to at any later time to detect small changes in the position or brightness of objects recorded. Large telescopes are, therefore, used as cameras to take photographs. They are also used to collect light for analysis with photometers, spectrographs, and other instruments. From such detailed analyses, one can determine temperatures, chemical compositions, velocities, and other properties of the objects under study.

In 1932 a German optician, Bernhard Schmidt, developed a new type of telescope which is a combination of a lens and a mirror, and which permits the photography of a large area of the sky on one plate. Thus, the 48-inch Schmidt telescope on Palomar Mountain was used to photograph the whole sky visible from the northern hemisphere on about 900 plates for the National Geographic Society-Palomar Observatory Sky Atlas.

The discovery, in the 1930s, that radio waves were coming from outside the atmosphere, led to the construction of radio telescopes for their study. Many of these radio telescopes are parabolic reflectors of metal sheet or screen, which are pointed at objects under study, and which concentrate the radio waves in the same manner that a reflecting telescope focuses light. The largest of these steerable reflectors is at Jodrell Bank, near Manchester, England, and has a diameter of 250 feet.

### LARGEST REFRACTING TELESCOPES

| DIAMETER OF LENS (In inches) | OBSERVATORY AND LOCATION | YEAR COMPLETED |
|---|---|---|
| 40.0........ | Yerkes Observatory, Williams Bay, Wisconsin | 1897 |
| 36.0........ | Lick Observatory, Mount Hamilton, California.... | 1888 |
| 32.7........ | Paris Observatory of Physical Astronomy, Meudon, France........ | 1889 |
| 32.0........ | Astrophysical Observatory, Potsdam, East Germany | 1899 |
| 30.0........ | Allegheny Observatory, Pittsburgh, Pennsylvania | 1914 |
| 30.0........ | Bischoffsheim Observatory at Mont Gros, Nice, France................ | 1886 |
| 30.0........ | Pulkovo Observatory, near Leningrad, U.S.S.R...... | 1885 |

### LARGE RADIO AND RADAR TELESCOPES

| DIAMETER OR MAXIMUM DIMENSIONS (In feet) | OBSERVATORY AND LOCATION | YEAR COMPLETED |
|---|---|---|
| 1600/1600... | Crimean Astrophysical Observatory, Simferopol, U.S.S.R................ | 1964 |
| 1500........ | Mullard Observatory, Cambridge, England.... | 1958 |
| 1000/1000... | Arecibo Ionospheric Observatory, Puerto Rico | 1964 |
| 350/70...... | Ohio State University Observatory, Columbus, Ohio.................. | 1963 |
| 350/10...... | Pulkovo Observatory, near Leningrad, U.S.S.R...... | 1958 |
| 300........ | National Radio Astronomy Observatory, Green Bank, West Virginia.......... | 1962 |
| 250........ | Nuffield Radio Astronomy Laboratory, Jodrell Bank, England........ | 1957 |

### LARGEST REFLECTING TELESCOPES

| DIAMETER OF MIRROR (In inches) | OBSERVATORY AND LOCATION | YEAR COMPLETED |
|---|---|---|
| 200........ | Hale, Palomar Mountain, near Pasadena, California | 1948 |
| 120........ | Lick Observatory, Mount Hamilton, California.... | 1959 |
| 102........ | Crimean Astrophysical Observatory, Simferopol, U.S.S.R................ | 1960 |
| 100........ | Hooker, Mount Wilson, Carnegie Institution, California.............. | 1917 |
| 98........ | Royal Greenwich Observatory, Herstmonceux Castle, Sussex, England....... | 1966 |
| 84........ | Kitt Peak National Observatory, Tucson, Arizona.............. | 1963 |
| 82.......... | McDonald Observatory, Universities of Texas and Chicago, Fort Davis, Texas................. | 1939 |
| 80.......... | Schwarzschild Observatory, Jena, East Germany..... | 1960 |
| 76........ | Haute-Provence Observatory, Saint-Michel, France.... | 1958 |
| 74.......... | Dunlap Observatory, Richmond Hill, Ontario, Canada........ | 1935 |
| 74.......... | Radcliffe Observatory, Pretoria, Republic of South Africa........... | 1938 |
| 74.......... | Mount Stromlo Observatory, Canberra, Australia..... | 1955 |
| 74.......... | Tokyo Astronomical Observatory, Mitaka, Japan................. | 1960 |
| 74.......... | Helwan Observatory, Helwan, Egypt......... | 1960 |
| 72.......... | Dominion Astrophysical Observatory, Royal Oak, British Columbia....... | 1919 |

# OUR SOLAR SYSTEM

Ancient man believed without question that the Earth was the center of the universe. This belief was shattered by the astronomers Copernicus (1473–1543) and Galileo (1564–1642), who proved that the Earth is but one of several planets that revolve around the Sun. Today we know that the Sun, although the source of life on Earth, is but one of a countless number and variety of stars in the universe. Many of these stars must have their own systems, some with planets that may support some kind of life.

Our solar system consists of the Sun, nine known planets and their 32 satellites, a belt of asteroids between Mars and Jupiter, and numerous meteors and comets. These celestial bodies revolve around the Sun, held in their orbits by mutual gravitation. Their elliptical orbital paths differ considerably on the basis of their mass, velocity, and distance from the Sun.

The four planets closest to the Sun (Mercury, Venus, Earth, and Mars) are dense rocky bodies and are called "earthlike." The four large outer planets (Jupiter, Saturn, Uranus, and Neptune) are composed mostly of such elements as hydrogen and helium. They are much bigger than the rocky planets and are flattened at their poles by rotation. They are called the "gas giants" or "starlike planets."

**The Sun:** Merely one of a vast number of similar bodies in our Milky Way Galaxy, the Sun is a fairly average star, approximately 864,000 miles in diameter and with a surface temperature of about 10,000° F. The main form of energy radiating from this sphere of seething gas is light. Other radiations include gamma rays, X-rays, infrared rays, energetic cosmic rays, radio waves, and what is known as the "solar wind," a continuous flow of charged particles, protons and electrons, that the Sun sprays out like a rotating water sprinkler.

The Sun is essentially a huge ball of hydrogen, but in its interior, where temperatures approach 25 million degrees F., this element is converted into helium. The nuclear conversion of hydrogen into helium results in the loss of mass and the release of immense quantities of energy, which is the source of life on Earth. Despite this great loss of matter, the Sun is large enough to exist for at least four to five billion years more. Probably the Sun has already burned in this same way for about five billion years.

The atmosphere of the Sun consists of several layers of gases cooler and less dense than those on the surface. The layer next to the surface is about 10,000 miles thick and is called the chromosphere. Enveloping this layer are the inner and outer coronas, some hundreds of thousands of miles thick. The corona is best seen during a total solar eclipse when the Moon blocks the Sun from view.

One of the most striking features of the Sun is the sunspots. They are dark, turbulent regions often seen within larger, brighter areas
*(continued)*

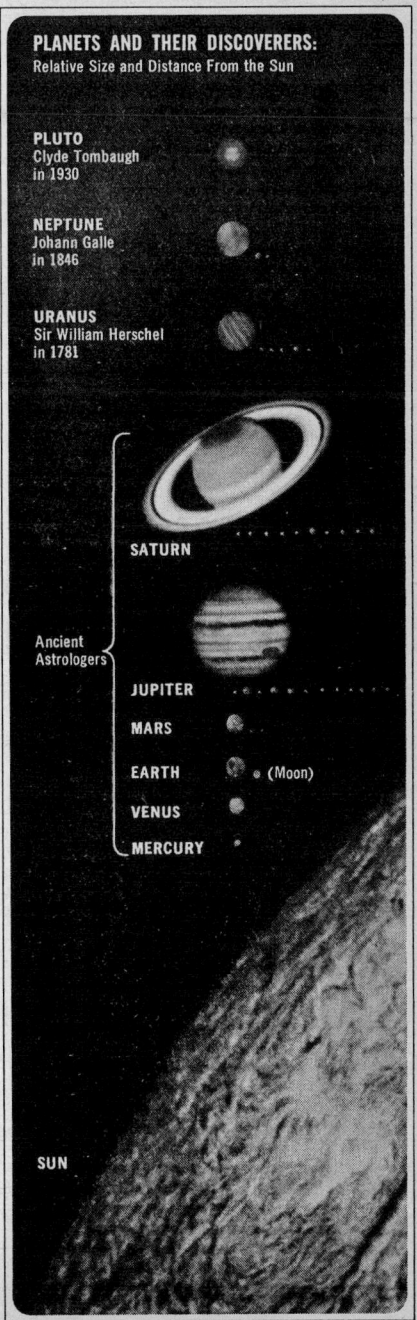

PLANETS AND THEIR DISCOVERERS:
Relative Size and Distance From the Sun

PLUTO
Clyde Tombaugh
in 1930

NEPTUNE
Johann Galle
in 1846

URANUS
Sir William Herschel
in 1781

SATURN

Ancient
Astrologers

JUPITER

MARS

EARTH        (Moon)

VENUS

MERCURY

SUN

**OUR SOLAR SYSTEM** (continued)

known as "flocculi" on the surface of the Sun. The presence of a sunspot is frequently accompanied by a sudden, intense surge of energy called a solar burst. These bursts are the cause of auroras, they often disrupt radio and telegraph communications on Earth, and they might endanger astronauts in space with their heavy radiation. Careful records of sunspots have been kept for many years, and they reveal that the intensity and frequency of solar bursts vary over an 11-year period. During 1964–65 the Sun passed through a period with a minimum of sunspots and solar bursts. Then the spots began to increase toward the maximum of the cycle.

Sunspots move across the surface of the Sun from left to right when viewed through a smoked-lens telescope. This shows that the Sun rotates on its axis from west to east, in the same manner as the Earth, with a mean period of 30 days.

**Mercury:** Mercury is the planet nearest the Sun. It is also the smallest, the fastest, and at the same time the hottest of the nine planets.

Since Mercury orbits between the Earth and the Sun, it is seen in phases like those of the Moon. Because of its eccentric orbit, it appears largest when in the crescent phases and much smaller when it is full. Recently radar telescopes have shown that Mercury rotates slowly with a period of about 59 days, two thirds of its period of revolution, in a direction opposite to that of the Sun.

Little is actually known about Mercury. It is so small, distant, and close to the Sun that optical telescopes are nearly useless in determining surface features. Most astronomers believe, however, that it is a dark, rocky planet with a surface somewhat like the Moon. There is little evidence that it has any significant atmosphere.

**Venus:** Venus is the planet closest to the Earth, and after the Sun and Moon, the brightest object in our view. Its diameter is 7,550 miles, only 377 miles less than the Earth's. It revolves about the Sun in a nearly circular orbit at a distance of 67 million miles. When Venus is closest to us, it is less than 25 million miles

away. Venus is so bright that it can sometimes be seen in the daytime and occasionally even casts shadows like the Moon.

From information transmitted by U.S. and U.S.S.R. space probes in 1967, scientists have determined that Venus has no strong magnetic field and that its surface temperature was about 530° F. lower than believed earlier. It was also suggested by the data that the atmospheric pressure on Venus is 15 to 22 times greater than that on Earth. The surface of Venus may be a vast hot desert blasted by fierce winds filled with dust. Radar observations have suggested that Venus' rotational period may be 245.1 Earth days, longer than its year of about 225 Earth days. Venus rotates in the same direction as the Earth, however.

**Mars:** Mars is the planet we know most about, and probably the most like the Earth. It has four seasons, a day just slightly longer than ours, polar caps, and possibly even vegetation. Because of its reddish color, which reminded the ancients of blood, it was named after the god of war. Its two tiny satellites are Deimos (Terror) and Phobos (Fear). Phobos, which is closest to Mars, revolves around Mars faster than Mars itself rotates, so that Phobos rises in the west and sets in the east.

Mars' atmosphere is thin, perhaps only one or two per cent of the Earth's, so we can see much of Mars' surface detail. It is believed to have frost-capped polar regions, which shrink during the Martian summer and expand again during its winter. With a telescope, the large Martian "deserts" look reddish, and dark patches elsewhere have been found to vary in shape and size. In summer, a wave of darkening moves down from the pole toward the equator as the ice cap shrinks. This changing color has been attributed to dust storms, volcanoes, and even plant growth, but it is most likely a seasonal change in rock coloration.

The summer temperature at the Martian equator is no more than 85° F. and the planet probably freezes each night. The force of gravity is only a little more than one third of that on Earth; a 180-pound man would weigh only 60 pounds on Mars. The atmosphere may be mostly nitrogen, carbon dioxide, and argon

## THE PLANETS OF OUR SOLAR SYSTEM

The planetary data included in the table are based on modern astronomical findings and will vary from the traditional and less up-to-date data.

| PLANET | DIAMETER | MASS | DENSITY | GRAVITY | ESCAPE VELOCITY | INCLI-NATION OF AXIS | ALBEDO OR REFLEC-TIVITY | SPEED IN SOLAR ORBIT |
|---|---|---|---|---|---|---|---|---|
| | (in miles) | (Earth = 1) | (water = 1) | (Earth = 1) | (in miles per sec.) | | | (in miles per sec.) |
| MERCURY | 3,100 | 0.056 | 5.13 | 0.36 | 2.6 | unknown | 0.056 | 29.8 |
| VENUS | 7,700 | 0.817 | 4.97 | 0.87 | 6.4 | 10° | 0.76 | 21.8 |
| EARTH | 7,926 | 1.00 | 5.52 | 1.00 | 7.0 | 23°4′ | 0.36 | 18.5 |
| MARS | 4,200 | 0.108 | 3.94 | 0.38 | 3.1 | 24° | 0.16 | 15.0 |
| JUPITER | 88,700 | 318.0 | 1.33 | 2.64 | 37.9 | 3°1′ | 0.73 | 8.1 |
| SATURN | 75,100 | 95.2 | 0.69 | 1.13 | 23.0 | 26°7′ | 0.76 | 6.0 |
| URANUS | 29,200 | 14.6 | 1.56 | 1.07 | 13.7 | 97°9′ | 0.93 | 4.2 |
| NEPTUNE | 27,700 | 17.3 | 2.27 | 1.41 | 15.5 | 28°8′ | 0.84 | 3.4 |
| PLUTO | 3,500? | 0.06? | 4.? | 0.3? | unknown | unknown | 0.14? | 2.9 |

gases, and very little oxygen or water vapor is detectable. However, this does not rule out the possibility of some kind of life on Mars.

Mars has been famed for its "canals." These supposed surface features were discovered in 1877 by Schiaparelli (1835–1910), an Italian astronomer. He called them channels (canali, in Italian), but others inferred the presence of intelligent life on Mars from such fine, straight lines. If such lines exist, it is now thought that they may be geologic faults, or cracks in the surface caused by meteoritic impacts.

The Mariner 4 space probe which flew by Mars in 1965 returned photographs showing a crater-pitted, Moonlike surface, without enough resolution of detail to settle many of the questions about Mars, although some questionable "lines" were apparent.

**Jupiter:** Jupiter, the largest of the planets of our solar system, has a diameter of 88,700 miles. It rotates vertically on its axis and has no seasons. It completes one revolution around the Sun in nearly 12 years at a mean distance of 483 million miles. This giant planet has a dense atmosphere which precludes surface telescopic examination. The atmosphere shows up in the form of light and dark bands in the midst of which the so-called Red Spot appears. It is reddish in color, and shifts its position occasionally, but no one knows just what it is.

Many astronomers believe that Jupiter may not have a true crust. It is possible that the atmosphere, which is composed largely of methane and ammonia, grades into a liquid zone. The water on Jupiter may have accumulated in a thick layer, beneath which the planet may be warmer than previously believed. Recent laboratory experiments with fungi and other primitive organisms, in an atmosphere similar to that believed to exist on Jupiter, have indicated that life of some kind may be able to exist even on this uninviting planet.

Jupiter has 12 satellites. Four of these are quite large and were discovered by Galileo in 1610. At least one, Io, probably has a thin atmosphere of its own. Io's position in relation to the Earth and Jupiter seems to trigger its most intense radio emissions.

Jupiter has recently been of special interest because it has been found to have a strong magnetic field and large Van Allen belts, and it emits natural radio waves. The exact significance of these emissions is still unknown.

**Saturn:** Saturn is the most beautiful planet in the solar system. This huge planet (75,100 miles in diameter) is encircled by three distinct thin rings, which are probably composed of billions of minute formaldehyde crystals associated perhaps with dust particles. Saturn's atmosphere consists mainly of methane and ammonia. The rings may be no more than one foot in thickness.

Ten satellites travel around Saturn. The largest, Titan, is larger than our Moon. The discovery of Janus, closest to Saturn, was announced January 3, 1967.

Saturn is most unusual in that its density is only two thirds that of water. Saturn is so light that it would float on water if placed in a large enough sea.

**Uranus:** Uranus is the only planet that does not spin more or less upright like a top. Its axis is tilted 98° from the vertical, so Uranus rolls on its side as it orbits the Sun.

Uranus was believed to be a star—or, at times, a comet—until 1781, when its orbit around the Sun was finally plotted. Study of the motion of Uranus revealed irregularities that eventually led to the discovery of Neptune.

**Neptune:** Neptune is the planet that was discovered by mathematics. In 1846 two astronomers, Adams in England and Leverrier in France, independently calculated the existence and probable position of this planet. In the same year, Galle, a German astronomer, pointed his telescope to the calculated position, and Neptune was discovered.

Neptune has an atmosphere of methane and ammonia. It has two satellites, one 2,000 miles in diameter, and one only 200 miles in diameter. The latter is so small and distant from the planet that it was not discovered until 1949.

**Pluto:** Pluto is the most distant known planet in the solar system, the last to be discovered, and the least known of the nine planets. It was discovered on a telescopic photograph in 1930 after a long search.

(continued)

| PERIOD OF ROTATION | | | | PERIOD OF REVOLUTION (in Earth days) | UNIT SOLAR RADIATION AVAILABLE (Earth = 1) | AVERAGE DISTANCE FROM SUN (in million miles) | MINIMUM DISTANCE FROM EARTH (in million miles) | AVERAGE TRAVEL TIME FROM EARTH | PLANET |
|---|---|---|---|---|---|---|---|---|---|
| days | hrs. | mins. | secs. | | | | | | |
| 58.65 | — | — | — | 88 days | 6.7 | 36.0 | 48 | 115 days | MERCURY |
| 245.1 | — | — | — | 224.7 days | 1.9 | 67.2 | 24 | 146 days | VENUS |
| — | 23 | 56 | 4 | 365.26 days | 1.00 | 92.9 | — | — | EARTH |
| — | 24 | 37 | 23 | 687 days | 0.43 | 141.5 | 34 | 237 days | MARS |
| — | 9 | 50 | 30 | 11.86 years | 0.04 | 483.4 | 366 | 2.6 years | JUPITER |
| — | 10 | 14 | — | 29.46 years | 0.01 | 886.0 | 743 | 5.6 years | SATURN |
| — | 10 | 49 | — | 84.01 years | 0.0031 | 1,782.0 | 1,606 | 15 years | URANUS |
| — | 14? | — | — | 164 8 years | 0.001 | 2,792.0 | 2,678 | 30 years | NEPTUNE |
| 6.387 | — | — | — | 247.7 years | 0.0006 | 3,664.0 | 2,650 | 30 years | PLUTO |

**OUR SOLAR SYSTEM** (*continued*)

Pluto is so distant, and so poorly illuminated, that we can only approximate its distance and diameter. Its distance from the Sun is estimated at 3.65 billion miles.

Pluto's period of revolution is 248 years. Although its period of rotation cannot be obtained very accurately, it has been calculated to be about six days. Pluto has the most eccentric orbit of all the planets; in fact, at perihelion it passes inside the path of Neptune, but it has been calculated that these two planets could not possibly collide for the next 120,000 years.

**The Asteroids:** The minor planets, or asteroids, are concentrated mainly between the paths of Mars and Jupiter. The asteroids are probably stony bodies, generally irregular in shape. They range in size from less than a mile to about 480 miles in diameter. Only one, Vesta, can be seen (rarely) with the unaided eye.

Ceres was the first to be discovered, in 1801, then Pallas, Juno, and Vesta were discovered between 1802 and 1807. When a fifth, Astraea, was found, astronomers began a systematic search that has yielded more than 1,600 whose orbits are known. Despite the large number involved, the total mass of all the asteroids appears to be less than 1/1000 of the mass of the Earth.

The origin of the asteroids remains a mystery, although two plausible theories have been advanced. One theory suggests that the asteroids are the debris of a planet that once orbited between Mars and Jupiter, but which was destroyed by some unknown catastrophe. The other theory, called the Planetesimal Hypothesis, holds that they are small bodies that were created at the same time as the larger nine planets of our solar system, but did not accumulate into a larger planet because of the gravitational effects of Jupiter, or because they were too widely scattered.

## NATURAL SATELLITES OF THE PLANETS

The Earth is one of six planets known to have satellites. Pluto, the darkest of the planets, may also have satellites, but if so they have never been seen.

An (R) after the satellite's name indicates that it revolves in a retrograde manner, opposite to the direction of its planet's rotation. The numbers given the satellites are noted, but the satellites follow the order of their distance from their primary planet.

| PLANET AND SATELLITE | | AVERAGE DISTANCE FROM PLANET (in miles) | DIAMETER (in miles) | PERIOD OF REVOLUTION AROUND PLANET days | hrs. | mins. | APPARENT MAGNITUDE | DISCOVERER AND DATE |
|---|---|---|---|---|---|---|---|---|
| **EARTH** | | | | | | | | |
| | Moon........... | 238,866 | 2,057.6 | 27 | 7 | 43 | −12.7 | ———— |
| **MARS** | | | | | | | | |
| | Phobos.......... | 5,825 | 5 | | 7 | 39 | 11.5 | Asaph Hall, 1877 |
| | Deimos.......... | 14,580 | 3 | 1 | 6 | 18 | 12.5 | Asaph Hall, 1877 |
| **JUPITER** | | | | | | | | |
| V | Amalthea... | 112,000 | 70 | | 11 | 57 | 13 | Edward Barnard, 1892 |
| I | Io......... | 261,900 | 2,020 | 1 | 18 | 28 | 5.5 | Galileo, 1610 |
| II | Europa..... | 416,600 | 1,790 | 3 | 13 | 14 | 5.8 | Galileo, 1610 |
| III | Ganymede... | 664,600 | 3,120 | 7 | 3 | 43 | 5.1 | Galileo, 1610 |
| IV | Callisto..... | 1,169,000 | 2,770 | 16 | 16 | 32 | 6.3 | Galileo, 1610 |
| VI | Hestia...... | 7,130,000 | 50? | 251 | — | — | 14 | Charles Perrine, 1904 |
| VII | Hera...... | 7,290,000 | 8? | 260 | — | — | 18 | Charles Perrine, 1905 |
| X | Demeter.... | 7,200,000 | 5? | 254 | — | — | 19 | Seth Nicholson, 1938 |
| XII | Adrastea (R) | 13,000,000 | 4? | 625 | — | — | 19 | Seth Nicholson, 1951 |
| XI | Pan (R).... | 14,300,000 | 6? | 714 | — | — | 19 | Seth Nicholson, 1938 |
| VIII | Poseidon (R) | 14,600,000 | 9? | 735 | — | — | 18.5 | P. J. Melotte, 1908 |
| IX | Hades (R).. | 14,700,000 | 6? | 758 | — | — | 19 | Seth Nicholson, 1914 |
| **SATURN** | | | | | | | | |
| X | Janus | 99,100 | 300 | | 17 | 59 | 14 | Audouin Dollfus, 1967 |
| I | Mimas..... | 115,200 | 400? | 0 | 22 | 37 | 12.1 | Sir William Herschel, 1789 |
| II | Enceladus.. | 147,700 | 500? | 1 | 8 | 53 | 11.7 | Sir William Herschel, 1789 |
| III | Tethys..... | 182,900 | 630 | 1 | 21 | 18 | 10.6 | Giovanni Cassini, 1684 |
| IV | Dione...... | 234,300 | 550 | 2 | 17 | 41 | 10.7 | Giovanni Cassini, 1684 |
| V | Rhea...... | 327,100 | 810 | 4 | 12 | 25 | 10.0 | Giovanni Cassini, 1672 |
| VI | Titan...... | 758,400 | 2,980 | 15 | 22 | 41 | 8.3 | Christiaan Huygens, 1655 |
| VII | Hyperion... | 918,700 | 100? | 21 | 6 | 38 | 14.5 | G. P. & W. C. Bond, 1848 |
| VIII | Iapetus.... | 2,210,000 | 500? | 79 | 7 | 55 | 11 | Giovanni Cassini, 1671 |
| IX | Phoebe (R) | 8,040,000 | 100? | 550 | 9 | — | 14 | William Pickering, 1898 |
| **URANUS** | | | | | | | | |
| V | Miranda.... | 80,700 | 200? | 1 | 9 | 56 | 16.9 | Gerard Kuiper, 1948 |
| I | Ariel....... | 119,100 | 500? | 2 | 12 | 29 | 14 | William Lassell, 1851 |
| II | Umbriel.... | 165,900 | 300? | 4 | 3 | 28 | 15 | William Lassell, 1851 |
| III | Titania..... | 272,100 | 600? | 8 | 16 | 56 | 13.8 | Sir William Herschel, 1787 |
| IV | Oberon..... | 363,900 | 500? | 13 | 11 | 7 | 14.0 | Sir William Herschel, 1787 |
| **NEPTUNE** | | | | | | | | |
| | Triton (R)........ | 219,500 | 2,300 | 5 | 21 | 3 | 13.6 | William Lassell, 1846 |
| | Nereid.......... | 3,461,000 | 200? | 359 | 10 | — | 19.7 | Gerard Kuiper, 1949 |

## METEORS, METEORITES, AND COMETS

While man's imagination is excited by reports of flying saucers and callers from other planets, he often forgets that the Earth daily receives millions of genuine visitors from interplanetary space. On any clear dark night in the country, well away from city lights, you stand an even chance of seeing from five to ten "falling stars," or meteors. Infrequently you may be privileged to see a spectacularly brilliant fireball—a bigger meteor. Very rarely you may be lucky enough to hear a rumble or sonic boom from an outstanding fireball. This gives warning that a meteor may have actually fallen to Earth as a meteorite without being completely vaporized in the Earth's atmosphere.

All these events give evidence of an immense clutter of small solid particles that travel in a maze of orbits about the Sun, and through which the Earth and other planets move. The Earth meets this cosmic sand and gravel at velocities from ten to forty-five miles per second. The small grains, up to a few ounces in weight, break up into dust and atoms through collision with the air. Some of the energy of collision produces the luminescence that makes meteors visible.

Most of the meteorites seem to be the remains of asteroids, small planets a few hundred miles in diameter that broke up millions of years ago. Their debris remains as a significant although not too serious space hazard.

The great majority of meteors are fragments of comets, hazy objects, often with long curved tails, that always point away from the Sun, and sometimes grace the night sky for a few days or weeks. Comets generally travel about the Sun in great elongated orbits. When the Earth crosses the path of a comet, an unusual number of meteors, or a meteor "shower," can be seen.

### ANNUAL METEOR SHOWERS: 1968

A few of the more important annual meteor showers are given in the table below. The dates of their greatest visibility are the evening dates for North America, and most showers can be seen for a few nights before and after the dates listed. Meteor showers can be seen anywhere in the sky once the constellation from which the name is derived is above the horizon. The speed of entry into the atmosphere is given in miles per second.

| SHOWER | MAXIMUM VISIBILITY | ENTRY SPEED |
|---|---|---|
| Quadrantids | January 3 | 25 |
| Lyrids | April 21 | 30 |
| Eta Aquarids | May 4 | 40 |
| Delta Aquarids | July 29 | 25 |
| Perseids | August 11 | 37 |
| Orionids | October 20 | 41 |
| Taurids | November 5 | 17 |
| Leonids | November 16 | 45 |
| Geminids | December 13 | 22 |
| Ursids | December 22 | 21 |

## IMPORTANT COMETS

Some of the more important and best-known comets are listed in the following table in order of the length of their periods of revolution about the Sun. Their periods are given in sidereal years (one sidereal year is equal to 365 days, 6 hours, 9 minutes, 9.54 seconds).

| NAME | DATE OF NEXT APPEARANCE | PERIOD OF REVOLUTION | NAME | DATE OF NEXT APPEARANCE | PERIOD OF REVOLUTION |
|---|---|---|---|---|---|
| Schwassmann-Wachmann II | February, 1968 | 6.5 | Schwassmann-Wachmann I | May, 1973 | 16.1 |
| Schaumasse | June, 1968 | 8.2 | Tempell II | September, 1973 | 5.3 |
| Pons-Winnecke | July, 1969 | 6.2 | Brooks II | March, 1974 | 6.6 |
| Comas Sola | August, 1969 | 8.6 | Oterma | March, 1974 | 7.9 |
| Faye | November, 1969 | 7.4 | Borrelly | June, 1974 | 6.9 |
| Whipple | December, 1969 | 7.5 | Neujmin I | November, 1984 | 17.97 |
| Encke | February, 1971 | 3.3 | Halley | March, 1986 | 76.03 |
| Grigg-Skjellerup | August, 1971 | 4.9 | Pons-Brooks | May, 2024 | 70.9 |
| Giacobini-Zinner | October, 1972 | 6.6 | Olbers | January, 2026 | 69.6 |

## LARGE METEORITIC CRATERS

Many terrestrial craters similar to those on the Moon may have been caused by the impact of large meteorites. Some of the major authenticated craters are given in the table.

| NAME AND LOCATION | LARGEST CRATER | FEATURES |
|---|---|---|
| Lac Couture, Quebec | 9.92 miles | Occupied by lake; identified in 1963 |
| Alice Springs, N.T., Australia | 2 miles | Largest of several found recently |
| Brent crater, Algonquin Park, Ontario | 2 miles | Fossil crater, perhaps 750 million years old |
| Holleford crater, Ontario | 1.25 miles | Contains part of village of Holleford |
| Barringer crater, Winslow, Arizona | 3,937 feet | Perhaps 25,000 years old |
| Odessa craters, Ector County, Texas | 530 feet | Two metallic meteorite craters |
| Campo del Cielo crater, Gran Chaco, Argentina | 184 feet | Many craters and large meteorites |

## LIFE ON OTHER PLANETS

When the solar system formed about 5 billion years ago it was composed, like the rest of the universe, largely of hydrogen. Since that time the Sun and the major planets—Jupiter, Saturn, Uranus, and Neptune—have retained their hydrogen, but the small planets close to the Sun—Mercury, Venus, the Earth, and Mars—have lost most of their hydrogen to interplanetary space. During the Earth's infancy, hydrogen-rich gases must have been abundant. When energy is supplied to such gas mixtures in the presence of sea water, complex organic molecules are produced. It is believed that the origin of life on Earth occurred after sunlight and lightning energized the primitive oceans and produced a system of molecules capable of reproducing itself.

Since very general chemical conditions and energy sources are all that seem required for life on other planets, it is possible that life-related molecules and even living organisms have been produced on other planets in our solar system. Because the environments of the other planets differ from the Earth's, we would not expect extraterrestrial organisms to resemble familiar life forms. Just as organisms are adapted to a wide range of environments on the Earth, an even larger range of adaptation can be expected on other worlds.

The day side of the planet Mercury and the entire surface of the planet Venus are probably too hot for life. Our Moon and most of the other satellites in the solar system are bathed in ultraviolet light, X-rays, and protons from the Sun, have no atmosphere, and experience great temperature extremes. We would not expect life on their surfaces.

But the surface of Mars, the warm atmospheric regions below the clouds of Jupiter, Saturn, and Neptune, may—just possibly—provide suitable habitats for life. No good direct evidence of life on these planets is available at this time, and the seasonal and other changes observed on Mars might be due to wind-blown dust rather than living organisms. It is interesting to note, however, that even most weather-satellite photographs of the Earth have shown no sign of life on our own planet.

The discovery of life on other planets would be of greatest interest to the biologist, giving him information on alternative evolutionary processes. But only by landing unmanned or manned space vehicles on other planets can we definitely investigate life on other worlds.

## INTERPLANETARY SPACE

Spacecraft observations during the past few years have completely revised our picture of interplanetary space, previously conceived of as an "empty void." The modern picture began to develop in the early 1950s when it was realized that the observed fact that the ionized tails of comets always point in a direction almost directly away from the Sun requires a pressure that could only be supplied by particles streaming from the Sun. Since these comet tails have been observed during all portions of the 11-year sunspot cycle, it was inferred that such particles streaming from the Sun should be present most or all of the time. This suggestion was confirmed in 1962 with a plasma detector operating on the Mariner 2 spacecraft during the interplanetary portion of its flight past Venus.

The solar wind plasma is nothing more than the outer portion of the solar corona, the outward streaming halo of particles around it. The energy flowing into the corona from lower layers of the Sun produces a pressure that cannot be balanced by the galactic pressure at the outer boundary of the solar system. This imbalance of pressure accelerates a portion of the solar corona so as to produce the solar wind. As the solar-wind plasma streams away from the Sun, it stretches the Sun's magnetic lines along with it so that the magnetic lines have a spiral form caused by a combination of the radial flow of the solar wind and the twisting effect of the solar rotation. The kinks in the interplanetary magnetic field lines cause some of the cosmic rays that enter the solar system from the nearby galaxy to be reflected and thereby kept out of the inner solar system.

Explosive bursts on the Sun can produce cosmic rays and energetic streams of plasma and shock waves that travel from the Sun to the Earth, causing geomagnetic storms and the auroras and interrupting radio communications. The geomagnetic field diverts the solar-wind plasma so that it flows around the Earth at a distance of approximately ten earth radii or more. The Moon, which has a very weak magnetic field, if any, does not receive this protection and may be bombarded by considerable streams of solar plasma.

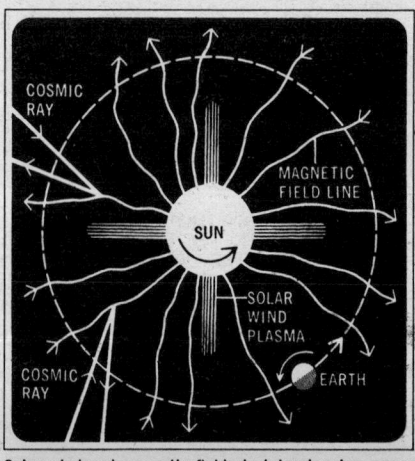

Solar wind and magnetic fields in interplanetary space (not drawn to scale).

# THE MOON

Our Moon, the only natural satellite of the Earth, revolves around us in an approximately elliptic orbit, which causes its mean distance of 239,000 miles from us to oscillate between 221,000 miles (perigee) and 253,000 miles (apogee) in a period of 27.322 days. This distance represents less than one per cent of that separating us from Venus or Mars at their closest approaches. Light or radio waves will cross it in 1.28 seconds; and an average spacecraft will take about 2.5 days to cross it. The Moon's rotation about its axis is exactly synchronized with its revolution, and this is why the Moon always shows us the same face. However, since its rate of rotation is uniform whereas that of its revolution is not (the Moon moving faster near perigee than around apogee), and also because its equator is inclined by 6.4 degrees to the plane of its orbit, more than one half (59 per cent) of its surface can be seen at different times from the Earth.

The mass of the Moon is a little less than one eightieth of that of the Earth, and its size is only about a quarter of that of the terrestrial globe. The Moon's mean density proves to be about 60 per cent that of our planet. The mean radius of the lunar globe is equal to 1,080 miles; the departures of its actual surface from a sphere are less than two miles, but apparently quite complicated. The gravitational acceleration on the lunar surface is only about one sixth of the terrestrial one. In consequence, the Moon cannot permanently retain any liquid on its surface, or any atmosphere above it.

The temperature of the Moon's visible surface is controlled solely by sunlight, and the absence of any atmosphere causes it to vary greatly between day and night. This variation ranges between 270 degrees Fahrenheit in the lunar tropics at noontime, to less than −300 degrees Fahrenheit before sunrise, that is, from a temperature in excess of that of boiling water to one of liquid air. These extremes make it necessary to shut off the cameras of the Surveyors during the two-week lunar night.

This large range in temperature is, however, experienced only on the exposed surface and vanishes almost completely at a subsurface depth of less than a yard, where a constant temperature of some −30 degrees Fahrenheit prevails day and night.

The surface of the Moon is highly diversified with innumerable markings, but consists essentially of two types of ground, easily distinguishable on the photographic map. One type of ground, rough and broken, is comparatively light (the "continents"); the other is darker (half as bright, on the average), smoother, and more gently rolling, similar to waterless "seas" (maria). The latter occupy almost 40 per cent of the visible face of the Moon, but the maria on the far side are both fewer and smaller. A closer look reveals that the dominant type of formations giving the lunar face its characteristic pockmarked ap-
*(continued)*

The region of the moon known as Oceanus Procellarum, as photographed by Lunar Orbiter III.

NASA

## THE MOON (continued)

pearance are the craters, representing essentially shallow local depressions of ground surrounded by ramparts whose height is, in general, a very small fraction of the diameter. The largest crater, Clavius, is more than 150 miles across. The number of those with diameters in excess of 0.6 of a mile is estimated to be more than 300,000 on the visible face of the Moon alone; smaller craters are countless.

Not all of these craters can be of the same origin. The preponderant type are the so-called impact craters, which have originated from collisions of the unprotected lunar surface with all the solid bodies that the Moon may have encountered on its perpetual journey through space. Such bodies have ranged from asteroids and comets, through meteorites, to the smallest interplanetary dust, producing impact craters running from hundreds of miles to fractions of an inch in size. Other craters, again, may be of internal (volcanic) origin or may have been formed by a gradual release of gaseous compounds. Indeed, the lunar surface must represent an "impact counter" of events that have occurred there since the formation of our satellite not less than 4.5 billion years ago; plus a "boundary condition" of the processes that may have been operative in the lunar interior during the same period of time. Since a complete absence of air or water gives all landmarks relative permanence, the Moon affords the best glimpse we possess into the conditions obtaining in this part of the solar system almost back to the very time of its formation. Some of the more recent impact craters on the Moon surrounded by bright rays reveal the extent of the splash of internal material thrown

out around them in different directions. For example, portions of the crater Kepler's ray system extend nearly across the near side of the Moon. There are many lunar mountain chains with peaks as high as 19,500 feet.

The light of the Moon is essentially sunlight falling on the lunar surface from different directions and returned by it in different forms. A relatively small part of the incoming sunlight (about seven per cent) is scattered in a way that preserves the white color of the light without much change. This gives rise to the "silvery moonlight" of song and romance. The bulk of the sunlight is, however, absorbed by the lunar surface and emitted by it as infrared heat waves, which are invisible to the eye but measurable with sensitive instruments. The balance sometimes produces the "cold light" of a luminescing surface, the intensity of which changes with time. On the whole, the Moon reflects but very little light. The Moon is about as dark in optical frequencies as volcanic ashes, largely as a result of radiation bombardment by the solar wind.

The brightness of the Moon increases rapidly toward full Moon, which is more than 11 times brighter than the First Quarter, although the illuminated area has merely doubled. Thereafter, the brightness diminishes with equal rapidity, indicating a very rough surface.

Photographs taken by the Soviet Zond III and the U.S. Lunar Orbiters have revealed some remarkable topography on the "hidden" or far side of the Moon. A gigantic "bullseye" 300 miles across is the largest of a new class of similar features, named thalassoids by the Russians. They may have been created when comets or asteroids hit the moon.

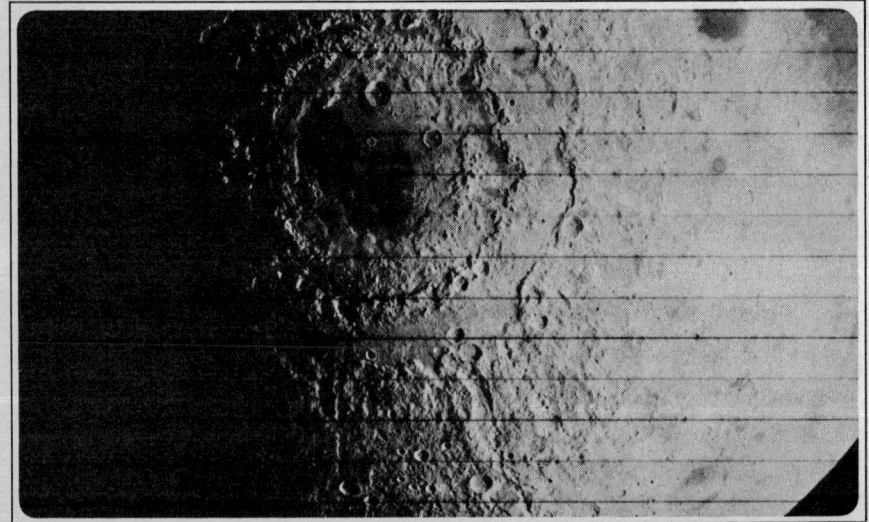

The target-shaped Orientale Basin, 600 miles across, was discovered in 1967 by Lunar Orbiter IV.

## PHASES OF THE MOON

The Moon shines only by reflected light. Its phases, or apparent changes in shape, result from the varying part of the sunlit hemisphere of the Moon visible to observers on Earth, because of the relative positions of the Moon, the Sun, and the Earth.

At New Moon, when the Moon is on the line between the Sun and the Earth, eclipses of the Sun by the Moon may occur, if the Moon is properly positioned. The Moon moves on in its orbit of the Earth from west to east. It passes through its waxing Crescent phase into First Quarter, when it is at Half Moon. Through the waxing Gibbous phase, it comes then to Full Moon, on the opposite side of the Earth from the Sun, when the Earth's shadow may be cast across the Moon in lunar eclipses. The Moon marches on through waning Gibbous into Last Quarter, then through the waning Crescent phase into New Moon again.

Recently the heaviest storms in the calendar month across the United States have been found to be significantly related to lunar phases. Such storms are more likely to occur, in the long run, from one to three days after New Moon and from three to five days after Full Moon, it has been shown. The magnetic disturbances that sometimes disrupt radio communications, and the beginning of hurricanes in the Caribbean have been found to be similarly related to lunar positions. The way in which these effects are produced is still a mystery. Similar relationships have been reported from a number of other countries.

Occasionally the unlighted portion of the Moon facing the Earth glows in the "earthshine" (sunlight reflected from the Earth to the Moon and back again). Portions of the Moon, like the bright crater Aristarchus, are very reflective. In the main, however, the Moon is a poor mirror, reflecting only seven per cent of the light it receives.

At perigee, the Moon approaches closest in its path to the Earth; at apogee the Moon is farthest distant. The phases of the Moon, as well as its perigee and apogee, are given here in Greenwich Mean Time (GMT). The conversion from Greenwich Mean Time to other times is explained under the "Standard Time of Astronomical Events," page 814.

### PHASES OF THE MOON: 1968

### MOON'S PERIGEE AND APOGEE: 1968

| NEW MOON | | | FIRST QUARTER | | | FULL MOON | | | LAST QUARTER | | | PERIGEE | | APOGEE | |
|---|---|---|---|---|---|---|---|---|---|---|---|---|---|---|---|
| day | hr. | min. | day | hr. | min. | day | hr. | min. | day | hr. | min. | day | hr. | day | hr. |
| Dec. 31 | 03 | 39 | Jan. 7 | 14 | 23 | Jan. 15 | 16 | 11 | Jan. 22 | 19 | 38 | Dec. 28 | 19 | Jan. 9 | 13 |
| Jan. 29 | 16 | 29 | Feb. 6 | 12 | 20 | Feb. 14 | 06 | 43 | Feb. 21 | 03 | 28 | Jan. 25 | 00 | Feb. 6 | 10 |
| Feb. 28 | 06 | 56 | Mar. 7 | 09 | 20 | Mar. 14 | 18 | 52 | Mar. 21 | 11 | 07 | Feb. 18 | 16 | Mar. 5 | 07 |
| Mar. 28 | 22 | 48 | Apr. 6 | 03 | 28 | Apr. 13 | 04 | 52 | Apr. 19 | 19 | 35 | Mar. 17 | 02 | Apr. 1 | 23 |
| Apr. 27 | 15 | 21 | May 5 | 17 | 54 | May 12 | 13 | 05 | May 19 | 05 | 44 | Apr. 14 | 07 | Apr. 29 | 09 |
| May 27 | 07 | 30 | June 4 | 04 | 47 | June 10 | 20 | 13 | June 17 | 18 | 14 | May 12 | 17 | May 26 | 12 |
| June 25 | 22 | 25 | July 3 | 12 | 42 | July 10 | 03 | 18 | July 17 | 09 | 11 | June 10 | 03 | June 22 | 19 |
| July 25 | 11 | 49 | Aug. 1 | 18 | 34 | Aug. 8 | 11 | 32 | Aug. 16 | 02 | 13 | July 8 | 09 | July 20 | 09 |
| Aug. 23 | 23 | 57 | Aug. 30 | 23 | 35 | Sept. 6 | 22 | 07 | Sept. 14 | 20 | 31 | Aug. 5 | 03 | Aug. 17 | 03 |
| Sept. 22 | 11 | 08 | Sept. 29 | 05 | 07 | Oct. 6 | 11 | 46 | Oct. 14 | 15 | 05 | Aug. 31 | 02 | Sept. 13 | 22 |
| Oct. 21 | 21 | 44 | Oct. 28 | 12 | 40 | Nov. 5 | 04 | 25 | Nov. 13 | 08 | 53 | Sept. 25 | 20 | Oct. 11 | 17 |
| Nov. 20 | 08 | 02 | Nov. 26 | 23 | 30 | Dec. 4 | 23 | 07 | Dec. 13 | 00 | 49 | Oct. 23 | 15 | Nov. 8 | 09 |
| Dec. 19 | 18 | 19 | Dec. 26 | 14 | 14 | Jan. 3 | 18 | 28 | Jan. 11 | 14 | 01 | Nov. 21 | 00 | Dec. 5 | 15 |
| | | | | | | | | | | | | Dec. 19 | 12 | Jan. 1 | 15 |

## ASTRONOMICAL TIME

**Anomalistic month:** the time of the Moon's revolution, measured from perigee to perigee.

= 27 days, 13 hours, 18 minutes, 33.2 seconds

**Anomalistic year:** the time of the Earth's revolution, measured from perihelion to perihelion.

= 365 days, 6 hours, 13 minutes, 53 seconds

**Draconitic month:** the time interval between two nodes of the Moon's orbit. The Draconitic month is also called the Nodical month.

= 27 days, 5 hours, 5 minutes, 36 seconds

**Eclipse year:** the time interval between two successive conjunctions of the Sun with nodes of the Moon's orbit.

= 364 days, 14 hours, 52 minutes, 53 seconds

**Lunar month:** the time required for the Moon to complete one revolution around the Earth, measured from the passing of two similar phases of the Moon. It is also called the Synodic month.

= 29 days, 12 hours, 44 minutes, 2.9 seconds

**Sidereal day:** the time required for a point on Earth to complete two successive passages in relation to any star other than the Sun.

= 23 hours, 56 minutes, 4.09892 seconds

**Sidereal month:** the time required for one revolution of the Moon about the Earth, measured by two successive passages of the Moon by a selected star.

= 27 days, 7 hours, 43 minutes, 11.5 seconds

**Sidereal year:** the time required for one complete revolution of the Earth around the Sun, relative to a selected star.

= 365 days, 6 hours, 9 minutes, 9.54 seconds

**Solar day:** the time interval from midnight to midnight, measured in sidereal time.

= 24 hours, 3 minutes, 56.555 seconds

**Tropical year:** the time required for one complete revolution of the Earth around the Sun, as reckoned from two successive passages of a point on Earth relative to the vernal equinox.

= 365 days, 5 hours, 48 minutes, 46.5 seconds

## STANDARD TIME OF ASTRONOMICAL EVENTS

Unless otherwise specified, all astronomical events listed in the *Almanac* are given in Greenwich Mean Time (GMT)—the international standard of time. In GMT the day begins at 00 hours 00 minutes (midnight) at the Greenwich meridian and is reckoned in hours and minutes through 23 hours 59 minutes, or one minute before start of the next day.

The United States uses seven standard time zones in which clocks differ from GMT by a fixed number of hours. To convert any given GMT to that of a local time zone, subtract from the GMT the applicable number of hours shown in the table below. The difference obtained after subtracting gives the local clock time in a particular time zone. If the difference is between 00 and 11 hours, the time is A.M.; if the difference is between 12 and 23 hours, the time is P.M. If the number of hours to be subtracted is greater than the GMT, then add

24 hours to the GMT before subtracting. In this case only, the local clock time is that of the preceding day.

Two examples are given below to show the method of subtraction.

**Example 1:** In 1968 the autumnal equinox occurs on September 22 at 23 hours 26 minutes GMT. To convert to Eastern Daylight Time, subtract 4 hours. The difference is 19 hours 26 minutes. Therefore the autumnal equinox occurs on September 22 at 7:26 P.M. Eastern Daylight Time.

**Example 2:** In 1968 a total eclipse of the Moon begins on April 13 at 04 hours 23 minutes GMT. To convert to Pacific Standard Time, first add 24 hours. From the resulting sum of 28 hours 23 minutes, subtract 8 hours. The difference is 20 hours 23 minutes. Therefore the eclipse begins on April 12 at 8:23 P.M. Pacific Standard Time.

| LOCAL TIME | CORRECTION FROM GMT |
|---|---|
| Eastern Daylight............ | Subtract 4 hours |
| Eastern Standard or Central Daylight.......... | Subtract 5 hours |
| Central Standard or Mountain Daylight......... | Subtract 6 hours |
| Mountain Standard or Pacific Daylight........... | Subtract 7 hours |

| LOCAL TIME | CORRECTION FROM GMT |
|---|---|
| Pacific Standard or Yukon Daylight........... | Subtract 8 hours |
| Yukon Standard or Alaska and Hawaii Daylight.................. | Subtract 9 hours |
| Alaska and Hawaii Standard................. | Subtract 10 hours |

## SKY-WATCHER'S CALENDAR: 1968

Listed below are some of the more interesting sky phenomena which you can observe in the year 1968. Time is given in GMT; see the table above for conversion to local times.

| DAY | HOUR | EVENT |
|---|---|---|
| Jan. 6 | 06 | Saturn is 1° south of the Moon. Both objects appear quite close during the evening hours. They are located in constellation of Pisces. |
| Feb. 20 | 11 | Jupiter is exactly opposite the Sun. It is of magnitude —2, rises at sunset and sets at sunrise. |
| Mar. 5 | 07 | Jupiter is 0.8° north of first-magnitude star Regulus in constellation of Leo. Planet is at bottom of sickle-shaped group of stars which marks the head and mane of the lion. |
| Mar. 20 | 13 | Vernal equinox; spring begins in northern hemisphere and autumn begins in southern hemisphere. Sun rises exactly in east and sets directly in west. |
| Apr. 13 | 05 | Total eclipse of the Moon is visible from entire United States. Total phase lasts 50 minutes. This is the most favorable eclipse in several years. See page 815 for additional data. |
| Apr. 16 | 06 | First-magnitude star Antares in constellation of Scorpius is hidden as gibbous Moon passes between Earth and Antares. Star disappears behind bright limb of Moon and reappears from behind dark limb. This phenomena is called an occultation. |
| May 24 | 01 | Mercury is at greatest elongation, 23° east of the Sun. For a week before and after this date the planet may be glimpsed low in the western sky about one hour after sunset. |

| DAY | HOUR | EVENT |
|---|---|---|
| June 10 | 03 | Antares is again occulted by the Moon. |
| Aug. 11 | — | Perseid meteor shower reaches its peak. Shooting stars appear to radiate from a small area in the constellation of Perseus, located in the northeastern sky. Shower lasts the entire night; over 50 per hour may appear after midnight. Meteors also are plentiful on August 10 and 12. |
| Sept. 7 | — | Harvest Moon occurs on this date. The Moon generally rises about 50 minutes later each night, but for several nights following the Harvest Moon it rises only about 20 minutes later. Presence of the Moon after sunset gives farmers extra light during harvest time. |
| Oct. 6 | 12 | Total eclipse of the Moon, lasting 64 minutes, is visible from the United States. |
| Oct. 15 | 09 | Saturn is exactly opposite the Sun. Planet is located in Pisces, below and to the right of triangle-shaped constellation of Aries. Saturn rises at sunset, remains visible all night, and sets at sunrise. |
| Nov. 6 | 08 | Mars is 0.3° north of Jupiter, an extremely close approach of the two planets. They are in the constellation of Virgo and rise about two hours before the Sun. |
| Dec. 12 | — | Geminid meteor shower reaches its peak. Meteors are visible all night; up to 50 per hour seem to radiate from an area in Gemini. Radiant point is almost overhead at 2:00 A.M. local time. Meteors also appear on nights of December 11 and 13. |

## ECLIPSES

Both the Earth and the Moon cast shadows out into space in the direction away from the Sun. The area of total darkness behind either body is cone-shaped and is called the umbra. Surrounding the umbra is a fan-shaped larger area of half-shadow called the penumbra. If the Moon's orbit coincided exactly with the plane of the Earth's orbit, two eclipses could be seen each month. A solar eclipse would occur every "new moon" when the tip of the Moon's umbra traveled across the sunlit hemisphere of the Earth, and a lunar eclipse would occur every "full moon" when the Moon passed through the umbra of the Earth's shadow.

Unfortunately for would-be eclipse-watchers, the plane of the Moon's orbit is inclined more than 5° to that of the Earth's. The orbital planes intersect only at two places called the nodes, and it is only when the Moon is at one of the nodes that an eclipse can take place. There are usually two time intervals during the year (occasionally three) when eclipses may occur. These periods are called eclipse seasons. The eclipse seasons shift through the year in a repeating cycle, so that if an eclipse occurs on a given date another eclipse of the same type will generally occur 18 years and 10 days later. (By using this "saros" cycle, the ancient Chaldeans were able to predict future eclipses of the Sun and Moon.)

A lunar eclipse occurs only when the Moon is at or near one of its nodes during the "full moon" phase, when the Sun is on the opposite side of the Earth from the Moon. If the Moon moves completely into the Earth's umbra, a total lunar eclipse results. If the Moon passes only partly through the umbra, a partial eclipse results. Occasionally the Moon only cuts through the penumbra, and in this case an appulse occurs. Appulses are generally difficult to detect.

A solar eclipse occurs at "new moon" time when the Sun and Moon are on the same side of the Earth. If a given point on the Earth's surface is within the Moon's umbra, a total solar eclipse results. At that point the Moon completely hides the disk of the Sun, allowing the beautiful and eerie corona to be seen. A partial eclipse is seen from all places on the Earth's surface that are in the Moon's penumbra. Total solar eclipses are important to scientists because they offer excellent conditions for observation and analysis of the Sun's corona, prominences, and other features.

Information about the four eclipses which occur in 1968 appears in the table below. Greenwich Mean Time is used in the table. Conversion into other times is explained in "Standard Times of Astronomical Events" on page 814.

### ECLIPSES OF THE SUN AND MOON: 1968

| DATE | TYPE OF ECLIPSE | REGIONS OF VISIBILITY AND TIMES OF OCCURENCE (GMT) |
|------|-----------------|----------------------------------------------------|
| March 28....... | Total Solar | Eclipse is visible from southern tip of South America and parts of Antarctica. Middle of eclipse occurs at 9:55 P.M. |
| April 13........ | Total Lunar | Eclipse is visible from North and South America. Moon enters penumbra at 2:12 A.M., enters umbra at 3:11 A.M., and total eclipse begins at 4:23 A.M. Middle of eclipse occurs at 4:48 A.M. Total eclipse ends at 5:13 A.M. Moon leaves umbra at 6:25 A.M. and leaves penumbra at 7:24 A.M. |
| September 22... | Total Solar | Total phase is visible from northern and western Siberia. Middle of eclipse occurs at 10:22 A.M. |
| October 6....... | Total Lunar | Beginning of total phase is visible from all of North America. End of total phase is visible from western part of North America. Moon enters penumbra at 8:45 A.M., enters umbra at 9:55 A.M., and total eclipse begins at 11:11 A.M. Middle of eclipse occurs at 11:42 A.M. Total eclipse ends at 12:15 P.M. Moon leaves umbra at 1:30 P.M., and leaves penumbra at 2:40 P.M. |

### EVENING AND MORNING STARS: 1968

We are accustomed to think of an Evening Star as one that can be seen in the western sky shortly after sunset and a Morning Star as one that is visible in the eastern sky before sunrise. The terms are actually inaccurate since we know that planets, rather than stars, are involved. To be more accurate, an Evening Star is any planet that is above the horizon at sunset and a Morning Star is any planet that is above the horizon at sunrise.

The table below lists the periods when the five planets visible to the naked eye are technically evening stars and morning stars. A given planet may often be invisible because it is so close to the Sun that it sets before the evening sky has become dark or rises after the

morning sky has become too bright. This is particularly true of Mercury. Venus and Mars also remain close to the Sun for much of 1968, but will be prominently visible in 1969.

| PLANET | EVENING STAR | MORNING STAR |
|--------|--------------|--------------|
| Mercury.... | Jan. 1 to Feb. 15<br>Apr. 24 to June 18<br>Aug. 7 to Oct. 15<br>Dec. 3 to Dec. 31 | Feb. 15 to Apr. 24<br>June 18 to Aug. 7<br>Oct. 15 to Dec. 3 |
| Venus...... | June 20 to Dec. 31 | Jan. 1 to June 20 |
| Mars....... | Jan. 1 to June 21 | June 21 to Dec. 31 |
| Jupiter..... | Feb. 20 to Sept. 9 | Jan. 1 to Feb. 20<br>Sept. 9 to Dec. 31 |
| Saturn..... | Jan. 1 to Apr. 5<br>Oct. 15 to Dec. 31 | Apr. 5 to Oct. 15 |

# LANDMARKS IN ASTRONOMY

**3000 B.C.:** Construction begun on Egyptian pyramids built and oriented toward the stars.

**2000:** The constellations were named by astrologers in the Near East.

**585:** Thales, one of the earliest astronomers, is said to have predicted the occurrence of an eclipse of the Sun.

**530:** Pythagoras stated that the Earth is a sphere that rotates on an axis.

**270:** Eratosthenes, Greek scientist, is credited with measuring the circumference and inclination of the Earth.

**130:** Hipparchus, Greek astronomer, recorded the motion of the Sun and Moon, and compiled a star catalogue of about 850 entries. Much of his research was used in Ptolemy's later work.

**140 A.D.:** Ptolemy, Greco-Egyptian, the last of the ancient astronomers, gathered all the astronomical knowledge of his time into one great work entitled the *Almagest*. He presented the theory that the Earth is the center of the universe and that the Sun, Moon, and other planets revolve around it. This principle was accepted until the 16th century.

**1543:** Nicholas Copernicus (1473–1543), the great Polish astronomer, stated that the Sun was the center around which the Earth and other planets revolved. The results of his observations were published in 1543 in *De revolutionibus orbium coelestium*. This treatise marked the beginning of modern astronomy.

**1609:** Galileo (1564–1642), the Italian astronomer, constructed the first astronomical telescope. It was a modification of a crude instrument invented the previous year by the Dutch optician, Lippershey. With this new device Galileo discovered four satellites of Jupiter, observed the surface of the Moon, and saw and studied sunspots and the phases of Venus. He confirmed the heretical Copernican theory of the universe, and in 1633 was forced to recant by the Church.

**1609:** Johannes Kepler (1571–1630), the German mathematician and astronomer, influenced by the Copernican theory, used the accurate planetary observations of the Danish astronomer, Tycho Brahe (1546–1601), to work out his laws of planetary motion.

**1668:** Sir Isaac Newton (1642–1727), the English scientist, constructed the first reflecting telescope. Earlier, in 1665 and 1666, he invented a system of calculus and worked out his law of gravitation.

**1675:** Olaus Roemer (1644–1710), a Danish astronomer, while observing eclipses of the satellites of Jupiter when the planet was at varying distances from the Earth, calculated the approximate speed of light. Previous scientists had generally accepted the idea that light was transmitted to any point in space instantaneously.

**1704:** Edmund Halley (1656–1742) applied the law of gravitation to comet orbits. "Halley's Comet" returned on schedule in 1758.

**1781:** Sir William Herschel (1738–1822), an English astronomer, discovered the planet Uranus. A great observer and telescope-maker, he also discovered the sixth and seventh satellites of Saturn, catalogued over 800 double stars and concluded that they were held together by mutual gravitation, and recorded over 2,500 nebulae.

**1823:** J. von Fraunhofer was the first to observe the dark (Fraunhofer) lines in star spectra.

**1846:** John Couch Adams (1819–1892) and Urbain J. J. Leverrier (1811–1877) calculated possible position of planet beyond Uranus. Neptune discovered in indicated position.

**1913:** H. N. Russell, American astronomer, constructed the Hertzsprung-Russell (H-R) Diagram, grouping the spectral classes of stars on the basis of their absolute magnitudes. This analysis yielded many ideas on stellar evolution.

**1916:** Albert Einstein (1879–1955) presented General Theory of Relativity.

**1923:** Edwin P. Hubble, American astronomer, discovered that many of the so-called nebulae are in fact galaxies. He also interpreted the red shift in the spectra of galaxies to mean that they were racing away from each other, giving rise to theory of expanding universe.

**1931:** Karl Jansky, American physicist, discovered radio waves from space and thus initiated radio astronomy.

**1938:** H. A. Bethe, American physicist, proposed the fusion of lighter into heavier elements as a source of stellar energy.

**1957:** Sputnik I, the world's first artificial satellite, was launched into orbit by the U.S.S.R., opening a new era in modern astronomy.

**1959:** The U.S.S.R. launched Luna II, the first space probe to impact on the Moon. Luna III transmitted the first photographs of the far side of the Moon back to earth.

**1962:** Mariner 2, U.S. space probe, first vehicle to fly past another planet, returned much information about Venus.

**1964–65:** U.S. probe Ranger 7 returned 4,300 closeup photos of the Moon before impacting on its surface. U.S.-launched Mariner 4 flew past Mars and transmitted first pictures taken from the vicinity of another planet.

**1965:** American astronomers identified "quasi-stellar radio sources," or quasars, as strange distant galaxies, and a hitherto unknown type of "blue" galaxy, which promised to alter man's concept of the universe.

**1966:** U.S.S.R. Luna IX and U.S. Surveyor 1 soft-landed on the moon and returned pictures of its surface. First satellites placed in lunar orbit by the U.S.S.R. and the U.S.

**1967:** Robert Dicke announced that the Sun is not quite spherical. This may make necessary a re-evaluation of Einstein's views.

**1967:** Lunar Orbiters mapped far side of Moon. Surveyor 5 made first chemical analysis of Moon material. U.S.S.R. Venus IV soft-landed on Venus.

# THE SPACE AGE

## Space Exploration · Records · Space Age Glossary

NASA

This moonscape, photographed by the wide-angle camera of Lunar Orbiter II, shows features similar in form and size to volcanic domes found in California and Oregon.

## SPACE EXPLORATION: 1967

The year 1967 was a year of tragedy for the manned space program. On January 27, three American astronauts, Colonel Virgil I. Grissom, Lieutenant Colonel Edward H. White II, and Lieutenant Commander Robert B. Chaffee, died in a fire in an oxygen-filled capsule undergoing ground tests for the first Apollo flight. On April 24, Russian cosmonaut Colonel Vladimir Komarov died while attempting to land his space capsule after a trouble-filled flight. Both the United States and the Soviet Union were forced to take another look at safety procedures—to pause and then proceed more slowly.

In unmanned exploration, however, the year brought dramatic successes. The secrets of our next-door neighbor, the Moon, are being uncloaked gradually, leaving fewer and fewer uncertainties for the astronauts who finally stand upon its surface.

In 1967 the Soviet probe Luna 10 analyzed

the gamma ray emission from the Moon's surface. Data from Luna 10 showed this emission to be very similar to that produced by the basalt layers of the Earth's crust. Thus portions of the Moon's surface seemed more like the Earth's ocean bottoms, which are basaltic, than like the continents, which are granitic.

The American probe, Surveyor 3, not only landed on the Moon's surface, as several earlier probes had done, but actually used a shovel to scoop up a portion of the Moon's crust. Scientists on Earth followed the process on television. Thus in 1967 men sent hands, as well as eyes, to the Moon. The force required to dig up the sample, and the appearance of that sample, showed the Moon's surface to be denser than scientists had thought from previous, less direct, evidence. Though it is bone dry, the "Moonsoil" behaves as if it were moist soil.

*(continued)*

**SPACE EXPLORATION: 1967** (continued)

The Lunar Orbiter series gave other kinds of valuable information. Photographs from Lunar Orbiter 2 showed volcanic domes, two to ten miles across and up to 1,500 feet high, in the midst of vast ash or lava flows. Few scientists could still deny that there had been volcanic activity on the Moon. In fact, there may still be occasional volcanic rumbles in the Moon's interior. This discovery, along with other evidence, has dispelled the old myth of the "changeless face" of the Moon.

What does a restless, ever-changing Moon signify? It means, first of all, that the Moon has had an eventful geological history, as has the Earth. In September, Surveyor 5 conducted a rough chemical analysis in the Moon's Sea of Tranquility. Results implied that as much as 20 per cent of the Moon's surface (that is, the area covered by the lunar "seas") had filled with basalt that was volcanic in origin. These lunar basaltic regions are similar to the volcano-riddled Hawaiian Islands, the Columbia Plateau around Mt. Ranier in Washington, and the Earth's ocean basins.

Curiously, these findings served to resurrect the name of a practically unknown Darwin—George Darwin, brother of Charles. In 1891 George Darwin had put forth the theory that the Moon had been "spawned" by the Earth. Darwin noted that the Earth's granitic crust (the continents) was incomplete and proposed that the Moon would be found to be made of the Earth's "missing" granite. While evidence from Surveyor 5 indicated not a granitic but a basaltic surface associated with volcanoes, this first-hand evidence does not at all disprove Darwin's central hypothesis of an Earth-spawned Moon.

If, as the current tests strongly imply, the Moon has undergone geological growing pains like the Earth, then geologists would expect the heavier basalt to be found in the low-lying lunar areas of the Moon, just as basalt (following the principle called *isostasy* or *isostatic balance*) is found on the Earth's ocean bottoms. Future probes will look for granite in the lunar highlands—if granite is found there, little doubt will remain that the Moon, born of a youthful Earth, underwent very similar geological changes.

In 1967 the Moon's measurements were refined, too. The orbits of the Lunar Orbiters, accurately measured as they whirled around the Moon, permitted the satellite's actual center of mass to be fixed with great accuracy. This, combined with the measurement of radar waves bouncing off the Moon, showed it to be slightly smaller than had been thought. But not much smaller, to be sure; some 2.4 miles were stripped from its diameter, which is now set at 2,057.6 miles rather than 2,060.

The same measurements showed the size of the Moon's central bulge. This small "pot-belly," pointed at the Earth, is undoubtedly due to the tidal influence of our planet upon our satellite. The bulge is 5,000 feet high in the Moon's lowlands and 15,000 feet high in its mountainous areas.

As a demonstration of man's new mastery of near space, the National Aeronautics and Space Administration released in October, 1967, a detailed chart of the far side of the Moon. This far side has never been seen by human eyes, but it has been photographed over and over again by Lunar probes. It is now better mapped than was the visible side of the Moon only a few years ago.

Lunar surface material disturbed by a footpad of Surveyor V (right) bears a surprising resemblance to the soil of the southwestern United States (left).

## "FIRE IN THE COCKPIT!"

After the Apollo space tragedy, window view shows dangling oxygen hoses over an astronaut's couch.

The horror of the last moments of the three astronauts trapped within Apollo Command Module 012 has been imprinted on the minds of all Americans. The deaths of Virgil Grissom, Edward White, and Roger Chaffee on Jan. 27, 1967, will continue to haunt the nation for many years. Some of the luster, some of the invincible rightness, some of the spirit of a gallant crusade has gone out of the space effort. All Americans—from national leaders to youngsters in school—will be watching our man-in-space program a little more closely, a little less confidently.

Hours after the tragedy, James E. Webb, Administrator of the National Aeronautics and Space Administration (NASA), set up a board to review what had gone wrong with Apollo Mission 204. On April 5, 1967, the Review Board presented its formal report. Sensing the doubts of the nation, the Board members wrote in a preface: "The Board is very concerned that its description of the defects in the Apollo Program . . . will be interpreted as an indictment of the entire manned space flight program. . . . Nothing is further from the Board's intent . . . . The Board has been greatly impressed by the integrity, candor, and dedication of those people upon whom the Board relied in conducting this investigation. All have felt a personal loss in this accident, and all are determined that a comparable tragedy shall not occur."

But mistakes had unquestionably been made: "In its devotion to the many difficult problems of space travel," the Board concluded, "the Apollo team failed to give adequate attention to vital questions of crew safety . . . . When these deficiencies are corrected the overall reliability of the Apollo Program will be increased greatly."

Clearly, the Apollo Review Board felt, a slowdown now might well save the lives of future Grissoms and Whites and Chaffees.

## CURRENT U.S. SPACE PROJECTS

The U.S. space program, along with all other non-defense programs, has suffered budget cutbacks for the fiscal year 1967–68. Thus some programs such as *Apollo Applications* and *Voyager* have been suspended. Listed are the principal projects being continued.

**Apollo:** This prime U.S. space program is to land two U.S. astronauts on the Moon and return them safely to Earth. Several other programs, such as the *Surveyor* series, are connected with this major project. Because of delays following the death of three astronauts in January, 1967, the first manned Earth-orbit test flights have been rescheduled for 1968.

This Saturn rocket, capped by the **Apollo 4** space vehicle, is 36 stories tall. Saturn 5 was launched Nov. 9, 1967.

**Applications Technology Satellite:** Evaluation of advanced techniques and equipment for future artificial satellites. Flights began in December, 1966.

**Biosatellite:** Earth-orbiting biological laboratories to develop space medicine by studying the effects of prolonged weightlessness and space radiation on living organisms. Initial launch in 1966 was unrecovered. *Biosatellite II,* in September, 1967, was highly successful.

**Explorer:** A continuing program, dating back to the first successful U.S. satellite, *Explorer I,* which was placed in orbit January 31, 1958. Separate Explorers probe the atmosphere, ionosphere, and interplanetary space.

**Lunar Orbiter:** Highly successful program to provide complete, high-resolution photography of both sides of the Moon. Its photographs and those of the Surveyor probes were used to select a suitable landing site for the Apollo project. Program also helped refine data on Moon's shape, environment, and origin. Series of five flights began in 1966 and ended in August, 1967.

**Mariner:** Program of U.S. planetary exploration. Began in 1962 with the launching of *Mariner II* toward Venus. *Mariner IV,* in 1965, returned photographs of Mars and data on its atmosphere. The second Venus probe, *Mariner V,* was launched in June, 1967, for an October rendezvous. The second Mars effort (a dual launch of *Mariners VI* and *VII*) is slated for 1969.

**Nimbus:** Weather research satellites placed in near-polar orbits to view each area of the Earth twice a day. Launchings began in 1964.

**Orbiting Astronomical Observatory (OAO):** Earth-orbiting spacecraft gathering information on the entire celestial sphere, including the brightness of 100,000 stars, ultraviolet rays, nebulae, and other features obscured by the Earth's atmosphere. Three more flights are planned.

**Orbiting Geophysical Observatory (OGO):** Investigates Earth's atmosphere, magnetic field, and interplanetary space. Flights began in 1964. Two flights (OGO 5 and 6) will complete the existing program.

**Orbiting Solar Observatory (OSO):** Earth-orbiting platform for data on physics of the Sun and for monitoring solar flares; placed in orbit in 1962.

**Pioneer:** Spacecraft placed in orbit of Sun to provide data on solar and interplanetary events. Program began in 1958, with three more flights planned after late 1967.

**Surveyor:** Soft landings on the Moon to photograph possible Apollo landing sites. *Surveyors I* and *III* successfully photographed and observed lunar surface material. *Surveyor V* yielded more pictures and the first chemical analysis of a celestial body other than Earth. Two remaining flights are scheduled.

**Tiros:** The basis of the first operational weather satellite system in the world, Tiros will eventually assist in worldwide weather forecasting. Program was initiated in 1960.

# FOCUS ON THE NEWS

## MORE ON MARS FROM MARINER 4

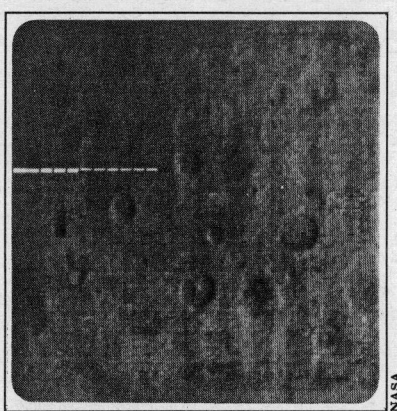

Original Mariner 4 photographs (1965) revealed craters on the surface of Mars.

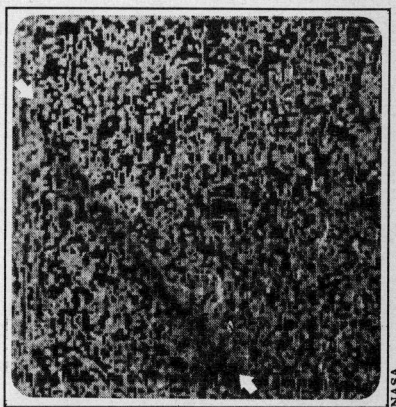

Computer-made "variance plot" (1967) showed 150-mile-long smooth area (**between arrows**).

More than two years after Mariner 4 flew by Mars, that pioneering U.S. space mission is still providing information. In July, 1965, when Mariner 4 photographed about one per cent of the Martian surface, the old dreams of Earth-like life on Mars were dealt a deathblow. Mars, it appeared, was much more like the Moon than like the Earth. About 70 craters, ranging from 3 to 75 miles in diameter, were recognized in the midst of what appeared to be a bleak and windblown desert. Mariner 4's report of a life-forbidding Mars was, in a way, a disappointment. But it was also a classic scientific triumph—years of dreaming and conjecture swept abruptly away by observed fact.

When the hubbub had subsided and the space program had gone on to new projects, scientists at the Jet Propulsion Laboratory and California Institute of Technology began a routine, but more detailed, re-examination of the 21 Martian pictures relayed by Mariner 4. Two years later, in August, 1967, these painstaking studies yielded new and startling information. Using the computer data that had produced the original pictures, the scientists "rebuilt" each of the pictures in a numerical form—each of 40,000 points (per photograph) was given a number representing the degree of light and shadow. The scientists made a number of other improvements in the pictures, including removal of background "noise," the same signal interference that causes a TV picture to become blurred and "snowy". A special computer-generated picture, called a *variance plot*, was also produced.

With these techniques the scientists were able to spot more than three times as many craters as had appeared on the original photographs. Possible fractures in the Martian crust, 100 to 200 miles long, could also be distinguished. Mars is just as pockmarked as the Moon; however, it has evidently suffered more from the ravages of erosion. The surface of the "Red Planet" is indeed reddish in color. Martian peaks and valleys, while equal in size to those on Earth, seem much smoother, perhaps buried beneath a blanket of wind-blown dust.

The most curious aspect of the computer-generated pictures (in which rough areas are white and smooth areas are black) is a long, smooth area about five to ten miles wide and about 150 miles long. Was this one of the once-popular "Martian canals"? Certainly not, said the scientists. But it was a remarkable surface feature nevertheless—and there had not been a trace of it on any of the original Mariner 4 photographs.

The lesson is clear: Continued and patient evaluation of data gleaned from space can yield new, unsuspected information long after a spacecraft has beeped its last sound.

# SPACE RECORDS

## SELECTED SUCCESSFUL SPACE LAUNCHES: 1957–1967

This list includes a selection of those space launches that have advanced man's knowledge of space and the universe. Minor launches, as well as classified U.S. and Soviet launches, are not included.

Under Launch Data, weight is payload in pounds. Unless otherwise specified, under Initial Orbital Data the period of earth satellites is given in minutes and perigee and apogee in miles.

| LAUNCH DATA | | | | INITIAL ORBITAL DATA | | | REMARKS |
| Date | Name | Country | Weight | Period | Perigee | Apogee | |
|---|---|---|---|---|---|---|---|
| Oct. 4, 1957 | Sputnik I | U.S.S.R. | 184 | 96.2 | 141 | 588 | First artificial satellite; transmitted for 21 days |
| Nov. 3, 1957 | Sputnik II | U.S.S.R. | 1,120 | 103.8 | 140 | 1,038 | First biological satellite; carried dog Laika; transmitted for seven days |
| Feb. 1, 1958 | Explorer 1 | U.S. | 31 | 114.8 | 224 | 1,573 | Discovered inner Van Allen radiation belt; provided micrometeorite impact data |
| July 26, 1958 | Explorer 4 | U.S. | 38 | 110.3 | 163 | 1,380 | Mapped radiation belts |
| Oct. 11, 1958 | Pioneer 1 | U.S. | 84 | reached dist. 70,715 mi. | | | Lunar probe; radiation, magnetic field, micrometeoroid data |
| Dec. 6, 1958 | Pioneer 3 | U.S. | 13 | reached dist. 63,581 mi. | | | Discovered outer Van Allen radiation belt |
| Dec. 18, 1958 | Atlas-Score | U.S. | 8,750 | 101.5 | 115 | 914 | First communications satellite; relayed taped messages for 13 days |
| Jan. 2, 1959 | Luna I | U.S.S.R. | 800 | Sun orbit | | | Lunar Probe; passed within 2,187 miles of Moon |
| Feb. 28, 1959 | Discoverer 1 | U.S. | 1,300 | 96 | 114 | 697 | First polar orbit |
| Aug. 7, 1959 | Explorer 6 | U.S. | 142 | 768 | 156 | 2,640 | First use of solar paddles; first TV photo of Earth; mapped radiation belts |
| Sept. 12, 1959 | Luna II | U.S.S.R. | 858 | 35 hrs. in flight | | | First probe to hit the Moon; detected lunar ionosphere but no magnetic field or radiation |
| Sept. 18, 1959 | Vanguard 3 | U.S. | 100 | 130.2 | 320 | 2,329 | Mapped Earth's magnetic field; radiation and micrometeoroid data |
| Oct. 4, 1959 | Luna III | U.S.S.R. | 614 | 16.2 | 24,856 | 298,272 | First crude photo of hidden side of Moon |
| Mar. 11, 1960 | Pioneer 5 | U.S. | 95 | Sun orbit | | | Space probe; data on magnetic field, solar wind, size of solar system |
| Apr. 1, 1960 | Tiros 1 | U.S. | 270 | 99.2 | 429 | 466 | First weather satellite; sent 22,952 photos |
| Apr. 13, 1960 | Transit 1B | U.S. | 265 | 96 | 233 | 479 | First navigation satellite; infrared data; piggyback payload |
| June 22, 1960 | Greb 1 | U.S. | 42 | 101.5 | 382 | 657 | First piggyback satellite; returned solar X-ray data |
| Aug. 10, 1960 | Discoverer 13 | U.S. | 1,700 | 94.1 | 161 | 436 | First space recovery—executed in ocean |
| Aug. 12, 1960 | Echo 1 | U.S. | 124 | 118.3 | 945 | 1,049 | First passive communications relay; voice and TV |
| Aug. 18, 1960 | Discoverer 14 | U.S. | 1,700 | 94.5 | 116 | 502 | First mid-air recovery—by C-119 aircraft off Hawaii |
| Aug. 19, 1960 | Sputnik V | U.S.S.R. | 10,120 | 90.7 | 190 | 211 | First Soviet recovery; carried dogs Belka and Strelka |
| Oct. 4, 1960 | Courier 1B | U.S. | 500 | 107 | 501 | 658 | First active-repeater comsat |
| Nov. 3, 1960 | Explorer 8 | U.S. | 90 | 112.7 | 258 | 1,423 | First U.S. ionospheric satellite; electron and ion density |
| Nov. 23, 1960 | Tiros 2 | U.S. | 280 | 98.4 | 387 | 453 | 36,156 cloud-cover and infrared photos |
| Feb. 12, 1961 | Venus I | U.S.S.R. | 1,419 | Sun orbit | | | Venus probe; in solar orbit; radio contact lost at 4.7 million miles |

| LAUNCH DATA | | | | INITIAL ORBITAL DATA | | | REMARKS |
| Date | Name | Country | Weight | Period | Perigee | Apogee | |
| --- | --- | --- | --- | --- | --- | --- | --- |
| Feb. 16, 1961 | Explorer 9 | U.S. | 80 | 118.3 | 395 | 1,605 | Optical tracking of 12-foot balloon; upper atmosphere density; solar activity |
| Mar. 9, 1961 | Sputnik IX | U.S.S.R. | 10,362 | 88.5 | 114 | 155 | Re-entry March 9, 1961; dog Chernushka recovered |
| Mar. 25, 1961 | Sputnik X | U.S.S.R. | 10,350 | 88.4 | 111 | 153 | Last unmanned Vostok test; re-entry March 26, 1961; dog Zvezdochka recovered |
| Mar. 25, 1961 | Explorer 10 | U.S. | 79 | 112 hrs. | 110 | 144,786 | Data on magnetic fields and solar wind |
| Apr. 27, 1961 | Explorer 11 | U.S. | 82 | 108.1 | 304 | 1,114 | Disproved part of steady-state evolution theory; gamma ray counts until Dec. 6, 1961 |
| June 29, 1961 | Transit 4A | U.S. | 175 | 103.7 | 534 | 623 | First nuclear power in space; employed radioisotope-fueled SNAP generator |
| July 12, 1961 | Tiros 3 | U.S. | 285 | 100.4 | 461 | 506 | First Tiros to photograph hurricanes; 35,033 photos up to Feb. 27, 1962 |
| Nov. 29, 1961 | Mercury (MA-5) | U.S. | 2,900 | 88.6 | 100 | 159 | Re-entry Nov. 29, 1961; Chimp Enos recovered after three orbits |
| Feb. 8, 1962 | Tiros 4 | U.S. | 285 | 100.4 | 440 | 525 | 32,593 cloud photos |
| Mar. 7, 1962 | OSO 1 | U.S. | 440 | 96.2 | 344 | 368 | Data on 75 solar flares, radiation |
| Apr. 26, 1962 | Ariel 1 | U.S./U.K. | 132 | 100.9 | 242 | 754 | First NASA international satellite; ionosphere, X-ray, and cosmic ray data |
| June 19, 1962 | Tiros 5 | U.S. | 285 | 100.5 | 367 | 604 | Good cloud-cover photos provided data during 1962 tropical storm season |
| July 10, 1962 | Telstar 1 | U.S. | 171 | 157.8 | 593 | 3,002 | Active-repeater comsat |
| Aug. 27, 1962 | Mariner 2 | U.S. | 449 | Sun orbit | | | First successful inter-planetary probe; passed within 21,594 miles of Venus; inter-planetary data |
| Sept. 18, 1962 | Tiros 6 | U.S. | 285 | 98.7 | 425 | 442 | Detected sandstorms, ice conditions, and 13 hurricanes; 67,000 cloud-cover photos |
| Sept. 28, 1962 | Alouette 1 | Canada | 320 | 105 | 620 | 650 | First Canadian satellite; ionospheric sounding |
| Oct. 2, 1962 | Explorer 14 | U.S. | 89 | 36.4 | 174 | 61,192 | Mapped shape of Earth's magnetosphere |
| Dec. 13, 1962 | Relay 1 | U.S. | 172 | 185.1 | 820 | 4,611 | First satellite transmissions to South America; active-repeater comsat |
| Dec. 16, 1962 | Explorer 16 | U.S. | 159 | 104.4 | 466 | 733 | First statistically significant meteoroid-penetration data |
| Apr. 3, 1963 | Explorer 17 | U.S. | 405 | 96.4 | 168 | 598 | First measurement of neutral hydrogen belt |
| May 7, 1963 | Telstar 2 | U.S. | 175 | 221.5 | 603 | 6,530 | Active-repeater comsat |
| June 19, 1963 | Tiros 7 | U.S. | 297 | 97.4 | 385 | 401 | Covered two hurricane seasons |
| June 28, 1963 | Geophysical Research Satellite | U.S. | 220 | 102.1 | 258 | 810 | Plasma experiments |
| July 26, 1963 | Syncom 2 | U.S. | 80 | 23.9 hrs. | 22,231 | 22,234 | Active-repeater synchronous comsat; communication tests successful |
| Nov. 1, 1963 | Polyot I | U.S.S.R. | — | 102.4 | 213 | 893 | First Soviet spacecraft reported to have extensive maneuver capability |
| Nov. 27, 1963 | Explorer 18 | U.S. | 138 | 94.4 hrs. | 192 | 106,635 | Discovered high-energy radiation region beyond Van Allen belts |
| Dec. 19, 1963 | Explorer 19 | U.S. | 94 | 115.8 | 368 | 1,482 | 12-foot balloon; atmospheric density studies in near-polar orbit |

*(continued)*

## SUCCESSFUL SPACE LAUNCHES (*continued*)

| LAUNCH DATA | | | | INITIAL ORBITAL DATA | | | REMARKS |
|---|---|---|---|---|---|---|---|
| Date | Name | Country | Weight | Period | Perigee | Apogee | |
| Jan. 21, 1964 | Relay 2 | U.S. | 183 | 194.7 | 1,298 | 4,606 | First Japan-France comsat link; active-repeater comsat |
| Jan. 25, 1964 | Echo 2 | U.S. | 565 | 109 | 642 | 816 | First cooperative program with U.S.S.R.; passive reflector comsat |
| Jan. 30, 1964 | Elektron I | U.S.S.R. | — | 169 | 252 | 4,412 | First dual Soviet launch; studies on inner and outer Van Allen radiation belts |
| | Elektron II | U.S.S.R. | — | 22.7 hrs. | 286 | 42,379 | |
| Mar. 27, 1964 | Ariel 2 | U.S./U.K. | 165 | 101.38 | 180 | 843 | Data on ozone, micrometeroids, and galactic noise |
| Apr. 12, 1964 | Polyot II | U.S.S.R. | — | 92.4 | 193 | 311 | Series of maneuver tests during first day in orbit |
| May 28, 1964 | Saturn 1 (SA-6) | U.S. | 38,900 | 88.56 | 62 | 76 | Unmanned Apollo module and second stage |
| July 10, 1964 | Elektron III | U.S.S.R. | — | 168 | 252 | 4,375 | Dual launch; simultaneous radiation measurements in outer belt and magnetosphere |
| | Elektron IV | U.S.S.R. | — | 21.9 hrs. | 285 | 41,158 | |
| July 17, 1964 | Vela 3 | U.S. | 319 | 100.3 hrs. | 63,369 | 65,024 | Identical experimental nuclear detection satellites |
| | Vela 4 | U.S. | 319 | 100.1 hrs. | 58,766 | 69,482 | |
| July 17, 1964 | ERS 13 | U.S. | 4.5 | 39.2 | 120 | 64,886 | Tetrahedral research satellite; radiation data |
| July 28, 1964 | Ranger 7 | U.S. | 806 | Flight time: 68 hrs. 36 min. | | | Impacted on Moon; 4,316 high-quality photos in last 13 minutes |
| Aug. 19, 1964 | Syncom 3 | U.S. | 83 | 692 | 702 | 23,577 | First synchronous comsat |
| Aug. 28, 1964 | Nimbus 1 | U.S. | 830 | 98.3 | 262 | 579 | Weather satellite; 27,000 photos |
| Sept. 5, 1964 | OGO 1 | U.S. | 1,073 | 64 hrs. | 176 | 92,850 | Data from 20 geophysical experiments |
| Oct. 10, 1964 | Explorer 22 | U.S. | 116 | 104.8 | 547 | 676 | Ionosphere and geodetic research satellite |
| Nov. 21, 1964 | Explorer 24 | U.S. | 19 | 116.15 | 326 | 1,549 | First NASA dual payload launch |
| | Explorer 25 | | 90 | 116.15 | 326 | 1,549 | Radiation satellite; results integrated with Explorer 24; air density data |
| Nov. 28, 1964 | Mariner 4 | U.S. | 575 | Sun orbit; flight time to Mars: 228 days | | | First successful major interplanetary space probe; 21 photos (1% of Martian surface) revealed surface similar to Moon |
| Nov. 30, 1964 | Zond II | U.S.S.R. | — | Sun orbit | | | Mars probe; tested plasma engine in flight |
| Dec. 15, 1964 | San Marco | Italy | 250 | 94.9 | 128 | 510 | Flight test of Italian ionosphere-air density satellite |
| Jan. 22, 1965 | Tiros 9 | U.S. | 305 | 119 | 440 | 1,600 | In Tiros weather series |
| Feb. 3, 1965 | OSO 2 | U.S. | 545 | 96.4 | 287 | 374 | Part of study of Sun throughout an 11-year solar cycle |
| Feb. 11, 1965 | Titan 3A | U.S. | 11,500 | 145.6 | 1,721 | 1,737 | First time U.S. rocket started and stopped in space three times; described three different orbits |
| Feb. 16, 1965 | Pegasus 1 | U.S. | 23,700 | 97 | 308 | 453 | To measure hazards of meteoroids in space; 96-foot wing span |
| Feb. 17, 1965 | Ranger 8 | U.S. | 808.8 | Flight time: 64.9 hrs. | | | Photographed portion of Moon's surface not photographed by Ranger 7; over 7,000 pictures during last 23 minutes of flight; impacted in Sea of Tranquillity |
| Mar. 21, 1965 | Ranger 9 | U.S. | 808.8 | Flight time: 64.5 hrs. | | | Last of Ranger series; first live TV pictures of Moon |
| Apr. 3, 1965 | Snapshot 1 | U.S. | 970 | 111.5 | 788 | 820 | First atomic-powered reactor used for a spacecraft; also 2.2-lb. non-nuclear ion engine aboard vehicle |

| LAUNCH DATA | | | | INITIAL ORBITAL DATA | | | REMARKS |
|---|---|---|---|---|---|---|---|
| Date | Name | Country | Weight | Period | Perigee | Apogee | |
| Apr. 6, 1965 | Early Bird "Comsat" | U.S. | 87 | 23.9 hrs. | 21,700 | 22,683 | First commercial communications satellite |
| Apr. 23, 1965 | Molniya I | U.S.S.R. | — | 11.8 hrs. | 308 | 24,454 | First Soviet communications satellite; broadcast to Moscow from Vladivostok |
| Apr. 29, 1965 | Explorer 27 | U.S. | 132 | 107.8 | 577 | 816 | Study of Earth's gravitational field; ionospheric data |
| July 16, 1965 | Proton I | U.S.S.R. | 27,000 | 92.5 | 118 | 390 | Heaviest Soviet payload ever launched; a "space platform" |
| July 18, 1965 | Zond III | U.S.S.R. | — | Sun orbit | | | Interplanetary exploration; photographed Moon |
| July 30, 1965 | Pegasus 3 | U.S. | 23,700 | 95.2 | 319 | 322 | Wings contained detachable panels that could be retrieved by an astronaut |
| Nov. 2, 1965 | Proton II | U.S.S.R. | 26,896 | 92.6 | 119 | 396 | A second "space platform" to study cosmic rays and danger to manned flight |
| Nov. 29, 1965 | A 1 | France | 92 | 108.7 | 328 | 1,099 | First French satellite; transmitted for two days |
| Nov. 29, 1965 | Alouette 2 | Canada- | 323 | 121.4 | 313 | 1,852 | Dual launch; ionospheric research |
| | Explorer 31 | U.S. | 218 | 121.3 | 313 | 1,846 | |
| Dec. 6, 1965 | FR-1A | France | 135 | 99.9 | 464 | 469 | Radio research satellite |
| Dec. 16, 1965 | Pioneer 6 | U.S. | 140 | Sun orbit | | | Solar and interplanetary data from solar orbit |
| Jan. 31, 1966 | Luna IX | U.S.S.R. | 220 | — | — | — | Soft landing on Moon; photos of surface for three days |
| Feb. 3, 1966 | ESSA 1 | U.S. | 305 | Sun orbit | | | First cartwheel weather satellite with automatic picture transmission |
| Feb. 28, 1966 | ESSA 2 | U.S. | 290 | Sun orbit | | | Completed first ESSA global system |
| Mar. 31, 1966 | Luna X | U.S.S.R. | 540 | Lunar orbit | | | First satellite to orbit Moon; lunar surface and circumlunar space data |
| May 30, 1966 | Surveyor 1 | U.S. | 596 | Flight time: 63.6 hrs. | | | Landed on Moon; photos of lunar surface |
| Aug. 10, 1966 | Lunar Orbiter 1 | U.S. | 853 | Lunar orbit | | | Lunar photography |
| Aug. 17, 1966 | Pioneer 7 | U.S. | 140 | Sun orbit | | | Solar and interplanetary experiments; data on magnetic field, solar plasma, cosmic rays |
| Aug. 24, 1966 | Luna XI | U.S.S.R. | — | Lunar orbit | | | Lunar space environment |
| Oct. 2, 1966 | ESSA 3 | U.S. | 325 | Sun orbit | | | Weather; excellent cloud-cover photos |
| Oct. 22, 1966 | Luna XII | U.S.S.R. | | Lunar orbit | | | First U.S.S.R. satellite to return photos of Moon |
| Oct. 26, 1966 | Intelsat 2A | U.S. | 192 | 669.6 | 185 | 23,342 | Communications commercial satellite; orbit allows eight hours of use per day |
| Nov. 6, 1966 | Lunar Orbiter 2 | U.S. | 850 | Lunar orbit | | | Lunar photography |
| Dec. 6, 1966 | ATS 1 | U.S. | 775 | 24.4 hrs. | 22,228 | 22,870 | Communications, spacecraft technology, meteorological tests; Earth disk photos |
| Dec. 20, 1966 | Luna XIII | U.S.S.R. | — | — | — | — | Landed on Moon in Ocean of Storms; photos, soil density data, radiation |
| Jan. 11, 1967 | Intelsat 2B | U.S. | 195 | 23.9 hrs. | 22,236 | 22,242 | Communications commercial satellite |
| Jan. 26, 1967 | ESSA 4 | U.S. | 290 | Nearly polar sun orbit | | | Operational weather satellite; good photos returned |
| Feb. 4, 1967 | Lunar Orbiter 3 | U.S. | 850 | Lunar orbit | | | Lunar photography |
| Mar. 8, 1967 | OSO 3 | U.S. | 627 | Solar orbit | | | Solar physics; data on solar flares; solar disk, corona |
| Mar. 23, 1967 | Intelsat 2-C | U.S. | 195 | 23.9 hrs. | 22,245 | 23,472 | Communications commercial satellite |
| April 6, 1967 | ATS 2 | U.S. | 715 | 204 | 116 | 6,222 | Satellite technology |
| April 17, 1967 | Surveyor 3 | U.S. | 625 | — | — | — | Lunar impact; soft landing; TV photography |
| April 20, 1967 | ESSA 5 | U.S. | 325 | Sun orbit | | | Operational weather; advanced camera |

(continued)

## SUCCESSFUL SPACE LAUNCHES (continued)

| LAUNCH DATA | | | | INITIAL ORBITAL DATA | | | REMARKS |
|---|---|---|---|---|---|---|---|
| Date | Name | Country | Weight | Period | Perigee | Apogee | |
| May 4, 1967 | Lunar Orbiter 4 | U.S. | 850 | Lunar orbit | | | Lunar photography; high resolution photos of over 99% of frontside of Moon |
| May 5, 1967 | Ariel 3 | U.S./U.K. | 198 | 95.6 | 311 | 372 | Atmospheric and ionospheric research |
| May 24, 1967 | Explorer 34 | U.S. | 163 | 105.9 hrs. | 150 | 133,218 | Cosmic ray research |
| June 13, 1967 | Venus IV | U.S.S.R. | 2,437 | Sun orbit | | | First soft landing on planet |
| June 14, 1967 | Mariner 5 | U.S. | 550 | Sun orbit | | | Venus flyby; planetary and interplanetary exploration |
| July 19, 1967 | Explorer 35 | U.S. | 230 | Lunar orbit | | | Interplanetary space research |
| July 28, 1967 | OGO 4 | U.S. | 1,240 | 97.8 | 256 | 564 | Sun's effect on Earth's environment |
| Aug. 1, 1967 | Lunar Orbiter 5 | U.S. | 850 | Lunar orbit | | | Lunar photography from lunar orbit |
| Sept. 7, 1967 | Biosatellite 2 | U.S. | 940 | In space 45 hrs. | | | Effects of space on life |
| Sept. 8, 1967 | Surveyor 5 | U.S. | 616 | — | — | — | Lunar photos and soil analysis; impact on Moon |
| Oct. 18, 1967 | OSO 4 | U.S. | 599 | 95 | 350 | 350 | Solar observation |
| Oct. 27 and Oct. 30, 1967 | Cosmos 186 and Cosmos 188 | U.S.S.R. | — | — | — | — | First unmanned docking between two satellites |

## PLANNED SPACE LAUNCHES: 1967–1968

| LAUNCH DATA | | | | INITIAL ORBITAL DATA (Est.) | | | REMARKS |
|---|---|---|---|---|---|---|---|
| Date | Name | Country | Weight | Period | Perigee | Apogee | |
| Nov. 1967 | Surveyor 6 | U.S. | 2,200 | Lunar soft landing | | | Lunar surface measurements; site selection |
| Nov. 1967 | ATS-C | U.S. | 801 | — | — | — | Spin stabilization; weather, communication, and radiation experiments |
| Nov. 1967 | TOS-D | U.S. | 285 | — | — | — | Weather satellite |
| Dec. 1967 | GEOS-B | U.S. | 450 | 107 | 600 | 800 | Geodetic explorer |
| Dec. 1967 | Pioneer C | U.S. | 145 | Sun orbit | | | Interplanetary data |
| 1968 | Nimbus B | U.S. | 1,280 | 105 | 600 | 600 | Weather satellite |
| 1968 | Surveyor 7 | U.S. | 2,200 | Lunar soft landing | | | Lunar surface measurements; site selection |
| 1968 | RAE-A | U.S. | 420 | — | 3,200 | 3,200 | To observe radio signals in space |
| 1968 | Air Density/ Injun Explorers | U.S. | 145 (Inj.) 20 (A.D. Balloon) | 117 | 350 | 1,600 | To be launched simultaneously. A.D. to measure atmospheric density and temperature; Inj. to measure particles in geomagnetic field |
| 1968 | Apollo | U.S. | — | — | — | — | First Apollo manned flight; earth orbital |
| 1968 | TOS-E | U.S. | — | — | — | — | Weather satellite |
| 1968 | OGO-E | U.S. | 1,300 | 64 hrs. | 150 | 80,000 | To study interplanetary space, the magnetosphere, and Earth's atmosphere |
| 1968 | IMP-G | U.S. | 156 | 96 hrs. | 105 | 110,000 | To study radiation, interplanetary magnetic field, Earth's magnetosphere |
| 1968 | RAM C-B | U.S. | 285 | — | — | — | Plasma density measurements |
| 1968 | TOS-F | U.S. | 285 | 109 | 770 | 770 | Weather satellite |
| 1968 | ATS-D | U.S. | 895 | — | — | — | Weather, communication, radiation damage experiments |
| 1968 | OSO-F | U.S. | 600 | 95 | 300 | 300 | To study solar physics |
| 1968 | TOS-G | U.S. | 325 | — | — | — | Weather satellite |
| 1968 | OWL-A OWL-B | U.S. | 125 | 96 | 350 | 350 | To study atmospheric data—aurorae, airglow, Van Allen belt |
| 1968 | Pioneer D | U.S. | 145 | Sun orbit | | | Interplanetary data |
| 1968 | ISIS-A | Canada-U.S. | 490 | 121 | 270 | 1,890 | Ionospheric data; continuation of joint U.S.-Canadian Alouette program |
| 1968 | TOS-H | U.S. | 285 | 109 | 770 | 770 | Weather satellite |
| 1968 | OAO-A2 | U.S. | 4,200 | 99 | 430 | 430 | Orbiting astronomical observatory |

## OFFICIAL WORLD SPACE RECORDS

Source: National Aeronautics and Space Administration

MANNED SPACECRAFT:

| | |
|---|---|
| Duration With Earth Orbit.....U.S.A. 190 hours 56 minutes | Duration of Sortie from Spacecraft |
| Distance With Earth Orbit...........U.S.A. 3,312,997 miles | in Earth Orbit.................U.S.S.R. 12 mins. 9 secs. |
| Greatest Altitude With Earth Orbit.....U.S.S.R. 309.25 miles | Greatest Altitude Without Earth Orbit.....U.S.A. 116.5 miles |
| Greatest Mass Lifted With Earth Orbit. .U.S.S.R. 11,728.59 lbs. | Greatest Mass Lifted Without Earth Orbit...U.S.A. 4,040 lbs. |

| | | | |
|---|---|---|---|
| August 21–29, 1965 | **Duration With Earth Orbit**............................... Lieut. Col. L. Gordon Cooper and Lieut. Comdr. Charles Conrad, Spacecraft U.S. Gemini 5; a total of 120 orbits around earth. | U.S.A. | 190 hrs. 56 mins. |
| August 21–29, 1965 | **Distance With Earth Orbit**............................... Lieutenant Colonel L. Gordon Cooper and Lieutenant Commander Charles Conrad, Spacecraft U.S. Gemini 5 | U.S.A. | 3,312,997 miles |
| March 18, 1965 | **Greatest Altitude With Earth Orbit**....................... Colonel Pavel I. Belyayev and Lieutenant Colonel Alexei A. Leonov, Spacecraft U.S.S.R. Voskhod II | U.S.S.R. | 309.25 miles |
| March 18, 1965 | **Duration of Sortie from Spacecraft in Earth Orbit**......... Lieut. Col. Alexei A. Leonov, Spacecraft U.S.S.R. Voskhod II | U.S.S.R. | 12 mins. 9 secs. |
| October 12–13, 1964 | **Greatest Mass Lifted With Earth Orbit**.................... Colonel Vladimir M. Komarov, Konstantin P. Feoktistov, and Dr. Boris B. Yegorov, Spacecraft U.S.S.R. Voskhod I | U.S.S.R. | 11,728.59 pounds |
| May 5, 1961 | **Greatest Altitude Without Earth Orbit**.................... Commander Alan B. Shepard, USN, McDonnell Spacecraft U.S. Freedom 7 From: Cape Canaveral, Florida To: 27° 13' 07'' N  75° 51' 14'' W (Gulf of Mexico) | U.S.A. | 116.5 miles |
| May 5, 1961 | **Greatest Mass Lifted Without Earth Orbit**................ Commander Alan B. Shepard, USN, McDonnell Spacecraft U.S. Freedom 7 From: Cape Canaveral, Florida To: 27° 13' 07'' N, 75° 51' 14'' W (Gulf of Mexico) | U.S.A. | 4,040 pounds |

OFFICIAL WORLD SPACE RECORDS (Female):

| | | | |
|---|---|---|---|
| June 16–19, 1963 | **Duration With Earth Orbit**............................... Valentina V. Terechkova, Vostok VI spacecraft 48 earth orbits | U.S.S.R. | 70 hr. 40 mins. 48 secs. |
| June 16–19, 1963 | **Distance With Earth Orbit**............................... Valentina V. Terechkova, Vostok VI spacecraft | U.S.S.R. | 1,223,716 miles |
| June 16–19, 1963 | **Greatest Altitude With Earth Orbit**....................... Valentina V. Terechkova, Vostok VI spacecraft | U.S.S.R. | 143.59 miles |
| June 16–19, 1963 | **Greatest Mass Lifted With Earth Orbit**.................... Valentina V. Terechkova, Vostok VI spacecraft | U.S.S.R. | 10,380.3 lbs. |

## CLAIMED WORLD SPACE RECORDS

Source: National Aeronautics and Space Administration

| | | | |
|---|---|---|---|
| December 4–18, 1965 | **Duration With Earth Orbit**............................... Lieut. Col. Frank Borman and Comdr. James A. Lovell, Jr., Spacecraft U.S. Gemini 7 | U.S.A. | 13 days 18 hrs. 35 mins. |
| December 4–18, 1965 | **Distance With Earth Orbit**............................... Lieut. Col. Frank Borman and Comdr. James A. Lovell, Jr., Spacecraft U.S. Gemini 7 | U.S.A. | 5,716,900 miles |
| December 15–16, 1965 | **Duration in Group Flight**................................ Capt. Walter M. Schirra, Major Thomas P. Stafford, Spacecraft U.S. Gemini 6 Lieut. Col. Frank Borman, Comdr. James A. Lovell, Jr. Spacecraft U.S. Gemini 7 | U.S.A. | 20 hrs. 22 mins. |
| December 15–16, 1965 | **Distance in Group Flight**............................... Capt. Walter M. Schirra and Major Thomas P. Stafford, Spacecraft U.S. Gemini 6; Lieut. Col. Frank Borman, Comdr. James A. Lovell, Jr., Spacecraft U.S. Gemini 7 | U.S.A. | 358,189.4 miles |
| July 21, 1966 | **Precision Landing** (Distance From Target)............... Comdr. John Young and Major Michael Collins, Spacecraft U.S. Gemini 10 | U.S.A. | 3.06 miles |
| September 12–15, 1966 | **Greatest Altitude With Earth Orbit**....................... Lieut. Comdr. Charles Conrad and Lieut. Comdr. Richard F. Gordon, Jr., Spacecraft U.S. Gemini 11 | U.S.A. | 850 miles |

## OUTSTANDING MANNED ORBITAL FLIGHTS

Source: National Aeronautics and Space Administration

In the seven years since Yuri Gagarin made a single orbit about the Earth, nearly 30 men, and one woman, have followed him into space, logging well over 1,000 hours "out there."

| ASTRONAUT, COUNTRY, AND DATE | ORBITS | ALTITUDE (in miles) | FLIGHT TIME | WEIGHT OF CRAFT (in pounds) | CRAFT NAME | ROCKET THRUST (in pounds) |
|---|---|---|---|---|---|---|
| Yuri A. Gagarin (U.S.S.R.) April 12, 1961......... | 1 | 112.5 to 203.2 | 1 hr. 48 mins. | 10,418 | Vostok I | 800,000 |
| Gherman S. Titov (U.S.S.R.) August 6, 1961........ | 17.5 | 111 to 160 | 25 hrs. 18 mins. | 10,430 | Vostok II | 800,000 |
| John H. Glenn (U.S.) February 20, 1962....... | 3 | 100.3 to 162.7 | 4 hrs. 55 mins. | 2,900 | Friendship 7 | 360,000 |
| M. Scott Carpenter (U.S.) May 24, 1962..... | 3 | 100 to 166.8 | 4 hrs. 56 mins. | 2,975 | Aurora 7 | 360,000 |
| Andrian G. Nikolayev (U.S.S.R.) August 11, 1962....... | 64 | 114 to 156 | 94 hrs. 35 mins. | 10,400 | Vostok III | 880,000 |
| Pavel R. Popovich (U.S.S.R.) August 12, 1962....... | 48 | 112 to 158 | 70 hrs. 57 mins. | 10,400 | Vostok IV | 880,000 |
| Walter M. Schirra (U.S.) October 3, 1962... | 6 | 100 to 176 | 9 hrs. 13 mins. | 2,900 | Sigma 7 | 360,000 |
| L. Gordon Cooper (U.S.) May 15, 1963..... | 22 | 100.2 to 166.1 | 34 hrs. 20 mins. | 2,900 | Faith 7 | 360,000 |
| Valery F. Bykovsky (U.S.S.R.) June 14, 1963......... | 81 | 109 to 138 | 119 hrs. 6 mins. | 10,360 | Vostok V | 800,000 |
| Valentina V. Tereshkova (U.S.S.R.) June 16, 1963..... | 48 | 114 to 145 | 70 hrs. 50 mins. | 10,360 | Vostok VI | 800,000 |
| Konstantin Feoktistov Vladimir Komarov Boris Yegorov (U.S.S.R.) October 12, 1964........ | 16 | 111 to 254 | 24 hrs. 17 mins. | 16,000 | Voskhod I | 900,000 |
| Pavel I. Belyayev Alexei A. Leonov (U.S.S.R.) March 18, 1965........ | 17 | 107 to 308 | 26 hrs. 2 mins. | 13,200 | Voskhod II | 1,433,000 |
| Virgil I. Grissom John W. Young (U.S.) March 23, 1965... | 3 | 100 to 139 | 4 hrs. 53 mins. | 7,111 | Gemini 3 | 530,000 |
| James A. McDivitt Edward H. White (U.S.) June 3, 1965..... | 62 | 100 to 175 | 97 hrs. 56 mins. | 7,879 | Gemini 4 | 530,000 |
| L. Gordon Cooper Charles Conrad, Jr. (U.S.) August 21, 1965.. | 120 | 101 to 217 | 7 days 22 hrs. 56 mins. | 7,947 | Gemini 5 | 530,000 |
| Frank Borman James A. Lovell, Jr. (U.S.) December 4, 1965 | 206 | 100 to 204 | 13 days 18 hrs. 35 mins. | 8,076 | Gemini 7 | 530,000 |
| Walter M. Schirra, Jr. Thomas P. Stafford (U.S.) December 15, 1965...... | 15 | 100 to 161 | 25 hrs. 51 mins. | 7,817 | Gemini 6 | 530,000 |
| Neil A. Armstrong David R. Scott (U.S.) March 16, 1966... | 6.6 | 99 to 164 | 10 hrs. 42 mins. | 7,116 | Gemini 8 | 530,000 |
| Thomas P. Stafford Eugene A. Cernan (U.S.) June 3, 1966..... | 44 | 167 to 169 | 72 hrs. 20 mins. | 8,100 | Gemini 9 | 530,000 |
| John W. Young Michael Collins (U.S.) July 18, 1966..... | 43 | 185 to 468 | 70 hrs. 46 mins. | 8,250 | Gemini 10 | 530,000 |
| Charles Conrad, Jr. Richard F. Gordon, Jr. (U.S.) Sept. 12, 1966.... | 44 | 180 to 850 | 71 hrs. 17 mins. | 8,260 | Gemini 11 | 530,000 |
| James A. Lovell, Jr. Edwin E. Aldrin, Jr. (U.S.) Nov. 11, 1966..... | 59 | 158 to 179 | 94 hrs. 34 mins. | 8,290 | Gemini 12 | 530,000 |

# SPACE AGE GLOSSARY

**Ablating materials:** Special plastic-like materials on the surface of the spacecraft or missile that vaporize or melt away during re-entry, thus dissipating the intense heat of atmospheric friction that would otherwise destroy the pay load.

**Abort:** To cut short an aerospace mission after the command to "fire" and before the mission has accomplished its objective.

**Acquisition:** The process of locating the path of a satellite or space probe so that earth-based instruments can "lock on" to their signals and begin gathering tracking or telemetry data.

**Aphelion:** The point at which an orbiting planet, comet, or artificial satellite is farthest from the Sun.

**Apogee:** The point at which the Moon or an artificial satellite in its orbit is farthest from Earth.

**Atmosphere:** The gaseous envelope surrounding any of the planets or their satellites. Earth's atmosphere consists of six ascending zones: *Troposphere,* between the Earth's surface and 10 miles above it; *Stratosphere,* between 10 and 16 miles above the surface; *Mesosphere,* between 16 and 50 miles above the surface (also called the Chemosphere); *Ionosphere,* between 40 to 50 and 175 to 250 miles above the surface; *Thermosphere,* between 250 and 300 miles above the surface; and *Exosphere,* between 300 and 1,000 miles above the surface.

**Attitude:** The position of an aerospace vehicle's axes in relation to some frame of reference, usually the Earth's surface. Attitude has three components: *Pitch,* rotation about an axis (Y) that is both perpendicular to the vehicle's longitudinal axis and horizontal with respect to the ground; *Roll,* rotation about a longitudinal (X) axis; and *Yaw,* rotation about a vertical (Z) axis.

**Axis** (pl. axes): In aircraft terminology, any of three straight lines, the first running through the center of the fuselage lengthwise (X); the second at right angles to this and parallel to the horizontal airfoils (Y); and the third perpendicular to the first two axes at their point of intersection (Z).

**Ballistics:** The science that deals with the motion, behavior, design, and launching of projectiles such as bullets and rockets. A ballistics flight is synonymous with suborbital space flight (less than one complete orbit). A ballistic missile travels through most of its flight as a free-falling body. It is set on the proper flight path by the adjustment of its rocket engines and by guidance devices. The ICBM (Intercontinental Ballistic Missile) has an approximate range of 6,500 miles. The IRBM (Intermediate Range Ballistic Missile) has an approximate range of between 200 and 1,500 miles. As weapons, ballistic missiles bear explosive warheads.

**Boilerplate:** A full-scale model that has the weight, size, and shape of the true item, but not all of its functional features.

**Booster:** Short for "booster rocket engine," the first auxiliary stage of a multistage launch vehicle that is fired at lift-off in order to boost the rocket to the proper speed necessary for prolonged flight.

**Burnout:** When combustion (and therefore *thrust*) ceases in a rocket engine.

**Capsule:** A small, sealed, pressurized cabin with an internal environment that will support human or animal life during extremely high-altitude flight or space flight. It forms the nose cone of a rocket and is referred to as the spacecraft.

**Destruct:** The destroying of a rocket vehicle after launch but before completion of its flight, usually as a safety measure or to terminate a test phase.

**Drogue parachute:** (1) A type of parachute attached to a spacecraft or missile to slow it down (also called *deceleration* or *drag* parachute). (2) A small parachute specially used to pull a larger parachute out of stowage.

**Entry Corridor:** During re-entry, the prescribed path of flight that allows safe recovery of a spacecraft.

**Escape velocity:** The velocity required for any rocket or other missile to overcome and "escape" the gravitational pull of Earth or other planetary bodies. Space probes designed to leave the Earth and travel beyond its gravitational field must exceed 25,000 miles per hour. The mass of each planet varies, and so each has a different escape velocity. Because the moon's mass is much less than Earth's, its escape velocity is only 5,292 miles per hour.

**Exobiology:** The science that deals with the detection and study of possible forms of life on celestial bodies other than the Earth.

**G:** An acceleration equal to the acceleration of *gravity* (approximately 32.2 feet per second per second at sea level) used as a unit for measuring the stress on bodies that are undergoing acceleration during high-speed or space flights.

**Gimballed Motor:** A rocket motor mounted on gimbals; i.e., on a contrivance having two mutually perpendicular axes of rotation to allow for pitch and yaw corrections.

**Glitch:** A foul-up, mistake, or interruption of plans. Glitches are generally said to occur with inanimate things such as computer programs or mechanical components, and cannot be traced to, or blamed on, any particular person.

**Guidance System:** A system which measures and evaluates flight information, correlates this with target data, converts the result into the conditions necessary to achieve the desired flight path, and communicates this data in the form of commands to the flight control system.

**Hypersonic:** Usually applied to velocities five times greater than the speed of sound (Mach 5). *Subsonic* velocities are less than the speed of sound (Mach 1), and *supersonic* flights are at velocities greater than Mach 1.

**Ice Frost:** A layer of ice that gathers on the outside of a rocket vehicle over surfaces super-
*(continued)*

**SPACE AGE GLOSSARY** (*continued*)

cooled by liquid oxygen (LOX) carried within the vehicle.

**Injection:** The process of placing a spacecraft into a calculated orbit.

**Jettison:** Separation of an instrument section or package from the remainder of the rocket vehicle by application of force stemming from inside the package.

**Launch window:** Precisely when and where a spacecraft must be launched to achieve a desired encounter, rendezvous, impact, or other mission. Spacecraft must find the proper "window" for re-entry as well.

**Liquid Hydrogen (LH$_2$):** A liquid rocket fuel that, when oxidized by liquid oxygen, provides about 40 per cent greater thrust than any previously used fuel.

**Mach number** (pronounced "mock"): A number representing the ratio of a vehicle's speed to the speed of sound. Thus Mach 5 is 5 times the speed of sound.

**Orbital flight:** Orbital flights, both manned and unmanned, are conducted for the purpose of space study, weather observation, and military surveillance. A satellite designed to orbit approximately 200 miles above the Earth's surface must travel at about 18,000 miles per hour. At that speed the satellite or spacecraft remains in orbit, balanced by its centrifugal thrust into space and the force of gravity drawing it back to earth. A *parking orbit* is a self-sustaining orbit achieved when these forces are equal. Such a maneuver is sometimes executed while data is relayed to Earth before the next experiment is begun. Once a parking orbit is achieved, no further power is needed to maintain it. When the object's orbital velocity slows so that gravity pulls it back to Earth (*orbital decay*), it falls back to Earth (re-enters), and may be recovered if it is not consumed by the heat of atmospheric friction.

**Oxidizer:** In a rocket propellant, a substance such as liquid oxygen or nitric acid that yields the oxygen necessary for the combustion of the actual fuel.

**Perigee:** The point at which the Moon or an artificial satellite in its orbit is closest to the Earth.

**Perihelion:** The point at which an orbiting planet, comet, or artificial satellite is closest to the Sun.

**Piggyback satellite:** A secondary satellite carried atop the main payload of a spacecraft. Once the primary satellite is in orbit, the piggyback is released to attain its own independent mission.

**Plasma:** A gaseous material. Much of the matter in the universe is in a plasma state, including the interior of the stars. A plasma sheath often surrounds an aerospace vehicle during re-entry or hypersonic speed as a result of atmospheric friction. It is a major cause of communications blackout.

**Retrorocket:** A rocket that gives thrust in a direction opposite to that of an object's motion. It is used to brake a vehicle for space maneuvers or for landings.

**Rocket cluster:** Two or more rocket engines bound together so as to function as one propulsive unit.

**Scrub:** To cancel out a scheduled launch either before or during countdown.

**Solar cell:** A type of battery used to convert sunlight into electrical energy. It can be either the main or auxiliary power source for many space experiments.

**Space:** Everything beyond Earth's atmosphere. In space there is an almost total lack of the molecules that make matter. In our atmosphere, "thin" air is really composed of molecules that are (relatively speaking) packed tightly together. In space there are only a few molecules per cubic foot, compared with millions in a cubic foot of the air we breathe on Earth. *Deep space* is sometimes used to refer to space other than that in the vicinity of Earth.

**Space probe:** An exploratory vehicle that travels through space or lands on a celestial body such as the Moon. It is designed to collect, and transmit to Earth stations, data concerning the environment it has encountered.

**Synchronous satellite:** An artificial satellite whose orbital speed, matched with the Earth's rotation, causes it to appear to remain at the same fixed point above the Earth.

**Telemetry:** A system for taking measurements on the ground or within an aerospace vehicle in flight and transmitting them by radio to another station.

**Thrust:** The force, expressed in pounds, that is developed by an aircraft or rocket engine. It is the force required to lift the vehicle and overcome Earth's gravitational pull. Saturn V, the largest U.S. rocket engine, develops about 7,500,000 pounds of thrust.

**Time Hack:** Space talk for "What time is it?" Because of the precision necessary, a time hack may be given in hundredths of a second—or even milliseconds.

**Tracking:** The process of following the movement of a satellite or other space vehicle by radar, radio, and photographic observations.

**Ullage:** The volume in a container above the surface of a stored liquid; also, the ratio of this volume to the total volume of the tank. Ullage does not exist without gravity. Thus, in space small rockets must be fired to create ullage—that is, to force the fuel to the bottom of the tank where it can feed into the engines.

**Van Allen Radiation Belt:** A zone of high-intensity radiation that begins at an altitude of about 500 miles and encircles the Earth. It may prove hazardous in deep space flights. The actual existence of the belt was discovered during the flight of U.S. Explorer I in 1958 and named for James Van Allen, American astrophysicist.

**Weightlessness:** A condition, experienced by astronauts in orbital flights, similar to floating without gravity. Weightlessness is the result of the lifting force of the rocket being nearly equal to the downward pull of gravity. On prolonged space flights beyond the Earth's gravitational field without artificial gravity in the capsule, this condition could prove hazardous since weightlessness seems to affect body metabolism.

# LIVELY ARTS

## Art • Books • Films • Theater • Music and Dance

The New York Times

The Metropolitan Opera Company's outdoor concerts, attended by huge crowds in New York City, were typical of cultural events drawing support from an increasingly large segment of the American public.

### THE ARTS IN AMERICA: 1967

Late in the summer of 1967, the National Council on the Arts submitted to Congress recommendations for the appropriation of $139 million in Federal funds for support of the arts. Earlier, Congress had appropriated $17.5 million for a three-year Federal arts program ending in June, 1968. If approved, the new appropriation could put into effect the most extensive program of Federal assistance to the arts in American history.

The National Council plan recommends, among other things, that Government aid be granted to museums, orchestras, and dance companies, and that assistance be given to individual painters, sculptors, novelists, poets, playwrights, and composers. The program also calls for establishment of some 50 permanent, professional dramatic companies in communities across the country, and the development of new experimental projects in the visual arts.

To many observers the National Council's extraordinarily ambitious proposals for development and expansion of the performing and visual arts on a nationwide scale reaffirmed the continuing growth of interest in and support for the arts throughout the United States. The action further suggested that the much-discussed American "culture explosion" had, indeed, emerged as a genuine, perhaps deep-rooted, and hopefully permanent phenomenon in the nation's development.

There is considerable evidence to support this view of increasing national involvement in the arts. Statistics show sharp increases in museum attendance, record sales, and publication of both hard-cover and paperback books; increases in the number and size of grants in the arts awarded by public *(continued)*

**THE ARTS IN AMERICA: 1967** (*continued*)

and private foundations, and a plethora of Standing Room Only signs at box offices across the country.

There were, of course, contrasting views of the situation. In some quarters, fears were expressed that quality might be diluted in order to win mass acceptance. And at least one much-discussed report, *Performing Arts—The Economic Dilemma,* published late in 1966 by the 20th Century Fund, challenged contentions of broad-based patronage by concluding that serious, continuing support for the arts derives from less than 3 per cent of the population. The report went on to suggest that most patrons of the arts represent a group highly atypical of the average urban dweller.

However, if the complexion and extent of support for the arts in America remained debatable, it was clear that an ever-increasing number of cultural activities had been staged during the year in virtually every city and town in the country.

In many areas, activities seemed to center more and more around newly established cultural centers. In addition, many museums offered programs that included film screenings, concerts, lectures, guided tours, and symposiums, frequently held in connection with exhibitions from their own collections, loan exhibits, and touring art shows.

One of the most widely circulated traveling shows was the exhibit of festival designs by Inigo Jones, the Jacobean theatrical designer who dazzled the monarchs of his era with lavish, dramatic entertainments. On loan from the Chatsworth Collection of the British Duke of Devonshire, the Inigo Jones show was scheduled for exhibition in more than a dozen American cities during 1967 and 1968.

In the world of more contemporary art idioms, big names made big news. Major retrospectives in various cities were devoted to the work of Aubrey Beardsley, Edgar Degas, Jean Auguste Dominique Ingres, Henry Moore, Pablo Picasso, Jackson Pollack, Raphael Soyer, Gilbert Stuart, and Andrew Wyeth, to mention but a few.

The Museum of Modern Art in New York City mounted a spectacular show of Picasso's sculpture. Comprising more than 200 pieces, the exhibition included many works on loan from the artist's private collection, which had been shown publicly only once in London and once in Paris. The show proved to be still another triumph for Picasso, drawing both critical acclaim and record crowds.

The literary world provided sensational news of a different kind with developments surrounding the publication of two extraordinary nonfiction books.

The first was William Manchester's *The Death of a President,* a detailed examination of the assassination of President John F. Kennedy. Manchester's book appeared in April, in the wake of a much-publicized controversy that involved members of the Kennedy family in a dispute with the author, the publisher, and magazine executives over the contents, serialization, and publication of the book.

The second was *Twenty Letters to a Friend,* Svetlana Alliluyeva's account of her life with her father, the Russian dictator Joseph Stalin. Mrs. Alliluyeva's book appeared in October, less than nine months after the author's spectacular, cloak-and-dagger defection from the Soviet Union and subsequent arrival in the United States had made front-page headlines around the world.

Buried in financial columns behind the headlines was the equally important news that during 1967 books rolled from publishers' presses in record quantities. Nonfiction outsold fiction, and biography clearly emerged as the strongest category of the year.

The theater season set records of a different kind. The number of new productions that opened on Broadway—47—was the smallest of any season since 1899–1900. Of the new productions that made it to Broadway, nine were musicals, five were revivals, four were reviews, three were Yiddish entertainments, and 26 were nonmusical plays. Ten of the nonmusical plays were hits imported from abroad. At the close of the season 13 of the new offerings were still running; 34 had closed, many after minimal runs.

A number of theater people blamed the bleak season on sharp increases in costs, which had made producers wary about risking substantial sums on any but proven stage vehicles, works by well-known playwrights, or productions featuring bona fide stars—any one of which might guarantee good box office business.

Some theatrical figures called the season the "worst in years." However, at least one more-optimistic observer suggested that, judging on the basis of quality rather than quantity, the season could be termed "excellent."

Most critics agreed that the best new play of the year was *The Homecoming,* by the British playwright, Harold Pinter. *Cabaret,* adapted from the play *I Am a Camera* by Fred Ebb, John Kander, and Joe Masteroff, was cited by most critics as the best new musical.

In contrast to the generally dismal scene on Broadway, Off-Broadway theaters in New York, as well as theaters in other parts of the country, seemed to be thriving. Hundreds of works by new playwrights were produced in dozens of makeshift theaters.

The Off-Broadway production of *You're a Good Man Charlie Brown* developed into a smash hit on the basis of generally warm reviews. At year's end a San Francisco company was performing the play, and plans for simultaneous productions in other American cities were under discussion.

Two controversial plays, *MacBird!* and *America Hurrah,* drew interested audiences after their New York openings. A number of other Off-Broadway productions received receptions sufficiently favorable to generate box office interest and repay their backers—no small feat in a segment of the theater hitherto more accustomed to deficit operations than to profit.

# ART: 1967

Virtually every museum in the United States presents one or more major new exhibitions each season. In addition, most museums present a number of smaller touring shows, as well as rotating exhibits drawn from permanent and loan collections.

**American Art of the 20th Century.** Drawing on its extensive permanent collection, the Whitney Museum of American Art in New York City assembled a major survey of contemporary art comprising some 300 paintings, watercolors, and sculpture by 269 American artists.

**American Sculpture of the Sixties.** An anthology of current idioms in sculpture comprising 166 works by 80 American sculptors, the exhibition was organized and shown first by the Los Angeles County Museum of Art; it later appeared in other American museums.

**The Art of India and Nepal: The Nasli and Alice Heeramaneck Collection.** Prior to permanent installation of the entire collection in the Museum of Fine Arts in Boston, 274 select pieces of Indian and Nepalese art were exhibited in five American cities.

**Art Treasures of Turkey.** Organized under the honorary patronage of the Presidents of Turkey and the United States, an exhibition comprising more than 280 art works and artifacts on loan from 15 Turkish museums toured American cities. The diverse store of treasures, dating from about 6000 B.C. to the mid-18th century, included jewel-encrusted weapons, richly embroidered sultans' robes, and ancient tapestries and sculpture.

**Aubrey Beardsley.** The Gallery of Modern Art in New York City presented a major show of the work of the 19th-century British artist. Many of the drawings, prints, and illustrations shown in New York had been shown at an earlier exhibition in London. Other items were lent by the John Hay Whitney Collection.

**British Watercolors, 1750–1850.** Lent by the Victoria and Albert Museum in London, 100 watercolors by such British masters as Constable and Turner were shown at the Worcester Art Museum in Massachusetts.

**Dada, Surrealism, and Their Heritage.** Scheduled to be shown first at the Museum of Modern Art in New York City and later at the Art Institute of Chicago and the Los Angeles County Museum of Art, the exhibition was to be the first in nearly 30 years to treat exclusively the Dada and Surrealist movements and their subsequent influence on art produced during the last two decades. Scheduled for inclusion in the show were paintings, sculpture, drawings, prints, book illustrations, theater designs, photographs, and objects—all dating from the beginnings of Dada in 1912 to the present.

**Drawings by Degas.** More than 150 Degas drawings dating from 1855 to 1905 and lent by European and American collections were shown at the City Art Museum of St. Louis, the Minneapolis Institute of Arts, and the Philadelphia Museum of Art in an exhibition marking the 50th anniversary of Degas' death.

**Fantastics and Eccentrics in Chinese Painting.** Examples of the revolutionary painting styles practiced in China during the 17th and 18th centuries were shown first at Asia House in New York City and later at museums in other cities.

**Festival Designs by Inigo Jones.** An exhibition of drawings, costume reconstructions, and plans for stage sets by the Jacobean theatrical designer was lent by the Chatsworth Collection of the British Duke of Devonshire for a tour of more than a dozen cities in the United States and Canada.

**Guggenheim International Exhibition 1967: Sculpture from Twenty Nations.** More than 100 works by 80 artists representing 20 countries were included in the current invitational exhibition held by the Solomon R. Guggenheim Museum in New York City. The show, comprising works conceived and executed since 1960, was scheduled for exhibition at the Art Gallery of Ontario, Toronto, Canada; the Montreal Museum of Fine Arts; and the National Gallery of Canada, Ottawa.

**Homage to Rodin.** Four days before the 50th anniversary of the French sculptor's death, the Los Angeles County Museum of Art opened an exhibition comprising 69 Rodin works—bronzes, plasters, and ceramics—on loan from the collection of B. Gerald Cantor. The show was scheduled for exhibition at the California Palace of the Legion of Honor, San Francisco; the Museum of Fine Arts, Houston; and museums in other cities.

**In the Presence of Kings.** Drawing on its permanent collection, the Metropolitan Museum of Art in New York City assembled an exhibition comprising more than 600 art works and objects originally commissioned by, or presented to monarchs, rulers, or members of royal courts over a period of 5,000 years.

**Ingres Centennial Exhibition.** More than 100 oil sketches, drawings, and watercolors by the French artist Jean Auguste Dominique Ingres were shown at the Fogg Art Museum, Harvard University, in an exhibition commemorating the centennial of the artist's death.

**The Sidney and Harriet Janis Collection.** The Museum of Modern Art in New York City exhibited a collection comprising 100 paintings and pieces of sculpture by 54 leading 20th-century artists, including Picasso, de Kooning, Leger, Kandinsky, Mondrian, Pollack, and Dubuffet. Valued at more than $2,000,000 and

Here follows a representative summary of major art exhibitions held or scheduled to be held in leading American museums during 1967 and 1968. A directory of major American art museums and their collections appears on pages 836–38.

(continued)

**ART: 1967** (*continued*)

donated to the Museum by the art dealer for which it is named, the collection was scheduled for exhibition in museums throughout the country during a two-year tour.

**Paul Klee Retrospective.** Organized by the Solomon R. Guggenheim Museum of New York and the Pasadena Art Museum and shown in several American cities, the exhibition included more than 150 works by the Swiss-born master—oils, watercolors, gouaches, prints, drawings, and paintings on glass—lent by European and American museums, collectors, and art dealers. Among the most important contributors to the exhibition were the artist's son, Felix Klee, and the Paul Klee Foundation of Berne.

**Masterpieces from Montreal.** A collection of 102 paintings, including works by Corot, Delacroix, El Greco, Gainsborough, Hogarth, Matisse, Monet, and Rembrandt, were lent by the Montreal Museum of Fine Arts for exhibition at the Albright Knox Art Gallery, Buffalo, New York; the Gallery of Fine Arts, Columbus, Ohio; the Gallery of Modern Art, New York City; the Memorial Art Gallery, Rochester, New York; the Museum of Art, Carnegie Institute, Pittsburgh; the North Carolina Museum of Art, Raleigh; and the John and Mable Ringling Museum of Art, Sarasota.

**Masters of Modern Italian Art.** The collection, comprising more than 100 paintings, drawings, and sculpture executed by Italian artists of the Futurist and Metaphysical schools between 1910 and 1935, was lent by the Gianni Mattioli Collection of Milan for exhibition in Washington, Chicago, Dallas, Minneapolis, St. Louis, and San Francisco.

**Louise Nevelson Retrospective.** More than 100 works by the American artist credited with the development of "environmental" sculpture were shown at the Whitney Museum of American Art in New York City.

**Paintings and Drawings from the Collection of Mr. and Mrs. Leigh Block.** Drawn from a private collection widely regarded as one of the most important in the United States, the exhibition included works by Braque, Gaugin, Degas, Cezanne, Picasso, and Van Gogh, and was shown at the National Gallery of Art in Washington, D.C., and the Los Angeles County Art Museum.

**Pittsburgh International Exhibition of Contemporary Painting and Sculpture.** More than 300 works by artists representing 34 nations were selected for exhibition in the Pittsburgh triennial, held at the Museum of Art, Carnegie Institute. Eleven prizes were awarded.

**Jackson Pollack.** The Museum of Modern Art in New York City staged the largest retrospective ever devoted to the paintings and drawings of the influential American abstract artist who died in 1956 at the age of 44. Among the 172 works shown were a number lent by the artist's widow.

**Romantic Art in Britain; Paintings and Drawings: 1760–1860.** Organized under the honorary patronage of Queen Elizabeth II of England and President Lyndon B. Johnson of the United States, the exhibit was shown at the Detroit Institute of Arts and the Philadelphia Museum of Art. Included were more than 200 paintings and drawings lent by the Royal Collection of Great Britain.

**Sculpture and Drawings by Henry Moore.** A major retrospective devoted to the work of the British sculptor included bronzes and drawings, many on loan from the collections of the artist and his family and never before exhibited in the United States. The show was scheduled for exhibition in ten American cities.

**The Sculpture of Picasso.** The Museum of Modern Art in New York City mounted a major survey of the Spanish artist's sculpture comprising more than 200 pieces executed in bronze, wood, terra cotta, painted sheet metal, and ceramics. Many pieces were from the artist's private collection and had been shown publicly only in London and Paris.

**Gilbert Stuart, Portraitist of the Young Republic.** The National Gallery of Art in Washington, D.C., mounted the first major exhibit in 40 years devoted to the work of the painter-laureate of young America. Included were more than 50 portraits of political, social, and artistic leaders of 18th-century America and Britain.

**Swiss Drawings, Masterpieces of Five Centuries.** More than 125 drawings executed by Swiss-born artists between the 16th and 20th centuries were shown at the National Gallery of Art, Washington, D.C.; the Pierpont-Morgan Library, New York City; the Art Institute of Chicago; and the M. H. de Young Memorial Museum in San Francisco.

**Treasures of Poland.** The exhibition, including paintings, sculpture, armour, tiles, period costumes and precious metals lent by Polish museums and never before seen outside Europe, was shown at the Philadelphia Museum of Art and the Art Institute of Chicago.

**The Triumph of Realism.** Comprising 98 paintings on loan from European and American museums—including 27 pictures from Germany never before exhibited in the United States—the show was designed to illustrate the chain of relationships that led to establishment of an international school of realistic painting during the 19th century. The exhibition was organized by the Brooklyn Museum and was also shown at the Virginia Museum of Fine Arts, Richmond, and the Palace of the Legion of Honor, San Francisco.

**Van Gogh: Drawings and Watercolors.** First seen in Paris, this exhibition comprising 90 works executed by Vincent Van Gogh between 1881 and 1890 was shown at the Philadelphia Museum of Art, the Dallas Museum of Fine Arts, the Toledo Museum of Art, and the National Gallery of Canada, Ottawa.

**Andrew Wyeth Retrospective Exhibition.** Described as the most comprehensive exhibition of the work of a living American artist, the Wyeth show included more than 200 paintings and drawings lent by more than 150 collectors. Organized and shown first by the Pennsylvania Academy of Fine Arts, Philadelphia, it was also shown in Baltimore and New York.

# FOCUS ON THE NEWS

## THE MIRACLE OF FLORENCE

A major casualty of the Florentine flood, Cimabue's 13th-century **Crucifix** was damaged beyond restoration.

Paris Match / Pictorial Parade

Early in November, 1966, floods ravaged much of northern Italy. Many died and thousands more were left homeless. Florence, symbol of Renaissance glory, was among the cities hardest hit. The Arno River, rain-swollen and choked with debris, surged over retaining walls and raged through streets and piazzas. Its waters poured into Florentine homes, shops, museums, and libraries, leaving buildings, statues, paintings, and books inundated with mud and a thick glaze of fuel oil that had burst from shattered tanks. The damage was incredible. "Worse than the war," many cried.

Yet, barely six months later, Florence had made a dazzling recovery. Refurbished hotels, restaurants, and shops had been opened. Artisans skilled in the medieval crafts of leatherwork, embroidery, and jewelry-making were back at their benches. And all but a fraction of the city's Renaissance treasures were back in museums.

Clearly, the near-miraculous recovery of Florence could be credited to the extraordinary fibre of the Tuscan character, acting in concert with an unprecedented outpouring of financial and technical assistance from all parts of the world.

In the first days after the flood, thousands of volunteers arrived in the city to help the people dig out and re-establish their homes and businesses, and to help salvage the contents of museums, churches, and libraries. The work was still going on late in 1967. Experts estimate that complete restoration of restorable buildings, sculptures, paintings, books, and manuscripts may take as long as two or three decades.

The people of Florence are confident of total recovery. The face their city now presents to the world is testimony to their courage. "Nothing," they declare with the force of will for which they are famous, "is beyond the power of a Florentine."

## FIFTY AMERICAN ART MUSEUMS AND THEIR COLLECTIONS

**Addison Gallery of American Art,** Andover, Mass. An outstanding small collection of American paintings, sculpture, prints, furniture, and silver.

**Art Institute of Chicago,** Chicago, Ill. One of the world's great sequences of 19th and 20th century French painting; extensive collections cover other major periods of Western art; primitive and Oriental art; prints and drawings; photographs; decorative arts.

**Atlanta Art Association Galleries,** Atlanta, Ga. Kress collection of Renaissance paintings and sculpture; American and Oriental art; representative European paintings, sculpture; graphic and decorative arts.

**Baltimore Museum of Art,** Baltimore, Md. Epstein and Jacobs collections of old masters and sculpture; Cone collection of 19th and 20th century French art; May collection of European paintings and sculpture; more than 100,000 prints dating from the 15th century to the present; tapestries; American, pre-Columbian, African, and Oriental art.

**Barnes Foundation,** Merion, Penn. A private museum houses the Barnes collection: more than 1,000 European and American paintings, dating from the Renaissance to the present; African sculpture; Chinese art; furniture; American artifacts; hinge and bolt collection.

**Birmingham Museum of Art,** Birmingham, Ala. European and American paintings; Kress collection of Italian art; Classical, Near Eastern, and Oriental antiquities; American Indian and pre-Columbian artifacts.

**Brooklyn Museum,** New York, N.Y. Fine collection of Egyptian art; art objects from many Near and Far Eastern countries; prehistoric and primitive art; Renaissance and Medieval paintings; 19th and 20th century European paintings; European and American sculpture; American paintings dating from colonial times to the present; period furniture and costumes; prints and drawings.

**Buffalo Fine Arts Academy, Albright-Knox Art Gallery,** Buffalo, N.Y. Good collection of 20th-century American and European paintings; sculpture dating from 3000 B.C. to the present; representative collections of European and American paintings, sculpture, drawings, and prints.

**California Palace of the Legion of Honor,** San Francisco, Calif. Rodin marbles and bronzes; European and American paintings and tapestries; decorative arts; Egyptian and Greek collections; furniture and porcelain.

**Carnegie Institute, Museum of Art,** Pittsburgh, Penn. Old masters and Impressionist paintings; American paintings and sculpture; outstanding international collection of contemporary paintings and sculpture; prints and drawings; Oriental and Western decorative and graphic arts.

**Cincinnati Art Museum,** Cincinnati, Ohio. European paintings dating from the 14th to the 20th century; Chinese paintings dating from the 13th to the 17th century; antiquities from the Near and Far East; musical instruments dating from the second to the 20th century; collections of primitive, ancient, and decorative arts from Western and Oriental cultures; 18th, 19th, and 20th century American paintings; period rooms.

**City Art Museum of St. Louis,** St. Louis, Mo. Comprehensive collections covering major periods of art history from ancient to modern times; both Oriental and Western civilizations are represented.

**Cleveland Museum of Art,** Cleveland, Ohio. Art from many cultures and periods, including important Chinese and Japanese collections; American paintings; fine collection of 17th and 19th century European paintings; prints, drawings, and textiles.

**Columbus Gallery of Fine Arts,** Columbus, Ohio. Schumacher collection of old masters; Howald collection of modern French and American paintings; Derby collection of English and Dutch portraiture; major collection of George Bellows paintings.

**Corcoran Gallery of Art,** Washington, D.C. Outstanding collection of 18th, 19th, and 20th century American paintings, sculpture, and drawings; collections of Dutch, Flemish, French, and English paintings; tapestries; sculpture, furniture, rugs, and decorative arts.

**Denver Art Museum,** Denver, Colo. The museum's five units house Oriental and Western folk arts; the Kress collection of Renaissance art; period rooms; Egyptian, Greek, Roman, and Medieval art; 19th and 20th century European and American art.

**Des Moines Art Center,** Des Moines, Iowa. Edmundson collection of American and European art; Rosenfeld collection of contemporary art; sculpture; drawings; graphic art.

**Detroit Institute of Arts,** Detroit, Mich. Representative examples of art of many cultures, dating from prehistoric times to the present; rich in Medieval and Renaissance Italian sculpture, and 17th-century Dutch paintings; period rooms; decorative and graphic arts.

**Fine Arts Gallery of San Diego,** San Diego, Calif. Extensive collection of European paintings dating from the Renaissance to the 19th century; Oriental art; large print collection; contemporary American paintings and sculpture.

**Frick Collection,** New York, N.Y. Henry Clay Frick, the American industrialist, amassed one of the world's great collections of European paintings, sculpture, prints, and drawings, dating from the 14th to the 19th century. Also displayed in Frick's baronial Fifth Avenue town house are Limoges enamels, French and Chinese porcelains, and period furniture.

**Gallery of Modern Art,** New York, N.Y. Huntington Hartford commissioned Edward Durell Stone to design the gallery that houses the Hartford collection of 19th and 20th century European and American paintings and sculpture; major collection of paintings by Salvador Dali, the Spanish Surrealist painter.

**Harvard University, Fogg Art Museum,** Cambridge, Mass. Collections illustrate the evolution of Oriental and Western art from ancient times to the present; representative collections of

## AMERICA'S LEONARDO: THE MOST EXPENSIVE PAINTING IN THE WORLD

Leonardo da Vinci (1452–1519) has always been considered one of the three great geniuses of the High Renaissance. Yet, unlike his younger contemporaries Michelangelo and Raphael, Leonardo's extraordinary talents were diffused over so vast a range of interests—including astronomy, medicine, architecture, and armaments, as well as painting—that he left few finished works. Only 15 paintings are generally accepted as his work, and some experts believe there may be as few as nine. Until 1967 none existed outside Europe. Now America has a Leonardo.

Late in February, 1967, the National Gallery of Art in Washington, D.C., announced the acquisition of Leonardo's portrait of Ginevra de Benci, believed to have been painted in Florence between 1474 and 1480.

The purchase price was not disclosed; however, knowledgeable estimates ranged between $5 million and $6 million—the highest price ever known to have been paid for a single picture. (The previous high was $2.3 million, paid by the Metropolitan Museum of Art at auction in 1961 for Rembrandt's *Aristotle Contemplating the Bust of Homer*.)

The seller was Prince Franz Josef II of Liechtenstein, one of the wealthiest men in Europe and the owner of a fabled collection of Old Masters.

The Leonardo sold to the National Gallery is believed to have been in the Liechtenstein Collection since 1733. Its whereabouts between that time and the time that it left the possession of the Benci family remain a mystery.

Ginevra de Benci belonged to a family of prominent, 15th-century Florentine merchants, whose palazzo still stands in Florence. The Benci had close ties with the Medici and were patrons of the arts. Ginevra's grandfather built the Cloister of the Suore Murate and commissioned Fra Filippo Lippi to paint three altarpieces for the building. Her father attended meetings of the Platonic Academy in Florence, and her brother Carlo was one of a group of Florentines actively engaged in the decoration of the facade of the city's cathedral.

The Benci family's closest ties with Leonardo da Vinci are believed to have been through Ginevra's brother Giovanni, who is known to have exchanged books and maps with the painter. Further, it is believed that Leonardo's unfinished *Adoration of the Magi*, now in the collection of the Uffizi Gallery in Florence, was at one time in the home of Giovanni's son, Amerigo.

Ginevra is known to have written poetry, and she, together with her sisters Tita and Lucrezia, was cited by a close family friend at the Papal Court in Rome as being exemplary of the qualities for which highborn Florentine ladies of the Renaissance were known.

In 1474, when Ginevra was 16, she was married to Luigi Niccolini, a member of a prominent Florentine family, who later became a high-ranking official in the Government of Florence. It was after her marriage that she became the subject of Leonardo's portrait.

The picture, measuring 15⅛ inches by 14½ inches, is painted in a mixed medium of oil, tempera, and resin on a three-eighths-inch-thick piece of Italian poplar wood—the same kind of wood on which the *Mona Lisa* is painted. Ginevra appears in three-quarter view, her head erect and turned with a placid gaze toward the viewer. She wears a brown dress laced with a blue ribbon and edged in gold, with a black stole over her shoulders. In the background is a thicket of juniper, behind which can be glimpsed a landscape of trees and shrubs, a stream, a church, and two slender towers.

The portrait of Ginevra is often called a counterpart of the *Mona Lisa*, painted more than 20 years later, because it has about it the same air of compelling, mysterious, enigmatic beauty.

Leonardo da Vinci was born in Vinci, a Tuscan hill village. His father was a Florentine notary, and his mother a peasant girl. Leonardo moved to Florence to begin his apprenticeship in the workshop of the painter Verrocchio about 1466. Six years later he was registered in the Florentine painters' guild. About 1482 Leonardo left Florence for the court of Ludovico Sforza, Duke of Milan, where he remained for 16 years.

paintings, sculpture, prints, drawings, silver, and decorative arts.

**Henry E. Huntington Library and Art Gallery,** San Marino, Calif. Excellent collection of 18th-century British portraits and landscapes; Italian and Flemish paintings of the 15th and 16th centuries; sculpture, tapestries, and furniture.

**Isabella Stewart Gardner Museum,** Boston, Mass. A great personal museum houses a trove of American and European paintings dating from the 14th to the 20th century; Classical, Romanesque, Gothic, and Renaissance sculpture; Oriental art; tapestries, furniture, tex-

tiles, ceramics, prints, and decorative arts.

**Joslyn Art Museum,** Omaha, Nebr. Classical, Renaissance, and modern European art; 19th and 20th century American art; frontier arts of the old West.

**Los Angeles County Museum of Art,** Los Angeles, Calif. Major periods, from ancient to modern times, are represented in this relatively new museum's collection; particularly strong in Renaissance and American art.

**M. H. De Young Memorial Museum,** San Francisco, Calif. Large collection of European and Amer-
(continued)

**AMERICAN ART MUSEUMS** (*continued*)

ican art; the Kress and Oakes collections of European paintings and sculpture; a new wing houses the Avery Brundage collection of Oriental art; tapestries, furniture, and period rooms.

**Metropolitan Museum of Art,** New York, N.Y. One of the great museums of the world, and the largest in the Western Hemisphere, the Metropolitan contains comprehensive collections covering 5,000 years of art history; outstanding collections of Classical art from Egypt, Greece, and Rome; Medieval art (located at the Cloisters in Fort Tryon Park, New York); old masters and European painting through the 19th century; important collections of decorative arts, prints, musical instruments, furniture, armor, and ceramics.

**Milwaukee Art Center, Inc.,** Milwaukee, Wis. Layton collection of late 19th and early 20th century American and European paintings; the collection of the former Milwaukee Art Institute is housed here, and contains an extensive selection of paintings, sculpture, drawings, prints, and decorative arts.

**Minneapolis Institute of Arts,** Minneapolis, Minn. Excellent collections of Chinese and pre-Columbian art; prints and drawings; tapestries; American and European decorative arts; European paintings and sculpture.

**Museum of Fine Arts,** Boston, Mass. Exceptionally fine collections of prints, Oriental art, and decorative arts; collections of Egyptian, Greek, and Roman art; old masters and 19th-century French paintings; American paintings; sculpture; furniture.

**Museum of Fine Arts of Houston, Texas.** Collection of paintings, sculpture, and decorative arts covering most major periods of art history; the Straus and Kress collections of Renaissance paintings; Classical art; sculpture; American art.

**Museum of Modern Art,** New York, N.Y. A major influence on contemporary art movements, the Museum of Modern Art contains one of the world's foremost collections of 19th and 20th century American and European paintings and sculpture, as well as extraordinary collections of prints, drawings, photographs, posters, architectural renderings, furniture, industrial design, and films.

**National Gallery of Art,** Washington, D.C. The Mellon, Kress, Widener, and Dale collections comprise an outstanding body of old masters; 19th-century paintings, sculpture, American art, tapestries, and decorative arts. The Rosenwald collection of prints and drawings, and the Garbisch collection of American primitive paintings are extensive and important.

**Newark Museum,** Newark, N.J. Large collection of American painting and sculpture from all periods; Oriental art, with a particularly good Tibetan collection; decorative arts.

**Philadelphia Museum of Art,** Philadelphia, Penn. Extensive, varied collections of art from many cultures, covering more than 2,000 years; of special importance are the collections of Medieval, Renaissance, and 20th-century European art, as well as exhibitions of Oriental art, period rooms, costumes, and prints.

**Phillips Collection,** Washington, D.C. Devoted principally to modern art, the Phillips Collection comprises paintings by 19th and 20th century American and European artists, as well as some earlier works of various periods.

**Rhode Island School of Design, Museum of Art,** Providence, R.I. Classical art; 19th-century paintings; Medieval, Renaissance, and Baroque paintings, sculpture, and prints; furniture; the Rockefeller collection of bird and flower prints; decorative arts.

**San Francisco Museum of Art,** San Francisco, Calif. Excellent collection of contemporary paintings, sculpture, prints, drawings, photographs, and decorative arts from Europe, the United States, and Latin America; works by San Francisco artists.

**Seattle Art Museum,** Seattle, Wash. Extensive collections of Classical and Oriental art; Kress collection of European paintings dating from the 14th to the 18th century; pre-Columbian and primitive art; period rooms; Backus collections of prints and paintings.

**Smithsonian Institution, Freer Gallery of Art,** Washington, D.C. Famed collections of Oriental art and Biblical manuscripts; 19th and 20th century American art.

**Smithsonian Institution, National Collection of Fine Arts,** Washington, D.C. An outstanding collection of American art; European and Oriental paintings; decorative arts; sculpture.

**Solomon R. Guggenheim Museum,** New York, N.Y. A collection of contemporary paintings and sculpture, including the world's largest collection of Kandinsky's work, is hung along a spiral ramp in one of the last buildings designed by Frank Lloyd Wright.

**Sterling and Francine Clark Art Institute,** Williamstown, Mass. European paintings dating from the 14th to the 19th century; impressive 19th-century French paintings; American paintings; old English silver.

**Toledo Museum of Art,** Toledo, Ohio. A large collection tracing the history of art from ancient Egypt to the 20th century; the most extensive glass collection in America.

**Virginia Museum of Fine Arts,** Richmond, Va. Most important periods, from ancient times to the present, are represented in a collection noteworthy for its Greek vases, archaic Chinese bronzes and jades, and Renaissance art.

**Walters Art Gallery,** Baltimore, Md. More than 25,000 objects comprise a collection noted for Byzantine and Medieval art, and Classical art of Egypt, Greece, and Rome.

**Whitney Museum of American Art,** New York, N.Y. A new building, designed by Marcel Breuer, houses a large collection of American paintings, sculpture, drawings, and prints.

**William Rockhill Nelson Gallery and Atkins Museum of Fine Arts,** Kansas City, Mo. Extensive collection of Oriental art from many periods and countries; Classical art; European and American painting, sculpture, and decorative arts.

**Worcester Art Museum,** Worcester, Mass. Especially strong in ancient and Classical sculpture, decorative arts, Medieval and Oriental art; European and American paintings and prints; furniture.

# BOOKS

Doubleday & Company

Book stores throughout the United States again reported increased reader interest and higher sales during 1967.

## BOOKS AND AUTHORS: 1967

For the world of books and authors, 1967 was a prosperous and productive year, if not a distinguished one. Books continued to pour from publishers' presses in a volume that promised new records in quantity. This was true in every category except poetry, which appears to have been in an apparently irreversible decline for years. However, notwithstanding the competition of television and other distractions, the gratifying fact remained that people seemed to be reading more books.

**Publishing Industry.** For the publishing industry it was a year of steady expansion. Though costs continued to rise, thus increasing book prices (the average novel now costs $5.95, as opposed to $4.95 a few years ago), sales of hard-cover books remained satisfactory. Paperback publishing, on the other hand, had a middling year, with heavy returns caused by overproduction. Like the price of hard-cover books, the price of paperbacks has steadily increased; the vast majority of titles now cost more than 50 cents a copy. Nevertheless, aggregate paperback sales during 1967 edged steadily closer to the impressive mark of 1,000,000 copies a day.

The much publicized explosions in population and learning, which statisticians plot in a sharply rising curve for the balance of the century, have focused the attention of Wall Street on book publishing as a growth investment. In recent years a number of book pub-

lishers have been acquired as subsidiaries by large corporations outside of publishing. The trend continued in 1967. Particularly significant was the entry of two large electronics corporations into the publishing field. Radio Corporation of America acquired Random House and its associated companies, Alfred A. Knopf, Inc. and Pantheon Books, and the Columbia Broadcasting System acquired Holt, Rinehart & Winston. These transactions pointed unmistakably to a future community of interest between books and electronic communications.

Some publishers believe that such mergers are not without hazard for their relatively small, individualistic industry. Book publishing, they point out, is not a push-button business in which production and quality can be achieved at will. Rather, the publishing industry is based upon the talents of writers and their sympathetic relationships with editors and publishers.

Indeed, two leading publishers uttered warnings during the year against the overmechanization of the industry. Victor Weybright, former president of New American Library and now head of Weybright & Talley, feared that "if more communications empires enter the field, it will tend to limit book publishing to 'sure things' only." And Cass Canfield, editorial head of Harper & Row until his retirement in 1967, echoed the warning: "The entry of com-

*(continued)*

munications corporations into book publishing holds out the possibility that in time the accountants may take over; accountants are able men, but they are not publishers."

Writers are, of necessity, an inward-oriented species, preoccupied with their craft. If writers saw any threat from the computer, they kept it to themselves; what mattered in 1967, as in any other year, was getting their books out.

**Notable Fiction.** Once again, in what has now developed into an unmistakable trend, fiction lagged behind nonfiction. There can no longer be any doubt that the novel is not flourishing today as it should. This most flexible of literary forms is passing through a difficult transition period as younger novelists, impatient with traditional linear narrative, experiment with newer approaches. These take the form of existential fiction, novels of the absurd, black humor, intellectual fantasy, and other innovations of a decidedly ephemeral nature.

Besides the obvious best sellers, the fiction most widely read and discussed came mostly from established writers. Heading the list was *The Eighth Day,* Thornton Wilder's first novel in many years, followed by William B. Styron's *The Confessions of Nat Turner,* which exhumed from history a long-forgotten slave uprising in Virginia. Written in semi-documentary form, the novel has been hailed as one of the finest by an American in recent years. Moreover, though long in preparation, it happened to appear at the very time when Negro civil aspirations had become militant.

Gore Vidal's *Washington, D.C.* was a bland and disappointing essay in political fiction. Philip Roth's *When She Was Good* was an interesting study of the female character, but well below his best work. Norman Mailer's *Why Are We in Vietnam,* a powerful lampoon on the Texas state of mind, provoked instant controversy; however, the novel was couched in such scatological language as to cast doubt on the author's seriousness about his craft.

Two notable volumes of short stories by two leading playwrights, Arthur Miller and Tennessee Williams, hinted at the possibility that as Broadway turns more and more to the production of musicals and comedy, serious playwrights may turn more and more to the writing of books.

**Nonfiction.** The nonfiction scene was dominated by two remarkable studies of world leaders. The first, William Manchester's exhaustive *The Death of a President,* was published April 7 in the wake of bitter controversy between the author and members of the Kennedy family. Manchester's account of the assassination of President John F. Kennedy in 1963 emerged as a massive literary autopsy that left no stone unturned and no clue unexplored in tracking down every participant and incident, however peripheral, in the tragic affair.

The second study was Svetlana Alliluyeva's *Twenty Letters to a Friend,* an account in epistolary form of her life with her father, the late Russian dictator Joseph Stalin. Written in a gentle, unemotional style, *Twenty Letters to a Friend* recorded the author's unhappy childhood with a ruthless parent who treated his family with little more consideration than he showed those with whom he was associated in public life. The book was published in translation from the Russian less than nine months after the author defected to the West from the Soviet Union. (For information about Mrs. Alliluyeva's defection, see page 32.)

Other noteworthy nonfiction books included John Kenneth Galbraith's *The New Industrial State,* in which the economist and former United States Ambassador to India presented a fresh view of the quality of American life and industrial society, and *Rousseau and Revolution,* with which Will and Ariel Durant, the historians, completed their forty-year, ten-volume study, *The Story of Civilization.*

A pioneer work likely to serve as a source-book in the future was David Kahn's *The Code-Breakers,* a monumental history of cryptology, which draws on many unpublished sources.

Civil rights, Negro unrest, and the steady decline in the quality of urban living generated a stream of books reflecting widespread concern. However, practical solutions to these vital national problems appeared to remain hidden.

As the 1968 elections drew near, the first wave of books on potential Presidential candidates began to appear. The several titles devoted to President Lyndon B. Johnson were, on the whole, unflattering. Major attention was given to Democratic Senator Robert F. Kennedy of New York in a score of books both pro and con.

Biography emerged as by far the strongest category of the year, with publication of at least five works of major stature. In *Old Bruin,* Samuel Eliot Morison, the historian and retired admiral, produced a first-rate life of Commodore Matthew Perry, the American naval commander who "opened" Japan to Western influence a century ago. *Old Bruin* impressed as a work fully comparable to Morison's prize-winning biographies of Christopher Columbus and John Paul Jones.

George E. Kennan's *Memoirs, 1925–1950* chronicled the distinguished diplomat's career in the Foreign Service during a period of historic crisis. W. A. Swanberg's *Pulitzer* did full justice to the journalistic genius who bestrode the newspaper world of his day like a colossus. Marcia Davenport's autobiography, *Too Strong for Fantasy,* re-created the so-called "Golden Age of Opera" in New York during the early decades of the 20th century, and threw new light on the mysterious death of the author's close friend, Czechoslovak statesman Jan Masaryk, in Prague in 1948.

Finally, it should be noted that 1967 was also the year in which Marshall McLuhan, Canadian high priest of the electronic tube, reiterated his dire prediction that books had become obsolete and were doomed to imminent demise. It is interesting to note that McLuhan's statement appeared in a book, and that it sent no noticeable tremors through the publishing industry.

## THE MANCHESTER CONTROVERSY

Principals in the controversy over publication of the book, **The Death of a President:** author William Manchester (left); Mrs. Jacqueline Kennedy; and Senator Robert F. Kennedy.

One of the literary furors of 1967 was over the publication of William Manchester's book, *The Death of a President.* Although the book had been commissioned by the Kennedy family as the authorized version of President John F. Kennedy's assassination, its publication involved the author and the family in a well-publicized controversy.

In December, 1966, Mrs. Jacqueline Kennedy announced that she was initiating legal action to halt publication of the book. It had been scheduled for publication by Harper and Row, and a condensed version was to be serialized by *Look* magazine.

On March 26, 1964—four months after the Dallas tragedy—the late President's brother, Robert F. Kennedy, signed the commissioning agreement with Manchester. The agreement stipulated that the completed Manchester manuscript was to be reviewed and approved by the Kennedy family.

However, in late 1966, when the book was nearly ready for publication, Mrs. Kennedy claimed breach of contract by Manchester. Mrs. Kennedy, who objected to the fact that several passages in the text did not have her approval, stated, "...to expose to all the world at this time all the private grief, personal thoughts, and painful reactions which my children and I endured in those terrible days does not seem to me to be essential to any current historical record."

*Look,* Harper and Row, and Manchester claimed that representatives of the Kennedy family had seen the manuscript and had suggested revisions, which subsequently had been made. As they seemed unwilling to make further revisions, a court battle appeared inevitable.

However, *Look,* scheduled to begin serialization in mid-January, quickly decided to come to terms and deleted several passages that Mrs. Kennedy considered painful. In January the Kennedys reached agreement with Harper and Row, and about 10,000 words were cut from the original 300,000-word text. But *Stern,* a German weekly magazine that had purchased the German-language rights from *Look,* published the original uncut version.

Harper and Row set April 7, 1967, as the official publication date for *The Death of a President.* The book became a best-seller and was generally acclaimed as a valuable historical record. The bulk of Harper and Row's profits—an estimated $2,000,000—is being turned over to the John F. Kennedy Memorial Library in Boston.

## REPRESENTATIVE BEST SELLERS: 1966–1967

### FICTION

*All in the Family,* Edwin O'Connor (Atlantic-Little, Brown) $6.95

*The Arrangement,* Elia Kazan (Stein & Day) $6.95

*The Beautiful Life,* Edwin Gilbert (G. P. Putnam's Sons) $5.95

*The Birds Fall Down,* Rebecca West (Viking Press) $5.95

*The Candlesticks and the Cross,* Ruth Freeman Solomon (G. P. Putnam's Sons) $5.95

*Capable of Honor,* Allen Drury (Doubleday & Co.) $5.95

*The Captain,* Jan de Hartog (Atheneum) $5.95

*The Chosen,* Chaim Potok (Simon and Schuster) $4.95

*Death Kit,* Susan Sontag (Farrar, Straus & Giroux) $5.75

*A Dream of Kings,* Harry Mark Petrakis (McKay & Co.) $4.50

*The Eighth Day,* Thornton Wilder (Harper & Row) $6.95

*Fathers,* Herbert Gold (Random House) $5.95

*Five Smooth Stones,* Ann Fairbairn (Crown) $6.95

*The Fixer,* Bernard Malamud (Farrar, Straus & Giroux) $5.75

*Go to the Widow Maker,* James Jones (Delacorte Press) $7.50

*The King,* Morton Cooper (Bernard Geis Associates) $5.95

*King of the Castle,* Victoria Holt (Doubleday & Co.) $4.95

*The Mask of Apollo,* Mary Renault (Pantheon Books) $5.95

*Night Falls on the City,* Sarah Gainham (Holt, Rinehart & Winston) $6.95

*A Night of Watching,* Elliott Arnold (Charles Scribner's Sons) $5.95

*An Operational Necessity,* Gwen Griffin (G. P. Putnam's Sons) $6.95

*The Plot,* Irving Wallace (Simon and Schuster) $6.95

*Rosemary's Baby,* Ira Levin (Random House) $4.95

*A Second-Hand Life,* Charles Jackson (Macmillan Co.) $6.95

*The Secret of Santa Vittoria,* Robert Crichton (Simon and Schuster) $5.95

*Silverhill,* Phyllis Whitney (Doubleday & Co.) $4.95

*Tai-Pan,* James Clavell (Atheneum) $6.95

*Tales of Manhattan,* Louis Auchincloss (Houghton Mifflin Co.) $4.95

*The Time Is Noon,* Pearl S. Buck (John Day Co.) $6.95

*Topaz,* Leon Uris (McGraw-Hill) $5.95

*Under the Eye of the Storm,* John Hersey (Alfred A. Knopf) $4.95

*Valley of the Dolls,* Jacqueline Susann (Bernard Geis Associates) $5.95

*Waiting for Winter,* John O'Hara (Random House) $5.95

*Washington, D. C.,* Gore Vidal (Little, Brown) $6.95

*When She Was Good,* Philip Roth (Random House) $5.95

### NONFICTION

*Anyone Can Make a Million,* Morton Shulman (McGraw-Hill) $4.95

*The Arrogance of Power,* Senator J. William Fulbright (Random House) $4.95

*At Ease: Stories I Tell to Friends,* Dwight D. Eisenhower (Doubleday & Co.) $6.95

*The Autobiography of Bertrand Russell,* Bertrand Russell (Atlantic-Little, Brown) $7.95

*The Boston Strangler,* Gerold Frank (New American Library) $5.95

*By-Line: Ernest Hemingway,* Edited by William White (Charles Scribner's Sons) $8.95

*The Death of a President,* William Manchester (Harper & Row) $10.00

*The Diaries and Letters of Harold Nicholson,* Edited by Nigel Nicholson (Atheneum) Volume I: 1930–1939, $7.50; Volume II: 1939–1945, $8.50

*Disraeli,* Robert Blake (St. Martin's Press) $12.50

*Division Street: America,* Studs Terkel (Pantheon Books) $5.95

*Edgar Cayce—The Sleeping Prophet,* Jess Stearn (Doubleday & Co.) $4.95

*Everything but Money,* Sam Levenson (Simon and Schuster) $4.95

*Games People Play,* Eric Berne, M.D. (Grove Press) $5.00

*How to Avoid Probate,* Norman F. Dacey (Crown) $4.95

*Incredible Victory,* Walter Lord (Harper & Row) $5.95

*Inside South America,* John Gunther (Harper & Row) $6.95

*The Jury Returns,* Louis Nizer (Doubleday & Co.) $6.95

*The Lawyers,* Martin Mayer (Harper & Row) $8.95

*Madame Sarah,* Cornelia Otis Skinner (Houghton Mifflin Co.) $6.95

*A Modern Priest Looks at His Outdated Church,* Father James Kavanaugh (Trident Press) $4.95

*The Natural World of San Francisco,* Harold Gilliam and Michael Bry (Doubleday & Co.) $6.95

*Nicholas and Alexandra,* Robert K. Massie (Atheneum) $10.00

*The New Industrial State,* John Kenneth Galbraith (Houghton Mifflin Co.) $6.95

*"Our Crowd": The Great Jewish Families of New York,* Stephen Birmingham (Harper & Row) $8.95

*Paper Lion,* George Plimpton (Harper & Row) $5.95

*The Passover Plot,* Hugh J. Schonfield (Bernard Geis Associates) $4.95

*The Random House Dictionary of the English Language,* Jess Stein, Editor-in-Chief; Laurence Urdang, Managing Editor (Random House) $25.00

*Twenty Letters to a Friend,* Svetlana Alliluyeva (Harper & Row) $5.95

*Winston S. Churchill: Youth, 1874–1900,* Randolph S. Churchill (Houghton Mifflin Co.) $10.00

# FILMS

Paul Scofield, the Academy Award-winning English actor, in a scene from **A Man for All Seasons**

## NOTABLE FILMS OF 1967

Any year is good that brings one film which seems really destined to last. The year 1967 could be termed a bonanza because of three such films—*Blow-Up, Persona,* and *How I Won the War.* These and other noteworthy films of 1967 are described below, and their general critical reception is summarized briefly.

**Noteworthy Films.** *Blow-Up,* the first feature film made in English by Italian director Michelangelo Antonioni, was the first film by a major foreign artist to gain immediate and widespread American distribution. It was set in London and photographed in such brilliant color that the city seems both real and fantastic. *Blow-Up* tells of a successful young fashion photographer who takes what he thinks is a picture of idyllic lovers in a park, and accidentally becomes a witness to a murder.

The film's theme is how man's consciousness is being expanded by technology without an equivalent ability to handle the expansion, and the impulse to escape from this increased consciousness into greater illusion. All this is placed in the middle of a youth-oriented culture. David Hemmings is forceful as the hero, and Vanessa Redgrave is beautifully intriguing as the mysterious girl in the park.

Like much good art, *Blow-Up* asks more questions than it answers, so it enraged many who are used to just the opposite in films. But the critical consensus was that *Blow-Up* ranks among Antonioni's better films, and thus is a part of film history.

The same was said of Ingmar Bergman's latest film, *Persona,* in which the Swedish director explores one manifestation of the loss of the will to live—withdrawal into the mind, into silence. *Persona* deals almost exclusively with a patient and a nurse. The former is a successful young actress who has suddenly stopped speaking; the latter is a young woman about the same age as the actress, who greatly resembles her. Isolated in a house by the sea, with the nurse the only one of the two who speaks, the two women become engaged in an enigmatic but deeply moving symbolic drama. The climax is a choice between withdrawal from life or willingness to face all the consequences of contemporary existence.

The two roles are finely played by Liv Ullman as the actress, and Bibi Andersson as the nurse. Sven Nykvist's black and white photography is exquisite.

*How I Won the War* is a British film directed by Richard Lester, the American who made the two Beatles films and *The Knack.* It is a brilliant anti-war comedy (yes, comedy) about a British Army platoon in World War II. The platoon is commanded by a good-hearted, thick-headed young lieutenant who, in the course of six years, manages to butcher *(continued)*

**NOTABLE FILMS OF 1967** (*continued*)

all of the men except the platoon coward and himself.

Embroidered with a dazzling display of cinematic pyrotechnics, *How I Won the War* is both bitter and funny. Michael Crawford as the lieutenant, Michael Hordern as a stuffy colonel, and John Lennon, Roy Kinnear, and Jack McGowran as soldiers give razor-keen performances. The script by Charles Wood is ingenious and well-written.

**Other Foreign Films.** Another good film about World War II came from Czechoslovakia: *Closely Watched Trains,* directed by Jiri Menzel. The film deals with the German occupation of Czechoslovakia, as seen through the eyes of a young Czech beginning his career as a rural railroad employee. By focusing on the hero's highly personal experiences in sex and love, in job ambitions, and in status hunger, Menzel portrays the grimness of Nazi occupation at an oblique but effective angle.

*Closely Watched Trains* is easily the best of the Czech "New Wave" films yet seen in America, being more subtle than *The Shop on Main Street* and more skillful than *Loves of a Blonde.*

The screenplay for the British film *Accident* was written by Harold Pinter and was based on a novel by Nicholas Moseley. Pinter's distinctive and evocative style is well used in many sequences, but some of the parts are better than the sum of all the parts of the film. Dirk Bogarde portrays a married Oxford University don who becomes infatuated with a student (Jacqueline Sassard). The student has an affair with another don, played by Stanley Baker, and becomes engaged to another student. Although there is a literal accident in the film, the girl is the "accident" that happens to all of the men and changes their lives. Much of Pinter's dialogue is excellent, and much of Joseph Losey's direction is adroit. Yet the film never really pulls itself together to reach the point toward which it seems to be heading.

Another British film, *Privilege,* also was more noteworthy for what it attempted than for what it accomplished. Peter Watkins, the director, wanted to show his audience just how the world of pop culture—in the person of a pop-singing idol—is manipulated in order to manipulate its audience. However, some critics found Watkins' direction so lurid, his handling of actors so inadequate and his whole tone so self-righteous that the effect on the viewer was to become more impatient with him than with the menace he is attacking.

*The Whisperers,* another British import, written and directed by Bryan Forbes, was criticized as a flabby, forced piece of writing and direction. But its subject, the loneliness of impoverished old people, provides a star role for the great English actress Dame Edith Evans, who gives a great performance.

One of the recurrent problems in films is how to adapt a stage production to the screen. The better the original, it seems, the more difficult is the transposition. However, this problem was handled with some brilliance by Peter Brook in making a film of his extraordinary Royal Shakespeare Company production of Peter Weiss's *Marat/Sade* (full title: *The Persecution and Assassination of Marat, as Performed by the Inmates of the Asylum of Charenton, Under the Direction of the Marquis de Sade*).

Without moving his camera from one room in the 19th-century Charenton asylum near Paris, Brook captures on film the tension between acting and reality in performances given by the inmates in the French Revolutionary drama written by their fellow inmate, the Marquis de Sade. Ian Richardson as Marat, Patrick Magee as the Marquis de Sade, and Glenda Jackson as Charlotte Corday are even better in the film than they were on the stage.

**American Films.** The best American film of the year was *Bonnie and Clyde,* directed by Arthur Penn and produced by Warren Beatty, who also starred in the film with Faye Dunaway. *Bonnie and Clyde* is an attempted folk epic, based loosely on the facts about Bonnie Parker and Clyde Barrow, a pair of bandit killers who operated in the southwestern United States during the early 1930s.

In its effort to render thudding violence as a metaphor of social desperation, *Bonnie and Clyde* is often successful. However, the superficial Freudian and proletarian overtones struck some critics as strained and hollow. With all its distinctions the film was regarded by many as a failure; yet, despite its deficiencies, it has real distinction.

The film contains a good deal of good acting, particularly by the two stars, and by Gene Hackman and Michael J. Pollard. Both the color camera work by Burnett Guffey and the editing by Dede Allen are first class.

*Two for the Road,* starring Audrey Hepburn and Albert Finney, was directed by Stanley Donen, who has a large reputation as a maker of musicals. This marital comedy-drama recounts the progress through the inevitable period of disappointment in a marriage after the romance wears off. To this essentially lightweight material Donen has applied some of the apparatus of the recent European art film: sexual frankness (watered down) and camera styles (patently counterfeited). The result was criticized as an old cornball in fairly flashy wrappings.

Two of James Joyce's novels were adapted for films which appeared in the United States during 1967. Joseph Strick, who directed *Ulysses* and co-authored the screenplay, concentrated in the film on the novel's sexual passages and, as an apparent plea for human brotherhood, the passages in which the Jewish hero is slurred. Strick reproduces these incidents faithfully. But in doing this he does not wholly reproduce the novel's complexity and intent. Some critics faulted Strick's directorial imagination, and only one of the performances —that of Barbara Jefford as Molly—was consistently praised as truly adequate.

The second film based upon a Joyce book is Mary Ellen Bute's *Passages from Finnegan's*

*Wake.* With modest means, this film does capture at least some of the spirit of its source. Although the picture is too long and the direction falters at times, Miss Bute's passionate understanding of the novel is, by and large, translated into a good cinematic equivalent.

*The Flim-Flam Man* is a spotty but unusual film that deals with two great American subjects: the "Free Life" and the "Big Con."

George C. Scott plays a confidence man in the South who plies his trade as one way of remaining outside the confines of a grubby, nine-to-five existence. If *The Flim-Flam Man* had stayed confidently with its subject, it might have emerged as a nice, off-beat, character comedy. Instead, it is marred by inserted slapstick and a melodramatic ending.

Scott gives a good-humored performance in the W. C. Fields tradition as the confidence man. Michael Sarrazin also gives a pleasant performance, and Harry Morgan is funny as a rube sheriff.

*Up the Down Staircase,* adapted from Bel Kaufman's best-selling novel, provides Sandy Dennis with her first solo starring film role. Miss Dennis' portrayal of a young, inexperienced school teacher is frequently touching, though somewhat repetitious in mannerism. The script deals with some problems in a slum school in New York City and faces them with unusual honesty. Unfortunately, however, when the screenplay has faced the problems long enough to get enough throbs and thrills for a full-length film, it just drops rather than solves them and tacks on a rosy ending.

On Broadway, *Barefoot in the Park* was a tasty meringue—as directed by Mike Nichols. Adapted for the screen by playwright Neil Simon and directed by Gene Saks, this tale of newlyweds in a Greenwich Village walk-up suffers considerably on film. Robert Redford is still adept in his original role of the young husband, but Mildred Natwick, his mother-in-law in the Broadway version, flounders in repeating her role on film. Charles Boyer, as her boyfriend, is also not at his best. Aside from some of the bright repartee, the film's chief asset is Jane Fonda's performance as the young wife. Miss Fonda proves yet again that in the right role, serious or light, she is one of the best young actresses on the screen.

*In the Heat of the Night,* starring Sidney Poitier and Rod Steiger, is a tricky thriller with a serious subject. A Negro stranger, arrested on suspicion of murder in a Deep South town, turns out to be a Philadelphia detective who specializes in homicide. The bigoted local police chief quickly becomes dependent upon the detective for help in solving the crime. This novel situation, however, is spoiled by the cliché-ridden mystery plot. But two elements are remarkable. Rod Steiger gives a shrewd performance as a gum-chewing, fat-bellied police chief. And Haskell Wexler's color photography makes this picture a feast for the eyes even when the mind is growing restless.

## ADDITIONAL NOTABLE FILMS OF 1967

**The Battle of Algiers.** Italian director Gillo Pontecorvo's documentary-style account of the guerrilla war waged by Algerian rebels against the French scored solidly when shown at the New York Film Festival and, later, in commercial theaters.

**Camelot.** The film version of the hit Broadway musical by Alan Jay Lerner and Frederick Loewe starred Richard Harris, Vanessa Redgrave, Franco Nero, David Hemmings, and Lionel Jeffries, under Joshua Logan's direction.

**The Climax.** Pietro Germi directed this Italian comedy starring Ugo Tognazzi.

**The Comedians.** British author Graham Greene wrote the screenplay for the film version of his best-selling novel; Richard Burton, Elizabeth Taylor, Alec Guinness, Peter Ustinov, Paul Ford, and Lillian Gish starred; Peter Glenville directed.

**The Exterminating Angel.** Luis Buñuel directed this widely discussed, Spanish-language, metaphorical comedy set in a house where a group of guests find themselves unable to leave a dinner party.

**The Family Way.** John Mills, Hayley Mills, and Hywel Bennet starred in this well-received British film about a young couple who are unable to consummate their marriage.

**A Guide for the Married Man.** Walter Matthau won critical praise for his performance in the starring role of this American comedy directed by Gene Kelly.

**Luv.** The film, based on Murray Schisgal's Broadway hit, starred Peter Falk, Jack Lemmon, and Elaine May.

**A Man for All Seasons.** Winner of the Academy Award for best picture of the year, Robert Bolt's adaptation of his successful stage drama was produced and directed by Fred Zinnemann. Paul Scofield, the British actor, won an Oscar for his performance in the leading role.

**Our Mother's House.** Dirk Bogarde starred, together with seven children, in this British chiller produced and directed by Jack Clayton.

**Reflections in a Golden Eye.** Elizabeth Taylor, Marlon Brando, Brian Keith, and Julie Harris starred in this drama based on a novel by Carson McCullers and directed by John Huston.

**The Taming of the Shrew.** Franco Zeffirelli directed this new production of Shakespeare's classic starring Elizabeth Taylor and Richard Burton.

**Thoroughly Modern Millie.** Julie Andrews, Mary Tyler Moore, Carol Channing, James Fox, John Gavin, and Beatrice Lillie starred in this Ross Hunter musical.

**The Tiger Makes Out.** Eli Wallach and Anne Jackson starred in this well-received adaptation of Murray Schisgal's Off-Broadway comedy, *The Tiger.*

**Wait Until Dark.** Adapted from the hit Broadway suspense drama about a blind girl terrorized by intruders, the film starred Audrey Hepburn, Alan Arkin, Richard Crenna, and Efram Zimbalist, Jr.

## LEADING MONEY-MAKING FILMS
Source: VARIETY

| MOTION PICTURE | STUDIO | YEAR | GROSS INCOME |
|---|---|---|---|
| Birth of a Nation | Mutual (D. W. Griffith) | 1915 | $50,000,000 |
| The Sound of Music | Fox | 1965 | 42,500,000 |
| Gone with the Wind | Metro-Goldwyn-Mayer | 1939 | 41,200,000 |
| The Ten Commandments | Paramount | 1957 | 40,000,000 |
| Ben-Hur | Metro-Goldwyn-Mayer | 1959 | 38,000,000 |
| Mary Poppins | Buena Vista | 1964 | 31,000,000 |
| My Fair Lady | Warner Brothers | 1964 | 30,000,000 |
| Thunderball | United Artists | 1965 | 26,000,000 |
| Cleopatra | 20th Century-Fox | 1963 | 23,500,000 |
| How the West Was Won | Metro-Goldwyn-Mayer | 1962 | 23,000,000 |
| Around the World in 80 Days | United Artists | 1957 | 22,000,000 |
| West Side Story | United Artists | 1961 | 22,000,000 |
| Goldfinger | United Artists | 1964 | 22,000,000 |
| It's a Mad, Mad, Mad, Mad World | United Artists | 1963 | 19,000,000 |
| The Robe | 20th Century Fox | 1953 | 17,500,000 |
| South Pacific | 20th Century-Fox | 1958 | 17,500,000 |
| The Bridge on the River Kwai | Columbia | 1958 | 17,195,000 |
| Tom Jones | United Artists | 1963 | 16,150,000 |
| The Longest Day | 20th Century-Fox | 1962 | 15,100,000 |
| This Is Cinerama | Cinerama | 1952 | 15,000,000 |
| Lawrence of Arabia | Columbia | 1963 | 15,000,000 |
| Doctor Zhivago | Metro-Goldwyn-Mayer | 1965 | 15,000,000 |
| The Carpetbaggers | Paramount | 1964 | 14,500,000 |
| Spartacus | Universal | 1961 | 14,000,000 |
| The Guns of Navarone | Columbia | 1961 | 13,000,000 |
| The Greatest Show on Earth | Paramount | 1952 | 12,800,000 |
| The Seven Wonders of the World | Cinerama | 1956 | 12,500,000 |
| From Here to Eternity | Columbia | 1953 | 12,200,000 |
| White Christmas | Paramount | 1954 | 12,000,000 |
| Cinerama Holiday | Cinerama | 1955 | 12,000,000 |
| El Cid | Allied Artists | 1962 | 12,000,000 |
| Irma la Douce | United Artists | 1963 | 12,000,000 |
| Those Magnificent Men in Their Flying Machines | 20th Century-Fox | 1965 | 12,000,000 |
| Quo Vadis | Metro-Goldwyn-Mayer | 1951 | 11,750,000 |
| Samson and Delilah | Paramount | 1950 | 11,500,000 |
| Duel in the Sun | Selznick Releasing Organization | 1947 | 11,300,000 |
| The Best Years of Our Lives | RKO | 1947 | 11,300,000 |
| Peyton Place | 20th Century-Fox | 1958 | 11,000,000 |
| Psycho | Paramount | 1960 | 11,000,000 |
| Sayonara | Warner Brothers | 1958 | 10,500,000 |
| Snow White (animated) | RKO-Buena Vista | 1937 | 10,400,000 |
| Who's Afraid of Virginia Woolf? | Warner Brothers | 1966 | 10,300,000 |
| The Parent Trap | Buena Vista | 1961 | 9,400,000 |
| The Apartment | United Artists | 1960 | 9,300,000 |
| Cat Ballou | Columbia | 1965 | 9,300,000 |
| Cinderella | RKO-Buena Vista | 1950 | 9,250,000 |
| That Damn Cat | Buena Vista | 1965 | 9,200,000 |
| The Absent-Minded Professor | Buena Vista | 1961 | 9,100,000 |
| Shane | Paramount | 1953 | 9,000,000 |
| Cat on a Hot Tin Roof | Metro-Goldwyn-Mayer | 1958 | 9,000,000 |
| Auntie Mame | Warner Brothers | 1959 | 9,000,000 |
| From Russia with Love | United Artists | 1964 | 9,000,000 |
| The Caine Mutiny | Columbia | 1954 | 8,700,000 |
| Exodus | United Artists | 1960 | 8,700,000 |
| Bambi | RKO-Buena Vista | 1942 | 8,600,000 |
| 20,000 Leagues Under the Sea | Buena Vista | 1955 | 8,600,000 |
| This Is the Army | Warner Brothers | 1943 | 8,500,000 |
| Mister Roberts | Warner Brothers | 1955 | 8,500,000 |
| The King and I | 20th Century-Fox | 1956 | 8,500,000 |
| Lover Come Back | Universal | 1962 | 8,500,000 |
| That Touch of Mink | Universal | 1962 | 8,500,000 |
| Lady and the Tramp (animated) | Buena Vista | 1955 | 8,300,000 |
| Some Like It Hot | United Artists | 1959 | 8,300,000 |
| What's New Pussycat? | United Artists | 1965 | 8,300,000 |
| Old Yeller | Buena Vista | 1958 | 8,200,000 |
| Swiss Family Robinson | Buena Vista | 1960 | 8,100,000 |
| The Bells of St. Mary's | RKO | 1945 | 8,000,000 |
| The Jolson Story | Columbia | 1947 | 8,000,000 |
| Battle Cry | Warner Brothers | 1955 | 8,000,000 |

# THEATER

Friedman-Abeles

Scene from **Cabaret**, the Tony Award-winning musical, set in pre-war Germany

## THE AMERICAN THEATER: 1966–1967

The negative aspects of the 1966–67 Broadway theater season were depressingly obvious. A new low of only 47 productions opened, and of these, only eight could be classified as new, serious dramas. Of the 12 new musicals, none was as impressive as the previous season's *Man of La Mancha*, and of the 19 new comedies, none was as entertaining as the previous season's *Cactus Flower*.

Threatening to impoverish Broadway still further were the reduction of New York City's major newspapers from four to three, a move within Actors Equity Association to increase restrictions against the importing of foreign actors, and the continuing upward spiral of production costs.

**Notable Broadway Plays.** There were a few bright spots in the generally bleak Broadway picture. The season's best play, British playwright Harold Pinter's *The Homecoming,* was magnificently performed by members of the Royal Shakespeare Company, and it overcame a cool initial reception in the daily press to win both the Antoinette Perry Award (Tony) and the New York Drama Critics' Circle Award for the best play of the 1966–67 season.

In *The Homecoming,* Pinter describes a British lower-middle-class family, comprising a father, an uncle, and two grown sons, that is fiercely determined to preserve itself. A third son and his wife pay an unexpected visit and are greeted with insults and abuse. Then the two unmarried brothers proceed to seduce their brother's wife. She, in self-defense, emasculates them and their father. At the end, her husband leaves her behind to become a prostitute, but the audience is left with the feeling that she is very much in control of both the family and her own destiny.

While the events of the play were sordid, *The Homecoming* was also deeply funny as it undermined the gentility with which we pretend to live.

Winning the Pulitzer Prize for the best American theater work was Edward Albee's drama, *A Delicate Balance.* With surprising compassion, Albee's play examined an affluent suburban couple named Tobias and Agnes, who live contentedly with a number of myths. Then in the course of one night, both husband and wife are forced into an awareness of their illusions. Through a parable, Tobias shows us that he now understands that love cannot be compelled. When a couple who are their best friends arrive and ask to move in, Tobias learns that there is a conflict between the idea of friendship and really liking people. And finally, Tobias sees that aging human beings are more restricted in their freedom of choice than they like to believe.

While *A Delicate Balance* received a mixed critical reception, the play impressed many as being more subtle than Albee's violently extroverted *Who's Afraid of Virginia Woolf?* All other serious plays of the season failed
**(continued)**

**THE AMERICAN THEATER** (*continued*)

on Broadway; however, there were a number of distinguished attempts. David Westheimer's *My Sweet Charlie* explored with fervent honesty one girl's progress from ignorance and racial prejudice to a degree of civilized awareness that is perhaps possible only when one can live temporarily outside society.

The girl, a 16-year-old Southerner thrown out of her home for having become pregnant by a white boy, finds herself forced to share an empty Gulf Coast house with a Northern Negro lawyer fleeing an anti-civil rights posse. Although the play ends fuzzily, perhaps the most moving moment of the Broadway season comes when the girl tells her new friend that she would like her baby to be like him. It is moving because it is a genuine assessment of the Negro's qualities, seen without the fantasy of color.

Frank D. Gilroy made the season's most ambitious effort in *That Summer—That Fall*, a play which wed the contemporary naturalism of a Brooklyn household to the Classical tragic tale of Phaedra and Hippolytus. Unfortunately, the small talk of today was disproportionate to the terse statement of the play's large and eternal passions.

Cartoonist Jules Feiffer's *Little Murders* here and there neatly satirized the violent atmosphere in which New Yorkers live, but the play's harassed characters emerged as strangely unsympathetic.

Peter Weiss's *The Investigation* grimly recited the Nazi atrocities that came to light during the 1965 Frankfurt trial of former concentration camp officials.

Of the season's five comedy hits, the two funniest were written by British playwrights: Peter Shaffer's *Black Comedy* and Frank Marcus' *The Killing of Sister George*. The latter featured fine performances by Beryl Reid, as an irascible, fading BBC star, and Eileen Atkins, as her young roommate.

The season's two best performances came in revivals. Maureen Stapleton in *The Rose Tattoo* lifted the grotesque confusion of the play's protagonist into something simultaneously comic and tragic. And Ethel Merman, in a revised version of *Annie Get Your Gun*, proved even funnier than she was in the original production. Most amazing of all, 78-year-old composer Irving Berlin turned out a new song, *Old Fashioned Wedding*, which stopped the show.

New musical comedies tended to thrive on Broadway, despite a lack of unanimous critical enthusiasm for any one of the offerings. Tom Jones and Harvey Schmidt did a highly respectable job of adapting *The Fourposter* into *I Do! I Do!* for Mary Martin and Robert Preston. Joe Masteroff, John Kander, and Fred Ebb made the smash hit musical *Cabaret* from *I Am a Camera*. In this vehicle, Joel Grey gives a remarkable performance as a pre–World War II Berlin nightclub entertainer.

Three Broadway personalities saved mediocre offerings from extinction. Melina Mercouri repeated her starring role in the film *Never on*

*Sunday* to make passable the musical stage version, *Illya Darling*. Leslie Uggams' beauty and talent gave zest to the ambitious but rather dull *Hallelujah, Baby!* And Barbara Harris brought her unique charm and humor to a mixed bag called *The Apple Tree*.

**Off-Broadway.** The most universally acclaimed hit of the season, however, was a simple, Off-Broadway musical called *You're a Good Man Charlie Brown*, based on Charles M. Schulz's comic strip, *Peanuts*. While none of the sketches or songs by John Gordon and Clark Gesner seemed outstanding, director Joseph Hardy's production was wonderfully successful in creating the special world of Charlie Brown, Snoopy, Lucy, Linus, et al.

Indeed, the whole Off-Broadway season was above average. Three short plays by Jean-Claude van Itallie, grouped under the title *America Hurrah!*, received the votes of two of the four major New York daily newspaper drama critics as the best play of the year on or off Broadway. Most startling of van Itallie's three plays was *Motel*, which dressed its characters as larger-than-life dolls. While a benign landlady doll boasted about her clean and well-equipped motel, vulgar man and woman dolls proceeded with an orgy in which they wrecked the motel and scrawled obscenities across the walls. Their final act of vandalism was to destroy the landlady doll, which turned out to be empty.

Perhaps the best full-length Off-Broadway play was Lanford Wilson's *The Rimers of Eldritch*, which described with great insight the poverty of spirit in a small, Midwestern town. And the best short play Off-Broadway was Rochelle Owens' *Futz*, performed at Cafe La Mama Experimental Theatre Club. It dealt with a backwoods community which persecuted one ignorant farmer for practicing bestiality.

Three other Off-Broadway plays achieved long runs: British playwright Henry Livings' *Eh?* found absurd fun in an inept young man's blithe but effective rebellion against a society which had reduced him to tending an automatic boiler. Canadian playwright John Herbert's *Fortune and Man's Eyes* proved a shocking exposé of homosexuality in prison. And a parody written by California housewife Barbara Garson, *MacBird!*, combined the *Macbeth* plot and the Kennedy assassination, with LBJ in the title role. Although *MacBird!* received generally disapproving reviews, the play struck many as being outrageously entertaining, provided one set aside the idea that literal truth was intended.

**Repertory Theater Companies.** The resident theater movement continued to flourish. New York City welcomed the APA Repertory Company in the APA-Phoenix's fourth consecutive season. The city's theatergoers also noted signs of improvement at Lincoln Center's Vivian Beaumont Theater, both in the repertory company's production of *Galileo* and in Peter Ustinov's *The Unknown Soldier and His Wife*.

Outside of New York City, several more new companies joined the expanding list of nonprofit institutions using a more or less resident nucleus of paid actors to offer high quality productions to their communities. Listed below are a number of such theater companies, including Shakespeare Festivals, in approximate order of their year of inauguration.

## RESIDENT THEATER COMPANIES OF THE UNITED STATES AND CANADA

| YEAR ESTAB-LISHED | THEATER COMPANY | YEAR ESTAB-LISHED | THEATER COMPANY |
|---|---|---|---|
| 1967 | Committee Theater, San Francisco, Calif. | 1962 | Great Lakes Shakespeare Festival Company, Lakewood, Ohio |
| | Inner City Repertory Company, Los Angeles, Calif. | | Marin Shakespeare Festival, San Rafael, Calif. |
| | John Fernald Company of the Meadow Brook Theatre, Rochester, Mich. | | Pocket Theatre, Atlanta, Ga. |
| | Purdue Professional Theatre Company, Lafayette, Ind. | | Shaw Festival, Niagara-on-the-Lake, Ontario |
| | | | Theater in the Street, New York, N.Y. |
| | Spingold Theater, Brandeis University, Waltham, Mass. | | Utah Shakespeare Festival, Cedar City, Utah |
| | | 1961 | National Repertory Theatre (Traveling) |
| | Springfield Theatre Company at Stage West, West Springfield, Mass. | | Shakespeare Summer Festival, Washington, D.C. |
| | Syracuse Repertory Theatre, Syracuse, N.Y. | | Southern Shakespeare Repertory Theatre, Coral Gables, Fla. |
| | Yale School of Drama Repertory Company, New Haven, Conn. | | Washington Theater Club, Washington, D.C. |
| 1966 | Garrick Players, Washington, D.C. | 1960 | APA, Association of Producing Artists (Traveling) |
| | Repertory Theatre of Loretto-Hilton Performing Arts Center, Webster Groves, Mo. | | Asolo Theater Festival, Sarasota, Fla. |
| | Repertory Theatre, New Orleans, La. | | McCarter Theatre Company, Princeton, N.J. |
| | Theatre Atlanta, Atlanta, Georgia | | Playhouse in the Park, Cincinnati, Ohio |
| | Theatre East, Rochester, N.Y. | 1959 | Champlain Shakespeare Festival, Burlington, Vt. |
| | Ypsilanti Greek Festival, Ypsilanti, Mich. (Inactive since 1966) | | Dallas Theater Center, Dallas, Texas |
| | | | San Francisco Mime Troupe, San Francisco, Calif. |
| 1965 | American Conservatory Theatre, Pittsburgh, Penn. San Francisco, Calif. (after 1966) | | Theatre Group, Los Angeles, Calif. (Operated as Center Theatre Group after 1966) |
| | Boston Herald-Traveler Theatre, Boston, Mass. | 1958 | Colorado Shakespeare Festival, Boulder, Colo. |
| | Citadel Theatre, Edmonton, Alberta | | Manitoba Theatre Centre, Winnipeg, Manitoba |
| | A Contemporary Theatre, Seattle, Wash. | | Pennsylvania State Festival Theatre, University Park, Penn. |
| | Eugene O'Neill Memorial Theatre Foundation, Waterford, Conn. | 1957 | Charles Playhouse, Boston, Mass. |
| | Indiana Theatre Company, Bloomington, Ind. | | Front Street Theatre, Memphis, Tenn. |
| | Long Wharf Theatre, New Haven, Conn. | 1956 | Academy Theatre, Atlanta, Ga. |
| | Morris Repertory Theater, Morristown, N.J. | | Cambridge Drama Festival, Cambridge, Mass. (Inactive since 1960) |
| | Pioneer Theatre, Salt Lake City, Utah | | Hollywood Shakespeare Festival, West Hollywood, Calif. |
| | Stanford Repertory Theater, Stanford, Calif. | | |
| | Studio Arena Theatre, Buffalo, N.Y. | | Millan Theatre Company, Detroit, Mich. (Operated as Detroit Repertory Theatre after 1965) |
| | Theatre of the Living Arts, Philadelphia, Penn. | | |
| | Vermont Theatre Company, Stowe, Vt. | 1955 | American Shakespeare Festival Theatre and Academy, Stratford, Conn. |
| 1964 | Actors Theatre of Louisville, Louisville, Ky. | | Fred Miller Theater, Milwaukee, Wis. (Operated as Milwaukee Repertory Theater after 1963) |
| | Arena House Theatre, Harrisburg, Penn. | | |
| | Arts Center Players, Little Rock, Ark. | 1954 | New York Shakespeare Festival, New York, N.Y. |
| | Free Southern Theater (Traveling) | 1953 | Phoenix Theatre, New York, N.Y. (Operated as APA-Phoenix after 1963) |
| | Hiberry Classic Theatre Repertory Company, Detroit, Mich. | | |
| | Missouri Repertory Theater, Kansas City, Mo. | | Stratford Shakespearean Festival Foundation of Canada, Stratford, Ontario |
| | Repertory Theater of Lincoln Center, New York, N.Y. | 1952 | Living Theatre, New York, N.Y. (Traveling abroad since 1964) |
| | Theatre St. Paul, St. Paul, Minn. (Operated by the Minnesota Theatre Company after 1966) | | San Francisco Actors Workshop, San Francisco, Calif. (Inactive since 1966.) |
| | Trinity Square Repertory Co., Providence, R.I. | | Shakespeare Under the Stars, Yellow Springs, Ohio (Inactive since 1957) |
| | University Theatre, Lawrence, Kans. | 1950 | Arena Stage, Washington, D.C. |
| 1963 | California Shakespeare Festival, Santa Clara, Calif. | 1949 | Brattle Theatre, Cambridge, Mass. (Inactive since 1952) |
| | Dartmouth Repertory Theater Company, Hanover, N.H. | | Mummers Theatre, Oklahoma City, Okla. |
| | Firehouse Theater Company, Minneapolis, Minn. | 1948 | Group 20, Wellesley, Mass. (Inactive since 1959) |
| | Hartford Stage Company, Hartford, Conn. | 1947 | Alley Theatre, Houston, Texas |
| | Minnesota Theatre Company, Minneapolis, Minn. | | Theatre 47, Dallas, Texas (Inactive since 1958) |
| | National Shakespeare Company (Traveling) | 1935 | National Shakespeare Festival, San Diego, Calif. |
| | Neptune Theatre, Halifax, Nova Scotia | | Oregon Shakespeare Festival, Ashland, Oreg. |
| | New Jersey Shakespeare Festival, Cape May, N.J. | 1934 | Pittsburgh Playhouse, Pittsburgh, Penn. |
| | The Playhouse Theater Company, Vancouver, B.C. | 1932 | Barter Theatre, Abingdon, Va. |
| | Seattle Repertory Theatre, Seattle, Wash. | 1925 | Goodman Theatre, Chicago, Ill. |
| | Theater Company of Boston, Boston, Mass. | 1917 | Pasadena Playhouse, Pasadena, Calif. |
| | Trident Theatre, Denver, Colo. | 1916 | Cleveland Playhouse, Cleveland, Ohio |

## THE BROADWAY SEASON: 1966–1967
Source: Celebrity Service, Inc.

*September 21* **Annie Get Your Gun.** Closing a successful run at City Center, this revival of the Irving Berlin-Dorothy Fields musical, starring Ethel Merman, moved to the Broadway Theatre, where it drew capacity crowds during a limited run.

*September 21* **A Hand on the Gate.** An all-Negro cast presented a program of poems, songs, and sketches portraying the struggles of the Negro people from slave days to present times. The critical consensus acknowledged moments of brilliance, but faulted the lack of a dramatic line of development.

*September 22* **A Delicate Balance.** The production of Edward Albee's wry comedy, starring the husband-and-wife team of Hume Cronyn and Jessica Tandy, proved to be the historic, if not the dramaturgic event of the theatrical season. Like the rest of Albee's plays, this one generated much discussion and controversy, but failed to achieve more than a moderate run. It won for its author the 1967 Pulitzer Prize in Drama.

*September 27* **Dinner at Eight.** Sir Tyrone Guthrie, lately of Minneapolis, directed this revival of the 1932 comedy hit by George S. Kaufman and Edna Ferber. Critics seemed less than impressed by the presence of ten major stars, and although audience response built to hit proportions in the second month of the play's run, it languished thereafter.

*September 29* **Help Stamp Out Marriage.** Imported by the Theatre Guild and directed expertly by George Abbott, the London hit by Keith Waterhouse and Willis Hall evoked little response and closed quickly.

*September 29* **The Country Girl.** City Center's revival of the Clifford Odets drama, with Jennifer Jones and Rip Torn in the starring roles, made no great splash during its limited engagement.

*October 4* **The Investigation.** Drawn from the court transcripts of the Frankfurt trials of Nazis accused of committing criminal acts at Auschwitz, Peter Weiss's play became more a subject of discussion than of popularity. Critics found the production impressive, if harrowing, but the public responded with interest sufficient only for a moderate run.

*October 5* **The Killing of Sister George.** Frank Marcus' drama had been a hit in London, but it fared less well in New York. However, all agreed that Beryl Reid was spectacular as the Sister George of the title—not a nurse or a nun, but a lesbian Miss Lonelyhearts.

*October 6* **The Loves of Cass McGuire.** With his production of Brian Freil's comedy about a Bowery barmaid returning to Ireland after a 40-year absence, David Merrick showed that even a master producer can falter. Critics found the play diverting, and all agreed that the presence of Ruth Gordon was a plus. However, the run was comparatively brief.

*October 13* **The Alchemist.** The Repertory Theatre of Lincoln Center opened its second season with a revival of Ben Jonson's 17th-century comedy. Critical and popular consensus found the offering less than pleasing.

*October 18* **The Apple Tree.** A trio of one-act musical plays based on stories by Mark Twain, Frank Stockton, and Jules Feiffer became the first true hit of the season. Barbara Harris, starring as Eve in all three plays, was hailed as the enchantress of the season.

*October 19* **We Have Always Lived in the Castle.** David Merrick came acropper again with the production of this excursion into 20th-century Gothic, based on the late Shirley Jackson's story. A strong cast and Garson Kanin's direction were not enough, and the play closed quickly.

*October 20* **The Rose Tattoo.** A revival of Tennessee Williams' comedy about an Italian-American widow was the second in a series of American plays presented by City Center. Handsomely mounted, with Maureen Stapleton and Harry Guardino in the leading roles, the production aroused only lukewarm response during its limited run.

*October 24* **How's the World Treating You?** Critics and public found this British comedy little more inspired than its title.

*October 27* **Under the Weather.** A trio of one-act plays by novelist Saul Bellow failed to impress.

*October 31* **Gilbert Becaud on Broadway.** The dynamic French *chanteur* played a successful two-week engagement at the Longacre Theatre.

*November 3* **Elizabeth the Queen.** City Center continued its series of American dramatic revivals with a production of Maxwell Anderson's study of Elizabeth I of England. Despite the presence of Judith Anderson in the leading role, critics found the play full of bombast and fustian.

*November 15* **The D'Oyly Carte Opera Company.** Under Sol Hurok's auspices the popular Gilbert and Sullivan Company from Britain played a month's engagement at City Center.

*November 16* **The Apparition Theatre of Prague.** Mixed genre—ballet, drama, and pantomime—presented by a Czech troupe in a limited engagement failed to overwhelm the critics.

*November 16* **Les Ballets Africains.** High-spirited goings-on, staged by a troupe from the Republic of New Guinea, won the approval of both critics and public during a limited engagement at the Ethel Barrymore Theatre.

*November 17* **Don't Drink the Water.** Woody Allen's comedy about a New Jersey caterer on vacation behind the Iron Curtain became a personal triumph for Lou Jacobi, the star. Produced by David Merrick, the show enjoyed a substantial run.

*November 20* **Cabaret.** Producer Harold Prince scored solidly with a musical set in pre-World War II Berlin. Joel Grey, Jill Haworth, and Lotte Lenya were the principals.

*November 21* **The School for Scandal.** The prestigious APA-Phoenix repertory company mounted a stylish revival of Richard Brinsley Sheridan's 18th-century comedy of manners.

*November 22* **Right You Are (If You Think You Are).** The APA-Phoenix followed Sheridan's play with a revival of Luigi Pirandello's modern classic. The production won critical praise and public support.

*November 24* **Those That Play the Clowns.** Michael Stewart's comedy involving the Shakespearean characters whom Hamlet employs to catch the king received a chilly reception and closed fast.

*November 26* **Walking Happy.** The musical version of the British comedy *Hobson's Choice* ran for several months. Norman Wisdom won praise for his performance.

*November 28* **Hail Scrawdyke!** David Halliwell's British comedy about the investigation of an art school in the North of England received a chilly reception and folded quickly.

*December 5* **I Do! I Do!** David Merrick brought in a winner with a musical version of Jan De Hartog's memorable *The Fourposter.* Mary Martin and Robert Preston were the felicitous stars in happy partnership, and the show enjoyed a substantial run.

*December 6* **My Sweet Charlie.** This drama involving two fugitives—one a young Negro fleeing Southern law, the other a pregnant white farm girl—won critical approval, but failed to last long.

*December 8* **Yerma.** The Repertory Theatre of Lincoln Center presented García Lorca's study of domestic frustration in Spain. Critical reception was cool, although the translation by W. S. Merwin, the poet, found favor.

*December 14* **Agatha Sue, I Love You.** This confection involving an innocent young girl folksinger and two bachelor horse players proved to be just another also-ran.

*December 15* **Carousel.** City Center mounted a pleasant revival of the Rodgers and Hammerstein classic. A powerful cast and elaborate staging pleased thousands.

*December 15* **A Joyful Noise.** A musical adaptation of the Borden Deal novel, *The Insolent Breed,* folded quickly.

*(continued)*

## LONGEST RUNS ON BROADWAY

| PLAY | NUMBER OF PERFORMANCES | PLAY | NUMBER OF PERFORMANCES | PLAY | NUMBER OF PERFORMANCES |
|---|---|---|---|---|---|
| Life with Father...... | 3,224 | The King and I....... | 1,246 | Bells Are Ringing..... | 924 |
| Tobacco Road........ | 3,182 | Fiddler on the Roof *.. | 1,240 | Luv.................. | 902 |
| My Fair Lady......... | 2,717 | Guys and Dolls....... | 1,200 | Can-Can............. | 892 |
| Abie's Irish Rose..... | 2,327 | Mister Roberts....... | 1,157 | Carousel............ | 890 |
| Oklahoma!.......... | 2,212 | Annie Get Your Gun... | 1,147 | Hats Off to Ice........ | 889 |
| Harvey.............. | 1,775 | The Seven Year Itch.. | 1,141 | Fanny............... | 888 |
| South Pacific........ | 1,694 | Pins and Needles..... | 1,108 | Follow the Girls....... | 882 |
| Born Yesterday...... | 1,642 | Kiss Me Kate........ | 1,070 | Camelot............. | 873 |
| Mary, Mary......... | 1,572 | Pajama Game........ | 1,063 | The Bat............. | 867 |
| The Voice of the Turtle | 1,557 | The Teahouse of the August Moon....... | 1,027 | My Sister Eileen...... | 865 |
| Barefoot in the Park.. | 1,532 | Damn Yankees....... | 1,019 | White Cargo.......... | 864 |
| Hello, Dolly! *........ | 1,523 | Never Too Late....... | 1,007 | Song of Norway...... | 860 |
| How to Succeed in Business Without Really Trying....... | 1,461 | Any Wednesday...... | 984 | A Streetcar Named Desire............. | 855 |
| Arsenic and Old Lace.. | 1,444 | A Funny Thing Happened on the Way to the Forum....... | 964 | Comedy in Music..... | 849 |
| The Sound of Music... | 1,443 | The Odd Couple...... | 965 | You Can't Take It with You........... | 837 |
| Hellzapoppin......... | 1,404 | Anna Lucasta........ | 957 | La Plume de Ma Tante | 835 |
| The Music Man....... | 1,375 | Kiss and Tell........ | 957 | Three Men on a Horse | 835 |
| Funny Girl........... | 1,348 | The Moon Is Blue..... | 924 | The Subject Was Roses | 832 |
| Angel Street......... | 1,295 | | | Inherit the Wind...... | 806 |
| Lightnin'............. | 1,291 | | | | |

## LONGEST RUNS OFF-BROADWAY

| PLAY | NUMBER OF PERFORMANCES | PLAY | NUMBER OF PERFORMANCES | PLAY | NUMBER OF PERFORMANCES |
|---|---|---|---|---|---|
| The Fantasticks*..... | 3,075 | The Connection...... | 722 | The Hostage......... | 545 |
| The Threepenny Opera | 2,611 | The Knack.......... | 685 | Krapp's Last Tape and The Zoo Story...... | 532 |
| The Blacks.......... | 1,408 | The Balcony........ | 672 | Six Characters in Search of an Author | 529 |
| Little Mary Sunshine.. | 1,143 | The Pocket Watch.... | 624 | Happy Ending and Day of Absence........ | 504 |
| Leave It to Jane...... | 928 | Hogan's Goat........ | 607 | The Boys from Syracuse | 500 |
| A View from the Bridge | 780 | The Trojan Women.... | 600 | | |
| The Boy Friend...... | 763 | The Crucible........ | 571 | | |
| The Mad Show....... | 760 | The Iceman Cometh... | 565 | | |
| Man of La Mancha.... | 751 | | | | |

*Still running; performances as of September 10, 1967.

**THE BROADWAY SEASON** (*continued*)

*December 20*  **We, Comrades Three.** The APA repertory group's attempt to effect a dramatic pastiche derived from Walt Whitman's poems failed to arouse much enthusiasm.

*December 21*  **The Star-Spangled Girl.** Arnold Saint Subber presented Neil Simon's new comedy with the film stars Tony Perkins and Connie Stevens in leading roles. The show ran well.

*December 27*  **At the Drop of Another Hat.** The inimitable British team of Michael Flanders and Donald Swann played to appreciative audiences during a limited engagement.

*January 3*  **Marat/Sade.** Peter Weiss's stunning play was given a second New York production by the National Players Company. The critics approved, and audience interest remained high.

*January 5*  **The Homecoming.** Harold Pinter's new play, performed by the British Royal Shakespeare Company, was hailed as the most distinguished offering of the new season.

*January 11*  **The Wild Duck.** The APA repertory company presented a moderately successful revival of Ibsen's drama, in a translation by Eva Le Gallienne.

*January 12*  **The Astrakhan Coat.** A melodrama in which three intellectuals plan the killing of an inoffensive waiter found little favor and folded quickly.

*January 26*  **Come Live with Me.** Soupy Sales, the television personality, made his stage debut in this comedy by Lee Minoff and Stanley Price. The play was short-lived, but Sales earned warm notices for his performance.

*February 7*  **Black Comedy.** Peter Shaffer's London hit scored well in New York. The presence of Lynn Redgrave and Geraldine Page, as well as the play's bitter humor and innovative lighting, pleased audiences.

*February 9*  **The Paisley Convertible.** No *Solid Gold Cadillac,* this vehicle departed swiftly.

*February 9*  **The East Wind.** The Repertory Theatre of Lincoln Center opened the second half of its season with Leo Lehman's study of two Polish refugees in London. The play, and several individual performances, aroused some critical interest.

*February 10*  **You Can't Take It with You.** The APA-Phoenix group came on strong with a delightful revival of the George S. Kaufman-Moss Hart comedy.

*February 13*  **Love in E-Flat.** Norman Krasna's comedy closed quickly.

*February 14*  **The Bristol Old Vic.** During a successful limited engagement, the Bristol Old Vic repertory company presented an all-Shakespeare program, including productions of *Hamlet, Romeo and Juliet,* and *Measure for Measure.* Inevitably, critics compared the Bristol troupe with the London Old Vic and found it a shade short of that mark. However, reaction was generally very favorable.

*February 18*  **Of Love Remembered.** Arnold Sundgaard's saga of a Norwegian family left all concerned cold.

*March 11*  **The Natural Look.** A highly talented cast toiled to no avail in this short-lived comedy about the cosmetics industry.

*March 13*  **You Know I Can't Hear You**

**When the Water's Running.** The success of four short plays by Robert Anderson proved again that new playwrights sometimes can be winners still. An immediate hit, Anderson's plays provided the vehicles for splendid performances by Martin Balsam.

*March 16*  **That Summer—That Fall.** A new play by Frank D. Gilroy fell far short of his earlier success, *The Subject Was Roses,* and folded quickly.

*March 21*  **War and Peace.** Erwin Piscator's adaptation of Tolstoy's classic novel was presented by the APA-Phoenix company. As in previous seasons, the new production proved again that if an adaptor is sufficiently gifted, the most unlikely sounding venture can emerge as a rousing success.

*March 28*  **Sherry!** *The Man Who Came to Dinner* came back once again, this time as a musical. The cast was good, and some of the music attractive, but appeal was lacking and the run was brief.

*April 4*  **Hello Solly!** A Yiddish-American musical review proved to be a clever diversion for large crowds during a limited engagement.

*April 5*  **Finian's Rainbow.** The City Center Light Opera Company's handsome revival gave nostalgic pleasure to theatergoers.

*April 11*  **Illya Darling.** Melina Mercouri sparked the musical stage version of her smash comedy film, *Never on Sunday,* making the play a solid hit despite critical reservations.

*April 13*  **Galileo.** The Repertory Theatre of Lincoln Center scored one of its more popular successes with its production of Bertolt Brecht's drama about the Renaissance astronomer.

*April 25*  **Little Murders.** The first Broadway offering by Jules Feiffer, the cartoonist, involved a satiric look at violence in America. The play had a short run in New York, but excited some interest in London.

*April 26*  **The Sound of Music.** The City Center Light Opera Company revived the Rodgers and Hammerstein musical for a limited engagement.

*April 26*  **Hallelujah, Baby!** An elaborate musical dealing with crises in a Negro couple's lives, the production established its star, Leslie Uggams, as a theatrical phenomenon to be reckoned with, and went on to enjoy a long run.

*May 1*  **The National Repertory Theatre.** The group, which usually tours, presented *The Imaginary Invalid* by Molière, *A Touch of the Poet* by O'Neill, and *Tonight at 8:30* by Noel Coward, during a highly successful limited engagement at the ANTA Theatre.

*May 11*  **Sing, Israel, Sing.** Michael Myerberg presented a musical, based on Yiddish and Israeli folklore, that dealt with the many different foreign strains that compromise the population of Israel. Performances were well attended during a limited engagement.

*May 17*  **Wonderful Town.** The City Center Light Opera Company presented a two-week revival of the Comden and Green-Leonard Bernstein hit musical.

*May 18*  **The Girl in the Freudian Slip.** William F. Brown's comedy closed quickly.

# MUSIC AND DANCE

Leonard Bernstein conducts the New York Philharmonic Orchestra in concert.

## THE 1966–1967 SEASON

If the opening of the new Metropolitan Opera House at Lincoln Center in New York City was the major single event of the 1966–67 music season on the North American continent —if not in the world—it was not the only important happening, not even at the Metropolitan itself.

**Opera.** The season had not been under way very long when the Metropolitan Opera Company announced that it faced one of the most serious financial crises in its history. Ticket prices were increased forthwith to a $15.50 top, and subscribers who had paid less for their tickets prior to the opening of the season were earnestly requested to send in more money.

Next, the Metropolitan announced that it would suspend operation of the National Company, its touring group, at the end of the season. The company had been formed under the direction of Risë Stevens two years earlier, and had had considerable success. It was felt generally that the financial predicament of the parent company, rather than the anticipated and modest deficits of the touring company, was to blame for the decision to disband the National Company.

The Metropolitan finally won the right to lease the site of the old opera house for an office building, which assured the company of a substantial annual rental. However, neither this development, nor the offer of $1,000,000 by Lila Acheson Wallace, co-founder of *The Reader's Digest,* made the company willing to continue the touring group.

Within a month of the Metropolitan's announcement of plans to dissolve the National Company, the National Council on the Arts, headed by Roger L. Stevens, declared that it "felt strongly that the country should have a national touring company." Almost as promptly, a grant of $350,000 in Federal funds to assist in the creation of such a company was announced.

The Metropolitan had said that it was too late to make plans for a 1967–68 touring company season. However, Sarah Caldwell, the extraordinary opera producer from Boston, agreed to create a company and to develop an enterprising repertory that would include Alban Berg's *Lulu* and Verdi's *Falstaff.* Sol Hurok agreed to book the company's tours. Thus the American National Opera Company made its debut in Indianapolis, Indiana, in September, 1967, and won high praise.

Meanwhile, in New York, the Metropolitan itself faced artistic if not box-office competition on its new home ground at Lincoln Center. The Metropolitan had selected the Samuel Barber-Franco Zefferelli production of *Antony and Cleopatra* to open its new opera house. From an artistic standpoint, the piece was a spectacular disaster.

The Met also invested a great deal in a colossal new production of Verdi's *La Traviata;* however, the general critical estimate was so-so.

Next door, at Lincoln Center's New York State Theater, the New York City Opera opened its season with a production of Handel's *Julius Caesar* (the Caesar in *Antony and Cleopatra* was only Octavius). The production emerged as a smashing success, evoking praise as a beautiful, stylized work. Shortly thereafter the New York City Opera presented its version of *La Traviata,* and Frank Corsaro's direction of the work was hailed as a milestone in the production history of the work.

Never was the opera business in New York as good as it was during the 1966–67 season. No matter what they put on, both major companies did splendidly at the box-office. Nearly all of the Metropolitan's productions were sold out in advance at extremely high prices.

North America hit a musical jackpot in the spring of the year when Expo 67 opened in Montreal, bringing before the public an array of visiting soloists, orchestras, and opera companies the like of which had never before been assembled in one place in so short a time. In swift succession, the Bolshoi, La Scala, and the Swedish and Vienna opera companies, among others, moved in and out of the Salle Pelletier at the Place des Arts, presenting a repertory of productions that was truly astounding. Any music lover with sufficient time, energy, and money could, if he wished, avail himself of the opportunity to see a panorama of international opera that in one way or another presented just about everything of value in the operatic tradition.

**Orchestras.** Also at Lincoln Center, the New York Philharmonic made big news by announcing that Leonard Bernstein would resign as music director of the orchestra when his (continued)

**MUSIC AND DANCE** (*continued*)

contract expired in 1969. This was a blow, for in the years since Bernstein took over the Philharmonic in 1958, he had transformed it from a dispirited ensemble into one that could take justifiable pride in its excellence.

Bernstein saw the New York Philharmonic safely through its move from Carnegie Hall to Lincoln Center, brought the orchestra fame through its celebrated music-appreciation programs on television, secured year-round employment for its musicians, and made the Philharmonic's programs reflect significant artistic trends of the present day.

The immediate sense of loss experienced by both the orchestra and its public when Bernstein's decision was announced was fully justified. No one believed that Bernstein could be replaced. He would be succeeded by a man of talent, of course; but his equivalent in dynamism, imagination, and dazzlement was not even hoped for.

One of the popular guessing games in the music business during 1967 had to do with the New York Philharmonic's probable choice of a successor to Bernstein. Speculation on the choice of a successor was made still more interesting when Jean Martinon and the Chicago Symphony Orchestra announced that they would part company after Martinon's current contract expired. In addition, there were recurrent rumors that Eugene Ormandy might be planning to retire from his post as conductor of the Philadelphia Orchestra. The competition for conducting talent was going to be intense.

The steadily increasing activities of all the major symphony orchestras made it apparent that the job of music director would be different in the future from what it had been in the past. Given the demands of the musicians for year-round employment, the orchestras have had to find ways and places to play concerts during the off-season months—usually May through September—that had until quite recently been symphonically silent in most cities. This meant that music directors would have to be more imaginative and active in the future than they had been previously.

The summer of 1967 saw the Washington (D.C.) National Symphony move into its new Merriweather Pavilion at Columbia, Maryland, for its first annual al fresco summer series. As part of its expansion program, the Chicago Symphony accepted an invitation to provide music for the new Fairlane Festival, sponsored by the University of Michigan, on the former estate of Henry Ford in Dearborn, Michigan. This put the Chicago Symphony right in the backyard of the Detroit Symphony, which holds its summer series on the Oakland University campus, northeast of Detroit. Since the Fairlane Festival was held in June and the Oakland concerts in July and August, there was no conflict between the two orchestras. Nevertheless, the Michigan situation did indicate that the time is fast approaching when orchestras may find themselves in head-on competition with each other.

**Ballet.** Developments in dance during the 1966–67 season had to do chiefly with stabilization and expansion of existing companies and institutions. Thus another season passed without the appearance of significant new talents in either performance or choreography.

The Robert Joffrey Ballet made the biggest news by becoming a constituent of the New York City Center. The company changed its name to the City Center Joffrey Ballet and played two short seasons, one in the fall and one in the spring, at the City Center.

A welcome artistic contribution by the company was its revival of *The Green Table,* the famed anti-war dance work created in 1931 by Kurt Jooss, a German exponent of modern dance.

The Joffrey company was the object of another adoption in 1967 when it was given a summer home in the State of Washington. The Pacific Northwest Ballet Association raised funds and arranged the collaboration of cultural leaders in several Pacific Northwest cities to make the project feasible. While in summer residence at the Pacific Lutheran College of Tacoma, the company rehearsed, prepared new works, and gave numerous performances in the area.

This move was significant because it extended the artist-in-residence principle to an entire dance company, and made it possible for both the company and the host region to benefit from the arrangement. The chances are that the idea will be adopted by other companies and other communities in the future.

On February 16, 1967, the American Ballet Theatre gave the first performance of its full-length production of *Swan Lake,* the Petipa-Ivanov ballet classic that had to wait until this occasion for a full-fledged mounting by an American company. David Blair of the Royal Ballet of England staged the work, and the result was unanimously hailed as a great success.

The first full-length ballet ever filmed in this country, George Balanchine's production of *A Midsummer Night's Dream,* had its premiere April 17 at the New York State Theater at Lincoln Center. At least one important critic described the effort as the "best film yet of a ballet."

In Washington, D.C., the National Ballet expanded its subscription season to include three series of seven performances each, in addition to a series of *Nutcracker* performances at Christmas. This company, organized in 1963 by Frederic Franklin, has increased its season during each of the last four years and expects to offer a ten-week subscription season by the time it moves into the John F. Kennedy Center in 1968 or 1969.

Similar expansions were noted in almost every American city that has a ballet company of its own (Philadelphia and Boston being two of the most prominent). Indications were that the dance was continuing to grow in popularity among the performing-arts public.

There were some suggestions that concert attendance, as opposed to opera attendance, might be falling off slightly in New York during the current season. However, the evidence was too slight and incomplete to be regarded as conclusive. It did become increasingly apparent, though, that the surest way to get the public into a music performance was to give the audience something—opera, dance, or a "staged" concert such as the New York Philharmonic Promenades or the Boston "Pops"—that it could look at as well as listen to. It could well be that concerts of the future will have to be "seen" as well as "heard" if they are to appeal to a wide segment of the public.

## MAJOR AMERICAN SYMPHONY ORCHESTRAS

| STATE | ORCHESTRA | CONDUCTOR |
|---|---|---|
| California | Los Angeles Philharmonic | Zubin Mehta |
| | San Francisco Symphony | Josef Krips |
| Colorado | Denver Symphony Orchestra | Vladimir Golschmann |
| Connecticut | Hartford Symphony Orchestra | Arthur Winograd |
| District of Columbia | Washington National Symphony Orchestra | Howard Mitchell |
| Georgia | Atlanta Symphony Orchestra | Robert Shaw |
| Illinois | Chicago Symphony Orchestra | Jean Martinon |
| Indiana | Indianapolis Symphony Orchestra | Izler Solomon |
| Kentucky | Louisville Symphony Orchestra | Robert Whitney |
| Louisiana | New Orleans Philharmonic Symphony Orchestra | Werner Torkanowsky |
| Maryland | Baltimore Symphony Orchestra | Peter Herman Adler |
| Massachusetts | Boston Symphony Orchestra | Erich Leinsdorf |
| Michigan | Detroit Symphony Orchestra | Sixten Ehrling |
| Minnesota | Minneapolis Symphony Orchestra | Stanislaw Skrowaczewski |
| Missouri | Kansas City Philharmonic | Hans Schweiger |
| | St. Louis Symphony | Eleazar de Carvalho |
| New York | American Symphony Orchestra (New York City) | Leopold Stokowski |
| | Buffalo Philharmonic Orchestra | Lukas Foss |
| | New York Philharmonic | Leonard Bernstein |
| | Rochester Philharmonic Orchestra | Laszlo Somogyi |
| Ohio | Cincinnati Symphony Orchestra | Max Rudolf |
| | Cleveland Orchestra | Georg Szell |
| Oklahoma | Oklahoma City Symphony Orchestra | Guy Fraser Harrison |
| Pennsylvania | Chamber Symphony of Philadelphia | Anshel Brusilow |
| | Philadelphia Orchestra | Eugene Ormandy |
| | Pittsburgh Symphony | William Steinberg |
| Texas | Dallas Symphony | Donald Johanos |
| | Houston Symphony Orchestra | Sir John Barbirolli |
| | San Antonio Symphony | Victor Alessandro |
| Utah | Utah Symphony Orchestra | Maurice Abravanel |
| Washington | Seattle Symphony Orchestra | Milton Katims |
| Wisconsin | Milwaukee Symphony Orchestra | Harry John Brown |

## MAJOR BALLET COMPANIES OF THE WORLD

Alwin Nikolais Ballet
  *Director: Alwin Nikolais*
American Ballet Theatre
  *Directors:*
  *Lucia Chase and Oliver Smith*
Australian Ballet
  *Director: Peggy van Praagh*
Bolshoi Ballet
  *Director: Mikhail Chulaki*
City Center Joffrey Ballet
  *Director: Robert Joffrey*
Festival Ballet (London)
  *Director: Julian Braunsweig*
Les Grands Ballets Canadiens
  *Director: Ludmilla Chiriaeff*
Harkness Ballet
  *Director: Brian MacDonald*
Kirov Ballet
  *Director: Pyotr Rachinsky*
Martha Graham Dance Company
  *Director: Martha Graham*

National Ballet of Canada
  *Director: Celia Franca*
National Ballet of Washington
  *Director: Frederic Franklin*
New York City Ballet
  *Directors:*
  *George Balanchine and Lincoln Kirstein*
Paris Opéra Ballet
  *Director: Michel Descombey*
Royal Ballet, Covent Garden
  *Director: Frederick Ashton*
Royal Danish Ballet
  *Director: Fleming Flindt*
Royal Swedish Ballet
  *Director: Erik Bruhn*
Royal Winnipeg Ballet
  *Director: Lew Christensen*
Scandinavian Ballet
  *Director: Eva-Marianne von Rosen*
Western Theatre Ballet (England)
  *Director: Peter Darrell*

## NOTABLES OF THE MUSICAL WORLD: PAST AND PRESENT

Albanese, Licia (1913– ), Italian soprano
Albéniz, Isaac (1860–1909), Spanish composer
Anderson, Marian (1902– ), American contralto
Ansermet, Ernest (1883– ), Swiss conductor
Arlen, Harold (1905– ), American composer
Arrau, Claudio (1903– ), Chilean pianist
Ashkenazy, Vladimir (1937– ), Russian pianist
Baccaloni, Salvatore (1900– ), Italian basso
Bach, Johann Sebastian (1685–1750), German composer
Bachauer, Gina (1913– ), Greek pianist
Backhaus, Wilhelm (1884– ), German pianist
Barber, Samuel (1910– ), American composer
Barbirolli, Sir John (1899– ), English conductor
Bartók, Béla (1881–1945), Hungarian composer
Beecham, Sir Thomas (1879–1961), English conductor
Beethoven, Ludwig van (1770–1827), German composer
Beinum, Eduard van (1901– ), Dutch conductor
Bellini, Vincenzo (1801–35), Italian composer
Berg, Alban (1885–1935), Austrian composer
Berlin, Irving (1888– ), American composer
Berlioz, Louis Hector (1803–69), French composer
Bernstein, Leonard (1918– ), American conductor and composer
Bing, Rudolf (1902– ), Austrian-American impresario
Bizet, Georges (1838–75), French composer
Björling, Jussi (1907–60), Swedish tenor
Blitzstein, Marc (1905–64), American composer
Bloch, Ernest (1880–1959), Swiss-American composer
Boccherini, Luigi (1743–1805), Italian composer
Borodin, Aleksandr (1833–87), Russian composer
Boulanger, Nadia (1887– ), French teacher and conductor
Boulez, Pierre (1925– ), French composer
Brahms, Johannes (1833–97), German composer
Britten, Benjamin (1913– ), English composer
Browning, John (1933– ), American pianist
Bruch, Max (1838–1920), German composer
Bruckner, Anton (1824–96), Austrian composer
Busoni, Feruccio (1866–1924), Italian composer
Buxtehude, Dietrich (1637?–1707), German organist and composer
Byrd, William (1543?–1623), English organist and composer
Cage, John (1912– ), American composer
Callas, Maria (1923– ), Greek-American soprano
Calvé, Emma (1858–1942), French soprano
Caruso, Enrico (1873–1921), Italian tenor
Casadesus, Robert (1899– ), French pianist

Casals, Pablo (1876– ), Spanish cellist and conductor
Chaliapin, Feodor (1873–1938), Russian basso
Chamlee, Mario (1892– ), American tenor
Charpentier, Gustave (1860–1956), French composer
Chausson, Ernest (1855–99), French composer
Chávez, Carlos (1899– ), Mexican composer and conductor
Cherubini, Luigi (1760–1842), Italian composer
Chopin, Frédéric (1810–49), Polish-French composer
Cimarosa, Domenico (1749–1801), Italian composer
Cliburn, Van (1934– ), American pianist
Copland, Aaron (1900– ), American composer
Corelli, Arcangelo (1653–1713), Italian composer
Corelli, Franco (1924– ), Italian tenor
Cortot, Alfred (1877–1962), French pianist
Couperin, François (1668–1733), French composer
Cowell, Henry (1897– ), American composer
Curzon, Clifford (1907– ), English pianist
Damrosch, Walter (1862–1950), American conductor
Debussy, Claude (1862–1918), French composer
Délibes, Léo (1836–91), French composer
Delius, Frederick (1862–1934), English composer
Dello Joio, Norman (1913– ), American composer
de los Angeles, Victoria (1923– ), Spanish soprano
De Reszke, Edouard (1853–1917), Polish bass
De Reszke, Jean (1850–1925), Polish tenor
De Reszke, Josephine (1855–91), Polish soprano
Diamond, David (1915– ), American composer
Dohnanyi, Ernst von (1877–1960), Hungarian composer
Donizetti, Gaetano (1797–1848), Italian composer
Dowland, John (1563–1626), English lutanist and composer
Dufay, Guillaume (1400?–74), Flemish composer
Dukas, Paul (1865–1935), French composer
Dvořák, Anton (1841–1904), Czechoslovakian composer
Eames, Emma (1865–1952), American soprano
Elgar, Sir Edward (1857–1934), British composer
Elias, Rosalind (1931– ), American soprano
Elman, Mischa (1891–1967), Russian-American violinist
Enesco, Georges (1881–1955), Romanian composer
Evans, David (1874–1948), Welsh composer
Falla, Manuel de (1876–1946), Spanish composer
Farrar, Geraldine (1882–1967), American soprano

**Farrell, Eileen** (1920–   ), American soprano
**Fauré, Gabriel** (1845–1924), French composer
**Ferrier, Kathleen** (1912–53), English contralto
**Firkušny, Rudolf** (1912–   ), Czech pianist
**Flagstad, Kirsten** (1895–1962), Norwegian soprano
**Flotow, Friedrich von** (1812–83), German composer
**Foster, Stephen** (1826–64), American composer
**Fox, Virgil** (1912–   ), American organist
**Francescatti, Zino** (1905–   ), French violinist
**Franck, César** (1822–90), Belgian-French composer
**Frescobaldi, Girolamo** (1583–1643), Italian composer
**Frijsh, Povla** (1875?–1960), Danish soprano
**Friml, Rudolf** (1879–   ), Bohemian-American composer
**Fromm, Herbert** (1905–   ), German composer
**Fürtwangler, Wilhelm** (1886–1954), German conductor
**Galli-Curci, Amelita** (1882–1963), Italian soprano
**Garden, Mary** (1877–1967), Scottish-American soprano
**Gershwin, George** (1898–1937), American composer
**Giannini, Dusolina** (1902–   ), American soprano
**Gieseking, Walter** (1895–1956), German pianist
**Gigli, Beniamino** (1890–1957), Italian tenor
**Gilels, Emil** (1916–   ), Russian pianist
**Giulini, Carlo Maria** (1914–   ), Italian conductor
**Glière, Reinhold** (1875–1956), Russian composer
**Glinka, Mikhail** (1804–57), Russian composer
**Gluck, Christoph von** (1714–87), German composer
**Godowsky, Leopold** (1870–1938), Polish-American pianist and composer
**Gould, Glenn** (1932–   ), Canadian pianist
**Gounod, Charles** (1818–93), French composer
**Grieg, Edvard Hagerup** (1843–1907), Norwegian composer
**Grofé, Ferde** (1892–   ), American composer
**Halévy, Jacques** (1799–1862), French composer
**Handel, George Frederick** (1685–1759), German-English composer
**Harris, Roy** (1898–   ), American composer
**Haydn, Franz Joseph** (1732–1809), Austrian composer
**Heifetz, Jascha** (1901–   ), Russian-American violinist
**Hendl, Walter** (1917–   ), American conductor
**Herbert, Victor** (1859–1924), Irish-American composer
**Hess, Dame Myra** (1890–1965), English pianist
**Hindemith, Paul** (1895–1963), German-American composer
**Hollander, Lorin** (1945–   ), American pianist
**Holst, Gustav Theodore** (1874–1934), English composer
**Honegger, Arthur** (1892–1955), Swiss-French composer

**Horowitz, Vladimir** (1904–   ), Russian-American pianist
**Humperdinck, Engelbert** (1854–1921), German composer
**Ibert, Jacques** (1890–1962), French composer
**Indy, Vincent d'** (1851–1931), French composer
**Ippolitov-Ivanov, Mikhail** (1859–1935), Russian composer
**Iturbi, José** (1895–   ), Spanish pianist and conductor
**Ives, Charles** (1874–1954), American composer
**Janáček, Leoš** (1854–1928), Moravian composer
**Janis, Byron** (1928–   ), American pianist
**Joachim, Joseph** (1831–1907), Hungarian violinist
**Jongen, Joseph** (1873–   ), Belgian composer
**Kabalevsky, Dmitri** (1904–   ), Russian composer
**Kapell, William** (1922–53), American pianist
**Karajan, Herbert von** (1908–   ), Austrian conductor
**Kates, Stephen** (1943–   ), American violinist and cellist
**Khachaturian, Aram** (1903–   ), Russian composer
**Kipnis, Alexander** (1891–   ), Russian bass
**Klemperer, Otto** (1885–   ), German conductor and composer
**Kodály, Zoltán** (1882–1967), Hungarian composer
**Koussevitzky, Serge** (1874–1951), Russian-American conductor
**Kraus, Lili** (1908–   ), American pianist
**Kreisler, Fritz** (1875–1962), Austrian-American violinist and composer
**Lalo, Edouard** (1823–92), French composer
**Landowska, Wanda** (1879–1959), Polish-French harpsichordist and pianist
**Lehmann, Lilli** (1848–1929), German soprano
**Lehmann, Lotte** (1888–   ), German soprano
**Leinsdorf, Erich** (1912–   ), German-American conductor
**Leoncavallo, Ruggiero** (1858–1919), Italian composer
**Lhevine, Josef** (1874–1944), Russian-American pianist and teacher
**Lhevine, Rosina** (1880–   ), Russian-American pianist and teacher
**Lind, Jenny** (1820–87), Swedish soprano
**Liszt, Franz** (1811–86), Hungarian composer
**Lully, Jean Baptiste** (1632–87), French composer
**MacDowell, Edward** (1861–1908), American composer and pianist
**Mahler, Gustav** (1860–1911), Austrian composer
**Mannes, David** (1866–1959), American violinist and conductor
**Martinelli, Giovanni** (1885–   ), Italian tenor
**Mascagni, Pietro** (1863–1945), Italian composer
**Massenet, Jules** (1842–1912), French composer
**McCormack, John** (1884–1945), Irish-American tenor

*(continued)*

**NOTABLES OF THE MUSIC WORLD** (*continued*)

Melba, Dame Nellie (1859–1931), Australian soprano

Melchior, Lauritz (1890–  ), Danish tenor

Mendelssohn, Felix (1809–47), German composer

Menotti, Gian-Carlo (1911–  ), Italian-American composer

Menuhin, Yehudi (1916–  ), American violinist

Merrill, Robert (1917–  ), American baritone

Meyerbeer, Giacomo (1791–1864), German composer

Miaskovsky, Nicolas (1881–  ), Russian composer

Milanov, Zinka (1906–  ), Yugoslavian soprano

Milhaud, Darius (1892–  ), French composer

Milstein, Nathan (1904–  ), American violinist

Mitropoulos, Dmitri (1896–1960), Greek-American conductor

Moffo, Anna (1934–  ), American soprano

Monteux, Pierre (1875–1964), French conductor

Monteverdi, Claudio (1567–1643), Italian composer

Moore, Grace (1901–47), American soprano

Morley Thomas (1557–1603?), English madrigal composer

Moussorgsky, Modest Petrovich (1839–91), Russian composer

Mozart, Wolfgang Amadeus (1756–91), Austrian composer

Münch, Charles (1891–  ), French conductor

Munsel, Patrice (1925–  ), American soprano

Muzio, Claudia (1892–1936), Italian soprano

Nadien, David (1926–  ), American violinist

Nevin, Ethelbert (1862–1901), American pianist and composer

Nielsen, Carl (1865–1931), Danish composer

Nilsson, Birgit (1922–  ), Swedish soprano

Nordica, Lillian (1857–1914), American soprano

Novaes, Guiomar (1895–  ), Brazilian pianist

Offenbach, Jacques (1819–80), German-French composer

Oistrakh, David (1908–  ), Russian violinist

Orff, Carl (1895–  ), German composer

Ormandy, Eugene (1899–  ), Hungarian-American conductor

Paderewski, Ignace Jan (1860–1941), Polish pianist and composer

Paganini, Niccolò (1782–1840), Italian violinist and composer

Palestrina, Giovanni Pierluigi da (1524?–94), Italian composer

Parker, Horatio (1863–1919), American composer

Partch, Harry (1901–  ), American composer

Patti, Adelina (1843–1919), Italian soprano

Peerce, Jan (1904–  ), American tenor

Peters, Roberta (1930–  ), American soprano

Pergolesi, Giovanni (1710–36), Italian composer

Piatigorsky, Gregor (1903–  ), Russian cellist

Pillois, Jacques (1877–1935), French composer

Pinkham, Daniel (1923–  ), American composer and harpsichordist

Pinza, Ezio (1892–1957), Italian-American bass

Piston, Walter (1894–  ), American composer

Ponchielli, Amilcare (1834–86), Italian composer

Pons, Lily (1904–  ), French-American soprano

Ponselle, Rosa (1897–  ), American soprano

Porter, Cole (1893–1964), American composer

Poulenc, Francis (1899–1963), French composer

Price, Leontyne (1927–  ), American soprano

Primrose, William (1903–  ), Scottish violist

Prokofiev, Serge (1891–1953), Russian composer

Puccini, Giacomo (1858–1924), Italian composer

Purcell, Henry (1659?–95), English composer

Rachmaninov, Sergei (1873–1943), Russian composer and pianist

Ravel, Maurice (1875–1937), French composer

Reger, Max (1873–1916), German composer and pianist

Reiner, Fritz (1888–1963), Hungarian-American conductor

Reisenberg, Nadia (1905–  ), Russian-American pianist

Renaud, Maurice (1861–1933), French baritone

Respighi, Ottorino (1879–1936), Italian composer

Reyer, Ernest (1823–1909), French composer and critic

Richter, Sviatoslav (1914–  ), Russian pianist

Riegger, Wallingford (1885–1961), American composer

Rimsky-Korsakov, Nikolai (1844–1908), Russian composer

Romberg, Sigmund (1887–1951), Hungarian-American composer

Rossini, Gioacchino (1792–1868), Italian composer

Roussel, Albert (1869–1937), French composer

Rubinstein, Anton (1829–94), Russian pianist and composer

Rubinstein, Artur (1886–  ), Polish-American pianist

Sabata, Victor de (1892–  ), Italian composer and conductor

Saint-Saëns, Charles Camille (1835–1921), French composer

Salieri, Antonio (1750–1825), Italian composer

Sarasate, Pablo (1844–1908), Spanish violinist

Satie, Erik (1866–1925), French composer

Scarlatti, Domenico (1685–1757), Italian composer and harpsichordist

Scherchen, Hermann (1891–1966), German conductor

Schipa, Tito (1889–1965), Italian tenor

Schippers, Thomas (1930–  ), American conductor

Schnabel, Artur (1882–1951), Austrian-American pianist

Schoenberg, Arnold (1874–1951), Austrian composer

Schubert, Franz (1797–1828), Austrian composer

Schuecker, Edmund (1860–1911), Austrian composer and harpist

Schuman, William (1910–  ), American composer

Schumann, Clara (1819–96), German pianist
Schumann, Elisabeth (1885–1952), German soprano
Schumann, Robert (1810–56), German composer
Schumann-Heink, Ernestine (1861–1936), Austrian-Czech contralto
Schuppanzigh, Ignaz (1776–1830), Austrian violinist, conductor, and teacher
Schütz, Heinrich (1585–1672), German composer
Schwarzkopf, Elisabeth (1915–  ), German soprano
Schwieger, Hans (1906–  ), German-American conductor
Scotti, Antonio (1866–1936), Italian baritone
Scovotti, Geanette (1933–  ), American soprano
Scriabin, Alexander (1872–1915), Russian composer
Searle, Humphrey (1915–  ), English composer
Segovia, Andrés (1893–  ), Spanish guitarist
Sembrich, Marcella (1858–1935), Austrian soprano
Serkin, Rudolf (1903–  ), Russian-American pianist
Sessions, Roger (1896–  ), American composer
Sgambati, Giovanni (1841–1914), Italian pianist, conductor, and composer
Shostakovitch, Dmitri (1906–  ), Russian composer
Sibelius, Jean (1865–1957), Finnish composer
Siloti, Alexander (1863–1945), Russian pianist and teacher
Smetana, Friedrich (1824–84), Czech composer
Sousa, John Philip (1854–1932), American composer and bandmaster
Stamitz, Johann (1717–57), German violinist and composer
Steber, Eleanor (1916–  ), American soprano
Steinberg, William (1899–  ), German-American conductor
Stern, Isaac (1920–  ), Russian-American violinist
Stevens, Halsey (1908–  ), American composer and writer
Stevens, Risë (1913–  ), American mezzo-soprano
Stockhausen, Karlheinz (1928–  ), German composer, teacher, and theorist
Stokowski, Leopold (1882–  ), American conductor
Strauss, Johann (1804–49), Austrian composer and conductor
Strauss, Johann, Jr. (1825–99), Austrian composer and conductor
Strauss, Richard (1864–1949), German composer
Stravinsky, Igor (1882–  ), Russian-French composer
Sullivan, Sir Arthur (1842–1900), British composer
Suppé, Franz von (1819–95), Austrian composer
Sutherland, Joan (1926–  ), Australian soprano
Svanholm, Set (1904–  ), Swedish tenor
Swarthout, Gladys (1904–  ), American contralto

Szell, Georg (1897–  ), Hungarian-American conductor
Szeryng, Henryk (1918–  ), Polish-Mexican violinist
Szigeti, Joseph (1892–  ), Hungarian violinist
Szymanowski, Karol (1882–1937), Polish composer
Tallis, Thomas (c.1505–85), British composer and organist
Tartini, Giuseppe (1692–1770), Italian violinist
Taylor, Deems (1885–1966), American composer
Tchaikovsky, Pëtr I. (1840–93), Russian composer
Tebaldi, Renata (1922–  ), Italian soprano
Telemann, Georg (1681–1767), German composer
Tetrazzini, Luisa (1871–1940), Italian soprano
Teyte, Dame Maggie (1888–  ), British soprano
Thomas, Ambroise (1811–96), French composer
Thomas, John Charles (1891–  ), American baritone
Thomas, Theodore (1835–1905), German-American conductor
Thomson, Virgil (1896–  ), American composer
Tibbett, Lawrence (1896–1960), American baritone
Toscanini, Arturo (1867–1957), Italian conductor
Tourel, Jennie (1910–  ), Canadian-American mezzo-soprano
Traubel, Helen (1903–  ), American soprano
Tucker, Richard (1914–  ), American tenor
Varèse, Edgard (1885–1965), French-American composer
Vaughan Williams, Ralph (1872–1958), English composer
Verdi, Giuseppe (1813–1901), Italian composer
Villa-Lobos, Heitor (1887–1959), Brazilian composer
Vivaldi, Antonio (c.1675–1741), Italian composer and violinist
Wagner, Richard (1813–83), German composer
Walter, Bruno (1876–1962), German-American conductor
Walton, Sir William (1902–  ), English composer
Warren, Leonard (1911–60), American baritone
Watts, André (1946–  ), American pianist
Weber, Carl Maria von (1786–1826), German composer
Webern, Anton (1883–1945), Austrian composer
Weill, Kurt (1900–50), German composer
Weingartner, Felix (1863–1942), German composer and conductor
Wolf, Hugo (1860–1903), Austrian composer
Wolf-Ferrari, Ermanno (1876–1948), Italian composer
Ysaÿe, Eugène (1858–1931), Belgian violinist and conductor
Zimbalist, Efrem (1889–  ), Russian-American violinist

## SOME NOTABLES OF THE DANCE

Adams, Diana (1926– ), dancer

Angiolini, Gasparo (1723–96), choreographer

Ashton, Sir Frederick (1906– ), dancer, choreographer, and director

Balanchine, George (1904– ), dancer, choreographer, and director

Baronova, Irina (1919– ), dancer

Blair, David (1932– ), dancer

Blasis, Carlo (1797–1878), dancer, choreographer, and teacher

Blum, René (1884–1944), director

Boris, Ruthanna (1918– ), dancer

Bournonville, August (1805–79), choreographer and teacher

Bruhn, Erik (1919– ), dancer and director

Camargo, Marie-Anne de (1710–1770), dancer

Cecchetti, Enrico (1850–1928), dancer

Chase, Lucia (1907– ), dancer and director

Christensen, Lew (1908– ), dancer and director

Cranko, John (1927– ), choreographer

Cunningham, Merce (1926– ), dancer and choreographer

Dalcroze, Emile-Jacques (1865–1950), teacher

d'Amboise, Jacques (1934– ), dancer

Danilova, Alexandra (1906– ), dancer

Dauberval, Jean (1724–1806), choreographer and teacher

Delsarte, François (1811–71), teacher

De Mille, Agnes (1909– ), dancer and choreographer

Diaghilev, Sergei (1872–1929), director

Didelot, Charles Louis (1767–1837), dancer and choreographer

Dolin, Anton (1904– ), dancer

Eglevsky, André (1917– ), dancer

Fokine, Mikhail (1880–1942), dancer, choreographer, and teacher

Fonteyn, Dame Margot (1919– ), dancer

Franklin, Frederic (1914– ), dancer and director

Genée, Adeline (1878– ), dancer and teacher of choreography

Geva, Tamara (1908– ), dancer

Gorsky, Alexander (1871–1924), dancer, choreographer, and teacher

Graham, Martha (1895– ), dancer, choreographer, director, and teacher

Grisi, Carlotta (1819–99), dancer

Hayden, Melissa (1928– ), dancer

Helpmann, Robert (1909– ), dancer and choreographer

Hightower, Rosella (1920– ), dancer

Humphrey, Doris (1895–1958), dancer and choreographer

Ivanov, Lev (1834–1901), choreographer

Joffrey, Robert (1930– ), dancer, choreographer, and director

Joos, Kurt (1901– ), dancer, choreographer, and director

Kelly, Gene (1912– ), dancer and choreographer

Kent, Allegra (1938– ), dancer

Kirstein, Lincoln (1907– ), director

Kreutzberg, Harald (1902– ), dancer

Kriza, John (1919– ), dancer

La Fontaine, Mlle. (1665–1728), dancer

Lavrovsky, Leonide (1905– ), choreographer

LeClercq, Tanaquil (1929– ), dancer

Lichine, David (1910– ), dancer

Lifar, Serge (1905– ), dancer and choreographer

Limón, José (1908– ), dancer, choreographer, teacher

Littlefield, Catherine (1908–51), choreographer

Loring, Eugene (1914– ), dancer

Macmillan, Kenneth (1930– ), choreographer

Magallanes, Nicholas (1919– ), dancer

Markova, Alicia (1910– ), dancer

Massine, Léonide (1894– ), dancer and choreographer

Moiseyev, Igor (1906– ), director

Mordkin, Michel (1881–1944), dancer and choreographer

Nijinska, Bronislava (1891– ), dancer and choreographer

Nijinsky, Vaslav (1890–1950), dancer

Noverre, Jean-Georges (1727–1810), choreographer and teacher

Nureyev, Rudolf (1938– ), dancer

Page, Ruth (1903?– ), dancer

Pavlova, Anna (1881–1931), dancer

Perrot, Jules (1810–92), dancer and choreographer

Petipa, Marius (1822–1910), dancer, choreographer, and teacher

Petit, Roland (1921– ), dancer and choreographer

Rambert, Dame Marie (1888– ), director and teacher

Riabouchinska, Tatiana (1917– ), dancer

Robbins, Jerome (1918– ), dancer and choreographer

Rubinstein, Ida (1884– ), dancer

Saint-Léon, Arthur (1821–70), dancer and choreographer

St. Denis, Ruth (1877– ), dancer and choreographer

Sallé, Marie (1707–56), dancer

Semenova, Marina (1909– ), dancer

Shawn, Ted (1891– ), dancer, choreographer, and teacher

Shearer, Moira (1926– ), dancer

Skibine, George (1920– ), dancer

Somes, Michael (1917– ), dancer

Spessivetzeva, Olga (1895– ), dancer

Taglioni, Filipo (1778–1871), choreographer

Taglioni, Marie (1804–84), dancer

Tallchief, Maria (1924– ), dancer

Taylor, Paul (1930– ), choreographer

Toumanova, Tamara (1919– ), dancer

Tudor, Antony (1909– ), dancer and choreographer

Ulanova, Galina (1910– ), dancer

Valois, Dame Ninette de (1898– ), dancer, director, and teacher

Villella, Edward (1931– ), dancer

Wall, David (1945– ), dancer

Weaver, John (1673–1760), dancer and teacher

Weidman, Charles (1901– ), dancer, choreographer, and director

Wigman, Mary (1886– ), dancer and director

Wilde, Patricia (1928– ), dancer

Youskevich, Igor (1912– ), dancer

## ARTISTS: PAST AND PRESENT

**Agasius of Ephesus** (first century B.C.), Greek sculptor

**Albers, Josef** (1888– ), American (German-born) painter

**Alberti, Leone Battista** (1404–72), Italian architect and painter

**Albright, Ivan** (1897– ), American painter

**Albright, Malvin Marr** (1897– ), American painter and sculptor

**Ammanati, Bartolomeo** (1511–92), Italian sculptor and architect

**Angelico, Fra** (c.1400–55), Italian painter

**Apollodorus** (fifth century B.C.), Greek painter

**Apollonius of Athens** (second century B.C.), Greek sculptor

**Arnolfo di Cambio** (c.1245–1310), Italian architect and sculptor

**Arp, Jean** (1887–1966), French painter and sculptor

**Barlach, Ernst** (1870–1938), German painter and sculptor

**Bartolomeo della Porta, Fra** (c.1474–1517), Italian painter

**Baskin, Leonard** (1922– ), American sculptor and etcher

**Beckmann, Max** (1884–1950), German painter

**Bellini, Gentile** (1429–1507), Italian painter

**Bellini, Giovanni** (c.1430–1516), Italian painter

**Bellini, Jacopo** (c.1400–70), Italian painter

**Bellows, George** (1882–1925), American painter and lithographer

**Benton, Thomas Hart** (1889– ), American painter

**Berenson, Bernard** (1865–1959), American art critic and connoisseur

**Bernini, Giovanni Lorenzo** (1598–1680), Italian architect and sculptor

**Blake, William** (1757–1827), English painter

**Boccioni, Umberto** (1882–1916), Italian sculptor and painter

**Bologna, Giovanni da** (1524–1608), Italian sculptor

**Bonnard, Pierre** (1867–1947), Flemish painter

**Borromini, Francesco** (1599–1677), Italian architect

**Bosch, Hieronymus** (c.1450–1516), Flemish painter

**Botticelli, Sandro** (c.1444–1510), Italian painter

**Boucher, François** (1703–70), French painter

**Bramante, Donato** (c.1444–1514), Italian architect and painter

**Brancusi, Constantin** (1876–1957), Romanian sculptor

**Braque, Georges** (1882–1963), French painter

**Breuer, Marcel** (1902– ), Hungarian-American architect

**Bronzino, Angelo** (1503–72), Italian painter

**Brouwer, Adriaen** (c.1606–38), Flemish painter

**Bruegel, Pieter, the elder** (c.1525–69), Flemish painter

**Brunelleschi, Filippo** (1377–1446), Italian architect

**Calder, Alexander** (1898– ), American sculptor

**Canaletto, Antonio (Giovanni)** (1697–1768), Italian painter

**Canova, Antonio** (1757–1882), Italian sculptor

**Caravaggio, Michelangelo Meris da** (1537–1610), Italian painter

**Cassatt, Mary** (1845–1926), American painter and etcher

**Castagno, Andrea del** (c.1423–57), Italian painter

**Cellini, Benvenuto** (1500–71), Italian sculptor

**Cézanne, Paul** (1839–1906), French painter

**Chagall, Marc** (1887– ), Russian painter

**Chardin, Jean-Baptiste** (1699–1779), French painter

**Chirico, Giorgio de** (1888– ), Italian painter

**Cimabue, Giovanni** (c.1240–1302), Italian painter

**Claude Lorrain** (1600–82), French painter

**Clodion** (1738–1814), French sculptor

**Cole, Thomas** (1801–48), American painter

**Constable, John** (1776–1837), English painter

**Copley, John Singleton** (1738–1815), American painter

**Corot, Jean Baptiste Camille** (1796–1875), French painter

**Correggio, Antonio** (1494–1534), Italian painter

**Courbet, Gustave** (1819–77), French painter

**Cranach, Lucas, the elder** (1472–1553), German painter and engraver

**Cranach, Lucas, the younger** (1515–86), German painter

**Crivelli, Carlo** (c.1430–93), Italian painter

**Dali, Salvador** (1904– ), Spanish painter

**Daumier, Honoré** (1808–79), French painter, sculptor, and caricaturist

**David, Jacques Louis** (1748–1825), French painter

**Degas, Edgar** (1834–1917), French painter and sculptor

**de Kooning, Willem** (1904– ), Dutch-American painter

**Delacroix, Eugène** (1798–1863), French painter

**Derain, André** (1880–1954), French painter

**Desiderio da Settignano** (1428–64), Italian sculptor

**Donatello** (c.1386–1466), Italian sculptor

**Duccio di Buoninsegna** (c.1255–1319), Italian painter

**Duchamp, Marcel** (1887– ), French painter

**Dufy, Raoul** (1877–1953), French painter

**Dürer, Albrecht** (1471–1528), German painter and engraver

**Eakins, Thomas** (1844–1916), American painter and sculptor

**Eiffel, Alexandre Gustave** (1832–1923), French architect

**Ensor, James** (1860–1949), Belgian painter and etcher

**Epstein, Sir Jacob** (1880–1959), English sculptor

**Ernst, Max** (1881– ), German painter

**Eyck, Hubert van** (c.1370–1426), Flemish painter

**Ezekius** (sixth century B.C.), Greek painter

**Falconet, Étienne-Maurice** (1716–91), French sculptor

(continued)

**ARTISTS: PAST AND PRESENT** (*continued*)

**Feininger, Lyonel** (1871–1956), American painter

**Fouquet, Jean** (c.1420–80), French painter

**Fragonard, Jean-Honoré** (1732–1806), French painter

**Fry, Roger E.** (1866–1934), English painter and art critic

**Gabo, Naum** (1890–   ), Russian sculptor and architect

**Gainsborough, Thomas** (1727–88), English painter

**Gaudí, Antonio** (1852–1926), Spanish architect

**Gauguin, Paul** (1848–1903), French painter

**Gentile da Fabriano** (c.1370–1427), Italian painter

**Géricault, Théodore** (1791–1824), French painter

**Ghiberti, Lorenzo** (c.1378–1455), Italian sculptor

**Ghirlandaio, Domenico** (1449–94), Italian painter

**Giacometti, Alberto** (1901–66), Swiss sculptor and painter

**Giorgio, Francesco di** (1439–1502), Italian architect, painter, and sculptor

**Giorgione** (c.1476–1510), Italian painter

**Giotto** (c.1266–1337), Italian painter and architect

**Giovanni di Paolo** (c.1403–83), Italian painter

**Giulio Romano** (c.1492–1546), Italian painter and architect

**Goujon, Jean** (c.1510–66), French sculptor and architect

**Goya y Lucientes, Francisco de** (1746–1828), Spanish painter and etcher

**Gozzoli, Benozzo** (1420–97), Italian painter

**Greco, El** (1541–1614), Spanish painter

**Gris, Juan** (1887–1927), Spanish painter

**Grosz, George** (1893–1959), German-American painter

**Guardi, Francesco** (1712–93), Italian painter

**Grünewald, Matthias** (c.1470–1528), German painter

**Hals, Frans** (c.1580–1666), Dutch painter

**Hepworth, Barbara** (1903–   ), English sculptor

**Hiroshige, Ando** (1797–1858), Japanese painter

**Hoffman, Hans** (1880–1966), German-American painter

**Hogarth, William** (1697–1764), English painter and engraver

**Hokusai, Katsushika** (1760–1849), Japanese painter and engraver

**Holbein, Hans, the elder** (c.1465–1524), German painter

**Holbein, Hans, the younger** (c.1497–1543), German painter

**Homer, Winslow** (1836–1910), American painter

**Hooch, Pieter de** (c.1629–1684), Dutch painter

**Hopper, Edward** (1882–1967), American painter and engraver

**Houdon, Jean Antoine** (1741–1828), French sculptor

**Ingres, Jean Auguste Dominique** (1780–1867), French painter

**Inness, George** (1825–94), American painter

**Isidorus of Miletus** (sixth century B.C.), Greek architect

**Johnson, Philip C.** (1906–   ), American architect

**Jones, Inigo** (1573–1652), English architect

**Kandinsky, Vassily** (1866–1944), Russian painter

**Klee, Paul** (1879–1940), Swiss painter

**Kokoshchka, Oskar** (1886–   ), Austrian painter

**Kollwitz, Käthe** (1867–1945), German painter and sculptor

**Lachaise, Gaston** (1882–1935), American sculptor

**La Tour, Georges de** (1593–1652), French painter

**Lebrun, Charles** (1619–90), French architect and painter

**Le Corbusier** (1887–1965), Franco-Swiss architect

**Léger, Fernand** (1881–1955), French painter

**Leonardo da Vinci** (1452–1519), Italian painter, architect, and sculptor

**Lescot, Pierre** (c.1510–78), French architect

**Lipchitz, Jacques** (1891–   ), French sculptor

**Lippi, Fra Filippo** (c.1406–69), Italian painter

**Li T'ang** (c.1050–1130), Chinese painter

**Lochner, Stefan** (d.1451), German painter

**Lorenzetti, Ambrogio** (died c.1348), Italian painter

**Lotto, Lorenzo** (c.1480–1556), Italian painter

**Lysippus of Sicyon** (fourth century B.C.), Greek sculptor

**Magritte, René** (1898–1967), Belgian-French painter

**Maillol, Aristide** (1861–1944), French sculptor, painter, and woodcut artist

**Manet, Édouard** (1832–83), French painter

**Mantegna, Andrea** (c.1431–1506), Italian painter

**Marc, Franz** (1880–1916), German painter

**Marin, John** (1870–1953), American painter

**Martini, Simone** (c.1284–1344), Italian painter

**Massaccio** (c.1401–28), Italian painter

**Matisse, Henri** (1869–1954), French painter, sculptor, and lithographer

**Matta Echaurren, Roberto** (1912–   ), Chilean painter

**Memling, Hans** (c.1430–94), Flemish painter

**Michelangelo Buonarroti** (1475–1564), Italian painter, sculptor, and architect

**Michelozzo Michelozzi** (1396–1472), Italian sculptor and architect

**Miës van der Rohe, Ludwig** (1886–   ), German-American architect

**Millet, Jean François** (1814–75), French painter

**Mino da Fiesole** (c.1429–84), Italian sculptor

**Miró, Joan** (1893–   ), Spanish painter

**Modigliani, Amedeo** (1884–1920), Italian painter

**Mondrian, Piet** (1872–1944), Dutch painter

**Monet, Claude** (1840–1926), French painter

**Moore, Henry** (1898–   ), English sculptor

**Morris, William** (1834–96), English architect and painter

**Motherwell, Robert** (1915–   ), American painter

**Munch, Edvard** (1863–1944), Norwegian painter
**Murillo, Bartolomé Estéban** (c.1617–82), Spanish painter
**Myron** (fifth century B.C.), Greek sculptor
**O'Keeffe, Georgia** (1887– ), American painter
**Orozco, José Clemente** (1883–1949), Mexican painter and lithographer
**Palladio, Andrea** (1508–80), Italian architect
**Perrault, Claude** (1613–88), French architect
**Perugino, Il** (c.1445–1523), Italian painter
**Phidias of Athens** (c.500–432 B.C.), Greek sculptor
**Picasso, Pablo** (1881– ), Spanish painter and sculptor
**Piero della Francesca** (c.1420–92), Italian painter
**Piranesi, Giovanni Battista** (1720–78), Italian architect and engraver
**Pisano, Andrea** (c.1290–1348), Italian sculptor
**Pisano, Nicolá** (c.1220–84), Italian sculptor
**Pissarro, Camille** (1830–1903), French painter
**Pollaiuolo, Antonio** (c.1429–98), Italian painter, sculptor, and engraver
**Pollock, Jackson** (1912–56), American painter
**Polycleitus of Argos** (fifth century B.C.), Greek sculptor
**Polygnotos of Thasos** (fifth century B.C.), Greek painter
**Poussin, Nicolas** (c.1593–1665), French painter
**Praxiteles** (fourth century B.C.), Greek sculptor
**Primaticcio, Francesco** (c.1504–70), Italian painter
**Prud'hon, Pierre Paul** (1758–1823), French painter
**Quercia, Jacopo della** (c.1374–1438), Italian sculptor
**Raeburn, Sir Henry** (1756–1823), Scottish painter
**Raphael Santi** or **Raphael Sanzio** (1483–1520), Italian painter
**Ray, Man** (1890– ), American painter and photographer
**Redon, Odilon** (1840–1916), French painter and lithographer
**Rembrandt van Rijn** (1606–69), Dutch painter
**Renoir, Pierre Auguste** (1841–1919), French painter and sculptor
**Reynolds, Sir Joshua** (1723–92), English painter
**Richardson, Henry Hobson** (1838–86), American architect
**Rivera, Diego** (1886–1957), Mexican painter
**Robbia, Lucca della** (1400–82), Italian painter
**Rodin, Auguste** (1840–1917), French sculptor
**Rossellino, Bernardo** (1409–64), Italian architect and sculptor
**Rosso, Giovanni Battista, "Il Rosso"** (1495–1540), Italian painter
**Rouault, Georges** (1871–1958), French painter
**Rousseau, Henri** (1844–1910), French painter
**Rubens, Peter Paul** (1577–1640), Flemish painter
**Rudolph, Paul** (1918– ), American architect
**Ruisdael, Jacob von** (c.1628–82), Dutch painter
**Saarinen, Eero** (1910–61), Finnish-American architect

**Saint-Gaudens, Augustus** (1848–1907), American sculptor
**Sansovino, Jacopo** (1486–1570), Italian architect and sculptor
**Sarto, Andrea del** (1486–1531), Italian painter
**Scopas** (fourth century B.C.), Greek sculptor
**Seurat, Georges** (1859–91), French painter
**Severini, Gino** (1893– ), Franco-Italian painter
**Shahn, Ben** (1898– ), American painter and photographer
**Sisley, Alfred** (1839–99), Anglo-French painter
**Sluter, Claus** (d.1406), Flemish painter
**Stieglitz, Alfred** (1864–1946), American photographer
**Stuart, Gilbert** (1755–1828), American painter
**Sullivan, Louis Henry** (1856–1924), American architect
**Tanguy, Yves** (1900–55), French painter
**Thorvaldsen, Albert Bertel** (1777–1844), Danish sculptor
**Tiepolo, Giovanni Battista** (1696–1770), Italian painter
**Tintoretto** (1518–94), Italian painter
**Titian** (c.1487–1576), Italian painter
**Toulouse-Lautrec, Henri de** (1864–1901), French painter and lithographer
**Turner, Joseph Mallord William** (1775–1851), English painter
**Utrillo, Maurice** (1883–1955), French painter
**Van der Goes, Hugo** (d.1482), Flemish painter
**Van der Heyden, Jan** (1637–1712), Dutch painter
**Van der Weyden, Rogier** (c.1399–1464), Flemish painter
**Van Dyck, Anthony** (1599–1641), Flemish painter and etcher
**Van Eyck, Jan** (mid-15th century), Flemish painter
**Van Gogh, Vincent** (1853–90), Dutch painter
**Vasari, Giorgio** (1511–74), Italian architect, writer, and painter
**Velázquez, Diego** (1599–1660), Portuguese-Spanish painter
**Vermeer, Jan** (1632–75), Dutch painter
**Veronese, Paolo** (c.1528–88), Italian painter
**Verrocchio, Andrea del** (c.1435–88), Italian painter and sculptor
**Viollet-le-Duc, Eugène Emmanuel** (1814–79), French architect and writer
**Vitruvius** (first century B.C.–first century A.D.), Roman architect
**Vlaminck, Maurice de** (1876–1958), French painter
**Vuillard, Edouard** (1868–1940), French painter
**Watteau, (Jean) Antoine** (1648–1721), French painter
**West, Benjamin** (1738–1820), American painter
**Whistler, James Abbott McNeill** (1834–1903), American painter and etcher
**Wood, Grant** (1891–1942), American painter
**Wren, Sir Christopher** (1632–1723), English architect
**Wright, Frank Lloyd** (1869–1959), American architect
**Wu Tao-tzu** (seventh century), Chinese painter
**Wyeth, Andrew** (1917– ), American painter
**Yamasaki, Minoru** (1912– ), American architect

## WRITERS: PAST AND PRESENT

**Adams, Henry** (1838–1918), American biographer, historian, and novelist
**Addison, Joseph** (1672–1719), English essayist
**Aeschylus** (c.524 B.C.–456 B.C.), Greek dramatist
**Aesop** (sixth century B.C.), Greek fabulist
**Aiken, Conrad** (1889–    ), American novelist and poet
**Alarcón, Juan Ruiz de** (1581?–1639), Mexican dramatist
**Alarcón, Pedro Antonio de** (1883–91), Spanish novelist
**Albee, Edward** (1928–    ), American dramatist
**Alcott, Louisa May** (1832–88), American novelist
**Aldington, Richard** (1892–1962), English novelist and poet
**Aleman, Mateo** (c.1547–1610), Spanish novelist
**Andersen, Hans Christian** (1805–75), Danish fantasy writer
**Anderson, Maxwell** (1888–1959), American dramatist
**Anderson, Sherwood** (1876–1941), American dramatist and novelist
**Andreyev, Leonid** (1871–1919), Russian dramatist and short-story writer
**Anouilh, Jean** (1910–    ), French dramatist
**Apollinaire, Guillaume** (1880–1918), French poet
**Apulius, Lucius** (c.125–175), Latin satirist
**Aristophanes** (c.448 B.C.–380 B.C.), Greek dramatist
**Aristotle** (c.384 B.C.–322 B.C.), Greek philosopher
**Arnold, Matthew** (1822–88), English poet and critic
**Asch, Sholem** (1880–1957), Polish novelist and short-story writer
**Auden, W. H.** (1907–    ), Anglo-American poet
**Austen, Jane** (1775–1817), English novelist
**Bacon, Sir Francis** (1561–1626), English essayist and philosopher
**Baldwin, James** (1924–    ), American novelist
**Balzac, Honoré de** (1799–1850), French novelist and dramatist
**Barrie, Sir James Matthew** (1860–1937), Scottish dramatist and novelist
**Barth, John** (1930–    ), American novelist
**Bashô, Matsuo** (1644–94), Japanese poet
**Baudelaire, Charles** (1821–67), French poet
**Beaumarchais, Pierre Augustin de** (1732–99), French dramatist
**Beaumont, Francis** (1584?–1616), English dramatist
**Beckett, Samuel** (1906–    ), French (Irish-born) dramatist and novelist
**Bécquer, Gustavo Adolfo** (1836–70), Spanish poet
**Bede** (673?–735), Anglo-Saxon historian
**Beerbohm, Sir Max** (1872–1956), English parodist and critic
**Bellay, Joachim du** (1552–60), French poet
**Belloc, Hilaire** (1870–1953), English novelist, essayist, and historian
**Bellow, Saul** (1915–    ), Canadian-American novelist

**Benét, Stephen Vincent** (1898–1943), American poet and short-story writer
**Bennett, Arnold** (1867–1931), English novelist
**Bernanos, Georges** (1888–1948), French novelist
**Bierce, Ambrose** (1842–1914), American critic and short-story writer
**Björnson, Björnstjerne** (1832–1910), Norwegian dramatist and novelist
**Blake, William** (1757–1827), English poet
**Blasco-Ibáñez, Vicente** (1867–1928), Spanish novelist
**Blunden, Edmund** (1896–    ), English poet and memoirist
**Boccaccio, Giovanni** (1313–75), Italian poet and storyteller
**Boswell, James** (1740–95), Scottish biographer and diarist
**Bowen, Elizabeth** (1899–    ), Anglo-Irish novelist
**Brecht, Bertolt** (1898–1956), German dramatist and poet
**Bridges, Robert** (1844–1930), English poet
**Brooks, Van Wyck** (1886–1963), American critic and historian
**Brontë, Charlotte** (1816–55), English novelist
**Brontë, Emily Jane** (1818–48), English novelist and poet
**Browne, Sir Thomas** (1605–82), English divine and metaphysician
**Browning, Elizabeth Barrett** (1806–61), English poet and translator
**Browning, Robert** (1812–89), English poet
**Bryant, William Cullen** (1794–1878), American poet
**Buck, Pearl S.** (1892–    ), American novelist
**Bunyan, John** (1628–88), English allegorist
**Burke, Edmund** (1729–97), English essayist and orator
**Burns, Robert** (1759–96), Scottish poet
**Butler, Samuel** (1835–1902), English novelist
**Byron, George Gordon,** Lord Byron (1788–1824), English poet
**Cable, George Washington** (1844–1925), American novelist and short-story writer
**Caedmon** (seventh century), Anglo-Saxon poet
**Caesar, Gaius Julius** (100 B.C.?–44 B.C.), Roman historian
**Calderón de la Barca, Pedro** (1600–81), Spanish dramatist and poet
**Callimachus** (c.310 B.C.–240 B.C.), Greek poet
**Camoëns, Luis Vaz de** (c.1524–79), Portuguese poet
**Campion, Thomas** (1567–1619?), English poet and critic
**Camus, Albert** (1913–60), French novelist and journalist
**Čapek, Karel** (1890–1938), Czechoslovakian dramatist and novelist
**Capote, Truman** (1924–    ), American novelist and short-story writer
**Carducci, Giosuè** (1835–1907), Italian poet
**Carlyle, Thomas** (1795–1881), Scottish essayist, critic, and historian
**Carroll, Lewis** (1832–98), English novelist
**Cary, Joyce** (1888–1957), Anglo-Irish novelist and critic

**Casanova, Giacomo** (1725–98), Italian memoirist

**Cather, Willa** (1886–1947), American novelist

**Catullus, Gaius Valerius** (c.84 B.C.–54 B.C.), Roman poet

**Cervantes Saavedra, Miguel de** (c.1547–1616), Spanish novelist

**Chateaubriand, François René de** (1768–1848), French novelist and essayist

**Chaucer, Geoffrey** (1343?–1400), English poet

**Chekhov, Anton** (1860–1904), Russian dramatist and short-story writer

**Chesterton, G. K.** (1874–1936), English novelist, poet, and critic

**Chikamatsu Monzaemon** (c.1653–1725), Japanese dramatist

**Chuang Tze** (fourth century B.C.), Chinese philosopher

**Churchill, Sir Winston** (1874–1965), English statesman and historian

**Cicero, Marcus Tullius** (106 B.C.–43 B.C.), Roman statesman and orator

**Claudel, Paul** (1868–     ), French poet and dramatist

**Clough, Arthur Hugh** (1819–61), English poet

**Cocteau, Jean** (1891–1963), French dramatist, novelist, and poet

**Coleridge, Samuel Taylor** (1772–1834), English poet and critic

**Colette** (1873–1954), French novelist

**Collins, Wilkie** (1824–89), English novelist

**Colum, Padraic** (1881–     ), American (Irishborn) poet, dramatist, and novelist

**Compton-Burnett, Ivy** (1892–     ), English novelist

**Congreve, William** (1670–1729), English dramatist

**Conrad, Joseph** (1857–1924), English (Polishborn) novelist and short-story writer

**Cooper, James Fenimore** (1789–1851), American novelist

**Corneille, Pierre** (1606–84), French dramatist

**Coward, Noel** (1899–     ), English playwright

**Cowley, Malcolm** (1898–     ), American poet and critic

**Cowper, William** (1731–1800), English poet

**Cozzens, James Gould** (1903–     ), American novelist

**Crabbe, George** (1754–1832), English poet

**Crane, Hart** (1899–1932), American poet

**Crane, Stephen** (1871–1900), American novelist and short-story writer

**Crashaw, Richard** (1613?–49), English poet

**cummings, e. e.** (1894–1962), American poet

**Cynewulf** (eighth century), Anglo-Saxon poet

**D'Annunzio, Gabriele** (1863–1938), Italian poet, novelist, and dramatist

**Dante Alighieri** (1265–1321), Italian poet

**Darwin, Charles** (1809–82), English essayist

**Daudet, Alphonse** (1840–97), French novelist, poet, and dramatist

**Defoe, Daniel** (1660–1731), English novelist and pamphleteer

**Dekker, Thomas** (c.1572–1632), English dramatist

**De la Mare, Walter** (1873–1956), English novelist and critic

**De la Roche, Mazo** (1885–1961), Canadian novelist and dramatist

**WILLIAM FAULKNER** (1897–1962), American novelist, poet, and short-story writer. Faulkner was the product of the environment and culture he re-created in his writing. He lived virtually his entire life in Mississippi. In his third novel, *Sartoris,* published in 1929, he turned to the theme that would occupy most of his literary attention: history's devastating effect upon the people of the old South. Faulkner often told his stories in reverse order, beginning in the present and moving back into the past, thus revealing many generations of Southern families and thought. He won the Nobel Prize for Literature in 1949, and the Pulitzer Prize in 1954. Faulkner's important works include *The Sound and the Fury* (1929), *As I Lay Dying* (1930), *Sanctuary* (1931), *Light in August* (1932), *Absalom, Absalom!* (1936), *Go Down, Moses* (1942), *Intruder in the Dust* (1948), *Requiem for a Nun* (1951), *A Fable* (1954), and *The Town* (1957).

**Demosthenes** (384 B.C.–332 B.C.), Greek orator

**De Quincey, Thomas** (1785–1859), English novelist and essayist

**Dickens, Charles** (1812–70), English novelist

**Dickey, James** (1923–     ), American poet

**Dickinson, Emily** (1830–86), American poet

**Diderot, Denis** (1713–84), French encyclopedist, novelist, and dramatist

**Dinesen, Isak** (1885–1962), Danish novelist

**Donne, John** (1572–1631), English poet and essayist

**Doolittle, Hilda, "H. D."** (1886–1961), American poet

**Dos Passos, John** (1896–     ), American novelist

**Dostoievski, Fyodor Mikhailovich** (1821–81), Russian novelist

**Doyle, Sir Arthur Conan** (1859–1930), Scottist mystery novelist

**Drayton, Michael** (1563–1631), English poet

**Dreiser, Theodore** (1871–1945), American novelist

**Drury, Alan** (1918–     ), American novelist

**Dryden, John** (1631–1700), English poet, dramatist, and critic

**Dumas, Alexandre, "père"** (1802–70), French novelist and dramatist

**Dumas, Alexandre, "fils"** (1824–95), French dramatist

**Durrell, Lawrence** (1910–     ), English novelist

**Eberhart, Richard** (1904–     ), American poet

**Echegaray y Eizaguirre, José** (1832–1916), Spanish dramatist and poet

**Ehrenburg, Ilya** (1891–1967), Russian novelist

**Eliot, George** (1819–80), English novelist

**Eliot, Thomas Stearns** (1888–1965), English poet, dramatist, and critic

**Ellis, Havelock** (1859–1939), English literary critic and essayist

**Ellison, Ralph** (1914–     ), American novelist

**Emerson, Ralph Waldo** (1803–82), American essayist and poet

*(continued)*

**WRITERS: PAST AND PRESENT** (*continued*)

**Empson, William** (1906–   ), English poet and critic

**Erasmus, Desiderius** (1466?–1536), Netherlandish theologian and philosopher

**Euripides** (c.485 B.C.–406 B.C.), Greek dramatist

**Farquhar, George** (1678–1707), English dramatist

**Farrell, James T.** (1904–   ), American novelist

**Faulkner, William** (1897–1962), American novelist (see biography on page 865)

**Feuchtwanger, Lion** (1884–1958), German novelist and dramatist

**Fielding, Henry** (1707–54), English novelist and dramatist

**FitzGerald, Edward** (1809–83), English poet and translator

**Fitzgerald, F. Scott** (1896–1940), American novelist and short-story writer

**Flaubert, Gustave** (1821–80), French novelist

**Fletcher, John** (1579–1625), English dramatist

**Ford, Ford Madox** (1873–1939), English novelist, critic, and poet

**Ford, John** (1586–1640?), English dramatist

**Forster, E. M.** (1879–   ), English novelist and critic

**France, Anatole** (1844–1924), French novelist and satirist

**Freytag, Gustav** (1816–95), German novelist and dramatist

**Froissart, Jean** (c.1338–1410), French historian and poet

**Frost, Robert** (1874–1963), American poet

**Fry, Christopher** (1907–   ), English dramatist and translator

**Galsworthy, John** (1867–1933), English novelist and dramatist

**Garland, Hamlin** (1860–1940), American novelist

---

**ERNEST HEMINGWAY** (1899–1961), American novelist and short-story writer. Born in Illinois. Hemingway was an ambulance driver during World War I. He joined the expatriate literati living in Paris during the 1920s, and, with publication of *The Sun Also Rises* in 1926, became known as spokesman of the disillusioned "lost generation." *For Whom the Bell Tolls* (1940) grew out of his experience as a correspondent in the Spanish Civil War. He also covered the Allied invasion of Europe during World War II. Hemingway lived in the United States and Cuba, and traveled extensively in Spain and Africa. After publication of *The Old Man and the Sea* in 1952, he won the Pulitzer and Nobel prizes for literature. Hemingway's other important works include the novels *A Farewell to Arms* (1929), *To Have and Have Not* (1937) and *Across the River and into the Trees* (1950); the nonfiction, *Death in the Afternoon* (1932) and *The Green Hills of Africa* (1935); numerous short stories, and a play, *The Fifth Column* (1938).

---

**Gaskell, Elizabeth** (1810–65), English novelist and biographer

**Gautier, Théophile** (1811–72), French novelist

**Gay, John** (1685–1732), English dramatist and poet

**Genêt, Jean** (1910–   ), French novelist and dramatist

**George, Stefan** (1868–1933), German poet

**Gibbon, Edward** (1737–94), English historian

**Gide, André** (1869–1951), French novelist, critic, and poet

**Giono, Jean** (1895–   ), French novelist

**Giraudoux, Jean** (1882–1944), French dramatist and novelist

**Gissing, George** (1857–1903), English novelist

**Goethe, Johann Wolfgang von** (1749–1832), German dramatist, poet, and novelist

**Gogol, Nikolai Vasilyevich** (1809–52), Russian novelist

**Golding, William** (1911–   ), English novelist

**Goldsmith, Oliver** (1728–74), Irish novelist, dramatist, and poet

**Gorki, Maxim** (1868–1936), Russian novelist, dramatist, and short-story writer

**Grahame, Kenneth** (1859–1932), Scottish fantasy writer and anthologist

**Grass, Günter** (1927–   ), German novelist

**Graves, Robert** (1895–   ), English poet, novelist, and critic

**Gray, Thomas** (1716–71), English poet

**Greene, Graham** (1904–   ), English novelist

**Gregory, Lady Augusta** (1852–1932), Irish dramatist

**Hāfiz** (c.1320–88), Persian poet

**Hamsun, Knut** (1859–1952), Norwegian novelist

**Hardy, Thomas** (1840–1928), English novelist, poet, and dramatist

**Harris, Joel Chandler** (1848–1908), American novelist and short-story writer

**Harte, Bret** (1836–1902), American novelist and short-story writer

**Hauptmann, Gerhart** (1862–1946), German dramatist and novelist

**Hawthorne, Nathaniel** (1804–64), American novelist and short-story writer

**Hazlitt, William** (1778–1830), English essayist and critic

**Hebbel, Friedrich** (1813–63), German dramatist and poet

**Heine, Heinrich** (1797–1856), German poet, essayist, and critic

**Hellman, Lillian** (1905–   ), American dramatist

**Hemingway, Ernest** (1899–1961), American novelist (see biography in adjoining column)

**Henry, O.** (1862–1910), American short-story writer

**Herbert, George** (1593–1633), English poet

**Hernández, José** (1834–86), Argentine epic poet

**Herodotus** (c.484 B.C.–425 B.C.), Greek historian

**Herrick, Robert** (1591–1674), English poet

**Hersey, John** (1914–   ), American novelist and journalist

**Hesiod** (eighth century B.C.), Greek poet

**Hesse, Hermann** (1877–1962), German novelist and poet

Heywood, Thomas (1574?–1641), English dramatist

Hoffmann, E. T. A. (1776–1822), German novelist and short-story writer

Holmes, Oliver Wendell (1809–94), American poet, novelist, and essayist

Homer (c. ninth century B.C.), Greek epic poet

Hopkins, Gerard Manley (1844–89), English poet

Horace (65 B.C.–8 B.C.), Latin poet

Housman, A. E. (1859–1936), English poet

Howells, William Dean (1837–1920), American novelist and literary critic

Hugo, Victor (1802–85), French novelist, poet, and dramatist

Huxley, Aldous (1894–1963), English novelist and essayist

Ibsen, Henrik (1828–1906), Norwegian dramatist

Inge, William (1913–    ), American dramatist

Ionesco, Eugène (1912–    ), French dramatist

Irving, Washington (1783–1859), American short-story writer, historian, and editor

Isherwood, Christopher (1904–    ), English dramatist and novelist

James, Henry (1843–1916), American novelist and short-story writer

Jeffers, Robinson (1887–1962), American poet and dramatist

Jiménez, Juan Ramón (1881–1958), Spanish poet

Johnson, Samuel (1709–84), English essayist, lexicographer, poet, and critic

Jonson, Ben (1573?–1637), English dramatist and poet

Joyce, James (1882–1941), Irish novelist, poet, and short-story writer

Juvenal (c.55–135), Roman satirical poet

Kafka, Franz (1883–1924), German novelist and short-story writer

Kazantzakis, Nikos (1883?–1957), Greek novelist

Keats, John (1795–1821), English poet

Keller, Gottfried (1819–90), Swiss novelist, poet, and short-story writer

Kingsley, Charles (1819–75), English novelist

Kipling, Rudyard (1865–1936), English poet, novelist, and short-story writer

Koestler, Arthur (1905–    ), Hungarian novelist

Kyd, Thomas (1558–94), English dramatist

La Fontaine, Jean de (1621–95), French fabulist and poet

Laforgue, Jules (1860–87), French poet

Lagerkvist, Pär (1891–    ), Swedish novelist, poet, and dramatist

Lagerlof, Selma (1858–1940), Swedish novelist

Lamartine, Alphonse (1790–1869), French poet

Lamb, Charles (1775–1834), English essayist and critic

Langland, William (c.1332–1400), English poet

Lanier, Sidney (1842–81), American poet and critic

Lardner, Ring (1885–1933), American satirist and short-story writer

La Rochefoucauld, François, Duc de (1613–80), French maximist

**HERMAN MELVILLE** (1819–91), American novelist and poet. Melville was born into a somewhat eminent New York family. However, his father went bankrupt in 1826 and died six years later, leaving his family quite poor. Melville first went to sea in 1837, as a cabin boy aboard a merchant ship bound for Liverpool. In 1841 he shipped out for the Pacific in the New Bedford whaler *Acushnet*. He returned to New York three years later, and wrote a series of popular travel romances based upon his sea experiences. Succeeding works with allegorical implications proved less popular. *Moby Dick*, now a literary landmark, was largely ignored for almost 70 years after publication in 1851. Melville served as a customs inspector in New York City between 1866 and 1885. His last work was *Billy Budd*, published in 1924.

Lawrence, D. H. (1885–1930), English novelist, poet, and essayist

Lessing, Gotthold Ephraim (1729–81), German dramatist and critic

Lewis, C. S. (1898–    ), English (Irish-born) essayist and novelist

Lewis, Cecil Day (1904–63), English poet

Lewis, Sinclair (1885–1951), American novelist

Lindsay, Vachel (1879–1931), American poet

Li Po (c.700–62), Chinese poet

Livy (59 B.C.–17 A.D.), Roman historian

London, Jack (1876–1916), American novelist and short-story writer

Longfellow, Henry Wadsworth (1807–82), American poet

Lorca, Federico García (1899–1936), Spanish poet and dramatist

Lovelace, Richard (1618–58), English poet

Lowell, James Russell (1819–91), American poet, editor, and essayist

Lowell, Robert (1917–    ), American poet and critic

Lucian (c.120–200), Greek satirist

Lucretius (98 B.C.?–55 B.C.), Roman poet

Lyly, John (1554?–1606), English dramatist

Macaulay, Thomas Babington (1800–59), English historian, essayist, and critic

Machiavelli, Niccolò (1469–1527), Italian essayist and dramatist

MacLeish, Archibald (1892–    ), American poet, dramatist, and critic

Maeterlinck, Maurice (1862–1949), Belgian dramatist and critic

Mailer, Norman (1923–    ), American novelist and essayist

Malamud, Bernard (1914–    ), American novelist

Mallarmé, Stéphane (1842–98), French poet

Malory, Sir Thomas (15th century), English Arthurian romance writer

Malraux, André (1901–    ), French novelist

Mann, Heinrich (1871–1950), German novelist

(continued)

**WRITERS: PAST AND PRESENT** (*continued*)

**Mann, Thomas** (1875–1955), German novelist, essayist, and short-story writer

**Mansfield, Katherine** (1888–1923), British short-story writer

**Markham, Edwin** (1852–1940), American poet

**Marlowe, Christopher** (1564–93), English dramatist and poet

**Martial** (c.40–104), Roman epigrammatist

**Marvell, Andrew** (1621–78), English poet

**Masefield, John** (1878–1967), English poet

**Masters, Edgar Lee** (1869–1950), American poet

**Maugham, W. Somerset** (1874–1965), English novelist, dramatist, and short-story writer

**Maupassant, Guy de** (1850–93), French novelist, dramatist, and short-story writer

**Mauriac, François** (1885–  ), French novelist

**Maurois, André** (1885–1967), French novelist, essayist, and biographer

**Melville, Herman** (1819–91), American novelist and poet (see biography on page 867)

**Menander** (c.342 B.C.–291 B.C.), Greek dramatist

**Mencken, H. L.** (1880–1956), American satirist, editor, and critic

**Meredith, George** (1828–1909), English novelist and historian

**Mérimée, Prosper** (1803–70), French novelist, dramatist, and poet

**Mill, John Stuart** (1806–73), English essayist and autobiographer

**Millay, Edna St. Vincent** (1892–1950), American poet

**Miller, Arthur** (1915–  ), American dramatist

**Miller, Henry** (1891–  ), American novelist

**Milne, A. A.** (1882–1956), English poet, dramatist, and writer of children's books

**Milton, John** (1608–74), English poet

**Molière, Jean Baptiste** (1622–73), French dramatist

**Molina, Tirsode** (1571?–1648), Spanish novelist and dramatist

**Molnar, Ferenc** (1878–1952), Hungarian dramatist and novelist

**Montaigne, Michel Eyquem de** (1533–92), French essayist

**Moore, George** (1852–1933), Irish novelist, poet, and playwright

**Moore, Marianne** (1887–  ), American poet

**Moore, Thomas** (1779–1852), Irish poet

**Moravia, Alberto** (1907–  ), Italian novelist

**More, Sir Thomas** (1478–1535), English historian and social critic

**Morley, Christopher** (1890–1957), American novelist, editor, and essayist

**Murdoch, Iris** (1919–  ), English novelist

**Musset, Alfred de** (1810–57), French poet and dramatist

**Nabokov, Vladimir** (1899–  ), Russian novelist and poet

**Nash, Thomas** (1567–1601), English satirist and dramatist

**Nerval, Gérard de** (1808–55), French poet, translator, and short-story writer

**Newman, John Henry, Cardinal** (1801–90), English novelist, essayist, and poet

**Nietzsche, Friedrich Wilhelm** (1844–1900), German philosopher

**Nievo, Ippolito** (1831–61), Italian novelist

**Norris, Frank** (1870–1902), American novelist

**O'Casey, Sean** (1884–1964), Irish dramatist

**Odets, Clifford** (1906–63), American dramatist

**O'Faoláin, Seán** (1900–  ), Irish novelist, short-story writer, and biographer

**O'Flaherty, Liam** (1896–  ), Irish novelist

**O'Hara, John** (1905–  ), American novelist and short-story writer

**Omar Khayyám** (11th century), Persian poet

**O'Neill, Eugene** (1888–1953), American dramatist

**Ortega y Gasset, José** (1883–1955), Spanish essayist and critic

**Orwell, George** (1903–50), English satirist

**Ostrovsky, Aleksandr** (1823–86), Russian dramatist

**Ovid** (43 B.C.–18 A.D.?), Latin poet

**Owen, Wilfred** (1893–1918), English poet

**Paine, Thomas** (1737–1809), American political essayist

**Parker, Dorothy** (1893–1967), American poet, short-story writer, and critic

**Pascal, Blaise** (1623–62), French philosopher

**Pater, Walter** (1839–94), English essayist and critic

**Paton, Alan Stewart** (1903–  ), South African novelist

**Peacock, Thomas Love** (1785–1866), English novelist and poet

**Pepys, Samuel** (1633–1703), English diarist

**Perse, St.-John** (1887–  ), French poet

**Petrarch, Francesco** (1304–74), Italian poet

**Petronius** (first century A.D.), Roman satirist

**Pindar** (c.518 B.C.–438 B.C.), Greek poet

**Pinero, Sir Arthur Wing** (1855–1934), English dramatist and novelist

**Pirandello, Luigi** (1867–1936), Italian dramatist

**Plato** (427 B.C.?–347 B.C.), Greek philosopher

**Plautus** (254 B.C.?–184 B.C.), Roman dramatist

**Pliny the Elder** (23–79), Roman historian

**Pliny the Younger** (c.62–113), Roman orator

**Plutarch** (c.45–125), Greek biographer and essayist

**Poe, Edgar Allan** (1809–49), American poet and short-story writer

---

**JOHN STEINBECK** (1902–  ), American novelist. Steinbeck was born in Salinas, California, studied at Stanford, and worked as a laborer in New York. His first literary success came with *Tortilla Flat*, published in 1935, followed by *In Dubious Battle* (1936), *Of Mice and Men* (1937), *The Grapes of Wrath* (1939), and *Cannery Row* (1945). He won the Pulitzer Prize in 1940, and the Nobel Prize for Literature in 1962. His writing reveals compassion for the exploited laboring classes and a somewhat skeptical view of the possibilities for reform. Other Steinbeck works include *The Wayward Bus* (1947), *East of Eden* (1952), and *The Winter of Our Discontent* (1961).

Pope, Alexander (1688–1744), English poet

Porter, Katherine Anne (1894–  ), American short-story writer and novelist

Pound, Ezra (1885–  ), American poet

Powers, J. F. (1917–  ), American novelist and short-story writer

Priestley, J. B. (1894–  ), English novelist, dramatist, and essayist

Prior, Matthew (1664–1721), English poet

Pritchett, V. S. (1900–  ), English novelist and critic

Proust, Marcel (1871–1922), French novelist

Pushkin, Aleksander Sergeyevich (1799–1837), Russian poet

Quasimodo, Salvatore (1901–  ), Italian poet

Quintilian (c.35–95), Roman rhetorician

Rabelais, François (c.1494–1553), French satirist

Racine, Jean Baptiste (1639–99), French dramatist

Ransom, John Crowe (1888–  ), American poet and critic

Reade, Charles (1814–84), English novelist and dramatist

Remarque, Erich Maria (1897–  ), German-American novelist

Richardson, Dorothy M. (1882–1957), English novelist

Richardson, Samuel (1689–1761), English novelist

Richter, Conrad (1890–  ), American novelist

Rilke, Rainer Maria (1875–1926), German poet

Rimbaud, Arthur (1854–91), French poet

Robinson, Edwin Arlington (1869–1935), American poet

Roethke, Theodore (1908–63), American poet

Rojas, Fernando de (c.1475–1541), Spanish novelist

Rolland, Romain (1866–1944), French novelist and biographer

Rölvaag, O. E. (1876–1931), Norwegian-American novelist

Ronsard, Pierre de (1524?–85), French poet

Rossetti, Christina (1830–94), English poet

Rossetti, Dante Gabriel (1828–82), English poet and translator

Rostand, Edmond (1868–1918), French dramatist and poet

Rousseau, Jean Jacques (1712–78), French philosopher, novelist, and essayist

Ruskin, John (1819–1900), English critic and essayist

Russell, George, "A. E." (1867–1935), Irish poet

Sainte-Beuve, Charles Augustin (1804–69), French critic and historian

Saint-Exupéry, Antoine de (1900–44), French novelist and essayist

Saki, (1870–1916), English short-story writer and novelist

Salinger, J. D. (1919–  ), American novelist and short-story writer

Sand, George (1804–76), French novelist and dramatist

Sandburg, Carl (1878–1967), American poet and biographer

Santayana, George (1863–1952), American poet, philosopher, and essayist

MARK TWAIN (Samuel Langhorne Clemens, 1835–1910), American writer and humorist. Mark Twain grew up in the haunts of Tom Sawyer and Huck Finn. Variously a riverboat pilot, journeyman printer, miner, lecturer, and journalist, he took his pen name from the river term for "two-fathom depth." A tall tale, *The Celebrated Jumping Frog of Calaveras County*, published in 1865, made him famous. *Innocents Abroad* (1869) confirmed his reputation as the nation's foremost humorist. Twain married in 1870, settled in Connecticut, and alternated between writing and delivering humorous lectures. In the last years of his life, bankruptcy and personal tragedy—the deaths of two of his daughters and the long illness and death of his wife—brought out a latent streak of pessimism and bitterness in his writing. Twain's important works include *The Gilded Age* (1873), *Tom Sawyer* (1876), *A Tramp Abroad* (1880), *The Prince and the Pauper* (1882), *Life on the Mississippi* (1883), *Huckleberry Finn* (1884), *A Connecticut Yankee in King Arthur's Court* (1889), and *The Tragedy of Pudd'nhead Wilson* (1894).

Sappho (early sixth century B.C.), Greek poet

Saroyan, William (1908–  ), American novelist, dramatist, and short-story writer

Sartre, Jean-Paul (1905–  ), French philosopher, novelist, and dramatist

Sassoon, Siegfried (1886–1967), English poet and memoirist

Schiller, Friedrich von (1759–1805), German dramatist, historian, and poet

Scott, Sir Walter (1771–1832), British novelist and poet

Seneca, Lucius Annaeus (34 B.C.?–65 A.D.), Roman dramatist

Shakespeare, William (1564–1616), English dramatist and poet

Shaw, George Bernard (1856–1950), British dramatist, novelist, and critic

Shelley, Mary W. Godwin (1797–1851), English novelist

Shelley, Percy Bysshe (1792–1822), English poet

Sheridan, Richard Brinsley (1751–1816), British dramatist

Sherwood, Robert E. (1896–1955), American dramatist

Sholokhov, Mikhail (1905–  ), Russian novelist

Sidney, Sir Philip (1554–86), English poet and essayist

Sienkiewicz, Henryk (1846–1916), Polish novelist

Sillanpää, Frans Eemil (1888–1964), Finnish novelist

Silone, Ignazio (1900–  ), Italian novelist

Sinclair, Upton (1878–  ), American novelist

Sitwell, Dame Edith (1887–1964), English poet and critic

(continued)

**WRITERS: PAST AND PRESENT** (*continued*)

**Smith, Lillian** (1897–1966), American novelist
**Sophocles** (c.496 B.C.–406 B.C.), Greek dramatist
**Southey, Robert** (1774–1843), English poet
**Spark, Muriel** (1918–  ), English novelist and short-story writer
**Spender, Stephen** (1909–  ), English poet, critic, and editor
**Spenser, Edmund** (1552?–99), English poet
**Steegmuller, Francis** (1906–  ), American novelist and biographer
**Steele, Sir Richard** (1672–1729), English essayist and dramatist
**Stein, Gertrude** (1874–1946), American poet, critic, and novelist
**Steinbeck, John** (1902–  ), American novelist (see biography on page 868)
**Stendhal** (1783–1842), French novelist
**Sterne, Laurence** (1713–68), British novelist
**Stevens, Wallace** (1879–1955), American poet
**Stevenson, Robert Louis** (1850–94), Scottish novelist and poet
**Stowe, Harriet Beecher** (1811–96), American novelist
**Strindberg, August** (1849–1912), Swedish dramatist and novelist
**Styron, William** (1925–  ), American novelist
**Swift, Jonathan** (1667–1745), English satirist, poet, and essayist
**Swinburne, Algernon Charles** (1837–1909), English poet and critic
**Symonds, John Addington** (1840–93), English cultural historian, critic, and translator
**Synge, John Millington** (1871–1909), Irish dramatist and poet
**Tacitus, Cornelius** (c.55–117), Roman historian
**Taine, Hippolyte** (1828–93), French critic and historian
**Tarkington, Booth** (1869–1946), American novelist
**Tate, Allen** (1899–  ), American poet and critic
**Tennyson, Alfred** (1809–92), English poet
**Thackeray, William Makepeace** (1811–63), English novelist
**Theocritus** (third century B.C.), Greek poet
**Thomas, Dylan** (1914–53), Welsh poet
**Thompson, Francis** (1859–1907), English poet
**Thoreau, Henry David** (1817–62), American essayist and poet
**Thucydides** (c.460 B.C.–400 B.C.), Greek historian
**Thurber, James** (1894–1961), American humorist, short-story writer, and cartoonist
**Tolstoy, Leo** (1828–1910), Russian novelist
**Tourneur, Cyril** (1575?–1626), English dramatist
**Toynbee, Arnold** (1889–  ), English historian
**Trilling, Lionel** (1905–  ), American critic
**Trollope, Anthony** (1815–82), English novelist
**Turgenev, Ivan** (1818–83), Russian novelist and dramatist
**Twain, Mark** (1835–1910), American writer (see biography on page 869)
**Undset, Sigrid** (1882–1949), Danish novelist
**Updike, John** (1932–  ), American novelist, poet, and short-story writer

**Valéry, Paul** (1871–1945), French poet and critic
**Van Doren, Mark** (1894–  ), American poet and critic
**Vega, Lope de** (1562–1635), Spanish dramatist
**Verne, Jules** (1828–1905), French novelist
**Vigny, Alfred de** (1797–1863), French novelist, poet, and dramatist
**Villon, François** (c.1431–63), French poet
**Virgil** (70 B.C.–19 B.C.), Roman poet
**Voltaire, François Marie Arouet de** (1694–1778), French novelist, dramatist, critic, and poet
**Walpole, Horace** (1717–97), English novelist
**Walton, Izaak** (1593–1683), English biographer and essayist
**Warren, Robert Penn** (1905–  ), American novelist, poet, editor, and biographer
**Wassermann, Jakob** (1873–1934), Austrian novelist and biographer
**Waugh, Evelyn** (1903–66), English novelist and satirist
**Webster, John** (c.1580–1625), English dramatist
**Webster, Noah** (1758–1843), American lexicographer
**Wells, H. G.** (1866–1946), English novelist, essayist, and historian
**Welty, Eudora** (1909–  ), American novelist and short-story writer
**Werfel, Franz** (1890–1945), Austrian novelist, dramatist, and poet
**West, Nathanael** (1902–40), American novelist
**West, Rebecca** (1892–  ), English novelist and journalist
**Wharton, Edith** (1862–1937), American novelist and short-story writer
**Whitman, Walt** (1819–92), American poet
**Whittier, John Greenleaf** (1807–92), American poet
**Wilde, Oscar** (1854–1900), British dramatist, novelist, poet, and essayist
**Wilder, Thornton** (1897–  ), American novelist and dramatist
**Williams, Tennessee** (1914–  ), American dramatist
**Williams, William Carlos** (1883–1963), American poet and novelist
**Wolfe, Thomas** (1900–38), American novelist
**Wolfram von Eschenbach** (c.1170–1220), German epic poet
**Woolf, Virginia** (1882–1941), English novelist and essayist
**Wordsworth, William** (1770–1850), English poet
**Wright, Richard** (1908–60), American novelist
**Wyatt, Sir Thomas** (1503?–42), English poet
**Wylie, Elinor** (1885–1928), American novelist and poet
**Xenophon** (c.430 B.C.–354 B.C.), Greek historian
**Yeats, William Butler** (1865–1939), Irish poet, dramatist, and essayist
**Yevtushenko, Yevgeny** (1933–  ), Russian poet
**Zola, Émile** (1840–1902), French novelist and critic

# CELEBRITIES OF ENTERTAINMENT

Abbott, Bud (1895– ), comedian
Abbott, George (1887– ), theatrical producer
Adams, Edie (1927– ), singer
Adams, Maude (1872–1953), actress
Addams, Charles (1912– ), cartoonist
Adler, Larry (1914– ), musician
Adler, Stella (c.1918– ), actress and teacher
Albert, Eddie (1908– ), actor
Alda, Allen (1931– ), actor
Allen, Fred (1895–1956), actor and comedian
Allen, Gracie (1906–64), comedienne
Allen, Steve (1921– ), entertainer
Allen, Woody (1935– ), actor, comedian, and writer
Allyson, June (1923– ), actress
Alpert, Herb (1937– ), musician
Ameche, Don (1908– ), actor
Amsterdam, Morey (1912– ), actor and comedian
Anderson, Eddie "Rochester" (1905– ), actor
Anderson, Dame Judith (1898– ), actress
Andress, Ursula (1936– ), actress
Andrews, Dana (1912– ), actor
Andrews, Julie (1935– ), actress and singer
Andrews, LaVerne (1915– ), singer
Andrews, Maxine (1918– ), singer
Andrews, Patti (1920– ), singer
Anka, Paul (1941– ), singer
Ann-Margret (1941– ), actress
Arden, Eve (1912– ), actress
Arlen, Richard (1900– ), actor
Arliss, George (1868–1946), actor
Armstrong, Louis (1900– ), musician
Arnaz, Desi (1917– ), actor and producer
Arness, James (1923– ), actor
Arno, Peter (1904– ), cartoonist
Arquette, Cliff (1905– ), comedian
Arthur, Jean (1908– ), actress
Ashley, Elizabeth (1940– ), actress
Astaire, Fred (1899– ), dancer
Astor, Mary (1906– ), actress
Attenborough, Richard (1924– ), actor
Autry, Gene (1907– ), singer
Avalon, Frankie (1940– ), singer
Ayres, Lew (1908– ), actor
Bacall, Lauren (1924– ), actress
Backus, Jim (1913– ), actor
Baez, Joan (1941– ), folk singer
Bailey, Pearl (1918– ), singer
Baker, Carroll (1935– ), actress
Baker, Josephine (1906– ), singer
Ball, Lucille (1911– ), comedienne
Ballard, Kaye (1926– ), actress and comedienne
Balsam, Martin (1919– ), actor
Bancroft, Anne (1931– ), actress
Bankhead, Tallulah (1903– ), actress
Bara, Theda (1890–1955), actress
Bardot, Brigitte (1934– ), actress
Barnum, Phineas T. (1819–91), showman
Barry, Gene (1922– ), actor
Barrymore, Ethel (1879–1959), actress
Barrymore, John (1882–1942), actor
Barrymore, Lionel (1878–1954), actor
Barthelmess, Richard (1895–1963), actor
Barton, James (1890–1963), actor

The singing group, The Mamas and the Papas

Basehart, Richard (1919– ), actor
Basie, Count (1904– ), musician
Baxter, Anne (1923– ), actress
Bean, Orson (1928– ), actor and comedian
Beaton, Cecil (1904– ), photographer and designer
Beatty, Warren (1937– ), actor
Bechet, Sidney (1897–1959), musician
Beery, Noah (1884–1946), actor
Beery, Noah, Jr. (1916– ), actor
Beery, Wallace (1889–1949), actor
Begley, Ed (1901– ), actor
Belafonte, Harry (1927– ), singer
Belasco, David (1854–1931), impresario
Bel Geddes, Barbara (1922– ), actress
Bel Geddes, Norman (1900–58), scenic designer, actor, and producer
Bellamy, Ralph (1904– ), actor
Belmondo, Jean Paul (1933– ), actor
Bendix, William (1906–64), actor
Bennett, Constance (1908–65), actress
Bennett, Joan (1910– ), actress
Bennett, Tony (1926– ), singer
Benny, Jack (1894– ), comedian
Berg, Gertrude (1899–1966), actress
Bergen, Candice (1946– ), actress
Bergen, Edgar (1903– ), ventriloquist
Bergen, Polly (1930– ), singer
Bergman, Ingmar (1917– ), film director
Bergman, Ingrid (1917– ), actress
Berle, Milton (1908– ), comedian

(continued)

**CELEBRITIES OF ENTERTAINMENT** (*continued*)

Berman, Shelley (1926– ), comedian
Bernardi, Herschel (1923– ), actor
Bernhardt, Sarah (1845–1923), tragedienne
Bernie, Ben (1893–1943), comedian
Bickford, Charles (1889–1967), actor
Bikel, Theodore (1924– ), actor, musician, and singer
Bishop, Joey (1931– ), comedian
Blackman, Honor (1926– ), actress
Blaine, Vivian (1923– ), singer and actress
Block, Herbert L. "Herblock" (1909– ), cartoonist
Blondell, Joan (1913– ), actress
Bloom, Claire (1931– ), actress
Bloomgarden, Kermit (1904– ), theatrical producer
Blue, Ben (1901– ), comedian
Blue, Monte (1889–1963), actor
Blythe, Anne (1928– ), actress
Bogarde, Dirk (1921– ), actor
Bogart, Humphrey (1899–1957), actor
Boland, Mary (1885–1965), actress
Bolger, Ray (1906– ), dancer and actor
Boone, Pat (1934– ), singer
Boone, Richard (1916– ), actor
Booth, Edwin (1833–93), actor
Booth, Shirley (1907– ), actress
Borge, Victor (1909– ), pianist and comedian
Borgnine, Ernest (1918– ), actor
Bow, Clara (1905–65), actress
Boyd, Stephen (1928– ), actor
Boyd, William (1898– ), actor
Boyer, Charles (1899– ), actor
Bracken, Eddie (1920– ), comedian
Brando, Marlon (1924– ), actor
Brazzi, Rossano (1916– ), actor
Brennan, Walter (1894– ), actor
Brewer, Theresa (1931– ), singer
Brice, Fanny (1891–1951), actress and singer
Bridges, Lloyd (1913– ), actor
Brinkley, David (1920– ), newscaster
Brisson, Frederick (1917– ), producer
Brown, Joe E. (1892– ), comedian
Brubeck, Dave (1920– ), musician
Brynner, Yul (1917– ), actor
Burke, Billie (1885– ), actress
Burnett, Carol (1935– ), comedienne
Burns, George (1896– ), comedian
Burr, Raymond (1917– ), actor
Burrows, Abe (1910– ), playwright and director
Burton, Richard (1925– ), actor
Bushman, Francis X. (1883–1966), actor
Buttons, Red (1919– ), actor and comedian
Byington, Spring (1898– ), actress
Caesar, Sid (1922– ), comedian
Cagney, James (1904– ), actor
Cahn, Sammy (1913– ), composer
Caine, Michael (1933– ), actor
Calhern, Louis (1895–1956), actor
Calloway, Cab (1907– ), musician
Campbell, Mrs. Patrick (1865–1940), actress
Canova, Judy (1916– ), actress
Cantor, Eddie (1892–1964), comedian
Capp, Al (1909– ), comic-strip artist
Capra, Frank (1897– ), film producer
Cardinale, Claudia (1939– ), actress
Carlisle, Kitty (1915– ), television personality

Carney, Art (1918– ), actor
Carnovsky, Morris (1898– ), actor
Caron, Leslie (1932– ), actress
Carradine, John (1906– ), actor
Carroll, Diahann (1935– ), singer
Carroll, Earl (1893–1948), theatrical producer
Carroll, Madeleine (1909– ), actress
Carson, Johnny (1925– ), television entertainer
Cass, Peggy (1926– ), actress and comedienne
Cerf, Bennett (1898– ), publisher and television panelist
Chamberlain, Richard (1935– ), actor
Champion, Gower (1926– ), dancer and theatrical director
Champion, Marge (1926– ), dancer
Chandler, Jeff (1918–1961), actor
Chaney, Lon (1883–1930), actor
Channing, Carol (1922– ), actress
Chaplin, Charles (1889– ), actor
Chaplin, Geraldine (1944– ), actress
Chaplin, Sydney (1926– ), actor
Charisse, Cyd (1923– ), actress and dancer
Charles, Ray (1932– ), musician
Chatterton, Ruth (1893–1961), actress
Chevalier, Maurice (1888– ), singer and entertainer
Christopher, Jordan (1941– ), actor and musician
Christy, Edwin P. (1815–62), showman and minstrel
Christie, Julie (1941– ), actress
Christy, June (1925– ), singer
Clair, René (1898– ), film director
Claire, Ina (1892– ), actress
Clark, Petula (1932– ), singer and actress
Clift, Montgomery (1920–66), actor
Clooney, Rosemary (1928– ), singer
Cobb, Lee J. (1911– ), actor
Coburn, Charles (1877–1961), actor
Coburn, James (1929– ), actor
Coca, Imogene (1920– ), comedienne
Cohan, George M. (1878–1942), musician, composer, and showman
Colbert, Claudette (1907– ), actress
Cole, Nat King (1919–65), singer
Collins, Joan (1933– ), actress
Collyer, Bud (1908– ) actor and television entertainer
Colman, Ronald (1891–1958), actor
Colonna, Jerry (1903– ), comedian
Coltrane, John (1926–67), musician
Columbo, Russ (1908–34), singer
Comden, Betty (1919– ), writer and performer
Como, Perry (1911– ), singer
Condon, Eddie (1905– ), musician
Connery, Sean (1930– ), actor
Connors, Chuck (1924– ), actor
Conreid, Hans (1917– ), actor
Coogan, Jackie (1914– ), actor
Cooper, Gary (1901–61), actor
Cooper, Gladys (1888– ), actress
Cooper, Jackie (1922– ), actor
Corey, Wendell (1914– ), actor
Cornell, Katharine (1898– ), actress
Correll, Charles "Andy" (1890– ), actor
Cosby, Bill (1938– ), actor and comedian
Costello, Lou (1906–59), comedian

Cotten, Joseph (1905–  ), actor
Coward, Noel (1899–  ), playwright, actor, and producer
Craven, Frank (1875–1945), actor
Crawford, Broderick (1911–  ), actor
Crawford, Joan (1908–  ), actress
Crenna, Richard (1927–  ), actor
Cronkite, Walter (1916–  ), radio and television newscaster
Cronyn, Hume (1911–  ), actor
Crosby, Bing (1904–  ), singer
Crosby, Bob (1903–  ), musician
Cugat, Xavier (1900–  ), musician
Cukor, George (1899–  ), director
Culp, Robert (1931–  ), actor
Cummings, Robert (1910–  ), actor
Curtis, Tony (1925–  ), actor
Curtiz, Michael (1890–1962), director
Dahl, Arlene (1927–  ), actress
Daly, John (1914–  ), television entertainer and newscaster
Damone, Vic (1928–  ), singer
Darin, Bobby (1937–  ), singer
Darnell, Linda (1921–65), actress
Darrieux, Danielle (1917–  ), actress
Da Silva, Howard (1909–  ), actor
Dassin, Jules (1911–  ), director, actor, and writer
Davies, Marion (1900?–61), actress
Davis, Bette (1908–  ), actress
Davis, Joan (1912–61), comedienne
Davis, Miles (1926–  ), musician
Davis, Ossie (1921–  ), playwright and actor
Davis, Sammy, Jr. (1925–  ), actor
Davis, Skeeter (1931–  ), singer
Day, Dennis (1917–  ), singer
Day, Doris (1924–  ), actress
Day, Laraine (1920–  ), actress
Dean, James (1931–55), actor
Dean, Jimmy (1928–  ), singer and entertainer
de Havilland, Olivia (1916–  ), actress
De Laurentiis, Dino (1919–  ), producer
Del Rio, Dolores (1905–  ), actress
Demarest, William (1892–  ), actor
De Mille, Cecil B. (1881–1959), director
Dennis, Sandy (1937–  ), actress
De Sica, Vittorio (1902–  ), actor and director
deWilde, Brandon (1942–  ), actor
Dickinson, Angie (1932–  ), actress
Dietrich, Marlene (1904–  ), actress
Diller, Phyllis (1917–  ), comedienne
Dillman, Bradford (1930–  ), actor
Disney, Walt (1901–66), producer and showman
Domino, Fats (1928–  ), musician and composer
Donat, Robert (1905–58), actor
Donlevy, Brian (1903–  ), actor
Dors, Diana (1931–  ), actress
Dorsey, Jimmy (1904–57), musician
Dorsey, Tommy (1905–56), musician
Douglas, Kirk (1916–  ), actor
Douglas, Melvyn (1901–  ), actor
Drake, Alfred (1914–  ), singer and actor
Dressler, Marie (1869–1934), actress
Duchin, Eddy (1905–51), musician
Duchin, Peter (1937–  ), musician
Dunaway, Faye (1942–  ), actress
Duncan, Isadora (1877–1927), dancer

Dunne, Irene (1904–  ), actress
Dunnock, Mildred (1904–  ), actress
Durante, Jimmy (1893–  ), comedian
Durbin, Deanna (1922–  ), actress
Duryea, Dan (1907–  ), actor
Dylan, Bob (1941–  ), folk singer
Eagels, Jeanne (1894–1929), actress
Eckstine, Billy (1914–  ), singer
Eddy, Nelson (1901–67), singer
Edwards, Ralph (1913–  ), entertainer
Edwards, Vince (1928–  ), actor
Eisenstein, Sergei (1898–1948), director
Eldridge, Florence (1901–  ), actress
Ellington, Duke (1899–  ), musician and composer
Evans, Dale (1912–  ), singer and actress
Evans, Dame Edith (1888–  ), actress
Evans, Maurice (1901–  ), actor
Evelyn, Judith (1913–67), actress
Ewell, Tom (1909–  ), actor
Fabian (1943–  ), singer
Fabray, Nanette (1920–  ), actress
Fairbanks, Douglas (1883–1939), actor
Fairbanks, Douglas, Jr. (1909–  ), actor
Falk, Peter (1927–  ), actor
Farrow, Mia (1945–  ), actress
Fay, Frank (1897–1960), actor
Faye, Alice (1915–  ), singer
Feiffer, Jules (1929–  ), cartoonist
Fellini, Federico (1920–  ), writer and director
Fernandel (1903–  ), comedian
Ferrer, José (1912–  ), actor and director
Ferrer, Mel (1917–  ), actor
Fetchit, Stepin (1902–  ), comedian
Field, Betty (1913–  ), actress
Fields, Gracie (1898–  ), singer and comedienne
Fields, Lew (1867–1941), vaudeville comedian
Fields, W. C. (1879–1946), comedian
Finney, Albert (1936–  ), actor
Fisher, Eddie (1928–  ), singer
Fitzgerald, Barry (1888–1961), actor
Fitzgerald, Ella (1918–  ), singer
Fitzgerald, Geraldine (1912–  ), actress
Flaherty, Robert (1884–1951), producer
Fleming, Rhonda (1922–  ), actress
Flippen, Jay C. (1898–  ), actor
Flynn, Errol (1909–59), actor
Fonda, Henry (1905–  ), actor
Fonda, Jane (1937–  ), actress
Fonda, Peter (1939–  ), actor
Fontaine, Frank (1920–  ), singer and comedian
Fontaine, Joan (1917–  ), actress
Fontanne, Lynn (1887?–  ), actress
Ford, Glenn (1916–  ), actor
Ford, John (1895–  ), director
Ford, Tennessee Ernie (1919–  ), singer
Forrest, Edwin (1806–72), actor
Forsythe, John (1918–  ), actor
Foster, Preston (1904–  ), actor
Foy, Eddie, Jr. (1905–  ), actor and dancer
Franciosa, Anthony (1928–  ), actor
Francis, Arlene (1908–  ), actress
Francis, Connie (1938–  ), singer
Freeman, Bud (1906–  ), musician
Frohmann, Charles (1860–1915), theatrical producer  (continued)

CELEBRITIES OF ENTERTAINMENT (continued)

Froman, Jane (1911–  ), singer and actress
Gabel, Martin (1912–  ), actor and producer
Gabin, Jean (1904–  ), actor
Gable, Clark (1901–60), actor
Gabor, Eva (1926–  ), actress
Gabor, Zsa Zsa (1923–  ), actress
Gam, Rita (1928–  ), actress
Garbo, Greta (1905–  ), actress
Gardner, Ava (1922–  ), actress
Garfield, John (1913–52), actor
Garland, Judy (1923–  ), singer
Garner, Erroll (1923–  ), musician
Garner, James (1928–  ), actor
Garroway, Dave (1913–  ), entertainer
Garson, Greer (1908–  ), actress
Gary, John (1932–  ), singer
Gassman, Vittorio (1922–  ), actor
Gaxton, William (1893–1963), actor
Gaynor, Janet (1906–  ), actress
Gaynor, Mitzi (1930–  ), actress and singer
Gazzara, Ben (1930–  ), actor
Gershwin, Ira (1896–  ), lyricist
Gielgud, Sir John (1904–  ), actor
Gilbert, Billy (1894–  ), actor and musician
Gilbert, John (1897–1936), actor
Gillespie, Dizzy (1917–  ), musician
Gingold, Hermione (1897–  ), actress and co-medienne
Gish, Dorothy (1898–  ), actress
Gish, Lillian (1899–  ), actress
Gleason, Jackie (1916–  ), musician and co-median
Gobel, George (1920–  ), comedian
Godard, Jean-Luc (1930–  ), director
Goddard, Paulette (1911–  ), actress
Godfrey, Arthur (1903–  ), entertainer
Goldberg, Rube (1883–  ), cartoonist
Goldwyn, Sam (1882–  ), director and pro-ducer
Goodman, Benny (1909–  ), musician
Gordon, Ruth (1896–  ), actress
Gormé, Eydie (1935–  ), singer
Gosden, Freeman "Amos" (1899–  ), actor
Gould, Chester (1900–  ), comic-strip artist
Goulet, Robert (1933–  ), singer
Grable, Betty (1916–  ), actress
Granger, Farley (1925–  ), actor
Granger, Stewart (1913–  ), actor
Grant, Cary (1904–  ), actor
Gray, Dolores (1924–  ), singer and actress
Green, Adolph (1915–  ), actor and lyricist
Greenstreet, Sidney (1879–1954), actor
Greenwood, Joan (1921–  ), actress and di-rector
Gregory, Dick (1932–  ), comedian
Grenfell, Joyce (1910–  ), actress
Grey, Joel (1932–  ), actor
Griffin, Merv (1925–  ), television entertainer
Griffith, Andy (1926–  ), actor
Griffith, David W. (1874–1948), director
Grimes, Tammy (1934–  ), actress
Grizzard, George (1928–  ), actor
Guinness, Sir Alec (1914–  ), actor
Guitry, Sacha (1885–1957), actor and singer
Guthrie, Sir Tyrone (1900–  ), actor and di-rector
Hackett, Buddy (1924–  ), comedian
Hagen, Uta (1919–  ), actress

Hamilton, George (1939–  ), actor
Hammerstein, Oscar, II (1895–1960), com-poser
Hampden, Walter (1879–1955), actor
Hampton, Lionel (1914–  ), musician
Handy, W. C. (1873–1958), composer
Harbach, Otto (1873–1958), librettist and lyr-icist
Harding, Anne (1904–  ), actress
Hardwicke, Sir Cedric (1893–1964), actor
Hardy, Oliver (1892–1957), comedian
Harlow, Jean (1911–37), actress
Harris, Barbara (1937–  ), actress
Harris, Julie (1925–  ), actress
Harris, Phil (1906–  ), actor
Harris, Richard (1933–  ), actor
Harris, Rosemary (1930–  ), actress
Harrison, George (1943–  ), singer and musi-cian
Harrison, Noel (1934–  ), actor
Harrison, Rex (1908–  ), actor
Hart, Lorenz (1895–1943), lyricist
Hart, William S. (1870–1946), actor
Hartman, Elizabeth (1941–  ), actress
Harvey, Laurence (1928–  ), actor
Harewood, Earl of (1923–  ), impresario
Hasso, Signe (1910–  ), actress
Haver, June (1926–  ), actress
Havoc, June (1916–  ), actress
Hawkins, Jack (1910–  ), actor
Haworth, Jill (1946–  ), actress
Hayakawa, Sessue (1890–  ), actor
Hayden, Sterling (1916–  ), actor
Hayes, Helen (1901–  ), actress
Hayward, Leland (1902–  ), producer
Hayward, Susan (1919–  ), actress
Heckart, Eileen (1919–  ), actress
Heflin, Van (1910–  ), actor
Henderson, Skitch (1918–  ), musician
Henreid, Paul (1908–  ), actor
Hepburn, Audrey (1929–  ), actress
Hepburn, Katherine (1909–  ), actress
Herbert, Victor (1859–1924), composer
Herman, Woody (1913–  ), musician
Hersholt, Jean (1886–1956), actor
Heston, Charlton (1924–  ), actor
Hildegarde (1906–  ), singer
Hiller, Wendy (1912–  ), actress
Hines, Mimi (1933–  ), actress and singer
Hirschfeld, Al (1903–  ), cartoonist
Hirt, Al (1922–  ), musician
Hitchcock, Alfred (1899–  ), director
Hodiak, John (1914–55), actor
Holden, William (1918–  ), actor
Holiday, Billie (1915–59), singer
Holliday, Judy (1923–65), actress
Holloway, Stanley (1890–  ), actor
Holm, Celeste (1919–  ), actress
Homolka, Oscar (1901–  ), actor
Hope, Bob (1904–  ), comedian
Hopkins, Miriam (1902–  ), actress
Hopper, Hedda (1890–1966), columnist
Horne, Lena (1918–  ), singer
Horton, Edward Everett (1888–  ), actor
Houdini, Harry (1874–1926), magician
Howard, Joe (1878?–1961), vaudevillian
Howard, Leslie (1893–1943), actor
Howard, Sidney Coe (1891–1939), dramatist
Howard, Trevor (1916–  ), actor

Hudson, Rock (1925– ), actor
Hunter, Kim (1922– ), actress
Huntley, Chet (1911– ), newscaster
Hurok, Sol (1888– ), impresario
Huston, John (1906– ), writer and director
Huston, Walter (1884–1950), actor
Hutton, Betty (1921– ), actress
Ives, Burl (1909– ), singer
Jackson, Anne (1926– ), actress
Jackson, Mahalia (1911– ), singer
James, Harry (1916– ), musician
Janssen, David (1930– ), actor
Jeanmaire, Renée (1925– ), dancer
Jens, Salome (1935– ), actress
Jessel, George E. (1898– ), entertainer
Johns, Glynis (1923– ), actress
Johnson, Chic (1892–1962), comedian
Johnson, Van (1916– ), actor
Jolson, Al (1880–1950), singer
Jones, Buck (1889–1942), actor
Jones, Carolyn (1933– ), singer
Jones, Jennifer (1919– ), actress
Jones, Spike (1911–65), musician and comedian
Jory, Victor (1902– ), actor
Jourdan, Louis (1920– ), actor
Karloff, Boris (1885– ), actor
Kaye, Danny (1913– ), dancer, singer, and actor
Kaye, Sammy (1910– ), musician
Kayser, Kay (1905– ), musician
Kazan, Elia (1909– ), director
Keaton, Buster (1895–1966), comedian
Kedrova, Lila (1918– ), actress
Keel, Howard (1919– ), actor and singer
Kelley, Walt (1913– ), cartoonist
Kelly, Emmett (1898– ), clown
Kelly, Gene (1912– ), dancer and actor
Kelly, Grace (1930– ), actress
Kennedy, Arthur (1914– ), actor
Kenton, Stan (1912– ), musician
Kern, Jerome (1885–1945), composer
Kerr, Deborah (1921– ), actress
Kerr, Walter (1913– ), drama critic
Ketcham, Hank (1920– ), cartoonist
Kiley, Richard (1922– ), actor and singer
King, Alan (1927– ), comedian
King, Dennis (1897– ), actor
King, Frank O. (1883– ), cartoonist
Knotts, Don (1924– ), actor
Kovacs, Ernie (1919–62), actor
Kramer, Stanley (1913– ), director
Ladd, Alan (1913–64), actor
Lahr, Bert (1895– ), comedian
Laine, Frankie (1913– ), singer
Lamarr, Hedy (1915– ), actress
Lamour, Dorothy (1914– ), actress
Lancaster, Burt (1913– ), actor
Lanchester, Elsa (1902– ), actress
Landis, Jessie Royce (1904– ), actress
Lang, Fritz (1890– ), director
Lang, Otto (1908– ), producer and director
Lang, Walter (1898– ), director
Langford, Frances (1913– ), singer
Langtry, Lily (1856–1929), actress
Lansbury, Angela (1925– ), actress
Lasky, Jesse L. (1881–1958), producer
Lauder, Sir Harry (1870–1950), comedian and singer

Laughton, Charles (1889–1962), actor
Laurel, Stan (1890–1965), comedian
Lawford, Peter (1923– ), actor
Lawrence, Carol (1935– ), dancer
Lawrence, Gertrude (1898–1952), actress and singer
Lawrence, Steve (1935– ), singer
Lean, David (1908– ), director
Ledbetter, Huddie "Lead Belly" (1888–1949), folk singer
Lee, Gypsy Rose (1914– ), ecdysiast
Lee, Peggy (1920– ), singer
Le Gallienne, Eva (1899– ), actress
Leigh, Janet (1927– ), actress
Leigh, Vivien (1913–67), actress
Leighton, Margaret (1922– ), actress
Lemmon, Jack (1925– ), actor
Lennon, John (1940– ), singer and musician
Lenya, Lotte (1905– ), singer
Leonard, Sheldon (1907– ), actor, director, and producer
Lerner, Alan Jay (1918– ), librettist and lyricist
LeRoy, Mervyn (1900– ), actor and director
Levant, Oscar (1906– ), musician and comedian
Levene, Sam (1907– ), actor
Levine, Joseph E. (1905– ), producer
Lewis, Jerry (1926– ), comedian
Lewis, Ted (1891– ), musician and vaudevillian
Liberace (1920– ), pianist
Lillie, Beatrice (1898– ), comedienne
Lindfors, Viveca (1920– ), actress
Lindsay, Howard (1889– ), playwright
Linkletter, Art (1912– ), entertainer
Lisi, Virna (1937– ), actress
Livingston, Jay (1915– ), composer
Livingstone, Mary (1909– ), actress
Lloyd, Harold (1893– ), comedian
Lockhart, Gene (1891–1957), actor
Lockhart, June (1925– ), actress
Lockwood, Margaret (1916– ), actress
Loesser, Frank (1910– ), composer
Loewe, Frederick (1904– ), composer
Logan, Joshua (1908– ), writer, director, and producer
Lollobrigida, Gina (1928– ), actress
Lombard, Carole (1909–42), actress
Lombardo, Guy (1902– ), musician
London, Julie (1927– ), singer and actress
Loos, Anita (1893– ), writer
Loren, Sophia (1934– ), actress
Lorre, Peter (1904–64), actor
Louise, Anita (1917– ), actress
Lovejoy, Frank (1912?–62), actor
Low, David (1891–1963), cartoonist
Loy, Myrna (1905– ), actress
Lubitsch, Ernst (1892–1947), producer and director
Lugosi, Bela (1886–1956), actor
Lukas, Paul (1895– ), actor
Lumet, Sidney (1924– ), director
Lundigan, William (1914– ), actor
Lunt, Alfred (1896– ), actor
Lupino, Ida (1918– ), actress and director
Lynn, Jeffrey (1909– ), actor
MacArthur, James (1937– ), actor

*(continued)*

**CELEBRITIES OF ENTERTAINMENT** (*continued*)

MacDonald, Jeanette (1907–65), singer
MacLaine, Shirley (1934–    ), actress
MacMurray, Fred (1908–    ), actor
MacRae, Gordon (1921–    ), singer
Madden, Donald (1933–    ), actor
Magnani, Anna (1909–    ), actress
Makeba, Miriam (1932–    ), singer
Malden, Karl (1924–    ), actor
Malone, Dorothy (1925–    ), actress
Mamoulian, Rouben (1897–    ), director
Mancini, Henry (1924–    ), musician and composer
Marceau, Marcel (1923–    ), pantomimist
March, Fredric (1897–    ), actor
Marshall, E. G. (1910–    ), actor
Marshall, Herbert (1890–1966), actor
Martin, Dean (1917–    ), singer
Martin, Mary (1913–    ), singer and actress
Martin, Tony (1912–    ), singer
Marvin, Lee (1924–    ), actor
Marx, Chico (1891–1961), comedian
Marx, Groucho (1895–    ), comedian
Marx, Harpo (1893–1964), comedian
Marx, Zeppo (1901–    ), comedian
Mason, James (1909–    ), actor
Massey, Raymond (1896–    ), actor
Mastroianni, Marcello (1924–    ), actor
Mathis, Johnny (1935–    ), singer
Matthau, Walter (1920–    ), actor
Mature, Victor (1916–    ), actor
Mauldin, Bill (1921–    ), cartoonist
May, Elaine (1932–    ), comedienne and playwright
Mayer, Louis B. (1885–1956), producer
Mayo, Virginia (1920–    ), actress
Maxwell, Marilyn (1922–    ), actress
McBride, Mary Margaret (1899–    ), radio personality
McCallum, David (1933–    ), actor
McCambridge, Mercedes (1918–    ), actress
McCartney, Paul (1942–    ), singer and musician
McClintic, Guthrie (1893–1961), producer and director
McCormick, Myron (1907–62), actor
McCoy, Tim (1891–    ), actor
McCrea, Joel (1905–    ), actor
McCutcheon, John T. (1870–1949), cartoonist
McDowall, Roddy (1928–    ), actor
McGavin, Darren (1925–    ), actor
McGee, Fibber (1896–    ), comedian
McGee, Molly (1898–1961), comedienne
McGuire, Dorothy (1919–    ), actress
McHugh, Frank (1899–    ), actor
McKenna, Siobhan (1923–    ), actress
McLaglen, Victor (1866–1959), actor
McMahon, Ed (1923–    ), actor
McQueen, Steve (1932–    ), actor
Meadows, Audrey (1929–    ), actress
Meadows, Jayne (1926–    ), actress
Meilziner, Jo (1901–    ), scenic designer
Menjou, Adolphe (1890–1963), actor
Menken, Helen (1901–66), actress
Mercer, Johnny (1909–    ), composer
Mercouri, Melina (1915–    ), actress
Meredith, Burgess (1909–    ), actor
Merkel, Una (1903–    ), actress
Merman, Ethel (1909–    ), singer and actress

Merrick, David (1911–    ), producer
Miles, Sarah (1941–    ), actress
Miles, Vera (1929–    ), actress
Milland, Ray (1908–    ), actor
Miller, Ann (1919–    ), dancer
Miller, Gilbert (1884–    ), producer
Miller, Glenn (1909–44), musician
Miller, Mitch (1911–    ), musician
Mills, Hayley (1946–    ), actress
Mills, John (1908–    ), actor
Minelli, Liza (1945–    ), singer
Mitchell, Cameron (1918–    ), actor
Mitchell, Thomas (1892–1962), actor
Mitchum, Robert (1917–    ), actor
Mix, Tom (1880–1944), actor
Monk, Thelonious (1918–    ), musician
Monroe, Marilyn (1926–62), actress
Monroe, Vaughan (1911–    ), musician
Montalban, Ricardo (1920–    ), actor
Montand, Yves (1921–    ), singer and actor
Montgomery, Elizabeth (1933–    ), actress
Montgomery, Robert (1904–    ), actor
Moore, Garry (1915–    ), radio and television entertainer
Moore, Mary Tyler (1937–    ), actress
Moore, Victor (1876–1962), actor
Moorhead, Agnes (1906–    ), actress
Moreau, Jeanne (1928–    ), actress
Moreno, Rita (1931–    ), actress
Morgan, Helen (1900–41), actress
Morgan, Henry (1915–    ), comedian
Morgan, Jane (1916–    ), singer
Morley, Robert (1908–    ), actor
Morton, Jelly Roll (1885–1941), musician
Mostel, Zero (1915–    ), actor
Muni, Paul (1897–1967), actor
Murray, Arthur (1895–    ), dancer
Murray, Kathryn (1906–    ), dancer
Naish, J. Carrol (1900–    ), actor
Nast, Thomas (1840–1902), cartoonist
Navarro, Ramon (1905–    ), actor
Negri, Pola (1899–    ), actress
Negulesco, Jean (1900–    ), director
Nelson, Barry (1925–    ), actor
Nelson, David (1936–    ), actor
Nelson, Ozzie (1906–    ), actor, musician, and comedian
Nelson, Ricky (1940–    ), actor and singer
Nesbitt, Cathleen (1888–    ), actress
Newhart, Bob (1929–    ), comedian
Newley, Anthony (1931–    ), actor, composer, and writer
Newman, Paul (1925–    ), actor
Nichols, Mike (1931–    ), comedian and director
Nichols, Red (1905–65), musician
Niven, David (1911–    ), actor
Nolan, Lloyd (1903–    ), actor
North, John Ringling (1903–    ), showman
Novak, Kim (1933–    ), actress
Nugent, Elliott (1900–    ), director and writer
Oakie, Jack (1903–    ), comedian
Oberon, Merle (1911–    ), actress
O'Brian, Hugh (1928–    ), actor
O'Brien, Edward (1925–    ), actor
O'Brien, Margaret (1937–    ), actress
O'Brien, Pat (1899–    ), actor
O'Connor, Donald (1925–    ), actor and dancer

Odetta (1930–   ), folk singer and actress
O'Hara, Maureen (1921–   ), actress
Olivier, Sir Laurence (1907–   ), actor
Olsen, Ole (1892–1963), vaudeville producer and comedian
O'Sullivan, Maureen (1911–   ), actress
O'Toole, Peter (1934–   ), actor
Paar, Jack (1918–   ), television entertainer
Page, Geraldine (1924–   ), actress
Palance, Jack (1920–   ), actor
Palmer, Betsy (1929–   ), actress
Parker, Charlie "Bird" (1920–55), musician
Parker, Eleanor (1922–   ), singer and actress
Parker, Fess (1927–   ), actor
Parsons, Louella (1893–   ), columnist
Partch, Virgil (1916–   ), cartoonist
Pasternak, Joseph (1901–   ), film producer
Payne, John (1912–   ), actor
Pearce, Alice (1917–66), actress and comedienne
Pearl, Minnie (1912–   ), country singer
Peck, Gregory (1916–   ), actor
Peppard, George (1933–   ), actor
Perkins, Tony (1932–   ), actor
Peterson, Oscar (1925–   ), musician
Piaf, Edith (1915–63), singer
Pickford, Mary (1893–   ), actress
Pidgeon, Walter (1898–   ), actor
Pitts, Zasu (1900–63), actress
Plummer, Christopher (1927–   ), actor
Poitier, Sidney (1924–   ), actor
Portman, Eric (1903–   ), actor
Powell, Dick (1904–63), actor
Powell, Eleanor (1913–   ), dancer and actress
Powell, Jane (1929–   ), dancer and singer
Power, Tyrone (1914–58), actor
Powers, Stefanie (1942–   ), actress
Preminger, Otto (1906–   ), director and producer
Prentiss, Paula (1939–   ), actress
Presley, Elvis (1935–   ), singer
Preston, Robert (1918–   ), actor
Purcell, Noel (1900–   ), actor
Quayle, Anthony (1913–   ), actor
Quinn, Anthony (1915–   ), actor
Quintero, José (1924–   ), director
Raft, George (1903–   ), actor
Rains, Claude (1890–1967), actor
Rainer, Luise (1912–   ), actress
Raines, Ella (1921–   ), actress
Rand, Sally (1904–   ), dancer
Randall, Tony (1920–   ), actor
Rathbone, Basil (1892–1967), actor
Raye, Martha (1916–   ), actress and comedienne
Raymond, Gene (1908–   ), actor
Redgrave, Sir Michael (1908–   ), actor
Redgrave, Vanessa (1937–   ), actress
Reed, Carol (1906–   ), director
Reed, Donna (1921–   ), actress
Reiner, Carl (1920–   ), actor, director, and comedian
Remick, Lee (1935–   ), actress
Rennie, Michael (1909–   ), actor
Renoir, Jean (1894–   ), director
Resnais, Alain (1922–   ), director
Reynolds, Debbie (1932–   ), actress
Rich, Buddy (1917–   ), musician
Richardson, Sir Ralph (1912–   ), actor

Richardson, Tony (1929–   ), director
Ritchard, Cyril (1898–   ), actor
Ritter, Thelma (1905–   ), actress
Ritz, Al (1903–   ), comedian
Ritz, Harry (1908–   ), comedian
Ritz, Jimmy (1905–   ), comedian
Rivera, Chita (1933–   ), dancer
Roach, Hal (1892–   ), director
Robards, Jason, Jr. (1922–   ), actor
Robeson, Paul (1898–   ), singer
Robertson, Cliff (1925–   ), actor
Robertson, Dale (1923–   ), actor
Robinson, Bill "Bojangles" (1878–1949), dancer and singer
Robinson, Edward G. (1893–   ), actor
Rodgers, Richard (1902–   ), composer and producer
Rogers, Ginger (1911–   ), actress and dancer
Rogers, Roy (1912–   ), actor
Rogers, Will (1879–1935), humorist
Roland, Gilbert (1905–   ), actor
Romero, Cesar (1907–   ), actor
Rooney, Mickey (1920–   ), actor
Rooney, Pat (1880–1962), dancer and songwriter
Rose, Billy (1899–1966), showman
Rose, David (1910–   ), musician
Rossellini, Roberto (1906–   ), director
Russell, Jane (1921–   ), actress
Russell, Lillian (1861–1922), actress
Russell, Rosalind (1912–   ), actress
Rutherford, Margaret (1892–   ), actress
Ryan, Robert (1913–   ), actor
Rydell, Bobby (1942–   ), singer
Sahl, Mort (1927–   ), comedian
Sanders, George (1906–   ), actor
Sands, Tommy (1937–   ), singer
Schary, Dore (1905–   ), writer, producer, and director
Schell, Maria (1926–   ), actress
Schell, Maximilian (1930–   ), actor
Schultze, Carl E. (1866–1939), cartoonist
Scofield, Paul (1922–   ), actor
Scott, George C. (1927–   ), actor
Scott, Lizabeth (1923–   ), actress
Scott, Martha (1916–   ), actress
Scott, Randolph (1903–   ), actor
Scott, Zachary (1914–65), actor
Searle, Ronald (1920–   ), cartoonist
Seberg, Jean (1938–   ), actress
Seeger, Pete (1919–   ), folk singer
Sellers, Peter (1925–   ), comedian
Selznick, David O. (1902–65), producer
Sennett, Mack (1884–1960), producer and director
Serling, Rod (1924–   ), writer
Shaw, Artie (1910–   ), musician
Shearer, Norma (1904–   ), actress
Shearing, George (1920–   ), musician
Shore, Dinah (1920–   ), singer
Shubert, Lee (1883–1953), impresario
Signoret, Simone (1921–   ), actress
Silvers, Phil (1912–   ), actor
Sim, Alistair (1900–   ), actor
Simone, Simone (1914–   ), actress
Sinatra, Frank (1915–   ), singer and actor
Sinatra, Nancy (1941–   ), singer and actress
Skelton, Red (1913–   ), comedian

(continued)

**CELEBRITIES OF ENTERTAINMENT** (*continued*)

Skinner, Cornelia Otis (1903–    ), actress and writer
Skinner, Otis (1858–1942), actor
Smith, Bessie (1898?–1937), singer
Smith, Kate (1909–    ), singer
Snow, Hank (1914–    ), country musician
Sobol, Louis (1896–    ), columnist
Soglow, Otto (1900–    ), comic-strip artist
Sommer, Elke (1941–    ), actress
Sothern, Ann (1915–    ), actress
Stack, Robert (1919–    ), actor
Stafford, Jo (1918–    ), singer
Stanley, Kim (1921–    ), actress
Stanwyck, Barbara (1907–    ), actress
Stapleton, Maureen (1925–    ), actress
Starr, Ringo (1940–    ), singer and musician
Steiger, Rod (1925–    ), actor
Stevens, Stella (c.1936–    ), actress
Stewart, James (1909–    ), actor
Strasberg, Lee (1901–    ), director
Strasberg, Susan (1938–    ), actress
Streisand, Barbra (1942–    ), singer
Stritch, Elaine (1925–    ), actress
Stroheim, Erich von (1885–1957), actor and director
Sturges, Preston (1898–1957), producer and director
Styne, Jules (1905–    ), composer
Sullavan, Margaret (1911–60), actress
Sullivan, Barry (1912–    ), actor
Sullivan, Ed (1902–    ), columnist and television personality
Susskind, David (1920–    ), television personality and producer
Swanson, Gloria (1899–    ), actress
Tandy, Jessica (1909–    ), actress
Taylor, Elizabeth (1932–    ), actress
Taylor, Laurette (1887–1946), actress
Taylor, Robert (1911–    ), actor
Taylor, Rod (1930–    ), actor
Teagarden, Jack (1905–64), musician
Temple, Shirley (1929–    ), actress
Templeton, Alec (1910–63), musician
Templeton, Fay (1865–1939), actress
Terry, Ellen (1848–1928), actress
Terry-Thomas (1911–    ), comedian
Thomas, Danny (1914–    ), comedian
Thorndike, Dame Sybil (1882–    ), actress
Tierney, Gene (1920–    ), actress
Tiffin, Pamela (1942–    ), actress
Tillstrom, Burr (1917–    ), puppeteer
Tone, Franchot (1906–    ), actor
Torn, Rip (1931–    ), actor
Tracy, Spencer (1900–67), actor
Treacher, Arthur (1894–    ), actor
Tree, Herbert Beerbohm (1853–1917), actor
Trevor, Claire (1909–    ), actress
Tucker, Forrest (1919–    ), actor
Tucker, Sophie (1884–1966), singer
Tufts, Sonny (1911–    ), actor
Turner, Lana (1921–    ), actress
Turpin, Ben (1847–1940), comedian
Tushingham, Rita (1940–    ), actress
Uggams, Leslie (1943–    ), singer and actress
Ure, Mary (1933–    ), actress
Ustinov, Peter (1921–    ), actor, writer, and director
Vadim, Roger (1927–    ), director

Valentino, Rudolph (1895–1926), actor
Vallee, Rudy (1901–    ), singer and actor
Van Dyke, Dick (1925–    ), actor
Van Fleet, Jo (1922–    ), actress
Vaughan, Robert (1933–    ), actor
Vaughan, Sarah (1922–    ), singer
Verdon, Gwen (1925–    ), singer and dancer
Vidor, King (1895–    ), director
Vitti, Monica (1933–    ), actress
Wald, Jerry (1919–62), film producer
Walker, Nancy (1922–    ), comedienne
Walker, Robert (1919–51), actor
Wallach, Eli (1915–    ), actor
Waller, Fats (1904–43), musician and composer
Walston, Ray (1918–    ), actor
Wanger, Walter (1894–    ), producer
Waring, Fred (1900–    ), musician
Warner, Jack L. (1892–    ), producer
Washington, Dinah (1924–64), singer
Waters, Ethel (1900–    ), actress
Wayne, John (1907–    ), actor
Webb, Clifton (1896–1966), actor
Webb, Jack (1920–    ), actor
Weber, Joe (1867–1942), vaudeville impresario
Webster, Margaret (1905–    ), theatrical producer
Welch, Raquel (1942–    ), actress
Welk, Lawrence (1904–    ), musician
Welles, Orson (1915–    ), actor, producer, and director
Werner, Oskar (1922–    ), actor
West, Mae (1892–    ), actress
White, Pearl (1889–1938), actress
Whiteman, Paul (1890–    ), musician
Widmark, Richard (1914–    ), actor
Wilder, Billy (1906–    ), producer and director
Williams, Andy (1930–    ), singer
Williams, Esther (1923–    ), actress
Williams, Hank (1923–53), country musician
Willson, Meredith (1902–    ), musician, composer, and conductor
Wilson, Don (1900–    ), radio and television announcer
Wilson, Earl (1907–    ), columnist
Winchell, Walter (1897–    ), columnist
Winters, Jonathan (1925–    ), comedian
Winters, Shelley (1922–    ), actress
Wise, Robert (1914–    ), director
Woodward, Joanne (1931–    ), actress
Woolley, Monty (1888–1963), actor
Wray, Fay (1907–    ), actress
Wyatt, Jane (1912–    ), actress
Wyler, William (1902–    ), director
Wyman, Jane (1914–    ), actress
Wynn, Ed (1886–1966), comedian
Wynn, Keenan (1916–    ), actor
York, Susannah (1942–    ), actress
Youmans, Vincent (1898–1946), composer and producer
Young, Alan (1919–    ), actor
Young, Chic (1901–    ), comic-strip artist
Young, Gig (1917–    ), actor
Young, Loretta (1913–    ), actress
Young, Robert (1907–    ), actor
Young, Roland (1887–1953), actor
Yurka, Blanche (1893–    ), actress
Zanuck, Darryl (1902–    ), producer
Ziegfeld, Florenz (1869–1932), showman

# PRIZES AND AWARDS

## Nobel Prizes · Pulitzer Prizes · Academy Awards · Other Selected Awards

National Book Committee

Novelist Bernard Malamud, author of **The Fixer**, accepts the National Book Award for fiction. Vice President Hubert H. Humphrey, who spoke at the award ceremonies, is at left. Other award winners are at right.

## THE NOBEL PRIZES

The Nobel Prizes, which rank among the most prestigious awards in the world, were established by Alfred Bernhard Nobel, the Swedish inventor, who died in 1896. Nobel's will provided that the interest on a multimillion-dollar fund was to be distributed annually in the form of prizes to "those who, during the preceding year, shall have conferred the greatest benefit on mankind" in each of five fields: physics, chemistry, physiology or medicine, literature, and peace. Nobel's will stipulated further that prize winners be selected without regard to nationality.

The Nobel Prizes were first awarded in 1901. In recent years the prize in each category has been valued at more than $50,000 (1967 prize: approximately $62,000), which may be shared by two or more winners.

Prizes in physiology or medicine are awarded by the Royal Caroline Medico-Chirurgical Institute, Stockholm; those in chemistry and physics by the Royal Academy of Science,

Stockholm; the prize in literature by the Swedish Academy, Stockholm; and the peace prize by the Nobel Committee of the Norwegian Storting (Parliament), Oslo.

Marie Curie, the French scientist, was the first person to be awarded the Nobel Prize in two categories: physics (1903), for a study of radiation phenomena (conducted with her husband, Pierre Curie), and chemistry (1911), for the discovery of radium and polonium. Linus Pauling, the American scientist, also won Nobel Prizes in two categories: chemistry (1954), for his studies of the structures and forces of molecules; and the peace prize (1962). The International Red Cross has been awarded the peace prize three times: in 1917, 1944, and 1963.

Nobel Prizes are formally presented on December 10, the anniversary of Alfred Nobel's death. No awards were made in any category from 1940 to 1942. No peace prize was awarded in 1966 or 1967.

**NOBEL PRIZES: PHYSICS**

| YEAR | NAME AND NATIONALITY | AWARDED FOR: |
|------|---------------------|--------------|
| 1967 | Hans A. Bethe, American.............. (German-born) | Contributions to the theory of nuclear reaction, especially his discoveries concerning energy production of stars. |
| 1966 | Alfred Kastler, French................. | Discovery and development of optical methods for studying Herzian resonances in atoms. |
| 1965 | Richard P. Feynman, American........ Julian S. Schwinger, American Shinichiro Tomanaga, Japanese | Research in quantum electrodynamics, which contributed to the understanding of elementary particles in high-energy physics. |
| 1964 | Nikolai G. Basov, Russian.............. Aleksander M. Prochorov, Russian Charles H. Townes, American | Fundamental work in the field of quantum electronics, leading to construction of maser-laser oscillators and amplifiers. |
| 1963 | Maria Goeppert-Mayer, American....... J. Hans D. Jensen, German............. Eugene P. Wigner, American | Discoveries concerning nuclear shell structure. Contribution to the theory of the atomic nucleus and elementary particles. |
| 1962 | Lev. D. Landau, Russian............... | Theories of condensed matter, especially liquid helium. |
| 1961 | Robert Hofstadter, American........... | Studies of electron scattering with resulting discoveries concerning the structure of the nucleons. |
| | Rudolf L. Mössbauer, German.......... | Studies of the resonance absorption of gamma radiation and the discovery of the Mössbauer effect. |
| 1960 | Donald A. Glaser, American............ | Invention of the bubble chamber. |
| 1959 | Owen Chamberlain, American.......... Emilio G. Segrè, American (Italian-born) | Discovery of the antiproton. |
| 1958 | Paval A. Čerenkov, Russian............ Ilya M. Frank, Russian Igor J. Tamm, Russian | Discovery and interpretation of the Čerenkov effect. |
| 1957 | Tsung-Dao Lee, American.............. (Chinese-born) Chen Ning Yang, American (Chinese-born) | Investigation of the parity laws, which has led to important discoveries regarding elementary particles. |
| 1956 | John Bardeen, American............... Walter H. Brattain, American William Shockley, American (British-born) | Research on semiconductors and discovery of the transistor effect. |
| 1955 | Polykarp Kusch, American............. (German-born) | Precise determination of the magnetic moment of the electron. |
| | Willis E. Lamb, American.............. | Discoveries concerning the fine structure of the hydrogen spectrum. |
| 1954 | Max Born, British...................... (German-born) | Fundamental research in quantum mechanics. |
| | Walther Bothe, German................ | The coincidence method of counting, used in nuclear and cosmic-ray research. |
| 1953 | Frits Zernike, Dutch................... | Demonstration of the phase contrast method, and invention of the phase contrast microscope. |
| 1952 | Felix Bloch, American................. (Swiss-born) Edward M. Purcell, American | Development of new methods for nuclear-magnetic precision measurements and related discoveries. |
| 1951 | Sir John D. Cockroft, British........... Ernest T. S. Walton, Irish | Research on the transmutation of atomic nuclei by artificially accelerated atomic particles. |
| 1950 | Cecil F. Powell, British............... | Development of photographic method of studying nuclear processes and resulting discoveries regarding mesons. |
| 1949 | Hideki Yukawa, Japanese.............. | Theoretical prediction of the existence of mesons. |
| 1948 | Patrick M. S. Blackett, British.......... | Development of the Wilson cloud chamber method and resulting discoveries in the fields of nuclear physics and cosmic radiation. |
| 1947 | Sir Edward V. Appleton, British........ | Investigations of the physics of the upper atmosphere and discovery of the Appleton layer. |
| 1946 | Percy Williams Bridgman, American.... | Discoveries in the field of high pressure physics. |
| 1945 | Wolfgang Pauli, American............. (Austro-Hungarian-born) | Discovery of the exclusion principle, also called the Pauli principle, in quantum physics. |
| 1944 | Isidor Isaac Rabi, American............ | Resonance method for recording the magnetic properties of atomic nuclei. |
| 1943 | Otto Stern, American.................. | Contribution to development of the molecular ray method and discovery of the magnetic moment of the proton. |
| 1942 | No award | |
| 1941 | No award | |
| 1940 | No award | |
| 1939 | Ernest O. Lawrence, American........ | Invention and development of the cyclotron and results obtained from its use in the investigation of artificial radioactive elements. |
| 1938 | Enrico Fermi, American ............... (Italian-born) | Demonstrations of existence of new radioactive elements produced by neutron irradiation, and discovery of nuclear reactions caused by slow neutrons. |
| 1937 | Clinton J. Davisson, American......... George P. Thomson, British | Experimental discovery of the diffraction of electrons by crystals. |

| YEAR | NAME AND NATIONALITY | AWARDED FOR: |
|------|---------------------|--------------|
| 1936 | Carl D. Anderson, American............ | Discovery of the positron. |
|      | Victor F. Hess, Austrian................ | Discovery of cosmic radiation. |
| 1935 | James Chadwick, British.............. | Discovery of the neutron. |
| 1934 | No award | |
| 1933 | Paul A. M. Dirac, British.............. | Extensions of atomic theory. |
|      | Erwin Schrödinger, Austrian | |
| 1932 | Werner Heisenberg, German........... | Creation of quantum mechanics, which led to the discovery of allotropic forms of hydrogen. |
| 1931 | No award | |
| 1930 | Sir Chandrasekhara V. Raman, Indian.. | Work on the scattering of light and discovery of the Raman effect. |
| 1929 | Prince Louis-Victor de Broglie, French | Discovery of the wave nature of electrons. |
| 1928 | Owen W. Richardson, British.......... | Work on thermionics, the phenomena associated with the emission of electrically charged particles by a heated body, and for discovery of Richardson's law. |
| 1927 | Arthur H. Compton, American......... | Discovery of the Compton effect. |
|      | Charles T. R. Wilson, British........... | Method of making the paths of electrically charged particles visible by condensation of vapor. |
|      | (Scotch-born) | |
| 1926 | Jean B. Perrin, French................ | Work on the discontinuous structure of matter, and especially for his discovery of sedimentation equilibrium. |
| 1925 | James Franck, German................ | Discovery of the laws governing the impact of an electron upon an atom. |
|      | Gustav Hertz, German | |
| 1924 | Karl M. G. Siegbahn, Swedish......... | Discoveries and research in the field of X-ray spectroscopy. |
| 1923 | Robert A. Millikan, American.......... | Work on the elementary charge of electricity and on the photoelectric effect. |
| 1922 | Niels Bohr, Danish................... | Investigation of atomic structure and radiation. |
| 1921 | Albert Einstein, American............. | Studies in theoretical physics, and especially for his discovery of the law of the photoelectric effect. |
|      | (German-born) | |
| 1920 | Charles E. Guillaume, French.......... | Discovery of anomalies in nickel steel alloys. |
|      | (Swiss-born) | |
| 1919 | Johannes Stark, German.............. | Discovery of the Doppler effect in canal rays and the splitting of spectral lines in electric fields. |
| 1918 | Max K. E. L. Planck, German........... | Discovery of energy quanta. |
| 1917 | Charles G. Barkla, British............. | Discovery of the characteristic Röntgen radiation of the elements. |
| 1916 | No award | |
| 1915 | Sir William H. Bragg, British.......... | The analysis of crystal structure by means of X-rays. |
|      | William L. Bragg, British | |
| 1914 | Max von Laue, German................ | Discovery of the diffraction of X-rays by crystals. |
| 1913 | Heike Kamerlingh-Onnes, Dutch....... | Investigations on the properties of matter at low temperatures, which led to the production of liquid helium. |
| 1912 | Nils G. Dalén, Swedish................ | Invention of automatic devices for illuminating lighthouses and buoys. |
| 1911 | Wilhelm Wien, German................ | Discoveries regarding the laws of heat radiation. |
| 1910 | Johannes D. van der Waals, Dutch...... | Work on the equation of state for gases and liquids. |
| 1909 | Carl F. Braun, German................ | Development of wireless telegraphy. |
|      | Guglielmo Marconi, Italian | |
| 1908 | Gabriel Lippmann, French............. | Method of reproducing colors photographically based on the phenomenon of interference. |
| 1907 | Albert A. Michelson, American......... | Optical precision instruments for spectroscopic and meteorological investigations. |
|      | (German-born) | |
| 1906 | Sir Joseph J. Thomson, British......... | Theoretical and experimental investigations on the conduction of electricity by gases. |
| 1905 | Philipp E. A. von Lenard, German...... | Work on cathode rays. |
|      | (Hungarian-born) | |
| 1904 | Rayleigh, Lord (John W. Strutt), British | Investigations of the densities of the most important gases and the discovery of argon. |
| 1903 | Antoine Henri Becquerel, French....... | Discovery of spontaneous radioactivity. |
|      | Marie Curie, French (Polish-born)...... | Joint researches on the radiation phenomena discovered by A. Henri Becquerel. |
|      | Pierre Curie, French | |
| 1902 | Hendrik A. Lorentz, Dutch............. | Researches into the influence of magnetism upon radiation phenomena. |
|      | Pieter Zeeman, Dutch | |
| 1901 | Wilhelm C. Röntgen, German.......... | Discovery of Röntgen rays (X-rays). |

## NOBEL PRIZES: CHEMISTRY

| YEAR | NAME AND NATIONALITY | AWARDED FOR: |
|------|---------------------|--------------|
| 1967 | Manfred Eigen, German ............... | Studies of extremely fast chemical reactions effected by disturbing the equilibrium by means of very short pulses of energy. |
|      | Ronald G. W. Norrish, British | |
|      | George Porter, British | |
| 1966 | Robert S. Mulliken, American.......... | Fundamental work on chemical bonds and the electronic structure of molecules by the molecular orbital method. |
| 1965 | Robert B. Woodward, American......... | Development of fundamental techniques for syntheses of complicated organic compounds. |
| 1964 | Dorothy Crowfoot Hodgkin, British..... | Discovery by X-Ray techniques of the structure of important biochemical substances. |

(continued)

**NOBEL PRIZES** (*continued*)

| YEAR | NAME AND NATIONALITY | AWARDED FOR: |
|---|---|---|
| 1963 | Giulio Natta, Italian.................. Karl Ziegler, German | Discoveries in the field of the chemistry and technology of high polymers. |
| 1962 | John C. Kendrew, British.............. Max F. Perutz, British (Austrian-born) | Studies of the structures of globular proteins. |
| 1961 | Melvin Calvin, American............... | Research on the carbon dioxide assimilation in plants. |
| 1960 | Willard F. Libby, American............ | Method to use carbon-14 for age determination in archeology, geology, geophysics, and other branches of science. |
| 1959 | Jaroslav Heyrovský, Czech............. | Discovery and development of polarographic methods of analysis. |
| 1958 | Frederick Sanger, British............. | Work on the structure of proteins, especially that of insulin. |
| 1957 | Sir Alexander R. Todd, British.......... | Work on nucleotides and nucleotide co-enzymes. |
| 1956 | Sir Cyril N. Hinshelwood, British....... Nikolai N. Semenov, Russian | Researches into the mechanism of chemical reactions. |
| 1955 | Vincent du Vigneaud, American........ | Work on biochemically important sulfur compounds, especially for the first synthesis of a polypeptide hormone. |
| 1954 | Linus C. Pauling, American............ | Research into the nature of the chemical bond and its application to the elucidation of the structure of complex substances. |
| 1953 | Hermann Staudinger, German.......... | Discoveries in the field of macromolecular chemistry. |
| 1952 | Archer J. P. Martin, British............ Richard L. M. Synge, British | Invention of partition chromatography, a method for the analysis of mixtures. |
| 1951 | Edwin M. McMillan, American.......... Glenn T. Seaborg, American | Discoveries in the chemistry of the transuranium elements. |
| 1950 | Kurt Alder, German................... Otto P. H. Diels, German | Discovery and development of the diene synthesis. |
| 1949 | William F. Giauque, American.......... | Contributions in the field of chemical thermodynamics, particularly the behavior of substances at extremely low temperatures. |
| 1948 | Arne W. K. Tiselius, Swedish........... | Research on electrophoresis and adsorption analysis, especially for discoveries concerning the complex nature of serum proteins. |
| 1947 | Sir Robert Robinson, British........... | Investigation of plant products of biological importance, especially the alkaloids. |
| 1946 | James B. Sumner, American............ John H. Northrop, American........... Wendell M. Stanley, American | Discovery that enzymes can be crystallized. Preparation of enzymes and virus proteins in a pure form. |
| 1945 | Artturi I. Virtanen, Finnish............ | Research and inventions in agricultural and nutrition chemistry, especially for his fodder preservation method. |
| 1944 | Otto Hahn, German................... | Discovery of the fission of heavy nuclei. |
| 1943 | Georg de Hevesy, Hungarian........... | Work on the use of isotopes as tracers in chemistry. |
| 1942 | No award | |
| 1941 | No award | |
| 1940 | No award | |
| 1939 | Adolf F. J. Butenandt, German......... | Work on sex hormones. (Prize declined under political pressure. Diploma and medal awarded subsequently.) |
| | Leopold Ružicka, Swiss............... (Austro-Hungarian-born) | Work on polymethylenes and higher terpenes. |
| 1938 | Richard Kuhn, German................. | Work on carotenoids and vitamins. (Prize declined under political pressure. Diploma and medal awarded subsequently.) |
| 1937 | Walter N. Haworth, British............. Paul Karrer, Swiss................... (Russian-born) | Research on carbohydrates and vitamin C. Investigations on carotenoids, flavin, and vitamins A and $B^2$. |
| 1936 | Peter J. W. Debye, Dutch.............. | Contributions to knowledge of molecular structure through studies of dipole moments and diffraction of X-rays and electrons in gases. |
| 1935 | Frédéric Joliot, French................ Iréne Joliot-Curie, French | Synthesis of new radioactive elements. |
| 1934 | Harold C. Urey, American.............. | Discovery of heavy hydrogen. |
| 1933 | No award | |
| 1932 | Irving Langmuir, American............. | Discoveries and investigations in surface chemistry. |
| 1931 | Friedrich Bergius, German............. Carl Bosch, German | Contributions to invention and development of chemical high pressure methods. |
| 1930 | Hans Fischer, German................. | Researches into the constitution of haemin and chlorophyll and especially for synthesis of haemin. |
| 1929 | Arthur Harden, British................ Hans K. A. S. von Euler-Chelpin, Swedish (German-born) | Investigations on the fermentation of sugar and fermentative enzymes. |
| 1928 | Adolf O. R. Windaus, German........... | Research into the constitution of the sterols and their connection with the vitamins. |
| 1927 | Heinrich O. Wieland, German........... | Studies of the constitution of the bile acids and related substances. |
| 1926 | Theodor Svedberg, Swedish............ | Work on disperse systems. |
| 1925 | Richard A. Zsigmondy, German......... | Demonstration of heterogeneous nature of colloid solutions and the methods used. |
| 1924 | No award | |
| 1923 | Fritz Pregl, Austrian.................. | Invention of method of microanalysis of organic substances. |

| YEAR | NAME AND NATIONALITY | AWARDED FOR: |
|------|----------------------|--------------|
| 1922 | Francis W. Aston, British............. | Discovery, by means of his mass spectrograph, of isotopes in a large number of nonradioactive elements, and for enunciation of the whole-number rule. |
| 1921 | Frederick Soddy, British.............. | Studies of chemistry of radioactive substances, and investigations into the origin and nature of isotopes. |
| 1920 | Walther H. Nernst, German........... | Work in thermochemistry. |
| 1919 | No award | |
| 1918 | Fritz Haber, German.................. | The synthesis of ammonia from its elements. |
| 1917 | No award | |
| 1916 | No award | |
| 1915 | Richard M. Willstätter, German........ | Researches on plant pigments, especially chlorophyll. |
| 1914 | Theodore W. Richards, American....... | Determinations of the atomic weight of many chemical elements. |
| 1913 | Alfred Werner, Swiss (German-born).... | Work on the linkage of atoms in molecules. |
| 1912 | Victor Grignard, French............... | Discovery of the Grignard reagent. |
|  | Paul Sabatier, French................. | Method of hydrogenating organic compounds in the presence of finely disintegrated metals. |
| 1911 | Marie Curie, French.................. (Polish-born) | Discovery of the elements radium and polonium, the isolation of radium and the study of its nature and compounds. |
| 1910 | Otto Wallach, German.................. | Pioneer work in the field of alicyclic compounds. |
| 1909 | Wilhelm Ostwald, German............. | Work on catalysis and studies of fundamental principles governing chemical equilibria and rates of reaction. |
| 1908 | Ernest Rutherford, British............ | Studies of disintegration of the elements, and chemistry of radioactive substances. |
| 1907 | Eduard Buchner, German............. | Biochemical researches and discovery of cell-free fermentation. |
| 1906 | Henri Moissan, French................ | Study and isolation of the element fluorine and for developing the electric furnace named after him. |
| 1905 | Johann F. W. A. von Baeyer, German... | Work on organic dyes and hydroaromatic compounds. |
| 1904 | Sir William Ramsay, British........... | Discovery of the inert gaseous elements in air (helium, neon, xenon, argon and krypton) and determination of their place in the periodic system. |
| 1903 | Svante A. Arrhenius, Swedish......... | Electrolytic theory of dissociation. |
| 1902 | Hermann E. Fischer, German.......... | Work on sugar and purine syntheses. |
| 1901 | Jacobus H. van't Hoff, Dutch.......... | Discovery of the laws of chemical dynamics and osmotic pressure in solutions. |

## NOBEL PRIZES: PHYSIOLOGY OR MEDICINE

| YEAR | NAME AND NATIONALITY | AWARDED FOR: |
|------|----------------------|--------------|
| 1967 | Ragnar Granit, Swedish............... (Finnish-born) Haldan Keffer Hartline, American George Wald, American | Discoveries concerning the primary chemical and physiological visual processes in the eye. |
| 1966 | Charles B. Huggins, American......... | Discoveries concerning hormonal treatment of cancer of the prostate gland. |
|  | Francis Peyton Rous, American....... | Discovery of tumor-inducing viruses in chickens. |
| 1965 | François Jacob, French............... André Lwoff, French Jacques Monod, French | Discovery of regulatory processes in body cells that contribute to genetic control of enzymes and virus synthesis. |
| 1964 | Konrad E. Bloch, American............ Feodor Lynen, German | Discoveries concerning the mechanism and regulation of the cholesterol and fatty acid metabolism. |
| 1963 | Sir John C. Eccles, Australian......... Alan L. Hodgkin, British Andrew F. Huxley, British | Discoveries concerning the nerve cell membrane. |
| 1962 | Francis H. C. Crick, British........... James D. Watson, American Maurice H. F. Wilkins, British | Discoveries concerning the molecular structure of nuclear acids and its significance for information transfer in living material. |
| 1961 | Georg von Bekesy, American.......... (Hungarian-born) | Discoveries of the physical mechanism of stimulation within the cochlea of the inner ear. |
| 1960 | Sir F. Macfarlane Burnet, Australian.... Peter B. Medawar, British (Brazilian-born) | Discovery of acquired immunological tolerance. |
| 1959 | Arthur Kornberg, American............ Severo Ochoa, American (Spanish-born) | Discovery of the mechanisms in the biological synthesis of RNA and DNA. |
| 1958 | George W. Beadle, American.......... Edward L. Tatum, American | Discovery that genes act by regulating definite chemical events. |
|  | Joshua Lederberg, American.......... | Discoveries concerning genetic recombination and the organization of the genetic material of bacteria. |
| 1957 | Daniel Bovet, Italian.................. (Swiss-born) | Discoveries relating to synthetic compounds that inhibit the action of certain body substances, and especially their action on the vascular system and the skeletal muscles. |
| 1956 | André F. Cournand, American.......... (French-born) | Discoveries concerning heart catheterization and pathological changes in the circulatory system. |

(continued)

| YEAR | NAME AND NATIONALITY | AWARDED FOR: |
|---|---|---|
| | Werner Forssmann, German | |
| | Dickinson W. Richards, Jr., American | |
| 1955 | Alex H. T. Theorell, Swedish........... | Discoveries concerning the nature and mode of action of oxidation enzymes. |
| 1954 | John F. Enders, American.............. | Discovery of the ability of poliomyelitis viruses to grow in cultures of various types of tissue. |
| | Frederick C. Robbins, American | |
| | Thomas H. Weller, American | |
| 1953 | Hans A. Krebs, British................ | Discovery of the citric acid cycle. |
| | (German-born) | |
| | Fritz A. Lipmann, American........... | Discovery of coenzyme A and its importance for intermediary metabolism. |
| | (German-born) | |
| 1952 | Selman A. Waksman, American........ | Discovery of streptomycin, the first antibiotic effective against tuberculosis. |
| | (Russian-born) | |
| 1951 | Max Theiler, American................ | Discoveries concerning yellow fever and how to combat it. |
| | (South-African-born) | |
| 1950 | Philip S. Hench, American............ | Discoveries relating to the hormones of the adrenal cortex, their structure and biological effects. |
| | Edward C. Kendall, American | |
| | Tadeus Reichstein, Swiss | |
| | (Polish-born) | |
| 1949 | Walter R. Hess, Swiss................ | Discovery of the functional organization of the interbrain as a coordinator of the activities of the internal organs. |
| | Antonio Moniz, Portuguese............ | Discovery of the therapeutic value of prefrontal lobotomy in certain psychoses. |
| 1948 | Paul H. Müller, Swiss................ | Discovery of the high efficiency of DDT as a contact poison against several arthropods. |
| 1947 | Carl F. Cori, American................ | Discovery of the course of the catalytic conversion of glycogen. |
| | (Czech-born) | |
| | Gerty T. Cori, American | |
| | (Czech-born) | |
| | Bernardo A. Houssay, Argentine........ | Discovery of the part played by the hormone of the anterior pituitary lobe in the metabolism of sugar. |
| 1946 | Hermann J. Muller, American......... | Discovery of the production of mutations by means of X-ray irradiation. |
| 1945 | Ernst B. Chain, British................ | Discovery of penicillin and its curative effect in various infectious diseases. |
| | (German-born) | |
| | Sir Alexander Fleming, British | |
| | (Scotch-born) | |
| | Sir Howard W. Florey, British | |
| | (Australian-born) | |
| 1944 | Joseph Erlanger, American............ | Discoveries relating to the highly differentiated functions of single nerve fibers. |
| | Herbert S. Gasser, American | |
| 1943 | Henrik C. P. Dam, Danish............. | Discovery of vitamin K. |
| | Edward A. Doisy, American............ | Discovery of the chemical nature of vitamin K. |
| 1942 | No award | |
| 1941 | No award | |
| 1940 | No award | |
| 1939 | Gerhard Domagk, German............. | Discovery of the antibacterial effects of the drug prontosil. (Prize declined under political pressure. Diploma and medal awarded subsequently.) |
| 1938 | Corneille J. F. Heymans, Belgian....... | Discovery of the role played by the sinus and aortic mechanisms in the regulation of respiration. |
| 1937 | Albert Szent-Györgyi von Nagyrapolt... | Studies in body metabolism with special reference to the role of vitamin C and fumaric acid. |
| | American (Hungarian-born) | |
| 1936 | Sir Henry H. Dale, British............. | Discoveries relating to the chemical transmission of nerve impulses. |
| | Otto Loewi, American | |
| | (Austrian born) | |
| 1935 | Hans Spemann, German............... | Discovery of the organizer effect in embryonic development. |
| 1934 | George R. Minot, American............ | Discoveries concerning liver therapy in cases of anemia. |
| | William P. Murphy, American | |
| | George H. Whipple, American | |
| 1933 | Thomas H. Morgan, American......... | Discoveries concerning the role of the chromosome in heredity. |
| 1932 | Edgar D. Adrian, British............... | Discoveries regarding the functions of nerve cells. |
| | Sir Charles S. Sherrington, British | |
| 1931 | Otto H. Warburg, German............. | Discovery of the nature and mode of action of the respiratory enzyme. |
| 1930 | Karl Landsteiner, American............ | Discovery of human blood groups. |
| | (Austrian-born) | |
| 1929 | Christiaan Eijkman, Dutch............ | Discovery of health effects due to vitamin B$_1$ deficiency. |
| | Sir Frederick G. Hopkins, British....... | Discovery of the growth-stimulating vitamins. |
| 1928 | Charles J. H. Nicolle, French........... | Work on typhus. |
| 1927 | Julius Wagner-Jauregg, Austrian....... | Use of malaria inoculation to treat paralysis and mental deterioration associated with syphilis. |
| 1926 | Johannes A. G. Fibiger, Danish........ | Experimental production of a cancerlike growth in rats. |

| YEAR | NAME AND NATIONALITY | AWARDED FOR: |
|---|---|---|
| 1925 | No award | |
| 1924 | Willem Einthoven, Dutch.............. | Discovery of the mechanism of the electrocardiogram. |
| 1923 | Frederick G. Banting, Canadian........ | Discovery of insulin. |
| | John J. R. Macleod, Canadian | |
| 1922 | Archibald V. Hill, British.............. | Discovery relating to the production of heat in the muscle. |
| | Otto F. Meyerhof, German............. | Discovery of the fixed relationship between the consumption of oxygen and the metabolism of lactic acid in the muscle. |
| 1921 | No award | |
| 1920 | Schack A. S. Krogh, Danish........... | Discovery of the capillary motor-regulating mechanism. |
| 1919 | Jules Bordet, Belgian................. | Discoveries relating to immunity. |
| 1918 | No award | |
| 1917 | No award | |
| 1916 | No award | |
| 1915 | No award | |
| 1914 | Robert Bárány, Hungarian............. | Work on the physiology and pathology of the vestibular apparatus of the inner ear. |
| | (Austrian-born) | |
| 1913 | Charles R. Richet, French............. | Work on anaphylaxis and allergies. |
| 1912 | Alexis Carrel, American............... | Work on vascular suture and the transplantation of blood vessels and organs. |
| 1911 | Allvar Gullstrand, Swedish............ | Work on the dioptrics of the eye. |
| 1910 | Albrecht Kossel, German.............. | Contributions to knowledge of cell chemistry made through his work on proteins, including the nucleic substances. |
| 1909 | Emil T. Kocher, Swiss................ | Work on the physiology, pathology, and surgery of the thyroid gland. |
| 1908 | Paul Éhrlich, German................. | Work on immunity. |
| | Elie Metchnikoff, French (Russian-born) | |
| 1907 | Charles L. A. Laveran, French.......... | Work on the role played by protozoa in causing diseases. |
| 1906 | Camillo Golgi, Italian................. | Work on the structure of the nervous system. |
| | Santiago Roman y Cajal, Spanish | |
| 1905 | Robert Koch, German................. | Investigations and discoveries in relation to tuberculosis. |
| 1904 | Ivan P. Pavlov, Russian............... | Work on the physiology of digestion. |
| 1903 | Niels R. Finsen, Danish............... | Contribution to treatment of tuberculous skin diseases, especially lupus vulgaris, with concentrated light radiation. |
| 1902 | Sir Ronald Ross, British............... | Investigation of how malaria parasites enter the body. |
| 1901 | Emil A. von Behring, German.......... | Work on serum therapy, especially its application against diphtheria. |

## LITERATURE

| | | | |
|---|---|---|---|
| 1967 | Miguel Angel Asturias, Guatemalan | 1941 | No award |
| 1966 | Samuel Joseph Agnon, Israeli | 1940 | No award |
| | (Austrian-born) | 1939 | Frans E. Sillanpää, Finnish |
| | Nelly Sachs, Swedish | 1938 | Pearl S. Buck, American |
| | (German-born) | 1937 | Roger Martin du Gard, French |
| 1965 | Mikhail Sholokhov, Russian | 1936 | Eugene O'Neill, American |
| 1964 | Jean Paul Sartre, French | 1935 | No award |
| | (Prize declined) | 1934 | Luigi Pirandello, Italian |
| 1963 | Giorgos Seferis, Greek | 1933 | Ivan A. Bunin, French |
| 1962 | John Steinbeck, American | | (Russian-born) |
| 1961 | Ivo Andríc, Yugoslavian | 1932 | John Galsworthy, British |
| 1960 | Saint-John Perse, French | 1931 | Erik A. Karlfeldt, Swedish |
| 1959 | Salvatore Quasimondo, Italian | 1930 | Sinclair Lewis, American |
| 1958 | Boris L. Pasternak, Russian | 1929 | Thomas Mann, German |
| | (Prize declined for political reasons.) | 1928 | Sigrid Undset, Norwegian |
| 1957 | Albert Camus, French | | (Danish-born) |
| 1956 | Juan Ramón Jiménez, Puerto Rican | 1927 | Henri Bergson, French |
| | (Spanish-born) | 1926 | Grazia Deledda, Italian |
| 1955 | Halldór K. Laxness, Icelandic | 1925 | George Bernard Shaw, British |
| 1954 | Ernest Hemingway, American | | (Irish-born) |
| 1953 | Sir Winston Churchill, British | 1924 | Wladyslaw S. Reymont, Polish |
| 1952 | François Mauriac, French | 1923 | William Butler Yeats, Irish |
| 1951 | Pär F. Lagerkvist, Swedish | 1922 | Jacinto Benavente, Spanish |
| 1950 | Bertrand Russell, British | 1921 | Anatole France, French |
| 1949 | William Faulkner, American | 1920 | Knut Hamsun, Norwegian |
| 1948 | T. S. Eliot, British | 1919 | Carl F. G. Spitteler, Swiss |
| | (American-born) | 1918 | No award |
| 1947 | André Gide, French | 1917 | Karl A. Gjellerup, Danish |
| 1946 | Herman Hesse, Swiss | | Henrik Pontoppidan, Danish |
| | (German-born) | 1916 | Carl G. von Heidenstam, Swedish |
| 1945 | Gabriela Mistral, Chilean | 1915 | Romain Rolland, French |
| 1944 | Johannes V. Jensen, Danish | 1914 | No award |
| 1943 | No award | 1913 | Rabindranath Tagore, Indian |
| 1942 | No award | 1912 | Gerhart Hauptmann, German |

(continued)

**NOBEL PRIZES** (*continued*)

| | | | |
|---|---|---|---|
| 1911 | Count Maurice Maeterlinck, Belgian | 1905 | Henryk Sienkiewicz, Polish |
| 1910 | Paul J. L. Heyse, German | 1904 | Frédéri Mistral, French |
| 1909 | Selma Lagerlof, Swedish | | José Echegaray, Spanish |
| 1908 | Rudolf C. Eucken, German | 1903 | Björnsterne Björnson, Norwegian |
| 1907 | Rudyard Kipling, British | 1902 | C. M. T. Mommsen, German |
| 1906 | Giosuè Carducci, Italian | 1901 | Sully-Prudhomme (René F. A. Prudhomme), French |

## PEACE

| | | | |
|---|---|---|---|
| 1967 | No award | 1931 | Jane Addams, American |
| 1966 | No award | | Nicholas Murray Butler, American |
| 1965 | The United Nations Children's Fund (UNICEF) | 1930 | Lars O. N. Söderblom, Swedish |
| 1964 | Martin Luther King, Jr., American | 1929 | Frank B. Kellogg, American |
| 1963 | International Committee of the Red Cross | 1928 | No award |
| | Red Cross Societies League | 1927 | Ferdinand E. Buisson, French |
| 1962 | Linus C. Pauling, American | | Ludwig Quidde, German |
| 1961 | Dag Hammarskjöld, Swedish | 1926 | Aristide Briand, French |
| | (Awarded posthumously) | | Gustav Stresemann, German |
| 1960 | Albert J. Luthuli, South African | 1925 | Sir J. Austen Chamberlain, British |
| 1959 | Philip J. Noel-Baker, British | | Charles G. Dawes, American |
| 1958 | Georges Pire, Belgian | 1924 | No award |
| 1957 | Lester B. Pearson, Canadian | 1923 | No award |
| 1956 | No award | 1922 | Fridtjof Nansen, Norwegian |
| 1955 | No award | 1921 | Karl H. Branting, Swedish |
| 1954 | Office of the United Nations High Commissioner | | Christian L. Lange, Norwegian |
| | for Refugees | 1920 | Léon V. A. Bourgeois, French |
| 1953 | George C. Marshall, American | 1919 | Woodrow Wilson, American |
| 1952 | Albert Schweitzer, French (German-born) | 1918 | No award |
| 1951 | Léon Jouhaux, French | 1917 | International Committee of the Red Cross |
| 1950 | Ralph J. Bunche, American | 1916 | No award |
| 1949 | Lord John Boyd Orr of Brechin, British | 1915 | No award |
| 1948 | No award | 1914 | No award |
| 1947 | Friends Service Council, British | 1913 | Henri La Fontaine, Belgian |
| | American Friends Service Committee, American | 1912 | Elihu Root, American |
| 1946 | Emily G. Balch, American | 1911 | Tobias M. C. Asser, Dutch |
| | John R. Mott, American | | Alfred H. Fried, Austrian |
| 1945 | Cordell Hull, American | 1910 | Permanent International Peace Bureau |
| 1944 | International Committee of the Red Cross | 1909 | Auguste M. F. Beernaert, Belgian |
| 1943 | No award | | Paul H. B. B. d'Estournelles de Constant, French |
| 1942 | No award | 1908 | Klas P. Arnoldson, Swedish |
| 1941 | No award | | Fredrik Bajer, Danish |
| 1940 | No award | 1907 | Ernesto T. Moneta, Italian |
| 1939 | No award | | Louis Renault, French |
| 1938 | Nasen International Office for Refugees | 1906 | Theodore Roosevelt, American |
| 1937 | Viscount Cecil of Chelwood | 1905 | Baroness Bertha von Suttner, Austrian |
| | (Lord Edgar A. R. G. Cecil), British | 1904 | Institute of International Law |
| 1936 | Carlos de Saavedra Lamas, Argentinian | 1903 | Sir William R. Cremer, British |
| 1935 | Carl von Ossietzky, German | 1902 | Élie Ducommun, Swiss |
| 1934 | Arthur Henderson, British | | Charles A. Gobat, Swiss |
| 1933 | Sir Norman Angell, British | 1901 | Jean H. Dunant, Swiss |
| 1932 | No award | | Frédéric Passy, French |

## DATA ON NOBEL PRIZE-WINNERS IN SCIENCE

The United States leads the world in the number of citizens who have been awarded Nobel Prizes in science. As of 1967, the number of American citizens who had been named Nobel laureates in the categories of physiology or medicine, chemistry, or physics, since 1901 stood at 74. The United Kingdom has the second largest concentration of Nobel science laureates, 47. Germany has 46; France, 20; the Netherlands, the Soviet Union, and Sweden, nine each.

A tabulation of academic institutions with which American prize winners have been associated follows.

| UNIVERSITY | LAUREATE DID DOCTORAL RESEARCH THERE | WORK DONE THERE | LAUREATE CURRENTLY ON STAFF | UNIVERSITY | LAUREATE DID DOCTORAL RESEARCH THERE | WORK DONE THERE | LAUREATE CURRENTLY ON STAFF |
|---|---|---|---|---|---|---|---|
| Harvard...... | 11 | 14 | 7 | Princeton..... | 6 | 1 | 1 |
| California (at | | | | Washington... | — | 6 | 1 |
| Berkeley)... | 6 | 7 | 8 | Cornell....... | 1 | 3 | 2 |
| Columbia..... | 9 | 9 | 2 | Johns Hopkins | 6 | — | — |
| Chicago....... | 4 | 6 | 2 | Rockefeller... | — | 3 | 3 |
| Cal Tech...... | 4 | 3 | 3 | All others..... | 13 | 18 | 9 |
| Stanford...... | — | 4 | 5 | | | | |

# THE PULITZER PRIZES

The Pulitzer Prizes in journalism, letters, and music were established under terms of the will of Joseph Pulitzer (1847–1911), the American newspaper publisher. The prizes have been awarded annually since 1917 by the Trustees of Columbia University, New York City, acting on the recommendations of an Advisory Board. The Board, in turn, receives recommendations from juries which examine the entries in each category.

Seven of the eight prizes in journalism carry awards of $1,000 each; the eighth is a gold medal awarded for meritorious public service. Prizes in letters and music carry awards of $500 each. Pulitzer Prizes are awarded for work completed or published during the preceding year, with the exception of prizes in music and drama, for which the deadline is extended to March 1 of the year in which the award is presented.

Following is a complete list of Pulitzer Prizes awarded through 1967.

## PRIZES IN JOURNALISM

### GENERAL REPORTING
(Discontinued category: awarded 1917–52)

1952 George de Carvalho (*San Francisco* [Calif.] *Chronicle*)
1951 Edward S. Montgomery (*San Francisco* [Calif.] *Examiner*)
1950 Meyer Berger (*The New York Times*)
1949 Malcolm Johnson (New York *Sun*)
1948 George E. Goodwin (*Atlanta* [Ga.] *Journal*)
1947 Frederick Woltman (*New York World-Telegram*)
1946 William Leonard Laurence (*The New York Times*)
1945 Jack S. McDowell (*Call-Bulletin,* San Francisco, Calif.)
1944 Paul Schoenstein and associates (*New York Journal-American*)
1943 George Weller (*Chicago* [Ill.] *Daily News*)
1942 Stanton Delaplane (*San Francisco* [Calif.] *Chronicle*)
1941 Westbrook Pegler (*New York World-Telegram*)
1940 S. Burton Heath (*New York World-Telegram*)
1939 Thomas Lunsford Stokes (Scripps-Howard Newspaper Alliance; for articles published in the *New York World-Telegram*)
1938 Raymond Sprigle (*Pittsburgh* [Penn.] *Post-Gazette*)
1937 John J. O'Neill (*New York Herald Tribune*) William Laurence (*The New York Times*) Howard W. Blakeslee (Associated Press) Gobind Behari Lal (Universal Service) David Dietz (Scripps-Howard Newspapers)
1936 Lauren D. Lyman (*The New York Times*)
1935 William H. Taylor (*New York Herald Tribune*)
1934 Royce Brier (*San Francisco* [Calif.] *Chronicle*)
1933 Francis A. Jamieson (Associated Press)
1932 W. C. Richards, D. D. Martin, J. S. Pooler, F. D. Webb, J. N. W. Sloan (*Detroit* [Mich.] *Free Press*)
1931 A. B. MacDonald (*Kansas City* [Mo.] *Star*)
1930 Russell D. Owen (*The New York Times*)
1929 Paul Anderson (*St. Louis Post-Dispatch*)
1928 No award
1927 John T. Rogers (*St. Louis* [Mo.] *Post-Dispatch*)
1926 William Burke Miller (*Courier-Journal,* Louisville, Ky.)

1925 James W. Mulroy (*Chicago* [Ill.] *Daily News*)
Alvin H. Goldstein (*Chicago* [Ill.] *Daily News*)
1924 Magner White (*San Diego* [Calif.] *Sun*)
1923 Alva Johnston (*The New York Times*)
1922 Kirke L. Simpson (Associated Press)
1921 Louis Seibold (New York *World*)
1920 John J. Leary, Jr. (New York *World*)
1919 No award
1918 Harold A. Littledale (*New York Evening Post*)
1917 Herbert Bayard Swope (New York *World*)

### GENERAL CORRESPONDENCE
(Discontinued category: awarded 1929–47)

1947 Brooks Atkinson (*The New York Times*)
1946 Arnaldo Cortesi (*The New York Times*)
1945 Harold V. Boyle (Associated Press)
1944 Ernest Taylor Pyle (Scripps-Howard Newspaper Alliance)
1943 Hanson W. Baldwin (*The New York Times*)
1942 Carlos P. Romulo (*Philippines Herald,* Manila, P.I.)
1941 In place of an individual Pulitzer Prize for foreign correspondence, the trustees approved the recommendation of the Advisory Board that a bronze plaque or scroll be designed and executed to recognize and symbolize the public services and the individual achievements of American news reporters in the war zones of Europe, Asia, and Africa, from the beginning of World War II.
1940 Otto D. Tolischus (*The New York Times*)
1939 Louis P. Lochner (Associated Press)
1938 Arthur Krock (*The New York Times*)
1937 Anne O'Hare McCormick (*The New York Times*)
1936 Wilfred C. Barber (*Chicago* [Ill.] *Tribune*)
1935 Arthur Krock (*The New York Times*)
1934 Frederick T. Birchall (*The New York Times*)
1933 Edgar Ansel Mowrer (*Chicago* [Ill.] *Daily News*)
1932 Walter Duranty (*The New York Times*)
Charles G. Ross (*St. Louis* [Mo.] *Post-Dispatch*)
1931 H. R. Knickerbocker (*Philadelphia* [Penn.] *Public Ledger and News*)

*(continued)*

PULITZER PRIZES (continued)

1930   Leland Stowe (New York Herald Tribune)
1929   Paul Scott Mowrer (Chicago [Ill.] Daily News)

**NATIONAL TELEGRAPHIC REPORTING**
(Discontinued category: awarded 1942–47)

1947   Edward T. Folliard (Washington [D.C.] Post)
1946   Edward A. Harris (St. Louis [Mo.] Post-Dispatch)
1945   James Reston (The New York Times)
1944   Dewey L. Fleming (Baltimore Sun)
1943   No award
1942   Louis Stark (The New York Times)

**INTERNATIONAL TELEGRAPHIC REPORTING**
(Discontinued category: awarded 1942–47)

1947   Eddy Gilmore (Associated Press)
1946   Homer Bigart (New York Herald Tribune)
1945   Mark S. Watson (Baltimore Sun)
1944   Daniel De Luce (Associated Press)
1943   Ira Wolfert (North American Newspaper Alliance)
1942   Laurence Edmund Allen (Associated Press)

**LOCAL REPORTING**
For an outstanding example of local reporting written without the pressure of a deadline.

1967   Gene Miller (Miami [Fla.] Herald)
1966   John A. Frasca (Tampa [Fla.] Tribune)
1965   Gene Goltz (Houston [Tex.] Post)
1964   James V. Magee, Albert V. Gaudiosi, and Frederick A. Meyer (Philadelphia [Penn.] Bulletin)
1963   Oscar O'Neal Griffin, Jr. (Pecos [Tex.] Independent and Enterprise)
1962   George Bliss (Chicago [Ill.] Tribune)
1961   Edgar May (Buffalo [N.Y.] Evening News)
1960   Miriam Ottenberg (Washington [D.C.] Evening Star)
1959   John Harold Brislin (Scranton [Penn.] Tribune and Scrantonian)
1958   George Beveridge (Washington [D.C.] Evening Star)
1957   Wallace Turner and William Lambert (Portland Oregonian)
1956   Arthur Daley (The New York Times)
1955   Roland K. Towery (Cuero [Tex.] Record)
1954   Alvin McCoy (Kansas City [Mo.] Star)
1953   Edward J. Mowery (New York World-Telegram & Sun)

**LOCAL REPORTING**
For a distinguished example of local reporting written under pressure of a deadline.

1967   Robert V. Cox (Chambersburg [Penn.] Public Opinion)
1966   Staff, Los Angeles (Calif.) Times
1965   Melvin H. Ruder (Hungry Horse [Mont.] News)
1964   Norman C. Miller (The Wall Street Journal)
1963   Sylvan Fox, Anthony Shannon, and William Longgood (New York World-Telegram & Sun)

1962   Robert D. Mullins (Deseret News, Salt Lake City, Utah)
1961   Sanche de Gramont (New York Herald Tribune)
1960   Jack Nelson (Atlanta [Ga.] Constitution)
1959   Mary Lou Werner (Washington [D.C.] Evening Star)
1958   Fargo (N.D.) Forum
1957   Salt Lake (Utah) Tribune
1956   Lee Hills (Detroit [Mich.] Free Press)
1955   Mrs. Caro Brown (Alice [Texas] Daily Echo)
1954   Vicksburg (Miss.) Sunday Post Herald
1953   Editorial Staff, Providence (R.I.) Journal and Evening Bulletin

**NATIONAL REPORTING**
For an exceptional example of reporting on national and domestic affairs.

1967   Monroe W. Karmin and Stanley W. Penn (The Wall Street Journal)
1966   Hayes Johnson (Washington [D.C.] Evening Star)
1965   Louis M. Kohlmeier (The Wall Street Journal)
1964   Merriman Smith (United Press International)
1963   Anthony Lewis (The New York Times)
1962   Nathan G. Caldwell and Gene S. Graham (Nashville Tennessean)
1961   Edward R. Cony (The Wall Street Journal)
1960   Vance Trimble (Scripps-Howard Newspaper Alliance)
1959   Howard Van Smith (Miami [Fla.] News)
1958   Relman Morin (Associated Press)
1957   James Reston (The New York Times)
1956   Charles L. Bartlett (Chattanooga [Tenn.] Times)
1955   Anthony Lewis (Washington [D.C.] Daily News)
1954   Richard Wilson (Cowles Newspapers)
1953   Don Whitehead (Associated Press)
1952   Anthony Leviero (The New York Times)
1951   The Advisory Board as a policy does not make any award to an individual member of the Board, and because the outstanding instance of national reporting in 1950 was the achievement of Arthur Krock of The New York Times in obtaining an exclusive interview with President Truman, no award was made in 1951.
1950   Edwin O. Guthman (Seattle [Wash.] Times)
1949   C. P. Trussell (The New York Times)
1948   Bert Andrews (New York Herald Tribune)
        Nat S. Finney (Minneapolis Tribune)

**INTERNATIONAL CORRESPONDENCE**
For a distinguished example of international reporting.

1967   R. John Hughes (Christian Science Monitor)
1966   Peter Arnett (Associated Press)
1965   J. A. Livingston (Philadelphia [Penn.] Bulletin)
1964   Malcolm W. Browne (Associated Press)
        David Halberstam (The New York Times)
1963   Hal Hendrix (Miami [Fla.] News)
1962   Walter Lippmann (New York Herald Tribune Syndicate)

| | |
|---|---|
| 1961 | Lynn Heinzerling (Associated Press) |
| 1960 | A. M. Rosenthal (*The New York Times*) |
| 1959 | Joseph Martin and Philip Santora (New York *Daily News*) |
| 1958 | *The New York Times* |
| 1957 | Russell Jones (United Press) |
| 1956 | William Randolph Hearst, Jr., Kingsbury Smith, and Frank Conniff (International News Service) |
| 1955 | Harrison E. Salisbury (*The New York Times*) |
| 1954 | Jim G. Lucas (Scripps-Howard Newspapers) |
| 1953 | Austin Wehrwein (*Milwaukee* [Wis.] *Journal*) |
| 1952 | John M. Hightower (Associated Press) |
| 1951 | Keyes Beech (*Chicago* [Ill.] *Daily News*) |
| | Homer Bigart (*New York Herald Tribune*) |
| | Marguerite Higgins (*New York Herald Tribune*) |
| | Relman Morin (Associated Press) |
| | Fred Sparks (*Chicago* [Ill.] *Daily News*) |
| | Don Whitehead (Associated Press) |

**EDITORIAL WRITING**
For editorial writing, the test of excellence being clearness of style, moral purpose, sound reasoning, and power to influence public opinion in what the writer conceives to be the right direction.

| | |
|---|---|
| 1967 | Eugene C. Patterson (*Atlanta* [Ga.] *Constitution*) |
| 1966 | Robert Lasch (*St. Louis* [Mo.] *Post-Dispatch*) |
| 1965 | John R. Harrison (*Gainesville* [Fla.] *Sun*) |
| 1964 | Hazel Brannon Smith (*Lexington* [Miss.] *Advertiser*) |
| 1963 | Ira B. Harkey, Jr. (*Pascagoula* [Miss.] *Chronicle*) |
| 1962 | Thomas M. Storke (*Santa Barbara* [Calif.] *News-Press*) |
| 1961 | William J. Dorvillier (*San Juan* [P.R.] *Star*) |
| 1960 | Lenoir Chambers (*Norfolk Virginian-Pilot*) |
| 1959 | Ralph McGill (*Atlanta* [Ga.] *Constitution*) |
| 1958 | Harry S. Ashmore (*Arkansas Gazette*, Little Rock, Ark.) |
| 1957 | Buford Boone (*Tuscaloosa* [Ala.] *News*) |
| 1956 | Lauren K. Soth (*Des Moines* [Iowa] *Register and Tribune*) |
| 1955 | Royce Howes (*Detroit* [Mich.] *Free Press*) |
| 1954 | Don Murray (*Boston* [Mass.] *Herald*) |
| 1953 | Vermont C. Royster (*The Wall Street Journal*) |
| 1952 | Louis LaCoss (*St. Louis* [Mo.] *Globe Democrat*) |
| 1951 | William Harry Fitzpatrick (*New Orleans* [La.] *States*) |
| 1950 | Carl M. Saunders (*Jackson* [Mich.] *Citizen Patriot*) |
| 1949 | John H. Crider (*Boston* [Mass.] *Herald*) |
| | Herbert Elliston (*Washington* [D.C.] *Post*) |
| 1948 | Virginius Dabney (*Richmond* [Va.] *Times-Dispatch*) |
| 1947 | William H. Grimes (*The Wall Street Journal*) |
| 1946 | Hodding Carter (*Delta Democrat-Times*, Greenville, Miss.) |
| 1945 | George W. Potter (*Providence* [R.I.] *Journal-Bulletin*) |
| 1944 | Henry J. Haskell (*Kansas City* [Mo.] *Star*) |

| | |
|---|---|
| 1943 | Forrest W. Seymour (*Register and Tribune*, Des Moines, Iowa) |
| 1942 | Geoffrey Parsons (*New York Herald Tribune*) |
| 1941 | Reuben Maury (New York *Daily News*) |
| 1940 | Bart Howard (*St. Louis Post-Dispatch*) |
| 1939 | Ronald G. Callvert (Portland *Oregonian*) |
| 1938 | W. W. Waymack (*Register and Tribune*, Des Moines, Iowa) |
| 1937 | John W. Owens (*Baltimore Sun*) |
| 1936 | Felix Morley (*Washington* [D.C.] *Post*) |
| | George B. Parker (Scripps-Howard Newspapers) |
| 1935 | No award |
| 1934 | E. P. Chase (*Atlantic* [Iowa] *News-Telegraph*) |
| 1933 | *Kansas City* (Mo.) *Star* |
| 1932 | No award |
| 1931 | Charles S. Ryckman (*Fremont* [Nebr.] *Tribune*) |
| 1930 | No award |
| 1929 | Louis I. Jaffe (*Norfolk Virginian-Pilot*) |
| 1928 | Grover Cleveland Hall (*Montgomery* [Ala.] *Advertiser*) |
| 1927 | *Boston* (Mass.) *Herald* (F. L. Bullard) |
| 1926 | *The New York Times* (Edward M. Kingsbury) |
| 1925 | *Charleston* (S.C.) *News and Courier* |
| 1924 | *Boston* (Mass.) *Herald* |
| | Special award: Frank I. Cobb (New York *World*) |
| 1923 | William Allen White (*Emporia* [Kans.] *Gazette*) |
| 1922 | Frank M. O'Brien (*New York Herald*) |
| 1921 | No award |
| 1920 | Harvey E. Newbranch (*Evening World-Herald*, Omaha, Nebr.) |
| 1919 | No award |
| 1918 | *Louisville* (Ky.) *Courier-Journal* |
| 1917 | *New York Tribune* |

**CARTOONS**
For the best example of a newspaper cartoonist's work.

| | |
|---|---|
| 1967 | Patrick B. Oliphant (*Denver* [Colo.] *Post*) |
| 1966 | Don Wright (*Miami* [Fla.] *News*) |
| 1965 | No award |
| 1964 | Paul Conrad (*Denver* [Colo.] *Post*) |
| 1963 | Frank Miller (*Des Moines* [Iowa] *Register*) |
| 1962 | Edmund S. Valtman (*Hartford* [Conn.] *Times*) |
| 1961 | Carey Orr (*Chicago* [Ill.] *Tribune*) |
| 1960 | No award |
| 1959 | William (Bill) Mauldin (*St. Louis* [Mo.] *Post-Dispatch*) |
| 1958 | Bruce M. Shanks (*Buffalo* [N.Y.] *Evening News*) |
| 1957 | Tom Little (*Nashville Tennessean*) |
| 1956 | Robert York (*Louisville* [Ky.] *Times*) |
| 1955 | Daniel R. Fitzpatrick (*St. Louis* [Mo.] *Post-Dispatch*) |
| 1954 | Herbert L. Block (Herblock) (*Washington* [D.C.] *Post & Times-Herald*) |
| 1953 | Edward D. Kuekes (*Cleveland* [Ohio] *Plain Dealer*) |
| 1952 | Fred L. Packer (*New York Mirror*) |
| 1951 | Reginald W. Manning (*Arizona Republic*, Phoenix, Ariz.) |

(continued)

**PULITZER PRIZES** (*continued*)

1950 James T. Berryman (*Washington* [D.C.] *Evening Star*)
1949 Lute Pease (*Newark* [N.J.] *Evening News*)
1948 Reuben L. (Rube) Goldberg (New York *Sun*)
1947 Vaughn Shoemaker (*Chicago Daily News*)
1946 Bruce Alexander Russell (*Los Angeles* [Calif.] *Times*)
1945 William (Bill) Mauldin (United Features Syndicate, Inc.)
1944 Clifford K. Berryman (*Washington* [D.C.] *Evening Star*)
1943 Jay Norwood Darling (*New York Herald Tribune*)
1942 Herbert L. Block (Herblock) (Newspaper Enterprise Association Service)
1941 Jacob Burck (*Chicago Times*)
1940 Edmund Duffy (*Baltimore Sun*)
1939 Charles G. Werner (*Daily Oklahoman*, Oklahoma City, Okla.)
1938 Vaughn Shoemaker (*Chicago Daily News*)
1937 Clarence Daniel Batchelor (New York *Daily News*)
1936 No award
1935 Ross A. Lewis (*Milwaukee* [Wis.] *Journal*)
1934 Edmund Duffy (*Baltimore Sun*)
1933 Harold Morton Talburt (*Washington* [D.C.] *Daily News*)
1932 John T. McCutcheon (*Chicago Tribune*)
1931 Edmund Duffy (*Baltimore Sun*)
1930 Charles R. Macauley (*Brooklyn* [N.Y.] *Daily Eagle*)
1929 Rollin Kirby (New York *World*)
1928 Nelson Harding (*Brooklyn* [N.Y.] *Daily Eagle*)
1927 Nelson Harding (*Brooklyn* [N.Y.] *Daily Eagle*)
1926 D. R. Fitzpatrick (*St. Louis* [Mo.] *Post-Dispatch*)
1925 Rollin Kirby (New York *World*)
1924 Jay Norwood Darling (*New York Tribune*)
1923 No award
1922 Rollin Kirby (New York *World*)

**NEWS PHOTOGRAPHY**

1967 Jack R. Thornell (Associated Press)
1966 Kyoichi Sawada (United Press International)
1965 Horst Faas (Associated Press)
1964 Robert H. Jackson (*Dallas* [Texas] *Times Herald*)
1963 Hector Rondon (*La Republica,* Caracas, Venezuela)
1962 Paul Vathis (Associated Press)
1961 Yasushi Nagao (Mainichi Newspapers, Tokyo, Japan)
1960 Andrew Lopez (United Press International)
1959 William Seaman (*Minneapolis Star*)
1958 William C. Beall (*Washington* [D.C.] *Daily News*)
1957 Harry A. Trask (*Boston* [Mass.] *Traveler*)
1956 New York *Daily News*
1955 John L. Gaunt, Jr. (*Los Angeles Times*)
1954 Mrs. Walter M. Schau (Photographer)
1953 William M. Gallagher (*Flint* [Mich.] *Journal*)
1952 John Robinson and Don Ultang (*Des Moines* [Iowa] *Register and Tribune*)

1951 Max Desfor (Associated Press)
1950 Bill Crouch (*Oakland* [Calif.] *Tribune*)
1949 Nathaniel Fein (*New York Herald Tribune*)
1948 Frank Cushing (*Boston* [Mass.] *Traveler*)
1947 Arnold Hardy (Amateur photographer)
1946 No award
1945 Joe Rosenthal (Associated Press)
1944 Frank Filan (Associated Press)
Earle L. Bunker (*World-Herald,* Omaha, Nebr.)
1943 Frank Noel (Associated Press)
1942 Milton Brooks (*Detroit* [Mich.] *News*)

**MERITORIOUS PUBLIC SERVICE**

A gold medal is awarded for meritorious public service rendered by an American newspaper.

1967 *Louisville* (Ky.) *Courier-Journal*
     *Milwaukee* (Wis.) *Journal*
1966 *Boston* (Mass.) *Globe*
1965 *Hutchinson* (Kans.) *News*
1964 *St. Petersburg* (Fla.) *Times*
1963 *Chicago* (Ill.) *Daily News*
1962 *Panama City* (Fla.) *News-Herald*
1961 *Amarillo* (Texas) *Globe-Times*
1960 *Los Angeles* (Calif.) *Times*
1959 *Utica* (N.Y.) *Observer-Dispatch*
     *Utica* (N.Y.) *Daily Press*
1958 *Arkansas Gazette,* Little Rock, Ark.
1957 *Chicago* (Ill.) *Daily News*
1956 *Watsonville* (Calif.) *Register-Pajaronian*
1955 *Columbus* (Ga.) *Ledger* and *Sunday Ledger-Enquirer*
1954 *Newsday,* Garden City, N.Y.
1953 *News Reporter,* Whiteville, N.C.
     *Tabor City* (N.C.) *Tribune*
1952 *St. Louis* (Mo.) *Post-Dispatch*
1951 *Miami* (Fla.) *Herald*
     *Brooklyn* (N.Y.) *Eagle*
1950 *Chicago* (Ill.) *Daily News*
     *St. Louis* (Mo.) *Post-Dispatch*
1949 *Nebraska State Journal*
1948 *St. Louis* (Mo.) *Post-Dispatch*
1947 *Baltimore Sun*
1946 *Scranton* (Penn.) *Times*
1945 *Detroit* (Mich.) *Free Press*
1944 *The New York Times*
1943 *World-Herald,* Omaha, Nebr.
1942 *Los Angeles* (Calif.) *Times*
1941 *St. Louis* (Mo.) *Post-Dispatch*
1940 *Waterbury* (Conn.) *Republican and American*
1939 *Miami* (Fla.) *Daily News*
1938 *Bismarck* (N.D.) *Tribune*
1937 *St. Louis* (Mo.) *Post-Dispatch*
1936 *Cedar Rapids* (Iowa) *Gazette*
1935 *Sacramento* (Calif.) *Bee*
1934 *Medford* (Ore.) *Mail Tribune*
1933 *New York World-Telegram*
1932 *Indianapolis* (Ind.) *News*
1931 *Atlanta* (Ga.) *Constitution*
1930 No award
1929 *Evening World,* New York
1928 *Indianapolis* (Ind.) *Times*
1927 *Canton* (Ohio) *Daily News*
1926 *Enquirer Sun,* Columbus, Ga.
1925 No award
1924 New York *World*
1923 *Memphis* (Tenn.) *Commercial Appeal*

1922 New York *World*
1921 *Boston* (Mass.) *Post*
1920 No award
1919 *Milwaukee* (Wis.) *Journal*
1918 *The New York Times*
1917 No award

**NEWSPAPER HISTORY AWARD**

1918 Minna Lewinson and Harry Beetle Hough, for their history of services rendered to the public by the American press during 1917. This award was made only in 1918.

**SPECIAL CITATIONS FOR JOURNALISM**

1964 Gannett Newspapers, Rochester, N.Y., for their program, *The Road to Integration*, a distinguished example of the use of a newspaper group's resources to complement the work of its individual newspapers.
1958 Walter Lippmann, nationally syndicated columnist of the *New York Herald Tribune*, for the wisdom, perception, and high sense of responsibility with which he has commented for many years on national and international affairs.
1953 *The New York Times*, for the section of its Sunday edition headed *Review of the Week*, which for 17 years has brought enlightened commentary to its readers.
1952 *Kansas City* (Mo.) *Star*, for the news coverage of the great regional flood of 1951 in Kansas and northwestern Missouri—a distinguished example of editing and reporting that also gave advance information that achieved the maximum of public protection.
Max Case, of the *New York Journal-American*, for his exclusive exposures of bribery and other forms of corruption in the popular American sport of basketball, which exposures tended to restore confidence in the game's integrity.
1951 Cyrus L. Sulzberger, of *The New York Times*, for his exclusive interview with Archbishop Aloysius Stepinac, Roman Catholic Primate of Yugoslavia.
1948 To Dr. Frank Diehl Fackenthal, a scroll indicating appreciation of his interest and service during the past years.
1947 (Pulitzer Centennial year)
Columbia University and the Graduate School of Journalism, for their efforts to maintain and advance the high standards governing the Pulitzer Prize awards.
The *St. Louis* (Mo.) *Post-Dispatch*, for its unswerving adherence to the public and professional ideals of its founder.
1945 The cartographers of the American press, whose maps of the war fronts helped notably to clarify and increase public information on the progress of the armies and navies engaged in World War II.
1944 To Mrs. William Allen White, a scroll indicating appreciation of Mr. White's interest and services during the past seven years as a member of the Advisory Board of the Graduate School of Journalism, Columbia University.

Byron Price, Director of the Office of Censorship, for the creation and administration of the newspaper and radio codes.
1941 *The New York Times*, for the public educational value of its foreign news reporting, exemplified by its scope, excellence of writing and presentation, and supplementary background information, illustration, and interpretation.
1938 To the *Edmonton* (Alberta) *Journal*, a special bronze plaque for editorial leadership in defense of the freedom of the press in the Province of Alberta, Canada.

**PRIZES IN LETTERS**

**FICTION**
For distinguished fiction, published in book form by an American author, preferably dealing with American life.

1967 *The Fixer*, by Bernard Malamud
1966 *The Collected Stories of Katherine Anne Porter*, by Katherine Anne Porter
1965 *The Keepers of the House*, by Shirley Ann Grau
1964 No award
1963 *The Reivers*, by William Faulkner
1962 *The Edge of Sadness*, by Edwin O'Connor
1961 *To Kill a Mockingbird*, by Harper Lee
1960 *Advise and Consent*, by Allen Drury
1959 *The Travels of Jaimie McPheeters*, by Robert Lewis Taylor
1958 *A Death in the Family*, by James Agee
1957 No award
1956 *Andersonville*, by MacKinlay Kantor
1955 *A Fable*, by William Faulkner
1954 No award
1953 *The Old Man and the Sea*, by Ernest Hemingway
1952 *The Caine Mutiny*, by Herman Wouk
1951 *The Town*, by Conrad Richter
1950 *The Way West*, by A. B. Guthrie, Jr.
1949 *Guard of Honor*, by James Gould Cozzens
1948 *Tales of the South Pacific*, by James Michener
1947 *All the King's Men*, by Robert Penn Warren
1946 No award
1945 *A Bell for Adano*, by John Hersey
1944 *Journey in the Dark*, by Martin Flavin
1943 *Dragon's Teeth*, by Upton Sinclair
1942 *In This Our Life*, by Ellen Glasgow
1941 No award
1940 *The Grapes of Wrath*, by John Steinbeck
1939 *The Yearling*, by Marjorie Kinnan Rawlings
1938 *The Late George Apley*, by John Marquand
1937 *Gone with the Wind*, by Margaret Mitchell
1936 *Honey in the Horn*, by Harold L. Davis
1935 *Now in November*, by Josephine Winslow Johnson
1934 *Lamb in His Bosom*, by Caroline Miller
1933 *The Store*, by T. S. Stribling
1932 *The Good Earth*, by Pearl S. Buck
1931 *Years of Grace*, by Margaret Ayer Barnes
1930 *Laughing Boy*, by Oliver LaFarge
1929 *Scarlet Sister Mary*, by Julia Peterkin
1928 *The Bridge of San Luis Rey*, by Thornton Wilder

*(continued)*

**PULITZER PRIZES** (continued)

1927 *Early Autumn*, by Louis Bromfield
1926 *Arrowsmith*, by Sinclair Lewis
1925 *So Big*, by Edna Ferber
1924 *The Able McLaughlins*, by Margaret Wilson
1923 *One of Ours*, by Willa Cather
1922 *Alice Adams*, by Booth Tarkington
1921 *The Age of Innocence*, by Edith Wharton
1920 No award
1919 *The Magnificent Ambersons*, by Booth Tarkington
1918 *His Family*, by Ernest Poole
1917 No award

**DRAMA**

For an American play, preferably original in its source, and dealing with an American theme.

1967 *A Delicate Balance*, by Edward Albee
1966 No award
1965 *The Subject Was Roses*, by Frank D. Gilroy
1964 No award
1963 No award
1962 *How to Succeed in Business Without Really Trying*, by Frank Loesser and Abe Burrows
1961 *All the Way Home*, by Tad Mosel
1960 *Fiorello!* book by Jerome Weidman and George Abbott, music by Jerry Bock, lyrics by Sheldon Harnick
1959 *J. B.*, by Archibald MacLeish
1958 *Look Homeward, Angel*, by Ketti Frings
1957 *Long Day's Journey Into Night*, by Eugene O'Neill
1956 *Diary of Anne Frank*, by Albert Hackett and Frances Goodrich
1955 *Cat on a Hot Tin Roof*, by Tennessee Williams
1954 *The Teahouse of the August Moon*, by John Patrick
1953 *Picnic*, by William Inge
1952 *The Shrike*, by Joseph Kramm
1951 No award
1950 *South Pacific*, by Richard Rodgers, Oscar Hammerstein II, and Joshua Logan
1949 *Death of a Salesman*, by Arthur Miller
1948 *A Streetcar Named Desire*, by Tennessee Williams
1947 No award
1946 *State of the Union*, by Russel Crouse and Howard Lindsay
1945 *Harvey*, by Mary Chase
1944 No award
1943 *The Skin of Our Teeth*, by Thornton Wilder
1942 No award
1941 *There Shall Be No Night*, by Robert E. Sherwood
1940 *The Time of Your Life*, by William Saroyan
1939 *Abe Lincoln in Illinois*, by Robert E. Sherwood
1938 *Our Town*, by Thornton Wilder
1937 *You Can't Take It With You*, by Moss Hart and George S. Kaufman
1936 *Idiot's Delight*, by Robert E. Sherwood
1935 *The Old Maid*, by Zoe Akins
1934 *Men in White*, by Sidney Kingsley
1933 *Both Your Houses*, by Maxwell Anderson
1932 *Of Thee I Sing*, by George S. Kaufman, Ira Gershwin, and Morrie Ryskind

1931 *Alison's House*, by Susan Glaspell
1930 *The Green Pastures*, by Marc Connelly
1929 *Street Scene*, by Elmer L. Rice
1928 *Strange Interlude*, by Eugene O'Neill
1927 *In Abraham's Bosom*, by Paul Green
1926 *Craig's Wife*, by George Kelly
1925 *They Knew What They Wanted*, by Sidney Howard
1924 *Hell-Bent for Heaven*, by Hatcher Hughes
1923 *Icebound*, by Owen Davis
1922 *Anna Christie*, by Eugene O'Neill
1921 *Miss Lulu Bett*, by Zona Gale
1920 *Beyond the Horizon*, by Eugene O'Neill
1919 No award
1918 *Why Marry?* by Jesse Lynch Williams
1917 No award

**HISTORY**

For an outstanding book on any aspect of the history of the United States.

1967 *Exploration and Empire: The Explorer and Scientist in the Winning of the American West*, by William H. Goetzmann
1966 *Life of the Mind in America: From the Revolution to the Civil War*, by Perry Miller
1965 *The Greenback Era*, by Irwin Unger
1964 *Puritan Village: The Formation of a New England Town*, by Sumner Chilton Powell
1963 *Washington: Village and Capital, 1800–1878*, by Constance McLaughlin Green
1962 *The Triumphant Empire: Thunder-Clouds Gather in the West*, by Lawrence H. Gipson
1961 *Between War and Peace: The Potsdam Conference*, by Herbert Feis
1960 *In the Days of McKinley*, by Margaret Leech
1959 *The Republican Era: 1869–1901*, by Leonard D. White, assisted by Jean Schneider
1958 *Banks and Politics in America—From the Revolution to the Civil War*, by Bray Hammond
1957 *Russia Leaves the War: Soviet-American Relations, 1917–1920*, by George F. Kennan
1956 *Age of Reform*, by Richard Hofstadter
1955 *Great River: The Rio Grande in North American History*, by Paul Horgan
1954 *A Stillness at Appomattox*, by Bruce Catton
1953 *The Era of Good Feelings*, by George Dangerfield
1952 *The Uprooted*, by Oscar Handlin
1951 *The Old Northwest: Pioneer Period, 1815–1840*, by R. Carlyle Buley
1950 *Art and Life in America*, by Oliver W. Larkin
1949 *The Disruption of American Democracy*, by Roy Franklin Nichols
1948 *Across the Wide Missouri*, by Bernard DeVoto
1947 *Scientists Against Time*, by James Phinney Baxter III
1946 *The Age of Jackson*, by Arthur M. Schlesinger, Jr.
1945 *Unfinished Business*, by Stephen Bonsal
1944 *The Growth of American Thought*, by Merle Curti
1943 *Paul Revere and the World He Lived In*, by Esther Forbes
1942 *Reveille in Washington*, by Margaret Leech

1941 *The Atlantic Migration, 1607–1860,* by Marcus Lee Hansen

1940 *Abraham Lincoln: The War Years,* by Carl Sandburg

1939 *A History of American Magazines,* by Frank Luther Mott

1938 *The Road to Reunion, 1865–1900,* by Paul Herman Buck

1937 *The Flowering of New England,* by Van Wyck Brooks

1936 *The Constitutional History of the United States,* by Andrew C. McLaughlin

1935 *The Colonial Period of American History,* by Charles McLean Andrews

1934 *The People's Choice,* by Herbert Agar

1933 *The Significance of Sections in American History,* by Frederick J. Turner

1932 *My Experiences in the World War,* by John J. Pershing

1931 *The Coming of the War: 1914,* by Bernadotte E. Schmitt

1930 *The War of Independence,* by Claude H. Van Tyne

1929 *The Organization and Administration of the Union Army, 1861–1865,* by Fred Albert Shannon

1928 *Main Currents in American Thought* (two volumes), by Vernon Louis Parrington

1927 *Pinckney's Treaty,* by Samuel Flagg Bemis

1926 *The History of the United States,* by Edward Channing

1925 *A History of the American Frontier,* by Frederic L. Paxson

1924 *The American Revolution—A Constitutional Interpretation,* by Charles Howard McIlwain

1923 *The Supreme Court in United States History,* by Charles Warren

1922 *The Founding of New England,* by James Truslow Adams

1921 *The Victory at Sea,* by William Sowden Sims and Burton J. Hendrick

1920 *The War with Mexico* (two volumes), by Justin H. Smith

1919 No award

1918 *A History of the Civil War, 1861–65,* by James Ford Rhodes

1917 *With Americans of Past and Present Days,* by J. J. Jusserand

### BIOGRAPHY OR AUTOBIOGRAPHY

1967 *Mr. Clemens and Mark Twain,* by Justin Kaplan

1966 *A Thousand Days,* by Arthur M. Schlesinger, Jr.

1965 *Henry Adams,* by Ernest Samuels

1964 *John Keats,* by Walter Jackson Bate

1963 *Henry James,* by Leon Edel

1962 No award

1961 *Charles Sumner and the Coming of the Civil War,* by David Donald

1960 *John Paul Jones,* by Samuel Eliot Morison

1959 *Woodrow Wilson, American Prophet,* by Arthur Walworth

1958 *George Washington, Volumes I–VI,* by Douglas Southall Freeman, and *Volume VII,* by Mary Wells Ashworth and John Alexander Carroll

1957 *Profiles in Courage,* by John F. Kennedy

1956 *Benjamin Henry Latrobe,* by T. F. Hamlin

1955 *The Taft Story,* by William S. White

1954 *The Spirit of St. Louis,* by Charles A. Lindbergh

1953 *Edmund Pendleton 1721–1803,* by David J. Mays

1952 *Charles Evans Hughes,* by Merlo J. Pusey

1951 *John C. Calhoun: American Portrait,* by Margaret Louise Coit

1950 *John Quincy Adams and the Foundations of American Foreign Policy,* by Samuel Flagg Bemis

1949 *Roosevelt and Hopkins,* by Robert E. Sherwood

1948 *Forgotten First Citizen: John Bigelow,* by Margaret Clapp

1947 *The Autobiography of William Allen White,* by William Allen White

1946 *Son of the Wilderness,* by Linnie M. Wolfe

1945 *George Bancroft: Brahmin Rebel,* by Russell Blaine Nye

1944 *The American Leonardo: The Life of Samuel F. B. Morse,* by Carleton Mabee

1943 *Admiral of the Ocean Sea,* by Samuel Eliot Morison

1942 *Crusader in Crinoline,* by Forrest Wilson

1941 *Jonathan Edwards,* by Ola E. Winslow

1940 *Woodrow Wilson, Life and Letters, Volumes VII and VIII,* by Ray Stannard Baker

1939 *Benjamin Franklin,* by Carl Van Doren

1938 *Pedlar's Progress,* by Odell Shepard
*Andrew Jackson,* by Marquis James

1937 *Hamilton Fish,* by Allan Nevins

1936 *The Thought and Character of William James,* by Ralph Barton Perry

1935 *R. E. Lee,* by Douglas Southall Freeman

1934 *John Hay,* by Tyler Dennett

1933 *Grover Cleveland,* by Allan Nevins

1932 *Theodore Roosevelt,* by Henry F. Pringle

1931 *Charles W. Eliot,* by Henry James

1930 *The Raven,* by Marquis James

1929 *The Training of an American: The Earlier Life and Letters of Walter H. Page,* by Burton J. Hendrick

1928 *The American Orchestra and Theodore Thomas,* by Charles Edward Russell

1927 *Whitman,* by Emory Holloway

1926 *The Life of Sir William Osler* (two volumes), by Harvey Cushing

1925 *Barrett Wendell and His Letters,* by M. A. DeWolfe Howe

1924 *From Immigrant to Inventor,* by Michael Idvorsky Pupin

1923 *The Life and Letters of Walter H. Page,* by Burton J. Hendrick

1922 *A Daughter of the Middle Border,* by Hamlin Garland

1921 *The Americanization of Edward Bok,* by Edward Bok

1920 *The Life of John Marshall* (four volumes), by Albert J. Beveridge

1919 *The Education of Henry Adams,* by Henry Adams

1918 *Benjamin Franklin, Self-Revealed,* by William Cabell Bruce

1917 *Julia Ward Howe,* by Laura E. Richards, Maude H. Elliot, and Florence H. Hall

(*continued*)

**PULITZER PRIZES** (continued)

**POETRY**

For distinguished verse by an American author.

1967   *Live or Die,* by Anne Sexton
1966   *Selected Poems,* by Richard Eberhart
1965   *77 Dream Songs,* by John Berryman
1964   *At the End of the Open Road,* by Louis Simpson
1963   *Pictures from Breughel,* by William Carlos Williams
1962   *Poems,* by Alan Dugan
1961   *Times Three: Selected Verse from Three Decades,* by Phyllis McGinley
1960   *Heart's Needle,* by W. D. Snodgrass
1959   *Selected Poems 1928–1958,* by Stanley Kunitz
1958   *Promises: Poems 1954–56,* by Robert Penn Warren
1957   *Things of This World,* by Richard Wilbur
1956   *Poems—North & South,* by Elizabeth Bishop
1955   *Collected Poems,* by Wallace Stevens
1954   *The Waking,* by Theodore Roethke
1953   *Collected Poems 1917–1952,* by Archibald MacLeish
1952   *Collected Poems,* by Marianne Moore
1951   *Complete Poems,* by Carl Sandburg
1950   *Annie Allen,* by Gwendolyn Brooks
1949   *Terror and Decorum,* by Peter Viereck
1948   *The Age of Anxiety,* by W. H. Auden
1947   *Lord Weary's Castle,* by Robert Lowell
1946   No award
1945   *V-Letter and Other Poems,* by Karl Shapiro
1944   *Western Star,* by Stephen Vincent Benét
1943   *A Witness Tree,* by Robert Frost
1942   *The Dust Which Is God,* by William Rose Benét
1941   *Sunderland Capture,* by Leonard Bacon
1940   *Collected Poems,* by Mark Van Doren
1939   *Selected Poems,* by John Gould Fletcher
1938   *Cold Morning Sky,* by Marya Zaturenska
1937   *A Further Range,* by Robert Frost
1936   *Strange Holiness,* by Robert P. Tristram Coffin
1935   *Bright Ambush,* by Audrey Wurdemann
1934   *Collected Verse,* by Robert Hillyer
1933   *Conquistador,* by Archibald MacLeish
1932   *The Flowering Stone,* by George Dillon
1931   *Collected Poems,* by Robert Frost
1930   *Selected Poems,* by Conrad Aiken
1929   *John Brown's Body,* by Stephen Vincent Benét
1928   *Tristram,* by Edwin Arlington Robinson
1927   *Fiddler's Farewell,* by Leonora Speyer
1926   *What's O'Clock,* by Amy Lowell
1925   *The Man Who Died Twice,* by Edwin Arlington Robinson
1924   *New Hampshire: A Poem with Notes and Grace Notes,* by Robert Frost
1923   *The Ballad of the Harp-Weaver; A Few Figs from Thistles; eight sonnets in American Poetry, 1922, A Miscellany,* by Edna St. Vincent Millay
1922   *Collected Poems,* by Edward Arlington Robinson

Prior to the establishment of the Pulitzer Poetry Prize in 1922, the following awards had been made from gifts provided by the Poetry Society:

1919   *Old Road to Paradise,* by Margaret Widdemer
       *Corn Huskers,* by Carl Sandburg
1918   *Love Songs,* by Sara Teasdale

**GENERAL NONFICTION**

For the best book by an American not eligible in any other category.

1967   *The Problem of Slavery in Western Culture,* by David Brion Davis
1966   *Wandering Through Winter,* by Edwin Way Teale
1965   *O Strange New World,* by Howard Mumford Jones
1964   *Anti-intellectualism in American Life,* by Richard Hofstadter
1963   *The Guns of August,* by Barbara W. Tuchman
1962   *The Making of the President 1960,* by Theodore H. White

**PRIZES IN MUSIC**

For musical composition in the forms of chamber, orchestral, or choral music, or for an operatic work (including ballet) performed or published by a composer of established residence in the United States.

1967   *Quartet No. 3,* by Leon Kirchner
1966   *Variations for Orchestra,* by Leslie Bassett
1965   No award
1964   No award
1963   *Piano Concerto No. 1,* by Samuel Barber
1962   *The Crucible,* by Robert Ward
1961   *Symphony No. 7,* by Walter Piston
1960   *Second String Quartet,* by Elliott Carter
1959   *Concerto for Piano and Orchestra,* by John La Montaine
1958   The score of *Vanessa,* by Samuel Barber
1957   *Meditations on Ecclesiastes,* by Norman Dello Joio
1956   *Symphony No. 3,* by Ernst Toch
1955   *The Saint of Bleecker Street,* by Gian-Carlo Menotti
1954   *Concerto for Two Pianos and Orchestra,* by Quincy Porter
1953   No award
1952   *Symphony Concertante,* by Gail Kubik
1951   *Giants in the Earth,* by Douglas S. Moore
1950   *The Consul,* by Gian-Carlo Menotti
1949   *Louisiana Story,* by Virgil Thomson
1948   *Symphony No. 3,* by Walter Piston
1947   *Symphony No. 3,* by Charles Ives
1946   *The Canticle of the Sun,* by Leo Sowerby
1945   *Appalachian Spring,* by Aaron Copland
1944   *Symphony No. 4,* by Howard Hanson
1943   *Secular Cantata No. 2, A Free Song,* by William Schuman

**SPECIAL CITATIONS**

1961   *The American Heritage Picture History of the Civil War*
1960   Garrett Mattingly, for *The Armada*
1957   Kenneth Roberts, for his historical novels which have long contributed to the creation of greater interest in early American history.
1944   *Oklahoma!* by Richard Rodgers and Oscar Hammerstein II

## THE NATIONAL BOOK AWARDS

The National Book Awards are presented annually to authors of "the most distinguished books written by Americans and published in the United States" during the preceding year. Established in 1950 and administered by the National Book Committee, the Awards carry considerable prestige in literary and publishing circles. A $1,000 prize, donated by the American Book Publishers Council, the American Booksellers Association, the Book Manufacturers' Institute, and the National Translation Center, accompanies each award.

### NATIONAL BOOK AWARD WINNERS: 1966–67

■ **FICTION**
**1967** Bernard Malamud, *The Fixer* (Farrar, Straus & Giroux). **Judges:** John K. Hutchens, Mark Schorer, Anthony West.
**1966** Katherine Anne Porter: *The Collected Stories of Katherine Anne Porter* (Harcourt, Brace & World). **Judges:** Paul Horgan, J. F. Powers, Glenway Wescott.

■ **POETRY**
**1967** James Merrill, *Nights and Days* (Atheneum). **Judges:** W. H. Auden, James Dickey, Howard Nemerov.
**1966** James Dickey, *Buckdancer's Choice* (Wesleyan University Press). **Judges:** Ben Belitt, Phyllis McGinley, Elder Olson.

■ **ARTS AND LETTERS**
**1967** Justin Kaplan, *Mr. Clemens and Mark Twain* (Simon and Schuster). **Judges:** Saul Maloff, Lon Tinkle, Aileen Ward.
**1966** Janet Flanner (Genêt), *Paris Journal of 1944–65* (Atheneum). **Judges:** Francis Fergusson, Walter Kerr, Norman Holmes Pearson.

■ **HISTORY AND BIOGRAPHY**
**1967** Peter Gay, *The Enlightenment: An Interpretation* (Alfred A. Knopf, Inc.). **Judges:** James MacGregor Burns, Leon Edel, C. Vann Woodward.
**1966** Arthur M. Schlesinger, Jr., *A Thousand Days* (Houghton Mifflin). **Judges:** Julian P. Boyd, Lyman Butterfield, Louis Fischer.

■ **SCIENCE, PHILOSOPHY, AND RELIGION**
**1967** Oscar Lewis, *La Vida* (Random House). **Judges:** Hannah Arendt, John Cogley, Gregory Vlastos.
**1966** No award. **Judges:** John Kenneth Galbraith, Ernest Nagel, James R. Newman.

■ **TRANSLATION** (Awards first made in 1967).
**Classic Work:** Willard Trask, *History of My Life,* by Giacomo Casanova (Harcourt, Brace & World—A Helen and Kurt Wolff Book).
**Contemporary Work:** Gregory Rabassa, *Hopscotch,* by Julio Cortázar (Pantheon).
**Judges:** William Arrowsmith, Clarence Brown, Stanley Burnshaw.

## THE GEORGE FOSTER PEABODY AWARDS

The George Foster Peabody Awards are presented annually for distinguished achievement in public service by radio and television. Following are awards made in 1966 and 1967.

■ **1966**
TELEVISION NEWS: Frank McGee, NBC; Morley Safer, CBS; KTLA, Los Angeles
TELEVISION ENTERTAINMENT: *The Julie Andrews Show,* NBC; *My Name Is Barbra,* CBS; *Frank Sinatra: A Man and His Music,* NBC
TELEVISION EDUCATION: National Educational Television (NET)
TELEVISION YOUTH AND CHILDREN'S PROGRAMS: *A Charlie Brown Christmas,* CBS
TELEVISION PUBLIC SERVICE: *CBS Reports: KKK—The Invisible Empire,* CBS
TELEVISION INNOVATION: *The National Driver's Test,* CBS
TELEVISION'S MOST INVENTIVE ART DOCUMENTARY: *The Mystery of Stonehenge,* CBS
TELEVISION SPECIAL AWARD: *A Visit to Washington with Mrs. Lyndon Johnson—On Behalf of a More Beautiful America,* ABC
TELEVISION CONTRIBUTIONS TO INTERNATIONAL UNDERSTANDING: Xerox Corporation (sponsor of *The Making of the President 1964, Let My People Go, The Louvre,* and United Nations dramas)
RADIO ENTERTAINMENT: *Music 'til Dawn,* CBS
RADIO PUBLIC SERVICE: WCCO Radio, Minneapolis

■ **1967**
TELEVISION NEWS: Harry Reasoner, CBS
TELEVISION ENTERTAINMENT: *A Christmas Memory: ABC Stage 67,* ABC
TELEVISION EDUCATION: National Geographic Specials, CBS; *American White Paper: Organized Crime in the United States,* NBC
TELEVISION YOUTH AND CHILDREN'S PROGRAM: *The World of Stuart Little,* NBC
TELEVISION-RADIO PUBLIC SERVICE: *The Dorothy Gordon Youth Forum: Youth and Narcotics—Who Has the Answer?,* WNBC-TV and NBC Radio
TELEVISION SPECIAL AWARDS: *Bell Telephone Hour,* NBC; Tom John, CBS, for *Death of a Salesman, The Strollin' Twenties,* and *Color Me Barbra; CBS Reports: The Poisoned Air,* CBS; National Educational Television (NET)
TELEVISION CONTRIBUTION TO INTERNATIONAL UNDERSTANDING: *ABC's Wide World of Sports,* ABC; *Siberia: A Day in Irkutsk,* NBC
TELEVISION LOCAL NEWS—ENTERTAINMENT: *Kup's Show,* WBKB-TV, Chicago
TELEVISION LOCAL MUSIC: *Artists' Showcase,* WGN-TV, Chicago; *A Polish Millennium Concert,* WTMJ-TV, Milwaukee, Wisconsin
TELEVISION LOCAL PUBLIC SERVICE: *Assignment Four,* KRON-TV, San Francisco
RADIO LOCAL PUBLIC SERVICE: Elmo Ellis, WSB, Atlanta, Georgia
RADIO NEWS: Edwin Newman, NBC
RADIO LOCAL EDUCATION: *Community Opinion,* WLIB, New York City

## THE ACADEMY AWARDS: 1927–66

The Academy Awards have been presented each year since 1927 by the Motion Picture Academy of Arts and Sciences for distinguished achievement in films released during the preceding year.

Following is a list of motion pictures that won Oscars as the best of their year, together with the names of those who won Academy Awards for best actor, best actress, and best director, for the years 1927–66.

| YEAR | BEST PICTURE | BEST ACTOR | BEST ACTRESS | BEST DIRECTOR |
|---|---|---|---|---|
| 1966 | "A Man for All Seasons" | Paul Scofield "A Man for All Seasons" | Elizabeth Taylor "Who's Afraid of Virginia Woolf?" | Fred Zinnemann "A Man for All Seasons" |
| 1965 | "Sound of Music" | Lee Marvin "Cat Ballou" | Julie Christie "Darling" | Robert Wise "Sound of Music" |
| 1964 | "My Fair Lady" | Rex Harrison "My Fair Lady" | Julie Andrews "Mary Poppins" | George Cukor "My Fair Lady" |
| 1963 | "Tom Jones" | Sidney Poitier "Lilies of the Field" | Patricia Neal "Hud" | Tony Richardson "Tom Jones" |
| 1962 | "Lawrence of Arabia" | Gregory Peck "To Kill a Mockingbird" | Anne Bancroft "The Miracle Worker" | David Lean "Lawrence of Arabia" |
| 1961 | "West Side Story" | Maximilian Schell "Judgment at Nuremberg" | Sophia Loren "Two Women" | Jerome Robbins, Robert Wise "West Side Story" |
| 1960 | "The Apartment" | Burt Lancaster "Elmer Gantry" | Elizabeth Taylor "Butterfield 8" | Billy Wilder "The Apartment" |
| 1959 | "Ben-Hur" | Charlton Heston "Ben-Hur" | Simone Signoret "Room at the Top" | William Wyler "Ben-Hur" |
| 1958 | "Gigi" | David Niven "Separate Tables" | Susan Hayward "I Want to Live" | Vincente Minnelli "Gigi" |
| 1957 | "The Bridge on the River Kwai" | Alec Guinness "The Bridge on the River Kwai" | Joanne Woodward "The Three Faces of Eve" | David Lean "The Bridge on the River Kwai" |
| 1956 | "Around the World in 80 Days" | Yul Brynner "The King and I " | Ingrid Bergman "Anastasia" | George Stevens "Giant" |
| 1955 | "Marty" | Ernest Borgnine "Marty" | Anna Magnani "The Rose Tattoo" | Delbert Mann "Marty" |
| 1954 | "On the Waterfront" | Marlon Brando "On the Waterfront" | Grace Kelly "The Country Girl" | Elia Kazan "On the Waterfront" |
| 1953 | "From Here to Eternity" | William Holden "Stalag 17" | Audrey Hepburn "Roman Holiday" | Fred Zinnemann "From Here to Eternity" |
| 1952 | "The Greatest Show on Earth" | Gary Cooper "High Noon" | Shirley Booth "Come Back, Little Sheba" | John Ford "The Quiet Man" |
| 1951 | "An American in Paris" | Humphrey Bogart "The African Queen" | Vivien Leigh "A Streetcar Named Desire" | George Stevens "A Place in the Sun" |
| 1950 | "All About Eve" | Jose Ferrer "Cyrano de Bergerac" | Judy Holliday "Born Yesterday" | Joseph L. Mankiewicz "All About Eve" |
| 1949 | "All the King's Men" | Broderick Crawford "All the King's Men" | Olivia de Havilland "The Heiress" | Joseph L. Mankiewicz "A Letter to Three Wives" |
| 1948 | "Hamlet" | Laurence Olivier "Hamlet" | Jane Wyman "Johnny Belinda" | John Huston "Treasure of Sierra Madre" |
| 1947 | "Gentleman's Agreement" | Ronald Colman "A Double Life" | Loretta Young "The Farmer's Daughter" | Elia Kazan "Gentleman's Agreement" |
| 1946 | "The Best Years of Our Lives" | Frederic March "The Best Years of Our Lives" | Olivia de Havilland "To Each His Own" | William Wyler "The Best Years of Our Lives" |
| 1945 | "The Lost Weekend" | Ray Milland "The Lost Weekend" | Joan Crawford "Mildred Pierce" | Billy Wilder "The Lost Weekend" |
| 1944 | "Going My Way" | Bing Crosby "Going My Way" | Ingrid Bergman "Gaslight" | Leo McCarey "Going My Way" |
| 1943 | "Casablanca" | Paul Lukas "Watch on the Rhine" | Jennifer Jones "The Song of Bernadette" | Michael Curtiz "Casablanca" |
| 1942 | "Mrs. Miniver" | James Cagney "Yankee Doodle Dandy" | Greer Garson "Mrs. Miniver" | William Wyler "Mrs. Miniver" |
| 1941 | "How Green Was My Valley" | Gary Cooper "Sergeant York" | Joan Fontaine "Suspicion" | John Ford "How Green Was My Valley" |
| 1940 | "Rebecca" | James Stewart "The Philadelphia Story" | Ginger Rogers "Kitty Foyle" | John Ford "The Grapes of Wrath" |
| 1939 | "Gone with the Wind" | Robert Donat "Goodbye, Mr. Chips" | Vivien Leigh "Gone with the Wind" | Victor Fleming "Gone with the Wind" |
| 1938 | "You Can't Take It with You" | Spencer Tracy "Boys Town" | Bette Davis "Jezebel" | Frank Capra "You Can't Take It with You" |

| YEAR | BEST PICTURE | BEST ACTOR | BEST ACTRESS | BEST DIRECTOR |
|---|---|---|---|---|
| 1937 | "The Life of Emile Zola" | Spencer Tracy "Captains Courageous" | Luise Rainer "The Good Earth" | Leo McCarey "The Awful Truth" |
| 1936 | "The Great Ziegfeld" | Paul Muni "The Story of Louis Pasteur" | Luise Rainer "The Great Ziegfeld" | Frank Capra "Mr. Deeds Goes to Town" |
| 1935 | "Mutiny on the Bounty" | Victor McLaglen "The Informer" | Bette Davis "Dangerous" | John Ford "The Informer" |
| 1934 | "It Happened One Night" | Clark Gable "It Happened One Night" | Claudette Colbert "Private Worlds" | Frank Capra "It Happened One Night" |
| 1932–33 | "Cavalcade" | Charles Laughton "The Private Life of Henry VIII" | Katherine Hepburn "Morning Glory" | Frank Lloyd "Cavalcade" |
| 1931–32 | "Grand Hotel" | Wallace Beery "The Champ" Frederic March "Dr. Jekyll and Mr. Hyde" | Helen Hayes "The Sin of Madelon Claudet" | Frank Borzage "Bad Girl" |
| 1930–31 | "Cimarron" | Lionel Barrymore "A Free Soul" | Marie Dressler "Min and Bill" | Norman Taurog "Skippy" |
| 1929–30 | "All Quiet on the Western Front" | George Arliss "Disraeli" | Norma Shearer "The Divorcee" | Lewis Milestone "All Quiet on the Western Front" |
| 1928–29 | "Broadway Melody" | Warner Baxter "In Old Arizona" | Mary Pickford "Coquette" | Frank Lloyd "The Divine Lady" |
| 1927–28 | "Wings" | Emil Jannings "The Last Command" "The Way of All Flesh" | Janet Gaynor "Seventh Heaven" "Street Angel" "Sunrise" | Frank Borzage "Seventh Heaven" Lewis Milestone "Two Arabian Knights" |

## THE HALL OF FAME FOR GREAT AMERICANS

Established in 1900, the Hall of Fame for Great Americans honors United States citizens who have made significant contributions to the nation's history and culture. Elections to the Hall of Fame are held every five years (the most recent was in 1965). Any American may nominate a candidate for membership; nominees must be approved by a College of Electors, a body generally comprising more than 100 prominent persons. No more than seven new members may be elected to membership on a single ballot; four persons were elected in 1965, bringing current membership to 93. For each member of the Hall of Fame, a bronze portrait bust and an inscribed bronze tablet are installed in an open-air colonnade on the New York University Bronx campus, high above the Hudson River.

**MEMBERS OF THE HALL OF FAME**  **ELECTED**

Adams, John (1735–1826), statesman and President — 1900

Adams, John Quincy (1767–1848), statesman and President — 1905

Addams, Jane (1860–1935), social reformer — 1965

Agassiz, Louis (1807–73), naturalist — 1915

Anthony, Susan B. (1820–1906), social reformer — 1950

Audubon, John James (1785–1851), ornithologist and artist — 1900

Bancroft, George (1800–91), historian and diplomat — 1910

Beecher, Henry Ward (1813–87), theologian and author — 1900

Bell, Alexander Graham (1847–1922), scientist and inventor — 1950

Boone, Daniel (1734–1820), frontiersman — 1915

Booth, Edwin (1833–93), actor — 1925

Brooks, Phillips (1835–93), theologian — 1910

Bryant, William Cullen (1794–1878), poet and editor — 1910

Channing, William Ellery (1780–1842), theologian — 1900

Choate, Rufus (1799–1859), lawyer and legislator — 1915

Clay, Henry (1777–1852), statesman — 1900

Clemens, Samuel (Mark Twain) (1835–1910), novelist — 1920

Cleveland, Grover (1837–1908), statesman and President — 1935

Cooper, James Fenimore (1789–1851), novelist — 1910

Cooper, Peter (1791–1883), philanthropist — 1900

Cushman, Charlotte Saunders (1816–76), actress — 1915

Eads, James Buchanan (1820–87), engineer — 1920

Edison, Thomas Alva (1847–1931), inventor — 1960

Edwards, Jonathan (1703–58), theologian — 1900

Emerson, Ralph Waldo (1803–82), poet and essayist — 1900

Farragut, David Glasgow (1801–70), naval commander — 1900

Foster, Stephen (1826–64), composer — 1940

(continued)

**MEMBERS OF THE HALL OF FAME** (*continued*)

| | |
|---|---|
| Franklin, Benjamin (*1706–90*), statesman and inventor | 1900 |
| Fulton, Robert (*1765–1815*), inventor | 1900 |
| Gibbs, Josiah (*1839–1903*), physicist | 1950 |
| Gorgas, William Crawford (*1854–1920*), physician and scientist | 1950 |
| Grant, Ulysses S. (*1822–85*), Union general and President | 1900 |
| Gray, Asa (*1810–88*), botanist | 1900 |
| Hamilton, Alexander (*1755?–1804*), statesman | 1915 |
| Hawthorne, Nathaniel (*1804–64*), novelist and short-story writer | 1900 |
| Henry, Joseph (*1797–1878*), physicist | 1915 |
| Henry, Patrick (*1736–99*), statesman | 1920 |
| Holmes, Oliver Wendell (*1809–94*), essayist and poet | 1910 |
| Holmes, Oliver Wendell, Jr. (*1841–1935*), Supreme Court justice | 1965 |

Hall of Fame, New York University

*New York University*

| | |
|---|---|
| Hopkins, Mark (*1802–87*), educator | 1915 |
| Howe, Elias (*1819–67*), inventor | 1915 |
| Irving, Washington (*1783–1859*), author and diplomat | 1900 |
| Jackson, Andrew (*1767–1845*), statesman and President | 1910 |
| Jackson, Thomas J. (Stonewall) (*1824–63*), Confederate general | 1955 |
| Jefferson, Thomas (*1743–1826*), statesman and President | 1900 |
| Jones, John Paul (*1747–92*), naval commander | 1925 |
| Kent, James (*1763–1847*), jurist | 1900 |
| Lanier, Sidney (*1842–81*), poet and musician | 1945 |
| Lee, Robert E. (*1807–70*), Confederate general | 1900 |
| Lincoln, Abraham (*1809–65*), statesman and President | 1900 |
| Longfellow, Henry Wadsworth (*1807–82*), poet | 1900 |
| Lowell, James Russell (*1819–91*), poet, critic, and editor | 1905 |
| Lyon, Mary (*1797–1849*), educator | 1905 |
| MacDowell, Edward Alexander (*1861–1908*), composer | 1960 |
| Madison, James (*1751–1836*), statesman and President | 1905 |
| Mann, Horace (*1796–1859*), educator | 1900 |
| Marshall, John (*1755–1835*), Supreme Court justice | 1900 |
| Maury, Matthew Fontaine (*1806–73*), naval officer and oceanographer | 1930 |
| Mitchell, Maria (*1818–89*), astronomer | 1905 |
| Monroe, James (*1758–1831*), statesman and President | 1930 |
| Morse, Samuel F. B. (*1791–1872*), inventor | 1900 |
| Morton, William Thomas Green (*1819–68*), dentist | 1920 |
| Motley, John Lothrop (*1814–77*), historian and diplomat | 1910 |
| Newcomb, Simon (*1835–1909*), astronomer | 1935 |
| Paine, Thomas (*1737–1809*), political writer and pamphleteer | 1945 |
| Palmer, Alice Freeman (*1855–1902*), educator | 1920 |

| | |
|---|---|
| Parkman, Francis (*1823–93*), historian | 1915 |
| Peabody, George (*1795–1869*), financier and philanthropist | 1900 |
| Penn, William (*1644–1718*), colonial leader and statesman | 1935 |
| Poe, Edgar Allan (*1809–49*), poet, short-story writer, and critic | 1910 |
| Reed, Walter (*1851–1902*), physician and scientist | 1945 |
| Roosevelt, Theodore (*1858–1919*), statesman and President | 1950 |
| Saint-Gaudens, Augustus (*1848–1907*), sculptor | 1920 |
| Sherman, William Tecumseh (*1820–91*), Union general | 1905 |
| Story, Joseph (*1779–1845*), Supreme Court justice | 1900 |
| Stowe, Harriet Beecher (*1811–96*), humanitarian and novelist | 1910 |
| Stuart, Gilbert C. (*1755–1828*), portrait painter | 1900 |
| Thayer, Sylvanus (*1785–1872*), soldier and educator | 1965 |
| Thoreau, Henry David (*1817–62*), essayist and poet | 1960 |
| Washington, Booker T. (*1856–1915*), educator | 1945 |
| Washington, George (*1732–99*), Revolutionary War general and President | 1900 |
| Webster, Daniel (*1782–1852*), statesman | 1900 |
| Westinghouse, George (*1846–1914*), inventor | 1955 |
| Whistler, James Abbott McNeill (*1834–1903*), painter | 1930 |
| Whitman, Walt (*1819–92*), poet | 1930 |
| Whitney, Eli (*1765–1825*), inventor | 1900 |
| Whittier, John Greenleaf (*1807–92*), poet | 1905 |
| Willard, Emma (*1787–1870*), educator | 1905 |
| Willard, Frances Elizabeth (*1839–98*), social reformer | 1910 |
| Williams, Roger (*1603?–83*), colonial leader and theologian | 1920 |
| Wilson, Woodrow (*1856–1924*), statesman and President | 1950 |
| Wright, Orville (*1871–1948*), inventor | 1965 |
| Wright, Wilbur (*1867–1912*), inventor | 1955 |

# SELECTED AWARDS IN VARIOUS FIELDS

Thousands of awards are conferred each year in the United States by civic, professional, academic, and government organizations in recognition of meritorious service or performance in a variety of professions and disciplines. The following list contains a selection of awards presented in 1967 that are of particular significance or importance in their fields.

## NATIONAL INSTITUTE OF ARTS AND LETTERS

The National Institute of Arts and Letters was founded in 1898 to foster excellence in literature and the fine arts in the United States. At present 250 American citizens noted for outstanding achievements in art, literature, or music are members.

Fifty members comprise the American Academy of Arts and Letters, the National Institute's guiding body.

It is a joint function of the Institute and the Academy to elect eminent foreign artists, writers, and composers as honorary members, in order to establish and retain cultural ties between the United States and other nations.

Each year both the National Institute and the American Academy confer awards designed to afford recognition and impetus to artistic endeavors in this country. Here follows a list of awards announced by the Institute and the Academy during 1967.

**Arts and Letters Grants** ($2,500), awarded by the Institute to honor and encourage distinguished artists, composers, and writers who are not members of the Institute.
ART: Byron Burford, Jared French, Stephen Greene, Leo Kenney, Dennis Leon, Hugh Townley, Louis Tytell.
LITERATURE: Philip Booth, Hortense Calisher, Daniel Hoffman, Stanley E. Hyman, Bernard M. W. Knox, Walker Percy, David Wagoner.
MUSIC: George H. Crumb, Donald Martino, Julian Orbon, Charles Wuorinen.
**Award of Merit in Painting** ($1,000), awarded by the Academy: John Heliker.
**The Gold Medal of the Institute in Fiction:** Katherine Anne Porter.
**The Gold Medal of the Institute in History and Biography:** Arthur M. Schlesinger, Jr.
**Richard and Hinda Rosenthal Foundation**

**Award in Literature** ($2,000), presented by the Institute for an American novel which, though not a commercial success, is a considerable literary achievement: Thomas Pynchon, *The Crying of Lot 49* (J. B. Lippincott Co.).
**Richard and Hinda Rosenthal Foundation Award in Painting** ($2,000), presented by the Institute to a young American painter of distinction who has not yet been accorded due recognition: Robert D'Arista.
**Traveling Fellowship in Literature** ($5,000), awarded by the Academy to a young American writer of great promise for one year of residence and travel abroad: A. R. Ammons.
**Marjorie Peabody Waite Award** ($1,500), conferred annually on an older artist, writer, or composer for continuing achievement and integrity in his art: Stringfellow Barr.

## ART AND ARCHITECTURE

**Benjamin Altman Awards,** presented by the National Academy of Design: William Thon, painter, Isabel Bishop, painter ($2,000 each); Paul W. Zimmerman, painter, Mary Fife, painter ($1,000 each).
**American Institute of Architects Awards**
FINE ARTS MEDAL, awarded for distinguished achievement in the fine arts related to architecture: Costantino Nivola, sculptor.
GOLD MEDAL, awarded for distinguished service to architecture or to the Institute: Wallace K. Harrison, architect.
HONOR AWARDS: Fred Bassetti & Co., Seattle, Washington, for Ridgeway Men's Dormitories, Phase III, Western Washington State College, Bellingham, Washington; Caudill Rowlett Scott and Partners, Houston, Texas, for Jesse H. Jones Hall for the Performing Arts, Houston, Texas; Hammel Green & Abrahamson, Inc., St. Paul, Minnesota, for St. Bede's Priory, Eau Claire, Wisconsin; Vincent G. Kling & Associates, Philadelphia, Pennsylvania, for the Municipal Services Building, Philadelphia; Ian Mackinlay AIA & Associates, Orinda, California, for Boreal Ridge, Truckee, California; Moore, Lyndon, Turnbull, Whitaker, Berkeley, California, for Sea Ranch Condominium I, Sonoma County, California; I. M. Pei & Partners, New York City, for University Plaza, New York University, New York City; Pomerance & Breines, New York City, for amphitheater and plaza, Jacob Riis Houses, New York City; Skidmore, Owings & Merrill, New York City, for the National Headquarters Building, American Republic Insurance Co., Des Moines, Iowa, the Banque Lambert Office Building and Residence, Brussels, Belgium, the Beinecke Rare Book and Manuscript Library, Yale University, New Haven, Connecticut, Mauna Kea Beach Hotel, Kamuela, Hawaii, and Vannevar Bush Center for Materials Science and Engineering, Massachusetts Institute of Technology, Cambridge, Massachusetts; Smith, Hinchman & (*continued*)

**SELECTED AWARDS** (*continued*)

Grylls Associates, Inc., Detroit, Michigan, for the First Federal Office Building, Detroit, Michigan; Neill Smith and Associates, San Francisco, California, for Redwood National Bank, Napa, California; Stickney & Hull, Berkeley, California, for Los Gatos Civic Center, Los Gatos, California; Edward Durell Stone, New York City, for Museo de Arte de Ponce, Ponce, Puerto Rico; The Architects Collaborative, Inc., Cambridge, Massachusetts, for Dormitory and Commons Building Quadrangle, Clark University, Worcester, Massachusetts, and C. Thurston Chase Learning Center, Eaglebrook School, Deerfield, Massachusetts; Toombs, Amisano & Wells, Atlanta, Georgia, for John Knox Presbyterian Church, Marietta, Georgia.

## LITERATURE

**Academy of American Poets Fellowship** ($5,000): John Berryman.

**Bancroft Prizes of Columbia University** ($4,000 each), for the year's best books on American history: Dr. James Sterling Young, *The Washington Community, 1800–1828* (Columbia University Press); Dr. Charles Sellers, *James K. Polk, Continentalist: 1843–1846* (Princeton University Press); Dr. William W. Freehling, *Prelude to Civil War: The Nullification Controversy in South Carolina, 1816–1836* (Harper & Row).

**Bollingen Prize in Poetry** ($5,000), awarded biennially by Yale University (1967): Robert Penn Warren.

**Brandeis University Creative Arts Awards** (medal and $1,000 each)
ARCHITECTURE: Ludwig Mies van der Rohe
MUSIC: Ross Lee Finney
POETRY: Conrad Aiken
THEATER: Jerome Robbins
NOTABLE CREATIVE ACHIEVEMENT: Kenneth Burke

**John Burroughs Association Medal,** for the year's outstanding book on natural history: Charlton Ogburn, Jr., *The Winter Beach* (William Morrow & Co.).

**Carey-Thomas Award,** for a distinguished project of creative publishing: George Braziller, Inc., *The Hours of Catherine of Cleves.*

**William Faulkner Foundation Award,** for a notable first novel by an American: Robert Coover, *The Origin of the Brunists* (G. P. Putnam's Sons).

**Friends of American Writers Award** ($1,000), for a distinguished novel: Frederick J. Lipp, *Rulers of Darkness* (World Publishing Co.).

**George Jean Nathan Award** ($4,000), for dramatic criticism: Eric Bentley, Columbia University, for work published in the *Tulane Drama Review.*

**National Catholic Book Awards,** presented by the Catholic Press Association for the year's best books of Catholic and general interest: Rev. John L. McKenzie, S. J., *Authority in the Church* (Sheed and Ward); Rev. Walter

M. Abbott, S. J., general editor, *The Documents of Vatican II* (Herder & Herder, Association Press); Leslie Dewart, *The Future of Belief* (Herder & Herder); Rev. Alexander Jones, general editor, *The Jerusalem Bible* (Doubleday & Co.); Rev. Christopher F. Mooney, *Teilhard de Chardin and the Mystery of Christ* (Harper & Row).

**National Medal for Literature,** presented by the National Book Committee: W. H. Auden, poet, essayist, and playwright.

**Francis Parkman Prize** ($500), awarded by the Society of American Historians for the best book on American history: William H. Goetzmann, *Exploration and Empire: The Explorer and Scientist in the Winning of the American West* (Alfred A. Knopf, Inc.).

**P.E.N. Translation Award** ($1,000): Harriet de Onis, for the translation from the Portuguese of João Guimaraes Rosa's *Sagarana* (Alfred A. Knopf, Inc.).

**Phi Beta Kappa Book Awards** ($1,000 each)
RALPH WALDO EMERSON AWARD, for a comprehensive study of the intellectual and cultural condition of man: John Herman Randall, Jr., *The Career of Philosophy: From the German Enlightenment to the Age of Darwin.* (Columbia University Press).
CHRISTIAN GAUSS AWARD, for literary scholarship or criticism: Wilfred Stone, *The Cave and the Mountain: A Study of E. M. Forster* (Stanford University Press).
PHI BETA KAPPA AWARD IN SCIENCE, for outstanding contributions to the literature of science: René Dubos, *Man Adapting* (Yale University Press).

**Edgar Allan Poe Award,** presented by the Mystery Writers of America for the best mystery novel of the year: Nicholas Freeling, *The King of the Rainy Country* (Harper & Row).

**Poetry Society of America Awards**
ALICE FAY DI CASTAGNOLA AWARD ($3,500), for a work in progress: Gustav Davidson.
MELVILLE CANE AWARD ($500), for the best published book of poems by an American poet: Lawrence Thompson, *Robert Frost: The Early Years* (Holt, Rinehart & Winston).

## MUSIC

**Anne Gannet Awards,** presented by the National Federation of Music Clubs: Wesley C. Flinn, baritone ($500); Bruce James Headlee, composer ($200).

**Grammy Awards,** presented by the National Academy of Recording Arts and Sciences.
RECORD OF THE YEAR: Frank Sinatra, *Strangers in the Night* (Reprise).
NONCLASSICAL ALBUM OF THE YEAR: Frank Sinatra, *A Man and His Music* (Reprise).
SONG OF THE YEAR: *Michelle,* written and composed by John Lennon and Paul McCartney (Capitol).
BEST INSTRUMENTAL THEME: *Batman Theme,* composed by Neil Hefti (RCA).
BEST FEMALE VOCAL PERFORMANCE: Eydie Gorme, *If He Walked into My Life* (Columbia).

BEST MALE VOCAL PERFORMANCE: Frank Sinatra, *Strangers in the Night* (Reprise).

BEST INSTRUMENTAL PERFORMANCE (other than jazz): Herb Alpert & the Tijuana Brass, *What Now My Love* (A&M).

BEST INSTRUMENTAL JAZZ PERFORMANCE: Wes Montgomery, *Goin' Out of My Head* (Verve).

BEST ORIGINAL JAZZ COMPOSITION: Duke Ellington, *In the Beginning God* (RCA).

BEST CONTEMPORARY SINGLE: Geoff Stephens, New Vaudeville Band, *Winchester Cathedral* (Fontana).

BEST CONTEMPORARY SOLO VOCAL PERFORMANCE: Paul McCartney (The Beatles), *Eleanor Rigby* (Capitol).

BEST CONTEMPORARY GROUP PERFORMANCE: The Mamas and The Papas, *Monday, Monday* (Dunhill).

BEST FOLK RECORDING: Cortelia Clark, *Blues in the Street* (RCA).

CLASSICAL ALBUM OF THE YEAR: Morton Gould conducting the Chicago Symphony Orchestra, *Ives: Symphony No. 1 in D Minor* (RCA).

BEST ORCHESTRA PERFORMANCE: Eric Leinsdorf conducting the Boston Symphony Orchestra, *Mahler: Symphony No. 6 in A Minor* (RCA).

BEST CHAMBER MUSIC PERFORMANCE: Boston Symphony Chamber Players, *Boston Symphony Chamber Players* (RCA).

BEST SOLO INSTRUMENT PERFORMANCE: Julian Bream, *Baroque Guitar* (RCA).

BEST PERFORMANCE BY A VOCAL SOLOIST: Leontyne Price, *Prima Donna* (RCA).

BEST OPERA RECORDING: Georg Solti conducting the Vienna Philharmonic Orchestra, *Wagner: Die Walküre* (London).

**Leventritt International Music Competition for Violin** (1967): Pinchas Zuckerman, Israel; Kyung Whachung, Korea ($1,000 each).

**Metropolitan Opera National Council Auditions**

FRANK CHAPMAN MEMORIAL AWARD ($2,000): Paula Page.

ROSLYN WEISBERG COMINSKY AWARD ($2,000): Sidney Johnson.

MILTON J. CROSS AWARD ($2,000): Costanza Cuccaro.

STEVENSON H. EVANS MEMORIAL AWARD ($2,000): Sung Sook Lee.

ELSE L. BERNARD JOSEPH MEMORIAL AWARD ($2,000): Valerie Hanlon.

ANNE ROSOFF MEMORIAL AWARD ($2,000): George Reid.

VIRGINIA MARVIN STOUGHTON AWARD ($2,000): Lauretta Young.

GLADYS AXMAN TAYLOR AWARD ($2,000): Sakiko Kanamori.

MRS. FREDERICK K. WEYERHAEUSER AWARD ($2,000): Noel Rogers.

**Phebe Ketchum Thorne Honorary Award** ($3,000): Harry Partch, composer.

## THEATER

**Clarence Derwent Acting Prizes,** for young performers in nonfeatured roles ($500): Reva Rose, *You're a Good Man, Charlie Brown*; Austin Pendleton, *Hail Scrawdyke*; Phillip Bosco, New York Shakespeare Company, the American Shakespeare Festival, and the Repertory Theater of Lincoln Center.

**New York Drama Critics' Circle Awards**

BEST PLAY: *The Homecoming*, by Harold Pinter.

BEST MUSICAL: *Cabaret*, by Joe Masteroff, John Kander, and Fred Ebb.

**Antoinette Perry (Tony) Awards**

BEST PLAY: *The Homecoming*, by Harold Pinter.

BEST MUSICAL: *Cabaret*, by Joe Masteroff, John Kander, and Fred Ebb.

BEST DRAMATIC STAR: Paul Rogers, *The Homecoming.*

BEST DRAMATIC ACTRESS: Beryl Reid, *The Killing of Sister George.*

BEST MUSICAL STAR: Robert Preston, *I Do! I Do!*

BEST MUSICAL ACTRESS: Barbara Harris, *The Apple Tree.*

BEST FEATURED DRAMATIC STAR: Ian Holm, *The Homecoming.*

BEST SUPPORTING DRAMATIC ACTRESS: Marian Seldes, *A Delicate Balance.*

BEST SUPPORTING MUSICAL STAR: Joel Grey, *Cabaret.*

BEST SUPPORTING MUSICAL ACTRESS: Peg Murray, *Cabaret.*

BEST DIRECTOR: Peter Hall, *The Homecoming.*

BEST MUSICAL DIRECTOR: Harold Prince, *Cabaret.*

BEST COMPOSER AND LYRICIST: Fred Ebb and John Kander, *Cabaret.*

BEST SCENIC DESIGNER: Boris Aronson, *Cabaret.*

BEST COSTUME DESIGNER: Patricia Zipprodt, *Cabaret.*

BEST CHOREOGRAPHER: Ronald Field, *Cabaret.*

**Vernon Rice Awards,** presented by the Drama Desk for excellence in the Off-Broadway Theater.

PLAYWRIGHTS: Jean Claude van Itallie, *America Hurrah*; Langford Wilson, *The Rimers of Eldritch.*

PERFORMERS: Bill Hinnant, *You're a Good Man, Charlie Brown*; Stacy Keach, *Mac Bird!*; Dustin Hoffman, *Eh?*; Will Lee, *The Deer Park.*

DIRECTOR: Joseph Hardy, *You're a Good Man, Charlie Brown.*

## DANCE

**Capezio Dance Award** ($1,000), "for vital and lasting contributions by an individual to the progress of the dance in America": Paul Taylor, dancer and choreographer.

## JOURNALISM

**Albert Lasker Medical Journalism Awards** ($2,500 in each category), presented by the
*(continued)*

**SELECTED AWARDS** (*continued*)

Albert and Mary Lasker Foundation for distinguished work in the mass media on medical research and public health: Barbara Yuncker. *New York Post*, for the series, "The Pill"; Lawrence Lessing, *Fortune*, for the series, "The Biology Revolution"; WABC-TV for "The Long Childhood of Timmy," a program on mental retardation; WXYZ-TV for "End Measles Sunday," a program that fostered a one-day mass inoculation drive against measles; Albert Rosenfeld, *Life*, for "the consistent excellence of *Life's* medical articles in recent years" and "leadership in medical journalism."

**Overseas Press Club Awards**

BEST DAILY NEWSPAPER OR WIRE SERVICE REPORTING FROM ABROAD: Hugh Mulligan, Associated Press.

BEST DAILY OR WIRE SERVICE INTERPRETATION OF FOREIGN AFFAIRS: Robert S. Elegant, *Los Angeles Times*.

BEST DAILY NEWSPAPER OR WIRE SERVICE PHOTOGRAPHIC REPORTING FROM ABROAD: Kyoichi Sawada, United Press International.

BEST PHOTOGRAPHIC REPORTING OR INTERPRETATION FROM ABROAD IN A MAGAZINE OR A BOOK: Marc Riboud, Magnum, for *The Three Banners of China* (Macmillan Co.)

BEST RADIO REPORTING FROM ABROAD: Sam Jaffe, ABC News.

BEST RADIO INTERPRETATION OF FOREIGN AFFAIRS: NBC News.

BEST TELEVISION REPORTING FROM ABROAD: Morley Safer, CBS News.

BEST TELEVISION INTERPRETATION OF FOREIGN AFFAIRS: Howard K. Smith, ABC News.

BEST MAGAZINE REPORTING FROM ABROAD: Sybille Bedford, for "Auschwitz: The Worst That Ever Happened," published in *The Saturday Evening Post*.

BEST MAGAZINE INTERPRETATION OF FOREIGN AFFAIRS: Eric Sevareid, for work appearing in *Look*.

BEST BOOK ON FOREIGN AFFAIRS: Welles Hagen, *The Muted Revolution* (Alfred A. Knopf, Inc.).

THE VISION MAGAZINE ED STOUT AWARD ($500), for the best article or report on Latin America in any medium: Georgie Anne Geyer, *The Chicago Daily News*.

THE E. W. FAIRCHILD AWARD ($500), for the best business news report from abroad in any medium: Lawrence Malkin, Associated Press.

THE ROBERT CAPA GOLD MEDAL AWARD for superlative still photography requiring exceptional courage and enterprise abroad: Henri Huet, Associated Press.

THE ASIA MAGAZINE AWARD, for the best article or report on Asia in any medium ($500): Harrison Salisbury, *The New York Times*.

THE GEORGE POLK MEMORIAL AWARD, for the best reporting in any medium requiring exceptional courage and enterprise abroad

($500): Ron Nessen and crew, NBC News.

SPECIAL AWARD, for outstanding work in journalism, given by the Overseas Press Club: Henry Luce, founder-publisher, *Time* and *Life* magazines.

**Page One Awards of the Newspaper Guild of New York,** for continuous journalistic excellence.

BEST CRUSADING NEWSPAPER: *New York Post*.

BEST LOCAL REPORTING: Edith Evans Asbury, *The New York Times*.

BEST FEATURE WRITING: Harold Phelan, Frank Sugrue, Mort Young, John Molleson, Patricia Smith, and Ara Piastro, *World Journal Tribune*.

BEST FEATURE CARTOON: Pierre E. Bellocq (PEB), *Morning Telegraph*.

BEST FEATURE PHOTOGRAPHY: Frank Hurley, *New York Daily News*.

BEST SPOT NEWS PHOTOGRAPHY: Mel Finkelstein, *World Journal Tribune*.

BEST SPORTS PHOTOGRAPHY: Walter Kelleher, *New York Daily News*.

BEST EDITORIAL CARTOON: Warren King, *New York Daily News*.

BEST NEWSMAGAZINE WRITING OF THE YEAR: Staff, *Newsweek*.

BEST NEWSMAGAZINE PHOTOGRAPHY: Douglas Jones, *Look*.

**George Polk Memorial Awards**

FOREIGN REPORTING: Harrison E. Salisbury, *The New York Times*.

NATIONAL REPORTING: *Richard Harwood, The Washington Post*.

LOCAL REPORTING: Cal Olson, *The Fargo* (North Dakota) *Forum*.

INTERPRETIVE REPORTING: Murray Kempton, *New York Post*.

MAGAZINE REPORTING: *Ramparts*.

CRITICISM: Alfred Kazin.

BOOK: *Modern American Usage*, by Wilson H. Follett.

NEWS PHOTOGRAPHY: Horst Faas, Associated Press.

SPECIAL AWARD: Arnold Gingrich, *Esquire*.

SPECIAL AWARD: Time Essay, *Time*.

**Sigma Delta Chi Society Awards,** for distinguished service in journalism.

GENERAL REPORTING: Stanley W. Penn and Monroe W. Karmin, *The Wall Street Journal*.

EDITORIAL WRITING: Duane Croft, *The Blade*, Toledo, Ohio.

WASHINGTON CORRESPONDENCE: Richard Harwood, *The Washington Post*.

FOREIGN CORRESPONDENCE: Robert S. Elegant, *Los Angeles Times*.

NEWS PHOTOGRAPHY: Ray Mews, *Sioux Falls* (South Dakota) *Argus-Leader*.

EDITORIAL CARTOONING: Patrick B. Oliphant, *Denver* (Colorado) *Post*.

NEWSPAPER PUBLIC SERVICE: *Los Angeles Times* and the *Long Island Press*.

MAGAZINE REPORTING: John G. Hubbell, *The Reader's Digest*.

MAGAZINE PUBLIC SERVICE: *Life*.

RADIO EDITORIALIZING: WAIT, Chicago.

RADIO REPORTING: KTBC Radio News, Austin, Texas.

RADIO PUBLIC SERVICE: WIBW Radio, Topeka, Kansas.

TELEVISION REPORTING: WSB-TV News, Atlanta, Georgia.

TELEVISION PUBLIC SERVICE: KLZ-TV, Denver, Colorado.

TELEVISION EDITORIALIZING: WFBM-TV, Indianapolis, Indiana.

JOURNALISM RESEARCH: Kenneth E. Olson, Northwestern University.

**Society of the Silurians Awards,** for excellence in newspaper journalism.

EDITORIAL WRITING AWARD: Joseph E. Evans, *The Wall Street Journal.*

SPOT NEWS AWARD: Theo Wilson, *New York Daily News.*

PUBLIC SERVICE AWARD: *The Record,* Hackensack, New Jersey.

FEATURE NEWS STORY AWARD: John D. Williams, *The Wall Street Journal.*

SPOT NEWS PHOTO AWARD: Richard Kraus, *Newsday.*

FEATURE PHOTO AWARD: Frank Hurley, *New York Daily News.*

CARTOONING AWARD: Warren King, *New York Daily News.*

CHARLES M. LINCOLN-CHARLES P. COOPER AWARD: Paul Brinkley-Rogers, Columbia University.

## RADIO AND TELEVISION

**Emmy Awards,** presented by the National Academy of Television Arts and Sciences.

BEST COMEDY SERIES: *The Monkees.*

BEST VARIETY SERIES: *The Andy Williams Show.*

BEST VARIETY SPECIAL: *The Sid Caesar, Imogene Coca, Carl Reiner, Howard Morris Special.*

BEST DRAMATIC SERIES: *Mission: Impossible.*

BEST SINGLE DRAMA: *Death of a Salesman.*

BEST SINGLE MUSICAL: *Brigadoon.*

BEST CHILDREN'S PROGRAM: *Jack and the Beanstalk.*

BEST ACTOR: Single Dramatic Performance, Leading Role: Peter Ustinov, *Barefoot in Athens,* on *Hallmark Hall of Fame;* Continuing Dramatic Performance, Leading Role: Bill Cosby, *I Spy;* Continuing Comic Performance, Leading Role: Don Adams, *Get Smart!;* Dramatic Performance, Supporting Role: Eli Wallach, *The Poppy Is Also a Flower,* a Xerox Special; Comic Performance, Supporting Role: Don Knotts, *Barney Comes to Mayberry,* on *The Andy Griffith Show.*

BEST ACTRESS: Single Dramatic Performance, Leading Role: Geraldine Page, *A Christmas Memory,* on *ABC Stage 67;* Continuing Dramatic Performance, Leading Role: Barbara Bain, *Mission: Impossible;* Continuing Comic Performance, Leading Role: Lucille Ball, *The Lucy Show;* Dramatic Performance, Supporting Role: Agnes Moorehead, *Night of the Vicious Valentine,*

on *Wild, Wild West;* Comic Performance, Supporting Role: Frances Bavier, *The Andy Griffith Show.*

BEST NEWS AND DOCUMENTARY: *China: The Roots of Madness, Hall of Kings, The Italians.*

BEST SPORTS PROGRAM: *ABC's Wide World of Sports.*

**National Association of Broadcasters Awards**

DISTINGUISHED SERVICE AWARD: Chet Huntley and David Brinkley, NBC News.

ENGINEERING ACHIEVEMENT AWARD: Robert Morris, staff consultant, ABC engineering department.

RADIO CODE AWARD OF MERIT: Alabama Broadcasters Association.

## FILMS

**New York Film Critics' Awards**

BEST PICTURE: *A Man for All Seasons.*

BEST ACTOR: Paul Scofield, *A Man for All Seasons.*

BEST ACTRESS: Elizabeth Taylor, *Who's Afraid of Virginia Woolf?,* and Lynn Redgrave, *Georgy Girl.*

BEST DIRECTOR: Fred Zinnemann, *A Man for All Seasons.*

BEST WRITER: Robert Bolt, *A Man for All Seasons.*

BEST FOREIGN-LANGUAGE FILM: *The Shop on Main Street* (Czechoslovakia).

## MEDICINE

**Banting Memorial Award** of the American Diabetes Association: Dr. Alexander Marble, Boston, Massachusetts.

**Banting Medal** of the American Diabetes Association: Dr. L. O. Underdahl, Rochester, Minnesota.

**Distinguished Service Award of the American Psychiatric Association:** Dr. Howard Potter, for outstanding contributions to the care of retarded children.

**Ramon Guiteras Award** ($5,000), of the American Urological Association, for outstanding work in urology: Dr. Reed M. Nesbit, University of Michigan.

**Albert Lasker Medical Research Awards** ($10,000 each), for distinguished work in medical research, or contributions to public health and public health administration.

BASIC RESEARCH AWARD: George E. Palade, Ph.D., for cellular research.

CLINICAL RESEARCH AWARD: Dr. Sidney Farber, for cancer research.

ALBERT LASKER PUBLIC SERVICE AWARD: Mrs. Eunice Kennedy Shriver, for meritorious work in mental retardation.

**Lederle Medical Faculty Awards,** to outstanding medical teachers and researchers (equal shares of a $250,000 grant): Dr. James W. West, University of Pennsylvania; Dr. William A. Peck, Rochester School of Medicine; Dr. John W. C. Johnson, Johns Hopkins University; Dr. Franklin Fuchs, Uni-

(*continued*)

**SELECTED AWARDS** (continued)

versity of Pittsburgh; Dr. Barry D. Lindley, Western Reserve University; Dr. Samuel L. Kountz, Stanford University; Dr. Leodis Davis, Howard University; Dr. Fred N. White, University of California Medical School; George J. Hill II, M.D., University of Colorado School of Medicine; Dr. Michael W. Rytel, University of Tennessee; Dr. William C. Govier, University of Texas Southwestern Medical School.

**Meltzer Award** of the Society for Experimental Biology and Medicine ($500), for the most meritorious work in experimental biology: Dr. Elliot Vesell, National Institute of Health, Bethesda, Maryland.

**Margaret Sanger Award** of the American Association of Planned Parenthood-World Population: President Lyndon B. Johnson, John D. Rockefeller III.

## SCIENCE

**Frederick Chandler Medal,** presented by Columbia University for outstanding achievement in pure or applied chemistry: Louis P. Hammett, Professor Emeritus, Columbia University.

**Enrico Fermi Award,** presented by the Atomic Energy Commission for "especially meritorious contributions to the development, use, or control of atomic energy" (equal shares of a $50,000 grant): Dr. Otto Hahn, Dr. Lise Meitner, and Dr. Fritz Strassman, German nuclear scientists, for their combined and separate work in the discovery of nuclear fission.

**E. O. Lawrence Memorial Awards** ($5,000 each), presented by the Atomic Energy Commission for outstanding contributions to the field of atomic energy: Dr. Mortimer M. Elkind, National Cancer Institute; Dr. John M. Googin, Oak Ridge Plant; Dr. Allan F. Henry, Bettis Atomic Power Laboratory; Dr. John O. Rasmussen, Lawrence Radiation Laboratory; Dr. Robert N. Thorn, Los Alamos Laboratory.

**National Academy of Sciences Awards**

UNITED STATES STEEL FOUNDATION AWARD, for distinguished work in molecular biology: Dr. Robert W. Holly, Cornell University.

J. LAWRENCE SMITH MEDAL, for outstanding work in the investigation of meteoric bodies: Dr. John H. Reynolds, University of California.

DANIEL GIRAUD ELLIOT MEDAL, for an outstanding published work in zoology or paleontology: Dr. Ernst Mayr, Harvard University, *Animal Species and Evolution* (Harvard University Press).

CHARLES DOOLITTLE WALCOTT MEDAL: Dr. Allison R. Palmer, State University of New York, Stony Brook, New York, for his outstanding work on animal fossils.

KIMBER GENETICS MEDAL: Dr. Barbara McClintock, Carnegie Institution of Washington, for studies on chromosome structure and function.

GIBBS BROTHERS MEDAL, for outstanding contributions in the field of naval architecture and marine engineering: Dr. Alfred A. H. Keil, Massachusetts Institute of Technology.

MARY CLARK THOMPSON MEDAL: Dr. Wendell Phillips Woodring, Smithsonian Institution, for research in geology and paleontology.

FOUNDERS' MEDAL, presented by the National Academy of Engineering: James S. McDonnell, McDonnell Aircraft Corporation, for outstanding contributions in design and development of military aircraft, and pioneer work in space technology.

**National Medals of Science of the United States,** presented by the President.

BIOLOGICAL SCIENCES: Edward F. Knipling, Department of Agriculture; Fritz A. Lipmann, Rockefeller University; William C. Rose, University of Illinois; Sewall Wright, University of Wisconsin.

ENGINEERING SCIENCES: Claude E. Shannon, Massachusetts Institute of Technology; Vladimir K. Zworykin, Radio Corporation of America.

MATHEMATICAL SCIENCES: John W. Milnor, Princeton University.

PHYSICAL SCIENCES: Jacob A. B. Bjerknes, University of California; Subrahmanyan Chandrasekhar, University of Chicago; Henry Eyring, University of Utah; John H. Van Vleck, Harvard University.

**Priestley Memorial Award** ($1,000), presented by Dickinson College for invention, discovery, or research benefiting mankind: Dr. George W. Beadle, University of Chicago.

## PUBLIC SERVICE

**American Council for Nationalities Service Golden Door Award,** to a foreign-born citizen who has made outstanding contributions to American life and culture: Frederic O. Hess, inventor and industrialist.

**Aspen Institute for Humanistic Studies Award** ($30,000), for the greatest contribution to the advancement of the humanities: Dr. Gilberto Freyre, Brazilian author.

**Freedom Award of the International Rescue Committee,** for lasting contributions to the cause of freedom: David Sarnoff, Radio Corporation of America.

**Freedom House Award:** Roy Wilkins, National Association for the Advancement of Colored People, for his intelligent guidance in the struggle for human rights.

**United States Department of Interior Conservation Service Awards,** presented annually for outstanding contributions in the safeguarding of the nation's natural resources: Maurice Arnold, Hinsdale, Montana; Dr. William S. Cooper, Boulder, Colorado; Robert McColly, Hinsdale, Montana; Ernest C. Oberholtzer, Ranier, Minnesota; Mrs. Dawn Peseau, Reedsport, Oregon; Dr. Eliot F. Porter, Santa Fe, New Mexico; Melvin Ruder, Columbia Falls, Montana; John W. Simmons, Orange, Texas; Walter A. Weber, Oakton, Virginia.

# SPORTS

## Olympic Games · Pan-American Games · Reviews and Records of Individual Sports

Site of the 1968 Olympic Games, this main stadium in Mexico City will seat 80,000 spectators.

### THE OLYMPIC GAMES

Although the Olympic Games have as their purpose the bringing together of the world's youth in fellowship and athletic rivalry, seldom have they been free of controversy and friction. The 1968 Games, to be held in Mexico City October 12-27, will be no exception. Ever since the International Olympic Committee (IOC) named Mexico as the host country for the XIX Olympiad, there has been heated debate over the possibly adverse effect on participating athletes of the rarefied air of Mexico City, with its 7,430-foot altitude.

Coaches in the 123 invited countries began early to search for training facilities at comparable altitudes. Potential United States Olympians spent training periods in Colorado, Arizona, New Mexico, and the mountainous sections of California. The Soviet Union established a basketball training camp high in the Urals. The trend became so general that the IOC finally decreed that no athlete could spend more than six weeks in such preparation and that no more than one month of it could take place immediately prior to the games.

Mexican officials have ridiculed the fears of the coaches, pointing out that the Pan-American Games athletes of 1955 suffered no ill effects and actually set one world record in track and field. However, they did promise to have their Olympic Village open by September 15 so that the athletes could acclimatize themselves.

The opening and closing ceremonies at Mexico City and all the track and field competition are to be held in the enlarged main stadium (shown above), originally built for the 1955 Pan-American Games. *(continued)*

Star U.S. athletes scheduled to compete in the 1968 Olympics include: Jim Ryun (left), record-holding miler; Claudia Kolb, AAU champion swimmer; and John Pennel, seven-foot-plus pole vaulter.

### THE OLYMPIC GAMES (*continued*)

Hollowed out of a lava bed, it now seats 80,000. The new Aztec Stadium, dedicated in May, 1966, has a capacity of 98,500 and is to be used for soccer only.

Also new is the Sports Palace, which can accommodate 24,000 for boxing or 16,000 for basketball and volleyball. Other new facilities are the outdoor, roofed swimming pool and the Veledrome for cycling. The Olympic Village is expected to house 8,000 athletes, coaches, officials, and newsmen. Built on a 98-acre tract by a government bank and loaned to the organizing committee, it will ultimately become an apartment complex.

The Mexican program calls for competition in 19 sports, one less than the number at Tokyo, where judo was included. Still on the schedule are track and field, basketball, boxing, canoeing, cycling, equestrianism, fencing, field hockey, gymnastics, modern pentathlon, rowing, shooting, soccer, swimming and diving, volleyball, water polo, weight lifting, wrestling, and yachting.

The field of contestants will be the most competent ever. In the past, countries could bring almost as many athletes as their own budgets permitted, although not more than two could compete in the individual events. However, for the Mexican games a stringent set of standards must be met before an athlete can become a resident of the Olympic Village. For instance, Henry Eriksson of Sweden won the 1,500-meter run (the metric mile) in 3 minutes, 49.8 seconds at London in 1948 when competition was revived after World War II. But to be accepted for the coming games, the runner must have an official tryout time of 3 minutes, 42 seconds.

With the world's record holder in the mile, Jim Ryun of the University of Kansas; the world's only 70-foot shot-putter, Randy Matson of Texas A&M; John Pennel and several other 17-foot pole-vaulters, and hordes of sprinters and hurdlers, the U.S. should continue to dominate in men's track and field. U.S. girls, always potent in the sprints, have improved in the longer distances and should score heavily. The U.S. also should be strong in basketball and swimming.

The U.S. has won every Olympic basketball title since the sport was added to the program in 1936. Thanks to the availability of seven-foot Lew Alcindor of UCLA, the U.S. will be favored once more in 1968.

Eleven new events have been added to the swimming and diving program, and this should boost the U.S. medal harvest. At Tokyo in 1964, the U.S. won 13 of 18 gold medals, with Don Schollander taking four of them. So fantastic has been the improvement in swimming since then that now Mark Spitz, a 17-year-old from Santa Clara, California, overshadows him. It is possible that the girls—led by 15-year-old Catie Ball of Jacksonville, Florida, 16-year-old Pamela Kruse of Fort Lauderdale, Florida, and 16-year-old Lillian ("Pokey") Watson and 17-year-old Claudia Kolb, both of Santa Clara, California—will take all 14 gold medals in their division.

While Mexico City's Olympic sites are a collection of old and new facilities, those at Grenoble, France, are new for the Winter Games, from February 6 to 18. The facilities have been built virtually from scratch at an estimated sum of $200,000,000, including the cost of a new city hall, a new railroad station, and a new communications system. A huge apartment house and a modernized road system are also included.

Sites of the various snow-and-ice sports are scattered all over the Grenoble area, which is in the French Alps, approximately 40 miles from the Italian border. An Ice Palace that seats 14,000 was built in Grenoble for figure skating and hockey, as was a speed-skating rink that is expected to become a children's playground after the Winter Games. The bobsledding runs are to be held at L'Alpe d'Huez, the luge (sledding) at Villard-de-Lans, and the 90-meter ski jump at Saint Nizier.

Medals in these events are relatively rare for the United States, except for figure skating. It is expected that the Scandinavians and the Russians will again dominate the Nordic events; France, Austria, and Switzerland will be hard to overcome in the Alpine spectaculars; and the Germans will continue strong in the exciting jumps.

# HISTORY OF THE OLYMPIC GAMES

The prime athletic meeting of ancient Greece, the Olympic Games were held in the summer, once every four years, at Olympia in honor of Zeus. They were, according to tradition, initiated in 776 B.C., when the first Olympiad—a four-year period in ancient Greece—began. The games were the greatest festival in the Greek world, and so seriously were they taken by the competing city-states that women not only were forbidden to participate but could not even watch the events. The games were intensely nationalistic and the city-states are said to have been prouder of Olympic victories than of winning battles.

In the early period, the chief events included foot racing, a marathon, the pentathlon, boxing and wrestling, chariot racing, and a foot race with armor.

After the Roman conquest of Greece in 146 B.C., the games deteriorated, and professional athletes made a travesty of the events. In 392 A.D., the Roman emperor Theodosius banned the Olympic games entirely.

The modern revival of the Olympic Games is due in large measure to the efforts of Pierre, Baron de Coubertin, a 19th-century French educator. In 1896, after an Olympic stadium was constructed—appropriately enough, near Athens—the first modern games were held. The meeting in Athens and those that followed in Paris (1900) and in St. Louis (1904) were limited by a lack of organization and the absence of worldwide representation. The first successful Olympic Games were held at London in 1908.

Through the years, the games have gradually developed, with more contestants and a greater variety of events. Women athletes first competed in 1900, and in 1924 at Chamonix, France, winter sports were added.

The First World War prevented the Olympic meeting of 1916 and the Second World War brought about the cancellation of the 1940 and 1944 games. Overall, the United States has the best all-time record in the Olympic games. But since 1952, when the U.S.S.R. began participating in the games, the dominance of the United States has been seriously challenged. In the 1960 games the U.S.S.R. won a total of 50 gold medals—for first places—to the United States' 37. In the 1964 Olympics, the U.S.S.R. won 41 gold medals and the United States 37, although the United States won 36 gold medals and the Soviets 30 in the Summer Games, held at Tokyo, Japan.

The Tokyo games were the first ever to be held in Asia. Preparations cost in excess of $1 billion, and the largest number of athletes (5,558) from the most nations (94) in Olympic history participated. Perhaps the most notable performances were those of the United States swimmers, both men and women, who broke a total of 10 world records while tying another. One United States swimmer, Don Schollander, who was only 18 years old, won a total of four gold medals; another, Sharon Stouder, then 15, won three gold medals. In the men's track and field competition the United States won 12 out of 24 events.

A list of major-event winners since 1896 is on the following pages. Information on events sometimes considered minor, such as canoeing, field hockey, etc., is available at the United States Olympic Committee, 57 Park Avenue, New York City. Olympic competition is under the control of the International Olympic Committee. National Olympic Committees, established by each country, select and sponsor the individual participating teams in the Olympic Games.

## SUMMER OLYMPIC GAMES: 1896–1968

| YEAR | SITE | ENTRIES | NATIONS | YEAR | SITE | ENTRIES | NATIONS |
|---|---|---|---|---|---|---|---|
| 1896 | Athens, Greece.......... | 285 | 13 | 1932 | Los Angeles, California... | 1,408 | 37 |
| 1900 | Paris, France........... | 1,066 | 20 | 1936 | Berlin, Germany......... | 4,069 | 49 |
| 1904 | St. Louis, Missouri....... | 496 | 11 | 1948 | London, England........ | 4,468 | 59 |
| 1908 | London, England........ | 2,059 | 22 | 1952 | Helsinki, Finland........ | 5,867 | 69 |
| 1912 | Stockholm, Sweden...... | 2,541 | 28 | 1956 [1] | Melbourne, Australia..... | 3,184 | 67 |
| 1920 | Antwerp, Belgium....... | 2,606 | 29 | 1960 | Rome, Italy............ | 5,396 | 84 |
| 1924 | Paris, France........... | 3,092 | 44 | 1964 | Tokyo, Japan........... | 5,558 | 94 |
| 1928 | Amsterdam, Holland..... | 3,015 | 46 | 1968 | Mexico City, Mexico..... | 7,000 [2] | 106 [2] |

[1] Because of an Australian quarantine on horses, equestrian competition was held in Stockholm.   [2] Estimated.

## WINTER OLYMPIC GAMES: 1924–1968

| YEAR | SITE | ENTRIES | NATIONS | YEAR | SITE | ENTRIES | NATIONS |
|---|---|---|---|---|---|---|---|
| 1924 | Chamonix, France........ | 293 | 16 | 1952 | Oslo, Norway........... | 960 | 30 |
| 1928 | St. Moritz, Switzerland... | 491 | 25 | 1956 | Cortina d'Ampezzo, Italy | 923 | 32 |
| 1932 | Lake Placid, New York... | 307 | 17 | 1960 | Squaw Valley, | | |
| 1936 | Garmisch-Partenkirchen, | | | | California............. | 693 | 30 |
| | Germany............. | 756 | 28 | 1964 | Innsbruck, Austria....... | 928 | 36 |
| 1948 | St. Moritz, Switzerland... | 878 | 28 | 1968 | Grenoble, France........ | 1,500 * | 38 * |

* Estimated.

# OLYMPIC GAMES CHAMPIONS: 1896–1964
(* Indicates Olympic event record)

## TRACK AND FIELD: MEN

| YEAR WINNER AND COUNTRY | TIME |
| --- | --- |
| **100 METER DASH** | |
| 1896—Thomas E. Burke, United States..... | 12.0 |
| 1900—Francis W. Jarvis, United States..... | 10.8 |
| 1904—Archie Hahn, United States......... | 11.0 |
| 1906—Archie Hahn, United States......... | 11.2 |
| 1908—Reginald E. Walker, South Africa.... | 10.8 |
| 1912—Ralph C. Craig, United States....... | 10.8 |
| 1920—Charles W. Paddock, United States.. | 10.8 |
| 1924—Harold M. Abrahams, Great Britain.. | 10.6 |
| 1928—Percy Williams, Canada............. | 10.8 |
| 1932—Eddie Tolan, United States.......... | 10.3 |
| 1936—Jesse Owens, United States......... | 10.3 |
| 1948—Harrison Dillard, United States...... | 10.3 |
| 1952—Lindy J. Remigino, United States.... | 10.4 |
| 1956—Bobby J. Morrow, United States..... | 10.5 |
| (Timed at 10.3 in semi-finals) | |
| 1960—Armin Hary, Germany.............. | 10.2 |
| 1964—Robert L. Hayes, United States...... | 10.0 * |
| **200 METER DASH** | |
| 1900—John W. B. Tewksbury, United States | 22.2 |
| 1904—Archie Hahn, United States......... | 21.6 |
| 1908—Robert Kerr, Canada................ | 22.6 |
| 1912—Ralph C. Craig, United States....... | 21.7 |
| 1920—Allan Woodring, United States...... | 22.0 |
| 1924—Jackson V. Scholz, United States.... | 21.6 |
| 1928—Percy Williams, Canada............. | 21.8 |
| 1932—Eddie Tolan, United States.......... | 21.2 |
| 1936—Jesse Owens, United States......... | 20.7 |
| 1948—Mel Patton, United States.......... | 21.1 |
| 1952—Andrew W. Stanfield, United States.. | 20.7 |
| 1956—Bobby J. Morrow, United States..... | 20.6 |
| 1960—Livio Berruti, Italy.................. | 20.5 |
| 1964—Henry Carr, United States.......... | 20.3 * |
| **400 METER DASH** | |
| 1896—Thomas E. Burke, United States..... | 54.2 |
| 1900—Maxey W. Long, United States...... | 49.4 |
| 1904—Harry I. Hillman, United States...... | 49.2 |
| 1906—Paul Pilgrim, United States......... | 53.2 |
| 1908—Wyndham Halswelle, Great Britain (walkover)..................... | 50.0 |
| 1912—Charles D. Reidpath, United States.. | 48.2 |
| 1920—Bevil G. D. Rudd, South Africa...... | 49.6 |
| 1924—Eric H. Liddell, Great Britain........ | 47.6 |
| 1928—Ray Barbuti, United States......... | 47.8 |
| 1932—William Carr, United States......... | 46.2 |
| 1936—Archie Williams, United States...... | 46.5 |
| 1948—Arthur Wint, Jamaica.............. | 46.2 |
| 1952—George Rhoden, Jamaica........... | 45.9 |
| 1956—Charles L. Jenkins, United States.... | 46.7 |
| 1960—Otis Davis, United States.......... | 44.9 * |
| 1964—Michael D. Larrabee, United States.. | 45.1 |
| **800 METER RUN** | |
| 1896—Edwin H. Flack, Australia........... | 2:11.0 |
| 1900—Alfred E. Tysoe, Great Britain....... | 2:01.4 |
| 1904—James D. Lightbody, United States... | 1:56.0 |
| 1906—Paul Pilgrim, United States......... | 2:01.2 |
| 1908—Melvin W. Sheppard, United States.. | 1:52.8 |
| 1912—James T. Meredith, United States... | 1:51.9 |
| 1920—Albert G. Hill, Great Britain........ | 1:53.4 |
| 1924—Douglas G. A. Lowe, Great Britain... | 1:52.4 |
| 1928—Douglas G. A. Lowe, Great Britain... | 1:51.8 |
| 1932—Thomas Hampson, Great Britain..... | 1:49.8 |
| 1936—John Woodruff, United States....... | 1:52.9 |
| 1948—Mal Whitfield, United States....... | 1:49.2 |

| YEAR WINNER AND COUNTRY | TIME |
| --- | --- |
| 1952—Mal Whitfield, United States........ | 1:49.2 |
| 1956—Thomas W. Courtney, United States.. | 1:47.7 |
| 1960—Peter Snell, New Zealand.......... | 1:46.3 |
| 1964—Peter Snell, New Zealand.......... | 1:45.1 |
| **1,500 METER RUN** | |
| 1896—Edwin H. Flack, Great Britain....... | 4:33.2 |
| 1900—Charles Bennett, Great Britain...... | 4:06.2 |
| 1904—James D. Lightbody, United States... | 4:05.4 |
| 1906—James D. Lightbody, United States... | 4:12.0 |
| 1908—Melvin W. Sheppard, United States.. | 4:03.4 |
| 1912—Arnold N. S. Jackson, Great Britain.. | 3:56.8 |
| 1920—Albert G. Hill, Great Britain........ | 4:01.8 |
| 1924—Paavo Nurmi, Finland............. | 3:53.6 |
| 1928—Harry E. Larva, Finland............ | 3:53.2 |
| 1932—Luigi Beccali, Italy................ | 3:51.2 |
| 1936—Jack E. Lovelock, New Zealand...... | 3:47.8 |
| 1948—Henry Eriksson, Sweden........... | 3:49.8 |
| 1952—Joseph Barthel, Luxembourg........ | 3:45.2 |
| 1956—Ron Delany, Ireland............... | 3:41.2 |
| 1960—Herbert Elliott, Australia........... | 3:35.6 * |
| 1964—Peter Snell, New Zealand.......... | 3:38.1 |
| **5,000 METER RUN** | |
| 1912—Hannes Kolehmainen, Finland....... | 14:36.6 |
| 1920—Joseph Guillemot, France.......... | 14:55.6 |
| 1924—Paavo Nurmi, Finland............. | 14:31.2 |
| 1928—Willie Ritola, Finland............. | 14:38.0 |
| 1932—Lauri Lehtinen, Finland............ | 14:30.0 |
| 1936—Gunnar Hockert, Finland........... | 14:22.2 |
| 1948—Gaston Reiff, Belgium............. | 14:17.6 |
| 1952—Emil Zatopek, Czechoslovakia...... | 14:06.6 |
| 1956—Vladimir Kuts, U.S.S.R............. | 13:39.6 * |
| 1960—Murray Halberg, New Zealand...... | 13:43.4 |
| 1964—Robert K. Schul, United States...... | 13:48.8 |
| **10,000 METER RUN** | |
| 1912—Hannes Kolehmainen, Finland....... | 31:20.8 |
| 1920—Paavo Nurmi, Finland............. | 31:45.8 |
| 1924—Willie Ritola, Finland............. | 30:23.2 |
| 1928—Paavo Nurmi, Finland............. | 30:18.8 |
| 1932—Janusz Kusocinski, Poland......... | 30:11.4 |
| 1936—Ilmari Salminen, Finland........... | 30:15.4 |
| 1948—Emil Zatopek, Czechoslovakia...... | 29:59.6 |
| 1952—Emil Zatopek, Czechoslovakia...... | 29:17.0 |
| 1956—Vladimir Kuts, U.S.S.R............. | 28:45.6 |
| 1960—Petr Bolotnikov, U.S.S.R........... | 28:32.2 |
| 1964—William M. Mills, United States...... | 28:24.4 * |
| **MARATHON** | |
| 1896—Spyros Loues, Greece.............. | 2:58:50.0 |
| 1900—Michel Theato, France............. | 2:59:45.0 |
| 1904—Thomas J. Hicks, United States..... | 3:28:53.0 |
| 1906—W. Sherring, Canada.............. | 2:51:23.6 |
| 1908—John J. Hayes, United States........ | 2:55:18.4 |
| 1912—Kenneth MacArthur, So. Africa...... | 2:36:54.8 |
| 1920—Hannes Kolehmainen, Finland...... | 2:32:35.8 |
| 1924—Albin Stenroos, Finland............ | 2:41:22.6 |
| 1928—El Ouafi, France.................. | 2:32:57.0 |
| 1932—Juan Zabala, Argentina............ | 2:31:36.0 |
| 1936—Kitei Son, Japan.................. | 2:29:19.2 |
| 1948—Delfo Cabrera, Argentina.......... | 2:34:51.6 |
| 1952—Emil Zatopek, Czechoslovakia...... | 2:23:03.2 |
| 1956—Alain Mimoun, France............. | 2:25:00.0 |
| 1960—Abebe Bikila, Ethiopia............. | 2:15:16.2 |
| 1964—Abebe Bikila, Ethiopia............. | 2:12:11.2 * |

| YEAR WINNER AND COUNTRY | TIME |
| --- | --- |

**110 METER HURDLES**
| | |
| --- | --- |
| 1896—Thomas P. Curtis, United States..... | 17.6 |
| 1900—Alvin E. Kraenzlein, United States... | 15.4 |
| 1904—Frederick W. Schule, United States.. | 16.0 |
| 1906—R. G. Leavitt, United States......... | 16.2 |
| 1908—Forrest Smithson, United States..... | 15.0 |
| 1912—Frederick W. Kelley, United States... | 15.1 |
| 1920—Earl J. Thomson, Canada........... | 14.8 |
| 1924—Daniel C. Kinsey, United States...... | 15.0 |
| 1928—Sydney Atkinson, South Africa...... | 14.8 |
| 1932—George Saling, United States........ | 14.6 |
| 1936—Forrest Towns, United States....... | 14.2 |
| 1948—William Porter, United States....... | 13.9 |
| 1952—Harrison Dillard, United States...... | 13.7 |
| 1956—Lee Q. Calhoun, United States..... | 13.5 * |
| 1960—Lee Q. Calhoun, United States...... | 13.8 |
| 1964—Hayes W. Jones, United States...... | 13.6 |

**400 METER HURDLES**
| | |
| --- | --- |
| 1900—John W. B. Tewksbury, United States | 57.6 |
| 1904—Harry L. Hillman, United States..... | 53.0 |
| 1908—Charles J. Bacon, United States..... | 55.0 |
| 1920—Frank F. Loomis, United States...... | 54.0 |
| 1924—F. Morgan Taylor, United States..... | 52.6 |
| 1928—Lord David Burgley, Great Britain... | 53.4 |
| 1932—Robert Tisdall, Ireland............. | 51.8 |
| 1936—Glenn Hardin, United States........ | 52.4 |
| 1948—Roy Cochran, United States........ | 51.1 |
| 1952—Charles Moore, United States....... | 50.8 |
| 1956—Glenn A. Davis, United States....... | 50.1 |
| (Ed Southern, United States, had 50.1 in semi-finals) | |
| 1960—Glenn A. Davis, United States....... | 49.3 * |
| 1964—Warren J. Cawley, United States..... | 49.6 |

**3,000 METER STEEPLECHASE**
| | |
| --- | --- |
| 1920—Percy Hodge, Great Britain......... | 10:00.4 |
| 1924—Willie Ritola, Finland............... | 9:33.6 |
| 1928—Toiva A. Loukola, Finland.......... | 9:21.8 |
| 1932—Volmari Iso-Hollo, Finland.......... | 10:33.4 |
| (3,460 meters—extra lap by error) | |
| 1936—Volmari Iso-Hollo, Finland.......... | 9:03.8 |
| 1948—Thore Sjostrand, Sweden........... | 9:04.6 |
| 1952—Horace Ashenfelter, United States... | 8:45.4 |
| 1956—Chris Brasher, Great Britain........ | 8:41.2 |
| 1960—Zdzislaw Krzyszkowiak, Poland..... | 8:34.2 |
| 1964—Gaston Roelants, Belgium.......... | 8:30.8 * |

**20,000 METER WALK**
| | |
| --- | --- |
| 1956—L. Spirine, U.S.S.R................ | 1:31.27 |
| 1960—Vladimir Golubnichy, U.S.S.R........ | 1:34:07.2 |
| 1964—Kenneth Mathews, Great Britain..... | 1:29:34.0 * |

**50,000 METER WALK**
| | |
| --- | --- |
| 1932—Thomas W. Green, Great Britain..... | 4:50:10.0 |
| 1936—Harold Whitlock, Great Britain...... | 4:30:41.4 |
| 1948—John A. Ljunggren, Sweden.......... | 4:41:52.0 |
| 1952—Giuseppe Dordoni, Italy........... | 4:28:07.8 |
| 1956—Norm. Read, N. Zealand........... | 4:30:42.8 |
| 1960—Donald Thompson, Great Britain..... | 4:25:30.0 |
| 1964—Abdon Pamich, Italy............... | 4:11:12.4 * |

**4 x 100 METER RELAY**
| | |
| --- | --- |
| 1912—Great Britain (D. H. Jacobs, H. M. Macintosh, Victor d'Arcy, William Applegarth)..................... | 42.4 |
| 1920—United States (Charles Paddock, Jackson Scholz, Morris Kirksey, Loren Murchison)................. | 42.2 |
| 1924—United States (Louis Clarke, Francis Hussey, Loren Murchison, Alfred Leconey)...................... | 41.0 |
| 1928—United States (Frank Wycoff, James | |

| YEAR WINNER AND COUNTRY | TIME |
| --- | --- |
| Quinn, Charles Borah, Henry Russell)........................ | 41.0 |
| 1932—United States (Robert Kiesel, Emmett Toppino, Hector Dyer, Frank Wycoff)................... | 40.0 |
| 1936—United States (Jesse Owens, Ralph Metcalfe, Foy Draper, Frank Wycoff)....................... | 40.0 |
| 1948—United States (Norwood Ewell, Lorenzo Wright, Harrison Dillard, Mel Patton).................... | 40.3 |
| 1952—United States (Dean Smith, Harrison Dillard, Lindy Remigino, Andrew Stanfield).................... | 40.1 |
| 1956—United States (I. J. Murchison, L. King, W. T. Baker, B. J. Morrow) | 39.0 |
| 1960—Germany (Bernd Cullman, Armin Hary, Walter Mahlendorf, Martin Lauer)........................ | 39.5 |
| 1964—United States (Paul Drayton, Gerald Ashworth, Richard Stebbins, Robert Hayes).................. | 39.0 * |

**4 x 400 METER RELAY**
| | |
| --- | --- |
| 1908—United States (William F. Hamilton, Nathan J. Cartmell, John Taylor, Melvin W. Sheppard) (200-200-400-800 m)............ | 3:29.4 |
| 1912—United States (Melvin W. Sheppard, Edward F. Lindberg, James T. Meredith, Charles D. Reidpath).... | 3:16.6 |
| 1920—Great Britain (Robert Lindsay, Guy Butler, John Ainsworth, Cecil Griffiths)...................... | 3:22.2 |
| 1924—United States (C. S. Cochran, William E. Stevenson, J. O. McDonald, Allen Helffrich)........ | 3:16.0 |
| 1928—United States (George Baird, Fred Alderman, Emerson Spencer, Ray Barbuti).................... | 3:14.2 |
| 1932—United States (Ivan Fuqua, Edgar Ablowich, Karl Warner, William Carr)...................... | 3:08.2 |
| 1936—Great Britain (Frederick Wolff, Godfrey Rampling, William Roberts, Godfrey Brown)........ | 3:09.0 |
| 1948—United States (Cliff Bourland, Art Harnden, Roy Cochran, Mal Whitfield)..................... | 3:10.4 |
| 1952—Jamaica (Herbert McKenley, Leslie Laing, Arthur Wint, George Rhoden)...................... | 3:03.9 |
| 1956—United States (C. L. Jenkins, L. Jones, J. Mashburn, T. J. Courtney)..................... | 3:04.8 |
| 1960—United States (Jack Yerman, Earl Young, Glenn Davis, Otis Davis)... | 3:02.2 |
| 1964—United States (Ollan Cassell, Michael Larrabee, Ulis Williams, Henry Carr)................... | 3:00.7 * |

| YEAR WINNER AND COUNTRY | HEIGHT |
| --- | --- |

**POLE VAULT**
| | |
| --- | --- |
| 1896—William W. Hoyt, United States...... | 10' 9¾'' |
| 1900—Irving K. Baxter, United States...... | 10' 9.9'' |
| 1904—Charles E. Dvorak, United States.... | 11' 6'' |
| 1906—Gouder, France.................... | 11' 6'' |
| 1908—Albert C. Gilbert, United States Edward T. Cook, Jr., United States... | 12' 2'' |
| 1912—Harry S. Babcock, United States.... | 12' 11½'' |
| 1920—Frank K. Foss, United States....... | 12' 5⁹⁄₁₆'' |
| 1924—Lee S. Barnes, United States........ | 12' 11½'' |

| YEAR WINNER AND COUNTRY | HEIGHT |
|---|---|
| 1928—Sabin W. Carr, United States | 13′9⅜″ |
| 1932—William Miller, United States | 14′ 1⅞″ |
| 1936—Earle Meadows, United States | 14′ 3¼″ |
| 1948—O. Guinn Smith, United States | 14′ 1¼″ |
| 1952—Robert Richards, United States | 14′ 11¼″ |
| 1956—Robert Richards, United States | 14′ 11½″ |
| 1960—Donald Bragg, United States | 15′ 5⅛″ |
| 1964—Fred M. Hansen, United States | 16′ 8¾″ * |

**RUNNING HIGH JUMP**

| | |
|---|---|
| 1896—Ellery Clark, United States | 5′ 11¼″ |
| 1900—Irving Baxter, United States | 6′ 2⅘″ |
| 1904—Samuel Jones, United States | 5′ 11″ |
| 1906—Con Leahy, Ireland | 5′ 9⅞″ |
| 1908—Harry Porter, United States | 6′ 3″ |
| 1912—Almer Richards, United States | 6′ 4″ |
| 1920—Richard Landon, United States | 6′ 4¼″ |
| 1924—Harold Osborn, United States | 6′ 5 15/16″ |
| 1928—Robert W. King, United States | 6′ 4⅜″ |
| 1932—Duncan McNaughton, Canada | 6′ 5⅝″ |
| 1936—Cornelius Johnson, United States | 6′ 7 15/16″ |
| 1948—John Winter, Australia | 6′ 6″ |
| 1952—Walter Davis, United States | 6′ 8¼″ |
| 1956—Charles E. Dumas, United States | 6′ 11¼″ |
| 1960—Robert Shavlakadze, U.S.S.R. | 7′ 1″ |
| 1964—Valery Brumel, U.S.S.R. | 7′ 1¾″ * |

| YEAR WINNER AND COUNTRY | DISTANCE |
|---|---|

**RUNNING LONG JUMP**

| | |
|---|---|
| 1896—Ellery Clark, United States | 20′ 10″ |
| 1900—Alvin Kraenzlein, United States | 23′ 6⅞″ |
| 1904—Myer Prinstein, United States | 24′ 1″ |
| 1906—Myer Prinstein, United States | 23′ 7½″ |
| 1908—Frank Irons, United States | 24′ 6½″ |
| 1912—Albert Gutterson, United States | 24′ 11¼″ |
| 1920—William Pettersson, Sweden | 23′ 5½″ |
| 1924—DeHart Hubbard, United States | 24′ 5⅛″ |
| 1928—Edward Hamm, United States | 25′ 4¾″ |
| 1932—Edward Gordon, United States | 25′ ¾″ |
| 1936—Jesse Owens, United States | 26′ 5⅜″ |
| 1948—Willie Steel, United States | 25′ 8″ |
| 1952—Jerome Biffle, United States | 24′ 10″ |
| 1956—Gregory C. Bell, United States | 25′ 8¼″ |
| 1960—Ralph Boston, United States | 26′ 7¾″ * |
| 1964—Lynn Davies, Great Britain | 26′ 5¾″ |

**RUNNING TRIPLE JUMP**

| | |
|---|---|
| 1896—James Connolly, United States | 45′ |
| 1900—Myer Prinstein, United States | 47′ 4¼″ |
| 1904—Myer Prinstein, United States | 47′ |
| 1906—P. O'Connor, Ireland | 46′ 2″ |
| 1908—Timothy Ahearne, Great Britain | 48′ 11¼″ |
| 1912—Gustaf Lindblom, Sweden | 48′ 5⅛″ |
| 1920—Vilho Tuulos, Finland | 47′ 6⅞″ |
| 1924—Archibald Winter, Australia | 50′ 11⅛″ |
| 1928—Mikio Oda, Japan | 49′ 10-13/16″ |
| 1932—Chuhei Nambu, Japan | 51′ 7″ |
| 1936—Naoto Tajima, Japan | 52′ 5⅞″ |
| 1948—Arne Ahman, Sweden | 50′ 6¼″ |
| 1952—Adhemar Ferreira da Silva, Brazil | 53′ 2½″ |
| 1956—Adhemar Ferreira da Silva, Brazil | 53′ 7½″ |
| 1960—Jozef Schmidt, Poland | 55′ 1¾″ |
| 1964—Jozef Schmidt, Poland | 55′ 3¼″ * |

**16 LB. SHOT PUT**

| | |
|---|---|
| 1896—Robert Garrett, United States | 36′ 9¾″ |
| 1900—Richard Sheldon, United States | 46′ 3⅛″ |
| 1904—Ralph Rose, United States | 48′ 7″ |
| 1906—M. J. Sheridan, United States | 40′ 4⅘″ |
| 1908—Ralph Rose, United States | 46′ 7½″ |
| 1912—Patrick McDonald, United States | 50′ 4″ |
| 1920—Ville Porhola, Finland | 48′ 7⅛″ |

| YEAR WINNER AND COUNTRY | DISTANCE |
|---|---|
| 1924—Clarence Houser, United States | 49′ 2½″ |
| 1928—John Kuck, United States | 52′ 11/16″ |
| 1932—Leo Sexton, United States | 52′ 6-3/16″ |
| 1936—Hans Woellke, Germany | 53′ 1¾″ |
| 1948—Wilbur Thompson, United States | 56′ 2″ |
| 1952—Parry O'Brien, Jr., United States | 57′ 1½″ |
| 1956—Parry O'Brien, Jr., United States | 60′ 11″ |
| 1960—William Nieder, United States | 64′ 6¾″ |
| 1964—Dallas C. Long, United States | 66′ 8¼″ * |

**DISCUS THROW**

| | |
|---|---|
| 1896—Robert Garrett, United States | 95′ 7½″ |
| 1900—Rudolf Bauer, Hungary | 118′ 2.9″ |
| 1904—Martin Sheridan, United States | 128′ 10½″ |
| 1906—Martin Sheridan, United States | 136′ ⅓″ |
| 1908—Martin Sheridan, United States | 134′ 2″ |
| 1912—Armas Taiple, Finland | 145′ 9/16″ |
| 1920—Elmer Ninklander, Finland | 146′ 7″ |
| 1924—Clarence Houser, United States | 151′ 5¼″ |
| 1928—Clarence Houser, United States | 155′ 2⅘″ |
| 1932—John Anderson, United States | 162′ 4⅞″ |
| 1936—Kenneth Carpenter, United States | 165′ 7½″ |
| 1948—Adolfo Consolini, Italy | 173′ 2″ |
| 1952—Sim Iness, United States | 180′ 6½″ |
| 1956—Alfred A. Oerter, United States | 184′ 10½″ |
| 1960—Alfred A. Oerter, United States | 194′ 2″ |
| 1964—Alfred A. Oerter, United States | 200′ 1½″ * |

**16 LB. HAMMER THROW**

| | |
|---|---|
| 1900—John Flanagan, United States | 167′ 4″ |
| 1904—John Flanagan, United States | 168′ 1″ |
| 1908—John Flanagan, United States | 170′ 4¼″ |
| 1912—Matthew McGrath, United States | 179′ 7⅛″ |
| 1920—Patrick Ryan, United States | 173′ 5⅝″ |
| 1924—Frederick Tootell, United States | 174′ 10¼″ |
| 1928—Patrick O'Callaghan, Ireland | 168′ 7½″ |
| 1932—Patrick O'Callaghan, Ireland | 176′ 11⅛″ |
| 1936—Karl Hein, Germany | 185′ 4¼″ |
| 1948—Imre Nemeth, Hungary | 183′ 11½″ |
| 1952—Jozsef Csermak, Hungary | 197′ 11¾″ |
| 1956—Harold Connolly, United States | 207′ 3½″ |
| 1960—Vasiliy Rudenkov, U.S.S.R. | 220′ 1⅝″ |
| 1964—Romuald Klim, U.S.S.R. | 228′ 9½″ * |

**JAVELIN THROW**

| | |
|---|---|
| 1906—Erik Lemming, Sweden | 175′ 6″ |
| 1908—Erik Lemming, Sweden | 179′ 10½″ |
| 1912—Erik Lemming, Sweden | 198′ 11¼″ |
| 1920—Jonni Myra, Finland | 215′ 9¾″ |
| 1924—Jonni Myra, Finland | 206′ 6¾″ |
| 1928—Erik Lundquist, Sweden | 218′ 6⅛″ |
| 1932—Matti Jarvinen, Finland | 238′ 7″ |
| 1936—Gerhard Stock, Germany | 235′ 8-5/16″ |
| 1948—Tapio Rautavaara, Finland | 228′ 10½″ |
| 1952—Cy C. Young, United States | 242′ ¾″ |
| 1956—E. Danielson, Norway | 281′ 2¼″ |
| 1960—Viktor Cybulenko, U.S.S.R. | 277′ 8⅛″ |
| 1964—Pauli Nevala, Finland | 271′ 2¼″ |

| YEAR WINNER AND COUNTRY | POINTS |
|---|---|

**DECATHLON**

| | |
|---|---|
| 1912—Hugo Wieslander, Sweden | 7724.49 |
| 1920—Helge Lovland, Norway | 6804.35 |
| 1924—Harold Osborn, United States | 7710.77 |
| 1928—Paavo Yrjola, Finland | 8053.23 |
| 1932—James Bausch, United States | 8462.23 |
| (Old point system, 1912 to 1932) | |
| 1936—Glenn Morris, United States | 7900.00 |
| 1948—Robert Mathias, United States | 7139.00 |
| 1952—Robert Mathias, United States | 7887.00 |
| 1956—Milton G. Campbell, United States | 7937.00 |

| YEAR WINNER AND COUNTRY | POINTS |
|---|---|
| 1960—Rafer Johnson, United States....... | 8392.00 * |
| 1964—Willi Holdorf, Germany............. | 7,887 * |
| (Scoring system revised) | |

## TRACK AND FIELD: WOMEN

| YEAR WINNER AND COUNTRY | TIME |
|---|---|

### 100 METER DASH
| | |
|---|---|
| 1928—Elizabeth Robinson, United States... | 12.2 |
| 1932—Stanislawa Walasiewiz, Poland...... | 11.9 |
| 1936—Helen Stephens, United States....... | 11.5 |
| 1948—Francina Blankers-Koen, Netherlands | 11.9 |
| 1952—Marjorie Jackson, Australia......... | 11.5 |
| 1956—Betty Cuthbert, Australia........... | 11.5 |
| 1960—Wilma Rudolph, United States....... | 11.0 * |
| 1964—Wyomia Tyus, United States........ | 11.4 |

### 200 METER DASH
| | |
|---|---|
| 1948—Francina Blankers-Koen, Netherlands.................... | 24.4 |
| 1952—Marjorie Jackson, Australia......... | 23.7 |
| 1956—Betty Cuthbert, Australia............ | 23.4 |
| 1960—Wilma Rudolph, United States....... | 24.0 |
| 1964—Edith McGuire, United States....... | 23.0 * |

### 400 METER DASH
| | |
|---|---|
| 1964—Betty Cuthbert, Australia............ | 52.0 |

### 800 METER RUN
| | |
|---|---|
| 1928—Linda Radke, Germany............. | 2:16.8 |
| 1960—Ljudmila Shevcova, U.S.S.R........ | 2:04.3 |
| 1964—Ann Packer, Great Britain......... | 2:01.1 * |

### 4 x 100 METER RELAY
| | |
|---|---|
| 1928—Canada............................ | 48.4 |
| 1932—United States..................... | 47.0 |
| 1936—United States..................... | 46.9 |
| 1948—Netherlands....................... | 47.5 |
| 1952—United States..................... | 45.9 |
| 1956—Australia......................... | 44.5 |
| 1960—United States..................... | 44.5 |
| 1964—Poland............................ | 43.6 * |

### 80 METER HURDLES
| | |
|---|---|
| 1932—Mildred Didrikson, United States.... | 11.7 |
| 1936—Trebisonda Villa, Italy.............. | 11.7 |
| 1948—Francina Blankers-Koen, Netherlands .................... | 11.2 |
| 1952—Shirley Strickland de la Hunty, Australia....................... | 10.9 |
| 1956—Shirley Strickland de la Hunty, Australia....................... | 10.7 |
| 1960—Irina Press, U.S.S.R................ | 10.8 |
| 1964—Karin Balzer, Germany............. | 10.5 * |

| YEAR WINNERS AND COUNTRY | HEIGHT |
|---|---|

### RUNNING HIGH JUMP
| | |
|---|---|
| 1928—Ethel Catherwood, Canada.......... | 5' 3'' |
| 1932—Jean Shiley, United States.......... | 5' 5¼'' |
| 1936—Ibolya Csak, Hungary.............. | 5' 3'' |
| 1948—Alice Coachman, United States...... | 5' 6⅛'' |
| 1952—Esther Brand, South Africa......... | 5' 5¾'' |
| 1956—Mildred L. McDaniel, United States.. | 5' 9¼'' |
| 1960—Iolanda Balas, Romania............ | 6' 0¼'' |
| 1964—Iolanda Balas, Romania............ | 6' 2¾'' * |

| YEAR WINNER AND COUNTRY | DISTANCE |
|---|---|

### LONG JUMP
| | |
|---|---|
| 1948—Olga Gyarmati, Hungary............ | 18' 8¼'' |
| 1952—Yvette Williams, New Zealand....... | 20' 5¾'' |

| YEAR WINNING COUNTRY | DISTANCE |
|---|---|
| 1956—E. Krzeskinska, Poland............. | 20' 9¾'' |
| 1960—Vyera Krepkina, U.S.S.R........... | 20' 10¾'' |
| 1964—Mary Rand, Great Britain.......... | 22' 2'' * |

### DISCUS THROW
| | |
|---|---|
| 1928—Helena Konopacka, Poland......... | 129' 11⅞'' |
| 1932—Lillian Copeland, United States...... | 133' 2'' |
| 1936—Gisela Mauermayer, Germany....... | 156' 3-³⁄₁₆'' |
| 1948—Micheline Ostermeyer, France....... | 137' 6½'' |
| 1952—Nina Romaschkova, U.S.S.R........ | 168' 8½'' |
| 1956—Olga Fikotova, Czechoslovakia....... | 176' 1½'' |
| 1960—Nina Ponomareva, U.S.S.R........ | 180' 8¼'' |
| 1964—Tamara Press, U.S.S.R............. | 187' 10¾'' * |

### 8 LB. 3 OZ. SHOT PUT
| | |
|---|---|
| 1948—Micheline Ostermeyer, France....... | 45' 1½'' |
| 1952—Galina Zybina, U.S.S.R............. | 50' 1½'' |
| 1956—T. Tishkyevich, U.S.S.R............. | 54' 5'' |
| 1960—Tamara Press, U.S.S.R............. | 56' 9¾'' |
| 1964—Tamara Press, U.S.S.R............. | 59' 6'' * |

### JAVELIN THROW
| | |
|---|---|
| 1932—Mildred Didrikson, United States.... | 143' 4'' |
| 1936—Tilly Fleischer, Germany........... | 148' 2¾'' |
| 1948—Herma Bauma, Austria............. | 149' 6'' |
| 1952—Dana Zatopekova, Czechoslovakia... | 165' 7'' |
| 1956—Inessa Janzeme, U.S.S.R........... | 176' 8'' |
| 1960—Elvira Ozolina, U.S.S.R........... | 183' 8'' |
| 1964—Mihaela Penes, Romania........... | 198' 7½'' [1] |

## SWIMMING AND DIVING: MEN

| YEAR WINNER AND COUNTRY | TIME |
|---|---|

### 100 METER FREE STYLE
| | |
|---|---|
| 1896—Alfred Hajos, Hungary............. | 1:22.2 |
| 1904—Zoltan de Halmay, Hungary (yds.)... | 1:02.8 |
| 1906—Charles Daniels, United States...... | 1:13.4 |
| 1908—Charles Daniels, United States...... | 1:05.6 |
| 1912—Duke Kahanamoku, United States... | 1:03.4 |
| 1920—Duke Kahanamoku, United States... | 1:01.4 |
| 1924—John Weissmuller, United States.... | 59.0 |
| 1928—John Weissmuller, United States.... | 58.6 |
| 1932—Yasuji Miyazaki, Japan............. | 58.2 |
| 1936—Ferenec Csik, Hungary............. | 57.6 |
| 1948—Walter Ris, United States........... | 57.3 |
| 1952—Clarke Scholes, United States....... | 57.4 |
| 1956—Jon Hendricks, Australia........... | 55.4 |
| 1960—John Devitt, Australia.............. | 55.2 |
| 1964—Donald A. Schollander, United States | 53.4 *[2] |

### 400 METER FREE STYLE
| | |
|---|---|
| 1896—Paul Neumann, Austria (500-m)..... | 8:12.6 |
| 1904—Charles Daniels, United States (440-yds).................... | 6:16.2 |
| 1906—Otto Scheff, Austria................. | 6:23.8 |
| 1908—Henry Taylor, Great Britain........ | 5:36.8 |
| 1912—George Hodgson, Canada.......... | 5:24.4 |
| 1920—Norman Ross, United States....... | 5:26.8 |
| 1924—John Weissmuller, United States.... | 5:04.2 |
| 1928—Albert Zorilla, Argentina.......... | 5:01.6 |
| 1932—Clarence Crabbe, United States..... | 4:48.4 |
| 1936—Jack Medica, United States........ | 4:44.5 |
| 1948—William Smith, United States....... | 4:41.0 |
| 1952—Jean Boiteux, France.............. | 4:30.7 |
| 1956—M. Rose, Australia................. | 4:27.3 |
| 1960—Murray Rose, Australia............ | 4:18.3 |
| 1964—Donald A. Schollander, United States | 4:12.2 * |

[1] Elena Gorchakova, U.S.S.R., set new record of 204' 8¾'' in qualifying round.
[2] Lance Larson, U.S., also credited with same record time although placed second.

| YEAR WINNER AND COUNTRY | TIME |
|---|---|

**1,500 METER FREE STYLE**

| | |
|---|---|
| 1896—Alfred Hajos, Hungary (1200-m)..... | 18:22.2 |
| 1900—John Jarvis, Great Britain (1000-m).. | 13:40.2 |
| 1904—Emil Rausch, Germany (1609-m)..... | 27:18.2 |
| 1906—H. Taylor, Great Britain (1609-m).... | 28:28.0 |
| 1908—Henry Taylor, Great Britain......... | 22:48.4 |
| 1912—George Hodgson, Canada........... | 22:00.0 |
| 1920—Norman Ross, United States........ | 22:23.2 |
| 1924—Andrew Charlton, Australia........ | 20:06.6 |
| 1928—Arne Borg, Sweden................ | 19:51.8 |
| 1932—Kusuo Kitamura, Japan............ | 19:12.4 |
| 1936—Noburo Terada, Japan............. | 19:13.7 |
| 1948—James P. McLane, United States..... | 19:18.5 |
| 1952—Ford Konno, United States.......... | 18:30.0 |
| 1956—M. Rose, Australia................. | 17:58.9 |
| 1960—John Konrads, Australia........... | 17:19.6 |
| 1964—Robert Windle, Australia........... | 17:07.1 * |

**200 METER BACKSTROKE**

| | |
|---|---|
| 1964—Jed R. Graef, United States......... | 2:10.3 * |

**200 METER BREASTSTROKE**

| | |
|---|---|
| 1908—Frederick Holman, Great Britain..... | 3:09.2 |
| 1912—Walter Bathe, Germany............. | 3:01.8 |
| 1920—Haken Malmroth, Sweden.......... | 3:04.4 |
| 1924—Robert Skelton, United States....... | 2:56.6 |
| 1928—Yoshiyuki Tsuruta, Japan........... | 2:48.8 |
| 1932—Yoshiyuki Tsuruta, Japan........... | 2:45.4 |
| 1936—Tetsuo Hamuro, Japan............. | 2:41.5 |
| 1948—Joseph Verdeur, United States...... | 2:39.3 |
| 1952—John Davies, Australia............. | 2:34.4 |
| 1956—Masura Furukawa, Japan..... | 2:34.7 |
| 1960—William Mulliken, United States..... | 2:37.4 |
| 1964—Ian O'Brien, Australia.............. | 2:27.8 * |

**200 METER BUTTERFLY**

| | |
|---|---|
| 1956—William Yorzyk, United States....... | 2:19.3 |
| 1960—Michael Troy, United States......... | 2:12.8 |
| 1964—Kevin Barry, Australia............. | 2:06.6 * |

**400 METER INDIVIDUAL MEDLEY**

| | |
|---|---|
| 1964—Richard W. Roth, United States...... | 4:45.4 * |

**4 x 100 FREE STYLE RELAY**

| | |
|---|---|
| 1964—United States.................... | 3:33.2 * |

**4 x 100 METER MEDLEY RELAY**

| | |
|---|---|
| 1960—United States.................... | 4:05.4 |
| 1964—United States.................... | 3:58.4 * |

**4 x 200 METER FREE STYLE RELAY**

| | |
|---|---|
| 1908—Great Britain...................... | 10:55.6 |
| 1912—Australia......................... | 10:11.6 |
| 1920—United States..................... | 10:04.4 |
| 1924—United States..................... | 9:53.4 |
| 1928—United States..................... | 9:36.2 |
| 1932—Japan............................ | 8:58.2 |
| 1936—Japan............................ | 8:51.5 |
| 1948—United States..................... | 8:31.1 |
| 1952—United States..................... | 8:31.1 |
| 1956—Australia......................... | 8:23.6 |
| 1960—United States..................... | 8:10.2 |
| 1964—United States..................... | 7:52.1 * |

| YEAR WINNER AND COUNTRY | POINTS |
|---|---|

**SPRINGBOARD DIVING**

| | |
|---|---|
| 1908—Albert Zurner, Germany........... | 85.50 |
| 1912—Paul Guenther, Germany........... | 79.23 |
| 1920—Louis Kuehn, United States....... | 675.00 |
| 1924—Albert C. White, United States...... | 696.40 |
| 1928—Pete Desjardins, United States..... | 185.04 |
| 1932—Michael Galitzen, United States.... | 161.38 |
| 1936—Richard Degener, United States..... | 163.57 |

| YEAR WINNER AND COUNTRY | POINTS |
|---|---|
| 1948—Bruce Harlan, United States........ | 163.64 |
| 1952—David Browning, United States...... | 205.29 |
| 1956—Robert L. Clotworthy, United States.. | 159.56 |
| 1960—Gary Tobian, United States......... | 170.00 |
| 1964—Kenneth R. Sitzberger, United States.................. | 159.90 |

**HIGH DIVING**

| | |
|---|---|
| 1904—Dr. G. E. Sheldon, United States..... | 12.75 |
| 1906—Gottlob Walz, Germany............. | 156.00 |
| 1908—Hjalmar Johansson, Sweden........ | 83.75 |
| 1912—Erik Adlerz, Sweden............... | 73.94 |
| 1920—Clarence Pinkston, United States.... | 100.67 |
| 1924—Albert White, United States........ | 97.46 |
| 1928—Pete Desjardins, United States...... | 98.74 |
| 1932—Harold Smith, United States....... | 124.80 |
| 1936—Marshall Wayne, United States..... | 113.58 |
| 1948—Dr. Samuel Lee, United States...... | 130.05 |
| 1952—Dr. Samuel Lee, United States...... | 156.28 |
| 1956—Joaquin Capilla, Mexico........... | 152.44 |
| 1960—Robert Webster, United States..... | 165.56 |
| 1964—Robert Webster, United States..... | 148.58 |

## SWIMMING AND DIVING: WOMEN

| YEAR WINNER AND COUNTRY | TIME |
|---|---|

**100 METER FREE STYLE**

| | |
|---|---|
| 1912—Fanny Durack, Australia........... | 1:22.2 |
| 1920—Ethelda Bleibtrey, United States..... | 1:13.6 |
| 1924—Ethel Lackie, United States........ | 1:12.4 |
| 1928—Albina Osipowich, United States..... | 1:11.0 |
| 1932—Helene Madison, United States..... | 1:06.8 |
| 1936—Hendrika Mastenbroek, Holland..... | 1:05.9 |
| 1948—Greta Andersen, Denmark......... | 1:06.3 |
| 1952—Katalin Szoke, Hungary........... | 1:06.8 |
| 1956—Dawn Fraser, Australia............ | 1:02.0 |
| 1960—Dawn Fraser, Australia............ | 1:01.2 |
| 1964—Dawn Fraser, Australia............ | 59.5 * |

**100 METER BACKSTROKE**

| | |
|---|---|
| 1924—Sybil Bauer, United States......... | 1:23.2 |
| 1928—Marie Braun, Holland.............. | 1:22.0 |
| 1932—Eleanor Holm, United States....... | 1:19.4 |
| 1936—Dina Senff, Holland............... | 1:18.9 |
| 1948—Karen Harup, Denmark........... | 1:14.4 |
| 1952—Joan Harrison, South Africa........ | 1:14.3 |
| 1956—J. Grinham, Great Britain.......... | 1:12.9 |
| 1960—Lynn Burke, United States.......... | 1:09.3 |
| 1964—Cathy Ferguson, United States..... | 1:07.7 * |

**100 METER BUTTERFLY**

| | |
|---|---|
| 1956—Shelley Mann, United States........ | 1:11.0 |
| 1960—Carolyn Schuler, United States..... | 1:09.5 |
| 1964—Sharon Stouder, United States..... | 1:04.7 * |

**400 METER FREE STYLE**

| | |
|---|---|
| 1920—Ethelda Bleibtrey, United States (300-m)...................... | 4:34.0 |
| 1924—Martha Norelius, United States...... | 6:02.2 |
| 1928—Martha Norelius, United States...... | 5:26.4 |
| 1932—Helene Madison, United States..... | 5:28.5 |
| 1936—Hendrika Mastenbroek, Holland..... | 5:26.4 |
| 1948—Ann Curtis, United States.......... | 5:17.8 |
| 1952—Valeria Gyenge, Hungary.......... | 5:12.1 |
| 1956—L. Crapp, Australia................ | 4:54.6 |
| 1960—S. Chris Von Saltza, United States... | 4:50.6 |
| 1964—Virginia Duenkel, United States..... | 4:43.3 * |

**200 METER BREASTSTROKE**

| | |
|---|---|
| 1924—Lucy Morton, Great Britain......... | 3:33.2 |
| 1928—Hilde Schrader, Germany.......... | 3:12.6 |
| 1932—Clare Dennis, Australia........... | 3:06.3 |
| 1936—Hideko Maehata, Japan........... | 3:03.6 |

| YEAR WINNER AND COUNTRY | TIME |
|---|---|
| 1948—Nel Van Vliet, Netherlands | 2:57.2 |
| 1952—Eva Szekely, Hungary | 2:51.7 |
| 1956—U. Happe, Germany | 2:53.1 |
| 1960—Anita Lonsbrough, Great Britain | 2:49.5 |
| 1964—Galina Prozumenschikova, U.S.S.R. | 2:46.4 * |

### 4 x 100 METER FREE STYLE RELAY

| | |
|---|---|
| 1912—Great Britain | 5:52.8 |
| 1920—United States | 5:11.6 |
| 1924—United States | 4:58.8 |
| 1928—United States | 4:47.6 |
| 1932—United States | 4:38.0 |
| 1936—Holland | 4:36.0 |
| 1948—United States | 4:29.2 |
| 1952—Hungary | 4:24.4 |
| 1956—Australia | 4:17.1 |
| 1960—United States | 4:08.9 |
| 1964—United States | 4:03.8 * |

### 4 x 100 METER MEDLEY RELAY

| | |
|---|---|
| 1964—United States | 4:33.9 * |

### 400 METER INDIVIDUAL MEDLEY

| | |
|---|---|
| 1960—United States | 4:41.1 * |
| 1964—Donna deVarona, United States | 5:18.7 |

| YEAR WINNER AND COUNTRY | POINTS |
|---|---|

### SPRINGBOARD DIVING

| | |
|---|---|
| 1920—Aileen Riggin, United States | 539.90 |
| 1924—Elizabeth Becker, United States | 474.50 |
| 1928—Helen Meany, United States | 78.62 |
| 1932—Georgia Coleman, United States | 87.52 |
| 1936—Marjorie Gestring, United States | 89.27 |
| 1948—Victoria Draves, United States | 108.74 |
| 1952—Patricia McCormick, United States | 147.30 |
| 1956—Patricia McCormick, United States | 142.36 |
| 1960—Ingrid Kramer, Germany | 155.81 |
| 1964—Ingrid Engle-Kramer, Germany | 145.00 |

### HIGH DIVING

| | |
|---|---|
| 1912—Greta Johansson, Sweden | 39.90 |
| 1920—Stefani Fryland-Clausen, Denmark | 34.60 |
| 1924—Caroline Smith, United States | 33.20 |
| 1928—Elizabeth Pinkston, United States | 31.60 |
| 1932—Dorothy Poynton, United States | 40.26 |
| 1936—Dorothy Poynton Hill, United States | 33.93 |
| 1948—Victoria Draves, United States | 68.87 |
| 1952—Patricia McCormick, United States | 79.37 |
| 1956—Patricia McCormick, United States | 84.85 |
| 1960—Ingrid Kramer, Germany | 91.28 |
| 1964—Lesley Bush, United States | 99.80 |

## WEIGHTLIFTING

| YEAR CHAMPION AND COUNTRY | POUNDS |
|---|---|

### BANTAMWEIGHT

| | |
|---|---|
| 1948—Joe N. DePietro, United States | 677.915 |
| 1952—Ivan Udovov, U.S.S.R. | 694 |
| 1956—Charles Vinci, United States | 754½ |
| 1960—Charles Vinci, United States | 760 |
| 1964—Alexey Vakhonin, U.S.S.R. | 788.14 * |

### FEATHERWEIGHT

| | |
|---|---|
| 1920—L. de Haes, Belgium | 485 |
| 1924—Paolo Gabetti, Italy | 887.35 [1] |
| 1928—Franz Andrysek, Austria | 633.822 |
| 1932—Raymond Suvigny, France | 633.822 |
| 1936—Anthony Terlazzo, United States | 688.937 |
| 1948—Mahmoud Fayad, Egypt | 733.02 |
| 1952—Rafael Chimishyan, U.S.S.R. | 743½ |
| 1956—Isaac Berger, United States | 776¾ |
| 1960—Evgeniy Minaev, U.S.S.R. | 821 |
| 1964—Yoshinobu, Miyake, Japan | 876.33 * |

| YEAR WINNER AND COUNTRY | POUNDS |
|---|---|

### LIGHTWEIGHT

| | |
|---|---|
| 1920—Alfred Neyland, Estonia | 567.68 |
| 1924—Edmond Decottignies, France | 970.02 [1] |
| 1928—Kurt Helbig, Germany, and Hans Hass, Austria | 710.98 |
| 1932—Rene Duverger, France | 716.495 |
| 1936—Mohammed Mesbah, Egypt | 755.085 |
| 1948—Ibrahim Shams, Egypt | 793.656 |
| 1952—Thomas Kono, United States | 798¾ |
| 1956—Igors Rybak, U.S.S.R. | 837 |
| 1960—Viktor Bushuev, U.S.S.R. | 876 |
| 1964—Waldemar Baszanowski, Poland | 953.49 * |

### MIDDLEWEIGHT

| | |
|---|---|
| 1920—B. Gance, France | 540.012 |
| 1924—Carlo Galimberti, Italy | 1085.725 [1] |
| 1928—Francois Roger, France | 738.54 |
| 1932—Rudolf Ismayr, Germany | 760.507 |
| 1936—Khadr El Touni, Egypt | 854.28 |
| 1948—Frank Spellman, United States | 859.794 |
| 1952—Peter George, United States | 881½ |
| 1956—F. Bogdanovskii, U.S.S.R. | 925½ |
| 1960—Alexander Kurynov, U.S.S.R. | 964¼ |
| 1964—Hans Zdrazila, Czechoslovakia | 981.05 * |

### LIGHT HEAVYWEIGHT

| | |
|---|---|
| 1920—E. Cadine, France | 639.334 |
| 1924—Charles Rigoulot, France | 1107.811 [1] |
| 1928—Saied Nosseir, Egypt | 782.63 |
| 1932—Louis Hostin, France | 804.679 |
| 1936—Louis Hostin, France | 821.213 |
| 1948—Stanley Stanczyk, United States | 920.42 |
| 1952—Trofim Lomakin, U.S.S.R. | 920¼ |
| 1956—Tommy Kono, United States | 986¼ |
| 1960—Ireneusz Palinski, Poland | 975¼ |
| 1964—Rudolf Plyukfeider, U.S.S.R. | 1047.19 * |

### MIDDLE HEAVYWEIGHT

| | |
|---|---|
| 1952—Norbert Schemansky, United States | 980¾ |
| 1956—A. Vorobiev, U.S.S.R. | 1019¼ |
| 1960—Arkakiy Vorobiev, U.S.S.R. | 1041¼ |
| 1964—Vladimir Golovanov, U.S.S.R. | 1074.74 * |

### HEAVYWEIGHT

| | |
|---|---|
| 1920—Filippo Bottini, Italy | 595.24 |
| 1924—Giuseppe Tonani, Italy | 1140.879 [1] |
| 1928—Joseph Strassberger, Germany | 821.213 |
| 1932—Jaroslaw Skobla, Czechoslovakia | 837.748 |
| 1936—Joseph Manger, Germany | 903.886 |
| 1948—John Davis, United States | 997.581 |
| 1952—John Davis, United States | 1013¾ |
| 1956—Paul E. Anderson, United States | 1102 |
| 1960—Yuriy Vlasov, U.S.S.R. | 1184¼ |
| 1964—Leonid Zhabotinsky, U.S.S.R. | 1272.13 * |

| YEAR WINNER AND COUNTRY | POINTS |
|---|---|

### MODERN PENTATHLON: INDIVIDUAL

| | |
|---|---|
| 1912—Gustaf Lilliehook, Sweden | 27.0 |
| 1920—Gustaf Dyrssen, Sweden | 18.0 |
| 1924—Bo Lindman, Sweden | 18.0 |
| 1928—Sevn Thofelt, Sweden | 47.0 |
| 1932—Johan Oxenstierna, Sweden | 32.0 |
| 1936—Gotthard Handrick, Germany | 31.5 |
| 1948—Capt. William Grut, Sweden | 16.0 |
| 1952—Lars Hall, Sweden | 32.0 |
| 1956—Lars Hall, Sweden | 4,833.0 |
| 1960—Ferenc Nemeth, Hungary | 5,024.0 |
| 1964—Ferenc Tork, Hungary | 5,116.0 |

[1] Special scoring system used only in 1924; does not conform to present method.

| YEAR WINNER AND COUNTRY | POINTS |
|---|---|
| **MODERN PENTATHLON: TEAM** | |
| 1952—Hungary | 166.0 |
| 1956—U.S.S.R. | 13,690.5 |
| 1960—Hungary | 14,863.0 |
| 1964—U.S.S.R. | 14,961.0 |

# ROWING

| YEAR WINNER AND COUNTRY | TIME |
|---|---|
| **SINGLE SCULLS** | |
| 1900—H. Barrelet, France | 7:35.6 |
| 1904—Frank Greer, United States (demonstration) (3218-m) | 10:08.5 |
| 1908—Harry Blackstaffe, Great Britain | 9:26.0 |
| 1912—William Kinnear, Great Britain | 7:47.6 |
| 1920—John Kelly, United States | 7:35.0 |
| 1924—Jack Beresford, Great Britain | 7:49.2 |
| 1928—Henry Pearce, Australia | 7:11.0 |
| 1932—Henry Pearce, Australia | 7:44.4 |
| 1936—Gustav Schafer, Germany | 8:21.5 |
| 1948—Mervyn Wood, Australia | 7:24.4 |
| 1952—Yuri Tjukalov, U.S.S.R. | 8:12.8 |
| 1956—V. Ivanov, U.S.S.R. | 8:02.5 |
| 1960—Vjacheslav Ivanov, U.S.S.R. | 7:13.96 |
| 1964—Vjacheslav Ivanov, U.S.S.R. | 8:22.51 |
| **DOUBLE SCULLS** | |
| 1904—United States (Demonstration) (3218-m) | 10:03.3 |
| 1920—United States, John Kelly, Paul V. Costello | 7:09.0 |
| 1924—United States, John Kelly, Paul V. Costello | 6:34.0 |
| 1928—United States, Paul V. Costello, Charles McIlvaine | 6:41.4 |
| 1932—United States, Kenneth Myers, Garrett Wm. Gilmore | 7:17.4 |
| 1936—Great Britain, Jack Beresford, Leslie Southwood | 7:20.8 |
| 1948—Great Britain, R. D. Burnell, B. H. Bushnell | 6:51.3 |
| 1952—Argentina, T. Cappozzo, E. Guerrero | 7:32.2 |
| 1956—U.S.S.R., A. Berkoutov, Turi Tiukalov | 7:24.0 |
| 1960—Czechoslovakia, Vaclav Kozak, Pavel Schmidt | 6:47.50 |
| 1964—U.S.S.R., Oleg Tiurin, Boris Dubrovsky | 7:10.66 |
| **COXSWAINLESS PAIRS** | |
| 1908—Great Britain, J. Fenning, G. Thompson | 9:41.0 |
| 1920—Italy, M. Olgeni, G. Scatturini | 7:56.0 |
| 1924—Holland, W. H. Rosingh, A. C. Beynen | 8:19.4 |
| 1928—Germany, K. Moeschter, B. Muller | 7:06.4 |
| 1932—Great Britain, L. Clive, H. R. A. Edwards | 8:00.0 |
| 1936—Germany, W. Eichhorn, Hugo Strauss | 8:16.1 |
| 1948—Great Britain, J. Wilson, W. Laurie | 7:21.1 |
| 1952—United States, C. P. Logg, T. S. Price | 8:20.7 |
| 1956—United States, James Fifer, Duvall Hecht | 7:55.4 |
| 1960—U.S.S.R., Valentin Boreiko, Oleg Golovanov | 7:02.01 |
| 1964—Canada, George Hungerford, Roger Jackson | 7:32.94 |
| **PAIRS WITH COXSWAIN** | |
| 1900—Holland, R. Klein, F. A. Brandt | 7:34.2 |
| 1906—Italy, Brunna, Fontanella, G. Cesana | 7:32.4 |
| 1924—Switzerland, M. Candeveau, A. Felber, E. Lachapelle | 8:39.0 |
| 1928—Switzerland, H. Schochlin, C. Schochlin-Bourquin | 7:42.6 |

| YEAR WINNER AND COUNTRY | TIME |
|---|---|
| 1932—United States, J. A. Schauers, C. M. Kieffer, E. F. Jennings | 8:25.8 |
| 1936—Germany, G. Gustmann, H. Adamski, Dieter Arend | 8:36.9 |
| 1948—Denmark, F. Pedersen, T. Henriksen, C. E. Andersen | 8:00.5 |
| 1952—France, Salles, Mercier, Malivoire | 8:28.6 |
| 1956—United States, Art Ayrault, Conn Findlay, Kurt Seiffert | 8:26.1 |
| 1960—Germany, Berhard Knubel, Heinz Renneberg, Klaus Zerta | 7:29.14 |
| 1964—United States, Edward Ferry, Conn Findlay, Kent Mitchell | 8:21.33 |
| **COXSWAINLESS FOURS** | |
| 1908—Great Britain | 8:34.0 |
| 1924—Great Britain | 7:08.6 |
| 1928—Great Britain | 6:36.0 |
| 1932—Great Britain | 6:58.2 |
| 1936—Germany | 7:01.8 |
| 1948—Italy | 6:39.0 |
| 1952—Yugoslavia | 7:16.0 |
| 1956—Canada | 7:08.8 |
| 1960—United States | 6:26.26 |
| 1964—Denmark | 6:59.30 |
| **FOURS WITH COXSWAIN** | |
| 1906—Italy | 8:13.0 |
| 1912—Germany | 6:59.4 |
| 1920—Switzerland | 6:54.0 |
| 1924—Switzerland | 7:18.4 |
| 1928—Italy | 6:47.8 |
| 1932—Germany | 7:19.0 |
| 1936—Germany | 7:16.2 |
| 1948—United States | 6:50.3 |
| 1952—Czechoslovakia | 7:33.4 |
| 1956—Italy | 7:19.4 |
| 1960—Germany | 6:39.12 |
| 1964—Germany | 7:00.44 |
| **EIGHT-OARED SHELL** | |
| 1900—United States (Vesper B.C.) | 6:09.8 |
| 1904—United States (demonstration) | |
| 1908—Great Britain | 7:52.0 |
| 1912—Great Britain | 6:15.0 |
| 1920—United States (Navy) | 6:02.6 |
| 1924—United States (Yale) | 6:33.4 |
| 1928—United States (California) | 6:03.2 |
| 1932—United States (California) | 6:37.6 |
| 1936—United States (Washington) | 6:25.4 |
| 1948—United States (California) | 5:56.7 |
| 1952—United States (Navy) | 6:25.9 |
| 1956—United States (Yale) | 6:35.2 |
| 1960—Germany | 5:57.18 |
| 1964—United States (Vesper B.C.) | 6:18.23 |

# BOXING

YEAR CHAMPION AND COUNTRY

**FLYWEIGHT**
1904—George V. Finnegan, United States
1920—Frank De Genaro, United States
1924—Fidel La Barba, United States
1928—Anton Kocsis, Hungary
1932—Stephen Enekes, Hungary
1936—Willi Kaiser, Germany
1948—Pascual Perez, Argentina
1952—Nathan Brooks, United States
1956—Terence Spinks, Great Britain
1960—Gyula Torok, Hungary
1964—Fernando Atzori, Italy

| YEAR CHAMPION AND COUNTRY | | YEAR CHAMPION AND COUNTRY |

## BANTAMWEIGHT
1904—O. L. Kirk, United States
1908—H. Thomas, Great Britain
1920—Clarence Walker, South Africa
1924—William Smith, South Africa
1928—Vittorio Tamagnini, Italy
1932—Horace Gwynne, Canada
1936—Ulderico Sergo, Italy
1948—Tibor Csik, Hungary
1952—Pentti Hamalainen, Finland
1956—Wolfgang Behrendt, Germany
1960—Oleg Grigoryev, U.S.S.R.
1964—Takao Sakurai, Japan

## FEATHERWEIGHT
1904—O. L. Kirk, United States
1908—R. K. Gunn, Great Britain
1920—Paul Fritsch, France
1924—John Fields, United States
1928—L. Van Klaveren, Holland
1932—Carmelo Robledo, Argentina
1936—Oscar Casanovas, Argentina
1948—Ernesto Formenti, Italy
1952—Jan Zachara, Czechoslovakia
1956—Vladimir Safronov, U.S.S.R.
1960—Francesco Musso, Italy
1964—Stanislav Stepashkin, U.S.S.R.

## LIGHTWEIGHT
1904—H. J. Spanger, United States
1908—F. Grace, Great Britain
1920—Samuel Mosberg, United States
1924—Harold Nielson, Denmark
1928—Carlo Orlandi, Italy
1932—Lawrence Stevens, South Africa
1936—Imre Harangi, Hungary
1948—Gerald Dreyer, South Africa
1952—Aureliano Bolognesi, Italy
1956—Richard McTaggart, Great Britain
1960—Kazimierz Pazdzior, Poland
1964—Jozef Grudzien, Poland

## LIGHT WELTERWEIGHT
1952—Charles Adkins, United States
1956—Vladimir Enguibarian, U.S.S.R.
1960—Bonumil Nemecek, Czechoslovakia
1964—Jerzy Kulej, Poland

## WELTERWEIGHT
1904—Albert Young, United States
1920—T. Schneider, Canada
1924—Jean Delarge, Belgium
1928—Edward Morgan, New Zealand
1932—Edward Flynn, United States
1936—Sten Suvio, Finland
1948—Julius Torma, Czechoslovakia
1952—Zigmunt Chycha, Poland
1956—Necalae Linca, Romania
1960—Giovanni Benvenuti, Italy
1964—Marian Kasprzyk, Poland

## LIGHT MIDDLEWEIGHT
1952—Laszlo Papp, Hungary
1956—Laszlo Papp, Hungary
1960—Wilbert McClure, United States
1964—Boris Lagutin, U.S.S.R.

## MIDDLEWEIGHT
1904—Charles Mayer, United States
1908—John Douglas, Great Britain
1920—Harry Mallin, Great Britain
1924—Harry Mallin, Great Britain
1928—Piero Toscani, Italy

1932—Carmen Barth, United States
1936—Jean Despeaux, France
1948—Laszlo Papp, Hungary
1952—Floyd Patterson, United States
1956—Guennadii Chatkov, U.S.S.R.
1960—Edward Crook, United States
1964—Valery Popenchenko, U.S.S.R.

## LIGHT HEAVYWEIGHT
1920—Edward Eagan, United States
1924—Harry Mitchell, Great Britain
1928—Victorio Avendano, Argentina
1932—David E. Carstens, South Africa
1936—Roger Michlot, France
1948—George Hunter, South Africa
1952—Nor.el Lee, United States
1956—James F. Boyd, United States
1960—Cassius Clay, United States
1964—Cosimo Pinto, Italy

## HEAVYWEIGHT
1904—Samuel Berger, United States
1908—A. L. Oldham, Great Britain
1920—R. Rawson, Great Britain
1924—Otto von Porath, Norway
1928—Rodriguez Jurado, Argentina
1932—Santiago A. Lovell, Argentina
1936—Herbert Runge, Germany
1948—Rafael Iglesias, Argentina
1952—Edward Sanders, United States
1956—Peter Rademacher, United States
1960—Francesco De Piccoli, Italy
1964—Joseph Frazier, United States

## BASKETBALL: TEAM CHAMPION

YEAR COUNTRY

1904—United States [1]
1936—United States
1948—United States
1952—United States
1956—United States
1960—United States
1964—United States

[1] Demonstration.

## SOCCER FOOTBALL: TEAM CHAMPION

YEAR COUNTRY

1900—Great Britain
1904—Canada
1906—Denmark
1908—Great Britain
1912—Great Britain
1920—Belgium
1924—Uruguay
1928—Uruguay
1936—Italy
1948—Sweden
1952—Hungary
1956—Russia
1960—Yugoslavia
1964—Hungary

## SKIING: ALPINE

| YEAR WINNER AND COUNTRY | TIME |

### MEN'S DOWNHILL
1948—Henry Oreiller, France.............    2:55.0

| YEAR WINNER AND COUNTRY | TIME |
|---|---|
| 1952—Zeno Colo, Italy | 2:30.8 |
| 1956—Anton Sailer, Austria | 2:52.2 |
| 1960—Jean Vuarnet, France | 2:06.0 |
| 1964—Egon Zimmermann, Austria | 2:18.16 |

**MEN'S GIANT SLALOM**

| | |
|---|---|
| 1952—Stein Eriksen, Norway | 2:25.0 |
| 1956—Anton Sailer, Austria | 3:00.1 |
| 1960—Roger Staub, Switzerland | 1:48.3 |
| 1964—Francois Bonlieu, France | 1:46.71 |

**MEN'S SLALOM**

| | |
|---|---|
| 1948—Edi Reinalter, Switzerland | 2:10.3 |
| 1952—Othmar Schneider, Austria | 2:00.0 |
| 1956—Anton Sailer, Austria | 194.7 pts. [1] |
| 1960—Ernst Hinterseer, Austria | 2:08.9 |
| 1964—Josef Stiegler, Austria | 2:11.13 |

| YEAR WINNER AND COUNTRY | POINTS |
|---|---|

**ALPINE COMBINATION DOWNHILL AND SLALOM**

| | |
|---|---|
| 1936—Franz Pfnur, Germany | 99.25 |
| 1948—Henri Oreiller, France | 3.27 |

| YEAR WINNER AND COUNTRY | TIME |
|---|---|

**WOMEN'S DOWNHILL**

| | |
|---|---|
| 1948—Hedi Schlunegger, Switzerland | 2:28.3 |
| 1952—True Jochum-Beiser, Austria | 1:47.1 |
| 1956—Madeleine Berthod, Switzerland | 1:40.7 |
| 1960—Heidi Biebl, Germany | 1:37.6 |
| 1964—Christl Haas, Austria | 1:55.39 |

**WOMEN'S GIANT SLALOM**

| | |
|---|---|
| 1952—Andrea Mead Lawrence, United States | 2:06.8 |
| 1956—Ossi Reichert, Germany | 1:56.5 |
| 1960—Yvonne Ruegg, Switzerland | 1:39.9 |
| 1964—Marielle Goitschel, France | 1:52.24 |

**WOMEN'S SLALOM**

| | |
|---|---|
| 1948—Gretchen Fraser, United States | 1:57.2 |
| 1952—Andrea Mead Lawrence, United States | 2:10.6 |
| 1956—Renee Colliard, Switzerland | 112.3 pts. [1] |
| 1960—Anne Heggtveigt, Canada | 1:49.6 |
| 1964—Christine Goitschel, France | 1:35.11 |

| YEAR WINNER AND COUNTRY | POINTS |
|---|---|

**ALPINE COMBINATION DOWNHILL AND SLALOM**

| | |
|---|---|
| 1936—Christel Cranz, Germany | 97.06 |
| 1948—Trude Beiser, Austria | 6.58 |

[1] Scoring system changed in 1956.

## SKIING: NORDIC

| YEAR WINNER AND COUNTRY | TIME |
|---|---|

**MEN'S 15-KILOMETER CROSS-COUNTRY**

| | |
|---|---|
| 1956—Hallgeir Brenden, Norway | 0:49:39.0 |
| 1960—Hakon Brusveen, Norway | 0:51:55.5 |
| 1964—Eero Mantyranta, Finland | 1:30:50.7 |

**MEN'S 18-KILOMETER**

| | |
|---|---|
| 1924—Thorlief Haug, Norway | 1:14:31.0 |
| 1928—Johan Grottumsbraaten, Norway | 1:37:01.0 [1] |
| 1932—Sven Utterstrom, Sweden | 1:23:07.0 [2] |
| 1936—Erik-August Larsson, Sweden | 1:14:38.0 |
| 1948—Martin Lundstroem, Sweden | 1:13:50.0 |
| 1952—Hallgeir Brenden, Norway | 1:01:34.0 |

**MEN'S 30-KILOMETER CROSS-COUNTRY**

| | |
|---|---|
| 1956—Veikko Hakulinen, Finland | 1:44:06.0 |
| 1960—Sixten Jernberg, Sweden | 1:51:03.9 |
| 1964—Eero Mantyranta, Finland | 0:50:54.1 |

**MEN'S 50-KILOMETER CROSS-COUNTRY**

| | |
|---|---|
| 1924—Thorlief Haug, Norway | 3:44:32.0 |
| 1928—Per E. Hedlund, Sweden | 4:52:03.0 |
| 1932—Veli Saarinen, Finland | 4:28:00.0 [3] |
| 1936—Elis Viklund, Sweden | 3:30:11.0 |
| 1948—Nils Karlsson, Sweden | 3:47:48.0 |
| 1952—Veikko Haukulinen, Finland | 3:33:33.0 |
| 1956—Sixten Jernberg, Sweden | 2:50:27.0 |
| 1960—Kalevi Hamalainen, Finland | 2:59:06.3 |
| 1964—Sixten Jernberg, Sweden | 2:43:52.6 |

**MEN'S 40-KILOMETER CROSS-COUNTRY RELAY**

| | |
|---|---|
| 1936—Finland | 2:41:33.0 |
| 1948—Sweden | 2:32:08.0 |
| 1952—Finland | 2:20:16.0 |
| 1956—U.S.S.R. | 2:15:30.0 |
| 1960—Finland | 2:18:45.6 |
| 1964—Sweden | 2:18:34.6 |

| YEAR WINNER AND COUNTRY | POINTS |
|---|---|

**MEN'S NORDIC COMBINED 15-KILOMETER CROSS-COUNTRY & JUMPING**

| | |
|---|---|
| 1924—Thorlief Haug, Norway | 453.800 |
| 1928—Johan Grottumsbraaten, Norway | 427.800 |
| 1932—Johan Grottumsbraaten, Norway | 446.200 |
| 1936—Oddbjorn Hagen, Norway | 430.300 |
| 1948—Heikki Hasu, Finland | 448.800 |
| 1952—Simon Slattvik, Norway | 451.621 |
| 1956—Sverre Stenersen, Norway | 455.000 |
| 1960—Georg Thoma, Germany | 457.952 |
| 1964—Tormod Knutsen, Norway | 469.280 |

| YEAR WINNER AND COUNTRY | TIME |
|---|---|

**WOMEN'S 5-KILOMETER CROSS-COUNTRY**

| | |
|---|---|
| 1964—Claudia Boyarskikh, U.S.S.R. | 17:50.5 |

**WOMEN'S 10-KILOMETER CROSS-COUNTRY**

| | |
|---|---|
| 1952—Lydia Wideman, Finland | 41:40.0 |
| 1956—Ljubovj Kozyreva, Russia | 38:11.0 |
| 1960—Marija Gusakova, U.S.S.R. | 39:46.6 |
| 1964—Claudia Boyarskikh, U.S.S.R. | 40:24.3 |

**WOMEN'S 15-KILOMETER CROSS-COUNTRY RELAY**

| | |
|---|---|
| 1956—Finland | 1:09:01.0 |
| 1960—Sweden | 1:04:21.4 |
| 1964—U.S.S.R. | 59:20.2 |

| YEAR WINNER AND COUNTRY | POINTS |
|---|---|

**SKI JUMPING**

| | |
|---|---|
| 1924—Jacob T. Thams, Norway | 227.5 |
| 1928—Alfred Andersen, Norway | 230.5 |
| 1932—Birger Ruud, Norway | 228.0 |
| 1936—Birger Ruud, Norway | 232.0 |
| 1948—Petter Hugsted, Norway | 228.1 |
| 1952—A. Bergmann, Norway | 226.0 |
| 1956—Antti Hyvarinen, Finland | 227.0 |
| 1960—Helmut Recknagel, Germany | 227.2 |
| 1964—Toralf Engan, Norway | 230.7 |

**70 METERS HILL**

| | |
|---|---|
| 1964—Veikko Kankkonen, Finland | 229.9 |

[1] 19,700 meter course.  [2] 18,214 meter course.  [3] 48,238 meter course.

| YEAR WINNER AND COUNTRY | POINTS |
|---|---|

# FIGURE SKATING

## MEN'S SINGLES

| | |
|---|---|
| 1908—Ulrich, Sweden | 2,641.00 |
| 1920—Gillis Grafstrom, Sweden | 2,838.50 |
| 1924—Gillis Grafstrom, Sweden | 2,575.25 |
| 1928—Gillis Grafstrom, Sweden | 2,698.25 |
| 1932—Karl Schaefer, Austria | 2,602.00 |
| 1936—Karl Schaefer, Austria | 2,959.00 |
| 1948—Richard T. Button, United States | 191.177 |
| 1952—Richard T. Button, United States | 192.256 |
| 1956—Hayes Alan Jenkins, United States | 166.430 |
| 1960—David W. Jenkins, United States | 1,440.2 |
| 1964—Manfred Schnelldorfer, Germany | 1,916.9 |

## WOMEN'S SINGLES

| | |
|---|---|
| 1908—Madge Syers, Great Britain | 1,767.50 |
| 1920—Madam Julin, Sweden | 1,278.90 |
| 1924—Mrs. Herma von Szabo-Planck, Austria | 2,094.25 |
| 1928—Sonja Henie, Norway | 2,452.25 |
| 1932—Sonja Henie, Norway | 2,302.50 |
| 1936—Sonja Henie, Norway | 2,971.40 |
| 1948—Barbara Ann Scott, Canada | 163.077 |
| 1952—Jeannette Altwegg, Great Britain | 161.756 |
| 1956—Tenley E. Albright, United States | 169.670 |
| 1960—Carol Heiss, United States | 1,490.1 |
| 1964—Sjoukje Dijkstra, Holland | 2,018.5 |

## PAIRS [1]

| | |
|---|---|
| 1908—Miss Hubler and H. Burger, Germany | 78.40 |
| 1920—Mr. & Mrs. Jacobsson, Finland | 80.70 |
| 1924—Helen Engelman and A. Berger, Austria | 74.50 |
| 1928—Andree Joly and Pierre Brunet, France | 78.20 |
| 1932—Andree and Pierre Brunet, France | 76.70 |
| 1936—Maxie Herber and Ernst Baier, Germany | 103.30 |
| 1948—Micheline Lannoy and Pierre Baugniet, Belgium | 11.227 |
| 1952—Ria and Paul Falk, Germany | 11.400 |
| 1956—Elizabeth Schwarz and Kurt Oppelt, Austria | 11.310 |
| 1960—Barbara A. Wagner and Robert Paul, Canada | 80.4 |
| 1964—Ludmilla Belousova and Oleg Protopopov, U.S.S.R. | 104.4 |

[1] Scoring systems have varied in different years in the Games.

# SPEED SKATING

| YEAR WINNER AND COUNTRY | TIME |
|---|---|

## MEN'S 500 METERS

| | |
|---|---|
| 1924—Charles Jewtraw, United States | 0:44.0 |
| 1928—Clas Thunberg, Finland and Bernt Evensen, Norway (tied) | 0:43.4 |
| 1932—John A. Shea, United States | 0:43.4 |
| 1936—Ivar Ballangrud, Norway | 0:43.4 |
| 1948—Finn Helgesen, Norway | 0:43.1 |
| 1952—Kenneth Henry, United States | 0:43.2 |
| 1956—Evgenij Grishin, U.S.S.R. | 0:40.2 |
| 1960—Evgenij Grishin, U.S.S.R. | 0:40.2 |
| 1964—R. Terrance McDermott, United States | 0:40.1 * |

## MEN'S 1500 METERS

| | |
|---|---|
| 1924—Clas Thunberg, Finland | 2:20.8 |
| 1928—Clas Thunberg, Finland | 2:21.1 |

| YEAR WINNER AND COUNTRY | TIME |
|---|---|
| 1932—John A. Shea, United States | 2:57.5 |
| 1936—Charles Mathisen, Norway | 2:19.2 |
| 1948—Sverre Farstad, Norway | 2:17.6 |
| 1952—Hjalmar Anderson, Norway | 2:20.4 |
| 1956—Evgenij Grishin, U.S.S.R. | 2:08.6 * |
| 1960—Edgar Roadaas, Norway | 2:10.4 |
| 1964—Ants Anston, U.S.S.R. | 2:10.3 |

## MEN'S 5,000 METERS

| | |
|---|---|
| 1924—Clas Thunberg, Finland | 8:39.0 |
| 1928—Ivar Ballangrud, Norway | 8:50.5 |
| 1932—Irving Jaffee, United States | 9:40.8 |
| 1936—Ivar Ballangrud, Norway | 8:19.6 |
| 1948—Reidar Liaklev, Norway | 8:29.4 |
| 1952—Hjalmar Anderson, Norway | 8:10.6 |
| 1956—Boris Shilkov, U.S.S.R. | 7:48.7 |
| 1960—Viktor Kosichkin, U.S.S.R. | 7:51.3 |
| 1964—Knut Johannesen, Norway | 7:38.4 * |

## MEN'S 10,000 METERS

| | |
|---|---|
| 1924—Julien Skutnabb, Finland | 18:04.8 |
| 1928—No decision, thawing of ice [1] | |
| 1932—Irving Jaffee, United States | 19:13.6 |
| 1936—Ivar Ballangrud, Norway | 17:24.3 |
| 1948—Ake Seyffarth, Norway | 17:26.3 |
| 1952—Hjalmar Anderson, Norway | 16:45.8 |
| 1956—Sigvard Ericsson, Sweden | 16:35.9 |
| 1960—Knut Johannesen, Norway | 15:46.6 * |
| 1964—Jonny Nilsson, Sweden | 15:50.1 |

[1] Irving Jaffee, representing the U.S., had the best time, 18:36.5.

| YEAR WINNER AND COUNTRY | TIME |
|---|---|

## WOMEN'S 500 METERS

| | |
|---|---|
| 1932—Jean Wilson, Canada | 0:58.0 [1] |
| 1960—Helga Haase, Germany | 0:45.9 |
| 1964—Lydia Skoblikova, U.S.S.R. | 0:45.0 * |

## WOMEN'S 1,000 METERS

| | |
|---|---|
| 1932—Elizabeth DuBois, United States | 2:04.0 [1] |
| 1960—Klara Guseva, U.S.S.R. | 1:34.1 |
| 1964—Lydia Skoblikova, U.S.S.R. | 1:33.2 * |

## WOMEN'S 1,500 METERS

| | |
|---|---|
| 1932—Kit Klein, United States | 3:06.0 [1] |
| 1960—Lydia Skoblikova, U.S.S.R. | 2:52.2 |
| 1964—Lydia Skoblikova, U.S.S.R. | 2:22.6 * |

## WOMEN'S 3,000 METERS

| | |
|---|---|
| 1960—Lydia Skoblikova, U.S.S.R. | 5:14.3 * |
| 1964—Lydia Skoblikova, U.S.S.R. | 5:14.9 |

[1] Women's events in 1932 were not credited as being official.

# ICE HOCKEY: CHAMPIONSHIP FINAL ROUND STANDINGS

| YEAR COUNTRY | RECORD |
|---|---|
| 1920—Canada | W-3 L-0 |
| 1924—Canada | W-2 L-0 |
| 1928—Canada | W-3 L-0 |
| 1932—Canada | W-5 L-0 T-1 |
| 1936—Great Britain | W-2 L-0 T-1 |
| 1948—Canada | W-7 L-0 T-1 |
| 1952—Canada | W-7 L-0 T-1 |
| 1956—U.S.S.R. | W-5 L-0 |
| 1960—United States | W-5 L-0 |
| 1964—U.S.S.R. | W-7 L-0 |

# PAN-AMERICAN GAMES: 1967

Canadian team parades into Winnipeg stadium during opening ceremonies of the 1967 Pan-American Games.

On July 23, 1967, some 2,400 athletes from 28 Western Hemisphere countries met in Winni-peg, Canada, to compete in the Fifth Pan-American Games. When the closing ceremonies were held on August 6, there was no doubt as to the tournament champion—the United States, winner of 120 gold medals (out of a total of 171), 63 silver, and 42 bronze ones.

Initiated shortly after World War II to foster better understanding among the nations of the Americas, the Games are held every four years, a year prior to the quadrennial Olympic Games.

Perhaps the most spectacular array of United States victories were in swimming. U.S. men and women swimmers captured 28 first places in 33 events and broke 14 world records. In track and field it was much the same—the U.S. placed first in 22 out of 24 men's events, while the women's team took 8 out of their 11 events. One of the individual gold medals for shooting went to Lieutenant Margaret Thompson of the U.S. Army, who outgunned the best shots of North and South America in the small bore rifle competition.

And for the first time in the history of the Games, a United States team won a gold medal in its own national sport—baseball.

Overall, the 1967 Games were an unqualified success for the United States. Yet the other participants had their triumphs, too.

## PAN-AMERICAN TEAMS: MEDALS WON, 1967

| COUNTRY | Gold | Silver | Bronze | COUNTRY | Gold | Silver | Bronze | COUNTRY | Gold | Silver | Bronze |
|---|---|---|---|---|---|---|---|---|---|---|---|
| U.S.A........ | 120 | 63 | 42 | Venezuela... | 1 | 4 | 5 | Ecuador..... | 0 | 1 | 2 |
| Canada...... | 12 | 37 | 43 | Colombia.... | 1 | 2 | 5 | Bermuda.... | 0 | 1 | 1 |
| Brazil....... | 11 | 10 | 5 | Puerto | | | | Barbados.... | 0 | 1 | 0 |
| Argentina... | 9 | 14 | 11 | Rico...... | 1 | 1 | 4 | Jamaica..... | 0 | 0 | 3 |
| Cuba........ | 8 | 14 | 23 | Chile........ | 1 | 1 | 3 | Guyana...... | 0 | 0 | 1 |
| Mexico...... | 5 | 14 | 24 | Peru........ | 0 | 2 | 1 | Netherlands | | | |
| Trinidad and | | | | Uruguay..... | 0 | 1 | 4 | Antilles... | 0 | 0 | 1 |
| Tobago.... | 2 | 2 | 3 | Panama..... | 0 | 1 | 3 | | | | |

## SUMMARY OF EVENTS: FIFTH PAN-AMERICAN GAMES

| EVENT, WINNER, AND COUNTRY | TIME | EVENT, WINNER, AND COUNTRY | TIME | EVENT, WINNER, AND COUNTRY | LENGTH |
|---|---|---|---|---|---|
| **Men's Running Events** | | 50,000-Meter Race Walk: | 4 hrs., | **Men's Field Events** | |
| 100 Meters: Henry | | Larry Young, U.S.A. | 26:20.8 | Pole Vault: Bob Seagren, | |
| Jerome, Canada | 10.2 | 110-Meter High Hurdles: | | U.S.A. | 16' 1'' * |
| 200 Meters: John Carlos, | | Earl McCulloch, U.S.A. | 13.4 * | High Jump: | |
| U.S.A. | 20.5 * | 400-Meter Intermediate | | Ed Caruthers, U.S.A. | 7' 2¼'' * |
| 400 Meters: Lee Evans, | | Hurdles: Ron Whitney, | | Long Jump: Ralph | |
| U.S.A. | 44.9 * | U.S.A. | 50.7 | Boston, U.S.A. | 27' 2½'' * |
| 800 Meters: Wade Bell, | | 3,000-Meter Steeple- | | Triple Jump: Charles | |
| U.S.A. | 1:49.2 | chase: Chris | | Craig, U.S.A. | 54' 3¼'' * |
| 1,500 Meters: Tom Von | | McCubbins, U.S.A. | 8:38.2 * | Shot Put: Randle | |
| Ruden, U.S.A. | 3:43.4 | 4 x 100-Meter Relay: | | Matson, U.S.A. | 65' 1'' |
| 5,000 Meters: Van | | U.S.A. (E. McCulloch, | | Discus: Gary Carlsen, | |
| Nelson, U.S.A. | 13:47.4 * | J. Bright, R. Copeland, | | U.S.A. | 188' 8'' |
| 10,000 Meters: Van | | W. Turner) | 39.0 * | Javelin: Frank Covelli, | |
| Nelson, U.S.A. | 29:17.4 * | 4 x 400-Meter Relay: | | U.S.A. | 243' 8'' |
| Marathon: Andrew | 2 hrs., | U.S.A. (E. Stinson, | | Hammer: Tom Gage, | |
| Boychuk, Canada | 23:2.4 | E. Taylor, V. Matthews, | | U.S.A. | 214' 4'' * |
| 20,000-Meter Race Walk: | 1 hr., | L. Evans) | 3:02.0 * | Decathlon: William | 8,044 |
| Ronald Laird, U.S.A. | 33:5.2 | | | Toomey, U.S.A. | pts. * |

\* Pan-American Games record.

| EVENT, WINNER, AND COUNTRY | TIME |
|---|---|
| **Women's Events** | |
| 100 Meters: Barbara Ferrell, U.S.A. | 11.5 |
| 200 Meters: Wyomia Tyus, U.S.A. | 23.7 |
| 800 Meters: Madeline Manning, U.S.A. | 2:02.3 * |
| 80-Meter Hurdles: Cherrie Sherrard, U.S.A. | 10.8 * |
| 4 x 100-Meter Relay: Cuba | 44.6 * |

| EVENT, WINNER, AND COUNTRY | LENGTH |
|---|---|
| High Jump: Eleanor Montgomery, U.S.A. | 5' 10'' * |
| Long Jump: Irene Martinez Tartabull, Cuba. | 20' 9'' * |
| Shot Put: Nancy McCredie, Canada | 49' 9¾'' |
| Discus: Carol Moseke, U.S.A. | 161' 7'' |
| Javelin: Barbara Friedrich, U.S.A. | 174' 9'' * |
| Pentathlon: Pat D. Winslow, U.S.A. (4,860 points) | |

## BASEBALL

**Gold Medal:** U.S.A.
**Silver Medal:** Cuba
**Bronze Medal:** Puerto Rico

## BASKETBALL: MEN

**Gold Medal:** U.S.A.
**Silver Medal:** Mexico
**Bronze Medal:** Panama

## BASKETBALL: WOMEN

**Gold Medal:** Brazil
**Silver Medal:** U.S.A.
**Bronze Medal:** Canada

## BOXING: EVENT, WINNER, AND COUNTRY

Flyweight: Francisco Rodriguez, Venezuela
Bantamweight: Juvencio Martinez Gonzalez, Mexico
Featherweight: Miguel Garcia, Argentina

Lightweight: Enrico Blanco, Cuba
Light Welterweight: James Wallington, U.S.A.
Welterweight: Andres Modina Casanola, Cuba
Light Middleweight: Rolando

Garbey, Cuba
Middleweight: Jorge Victor Ahumada, Argentina
Light Heavyweight: Arthur Redden, U.S.A.
Heavyweight: Forest Ward, U.S.A.

## CYCLING

| EVENT, WINNER, AND COUNTRY | TIME |
|---|---|
| Two-Lap Sprints: Roger Gibbon, Trinidad and Tobago | — |
| 1,000-Meter Time Trial: Roger Gibbon, Trinidad and Tobago | 1:09.33 |
| 4,000-Meter Individual Pursuit Final: Martin Rodriguez, Colombia | 4:58.31 |

| EVENT, WINNER, AND COUNTRY | TIME |
|---|---|
| 4,000-Meter Team Pursuit Final: Argentina | 4:44.58 |
| 10-Mile Scratch Race: Carlos Alvarez, Argentina | 23:11.4 |
| 100-Kilometer Team Time Trial: Argentina | 2 hours, 20:49 |
| 110-Mile Road Race: Marcel Roy, Canada | 5 h., 3:5 |

## FENCING: EVENT, WINNER, AND COUNTRY

Individual Epée: Arthur Telles, Brazil
Team Epée: U.S.A.
Individual Foil: Guillermo Sau-

cedo, Argentina
Team Foil: Argentina
Individual Sabre: Anthony Keane, U.S.A.

Team Sabre: U.S.A.
Women's Individual Foil: Pilar Roldan, Mexico
Women's Team Foil: U.S.A.

## EQUESTRIAN

**Team Final Standings:** (1) Brazil (2) United States (3) Canada

## FIELD HOCKEY

**Team Final Standings:** (1) Argentina (2) Trinidad and Tobago (3) United States

## GYMNASTICS

| EVENT, WINNER, AND COUNTRY | POINTS |
|---|---|
| **Men's Individual Final Standings** | |
| All Around: Fred Rothlisberger, U.S.A. | 110.75 |
| Horizontal Bar: Rothlisberger, U.S.A. | 18.85 |
| Parallel Bars: Rothlisberger, R. Loyd, U.S.A. | 18.95 |

| EVENT, WINNER, AND COUNTRY | POINTS |
|---|---|
| Pommel (Side) Horse: Mark Cohn, U.S.A. | 19.15 |
| Floor Exercises: Hector Ramirez, Cuba | 18.45 |
| Still Rings: Armando Valles, Mexico | 18.90 |
| Long Horse Vault: Jorge Rodriguez, Cuba | 18.60 |

**Men's Team Final Standings:** (1) United States, 548.55 (2) Cuba, 536.55 (3) Mexico, 529.40 (4) Canada, 519.05 (5) Ecuador, 402.45 (6) Argentina, 210.75

| | POINTS |
|---|---|
| **Women's Individual Final Standings** | |
| All Around: Linda Metheny, U.S.A. | 74.03 |
| Floor Exercises: Linda Metheny, U.S.A. | 19.107 |
| Side Horse Vault: Linda Metheny, U.S.A. | 18.500 |

| | POINTS |
|---|---|
| Balance Beam: Linda Metheny, U.S.A. | 18.691 |
| Uneven Parallel Bars: Susan McDonnell, Canada | 18.641 |

**Women's Team Final Standings:** (1) United States, 362.377 (2) Canada, 336.75 (3) Cuba, 334.526 (4) Mexico, 289.130 (5) Brazil, 112.231

## JUDO

Open: D. Rogers, Canada
Heavyweight: A. Coage, U.S.A.

Lt. Heavywt.: M. Johnson, Canada
Middleweight: H. Nishioka, U.S.A.

Lightweight: T. Miura, Brazil
Featherweight: A. Ono, Brazil

\* Pan-American Games record.

**PAN-AMERICAN GAMES** (*continued*)
## ROWING

| EVENT, WINNER, AND COUNTRY | TIME | EVENT, WINNER, AND COUNTRY | TIME |
|---|---|---|---|
| Eights with Coxswain: U.S.A. | 6:30.86 | Pairs Without Coxswain: U.S.A. | 7:20.24 |
| Four Oars with Coxswain: U.S.A. | 6:47.91 | Singles Sculls: Alberto Demiddi, Argentina.... | 7:42.18 |
| Four Oars Without Coxswain: U.S.A. | 6:46.99 | Double Sculls: U.S.A. | 7:26.67 |
| Pairs with Coxswain: U.S.A. | 8:00.14 | | |

### SHOOTING: EVENT AND WINNER

**Free Pistol:** Team—United States (2,171 points [1])
 Individual—Hershel Anderson, U.S.A. (548 points)
**Small Bore Rifle** [2]**:** Team— United States (2,379 points [3])
 Individual—Alf Mayer, Canada (598 points [4])
**Rapid Fire Pistol:** Team—United States (2,307 points)
 Individual—Maj. Wm. McMillan, U.S.A. (581 points)

**Small Bore Rifle** [5]**:** Team—United States (4,571 points [1])
 Individual—Lt. Margaret Thompson, U.S.A. (1,152 pts [1])
**Center Fire Pistol:** Team—United States (2,342 points)
 Individual—Francis Higginson, U.S.A. (593 points)
**Skeet Shooting:** Team—United States (379/400 points)
 Individual—Lt. Allen Morrison, U.S.A. (195 points)

### SWIMMING AND DIVING

**Men**

| EVENT, WINNER, AND COUNTRY | TIME | EVENT, WINNER, AND COUNTRY | TIME |
|---|---|---|---|
| 100-Meter Freestyle: D. Havens, U.S.A. | 0:53.79[1] | 100-Meter Butterfly: M. Spitz, U.S.A. | 0:56.20[1] |
| 200-Meter Freestyle: D. Schollander, U.S.A.... | 1:56.01[1] | 200-Meter Butterfly: M. Spitz, U.S.A. | 2:06.42[1] |
| 400-Meter Freestyle: G. Charlton, U.S.A. | 4:10.23[1] | 200-Meter Indiv. Medley: D. Russell, U.S.A... | 2:13.22[1] |
| 1,500-Meter Freestyle: M. Burton, U.S.A. | 16:44.40[1] | 400-Meter Individual Medley: W. Utley, U.S.A. | 4:48.12[1] |
| 100-Meter Backstroke: C. Hickcox, U.S.A. | 1:01.19[1] | 400-Meter Freestyle Relay: United States..... | 3:34.08[1] |
| 200-Meter Backstroke: R. Hutton, Canada..... | 2:12.55[1] | 800-Meter Freestyle Relay: United States..... | 8:00.46[1] |
| 100-Meter Breaststroke: J. Fiolo, Brazil....... | 1:07.52[1] | 400-Meter Medley Relay: United States....... | 3:59.31[1] |
| 200-Meter Breaststroke: J. Fiolo, Brazil....... | 2:30.42[1] | Diving, Springboard: B. Wrightson, U.S.A. | |
| | | Diving, Platform: W. Young, U.S.A. | |

**Women**

| EVENT, WINNER, AND COUNTRY | TIME | EVENT, WINNER, AND COUNTRY | TIME |
|---|---|---|---|
| 100-Meter Freestyle: E. Bricker, U.S.A. | 1:00.89 | 100-Meter Butterfly: E. Daniel, U.S.A. | 1:05.24[1] |
| 200-Meter Freestyle: P. Kruse, U.S.A. | 2:11.91[1] | 200-Meter Butterfly: C. Kolb, U.S.A. | 2:25.49[1] |
| 400-Meter Freestyle: D. Meyer, U.S.A. | 4:32.64[1] | 200-Meter Individual Medley: C. Kolb, U.S.A... | 2:26.06[1] |
| 800-Meter Freestyle: D. Meyer, U.S.A. | 9:22.86[1] | 400-Meter Individual Medley: C. Kolb, U.S.A... | 5:09.68[1] |
| 100-Meter Backstroke: E. Tanner, Canada..... | 1:07.32[1] | 400-Meter Freestyle Relay: United States..... | 4:04.57[1] |
| 200-Meter Backstroke: E. Tanner, Canada..... | 2:24.55[1] | 400-Meter Medley Relay: United States....... | 4:30.0[1] |
| 100-Meter Breaststroke: C. Ball, U.S.A. | 1:14.80[1] | Diving, Springboard: S. Gossick, U.S.A. | |
| 200-Meter Breaststroke: C. Ball, U.S.A. | 2:42.18[4] | Diving, Platform: L. Bush, U.S.A. | |

### TENNIS

**Men's Singles:** Thomas Koch, Brazil
**Men's Doubles:** Edson Mandarino and Thomas Koch, Brazil
**Mixed Doubles:** Jane Albert and Lt. Albert Ashe, U.S.A.
**Women's Singles:** Elena Subirats, Mexico
**Women's Doubles:** Jane Albert and Patsy Rippy, U.S.A.

### VOLLEYBALL

**Team Final Standings:**
**Men's:** (1) United States (2) Brazil (3) Cuba
**Women's:** (1) United States (2) Peru (3) Cuba

### WATER POLO

**Team Final Standings:**
(1) United States (2) Brazil (3) Mexico

### WEIGHTLIFTING

| EVENT, WINNER, AND COUNTRY | POUNDS | EVENT, WINNER, AND COUNTRY | POUNDS |
|---|---|---|---|
| Bantamweight: Fernando Baez, Puerto Rico... | 735½[1] | Light Heavyweight: Joseph Puelo, U.S.A. | 992[1] |
| Featherweight: Walter Imahara, U.S.A. | 777 | Middle Heavywt.: Phillip Grippaldi, U.S.A.... | 1,047[1] |
| Lightweight: Pastor Rodriguez, Cuba. | 848[1] | Heavyweight: Joseph Dube, U.S.A. | 1,163[1] |
| Middleweight: Russel Knipp, U.S.A. | 948[1] | | |

### WRESTLING

Flyweight: Richard Sofman, U.S.A.
Bantamweight: Richard Sanders, U.S.A.
Featherweight: Mike Young, U.S.A.
Lightweight: Gerald Bell, U.S.A.

Welterweight: Patrick Kelly, U.S.A.
Middleweight: Lt. Wayne Baughman, U.S.A.
Light Heavyweight: Harry Houska, U.S.A.
Heavyweight: Larry Kristoff, U.S.A.

### YACHTING

**Lightning Class:** U.S.A.; **Flying Dutchman Class:** U.S.A.; **Finn Class:** Brazil; **Snipe Class:** Brazil

[1] Pan-American Games record.　　[2] 50 Meters.　　[3] World record.　　[4] Tied world record.　　[5] Prone, Kneeling, Standing.

## ATHLETE OF THE YEAR

Each year a nationwide poll is conducted by the Associated Press among sportswriters, editors, and other notables to select the year's outstanding male and female athletes. Winners:

MALE
1934—Dizzy Dean, Baseball
1935—Joe Louis, Boxing
1936—Jesse Owens, Track
1937—Don Budge, Tennis
1938—Don Budge, Tennis
1939—Nile Kinnick, Football
1940—Tommy Harmon, Football
1941—Joe DiMaggio, Baseball
1942—Frank Sinkwich, Football
1943—Gunder Haegg, Track
1944—Byron Nelson, Golf
1945—Byron Nelson, Golf
1946—Glenn Davis, Football
1947—Johnny Lujack, Football
1948—Lou Boudreau, Baseball
1949—Leon Hart, Football
1950—Jim Konstanty, Baseball
1951—Dick Kazmaier, Football
1952—Bob Mathias, Track and Football
1953—Ben Hogan, Golf
1954—Willie Mays, Baseball
1955—Hopalong Cassady, Football
1956—Mickey Mantle, Baseball
1957—Ted Williams, Baseball
1958—Herb Elliott, Track
1959—Ingemar Johansson, Boxing
1960—Rafer Johnson, Decathlon
1961—Roger Maris, Baseball
1962—Maury Wills, Baseball
1963—Sandy Koufax, Baseball
1964—Don Schollander, Swimming
1965—Sandy Koufax, Baseball
1966—Frank Robinson, Baseball

FEMALE
1934—Virginia Van Wie, Golf
1935—Helen Wills Moody, Tennis
1936—Helen Stephens, Track
1937—Katherine Rawls, Swimming
1938—Patty Berg, Golf
1939—Alice Marble, Tennis
1940—Alice Marble, Tennis
1941—Betty Hicks Newell, Golf
1942—Gloria Callen, Swimming
1943—Patty Berg, Golf
1944—Ann Curtis, Swimming
1945—Babe Didrikson Zaharias, Golf
1946—Babe Didrikson Zaharias, Golf
1947—Babe Didrikson Zaharias, Golf
1948—Fanny Blankers-Koen, Track
1949—Marlene Bauer, Golf
1950—Babe Didrikson Zaharias, Golf
1951—Maureen Connolly, Tennis
1952—Maureen Connolly, Tennis
1953—Maureen Connolly, Tennis
1954—Babe Didrikson Zaharias, Golf
1955—Patty Berg, Golf
1956—Pat McCormick, Diving
1957—Althea Gibson, Tennis
1958—Althea Gibson, Tennis
1959—Maria Bueno, Tennis
1960—Wilma Rudolph, Track
1961—Wilma Rudolph, Track
1962—Dawn Fraser, Swimming
1963—Mickey Wright, Golf
1964—Mickey Wright, Golf
1965—Kathy Whitworth, Golf
1966—Kathy Whitworth, Golf

## JAMES E. SULLIVAN MEMORIAL TROPHY

Given since 1930 in honor of James E. Sullivan of New York City, a former president of the Amateur Athletic Union, the James E. Sullivan Memorial Trophy is awarded to the "amateur athlete who, by performance, example, and good influence, did the most to advance the cause of good sportsmanship during the year." Athletes from every sport are considered for the award. Winners are selected by outstanding sports authorities in a nationwide poll.

Here follows a listing of Sullivan Award winners from 1936:

| YEAR | ATHLETE | SPORT |
|------|---------|-------|
| 1936 | Glenn Morris | Track and Field (Decathlon) |
| 1937 | Don Budge | Tennis |
| 1938 | Donald R. Lash | Track and Field (Distance Runner) |
| 1939 | Joe Burk | Rowing |
| 1940 | Greg Rice | Track and Field (Distance Runner) |
| 1941 | Leslie MacMitchell | Track and Field (Middle Distance Runner) |
| 1942 | Cornelius Warmerdam | Track and Field (Pole Vaulter) |
| 1943 | Gil Dodds | Track and Field (Distance Runner) |
| 1944 | Ann Curtis | Swimming |
| 1945 | Doc Blanchard | Football |
| 1946 | Arnold Tucker | Football |
| 1947 | Jack Kelly, Jr. | Rowing |
| 1948 | Bob Mathias | Track and Field (Decathlon) |
| 1949 | Dick Button | Figure Skating |
| 1950 | Fred Wilt | Track and Field (Distance Runner) |
| 1951 | Bob Richards | Track and Field (Pole Vaulter) |

| YEAR | ATHLETE | SPORT |
|------|---------|-------|
| 1952 | Horace Ashenfelter | Track and Field (Distance Runner) |
| 1953 | Sammy Lee | Diving |
| 1954 | Mal Whitfield | Track and Field (Middle Distance Runner) |
| 1955 | Harrison Dillard | Track and Field (Sprinter) |
| 1956 | Patricia McCormick | Diving |
| 1957 | Bobby Joe Morrow | Track and Field (Sprinter) |
| 1958 | Glenn Davis | Track and Field (Mid. Distance Runner; Sprinter) |
| 1959 | Parry O'Brien | Track and Field (Shot Putter) |
| 1960 | Rafer Johnson | Track and Field (Decathlon) |
| 1961 | Wilma Rudolph | Track and Field (Sprinter) |
| 1962 | Jim Beatty | Track and Field (Middle Distance Runner) |
| 1963 | John Pennel | Track and Field (Pole Vaulter) |
| 1964 | Don Schollander | Swimming |
| 1965 | Bill Bradley | Basketball |
| 1966 | Jim Ryun | Track (Mile Runner) |

# SPORTS ORGANIZATIONS

**Amateur Fencers League of America:** 33 62d Street, West New York, New Jersey 07093; William J. Latzko, Secretary. Founded in 1891, the League has 4,000 members in 52 local divisions. It is responsible for the selection of fencers for the U.S. Olympic fencing team and for national fencing competition.

**Amateur Softball Association of America:** 1351 Skirvin Tower, Oklahoma City, Oklahoma 73101; D. E. Porter, Executive Secretary. The ruling body of amateur softball in the United States, it has some 4,500,000 members.

**American Amateur Baseball Congress (AABC):** P.O. Box 5332, Akron, Ohio 44313; Lincoln Hackim, President. Founded in 1935, the AABC is a federation of 44 state and regional baseball associations with 2,000 teams in two league divisions. The group sponsors the annual Stan Musial (unlimited age) and the Connie Mack (under 19 years) World Series.

**American Bowling Congress (ABC):** 1572 East Capitol Drive, Milwaukee, Wisconsin 53211; Frank K. Baker, Executive Secretary. Organized in 1895, the ABC sponsors major bowling competitions for men in the United States and has almost 5,000,000 members.

**American Casting Association:** P.O. Box 51, Nashville, Tennessee 37202; Paul N. Jones, Executive Secretary. The governing body of tournament fly and bait casting in the United States, this Association has a membership of 6,000.

**American Football League (AFL):** 200 Park Avenue, New York, New York 10017; Milt Woodard, President. Founded in 1960, the nine-member League is divided into two divisions: The Eastern Division has professional football teams in Boston, Buffalo, Houston, Miami, and New York City; the Western Division has teams in Denver, Kansas City, Oakland, and San Diego. A championship play-off is held at the end of each season.

**American League of Professional Baseball Clubs (AL):** 520 Boylston Street, Boston, Massachusetts 02130; Joseph E. Cronin, President. Founded in 1900, the American League is composed of major league baseball teams in Baltimore, Boston, California, Chicago, Cleveland, Detroit, Kansas City, Minneapolis-St. Paul, New York City, and Washington, D.C.

**American Power Boat Association:** The Whittier, 415 Burns Drive, Detroit, Michigan 48214; Harry Smith, Jr., Executive Secretary. Founded in 1903, it is the governing body of U.S. powerboat racing and has 6,000 members.

**Babe Ruth League:** 524½ Hamilton Avenue, Trenton, New Jersey 08609; Richard W. Case, Executive Vice President. The Babe Ruth League was formed in 1952 to provide supervised regulation baseball for boys 13 through 15 years of age. In 1966 Babe Ruth 16–18 Baseball was formed for boys of this older age group. Total 1967 participation: 169,064.

**Eastern Association of Rowing Colleges:** Hotel Manhattan, Eighth Avenue and 44th Street, New York, New York 10036; Ralph Furey, President. The 15-member association organizes regattas and championships.

**Eastern College Athletic Conference:** Hotel Manhattan, Eighth Avenue and 44th Street, New York, New York 10036; Asa S. Bushnell, Commissioner. The group includes 161 colleges and universities in 12 New England and Mid-Atlantic states and Washington, D.C.

**Intercollegiate Association of Amateur Athletes of America (ICAA):** Hotel Manhattan, Eighth Avenue and 44th Street, New York, New York 10036; Hugh G. McCurdy, President. Founded in 1875, the organization has 78 member colleges, and is a governing body of intercollegiate track and field events.

**Intercollegiate (Big Ten) Conference of Faculty Representatives:** Sheraton Chicago Hotel, Chicago, Illinois 60611; William R. Reed, Commissioner. Founded in 1895, the Big Ten includes nine state universities and one private university in the Middle West.

**Intercollegiate Fencing Association:** Hotel Manhattan, Eighth Avenue and 44th Street, New York, New York 10036; Albert W. Twitchell, President. The 12 members of this group, founded in 1894, are C.C.N.Y., Columbia, Cornell, Harvard, M.I.T., Navy, New York University, Penn State, Pennsylvania, Princeton, Rutgers, and Yale.

**International 5.5-Metre Class Association of the U.S.A.:** Ives Building, Narberth, Pennsylvania 19072; Victor F. Sheronas, Secretary. Formed in 1956, this organization governs and selects the yachtsmen who represent the United States in the Olympics, Pan-American Games, and other important sailing regattas.

**International Olympic Committee:** 10 North La Salle Street, Chicago, Illinois 60602; Avery Brundage, President. Founded in 1894, the Committee has representatives in the countries participating in the games, and selects the site of winter and summer Olympic Games.

**Jockey Club:** 300 Park Avenue, New York, New York 10022; John F. Kennedy, Executive Secretary. Founded in 1894, the organization encourages the development of thoroughbred horses, establishes the regulations governing horse races throughout the nation, and licenses jockeys and trainers.

**Ladies Professional Golf Association (LPGA):** 1172 West Galbraith Road, Cincinnati, Ohio 45231; Leonard F. Wirtz, Tournament Director. Formed in 1950 for professional women golfers, the LPGA sponsors tournaments.

**Little League Baseball:** Williamsport, Pennsylvania; Peter J. McGovern, President. Founded in 1939 to provide a baseball program for boys between the ages of 10 and 15, the Little League has 7,000 leagues in 28 countries.

**National Archery Association of the U.S.:** 2833 Lincoln Highway East, Ronks, Pennsylvania; Clayton B. Shenk, Executive Secretary. The governing body of amateur archery, it standardizes tournament rules and procedures and maintains official records.

**National Association of Intercollegiate Athletics (NAIA):** 106 West 12th Street, Kansas City, Missouri 64152; A. O. Duer, Executive Secretary-Treasurer. Formed in 1940, the NAIA has 505 member colleges.

**National Association of Professional Baseball Leagues:** 720 East Broad Street, Columbus, Ohio 43215; Phillip Piton, President. Comprised of all professional baseball minor leagues, the group includes 141 teams in 19 leagues and was organized in 1901.

**National Association of Stock Car Automobile Racing (NASCAR):** 1801 Volusia Avenue, Daytona Beach, Florida 32015; William H. G. France, President. Founded in 1947, NASCAR has more than 14,000 members and sanctions and supervises stock car races.

**National Basketball Association (NBA):** 350 Fifth Avenue, New York, New York 10001; J. Walter Kennedy, Commissioner. Comprised of 12 teams in two divisions: the Eastern Division has teams in Baltimore, Boston, Cincinnati, Detroit, New York, and Philadelphia; the Western Division has teams in Chicago, Los Angeles, St. Louis, San Diego, San Francisco, and Seattle. The NBA, organized in 1949, governs professional basketball play.

**National Collegiate Athletic Association (NCAA):** Midland Building, Kansas City, Missouri 64105; Walter Byers, Executive Director. Founded in 1906, the Association includes universities, colleges, and allied educational and athletic associations devoted to the administration of intercollegiate athletics.

**National Football League (NFL):** 1 Rockefeller Plaza, New York, New York 10020; Pete Roselle, Commissioner. Composed of 16 teams organized in two conferences, each having two divisions. Eastern Conference teams, Capitol Division: Dallas, New Orleans, Philadelphia, Washington; Century Division: Cleveland, New York, Pittsburgh, St. Louis. Western Conference teams, Coastal Division: Atlanta, Baltimore, Los Angeles, San Francisco; Central Division: Chicago, Detroit, Green Bay, Minnesota.

**National Hockey League (NHL):** Sun Life Building, Montreal, Canada; Clarence Campbell, President. Founded in 1917 in Montreal, the League is comprised of 12 professional teams: Boston, California, Chicago, Detroit, Los Angeles, Minnesota, Montreal, New York, Philadelphia, Pittsburgh, St. Louis, and Toronto.

**National League of Professional Baseball Clubs (NL):** 2601 Carew Tower, Cincinnati, Ohio 45202; Warren C. Giles, President. Founded in 1876, the National League is composed of teams in Atlanta, Chicago, Cincinnati, Houston, Los Angeles, New York, Philadelphia, Pittsburgh, St. Louis, and San Francisco.

**National Rifle Association of America (NRA):** 1600 Rhode Island Avenue, N.W., Washington, D.C. 20036; Louis F. Lucas, Executive Director. Founded in 1871, the group sponsors U.S. Olympic rifle teams and has 850,000 members.

**Professional Golfers Association (PGA):** Box 12458, Palm Beach Gardens, Florida; Robert T. Creasey, Director. Founded in 1916, the PGA has a membership of 6,000 golf professionals. It sponsors the PGA Championship, the Ryder Cup Matches, National Golf Day, and other tournaments.

**United States Golf Association (USGA):** 40 East 38th Street, New York, New York 10016; Joe Dey, Executive Director. Founded in 1894, the USGA is a voluntary association of golf clubs and courses. It is the governing body for golf in the United States, conducts annual championships, and provides data on rules, handicapping, and amateur status.

**United States Handball Association (USHA):** 4101 Dempster Street, Skokie, Illinois; Mort Leve, Executive Secretary. Founded in 1951, it has 6,000 members, all handball players and coaches. The group sponsors handball tournaments and establishes rules.

**United States Lawn Tennis Association (USLTA):** 51 East 42d Street, New York, New York 10017; Robert S. Malaga, Executive Director. Founded in 1881, the USLTA governs tennis in the United States and sanctions tennis tournaments for players of all ages. It sponsors U.S. championships for top-ranking amateurs from all over the world.

**United States Olympic Committee:** 57 Park Avenue, New York, New York 10016; Douglas F. Roby, President. Founded in 1921, it organizes and finances U.S. Olympic teams.

**United States Ski Association:** The Broadmoor, Colorado Springs, Colorado 80906; Gloria Chadwick, Executive Secretary. Formed in 1904, the Association has 100,000 members. It rules over U.S. amateur skiing competition, decides eligibility rules, and maintains a skiing Hall of Fame at Ishpeming, Michigan.

**United States Soccer Football Association:** 350 Fifth Avenue, New York, New York 10001; Joseph J. Barriskill, Executive Secretary. Founded in 1913, the Association sponsors all soccer tournament competitions in the United States, as well as a National Challenge Cup competition for soccer teams from all over the United States.

**United States Trotting Association (USTA):** 750 Michigan Avenue, Columbus, Ohio 43215; Edward F. Hackett, Executive Vice President. Founded in 1938, the group establishes rules and regulations for harness racing, registers trotters, and maintains records.

**Woman's International Bowling Congress (WIBC):** 1225 Dublin Road, Columbus, Ohio 43212; Freda Botkin, Executive Secretary. Founded in 1916, the group sponsors championship bowling for its nearly 3,000,000 women members in the United States and Canada.

**World Boxing Association of America (WBA):** 6501 North 17th Avenue, Phoenix, Arizona 85015; Jay Edson, Executive Secretary. The regulating body of professional boxing, it was formed in 1920 and comprises state and city boxing commissioners in all boxing states except New York, Massachusetts, and Michigan. It was formerly called the National Boxing Association of America.

# AUTOMOBILE RACING

## WORLD DRIVING CHAMPIONSHIP: 1967

Dennis Hulme of New Zealand came in first in 1967 in only two major Grand Prix point races for Formula One cars—Monaco and West Germany. But he scored enough points in the season's 11 events to earn the 1967 World Driving Championship title, edging out runner-up and three-time champion Jack Brabham by 51 points to 48. Jim Clark, twice world champion and winner of four races, including the Mexico City windup, ended the season in third place.

| GRAND PRIX RACE | DRIVER | TOTAL MILES | CAR | AVERAGE MPH |
|---|---|---|---|---|
| South Africa (Johannesburg, Jan. 2) | Pedro Rodriguez, Mexico | 203.8 | Cooper-Maserati | 97.09 |
| Monaco (Monte Carlo, May 7) | Dennis Hulme, New Zealand | 190 | Brabham-Repco | 75.9 |
| Netherlands (Zandvoort, June 4) | Jim Clark, Scotland | 234.4 | Lotus-Ford | 104.4 |
| Belgium (Spa, June 18) | Dan Gurney, United States | 245.3 | American Eagle | 145.98 |
| France (Le Mans, July 2) | Jack Brabham, Australia | 224 | Brabham-Repco | 98.9 |
| Great Britain (Silverstone, July 15) | Jim Clark, Scotland | 240 | Lotus-Ford | 117.64 |
| West Germany (Adenau, August 2) | Dennis Hulme, New Zealand | 213 | Brabham-Repco | 101.4 |
| Canada (Mosport, Ont., August 26) | Jack Brabham, Australia | 220.5 | Brabham-Repco | 131.5 |
| Italy (Monza, September 10) | John Surtees, England | 243 | Honda | 140.5 |
| U.S. (Watkins Glen, N.Y., Oct. 1) | Jim Clark, Scotland | 248 | Lotus-Ford | 120.95 |
| Mexico (Mexico City, October 22) | Jim Clark, Scotland | 201 | Lotus-Ford | 101.5 |

## STOCK CAR RACING: 1967

Thirty-year-old Richard Petty, the 1964 NASCAR (National Association for Stock Car Auto Racing) Grand National Champion, far outpointed all competitors to take the title again in 1967. In addition to upholding a family tradition (his father, Lee, won the NASCAR championship three times), Petty had a sensational year in other respects: a record number of career wins (75); the most wins ever tallied in one season (27); an unparalleled ten straight wins in the period between the Dixie 500 and the National 500; and the highest single season earnings record. Donnie Allison was named NASCAR Rookie-of-the-Year for 1967.

| MAJOR NASCAR RACES | DRIVER | CAR | AVERAGE MPH |
|---|---|---|---|
| Riverside 500 (January 22) | Parnelli Jones | '67 Ford | 91.08 |
| Daytona 500 (February 26) | Mario Andretti | '67 Ford | 146.926 |
| Atlanta 500 (April 2) | Cale Yarborough | '67 Ford | 131.238 |
| Rebel 400 (May 13) | Richard Petty | '67 Plymouth | 125.738 |
| World 600 (May 28) | Jim Paschal | '67 Plymouth | 135.823 |
| Carolina 500 (June 18) | Richard Petty | '67 Plymouth | 104.682 |
| Firecracker 400 (July 4) | Cale Yarborough | '67 Ford | 143.583 |
| Dixie 500 (August 6) | Dick Hutcherson | '67 Ford | 132.286 |
| Southern 500 (September 4) | Richard Petty | '67 Plymouth | 130.423 |
| National 500 (October 15) | Buddy Baker | '67 Dodge | 130.317 |
| American 500 (October 29) | Bobby Allison | '67 Ford | 98.420 |

## OUTSTANDING LAND-SPEED RECORDS

Craig Breedlove drove his jet-powered $250,000 *Spirit of America* to a record 600.601 mph on November 15, 1965 at the Bonneville Salt Flats in Utah.

Mrs. Craig Breedlove, driving her husband's *Spirit of America*, set a land-speed record for women—308.56 mph—on November 4, 1965. Neither record was broken in 1967.

| YEAR | DRIVER | CAR | AVERAGE MPH |
|---|---|---|---|
| 1931 | Sir Malcolm Campbell | Napier-Campbell | 246.086 |
| 1935 | Sir Malcolm Campbell | Bluebird Special | 301.130 |
| 1938 | Capt. G. E. T. Eyston | Thunderbolt | 345.500 |
| 1938 | John Cobb | Railton | 350.200 |
| 1938 | Capt. G. E. T. Eyston | Thunderbolt | 357.500 |
| 1939 | John Cobb | Railton | 368.900 |
| 1947 | John Cobb | Railton-Mobil | 394.200 |
| 1964 | Donald Campbell | Bluebird | 403.000 |
| 1964 | Craig Breedlove | Spirit of America | 526.260 |
| 1964 | Art Arfons | Green Monster | 536.710 |
| 1965 | Craig Breedlove | Spirit of America | 555.127 |
| 1965 | Art Arfons | Green Monster | 576.553 |
| 1965 | Craig Breedlove | Spirit of America | 600.601 |

## INDIANAPOLIS 500 AND U.S.A.C. CHAMPIONSHIP

Only four times has the weather forced a postponement of the Indianapolis 500. Memorial Day, 1967, was one of those days, and rain halted the 51st running of the race after 18 laps.

In that time, however, Parnelli Jones's STP Turbine Special (which created a sensation when it first appeared at the track earlier in May) proved a record-setter. And as the race resumed on May 31, any hope that another car would be the winner dwindled with each circuit of the 2.5-mile track. After 196 laps, Jones, 45 seconds ahead of his nearest piston-powered rival, seemed unbeatable. Then the STP developed gear trouble. As Jones said later, he "all of a sudden dropped from a 151-m.p.h. leader to a non-finishing also-ran." A. J. Foyt took the lead and the winner's $171,277 prize money. Foyt's triumph was his third in the 500; only three other drivers have scored such a record.

The 500 is the major race on the United States Auto Club championship trail. Foyt, more than 700 points in the lead for the 1967 U.S.A.C. championship as the season neared its end, appeared well on his way to the title.

### INDIANAPOLIS 500 WINNERS

| YEAR | WINNER | CAR | TIME (hr., min., sec.) | AVERAGE SPEED (m.p.h.) |
|------|--------|-----|------------------------|------------------------|
| 1911 | Ray Harroun | Marmon | 6:42:08 | 74.590 |
| 1912 | Joe Dawson | National | 6:21:06 | 78.720 |
| 1913 | Jules Goux | Peugeot | 6:35:05 | 75.930 |
| 1914 | Rene Thomas | Delage | 6:03:45 | 82.470 |
| 1915 | Ralph De Palma | Mercedes | 5:33:55.51 | 89.840 |
| 1916 | Davis Resta | Peugeot | 3:34:17 [1] | 84.000 |
| 1919 | Howard Wilcox | Peugeot | 5:40:42.87 | 88.050 |
| 1920 | Gaston Chevrolet | Monroe | 5:38:32.00 | 88.620 |
| 1921 | Tommy Milton | Frontenac | 5:34:44.65 | 89.620 |
| 1922 | Jim Murphy | Murphy Special | 5:17:30.79 | 94.480 |
| 1923 | Tommy Milton | H.C.S. Special | 5:29:50.17 | 90.950 |
| 1924 | L. L. Corum, Joe Boyer | Duesenberg Special | 5:05:23.51 | 98.230 |
| 1925 | Peter De Paolo | Duesenberg Special | 4:56:39.46 | 101.130 |
| 1926 | Frank Lockhart | Miller Special | 4:10:14.95 [2] | 95.900 |
| 1927 | George Souders | Duesenberg | 5:07:33.08 | 97.540 |
| 1928 | Louis Meyer | Miller Special | 5:01:33.75 | 99.480 |
| 1929 | Ray Keech | Simplex Special | 5:07:25.42 | 97.580 |
| 1930 | Billy Arnold | Hartz-Miller | 4:58:39.72 | 100.440 |
| 1931 | Louis Schneider | Bowes Special | 5:10:27.93 | 96.620 |
| 1932 | Fred Frame | Miller Special | 4:48:03.79 | 104.140 |
| 1933 | Louis Meyer | Miller Special | 4:48:00.75 | 104.160 |
| 1934 | Bill Cummings | Miller Special | 4:46:05.20 | 104.860 |
| 1935 | Kelly Petillo | Gilmore Special | 4:42:22.71 | 106.240 |
| 1936 | Louis Meyer | Ring Free Special | 4:35:03.39 | 109.060 |
| 1937 | Wilbur Shaw | Shaw-Gilmore Special | 4:24:07.80 | 113.580 |
| 1938 | Floyd Roberts | Burd Piston Reg. Special | 4:15:58.40 | 117.200 |
| 1939 | Wilbur Shaw | Boyle Special | 4:20:47.39 | 115.030 |
| 1940 | Wilbur Shaw | Boyle Special | 4:22:31.17 | 114.270 |
| 1941 | Mauri Rose, Floyd Davis | Noc-Out Hose Clamp Special | 4:20:36.24 | 115.110 |
| 1946 | George Robson | Thorne Eng. Special | 4:21:26.70 | 114.820 |
| 1947 | Mauri Rose | Blue Crown Special | 4:17:52.17 | 116.330 |
| 1948 | Mauri Rose | Blue Crown Special | 4:10:23.33 | 119.810 |
| 1949 | Bill Holland | Blue Crown Special | 4:07:15.97 | 121.320 |
| 1950 | Johnny Parsons | Wynn's Special | 2:46:55.97 [3] | 124.000 |
| 1951 | Lee Wallard | Belanger Special | 3:57:38.05 | 126.240 |
| 1952 | Troy Ruttman | Agajanian Special | 3:52:41.88 | 128.920 |
| 1953 | Bill Vukovich | Fuel Injection Special | 3:53:01.69 | 128.740 |
| 1954 | Bill Vukovich | Fuel Injection Special | 3:49:17.27 | 130.840 |
| 1955 | Bob Sweikert | John Zink Special | 3:53:59.13 | 128.209 |
| 1956 | Pat Flaherty | John Zink Special | 3:53:28.84 | 128.490 |
| 1957 | Sam Hanks | Belond Exhaust Special | 3:41:14.25 | 135.601 |
| 1958 | Jimmy Bryan | Belond AP Special | 3:44:13.80 | 133.791 |
| 1959 | Rodger Ward | Leader Card 500 | 3:40:49.20 | 135.857 |
| 1960 | Jim Rathman | Ken-Paul Special | 3:36:11.36 | 138.767 |
| 1961 | A. J. Foyt | Bowes Seal Special | 3:35:37.49 | 139.130 |
| 1962 | Rodger Ward | Leader Card 500 | 3:33:50.33 | 140.293 |
| 1963 | Parnelli Jones | Agajanian-Willard Battery Special | 3:29:35.36 | 143.137 |
| 1964 | A. J. Foyt | Sheraton-Thompson Watson Offenhauser | 3:23:35.81 | 147.350 |
| 1965 | Jim Clark | Lotus-Ford | 3:19:05.34 | 150.686 |
| 1966 | Graham Hill | Lotus-Ford | 3:27:52.53 | 144.317 |
| 1967 | A. J. Foyt | Coyote Ford | 3:18:24.22 | 151.207 [4] |

[1] 300 miles.    [2] 400 miles.    [3] 345 miles.    [4] Track record.

# BASEBALL

Heroes of the 1967 World Series included: Carl Yastrzemski (left), hitting one of his three Series' homers for Boston; Lou Brock (center), St. Louis outfielder, scoring in sixth game; and Cardinal pitcher Bob Gibson, who won three games.

## BASEBALL: 1967

In the "Year of the Yaz," baseball was dominated by the underdog and dazzled by the upset. Sandy Koufax had retired, the New York Yankees were still downtrodden, and the Baltimore Orioles plunged from the pinnacle of their 1966 success.

The vacancies left by these giants of the past were filled in 1967 by a spectacular array of unknowns, newcomers, and reincarnated figures from other years. Leo Durocher led the Chicago Cubs from last place in the National League to third. He got outstanding pitching from Ken Holtzman, an Army inductee who was available mostly on weekends, and from Ferguson Jenkins, a Canadian who won 20 games. Mike McCormick, a retread from the American League, won 22 games and helped pitch the San Francisco Giants into second place. Earl Wilson won 22 for the Detroit Tigers, and hitters named Jim Wynn and Rusty Staub raised a rumpus under the great domed roof of Houston's Astrodome.

But the greatest rags-to-riches stories were produced by the St. Louis Cardinals, who went from sixth place to first and won the National League pennant by 10½ games, and by the Boston Red Sox, who rose from ninth to first and won the American League pennant in the 162d and last game.

The Red Sox, the longest of 100-to-1 long shots, completed their "Cinderella story" by defeating the Minnesota Twins twice on the final weekend to finish first in the tightest race in the league's 67-year history. Minnesota, Detroit, and Chicago were bunched behind within a three-game spread. Then the Cinderella team met the Cardinals in the 64th World Series and carried them to the full seven games before losing.

Bob Gibson, recovered from a broken shinbone, won the opening game for St. Louis, 2–1. Jim Lonborg took the second game for Boston, 5–0, pitching no-hit ball for 8⅔ innings. The Red Sox lost the next two games by 5–2 and 6–0, with Gibson shutting them out, and St.

Louis took a lead of three games to one.

But then the Cinderella team enjoyed perhaps its finest hour. Lonborg pitched a 3–1 three-hitter, and an obscure rookie named Gary Waslewski worked six strong innings in an 8–4 victory marked by three Boston home runs in one inning. And now the World Series was tied with the championship riding on one final game: a duel between Gibson and Lonborg.

Working after three days of rest, Gibson won his third game of the series by outpitching Lonborg, who worked after only two days of rest. The score was 7–2. And so St. Louis succeeded Baltimore as the master of baseball.

But the lasting memory of 1967 was the success story of the Red Sox and their triple-threat hero, Carl Yastrzemski. Yaz led the league in batting average (.326), runs batted in (121), and home runs (44), and he hit .400 in the World Series with three more home runs. For St. Louis, Lou Brock hit .414 and stole seven bases, and Gibson was voted the outstanding performer in the Series. But the Red Sox and Yaz captured the imagination of the country and gave baseball a year to remember.

Yastrzemski's feat in winning the Triple Crown was underscored by the fact that the National League's batting honors were divided three ways: Roberto Clemente led in batting average with .357; Henry Aaron in home runs with 39; and Orlando Cepeda in runs batted in with 111.

While Dick Williams of Boston and Red Schoendienst of St. Louis thrived as the winning managers, the hectic season took a heavy toll of skippers. Harry Walker of Pittsburgh, Billy Hitchcock of Atlanta, Wes Westrum of the New York Mets, Sam Mele of Minnesota, Joe Adcock of Cleveland, and Alvin Dark of Kansas City all departed as managers. Dark became manager of the Cleveland club, and Gil Hodges also changed managerial posts, moving from Washington to the New York Mets.

The Kansas City franchise was shifted to Oakland, beginning with the 1968 season.

## 1967 WORLD SERIES

### FIRST GAME

|          | | | | | | | | | | | R | H | E |
|----------|-|-|-|-|-|-|-|-|-|-|---|---|---|
| Cardinals | 0 | 0 | 1 | 0 | 0 | 0 | 1 | 0 | 0 | 2 | 10 | 0 |
| Red Sox   | 0 | 0 | 1 | 0 | 0 | 0 | 0 | 0 | 0 | 1 | 6 | 0 |

Batteries—B. Gibson and McCarver; Santiago, Wyatt (8)
and R. Gibson, Howard (8).
Losing pitcher—Santiago.
Home run—Red Sox: Santiago.

### SECOND GAME

|          | | | | | | | | | | | R | H | E |
|----------|-|-|-|-|-|-|-|-|-|-|---|---|---|
| Cardinals | 0 | 0 | 0 | 0 | 0 | 0 | 0 | 0 | 0 | 0 | 1 | 1 |
| Red Sox   | 0 | 0 | 0 | 1 | 0 | 1 | 3 | 0 | x | 5 | 9 | 0 |

Batteries—Hughes, Willis (6), Hoerner (7), Lamabe (7)
and McCarver; Lonborg and Howard.
Losing pitcher—Hughes.
Home runs—Red Sox: Yastrzemski 2.

### THIRD GAME

|          | | | | | | | | | | | R | H | E |
|----------|-|-|-|-|-|-|-|-|-|-|---|---|---|
| Red Sox   | 0 | 0 | 0 | 0 | 0 | 1 | 1 | 0 | 0 | 2 | 7 | 1 |
| Cardinals | 1 | 2 | 0 | 0 | 0 | 1 | 0 | 1 | x | 5 | 10 | 0 |

Batteries—Bell, Waslewski (3), Stange (6), Osinski (8)
and Howard; Briles and McCarver.
Losing pitcher—Bell.
Home runs—Red Sox: Smith. Cardinals: Shannon.

### FOURTH GAME

|          | | | | | | | | | | | R | H | E |
|----------|-|-|-|-|-|-|-|-|-|-|---|---|---|
| Red Sox   | 0 | 0 | 0 | 0 | 0 | 0 | 0 | 0 | 0 | 0 | 5 | 0 |
| Cardinals | 4 | 0 | 2 | 0 | 0 | 0 | 0 | 0 | x | 6 | 9 | 0 |

Batteries—Santiago, Bell (1), Stephenson (3), Morehead (5),
Brett (8) and Howard, Ryan (5); B. Gibson and
McCarver.
Losing pitcher—Santiago.

### FIFTH GAME

|          | | | | | | | | | | | R | H | E |
|----------|-|-|-|-|-|-|-|-|-|-|---|---|---|
| Red Sox   | 0 | 0 | 1 | 0 | 0 | 0 | 0 | 0 | 2 | 3 | 6 | 1 |
| Cardinals | 0 | 0 | 0 | 0 | 0 | 0 | 0 | 0 | 1 | 1 | 3 | 2 |

Batteries—Lonborg and Howard; Carlton,
Washburn (7), Willis (9), Lamabe (9),
and McCarver.
Losing pitcher—Carlton.
Home run—Cardinals: Maris.

### SIXTH GAME

|          | | | | | | | | | | | R | H | E |
|----------|-|-|-|-|-|-|-|-|-|-|---|---|---|
| Cardinals | 0 | 0 | 2 | 0 | 0 | 0 | 2 | 0 | 0 | 4 | 8 | 0 |
| Red Sox   | 0 | 1 | 0 | 3 | 0 | 0 | 4 | 0 | x | 8 | 12 | 1 |

Batteries—Hughes, Willis (4), Briles (5), Lamabe (7),
Hoerner (7), Jaster (7), Washburn (7), Woodeshick (8) and
McCarver; Waslewski, Wyatt (6), Bell (8) and Howard.
Losing pitcher—Lamabe.
Home runs—Cardinals: Brock. Red Sox: Petrocelli 2,
Yastrzemski, Smith.

### SEVENTH GAME

|          | | | | | | | | | | | R | H | E |
|----------|-|-|-|-|-|-|-|-|-|-|---|---|---|
| Cardinals | 0 | 0 | 2 | 0 | 2 | 3 | 0 | 0 | 0 | 7 | 12 | 1 |
| Red Sox   | 0 | 0 | 0 | 0 | 1 | 0 | 0 | 1 | 0 | 2 | 3 | 1 |

Batteries—B. Gibson and McCarver; Lonborg, Santiago (7),
Morehead (9), Osinski (9), Brett (9) and Howard,
R. Gibson (9).
Losing pitcher—Lonborg.
Home runs—Cardinals: B. Gibson, Javier.

### SERIES FINANCIAL FIGURES—SEVEN-GAME DATA

Paid Attendance..............................304,085
Net receipts.............................$2,350,607.10
Commissioner's share.........................$352,591.08
Players' share...............................$705,878.44
Clubs' and Leagues' share....................$323,034.09
St. Louis Cardinals player's share ............. $8,314.81
Boston Red Sox player's share ................ $5,115.23

## WORLD SERIES SCORES

| YEAR | CLUBS AND GAMES WON | YEAR | CLUBS AND GAMES WON | YEAR | CLUBS AND GAMES WON |
|------|---------------------|------|---------------------|------|---------------------|
| 1903 * | Bos. (A) 5, Pitts. 3 | 1925 | Pitts. (N) 4, Wash. (A) 3 | 1947 | N.Y. (A) 4, Bklyn. (N) 3 |
| 1904 | Not played | 1926 | St. L. (N) 4, N.Y. (A) 3 | 1948 | Clev. (A) 4, Bos. (N) 2 |
| 1905 | N.Y. (N) 4, Phil. (A) 1 | 1927 | N.Y. (A) 4, Pitts. (N) 0 | 1949 | N.Y. (A) 4, Bklyn. (N) 1 |
| 1906 | Chi. (A) 4, Chi. (N) 2 | 1928 | N.Y. (A) 4, St. L. (N) 0 | 1950 | N.Y. (A) 4, Phila. (N) 0 |
| 1907 † | Chi. (N) 4, Det. (A) 0 | 1929 | Phila. (A) 4, Chi. (N) 1 | 1951 | N.Y. (A) 4, N.Y. (N) 2 |
| 1908 | Chi. (N) 4, Det. (A) 1 | 1930 | Phila. (A) 4, St. L. (N) 2 | 1952 | N.Y. (A) 4, Bklyn. (N) 3 |
| 1909 | Pitts. (N) 4, Det. (A) 3 | 1931 | St. L. (N) 4, Phila. (A) 3 | 1953 | N.Y. (A) 4, Bklyn. (N) 2 |
| 1910 | Phil. (A) 4, Chi. (N) 1 | 1932 | N.Y. (A) 4, Chi. (N) 0 | 1954 | N.Y. (N) 4, Clev. (A) 0 |
| 1911 | Phil. (A) 4, N.Y. (N) 2 | 1933 | N.Y. (N) 4, Wash. (A) 1 | 1955 | Bklyn. (N) 4, N.Y. (A) 3 |
| 1912 † | Bos. (A) 4, N.Y. (N) 3 | 1934 | St. L. (N) 4, Det. (A) 3 | 1956 | N.Y. (A) 4, Bklyn. (N) 3 |
| 1913 | Phil. (A) 4, N.Y. (N) 1 | 1935 | Det. (A) 4, Chi. (N) 2 | 1957 | Milw. (N) 4, N.Y. (A) 3 |
| 1914 | Bos. (N) 4, Phil. (A) 0 | 1936 | N.Y. (A) 4, N.Y. (N) 2 | 1958 | N.Y. (A) 4, Milw. (N) 3 |
| 1915 | Bos. (A) 4, Phil. (N) 1 | 1937 | N.Y. (A) 4, N.Y. (N) 1 | 1959 | L.A. (N) 4, Chi. (A) 2 |
| 1916 | Bos. (A) 4, Bklyn. (N) 1 | 1938 | N.Y. (A) 4, Chi. (N) 0 | 1960 | Pitts. (N) 4, N.Y. (A) 3 |
| 1917 | Chi. (A) 4, N.Y. (N) 2 | 1939 | N.Y. (A) 4, Cinc. (N) 0 | 1961 | N.Y. (A) 4, Cinc. (N) 1 |
| 1918 | Bos. (A) 4, Chi. (N) 2 | 1940 | Cinc. (N) 4, Det. (A) 3 | 1962 | N.Y. (A) 4, S.F. (N) 3 |
| 1919 * | Cinc. (N) 5, Chi. (A) 3 | 1941 | N.Y. (A) 4, Bklyn. (N) 1 | 1963 | L.A. (N) 4, N.Y. (A) 0 |
| 1920 * | Clev. (A) 5, Bklyn. (N) 2 | 1942 | St. L. (N) 4, N.Y. (A) 1 | 1964 | St. L. (N) 4, N.Y. (A) 3 |
| 1921 * | N.Y. (N) 5, N.Y. (A) 3 | 1943 | N.Y. (A) 4, St. L. (N) 1 | 1965 | L.A. (N) 4, Minn. (A) 3 |
| 1922 † | N.Y. (N) 4, N.Y. (A) 0 | 1944 | St. L. (N) 4, St. L. (A) 2 | 1966 | Balt. (A) 4, L.A. (N) 0 |
| 1923 | N.Y. (A) 4, N.Y. (N) 2 | 1945 | Det. (A) 4, Chi. (N) 3 | 1967 | St. L. (N) 4, Bos. (A) 3 |
| 1924 | Wash. (A) 4, N.Y. (N) 3 | 1946 | St. L. (N) 4, Bos. (A) 3 | | |

* A nine-game World Series was played.   † One tie game played.

## COMPOSITE SCORE OF 1967 WORLD SERIES GAMES

| ST. LOUIS (NL) | G | AB | R | H | 2B | 3B | HR | RBI | SO | BB | Bat. Avg. | PO | A | E | Fldg. Avg. |
|---|---|---|---|---|---|---|---|---|---|---|---|---|---|---|---|
| Brock, lf........ | 7 | 29 | 8 | 12 | 2 | 1 | 1 | 3 | 3 | 2 | .414 | 13 | 0 | 0 | 1.000 |
| Flood, cf...... | 7 | 28 | 2 | 5 | 1 | 0 | 0 | 3 | 3 | 3 | .179 | 15 | 0 | 0 | 1.000 |
| Maris, rf....... | 7 | 26 | 3 | 10 | 1 | 0 | 1 | 7 | 1 | 3 | .385 | 15 | 0 | 1 | .937 |
| Cepeda, 1b...... | 7 | 29 | 1 | 3 | 2 | 0 | 0 | 1 | 4 | 0 | .103 | 53 | 4 | 0 | 1.000 |
| McCarver, c..... | 7 | 24 | 3 | 3 | 1 | 0 | 0 | 2 | 2 | 2 | .125 | 55 | 4 | 0 | 1.000 |
| Shannon, 3b..... | 7 | 24 | 3 | 5 | 1 | 0 | 1 | 2 | 4 | 1 | .208 | 5 | 13 | 2 | .900 |
| Javier, 2b...... | 7 | 25 | 2 | 9 | 3 | 0 | 1 | 4 | 6 | 0 | .360 | 11 | 19 | 1 | .968 |
| Maxvill, ss..... | 7 | 19 | 1 | 3 | 0 | 1 | 0 | 1 | 1 | 4 | .158 | 13 | 17 | 0 | 1.000 |
| Tolan *......... | 3 | 2 | 1 | 0 | 0 | 0 | 0 | 0 | 1 | 1 | .000 | 0 | 0 | 0 | .000 |
| Bressoud, ss.... | 1 | 0 | 0 | 0 | 0 | 0 | 0 | 0 | 0 | 0 | .000 | 0 | 0 | 0 | .000 |
| B. Gibson, p..... | 3 | 11 | 1 | 1 | 0 | 0 | 1 | 1 | 2 | 1 | .091 | 2 | 3 | 0 | 1.000 |
| Hughes, p....... | 2 | 3 | 0 | 0 | 0 | 0 | 0 | 0 | 3 | 0 | .000 | 1 | 0 | 0 | 1.000 |
| Willis, p........ | 3 | 0 | 0 | 0 | 0 | 0 | 0 | 0 | 0 | 0 | .000 | 0 | 0 | 0 | .000 |
| Spiezio *........ | 1 | 1 | 0 | 0 | 0 | 0 | 0 | 0 | 0 | 0 | .000 | 0 | 0 | 0 | .000 |
| Jaster, p........ | 1 | 0 | 0 | 0 | 0 | 0 | 0 | 0 | 0 | 0 | .000 | 0 | 0 | 0 | .000 |
| Hoerner, p...... | 2 | 0 | 0 | 0 | 0 | 0 | 0 | 0 | 0 | 0 | .000 | 0 | 0 | 0 | .000 |
| Lamabe, p...... | 2 | 0 | 0 | 0 | 0 | 0 | 0 | 0 | 0 | 0 | .000 | 0 | 1 | 0 | 1.000 |
| Ricketts *........ | 3 | 3 | 0 | 0 | 0 | 0 | 0 | 0 | 0 | 0 | .000 | 0 | 0 | 0 | .000 |
| Briles, p......... | 2 | 3 | 0 | 0 | 0 | 0 | 0 | 0 | 0 | 0 | .000 | 0 | 4 | 0 | 1.000 |
| Gagliano *....... | 1 | 1 | 0 | 0 | 0 | 0 | 0 | 0 | 0 | 0 | .000 | 0 | 0 | 0 | .000 |
| Washburn, p..... | 1 | 0 | 0 | 0 | 0 | 0 | 0 | 0 | 0 | 0 | .000 | 0 | 1 | 0 | 1.000 |
| Woodeshick, p.... | 1 | 0 | 0 | 0 | 0 | 0 | 0 | 0 | 0 | 0 | .000 | 0 | 1 | 0 | 1.000 |
| Carlton, p....... | 1 | 0 | 0 | 0 | 0 | 0 | 0 | 0 | 0 | 0 | .000 | 0 | 0 | 0 | .000 |
| Total........ | 7 | 229 | 25 | 51 | 11 | 2 | 5 | 24 | 30 | 17 | .223 | 183 | 67 | 4 | .984 |

| BOSTON (AL) | G | AB | R | H | 2B | 3B | HR | RBI | SO | BB | Bat. Avg. | PO | A | E | Fldg. Avg. |
|---|---|---|---|---|---|---|---|---|---|---|---|---|---|---|---|
| Adair, 2b........ | 5 | 16 | 0 | 2 | 0 | 0 | 0 | 1 | 3 | 0 | .125 | 7 | 10 | 0 | 1.000 |
| Jones, 3b........ | 6 | 18 | 2 | 7 | 0 | 0 | 0 | 1 | 3 | 1 | .389 | 4 | 8 | 0 | 1.000 |
| Yastrzemski, lf.. | 7 | 25 | 4 | 10 | 0 | 0 | 3 | 5 | 1 | 4 | .400 | 16 | 2 | 0 | 1.000 |
| Harrelson, rf..... | 4 | 13 | 0 | 1 | 0 | 0 | 0 | 1 | 3 | 1 | .077 | 5 | 0 | 0 | 1.000 |
| Wyatt, p........ | 2 | 0 | 0 | 0 | 0 | 0 | 0 | 0 | 0 | 0 | .000 | 0 | 0 | 0 | .000 |
| Foy, 3b *........ | 6 | 15 | 2 | 2 | 1 | 0 | 0 | 1 | 5 | 1 | .133 | 6 | 6 | 1 | .923 |
| Scott, 1b........ | 7 | 26 | 3 | 6 | 1 | 1 | 0 | 0 | 6 | 3 | .231 | 70 | 3 | 0 | 1.000 |
| Petrocelli, ss.... | 7 | 20 | 3 | 4 | 1 | 0 | 2 | 3 | 8 | 3 | .200 | 11 | 21 | 2 | .941 |
| Morehead, p..... | 2 | 0 | 0 | 0 | 0 | 0 | 0 | 0 | 0 | 0 | .000 | 0 | 0 | 0 | .000 |
| Brett, p......... | 2 | 0 | 0 | 0 | 0 | 0 | 0 | 0 | 0 | 0 | .000 | 0 | 0 | 0 | .000 |
| Andrews, 2b *.... | 5 | 13 | 2 | 4 | 0 | 0 | 0 | 1 | 1 | 0 | .308 | 2 | 6 | 0 | 1.000 |
| R. Smith, cf...... | 7 | 24 | 3 | 6 | 1 | 0 | 2 | 3 | 3 | 2 | .250 | 14 | 0 | 0 | 1.000 |
| R. Gibson, c..... | 2 | 2 | 0 | 0 | 0 | 0 | 0 | 0 | 2 | 0 | .000 | 9 | 0 | 0 | 1.000 |
| Siebern, rf *..... | 3 | 3 | 0 | 1 | 0 | 0 | 0 | 1 | 0 | 0 | .333 | 0 | 0 | 0 | .000 |
| Tartabull, rf *.... | 7 | 13 | 1 | 2 | 0 | 0 | 0 | 0 | 2 | 1 | .154 | 7 | 0 | 0 | 1.000 |
| Santiago, p...... | 3 | 2 | 1 | 1 | 0 | 0 | 1 | 1 | 1 | 0 | .500 | 0 | 0 | 0 | .000 |
| Howard, c....... | 7 | 18 | 0 | 2 | 0 | 0 | 0 | 1 | 1 | 1 | .111 | 23 | 1 | 0 | 1.000 |
| Lonborg, p...... | 3 | 9 | 0 | 0 | 0 | 0 | 0 | 0 | 7 | 0 | .000 | 1 | 2 | 0 | 1.000 |
| Bell, p.......... | 3 | 0 | 0 | 0 | 0 | 0 | 0 | 0 | 0 | 0 | .000 | 0 | 2 | 0 | 1.000 |
| Thomas, rf *..... | 2 | 2 | 0 | 0 | 0 | 0 | 0 | 0 | 0 | 0 | .000 | 1 | 0 | 0 | 1.000 |
| Waslewski, p..... | 2 | 1 | 0 | 0 | 0 | 0 | 0 | 0 | 1 | 0 | .000 | 2 | 0 | 0 | 1.000 |
| Stange, p....... | 1 | 0 | 0 | 0 | 0 | 0 | 0 | 0 | 0 | 0 | .000 | 0 | 0 | 1 | .000 |
| Osinski, p....... | 2 | 0 | 0 | 0 | 0 | 0 | 0 | 0 | 0 | 0 | .000 | 0 | 0 | 0 | .000 |
| Stephenson, p.... | 1 | 0 | 0 | 0 | 0 | 0 | 0 | 0 | 0 | 0 | .000 | 0 | 0 | 0 | .000 |
| Ryan, c......... | 1 | 2 | 0 | 0 | 0 | 0 | 0 | 0 | 1 | 0 | .000 | 4 | 0 | 0 | .000 |
| Total........ | 7 | 222 | 21 | 48 | 6 | 1 | 8 | 19 | 48 | 17 | .216 | 182 | 61 | 4 | .984 |

\* Pinch hitter.

### PITCHING SUMMARY

| ST. LOUIS | G | IP | H | R | BB | SO | W | L | ERA | BOSTON | G | IP | H | R | BB | SO | W | L | ERA |
|---|---|---|---|---|---|---|---|---|---|---|---|---|---|---|---|---|---|---|---|
| B. Gibson... | 3 | 27 | 14 | 3 | 5 | 26 | 3 | 0 | 1.00 | Santiago.... | 3 | 9⅔ | 16 | 6 | 3 | 6 | 0 | 2 | 5.40 |
| Hughes..... | 2 | 9 | 9 | 6 | 3 | 7 | 0 | 1 | 5.00 | Wyatt...... | 2 | 3⅔ | 1 | 2 | 3 | 1 | 1 | 0 | 6.00 |
| Willis....... | 3 | 1 | 2 | 4 | 4 | 1 | 0 | 0 | 27.00 | Lonborg.... | 3 | 24 | 14 | 8 | 2 | 11 | 2 | 1 | 2.63 |
| Hoerner.... | 2 | ⅔ | 2 | 3 | 1 | 0 | 0 | 0 | 27.00 | Bell........ | 3 | 5⅓ | 8 | 3 | 1 | 1 | 0 | 1 | 5.40 |
| Lamabe.... | 3 | 2⅔ | 5 | 2 | 0 | 4 | 0 | 1 | 6.00 | Waslewski.. | 2 | 8⅓ | 4 | 2 | 2 | 7 | 0 | 0 | 2.25 |
| Briles...... | 2 | 11 | 7 | 2 | 1 | 3 | 1 | 0 | 1.64 | Stange..... | 1 | 2 | 3 | 1 | 0 | 0 | 0 | 0 | 0.00 |
| Carlton..... | 1 | 6 | 3 | 1 | 2 | 5 | 0 | 1 | 0.00 | Osinski..... | 2 | 1⅓ | 2 | 1 | 0 | 0 | 0 | 0 | 9.00 |
| Washburn... | 2 | 2⅓ | 1 | 0 | 1 | 2 | 0 | 0 | 0.00 | Stephenson | 1 | 2 | 3 | 2 | 1 | 0 | 0 | 0 | 9.00 |
| Jaster...... | 1 | ⅓ | 2 | 0 | 0 | 0 | 0 | 0 | 0.00 | Morehead... | 2 | 3⅓ | 0 | 0 | 4 | 3 | 0 | 0 | 0.00 |
| Woodeshick | 1 | 1 | 1 | 0 | 0 | 0 | 0 | 0 | 0.00 | Brett....... | 2 | 1⅓ | 0 | 0 | 1 | 1 | 0 | 0 | 0.00 |
| Total.... | 7 | 61 | 48 | 21 | 17 | 48 | 4 | 3 | 2.66 | Total.... | 7 | 61 | 51 | 25 | 17 | 30 | 3 | 4 | 3.39 |

## NATIONAL LEAGUE STADIUMS

The numbers in the drawings indicate the distances from home plate to left field, center field, and right field.

Capacity of stadiums by rank:

1. Dodger Stadium
   56,000
2. Shea Stadium
   55,300
3. Atlanta Stadium
   50,893
4. Busch Memorial Stadium
   49,450
5. Astrodome
   44,500

6. Candlestick Park
   42,561
7. Wrigley Field
   36,645
8. Forbes Field
   35,000
9. Connie Mack Stadium
   33,608
10. Crosley Field
    29,468

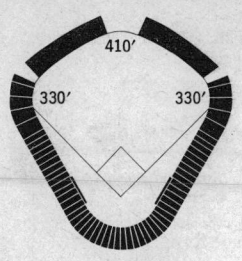

**LOS ANGELES**
DODGER STADIUM
Capacity 56,000

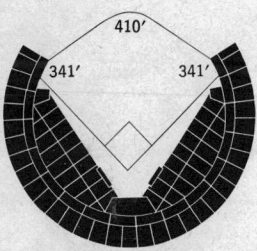

**NEW YORK**
WILLIAM A. SHEA STADIUM
Capacity 55,300

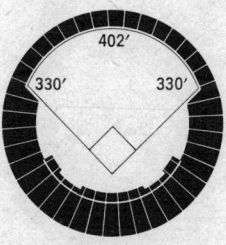

**ATLANTA**
ATLANTA STADIUM
Capacity 50,893

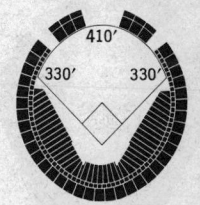

**ST. LOUIS**
BUSCH MEMORIAL STADIUM
Capacity 49,450

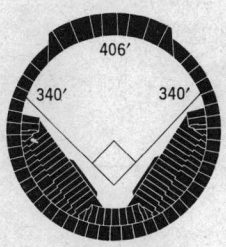

**HOUSTON**
ASTRODOME
Capacity 44,500

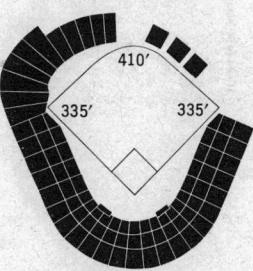

**SAN FRANCISCO**
CANDLESTICK PARK
Capacity 42,561

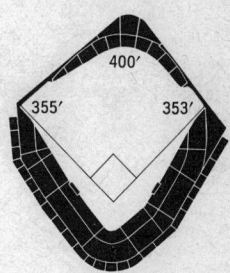

**CHICAGO**
WRIGLEY FIELD
Capacity 36,645

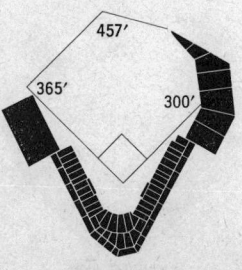

**PITTSBURGH**
FORBES FIELD
Capacity 35,000

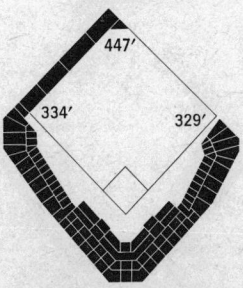

**PHILADELPHIA**
CONNIE MACK STADIUM
Capacity 33,608

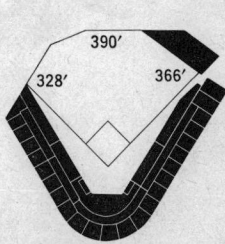

**CINCINNATI**
CROSLEY FIELD
Capacity 29,468

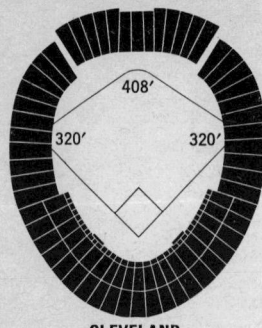

**CLEVELAND**
MUNICIPAL STADIUM
Capacity 74,056

## AMERICAN LEAGUE STADIUMS

The numbers in the drawings indicate the distances from home plate to left field, center field, and right field.

Capacity of stadiums by rank:

1. Cleveland Municipal Stadium
   74,056
2. Yankee Stadium
   67,338
3. Tiger Stadium
   53,089
4. Memorial Stadium
   52,185
5. Comiskey Park
   46,550

6. Metropolitan Stadium
   45,182
7. District of Columbia Stadium
   45,016
8. Anaheim Stadium
   43,204
9. Fenway Park
   33,524
10. Kansas City Municipal Stadium
    32,561

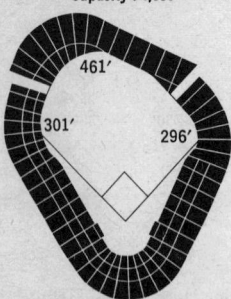

**NEW YORK**
YANKEE STADIUM
Capacity 67,338

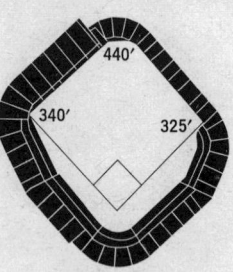

**DETROIT**
TIGER STADIUM
Capacity 53,089

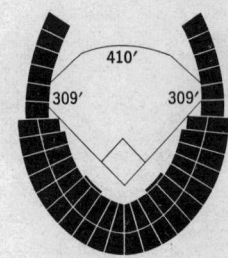

**BALTIMORE**
MEMORIAL STADIUM
Capacity 52,185

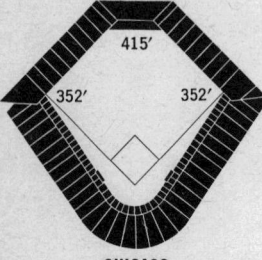

**CHICAGO**
COMISKEY PARK
Capacity 46,550

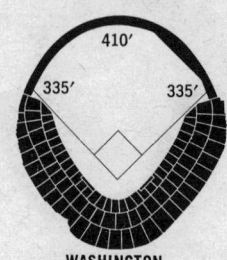

**WASHINGTON**
DISTRICT OF COLUMBIA STADIUM
Capacity 45,016

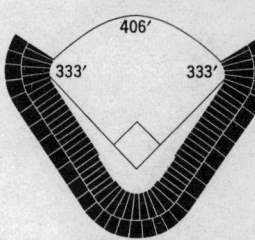

**CALIFORNIA ANGELS**
ANAHEIM STADIUM
Capacity 43,204

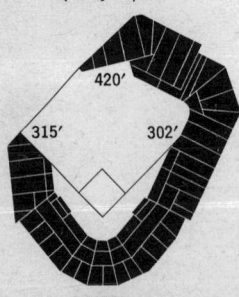

**BOSTON**
FENWAY PARK
Capacity 33,524

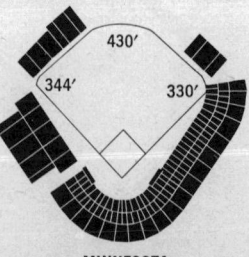

**MINNESOTA**
METROPOLITAN STADIUM
Capacity 45,182

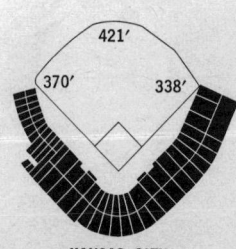

**KANSAS CITY**
MUNICIPAL STADIUM
Capacity 32,561

# MAJOR LEAGUE PENNANT WINNERS

**National League**     **American League**

| YEAR | CLUB | W | L | PCT | MANAGER | YEAR | CLUB | W | L | PCT | MANAGER |
|---|---|---|---|---|---|---|---|---|---|---|---|
| 1903 | Pittsburgh | 91 | 49 | .650 | F. Clarke | 1903 | Boston | 91 | 47 | .659 | J. Collins |
| 1904 | New York | 106 | 47 | .693 | J. McGraw | 1904 | Boston | 95 | 59 | .617 | J. Collins |
| 1905 | New York | 105 | 48 | .686 | J. McGraw | 1905 | Philadelphia | 92 | 56 | .622 | C. Mack |
| 1906 | Chicago | 116 | 36 | .763 | F. Chance | 1906 | Chicago | 93 | 58 | .616 | F. Jones |
| 1907 | Chicago | 107 | 45 | .704 | F. Chance | 1907 | Detroit | 92 | 58 | .613 | H. Jennings |
| 1908 | Chicago | 99 | 55 | .643 | F. Chance | 1908 | Detroit | 90 | 63 | .588 | H. Jennings |
| 1909 | Pittsburgh | 110 | 42 | .724 | F. Clarke | 1909 | Detroit | 98 | 54 | .645 | H. Jennings |
| 1910 | Chicago | 104 | 50 | .675 | F. Chance | 1910 | Philadelphia | 102 | 48 | .680 | C. Mack |
| 1911 | New York | 99 | 54 | .647 | J. McGraw | 1911 | Philadelphia | 101 | 50 | .669 | C. Mack |
| 1912 | New York | 103 | 48 | .682 | J. McGraw | 1912 | Boston | 105 | 47 | .691 | J. Stahl |
| 1913 | New York | 101 | 51 | .664 | J. McGraw | 1913 | Philadelphia | 96 | 57 | .627 | C. Mack |
| 1914 | Boston | 94 | 59 | .614 | G. Stallings | 1914 | Philadelphia | 99 | 53 | .651 | C. Mack |
| 1915 | Philadelphia | 90 | 62 | .592 | P. Moran | 1915 | Boston | 101 | 50 | .669 | W. Carrigan |
| 1916 | Brooklyn | 94 | 60 | .610 | W. Robinson | 1916 | Boston | 91 | 63 | .591 | W. Carrigan |
| 1917 | New York | 98 | 56 | .636 | J. McGraw | 1917 | Chicago | 100 | 54 | .649 | C. Rowland |
| 1918 | Chicago | 84 | 45 | .651 | F. Mitchell | 1918 | Boston | 75 | 51 | .595 | E. Barrow |
| 1919 | Cincinnati | 96 | 44 | .686 | P. Moran | 1919 | Chicago | 88 | 52 | .629 | W. Gleason |
| 1920 | Brooklyn | 93 | 61 | .604 | W. Robinson | 1920 | Cleveland | 98 | 56 | .636 | T. Speaker |
| 1921 | New York | 94 | 59 | .614 | J. McGraw | 1921 | New York | 98 | 55 | .641 | M. Huggins |
| 1922 | New York | 93 | 61 | .604 | J. McGraw | 1922 | New York | 94 | 60 | .610 | M Huggins |
| 1923 | New York | 95 | 58 | .621 | J. McGraw | 1923 | New York | 98 | 54 | .645 | M. Huggins |
| 1924 | New York | 93 | 60 | .608 | J. McGraw | 1924 | Washington | 92 | 62 | .597 | S. Harris |
| 1925 | Pittsburgh | 95 | 58 | .621 | W. McKechnie | 1925 | Washington | 96 | 55 | .636 | S. Harris |
| 1926 | St. Louis | 89 | 65 | .578 | R. Hornsby | 1926 | New York | 91 | 63 | .591 | M. Huggins |
| 1927 | Pittsburgh | 94 | 60 | .610 | O. Bush | 1927 | New York | 110 | 44 | .714 | M. Huggins |
| 1928 | St. Louis | 95 | 59 | .617 | W. McKechnie | 1928 | New York | 101 | 53 | .656 | M. Huggins |
| 1929 | Chicago | 98 | 54 | .645 | J. McCarthy | 1929 | Philadelphia | 104 | 46 | .693 | C. Mack |
| 1930 | St. Louis | 92 | 62 | .597 | C. Street | 1930 | Philadelphia | 102 | 52 | .662 | C. Mack |
| 1931 | St. Louis | 101 | 53 | .656 | C. Street | 1931 | Philadelphia | 107 | 45 | .704 | C. Mack |
| 1932 | Chicago | 90 | 64 | .584 | C. Grimm | 1932 | New York | 107 | 47 | .695 | J. McCarthy |
| 1933 | New York | 91 | 61 | .599 | W. Terry | 1933 | Washington | 99 | 53 | .651 | J. Cronin |
| 1934 | St. Louis | 95 | 58 | .621 | F. Frisch | 1934 | Detroit | 101 | 53 | .656 | G. Cochrane |
| 1935 | Chicago | 100 | 54 | .649 | C. Grimm | 1935 | Detroit | 93 | 58 | .616 | G. Cochrane |
| 1936 | New York | 92 | 62 | .597 | W. Terry | 1936 | New York | 102 | 51 | .667 | J. McCarthy |
| 1937 | New York | 95 | 57 | .625 | W. Terry | 1937 | New York | 102 | 52 | .662 | J. McCarthy |
| 1938 | Chicago | 89 | 63 | .586 | C. Hartnett | 1938 | New York | 99 | 53 | .651 | J. McCarthy |
| 1939 | Cincinnati | 97 | 57 | .630 | W. McKechnie | 1939 | New York | 106 | 45 | .702 | J. McCarthy |
| 1940 | Cincinnati | 100 | 53 | .654 | W. McKechnie | 1940 | Detroit | 90 | 64 | .584 | D. Baker |
| 1941 | Brooklyn | 100 | 54 | .649 | L. Durocher | 1941 | New York | 101 | 53 | .656 | J. McCarthy |
| 1942 | St. Louis | 106 | 48 | .688 | W. Southworth | 1942 | New York | 103 | 51 | .669 | J. McCarthy |
| 1943 | St. Louis | 105 | 49 | .682 | W. Southworth | 1943 | New York | 98 | 56 | .636 | J. McCarthy |
| 1944 | St. Louis | 105 | 49 | .682 | W. Southworth | 1944 | St. Louis | 89 | 65 | .578 | J. Sewell |
| 1945 | Chicago | 98 | 56 | .636 | C. Grimm | 1945 | Detroit | 88 | 65 | .575 | S. O'Neill |
| 1946 | St. Louis¹ | 98 | 58 | .628 | E. Dyer | 1946 | Boston | 104 | 50 | .675 | J. Cronin |
| 1947 | Brooklyn | 94 | 60 | .610 | B. Shotton | 1947 | New York | 97 | 57 | .630 | S. Harris |
| 1948 | Boston | 91 | 62 | .595 | W. Southworth | 1948 | Cleveland⁵ | 97 | 58 | .626 | L. Boudreau |
| 1949 | Brooklyn | 97 | 57 | .630 | B. Shotton | 1949 | New York | 97 | 57 | .630 | C. Stengel |
| 1950 | Philadelphia | 91 | 63 | .591 | E. Sawyer | 1950 | New York | 98 | 56 | .636 | C. Stengel |
| 1951 | New York² | 98 | 59 | .624 | L. Durocher | 1951 | New York | 98 | 56 | .636 | C. Stengel |
| 1952 | Brooklyn | 96 | 57 | .627 | C. Dressen | 1952 | New York | 95 | 59 | .617 | C. Stengel |
| 1953 | Brooklyn | 105 | 49 | .682 | C. Dressen | 1953 | New York | 99 | 52 | .656 | C. Stengel |
| 1954 | New York | 97 | 57 | .630 | L. Durocher | 1954 | Cleveland | 111 | 43 | .721 | A. Lopez |
| 1955 | Brooklyn | 98 | 55 | .641 | W. Alston | 1955 | New York | 96 | 58 | .623 | C. Stengel |
| 1956 | Brooklyn | 93 | 61 | .604 | W. Alston | 1956 | New York | 97 | 57 | .630 | C. Stengel |
| 1957 | Milwaukee | 95 | 59 | .617 | F. Haney | 1957 | New York | 98 | 56 | .636 | C. Stengel |
| 1958 | Milwaukee | 92 | 62 | .597 | F. Haney | 1958 | New York | 92 | 62 | .597 | C. Stengel |
| 1959 | Los Angeles³ | 88 | 68 | .564 | W. Alston | 1959 | Chicago | 94 | 60 | .610 | A. Lopez |
| 1960 | Pittsburgh | 95 | 59 | .617 | D. Murtaugh | 1960 | New York | 97 | 57 | .630 | C. Stengel |
| 1961 | Cincinnati | 93 | 61 | .604 | F. Hutchinson | 1961 | New York | 109 | 53 | .673 | R. Houk |
| 1962 | San Fran.⁴ | 103 | 62 | .624 | A. Dark | 1962 | New York | 96 | 66 | .593 | R. Houk |
| 1963 | Los Angeles | 99 | 63 | .611 | W. Alston | 1963 | New York | 104 | 57 | .646 | R. Houk |
| 1964 | St. Louis | 93 | 69 | .574 | J. Keane | 1964 | New York | 99 | 63 | .611 | L. Berra |
| 1965 | Los Angeles | 97 | 65 | .599 | W. Alston | 1965 | Minnesota | 102 | 60 | .630 | S. Mele |
| 1966 | Los Angeles | 95 | 67 | .586 | W. Alston | 1966 | Baltimore | 97 | 63 | .606 | H. Bauer |
| 1967 | St. Louis | 101 | 60 | .627 | A. Schoendienst | 1967 | Boston | 92 | 70 | .568 | R. Williams |

¹Defeated Brooklyn Dodgers in a play-off. ²Defeated Brooklyn Dodgers in a play-off. ³Defeated Milwaukee Braves in a play-off. ⁴Defeated Los Angeles Dodgers in a play-off. ⁵Defeated Boston Red Sox in a play-off.

## FINAL STANDINGS IN MAJOR LEAGUES: 1967

In the American League the pennant remained in contention between four teams—Boston, Detroit, Minnesota, and Chicago—until the last week of the season. On the season's last day Boston won the pennant and entered the World Series with the lowest won-lost percentage (.568) of any American League club in Series history.

| NATIONAL LEAGUE | ST. LOUIS | SAN FRANCISCO | CHICAGO | CINCINNATI | PHILADELPHIA | PITTSBURGH | ATLANTA | LOS ANGELES | HOUSTON | NEW YORK | WON | LOST | PERCENTAGE | GAMES BEHIND |
|---|---|---|---|---|---|---|---|---|---|---|---|---|---|---|
| St. Louis......... | — | 11 | 11 | 13 | 12 | 7 | 12 | 12 | 12 | 11 | 101 | 60 | .627 | — |
| San Francisco..... | 7 | — | 8 | 10 | 10 | 10 | 8 | 13 | 12 | 13 | 91 | 71 | .562 | 10½ |
| Chicago.......... | 6 | 10 | — | 12 | 11 | 11 | 7 | 9 | 8 | 13 | 87 | 74 | .540 | 14 |
| Cincinnati........ | 5 | 8 | 6 | — | 10 | 10 | 13 | 8 | 15 | 12 | 87 | 75 | .537 | 14½ |
| Philadelphia...... | 6 | 8 | 7 | 8 | — | 8 | 8 | 12 | 11 | 14 | 82 | 80 | .506 | 19½ |
| Pittsburgh........ | 11 | 8 | 7 | 8 | 10 | — | 10 | 11 | 9 | 7 | 81 | 81 | .500 | 20½ |
| Atlanta........... | 6 | 10 | 11 | 5 | 10 | 8 | — | 8 | 11 | 8 | 77 | 85 | .475 | 24½ |
| Los Angeles...... | 6 | 5 | 9 | 10 | 6 | 7 | 10 | — | 8 | 12 | 73 | 89 | .451 | 28½ |
| Houston.......... | 6 | 6 | 10 | 3 | 7 | 9 | 7 | 10 | — | 11 | 69 | 93 | .426 | 32½ |
| New York........ | 7 | 5 | 5 | 6 | 4 | 11 | 10 | 6 | 7 | — | 61 | 101 | .377 | 40½ |

| AMERICAN LEAGUE | BOSTON | DETROIT | MINNESOTA | CHICAGO | CALIFORNIA | BALTIMORE | WASHINGTON | CLEVELAND | NEW YORK | KANSAS CITY | WON | LOST | PERCENTAGE | GAMES BEHIND |
|---|---|---|---|---|---|---|---|---|---|---|---|---|---|---|
| Boston........... | — | 11 | 7 | 8 | 10 | 8 | 11 | 13 | 12 | 12 | 92 | 70 | .568 | — |
| Detroit.......... | 7 | — | 8 | 10 | 10 | 15 | 9 | 10 | 10 | 12 | 91 | 71 | .562 | 1 |
| Minnesota....... | 11 | 10 | — | 9 | 11 | 10 | 10 | 8 | 12 | 10 | 91 | 71 | .562 | 1 |
| Chicago.......... | 10 | 8 | 9 | — | 11 | 11 | 8 | 12 | 12 | 8 | 89 | 73 | .549 | 3 |
| California........ | 8 | 8 | 7 | 7 | — | 11 | 6 | 14 | 9 | 14 | 84 | 77 | .522 | 7½ |
| Baltimore....... | 10 | 3 | 8 | 7 | 6 | — | 10 | 9 | 13 | 10 | 76 | 85 | .472 | 15½ |
| Washington...... | 7 | 9 | 8 | 10 | 12 | 8 | — | 5 | 6 | 11 | 76 | 85 | .472 | 15½ |
| Cleveland....... | 5 | 8 | 10 | 6 | 4 | 9 | 13 | — | 9 | 11 | 75 | 87 | .463 | 17 |
| New York....... | 6 | 8 | 6 | 6 | 9 | 5 | 12 | 9 | — | 11 | 72 | 90 | .444 | 20 |
| Kansas City...... | 6 | 6 | 8 | 10 | 4 | 8 | 6 | 7 | 7 | — | 62 | 99 | .385 | 29½ |

## MAJOR LEAGUE AVERAGES: 1967

### ■ CLUB BATTING

| NATIONAL LEAGUE | G | AB | R | H | 2B | 3B | HR | SB | ShO | PCT |
|---|---|---|---|---|---|---|---|---|---|---|
| Pittsburgh.............. | 163 | 5724 | 679 | 1585 | 193 | 62 | 91 | 79 | 6 | .277 |
| St. Louis................ | 161 | 5566 | 695 | 1462 | 225 | 40 | 115 | 102 | 15 | .263 |
| Chicago................. | 162 | 5463 | 702 | 1373 | 211 | 49 | 128 | 61 | 9 | .251 |
| Houston................ | 162 | 5506 | 626 | 1372 | 259 | 46 | 93 | 87 | 13 | .249 |
| Cincinnati.............. | 162 | 5520 | 604 | 1366 | 252 | 54 | 109 | 88 | 11 | .247 |
| San Francisco.......... | 162 | 5524 | 652 | 1354 | 200 | 39 | 140 | 22 | 7 | .245 |
| Philadelphia............ | 162 | 5401 | 612 | 1306 | 223 | 47 | 103 | 79 | 9 | .242 |
| Atlanta................. | 162 | 5450 | 631 | 1307 | 191 | 29 | 158 | 53 | 26 | .240 |
| New York............... | 162 | 5417 | 498 | 1288 | 178 | 23 | 83 | 58 | 10 | .238 |
| Los Angeles............ | 162 | 5456 | 519 | 1285 | 203 | 38 | 82 | 56 | 15 | .236 |

| AMERICAN LEAGUE | G | AB | R | H | 2B | 3B | HR | SB | ShO | PCT |
|---|---|---|---|---|---|---|---|---|---|---|
| Boston.................. | 162 | 5471 | 722 | 1394 | 216 | 39 | 158 | 68 | 15 | .255 |
| Detroit................. | 163 | 5411 | 683 | 1315 | 193 | 36 | 152 | 37 | 15 | .243 |
| Baltimore............... | 161 | 5456 | 654 | 1312 | 215 | 44 | 138 | 54 | 14 | .240 |
| Minnesota.............. | 164 | 5458 | 671 | 1309 | 216 | 48 | 131 | 55 | 11 | .240 |
| California............... | 161 | 5307 | 566 | 1265 | 170 | 37 | 114 | 40 | 15 | .238 |
| Cleveland............... | 162 | 5461 | 559 | 1282 | 213 | 35 | 131 | 53 | 16 | .235 |
| Kansas City............. | 161 | 5349 | 533 | 1244 | 212 | 50 | 69 | 132 | 19 | .233 |
| New York............... | 163 | 5443 | 522 | 1225 | 166 | 17 | 100 | 64 | 18 | .225 |
| Chicago................. | 162 | 5383 | 531 | 1209 | 181 | 34 | 89 | 124 | 13 | .225 |
| Washington............. | 161 | 5441 | 550 | 1211 | 168 | 25 | 115 | 53 | 17 | .223 |

# ■ INDIVIDUAL BATTING

## National League

| PLAYER AND CLUB | AB | R | H | HR | RBI | PCT |
|---|---|---|---|---|---|---|
| Clemente, Pitts..... | 585 | 103 | 209 | 23 | 110 | .357 |
| Gonzalez, Phila.... | 508 | 74 | 172 | 9 | 59 | .339 |
| M. Alou, Pitts...... | 550 | 87 | 186 | 2 | 28 | .338 |
| Flood, St. L........ | 514 | 68 | 172 | 5 | 50 | .335 |
| Staub, Hous........ | 546 | 71 | 182 | 10 | 75 | .333 |
| Cepeda, St. L...... | 563 | 91 | 183 | 25 | 111 | .325 |
| Mota, Pitts........ | 349 | 53 | 112 | 4 | 57 | .321 |
| Aaron, Atl........ | 600 | 113 | 184 | 39 | 109 | .307 |
| R. Allen, Phila..... | 463 | 89 | 142 | 23 | 77 | .307 |
| Wills, Pitts........ | 616 | 92 | 186 | 3 | 45 | .302 |
| T. Davis, N.Y...... | 577 | 72 | 174 | 16 | 74 | .302 |
| Rose, Cinc........ | 585 | 86 | 176 | 12 | 76 | .301 |
| Brock, St. L....... | 689 | 113 | 206 | 21 | 76 | .299 |
| Santo, Chi........ | 586 | 107 | 175 | 31 | 98 | .299 |
| McCarver, St. L.... | 471 | 68 | 139 | 14 | 69 | .295 |
| Aspromonte, Hous... | 486 | 51 | 143 | 6 | 58 | .294 |
| J. Alou, S.F....... | 510 | 55 | 149 | 5 | 30 | .292 |
| Perez, Cinc........ | 600 | 78 | 174 | 26 | 102 | .290 |
| Hart, S.F.......... | 578 | 98 | 167 | 29 | 99 | .289 |
| Pinson, Cinc...... | 650 | 90 | 187 | 18 | 66 | .288 |
| Alley, Pitts........ | 550 | 59 | 158 | 6 | 54 | .287 |
| Swoboda, N.Y..... | 449 | 47 | 126 | 13 | 53 | .281 |
| Javier, St. L...... | 521 | 68 | 146 | 14 | 64 | .280 |
| Beckert, Chi....... | 597 | 97 | 167 | 5 | 40 | .280 |
| Williams, Chi...... | 634 | 92 | 176 | 28 | 84 | .278 |
| Torre, Atl......... | 477 | 67 | 132 | 20 | 68 | .277 |
| Ferrara, L.A....... | 347 | 41 | 96 | 16 | 50 | .277 |
| McCovey, S.F...... | 456 | 73 | 126 | 31 | 91 | .276 |
| Banks, Chi........ | 573 | 68 | 158 | 23 | 94 | .276 |
| Morgan, Hous...... | 495 | 73 | 136 | 6 | 42 | .275 |
| Davenport, S.F..... | 295 | 41 | 81 | 5 | 30 | .275 |
| Helms, Cinc........ | 497 | 40 | 136 | 2 | 35 | .274 |
| F. Alou, Atl....... | 574 | 76 | 157 | 15 | 43 | .274 |
| Roseboro, L.A...... | 334 | 37 | 91 | 4 | 24 | .272 |
| J. May, Pitts...... | 325 | 23 | 88 | 3 | 22 | .271 |
| L. Johnson, L.A.... | 330 | 39 | 89 | 11 | 41 | .270 |
| Kranepool, N.Y.... | 469 | 37 | 126 | 10 | 53 | .269 |
| Stargell, Pitts...... | 462 | 54 | 124 | 20 | 73 | .268 |
| Phillips, Chi....... | 448 | 66 | 120 | 17 | 70 | .268 |
| Hundley, Chi...... | 539 | 68 | 144 | 14 | 60 | .267 |
| Brown, S.F........ | 412 | 44 | 110 | 13 | 53 | .267 |
| L. May, Cinc...... | 438 | 54 | 116 | 12 | 57 | .265 |
| Hunt, L.A......... | 387 | 44 | 102 | 3 | 33 | .264 |
| Mays, S.F......... | 486 | 83 | 128 | 22 | 68 | .263 |
| Mazeroski, Pitts.... | 640 | 62 | 168 | 9 | 77 | .263 |
| Lefebvre, L.A...... | 494 | 51 | 129 | 8 | 50 | .261 |
| Maris, St. L....... | 410 | 65 | 107 | 9 | 55 | .261 |
| Callison, Phila..... | 556 | 52 | 145 | 14 | 64 | .261 |
| Rojas, Phila....... | 528 | 60 | 137 | 4 | 45 | .259 |
| W. Davis, L.A..... | 569 | 65 | 146 | 6 | 41 | .257 |
| R. Davis, Hous..... | 285 | 31 | 73 | 7 | 38 | .256 |
| Cardenas, Cinc..... | 379 | 30 | 97 | 2 | 22 | .256 |
| Carty, Atl......... | 443 | 41 | 113 | 15 | 63 | .255 |

## American League

| PLAYER AND CLUB | AB | R | H | HR | RBI | PCT |
|---|---|---|---|---|---|---|
| Yastrzemski, Bos.... | 579 | 112 | 189 | 44 | 121 | .326 |
| F. Robinson, Balt.... | 479 | 83 | 149 | 30 | 94 | .311 |
| Kaline, Det........ | 453 | 93 | 140 | 25 | 78 | .309 |
| Scott, Bos......... | 565 | 74 | 171 | 19 | 82 | .303 |
| Blair, Balt......... | 552 | 72 | 162 | 11 | 64 | .293 |
| Carew, Minn........ | 514 | 66 | 150 | 8 | 51 | .292 |
| Oliva, Minn........ | 557 | 76 | 161 | 17 | 83 | .289 |
| Davalillo, Clev...... | 358 | 47 | 103 | 2 | 22 | .288 |
| Fregosi, Cal........ | 585 | 73 | 168 | 8 | 53 | .287 |
| Conigliaro, Bos..... | 349 | 59 | 100 | 20 | 67 | .287 |
| T. Horton, Clev..... | 402 | 37 | 114 | 10 | 53 | .284 |
| Freehan, Det....... | 515 | 66 | 146 | 20 | 73 | .283 |
| Donaldson, K.C.... | 377 | 27 | 104 | 0 | 28 | .276 |
| W. Horton, Det..... | 399 | 46 | 110 | 19 | 67 | .276 |
| Adair, Bos......... | 415 | 47 | 113 | 3 | 35 | .272 |
| Clarke, N.Y....... | 588 | 74 | 160 | 3 | 29 | .272 |
| Cater, K.C........ | 529 | 55 | 143 | 4 | 46 | .270 |
| Northrup, Det...... | 492 | 62 | 133 | 9 | 58 | .270 |
| Mincher, Cal....... | 482 | 79 | 130 | 25 | 75 | .270 |
| B. Robinson, Balt... | 610 | 88 | 164 | 22 | 77 | .269 |
| Killebrew, Minn..... | 547 | 105 | 147 | 44 | 113 | .269 |
| Tovar, Minn....... | 650 | 98 | 173 | 6 | 47 | .266 |
| Reichardt, Cal...... | 493 | 55 | 131 | 17 | 68 | .266 |
| Andrews, Bos....... | 494 | 79 | 130 | 8 | 40 | .263 |
| Petrocelli, Bos..... | 491 | 53 | 127 | 17 | 66 | .259 |
| Maye, Clev........ | 298 | 43 | 77 | 9 | 27 | .258 |
| Allison, Minn....... | 496 | 73 | 126 | 24 | 75 | .258 |
| Uhlaender, Minn.... | 415 | 41 | 107 | 6 | 49 | .258 |
| F. Howard, Wash.... | 519 | 71 | 133 | 36 | 89 | .256 |
| Wert, Det......... | 531 | 60 | 136 | 6 | 40 | .256 |
| Webster, K.C....... | 360 | 41 | 92 | 11 | 50 | .256 |
| Alvis, Clev........ | 638 | 66 | 163 | 21 | 69 | .255 |
| Harrelson, Bos...... | 334 | 42 | 85 | 12 | 54 | .254 |
| Hershberger, K.C.... | 480 | 55 | 122 | 1 | 48 | .254 |
| Pepitone, N.Y....... | 501 | 45 | 126 | 13 | 64 | .251 |
| Monday, K.C....... | 406 | 52 | 102 | 14 | 57 | .251 |
| Foy, Bos.......... | 446 | 70 | 112 | 16 | 48 | .251 |
| Azcue, Clev........ | 295 | 33 | 74 | 11 | 34 | .251 |
| Hall, Cal.......... | 398 | 53 | 99 | 16 | 54 | .249 |
| Casanova, Wash..... | 528 | 47 | 131 | 9 | 53 | .248 |
| Campaneris, K.C.... | 601 | 85 | 149 | 3 | 32 | .248 |
| Johnson, Balt....... | 510 | 62 | 126 | 10 | 64 | .247 |
| Hinton, Clev....... | 497 | 55 | 122 | 10 | 37 | .245 |
| Mantle, N.Y....... | 440 | 63 | 108 | 22 | 55 | .245 |
| Repoz, Cal........ | 261 | 34 | 64 | 7 | 27 | .245 |
| McMullen, Wash.... | 563 | 73 | 138 | 16 | 67 | .245 |
| Rollins, Minn....... | 339 | 31 | 83 | 6 | 39 | .245 |
| Knoop, Cal........ | 507 | 50 | 124 | 9 | 37 | .245 |
| R. Smith, Bos...... | 536 | 73 | 131 | 14 | 56 | .244 |
| Whitaker, N.Y...... | 441 | 37 | 107 | 11 | 50 | .243 |
| Wagner, Clev....... | 434 | 56 | 105 | 15 | 54 | .242 |
| Blefary, Balt....... | 554 | 68 | 134 | 22 | 81 | .242 |
| Cash, Det......... | 488 | 64 | 118 | 22 | 72 | .242 |

# ■ CLUB PITCHING

## National League

| CLUB | G | CG | IP | H | R | BB | SO | ShO | ERA |
|---|---|---|---|---|---|---|---|---|---|
| San Francisco........... | 162 | 64 | 1485 | 1283 | 551 | 453 | 990 | 17 | 2.90 |
| Cincinnati.............. | 162 | 34 | 1468 | 1328 | 563 | 498 | 1065 | 18 | 3.05 |
| St. Louis............... | 161 | 44 | 1465 | 1313 | 557 | 431 | 956 | 17 | 3.05 |
| Philadelphia............ | 162 | 46 | 1455 | 1372 | 581 | 403 | 967 | 17 | 3.10 |
| Los Angeles............. | 162 | 41 | 1474 | 1421 | 595 | 393 | 965 | 17 | 3.21 |
| Atlanta................. | 162 | 35 | 1462 | 1377 | 640 | 449 | 862 | 5 | 3.45 |
| Chicago................ | 162 | 47 | 1457 | 1352 | 624 | 463 | 888 | 7 | 3.48 |
| New York............... | 162 | 36 | 1434 | 1369 | 672 | 536 | 894 | 10 | 3.73 |
| Pittsburgh.............. | 163 | 35 | 1458 | 1439 | 693 | 561 | 820 | 5 | 3.74 |
| Houston................ | 162 | 35 | 1446 | 1444 | 742 | 485 | 1059 | 8 | 4.03 |

## CLUB PITCHING (*continued*)

| American League | G | CG | IP | H | R | BB | SO | ShO | ERA |
|---|---|---|---|---|---|---|---|---|---|
| Chicago.............. | 162 | 36 | 1490 | 1197 | 491 | 465 | 927 | 24 | 2.45 |
| Minnesota............. | 164 | 58 | 1461 | 1336 | 590 | 396 | 1089 | 18 | 3.14 |
| California............. | 161 | 19 | 1430 | 1246 | 587 | 525 | 892 | 14 | 3.19 |
| New York............. | 163 | 37 | 1480 | 1375 | 621 | 480 | 898 | 16 | 3.24 |
| Cleveland............. | 162 | 49 | 1477 | 1258 | 613 | 559 | 1189 | 14 | 3.25 |
| Baltimore............. | 161 | 29 | 1457 | 1218 | 592 | 566 | 1034 | 17 | 3.32 |
| Detroit................ | 163 | 46 | 1443 | 1230 | 587 | 472 | 1038 | 17 | 3.32 |
| Boston................ | 162 | 41 | 1459 | 1307 | 614 | 477 | 1010 | 9 | 3.36 |
| Washington............ | 161 | 24 | 1473 | 1334 | 637 | 495 | 878 | 14 | 3.38 |
| Kansas City........... | 161 | 26 | 1428 | 1265 | 660 | 558 | 990 | 10 | 3.68 |

## ■ INDIVIDUAL PITCHING

| National League PITCHER AND CLUB | IP | H | BB | SO | W | L | ERA | American League PITCHER AND CLUB | IP | H | BB | SO | W | L | ERA |
|---|---|---|---|---|---|---|---|---|---|---|---|---|---|---|---|
| Abernathy, Cin. | 106 | 63 | 41 | 88 | 6 | 3 | 1.27 | Wilhelm, Chi.... | 89 | 58 | 33 | 76 | 8 | 3 | 1.31 |
| Linzy, S.F...... | 96 | 67 | 34 | 38 | 7 | 7 | 1.50 | Drabowsky, Balt. | 95 | 66 | 25 | 96 | 7 | 5 | 1.61 |
| Niekro, Atl..... | 207 | 164 | 55 | 129 | 11 | 9 | 1.87 | McMahon, Chi... | 109 | 68 | 40 | 84 | 6 | 2 | 1.98 |
| Nottebart, Cin... | 80 | 75 | 19 | 48 | 0 | 3 | 1.91 | Gladding, Det.. | 77 | 62 | 19 | 63 | 6 | 4 | 1.99 |
| Hall, Phil...... | 86 | 83 | 12 | 49 | 10 | 8 | 2.20 | Horlen, Chi..... | 259 | 188 | 58 | 103 | 19 | 7 | 2.05 |
| Bunning, Phil... | 302 | 241 | 73 | 253 | 17 | 15 | 2.29 | Locker, Chi..... | 125 | 102 | 23 | 80 | 7 | 5 | 2.09 |
| Farrell, Hou.–Phil..... | 104 | 87 | 22 | 78 | 10 | 6 | 2.34 | Watt, Balt...... | 104 | 67 | 37 | 93 | 3 | 5 | 2.25 |
| Taylor, N.Y..... | 73 | 60 | 22 | 46 | 4 | 6 | 2.34 | Hardin, Balt.... | 111 | 85 | 27 | 64 | 8 | 3 | 2.27 |
| Short, Phil..... | 199 | 163 | 74 | 142 | 9 | 11 | 2.40 | Peters, Chi..... | 260 | 187 | 91 | 215 | 16 | 11 | 2.28 |
| Face, Pitt...... | 74 | 62 | 22 | 39 | 7 | 5 | 2.43 | Siebert, Clev... | 185 | 136 | 54 | 136 | 10 | 12 | 2.29 |
| Briles, St. L..... | 155 | 139 | 40 | 94 | 14 | 5 | 2.44 | Monbouquette, N.Y.......... | 135 | 123 | 17 | 55 | 6 | 5 | 2.33 |
| Perranoski, L.A. | 110 | 97 | 45 | 75 | 6 | 7 | 2.45 | Womack, N.Y.... | 97 | 80 | 35 | 57 | 5 | 6 | 2.41 |
| Hands, Chi..... | 150 | 134 | 48 | 84 | 7 | 8 | 2.46 | Rojas, Calif.... | 122 | 106 | 38 | 83 | 12 | 9 | 2.43 |
| Holtzman, Chi... | 93 | 76 | 44 | 62 | 9 | 0 | 2.52 | Wood, Chi...... | 95 | 95 | 28 | 47 | 4 | 2 | 2.46 |
| McBean, Pitt... | 131 | 118 | 43 | 54 | 7 | 4 | 2.54 | John, Chi...... | 178 | 143 | 47 | 110 | 10 | 13 | 2.48 |
| Nolan, Cin...... | 227 | 193 | 62 | 206 | 14 | 8 | 2.58 | Merritt, Minn... | 226 | 195 | 29 | 161 | 13 | 7 | 2.51 |
| Perry, S.F...... | 293 | 231 | 84 | 230 | 15 | 17 | 2.61 | S. Miller, Balt... | 81 | 63 | 36 | 60 | 3 | 10 | 2.56 |
| Singer, L.A..... | 204 | 185 | 61 | 169 | 12 | 8 | 2.65 | Clark, Calif..... | 174 | 144 | 69 | 81 | 12 | 11 | 2.59 |
| Brewer, L.A..... | 101 | 78 | 31 | 74 | 5 | 4 | 2.67 | Wyatt, Bstn..... | 93 | 71 | 39 | 68 | 10 | 7 | 2.61 |
| Willis, St. L..... | 81 | 76 | 43 | 42 | 6 | 5 | 2.67 | Hargan, Clev.... | 223 | 180 | 72 | 141 | 14 | 13 | 2.62 |
| Hughes, St. L... | 222 | 164 | 48 | 161 | 16 | 6 | 2.67 | Downing, N.Y... | 202 | 158 | 61 | 171 | 14 | 10 | 2.63 |
| Drysdale, L.A... | 282 | 269 | 60 | 196 | 13 | 16 | 2.74 | Knowles, Wash.. | 113 | 91 | 52 | 85 | 6 | 8 | 2.71 |
| Johnson, Atl.... | 210 | 191 | 41 | 86 | 13 | 9 | 2.74 | Wickersham, Det. | 85 | 72 | 33 | 44 | 4 | 5 | 2.72 |
| Seaver, N.Y..... | 251 | 224 | 78 | 171 | 16 | 13 | 2.76 | Chance, Minn... | 283 | 244 | 68 | 220 | 20 | 14 | 2.73 |
| Marichal, S.F... | 202 | 195 | 42 | 166 | 14 | 10 | 2.76 | Tiant, Clev..... | 214 | 177 | 67 | 219 | 12 | 9 | 2.73 |
| Queen, Cin..... | 196 | 155 | 52 | 154 | 14 | 8 | 2.76 | Williams, Clev... | 79 | 64 | 24 | 75 | 6 | 4 | 2.73 |
| Sadecki, St. L... | 188 | 165 | 58 | 145 | 12 | 6 | 2.78 | Stange, Bstn.... | 182 | 170 | 32 | 101 | 8 | 10 | 2.77 |
| Selma, N.Y..... | 81 | 71 | 36 | 52 | 2 | 4 | 2.78 | Hunter, K.C.... | 260 | 209 | 84 | 196 | 13 | 17 | 2.80 |
| Wilson, Hou..... | 184 | 141 | 69 | 159 | 10 | 9 | 2.79 | Worthington, Min. | 92 | 77 | 38 | 80 | 8 | 9 | 2.84 |
| Jenkins, Chi.... | 289 | 230 | 83 | 236 | 20 | 13 | 2.80 | Verbanic, N.Y... | 80 | 74 | 21 | 39 | 4 | 3 | 2.93 |
| McCormick, S.F. | 262 | 220 | 81 | 150 | 22 | 10 | 2.85 | Stottlemyre, N.Y. | 255 | 235 | 88 | 151 | 15 | 15 | 2.96 |
| Carlton, St. L... | 193 | 173 | 62 | 168 | 14 | 9 | 2.98 | Cox, Wash...... | 73 | 67 | 21 | 32 | 7 | 4 | 2.96 |
| Gibson, St. L.... | 175 | 151 | 40 | 147 | 13 | 7 | 2.98 | McGlothlin, Calif. | 197 | 163 | 56 | 137 | 12 | 8 | 2.97 |
| Regan, L.A..... | 96 | 108 | 32 | 53 | 6 | 9 | 3.00 | Bertaina, Wash.. | 117 | 107 | 51 | 86 | 7 | 6 | 3.00 |
| Jaster, St. L.... | 152 | 141 | 44 | 87 | 9 | 7 | 3.02 | Perry, Minn..... | 131 | 123 | 50 | 93 | 8 | 7 | 3.02 |
| Cuellar, Hou.... | 246 | 233 | 63 | 202 | 16 | 11 | 3.04 | Ortega, Wash... | 220 | 189 | 57 | 122 | 10 | 10 | 3.03 |
| Herbel, S.F..... | 126 | 125 | 35 | 52 | 4 | 5 | 3.07 | Pierce, K.C..... | 98 | 79 | 30 | 61 | 3 | 4 | 3.03 |
| Gibbon, S.F..... | 82 | 65 | 33 | 63 | 6 | 2 | 3.07 | Lolich, Det...... | 204 | 165 | 56 | 174 | 14. | 13 | 3.04 |
| L. Jackson, Phil. | 262 | 242 | 54 | 139 | 13 | 15 | 3.09 | Kaat, Minn..... | 263 | 269 | 42 | 211 | 16 | 13 | 3.05 |

* 75 and more total innings pitched.

## LITTLE LEAGUE WORLD SERIES: 1967

For the third time in history a team from outside the United States won the 21st Little League World Series at Williamsport, Pennsylvania. A team from West Tokyo, Japan, defeated the North Roseland (Chicago) nine by a score of 4 to 1 in the final game of the series, on August 26, before about 15,000 fans. This was the first Japanese team to play in the finals of any Little League series.

Six other teams participated in the games. Newton-Edgmont, Pennsylvania, finished third, and Linares, Mexico, placed fourth. The remaining teams were from Northridge, California; West Tampa, Florida; East Trail, British Columbia; and Rota, Spain—children of U.S. military personnel. North Roseland's pitcher Bob Stratta hurled a no-run, no-hit game against the Rota team on August 23.

## BASEBALL'S MOST VALUABLE PLAYER AWARDS

Source: Baseball Writers' Association

In 1911 the first Most Valuable Player awards were presented to Frank Schulte of the Chicago Cubs (National League) and Ty Cobb of the Detroit Tigers (American League). The award was called the Chalmers Award. The Baseball Writers' Association awards began in 1931.

### National League / American League

| YEAR | PLAYER | CLUB | YEAR | PLAYER | CLUB |
|------|--------|------|------|--------|------|
| 1931 | Frisch, Frank | St. Louis | 1931 | Grove, Robert (Lefty) | Philadelphia |
| 1932 | Klein, Chuck | Philadelphia | 1932 | Foxx, Jimmy | Philadelphia |
| 1933 | Hubbell, Carl | New York | 1933 | Foxx, Jimmy | Philadelphia |
| 1934 | Dean, Jerome (Dizzy) | St. Louis | 1934 | Cochrane, Gordon (Mickey) | Detroit |
| 1935 | Hartnett, Charles (Gabby) | Chicago | 1935 | Greenberg, Hank | Detroit |
| 1936 | Hubbell, Carl | New York | 1936 | Gehrig, Henry (Lou) | New York |
| 1937 | Medwick, Joe (Ducky) | St. Louis | 1937 | Gehringer, Charley | Detroit |
| 1938 | Lombardi, Ernie | Cincinnati | 1938 | Foxx, Jimmy | Boston |
| 1939 | Walters, William (Bucky) | Cincinnati | 1939 | DiMaggio, Joe | New York |
| 1940 | McCormick, Frank | Cincinnati | 1940 | Greenberg, Hank | Detroit |
| 1941 | Camilli, Dolph | Brooklyn | 1941 | DiMaggio, Joe | New York |
| 1942 | Cooper, Mort | St. Louis | 1942 | Gordon, Joe | New York |
| 1943 | Musial, Stan | St. Louis | 1943 | Chandler, Spurgeon (Spud) | New York |
| 1944 | Marion, Marty | St. Louis | 1944 | Newhouser, Hal | Detroit |
| 1945 | Cavarretta, Phil | Chicago | 1945 | Newhouser, Hal | Detroit |
| 1946 | Musial, Stan | St. Louis | 1946 | Williams, Ted | Boston |
| 1947 | Elliott, Bob | Boston | 1947 | DiMaggio, Joe | New York |
| 1948 | Musial, Stan | St. Louis | 1948 | Boudreau, Lou | Cleveland |
| 1949 | Robinson, Jackie | Brooklyn | 1949 | Williams, Ted | Boston |
| 1950 | Konstanty, Jim | Philadelphia | 1950 | Rizzuto, Phil | New York |
| 1951 | Campanella, Roy | Brooklyn | 1951 | Berra, Larry (Yogi) | New York |
| 1952 | Sauer, Hank | Chicago | 1952 | Shantz, Bobby | Philadelphia |
| 1953 | Campanella, Roy | Brooklyn | 1953 | Rosen, Al | Cleveland |
| 1954 | Mays, Willie | New York | 1954 | Berra, Larry (Yogi) | New York |
| 1955 | Campanella, Roy | Brooklyn | 1955 | Berra, Larry (Yogi) | New York |
| 1956 | Newcombe, Don | Brooklyn | 1956 | Mantle, Mickey | New York |
| 1957 | Aaron, Hank | Milwaukee | 1957 | Mantle, Mickey | New York |
| 1958 | Banks, Ernie | Chicago | 1958 | Jensen, Jackie | Boston |
| 1959 | Banks, Ernie | Chicago | 1959 | Fox, Nelson (Nellie) | Chicago |
| 1960 | Groat, Dick | Pittsburgh | 1960 | Maris, Roger | New York |
| 1961 | Robinson, Frank | Cincinnati | 1961 | Maris, Roger | New York |
| 1962 | Wills, Maury | Los Angeles | 1962 | Mantle, Mickey | New York |
| 1963 | Koufax, Sanford (Sandy) | Los Angeles | 1963 | Howard, Elston | New York |
| 1964 | Boyer, Ken | St. Louis | 1964 | Robinson, Brooks | Baltimore |
| 1965 | Mays, Willie | San Francisco | 1965 | Versalles, Zoilo | Minnesota |
| 1966 | Clemente, Roberto | Pittsburgh | 1966 | Robinson, Frank | Baltimore |
| 1967 | Cepeda, Orlando | St. Louis | 1967 | Yastrzemski, Carl | Boston |

## ROOKIE OF THE YEAR AWARDS

### National League / American League

| YEAR | PLAYER AND POSITION | CLUB | YEAR | PLAYER AND POSITION | CLUB |
|------|---------------------|------|------|---------------------|------|
| 1949 | Don Newcombe, pitcher | Brooklyn | 1949 | Roy Sievers, outfielder | St. Louis |
| 1950 | Sam Jethroe, outfielder | Boston | 1950 | Walt Dropo, first baseman | Boston |
| 1951 | Willie Mays, outfielder | New York | 1951 | Gil McDougald, third baseman | New York |
| 1952 | Joe Black, pitcher | Brooklyn | 1952 | Harry Byrd, pitcher | Philadelphia |
| 1953 | Jim Gilliam, second baseman | Brooklyn | 1953 | Harvey Kuenn, shortstop | Detroit |
| 1954 | Wally Moon, outfielder | St. Louis | 1954 | Bob Grim, pitcher | New York |
| 1955 | Bill Virdon, outfielder | St. Louis | 1955 | Herb Score, pitcher | Cleveland |
| 1956 | Frank Robinson, outfielder | Cincinnati | 1956 | Luis Aparicio, shortstop | Chicago |
| 1957 | John Sanford, pitcher | Philadelphia | 1957 | Tony Kubek, infielder | New York |
| 1958 | Orlando Cepeda, first baseman | San Francisco | 1958 | Albie Pearson, outfielder | Washington |
| 1959 | Willie McCovey, first baseman | San Francisco | 1959 | Bob Allison, outfielder | Washington |
| 1960 | Frank Howard, outfielder | Los Angeles | 1960 | Ronnie Hansen, shortstop | Baltimore |
| 1961 | Billy Williams, outfielder | Chicago | 1961 | Don Schwall, pitcher | Boston |
| 1962 | Ken Hubbs, second baseman | Chicago | 1962 | Tommy Tresh, outfielder-shortstop | New York |
| 1963 | Pete Rose, second baseman | Cincinnati | 1963 | Gary Peters, pitcher | Chicago |
| 1964 | Richie Allen, third baseman | Philadelphia | 1964 | Tony Oliva, outfielder | Minnesota |
| 1965 | Jim Lefebvre, second baseman | Los Angeles | 1965 | Curt Blefary, outfielder | Baltimore |
| 1966 | Tommy Helms, third baseman | Cincinnati | 1966 | Tommie Agee, outfielder | Chicago |
| 1967 | Tom Seaver, pitcher | New York | 1967 | Rod Carew, second baseman | Minnesota |

## MAJOR LEAGUE BATTING CHAMPIONS: 1908–1967

Rogers Hornsby of the St. Louis Cardinals, the National League's leading batter, set a one-season modern major league record in 1924 with a batting average of .424. Ty Cobb of the Detroit Tigers, the American League's greatest batter, won the championship 12 times in all.

In 1966 Frank Robinson won baseball's triple crown: highest batting average, most home runs, and most runs batted in. Carl Yastrzemski won this crown in 1967.

### National League

| YEAR | PLAYER AND CLUB | PCT |
|------|-----------------|-----|
| 1908 | Wagner, John (Honus), Pittsburgh | .354 |
| 1909 | Wagner, John (Honus), Pittsburgh | .339 |
| 1910 | Magee, Sherwood, Philadelphia | .331 |
| 1911 | Wagner, John (Honus), Pittsburgh | .334 |
| 1912 | Zimmerman, Henry (Heinie), Chicago | .372 |
| 1913 | Daubert, Jake, Brooklyn | .350 |
| 1914 | Daubert, Jake, Brooklyn | .329 |
| 1915 | Doyle, Larry, New York | .320 |
| 1916 | Chase, Hal, Cincinnati | .339 |
| 1917 | Roush, Edd, Cincinnati | .341 |
| 1918 | Wheat, Zack, Brooklyn | .335 |
| 1919 | Roush, Edd, Cincinnati | .321 |
| 1920 | Hornsby, Rogers, St. Louis | .370 |
| 1921 | Hornsby, Rogers, St. Louis | .397 |
| 1922 | Hornsby, Rogers, St. Louis | .401 |
| 1923 | Hornsby, Rogers, St. Louis | .384 |
| 1924 | Hornsby, Rogers, St. Louis | .424 |
| 1925 | Hornsby, Rogers, St. Louis | .403 |
| 1926 | Hargrave, Gene, Cincinnati | .353 |
| 1927 | Waner, Paul, Pittsburgh | .380 |
| 1928 | Hornsby, Rogers, Boston | .387 |
| 1929 | O'Doul, Frank (Lefty), Philadelphia | .398 |
| 1930 | Terry, Bill, New York | .401 |
| 1931 | Hafey, Charles (Chick), St. Louis | .349 * |
| 1932 | O'Doul, Frank (Lefty), Brooklyn | .368 |
| 1933 | Klein, Chuck, Philadelphia | .368 |
| 1934 | Waner, Paul, Pittsburgh | .362 |
| 1935 | Vaughan, Joseph (Arky), Pittsburgh | .385 |
| 1936 | Waner, Paul, Pittsburgh | .373 |
| 1937 | Medwick, Joe (Ducky), St. Louis | .374 |
| 1938 | Lombardi, Ernie, Cincinnati | .342 |
| 1939 | Mize, Johnny, St. Louis | .349 |
| 1940 | Garms, Debs, Pittsburgh | .355 |
| 1941 | Reiser, Pete, Brooklyn | .343 |
| 1942 | Lombardi, Ernie, Boston | .330 |
| 1943 | Musial, Stan, St. Louis | .357 |
| 1944 | Walker, Fred (Dixie), Brooklyn | .357 |
| 1945 | Cavarretta, Phil, Chicago | .355 |
| 1946 | Musial, Stan, St. Louis | .365 |
| 1947 | Walker, Harry, St. Louis-Philadelphia | .363 |
| 1948 | Musial, Stan, St. Louis | .376 |
| 1949 | Robinson, Jackie, Brooklyn | .342 |
| 1950 | Musial, Stan, St. Louis | .346 |
| 1951 | Musial, Stan, St. Louis | .355 |
| 1952 | Musial, Stan, St. Louis | .336 |
| 1953 | Furillo, Carl, Brooklyn | .344 |
| 1954 | Mays, Willie, New York | .345 |
| 1955 | Ashburn, Richie, Philadelphia | .338 |
| 1956 | Aaron, Hank, Milwaukee | .328 |
| 1957 | Musial, Stan, St. Louis | .351 |
| 1958 | Ashburn, Richie, Philadelphia | .350 |
| 1959 | Aaron, Hank, Milwaukee | .355 |
| 1960 | Groat, Dick, Pittsburgh | .325 |
| 1961 | Clemente, Roberto, Pittsburgh | .351 |
| 1962 | Davis, Tommy, Los Angeles | .346 |
| 1963 | Davis, Tommy, Los Angeles | .326 |
| 1964 | Clemente, Roberto, Pittsburgh | .339 |
| 1965 | Clemente, Roberto, Pittsburgh | .329 |
| 1966 | Alou, Matty, Pittsburgh | .342 |
| 1967 | Clemente, Roberto, Pittsburgh | .357 |

### American League

| YEAR | PLAYER AND CLUB | PCT |
|------|-----------------|-----|
| 1908 | Cobb, Ty, Detroit | .324 |
| 1909 | Cobb, Ty, Detroit | .377 |
| 1910 | Cobb, Ty, Detroit | .385 |
| 1911 | Cobb, Ty, Detroit | .420 |
| 1912 | Cobb, Ty, Detroit | .410 |
| 1913 | Cobb, Ty, Detroit | .390 |
| 1914 | Cobb, Ty, Detroit | .368 |
| 1915 | Cobb, Ty, Detroit | .369 |
| 1916 | Speaker, Tris, Cleveland | .386 |
| 1917 | Cobb, Ty, Detroit | .383 |
| 1918 | Cobb, Ty, Detroit | .382 |
| 1919 | Cobb, Ty, Detroit | .384 |
| 1920 | Sisler, George, St. Louis | .407 |
| 1921 | Heilmann, Harry, Detroit | .394 |
| 1922 | Sisler, George, St. Louis | .420 |
| 1923 | Heilmann, Harry, Detroit | .403 |
| 1924 | Ruth, George (Babe), New York | .378 |
| 1925 | Heilmann, Harry, Detroit | .393 |
| 1926 | Manush, Henry (Heinie), Detroit | .378 |
| 1927 | Heilmann, Harry, Detroit | .398 |
| 1928 | Goslin, Leon (Goose), Washington | .379 |
| 1929 | Fonseca, Lew, Cleveland | .369 |
| 1930 | Simmons, Al, Philadelphia | .381 |
| 1931 | Simmons, Al, Philadelphia | .390 |
| 1932 | Alexander, Dale, Detroit-Boston | .367 |
| 1933 | Foxx, Jimmy, Philadelphia | .356 |
| 1934 | Gehrig, Henry (Lou), New York | .363 |
| 1935 | Myer, Charles (Buddy), Washington | .349 |
| 1936 | Appling, Luke, Chicago | .388 |
| 1937 | Gehringer, Charley, Detroit | .371 |
| 1938 | Foxx, Jimmy, Boston | .349 |
| 1939 | DiMaggio, Joe, New York | .381 |
| 1940 | DiMaggio, Joe, New York | .352 |
| 1941 | Williams, Ted, Boston | .406 |
| 1942 | Williams, Ted, Boston | .356 |
| 1943 | Appling, Luke, Chicago | .328 |
| 1944 | Boudreau, Lou, Cleveland | .327 |
| 1945 | Sternweiss, George (Snuffy), New York | .309 |
| 1946 | Vernon, James (Mickey), Washington | .353 |
| 1947 | Williams, Ted, Boston | .343 |
| 1948 | Williams, Ted, Boston | .369 |
| 1949 | Kell, George, Detroit | .343† |
| 1950 | Goodman, Billy, Boston | .354 |
| 1951 | Fain, Ferris, Philadelphia | .344 |
| 1952 | Fain, Ferris, Philadelphia | .327 |
| 1953 | Vernon, James (Mickey), Washington | .337 |
| 1954 | Avila, Bobby, Cleveland | .341 |
| 1955 | Kaline, Al, Detroit | .340 |
| 1956 | Mantle, Mickey, New York | .353 |
| 1957 | Williams, Ted, Boston | .388 |
| 1958 | Williams, Ted, Boston | .328 |
| 1959 | Kuenn, Harvey, Detroit | .353 |
| 1960 | Runnels, James (Pete), Boston | .320 |
| 1961 | Cash, Norm, Detroit | .361 |
| 1962 | Runnels, James (Pete), Boston | .326 |
| 1963 | Yastrzemski, Carl, Boston | .321 |
| 1964 | Oliva, Tony, Minnesota | .323 |
| 1965 | Oliva, Tony, Minnesota | .321 |
| 1966 | Robinson, Frank, Baltimore | .316 |
| 1967 | Yastrzemski, Carl, Boston | .326 |

* In 1931, Hafey compiled an average of .3489. Bill Terry of New York was second with .3486, and Jim Bottomley of St. Louis was third with .3482.    † In 1949, Kell compiled an average of .3429. Ted Williams of Boston was second with .3427.

## HOME RUN CHAMPIONS: 1915–1967

Babe Ruth, the greatest home run hitter in major league history, hit 714 home runs in his 22-year career, an unrivaled record. Other former all-time home run hitters include Jimmy Foxx, Philadelphia Athletics, 534; Ted Williams, Boston Red Sox, 521; Mel Ott, New York Giants, 511; Lou Gehrig, New York Yankees, 493; and Stan Musial, St. Louis Cardinals, 463.

### National League

| YEAR | PLAYER AND CLUB | NUMBER OF HOME RUNS |
|---|---|---|
| 1915 | Cravath, Cliff, Philadelphia | 24 |
| 1916 | Robertson, Davis, New York | 12 |
|  | Williams, Fred, Chicago | 12 |
| 1917 | Robertson, Davis, New York | 12 |
|  | Cravath, Cliff, Philadelphia | 12 |
| 1918 | Cravath, Cliff, Philadelphia | 8 |
| 1919 | Cravath, Cliff, Philadelphia | 12 |
| 1920 | Williams, Fred (Cy), Philadelphia | 15 |
| 1921 | Kelly, George, New York | 23 |
| 1922 | Hornsby, Rogers, St. Louis | 42 |
| 1923 | Williams, Fred (Cy), Philadelphia | 41 |
| 1924 | Fournier, Jacques, Brooklyn | 27 |
| 1925 | Hornsby, Rogers, St. Louis | 39 |
| 1926 | Wilson, Lewis (Hack), Chicago | 21 |
| 1927 | Wilson, Lewis (Hack), Chicago | 30 |
|  | Williams, Fred (Cy), Philadelphia | 30 |
| 1928 | Wilson, Lewis (Hack), Chicago | 31 |
|  | Bottomley, Jim, St. Louis | 31 |
| 1929 | Klein, Chuck, Philadelphia | 43 |
| 1930 | Wilson, Lewis (Hack), Chicago | 56 |
| 1931 | Klein, Chuck, Philadelphia | 31 |
| 1932 | Klein, Chuck, Philadelphia | 38 |
|  | Ott, Mel, New York | 38 |
| 1933 | Klein, Chuck, Philadelphia | 28 |
| 1934 | Ott, Mel, New York | 35 |
|  | Collins, James (Rip), St. Louis | 35 |
| 1935 | Berger, Wally, Boston | 34 |
| 1936 | Ott, Mel, New York | 33 |
| 1937 | Ott, Mel, New York | 31 |
|  | Medwick, Joe (Ducky), St. Louis | 31 |
| 1938 | Ott, Mel, New York | 36 |
| 1939 | Mize, Johnny, St. Louis | 28 |
| 1940 | Mize, Johnny, St. Louis | 43 |
| 1941 | Camilli, Dolph, Brooklyn | 34 |
| 1942 | Ott, Mel, New York | 30 |
| 1943 | Nicholson, Bill (Swish), Chicago | 29 |
| 1944 | Nicholson, Bill (Swish), Chicago | 33 |
| 1945 | Holmes, Tommy, Boston | 28 |
| 1946 | Kiner, Ralph, Pittsburgh | 23 |
| 1947 | Kiner, Ralph, Pittsburgh | 51 |
|  | Mize, Johnny, New York | 51 |
| 1948 | Kiner, Ralph, Pittsburgh | 40 |
|  | Mize, Johnny, New York | 40 |
| 1949 | Kiner, Ralph, Pittsburgh | 54 |
| 1950 | Kiner, Ralph, Pittsburgh | 47 |
| 1951 | Kiner, Ralph, Pittsburgh | 42 |
| 1952 | Kiner, Ralph, Pittsburgh | 37 |
|  | Sauer, Hank, Chicago | 37 |
| 1953 | Mathews, Eddie, Milwaukee | 47 |
| 1954 | Kluszewski, Ted, Cincinnati | 49 |
| 1955 | Mays, Willie, New York | 51 |
| 1956 | Snider, Edwin (Duke), Brooklyn | 43 |
| 1957 | Aaron, Hank, Milwaukee | 44 |
| 1958 | Banks, Ernie, Chicago | 47 |
| 1959 | Mathews, Eddie, Milwaukee | 46 |
| 1960 | Banks, Ernie, Chicago | 41 |
| 1961 | Cepeda, Orlando, San Francisco | 46 |
| 1962 | Mays, Willie, San Francisco | 49 |
| 1963 | Aaron, Hank, Milwaukee | 44 |
|  | McCovey, Willie, San Francisco | 44 |
| 1964 | Mays, Willie, San Francisco | 47 |
| 1965 | Mays, Willie, San Francisco | 52 |
| 1966 | Aaron, Hank, Atlanta | 44 |
| 1967 | Aaron, Hank, Atlanta | 39 |

### American League

| YEAR | PLAYER AND CLUB | NUMBER OF HOME RUNS |
|---|---|---|
| 1915 | Roth, Robert, Chicago-Cleveland | 7 |
| 1916 | Pipp, Wally, New York | 12 |
| 1917 | Pipp, Wally, New York | 9 |
| 1918 | Ruth, George (Babe), Boston | 11 |
|  | Walker, Clarence, Philadelphia | 11 |
| 1919 | Ruth, George (Babe), Boston | 29 |
| 1920 | Ruth, George (Babe), New York | 54 |
| 1921 | Ruth, George (Babe), New York | 59 |
| 1922 | Williams, Kenneth R., St. Louis | 39 |
| 1923 | Ruth, George (Babe), New York | 41 |
| 1924 | Ruth, George (Babe), New York | 46 |
| 1925 | Meusel, Bob, New York | 33 |
| 1926 | Ruth, George (Babe), New York | 47 |
| 1927 | Ruth, George (Babe), New York | 60 |
| 1928 | Ruth, George (Babe), New York | 54 |
| 1929 | Ruth, George (Babe), New York | 46 |
| 1930 | Ruth, George (Babe), New York | 49 |
| 1931 | Ruth, George (Babe), New York | 46 |
|  | Gehrig, Henry (Lou), New York | 46 |
| 1932 | Foxx, Jimmy, Philadelphia | 58 |
| 1933 | Foxx, Jimmy, Philadelphia | 48 |
| 1934 | Gehrig, Henry (Lou), New York | 49 |
| 1935 | Foxx, Jimmy, Philadelphia | 36 |
|  | Greenberg, Hank, Detroit | 36 |
| 1936 | Gehrig, Henry (Lou), New York | 49 |
| 1937 | DiMaggio, Joe, New York | 46 |
| 1938 | Greenberg, Hank, Detroit | 58 |
| 1939 | Foxx, Jimmy, Boston | 35 |
| 1940 | Greenberg, Hank, Detroit | 41 |
| 1941 | Williams, Ted, Boston | 37 |
| 1942 | Williams, Ted, Boston | 36 |
| 1943 | York, Rudy, Detroit | 34 |
| 1944 | Etten, Nick, New York | 22 |
| 1945 | Stephens, Vernon, St. Louis | 24 |
| 1946 | Greenberg, Hank, Detroit | 44 |
| 1947 | Williams, Ted, Boston | 32 |
| 1948 | DiMaggio, Joe, New York | 39 |
| 1949 | Williams, Ted, Boston | 43 |
| 1950 | Rosen, Al, Cleveland | 37 |
| 1951 | Zernial, Gus, Chicago-Philadelphia | 33 |
| 1952 | Doby, Larry, Cleveland | 32 |
| 1953 | Rosen, Al, Cleveland | 43 |
| 1954 | Doby, Larry, Cleveland | 32 |
| 1955 | Mantle, Mickey, New York | 37 |
| 1956 | Mantle, Mickey, New York | 52 |
| 1957 | Sievers, Roy, Washington | 42 |
| 1958 | Mantle, Mickey, New York | 42 |
| 1959 | Colavito, Rocky, Cleveland | 42 |
|  | Killebrew, Harmon, Washington | 42 |
| 1960 | Mantle, Mickey, New York | 40 |
| 1961 | Maris, Roger, New York | 61 |
| 1962 | Killebrew, Harmon, Minnesota | 48 |
| 1963 | Killebrew, Harmon, Minnesota | 45 |
| 1964 | Killebrew, Harmon, Minnesota | 49 |
| 1965 | Conigliaro, Tony, Boston | 32 |
| 1966 | Robinson, Frank, Baltimore | 49 |
| 1967 | Yastrzemski, Carl, Boston | 44 |
|  | Killebrew, Harmon, Minnesota | 44 |

## MAJOR LEAGUE RUNS-BATTED-IN LEADERS

Lewis (Hack) Wilson of the Chicago Cubs holds the National League runs-batted-in season record of 190, which he set in 1930. This is also the major league record. Lou Gehrig of the New York Yankees established the American League mark of 184 in 1931.

### National League

### American League

| YEAR | PLAYER AND CLUB | RBI | YEAR | PLAYER AND CLUB | RBI |
|---|---|---|---|---|---|
| 1912 | Zimmerman, Henry (Heinie), Chicago... | 98 | 1912 | Baker, Frank, Philadelphia............ | 133 |
| 1913 | Cravath, Cliff, Philadelphia............ | 129 | 1913 | Baker, Frank, Philadelphia............ | 126 |
| 1914 | Magee, Sherwood, Philadelphia........ | 101 | 1914 | Crawford, Sam, Detroit................ | 112 |
| 1915 | Cravath, Cliff, Philadelphia............ | 118 | 1915 | Crawford, Sam, Detroit................ | 116 |
| 1916 | Chase, Hal, Cincinnati................ | 84 | 1916 | Pipp, Wally, New York................ | 99 |
| 1917 | Zimmerman, Henry (Heinie), New York.. | 100 | 1917 | Veach, Robert, Detroit................ | 115 |
| 1918 | Merkle, Frederick, Chicago........... | 71 | 1918 | Burns, George, Philadelphia........... | 74 |
|  |  |  |  | Veach, Robert, Detroit................ | 74 |
| 1919 | Myers, Henry (Hi), Brooklyn........... | 72 | 1919 | Ruth, George (Babe), Boston........ | 112 |
| 1920 | * { Kelly, George, New York............ | 94 | 1920 | Ruth, George (Babe), New York........ | 137 |
|  | { Hornsby, Rogers, St. Louis.......... | 94 |  |  |  |
| 1921 | Hornsby, Rogers, St. Louis............ | 126 | 1921 | Ruth, George (Babe), New York........ | 170 |
| 1922 | Hornsby, Rogers, St. Louis............ | 152 | 1922 | Williams, Ken, St. Louis............... | 155 |
| 1923 | Meusel, Emil (Irish), New York........ | 125 | 1923 | * { Speaker, Tris, Cleveland........... | 130 |
|  |  |  |  | { Ruth, George (Babe), New York..... | 130 |
| 1924 | Kelly, George, New York.............. | 136 | 1924 | Goslin, Leon (Goose), Washington...... | 129 |
| 1925 | Hornsby, Rogers, St. Louis............ | 143 | 1925 | Meusel, Bob, New York............... | 138 |
| 1926 | Bottomley, Jim, St. Louis............. | 120 | 1926 | Ruth, George (Babe), New York........ | 155 |
| 1927 | Waner, Paul, Pittsburgh............... | 131 | 1927 | Gehrig, Henry (Lou), New York......... | 175 |
| 1928 | Bottomley, Jim, St. Louis............. | 136 | 1928 | * { Ruth, George (Babe), New York..... | 142 |
|  |  |  |  | { Gehrig, Henry (Lou), New York...... | 142 |
| 1929 | Wilson, Lewis (Hack), Chicago........ | 159 | 1929 | Simmons, Al, Philadelphia............. | 157 |
| 1930 | Wilson, Lewis (Hack), Chicago........ | 190 | 1930 | Gehrig, Henry (Lou), New York........ | 174 |
| 1931 | Klein, Chuck, Philadelphia............ | 121 | 1931 | Gehrig, Henry (Lou), New York........ | 184 |
| 1932 | Hurst, Frank, Philadelphia............ | 143 | 1932 | Foxx, Jimmy, Philadelphia............ | 169 |
| 1933 | Klein, Chuck, Philadelphia............ | 120 | 1933 | Foxx, Jimmy, Philadelphia............ | 163 |
| 1934 | Ott, Mel, New York................... | 135 | 1934 | Gehrig, Henry (Lou), New York........ | 165 |
| 1935 | Berger, Wally, Boston................ | 130 | 1935 | Greenberg, Hank, Detroit............. | 170 |
| 1936 | Medwick, Joe (Ducky), St. Louis...... | 138 | 1936 | Trosky, Hal, Cleveland................ | 162 |
| 1937 | Medwick, Joe (Ducky), St. Louis...... | 154 | 1937 | Greenberg, Hank, Detroit............. | 183 |
| 1938 | Medwick, Joe (Ducky), St. Louis...... | 122 | 1938 | Foxx, Jimmy, Boston.................. | 175 |
| 1939 | McCormick, Frank, Cincinnati......... | 128 | 1939 | Williams, Ted, Boston................ | 145 |
| 1940 | Mize, Johnny, St. Louis............... | 137 | 1940 | Greenberg, Hank, Detroit............. | 150 |
| 1941 | Camilli, Dolph, Brooklyn.............. | 120 | 1941 | DiMaggio, Joe, New York.............. | 125 |
| 1942 | Mize, Johnny, New York.............. | 110 | 1942 | Williams, Ted, Boston................ | 137 |
| 1943 | Nicholson, Bill, Chicago.............. | 128 | 1943 | York, Rudy, Detroit.................. | 118 |
| 1944 | Nicholson, Bill, Chicago.............. | 122 | 1944 | Stephens, Vernon, St. Louis........... | 109 |
| 1945 | Walker, Fred (Dixie), Brooklyn........ | 124 | 1945 | Etten, Nick, New York................ | 111 |
| 1946 | Slaughter, Enos, St. Louis............ | 130 | 1946 | Greenberg, Hank, Detroit............. | 127 |
| 1947 | Mize, Johnny, New York.............. | 138 | 1947 | Williams, Ted, Boston................ | 114 |
| 1948 | Musial, Stan, St. Louis............... | 131 | 1948 | DiMaggio, Joe, New York.............. | 155 |
| 1949 | Kiner, Ralph, Pittsburgh.............. | 127 | 1949 | * { Williams, Ted, Boston............. | 159 |
|  |  |  |  | { Stephens, Vernon, Boston........... | 159 |
| 1950 | Ennis, Del, Philadelphia.............. | 126 | 1950 | * { Stephens, Vernon, Boston.......... | 144 |
|  |  |  |  | { Dropo, Walt, Boston............... | 144 |
| 1951 | Irvin, Monford (Monte), New York...... | 121 | 1951 | Zernial, Gus, Chicago–Philadelphia...... | 129 |
| 1952 | Sauer, Hank, Chicago................ | 121 | 1952 | Rosen, Al, Cleveland................. | 105 |
| 1953 | Campanella, Roy, Brooklyn............ | 142 | 1953 | Rosen, Al, Cleveland................. | 145 |
| 1954 | Kluszewski, Ted, Cincinnati........... | 141 | 1954 | Doby, Larry, Cleveland............... | 126 |
| 1955 | Snider, Edwin (Duke), Brooklyn....... | 136 | 1955 | * { Boone, Raymond, Detroit.......... | 116 |
|  |  |  |  | { Jensen, Jackie, Boston............. | 116 |
| 1956 | Musial, Stan, St. Louis............... | 109 | 1956 | Mantle, Mickey, New York............. | 130 |
| 1957 | Aaron, Hank, Milwaukee.............. | 132 | 1957 | Sievers, Roy, Washington............. | 114 |
| 1958 | Banks, Ernie, Chicago................ | 129 | 1958 | Jensen, Jackie, Boston............... | 122 |
| 1959 | Banks, Ernie, Chicago................ | 143 | 1959 | Jensen, Jackie, Boston............... | 112 |
| 1960 | Aaron, Hank, Milwaukee.............. | 126 | 1960 | Maris, Roger, New York............... | 112 |
| 1961 | Cepeda, Orlando, San Francisco........ | 142 | 1961 | Maris, Roger, New York............... | 142 |
| 1962 | Davis, Tommy, Los Angeles............ | 153 | 1962 | Killebrew, Harmon, Minnesota......... | 126 |
| 1963 | Aaron, Hank, Milwaukee.............. | 130 | 1963 | Stuart, Dick, Boston................. | 118 |
| 1964 | Boyer, Ken, St. Louis................ | 119 | 1964 | Robinson, Brooks, Baltimore........... | 118 |
| 1965 | Johnson, Deron, Cincinnati............ | 130 | 1965 | Colavito, Rocky, Cleveland............ | 108 |
| 1966 | Aaron, Hank, Atlanta................. | 121 | 1966 | Robinson, Frank, Baltimore............ | 122 |
| 1967 | Cepeda, Orlando, St. Louis............ | 111 | 1967 | Yastrzemski, Carl, Boston............. | 121 |

*Indicates a tie.

## GREAT MAJOR LEAGUE PITCHERS

There are several standards by which baseball pitchers are judged, but most authorities agree that a pitcher's earned run average and his won and lost record are the legitimate measures of his effectiveness.

Some great pitchers prior to 1940 were: Hubert (Dutch) Leonard, who recorded in 1914 the lowest earned run average—1.01—in major league baseball; Walter Johnson, with an earned run average of 1.09 in 1913; and Grover Cleveland Alexander, who in 1915 had an earned run average of 1.22.

Here follows a listing of pitchers with outstanding earned run averages since 1947.

| | National League | | | American League | | |
|---|---|---|---|---|---|---|
| YEAR | PITCHER AND CLUB | INNINGS PITCHED | ERA | PITCHER AND CLUB | INNINGS PITCHED | ERA |
| 1947 | Spahn, Warren, Boston | 290 | 2.33 | Chandler, Spurgeon (Spud), New York | 128 | 2.46 |
| 1948 | Brecheen, Harry, St. Louis | 233 | 2.24 | Bearden, Gene, Cleveland | 230 | 2.43 |
| 1949 | Koslo, Dave, New York | 212 | 2.50 | Parnell, Mel, Boston | 295 | 2.78 |
| 1950 | Hearn, Jim, St. Louis-New York | 134 | 2.49 | Wynn, Early, Cleveland | 214 | 3.20 |
| 1951 | Nichols, Chet, Boston | 156 | 2.88 | Rogovin, Saul, Detroit-Chicago | 217 | 2.78 |
| 1952 | Wilhelm, Hoyt, New York | 159 | 2.43 | Reynolds, Allie, New York | 244 | 2.07 |
| 1953 | Spahn, Warren, Milwaukee | 266 | 2.10 | Lopat, Eddie, New York | 178 | 2.43 |
| 1954 | Antonelli, John, New York | 259 | 2.29 | Garcia, Mike, Cleveland | 259 | 2.64 |
| 1955 | Friend, Bob, Pittsburgh | 200 | 2.84 | Pierce, Billy, Chicago | 206 | 1.97 |
| 1956 | Burdette, Lew, Milwaukee | 256 | 2.71 | Ford, Edward (Whitey), New York | 226 | 2.47 |
| 1957 | Podres, John, Brooklyn | 196 | 2.66 | Shantz, Bobby, New York | 173 | 2.45 |
| 1958 | Miller, Stu, San Francisco | 182 | 2.47 | Ford, Edward (Whitey), New York | 219 | 2.01 |
| 1959 | Jones, Sam, San Francisco | 271 | 2.82 | Wilhelm, Hoyt, Baltimore | 226 | 2.19 |
| 1960 | McCormick, Mike, San Francisco | 253 | 2.70 | Baumann, Frank, Chicago | 185 | 2.68 |
| 1961 | Spahn, Warren, Milwaukee | 263 | 3.01 | Donovan, Dick, Washington | 169 | 2.40 |
| 1962 | Koufax, Sanford (Sandy), Los Angeles | 184 | 2.54 | Aguirre, Hank, Detroit | 216 | 2.21 |
| 1963 | Koufax, Sanford (Sandy), Los Angeles | 311 | 1.88 | Peters, Gary, Chicago | 243 | 2.33 |
| 1964 | Koufax, Sanford (Sandy), Los Angeles | 223 | 1.74 | Chance, Dean, Los Angeles | 278 | 1.65 |
| 1965 | Koufax, Sanford (Sandy), Los Angeles | 336 | 2.04 | McDowell, Sam, Cleveland | 274 | 2.17 |
| 1966 | Koufax, Sanford (Sandy), Los Angeles | 323 | 1.73 | Peters, Gary, Chicago | 204 | 2.03 |
| 1967 | Niekro, Philip, Atlanta | 207 | 1.96 | Horlen, Joel, Chicago | 258 | 2.06 |

## PITCHERS WITH HIGHEST WON-LOST PERCENTAGES: 1942–1967

| | National League | GAMES | | PER-CENT-AGE | American League | GAMES | | PER-CENT-AGE |
|---|---|---|---|---|---|---|---|---|
| YEAR | PITCHER AND CLUB | Won | Lost | | PITCHER AND CLUB | Won | Lost | |
| 1942 | Krist, Howard, St. Louis | 13 | 3 | .813 | Bonham, Ernie, New York | 21 | 5 | .808 |
| 1943 | Shoun, Clyde, Cincinnati | 14 | 5 | .737 | Chandler, Spurgeon (Spud), | | | |
| | Wyatt, Whitlow, Brooklyn | 14 | 5 | .737 | New York | 20 | 4 | .833 |
| 1944 | Wilks, Ted, St. Louis | 17 | 4 | .810 | Hughson, Cecil (Tex), Boston | 18 | 5 | .783 |
| 1945 | Brecheen, Harry, St. Louis | 15 | 4 | .789 | Muncrief, Bob, St. Louis | 13 | 4 | .765 |
| 1946 | Rowe, Lynwood (Schoolboy), | | | | Ferriss, Dave, Boston | 25 | 6 | .806 |
| | Philadelphia | 11 | 4 | .733 | | | | |
| 1947 | Jansen, Larry, New York | 21 | 5 | .808 | Shea, Frank, New York | 14 | 5 | .737 |
| 1948 | Sewell, Truett (Rip), Pittsburgh | 13 | 3 | .813 | Kramer, Jack, Boston | 18 | 5 | .783 |
| 1949 | Branca, Ralph, Brooklyn | 13 | 5 | .722 | Kinder, Ellis, Boston | 23 | 6 | .793 |
| 1950 | Maglie, Sal, New York | 18 | 4 | .818 | Raschi, Vic, New York | 21 | 8 | .724 |
| 1951 | Roe, Elwin (Preacher), Brooklyn | 22 | 3 | .880 | Feller, Bob, Cleveland | 22 | 8 | .733 |
| | | | | | Martin, Morrie, Philadelphia | 11 | 4 | .733 |
| 1952 | Wilhelm, Hoyt, New York | 15 | 3 | .833 | Shantz, Bobby, Philadelphia | 24 | 7 | .774 |
| 1953 | Erskine, Carl, Brooklyn | 20 | 6 | .769 | Lopat, Eddie, New York | 16 | 4 | .800 |
| 1954 | Antonelli, John, New York | 21 | 7 | .750 | Consuegra, Sandalio (Sandy), | | | |
| | Wilhelm, Hoyt, New York | 12 | 4 | .750 | Chicago | 16 | 3 | .842 |
| 1955 | Newcombe, Don, Brooklyn | 20 | 5 | .800 | Byrne, Tommy, New York | 16 | 5 | .762 |
| 1956 | Newcombe, Don, Brooklyn | 27 | 7 | .794 | Ford, Edward (Whitey), New York | 19 | 6 | .760 |
| 1957 | Buhl, Bob, Milwaukee | 18 | 7 | .720 | Donovan, Dick, Chicago | 16 | 6 | .727 |
| 1958 | Spahn, Warren, Milwaukee | 22 | 11 | .667 | Sturdivant, Tom, New York | 16 | 6 | .727 |
| | Burdette, Lew, Milwaukee | 20 | 10 | .667 | Turley, Bob, New York | 21 | 7 | .750 |
| 1959 | Face, Elroy, Pittsburgh | 18 | 1 | .947 | Shaw, Bob, Chicago | 18 | 6 | .750 |
| 1960 | McDaniel, Lindy, St. Louis | 12 | 4 | .750 | Coates, Jim, New York | 13 | 3 | .813 |
| 1961 | Podres, Johnny, Los Angeles | 18 | 5 | .783 | Ford, Edward (Whitey), New York | 25 | 4 | .862 |
| 1962 | Purkey, Bob, Cincinnati | 23 | 5 | .821 | Herbert, Ray, Chicago | 20 | 9 | .690 |
| 1963 | Perranoski, Ron, Los Angeles | 16 | 3 | .842 | Ford, Edward (Whitey), New York | 24 | 7 | .774 |
| 1964 | Koufax, Sanford (Sandy), L.A. | 19 | 5 | .792 | Bunker, Wally, Baltimore | 19 | 5 | .792 |
| 1965 | Koufax, Sanford (Sandy), L.A. | 26 | 8 | .765 | Grant, Jim (Mudcat), Minnesota | 21 | 7 | .750 |
| 1966 | Marichal, Juan, San Francisco | 25 | 6 | .806 | Boswell, Dave, Minnesota | 12 | 5 | .706 |
| 1967 | Briles, Nelson, St. Louis | 14 | 5 | .736 | Horlen, Joel, Chicago | 19 | 7 | .730 |

## INDIVIDUAL MAJOR LEAGUE RECORDS: 1900–1967

### BATTING

**Highest Batting Average, Season:**
(NL) .424, Rogers Hornsby, *St. Louis*—1924
(AL) .422, Napoleon Lajoie, *Phila.*—1901

**Most Years Led League in Batting:**
(AL) 12, Ty Cobb, *Detroit*—1907–15; 1917–19
(NL) 8, Honus Wagner, *Pittsburgh*—1900;
1903–04; 1906–09; 1911

**Most Hits, Lifetime:**
(AL) 4,191, Ty Cobb, *Detroit and Philadelphia*—1905–28
(NL) 3,630, Stan Musial, *St. Louis*—1941–44;
1946–63

**Most Hits, Season:**
(AL) 257, George Sisler, *St. Louis*—1920
(NL) 254, Lefty O'Doul, *Philadelphia*—1929
(NL) 254, Bill Terry, *New York*—1930

**Most Hits in Succession:**
(AL) 12, Mike Higgens, *Boston*—1938
(AL) 12, Walt Dropo, *Detroit*—1952
(NL) 10, held by eight League players

**Most Consecutive Games Hit Safely In:**
(AL) 56, Joe DiMaggio, *New York*—1941
(NL) 37, Tommy Holmes, *Boston*—1945

**Most Runs, Lifetime:**
(AL) 2,244, Ty Cobb, *Detroit, Philadelphia*—1905–28
(NL) 1,949, Stan Musial, *St. Louis*—1941–44;
1946–63

**Most Runs, Season:**
(AL) 177, Babe Ruth, *New York*—1921
(NL) 158, Chuck Klein, *Philadelphia*—1930

**Most Runs Batted In, Lifetime:**
(AL) 2,209, Babe Ruth, *New York and Boston* (including 12 games with Boston [NL] in 1935)—1914–35
(NL) 1,951, Stan Musial, *St. Louis*—1941–44;
1946–63

**Most Runs Batted In, Season:**
(NL) 190, Hack Wilson, *Chicago*—1930
(AL) 184, Lou Gehrig, *New York*—1931

**Most Runs Batted In, Game:**
(NL) 12, Jim Bottomley, *St. Louis*—1924
(AL) 11, Tony Lazzeri, *New York*—1936

**Most Home Runs, Lifetime:**
(AL) 714, Babe Ruth, *Boston and New York* (AL)—1914–34, *Boston* (NL)—1935
(NL) 511, Mel Ott, *New York*—1926–47

**Most Home Runs, Season:**
(AL) 61, Roger Maris, *New York*—1961 (162 games)
(AL) 60, Babe Ruth, *New York*—1927 (151 games)
(NL) 56, Hack Wilson, *Chicago*—1930 (155 games)

**Most Home Runs, 9-Inning Game:**
(NL) 4, Gil Hodges, *Brooklyn*—1950; Joe Adcock, *Milwaukee*—1954; Willie Mays, *San Francisco*—1961
(AL) 4, Lou Gehrig, *New York*—1932; Rocky Colavito, *Cleveland*—1959

**Most Home Runs with Bases Loaded, Lifetime:**
(AL) 23, Lou Gehrig, *New York*—1927–38

(NL) 14, Gil Hodges, *Brooklyn*—1943–57;
*Los Angeles*—1958

**Most 2-Base Hits, Lifetime:**
(AL) 793, Tris Speaker, *Cleveland, Washington, Philadelphia, Boston*—1907–28
(NL) 725, Stan Musial, *St. Louis*—1941–63

**Most 3-Base Hits, Lifetime:**
312, Sam Crawford, *Cincinnati* (NL), 1899–1902, *and Detroit* (AL)—1903–17
(AL) 297, Ty Cobb, *Detroit and Philadelphia*—1905–28
(NL) 252, Honus Wagner, *Louisville*, 1897–99 *and Pittsburgh*—1900–17

**Most Games Played, Lifetime:**
(AL) 3,033, Ty Cobb, *Detroit*, 1905–26 *and Philadelphia*—1927–28
(NL) 3,026, Stan Musial, *St. Louis*—1941–44;
1946–63

**Most Consecutive Games Played:**
(AL) 2,130, Lou Gehrig, *New York*—1925–39
(NL) 895, Stan Musial, *St. Louis*—1952–57

**Most Bases on Balls, Lifetime:**
(AL) 2,056, Babe Ruth, *Boston and New York; Boston* (NL)—1914–35
(NL) 1,708, Mel Ott, *New York*—1926–47

### PITCHING

**Most Games Won, Lifetime:**
511, Cy Young, *Cleveland* (NL), *St. Louis* (NL), *Boston* (AL), *Cleveland* (AL), *Boston* (NL)—1890–1911
(AL) 416, Walter Johnson, *Washington*—1907–27
(NL) 373, Christy Mathewson, *New York and Cincinnati*—1900–16
(NL) 373, Grover Alexander, *Philadelphia, Chicago, and St. Louis*—1911–30

**Most Games Won, Season:**
(AL) 41, Jack Chesbro, *New York*—1904
(NL) 37, Christy Mathewson, *New York*—1908

**Most Consecutive Games Won, Season:**
(NL) 19, Rube Marquard, *New York*—1912
(AL) 16, Joe Wood, *Boston*—1912
(AL) 16, Walter Johnson, *Washington*—1912
(AL) 16, Lefty Grove, *Philadelphia*—1931
(AL) 16, Schoolboy Rowe, *Detroit*—1934

**Most Shutouts, Lifetime:**
(AL) 113, Walter Johnson, *Washington*—1907–27
(NL) 90, Grover Alexander, *Philadelphia, Chicago, and St. Louis*—1911–29

**Most Shutouts, Season:**
(NL) 16, Alexander, *Philadelphia*—1916
(AL) 13, Jack Coombs, *Philadelphia*—1910

**Most Consecutive Shutouts:**
(AL) 5, Harris White, *Chicago*—1904
(NL) 4, held by five League pitchers

**Most Strikeouts, Season:**
(NL) 382, Sandy Koufax, *Los Angeles*—1965
(AL) 348, Bob Feller, *Cleveland*—1946

**Most Strikeouts, 9-Inning Game:**
(AL) 18, Bob Feller, *Cleveland*—1938
(NL) 18, Sandy Koufax, *Los Angeles*—1959
18, Sandy Koufax, *Los Angeles*—1962

## NEW BASEBALL FRANCHISES IN THE MAJOR LEAGUES

**1953** The Boston Braves of the National League moved to Milwaukee and became the Milwaukee Braves.

**1954** The St. Louis Browns of the American League moved to Baltimore and took the name Baltimore Orioles.

**1955** The Philadelphia Athletics of the American League moved to Kansas City and became the Kansas City Athletics.

**1958** The Brooklyn Dodgers and the New York Giants of the National League moved to California, where they became, respectively, the Los Angeles Dodgers and the San Francisco Giants.

**1961** The American League expanded to ten teams with the addition of the Los Angeles Angels and the new Washington Senators. The old Washington Senators moved to Minnesota and became the Minnesota Twins.

**1962** The National League expanded to ten teams with the addition of the Houston Colts and the New York Mets.

**1965** The Houston Colts changed their name to the Houston Astros, and the Los Angeles Angels became the California Angels.

**1966** The Milwaukee Braves moved to Atlanta and became the Atlanta Braves.

## MAJOR LEAGUE ATTENDANCE RECORDS
Largest Total Season Attendance at Home

| NATIONAL LEAGUE | ATTENDANCE | YEAR | AMERICAN LEAGUE | ATTENDANCE | YEAR |
|---|---|---|---|---|---|
| Los Angeles | 2,755.184 | 1962 | Cleveland | 2,620,627 | 1948 |
| Milwaukee | 2,215,404 | 1957 | New York | 2,373,901 | 1948 |
| Houston | 2,151,470 | 1965 | Detroit | 1,951,474 | 1950 |
| St. Louis | 2,100,838 | 1967 | Boston | 1,692,339 | 1967 |
| New York | 1,933,693 | 1966 | Chicago | 1,644,460 | 1960 |
| San Francisco | 1,795,356 | 1960 | Minnesota | 1,483,421 | 1967 |
| Pittsburgh | 1,705,828 | 1960 | California | 1,400,321 | 1966 |
| Chicago | 1,485,166 | 1929 | Kansas City | 1,393,054 | 1955 |
| Philadelphia | 1,425,891 | 1964 | Baltimore | 1,187,849 | 1960 |
| Cincinnati | 1,125,928 | 1956 | Washington | 770,888 | 1967 |

## THE ALL-STAR GAMES

Originated in 1933 by Arch Ward, sports editor of the *Chicago Tribune*, the All-Star game is played annually for the benefit of the baseball players' pension fund. Prior to 1958 the participants were chosen by popular vote. Since then, however, the lineup has been selected by professional baseball players, managers, and coaches. The site alternates annually between an American and a National League stadium.

Stan Musial of the National League holds the record for service in the most All-Star games with 24. The highest batting average belongs to Charley Gehringer of the American League with .500 in six All-Star games.

## ALL-STAR GAME RESULTS

| YEAR | PARK | WINNER | SCORE | YEAR | PARK | WINNER | SCORE |
|---|---|---|---|---|---|---|---|
| 1933 | Comiskey Park, Chicago | AL | 4-2 | 1956 | Griffith Stadium, Washington, D.C. | NL | 7-3 |
| 1934 | Polo Grounds, New York | AL | 9-7 | 1957 | Busch Stadium, St. Louis | AL | 6-5 |
| 1935 | Municipal Stadium, Cleveland | AL | 4-1 | 1958 | Memorial Stadium, Baltimore | AL | 4-3 |
| 1936 | Braves Field, Boston | NL | 4-3 | 1959 | Forbes Field, Pittsburgh | NL | 5-4 |
| 1937 | Griffith Stadium, Washington, D.C. | AL | 8-3 | | Memorial Coliseum, Los Angeles | AL | 5-3 |
| 1938 | Crosley Field, Cincinnati | NL | 4-1 | 1960 | Municipal Stadium, Kansas City | NL | 5-3 |
| 1939 | Yankee Stadium, New York | AL | 3-1 | | Yankee Stadium, New York | NL | 6-0 |
| 1940 | Sportsman's Park, St. Louis | NL | 4-0 | 1961 | Candlestick Park, San Francisco [5] | NL | 5-4 |
| 1941 | Briggs Stadium, Detroit | AL | 7-5 | | Fenway Park, Boston [6] | Tie | 1-1 |
| 1942 | Polo Grounds. New York | AL | 3-1 | 1962 | D.C. Stadium, Washington, D.C. | NL | 3-1 |
| 1943 | Shibe Park, Philadelphia [1] | AL | 5-3 | | Wrigley Field, Chicago | AL | 9-4 |
| 1944 | Forbes Field, Pittsburgh [1] | NL | 7-1 | 1963 | Municipal Stadium, Cleveland | NL | 5-3 |
| 1945 | Not played | — | — | 1964 | Shea Stadium, New York | NL | 7-4 |
| 1946 | Fenway Park, Boston | AL | 12-0 | 1965 | Metropolitan Stadium, Bloomington, Minnesota | NL | 6-5 |
| 1947 | Wrigley Field, Chicago | AL | 2-1 | | | | |
| 1948 | Sportsman's Park, St. Louis | AL | 5-2 | | | | |
| 1949 | Ebbets Field, Brooklyn | AL | 11-7 | | | | |
| 1950 | Comiskey Park, Chicago [2] | NL | 4-3 | 1966 | Busch Stadium, St. Louis, Missouri | NL | 2-1 |
| 1951 | Briggs Stadium, Detroit | NL | 8-3 | 1967 | Anaheim Stadium, Anaheim, California [7] | NL | 2-1 |
| 1952 | Shibe Park, Philadelphia [3] | NL | 3-2 | | | | |
| 1953 | Crosley Field, Cincinnati | NL | 5-1 | | | | |
| 1954 | Municipal Stadium, Cleveland | AL | 11-9 | | | | |
| 1955 | Milwaukee Cnty. Stadium [4] | NL | 6-5 | | | | |

[1] Indicates a night game. [2] Ended after 14 innings of play. [3] Rain halted the game at the end of five innings. [4] Play ended after 12 innings. [5] A ten-inning game. [6] Rain halted play in the ninth inning. [7] Ended after record 15 innings.

## MEMBERS OF THE BASEBALL HALL OF FAME

The National Baseball Hall of Fame and Museum, dedicated at Cooperstown, New York, on June 12, 1939, commemorates baseball's greatest figures. It is situated near the Abner Doubleday Field, which, according to tradition, was the site of the first baseball game (1839).

| PITCHERS | CAREER | Won | Lost |
|---|---|---|---|
| Alexander, Grover | 1911–1930 | 373 | 208 |
| Bender, Charles (Chief) | 1903–1925 | 212 | 128 |
| Brown, Mordecai (Three-finger) | 1903–1916 | 239 | 130 |
| Chesbro, Jack | 1899–1909 | 199 | 128 |
| Clarkson, John | 1882–1894 | 328 | 175 |
| Cummings, W. A. * | 1872–1877 | 146 | 92 |
| Dean, Jerome (Dizzy) | 1930–1947 | 150 | 83 |
| Faber, Urban (Red) | 1914–1933 | 253 | 211 |
| Feller, Bob | 1936–1956 | 266 | 162 |
| Galvin, James (Pud) | 1876–1892 | 365 | 309 |
| Griffith, Clark | 1891–1914 | 237 | 140 |
| Grimes, Burleigh | 1916–1934 | 270 | 212 |
| Grove, Robert (Lefty) | 1925–1941 | 300 | 141 |
| Hubbell, Carl | 1928–1943 | 253 | 154 |
| Johnson, Walter | 1907–1927 | 416 | 279 |
| Keefe, Tim | 1880–1893 | 346 | 225 |
| Lyons, Ted | 1923–1946 | 260 | 230 |
| McGinnity, Joe | 1899–1908 | 247 | 142 |
| Mathewson, Christy | 1900–1916 | 373 | 188 |
| Nichols, Charles (Kid) | 1890–1906 | 360 | 202 |
| Pennock, Herb | 1912–1934 | 241 | 163 |
| Plank, Eddie | 1901–1917 | 325 | 190 |
| Radbourne, Charles (Old Hoss) | 1880–1891 | 308 | 191 |
| Rixey, Eppa | 1912–1933 | 266 | 251 |
| Ruffing, Charles (Red) | 1924–1947 | 273 | 225 |
| Spalding, A. G. * | 1871–1877 | 252 | 68 |
| Vance, Arthur (Dazzy) | 1915–1935 | 197 | 140 |
| Waddell, George (Rube) | 1897–1910 | 193 | 140 |
| Walsh, Ed | 1904–1917 | 195 | 126 |
| Ward, John | 1878–1894 | 158 | 102 |
| Young, Denton T. (Cy) | 1890–1911 | 511 | 315 |

| CATCHERS | CAREER | AVERAGE |
|---|---|---|
| Bresnahan, Roger | 1897–1915 | .279 |
| Cochrane, Gordon (Mickey) | 1925–1937 | .320 |
| Dickey, Bill | 1928–1946 | .313 |
| Ewing, William (Buck) | 1880–1897 | .311 |
| Hartnett, Charles (Gabby) | 1922–1941 | .297 |
| Kelly, Mike | 1878–1893 | .315 |
| Mack, Connie | 1886–1896 | .249 |
| Robinson, Wilbert | 1886–1902 | .280 |
| Schalk, Ray | 1912–1929 | .253 |

| FIRST BASEMEN | CAREER | AVERAGE |
|---|---|---|
| Anson, Adrian | 1876–1897 | .339 |
| Brouthers, Dennis (Dan) | 1879–1896 | .348 |
| Chance, Frank | 1898–1914 | .297 |
| Comiskey, Charles | 1882–1894 | .269 |
| Foxx, Jimmy | 1925–1945 | .325 |
| Gehrig, Henry (Lou) | 1923–1939 | .340 |
| Greenberg, Hank | 1933–1947 | .313 |
| Sisler, George | 1915–1930 | .340 |
| Terry, Bill | 1923–1936 | .341 |

| SECOND BASEMEN | CAREER | AVERAGE |
|---|---|---|
| Collins, Eddie | 1906–1930 | .333 |
| Evers, Johnny | 1902–1919 | .270 |
| Frisch, Frank | 1919–1937 | .316 |
| Gehringer, Charles | 1924–1942 | .321 |
| Hornsby, Rogers | 1915–1937 | .358 |
| Lajoie, Napoleon | 1896–1916 | .339 |
| Robinson, Jackie | 1947–1956 | .311 |

| THIRD BASEMEN | CAREER | AVERAGE |
|---|---|---|
| Baker, Frank (Home Run) | 1908–1922 | .307 |
| Collins, Jimmy | 1895–1908 | .294 |
| McGraw, John | 1891–1906 | .334 |
| Traynor, Harold (Pie) | 1920–1937 | .320 |

| SHORTSTOPS | CAREER | AVERAGE |
|---|---|---|
| Appling, Luke | 1930–1950 | .310 |
| Cronin, Joe | 1926–1945 | .302 |
| Jennings, Hugh | 1891–1918 | .314 |
| Maranville, Walter (Rabbit) | 1912–1935 | .258 |
| Tinker, Joe | 1902–1916 | .264 |
| Wagner, John (Honus) | 1897–1917 | .329 |
| Wallace, Roderick (Bobby) | 1894–1918 | .267 |
| Wright, George * | 1876–1882 | .251 |

| OUTFIELDERS | CAREER | AVERAGE |
|---|---|---|
| Burkett, Jesse | 1890–1905 | .342 |
| Carey, Max | 1910–1929 | .285 |
| Clarke, Fred | 1894–1915 | .315 |
| Cobb, Ty | 1905–1928 | .367 |
| Crawford, Sam | 1899–1917 | .309 |
| Delahanty, Ed | 1888–1903 | .346 |
| DiMaggio, Joe | 1936–1951 | .325 |
| Duffy, Hugh | 1888–1906 | .330 |
| Flick, Elmer | 1898–1910 | .315 |
| Hamilton, Billy | 1888–1901 | .344 |
| Heilmann, Harry | 1914–1932 | .342 |
| Keeler, Willie | 1892–1910 | .345 |
| Manush, Henry (Heinie) | 1923–1939 | .330 |
| McCarthy, Thomas | 1884–1896 | .294 |
| O'Rourke, James | 1876–1894 | .315 |
| Ott, Mel | 1926–1947 | .304 |
| Rice, Edgar (Sam) | 1915–1934 | .322 |
| Roush, Edd | 1913–1931 | .323 |
| Ruth, George (Babe) | 1914–1935 | .342 |
| Simmons, Al | 1924–1944 | .334 |
| Speaker, Tris | 1907–1928 | .344 |
| Waner, Lloyd | 1927–1945 | .316 |
| Waner, Paul | 1926–1945 | .333 |
| Wheat, Zack | 1909–1927 | .317 |
| Williams, Ted | 1939–1960 | .344 |

### OTHERS ELECTED FOR MERITORIOUS SERVICE

**Morgan G. Bulkeley,** first National League president
**Ban Johnson,** first American League president
**Henry Chadwick,** who wrote the first baseball rule book
**Alexander J. Cartwright,** who organized the first baseball club
**Kenesaw M. Landis,** baseball's first commissioner
**Bill Klem,** National League umpire for 46 years
**Tom Connolly,** American League umpire for 52 years
**Harry Wright,** National League manager for 30 years
**Edward G. Barrow,** American League club executive and manager
**Joe McCarthy,** managed the New York Yankees to nine pennants and won seven World Series
**Bill McKechnie,** managed three different clubs to pennants
**Miller Huggins,** managed the New York Yankees to six pennants
**Casey Stengel,** New York Yankees' manager
**Branch Rickey,** executive of 3 National League clubs

* Elected for meritorious service.

# BASKETBALL

### COLLEGE BASKETBALL: 1967

When the 1966–67 college basketball season ended there was no question that of all the 889 participating teams, the Bruins of the University of California, Los Angeles, rated the number one slot. U.C.L.A. had completed the regular season with a spectacular 26–0 record to become the sixth undefeated major college basketball team in history. In addition, they had in their ranks the one and only Lew Alcindor, a player who completely dominated the hardwood scene.

Alcindor, a 7-foot, 1⅜-inch sophomore, made his varsity debut as the most publicized collegiate prospect since Wilt Chamberlain went to Kansas a decade earlier. In his first game against the University of Southern California, Alcindor ran up an impressive total of 56 points, many of them coming on his patented "stuff" shots—a showy scoring maneuver that has since been outlawed.

Coach John Wooden took U.C.L.A. to the National Collegiate Athletic Association tournament at Louisville, Kentucky, where the Bruins won all three divisional games before meeting the Flyers of Dayton in the finals on March 25. U.C.L.A. captured the big game by a score of 79 to 64, with Alcindor ringing up 20 points and snagging 14 rebounds. The victory enabled U.C.L.A. to end the year with an impressive 30–0 game total.

In the Associated Press poll U.C.L.A. received all 300 votes for the nation's top college basketball team. One lone vote for Louisville in the United Press International poll marred their perfect record.

Southern Illinois (Carbondale, Illinois) was named as the top small college team. The Salukis received a bid to the big post-season play-off in New York, the National Invitation Tournament. Led by Walt Frazier, their 6-foot, 3-inch guard, Southern Illinois trimmed Marquette University in the finals on March 18 by the

UCLA star Lew Alcindor making his famous "stuff" shot

score of 71–56.

The honor of leading the nation in scoring went to Jimmy Walker, of Providence, with a 30.4 point-per-game average. Lew Alcindor placed a close second, with a 29.0 average. Mal Graham of New York University was third with a 28.7 average.

Named to the first-string All-American team by both the Associated Press and United Press International were Alcindor, Walker, Westley Unseld of Louisville, and Elvin Hayes of Houston. Clem Haskins of Western Kentucky was picked by the AP poll, and Bob Lloyd of Rutgers (New Brunswick, New Jersey) was selected in the UPI poll.

### LEADING COLLEGE BASKETBALL TEAMS: 1966–67 SEASON

The major American news services—The Associated Press and United Press International—conduct a poll each year to determine the top college teams in the United States.

The AP poll is based on a survey of sportswriters' selections made at the end of each season, while UPI conducts a poll of college basketball coaches.

**Associated Press**

| RANK | TEAM | WON | LOST |
|------|------|-----|------|
| 1 | U.C.L.A. | 26 | 0 |
| 2 | Louisville | 23 | 3 |
| 3 | Kansas | 20 | 3 |
| 4 | North Carolina | 21 | 4 |
| 5 | Princeton | 23 | 2 |
| 6 | Western Kentucky | 23 | 2 |
| 7 | Houston | 23 | 3 |
| 8 | Tennessee | 20 | 5 |
| 9 | Boston College | 19 | 2 |
| 10 | Texas Western | 20 | 5 |

**United Press International**

| RANK | TEAM | WON | LOST |
|------|------|-----|------|
| 1 | U.C.L.A. | 26 | 0 |
| 2 | Louisville | 23 | 3 |
| 3 | North Carolina | 21 | 4 |
| 4 | Kansas | 20 | 3 |
| 5 | Princeton | 23 | 2 |
| 6 | Houston | 23 | 3 |
| 7 | Western Kentucky | 23 | 2 |
| 8 | Texas Western | 20 | 5 |
| 9 | Tennessee | 20 | 5 |
| 10 | Boston College | 19 | 2 |

## RANKING COLLEGIATE BASKETBALL SCORERS: 1966–1967 SEASON

| PLAYER AND SCHOOL | G[1] | FG[2] | FT[3] | PTS[4] | AVG[5] | PLAYER AND SCHOOL | G[1] | FG[2] | FT[3] | PTS[4] | AVG[5] |
|---|---|---|---|---|---|---|---|---|---|---|---|
| 1. Walker, Providence... | 28 | 323 | 205 | 851 | 30.4 | 10. Tillman, Loyola...... | 22 | 219 | 115 | 553 | 25.1 |
| 2. Alcindor, U.C.L.A..... | 30 | 346 | 178 | 870 | 29.0 | 11. Moates, Richmond... | 23 | 219 | 136 | 574 | 25.0 |
| 3. Graham, New York | | | | | | 12. Kondla, Minnesota... | 24 | 232 | 133 | 597 | 24.9 |
| University.......... | 24 | 250 | 188 | 688 | 28.7 | 13. Hollines, Denver..... | 25 | 237 | 147 | 621 | 24.8 |
| 4. Hayes, Houston.... | 31 | 373 | 135 | 881 | 28.4 | 14. Smith, Iowa State.... | 25 | 222 | 175 | 619 | 24.8 |
| 5. Bialosuknia, Conn..... | 24 | 257 | 159 | 673 | 28.0 | 15. Stone, Marshall...... | 28 | 284 | 116 | 684 | 24.4 |
| 6. Lloyd, Rutgers........ | 29 | 277 | 255 | 809 | 27.9 | 16. Barnett, Delaware.... | 12 | 126 | 40 | 292 | 24.3 |
| 7. Gray, Okla. City..... | 26 | 298 | 119 | 715 | 27.5 | 17. Sidle, Oklahoma..... | 25 | 206 | 180 | 592 | 23.7 |
| 8. Anderson, St. Joseph's | | | | | | 18. Halimon, Utah State.. | 26 | 247 | 119 | 613 | 23.6 |
| (Ind.)............... | 26 | 243 | 204 | 690 | 26.5 | 19. Lechman, Gonzaga... | 25 | 196 | 186 | 578 | 23.1 |
| 9. Verga, Duke........ | 27 | 283 | 139 | 705 | 26.1 | 20. Mix, Toledo......... | 25 | 227 | 122 | 576 | 23.0 |

[1] Games.  [2] Field goals.  [3] Free throws.  [4] Points.  [5] Average points per game.

## NATIONAL INVITATION TOURNAMENT: 1938–1967

| YEAR | CHAMPION | COACH | YEAR | CHAMPION | COACH |
|---|---|---|---|---|---|
| 1938 | Temple.................. | Jim Usilton | 1953 | Seton Hall................ | John Russell |
| 1939 | Long Island University...... | Clair Bee | 1954 | Holy Cross................ | Lester Sheary |
| 1940 | Colorado................. | Forest Cox | 1955 | Duquesne................ | Donald Moore |
| 1941 | Long Island University...... | Clair Bee | 1956 | Louisville................ | Bernard Hickman |
| 1942 | West Virginia............. | Byke Raese | 1957 | Bradley.................. | Chuck Orsborn |
| 1943 | St. John's (Brooklyn, N.Y.).. | Joe Lapchick | 1958 | Xavier of Ohio............ | James McCafferty |
| 1944 | St. John's (Brooklyn, N.Y.).. | Joe Lapchick | 1959 | St. John's (Brooklyn, N.Y.).. | Joe Lapchick |
| 1945 | DePaul (Chicago, Illinois).... | Raymond Meyer | 1960 | Bradley.................. | Chuck Orsborn |
| 1946 | Kentucky................. | Adolph Rupp | 1961 | Providence College......... | Joe Mullaney |
| 1947 | Utah..................... | Vadal Peterson | 1962 | Dayton.................. | Tom Blackburn |
| 1948 | St. Louis................. | Edward Hickey | 1963 | Providence College......... | Joe Mullaney |
| 1949 | San Francisco............. | Peter Newell | 1964 | Bradley.................. | Chuck Orsborn |
| 1950 | City College of New York.... | Nat Holman | 1965 | St. John's (Brooklyn, N.Y.).. | Joe Lapchick |
| 1951 | Brigham Young............ | Stanley Watts | 1966 | Brigham Young............ | Stanley Watts |
| 1952 | La Salle................. | Kenneth Loeffler | 1967 | Southern Illinois........... | Jack Hartman |

## NATIONAL COLLEGIATE ATHLETIC ASSOCIATION TOURNAMENT: 1939–1967

| YEAR | CHAMPION | COACH | YEAR | CHAMPION | COACH |
|---|---|---|---|---|---|
| 1939 | Oregon.................. | Howard Hobson | 1954 | La Salle.................. | Kenneth Loeffler |
| 1940 | Indiana.................. | Branch McCracken | 1955 | San Francisco............. | Phil Woolpert |
| 1941 | Wisconsin................ | Harold Foster | 1956 | San Francisco............. | Phil Woolpert |
| 1942 | Stanford................. | Everett Dean | 1957 | North Carolina............. | Frank McGuire |
| 1943 | Wyoming................. | Everett Shelton | 1958 | Kentucky................ | Adolph Rupp |
| 1944 | Utah.................... | Vadal Peterson | 1959 | California................ | Pete Newell |
| 1945 | Oklahoma A & M.......... | Henry Iba | 1960 | Ohio State................ | Fred Taylor |
| 1946 | Oklahoma A & M.......... | Henry Iba | 1961 | Cincinnati................ | Edward Jucker |
| 1947 | Holy Cross................ | Alvin Julian | 1962 | Cincinnati................ | Edward Jucker |
| 1948 | Kentucky................ | Adolph Rupp | 1963 | Loyola (Chicago)........... | George Ireland |
| 1949 | Kentucky................ | Adolph Rupp | 1964 | UCLA................... | John Wooden |
| 1950 | City College of New York.... | Nat Holman | 1965 | UCLA................... | John Wooden |
| 1951 | Kentucky................ | Adolph Rupp | 1966 | Texas Western College (of the University of Texas)... | Donald Haskins |
| 1952 | Kansas.................. | Forest C. Allen | 1967 | UCLA................... | John Wooden |
| 1953 | Indiana.................. | Branch McCracken | | | |

## COLLEGIATE ALL-AMERICA TEAMS: 1966–1967 SEASON

United Press International

**First Team**
Lew Alcindor, U.C.L.A.
Jim Walker, Providence
Elvin Hayes, Houston
Westley Unseld, Louisville
Bob Lloyd, Rutgers
**Second Team**
Bob Verga, Duke
Clem Haskins, Western Ky.
Mel Daniels, New Mexico
Al ("Butch") Beard, Louisville
Lloyd ("Sonny") Dove, St. John's

Associated Press

**First Team**
Lew Alcindor, U.C.L.A.
Jim Walker, Providence
Elvin Hayes, Houston
Westley Unseld, Louisville
Clem Haskins, Western Ky.
**Second Team**
Bob Verga, Duke
Ron Widby, Tennessee
Larry Miller, N. Carolina
Bob Lloyd, Rutgers
Louie Dampier, Kentucky

# PROFESSIONAL BASKETBALL

The Boston Celtics' domination of professional basketball ended on April 11, 1967, when they were humbled by the younger Philadelphia 76ers in the semifinals of the National Basketball Association (NBA) play-offs. Boston, which had won eight straight league titles, lost four out of five games to the Wilt Chamberlain-led 76ers.

Philadelphia set an NBA winning-percentage record of .840 with 68 victories and 13 losses during the regular season. Much of the 76ers' success can be attributed to the changed attitude of Chamberlain. In past years he led the league in scoring, but in 1967 he became more of a playmaker. With a 30.5 points-per-game average, he was the second-leading NBA scorer; Rick Barry of the San Francisco Warriors was first with 35.6.

In the NBA finals Chamberlain and Barry met head on. Despite a 44-point performance by Barry, the 76ers defeated the Warriors, 125–122, on April 4, taking the series four games to two.

Chamberlain, who during 1966–67 set an NBA record for the highest field goal average, was named the most valuable player. Wilt, Barry, Oscar Robertson of the Cincinnati Royals, and Elgin Baylor and Jerry West of the Los Angeles Lakers were selected for the all-star team.

Dave Bing of the Detroit Pistons was picked as rookie of the year. Bill Bradley, a former Princeton star and Rhodes scholar signed by New York to a four-year, $500,000 contract, was scheduled to begin play for the Knickerbockers in January, 1968.

With the start of the 1967–68 season the new American Basketball Association swung into action with 11 franchised teams, extending from New Jersey to California. The NBA brought Seattle and San Diego into its fold.

■ **FINAL NBA STANDINGS: 1966–1967**

| TEAM | WON | LOST | PERCENTAGE | SCORING | |
|---|---|---|---|---|---|
| | | | | For | Against |
| **Eastern Division** | | | | | |
| Philadelphia.............. | 68 | 13 | .840 | 10,143 | 9,378 |
| Boston................... | 60 | 21 | .741 | 9,664 | 9,012 |
| Cincinnati................ | 39 | 42 | .481 | 9,487 | 9,507 |
| New York................. | 36 | 45 | .444 | 9,425 | 9,672 |
| Baltimore................ | 20 | 61 | .247 | 9,353 | 9,881 |
| **Western Division** | | | | | |
| San Francisco............ | 44 | 37 | .543 | 9,911 | 9,679 |
| St. Louis................. | 39 | 42 | .481 | 9,204 | 9,334 |
| Los Angeles.............. | 36 | 45 | .444 | 9,764 | 9,736 |
| Chicago.................. | 33 | 48 | .407 | 9,167 | 9,407 |
| Detroit.................. | 30 | 51 | .370 | 9,015 | 9,163 |

■ **NBA CHAMPIONSHIP FINALS: 1950–1967**

| YEAR | CHAMPION | SERIES (in games) | YEAR | CHAMPION | SERIES (in games) |
|---|---|---|---|---|---|
| 1950 | Minneapolis over Syracuse...... | 4-2 | 1959 | Boston over Minneapolis........ | 4-0 |
| 1951 | Rochester over New York...... | 4-3 | 1960 | Boston over St. Louis.......... | 4-3 |
| 1952 | Minneapolis over New York...... | 4-3 | 1961 | Boston over St. Louis.......... | 4-1 |
| 1953 | Minneapolis over New York...... | 4-1 | 1962 | Boston over Los Angeles........ | 4-3 |
| 1954 | Minneapolis over Syracuse...... | 4-3 | 1963 | Boston over Los Angeles........ | 4-2 |
| 1955 | Syracuse over Fort Wayne...... | 4-3 | 1964 | Boston over San Francisco...... | 4-1 |
| 1956 | Philadelphia over Fort Wayne.... | 4-1 | 1965 | Boston over Los Angeles........ | 4-1 |
| 1957 | Boston over St. Louis.......... | 4-3 | 1966 | Boston over Los Angeles........ | 4-3 |
| 1958 | St. Louis over Boston........... | 4-2 | 1967 | Philadelphia over San Francisco.. | 4-2 |

■ **NBA TEAM STATISTICS: 1966–1967**

| TEAM | GAMES | FIELD GOALS | | | FREE THROWS | | | SCORING AVERAGE | | |
|---|---|---|---|---|---|---|---|---|---|---|
| | | Made | Attempts | Percentage | Made | Attempts | Percentage | For | Against | Difference |
| Philadelphia.... | 81 | 3,912 | 8,103 | .483 | 2,319 | 3,411 | .680 | 125.2 | 115.8 | +9.4 |
| Boston......... | 81 | 3,724 | 8,325 | .447 | 2,216 | 2,963 | .748 | 119.3 | 111.3 | +8.0 |
| San Francisco.. | 81 | 3,814 | 8,818 | .433 | 2,283 | 3,021 | .758 | 122.4 | 119.5 | +2.9 |
| Los Angeles.... | 81 | 3,786 | 8,466 | .447 | 2,192 | 2,917 | .751 | 120.5 | 120.2 | +0.3 |
| Cincinnati...... | 81 | 3,654 | 8,137 | .449 | 2,179 | 2,806 | .777 | 117.1 | 117.4 | −0.3 |
| St. Louis....... | 81 | 3,547 | 8,004 | .443 | 2,110 | 2,979 | .708 | 113.6 | 115.2 | −1.6 |
| New York....... | 81 | 3,637 | 8,025 | .453 | 2,151 | 2,980 | .722 | 116.4 | 119.4 | −3.0 |
| Chicago........ | 81 | 3,565 | 8,505 | .419 | 2,037 | 2,784 | .732 | 113.2 | 116.9 | −3.7 |
| Detroit......... | 81 | 3,523 | 8,542 | .412 | 1,969 | 2,725 | .723 | 111.3 | 116.8 | −5 5 |
| Baltimore...... | 81 | 3,664 | 8,578 | .427 | 2,025 | 2,771 | .731 | 115.5 | 122.0 | −6.5 |

## NBA SCORING LEADERS: 1949-1967

| SEASON | PLAYER AND TEAM | G[1] | FG[2] | FT[3] | TP[4] | AVG.[5] |
|--------|-----------------|------|-------|-------|-------|---------|
| 1949-50 | George Mikan, Minneapolis Lakers | 68 | 649 | 567 | 1,865 | 27.4 |
| 1950-51 | George Mikan, Minneapolis Lakers | 68 | 678 | 576 | 1,932 | 28.4 |
| 1951-52 | Paul Arizin, Philadelphia Warriors | 66 | 548 | 578 | 1,674 | 25.4 |
| 1952-53 | Neil Johnston, Philadelphia Warriors | 70 | 504 | 556 | 1,564 | 22.3 |
| 1953-54 | Neil Johnston, Philadelphia Warriors | 72 | 591 | 577 | 1,759 | 24.4 |
| 1954-55 | Neil Johnston, Philadelphia Warriors | 72 | 521 | 589 | 1,631 | 22.7 |
| 1955-56 | Bob Pettit, St. Louis Hawks | 72 | 646 | 557 | 1,849 | 25.7 |
| 1956-57 | Paul Arizin, Philadelphia Warriors | 71 | 613 | 591 | 1,817 | 25.6 |
| 1957-58 | George Yardley, Detroit Pistons | 72 | 673 | 655 | 2,001 | 27.8 |
| 1958-59 | Bob Pettit, St. Louis Hawks | 72 | 719 | 667 | 2,105 | 29.2 |
| 1959-60 | Wilt Chamberlain, Philadelphia Warriors | 72 | 1,065 | 577 | 2,707 | 37.6 |
| 1960-61 | Wilt Chamberlain, Philadelphia Warriors | 79 | 1,251 | 531 | 3,033 | 38.4 |
| 1961-62 | Wilt Chamberlain, Philadelphia Warriors | 80 | 1,597 | 835 | 4,029 | 50.4 |
| 1962-63 | Wilt Chamberlain, San Francisco Warriors | 80 | 1,463 | 660 | 3,586 | 44.8 |
| 1963-64 | Wilt Chamberlain, San Francisco Warriors | 80 | 1,204 | 540 | 2,948 | 36.5 |
| 1964-65 | Wilt Chamberlain, Philadelphia 76ers | 73 | 1,063 | 408 | 2,534 | 34.7 |
| 1965-66 | Wilt Chamberlain, Philadelphia 76ers | 79 | 1,074 | 501 | 2,649 | 33.5 |
| 1966-67 | Rick Barry, San Francisco Warriors | 78 | 1,011 | 753 | 2,775 | 35.6 |

[1] Games. [2] Field Goals. [3] Free Throws. [4] Total Points. [5] Average per Game.

| ■ NBA FIELD GOAL LEADERS | FG | FGA | PCT. |
|--------------------------|-----|------|------|
| W. Chamberlain, Philadelphia... | 785 | 1,150 | .683 |
| W. Bellamy, New York | 565 | 1,084 | .521 |
| B. Howell, Boston | 636 | 1,242 | .512 |
| O. Robertson, Cincinnati | 838 | 1,699 | .493 |
| W. Reed, New York | 635 | 1,298 | .490 |
| C. Walker, Philadelphia | 561 | 1,150 | .488 |
| B. Boozer, Chicago | 538 | 1,104 | .487 |
| T. Hawkins, Los Angeles | 275 | 572 | .481 |
| H. Hairston, Cincinnati | 461 | 962 | .479 |
| D. Barnett, New York | 454 | 949 | .478 |

| ■ NBA FREE THROW LEADERS | FT | FTA | PCT. |
|--------------------------|-----|------|------|
| A. Smith, Cincinnati | 343 | 380 | .903 |
| R. Barry, San Francisco | 753 | 852 | .884 |
| J. West, Los Angeles | 602 | 686 | .878 |
| O. Robertson, Cincinnati | 736 | 843 | .873 |
| S. Jones, Boston | 318 | 371 | .857 |
| L. Siegfried, Boston | 294 | 347 | .847 |
| W. Jones, Philadelphia | 223 | 266 | .838 |
| J. Havlicek, Boston | 365 | 441 | .828 |
| K. Loughery, Baltimore | 340 | 412 | .825 |
| E. Baylor, Los Angeles | 440 | 541 | .813 |

## PROFESSIONAL BASKETBALL RECORDS

### New Individual and Team Records: 1966-67

| | |
|---|---|
| Most Games Won | 68 (Philadelphia) |
| Highest Winning Percentage | .840 (Philadelphia) |
| Most Points Scored in a Season | 10,143 (Philadelphia) |
| Most Points Scored Against | 9,881 (Baltimore) |
| Highest Team Field Goal Average | .483 (Philadelphia) |
| Most Free Throws Attempted | 3,411 (Philadelphia) |
| Most Games 100 Points | 80 each (N.Y.; Phila.; San Francisco) |
| Most Players Averaging Double Figures | 7 each (New York, San Francisco) |
| Team Having Most Players with over 100 Rebounds | New York (W. Reed, 1,136; W. Bellamy, 1,064) |
| Highest Field Goal Average | .683 (W. Chamberlain, Philadelphia) |
| Most Consecutive Field Goals Made | 35 (W. Chamberlain, Philadelphia) |
| Most Assists in a Season | 908 (G. Rodgers, Chicago) |
| Most Assists by a Center in a Season | 630 (W. Chamberlain, Philadelphia) |
| Most Consecutive Games no Disqualifications | 624 (W. Chamberlain, Philadelphia) |
| All-Time League High Scorer | W. Chamberlain, Philadelphia (23,442) |

### Standing Individual and Team Records

| | |
|---|---|
| Most Points in One Game | 100 (Chamberlain, Phila. Warriors, Mar. 2, 1962) |
| Most Assists in One Game | 28 each (Bob Cousy, Boston Celtics, Feb. 27, 1959; G. Rodgers, S. F. Warriors, Mar. 14, 1963) |
| Most Rebounds in One Game | 55 (Chamberlain, Phila. Warriors, Nov. 24, 1960) |
| Most Games in Career | 1,059 (Dolph Schayes, 1948-64) |
| Most Team Points in One Game | 173 (Boston Celtics, Feb. 27, 1959) |
| Most Team Assists in One Game | 60 (Syracuse Nationals, Nov. 15, 1952) |
| Most Team Rebounds in One Game | 112 (Philadelphia Warriors, Nov. 8, 1959; Boston Celtics, December 24, 1960) |
| Most Consecutive Games Won | 17 (Washington Capitols, Nov. 16-Dec. 30, 1946; Boston Celtics, Nov. 28-Dec. 30, 1959) |
| Most Consecutive Games Lost | 17 (S. F. Warriors, Dec. 20, 1964-Jan. 26, 1965) |
| Most Games Lost | 63 (San Francisco Warriors, 1964-65) |

# BOWLING

Nine-pin bowling was introduced to New Amsterdam by the Dutch before 1700. The American Bowling Congress, founded in 1895, revived the sport as a ten-pin game, and held its first tournament at Chicago in 1901. ABC national membership is about 5,000,000.

## AMERICAN BOWLING CONGRESS CHAMPIONSHIPS

### Singles—Regular Division

| YEAR | CHAMPION | SCORE |
|---|---|---|
| 1930... | Larry Shotwell, Covington, Ky........ | 774 |
| 1931... | Walter Lachowski, Erie, Penn......... | 712 |
| 1932... | Otto Nitschke, Cleveland, Ohio....... | 731 |
| 1933... | Earl Hewitt, Erie, Penn.............. | 724 |
| 1934... | Jerry Vidro, Grand Rapids, Mich...... | 721 |
| 1935... | Don Brokaw, Canton, Ohio........... | 733 |
| 1936... | Charles Warren, Springfield, Ill...... | 735 |
| 1937... | Eugene Gagliardi, Mt. Vernon, N.Y.... | 749 |
| 1938... | Knute Anderson, Moline, Ill......... | 746 |
| 1939... | James Danek, Forest Park, Ill........ | 730 |
| 1940... | Ray Brown, Terre Haute, Ind......... | 742 |
| 1941... | Fred Ruff, Belleville, Ill............. | 745 |
| 1942... | John Stanley, Cleveland, Ohio........ | 756 |
| 1946... | Leo Rollick, Santa Monica, Calif...... | 737 |
| 1947... | Junie McMahon, Chicago, Ill......... | 740 |
| 1948... | Lincoln Protich, Akron, Ohio........ | 721 |
| 1949... | Bernard Rusche, St. Bernard, Ohio... | 716 |
| 1950... | Everett Leins, Aurora, Ill........... | 757 |
| 1951... | Lee Jouglard, Detroit, Mich......... | 775 |
| 1952... | Al Sharkey, Chicago, Ill............. | 758 |
| 1953... | Frank Santore, New York, N.Y....... | 749 |
| 1954... | Tony Sparando, Newark, N.J........ | 723 |
| 1955... | Edward Gerzine, Milwaukee, Wis..... | 738 |
| 1956... | George Wade, Steubenville, Ohio..... | 744 |
| 1957... | Bob Allen, Yonkers, N.Y............ | 729 |
| 1958... | Ed Shay, Chester, Penn............. | 733 |
| 1959... | Ed Lubanski, Detroit, Mich.......... | 764 |
| 1960... | Paul Kulbaga, Cleveland, Ohio....... | 726 |
| 1961... | Lyle Spooner, St. Cloud, Minn....... | 726 |
| 1962... | Andrew Renaldy, Youngstown, Ohio.. | 720 |
| 1963... | Fred Delello, Oneonta, N.Y......... | 744 |
| 1964... | Jim Stefanich, Chicago, Ill.......... | 726 |
| 1965... | Kenneth Roeth, Dubuque, Iowa...... | 700 |
| 1966... | Don Chapman, Scranton, Penn....... | 761 |
| 1967... | Frank Perry, Lorain, Ohio .......... | 723 |

### All-Events—Regular Division

| YEAR | CHAMPION | SCORE |
|---|---|---|
| 1930... | George Morrison, Chicago, Ill........ | 1985 |
| 1931... | Michael Mauser, Youngstown, Ohio... | 1966 |
| 1932... | Hugh Stewart, Cincinnati, Ohio....... | 1980 |
| 1933... | Gil Zunker, Milwaukee, Wis.......... | 2060 |
| 1934... | Walter Reppenhagen, Detroit, Mich.... | 1972 |
| 1935... | Ora Mayer, San Francisco, Calif....... | 2022 |
| 1936... | John Murphy, Indianapolis, Ind....... | 2006 |
| 1937... | Max Stein, Belleville, Ill............. | 2070 |
| 1938... | Donald L. Beatty, Jackson, Mich...... | 1978 |
| 1939... | Joe Wilman, Chicago, Ill............. | 2028 |
| 1940... | Fred Fischer, Buffalo, N.Y........... | 2001 |
| 1941... | Harold Kelly, South Bend, Ind....... | 2013 |
| 1942... | Stanley Moskal, Saginaw, Mich....... | 1973 |
| 1946... | Joe Wilman, Chicago, Ill............. | 2054 |
| 1947... | Junie McMahon, Chicago, Ill.......... | 1965 |
| 1948... | Ned Day, West Allis, Wis............ | 1979 |
| 1949... | John Small, Chicago, Ill............. | 1941 |
| 1950... | Frank Santore, New York, N.Y....... | 1981 |
| 1951... | Tony Lindemann, Detroit, Mich....... | 2005 |
| 1952... | Steve Nagy, Cleveland, Ohio......... | 2065 |
| 1953... | Frank Santore, New York, N.Y....... | 1994 |
| 1954... | Brad Lewis, Ashland, Ohio........... | 1985 |
| 1955... | Fred Bujack, Detroit, Mich........... | 1993 |
| 1956... | Bill Lillard, Chicago, Ill............. | 2018 |
| 1957... | Jim Spalding, Louisville, Ky.......... | 2088 |
| 1958... | Al Faragalli, Paterson, N.J........... | 2043 |
| 1959... | Ed Lubanski, Detroit, Mich.......... | 2116 |
| 1960... | Vince Lucci, Trenton, N.J............ | 1985 |
| 1961... | Luke Karan, Detroit, Mich........... | 1960 |
| 1962... | Billy Young, Tulsa, Okla............. | 2015 |
| 1963... | Wilford (Bus) Oswalt, Fort Wayne, Ind. | 2055 |
| 1964... | Les Zikes, Jr., Chicago, Ill........... | 2001 |
| 1965... | Tom Hathaway, Los Angeles, Calif.... | 1922 |
| 1966... | John Wilcox, Williamsport, Penn...... | 2004 |
| 1967... | Gary Lewis, Chicago, Ill............. | 2010 |

## ABC MASTERS TOURNAMENT *

| YEAR | CHAMPION | RUNNER-UP | MATCHES Won | Lost | AVERAGE |
|---|---|---|---|---|---|
| 1951 | Lee Jouglard, Detroit, Mich............ | Joe Wilman, Chicago, Ill.............. | 6 | 1 | 201-8 |
| 1952 | Willard Taylor, Charleston, W. Va...... | Andy Varipapa, Hempstead, N.Y....... | 8 | 1 | 200-32 |
| 1953 | Rudy Habetler, Chicago, Ill.......... | Ed Brosius, Chicago, Ill............. | 10 | 1 | 200-13 |
| 1954 | Eugene Elkins, San Carlos, Calif....... | Willard Taylor, Charleston, W. Va..... | 7 | 0 | 205-19 |
| 1955 | Buzz Fazio, Detroit, Mich............. | Joe Kristof, Chicago, Ill.............. | 7 | 0 | 204-13 |
| 1956 | Dick Hoover, Akron, Ohio............. | Ray Bluth, St. Louis, Mo............. | 7 | 1 | 209-9 |
| 1957 | Dick Hoover, Akron, Ohio............. | Bill Lillard, Dallas, Texas........... | 9 | 1 | 216-39 |
| 1958 | Tom Hennessey, St. Louis, Mo......... | Lou Frantz, Louisville, Ky............ | 7 | 0 | 209-15 |
| 1959 | Ray Bluth, St. Louis, Mo............. | Bill Golembiewski, Detroit, Mich...... | 7 | 0 | 214-26 |
| 1960 | Bill Golembiewski, Detroit, Mich....... | Steve Nagy, St. Louis, Mo........... | 7 | 0 | 206-13 |
| 1961 | Don Carter, St. Louis, Mo............. | Dick Hoover, St. Louis, Mo............. | 8 | 1 | 211-18 |
| 1962 | Bill Golembiewski, Detroit, Mich....... | Ron Winger, Los Angeles, Calif....... | 7 | 0 | 223-12 |
| 1963 | Harry Smith, St. Louis, Mo............. | Bobby Meadows, Dallas, Texas........ | 7 | 0 | 219-3 |
| 1964 | Billy Welu, St. Louis, Mo............. | Harry Smith, Baltimore, Md.......... | 7 | 0 | 227 |
| 1965 | Billy Welu, St. Louis, Mo............. | Don Ellis, Houston, Texas............ | 9 | 1 | 202-12 |
| 1966 | Bob Strampe, Detroit, Mich........... | Al Thompson, Cleveland, Ohio........ | 7 | 0 | 219-8 |
| 1967 | Lou Scalia, Miami, Fla................ | Bill Johnson, New Orleans, La........ | 7 | 0 | 216-9 |

* First held in 1951. The Masters champion receives about $4,000 in prize money.

# BOXING

One of the oldest sports, boxing was included in the original Olympic Games. Centuries later, in England, bareknuckle boxing took a strong hold with the support of royal patronage. In 1743, Jack Broughton drew up the first set of London prize-ring rules.

Broughton's rules were superseded when the Marquess of Queensberry introduced his celebrated code of boxing rules in 1865. By 1889 these rules were standardized and called for boxing gloves and a limited number of three-minute rounds, outlawed gouging and wrestling, and required a ten-second count before a floored boxer was declared the loser. In the United States, boxing was illegal for many years. New York State was the first to legalize

## HEAVYWEIGHT CHAMPIONSHIP TITLE FIGHTS [1]

| DATE OF FIGHT | SITE | DEFENDING CHAMPION | WEIGHT | AGE | BIRTH-PLACE | CHALLENGER |
|---|---|---|---|---|---|---|
| July 8, 1889.......... | Richburg, Mississippi | John L. Sullivan... | 205 | 30 | U.S. | Jake Kilrain...... |
| September 7, 1892.... | New Orleans, Louisiana | John L. Sullivan... | 212 | 33 | U.S. | James J. Corbett.. |
| March 17, 1897....... | Carson City, Nevada | James J. Corbett.. | 180 | 29 | U.S. | Bob Fitzsimmons.. |
| June 9, 1899.......... | Coney Island, New York | Bob Fitzsimmons.. | 175 | 37 | England | James J. Jeffries.. |
| February 23, 1906..... | Los Angeles, California | Marvin Hart...... | 190 | 29 | U.S. | Tommy Burns..... |
| December 26, 1908.... | Sydney, Australia | Tommy Burns..... | 176 | 27 | Canada | Jack Johnson..... |
| April 5, 1915......... | Havana, Cuba | Jack Johnson..... | 205½ | 37 | U.S. | Jess Willard...... |
| July 4, 1919.......... | Toledo, Ohio | Jess Willard...... | 245 | 35 | U.S. | Jack Dempsey.... |
| September 23, 1926... | Philadelphia, Pennsylvania | Jack Dempsey.... | 190 | 31 | U.S. | Gene Tunney...... |
| June 12, 1930........ | New York City | Jack Sharkey..... | 197 | 27 | U.S. | Max Schmeling.... |
| June 21, 1932........ | Long Island City, New York | Max Schmeling.... | 188 | 26 | Germany | Jack Sharkey..... |
| June 29, 1933........ | Long Island City, New York | Jack Sharkey..... | 201 | 30 | U.S. | Primo Carnera.... |
| June 14, 1934........ | Long Island City, New York | Primo Carnera.... | 263¼ | 27 | Italy | Max Baer......... |
| June 13, 1935........ | Long Island City, New York | Max Baer......... | 209½ | 26 | U.S. | Jim Braddock..... |
| June 22, 1937........ | Chicago, Illinois | Jim Braddock..... | 197 | 31 | U.S. | Joe Louis......... |
| June 22, 1949........ | Chicago, Illinois | Ezzard Charles.... | 181¾ | 28 | U.S. | Jersey Joe Walcott. |
| September 27, 1950... | New York City | Ezzard Charles.... | 184½ | 29 | U.S. | Joe Louis......... |
| July 18, 1951......... | Pittsburgh, Pennsylvania | Ezzard Charles.... | 182 | 30 | U.S. | Jersey Joe Walcott. |
| September 23, 1952... | Philadelphia, Pennsylvania | Jersey Joe Walcott. | 196 | 38 | U.S. | Rocky Marciano... |
| November 30, 1956... | Chicago, Illinois | Floyd Patterson... | 182¼ | 21 | U.S. | Archie Moore..... |
| June 26, 1959........ | New York City | Floyd Patterson... | 182 | 24 | U.S. | Ingemar Johansson |
| June 20, 1960......... | New York City | Ingemar Johansson | 194¾ | 27 | Sweden | Floyd Patterson... |
| September 25, 1962... | Chicago, Illinois | Floyd Patterson... | 189 | 27 | U.S. | Sonny Liston...... |
| February 25, 1964..... | Miami Beach, Florida | Sonny Liston...... | 218 | 30[2] | U.S. | Cassius Clay ..... |

[1] Includes only those bouts in which the title changed hands.

it, in 1896. Athletic or boxing commissions regulate the sport in each state, and most of these are members of the World Boxing Association (WBA), formerly the National Boxing Association (NBA). Several states do not accept WBA rulings and as a result, on occasion, there is more than one champion. During 1965, for example, the WBA recognized Ernie Terrell as world heavyweight champion.

Prize fighting reached its peak of popularity during the 1920s and 1930s; since World War II, scandals, ring injuries, deaths, investigations, and monopolistic practices by promoters have all contributed to its decay as a spectator sport. Major championship fights are now generally telecast only on closed-circuit networks, which pay substantial fees for the privilege to the fight promoters and the boxers.

| WEIGHT | AGE | BIRTH-PLACE | RESULTS |
|---|---|---|---|
| 195 | 31 | U.S. | Sullivan defeated Kilrain in the 75th round when Kilrain's chief second threw in the sponge. This was the last major bareknuckle bout in America. |
| 178 | 25 | U.S. | For a purse of $25,000, winner take all, Corbett knocked out Sullivan in the 21st round. This was the first world championship fight under Marquess of Queensberry rules. |
| 156½ | 34 | England | The first championship fight of which movies were taken, and the first staged in a specifically built open-air area. Fitzsimmons knocked out Corbett in the 14th round. |
| 206 | 24 | U.S. | Jeffries scored a knockout over Fitzsimmons in the 11th round. Fitzsimmons was the last English-born heavyweight champion. |
| 180 | 24 | Canada | Jeffries retired as champion in 1905. He named a lackluster heavyweight, Marvin Hart, to take his place. In this fight Hart, the alleged champion, was soundly beaten in a 20-round decision bout by Tommy Burns. |
| 196 | 30 | U.S. | The bout was stopped in the 14th round because of the beating Johnson administered to Burns. Johnson became the world's first Negro heavyweight champion. |
| 230 | 31 | U.S. | Willard, "the white hope," knocked out Johnson in the 26th round to become heavyweight champion. |
| 187 | 24 | U.S. | After three rounds, Willard's seconds threw in the towel in what has come to be regarded as the worst beating ever taken by a heavyweight champion. |
| 189½ | 28 | U.S. | An all-time record crowd of 120,000 people saw Tunney outpoint Dempsey in ten rounds. After defeating Dempsey again a year later in the "Battle of the Long Count," Tunney went on to knock out Tom Heeney of Australia before retiring undefeated July 28, 1928. |
| 188 | 24 | Germany | Schmeling took the title when officials contended that Sharkey had committed a foul in the fourth round. Movies later revealed that Sharkey did not commit a foul and a year later the New York Commission reversed its decision in favor of Sharkey. |
| 205 | 29 | U.S. | After 15 rounds of tedious sparring, the decision went to Sharkey, dumbfounding not only everyone in the arena, but the two fighters as well. |
| 260½ | 26 | Italy | Carnera knocked out Sharkey in the sixth round with a blow that has come to be called "the invisible punch." |
| 209½ | 25 | U.S. | Carnera went down 12 times before referee Arthur Donovan stopped the fight in the 11th round. |
| 193¾ | 29 | U.S. | Braddock, who went into the fight with 10 to 1 odds against him, was awarded the decision at the end of the 15-round bout. |
| 197¼ | 23 | U.S. | Louis knocked out Braddock in the eighth round. |
| 195½ | 35 | U.S. | After Louis' retirement in 1949, an elimination tournament was held. Charles was awarded the decision in the drab 15-round sparring match and named world champion by the National Boxing Association. |
| 218 | 36 | U.S. | After 15 bruising rounds, Charles received the unanimous decision and by defeating Louis, who came out of retirement to reclaim his title, Charles was universally recognized as champion. |
| 194 | 37 | U.S. | In his fifth try at the title, Walcott unexpectedly knocked out Charles in the seventh round with a left hook to the jaw and became the oldest man ever to win the heavyweight championship. |
| 184 | 28 | U.S. | Marciano, far behind in points, knocked the champion out with one punch in the 13th round. The new champion retired from boxing on April 27, 1956, the only heavyweight champion to retire undefeated in a total professional career. |
| 187¾ | 39 | U.S. | In an elimination bout, held after Marciano's retirement, Patterson knocked out Moore in the fifth round and became the youngest heavyweight champion in history. |
| 198 | 26 | Sweden | The first Swede to win the heavyweight championship, Johansson knocked out Patterson in the third round. |
| 190 | 25 | U.S. | Patterson knocked out Johansson in the fifth round and became the first heavyweight champion to regain his lost title. |
| 214 | 28[2] | U.S. | Liston knocked out Patterson in two minutes, six seconds of the first round with a left hook. |
| 210½ | 22 | U.S. | Clay[3] took the championship when Liston sat on his stool in the opposite corner and refused to come out for the seventh round. Liston later claimed he had hurt his left arm. (In 1967 Clay was shorn of his title by the World Boxing Association and the New York Athletic Commission for failure to answer a draft call. The championship is still open.) |

[2] Liston's actual age is uncertain.    [3] Also known as Muhammad Ali.

## THE CHAMP WHO LOST HIS CROWN

"What's my name?" taunts Cassius Clay during victorious championship bout with Ernie Terrell.

As 1967 drew to a close Cassius Marcellus Clay (who calls himself Muhammad Ali) was seen in a strange role—defending himself in court, not in the ring. Convicted on government charges of refusal to be inducted into the armed forces of the United States, Clay appealed, claiming exception on the grounds that he is a Muslim minister. Earlier, his stand on the draft had caused boxing authorities to strip him of his heavyweight title.

Born in Louisville, Kentucky, January 12, 1942, Clay began boxing in his early teens. After capturing the Golden Gloves heavyweight title and the Olympic gold medal (1960), he turned professional. In 1964 he became world champion when he defeated Sonny Liston, but was shorn of his title for planning a rematch in violation of WBA rules. Clay defeated a string of challengers and regained his crown in February, 1967, by outpointing the WBA-sanctioned champion, Ernie Terrell.

Whatever the result of his present legal tangle may be, the career of the irrepressible Cassius Clay seems to be headed for a technical knockout.

## BOXING CHAMPIONS: 1967

| DIVISION | WEIGHT CLASS | CHAMPION | DIVISION | WEIGHT CLASS | CHAMPION |
|---|---|---|---|---|---|
| Heavyweight | 175 lbs. and up | Cassius Clay, Houston, Texas | Junior Welterweight | 138–140 lbs. | Paul Fujii, Honolulu |
| Light-Heavyweight | 160–175 lbs. | Dick Tiger, Nigeria | Lightweight | 126–135 lbs. | Carlos Ortiz, N.Y. |
| Middleweight | 147–160 lbs. | Emile Griffith, New York City | Junior Lightweight | 128–130 lbs. | Yoshiaki Numata, Japan |
| Junior Middleweight | 150–154 lbs. | Ki Soo Kim, South Korea | Featherweight | 118–126 lbs. | Vicente Saldivar, Mexico |
| Welterweight | 135–147 lbs. | Curtis Cokes, Dallas, Texas | Bantamweight | 112–118 lbs. | Masahiko Harada, Japan |
| | | | Flyweight | 112 lbs. (max.) | Chartchai Chionoi, Thailand |

## LIGHT-HEAVYWEIGHT CHAMPIONS

The light-heavyweight division was created about 1900. Here follows a listing of light-heavyweight champions, many of whom later became contenders for the heavyweight crown.

| YEAR | CHAMPION | REIGN | YEAR | CHAMPION | REIGN |
|---|---|---|---|---|---|
| 1903... | George Gardner | 1903 | 1934... | Bob Olin | 1934–35 |
| 1903... | Bob Fitzsimmons | 1903–05 | 1935... | John Henry Lewis | 1935–38 |
| 1905... | "Philadelphia" Jack O'Brien [1] | 1905–12 | 1939... | Melio Bettina [6] | 1939 |
| 1912... | Jack Dillon [2] | 1912–16 | 1939... | Billy Conn | 1939–40 |
| 1916... | Battling Levinsky | 1916–20 | 1941... | Anton Christoforidis [7] | 1941 |
| 1920... | Georges Carpentier [3] | 1920–22 | 1941... | Gus Lesnevich | 1941–48 |
| 1922... | Battling Siki | 1922–23 | 1948... | Freddie Mills | 1948–50 |
| 1923... | Mike McTigue | 1923–25 | 1950... | Joey Maxim | 1950–52 |
| 1925... | Paul Berlenbach | 1925–26 | 1952... | Archie Moore | 1952–61 |
| 1926... | Jack Delaney | 1926–27 | 1961... | Harold Johnson [8] | 1961–63 |
| 1927... | Mike McTigue [4] | 1927 | 1963... | Willie Pastrano | 1963–65 |
| 1927... | Tommy Loughran | 1927–29 | 1965... | Jose Torres | 1965-66 |
| 1930... | Maxie Rosenbloom [5] | 1930–34 | 1966... | Dick Tiger | 1966– |

[1] Tommy Burns defeated O'Brien in 1907 but made no claim to the title.   [2] Dillon defeated all men in his weight class in 1912 and so claimed the title.   [3] Carpentier, light-heavyweight champion of France, became the first world champion with his defeat of Levinsky.   [4] Delaney resigned the crown and McTigue reclaimed it in 1927.   [5] Loughran resigned the title and Rosenbloom became champion.   [6] Bettina was the victor in an elimination tournament after Lewis resigned as title-holder.   [7] Conn moved into the heavyweight division, and Christoforidis was named champion by the NBA.   [8] Moore was stripped of his title by the NBA. Johnson knocked out Jesse Bowdry and became the new light-heavyweight champion.

## MIDDLEWEIGHT CHAMPIONS

The middleweight class, today called the middleweight division, was officially recognized in 1884. Until 1915 the maximum weight limit was 158 pounds; today it is 160.

| YEAR | CHAMPION | REIGN | YEAR | CHAMPION | REIGN |
|------|----------|-------|------|----------|-------|
| 1884... | Jack (Nonpareil) Dempsey..... | 1884–91 | 1949... | Jake LaMotta................. | 1949–51 |
| 1891... | Bob Fitzsimmons............. | 1891–97 | 1951... | Sugar Ray Robinson.......... | 1951 |
| 1897... | Tommy Ryan [1]............... | 1897–1907 | 1951... | Randy Turpin................. | 1951 |
| 1908... | Stanley Ketchel [2]........... | 1908 | 1951... | Sugar Ray Robinson.......... | 1951–52 |
| 1908... | Billy Papke.................. | 1908 | 1953... | Bobo Olson [5]............... | 1953–55 |
| 1908... | Stanley Ketchel.............. | 1908–10 | 1955... | Sugar Ray Robinson [5]........ | 1955–57 |
| 1913... | Frank Klaus [3]............... | 1913 | 1957... | Gene Fullmer................. | 1957 |
| 1913... | George Chip................. | 1913–14 | 1957... | Sugar Ray Robinson.......... | 1957 |
| 1914... | Al McCoy.................... | 1914–17 | 1957... | Carmen Basilio.............. | 1957–58 |
| 1917... | Mike O'Dowd................ | 1917–20 | 1958... | Sugar Ray Robinson [6]........ | 1958–60 |
| 1920... | Johnny Wilson............... | 1920–23 | 1959... | Gene Fullmer [7]............. | 1959–62 |
| 1923... | Harry Greb.................. | 1923–26 | 1960... | Paul Pender................. | 1960–62 |
| 1926... | Tiger Flowers................ | 1926 | 1962... | Dick Tiger................... | 1962–63 |
| 1926... | Mickey Walker [4].............. | 1926–31 | 1963... | Joey Giardello.............. | 1963–65 |
| 1941... | Tony Zale................... | 1941–47 | 1965... | Dick Tiger................... | 1965–66 |
| 1947... | Rocky Graziano.............. | 1947–48 | 1966... | Emile Griffith............... | 1966–67 |
| 1948... | Tony Zale................... | 1948 | 1967... | Nino Benvenuti.............. | 1967 |
| 1948... | Marcel Cerdan............... | 1948–49 | 1967... | Emile Griffith............... | 1967– |

[1] In 1897 there were many claimants to the middleweight title. It is generally considered, however, that Ryan had the best claim. [2] Ketchel and Jack Sullivan both claimed the title. Ketchel clinched it by knocking out Sullivan. [3] Ketchel was shot and killed in 1910. Papke reclaimed the title and Klaus defeated him in 1913 to gain the middleweight crown. [4] Walker relinquished the title in 1931. The NBA and New York State Athletic Commission each sponsored separate tournaments to determine a new champion. During the next ten years Gorilla Jones, Ben Jeby, Marcel Thil, Lou Brouillard, Vince Dundee, Teddy Yarosz, Babe Risko, Freddy Steele, Al Hostak, Solly Krieger, Fred Apostoli, Ceferino Garcia, Ken Overlin, and Billy Soose were all recognized as champions. [5] Robinson retired from the ring in 1952. Olson outpointed Randy Turpin to become world champion in 1953. Robinson returned to the ring in 1955. [6] Robinson's defeat of Basilio in 1958 made him the first boxer ever to win a division title five times. [7] The NBA vacated Robinson's title in 1959 and Fullmer fought Basilio for the title. When, in 1962, he defeated Pender, who outpointed Robinson in 1960, he was universally recognized as champion.

## WELTERWEIGHT CHAMPIONS

Welterweight boxing began in England in 1792. The name "welter" was adopted from an English horse racing weight term. The maximum weight for the division today is 147 pounds.

| YEAR | CHAMPION | REIGN | YEAR | CHAMPION | REIGN |
|------|----------|-------|------|----------|-------|
| 1892... | "Mysterious" Billy Smith...... | 1892–94 | 1934... | Barney Ross................. | 1934 |
| 1894... | Tommy Ryan................. | 1894–96 | 1934... | Jimmy McLarnin............. | 1934–35 |
| 1897... | "Mysterious" Billy Smith [1].... | 1897–1900 | 1935... | Barney Ross................. | 1935–38 |
| 1900... | Rube Ferns.................. | 1900 | 1938... | Henry Armstrong............ | 1938–40 |
| 1900... | Matty Matthews.............. | 1900–01 | 1940... | Fritzie Zivic................. | 1940–41 |
| 1901... | Rube Ferns.................. | 1901 | 1941... | Freddie Cochrane............ | 1941–46 |
| 1901... | Joe Walcott................. | 1901–04 | 1946... | Marty Servo................. | 1946 |
| 1904... | Dixie Kid [2]................. | 1904 | 1946... | Sugar Ray Robinson [4]......... | 1946–51 |
| 1904... | Joe Walcott................. | 1904–06 | 1951... | Johnny Bratton.............. | 1951 |
| 1906... | Honey Mellody.............. | 1906–07 | 1951... | Kid Gavilan [5].............. | 1951–54 |
| 1907... | Mike (Twin) Sullivan [3]....... | 1907–10 | 1954... | Johnny Saxton.............. | 1954–55 |
| 1915... | Ted Lewis................... | 1915–19 | 1955... | Tony DeMarco............... | 1955 |
| 1919... | Jack Britton................. | 1919–22 | 1955... | Carmen Basilio.............. | 1955–56 |
| 1922... | Mickey Walker.............. | 1922–26 | 1956... | Johnny Saxton.............. | 1956 |
| 1926... | Pete Latzo.................. | 1926–27 | 1956... | Carmen Basilio.............. | 1956–57 |
| 1927... | Joe Dundee................. | 1927–29 | 1958... | Virgil Akins [6]............. | 1958 |
| 1929... | Jackie Fields................ | 1929–30 | 1958... | Don Jordan................. | 1958–60 |
| 1930... | Young Jack Thompson........ | 1930 | 1960... | Benny (Kid) Paret........... | 1960–61 |
| 1930... | Tommy Freeman............. | 1930–31 | 1961... | Emile Griffith............... | 1961 |
| 1931... | Young Jack Thompson........ | 1931 | 1961... | Benny (Kid) Paret........... | 1961–62 |
| 1931... | Lou Brouillard............... | 1931–32 | 1962... | Emile Griffith [7]............ | 1962–63 |
| 1932... | Jackie Fields................ | 1932–33 | 1963... | Luis Rodriguez.............. | 1963 |
| 1933... | Young Corbett, 3rd.......... | 1933 | 1963... | Emile Griffith............... | 1963–66 |
| 1933... | Jimmy McLarnin............. | 1933–34 | 1966... | Curtis Cokes [8]............. | 1966– |

[1] Tommy Ryan vacated his title and Smith reclaimed it in 1897. [2] Although the Dixie Kid won on a foul from Walcott, only a few ring experts recognized him as champion. [3] Sullivan vacated his title in 1910 by becoming a middleweight. Lewis, the British champion, was generally recognized as the titleholder when he defeated Jack Britton, outstanding U.S. welterweight, in 1915. [4] Because Servo refused to fight Robinson, the New York State Commission declared his title vacant. Robinson beat Tommy Bell in a 15-round bout in New York City and gained recognition as the world champion. [5] Robinson gave up the crown in 1951 after winning the middleweight title. Kid Gavilan became champion after defeating Johnny Bratton, the NBA champion, and Billy Graham. [6] Basilio vacated the 147-pound championship in 1957. Akins' knockout of Vince Martinez in 1958 gained him the title. [7] Griffith knocked out Paret to regain the title. Paret died of injuries shortly after the bout. [8] Cokes was accepted as titleholder when Griffith became middleweight champion.

## LIGHTWEIGHT CHAMPIONS

The lightweight division of boxing gained recognition in the United States in 1868 when Abe Hicken defeated Pete McGuire. The two fighters called themselves "lightweights" and Hicken claimed the title after the bout. Following Hicken's retirement there was only irregular activity in the lightweight division until 1896, when Kid Lavigne's claim to the title was generally recognized after his defeat of the British champion, Dick Burge.

| YEAR | CHAMPION | REIGN | YEAR | CHAMPION | REIGN |
|------|----------|-------|------|----------|-------|
| 1899... | Frank Erne | 1899–1901 | 1938... | Henry Armstrong | 1938–39 |
| 1901... | Joe Gans | 1901–08 | 1939... | Lou Ambers | 1939–40 |
| 1908... | Battling Nelson | 1908–10 | 1940... | Lew Jenkins | 1940–41 |
| 1910... | Ad Wolgast [1] | 1910–12 | 1941... | Sammy Angott [4] | 1941–42 |
| 1912... | Willie Ritchie | 1912–14 | 1947... | Ike Williams | 1947–51 |
| 1914... | Freddie Welsh | 1914–17 | 1951... | Jimmy Carter | 1951–52 |
| 1917... | Benny Leonard [2] | 1917–24 | 1952... | Lauro Salas | 1952 |
| 1925... | Jimmy Goodrich | 1925 | 1952... | Jimmy Carter | 1952–54 |
| 1925... | Rocky Kansas | 1925–26 | 1954... | Paddy DeMarco | 1954 |
| 1926... | Sammy Mandell | 1926–30 | 1954... | Jimmy Carter | 1954–55 |
| 1930... | Al Singer | 1930 | 1955... | Wallace (Bud) Smith | 1955–56 |
| 1930... | Tony Canzoneri | 1930–33 | 1956... | Joe Brown | 1956–62 |
| 1933... | Barney Ross | 1933–35 | 1962... | Carlos Ortiz | 1962–65 |
| 1935... | Tony Canzoneri [3] | 1935–36 | 1965... | Ismael Laguna | 1965 |
| 1936... | Lou Ambers | 1936–38 | 1965... | Carlos Ortiz | 1965– |

[1] After the 40th round of a 45-round fight, the referee intervened to proclaim Wolgast the winner and save Nelson from further battering.   [2] Leonard retired undefeated. Goodrich was the survivor of an elimination tournament and was acclaimed champion.   [3] Ross, unable to make the weight, relinquished his title. Canzoneri defeated Lou Ambers and took Ross's crown in 1935.   [4] Angott resigned his title in 1942. From 1943 to 1947, the NBA and the New York State Commission recognized different champions. According to New York, champions were Beau Jack (1942–44) and Bob Montgomery (1944–47). According to the NBA, champions were Sammy Angott (returned to ring, 1943–44), Juan Zurita (1944–45), and Ike Williams (1945–47). The dispute was settled in 1947 when Williams defeated Montgomery.

## FEATHERWEIGHT CHAMPIONS

In its earliest years the featherweight division had a variety of claimants to the title. In 1890 George Dixon, an American Negro, knocked out Nunce Wallace of England. Dixon is generally considered the world's first featherweight champion. Since then the champions have been:

| YEAR | CHAMPION | REIGN | YEAR | CHAMPION | REIGN |
|------|----------|-------|------|----------|-------|
| 1890... | George Dixon | 1890–99 | 1933... | Freddie Miller | 1933–36 |
| 1899... | Terry McGovern | 1899–1901 | 1936... | Petey Sarron | 1936–37 |
| 1901... | Young Corbett [1] | 1901–04 | 1937... | Henry Armstrong | 1937–38 |
| 1904... | Abe Attell | 1904 | 1938... | Joey Archibald [4] | 1938–40 |
| 1904... | "Brooklyn" Tommy Sullivan... | 1904–08 | 1940... | Harry Jeffra | 1940–41 |
| 1908... | Abe Attell | 1908–12 | 1941... | Joey Archibald | 1941 |
| 1912... | Johnny Kilbane | 1912–23 | 1941... | Chalky Wright | 1941–42 |
| 1923... | Eugene Criqui | 1923 | 1942... | Willie Pep | 1942–48 |
| 1923... | Johnny Dundee | 1923–25 | 1948... | Sandy Saddler | 1948–49 |
| 1926... | Louis (Kid) Kaplan [2] | 1926–27 | 1949... | Willie Pep | 1949–50 |
| 1927... | Benny Bass [2] | 1927–28 | 1950... | Sandy Saddler | 1950–57 |
| 1928... | Tony Canzoneri | 1928 | 1957... | Kid Bassey [5] | 1957–59 |
| 1928... | Andre Routis | 1928–29 | 1959... | Davey Moore | 1959–63 |
| 1929... | Battling Battalino | 1929–32 | 1963... | Sugar Ramos | 1963–64 |
| 1932... | Tommy Paul [3] | 1932 | 1964... | Vicente Saldivar | 1964– |
| 1932... | Kid Chocolate [3] | 1932–34 | | | |

[1] Corbett never actually made claim to the title although he did knock out McGovern in 1901. Corbett retired from the division in 1904, and the title went to Abe Attell, a leading contender who was within the weight limit.   [2] In 1927, Kaplan outgrew the division and retired. Bass was recognized as champion by the NBA when he defeated Red Chapman.   [3] Battalino relinquished the title in 1932. The NBA held an elimination tournament and Tommy Paul was the winner. The New York State Commission's elimination tournament named Kid Chocolate the winner. In 1934, Chocolate retired from the division, and Freddie Miller, who defeated Paul in 1933, stood alone as champion.   [4] With Armstrong's retirement in 1938, Archibald became champion after defeating the other highest contender, Mike Belloise in 1957.   [5] Saddler vacated his title after an automobile accident in 1957. Bassey won the elimination tournament.

## AMERICAN BAREKNUCKLE BOXING

Jacob Hyer's defeat of Tom Beasley in 1816 marks the first official bareknuckle fight on American soil. Hyer's son, Tom, inherited his father's title and retired after defeating English slugger Yankee Sullivan in 1849. Hyer was succeeded by John C. Morrissey.

Bareknuckle boxing came to an end in the United States in the 1880s. On February 7, 1882, John L. Sullivan knocked out Paddy Ryan in the ninth round at Mississippi City, Mississippi, thus becoming the last of the bareknuckle champions.

# BRIDGE

With a history dating back about 500 years to the early English game of "whisk," bridge is today one of the most popular games in the world. There are an estimated 40,000,000 players in the U.S. and Canada alone.

U.S. tournament bridge is conducted by the American Contract Bridge League, which was organized in 1927. The League has more than 180,000 members in approximately 5,000 affiliated clubs. Three national tournaments are scheduled for 1968: March 8–17 at the Americana Hotel in New York City; July 26–August 4 at the Leamington Hotel in Minneapolis; and November 29–December 8 at the Del Co-ronado Hotel in Coronado, California.

The World Contract Bridge Team Olympiad, held every four years and conducted by the World Bridge Federation, will be played in Deauville, France, in June, 1968. U.S. representatives will be Arthur Robinson and Robert Jordan, William Root and Alvin Roth, Edgar Kaplan and Norman Kay, and alternates Philip Feldesman and Ira Rubin. Italy won the 1964 competition.

The Bermuda Bowl series, an international event that was held in Miami in 1967, was won by Italy for the ninth straight time; the U.S. was second for the ninth straight time.

# CHESS

Chess, a game that has fascinated men for centuries, probably originated in India, spread to Persia, and may have been introduced into Europe by the Moors. By the 13th century it was played widely in western Europe. The first recorded chess tournament was held in 1562 between Spanish and Italian players. Among the players who attained particular distinction between 1750 and 1850 were François Philidor, Alexandre Deschappelles, and Louis de la Bourdonnais of France, and Howard Staunton of England. The first international chess tournament was held in London in 1851 and was won by Adolphe Anderssen.

The first American world chess champion was 20-year-old Paul C. Morphy of New Orleans, Louisiana, who was the first-prize winner in the American Chess Congress international tournament held in 1857. During this championship Morphy's opponent, Louis Paulsen, contemplated for 14 hours and 28 minutes before making one move.

## WORLD CHESS CHAMPIONS

| YEARS | CHAMPION | COUNTRY | YEARS | CHAMPION | COUNTRY |
|---|---|---|---|---|---|
| 1851–58 | Adolph Anderssen ..... | Germany | 1937–46 | Alexander A. Alekhine*. | France |
| 1858–62 | Paul C. Morphy........ | United States | 1948–57 | Mikhail Botvinnik...... | U.S.S.R. |
| 1862–66 | Adolph Anderssen...... | Germany | 1957–58 | Vassily Smyslov........ | U.S.S.R. |
| 1866–94 | Wilhelm Steinitz........ | Austria, U.S. | 1958–60 | Mikhail Botvinnik...... | U.S.S.R. |
| 1894–1921 | Emanuel Lasker........ | Germany | 1960–61 | Mikhail Tal............ | U.S.S.R. |
| 1921–27 | José R. Capablanca..... | Cuba | 1961–62 | Mikhail Botvinnik...... | U.S.S.R. |
| 1927–35 | Alexander A. Alekhine.. | France | 1962– | Tigran Petrosyan....... | U.S.S.R. |
| 1935–37 | Max Euwe............. | The Netherlands | | | |

* Dr. Alekhine died in 1946, leaving the title vacant for two years.

## U.S. CHESS CHAMPIONS

Before 1936 the U.S. chess championship was decided by a match between the recognized champion and a challenger. Since then tournament play, or a kind of round robin, has determined the U.S. champion. Robert (Bobby) Fischer is the current champion.

| YEARS | CHAMPION | YEARS | CHAMPION |
|---|---|---|---|
| 1852–62 | Paul C. Morphy | 1936–44 | Samuel Reshevsky |
| 1871–87 | George H. Mackenzie | 1944–46 | Arnold S. Denker |
| 1887–92 | Max Judd | 1948 * | Herman Steiner |
| 1892–94 | Simon Lipschultz | 1951–53 | Larry Evans |
| 1894 | Albert B. Hodges | 1954–57 | Arthur B. Bisguier |
| 1894–97 | Jackson W. Showalter | 1958–61 | Robert Fischer |
| 1897–1906 | Harry Nelson Pillsbury | 1962 | Larry Evans |
| 1906–09 | Jackson W. Showalter | 1964– | Robert Fischer |
| 1909–36 | Frank J. Marshall | | |

* The U.S. chess championship tournament was not held from 1948 to 1951 nor in 1965.

# FISHING

## WORLD FRESH-WATER FISHING RECORDS

The table below, listing the current world fresh-water fishing records (in alphabetical order) and record-holders, was prepared from information supplied by *Field & Stream* magazine.

| SPECIES | WEIGHT (lbs.-ozs.) | LENGTH (inches) | GIRTH (inches) | WHERE CAUGHT | DATE | ANGLER |
|---|---|---|---|---|---|---|
| Bass, Largemouth.... | 22-4 | 32½ | 28½ | Montgomery Lake, Ga. | June 2, 1932 | George W. Perry |
| Bass, Smallmouth... | 11-15 | 27 | 21⅔ | Dale Hollow Lake, Ky. | July 9, 1955 | David L. Hayes |
| Bass, Spotted....... | 8 | 24 | 18¼ | Smith Lake, Alabama.. | Mar. 7, 1966 | Bob Hamilton |
| Bass, White......... | 5-2 | 19 | 15½ | Grenada Dam, Miss.... | July 9, 1960 | Eddy Vaughn |
| Bluegill............. | 4-12 | 15 | 18¼ | Ketona Lake, Ala...... | Apr. 9, 1950 | T. S. Hudson |
| Bullhead, Black..... | 8 | 24 | 17¾ | Lake Waccabuc, N.Y.... | Aug. 1, 1951 | Kani Evans |
| Carp............... | 55-5 | 42 | 31 | Clearwater Lake, Minn. | July 10, 1952 | Frank J. Ledwein |
| Catfish, Blue....... | 97 | 57 | 37 | Missouri River, S. Dak.. | Sept. 16, 1959 | Edward B. Elliott |
| Catfish, Channel..... | 58 | 47¼ | 29⅛ | Santee-Cooper Res., South Carolina...... | July 7, 1964 | W. B. Whaley |
| Char, Arctic........ | 27-4 | 40¼ | 26½ | Tree River, N.W.T...... | Sept. 2, 1963 | William Murphy |
| Crappie, Black...... | 5 | 19¼ | 18⅝ | Santee-Cooper Res., South Carolina...... | Mar. 15, 1957 | Paul E. Foust |
| Crappie, White...... | 5-3 | 21 | 19 | Enid Dam, Miss........ | July 31, 1957 | Fred L. Bright |
| Dolly Varden........ | 32 | 40½ | 29¾ | L. Pend Oreille, Idaho.. | Oct. 27, 1949 | N. L. Higgins |
| Gar, Alligator....... | 279 | 93 | — | Rio Grande, Texas..... | Dec. 2, 1951 | Bill Valverde |
| Gar, Longnose....... | 50-5 | 72¼ | 22¼ | Trinity River, Texas.... | July 30, 1954 | Townsend Miller |
| Grayling, Arctic...... | 5 | 21 | 11 | Great Slave L., N.W.Territories, Canada | Aug. 5, 1959 | William G. Clark |
| Muskellunge........ | 69-15 | 64½ | 31¾ | St. Lawrence R., N.Y... | Sept. 22, 1957 | Arthur Lawton |
| Perch, White........ | 4-12 | 19½ | 13 | Messalonskee Lake, Me. | June 4, 1949 | Mrs. Earl Small |
| Perch, Yellow....... | 4-3½ | — | — | Bordentown, N.J....... | May 1865 | Dr. C. C. Abbot |
| Pickerel, Chain...... | 9-6 | 31 | 14 | Homerville, Georgia... | Feb. 17, 1961 | Baxley McQuaig, Jr. |
| Pike, Northern...... | 46-2 | 52½ | 25 | Sacandaga Res., N.Y... | Sept. 15, 1940 | Peter Dubuc |
| Salmon, Atlantic.... | 79-2 | — | — | Tana River, Norway.... | 1928 | Henrik Henriksen |
| Salmon, Chinook.... | 92 | 58½ | 36 | Skeena River, B.C..... | July 19, 1959 | Heinz Wichmann |
| Salmon, Landlocked | 22-8 | 36 | — | Sebago Lake, Maine... | Aug. 1, 1907 | Edward Blakely |
| Salmon, Coho or Silver | 31 | — | — | Cowichan Bay, B.C..... | Oct. 11, 1947 | Mrs. Lee Hallberg |
| Sauger............. | 8-5 | 28 | — | Niobrara, Nebraska.... | Oct. 22, 1961 | Mrs. Petty Tepner |
| Sturgeon, White..... | 360 | 111 | 86 | Snake River, Idaho.... | Apr. 24, 1956 | Willard Cravens |
| Trout, Brook........ | 14-8 | 31½ | 11½ | Nipigon River, Ontario. | July 1916 | Dr. W. J. Cook |
| Trout, Brown........ | 39-8 | — | — | Loch Awe, Scotland.... | 1866 | W. Muir |
| Trout, Cutthroat..... | 41 | 39 | — | Pyramid Lake, Nevada............ | Dec. 1925 | John Skimmerhorn |
| Trout, Golden....... | 11 | 28 | 16 | Cook's Lake, Wyoming. | Aug. 5, 1948 | Chas. S. Reed |
| Trout, Lake......... | 63-2 | 51½ | 32¾ | Lake Superior......... | May 25, 1952 | Hubert Hammers |
| Trout, Rainbow, Steelhead, or Kamloops......... | 37 | 40½ | 28 | L. Pend Oreille, Idaho. | Nov. 25, 1947 | Wes Hamlet |
| Trout, Sunapee...... | 11-8 | 33 | 17¼ | Lake Sunapee, N.H.... | Aug. 1, 1954 | Ernest Theoharis |
| Walleye............. | 25 | 41 | 29 | Old Hickory Lake, Tenn................ | Aug. 1, 1960 | Mabry Harper |
| Whitefish, Mountain.. | 5 | 19 | 14 | Athabasca R., Alberta. | June 3, 1963 | Orville Welch |

## FLY AND BAIT CASTING NATIONAL CHAMPIONS: 1967

American Casting Association, 59th Annual Tournament, Nashville, Tennessee

| OFFICIAL EVENTS—MEN | COMBINED CHAMPION | SCORE |
|---|---|---|
| All Around.............................. | Zack Willson, Jr., St. Charles, Missouri................ | — |
| All Distance............................. | Zack Willson, Jr., St. Charles, Missouri................ | 3,316 ft.[1] |
| All Accuracy............................. | Zack Willson, Jr., St. Charles, Missouri................ | 392 points |
| Distance Baits.......................... | Zack Willson, Jr., St. Charles, Missouri................ | 2,333 ft.[2] |
| Distance Flies.......................... | Dave Cohen, San Francisco, California................ | 1,011 ft.[3] |
| Accuracy Baits.......................... | Zack Willson, Jr., St. Charles, Missouri................ | 194 points |
| Accuracy Flies.......................... | Eugene Lentz, St. Louis, Missouri..................... | 199 points |
| OFFICIAL EVENTS—WOMEN | | |
| All Accuracy............................. | Mel Gavin, St. Louis, Missouri........................ | 389 points |
| Accuracy Baits.......................... | Mel Gavin, St. Louis, Missouri........................ | 193 points |
| | Mollie Schneider, Jeffersonville, Indiana.............. | 193 points |
| Accuracy Flies.......................... | Mel Gavin, St. Louis, Missouri........................ | 192 points |

[1] Total measure of 12 casts. [2] Total measure of six casts. [3] Total measure of the six best casts.

## SALTWATER FISHING ALL-TACKLE RECORDS

The appeal of saltwater fishing continues to grow as the number of powerboat owners increases. The records below were supplied by the International Game Fish Association.

| SPECIES | WEIGHT (in lbs. and oz.) | LENGTH (in ft. and in.) | GIRTH (in inches) | WHERE CAUGHT | DATE | ANGLER |
|---|---|---|---|---|---|---|
| Albacore............ | 69–2 | 3′ 10″ | 32 | Montauk, New York... | Aug. 21, 1964 | Larry R. Kranz |
| (Three-way tie) | 69–1 | 4′ ¼″ | 33¼ | Hudson Canyon, N. J... | Oct. 8, 1961 | Walter C. Timm |
| | 69 | 3′ 6″ | 32½ | St. Helena, Atlantic Ocean............ | Apr. 7, 1956 | P. Allen |
| Amberjack.......... | 149 | 5′ 11″ | 41¾ | Bermuda............ | June 21, 1964 | Peter Simons |
| Barracuda.......... | 103–4 | 5′ 6″ | 31¼ | West End, Bahamas.... | Aug. 11, 1932 | C. E. Benet |
| California Black Sea Bass.......... | 557–3 | 7′ 4¼″ | 78 | Catalina Island, Calif... | July 1, 1962 | Richard M. Lane |
| California White Sea Bass.......... | 83–12 | 5′ 5½″ | 34 | San Felipe, Mexico.... | Mar. 31, 1953 | L. C. Baumgardner |
| Channel Bass........ | 83 | 4′ 4″ | 29 | Cape Charles, Virginia . | Aug. 5, 1949 | Zack Waters, Jr. |
| Giant Sea Bass....... | 680 | 7′ 1½″ | 66 | Fernandina Beach, Fla. | May 20, 1961 | Lynn Joyner |
| Sea Bass........... | 8 | 1′ 10″ | 19 | Nantucket Sound, Massachusetts...... | May 13, 1951 | H. R. Rider |
| Striped Bass......... | 73 | 5′ | 30½ | Vineyard Sound, Mass. | Aug. 17, 1913 | C. B. Church |
| Blackfish or Tautog... | 21–6 | 2′ 7½″ | 23½ | Cape May, New Jersey | June 12, 1954 | R. N. Sheafer |
| Bluefish............ | 24–3 | 3′ 5″ | 22 | San Miguel, Azores.... | Aug. 27, 1953 | M. A. da Silva Veloso |
| Bonefish............ | 19 | 3′ 3⅝″ | 17 | Zululand, South Africa | May 26, 1962 | Brian W. Batchelor |
| Oceanic Bonito....... | 39–15 | 3′ 3″ | 28 | Walker Cay, Bahamas.. | Jan. 21, 1952 | F. Drowley |
| Cobia.............. | 102 | 5′ 10″ | 34 | Cape Charles, Virginia | July 3, 1938 | J. E. Stansbury |
| Cod............... | 81 | 4′ 6⅞″ | 35½ | Brielle, N.J........... | Mar. 15, 1967 | Joseph Chesla |
| Dolphin............ | 76–12 | 5′ 10½″ | 35 | Bimini Bahamas...... | May 28, 1964 | Charles J. Costello |
| Black Drum.......... | 92–8 | 4′ 5″ | 40 | Willis Wharf, Va....... | June 12, 1967 | Gary Hilton Kelley |
| Flounder............ | 22–1 | 3′ 1″ | 35 | Caleta Horcon, Chile... | Dec. 8, 1965 | S. I. Aguirrezabal |
| Kingfish or Tanguigue | 81 | 5′ 11½″ | 29¼ | Karachi, Pakistan..... | Aug. 27, 1960 | George E. Rusinak |
| Black Marlin......... | 1,560 | 14′ 6″ | 81 | Cabo Blanco, Peru..... | Aug. 4, 1953 | Alfred C. Glassell, Jr. |
| Blue Marlin......... | 814 | 13′ 8″ | 69 | St. Thomas, Virgin Is... | July 26, 1964 | John Battles |
| Pacific Blue Marlin.... | 1,100 | 13′ 9½″ | 79½ | Le Morne, Mauritius... | Feb. 20, 1966 | Andre D'Hotman |
| (Tie) | 1,100 | 14′ 4¾″ | 72½ | Kailua Kona, Hawaii... | May 23, 1967 | Hale L. Erickson |
| Striped Marlin........ | 465 | 10′ 6″ | 65 | Mayor Island, New Zealand........... | Feb. 27, 1948 | James Black |
| White Marlin......... | 161 | 8′ 8″ | 33 | Miami Beach, Florida.. | Mar. 20, 1938 | L. F. Hooper |
| Permit............. | 50 | 3′ 7″ | 34½ | Miami, Florida........ | Mar. 27, 1965 | Robert F. Miller |
| Pollack............. | 43 | 4′ | 29 | Brielle, New Jersey.... | Oct. 21, 1964 | Philip Barlow |
| Rainbow Runner...... | 30–15 | 3′ 11″ | 22 | Kauai, Hawaii......... | Apr. 27, 1963 | Holbrook Goodale |
| Roosterfish.......... | 114 | 5′ 4″ | 33 | La Paz, Mexico........ | June 1, 1960 | Abe Sackheim |
| Atlantic Sailfish...... | 141–1 | 8′ 5″ | — | Ivory Coast, Africa..... | Jan. 26, 1961 | Tony Burnand |
| Pacific Sailfish........ | 221 | 10′ 9″ | — | Santa Cruz Island, Galápagos Islands... | Feb. 12, 1947 | C. W. Stewart |
| Blue Shark.......... | 410 | 11′ 6″ | 52 | Rockport, Mass........ | Sept. 1, 1960 | Richard C. Webster |
| Mako Shark.......... | 1,000 | 12′ | — | Mayor Island, New Zealand........... | Mar. 14, 1943 | B. D. H. Ross |
| Man-Eater or White Shark....... | 2,664 | 16′ 10″ | 114 | Ceduna, So. Australia.. | Apr. 21, 1959 | Alfred Dean |
| Porbeagle Shark...... | 400–8 | 7′ 9½″ | 57½ | Fire Island, New York.. | May 16, 1965 | James T. Kirkup |
| Thresher Shark....... | 922 | — | — | Bay of Islands, New Zealand........... | Mar. 21, 1937 | W. W. Dowding |
| Tiger Shark.......... | 1,780 | 13′ 10½″ | 103 | Cherry Grove, S.C...... | June 14, 1964 | Walter Maxwell |
| Snook or Robalo...... | 52–6 | 4′ 1½″ | 26 | La Paz, Mexico........ | Jan. 9, 1963 | Jane Haywood |
| Swordfish........... | 1,182 | 14′ 11¼″ | 78 | Iquique, Chile......... | May 7, 1953 | L. Marron |
| Tarpon............. | 283 | 7′ 2⅗″ | — | Lake Maracaibo, Venezuela......... | Mar. 19, 1956 | M. Salazar |
| Allison or Yellowfin Tuna............. | 269–8 | 6′ 9″ | 53 | Hanalei, Hawaii....... | May 30, 1962 | Henry Nishikawa |
| Atlantic Big-Eyed Tuna | 295 | 6′ 6½″ | 40 | San Miguel, Azores.... | July 8, 1960 | Dr. Arsenio Cordeiro |
| Pacific Big-Eyed Tuna | 435 | 7′ 9″ | 63½ | Cabo Blanco, Peru..... | Apr. 17, 1957 | Dr. Russel V. A. Lee |
| Blackfin Tuna........ | 36–4 | 3′ 1½″ | 28⅛ | Challenger Bank, Bermuda............ | Aug. 6, 1967 | Raymond C. McPherson |
| (Tie) | 36 | 3′ ¼″ | 28⅞ | Bermuda............ | July 14, 1963 | Joseph E. Baptiste, Jr. |
| Bluefin Tuna......... | 977 | 9′ 8″ | 94½ | St. Ann Bay, Nova Scotia............. | Sept. 4, 1950 | D. Mcl. Hodgson |
| Wahoo.............. | 149 | 6′ 7¾″ | 37½ | Cat Cay, Bahamas..... | June 15, 1962 | John Pirovano |
| Weakfish............ | 19–8 | 3′ 1″ | 23¾ | Trinidad, West Indies.. | Apr. 13, 1962 | Dennis B. Hall |
| Spotted Weakfish..... | 15–3 | 2′ 10½″ | 20½ | Ft. Pierce, Florida..... | Jan. 13, 1949 | C. W. Hubbard |
| Yellowtail........... | 111 | 5′ 2″ | 38 | Bay of Islands, New Zealand........... | June 11, 1961 | A. F. Plim |

# FOOTBALL (PROFESSIONAL)

On June 8, 1966, the American and National Football Leagues decided to end their competition for talent and form a merged structure. The NFL, founded in 1922, and the AFL, started in 1960, appointed Pete Roselle as "Football Czar" of a potential 28-team, four-division league that is to take shape in 1970.

The only loser will be the college player, who for the past six years has been able to extract large bonus payments from both leagues. Joe Namath, University of Alabama quarterback, reportedly received $400,000 from the New York Jets (AFL) in 1965, and Donny Anderson, Texas Tech running back, signed a record $700,000 contract wtih the NFL's Green Bay Packers.

The merger movement accelerated when the NFL's New York Giants signed Pete Gogolak, a free agent place-kicker who left the Buffalo Bills of the rival league. The AFL retaliated by signing John Brodie, quarterback of the San Francisco 49ers of the NFL. Brodie intended to play for the Houston Oilers for a reported $750,000 but returned to the 49ers.

Conditions of the merger called for the AFL to pay an indemnity of $18 million over 20 years. An unnamed tenth AFL team will have to pay an entrance fee of $7.5 million.

On January 15, 1967, the NFL champions, the Green Bay Packers, met the AFL's top team, the Kansas City Chiefs, in the "Super Bowl." The game, perhaps the most talked about ever, was played in the Los Angeles Coliseum before 63,036 fans. The Packers led at half time by the thin margin of 14–10. Carrying the prestige of the older league into the game, the Packers swiftly scored two touchdowns at the outset of the second half and went on to a 35 to 10 win.

The Super Bowl game was one of the richest events in the history of American team sports. Gate receipts totaled $750,000 and an additional $2 million was paid for the rights to televise the game. Each Packer player received $15,000 and each Chief got $7,500.

Green Bay quarterback Bart Starr was named NFL Player of the Year. Tom Landry of Dallas was voted Coach of the Year.

In the AFL, Jim Nance of the Boston Patriots was the choice for Player of the Year. Mike Holovak of Boston and Hank Stram of Kansas were jointly named Coach of the Year.

## NFL CONFERENCE CHAMPIONS

| YEAR | EASTERN CONFERENCE CHAMPIONS | W | L | T | YEAR | WESTERN CONFERENCE CHAMPIONS | W | L | T |
|---|---|---|---|---|---|---|---|---|---|
| 1933 | New York Giants | 11 | 3 | 0 | 1933 | Chicago Bears | 10 | 2 | 1 |
| 1934 | New York Giants | 8 | 5 | 0 | 1934 | Chicago Bears | 13 | 0 | 0 |
| 1935 | New York Giants | 9 | 3 | 0 | 1935 | Detroit Lions | 7 | 3 | 2 |
| 1936 | Boston Redskins | 7 | 5 | 0 | 1936 | Green Bay Packers | 10 | 1 | 1 |
| 1937 | Washington Redskins | 8 | 3 | 0 | 1937 | Chicago Bears | 9 | 1 | 1 |
| 1938 | New York Giants | 8 | 2 | 1 | 1938 | Green Bay Packers | 8 | 3 | 0 |
| 1939 | New York Giants | 9 | 1 | 1 | 1939 | Green Bay Packers | 9 | 2 | 0 |
| 1940 | Washington Redskins | 9 | 2 | 0 | 1940 | Chicago Bears | 8 | 3 | 0 |
| 1941 | New York Giants | 8 | 3 | 0 | 1941 | Chicago Bears | 10 | 1 | 1* |
| 1942 | Washington Redskins | 10 | 1 | 1 | 1942 | Chicago Bears | 11 | 0 | 0 |
| 1943 | Washington Redskins | 6 | 3 | 1* | 1943 | Chicago Bears | 8 | 1 | 1 |
| 1944 | New York Giants | 8 | 1 | 1 | 1944 | Green Bay Packers | 8 | 2 | 0 |
| 1945 | Washington Redskins | 8 | 2 | 0 | 1945 | Cleveland Rams | 9 | 1 | 0 |
| 1946 | New York Giants | 7 | 3 | 1 | 1946 | Chicago Bears | 8 | 2 | 1 |
| 1947 | Philadelphia Eagles | 8 | 4 | 0* | 1947 | Chicago Cardinals | 9 | 3 | 0 |
| 1948 | Philadelphia Eagles | 9 | 2 | 1 | 1948 | Chicago Cardinals | 11 | 1 | 0 |
| 1949 | Philadelphia Eagles | 11 | 1 | 0 | 1949 | Los Angeles Rams | 8 | 2 | 2 |
| 1950 | Cleveland Browns | 10 | 2 | 0* | 1950 | Los Angeles Rams | 9 | 3 | 0* |
| 1951 | Cleveland Browns | 11 | 1 | 0 | 1951 | Los Angeles Rams | 8 | 4 | 0 |
| 1952 | Cleveland Browns | 8 | 4 | 0 | 1952 | Detroit Lions | 9 | 3 | 0* |
| 1953 | Cleveland Browns | 11 | 1 | 0 | 1953 | Detroit Lions | 10 | 2 | 0 |
| 1954 | Cleveland Browns | 9 | 3 | 0 | 1954 | Detroit Lions | 9 | 2 | 1 |
| 1955 | Cleveland Browns | 9 | 2 | 1 | 1955 | Los Angeles Rams | 8 | 3 | 1 |
| 1956 | New York Giants | 8 | 3 | 1 | 1956 | Chicago Bears | 9 | 2 | 1 |
| 1957 | Cleveland Browns | 9 | 2 | 1 | 1957 | Detroit Lions | 8 | 4 | 0* |
| 1958 | New York Giants | 9 | 3 | 0* | 1958 | Baltimore Colts | 9 | 3 | 0 |
| 1959 | New York Giants | 10 | 2 | 0 | 1959 | Baltimore Colts | 9 | 3 | 0 |
| 1960 | Philadelphia Eagles | 10 | 2 | 0 | 1960 | Green Bay Packers | 8 | 4 | 0 |
| 1961 | New York Giants | 10 | 3 | 1 | 1961 | Green Bay Packers | 11 | 3 | 0 |
| 1962 | New York Giants | 12 | 2 | 0 | 1962 | Green Bay Packers | 13 | 1 | 0 |
| 1963 | New York Giants | 11 | 3 | 0 | 1963 | Chicago Bears | 11 | 1 | 2 |
| 1964 | Cleveland Browns | 10 | 3 | 1 | 1964 | Baltimore Colts | 12 | 2 | 0 |
| 1965 | Cleveland Browns | 11 | 3 | 0 | 1965 | Green Bay Packers | 10 | 3 | 1 |
| 1966 | Dallas Cowboys | 10 | 3 | 1 | 1966 | Green Bay Packers | 12 | 2 | 0 |

* Division playoff winner.

Green Bay quarterback Bart Starr led Packers to 35-10 victory over Kansas City Chiefs in 1967 Super Bowl game.

## NFL CHAMPIONSHIP PLAYOFFS

| | | | | | |
|---|---|---|---|---|---|
| 1933 | Chicago Bears 23, New York 21 | 1945 | Cleveland 15, Washington 14 | 1955 | Cleveland 38, Los Angeles 14 |
| 1934 | New York 30, Chicago Bears 13 | 1946 | Chicago Bears 24, New York 14 | 1956 | New York 47, Chicago Bears 7 |
| 1935 | Detroit 26, New York 7 | 1947 | Chicago Cardinals 28, | 1957 | Detroit 59, Cleveland 14 |
| 1936 | Green Bay 21, Boston 6 | | Philadelphia 21 | 1958 | Baltimore 23, New York 17* |
| 1937 | Washington 28, Chicago Bears 21 | 1948 | Philadelphia 7, Chicago | 1959 | Baltimore 31, New York 16 |
| 1938 | New York 23, Green Bay 17 | | Cardinals 0 | 1960 | Philadelphia 17, Green Bay 13 |
| 1939 | Green Bay 27, New York 0 | 1949 | Philadelphia 14, Los Angeles 0 | 1961 | Green Bay 37, New York 0 |
| 1940 | Chicago Bears 73, Washington 0 | 1950 | Cleveland 30, Los Angeles 28 | 1962 | Green Bay 16, New York 7 |
| 1941 | Chicago Bears 37, New York 9 | 1951 | Los Angeles 24, Cleveland 17 | 1963 | Chicago 14, New York 10 |
| 1942 | Washington 14, Chicago Bears 6 | 1952 | Detroit 17, Cleveland 7 | 1964 | Cleveland 27, Baltimore 0 |
| 1943 | Chicago Bears 41, Washington 21 | 1953 | Detroit 17, Cleveland 16 | 1965 | Green Bay 23, Cleveland 12 |
| 1944 | Green Bay 14, New York 7 | 1954 | Cleveland 56, Detroit 10 | 1966 | Green Bay 34, Dallas 27 |

* Won at 8:15 of "sudden death" overtime period.

## STARS OF THE NATIONAL FOOTBALL LEAGUE

| YEAR | LEADING PASSER AND TEAM | A[1] | C[2] | YG[3] | YEAR | LEADING PASSER AND TEAM | A[1] | C[2] | YG[3] |
|---|---|---|---|---|---|---|---|---|---|
| 1932 | Arnie Herber, Green Bay..... | 101 | 37 | 639 | 1950 | Norm Van Brocklin, L.A...... | 233 | 127 | 2,061 |
| 1933 | Harry Newman, New York.... | 132 | 53 | 963 | 1951 | Bob Waterfield, L.A.......... | 176 | 88 | 1,556 |
| 1934 | Arnie Herber, Green Bay..... | 115 | 42 | 799 | 1952 | Norm Van Brocklin, L.A...... | 205 | 113 | 1,736 |
| 1935 | Ed Danowski, New York...... | 113 | 57 | 795 | 1953 | Otto Graham, Cleveland...... | 258 | 167 | 2,722 |
| 1936 | Arnie Herber, Green Bay..... | 173 | 77 | 1,239 | 1954 | Norm Van Brocklin, L.A...... | 260 | 139 | 2,637 |
| 1937 | Sammy Baugh, Washington... | 171 | 81 | 1,127 | 1955 | Otto Graham, Cleveland...... | 185 | 98 | 1,721 |
| 1938 | Ed Danowski, New York...... | 129 | 70 | 848 | 1956 | Ed Brown, Chicago Bears..... | 168 | 96 | 1,667 |
| 1939 | Parker Hall, Cleveland....... | 208 | 106 | 1,227 | 1957 | Tom O'Connell, Cleveland.... | 110 | 63 | 1,229 |
| 1940 | Sammy Baugh, Washington... | 177 | 111 | 1,367 | 1958 | Eddie LeBaron, Washington... | 145 | 79 | 1,365 |
| 1941 | Cecil Isbell, Green Bay....... | 206 | 117 | 1,479 | 1959 | Charley Conerly, New York... | 194 | 113 | 1,706 |
| 1942 | Cecil Isbell, Green Bay....... | 268 | 146 | 2,021 | 1960 | Milt Plum, Cleveland........ | 250 | 151 | 2,297 |
| 1943 | Sammy Baugh, Washington... | 239 | 133 | 1,754 | 1961 | Milt Plum, Cleveland........ | 302 | 177 | 2,416 |
| 1944 | Frank Filchock, Washington... | 147 | 84 | 1,139 | 1962 | Bart Starr, Green Bay........ | 285 | 178 | 2,438 |
| 1945 | Sammy Baugh, Washington... | 182 | 128 | 1,669 | 1963 | Y. A. Tittle, New York....... | 367 | 221 | 3,145[4] |
| 1946 | Bob Waterfield, Los Angeles... | 251 | 127 | 1,747 | 1964 | Bart Starr, Green Bay....... | 272 | 163 | 2,144 |
| 1947 | Sammy Baugh, Washington... | 354 | 210 | 2,938 | 1965 | Rudy Bukich, Chicago Bears.. | 312 | 176 | 2,641 |
| 1948 | Tom Thompson, Philadelphia | 246 | 141 | 1,965 | 1966 | Bart Starr, Green Bay........ | 251 | 156 | 2,257 |
| 1949 | Sammy Baugh, Washington... | 255 | 145 | 1,903 | | | | | |

[1] Attempts.   [2] Completions.   [3] Yards gained.   [4] Record.

STARS OF THE NATIONAL FOOTBALL LEAGUE (*continued*)

| YEAR | LEADING PASS RECEIVER AND TEAM | PASSES RECEIVED | YEAR | LEADING PASS RECEIVER AND TEAM | PASSES RECEIVED |
|------|-------------------------------|-----------------|------|-------------------------------|-----------------|
| 1932 | Luke Johnsos, Chicago Bears | 24 | 1950 | Tom Fears, Los Angeles | 84 |
| 1933 | John Kelley, Brooklyn | 21 | 1951 | Elroy Hirsch, Los Angeles | 66 |
| 1934 | Joe Carter, Philadelphia | 16 | 1952 | Mac Speedie, Cleveland | 62 |
| 1935 | Tod Goodwin, New York | 26 | 1953 | Pete Pihos, Philadelphia | 63 |
| 1936 | Don Hutson, Green Bay | 34 | 1954 | Pete Pihos, Philadelphia [1] | 60 |
| 1937 | Don Hutson, Green Bay | 41 |  | Billy Wilson, San Francisco [1] | 60 |
| 1938 | Gaynell Tinsley, Chicago Cardinals | 41 | 1955 | Pete Pihos, Philadelphia | 62 |
| 1939 | Don Hutson, Green Bay | 34 | 1956 | Billy Wilson, San Francisco | 60 |
| 1940 | Don Looney, Philadelphia | 58 | 1957 | Billy Wilson, San Francisco | 52 |
| 1941 | Don Hutson, Green Bay | 58 | 1958 | Ray Berry, Baltimore [1] | 56 |
| 1942 | Don Hutson, Green Bay | 74 |  | Pete Retzlaff, Philadelphia [1] | 56 |
| 1943 | Don Hutson, Green Bay | 47 | 1959 | Ray Berry, Baltimore | 66 |
| 1944 | Don Hutson, Green Bay | 58 | 1960 | Ray Berry, Baltimore | 74 |
| 1945 | Don Hutson, Green Bay | 47 | 1961 | Jim Phillips, Los Angeles | 78 |
| 1946 | Jim Benton, Los Angeles | 63 | 1962 | Bobby Mitchell, Washington | 72 |
| 1947 | Jim Keane, Chicago Bears | 64 | 1963 | Bobby Joe Conrad, St. Louis | 73 |
| 1948 | Tom Fears, Los Angeles | 51 | 1964 | Johnny Morris, Chicago Bears | 93 [2] |
| 1949 | Tom Fears, Los Angeles | 77 | 1965 | Dave Parks, San Francisco | 80 |
|  |  |  | 1966 | Charles Taylor, Washington | 72 |

[1] Tie.   [2] Record.

| YEAR | RUSHING LEADER AND TEAM | YARDS GAINED | YEAR | RUSHING LEADER AND TEAM | YARDS GAINED |
|------|------------------------|--------------|------|------------------------|--------------|
| 1932 | Bob Campiglio, Stapleton, New York | 504 | 1950 | Marion Motley, Cleveland | 810 |
| 1933 | Cliff Battles, Boston | 737 | 1951 | Eddie Price, New York | 971 |
| 1934 | Beattie Feathers, Chicago Bears | 1,004 | 1952 | Dan Towler, Los Angeles | 894 |
| 1935 | Doug Russell, Chicago Cardinals | 499 | 1953 | Joe Perry, San Francisco | 1,018 |
| 1936 | Tuffy Leemans, New York | 830 | 1954 | Joe Perry, San Francisco | 1,049 |
| 1937 | Cliff Battles, Washington | 874 | 1955 | Alan Ameche, Baltimore | 961 |
| 1938 | Whizzer White, Pittsburgh | 567 | 1956 | Rick Casares, Chicago Bears | 1,126 |
| 1939 | Bill Osmanski, Chicago Bears | 699 | 1957 | Jimmy Brown, Cleveland | 942 |
| 1940 | Whizzer White, Detroit | 514 | 1958 | Jimmy Brown, Cleveland | 1,527 |
| 1941 | Pug Manders, Brooklyn | 486 | 1959 | Jimmy Brown, Cleveland | 1,329 |
| 1942 | Bill Dudley, Pittsburgh | 696 | 1960 | Jimmy Brown, Cleveland | 1,257 |
| 1943 | Bill Paschal, New York | 572 | 1961 | Jimmy Brown, Cleveland | 1,408 |
| 1944 | Bill Paschal, New York | 737 | 1962 | Jim Taylor, Green Bay | 1,474 |
| 1945 | Steve Van Buren, Philadelphia | 832 | 1963 | Jimmy Brown, Cleveland | 1,863 [1] |
| 1946 | Bill Dudley, Pittsburgh | 604 | 1964 | Jimmy Brown, Cleveland | 1,446 |
| 1947 | Steve Van Buren, Philadelphia | 1,008 | 1965 | Jimmy Brown, Cleveland | 1,544 |
| 1948 | Steve Van Buren, Philadelphia | 845 | 1966 | Gale Sayers, Chicago Bears | 1,231 |
| 1949 | Steve Van Buren, Philadelphia | 1,146 |  |  |  |

[1] Record.

| YEAR | SCORING LEADER AND TEAM | POINTS | YEAR | SCORING LEADER AND TEAM | POINTS |
|------|------------------------|--------|------|------------------------|--------|
| 1932 | Earl Clark, Portsmouth | 39 |  | Gene Roberts, New York [1] | 102 |
| 1933 | Ken Strong, New York [1] | 64 | 1950 | Doak Walker, Detroit | 128 |
|  | Glenn Presnell, Portsmouth [1] | 64 | 1951 | Elroy Hirsch, Los Angeles | 102 |
| 1934 | Jack Manders, Chicago Bears | 79 | 1952 | Gordon Soltau, San Francisco | 94 |
| 1935 | Earl Clark, Detroit | 55 | 1953 | Gordon Soltau, San Francisco | 114 |
| 1936 | Earl Clark, Detroit | 73 | 1954 | Bob Walston, Philadelphia | 114 |
| 1937 | Jack Manders, Chicago Bears | 69 | 1955 | Doak Walker, Detroit | 96 |
| 1938 | Clark Hinkle, Green Bay | 58 | 1956 | Bobby Lane, Detroit | 99 |
| 1939 | Andy Farkas, Washington | 68 | 1957 | Sam Baker, Washington [1] | 77 |
| 1940 | Don Hutson, Green Bay | 57 |  | Lou Groza, Cleveland [1] | 77 |
| 1941 | Don Hutson, Green Bay | 95 | 1958 | Jimmy Brown, Cleveland | 108 |
| 1942 | Don Hutson, Green Bay | 138 | 1959 | Paul Hornung, Green Bay | 94 |
| 1943 | Don Hutson, Green Bay | 117 | 1960 | Paul Hornung, Green Bay | 176 [2] |
| 1944 | Don Hutson, Green Bay | 85 | 1961 | Paul Hornung, Green Bay | 146 |
| 1945 | Steve Van Buren, Philadelphia Eagles | 110 | 1962 | Jim Taylor, Green Bay | 114 |
| 1946 | Ted Fritsch, Green Bay | 100 | 1963 | Don Chandler, New York | 106 |
| 1947 | Pat Harder, Chicago Cardinals | 102 | 1964 | Lenny Moore, Baltimore | 120 |
| 1948 | Pat Harder, Chicago Cardinals | 110 | 1965 | Gale Sayers, Chicago Bears | 132 |
| 1949 | Pat Harder, Chicago Cardinals [1] | 102 | 1966 | Bruce Gossett, Los Angeles | 113 |

[1] Tie.   [2] Record.

## NFL ANNUAL AWARDS

### Jim Thorpe Memorial Trophy Winners

1966 Bart Starr, Quarterback, Green Bay Packers
1965 Jim Brown, Fullback, Cleveland Browns
1964 Lenny Moore, Halfback, Baltimore Colts
1963 Y. A. Tittle, Quarterback, New York Giants
Jim Brown, Fullback, Cleveland Browns
1962 Jim Taylor, Fullback, Green Bay Packers
1961 Y. A. Tittle, Quarterback, New York Giants
1960 Norm Van Brocklin, Quarterback, Phila. Eagles
1959 Charley Conerly, Quarterback, New York Giants
1958 Jim Brown, Fullback, Cleveland Browns
1957 John Unitas, Quarterback, Baltimore Colts
1956 Frank Gifford, Halfback, New York Giants

1955 Harlon Hill, End, Chicago Bears

### Joe Carr Memorial Trophy Winners
(This award was discontinued after 1946)

1946 Bill Dudley, Halfback, Pittsburgh Steelers
1945 Bob Waterfield, Quarterback, Cleveland Rams
1944 Frank Sinkwich, Quarterback, Detroit Lions
1943 Sid Luckman, Quarterback, Chicago Bears
1942 Don Hutson, End, Green Bay Packers
1941 Don Hutson, End, Green Bay Packers
1940 Ace Parker, Halfback, Brooklyn Dodgers
1939 Parker Hall, Halfback, Cleveland Rams
1938 Mel Hein, Center, New York Giants

## AMERICAN FOOTBALL LEAGUE

| YEAR | EASTERN DIVISION CHAMPIONS | W | L | T | YEAR | WESTERN DIVISION CHAMPIONS | W | L | T |
|------|----------------------------|----|---|---|------|----------------------------|----|---|---|
| 1960 | Houston Oilers | 10 | 4 | 0 | 1960 | Los Angeles Chargers | 10 | 4 | 0 |
| 1961 | Houston Oilers | 10 | 3 | 1 | 1961 | San Diego Chargers | 12 | 2 | 0 |
| 1962 | Houston Oilers | 11 | 3 | 0 | 1962 | Dallas Texans | 11 | 3 | 0 |
| 1963 | Boston Patriots * | 8 | 6 | 1 | 1963 | San Diego Chargers | 11 | 3 | 0 |
| 1964 | Buffalo Bills | 12 | 2 | 0 | 1964 | San Diego Chargers | 8 | 5 | 1 |
| 1965 | Buffalo Bills | 10 | 3 | 1 | 1965 | San Diego Chargers | 9 | 2 | 3 |
| 1966 | Buffalo Bills | 9 | 4 | 1 | 1966 | Kansas City Chiefs | 11 | 2 | 1 |

* Won divisional playoff.

### AFL CHAMPIONSHIP PLAYOFFS

1960 Houston 24, Los Angeles 16
1961 Houston 10, San Diego 3
1962 * Dallas 20, Houston 17
1963 San Diego 51, Boston 10
1964 Buffalo 20, San Diego 7
1965 Buffalo 23, San Diego 0
1966 Kansas City 31, Buffalo 7

* Won at 2:45 of the second "sudden death" period.

### STARS OF THE AMERICAN FOOTBALL LEAGUE

| YEAR | LEADING PASSER AND TEAM | A[1] | C[2] | YG[3] | YEAR | LEADING PASSER AND TEAM | A[1] | C[2] | YG[3] |
|------|-------------------------|------|------|-------|------|-------------------------|------|------|-------|
| 1960 | Jack Kemp, Los Angeles | 406 | 211 | 3,018 | 1964 | Len Dawson, Kansas City | 354 | 199 | 2,879 |
| 1961 | George Blanda, Houston | 362 | 187 | 3,330 | 1965 | John Hadl, San Diego | 348 | 174 | 2,798 |
| 1962 | Len Dawson, Dallas | 310 | 189 | 2,749 | 1966 | Len Dawson, Kansas City | 284 | 159 | 2,527 |
| 1963 | Tobin Rote, San Diego | 287 | 170 | 2,510 | | | | | |

| YEAR | LEADING PASS RECEIVER AND TEAM | PASSES RECEIVED | YEAR | RUSHING LEADER AND TEAM | YARDS GAINED |
|------|-------------------------------|-----------------|------|-------------------------|--------------|
| 1960 | Lionel Taylor, Denver | 92 | 1960 | Abner Haynes, Dallas | 875 |
| 1961 | Lionel Taylor, Denver | 100 | 1961 | Billy Cannon, Houston | 948 |
| 1962 | Lionel Taylor, Denver | 77 | 1962 | Cookie Gilchrist, Buffalo | 1,096 |
| 1963 | Lionel Taylor, Denver | 78 | 1963 | Clem Daniels, Oakland | 1,098 |
| 1964 | Charley Hennigan, Houston | 101 | 1964 | Cookie Gilchrist, Buffalo | 981 |
| 1965 | Lionel Taylor, Denver | 85 | 1965 | Paul Lowe, San Diego | 1,121 |
| 1966 | Lance Alworth, San Diego | 73 | 1966 | Jim Nance, Boston | 1,458 |

| YEAR | SCORING LEADER AND TEAM | POINTS | YEAR | MOST VALUABLE PLAYER [4] | POSITION |
|------|-------------------------|--------|------|--------------------------|----------|
| 1960 | Gene Mingo, Denver | 123 | 1960 | Abner Haynes, Dallas | Halfback |
| 1961 | Gino Cappelletti, Boston | 147 | 1961 | George Blanda, Houston | Quarterback |
| 1962 | Gene Mingo, Denver | 137 | 1962 | Len Dawson, Dallas | Quarterback |
| 1963 | Gino Cappelletti, Boston | 113 | 1963 | Clem Daniels, Oakland | Fullback |
| 1964 | Gino Cappelletti, Boston | 155 | 1964 | Gino Cappelletti, Boston | End |
| 1965 | Gino Cappelletti, Boston | 132 | 1965 | Jack Kemp, Buffalo | Quarterback |
| 1966 | Gino Cappelletti, Boston | 119 | 1966 | Jim Nance, Boston | Fullback |

[1] Attempts.    [2] Completions.    [3] Yards gained.    [4] Award based on poll of AP and UPI sportswriters.

# FOOTBALL (COLLEGE)

The two top college football teams of 1966, Notre Dame and Michigan State, collided on October 28, 1967, at South Bend, Indiana. Notre Dame won by a score of 24 to 12. Above, Irish back Bob Bleier hurtles into line.

Originally a blend of soccer and rugby, football was first played by collegiate teams in 1869, when Rutgers faced Princeton at New Brunswick, New Jersey. The foundation for further intercollegiate football matches was laid by Princeton, Rutgers, Columbia, and Yale, who met in 1873 to draft a football code. These rules, based on soccer, were considerably revised after Harvard played McGill University of Canada in 1874. Football drew nearer to rugby in 1876, the year the American Intercollegiate Football Association was organized by Princeton, Rutgers, Columbia, Harvard, and Yale. During the 1880s new rules were introduced, and by the 1890s, college football coaching had become professionalized.

The forward pass, a major innovation, was introduced as a result of President Theodore Roosevelt's outrage over an especially brutal football game. Roosevelt announced his intention to ban football by executive edict if rough play continued. To appease the President, the Rules Committee of Football met in 1906 and prohibited hurdling and mass formations, such as "the flying wedge," and legalized the forward pass. Yale was the first major college team to employ the new device successfully as an offensive weapon. However, it was not until 1913 when the now famous combination of Knute Rockne and Gus Dorais led a little-known Notre Dame team to an overwhelming victory over heavily favored Army that the forward pass came into its own.

Later in the 20th century, college football turned into big business. Gate receipts from football often finance other college sports, and games are frequently played before crowds of 70,000 or more in university-owned stadiums.

The two top college teams in 1966, Notre Dame and Michigan State, clashed in an unforgettable game which ended in a 10–10 tie. Notre Dame was named national champion by the polls, with Michigan State second.

In one of the big games of the 1967 season, Southern California beat UCLA by the score of 21 to 20 on November 18. Trojan Tailback O. J. Simpson scored two touchdowns, including the decisive one on a 64-yard run. UCLA Quarterback Gary Beban completed 16 of 24 passes for 301 yards and two touchdowns.

# COLLEGE CONFERENCE STANDINGS: 1967

| TEAM | CONFERENCE GAMES | | | ALL GAMES | | |
|---|---|---|---|---|---|---|
| | W | L | T | W | L | T |
| **Ivy League** | | | | | | |
| Yale | 7 | 0 | 0 | 8 | 1 | 0 |
| Dartmouth | 5 | 2 | 0 | 7 | 2 | 0 |
| Cornell | 4 | 2 | 1 | 6 | 2 | 1 |
| Princeton | 4 | 3 | 0 | 6 | 3 | 0 |
| Harvard | 4 | 3 | 0 | 6 | 3 | 0 |
| Pennsylvania | 2 | 5 | 0 | 3 | 6 | 0 |
| Brown | 1 | 5 | 1 | 2 | 6 | 1 |
| Columbia | 0 | 7 | 0 | 2 | 7 | 0 |
| **Big Eight** | | | | | | |
| Oklahoma | 7 | 0 | 0 | 9 | 1 | 0 |
| Colorado | 5 | 2 | 0 | 8 | 2 | 0 |
| Kansas | 5 | 2 | 0 | 5 | 5 | 0 |
| Missouri | 4 | 3 | 0 | 7 | 3 | 0 |
| Oklahoma State | 3 | 4 | 0 | 4 | 5 | 1 |
| Nebraska | 3 | 4 | 0 | 6 | 4 | 0 |
| Iowa State | 1 | 6 | 0 | 2 | 8 | 0 |
| Kansas State | 0 | 7 | 0 | 1 | 9 | 0 |
| **Southern** | | | | | | |
| West Virginia | 4 | 0 | 1 | 5 | 4 | 1 |
| East Carolina | 4 | 1 | 0 | 8 | 2 | 0 |
| Richmond | 5 | 2 | 0 | 5 | 5 | 0 |
| William & Mary | 2 | 2 | 1 | 5 | 4 | 1 |
| Va. Military Inst. | 2 | 3 | 0 | 6 | 4 | 0 |
| Furman | 2 | 3 | 0 | 5 | 5 | 0 |
| Citadel | 2 | 4 | 0 | 5 | 5 | 0 |
| Davidson | 1 | 5 | 0 | 4 | 5 | 0 |
| **Atlantic Coast** | | | | | | |
| Clemson | 6 | 0 | 0 | 6 | 4 | 0 |
| No. Carolina St. | 5 | 1 | 0 | 8 | 2 | 0 |
| South Carolina | 4 | 2 | 0 | 5 | 5 | 0 |
| Virginia | 3 | 3 | 0 | 5 | 5 | 0 |
| Wake Forest | 3 | 4 | 0 | 4 | 6 | 0 |
| Duke | 2 | 4 | 0 | 4 | 6 | 0 |
| North Carolina | 2 | 5 | 0 | 2 | 8 | 0 |
| Maryland | 0 | 6 | 0 | 0 | 9 | 0 |
| **Southwest** | | | | | | |
| Texas A & M | 6 | 1 | 0 | 6 | 4 | 0 |
| Texas Tech | 5 | 2 | 0 | 6 | 4 | 0 |
| Texas Christian | 4 | 3 | 0 | 4 | 6 | 0 |
| Texas | 4 | 3 | 0 | 6 | 4 | 0 |
| Arkansas | 3 | 3 | 1 | 4 | 5 | 1 |
| So. Methodist | 3 | 4 | 0 | 3 | 7 | 0 |
| Rice | 2 | 5 | 0 | 4 | 6 | 0 |
| Baylor | 0 | 6 | 1 | 1 | 8 | 1 |
| **Big Ten** | | | | | | |
| Indiana | 6 | 1 | 0 | 9 | 1 | 0 |
| Minnesota | 6 | 1 | 0 | 8 | 2 | 0 |
| Purdue | 6 | 1 | 0 | 8 | 2 | 0 |
| Ohio State | 5 | 2 | 0 | 6 | 3 | 0 |
| Michigan State | 3 | 4 | 0 | 3 | 7 | 0 |
| Illinois | 3 | 4 | 0 | 4 | 6 | 0 |
| Michigan | 3 | 4 | 0 | 4 | 6 | 0 |
| Northwestern | 2 | 5 | 0 | 3 | 7 | 0 |
| Iowa | 0 | 6 | 1 | 1 | 8 | 1 |
| Wisconsin | 0 | 6 | 1 | 0 | 9 | 1 |
| **Southeastern** | | | | | | |
| Tennessee | 6 | 0 | 0 | 9 | 1 | 0 |
| Alabama | 5 | 1 | 0 | 8 | 1 | 1 |
| Georgia | 4 | 2 | 0 | 7 | 3 | 0 |
| Florida * | 4 | 2 | 0 | 6 | 3 | 0 |
| Mississippi | 4 | 2 | 1 | 6 | 3 | 1 |
| Louisiana State | 3 | 2 | 1 | 6 | 3 | 1 |
| Auburn | 3 | 3 | 0 | 6 | 4 | 0 |
| Kentucky | 1 | 6 | 0 | 2 | 8 | 0 |
| Vanderbilt | 0 | 6 | 0 | 2 | 7 | 1 |
| Mississippi St. | 0 | 6 | 0 | 1 | 9 | 0 |
| **AAWU** | | | | | | |
| So. California | 6 | 1 | 0 | 9 | 1 | 0 |
| UCLA | 4 | 1 | 1 | 7 | 2 | 1 |
| Oregon State | 4 | 1 | 1 | 7 | 2 | 1 |
| Stanford | 3 | 4 | 0 | 5 | 5 | 0 |
| Washington | 3 | 4 | 0 | 5 | 5 | 0 |
| California | 2 | 3 | 0 | 5 | 5 | 0 |
| Oregon | 1 | 5 | 0 | 2 | 8 | 0 |
| Washington St. | 1 | 5 | 0 | 2 | 8 | 0 |
| **Mid-American** | | | | | | |
| Toledo | 5 | 1 | 0 | 9 | 1 | 0 |
| Ohio University | 5 | 1 | 0 | 6 | 4 | 0 |
| Miami (Ohio) | 4 | 2 | 0 | 6 | 4 | 0 |
| Western Michigan | 4 | 2 | 0 | 5 | 4 | 0 |
| Bowling Green | 2 | 4 | 0 | 6 | 4 | 0 |
| Kent State | 1 | 5 | 0 | 4 | 6 | 0 |
| Marshall | 0 | 6 | 0 | 0 | 10 | 0 |
| **Missouri Valley** | | | | | | |
| No. Texas State | 4 | 0 | 0 | 7 | 1 | 1 |
| Tulsa | 3 | 1 | 0 | 7 | 3 | 0 |
| Cincinnati | 2 | 2 | 0 | 3 | 6 | 0 |
| Louisville | 1 | 3 | 0 | 5 | 5 | 0 |
| Wichita | 0 | 4 | 0 | 2 | 7 | 1 |
| Memphis State | 0 | 0 | 0 | 6 | 3 | 0 |
| **Middle Atlantic (UNIVERSITY DIVISION)** | | | | | | |
| Temple | 4 | 0 | 0 | 7 | 2 | 0 |
| Hofstra | 3 | 1 | 0 | 8 | 2 | 0 |
| Bucknell | 3 | 2 | 0 | 4 | 6 | 0 |
| Delaware | 2 | 3 | 0 | 2 | 7 | 0 |
| Gettysburg | 2 | 3 | 0 | 4 | 5 | 0 |
| Lafayette | 2 | 3 | 0 | 4 | 5 | 0 |
| Lehigh | 0 | 4 | 0 | 1 | 8 | 0 |
| West Chester | 0 | 0 | 0 | 10 | 0 | 0 |
| **(COLLEGE DIV., NORTH)** | | | | | | |
| Wilkes | 8 | 0 | 0 | 8 | 0 | 0 |
| Juniata | 5 | 0 | 0 | 7 | 1 | 1 |
| Wagner | 5 | 0 | 0 | 9 | 0 | 0 |
| Delaware Valley | 5 | 2 | 0 | 6 | 2 | 0 |
| Albright | 4 | 3 | 0 | 5 | 4 | 0 |
| Upsala | 4 | 4 | 0 | 4 | 4 | 0 |
| Lycoming | 3 | 5 | 0 | 3 | 5 | 0 |
| Moravian | 3 | 6 | 0 | 3 | 6 | 0 |
| Susquehanna | 0 | 3 | 0 | 1 | 8 | 0 |
| **(COLLEGE DIV., SOUTH)** | | | | | | |
| Johns Hopkins | 6 | 0 | 0 | 6 | 1 | 0 |
| Western Maryland | 3 | 2 | 0 | 6 | 3 | 0 |
| Franklin & Marshall | 4 | 3 | 0 | 4 | 4 | 0 |
| Lebanon Valley | 3 | 5 | 0 | 3 | 5 | 0 |
| Swarthmore | 3 | 5 | 0 | 3 | 5 | 0 |
| Dickinson | 3 | 5 | 0 | 3 | 5 | 0 |

* Includes games as of December 2.

| TEAM | CONFERENCE GAMES | | | ALL GAMES | | | TEAM | CONFERENCE GAMES | | | ALL GAMES | | |
|---|---|---|---|---|---|---|---|---|---|---|---|---|---|
| | W | L | T | W | L | T | | W | L | T | W | L | T |
| PMC Colleges.... | 3 | 5 | 0 | 3 | 6 | 0 | New Mexico State | — | — | — | 7 | 2 | 1 |
| Haverford........ | 2 | 4 | 0 | 2 | 5 | 0 | Florida State..... | — | — | — | 7 | 2 | 1 |
| Muhlenberg...... | 2 | 5 | 1 | 2 | 5 | 1 | Utah State....... | — | — | — | 7 | 2 | 1 |
| Drexel.......... | 1 | 5 | 0 | 3 | 5 | 0 | Houston......... | — | — | — | 7 | 3 | 0 |
| Ursinus.......... | 1 | 6 | 1 | 1 | 6 | 1 | Virginia Tech..... | — | — | — | 7 | 3 | 0 |
| **Yankee** | | | | | | | W. Texas State... | — | — | — | 7 | 3 | 0 |
| Massachusetts.... | 5 | 0 | 0 | 7 | 2 | 0 | Texas (El Paso)... | — | — | — | 6 | 2 | 1 |
| Connecticut...... | 4 | 1 | 0 | 5 | 4 | 0 | Dayton.......... | — | — | — | 6 | 2 | 1 |
| Rhode Island..... | 2 | 2 | 1 | 6 | 2 | 1 | Miami (Florida) *. | — | — | — | 6 | 3 | 0 |
| New Hampshire.. | 2 | 3 | 0 | 5 | 3 | 0 | Southern Miss.... | — | — | — | 6 | 3 | 0 |
| Vermont......... | 1 | 3 | 1 | 2 | 6 | 1 | Xavier (Ohio).... | — | — | — | 6 | 3 | 1 |
| Maine........... | 0 | 5 | 0 | 0 | 8 | 0 | Buffalo.......... | — | — | — | 6 | 4 | 0 |
| **Western Athletic** | | | | | | | Navy........... | — | — | — | 5 | 4 | 1 |
| Wyoming........ | 5 | 0 | 0 | 10 | 0 | 0 | Holy Cross....... | — | — | — | 5 | 5 | 0 |
| Arizona State..... | 4 | 1 | 0 | 8 | 2 | 0 | Pacific (Calif.).... | — | — | — | 4 | 5 | 0 |
| Brigham Young... | 3 | 2 | 0 | 6 | 4 | 0 | Rutgers.......... | — | — | — | 4 | 5 | 0 |
| Utah............ | 2 | 3 | 0 | 4 | 7 | 0 | Villanova........ | — | — | — | 4 | 6 | 0 |
| Arizona......... | 1 | 4 | 0 | 3 | 6 | 1 | Georgia Tech..... | — | — | — | 4 | 6 | 0 |
| New Mexico...... | 0 | 5 | 0 | 1 | 9 | 0 | Boston College... | — | — | — | 4 | 6 | 0 |
| **Major Independents** | | | | | | | Colorado State... | — | — | — | 3 | 5 | 1 |
| Army........... | — | — | — | 8 | 2 | 0 | Tulane.......... | — | — | — | 3 | 7 | 0 |
| Notre Dame...... | — | — | — | 8 | 2 | 0 | Air Force........ | — | — | — | 2 | 6 | 2 |
| Penn State...... | — | — | — | 8 | 2 | 0 | Colgate......... | — | — | — | 2 | 8 | 0 |
| Syracuse......... | — | — | — | 8 | 2 | 0 | San Jose State... | — | — | — | 1 | 7 | 0 |
| | | | | | | | Pittsburgh....... | — | — | — | 1 | 9 | 0 |

*Includes games as of December 2.

## COLLEGE FOOTBALL CHAMPIONS

Various groups have picked the annual college football team champion since 1924. The Associated Press started polling sportswriters in 1936 to determine the team winner; in 1950 United Press International began to poll football coaches. The NCAA recognizes both polls.

| | | | | | | | |
|---|---|---|---|---|---|---|---|
| 1924 | Notre Dame | 1934 | Minnesota | 1946 | Notre Dame | 1957 | Auburn (AP); |
| 1925 | Dartmouth | 1935 | Southern Methodist | 1947 | Notre Dame | | Ohio State (UPI) |
| 1926 | Stanford | 1936 | Minnesota | 1948 | Michigan | 1958 | Louisiana State |
| 1927 | Illinois | 1937 | Pittsburgh | 1949 | Notre Dame | 1959 | Syracuse |
| 1928 | Southern | 1938 | Texas Christian | 1950 | Oklahoma | 1960 | Minnesota |
| | California | 1939 | Texas A & M | 1951 | Tennessee | 1961 | Alabama |
| 1929 | Notre Dame | 1940 | Minnesota | 1952 | Michigan State | 1962 | So. California |
| 1930 | Notre Dame | 1941 | Minnesota | 1953 | Maryland | 1963 | Texas |
| 1931 | Southern | 1942 | Ohio State | 1954 | Ohio State (AP); | 1964 | Alabama |
| | California | 1943 | Notre Dame | | UCLA (UPI) | 1965 | Alabama |
| 1932 | Michigan | 1944 | Army | 1955 | Oklahoma | 1966 | Notre Dame |
| 1933 | Michigan | 1945 | Army | 1956 | Oklahoma | 1967 | So. California |

## COLLEGE FOOTBALL CONFERENCE CHAMPIONS

■ ATHLETIC ASSOCIATION OF WESTERN UNIVERSITIES

The Pacific Coast Conference, formed in 1916, disbanded in 1958 and reorganized as the Athletic Association of Western Universities.

CHAMPIONS

| | | | |
|---|---|---|---|
| 1935* | California—Stanford— | 1945 | Southern California |
| | UCLA | 1946 | UCLA |
| 1936* | Washington—Southern | 1947 | Southern California |
| | California | 1948* | Oregon—California |
| 1937 | California | 1949 | California |
| 1938* | California—Southern | 1950 | California |
| | California | 1951 | Stanford |
| 1939 | Southern California | 1952 | Southern California |
| 1940 | Stanford | 1953 | UCLA |
| 1941 | Oregon State | 1954 | UCLA |
| 1942 | UCLA | 1955 | UCLA |
| 1943 | Southern California | 1956 | Oregon State |
| 1944 | Southern California | 1957* | Oregon State—Oregon |

* Tie.

| | |
|---|---|
| 1958 | California |
| 1959* | Washington—Southern California—UCLA |
| 1960 | Washington |
| 1961 | UCLA |
| 1962 | Southern California |
| 1963 | Washington |
| 1964* | Oregon State—Southern California |
| 1965 | UCLA |
| 1966 | Southern California |
| 1967 | Southern California |

■ THE BIG TEN (WESTERN CONFERENCE)

The Big Ten was formed in 1895.

CHAMPIONS

| | | | |
|---|---|---|---|
| 1935* | Minnesota—Ohio State | 1944 | Ohio State |
| 1936 | Northwestern | 1945 | Indiana |
| 1937 | Minnesota | 1946 | Illinois |
| 1938 | Minnesota | 1947 | Michigan |
| 1939 | Ohio State | 1948 | Michigan |
| 1940 | Minnesota | 1949* | Ohio State—Michigan |
| 1941 | Minnesota | 1950 | Michigan |
| 1942 | Ohio State | 1951 | Illinois |
| 1943* | Michigan—Purdue | 1952* | Wisconsin—Purdue |

| 1953* | Illinois—Mich. State | 1961 | Ohio State |
|---|---|---|---|
| 1954 | Ohio State | 1962 | Wisconsin |
| 1955 | Ohio State | 1963 | Illinois |
| 1956 | Iowa | 1964 | Michigan |
| 1957 | Ohio State | 1965 | Michigan State |
| 1958 | Iowa | 1966 | Michigan State |
| 1959 | Wisconsin | 1967* | Indiana—Purdue— |
| 1960* | Minnesota—Iowa | | Minnesota |

## ■ THE IVY LEAGUE

The Ivy League became a formal conference with specific teams in 1956.

| CHAMPIONS | | 1962 | Dartmouth |
|---|---|---|---|
| 1956 | Yale | 1963* | Dartmouth—Princeton |
| 1957 | Princeton | 1964 | Princeton |
| 1958 | Dartmouth | 1965 | Dartmouth |
| 1959 | Pennsylvania | 1966* | Dartmouth—Harvard |
| 1960 | Yale | | —Princeton |
| 1961* | Columbia—Harvard | 1967 | Yale |

## ■ SOUTHEASTERN CONFERENCE

This conference began in 1922.

| CHAMPIONS | | | |
|---|---|---|---|
| 1934 | Tulane | 1951* | Georgia Tech—Tenn. |
| 1935 | LSU | 1952 | Georgia Tech |
| 1936 | LSU | 1953 | Alabama |
| 1937 | Alabama | 1954 | Mississippi |
| 1938 | Tennessee | 1955 | Mississippi |
| 1939* | Tennessee—Ga. Tech | 1956 | Tennessee |
| 1940 | Tennessee | 1957 | Auburn |
| 1941 | Mississippi State | 1958 | LSU |
| 1942 | Georgia | 1959 | Georgia |
| 1943 | Georgia Tech | 1960 | Mississippi |
| 1944 | Georgia Tech | 1961* | Alabama—LSU |
| 1945 | Alabama | 1962 | Mississippi |
| 1946* | Georgia—Tennessee | 1963 | Mississippi |
| 1947 | Mississippi | 1964 | Alabama |
| 1948 | Georgia | 1965 | Alabama |
| 1949 | Tulane | 1966* | Georgia—Alabama |
| 1950 | Kentucky | 1967 | Tennessee |

## ■ SOUTHWEST CONFERENCE

The Southwest Conference was formed in 1915.

| CHAMPIONS | | | |
|---|---|---|---|
| 1936 | Arkansas | 1952 | Texas |
| 1937 | Rice | 1953* | Rice—Texas |
| 1938 | TCU | 1954 | Arkansas |
| 1939 | Texas A & M | 1955 | Texas |
| 1940* | Texas A & M—SMU | 1956 | Texas A & M |
| 1941 | Texas A & M | 1957 | Rice |
| 1942 | Texas | 1958 | TCU |
| 1943 | Texas | 1959* | Texas—TCU—Ark. |
| 1944 | TCU | 1960 | Arkansas |
| 1945 | Texas | 1961* | Texas—Arkansas |
| 1946* | Arkansas—Rice | 1962 | Texas |
| 1947 | SMU | 1963 | Texas |
| 1948 | SMU | 1964 | Arkansas |
| 1949 | Rice | 1965 | Arkansas |
| 1950 | Texas | 1966 | SMU |
| 1951 | TCU | 1967 | Texas A & M |

## ■ BIG EIGHT CONFERENCE

| CHAMPIONS | | | |
|---|---|---|---|
| 1935 | Nebraska | 1941 | Missouri |
| 1936 | Nebraska | 1942 | Missouri |
| 1937 | Nebraska | 1943 | Oklahoma |
| 1938 | Oklahoma | 1944 | Oklahoma |
| 1939 | Missouri | 1945 | Missouri |
| 1940 | Nebraska | 1946* | Oklahoma—Kansas |

* Tie.

| 1947* | Oklahoma—Kansas | 1963 | Nebraska |
|---|---|---|---|
| 1948 to 1959 | Oklahoma | 1964 | Nebraska |
| 1960 | Missouri | 1965 | Nebraska |
| 1961 | Colorado | 1966 | Nebraska |
| 1962 | Oklahoma | 1967 | Oklahoma |

## ■ ATLANTIC COAST CONFERENCE

Established in 1952 by eight colleges formerly with the Southern Conference.

| CHAMPIONS | | | |
|---|---|---|---|
| 1954 | Duke | 1961 | Duke |
| 1955* | Maryland—Duke | 1962 | Duke |
| 1956 | Clemson | 1963 | North Carolina State |
| 1957 | North Carolina State | 1964 | North Carolina State |
| 1958 | Clemson | 1965 | Duke |
| 1959 | Clemson | 1966 | Clemson |
| 1960 | Duke | 1967 | Clemson |

## ■ MID-AMERICAN CONFERENCE

| CHAMPIONS | | 1958 | Miami (Ohio) |
|---|---|---|---|
| 1947 | Cincinnati | 1959 | Bowling Green |
| 1948 | Miami (Ohio) | 1960 | Ohio University |
| 1949 | Cincinnati | 1961 | Bowling Green |
| 1950 | Miami (Ohio) | 1962 | Bowling Green |
| 1951 | Cincinnati | 1963 | Ohio University |
| 1952 | Cincinnati | 1964 | Bowling Green |
| 1953 | Ohio University | 1965* | Miami (Ohio)—Bowling |
| 1954 | Miami (Ohio) | | Green |
| 1955 | Miami (Ohio) | 1966* | Miami (Ohio)—Western |
| 1956 | Bowling Green | | Michigan |
| 1957 | Miami (Ohio) | 1967* | Toledo—Ohio Univ. |

## ■ MISSOURI VALLEY CONFERENCE

| CHAMPIONS | | 1952 | Houston |
|---|---|---|---|
| 1936* | Creighton—Tulsa | 1953* | Oklahoma A & M— |
| 1937 | Tulsa | | Detroit |
| 1938 | Tulsa | 1954 | Wichita |
| 1939 | Washington | 1955* | Detroit—Wichita |
| 1940 | Tulsa | 1956 | Houston |
| 1941 | Tulsa | 1957 | Houston |
| 1942 | Tulsa | 1958 | North Texas |
| 1943 | Tulsa | 1959* | North Texas—Houston |
| 1944 | Oklahoma A & M | 1960 | Wichita |
| 1945 | Oklahoma A & M | 1961 | Wichita |
| 1946 | Tulsa | 1962 | Tulsa |
| 1947 | Tulsa | 1963* | Cincinnati—Wichita |
| 1948 | Oklahoma A & M | 1964 | Cincinnati |
| 1949 | Detroit | 1965 | Tulsa |
| 1950 | Tulsa | 1966* | North Texas—Tulsa |
| 1951 | Tulsa | 1967 | North Texas |

## ■ SOUTHERN CONFERENCE

| CHAMPIONS | | | |
|---|---|---|---|
| 1933 | Duke | 1951* | Maryland—VMI |
| 1934 | Washington & Lee | 1952 | Duke |
| 1935 | Duke | 1953 | West Virginia |
| 1936 | Duke | 1954 | West Virginia |
| 1937 | Maryland | 1955 | West Virginia |
| 1938 | Duke | 1956 | West Virginia |
| 1939 | Duke | 1957 | VMI |
| 1940 | Clemson | 1958 | West Virginia |
| 1941 | Duke | 1959 | VMI |
| 1942 | William & Mary | 1960 | VMI |
| 1943 | Duke | 1961 | Citadel |
| 1944 | Duke | 1962 | VMI |
| 1945 | Duke | 1963 | Virginia Tech |
| 1946 | North Carolina | 1964 | West Virginia |
| 1947 | William & Mary | 1965 | West Virginia |
| 1948 | Clemson | 1966* | William & Mary— |
| 1949 | North Carolina | | East Carolina |
| 1950 | Washington & Lee | 1967 | West Virginia |

# HISTORY OF THE FIVE MAJOR BOWL GAMES

## ■ THE ROSE BOWL

Although there was a postseason bowl game at Pasadena, California, in 1902, Rose Bowl history actually dates from 1915, when the Pacific Coast Conference champion, Washington State, invited Brown University to play in the Pasadena Bowl on January 1, 1916. Brown was defeated 14 to 0.

Since then the Rose Bowl game has been played annually in association with the city's Tournament of Roses; in 1923 a new stadium was built at Pasadena. In 1946 it was ruled that in the following years the Rose Bowl game would be played annually between the Pacific Coast and Big Ten Conference champions.

RESULTS

| | | | | | |
|---|---|---|---|---|---|
| 1902 | Michigan 49, Stanford 0 | 1932 | Southern California 21, Tulane 12 | 1948 | Michigan 49, Southern California 0 |
| 1916 | Washington State 14, Brown 0 | | | | |
| 1917 | Oregon 14, Pennsylvania 0 | 1933 | Southern California 35, Pittsburgh 0 | 1949 | Northwestern 20, California 14 |
| 1918 | Mare Island Marines 19, Camp Lewis (Army) 7 | 1934 | Columbia 7, Stanford 0 | 1950 | Ohio State 17, California 14 |
| 1919 | Great Lakes (Navy) 17, Mare Island Marines 0 | 1935 | Alabama 29, Stanford 13 | 1951 | Michigan 14, California 6 |
| | | 1936 | Stanford 7, SMU 0 | 1952 | Illinois 40, Stanford 7 |
| 1920 | Harvard 7, Oregon 6 | 1937 | Pittsburgh 21, Washington 0 | 1953 | Southern California 7, Wisconsin 0 |
| 1921 | California 28, Ohio State 0 | 1938 | California 13, Alabama 0 | | |
| 1922 | Washington and Jefferson 0, California 0 | 1939 | Southern California 7, Duke 3 | 1954 | Michigan State 28, UCLA 20 |
| | | 1940 | Southern California 14, Tennessee 0 | 1955 | Ohio State 20, So. Calif. 7 |
| 1923 | Southern California 14, Penn State 3 | 1941 | Stanford 21, Nebraska 13 | 1956 | Michigan State 17, UCLA 14 |
| 1924 | Navy 14, Washington 14 | 1942 | Oregon State 20, Duke 16 * | 1957 | Iowa 35, Oregon State 19 |
| 1925 | Notre Dame 27, Stanford 10 | 1943 | Georgia 9, UCLA 0 | 1958 | Ohio State 10, Oregon 7 |
| 1926 | Alabama 20, Washington 19 | 1944 | Southern California 29, Washington 0 † | 1959 | Iowa 38, California 12 |
| 1927 | Alabama 7, Stanford 7 | | | 1960 | Washington 44, Wisconsin 8 |
| 1928 | Stanford 7, Pittsburgh 6 | 1945 | Southern California 25, Tennessee 0 | 1961 | Washington 17, Minnesota 7 |
| 1929 | Georgia Tech 8, California 7 | | | 1962 | Minnesota 21, UCLA 3 |
| 1930 | Southern California 47, Pittsburgh 14 | 1946 | Alabama 34, Southern California 14 | 1963 | So. Calif. 42, Wisconsin 37 |
| | | 1947 | Illinois 45, UCLA 14 | 1964 | Illinois 17, Washington 7 |
| 1931 | Alabama 24, Washington State 0 | | | 1965 | Michigan 34, Oregon State 7 |
| | | | | 1966 | UCLA 14, Michigan State 12 |
| | | | | 1967 | Purdue 14, So. Calif. 13 |

* Because of World War II restrictions, the 1942 Rose Bowl game was played at Duke Stadium, Durham, North Carolina.
† The only Rose Bowl game between two Pacific Coast Conference teams.

## ■ THE ORANGE BOWL

Played each New Year's Day at Miami, Florida, since 1933, the Orange Bowl game was originally called the Palm Festival game. Since 1958 the Orange Bowl has been invitational,

open to any two top-ranked teams in the country. Florida won the 1967 bowl game as tailback Larry Smith set an Orange Bowl record of 187 yards for total rushing.

RESULTS

| | | | | | |
|---|---|---|---|---|---|
| 1933 | Miami (Fla.) 7, Manhattan 0 | 1943 | Alabama 37, Boston College 21 | 1956 | Oklahoma 20, Maryland 6 |
| 1934 | Duquesne 33, Miami (Fla.) 7 | 1944 | LSU 19, Texas A & M 14 | 1957 | Colorado 27, Clemson 21 |
| 1935 | Bucknell 26, Miami (Fla.) 0 | 1945 | Tulsa 26, Georgia Tech 12 | 1958 | Oklahoma 48, Duke 21 |
| 1936 | Catholic University 20, Mississippi 19 | 1946 | Miami (Fla.) 13, Holy Cross 6 | 1959 | Oklahoma 21, Syracuse 6 |
| | | 1947 | Rice 8, Tennessee 0 | 1960 | Georgia 14, Missouri 0 |
| 1937 | Duquesne 13, Mississippi State 12 | 1948 | Georgia Tech 20, Kansas 14 | 1961 | Missouri 21, Navy 14 |
| | | 1949 | Texas 41, Georgia 28 | 1962 | LSU 25, Colorado 7 |
| 1938 | Alabama Poly 6, Michigan State 0 | 1950 | Santa Clara 21, Kentucky 13 | 1963 | Alabama 17, Oklahoma 0 |
| 1939 | Tennessee 17, Oklahoma 0 | 1951 | Clemson 15, Miami 14 | 1964 | Nebraska 13, Auburn 7 |
| 1940 | Georgia Tech 21, Missouri 7 | 1952 | Georgia Tech 17, Baylor 14 | 1965 | Texas 21, Alabama 17 |
| 1941 | Mississippi State 14, Georgetown 7 | 1953 | Alabama 61, Syracuse 6 | 1966 | Alabama 39, Nebraska 28 |
| | | 1954 | Oklahoma 7, Maryland 0 | 1967 | Florida 27, Georgia Tech 12 |
| 1942 | Georgia 40, Texas Christian 26 | 1955 | Duke 36, Nebraska 7 | | |

## ■ THE SUGAR BOWL

First played in 1935, the Sugar Bowl game is held annually at New Orleans, Louisiana. The Sugar Bowl usually has the champion of the Southeastern Conference pitted against a first-ranked team from another part of the country.

The Alabama team won only third place in the U.S. press services' final 1966 polls. But in the January 2, 1967, game the team played like champions and swamped the Nebraska Cornhuskers by the score of 34 to 7.

RESULTS

| | | | | | |
|---|---|---|---|---|---|
| 1935 | Tulane 20, Temple 14 | 1937 | Santa Clara 21, Louisiana State 14 | 1939 | Texas Christian 15, Carnegie Tech 7 |
| 1936 | Texas Christian 3, Louisiana State 2 | 1938 | Santa Clara 6, Louisiana State 0 | 1940 | Texas A & M 14, Tulane 13 |

| 1941 | Boston College 19, Tennessee 13 | 1949 | Oklahoma 14, North Carolina 6 | 1959 | Louisiana State 7, Clemson 0 |
|------|------|------|------|------|------|
| 1942 | Fordham 2, Missouri 0 | 1950 | Oklahoma 35, Louisiana State 0 | 1960 | Mississippi 21, Louisiana State 0 |
| 1943 | Tennessee 14, Tulsa 7 | 1951 | Kentucky 13, Oklahoma 7 | | |
| 1944 | Georgia Tech 20, Tulsa 18 | 1952 | Maryland 28, Tennessee 13 | 1961 | Mississippi 14, Rice 6 |
| 1945 | Duke 29, Alabama 26 | 1953 | Georgia Tech 24, Mississippi 7 | 1962 | Alabama 10, Arkansas 3 |
| 1946 | Oklahoma A & M 33, St. Mary's (Calif.) 13 | 1954 | Georgia Tech 42, West Virginia 19 | 1963 | Mississippi 17, Arkansas 13 |
| | | 1955 | Navy 21, Mississippi 0 | 1964 | Alabama 12, Mississippi 7 |
| 1947 | Georgia 20, North Carolina 10 | 1956 | Georgia Tech 7, Pittsburgh 0 | 1965 | Louisiana State 13, Syracuse 10 |
| 1948 | Texas 27, Alabama 7 | 1957 | Baylor 13, Tennessee 7 | 1966 | Missouri 20, Florida 18 |
| | | 1958 | Mississippi 39, Texas 7 | 1967 | Alabama 34, Nebraska 7 |

## ■ THE COTTON BOWL

Held annually at Dallas, Texas, since 1937, the Cotton Bowl pits the winner of the Southwestern Conference against another top team. Georgia's victory in the 1967 bowl classic was no surprise, but in the preceding year's game college football's longest winning streak in recent times—22 games—was ended by Louisiana State's defeat of Arkansas.

### RESULTS

| 1937 | Texas Christian 16, Marquette 6 | 1947 | Louisiana State 0, Arkansas 0 | 1956 | Mississippi 14, Texas Christian 13 |
|------|------|------|------|------|------|
| 1938 | Rice 28, Colorado 14 | 1948 | Southern Methodist 13, Penn State 13 | 1957 | Texas Christian 28, Syracuse 27 |
| 1939 | St. Mary's (Calif.) 20, Texas Tech 13 | 1949 | Southern Methodist 21, Oregon 13 | 1958 | Navy 20, Rice 7 |
| 1940 | Clemson 6, Boston College 3 | | | 1959 | Air Force 0, Texas Christian 0 |
| 1941 | Texas A & M 13, Fordham 12 | 1950 | Rice 27, North Carolina 13 | 1960 | Syracuse 23, Texas 14 |
| 1942 | Alabama 29, Texas A & M 21 | 1951 | Tennessee 20, Texas 14 | 1961 | Duke 7, Arkansas 6 |
| 1943 | Texas 14, Georgia Tech 7 | 1952 | Kentucky 20, Texas Christian 7 | 1962 | Texas 12, Mississippi 7 |
| 1944 | Randolph Field 7, Texas 7 | | | 1963 | Louisiana State 13, Texas 0 |
| 1945 | Oklahoma A & M 34, Texas Christian 0 | 1953 | Texas 16, Tennessee 0 | 1964 | Texas 28, Navy 6 |
| | | 1954 | Rice 28, Alabama 6 | 1965 | Arkansas 10, Nebraska 7 |
| 1946 | Texas 40, Missouri 27 | 1955 | Georgia Tech 14, Arkansas 6 | 1966 | Louisiana State 14, Arkansas 7 |
| | | | | 1967 | Georgia 24, So. Methodist 9 |

## ■ THE GATOR BOWL

First played in 1946, the Gator Bowl is the youngest of the five major bowl games. Leading college teams are invited to play in this annual event at Jacksonville, Florida.

### RESULTS

| 1946 | Wake Forest 26, South Carolina 14 | 1952 | Miami (Fla.) 14, Clemson 0 | 1960 | Arkansas 14, Georgia Tech 7 |
|------|------|------|------|------|------|
| | | 1953 | Florida 14, Tulsa 13 | 1961 | Florida 13, Baylor 12 |
| 1947 | Oklahoma 34, North Carolina State 13 | 1954 | Texas Tech 35, Auburn 13 | 1962 | Penn State 30, Georgia Tech 15 |
| | | 1955 | Auburn 33, Baylor 13 | 1963 | Florida 17, Penn State 7 |
| 1948 | Maryland 20, Georgia 20 | 1956 | Vanderbilt 25, Auburn 13 | 1964 | North Carolina 35, Air Force 0 |
| 1949 | Clemson 24, Missouri 23 | 1957 | Georgia Tech 21, Pittsburgh 14 | 1965 | Florida State 36, Oklahoma 19 |
| 1950 | Maryland 20, Missouri 7 | 1958 | Tennessee 3, Texas A & M 0 | 1966 | Georgia Tech 31, Texas Tech 21 |
| 1951 | Wyoming 20, Washington & Lee 7 | 1959 | Mississippi 7, Florida 3 | 1967 | Tennessee 18, Syracuse 12 |

## THE HEISMAN MEMORIAL TROPHY

The John W. Heisman Memorial Trophy is awarded annually to the nation's leading college football player. The award was originated in 1935 by the Downtown Athletic Club of New York and is decided by votes of sportswriters throughout the country.

| YEAR | PLAYER | POSITION | TEAM | YEAR | PLAYER | POSITION | TEAM |
|------|--------|----------|------|------|--------|----------|------|
| 1935 | Jay Berwanger.... | Back | Chicago | 1951 | Dick Kazmaier.... | Back | Princeton |
| 1936 | Larry Kelley...... | End | Yale | 1952 | Billy Vessels....... | Back | Oklahoma |
| 1937 | Clint Frank....... | Quarterback | Yale | 1953 | Johnny Lattner.... | Back | Notre Dame |
| 1938 | Davey O'Brien.... | Quarterback | Texas Christian | 1954 | Alan Ameche..... | Back | Wisconsin |
| | | | | 1955 | Howard Cassady... | Back | Ohio State |
| 1939 | Nile Kinnick...... | Back | Iowa | 1956 | Paul Hornung..... | Quarterback | Notre Dame |
| 1940 | Tom Harmon...... | Back | Michigan | 1957 | John Crow....... | Back | Texas A & M |
| 1941 | Bruce Smith...... | Back | Minnesota | 1958 | Pete Dawkins..... | Back | Army |
| 1942 | Frank Sinkwich.... | Back | Georgia | 1959 | Billy Cannon...... | Back | Louisiana State |
| 1943 | Angelo Bertelli.... | Quarterback | Notre Dame | | | | |
| 1944 | Leslie Horvath.... | Quarterback | Ohio State | 1960 | Joe Bellino....... | Back | Navy |
| 1945 | Felix Blanchard.... | Back | Army | 1961 | Ernie Davis....... | Back | Syracuse |
| 1946 | Glenn Davis....... | Back | Army | 1962 | Terry Baker...... | Back | Oregon State |
| 1947 | Johnny Lujack.... | Quarterback | Notre Dame | 1963 | Roger Staubach... | Quarterback | Navy |
| 1948 | Doak Walker...... | Back | Southern Methodist | 1964 | John Huarte...... | Quarterback | Notre Dame |
| | | | | 1965 | Mike Garrett...... | Quarterback | So. Calif. |
| 1949 | Leon Hart........ | End | Notre Dame | 1966 | Steve Spurrier.... | Quarterback | Florida |
| 1950 | Vic Janowicz...... | Back | Ohio State | 1967 | Gary Beban....... | Quarterback | UCLA |

# GOLF

Wide World

A happy Jack Nicklaus picks up his ball after beating Arnold Palmer (right) to win the 1967 U.S. Open.

Jack Nicklaus had a lot going against him in the final round of the U.S. Open Golf Championship at the Baltusrol Golf Club, Springfield, New Jersey, on June 18, 1967. Not only was he having a disastrous season with one lone tournament win to his credit (the Bing Crosby) but he was pitted against Arnold Palmer and a contingent of Arnie's Army. For all of that Jack came through, beating Palmer by four strokes to win $30,000 and the championship with a five-under-par 275. In addition, he broke the hitherto impregnable Open record of 276 set by Ben Hogan in 1948. Big Jack went on to win the World Series of Golf and a trio of other big ones.

Other golfers were also busily picking up titles. Gay Brewer took the Masters, Don January copped the PGA, and the U.S. men's amateur crown went to Bob Dickson.

Perhaps the biggest upset of the year came when 22-year-old Catherine Lacoste of France won the Women's U.S. Open to become the first foreigner, as well as the youngest, to take the event. A still younger girl, Lou Dill, 19, won the USGA Women's National Amateur.

## PROFESSIONAL GOLF'S LEADING MONEY WINNERS: 1967*

| RANK | GOLFER | OFFICIAL | UNOFFICIAL | TOTAL WINNINGS |
|------|--------|----------|------------|----------------|
| 1 | Arnold Palmer | $182,393.96 | $ 9,848.95 | $192,242.91 |
| 2 | Jack Nicklaus | 168,998.08 | 22,568.58 | 191,566.66 |
| 3 | Julius Boros | 123,810.69 | 2,743.63 | 126,554.32 |
| 4 | Billy Casper | 116,902.12 | 14,250.29 | 131,152.41 |
| 5 | Dan Sikes | 111,508.65 | 1,766.23 | 113,274.88 |
| 6 | Doug Sanders | 103,783.95 | 15,838.44 | 119,622.39 |
| 7 | Frank Beard | 101,412.20 | 4,496.30 | 105,908.50 |
| 8 | George Archer | 81,698.28 | 6,418.79 | 88,117.07 |
| 9 | Gay Brewer | 77,823.99 | 3,453.06 | 81,277.05 |
| 10 | Bob Goalby | 74,906.85 | 5,323.92 | 80,230.77 |

* Through October 2, 1967.

## LEADING MONEY WINNERS: PROFESSIONAL GOLFERS' ASSOCIATION

| YEAR | PLAYER | TOTAL MONEY [1] | YEAR | PLAYER | TOTAL MONEY [1] |
|------|--------|-----------------|------|--------|-----------------|
| 1936 | Horton Smith | $ 7,682 | 1952 | Julius Boros | $ 37,032 |
| 1937 | Harry Cooper | 14,138 | 1953 | Lew Worsham | 34,002 |
| 1938 | Sam Snead | 19,543 | 1954 | Bob Toski | 65,819 |
| 1939 | Henry Picard | 10,303 | 1955 | Julius Boros | 65,121 |
| 1940 | Ben Hogan | 10,656 | 1956 | Ted Kroll | 72,835 |
| 1941 | Ben Hogan | 18,358 | 1957 | Dick Mayer | 65,835 |
| 1942 | Ben Hogan | 13,143 | 1958 | Arnold Palmer | 42,407 |
| 1943 | Byron Nelson | No Record | 1959 | Art Wall, Jr. | 53,167 |
| 1944 | Byron Nelson | 35,005 | 1960 | Arnold Palmer | 75,262 |
| 1945 | Byron Nelson | 52,511 | 1961 | Gary Player | 64,540 |
| 1946 | Ben Hogan | 42,556 | 1962 | Arnold Palmer | 81,448 |
| 1947 | Jimmy Demaret | 27,936 | 1963 | Arnold Palmer | 128,230 |
| 1948 | Ben Hogan | 36,812 | 1964 | Jack Nicklaus [2] | 113,284 |
| 1949 | Sam Snead | 31,593 | 1965 | Jack Nicklaus | 140,752 |
| 1950 | Sam Snead | 35,758 | 1966 | Billy Casper | 121,944 |
| 1951 | Lloyd Mangrum | 26,088 | 1967 | Arnold Palmer | 182,394 [3] |

[1] Total money does not include the numerous tournaments that are not recognized as official by the PGA, and these winnings are not included in PGA figures.   [2] Arnold Palmer earned $113,203 in 1964, only $81 less than Nicklaus. Palmer, however, did win $3,214 in unofficial tournaments, while Nicklaus took in $2,794 in unofficial game money. Thus, Palmer's unofficial total was $116,417 while that for Nicklaus was $116,079.   [3] As of October 10, 1967.

## PGA CHAMPIONS

| YEAR | SITE | WINNER | RUNNER-UP | SCORE |
|------|------|--------|-----------|-------|
| 1920 | Flossmoor (Ill.) C.C. | Jock Hutchison... | J. D. Edgar | 1 up |
| 1921 | Inwood C.C., Far Rockaway, N.Y. | Walter Hagen.... | J. Barnes | 3 and 2 |
| 1922 | Oakmont (Penn.) C.C. | Gene Sarazen.... | E. French | 4 and 3 |
| 1923 | Pelham (N.Y.) C.C. | Gene Sarazen.... | W. Hagen | 1 up, 38 holes |
| 1924 | French Lick Springs (Ind.) G.C. | Walter Hagen.... | J. Barnes | 2 up |
| 1925 | Olympia Fields (Ill.) C.C. | Walter Hagen.... | B. Mehlhorn | 6 and 5 |
| 1926 | Salisbury G.C., Westbury, L.I., N.Y. | Walter Hagen.... | L. Diegel | 5 and 3 |
| 1927 | Cedar Crest C.C., Dallas, Texas | Walter Hagen.... | J. Turnesa | 1 up |
| 1928 | Baltimore (Md.) C.C. | Leo Diegel | Al Espinosa | 6 and 5 |
| 1929 | Hillcrest C.C., Los Angeles, Calif. | Leo Diegel | J. Farrell | 6 and 4 |
| 1930 | Fresh Meadows C.C., Flushing, N.Y. | Tommy Armour.. | G. Sarazen | 1 up |
| 1931 | Wannamoisett C.C., Rumford, R.I. | Tom Creavy | D. Shute | 2 and 1 |
| 1932 | Keller G.C., St. Paul, Minn. | Olin Dutra | F. Walsh | 4 and 3 |
| 1933 | Blue Mound C.C., Milwaukee, Wis. | Gene Sarazen | W. Goggin | 5 and 4 |
| 1934 | Park C.C., Williamsville, N.Y. | Paul Runyan | C. Wood | 1 up, 38 holes |
| 1935 | Twin Hills C.C., Oklahoma City, Okla. | Johnny Revolta | T. Armour | 5 and 4 |
| 1936 | Pinehurst (N.C.) C.C. | Denny Shute | J. Thomson | 3 and 2 |
| 1937 | Pittsburgh F.C., Aspinwall, Penn. | Denny Shute | H. McSpaden | 1 up, 37 holes |
| 1938 | Shawnee C.C., Shawnee-on-Delaware, Penn. | Paul Runyan | S. Snead | 8 and 7 |
| 1939 | Pomonok C.C., Flushing, N.Y. | Henry Picard | B. Nelson | 1 up, 37 holes |
| 1940 | Hershey (Penn.) C.C. | Byron Nelson | S. Snead | 1 up |
| 1941 | Cherry Hills C.C., Denver, Colo. | Vic Ghezzi | B. Nelson | 1 up, 38 holes |
| 1942 | Seaview C.C., Atlantic City, N.J. | Sam Snead | J. Turnesa | 2 and 1 |
| 1944 | Manito G. & C.C., Spokane, Wash. | Bob Hamilton | B. Nelson | 1 up |
| 1945 | Moraine C.C., Dayton, Ohio | Byron Nelson | S. Byrd | 4 and 3 |
| 1946 | Portland (Oreg.) C.C. | Ben Hogan | E. Oliver | 6 and 4 |
| 1947 | Plum Hollow C.C., Detroit, Mich. | Jim Ferrier | C. Harbert | 2 and 1 |
| 1948 | Norwood Hills C.C., St. Louis, Mo. | Ben Hogan | M. Turnesa | 7 and 6 |
| 1949 | Hermitage C.C., Richmond, Va. | Sam Snead | J. Palmer | 3 and 2 |
| 1950 | Scioto C.C., Columbus, Ohio | Chandler Harper. | H. Williams, Jr. | 4 and 3 |
| 1951 | Oakmont (Penn.) C.C. | Sam Snead | W. Burkemo | 7 and 6 |
| 1952 | Big Spring C.C., Louisville, Ky. | Jim Turnesa | C. Harbert | 1 up |
| 1953 | Birmingham (Mich.) C.C. | Walter Burkemo. | F. Torza | 2 and 1 |
| 1954 | Keller G.C., St. Paul, Minn. | Chick Harbert | W. Burkemo | 4 and 3 |
| 1955 | Meadow Brook C.C., Northville, Mich. | Doug Ford | C. Middlecoff | 4 and 3 |
| 1956 | Blue Hill C.C., Canton, Mass. | Jack Burke | T. Kroll | 3 and 2 |
| 1957 | Miami Valley C.C., Dayton, Ohio. | Lionel Hebert | D. Finsterwald | 2 and 1 |
| 1958 | Llanerch C.C., Haverford, Penn. | Dow Finsterwald. | Bill Casper | 276–278 |
| 1959 | Minneapolis G.C., St. Louis Park, Minn. | Bob Rosburg | Jerry Barber Doug Sanders | 277–278 |
| 1960 | Firestone C.C., Akron, Ohio. | Jay Hebert | Jim Ferrier | 281–282 |
| 1961 | Olympia Fields (Ill.) C.C. | Jerry Barber | Don January | 277–67, 277–68 |
| 1962 | Aronimink G.C., Newtown Square, Penn. | Gary Player | Bob Goalby | 278–279 |
| 1963 | Dallas C.C., Dallas, Texas. | Jack Nicklaus | Dave Ragen | 279–281 |
| 1964 | Columbus C.C., Columbus, Ohio. | Bobby Nichols | Arnold Palmer Jack Nicklaus | 271–274 |
| 1965 | Laurel Valley G.C., Ligonier, Penn. | Dave Marr | Bill Casper Jack Nicklaus | 280–282 |
| 1966 | Firestone C.C., Akron, Ohio. | Al Geiberger | Dudley Wysong | 280–284 |
| 1967 | Colombine C.C., Denver, Colo. | Don January | Don Massengale | 281–69, 281–71 |

## THE MASTERS CHAMPIONSHIP

The Masters is played annually at Augusta National Golf Club, Augusta, Georgia, among leading professional golfers. In 1967 the winner's share of the tournament money was $20,000. Arnold Palmer is the only golfer to have won the Masters four times.

| YEAR | WINNER | SCORE | YEAR | WINNER | SCORE | YEAR | WINNER | SCORE |
|------|--------|-------|------|--------|-------|------|--------|-------|
| 1935 | Gene Sarazen[1] | 282 | 1948 | Claude Harmon | 279 | 1958 | Arnold Palmer | 284 |
| 1936 | Horton Smith | 285 | 1949 | Sam Snead | 282 | 1959 | Art Wall, Jr. | 284 |
| 1937 | Byron Nelson | 283 | 1950 | Jimmy Demaret | 283 | 1960 | Arnold Palmer | 282 |
| 1938 | Henry Picard | 285 | 1951 | Ben Hogan | 280 | 1961 | Gary Player | 280 |
| 1939 | Ralph Guldahl | 279 | 1952 | Sam Snead | 286 | 1962 | Arnold Palmer[1] | 280 |
| 1940 | Jimmy Demaret | 280 | 1953 | Ben Hogan | 274 | 1963 | Jack Nicklaus | 286 |
| 1941 | Craig Wood | 280 | 1954 | Sam Snead[1] | 289 | 1964 | Arnold Palmer | 276 |
| 1942 | Byron Nelson[1] | 280 | 1955 | Cary Middlecoff | 279 | 1965 | Jack Nicklaus | 271[2] |
| 1946 | Herman Keiser | 282 | 1956 | Jack Burke | 289 | 1966 | Jack Nicklaus[1] | 288 |
| 1947 | Jimmy Demaret | 281 | 1957 | Doug Ford | 283 | 1967 | Gay Brewer | 280 |

[1] Won in playoff. [2] Lowest score ever recorded in the Masters.

## OTHER SELECTED PROFESSIONAL GOLF TOURNAMENTS: 1967

| EVENT | PURSE | WINNER | WINNER'S SHARE | COURSE |
|---|---|---|---|---|
| American Golf Classic..... | $100,000 | Arnold Palmer....... | $20,000 | Firestone C.C., Akron, Ohio |
| Atlanta Classic.......... | 110,000 | Bob Charles......... | 22,000 | Atlanta C.C., Atlanta, Georgia |
| Bing Crosby National..... | 80,000 | Jack Nicklaus........ | 16,000 | Pebble Beach G.C., Cypress Point G.C., and Spy Glass Hill C.C., California |
| Bob Hope Desert Classic.. | 88,000 | Tom Nieporte........ | 17,600 | Four California courses |
| Buick Open............. | 100,000 | Julius Boros......... | 20,000 | Warwick Hills C.C., Grand Blanc, Michigan |
| Canadian Open.......... | 200,000 | Billy Casper......... | 30,000 | Vancouver C.C., Vancouver, Canada |
| Carling World Open...... | 200,000 | Billy Casper......... | 35,000 | Board of Trade C.C., Toronto, Canada |
| Cleveland Open.......... | 103,500 | Gardner Dickinson.... | 20,700 | Lakewood C.C., Cleveland, Ohio |
| Colonial Invitational...... | 115,000 | Dave Stockton....... | 23,000 | Colonial C.C., Fort Worth, Texas |
| Dallas Open............. | 100,000 | Bert Yancey......... | 20,000 | Oak Cliff C.C., Dallas, Texas |
| Doral Open............. | 100,000 | Doug Sanders........ | 20,000 | Doral C.C., Miami, Florida |
| 500 Festival Open........ | 100,000 | Frank Beard......... | 20,000 | Speedway G.C., Indianapolis, Indiana |
| Florida Citrus Open...... | 115,000 | Julius Boros......... | 23,000 | Rio Pinar C.C., Orlando, Florida |
| Greater Hartford Open.... | 100,000 | Charles Sifford....... | 20,000 | Wethersfield C.C., Wethersfield, Connecticut |
| Greensboro Open......... | 125,000 | George Archer....... | 25,000 | Sedgefield C.C., Greensboro, North Carolina |
| Houston Champions International.......... | 115,000 | Frank Beard......... | 23,000 | Champions G.C., Houston, Texas |
| Jacksonville Open........ | 100,000 | Dan Sikes........... | 20,000 | Selva Marina C.C., Jacksonville, Florida |
| Los Angeles Open........ | 100,000 | Arnold Palmer....... | 20,000 | Rancho Park Municipal Course, Los Angeles, California |
| Memphis Open.......... | 100,000 | Dave Hill........... | 20,000 | Colonial C.C., Memphis, Tennessee |
| Minnesota Classic........ | 100,000 | Lou Graham......... | 20,000 | Medinah C.C., Medinah, Minnesota |
| New Orleans Open....... | 100,000 | George Knudson...... | 20,000 | Lakewood C.C., New Orleans, Louisiana |
| Pensacola Open......... | 75,000 | Gay Brewer......... | 15,000 | Pensacola C.C., Pensacola, Florida |
| Philadelphia Classic...... | 110,000 | Dan Sikes.......... | 22,000 | Whitemarsh C.C., Whitemarsh, Pennsylvania |
| Phoenix Open........... | 70,000 | Julius Boros......... | 14,000 | Arizona C.C., Phoenix, Arizona |
| Sahara Tournament...... | 100,000 | Jack Nicklaus....... | 20,000 | Paradise C.C., Las Vegas, Nevada |
| San Diego Open.......... | 66,000 | Bob Goalby.......... | 13,200 | Stardust C.C., San Diego, California |
| Texas Open............. | 100,000 | Juan Rodriguez...... | 20,000 | Oak Hills C.C., San Antonio, Texas |
| Thunderbird Classic...... | 150,000 | Arnold Palmer....... | 30,000 | Upper Montclair C.C., Montclair, New Jersey |
| Tournament of Champions | 100,000 | Frank Beard......... | 20,000 | Desert Inn C.C., Las Vegas, Nevada |
| Tucson Open............ | 60,000 | Arnold Palmer....... | 12,000 | Tucson National C.C., Tucson, Arizona |
| Westchester Classic...... | 250,000 | Jack Nicklaus........ | 50,000 | Westchester C.C., Harrison, New York |
| Western Open........... | 102,000 | Jack Nicklaus........ | 20,000 | Tam O'Shanter C.C., Chicago, Illinois |
| World Series of Golf...... | 77,500 | Jack Nicklaus........ | 50,000 | Firestone C.C., Akron, Ohio |

## THE WALKER CUP

The oldest international amateur golf team match, the Walker Cup competition is played between teams representing the United States and Great Britain. The Cup was presented by G. Herbert Walker, former president of the United States Golf Association, and the first competition was held in 1922. Since 1924 the match has taken place every two years.

| YEAR | RESULTS | COURSE AND LOCATION |
|---|---|---|
| 1922 | United States, 8; Great Britain, 4.................... | National Golf Links of America, Southampton, N.Y. |
| 1923 | United States, 6; Great Britain, 5; one match halved... | St. Andrews, Scotland |
| 1924 | United States, 9; Great Britain, 3.................... | Garden City Golf Club, Garden City, N.Y. |
| 1926 | United States, 6; Great Britain, 5; one match halved... | St. Andrews, Scotland |
| 1928 | United States, 11; Great Britain, 1................... | Chicago Golf Club, Wheaton, Ill. |
| 1930 | United States, 10; Great Britain, 2.................. | Royal St. George's G.C., Sandwich, England |
| 1932 | United States, 8; Great Britain, 1; three matches halved | The Country Club, Brookline, Mass. |
| 1934 | United States, 9; Great Britain, 2; one match halved... | St. Andrews, Scotland |
| 1936 | United States, 9; Great Britain, 0; three matches halved | Pine Valley Golf Club, Clementon, N.J. |
| 1938 | Great Britain, 7; United States, 4; one match halved... | St. Andrews, Scotland |
| 1947 * | United States, 8; Great Britain, 4................... | St. Andrews, Scotland |
| 1949 | United States, 10; Great Britain, 2.................. | Winged Foot G.C., Mamaroneck, N.Y. |
| 1951 | United States, 6; Great Britain, 3; three matches halved | Birkdale Golf Club, Southport, England |
| 1953 | United States, 9; Great Britain, 3................... | Kittansett Club, Marion, Mass. |
| 1955 | United States, 10; Great Britain, 2.................. | St. Andrews, Scotland |
| 1957 | United States, 8; Great Britain, 3; one match halved... | Minikahda Club, Minneapolis, Minn. |
| 1959 | United States, 9; Great Britain, 3................... | Honourable Company of Edinburgh Golfers, Muirfield, Scotland |
| 1961 | United States, 11; Great Britain, 1.................. | Seattle Golf Club, Seattle, Wash. |
| 1963 | United States, 12; Great Britain, 8; four matches halved. | Turnberry, Scotland |
| 1965 | United States, 11; Great Britain, 11................. | Baltimore Country Club, Baltimore, Md. |
| 1967 | United States, 13; Great Britain, 7.................. | Royal St. George's G.C., Sandwich, England |

* No competition, 1940–45, because of World War II.

## USGA AMATEUR CHAMPIONS

The United States Golf Association (USGA) conducted its first amateur men's championship in 1895. Today, amateurs with handicaps of three strokes or less, who qualify on a 36-hole round, are eligible to play in the championship matches. The winner is awarded a silver trophy. In 1965 the USGA shifted the Amateur from match to stroke play.

| YEAR | ENTRIES | COURSE AND LOCATION | CHAMPION | RUNNER-UP | SCORE |
|------|---------|---------------------|----------|-----------|-------|
| 1921 | 159 | St. Louis C.C., Clayton, Mo............. | Jesse P. Guilford..... | Robert A. Gardner.. | 7 and 6 |
| 1922 | 161 | The Country Club, Brookline, Mass...... | Jess W. Sweetser..... | Charles Evans, Jr... | 3 and 2 |
| 1923 | 143 | Flossmoor C.C., Flossmoor, Ill......... | Max R. Marston..... | Jess W. Sweetser... | 1 up, 38 holes |
| 1924 | 154 | Merion Cricket C., Haverford, Penn...... | Robert T. Jones, Jr.... | George Von Elm.... | 9 and 8 |
| 1925 | 141 | Oakmont C.C., Oakmont, Penn.......... | Robert T. Jones, Jr.... | Watts Gunn........ | 8 and 7 |
| 1926 | 157 | Baltusrol G.C., Short Hills, N.J......... | George Von Elm...... | Robert T. Jones, Jr. | 2 and 1 |
| 1927 | 174 | Minikahda Club, Minneapolis, Minn.... | Robert T. Jones, Jr.... | Charles Evans, Jr... | 8 and 7 |
| 1928 | 158 | Brae Burn C.C., West Newton, Mass..... | Robert T. Jones, Jr.... | T. Phillip Perkins... | 10 and 9 |
| 1929 | 162 | Del Monte Golf & C.C., Del Monte, Calif. | Harrison R. Johnston | Dr. O. F. Willing.... | 4 and 3 |
| 1930 | 175 | Merion Cricket C., Ardmore, Penn...... | Robert T. Jones, Jr.... | Eugene V. Homans.. | 8 and 7 |
| 1931 | 583 | Beverly C.C., Chicago, Ill.............. | Francis Ouimet....... | Jack Westland..... | 6 and 5 |
| 1932 | 600 | Baltimore C.C., Five Farms Course, Md. | C. Ross Somerville.. | John Goodman..... | 2 and 1 |
| 1933 | 601 | Kenwood C.C., Cincinnati, Ohio....... | George T. Dunlap, Jr. | Max R. Marston.... | 6 and 5 |
| 1934 | 758 | The Country Club, Brookline, Mass...... | W. Lawson Little, Jr... | David Goldman..... | 8 and 7 |
| 1935 | 945 | The Country Club, Cleveland, Ohio..... | W. Lawson Little, Jr... | Walter Emery...... | 4 and 2 |
| 1936 | 1,118 | Garden City G.C., Garden City, N.Y..... | John W. Fischer...... | Jack McLean...... | 1 up, 37 holes |
| 1937 | 619 | Alderwood C.C., Portland, Oreg........ | John Goodman....... | Raymond E. Billows.. | 2 up |
| 1938 | 871 | Oakmont C.C., Oakmont, Penn........ | William P. Turnesa... | B. Patrick Abbott... | 8 and 7 |
| 1939 | 826 | North Shore C.C., Glenview, Ill........ | Marvin H. Ward..... | Raymond E. Billows | 7 and 5 |
| 1940 | 755 | Winged Foot G.C., Mamaroneck, N.Y.... | Richard D. Chapman.. | W. B. McCullough, Jr. | 11 and 9 |
| 1941 | 637 | Omaha Field C., Omaha, Nebr........ | Marvin H. Ward..... | B. Patrick Abbott... | 4 and 3 |
| 1946 | 899 | Baltusrol G.C., Springfield, N.J......... | Stanley E. (Ted) Bishop | Smiley L. Quick..... | 1 up, 37 holes |
| 1947 | 1,048 | Del Monte Golf & C.C., Del Monte, Calif. | Robert H. (Skee) Riegel | John W. Dawson.... | 2 and 1 |
| 1948 | 1,220 | Memphis C.C., Memphis, Tenn......... | William P. Turnesa... | Raymond E. Billows | 2 and 1 |
| 1949 | 1,060 | Oak Hill C.C., Rochester, N.Y......... | Charles R. Coe...... | Rufus King....... | 11 and 10 |
| 1950 | 1,025 | Minneapolis G.C., Minneapolis, Minn.... | Sam Urzetta........ | Frank Stranahan... | 1 up, 39 holes |
| 1951 | 1,416 | Saucon Valley C.C., Bethlehem, Penn.... | Billy Maxwell....... | Joseph F. Gagliardi.. | 4 and 3 |
| 1952 | 1,029 | Seattle G.C., Seattle, Wash........... | Jack Westland....... | Al Mengert........ | 3 and 2 |
| 1953 | 1,284 | Oklahoma City G. & C.C., Oklahoma City, Okla...................... | Gene A. Littler....... | Dale Morey........ | 1 up |
| 1954 | 1,278 | C.C. of Detroit, Grosse Pointe Farms, Mich...................... | Arnold D. Palmer.... | Robert Sweeny..... | 1 up |
| 1955 | 1,493 | C.C. of Virginia, Richmond, Va........ | E. Harvie Ward, Jr... | Wm. Hyndman, III.. | 9 and 8 |
| 1956 | 1,600 | Knollwood C.C., Lake Forest, Ill........ | E. Harvie Ward, Jr... | Charles Kocsis..... | 5 and 4 |
| 1957 | 1,578 | The Country Club, Brookline, Mass...... | Hillman Robbins, Jr... | Dr. Frank M. Taylor | 5 and 4 |
| 1958 | 1,472 | Olympic C.C., San Francisco, Calif...... | Charles R. Coe...... | Thomas D. Aaron... | 5 and 4 |
| 1959 | 1,696 | Broadmoor G.C., Colorado Springs, Colo. | Jack W. Nicklaus..... | Charles R. Coe..... | 1 up |
| 1960 | 1,737 | St. Louis C.C., Clayton, Mo............. | Deane R. Beman..... | Robert W. Gardner.. | 6 and 4 |
| 1961 | 1,995 | Pebble Beach Golf Links, Pebble Beach, Calif...................... | Jack W. Nicklaus..... | Dudley Wysong..... | 8 and 6 |
| 1962 | 2,044 | Pinehurst C.C., Pinehurst, N.C......... | Labron Harris, Jr..... | Downing Gray...... | 1 up |
| 1963 | 1,768 | Wakonda Club, Des Moines, Iowa....... | Deane R. Beman..... | Dan Sikes........ | 2 and 1 |
| 1964 | 1,562 | Canterbury C.C., Cleveland, Ohio....... | William Campbell.... | Edgar Tutwiler..... | 1 up |
| 1965 | 1,476 | Southern Hills C.C., Tulsa, Okla........ | Robert J. Murphy, Jr.. | Bob Dickson...... | 291–292 |
| 1966 | 1,902 | Merion G.C., Ardmore, Penn........... | Gary Cowan......... | Deane R. Beman.... | 285–285 * |
| 1967 | 1,818 | Broadmoor G.C., Colorado Springs, Colo. | Robert B. Dickson.... | Marvin Giles, III... | 285–286 |

\* Play-off; Cowan–75, Beman–76.

## THE AMERICAS CUP GOLF MATCH

Presented in 1952, the Americas Cup is played for by men's amateur golf teams represent- ing the United States, Mexico, and Canada. Matches are held every two years.

| YEAR | RESULTS | COURSE AND LOCATION |
|------|---------|---------------------|
| 1952 | United States, 12; Canada, 10; Mexico, 5........... | Seattle Golf Club, Seattle, Washington |
| 1954 | United States, 14; Canada, 13; Mexico, 0........... | London Hunt and Country Club, London, Ontario, Canada |
| 1956 | United States, 29½; Mexico, 13; Canada, 11½...... | Club Campestre de la Ciudad de Mexico, D. F. |
| 1958 | United States, 30; Canada, 17; Mexico, 7.......... | Olympic C.C. (Lake Course), San Francisco, California |
| 1960 | United States, 21½; Canada, 20; Mexico, 12½...... | Ottawa Hunt and Golf Club, Ottawa, Canada |
| 1961 | United States, 29; Mexico, 14; Canada, 11........ | Club Campestre Monterrey, A. C., Monterrey City, Mex. |
| 1963 | United States, 26½; Canada, 19½; Mexico, 8....... | Wakonda Club, Des Moines, Iowa |
| 1965 | Canada, 22; United States, 19½; Mexico, 12½...... | St. Charles C.C., Winnipeg, Manitoba, Canada |
| 1967 | United States, 14½; Canada, 11½; Mexico, 10...... | Guadalajara C.C., Guadalajara Jal, Mexico |

## UNITED STATES GOLF ASSOCIATION OPEN

The first USGA Open was held in 1895 at the Newport (Rhode Island) Golf Club, with a field of ten professionals and one amateur. The 36-hole, one-day competition was won by Horace Rawlins, an English professional; at 19, he was the youngest golfer ever to win the U.S. Open.

Today the tournament is a 72-hole, 4-day competition. The Open champion is awarded a silver trophy, custody of the Championship Cup, and a first prize of about $25,000.

### U.S. OPEN GOLF FINISHES: 1927–67

**1927** Oakmont, Pennsylvania, Tommy Armour and Harry Cooper tied at 301. Armour won playoff, 76-79.

**1928** Mateson, Illinois, Johnny Farrell and Robert T. Jones, Jr. tied at 294. Farrell won playoff, 143-144.

**1929** Mamaroneck, New York, Robert T. Jones, Jr. and Al Espinosa tied at 294. Jones won play-off, 141-164.

**1930** Minneapolis, Minn., Robert T. Jones, Jr. 287, Macdonald Smith 289.

**1931** Toledo, Ohio, Billy Burke and George Von Elm tied at 292. Tied playoff at 149. Burke won second playoff, 148-149.

**1932** Flushing, N.Y., Gene Sarazen 286, two tied at 289.

**1933** Glenn View, Ill., Johnny Goodman 287, Ralph Guldahl 288.

**1934** Ardmore, Penn., Olin Dutra 293, Gene Sarazen 294.

**1935** Oakmont, Penn., Sam Parks, Jr. 299, Jimmy Thomson 301.

**1936** Baltusrol, N.J., Tony Manero 282, Harry Cooper 284.

**1937** Birmingham, Mich., Ralph Guldahl 281, Sam Snead 283.

**1938** Denver, Colo., Ralph Guldahl 284, Dick Metz 290.

**1939** Philadelphia, Byron Nelson, Craig Wood, and Denny Shute tied at 284. Nelson and Wood tied in first playoff at 68. Nelson won second play-off, 70-73.

**1940** Warrensville, Ohio, Lawson Little and Gene Sarazen tied at 287. Little won playoff, 70-73.

**1941** Fort Worth, Texas, Craig Wood 284, Denny Shute 287.

**1942-45** World War II.: no tournaments held.

**1946** Cleveland, Ohio, Lloyd Mangrum, Byron Nelson, and Vic Ghezzi tied at 284. Mangrum won the playoff, 72-73-73.

**1947** St. Louis, Mo., Lew Worsham and Sam Snead tied at 282. Worsham won playoff, 69-70.

**1948** Los Angeles, Calif., Ben Hogan 276, Jimmy Demaret 278.

**1949** Medinah, Ill., Cary Middlecoff 286, two tied at 287.

**1950** Ardmore, Penn., Ben Hogan, Lloyd Mangrum, and George Fazio tied at 287. Hogan won play-off, 69-73-75.

**1951** Birmingham, Mich., Ben Hogan 287, Clayton Heafner 289.

**1952** Dallas, Texas, Julius Boros 281, Ed Oliver 285.

**1953** Oakmont, Penn., Ben Hogan 283, Sam Snead 289.

**1954** Baltusrol, N.J., Ed Furgol 284, Gene Littler 285.

**1955** San Francisco, Calif., Jack Fleck and Ben Hogan tied at 287. Fleck won the eighteen-hole playoff, 69-72.

**1956** Rochester, N.Y., Cary Middlecoff 281, two tied at 282.

**1957** Toledo, Ohio, Dick Mayer and Cary Middlecoff tied at 282. Mayer won playoff, 72-79.

**1958** Tulsa, Okla., Tommy Bolt 283, Gary Player 287.

**1959** Mamaroneck, N.Y., Bill Casper 282, Bob Ros-burg 283.

**1960** Denver, Colo., Arnold Palmer 280, Jack Nicklaus 282.

**1961** Birmingham, Mich., Gene Littler 281, two tied at 282.

**1962** Oakmont, Penn., Jack Nicklaus and Arnold Palmer tied at 283. Nicklaus won playoff, 71-74.

**1963** Brookline, Mass., Julius Boros, Jacky Cupit, and Arnold Palmer tied at 293. Boros won play-off, 70-73-76.

**1964** Washington, D.C., Ken Venturi 278, Tommy Jacobs 282.

**1965** St. Louis, Mo., Gary Player and Kel Nagle tied at 282. Player won playoff, 71-74.

**1966** San Francisco, Calif., Billy Casper and Arnold Palmer tied at 278. Casper won playoff, 69-73.

**1967** Springfield, N.J., Jack Nicklaus 275, Arnold Palmer 279.

## WOMEN'S AMATEUR GOLF CHAMPIONSHIP

First held in 1895, and sponsored by the United States Golf Association (USGA), the Women's Amateur tournament since 1896 has been set at match play. Mrs. Edwin H. Vare, Jr. (Glenna Collett) is the only woman ever to have taken the amateur title six times.

| YEAR | COURSE AND LOCATION | CHAMPION | RUNNER-UP | SCORE |
|---|---|---|---|---|
| 1923 | Westchester-Biltmore C.C., Rye, N.Y......... | Edith Cummings......... | Alexa Stirling........ | 3 and 2 |
| 1924 | Rhode Island C.C., Nyatt, R.I............. | Dorothy Campbell Hurd. | Mary K. Browne...... | 7 and 6 |
| 1925 | St. Louis C.C., Clayton, Mo................. | Glenna Collett.......... | Mrs. W. G. Fraser..... | 9 and 8 |
| 1926 | Merion Cricket C., Haverford, Penn.......... | Mrs. G. Henry Stetson... | Mrs. W. D. Goss, Jr.... | 3 and 1 |
| 1927 | Cherry Valley Club, Garden City, N.Y....... | Miriam Burns Horn..... | Maureen Orcutt...... | 5 and 4 |
| 1928 | Hot Springs G. & T.C., Hot Springs, Va....... | Glenna Collett.......... | Virginia Van Wie..... | 13 and 12 |
| 1929 | Oakland Hills C.C., Birmingham, Mich........ | Glenna Collett.......... | Mrs. Leona Pressler... | 4 and 3 |
| 1930 | Los Angeles C.C., Beverly Hills, Calif......... | Glenna Collett.......... | Virginia Van Wie..... | 6 and 5 |
| 1931 | C.C. of Buffalo, Williamsville, N.Y........... | Helen Hicks .......... | Glenna Collett....... | 2 and 1 |
| 1932 | Salem C.C., Peabody, Mass................. | Virginia Van Wie...... | Glenna Collett Vare... | 10 and 8 |
| 1933 | Exmoor C.C., Highland Park, Ill............. | Virginia Van Wie...... | Helen Hicks........ | 4 and 3 |
| 1934 | Whitemarsh Valley C.C., Chestnut Hill, Penn.... | Virginia Van Wie...... | Dorothy Traung...... | 2 and 1 |

| YEAR | COURSE AND LOCATION | CHAMPION | RUNNER-UP | SCORE |
|---|---|---|---|---|
| 1935 | Interlachen C.C., Hopkins, Minn.............. | Glenna Collett Vare..... | Patty Berg........... | 3 and 2 |
| 1936 | Canoe Brook C.C., Summit, N.J.............. | Pamela Barton........ | Maureen Orcutt Crews | 4 and 3 |
| 1937 | Memphis C.C., Memphis, Tenn............... | Mrs. Julius A. Page, Jr. | Patty Berg........... | 7 and 6 |
| 1938 | Westmoreland C.C., Wilmette, Ill............. | Patty Berg............. | Mrs. Julius A. Page, Jr. | 6 and 5 |
| 1939 | Wee Burn Club, Darien, Conn. | Betty Jameson........ | Dorothy Kirby........ | 3 and 2 |
| 1940 | Del Monte G. & C.C., Del Monte, Calif....... | Betty Jameson........ | Jane Cothran......... | 6 and 5 |
| 1941 | The Country Club, Brookline, Mass........... | Mrs. Frank Newell...... | Helen Sigel.......... | 5 and 3 |
| 1946 | Southern Hills C.C., Tulsa, Okla............. | Babe Didrikson Zaharias | Mrs. Clara Sherman.. | 11 and 9 |
| 1947 | Franklin Hills C.C., Franklin, Mich........... | Louise Suggs.......... | Dorothy Kirby........ | 2 up |
| 1948 | Del Monte G. & C.C., Del Monte, Calif........ | Grace S. Lenczyk...... | Helen Sigel.......... | 4 and 3 |
| 1949 | Merion G.C., Ardmore, Penn................ | Mrs. Mark A. Porter.... | Dorothy Kielty....... | 3 and 2 |
| 1950 | Atlanta A.C. (East Lake), Atlanta, Ga......... | Beverly Hanson........ | Mae Murray........ | 6 and 4 |
| 1951 | Town C.C., St. Paul, Minn.................. | Dorothy Kirby......... | Claire Doran........ | 2 and 1 |
| 1952 | Waverley C.C., Portland, Oreg.............. | Mrs. Jacqueline Pung... | Shirley McFedters.... | 2 and 1 |
| 1953 | Rhode Island C.C., West Barrington, R.I....... | Mary Lena Faulk...... | Polly Riley......... | 3 and 2 |
| 1954 | Allegheny C.C., Sewickley, Penn............. | Barbara Romack....... | Mary K. Wright...... | 4 and 2 |
| 1955 | Myers Park C.C., Charlotte, N.C............. | Patricia A. Lesser..... | Jane Nelson....... | 7 and 6 |
| 1956 | Meridian Hills C.C., Indianapolis, Ind......... | Marlene Stewart...... | JoAnne Gunderson.... | 2 and 1 |
| 1957 | Del Paso C.C., Sacramento, Calif............. | JoAnne Gunderson...... | Mrs. Les Johnstone.... | 8 and 6 |
| 1958 | Wee Burn C.C., Darien, Conn............... | Anne Quast............ | Barbara Romack..... | 3 and 2 |
| 1959 | Congressional C.C., Washington, D.C......... | Barbara McIntire...... | Joanne Goodwin..... | 4 and 3 |
| 1960 | Tulsa C.C., Tulsa, Okla.................... | JoAnne Gunderson..... | Jean Ashley......... | 6 and 5 |
| 1961 | Tacoma C. & G.C., Tacoma, Wash............ | Anne Quast Decker.... | Phyllis Preuss....... | 14 and 13 |
| 1962 | C.C. of Rochester, Rochester, N.Y........... | JoAnne Gunderson..... | Ann Baker.......... | 9 and 8 |
| 1963 | Taconic G.C., Williamstown, Mass............ | Anne Quast Welts...... | Peggy Conley....... | 2 and 1 |
| 1964 | Prairie Dunes C.C., Hutchinson, Kans......... | Barbara McIntire...... | JoAnne Gunderson.... | 3 and 2 |
| 1965 | Lakewood C.C., Denver, Colo............... | Jean Ashley.......... | Anne Quast Welts.... | 5 and 4 |
| 1966 | Sewickley Heights G.C., Sewickley, Penn....... | Mrs. JoAnne G. Carner.. | Mrs. J. Douglas Streit. | 41 holes |
| 1967 | Annandale G.C., Pasadena, Calif............. | Lou Dill.............. | Jean Ashley......... | 5 and 4 |

## WOMEN'S OPEN GOLF CHAMPIONSHIP

First held in 1946, the Women's Open is a major golf tournament. Betsy Rawls and Mickey Wright are the only women ever to have won four Open championships.

| YEAR | COURSE | WINNER | SCORE | RUNNER-UP | SCORE |
|---|---|---|---|---|---|
| **Conducted by Women's Professional Golfers' Association** | | | | | |
| 1946 | Spokane C.C., Spokane, Wash......... | Patty Berg............ | 5 and 4 [1] | Betty Jameson........ | — |
| 1947 | Starmount Forest C.C., Greensboro, N.C. | Betty Jameson........ | 295 | Sally Sessions [2]....... | 301-4 [4] |
| | | | | Polly Riley [2].......... | 301-5 [4] |
| 1948 | Atlantic City C.C., Northfield, N.J... | Babe Didrikson Zaharias | 300 | Betty Hicks.......... | 308 |
| **Conducted by Ladies' Professional Golfers' Association** | | | | | |
| 1949 | Prince Georges G. & C.C., Landover, Md. | Louise Suggs......... | 291 | Babe Didrikson Zaharias | 305 |
| 1950 | Rolling Hills C.C., Wichita, Kans........ | Babe Didrikson Zaharias | 291 | Betsy Rawls [2]........ | 300 |
| 1951 | Druid Hills G.C., Atlanta, Ga............ | Betsy Rawls.......... | 293 | Louise Suggs......... | 298 |
| 1952 | Bala G.C., Philadelphia, Penn.......... | Louise Suggs......... | 284 | Marlene Bauer....... | 291 |
| | | | | Betty Jameson........ | 291 |
| **Conducted by United States Golf Association** | | | | | |
| 1953 | C.C. of Rochester, Rochester, N.Y...... | Betsy Rawls.......... | 302-71 [3] | Jacqueline Pung....... | 302-77 |
| 1954 | Salem C.C., Peabody, Mass........... | Babe Didrikson Zaharias | 291 | Betty Hicks.......... | 303 |
| 1955 | Wichita C.C., Wichita, Kans............ | Fay Crocker.......... | 299 | Louise Suggs......... | 303 |
| | | | | Mary Lena Faulk...... | 303 |
| 1956 | Northland C.C., Duluth, Minn.......... | Kathy Cornelius....... | 302-75 [3] | Barbara McIntire [2]..... | 302-82 |
| 1957 | Winged Foot G.C., Mamaroneck, N.Y.... | Betsy Rawls.......... | 299 | Patty Berg........... | 305 |
| 1958 | Forest Lake C.C., Bloomfield Hills, Mich. | Mickey Wright........ | 290 | Louise Suggs......... | 295 |
| 1959 | Churchill Valley C.C., Pittsburgh, Penn. . | Mickey Wright........ | 287 | Louise Suggs......... | 289 |
| 1960 | Worcester C.C., Worcester, Mass........ | Betsy Rawls.......... | 292 | Joyce Ziske......... | 293 |
| 1961 | Baltusrol G.C., Springfield, N.J......... | Mickey Wright........ | 293 | Betsy Rawls......... | 299 |
| 1962 | Dunes G.C., Myrtle Beach, S.C.......... | Murle Lindstrom...... | 301 | Ruth Jessen......... | 303 |
| | | | | JoAnn Prentice....... | 303 |
| 1963 | Kenwood C.C., Cincinnati, Ohio........ | Mary Mills........... | 289 | Sandra Haynie....... | 292 |
| | | | | Louise Suggs......... | 292 |
| 1964 | Chula Vista C.C., Chula Vista, Calif..... | Mickey Wright........ | 290-70 [3] | Ruth Jessen......... | 290-72 |
| 1965 | Southern Hills C.C., Tulsa, Okla........ | Carol Mann........... | 290 | Cathy Cornelius...... | 292 |
| 1966 | Hazeltine Nat'l G.C., Chaska, Minn...... | Sandra Spuzich....... | 297 | Carol Mann.......... | 298 |
| 1967 | Hot Springs G. & T.C., Hot Springs, Va... | Catherine Lacoste..... | 294 | Susie Maxwell....... | 296 |
| | | | | Beth Stone.......... | 296 |

[1] Match play. After 1946 tournament was set at medal play.　　[2] Amateur.　　[3] Won playoff.　　[4] Sudden-death playoff.

# GYMNASTICS

The activities at gymnasia in ancient Greece involved far more than just the skilled exercises now associated with competitive gymnastics. Youths not only engaged in all the sports of the day (many of which are classed today as track and field events) but heard lectures and took part in learned discussions.

Despite the physical demands of modern competitive gymnastics—feats of endurance, coordination, and strength equal to or greater than those required by practically any sport—they have not garnered the headlines of other spectator sports in the United States. However, interest in gymnastics is growing in America (it already exists to a much greater degree abroad). The results of two major national championship contests and that for the world championship are given below.

## AAU CHAMPIONSHIP: 1967
(at Nachitoches, Louisiana, May 5–6)

| EVENT | WINNER |
|---|---|
| **Men** | |
| Free Exercise...... | Makato Sakamoto, U. of Southern California |
| Side Horse........ | Arnold Lascari, University of Wisconsin |
| Parallel Bars...... | Yoshi Hayasaki, University of Washington |
| Rings............. | Sei Ito, Northwestern Louisiana State College |
| Horizontal Bar..... | Makato Sakamoto, U. of Southern California |
| Long Horse........ | Sei Ito, Northwestern Louisiana State College |
| Tumbling......... | Tom Proux, Pasadena College |
| Trampoline........ | David Jacobs, University of Michigan |
| All-Around........ | Yoshi Hayasaki, University of Wisconsin |

| EVENT | WINNER |
|---|---|
| Team............. | Northwestern Louisiana State College |
| **Women** | |
| Free Exercise...... | Linda Metheny, University of Illinois |
| Horse Vault....... | Carolyn Hacker, Southern Connecticut State |
| Balance Beam..... | Carolyn Hacker, Southern Connecticut State |
| Uneven Bars...... | Linda Metheny, University of Illinois |
| Tumbling......... | Judy Wills, Southern Illinois University |
| Trampoline........ | Judy Wills, Southern Illinois University |
| All-Around........ | Carolyn Hacker, Southern Connecticut State |
| Team Title........ | Southern Illinois University |

## NCAA CHAMPIONSHIPS: 1967
(at Carbondale, Illinois, March 31–April 1)

| EVENT | WINNER | POINTS |
|---|---|---|
| Floor Exercise............ | Dave Jacobs, University of Michigan........ | 9.450 |
| Side Horse................ | Keith McCanless, University of Iowa........ | 9.600 |
| Horizontal Bar............ | Rich Grigsby, San Fernando Valley State College........ | 9.500 |
| Long Horse Vault.......... | Paul Mayer, Southern Illinois University........ | 9.512 |
| Parallel Bars............. | Makato Sakamoto, University of Southern California....... | 9.525 |
| Still Rings............... | Josh Robison, University of California (Berkeley)........ | 9.600 |
| Trampoline............... | Dave Jacobs, University of Michigan........ | 9.500 |
| All-Around............... | Steve Cohen, Pennsylvania State University........ | 55.750 |
| Team.................... | Southern Illinois University........ | 189.550 |

## WORLD CHAMPIONSHIP

The Federation Internationale de Gymnastique (FIG) determines the rules, exercises, and equipment used in international gymnastic events (the AAU of the U.S., a FIG member, runs its meets under their rules). It also is responsible for the conduct of Olympic gymnastic competition and holds contests in the second year after each Olympic games. The results of the last FIG championship (at Dortmund, Germany, July, 1966) are listed below.

| EVENT | WINNER |
|---|---|
| **Men** | |
| Floor Exercise..... | Akinori Nakayama, Japan |
| Side Horse........ | Miroslav Cernar, Yugoslavia |
| Rings............. | Mikhail Voronine, USSR |
| Long Horse Vault... | Haruhio Matsuda, Japan |
| Parallel Bars...... | Sergei Diamidov, USSR |
| Horizontal Bar..... | Akinori Nakayama, Japan |
| All-Around........ | Mikhail Voronine, USSR |
| Team............. | Japan |

| EVENT | WINNER |
|---|---|
| **Women** | |
| Floor Exercise..... | Natalia Koutchinskaia, USSR |
| Balance Beam..... | Natalia Koutchinskaia, USSR |
| Uneven Parallel Bars...... | Natalia Koutchinskaia, USSR |
| Side Horse Vault... | Vera Casoavska, Czechoslovakia |
| All-Around........ | Vera Casoavska, Czechoslovakia |
| Team............. | Czechoslovakia |

# HOCKEY

Ice hockey probably originated in Kingston, Ontario, around 1860, although several other Canadian cities claim the invention of the sport. In any case, by the 1890s hockey leagues and associations had formed, and the first Stanley Cup was awarded in 1893 to the team winning the championship of Canada.

Hockey turned into a professional sport in the early 20th century, with teams in Canada and the United States. The National Hockey League (NHL) was organized in 1917, and a few years later the Stanley Cup, symbol of world supremacy in professional hockey, came into the possession of the NHL.

In the past decade the only team to break the domination of the Cup by the Montreal Canadiens and Toronto Maple Leafs was the 1960–61 Chicago Black Hawks under coach Rudy Pilous.

The NHL expansion draft began on June 6, 1967. Each of the six new officially franchised members of the NHL received 20 players from the six current teams, which will be known as the Eastern Division. The new teams, which will constitute the Western Division, are: Minnesota North Stars; Pittsburgh Penguins; Los Angeles Kings; California Seals; St. Louis Blues; and Philadelphia Flyers.

## STANLEY CUP CHAMPIONS

The Stanley Cup, which signifies world professional hockey supremacy, is awarded each year to the winner of the playoff among the four top teams of the National Hockey League.

| YEAR | TEAM | COACH | YEAR | TEAM | COACH |
|---|---|---|---|---|---|
| 1945–46 | Montreal Canadiens | Dick Irvin | 1956–57 | Montreal Canadiens | Hector (Toe) Blake |
| 1946–47 | Toronto Maple Leafs | Clarence (Hap) Day | 1957–58 | Montreal Canadiens | Hector (Toe) Blake |
| 1947–48 | Toronto Maple Leafs | Clarence (Hap) Day | 1958–59 | Montreal Canadiens | Hector (Toe) Blake |
| 1948–49 | Toronto Maple Leafs | Clarence (Hap) Day | 1959–60 | Montreal Canadiens | Hector (Toe) Blake |
| 1949–50 | Detroit Red Wings | Tommy Ivan | 1960–61 | Chicago Black Hawks | Rudy Pilous |
| 1950–51 | Toronto Maple Leafs | Joe Primeau | 1961–62 | Toronto Maple Leafs | George (Punch) Imlach |
| 1951–52 | Detroit Red Wings | Tommy Ivan | 1962–63 | Toronto Maple Leafs | George (Punch) Imlach |
| 1952–53 | Montreal Canadiens | Dick Irvin | 1963–64 | Toronto Maple Leafs | George (Punch) Imlach |
| 1953–54 | Detroit Red Wings | Tommy Ivan | 1964–65 | Montreal Canadiens | Hector (Toe) Blake |
| 1954–55 | Detroit Red Wings | Jimmy Skinner | 1965–66 | Montreal Canadiens | Hector (Toe) Blake |
| 1955–56 | Montreal Canadiens | Hector (Toe) Blake | 1966–67 | Toronto Maple Leafs | George (Punch) Imlach |

## STANLEY CUP PLAYOFFS: 1967
(Best four out of seven games)

**Semifinals: Toronto v. Chicago**

| April 6 | Toronto 2....................Chicago 5 |
|---|---|
| April 9 | Toronto 3....................Chicago 1 |
| April 11 | Toronto 3....................Chicago 1 |
| April 13 | Toronto 3....................Chicago 4 |
| April 15 | Toronto 4....................Chicago 2 |
| April 18 | Toronto 3....................Chicago 1 |
| | Toronto wins series, 4–2 |

**Semifinals: Montreal v. New York**

| April 6 | Montreal 6...................New York 4 |
|---|---|
| April 8 | Montreal 3...................New York 1 |

| April 11 | Montreal 3...................New York 2 |
|---|---|
| April 13 | Montreal 2...................New York 1 |
| | Montreal wins series, 4–0 |

**Championship: Toronto v. Montreal**

| April 20 | Toronto 2....................Montreal 6 |
|---|---|
| April 22 | Toronto 3....................Montreal 0 |
| April 25 | Toronto 3....................Montreal 2 |
| April 27 | Toronto 2....................Montreal 6 |
| April 29 | Toronto 4....................Montreal 1 |
| May 2 | Toronto 3....................Montreal 1 |
| | Toronto wins Stanley Cup, 4–2 |

## NATIONAL HOCKEY LEAGUE FINAL STANDINGS: 1966–67

| TEAM | WON | LOST | TIE | PTS. | GOALS For | Agst. | TEAM | WON | LOST | TIE | PTS. | GOALS For | Agst. |
|---|---|---|---|---|---|---|---|---|---|---|---|---|---|
| Chicago...... | 41 | 17 | 12 | 94 | 264 | 170 | New York.... | 30 | 28 | 12 | 72 | 188 | 189 |
| Montreal..... | 32 | 25 | 13 | 77 | 202 | 188 | Detroit...... | 27 | 39 | 4 | 58 | 212 | 241 |
| Toronto...... | 32 | 27 | 11 | 75 | 204 | 211 | Boston...... | 17 | 43 | 10 | 44 | 182 | 253 |

## NATIONAL HOCKEY LEAGUE CHAMPIONS

| 1949–50 | Detroit Red Wings | 1955–56 | Montreal Canadiens | 1961–62 | Montreal Canadiens |
|---|---|---|---|---|---|
| 1950–51 | Detroit Red Wings | 1956–57 | Detroit Red Wings | 1962–63 | Toronto Maple Leafs |
| 1951–52 | Detroit Red Wings | 1957–58 | Montreal Canadiens | 1963–64 | Montreal Canadiens |
| 1952–53 | Detroit Red Wings | 1958–59 | Montreal Canadiens | 1964–65 | Detroit Red Wings |
| 1953–54 | Detroit Red Wings | 1959–60 | Montreal Canadiens | 1965–66 | Montreal Canadiens |
| 1954–55 | Detroit Red Wings | 1960–61 | Montreal Canadiens | 1966–67 | Chicago Black Hawks |

## PROFESSIONAL HOCKEY'S LEADING SCORERS

| YEAR | PLAYER | GAMES PLAYED | GOALS | ASSISTS | POINTS | YEAR | PLAYER | GAMES PLAYED | GOALS | ASSISTS | POINTS |
|------|--------|-----|-----|-----|-----|------|--------|-----|-----|-----|-----|
| 1940–41 | Bill Cowley, Boston...... | 46 | 17 | 45 | 62 | 1954–55 | Bernie Geoffrion, Montreal | 70 | 38 | 37 | 75 |
| 1941–42 | Bryan Hextall, New York. | 48 | 24 | 32 | 56 | 1955–56 | Jean Beliveau, Montreal.. | 70 | 47 | 41 | 88 |
| 1942–43 | Doug Bentley, Chicago... | 50 | 33 | 40 | 73 | 1956–57 | Gordie Howe, Detroit..... | 70 | 44 | 45 | 89 |
| 1943–44 | Herbie Cain, Boston...... | 48 | 36 | 46 | 82 | 1957–58 | Dickie Moore, Montreal... | 70 | 36 | 48 | 84 |
| 1944–45 | Elmer Lach, Montreal.... | 50 | 26 | 54 | 80 | 1958–59 | Dickie Moore, Montreal... | 70 | 41 | 55 | 96 |
| 1945–46 | Max Bentley, Chicago.... | 47 | 31 | 30 | 61 | 1959–60 | Bobby Hull, Chicago..... | 70 | 39 | 42 | 81 |
| 1946–47 | Max Bentley, Chicago.... | 60 | 29 | 43 | 72 | 1960–61 | Bernie Geoffrion, | | | | |
| 1947–48 | Elmer Lach, Montreal.... | 60 | 30 | 31 | 61 |  | Montreal............. | 64 | 50 | 45 | 95 |
| 1948–49 | Roy Conacher, Chicago... | 60 | 26 | 42 | 68 | 1961–62 | Bobby Hull, Chicago..... | 70 | 50 | 34 | 84 |
| 1949–50 | Ted Lindsay, Detroit..... | 69 | 23 | 55 | 78 | 1962–63 | Gordie Howe, Detroit..... | 70 | 38 | 48 | 86 |
| 1950–51 | Gordie Howe, Detroit..... | 70 | 43 | 43 | 86 | 1963–64 | Stan Mikita, Chicago..... | 70 | 39 | 50 | 89 |
| 1951–52 | Gordie Howe, Detroit..... | 70 | 47 | 39 | 86 | 1964–65 | Stan Mikita, Chicago..... | 70 | 28 | 59 | 87 |
| 1952–53 | Gordie Howe, Detroit..... | 70 | 49 | 46 | 95 | 1965–66 | Bobby Hull, Chicago..... | 65 | 54 | 43 | 97 |
| 1953–54 | Gordie Howe, Detroit..... | 70 | 33 | 48 | 81 | 1966–67 | Stan Mikita, Chicago..... | 70 | 35 | 62 | 97 |

## HOCKEY TROPHY WINNERS

### HART MEMORIAL TROPHY (Most valuable player)

| | | | | | |
|---|---|---|---|---|---|
| 1940–41 | Bill Cowley, Boston | 1948–49 | Sid Abel, Detroit | 1957–58 | Gordie Howe, Detroit |
| 1941–42 | Tommy Anderson, | 1949–50 | Chuck Rayner, | 1958–59 | Andy Bathgate, New York |
|  | New York Americans |  | New York Rangers | 1959–60 | Gordie Howe, Detroit |
| 1942–43 | Bill Cowley, Boston | 1950–51 | Milt Schmidt, Boston | 1960–61 | Bernie Geoffrion, Montreal |
| 1943–44 | Walter Pratt, Toronto | 1951–52 | Gordie Howe, Detroit | 1961–62 | Jacques Plante, Montreal |
| 1944–45 | Elmer Lach, Montreal | 1952–53 | Gordie Howe, Detroit | 1962–63 | Gordie Howe, Detroit |
| 1945–46 | Max Bentley, Chicago | 1953–54 | Al Rollins, Chicago | 1963–64 | Jean Beliveau, Montreal |
| 1946–47 | Maurice Richard, Montreal | 1954–55 | Ted Kennedy, Toronto | 1964–65 | Bobby Hull, Chicago |
| 1947–48 | Herbert O'Connor, | 1955–56 | Jean Beliveau, Montreal | 1965–66 | Bobby Hull, Chicago |
|  | New York Rangers | 1956–57 | Gordie Howe, Detroit | 1966–67 | Stan Mikita, Chicago |

### VEZINA TROPHY (Best goalkeeper record)

| | | | | | |
|---|---|---|---|---|---|
| 1940–41 | Walter Broda, Toronto | 1950–51 | Al Rollins, Toronto | 1960–61 | Johnny Bower, Toronto |
| 1941–42 | Frank Brimsek, Boston | 1951–52 | Terry Sawchuk, Detroit | 1961–62 | Jacques Plante, Montreal |
| 1942–43 | Johnny Mowers, Detroit | 1952–53 | Terry Sawchuk, Detroit | 1962–63 | Glenn Hall, Chicago |
| 1943–44 | Bill Durnan, Montreal | 1953–54 | Harry Lumley, Toronto | 1963–64 | Charlie Hodge, Montreal |
| 1944–45 | Bill Durnan, Montreal | 1954–55 | Terry Sawchuk, Detroit | 1964–65 | Terry Sawchuk and |
| 1945–46 | Bill Durnan, Montreal | 1955–56 | Jacques Plante, Montreal |  | Johnny Bower, Toronto |
| 1946–47 | Bill Durnan, Montreal | 1956–57 | Jacques Plante, Montreal | 1965–66 | Lorne Worsley and |
| 1947–48 | Walter Broda, Toronto | 1957–58 | Jacques Plante, Montreal |  | Charlie Hodge, Montreal |
| 1948–49 | Bill Durnan, Montreal | 1958–59 | Jacques Plante, Montreal | 1966–67 | Denis De Jordy and |
| 1949–50 | Bill Durnan, Montreal | 1959–60 | Jacques Plante, Montreal |  | Glenn Hall, Chicago |

### CALDER MEMORIAL TROPHY (Rookie of the year)

| | | | | | |
|---|---|---|---|---|---|
| 1940–41 | Johnny Quilty, Montreal | 1949–50 | Jack Gelineau, Boston | 1958–59 | Ralph Backstrom, Montreal |
| 1941–42 | Grant Warwick, New York | 1950–51 | Terry Sawchuk, Detroit | 1959–60 | Bill Hay, Chicago |
| 1942–43 | Gaye Stewart, Toronto | 1951–52 | Bernie Geoffrion, Montreal | 1960–61 | Dave Keon, Toronto |
| 1943–44 | Gus Bodnar, Toronto | 1952–53 | Lorne Worsley, New York | 1961–62 | Bobby Rousseau, Montreal |
| 1944–45 | Frank McCool, Toronto | 1953–54 | Camille Henry, New York | 1962–63 | Kent Douglas, Toronto |
| 1945–46 | Edgar Laprade, New York | 1954–55 | Ed Litzenberger, Chicago | 1963–64 | Jacques Laperriere, Montreal |
| 1946–47 | Howie Meeker, Toronto | 1955–56 | Glenn Hall, Detroit | 1964–65 | Roger Crozier, Detroit |
| 1947–48 | Jimmy McFadden, Detroit | 1956–57 | Larry Regan, Boston | 1965–66 | Brit Selby, Toronto |
| 1948–49 | Pentti Lund, New York | 1957–58 | Frank Mahovlich, Toronto | 1966–67 | Bobby Orr, Boston |

### LADY BYNG MEMORIAL TROPHY (For skillful and sportsmanlike play)

| | | | | | |
|---|---|---|---|---|---|
| 1940–41 | Bobby Bauer, Boston | 1949–50 | Edgar Laprade, New York | 1958–59 | Alex Delvecchio, Detroit |
| 1941–42 | Syl Apps, Toronto | 1950–51 | Leonard Kelly, Detroit | 1959–60 | Don McKenney, Boston |
| 1942–43 | Max Bentley, Chicago | 1951–52 | Sid Smith, Toronto | 1960–61 | Leonard Kelly, Toronto |
| 1943–44 | Clint Smith, Chicago | 1952–53 | Leonard Kelly, Detroit | 1961–62 | Dave Keon, Toronto |
| 1944–45 | Bill Mosienko, Chicago | 1953–54 | Leonard Kelly, Detroit | 1962–63 | Dave Keon, Toronto |
| 1945–46 | Hector Blake, Montreal | 1954–55 | Sid Smith, Toronto | 1963–64 | Ken Wharram, Chicago |
| 1946–47 | Bobby Bauer, Boston | 1955–56 | Earl Reibel, Detroit | 1964–65 | Bobby Hull, Chicago |
| 1947–48 | Herbert O'Connor, New York | 1956–57 | Andy Hebenton, New York | 1965–66 | Alex Delvecchio, Detroit |
| 1948–49 | Bill Quackenbush, Detroit | 1957–58 | Camille Henry, New York | 1966–67 | Stan Mikita, Chicago |

### JAMES NORRIS MEMORIAL TROPHY (Outstanding defenseman)

| | | | | | |
|---|---|---|---|---|---|
| 1953–54 | Red Kelly, Detroit | 1958–59 | Tom Johnson, Montreal | 1963–64 | Pierre Pilote, Chicago |
| 1954–55 | Doug Harvey, Montreal | 1959–60 | Doug Harvey, Montreal | 1964–65 | Pierre Pilote, Chicago |
| 1955–56 | Doug Harvey, Montreal | 1960–61 | Doug Harvey, Montreal | 1965–66 | Jacques Laperriere, |
| 1956–57 | Doug Harvey, Montreal | 1961–62 | Doug Harvey, New York |  | Montreal |
| 1957–58 | Doug Harvey, Montreal | 1962–63 | Pierre Pilote, Chicago | 1966–67 | Harry Howell, New York |

# HORSE RACING

Horse racing, often referred to as the Sport of Kings, has been showing yearly increase in popularity. The Smithfield Track in London, first of the public race courses, was built about 1174. In this country the first known turf race took place in New York in 1665.

## HORSE RACING'S TRIPLE CROWN

The Kentucky Derby, the Preakness Stakes, and the Belmont Stakes, run each spring in that order, make up horse racing's Triple Crown. Only eight horses have won the Triple Crown: Sir Barton (1919), Gallant Fox (1930), Omaha (1935), War Admiral (1937), Whirlaway (1941), Count Fleet (1943), Assault (1946), and Citation (1948).

### THE KENTUCKY DERBY

Held annually at Churchill Downs, Louisville, Kentucky, the Kentucky Derby was first run in 1875. The distance was a mile and a half until 1896, when it was shortened to a mile and a quarter. Since 1920 the weight has been set at 126 pounds, except for fillies, who are given a five-pound advantage. Eddie Arcaro is the only jockey ever to ride five Derby winners.

| YEAR | WINNER | TIME | MONEY | JOCKEY | WEIGHT | OWNER |
|---|---|---|---|---|---|---|
| 1917 | Omar Khayyam....... | 2:04⅗ | $ 16,600 | C. Borel............. | 117 | Billings and Johnson |
| 1918 | Exterminator.......... | 2:10⅘ | 14,700 | W. Knapp............ | 114 | W. S. Kilmer |
| 1919 | Sir Barton............ | 2:09⅘ | 28,825 | J. Loftus............ | 112½ | J. K. L. Ross |
| 1920 | Paul Jones............ | 2:09 | 30,375 | T. Rice............. | 126 | Ral Parr |
| 1921 | Behave Yourself....... | 2:04⅕ | 38,450 | C. Thompson......... | 126 | E. R. Bradley |
| 1922 | Morvich............. | 2:04⅗ | 46,775 | A. Johnson........... | 126 | Ben Block |
| 1923 | Zev................ | 2:05⅖ | 53,600 | E. Sande............ | 126 | H. F. Sinclair |
| 1924 | Black Gold........... | 2:05⅕ | 52,775 | J. D. Mooney......... | 126 | Mrs. R. M. Hoots |
| 1925 | Flying Ebony.......... | 2:07⅗ | 52,950 | E. Sande............ | 126 | G. A. Cochran |
| 1926 | Bubbling Over........ | 2:03⅘ | 50,075 | A. Johnson........... | 126 | E. R. Bradley |
| 1927 | Whiskery............ | 2:06 | 51,000 | L. McAtee........... | 126 | H. P. Whitney |
| 1928 | Reigh Count.......... | 2:10⅖ | 55 375 | C. Lang............. | 126 | Mrs. John D. Hertz |
| 1929 | Clyde Van Dusen...... | 2:10⅘ | 53,950 | L. McAtee........... | 126 | H. P. Gardner |
| 1930 | Gallant Fox.......... | 2:07⅗ | 50,725 | E. Sande............ | 126 | William Woodward |
| 1931 | Twenty Grand......... | 2:01⅘ | 48,725 | C. Kurtsinger........ | 126 | Mrs. Payne Whitney |
| 1932 | Burgoo King.......... | 2:05⅕ | 52,350 | E. James............ | 126 | E. R. Bradley |
| 1933 | Brokers Tip.......... | 2:06⅘ | 48,925 | D. Meade............ | 126 | E. R. Bradley |
| 1934 | Cavalcade........... | 2:04 | 28,175 | M. Garner........... | 126 | Mrs. Dodge Sloane |
| 1935 | Omaha.............. | 2:05 | 39,525 | W. Saunders.......... | 126 | William Woodward |
| 1936 | Bold Venture......... | 2:03⅗ | 37,725 | I. Hanford........... | 126 | M. L. Schwartz |
| 1937 | War Admiral.......... | 2:03⅕ | 52,050 | C. Kurtsinger........ | 126 | S. D. Riddle |
| 1938 | Lawrin.............. | 2:04⅘ | 47,050 | E. Arcaro........... | 126 | Herbert M. Woolf |
| 1939 | Johnstown........... | 2:03⅖ | 46,350 | J. Stout............ | 126 | William Woodward |
| 1940 | Gallahadion.......... | 2:05 | 60,150 | C. Bierman.......... | 126 | Mrs. Ethel V. Mars |
| 1941 | Whirlaway........... | 2:01⅖ | 61,275 | E. Arcaro........... | 126 | Calumet Farm |
| 1942 | Shut Out............ | 2:04⅖ | 64,225 | W. Wright........... | 126 | Mrs. Payne Whitney |
| 1943 | Count Fleet.......... | 2:04 | 60,725 | J. Longden.......... | 126 | Mrs. John D. Hertz |
| 1944 | Pensive............. | 2:04⅕ | 64,675 | C. McCreary......... | 126 | Calumet Farm |
| 1945 | Hoop Jr............. | 2:07 | 64,850 | E. Arcaro........... | 126 | F. W. Hooper |
| 1946 | Assault............. | 2:06⅗ | 96,400 | W. Mehrtens......... | 126 | R. J. Kleberg |
| 1947 | Jet Pilot............ | 2:06⅘ | 92,160 | E. Guerin........... | 126 | Mrs. E. Graham |
| 1948 | Citation............ | 2:05⅖ | 83,400 | E. Arcaro........... | 126 | Calumet Farm |
| 1949 | Ponder............. | 2:04⅕ | 91,600 | S. Brooks........... | 126 | Calumet Farm |
| 1950 | Middleground......... | 2:01⅗ | 92,650 | W. Boland........... | 126 | R. J. Kleberg |
| 1951 | Count Turf .......... | 2:02⅗ | 98,050 | C. McCreary......... | 126 | J. J. Amiel |
| 1952 | Hill Gail............ | 2:01⅗ | 96,300 | E. Arcaro........... | 126 | Calumet Farm |
| 1953 | Dark Star........... | 2:02 | 90,050 | H. Moreno........... | 126 | H. F. Guggenheim |
| 1954 | Determine........... | 2:03 | 102,050 | R. York............. | 126 | A. J. Crevolin |
| 1955 | Swaps.............. | 2:01⅘ | 108,400 | W. Shoemaker........ | 126 | R. C. Ellsworth |
| 1956 | Needles............ | 2:03⅖ | 123,450 | D. Erb............. | 126 | J. Dudley & B. Heath |
| 1957 | Iron Liege........... | 2:02⅕ | 109,550 | W. Hartack.......... | 126 | Calumet Farm |
| 1958 | Tim Tam............ | 2:05 | 116,400 | I. Valenzuela......... | 126 | Calumet Farm |
| 1959 | Tomy Lee........... | 2:02⅕ | 119,650 | W. Shoemaker........ | 126 | F. Turner |
| 1960 | Venetian Way......... | 2:02⅖ | 114,850 | W. Hartack.......... | 126 | Isaac Blumberg |
| 1961 | Carry Back.......... | 2:04 | 120,500 | J. Sellers........... | 126 | Mrs. K. Price |
| 1962 | Decidedly........... | 2:00⅖ | 119,650 | W. Hartack.......... | 126 | George A. Pope, Jr. |
| 1963 | Chateaugay.......... | 2:01⅘ | 108,900 | B. Baeza........... | 126 | J. W. Galbreath |
| 1964 | Northern Dancer...... | 2:00 | 114,300 | W. Hartack.......... | 126 | E. P. Taylor |
| 1965 | Lucky Debonair....... | 2:01⅕ | 112,000 | W. Shoemaker........ | 126 | Mrs. A. L. Rice |
| 1966 | Kauai King.......... | 2:02 | 120,500 | D. Brumfield......... | 126 | Ford Stable |
| 1967 | Proud Clarion......... | 2:00⅗ | 119,700 | B. Ussery........... | 126 | J. W. Galbreath |

## THE PREAKNESS STAKES

First run in 1873, the Preakness is the second of the Triple Crown classics and is held at Pimlico in Baltimore, Maryland. Weight was set at 126 pounds in 1925, but fillies have a five-pound advantage. In 1925 the distance was set at a mile and three-sixteenths. The Preakness was not held from 1890 to 1893; from 1894 to 1908 it was run at Gravesend, Brooklyn, N.Y.

| YEAR | WINNER | TIME | MONEY | JOCKEY | WEIGHT | OWNER |
|---|---|---|---|---|---|---|
| 1918 | War Cloud | 1:53⅗ | $ 12,250 | J. Loftus | 117 | A. K. Macomber |
| 1919 | Sir Barton | 1:53 | 24,500 | J. Loftus | 126 | J. K. L. Ross |
| 1920 | Man o' War | 1:51⅗ | 23,000 | C. Kummer | 126 | S. D. Riddle |
| 1921 | Broomspun | 1:54⅕ | 43,000 | F. Coltiletti | 114 | H. P. Whitney |
| 1922 | Pillory | 1:51⅗ | 51,000 | L. Morris | 114 | R. T. Wilson, Jr. |
| 1923 | Vigil | 1:53⅗ | 52,000 | B. Marinelli | 114 | W. J. Salmon |
| 1924 | Nellie Morse | 1:57⅕ | 54,000 | J. Merimee | 121 | H. C. Fisher |
| 1925 | Coventry | 1:59 | 52,700 | C. Kummer | 126 | G. A. Cochran |
| 1926 | Display | 1:59⅘ | 53,625 | J. Maiben | 126 | W. J. Salmon |
| 1927 | Bostonian | 2:01⅗ | 53,100 | A. Abel | 126 | H. P. Whitney |
| 1928 | Victorian | 2:00⅕ | 60,000 | R. Workman | 126 | H P. Whitney |
| 1929 | Dr. Freeland | 2:01⅗ | 52,325 | L. Schaefer | 126 | W. J. Salmon |
| 1930 | Gallant Fox | 2:00⅗ | 51,925 | E. Sande | 126 | William Woodward |
| 1931 | Mate | 1:59 | 48,225 | G. Ellis | 126 | A. C. Bostwick |
| 1932 | Burgoo King | 1:59⅘ | 50,375 | E. James | 126 | E. R. Bradley |
| 1933 | Head Play | 2:02 | 26,850 | C. Kurtsinger | 126 | Mrs. S. B. Mason |
| 1934 | High Quest | 1:58⅕ | 25,175 | R. Jones | 126 | Mrs. I. D. Sloane |
| 1935 | Omaha | 1:58⅖ | 25,325 | W. Saunders | 126 | William Woodward |
| 1936 | Bold Venture | 1:59 | 27,325 | G. Woolf | 126 | M. Schwartz |
| 1937 | War Admiral | 1:58⅖ | 45,600 | C. Kurtsinger | 126 | S. D. Riddle |
| 1938 | Dauber | 1:59⅘ | 51,875 | M. Peters | 126 | Foxcatcher Farms |
| 1939 | Challedon | 1:59⅘ | 53,710 | G. Seabo | 126 | W. L. Brann |
| 1940 | Bimelech | 1:58⅗ | 53,230 | F. A. Smith | 126 | E. R. Bradley |
| 1941 | Whirlaway | 1:58⅘ | 49,365 | E. Arcaro | 126 | Calumet Farm |
| 1942 | Alsab | 1:57 | 58,175 | B. James | 126 | Mrs. A. Sabath |
| 1943 | Count Fleet | 1:57⅖ | 43,190 | J. Longden | 126 | Mrs. John D. Hertz |
| 1944 | Pensive | 1:59⅕ | 60,075 | C. McCreary | 126 | Calumet Farm |
| 1945 | Polynesian | 1:58⅘ | 66,170 | W. D. Wright | 126 | Mrs. P. A. B. Widener |
| 1946 | Assault | 2:01⅖ | 96,620 | W. Mehrtens | 126 | R. J. Kleberg |
| 1947 | Faultless | 1:59 | 98,005 | D. Dodson | 126 | Calumet Farm |
| 1948 | Citation | 2:02⅖ | 91,870 | E. Arcaro | 126 | Calumet Farm |
| 1949 | Capot | 1:56 | 79,985 | T. Atkinson | 126 | Greentree Stable |
| 1950 | Hill Prince | 1:59⅕ | 56,115 | E. Arcaro | 126 | C. T. Chenery |
| 1951 | Bold | 1:56⅖ | 83,110 | E. Arcaro | 126 | Mrs. I. D. Sloane |
| 1952 | Blue Man | 1:57⅖ | 86,135 | C. McCreary | 126 | White Oak Stable |
| 1953 | Native Dancer | 1:57⅘ | 65,200 | E. Guerin | 126 | A. G. Vanderbilt |
| 1954 | Hasty Road | 1:57⅖ | 91,600 | J. Adams | 126 | Hasty House Farm |
| 1955 | Nashua | 1:54⅗ | 67,550 | E. Arcaro | 126 | William Woodward |
| 1956 | Fabius | 1:58⅖ | 84,250 | W. Hartack | 126 | Calumet Farm |
| 1957 | Bold Ruler | 1:56⅕ | 65,250 | E. Arcaro | 126 | Mrs. H. C. Phipps |
| 1958 | Tim Tam | 1:57⅕ | 97,900 | I. Valenzuela | 126 | Calumet Farm |
| 1959 | Royal Orbit | 1:57 | 136,200 | W. Harmatz | 126 | Estate of J. Braunstein |
| 1960 | Ballyache | 1:57⅗ | 121,000 | R. Ussery | 126 | Turfland |
| 1961 | Carry Back | 1:57⅗ | 126,200 | J. Sellers | 126 | Mrs. K. Price |
| 1962 | Greek Money | 1:56⅕ | 135,800 | J. L. Rotz | 126 | Brandywine Stable |
| 1963 | Candy Spots | 1:56⅕ | 127,500 | W. Shoemaker | 126 | R. C. Ellsworth |
| 1964 | Northern Dancer | 1:56⅘ | 124,200 | W. Hartack | 126 | E. P. Taylor |
| 1965 | Tom Rolfe | 1:56⅕ | 128,100 | R. Turcotte | 126 | R. Guest |
| 1966 | Kauai King | 1:55⅖ | 129,000 | D. Brumfield | 126 | Ford Stable |
| 1967 | Damascus | 1:55⅕ | 141,500 | W. Shoemaker | 126 | Mrs. E. Bancroft |

## THE BELMONT STAKES

Oldest of the Triple Crown classics, the Belmont was first run in 1867, at a distance of a mile and five-eighths. In 1926, when the race was being run at Belmont Park, Elmont, New York, the distance was set at a mile and a half. At the close of the 1962 season the race was moved from Belmont Park to Aqueduct, New York City, where it has been run since.

| YEAR | WINNER | TIME | MONEY | JOCKEY | WEIGHT | OWNER |
|---|---|---|---|---|---|---|
| 1918 | Johren | 2:20⅖ | $ 8,950 | F. Robinson | 126 | H. P. Whitney |
| 1919 | Sir Barton | 2:17⅖ | 11,950 | J. Loftus | 126 | J. K. L. Ross |
| 1920 | Man o' War | 2:14⅕ | 7,950 | C. Kummer | 126 | Glen Riddle Farms |
| 1921 | Grey Lag | 2:16⅘ | 8,650 | E. Sande | 126 | Rancocas Stable |
| 1922 | Pillory | 2:18⅘ | 39,200 | C. H. Miller | 126 | R. T. Wilson |

*(continued)*

**THE BELMONT STAKES** *(continued)*

| YEAR | WINNER | TIME | MONEY | JOCKEY | WEIGHT | OWNER |
|---|---|---|---|---|---|---|
| 1923 | Zev | 2:19 | $ 38,000 | E. Sande | 126 | Rancocas Stable |
| 1924 | Mad Play | 2:18⅘ | 42,880 | E. Sande | 126 | Rancocas Stable |
| 1925 | American Flag | 2:16⅘ | 38,500 | A. Johnson | 126 | Glen Riddle Farms |
| 1926 | Crusader | 2:32⅕ | 48,550 | A. Johnson | 126 | Glen Riddle Farms |
| 1927 | Chance Shot | 2:32⅖ | 60,910 | E. Sande | 126 | J. E. Widener |
| 1928 | Vito | 2:33⅕ | 63,430 | C. Kummer | 126 | A. H. Cosden |
| 1929 | Blue Larkspur | 2:32⅘ | 59,650 | M. Garner | 126 | E. R. Bradley |
| 1930 | Gallant Fox | 2:31⅗ | 66,040 | E. Sande | 126 | William Woodward |
| 1931 | Twenty Grand | 2:29⅗ | 58,770 | C. Kurtsinger | 126 | Greentree Stable |
| 1932 | Faireno | 2:32⅘ | 55,120 | T. Malley | 126 | William Woodward |
| 1933 | Hurryoff | 2:32⅗ | 49,490 | M. Garner | 126 | J. E. Widener |
| 1934 | Peace Chance | 2:29⅕ | 43,410 | W. D. Wright | 126 | J. E. Widener |
| 1935 | Omaha | 2:30⅗ | 35,480 | W. Saunders | 126 | William Woodward |
| 1936 | Granville | 2:30 | 29,800 | J. Stout | 126 | William Woodward |
| 1937 | War Admiral | 2:28⅗ | 38,020 | C. Kurtsinger | 126 | Glen Riddle Farms |
| 1938 | Pasteurized | 2:29⅖ | 34,530 | J. Stout | 126 | Mrs. W. P. Stewart |
| 1939 | Johnstown | 2:29⅗ | 37,020 | J. Stout | 126 | William Woodward |
| 1940 | Bimelech | 2:29⅗ | 35,030 | F. A. Smith | 126 | E. R. Bradley |
| 1941 | Whirlaway | 2:31 | 39,770 | E. Arcaro | 126 | Calumet Farm |
| 1942 | Shut Out | 2:29⅕ | 44,520 | E. Arcaro | 126 | Greentree Stable |
| 1943 | Count Fleet | 2:28⅕ | 35,340 | J. Longden | 126 | Mrs. John D Hertz |
| 1944 | Bounding Home | 2:32⅕ | 55,000 | G. L. Smith | 126 | W. Ziegler, Jr. |
| 1945 | Pavot | 2:30⅕ | 52,675 | E. Arcaro | 126 | W. M. Jeffords |
| 1946 | Assault | 2:30⅘ | 75,400 | W. Mehrtens | 126 | King Ranch |
| 1947 | Phalanx | 2:29⅖ | 78,900 | R. Donoso | 126 | C. V. Whitney |
| 1948 | Citation | 2:28⅕ | 77,700 | E. Arcaro | 126 | Calumet Farm |
| 1949 | Capot | 2:30⅕ | 60,900 | T. Atkinson | 126 | Greentree Stable |
| 1950 | Middleground | 2:28⅗ | 61,350 | W. Boland | 126 | King Ranch |
| 1951 | Counterpoint | 2:29 | 82,000 | D. Gorman | 126 | C. V. Whitney |
| 1952 | One Count | 2:30⅕ | 82,400 | E. Arcaro | 126 | Mrs. W. M. Jeffords |
| 1953 | Native Dancer | 2:28⅗ | 82,500 | E. Guerin | 126 | A. G. Vanderbilt |
| 1954 | High Gun | 2:30⅘ | 89,000 | E. Guerin | 126 | King Ranch |
| 1955 | Nashua | 2:29 | 83,700 | E. Arcaro | 126 | William Woodward |
| 1956 | Needles | 2:29⅘ | 83,600 | D. Erb | 126 | D. & H. Stable |
| 1957 | Gallant Man | 2:26⅗ | 77,300 | W. Shoemaker | 126 | Ralph Lowe |
| 1958 | Cavan | 2:30⅕ | 73,440 | P. Anderson | 126 | J. E. O'Connell |
| 1959 | Sword Dancer | 2.28⅖ | 93,525 | W. Shoemaker | 126 | Brookmeade Stable |
| 1960 | Celtic Ash | 2:29⅗ | 96,785 | W. Hartack | 126 | J. E. O'Connell |
| 1961 | Sherluck | 2:29⅕ | 104,900 | B. Baeza | 126 | J. Sher |
| 1962 | Jaipur | 2:28⅘ | 109,550 | W. Shoemaker | 126 | George D. Widener |
| 1963 | Chateaugay | 2:30⅕ | 101,700 | B. Baeza | 126 | John W. Galbreath |
| 1964 | Quadrangle | 2:28⅖ | 110,850 | M. Ycaza | 126 | Paul Mellon |
| 1965 | Hail to All | 2:28⅖ | 104,150 | J. Sellers | 126 | Mrs. Ben Cohen |
| 1966 | Amberoid | 2:29⅗ | 117,700 | W. Boland | 126 | Reginald N. Webster |
| 1967 | Damascus | 2:28⅘ | 104,950 | W. Shoemaker | 126 | Mrs. E. Bancroft |

## LEADING MONEY-WINNING JOCKEYS

| YEAR | JOCKEY | WINNERS | AMOUNT WON * | YEAR | JOCKEY | WINNERS | AMOUNT WON * |
|---|---|---|---|---|---|---|---|
| 1931 | C. Kurtsinger | 93 | $ 392,095 | 1949 | S. Brooks | 209 | $1,316,817 |
| 1932 | R. Workman | 87 | 385,070 | 1950 | E. Arcaro | 195 | 1,410,160 |
| 1933 | R. Jones | 63 | 226,285 | 1951 | W. Shoemaker | 257 | 1,329,890 |
| 1934 | W. Wright | 174 | 287,185 | 1952 | E. Arcaro | 188 | 1,859,591 |
| 1935 | S. Coucci | 141 | 319,760 | 1953 | W. Shoemaker | 485 | 1,784,187 |
| 1936 | W. Wright | 100 | 264,000 | 1954 | W. Shoemaker | 380 | 1,876,760 |
| 1937 | C. Kurtsinger | 120 | 384,202 | 1955 | E. Arcaro | 158 | 1,864,796 |
| 1938 | N. Wall | 97 | 385,161 | 1956 | W. Hartack | 347 | 2,343,955 |
| 1939 | B. James | 191 | 353,333 | 1957 | W. Hartack | 341 | 3,060,501 |
| 1940 | E. Arcaro | 132 | 343,661 | 1958 | W. Shoemaker | 300 | 2,961,693 |
| 1941 | D. Meade | 210 | 398,627 | 1959 | W. Shoemaker | 347 | 2,843,133 |
| 1942 | E. Arcaro | 123 | 481,949 | 1960 | W. Shoemaker | 274 | 2,123,961 |
| 1943 | J. Longden | 173 | 573,276 | 1961 | W. Shoemaker | 304 | 2,690,819 |
| 1944 | T. Atkinson | 287 | 899,101 | 1962 | W. Shoemaker | 311 | 2,916,844 |
| 1945 | J. Longden | 180 | 981,977 | 1963 | W. Shoemaker | 271 | 2,526,925 |
| 1946 | T. Atkinson | 233 | 1,036,825 | 1964 | W. Shoemaker | 246 | 2,649,553 |
| 1947 | D. Dodson | 141 | 1,429,949 | 1965 | B. Baeza | 270 | 2,582,000 |
| 1948 | E. Arcaro | 188 | 1,686,230 | 1966 | B. Baeza | 298 | 2,951,022 |

*** Total purses.**

## LEADING MONEY-WINNING HORSES

In the early days of horse racing the value of an animal was usually estimated by his earnings. The values of stakes were so standardized that the winnings of a horse in one season, or even in a lifetime, were something of a gauge by which he could be judged.

| YEAR | HORSE | AGE (in years) | STARTS | FIRSTS | SECONDS | THIRDS | AMOUNT WON |
|---|---|---|---|---|---|---|---|
| 1920 | Man o' War | 3 | 11 | 11 | 0 | 0 | $166,140 |
| 1921 | Morvich | 2 | 11 | 11 | 0 | 0 | 115,234 |
| 1922 | Pillory | 3 | 7 | 4 | 1 | 1 | 96,654 |
| 1923 | Zev | 3 | 14 | 12 | 1 | 0 | 272,008 |
| 1924 | Sarazen | 3 | 12 | 8 | 1 | 1 | 95,640 |
| 1925 | Pompey | 2 | 10 | 7 | 2 | 0 | 121,630 |
| 1926 | Crusader | 3 | 15 | 9 | 4 | 0 | 166,033 |
| 1927 | Anita Peabody | 2 | 7 | 6 | 0 | 1 | 111.905 |
| 1928 | High Strung | 2 | 6 | 5 | 0 | 0 | 153.590 |
| 1929 | Blue Larkspur | 3 | 6 | 4 | 1 | 0 | 153,450 |
| 1930 | Gallant Fox | 3 | 10 | 9 | 1 | 0 | 308,275 |
| 1931 | Top Flight | 2 | 7 | 7 | 0 | 0 | 219,000 |
| 1932 | Gusto | 3 | 16 | 4 | 3 | 2 | 145,940 |
| 1933 | Singing Wood | 2 | 9 | 3 | 2 | 2 | 88,050 |
| 1934 | Cavalcade | 3 | 7 | 6 | 1 | 0 | 111,235 |
| 1935 | Omaha | 3 | 9 | 6 | 1 | 2 | 142,255 |
| 1936 | Granville | 3 | 11 | 7 | 3 | 0 | 110,295 |
| 1937 | Seabiscuit | 4 | 15 | 11 | 2 | 2 | 168,580 |
| 1938 | Stagehand | 3 | 15 | 8 | 2 | 3 | 189,710 |
| 1939 | Challedon | 3 | 15 | 9 | 2 | 3 | 184,535 |
| 1940 | Bimelech | 3 | 7 | 4 | 2 | 1 | 110,005 |
| 1941 | Whirlaway | 3 | 20 | 13 | 5 | 2 | 272,386 |
| 1942 | Shut Out | 3 | 12 | 8 | 2 | 0 | 238,872 |
| 1943 | Count Fleet | 3 | 6 | 6 | 0 | 0 | 174,055 |
| 1944 | Pavot | 2 | 8 | 8 | 0 | 0 | 179,040 |
| 1945 | Busher | 3 | 13 | 10 | 2 | 1 | 273,735 |
| 1946 | Assault | 3 | 15 | 8 | 2 | 3 | 424,195 |
| 1947 | Armed | 6 | 17 | 11 | 4 | 1 | 376,325 |
| 1948 | Citation | 3 | 20 | 19 | 1 | 0 | 709,470 |
| 1949 | Ponder | 3 | 21 | 9 | 5 | 2 | 321,825 |
| 1950 | Noor | 5 | 12 | 7 | 4 | 1 | 346,940 |
| 1951 | Counterpoint | 3 | 15 | 7 | 2 | 1 | 250,525 |
| 1952 | Crafty Admiral | 4 | 16 | 9 | 4 | 1 | 277,225 |
| 1953 | Native Dancer | 3 | 10 | 9 | 1 | 0 | 513,425 |
| 1954 | Determine | 3 | 15 | 10 | 3 | 2 | 328,700 |
| 1955 | Nashua | 3 | 12 | 10 | 1 | 1 | 752,550 |
| 1956 | Needles | 3 | 8 | 4 | 2 | 0 | 440,850 |
| 1957 | Round Table | 3 | 22 | 15 | 1 | 3 | 600,383 |
| 1958 | Round Table | 4 | 20 | 14 | 4 | 0 | 662,780 |
| 1959 | Sword Dancer | 3 | 13 | 8 | 4 | 0 | 537,004 |
| 1960 | Ballyache | 3 | 15 | 10 | 3 | 1 | 455,045 |
| 1961 | Carry Back | 3 | 16 | 9 | 1 | 3 | 565,349 |
| 1962 | Never Bend | 2 | 10 | 7 | 1 | 2 | 402,969 |
| 1963 | Candy Spots | 3 | 12 | 7 | 2 | 1 | 604,481 |
| 1964 | Gun Bow | 4 | 16 | 8 | 4 | 2 | 580,100 |
| 1965 | Roman Brother | 4 | 14 | 5 | 2 | 2 | 257,520 |
| 1966 | Buckpasser | 3 | 14 | 13 | 1 | 0 | 669,078 |

### ■ HIGHEST DAILY DOUBLE

| AMOUNT | BET | DATE | COMBINATION | TRACK |
|---|---|---|---|---|
| $12,724.80 | $2.00 | July 4, 1954 | Rocklite and Slick Trick | Caliente Race Track, Agua Caliente, Mexico |
| 10,772.40 | $2.00 | Aug. 14, 1939 | Joy Bet and Merry Caroline | Washington Park, Homewood, Illinois |
| 9,826.80 | $2.00 | Aug. 16, 1964 | Warcreus and Johnny Green | Caliente Race Track, Agua Caliente, Mexico |

### ■ FAMOUS MATCH RACES

| WINNER | SECOND PLACE | DATE | PURSE | DISTANCE (in miles) | TRACK | TIME |
|---|---|---|---|---|---|---|
| Nashua | Swaps | Aug. 31, 1955 | $100,000 | 1¼ | Washington Park, Homewood, Illinois | 2:04⅕ |
| Armed | Assault | Sept. 27, 1947 | 100,000 | 1¼ | Belmont, New York | 2:02⅗ |
| Sea Biscuit | War Admiral | Nov. 1, 1938 | 15,000 | 1³⁄₁₆ | Pimlico, Maryland | 1:56⅗ |
| Zev | Papyrus | Oct. 20, 1923 | 85,000 | 1½ | Belmont, New York | 2:35⅖ |
| Man o' War | Sir Barton | Oct. 12, 1920 | 80,000 | 1¼ | Kenilworth Park, Windsor, Ontario | 2:03 |

## HARNESS RACING

Harness racing has grown into one of the country's most popular spectator sports. A major reason is that harness tracks now feature nighttime racing. In 1966 total attendance was over 27 million while total pari-mutuel betting was more than $1.46 billion. The United States Trotting Association governs the sport.

Three-year-old trotters have three classic races each year, known as Trotting's Triple Crown. Most important is the Hambletonian. First raced at Syracuse, N.Y., in 1926, it was moved to Du Quoin, Illinois, in 1957. Next and oldest is the Kentucky Futurity, raced each autumn since 1893 at Lexington, Ky. Yonkers Raceway, Yonkers, N.Y. is the home of the Yonkers Futurity, first held in 1955.

### ■ THE HAMBLETONIAN

| YEAR | PURSE | WINNER | DRIVER | FASTEST HEAT |
|---|---|---|---|---|
| 1948 | 59,941.18 | Demon Hanover | Harrison Hoyt | 2:02 |
| 1949 | 69,791.08 | Miss Tilly | Fred Egan | 2:01⅖ |
| 1950 | 75,209.12 | Lusty Song | Del Miller | 2:02 |
| 1951 | 95,263.93 | Mainliner | Guy Crippen | 2:02⅗ |
| 1952 | 87,637.55 | Sharp Note | Bion Shively | 2:02⅗ |
| 1953 | 117,117.98 | Helicopter | Harry Harvey | 2:01⅗ |
| 1954 | 106,830.68 | Newport Dream | Del Cameron | 2:02⅘ |
| 1955 | 86,863.32 | Scott Frost | Joe O'Brien | 2:00⅗ |
| 1956 | 100,603.99 | The Intruder | Ned Bower | 2:01⅖ |
| 1957 | 111,126.25 | Hickory Smoke | John Simpson | 2:00⅕ |
| 1958 | 106,719.24 | Emily's Pride | Flave Nipe | 1:59⅘ |
| 1959 | 125,283.98 | Diller Hanover | Frank Ervin | 2:01⅕ |
| 1960 | 147,481.94 | Blaze Hanover | Joe O'Brien | 1:59⅗ |
| 1961 | 131,573.01 | Harlan Dean | James Arthur | 1:58⅖ |
| 1962 | 116,612.78 | A. C.'s Viking | Sanders Russell | 1:59⅗ |
| 1963 | 115,549.28 | Speedy Scot | Ralph Baldwin | 1:57⅗ |
| 1964 | 115,281.40 | Ayres | John Simpson | 1:56⅘ (R) |
| 1965 | 122,245.76 | Egyptian Candor | Del Cameron | 2:01⅕ |
| 1966 | 122,540.00 | Kerry Way | Frank Ervin | 1:58⅘ |
| 1967 | 122,650.00 | Speedy Streak | Del Cameron | 1:59⅖ |

### ■ THE KENTUCKY FUTURITY

| YEAR | PURSE | WINNER | DRIVER | FASTEST HEAT |
|---|---|---|---|---|
| 1948 | 50,071.00 | Egan Hanover | Ralph Baldwin | 2:03⅖ |
| 1949 | 57,154.76 | Bangaway | Ralph Baldwin | 2:05⅖ |
| 1950 | 54,665.08 | Star's Pride | Harry Pownall, Sr. | 2:02 |
| 1951 | 66,659.57 | Ford Hanover | John Simpson | 2:01⅖ |
| 1952 | 66,231.89 | Sharp Note | Bion Shively | 2:00 |
| 1953 | 67,485.05 | Kimberly Kid | Thomas Berry | 2:00⅗ |
| 1954 | 63,121.84 | Harlan | Del Miller | 2:01 |
| 1955 | 62,702.60 | Scott Frost | Joe O'Brien | 2:00⅗ |
| 1956 | 53,731.74 | Nimble Colby | Ralph Baldwin | 2:02 |
| 1957 | 50,460.00 | Cassin Hanover | Fred Egan | 2:02⅕ |
| 1958 | 53,330.00 | Emily's Pride | Flave Nipe | 1:59⅕ |
| 1959 | 53,810.00 | Diller Hanover | Ralph Baldwin | 2:01⅕ |
| 1960 | 64,040.00 | Elaine Rodney | Clint Hodgins | 1:58⅗ |
| 1961 | 59,330.00 | Duke Rodney | Eddie Wheeler | 1:58⅕ |
| 1962 | 55,230.00 | Safe Mission | Joe O'Brien | 1:59⅕ |
| 1963 | 61,128.82 | Speedy Scot | Ralph Baldwin | 1:57⅕ (R) |
| 1964 | 57,096.21 | Ayres | John Simpson | 1:58⅕ |
| 1965 | 65,133.93 | Armbro Flight | Joe O'Brien | 1:59⅗ |
| 1966 | 61,602.18 | Governor Armbro | Joe O'Brien | 2:00⅖ |
| 1967 | 58,642.37 | Speed Model | Art Hult | 2:01⅖ |

### ■ THE YONKERS FUTURITY *

| YEAR | PURSE | WINNER | DRIVER | FASTEST HEAT |
|---|---|---|---|---|
| 1955 | $ 73,840.00 | Scott Frost | Joe O'Brien | 2:12 |
| 1956 | 77,170.00 | Add Hanover | John Simpson | 2:12⅘ |
| 1957 | 57,812.50 | Hoot Song | Ralph Baldwin | 2:16⅕ |
| 1958 | 56,157.50 | Spunky Hanover | Howard Camper | 2:13⅗ |
| 1959 | 56,397.50 | John A. Hanover | Stanley Dancer | 2:11 |
| 1960 | 74,265.00 | Duke of Decatur | Del Miller | 2:13⅗ |
| 1961 | 100,330.00 | Duke Rodney | Eddie Wheeler | 2:10⅗ |
| 1962 | 105,422.50 | A. C.'s Viking | Sanders Russell | 2:10⅘ |
| 1963 | 135,127.50 | Speedy Scot | Ralph Baldwin | 2:03⅗ |
| 1964 | 116,691.25 | Ayres | John Simpson | 2:01⅗ (R) |
| 1965 | 122,236.00 | Noble Victory | Stanley Dancer | 2:02 |
| 1966 | 123,375.00 | Polaris | George Sholty | 2:06 |
| 1967 | 150,000.00 | Pomp | Harry Pownall | 2:04⅖ |

R = record. * 1 1/16-mile race before 1963.

## PACING'S TRIPLE CROWN

The Little Brown Jug (at Delaware, Ohio), the Cane Futurity (at Yonkers Raceway, Yonkers, N.Y.), and the Messenger Stake (at Roosevelt Raceway, Westbury, Long Island, N.Y.) are the three major purse attractions for the nation's three-year-old pacers. The "Jug" classic was first run at Delaware in 1946, and ten years later the companion pacing events were begun.

### ■ LITTLE BROWN JUG

| YEAR | PURSE | WINNER | DRIVER | FASTEST HEAT |
|---|---|---|---|---|
| 1947 | $38,200.00 | Forbes Chief | Del Cameron | 2:05 |
| 1948 | 47,528.58 | Knight Dream | Frank Safford | 2:07⅕ |
| 1949 | 58,281.30 | Good Time | Frank Ervin | 2:03⅖ |
| 1950 | 56,525.47 | Dudley Hanover | Del Miller | 2:02⅗ |
| 1951 | 66,280.55 | Tar Heel | Del Cameron | 2:00 |
| 1952 | 60,463.35 | Meadow Rice | Wayne Smart | 2:01⅗ |
| 1953 | 54,972.21 | Keystoner | Frank Ervin | 2:02⅗ |
| 1954 | 69,332.06 | Adios Harry | Morris MacDonald | 2:01⅖ |
| 1955 | 66,608.83 | Quick Chief | Billy Haughton | 2:00 |
| 1956 | 52,666.05 | Noble Adios | John Simpson | 2:00⅘ |
| 1957 | 73,528.15 | Torpid | John Simpson | 2:00⅘ |
| 1958 | 65,252.94 | Shadow Wave | Joe O'Brien | 2:01 |
| 1959 | 76,582.00 | Adios Butler | Clint Hodgins | 1:59⅖ |
| 1960 | 66,510.89 | Bullet Hanover | John Simpson | 1:58⅗ |
| 1961 | 70,069.14 | Henry T. Adios | Stanley Dancer | 1:58⅘ |
| 1962 | 75,038.80 | Lehigh Hanover | Stanley Dancer | 1:58⅘ |
| 1963 | 68,294.90 | Overtrick | John Patterson | 1:57⅕ |
| 1964 | 66,590.79 | Vicar Hanover | Billy Haughton | 2:00⅘ |
| 1965 | 70,000.00 | Bret Hanover | Frank Ervin | 1:57(R) |
| 1966 | 74,616.69 | Romeo Hanover | George Sholty | 1:59⅗ |
| 1967 | 84,778.00 | Best of All | Jim Hackett | 1:59⅕ |

### ■ THE WILLIAM H. CANE FUTURITY *

| YEAR | PURSE | WINNER | DRIVER | TIME |
|---|---|---|---|---|
| 1956 | $ 71,570.00 | Noble Adios | John Simpson | 2:09⅖ |
| 1957 | 66,952.50 | Torpid | John Simpson | 2:09⅕ |
| 1958 | 60,457.50 | Raider Frost | Hugh Bell | 2:08⅕ |
| 1959 | 64,457.50 | Adios Butler | Clint Hodgins | 2:09 |
| 1960 | 65,245.00 | Countess Adios | Del Miller | 2:08 |
| 1961 | 110,950.00 | Cold Front | Clint Hodgins | 2:08⅗ |
| 1962 | 117,542.50 | Ranger Knight | Clint Hodgins | 2:13⅕ |
| 1963 | 163,187.50 | Meadow Skipper | Earle Avery | 1:58⅘(R) |
| 1964 | 123,191.25 | Race Time | George Sholty | 2:01⅘ |
| 1965 | 125,236.00 | Bret Hanover | Frank Ervin | 2:01 |
| 1966 | 126,915.00 | Romeo Hanover | William Myer | 1:59⅘ |
| 1967 | 150,000.00 | Meadow Paige | Billy Haughton | 2:03 |

### ■ THE MESSENGER STAKE

| YEAR | PURSE | WINNER | DRIVER | TIME |
|---|---|---|---|---|
| 1957 | $100,084.31 | Meadow Lands | Del Miller | 2:04⅘ |
| 1958 | 108,565.52 | O'Brien Hanover | James Jordan | 2:01⅘ |
| 1959 | 110,994.29 | Adios Butler | Clint Hodgins | 2:00⅕ |
| 1960 | 142,786.15 | Countess Adios | Del Miller | 2:02⅕ |
| 1961 | 145,377.96 | Adios Don | Howard Camper | 2:02⅘ |
| 1962 | 169,430.93 | Thor Hanover | John Simpson | 2:01⅕ |
| 1963 | 146,324.87 | Overtrick | John Patterson | 2:00⅘ |
| 1964 | 150,960.41 | Race Time | Ralph Baldwin | 2:01⅖ |
| 1965 | 151,252.05 | Bret Hanover | Frank Ervin | 2:02 |
| 1966 | 169,885.23 | Romeo Hanover | George Sholty | 2:01 |
| 1967 | 178,064.00 † | Romulus Hanover | Bill Haughton | 1:59⅒(R) |

## 1966 HARNESS HORSE OF THE YEAR BALLOTING

**(By 198 harness writers and sportscasters on a 10-5-3-2-1 basis)**

| HORSE | 1sts | POINTS | HORSE | 1sts | POINTS |
|---|---|---|---|---|---|
| 1. Bret Hanover | 161 | 1,663 | 6. Cardigan Bay | 0 | 125 |
| 2. Romeo Hanover | 28 | 922 | 7. Adios Vic | 0 | 124 |
| 3. Noble Victory | 1 | 310 | 8. Bonjour Hanover | 2 | 109 |
| 4. True Duane | 1 | 159 | 9. Kerry Way | 0 | 99 |
| 5. Armbro Flight | 0 | 146 | 10. Best of All | 0 | 99 |

**(Also receiving first place votes: Roquepine, 2; Murdock Hanover, 1)**

*** 1 1/16-mile race before 1963. † Biggest purse in harness-racing history. R = record.**

## HARNESS HORSE RACING FACTS

### FAMOUS HORSES

**Adios.** He is considered the greatest pacing sire of all time. His offspring hold race records in all age groups on one-mile tracks: Bullet Hanover (2-year-old and 3-year-old); Adios Harry (4-year-old and all-age). Adios Butler, another offspring, was clocked at 1:54.6, the fastest of all.

**Dan Patch.** One of the most famous harness racers, he performed at the turn of the century. Dan Patch never lost a race and lost only two of 56 heats; in both instances he won the second heat and the decision. He retired after a 1909 exhibition with nine world records and died in July, 1916.

**Hambletonian.** Although he rarely appeared in harness, Hambletonian sired 1,331 foals from 1851 to 1874, an unprecedented feat in harness horse history. The most famous trotting race, the Hambletonian classic, is named after this great stallion.

### RECORD-BREAKING HORSES

| HORSE | DRIVER | YEAR | TRACK | TIME |
|---|---|---|---|---|
| **Trotters—Mile Track** | | | | |
| Greyhound | Sep Palin | 1938 | Lexington | 1:55¼ |
| Noble Victory | Stanley Dancer | 1966 | Du Quoin | 1:55⅗ |
| Matastar | Harry Pownall, Sr. | 1962 | Lexington | 1:55⅘ |
| Peter Manning | T. W. Murphy | 1922 | Lexington | 1:56¾ |
| Rosalind | Ben F. White | 1938 | Lexington | 1:56¾ |
| Speedy Scot [1] | Ralph Baldwin | 1963 | Lexington | 1:56⅘ |
| Ayres [1] | John Simpson | 1964 | Du Quoin | 1:56⅘ |
| **Pacers—Mile Track** | | | | |
| Bret Hanover [1] | Frank Ervin | 1966 | Lexington | 1:53⅗(R) |
| Adios Butler [1] | Page West | 1960 | Lexington | 1:54⅗ |
| Billy Direct [1] | Vic Fleming | 1938 | Lexington | 1:55 |
| Adios Harry [2] | Luther Lyons | 1955 | Vernon Downs | 1:55 |
| Bret Hanover | Frank Ervin | 1965 | Indiana State Fairgrounds | 1:55 |
| Meadow Skipper [1] | Earle Avery | 1963 | Lexington | 1:55⅕ |
| Dan Patch | H. C. Hersey | 1905 | Lexington | 1:55¼ |
| **Trotters—Half-Mile Track** | | | | |
| Speedy Rodney | Del Insko | 1966 | Yonkers | 1:58⅗ |
| Matastar [1] | Harry Pownall, Sr. | 1963 | Delaware | 1:58⅗ |
| Armbro Flight | Joe O'Brien | 1965 | Delaware | 1:59⅕ |
| Duke Rodney [1] | Billy Haughton | 1963 | Saratoga | 1:59⅗ |
| Greyhound [1] | Sep Palin | 1937 | Goshen | 1:59¾ |
| Darn Safe | James Arthur | 1957 | Saratoga | 1:59⅘ |
| Su Mac Lad | Harold Dancer, Sr. | 1961 | Yonkers | 2:00 |
| **Pacers—Half-Mile Track** | | | | |
| Adios Butler [1] | Eddie Cobb | 1961 | Delaware | 1:55⅗ |
| Bret Hanover | Frank Ervin | 1965 | Delaware | 1:57 |
| Overtrick | John Patterson | 1963 | Delaware | 1:57⅕ |
| Bye Bye Byrd | Clint Hodgins | 1959 | Roosevelt | 1:57⅘ |
| Adios Butler | Eddie Cobb | 1961 | Roosevelt | 1:57⅘ |
| Cardigan Bay | Vernon Dancer | 1964 | Yonkers | 1:58⅕ |

[1] Time trial. [2] Three-quarter-mile track. R = record.

### HORSES WITH MOST TWO-MINUTE MILES

| HORSE AND GAIT | YEARS RACED | NUMBER |
|---|---|---|
| Bret Hanover, pacer | 1964–66 | 31 |
| Dan Patch, pacer | 1900–09 | 30 |
| Greyhound, trotter | 1934–40 | 25 |
| Adios Butler, pacer | 1958–61 | 20 |
| Henry T. Adios, pacer | 1960–64 | 20 |
| Bye Bye Byrd, pacer | 1957–61 | 19 |

### HARNESS HORSE OF THE YEAR

| YEAR | HORSE | GAIT |
|---|---|---|
| 1949 | Good Time | pacer |
| 1950 | Proximity | trotter |
| 1951 | Pronto Don | trotter |
| 1952 | Good Time | pacer |
| 1953 | Hi-Lo's Forbes | pacer |
| 1954 | Stenographer | trotter |
| 1955 | Scott Frost | trotter |
| 1956 | Scott Frost | trotter |
| 1957 | Torpid | pacer |
| 1958 | Emily's Pride | trotter |
| 1959 | Bye Bye Byrd | pacer |
| 1960 | Adios Butler | pacer |
| 1961 | Adios Butler | pacer |
| 1962 | Su Mac Lad | trotter |
| 1963 | Speedy Scot | trotter |
| 1964 | Bret Hanover | pacer |
| 1965 | Bret Hanover | pacer |
| 1966 | Bret Hanover | pacer |

# ROWING

For centuries, boats propelled by oars were used only for transportation, maritime trade, or war. Today, rowing is a major intercollegiate sport in the United States, as well as a prominent sport in several European countries.

A variety of races are open to rowing competitors; the most popular is probably crew. In crew racing a coxswain steers the eight-oared shell by means of tiller ropes attached to a rudder, and directs the crew. The most famous of all crew races, the Henley-on-Thames Royal Regatta, began in 1839 at Henley, England.

The first collegiate regatta in the United States was staged in 1852 between Harvard and Yale. Since then, this annual meet has come to be regarded by experts as America's classic.

All rowing in the United States is governed by the National Association of Amateur Oarsmen.

## HENLEY-ON-THAMES ROYAL REGATTA

Held each year at Henley, England, the Royal Regatta is rowed on the Thames River over a course set at one mile, 550 yards. A listing of the 1967 Henley champions follows.

| RACE | WINNER | TIME |
|---|---|---|
| Grand Challenge Cup (for eights)......... | S. C. Wissenschaft, Leipzig, East Germany...................... | 6:46 |
| Diamond Sculls.......................... | M. Studach (Grasshopper Club), Zurich, Switzerland............. | 8:27 |
| Silver Goblet (for pairs)................. | M. Gelpke and K. Jacob, Dresden, East Germany................. | 8:18 |
| Double Sculls........................... | M. Studach and M. Burgin, Zurich, Switzerland................. | 7:47 |
| Prince Philip Cup (fours with coxswain).... | A. S. K. Vorwartz, Rostock, East Germany...................... | 7:39 |
| Princess Elizabeth Cup (schoolboy eights).. | Eton College, England.......................... | 7:03 |
| Thames Challenge Cup (for eights)....... | Cornell University, United States...................... | 7:06 |
| Stewards' Challenge Cup (for fours)....... | S. G. Dynamo, Potsdam, East Germany........................ | 7:31 |

## INTERCOLLEGIATE ROWING ASSOCIATION REGATTA

The first official Intercollegiate Rowing Association (IRA) Regatta was held on the Hudson River near Poughkeepsie, New York, in 1900. Since 1952 this major intercollegiate rowing event has been held at Onondaga Lake, Syracuse, New York. Here the nation's outstanding collegiate crews come to compete for the national intercollegiate title. Harvard and Yale are the only major crews that do not participate in the IRA Regatta.

| YEAR | WINNER | TIME | YEAR | WINNER | TIME | YEAR | WINNER | TIME |
|---|---|---|---|---|---|---|---|---|
| 1908 | Syracuse...... | 19:24.2 | 1928 | California...... | 18:35.8 | 1951 | Wisconsin..... | 7:50.5 |
| 1909 | Cornell........ | 19:02.0 | 1929 | Columbia...... | 22:58.0 | 1952 [5] | Navy.......... | 15:08.5 |
| 1910 | Cornell........ | 20:42.2 | 1930 | Cornell........ | 21:42.0 | 1953 | Navy.......... | 15:29.6 |
| 1911 | Cornell........ | 20:10.8 | 1931 | Navy.......... | 18:54.2 | 1954 | Navy.......... | 16:04.1 |
| 1912 | Cornell........ | 19:31.4 | 1932 | California...... | 19:55.0 | 1955 | Cornell........ | 15:49.9 |
| 1913 | Syracuse...... | 19:28.6 | 1934 | California...... | 19:44.0 | 1956 | Cornell........ | 16:22.4 |
| 1914 | Columbia...... | 19:37.8 | 1935 | California...... | 18:52.0 | 1957 | Cornell........ | 15:26.2 |
| 1915 | Cornell........ | 19:36.8 | 1936 | Washington.... | 19:06.0 | 1958 | Cornell........ | 17:12.1 |
| 1916 | Syracuse...... | 20:15.4 | 1937 | Washington.... | 18:33.6 | 1959 | Wisconsin..... | 18:01.7 |
| 1920 [1] | Syracuse...... | 11:02.6 | 1938 | Navy.......... | 18:19.0 | 1960 | California...... | 15:57.0 |
| 1921 | Navy.......... | 14:07.0 | 1939 | California...... | 18:12.6 | 1961 | California...... | 16:49.2 |
| 1922 | Navy.......... | 13:33.6 | 1940 | Washington.... | 22:42.0 | 1962 | Cornell........ | 17:02.9 |
| 1923 | Washington.... | 14:03.2 | 1941 | Washington.... | 18:53.3 | 1963 | Cornell........ | 17:24.0 |
| 1924 | Washington.... | 15:02.0 | 1947 [3] | Navy.......... | 13:59.2 | 1964 [6] | California...... | 6:31.1 |
| 1925 [2] | Navy.......... | 19:24.8 | 1948 | Washington.... | 14:06.4 | 1965 | Navy.......... | 16:51.4 |
| 1926 | Washington.... | 19:28.6 | 1949 | California...... | 14:42.6 | 1966 | Wisconsin..... | 16:03.4 |
| 1927 | Columbia...... | 20:57.0 | 1950 [4] | Washington.... | 8:07.5 | 1967 | Pennsylvania.. | 16:13.9 |

[1] No competition, 1917–19. The original four-mile run was cut to two miles in 1920, and the race was held at Lake Cayuga, Ithaca, New York. In 1921 it returned to Poughkeepsie and was set at three miles until 1925. [2] A four-mile race until 1950. [3] No competition, 1942–46. [4] The 1950-51 regattas were moved to Marietta, Ohio, and cut to two miles. [5] In 1952 the race was set at three miles and permanently moved to Onondaga Lake, Syracuse, New York. [6] The 1964 regatta was cut to 2,000 meters. In 1965 it returned to a three-mile course.

## HARVARD-YALE REGATTA

| YEAR | WINNER | TIME | YEAR | WINNER | TIME | YEAR | WINNER | TIME |
|---|---|---|---|---|---|---|---|---|
| 1953 | Harvard....... | 20:09 | 1958 | Yale.......... | 22:39 | 1963 | Harvard....... | 19:47 |
| 1954 | Yale.......... | 21:58.4 | 1959 | Harvard....... | 19:52 | 1964 | Harvard....... | 20:48.2 |
| 1955 | Yale.......... | 20:05 | 1960 | Harvard....... | 19:41.2 | 1965 | Harvard....... | 19:41.6 |
| 1956 | Yale.......... | 19:26 | 1961 | Harvard....... | 22:0 | 1966 | Harvard....... | 19:44 |
| 1957 | Yale.......... | 20:35 | 1962 | Yale.......... | 21:26 | 1967 | Harvard....... | 22:43.2 |

# SKATING

## FIGURE ICE SKATING

Traditionally, the Scandinavians are credited with being the first people to use ice skates. However, an American, Jackson Haines, first came up with the idea of figure skating that later turned the sport into an art. A ballet master, Haines opened figure skating schools in Vienna, and by the late 1870s he had developed the international style of figure skating. Louis Rubenstein, a Canadian pupil of Haines, was the first famous figure skater in North America and introduced the art here.

Probably the most famous of figure skaters was Norway's Sonja Henie, who won the world figure skating championship ten times (1927–36), the European title eight times (1929–36), the Norwegian title six times (1924–29), and three Olympic gold medals (1928, 1932, and 1936), before turning professional in 1936.

The great American figure skater Dick Button won the U.S. championship in 1946 at 16 years of age. He went on to win five consecutive world championships, seven straight U.S. men's titles, and two Olympic gold medals before turning professional in 1952.

## WORLD FIGURE SKATING CHAMPIONS: 1967

The world championships of figure skating are conducted by the International Skating Union, the governing body of all international amateur figure skating events. The 1967 championships were held in Vienna, Austria, from February 28 to March 5.

Men's Singles: Emmerich Danzer, Austria
Ladies' Singles: Peggy Fleming, U.S.
Pairs: Ljudmila Belousova and Oleg Protopopov, U.S.S.R.
Ice Dance: Diane Towler and Bernard Ford, Great Britain

## NATIONAL FIGURE SKATING CHAMPIONS: 1967

The United States Figure Skating Association, governing body of amateur figure skating on ice, conducts national figure skating championships each year. The 1967 national championships were held in Omaha, Nebraska, from January 18 to 21.

Senior Men's Singles: Gary Visconti, Detroit Skating Club, Detroit, Mich.
Senior Ladies' Singles: Peggy Fleming, Broadmoor Skating Club, Colorado Springs, Colo.
Junior Men's Singles: Roger Bass, Arctic Blades Figure Skating Club, Los Angeles, Calif.
Junior Ladies' Singles: Julie Holmes, Arctic Blades Figure Skating Club, Los Angeles, Calif.
Senior Pairs: Cynthia and Ronald Kauffman, Seattle Skating Club, Seattle, Wash.
Junior Pairs: Jo Jo Starbuck and Kenneth Shelley, Arctic Blades Figure Skating Club, Los Angeles, Calif.
Dance: Lorna Dyer and John Carrell, Broadmoor Skating Club, Colorado Springs, Colo.
Silver Dance: Debbi Gerken, Skating Club of Lake Placid, N.Y., and Keith Galgot, Town of Watertown, Conn.

## SPEED SKATING

The International Skating Union sponsored the first world speed skating championships in 1893, while the United States speed championships were first held in 1921. For many years Norwegian and Finnish skaters dominated the sport of speed skating, but in recent years Russian skaters have taken more and more international titles. Hjalmar Andersen of Norway is the only man ever to win the world title three years in succession.

## WORLD SPEED SKATING CHAMPIONS: 1967

Men's (Championships held in Oslo, Norway, from February 11–12): Kees Verkerk, Netherlands
Women's (Championships held in Deventer, Netherlands, from February 18–19): Stien Kaiser, Netherlands

## NATIONAL OUTDOOR SPEED SKATING CHAMPIONS: 1967

Senior Men: Michael Passarella, Chicago, Ill.
Intermediate Boys: Barth Levy, Middle Atlantic
Junior Boys: Dennis Berry, Minneapolis, Minn.
Juvenile Boys: Thomas Klanchnik, Minneapolis, Minn.
Midget Boys: Lee Mazzilli, New York; William Anderson, Ill. (Tie)
Senior Women: Jeanne Ashworth, Northern New York Skating Association

Intermediate Girls: Jenny Fish, Strongville, Ohio
Junior Girls: Donna Peterson, Minneapolis
Juvenile Girls: Kay Lancour, Wis.
Midget Girls: Carol Trombley, Minneapolis, Minn.

## NATIONAL INDOOR SPEED SKATING CHAMPIONS: 1967

Senior Men: Bill Lanigan, Middle Atlantic
Intermediate Boys: Jim Keane, Ohio
Junior Boys: Mark McDonald, Middle Atlantic
Juvenile Boys: John Siempeckamp, Mo.
Midget Boys: Ken Kresge, Ohio
Senior Women: Sally Blatchford, Ill.
Intermediate Girls: Jenny Fish, Ohio
Junior Girls: Debbie Fish, Ohio
Juvenile Girls: Kim Vala, Ill.
Midget Girls: Ann Henning, Ill.

# SKIING

Skiing was first organized as a sport in the mid-19th century when the Norwegians initiated local ski festivals. The idea caught on, and by the late 19th century most European countries had established national skiing championships. The sport was brought to America by Scandinavians who organized ski clubs in Pennsylvania, Minnesota, New Hampshire, and Michigan. The National Ski Association, later the United States Ski Association, was formed in 1904 to govern the sport in this country. The 1932 Winter Olympics, held at Lake Placid, New York, was the first international skiing event in the United States.

Popular interest in competitive skiing did not develop in the United States until the 1950s. One of the most famous American skiing stars, Andrea Mead Lawrence, won two gold medals in the 1952 Olympic Games. In 1960 the Winter Olympics were held at Squaw Valley, California, and televised throughout the nation. The first American men to win Olympic medals in skiing were Billy Kidd and Jimmy Heuga in the 1964 Olympics.

Major skiing championships combine two categories of competitive skiing: Alpine events (slalom, giant slalom, and downhill); and Nordic skiing (cross-country and jumping).

## 1967 NATIONAL SKI CHAMPIONSHIPS
Source: United States Ski Association

### JUMPING
Men's Class A: Gene Kotlarek, Duluth, Minnesota, 216.7 points
Men's Veteran Class: Leonard Johnson, Leavenworth, Washington, 153.2 points
Boy's Class C: Gary Sparpana, Leavenworth, Washington, 178.0 points

### ALPINE, MEN
Giant Slalom: Dumeng Giovanoli, Switzerland, 1 minute, 48.68 seconds
Slalom: Jim Heuga, Squaw Valley, California, 1 minute, 38.24 seconds
Downhill: Dennis McCoy, Denver (Colorado) University, 1 minute, 42.14 seconds
Combined: Dumeng Giovanoli, Switzerland, 27.29 points

### ALPINE, WOMEN
Giant Slalom: Sandra Shellworth, Bogus Basin, Idaho, 1 minute, 55.75 seconds
Slalom: Penny McCoy, Mammoth Mountain, California, 1 minute, 39.94 seconds
Downhill: Nancy Greene, Canada, 2 minutes, 1.66 seconds
Combined: Karen Budge, Jackson, Wyoming, 42.82 points

### NORDIC
Cross-Country: Mike Gallagher, Killington, Vermont, 49.07 points
Combined Cross-Country and Jumping: John Bower, Auburn, Maine, 500.25 points

## SKI JUMPING RECORDS
Source: United States Ski Association

| DATE | SKIER | SITE | RECORD |
|------|-------|------|--------|
| 1964 | Nino Zandanel, Italy | Obertsdorf, West Germany | 472 feet |
| 1967 | Bjorn Wirkola, Norway | Leavenworth, Washington | 335 feet |
| 1965 | John Balfanz, Stockton, Illinois | Iron Mountain, Michigan | 325 feet |
| 1965 | Toralf Engan, Norway | Leavenworth, Washington | 324 feet |
| 1963 | Gene Kotlarek, Duluth, Minnesota | Steamboat Springs, Colorado | 318–322 feet * |
| 1962 | John Balfanz, Minneapolis, Minnesota | Westby, Wisconsin | 317 feet |

* Undecided.

## NCAA SKIING CHAMPIONS: 1967

The National Collegiate Athletic Association (NCAA) annually plans and sponsors national intercollegiate skiing championships. The 14th annual NCAA Skiing Championships were held at Sugarloaf Mountain in Maine from March 2 to March 4, 1967.

Slalom: Rick Chaffee, University of Denver, 81.96 seconds
Downhill: Dennis McCoy, University of Denver, 2 minutes, 11.20 seconds
Alpine Combined: Terje Overland, University of Denver, 265.83 points
Cross-Country: Ned Gillette, Dartmouth College, 1 hour, 4 minutes, 7 seconds

Scoring firsts in the slalom, downhill, and Alpine combined, coach Willy Schaeffler's University of Denver team edged past the University of Wyoming by eight-tenths of a point to take its seventh consecutive championship.

Following is a list of the 1967 winners.

Jumping: Bjorn Loken, University of Utah, 213.5 points
Nordic Combined: Matz Jenssen, University of Utah, 430.5 points
Skimeister Award (all events): Matz Jenssen, University of Utah, 365.2 points
Team Scoring: University of Denver, 376.7; University of Wyoming, 375.9.

# SOCCER

The principal national game in well over 100 countries, soccer comes closest to being a truly international sport.

Few spectator games, if any, have ever equalled soccer in arousing such passions. There are instances where "kill the umpire" has turned into more than an angry shout from the fans, and numerous cases of emotion-ridden fans violently attacking each other or the players, as well as spurts of flaring tempers between members of opposing teams.

Because of the intense loyalties that soccer can provoke, stadiums in many countries have barriers erected between the stands and the playing fields. In Rio de Janeiro, Brazil, for example, the Maracãna Stadium (where crowds of more than 200,000 are not unusual) has a supposedly fan-proof moat circling the field.

The United States is one of the few nations where soccer has not yet won a large following, despite the number of schools that include it in their sports activities. One reason soccer has not had more appeal for most Americans is that they have a far wider choice of sports in which to become interested than do the citizens of any other country.

## UNITED SOCCER ASSOCIATION (USA) TEAM STANDINGS: 1967

| EASTERN DIVISION | W | L | T | P[1] | GF[2] | GA[3] | WESTERN DIVISION | W | L | T | P[1] | GF[2] | GA[3] |
|---|---|---|---|---|---|---|---|---|---|---|---|---|---|
| Washington Whips | 5 | 2 | 5 | 15 | 19 | 11 | Los Angeles Wolves | 5 | 2 | 5 | 15 | 21 | 14 |
| Cleveland Stokers | 5 | 3 | 4 | 14 | 19 | 13 | San Francisco Gales | 5 | 4 | 3 | 13 | 25 | 19 |
| Toronto | 4 | 3 | 5 | 13 | 23 | 17 | Chicago Mustangs | 3 | 2 | 7 | 13 | 20 | 14 |
| Detroit Cougars | 3 | 3 | 6 | 12 | 11 | 18 | Houston Stars | 4 | 4 | 4 | 12 | 19 | 18 |
| New York Skyliners | 2 | 4 | 6 | 10 | 15 | 17 | Vancouver Royal Canadians | 3 | 4 | 5 | 11 | 20 | 28 |
| Boston Rovers | 2 | 7 | 3 | 7 | 12 | 26 | Dallas Tornado | 3 | 6 | 3 | 9 | 14 | 23 |

[1] Points (based on FIFA scoring system).   [2] Goals for.   [3] Goals against.

## USA SCORING LEADERS: 1967

| PLAYER AND CLUB | GOALS | ASSISTS | POINTS | PLAYER AND CLUB | GOALS | ASSISTS | POINTS |
|---|---|---|---|---|---|---|---|
| Roberto Boninsegna, Chicago | 10 | 1 | 21 | Peter Cormack, Toronto | 6 | 1 | 13 |
| Henk Houwaart, San Francisco | 9 | 2 | 20 | Benedicto Ribiero, New York | 5 | 2 | 12 |
| Paulo Borges, Houston | 6 | 3 | 15 | Colin Stein, Toronto | 5 | 1 | 11 |
| Peter Dobing, Cleveland | 7 | 0 | 14 | Jim Storrie, Washington | 5 | 1 | 11 |
| Rene Pas, San Francisco | 6 | 2 | 14 | Aladim Luciano, Houston | 4 | 2 | 10 |

## NATIONAL PROFESSIONAL SOCCER LEAGUE (NPSL) TEAM STANDINGS: 1967

| EASTERN DIVISION | W | L | T | P[1] | GF[2] | GA[3] | WESTERN DIVISION | W | L | T | P[1] | GF[2] | GA[3] |
|---|---|---|---|---|---|---|---|---|---|---|---|---|---|
| Baltimore Bays | 14 | 9 | 9 | 162 | 53 | 47 | Oakland Clippers | 19 | 8 | 5 | 185 | 64 | 34 |
| Philadelphia Spartans | 14 | 9 | 9 | 157 | 53 | 43 | St. Louis Stars | 14 | 11 | 7 | 156 | 54 | 57 |
| New York Generals | 11 | 13 | 8 | 143 | 60 | 58 | Chicago Spurs | 10 | 11 | 11 | 142 | 50 | 55 |
| Atlanta Chiefs [4] | 10 | 12 | 9 | 135 | 51 | 46 | Toronto Falcons | 10 | 17 | 5 | 127 | 59 | 70 |
| Pittsburgh Phantoms [4] | 10 | 14 | 7 | 132 | 59 | 74 | Los Angeles Toros | 7 | 15 | 10 | 113 | 42 | 61 |

[1] Points (based on NPSL scoring system).   [2] Goals for.   [3] Goals against.   [4] Last game cancelled by rain.

## NPSL SCORING LEADERS: 1967

| PLAYER AND CLUB | GOALS | ASSISTS | POINTS | PLAYER AND CLUB | GOALS | ASSISTS | POINTS |
|---|---|---|---|---|---|---|---|
| Yanko Daucik, Toronto | 20 | 8 | 48 | Oscar Lopez, Toronto | 13 | 5 | 31 |
| Willie Roy, Chicago | 17 | 5 | 39 | Bara Kostic, St. Louis | 13 | 5 | 31 |
| Eli Durante, Los Angeles | 15 | 5 | 35 | George Kirby, New York | 14 | 2 | 30 |
| Rudi Kolbl, St. Louis | 13 | 8 | 34 | Ilija Mitic, Oakland | 13 | 3 | 29 |
| Manfred Rummell, Pittsburgh | 14 | 4 | 32 | Ernie Winchester, Chicago | 13 | 2 | 28 |

## THE WORLD CUP SOCCER CHAMPIONSHIP

The fervid international interest in soccer is well-illustrated by the World Championship playoffs, the sport's World Series (held every four years, except 1942 and 1946, since 1930).

Over 1.6 million fans attended the 1966 games in England, while an estimated worldwide audience of 400 million saw the action on television. Cup winners are listed below.

| | | | |
|---|---|---|---|
| 1930 Uruguay | 1938 Italy | 1954 Germany | 1962 Brazil |
| 1934 Italy | 1950 Uruguay | 1958 Brazil | 1966 England |

# FOCUS ON THE NEWS

## BIG-LEAGUE SOCCER COMES TO U.S.

The fast, exciting game of professional soccer often sees collisions between players, as (above) during a game between the Chicago Spurs and St. Louis Stars, who won 2-1. Diagram of a soccer field is at right.

The latest sport to kick up a storm in the United States is professional soccer—or, as most of the world calls it, football. Known as a game that incites fans in other lands to acts of violence, it has already embroiled two fledgling American leagues in a bitter legal battle that threatens to eclipse the sport almost before it can be introduced.

One league, the United Soccer Association (USA), has been sanctioned by the Federation Internationale de Football Association (FIFA), the governing body of world football. The other league, the National Professional Soccer League (NPSL), has been refused recognition. Ineligible to enter international competition and faced with other crippling restrictions, the NPSL lodged an $18 million suit against FIFA and United, claiming restraint of trade.

Actual pro soccer play got under way across the nation in April. The NPSL began operating with franchised clubs in New York, Toronto, Baltimore, Philadelphia, Pittsburgh, Chicago, St. Louis, Oakland, Los Angeles, and Atlanta (a Boston team is scheduled to join the NPSL in 1968). The

12 clubs of the USA league also took to the field (or pitch, as it is called) in New York, Boston, Toronto, Washington, Cleveland, Detroit, Chicago, Vancouver, Los Angeles, San Francisco, Dallas, and Houston.

Making use of its sanction rights, United imported complete teams from the other 136 FIFA countries to represent its cities. Lacking such authorization, the NPSL was forced to construct its clubs from a mixture of foreign and domestic talent. But the outlawed league did have the advantage of a national television contract (CBS) to show weekly games from coast to coast.

Championship play-offs were held at the end of the 1967 season. The Oakland Clippers defeated the Baltimore Bays in two straight games for the NPSL championship; Los Angeles downed Washington, 6-5, to take the United Soccer Association title.

Serious merger negotiations are rumored to be on the verge of blending the two divergent groups into one major North American league. Team sponsors hope that soccer will eventually flourish as a professional sport on American soil.

# SURFING

Surfing, once limited to a few beaches in California and Hawaii (where the sport existed when Captain Cook discovered the islands in 1778), has become increasingly popular in the United States since World War II. At the October (1966) World Championship in San Diego, entrants from as far away as Australia and France competed for prizes, and a low-budget surfing documentary, *The Endless Summer*, became one of the surprise money-making film hits of 1967.

Although Atlantic Ocean beaches have smaller—but trickier—surf than do those on the Pacific, the enthusiasm and skill of the sport's Eastern followers is proving a match for their West Coast counterparts; an intense rivalry exists between the two regions.

Now somewhat shorn of the rebellious image that colored its earlier days, surfing is rapidly becoming an established sport.

## MAJOR SURFING CHAMPIONSHIP CONTESTS: 1967
Source: United States Surfing Association

### EVENT AND WINNER

**Peru International,** Lima, Peru
Corky Carroll, Dana Point, California

**Laguna Masters,** Redondo Beach, California
Men: Skip Frye, San Diego, California
Juniors: Mike Tabeling, Cocoa Beach, Florida
Women: Joyce Hoffman, Capistrano Beach, Calif.
Boys: Rolf Aurness, Pacific Palisades, Calif.
Seniors: Les Williams, Dana Point, California
Tandem: Pete Peterson and Barrie Algaw,
    Santa Monica, California

**Men's Invitational,** Oceanside, California
Mike Purpus, Hermosa Beach, California

**Carlsbad Open,** Carlsbad, California
Men: Steve Bigler, Newport Beach, California
Juniors: Charles Quesnel, Hermosa Beach, Calif.
Women: Joyce Hoffman, Capistrano Beach, Calif.
Boys: Bobby Burnside, Malibu, California
Seniors: Bob Moore, Hawaii
Tandem: Pete Peterson and Barrie Algaw,
    Santa Monica, California

**Fiesta de la Marina Invitational,** Ventura, California
Men: Greg Tucker, Long Beach, California
Juniors: Dru Harrison, Hermosa Beach, California
Women: Joey Hamasaki, Venice, California
Boys: Rolf Aurness, Pacific Palisades, Calif.
Seniors: Kit Horn, Fullerton, California
Tandem: Wesley Thomas and Sally Reid,
    San Clemente, California

**United States,** Huntington Beach, California
Men: Corky Carroll, Dana Point, California
Juniors: Dru Harrison, Hermosa Beach, Calif.
Women: Joyce Hoffman, Capistrano Beach, Calif.
Seniors: Bob Holland, Virginia Beach, Va.
Tandem: Don Hansen and Diana Bolton,
    Cardiff, California

### EVENT AND WINNER

**Ocean Beach Open,** Ocean Beach, California
Men: Corky Carroll, Dana Point, California
Juniors: Mike Tabeling, Cocoa Beach, Florida
Women: Joyce Hoffman, Capistrano Beach, Calif.
Boys: Rolf Aurness, Pacific Palisades, Calif.
Seniors: Phil Vedder, Dana Point, California
Tandem: Wesley Thomas and Sally Reid,
    San Clemente, California

**Atlantic States,** Seaside Heights, N.J.
Men: Skip Frye, San Diego, California
Juniors: Bobby Michel, Manhattan Beach, Calif.
Women: Joey Hamasaki, Venice, California
Boys: Vincent Roland, Cocoa Beach, Florida
Midgets: Harold Fitzpatrick, Seaside Heights,
    New Jersey

**East Coast,** Virginia Beach, Virginia
Men: Steve Bigler, Newport Beach, California
Juniors: Mike Tabeling, Cocoa Beach, Florida
Women: Joey Hamasaki, Venice, California
Boys: Fletcher Sharpe, Cocoa Beach, Florida
Midgets: Jimbo Brothers, Virginia Beach, Va.
Seniors: Les Williams, Dana Point, Calif.
Tandem: Don Hansen and Diana Bolton,
    Cardiff, California

**Eastern Surfing Association,** Rincon, Puerto Rico
Eastern Men: Claude Codgen, Cocoa Beach, Fla.
Eastern Women: Mimi Munro, Ormond Beach, Fla.
International Men: Corky Carroll, Dana Point,
    California

**Hawaii State,** Ala Moana, Hawaii
Men: Jock Sutherland, Hawaii
Juniors: Randy Rarich, Hawaii
Women: Sharron Weber, Hawaii

## SOME POPULAR SURFING BEACHES

The following list represents only a few of the more popular surfing beaches scattered throughout the world. Southern California reportedly has almost 300 beaches where surfers practice their sport. Probably every surfing devotee has his own favorite area or areas, and the search for the beach with the perfect wave is never-ending.

| | | |
|---|---|---|
| Malibu, California | Waikiki Beach, Hawaii | Kitty Hawk, North Carolina |
| Rincon, California | Ala Moana, Hawaii | Punta Rocas, Peru |
| San Onofre, California | Makaha Beach, Hawaii | Rincon, Puerto Rico |
| Sunset Cliffs, California | Sunset Beach, Hawaii | Cape St. Francis, South Africa |
| Biarritz, France | Gilgo Beach (L.I.), New York | Virginia Beach, Virginia |

# SWIMMING

Speed swimming was included in the program of the first modern Olympic Games of 1896, and swimming clubs in the United States and in Europe were organized to train athletes to compete in this great meet. In the 1904 Olympics the United States won its first international swimming event when Charles M. Daniels swam the 440-yard (today 400-meter) race.

Duke Kahanamoku and Johnny Weissmuller were among the outstanding American swimmers of the early decades of the 20th century. Today, British, American, and Australian swimmers are setting new world records in almost every major national and international meet. Among the outstanding American swimmers is Don Schollander, who won four 1964

Olympic gold medals.

Amateur swimming in this country is under the jurisdiction of the Amateur Athletic Union, although the National Collegiate Athletic Association also holds annual championships. All world records are subject to the approval of the International Amateur Swimming Federation. In December, 1962, the International Amateur Swimming Federation decided to approve only those world records achieved over either a 50-meter or 55-yard course.

At the 1967 National AAU Women's outdoor and indoor swimming championships, Claudia Kolb emerged as individual point leader. The Santa Clara Swim Club ace set two world records.

## AAU OUTDOOR SWIMMING AND DIVING CHAMPIONSHIPS: 1967

### MEN'S EVENTS
(at Oak Park, Illinois)

■ **Freestyle**
100-Meter: Don Schollander, Santa Clara (Calif.) Swim Club, 0:53.3
200-Meter: Don Schollander, Santa Clara (Calif.) Swim Club, 1:55.7 [1]
400-Meter: Greg Charlton, Santa Clara (Calif.) Swim Club, 4:09.8 [1]
400-Meter Relay: Los Angeles Athletic Club, A Team (R. Kidder, B. Boag, Z. Zorn, D. Havens), 3:36.4
800-Meter Relay: Santa Clara (Calif.) Swim Club, A Team (G. Ilman, M. Wall, M. Spitz, D. Schollander), 7:52.1 [1]
1,500-Meter: Mike Burton, Arden Hills (Calif.) Swim Club, 16:34.1 [1]

■ **Breaststroke**
100-Meter: Ken Merten, Los Angeles (Calif.) Athletic Club, 1:08.9
200-Meter: Ken Merten, Los Angeles (Calif.) Athletic Club, 2:30.8

■ **Butterfly**
100-Meter: Mark Spitz, Santa Clara (Calif.) Swim Club, 0:56.7 [1]

200-Meter: Mark Spitz, Santa Clara (Calif.) Swim Club, 2:06.4 [1]

■ **Backstroke**
100-Meter: Charles Hickcox, Indiana Aquatic Club, 0:59.7
200-Meter: Charles Hickcox, Indiana Aquatic Club, 2:12.3

■ **Medley**
200-Meter Individual: Greg Buckingham, Santa Clara (Calif.) Swim Club, 2:11.3 [1]
400-Meter Individual: Peter Williams, Spartan Swim Club, Mich., 4:50.8
400-Meter Relay: Santa Clara (Calif.) Swim Club, A Team (F. Haywood, W. Anderson, M. Spitz, D. Schollander), 3:59.7 [2]

■ **Diving**
One-Meter: Jim Henry, Indiana Aquatic Club, 489.85 points
Three-Meter: Keith Russell, Dick Smith Swim Gym, Phoenix, Ariz. 557.10 points
Ten-Meter Platform: Keith Russell, Dick Smith Swim Gym, Phoenix, Ariz. 576.95 points

■ **Team Champion:** Santa Clara (Calif.) Swim Club, 208 points

### WOMEN'S EVENTS
(at Philadelphia, Pennsylvania)

■ **Freestyle**
100-Meter: Jane Barkman, Vesper Boat Club, Philadelphia, Penn., 0:59.8 [2]
200-Meter: Pam Kruse, Fort Lauderdale (Fla.) Swimming Association, 2:09.7 [1]
400-Meter: Debbie Meyer, Arden Hills (Calif.) Swim Club, 4:29.0 [1]
1,500-Meter: Debbie Meyer, Arden Hills (Calif.) Swim Club, 17:50.2 [1]
400-Meter Relay: Santa Clara (Calif.) Swim Club (L. Gustavson, N. Ryan, L. Fritz, P. Watson), 4:03.5 [1]
800-Meter Relay: Santa Clara (Calif) Swim Club, A Team (N. Ryan, L. Gustavson, C. Kolb, P. Watson), 8:53.0 [1]

■ **Breaststroke**
100-Meter: Catie Ball, Jacksonville, Fla., 1:14.6 [1]
200-Meter: Catie Ball, Jacksonville, Fla., 2:39.5 [1]

■ **Butterfly**
100-Meter: Ellie Daniel, Vesper Boat Club, Philadelphia, Penn., 1:05.7

200-Meter: Toni Hewitt, Corona Del Mar (Calif.) Swim Club, 2:23 6 [1]

■ **Backstroke**
100-Meter: Kendis Moore, Arizona Desert Rats, 1:09.2
200-Meter: Kendis Moore, Arizona Desert Rats, 2:28.1

■ **Medley**
200-Meter Individual: Claudia Kolb, Santa Clara (Calif.) Swim Club, 2:25.0 [1]
400-Meter Individual: Claudia Kolb, Santa Clara (Calif.) Swim Club, 5:08.2 [1]
400-Meter Relay: Santa Clara (Calif.) Swim Club (L. Gustavson, L. Davis, C. Kolb, P. Watson), 4:34.6 [2]

■ **Diving**
One-Meter: Micki King, Ann Arbor, Mich., 407.80 points
Three-Meter: Micki King, Ann Arbor, Mich., 466.90 points
Ten-Meter Platform: Lesley Bush, Princeton, N.J., 377.10 points

■ **Team Champion:** Santa Clara (Calif.) Swim Club, 203 points

[1] Set a world record.  [2] Set a U.S. record.

## AAU INDOOR SWIMMING AND DIVING CHAMPIONSHIPS: 1967

**MEN'S EVENTS**
(at Dallas, Texas)

■ **Freestyle**
100-Yard: Donald Havens, Southern California,
0:46.0
200-Yard: Don Schollander, Yale, 1:41.2 [1]
500-Yard: Mike Burton, UCLA, 4:37.0 [2]
1,650-Yard: Mike Burton, UCLA, 16:08.0 [1]
400-Yard Relay: Yale University Varsity
(R. Waples, M. Ahern, D. Kennedy,
D. Schollander), 3:06.5
800-Yard Relay: Yale University Varsity
(R. Waples, R. Schneider, D. Kennedy,
D. Schollander), 6:56.2
■ **Breaststroke**
100-Yard: Ken Merten, Southern Methodist, 0:58.9
200-Yard: Ken Merten, Southern Methodist, 2:10.4
■ **Backstroke**
100-Yard: Fred Haywood, unattached, Santa Clara,
Calif., 0:52.6
200-Yard: Mark Mader, Southern California Frosh,
1:54.4 [1]

■ **Butterfly**
100-Yard: Mark Spitz, unattached, Santa Clara,
Calif., 0:49.9 [1]
200-Yard: Mark Spitz, unattached, Santa Clara,
Calif., 1:50.6 [1]
■ **Medley**
200-Yard Individual: William Utley, Indiana University,
1:55.9 [1]
400-Yard Individual: Dick Roth, Santa Clara (Calif.)
Swim Club, 4:09.5
400-Yard Relay: Santa Clara (Calif.) Swim Club "A"
(J. Malley, R. Momsen, L. Nicolao, W. Meyer), 3:30.4
■ **Diving** (at Arlington, Texas)
One-Meter: Luis Rivero, Indiana University, 516.70 points
Three-Meter: Keith Russell, Dick Smith Swim Gym, Phoenix,
Ariz. 509.70 points
Ten-Meter Platform: Keith Russell, Dick Smith Swim
Gym, Phoenix, Ariz. 548.90 points
■ **Team Champion:** Santa Clara (Calif.) Swim Club, 65
points

**WOMEN'S EVENTS**
(at Fairview Park, Ohio)

■ **Freestyle**
100-Yard: Erika Bricker, unattached, Visalia,
Calif., 0:53.3 [1]
200-Yard: Pokey Watson, Santa Clara (Calif.)
Swim Club, 1:54.1 [1]
500-Yard: Pam Kruse, Fort Lauderdale (Florida)
Swim Association, 5:06.9 [1]
1,650-Yard: Debbie Meyer, Arden Hills (Calif.) Swim Club,
17:38.1 [1]
400-Yard Relay: Santa Clara (Calif.) Swim Club "A"
(L. Gustavson, N. Ryan, C. Kolb, P. Watson),
3:37.1 [1]
800-Yard Relay: Santa Clara (Calif.) Swim Club "A"
(L. Gustavson, N. Ryan, C. Kolb, P. Watson), 7:53.7 [1]
■ **Breaststroke**
100-Yard: Catie Ball, unattached, Jacksonville, Fla.,
1:06.6 [1]
200-Yard: Catie Ball, unattached, Jacksonville, Fla.,
2:25.2
■ **Backstroke**
100-Yard: Kay Hall, Tacoma (Wash.) Swim Club, 1:01.6
200-Yard: Kendis Moore, Arizona Desert Rats, 2:10.2 [1]

■ **Butterfly**
100-Yard: Lee Davis, unattached, Saratoga, Calif.,
0:58.4 [1]
200-Yard: Lee Davis, unattached, Saratoga, Calif.,
2:07.9 [1]
■ **Medley**
200-Yard Individual: Claudia Kolb, Santa Clara
(Calif.) Swim Club, 2:09.7
400-Yard Individual: Sue Pedersen, Arden Hills
Swim Club, 4:37.0 [1]
400-Yard Relay: Santa Clara (Calif.) Swim Club "A"
(P. Watson, C. Kolb, L. Hildreth, L. Gustavson),
4:05.4 [1]
■ **Diving** (at Arlington, Texas)
One-Meter: Lesley Bush, unattached, Bloomington,
Ind., 443.10 points
Three-Meter: Sue Gossick, unattached, Tarzana, Calif.,
416.40 points
Ten-Meter Platform: Patty Simms, unattached, Arcadia,
Calif., 266.25 points
■ **Team Champion:** Santa Clara (Calif.) Swim Club,
136 points

## NCAA SWIMMING AND DIVING CHAMPIONSHIPS: 1967

**MEN'S EVENTS**
(at East Lansing, Michigan)

■ **Freestyle**
50-Yard: Zack Zorn, UCLA, 0:21.12
100-Yard: Ken Walsh, Michigan State, 0:45.6 [2]
200-Yard: Greg Buckingham, Stanford, 1:41.3
500-Yard: Greg Buckingham, Stanford, 4:37.0 [1]
1,650-Yard: Mike Burton, UCLA, 16:17.5
400-Yard Relay: Stanford (L. Nicolao, B. Meyer,
M. Manning, J. Laney), 3:04.9 [1]
800-Yard Relay: Stanford (D. Roth, P. Siebert,
M. Wall, G. Buckingham), 6:54.5 [1]
■ **Breaststroke**
100-Yard: Ken Merten, Southern Methodist, 0:58.4 [1]
200-Yard: Ken Merten, Southern Methodist, 2:07.9 [1]
■ **Backstroke**
100-Yard: Charles Hickcox, Indiana University, 0:53.17
200-Yard: Charles Hickcox, Indiana University, 1:55.3

■ **Butterfly**
100-Yard: Ross Wales, Princeton, 0:50.2
200-Yard: Carl Robie, Michigan State, 1:52.59
■ **Medley**
200-Yard Individual: Dick Roth, Stanford,
1:56.0
400-Yard Individual: Dick Roth, Stanford,
4:12.0
400-Yard Relay: UCLA (M. Berger, R. Webb, S. Cole,
Z. Zorn), 3:29.5
■ **Diving**
One-Meter: Ken Sitzenberger, Indiana University,
510.25 points
Three-Meter: Ken Sitzenberger, Indiana University,
572.65 points
■ **Team Champion:** Stanford, 275 points

[1] Set a U.S. record.   [2] Tied a U.S. record.

# WORLD SWIMMING RECORDS

For years English, Australian, and Japanese swimmers dominated world swimming. In 1948 the Americans swept the Olympic swimming competition, and today the U.S. and Australia generally dominate. The International Amateur Swimming Federation approves world records.

The four strokes recognized are the freestyle, backstroke, butterfly, and breaststroke.

As a result of the 1967 swimming competitions, over 50 per cent of the women's swimming records were broken and more than 30 per cent of the men's records were toppled.

## Men's Events

| EVENT | TIME | SWIMMER | NATION | DATE | SITE |
|---|---|---|---|---|---|
| 100-Meter Freestyle | 0:52.6 | Ken Walsh | U.S.A. | 7-27-67 | Winnipeg |
| 110-Yard Freestyle | 0:53.5 | Bob McGregor | Britain | 9-10-66 | Blackpool, England |
| 200-Meter Freestyle | 1:55.7 | Don Schollander | U.S.A. | 8-12-67 | Oak Park, Ill. |
| 220-Yard Freestyle | 1:57.0 | Don Schollander | U.S.A. | 8-27-66 | Vancouver, B.C. |
| 400-Meter Freestyle | 4:08.2 | Greg Charlton | U.S.A. | 8-28-67 | Tokyo |
| 440-Yard Freestyle | 4:12.2 | Greg Charlton | U.S.A. | 8-26-66 | Vancouver, B.C. |
| 800-Meter Freestyle | 8:42.0 | Francis Luyce | France | 7-21-67 | Dinard, France |
| 880-Yard Freestyle | 8:55.5 | S. Murray Rose | Australia | 9-5-64 | Vancouver, B.C. |
| 1,500-Meter Freestyle | 16:34.1 | Mike Burton | U.S.A. | 8-13-67 | Oak Park, Ill. |
| 1,650-Yard Freestyle | 17:11.0 | John Konrads | Australia | 2-27-60 | Sydney |
| 100-Meter Breaststroke | 1:06.9 | Georgy Prokopenko | U.S.S.R. | 9-3-64 | Moscow |
| 110-Yard Breaststroke | 1:08.2 | Ian O'Brien | Australia | 8-12-66 | Jamaica |
| 200-Meter Breaststroke | 2:27.8 | Ian O'Brien | Australia | 10-15-64 | Tokyo |
| 220-Yard Breaststroke | 2:28.0 | Ian O'Brien | Australia | 8-6-66 | Jamaica |
| 100-Meter Butterfly | 0:56.3 | Mark Spitz | U.S.A. | 7-31-67 | Winnipeg |
|  | 0:56.3 | Doug Russels | U.S.A. | 8-29-67 | Tokyo |
| 110-Yard Butterfly | 0:58.1 | Dan Sherry | Canada | 8-12-65 | Blackpool, England |
| 200-Meter Butterfly | 2:06.0 | John Ferris | U.S.A. | 8-30-67 | Tokyo |
| 220-Yard Butterfly | 2:08.4 | Kevin Berry | Australia | 1-12-63 | Sydney |
| 100-Meter Backstroke | 0:59.1 | Charles Hickcox | U.S.A. | 8-31-64 | Tokyo |
| 110-Yard Backstroke | 1:01.5 | John Monckton | Australia | 2-15-58 | Melbourne |
| 200-Meter Backstroke | 2:09.4 | Charles Hickcox | U.S.A. | 8-29-67 | Tokyo |
| 220-Yard Backstroke | 2:12.0 | Peter Reynolds | Australia | 8-9-66 | Jamaica |
| 200-Meter Individual Medley | 2:11.3 | Greg Buckingham | U.S.A. | 8-13-67 | Oak Park, Ill. |
| 400-Meter Individual Medley | 4:45.4 | Dick Roth | U.S.A. | 10-14-64 | Tokyo |
| 440-Yard Individual Medley | 4:50.8 | Peter Reynolds | Australia | 8-8-66 | Jamaica |

## Women's Events

| EVENT | TIME | SWIMMER | NATION | DATE | SITE |
|---|---|---|---|---|---|
| 100-Meter Freestyle | 0:58.9 | Dawn Fraser | Australia | 2-29-64 | Sydney |
| 110-Yard Freestyle | 0:59.5 | Dawn Fraser | Australia | 11-24-62 | Perth |
| 200-Meter Freestyle | 2:09.7 | Pam Kruse | U.S.A. | 8-19-67 | Philadelphia |
| 220-Yard Freestyle | 2:11.6 | Dawn Fraser | Australia | 2-27-60 | Sydney |
| 400-Meter Freestyle | 4:29.0 | Debbie Meyer | U.S.A. | 8-18-67 | Philadelphia |
| 440-Yard Freestyle | 4:38.8 | Kathy Wainwright | Australia | 8-12-66 | Jamaica |
| 800-Meter Freestyle | 9:22.9 | Debbie Meyer | U.S.A. | 7-29-67 | Winnipeg |
| 880-Yard Freestyle | 9:50.3 | Kathy Wainwright | Australia | 11-19-66 | Victoria Park, Australia |
| 1,500-Meter Freestyle | 17:50.2 | Debbie Meyer | U.S.A. | 8-20-67 | Philadelphia |
| 1,650-Yard Freestyle | 18:51.1 | Pat Caretto | U.S.A. | 8-20-65 | Cardiff, Wales |
| 100-Meter Breaststroke | 1:14.6 | Catie Ball | U.S.A. | 8-19-67 | Philadelphia |
| 110-Yard Breaststroke | 1:18.3 | Sue Jones | U.S.A. | 8-25-66 | Vancouver, B.C. |
| 200-Meter Breaststroke | 2:39.5 | Catie Ball | U.S.A. | 8-20-67 | Philadelphia |
| 220-Yard Breaststroke | 2:47.7 | Galina Prozumenshikova | U.S.S.R. | 4-11-64 | Blackpool, England |
| 100-Meter Butterfly | 1:04.5 | Ada Kok | Netherlands | 8-14-65 | Budapest |
| 110-Yard Butterfly | 1:05.1 | Ada Kok | Netherlands | 5-30-64 | Blackpool, England |
| 200-Meter Butterfly | 2:21.0 | Ada Kok | Netherlands | 8-25-67 | Blackpool, England |
| 220-Yard Butterfly | 2:21.0 | Ada Kok | Netherlands | 8-25-67 | Blackpool, England |
| 100-Meter Backstroke | 1:07.1 | Elaine Tanner | Canada | 7-30-67 | Winnipeg |
| 110-Yard Backstroke | 1:07.5 | Karen Muir | South Africa | 7-22-67 | Coventry, England |
| 200-Meter Backstroke | 2:24.4 | Elaine Tanner | Canada | 7-26-67 | Winnipeg |
| 220-Yard Backstroke | 2:27.7 | Karen Muir | South Africa | 1-28-67 | Pretoria |
| 200-Meter Individual Medley | 2:25.0 | Claudia Kolb | U.S.A. | 8-18-67 | Philadelphia |
| 400-Meter Individual Medley | 5:08.2 | Claudia Kolb | U.S.A. | 8-19-67 | Philadelphia |
| 440-Yard Individual Medley | 5:25.1 | Mary E. Olcese | U.S.A. | 8-21-65 | Cardiff, Wales |

# TENNIS

A descendant of court (indoor) tennis, lawn tennis was first introduced in 1873 by Walter C. Wingfield at a lawn party in Wales. In the following year, several grass tennis courts were built in England and the game's popularity grew rapidly. Lawn tennis spread to all parts of the British Empire and before long took root in the United States where the United States Lawn Tennis Association (USLTA) was formed in 1881 to standardize the rules of play. The International Lawn Tennis Association regulates international competition.

The standard area of a court for singles (two players) measures 78 feet by 27 feet; for doubles (four players), the court measures 78 feet by 36 feet. The court is divided in half by a net three feet high.

Since 1945, Australia has dominated amateur lawn tennis, particularly in Davis Cup play. In 1962, Rod Laver of Australia completed the "grand slam" of tennis, winning the Wimbledon, U.S., French, and Australian singles titles. He was the first to win all major championships since an American, Don Budge, in 1938.

## U.S. OUTDOOR TENNIS CHAMPIONSHIP

Sponsored by the United States Lawn Tennis Association (USLTA), the first national men's lawn tennis tournament was held in 1881 and was open to "all comers." Today it is considered one of the four major tennis championships in the world, and players from all countries come to the United States to join in the competition.

The first national women's championship was held in the United States in 1887, and subsequently doubles championships for both men and women were added, as well as a mixed doubles championship. Play is held each year at the Forest Hills Stadium in New York City, the American counterpart to Wimbledon.

### ■ U.S. MEN'S SINGLES CHAMPIONS

| | | | | | |
|---|---|---|---|---|---|
| 1901–02 | William A. Larned (U.S.A.) | 1928 | Henri Cochet (France) | 1948 | Pancho Gonzales (U.S.A.) |
| 1903 | Hugh L. Doherty (England) | 1929 | Bill Tilden (U.S.A.) | 1949 | Pancho Gonzales (U.S.A.) |
| 1904 | Holcombe Ward (U.S.A.) | 1930 | John Doeg (U.S.A.) | 1950 | Art Larsen (U.S.A.) |
| 1905 | Beals C. Wright (U.S.A.) | 1931 | Ellsworth Vines (U.S.A.) | 1951 | Frank Sedgman (Australia) |
| 1906 | William J. Clothier (U.S.A.) | 1932 | Ellsworth Vines (U.S.A.) | 1952 | Frank Sedgman (Australia) |
| 1907–11 | William A. Larned (U.S.A.) | 1933 | Fred Perry (England) | 1953 | Tony Trabert (U.S.A.) |
| 1912–13 | Maurice E. McLoughlin (U.S.A.) | 1934 | Fred Perry (England) | 1954 | Vic Seixas (U.S.A.) |
| 1914 | R. Norris Williams II (U.S.A.) | 1935 | Wilmer Allison (U.S.A.) | 1955 | Tony Trabert (U.S.A.) |
| 1915 | William M. Johnston (U.S.A.) | 1936 | Fred Perry (England) | 1956 | Ken Rosewall (Australia) |
| 1916 | R. Norris Williams II (U.S.A.) | 1937 | Don Budge (U.S.A.) | 1957 | Mal Anderson (Australia) |
| 1917–18 | R. Lindley Murray (U.S.A.) | 1938 | Don Budge (U.S.A.) | 1958 | Ashley Cooper (Australia) |
| 1919 | William M. Johnston (U.S.A.) | 1939 | Bobby Riggs (U.S.A.) | 1959 | Neale Fraser (Australia) |
| 1920 | Bill Tilden (U.S.A.) | 1940 | Don McNeill (U.S.A.) | 1960 | Neale Fraser (Australia) |
| 1921 | Bill Tilden (U.S.A.) | 1941 | Bobby Riggs (U.S.A.) | 1961 | Roy Emerson (Australia) |
| 1922 | Bill Tilden (U.S.A.) | 1942 | Ted Schroeder (U.S.A.) | 1962 | Rod Laver (Australia) |
| 1923 | Bill Tilden (U.S.A.) | 1943 | Joe Hunt (U.S.A.) | 1963 | Rafael Osuna (Mexico) |
| 1924 | Bill Tilden (U.S.A.) | 1944 | Frank Parker (U.S.A.) | 1964 | Roy Emerson (Australia) |
| 1925 | Bill Tilden (U.S.A.) | 1945 | Frank Parker (U.S.A.) | 1965 | Manuel Santana (Spain) |
| 1926 | Rene Lacoste (France) | 1946 | Jack Kramer (U.S.A.) | 1966 | Fred Stolle (Australia) |
| 1927 | Rene Lacoste (France) | 1947 | Jack Kramer (U.S.A.) | 1967 | John Newcombe (Australia) |

### ■ U.S. WOMEN'S SINGLES CHAMPIONS

| | | | | | |
|---|---|---|---|---|---|
| 1903 | Elisabeth H. Moore (U.S.A.) | 1927 | Helen Wills (U.S.A.) | 1948 | Margaret Osborne du Pont (U.S.A.) |
| 1904 | May G. Sutton (U.S.A.) | 1928 | Helen Wills (U.S.A.) | 1949 | Margaret Osborne du Pont (U.S.A.) |
| 1905 | Elisabeth H. Moore (U.S.A.) | 1929 | Helen Wills (U.S.A.) | 1950 | Margaret Osborne du Pont (U.S.A.) |
| 1906 | Helen Homans (U.S.A.) | 1930 | Betty Nuthall (England) | 1951 | Maureen Connolly (U.S.A.) |
| 1907 | Evelyn Sears (U.S.A.) | 1931 | Helen Wills Moody (U.S.A.) | 1952 | Maureen Connolly (U.S.A.) |
| 1908 | Mrs. Maud Bargar-Wallach (U.S.A.) | 1932 | Helen Hull Jacobs (U.S.A.) | 1953 | Maureen Connolly (U.S.A.) |
| | | 1933 | Helen Hull Jacobs (U.S.A.) | 1954 | Doris Hart (U.S.A.) |
| 1909 | Hazel V. Hotchkiss (U.S.A.) | 1934 | Helen Hull Jacobs (U.S.A.) | 1955 | Doris Hart (U.S.A.) |
| 1910 | Hazel V. Hotchkiss (U.S.A.) | 1935 | Helen Hull Jacobs (U.S.A.) | 1956 | Shirley Fry (U.S.A.) |
| 1911 | Hazel V. Hotchkiss (U.S.A.) | 1936 | Alice Marble (U.S.A.) | 1957 | Althea Gibson (U.S.A.) |
| 1912 | Mary K. Browne | 1937 | Anita Lizana (Chile) | 1958 | Althea Gibson (U.S.A.) |
| 1913 | Mary K. Browne | 1938 | Alice Marble (U.S.A.) | 1959 | Maria Bueno (Brazil) |
| 1914 | Mary K. Browne | 1939 | Alice Marble (U.S.A.) | 1960 | Darlene Hard (U.S.A.) |
| 1919 | Mrs. Hazel Hotchkiss Wightman | 1940 | Alice Marble (U.S.A.) | 1961 | Darlene Hard (U.S.A.) |
| 1920 | Molla Bjurstedt Mallory (U.S.A.) | 1941 | Sarah Palfrey Cooke (U.S.A.) | 1962 | Margaret Smith (Australia) |
| 1921 | Molla Bjurstedt Mallory (U.S.A.) | 1942 | Pauline Betz (U.S.A.) | 1963 | Maria Bueno (Brazil) |
| 1922 | Molla Bjurstedt Mallory (U.S.A.) | 1943 | Pauline Betz (U.S.A.) | 1964 | Maria Bueno (Brazil) |
| 1923 | Helen Wills (U.S.A.) | 1944 | Pauline Betz (U.S.A.) | 1965 | Margaret Smith (Australia) |
| 1924 | Helen Wills (U.S.A.) | 1945 | Sarah Palfrey Cooke (U.S.A.) | 1966 | Maria Bueno (Brazil) |
| 1925 | Helen Wills (U.S.A.) | 1946 | Pauline Betz (U.S.A.) | 1967 | Billie Jean King (U.S.A.) |
| 1926 | Molla Bjurstedt Mallory (U.S.A.) | 1947 | Louise Brough (U.S.A.) | | |

## THE DAVIS CUP

The most highly prized trophy of international men's team tennis, the Davis Cup, was put up in 1900 by Dwight F. Davis, an outstanding sportsman and U.S. public official.

In the early years of play, the United States, England, and Australasia (Australia and New Zealand) held a monopoly on the trophy.

By 1927, however, France, and then other nations, developed high-caliber teams. Recently Australia has dominated the matches. The annual Davis Cup Challenge Round is played in the country of the defending champion.

### DAVIS CUP CHALLENGE ROUND

| YEAR | WINNER | LOSER | SCORE | YEAR | WINNER | LOSER | SCORE |
|------|--------|-------|-------|------|--------|-------|-------|
| 1900 | U.S.A. | England | 5-0 | 1933 | England | France | 3-2 |
| 1901 | Not held | — | | 1934 | England | U.S.A. | 4-1 |
| 1902 | U.S.A. | England | 3-2 | 1935 | England | U.S.A. | 5-0 |
| 1903 | England | U.S.A. | 4-1 | 1936 | England | Australia | 3-2 |
| 1904 | England | Belgium | 5-0 | 1937 | U.S.A. | England | 4-1 |
| 1905 | England | U.S.A. | 5-0 | 1938 | U.S.A. | Australia | 3-2 |
| 1906 | England | U.S.A. | 5-0 | 1939 | Australia | U.S.A. | 3-2 |
| 1907 | Australia | England | 3-2 | 1940-45 | Not held | — | — |
| 1908 | Australia | U.S.A. | 3-2 | 1946 | U.S.A. | Australia | 5-0 |
| 1909 | Australasia | U.S.A. | 5-0 | 1947 | U.S.A. | Australia | 4-1 |
| 1910 | Not held | — | | 1948 | U.S.A. | Australia | 5-0 |
| 1911 | Australasia | U.S.A. | 5-0 | 1949 | U.S.A. | Australia | 4-1 |
| 1912 | England | Australasia | 3-2 | 1950 | Australia | U.S.A. | 4-1 |
| 1913 | U.S.A. | England | 3-2 | 1951 | Australia | U.S.A. | 3-2 |
| 1914 | Australasia | U.S.A. | 3-2 | 1952 | Australia | U.S.A. | 4-1 |
| 1915-18 | Not held | — | | 1953 | Australia | U.S.A. | 3-2 |
| 1919 | Australasia | England | 4-1 | 1954 | U.S.A. | Australia | 3-2 |
| 1920 | U.S.A. | Australasia | 5-0 | 1955 | Australia | U.S.A. | 5-0 |
| 1921 | U.S.A. | Japan | 5-0 | 1956 | Australia | U.S.A. | 5-0 |
| 1922 | U.S.A. | Australasia | 4-1 | 1957 | Australia | U.S.A. | 3-2 |
| 1923 | U.S.A. | Australasia | 4-1 | 1958 | U.S.A. | Australia | 3-2 |
| 1924 | U.S.A. | Australasia | 5-0 | 1959 | Australia | U.S.A. | 3-2 |
| 1925 | U.S.A. | France | 5-0 | 1960 | Australia | Italy | 4-1 |
| 1926 | U.S.A. | France | 4-1 | 1961 | Australia | Italy | 5-0 |
| 1927 | France | U.S.A. | 3-2 | 1962 | Australia | Mexico | 5-0 |
| 1928 | France | U.S.A. | 4-1 | 1963 | U.S.A. | Australia | 3-2 |
| 1929 | France | U.S.A. | 3-2 | 1964 | Australia | U.S.A. | 3-2 |
| 1930 | France | U.S.A. | 4-1 | 1965 | Australia | Spain | 4-1 |
| 1931 | France | England | 3-2 | 1966 | Australia | India | 4-1 |
| 1932 | France | U.S.A. | 3-2 | | | | |

## THE WIGHTMAN CUP

Donated in 1923 by Mrs. Hazel Wightman, an American tennis champion and socialite, the Wightman Cup is the premier prize in women's international competition. Teams from the U.S. and England compete for the trophy; the site alternates between the two countries.

| YEAR | WINNER | SCORE | YEAR | WINNER | SCORE | YEAR | WINNER | SCORE |
|------|--------|-------|------|--------|-------|------|--------|-------|
| 1923 | United States | 7-0 | 1937 | United States | 6-1 | 1956 | United States | 5-2 |
| 1924 | England | 6-1 | 1938 | United States | 5-2 | 1957 | United States | 6-1 |
| 1925 | England | 4-3 | 1939 | United States | 5-2 | 1958 | England | 4-3 |
| 1926 | United States | 4-3 | 1940-45 | Not held | — | 1959 | United States | 4-3 |
| 1927 | United States | 5-2 | 1946 | United States | 7-0 | 1960 | England | 4-3 |
| 1928 | England | 4-3 | 1947 | United States | 7-0 | 1961 | United States | 6-1 |
| 1929 | United States | 4-3 | 1948 | United States | 6-1 | 1962 | United States | 4-3 |
| 1930 | England | 4-3 | 1949 | United States | 7-0 | 1963 | United States | 6-1 |
| 1931 | United States | 5-2 | 1950 | United States | 7-0 | 1964 | United States | 5-2 |
| 1932 | United States | 4-3 | 1951 | United States | 6-1 | 1965 | United States | 5-2 |
| 1933 | United States | 4-3 | 1952 | United States | 7-0 | 1966 | United States | 4-3 |
| 1934 | United States | 5-2 | 1953 | United States | 7-0 | 1967 | United States | 6-1 |
| 1935 | United States | 4-3 | 1954 | United States | 6-0 * | | | |
| 1936 | United States | 4-3 | 1955 | United States | 6-1 | | | |

* One doubles match was not played because of rain.

## WIMBLEDON CHAMPIONS

The scene of one of the four major championship tournaments in the world, Wimbledon is the headquarters of tennis in England and one of the great shrines of international tennis. Here, each year, the great names of amateur tennis gather to compete for what is regarded as the world championship of tennis. The first men's singles championship was held at Wimbledon in 1877. Seven years later the women's singles championship was inaugurated. The first men's double matches of the tournament were played in 1879, and women's doubles were arranged in 1913. No matches were played during the war years, 1940–45.

## ■ WIMBLEDON MEN'S SINGLES CHAMPIONS

| | | | |
|---|---|---|---|
| 1938 | Don Budge (U.S.A.) | 1952 | Frank Sedgman (Australia) |
| 1939 | Bobby Riggs (U.S.A.) | 1953 | Vic Seixas (U.S.A.) |
| 1946 | Yvon Petra (France) | 1954 | Jaroslav Drobny (Egypt) |
| 1947 | Jack Kramer (U.S.A.) | 1955 | Tony Trabert (U.S.A.) |
| 1948 | Bob Falkenburg (U.S.A.) | 1956 | Lew Hoad (Australia) |
| 1949 | Ted Schroeder (U.S.A.) | 1957 | Lew Hoad (Australia) |
| 1950 | Budge Patty (U.S.A.) | 1958 | Ashley Cooper (Australia) |
| 1951 | Dick Savitt (U.S.A.) | 1959 | Alex Olmedo (U.S.A.) |

| 1960 | Neale Fraser (Australia) |
|---|---|
| 1961 | Rod Laver (Australia) |
| 1962 | Rod Laver (Australia) |
| 1963 | Chuck McKinley (U.S.A.) |
| 1964 | Roy Emerson (Australia) |
| 1965 | Roy Emerson (Australia) |
| 1966 | Manuelo Santana (Spain) |
| 1967 | John Newcombe (Australia) |

## ■ WIMBLEDON WOMEN'S SINGLES CHAMPIONS

| | | | |
|---|---|---|---|
| 1938 | Helen Wills Moody (U.S.A.) | 1952 | Maureen Connolly (U.S.A.) |
| 1939 | Alice Marble (U.S.A.) | 1953 | Maureen Connolly (U.S.A.) |
| 1946 | Pauline Betz (U.S.A.) | 1954 | Maureen Connolly (U.S.A.) |
| 1947 | Margaret Osborne (U.S.A.) | 1955 | Louise Brough (U.S.A.) |
| 1948 | Louise Brough (U.S.A.) | 1956 | Shirley Fry (U.S.A.) |
| 1949 | Louise Brough (U.S.A.) | 1957 | Althea Gibson (U.S.A.) |
| 1950 | Louise Brough (U.S.A.) | 1958 | Althea Gibson (U.S.A.) |
| 1951 | Doris Hart (U.S.A.) | 1959 | Maria Bueno (Brazil) |

| 1960 | Maria Bueno (Brazil) |
|---|---|
| 1961 | Angela Mortimer (England) |
| 1962 | Karen Hantze Susman (U.S.A.) |
| 1963 | Margaret Smith (Australia) |
| 1964 | Maria Bueno (Brazil) |
| 1965 | Margaret Smith (Australia) |
| 1966 | Billie Jean King (U.S.A.) |
| 1967 | Billie Jean King (U.S.A.) |

## ■ WIMBLEDON MEN'S DOUBLES CHAMPIONS

| | |
|---|---|
| 1938 | Don Budge and Gene Mako (U.S.A.) |
| 1939 | Bobby Riggs and Elwood Cooke (U.S.A.) |
| 1946 | Jack Kramer and Tom Browne (U.S.A.) |
| 1947 | Jack Kramer and Bob Falkenburg (U.S.A.) |
| 1948 | John Bromwich and Frank Sedgman (Australia) |
| 1949 | Frank Parker and Pancho Gonzales (U.S.A.) |
| 1950 | John Bromwich and Adrian Quist (Australia) |
| 1951 | Frank Sedgman and Ken McGregor (Australia) |
| 1952 | Frank Sedgman and Ken McGregor (Australia) |
| 1953 | Ken Rosewall and Lew Hoad (Australia) |
| 1954 | Rex Hartwig and Mervyn Rose (Australia) |
| 1955 | Rex Hartwig and Mervyn Rose (Australia) |

| | |
|---|---|
| 1956 | Lew Hoad and Ken Rosewall (Australia) |
| 1957 | Gardnar Mulloy and Budge Patty (U.S.A.) |
| 1958 | Sven Davidson and Ulf Schmidt (Sweden) |
| 1959 | Neale Fraser and Roy Emerson (Australia) |
| 1960 | Rafael Osuna (Mexico) and Dennis Ralston (U.S.A.) |
| 1961 | Neale Fraser and Roy Emerson (Australia) |
| 1962 | Fred Stolle and Bob Hewitt (Australia) |
| 1963 | Rafael Osuna and Antonio Palafox (Mexico) |
| 1964 | Fred Stolle and Bob Hewitt (Australia) |
| 1965 | John Newcombe and Tony Roche (Australia) |
| 1966 | Ken Fletcher and John Newcombe (Australia) |
| 1967 | Bob Hewitt and Frew McMillan (South Africa) |

## ■ WIMBLEDON WOMEN'S DOUBLES CHAMPIONS

| | |
|---|---|
| 1938 | Alice Marble and Sarah Palfrey Fabyan (U.S.A.) |
| 1939 | Alice Marble and Sarah Palfrey Fabyan (U.S.A.) |
| 1946 | A. Louise Brough and Margaret Osborne (U.S.A.) |
| 1947 | Doris Hart and Patricia Canning Todd (U.S.A.) |
| 1948 | A. Louise Brough and Margaret Osborne du Pont (U.S.A.) |
| 1949 | A. Louise Brough and Margaret Osborne du Pont (U.S.A.) |
| 1950 | A. Louise Brough and Margaret Osborne du Pont (U.S.A.) |
| 1951 | Doris Hart and Shirley Fry (U.S.A.) |
| 1952 | Doris Hart and Shirley Fry (U.S.A.) |
| 1953 | Doris Hart and Shirley Fry (U.S.A.) |
| 1954 | A. Louise Brough and Margaret Osborne du Pont (U.S.A.) |

| | |
|---|---|
| 1955 | Angela Mortimer and Ann Shilcock (England) |
| 1956 | Angela Buxton (England) and Althea Gibson (U.S.A.) |
| 1957 | Althea Gibson and Darlene Hard (U.S.A.) |
| 1958 | Althea Gibson (U.S.A.) and Maria Bueno (Brazil) |
| 1959 | Jeanne Arth and Darlene Hard (U.S.A.) |
| 1960 | Maria Bueno (Brazil) and Darlene Hard (U.S.A.) |
| 1961 | Karen Hantze and Billie Jean Moffitt (U.S.A.) |
| 1962 | Karen Hantze Susman and Billie Jean Moffitt (U.S.A.) |
| 1963 | Darlene Hard (U.S.A.) and Maria Bueno (Brazil) |
| 1964 | Margaret Smith and Lesley Turner (Australia) |
| 1965 | Billie Jean Moffitt (U.S.A.) and Maria Bueno (Brazil) |
| 1966 | Maria Bueno (Brazil) and Nancy Richey (U.S.A.) |
| 1967 | Billie Jean King and Rosemary Casals (U.S.A.) |

## ■ WIMBLEDON MIXED DOUBLES CHAMPIONS

| | |
|---|---|
| 1938 | Alice Marble and J. Donald Budge (U.S.A.) |
| 1939 | Alice Marble and Robert L. Riggs (U.S.A.) |
| 1946 | A. Louise Brough and Thomas P. Brown, Jr. (U.S.A.) |
| 1947 | A. Louise Brough and John E. Bromwich (U.S.A.) |
| 1948 | A. Louise Brough and John E. Bromwich (U.S.A.) |
| 1949 | Mrs. Sheila Summers (U.S.A.) and Eric Sturgess (South Africa) |
| 1950 | A. Louise Brough (U.S.A.) and Eric Sturgess (South Africa) |
| 1951 | Doris Hart (U.S.A.) and Frank A. Sedgman (Australia) |
| 1952 | Doris Hart (U.S.A.) and Frank A. Sedgman (Australia) |
| 1953 | Doris Hart and E. Victor Seixas, Jr. (U.S.A.) |
| 1954 | Doris Hart and E. Victor Seixas, Jr. (U.S.A.) |
| 1955 | Doris Hart and E. Victor Seixas, Jr. (U.S.A.) |

| | |
|---|---|
| 1956 | Shirley J. Fry and E. Victor Seixas, Jr. (U.S.A.) |
| 1957 | Darlene Hard (U.S.A.) and Mervyn Rose (Australia) |
| 1958 | Lorraine Coughlan and Robert Howe (Australia) |
| 1959 | Darlene Hard (U.S.A.) and Rodney Laver (Australia) |
| 1960 | Darlene Hard (U.S.A.) and Rodney Laver (Australia) |
| 1961 | Lesley Turner and Fred Stolle (Australia) |
| 1962 | Margaret Osborne du Pont (U.S.A.) and Neale Fraser (Australia) |
| 1963 | Margaret Smith and Ken Fletcher (Australia) |
| 1964 | Lesley Turner and Fred Stolle (Australia) |
| 1965 | Margaret Smith and Ken Fletcher (Australia) |
| 1966 | Margaret Smith and Ken Fletcher (Australia) |
| 1967 | Billie Jean King (U.S.A.) and Owen Davidson (Australia) |

# TRACK AND FIELD

The Intercollegiate Association of Amateur Athletes of America (the pioneer national athletic group) in 1876 held the first U.S. collegiate track and field meet; 12 years later the Amateur Athletic Union of the U.S.A. held its first contests. These two groups and the National Collegiate Athletic Association regulate U.S. track and field events.

## AAU INDOOR CHAMPIONSHIPS: 1967
(at Oakland, Calif., March 3–4)

### Men's Running Events
60-Yard Dash: Bill Gaines, Mullica Hill, N.J., 0:06.0
60-Yard High Hurdles: Willie Davenport, unattached, 0:07.0
600-Yard Run: Jim Kemp, Long Beach 49ers Track Club, 1:10.6
1,000-Yard Run: Preston Davis, Long Beach 49ers Track Club, 2:09.4
One-Mile Run: Sam Bair, Kent State, 4:03.2
Three-Mile Run: Tracy Smith, unattached, 13:16.2
One-Mile Relay: San Jose State College (K. Schackelford, J. Bambury, L. Evans, T. Smith), 3:14.9
Two-Mile Relay: Long Beach 49ers T.C., 7:36.9
Sprint Medley Relay: S.C. Striders (R. Hodge, B. Frey, B. Toomey, L. Dunn), 1:51.6

### Men's Field Events
High Jump: John Rambo, Long Beach 49ers Track Club, 7' 1''
Long Jump: Bob Beamon, Texas Western Track Club, 26' 11½'' [1,2]
Triple Jump: Art Walker, S.C. Striders, 52' 10¼''
Pole Vault: Bob Seagren, S.C. Striders, 17' ¾'' [1]
35-Pound Weight Throw: Ed Burke, S.C. Striders, 69' 2''
Shot Put: George Wood, So. Ill., 63' 11''
Team: Southern California Striders, 34 points

### Women's Running Events
60-Yard Dash: Wyomia Tyus, Tenn. State, 0:06.7
220-Yard Dash: Una Morris, Tenn. State, 0:25.0
440-Yard Dash: Kathy Hammond, Wills Spikettes, 0:55.2
880-Yard Run: Madeline Manning, Tenn. State, 2:08.4 [3]
Mile Run: Doris Brown, Seattle Falcons, 4:43.3
Sprint Medley: Tenn. State (M. Manning, M. Render, M. Daniel, W. Tyus), 1:46.6 [1]
4 x 160 Relay: Detroit T.C. (C. Coleman, D. Barbridge, L. White, K. Dennis), 1:12.4
60-Yard Hurdles: Pat Van Wolvelaere, Angels Track Club, 0:07.7

### Women's Field Events
Shot Put: Lynn Graham, L.A. Mercurettes, 46' 4¾''
Basketball Throw: Barbara Friedrich, Shore Athletic Club, 131' 1½''
Long Jump: Martha Watson, Tenn. State, 20' 6½''
High Jump: Eleanor Montgomery, Tenn. State, 5' 9''
Team: Tennessee State, 33 points

## AAU OUTDOOR CHAMPIONSHIPS: 1967
at Bakersfield, Calif., June 22–23)

### Running Events
100-Yard Dash: James Hines, Texas So., 0:09.3
220-Yard Dash: Tommie Smith, Santa Clara Youth Village, 0:20.4
440-Yard Dash: Lee Evans, Santa Clara Youth Village, 0:45.3 [1]
880-Yard Run: Wade Bell, Oregon U., 1:46.1 [1]
(continued)

One-Mile Run: Jim Ryun, Jayhawk Track Club, 3:51.1 [4]
Three-Mile Run: Gerry Lindgren, Washington State, 13:10.6
Six-Mile Run: Van Nelson, St. Cloud State College, 28:18.8
Two-Mile Walk: Ron Laird, New York Athletic Club, 13:41.4 [1]
120-Yard High Hurdles: Willie Davenport, Southern University, 0:13.3 [5]
440-Yard Intermediate Hurdles: Ron Whitney, So. Calif. Striders, 0:50.3
3,000-Meter Steeplechase: Pat Traynor, U.S. Air Force, 8:42.0

### Field Events
Long Jump: Jerry Proctor, Pasadena Athletic Association, 26' ¾''
Triple Jump: Charles Craig, Long Beach 49ers Track Club, 53' 1½''
Pole Vault: Paul Wilson, Southern California Striders, 17' 8'' [4]
Shot Put: Randy Matson, Texas A&M, 66' 11'' [1]
High Jump: Otis Burrell, unattached, 7' ¼''
Discus Throw: Gary Carlsen, unatt., 205' 10'' [1]
Javelin: Delmon McNabb, Louisiana State University, 268' 3''
Hammer Throw: Ed Burke, Southern California Striders, 235' 11'' [2]
Team: Southern California Striders, 64 points

## AAU SR. WOMEN'S OUTDOOR CHAMPIONSHIPS
(at Santa Barbara, Calif., July 1–2)

### Running Events
100 Meters: Barbara Ferrell, Los Angeles Mercurettes, 0:11.1 [3]
200 Meters: Diana Wilson, Tennessee State, 0:23.6
400 Meters: Charlotte Cook, unattached, Washington, D.C., 0:52.5 [1,2]
800 Meters: Madeline Manning, Tennessee State, 2:03.6 [1,2]
1,500 Meters: Natalia Rocha, Wills Spikettes, 4:29.0
200-Meter Hurdles: Pat Van Wolvelaere, Angels Track Club, 0:27.8
80-Meter Hurdles: Mamie Rallins, Mayor Daley Youth Foundation, 0:10.9
400-Meter Relay: Texas Southern, 0:46.3
800-Meter Medley Relay: Tennessee State, 1:41.7 [1,2]

### Field Events
Javelin: RaNae Bair, San Diego Mission Belles, 196' 3'' [1]
Shot Put: Maren Seidler, Shore Athletic Club, 46' 10''
Long Jump: Pat Winslow, Millbrae Lions, 20' 8¼''
Discus Throw: Carol Moseke, Nebraska Track Club, 152' 5''
High Jump: Eleanor Montgomery, Tennessee State, 5' 6¼''

---

[1] AAU record.    [2] U.S. record.    [3] Equaled world record.    [4] World record.    [5] Equaled AAU record.

## NCAA INDOOR CHAMPIONSHIPS: 1967
(at Detroit, Michigan, March 10–11)

### Running Events
60-Yard Dash: Charles Greene, University
of Nebraska, 0:06.0 [1]
60-Yard High Hurdles: Earl McCullouch,
Southern California, 0:07.0 [2]
440-Yard Run: Bill Calhoun, Oklahoma,
0:48.9
600-Yard Run: Steve Carson, Iowa State,
1:10.2
880-Yard Run: Dave Patrick, Villanova, 1:48.9 [2]
1,000-Yard Run: Ray Arrington, Wisconsin,
2:07.8 [2]
Mile Run: Jim Ryun, Kansas, 3:58.6 [2]
Invitational Mile: Art Dulong, Holy Cross, 4:04.8
(continued)

Two-Mile Run: Gerry Lindgren, Washington State, 8:34.7 [2]
Mile Relay: Oklahoma (J. Shields, J. Hardwick,
T. Melton, B. Calhoun), 3:15.6 [2]
Two-Mile Relay: So. Cal. (R. Joyce, D. Buck,
D. Carr, C. Trentadue), 7:30.1
Distance Medley Relay: Kansas St. (C. Harper,
J. Holbrook, W. Dutton, C. Nightingale), 9:44.6

### Field Events
High Jump: Ted Downing, Miami (Ohio), 7' [1]
Pole Vault: Bob Seagren, So. Cal., 17' ¼'' [2]
Long Jump: Aaron Hopkins, Toledo, 24' 7¾''
Shot Put: Ken Patera, Brigham Young U., 59' 6''
35-Pound Weight Throw: Gower Yuen, Connecticut, 61' 9¾'' [2]
Team: University of Southern California, 26 points

[1] Equaled indoor record.   [2] NCAA indoor record.

## NCAA OUTDOOR CHAMPIONSHIPS: 1967
(at Provo, Utah, June 15–17)

### Running Events
100-Yard Dash: Charles Greene, University
of Nebraska, 0:09.2
220-Yard Dash: Tommie Smith, San Jose
State, 0:20.2 [1]
440-Yard Run: Emmet Taylor, Ohio U., 0:45.9
880-Yard Run: Wade Bell, Oregon, 1:47.6
One-Mile Run: Jim Ryun, University of
Kansas, 4:03.5
Three-Mile Run: Gerry Lindgren, Washington
State, 13:47.8
Six-Mile Run: Gerry Lindgren, Washington
State, 28:44.0
3,000-Meter Steeplechase: Chris McCubbins,
Oklahoma State, 8:51.4
120-Yard High Hurdles: Earl McCullouch,
Southern California, 0:13.4 [1]
440-Yard Hurdles: Bob Steele,
Michigan State, 0:50.2
(continued)

440-Yard Relay: Southern California
(E. McCullouch, F. Kuller, O. Simpson,
L. Miller), 0:38.6 [2]
One-Mile Relay: Iowa (F. Ferree, C. Frazier,
J. Reimer, M. Mondane), 3:06.8 [3]

### Field Events
High Jump: Steve Brown, Idaho, 7' 1''
Pole Vault: Bob Seagren, So. Cal., 17' 4'' [4]
Long Jump: Gary Ard, Kansas, 25' 9''
Triple Jump: Art Baxter, New Mexico, 52' 4½'' [3]
Shot Put: Randy Matson, Texas A&M,
67' 9¼'' [3]
Discus Throw: Randy Matson, Texas A&M,
190' 4''
Javelin Throw: Delmon McNabb, Louisiana
State University, 263' 5''
Hammer Throw: Bob Narcessian, Rhode
Island, 197' ½''
Team: University of Southern California, 86 points

[1] Equaled meet record.   [2] World record.   [3] Meet record.   [4] Collegiate record.

## HISTORY OF THE MILE RECORD

The mile run, one of the most exciting and best-known events in track and field, has historical precedence in the early Grecian Olympic games. The first record-holder in modern times was Charles Lawes of Britain, clocked at 4:56.0 in 1864. The mythical four-minute barrier was cracked by Britain's Roger Bannister in 1954; since then the mark has dropped to the new 1967 low of 3:51.1 set by the University of Kansas's record-breaking Jim Ryun.

| TIME | RUNNER AND COUNTRY | YEAR | TIME | RUNNER AND COUNTRY | YEAR |
|---|---|---|---|---|---|
| 4:56 | Charles Lawes, Britain | 1864 | 4:06.8 | Glenn Cunningham, U.S. | 1934 |
| 4:36.5 | Richard Webster, Britain | 1865 | 4:06.4 | Sydney Wooderson, Britain | 1937 |
| 4:29 | William Chinnery, Britain | 1868 | 4:06.2 | Gunder Haegg, Sweden | 1942 |
| 4:28.8 | W. C. Gibbs, Britain | 1868 | 4:06.2 | Arne Andersson, Sweden | 1942 |
| 4:26 | Walter Slade, Britain | 1874 | 4:04.6 | Gunder Haegg, Sweden | 1942 |
| 4:24.5 | Walter Slade, Britain | 1875 | 4:02.6 | Arne Andersson, Sweden | 1943 |
| 4:23.2 | Walter George, Britain | 1880 | 4:01.6 | Arne Andersson, Sweden | 1944 |
| 4:21.4 | Walter George, Britain | 1882 | 4:01.4 | Gunder Haegg, Sweden | 1945 |
| 4:18.4 | Walter George, Britain | 1884 | 3:59.4 | Roger Bannister, Britain | 1954 |
| 4:18.2 | Fred Bacon, Scotland | 1894 | 3:58 | John Landy, Australia | 1954 |
| 4:17 | Fred Bacon, Scotland | 1895 | 3:57.2 | Derek Ibbotson, Britain | 1957 |
| 4:15.6 | Thomas Connett, U.S. | 1911 | 3:54.5 | Herb Elliott, Australia | 1958 |
| 4:15.4 | John Paul Jones, U.S. | 1911 | 3:54.4 | Peter Snell, New Zealand | 1962 |
| 4:14.6 | John Paul Jones, U.S. | 1913 | 3:54.1 | Peter Snell, New Zealand | 1964 |
| 4:12.6 | Norman Taber, U.S. | 1915 | 3:53.6 | Michel Jazy, France | 1965 |
| 4:10.4 | Paavo Nurmi, Finland | 1923 | 3:51:3 | Jim Ryun, U.S. | 1966 |
| 4:09.2 | Jules Ladoumegue, France | 1931 | 3:51.1 | Jim Ryun, U.S. | 1967 |
| 4:07.6 | Jack Lovelock, New Zealand | 1933 | | | |

## WORLD TRACK AND FIELD RECORDS

The International Amateur Athletic Federation approves world amateur track and field records.

| EVENT | TIME OR DISTANCE | RUNNER | NATION | DATE | SITE |
|---|---|---|---|---|---|
| **Running** | | | | | |
| 100 Yards......... | 0:09.1 | R. Hayes........ | U.S.A........... | 6-21-63 | St. Louis, Missouri |
| | | H. W. Jerome.... | Canada......... | 7-15-66 | Edmonton, Alberta, Canada |
| 220 Yards......... | 0:19.5 | T. Smith........ | U.S.A.......... | 5-7-66 | San Jose, California |
| 220 Yards (Bend)... | 0:20.0 | T. Smith........ | U.S.A.......... | 6-11-66 | Sacramento, California |
| 440 Yards......... | 0:44.9 | A. Plummer..... | U.S.A.......... | 5-25-63 | Tempe, Arizona |
| 880 Yards......... | 1:45.1 | P. Snell........ | New Zealand... | 2-3-62 | Christchurch, New Zealand |
| 1 Mile............. | 3:51.1 | J. Ryun......... | U.S.A.......... | 6-23-67 | Bakersfield, California |
| 2 Miles........... | 8:22.6 | M. Jazy........ | France......... | 6-23-65 | Melun, France |
| 3 Miles........... | 12:50.4 | R. Clarke....... | Australia....... | 7-5-66 | Stockholm, Sweden |
| 6 Miles........... | 26:47.0 | R. Clarke....... | Australia....... | 7-14-65 | Oslo, Norway |
| 10 Miles.......... | 47:12.8 | R. Clarke....... | Australia....... | 3-3-65 | Victoria, Australia |
| 15 Miles.......... | 1 hr. 12:48.2 | R. Hill......... | Britain......... | 7-21-65 | Bolton, Lancs., England |
| 1 Hour............ | 12 mi., 1,478 yd. | G. Roelants..... | Belgium........ | 10-28-66 | Leuven, Belgium |
| 100 Meters....... | 0:10.0 | A. Hary........ | Germany....... | 6-21-60 | Zurich, Switzerland |
| | 0:10.0 | H. Jerome....... | Canada........ | 7-15-60 | Saskatoon, Saskatchewan, Canada |
| | 0:10.0 | H. Esteves....... | Venezuela...... | 8-15-64 | Caracas, Venezuela |
| | 0:10.0 | R. Hayes....... | U.S.A......... | 10-15-64 | Tokyo, Japan |
| 200 Meters........ | 0:19.5 | T. Smith........ | U.S.A......... | 5-7-66 | San Jose, California |
| 200 Meters (Bend).. | 0:20.0 | T. Smith........ | U.S.A......... | 6-11-66 | Sacramento, California |
| 400 Meters........ | 0:44.9 | O. Davis....... | U.S.A......... | 9-6-60 | Rome, Italy |
| | 0:44.9 | C. Kaufmann.... | Germany....... | 9-6-60 | Rome, Italy |
| | 0:44.9 | A. Plummer..... | U.S.A......... | 5-25-63 | Tempe, Arizona |
| | 0:44.9 | M. Larrabee..... | U.S.A......... | 9-12-64 | Los Angeles, California |
| 800 Meters........ | 1:44.3 | P. Snell........ | New Zealand.... | 2-3-62 | Christchurch, New Zealand |
| 1,000 Meters...... | 2:16.2 | J. May......... | East Germany... | 7-20-65 | Erfurt, East Germany |
| 1,500 Meters...... | 3:35.6 | H. Elliott...... | Australia....... | 9-6-60 | Rome, Italy |
| 2,000 Meters...... | 4:56.2 | M. Jazy........ | France......... | 10-12-66 | St. Maur les Fossés, France |
| 3,000 Meters...... | 7:39.6 | K. Keino....... | Kenya.......... | 8-27-65 | Halsingborg, Sweden |
| 3,000-Meter Steeplechase..... | 8:26.4 | G. Roelants..... | Belgium........ | 8-7-65 | Brussels, Belgium |
| 5,000 Meters...... | 13:16.6 | R. Clarke....... | Australia....... | 7-5-66 | Stockholm, Sweden |
| 10 000 Meters...... | 27:39.4 | R. Clarke....... | Australia....... | 7-14-65 | Oslo, Norway |
| 20,000 Meters...... | 58:06.2 | G. Roelants..... | Belgium........ | 10-28-66 | Leuven, Belgium |
| 25,000 Meters...... | 1 hr. 15:22.6 | R. Hill......... | Britain......... | 7-21-65 | Bolton, Lancs., England |
| 30,000 Meters...... | 1 hr. 32:25.4 | J. Hogan....... | Britain......... | 11-12-66 | Walton-on-Thames, England |
| **Hurdles** | | | | | |
| 120 Yards......... | 0:13.2 | M. Lauer........ | Germany........ | 7-7-59 | Zurich, Switzerland |
| | 0:13.2 | L. Calhoun...... | U.S.A.......... | 8-21-60 | Berne, Switzerland |
| 220 Yards......... | 0:21.9 | D. Styron....... | U.S.A.......... | 4-2-60 | Baton Rouge, Louisiana |
| 440 Yards......... | 0:49.3 | G. Potgieter..... | S. Africa....... | 4-16-60 | Bloemfontein, S. África |
| 110 Meters........ | 0:13.2 | M. Lauer....... | Germany........ | 7-7-59 | Zurich, Switzerland |
| | 0:13.2 | L. Calhoun...... | U.S.A.......... | 8-21-60 | Berne, Switzerland |
| 200 Meters........ | 0:21.9 | D. Styron....... | U.S.A.......... | 4-2-60 | Baton Rouge, Louisiana |
| 200 Meters (Bend).. | 0:22.5 | M. Lauer....... | Germany........ | 7-7-59 | Zurich, Switzerland |
| | 0:22.5 | G. Davis....... | U.S.A.......... | 8-20-60 | Berne, Switzerland |
| 400 Meters........ | 0:49.1 | R. Cawley....... | U.S.A.......... | 9-13-64 | Los Angeles, California |
| **Walking** | | | | | |
| 20 Miles.......... | 2 hr. 31:33 | A. Vedjakov..... | U.S.S.R........ | 8-23-58 | Moscow, U.S.S.R. |
| 30 Miles.......... | 4 hr. 02:33 | C. Hohne........ | East Germany.... | 5-16-65 | Potsdam, East Germany |
| 2 Hours........... | 16 mi., 743 yd. | A. Egorov....... | U.S.S.R........ | 7-15-59 | Leningrad, U.S.S.R. |
| 20,000 Meters...... | 1 hr. 27:05 | V. Golubnichiy... | U.S.S.R........ | 9-23-58 | Simferopol, U.S.S.R. |
| 30,000 Meters...... | 2 hr. 17:16.8 | A. Egorov....... | U.S.S.R........ | 7-15-59 | Leningrad, U.S.S.R. |
| 50,000 Meters...... | 4 hr. 10:51.8 | C. Hohne........ | East Germany.... | 5-16-65 | Potsdam, East Germany |
| **Jumping** | | | | | |
| High Jump......... | 7′ 5¾″ | V. Brumel....... | U.S.S.R........ | 7-22-63 | Moscow, U.S.S.R. |
| Long Jump........ | 27′ 4¾″ | R. Boston....... | U.S.A.......... | 5-29-65 | Modesto, California |
| Triple Jump....... | 55′ 10¼″ | J. Schmidt....... | Poland......... | 8-5-60 | Olsztyn, Poland |
| Pole Vault........ | 17′ 8″ | P. Wilson....... | U.S.A.......... | 6-23-67 | Bakersfield, California |
| **Throwing** | | | | | |
| Shot.............. | 70′ 7¼″ | R. Matson...... | U.S.A.......... | 5-8-65 | Texas |
| Discus............ | 213′ 11¾″ | L. Danek....... | Czechoslovakia... | 10-12-65 | Sokolov, Czechoslovakia |
| Javelin............ | 300′ 11″ | T. Pedersen..... | Norway........ | 9-2-64 | Oslo, Norway |
| Hammer........... | 241′ 11″ | G. Zsivotsky..... | Hungary........ | 9-4-65 | Debrecen, Hungary |
| Decathlon........ | 9,121 pts. | C. K. Yang...... | Taiwan......... | 4-28-63 | Walnut, California |

# WEIGHT LIFTING *

## WORLD CHAMPIONS: 1962–1966 [1]

| YEAR | CLASS | COUNTRY | TOTAL[2] | YEAR | CLASS | COUNTRY | TOTAL[2] |
|---|---|---|---|---|---|---|---|
| | **123½ Pounds** | | | | **165¼ Pounds** (*cont.*) | | |
| 1962 | Y. Miyake.............. | Japan | 777 | 1965 | V. Kurentsov........... | U.S.S.R. | 963½ |
| 1963 | A. Vakhonin........... | U.S.S.R. | 760½ | 1966 | V. Kurentsov........... | U.S.S.R. | 991¾ |
| 1965 | I. Foldi................. | Hungary | 793 | | **181¾ Pounds** | | |
| 1966 | A. Vakhonin........... | U.S.S.R. | 799 | 1962 | G. Veres................ | Hungary | 1,014 |
| | **132¼ Pounds** | | | 1963 | G. Veres................ | Hungary | 1,052½ |
| 1962 | E. Minaev.............. | U.S.S.R. | 799 | 1965 | N. Ozimek.............. | Poland | 1,040 |
| 1963 | Y. Miyake.............. | Japan | 826½ | 1966 | V. Belyaev............. | U.S.S.R. | 1,068¾ |
| 1965 | Y. Miyake.............. | Japan | 847½ | | **198¼ Pounds** | | |
| 1966 | Y. Miyake.............. | Japan | 847½ | 1962 | L. Martin.............. | England | 1,058 |
| | **148¾ Pounds** | | | 1963 | L. Martin.............. | England | 1,058 |
| 1962 | V. Kaplunov........... | U.S.S.R. | 914¾ | 1965 | L. Martin.............. | England | 1,074 |
| 1963 | M. Zielinski........... | Poland | 920¼ | 1966 | G. Toth................ | Hungary | 1,074½ |
| 1965 | W. Baszanowski........ | Poland | 940½ | | **Heavyweight** | | |
| 1966 | E. Katsura............. | U.S.S.R. | 964¼ | 1962 | J. Vlasov.............. | U.S.S.R. | 1,190¼ |
| | **165¼ Pounds** | | | 1963 | J. Vlasov.............. | U.S.S.R. | 1,229 |
| 1962 | A. Kourinov........... | U.S.S.R. | 931¼ | 1965 | L. Zhabotinsky......... | U.S.S.R. | 1,217 |
| 1963 | A. Kourinov........... | U.S.S.R. | 964½ | 1966 | L. Zhabotinsky......... | U.S.S.R. | 1,250¾ |

[1] No competition held in 1967; list excludes 1964 Olympics champions.　　[2] In pounds.

## AAU SENIOR NATIONAL CHAMPIONSHIPS: 1967

| WINNER | PRESS[1] | SNATCH[1] | C&J[1,2] | TOTAL[1] | WINNER | PRESS[1] | SNATCH[1] | C&J[1,2] | TOTAL[1] |
|---|---|---|---|---|---|---|---|---|---|
| **123½-pound Class** | | | | | (*continued*) | | | | |
| Gary H. Hanson, | | | | | Pittsburgh, Penn. | 330 | 265 | 360 | 955 |
| N.Y............. | 205 | 205 | 280 | 690 | **181¾-pound Class** | | | | |
| **132¼-pound Class** | | | | | Joseph Puleo, | | | | |
| Walter Imahara, | | | | | Detroit, Michigan | 310 | 280 | 365 | 955 |
| Baton Rouge, La. | 250 | 235 | 290 | 775 | **198¼-pound Class** | | | | |
| **148¾-pound Class** | | | | | Phillip Grippaldi, | | | | |
| Homer Brannum, | | | | | Belleville, N.J.... | 350[3] | 295 | 390 | 1,035[4] |
| U.S.A.F........ | 285 | 240 | 310 | 835 | **Heavyweight Class** | | | | |
| **165¼-pound Class** | | | | | Robert Bednarski, | | | | |
| Russell Knipp, | | | | | York, Penn...... | 410 | 330 | 435 | 1,175 |

[1] In pounds.　　[2] Clean and jerk.　　[3] New Senior National press record.　　[4] New Senior National total.

# WRESTLING *

**World Greco-Roman Champions: 1967**
**114½-pound Class**
Viktor Bakulin, U.S.S.R.
**125½-pound Class**
Ion Baciv, Romania
**138½-pound Class**
Roman Rurua, U.S.S.R.
**154-pound Class**
Eere Tapio, Finland
**171½-pound Class**
Viktor Igoumenev, U.S.S.R.
**191½-pound Class**
Laszle Sillay, Hungary
**213½-pound Class**
Nikolai Iacevence, U.S.S.R.
**Heavyweight Class**
Istuan Kosma, Hungary
**AAU Greco-Roman Champions: 1967**
**114½-pound Class**
Dave Hazewinkel, Minnesota
**125½-pound Class**
Tomino Michio, New York

**138½-pound Class**
Charles Coffee, Minnesota
**154-pound Class**
Ben Northrup, California
**171½-pound Class**
Rudy Williams, Michigan
**191½-pound Class**
Wayne Baughman, U.S. Air Force
**213½-pound Class**
Gary Stensland, Oregon
**Heavyweight Class**
Larry Kristoff, Illinois
**World Free-Style Champions: 1967**
**114½-pound Class**
Shigeo Nakata, Japan
**125½-pound Class**
Ali Aliev, U.S.S.R.
**138½-pound Class**
Massaki Kaneko, Japan
**154-pound Class**
Abdulla Movahed, Iran
**171½-pound Class**
Daniel Sauton-Robin, France

**191½-pound Class**
Boris Gurevitch, U.S.S.R.
**213½-pound Class**
Ahmed Ayik, Turkey
**Heavyweight Class**
Alexandre Medved, U.S.S.R.
**AAU Free-Style Champions: 1967**
**114½-pound Class**
Noriyuki Suzuki, Japan
**125½-pound Class**
Rich Sanders, Oregon
**138½-pound Class**
Bob Buzzard, Michigan
**154-pound Class**
Bobby Douglas, Michigan
**171½-pound Class**
Pat Kelly, Illinois
**191½-pound Class**
Bill Harlow, Michigan
**213½-pound Class**
Henk Schenk, U.S. Army
**Heavyweight Class**
Larry Kristoff, Illinois

* Source: Amateur Athletic Union of the United States.

# YACHTING

## THE AMERICA'S CUP

A feature of the London Exhibition of 1851 was a 58-mile yacht race around the Isle of Wight. Among the entries was a 100-foot schooner from the United States, named the *America* and sponsored by members of the New York Yacht Club. The *America* won the race, defeating 14 English cutters and schooners, and was awarded a trophy called the Hundred-Guineas Cup, which had been donated by the Royal Yacht Squadron.

The *America* was sold and left in England, but the cup was brought back to the U.S. and presented to the New York Yacht Club. Used as a trophy for international yacht racing, it ultimately became known as the America's Cup, after the name of its original winner.

The first international challenge race took place in 1870 and set a pattern that is still followed. In the first contest the America's Cup was successfully defended, as were 19 successive challenges over the years. The last

—the 20th challenge—was made in 1967 by the Royal Sydney Yacht Squadron of Australia, with the yacht *Dame Pattie*. Selected to defend the Cup was the *Intrepid,* a 12-Meter yacht designed by Olin Stephens and skippered by Emil (Bus) Mosbacher, Jr.

In the opening race of the best-of-seven series, the *Intrepid* sped over the six-sided 24.3-mile course on Rhode Island Sound to far out-distance *Dame Pattie*. In the subsequent three races the *Intrepid* proved overwhelmingly superior.

Once again a foreign challenger had been turned back, and the America's Cup remained safely in possession of the New York Yacht Club for at least another three years. Yet, scarcely had the toasts been raised to the victorious U.S. crew than new challenges for 1970 were submitted by the Royal Dorset Yacht Club of Weymouth, England, and France's Club d'Hyères.

### ■ AMERICA'S CUP WINNERS AND CHALLENGERS

| YEAR | WINNER | OWNER | COUNTRY | CHALLENGER | OWNER | COUNTRY |
|------|--------|-------|---------|------------|-------|---------|
| 1870 | Magic........ | Franklin Osgood | United States | Cambria [1] ..... | James Ashbury | England |
| 1871 | Columbia [2] ... | Franklin Osgood | United States | Livonia........ | James Ashbury | England |
|      | Sappho [2] ..... | William P. Douglass | United States | | | |
| 1876 | Madeleine.... | John S. Dickerson | United States | Countess of Dufferin..... | Charles Gifford | Canada |
| 1881 | Mischief...... | J. R. Busk | United States | Atlanta........ | Alexander Cuthbert | Canada |
| 1885 | Puritan....... | J. M. Forbes, Charles Paine | United States | Genesta....... | Sir Richard Sutton | England |
| 1886 | Mayflower.... | Charles Paine | United States | Galatea........ | William Henn | England |
| 1887 | Volunteer..... | Charles Paine | United States | Thistle........ | James Bell | England |
| 1893 | Vigilant...... | Oliver Iselin | United States | Valkyrie II..... | Lord Dunraven | England |
| 1895 | Defender..... | Oliver Iselin, E. D. Morgan, W. K. Vanderbilt | United States | Valkyrie III.... | Lord Dunraven, Lord Lonsdale, Lord Wolverton | England |
| 1899 | Columbia..... | Oliver Iselin, J. P. Morgan | United States | Shamrock I.... | Sir Thomas Lipton | Ireland |
| 1901 | Columbia.... | E. D. Morgan | United States | Shamrock II... | Sir Thomas Lipton | Ireland |
| 1903 | Reliance...... | Cornelius Vanderbilt | United States | Shamrock III.. | Sir Thomas Lipton | Ireland |
| 1920 | Resolute...... | Harry Walters | United States | Shamrock IV.. | Sir Thomas Lipton | Ireland |
| 1930 | Enterprise.... | Harold S. Vanderbilt | United States | Shamrock V... | Sir Thomas Lipton | Ireland |
| 1934 | Rainbow...... | Harold S. Vanderbilt | United States | Endeavour..... | T. O. M. Sopwith | England |
| 1937 | Ranger....... | Harold S. Vanderbilt | United States | Endeavour II... | T. O. M. Sopwith | England |
| 1958 | Columbia.... | Henry Sears | United States | Sceptre....... | Hugh Goodson | England |
| 1962 | Weatherly.... | Henry Mercer | United States | Gretel........ | Sir Frank Packer | Australia |
| 1964 | Constellation.. | Walter Gubelmann | United States | Sovereign..... | Anthony Boyden | England |
| 1967 | Intrepid...... | N.Y. Yacht Club's Intrepid Syndicate | United States | Dame Pattie... | Royal Sydney Yacht Squadron's Syndicate | Australia |

[1] *Cambria,* the only English schooner in the race, finished tenth in a field of 24.   [2] After winning the first two races, the *Columbia* was disabled. *Sappho* substituted and won the fourth and fifth races.

## NORTH AMERICAN CHAMPIONSHIPS

The North American Yacht Racing Union, founded in 1925, sponsors North American championships each year, and awards an appropriate cup to the winner. Following are the 1967 results:

**Mallory Cup** (for men): Clifford W. Campbell, Toms River Yacht Club, New Jersey

**Adams Cup** (for women): Mrs. William H. Foulk, Indian Harbor Yacht Club, Greenwich, Connecticut

**Sears Cup** (for juniors): John Dane, Southern Yacht Club, New Orleans, Louisiana

**O'Day Trophy:** Charles Barthrop, Area I, Intercollegiate Yacht Racing Association, Kings Point, New York

## SIR FRANCIS CHICHESTER AND GIPSY MOTH IV

Francis Chichester aboard the ketch **Gipsy Moth IV** after his famous solo journey around the world.

L D E / Pictorial Parade

The imagination of the world was captured in 1967 by the daring of a 65-year-old Englishman who successfully sailed alone around the world in a 53-foot ketch. Lanky, bespectacled Francis Chichester left Plymouth, England, on August 27, 1966. Some 226 days later, after covering 28,500 watery miles, he brought his *Gipsy Moth IV* triumphantly back into Plymouth Harbor and received a wild welcome.

Adventure has always beckoned to Francis Chichester. The son of an English clergyman, he left school at 17 and made his way to New Zealand, where he worked as a coal miner, lumberjack, gold prospector, and land speculator. Returning to England about ten years later (1929), Chichester took flying lessons and later made a solo flight to Australia in a Gipsy Moth, a fabric-and-wood biplane of the period.

His interest turned to sailing after the Second World War when he bought a small sloop, which he named *Gipsy Moth II* in memory of his old airplane. Later, in *Gipsy Moth III,* he won a trans-Atlantic sailing race to New York and began to dream of the greatest adventure of all — circumnavigating the globe.

With the aid of private financial backing, Chichester fitted out a new boat, *Gipsy Moth IV,* and began his epic voyage. After a series of hair-raising experiences he reached Sydney, Australia, on Dec. 12, 1966. Six weeks later the wiry Englishman re-embarked for the trip home. Rounding Cape Horn at the tip of South America, *Gipsy Moth IV* was almost torn apart by a hurricane, but the skipper's courage and persistence prevailed. On May 28, 1967, to the clanging of church bells and cheers of the crowd, Francis Chichester entered Plymouth Harbor.

Perhaps the courageous mariner's greatest accolade came when Queen Elizabeth II knighted him and said: "Rise, Sir Francis."

# INDEX